2013 Conference of the North American Chapter of the Association for Computational Linguistics: Human Language Technologies

(NAACL HLT 2013)

Atlanta, Georgia, USA
9-14 June 2013

Volume 1 of 2

ISBN: 978-1-62748-838-9

Printed from e-media with permission by:

Curran Associates, Inc.
57 Morehouse Lane
Red Hook, NY 12571

Some format issues inherent in the e-media version may also appear in this print version.

Printed by Curran Associates, Inc. (2013)

For permission requests, please contact the Association for Computational Linguistics at the address below.

Association for Computational Linguistics
209 N. Eighth Street
Stroudsburg, Pennsylvania 18360

Phone: 1-570-476-8006
Fax: 1-570-476-0860

acl@aclweb.org

Additional copies of this publication are available from:

Curran Associates, Inc.
57 Morehouse Lane
Red Hook, NY 12571 USA
Phone: 845-758-0400
Fax: 845-758-2634
Email: curran@proceedings.com
Web: www.proceedings.com

NAACL HLT 2013

The 2013 Conference of the North American Chapter of the Association for Computational Linguistics: Human Language Technologies

Proceedings of the Main Conference

9–14 June 2013
Westin Peachtree Plaza Hotel
Atlanta, Georgia

Sponsors

NAACL HLT 2013 gratefully acknowledges the following sponsors for their support.

Gold Level

Google

Microsoft® Research

Bronze Level

ETS® Listening. Learning. Leading.®

Rakuten

Appen ButlerHill

Student Best Paper Award and Student Lunch Sponsor

IBM Research

Student Volunteer Sponsor

AI @ ISI

Conference Bags

SDL Research

General Chair Preface

Welcome everyone!

It is my pleasure to welcome you all to Atlanta, Georgia, for the 2013 NAACL Human Language Technologies conference. This is a great opportunity to reconnect with old friends and make new acquaintances, learn the latest in your own field and become curious about new areas, and also to experience Atlanta's warm southern hospitality. That hospitality starts with Priscilla Rasmussen! Priscilla thinks about everything that we all take for granted: the registration that just took place, the rooms in which we sit, the refreshments that keep us energized, and the social events that make this conference so fun, and many other details that you would miss if they weren't there. Please introduce yourself and say hi. Priscilla is the backbone of the NAACL organization. Thank you!

This conference started a year ago, when Hal Daumé III and Katrin Kirchhoff graciously agreed to be program co-chairs. It is no exaggeration to say how much their dedication has shaped this conference and how grateful I am for their initiative and hard work. Thank you Hal and Katrin, especially for all the fun discussion that made the work light and the year go by fast! This conference could not have happened with you.

Thanks go to the entire organizing committee. As I am writing this to be included in the proceedings, I am grateful for the fantastic detailed and proactive work by Colin Cherry and Matt Post, the publications chairs. The tutorials chairs, Katrin Erk and Jimmy Lin, selected, and solicited, 6 tutorials to present in depth material on some of the diverse topics represented in our community. Chris Dyer and Derrick Higgins considered which projects shine best when shown as a demonstration. The workshops chairs for NAACL, Sujith Ravi and Luke Zettlemoyer, worked jointly with ACL and EMNLP to select the workshops to be held at NAACL. They also worked with ICML 2013 to co-host workshops that bridge the two communities, in addition to the Joint NAACL/ICML symposium.

Posters from the student research workshop are part of the poster and demonstrations session on Monday night. This is a great opportunity for the students to be recognized in the community and to benefit from lively discussion of their presentations (attendees take note!) Annie Louis and Richard Socher are the student research workshop chairs, and Julia Hockenmaier and Eric Ringger generously share their wisdom as the faculty advisors. The student research workshop itself will be held on the first day of workshops. There are so many people who contribute their time to the behind-the-scenes organization of the conference, without which the conference cannot take place. Asking for money is probably not a natural fit for anyone, but Chris Brew worked on local sponsorship, and Dan Bikel and Patrick Pantel worked to obtain sponsorship across the ACL conferences this year - thank you! Jacob Eisenstein had the more fun role of distributing money as the student volunteer coordinator, and we thank all of the student volunteers who will be helping to run a smooth conference. Kristy Boyer kept the communication "short and tweet" using a variety of social media (and old-fashioned media too). An important part of the behind-the-scenes efforts that enable a conference like NAACL to come together are the sponsors. We thank all of the sponsors for the contributions to the conference , both for the general funding made available as well as the specific programs that are funded through sponsorship. You can read more about these sponsors in our conference handbook.

This year there are several initiatives, and if successful, we hope they'll be part of NAACL conferences in the future. One is to make the proceedings available prior to the conference; we hope you will benefit from the extra time to read the papers beforehand. Another is for tutorials and all oral presentations to be recorded on video and made available post-conference. We are also delighted to host presentations, in both oral and poster formats, from the new Transactions of the ACL journal, to enhance the impact these will already have as journal publications. Finally, Matt Post is creating a new digital form of conference handbook to go with our digital age; thanks also go to Alex Clemmer who has prepared the paper copy that you may be reading right now. We hope you use the #NAACL2013 tag when you are tweeting about the conference or papers at the conference; together, we'll be creating a new social media corpus to explore.

Once again, we are pleased to be co-located with *SEM conference, and the SemEval workshop. We are lucky to have ICML 2013 organized so close in time and place. Several researchers who span the two communities have reconvened the Joint NAACL/ICML symposium on June 15, 2013. In addition, two workshops that address areas of interest to both NAACL and ICML members have been organized on June 16th, as part of the ICML conference.

NAACL 2013 has given me a great appreciation for the volunteering that is part of our culture. Besides the organizing committee itself, we are guided by the NAACL executive board, who think about questions with a multi-year perspective. I also want to recognize the members who first initiated and now maintain the ACL Anthology, where all of our published work will be available to all in perpetuity, a fabulous contribution and one that distinguishes our academic community.

Have a fun conference!

Lucy Vanderwende, Microsoft Research
NAACL HLT 2013 General Chair

Program Chair Preface

Welcome to NAACL HLT 2013 in Atlanta, Georgia. We have an exciting program consisting of six tutorials, 24 sessions of talks (both for long and short papers), an insane poster madness session that includes posters from the newly revamped student research workshop, ten workshops and two additional cross-pollination workshops held jointly with ICML (occurring immediately after NAACL HLT, just one block away). There are a few innovations in the conference this year, the most noticeable of which is the twitter channel #naacl2013 and the fact that we are the first conference to host papers published in the Transactions of the ACL journal – there are six such papers in our program, marked as [TACL]. We are very excited about our two invited talks, one on Monday morning and one Wednesday morning. The first is by Gina Kuperberg, who will talk about "Predicting Meaning: What the Brain tells us about the Architecture of Language Comprehension." The second presenter is our own Kathleen KcKeown, who will talk about "Natural Language Applications from Fact to Fiction."

The morning session on Tuesday includes the presentation of best paper awards to two worthy recipients. The award for Best Short Paper goes to Marta Recasens, Marie-Catherine de Marneffe and Christopher Potts for their paper "The Life and Death of Discourse Entities: Identifying Singleton Mentions" The award for Best Student Paper goes to the long paper "Automatic Generation of English Respellings" by Bradley Hauer and Greg Kondrak. We gratefully acknowledge IBM's support for the Student Best Paper Award. Finally, many thanks to the Best Paper Committee for selecting these excellent papers!

The complete program includes 95 long papers (of which six represent presentations from the journal Transactions of the ACL, a first for any ACL conference!) and 51 short papers. We are excited that the conference is able to present such a dynamic array of papers, and would like to thank the authors for their great work. We worked hard to keep the conference to three parallel sessions at any one time to hopefully maximize a participant's ability to see everything she wants! This represents an acceptance rate of 30% for long papers and 37% for short papers. More details about the distribution across areas and other statistics will be made available in the NAACL HLT Program Chair report on the ACL wiki: `http://aclweb.org/adminwiki/index.php?title=Reports`

The review process for the conference was double-blind, and included an author response period for clarifying reviewers' questions. We were very pleased to have the assistance of 350 reviewers, each of whom reviewed an average of 3.7 papers, in deciding the program. We are especially thankful for the reviewers who spent time reading the author responses and engaging other reviewers in the discussion board. Assigning reviewers would not have been possible without the hard work of Mark Dredze and his miracle assignment scripts. Furthermore, constructing the program would not have been possible without 22 excellent area chairs forming the Senior Program Committee: Eugene Agichtein, Srinivas Bangalore, David Bean, Phil Blunsom, Jordan Boyd-Graber, Marine Carpuat, Joyce Chai, Vera Demberg, Bill Dolan, Doug Downey, Mark Dredze, Markus Dreyer, Sanda Harabagiu, James Henderson, Guy Lapalme, Alon Lavie, Percy Liang, Johanna Moore, Ani Nenkova, Joakim Nivre, Bo Pang, Zak Shafran, David Traum, Peter Turney, and Theresa Wilson. Area chairs were responsible for managing paper assignments, collating reviewer responses, handling papers for other area chairs or program chairs who had conflicts of interest, making recommendations for paper acceptance or rejection, and nominating best papers from their areas. We are very grateful for the time and energy that they have put into the program.

There are a number of other people that we interacted with who deserve a hearty thanks for the success of the program. Rich Gerber and the START team at Softconf have been invaluable for helping us with the mechanics of the reviewing process. Matt Post and Colin Cherry, as publications co-chairs, have been very helpful in assembling the final program and coordinating the publications of the workshop proceedings. There are several crucial parts of the overall program that were the responsibility of various contributors, including Annie Louis, Richard Socher, Julia Hockenmaier and Eric Ringger (Student Research Workshop chairs, who did an amazing job revamping the SRW); Jimmy Lin and Katrin Erk (Tutorial Chairs); Luke Zettlemoyer and Sujith Ravi (Workshop Chairs); Chris Dyer and Derrick Higgins (Demo Chairs); Jacob Eisenstein (Student Volunteer Coordinator); Chris Brew (Local Sponsorship Chair); Patrick Pantel and Dan Bikel (Sponsorship Chairs); and the new-founded Publicity chair who handled #naacl2013 tweeting among other things, Kristy Boyer.

We would also like to thank Chris Callison-Burch and the NAACL Executive Board for guidance during the process. Michael Collins was amazingly helpful in getting the inaugural TACL papers into the NAACL HLT conference. Priscilla Rasmussen deserves, as always, special mention and warmest thanks as the local arrangements chair and general business manager. Priscilla is amazing and everyone who sees her at the conference should thank her.

Finally, we would like to thank our General Chair, Lucy Vanderwende, for both her trust and guidance during this process. She helped turn the less-than-wonderful parts of this job to roses, and her ability to organize an incredibly complex event is awe inspiring. None of this would have happened without her.

We hope that you enjoy the conference!

Hal Daumé III, University of Maryland
Katrin Kirchhoff, University of Washington

Organizing Committee

General Conference Chair

Lucy Vanderwende, Microsoft Research

Program Committee Chairs

Hal Daumé III, University of Maryland
Katrin Kirchhoff, University of Washington

Local Arrangements

Priscilla Rassmussen

Workshop Chairs

Luke Zettlemoyer, University of Washington
Sujith Ravi, Google

Tutorial Chairs

Jimmy Lin, University of Maryland
Katrin Erk, University of Texas at Austin

Student Research Workshop

Chairs:
Annie Louis, University of Pennsylvania
Richard Socher, Stanford University
Faculty Advisors:
Julia Hockenmaier, University of Illinois at Urbana-Champaign
Eric Ringger, Brigham Young University

Student Volunteer Coordinator

Jacob Eisenstein, School of Interactive Computing, Georgia Tech

Demonstrations Chairs

Chris Dyer, Carnegie Mellon University
Derrick Higgins, Educational Testing Service

Local Sponsorship Chair

Chris Brew, Educational Testing Service

NAACL Sponsorship Chairs

Patrick Pantel, Microsoft Research
Dan Bikel, Google

Publications Chairs

Matt Post, Johns Hopkins University
Colin Cherry, National Research Council, Canada

Publicity Chair

Kristy Boyer, North Carolina State University

Program Committee

Program Committee Chairs

Hal Daumé III, University of Maryland
Katrin Kirchhoff, University of Washington

Area Chairs

Phonology and Morphology, Word Segmentation
Markus Dreyer (SDL Language Weaver)
Syntax, Tagging, Chunking and Parsing
Joakim Nivre (Uppsala University)
James Henderson (Université de Genève)
Semantics
Percy Liang (Stanford University)
Peter Turney (National Research Council of Canada)
Multimodal NLP
Srinivas Bangalore (AT&T)
Discourse, Dialogue, Pragmatics
David Traum (Institute for Creative Technologies)
Joyce Chai (Michigan State University)
Linguistic Aspects of CL
Vera Demberg (Saarland University)
Summarization
Guy Lapalme (Université de Montréal)
Generation
Johanna Moore (University of Edinburgh)
ML for Language Processing
Phil Blunsom (University of Oxford)
Mark Dredze (Johns Hopkins University)

Machine Translation
Alon Lavie (Carnegie Mellon University)
Marine Carpuat (National Research Council of Canada)
Information Retrieval and QA
Eugene Agichtein (Emory University)
Information Extraction
Doug Downey (Northwestern University)
Sanda Harabagiu (University of Texas at Dallas)
Spoken Language Processing
Zak Shafran (Oregon Health and Science University)
Sentiment Analysis and Opinion Mining
Bo Pang (Cornell University)
Theresa Wilson (Johns Hopkins University)
NLP-enabled Technology
David Bean (TDW)
Document Categorization and Topic Clustering
Jordan Boyd-Graber (University of Maryland)
Social Media Analysis and Processing
Bill Dolan (Microsoft Research)
Language Resources and Evaluation Methods
Ani Nenkova (University of Pennsylvania)

Primary Reviewers

Ahmed Abbasi
Mikhail Ageev
Eneko Agirre
Gregory Aist
Jan Alexandersson
Nicholas Andrews
David Andrzejewski
Gabor Angeli
Yoav Artzi
Michael Auli
Michiel Bacchiani
Anton Bakalov
Kirk Baker
Tyler Baldwin
Marco Baroni
Roberto Basili
Beata Beigman Klebanov
Kedar Bellare
Patrice Bellot
Emily M. Bender
Jonathan Berant
Justin Betteridge
Chandra Bhagavatula
Arianna Bisazza
Nathan Bodenstab
Danushka Bollegala
Alexandre Bouchard
Jordan Boyd-Graber
S.R.K. Branavan
Thorsten Brants
Chris Brew
Wray Buntine
David Burkett
Jill Burstein
Aoife Cahill
Chris Callison-Burch
Nicoletta Calzolari
Nicola Cancedda
Sandra Carberry
Claire Cardie
Xavier Carreras
Daniel Cer
Nate Chambers
Ming-Wei Chang
Boxing Chen
Chen Chen
David Chen
Colin Cherry
David Chiang
Yejin Choi
Jennifer Chu-Carroll
Stephen Clark
James Clarke
Martin Cmejrek
Shay Cohen
Trevor Cohn
Kevyn Collins-Thompson
John Conroy
Aron Culotta
James Cussens
Lyne Da Sylva
Ido Dagan
Robert Daland
Bhavana Dalvi
William Darling
Dipanjan Das

Pradipto Das
Eric De La Clergerie
Steve DeNeefe
John DeNero
David DeVault
Michael Denkowski
Jacob Devlin
Laura Dietz
Gregory Druck
Lan Du
Chris Dyer
Koji Eguchi
Vladimir Eidelman
Jacob Eisenstein
Jason Eisner
Ahmad Emami
Andrea Esuli
Anthony Fader
Atefeh Farzindar
Anna Feldman
Radu Florian
George Foster
Jennifer Foster
Mary Ellen Foster
Bob Frank
Dayne Freitag
Michel Galley
Michael Gamon
Sudeep Gandhe
Kavita Ganesan
Claire Gardent
Matt Gardner
Niyu Ge
Matthew Gerber
George Giannakopoulos
Daniel Gildea
Daniel Gillick
Kevin Gimpel
Filip Ginter
Yoav Goldberg
Dan Goldwasser
Sharon Goldwater
Dave Golland
Kyle Gorman
Cyril Goutte
Amit Goyal
Joao Graca
Brigitte Grau
Edward Grefenstette
Justin Grimmer
Carlos Gómez-Rodríguez
Nizar Habash
Barry Haddow
Eva Hajicova
John Hale
David Hall
Keith Hall
Greg Hanneman
Claudia Hauff
Xiaodong He
Kenneth Heafield
James Henderson
John Henderson
Ulf Hermjakob
Derrick Higgins
Graeme Hirst
Anna Hjalmarsson
Hieu Hoang
Julia Hockenmaier
Matthew Hoffman
Kristy Hollingshead
Yuening Hu
Fei Huang
Liang Huang
Minlie Huang
Zhongqiang Huang
Rebecca Hwa
Diana Inkpen
Ann Irvine
Abe Ittycheriah
Jagadeesh Jagarlamudi
Jiarong Jiang
Howard Johnson
Michael Johnston
David Jurgens
Alexander Kain
Pallika Kanani
Anna Kazantseva
Alistair Kennedy
Tracy Holloway King
Brian Kingsbury
Alexandre Klementiev
Philipp Koehn
Rob Koeling
Moshe Koppel
Alexander Kotov
Jayant Krishnamurthy
Sandra Kuebler
Marco Kuhlmann
Jonas Kuhn
Roland Kuhn
Seth Kulick
Shankar Kumar
Oren Kurland
Tom Kwiatkowski
Yoong Keok Lee
Maider Lehr
Alessandro Lenci
Gregor Leusch
Rivka Levitan
Fangtao Li
Mu Li
Shoushan Li
Percy Liang
Jimmy Lin
Xiao Ling
Diane Litman
Ding Liu
Qun Liu
Yang Liu
Adam Lopez
Annie Louis
Xiaofei Lu
Yue Lu
Michael Lucas
Xiaoqiang Luo
Klaus Macherey
Wolfgang Macherey
Nitin Madnani
Suresh Manandhar
Gideon Mann
Lluis Marquez
Erwin Marsi
Andre Martins
Yuval Marton

Sameer Maskey
Yuji Matsumoto
Evgeny Matusov
Arne Mauser
Diana McCarthy
David McClosky
Arul Menezes
Florian Metze
Donald Metzler
Haitao Mi
Rada Mihalcea
Minel Minel
Margaret Mitchell
Yusuke Miyao
Saif Mohammad
Taesun Moon
Robert Moore
Roser Morante
Louis-Philippe Morency
Preslav Nakov
Nava Nava
Roberto Navigli
Mark-Jan Nederhof
Hwee Tou Ng
Vincent Ng
Patrick Nguyen
Viet-An Nguyen
Joakim Nivre
Brendan O'Connor
Stephan Oepen
Miles Osborne
Myle Ott
Karolina Owczarzak
Martha Palmer
Sinno J. Pan
Bo Pang
Rebecca J. Passonneau
Siddharth Patwardhan
Michael Paul
Lisa Pearl
Ted Pedersen
Gerald Penn
Slav Petrov
Thierry Poibeau
Heather Pon-Barry
Hoifung Poon
Andrei Popescu-Belis
Matthew Purver
Chris Quirk
Reinhard Rapp
Roi Reichart
Ehud Reiter
Jason Riesa
Stefan Riezler
Ellen Riloff
Eric Ringger
Alan Ritter
Brian Roark
Antonio Roque
Carolyn Rose
Andrew Rosenberg
Markus Saers
Alicia Sagae
Kenji Sagae
Horacio Saggion
Saurav Sahay
Mark Sammons
Murat Saraclar
Anoop Sarkar
Giorgio Satta
Roser Saurí
Asad Sayeed
David Schlangen
Judith Schlesinger
Lane Schwartz
Holger Schwenk
Hendra Setiawan
Zak Shafran
Libin Shen
Wade Shen
Michel Simard
Sameer Singh
Jason Smith
Nathaniel Smith
Noah A. Smith
Swapna Somasundaran
Lucia Specia
Valentin Spitkovsky
Caroline Sporleder
Vivek Srikumar
Keith Stevens
Mark Stevenson
Matthew Stone
Veselin Stoyanov
Fabian Suchanek
Ang Sun
Mihai Surdeanu
Jun Suzuki
Stan Szpakowicz
Partha Talukdar
Christoph Tillmann
Ivan Titov
Kristina Toutanova
Reut Tsarfaty
Oren Tsur
Benjamin Van Durme
Josef van Genabith
Vincent Vanhoucke
Enrique Vidal
Karthik Visweswariah
Adam Vogel
Stephan Vogel
Xiaojun Wan
Haifeng Wang
Taro Watanabe
Bonnie Webber
David Weir
Michael White
Jan Wiebe
Shuly Wintner
Kristian Woodsend
Bing Xiang
Peng Xu
Hui Yang
Muyun Yang
Yi Yang
Tae Yano
Limin Yao
Mahsa Yarmohammadi
Alexander Yates
Wen-tau Yih
Yisong Yue
Rabih Zbib
Richard Zens
Luke Zettlemoyer

Ke Zhai
Congle Zhang
Lei Zhang
Min Zhang
Shiqi Zhao
Tiejun Zhao
Bowen Zhou
Jun Zhu
Xiaodan Zhu
Chengqing Zong
Geoffrey Zweig

Secondary Reviewers

JH
Karteek Addanki
Neil Ashton
Daniel Blanchard
Hailong Cao
Dave Carter
Glen Coppersmith
Daniel Dahlmeier
David Etter
Paul Felt
Francisco Guzman
Robbie Haertel
Khairun Nisa Hassanali
Kriste Krstovski
Jun Lang
Wang Ling
Hito Matsushita
Hans Moen
Kevin Seppi
Jun Sun
Xavier Tannier
Svitlana Volkova
Haochang Wang
Xinglong Wang
Mo Yu
Feifei Zhai
Bo Zhao
Kai Zhao
Xiaoning Zhu

Table of Contents

Conference Program

Monday, June 10, 2013

8:45–9:00 Welcome to NAACL 2013!

9:00–10:10 Invited talk by Gina Kuperberg – Predicting Meaning: What the Brain tells us about the Architecture of Language Comprehension

10:10–10:40 Break

M1a: Machine Translation

10:40-11:05 *Model With Minimal Translation Units, But Decode With Phrases*
Nadir Durrani, Alexander Fraser and Helmut Schmid

11:05-11:30 *Beyond Left-to-Right: Multiple Decomposition Structures for SMT*
Hui Zhang, Kristina Toutanova, Chris Quirk and Jianfeng Gao

11:30-11:55 *Improved Reordering for Phrase-Based Translation using Sparse Features*
Colin Cherry

11:55-12:20 *Simultaneous Word-Morpheme Alignment for Statistical Machine Translation*
Elif Eyigöz, Daniel Gildea and Kemal Oflazer

M1b: Information Extraction

10:40-11:05 *Multi-faceted Event Recognition with Bootstrapped Dictionaries*
Ruihong Huang and Ellen Riloff

11:05-11:30 *Named Entity Recognition with Bilingual Constraints*
Wanxiang Che, Mengqiu Wang, Christopher D. Manning and Ting Liu

11:30-11:55 *Minimally Supervised Method for Multilingual Paraphrase Extraction from Definition Sentences on the Web*
Yulan Yan, Chikara Hashimoto, Kentaro Torisawa, Takao Kawai, Jun'ichi Kazama and Stijn De Saeger

11:55-12:20 *Relation Extraction with Matrix Factorization and Universal Schemas*
Sebastian Riedel, Limin Yao, Andrew McCallum and Benjamin M. Marlin

Monday, June 10, 2013 (continued)

M2b: Topic Modeling and Text Mining

2:00-2:25 *Representing Topics Using Images*
Nikolaos Aletras and Mark Stevenson

2:25-2:50 *Drug Extraction from the Web: Summarizing Drug Experiences with Multi-Dimensional Topic Models*
Michael J. Paul and Mark Dredze

2:50-3:15 *Towards Topic Labeling with Phrase Entailment and Aggregation*
Yashar Mehdad, Giuseppe Carenini, Raymond T. Ng and Shafiq Joty

3:15-3:40 *Topic Segmentation with a Structured Topic Model*
Lan Du, Wray Buntine and Mark Johnson

M2c: Spoken Language Processing

2:00-2:25 *Text Alignment for Real-Time Crowd Captioning*
Iftekhar Naim, Daniel Gildea, Walter Lasecki and Jeffrey P. Bigham

2:25-2:50 *Discriminative Joint Modeling of Lexical Variation and Acoustic Confusion for Automated Narrative Retelling Assessment*
Maider Lehr, Izhak Shafran, Emily Prud'hommeaux and Brian Roark

2:50-3:15 *Using Out-of-Domain Data for Lexical Addressee Detection in Human-Human-Computer Dialog*
Heeyoung Lee, Andreas Stolcke and Elizabeth Shriberg

3:15-3:40 *Segmentation Strategies for Streaming Speech Translation*
Vivek Kumar Rangarajan Sridhar, John Chen, Srinivas Bangalore, Andrej Ljolje and Rathinavelu Chengalvarayan

3:40–4:10 Break

4:10–6:00 Poster madness!

Enforcing Subcategorization Constraints in a Parser Using Sub-parses Recombining
Seyed Abolghasem Mirroshandel, Alexis Nasr and Benoît Sagot

Large-Scale Discriminative Training for Statistical Machine Translation Using Held-Out Line Search
Jeffrey Flanigan, Chris Dyer and Jaime Carbonell

Monday, June 10, 2013 (continued)

Measuring Term Informativeness in Context
Zhaohui Wu and C. Lee Giles

Unsupervised Learning Summarization Templates from Concise Summaries
Horacio Saggion

Classification of South African languages using text and acoustic based methods: A case of six selected languages
Peleira Nicholas Zulu

Improving Syntax-Augmented Machine Translation by Coarsening the Label Set
Greg Hanneman and Alon Lavie

Keyphrase Extraction for N-best Reranking in Multi-Sentence Compression
Florian Boudin and Emmanuel Morin

Development of a Persian Syntactic Dependency Treebank
Mohammad Sadegh Rasooli, Manouchehr Kouhestani and Amirsaeid Moloodi

Improving reordering performance using higher order and structural features
Mitesh M. Khapra, Ananthakrishnan Ramanathan and Karthik Visweswariah

Massively Parallel Suffix Array Queries and On-Demand Phrase Extraction for Statistical Machine Translation Using GPUs
Hua He, Jimmy Lin and Adam Lopez

Discriminative Training of 150 Million Translation Parameters and Its Application to Pruning
Hendra Setiawan and Bowen Zhou

Applying Pairwise Ranked Optimisation to Improve the Interpolation of Translation Models
Barry Haddow

Dialectal Arabic to English Machine Translation: Pivoting through Modern Standard Arabic
Wael Salloum and Nizar Habash

What to do about bad language on the internet
Jacob Eisenstein

Monday, June 10, 2013 (continued)

Minibatch and Parallelization for Online Large Margin Structured Learning
Kai Zhao and Liang Huang

Improved Part-of-Speech Tagging for Online Conversational Text with Word Clusters
Olutobi Owoputi, Brendan O'Connor, Chris Dyer, Kevin Gimpel, Nathan Schneider and Noah A. Smith

Parser lexicalisation through self-learning
Marek Rei and Ted Briscoe

Mining User Relations from Online Discussions using Sentiment Analysis and Probabilistic Matrix Factorization
Minghui Qiu, Liu Yang and Jing Jiang

Focused training sets to reduce noise in NER feature models
Amber McKenzie

Learning to Relate Literal and Sentimental Descriptions of Visual Properties
Mark Yatskar, Svitlana Volkova, Asli Celikyilmaz, Bill Dolan and Luke Zettlemoyer

Morphological Analysis and Disambiguation for Dialectal Arabic
Nizar Habash, Ryan Roth, Owen Rambow, Ramy Eskander and Nadi Tomeh

Using a Supertagged Dependency Language Model to Select a Good Translation in System Combination
Wei-Yun Ma and Kathleen McKeown

Dudley North visits North London: Learning When to Transliterate to Arabic
Mahmoud Azab, Houda Bouamor, Behrang Mohit and Kemal Oflazer

Better Twitter Summaries?
Joel Judd and Jugal Kalita

Training MRF-Based Phrase Translation Models using Gradient Ascent
Jianfeng Gao and Xiaodong He

Automatic Morphological Enrichment of a Morphologically Underspecified Treebank
Sarah Alkuhlani, Nizar Habash and Ryan Roth

Embracing Ambiguity: A Comparison of Annotation Methodologies for Crowdsourcing Word Sense Labels
David Jurgens

Compound Embedding Features for Semi-supervised Learning
Mo Yu, Tiejun Zhao, Daxiang Dong, Hao Tian and Dianhai Yu

On Quality Ratings for Spoken Dialogue Systems – Experts vs. Users
Stefan Ultes, Alexander Schmitt and Wolfgang Minker

Overcoming the Memory Bottleneck in Distributed Training of Latent Variable Models of Text
Yi Yang, Alexander Yates and Doug Downey

Processing Spontaneous Orthography
Ramy Eskander, Nizar Habash, Owen Rambow and Nadi Tomeh

Purpose and Polarity of Citation: Towards NLP-based Bibliometrics
Amjad Abu-Jbara, Jefferson Ezra and Dragomir Radev

Estimating effect size across datasets
Anders Søgaard

Systematic Comparison of Professional and Crowdsourced Reference Translations for Machine Translation
Rabih Zbib, Gretchen Markiewicz, Spyros Matsoukas, Richard Schwartz and John Makhoul

Down-stream effects of tree-to-dependency conversions
Jakob Elming, Anders Johannsen, Sigrid Klerke, Emanuele Lapponi, Hector Martinez Alonso and Anders Søgaard

6:00–6:30 Break

6:30–8:30 Poster and Demonstrations Session

Tuesday, June 11, 2013

9:15–9:25 Best paper awards

Best Short Paper

9:25–9:45 *The Life and Death of Discourse Entities: Identifying Singleton Mentions*
Marta Recasens, Marie-Catherine de Marneffe and Christopher Potts

IBM Best Student Paper

9:45–10:15 *Automatic Generation of English Respellings*
Bradley Hauer and Grzegorz Kondrak

10:15–10:45 Break

T1a: Machine Translation and Multilinguality

10:45-11:00 *A Simple, Fast, and Effective Reparameterization of IBM Model 2*
Chris Dyer, Victor Chahuneau and Noah A. Smith

11:00-11:15 *Phrase Training Based Adaptation for Statistical Machine Translation*
Saab Mansour and Hermann Ney

11:15-11:30 *Translation Acquisition Using Synonym Sets*
Daniel Andrade, Masaki Tsuchida, Takashi Onishi and Kai Ishikawa

11:30-11:45 *Supersense Tagging for Arabic: the MT-in-the-Middle Attack*
Nathan Schneider, Behrang Mohit, Chris Dyer, Kemal Oflazer and Noah A. Smith

11:45-12:00 *Zipfian corruptions for robust POS tagging*
Anders Søgaard

Tuesday, June 11, 2013 (continued)

T1b: Sentiment Analysis and Topic Modeling

10:45-11:00 *A Multi-Dimensional Bayesian Approach to Lexical Style*
Julian Brooke and Graeme Hirst

11:00-11:15 *Unsupervised Domain Tuning to Improve Word Sense Disambiguation*
Judita Preiss and Mark Stevenson

11:15-11:30 *What's in a Domain? Multi-Domain Learning for Multi-Attribute Data*
Mahesh Joshi, Mark Dredze, William W. Cohen and Carolyn P. Rosé

11:30-11:45 *An opinion about opinions about opinions: subjectivity and the aggregate reader*
Asad Sayeed

11:45-12:00 *An Examination of Regret in Bullying Tweets*
Jun-Ming Xu, Benjamin Burchfiel, Xiaojin Zhu and Amy Bellmore

T1c: Spoken Language Processing

10:45-11:00 *A Cross-language Study on Automatic Speech Disfluency Detection*
Wen Wang, Andreas Stolcke, Jiahong Yuan and Mark Liberman

11:00-11:15 *Distributional semantic models for the evaluation of disordered language*
Masoud Rouhizadeh, Emily Prud'hommeaux, Brian Roark and Jan van Santen

11:15-11:30 *Atypical Prosodic Structure as an Indicator of Reading Level and Text Difficulty*
Julie Medero and Mari Ostendorf

11:30-11:45 *Using Document Summarization Techniques for Speech Data Subset Selection*
Kai Wei, Yuzong Liu, Katrin Kirchhoff and Jeff Bilmes

11:45-12:00 *Semi-Supervised Discriminative Language Modeling with Out-of-Domain Text Data*
Arda Çelebi and Murat Saraçlar

12:00–2:00 Lunch (and Business Meeting 1-2)

T2a: Semantics

T2b: Information Extraction

Tuesday, June 11, 2013 (continued)

T2c: Discourse and Dialog

2:00-2:15 *Differences in User Responses to a Wizard-of-Oz versus Automated System*
Jesse Thomason and Diane Litman

2:15-2:30 *Improving the Quality of Minority Class Identification in Dialog Act Tagging*
Adinoyi Omuya, Vinodkumar Prabhakaran and Owen Rambow

2:30-2:45 *Discourse Connectors for Latent Subjectivity in Sentiment Analysis*
Rakshit Trivedi and Jacob Eisenstein

2:45-3:00 *Coherence Modeling for the Automated Assessment of Spontaneous Spoken Responses*
Xinhao Wang, Keelan Evanini and Klaus Zechner

3:00-3:15 *Disfluency Detection Using Multi-step Stacked Learning*
Xian Qian and Yang Liu

3:15–3:45 Break

T3a: Semantics

4:10-4:35 *Using Semantic Unification to Generate Regular Expressions from Natural Language*
Nate Kushman and Regina Barzilay

4:35-5:00 *Probabilistic Frame Induction*
Jackie Chi Kit Cheung, Hoifung Poon and Lucy Vanderwende

5:00–5:25 *A Quantum-Theoretic Approach to Distributional Semantics*
William Blacoe, Elham Kashefi and Mirella Lapata

Tuesday, June 11, 2013 (continued)

T3b: Information Extraction

3:45-4:10 *Answer Extraction as Sequence Tagging with Tree Edit Distance*
Xuchen Yao, Benjamin Van Durme, Chris Callison-Burch and Peter Clark

4:10-4:35 *Open Information Extraction with Tree Kernels*
Ying Xu, Mi-Young Kim, Kevin Quinn, Randy Goebel and Denilson Barbosa

4:35-5:00 *Finding What Matters in Questions*
Xiaoqiang Luo, Hema Raghavan, Vittorio Castelli, Sameer Maskey and Radu Florian

5:00-5:25 *A Just-In-Time Keyword Extraction from Meeting Transcripts*
Hyun-Je Song, Junho Go, Seong-Bae Park and Se-Young Park

T3c: Discourse

3:45-4:10 *Same Referent, Different Words: Unsupervised Mining of Opaque Coreferent Mentions*
Marta Recasens, Matthew Can and Daniel Jurafsky

4:10-4:35 *Global Inference for Bridging Anaphora Resolution*
Yufang Hou, Katja Markert and Michael Strube

4:35-5:00 *Classifying Temporal Relations with Rich Linguistic Knowledge*
Jennifer D'Souza and Vincent Ng

5:00-5:25 *Improved Information Structure Analysis of Scientific Documents Through Discourse and Lexical Constraints*
Yufan Guo, Roi Reichart and Anna Korhonen

7:00–9:30 Banquet

Wednesday, June 12, 2013

9:00–10:10 Invited talk by Kathleen McKeown – Natural Language Applications from Fact to Fiction

10:10–10:40 Break

W1a: Machine Translation

10:40-11:05 *Adaptation of Reordering Models for Statistical Machine Translation*
Boxing Chen, George Foster and Roland Kuhn

11:05-11:30 *Multi-Metric Optimization Using Ensemble Tuning*
Baskaran Sankaran, Anoop Sarkar and Kevin Duh

11:30-11:55 *Grouping Language Model Boundary Words to Speed K–Best Extraction from Hypergraphs*
Kenneth Heafield, Philipp Koehn and Alon Lavie

11:55-12:20 *A Systematic Bayesian Treatment of the IBM Alignment Models*
Yarin Gal and Phil Blunsom

W1b: Semantics

10:40-11:05 *Unsupervised Metaphor Identification Using Hierarchical Graph Factorization Clustering*
Ekaterina Shutova and Lin Sun

11:05-11:30 *Three Knowledge-Free Methods for Automatic Lexical Chain Extraction*
Steffen Remus and Chris Biemann

11:30-11:55 *Combining Heterogeneous Models for Measuring Relational Similarity*
Alisa Zhila, Wen-tau Yih, Christopher Meek, Geoffrey Zweig and Tomas Mikolov

Wednesday, June 12, 2013 (continued)

W1c: Social Media Processing

10:40-11:05 *Broadly Improving User Classification via Communication-Based Name and Location Clustering on Twitter*
Shane Bergsma, Mark Dredze, Benjamin Van Durme, Theresa Wilson and David Yarowsky

11:05-11:30 *To Link or Not to Link? A Study on End-to-End Tweet Entity Linking*
Stephen Guo, Ming-Wei Chang and Emre Kiciman

11:30-11:55 *A Latent Variable Model for Viewpoint Discovery from Threaded Forum Posts*
Minghui Qiu and Jing Jiang

11:55-12:20 *Identifying Intention Posts in Discussion Forums*
Zhiyuan Chen, Bing Liu, Meichun Hsu, Malu Castellanos and Riddhiman Ghosh

12:20–2:00 Lunch

W2a: Parsing and Syntax

2:25-2:50 *Dependency-based empty category detection via phrase structure trees*
Nianwen Xue and Yaqin Yang

2:50-3:15 *Target Language Adaptation of Discriminative Transfer Parsers*
Oscar Täckström, Ryan McDonald and Joakim Nivre

W2b: Dialog

2:00-2:25 *Emergence of Gricean Maxims from Multi-Agent Decision Theory*
Adam Vogel, Max Bodoia, Christopher Potts and Daniel Jurafsky

2:25-2:50 *Open Dialogue Management for Relational Databases*
Ben Hixon and Rebecca J. Passonneau

2:50-3:15 *A method for the approximation of incremental understanding of explicit utterance meaning using predictive models in finite domains*
David DeVault and David Traum

Wednesday, June 12, 2013 (continued)

W2c: Annotation and Language Resources

2:00-2:25 *Paving the Way to a Large-scale Pseudosense-annotated Dataset*
Mohammad Taher Pilehvar and Roberto Navigli

2:25-2:50 *Labeling the Languages of Words in Mixed-Language Documents using Weakly Supervised Methods*
Ben King and Steven Abney

2:50-3:15 *Learning Whom to Trust with MACE*
Dirk Hovy, Taylor Berg-Kirkpatrick, Ashish Vaswani and Eduard Hovy

3:15–3:45 Break

W3a: Semantics and Syntax

3:45-4:10 *Supervised All-Words Lexical Substitution using Delexicalized Features*
György Szarvas, Chris Biemann and Iryna Gurevych

4:10-4:35 *A Tensor-based Factorization Model of Semantic Compositionality*
Tim Van de Cruys, Thierry Poibeau and Anna Korhonen

W3b: Summarization and Generation

3:45-4:10 *A Participant-based Approach for Event Summarization Using Twitter Streams*
Chao Shen, Fei Liu, Fuliang Weng and Tao Li

4:10-4:35 *Towards Coherent Multi-Document Summarization*
Janara Christensen, Mausam, Stephen Soderland and Oren Etzioni

4:35-5:00 *Generating Expressions that Refer to Visible Objects*
Margaret Mitchell, Kees van Deemter and Ehud Reiter

W3c: Morphology and Phonology

Model With Minimal Translation Units, But Decode With Phrases

Nadir Durrani*
University of Edinburgh
dnadir@inf.ed.ac.uk

Alexander Fraser **Helmut Schmid**
University of Stuttgart
fraser,schmid@ims.uni-stuttgart.de

Abstract

N-gram-based models co-exist with their phrase-based counterparts as an alternative SMT framework. Both techniques have pros and cons. While the N-gram-based framework provides a better model that captures both source and target contexts and avoids spurious phrasal segmentation, the ability to memorize and produce larger translation units gives an edge to the phrase-based systems during decoding, in terms of better search performance and superior selection of translation units. In this paper we combine N-gram-based modeling with phrase-based decoding, and obtain the benefits of both approaches. Our experiments show that using this combination not only improves the search accuracy of the N-gram model but that it also improves the BLEU scores. Our system outperforms state-of-the-art phrase-based systems (Moses and Phrasal) and N-gram-based systems by a significant margin on German, French and Spanish to English translation tasks.

1 Introduction

Statistical Machine Translation advanced from word-based models (Brown et al., 1993) towards more sophisticated models that take contextual information into account. Phrase-based (Och and Ney, 2004; Koehn et al., 2003) and N-gram-based (Mariño et al., 2006) models are two instances of such frameworks. While the two models have some common properties, they are substantially different.

Phrase-based systems employ a simple and effective machinery by learning larger chunks of translation called phrases[1]. Memorizing larger units enables the phrase-based model to learn local dependencies such as short reorderings, idioms, insertions and deletions, etc. The model however, has the following drawbacks: i) it makes independence assumptions over phrases ignoring the contextual information outside of phrases ii) it has issues handling long-distance reordering iii) it has the spurious phrasal segmentation problem which allows multiple derivations of a bilingual sentence pair having different model scores for each segmentation.

Modeling with minimal translation units helps address some of these issues. The N-gram-based SMT framework is based on tuples. Tuples are minimal translation units composed of source and target cepts[2]. N-gram-based models are Markov models over sequences of tuples (Mariño et al., 2006; Crego and Mariño, 2006) or operations encapsulating tuples (Durrani et al., 2011). This mechanism has several useful properties. Firstly, no phrasal independence assumption is made. The model has access to both source and target context outside of phrases. Secondly the model learns a unique derivation of a bilingual sentence given its alignment, thus avoiding the spurious segmentation problem.

Using minimal translation units, however, results in a higher number of search errors because of i)

*Much of the work presented here was carried out while the first author was at the University of Stuttgart.

[1] A phrase-pair in PBSMT is a sequence of source and target words that is translation of each other, and is not necessarily a linguistic constituent. Phrases are built by combining minimal translation units and ordering information.

[2] A cept is a group of words in one language that is translated as a minimal unit in one specific context (Brown et al., 1993).

poor translation selection, ii) inaccurate future-cost estimates and iii) incorrect early pruning of hypotheses that would produce better model scores if allowed to continue. In order to deal with these problems, search is carried out only on a graph of pre-calculated orderings, and ad-hoc reordering limits are imposed to constrain the search space (Crego et al., 2005; Crego and Mariño, 2006), or a higher beam size is used in decoding (Durrani et al., 2011). The ability to memorize and produce larger translation chunks during decoding, on the other hand, gives a distinct advantage to the phrase-based system during search. Phrase-based systems i) have access to uncommon translations, ii) do not require higher beam sizes, iii) have more accurate future-cost estimates because of the availability of phrase-internal language model context before search is started. To illustrate this consider the German-English phrase-pair "schoß ein Tor – scored a goal", composed from the tuples (cept-pairs) "schoß – scored", "ein – a" and "Tor – goal". It is likely that the N-gram system does not have the tuple "schoß – scored" in its n-best translation options because "scored" is an uncommon translation for "schoß" outside the sports domain. Even if "schoß – scored" is hypothesized, it will be ranked quite low in the stack until "ein" and "Tor" are generated in the next steps. A higher beam is required to prevent it from getting pruned. Phrase-based systems, on the other hand, are likely to have access to the phrasal unit "schoß ein Tor – scored a goal" and can generate it in a single step. Moreover, a more accurate future-cost estimate can be computed because of the available context internal to the phrase.

In this work, we extend the N-gram model, based on operation sequences (Durrani et al., 2011), to use phrases during decoding. The main idea is to study whether a combination of modeling with minimal translation units and using phrasal information during decoding helps to solve the above-mentioned problems.

The remainder of this paper is organized as follows. The next two sections review phrase-based and N-gram-based SMT. Section 2 provides a comparison of phrase-based and N-gram-based SMT. Section 3 summarizes the operation sequence model (OSM), the main baseline for this work. Section 4 analyzes the search problem when decoding with minimal units. Section 5 discusses how information available in phrases can be used to improve search performance. Section 6 presents the results of this work. We conducted experiments on the German-to-English and French-to-English translation tasks and found that using phrases in decoding improves both search accuracy and BLEU scores. Finally we compare our system with two state-of-the-art phrase-based systems (Moses and Phrasal) and two state-of-the-art N-gram-based systems (Ncode and OSM) on standard translation tasks.

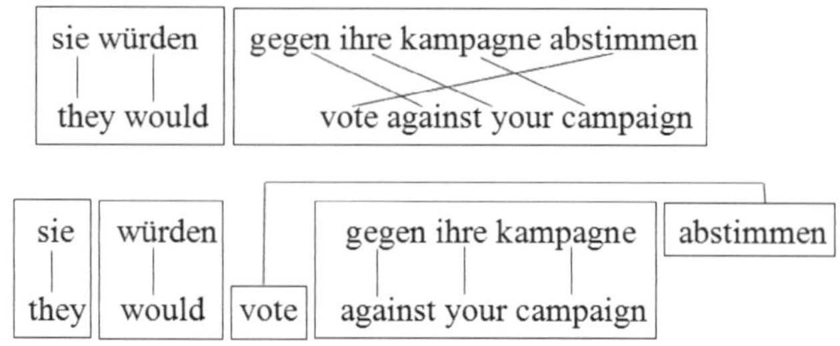

Figure 1: Different Segmentations of a Bilingual Sentence Pair

2 Previous Work

Phrase-based and N-gram-based SMT are alternative frameworks for string-to-string translation. Phrase-based SMT segments a bilingual sentence pair into phrases that are continuous sequences of words (Och and Ney, 2004; Koehn et al., 2003) or discontinuous sequences of words (Galley and Manning, 2010). These phrases are then reordered through a lexicalized reordering model that takes into account the orientation of a phrase with respect to its previous phrase (Tillmann and Zhang, 2005) or block of phrases (Galley and Manning, 2008).

There are several drawbacks of the phrase-based model. Firstly it makes an independence assumption over phrases, according to which phrases are translated independently of each other, thus ignoring the contextual information outside of the phrasal boundary. This problem is corrected by the monolingual language model that takes context into account. But often the language model cannot compensate for the dispreference of the translation model for nonlocal dependencies. The second problem is that the model is unaware of the actual phrasal segmentation of a sentence during training. It therefore learns all possible ways of segmenting a bilingual sentence. Different segmentations of a bilingual sentence result in different probability scores for the translation and reordering models, causing spurious ambiguity in the model. See Figure 1. In the first segmentation, the model learns the lexical and reordering probabilities of the phrases "sie würden – they would" and "gegen ihre kampagne abstimmen – vote against your campaign". In the second segmentation, the model learns the lexical and reordering probabilities of the phrases "sie – they" "würden – would", "abstimmen – vote", "gegen ihre kampagne – against your campaign". Both segmentations result in different translation and reordering scores. This kind of ambiguity in the model subsequently results in the presence of many different equivalent segmentations in the search space. Also note that the two segmentations contain different information. From the first segmentation the model learns the dependency between the verb "abstimmen – vote" and the phrase "gegen ihre kampagne – against your campaign". The second segmentation allows the model to capture the reordering of the complex verb predicate "würden – would" and "abstimmen – vote" by learning that the verb "abstimmen – vote" is discontinuous with respect to the auxiliary. This information cannot be captured in the first segmentation because of the phrasal independence assumption and stiff phrasal boundaries. The model loses one of the dependencies depending upon which segmentation it chooses during decoding.

N-gram-based SMT is an instance of a joint model that generates source and target strings together in bilingual translation units called tuples. Tuples are essentially phrases but they are atomic units that cannot be decomposed any further. This condition of atomicity results in a unique segmentation of the bilingual sentence pair given its alignments. The model does not make any phrasal independence assumption and generates a tuple by looking at a context of $n-1$ previous tuples (or operations). This allows the N-gram model to model all the dependencies through a single derivation.

The main drawback of N-gram-based SMT is its poor search mechanism which is inherent from using minimal translation units during search. Decoding with tuples has problems with a high number of search errors caused by lower translation coverage, inaccurate future-cost estimation and pruning of correct hypotheses (see Section 4.2 for details). Crego and Mariño (2006) proposed a way to couple reordering and search through POS-based rewrite rules. These rules are learned during training when units with crossing alignments are unfolded through source linearization to form minimal tuples. For example, in Figure 1, the N-gram-based MT will linearize the word sequence "gegen ihre kampagne abstimmen" to "abstimmen gegen ihre kampagne", so that it is in the same order as the English words. It also learns a POS-rule "IN PRP NN VB $\rightarrow$ VB IN PRP NN". The POS-based rewrite rules serve to precompute the orderings that are hypothesized during decoding. Coupling reordering and search allows the N-gram model to arrange hypotheses in 2^m stacks (for an m word source sentence), each containing hypotheses that cover exactly the same foreign words. This removes the need for future-cost estimation[3]. Secondly, memorizing POS-based rules enables phrase-based like reordering, however without lexical selection. There are three drawbacks of this approach. Firstly, lexical generation and reordering are decoupled. Search is only performed on a small number of reorderings, pre-calculated using the source side and completely ignoring the target-side. And lastly, the POS-based rules face data sparsity problems especially in the case of long distance reorderings.

Durrani et al. (2011) recently addressed these problems by proposing an operation sequence N-gram model which strongly couples translation and reordering, hypothesizes all possible reorderings and does not require POS-based rules. Representing bilingual sentences as a sequence of operations enables them to memorize phrases and lexical reordering triggers like PBSMT. However, using minimal units during decoding and searching over all possible reorderings means that hypotheses can no longer be arranged in 2^m stacks. The problem of inaccurate future-cost estimates resurfaces resulting in more search errors. A higher beam size of 500 is therefore used to produce translation units in comparison to phrase-based systems. This, however, still does not eliminate all search errors. This paper shows that using phrases instead of cepts in de-

[3]Using m stacks with future-cost estimation is a more efficient solution but is not used "due to the complexity of accurately computing these estimations in the N-gram architecture" (Crego et al., 2011).

coding improves the search accuracy and translation quality. It also shows that using some phrasal information in cept-based decoding captures some of these improvements.

3 Operation Sequence Model

The N-gram model with integrated reordering models a *sequence of operations* obtained through the transformation of a bilingual sentence pair. An operation can either be to i) generate a sequence of source and target words, ii) to insert a gap as a placeholder for skipped words, iii) or to jump forward and backward in a sentence to translate words discontinuously. The translate operation Generate(X,Y) encapsulates the translation tuple (X,Y). It generates source and target translations simultaneously[4]. This is similar to N-gram-based SMT except that the tuples in the N-gram-based model are generated monotonically, whereas in this case lexical generation and reordering information is strongly coupled in an operation sequence.

Consider the phrase pair:

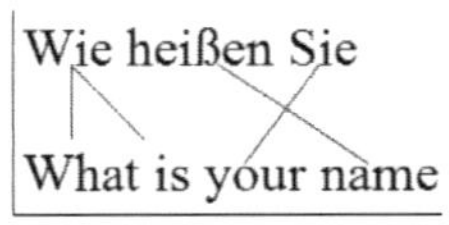

The model memorizes it through the sequence:

Generate(Wie, What is) → Gap → Generate (Sie, your) → Jump Back (1) → Generate (heissen, name)

Let $O = o_1, \ldots, o_{j-1}$ be a sequence of operations as hypothesized by the translator to generate the bilingual sentence pair $\langle F, E \rangle$ with an alignment function A. The translation model is defined as:

$$p(F, E, A) = p(o_1^J) = \prod_{j=1}^{J} p(o_j | o_{j-n+1}, ..., o_{j-1})$$

where n indicates the amount of context used. The translation model is implemented as an N-gram model of operations using SRILM-Toolkit (Stolcke, 2002) with Kneser-Ney smoothing. A 9-gram model is used. Several count-based features such as gap and open gap penalties and distance-based features such as gap-width and reordering distance are added to the model, along with the lexical weighting and length penalty features in a standard log-linear framework (Durrani et al., 2011).

[4]The generation is carried out in the order of the target language E.

4 Search

4.1 Overview of Decoding Framework

The decoding framework used in the operation sequence model is based on Pharaoh (Koehn, 2004a). The decoder uses beam search to build up the translation from left to right. The hypotheses are arranged in m stacks such that stack i maintains hypotheses that have already translated i many foreign words. The ultimate goal is to find the best scoring hypothesis, that has translated all the words in the foreign sentence. The overall process can be roughly divided into the following steps: i) extraction of translation units ii) future-cost estimation, iii) hypothesis extension iv) recombination and pruning.

During the hypothesis extension each extracted phrase is translated into a sequence of operations. The reordering operations (gaps and jumps) are generated by looking at the position of the translator, the last foreign word generated etc. (Refer to Algorithm 1 in Durrani et al. (2011)). The probability of an operation depends on the $n-1$ previous operations. The model backs-off to the smaller n-grams of operations if the full history is unknown. We use Kneser-Ney smoothing to handle back-off[5].

4.2 Drawbacks of Cept-based Decoding

One of the main drawbacks of the operation sequence model is that it has a more difficult search problem than the phrase-based model. The operation model, although based on minimal translation units, can learn larger translation chunks by memorizing a sequence of operations. However, using cepts during decoding has the following drawbacks: i) the cept-based decoder does not have access to all the translation units that a phrase-based decoder uses as part of a larger phrase. ii) it requires a higher beam size to prevent early pruning of better hypotheses that lead toward higher model scores when allowed to continue and iii) it uses worse future-cost estimates than the phrase-based decoder.

Recall the example from the last section. For the cept-based decoder to generate the same phrasal translation, it requires three separate tuple translations “Wie – what is”, “Sie – your” and “heißen – name”. Here we are faced with three challenges.

[5]We also tried Witten-Bell and Good Turing methods of discounting and found Kneser-Ney smoothing to produce the best results.

Translation Coverage: The first problem is that the N-gram model does not have the same coverage of translation options. The English cepts "what is", "your" and "name" are not good candidate translations for the German cepts "Wie", "Sie" and "heißen", respectively. When extracting tuple translations for these cepts from the Europarl data for our system, the tuple "Wie – what is" is ranked 124th, "heißen – name" is ranked 56th, and "Sie – your" is ranked 9th in the list of n-best translation candidates. Typically only the 20 best translation options are used, to reduce the decoding time, and such phrasal units with less frequent cept translations are never hypothesized in the N-gram-based systems. The phrase-based system on the other hand can extract the phrase "Wie heißen Sie – what is your name" even if it is observed only once during training. A similar problem is also reported in Costa-jussà et al. (2007). When trying to reproduce the sentences in the n-best translation output of the phrase-based system, the N-gram-based system was only able to produce 37.5% of the sentences in the Spanish-to-English and 37.2% in the English-to-Spanish translation tasks. In comparison the phrase-based system was able to reproduce 57.5% and 48.6% of the sentences in the n-best translation output of the Spanish-to-English and English-to-Spanish N-gram-based systems.

Larger Beam Size: A related problem is that a higher beam size is required in cept-based decoding to prevent uncommon translations from getting pruned. The phrase-based system can generate the phrase-pair "Wie heißen Sie – what is your name" in a single step placing it directly into the stack three words to the right. The cept-based decoder generates this phrase in three stacks with the tuple translations "Wie – What is", "Sie – your" and "heißen – name". A very large stack size is required during decoding to prevent the pruning of "Wie – What is" which is ranked quite low in the stack until the tuple "Sie – your" is hypothesized in the next stack. Costa-jussà et al. (2007) reports a significant drop in the performance of N-gram-based SMT when a beam size of 10 is used instead of 50 in their experiments. For the (cept-based) operation sequence model, Durrani et al. (2011) required a stack size of 500. In comparison, the translation quality achieved by phrase-based SMT remains the same when varying the beam size between 5 and 50.

Future-Cost Estimation: A third problem is caused by inaccurate future-cost estimation. Using phrases helps phrase-based SMT to better estimate the future language model cost because of the larger context available, and allows the decoder to capture local (phrase-internal) reorderings in the future cost. In comparison the future cost for tuples is mostly unigram probabilities. The future-cost estimate for the phrase pair "Wie heißen Sie – What is your name" is estimated by calculating the cost of each feature. The language model cost, for example, is estimated in the phrase-based system as follows:

$$\mathrm{p_{lm}} = \mathrm{p(What)} \times \mathrm{p(is|What)} \times \mathrm{p(your|What\ is)} \times \mathrm{p(name|What\ is\ your)}$$

The cost of the direct phrase translation probability, one of the features used in the phrase translation model, is estimated as:

$$\mathrm{p_{tm}} = \mathrm{p(What\ is\ your\ name|Wie\ heißen\ Sie)}$$

Phrase-based SMT is aware during the preprocessing step that the words "Wie heißen Sie" may be translated as a phrase. This is helpful for estimating a more accurate future cost because the phrase-internal context is already available. The same is not true for the operation sequence model, to which only minimal units are available. The operation model does not have the information that "Wie heißen Sie" may be translated as a phrase during decoding. The future-cost estimate available to the operation model for the span covering "Wie heißen Sie" will have unigram probabilities for both the translation and language model:

$$\mathrm{p_{lm}} = \mathrm{p(What)} \times \mathrm{p(is|What)} \times \mathrm{p(your)} \times \mathrm{p(name)}$$

$$\mathrm{p_{tm}} = \mathrm{p(Generate(Wie,\ What\ is))} \times \mathrm{p(Generate(heißen,name))} \times \mathrm{p(Generate(Sie,\ your))}$$

Thus the future-cost estimate in the operation model is much worse than that of the phrase-based model. The poor future-cost estimation leads to search errors, causing a drop in the translation quality. A more accurate future-cost estimate for the translation model cost would be:

$$p_{tm} = \text{p(Generate(Wie,What is))} \times \text{p(Insert Gap|C)}$$
$$\times \text{ p(Generate(Sie,your)|C)} \times \text{p(Jump Back(1)|C)}$$
$$\text{p(Generate(heißen,name)|C)}$$

where C is the context, i.e., the $n-1$ previously generated operations. The future-cost estimates computed in this manner are much more accurate because they not only consider context, but also take the reordering operations into account.

5 N-gram Model with Phrase-based Decoding

In the last section we discussed the disadvantages of using cepts during search in a left-to-right decoding framework. We now define a method to empirically study the mentioned drawbacks and whether using information available in phrase-pairs during decoding can help improve search accuracy and translation quality.

5.1 Training

We extended the training steps in Durrani et al. (2011) to extract a phrase lexicon from the parallel data. We extract all phrase pairs of length 6 and below, that are consistent (Och et al., 1999) with the word alignments. Only continuous phrases as used in a traditional phrase-based system are extracted thus allowing only inside-out (Wu, 1997) type of alignments. The future cost of each feature component used in the log-linear model is calculated. The operation sequence required to hypothesize each phrase is generated and its future cost is calculated. The future costs of other features such as language models, lexicalized probability features, etc. are also estimated. The estimates of the count-based reordering penalties (gap penalty and open gap penalty) and the distance-based features (gap-width and reordering distance) could not be estimated previously with cepts but are available when using phrases.

5.2 Decoding

We extended the decoder developed by Durrani et al. (2011) and tried three ideas. In our primary experiments we enabled the decoder to use phrases instead of cepts. This allows the decoder to i) use phrase-internal context when computing the future-cost estimates, ii) hypothesize translation options not available to the cept-based decoder iii) cover multiple source words in a single step subsequently improving translation coverage and search. Note that using phrases instead of cepts during decoding, does not reintroduce the spurious phrasal segmentation problem as is present in the phrase-based system, because the model is built on minimal units which avoids segmentation ambiguity. Different compositions of the same phrasal unit lead to exactly the same model score. We therefore do not create any alternative compositions of the same phrasal unit during decoding. This option is not available in phrase-based decoding, because an alternative composition may lead towards a better model score.

In our secondary set of experiments, we used cept-based decoding but modified the decoder to use information available from the phrases extracted for the test sentences. Firstly, we used future-cost estimates from the extracted phrases (see system cept.500.fc in Table1). This however, leads to inconsistency in the cases where the future cost is estimated from some phrasal unit that cannot be generated through the available cept translations. For example, say the best cost to cover the sequence "Wie heißen Sie" is given by the phrase "What is your name". The 20-best translation options in cept-based system, however, do not have tuples "Wie – What" and "heißen – name". To remove this discrepancy, we add all such tuples that are used in the extracted phrases, to the list of extracted cepts (system cept.500.fc.t). We also studied how much gain we obtain by only adding tuples from phrases and using cept-based future-cost estimates (system cept.500.t).

5.3 Evaluation Method

To evaluate our modifications we apply a simple strategy. We hold the model constant and change the search to use the baseline decoder, which uses minimal translation units, or the modified decoders that use phrasal information during decoding. The model parameters are optimized by running MERT (minimum error rate training) for the baseline decoder on the dev set. After we have the optimized weights, we run the baseline decoder and our modifications on the test. Note that because all the decoding runs use the same feature vector, the model stays constant, only search changes. This allows us to compare different decoding runs, obtained using the same parameters, but different search strategies, in terms of model scores. We compute a search accuracy and translation quality for each run.

Search accuracy is computed by comparing translation hypotheses from the different decoding runs. We form a collection of the best scoring hypotheses by traversing through all the runs and selecting the sentences with highest model score. For each input sentence we select a single best scoring hypothesis. The best scoring hypothesis can be contributed from several runs. In this case all these runs will be given a credit for that particular sentence when computing the search accuracy. The search accuracy of a decoding run is defined as the percentage of hypotheses that were contributed from this run, when forming a list of best scoring hypotheses. For example, for a test set of 1000 sentences, the accuracy of a decoding run would be 30% if it was able to produce the best scoring hypothesis for 300 sentences in the test set. Translation quality is measured through BLEU (Papineni et al., 2002).

6 Experimental Setup

We initially experimented with two language pairs: German-to-English (G-E) and French-to-English (F-E). We trained our system and the baseline systems on most of the data[6] made available for the translation task of the *Fourth Workshop on Statistical Machine Translation*.[7] We used 1M bilingual sentences, for the estimation of the translation model and 2M sentences from the monolingual corpus (news commentary) which also contains the English part of the bilingual corpus. Word alignments are obtained by running GIZA++ (Och and Ney, 2003) with the grow-diag-final-and (Koehn et al., 2005) symmetrization heuristic. We follow the training steps described in Durrani et al. (2011), consisting of i) post-processing the alignments to remove discontinuous and unaligned target cepts, ii) conversion of bilingual alignments into operation sequences, iii) estimation of the n-gram language models.

[6]We did not use all the available data due to scalability issues. The scores reported are therefore well below those obtained by the systems submitted to the WMT evaluation series.

[7]http://www.statmt.org/wmt09/translation-task.html

6.1 Search Accuracy Results

We divided our evaluation into two halves. In the first half we carried out experiments to measure search accuracy and translation quality of our decoders against the baseline cept-based OSM (cept.500) that uses minimal translation units with a stack size of 500. We used the version of the cept-based OSM system that does not allow discontinuous[8] source cepts. To increase the speed of the system we used a hard reordering limit of 15[9], in the baseline decoder and our modifications, disallowing jumps that are beyond 15 words from the first open gap. For each extracted cept or phrase 10-best translation options are extracted.

Using phrases in search reduces the decoding speed. In order to make a fair comparison, both the phrase-based and the baseline cept-based decoders should be allowed to run for the same amount of time. We therefore reduced the stack size in the phrase-based decoder so that it runs in the same amount of time as the cept-based decoder. We found that using a stack size of 200[10] for the phrase-based decoder was comparable in speed to using a stack-size of 500 in the cept-based decoding.

We first tuned the baseline on dev[11] to obtain an optimized weight vector. We then ran the baseline and our decoders as discussed in Section 5.2 on the dev-test. Then we repeated this experiment by tuning the weights with our phrase-based decoder (using a stack size of 100) and ran all the decoders again using the new weights.

Table 1 shows the average search accuracies and BLEU scores of the two experiments. Using phrases during decoding in the G-E experiments resulted in a statistically significant[12] 0.69 BLEU points gain comparing our best system phrase.200 with the baseline system cept.500. We mark a result as sig-

[8]Discontinuous source-side units did not lead to any improvements in (Durrani et al., 2011) and increased the decoding times by multiple folds. We also found these to be less useful.

[9]Imposing a hard reordering limit significantly reduced the decoding time and also slightly increased the BLEU scores.

[10]Higher stack sizes leads to improvement in model scores for both German-English and French-English and slight improvement of BLEU in the case of the former.

[11]We used news-dev2009a as dev and news-dev2009b as dev-test and tuned the weights with Z-MERT (Zaidan, 2009).

[12]We use bootstrap resampling (Koehn, 2004b) to test our results against the baseline result.

System	German		French	
	Acc.	BLEU	Acc.	BLEU
Baseline System cept.stack-size				
cept.50	25.95%	19.50	42.10%	21.44
cept.100	30.04%	19.79	47.32%	21.70
cept.200	35.17%	19.98	51.47%	21.82
cept.500	41.56%	20.14	54.93%	21.87
Our Cept-based Decoders				
cept.500.fc	48.44%	20.52*	54.73%	21.86
cept.500.t	52.24%	20.34	67.95%	22.00
cept.500.fc.t	61.81%	20.53*	67.76%	21.96
Our Phrase-based Decoders				
phrase.50	58.88%	20.58*	80.83%	22.04
phrase.100	69.85%	20.73*	88.34%	22.13
phrase.200	79.71%	20.83*	92.93%	22.17*

Table 1: Search Accuracies (Acc.) and BLEU scores of the Baseline and Our Decoders with different Stack Sizes (fc = Future Cost Estimated from Phrases, t = Cept Translation Options enriched from Phrases)

nificant if the improvement shown by our decoder over the baseline decoder (cept.500) is significant at the $p \leq 0.05$ level, in both the runs. All the outputs that show statistically significant improvements over the baseline decoder (cept.500) in Table 1 are marked with an asterisk.

The search accuracy of our best system (phrase.200), in G-E experiments is roughly 80%, which means that 80% of the times the phrase-based decoder (using stack size 200) was able to produce the same model score or a better model score than the cept-based decoders (using a stack size of 500). Our F-E experiments also showed improvements in BLEU and model scores. The search accuracy of our best system phrase.200 is roughly 93% as compared with 55% in the baseline decoder (cept.500) giving a BLEU point gain of +0.30 over the baseline.

Our modifications to the cept-based decoder also showed improvements. We found that extending the cept translation table (cept.500.t) using phrases helps both in G-E and F-E experiments by extending the list of n-best translation options by 18% and 18.30% respectively. Using future costs estimated from phrases (cept.500.fc) improved both search accuracy and BLEU scores in G-E experiments, but does not lead to any improvements in the F-E experiments, as both BLEU and model scores drop slightly. We looked at a few examples where the model score dropped and found that in these cases, the best scoring hypotheses are ranked very low earlier in the decoding and make their way to the top gradually in subsequent steps. A slight difference in the future-cost estimate prunes these hypotheses in one or the other decoder. We found future cost to be more critical in G-E than F-E experiments. This can be explained by the fact that more reordering is required in G-E and it is necessary to account for the reordering operations and jump-based features (gap-based penalties, reordering distance and gap-width) in the future-cost estimation. F-E on the other hand is largely monotonic except for a few short distance reorderings such as flipping noun and adjective.

6.2 Comparison with other Baseline Systems

In the second half of our evaluation we compared our best system phrase.200 with the baseline system cept.500, and other state-of-the-art phrase-based and N-gram-based systems on German-to-English, French-to-English, and Spanish-to-English tasks[13]. We used the official evaluation data (news-test sets) from the Statistical Machine Translation Workshops 2009-2011 for all three language pairs (German, Spanish and French). The feature weights for all the systems are tuned using the dev set news-dev2009a. We separately tune the baseline system (cept.500) and the phrase-based system (phrase.200) and do not hold the lambda vector constant like before.

Baseline Systems: We also compared our system with i) Moses (Koehn et al., 2007), ii) Phrasal[14] (Cer et al., 2010), and iii) Ncode (Crego et al., 2011).

We used the default stack sizes of 100 for Moses[15], 200 for Phrasal, 25 for Ncode (with 2^m stacks). A 5-gram English language model is used. Both phrase-based systems use 20-best phrases for translation, Ncode uses 25-best tuple translations. The training and test data for Ncode was tagged using *TreeTagger* (Schmid, 1994). All the baseline systems used lexicalized reordering model. A hard reordering limit[16] of 6 words is used as a default in

[13] We did not include the results of Spanish in the previous section due to space limitations but these are similar to those of the French-to-English translation task.

[14] Phrasal provides two extensions to Moses: i) hierarchical reordering model (Galley and Manning, 2008) and ii) discontinuous phrases (Galley and Manning, 2010).

[15] Using stacks sizes from $200-1000$ did not improve results.

[16] We tried to increase the distortion limit in the baseline sys-

both the baseline phrase-based systems. Amongst the other defaults we retained the hard source gap penalty of 15 and a target gap penalty of 7 in Phrasal. We provide Moses and Ncode with the same post-edited alignments[17] from which we removed target-side discontinuities. We feed the original alignments to Phrasal because of its ability to learn discontinuous source and target phrases. All the systems use MERT for the optimization of the weight vector.

	$\mathbf{M_s}$	$\mathbf{P_d}$	$\mathbf{N_c}$	$\mathbf{C_{500}}$	$\mathbf{P_{200}}$
German-to-English					
MT09	18.73*	19.00*	18.37*	19.06*	19.66
MT10	18.58*	18.96*	18.64*	19.12*	19.70
MT11	17.38*	17.58*	17.49*	17.87*	18.19
French-to-English					
MT09	24.61*	24.73*	24.28*	24.94*	25.27
MT10	23.69*	23.09*	23.96	23.90*	24.25
MT11	25.17*	25.55*	24.92*	25.40*	25.92
Spanish-to-English					
MT09	24.38*	24.63	24.72	24.48*	24.72
MT10	25.55*	25.66*	25.87	25.68*	26.10
MT11	25.72*	26.17*	26.36*	26.48	26.67

Table 2: Comparison on 3-Test Sets – $\mathbf{M_s}$ = Moses, $\mathbf{P_d}$ = Phrasal (Discontinuous Phrases), $\mathbf{N_c}$ = Ncode, $\mathbf{C_{500}}$ = Cept.500, $\mathbf{P_{200}}$ = Phrase.200

Table 2 compares the performance of our phrase-based decoder against the baselines. Our system shows an improvement over all the baseline systems for the G-E pair, in 11 out of 12 cases in the F-E pair and in 8 out of 12 cases in the S-E language pair. We mark a baseline with "*" to indicate that our decoder shows an improvement over this baseline result which is significant at the $p \leq 0.05$ level.

7 Conclusion and Future Work

We proposed a combination of using a model based on minimal units and decoding with phrases. Modeling with minimal units enables us to learn local and non-local dependencies in a unified manner and avoid spurious segmentation ambiguities. However, using minimal units also in the search presents a significant challenge because of the poor translation coverage, inaccurate future-cost estimates and the pruning of the correct hypotheses. Phrase-based SMT on the other hand overcomes these drawbacks by using larger translation chunks during search. However, the drawback of the phrase-based model is the phrasal independence assumption, spurious ambiguity in segmentation and a weak mechanism to handle non-local reorderings. We showed that combining a model based on minimal units with phrase-based decoding can improve both search accuracy and translation quality. We also showed that the phrasal information can be indirectly used in cept-based decoding with improved results. We tested our system against the state-of-the-art phrase-based and N-gram-based systems, for German-to-English, French-to-English, and Spanish-to-English for three standard test sets. Our system showed statistically significant improvements over all the baseline systems in most of the cases. We have shown the benefits of using phrase-based search with a model based on minimal units. In future work, we would like to study whether a phrase-based system like Moses or Phrasal can profit from an OSM-style or N-gram-style feature. Feng et al. (2010) previously showed that adding a linearized source-side language model in a phrase-based system helped. It would also be interesting to study whether the insight of using minimal units for modeling and phrase-based search would hold for hierarchical SMT. Vaswani et al. (2011) recently showed that a Markov model over the derivation history of minimal rules can obtain the same translation quality as using grammars formed with composed rules.

Acknowledgments

We would like to thank the anonymous reviewers for their helpful feedback and suggestions. Nadir Durrani and Alexander Fraser were funded by Deutsche Forschungsgemeinschaft grant Models of Morphosyntax for Statistical Machine Translation. Nadir Durrani was partially funded by the European Union Seventh Framework Programme (FP7/2007-2013) under grant agreement n° 287658. Helmut Schmid was supported by Deutsche Forschungsgemeinschaft grant SFB 732. This work was supported in part by the IST Programme of the European Community, under the PASCAL2 Network of Excellence, IST-2007-216886. This publication only reflects the authors' views.

tems to 15 (in G-E experiments) as used in our systems but the results dropped significantly in case of Moses and slightly for Phrasal so we used the default limits for both decoders.

[17]Using post-processed alignments gave slightly better results than the original alignments for these baseline systems. Details are omitted due to space limitation.

References

Peter F. Brown, Stephen A. Della Pietra, Vincent J. Della Pietra, and R. L. Mercer. 1993. The Mathematics of Statistical Machine Translation: Parameter Estimation. *Computational Linguistics*, 19(2):263–311.

Daniel Cer, Michel Galley, Daniel Jurafsky, and Christopher D. Manning. 2010. Phrasal: A Statistical Machine Translation Toolkit for Exploring New model Features. In *Proceedings of the NAACL HLT 2010 Demonstration Session*, pages 9–12, Los Angeles, California, June.

Marta R. Costa-jussà, Josep M. Crego, David Vilar, José A.R. Fonollosa, José B. Mariño, and Hermann Ney. 2007. Analysis and System Combination of Phrase- and N-Gram-Based Statistical Machine Translation Systems. In *Human Language Technologies 2007: The Conference of the North American Chapter of the Association for Computational Linguistics; Companion Volume, Short Papers*, pages 137–140, Rochester, New York, April.

Josep M. Crego and José B. Mariño. 2006. Improving Statistical MT by Coupling Reordering and Decoding. *Machine Translation*, 20(3):199–215.

Josep M. Crego, José B. Mariño, and Adrià de Gispert. 2005. Reordered Search and Unfolding Tuples for N-Gram-Based SMT. In *Proceedings of the 10th Machine Translation Summit (MT Summit X)*, pages 283–289, Phuket, Thailand.

Josep M. Crego, François Yvon, and José B. Mariño. 2011. Ncode: an Open Source Bilingual N-gram SMT Toolkit. *The Prague Bulletin of Mathematical Linguistics*, (96):49–58.

Nadir Durrani, Helmut Schmid, and Alexander Fraser. 2011. A Joint Sequence Translation Model with Integrated Reordering. In *Proceedings of the 49th Annual Meeting of the Association for Computational Linguistics: Human Language Technologies*, pages 1045–1054, Portland, Oregon, USA, June.

Minwei Feng, Arne Mauser, and Hermann Ney. 2010. A Source-side Decoding Sequence Model for Statistical Machine Translation. In *Conference of the Association for Machine Translation in the Americas 2010*, Denver, Colorado, USA, October.

Michel Galley and Christopher D. Manning. 2008. A Simple and Effective Hierarchical Phrase Reordering Model. In *Proceedings of the 2008 Conference on Empirical Methods in Natural Language Processing*, pages 848–856, Honolulu, Hawaii, October.

Michel Galley and Christopher D. Manning. 2010. Accurate Non-Hierarchical Phrase-Based Translation. In *Human Language Technologies: The 2010 Annual Conference of the North American Chapter of the Association for Computational Linguistics*, pages 966–974, Los Angeles, California, June. Association for Computational Linguistics.

Philipp Koehn, Franz J. Och, and Daniel Marcu. 2003. Statistical Phrase-Based Translation. In *Proceedings of HLT-NAACL*, pages 127–133, Edmonton, Canada.

Philipp Koehn, Amittai Axelrod, Alexandra Birch Mayne, Chris Callison-Burch, Miles Osborne, and David Talbot. 2005. Edinburgh System Description for the 2005 IWSLT Speech Translation Evaluation. In *International Workshop on Spoken Language Translation 2005*.

Philipp Koehn, Hieu Hoang, Alexandra Birch, Chris Callison-Burch, Marcello Federico, Nicola Bertoldi, Brooke Cowan, Wade Shen, Christine Moran, Richard Zens, Chris Dyer, Ondrej Bojar, Alexandra Constantin, and Evan Herbst. 2007. Moses: Open source toolkit for statistical machine translation. In *ACL 2007 Demonstrations*, Prague, Czech Republic.

Philipp Koehn. 2004a. Pharaoh: A Beam Search Decoder for Phrase-Based Statistical Machine Translation Models. In *AMTA*, pages 115–124.

Philipp Koehn. 2004b. Statistical Significance Tests for Machine Translation Evaluation. In Dekang Lin and Dekai Wu, editors, *Proceedings of EMNLP 2004*, pages 388–395, Barcelona, Spain, July.

José B. Mariño, Rafael E. Banchs, Josep M. Crego, Adrià de Gispert, Patrik Lambert, José A. R. Fonollosa, and Marta R. Costa-jussà. 2006. N-gram-Based Machine Translation. *Computational Linguistics*, 32(4):527–549.

Franz J. Och and Hermann Ney. 2003. A Systematic Comparison of Various Statistical Alignment Models. *Computational Linguistics*, 29(1):19–51.

Franz J. Och and Hermann Ney. 2004. The Alignment Template Approach to Statistical Machine Translation. *Computational Linguistics*, 30(1):417–449.

Franz J. Och, Christoph Tillmann, and Hermann Ney. 1999. Improved alignment models for statistical machine translation. In *Joint SIGDAT Conf. on Empirical Methods in Natural Language Processing and Very Large Corpora*, pages 20–28, University of Maryland, College Park, MD.

Kishore Papineni, Salim Roukos, Todd Ward, and Wei-Jing Zhu. 2002. BLEU: a method for automatic evaluation of machine translation. In *Proceedings of the 40th Annual Meeting on Association for Computational Linguistics*, ACL '02, pages 311–318, Morristown, NJ, USA.

Helmut Schmid. 1994. Probabilistic part-of-speech tagging using decision trees. In *International Conference on New Methods in Language Processing*, pages 44–49, Manchester, UK.

Andreas Stolcke. 2002. SRILM - An Extensible Language Modeling Toolkit. In *Intl. Conf. Spoken Language Processing*, Denver, Colorado.

Christoph Tillmann and Tong Zhang. 2005. A Localized Prediction Model for Statistical Machine Translation. In *Proceedings of the 43rd Annual Meeting of the Association for Computational Linguistics (ACL'05)*, pages 557–564, Ann Arbor, Michigan, June.

Ashish Vaswani, Haitao Mi, Liang Huang, and David Chiang. 2011. Rule Markov Models for Fast Tree-to-String Translation. In *Proceedings of the 49th Annual Meeting of the Association for Computational Linguistics: Human Language Technologies*, pages 856–864, Portland, Oregon, USA, June.

Dekai Wu. 1997. Stochastic Inversion Transduction Grammars and Bilingual Parsing of Parallel Corpora. *Computational Linguistics*, 23(3):377–403.

Omar F. Zaidan. 2009. Z-MERT: A Fully Configurable Open Source Tool for Minimum Error Rate Training of Machine Translation Systems. *The Prague Bulletin of Mathematical Linguistics*, 91:79–88.

Beyond Left-to-Right: Multiple Decomposition Structures for SMT

Hui Zhang*
USC/ISI
Los Angeles, CA 90089
hzhang@isi.edu

Kristina Toutanova
Microsoft Research
Redmond, WA 98502
kristout@microsoft.com

Chris Quirk
Microsoft Research
Redmond, WA 98502
chrisq@microsoft.com

Jianfeng Gao
Microsoft Research
Redmond, WA 98502
jfgao@microsoft.com

Abstract

Standard phrase-based translation models do not explicitly model context dependence between translation units. As a result, they rely on large phrase pairs and target language models to recover contextual effects in translation. In this work, we explore n-gram models over Minimal Translation Units (MTUs) to explicitly capture contextual dependencies across phrase boundaries in the channel model. As there is no single best direction in which contextual information should flow, we explore multiple decomposition structures as well as dynamic bidirectional decomposition. The resulting models are evaluated in an intrinsic task of lexical selection for MT as well as a full MT system, through n-best reranking. These experiments demonstrate that additional contextual modeling does indeed benefit a phrase-based system and that the direction of conditioning is important. Integrating multiple conditioning orders provides consistent benefit, and the most important directions differ by language pair.

1 Introduction

The translation procedure of a classical phrase-based translation model (Koehn et al., 2003) first divides the input sentence into a sequence of phrases, translates each phrase, explores reorderings of these translations, and then scores the resulting candidates with a linear combination of models. Conventional models include phrase-based channel models that effectively model each phrase as a large unigram, reordering models, and target language models. Of these models, only the target language model (and, to some weak extent, the lexicalized reordering model) captures some lexical dependencies that span phrase boundaries, though it is not able to model information from the source side. Larger phrases capture more contextual dependencies within a phrase, but individual phrases are still translated almost independently.

To address this limitation, several researchers have proposed bilingual n-gram Markov models (Marino et al., 2006) to capture contextual dependencies between phrase pairs. Much of their work is limited by the requirement "that the source and target side of a tuple of words are synchronized, i.e. that they occur in the same order in their respective languages" (Crego and Yvon, 2010).

For language pairs with significant typological divergences, such as Chinese-English, it is quite difficult to extract a synchronized sequence of units; in the limit, the smallest synchronized unit may be the whole sentence. Other approaches explore incorporation into syntax-based MT systems or replacing the phrasal translation system altogether.

We investigate the addition of MTUs to a phrasal translation system to improve modeling of context and to provide more robust estimation of long phrases. However, in a phrase-based system there is no single synchronized traversal order; instead, we may consider the translation units in many possible orders: left-to-right or right-to-left according to either the source or the target are natural choices. Alternatively we consider translating a particularly unambiguous unit in the middle of the sentence and building outwards from there. We investigate both consistent and dynamic decomposition orders in several language pairs, looking at distinct orders in isolation and combination.

*This research was conducted during the author's internship at Microsoft Research

2 Related work

Marino et al. (2006) proposed a translation model using a Markov model of bilingual n-grams, demonstrating state-of-the-art performance compared to conventional phrase-based models. Crego and Yvon (2010) further explored factorized n-gram approaches, though both models considered rather large n-grams; this paper focuses on small units with asynchronous orders in source and target. Durrani et al. (2011) developed a joint model that captures translation of contiguous and gapped units as well as reordering. Two prior approaches explored similar models in syntax based systems. MTUs have been used in dependency translation models (Quirk and Menezes, 2006) to augment syntax directed translation systems. Likewise in target language syntax systems, one can consider Markov models over minimal rules, where the translation probability of each rule is adjusted to include context information from parent rules (Vaswani et al., 2011).

Most prior work tends to replace the existing probabilities rather than augmenting them. We believe that Markov rules provide an additional signal but are not a replacement. Their distributions should be more informative than the so-called "lexical weighting" models, and less sparse than relative frequency estimates, though potentially not as effective for truly non-compositional units. Therefore, we explore the inclusion of all such information. Also, unlike prior work, we explore combinations of multiple decomposition orders, as well as dynamic decompositions. The most useful context for translation differs by language pair, an important finding when working with many language pairs.

We build upon a standard phrase-based approach (Koehn et al., 2003). This acts as a proposal distribution for translations; the MTU Markov models provide additional signal as to which translations are correct.

3 MTU n-gram Markov models

We begin by defining Minimal Translation Units (MTUs) and describing how to identify them in word-aligned text. Next we define n-gram Markov models over MTUs, which requires us to define traversal orders over MTUs.

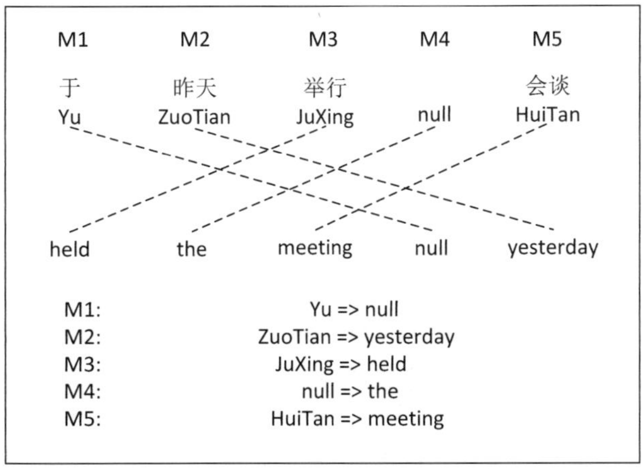

Figure 1: Word alignment and minimum translation units.

3.1 Definition of an MTU

Informally, the notion of a minimal translation unit is simple: it is a translation rule that cannot be broken down any further without violating the constraints of the rules. We restrict ourselves to *contiguous* MTUs. They are similar to small phrase pairs, though unlike phrase pairs we allow MTUs to have either an empty source or empty target side, thereby allowing insertion and deletion phrases. Conventional phrase pairs may be viewed as compositions of these MTUs up to a given size limit.

Consider a word-aligned sentence pair consisting of a sequence of source words $\mathbf{s} = s_1 \ldots s_m$, a sequence of target words $\mathbf{t} = t_1 \ldots t_n$, and a word alignment relation between the source and target words $\sim \subseteq \{1..m\} \times \{1..n\}$. A translation unit is a sequence of source words $s_i..s_j$ and a sequence of target words $t_k..t_l$ (one of which may be empty) such that for all aligned pairs $i' \sim k'$, we have $i \le i' \le j$ if and only if $k \le k' \le l$. This definition, nearly identical to that of a phrase pair (Koehn et al., 2003), relaxes the constraint that one aligned word must be present.

A set of translation units is a partition of the sentence pair if each source and target word is covered exactly once. *Minimal translation units* is the partition with the smallest average unit size, or, equivalently, the largest number of units. For example, Figure 1 shows a word-aligned sentence pair and its corresponding set of MTUs. We extract these minimal translation units with an algorithm similar to that of phrase extraction.

We train n-gram Markov models only over minimal rules for two reasons. First, the segmentation of the sentence pair is not unique under composed rules, which makes probability estimation complicated. Second, some phrase pairs are very large, which results in sparse data issues and compromises the model quality. Therefore, training an n-gram model over minimal translation units turns out to be a simple and clean choice: the resulting segmentation is unique, and the distribution is smooth. If we want to capture more context, we can simply increase the order of the Markov model.

Such Markov models address issues in large phrase-based translation approaches. Where standard phrase-based models rely upon large unigrams to capture contextual information, n-grams of minimal translation units allow a robust contextual model that is less constrained by segmentation.

3.2 MTU enumeration orders

When defining a joint probability distribution over MTUs of an aligned sentence pair, it is necessary to define a decomposition, or generation order for the sentence pair. For a single sequence in language modeling or synchronized sequences in channel modeling, the default enumeration order has been left-to-right.

Different decomposition orders have been used in part-of-speech tagging and named entity recognition (Tsuruoka and Tsujii, 2005). Intuitively, information from the left or right could be more useful for particular disambiguation choices. Our research on different decomposition orders was motivated by this work. When applying such ideas to machine translation, there are additional challenges and opportunities. The task exhibits much more ambiguity – the number of possible MTUs is in the millions. An opportunity arises from the reordering phenomenon in machine translation: while in POS tagging the natural decomposition orders to study are only left-to-right and right-to-left, in machine translation we can further distinguish source and target sentence orders.

We first define the source left-to-right and the target left-to-right orders of the aligned sets of MTUs. The definition is straightforward when there are no inserted or deleted word. To place the nulls corresponding to such word we use the following definition: the source position of the null for a target inserted word is just after the position of the last source word aligned to the closest preceding non-null aligned target word. The target position for a null corresponding to a source deleted MTU is defined analogously. In Figure 1 we define the position of M4 to be right after M3 (because "the" is after "held" in left-to-right order on the target side).

The complete MTU sequence in source left-to-right order is M1-M2-M3-M4-M5. The sequence in target left-to-right order is M3-M4-M5-M1-M2. This illustrates that decomposition structure may differ significantly depending on which language is used to define the enumeration order.

Once a sentence pair is represented as a sequence of MTUs, we can define the probability of the sentence pair using a conventional n-gram Markov model (MM) over MTUs. For example, the 3-gram MM probability of the sentence pair in Figure 1 under the source left-to-right order is as follows: $P(M1) \cdot P(M2|M1) \cdot P(M3|M1, M2) \cdot P(M4|M2, M3) \cdot P(M5|M3, M4)$.

Different decomposition orders use different context for disambiguation and it is not clear apriori which would perform best. We compare all four decomposition orders (source order left-to-right and right-to-left, and target order left-to-right and right-to-left). Although the independence assumptions of left-to-right and right-to-left are the same, the resulting models may be different due to smoothing.

In addition to studying these four basic decomposition orders, we report performance of two cyclic orders: cyclic in source or target sentence order. These models are inspired by the cyclic dependency network model proposed for POS tagging (Toutanova et al., 2003) and also used as a baseline in previous work on dynamic decomposition orders (Tsuruoka and Tsujii, 2005). [1]

The probability according to the cyclic orders is defined by conditioning each MTU on both its left and right neighbor MTUs. For example, the probability of the sentence pair in Figure 1 under the source cyclic order, using a 3-gram model is defined as: $P(M1|M2) \cdot P(M2|M1, M3) \cdot P(M3|M2, M4) \cdot P(M4|M3, M5) \cdot P(M5|M4)$.

All n-gram Markov models over MTUs are esti-

[1]The correct application of such models requires sampling to find the highest scoring sequence, but we apply the max product approximation as done in previous work.

mated using Kneser-Ney smoothing. Each MTU is treated as an atomic unit in the vocabulary of the n-gram model. Counts of all n-grams are obtained from the parallel MT training data, using different MTU enumeration orders.

Note that if we use a target-order decomposition, the model provides a distribution over target sentences and the corresponding source sides of MTUs, albeit unordered. Likewise source order based models provide distributions over source sentences and unordered target sides of MTUs. We attempted to introduce reordering models to predict an order over the resulting MTU sequences using approaches similar to reordering models for phrases. Although these models produced gains in some language pairs when used without translation MTU MMs, there were no additional gains over a model using multiple translation MTU MMs.

4 Lexical selection

We perform an empirical evaluation of different MTU decomposition orders on a simplified machine translation task: lexical selection. In this task we assume that the source sentence segmentation into minimal translation units is given and that the order of the corresponding target sides of the minimal translation units is also given. The problem is to predict the target sides of the MTUs, called target MTUs for brevity (see Figure 2). The lexical selection task is thus similar to sequence tagging tasks like part-of-speech tagging, though much more difficult: the predicted variables are sequences of target language words with millions of possible outcomes.

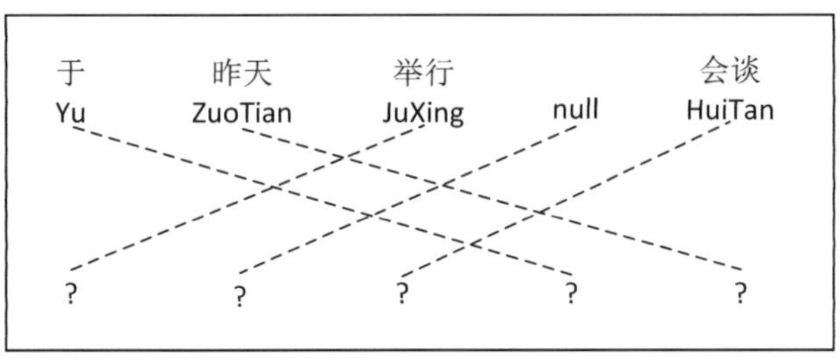

Figure 2: Lexical selection.

We use this constrained MT setting to evaluate the performance of models using different MTU decomposition orders and models using combinations of decomposition orders. The simplified setting allows controlled experimentation while lessening the impact of complicating factors in a full machine translation setting (search error, reordering limits, phrase table pruning, interaction with other models).

To perform the tagging task, we use trigram MTU models. The four basic decomposition orders for MTU Markov models we use are left-to-right in target sentence order, right-to-left in target sentence order, left-to-right in source sentence order, and right-to-left in source sentence order. We also consider cyclic orders in source and target.

Regardless of the decomposition order used, we perform decoding using a beam search decoder, similar to ones used in phrase-based machine translation. The decoder builds target hypotheses in left-to-right target sentence order. At each step, it fills in the translation of the next source MTU, in the context of the already predicted MTUs to its left. The top scoring complete hypotheses covering the first m MTUs are maintained in a beam. When scoring with a target left-to-right MTU Markov model (L2RT), we can score each partial hypothesis exactly at each step. When scoring using a R2LT model or a source order model, we use lower-order approximations to the trigram MTU Markov model scores as future scores, since not all needed context is available for a hypothesis at the time of construction. As additional context becomes available, the exact score can be computed. [2]

4.1 Basic decomposition order combinations

We first introduce two methods of combining different decomposition orders: *product* and *system combination*.

The *product* method arises naturally in the machine translation setting, where probabilities from different models are multiplied together and further weighted to form the log-linear model for machine translation (Och and Ney, 2002). We define a similar scoring function using a set of MTU Markov models $MM_1, ..., MM_k$ for a hypothesis h as follows:

$$\text{Score}(h) = \lambda_1 logP_{MM_1}(h) + ... + \lambda_k logP_{MM_k}(h)$$

[2]We apply hypothesis recombination, which can merge hypotheses that are indistinguishable with respect to future continuations. This is similar to recombination in a standard-phrase based decoder with the difference that it is not always the last two target MTUs that define the context needed by future extensions.

The weights λ of different models are trained on a development set using MER training to maximize the BLEU score of the resulting model. Note that this method of model combination was not considered in any of the previous works comparing different decompositions.

The *system combination* method is motivated by prior work in machine translation which combined left-to-right and right-to-left machine translation systems (Finch and Sumita, 2009). Similarly, we perform sentence-level system combination between systems using different MTU Markov models to come up with most likely translations. If we have k systems guessing hypotheses based on $MM_1, \ldots, MM_k$ respectively, we generate 1000-best lists from each system, resulting in a pool of up to $1000k$ possible distinct translations. Each of the candidate hypotheses from MM_i is scored with its Markov model log-probability $logP_{MM_i}(h)$. We compute normalized probabilities for each system's n-best by exponentiating and normalizing: $P_i(h) \propto P_{MM_i}(h)$. If a hypothesis h is not in system i's n-best list, we assume its probability is zero according to that system. The final scoring function for each hypothesis in the combined list of candidates is:

$$\text{Score}(h) = \lambda_1 P_1(h) + \ldots + \lambda_k P_k(h)$$

The weights λ for the combination are tuned using MERT as for the product model.

4.2 Dynamic decomposition orders

A more complex combination method chooses the best possible decomposition order for each translation dynamically, using a set of constraints to define the possible decomposition orders, and a set of features to score the candidate decompositions. We term this method *dynamic combination*. The score of each translation is defined as its score according to the highest-scoring decomposition order for that translation.

This method is very similar to the bidirectional tagging approach of Tsuruoka and Tsujii (2005). For this approach we only explored combinations of target language orders (L2RT, CycT, and R2LT). If source language orders were included, the complexity of decoding would increase substantially.

Figure 3 shows two possible decompositions for a short MTU sequence. The structures displayed are

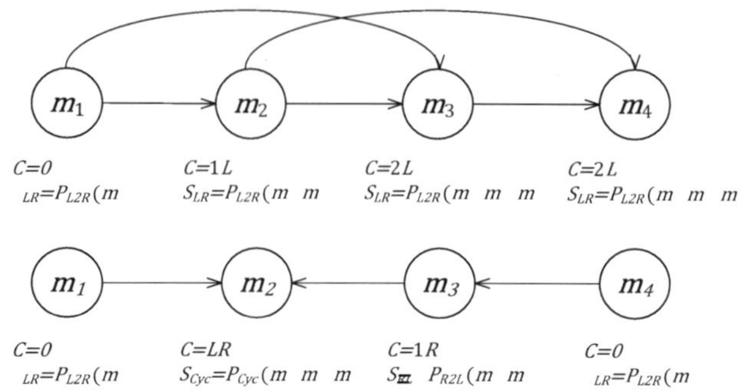

Figure 3: Different decompositions.

directed graphical models. They define the set of parents (context) used to predict each target MTU. The decomposition structures we consider are limited to acyclic graphs where each node can have one of the following parent configurations: no parents ($C = 0$ in the Figure), one left parent ($C = 1L$), one right parent ($C = 1R$), one left and one right parent ($C = LR$), two left parents ($C = 2L$), and two right parents ($C = 2R$). If all nodes have two left parents, we recover the left-to-right decomposition order, and if all nodes have two right parents, the right-to-left decomposition order. A mixture of parent configurations defines a mixed, dynamic decomposition order. The decomposition order chosen varies from translation to translation.

A directed graphical model defines the probability of an assignment of MTUs to the variable nodes as a product of local probabilities of MTUs given their parents. Here we extend this definition to scores of assignments by using a linear model with configuration features and log-probability features. The configuration features are indicators of which parent configuration is active at a node and the settings of these features for the decompositions in Figure 3 are shown as assignments to the C variables. The log-probability feature values are obtained by querying the appropriate n-gram model: L2RT, CycT, or R2LT. For a node with one or two left parents, the log-probability is computed according to the L2RT model. For a node with one or two right parents, the R2LT model is queried. The CycT model is used for nodes with one left and one right parent.

To find the best translation of a sentence the model now searches over hidden decomposition orders in addition to assignments to target MTUs. The final score of a translation and decomposition is a linear combination of the two types of feature values – model log-probabilities and configuration types. There is one feature weight for each parent configuration (six configuration weights) and one feature weight for each component model (three model weights). The final score of the second decomposition and assignment in Figure 3 is:

$$\begin{aligned} &\text{Score}(h) \\ &= 2 * w_{C_0} + w_{C_{LR}} + w_{C_{1R}} \\ &+ w_{L2R} log P_{LR}(m_1) + w_{Cyc} log P_{Cyc}(m_2|m_1, m_3) \\ &+ w_{R2L} log P_{RL}(m_3|m_4) + w_{L2R} log P_{LR}(m_4) \end{aligned}$$

There are two main differences between our approach and that of Tsuruoka and Tsujii (2005): we perform beam search with hypothesis recombination instead of exact decoding (due to the larger size of the hypothesis set), and we use parameters to be able to globally weight the probabilities from different models and to develop preferences for using certain types of decompositions. For example, the model can learn to prefer right-to-left decompositions for one language pair, and left-to-right decompositions for another. An additional difference from prior work is the definition of the possible decomposition orders that are searched over.

Compared to the structures allowed in (Tsuruoka and Tsujii, 2005) for a trigram baseline model, our allowed structures are a subset; in (Tsuruoka and Tsujii, 2005) there are sixteen possible parent configurations (up to two left and two right parents), whereas we allow only six. We train and use only three n-gram Markov models to assign probabilities: L2RT, R2LT, and CycT, whereas the prior work used sixteen models. One could potentially see additional gains from considering a larger space of structures but the training time and runtime memory requirements might become prohibitive for the machine translation task.

Because of the maximization over decomposition structures, the score of a translation is not a simple linear function of the features, but rather a maximum over linear functions. The score of a translation for a fixed decomposition is a linear function of the features, but the score of a translation is a maximum of linear functions (over decompositions). Therefore, if we define hypotheses as just containing translations, MERT training does not work directly for optimizing the weights of the dynamic combination method. [3] We used a combination of approaches; we did MERT training followed by local simplex-method search starting from three starting points: the MERT solution, a weight vector that strongly prefers left-to-right decompositions, and a weight-vector that strongly prefers right-to-left decompositions. In the Experiments section, we report results for the weights that achieved the best development set performance.

5 N-best reranking

To evaluate the impact of these models in a full MT system, we investigate n-best reranking. We use a phrase-based MT system to output 1000-best candidate translations. For each candidate translation, we have access to the phrase pairs it used as well as the alignments inside each phrase pair. Thus, each source sentence and its candidate translation form a word-aligned parallel sentence pair. We can extract MTU sequences from this sentence pair and compute its probability according to MTU Markov models. These MTU MM log-probabilities are appended to the original MT features and used to rerank the 1000-best list. The weight vectors for systems using the original features along with one or more MTU Markov model log-probabilities are trained on the development set using MERT.

6 Experiments

We report experimental results on the lexical selection task and the reranking task on three language pairs. The datasets used for the different languages are described in detail in Section 6.2.

6.1 Lexical selection experiments

The data used for the lexical selection experiments consists of the training portion of the datasets used for MT. These training sets are split into three sections: - , for training MTU Markov models and extracting possible translations for each source

[3] If we include the decompositions in the hypotheses we could use MERT but then the n-best lists used for training might not contain much variety in terms of translation options. This is an interesting direction for future research.

Model	Chs-En		Deu-En		En-Bgr	
	Dev	Test	Dev	Test	Dev	Test
Baseline	06.45	06.30	11.60	10.98	15.09	14.40
Oracle	69.79	70.78	72.28	75.39	85.15	84.32
L2RT	24.02	25.09	28.69	28.70	**49.86**	46.45
R2LT	23.79	24.91	**30.14**	**30.14***	49.22	**46.58**
CycT	18.59	20.33	25.91	26.83	41.30	38.85
L2RS	25.81	27.89*	25.52	25.10	45.69	43.98
R2LS	**26.48**	**27.96***	26.03	26.30	47.36	43.91
CycS	21.62	23.38	22.68	23.58	39.11	36.44

Table 1: Lexical selection results for individual MTU Markov models.

Model	Chs-En		Deu-En		En-Bgr	
	Dev	Test	Dev	Test	Dev	Test
Baseline-1	24.04	25.09	30.14	30.14	49.86	46.45
TgtProduct	**25.27**	**25.84***	30.47	**30.49**	**51.04**	**47.27***
TgtSysComb	24.49	25.27	30.20	30.15	50.46	46.31
TgtDynamic	24.07	25.10	**30.60**	30.41	49.99	46.52
Baseline-2	26.48	27.96	30.14	30.14	49.86	46.45
AllProduct	**28.68**	**29.59***	**31.54**	**31.36***	**51.50**	**48.10***
AllSyscomb	27.02	28.30	30.20	30.17	50.90	46.53

Table 2: Lexical selection results for combinations of MTU Markov models.

MTU, - for tuning combination weights for systems using several MTU MMs, and - , for final evaluation results. The possible translations for each source MTU are defined as the most frequent 100 translations seen in - . The - sets contain 200 sentence pairs each and the - sets contains 1000 sentence pairs each. These development and test sets consist of equally spaced sentences taken from the full MT training sets.

We start by reporting BLEU scores of the six individual MTU MMs on the three language pairs in Table 1. The baseline predicts the most frequent target MTU for each source MTU (unigram MM not using context). The oracle looks at the correct translation and always chooses the correct target MTU if it is in the vocabulary of available MTUs.

We can see that there is a large difference between the baseline and oracle performance, underscoring the importance of modeling context for accurate prediction. The best decomposition order varies from language to language: right-to-left in source order is best for Chinese-English, right-to-left in target order is best for German-English and left-to-right or right-to-left in target order are best in English-Bulgarian. We computed statistical significance tests, testing the difference between the L2RT model (the standard in prior work) and models achieving higher test set performance. The models that are significantly better at significance $\alpha < 0.01$ are marked with a star in the table. We used a paired bootstrap test with 10,000 trials (Koehn, 2004).

Next we evaluate the methods for combining decomposition orders introduced in Sections 4.1 and 4.2. The results are reported in Table 2. The upper part of the table focuses on combining different target-order decompositions. The lower part of the table looks at combining all six decomposition orders. The baseline for the target order combinations, Baseline-1, is the best single target MTU Markov model from Table 1. Baseline-2 in the lower part of the table is the best individual model out of all six. We can see that the product models TgtProduct (a product of the three target-order MTU MMs) and AllProduct (a product of all six MTU MMs) are consistently best. The dynamic decomposition models TgtDynamic achieve slight but not significant gains over the baseline. The combination models that are statistically significantly better than corresponding baselines ($\alpha < 0.01$) are marked with a star.

Our takeaway from these experiments is that multiple decomposition orders are good, and thus taking a product (which encourages agreement among the models) is a good choice for this task. The dynamic decomposition method shows some promise, but it does not outperform the simpler product approach. Perhaps a lager space of decompositions would achieve better results, especially given a larger parameter set to trade off decompositions and better tuning for those parameters.

6.2 Datasets and reranking settings

For Chinese-English, the training corpus consists of 1 million sentence pairs from the FBIS and HongKong portions of the LDC data for the NIST MT evaluation. We used the union of the NIST 2002 and 2003 test sets as the development set and the NIST 2005 test set as our test set. The baseline phrasal system uses a 5-gram language model with modified Kneser-Ney smoothing (Kenser and Ney, 1995), trained on the Xinhua portion of the English Gigaword corpus (238M English words).

For German-English we used the dataset from

Language	Training	Dev	Test
Chs-En	1 Mln	NIST02+03	NIST05
Deu-En	751 K	WMT06dev	WMT06test
En-Bgr	4 Mln	1,497	2,498

Table 3: Data sets for different language pairs.

the WMT 2006 shared task on machine translation (Koehn and Monz, 2006). The parallel training set contains approximately 751K sentences. We also used the English monolingual data of around 1 million sentences for language model training. The development set contains 2000 sentences. The final test set (the in-domain test set for the shared task) also contains 2000 sentences. Two Kneser-Ney language models were used as separate features: a 4-gram LM trained on the parallel portion of the data, and a 5-gram LM trained on the monolingual corpus.

For English-Bulgarian we used a dataset containing sentences from several data sources: JRC-Acquis (Steinberger et al., 2006), TAUS[4], and web-scraped data. The development set consists of 1,497 sentences, the English side from WMT 2009 news test data, and the Bulgarian side a human translation thereof. The test set comes from the same mixture of sources as the training set. For this system we used a single four-gram target language model trained on the target side of the parallel corpus.

All systems used phrase tables with a maximum length of seven words on either side and lexicalized reordering models. For the Chinese-English system we used GIZA++ alignments, and for the other two we used alignments by an HMM model augmented with word-based distortion (He, 2007). The alignments were symmetrized and then combined with the heuristics "grow-diag-final-and". [5] We tune parameters using MERT (Och, 2003) with random restarts (Moore and Quirk, 2008) on the development set. Case-insensitive BLEU-4 is our evaluation metric (Papineni et al., 2002).

Model	3-gram models Dev	3-gram models Test	5-gram models Dev	5-gram models Test
Baseline	32.58	31.78	32.58	31.78
L2RT	33.05	32.78*	33.16	32.88*
R2LT	33.05	32.96*	33.16	32.81*
L2RS	32.90	33.00*	32.98	32.98*
R2LS	32.94	32.98*	33.09	32.96*
4 MMs	33.22	33.07*	33.37	33.00*
4 MMs phrs	32.58	31.78	32.58	31.78

Table 4: Reranking with 3-gram and 5-gram MTU translation models on Chinese-English. Starred results on the test set indicate significantly better performance than the baseline.

6.3 MT reranking experiments

We first report detailed experiments on Chinese-English, and then verify our main conclusions on the other language pairs. Table 4 looks at the impact of individual 3-gram and 5-gram MTU Markov models and their combination. Amongst the decomposition orders tested (L2RT, R2LT, L2RS, and R2LS), each of the individual MTU MMs was able to achieve significant improvement over the baseline, around 1 BLEU point.[6] The results achieved by the individual models differ, and the combination of four directions is better than the best individual direction, but the difference is not statistically significant.

We ran an additional experiment to test whether MTU MMs make effective use of context across phrase boundaries, or whether they simply provide better smoothed estimates of phrasal translation probabilities. The last row of the table reports the results achieved by a combination of MTU MMs that do not use context across the phrasal boundaries. Since an MTU MM limited to look only inside phrases can provide improved smoothing compared to whole phrase relative frequency counts, it is conceivable it could provide a large improvement. However, there is no improvement in practice for this language pair; the additional improvements from MTU MMs stem from modeling cross-phrase context.

[4] www.tausdata.org

[5] The combination heuristic was further refined to disallow crossing one-to-many alignments, which would result in the extraction of larger minimum translation units. We found that this further refinement on the combination heuristic consistently improved the BLEU scores by between 0.3 and 0.7.

[6] Here again we call a difference significant if the paired bootstrap p-value is less than 0.01.

Table 5 shows the test set results of individual 3-gram MTU Markov models and the combination of 3-gram and 5-gram models on the English-Bulgarian and German-English datasets. For English-Bulgarian all individual 3-gram Markov models achieve significant improvements of close to one point; their combination is better than the best individual model (but not significantly). The individual 5-gram models and their combination bring much larger improvement, for a total increase of 2.82 points over the baseline. We believe the 5-gram models were more effective in this setting because the larger training set allowed for successful training of models of larger capacity. Also the increased context size helps to resolve ambiguity in the forms of morphologically-rich Bulgarian words. For German-English we see a similar pattern, with the combination of models outperforming the individual ones, and the 5-gram models being better than the 3-gram. Here the individual 3-gram models are better than the baseline at significance level 0.02 and their combination is better than the baseline at our earlier defined threshold of 0.01. The within-phrase MTU MMs (results shown in the last two rows) improve upon the baseline slightly, but here again the improvements mostly stem from the use of context across phrase boundaries. Our final results on German-English are better than the best result of 27.30 from the shared task (Koehn and Monz, 2006).

Thanks to the reviewers for referring us to recent work by (Clark et al., 2011) that pointed out problems with significance tests for machine translation, where the randomness and local optima in the MERT weight tuning method lead to a large variance in development and test set performance across different runs of optimization (using a different random seed or starting point). (Clark et al., 2011) proposed a stratified approximate randomization statistical significance test, which controls for optimizer instability. Using this test, for the English-Bulgarian system, we confirmed that the combination of four 3-gram MMs and the combination of 5-gram MMs is better than the baseline ($p = .0001$ for both, using five runs of parameter tuning). We have not run the test for the other language pairs.

Model	En-Bgr	Deu-En
Baseline	45.75	27.92
L2RT 3-gram	47.07*	28.15
R2LT 3-gram	47.06*	28.19
L2RS 3-gram	46.44*	28.15
R2LS 3-gram	47.04*	28.18
4 3-gram	47.17*	28.37*
4 5-gram	**48.57***	28.47*
4 3-gram phrs	46.08	27.92
4 5-gram phrs	46.17*	27.93

Table 5: English-Bulgarian and German-English test set results: reranking with MTU translation models.

7 Conclusions

We introduced models of Minimal Translation Units for phrasal systems, and showed that they make a substantial and statistically significant improvement on three distinct language-pairs. Additionally we studied the importance of decomposition order when defining the probability of MTU sequences. In a simplified lexical selection task, we saw that there were large differences in performance among the different decompositions, with the best decompositions differing by language. We investigated multiple methods to combine decompositions and found that a simple product approach was most effective. Results in the lexical selection task were consistent with those obtained in a full MT system, although the differences among decompositions were smaller.

In future work, perhaps we would see larger gains by including additional decomposition orders (e.g., top-down in a dependency tree), and taking this idea deeper into the machine translation model, down to the word-alignment and language-modeling levels.

We were surprised to find n-best reranking so effective. We are incorporating the models into first pass decoding, in hopes of even greater gains.

References

Jonathan H. Clark, Chris Dyer, Alon Lavie, and Noah A. Smith. 2011. Better hypothesis testing for statistical machine translation: Controlling for optimizer instability. In *Proc. ACL-11*.

JM Crego and F Yvon. 2010. Factored bilingual n-gram language models for statistical machine translation. *Machine Translation, Special Issue: Pushing the frontiers of SMT*, 24(2):159–175.

Nadir Durrani, Helmut Schmid, and Alexander Fraser. 2011. A joint sequence translation model with integrated reordering. In *Proceedings of the 49th Annual Meeting of the Association for Computational Linguistics: Human Language Technologies*, pages 1045–1054, Portland, Oregon, USA, June. Association for Computational Linguistics.

Andrew Finch and Eiichiro Sumita. 2009. Bidirectional phrase-based machine translation. In *In proceedings of EMNLP*.

Xiaodong He. 2007. Using word-dependent transition models in hmm based word alignment for statistical machine translation. In *WMT workshop*.

Reinhard Kenser and Hermann Ney. 1995. Improved backing-off for m-gram language modeling. In *Proc. ICASSP 1995*, pages 181–184.

Philipp Koehn and Christof Monz. 2006. Manual and automatic evaluation of machine translation between european languages. In *Proceedings on the Workshop on Statistical Machine Translation*, pages 102–121, June.

Philipp Koehn, Franz Josef Och, and Daniel Marcu. 2003. Statistical phrase-based translation. In *Proc. HLT-NAACL 2003*, pages 127–133.

Philipp Koehn. 2004. Statistical significance tests for machine translation evaluation. In *In Proceedings of EMNLP*.

JB Marino, RE Banchs, JM Crego, A de Gispert, P Lambert, JA Fonollosa, and MR Costa-Jussa. 2006. N-gram-based machine translation. *Computational Linguistics*, 32(4):527–549.

Robert C. Moore and Chris Quirk. 2008. Random restarts in minimum error training for statistical machine translation. In *Proc. Coling-08*.

Franz Josef Och and Hermann Ney. 2002. Discriminative training and maximum entropy models for statistical machine translation. In *In Proceedings of ACL*, pages 295–302.

Franz Joseph Och. 2003. Minimum error training in statistical machine translation. In *Proc. ACL-03*.

Kishore Papineni, Salim Roukos, Todd Ward, and Wei-Jing Zhu. 2002. B : a method for automatic evaluation of machine translation. In *Proc. 40th Annual Meeting of the ACL*, pages 311–318.

Chris Quirk and Arul Menezes. 2006. Do we need phrases? challenging the conventional wisdom in statistical machine translation. In *Proceedings of the Human Language Technology Conference of the NAACL, Main Conference*, pages 9–16, New York City, USA, June. Association for Computational Linguistics.

Ralf Steinberger, Bruno Pouliquen, Anna Widiger, Camelia Ignat, Toma Erjavec, Dan Tufis, and Dniel Varga. 2006. The JRC-Acquis: A multilingual aligned parallel corpus with 20+ languages. In *LREC*, Genoa, Italy.

Kristina Toutanova, Dan Klein, Christopher D. Manning, and Yoram Singer. 2003. Feature-rich part-of-speech tagging with a cyclic dependency network. In *In Proceedings of HLT-NAACL*.

Yoshimasa Tsuruoka and Jun'ichi Tsujii. 2005. Bidirectional inference with the easiest-first strategy for tagging sequence data. In *In proceedings of HLT/EMNLP*.

Ashish Vaswani, Haitao Mi, Liang Huang, and David Chiang. 2011. Rule markov models for fast tree-to-string translation. In *Proceedings of the 49th Annual Meeting of the Association for Computational Linguistics: Human Language Technologies*, pages 856–864, Portland, Oregon, USA, June. Association for Computational Linguistics.

Improved Reordering for Phrase-Based Translation using Sparse Features

Colin Cherry
National Research Council Canada
Colin.Cherry@nrc-cnrc.gc.ca

Abstract

There have been many recent investigations into methods to tune SMT systems using large numbers of sparse features. However, there have not been nearly so many examples of helpful sparse features, especially for phrase-based systems. We use sparse features to address reordering, which is often considered a weak point of phrase-based translation. Using a hierarchical reordering model as our baseline, we show that simple features coupling phrase orientation to frequent words or word-clusters can improve translation quality, with boosts of up to 1.2 BLEU points in Chinese-English and 1.8 in Arabic-English. We compare this solution to a more traditional maximum entropy approach, where a probability model with similar features is trained on word-aligned bitext. We show that sparse decoder features outperform maximum entropy handily, indicating that there are major advantages to optimizing reordering features directly for BLEU with the decoder in the loop.

1 Introduction

With the growing adoption of tuning algorithms that can handle thousands of features (Chiang et al., 2008; Hopkins and May, 2011), SMT system designers now face a choice when incorporating new ideas into their translation models. Maximum likelihood models can be estimated from large word-aligned bitexts, creating a small number of highly informative decoder features; or the same ideas can be incorporated into the decoder's linear model directly. There are trade-offs to each approach. Maximum likelihood models can be estimated from millions of sentences of bitext, but optimize a mismatched objective, predicting events observed in word aligned bitext instead of optimizing translation quality. Sparse decoder features have the opposite problem; with the decoder in the loop, we can only tune on small development sets,[1] but a translation error metric directly informs training.

We investigate this trade-off in the context of reordering models for phrase-based decoding. Starting with the intuition that most lexicalized reordering models do not smooth their orientation distributions intelligently for low-frequency phrase-pairs, we design features that track the first and last words (or clusters) of the phrases in a pair. These features are incorporated into a maximum entropy reordering model, as well as sparse decoder features, to see which approach best complements the now-standard relative-frequency lexicalized reordering model.

We also view our work as an example of strong sparse features for phrase-based translation. Features from hierarchical and syntax-based translation (Chiang et al., 2009) do not easily transfer to the phrase-based paradigm, and most work that has looked at large feature counts in the context of phrase-based translation has focused on the learning method, and not the features themselves (Hopkins and May, 2011; Cherry and Foster, 2012; Gimpel and Smith, 2012). We show that by targeting reordering, large gains can be made with relatively simple features.

2 Background

Phrase-based machine translation constructs its target sentence from left-to-right, with each translation operation selecting a source phrase and appending its translation to the growing target sentence, until

[1] Some systems tune for BLEU on much larger sets (Simianer et al., 2012; He and Deng, 2012), but these require exceptional commitments of resources and time.

all source words have been covered exactly once. The first phrase-based translation systems applied only a distortion penalty to model reordering (Koehn et al., 2003; Och and Ney, 2004). Any deviation from monotone translation is penalized, with a single linear weight determining how quickly the penalty grows.

2.1 Lexicalized Reordering

Implemented in a number of phrase-based decoders, the lexicalized reordering model (RM) uses word-aligned data to determine how each phrase-pair tends to be reordered during translation (Tillmann, 2004; Koehn et al., 2005; Koehn et al., 2007).

The core idea in this RM is to divide reordering events into three orientations that can be easily determined both during decoding and from word-aligned data. The orientations can be described in terms of the previously translated source phrase (*prev*) and the next source phrase to be translated (*next*):

- Monotone (M): *next* immediately follows *prev*.
- Swap (S): *prev* immediately follows *next*.
- Discontinuous (D): *next* and *prev* are not adjacent in the source.

Note that *prev* and *next* can be defined for constructing a translation from left-to-right or from right-to-left. Most decoders incorporate RMs for both directions; our discussion will generally only cover left-to-right, with the right-to-left case being implicit and symmetrical.

As the decoder extends its hypothesis by translating a source phrase, we can assess the implied orientations to determine if the resulting reordering makes sense. This is done using the probability of an orientation given the phrase pair $pp = [src, tgt]$ extending the hypothesis:[2]

$$P(o|pp) \approx \frac{cnt(o, pp)}{\sum_o cnt(o, pp)} \quad (1)$$

where $o \in \{M, S, D\}$, cnt uses simple heuristics on word-alignments to count phrase pairs and their orientations, and the $\approx$ symbol allows for smoothing. The log of this probability is easily folded into the linear models that guide modern decoders. Better performance is achieved by giving each orientation its own log-linear weight (Koehn et al., 2005).

2.2 Hierarchical Reordering

Introduced by Galley and Manning (2008), the hierarchical reordering model (HRM) also tracks statistics over orientations, but attempts to increase the consistency of orientation assignments. To do so, they remove the emphasis on the previously translated phrase ($prev$), and instead determine orientation using a compact representation of the full translation history, as represented by a shift-reduce stack. Each source span is shifted onto the stack as it is translated; if the new top is adjacent to the span below it, then a reduction merges the two.

Orientations are determined in terms of the top of this stack,[3] rather than the previously translated phrase *prev*. The resulting orientations are more consistent across different phrasal decompositions of the same translation, and more consistent with the statistics extracted from word aligned data. This results in a general improvement in performance. We assume the HRM as our baseline reordering model.

It is important to note that although our maximum entropy and sparse reordering solutions build on the HRM, the features in this paper can still be applied without a shift-reduce stack, by using the previously translated phrase where we use the top of the stack.

2.3 Maximum Entropy Reordering

One frequent observation regarding both the RM and the HRM is that the statistics used to grade orientations are very sparse. Each orientation prediction $P(o|pp)$ is conditioned on an entire phrase pair. Koehn et al. (2005) experiment with alternatives, such as conditioning on only the source or the target, but using the entire pair generally performs best. The vast majority of phrase pairs found in bitext with standard extraction heuristics are singletons (more than 92% in our Arabic-English bitext), and the corresponding $P(o|pp)$ estimates are based on a single observation. Because of these heavy tails, there have been several attempts to use maximum entropy to create more flexible distributions.

One straight-forward way to do so is to continue predicting orientations on phrases, but to use maxi-

[2] *pp* corresponds to the phrase pair translating *next* for the left-to-right model, and *prev* for right-to-left.

[3] In the case of the right-to-left model, an approximation of the top of the stack is used instead.

mum entropy to consider features of the phrase pair. This is the approach taken by Xiong et al. (2006); their maximum entropy model chooses between M and S orientations, which are the only two options available in their chart-based ITG decoder. Nguyen et al. (2009) build a similar model for a phrase-based HRM, using syntactic heads and constituent labels to create a rich feature set. They show gains over an HRM baseline, albeit on a small training set.

A related approach is to build a reordering model over words, which is evaluated at phrase boundaries at decoding time. Zens and Ney (2006) propose one such model, with jumps between words binned very coarsely according to their direction and distance, testing models that differentiate only left jumps from right, as well as the cross-product of {left, right} × {adjacent, discontinuous}. Their features consider word identity and automatically-induced clusters. Green et al. (2010) present a similar approach, with finer-grained distance bins, using word-identity and part-of-speech for features. Yahyaei and Monz (2010) also predict distance bins, but use much more context, opting to look at both sides of a reordering jump; they also experiment with hard constraints based on their model.

Tracking word-level reordering simplifies the extraction of complex models from word alignments; however, it is not clear if it is possible to enhance a word reordering model with the stack-based histories used by HRMs. In this work, we construct a phrase orientation maximum entropy model.

3 Methods

Our primary contribution is a comparison between the standard HRM and two feature-based alternatives. Since a major motivating concern is smoothing, we begin with a detailed description of our HRM baseline, followed by our maximum entropy HRM and our novel sparse reordering features.

3.1 Relative Frequency Model

The standard HRM uses relative frequencies to build smoothed maximum likelihood estimates of orientation probabilities. Orientation counts for phrase pairs are collected from bitext, using the method described by Galley and Manning (2008). The probability model $P(o|pp = [src, tgt])$ is estimated using recursive MAP smoothing:

$$P(o|pp) = \frac{cnt(o,pp) + \alpha_s P_s(o|src) + \alpha_t P_t(o|tgt)}{\sum_o cnt(o,pp) + \alpha_s + \alpha_t}$$

$$P_s(o|src) = \frac{\sum_{tgt} cnt(o,src,tgt) + \alpha_g P_g(o)}{\sum_{o,tgt} cnt(o,src,tgt) + \alpha_g}$$

$$P_t(o|tgt) = \frac{\sum_{src} cnt(o,src,tgt) + \alpha_g P_g(o)}{\sum_{o,src} cnt(o,src,tgt) + \alpha_g}$$

$$P_g(o) = \frac{\sum_{pp} cnt(o,pp) + \alpha_u/3}{\sum_{o,pp} cnt(o,pp) + \alpha_u} \tag{2}$$

where the various α parameters can be tuned empirically. In practice, the model is not particularly sensitive to these parameters.[4]

3.2 Maximum Entropy Model

Next, we describe our implementation of a maximum entropy HRM. Our goal with this system is to benefit from modeling features of a phrase pair, while keeping the system architecture as simple and replicable as possible. To simplify training, we learn our model from the same orientation counts that power the relative-frequency HRM. To simplify decoder integration, we limit our feature space to information from a single phrase pair.

In a maximum entropy model, the probability of an orientation o given a phrase pair pp is given by a log-linear model:

$$P(o|pp) = \frac{\exp(w \cdot f(o,pp))}{\sum_{o'} \exp(w \cdot f(o',pp))} \tag{3}$$

where $f(o, pp)$ returns features of a phrase-pair, and w is the learned weight vector. We build two models, one for left-to-right translation, and one for right-to-left. As with the relative frequency model, we limit our discussion to the left-to-right model, with the other direction being symmetrical.

We construct a training example for each unique phrase-pair type (as opposed to token) found in our bitext. We use the orientation counts observed for a phrase pair pp_i to construct its example weight: $c_i = \sum_o cnt(o, pp_i)$. The same counts are used to construct a target distribution $\tilde{P}(o|pp_i)$, using the

[4]We use a historically good setting of $\alpha_* = 10$ throughout.

Base:
$bias$; $src \wedge tgt$; src; tgt
$src.first$; $src.last$; $tgt.first$; $tgt.last$
$clust_{50}(src.first)$; $clust_{50}(src.last)$
$clust_{50}(tgt.first)$; $clust_{50}(tgt.last)$
$\times$ Orientation $\{M, S, D\}$

Table 1: Features for the Maximum Entropy HRM.

unsmoothed relative frequency estimate in Equation 1. We then train our weight vector to minimize:

$$\frac{1}{2}||w||^2 + C\sum_i c_i \left[\begin{array}{l} \log \sum_o \exp\left(w \cdot f(o, pp_i)\right) \\ -\sum_o \tilde{P}(o|pp_i)\left(w \cdot f(o, pp_i)\right) \end{array} \right] \quad (4)$$

where C is a hyper-parameter that controls the amount of emphasis placed on minimizing loss versus regularizing w.[5] Note that this objective is a departure from previous work, which tends to create an example for each phrase-pair token, effectively assigning $\tilde{P}(o|pp) = 1$ to a single gold-standard orientation. Instead, our model attempts to reproduce the target distribution $\tilde{P}$ for the entire type, where the penalty c_i for missing this target is determined by the frequency of the phrase pair. The resulting model will tend to match unsmoothed relative frequency estimates for very frequent phrase pairs, and will smooth intelligently using features for less frequent phrase pairs.

All of the features returned by $f(o|pp)$ are derived from the phrase pair $pp = [src, tgt]$, with the goal of describing the phrase pair at a variety of granularities. Our features are described in Table 1, using the following notation: the operators *first* and *last* return the first and last words of phrases,[6] while the operator $clust_{50}$ maps a word onto its corresponding cluster from an automatically-induced, deterministic 50-word clustering provided by `mkcls` (Och, 1999). Our use of words at the corners of phrases (as opposed to the syntactic head, or the last aligned word) follows Xiong et al. (2006), while our use of word clusters follows Zens and Ney (2006). Each feature has the orientation o appended onto it.

To help scale and to encourage smoothing, we only allow features that occur in at least 5 phrase pair

[5]Preliminary experiments indicated that the model is robust to the choice of C; we use $C = 0.1$ throughout.

[6]$first = last$ for a single-word phrase

Base:
$src.first$; $src.last$; $tgt.first$; $tgt.last$
$top.src.first$; $top.src.last$; $top.tgt.last$
$between\_words$
$\times$ Representation
{80-words, 50-clusters, 20-clusters}
$\times$ Orientation
$\{M, S, D\}$

Table 2: Features for the Sparse Feature HRM.

tokens. Furthermore, to deal with the huge number of extracted phrase pairs (our Arabic system extracts roughly 88M distinct phrase pair types), we subsample pairs that have been observed only once, keeping only 10% of them. This reduces the number of training examples from 88M to 19M.

3.3 Sparse Reordering Features

The maximum entropy approach uses features to model the distribution of orientations found in word alignments. Alternatively, a number of recent tuning methods, such as MIRA (Chiang et al., 2008) or PRO (Hopkins and May, 2011), can handle thousands of features. These could be used to tune similar features to maximize BLEU directly.

Given the appropriate tuning architecture, the sparse feature approach is actually simpler in many ways than the maximum entropy approach. There is no need to scale to millions of training examples, and there is no question of how to integrate the trained model into the decoder. Instead, one simply implements the desired features in the decoder's feature API and then tunes as normal. The challenge is to design features so that the model can be learned from small tuning sets.

The standard approach for sparse feature design in SMT is to lexicalize only on extremely frequent words, such as the top-80 words from each language (Chiang et al., 2009; Hopkins and May, 2011). We take that approach here, but we also use deterministic clusters to represent words from both languages, as provided by `mkcls`. These clusters mirror parts-of-speech quite effectively (Blunsom and Cohn, 2011), without requiring linguistic resources. They should provide useful generalization for reordering decisions. Inspired by recent successes in semi-supervised learning (Koo et al., 2008;

corpus	sentences	words (ar)	words (en)
train	1,490,514	46,403,734	47,109,486
dev	1,663	45,243	50,550
mt08	1,360	45,002	51,341
mt09	1,313	40,684	46,813

Table 3: Arabic-English Corpus. For English dev and test sets, word counts are averaged across 4 references.

corpus	sentences	words (ch)	words (en)
train	3,505,529	65,917,610	69,453,695
dev	1,894	48,384	53,584
mt06	1,664	39,694	47,143
mt08	1,357	33,701	40,893

Table 4: Chinese-English Corpus. For English dev and test sets, word counts are averaged across 4 references.

Lin and Wu, 2009), we cluster at two granularities (20 clusters and 50 clusters), and allow the discriminative tuner to determine how to best employ the various representations.

We add the sparse features in Table 2 to our decoder to help assess reordering decisions. As with the maximum entropy model, orientation is appended to each feature. Furthermore, each feature has a different version for each of our three word representations. Like the maximum entropy model, we describe the phrase pair being added to the hypothesis in terms of the first and last words of its phrases. Unlike the maximum entropy model, we make no attempt to use entire phrases or phrase-pairs as features, as they would be far too sparse for our small tuning sets. However, due to the sparse features' direct decoder integration, we have access to a fair amount of extra context. We represent the current top of the stack (top) using its first and last source words (accessible from the HRM stack), and its last target word (accessible using language model context). Furthermore, for discontinuous (D) orientations, we can include an indicator for each source word between the current top of the stack and the phrase being added.

Because the sparse feature HRM has no access to phrase-pair or monolingual phrase features, and because it completely ignores our large supply of word-aligned training data, we view it as complimentary to the relative frequency HRM. We always include both when tuning and decoding. Furthermore, we only include sparse features in the left-to-right translation direction, as the features already consider context (top) as well as the next phrase.

4 Experimental Design

We test our reordering models in Arabic to English and Chinese to English translation tasks. Both systems are trained on data from the NIST 2012 MT evaluation; the Arabic system is summarized in Table 3 and the Chinese in Table 4. The Arabic system's development set is the NIST mt06 test set, and its test sets are mt08 and mt09. The Chinese system's development set is taken from the NIST mt05 evaluation set, augmented with some material reserved from our NIST training corpora in order to better cover newsgroup and weblog domains. Its test sets are mt06 and mt08.

4.1 Baseline System

For both language pairs, word alignment is performed by GIZA++ (Och and Ney, 2003), with 5 iterations of Model 1, HMM, Model 3 and Model 4. Phrases are extracted with a length limit of 7 from alignments symmetrized using grow-diag-final-and (Koehn et al., 2003). Conditional phrase probabilities in both directions are estimated from relative frequencies, and from lexical probabilities (Zens and Ney, 2004). 4-gram language models are estimated from the target side of the bitext with Kneser-Ney smoothing. Relative frequency and maximum entropy RMs are represented with six features, with separate weights for M, S and D in both directions (Koehn et al., 2007). HRM orientations are determined using an unrestricted shift-reduce parser (Cherry et al., 2012). We also employ a standard distortion penalty incorporating the minimum completion cost described by Moore and Quirk (2007). Our multi-stack phrase-based decoder is quite similar to Moses (Koehn et al., 2007).

For all systems, parameters are tuned with a batch-lattice variant of hope-fear MIRA (Chiang et al., 2008; Cherry and Foster, 2012). Preliminary experiments suggested that the sparse reordering features have a larger impact when tuned with lattices as opposed to n-best lists.

4.2 Evaluation

We report lower-cased BLEU (Papineni et al., 2002), evaluated using the same English tokenization used in training. For our primary results, we perform random replications of parameter tuning, as suggested by Clark et al. (2011). Each replication uses a different random seed to determine the order in which MIRA visits tuning sentences. We test for significance using Clark et al.'s MultEval tool, which uses a stratified approximate randomization test to account for multiple replications.

5 Results

We begin with a comparison of the reordering models described in this paper: the hierarchical reordering model (**HRM**), the maximum entropy HRM (**Maxent HRM**) and our sparse reordering features (**Sparse HRM**). Results are shown in Table 5.

Our three primary points of comparison have been tested with 5 replications. We report BLEU scores averaged across replications as well as standard deviations, which indicate optimizer stability. We also provide unreplicated results for two systems, one using only the distortion penalty (**No RM**), and one using a non-hierarchical reordering model (**RM**). These demonstrate that our baseline already has quite mature reordering capabilities.

The Maxent HRM has very little effect on translation performance. We found this surprising; we expected large gains from improving the reordering distributions of low-frequency phrase-pairs. See §5.1 for further exploration of this result.

The Sparse HRM, on the other hand, performs very well. It produces significant BLEU score improvements on all test sets, with improvements ranging between 1 and 1.8 BLEU points. Even with millions of training sentences for our HRM, there is a large benefit in building HRM-like features that are tuned to optimize the decoder's BLEU score on small tuning sets. We examine the impact of subsets of these features in §5.2.

The test sets' standard deviations increase from 0.1 under the baseline to 0.3 under the Sparse HRM for Chinese-English, indicating a decrease in optimizer stability. With so many features trained on so few sentences, this is not necessarily surprising. Fortunately, looking at the actual replications (not shown), we confirmed that if a replication produced low scores in one test, it also produced low scores in the other. This means that one should be able to outperform the average case by using a dev-test set to select among replications.

Base:
$src.first$; $src.last$; $tgt.first$; $tgt.last$
× Representation
{80-words, 50-clusters}
× Orientation
$\{M, S, D\}$

Table 6: Intersection of Maxent & Sparse HRM features.

5.1 Maximum Entropy Analysis

The next two sections examine our two solutions in detail, starting with the Maxent HRM. To avoid excessive demands on our computing resources, all experiments report tuning with a single replication with the same seed. We select Arabic-English for our analysis, as this pair has high optimizer stability and fast decoding speeds.

Why does the Maxent HRM help so little? We begin by investigating some design decisions. One possibility is that our subsampling of frequency-1 training pairs (see §3.2) harmed performance. To test the impact of this decision, we train a Maxent HRM without subsampling, taking substantially longer. The resulting BLEU scores (not shown) are well within the projected standard deviations for optimizer instability (0.1 BLEU from Table 5). This indicates that subsampling is not the problem. To confirm our choice of hyperparameters, we conduct a grid search over the Maxent HRM's regularization parameter C (see Equation 4), covering the set $\{1, 0.1, 0.01, 0.001\}$, where $C = 0.1$ is the value used throughout this paper. Again, the resulting BLEU scores (not shown) are all within 0.1 of the means reported in Table 5.

Another possibility is that the Maxent HRM has an inferior feature set. We selected features for our Maxent and Sparse HRMs to be similar, but also to play to the strengths of each method. To level the playing field, we train and test both systems with the feature set shown in Table 6, which is the intersection of the features from Tables 1 and 2. The resulting average BLEU scores are shown in Table 7. With

Method	n	Chinese-English tune	std	mt06	std	mt08	std	Arabic-English tune	std	mt08	std	mt09	std
No RM	1	24.3	–	32.0	–	26.4	–	41.7	–	41.4	–	44.1	–
RM	1	25.2	–	33.3	–	27.4	–	42.4	–	42.6	–	45.2	–
HRM (baseline)	5	25.6	0.0	34.2	0.1	28.0	0.1	42.9	0.0	42.9	0.1	45.5	0.0
HRM + Maxent HRM	5	25.6	0.0	34.3	0.1	28.1	0.1	43.0	0.0	42.9	0.0	45.6	0.1
HRM + Sparse HRM	5	28.0	0.1	**35.4**	0.3	**29.0**	0.3	47.0	0.1	**44.6**	0.1	**47.3**	0.1

Table 5: Comparing reordering methods according to BLEU score. n indicates the number of tuning replications, while standard deviations (std) indicate optimizer stability. Test scores that are significantly higher ($p < 0.01$) than the HRM baseline are highlighted in bold.

Method		−HRM	+HRM
HRM (baseline)		–	44.2
Original	Maxent HRM	44.2	44.2
	Sparse HRM	45.4	46.0
Intersection	Maxent HRM	43.8	44.2
	Sparse HRM	45.2	46.0

Table 7: Arabic-English BLEU scores with each system's original feature set versus the intersection of the two feature sets, with and without the relative frequency HRM. BLEU is averaged across mt08 and mt09.

the baseline HRM included, performance does not change for either system with the intersected feature set. Sparse features continue to help, while the maximum entropy model does not. Without the HRM, both systems degrade under the intersection, though the Sparse HRM still improves over the baseline.

Finally, we examine Maxent HRM performance as a function of the amount of word-aligned training data. To do so, we hold all aspects of our system constant, except for the amount of bitext used to train either the baseline HRM or the Maxent HRM. Importantly, the phrase table always uses the complete bitext. For our reordering training set, we hold out the final two thousand sentences of bitext to calculate perplexity. This measures the model's surprise at reordering events drawn from previously unseen alignments; lower values are better. We proceed to subsample sentence pairs from the remaining bitext, in order to produce a series of training bitexts of increasing size. We subsample with the probability of accepting a sentence pair, P_a, set to $\{0.001, 0.01, 0.1, 1\}$. It is important to not confuse this subsampling of sentence pairs with the subsampling of low-frequency phrase pairs (see §3.2), which is still carried out by the Maxent HRM for each training scenario.

Figure 1 shows how BLEU (averaged across both test sets) and perplexity vary as training data increases from 1.5K sentences to the full 1.5M. At $P_a < 0.1$, corresponding to less than 150K sentences, the maximum entropy model actually makes a substantial difference in terms of BLEU. However, these deltas narrow to nothing as we reach millions of training sentences. This is consistent with the results of Nguyen et al. (2009), who report that maximum entropy reordering outperforms a similar baseline, but using only 50K sentence pairs.

A related observation is that held-out perplexity does not seem to predict BLEU in any useful way. In particular, perplexity does not predict that the two systems will become similar as data grows, nor does it predict that maxent's performance will level off. Predicting the orientations of unseen alignments is not the same task as predicting the orientation for a phrase during translation. We suspect that perplexity places too much emphasis on rare or previously unseen phrase pairs, due to phrase extraction's heavy tails. Preliminary attempts to correct for this using absolute discounting on the test counts did not resolve these issues. Unfortunately, in maximizing (regularized or smoothed) likelihood, both maxent and relative frequency HRMs are chasing the perplexity objective, not the BLEU objective.

5.2 Sparse Feature Analysis

The results in Table 7 from §5.1 already provide us with a number of insights regarding the Sparse HRM. First, note that the intersected feature set uses only information found within a single phrase. The fact that the Sparse HRM performs so well with

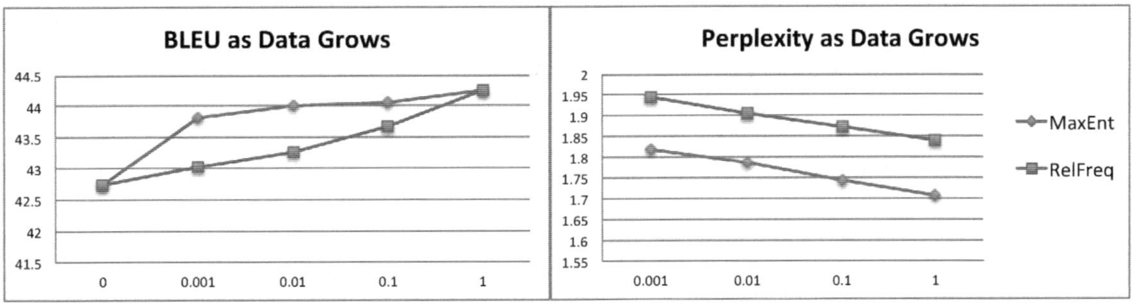

Figure 1: Learning curves for Relative Frequency and Maximum Entropy reordering models on Arabic-English.

Feature Group	Count	BLEU
No Sparse HRM	0	44.2
Between	312	44.4
Stack	1404	45.2
Phrase	1872	45.9
20 Clusters	506	45.4
50 Clusters	1196	45.8
80 Words	1886	45.8
Full Sparse HRM	3588	46.0

Table 8: Versions of the Sparse HRM built using organized subsets of the complete feature set for Arabic-English. Count is the number of distinct features, while BLEU is averaged over mt08 and mt09.

intersected features indicates that modeling context outside a phrase is not essential for strong performance. Furthermore, the −**HRM** portion of the table indicates that the sparse HRM does not require the baseline HRM to be present in order to outperform it. This is remarkable when one considers that the Sparse HRM uses less than 4k features to model phrase orientations, compared to the 530M probabilities[7] maintained by the baseline HRM's relative frequency model.

To determine which feature groups are most important, we tested the Sparse HRM on Arabic-English with a number of feature subsets. We report BLEU scores averaged over both test sets in Table 8. First, we break our features into three groups according to what part of the hypothesis is used to assess orientation. For each of these location groups, all forms of word representation (clusters or frequent words) are employed. The groups consist of **Between**: the words between the top of the stack and the phrase to be added; **Stack**: words describing the current top of the stack; and **Phrase**: words describing the phrase pair being added to the hypothesis. Each group was tested alone to measure its usefulness. This results in a clear hierarchy, with the phrase features being the most useful (nearly as useful as the complete system), and the between features being the least. Second, we break our features into three groups according to how words are represented. For each of these representation groups, all location groups (Between, Stack and Phrase) are employed. The groups are quite intuitive: **20 Clusters**, **50 Clusters** or **80 Words**. The differences between representations are much less dramatic than the location groups. All representations perform well on their own, with the finer-grained ones performing better. Including multiple representations provides a slight boost, but these experiments suggest that a leaner model could certainly drop one or two representations with little impact.

In its current implementation, the Sparse HRM is roughly 4 times slower than the baseline decoder. Our sparse feature infrastructure is designed for flexibility, not speed. To affect reordering, each sparse feature template is re-applied with each hypothesis extension. However, the intersected feature set from §5.1 is only 2 times slower, and could be made faster still. That feature set uses only within-phrase features to asses orientations; therefore, the total weight for each orientation for each phrase-pair could be pre-calculated, making its cost comparable to the baseline.

[7] 88.4M phrase pairs × 3 orientations (M, S and D) × 2 translation directions (left-to-right and right-to-left).

Chinese-English	tune	mt06	mt08
Base	27.7	39.9	33.7
+Sparse HRM	29.2	41.0	34.1

Arabic-English	tune	mt08	mt09
Base	49.6	49.1	51.6
+Sparse HRM	51.7	49.9	52.2

Table 9: The effect of Sparse HRMs on complex systems.

5.3 Impact on Competition-Grade SMT

Thus far, we have employed a baseline that has been designed for both translation quality and replicability. We now investigate the impact of our Sparse HRM on a far more complex baseline: our internal system used for MT competitions such as NIST.

The Arabic system uses roughly the same bilingual data as our original baseline, but also includes a 5-gram language model learned from the English Gigaword. The Chinese system adds the UN bitext as well as the English Gigaword. Both systems make heavy use of linear mixtures to create refined translation and language models, mixing across sources of corpora, genre and translation direction (Foster and Kuhn, 2007; Goutte et al., 2009). They also mix many different sources of word alignments, with the system adapting across alignment sources using either binary indicators or linear mixtures. Importantly, these systems already incorporate thousands of sparse features as described by Hopkins and May (2011). These provide additional information for each phrase pair through frequency bins, phrase-length bins, and indicators for frequent alignment pairs. Both systems include a standard HRM.

The result of adding the Sparse HRM to these systems is shown in Table 9. Improvements range from 0.4 to 1.1 BLEU, but importantly, all four test sets improve. The impact of these reordering features is reduced slightly in the presence of more carefully tuned translation and language models, but they remain a strong contributor to translation quality.

6 Conclusion

We have shown that sparse reordering features can improve the quality of phrase-based translations, even in the presence of lexicalized reordering models that track the same orientations. We have compared this solution to a maximum entropy model, which does not improve our HRM baseline. Our analysis of the maximum entropy solution indicates that smoothing the orientation estimates is not a major concern in the presence of millions of sentences of bitext. This implies that our sparse features are achieving their improvement because they optimize BLEU with the decoder in the loop, side-stepping the objective mismatch that can occur when training on word-aligned data. The fact that this is possible with such small tuning corpora is both surprising and encouraging.

In the future, we would like to investigate how to incorporate useful future cost estimates for our sparse reordering features. Previous work has shown future distortion penalty estimates to be important for both translation speed and quality (Moore and Quirk, 2007; Green et al., 2010), but we have ignored future costs in this work. We would also like to investigate features inspired by transition-based parsing, such as features that look further down the reordering stack. Finally, as there is evidence that ideas from lexicalized reordering can help hierarchical phrase-based SMT (Huck et al., 2012), it would be interesting to explore the use of sparse RMs in that setting.

Acknowledgments

Thanks to George Foster, Roland Kuhn and the anonymous reviewers for their valuable comments on an earlier draft.

References

Phil Blunsom and Trevor Cohn. 2011. A hierarchical pitman-yor process hmm for unsupervised part of speech induction. In *ACL*, pages 865–874, Portland, Oregon, USA, June.

Colin Cherry and George Foster. 2012. Batch tuning strategies for statistical machine translation. In *HLT-NAACL*, pages 427–436, Montréal, Canada, June.

Colin Cherry, Robert C. Moore, and Chris Quirk. 2012. On hierarchical re-ordering and permutation parsing for phrase-based decoding. In *Proceedings of the Workshop on Statistical Machine Translation*, pages 200–209, Montréal, Canada, June.

David Chiang, Yuval Marton, and Philip Resnik. 2008. Online large-margin training of syntactic and structural translation features. In *EMNLP*, pages 224–233.

David Chiang, Kevin Knight, and Wei Wang. 2009. 11,001 new features for statistical machine translation. In *HLT-NAACL*, pages 218–226.

Jonathan H. Clark, Chris Dyer, Alon Lavie, and Noah A. Smith. 2011. Better hypothesis testing for statistical machine translation: Controlling for optimizer instability. In *ACL*, pages 176–181.

George Foster and Roland Kuhn. 2007. Mixture-model adaptation for SMT. In *Proceedings of the Workshop on Statistical Machine Translation*, pages 128–135.

Michel Galley and Christopher D. Manning. 2008. A simple and effective hierarchical phrase reordering model. In *EMNLP*, pages 848–856, Honolulu, Hawaii.

Kevin Gimpel and Noah A. Smith. 2012. Structured ramp loss minimization for machine translation. In *HLT-NAACL*, Montreal, Canada, June.

Cyril Goutte, David Kurokawa, and Pierre Isabelle. 2009. Improving SMT by learning the translation direction. In *EAMT Workshop on Statistical Multilingual Analysis for Retrieval and Translation*.

Spence Green, Michel Galley, and Christopher D. Manning. 2010. Improved models of distortion cost for statistical machine translation. In *HLT-NAACL*, pages 867–875, Los Angeles, California, June.

Xiaodong He and Li Deng. 2012. Maximum expected bleu training of phrase and lexicon translation models. In *Proceedings of the 50th Annual Meeting of the Association for Computational Linguistics (Volume 1: Long Papers)*, pages 292–301, Jeju Island, Korea, July.

Mark Hopkins and Jonathan May. 2011. Tuning as ranking. In *EMNLP*, pages 1352–1362.

Matthias Huck, Stephan Peitz, Markus Freitag, and Hermann Ney. 2012. Discriminative reordering extensions for hierarchical phrase-based machine translation. In *Proceedings of the 16th Annual Conference of the European Association for Machine Translation (EAMT)*, pages 313–320, Trento, Italy, May.

Philipp Koehn, Franz Joesef Och, and Daniel Marcu. 2003. Statistical phrase-based translation. In *HLT-NAACL*, pages 127–133.

Philipp Koehn, Amittai Axelrod, Alexandra Birch Mayne, Chris Callison-Burch, Miles Osborne, and David Talbot. 2005. Edinburgh system description for the 2005 IWSLT speech translation evaluation. In *Proceedings to the International Workshop on Spoken Language Translation (IWSLT)*.

Philipp Koehn, Hieu Hoang, Alexandra Birch, Chris Callison-Burch, Marcello Federico, Nicola Bertoldi, Brooke Cowan, Wade Shen, Christine Moran, Richard Zens, Chris Dyer, Ondrej Bojar, Alexandra Constantin, and Evan Herbst. 2007. Moses: Open source toolkit for statistical machine translation. In *ACL*, pages 177–180, Prague, Czech Republic, June.

Terry Koo, Xavier Carreras, and Michael Collins. 2008. Simple semi-supervised dependency parsing. In *ACL*, pages 595–603, Columbus, Ohio, June.

Dekang Lin and Xiaoyun Wu. 2009. Phrase clustering for discriminative learning. In *Proceedings of the Joint Conference of the ACL and the AFNLP*, pages 1030–1038, Singapore, August.

Robert C. Moore and Chris Quirk. 2007. Faster beam-search decoding for phrasal statistical machine translation. In *MT Summit XI*, September.

Vinh Van Nguyen, Akira Shimazu, Minh Le Nguyen, and Thai Phuong Nguyen. 2009. Improving a lexicalized hierarchical reordering model using maximum entropy. In *MT Summit XII*, Ottawa, Canada, August.

Franz Josef Och and Hermann Ney. 2003. A systematic comparison of various statistical alignment models. *Computational Linguistics*, 29(1), March.

Franz Josef Och and Hermann Ney. 2004. The alignment template approach to statistical machine translation. *Computational Linguistics*, 30(4), December.

Franz Josef Och. 1999. An efficient method for determining bilingual word classes. In *EACL*.

Kishore Papineni, Salim Roukos, Todd Ward, and Wei-Jing Zhu. 2002. BLEU: a method for automatic evaluation of machine translation. In *ACL*, pages 311–318.

Patrick Simianer, Stefan Riezler, and Chris Dyer. 2012. Joint feature selection in distributed stochastic learning for large-scale discriminative training in smt. In *ACL*, pages 11–21, Jeju Island, Korea, July.

Christoph Tillmann. 2004. A unigram orientation model for statistical machine translation. In *HLT-NAACL*, pages 101–104, Boston, USA, May.

Deyi Xiong, Qun Liu, and Shouxun Lin. 2006. Maximum entropy based phrase reordering model for statistical machine translation. In *COLING-ACL*, pages 521–528, Sydney, Australia, July.

Sirvan Yahyaei and Christof Monz. 2010. Dynamic distortion in a discriminative reordering model for statistical machine translation. In *Proceedings of the International Workshop on Spoken Language Translation (IWSLT)*, pages 353–360.

Richard Zens and Hermann Ney. 2004. Improvements in phrase-based statistical machine translation. In *HLT-NAACL*, pages 257–264, Boston, USA, May.

Richard Zens and Hermann Ney. 2006. Discriminative reordering models for statistical machine translation. In *Proceedings on the Workshop on Statistical Machine Translation*, pages 55–63, New York City, June.

Simultaneous Word-Morpheme Alignment for Statistical Machine Translation

Elif Eyigöz
Computer Science
University of Rochester
Rochester, NY 14627

Daniel Gildea
Computer Science
University of Rochester
Rochester, NY 14627

Kemal Oflazer
Computer Science
Carnegie Mellon University
PO Box 24866, Doha, Qatar

Abstract

Current word alignment models for statistical machine translation do not address morphology beyond merely splitting words. We present a two-level alignment model that distinguishes between words and morphemes, in which we embed an IBM Model 1 inside an HMM based word alignment model. The model jointly induces word and morpheme alignments using an EM algorithm. We evaluated our model on Turkish-English parallel data. We obtained significant improvement of BLEU scores over IBM Model 4. Our results indicate that utilizing information from morphology improves the quality of word alignments.

1 Introduction

All current state-of-the-art approaches to SMT rely on an automatically word-aligned corpus. However, current alignment models do not take into account the morpheme, the smallest unit of syntax, beyond merely splitting words. Since morphology has not been addressed explicitly in word alignment models, researchers have resorted to tweaking SMT systems by manipulating the content and the form of what should be the so-called "word".

Since the word is the smallest unit of translation from the standpoint of word alignment models, the central focus of research on translating morphologically rich languages has been decomposition of morphologically complex words into tokens of the right granularity and representation for machine translation. Chung and Gildea (2009) and Naradowsky and Toutanova (2011) use unsupervised methods to find word segmentations that create a one-to-one mapping of words in both languages. Al-Onaizan et al. (1999), Čmejrek et al. (2003), and Goldwater and McClosky (2005) manipulate morphologically rich languages by selective lemmatization. Lee (2004) attempts to learn the probability of deleting or merging Arabic morphemes for Arabic to English translation. Niessen and Ney (2000) split German compound nouns, and merge German phrases that correspond to a single English word. Alternatively, Yeniterzi and Oflazer (2010) manipulate words of the morphologically poor side of a language pair to mimic having a morphological structure similar to the richer side via exploiting syntactic structure, in order to improve the similarity of words on both sides of the translation.

We present an alignment model that assumes internal structure for words, and we can legitimately talk about words and their morphemes in line with the linguistic conception of these terms. Our model avoids the problem of collapsing words and morphemes into one single category. We adopt a two-level representation of alignment: the first level involves word alignment, the second level involves morpheme alignment in the scope of a given word alignment. The model jointly induces word and morpheme alignments using an EM algorithm.

We develop our model in two stages. Our initial model is analogous to IBM Model 1: the first level is a bag of words in a pair of sentences, and the second level is a bag of morphemes. In this manner, we embed one IBM Model 1 in the scope of another IBM Model 1. At the second stage, by introducing distortion probabilities at the word level, we develop an HMM extension of the initial model.

We evaluated the performance of our model on the

Turkish-English pair both on hand-aligned data and by running end-to-end machine translation experiments. To evaluate our results, we created gold word alignments for 75 Turkish-English sentences. We obtain significant improvement of AER and BLEU scores over IBM Model 4. Section 2.1 introduces the concept of morpheme alignment in terms of its relation to word alignment. Section 2.2 presents the derivation of the EM algorithm and Section 3 presents the results of our experiments.

2 Two-level Alignment Model (TAM)

2.1 Morpheme Alignment

Following the standard alignment models of Brown et al. (1993), we assume one-to-many alignment for both words and morphemes. A word alignment a_w (or only a) is a function mapping a set of word positions in a source language sentence to a set of word positions in a target language sentence. A morpheme alignment a_m is a function mapping a set of morpheme positions in a source language sentence to a set of morpheme positions in a target language sentence. A morpheme position is a pair of integers (j, k), which defines a word position j and a relative morpheme position k in the word at position j. The alignments below are depicted in Figures 1 and 2.

$$a_w(1) = 1 \quad a_m(2,1) = (1,1) \quad a_w(2) = 1$$

Figure 1 shows a word alignment between two sentences. Figure 2 shows the morpheme alignment between same sentences. We assume that all unaligned morphemes in a sentence map to a special null morpheme.

A morpheme alignment a_m and a word alignment a_w are *compatible* if and only if they satisfy the following conditions: If the morpheme alignment a_m maps a morpheme of e to a morpheme of f, then the word alignment a_w maps e to f. If the word alignment a_w maps e to f, then the morpheme alignment a_m maps at least one morpheme of e to a morpheme of f. If the word alignment a_w maps e to null, then all of its morphemes are mapped to null. In sum, a morpheme alignment a_m and a word alignment a_w are *compatible* if and only if:

$$\begin{aligned} &\forall j,k,m,n \in \mathbb{N}^+,\ \exists s,t \in \mathbb{N}^+ \\ &[a_m(j,k) = (m,n) \Rightarrow a_w(j) = m] \wedge \\ &\qquad [a_w(j) = m \Rightarrow a_m(j,s) = (m,t)] \wedge \\ &\qquad\quad [a_w(j) = \text{null} \Rightarrow a_m(j,k) = \text{null}] \end{aligned} \quad (1)$$

Please note that, according to this definition of compatibility, '$a_m(j,k) = \text{null}$' does not necessarily imply '$a_w(j) = \text{null}$'.

A word alignment induces a set of compatible morpheme alignments. However, a morpheme alignment induces a unique word alignment. Therefore, if a morpheme alignment a_m and a word alignment a_w are compatible, then the word alignment is a_w is recoverable from the morpheme alignment a_m.

The two-level alignment model (TAM), like IBM Model 1, defines an alignment between words of a sentence pair. In addition, it defines a morpheme alignment between the morphemes of a sentence pair.

The problem domain of IBM Model 1 is defined over alignments between words, which is depicted as the gray box in Figure 1. In Figure 2, the smaller boxes embedded inside the main box depict the new problem domain of TAM. Given the word alignments in Figure 1, we are presented with a new alignment problem defined over their morphemes. The new alignment problem is constrained by the given word alignment. We, like IBM Model 1, adopt a bag-of-morphemes approach to this new problem. We thus embed one IBM Model 1 into the scope of another IBM Model 1, and formulate a second-order interpretation of IBM Model 1.

TAM, like IBM Model 1, assumes that words and morphemes are translated independently of their context. The units of translation are both words and morphemes. Both the word alignment a_w and the morpheme alignment a_m are hidden variables that need to be learned from the data using the EM algorithm.

In IBM Model 1, $p(\mathbf{e}|\mathbf{f})$, the probability of translating the sentence $\mathbf{f}$ into $\mathbf{e}$ with any alignment is computed by summing over all possible word alignments:

$$p(\mathbf{e}|\mathbf{f}) = \sum_a p(a, \mathbf{e}|\mathbf{f})$$

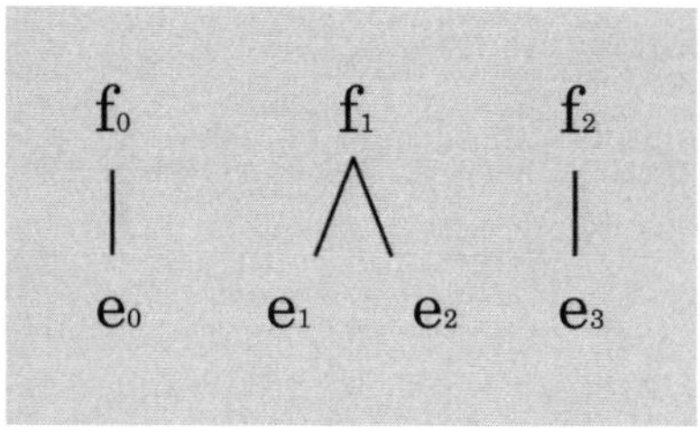

Figure 1: Word alignment

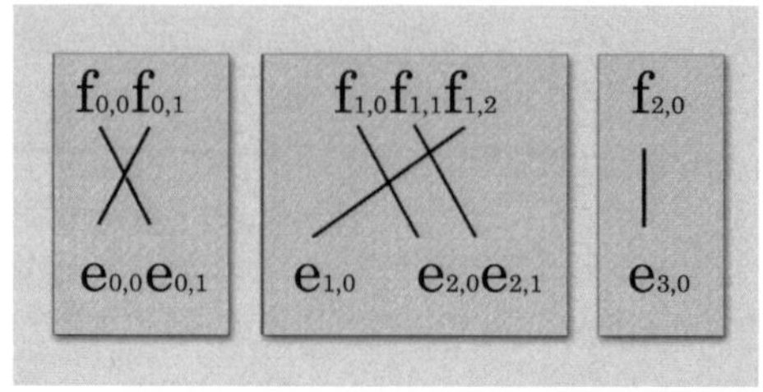

Figure 2: Morpheme alignment

In TAM, the probability of translating the sentence $\mathbf{f}$ into $\mathbf{e}$ with any alignment is computed by summing over all possible word alignments and all possible morpheme alignments that are compatible with a given word alignment a_w:

$$p(\mathbf{e}|\mathbf{f}) = \sum_{a_w} p(a_w, \mathbf{e}|\mathbf{f}) \sum_{a_m} p(a_m, \mathbf{e}|a_w, \mathbf{f}) \quad (2)$$

where a_m stands for a morpheme alignment. Since the morpheme alignment a_m is in the scope of a given word alignment a_w, a_m is constrained by a_w.

In IBM Model 1, we compute the probability of translating the sentence $\mathbf{f}$ into $\mathbf{e}$ by summing over all possible word alignments between the words of $\mathbf{f}$ and $\mathbf{e}$:

$$p(\mathbf{e}|\mathbf{f}) = R(\mathbf{e}, \mathbf{f}) \prod_{j=1}^{|\mathbf{e}|} \sum_{i=0}^{|\mathbf{f}|} t(e_j|f_i) \quad (3)$$

where $t(e_j \mid f_i)$ is the word translation probability of e_j given f_i. $R(\mathbf{e}, \mathbf{f})$ substitutes $\frac{P(l_\mathbf{e}|l_\mathbf{f})}{(l_\mathbf{f}+1)^{l_\mathbf{e}}}$ for easy readability.[1]

In TAM, the probability of translating the sentence $\mathbf{f}$ into $\mathbf{e}$ is computed as follows:

$$\underbrace{R(\mathbf{e}, \mathbf{f}) \prod_{j=1}^{|\mathbf{e}|} \sum_{i=0}^{|\mathbf{f}|} \Bigg(t(e_j|f_i)}_{\text{Word}} \; \underbrace{R(e_j, f_i) \prod_{k=1}^{|e_j|} \sum_{n=0}^{|f_i|} t(e_j^k|f_i^n) \Bigg)}_{\text{Morpheme}}$$

where f_i^n is the nth morpheme of the word at position i. The right part of this equation, the contribution of morpheme translation probabilities, is in the scope of the left part. In the right part, we compute the probability of translating the word f_i into the word e_j by summing over all possible morpheme alignments between the morphemes of e_j and f_i. $R(e_j, f_i)$ is equivalent to $R(\mathbf{e}, \mathbf{f})$ except for the fact that its domain is not the set of sentences but the set of words. The length of words e_j and f_i in $R(e_j, f_i)$ are the number of morphemes of e_j and f_i.

The left part, the contribution of word translation probabilities alone, equals Eqn. 3. Therefore, canceling the contribution of morpheme translation probabilities reduces TAM to IBM Model 1. In our experiments, we call this reduced version of TAM 'word-only' (IBM). TAM with the contribution of both word and morpheme translation probabilities, as the equation above, is called 'word-and-morpheme'. Finally, we also cancel out the contribution of word translation probabilities, which is called 'morpheme-only'. In the 'morpheme-only' version of TAM, $t(e_j|f_i)$ equals 1. Bellow is the equation of $p(\mathbf{e}|\mathbf{f})$ in the morpheme-only model.

$$p(\mathbf{e}|\mathbf{f}) = R(\mathbf{e}, \mathbf{f}) \prod_{j=1}^{|\mathbf{e}|} \sum_{i=0}^{|\mathbf{f}|} \prod_{k=1}^{|e_j|} \sum_{n=0}^{|f_i|} R(e_j, f_i) t(e_j^k|f_i^n) \quad (4)$$

Please note that, although this version of the two-level alignment model does not use word translation probabilities, it is also a word-aware model, as morpheme alignments are restricted to correspond to a valid word alignment according to Eqn. 1. When presented with words that exhibit no morphology, the morpheme-only version of TAM is equivalent to IBM Model 1, as every single-morpheme word is itself a morpheme.

Deficiency and Non-Deficiency of TAM We present two versions of TAM, the word-and-

[1] $l_\mathbf{e} = |\mathbf{e}|$ is the number of words in sentence $\mathbf{e}$ and $l_\mathbf{f} = |\mathbf{f}|$.

morpheme and the morpheme-only versions. The word-and-morpheme version of the model is deficient whereas the morpheme-only model is not.

The word-and-morpheme version is deficient, because some probability is allocated to cases where the morphemes generated by the morpheme model do not match the words generated by the word model. Moreover, although most languages exhibit morphology to some extent, they can be input to the algorithm without morpheme boundaries. This also causes deficiency in the word-and-morpheme version, as single morpheme words are generated twice, as a word and as a morpheme.

Nevertheless, we observed that the deficient version of TAM can perform as good as the non-deficient version of TAM, and sometimes performs better. This is not surprising, as deficient word alignment models such as IBM Model 3 or discriminative word alignment models work well in practice.

Goldwater and McClosky (2005) proposed a morpheme aware word alignment model for language pairs in which the source language words correspond to only one morpheme. Their word alignment model is:

$$P(e|f) = \prod_{k=0}^{K} P(e^k|f)$$

where e^k is the kth morpheme of the word e. The morpheme-only version of our model is a generalization of this model. However, there are major differences in their and our implementation and experimentation. Their model assumes a fixed number of possible morphemes associated with any stem in the language, and if the morpheme e^k is not present, it is assigned a null value.

The null word on the source side is also a null morpheme, since every single morpheme word is itself a morpheme. In TAM, the null word is the null morpheme that all unaligned morphemes align to.

2.2 Second-Order Counts

In TAM, we collect counts for both word translations and morpheme translations. Unlike IBM Model 1, $R(e, f) = \frac{P(l_e|l_f)}{(l_f+1)^{l_e}}$ does not cancel out in the counts of TAM. To compute the conditional probability $P(l_e|l_f)$, we assume that the length of word e (the number of morphemes of word e) varies according to a Poisson distribution with a mean that is linear with length of the word f.

$$\begin{aligned} P(l_e|l_f) &= F_{\text{Poisson}}(l_e, r \cdot l_f) \\ &= \frac{\exp(-r \cdot l_f)(r \cdot l_f)^{l_e}}{l_e!} \end{aligned}$$

$F_{\text{Poisson}}(l_e, r \cdot l_f)$ expresses the probability that there are l_e morphemes in e if the expected number of morphemes in e is $r \cdot l_f$, where $r = \frac{\mathbb{E}[l_e]}{\mathbb{E}[l_f]}$ is the rate parameter. Since l_f is undefined for null words, we omit $R(e, f)$ for null words.

We introduce $T(e|f)$, the translation probability of e given f with all possible morpheme alignments, as it will occur frequently in the counts of TAM:

$$T(e|f) = t(e|f)R(e, f) \prod_{k=1}^{|e|} \sum_{n=0}^{|f|} t(e^k|f^n)$$

The role of $T(e|f)$ in TAM is very similar to the role of $t(e|f)$ in IBM Model 1. In finding the Viterbi alignments, we do not take max over the values in the summation in $T(e|f)$.

2.2.1 Word Counts

Similar to IBM Model 1, we collect counts for word translations over all possible alignments, weighted by their probability. In Eqn. 5, the count function collects evidence from a sentence pair $(\mathbf{e}, \mathbf{f})$ as follows: For all words e_j of the sentence $\mathbf{e}$ and for all word alignments $a_w(j)$, we collect counts for a particular input word f and an output word e iff $e_j = e$ and $f_{a_w(j)} = f$.

$$c_w(e|f; \mathbf{e}, \mathbf{f}, a_w) = \sum_{\substack{1 \leq j \leq |\mathbf{e}| \\ \text{s.t.} \\ e = e_j \\ f = f_{a_w(j)}}} \frac{T(e|f)}{\sum_{i=0}^{|f|} T(e|f_i)} \quad (5)$$

2.2.2 Morpheme Counts

As for morpheme translations, we collect counts over all possible word and morpheme alignments, weighted by their probability. The morpheme count function below collects evidence from a word pair (e, f) in a sentence pair $(\mathbf{e}, \mathbf{f})$ as follows: For all words e_j of the sentence $\mathbf{e}$ and for all word alignments $a_w(j)$, for all morphemes e_j^k of the word e_j and for all morpheme alignments $a_m(j, k)$, we collect counts for a particular input morpheme g and an output morpheme h iff $e_j = e$ and $f_{a_w(j)} = f$ and $h = e_j^k$ and $g = f_{a_m(j,k)}$.

$$c_m(h|g; \mathbf{e}, \mathbf{f}, a_w, a_m) = \sum_{\substack{1 \le j \le |\mathbf{e}| \\ \text{s.t.} \\ e=e_j \\ f=f_{a_w(j)}}} \sum_{\substack{1 \le k \le |e| \\ \text{s.t.} \\ h=e_j^k \\ g=f_{a_m(j,k)}}} \frac{T(e|f)}{\sum_{i=0}^{|\mathbf{f}|} T(e|f_i)} \frac{t(h|g)}{\sum_{i=1}^{|f|} t(h|f^i)}$$

The left part of the morpheme count function is the same as the word-counts in Eqn. 5. Since it does not contain h or g, it needs to be computed only once for each word. The right part of the equation is familiar from the IBM Model 1 counts.

2.3 HMM Extension

We implemented TAM with the HMM extension (Vogel et al., 1996) at the word level. We redefine $p(\mathbf{e}|\mathbf{f})$ as follows:

$$R(\mathbf{e}, \mathbf{f}) \sum_{a_w} \prod_{j=1}^{|e|} \Bigg(p(s(j)\ |C(f_{a_w(j-1)}))\ t(e_j|f_{a_w(j)}) \\ R(e_j, f_{a_w(j)}) \sum_{a_m} \prod_{k=1}^{|e_j|} t(e_j^k|f_{a_m(j,k)}) \Bigg)$$

where the distortion probability depends on the relative jump width $s(j) = a_w(j-1) - a_w(j)$, as opposed to absolute positions. The distortion probability is conditioned on class of the previous aligned word $C(f_{a_w(j-1)})$. We used the `mkcls` tool in GIZA (Och and Ney, 2003) to learn the word classes.

We formulated the HMM extension of TAM only at the word level. Nevertheless, the morpheme-only version of TAM also has an HMM extension, as it is also a word-aware model. To obtain the HMM extension of the morpheme-only version, substitute $t(e_j|f_{a_w(j)})$ with 1 in the equation above.

For the HMM to work correctly, we must handle jumping to and jumping from null positions. We learn the probabilities of jumping to a null position from the data. To compute the jump probability from a null position, we keep track of the nearest previous source word that does not align to null, and use the position of the previous non-null word to calculate the jump width. For this reason, we use a total of $2l_{\mathbf{f}} - 1$ words for the HMM model, the positions $> l_f$ stand for null positions between the words of f (Och and Ney, 2003). We do not allow null to null jumps. In sum, we enforce the following constraints:

$$P(i + l_f + 1|i') = p(null|i')$$
$$P(i + l_f + 1|i' + l_f + 1) = 0$$
$$P(i|i' + l_f + 1) = p(i|i')$$

In the HMM extension of TAM, we perform forward-backward training using the word counts in Eqn. 5 as the emission probabilities. We calculate the posterior word translation probabilities for each e_j and f_i such that $1 \le j \le l_{\mathbf{e}}$ and $1 \le i \le 2l_{\mathbf{f}} - 1$ as follows:

$$\gamma_j(i) = \frac{\alpha_j(i)\beta_j(i)}{\sum_{m=1}^{2l_f-1} \alpha_j(m)\beta_j(m)}$$

where α is the forward and β is the backward probabilities of the HMM. The HMM word counts, in turn, are the posterior word translation probabilities obtained from the forward-backward training:

$$c_w(e|f; \mathbf{e}, \mathbf{f}, a_w) = \sum_{\substack{1 \le j \le |\mathbf{e}| \\ \text{s.t.} \\ e=e_j \\ f=f_{a_w(j)}}} \gamma_j(a_w(j))$$

Likewise, we use the posterior probabilities in HMM morpheme counts:

$$c_m(h|g; \mathbf{e}, \mathbf{f}, a_w, a_m) = \sum_{\substack{1 \le j \le |\mathbf{e}| \\ \text{s.t.} \\ e=e_j \\ f=f_{a_w(j)}}} \sum_{\substack{1 \le k \le |e| \\ \text{s.t.} \\ h=e_j^k \\ g=f_{a_m(j,k)}}} \gamma_j(a_w(j)) \frac{t(h|g)}{\sum_{i=1}^{|f|} t(h|f^i)}$$

The complexity of the HMM extension of TAM is $O(n^3m^2)$, where n is the number of words, and m is the number of morphemes per word.

2.4 Variational Bayes

Moore (2004) showed that the EM algorithm is particularly susceptible to overfitting in the case of rare words when training IBM Model 1. In order to prevent overfitting, we use the Variational Bayes extension of the EM algorithm (Beal, 2003). This

(a)	Kasım 1996'da, Türk makamları, İçişleri Bakanlığı bünyesinde bir kayıp kişileri arama birimi oluşturdu.
(b)	Kasım+Noun 1996+Num–Loc ,+Punc Türk+Noun makam+Noun–A3pl–P3sg ,+Punc İçişi+Noun–A3pl–P3sg Bakanlık+Noun–P3sg bünye+Noun–P3sg–Loc bir+Det kayıp+Adj kişi+Noun–A3pl–Acc ara+Verb–Inf2 birim+Noun–P3sg oluş+Verb–Caus–Past .+Punc
(c)	In November 1996 the Turkish authorities set up a missing persons search unit within the Ministry of the Interior.
(d)	in+IN November+NNP 1996+CD the+DT Turkish+JJ **author+NN–ity+N|N.–NNS** set+VB–VBD up+RP a+DT miss+VB–VBG+JJ **person+NN–NNS** search+NN unit+NN within+IN the+DT minister+NN–y+N|N. of+IN the+DT interior+NN .+.
(e)	In+IN November+NNP 1996+CD the+DT Turkish+JJ authorities+NNS set+VBD up+RP a+DT missing+JJ persons+NNS search+NN unit+NN within+IN the+DT Ministry+NNP of+IN the+DT Interior+NNP .+.

Figure 3: Turkish-English data examples

amounts to a small change to the M step of the original EM algorithm. We introduce Dirichlet priors α to perform an inexact normalization by applying the function $f(v) = \exp(\psi(v))$ to the expected counts collected in the E step, where ψ is the digamma function (Johnson, 2007).

$$\theta_{x|y} = \frac{f(E[c(x|y)] + \alpha)}{f(\sum_j E[c(x_j|y)] + \alpha)}$$

We set α to 10^{-20}, a very low value, to have the effect of anti-smoothing, as low values of α cause the algorithm to favor words which co-occur frequently and to penalize words that co-occur rarely.

3 Experimental Setup

3.1 Data

We trained our model on a Turkish-English parallel corpus of approximately 50K sentences, which have a maximum of 80 morphemes. Our parallel data consists mainly of documents in international relations and legal documents from sources such as the Turkish Ministry of Foreign Affairs, EU, etc. We followed a heavily supervised approach in morphological analysis. The Turkish data was first morphologically parsed (Oflazer, 1994), then disambiguated (Sak et al., 2007) to select the contextually salient interpretation of words. In addition, we removed morphological features that are not explicitly marked by an overt morpheme — thus each feature symbol beyond the root part-of-speech corresponds to a morpheme. Line (b) of Figure 3 shows an example of a segmented Turkish sentence. The root is followed by its part-of-speech tag separated by a '+'. The derivational and inflectional morphemes that follow the root are separated by '–'s. In all experiments, we used the same segmented version of the Turkish data, because Turkish is an agglutinative language.

For English, we used the CELEX database (Baayen et al., 1995) to segment English words into morphemes. We created two versions of the data: a segmented version that involves both derivational and inflectional morphology, and an unsegmented POS tagged version. The CELEX database provides tags for English derivational morphemes, which indicate their function: the part-of-speech category the morpheme attaches to and the part-of-speech category it returns. For example, in 'sparse+ity' = 'sparsity', the morpheme *-ity* attaches to an adjective to the right and returns a noun. This behavior is represented as 'N|A.' in CELEX, where '.' indicates the attachment position. We used these tags in addition to the surface forms of the English morphemes, in order to disambiguate multiple functions of a single surface morpheme.

The English sentence in line (d) of Figure 3 exhibits both derivational and inflectional morphology. For example, 'author+ity+s'='authorities' has both an inflectional suffix *-s* and a derivational suffix *-ity*, whereas 'person+s' has only an inflectional suffix *-s*.

For both English and Turkish data, the dashes in Figure 3 stand for morpheme boundaries, therefore the strings between the dashes are treated as indi-

	Words		Morphemes	
	Tokens	Types	Tokens	Types
English Der+Inf	1,033,726	27,758	1,368,188	19,448
English POS	1,033,726	28,647	1,033,726	28,647
Turkish Der+Inf	812,374	57,249	1,484,673	16,713

Table 1: Data statistics

visible units. Table 1 shows the number of words, the number of morphemes and the respective vocabulary sizes. The average number of morphemes in segmented Turkish words is 2.69, and the average length of segmented English words is 1.57.

3.2 Experiments

We initialized our baseline word-only model with 5 iterations of IBM Model 1, and further trained the HMM extension (Vogel et al., 1996) for 5 iterations. We call this model 'baseline HMM' in the discussions. Similarly, we initialized the two versions of TAM with 5 iterations of the model explained in Section 2.2, and then trained the HMM extension of it as explained in Section 2.3 for 5 iterations.

To obtain BLEU scores for TAM models and our implementation of the word-only model, i.e. baseline-HMM, we bypassed GIZA++ in the Moses toolkit (Och and Ney, 2003). We also ran GIZA++ (IBM Model 1–4) on the data. We translated 1000 sentence test sets.

4 Results and Discussion

We evaluated the performance of our model in two different ways. First, we evaluated against gold word alignments for 75 Turkish-English sentences. Second, we used the word Viterbi alignments of our algorithm to obtain BLEU scores.

Table 2 shows the AER (Och and Ney, 2003) of the word alignments of the Turkish-English pair and the translation performance of the word alignments learned by our models. We report the grow-diag-final (Koehn et al., 2003) of the Viterbi alignments. In Table 2, results obtained with different versions of the English data are represented as follows: 'Der' stands for derivational morphology, 'Inf' for inflectional morphology, and 'POS' for part-of-speech tags. 'Der+Inf' corresponds to the example sentence in line (d) in Figure 3, and 'POS' to line (e). 'DIR' stands for models with Dirichlet priors, and 'NO DIR' stands for models without Dirichlet priors. All reported results are of the HMM extension of respective models.

Table 2 shows that using Dirichlet priors hurts the AER performance of the word-and-morpheme model in all experiment settings, and benefits the morpheme-only model in the POS tagged experiment settings.

In order to reduce the effect of nondeterminism, we run Moses three times per experiment setting, and report the highest BLEU scores obtained. Since the BLEU scores we obtained are close, we did a significance test on the scores (Koehn, 2004). Table 2 visualizes the partition of the BLEU scores into statistical significance groups. If two scores within the same column have the same background color, or the border between their cells is removed, then the difference between their scores is not statistically significant. For example, the best BLEU scores, which are in bold, have white background. All scores in a given experiment setting without white background are significantly worse than the best score in that experiment setting, unless there is no border separating them from the best score.

In all experiment settings, the TAM Models perform better than the baseline-HMM. Our experiments showed that the baseline-HMM benefits from Dirichlet priors to a larger extent than the TAM models. Dirichlet priors help reduce the overfitting in the case of rare words. The size of the word vocabulary is larger than the size of the morpheme vocabulary. Therefore the number of rare words is larger for words than it is for morphemes. Consequently, baseline-HMM, using only the word vocab-

			BLEU EN to TR		BLEU TR to EN		AER	
			Der+Inf	POS	Der+Inf	POS	Der+Inf	POS
NO DIR	TAM	Morph only	**22.57**	**22.54**	**29.30**	**29.45**	0.293	0.276
		Word & Morph	21.95	22.37	28.81	29.01	0.286	0.282
	WORD	IBM 4	21.82	21.82	27.91	27.91	0.357	0.370
		Base-HMM	21.78	21.38	28.22	28.02	0.381	0.375
		IBM 4 Morph	17.15	17.94	25.70	26.33	N/A	N/A
DIR	TAM	Morph only	22.18	**22.52**	**29.32**	**29.98**	0.304	0.256
		Word & Morph	**22.43**	21.62	29.21	29.11	0.338	0.317
	WORD	IBM 4	21.82	21.82	27.91	27.91	0.357	0.370
		Base-HMM	21.69	21.95	28.76	29.13	0.381	0.377
		IBM 4 Morph	17.15	17.94	25.70	26.33	N/A	N/A

Table 2: AER and BLEU Scores

ulary, benefits from the use of Dirichlet priors more than the TAM models.

In four out of eight experiment settings, the morpheme-only model performs better than the word-and-morpheme version of TAM. However, please note that our extensive experimentation with TAM models revealed that the superiority of the morpheme-only model over the word-and-morpheme model is highly dependent on segmentation accuracy, degree of segmentation, and morphological richness of languages.

Finally, we treated morphemes as words and trained IBM Model 4 on the morpheme segmented versions of the data. To obtain BLEU scores, we had to unsegment the translation output: we concatenated the prefixes to the morpheme to the right, and suffixes to the morpheme to the left. Since this process creates malformed words, the BLEU scores obtained are much lower than the scores obtained by IBM Model 4, the baseline and the TAM Models.

5 Conclusion

We presented two versions of a two-level alignment model for morphologically rich languages. We observed that information provided by word translations and morpheme translations interact in a way that enables the model to be receptive to the partial information in rarely occurring words through their frequently occurring morphemes. We obtained significant improvement of BLEU scores over IBM Model 4. In conclusion, morphologically aware word alignment models prove to be superior to their word-only counterparts.

Acknowledgments Funded by NSF award IIS-0910611. Kemal Oflazer acknowledges the generous support of the Qatar Foundation through Carnegie Mellon University's Seed Research program. The statements made herein are solely the responsibility of this author(s), and not necessarily that of Qatar Foundation.

References

Yaser Al-Onaizan, Jan Curin, Michael Jahr, Kevin Knight, John Lafferty, Dan Melamed, Franz-Josef Och, David Purdy, Noah A. Smith, and David Yarowsky. 1999. Statistical machine translation.

Technical report, Final Report, JHU Summer Workshop.

R.H. Baayen, R. Piepenbrock, and L. Gulikers. 1995. *The CELEX Lexical Database (Release 2) [CD-ROM]*. Linguistic Data Consortium, University of Pennsylvania [Distributor], Philadelphia, PA.

Matthew J. Beal. 2003. *Variational Algorithms for Approximate Bayesian Inference*. Ph.D. thesis, University College London.

Peter F. Brown, Stephen A. Della Pietra, Vincent J. Della Pietra, and Robert L. Mercer. 1993. The mathematics of statistical machine translation: Parameter estimation. *Computational Linguistics*, 19(2):263–311.

Tagyoung Chung and Daniel Gildea. 2009. Unsupervised tokenization for machine translation. In *EMNLP*, pages 718–726.

Martin Čmejrek, Jan Cuřín, and Jiří Havelka. 2003. Czech-English dependency-based machine translation. In *EACL*, pages 83–90, Morristown, NJ, USA. Association for Computational Linguistics.

Sharon Goldwater and David McClosky. 2005. Improving statistical MT through morphological analysis. In *HLT-EMNLP*.

Mark Johnson. 2007. Why doesn't EM find good HMM POS-taggers? In *EMNLP-CoNLL*, pages 296–305, Prague, Czech Republic, June. Association for Computational Linguistics.

Philipp Koehn, Franz Josef Och, and Daniel Marcu. 2003. Statistical phrase-based translation. In *HLT-NAACL*.

Philipp Koehn. 2004. Statistical significance tests for machine translation evaluation. In *EMNLP*, pages 388–395.

Young-suk Lee. 2004. Morphological analysis for statistical machine translation. In *HLT-NAACL*, pages 57–60.

Robert C. Moore. 2004. Improving IBM word alignment model 1. In *ACL*, pages 518–525, Barcelona, Spain, July.

Jason Naradowsky and Kristina Toutanova. 2011. Unsupervised bilingual morpheme segmentation and alignment with context-rich Hidden Semi-Markov Models. In *Proceedings of the 49th Annual Meeting of the Association for Computational Linguistics: Human Language Technologies*, pages 895–904, Portland, Oregon, USA, June. Association for Computational Linguistics.

Sonja Niessen and Hermann Ney. 2000. Improving SMT quality with morpho-syntactic analysis. In *Computational Linguistics*, pages 1081–1085, Morristown, NJ, USA. Association for Computational Linguistics.

Franz Josef Och and Hermann Ney. 2003. A systematic comparison of various statistical alignment models. *Computational Linguistics*, 29(1):19–51.

Kemal Oflazer. 1994. Two-level description of Turkish morphology. *Literary and Linguistic Computing*, 9(2).

Haşim Sak, Tunga Güngör, and Murat Saraçlar. 2007. Morphological disambiguation of Turkish text with perceptron algorithm. In *CICLing*, pages 107–118, Berlin, Heidelberg. Springer-Verlag.

Stephan Vogel, Hermann Ney, and Christoph Tillmann. 1996. HMM-based word alignment in statistical translation. In *COLING*, pages 836–841.

Reyyan Yeniterzi and Kemal Oflazer. 2010. Syntax-to-morphology mapping in factored phrase-based statistical machine translation from English to Turkish. In *ACL*, pages 454–464, Stroudsburg, PA, USA. Association for Computational Linguistics.

Multi-faceted Event Recognition with Bootstrapped Dictionaries

Ruihong Huang and Ellen Riloff
School of Computing
University of Utah
Salt Lake City, UT 84112
{huangrh, riloff}@cs.utah.edu

Abstract

Identifying documents that describe a specific type of event is challenging due to the high complexity and variety of event descriptions. We propose a *multi-faceted event recognition* approach, which identifies documents about an event using event phrases as well as defining characteristics of the event. Our research focuses on civil unrest events and learns civil unrest expressions as well as phrases corresponding to potential agents and reasons for civil unrest. We present a bootstrapping algorithm that automatically acquires event phrases, agent terms, and purpose (reason) phrases from unannotated texts. We use the bootstrapped dictionaries to identify civil unrest documents and show that multi-faceted event recognition can yield high accuracy.

1 Introduction

Many people are interested in following news reports about events. Government agencies are keenly interested in news about civil unrest, acts of terrorism, and disease outbreaks. Companies want to stay on top of news about corporate acquisitions, high-level management changes, and new joint ventures. The general public is interested in articles about crime, natural disasters, and plane crashes. We will refer to the task of identifying documents that describe a specific type of event as *event recognition*.

It is tempting to assume that event keywords are sufficient to identify documents that discuss instances of an event. But event words are rarely reliable on their own. For example, consider the challenge of finding documents about civil unrest. The words *"strike"*, *"rally"*, and *"riot"* refer to common types of civil unrest, but they frequently refer to other things as well. A strike can refer to a military event or a sporting event (e.g., *"air strike"*, *"bowling strike"*), a rally can be a race or a spirited exchange (e.g.,*"car rally"*, *"tennis rally"*), and a riot can refer to something funny (e.g., *"she's a riot"*). Event keywords also appear in general discussions that do not mention a specific event (e.g., *"37 states prohibit teacher strikes"* or *"The fine for inciting a riot is $1,000"*). Furthermore, many relevant documents are not easy to recognize because events can be described with complex expressions that do not include event keywords. For example, *"took to the streets"*, *"walked off their jobs"* and *"stormed parliament"* often describe civil unrest.

The goal of our research is to recognize event descriptions in text by identifying event expressions as well as defining characteristics of the event. We propose that *agents* and *purpose* are characteristics of an event that are essential to distinguish one type of event from another. The agent responsible for an action often determines how we categorize the action. For example, natural disasters, military operations, and terrorist attacks can all produce human casualties and physical destruction. But the agent of a natural disaster must be a natural force, the agent of a military incident must be military personnel, and the agent of a terrorist attack is never a natural force and rarely military personnel. There may be other important factors as well, but the agent is often an essential part of an event definition.

The purpose of an event is also a crucial factor in distinguishing between event types. For example, civil unrest events and sporting events both involve large groups of people amassing at a specific site. But the purpose of civil unrest gatherings is to protest against socio-political problems, while sporting events are intended as entertainment. As another example, terrorist events and military incidents can both cause casualties, but the purpose of terrorism is to cause widespread fear, while the purpose of military actions is to protect national security interests.

Our research explores the idea of *multi-faceted event recognition*: using event expressions as well as facets of the event (agents and purpose) to identify documents about a specific type of event. We present a bootstrapping framework to automatically create event phrase, agent, and purpose dictionaries. The learning process uses unannotated texts, a few event keywords, and seed terms for common agents and purpose phrases associated with the event type.

Our bootstrapping algorithm exploits the observation that event expressions, agents, and purpose phrases often appear together in sentences that introduce an event. In the first step, we extract event expressions based on dependency relations with an agent and purpose phrase. The harvested event expressions are added to an event phrase dictionary. In the second step, new agent terms are extracted from sentences containing an event phrase and a purpose phrase, and new purpose phrases are harvested from sentences containing an event phrase and an agent. These harvested terms are added to agent and purpose dictionaries. The bootstrapping algorithm ricochets back and forth, alternately learning new event phrases and learning new agent/purpose phrases, in an iterative process.

We explore several ways of using these bootstrapped dictionaries. We conclude that finding at least two different types of event information produces high accuracy (88% precision) with good recall (71%) on documents that contain an event keyword. We also present experiments with documents that do not contain event keywords, and obtain 74% accuracy when matching all three types of event information.

2 Related Work

Event recognition has been studied in several different contexts. There has been a lot of research on event extraction, where the goal is to extract facts about events from text (e.g., (ACE Evaluations, 2006; Appelt et al., 1993; Riloff, 1996; Yangarber et al., 2000; Chieu and Ng, 2002; Califf and Mooney, 2003; Sudo et al., 2003; Stevenson and Greenwood, 2005; Sekine, 2006)). Although our research does not involve extracting facts, event extraction systems can also be used to identify stories about a specific type of event. For example, the MUC-4 evaluation (MUC-4 Proceedings, 1992) included "text filtering" results that measured the performance of event extraction systems at identifying event-relevant documents. The best text filtering results were high (about 90% F score), but relied on hand-built event extraction systems. More recently, some research has incorporated event region detectors into event extraction systems to improve extraction performance (Gu and Cercone, 2006; Patwardhan and Riloff, 2007; Huang and Riloff, 2011).

There has been recent work on event detection from social media sources (Becker et al., 2011; Popescu et al., 2011). Some research identifies specific types of events in tweets, such as earthquakes (Sakaki et al., 2010) and entertainment events (Benson et al., 2011). There has also been work on event trend detection (Lampos et al., 2010; Mathioudakis and Koudas, 2010) and event prediction through social media, such as predicting elections (Tumasjan et al., 2010; Conover et al., 2011) or stock market indicators (Zhang et al., 2010). (Ritter et al., 2012) generated a calendar of events mentioned on twitter. (Metzler et al., 2012) proposed structured retrieval of historical event information over microblog archives by distilling high quality event representations using a novel temporal query expansion technique.

Some text classification research has focused on event categories. (Riloff and Lehnert, 1994) used an information extraction system to generate *relevancy signatures* that were indicative of different event types. This work originally relied on manually labeled patterns and a hand-crafted semantic dictionary. Later work (Riloff and Lorenzen, 1999) eliminated the need for the dictionary and labeled patterns, but still assumed the availability of relevant/irrelevant training texts.

Event recognition is also related to Topic Detection and Tracking (TDT) (Allan et al., 1998; Allan,

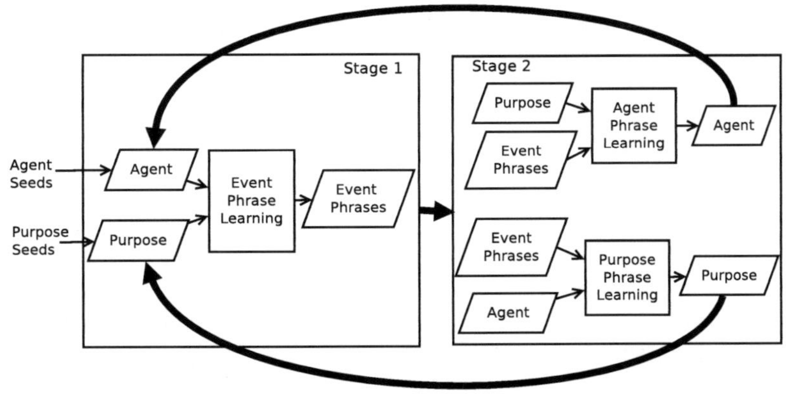

Figure 1: Bootstrapped Learning of Event Dictionaries

2002) which addresses event-based organization of a stream of news stories. Event recognition is similar to New Event Detection, also called First Story Detection, which is considered the most difficult TDT task (Allan et al., 2000a). Typical approaches reduce documents to a set of features, either as a word vector (Allan et al., 2000b) or a probability distribution (Jin et al., 1999), and compare the incoming stories to stories that appeared in the past by computing similarities between their feature representations. Recently, event paraphrases (Petrovic et al., 2012) have been explored to deal with the diversity of event descriptions. However, the New Event Detection task differs from our event recognition task because we want to find all stories describing a certain type of event, not just new events.

3 Bootstrapped Learning of Event Dictionaries

Our bootstrapping approach consists of two stages of learning as shown in Figure 1. The process begins with a few agent seeds, purpose phrase patterns, and unannotated articles selected from a broad-coverage corpus using event keywords. In the first stage, event expressions are harvested from the sentences that have both an agent and a purpose phrase in specific syntactic positions. In the second stage, new purpose phrases are harvested from sentences that contain both an event phrase and an agent, while new agent terms are harvested from sentences that contain both an event phrase and a purpose phrase. The new terms are added to growing event dictionaries, and the bootstrapping process repeats. Our work focuses on civil unrest events.

3.1 Stage 1: Event Phrase Learning

We first extract potential civil unrest stories from the English Gigaword corpus (Parker et al., 2011) using six civil unrest keywords. As explained in Section 1, event keywords are not sufficient to obtain relevant documents with high precision, so the extracted stories are a mix of relevant and irrelevant articles. Our algorithm first selects sentences to use for learning, and then harvests event expressions from them.

3.1.1 Event Sentence Identification

The input in stage 1 consists of a few agent terms and purpose patterns for seeding. The agent seeds are single nouns, while the purpose patterns are verbs in infinitive or present participle forms. Table 1 shows the agent terms and purpose phrases used in our experiments. The agent terms were manually selected by inspecting the most frequent nouns in the documents with civil unrest keywords. The purpose patterns are the most common verbs that describe the reason for a civil unrest event. We identify *probable event sentences* by extracting all sentences that contain at least one agent term and one purpose phrase.

Agents	protesters, activists, demonstrators, students, groups, crowd, workers, palestinians, supporters, women
Purpose Phrases	demanding, to demand, protesting, to protest

Table 1: Agent and Purpose Phrases Used for Seeding

3.1.2 Harvesting Event Expressions

To constrain the learning process, we require event expressions and purpose phrases to match certain syntactic structures. We apply the Stanford dependency parser (Marneffe et al., 2006) to the probable event sentences to identify verb phrase candidates and to enforce syntactic constraints between the different types of event information.

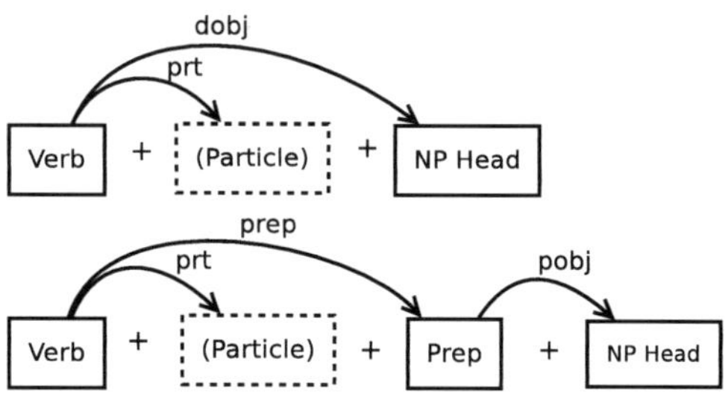

Figure 2: Phrasal Structure of Event & Purpose Phrases

Figure 2 shows the two types of verb phrases that we learn. One type consists of a verb paired with the head noun of its direct object. For example, event phrases can be *"stopped work"* or *"occupied offices"*, and purpose phrases can be *"show support"* or *"condemn war"*. The second type consists of a verb and an attached prepositional phrase, retaining only the head noun of the embedded noun phrase. For example, *"took to street"* and *"scuffled with police"* can be event phrases, while *"call for resignation"* and *"press for wages"* can be purpose phrases. In both types of verb phrases, a particle can optionally follow the verb.

Event expressions, agents, and purpose phrases must appear in specific dependency relations, as illustrated in Figure 3. An agent must be the syntactic subject of the event phrase. A purpose phrase must be a complement of the event phrase, specifically, we require a particular dependency relation, "xcomp"[1], between the two verb phrases. For example, in the sentence *"Leftist activists took to the streets in the Nepali capital Wednesday protesting higher fuel prices."*, the dependency relation "xcomp" links *"took to the streets"* with *"protesting higher fuel prices"*.

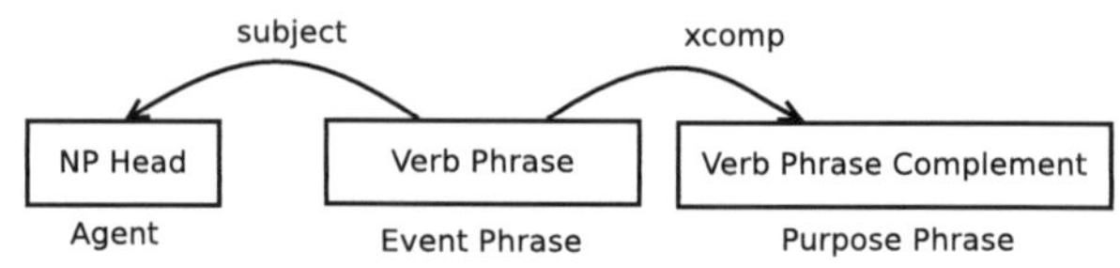

Figure 3: Syntactic Dependencies between Agents, Event Phrases, and Purpose Phrases

Given the syntactic construction shown in Figure 3, with a known agent and purpose phrase, we extract the head verb phrase of the "xcomp" dependency relation as an event phrase candidate. The event phrases that co-occur with at least two unique agent terms and two unique purposes phrases are saved in our event phrase dictionary.

3.2 Stage 2: Learning Agent and Purpose Phrases

In the second stage of bootstrapping, we learn new agent terms and purpose phrases. Our rationale is that if a sentence contains an event phrase and one other important facet of the event (agent or purpose), then the sentence probably describes a relevant event. We can then look for additional facets of the event in the same sentence. We learn both agent and purpose phrases simultaneously in parallel learning processes. As before, we first identify probable event sentences and then harvest agent and purpose phrases from these sentences.

3.2.1 Event Sentence Identification

We identify probable event sentences by extracting sentences that contain at least one event phrase (based on the dictionary produced in the first stage of bootstrapping) and an agent term or a purpose phrase. As before, the event information must occur in the sentential dependency structures shown in Figure 3.

3.2.2 Harvesting Agent and Purpose Phrases

The sentences that contain an event phrase and an agent are used to harvest more purpose phrases, while the sentences that contain an event phrase and a purpose phrase are used to harvest more agent terms. Purpose phrases are extracted from the phrasal structures shown in Figure 2. In the learning process for agents, if a sentence has an event

[1] In the dependency parser, "xcomp" denotes a general relation between a VP or an ADJP and its open clausal complement. For example, in the sentence *"He says that you like to swim."*, the "xcomp" relation will link "like" (head) and "swim" (dependent). With our constraints on the verb phrase forms, the dependent verb phrase in this construction tends to describe the purpose of the verb phrase.

phrase as the head of the "xcomp" dependency relation and a purpose phrase as the dependent clause of the "xcomp" dependency relation, then the head noun of the syntactic subject of the event phrase is harvested as a candidate agent term. We also record the modifiers appearing in all of the noun phrases headed by an agent term. Agent candidates that co-occur with at least two unique event phrases and at least two different modifiers of known agent terms are selected as new agent terms.

The learning process for purpose phrases is analogous. If the syntactic subject of an event phrase is an agent and the event phrase is the head of the "xcomp" dependency relation, then the dependent clause of the "xcomp" dependency relation is harvested as a candidate purpose phrase. Purpose phrase candidates that co-occur with at least two different event phrases are selected as purpose phrases.

The bootstrapping process then repeats, ricocheting back and forth between learning event phrases and learning agent and purpose phrases.

3.3 Domain Relevance Criteria

To avoid domain drift during bootstrapping, we use two additional criteria to discard phrases that are not necessarily associated with the domain.

For each event phrase and purpose phrase, we estimate its *domain-specificity* as the ratio of its prevalence in domain-specific texts compared to broad-coverage texts. The goal is to discard phrases that are common across many types of documents, and therefore not specific to the domain. We define the domain-specificity of phrase p as:

$$\text{domain-specificity(p)} = \frac{\text{frequency of p in domain-specific corpus}}{\text{frequency of p in broad-coverage corpus}}$$

We randomly sampled 10% of the Gigaword texts that contain a civil unrest event keyword to create the "domain-specific" corpus, and randomly sampled 10% of the remaining Gigaword texts to create the "broad-coverage" corpus.[2] Keyword-based sampling is an approximation to domain-relevance, but gives us a general idea about the prevalance of a phrase in different types of texts.

For agent terms, our goal is to identify people who participate as agents of civil unrest events. Other types of people may be commonly mentioned in civil unrest stories too, as peripheral characters. For example, police may provide security and reporters may provide media coverage of an event, but they are not the agents of the event. We estimate the *event-specificity* of each agent term as the ratio of the phrase's prevalence in event sentences compared to all the sentences in the domain-specific corpus. We define an event sentence as one that contains both a learned event phrase and a purpose phrase, based on the dictionaries at that point in time. Therefore, the number of event sentences increases as the bootstrapped dictionaries grow. We define the event-specificity of phrase p as:

$$\text{event-specificity(p)} = \frac{\text{frequency of p in event sentences}}{\text{frequency of p in all sentences}}$$

In our experiments we required event and purpose phrases to have *domain-specificity* $\geq .33$ and agent terms to have *event-specificity* $\geq .01$.[3]

4 Evaluation

4.1 Data

We conducted experiments to evaluate the performance of our bootstrapped event dictionaries for recognizing civil unrest events. Civil unrest is a broad term typically used by the media or law enforcement to describe a form of public disturbance that involves a group of people, usually to protest or promote a cause. Civil unrest events include strikes, protests, occupations, rallies, and similar forms of obstructions or riots. We chose six *event keywords* to identify potential civil unrest documents: "protest", "strike", "march", "rally", "riot" and "occupy". We extracted documents from the English Gigaword corpus (Parker et al., 2011) that contain at least one of these event keywords, or a morphological variant of a keyword.[4] This process extracted nearly one million documents, which we will refer to as our *event-keyword corpus*.

We randomly sampled 400 documents[5] from the event-keyword corpus and asked two annotators to determine whether each document mentioned a civil

[2]The random sampling was simply for efficiency reasons.

[3]This value is so small because we simply want to filter phrases that virtually never occur in the event sentences, and we can recognize very few event sentences in the early stages of bootstrapping.

[4]We used "marched" and "marching" as keywords but did not use "march" because it often refers to a month.

[5]These 400 documents were excluded from the unannotated data used for dictionary learning.

unrest event. We defined annotation guidelines and conducted an inter-annotator agreement study on 100 of these documents. The annotators achieved a κ score of .82. We used these 100 documents as our *tuning set*. Then each annotator annotated 150 more documents to create our *test set* of 300 documents.

4.2 Baselines

The first row of Table 2 shows event recognition accuracy when only the event keywords are used. All of our documents were obtained by searching for a keyword, but only 101 of the 300 documents in our test set were labeled as relevant by the annotators (i.e., 101 describe a civil unrest event). This means that using only the event keywords to identify civil unrest documents yields about 34% precision. In a second experiment, **KeywordTitle**, we required the event keyword to be in the title (headline) of the document. The KeywordTitle approach produced better precision (66%), but only 33% of the relevant documents had a keyword in the title.

Method	Recall	Precision	F
Keyword Accuracy			
Keyword	-	34	-
KeywordTitle	33	66	44
Supervised Learning			
Unigrams	62	66	64
Unigrams+Bigrams	55	71	62
Bootstrapped Dictionary Lookup			
Event Phrases (EV)	60	79	69
Agent Phrases (AG)	98	42	59
Purpose Phrases (PU)	59	67	63
All Pairs	71	**88**	**79**

Table 2: Experimental Results

The second section of Table 2 shows the results of two supervised classifiers based on 10-fold cross validation with our test set. Both classifiers were trained using support vector machines (SVMs) (Joachims, 1999) with a linear kernel (Keerthi and DeCoste, 2005). The first classifier used unigrams as features, while the second classifier used both unigrams and bigrams. All the features are binary. The evaluation results show that the unigram classifier has an F-score of .64. Using both unigram and bigram features increased precision to 71% but recall fell by 7%, yielding a slightly lower F-score of .62.

4.3 Event Recognition with Bootstrapped Dictionaries

Next, we used our bootstrapped dictionaries for event recognition. The bootstrapping process ran for 8 iterations and then stopped because no more phrases could be learned. The quality of bootstrapped data often degrades as bootstrapping progresses, so we used the tuning set to evaluate the dictionaries after each iteration. The best performance[6] on the tuning set resulted from the dictionaries produced after four iterations, so we used these dictionaries for our experiments. Table 3 shows the

	Event Phrases	Agent Terms	Purpose Phrases
Iter #1	145	67	124
Iter #2	410	106	356
Iter #3	504	130	402
Iter #4	623	139	569

Table 3: Dictionary Sizes after Several Iterations

number of event phrases, agents and purpose phrases learned after each iteration. All three lexicons were significantly enriched after each iteration. The final bootstrapped dictionaries contain *623* event phrases, *569* purpose phrases and *139* agent terms. Table 4 shows samples from each event dictionary.

Event Phrases: went on strike, took to street, chanted slogans, gathered in capital, formed chain, clashed with police, staged rally, held protest, walked off job, burned flags, set fire, hit streets, marched in city, blocked roads, carried placards
Agent Terms: employees, miners, muslims, unions, protestors, journalists, refugees, prisoners, immigrants, inmates, pilots, farmers, followers, teachers, drivers
Purpose Phrases: accusing government, voice anger, press for wages, oppose plans, urging end, defying ban, show solidarity, mark anniversary, calling for right, condemning act, pressure government, mark death, push for hike, call attention, celebrating withdrawal

Table 4: Examples of Dictionary Entries

The third section of Table 2 shows the results when using the bootstrapped dictionaries for event recognition. We used a simple dictionary look-up approach that searched for dictionary entries in each document. Our phrases were generated based on

[6] Based on the performance for the **All Pairs** approach.

syntactic analysis and only head words were retained for generality. But we wanted to match dictionary entries without requiring syntactic analysis of new documents. So we used an approximate matching scheme that required each word to appear within 5 words of the previous word. For example, "held protest" would match "held a large protest" and "held a very large political protest". In this way, we avoid the need for syntactic analysis when using the dictionaries for event recognition.

First, we labeled a document as relevant if it contained any Event Phrase (EV) in our dictionary. The event phrases achieved better performance than all of the baselines, yielding an F-score of 69%. The best baseline was the unigram classifier, which was trained with supervised learning. The bootstrapped event phrase dictionary produced much higher precision (79% vs. 66%) with only slightly lower recall (60% vs. 62%), and did not require annotated texts for training. Statistical significance testing shows that the Event Phrase lookup approach works significantly better than the unigram classifier ($p < 0.05$, paired bootstrap (Berg-Kirkpatrick et al., 2012)).

For the sake of completeness, we also evaluated the performance of dictionary look-up using our bootstrapped Agent (AG) and Purpose (PU) dictionaries, individually. The agents terms produced 42% precision with 98% recall, demonstrating that the learned agent list has extremely high coverage but (unsurprisingly) does not achieve high precision on its own. The purpose phrases achieved a better balance of recall and precision, producing an F-score of 63%, which is nearly the same as the supervised unigram classifier.

Our original hypothesis was that a single type of event information is not sufficient to accurately identify event descriptions. Our goal was high-accuracy event recognition by requiring that a document contain multiple clues pertaining to different facets of an event (*multi-faceted event recognition*). The last row of Table 2 (**All Pairs**) shows the results when requiring matches from at least two different bootstrapped dictionaries. Specifically, we labeled a document as relevant if it contained at least one phrase from each of two different dictionaries and these phrases occurred in the same sentence. Table 2 shows that multi-faceted event recognition achieves 88% precision with reasonably good recall of 71%, yielding an F-score of 79%. This multi-faceted approach with simple dictionary look-up outperformed all of the baselines, and each dictionary used by itself. Statistical significance testing shows that the All Pairs approach works significantly better than the unigram classifier ($p < 0.001$, paired bootstrap). The All Pairs approach is significantly better than the Event Phrase (EV) lookup approach at the $p < 0.1$ level.

Method	Recall	Precision	F-score
EV + PU	14	100	24
EV + AG	47	94	62
AG + PU	50	85	63
All Pairs	71	88	79

Table 5: Analysis of Dictionary Combinations

Table 5 takes a closer look at how each pair of dictionaries performed. The first row shows that requiring a document to have an event phrase and a purpose phrase produces the best precision (100%) but with low recall (14%). The second row reveals that requiring a document to have an event phrase and an agent term yields better recall (47%) and high precision (94%). The third row shows that requiring a document to have a purpose phrase and an agent term produces the best recall (50%) but with slightly lower precision (85%). Finally, the last row of Table 5 shows that taking the union of these results (i.e., any combination of dictionary pairs is sufficient) yields the best recall (71%) with high precision (88%), demonstrating that we get the best coverage by recognizing multiple combinations of event information.

Lexicon	Recall	Precision	F-score
Seeds	13	87	22
Iter #1	50	88	63
Iter #2	63	89	74
Iter #3	68	88	77
Iter #4	71	88	79

Table 6: **All Pairs** Lookup Results using only Seeds and the Lexicons Learned after each Iteration, on the Test Set

Table 6 shows the performance of the lexicon lookup approach using the **All Pairs** criteria during the bootstrapping process. The first row shows the results using only 10 agent seeds and 4 purpose seeds as shown in Table 1. The following four rows in the table show the performance of **All Pairs** using the lexicons learned after each bootstrapping iteration. We can see that the recall increases steadily and that precision is maintained at a high level throughout the bootstrapping process.

Event recognition can be formulated as an information retrieval (IR) problem. As another point of comparison, we ran an existing IR system, Terrier (Ounis et al., 2007), on our test set. We used Terrier to rank these 300 documents given our set of event keywords as the query [7], and then generated a recall/precision curve (Figure 4) by computing the precisions at different levels of recall, ranging from 0 to 1 in increments of *.10*. Terrier was run with the

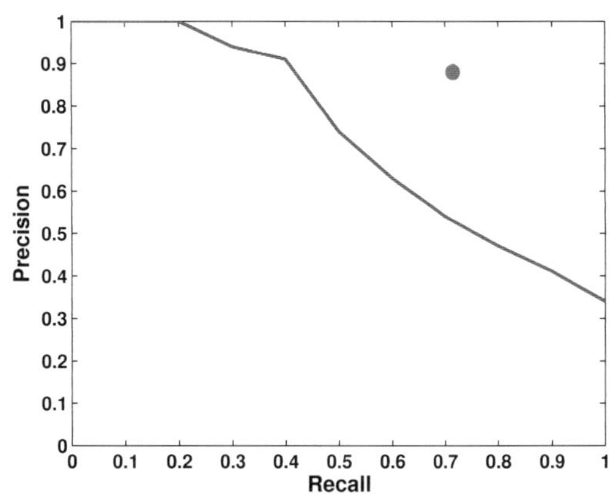

Figure 4: Comparison with the Terrier IR system

parameter PL2 which refers to an advanced Divergence From Randomness weighting model (Amati and Van Rijsbergen, 2002). In addition, Terrier used automatic query expansion. We can see that Terrier identified the first 60 documents (20% recall) with 100% precision. But precision dropped sharply after that. The circle in Figure 4 shows the performance of our bootstrapped dictionaries using the **All Pairs** approach. At comparable level of precision (88%), Terrier achieved about 45% recall versus 71% recall produced with the bootstrapped dictionaries.

4.4 Supervised Classifiers with Bootstrapped Dictionaries

We also explored the idea of using the bootstrapped dictionaries as features for a classifier to see if a supervised learner could make better use of the dictionaries. We created five SVM classifiers and performed 10-fold cross validation on the test set.

Method	Recall	Precision	F-score
TermLex	66	85	74
PairLex	10	91	18
TermSets	59	83	69
PairSets	68	84	75
AllSets	70	84	76

Table 7: Supervised classifiers using the dictionaries

Table 7 shows the results for the five classifiers. **TermLex** encodes a binary feature for every phrase in any of our dictionaries. **PairLex** encodes a binary feature for each pair of phrases from two different dictionaries and requires them to occur in the same sentence. The TermLex classifier achieves good performance (74% F-score), but is not as effective as our All Pairs dictionary look-up approach (79% F-score). The PairLex classifier yield higher precision but very low recall, undoubtedly due to sparsity issues in matching specific pairs of phrases.

One of the strengths of our bootstrapping method is that it creates dictionaries from large volumes of unannotated documents. A limitation of supervised learning with lexical features is that the classifier can not benefit from terms in the bootstrapped dictionaries that do not appear in its training documents. To address this issue, we also tried encoding the dictionaries as set-based features. The **TermSets** classifier encodes three binary features, one for each dictionary. A feature gets a value of 1 if a document contains any word in the corresponding dictionary. The **PairSets** classifier also encodes three binary features, but each feature represents a different pair of dictionaries (EV+AG, EV+PU, or AG+PU). A feature gets a value of 1 if a document contains at least one term from each of the two dictionaries in the same sentence. The **AllSets** classifier encodes 7 set-based features: the previous six features and one additional feature that requires a sentence to contain at least one entry from all three dictionaries.

The **All Sets** classifier yields the best performance with an F-score of 76%. However, our straightforward dictionary look-up approach still performs better (79% F-score), and does not require annotated documents for training.

[7] We gave Terrier one query with all of the event keywords.

4.5 Finding Articles with no Event Keyword

The learned event dictionaries have the potential to recognize event-relevant documents that do not contain any human-selected event keywords. This can happen in two ways. First, *378* of the *623* learned event phrases do not contain any of the original event keywords. Second, we expect that some event descriptions will contain a known agent and purpose phrase, even if the event phrase is unfamiliar.

We performed an additional set of experiments with documents in the Gigaword corpus that contain no human-selected civil unrest keyword. Following our multi-faceted approach to event recognition, we collected all documents that contain a sentence that matches phrases in at least two of our bootstrapped event dictionaries. This process retrieved 178,197 documents. The first column of Table 8 shows the number of documents that had phrases found in two different dictionaries (EV+AG, EV+PU, AG+PU) or in all three dictionaries (EV+AG+PU).

	Total	Samples	Accuracy
EV+AG	67,796	50	44%
EV+PU	2,375	50	54%
AG+PU	101,173	50	18%
EV+AG+PU	6,853	50	**74%**

Table 8: Evaluation of articles with no event keyword

We randomly sampled 50 documents from each category and had them annotated. The accuracies are shown in the third column. Finding all three types of phrases produced the best accuracy, 74%. Furthermore, we found over 6,800 documents that had all three types of event information using our learned dictionaries. This result demonstrates that the bootstrapped dictionaries can recognize many event descriptions that would have been missed by searching only with manually selected keywords. This experiment also confirms that multi-facted event recognition using all three learned dictionaries achieves good accuracy even for documents that do not contain the civil unrest keywords.

5 Conclusions

We proposed a *multi-faceted* approach to event recognition and presented a bootstrapping technique to learn event phrases as well as agent terms and purpose phrases associated with civil unrest events. Our results showed that *multi-faceted event recognition* using the learned dictionaries achieved high accuracy and performed better than several other methods. The bootstrapping approach can be easily trained for new domains since it requires only a large collection of unannotated texts and a few event keywords, agent terms, and purpose phrases for the events of interest. Furthermore, although the training phase requires syntactic parsing to learn the event dictionaries, the dictionaries can then be used for event recognition without needing to parse the documents.

An open question for future work is to investigate whether the same multi-faceted approach to event recognition will work well for other types of events. Our belief is that many different types of events have characteristic agent terms, but additional types of facets will need to be defined to cover a broad array of event types. The syntactic constructions used to harvest dictionary items may also vary depending on the types of event information that must be learned. In future research, we plan to explore these issues in more depth to design a more general multi-faceted event recognition system, and we plan to investigate new ways to use these event dictionaries for event extraction as well.

6 Acknowledgments

This research was supported by the Intelligence Advanced Research Projects Activity (IARPA) via Department of Interior National Business Center (DoI / NBC) contract number D12PC00285 and by the National Science Foundation under grant IIS-1018314. The U.S. Government is authorized to reproduce and distribute reprints for Governmental purposes notwithstanding any copyright annotation thereon. The views and conclusions contained herein are those of the authors and should not be interpreted as necessarily representing the official policies or endorsements, either expressed or implied, of IARPA, DoI/NBE, NSF, or the U.S. Government.

References

ACE Evaluations. 2006. *http://www.itl.nist.gov/iad/mig/tests/ace/.*

J. Allan, J. Carbonell, G. Doddington, J. Yamron, and Y. Yang. 1998. Topic Detection and Tracking Pilot Study: Final Report. In *Proceedings of DARPA Broadcast News Transcription and Understanding Workshop*.

J. Allan, V. Lavrenko, and H. Jin. 2000a. First Story Detection in TDT is Hard. In *Proceedings of the 2000 ACM CIKM International Conference on Information and Knowledge Management*.

J. Allan, Victor Lavrenko, Daniella Malin, and Russell Swan. 2000b. Detections, Bounds, and Timelines: UMass and TDT-3. In *Proceedings of Topic Detection and Tracking Workshop*.

J. Allan, 2002. *Topic Detection and Tracking: Event Based Information Organization*. Kluwer Academic Publishers.

G. Amati and C. J. Van Rijsbergen. 2002. Probabilistic Models of Information Retrieval based on Measuring Divergence from Randomness. *ACM Transactions on Information Systems*, 20(4):357–389.

D. Appelt, J. Hobbs, J. Bear, D. Israel, and M. Tyson. 1993. FASTUS: a finite-state processor for information extraction from real-world text. In *Proceedings of the Thirteenth International Joint Conference on Artificial Intelligence*.

H. Becker, M. Naaman, and L. Gravano. 2011. Beyond trending topics: Real-world event identification on twitter. In *Proceedings of the Fifth International AAAI Conference on Weblogs and Social Media*.

E. Benson, A. Haghighi, and R. Barzilay. 2011. Event discovery in social media feeds.

T. Berg-Kirkpatrick, D. Burkett, and D. Klein. 2012. An Empirical Investigation of Statistical Significance in NLP. In *Proceedings of the 2012 Conference on Empirical Methods in Natural Language Processing*.

M.E. Califf and R. Mooney. 2003. Bottom-up Relational Learning of Pattern Matching rules for Information Extraction. *Journal of Machine Learning Research*, 4:177–210.

H.L. Chieu and H.T. Ng. 2002. A Maximum Entropy Approach to Information Extraction from Semi-Structured and Free Text. In *Proceedings of the 18th National Conference on Artificial Intelligence*.

M. D. Conover, J. Ratkiewicz, M. Francisco, B. Goncalves, A. Flammini, and F. Menczer. 2011. Political Polarization on Twitter. In *Proceedings of the Fifth International AAAI Conference on Weblogs and Social Media*.

Z. Gu and N. Cercone. 2006. Segment-Based Hidden Markov Models for Information Extraction. In *Proceedings of the 21st International Conference on Computational Linguistics and 44th Annual Meeting of the Association for Computational Linguistics*, pages 481–488, Sydney, Australia, July.

R. Huang and E. Riloff. 2011. Peeling Back the Layers: Detecting Event Role Fillers in Secondary Contexts.

H. Jin, R. Schwartz, S. Sista, and F. Walls. 1999. Topic Tracking for Radio, TV broadcast, and Newswire. In *EUROSPEECH*.

T. Joachims. 1999. Making Large-Scale Support Vector Machine Learning Practical. In A. Smola B. Schölkopf, C. Burges, editor, *Advances in Kernel Methods: Support Vector Machines*. MIT Press, Cambridge, MA.

S. Keerthi and D. DeCoste. 2005. A Modified Finite Newton Method for Fast Solution of Large Scale Linear SVMs. *Journal of Machine Learning Research*.

V. Lampos, T. D. Bie, and N. Cristianini. 2010. Flu Detector - Tracking Epidemics on Twitter. In *ECML PKDD*.

M. d. Marneffe, B. MacCartney, and C. D. Manning. 2006. Generating Typed Dependency Parses from Phrase Structure Parses. In *Proceedings of the Fifth Conference on Language Resources and Evaluation (LREC-2006)*.

M. Mathioudakis and N. Koudas. 2010. TwitterMonitor: trend detection over the twitter stream. In *Proceedings of the 2010 international conference on Management of data*, page 11551158. ACM.

D. Metzler, C. Cai, and E. Hovy. 2012. Structured Event Retrieval over Microblog Archives. In *Proceedings of The 2012 Conference of the North American Chapter of the Association for Computational Linguistics: Human Language Technologies*.

MUC-4 Proceedings. 1992. *Proceedings of the Fourth Message Understanding Conference (MUC-4)*. Morgan Kaufmann.

I. Ounis, C. Lioma, C. Macdonald, and V. Plachouras. 2007. Research Directions in Terrier. *Novatica/UPGRADE Special Issue on Web Information Access, Ricardo Baeza-Yates et al. (Eds), Invited Paper*.

R. Parker, D. Graff, J. Kong, K. Chen, and Kazuaki M. 2011. English Gigaword. In *Linguistic Data Consortium*.

S. Patwardhan and E. Riloff. 2007. Effective Information Extraction with Semantic Affinity Patterns and Relevant Regions. In *Proceedings of 2007 the Conference on Empirical Methods in Natural Language Processing (EMNLP-2007)*.

S. Petrovic, M. Osborne, and V. Lavrenko. 2012. Using Paraphrases for Improving First Story Detection in

News and Twitter. In *Proceedings of The 2012 Conference of the North American Chapter of the Association for Computational Linguistics: Human Language Technologies*.

A.-M. Popescu, M. Pennacchiotti, and D. A. Paranjpe. 2011. Extracting events and event descriptions from twitter.

E. Riloff and W. Lehnert. 1994. Information Extraction as a Basis for High-Precision Text Classification. *ACM Transactions on Information Systems*, 12(3):296–333, July.

E. Riloff and J. Lorenzen. 1999. Extraction-based text categorization: Generating domain-specific role relationships automatically. In Tomek Strzalkowski, editor, *Natural Language Information Retrieval*. Kluwer Academic Publishers.

E. Riloff. 1996. Automatically Generating Extraction Patterns from Untagged Text. In *Proceedings of the Thirteenth National Conference on Artificial Intelligence*, pages 1044–1049. The AAAI Press/MIT Press.

A. Ritter, Mausam, O. Etzioni, and S. Clark. 2012. Open domain event extraction from twitter. In *The Proceedings of The 18th ACM SIGKDD Conference on Knowledge Discovery and Data Mining*.

T. Sakaki, M. Okazaki, and Y. Matsuo. 2010. Earthquake shakes twitter users: real-time event detection by social sensors.

S. Sekine. 2006. On-demand Information Extraction. In *Proceedings of Joint Conference of the International Committee on Computational Linguistics and the Association for Computational Linguistics (COLING/ACL-06)*.

M. Stevenson and M. Greenwood. 2005. A Semantic Approach to IE Pattern Induction. In *Proceedings of the 43rd Annual Meeting of the Association for Computational Linguistics*, pages 379–386, Ann Arbor, MI, June.

K. Sudo, S. Sekine, and R. Grishman. 2003. An Improved Extraction Pattern Representation Model for Automatic IE Pattern Acquisition. In *Proceedings of the 41st Annual Meeting of the Association for Computational Linguistics (ACL-03)*.

A. Tumasjan, T. O. Sprenger, P. G. Sandner, and I. M. Welpe. 2010. Predicting Elections with Twitter: What 140 Characters Reveal about Political Sentiment. In *Proceedings of the 4th International AAAI Conference on Weblogs and Social Media*.

R. Yangarber, R. Grishman, P. Tapanainen, and S. Huttunen. 2000. Automatic Acquisition of Domain Knowledge for Information Extraction. In *Proceedings of the Eighteenth International Conference on Computational Linguistics (COLING 2000)*.

X. Zhang, H. Fuehres, and P. A. Gloor. 2010. Predicting Stock Market Indicators Through Twitter "I hope it is not as bad as I fear". In *COINs*.

Named Entity Recognition with Bilingual Constraints

Wanxiang Che[†] **Mengqiu Wang**[‡] **Christopher D. Manning**[‡] **Ting Liu**[†]

[†]{car, tliu}@ir.hit.edu.cn
School of Computer Science and Technology
Harbin Institute of Technology
Harbin, China, 150001

[‡]{mengqiu, manning}@stanford.edu
Computer Science Department
Stanford University
Stanford, CA, 94305

Abstract

Different languages contain complementary cues about entities, which can be used to improve Named Entity Recognition (NER) systems. We propose a method that formulates the problem of exploring such signals on unannotated bilingual text as a simple Integer Linear Program, which encourages entity tags to agree via bilingual constraints. Bilingual NER experiments on the large OntoNotes 4.0 Chinese-English corpus show that the proposed method can improve strong baselines for both Chinese and English. In particular, Chinese performance improves by over 5% absolute F_1 score. We can then annotate a large amount of bilingual text (80k sentence pairs) using our method, and add it as up-training data to the original monolingual NER training corpus. The Chinese model retrained on this new combined dataset outperforms the strong baseline by over 3% F_1 score.

1 Introduction

Named Entity Recognition (NER) is an important task for many applications, such as information extraction and machine translation. State-of-the-art supervised NER methods require large amounts of annotated data, which are difficult and expensive to produce manually, especially for resource-poor languages.

A promising approach for improving NER performance without annotating more data is to exploit unannotated bilingual text (bitext), which are relatively easy to obtain for many language pairs, borrowing from the resources made available by statistical machine translation research.[1] Different languages contain complementary cues about entities. For example, in Figure 1, the word "本 (Ben)" is common in Chinese but rarely appears as a translated foreign name. However, its aligned word on the English side ("Ben") provides a strong clue that this is a person name. Judicious use of this type of bilingual cues can help to recognize errors a monolingual tagger would make, allowing us to produce more accurately tagged bitext. Each side of the tagged bitext can then be used to expand the original monolingual training dataset, which may lead to higher accuracy in the monolingual taggers.

Previous work such as Li et al. (2012) and Kim et al. (2012) demonstrated that bilingual corpus annotated with NER labels can be used to improve monolingual tagger performance. But a major drawback of their approaches are the need for manual annotation efforts to create such corpora. To avoid this requirement, Burkett et al. (2010) suggested a "multi-view" learning scheme based on re-ranking. Noisy output of a "strong" tagger is used as training data to learn parameters of a log-linear re-ranking model with additional bilingual features, simulated by a "weak" tagger. The learned parameters are then reused with the "strong" tagger to re-rank its own outputs for unseen inputs. Designing good "weak" taggers so that they complement the "view" of bilingual features in the log-linear re-ranker is crucial to the success of this algorithm. Unfortunately there is no principled way of designing such "weak" taggers.

In this paper, we would like to explore a conceptually much simpler idea that can also take advantage

[1] opus.lingfil.uu.se

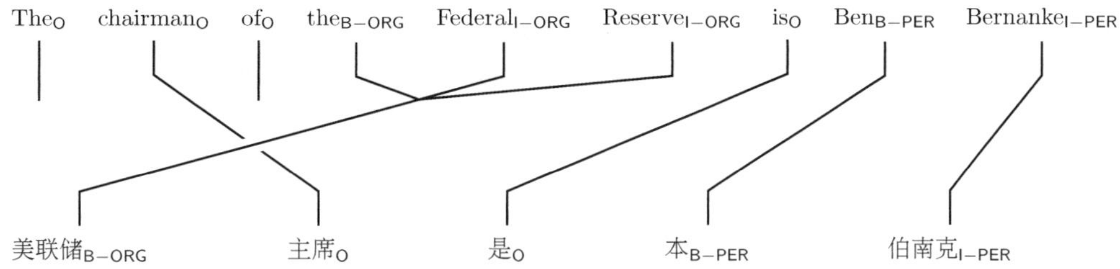

Figure 1: Example of NER labels between two word-aligned bilingual parallel sentences.

of the large amount of unannotated bitext, without complicated machinery. More specifically, we introduce a joint inference method that formulates the bilingual NER tagging problem as an Integer Linear Program (ILP) and solves it during decoding. We propose a set of intuitive and effective bilingual constraints that encourage NER results to agree across the two languages.

Experimental results on the OntoNotes 4.0 named entity annotated Chinese-English parallel corpus show that the proposed method can improve the strong Chinese NER baseline by over 5% F_1 score and also give small improvements over the English baseline. Moreover, by adding the automatically tagged data to the original NER training corpus and retraining the monolingual model using an up-training regimen (Petrov et al., 2010), we can improve the monolingual Chinese NER performance by over 3% F_1 score.

2 Constraint-based Monolingual NER

NER is a sequence labeling task where we assign a named entity tag to each word in an input sentence. One commonly used tagging scheme is the BIO scheme. The tag B-X (Begin) represents the first word of a named entity of type X, for example, PER (Person) or LOC (Location). The tag I-X (Inside) indicates that a word is part of an entity but not first word. The tag O (Outside) is used for all non-entity words.[2] See Figure 1 for an example tagged sentence.

Conditional Random Fields (CRF) (Lafferty et al., 2001) is a state-of-the-art sequence labeling model widely used in NER. A first-order linear-chain CRF defines the following conditional probability:

$$P_{CRF}(\mathbf{y}|\mathbf{x}) = \frac{1}{Z(\mathbf{x})}\prod_i M_i(y_i, y_{i-1}|\mathbf{x}) \quad (1)$$

where $\mathbf{x}$ and $\mathbf{y}$ are the input and output sequences, respectively, $Z(\mathbf{x})$ is the partition function, and M_i is the clique potential for edge clique i. Decoding in CRF involves finding the most likely output sequence that maximizes this objective, and is commonly done by the Viterbi algorithm.

Roth and Yih (2005) proposed an ILP inference algorithm, which can capture more task-specific and global constraints than the vanilla Viterbi algorithm. Our work is inspired by Roth and Yih (2005). But instead of directly solving the shortest-path problem in the ILP formulation, we re-define the conditional probability as:

$$P_{MAR}(\mathbf{y}|\mathbf{x}) = \prod_i P(y_i|\mathbf{x}) \quad (2)$$

where $P(y_i|\mathbf{x})$ is the marginal probability given by an underlying CRF model computed using *forward-backward* inference. Since the early HMM literature, it has been well known that using the marginal distributions at each position works well, as opposed to Viterbi MAP sequence labeling (Mérialdo, 1994). Our experimental results also supports this claim, as we will show in Section 6. Our objective is to find an optimal NER tag sequence:

$$\begin{aligned}\hat{\mathbf{y}} &= \arg\max_{\mathbf{y}} P_{MAR}(\mathbf{y}|\mathbf{x}) \\ &= \arg\max_{\mathbf{y}} \sum_i \log P(y_i|\mathbf{x}) \quad (3)\end{aligned}$$

Then an ILP can be used to solve the inference problem as classification problem with constraints.

[2]While the performance of NER is measured at the entity level (not the tag level).

The objective function is:

$$\max \sum_{i=1}^{|\mathbf{x}|} \sum_{y \in Y} z_i^y \log P_i^y \tag{4}$$

where Y is the set of all possible named entity tags. $P_i^y = P(y_i = y|\mathbf{x})$ is the CRF marginal probability that the ith word is tagged with y, and z_i^y is an indicator that equals 1 *iff* the ith word is tagged y; otherwise, z_i^y is 0.

If no constraints are identified, then Eq. (4) achieves maximum when all z_i^y are assigned to 1, which violates the condition that each word should only be assigned a single entity tag. We can express this with constraints:

$$\forall i : \sum_{y \in Y} z_i^y = 1 \tag{5}$$

After adding the constraints, the probability of the sequence is maximized when each word is assigned the tag with highest probability. However, some invalid results may still exist. For example a tag O may be wrongly followed by a tag I-X, although a named entity cannot start with I-X. Therefore, we can add the following constraints:

$$\forall i, \forall \mathsf{X} : z_{i-1}^{\mathsf{B\text{-}X}} + z_{i-1}^{\mathsf{I\text{-}X}} - z_i^{\mathsf{I\text{-}X}} \geq 0 \tag{6}$$

which specifies that when the ith word is tagged with I-X ($z_i^{\mathsf{I\text{-}X}} = 1$), then the previous word can only be tagged with B-X or I-X ($z_{i-1}^{\mathsf{B\text{-}X}} + z_{i-1}^{\mathsf{I\text{-}X}} \geq 1$).

3 NER with Bilingual Constraints

This section demonstrates how to jointly perform NER for two languages with bilingual constraints. We assume sentences have been aligned into pairs, and the word alignment between each pair of sentences is also given.

3.1 Hard Bilingual Constraints

We first introduce the simplest *hard* constraints, i.e., each word alignment pair should have the same named entity tag. For example, in Figure 1, the Chinese word "美联储" was aligned with the English words "the", "Federal" and "Reserve". Therefore, they have the same named entity tags ORG.[3]

[3]The prefix B- and I- are ignored.

Similarly, "本" and "Ben" as well as "伯南克" and "Bernanke" were all tagged with the tag PER.

The objective function for bilingual NER can be expressed as follows:

$$\max \sum_{i=1}^{|\mathbf{x}_c|} \sum_{y \in Y} z_i^y \log P_i^y + \sum_{j=1}^{|\mathbf{x}_e|} \sum_{y \in Y} z_j^y \log P_j^y \tag{7}$$

where P_i^y and P_j^y are the probabilities of the ith Chinese word and j^{th} English word to be tagged with y, respectively. $\mathbf{x}_c$ and $\mathbf{x}_e$ are respectively the Chinese and English sentences.

Similar to monolingual constrained NER (Section 2), monolingual constraints are added for each language as shown in Eqs. (8) and (9):

$$\forall i : \sum_{y \in Y} z_i^y = 1; \forall j : \sum_{y \in Y} z_j^y = 1 \tag{8}$$

$$\forall i, \forall \mathsf{X} : z_i^{\mathsf{B\text{-}X}} + z_i^{\mathsf{I\text{-}X}} - z_{i+1}^{\mathsf{B\text{-}X}} \geq 0 \tag{9}$$
$$\forall j, \forall \mathsf{X} : z_j^{\mathsf{B\text{-}X}} + z_j^{\mathsf{I\text{-}X}} - z_{j+1}^{\mathsf{B\text{-}X}} \geq 0$$

Bilingual constraints are added in Eq. (10):

$$\forall (i,j) \in A, \forall \mathsf{X} : z_i^{\mathsf{B\text{-}X}} + z_i^{\mathsf{I\text{-}X}} = z_j^{\mathsf{B\text{-}X}} + z_j^{\mathsf{I\text{-}X}} \tag{10}$$

where $A = \{(i,j)\}$ is the word alignment pair set, i.e., the ith Chinese word and the jth English word were aligned together. Chinese word i is tagged with a named entity type X ($z_i^{\mathsf{B\text{-}X}} + z_i^{\mathsf{I\text{-}X}} = 1$), *iff* English word j is tagged with X ($z_j^{\mathsf{B\text{-}X}} + z_j^{\mathsf{I\text{-}X}} = 1$). Therefore, these *hard* bilingual constraints guarantee that when two words are aligned, they are tagged with the same named entity tag.

However, in practice, aligned word pairs do not always have the same tag because of the difference in annotation standards across different languages. For example, in Figure 2(a), the Chinese word "开发区" is a location. However, it is aligned to the words, "development" and "zone", which are not named entities in English. Word alignment error is another serious problem that can cause violation of hard constraints. In Figure 2(b), the English word "Agency" is wrongly aligned with the Chinese word "电 (report)". Thus, these two words cannot be assigned with the same tag.

To address these two problems, we present a probabilistic model for bilingual NER which can lead to

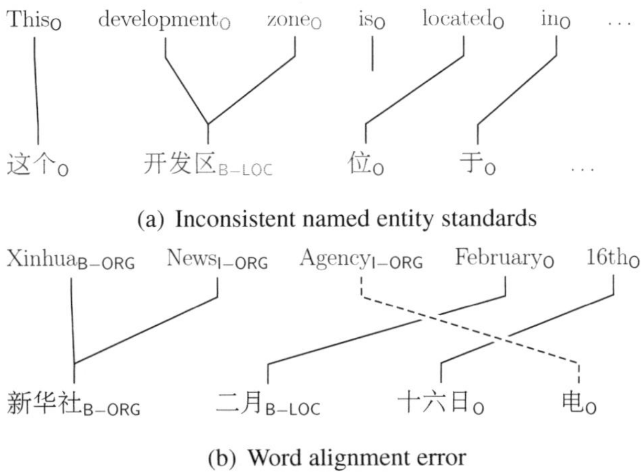

Figure 2: Errors of hard bilingual constraints method.

an optimization problem with two *soft* bilingual constraints:

1) allow word-aligned pairs to have different named entity tags; 2) consider word alignment probabilities to reduce the influence of wrong word alignments.

3.2 Soft Constraints with Tag Uncertainty

The new probabilistic model for bilingual NER is:

$$\begin{aligned} P(\mathbf{y}_c, \mathbf{y}_e | \mathbf{x}_c, \mathbf{x}_e, A) &= \frac{P(\mathbf{y}_c, \mathbf{y}_e, \mathbf{x}_c, \mathbf{x}_e, A)}{P(\mathbf{x}_c, \mathbf{x}_e, A)} \\ &= \frac{P(\mathbf{y}_c, \mathbf{x}_c, \mathbf{x}_e, A)}{P(\mathbf{x}_c, \mathbf{x}_e, A)} \cdot \frac{P(\mathbf{y}_e, \mathbf{x}_c, \mathbf{x}_e, A)}{P(\mathbf{x}_c, \mathbf{x}_e, A)} \\ &\quad \cdot \frac{P(\mathbf{y}_c, \mathbf{y}_e, \mathbf{x}_c, \mathbf{x}_e, A) P(\mathbf{x}_c, \mathbf{x}_e, A)}{P(\mathbf{y}_c, \mathbf{x}_c, \mathbf{x}_e, A) P(\mathbf{y}_e, \mathbf{x}_c, \mathbf{x}_e, A)} \quad (11) \\ &\approx P(\mathbf{y}_c | \mathbf{x}_c) P(\mathbf{y}_e | \mathbf{x}_e) \frac{P(\mathbf{y}_c, \mathbf{y}_e | A)}{P(\mathbf{y}_c | A) P(\mathbf{y}_e | A)} \quad (12) \end{aligned}$$

where $\mathbf{y}_c$ and $\mathbf{y}_e$ respectively denotes Chinese and English named entity output sequences. A is the set of word alignment pairs.

If we assume that named entity tag assignments in Chinese is only dependent on the observed Chinese sentence, then we can drop the A and $\mathbf{x}_e$ term in the first factor of Eq. (11), and arrive at the first factor of Eq. (12); similarly we can use the same assumption to derive the second factor in Eq. (12) for English; alternatively, if we assume the named entity tag assignments are only dependent on the cross-lingual word associations via word alignment, then we can drop $\mathbf{x}_c$ and $\mathbf{x}_e$ terms in the third factor of Eq. (11) and arrive at the third factor of Eq. (12). These factors represent the two major sources of information in the model: monolingual surface observation, and cross-lingual word associations.

The first two factors of Eq. (12) can be further decomposed into the product of probabilities of all words in each language sentence like Eq. (2).

Assuming that the tags are independent between different word alignment pairs, then the last factor of Eq. (12) can be decomposed into:

$$\begin{aligned} \frac{P(\mathbf{y}_c, \mathbf{y}_e | A)}{P(\mathbf{y}_c | A) P(\mathbf{y}_e | A)} &= \prod_{a \in A} \frac{P(y_{c_a} y_{e_a})}{P(y_{c_a}) P(y_{e_a})} \\ &= \prod_{a \in A} \lambda_a^{y_c y_e} \quad (13) \end{aligned}$$

where y_{c_a} and y_{e_a} respectively denotes Chinese and English named entity tags in a word alignment pair a. $\lambda^{y_c y_e} = \frac{P(y_c y_e)}{P(y_c) P(y_e)}$ is the pointwise mutual information (PMI) score between a Chinese named entity tag y_c and an English named entity tag y_e. If $y_c = y_e$, then the score will be high; otherwise the score will be low. A number of methods for calculating the scores are provided at the end of this section.

We use ILP to maximize Eq. (12). The new objective function is expressed as follow:

$$\begin{aligned} \max \sum_{i=1}^{|\mathbf{x}_c|} \sum_{y \in Y} z_i^y \log P_i^y + \sum_{j=1}^{|\mathbf{x}_e|} \sum_{y \in Y} z_j^y \log P_j^y \\ + \sum_{a \in A} \sum_{y_c \in Y} \sum_{y_e \in Y} z_a^{y_c y_e} \log \lambda_a^{y_c y_e} \quad (14) \end{aligned}$$

where $z_a^{y_c y_e}$ is an indicator that equals 1 *iff* the Chinese and English named entity tags are y_c and y_e respectively, given a word alignment pair a; otherwise, $z_a^{y_c y_e}$ is 0.

Monolingual constraints such as Eqs. (8) and (9) need to be added. In addition, one and only one possible named entity tag pair exists for a word alignment pair. This condition can be expressed as the following constraints:

$$\forall a \in A : \sum_{y_c \in Y} \sum_{y_e \in Y} z_a^{y_c y_e} = 1 \quad (15)$$

When the tag pair of a word alignment pair is determined, the corresponding monolingual named entity tags can also be identified. This rule can be expressed by the following constraints:

$$\forall a = (i,j) \in A : z_a^{y_c y_e} \le z_i^{y_c}, z_a^{y_c y_e} \le z_j^{y_e} \quad (16)$$

Thus, if $z_a^{y_c y_e} = 1$, then $z_i^{y_c}$ and $z_j^{y_e}$ must be both equal to 1. Here, the ith Chinese word and the jth English word are aligned together.

In contrast to hard bilingual constraints, inconsistent named entity tags for an aligned word pair are allowed in soft bilingual constraints, but are given lower $\lambda^{y_c y_e}$ scores.

To calculate the $\lambda^{y_c y_e}$ score, an annotated bilingual NER corpus is consulted. We count from all word alignment pairs the number of times y_c and y_e occur together ($C(y_c y_e)$) and separately ($C(y_c)$ and $C(y_e)$). Afterwards, $\lambda^{y_c y_e}$ is calculated with maximum likelihood estimation as follows:

$$\lambda^{y_c y_e} = \frac{P(y_c y_e)}{P(y_c)P(y_e)} = \frac{N \times C(y_c y_e)}{C(y_c)C(y_e)} \quad (17)$$

where N is the total number of word alignment pairs.

However, in this paper, we assume that no named entity annotated bilingual corpus is available. Thus, the above method is only used as `Oracle`. A realistic method for calculating the $\lambda^{y_c y_e}$ score requires the use of two initial monolingual NER models, such as baseline CRF, to predict named entity tags for each language on an unannotated bitext. We count from this automatically tagged corpus the statistics mentioned above. This method is henceforth referred to as `Auto`.

A simpler approach is to manually set the value of $\lambda^{y_c y_e}$: if $y_c = y_e$ then we assign a larger value to $\lambda^{y_c y_e}$; else we assign an ad-hoc smaller value. In fact, if we set $\lambda^{y_c y_e} = 1$ *iff* $y_c = y_e$; otherwise, $\lambda^{y_c y_e} = 0$, then the soft constraints backs off to hard constraints. We refer to this set of soft constraints as `Soft-tag`.

3.3 Constraints with Alignment Uncertainty

So far, we assumed that a word alignment set A is known. In practice, only the word alignment probability P_a for each word pair a is provided. We can set a threshold θ for P_a to tune the set A: $a \in A$ *iff* $P_a \ge \theta$. This condition can be regarded as a kind of *hard word alignment*. However, the following problem exists: the smaller the θ, the noisier the word alignments are; the larger the θ, the more possible word alignments are lost. To ameliorate this problem, we introduce another set of soft bilingual constraints.

We can re-express Eq. (13) as follows:

$$\prod_{a \in A} \lambda_a^{y_c y_e} = \prod_{a \in \mathscr{A}} (\lambda_a^{y_c y_e})^{I_a} \quad (18)$$

where $\mathscr{A}$ is the set of all word pairs between two languages. $I_a = 1$ *iff* $P_a \ge \theta$; otherwise, $I_a = 0$.

We can then replace the hard indicator I_a with the word alignment probability P_a, Eq. (14) is then transformed into the following equation:

$$\max \sum_i^{|W_c|} \sum_{y \in Y} z_i^y \log P_i^y + \sum_j^{|W_e|} \sum_{y \in Y} z_j^y \log P_j^y + \sum_{a \in \mathscr{A}} \sum_{y_c \in Y} \sum_{y_e \in Y} z_a^{y_c y_e} P_a \log \lambda_a^{y_c y_e} \quad (19)$$

We name the set of constraints above `Soft-align`, which has the same constraints as `Soft-tag`, i.e., Eqs. (8), (9), (15) and (16).

4 Experimental Setup

We conduct experiments on the latest OntoNotes 4.0 corpus (LDC2011T03). OntoNotes is a large, manually annotated corpus that contains various text genres and annotations, such as part-of-speech tags, named entity labels, syntactic parse trees, predicate-argument structures and co-references (Hovy et al., 2006). Aside from English, this corpus also contains several Chinese and Arabic corpora. Some of these corpora contain bilingual parallel documents. We used the Chinese-English parallel corpus with named entity labels as our development and test data. This corpus includes about 400 document pairs (chtb_0001-0325, ectb_1001-1078). We used odd-numbered documents as development data and even-numbered documents as test data. We used all other portions of the named entity annotated corpus as training data for the monolingual systems. There were a total of ~660 Chinese documents (~16k sentences) and ~1,400 English documents (~39k sentences). OntoNotes annotates 18 named entity types, such as person, location, date and money. In this paper, we selected the four most common named entity types, i.e., PER (Person), LOC (Location),

Chinese NER Templates
00: 1 (class bias param)
01: $w_{i+k}, -1 \leq k \leq 1$
02: $w_{i+k-1} \circ w_{i+k}, 0 \leq k \leq 1$
03: $\mathsf{shape}(w_{i+k}), -4 \leq k \leq 4$
04: $\mathsf{prefix}(w_i, k), 1 \leq k \leq 4$
05: $\mathsf{prefix}(w_{i-1}, k), 1 \leq k \leq 4$
06: $\mathsf{suffix}(w_i, k), 1 \leq k \leq 4$
07: $\mathsf{suffix}(w_{i-1}, k), 1 \leq k \leq 4$
08: $\mathsf{radical}(w_i, k), 1 \leq k \leq \mathsf{len}(w_i)$
Unigram Features
$y_i \circ$ 00 – 08
Bigram Features
$y_{i-1} \circ y_i \circ$ 00 – 08

Table 1: Basic features of Chinese NER.

ORG (Organization) and GPE (Geo-Political Entities), and discarded the others.

Since the bilingual corpus is only aligned at the document level, we performed sentence alignment using the Champollion Tool Kit (CTK).[4] After removing sentences with no aligned sentence, a total of 8,249 sentence pairs were retained.

We used the BerkeleyAligner,[5] to produce word alignments over the sentence-aligned datasets. BerkeleyAligner also gives posterior probabilities P_a for each aligned word pair.

We used the CRF-based Stanford NER tagger (using Viterbi decoding) as our baseline monolingual NER tool.[6] English features were taken from Finkel et al. (2005). Table 1 lists the basic features of Chinese NER, where $\circ$ means string concatenation and y_i is the named entity tag of the ith word w_i. Moreover, $\mathsf{shape}(w_i)$ is the shape of w_i, such as date and number. $\mathsf{prefix/suffix}(w_i, k)$ denotes the k-characters prefix/suffix of w_i. $\mathsf{radical}(w_i, k)$ denotes the radical of the kth Chinese character of w_i.[7] $\mathsf{len}(w_i)$ is the number of Chinese characters in w_i.

To make the baseline CRF taggers stronger, we added word clustering features to improve generalization over unseen data for both Chinese and English. Word clustering features have been successfully used in several English tasks, including NER (Miller et al., 2004) and dependency parsing (Koo et al., 2008). To our knowledge, this work is the first use of word clustering features for Chinese NER. A C++ implementation of the Brown word clustering algorithms (Brown et al., 1992) was used to obtain the word clusters (Liang, 2005).[8] Raw text was obtained from the fifth edition of Chinese Gigaword (LDC2011T13). One million paragraphs from Xinhua news section were randomly selected, and the Stanford Word Segmenter with LDC standard was applied to segment Chinese text into words.[9] About 46 million words were obtained which were clustered into 1,000 word classes.

5 Threshold Tuning

During development, we tuned the word alignment probability thresholds to find the best value. Figure 3 shows the performance curves.

When the word alignment probability threshold θ is set to 0.9, the hard bilingual constraints perform well for both Chinese and English. But as the thresholds value gets smaller, and more noisy word alignments are introduced, we see the hard bilingual constraints method starts to perform badly.

In `Soft-tag` setting, where inconsistent tag assignments within aligned word pairs are allowed but penalized, different languages have different optimal threshold values. For example, Chinese has an optimal threshold of 0.7, whereas English has 0.2. Thus, the optimal thresholds for different languages need to be selected with care when `Soft-tag` is applied in practice.

`Soft-align` eliminates the need for careful tuning of word alignment thresholds, and therefore can be more easily used in practice. Experimental results of `Soft-align` confirms our hypothesis – the performance of both Chinese and English NER systems improves with decreasing threshold. However, we can still improve efficiency by setting a low threshold to prune away very unlikely word alignments. We set the threshold to 0.1 for `Soft-align` to increase speed, and we observed very minimal performance lost when doing so.

We also found that automatically estimated bilingual tag PMI scores (`Auto`) gave comparable results

[4] champollion.sourceforge.net

[5] code.google.com/p/berkeleyaligner

[6] nlp.stanford.edu/software/CRF-NER.shtml, which has included our English and Chinese NER implementations.

[7] The radical of a Chinese character can be found at: www.unicode.org/charts/unihan.html

[8] github.com/percyliang/brown-cluster

[9] nlp.stanford.edu/software/segmenter.shtml

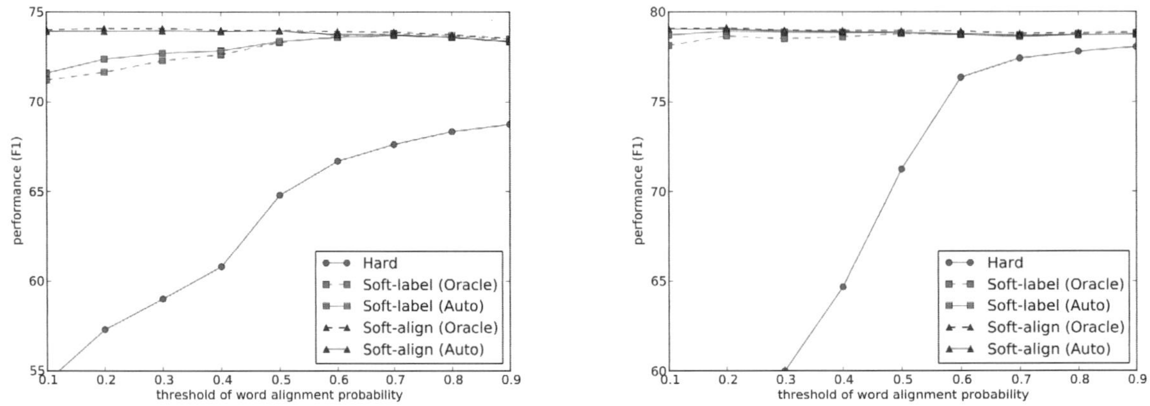

(a) Chinese

(b) English

Figure 3: Performance curves of different bilingual constraints methods on development set.

to `Oracle`. Therefore this technique is effective for computing the PMI scores, avoiding the need of manually annotating named entity bilingual corpus.

6 Bilingual NER Results

The main results on Chinese and English test sets with the optimal word alignment threshold for each method are shown in Table 2.

The CRF-based Chinese NER with and without word clustering features are compared here. The word clustering features significantly ($p < 0.01$) improved the performance of Chinese NER, [10] giving us a strong Chinese NER baseline.[11] The effectiveness of word clustering for English NER has been proved in previous work.

The performance of ILP with only monolingual constraints is quite comparable with the CRF results, especially on English. The greater ILP performance on English is probably due to more accurate marginal probabilities estimated by the English CRF model.

The ILP model with hard bilingual constraints gives a slight performance improvement on Chinese, but affects performance negatively on English. Once we introduced tagging uncertainties into the `Soft-tag` bilingual constraints, we see a very significant ($p < 0.01$) performance boost on Chinese. This method also improves the recall on English, with a smaller decrease in precision. Overall, it improves English F_1 score by about 0.4%, which is unfortunately not statistically significant.

Compared with `Soft-tag`, the final `Soft-align` method can further improve performance on both Chinese and English. This is likely to be because: 1) `Soft-align` includes more word alignment pairs, thereby improving recall; and 2) uses probabilities to cut wrong word alignments, thereby improving precision. In particular, compared with the strong CRF baseline, the gain on Chinese side is almost 5.5% in absolute F_1 score.

Decoding/inferenc efficiency of different methods are shown in the last column of Table 2.[12] Compared with Viterbi decoding in CRF, monolingual ILP decoding is about 2.3 times slower. Bilingual ILP decoding, with either hard or soft constraints, is significantly slower than the monolingual methods. The reason is that the number of monolingual ILP constraints doubles, and there are additionally many more bilingual constraints. The difference in speed between the `Soft-tag` and `Soft-align` methods is attributed to the difference in number of word alignment pairs.

Since each sentence pair can be decoded indepen-

[10] We use paired bootstrap resampling significance test (Efron and Tibshirani, 1993).

[11] To the best of our knowledge, there was no performance report of state-of-the-art NER results on the latest OntoNotes dataset.

[12] CPU: Intel Xeon E5-2660 2.20GHz. And the speed calculation of ILP inference methods exclude the time needed to obtain marginal probabilities from the CRF models.

	Chinese			English			Speed
	P	R	F_1	P	R	F_1	#sent/s
CRF (No Cluster)	74.74	56.17	64.13	–	–	–	–
CRF (Word Cluster)	76.90	63.32	69.45	**82.95**	76.67	79.68	317.3
Monolingual ILP	76.20	63.06	69.01	82.88	76.68	79.66	138.0
Hard	74.38	65.78	69.82	82.66	75.36	78.84	21.1
`Soft-tag` (Auto)	77.37	71.14	74.13	81.36	**78.74**	80.03	5.9
`Soft-align` (Auto)	**77.71**	**72.51**	**75.02**	81.94	78.35	**80.10**	1.5

Table 2: Results on bilingual parallel test set.

dently, parallelization the decoding process can result in significant speedup.

7 Semi-supervised NER Results

The above results show the usefulness of our method in a bilingual setting, where we are presented with sentence aligned data, and are tagging both languages at the same time. To have a greater impact on general monolingual NER systems, we employ a semi-supervised learning setting. First, we tag a large amount of unannotated bitext with our bilingual constraint-based NER tagger. Then we mix the automatically tagged results with the original monolingual Chinese training data to train a new model.

Our bitext is derived from the Chinese-English part of the Foreign Broadcast Information Service corpus (FBIS, LDC2003E14). The best performing bilingual model `Soft-align` with threshold $\theta = 0.1$ was used under the same experimental setting as described in Section 4

Method	#sent	P	R	F_1
CRF	~16k	76.90	63.32	69.45
Semi	10k	77.60	66.51	71.62
	20k	77.28	67.26	71.92
	40k	77.40	67.81	72.29
	80k	77.44	68.64	72.77

Table 3: Semi-supervised results on Chinese test set.

Table 3 shows that the performance of the semi-supervised method improves with more additional data. We simply appended these data to the original training data. We also have done the experiments to down weight the additional training data by duplicating the original training data. There was some slight improvements, but not very significant. Finally, when we add 80k sentences, the F_1 score is improved by 3.32%, which is significantly ($p < 0.01$) better than the baseline, and most of the contribution comes from recall improvement.

Before the end of experimental section, let us summarize the usage of different kinds of data resources used in our experiments, as shown in Table 4, where ✓ and × denote whether the corresponding resources are required. In the bilingual case, during training, only the monolingual named entity annotated data (NE-mono) is necessary to train a monolingual NER tagger. During the test, unannotated bitext (Bitext) is required by the word aligner and our bilingual NER tagger. Named entity annotated bitext (NE-bitext) is used to evaluate our bilingual model. In the semi-supervised case, besides the original NE-mono data, the Bitext is used as input to our bilingual NER tagger to product additional training data. To evaluate the final NER model, only NE-mono is needed.

		NE-mono	Bitext	NE-bitext
Bilingual	train	✓	×	×
	test	×	✓	✓
Semi	train	✓	✓	×
	test	✓	×	×

Table 4: Summarization of the data resource usage

8 Related Work

Previous work explored the use of bilingual corpora to improve existing monolingual analyzers. Huang et al. (2009) proposed methods to improve parsing performance using bilingual parallel corpus. Li et al. (2012) jointly labeled bilingual named entities with a cyclic CRF model, where approximate inference was done using loopy belief propagation. These methods require manually annotated bilingual corpora, which are expensive to construct, and hard to obtain. Kim et al. (2012) proposed a method of labeling bilingual corpora with named entity labels automatically based on Wikipedia. However, this method is restricted to topics covered by Wikipedia.

Similar to our work, Burkett et al. (2010) also assumed that annotated bilingual corpora are scarce. Beyond the difference discussed in Section 1, their re-ranking strategy may lose the correct named entity results if they are not included in the top-N outputs. Furthermore, we consider the word alignment probabilities in our method which can reduce the influence of word alignment errors. Finally, we test our method on a large standard publicly available corpus (8,249 sentences), while they used a much smaller (200 sentences) manually annotated bilingual NER corpus for results validation.

In addition to bilingual corpora, bilingual dictionaries are also useful resources. Huang and Vogel (2002) and Chen et al. (2010) proposed approaches for extracting bilingual named entity pairs from unannotated bitext, in which verification is based on bilingual named entity dictionaries. However, large-scale bilingual named entity dictionaries are difficult to obtain for most language pairs.

Yarowsky and Ngai (2001) proposed a projection method that transforms high-quality analysis results of one language, such as English, into other languages on the basis of word alignment. Das and Petrov (2011) applied the above idea to part-of-speech tagging with a more complex model. Fu et al. (2011) projected English named entities onto Chinese by carefully designed heuristic rules. Although this type of method does not require manually annotated bilingual corpora or dictionaries, errors in source language results, wrong word alignments and inconsistencies between the languages limit application of this method.

Constraint-based monolingual methods by using ILP have been successfully applied to many natural language processing tasks, such as Semantic Role Labeling (Punyakanok et al., 2004), Dependency Parsing (Martins et al., 2009) and Textual Entailment (Berant et al., 2011). Zhuang and Zong (2010) proposed a joint inference method for bilingual semantic role labeling with ILP. However, their approach requires training an alignment model with a manually annotated corpus.

9 Conclusions

We proposed a novel ILP based inference algorithm with bilingual constraints for NER. This method can jointly infer bilingual named entities without using any annotated bilingual corpus. We investigate various bilingual constraints: hard and soft constraints. Out empirical study on large-scale OntoNotes Chinese-English parallel NER data showed that `Soft-align` method, which allows inconsistent named entity tags between two aligned words and considers word alignment probabilities, can significantly improve over the performance of a strong Chinese NER baseline. Our work is the first to evaluate performance on a large-scale standard dataset. Finally, we can also improve monolingual Chinese NER performance significantly, by combining the original monolingual training data with new data obtained from bitext tagged by our method. The final ILP-based bilingual NER tagger with soft constraints is publicly available at: `github.com/carfly/bi_ilp`

Future work could apply the bilingual constraint-based method to other tasks, such as part-of-speech tagging and relation extraction.

Acknowledgments

The authors would like to thank Rob Voigt and the three anonymous reviewers for their valuable comments and suggestions. We gratefully acknowledge the support of the National Natural Science Foundation of China (NSFC) via grant 61133012, the National "863" Project via grant 2011AA01A207 and 2012AA011102, the Ministry of Education Research of Social Sciences Youth funded projects via grant 12YJCZH304, the Defense Advanced Research Projects Agency (DARPA) Machine Reading Program under Air Force Research Laboratory (AFRL) prime contract no. FA8750-09-C-0181 and the support of the DARPA Broad Operational Language Translation (BOLT) program through IBM.

Any opinions, findings, and conclusion or recommendations expressed in this material are those of the authors and do not necessarily reflect the view of the DARPA, AFRL, or the US government.

References

Jonathan Berant, Ido Dagan, and Jacob Goldberger. 2011. Global learning of typed entailment rules. In *Proceedings of the 49th Annual Meeting of the Association for Computational Linguistics: Human Language Technologies*, pages 610–619, Portland, Oregon, USA, June. Association for Computational Linguistics.

Peter F. Brown, Peter V. deSouza, Robert L. Mercer, Vincent J. Della Pietra, and Jenifer C. Lai. 1992. Class-based n-gram models of natural language. *Comput. Linguist.*, 18(4):467–479, December.

David Burkett, Slav Petrov, John Blitzer, and Dan Klein. 2010. Learning better monolingual models with unannotated bilingual text. In *Proceedings of the Fourteenth Conference on Computational Natural Language Learning*, pages 46–54, Uppsala, Sweden, July. Association for Computational Linguistics.

Yufeng Chen, Chengqing Zong, and Keh-Yih Su. 2010. On jointly recognizing and aligning bilingual named entities. In *Proceedings of the 48th Annual Meeting of the Association for Computational Linguistics*, pages 631–639, Uppsala, Sweden, July. Association for Computational Linguistics.

Dipanjan Das and Slav Petrov. 2011. Unsupervised part-of-speech tagging with bilingual graph-based projections. In *Proceedings of the 49th Annual Meeting of the Association for Computational Linguistics: Human Language Technologies*, pages 600–609, Portland, Oregon, USA, June. Association for Computational Linguistics.

B. Efron and R. J. Tibshirani. 1993. *An Introduction to the Bootstrap*. Chapman & Hall, New York.

Jenny Rose Finkel, Trond Grenager, and Christopher Manning. 2005. Incorporating non-local information into information extraction systems by gibbs sampling. In *Proceedings of the 43rd Annual Meeting of the Association for Computational Linguistics (ACL'05)*, pages 363–370, Ann Arbor, Michigan, June. Association for Computational Linguistics.

Ruiji Fu, Bing Qin, and Ting Liu. 2011. Generating chinese named entity data from a parallel corpus. In *Proceedings of 5th International Joint Conference on Natural Language Processing*, pages 264–272, Chiang Mai, Thailand, November. Asian Federation of Natural Language Processing.

Eduard Hovy, Mitchell Marcus, Martha Palmer, Lance Ramshaw, and Ralph Weischedel. 2006. Ontonotes: the 90% solution. In *Proceedings of the Human Language Technology Conference of the NAACL, Companion Volume: Short Papers*, NAACL-Short '06, pages 57–60, Stroudsburg, PA, USA. Association for Computational Linguistics.

Fei Huang and Stephan Vogel. 2002. Improved named entity translation and bilingual named entity extraction. In *Proceedings of the 4th IEEE International Conference on Multimodal Interfaces*, ICMI 2002, Washington, DC, USA. IEEE Computer Society.

Liang Huang, Wenbin Jiang, and Qun Liu. 2009. Bilingually-constrained (monolingual) shift-reduce parsing. In *Proceedings of the 2009 Conference on Empirical Methods in Natural Language Processing*, pages 1222–1231, Singapore, August. Association for Computational Linguistics.

Sungchul Kim, Kristina Toutanova, and Hwanjo Yu. 2012. Multilingual named entity recognition using parallel data and metadata from wikipedia. In *Proceedings of the 50th Annual Meeting of the Association for Computational Linguistics (Volume 1: Long Papers)*, pages 694–702, Jeju Island, Korea, July. Association for Computational Linguistics.

Terry Koo, Xavier Carreras, and Michael Collins. 2008. Simple semi-supervised dependency parsing. In *Proceedings of ACL-08: HLT*, pages 595–603, Columbus, Ohio, June. Association for Computational Linguistics.

Shankar Kumar. 2005. *Minimum bayes-risk techniques in automatic speech recognition and statistical machine translation*. Ph.D. thesis, Baltimore, MD, USA. AAI3155633.

John D. Lafferty, Andrew McCallum, and Fernando C. N. Pereira. 2001. Conditional random fields: Probabilistic models for segmenting and labeling sequence data. In *Proceedings of the Eighteenth International Conference on Machine Learning*, ICML '01, pages 282–289, San Francisco, CA, USA. Morgan Kaufmann Publishers Inc.

Qi Li, Haibo Li, Heng Ji, Wen Wang, Jing Zheng, and Fei Huang. 2012. Joint bilingual name tagging for parallel corpora. In *Proceedings of the 21st ACM International Conference on Information and Knowledge Management (CIKM 2012)*, Honolulu, Hawaii, October.

Percy Liang. 2005. Semi-supervised learning for natural language. Master's thesis, MIT.

Andre Martins, Noah Smith, and Eric Xing. 2009. Concise integer linear programming formulations for dependency parsing. In *Proceedings of the Joint Conference of the 47th Annual Meeting of the ACL and the 4th International Joint Conference on Natural Language Processing of the AFNLP*, pages 342–350, Suntec, Singapore, August. Association for Computational Linguistics.

Bernard Mérialdo. 1994. Tagging english text with a probabilistic model. *Comput. Linguist.*, 20(2):155–171.

Scott Miller, Jethran Guinness, and Alex Zamanian. 2004. Name tagging with word clusters and discriminative training. In Daniel Marcu Susan Dumais and Salim Roukos, editors, *HLT-NAACL 2004: Main Proceedings*, pages 337–342, Boston, Massachusetts, USA, May 2 - May 7. Association for Computational Linguistics.

Slav Petrov, Pi-Chuan Chang, Michael Ringgaard, and Hiyan Alshawi. 2010. Uptraining for accurate deterministic question parsing. In *Proceedings of the 2010 Conference on Empirical Methods in Natural Language Processing*, pages 705–713, Cambridge, MA, October. Association for Computational Linguistics.

Vasin Punyakanok, Dan Roth, Wen-tau Yih, and Dav Zimak. 2004. Semantic role labeling via integer linear programming inference. In *Proceedings of Coling 2004*, pages 1346–1352, Geneva, Switzerland, Aug 23–Aug 27. COLING.

Dan Roth and Wen-tau Yih. 2005. Integer linear programming inference for conditional random fields. In *Proceedings of the 22nd international conference on Machine learning*, ICML '05, pages 736–743, New York, NY, USA. ACM.

David Yarowsky and Grace Ngai. 2001. Inducing multilingual POS taggers and NP bracketers via robust projection across aligned corpora. In *Proceedings of the second meeting of the North American Chapter of the Association for Computational Linguistics on Language technologies*, NAACL '01, pages 1–8, Stroudsburg, PA, USA. Association for Computational Linguistics.

Tao Zhuang and Chengqing Zong. 2010. Joint inference for bilingual semantic role labeling. In *Proceedings of the 2010 Conference on Empirical Methods in Natural Language Processing*, pages 304–314, Cambridge, MA, October. Association for Computational Linguistics.

Minimally Supervised Method for Multilingual Paraphrase Extraction from Definition Sentences on the Web

Yulan Yan[*] Chikara Hashimoto[‡] Kentaro Torisawa[§]
Takao Kawai[¶] Jun'ichi Kazama[‖] Stijn De Saeger[**]
[* ‡ § ¶ ‖ **] Information Analysis Laboratory
Universal Communication Research Institute
National Institute of Information and Communications Technology (NICT)
{[*]yulan, [‡]ch, [§]torisawa, [**]stijn}@nict.go.jp

Abstract

We propose a minimally supervised method for multilingual paraphrase extraction from definition sentences on the Web. Hashimoto et al. (2011) extracted paraphrases from Japanese definition sentences on the Web, assuming that definition sentences defining the same concept tend to contain paraphrases. However, their method requires manually annotated data and is language dependent. We extend their framework and develop a minimally supervised method applicable to multiple languages. Our experiments show that our method is comparable to Hashimoto et al.'s for Japanese and outperforms previous unsupervised methods for English, Japanese, and Chinese, and that our method extracts 10,000 paraphrases with 92% precision for English, 82.5% precision for Japanese, and 82% precision for Chinese.

1 Introduction

Automatic paraphrasing has been recognized as an important component for NLP systems, and many methods have been proposed to acquire paraphrase knowledge (Lin and Pantel, 2001; Barzilay and McKeown, 2001; Shinyama et al., 2002; Barzilay and Lee, 2003; Dolan et al., 2004; Callison-Burch, 2008; Hashimoto et al., 2011; Fujita et al., 2012).

We propose a minimally supervised method for multilingual paraphrase extraction. Hashimoto et al. (2011) developed a method to extract paraphrases from definition sentences on the Web, based on their observation that definition sentences defining the same concept tend to contain many paraphrases. Their method consists of two steps; they extract definition sentences from the Web, and extract phrasal paraphrases from the definition sentences. Both steps require supervised classifiers trained by manually annotated data, and heavily depend on their target language. However, the basic idea is actually language-independent. Figure 1 gives examples of definition sentences on the Web that define the same concept in English, Japanese, and Chinese (with English translation). As indicated by underlines, each definition pair has a phrasal paraphrase.

(1) a. Paraphrasing is the use of your own words to express the author's ideas without changing the meaning.
b. Paraphrasing is defined as a process of transforming an expression into another while keeping its meaning intact.

(2) a. 言い換えとは、ある表現をその意味内容を変えずに別の表現に置き換えることを言います。 (Paraphrasing refers to the replacement of an expression into another without changing the semantic content.)
b. 言い換えとは、ある言語表現をできるだけ意味や内容を保ったまま同一言語の別の表現に変換する処理である。 (Paraphrasing is a process of transforming an expression into another of the same language while preserving the meaning and content as much as possible.)

(3) a. 意译是指译者在不改变原文意思的前提下，完全改变原文的句子结构。 (Paraphrasing refers to the transformation of sentence structure by the translator without changing the meaning of original text.)
b. 意译是指只保持原文内容，不保持原文形式的翻译方法。 (Paraphrasing is a translation method of keeping the content of original text but not keeping the expression.)

Figure 1: Multilingual definition pairs on "paraphrasing."

We aim at extending Hashimoto et al.'s method to a minimally supervised method, thereby enabling acquisition of phrasal paraphrases within one language, but in different languages without manually annotated data. The first contribution of our work is to develop a minimally supervised method for multilingual definition extraction that uses a classifier distinguishing definition from non-definition. The classifier is learnt from the first sentences in

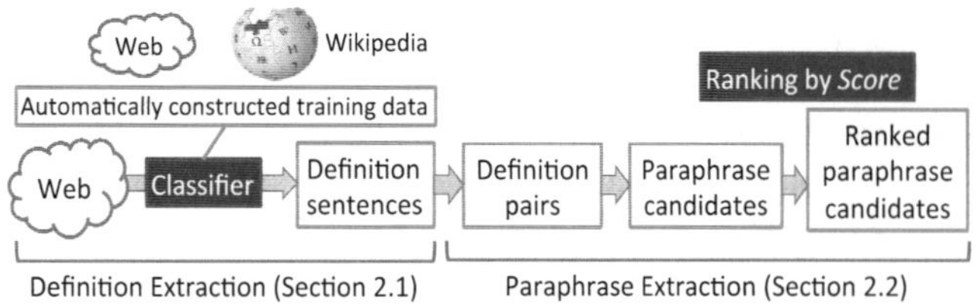

Figure 2: Overall picture of our method.

Wikipedia articles, which can be regarded as the definition of the title of Wikipedia article (Kazama and Torisawa, 2007) and hence can be used as positive examples. Our method relies on a POS tagger, a dependency parser, a NER tool, noun phrase chunking rules, and frequency thresholds for each language, in addition to Wikipedia articles, which can be seen as a manually annotated knowledge base. However, our method needs no additional manual annotation particularly for this task and thus we categorize our method as a minimally supervised method. On the other hand, Hashimoto et al.'s method heavily depends on the properties of Japanese like the assumption that characteristic expressions of definition sentences tend to appear at the end of sentence in Japanese. We show that our method is applicable to English, Japanese, and Chinese, and that its performance is comparable to state-of-the-art supervised methods (Navigli and Velardi, 2010). Since the three languages are very different we believe that our definition extraction method is applicable to any language as long as Wikipedia articles of the language exist.

The second contribution of our work is to develop a minimally supervised method for multilingual paraphrase extraction from definition sentences. Again, Hashimoto et al.'s method utilizes a supervised classifier trained with annotated data particularly prepared for this task. We eliminate the need for annotation and instead introduce a method that uses a novel similarity measure considering the occurrence of phrase fragments in global contexts. Our paraphrase extraction method is mostly language-independent and, through experiments for the three languages, we show that it outperforms unsupervised methods (Paşca and Dienes, 2005; Koehn et al., 2007) and is comparable to Hashimoto et al.'s supervised method for Japanese.

Previous methods for paraphrase (and entailment) extraction can be classified into a distributional similarity based approach (Lin and Pantel, 2001; Geffet and Dagan, 2005; Bhagat et al., 2007; Szpektor and Dagan, 2008; Hashimoto et al., 2009) and a parallel corpus based approach (Barzilay and McKeown, 2001; Shinyama et al., 2002; Barzilay and Lee, 2003; Dolan et al., 2004; Callison-Burch, 2008). The former can exploit large scale monolingual corpora, but is known to be unable to distinguish paraphrase pairs from antonymous pairs (Lin et al., 2003). The latter rarely mistakes antonymous pairs for paraphrases, but preparing parallel corpora is expensive. As with Hashimoto et al. (2011), our method is a kind of parallel corpus approach in that it uses definition pairs as a parallel corpus. However, our method does not suffer from a high labor cost of preparing parallel corpora, since it can automatically collect definition pairs from the Web on a large scale. The difference between ours and Hashimoto et al.'s is that our method requires no manual labeling of data and is mostly language-independent.

2 Proposed Method

Our method first extracts definition sentences from the Web, and then extracts paraphrases from the definition sentences, as illustrated in Figure 2.

2.1 Definition Extraction

2.1.1 Automatic Construction of Training Data

Our method learns a classifier that classifies sentences into definition and non-definition using automatically constructed training data, *TrDat*. *TrDat*'s positive examples, *Pos*, are the first sentences of Wikipedia articles and the negative examples, *Neg*, are randomly sampled Web sentences. The former can be seen as definition, while the chance that the sentences in the latter are definition is quite small.

Our definition extraction not only distinguishes definition from non-definition but also identities the defined term of a definition sentence, and in the paraphrase extraction step our method couples two definition sentences if their defined terms are identical. For example, the defined terms of (1a) and (1b) in Figure 1 are both "Paraphrasing" and thus the two definition sentences are coupled. For *Pos*, we mark up the title of Wikipedia article as the defined term. For *Neg*, we randomly select a noun phrase in a sen-

	N-gram definition pattern	N-gram non-definition pattern
(A)	^ [term] is the	[term] may be
	[term] is a type of	[term] is not

	Subsequence definition pattern	Subsequence non-definition pattern
(B)	[term] is * which is located	you may * [term]
	[term] is a * in the	was [term] * , who is

	Subtree definition pattern	Subtree non-definition pattern
(C)	[term] is defined as the NP	[term] will not be

Table 1: Examples of English patterns.

		English		Japanese		Chinese	
Type	Representation	*Pos*	*Neg*	*Pos*	*Neg*	*Pos*	*Neg*
N-gram	Surface	120	400	30	100	20	100
	Base	120	400	30	100	—	—
	POS	2,000	4,000	500	500	100	400
Subsequence	Surface	120	400	30	100	20	40
	Base	120	400	30	100	—	—
	POS	2,000	2,000	500	500	200	400
Subtree	Surface	5	10	5	10	5	5
	Base	5	10	5	10	—	—
	POS	25	50	25	50	25	50

Table 2: Values of frequency threshold.

tence and mark it up as a (false) defined term. Any marked term is uniformly replaced with [term].

2.1.2 Feature Extraction and Learning

As features, we use patterns that are characteristic of definition (definition patterns) and those that are unlikely to be a part of definition (non-definition patterns). Patterns are either *N-grams*, *subsequences*, or *dependency subtrees*, and are mined automatically from *TrDat*. Table 1 shows examples of patterns mined by our method. In (A) of Table 1, "^" is a symbol representing the beginning of a sentence. In (B), "*" represents a wildcard that matches any number of arbitrary words. Patterns are represented by either their words' surface form, base form, or POS. (Chinese words do not inflect and thus we do not use the base form for Chinese.)

We assume that definition patterns are frequent in *Pos* but are infrequent in *Neg*, and non-definition patterns are frequent in *Neg* but are infrequent in *Pos*. To see if a given pattern ϕ is likely to be a definition pattern, we measure ϕ's probability rate $Rate(\phi)$. If the probability rate of ϕ is large, ϕ tends to be a definition pattern. The probability rate of ϕ is:

$$Rate(\phi) = \frac{freq(\phi, Pos)/|Pos|}{freq(\phi, Neg)/|Neg|}, if freq(\phi, Neg) \neq 0.$$

Here, $freq(\phi, Pos) = |\{s \in Pos : \phi \subseteq s\}|$ and $freq(\phi, Neg) = |\{s \in Neg : \phi \subseteq s\}|$. We write $\phi \subseteq s$ if sentence s contains ϕ. If $freq(\phi, Neg) = 0$, $Rate(\phi)$ is set to the largest value of all the patterns' $Rate$ values. Only patterns whose $Rate$ is more than or equal to a $Rate$ threshold ρ_{pos} and whose $freq(\phi, Pos)$ is more than or equal to a frequency threshold are regarded as definition patterns. Similarly, we check if ϕ is likely to be a non-definition pattern. Only patterns whose $Rate$ is less or equal to a $Rate$ threshold ρ_{neg} and whose $freq(\phi, Neg)$ is more than or equal to a frequency threshold are regarded as non-definition patterns. The probability rate is based on the growth rate (Dong and Li, 1999).

ρ_{pos} and ρ_{neg} are set to 2 and 0.5, while the frequency threshold is set differently according to languages, pattern types (N-gram, subsequence, and subtree), representation (surface, base, and POS), and data (*Pos* and *Neg*), as in Table 2. The thresholds in Table 2 were determined manually, but not really arbitrarily. Basically they were determined according to the frequency of each pattern in our data (e.g. how frequently the surface N-gram of English appears in English positive training samples (*Pos*)).

Below, we detail how patterns are acquired. First, we acquire N-gram patterns. Then, subsequence patterns are acquired using the N-gram patterns as input. Finally, subtree patterns are acquired using the subsequence patterns as input.

N-gram patterns We collect N-gram patterns from *TrDat* with N ranging from 2 to 6. We filter out N-grams using thresholds on the $Rate$ and frequency, and regard those that are kept as definition or non-definition N-grams.

Subsequence patterns We generate subsequence patterns as ordered combinations of N-grams with the wild card "*" inserted between them (we use two or three N-grams for a subsequence). Then, we check each of the generated subsequences and keep it if there exists a sentence in *TrDat* that contains the subsequence and whose root node is contained in the subsequence. For example, subsequence "[term] is a * in the" is kept if a term-marked sentence like "[term] is a baseball player in the Dominican Republic." exists in *TrDat*. Then, patterns are filtered out using thresholds on the $Rate$ and frequency as we did for N-grams.

Subtree patterns For each definition and non-definition subsequence, we retrieve all the term-marked sentences that contain the subsequence from *TrDat*, and extract a minimal dependency subtree that covers all the words of the subsequence from each retrieved sentence. For example, assume that we retrieve a term-marked sentence "`[term]` is usually defined as the way of life of a group of people." for subsequence "`[term]` is * defined as the". Then we extract from the sentence the minimal dependency subtree in the left side of (C) of Table 1. Note that all the words of the subsequence are contained in the subtree, and that in the subtree a node ("way") that is not a part of the subsequence is replaced with its dependency label ("NP") assigned by the dependency parser. The patterns are filtered out using thresholds on the $Rate$ and frequency.

We train a SVM classifier[1] with a linear kernel, using binary features that indicate the occurrence of the patterns described above in a target sentence.

In theory, we could feed all the features to the SVM classifier and let the classifier pick informative features. But we restricted the feature set for practical reasons: the number of features would become tremendously large. There are two reasons for this. First, the number of sentences in our automatically acquired training data is huge (2,439,257 positive sentences plus 5,000,000 negative sentences for English, 703,208 positive sentences plus 1,400,000 negative sentences for Japanese and 310,072 positive sentences plus 600,000 negative sentences for Chinese). Second, since each subsequence pattern is generated as a combination of two or three N-gram patterns and one subsequence pattern can generate one or more subtree patterns, using all possible features leads to a combinatorial explosion of features. Moreover, since the feature vector will be highly sparse with a huge number of infrequent features, SVM learning becomes very time consuming. In preliminary experiments we observed that when using all possible features the learning process took more than one week for each language. We therefore introduced the current feature selection method, in which the learning process finished in one day but still obtains good results.

[1]`http://svmlight.joachims.org.`

Original Web sentence: Albert Pujols is a baseball player.
Term-marked sentence 1: `[term]` is a baseball player.
Term-marked sentence 2: Albert Pujols is a `[term]`.

Figure 3: Term-marked sentences from a Web sentence.

2.1.3 Definition Extraction from the Web

We extract a large amount of definition sentences by applying this classifier to sentences in our Web archive. Because our classifier requires term-marked sentences (sentences in which the term being defined is marked) as input, we first have to identify all such defined term candidates for each sentence. For example, Figure 3 shows a case where a Web sentence has two NPs (two candidates of defined term). Basically we pick up NPs in a sentence by simple heuristic rules. For English, NPs are identified using TreeTagger (Schmid, 1995) and two NPs are merged into one when they are connected by "for" or "of". After applying this procedure recursively, the longest NPs are regarded as candidates of defined terms and term-marked sentences are generated. For Japanese, we first identify nouns that are optionally modified by adjectives as NPs, and allow two NPs connected by "の" (*of*), if any, to form a larger NP. For Chinese, nouns that are optionally modified by adjectives are considered as NPs.

Then, each term-marked sentence is given a feature vector and classified by the classifier. The term-marked sentence whose SVM score (the distance from the hyperplane) is the largest among those from the same original Web sentence is chosen as the final classification result for the original Web sentence.

2.2 Paraphrase Extraction

We use all the Web sentences classified as definition and all the sentences in *Pos* for paraphrase extraction. First, we couple two definition sentences whose defined term is the same. We filter out definition sentence pairs whose cosine similarity of content word vectors is less than or equal to threshold C, which is set to 0.1. Then, we extract phrases from each definition sentence, and generate all possible phrase pairs from the coupled sentences. In this study, phrases are restricted to predicate phrases that consist of at least one dependency relation and in which all the constituents are consecutive in a

f_1	The ratio of the number of words shared between two candidate phrases to the number of all of the words in the two phrases. Words are represented by either their surface form ($f_{1,1}$), base form ($f_{1,2}$) or POS ($f_{1,3}$).
f_2	The identity of the leftmost word (surface form ($f_{2,1}$), base form ($f_{2,2}$) or POS ($f_{2,3}$)) between two candidate phrases.
f_3	The same as f_2 except that we use the rightmost word. There are three corresponding subfunctions ($f_{3,1}$ to $f_{3,3}$).
f_4	The ratio of the number of words that appear in a candidate phrase segment of a definition sentence s_1 and in a segment that is NOT a part of the candidate phrase of another definition sentence s_2 to the number of all the words of s_1's candidate phrase. Words are in their base form ($f_{4,1}$).
f_5	The reversed ($s_1 \leftrightarrow s_2$) version of $f_{4,1}$ ($f_{5,1}$).
f_6	The ratio of the number of words (the surface form) of a shorter candidate phrase to that of a longer one ($f_{6,1}$).
f_7	Cosine similarity between two definition sentences from which two candidate phrases are extracted. Only content words in the base form are used ($f_{7,1}$).
f_8	The ratio of the number of parent dependency subtrees that are shared by two candidate phrases to the number of all the parent dependency subtrees. The parent dependency subtrees are adjacent to the candidate phrases and represented by their surface form ($f_{8,1}$), base form ($f_{8,2}$), or POS ($f_{8,3}$).
f_9	The same as f_8 except that we use child dependency subtrees. There are 3 subfunctions ($f_{9,1}$ to $f_{9,3}$) of f_9 type.
f_{10}	The ratio of the number of context N-grams that are shared by two candidate phrases to the number of all the context N-grams of both candidate phrases. The context N-grams are adjacent to the candidate phrases and represented by either the surface form, the base form, or POS. The N ranges from 1 to 3, and the context is either left-side or right-side. Thus, there are 18 subfunctions ($3 \times 3 \times 2$).

Table 3: Local similarity subfunctions, $f_{1,1}$ to $f_{10,18}$.

sentence. Accordingly, if two definition sentences that are coupled have three such predicate phrases respectively, we get nine phrase pairs, for instance. A phrase pair extracted from a definition pair is a paraphrase candidate and is given a score that indicates the likelihood of being a paraphrase, *Score*. It consists of two similarity measures, *local similarity* and *global similarity*, which are detailed below.

Local similarity Following Hashimoto et al., we assume that two candidate phrases (p_1, p_2) tend to be a paraphrase if they are similar enough and/or their surrounding contexts are sufficiently similar. Then, we calculate the local similarity (*localSim*) of (p_1, p_2) as the weighted sum of 37 similarity subfunctions that are grouped into 10 types (Table 3.) For example, the f_1 type consists of three subfunctions, $f_{1,1}$, $f_{1,2}$, and $f_{1,3}$. The 37 subfunctions are inspired by Hashimoto et al.'s features. Then, *localSim* is defined as:

$$\textit{localSim}(p_1, p_2) = \max_{(d_l, d_m) \in DP(p_1, p_2)} ls(p_1, p_2, d_l, d_m).$$

Here, $ls(p_1, p_2, d_l, d_m) = \sum_{i=1}^{10} \sum_{j=1}^{k_i} \frac{w_{i,j} \times f_{i,j}(p_1, p_2, d_l, d_m)}{k_i}$. $DP(p_1, p_2)$ is the set of all definition sentence pairs that contain (p_1, p_2). (d_l, d_m) is a definition sentence pair containing (p_1, p_2). k_i is the number of subfunctions of f_i type. $w_{i,j}$ is the weight for $f_{i,j}$. $w_{i,j}$ is *uniformly* set to 1 except for $f_{4,1}$ and $f_{5,1}$, whose weight is set to -1 since they indicate the unlikelihood of (p_1, p_2)'s being a paraphrase. As the formula indicates, if there is more than one definition sentence pair that contains (p_1, p_2), *localSim* is calculated from the definition sentence pair that gives the maximum value of $ls(p_1, p_2, d_l, d_m)$. *localSim* is local in the sense that it is calculated based on only one definition pair from which (p_1, p_2) are extracted.

Global similarity The global similarity (*globalSim*) is our novel similarity function. We decompose a candidate phrase pair (p_1, p_2) into *Comm*, the common part between p_1 and p_2, and *Diff*, the difference between the two. For example, *Comm* and *Diff* of ("keep the meaning intact", "preserve the meaning") is ("the meaning") and ("keep, intact", "preserve"). *globalSim* measures the semantic similarity of the *Diff* of a phrase pair. It is proposed based on the following intuition: phrase pair (p_1, p_2) tend to be a paraphrase if their surface difference (i.e. *Diff*) have the same meaning. For example, if "keep, intact" and "preserve" mean the same, then ("keep the meaning intact", "preserve the meaning") is a paraphrase.

globalSim considers the occurrence of *Diff* in global contexts (i.e., all the paraphrase candidates from all the definition pairs). The *globalSim* of a given phrase pair (p_1, p_2) is measured by basically counting how many times the *Diff* of (p_1, p_2) appears in all the candidate phrase pairs from all the definition pairs. The assumption is that *Diff* tends to share the same meaning if it appears repeatedly in paraphrase candidates from all definition sentence pairs, i.e., our parallel corpus. Each occurrence of *Diff* is weighted by the *localSim* of the phrase pair in which *Diff* occurs. Precisely, *globalSim* is defined as:

Threshold	The frequency threshold of Table 2 (Section 2.1.2).
NP rule	Rules for identifying NPs in sentences (Section 2.1.3).
POS list	The list of content words' POS (Section 2.2).
Tagger/parser	POS taggers, dependency parsers and NER tools.

Table 4: Language-dependent components.

$$globalSim(p_1, p_2) = \sum_{(p_i,p_j) \in PP(p_1,p_2)} \frac{localSim(p_i, p_j)}{M}.$$

$PP(p_1, p_2)$ is the set of candidate phrase pairs whose *Diff* is the same as (p_1, p_2).[2] M is the number of similarity subfunction types whose weight is 1, i.e. $M = 8$ (all the subfunction types except f_4 and f_5). It is used to normalize the value of each occurrence of *Diff* to [0, 1].[3] *globalSim* is global in the sense that it considers all the definition pairs that have a phrase pair with the same *Diff* as a target candidate phrase pair (p_1, p_2).

The final score for a candidate phrase pair is:

$$Score(p_1, p_2) = localSim(p_1, p_2) + \ln globalSim(p_1, p_2).$$

The way of combining the two similarity functions has been determined empirically after testing several other ways of combining them. This ranks all the candidate phrase pairs.

Finally, we summarize language-dependent components that we fix manually in Table 4.

3 Experiments

3.1 Experiments of Definition Extraction

We show that our unsupervised definition extraction method is competitive with state-of-the-art supervised methods for English (Navigli and Velardi, 2010), and that it extracts a large number of definitions reasonably accurately for English (3,216,121 definitions with 70% precision), Japanese (651,293 definitions with 62.5% precision), and Chinese (682,661 definitions with 67% precision).

[2]If there are more than one (p_i, p_j) in a definition pair, we use only one of them that has the largest *localSim* value.

[3]Although we claim that our idea of using *globalSim* is effective, we do not claim that the above formula for calculating is the optimal way to implement the idea. Currently we are investigating a more mathematically well-motivated model.

3.1.1 Preparing Corpora

First we describe *Pos*, *Neg*, and the Web corpus from which definition sentences are extracted. As the source of *Pos*, we used the English Wikipedia of April 2011 (3,620,149 articles), the Japanese Wikipedia of October 2011 (830,417 articles), and the Chinese Wikipedia of August 2011 (365,545 articles). We removed category articles, template articles, list articles and so on from them. Then the number of sentences of *Pos* was 2,439,257 for English, 703,208 for Japanese, and 310,072 for Chinese. We verified our assumption that Wikipedia first sentences can mostly be seen as definition by manually checking 200 random samples from *Pos*. 96.5% of English *Pos*, 100% of Japanese *Pos*, and 99.5% of Chinese *Pos* were definitions.

As the source of *Neg*, we used 600 million Japanese Web pages (Akamine et al., 2010) and the ClueWeb09 corpus for English (about 504 million pages) and Chinese (about 177 million pages).[4] From each Web corpus, we collected the sentences satisfying following conditions: 1) they contain 5 to 50 words and at least one verb, 2) less than half of their words are numbers, and 3) they end with a period. Then we randomly sampled sentences from the collected sentences as *Neg* so that $|Neg|$ was about twice as large as $|Pos|$: 5,000,000 for English, 1,400,000 for Japanese, and 600,000 for Chinese.

In Section 3.1.3, we use 10% of the Web corpus as the input to the definition classifier. The number of sentences are 294,844,141 for English, 245,537,860 for Japanese, and 68,653,130 for Chinese.

All the sentences were POS-tagged and parsed. We used TreeTagger and MSTParser (McDonald et al., 2006) for English, JUMAN (Kurohashi and Kawahara, 2009a) and KNP (Kurohashi and Kawahara, 2009b) for Japanese, MMA (Kruengkrai et al., 2009) and CNP (Chen et al., 2009) for Chinese.

3.1.2 Comparison with Previous Methods

We compared our method with the state-of-the-art supervised methods proposed by Navigli and Velardi (2010), using their WCL datasets v1.0 (`http://lcl.uniroma1.it/wcl/`), definition and non-definition datasets for English (Navigli et al., 2010). Specifically, we used its training data ($TrDat_{wcl}$, hereafter), which consisted of 1,908 definition and

[4]`http://lemurproject.org/clueweb09.php/`

Method	Precision	Recall	F1	Accuracy
Proposed$_{def}$	86.79	**86.97**	**86.88**	**89.18**
WCL-1	**99.88**	42.09	59.22	76.06
WCL-3	98.81	60.74	75.23	83.48

Table 5: Definition classification results on $TrDat_{wcl}$.

2,711 non-definition sentences, and compared the following three methods. WCL-1 and WCL-3 are methods proposed by Navigli and Velardi (2010). They were trained and tested with 10 fold cross validation using $TrDat_{wcl}$. *Proposed*$_{def}$ is our method, which used *TrDat* for acquiring patterns (Section 2.1.2) and training. We tested *Proposed*$_{def}$ on each of $TrDat_{wcl}$'s 10 folds and averaged the results. Note that, for *Proposed*$_{def}$, we removed sentences in $TrDat_{wcl}$ from *TrDat* in advance for fairness. Table 5 shows the results. The numbers for *WCL-1* and *WCL-3* are taken from Navigli and Velardi (2010). *Proposed*$_{def}$ outperformed both methods in terms of recall, F1, and accuracy. Thus, we conclude that *Proposed*$_{def}$ is comparable to *WCL-1/WCL-3*.

We conducted ablation tests of our method to investigate the effectiveness of each type of pattern. When using only N-grams, F1 was 85.41. When using N-grams and subsequences, F1 was 86.61. When using N-grams and subtrees, F1 was 86.85. When using all the features, F1 was 86.88. The results show that each type of patterns contribute to the performance, but the contributions of subsequence patterns and subtree patterns do not seem very significant.

3.1.3 Experiments of Definition Extraction

We extracted definitions from 10% of the Web corpus. We applied *Proposed*$_{def}$ to the corpus of each language, and the state-of-the-art supervised method for Japanese (Hashimoto et al., 2011) (*Hashi*$_{def}$, hereafter) to the Japanese corpus. *Hashi*$_{def}$ was trained on their training data that consisted of 2,911 sentences, 61.1% of which were definitions. Note that we removed sentences in *TrDat* from 10% of the Web corpus in advance, while we did not remove Hashimoto et al.'s training data from the corpus. This means that, for *Hashi*$_{def}$, the training data is included in the test data.

For each method, we filtered out its positive outputs whose defined term appeared more than 1,000 times in 10% of the Web corpus, since those terms tend to be too vague to be a defined term or refer to an entity outside the definition sentence. For example, if "the college" appears more than 1,000 times in 10% of the corpus, we filter out sentences like "The college is one of three colleges in the Coast Community College District and was founded in 1947." For *Proposed*$_{def}$, the number of remaining positive outputs is 3,216,121 for English, 651,293 for Japanese, and 682,661 for Chinese. For *Hashi*$_{def}$, the number of positive outputs is 523,882.

For *Proposed*$_{def}$ of each language, we randomly sampled 200 sentences from the remaining positive outputs. For *Hashi*$_{def}$, we first sorted its output by the SVM score in descending order and then randomly sampled 200 from the top 651,293, i.e., the same number as the remaining positive outputs of *Proposed*$_{def}$ of Japanese, out of all the remaining sentences of *Hashi*$_{def}$.

For each language, after shuffling all the samples, two human annotators evaluated each sample. The annotators for English and Japanese were not the authors, while one of the Chinese annotators was one of the authors. We regarded a sample as a definition if it was regarded as a definition by both annotators. Cohen's kappa (Cohen, 1960) was 0.55 for English (moderate agreement (Landis and Koch, 1977)), 0.73 for Japanese (substantial agreement), and 0.69 for Chinese (substantial agreement).

For English, *Proposed*$_{def}$ achieved 70% precision for the 200 samples. For Japanese, *Proposed*$_{def}$ achieved 62.5% precision for the 200 samples, while *Hashi*$_{def}$ achieved 70% precision for the 200 samples. For Chinese, *Proposed*$_{def}$ achieved 67% precision for the 200 samples. From these results, we conclude that *Proposed*$_{def}$ can extract a large number of definition sentences from the Web moderately well for the three languages.

Although the precision is not very high, our experiments in the next section show that we can still extract a large number of paraphrases with high precision from these definition sentences, due mainly to our similarity measures, *localSim* and *globalSim*.

3.2 Experiments of Paraphrase Extraction

We show (1) that our paraphrase extraction method outperforms unsupervised methods for the three languages, (2) that *globalSim* is effective, and (3) that our method is comparable to the state-of-the-art su-

***Proposed$_{Score}$*:** Our method. Outputs are ranked by *Score*.

***Proposed$_{local}$*:** This is the same as *Proposed$_{Score}$* except that it ranks outputs by *localSim*. The performance drop from *Proposed$_{Score}$* shows *globalSim*'s effectiveness.

***Hashi$_{sup}$*:** Hashimoto et al.'s supervised method. Training data is the same as Hashimoto et al. Outputs are ranked by the SVM score (the distance from the hyperplane). This is for Japanese only.

***Hashi$_{uns}$*:** The unsupervised version of *Hashi$_{sup}$*. Outputs are ranked by the sum of feature values. Japanese only.

***SMT*:** The phrase table construction method of Moses (Koehn et al., 2007). We assume that Moses should extract a set of two phrases that are paraphrases of each other, if we input monolingual parallel sentence pairs like our definition pairs. We used default values for all the parameters. Outputs are ranked by the product of two phrase translation probabilities of both directions.

***P&D*:** The distributional similarity based method by Paşca and Dienes (2005) (their "N-gram-Only" method). Outputs are ranked by the number of contexts two phrases share. Following Paşca and Dienes (2005), we used the parameters $LC = 3$ and $MaxP = 4$, while $MinP$, which was 1 in Paşca and Dienes (2005), was set to 2 since our target was phrasal paraphrases.

Table 6: Evaluated paraphrase extraction methods.

pervised method for Japanese.

3.2.1 Experimental Setting

We extracted paraphrases from definition sentences in *Pos* and those extracted by *Proposed$_{def}$* in Section 3.1.3. First we coupled two definition sentences whose defined term was the same. The number of definition pairs was 3,208,086 for English, 742,306 for Japanese, and 457,233 for Chinese.

Then we evaluated six methods in Table 6.[5] All the methods except *P&D* took the same definition pairs as input, while *P&D*'s input was 10% of the Web corpus. The input can be seen as the same for all the methods, since the definition pairs were derived from that 10% of the Web corpus. In our experiments *Exp1* and *Exp2* below, all evaluation samples were shuffled so that human annotators could not know which sample was from which method. Annotators were the same as those who conducted the evaluation in Section 3.1.3. Cohen's kappa (Cohen, 1960) was 0.83 for English, 0.88 for Japanese, and 0.85 for Chinese, all of which indicated reasonably good (Landis and Koch, 1977). We regarded a candidate phrase pair as a paraphrase if both annotators regarded it as a paraphrase.

Exp1 We compared the methods that take definition pairs as input, i.e. *Proposed$_{Score}$*, *Proposed$_{local}$*, *Hashi$_{sup}$*, *Hashi$_{uns}$*, and *SMT*. We randomly sampled 200 phrase pairs from the top 10,000 for each method for evaluation. The evaluation of each candidate phrase pair (p_1, p_2) was based on bidirectional checking of entailment relation, $p_1 \rightarrow p_2$ and $p_2 \rightarrow p_1$, with p_1 and p_2 embedded in contexts, as Hashimoto et al. (2011) did. Entailment relation of both directions hold if (p_1, p_2) is a paraphrase. We used definition pairs from which candidate phrase pairs were extracted as contexts.

Exp2 We compared *Proposed$_{Score}$* and *P&D*. Since *P&D* restricted its output to phrase pairs in which each phrase consists of two to four words, we restricted the output of *Proposed$_{Score}$* to 2-to-4-words phrase pairs, too. We randomly sampled 200 from the top 3,000 phrase pairs from each method for evaluation, and the annotators checked entailment relation of both directions between two phrases using Web sentence pairs that contained the two phrases as contexts.

3.2.2 Results

From ***Exp1***, we obtained precision curves in the upper half of Figure 4. The curves were drawn from the 200 samples that were sorted in descending order by their score, and we plotted a dot for every 5 samples. *Proposed$_{Score}$* outperformed *Proposed$_{local}$* for the three languages, and thus *globalSim* was effective. *Proposed$_{Score}$* outperformed *Hashi$_{sup}$*. However, we observed that *Proposed$_{Score}$* acquired many candidate phrase pairs (p_1, p_2) for which p_1 and p_2 consisted of the same content words like "send a postcard to the author" and "send the author a postcard," while the other methods tended to acquire more content word variations like "have a *chance*" and "have an *opportunity*." Then we evaluated all the methods in terms of how many paraphrases with content word variations were extracted. We extracted from the evaluation samples only candidate phrase pairs whose *Diff* contained a content word (*content word variation pairs*), to see how many

[5] We filtered out phrase pairs in which one phrase contained a named entity but the other did not contain the named entity from the output of *Proposed$_{Score}$*, *Proposed$_{local}$*, *SMT*, and *P&D*, since most of them were not paraphrases. We used Stanford NER (Finkel et al., 2005) for English named entity recognition (NER), KNP for Japanese NER, and BaseNER (Zhao and Kit, 2008) for Chinese NER. *Hashi$_{sup}$* and *Hashi$_{uns}$* did the named entity filtering of the same kind (footnote 3 of Hashimoto et al. (2011)), and thus we did not apply the filter to them any further.

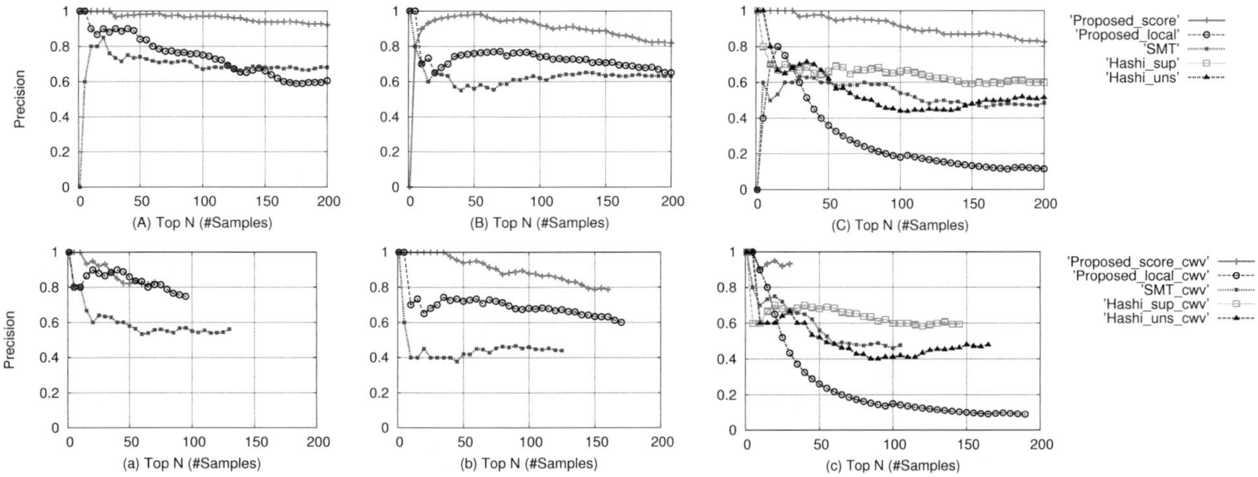

Figure 4: Precision curves of *Exp1*: English (A)(a), Chinese (B)(b), and Japanese (C)(c).

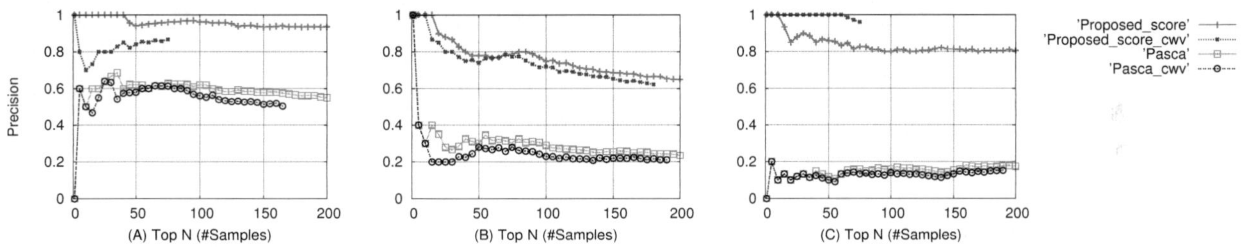

Figure 5: Precision curves of *Exp2*: English (A), Chinese (B), and Japanese (C).

of them were paraphrases. The lower half of Figure 4 shows the results (curves labeled with _*cwv*). The number of samples for $Proposed_{Score}$ reduced drastically compared to the others for English and Japanese, though precision was kept at a high level. It is due mainly to the *globalSim*; the *Diff* of the non-content word variation pairs appears frequently in paraphrase candidates, and thus their *globalSim* scores are high.

From ***Exp2***, precision curves in Figure 5 were obtained. *P&D* acquired more content word variation pairs as the curves labeled by _*cwv* indicates. However, $Proposed_{Score}$'s precision outperformed *P&D*'s by a large margin for the three languages.

From all of these results, we conclude (1) that our paraphrase extraction method outperforms unsupervised methods for the three languages, (2) that *globalSim* is effective, and (3) that our method is comparable to the state-of-the-art supervised method for Japanese, though our method tends to extract fewer content word variation pairs than the others.

Table 7 shows examples of English paraphrases extracted by $Proposed_{Score}$.

is based in Halifax = is headquartered in Halifax
used for treating HIV = used to treat HIV
is a rare form = is an uncommon type
is a set = is an unordered collection
has an important role = plays a key role

Table 7: Examples of extracted English paraphrases.

4 Conclusion

We proposed a minimally supervised method for multilingual paraphrase extraction. Our experiments showed that our paraphrase extraction method outperforms unsupervised methods (Paşca and Dienes, 2005; Koehn et al., 2007; Hashimoto et al., 2011) for English, Japanese, and Chinese, and is comparable to the state-of-the-art language dependent supervised method for Japanese (Hashimoto et al., 2011).

References

Susumu Akamine, Daisuke Kawahara, Yoshikiyo Kato, Tetsuji Nakagawa, Yutaka I. Leon-Suematsu, Takuya Kawada, Kentaro Inui, Sadao Kurohashi, and Yutaka Kidawara. 2010. Organizing information on the web to support user judgments on information credibility. In *Proceedings of 2010 4th International Universal Communication Symposium Proceedings (IUCS 2010)*, pages 122–129.

Regina Barzilay and Lillian Lee. 2003. Learning to paraphrase: An unsupervised approach using multiple-sequence alignment. In *Proceedings of HLT-NAACL 2003*, pages 16–23.

Regina Barzilay and Kathleen R. McKeown. 2001. Extracting paraphrases from a parallel corpus. In *Proceedings of the 39th Annual Meeting of the ACL joint with the 10th Meeting of the European Chapter of the ACL (ACL/EACL 2001)*, pages 50–57.

Rahul Bhagat, Patrick Pantel, and Eduard Hovy. 2007. Ledir: An unsupervised algorithm for learning directionality of inference rules. In *Proceedings of Conference on Empirical Methods in Natural Language Processing (EMNLP2007)*, pages 161–170.

Chris Callison-Burch. 2008. Syntactic constraints on paraphrases extracted from parallel corpora. In *Proceedings of the 2008 Conference on Empirical Methods in Natural Language Processing*, pages 196–205.

Wenliang Chen, Jun'ichi Kazama, Kiyotaka Uchimoto, and Kentaro Torisawa. 2009. Improving dependency parsing with subtrees from auto-parsed data. In *Proceedings of the 2009 Conference on Empirical Methods in Natural Language Processing*, EMNLP '09, pages 570–579, Singapore. Association for Computational Linguistics.

Jacob Cohen. 1960. Coefficient of agreement for nominal scales. In *Educational and Psychological Measurement*, pages 37–46.

Bill Dolan, Chris Quirk, and Chris Brockett. 2004. Unsupervised construction of large paraphrase corpora: exploiting massively parallel news sources. In *Proceedings of the 20th international conference on Computational Linguistics (COLING 2004)*, pages 350–356, Geneva, Switzerland, Aug 23–Aug 27.

Guozhu Dong and Jinyan Li. 1999. Efficient mining of emerging patterns: discovering trends and differences. In *Proceedings of the fifth ACM SIGKDD international conference on Knowledge discovery and data mining*, KDD '99, pages 43–52, San Diego, California, United States.

Jenny Rose Finkel, Trond Grenager, and Christopher Manning. 2005. Incorporating non-local information into information extraction systems by gibbs sampling. In *Proceedings of the 43nd Annual Meeting of the Association for Computational Linguistics (ACL 2005)*, pages 363–370.

Atsushi Fujita, Pierre Isabelle, and Roland Kuhn. 2012. Enlarging paraphrase collections through generalization and instantiation. In *Proceedings of the 2012 Joint Conference on Empirical Methods in Natural Language Processing and Computational Natural Language Learning (EMNLP-CoNLL 2012)*, pages 631–642.

Maayan Geffet and Ido Dagan. 2005. The distributional inclusion hypotheses and lexical entailment. In *Proceedings of the 43rd Annual Meeting of the Association for Computational Linguistics (ACL 2005)*, pages 107–114.

Chikara Hashimoto, Kentaro Torisawa, Kow Kuroda, Stijn De Saeger, Masaki Murata, and Jun'ichi Kazama. 2009. Large-scale verb entailment acquisition from the web. In *Proceedings of the 2009 Conference on Empirical Methods in Natural Language Processing (EMNLP 2009)*, pages 1172–1181.

Chikara Hashimoto, Kentaro Torisawa, Stijn De Saeger, Jun'ichi Kazama, and Sadao Kurohashi. 2011. Extracting paraphrases from definition sentences on the web. In *Proceedings of the 49th Annual Meeting of the Association for Computational Linguistics: Human Language Technologies*, pages 1087–1097, Portland, Oregon, USA, June. Association for Computational Linguistics.

Jun'ichi Kazama and Kentaro Torisawa. 2007. Exploiting Wikipedia as external knowledge for named entity recognition. In *Proceedings of the 2007 Joint Conference on Empirical Methods in Natural Language Processing and Computational Natural Language Learning (EMNLP-CoNLL)*, pages 698–707, Prague, Czech Republic, June. Association for Computational Linguistics.

Philipp Koehn, Hieu Hoang, Alexandra Birch, Chris Callison-Burch, Marcello Federico, Nicola Bertoldi, Brooke Cowan, Wade Shen, Christine Moran, Richard Zens, Chris Dyer, Ondřej Bojar, Alexandra Constantin, and Evan Herbst. 2007. Moses: Open source toolkit for statistical machine translation. In *Proceedings of the 45th Annual Meeting of the Association for Computational Linguistics Companion Volume Proceedings of the Demo and Poster Sessions*, pages 177–180, Prague, Czech Republic, June. Association for Computational Linguistics.

Canasai Kruengkrai, Kiyotaka Uchimoto, Jun'ichi Kazama, Yiou Wang, Kentaro Torisawa, and Hitoshi Isahara. 2009. An error-driven word-character hybrid model for joint chinese word segmentation and pos tagging. In *Proceedings of the Joint Conference of the*

47th Annual Meeting of the ACL and the 4th International Joint Conference on Natural Language Processing of the AFNLP, pages 513–521, Suntec, Singapore, August. Association for Computational Linguistics.

Sadao Kurohashi and Daisuke Kawahara. 2009a. Japanese morphological analyzer system juman version 6.0 (in japanese). Kyoto University, http://nlp.ist.i.kyoto-u.ac.jp/EN/index.php?JUMAN.

Sadao Kurohashi and Daisuke Kawahara. 2009b. Japanese syntax and case analyzer knp version 3.0 (in japanese). Kyoto University, http://nlp.ist.i.kyoto-u.ac.jp/EN/index.php?KNP.

J. Richard Landis and Gary G. Koch. 1977. Measurement of observer agreement for categorical data. *Biometrics*, 33(1):159–174.

Dekang Lin and Patrick Pantel. 2001. Discovery of inference rules for question answering. *Natural Language Engineering*, 7(4):343–360.

Dekang Lin, Shaojun Zhao Lijuan Qin, and Ming Zhou. 2003. Identifying synonyms among distributionally similar words. In *Proceedings of the 18th International Joint Conference on Artificial Intelligence (IJCAI-03)*, pages 1492–1493.

Ryan McDonald, Kevin Lerman, and Fernando Pereira. 2006. Multilingual dependency analysis with a two-stage discriminative parser. In *Proceedings of the Tenth Conference on Computational Natural Language Learning*, CoNLL-X '06, pages 216–220, New York City, New York.

Roberto Navigli and Paola Velardi. 2010. Learning word-class lattices for definition and hypernym extraction. In *Proceedings of the 48th Annual Meeting of the Association for Computational Linguistics*, pages 1318–1327, Uppsala, Sweden, July. Association for Computational Linguistics.

Roberto Navigli, Paola Velardi, and Juana María Ruiz-Martínez. 2010. An annotated dataset for extracting definitions and hypernyms from the web. In *Proceedings of LREC 2010*, pages 3716–3722.

Marius Paşca and Péter Dienes. 2005. Aligning needles in a haystack: paraphrase acquisition across the web. In *Proceedings of the Second international joint conference on Natural Language Processing*, IJCNLP'05, pages 119–130, Jeju Island, Korea.

Helmut Schmid. 1995. Improvements in part-of-speech tagging with an application to german. In *Proceedings of the ACL SIGDAT-Workshop*, pages 47–50.

Yusuke Shinyama, Satoshi Sekine, and Kiyoshi Sudo. 2002. Automatic paraphrase acquisition from news articles. In *Proceedings of the 2nd international Conference on Human Language Technology Research (HLT2002)*, pages 313–318.

Idan Szpektor and Ido Dagan. 2008. Learning entailment rules for unary template. In *Proceedings of the 22nd International Conference on Computational Linguistics (COLING2008)*, pages 849–856.

Hai Zhao and Chunyu Kit. 2008. Unsupervised segmentation helps supervised learning of character tagging for word segmentation and named entity recognition. In *Proceedings of the Sixth SIGHAN Workshop on Chinese Language Processing*, pages 106–111, Hyderabad, India.

Relation Extraction with Matrix Factorization and Universal Schemas

Sebastian Riedel
Department of Computer Science
University College London
s.riedel@ucl.ac.uk

Limin Yao, Andrew McCallum, Benjamin M. Marlin
Department of Computer Science
University of Massachusetts at Amherst
{lmyao,mccallum,marlin}@cs.umass.edu

Abstract

Traditional relation extraction predicts relations within some fixed and finite target schema. Machine learning approaches to this task require either manual annotation or, in the case of distant supervision, existing structured sources of the same schema. The need for existing datasets can be avoided by using a *universal schema*: the union of all involved schemas (surface form predicates as in OpenIE, and relations in the schemas of pre-existing databases). This schema has an almost unlimited set of relations (due to surface forms), and supports integration with existing structured data (through the relation types of existing databases). To populate a database of such schema we present matrix factorization models that learn latent feature vectors for entity tuples and relations. We show that such latent models achieve substantially higher accuracy than a traditional classification approach. More importantly, by operating simultaneously on relations observed in text and in pre-existing structured DBs such as Freebase, we are able to reason about unstructured and structured data in mutually-supporting ways. By doing so our approach outperforms state-of-the-art distant supervision.

1 Introduction

Most previous work in relation extraction uses a predefined, finite and fixed schema of relation types (such as *born-in* or *employed-by*). Usually some textual data is labeled according to this schema, and this labeling is then used in supervised training of an automated relation extractor, e.g. Culotta and Sorensen (2004). However, labeling textual relations is time-consuming and difficult, leading to significant recent interest in distantly-supervised learning. Here one aligns existing database records with the sentences in which these records have been "rendered"—effectively labeling the text—and from this labeling we can train a machine learning system as before (Craven and Kumlien, 1999; Mintz et al., 2009; Bunescu and Mooney, 2007; Riedel et al., 2010). However, this method relies on the availability of a large database that has the desired schema.

The need for pre-existing datasets can be avoided by using language itself as the source of the schema. This is the approach taken by OpenIE (Etzioni et al., 2008). Here surface patterns between mentions of concepts serve as relations. This approach requires no supervision and has tremendous flexibility, but lacks the ability to generalize. For example, OpenIE may find FERGUSON–*historian-at*–HARVARD but does not know FERGUSON–*is-a-professor-at*–HARVARD. OpenIE has traditionally relied on a large diversity of textual expressions to provide good coverage. But this diversity is not always available, and, in any case, the lack of generalization greatly inhibits the ability to support reasoning.

One way to gain generalization is to cluster textual surface forms that have similar meaning (Lin and Pantel, 2001; Pantel et al., 2007; Yates and Etzioni, 2009; Yao et al., 2011). While the clusters discovered by all these methods usually contain semantically related items, closer inspection invariably shows that they do not provide reliable implicature. For example, a typical representative cluster may include *historian-at*, *professor-at*, *scientist-at*, *worked-at*. Although these relation types are indeed semantically related, note that *scientist-at* does not necessarily imply *professor-at*, and *worked-at* certainly does not imply *scientist-at*. In fact, we contend that any relational schema would inherently be brittle and ill-defined—having ambiguities, problematic boundary cases, and incompleteness.[1] For example, Freebase, in spite of its extensive effort towards high coverage, has no *critized* nor *scientist-at* relation.

In response to this problem, we present a new approach: implicature with *universal schemas*. Here we embrace the diversity and ambiguity of original inputs; we avoid forcing textual meaning into predefined boxes. This is accomplished by defining our schema to be the union of all source schemas: original input forms, e.g. variants of surface patterns similarly to OpenIE, as well as relations in the schemas of many available pre-existing structured databases. But then, unlike OpenIE, our focus lies on learning asymmetric implicature among relations. This allows us to probabilistically "fill in" inferred unobserved entity-entity relations in this union. For example, after observing FERGUSON–*historian-at*–HARVARD our system infers that FERGUSON–*professor-at*–HARVARD, but not vice versa.

At the heart of our approach is the hypothesis that we should concentrate on predicting source data—a relatively well defined task that can be evaluated and optimized—as opposed to modeling semantic equivalence, which we believe will always be illusive.

Note that by operating simultaneously on relations observed in text and in pre-existing structured databases such as Freebase, we are able to reason about unstructured and structured data in mutually-supporting ways. For example, we can predict surface pattern relations that effectively serve as additional features when predicting Freebase relations, hence improving generalization. Also notice that users of our system will not have to study and understand the complexities of a particular schema in order to issue queries; they can ask in whatever form naturally occurs to them, and our system will likely already have that relation in our universal schema.

Our technical approach is based on extensions to probabilistic models of matrix factorization and collaborative filtering (Collins et al., 2001; Koren, 2008; Rendle et al., 2009). We represent the probabilistic knowledge base as a matrix with entity-entity pairs in the rows and relations in the columns (see figure 1). The rows come from running cross-document entity resolution across pre-existing structured databases and textual corpora. The columns come from the union of surface forms and DB relations. We present a series of models that learn lower dimensional manifolds for tuples, relations and entities, and a set of weights that capture direct correlations between relations. Weights and lower dimensional representations act, through dot products, as the natural parameters of a single log-linear model to derive per-cell probabilities.

In experiments we show that our models can accurately predict surface patterns relationships which do not appear explicitly in text, and that learning latent representations of entities, tuples and relations substantially improves results over a traditional classifier approach. Moreover, we can improve accuracy by simultaneously operating on relations observed in the New York Times corpus and in Freebase. In particular, our model outperforms the current state-of-the-art distant supervision method (Surdeanu et al., 2012) by 10% points Mean Average Precision through joint implicature among surface patterns and Freebase relations.

2 Model

Before we present our approach in more detail, we briefly introduce some notation. We use $\mathcal{R}$ to denote the set of relations we seek to predict (such as *works-written* in Freebase, or the X–*historian-at*–Y pattern), and $\mathcal{T}$ to denote the set of input tuples. For simplicity we assume each relation to be binary, although our approach can be easily generalized to the n-ary case. Given a relation $r \in \mathcal{R}$ and a tuple $t \in \mathcal{T}$ the pair $\langle r, t \rangle$ is a *fact*, or relation instance. The input to our model is a set of observed facts $\mathcal{O}$, and the observed facts for a given tuple is denoted by $\mathcal{O}_t := \{\langle r, t \rangle \in \mathcal{O}\}$.

Our goal is a model that can estimate, for a given relation r (such as X–*historian-at*–Y) and a given tuple t (such as <FERGUSON,HARVARD>), the probability $p(y_{r,t} = 1)$ where $y_{r,t}$ is a binary random variable that is true iff t is in relation r. We

[1] At NAACL 2012 Lucy Vanderwende asked "Where do the relation types come from?" There was no satisfying answer. At the same meeting, and in line with Brachman (1983), Ed Hovy stated "We don't even know what is-a means."

Figure 1 (diagram; its own text is given below):

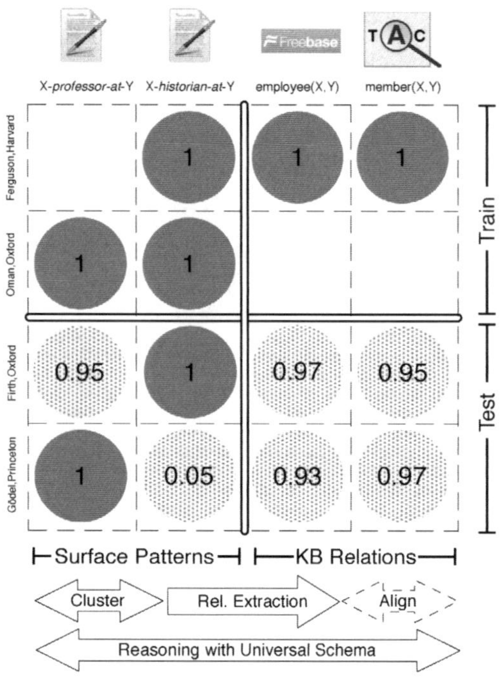

Figure 1: Filling up a database of universal schema. Dark circles are observed facts, shaded circles are inferred facts. Relation Extraction (RE) maps surface pattern relations (and other features) to structured relations. Surface form clustering models correlations between patterns, and can be fed into RE (Yao et al., 2011). Database alignment and integration models correlations between structured relations (not done in this work). Reasoning with the universal schema incorporates these tasks in a joint fashion.

introduce a series of exponential family models that estimate this probability using a *natural parameter* $\theta_{r,t}$ and the logistic function:

$$p(y_{r,t}=1|\theta_{r,t}) := \sigma(\theta_{r,t}) = \frac{1}{1+\exp(-\theta_{r,t})}.$$

We will first describe our models through different definitions of the natural parameter $\theta_{r,t}$. In each case $\theta_{r,t}$ will be a function of r, t and a set of weights and/or latent feature vectors. In section 2.5 we will then show how these weights and vectors can be estimated based on the observed facts $\mathcal{O}$.

Notice that we can interpret $p(y_{r,t}=1)$ as the probability that a customer t likes product r. This analogy allows us to draw from a large body of work in collaborative filtering, such as work in probabilistic matrix factorization and implicit feedback.

2.1 Latent Feature Model

One way to define $\theta_{r,t}$ is through a latent feature model F. Here we measure compatibility between relation r and tuple t as dot product of two latent feature representations of size K^{F}: $\mathbf{a}_r$ for relation r, and $\mathbf{v}_t$ for tuple t. This gives:

$$\theta^{\mathrm{F}}_{r,t} := \sum_{k}^{K^{\mathrm{F}}} a_{r,k} v_{t,k}.$$

This corresponds to generalized PCA (Collins et al., 2001), a model were the matrix $\Theta = (\theta_{r,t})$ of natural parameters is defined as the low rank factorization $\mathbf{AV}$.

Notice that we intentionally omit any per-relation bias-terms. In section 4 we evaluate ranked answers to queries on a per-relation basis, and a per-relation bias term will have no effect on ranking facts of the same relation. Also consider that such latent feature models can capture asymmetry by assigning more peaked vectors to specific relations, and more uniform vectors to general relations.

2.2 Neighborhood Model

We can interpolate the confidence for a given tuple and relation based on the trueness of other similar relations for the same tuple. In collaborative filtering this is referred to as a *neighborhood-based* approach (Koren, 2008). In terms of our natural parameter, we implement a neighborhood model N via a set of *weights* $w_{r,r'}$, where each corresponds to a directed association strength between relations r and r'. For a given tuple t and relation r we then sum up the weights corresponding to all relations r' that have been observed for tuple t:

$$\theta^{\mathrm{N}}_{r,t} := \sum_{(r',t)\in\mathcal{O}\setminus\{(r,t)\}} w_{r,r'}.$$

Notice that the neighborhood model amounts to a collection of local log-linear classifiers, one for each relation r with feature functions $f_{r,r'}(t) = \mathbb{I}[r' \neq r \wedge (r',t) \in \mathcal{O}]$ and weights $\mathbf{w}_r$. This means that in contrast to model F, this model cannot harness any synergies between textual and pre-existing DB relations.

2.3 Entity Model

Relations have selectional preferences: they allow only certain types in their argument slots. While knowledge bases such as Freebase or DBPedia have extensive ontologies of types of entities, these are often not sufficiently fine to allow relations to discriminate (Yao et al., 2012b). Hence, instead of using a predetermined set of entity types, in our *entity model* E we learn a latent entity representation from data. More concretely, for each entity e we introduce a latent feature vector $\mathbf{t}_e$ of dimension K^{E}. In addition, for each relation r and argument slot i we introduce a feature vector $\mathbf{d}_i$ of the same dimension. For example, binary relations have feature representations $\mathbf{d}_1$ for argument 1, and $\mathbf{d}_2$ for argument 2. Measuring compatibility of an entity tuple and relation amounts to measuring, and summing up, compatibility between each argument slot representation and the corresponding entity representation. This leads to:

$$\theta^{\mathrm{E}}_{r,t} := \sum_{i=1}^{\mathrm{arity}(r)} \sum_{k}^{K^{\mathrm{E}}} d_{i,k} t_{t_i,k}.$$

Note that due to entity resolution, tuples may share entities, and hence parameters are shared across rows.

2.4 Combined Model

In practice all the above models can capture important aspects of the data. Hence we also use various combinations, such as:

$$\theta^{\mathrm{NFE}}_{r,t} := \theta^{N}_{r,t} + \theta^{\mathrm{F}}_{r,t} + \theta^{\mathrm{E}}_{r,t}.$$

2.5 Parameter Estimation

Our models are parametrized through weights and latent component vectors. We could estimate these parameters by maximizing the loglikelihood of the observed data akin to Collins et al. (2001). However, as we do not have access to negative facts, the model would simply learn to predict all facts to be true. In our initial attempt to overcome this issue we sampled a set of unobserved facts as designated negative facts, as is done in related distant supervision approaches. However, we found that (a) our results were sensitive to the choice of negative data and (b) runtime was increased substantially because of a large number of required negative facts.

In collaborative filtering positive-only data is also known as *implicit feedback*. This type of feedback arises, for example, when users buy but not rate items. One successful approach to learning with implicit feedback is based on the observation that the actual task is not necessarily one of prediction (here: to predict a number between 0 and 1) but one of (generally simpler) ranking: to give true "user-item" cells higher scores than false ones. *Bayesian Personalized Ranking* (BPR) uses a variant of this ranking: giving observed true facts higher scores than unobserved (true or false) facts (Rendle et al., 2009). This relaxed constraint is to be contrasted with the log-likelihood setting that essentially requires (randomly sampled) negative facts to score below a globally defined threshold.

2.5.1 Objective

We first create a dataset of *ranked pairs*: for each relation r and each observed fact $f^+ := \langle r, t^+\rangle \in \mathcal{O}$ we choose all tuples t^- such that $f^- := \langle r, t^-\rangle \notin \mathcal{O}$—that is, tuples we have not observed to be in relation r. For each pair of facts f^+ and f^- we want $p(f^+) > p(f^-)$ and hence $\theta_{f^+} > \theta_{f^-}$. In BPR this is achieved by maximizing a sum terms of the form $\mathrm{Obj}_{f^+,f^-} := \log\left(\sigma\left(\theta_{f^+} - \theta_{f^-}\right)\right)$, one for each ranked pair:

$$\mathrm{Obj} := \sum_{\langle r,t^+\rangle \in \mathcal{O}} \sum_{\langle r,t^-\rangle \notin \mathcal{O}} \mathrm{Obj}_{\langle r,t^+\rangle,\langle r,t^-\rangle}. \quad (1)$$

Notice that this objective differs slightly from the one used by Rendle et al. (2009). Consider tuples as users and items as relations. We rank different users with respect to the same item, while BPR ranks items with respect to the same user. Also notice that the BPR objective is an approximation to the per-relation AUC (area under the ROC curve), and hence directly correlated to what we want to achieve: well-ranked tuples per relation.

Note that all parameters are regularized with quadratic penalty which we omit here for brevity.

2.5.2 Optimization

To maximize the objective[2] in equation 1 we follow Rendle et al. (2009) and employ Stochastic Gradient Descent (SGD). In particular, in each epoch

[2]This objective is non-convex for all models excluding the N model.

we sample $|\mathcal{O}|$ facts with replacement from $\mathcal{O}$. For each sampled fact $\langle r, t^+ \rangle$ we then sample a tuple $t^- \in \mathcal{T}$ such that $\langle r, t^- \rangle \notin \mathcal{O}$ is not an observed fact. This gives us $|\mathcal{O}|$ fact pairs $\langle f^+, f^- \rangle$, and for each pair we do an SGD update using the corresponding gradients of Obj_{f^+, f^-}. For the F model the gradients correspond to those presented by Rendle et al. (2009). The remaining gradients are easy to derive; we omit details for brevity.

3 Related Work

This work extends a previous workshop paper (Yao et al., 2012a) by introducing the neighborhood and entity model, by working with the BPR objective, and by more extensive experiments.

Relational Clustering There is a large body of work aiming to discover latent relations by clustering surface patterns (Hasegawa et al., 2004; Shinyama and Sekine, 2006; Kok and Domingos, 2008; Yao et al., 2011; Takamatsu et al., 2011), or by inducing synonymy relationships between patterns independently of the entities (Yates and Etzioni, 2009; Pantel et al., 2007; Lin and Pantel, 2001). Our approach has a fundamentally different objective: we are not (primarily) interested in clusters of patterns or their semantic representation, but in predicting patterns where they are not observed. Moreover, these related methods rely on a *symmetric* notion of synonymy in which clustered patterns are assumed to have the same meaning. Our approach rejects this assumption in favor of a model which learns that certain patterns, or combinations thereof, *entail* others in one direction, but not necessarily the other. This is similar in spirit to work on learning entailment rules (Szpektor et al., 2004; Zanzotto et al., 2006; Szpektor and Dagan, 2008). However, for us even entailment rules are just a by-product of our goal to improve prediction, and it is this goal we directly optimize for and evaluate.

Matrix Factorization Our approach is also related to work on factorizing YAGO to predict new links (Nickel et al., 2012). The primary differences are that we include surface patterns in our schema, use a ranking objective, and learn latent vectors for entities and tuples. Likewise, matrix factorization in various flavors has received significant attention in the lexical semantics community, from LSA to recent work on non-negative sparse embeddings (Murphy et al., 2012). In our problem columns correspond to relations, and rows correspond to entity tuples. By contrast, there columns are words, and rows are contextual features such as "words in a local window." Consequently, our objective is to *complete* the matrix, whereas their objective is to learn better latent embeddings of words (which by themselves again cannot capture any sense of asymmetry).

OpenIE Open IE (Etzioni et al., 2008) extracts facts mentioned in text, but does not predict potential facts not mentioned in text. Finding answers requires explicit mentions, and hence suffers from lower recall for not-so-frequently mentioned facts. Methods that learn rules between textual patterns in OpenIE aim at a similar goal as our proposed approach (Schoenmackers et al., 2008; Schoenmackers et al., 2010). However, their approach is substantially more complex, requires a categorization of entities into fine grained entity types, and needs inference in high tree-width Markov Networks. By contrast, our approach is based on a single unified model, requires no entity types, and for us inferring a fact amounts to not more than a few dot products. In addition, in our Universal Schema approach OpenIE surface patterns are just one kind of relations, and our aim is populate relations of all kinds. In the future we may even include relations between entities and continuous attributes (say, gene expression measurements).

Distant Supervision In Distant Supervision (DS) a set of facts from pre-existing structured sources is aligned with surface patterns mentioned in text (Bunescu and Mooney, 2007; Mintz et al., 2009; Riedel et al., 2010; Hoffmann et al., 2011; Surdeanu et al., 2012), and this alignment is then used to train a relation extractor. A core difference to our approach is the number of target relations: In DS it is the relatively small schema size of the knowledge base, while we also include surface patterns. This allows us to answer more expressive queries. Moreover, by learning from surface-pattern correlations, our latent models induce feature representations for patterns that do not appear in the DS training set. As we will see in section 4, this allows us to outperform state-of-the-art DS models.

Never-Ending Learning and Bootstrapping Our latent feature models are capable of never-ending learning (Carlson et al., 2010). That is, we can continue to train these models with incoming data, even if no structured annotation is available. In bootstrapping approaches the current model is used to predict new relations, and these hypothesized relations are used as new supervision targets (i.e. self-training). By contrast, our model only strengthens the correlations between incoming co-occurring observations. This has the advantage that wrong predictions are less likely be reinforced, hence reducing the risk of semantic drift.

4 Experiments

How accurately can we fill a database of Universal Schema, and does reasoning jointly across a universal schema help to improve over more isolated approaches? In the following we seek to answer this question empirically. To this end we train our models on observed facts in a newswire corpus and Freebase, and then manually evaluate ranked predictions: first for structured relations and then for surface form relations.

4.1 Data

Following previous work (Riedel et al., 2010), our documents are taken from the NYTimes corpus (Sandhaus, 2008). Articles after 2000 are used as training corpus, articles from 1990 to 1999 as test corpus. We also split Freebase facts 50/50 into train and test facts, and their corresponding tuples into train and test tuples. Then we align training tuples with the training corpus, and test tuples with the test corpus. This alignment relies on a preprocessing step that links NER mentions in text with entities in Freebase. In our case we use a simple string-match heuristic to find this linking. Now we align an entity tuple $\langle t_1, t_2 \rangle$ with a pair of mentions $\langle m_1, m_2 \rangle$ in the same sentence if m_1 is linked to t_1 and m_2 to t_2. Based on this alignment we filter out all relations for which we find fewer than 10 tuples with mentions in text.

The above alignment and filtering process reduces the total number of tuples related according to Freebase to 16k: approximately 8k tuples with facts mentioned in the training set, and approximately 8k such tuples for the test set. In addition we have a set of approximately 200k training tuples for which both arguments appear in the same sentence and both can be linked to Freebase entities, but for which no Freebase fact is recorded. This can either be because they are not related, or simply because Freebase does not contain the relationship yet. We also have about 200k such tuples in the test set. To simplify evaluation, we create a *subsampled test set* by randomly choosing 10k of the original test set tuples.

The above alignment allows us to determine, for each tuple t, the observed facts $\mathcal{O}_t$ as follows. To find the surface pattern facts $\mathcal{O}_t^{\text{PAT}}$ for the tuple $t = \langle t_1, t_2 \rangle$ we extract, for each mention $m = \langle m_1, m_2 \rangle$ of t, the *lexicalized dependency path* p between m_1 and m_2. Then we add $\langle p, t \rangle$ to $\mathcal{O}_t^{\text{PAT}}$. For example, we get "<-*subj*<-head->*obj*->" for "M1 heads M2." Filtering out patterns with fewer than 10 mentions in text yields approximately 4k patterns. For training tuples we add as Freebase facts $\mathcal{O}_t^{\text{FB}}$ all facts $\langle r, t \rangle$ that appear in Freebase, and for which r has not been filtered out beforehand. For the test set $\mathcal{O}_t^{\text{FB}}$ remains empty. The total set of observed facts $\mathcal{O}_t$ is $\mathcal{O}_t^{\text{FB}} \cup \mathcal{O}_t^{\text{PAT}}$, and their union over all tuples forms the set of observed facts $\mathcal{O}$.

4.2 Evaluation

For evaluation we use collections of relations: surface patterns in one experiment and Freebase relations in the other. In either case we compare the competing systems with respect to their ranked results for each relation in the collection. Given this ranking task, our evaluation is inspired by the TREC competitions and work in information retrieval (Manning et al., 2008). That is, we treat each relation as query and receive the top 1000 (*run depth*) entity pairs from each system. Then we pool the top 100 (*pool depth*) answers from each system and manually judge their relevance or "truth." This gives a set of relevant results that we can use to calculate recall and precision measures. In particular, we can use these annotations to measure an *average precision* across the precision-recall curve, and an aggregate *mean average precision* (MAP) across all relations. This metric has shown to be very robust and stable (Manning et al., 2008). In addition we also present a weighted version of MAP (weighted MAP) in which the average precision for each re-

Relation	#	MI09	YA11	SU12	N	F	NF	NFE
person/company	103	0.67	0.64	0.70	0.73	0.75	0.76	**0.79**
location/containedby	74	0.48	0.51	0.54	0.43	0.68	0.67	**0.69**
author/works_written	29	0.50	0.51	0.52	0.45	0.61	0.63	**0.69**
person/nationality	28	0.14	**0.40**	0.13	0.13	0.19	0.18	0.21
parent/child	19	0.14	0.25	0.62	0.46	0.76	**0.78**	0.76
person/place_of_death	19	0.79	0.79	0.86	**0.89**	0.83	0.85	0.86
person/place_of_birth	18	0.78	0.75	0.82	0.50	0.83	0.81	**0.89**
neighborhood/neighborhood_of	12	0.00	0.00	0.08	0.43	0.65	0.66	**0.72**
person/parents	7	0.24	0.27	0.58	0.56	0.53	**0.58**	0.39
company/founders	4	0.25	0.25	0.53	0.24	0.77	**0.80**	0.68
film/directed_by	4	0.06	0.15	0.25	0.09	0.26	0.26	**0.30**
sports_team/league	4	0.00	0.43	0.18	0.21	0.59	**0.70**	0.63
team/arena_stadium	3	0.00	0.06	0.06	0.03	0.08	**0.09**	0.08
team_owner/teams_owned	2	0.00	0.50	0.70	0.55	0.38	0.61	**0.75**
roadcast/area_served	2	*1.00*	0.50	*1.00*	0.58	0.58	0.83	*1.00*
structure/architect	2	0.00	0.00	*1.00*	0.27	*1.00*	*1.00*	*1.00*
composer/compositions	2	0.00	0.00	0.00	0.50	0.67	**0.83**	0.12
person/religion	1	0.00	*1.00*	*1.00*	0.50	*1.00*	*1.00*	*1.00*
film/produced_by	1	*1.00*	*1.00*	*1.00*	*1.00*	0.50	0.50	0.33
MAP		0.32	0.42	0.56	0.45	0.61	0.66	0.63
Weighted MAP		0.48	0.52	0.57	0.52	0.66	0.67	0.69

Table 1: Average and (weighted) Mean Average Precisions for Freebase relations based on pooled results. The # column shows the number of true facts in the pool. NFE is statistically different to all but NF and F according to the sign test. Bold faced are winners per relation, italics indicate ties.

lation is weighted by the relation's number of true facts.

Notice that we deviate from previous work in distant supervision that (a) combines the results from several relations in a single precision recall curve, and (b) uses held-out evaluation to measure how well the predictions match existing Freebase facts. This has several benefits. First, when aggregating across relations results are often dominated by a few very frequent relations, such as *containedby*, providing little information about how the models perform across the board. Second, evaluating with Freebase held-out data is biased. For example, we find that frequently mentioned entity pairs are more likely to have relations in Freebase. Systems that rank such tuples higher receives higher precision than those that do not have such bias, regardless of how correct their predictions are. Third, we can aggregate per-relation comparisons to establish statistical significance, for example via the sign test.

Also note that while we run our models on the complete training and test set, evaluation is restricted to the subsampled test set.

4.3 Predicting Freebase Relations

Table 1 shows our results for Freebase relations, omitting those for which none of the systems can find any relevant facts. Our first baseline is MI09, a distantly supervised classifier based on the work of Mintz et al. (2009). This classifier only learns from observed pattern-relation pairs in the training set (of which we only have about 8k). By contrast, our latent feature models can learn pattern-pattern correlations both on the unlabeled training and test set (comparable to bootstrapping). We hence also compare against YA11, a version of MI09 that uses preprocessed cluster features according to Yao et al. (2011). The third baseline is SU12, the state-of-the-art Multi-Instance Multi-Label system by Surdeanu et al. (2012).

The remaining systems are our neighborhood

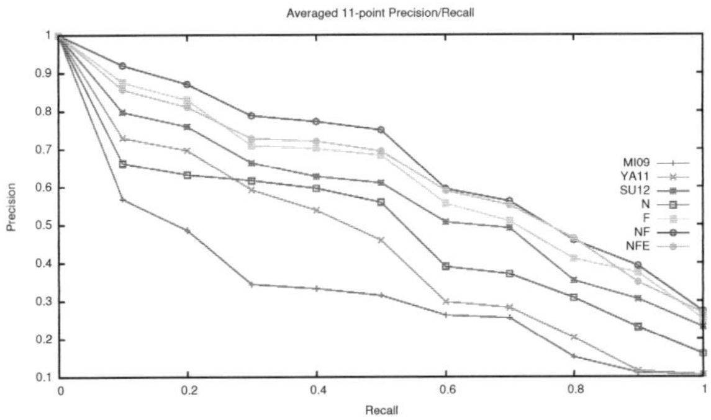

Figure 2: Averaged 11-point precision recall curve for Freebase relations in table 1.

model (N), the factorized model (F), their combination (NF) and the combined model with a latent entity representation (NFE). For all our models we use the same number of components when applicable ($K^{\text{F}} = K^{\text{E}} = 100$), 1000 epochs, and 0.01 as regularizer for component weights and 0.1 for neighborhood weights.

Table 1 shows that adding pattern cluster features (and hence incorporating more data) helps YA11 to improve over MI09. Likewise, we see that the factorized model F improves over N, again learning from unlabeled data. This improvement is bigger than the corresponding change between MI09 and YA11, possibly indicating that our latent representations are optimized directly towards improving prediction performance. The combination of N, F and E outperforms all other models in terms of weighted MAP, indicating the power of selectional preferences learned from data. Note that NFE is significantly different ($p \ll 0.05$ in sign test) to all but the NF and F models. In terms of MAP the NF model outperforms NFE, indicating that it does not do as well for frequent relations, but better for infrequent ones.

Figure 2 shows an averaged 11-point precision recall graph (Manning et al., 2008) for Freebase relations. We notice that our latent models outperform all remaining models across all recall levels, and that combining neighborhood and latent models is helpful. This finding is consistent with our MAP results. Figure 3 shows the recall-precision curve for the *works_written* relation with respect to our three baselines and the NFE model. Observe how precision drops for both MI09 and SU12 at about 50% recall. At this point the remaining unretrieved facts have patterns that have not been seen together with *works_written* in the training set. By using cluster features, YA11 can overcome this problem partly, but not as dramatically as NFE—a pattern we observe for many relations.

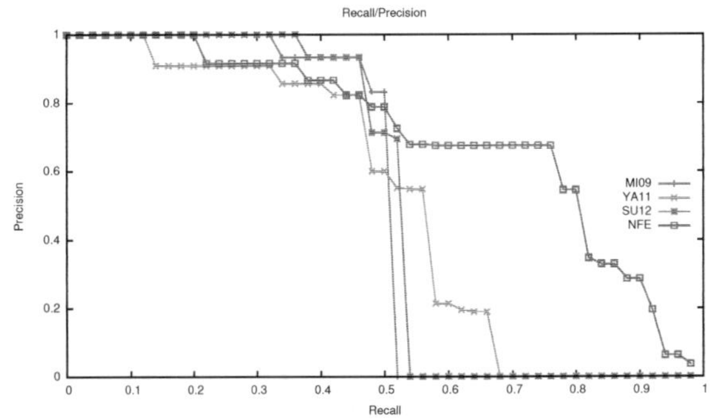

Figure 3: Precision and recall for *works_written*(X,Y).

Relation	#	N	F	NF	NFE
visit	80	0.19	**0.68**	0.49	0.42
attend	69	**0.23**	0.10	0.07	0.10
base	61	0.46	**0.87**	0.81	0.68
head	38	0.47	0.67	**0.70**	0.68
scientist	36	0.25	**0.84**	0.79	0.73
support	18	0.16	0.29	0.32	**0.38**
adviser	11	0.19	0.15	0.19	**0.28**
criticize	9	0.09	0.60	**0.67**	0.64
praise	4	0.01	0.03	0.05	**0.10**
vote	3	0.18	0.18	**0.34**	0.34
MAP		0.22	0.44	0.44	0.43
Weighted MAP		0.28	0.56	0.50	0.46

Table 2: Average and (weighted) Mean Average Precisions for surface patterns.[2]

All our models are fast to train. The slowest model trains in just 45 minutes. By contrast, training the topic model in YA11 alone takes 4 hours. Training SU12 takes two hours (on less data). Also notice that our models not only learn to predict Freebase relations, but also approximately 4k surface pattern relations.

4.4 Predicting Surface Patterns

Table 2 presents a comparison of our models with respect to 10 surface pattern relations. These relations

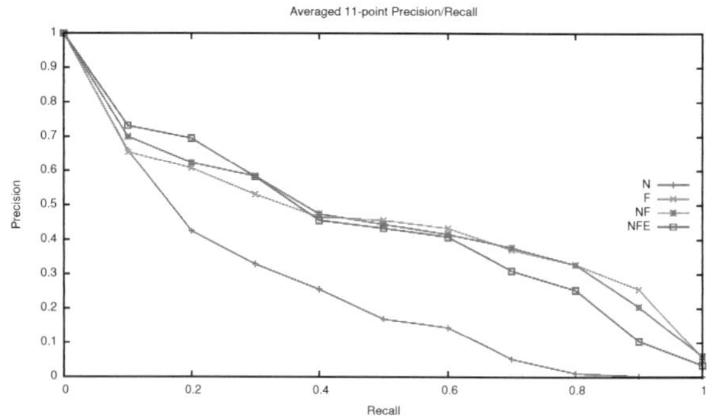

Figure 4: Averaged 11-point precision recall curve for surface pattern relations in table 2.

were chosen according to what we believe are interesting questions not currently captured in Freebase. We again see that learning a latent representation (F, NF and NFE) from additional data helps quite substantially over the N model. For in the weighted MAP metric we note that incorporating entity representations (in the NFE model) in fact hurts total performance.[3] One reason may be the fact that Freebase relations are typed—they require very specific types of entities as arguments. By contrast, for a surface pattern like "X visits Y" X could be a person or organization, and Y could be a location, organization or person. However, in terms of MAP score this time there is no obvious winner among the latent models. This is also confirmed by the averaged 11-point precision recall curve in figure 4.

Notice that we can accurately predict the X–*scientist-at*–Y surface pattern relation in table 2, as well as the more general *person/company* (employedBy) relation in table 1. This indicates that our models can capture asymmetry—a symmetric model would either over-predict X–*scientist-at*–Y or under-predict *person/company*.

5 Conclusion

We present relation extraction into universal schemas. Such schemas contain surface patterns as relations, as well as relations from structured sources. By predicting missing tuples for surface pattern relations we can populate a database without any labelled data, and answer questions not supported by the structured schema alone. By predicting missing tuples in the structured schema we can expand a knowledge base of fixed schema, and only require a set of existing facts from this schema. Crucially, by predicting and modeling both surface patterns and structured relations *simultaneously* we can improve performance. We show this experimentally by contrasting a series of the popular weakly supervised models to our collaborative filtering models that learn latent feature representations across surface patterns and structured relations. Moreover, our models are computationally efficient, requiring less time than comparable methods, while learning more relations.

Reasoning with universal schemas is not merely a tool for information extraction. It can also serve as a framework for various data integration tasks. For example, we could integrate facts from one schema (say, Freebase) into another (say, the TAC KBP schema) by adding both sets of relations to the set of surface patterns. Reasoning with this schema will mean populating each database with facts from the other, and would leverage information in surface patterns to improve integration. In future work we also plan to integrate universal entity types and attributes into the model.

The source code of our system, its output, and all data annotations are available at `http://www.riedelcastro.org/uschema`.

Acknowledgments

We thank the reviewers for very helpful comments. This work was supported in part by the Center for Intelligent Information Retrieval and the University of Massachusetts, in part by UPenn NSF medium IIS-0803847, in part by DARPA under agreement number FA8750-13-2-0020 and FA8750-09-C-0181, and in part by an award from Google. Any opinions, findings, and conclusion or recommendations expressed in this material are those of the authors and do not necessarily reflect the view of DARPA, AFRL, or the US government.

References

Ronald J. Brachman. 1983. What is-a is and isn t: An analysis of taxonomic links in semantic networks. *IEEE Computer*, 16(10):30–36.

[3]Due to the small set of relations only N is significantly different to F, NF and NFE ($p \ll 0.05$ in sign test).

Razvan C. Bunescu and Raymond J. Mooney. 2007. Learning to extract relations from the web using minimal supervision. In *Proceedings of the 45th Annual Meeting of the Association for Computational Linguistics (ACL '07)*.

Andrew Carlson, Justin Betteridge, Bryan Kisiel, Burr Settles, Estevam R. Hruschka, and Tom M. Mitchell. 2010. Toward an architecture for never-ending language learning. In *Proceedings of the 25th AAAI Conference on Artificial Intelligence (AAAI '10)*.

Michael Collins, Sanjoy Dasgupta, and Robert E. Schapire. 2001. A generalization of principal component analysis to the exponential family. In *Proceedings of NIPS*.

M. Craven and J. Kumlien. 1999. Constructing biological knowledge-bases by extracting information from text sources. In *Proceedings of the Seventh International Conference on Intelligent Systems for Molecular Biology*, pages 77–86, Germany.

Aron Culotta and Jeffery Sorensen. 2004. Dependency tree kernels for relation extraction. In *Proceedings of ACL*, Barcelona, Spain.

Oren Etzioni, Michele Banko, Stephen Soderland, and Daniel S. Weld. 2008. Open information extraction from the web. *Commun. ACM*, 51(12):68–74.

T. Hasegawa, S. Sekine, and R. Grishman. 2004. Discovering Relations among Named Entities from Large Corpora. *Proceedings of the 42nd Annual Meeting of the Association for Computational Linguistics (ACL '04)*, pages 415–422.

Raphael Hoffmann, Congle Zhang, Xiao Ling, Luke Zettlemoyer, and Daniel S. Weld. 2011. Knowledge-based weak supervision for information extraction of overlapping relations. In *Proceedings of ACL*.

Stanley Kok and Pedro Domingos. 2008. Extracting Semantic Networks from Text Via Relational Clustering. In *ECML*.

Yehuda Koren. 2008. Factorization meets the neighborhood: a multifaceted collaborative filtering model. In *Proceedings of the 14th ACM SIGKDD international conference on Knowledge discovery and data mining*, KDD '08, pages 426–434, New York, NY, USA. ACM.

Dekang Lin and Patrick Pantel. 2001. DIRT - discovery of inference rules from text. In *Knowledge Discovery and Data Mining*, pages 323–328.

Christopher D. Manning, Prabhakar Raghavan, and Hinrich Schütze. 2008. *Introduction to Information Retrieval*. Cambridge University Press, Cambridge, UK.

Mike Mintz, Steven Bills, Rion Snow, and Daniel Jurafsky. 2009. Distant supervision for relation extraction without labeled data. In *Proceedings of the Joint Conference of the 47th Annual Meeting of the ACL and the 4th International Joint Conference on Natural Language Processing of the AFNLP (ACL '09)*, pages 1003–1011. Association for Computational Linguistics.

Brian Murphy, Partha Pratim Talukdar, and Tom Mitchell. 2012. Learning effective and interpretable semantic models using non-negative sparse embedding. In *COLING*, pages 1933–1950.

Maximilian Nickel, Volker Tresp, and Hans-Peter Kriegel. 2012. Factorizing yago: scalable machine learning for linked data. In *Proceedings of the 21st international conference on World Wide Web*, WWW '12, pages 271–280, New York, NY, USA. ACM.

Patrick Pantel, Rahul Bhagat, Bonaventura Coppola, Timothy Chklovski, and Eduard Hovy. 2007. ISP: Learning Inferential Selectional Preferences. In *Proceedings of NAACL HLT*.

Steffen Rendle, Christoph Freudenthaler, Zeno Gantner, and Lars Schmidt-Thieme. 2009. Bpr: Bayesian personalized ranking from implicit feedback. In *Proceedings of the Twenty-Fifth Conference on Uncertainty in Artificial Intelligence*, UAI '09, pages 452–461, Arlington, Virginia, United States. AUAI Press.

Sebastian Riedel, Limin Yao, and Andrew McCallum. 2010. Modeling relations and their mentions without labeled text. In *Proceedings of the European Conference on Machine Learning and Knowledge Discovery in Databases (ECML PKDD '10)*.

Evan Sandhaus, 2008. *The New York Times Annotated Corpus*. Linguistic Data Consortium, Philadelphia.

Stefan Schoenmackers, Oren Etzioni, and Daniel S. Weld. 2008. Scaling textual inference to the web. In *EMNLP '08: Proceedings of the Conference on Empirical Methods in Natural Language Processing*, pages 79–88, Morristown, NJ, USA. Association for Computational Linguistics.

Stefan Schoenmackers, Oren Etzioni, Daniel S. Weld, and Jesse Davis. 2010. Learning first-order horn clauses from web text. In *Proceedings of the 2010 Conference on Empirical Methods in Natural Language Processing*, EMNLP '10, pages 1088–1098, Stroudsburg, PA, USA. Association for Computational Linguistics.

Yusuke Shinyama and Satoshi Sekine. 2006. Preemptive information extraction using unrestricted relation discovery. In *Proceedings of the main conference on Human Language Technology Conference of the North American Chapter of the Association of Computational Linguistics*, HLT-NAACL '06, pages 304–311, Stroudsburg, PA, USA. Association for Computational Linguistics.

Mihai Surdeanu, Julie Tibshirani, Ramesh Nallapati, and Christopher D. Manning. 2012. Multi-instance multi-label learning for relation extraction. In *Proceedings of the Conference on Empirical methods in natural language processing (EMNLP '12)*, pages 455–465.

Idan Szpektor and Ido Dagan. 2008. Learning entailment rules for unary templates. In *Proceedings of the 22nd International Conference on Computational Linguistics - Volume 1*, COLING '08, pages 849–856, Stroudsburg, PA, USA. Association for Computational Linguistics.

Idan Szpektor, Hristo Tanev, Ido Dagan, and Bonaventura Coppola. 2004. Scaling web-based acquisition of entailment relations. In *Proceedings of EMNLP*.

Shingo Takamatsu, Issei Sato, and Hiroshi Nakagawa. 2011. Probabilistic matrix factorization leveraging contexts for unsupervised relation discovery. In *Proceedings of PAKDD*.

Limin Yao, Aria Haghighi, Sebastian Riedel, and Andrew McCallum. 2011. Structured relation discovery using generative models. In *Proceedings of the Conference on Empirical methods in natural language processing (EMNLP '11)*, July.

Limin Yao, Sebastian Riedel, and Andrew McCallum. 2012a. Probabilistic databases of universal schema. In *Proceedings of the AKBC-WEKEX Workshop at NAACL 2012*, June.

Limin Yao, Sebastian Riedel, and Andrew McCallum. 2012b. Unsupervised relation discovery with sense disambiguation. In *Proceedings of the 50th Annual Meeting of the Association for Computational Linguistics (ACL '12)*, July.

Alexander Yates and Oren Etzioni. 2009. Unsupervised methods for determining object and relation synonyms on the web. *Journal of Artificial Intelligence Research*, 34:255–296.

Fabio Massimo Zanzotto, Marco Pennacchiotti, and Maria Teresa Pazienza. 2006. Discovering asymmetric entailment relations between verbs using selectional preferences. In *Proceedings of the 44th Annual Meeting of the Association for Computational Linguistics (ACL '06)*.

Extracting the Native Language Signal for Second Language Acquisition

Ben Swanson
Brown University
Providence, RI
chonger@cs.brown.edu

Eugene Charniak
Brown University
Providence, RI
ec@cs.brown.edu

Abstract

We develop a method for effective extraction of linguistic patterns that are differentially expressed based on the native language of the author. This method uses multiple corpora to allow for the removal of data set specific patterns, and addresses both feature relevancy and redundancy. We evaluate different relevancy ranking metrics and show that common measures of relevancy can be inappropriate for data with many rare features. Our feature set is a broad class of syntactic patterns, and to better capture the signal we extend the Bayesian Tree Substitution Grammar induction algorithm to a supervised mixture of latent grammars. We show that this extension can be used to extract a larger set of relevant features.

1 Introduction

Native Language Identification (NLI) is a classification task in which a statistical signal is exploited to determine an author's native language (L1) from their writing in a second language (L2). This academic exercise is often motivated not only by fraud detection or authorship attribution for which L1 can be an informative feature, but also by its potential to assist in Second Language Acquisition (SLA).

Our work focuses on the latter application and on the observation that the actual ability to automatically determine L1 from text is of limited utility in the SLA domain, where the native language of a student is either known or easily solicited. Instead, the likely role of NLP in the context of SLA is to provide a set of linguistic patterns that students with certain L1 backgrounds use with a markedly unusual frequency. Experiments have shown that such L1 specific information can be incorporated into lesson plans that improve student performance (Laufer and Girsai, 2008; Horst et al, 2008).

This is essentially a feature selection task with the additional caveat that features should be individually discriminative between native languages in order to facilitate the construction of focused educational excersizes. With this goal, we consider metrics for data set dependence, relevancy, and redundancy. We show that measures of relevancy based on mutual information can be inappropriate in problems such as ours where rare features are important.

While the majority of the methods that we consider generalize to any of the various feature sets employed in NLI, we focus on the use of Tree Substitution Grammar rules as features. Obtaining a compact feature set is possible with the well known Bayesian grammar induction algorithm (Cohn and Blunsom, 2010), but its rich get richer dynamics can make it difficult to find rare features. We extend the induction model to a supervised mixture of latent grammars and show how it can be used to incorporate linguistic knowledge and extract discriminative features more effectively.

The end result of this technique is a filtered list of patterns along with their usage statistics. This provides an enhanced resource for SLA research such as Jarvis and Crossley (2012) which tackles the manual connection of highly discriminative features with plausible linguistic transfer explanations. We output a compact list of language patterns that are empirically associated with native language labels, avoiding redundancy and artifacts from the corpus creation process. We release this list for use by the linguistics and SLA research communities, and plan to expand it with upcoming releases of L1 labeled corpora[1].

2 Related Work

Our work is closely related to the recent surge of research in NLI. Beginning with Koppel et al (2005), several papers have proposed different feature sets to be used as predictors of L1 (Tsur and Rappaport, 2007; Wong and Dras, 2011a; Swanson and Charniak, 2012). However, due to the ubiquitous use of random subsamples, different data preparation methods, and severe topic and annotation biases of the data set employed, there is little consensus on which feature sets are ideal or sufficient, or if any reported accuracies reflect some generalizable truth of the problem's difficulty. To combat the bias of a single data set, a new strain of work has emerged in which train and test documents come from different corpora (Brooke and Hirst, 2012; Tetreault et al, 2012; Bykh and Meurers, 2012). We follow this cross corpus approach, as it is crucial to any claims of feature relevance.

Feature selection itself is a well studied problem, and the most thorough systems address both relevancy and redundancy. While some work tackles these problems by optimizing a metric over both simultaneously (Peng et al, 2005), we decouple the notions of relevancy and redundancy to allow ad-hoc metrics for either, similar to the method of Yu and Liu (2004). The measurement of feature relevancy in NLI has to this point been handled primarily with Information Gain, and elimination of feature redundancy has not been considered.

Tree Substitution Grammars have recently been successfully applied in several domains using the induction algorithm presented by Cohn and Blunsom (2010). Our hierarchical treatment builds on this work by incorporating supervised mixtures over latent grammars into this induction process. Latent mixture techniques for NLI have been explored with other feature types (Wong and Dras, 2011b; Wong and Dras, 2012), but have not previously led to measurable empirical gains.

[1]bllip.cs.brown.edu/download/nli_corpus.pdf

3 Corpus Description

We first make explicit our experimental setup in order to provide context for the discussion to follow. We perform analysis of English text from Chinese, German, Spanish, and Japanese L1 backgrounds drawn from four corpora. The first three consist of responses to essay prompts in educational settings, while the fourth is submitted by users in an internet forum.

The first corpus is the International Corpus of Learner English (ICLE) (Granger et al, 2002), a mainstay in NLI that has been shown to exhibit a large topic bias due to correlations between L1 and the essay prompts used (Brooke and Hirst, 2011). The second is the International Corpus of Crosslinguistic Interlanguage (ICCI) (Tono et al, 2012), which is annotated with sentence boundaries and has yet to be used in NLI. The third is the public sample of the Cambridge International Corpus (FCE), and consists of short prompted responses. One quirk of the FCE data is that several responses are written in the form of letters, leading to skewed distributions of the specialized syntax involved with use of the second person. The fourth is the Lang8 data set introduced by Brooke and Hirst (2011). This data set is free of format, with no prompts or constraints on writing aids. The samples are often very short and are qualitatively the most noisy of the four data sets.

One distinctive experimental decision is to treat each sentence as an individual datum. As document length can vary dramatically, especially across corpora, this gives increased regularity to the number of features per data item. More importantly, this creates a rough correspondence between feature co-occurrence and the expression of the same underlying linguistic phenomenon, which is desirable for automatic redundancy metrics.

We automatically detect sentence boundaries when they are not provided, and parse all corpora with the 6-split Berkeley Parser. As in previous NLI work, we then replace all word tokens that do not occur in a list of 614 common words with an unknown word symbol, UNK.

While these are standard data preprocessing steps, from our experience with this problem we propose additional practical considerations. First, we filter the parsed corpora, retaining only sentences that are parsed to a Clause Level[2] tag. This is primarily due to the fact that automatic sentence boundary detectors must be used on the ICLE, Lang8, and FCE data sets, and false positives lead to sentence fragments that are parsed as NP, VP, FRAG, etc. The wild internet text found in the Lang8 data set also yields many non-Clause Level parses from non-English text or emotive punctuation. Sentence detection false negatives, on the other hand, lead to run-on sentences, and so we additionally remove sentences with more than 40 words.

We also impose a simple preprocessing step for better treatment of proper nouns. Due to the geographic distribution of languages, the proper nouns used in a writer's text naturally present a strong L1 signal. The obvious remedy is to replace all proper nouns with UNK, but this is unfortunately insufficient as the structure of the proper noun itself can be a covert signal of these geographical trends. To fix this, we also remove all proper noun left sisters of proper nouns. We choose to retain the rightmost sister node in order to preserve the plurality of the noun phrase, as the rightmost noun is most likely the lexical head.

From these parsed, UNKed, and filtered corpora we draw 2500 sentences from each L1 background at random, for a total of 10000 sentences per corpus. The exception is the FCE corpus, from which we draw 1500 sentences per L1 due to its small size.

4 Tree Substitution Grammars

A Tree Substitution Grammar (TSG) is a model of parse tree derivations that begins with a single ROOT nonterminal node and iteratively rewrites nonterminal leaves until none remain. A TSG rewrite rule is a tree of any depth, as illustrated in Figure 1, and can be used as a binary feature of a parsed sentence that is triggered if the rule appears in any derivation of that sentence.

Related NLI work compares a plethora of suggested feature sets, ranging from character n-grams to latent topic activations to labeled dependency arcs, but TSG rules are best able to represent complex lexical and syntactic behavior in a homogeneous feature type. This property is summed up nicely by the desire for features that capture rather than cover linguistic phenomena (Johnson, 2012); while features such as character n-grams, POS tag sequences, and CFG rules may provide a usable L1 signal, each feature is likely covering some component of a pattern instead of capturing it in full. TSG rules, on the other hand, offer remarkable flexibility in the patterns that they can represent, potentially capturing any contiguous parse tree structure.

[2] S, SINV, SQ, SBAR, or SBARQ

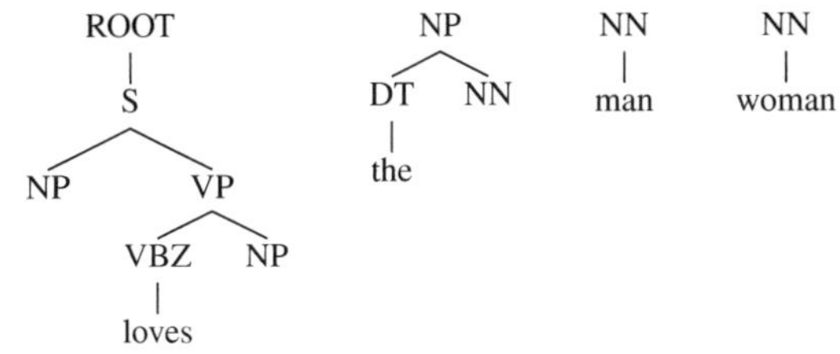

Figure 1: A Tree Substitution Grammar capable of describing the feelings of people of all sexual orientations.

As it is intractable to rank and filter the entire set of possible TSG rules given a corpus, we start with the large subset produced by Bayesian grammar induction. The most widely used algorithm for TSG induction uses a Dirichlet Process to choose a subset of frequently reoccurring rules by repeatedly sampling derivations for a corpus of parse trees (Cohn and Blunsom, 2010). The rich get richer dynamic of the DP leads to the use of a compact set of rules that is an effective feature set for NLI (Swanson and Charniak, 2012). However, this same property makes rare rules harder to find.

To address this weakness, we define a general model for TSG induction in labeled documents that combines a Hierarchical Dirichlet Process (Teh et al, 2005), with supervised labels in a manner similar to upstream supervised LDA (Mimno and McCallum, 2008). In the context of our work the document label η indicates both its authors native language L and data set D. Each η is associated with an observed Dirichlet prior ν_η, and a hidden multinomial θ_η over grammars is drawn from this prior. The traditional grammatical model of nonterminal expansion is augmented such that to rewrite a symbol we first choose a grammar from the document's θ_η and then choose a rule from that grammar.

For those unfamiliar with these models, the basic idea is to jointly estimate a mixture distribution over grammars for each η, as well as the parameters of these grammars. The HDP is necessary as the size of each of these grammars is essentially infinite. We can express the generative model formally by defining the probability of a rule r expanding a symbol s in a sentence labeled η as

$$\begin{aligned} \theta_\eta &\sim Dir(\nu_\eta) \\ z_{i\eta} &\sim Mult(\theta_\eta) \\ H_s &\sim DP(\gamma, P_0(\bullet|s)) \\ G_{ks} &\sim DP(\alpha_s, H_s) \\ r_{i\eta s} &\sim G_{z_{i\eta} s} \end{aligned}$$

This is closely related to the application of the Hierarchical Pitman Yor Process used in (Blunsom and Cohn, 2010) and (Shindo et al, 2012), which interpolates between multiple coarse and fine mappings of the data items being clustered to deal with sparse data. While the underlying Chinese Restaurant Process sampling algorithm is quite similar, our approach differs in that it models several different distributions with the same support that share a common prior.

By careful choice of the number of grammars K, the Dirichlet priors ν, and the backoff concentration parameter γ, a variety of interesting models can easily be defined, as demonstrated in our experiments.

5 Feature Selection

5.1 Dataset Independence

The first step in our L1 signal extraction pipeline controls for patterns that occur too frequently in certain combinations of native language and data set. Such patterns arise primarily from the reuse of essay prompts in the creation of certain corpora, and we construct a hard filter to exclude features of this type.

A simple first choice would be to rank the rules in order of dependence on the corpus, as we expect an irregularly represented topic to be confined to a single data set. However, this misses the subtle but important point that corpora have different qualities such as register and author proficiency. Instead we treat the set of sentences containing an arbitrary feature X as a set of observations of a pair of categorical random variables L and D, representing native language and data set respectively.

To see why this treatment is superior, consider the outcomes for the two hypothetical features shown in Figure 2. The left table has a high data set dependence but exhibits a clean twofold preference for L_1 in both data sets, making it a desirable feature to retain. Conversely, the right table shows a feature where the distribution is uniform over data sets, but has language preference in only one. This is a sign of either a large variance in usage or some data set specific tendency, and in either case we can not make confident claims as to this feature's association with any native language.

	L_1	L_2
D_1	1000	500
D_2	100	50

	L_1	L_2
D_1	1000	500
D_2	750	750

Figure 2: Two hypothetical feature profiles that illustrate the problems with filtering only on data set independence, which prefers the right profile over the left. Our method has the opposite preference.

The L-D dependence can be measured with Pearson's χ^2 test, although the specifics of its use as a filter deserve some discussion. As we eliminate the features for which the null hypothesis of independence is rejected, our noisy data will cause us to overzealously reject. In order to prevent the unneccesary removal of interesting patterns, we use a very small p value as a cutoff point for rejection. In all of our experiments the χ^2 value corresponding to $p < .001$ is in the twenties; we use $\chi^2 > 100$ as our criteria for rejection.

Another possible source of error is the sparsity of some features in our data. To avoid making predictions of rules for which we have not observed a sufficient number of examples, we automatically exclude any rule with a count less than five for any L-D combination η. This also satisfies the common requirements for validity of the χ^2 test that require a minimum number of 5 expected counts for every outcome.

5.2 Relevancy

We next rank the features in terms of their ability to discriminate between L1 labels. We consider three relevancy ranking metrics: Information Gain (IG), Symmetric Uncertainty (SU), and χ^2 statistic.

	IG	SU	χ^2
r	.84	.72	.15

Figure 3: Sample Pearson correlation coefficients between different ranking functions and feature frequency over a large set of TSG features.

$$IG(L, X_i) = H(L) - H(L|X_i)$$

$$SU(L, X_i) = 2\frac{IG(L, X_i)}{H(L) + H(X_i)}$$

$$\chi^2(X_i) = \sum_m \frac{(n_{im} - \frac{N_i}{M})^2}{\frac{N_i}{M}}$$

We define L as the Multinomial distributed L1 label taking values in $\{1, ..., M\}$ and X_i as a Bernoulli distributed indicator of the presence or absence of the ith feature, which we represent with the events X_i^+ and X_i^- respectively. We use the Maximum Likelihood estimates of these distributions from the training data to compute the necessary entropies for IG and SU. For the χ^2 metric we use n_{im}, the count of sentences with L1 label m that contain feature X_i, and their sum over classes N_i.

While SU is often preferred over IG in feature selection for several reasons, their main difference in the context of selection of binary features is the addition of $H(X_i)$ in the denominator, leading to higher values for rare features under SU. This helps to counteract a subtle preference for common features that these metrics can exhibit in data such as ours, as shown in Figure 3. The source of this preference is the overwhelming contribution of $p(X_i^-)H(L|X_i^-)$ in $IG(L, X_i)$ for rare features, which will be essentially the maximum value of $\log(M)$. In most classification problems a frequent feature bias is a desirable trait, as a rare feature is naturally less likely to appear and contribute to decision making.

We note that binary features in sentences are sparsely observed, as the opportunity for use of the majority of patterns will not exist in any given sentence. This leads to a large number of rare features that are nevertheless indicative of their author's L1. The χ^2 statistic we employ is better suited to retain such features as it only deals with counts of sentences containing X_i.

The ranking behavior of these metrics is highlighted in Figure 4. We expect that features with profiles like X_a and X_b will be more useful than those like X_d, and only χ^2 ranks these features accordingly. Another view of the difference between the metrics is taken in Figure 5. As shown in the left plot, IG and SU are nearly identical for the most highly ranked features and significantly different from χ^2.

	L_1	L_2	L_3	L_4	IG	SU	χ^2
X_a	20	5	5	5	**.0008**	**.0012**	**19.29**
X_b	40	20	20	20	.0005	.0008	**12.0**
X_c	2000	500	500	500	**.0178**	**.0217**	**385.7**
X_d	1700	1800	1700	1800	**.0010**	**.0010**	5.71

Figure 4: Four hypothetical features in a 4 label classification problem, with the number of training items from each class using the feature listed in the first four columns. The top three features under each ranking are shown in bold.

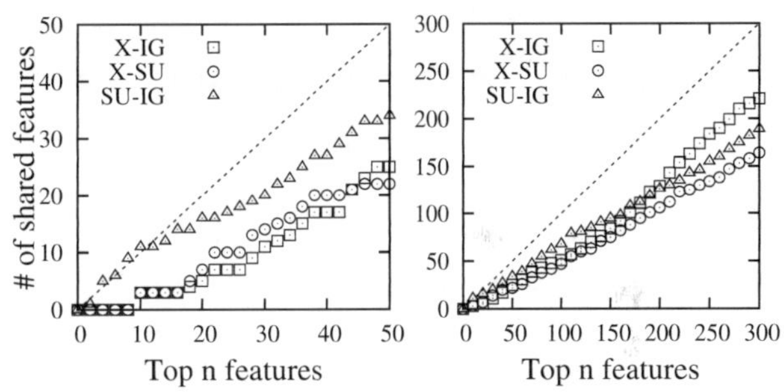

Figure 5: For all pairs of relevancy metrics, we show the number of features that appear in the top n of both. The result for low n is highlighted in the left plot, showing a high similarity between SU and IG.

5.3 Redundancy

The second component of thorough feature selection is the removal of redundant features. From an experimental point of view, it is inaccurate to compare feature selection systems under evaluation of the top n features or the number of features with ranking statistic at or beyond some threshold if redundancy has not been taken into account. Furthermore, as our stated goal is a list of discriminative patterns, multiple representations of the same pattern clearly degrade the quality of our output. This is especially necessary when using TSG rules as features, as it is possible to define many slightly different rules that essentially represent the same linguistic act.

Redundancy detection must be able to both determine that a set of features are redundant and also select the feature to retain from such a set. We use a greedy method that allows us to investigate different relevancy metrics for selection of the representative feature for a redundant set (Yu and Liu, 2004). The algorithm begins with a list S containing the full list of features, sorted by an arbitrary metric of relevancy. While S is not empty, the most relevant feature X^* in S is selected for retention, and all features X_i are removed from S if $R(X^*, X_i) > \rho$ for some redundancy metric R and some threshold ρ.

We consider two probabilistic metrics for redundancy detection, the first being SU, as defined in the previous section. We contrast this metric with Normalized Pointwise Mutual Information (NPMI) which uses only the events $A = X_a^+$ and $B = X_b^+$ and has a range of [-1,1].

$$\text{NPMI}(X_a, X_b) = \frac{\log(P(A|B)) - \log(P(A))}{-\log(P(A,B))}$$

Another option that we explore is the structural redundancy between TSG rules themselves. We define a 0-1 redundancy metric such that $R(X_a, X_b)$ is one if there exists a fragment that contains both X_a and X_b with a total number of CFG rules less than the sum of the number of CFG rules in X_a and X_b. The latter constraint ensures that X_a and X_b overlap in the containing fragment. Note that this is not the same as a nonempty set intersection of CFG rules, as can be seen in Figure 6.

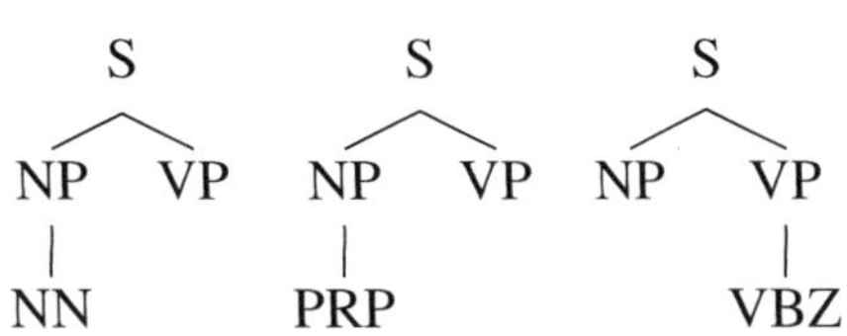

Figure 6: Three similar fragments that highlight the behavior of the structural redundancy metric; the first two fragments are not considered redundant, while the third is made redundant by either of the others.

6 Experiments

6.1 Relevancy Metrics

The traditional evaluation criterion for a feature selection system such as ours is classification accuracy or expected risk. However, as our desired output is not a set of features that capture a decision boundary as an ensemble, a per feature risk evaluation better quantifies the performance of a system for our purposes. We plot average risk against number of predicted features to view the rate of quality degradation under a relevancy measure to give a picture of a each metric's utility.

The per feature risk for a feature X is an evaluation of the ML estimate of $P_X(L) = P(L|X^+)$ from the training data on T_X, the test sentences that contain the feature X. The decision to evaluate only sentences in which the feature occurs removes an implicit bias towards more common features.

We calculate the expected risk $\mathcal{R}(X)$ using a 0-1 loss function, averaging over T_X.

$$\mathcal{R}(X) = \frac{1}{|T_X|} \sum_{t \in T_X} P_X(L \neq L_t^*)$$

where L_t^* is the gold standard L1 label of test item t. This metric has two important properties. First, given any true distribution over class labels in T_X, the best possible $P_X(L)$ is the one that matches these proportions exactly, ensuring that preferred features make generalizable predictions. Second, it assigns less risk to rules with lower entropy, as long as their predictions remain generalizable. This corresponds to features that find larger differences in usage frequency across L1 labels.

The alternative metric of per feature classification accuracy creates a one to one mapping between features and native languages. This unnecessarily penalizes features that are associated with multiple native languages, as well as features that are selectively dispreferred by certain L1 speakers. Also, we wish to correctly quantify the distribution of a feature over all native languages, which goes beyond correct prediction of the most probable.

Using cross validation with each corpus as a fold, we plot the average $\mathcal{R}(X)$ for the best n features against n for each relevancy metric in Figure 7. This clearly shows that for highly ranked features χ^2 is

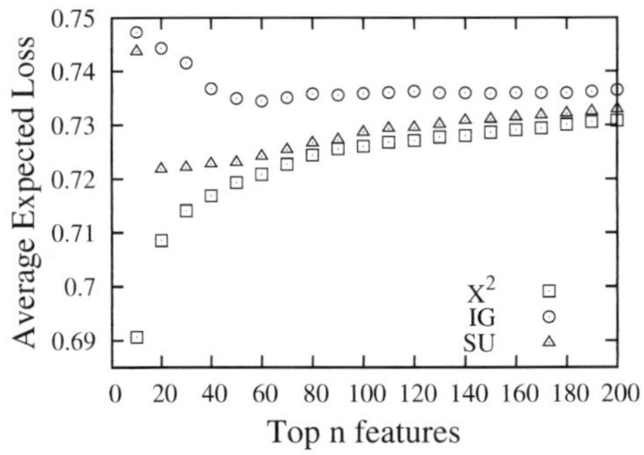

Figure 7: Per-feature Average Expected Loss plotted against top N features using χ^2, IG, and SU as a relevancy metric

able to best single out the type of features we desire. Another point to be taken from the plot is that it is that the top ten features under SU are remarkably inferior. Inspection of these rules reveals that they are precisely the type of overly frequent but only slightly discriminative features that we predicted would corrupt feature selection using IG based measures.

6.2 Redundancy Metrics

We evaluate the redundancy metrics by using the top n features retained by redundancy filtering for ensemble classification. Under this evaluation, if redundancy is not being effectively eliminated performance should increase more slowly with n as the set of test items that can be correctly classified remains relatively constant. Additionally, if the metric is overzealous in its elimination of redundancy, useful patterns will be eliminated leading to diminished increase in performance. Figure 8 shows the tradeoff between Expected Loss on the test set and the number of features used with SU, NPMI, and the overlap based structural redundancy metric described above. We performed a coarse grid search to find the optimal values of ρ for SU and NPMI.

Both the structural overlap hueristic and SU perform similarly, and outperform NPMI. Analysis reveals that NPMI seems to overstate the similarity of large fragments with their small subcomponents. We choose to proceed with SU, as it is not only faster in our implementation but also can generalize to feature types beyond TSG rules.

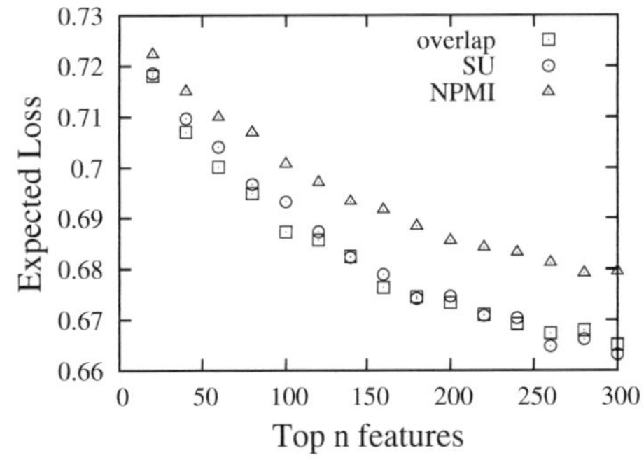

Figure 8: The effects of redundancy filtering on classification performance using different redundancy metrics. The cutoff values (ρ) used for SU and NPMI are .2 and .7 respectively.

6.3 TSG Induction

We demonstrate the flexibility and effectiveness of our general model of mixtures of TSGs for labeled data by example. The tunable parameters are the number of grammars K, the Dirichlet priors ν_η over grammar distributions for each label η, and the concentration parameter γ of the smoothing DP.

For a first baseline we set the number of grammars $K = 1$, making the Dirichlet priors ν irrelevant. With a large $\gamma = 10^{20}$, we essentially recover the basic block sampling algorithm of Cohn and Blunsom (2010). We refer to this model as M1. Our second baseline model, M2, sets K to the number of native language labels, and sets the ν variables such that each η is mapped to a single grammar by its L1 label, creating a naive Bayes model. For M2 and the subsequent models we use $\gamma = 1000$ to allow moderate smoothing.

We also construct a model (M3) in which we set $K = 9$ and ν_η is such that three grammars are likely for any single η; one shared by all η with the same L1 label, one shared by all η with the same corpus label, and one shared by all η. We compare this with another $K = 9$ model (M4) where the ν are set to be uniform across all 9 grammars.

We evaluate these systems on the percent of their resulting grammar that rejects the hypothesis of language independence using a χ^2 test. Slight adjustments were made to α for these models to bring their output grammar size into the range of approximately 12000 rules. We average our results for each model over single states drawn from five indepen-

	$p < .1$	$p < .05$	$p < .01$	$p < .001$
M1	56.5(3.1)	54.5(3.0)	49.8(2.7)	45.1(2.5)
M2	55.3(3.7)	53.7(3.6)	49.1(3.3)	44.7(3.0)
M3	**59.0(4.1)**	**57.2(4.1)**	**52.4(3.6)**	**48.4(3.3)**
M4	58.9(3.8)	57.0(3.7)	51.9(3.4)	47.2(3.1)

Figure 9: The percentage of rules from each model that reject L1 independence at varying levels of statistical significance. The first number is with respect to the number rules that pass the L1/corpus independence and redundancy tests, and the second is in proportion to the full list returned by grammar induction.

dent Markov chains.

Our results in Figure 9 show that using a mixture of grammars allows the induction algorithm to find more patterns that fit arbitrary criteria for language dependence. The intuition supporting this is that in simpler models a given grammar must represent a larger amount of data that is better represented with more vague, general purpose rules. Dividing the responsibility among several grammars lets rare patterns form clusters more easily. The incorporation of informed structure in M3 further improves the performance of this latent mixture technique.

7 Discussion

Using these methods, we produce a list of L1 associated TSG rules that we release for public use. We perform grammar induction using model M3, apply our data dependence and redundancy filters, rank for relevancy using χ^2 and filter at the level of $p < .1$ statistical significance for relevancy. Each entry consists of a TSG rule and its matrix of counts with each η. We provide the total for each L1 label, which shows the overall prediction of the proportional use of that item. We also provide the χ^2 statistics for L1 dependence and the dependence of L1 and corpus.

It is speculative to assign causes to the discriminative rules we report, and we leave quantification of such statements to future work. However, the strength of the signal, as evidenced by actual counts in data, and the high level interpretation that can be easily assigned to the TSG rules is promising. As understanding the features requires basic knowledge of Treebank symbols, we provide our interpretations for some of the more interesting rules and summarize their L1 distributions. Note that by describing a rule as being preferred by a certain set of L1 labels, our claim is relative to the other labels only; the true cause could also be a dispreference in the complement of this set.

One interesting comparison made easy by our method is the identification of similar structures that have complementary L1 usage. An example is the use of a prepositional phrase just before the first noun phrase in a sentence, which is preferred in German and Spanish, especially in the former. However, German speakers disprefer a prepositional phrase followed by a comma at the beginning of the sentence, and Chinese speakers use this pattern more frequently than the other L1s. Another contrastable pair is the use of the word "because" with upper or lower case, signifying sentence initial or medial use. The former is preferred in Chinese and Japanese text, while the latter is preferred in German and even more so in Spanish L1 data.

As these examples suggest, the data shows a strong division of preference between European and Asian languages, but many patterns exist that are uniquely preferred in single languages as well. Japanese speakers are seen to frequently use a personal pronoun as the subject of the sentence, while Spanish speakers use the phrase "the X of Y", the verb "go", and the determiner "this" with markedly higher frequency. Germans tend to begin sentences with adverbs, and various modal verb constructions are popular with Chinese speakers. We suspect these patterns to be evidence of preference in the specified language, rather than dispreference in the other three.

Our strategy in regard to the hard filters for L1-corpus dependence and redundancy has been to prefer recall to precision, as false positives can be easily ignored through subsequent inspection of the data we supply. This makes the list suitable for human qualitative analysis, but further work is required for its use in downstream automatic systems.

8 Conclusion

This work contributes to the goal of leveraging NLI data in SLA applications. We provide evidence for our hypothesis that relevancy metrics based on mutual information are ill-suited for this task, and recommend the use of the χ^2 statistic for rejecting the hypothesis of language independence. Explicit controls for dependence between L1 and corpus are proposed, and redundancy between features are addressed as well. We argue for the use of TSG rules as features, and develop an induction algorithm that is a supervised mixture of hierarchical grammars. This generalizable formalism is used to capture linguistic assumptions about the data and increase the amount of relevant features extracted at several thresholds.

This project motivates continued incorporation of more data and induction of TSGs over these larger data sets. This will improve the quality and scope of the resulting list of discriminative syntax, allowing broader use in linguistics and SLA research. The prospect of high precision and recall in the extraction of such patterns suggests several interesting avenues for future work, such as determination of the actual language transfer phenomena evidenced by an arbitrary count profile. To achieve the goal of automatic detection of plausible transfer the native languages themselves must be considered, as well as a way to distinguish between preference and dispreference based on usage statistics. Another exciting application of such a refined list of patterns is the automatic integration of its features in L1 targeted SLA software.

References

Phil Blunsom and Trevor Cohn. 2010. Unsupervised Induction of Tree Substitution Grammars for Dependency Parsing. *Empirical Methods in Natural Language Processing*.

Julian Brooke and Graeme Hirst. 2011. Native language detection with 'cheap' learner corpora. *Conference of Learner Corpus Research*.

Julian Brooke and Graeme Hirst. 2012. Measuring Interlanguage: Native Language Identification with L1-influence Metrics. *LREC*

Julian Brooke and Graeme Hirst. 2012. Robust, Lexicalized Native Language Identification. *COLING*.

Serhiy Bykh and Detmar Meurers. 2012. Native Language Identification Using Recurring N-grams - Investigating Abstraction and Domain Dependence. *COLING*.

Trevor Cohn, Sharon Goldwater, and Phil Blunsom. 2009. Inducing Compact but Accurate Tree-Substitution Grammars. In *Proceedings NAACL*.

Trevor Cohn, and Phil Blunsom. 2010. Blocked inference in Bayesian tree substitution grammars. *Association for Computational Linguistics*.

Gilquin, Gaëtanelle and Granger, Sylviane. 2011. From EFL to ESL: Evidence from the International Corpus of Learner English. *Exploring Second-Language Varieties of English and Learner Englishes: Bridging a Paradigm Gap (Book Chapter)*.

Joshua Goodman. 2003. Efficient parsing of DOP with PCFG-reductions. *In Bod et al. chapter 8.*.

S. Granger, E. Dagneaux and F. Meunier. 2002. *International Corpus of Learner English*, (ICLE).

Horst M., White J., Bell P. 2010. First and second language knowledge in the language classroom. *International Journal of Bilingualism*.

Scott Jarvis and Scott Crossley 2012. Approaching Language Transfer through Text Classification.

Mark Johnson 2011. How relevant is linguistics to computational linguistics?. *Linguistic Issues in Language Technology*.

Ekaterina Kochmar. 2011. Identification of a writer's native language by error analysis. *Master's Thesis*.

Koppel, Moshe and Schler, Jonathan and Zigdon, Kfir. 2005. Determining an author's native language by mining a text for errors. *Proceedings of the eleventh ACM SIGKDD international conference on Knowledge discovery in data mining*.

Laufer, B and Girsai, N. 2008. Form-focused Instruction in Second Language Vocabulary Learning: A Case for Contrastive Analysis and Translation. *Applied Linguistics*.

David Mimno and Andrew McCallum. 2008. Topic Models Conditioned on Arbitrary Features with Dirichlet-multinomial Regression. *UAI*.

Hanchuan Peng and Fuhui Long and Chris Ding. 2005. Feature selection based on mutual information criteria of max-dependency, max-relevance, and min-redundancy. *IEEE Transactions on Pattern Analysis and Machine Intelligence*.

Slav Petrov, Leon Barrett, Romain Thibaux, and Dan Klein. 2006. Learning Accurate, Compact, and Interpretable Tree Annotation. *Association for Computational Linguistics*.

Matt Post and Daniel Gildea. 2009. Bayesian Learning of a Tree Substitution Grammar. *Association for Computational Linguistics*.

Tono, Y., Kawaguchi, Y. & Minegishi, M. (eds.) . 2012. *Developmental and Cross-linguistic Perspectives in Learner Corpus Research.*.

Oren Tsur and Ari Rappoport. 2007. Using classifier features for studying the effect of native language on the choice of written second language words. *CACLA*.

Shindo, Hiroyuki and Miyao, Yusuke and Fujino, Akinori and Nagata, Masaaki 2012. Bayesian Symbol-Refined Tree Substitution Grammars for Syntactic Parsing. *Association for Computational Linguistics.*

Ben Swanson and Eugene Charniak. 2012. Native Language Detection with Tree Substitution Grammars. *Association for Computational Linguistics.*

Yee Whye Teh, Michael I. Jordan, Matthew J. Beal, and David M. Blei. 2005. Hierarchical Dirichlet Processes. *Journal of the American Statistical Association.*

Joel Tetreault, Daniel Blanchard, Aoife Cahill, Beata Beigman-Klebanov and Martin Chodorow. 2012. Native Tongues, Lost and Found: Resources and Empirical Evaluations in Native Language Identification. *COLING.*

Sze-Meng Jojo Wong and Mark Dras. 2009. Contrastive analysis and native language identification. *Proceedings of the Australasian Language Technology Association Workshop.*

Sze-Meng Jojo Wong and Mark Dras. 2011. Exploiting Parse Structures for Native Language Identification. *Proceedings of the 2011 Conference on Empirical Methods in Natural Language Processing.*

Sze-Meng Jojo Wong and Mark Dras. 2011. Topic Modeling for Native Language Identification. *Proceedings of the Australasian Language Technology Association Workshop.*

Sze-Meng Jojo Wong, Mark Dras, Mark Johnson. 2012. Exploring Adaptor Grammars for Native Language Identification. *EMNLP-CoNLL.*

Lei Yu and Huan Liu. 2004. Efficient Feature Selection via Analysis of Relevance and Redundancy. *Journal of Machine Learning Research.*

An Analysis of Frequency- and Memory-Based Processing Costs

Marten van Schijndel
The Ohio State University
vanschm@ling.osu.edu

William Schuler
The Ohio State University
schuler@ling.osu.edu

Abstract

The frequency of words and syntactic constructions has been observed to have a substantial effect on language processing. This begs the question of what causes certain constructions to be more or less frequent. A theory of grounding (Phillips, 2010) would suggest that cognitive limitations might cause languages to develop frequent constructions in such a way as to avoid processing costs. This paper studies how current theories of working memory fit into theories of language processing and what influence memory limitations may have over reading times. Measures of such limitations are evaluated on eye-tracking data and the results are compared with predictions made by different theories of processing.

1 Introduction

Frequency effects in language have been isolated and observed in many studies (Trueswell, 1996; Jurafsky, 1996; Hale, 2001; Demberg and Keller, 2008). These effects are important because they illuminate the ontogeny of language (how individual speakers have acquired language), but they do not answer questions about the phylogeny of language (how the language came to its current form).

Phillips (2010) has hypothesized that grammar rule probabilities may be grounded in memory limitations. Increased delays in processing center-embedded sentences as the number of embeddings increases, for example, are often explained in terms of a complexity cost associated with maintaining incomplete dependencies in working memory (Gibson, 2000; Lewis and Vasishth, 2005). Other studies have shown a link between processing delays and the low frequency of center-embedded constructions like object relatives (Hale, 2001), but they have not explored the source of this low frequency. A grounding hypothesis would claim that the low probability of generating such a structure may arise from an associated memory load. In this account, while these complexity costs may involve language-specific concepts such as referent or argument linking, the underlying explanation would be one of memory limitations (Gibson, 2000) or neural activation (Lewis and Vasishth, 2005).

This paper seeks to explore the different predictions made by these theories on a broad-coverage corpus of eye-tracking data (Kennedy et al., 2003). In addition, the current experiment seeks to isolate memory effects from frequency effects in the same task. The results show that memory load measures are a significant factor even when frequency measures are residualized out.

The remainder of this paper is organized as follows: Sections 2 and 3 describe several frequency and memory measures. Section 4 describes a probabilistic hierarchic sequence model that allows all of these measures to be directly computed. Section 5 describes how these measures were used to predict reading time durations on the Dundee eye-tracking corpus. Sections 6 and 7 present results and discuss.

2 Frequency Measures

2.1 Surprisal

One of the strongest predictors of processing complexity is surprisal (Hale, 2001). It has been shown in numerous studies to have a strong correlation with reading time durations in eye-tracking and self-paced reading studies when calculated with a variety of models (Levy, 2008; Roark et al., 2009; Wu et al., 2010).

Surprisal predicts the integration difficulty that a word x_t at time step t presents given the preceding context and is calculated as follows:

$$surprisal(x_t) = -\log_2 \left(\frac{\sum_{s \in S(x_1 \ldots x_t)} P(s)}{\sum_{s \in S(x_1 \ldots x_{t-1})} P(s)} \right) \quad (1)$$

where $S(x_1 \ldots x_t)$ is the set of syntactic trees whose leaves have $x_1 \ldots x_t$ as a prefix.[1]

In essence, surprisal measures how unexpected constructions are in a given context. What it does not provide is an explanation for why certain constructions would be less common and thus more surprising.

2.2 Entropy Reduction

Processing difficulty can also be measured in terms of entropy (Shannon, 1948). A larger entropy over a random variable corresponds to greater uncertainty over the observed value it will take. The entropy of a syntactic derivation over the sequence $x_1 \ldots x_t$ is calculated as:[2]

$$H(x_{1 \ldots t}) = \sum_{s \in S(x_1 \ldots x_t)} -P(s) \cdot \log_2 P(s) \quad (2)$$

Reduction in entropy has been found to predict processing complexity (Hale, 2003; Hale, 2006; Roark et al., 2009; Wu et al., 2010; Hale, 2011):

$$\Delta H(x_{1 \ldots t}) = \max(0, H(x_{1 \ldots t-1}) - H(x_{1 \ldots t})) \quad (3)$$

This measures the change in uncertainty about the discourse as each new word is processed.

3 Memory Measures

3.1 Dependency Locality

In Dependency Locality Theory (DLT) (Gibson, 2000), complexity arises from intervening referents introduced between a predicate and its argument. Under the original formulation of DLT, there is a *storage* cost for each new referent introduced and an *integration* cost for each referent intervening in a dependency projection. This is a simplification made for ease of computation, and subsequent work has found DLT to be more accurate cross-linguistically if the intervening elements are structurally defined rather than defined in terms of referents (Kwon et al., 2010). That is, simply having a particular referent intervene in a dependency projection may not have as great an effect on processing complexity as the syntactic construction the referent appears in. Therefore, this work reinterprets the costs of dependency locality to be related to the events of beginning a center embedding (storage) and completing a center embedding (integration). Note that anti-locality effects (where longer dependencies are easier to process) have also been observed in some languages, and DLT is unable to account for these phenomena (Vasishth and Lewis, 2006).

3.2 ACT-R

Processing complexity has also been attributed to confusability (Lewis and Vasishth, 2005) as defined in domain-general cognitive models like ACT-R (Anderson et al., 2004).

ACT-R is based on theories of neural activation. Each new word is *encoded* and stored in working memory until it is *retrieved* at a later point for modification before being re-encoded into the parse. A newly observed sign (word) associatively activates any appropriate arguments from working memory, so multiple similarly appropriate arguments would slow processing as the parser must choose between the highly activated hypotheses. Any intervening signs (words or phrases) that modify a previously encoded sign re-activate it and raise its resting activation potential. This can ease later retrieval of that sign in what is termed an *anti-locality* effect, contra predictions of DLT. In this way, returning out of an embedded clause can actually speed processing by having primed the retrieved sign before it was needed. ACT-R attributes locality phenomena to frequency effects (e.g. unusual constructions) overriding such priming and to activation decay if embedded signs do not prime the target sign through modification (as in parentheticals). Finally, ACT-R predicts something like DLT's storage cost due to the need to differentiate each newly encoded sign from

[1]The parser in this study uses a beam. However, given high parser accuracy, Roark (2001) showed that calculating complexity metrics over a beam should obtain similar results to the full complexity calculation.

[2]The incremental formulation used here was first proposed in Wu et al. (2010).

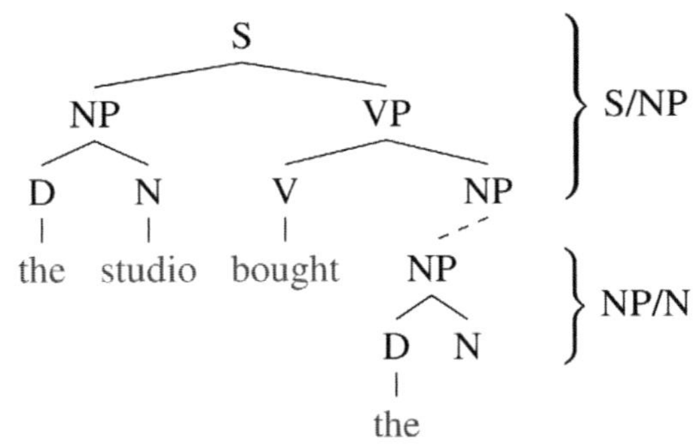

Figure 1: Two disjoint connected components of a phrase structure tree for the sentence *The studio bought the publisher's rights,* shown immediately prior to the word *publisher*.

those previously encoded (similarity-based encoding interference) (Lewis et al., 2006).

3.3 Hierarchic Sequential Prediction

Current models of working memory in structured tasks are defined in terms of hierarchies of sequential processes, in which superordinate sequences can be interrupted by subordinate sequences and resume when the subordinate sequences have concluded (Botvinick, 2007). These models rely on *temporal* cueing as well as content-based cueing to explain how an interrupted sequence may be recalled for continuation.

Temporal cueing is based on a context of temporal features for the current state (Howard and Kahana, 2002). The temporal context in which the subordinate sequence concludes must be similar enough to the temporal context in which it was initiated to recall where in the superordinate sequence the subordinate sequence occurred. For example, the act of making breakfast may be interrupted by a phone call. Once the call is complete, the temporal context is sufficiently similar to when the call began that one is able to continue preparing breakfast. The association between the current temporal context and the temporal context prior to the interruption is strong enough to cue the next action.

Temporal cueing is complemented by *sequential* (content-based) cueing (Botvinick, 2007) in which the content of an individual element is associated with, and thus cues, the following element. For example, recalling the 20th note of a song is difficult, but when playing the song, each note cues the following note, leading one to play the 20th note without difficulty.

Hierarchic sequential prediction may be directly applicable to processing syntactic center embeddings (van Schijndel et al., in press). An ongoing parse may be viewed graph-theoretically as one or more connected components of incomplete phrase structure trees (see Figure 1). Beginning a new subordinate sequence (a center embedding) introduces a new connected component, disjoint from that of the superordinate sequence. As the subordinate sequence proceeds, the new component gains associated discourse referents, each sequentially cued from the last, until finally it merges with the superordinate connected component at the end of the embedded clause, forming a single connected component representing the parse up to that point. Since it is not connected to the subordinate connected component prior to merging, the superordinate connected component must be recalled through temporal cueing.

McElree (2001; 2006) has found that retrieval of any non-focused (or in this case, unconnected) element from memory leads to slower processing. Therefore, integrating two disjoint connected components should be expected to incur a processing cost due to the need to recall the current state of the superordinate sequence to continue the parse. Such a cost would corroborate a DLT-like theory where integration slows processing.

3.4 Dynamic Recruitment of Additional Processing Resources

Language processing is typically centered in the left hemisphere of the brain (for right-handed individuals). Just and Varma (2007) provide fMRI results suggesting readers dynamically recruit additional processing resources such as the right-side homologues of the language processing areas of the brain when processing center-embedded constructions. Once an embedded construction terminates, the reader may still have temporary access to these extra processing resources, which may briefly speed processing.

This hypothesis would, therefore, predict an *encoding* cost when a center embedding is initiated. The resulting inhibition would trigger recruitment of additional processing resources, which would then allow the rest of the embedded structure to be processed at the usual speed. Upon completing an embedding, the difficulty arising from memory retrieval (McElree, 2001) would be ameliorated by these extra processing resources, and the reduced processing complexity arising from reduced memory load would yield a temporary *facilitation* in processing. No longer requiring the additional resources to cope with the increased embedding, the processor would release them, returning the processor to its usual speed. Unlike anti-locality, where processing is facilitated in longer passages due to accumulating probabilistic evidence, a model of dynamic recruitment of additional processing resources would predict universal facilitation after a center embedding of any length, modulo frequency effects.

3.5 Embedding Difference

Wu et al. (2010) propose an explicit measure of the difficulty associated with processing center-embedded constructions, which is similar to the predictions of dynamic recruitment and is defined in terms of changes in memory load. They calculate a probabilistically-weighted average embedding depth as follows:

$$\mu_{emb}(x_1 \ldots x_t) = \sum_{s \in S(x_1 \ldots x_t)} d(s) \cdot P(s) \tag{4}$$

where $d(s)$ returns the embedding depth of the derivation s at x_t in a variant of a left-corner parsing process.[3] Embedding difference may then be derived as:

$$\mathit{EmbDiff}(x_1 \ldots x_t) = \mu_{emb}(x_1 \ldots x_t) - \mu_{emb}(x_1 \ldots x_{t-1}) \tag{5}$$

This is hypothesized to correlate positively with processing load: increasing the embedding depth increases processing load and decreasing it reduces processing load. Note that embedding difference makes the opposite prediction from DLT in that integrating an embedded clause is predicted to speed processing. In fact, the predictions of embedding difference are such that it may be viewed as an implementation of the predictions of a hierarchic sequential processing model with dynamic recruitment of additional resources.

4 Model

This paper uses a hierarchic sequence model implementation of a left-corner parser variant (van Schijndel et al., in press), which represents connected components of phrase structure trees in hierarchies of hidden random variables. This requires, at each time step t:

- a hierarchically-organized set of N connected component states q_t^n, each consisting of an active sign of category $a_{q_t^n}$, and an awaited sign of category $b_{q_t^n}$, separated by a slash '/'; and
- an observed word x_t.

Each connected component state in this model then represents a contiguous portion of a phrase structure tree (see Figure 1 on preceding page).

The operations of this parser can be defined as a deductive system (Shieber et al., 1995) with an input sequence consisting of a top-level connected component state $\top/\top$, corresponding to an existing discourse context, followed by a sequence of observed words $x_1, x_2, \ldots$[4] If an observation x_t can attach as the awaited sign of the most recent (most subordinate) connected component a/b, it is hypothesized to do so, turning this incomplete sign into a complete sign a (F–, below); or if the observation can serve as a lower descendant of this awaited sign, it is hypothesized to form the first complete sign a' in a newly initiated connected component (F+):

$$\frac{a/b \quad x_t}{a}\; b \rightarrow x_t \tag{F–}$$

$$\frac{a/b \quad x_t}{a/b \quad a'}\; b \xrightarrow{+} a' \ldots ;\quad a' \rightarrow x_t \tag{F+}$$

Then, if either of these complete signs (a or a' above, matched to a'' below) can attach as an initial

[3] As pointed out by Wu et al. (2010), in practice this can be computed over a beam of potential parses in which case it must be normalized by the total probability of the beam.

[4] A deductive system consists of inferences or productions of the form: $\frac{P}{Q}R$, meaning premise P entails conclusion Q according to rule R.

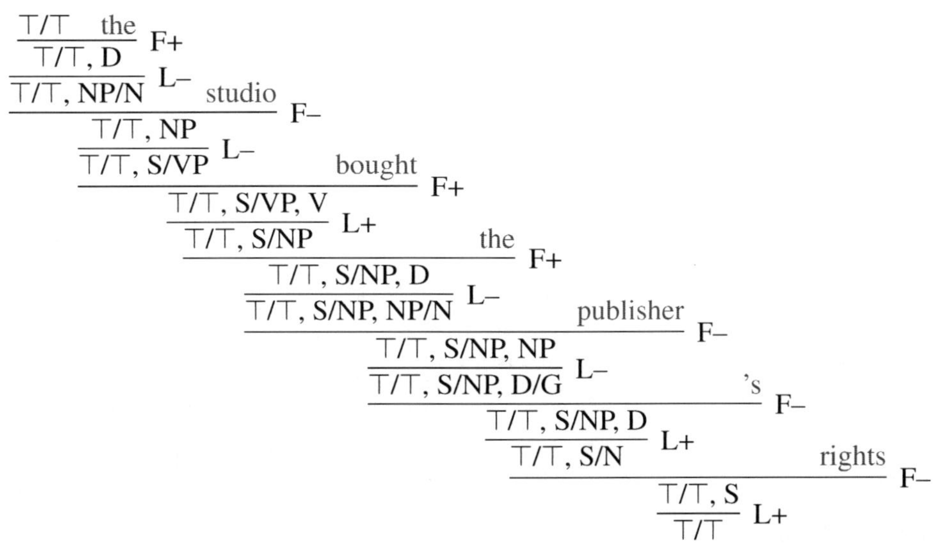

Figure 2: Example parse (in the form of a deductive proof) of the sentence *The studio bought the publisher's rights,* using F+, F–, L+, and L– productions. Each pair of deductions combines a context of one or more connected component states with a sign (word) observed in that context. By applying the F and L rules to the observed sign and context, the parser is able to generate a consequent context. Initially, the context corresponds to a connected pre-sentential dialogue state T/T. When *the* is observed, the parser applies F+ to begin a new connected component state D. By applying L–, the parser determines that this new connected component is unfinished and generates an appropriate incomplete connected component state NP/N, encoding the superordinate state T/T for later retrieval. Further on, the parser observes *'s* and uses F– to avoid generating a new connected component, which completes the sign D. The parser follows this up with L+ to recall the superordinate connected component state S/NP and integrate it into the most deeply embedded connected component, which results in a less deeply embedded structure.

child of the awaited sign of the immediately superordinate connected component state a/b, it is hypothesized to do so and terminate the subordinate connected component state, with x_t as the last observation of the terminated connected component (L+); or if the observation can serve as a lower descendant of this awaited sign, it is hypothesized to remain disjoint and form its own connected component (L–):

$$\frac{a/b \quad a''}{a/b''} \; b \rightarrow a'' \; b'' \qquad \text{(L+)}$$

$$\frac{a/b \quad a''}{a/b \quad a'/b''} \; b \xrightarrow{+} a' \; ... \; ; \quad a' \rightarrow a'' \; b'' \qquad \text{(L–)}$$

These operations can be made probabilistic. The probability σ of a transition at time step t is defined in terms of (i) a probability ϕ of initiating a new connected component state with x_t as its first observation, multiplied by (ii) the probability λ of terminating a connected component state with x_t as its last observation, multiplied by (iii) the probabilities α and β of generating categories for active and awaited signs $a_{q_t^n}$ and $b_{q_t^n}$ in the resulting most subordinate connected component state q_t^n. This kind of model can be defined directly on PCFG probabilities and trained to produce state-of-the-art accuracy by using the latent variable annotation of Petrov et al. (2006) (van Schijndel et al., in press).[5]

An example parse is shown in Figure 2. Since two binary structural decisions (F and L) must be made in order to generate each word, there are four possible structures that may be generated (see Table 1). The F+L– transition initiates a new level of embedding at word x_t and so requires the superordinate state to be encoded for later retrieval (e.g. on observing *the* in Figure 2). The F–L+ transition completes the deepest level of embedding and therefore requires the recall of the current superordinate connected component state with which the

[5]The model has been shown to achieve an F-score of 87.8, within .2 points of the Petrov and Klein (2007) parser, which obtains an F-score of 88.0 on the same task. Because the sequence model is defined over binary-branching phrase structure, both parsers were evaluated on binary-branching phrase structure trees to provide a fair comparison.

F–L–	Cue Active Sign
F+L–	Initiate/Encode
F–L+	Terminate/Integrate
F+L+	Cue Awaited Sign

Table 1: The hierarchical structure decisions and the operations they represent. F+L– initiates a new connected component, F–L+ integrates two disjoint connected components into a single connected component, and F–L– and F+L+ sequentially cue, respectively, a new active sign (along with an associated awaited sign) and a new awaited sign from the most recent connected component.

Theory	F+L–	F–L+
DLT	positive	positive
ACT-R	positive	positive
Hier. Sequential Prediction		positive
Dynamic Recruitment	positive	negative
Embedding Difference	positive	negative

Table 2: Each theory's prediction of the direction of the correlation between each hierachical structure predictor and reading times. Hierarchic sequential prediction is agnostic about the processing speed of F+L– operations, and none of the theories make any predictions as to the sign associated with the within-embedding measures F–L– and F+L+.

subordinate connected component state will be integrated. For example, in Figure 2, upon observing *'s*, the parser must use temporal cueing to recall that it is in the middle of processing an NP (to complete an S), which sequentially cues a prediction of N. F–L– transitions complete the awaited sign of the most subordinate state and so sequentially cue a following connected component state at the same tier of the hierarchy. For example, in Figure 2, after observing *studio*, the parser uses the completed NP to sequentially cue the prediction that it has finished the left child of an S. F+L+ transitions locally expand the awaited sign of the most subordinate state and so should also not require any recall or encoding. For example, in Figure 2, observing *bought* while awaiting a VP sequentially cues a prediction of NP.

F+L–, then, loosely corresponds to a *storage* action under DLT as more hierarchic levels must now be maintained at each future step of the parse. As stated before, it differs from DLT in that it is sensitive to the depth of embedding rather than a particular subset of syntactic categories. Wu et al. (2010) found that increasing the embedding depth led to longer reading times in a self-paced reading experiment. In ACT-R terms, F+L– corresponds to an *encoding* action, potentially causing processing difficulty resulting from the similarity of the current sign to previously encoded signs.

F–L+, by contrast, is similar to DLT's *integration* action since a subordinate connected component is integrated into the rest of the parse structure. This represents a temporal cueing event in which the awaited category of the superordinate connected component is recalled. In contrast to DLT, embedding difference and dynamic recruitment would predict a *shorter* reading time in the F–L+ case because of the reduction in memory load. In an ACT-R framework, reading time durations can increase at the retrieval site because the retrieval causes competition among similarly encoded signs in the context set. While it is possible for reading times to decrease when completing a center embedding in ACT-R (Vasishth and Lewis, 2006), this would be expressed as a frequency effect due to certain argument types commonly foreshadowing their predicates (Jaeger et al., 2008). Since frequency effects are factored separately from memory effects in this study, ACT-R would predict longer residual (memory-based) reading times when completing an embedding.

Predicted correlations to reading times for the F and L transitions are summarized in Table 2.

5 Eye-tracking

Eye-tracking and reading time data are often used to test complexity measures (Gibson, 2000; Demberg and Keller, 2008; Roark et al., 2009) under the assumption that readers slow down when reading more complex passages. Readers saccade over portions of text and regress back to preceding text in complex patterns, but studies have correlated certain measures with certain processing constraints (see Clifton et al. 2007 for a review). For example, the initial length of time fixated on a single word is correlated with word identification time; whereas regression durations after a word is fixated (but prior to a fixation in a new region) are hypothesized to correlate with integration difficulty.

Since this work focuses on incremental processing, all processing that occurs up to a given point in the sentence is of interest. Therefore, in this study, predictions will be compared to *go-past durations*. Go-past durations are calculated by summing all fixations in a region of text, including regressions, until a new region is fixated, which accounts for additional processing that may take place after initial lexical access, but before the next region is processed. For example, if one region ends at word 5 in a sentence, and the next fixation lands on word 8, then the *go-past region* consists of words 6-8 and the *go-past duration* sums all fixations until a fixation occurs after word 8.

6 Evaluation

The measures presented in this paper were evaluated on the Dundee eye-tracking corpus (Kennedy et al., 2003). The corpus consists of 2388 sentences of naturally occurring news text written in standard British English. The corpus also includes eye-tracking data from 10 native English speakers, which provides a test corpus of 260,124 subject-duration pairs of reading time data. Of this, any fixated words appearing fewer than 5 times in the training data were considered unknown and were filtered out to obtain accurate predictions. Fixations on the first or last words of a line were also filtered out to avoid any 'wrap-up' effects resulting from preparing to saccade to the beginning of the next line or resulting from orienting to a new line. Additionally, following Demberg and Keller (2008), any fixations that skip more than 4 words were attributed to track loss by the eyetracker or lack of attention of the reader and so were excluded from the analysis. This left the final evaluation corpus with 151,331 subject-duration pairs.

The evaluation consisted of fitting a linear mixed-effects model (Baayen et al., 2008) to reading time durations using the *lmer* function of the *lme4* R package (Bates et al., 2011; R Development Core Team, 2010). This allowed by-subject and by-item variation to be included in the initial regression as random intercepts in addition to several baseline predictors.[6] Before fitting, the durations extracted from the corpus were log-transformed, producing more normally distributed data to obey the assumptions of linear mixed effects models.[7]

Included among the fixed effects were the position in the sentence that initiated the go-past region (SENTPOS) and the number of characters in the initiating word (NRCHAR). The difficulty of integrating a word may be seen in whether the immediately following word was fixated (NEXTISFIX), and similarly if the immediately previous word was fixated (PREVISFIX) the current word probably need not be fixated for as long. Finally, unigram (LOGPROB) and bigram probabilities are included. The bigram probabilities are those of the current word given the previous word (LOGFWPROB) and the current word given the following word (LOGBWPROB). Fossum and Levy (2012) showed that for n-gram probabilities to be effective predictors on the Dundee corpus, they must be calculated from a wide variety of texts, so following them, this study used the Brown corpus (Francis and Kucera, 1979), the WSJ Sections 02-21 (Marcus et al., 1993), the written text portion of the British National Corpus (BNC Consortium, 2007), and the Dundee corpus (Kennedy et al., 2003). This amounted to an n-gram training corpus of roughly 87 million words. These statistics were smoothed using the SRILM (Stolcke, 2002) implementation of modified Kneser-Ney smoothing (Chen and Goodman, 1998). Finally, total surprisal (SURP) was included to account for frequency effects in the baseline.

The preceding measures are commonly used in baseline models to fit reading time data (Demberg and Keller, 2008; Frank and Bod, 2011; Fossum and Levy, 2012) and were calculated from the final word of each go-past region. The following measures create a more sophisticated baseline by accumulating over the entire go-past region to capture what must be integrated into the discourse to continue the parse. One factor (CWDELTA) simply counts the number of words in each go-past region. Cumula-

[6]Each fixed effect was centered to reduce collinearity.

[7]In particular, these models assume the noise in the data is normally distributed. Initial exploratory trials showed that the residuals of fitting any sensible baseline also become more normally distributed if the response variable is log-transformed. Finally, the directions of the effects remain the same whether or not the reading times are log-transformed, though significance cannot be ascertained without the transform.

tive total surprisal (CUMUSURP) and cumulative entropy reduction (ENTRED) give the surprisal (Hale, 2001) and entropy reduction (Hale, 2003) summed over the go-past region. To avoid convergence issues, each of the cumulative measures is residualized from the next simpler model in the following order: CWDELTA from the standard baseline, CUMUSURP from the baseline with CWDELTA, and ENTRED from the baseline with all other effects.

Residualization was accomplished by using the simpler mixed-effects model to fit the measure of interest. The residuals from that model fit were then used in place of the factor of interest. All joint interactions were included in the baseline model as well. Finally, to account for spillover effects (Just et al., 1982) where processing from a previous region contributes to the following duration, the above baseline predictors from the previous go-past region were included as factors for the current region.

Having SURP as a predictor with CUMUSURP may seem redundant, but initial analyses showed SURP was a significant predictor over CUMUSURP when CWDELTA was a separate factor in the baseline (current: $p = 2.2 \cdot 10^{-16}$ spillover: $p = 2 \cdot 10^{-15}$) and vice versa (current: $p = 2.2 \cdot 10^{-16}$ spillover: $p = 6 \cdot 10^{-5}$). One reason for this could be that go-past durations conflate complexity experienced when initially fixating on a region with the difficulty experienced during regressions. By including both versions of surprisal, the model is able to account for frequency effects occurring in both conditions.

This study is only interested in how well the proposed memory-based measures fit the data over the baseline, so to avoid fitting to the test data or weakening the baseline by overfitting to training data, the full baseline was used in the final evaluation.

Each measure proposed in this paper was summed over go-past regions to make it cumulative and was residualized from all non-spillover factors before being included on top of the full baseline as a main effect. Likewise, the spillover version of each proposed measure was residualized from the other spillover factors before being included as a main effect. Only a single proposed measure (or its spillover corrollary) was included in each model. The results shown in Table 3 reflect the probability of the full model fit being obtained by the model lacking each factor of interest. This was found via posterior sampling of each factor using the Markov chain Monte Carlo implementation of the *languageR* R package (Baayen, 2008).

Factor	Operation	t-score	p-value
F–L–	Cue Active	0.60	0.55
F+L–	Initiate	7.10	$2.22{\cdot}10^{-14}$
F–L+	Integrate	-5.44	$5.23{\cdot}10^{-8}$
F+L+	Cue Awaited	-1.55	0.12

Table 3: Significance of each of the structure generation outcomes at predicting log-transformed durations when added to the baseline as a main effect after being residualized from it. The sign of the t-score indicates the direction of the correlation between the residualized factor and go-past durations. Note that these factors are all based on the current go-past region; the spillover corollaries of these were not significant predictors of reading times.

The results indicate that the F+L– and F–L+ measures were both significant predictors of duration as expected. Further, F–L– and F+L+, which both simply reflect sequential cueing, were not significant predictors of go-past duration, also as expected.

7 Discussion and Conclusion

The fact that F+L– was strongly predictive over the baseline is encouraging as it suggests that memory limitations could provide at least a partial explanation of *why* certain constructions are less frequent in corpora and thus yield a high surprisal. Moreover, it indicates that the model corroborates the shared prediction of most of the memory-based models that initiating a new connected component slows processing.

The fact that F–L+ is predictive but has a negative coefficient could be evidence of anti-locality, or it could be an indication of some sort of processing momentum due to dynamic recruitment of additional processing resources (Just and Varma, 2007). Since anti-locality is an expectation-based frequency effect, and since this study controlled for frequency effects with n-grams, surprisal, and entropy reduction, an anti-locality explanation would rely on either (i) more precise variants of the metrics used in this study or (ii) other frequency metrics altogether. Future work could investigate the possibility of anti-locality by looking at the distance between an encoding operation and its corresponding integration action to see if the integration facilitation observed in this study is driven by longer embeddings or if there is simply a general facilitation effect when completing embeddings.

The finding of a negative integration cost was previously observed by Wu et al. (2010) as well as Demberg and Keller (2008), although Demberg and Keller calculated it using the original referent-based definitions of Gibson (1998; 2000) and varied which parts of speech counted for calculating integration cost. Ultimately, Demberg and Keller (2008) concluded that the negative coefficient was evidence that integration cost was not a good broad-coverage predictor of reading times; however, this study has replicated the effect and showed it to be a very strong predictor of reading times, albeit one that is correlated with facilitation rather than inhibition.

It is interesting that many studies have found negative integration cost using naturalistic stimuli while others have consistently found positive integration cost when using constructed stimuli with multiple center embeddings presented without context (Gibson, 2000; Chen et al., 2005; Kwon et al., 2010). It may be the case that any dynamic recruitment is overwhelmed by the memory demands of multiply center-embedded stimuli. Alternatively, it may be that the difficulty of processing multiply center-embedded sentences containing ambiguities produces anxiety in subjects, which slows processing at implicit prosodic boundaries (Fodor, 2002; Mitchell et al., 2008). In any case, the source of this discrepancy presents an attractive target for future research.

In general, sequential prediction does not seem to present people with any special ease or difficulty as evidenced by the lack of significance of F–L– and F+L+ predictions when frequency effects are factored out. This supports a theory of sequential, content-based cueing (Botvinick, 2007) that predicts that certain states would directly cue other states and thus avoid recall difficulty. An example of this may be seen in the case of a transitive verb triggering the prediction of a direct object. This kind of cueing would show up as a frequency effect predicted by surprisal rather than as a memory-based cost, due to frequent occurrences becoming ingrained as a learned skill. Future work could use these sequential cueing operations to investigate further claims of the dynamic recruitment hypothesis. One of the implications of the hypothesis is that recruitment of resources alleviates the initial encoding cost, which allows the parser to continue on as before the embedding. DLT, on the other hand, predicts that there is a storage cost for maintaining unresolved dependencies during a parse (Gibson, 2000). By weighting each of the sequential cueing operations with the embedding depth at which it occurs, an experiment may be able to test these two predictions.

This study has shown that measures based on working memory operations have strong predictivity over other previously proposed measures including those associated with frequency effects. This suggests that memory limitations may provide a partial explanation of what gives rise to frequency effects. Lastly, this paper provides evidence that there is a robust facilitation effect in English that arises from completing center embeddings.

The hierarchic sequence model, all evaluation scripts, and regression results for all baseline predictors used in this paper are freely available at http://sourceforge.net/projects/modelblocks/.

Acknowledgements

Thanks to Peter Culicover, Micha Elsner, and three anonymous reviewers for helpful suggestions. This work was funded by an OSU Department of Linguistics Targeted Investment for Excellence (TIE) grant for collaborative interdisciplinary projects conducted during the academic year 2012-13.

References

John R. Anderson, Dan Bothell, Michael D. Byrne, S. Douglass, Christian Lebiere, and Y. Qin. 2004. An integrated theory of the mind. *Psychological Review*, 111(4):1036–1060.

R. Harald Baayen, D. J. Davidson, and Douglas M. Bates. 2008. Mixed-effects modeling with crossed random effects for subjects and items. *Journal of Memory and Language*, 59:390–412.

R. Harald Baayen. 2008. *Analyzing Linguistic Data: A Practical Introduction to Statistics using R*. Cambridge University Press, New York, NY.

Douglas Bates, Martin Maechler, and Ben Bolker, 2011. *lme4: Linear mixed-effects models using S4 classes.*

BNC Consortium. 2007. The british national corpus.

Matthew Botvinick. 2007. Multilevel structure in behavior and in the brain: a computational model of Fuster's hierarchy. *Philosophical Transactions of the Royal Society, Series B: Biological Sciences*, 362:1615–1626.

Stanley F. Chen and Joshua Goodman. 1998. An empirical study of smoothing techniques for language modeling. Technical report, Harvard University.

Evan Chen, Edward Gibson, and Florian Wolf. 2005. Online syntactic storage costs in sentence comprehension. *Journal of Memory and Language*, 52(1):144–169.

Charles Clifton, Adrian Staub, and Keith Rayner. 2007. Eye movements in reading words and sentences. In *Eye movements: A window on mind and brain*, pages 341–372. Elsevier.

Vera Demberg and Frank Keller. 2008. Data from eye-tracking corpora as evidence for theories of syntactic processing complexity. *Cognition*, 109(2):193–210.

Janet Fodor. 2002. Prosodic disambiguation in silent reading. In M. Hirotani, editor, *In Proceedings of NELS 32*.

Victoria Fossum and Roger Levy. 2012. Sequential vs. hierarchical syntactic models of human incremental sentence processing. In *Proceedings of CMCL-NAACL 2012*. Association for Computational Linguistics.

W. Nelson Francis and Henry Kucera. 1979. The brown corpus: A standard corpus of present-day edited american english.

Stefan Frank and Rens Bod. 2011. Insensitivity of the human sentence-processing system to hierarchical structure. *Psychological Science*.

Edward Gibson. 1998. Linguistic complexity: Locality of syntactic dependencies. *Cognition*, 68(1):1–76.

Edward Gibson. 2000. The dependency locality theory: A distance-based theory of linguistic complexity. In *Image, language, brain: Papers from the first mind articulation project symposium*, pages 95–126.

John Hale. 2001. A probabilistic earley parser as a psycholinguistic model. In *Proceedings of the second meeting of the North American chapter of the Association for Computational Linguistics*, pages 159–166, Pittsburgh, PA.

John Hale. 2003. *Grammar, Uncertainty and Sentence Processing*. Ph.D. thesis, Cognitive Science, The Johns Hopkins University.

John Hale. 2006. Uncertainty about the rest of the sentence. *Cognitive Science*, 30(4):609–642.

John Hale. 2011. What a rational parser would do. *Cognitive Science*, 35(3):399–443.

Marc W. Howard and Michael J. Kahana. 2002. A distributed representation of temporal context. *Journal of Mathematical Psychology*, 45:269–299.

F. T. Jaeger, E. Fedorenko, P. Hofmeister, and E. Gibson. 2008. Expectation-based syntactic processing: Antilocality outside of head-final languages. In *The 21st CUNY Sentence Processing Conference*.

Daniel Jurafsky. 1996. A probabilistic model of lexical and syntactic access and disambiguation. *Cognitive Science: A Multidisciplinary Journal*, 20(2):137–194.

Marcel Adam Just and Sashank Varma. 2007. The organization of thinking: What functional brain imaging reveals about the neuroarchitecture of complex cognition. *Cognitive, Affective, & Behavioral Neuroscience*, 7:153–191.

Marcel Adam Just, Patricia A. Carpenter, and Jacqueline D. Woolley. 1982. Paradigms and processes in reading comprehension. *Journal of Experimental Psychology: General*, 111:228–238.

Alan Kennedy, James Pynte, and Robin Hill. 2003. The Dundee corpus. In *Proceedings of the 12th European conference on eye movement*.

Nayoung Kwon, Yoonhyoung Lee, Peter C. Gordon, Robert Kluender, and Maria Polinsky. 2010. Cognitive and linguistic factors affecting subject/object asymmetry: An eye-tracking study of pre-nominal relative clauses in korean. *Language*, 86(3):561.

Roger Levy. 2008. Expectation-based syntactic comprehension. *Cognition*, 106(3):1126–1177.

Richard L. Lewis and Shravan Vasishth. 2005. An activation-based model of sentence processing as skilled memory retrieval. *Cognitive Science*, 29(3):375–419.

Richard L. Lewis, Shravan Vasishth, and Jane A. Van Dyke. 2006. Computational principles of working memory in sentence comprehension. *Trends in Cognitive Science*, 10(10):447–454.

Mitchell P. Marcus, Beatrice Santorini, and Mary Ann Marcinkiewicz. 1993. Building a large annotated corpus of English: the Penn Treebank. *Computational Linguistics*, 19(2):313–330.

Brian McElree. 2001. Working memory and focal attention. *Journal of Experimental Psychology, Learning Memory and Cognition*, 27(3):817–835.

Brian McElree. 2006. Accessing recent events. *The Psychology of Learning and Motivation*, 46:155–200.

D. Mitchell, X. Shen, M. Green, and T. Hodgson. 2008. Accounting for regressive eye-movements in models of sentence processing: A reappraisal of the selective reanalysis hypothesis. *Journal of Memory and Language*, 59:266–293.

Slav Petrov and Dan Klein. 2007. Improved inference for unlexicalized parsing. In *Proceedings of NAACL HLT 2007*, pages 404–411, Rochester, New York, April. Association for Computational Linguistics.

Slav Petrov, Leon Barrett, Romain Thibaux, and Dan Klein. 2006. Learning accurate, compact, and interpretable tree annotation. In *Proceedings of the 44th Annual Meeting of the Association for Computational Linguistics (COLING/ACL'06)*.

Colin Phillips. 2010. Some arguments and non-arguments for reductionist accounts of syntactic phenomena. *Language and Cognitive Processes*, 28:156–187.

R Development Core Team, 2010. *R: A Language and Environment for Statistical Computing*. R Foundation for Statistical Computing, Vienna, Austria. ISBN 3-900051-07-0.

Brian Roark, Asaf Bachrach, Carlos Cardenas, and Christophe Pallier. 2009. Deriving lexical and syntactic expectation-based measures for psycholinguistic modeling via incremental top-down parsing. *Proceedings of the 2009 Conference on Empirical Methods in Natural Langauge Processing*, pages 324–333.

Brian Roark. 2001. Probabilistic top-down parsing and language modeling. *Computational Linguistics*, 27(2):249–276.

Claude Shannon. 1948. A mathematical theory of communication. *Bell System Technical Journal*, 27:379–423, 623–656.

Stuart M. Shieber, Yves Schabes, and Fernando C.N. Pereira. 1995. Principles and implementation of deductive parsing. *Journal of Logic Programming*, 24:3–36.

Andreas Stolcke. 2002. Srilm – an extensible language modeling toolkit. In *Seventh International Conference on Spoken Language Processing*.

John Trueswell. 1996. The role of lexical frequency in syntactic ambiguity resolution. *Journal of Memory and Language*, 35:566–585.

Marten van Schijndel, Andy Exley, and William Schuler. in press. A model of language processing as hierarchic sequential prediction. *Topics in Cognitive Science*.

Shravan Vasishth and Richard L. Lewis. 2006. Argument-head distance and processing complexity: Explaining both locality and antilocality effects. *Language*, 82(4):767–794.

Stephen Wu, Asaf Bachrach, Carlos Cardenas, and William Schuler. 2010. Complexity metrics in an incremental right-corner parser. In *Proceedings of the 48th Annual Meeting of the Association for Computational Linguistics (ACL'10)*, pages 1189–1198.

Cross-Lingual Semantic Similarity of Words as the Similarity of Their Semantic Word Responses

Ivan Vulić and Marie-Francine Moens
Department of Computer Science
KU Leuven
Celestijnenlaan 200A
Leuven, Belgium
{ivan.vulic,marie-francine.moens}@cs.kuleuven.be

Abstract

We propose a new approach to identifying semantically similar words across languages. The approach is based on an idea that two words in different languages are similar if they are likely to generate similar words (which includes both source and target language words) as their top semantic word responses. Semantic word responding is a concept from cognitive science which addresses detecting most likely words that humans output as free word associations given some cue word. The method consists of two main steps: (1) it utilizes a probabilistic multilingual topic model trained on comparable data to learn and quantify the semantic word responses, (2) it provides ranked lists of similar words according to the similarity of their semantic word response vectors. We evaluate our approach in the task of bilingual lexicon extraction (BLE) for a variety of language pairs. We show that in the cross-lingual settings without any language pair dependent knowledge the response-based method of similarity is more robust and outperforms current state-of-the art methods that directly operate in the semantic space of latent cross-lingual concepts/topics.

1 Introduction

Cross-lingual semantic word similarity addresses the task of detecting words that refer to similar semantic concepts and convey similar meanings across languages. It ultimately boils down to the automatic identification of translation pairs, that is, bilingual lexicon extraction (BLE). Such lexicons and semantically similar words serve as important resources in cross-lingual knowledge induction (e.g., Zhao et al. (2009)), statistical machine translation (Och and Ney, 2003) and cross-lingual information retrieval (Ballesteros and Croft, 1997; Levow et al., 2005).

From parallel corpora, semantically similar words and bilingual lexicons are induced on the basis of word alignment models (Brown et al., 1993; Och and Ney, 2003). However, due to a relative scarceness of parallel texts for many language pairs and domains, there has been a recent growing interest in mining semantically similar words across languages on the basis of comparable data readily available on the Web (e.g., Wikipedia, news stories) (Haghighi et al., 2008; Hassan and Mihalcea, 2009; Vulić et al., 2011; Prochasson and Fung, 2011).

Approaches to detecting semantic word similarity from comparable corpora are most commonly based on an idea known as the *distributional hypothesis* (Harris, 1954), which states that words with similar meanings are likely to appear in similar contexts. Each word is typically represented by a high-dimensional vector in a feature vector space or a so-called *semantic space*, where the dimensions of the vector are its *context features*. The semantic similarity of two words, w_1^S given in the source language L_S with vocabulary V^S and w_2^T in the target language L_T with vocabulary V^T is then:

$$Sim(w_1^S, w_2^T) = SF(cv(w_1^S), cv(w_2^T)) \quad (1)$$

$cv(w_1^S) = [sc_1^S(c_1), \ldots, sc_1^S(c_N)]$ denotes a context vector for w_1^S with N context features c_k, where $sc_1^S(c_k)$ denotes the score for w_1^S associated with context feature c_k (similar for w_2^T). SF is a similarity function (e.g., cosine, the Kullback-Leibler divergence, the Jaccard index) operating on the context vectors (Lee, 1999; Cha, 2007).

In order to compute cross-lingual semantic word similarity, one needs to design the context features of words given in two different languages that span a shared cross-lingual semantic space. Such cross-lingual semantic spaces are typically spanned by: (1) bilingual lexicon entries (Rapp, 1999; Gaussier et al., 2004; Laroche and Langlais, 2010; Tamura et al., 2012), or (2) latent language-independent semantic concepts/axes (e.g., latent cross-lingual topics) induced by an algebraic model (Dumais et al., 1996), or more recently by a generative probabilistic model (Haghighi et al., 2008; Daumé III and Jagarlamudi, 2011; Vulić et al., 2011). Context vectors $cv(w_1^S)$ and $cv(w_2^T)$ for both source and target words are then compared in the semantic space independently of their respective languages.

In this work, we propose a new approach to constructing the shared cross-lingual semantic space that relies on a paradigm of *semantic word responding* or *free word association*. We borrow that concept from the psychology/cognitive science literature. Semantic word responding addresses a task that requires participants to produce first words that come to their mind that are related to a presented cue word (Nelson et al., 2000; Steyvers et al., 2004).

The new cross-lingual semantic space is spanned *by all vocabulary words in the source and the target language*. Each axis in the space denotes a semantic word response. The similarity between two words is then computed as the similarity between the vectors comprising their semantic word responses using any of existing SF-s. *Two words are considered semantically similar if they are likely to generate similar semantic word responses and assign similar importance to them.*

We utilize a shared semantic space of latent cross-lingual topics learned by a multilingual probabilistic topic model to obtain semantic word responses and quantify the strength of association between any cue word and its responses monolingually and across languages, and, consequently, to build *semantic response vectors*. That effectively translates the task of word similarity from the semantic space spanned by latent cross-lingual topics to the semantic space spanned by all vocabulary words in both languages.

The main contributions of this article are:

- We propose a new approach to modeling cross-lingual semantic similarity of words based on the similarity of their semantic word responses.
- We present how to estimate and quantify semantic word responses by means of a multilingual probabilistic topic model.
- We demonstrate how to employ our novel paradigm that relies on semantic word responding in the task of bilingual lexicon extraction (BLE) from comparable data.
- We show that the response-based model of similarity is more robust and obtains better results for BLE than the models that operate in the semantic space spanned by latent semantic concepts, i.e., cross-lingual topics directly.

The following sections first review relevant prior work and provide a very short introduction to multilingual probabilistic topic modeling, then describe our response-based approach to modeling cross-lingual semantic word similarity, and finally present our evaluation and results on the BLE task for a variety of language pairs.

2 Related Work

When dealing with the cross-lingual semantic word similarity, the focus of the researchers is typically on BLE, since usually the most similar words across languages are direct translations of each other. Numerous approaches emerged over the years that try to induce bilingual word lexicons on the basis of distributional information. Especially challenging is the task of mining semantically similar words from comparable data without any external knowledge source such as machine-readable seed bilingual lexicons used in (Fung and Yee, 1998; Rapp, 1999; Fung and Cheung, 2004; Gaussier et al., 2004; Morin et al., 2007; Andrade et al., 2010; Tamura et al., 2012), predefined explicit ontology or category knowledge used in (Déjean et al., 2002; Hassan and Mihalcea, 2009; Agirre et al., 2009), or orthographic clues as used in (Koehn and Knight, 2002; Haghighi et al., 2008; Daumé III and Jagarlamudi, 2011). This work addresses that particularly difficult setting which does not assume any language pair dependent background knowledge. It makes methods developed in such a setting applicable even on distant language pairs with scarce resources.

Recently, Griffiths et al. (2007), and Steyvers and Griffiths (2007) proposed models of free word association and semantic word similarity in the monolingual settings based on per-topic word distributions from probabilistic topic models such as pLSA (Hofmann, 1999) and LDA (Blei et al., 2003). Additionally, Vulić et al. (2011) constructed several models that utilize a shared cross-lingual topical space obtained by a multilingual topic model (Mimno et al., 2009; De Smet and Moens, 2009; Boyd-Graber and Blei, 2009; Ni et al., 2009; Jagarlamudi and Daumé III, 2010; Zhang et al., 2010) to identify potential translation candidates in the cross-lingual settings without any background knowledge. In this paper, we show that a transition from their semantic space spanned by cross-lingual topics to a semantic space spanned by all vocabulary words yields more robust models of cross-lingual semantic word similarity.

3 Modeling Word Similarity as the Similarity of Semantic Word Responses

This section contains a detailed description of our semantic word similarity method that relies on semantic word responses. Since the method utilizes the concept of multilingual probabilistic topic modeling, we first provide a very short overview of that concept, then present the intuition behind the approach, and finally describe our method in detail.

3.1 Multilingual Probabilistic Topic Modeling

Assume that we are given a *multilingual corpus* $\mathcal{C}$ of l languages, and $\mathcal{C}$ is a set of text collections $\{\mathcal{C}_1, \ldots, \mathcal{C}_l\}$ in those languages. A *multilingual probabilistic topic model* (Mimno et al., 2009; De Smet and Moens, 2009; Boyd-Graber and Blei, 2009; Ni et al., 2009; Jagarlamudi and Daumé III, 2010; Zhang et al., 2010) of a multilingual corpus $\mathcal{C}$ is defined as a set of semantically coherent multinomial distributions of words with values $P_j(w_i^j|z_k)$, $j = 1, \ldots, l$, for each vocabulary $V^1, \ldots, V^j, \ldots, V^l$ associated with text collections $\mathcal{C}_1, \ldots, \mathcal{C}_j, \ldots, \mathcal{C}_l \in \mathcal{C}$ given in languages $L_1, \ldots, L_j, \ldots, L_l$. $P_j(w_i^j|z_k)$ is calculated for each $w_i^j \in V^j$. The probability scores $P_j(w_i^j|z_k)$ build *per-topic word distributions*, and they constitute a language-specific representation (e.g., a probability value is assigned only for words from V^j) of a language-independent cross-lingual latent concept, that is, latent cross-lingual topic $z_k \in \mathcal{Z}$. $\mathcal{Z} = \{z_1, \ldots, z_K\}$ represents the set of all K latent cross-lingual topics present in the multilingual corpus. Each document in the multilingual corpus is thus considered a mixture of K cross-lingual topics from the set $\mathcal{Z}$. That mixture for some document $d_i^j \in \mathcal{C}_j$ is modeled by the probability scores $P_j(z_k|d_i^j)$ that altogether build *per-document topic distributions*.

Each cross-lingual topic from the set $\mathcal{Z}$ can be observed as a latent language-independent concept present in the multilingual corpus, but each language in the corpus uses only words from its own vocabulary to describe the content of that concept. For instance, having a multilingual collection in English, Spanish and Dutch and discovering a topic on *Soccer*, that cross-lingual topic would be represented by words (actually probabilities over words) {*player, goal, coach, ...*} in English, {*balón (ball), futbolista (soccer player), goleador (scorer), ...*} in Spanish, and {*wedstrijd (match), elftal (soccer team), doelpunt (goal), ...*} in Dutch. We have $\sum_{w_i^j \in V^j} P_j(w_i^j|z_k) = 1$, for each vocabulary V^j representing language L_j, and for each topic $z_k \in \mathcal{Z}$. Therefore, the latent cross-lingual topics also span a shared cross-lingual semantic space.

3.2 The Intuition Behind the Approach

Imagine the following thought experiment. A group of human subjects who have been raised bilingually and thus are native speakers of two languages L_S and L_T, is playing a game of word associations. The game consists of possibly an infinite number of iterations, and each iteration consists of 4 rounds. In the first round (the *S-S round*), given a word in the language L_S, the subject has to generate a list of words in the same language L_S that first occur to her/him as semantic word responses to the given word. The list is in descending order, with more prominent word responses occurring higher in the list. In the second round (the *S-T round*), the subject repeats the procedure, and generates the list of word responses to the same word from L_S, but now in the other language L_T. The third (the *T-T round*) and the fourth round (the *T-S round*) are similar to the first and the second round, but now a list of word responses in both L_S and L_T has to be generated for some cue word from L_T. The process of generating the lists of semantic responses then continues with other cue words and other human subjects.

As the final result, for each word in the source language L_S, and each word in the target language L_T, we obtain a single list of semantic word responses comprising words in both languages. All lists are sorted in descending order, based on some association score that takes into account both the number of times a word has occurred as an associative response, as well as the position in the list in each round. We can now measure the similarity of any two words, regardless of their corresponding languages, according to the similarity of their corresponding lists that contain their word responses. Words that are equally likely to trigger the same associative responses in the human brain, and moreover assign equal importance to those responses, as provided in the lists of associative responses, are very likely to be closely semantically similar. Additionally, for a given word w_1^S in the source language L_S, some word w_2^T in L_T that has the highest similarity score among all words in L_T should be a direct word-to-word translation of w_1^S.

3.3 Modeling Semantic Word Responses via Cross-Lingual Topics

Cross-lingual topics provide a sound framework to construct a probabilistic model of the aforementioned experiment. To model semantic word responses via the shared space of cross-lingual topics, we have to set a probabilistic mass that quantifies the degree of association. Given two words $w_1, w_2 \in V^S \cup V^T$, a natural way of expressing the *asymmetric semantic association* is by modeling the probability $P(w_2|w_1)$ (Griffiths et al., 2007), that is, the probability to generate word w_2 as a response given word w_1. After the training of a multilingual topic model on a multilingual corpus, we obtain per-topic word distributions with scores $P_S(w_i^S|z_k)$ and $P_T(w_i^T|z_k)$ (see Sect. 3.1).[1] The probability $P(w_2|w_1)$ is then decomposed as follows:

$$Resp(w_1, w_2) = P(w_2|w_1) = \sum_{k=1}^{K} P(w_2|z_k)P(z_k|w_1) \quad (2)$$

The probability scores $P(w_2|z_k)$ select words that are highly descriptive for each particular topic. The probability scores $P(z_k|w_1)$ ensure that topics z_k that are semantically relevant to the given word w_1 dominate the sum, so the overall high score $Resp(w_1, w_2)$ of the semantic word response is assigned only to highly descriptive words of the semantically related topics. Using the shared space of cross-lingual topics, semantic response scores can be derived for any two words $w_1, w_2 \in V^S \cup V^T$.[1]

The generative model closely resembles the actual process in the human brain - when we generate semantic word responses, we first tend to associate that word with a related semantic/cognitive concept, in this case a cross-lingual topic (the factor $P(z_k|w_1)$), and then, after establishing the concept, we output a list of words that we consider the most prominent/descriptive for that concept (words with high scores in the factor $P(w_2|z_k)$) (Nelson et al., 2000; Steyvers et al., 2004). Due to such modeling properties, this model of semantic word responding tends to assign higher association scores for *high frequency words*. It eventually leads to *asymmetric associations/responses*. We have detected that phenomenon both monolingually and across languages. For instance, the first response to Spanish word *mutación (mutation)* is English word *gene*. Other examples include *caldera (boiler)-steam*, *deportista (sportsman)-sport*, *horario (schedule)-hour* or *pescador (fisherman)-fish*. In the other association direction, we have detected top responses such as *merchant-comercio (trade)* or *neologism-palabra (word)*. In the monolingual setting, we acquire English pairs such as *songwriter-music*, *discipline-sport*, or Spanish pairs *gripe (flu)-enfermedad (disease)*, *cuenca (basin)-río (river)*, etc.

3.4 Response-Based Model of Similarity

Eq. (2) provides a way to measure the strength of semantic word responses. In order to establish the

[1]A remark on notation throughout the paper: Since the shared space of cross-lingual topics allows us to construct a uniform representation for all words regardless of a vocabulary they belong to, due to simplicity and to stress the uniformity, we sometimes use notation $P(w_i|z_k)$ and $P(z_k|w_i)$ instead of $P_S(w_i|z_k)$ or $P_S(z_k|w_i)$ (similar for subscript T). However, the reader must be aware that, for instance, $P(w_i|z_k)$ actually means $P_S(w_i|z_k)$ if $w_i \in V^S$, and $P_T(w_i|z_k)$ if $w_i \in V^T$.

Semantic responses						Response-based similarity
dramaturgo (playwright)		play		playwright		dramaturgo
obra (play)	.101	play	.142	play	.122	playwright
escritor (writer)	.083	obra (play)	.111	escritor (writer)	.087	dramatist
play	.066	player	.033	obra (play)	.073	tragedy
writer	.050	escena (scene)	.031	writer	.060	play
poet	.047	jugador (player)	.026	poeta (poet)	.055	essayist
autor (author)	.041	adaptation	.025	poet	.053	novelist
poeta (poet)	.039	stage	.024	autor (author)	.046	drama
teatro (theatre)	.030	game	.022	teatro (theatre)	.043	tragedian
drama	.026	juego (game)	.021	tragedy	.031	satirist
contribution	.025	teatro (theatre)	.019	drama	.026	writer

Table 1: An example of top 10 semantic word responses and the final response-based similarity for some Spanish and English words. The responses are estimated from Spanish-English Wikipedia data by bilingual LDA. We can observe several interesting phenomena: (1) High-frequency words tend to appear higher in the lists of semantic responses (e.g., *play* and *obra* for all 3 words), (2) Due to the modeling properties that give preference to high-frequency words (Sect. 3.3), a word might not generate itself as the top semantic response (e.g., *playwright-play*), (3) Both source and target language words occur as the top responses in the lists, (4) Although *play* is the top semantic response in English for both *dramaturgo* and *playwright*, its list of top semantic responses is less similar to the lists of those two words, (5) Although the English word *playwright* does not appear in the top 10 semantic responses to *dramaturgo*, and *dramaturgo* does not appear in the top 10 responses to *playwright*, the more robust response-based similarity method detects that the two words are actually very similar based on their lists of responses, (6) *dramaturgo* and *playwright* have very similar lists of semantic responses which ultimately leads to detecting that *playwright* is the most semantically similar word to *dramaturgo* across the two languages (the last column), i.e., they are direct one-to-one translations of each other, (7) Another English word *dramatist* very similar to Spanish *dramaturgo* is also pushed higher in the final list, although it is not found in the list of top semantic responses to *dramaturgo*.

final similarity between two words, we have to compare their *semantic response vectors*, that is, their semantic response scores over all words in both vocabularies. The final model of word similarity closely mimics our thought experiment. First, for each word $w_i^S \in V^S$, we generate probability scores $P(w_j^S|w_i^S)$ for all words $w_j^S \in V^S$ (the *S-S* rounds). Note that $P(w_i^S|w_i^S)$ is also defined by Eq. (2). Following that, for each word $w_i^S \in V^S$, we generate probability scores $P(w_j^T|w_i^S)$, for all words $w_j^T \in V^T$ (the *S-T* rounds). Similarly, we calculate probability scores $P(w_j^T|w_i^T)$ and $P(w_j^S|w_i^T)$, for each $w_i^T, w_j^T \in V^T$, and for each $w_j^S \in V^S$ (the *T-T* and *T-S* rounds).

Now, each word $w_i \in V^S \cup V^T$ may be represented by a $(|V^S| + |V^T|)$-dimensional context vector $cv(w_i)$ as follows:[2]
$[P(w_1^S|w_i), \ldots, P(w_{|V^S|}^S|w_i), \ldots, P(w_{|V^T|}^T|w_i)]$.
We have created a language-independent cross-lingual semantic space spanned by all vocabulary words in both languages. Each feature corresponds to one word from vocabularies V^S and V^T, while the exact score for each feature in the context vector $cv(w_i)$ is precisely the probability that this word/feature will be generated as a word response given word w_i. The degree of similarity between two words is then computed on the basis of similarity between their feature vectors using some of the standard similarity functions (Cha, 2007).

The novel response-based approach of similarity removes the effect of high-frequency words that tend to appear higher in the lists of semantic word responses. Therefore, the real synonyms and translations should occur as top candidates in the lists of similar words obtained by the response-based method. That property may be exploited to identify one-to-one translations across languages and build a bilingual lexicon (see Table 1).

4 Experimental Setup

4.1 Data Collections

We work with the following corpora:

[2]We assume that the two sets V^S and V^T are disjunct. It means that, for instance, Spanish word *pie (foot)* from V^S and English word *pie* from V^T are treated as two different word types. In that case, it holds $|V^S \cup V^T| = |V^S| + |V^T|$.

- IT-EN-W: A collection of 18,898 Italian-English Wikipedia article pairs previously used by Vulić et al. (2011).

- ES-EN-W: A collection of 13,696 Spanish-English Wikipedia article pairs.

- NL-EN-W: A collection of 7,612 Dutch-English Wikipedia article pairs.

- NL-EN-W+EP: The NL-EN-W corpus augmented with 6,206 Dutch-English document pairs from Europarl (Koehn, 2005). Although Europarl is a parallel corpus, no explicit use is made of sentence-level alignments.

All corpora are theme-aligned, that is, the aligned document pairs discuss similar subjects, but are in general not direct translations (except the Europarl document pairs). NL-EN-W+EP serves to test whether better semantic responses could be learned from data of higher quality, and to measure how it affects the response-based similarity method and the quality of induced lexicons. Following (Koehn and Knight, 2002; Haghighi et al., 2008; Prochasson and Fung, 2011), we consider only noun word types. We retain only nouns that occur at least 5 times in the corpus. We record the lemmatized form when available, and the original form otherwise. Again following their setup, we use TreeTagger (Schmid, 1994) for POS tagging and lemmatization.

4.2 Multilingual Topic Model

The multilingual probabilistic topic model we use is a straightforward multilingual extension of the standard Blei et al.'s LDA model (Blei et al., 2003) called bilingual LDA (Mimno et al., 2009; Ni et al., 2009; De Smet and Moens, 2009). For the details regarding the modeling assumptions, generative story, training and inference procedure of the bilingual LDA model, we refer the interested reader to the aforementioned relevant literature. The potential of the model in the task of bilingual lexicon extraction was investigated before (Mimno et al., 2009; Vulić et al., 2011), and it was also utilized in other cross-lingual tasks (e.g., Platt et al. (2010); Ni et al. (2011)). We use Gibbs sampling for training. In a typical setting for mining semantically similar words using latent topic models in both monolingual (Griffiths et al., 2007; Dinu and Lapata, 2010) and cross-lingual setting (Vulić et al., 2011), the best results are obtained with the number of topics set to a few thousands (≈ 2000). Therefore, our bilingual LDA model on all corpora is trained with the number of topics $K = 2000$. Other parameters of the model are set to the standard values according to Steyvers and Griffiths (2007): $\alpha = 50/K$ and $\beta = 0.01$. We are aware that different hyper-parameter settings (Asuncion et al., 2009; Lu et al., 2011), might have influence on the quality of learned cross-lingual topics, but that analysis is out of the scope of this paper.

4.3 Compared Methods

We evaluate and compare the following word similarity approaches in all our experiments:

1) The method that regards the lists of semantic word responses across languages obtained by Eq. (2) directly as the lists of semantically similar words (**Direct-SWR**).

2) The state-of-the-art method that employs a similarity function (SF) on the K-dimensional word vectors $cv(w_i)$ in the semantic space of latent cross-lingual topics. The dimensions of the vectors are conditional topic distribution scores $P(z_k|w_i)$ that are obtained by the multilingual topic model directly (Steyvers and Griffiths, 2007; Vulić et al., 2011). We have tested different SF-s (e.g., the Kullback-Leibler and the Jensen-Shannon divergence, the cosine measure), and have detected that in general the best scores are obtained when using the Bhattacharyya coefficient (BC) (Bhattacharyya, 1943; Kazama et al., 2010) (**Topic-BC**).

3) The best scoring similarity method from Vulić et al. (2011) named **TI+Cue**. This state-of-the-art method also operates in the semantic space of latent cross-lingual concepts/topics.

4) The response-based similarity described in Sect. 3. As for *Topic-BC*, we again use BC as the similarity function, but now on $|V^S \cup V^T|$-dimensional context vectors in the semantic space spanned by all words in both vocabularies that represent semantic word responses (**Response-BC**). Given two N-dimensional word vectors $cv(w_1^S)$ and $cv(w_2^T)$, the BC or the *fidelity* measure (Cha, 2007) is defined as:

$$BC(cv(w_1^S), cv(w_2^T)) = \sum_{n=1}^{N} \sqrt{sc_1^S(c_n) \cdot sc_2^T(c_n)} \quad (3)$$

Corpus:	IT-EN-W			ES-EN-W			NL-EN-W			NL-EN-W+EP		
Method	Acc_1	MRR	Acc_{10}	Acc_1	MRR	Acc_{10}	Acc_1	MRR	Acc_{10}	Acc_1	MRR	Acc_{10}
Direct-SWR	.501	.576	.740	.332	.437	.675	.186	.254	.423	.344	.450	.652
Topic-BC	.578	.667	.834	.433	.576	.843	**.237**	.314	.489	.534	.630	.836
TI+Cue	.597	.702	**.897**	.429	.569	.828	.225	.296	.459	.446	.569	.808
Response-BC	**.622**	**.729**	.882	**.517**	**.635**	**.891**	.236	**.320**	**.511**	**.574**	**.653**	**.864**

Table 2: BLE performance of all the methods for Italian-English, Spanish-English and Dutch-English (with 2 different corpora utilized for the training of bilingual LDA and the estimation of semantic word responses for Dutch-English).

For the *Topic-BC* method $N = K$, while $N = |V^S \cup V^T|$ for *Response-BC*. Additionally, since $P(z_k|w_i) > 0$ and $P(w_k|w_i) > 0$ for each $z_k \in \mathcal{Z}$ and each $w_k \in V^S \cup V^T$, a lot of probability mass is assigned to topics and semantic responses that are completely irrelevant to the given word. Reducing the dimensionality of the semantic representation a posteriori to only a smaller number of most important semantic axes in the semantic spaces should decrease the effects of that statistical noise, and even more firmly emphasize the latent correlation among words. The utility of such *semantic space truncating* or *feature pruning* in monolingual settings (Reisinger and Mooney, 2010) was also detected previously for LSA and LDA-based models (Landauer and Dumais, 1997; Griffiths et al., 2007). Therefore, unless noted otherwise, we perform all our calculations over the best scoring 200 cross-lingual topics and the best scoring 2000 semantic word responses.[3]

4.4 Evaluation

Ground truth translation pairs.[4] Since our task is bilingual lexicon extraction, we designed a set of ground truth one-to-one translation pairs for all 3 language pairs as follows. For Dutch-English and Spanish-English, we randomly sampled a set of Dutch (Spanish) nouns from our Wikipedia corpora. Following that, we used the *Google Translate* tool plus an additional annotator to translate those words to English. The annotator manually revised the lists and retained only words that have their corresponding translation in the English vocabulary. Additionally, only one possible translation was annotated as correct. When more than 1 translation is possible, the annotator marked as correct the translation that occurs more frequently in the English Wikipedia data. Finally, we built a set of 1000 one-to-one translation pairs for Dutch-English and Spanish-English. The same procedure was followed for Italian-English, but there we obtained the ground truth one-to-one translation pairs for 1000 most frequent Italian nouns in order to test the effect of word frequency on the quality of semantic word responses and the overall lexicon quality.

Evaluation metrics. All the methods under consideration actually retrieve ranked lists of semantically similar words that could be observed as potential translation candidates. We measure the performance on BLE as *Top M* accuracy (Acc_M). It denotes the number of source words from ground truth translation pairs whose top M semantically similar words contain the correct translation according to our ground truth over the total number of ground truth translation pairs (=*1000*) (Tamura et al., 2012). Additionally, we compute the *mean reciprocal rank (MRR)* scores (Voorhees, 1999).

5 Results and Discussion

Table 2 displays the performance of each compared method on the BLE task. It shows the difference in results for different language pairs and different corpora used to extract latent cross-lingual topics and estimate the lists of semantic word responses. Example lists of semantically similar words over all 3 language pairs are shown in Table 3. Based on these results, we are able to derive several conclusions:

(i) *Response-BC* performs consistently better than the other 3 methods over all corpora and all language pairs. It is more robust and is able to find some cross-lingual similarities omitted by the other meth-

[3]The values are set empirically. Calculating similarity $Sim(w_1^S, w_2^T)$ may be interpreted as: "Given word w_1^S detect how similar word w_2^T is to the word w_1^S." Therefore, when calculating $Sim(w_1^S, w_2^T)$, even when dealing with symmetric similarity functions such as BC, we always consider only the scores $P(\cdot|w_1^S)$ for truncating.

[4]Available online: http://people.cs.kuleuven.be/∼ivan.vulic/software/

Italian-English (IT-EN)			Spanish-English (ES-EN)			Dutch-English (NL-EN)		
(1) **affresco** (fresco)	(2) **spigolo** (edge)	(3) **coppa** (cup)	(1) **caza** (hunting)	(2) **discurso** (speech)	(3) **comprador** (buyer)	(1) **behoud** (conservation)	(2) **schroef** (screw)	(3) **spar** (fir)
fresco	polyhedron	club	*hunting*	rhetoric	purchase	*conservation*	socket	conifer
mural	polygon	competition	hunt	oration	seller	preservation	wire	pine
nave	vertices	final	hunter	*speech*	tariff	heritage	wrap	firewood
wall	diagonal	champion	hound	discourse	market	diversity	wrench	seedling
testimonial	*edge*	football	safari	dialectic	bidding	emphasis	*screw*	weevil
apse	vertex	trophy	huntsman	rhetorician	auction	consequence	pin	chestnut
rediscovery	binomial	team	wildlife	oratory	bid	danger	fastener	acorn
draughtsman	solid	relegation	animal	wisdom	microeconomics	contribution	torque	girth
ceiling	graph	tournament	ungulate	oration	trade	decline	pipe	lumber
palace	modifier	soccer	chase	persuasion	listing	framework	routing	bark

Table 3: Example lists of top 10 semantically similar words across all 3 language pairs according to our *Response-BC* similarity method, where the correct translation word is: (col. 1) found as the most similar word, (2) contained lower in the list, and (3) not found in the top 10 words.

IT-EN	ES-EN	NL-EN
direttore-director	flauta-flute	kustlijn-coastline
radice-root	eficacia-efficacy	begrafenis-funeral
sintomo-symptom	empleo-employment	mengsel-mixture
perdita-loss	descubierta-discovery	lijm-glue
danno-damage	desalojo-eviction	kijker-viewer
battaglione-battalion	miedo-fear	oppervlak-surface

Table 4: Example translations found by the *Response-BC* method, but missed by the other 3 methods.

ods (see Table 4). The overall quality of the cross-lingual word similarities and lexicons extracted by the method is dependent on the quality of estimated semantic response vectors. The quality of these vectors is of course further dependent on the quality of multilingual training data. For instance, for Dutch-English, we may observe a rather spectacular increase in overall scores (the tests are performed over the same set of 1000 words) when we augment Wikipedia data with Europarl data (compare the scores for NL-EN-W and NL-EN-W+EP).

(ii) A transition from a semantic space spanned by cross-lingual topics (*Topic-BC*) to a semantic space spanned by vocabulary words (*Response-BC*) leads to better results over all corpora and language pairs. The difference is less visible when using training data of lesser quality (the scores for NL-EN-W). Moreover, since the shared space of cross-lingual topics is used to obtain and quantify semantic word responses, the quality of learned cross-lingual topics influences the quality of semantic word responses. If the semantic coherence of the cross-lingual topical space is unsatisfying, the method is unable to generate good semantic response vectors, and ultimately unable to correctly identify semantically similar words across languages.

(iii) Due to its modeling properties that assign more importance to high-frequency words, *Direct-SWR* produces reasonable results in the BLE task only for high-frequency words (see results for IT-EN-W). Although Eq. (2) models the concept of semantic word responding in a sound way (Griffiths et al., 2007), using the semantic word responses directly is not suitable for the actual BLE task.

(iv) The effect of word frequency is clearly visible when comparing the results obtained on IT-EN-W with the results obtained on the other Wikipedia corpora. High-frequency words produce more redundancies in training data that are captured by statistical models such as latent topic models. High-frequency words then obtain better estimates of their semantic response vectors which consequently leads to better overall scores. The effect of word frequency on statistical methods in the BLE task was investigated before (Pekar et al., 2006; Prochasson and Fung, 2011; Tamura et al., 2012), and we also confirm their findings.

(v) Unlike (Koehn and Knight, 2002; Haghighi et al., 2008), our response-based method does not rely on any orthographic features such as cognates or words shared across languages. It is a pure statistical method that only relies on word distributions over a multilingual corpus. Based on these distributions, it performs the initial shallow semantic analysis of the corpus by means of a multilingual probabilistic model. The method then builds, via the concept of semantic word responding, a language-independent semantic space spanned by all vocabulary words/responses in both languages. That makes the method portable to distant language pairs. However, for similar languages, including more evidence such as orthographic clues might lead to further increase in scores, but we leave that for future work.

6 Conclusion

We have proposed a new statistical approach to identifying semantically similar words across languages that relies on the paradigm of semantic word responding previously defined in cognitive science. The proposed approach is robust and does not make any additional language-pair dependent assumptions (e.g., it does not rely on a seed lexicon, orthographic clues or predefined concept categories). That effectively makes it applicable to any language pair. Our experiments on the task of bilingual lexicon extraction for a variety of language pairs have proved that the response-based approach is more robust and outperforms the methods that operate in the semantic space of latent concepts (e.g., cross-lingual topics) directly.

Acknowledgments

We would like to thank Steven Bethard and the anonymous reviewers for their useful suggestions. This research has been carried out in the framework of the TermWise Knowledge Platform (IOF-KP/09/001) funded by the Industrial Research Fund, KU Leuven, Belgium.

References

Eneko Agirre, Enrique Alfonseca, Keith Hall, Jana Kravalova, Marius Pasca, and Aitor Soroa. 2009. A study on similarity and relatedness using distributional and WordNet-based approaches. In *Proceedings of NAACL-HLT*, pages 19–27.

Daniel Andrade, Tetsuya Nasukawa, and Junichi Tsujii. 2010. Robust measurement and comparison of context similarity for finding translation pairs. In *Proceedings of COLING*, pages 19–27.

Arthur Asuncion, Max Welling, Padhraic Smyth, and Yee Whye Teh. 2009. On smoothing and inference for topic models. In *Proceedings of UAI*, pages 27–34.

Lisa Ballesteros and W. Bruce Croft. 1997. Phrasal translation and query expansion techniques for cross-language information retrieval. In *Proceedings of SIGIR*, pages 84–91.

A. Bhattacharyya. 1943. On a measure of divergence between two statistical populations defined by their probability distributions. *Bulletin of the Calcutta Mathematical Society*, 35:199–209.

David M. Blei, Andrew Y. Ng, and Michael I. Jordan. 2003. Latent Dirichlet Allocation. *Journal of Machine Learning Research*, 3:993–1022.

Jordan Boyd-Graber and David M. Blei. 2009. Multilingual topic models for unaligned text. In *Proceedings of UAI*, pages 75–82.

Peter F. Brown, Vincent J. Della Pietra, Stephen A. Della Pietra, and Robert L. Mercer. 1993. The mathematics of statistical machine translation: parameter estimation. *Computational Linguistics*, 19(2):263–311.

Sung-Hyuk Cha. 2007. Comprehensive survey on distance/similarity measures between probability density functions. *International Journal of Mathematical Models and Methods in Applied Sciences*, 1(4):300–307.

Hal Daumé III and Jagadeesh Jagarlamudi. 2011. Domain adaptation for machine translation by mining unseen words. In *Proceedings of ACL*, pages 407–412.

Wim De Smet and Marie-Francine Moens. 2009. Cross-language linking of news stories on the Web using interlingual topic modeling. In *CIKM Workshop on Social Web Search and Mining (SWSM)*, pages 57–64.

Hervé Déjean, Eric Gaussier, and Fatia Sadat. 2002. An approach based on multilingual thesauri and model combination for bilingual lexicon extraction. In *Proceedings of COLING*, pages 1–7.

Georgiana Dinu and Mirella Lapata. 2010. Topic models for meaning similarity in context. In *Proceedings of COLING*, pages 250–258.

Susan T. Dumais, Thomas K. Landauer, and Michael Littman. 1996. Automatic cross-linguistic information retrieval using Latent Semantic Indexing. In *Proceedings of the SIGIR Workshop on Cross-Linguistic Information Retrieval*, pages 16–23.

Pascale Fung and Percy Cheung. 2004. Mining very-non-parallel corpora: Parallel sentence and lexicon extraction via bootstrapping and EM. In *Proceedings of EMNLP*, pages 57–63.

Pascale Fung and Lo Yuen Yee. 1998. An IR approach for translating new words from nonparallel, comparable texts. In *Proceedings of COLING*, pages 414–420.

Eric Gaussier, Jean-Michel Renders, Irina Matveeva, Cyril Goutte, and Hervé Déjean. 2004. A geometric view on bilingual lexicon extraction from comparable corpora. In *Proceedings of ACL*, pages 526–533.

Thomas L. Griffiths, Mark Steyvers, and Joshua B. Tenenbaum. 2007. Topics in semantic representation. *Psychological Review*, 114(2):211–244.

Aria Haghighi, Percy Liang, Taylor Berg-Kirkpatrick, and Dan Klein. 2008. Learning bilingual lexicons from monolingual corpora. In *Proceedings of ACL*, pages 771–779.

Zellig S. Harris. 1954. Distributional structure. *Word*, 10(23):146–162.

Samer Hassan and Rada Mihalcea. 2009. Cross-lingual semantic relatedness using encyclopedic knowledge. In *Proceedings of EMNLP*, pages 1192–1201.

Thomas Hofmann. 1999. Probabilistic Latent Semantic Indexing. In *Proceedings of SIGIR*, pages 50–57.

Jagadeesh Jagarlamudi and Hal Daumé III. 2010. Extracting multilingual topics from unaligned comparable corpora. In *Proceedings of ECIR*, pages 444–456.

Jun'ichi Kazama, Stijn De Saeger, Kow Kuroda, Masaki Murata, and Kentaro Torisawa. 2010. A Bayesian method for robust estimation of distributional similarities. In *Proceedings of ACL*, pages 247–256.

Philipp Koehn and Kevin Knight. 2002. Learning a translation lexicon from monolingual corpora. In *ACL Workshop on Unsupervised Lexical Acquisition*, pages 9–16.

Philipp Koehn. 2005. Europarl: A parallel corpus for statistical machine translation. In *Proceedings of MT Summit*, pages 79–86.

Thomas K. Landauer and Susan T. Dumais. 1997. Solutions to Plato's problem: The Latent Semantic Analysis theory of acquisition, induction, and representation of knowledge. *Psychological Review*, 104(2):211–240.

Audrey Laroche and Philippe Langlais. 2010. Revisiting context-based projection methods for term-translation spotting in comparable corpora. In *Proceedings of COLING*, pages 617–625.

Lillian Lee. 1999. Measures of distributional similarity. In *Proceedings of ACL*, pages 25–32.

Gina-Anne Levow, Douglas W. Oard, and Philip Resnik. 2005. Dictionary-based techniques for cross-language information retrieval. *Information Processing and Management*, 41:523–547.

Yue Lu, Qiaozhu Mei, and ChengXiang Zhai. 2011. Investigating task performance of probabilistic topic models: an empirical study of PLSA and LDA. *Information Retrieval*, 14(2):178–203.

David Mimno, Hanna M. Wallach, Jason Naradowsky, David A. Smith, and Andrew McCallum. 2009. Polylingual topic models. In *Proceedings of EMNLP*, pages 880–889.

Emmanuel Morin, Béatrice Daille, Koichi Takeuchi, and Kyo Kageura. 2007. Bilingual terminology mining - using brain, not brawn comparable corpora. In *Proceedings of ACL*, pages 664–671.

Douglas L. Nelson, Cathy L. McEvoy, and Simon Dennis. 2000. What is free association and what does it measure? *Memory and Cognition*, 28:887–899.

Xiaochuan Ni, Jian-Tao Sun, Jian Hu, and Zheng Chen. 2009. Mining multilingual topics from Wikipedia. In *Proceedings of WWW*, pages 1155–1156.

Xiaochuan Ni, Jian-Tao Sun, Jian Hu, and Zheng Chen. 2011. Cross lingual text classification by mining multilingual topics from Wikipedia. In *Proceedings of WSDM*, pages 375–384.

Franz Josef Och and Hermann Ney. 2003. A systematic comparison of various statistical alignment models. *Computational Linguistics*, 29(1):19–51.

Viktor Pekar, Ruslan Mitkov, Dimitar Blagoev, and Andrea Mulloni. 2006. Finding translations for low-frequency words in comparable corpora. *Machine Translation*, 20(4):247–266.

John C. Platt, Kristina Toutanova, and Wen-Tau Yih. 2010. Translingual document representations from discriminative projections. In *Proceedings of EMNLP*, pages 251–261.

Emmanuel Prochasson and Pascale Fung. 2011. Rare word translation extraction from aligned comparable documents. In *Proceedings of ACL*, pages 1327–1335.

Reinhard Rapp. 1999. Automatic identification of word translations from unrelated English and German corpora. In *Proceedings of ACL*, pages 519–526.

Joseph Reisinger and Raymond J. Mooney. 2010. A mixture model with sharing for lexical semantics. In *Proceedings of EMNLP*, pages 1173–1182.

Helmut Schmid. 1994. Probabilistic part-of-speech tagging using decision trees. In *International Conference on New Methods in Language Processing*.

Mark Steyvers and Tom Griffiths. 2007. Probabilistic topic models. *Handbook of Latent Semantic Analysis*, 427(7):424–440.

Mark Steyvers, Richard M. Shiffrin, and Douglas L. Nelson. 2004. Word association spaces for predicting semantic similarity effects in episodic memory. In *Experimental Cognitive Psychology and Its Applications*, pages 237–249.

Akihiro Tamura, Taro Watanabe, and Eiichiro Sumita. 2012. Bilingual lexicon extraction from comparable corpora using label propagation. In *Proceedings of EMNLP*, pages 24–36.

Ellen M. Voorhees. 1999. The TREC-8 question answering track report. In *Proceedings of TREC*, pages 77–82.

Ivan Vulić, Wim De Smet, and Marie-Francine Moens. 2011. Identifying word translations from comparable corpora using latent topic models. In *Proceedings of ACL*, pages 479–484.

Duo Zhang, Qiaozhu Mei, and ChengXiang Zhai. 2010. Cross-lingual latent topic extraction. In *Proceedings of ACL*, pages 1128–1137.

Hai Zhao, Yan Song, Chunyu Kit, and Guodong Zhou. 2009. Cross language dependency parsing using a bilingual lexicon. In *Proceedings of ACL*, pages 55–63.

Combining multiple information types in Bayesian word segmentation

Gabriel Doyle and **Roger Levy**
Department of Linguistics
University of California, San Diego
La Jolla, CA 92093, USA
{gdoyle,rlevy}@ucsd.edu

Abstract

Humans identify word boundaries in continuous speech by combining multiple cues; existing state-of-the-art models, though, look at a single cue. We extend the generative model of Goldwater et al (2006) to segment using syllable stress as well as phonemic form. Our new model treats identification of word boundaries and prevalent stress patterns in the language as a joint inference task. We show that this model improves segmentation accuracy over purely segmental input representations, and recovers the dominant stress pattern of the data. Additionally, our model retains high performance even without single-word utterances. We also demonstrate a discrepancy in the performance of our model and human infants on an artificial-language task in which stress cues and transition-probability information are pitted against one another. We argue that this discrepancy indicates a bound on rationality in the mechanisms of human segmentation.

1 Introduction

For an adult speaker of a language, word segmentation from fluid speech may seem so easy that it barely needed to be learned. However, pauses in speech and word boundaries are not well correlated (Cole & Jakimik, 1980), word boundaries are marked by a conspiracy of partially-informative cues (Johnson & Jusczyk, 2001), and different languages mark their boundaries differently (Cutler & Carter, 1987). This makes the problem of unsupervised word segmentation acquisition, whether by a computational model or an infant, a daunting task.

Effective segmentation relies on the flexible integration of multiple types of segmentation cues, among them statistical regularities in phonemes and prosody, coarticulation, and allophonic variation. Infants begin using multiple segmentation cues within their first year of life (Johnson & Jusczyk, 2001). Despite this, many state-of-the-art models look at only one type of information: phonemes.

In this study, we expand an existing model to incorporate multiple cues, leading to an improvement in segmentation performance and opening new ways of investigating human segmentation acquisition. On the latter point, we show that rational learners can learn to segment without encountering words in isolation, and that human learners deviate from rationality in certain segmentation tasks.

2 Previous work

The prevailing unsupervised word segmentation systems (e.g., Brent, 1999; Goldwater, Griffiths, & Johnson, 2006; Blanchard & Heinz, 2008) use only phonemic information to segment speech. However, human segmenters use additional information types, notably stress information, in their segmentation. We present an overview of these phonemic models here before discussing the prosodic model expansion. A more complete review is available in Goldwater (2007).

2.1 Goldwater et al (2006)

The Goldwater et al model is related to Brent (1999)'s model, both of which use strictly phonemic information to segment. The model assumes that the corpus is generated by a Dirichlet process over word bigrams.[1] We present a basic overview here, based on Sect. 5.5 of Goldwater, 2007. To generate the word w_i given the preceding word w_{i-1}:

1. Decide if bigram $b_i = \langle w_{i-1}, w_i \rangle$ is novel
2. If b_i non-novel, draw b_i from bigram lexicon
3. If b_i novel, decide whether w_i is novel
   a. If w_i non-novel, draw w_i from word lexicon
   b. If w_i novel, draw w_i from word-generating distribution P_0.

The Dirichlet process first decides whether to draw a non-novel ("nn") bigram, with probability proportional to the number of times the previous word has appeared in the corpus:

$$p(\langle w_{i-1}, w_i \rangle \text{ nn} | w_{i-1}) = \frac{n_{\langle w_{i-1}, \cdot \rangle}}{n_{\langle w_{i-1}, \cdot \rangle} + \alpha_1}, \quad (1)$$

where $n_{\langle x,y \rangle}$ is the token count for bigram $\langle x, y \rangle$. If the bigram is non-novel, word w_i is drawn in proportion to the number of times it has appeared after w_{i-1} in the corpus:

$$p(w_i = x | \langle w_{i-1}, w_i \rangle \text{ nn}) = \frac{n_{\langle w_{i-1}, x \rangle}}{n_{\langle w_{i-1}, \cdot \rangle}} \quad (2)$$

If the bigram is novel, this could either be due to w_i being a novel word or due to w_i being an existing word that had not appeared with w_{i-1} before. The probability of w_i being a non-novel word x is

$$p(w_i = x, w_i \text{ nn} | \begin{matrix} \langle w_{i-1}, w_i \rangle \\ \text{novel} \end{matrix}) = \frac{b_{\langle \cdot, w_i \rangle}}{(b_{\langle \cdot, \cdot \rangle} + \alpha_0)}, \quad (3)$$

where $b_{\langle \cdot, \cdot \rangle}$ is the count of word bigram types. Finally, if w_i is a new word, its phonemic form is generated from a distribution P_0. In the Goldwater et al model, this distribution is simply the product of the unigram probabilities of the phonemes, $P(\sigma_j)$, times the probability of a word boundary, $p_\#$, to end the word:

$$p(w_i = \sigma_1 \cdots \sigma_M | \begin{matrix} w_i \\ \text{novel} \end{matrix}) = p_\# (1 - p_\#)^{M-1} \prod P(\sigma_j) \quad (4)$$

To segment an observed corpus, the model Gibbs samples over the possible word boundaries (utterance boundaries are assumed to be word boundaries).[2] The exchangability of draws from a Dirichlet process allows for Gibbs sampling of each possible boundary given all the others.

2.2 A cognitively-plausible variant

Phillips and Pearl (2012) make these Bayesian segmentation models more cognitively plausible in two ways. The first is to move from phonemes to syllables as the base representational unit from which words are constructed, as infants learn to categorize syllables before phonemes (Eimas, 1999). The second is to add memory and processing constraints on the learner. They find that syllable-based segmentation is better than phoneme-based segmentation in the bigram model (though worse in the unigram model), and that, counter-intuitively, the constrained learner outperforms the unconstrained learner. This improvement appears to be driven by better performance in segmenting more common words. In this work, we adopt the syllabified representation but retain the unconstrained rational learner assumption.

2.3 Other multiple-cue models

Some previous models have incorporated multiple cues, specifically the phonemic and stress information that our model will use. Two prominent examples are Christiansen, Allen, and Seidenberg (1998)'s connectionist model and Gambell and Yang (2006)'s algebraic model. The connectionist model places word boundaries where the combination of phonemic and stress information predict likely utterance boundaries, but does not include an explicit sense of "word", and performs only modestly on the segmentation task (boundary F-scores of .40-.45). The algebraic model also underperforms the Bayesian model (Phillips & Pearl, 2012) unless it includes the heuristic that there is a word boundary between any two stressed syllables. Our model presents a more general and completely unsupervised approach to segmentation with multiple cue-types.

[1] We will only discuss the bigram model here because it is more appropriate from both a cognitive perspective (it posits latent hierarchical structure) and engineering perspective (it segments more accurately) than the unigram model.

[2] The model assumes that utterance boundaries are generated just like other words, and includes an adjustable parameter $p_\$$ to account for their frequency.

In general, joint inference is becoming more common in language acquisition problems and has been shown to improve performance over single-feature inference. Examples include joint inference of a lexicon and phonetic categories (Feldman, Griffiths, & Morgan, 2009), joint inference of syntactic word order and word reference (Maurits, Perfors, & Navarro, 2009), and joint inference of word meanings and speaker intentions in child-directed speech (Frank, Goodman, & Tenenbaum, 2009).

3 Model design

Our model changes P_0 from a single-cue distribution, generating only phonemes, to a multiple-cue distribution that generates a stress form as well. This can improve segmentation performance and allows the investigation of rational segmentation behavior in a multiple-cue world.

In the original model, $P_0(w_i = \sigma_1 \cdots \sigma_M) \propto \prod_j P(\sigma_j)$, where $P(\sigma_j)$ is the frequency of the phoneme σ_j. In the multiple-cue model, we first generate a phonemic form w_i, then assign a stress pattern s_i to it.

$$\begin{aligned} P_0(w_i, s_i) &= P_W(w_i) P_S(s_i|M) \\ &= p_\#(1-p_\#)^{M-1} \prod_j^M P(\sigma_j) P_S(s_i|M) \quad (5) \end{aligned}$$

The phonemic form w_i has the same product-of-segments probability as the Goldwater et al model, but σ_j are now syllables instead of phonemes. We discuss the rationale behind this change in the next section.

The phonemic form is generated first, and the stress form is then drawn as a multinomial over all possible stress patterns with the same number of syllables as w_i. The stress distribution P_S is a multinomial distribution over word-length stress templates. P_S can be learned by the model based on a Dirichlet prior, but for simplicity in the present implementation, we estimate P_S as the plus-one-smoothed frequency of the stress patterns in the current segmentation. There are two stress levels (stressed or unstressed), and 2^M possible stress templates for a word of length M.[3]

Unlike phonemic forms, stress patterns are drawn as a whole word. This allows the model to capture a wide range of stress biases, although it prevents the model from generalizing biases across different word lengths. A potential future change to P_S that would allow for better generalization is discussed in Section 6.

3.1 On syllabification and stress

We change from segmenting on phonemes to segmenting on syllables in order to more easily implement stress information, which is a supersegmental feature most appropriately located on syllables. Syllabified data has been used in some previous models of segmentation, especially those using stress information or syllable-level transition probabilities (Christiansen et al., 1998; Swingley, 2005; Gambell & Yang, 2006; Phillips & Pearl, 2012).

For studying human word segmentation, Phillips and Pearl argue syllabified speech may be a more cognitively plausible testing ground. 3-month-old infants appear to have categorical representations of syllables (Eimas, 1999), three months before word segmentation appears (Borfeld, Morgan, Golinkoff, & Rathbun, 2005), and seven months before phoneme categorization (Werker & Tees, 1984). In addition, syllabification is assumed in much work on human word segmentation, especially in artificial-language studies (e.g., Thiessen & Saffran, 2003), which calculate statistical cues at the syllable level.

The assumption that syllable boundaries are known affects the baseline performance of the model, as it reduces the number of possible word boundary locations (since a word boundary is necessarily a syllable boundary). As such performance over syllabified data cannot be directly compared to performance on non-syllabified data.

It may seem that syllabification is so closely tied to word segmentation that including the former in a model of the latter leaves little to the model. However, the determinants of syllable boundaries are not the same as those for word boundaries. The prob-

[3]We do not assume that each word has one and only one stressed syllable, which would reduce the number of possible stress templates to M, for two reasons. First, in the current corpus, some words have citation forms with multiple stressed syllables. Second, in actual speech this assumption will not hold (e.g., many function words go unstressed).

lem of assigning syllable boundaries is a question of deciding where a boundary goes between two syllable nuclei, with the assumption that there must be a boundary there. The problem of assigning word boundaries is a question of deciding whether there is a boundary between two syllable nuclei, and if so, where it is. Knowing the syllable boundaries reduces the set of possible word boundaries, but does not directly address the question of how likely a boundary is. The difference in these tasks is supported by the three-month gap between syllable and word identification in infants.

4 Data

We use the Korman (1984) training corpus, as compiled by Christiansen et al. (1998), in this study. This is a 24493-word corpus of English spoken by adults to infants aged 6–16 weeks.[4] Phonemes, stresses, and syllable boundaries are the same as those used by Christiansen et al, which were based on citation forms in the MRC Psycholinguistic Database. All monosyllabic words were coded as stressed. Only utterances for which all words had citation forms were included.

This corpus is largely monosyllabic (87.3% of all word tokens), and heavily biased toward initial stress (89.2% of all multisyllable word tokens). No word is longer than three syllables, and most words have only one stressed syllable. A breakdown of the corpus by stress pattern is given in Table 1. This monosyllabic bias is an inherent property of English, not idiosyncratic to this corpus. The Bernstein-Ratner child-directed corpus is also over 80% monosyllabic. We expect that the results of segmentation on child-directed data will extend to adult speech, as the adult-directed corpus used by Gambell and Yang (2006) has an average word length of 1.17 syllables.

5 Experiments

We test the model on three problems. First, we show that the addition of stress information improves segmentation performance compared to a stress-less model. Next, we apply the model to a question in human segmentation acquisition. Finally, we look at a task where the rational model deviates from human performance.

[4] Approximately 150 word tokens from the original corpus were omitted in our version of the corpus due to a disparity between recorded number of syllables and number of stresses.

Types		Tokens	
Stress pattern	Count	Stress pattern	Count
S	21402	S	523
SW	2231	SW	208
SS	389	WS	40
WS	284	SWW	24
SWW	182	SS	7
WSW	33	WSW	7
Other	5	Other	2

Table 1: Corpus stress patterns by types and tokens, showing an initial-stress bias in all lengths.

5.1 Parameter setting

The model has four free parameters: α_0 and α_1, which affect the likelihood of new words and bigrams, respectively, and $p_{\#}$ and $p_{\$}$, which affect the expected likelihood of word and utterance boundaries. Following Goldwater, Griffiths, and Johnson (2009), we set $\alpha_0 = 20$, $\alpha_1 = 100$, $p_{\#} = 0.8$ and $p_{\$} = 0.5$ in all experiments.[5]

In all cases, the model performed five independent runs of 20000 iterations of Gibbs sampling the boundaries for the full corpus. Simulated annealing was performed during the burn-in period to improve convergence. All performance measures are reported as the mean of these five runs.

Performance is measured as word, boundary, and lexicon precision, recall, and F-scores. A word is matched iff both of its true boundaries are marked as boundaries and no internal boundaries are marked as word boundaries. Boundary counts omit utterance boundaries, which are assumed to be word boundaries. Lexical counts are based on word type counts.

5.2 Stress improves performance

We begin by showing that including a second cue type improves segmentation performance. We compare segmentation on a corpus with the attested stress patterns to that of a corpus without stress. With stress information included in the model, word/boundary/lexicon F-scores are

[5] Performance was similar for a range of settings between 1 and 100 for α_0 and between 10 and 200 for α_1.

	With stress			Without stress		
	Word	Bnd	Lex	Word	Bnd	Lex
Prec	.76	.99	.75	.76	.99	.72
Rec	.61	.70	.87	.60	.69	.84
F	.68	.82	.80	.67	.82	.77

Table 2: Precision, recall, and F-score over corpora with and without stress information available. Stress information especially improves lexical performance.

.68/.82/.80. Without stress, performance drops to .67/.82/.77.[6] Full results are given in Table 2.

Stress information primarily improves lexicon performance, along with a small improvement in token segmentation. Accounting for stress reduces both false positives and negatives in the lexicon; the fact that the lexical improvement is greater than that for words or boundaries suggests that much of the improvement rests is on rare words.

These effects are small but significant. For word token performance, we performed a paired *t*-test on utterance token F-scores between the with- and without-stress models. This difference was significant ($t = 11.28, df = 8125, p < .001$). We performed a similar utterance-by-utterance test on boundaries; again a small singificant improvement was found ($t = 8.92, df = 6084, p < .001$). To assess lexicon performance, we calculated for each word type in the gold-standard lexicon the proportion of the five trials in which that word appeared in the learned lexicon for the two models. We then examined the words where the proportions differed between the models. 89 true words appeared more often in the with-stress lexicons; 40 appeared more often in the without-stress lexicons. (683 appeared equally often in both.) By a sign test, this is significant at $p < .001$. We also tested lexicon performance with a binomial test on the two models' lexicon accuracy; this result was marginal ($p = .06$).

The explicit tracking of stress information also improves the model's acquisition of the stress bias of the language. Acquisition of the stress bias is potentially useful for generalization; stress patterns can be used for an initial segmentation if few or none of the words are familiar. In practice, we see children use their stress biases to segment new words from English speech (Jusczyk, Houston, & Newsome, 1999) as well as artificial languages (Thiessen & Saffran, 2003).

We assess the learned stress bias by dividing up the corpus as the model has segmented it, and count the number of tokens with SW versus WS stress patterns.[7] With stress representation, the learned stress bias is 6.77:1, and without stress representation, the stress bias is lower, at 6.33:1. Although these are both underestimates of the corpus's true stress bias (7.86:1), the stressed model is stronger and a better estimate of the true value.

The model's performance can be compared to various baselines, but perhaps the strongest is one with every syllable boundary being a word boundary. This baseline represents a shift from boundary *precision* being at ceiling (as in the model) to boundary *recall* being at ceiling. In fact, due to the preponderance of monosyllabic words in English child-directed speech, this baseline outperforms the model on word and boundary F-scores (.68 and .82 in the model, .82 and .91 in the baseline). However, the baseline's lexicon is much worse than the model's (F=.80 in the with-stress model, F=.64 in the baseline), and the baseline fails to learn anything about the language's stress biases. In addition, the baseline oversegments, whereas both the model and infant segmenters undersegment (Peters, 1983). This raises an important question about what the model should seek to optimize: though the baseline is more accurate by token, no structure is learned; type performance is more important if we want to learn the underlying structure.

5.3 Are isolated words necessary?

We next use this model to test the necessity of isolated words in rational word segmentation. It is not immediately obvious how human learners begin to segment words from fluid speech. Stress biases and other phonological cues are dominant in all but the earliest of infant word segmentation (Johnson & Jusczyk, 2001). This raises a chicken-and-egg problem; if the cues infants favor to segment words, such as stress biases, are dependent on the words of the

[6] Recall that due to the syllabified data, these results are not directly comparable to unsyllabified results in previous work.

[7] Note this defines a stress bias for the stressless model as well.

language, how do they learn enough words to determine the cues' biases?

One existing proposal is that human learners develop their stress biases based on words frequently heard in isolation (Jusczyk et al., 1999). In English, these include names and common diminutives (e.g., *mommy*, *kitty*) that generally have initial stress. These single-word utterances could offer the segmenter an initial guess of the stress bias, by supposing that short utterances are single words and recording their stress patterns. The most common stress patterns in short utterances could then be used as an initial guess at the stress bias to bootstrap other words and thereby improve the learned stress bias.

We test the rational learner's need for such explicit bootstrapping by learning to segment a corpus with all single-word utterances removed. The corpus is produced by excising all single-word utterances from the Korman corpus. This results in a 22081-word corpus, 10% fewer tokens than in the original. However, it does not substantially change the lexicon; the number of distinct word types only drops from 811 to 806.

We compare performance only on ambiguous boundaries and lexicon, as these are comparable between the corpora, and find that the model performs almost equally well. Without single-word utterances, boundary and lexical F-scores are .81 and .80, compared to .82 and .80 with single-word utterances. This shows that rational learners are able to segment even without the possibility of bootstrapping stress patterns from single-word utterances.

5.4 Bounded rationality in human segmentation

Lastly, we use this model to examine rational performance in a multiple-cue segmentation task. We show that humans' segmentation does not adhere to these predictions, suggesting a bound on human rationality in word segmentation.

We consider an artificial language study by Thiessen and Saffran (2003). In this study, infants are exposed to an artificial language consisting of four bisyllabic word types uttered repeatedly without pauses. Each syllable appears in only one word type, so within-word transition probabilities are always 1, while across-word transition probabilities are less than 0.5. Segmentation strategies that hypothesize word boundaries at low transition probabilities or that seek to minimize the lexicon size will segment out the four word types as expected.

Against bias, with TP			
AB	CD	CD	AB
WS	WS	WS	WS

With bias, against TP				
A	BC	DC	DA	B
W	SW	SW	SW	S

Table 3: Examples of segmenting an artificial language according to transition probabilities (top) or stress bias (bottom), when the true words have weak-strong stress. Vertical lines represent word boundaries. The top segmentation produces a smaller lexicon, but the bottom segmentation produces primarily words with the preferred stress pattern.

Segmentation in the experiment is complicated by the presence of stress in the artificial language. Depending on the condition, the words are either all strong-weak or all weak-strong. In the first condition, segmenting according to transition probabilities, lexicon size, or English stress bias favors the same segmentation. In the second condition, though, segmenting by the English stress bias to yield a lexicon of strong-weak words requires boundaries in the middle of the words. The segmenter must decide whether transition probabilities or preferred stress patterns are more important in segmentation. This situation is illustrated in Table 3, with a corpus consisting of two word types, AB and CD, each with weak-strong stress.

Thiessen and Saffran found that seven-month-old English-learning infants consistently segmented according to the transition probabilities, regardless of stress. However, nine-month-olds segmented according to the English stress bias, even if this meant going against the transition probabilities.

Intuitively, this could be rational behavior according to our model. A child's increasing age means more exposure to data, potentially leading the child to develop more confidence in the stress bias. As confidence in the stress bias increases, the cost of segmenting against it increases as well. A sufficiently strong stress preference could lead the segmenter to accept a large lexicon, all of whose words have the preferred stress pattern, over a small lexicon, all of whose words have the dispreferred stress pattern.

To judge by the Korman corpus, English has a stress bias of approximately 7:1 in favor of SW bisyllabic stress over WS.[8] If human segmentation behavior follows the rational model, the model should predict segmentation to favor strong-weak words over the transition probabilities when the stress bias is approximately this strong.

We test this rationality hypothesis with a smaller version of the Thiessen and Saffran artificial language, consisting of 48 tokens.[9] In one version, all tokens have the preferred SW pattern, and in the other all tokens have the dispreferred WS pattern. We then adjust the P_S distribution such that $P_S(SW|M=2) = b * P_S(WS|M=2)$, where b is the bias ratio. We run the model otherwise the same as in the previous experiments, except with 10 runs instead of 5.

Contrary to this hypothesis, the model's segmentation with $b = 7$ was the same whether the true words were strong-weak or weak-strong. In all ten runs, transition probabilities dictated the segmentation. To switch to stress-based segmentation, the bias must be orders of magnitude greater than the English bias. Figure 1 shows the proportions of runs in the weak-strong condition that show segmentation according to the stress bias, as the bias increases by factors of 10. When $b = 10000$, three of the ten runs segmented according to the stress bias; below that, the stress bias did not affect the rational model's segmentation.

Why is this? In the Bayesian model, the stress bias of a language affects only the $P_S(s_i|M)$ term in the P_0 distribution, so non-novel words are not penalized for their stress pattern. The model pays only once to create a word; once the word is generated, no matter how a priori implausible the word was, it may be cheaply drawn again as a non-novel word. This effect can be illustrated with a brief calculation.

Consider a corpus built from four bisyllabic word types (AB, CD, EF, GH), each appearing N times. If the corpus is segmented against the transition probabilities, the resulting lexicon will have 16 bisyllabic word types (BA, BC, BE, BG, DA, etc.), each occurring approximately $\frac{N}{4}$ times.

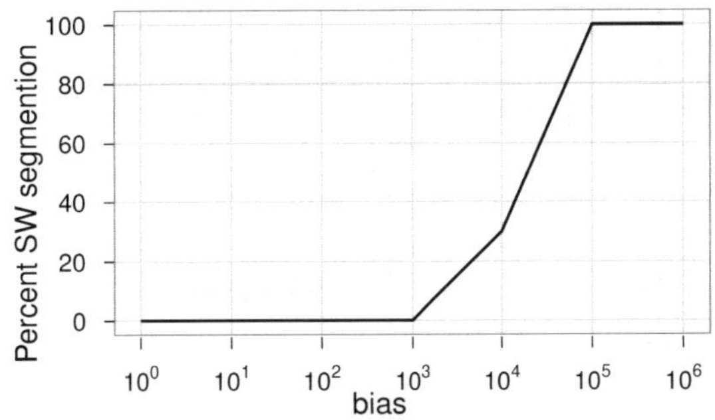

Figure 1: Percentage of runs segmented with the stress bias, against transition probabilities, as bias varies. At English-level biases, the rational model still overrules the stress bias when segmenting.

The probability of the against-bias corpus (C_{WS}) is proportional to the probability of generating the four word types, and then drawing them non-novelly from the lexicon.[10] (To simplify the calculations, we use the unigram version of the Goldwater et al model.)

$$p(C_{WS}) \propto P_W^4 P_S(WS)^4 (N!)^4 \frac{1}{4N!} \qquad (6)$$

The first two terms are the probability of generating the four word types (Eqn. 5);[11] the second two terms are the Dirichlet process draws from the existing lexicon N times each (Eqn. 2). By comparison, the probability of the with-bias corpus C_{SW} depends on generating the 16 word types, and drawing each non-novelly $\frac{N}{4}$ times.

$$p(C_{SW}) \propto P_W^{16} P_S(SW)^{16} \left(\frac{N}{4}!\right)^{16} \frac{1}{4N!} \qquad (7)$$

Given an SW bias b and a uniform distribution over syllables (so $P_W = \frac{1}{64}$), we find:

$$\frac{p(C_{WS})}{p(C_{SW})} = 64^{12} \frac{(b+1)^{12}}{b^{16}} \frac{(N!)^4}{(\frac{N}{4}!)^{16}} \qquad (8)$$

[8] The specific bias varies from corpus to corpus, but this appears to be a representative value.

[9] The 48 tokens come from four word types, with two types appearing 16 times and the other two appearing 8 times, mimicking the relative frequencies of Thiessen and Saffran's languages. Their test language had 270 tokens.

[10] It is also possible to generate this corpus by re-drawing the words novelly, but this is much less likely than non-novel draws.

[11] Because all syllables have equal unigram probabilities, the probability of all words' phonemic forms are equal, and will be written as P_W.

This equation shows that the rational model is heavily biased toward the segmentation that fits the transition probabilities. Increasing the stress bias b or decreasing the number of observed word tokens makes the rational model more likely to segment with the stress bias (against transition probabilities), but as we see in the experimental results, the stress bias must be very strong to overcome the efficient lexicon that the transition probability segmentation provides.

Since humans do not show this same inherent bias (or quickly lose it as they acquire the stress bias), we can ask how humans deviate from rationality. One possibility is that humans simply do not segment in this Bayesian manner. However, previous work (Frank, Goldwater, Griffiths, & Tenenbaum, 2010) has shown that human word segmentation shows similar behavior to a resource-limited Bayesian model. Equation 8 suggests that human segmentation could deviate from rationality by having an effectively stronger bias than English would suggest (reducing the first fraction)[12] or, as with Phillips and Pearl's constrained learners, by having effectively less input than the model assumes (reducing the second fraction).

6 Future work

Introducing stress into the Bayesian segmentation model suggests a few additional expansions. One possibility is to add other cues into the generative model via P_0. Any cue that is based on the word itself can be added in this way, with little change to the general model structure. Phonotactics can be added using an n-gram distribution for P_0 (Blanchard & Heinz, 2008). Coarticulation between adjacent phonemes is also used in human segmentation (Johnson & Jusczyk, 2001), so the P_0 distribution could predict higher within-word coarticulation. Integrating additional cues used by human segmenters extends the investigation of the bounds on rationality in human segmentation and in balancing multiple conflicting cues.

[12] A potential source of an inflated bias is infants' preference for strong-weak patterns. Jusczyk, Cutler, and Redanz (1993) found English-hearing infants listened longer to strong-weak patterns than weak-strong. This could lead to overestimation of the stress bias by making possible strong-weak segmentations more prominent in the segmenter's mind.

A more complex view of the stress system of a language may also be useful. One possibility is to place a Dirichlet prior over the stress templates and allow P_S to be learned as a latent variable in the model. Another possibility is to treat the stress templates more generally; in the present implementation, knowledge of the preferred stress patterns for word of one length tells the segmenter nothing about preferred stress patterns in another length. Cross-linguistically common stress rules (e.g., those that place stress a certain number of syllables from the left or right edge of a word) can be coded into P_S to improve generalization. Each rule dictates a specific stress pattern for each word length. When a word is generated in the Dirichlet process, the generative model would decide whether to assign stress according to one of these rules or to assign lexical stress from a default multinomial distribution. (This "default" distribution would handle idiosyncratic stress assignments, as one might see with names or morphologically complex words, like Spanish reflexive verbs.) A sparse prior over these rules, asymmetrically weighted against the default category, will encourage the model to explain as much of the observed stress patterns as possible with a few dominant rules, improving the phonological structure that the segmenter learns.

Improving the realism of the data is also important. The corpora used in much of segmentation research are idealized representations of the true data, and the dictionary-based phoneme and stress patterns used in this study are no exception. This ideal setting may paint a skewed picture of the segmentation problem, by providing a more consistent and learnable data source than humans actually receive. Elsner, Goldwater, and Eisenstein (2012)'s model unifying lexical and phonetic acquisition takes a significant step in showing that a rational segmenter can handle noisy input by recognizing phonetic variants of a base form. In terms of stress representations, dictionary-based stress has been standard in previous work (Christiansen et al., 1998; Gambell & Yang, 2006; Rytting, Brew, & Fosler-Lussier, 2010), but it is important to confirm such results against a (currently nonexistent) corpus with stresses based on the actual utterances. Effective use of stress in a less idealized setting may require a more complex representation of stress in the model.

7 Conclusion

Effective word segmentation combines multiple factors to make predictions about word boundaries. We extended an existing Bayesian segmentation model to account for two factors, phonemes and stress, when segmenting. This improves segmentation performance and opens up new possibilities for comparing rational segmentation and human segmentation.

Acknowledgments

This research was partially supported by an Alfred P. Sloan Fellowship to RL and by NSF award 0830535. We also appreciate the feedback of the reviewers and the members of the UCSD Computational Psycholinguistics Lab.

References

Blanchard, D., & Heinz, J. (2008). Improving word segmentation by simultaneously learning phonotactics. In *Proceedings of CoNLL* (pp. 65–72).

Borfeld, H., Morgan, J., Golinkoff, R., & Rathbun, K. (2005). Mommy and me: familiar names help launch babies into speech-stream segmentation. *Psychological Science*, *16*(4), 298–304.

Brent, M. R. (1999). An efficient, probabilistically sound algorithm for segmentation and word discovery. *Machine Learning*, *34*, 71–105.

Christiansen, M. H., Allen, J., & Seidenberg, M. S. (1998). Learning to segment speech using multiple cues: A connectionist model. *Language and Cognitive Processes*, *13*, 221–268.

Cole, R., & Jakimik, J. (1980). A model of speech perception. In *Perception and production of fluent speech* (pp. 136–163). Hillsdale, NJ: Erlbaum.

Cutler, A., & Carter, D. (1987). The predominance of strong initial syllables in the English vocabulary. *Comp. Speech Lang.*, *2*, 133–142.

Eimas, P. (1999). Segmental and syllabic representations in the perception of speech by young infants. *Journal of the Acoustic Society of America*, *105*, 1901–1911.

Elsner, M., Goldwater, S., & Eisenstein, J. (2012). Bootstrapping a unified model of lexical and phonetic acquisition. In *Proceedings of the 50th annual meeting of the ACL.*

Feldman, N., Griffiths, T., & Morgan, J. (2009). Learning phonetic categories by learning a lexicon. In *Proceedings of the 31st annual conference on cognitive science.*

Frank, M., Goldwater, S., Griffiths, T., & Tenenbaum, J. (2010). Modeling human performance in statistical word segmentation. *Cognition.*

Frank, M., Goodman, N., & Tenenbaum, J. (2009). Using speakers' referential intentions to model early cross-situational word learning. *Psychological Science*, *20*, 579–585.

Gambell, T., & Yang, C. (2006). *Word segmentation: Quick but not dirty.* (Unpublished manuscript)

Goldwater, S. (2007). *Nonparametric Bayesian models of lexical acquisition.* Unpublished doctoral dissertation, Brown Univ.

Goldwater, S., Griffiths, T., & Johnson, M. (2006). Contextual dependencies in unsupervised word segmentation. In *Proceedings of Coling/ACL.*

Goldwater, S., Griffiths, T. L., & Johnson, M. (2009). A Bayesian framework for word segmentation: Exploring the effects of context. *Cognition*, *112*, 21–54.

Johnson, E., & Jusczyk, P. (2001). Word segmentation by 8-month-olds: When speech cues count more than statistics. *J. of Memory and Language*, *44*, 548–567.

Jusczyk, P., Cutler, A., & Redanz, N. (1993). Preference for predominant stress patterns of English words. *Child Development*, *64*, 675–687.

Jusczyk, P., Houston, D., & Newsome, M. (1999). The beginnings of word segmentation in English-learning infants. *Cognitive Psychology*, *39*, 159–207.

Korman, M. (1984). Adaptive aspects of maternal vocalizations in differing contexts at ten weeks. *First language*, *5*, 44–45.

Maurits, L., Perfors, A., & Navarro, D. (2009). Joint acquisition of word order and word reference. In *Proceedings of 31st annual conference of the Cognitive Science Society.*

Peters, A. (1983). *The units of language acqui-*

sition: Monographs in applied psycholinguistics. Cambridge Univ. Press.

Phillips, L., & Pearl, L. (2012). "less is more" in Bayesian word segmentation: When cognitively plausible learners outperform the ideal. In *Proceedings of the 34th annual conference of the cognitive science society.*

Rytting, C. A., Brew, C., & Fosler-Lussier, E. (2010). Segmenting words from natural speech: subsegmental variation in segmental cues. *Journal of Child Language*, *37*, 513–543.

Swingley, D. (2005). Statistical clustering and the contents of the infant vocabulary. *Cognitive Psychology*, *50*, 86–132.

Thiessen, E. D., & Saffran, J. R. (2003). When cues collide: Use of stress and statistical cues to word boundaries by 7- to 9-month-old infants. *Developmental Psychology*, *39*(4), 706–716.

Werker, J., & Tees, R. (1984). Cross-language speech perception: Evidence for perceptual reorganization during the first year of life. *Infant Behavior and Development*, *7*, 49–63.

Training Parsers on Incompatible Treebanks

Richard Johansson
Språkbanken, Department of Swedish, University of Gothenburg
Box 200, SE-40530 Gothenburg, Sweden
richard.johansson@gu.se

Abstract

We consider the problem of training a statistical parser in the situation when there are multiple treebanks available, and these treebanks are annotated according to different linguistic conventions. To address this problem, we present two simple adaptation methods: the first method is based on the idea of using a shared feature representation when parsing multiple treebanks, and the second method on guided parsing where the output of one parser provides features for a second one.
To evaluate and analyze the adaptation methods, we train parsers on treebank pairs in four languages: German, Swedish, Italian, and English. We see significant improvements for all eight treebanks when training on the full training sets. However, the clearest benefits are seen when we consider smaller training sets. Our experiments were carried out with unlabeled dependency parsers, but the methods can easily be generalized to other feature-based parsers.

1 Introduction

When developing a data-driven syntactic parser, we need to fit the parameters of its statistical model on a collection of syntactically annotated sentences – a *treebank*. Generally speaking, a larger collection of examples in the training treebank will give a higher quality of the resulting parser, but the cost in time and effort of annotating training sentences is fairly high. Most existing treebanks are in the range of a few thousand sentences.

However, there is an abundance of theoretical models of syntax and there is no consensus on how treebanks should be annotated. For some languages, there exist multiple treebanks annotated according to different syntactic theories. Apart from German, Swedish, and Italian, which will be considered in this paper, there are important examples among the world's major languages, such as Arabic and Chinese.

To exemplify how syntactic annotation conventions may differ in even such a simple case as unlabeled dependency annotation, consider the Italian sentence fragment *la sospensione o l'interruzione* ('the suspension or the interruption') in Figure 1. As we will see in detail in §3.1.3, there are two Italian treebanks: the ISST and TUT. If annotating as in the ISST treebank (drawn above the sentence) determiners (*la, l'*) are annotated as dependents of the following nouns (*sospensione, interruzione*); in TUT (drawn below the sentence), we have the reverse situation. There are also differences in how coordinate structures are represented: in ISST, the two conjuncts are directly conjoined and the conjunction attached to the first of them, while in TUT the conjunction acts as a link between the conjuncts.

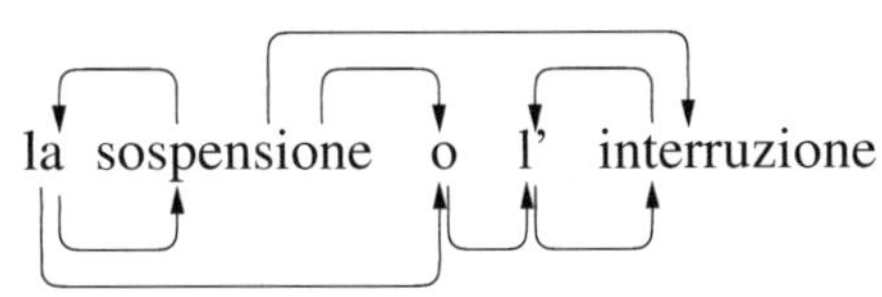

Figure 1: Differences in dependency annotation styles.

Given the high cost of treebank annotation and the importance of a proper amount of data for parser development, this situation is frustrating. How could we then make use of multiple treebanks when training a parser? A naïve way would be simply to concatenate them, but as we will see this results in a parser that performs badly on all the treebanks.

In this paper, we investigate two simple adaptation methods to bridge the gap between differing syntactic annotation styles, allowing us to use more data for parser training. The first approach treats the problem of parsing with multiple syntactic annotation styles as a multiview learning problem and addresses it by using feature representation that is partly shared between the views. In the second one we use a parser trained on one treebank to guide a new parser trained on another treebank. We evaluate these methods as well as their combination on four languages: German, Swedish, Italian, and English. In all four languages, we see a similar picture: the shared features approach is generally better when one of the treebanks is very small, while the guided parsing approach is better when the treebanks are more similar in size. However, for most training set sizes the combination of the the two methods achieves a higher performance than either of them individually.

2 Methods for Training Parsers on Multiple Treebanks

We now describe the two adaptation methods to leverage multiple treebanks for parser training. For clarity of presentation, we assume that there are two treebanks, although we can easily generalize to more. We use a common graph-based parsing technique (Carreras, 2007); the approaches described here could be used in transition-based parsing as well.

In a graph-based parser, for a given sentence x the task of finding the top-scoring parse $\hat{y}$ is stated as an optimization problem of maximizing a linear objective function:

$$\hat{y} = \arg\max_{y} w \cdot f(x, y).$$

Here w is a weight vector produced by some learning algorithm and $f(x, y)$ a *feature representation* that maps the sentence x with a parse tree y to a high-dimensional vector; the adaptation methods presented in this work is implemented as modifications of the feature representation function f. Since the search space is too large to be enumerated, the maximization must be handled carefully, and how this is done determines the expressivity of the feature representation f. In the parser by Carreras (2007) the maximization is carried out by a dynamic programming procedure relying on crucial independence assumptions to break down the search space into tractable parts. The factorization used in this approach allows f to express features extracted not only from single edges, as McDonald et al. (2005), but also from sibling and grandchild edges.

To understand the machine learning problem of training parsers on incompatible treebanks, we compare it to the related problem of domain adaptation: training a system for a target domain, using a large collection of training data from a source domain combined with a small labeled or large unlabeled set from the target domain. Some algorithms for domain adaptation rely on the assumption that the differences between source and target distributions P_s and P_t can be explained in terms of a *covariate shift*: $P_s(y|x) = P_t(y|x)$ for all x, y, but $P_s(x) \neq P_t(x)$ for some x. In our case, we have the reverse situation: the input distribution is at least in theory unchanged between the two treebanks, while the input–output relation (i.e. the treebank annotation style) is different. However, domain adaptation and cross-treebank training can be seen as instances of the more general problem of *multitask learning* (Caruana, 1997). Indeed, one of the simplest and most well-known approaches to domain adaptation (Daumé III, 2007), which will also be considered in this paper, should more correctly be seen as a trick to handle multitask learning with any machine learning algorithm. On the other hand, there is no point in trying to use domain adaptation methods assuming a covariate shift, e.g. instance weighting, or any method in which the target data is unlabeled (Blitzer et al., 2007; Ben-David et al., 2010).

2.1 Sharing Feature Representations

Our first adaptation method relies on the intuition that some properties of two treebanks are shared, while others are unique to each of them. For instance, as we have seen in Figure 1 the two Italian treebanks annotate coordination differently; on the other hand, these treebanks also annotate several other linguistic phenomena in the same way. This observation can then be used to devise a model where we train two parsers at the same time and use a feature representation that is partly shared between the two models, allowing the machine learning algorithm to automatically determine which properties of the two datasets are common and which are different. The idea of using features that are shared between the source and target training sets is a slight generalization of a well-known method for supervised domain adaptation (Daumé III, 2007).

In practice, this is implemented as follows. Assume that originally a sentence x with a parse tree y was represented as $f_1(x, y)$ if it came from the first treebank, and $f_2(x, y)$ if from the second treebank. We then add a *shared feature representation* f_s to f_1 and f_2, and embed them into a single feature space. The resulting feature vectors then become

$$f_1(x, y) \oplus \mathbf{0}_2 \oplus f_s(x, y) \quad (1)$$

for a sentence from the first treebank, and

$$\mathbf{0}_1 \oplus f_2(x, y) \oplus f_s(x, y) \quad (2)$$

for the second treebank. Here, $\mathbf{0}_1$ means an all-zero vector with the dimensionality of the feature space of f_1, and $\oplus$ is vector concatenation. Using this new representation, the two datasets are combined and a single model trained. The hope is then that the learning algorithm will store the information about the respective particularities in the weights for f_1 and f_2, and about the commonalities in the weights for f_s. The result of this process is a symmetric parser that can handle both treebank formats: when we parse a sentence at test time, we just use the representation (1) if we want an output according to the first treebank and (2) for the second treebank.

In this work, f_1, f_2, and f_s are identical: all of them correspond to the feature set described by Carreras (2007). However, it is certainly imaginable that f_s could consist of specially tailored features that make generalization easier. In particular, using a generalized f_s would allow us to use this approach in more complex cases than considered here, for instance if the dependencies would be labeled with two different sets of grammatical function labels, or if one of the treebanks would use constituents rather than dependencies.

2.2 Using One Parser to Guide Another

The second method is inspired by work in parser combination, an idea that has been applied successfully several times and relies on the fact that different parsing methods have different strengths and weaknesses (McDonald and Nivre, 2007), so that combining them may result in a better overall parsing accuracy. There are several ways to combine parsers; one of the simplest and most successful methods of parsing combination uses one parser as a *guide* for a second parser. This is normally implemented as a pipeline where the second parser extracts features based on the output of the first parser. Nivre and McDonald (2008) used this approach for combining a graph-based and a transition-based parser and achieved excellent results on test sets for several languages, and similar ideas were proposed by Martins et al. (2008).

We added guide features to the parser feature representation. However, the features by Nivre and McDonald (2008) are slightly too simple since they only describe whether two words are directly connected or not. That makes sense if the two parsers are trying to predict the same type of representation, but will not help us if there are systematic annotation differences between the two treebanks, for instance in whether to annotate a function word or a lexical word as the head. Instead, following work in semantic role labeling and similar areas, we use a generalized notion of syntactic relationship that we encode by determining a *path* between two nodes in a syntactic tree. We defined the function Path(x, y) as a representation describing the steps required to traverse the parse tree from x to y, first the steps up from x to the common ancestor a and then down from a to y. Since we are working with unlabeled trees, the path can be represented as just two integers; to generalize to labeled dependency parsing, we could have used a full path representation as commonly used in dependency-based semantic role labeling (Johansson and Nugues, 2008).

We added the following path-based feature templates, assuming we have a potential head h with dependent d, a sibling dependent s and grandchild (dependent-of-dependent) g:

- POS(h)+POS(d)+Path(h, d)
- POS(h)+POS(s)+Path(h, s)
- POS(h)+POS(d)+POS(s)+Path(h, s)
- POS(h)+POS(g)+Path(h, g)
- POS(h)+POS(d)+POS(g)+Path(h, g)

To exemplify, consider again the example *la sospensione o l'interruzione* shown in Figure 1. Assume that we are parsing according to the ISST representation (drawn above the sentence) and we consider adding an edge with *sospensione* as head and *la* as dependent, and another parser following the TUT representation (below the sentence) has created an edge in the opposite direction. The first feature template above would then result in a feature NOUN+DET+(1,0), where (1,0) represents the path relationship between the two words in the TUT tree (one step up, no step down). Similarly, when the ISST parser adds the coordination edge between *sospensione* and *interruzione*, it can make use of the information that these two nouns are *indirectly* connected in the output by the TUT parser; this is represented as a path (1,3). This is an example of a situation where we have a systematic correspondence where a single edge in one representation corresponds to several edges in the other.

Like the multiview approach described above, this method is trivially adaptable to more complex situations such as labeled dependency parsers with differing label sets, or dependency/constituent parsing.

2.3 Combining Methods

The two adaptation methods are orthogonal and can easily be combined. When trying to improve the performance of a parser trained on the primary treebank T_1 by leveraging a supporting treebank T_2, we then use T_2 in two different ways: first by training a guide parser, and secondly by concatenating it to T_1 using a shared feature representation.

3 Experiments

We carried out experiments to evaluate the cross-framework adaptation methods. The evaluations were carried out using the official CoNLL-X evaluation script using the default parameters. Since our parsers do not predict edge labels, we report unlabeled attachment scores in all tables and plots.

3.1 Treebanks Used in the Experiments

In our experiments, we used four languages: German, Swedish, Italian, and English. For each language, we had two treebanks. Our approaches currently require that the treebanks use the same tokenization conventions, so for Italian and Swedish we automatically retokenized the treebanks. We also made sure that the two treebanks for one language used the same part-of-speech tag sets, by applying an automatic tagger when necessary.

3.1.1 German: Tiger and TüBa-D/Z

For German, there are two treebanks available: Tiger (Brants et al., 2002) and TüBa-D/Z (Telljohann et al., 2004). These treebanks are constituent treebanks, but dependency versions are available: TüBa-D/Z (version 7.0) includes the dependency version in the distribution, while for Tiger we used the version from CoNLL-X (Buchholz and Marsi, 2006). The constituent annotation styles in the two treebanks are radically different: Tiger uses a very flat structure with a minimal amount of intermediate nodes, while TüBa-D/Z uses a more elaborate structure including topological field information. However, the dependency versions are actually quite similar, at least with respect to attachment. The most common systematic difference we observed is in the annotation of coordination.

Both treebanks are large: for Tiger, the training set was 31,243 sentences and the test set 7,973 sentences, and for TüBa-D/Z 40,000 and 11,428 sentences respectively. We did not use the Tiger test set from the CoNLL-X shared task since it is very small. We applied the TreeTagger POS tagger (Schmid, 1994) to both treebanks, using the pre-trained German model.

3.1.2 Swedish: Talbanken05 and Syntag

As previously noted by Nivre (2002) *inter alia*, Swedish has a venerable tradition in treebanking: there are not only one but two treebanks which must be counted among the earliest efforts of that kind. The oldest one is the Talbanken or MAMBA treebank (Einarsson, 1976), which has later been reprocessed for modern use (Nilsson et al., 2005). The original annotation is a function-tagged constituent syntax without phrase labels, but the reprocessed release includes a version converted to dependency syntax. The dependency treebank was used in the CoNLL-X Shared Task (Buchholz and Marsi, 2006), and we used that version version in this work.

The second treebank is called Syntag (Järborg, 1986). Similar to Talbanken, its representation uses function-tagged constituents but no phrase labels. We developed a conversion to dependency trees, which was straightforward since many constituents have explicitly defined heads (Johansson, 2013).

The two treebank annotation styles have significant differences. Most prominently, the Syntag annotation is fairly semantically oriented in its treatment of function words such as prepositions and subordinating conjunctions: in Talbanken, a preposition is the head of a prepositional phrase, while in Syntag the head is the prepositional complement. There are also some domain differences: Talbanken consists of student essays and public information, while Syntag consists of news text.

To make the two treebanks compatible on the token level, we retokenized Syntag – which handles punctuation in an idiosyncratic way – and applied a POS tagger trained on the Stockholm–Umeå Corpus (Gustafson-Capková and Hartmann, 2006) to both treebanks. For Talbanken, we used 7,362 sentences for training and set aside a new test set of 3,680 sentences since the CoNLL-X test set is too small for serious experimental purposes – only 389 sentences. For Syntag, we split the treebank into 3,524 sentences for training and 1,763 sentences for testing.

3.1.3 Italian: ISST and TUT

There are two Italian treebanks. The first is the Italian Syntactic–Semantic Treebank or ISST (Montemagni et al., 2003). Here, we used the version that was prepared (Montemagni and Simi, 2007) for the CoNLL-2007 Shared Task (Nivre et al., 2007).

The TUT treebank[1] is a more recent effort. This treebank is available in multiple constituent and dependency formats, and we have used the CoNLL-formatted dependency version in this work. The representation used in TUT is inspired by the Word Grammar theory (Hudson, 1984) and tends to be more surface-oriented than that of ISST. For instance, as pointed out above in the discussion of Figure 1, TUT differs from ISST in its treatment of determiner–noun constructions and coordination. It has been noted (Bosco and Lavelli, 2010; Bosco et al., 2010) that the TUT representation is easier to parse than the ISST representation.

We simplified the tokenization of both treebanks. In ISST, we split multiwords into separate tokens and reattached clitics to nonfinite verb forms. For instance, a single token *a_causa_di* was converted into three tokens *a, causa, di*, and the three tokens *trovar-se-lo* into a single token *trovarselo*. In TUT, we applied the same conversions and also recomposed preposition–article and multiple-clitic contractions that had been split by the annotators, e.g. *della, glielo* etc.[2] After changing the tokenization, we applied the TreeTagger POS tagger (Schmid, 1994) to both treebanks, using the pre-trained Italian model with the Baroni tagset[3].

After preprocessing the data, we created training and test sets. For ISST, the training set was 2,239 and the test set 1,120 sentences, while for TUT the training set was 1,906 and the test set 954 sentences.

3.1.4 English: Two Different Conversions of the Penn Treebank

For English, there is no significant dependency treebank so we followed most previous work in using dependency trees automatically derived from constituent trees in the large Penn Treebank WSJ corpus (Marcus et al., 1993). Due to the fact that there is a highly parametrizable constituent-to-dependency conversion tool available (Johansson and Nugues, 2007), we could create two dependency treebanks with very different annotation styles.

The first training set was created from sections 02–12 of the WSJ corpus. By default, the conversion tool outputs a treebank using the annotation style of the CoNLL-2008 Shared Task (Surdeanu et al., 2008); however we wanted to create a more surface-oriented style for this treebank, so we turned on options to make *wh*-words heads of relative clauses, and possessive markers heads of noun phrases. This corpus had 20,706 sentences, and will be referred to as WSJ Part 1 in the experimental section.

The second training treebank was built from sections 13–22. For this treebank, we inverted the value of most options in order to get a more semantically oriented treebank where content words are connected directly. In this treebank, we also used "Prague-style" annotation of coordination: the conjuncts are annotated as dependents of the conjunction. This set contained 20,826 sentences, and will

[1] http://www.di.unito.it/~tutreeb/

[2] It should be noted that these conversions also make sense from a practical NLP point of view, since a number of contractions are homonymic with other words.

[3] http://sslmit.unibo.it/~baroni/collocazioni/itwac.tagset.txt

be called WSJ Part 2.

We finally applied both conversion methods to sections 24 and 23 to create development and test sets. The development set contained 1,346 and the test set 2,416 sentences. We did not change the tokenization or part-of-speech tags of the WSJ corpora. Here, we should note that we have a slightly more synthetic and controlled experimental setting than for Swedish and German: the parsers are evaluated on the same test set, so we know that there is no difference in test set difficulty. We also know *a priori* that performance differences are not due to any significant differences in genre, since all texts come from the same source (the Wall Street Journal) and tend to focus on business-oriented news.

3.2 Baseline Parsing Performance

As a starting point, we trained parsers on all treebanks. In addition, we created a parser using a naïve adaptation method by combining the training sets for each language, and training parsers on those three sets. We then applied all three parsers for every language on both test sets for that language. The results for German, Swedish, Italian, and English are presented in Table 1.

Every parser performed well on the test set annotated in the same annotation style as its training set. As has been observed previously, surface-oriented styles are easier to parse than semantically oriented styles: The Talbanken and WSJ Part 1 parsers all achieve much higher performance on their respective test sets than the Syntag and WSJ Part 2 parsers. The better performance of the Talbanken parser is also partly explainable by the fact that its training set is more than twice as large as the Syntag training set. Similarly for German, we see slightly higher performance for TüBa-D/Z than for Tiger.

However, as can be expected every parser performed very poorly when applied to the test set using the annotation style it was not trained on. For Swedish and English, the accuracy figures are in the range of 50-60, while the figure are a bit less poor for German since the two treebanks are more similar. We also see, again unsurprisingly, that the naïve combination baseline performs poorly in all situations: we just get a "worst-of-both-worlds" parser that performs badly on both test sets.

GERMAN	Acc. on Tiger	Acc. on TBDZ
Tiger	87.8	72.0
TüBa-D/Z	71.8	89.4
Tiger+TBDZ	77.7	87.7

SWEDISH	Acc. on ST	Acc. on TB
Syntag	81.4	52.6
Talbanken	50.3	88.2
Syntag+Talbanken	61.8	82.7

ITALIAN	Acc. on ISST	Acc. on TUT
ISST	81.1	57.4
TUT	55.9	84.0
ISST+TUT	73.9	71.6

ENGLISH	Acc. on WSJ 1	Acc. on WSJ 2
WSJ part 1	92.6	57.4
WSJ part 2	57.4	89.5
WSJ parts 1+2	75.3	72.1

Table 1: Baseline performance figures.

3.3 Evaluation on the Full Training Sets

We trained new parsers using the shared features and guided parsing adaptation methods described in §2. Additionally, we trained parsers using both methods at the same time; we refer to these parsers as *combined*. Including the baseline parsers, this gave us 24 parsers to evaluate on their respective test sets.

The results for German are given in Table 2. Here, we see that all three adaptation methods give statistically significant[4] improvements over the baseline when parsing the Tiger treebank. In particular, the combined method gives a strong 0.7-point improvement, a 6% error reduction. For TüBa-D/Z, the improvements are smaller, although still significant except for the guided parsing method.

Method	Acc. on Tiger	Acc. on TüBa-D/Z
Baseline	87.8	89.4
Shared	**88.1**	**89.6**
Guided	**88.4**	89.5
Combined	**88.5**	**89.6**

Table 2: Performance figures for the German adapted parsers. Results that are significantly different from the baseline performances are written in boldface.

[4]At the 95% level. The significance levels of differences were computed using permutation tests.

Method	Acc. on ST	Acc. on TB
Baseline	81.4	88.2
Shared	81.3	88.3
Guided	**82.5**	**88.4**
Combined	**82.5**	**88.5**

Table 3: Performance of the Swedish adapted parsers.

For Swedish, we have a similar story: we see stronger improvements in the weak parser. Since the Talbanken treebank is twice as large as the Syntag treebank and has a surface-oriented representation that is easier to parse, this parser is useful as a guide for the Syntag parser: the improvements of the guided and combined Syntag parsers are statistically significant. However, it is harder to improve the Talbanken parser, for which the baseline is much stronger. 3 shows the results for the Swedish parsers.

Method	Acc. on ISST	Acc. on TUT
Baseline	81.1	84.0
Shared	**81.5**	**84.4**
Guided	**81.7**	**84.3**
Combined	**81.8**	**84.7**

Table 4: Performance of the Italian adapted parsers.

When we turn to the English corpora, the adaptation methods again gave us a number of very large improvements. The results are shown in Table 5. The shared features and combined methods gave statistically significant improvements for the WSJ Part 1 parser, and the guided parsing method an improvement that is nearly significant. However the most dramatic change is the 1.2-point improvement of the WSJ Part 2 parser, given by the guided parsing and combined methods. It is possible that this result partly can be explained by the fact that this experiment is a bit cleaner: in particular, as outlined in §3.1.4, there are no domain differences.

Method	Acc. on WSJ 1	Acc. on WSJ 2
Baseline	92.6	89.5
Shared	**92.8**	89.5
Guided	92.8	**90.7**
Combined	**92.9**	**90.7**

Table 5: Performance of the English adapted parsers.

For WSJ Part 2, we analyzed the differences between the baseline and the best adapted parser. While there were improvements for all POS tags, the most notable one was in the attachment of conjunctions, where we got an increase from 69% to 75% in attachment accuracy, an 18% relative error reduction. Here we saw a very clear benefit of guided parsing: since this treebank uses "Prague-style" coordination annotation (i.e. the conjunction governs the conjuncts), it is hard for the parser to handle valencies and selectional preferences when there is a conjunction involved. It has been noted (Nilsson et al., 2007) that this style of annotating coordination is hard to parse. Since the WSJ Part 1 parser uses a coordination style that is easier to parse, the WSJ Part 2 parser can rely on its judgment.

Although conclusions must be very tentative since we are testing on just four languages, we can make a few general observations.

- The largest improvements (absolute and relative) all happen in treebanks that are harder to parse. In particular, Syntag and WSJ Part 2 are harder to parse due to their representation, and to some extent this may be true for Tiger as well – its learning curve rises more slowly than for TüBa-D/Z. Of course, in some cases (in particular Syntag, but also Tiger) this may partly be explained by the training set being smaller, but not for WSJ Part 2. In these cases, the guided parsing method seems to be more effective.
- The languages where the shared features method gives significant improvement for both treebanks are German and Italian, where we do not have the situation that one treebank is much larger or much easier to parse.
- The combination of the two methods gave significant improvements in all eight cases, and had the highest performance in six cases.

3.4 The Effect of the Training Set Size

In order to better understand the differences between the adaptation methods, we analyzed the impact of training set size on the improvement given by the respective methods. Let us refer to the training treebank annotated according to the same style as the test set as the *primary treebank*, and the other one as the *supporting treebank*. We carried out the experiments in this section by varying the number of

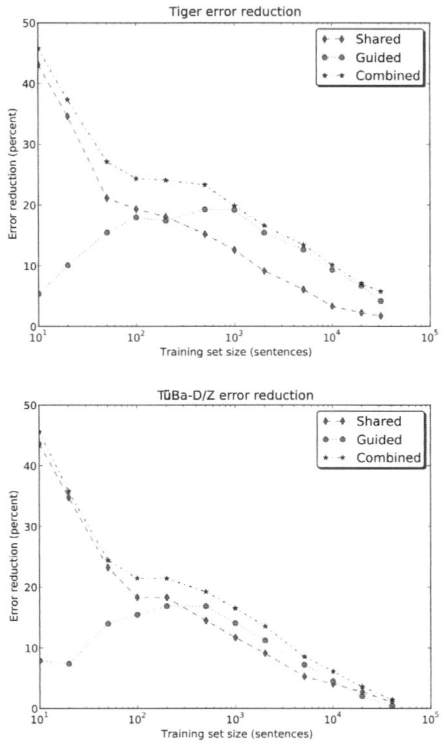

Figure 2: Error reduction by training set size, German.

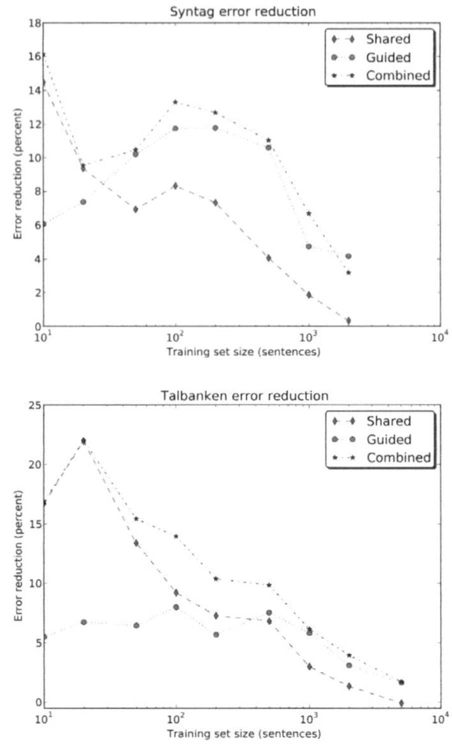

Figure 3: Error reduction by training set size, Swedish.

training sentences in the primary treebank and keeping the size of the supporting treebank constant.

In order to highlight the differences between the three adaptation methods, we show error reduction plots in Figures 2, 3, 4, and 5 for German, Swedish, Italian, and English respectively. For each training set size on the x axis, the plot shows the reduction in relative error with respect to the baseline.

We note that *every single one* of the 24 adapted parsers learns faster than the corresponding baseline parser. While we saw a number of significant improvements in §3.3 when using the full training sets, the relative improvements are much stronger when the training sets are small- and medium-sized.

These plots illustrate the different properties of the two methods. Using a shared feature representation tends to be very effective when the primary treebank is small: the error reductions are over 40 percent for German and over 25 percent for English. Guided parsing works best for mid-sized sets, and the relative effectiveness of both methods decreases as the size of the primary treebank increases. Again, we see that guided parsing is less effective if the guide uses an annotation style that is hard to parse.

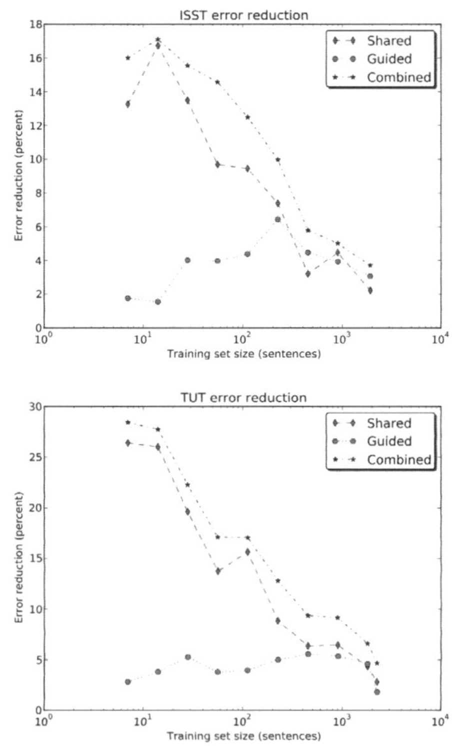

Figure 4: Error reduction by training set size, Italian.

In particular, for Swedish the Syntag parser never gives a very large improvement when guiding the Talbanken parser, and this is also true of both Italian parsers. To a smaller extent, this also holds for English and German: the WSJ Part 2 and Tiger parsers are less useful as guides than their counterparts.

The combination method generally performs very well: in all eight experiments, it outperforms the other two for almost every training set size. Its performance is very close to that of the guided parsing method for larger training sets, when the effect of the shared features method is less pronounced.

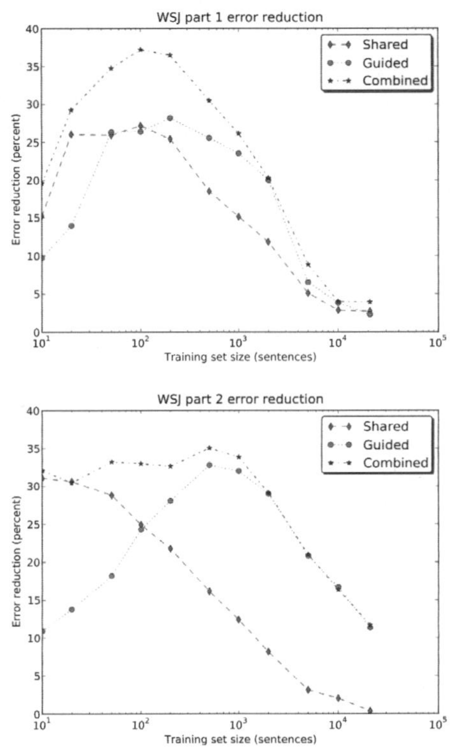

Figure 5: Error reduction by training set size, English.

4 Conclusion

We have considered the problem of training a dependency parser on incompatible treebanks, and we studied two very simple methods for addressing this problem, the shared features and guided parsing methods. These methods allow us to use more than one treebank when training dependency parsers. We evaluated the methods on eight treebanks in four languages, and had statistically significant improvements in all eight cases. In particular, for English we saw a strong 1.2-point absolute improvement (an 11% relative error reduction) in the performance of a semantically oriented parser when trained on the full training set. For German, we also had very strong results for the Tiger treebank: a 6% error reduction. For Swedish, the parser trained on the small Syntag treebank got a boost from a guide parser trained on the larger Talbanken. In general, it seems to be easier to improve parsers that use representations that are harder to parse.

For all eight treebanks, both methods achieved large improvements for small training set sizes, while the effect gradually diminished as the training set size increased. The shared features method was the most effective for very small training sets, while guided parsing surpassed it when training sets got larger. The combination of the two methods was also effective, in most cases outperforming both methods on their own. In particular, when using the full training sets, this was the only method that had statistically significant improvements for all treebanks.

While this work used an unlabeled graph-based dependency parser, our methods generalize naturally to other parsing approaches, including transition-based dependency parsing. Labeled parsing with incompatible label sets is easy to implement in the shared features framework by removing the label information from the shared feature representation f_s, and similar modifications of f_s could be carried out to handle more complex situations such as combined constituent and dependency parsing. Furthermore, the paths used by the feature extractor in the guided parser can be extended without much effort as well. The models presented here are very simple, and in future work we would like to explore more complex approaches such as quasi-synchronous grammars (Smith and Eisner, 2009; Li et al., 2012) or automatic treebank transformation (Niu et al., 2009).

Acknowledgements

I am grateful to the anonymous reviewers, whose feedback has helped to clarify the description of the methods. This research was supported by University of Gothenburg through its support of the Centre for Language Technology and Språkbanken. It has been partly funded by the Swedish Research Council under grant number 2012-5738.

References

Shai Ben-David, John Blitzer, Koby Crammer, Alex Kulesza, Fernando Pereira, and Jennifer Wortman Vaughan. 2010. A theory of learning from different domains. *Machine Learning*, 2010(79):151–175.

John Blitzer, Mark Dredze, and Fernando Pereira. 2007. Biographies, Bollywood, Boom-boxes and Blenders: Domain adaptation for sentiment classification. In *Proceedings of the 45th Annual Meeting of the Association of Computational Linguistics*, pages 440–447, Prague, Czech Republic.

Cristina Bosco and Alberto Lavelli. 2010. Annotation schema oriented validation for dependency parsing evaluation. In *Proceedings of the Ninth Workshop on Treebanks and Linguistic Theories (TLT9)*, Tartu, Estonia.

Cristina Bosco, Simonetta Montemagni, Alessandro Mazzei, Vincenzo Lombardo, Felice Dell'Orletta, Alessandro Lenci, Leonardo Lesmo, Giuseppe Attardi, Maria Simi, Alberto Lavelli, Johan Hall, Jens Nilsson, and Joakim Nivre. 2010. Comparing the influence of different treebank annotations on dependency parsing. In *Proceedings of the Seventh International Conference on Language Resources and Evaluation (LREC'10)*, pages 1794–1801, Valletta, Malta.

Sabine Brants, Stefanie Dipper, Silvia Hansen, Wolfgang Lezius, and George Smith. 2002. The TIGER treebank. In *Proceedings of the Workshop on Treebanks and Linguistic Theory*, pages 24–41, Sozopol, Bulgaria.

Sabine Buchholz and Erwin Marsi. 2006. CoNLL-X shared task on multilingual dependency parsing. In *Proceedings of the Tenth Conference on Computational Natural Language Learning (CoNLL-X)*, pages 149–164, New York City, United States.

Xavier Carreras. 2007. Experiments with a higher-order projective dependency parser. In *Proceedings the CoNLL Shared Task*, pages 957–961, Prague, Czech Republic.

Rich Caruana. 1997. Multitask learning. *Machine Learning*, 28(1):41–75.

Hal Daumé III. 2007. Frustratingly easy domain adaptation. In *Proceedings of the 45th Annual Meeting of the Association of Computational Linguistics*, pages 256–263, Prague, Czech Republic.

Jan Einarsson. 1976. Talbankens skriftspråkskonkordans. Department of Scandinavian Languages, Lund University.

Sofia Gustafson-Capková and Britt Hartmann. 2006. Manual of the Stockholm Umeå Corpus version 2.0. Stockholm University.

Richard Hudson. 1984. *Word Grammar*. Blackwell.

Jerker Järborg. 1986. Manual för syntaggning. Department of Linguistic Computation, University of Gothenburg.

Richard Johansson and Pierre Nugues. 2007. Extended constituent-to-dependency conversion for English. In *NODALIDA 2007 Conference Proceedings*, pages 105–112, Tartu, Estonia.

Richard Johansson and Pierre Nugues. 2008. The effect of syntactic representation on semantic role labeling. In *Proceedings of the 22nd International Conference on Computational Linguistics (Coling 2008)*, pages 393–400, Manchester, United Kingdom.

Richard Johansson. 2013. Bridging the gap between two Swedish treebanks. *Northern European Journal of Language Technology*. Submitted.

Zhenghua Li, Ting Liu, and Wanxiang Che. 2012. Exploiting multiple treebanks for parsing with quasi-synchronous grammars. In *Proceedings of the 50th Annual Meeting of the Association for Computational Linguistics (Volume 1: Long Papers)*, pages 675–684, Jeju Island, Korea.

Mitchell P. Marcus, Beatrice Santorini, and Mary Ann Marcinkiewicz. 1993. Building a large annotated corpus of English: the Penn Treebank. *Computational Linguistics*, 19(2):313–330.

André F. T. Martins, Dipanjan Das, Noah A. Smith, and Eric P. Xing. 2008. Stacking dependency parsers. In *Proceedings of the 2008 Conference on Empirical Methods in Natural Language Processing*, pages 157–166, Honolulu, United States.

Ryan McDonald and Joakim Nivre. 2007. Characterizing the errors of data-driven dependency parsing models. In *Proceedings of the 2007 Joint Conference on Empirical Methods in Natural Language Processing and Computational Natural Language Learning (EMNLP-CoNLL)*, pages 122–131, Prague, Czech Republic.

Ryan McDonald, Koby Crammer, and Fernando Pereira. 2005. Online large-margin training of dependency parsers. In *Proceedings of 43rd Annual Meeting of the Association for Computational Linguistics (ACL'05)*, pages 91–98, Ann Arbor, United States.

Simonetta Montemagni and Maria Simi. 2007. The Italian dependency annotated corpus developed for the CoNLL-2007 shared task. Technical report, ILC-CNR.

Simonetta Montemagni, Francesco Barsotti, Marco Battista, Nicoletta Calzolari, Ornella Corazzari, Alessandro Lenci, Antonio Zampolli, Francesca Fanciulli, Maria Massetani, Remo Raffaelli, Roberto Basili, Maria Teresa Pazienza, Dario Saracino, Fabio Zanzotto, Nadia Mana, Fabio Pianesi, and Rodolfo Delmonte. 2003. Building the Italian Syntactic–Semantic

Treebank. In Anne Abeillé, editor, *Building and Using Syntactically Annotated Corpora*. Kluwer, Dordrecht.

Jens Nilsson, Johan Hall, and Joakim Nivre. 2005. MAMBA meets TIGER: Reconstructing a Swedish treebank from antiquity. In *Proceedings of NODALIDA Special Session on Treebanks*.

Jens Nilsson, Joakim Nivre, and Johan Hall. 2007. Generalizing tree transformations for inductive dependency parsing. In *Proceedings of the 45th Annual Meeting of the Association of Computational Linguistics*, pages 968–975, Prague, Czech Republic.

Zheng-Yu Niu, Haifeng Wang, and Hua Wu. 2009. Exploiting heterogeneous treebanks for parsing. In *Proceedings of the Joint Conference of the 47th Annual Meeting of the ACL and the 4th International Joint Conference on Natural Language Processing of the AFNLP*, pages 46–54, Suntec, Singapore.

Joakim Nivre and Ryan McDonald. 2008. Integrating graph-based and transition-based dependency parsers. In *Proceedings of ACL-08: HLT*, pages 950–958, Columbus, United States.

Joakim Nivre, Johan Hall, Sandra Kübler, Ryan McDonald, Jens Nilsson, Sebastian Riedel, and Deniz Yuret. 2007. The CoNLL 2007 shared task on dependency parsing. In *Proceedings of the CoNLL Shared Task Session of EMNLP-CoNLL 2007*, pages 915–932, Prague, Czech Republic.

Joakim Nivre. 2002. What kinds of trees grow in Swedish soil? A comparison of four annotation schemes for Swedish. In *Proceedings of the First Workshop on Treebanks and Linguistic Theories (TLT2002)*, Sozopol, Bulgaria.

Helmut Schmid. 1994. Probabilistic part-of-speech tagging using decision trees. In *Proceedings of International Conference on New Methods in Language Processing*, Manchester, United Kingdom.

David A. Smith and Jason Eisner. 2009. Parser adaptation and projection with quasi-synchronous grammar features. In *Proceedings of the 2009 Conference on Empirical Methods in Natural Language Processing*, pages 822–831, Suntec, Singapore.

Mihai Surdeanu, Richard Johansson, Adam Meyers, Lluís Màrquez, and Joakim Nivre. 2008. The CoNLL-2008 shared task on joint parsing of syntactic and semantic dependencies. In *CoNLL 2008: Proceedings of the Twelfth Conference on Natural Language Learning*, pages 159–177, Manchester, United Kingdom.

Heike Telljohann, Erhard Hinrichs, and Sandra Kbler. 2004. The Tüba-D/Z treebank: Annotating German with a context-free backbone. In *In Proceedings of the Fourth International Conference on Language Resources and Evaluation (LREC 2004)*, pages 2229–2235.

Learning a Part-of-Speech Tagger from Two Hours of Annotation

Dan Garrette
Department of Computer Science
The University of Texas at Austin
dhg@cs.utexas.edu

Jason Baldridge
Department of Linguistics
The University of Texas at Austin
jbaldrid@utexas.edu

Abstract

Most work on weakly-supervised learning for part-of-speech taggers has been based on unrealistic assumptions about the amount and quality of training data. For this paper, we attempt to create true low-resource scenarios by allowing a linguist just two hours to annotate data and evaluating on the languages Kinyarwanda and Malagasy. Given these severely limited amounts of either type supervision (tag dictionaries) or token supervision (labeled sentences), we are able to dramatically improve the learning of a hidden Markov model through our method of automatically generalizing the annotations, reducing noise, and inducing word-tag frequency information.

1 Introduction

The high performance achieved by part-of-speech (POS) taggers trained on plentiful amounts of labeled word tokens is a success story of computational linguistics (Manning, 2011). However, research on learning taggers using type supervision (e.g. tag dictionaries or morphological transducers) has had a more checkered history. The setting is a seductive one: by labeling the possible parts-of-speech for high frequency words, one might learn accurate taggers by incorporating the type information as constraints to a semi-supervised generative learning model like a hidden Markov model (HMM). Early work showed much promise for this strategy (Kupiec, 1992; Merialdo, 1994), but successive efforts in recent years have continued to peel away and address layers of unrealistic assumptions about the size, coverage, and quality of the tag dictionaries that had been used (Toutanova and Johnson, 2008; Ravi and Knight, 2009; Hasan and Ng, 2009; Garrette and Baldridge, 2012). This paper attempts to strip away further layers so we can build better intuitions about the effectiveness of type-supervised and token-supervised strategies in a realistic setting of POS-tagging for low-resource languages.

In most previous work, tag dictionaries are extracted from a corpus of annotated tokens. To explore the type-supervised scenario, these have been used as a proxy for dictionaries produced by linguists. However, this overstates their effectiveness. Researchers have often manually *pruned* tag dictionaries by removing low-frequency word/tag pairs; this violates the assumption that frequency information is not available. Others have also created tag dictionaries by extracting every word/tag pair in a large, labeled corpus, *including the test data*—even though actual applications would never have such complete lexical knowledge. Dictionaries extracted from corpora are also biased towards including only the most likely tag for each word type, resulting in a cleaner dictionary than one would find in real scenario. Finally, tag dictionaries extracted from annotated tokens benefit from the annotation process of labeling *and* review *and* refinement over an extended collaboration period. Such high quality annotations are simply not available for most low-resource languages.

This paper describes an approach to learning a POS-tagger that can be applied in a truly low-resource scenario. Specifically, we discuss techniques that allow us to learn a tagger given only the amount of labeled data that a human annotator could provide in *two hours*. Here, we evaluate on the languages Malagasy and Kinyarwanda, as well as English as a control language. Furthermore, we are interested in whether type-supervision or token-supervision is more effective, given the strict time constraint; accordingly, we had annotators produce both a tag dictionary and a set of labeled sentences.

The data produced under our conditions differs in several ways from the labeled data used in previous work. Most obviously, there is less of it. Instead of using hundreds of thousands of labeled tokens to construct a tag dictionary (and hundreds of thousands more as unlabeled (raw) data for training), we only use the 1k-2k labeled tokens or types provided by our annotators within the timeframe. Our training data is also much noisier than the data from a typical corpus: the annotations were produced by a single non-native-speaker working alone for two hours. Therefore, dealing with the size and quality of training data were core challenges to our task.

To learn a POS-tagger from so little labeled data, we developed an approach that starts by generalizing the initial annotations to the entire raw corpus. Our approach uses label propagation (LP) (Talukdar and Crammer, 2009) to infer tag distributions on unlabeled tokens. We then apply a novel *weighted* variant of the model minimization procedure originally developed by Ravi and Knight (2009) to estimate sequence and word-tag frequency information from an unlabeled corpus by approximating the minimal set of tag bigrams needed to explain the data. This combination of techniques turns a tiny, unweighted, initial tag dictionary into a weighted tag dictionary that covers the entire corpus's vocabulary. This weighted information limits the potential damage of tag dictionary noise and bootstraps frequency information to approximate a good starting point for the learning of an HMM using expectation-maximization (EM), and far outperforms just using EM on the raw annotations themselves.

2 Data

Our experiments use Kinyarwanda (KIN), Malagasy (MLG), and English (ENG). KIN is a Niger-Congo language spoken in Rwanda. MLG is an Austronesian language spoken in Madagascar. Both KIN and MLG are low-resource and KIN is morphologically-rich. For each language, the word tokens are divided into four sets: training data to be labeled by annotators, raw training data, development data, and test data. For consistency, we use 100k raw tokens for each language.

Data sources For ENG, we used the Penn Treebank (PTB) (Marcus et al., 1993). Sections 00-04 were used as raw data, 05-14 as a dev set, and 15-24 (473K tokens) as a test set. The PTB uses 45 distinct POS tags. The KIN texts are transcripts of testimonies by survivors of the Rwandan genocide provided by the Kigali Genocide Memorial Center. The MLG texts are articles from the websites[1] *Lakroa* and *La Gazette* and Malagasy Global Voices,[2] a citizen journalism site.[3] Texts in both KIN and MLG were tokenized and labeled with POS tags by two linguistics graduate students, each of which was studying one of the languages. The KIN and MLG data have 14 and 24 distinct POS tags, respectively, and were developed by the annotators.

Time-bounded annotation One of our main goals is to evaluate POS-tagging for low-resource languages in experiments that correspond better to a real-world scenario than previous work. As such, we collected two forms of annotation, each constrained by a two-hour time limit. The annotations were done by the same linguists who had annotated the KIN and MLG data mentioned above. Our experiments are thus relevant to the reasonable context in which one has access to a linguist who is familiar with the target language and a given set of POS tags.

The first annotation task was to directly produce a dictionary of words to their possible POS tags—i.e., collecting an actual tag dictionary of the form that is typically *simulated* in POS-tagging experiments. For each language, we compiled a list of word types, ordered starting with most frequent, and presented it to the annotator with a list of admissible POS tags. The annotator had two hours to specify POS tags for as many words as possible. The word types and frequencies used for this task were taken from the raw training data and did not include the test sets. This

[1] www.lakroa.mg and www.lagazette-dgi.com

[2] mg.globalvoicesonline.org/

[3] The public-domain data is available at github.com/dhgarrette/low-resource-pos-tagging-2013

data is used for what will call *type-supervised* training. The second task was annotating full sentences with POS tags, again for two hours. We refer to this as *token-supervised* training.

Having both sets of annotations allows us to investigate the relative value of each with respect to training taggers. Token-supervision provides valuable frequency and tag context information, but type-supervision produces larger dictionaries. This can be seen in Table 1, where the dictionary size column in the table gives the number of unique word/tag pairs derived from the data.

We also wanted to directly compare the two annotators to see how the differences in their relative annotation speeds and quality would affect the overall ability to learn an accurate tagger. We thus had them complete the same two tasks for English. As can be seen in Table 1, there are clear differences between the two annotators. Most notably, annotator B was faster at annotating full sentences while annotator A was faster at annotating word types.

	sent.	tok.	dict.
KIN human sentences A	90	1537	750
KIN human TD A			1798
MLG human sentences B	92	1805	666
MLG human TD B			1067
ENG human sentences A	86	1897	903
ENG human TD A			1644
ENG human sentences B	107	2650	959
ENG human TD B			1090

Table 1: Statistics for Kinyarwanda, Malagasy, and English data annotated by annotators A and B.

3 Approach

Our approach to learning POS-taggers is based on Garrette and Baldridge (2012), which properly separated test data from learning data, unlike much previous work. The input to our system is a raw corpus and either a human-generated tag dictionary or human-tagged sentences. The majority of the system is the same for both kinds of labeled training data, but the following description will point out differences. The system has four main parts, in order:

1. Tag dictionary expansion
2. Weighted model minimization
3. Expectation maximization (EM) HMM training
4. MaxEnt Markov Model (MEMM) training

3.1 Tag dictionary expansion

In a low-resource setting, most word types will not be found in the initial tag dictionary. EM-HMM training uses the tag dictionary to limit ambiguity, so a sparse tag dictionary is problematic because it does not sufficiently confine the parameter space.[4] Small dictionaries also interact poorly with the model minimization of Ravi et al. (2010): if there are too many unknown words, and every tag must be considered for them, then the minimal model will simply be the one that assumes that they all have the same tag.

For these reasons, we automatically *expand* an initial small dictionary into one that has coverage for most of the vocabulary. We use label propagation (LP)—specifically, the Modified Adsorption (MAD) algorithm (Talukdar and Crammer, 2009)[5]—which is a graph-based technique for spreading labels between related items. Our graphs connect token nodes to each other via feature nodes and are seeded with POS-tag labels from the human-annotated data.

Defining the LP graph Our LP graph has several types of nodes, as shown in Figure 1. The graph contains a TOKEN node for each token of the labeled corpus (when available) and raw corpus. Each word type has one TYPE node that is connected to its TOKEN nodes. Both kinds of nodes are connected with *feature* nodes. The PREVWORD_x and NEXTWORD_x nodes represent the features of a token being preceded by or followed by word type x in the corpus. These *bigram* features capture extremely simple syntactic information. To capture shallow morphological relatedness, we use *prefix* and *suffix* nodes that connect word types that share prefix or suffix character sequences up to length 5. For each node-feature pair, the connecting edge is weighted as $1/N$ where N is the number of nodes connected to the particular feature.

[4]This is of course not the case for purely unsupervised taggers, though we also note that it is not at all clear they are actually learning taggers for part-of-speech.

[5]The open-source MAD implementation is provided through Junto: `github.com/parthatalukdar/junto`

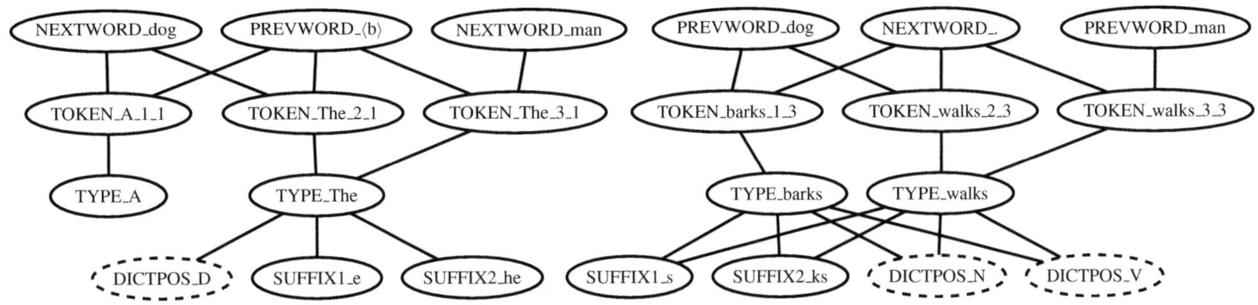

Figure 1: Subsets of the LP graph showing regions of connected nodes. Graph represents the sentences "A dog barks .", "The dog walks .", and "The man walks ."

We also explored the effectiveness of using an external dictionary in the graph since this is one of the few available sources of information for many low-resource languages. Though a standard dictionary probably will not use the same POS tag set that we are targeting, it nevertheless provides information about the relatedness of various word types. Thus, we use nodes DICTPOS_p that indicate that a particular word type is listed as having POS p in the dictionary. Crucially, *these tags bear no particular connection to the tags we are predicting*: we still target the tags defined by the linguist who annotated the types or tokens used, which may be more or less granular than those provided in the dictionary. As external dictionaries, we use English Wiktionary (614k entries), `malagasyworld.org` (78k entries), and `kinyarwanda.net` (3.7k entries).[6]

Seeding the graph is straightforward. With token-supervision, labels for tokens are injected into the corresponding TOKEN nodes with a weight of 1.0. In the type-supervised case, any TYPE node that appears in the tag dictionary is injected with a uniform distribution over the tags in its tag dictionary entry.

Toutanova and Johnson (2008) (also, Ravi and Knight (2009)) use a simple method for predicting possible tags for unknown words: a set of 100 most common suffixes are extracted and then models of *P(tag|suffix)* are built and applied to unknown words. However, these models suffer with an extremely small set of labeled data. Our method uses character affix feature nodes along with *sequence* feature nodes in the LP graph to get distributions over unknown words. Our technique thus subsumes theirs as it can infer tag dictionary entries for words whose suffixes do not show up in the labeled data (or with enough frequency to be reliable predictors).

Extracting a result from LP LP assigns a label distribution to every node. Importantly, each individual TOKEN gets its own distribution instead of sharing an aggregation over the entire word type. From this graph, we extract a new version of the raw corpus that contains tags for each token. This provides the input for model minimization.

We seek a small set of likely tags for each token, but LP gives each token a distribution over the entire set of tags. Most of the tags are simply noise, some of which we remove by normalizing the weights and excluding tags with probability less than 0.1. After applying this cutoff, the weights of the remaining tags are re-normalized. We stress that this tag dictionary cutoff is not like those used in past research, which were done with respect to frequencies obtained from labeled tokens: we use either no word-tag frequency information (type-supervision) or very small amounts of word-tag frequency information indirectly through LP (token-supervision).[7]

Some tokens might not have any associated tag labels after LP. This occurs when there is no path from a TOKEN node to any seeded nodes or when all tags for the TOKEN node have weights less than the threshold. Since we require a distribution for every token, we use a default distribution for such cases. Specifically, we use the unsupervised emission probability initialization of Garrette and Baldridge (2012), which captures both the estimated *frequency* of a tag and its *openness* using only a

[6] Wiktionary (`wiktionary.org`) has only 3,365 entries for Malagasy and 9 for Kinyarwanda.

[7] See Banko and Moore (2004) for further discussion of these issues.

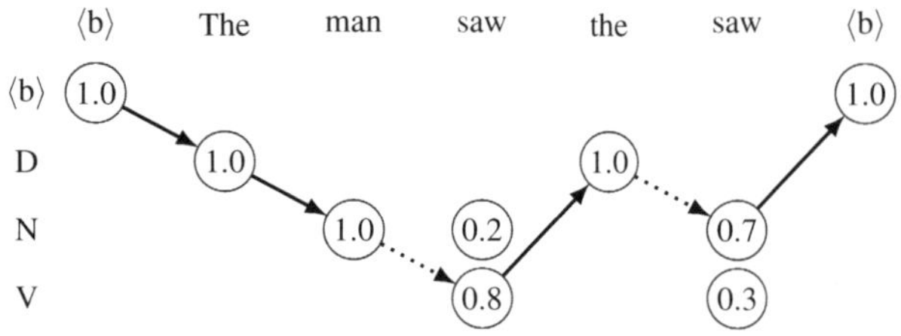

Figure 2: Weighted, greedy model minimization graph showing a potential state between the stages of the tag bigram choosing algorithm. Solid edges: selected bigrams. Dotted edges: holes in the path.

small tag dictionary and unlabeled text.

Finally, we ensure that tokens of words in the original tag dictionary are only assigned tags from its entry. With this filter, LP of course does not add new tags to known words (without it, we found performance drops). If the intersection of the small tag dictionary entry and the token's resulting distribution from LP (after thresholding) is empty, we fall back to the filtered and renormalized *default* distribution for that token's type.

The result of this process is a sequence of (initially raw) tokens, each associated with a distribution over a subset of tags. From this we can extract an *expanded* tag dictionary for use in subsequent stages that, crucially, provides tag information for words not covered by the human-supplied tag dictionary. This expansion is simple: an unknown word type's set of tags is the union of all tags assigned to its tokens. Additionally, we add the full entries of word types given in the original tag dictionary.

3.2 Weighted model minimization

EM-HMM training depends crucially on having a clean tag dictionary and a good starting point for the emission distributions. Given only raw text and a tag dictionary, these distributions are difficult to estimate, especially in the presence of a very sparse or noisy tag dictionary. Ravi and Knight (2009) use model minimization to remove tag dictionary noise and induce tag frequency information from raw text. Their method works by finding a minimal set of tag bigrams needed to explain a raw corpus.

Model minimization is a natural fit for our system since we start with little or no frequency information and automatic dictionary expansion introduces noise. We extend the greedy model minimization procedure of Ravi et al. (2010), and its enhancements by Garrette and Baldridge (2012), to develop a novel *weighted* minimization procedure that uses the tag weights from LP to find a minimal model that is biased toward keeping tag bigrams that have consistently high weights across the entire corpus. The new weighted minimization procedure fits well in our pipeline by allowing us to carry the tag distributions forward from LP instead of simply throwing that information away and using a traditional tag dictionary.

In brief, the procedure works by creating a graph such that each possible tag of each raw-corpus token is a vertex (see Figure 2). Any edge that would connect two tags of adjacent tokens is a potential tag bigram choice. The algorithm first selects tag bigrams until every token is covered by at least one bigram, then selects tag bigrams that fill gaps between existing edges until there is a complete bigram path for every sentence in the raw corpus.[8]

Ravi et al. (2010) select tag bigrams that cover the most new words (stage 1) or fill the most holes in the tag paths (stage 2). Garrette and Baldridge (2012) introduced the tie-breaking criterion that bigram choices should seek to introduce the smallest number of new *word/tag pairs* possible into the paths. Our criteria adds to this by using the tag weights on each token: a tag bigram b is chosen by summing up the node weights of any not-yet covered words touched by the tag bigram b, dividing this sum by one plus the number of *new* word/tag pairs that would be added by b, and choosing the b that maximizes this value.[9]

Summing node weights captures the intuition of Ravi et al. (2010) that good bigrams are those which have high coverage of new words: each newly covered node contributes additional (partial) counts. However, by using the weights instead of full counts, we also account for the confidence assigned by LP. Dividing by the number of new word/tag pairs added focuses on bigrams that reuse existing tags for words

[8]Ravi et al. (2010) include a third phase of iterative model fitting; however, we found this stage to be not only expensive, but also unhelpful because it frequently yields negative results.

[9]In the case of token-supervision, we pre-select all tag bigrams appearing in the labeled corpus since these are assumed to be known high-quality tag bigrams and word/tag pairs.

and thereby limits the addition of new tags for each word type.

At the start of model minimization, there are no selected tag bigrams, and thus no valid path through any sentence in the corpus. As bigrams are selected, we can begin to cover subsequences and eventually full sentences. There may be multiple valid taggings for a sentence, so after each new bigram is selected, we run the Viterbi algorithm over the raw corpus using the set of selected tag bigrams as a hard constraint on the allowable transitions. This efficiently identifies the highest-weight path through each sentence, if one exists. If such a path is found, we remove the sentence from the corpus and store the tags from the Viterbi tagging. The algorithm terminates when a path is found for every raw corpus sentence. The result of weighted model minimization is this set of tag paths. Since each path represents a valid tagging of the sentence, we use this output as a noisily labeled corpus for initializing EM in stage three.

3.3 Tagger training

Stage one provides an expansion of the initial labeled data and stage two turns that into a corpus of noisily labeled sentences. Stage three uses the EM algorithm initialized by the noisy labeling and constrained by the expanded tag dictionary to produce an HMM.[10] The initial distributions are smoothed with one-count smoothing (Chen and Goodman, 1996). If human-tagged sentences are available as training data, then we use their counts to supplement the noisy labeled text for initialization and we add their counts into every iteration's result.

The HMM produced by stage three is not used directly for tagging since it will contain zero-probabilities for test-corpus words that were unseen during training. Instead, we use it to provide a Viterbi labeling of the raw corpus, following the "auto-supervision" step of Garrette and Baldridge (2012). This material is then concatenated with the token-supervised corpus (when available), and used to train a Maximum Entropy Markov Model tagger.[11] The MEMM exploits subword features and generally produces 1-2% better results than an HMM trained on the same material.

4 Experiments[12]

Experimental results are shown in Table 2. Each experiment starts with an initial data set provided by annotator A or B. Experiment (1) simply uses EM with the initial small tag dictionary to learn a tagger from the raw corpus. (2) uses LP to infer an expanded tag dictionary and tag distributions over raw corpus tokens, but then takes the highest-weighted tag from each token for use as noisily-labeled training data to initialize EM. (3) performs greedy model-minimization on the LP output to derive that noisily-labeled corpus. Finally, (4) is the same as (3), but additionally uses external dictionary nodes in the LP graph. In the case of token-supervision, we also include (0), in which we simply used the tagged sentences as supervised data for an HMM without EM (followed by MEMM training).

The results show that performance improves with our LP and minimization techniques compared to basic EM-HMM training. LP gives large across-the-board improvements over EM training with only the original tag dictionary (compare columns 1 & 2). Weighted model minimization further improves results for type-supervision settings, but not for token supervision (compare 2 & 3).

Using an external dictionary in the LP graph has little effect for KIN, probably due to the available dictionary's very small size. However, MLG with its larger dictionary obtains an improvement in both scenarios. Results on ENG are mixed; this may be because the PTB tagset has 45 tags (far more than the dictionary) so the external dictionary nodes in the LP graph may consequently serve to collapse distinctions (e.g. singular and plural) in the larger set.

Our results show differences between token- and type-supervised annotations. Tag dictionary expansion is helpful no matter what the annotations look like: in both cases, the initial dictionary is too small for effective EM learning, so expansion is necessary. However, model minimization only benefits the type-supervised scenarios, leaving token-supervised performance unchanged. This suggests

[10]An added benefit of this strategy is that the EM algorithm with the expanded dictionary runs much more quickly than without it since it does not have to consider every possible tag for unknown words, averaging 20x faster on PTB experiments.

[11]We use OpenNLP: opennlp.apache.org.

[12]Our code is available at github.com/dhgarrette/low-resource-pos-tagging-2013

Human Annotations	0. No EM			1. EM only			2. With LP			3. LP+min			4. LP(ed)+min		
Initial data	T	K	U	T	K	U	T	K	U	T	K	U	T	K	U
KIN tokens A	**72**	90	58	55	82	32	71	86	58	71	86	58	71	86	58
KIN types A				63	77	32	78	83	69	**79**	83	70	**79**	83	70
MLG tokens B	74	89	49	68	87	39	74	89	49	74	89	49	**76**	90	53
MLG types B				71	87	46	72	81	57	74	86	56	**76**	86	60
ENG tokens A	63	83	38	62	83	37	**72**	85	55	**72**	85	55	**72**	85	56
ENG types A				66	76	37	75	81	56	**76**	83	56	74	81	55
ENG tokens B	70	87	44	70	87	43	**78**	90	60	**78**	90	60	**78**	89	61
ENG types B				69	83	38	75	82	61	**78**	85	61	**78**	86	61

Table 2: Experimental results. Three languages are shown: Kinyarwanda (KIN), Malagasy (MLG), and English (ENG). The letters A and B refer to the annotator. LP(ed) refers to label propagation including nodes from an external dictionary. Each result given as percentages for Total (T), Known (K), and Unknown (U).

that minimization is working as intended: it induces frequency information when none is provided. With token-supervision, the annotator provides some information about which tag transitions are best and which emissions are most likely. This is missing with type-supervision, so model minimization is needed to bootstrap word/tag frequency guesses.

This leads to perhaps our most interesting result: in a time-critical annotation scenario, it seems better to collect a simple tag dictionary than tagged sentences. While the tagged sentences certainly contain useful information regarding tag frequencies, our techniques can learn this missing information automatically. Thus, having wider coverage of word type information, and having that information be focused on the most frequent words, is more important. This can be seen as a validation of the last two decades of work on (simulated) type-supervision learning for POS-tagging—with the caveat that the additional effort we do is needed to realize the benefit.

Our experiments also allow us to compare how the data from different annotators affects the quality of taggers learned. Looking at the direct comparison on English data, annotator B was able to tag more sentences than A, but A produced more tag dictionary entries in the type-supervision scenario. However, it appears, based on the EM-only training, that the annotations provided by B were of higher quality and produced more accurate taggers in both scenarios. Regardless, our full training procedure is able to substantially improve results in all scenarios.

Table 3 gives the recall and precision of the tag dictionaries for MLG for settings 1, 2 and 3. The initial, human-provided tag dictionary unsurprisingly has the highest precision and lowest recall. LP expands that data to greatly improve recall with a large drop in precision. Minimization culls many entries and improves precision with a small relative loss in recall. Of course, this is only a rough indicator of the quality of the tag dictionaries since the word/tag pairs of the test set only partially overlap with the raw training data and annotations.

Tag Dictionary Source	R	P
(1) human-annotated TD	18.42	29.33
(2) LP output	35.55	2.62
(3) model min output	30.49	4.63

Table 3: Recall (R) and precision (P) for tag dictionaries versus the test data in a "MLG types B" run.

Because gold-standard annotations are available for the English sentences, we also ran *oracle* experiments using labels from the PTB corpus (essentially, the kind of data used in previous work). We selected the same amount of labeled tokens or word/tag pairs as were obtained by the annotators. We found similar patterns of improved performance by using LP expansion and model minimization, and all accuracies are improved compared to their human-annotator equivalents (about 2-6%). Overall accuracy for both type and token supervision comes to 78-80%.

#Errors	11k	6k	5k	4k	3k
Gold	TO	NNP	NN	JJ	NNP
Model	IN	NN	JJ	NN	JJ

Table 4: Top errors from an "ENG types B" run.

Error Analysis One potential source of errors comes directly from the annotators themselves. Though our approach is designed to be robust to annotation errors, it cannot correct all mistakes. For example, for the "ENG types B" experiment, the annotator listed IN (preposition) as the only tag for word type "to". However, the test set only ever assigns tag TO for this type. This single error accounts for a 2.3% loss in overall tagging accuracy (Table 4).

In many situations, however, we are able to automatically remove improbable tag dictionary entries, as shown in Table 5. Consider the word type "for". The annotator has listed RP (particle) as a potential tag, but only five out of 4k tokens have this tag. With RP included, EM becomes confused and labels a majority of the tokens as RP when nearly all should be labeled IN. We are able to eliminate RP as a possibility, giving excellent overall accuracy for the type. Likewise for the comma type, the annotator has incorrectly given ":" as a valid tag, and LP, which uses the tag dictionary, pushes this label to many tokens with high confidence. However, minimization is able to correct the problem.

Finally, the word type "opposition" provides an example of the expected behavior for unknown words. The type is not in the tag dictionary, so EM assumes all tags are valid and uses many labels. LP expands the starting dictionary to cover the type, limiting it to only two tags. Minimization then determines that NN is the best tag for each token.

for	*IN	*RP	JJ	NN	CD
(1) EM	1,221	2764		9	5
(2) LP	4,003				
(3) min	4,004		1		
gold	3,999	5			

, (comma)	*,	*:	JJS	PTD	VBP
(1) EM	24,708		4	3	3
(2) LP	15,505	9226			1
(3) min	24,730				
gold	24,732				

opposition	NN	JJ	DT	NNS	VBP
(1) EM	24	4	1	4	4
(2) LP	41	4			
(3) min	45				
gold	45				

Table 5: Tag assignments in different scenarios. A star indicates an entry in the human-provided TD.

5 Related work

Goldberg et al. (2008) trained a tagger for Hebrew using a manually-created lexicon which was not derived from an annotated corpus. However, their lexicon was constructed by trained lexicographers over a long period of time and achieves very high coverage of the language with very good quality. In contrast, our annotated data was created by untrained linguistics students working alone for just two hours.

Cucerzan and Yarowsky (2002) learn a POS-tagger from existing linguistic resources, namely a dictionary and a reference grammar, but these resources are not available, much less digitized, for most under-studied languages.

Subramanya et al. (2010) apply LP to the problem of tagging for domain adaptation. They construct an LP graph that connects tokens in low- and high-resource domains, and propagate labels from high to low. This approach addresses the problem of learning appropriate tags for unknown words within a language, but it requires that the language have at least one high-resource domain as a source of high quality information. For low-resource languages that have no significant annotated resources available in *any* domain, this technique cannot be applied.

Das and Petrov (2011) and Täckström et al. (2013) learn taggers for languages in which there are no POS-annotated resources, but for which parallel texts are available between that language and a high-resource language. They project tag information from the high-resource language to the lower-resource language via alignments in the parallel text. However, large parallel corpora are not available for most low-resource languages. These are also expensive resources to create and would take considerably more effort to produce than the monolingual resources that our annotators were able to generate in a two-hour timeframe. Of course, if they are available, such parallel text links could be incorporated into our approach.

Furthermore, their approaches require the use of a universal tag set shared between both languages. As such, their approach is only able to induce POS tags for the low-resource language if the same tag set is used to tag the high-resource language. Our approach does not rely on any such universal tag set; we learn whichever tags the human annotator chooses to use when they provide their annotations. In fact, in our experiments we learn much more detailed tag sets than the fairly coarse universal tag set used by Das and Petrov (2011) or Täckström et al. (2013): we learn a tagger for the full Penn Treebank tag set of 45 tags versus the 12 tags in the universal set.

Ding (2011) constructed an LP graph for learning POS tags on Chinese text by propagating labels from an initial tag dictionary to a larger set of data. This LP graph contained Wiktionary word/POS relationships as features as well as Chinese-English word alignment information and used it to directly estimate emission probabilities to initialize an EM training of an HMM.

Li et al. (2012) train an HMM using EM and an initial tag dictionary derived from Wiktionary. Like Das and Petrov (2011), they use a universal POS tag set, so Wiktionary can be directly applied as a wide-coverage tag dictionary in their case. Additionally, they evaluate their approach on languages for which Wiktionary has high coverage—which would certainly not get far with Kinyarwanda (9 entries). Our approach does not rely on a high-coverage tag dictionary nor is it restricted to use with a small tag set.

6 Conclusions and future work

With just two hours of annotation, we obtain 71-78% accuracy for POS-tagging across three languages using both type and token supervision. Without tag dictionary expansion and model minimization, performance is much worse, from 63-74%. We dramatically improve performance on unknown words: the range of 37-58% improves to 53-70%.

We also have a provisional answer to whether annotation should be on types or tokens: use type-supervision if you also expand and minimize. These methods can identify missing word/tag entries and estimate frequency information, and they produce as good or better results compared to starting with token supervision. The case of Kinyarwanda was most dramatic: 71% accuracy for token-supervision compared to 79% for type-supervision. Studies using more annotators and across more languages would be necessary to make any stronger claim about the relative efficacy of the two strategies.

Acknowledgements

We thank Kyle Jerro, Vijay John, Katrin Erk, Yoav Goldberg, Ray Mooney, Slav Petrov, Oscar Täckström, and the reviewers for their assistance and feedback. This work was supported by the U.S. Department of Defense through the U.S. Army Research Office (grant number W911NF-10-1-0533) and via a National Defense Science and Engineering Graduate Fellowship for the first author. Experiments were run on the UTCS Mastodon Cluster, provided by NSF grant EIA-0303609.

References

Michele Banko and Robert C. Moore. 2004. Part-of-speech tagging in context. In *Proceedings of COLING*, Geneva, Switzerland.

Stanley F. Chen and Joshua Goodman. 1996. An empirical study of smoothing techniques for language modeling. In *Proceedings of ACL*, Santa Cruz, California, USA.

Silviu Cucerzan and David Yarowsky. 2002. Bootstrapping a multilingual part-of-speech tagger in one person-day. In *Proceedings of CoNLL*, Taipei, Taiwan.

Dipanjan Das and Slav Petrov. 2011. Unsupervised part-of-speech tagging with bilingual graph-based projections. In *Proceedings of ACL-HLT*, Portland, Oregon, USA.

Weiwei Ding. 2011. Weakly supervised part-of-speech tagging for Chinese using label propagation. Master's thesis, University of Texas at Austin.

Dan Garrette and Jason Baldridge. 2012. Type-supervised hidden Markov models for part-of-speech tagging with incomplete tag dictionaries. In *Proceedings of EMNLP*, Jeju, Korea.

Yoav Goldberg, Meni Adler, and Michael Elhadad. 2008. EM can find pretty good HMM POS-taggers (when given a good start). In *Proceedings ACL*.

Kazi Saidul Hasan and Vincent Ng. 2009. Weakly supervised part-of-speech tagging for morphologically-rich, resource-scarce languages. In *Proceedings of EACL*, Athens, Greece.

Julian Kupiec. 1992. Robust part-of-speech tagging using a hidden Markov model. *Computer Speech & Language*, 6(3).

Shen Li, João Graça, and Ben Taskar. 2012. Wiki-ly supervised part-of-speech tagging. In *Proceedings of EMNLP*, Jeju Island, Korea.

Christopher D. Manning. 2011. Part-of-speech tagging from 97% to 100%: Is it time for some linguistics? In *Proceedings of CICLing*.

Mitchell P. Marcus, Beatrice Santorini, and Mary Ann Marcinkiewicz. 1993. Building a large annotated corpus of English: The Penn Treebank. *Computational Linguistics*, 19(2).

Bernard Merialdo. 1994. Tagging English text with a probabilistic model. *Computational Linguistics*, 20(2).

Sujith Ravi and Kevin Knight. 2009. Minimized models for unsupervised part-of-speech tagging. In *Proceedings of ACL-AFNLP*.

Sujith Ravi, Ashish Vaswani, Kevin Knight, and David Chiang. 2010. Fast, greedy model minimization for unsupervised tagging. In *Proceedings of COLING*.

Amarnag Subramanya, Slav Petrov, and Fernando Pereira. 2010. Efficient graph-based semi-supervised learning of structured tagging models. In *Proceedings EMNLP*, Cambridge, MA.

Oscar Täckström, Dipanjan Das, Slav Petrov, Ryan McDonald, and Joakim Nivre. 2013. Token and type constraints for cross-lingual part-of-speech tagging. In *Transactions of the ACL*. Association for Computational Linguistics.

Partha Pratim Talukdar and Koby Crammer. 2009. New regularized algorithms for transductive learning. In *Proceedings of ECML-PKDD*, Bled, Slovenia.

Kristina Toutanova and Mark Johnson. 2008. A Bayesian LDA-based model for semi-supervised part-of-speech tagging. In *Proceedings of NIPS*.

Experiments with Spectral Learning of Latent-Variable PCFGs

Shay B. Cohen[1], Karl Stratos[1], Michael Collins[1], Dean P. Foster[2], and Lyle Ungar[3]
[1]Dept. of Computer Science, Columbia University
[2]Dept. of Statistics/[3]Dept. of Computer and Information Science, University of Pennsylvania
{scohen,stratos,mcollins}@cs.columbia.edu, foster@wharton.upenn.edu, ungar@cis.upenn.edu

Abstract

Latent-variable PCFGs (L-PCFGs) are a highly successful model for natural language parsing. Recent work (Cohen et al., 2012) has introduced a spectral algorithm for parameter estimation of L-PCFGs, which—unlike the EM algorithm—is guaranteed to give consistent parameter estimates (it has PAC-style guarantees of sample complexity). This paper describes experiments using the spectral algorithm. We show that the algorithm provides models with the same accuracy as EM, but is an order of magnitude more efficient. We describe a number of key steps used to obtain this level of performance; these should be relevant to other work on the application of spectral learning algorithms. We view our results as strong empirical evidence for the viability of spectral methods as an alternative to EM.

1 Introduction

Latent-variable PCFGS (L-PCFGs) are a highly successful model for natural language parsing (Matsuzaki et al., 2005; Petrov et al., 2006). Recent work (Cohen et al., 2012) has introduced a spectral learning algorithm for L-PCFGs. A crucial property of the algorithm is that it is guaranteed to provide consistent parameter estimates—in fact it has PAC-style guarantees of sample complexity.[1] This is in contrast to the EM algorithm, the usual method for parameter estimation in L-PCFGs, which has the weaker guarantee of reaching a local maximum of the likelihood function. The spectral algorithm is relatively simple and efficient, relying on a singular value decomposition of the training examples, followed by a single pass over the data where parameter values are calculated.

Cohen et al. (2012) describe the algorithm, and the theory behind it, but as yet no experimental results have been reported for the method. This paper describes experiments on natural language parsing using the spectral algorithm for parameter estimation. The algorithm provides models with slightly higher accuracy than EM (88.05% F-measure on test data for the spectral algorithm, vs 87.76% for EM), but is an order of magnitude more efficient (9h52m for training, compared to 187h12m, a speed-up of 19 times).

We describe a number of key steps in obtaining this level of performance. A simple backed-off smoothing method is used to estimate the large number of parameters in the model. The spectral algorithm requires functions mapping inside and outside trees to feature vectors—we make use of features corresponding to single level rules, and larger tree fragments composed of two or three levels of rules. We show that it is important to scale features by their inverse variance, in a manner that is closely related to methods used in canonical correlation analysis. Negative values can cause issues in spectral algorithms, but we describe a solution to these problems.

In recent work there has been a series of results in spectral learning algorithms for latent-variable models (Vempala and Wang, 2004; Hsu et al., 2009; Bailly et al., 2010; Siddiqi et al., 2010; Parikh et al., 2011; Balle et al., 2011; Arora et al., 2012; Dhillon et al., 2012; Anandkumar et al., 2012). Most of these results are theoretical (although see Luque et al. (2012) for empirical results of spectral learning for dependency parsing). While the focus of our experiments is on parsing, our findings should be relevant to the application of spectral methods to other latent-variable models. We view our results as strong empirical evidence for the viability of spectral methods as an alternative to EM.

2 Background

In this section we first give basic definitions for L-PCFGs, and then describe the spectral learning algorithm of Cohen et al. (2012).

[1]under assumptions on certain singular values in the model; see section 2.3.1.

2.1 L-PCFGs: Basic Definitions

We follow the definition in Cohen et al. (2012) of L-PCFGs. An L-PCFG is an 8-tuple $(\mathcal{N}, \mathcal{I}, \mathcal{P}, m, n, \pi, t, q)$ where:

- $\mathcal{N}$ is the set of non-terminal symbols in the grammar. $\mathcal{I} \subset \mathcal{N}$ is a finite set of *in-terminals*. $\mathcal{P} \subset \mathcal{N}$ is a finite set of *pre-terminals*. We assume that $\mathcal{N} = \mathcal{I} \cup \mathcal{P}$, and $\mathcal{I} \cap \mathcal{P} = \emptyset$. Hence we have partitioned the set of non-terminals into two subsets.

- $[m]$ is the set of possible hidden states.[2]

- $[n]$ is the set of possible words.

- For all $a \in \mathcal{I}$, $b, c \in \mathcal{N}$, $h_1, h_2, h_3 \in [m]$, we have a context-free rule $a(h_1) \rightarrow b(h_2)\ \ c(h_3)$. The rule has an associated parameter $t(a \rightarrow b\ c, h_2, h_3 | a, h_1)$.

- For all $a \in \mathcal{P}$, $h \in [m]$, $x \in [n]$, we have a context-free rule $a(h) \rightarrow x$. The rule has an associated parameter $q(a \rightarrow x | a, h)$.

- For all $a \in \mathcal{I}$, $h \in [m]$, $\pi(a, h)$ is a parameter specifying the probability of $a(h)$ being at the root of a tree.

A *skeletal tree* (s-tree) is a sequence of rules $r_1 \ldots r_N$ where each r_i is either of the form $a \rightarrow b\ c$ or $a \rightarrow x$. The rule sequence forms a top-down, left-most derivation under a CFG with skeletal rules.

A *full tree* consists of an s-tree $r_1 \ldots r_N$, together with values $h_1 \ldots h_N$. Each h_i is the value for the hidden variable for the left-hand-side of rule r_i. Each h_i can take any value in $[m]$.

For a given skeletal tree $r_1 \ldots r_N$, define a_i to be the non-terminal on the left-hand-side of rule r_i. For any $i \in [N]$ such that r_i is of the form $a \rightarrow b\ c$, define $h_i^{(2)}$ and $h_i^{(3)}$ as the hidden state value of the left and right child respectively. The model then defines a probability mass function (PMF) as

$$p(r_1 \ldots r_N, h_1 \ldots h_N) =$$
$$\pi(a_1, h_1) \prod_{i: a_i \in \mathcal{I}} t(r_i, h_i^{(2)}, h_i^{(3)} | a_i, h_i) \prod_{i: a_i \in \mathcal{P}} q(r_i | a_i, h_i)$$

The PMF over skeletal trees is $p(r_1 \ldots r_N) = \sum_{h_1 \ldots h_N} p(r_1 \ldots r_N, h_1 \ldots h_N)$.

[2]For any integer n, we use $[n]$ to denote the set $\{1, 2, \ldots n\}$.

The parsing problem is to take a sentence as input, and produce a skeletal tree as output. A standard method for parsing with L-PCFGs is as follows. First, for a given input sentence $x_1 \ldots x_n$, for any triple (a, i, j) such that $a \in \mathcal{N}$ and $1 \leq i \leq j \leq n$, the marginal $\mu(a, i, j)$ is defined as

$$\mu(a, i, j) = \sum_{t:(a,i,j) \in t} p(t) \qquad (1)$$

where the sum is over all skeletal trees t for $x_1 \ldots x_n$ that include non-terminal a spanning words $x_i \ldots x_j$. A variant of the inside-outside algorithm can be used to calculate marginals. Once marginals have been computed, Goodman's algorithm (Goodman, 1996) is used to find $\arg\max_t \sum_{(a,i,j) \in t} \mu(a, i, j)$.[3]

2.2 The Spectral Learning Algorithm

We now give a sketch of the spectral learning algorithm. The training data for the algorithm is a set of skeletal trees. The output from the algorithm is a set of parameter estimates for t, q and π (more precisely, the estimates are estimates of linearly transformed parameters; see Cohen et al. (2012) and section 2.3.1 for more details).

The algorithm takes two inputs in addition to the set of skeletal trees. The first is an integer m, specifying the number of latent state values in the model. Typically m is a relatively small number; in our experiments we test values such as $m = 8, 16$ or 32. The second is a pair of functions ϕ and ψ, that respectively map *inside* and *outside trees* to feature vectors in $\mathbb{R}^d$ and $\mathbb{R}^{d'}$, where d and d' are integers. Each non-terminal in a skeletal tree has an associated inside and outside tree. The inside tree for a node contains the entire subtree below that node; the outside tree contains everything in the tree excluding the inside tree. We will refer to the node above the inside tree that has been removed as the "foot" of the outside tree. See figure 1 for an example.

Section 3.1 gives definitions of $\phi(t)$ and $\psi(o)$ used in our experiments. The definitions of $\phi(t)$ and

[3]In fact, in our implementation we calculate marginals $\mu(a \rightarrow b\ c, i, k, j)$ for $a, b, c \in \mathcal{N}$ and $1 \leq i \leq k < j$, and $\mu(a, i, i)$ for $a \in \mathcal{N}$, $1 \leq i \leq n$, then apply the CKY algorithm to find the parse tree that maximizes the sum of the marginals. For simplicity of presentation we will refer to marginals of the form $\mu(a, i, j)$ in the remainder of this paper.

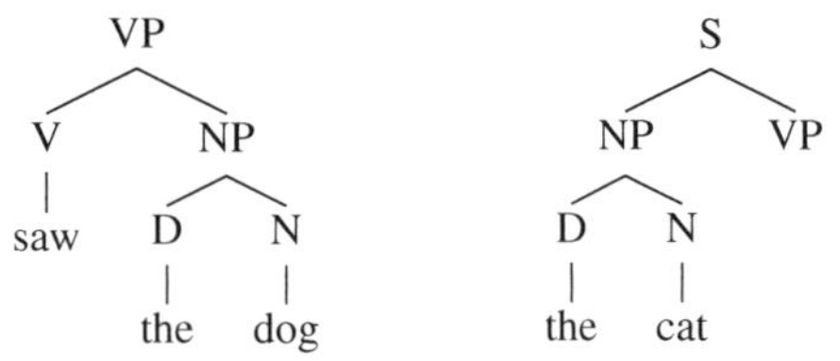

Figure 1: The inside tree (shown left) and outside tree (shown right) for the non-terminal VP in the parse tree [S [NP [D the] [N cat]] [VP [V saw] [NP [D the] [N dog]]]]

$\psi(o)$ are typically high-dimensional, sparse feature vectors, similar to those in log-linear models. For example ϕ might track the rule immediately below the root of the inside tree, or larger tree fragments; ψ might include similar features tracking rules or larger rule fragments above the relevant node.

The spectral learning algorithm proceeds in two steps. In step 1, we learn an m-dimensional representation of inside and outside trees, using the functions ϕ and ψ in combination with a projection step defined through singular value decomposition (SVD). In step 2, we derive parameter estimates directly from training examples.

2.2.1 Step 1: An SVD-Based Projection

For a given non-terminal $a \in \mathcal{N}$, each instance of a in the training data has an associated outside tree, and an associated inside tree. We define O^a to be the set of pairs of inside/outside trees seen with a in the training data: each member of O^a is a pair (o, t) where o is an outside tree, and t is an inside tree.

Step 1 of the algorithm is then as follows:

1. For each $a \in \mathcal{N}$ calculate $\hat{\Omega}^a \in \mathbb{R}^{d \times d'}$ as

$$[\hat{\Omega}^a]_{i,j} = \frac{1}{|O^a|} \sum_{(o,t) \in O^a} \phi_i(t)\psi_j(o)$$

2. Perform an SVD on $\hat{\Omega}^a$. Define $U^a \in \mathbb{R}^{d \times m}$ ($V^a \in \mathbb{R}^{d' \times m}$) to be a matrix containing the m left (right) singular vectors corresponding to the m largest singular values; define $\Sigma^a \in \mathbb{R}^{m \times m}$ to be the diagonal matrix with the m largest singular values on its diagonal.

3. For each inside tree in the corpus with root label a, define

$$Y(t) = (U^a)^\top \phi(t)$$

For each outside tree with a foot node labeled a, define

$$Z(o) = (\Sigma^a)^{-1} (V^a)^\top \psi(o)$$

Note that $Y(t)$ and $Z(o)$ are both m-dimensional vectors; thus we have used SVD to project inside and outside trees to m-dimensional vectors.

2.3 Step 2: Parameter Estimation

We now describe how the functions $Y(t)$ and $Z(o)$ are used in estimating parameters of the model. First, consider the $t(a \to b\ c, h_2, h_3 | a, h_1)$ parameters. Each instance of a given rule $a \to b\ c$ in the training corpus has an outside tree o associated with the parent labeled a, and inside trees t^2 and t^3 associated with the children labeled b and c. For any rule $a \to b\ c$ we define $Q^{a \to b\ c}$ to be the set of triples $(o, t^{(2)}, t^{(3)})$ occurring with that rule in the corpus. The parameter estimate is then

$$\hat{c}(a \to b\ c, j, k | a, i) \quad = \quad \frac{\text{count}(a \to b\ c)}{\text{count}(a)} \times E^{a \to b\ c}_{i,j,k} \tag{2}$$

where

$$E^{a \to b\ c}_{i,j,k} = \frac{\sum_{\substack{(o,t^{(2)},t^{(3)}) \\ \in Q^{a \to b\ c}}} Z_i(o) \times Y_j(t^{(2)}) \times Y_k(t^{(3)})}{|Q^{a \to b\ c}|}$$

Here we use count$(a \to b\ c)$ and count(a) to refer to the count of the rule $a \to b\ c$ and the non-terminal a in the corpus. Note that once the SVD step has been used to compute representations $Y(t)$ and $Z(o)$ for each inside and outside tree in the corpus, calculating the parameter value $\hat{c}(a \to b\ c, j, k | a, i)$ is a very simple operation.

Similarly, for any rule $a \to x$, define $Q^{a \to x}$ to be the set of outside trees seen with that rule in the training corpus. The parameter estimate is then

$$\hat{c}(a \to x | a, i) \quad = \quad \frac{\text{count}(a \to x)}{\text{count}(a)} \times E^{a \to x}_i \tag{3}$$

where $E^{a \to x}_i = \sum_{o \in Q^{a \to x}} Z_i(o) / |Q^{a \to x}|$.

A similar method is used for estimating parameters $\hat{c}(a, i)$ that play the role of the π parameters (details omitted for brevity; see Cohen et al. (2012)).

2.3.1 Guarantees for the Algorithm

Once the $\hat{c}(a \to b\ c, j, k | a, i)$, $\hat{c}(a \to x | a, i)$ and $\hat{c}(a, i)$ parameters have been estimated from the training corpus, they can be used in place of the t, q and π parameters in the inside-outside algorithm for computing marginals (see Eq. 1). Call the resulting marginals $\hat{\mu}(a, i, j)$. The guarantees for the parameter estimation method are as follows:

- Define $\Omega^a = \mathbf{E}[\phi(T)(\psi(O))^\top | A = a]$ where A, O, T are random variables corresponding to the non-terminal label at a node, the outside tree, and the inside tree (see Cohen et al. (2012) for a precise definition). Note that $\hat{\Omega}^a$, as defined above, is an estimate of Ω^a. Then if Ω^a has rank m, the marginals $\hat{\mu}$ will converge to the true values μ as the number of training examples goes to infinity, assuming that the training samples are i.i.d. samples from an L-PCFG.

- Define σ to be the m'th largest singular value of Ω^a. Then the number of samples required for $\hat{\mu}$ to be ϵ-close to μ with probability at least $1 - \delta$ is polynomial in $1/\epsilon$, $1/\delta$, and $1/\sigma$.

Under the first assumption, (Cohen et al., 2012) show that the $\hat{c}$ parameters converge to values that are linear transforms of the original parameters in the L-PCFG. For example, define $c(a \to b\ c, j, k | a, i)$ to be the value that $\hat{c}(a \to b\ c, j, k | a, i)$ converges to in the limit of infinite data. Then there exist invertible matrices $G^a \in \mathbb{R}^{m \times m}$ for all $a \in \mathcal{N}$ such that for any $a \to b\ c$, for any $h_1, h_2, h_3 \in \mathbb{R}^m$,

$$t(a \to b\ c, h_2, h_3 | a, h_1) = \sum_{i,j,k} [G^a]_{i,h_1} [(G^b)^{-1}]_{j,h_2} [(G^c)^{-1}]_{k,h_3} c(a \to b\ c, j, k | a, i)$$

The transforms defined by the G^a matrices are benign, in that they cancel in the inside-outside algorithm when marginals $\mu(a, i, j)$ are calculated. Similar relationships hold for the π and q parameters.

3 Implementation of the Algorithm

Cohen et al. (2012) introduced the spectral learning algorithm, but did not perform experiments, leaving several choices open in how the algorithm is implemented in practice. This section describes a number of key choices made in our implementation of the algorithm. In brief, they are as follows:

The choice of functions ϕ and ψ. We will describe basic features used in ϕ and ψ (single-level rules, larger tree fragments, etc.). We will also describe a method for scaling different features in ϕ and ψ by their variance, which turns out to be important for empirical results.

Estimation of $E^{a\to b\ c}_{i,j,k}$ and $E^{a\to x}_i$. There are a very large number of parameters in the model, leading to challenges in estimation. The estimates in Eqs. 2 and 3 are unsmoothed. We describe a simple backed-off smoothing method that leads to significant improvements in performance of the method.

Handling positive and negative values. As defined, the $\hat{c}$ parameters may be positive or negative; as a result, the $\hat{\mu}$ values may also be positive or negative. We find that negative values can be a significant problem if not handled correctly; but with a very simple fix to the algorithm, it performs well.

We now turn to these three issues in more detail. Section 4 will describe experiments measuring the impact of the different choices.

3.1 The Choice of Functions ϕ and ψ

Cohen et al. (2012) show that the choice of feature definitions ϕ and ψ is crucial in two respects. First, for all non-terminals $a \in \mathcal{N}$, the matrix Ω^a must be of rank m: otherwise the parameter-estimation algorithm will not be consistent. Second, the number of samples required for learning is polynomial in $1/\sigma$, where $\sigma = \min_{a \in \mathcal{N}} \sigma_m(\Omega^a)$, and $\sigma_m(\Omega^a)$ is the m'th smallest singular value of Ω^a. (Note that the second condition is stronger than the first; $\sigma > 0$ implies that Ω^a is of rank m for all a.) The choice of ϕ and ψ has a direct impact on the value for σ: roughly speaking, the value for σ can be thought of as a measure of how informative the functions ϕ and ψ are about the hidden state values.

With this in mind, our goal is to define a relatively simple set of features, which nevertheless provide significant information about hidden-state values, and hence provide high accuracy under the model. The inside-tree feature function $\phi(t)$ makes use of the following indicator features (throughout these definitions assume that $a \to b\ c$ is at the root of the inside tree t):

- The pair of nonterminals (a, b). E.g., for the inside tree in figure 1 this would be the pair `(VP, V)`.

• The pair (a, c). E.g., `(VP, NP)`.

• The rule $a \rightarrow b\ c$. E.g., `VP → V NP`.

• The rule $a \rightarrow b\ c$ paired with the rule at the root of $t^{(i,2)}$. E.g., for the inside tree in figure 1 this would correspond to the tree fragment `(VP (V saw) NP)`.

• The rule $a \rightarrow b\ c$ paired with the rule at the root of $t^{(i,3)}$. E.g., the tree fragment `(VP V (NP D N))`.

• The head part-of-speech of $t^{(i,1)}$ paired with a.[4] E.g., the pair `(VP, V)`.

• The number of words dominated by $t^{(i,1)}$ paired with a (this is an integer valued feature).

In the case of an inside tree consisting of a single rule $a \rightarrow x$ the feature vector simply indicates the identity of that rule.

To illustrate the function ψ, it will be useful to make use of the following example outside tree:

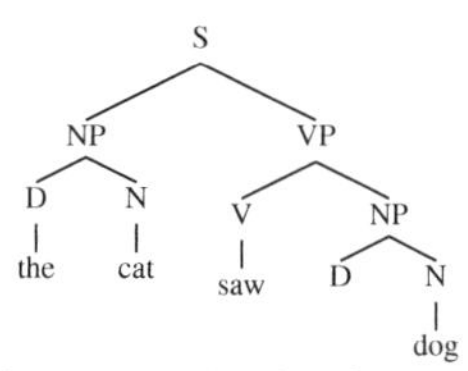

Note that in this example the foot node of the outside tree is labeled `D`. The features are as follows:

• The rule above the foot node. We take care to mark which non-terminal is the foot, using a $\star$ symbol. In the above example this feature is `NP → D* N`.

• The two-level and three-level rule fragments above the foot node. In the above example these features would be

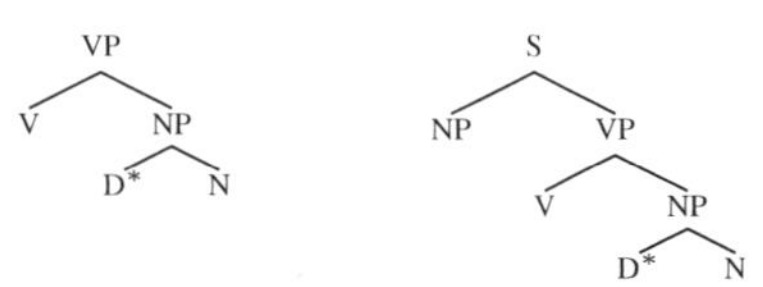

• The label of the foot node, together with the label of its parent. In the above example this is `(D, NP)`.

• The label of the foot node, together with the label of its parent and grandparent. In the above example this is `(D, NP, VP)`.

• The part of speech of the first head word along the path from the foot of the outside tree to the root of the tree which is different from the head node of the foot node. In the above example this is `N`.

• The width of the span to the left of the foot node, paired with the label of the foot node.

• The width of the span to the right of the foot node, paired with the label of the foot node.

Scaling of features. The features defined above are almost all binary valued features. We scale the features in the following way. For each feature $\phi_i(t)$, define count(i) to be the number of times the feature is equal to 1, and M to be the number of training examples. The feature is then redefined to be

$$\phi_i(t) \times \sqrt{\frac{M}{\text{count}(i) + \kappa}}$$

where κ is a smoothing term (the method is relatively insensitive to the choice of κ; we set $\kappa = 5$ in our experiments). A similar process is applied to the ψ features. The method has the effect of decreasing the importance of more frequent features in the SVD step of the algorithm.

The SVD-based step of the algorithm is very closely related to previous work on CCA (Hotelling, 1936; Hardoon et al., 2004; Kakade and Foster, 2009); and the scaling step is derived from previous work on CCA (Dhillon et al., 2011). In CCA the ϕ and ψ vectors are "whitened" in a preprocessing step, before an SVD is applied. This whitening process involves calculating covariance matrices $C_x = \mathbf{E}[\phi\phi^\top]$ and $C_y = \mathbf{E}[\psi\psi^\top]$, and replacing ϕ by $(C^x)^{-1/2}\phi$ and ψ by $(C^y)^{-1/2}\psi$. The exact calculation of $(C^x)^{-1/2}$ and $(C^y)^{-1/2}$ is challenging in high dimensions, however, as these matrices will not be sparse; the transformation described above can be considered an approximation where off-diagonal members of C_x and C_y are set to zero. We will see that empirically this scaling gives much improved accuracy.

3.2 Estimation of $E^{a \rightarrow b\ c}_{i,j,k}$ and $E^{a \rightarrow x}_{i}$

The number of $E^{a \rightarrow b\ c}_{i,j,k}$ parameters is very large, and the estimation method described in Eqs. 2–3 is unsmoothed. We have found significant improvements in performance using a relatively simple backoff smoothing method. The intuition behind this method is as follows: given two random variables X and Y, under the assumption that the random variables are independent, $\mathbf{E}[XY] = \mathbf{E}[X] \times \mathbf{E}[Y]$. It

[4] We use the English head rules from the Stanford parser (Klein and Manning, 2003).

makes sense to define "backed off" estimates which make increasingly strong independence assumptions of this form.

Smoothing of binary rules For any rule $a \rightarrow b\ c$ and indices $i, j \in [m]$ we can define a second-order moment as follows:

$$E_{i,j,\cdot}^{a \rightarrow b\ c} = \frac{\sum_{\substack{(o,t^{(2)},t^{(3)}) \\ \in Q^{a \rightarrow b\ c}}} Z_i(o) \times Y_j(t^{(2)})}{|Q^{a \rightarrow b\ c}|}$$

The definitions of $E_{i,\cdot,k}^{a \rightarrow b\ c}$ and $E_{\cdot,j,k}^{a \rightarrow b\ c}$ are analogous. We can define a first-order estimate as follows:

$$E_{\cdot,\cdot,k}^{a \rightarrow b\ c} = \frac{\sum_{\substack{(o,t^{(2)},t^{(3)}) \\ \in Q^{a \rightarrow b\ c}}} Y_k(t^{(3)})}{|Q^{a \rightarrow b\ c}|}$$

Again, we have analogous definitions of $E_{i,\cdot,\cdot}^{a \rightarrow b\ c}$ and $E_{\cdot,j,\cdot}^{a \rightarrow b\ c}$. Different levels of smoothed estimate can be derived from these different terms. The first is

$$E_{i,j,k}^{2,a \rightarrow b\ c} = \frac{E_{i,j,\cdot}^{a \rightarrow b\ c} \times E_{\cdot,\cdot,k}^{a \rightarrow b\ c} + E_{i,\cdot,k}^{a \rightarrow b\ c} \times E_{\cdot,j,\cdot}^{a \rightarrow b\ c} + E_{\cdot,j,k}^{a \rightarrow b\ c} \times E_{i,\cdot,\cdot}^{a \rightarrow b\ c}}{3}$$

Note that we give an equal weight of $1/3$ to each of the three backed-off estimates seen in the numerator. A second smoothed estimate is

$$E_{i,j,k}^{3,a \rightarrow b\ c} = E_{i,\cdot,\cdot}^{a \rightarrow b\ c} \times E_{\cdot,j,\cdot}^{a \rightarrow b\ c} \times E_{\cdot,\cdot,k}^{a \rightarrow b\ c}$$

Using the definition of O^a given in section 2.2.1, we also define

$$F_i^a = \frac{\sum_{(o,t) \in O^a} Y_i(t)}{|O^a|} \qquad H_i^a = \frac{\sum_{(o,t) \in O^a} Z_i(o)}{|O^a|}$$

and our next smoothed estimate as $E_{i,j,k}^{4,a \rightarrow b\ c} = H_i^a \times F_j^b \times F_k^c$.

Our final estimate is

$$\lambda E_{i,j,k}^{a \rightarrow b\ c} + (1 - \lambda) \left(\lambda E_{i,j,k}^{2,a \rightarrow b\ c} + (1 - \lambda) K_{i,j,k}^{a \rightarrow b\ c} \right)$$

where $K_{i,j,k}^{a \rightarrow b\ c} = \lambda E_{i,j,k}^{3,a \rightarrow b\ c} + (1 - \lambda) E_{i,j,k}^{4,a \rightarrow b\ c}$.

Here $\lambda \in [0, 1]$ is a smoothing parameter, set to $\sqrt{|Q^{a \rightarrow b\ c}|}/(C + \sqrt{|Q^{a \rightarrow b\ c}|})$ in our experiments, where C is a parameter that is chosen by optimization of accuracy on a held-out set of data.

Smoothing lexical rules We define a similar method for the $E_i^{a \rightarrow x}$ parameters. Define

$$E_i^a = \frac{\sum_{x'} \sum_{o \in Q^{a \rightarrow x'}} Z_i(o)}{\sum_{x'} |Q^{a \rightarrow x'}|}$$

hence E_i^a ignores the identity of x in making its estimate. The smoothed estimate is then defined as $\nu E_i^{a \rightarrow x} + (1 - \nu) E_i^a$. Here, ν is a value in $[0, 1]$ which is tuned on a development set. We only smooth lexical rules which appear in the data less than a fixed number of times. Unlike binary rules, for which the estimation depends on a high order moment (third moment), the lexical rules use first-order moments, and therefore it is not required to smooth rules with a relatively high count. The maximal count for this kind of smoothing is set using a development set.

3.3 Handling Positive and Negative Values

As described before, the parameter estimates may be positive or negative, and as a result the marginals computed by the algorithm may in some cases themselves be negative. In early experiments we found this to be a signficant problem, with some parses having a very large number of negatives, and being extremely poor in quality. Our fix is to define the output of the parser to be $\arg\max_t \sum_{(a,i,j) \in t} |\mu(a, i, j)|$ rather than $\arg\max_t \sum_{(a,i,j) \in t} \mu(a, i, j)$ as defined in Goodman's algorithm. Thus if a marginal value $\mu(a, i, j)$ is negative, we simply replace it with its absolute value. This step was derived after inspection of the parsing charts for bad parses, where we saw evidence that in these cases the entire set of marginal values had been negated (and hence decoding under Eq. 1 actually leads to the *lowest* probability parse being output under the model). We suspect that this is because in some cases a dominant parameter has had its sign flipped due to sampling error; more theoretical and empirical work is required in fully understanding this issue.

4 Experiments

In this section we describe parsing experiments using the L-PCFG estimation method. We give comparisons to the EM algorithm, considering both speed of training, and accuracy of the resulting model; we also give experiments investigating the various choices described in the previous section.

We use the Penn WSJ treebank (Marcus et al., 1993) for our experiments. Sections 2–21 were used as training data, and sections 0 and 22 were used as development data. Section 23 is used as the final test set. We binarize the trees in training data using the same method as that described in Petrov et al. (2006). For example, the non-binary rule `VP → V NP PP SBAR` would be converted to the structure `[VP [@VP [@VP V NP] PP] SBAR]` where `@VP` is a new symbol in the grammar. Unary rules are removed by collapsing non-terminal chains: for example the unary rule `S → VP` would be replaced by a single non-terminal `S|VP`.

For the EM algorithm we use the initialization method described in Matsuzaki et al. (2005). For efficiency, we use a coarse-to-fine algorithm for parsing with either the EM or spectral derived grammar: a PCFG without latent states is used to calculate marginals, and dynamic programming items are removed if their marginal probability is lower than some threshold (0.00005 in our experiments).

For simplicity the parser takes part-of-speech tagged sentences as input. We use automatically tagged data from Turbo Tagger (Martins et al., 2010). The tagger is used to tag both the development data and the test data. The tagger was retrained on sections 2–21. We use the F_1 measure according to the Parseval metric (Black et al., 1991). For the spectral algorithm, we tuned the smoothing parameters using section 0 of the treebank.

4.1 Comparison to EM: Accuracy

We compare models trained using EM and the spectral algorithm using values for m in $\{8, 16, 24, 32\}$.[5]

For EM, we found that it was important to use development data to choose the number of iterations of training. We train the models for 100 iterations, then test accuracy of the model on section 22 (development data) at different iteration numbers. Table 1 shows that a peak level of accuracy is reached for all values of m, other than $m = 8$, at iteration 20–30, with sometimes substantial overtraining beyond that point.

The performance of a regular PCFG model, estimated using maximum likelihood and with no latent states, is 68.62%.

	section 22		section 23	
	EM	spectral	EM	spectral
$m = 8$	86.87	85.60	—	—
$m = 16$	88.32	87.77	—	—
$m = 24$	88.35	88.53	—	—
$m = 32$	88.56	88.82	87.76	88.05

Table 2: Results on the development data (section 22, with machine-generated POS tags) and test data (section 23, with machine-generated POS tags).

Table 2 gives results for the EM-trained models and spectral-trained models. The spectral models give very similar accuracy to the EM-trained model on the test set. Results on the development set with varying m show that the EM-based models perform better for $m = 8$, but that the spectral algorithm quickly catches up as m increases.

4.2 Comparison to EM: Training Speed

Table 3 gives training times for the EM algorithm and the spectral algorithm for $m \in \{8, 16, 24, 32\}$. All timing experiments were done on a single Intel Xeon 2.67GHz CPU. The implementations for the EM algorithm and the spectral algorithm were written in Java. The spectral algorithm also made use of Matlab for several matrix calculations such as the SVD calculation.

For EM we show the time to train a single iteration, and also the time to train the optimal model (time for 30 iterations of training for $m = 8, 16, 24$, and time for 20 iterations for $m = 32$). Note that this latter time is optimistic, as it assumes an oracle specifying exactly when it is possible to terminate EM training with no loss in performance. The spectral method is considerably faster than EM: for example, for $m = 32$ the time for training the spectral model is just under 10 hours, compared to 187 hours for EM, a factor of almost 19 times faster.[6]

The reason for these speed ups is as follows. Step 1 of the spectral algorithm (feature calculation, transfer + scaling, and SVD) is not required by EM, but takes a relatively small amount of time (about 1.2 hours for all values of m). Once step 1 has been completed, step 2 of the spectral algorithm takes a

[5]Lower values of m, such as 2 or 4, lead to substantially lower performance for both models.

[6]In practice, in order to overcome the speed issue with EM training, we parallelized the E-step on multiple cores. The spectral algorithm can be similarly parallelized, computing statistics and parameters for each nonterminal separately.

	10	20	30	40	50	60	70	80	90	100
$m = 8$	83.51	86.45	86.68	86.69	86.63	86.67	86.70	86.82	**86.87**	86.83
$m = 16$	85.18	87.94	**88.32**	88.21	88.10	87.86	87.70	87.46	87.34	87.24
$m = 24$	83.62	88.19	**88.35**	88.25	87.73	87.41	87.35	87.26	87.02	86.80
$m = 32$	83.23	**88.56**	88.52	87.82	87.06	86.47	86.38	85.85	85.75	85.57

Table 1: Results on section 22 for the EM algorithm, varying the number of iterations used. Best results in each row are in boldface.

	single	EM	spectral algorithm					
	EM iter.	best model	total	feature	transfer + scaling	SVD	$a \rightarrow b\ c$	$a \rightarrow x$
$m = 8$	6m	3h	3h32m	22m	49m	36m	1h34m	10m
$m = 16$	52m	26h6m	5h19m			34m	3h13m	19m
$m = 24$	3h7m	93h36m	7h15m			36m	4h54m	28m
$m = 32$	9h21m	187h12m	9h52m			35m	7h16m	41m

Table 3: Running time for the EM algorithm and the various stages in the spectral algorithm. For EM we show the time for a single iteration, and the time to train the optimal model (time for 30 iterations of training for $m = 8, 16, 24$, time for 20 iterations of training for $m = 32$). For the spectral method we show the following: "total" is the total training time; "feature" is the time to compute the ϕ and ψ vectors for all data points; "transfer + scaling" is time to transfer the data from Java to Matlab, combined with the time for scaling of the features; "SVD" is the time for the SVD computation; $a \rightarrow b\ c$ is the time to compute the $\hat{c}(a \rightarrow b\ c, h_2, h_3|a, h_1)$ parameters; $a \rightarrow x$ is the time to compute the $\hat{c}(a \rightarrow x, h|a, h)$ parameters. Note that "feature" and "transfer + scaling" are the same step for all values of m, so we quote a single runtime for these steps.

single pass over the data: in contrast, EM requires a few tens of passes (certainly more than 10 passes, from the results in table 1). The computations performed by the spectral algorithm in its single pass are relatively cheap. In contrast to EM, the inside-outside algorithm is not required; however various operations such as calculating smoothing terms in the spectral method add some overhead. The net result is that for $m = 32$ the time for training the spectral method takes a very similar amount of time to a single pass of the EM algorithm.

4.3 Smoothing, Features, and Negatives

We now describe experiments demonstrating the impact of various components described in section 3.

The effect of smoothing (section 3.2) Without smoothing, results on section 22 are 85.05% ($m = 8$, -1.82), 86.84% ($m = 16$, -1.48), 86.47% ($m = 24$, -1.88), 86.47% ($m = 32$, -2.09) (in each case we show the decrease in performance from the results in table 2). Smoothing is clearly important.

Scaling of features (section 3.1) Without scaling of features, the accuracy on section 22 with $m = 32$ is 84.40%, a very significant drop from the 88.82% accuracy achieved with scaling.

Handling negative values (section 3.3) Replacing marginal values $\mu(a, i, j)$ with their absolute values is also important: without this step, accuracy on section 22 decreases to 80.61% ($m = 32$). 319 sentences out of 1700 examples have different parses when this step is implemented, implying that the problem with negative values described in section 3.3 occurs on around 18% of all sentences.

The effect of feature functions To test the effect of features on accuracy, we experimented with a simpler set of features than those described in section 3.1. This simple set just includes an indicator for the rule below a nonterminal (for inside trees) and the rule above a nonterminal (for outside trees). Even this simpler set of features achieves relatively high accuracy ($m = 8$: 86.44 , $m = 16$: 86.86, $m = 24$: 87.24 , $m = 32$: 88.07).

This set of features is reminiscent of a PCFG model where the nonterminals are augmented their parents (vertical Markovization of order 2) and binarization is done while retaining sibling information (horizontal Markovization of order 1). See Klein and Manning (2003) for more information. The performance of this Markovized PCFG model lags behind the spectral model: it is 82.59%. This is probably due to the complexity of the grammar which causes ovefitting. Condensing the sibling and parent information using latent states as done in the spectral model leads to better generalization.

It is important to note that the results for both EM and the spectral algorithm are comparable to state of the art, but there are other results previously reported in the literature which are higher. For example, Hiroyuki et al. (2012) report an accuracy of 92.4 F_1 on section 23 of the Penn WSJ treebank using a Bayesian tree substitution grammar; Charniak and Johnson (2005) report accuracy of 91.4 using a discriminative reranking model; Carreras et al. (2008) report 91.1 F_1 accuracy for a discriminative, perceptron-trained model; Petrov and Klein (2007) report an accuracy of 90.1 F_1, using L-PCFGs, but with a split-merge training procedure. Collins (2003) reports an accuracy of 88.2 F_1, which is comparable to the results in this paper.

5 Conclusion

The spectral learning algorithm gives the same level of accuracy as EM in our experiments, but has significantly faster training times. There are several areas for future work. There are a large number of parameters in the model, and we suspect that more sophisticated regularization methods than the smoothing method we have described may improve performance. Future work should also investigate other choices for the functions ϕ and ψ. There are natural ways to extend the approach to semi-supervised learning; for example the SVD step, where representations of outside and inside trees are learned, could be applied to unlabeled data parsed by a first-pass parser. Finally, the methods we have described should be applicable to spectral learning for other latent variable models.

Acknowledgements

Columbia University gratefully acknowledges the support of the Defense Advanced Research Projects Agency (DARPA) Machine Reading Program under Air Force Research Laboratory (AFRL) prime contract no. FA8750-09-C-0181. Any opinions, findings, and conclusions or recommendations expressed in this material are those of the author(s) and do not necessarily reflect the view of DARPA, AFRL, or the US government. Shay Cohen was supported by the National Science Foundation under Grant #1136996 to the Computing Research Association for the CIFellows Project. Dean Foster was supported by National Science Foundation grant 1106743.

References

A. Anandkumar, R. Ge, D. Hsu, S. M. Kakade, and M. Telgarsky. 2012. Tensor decompositions for learning latent-variable models. arXiv:1210.7559.

S. Arora, R. Se, and A. Moitra. 2012. Learning topic models - going beyond SVD. In *Proceedings of FOCS*.

R. Bailly, A. Habrar, and F. Denis. 2010. A spectral approach for probabilistic grammatical inference on trees. In *Proceedings of ALT*.

B. Balle, A. Quattoni, and X. Carreras. 2011. A spectral learning algorithm for finite state transducers. In *Proceedings of ECML*.

E. Black, S. Abney, D. Flickenger, C. Gdaniec, R. Grishman, P Harrison, D. Hindle, R. Ingria, F. Jelinek, J. Klavans, M. Liberman, M. Marcus, S. Roukos, B. Santorini, and T. Strzalkowski. 1991. A procedure for quantitatively comparing the syntactic coverage of English grammars. In *Proceedings of DARPA Workshop on Speech and Natural Language*.

X. Carreras, M. Collins, and T. Koo. 2008. TAG, Dynamic Programming, and the Perceptron for Efficient, Feature-rich Parsing. In *Proceedings of CoNLL*, pages 9–16.

E. Charniak and M. Johnson. 2005. Coarse-to-fine n-best parsing and maxent discriminative reranking. In *Proceedings of ACL*.

S. B. Cohen, K. Stratos, M. Collins, D. F. Foster, and L. Ungar. 2012. Spectral learning of latent-variable PCFGs. In *Proceedings of ACL*.

M. Collins. 2003. Head-driven statistical models for natural language processing. *Computational Linguistics*, 29:589–637.

P. Dhillon, D. P. Foster, and L. H. Ungar. 2011. Multi-view learning of word embeddings via CCA. In *Proceedings of NIPS*.

P. Dhillon, J. Rodu, M. Collins, D. P. Foster, and L. H. Ungar. 2012. Spectral dependency parsing with latent variables. In *Proceedings of EMNLP*.

J. Goodman. 1996. Parsing algorithms and metrics. In *Proceedings of ACL*.

D. Hardoon, S. Szedmak, and J. Shawe-Taylor. 2004. Canonical correlation analysis: An overview with application to learning methods. *Neural Computation*, 16(12):2639–2664.

S. Hiroyuki, M. Yusuke, F. Akinori, and N. Masaaki. 2012. Bayesian symbol-refined tree substitution grammars for syntactic parsing. In *Proceedings of ACL*, pages 440–448.

H. Hotelling. 1936. Relations between two sets of variants. *Biometrika*, 28:321–377.

D. Hsu, S. M. Kakade, and T. Zhang. 2009. A spectral algorithm for learning hidden Markov models. In *Proceedings of COLT*.

S. M. Kakade and D. P. Foster. 2009. Multi-view regression via canonical correlation analysis. In *COLT*.

D. Klein and C. D. Manning. 2003. Accurate unlexicalized parsing. In *Proc. of ACL*, pages 423–430.

F. M. Luque, A. Quattoni, B. Balle, and X. Carreras. 2012. Spectral learning for non-deterministic dependency parsing. In *Proceedings of EACL*.

M. P. Marcus, B. Santorini, and M. A. Marcinkiewicz. 1993. Building a large annotated corpus of English: The Penn treebank. *Computational Linguistics*, 19:313–330.

A. F. T. Martins, N. A. Smith, E. P. Xing, M. T. Figueiredo, and M. Q. Aguiar. 2010. TurboParsers: Dependency parsing by approximate variational inference. In *Proceedings of EMNLP*.

T. Matsuzaki, Y. Miyao, and J. Tsujii. 2005. Probabilistic CFG with latent annotations. In *Proceedings of ACL*.

A. Parikh, L. Song, and E. P. Xing. 2011. A spectral algorithm for latent tree graphical models. In *Proceedings of The 28th International Conference on Machine Learningy (ICML 2011)*.

S. Petrov and D. Klein. 2007. Improved inference for unlexicalized parsing. In *Proc. of HLT-NAACL*.

S. Petrov, L. Barrett, R. Thibaux, and D. Klein. 2006. Learning accurate, compact, and interpretable tree annotation. In *Proceedings of COLING-ACL*.

S. Siddiqi, B. Boots, and G. Gordon. 2010. Reduced-rank hidden markov models. *JMLR*, 9:741–748.

S. Vempala and G. Wang. 2004. A spectral algorithm for learning mixtures of distributions. *Journal of Computer and System Sciences*, 68(4):841–860.

Representing Topics Using Images

Nikolaos Aletras and **Mark Stevenson**
Department of Computer Science
University of Sheffield
Regent Court, 211 Portobello
Sheffield, S1 4DP, UK
{n.aletras, m.stevenson}@dcs.shef.ac.uk

Abstract

Topics generated automatically, e.g. using LDA, are now widely used in Computational Linguistics. Topics are normally represented as a set of keywords, often the n terms in a topic with the highest marginal probabilities. We introduce an alternative approach in which topics are represented using images. Candidate images for each topic are retrieved from the web by querying a search engine using the top n terms. The most suitable image is selected from this set using a graph-based algorithm which makes use of textual information from the metadata associated with each image and features extracted from the images themselves. We show that the proposed approach significantly outperforms several baselines and can provide images that are useful to represent a topic.

1 Introduction

Topic models are statistical methods for summarising the content of a document collection using latent variables known as topics (Hofmann, 1999; Blei et al., 2003). Within a model, each topic is a multinomial distribution over words in the collection while documents are represented as distributions over topics. Topic modelling is now widely used in Natural Language Processing (NLP) and has been applied to a range of tasks including word sense disambiguation (Boyd-Graber et al., 2007), multi-document summarisation (Haghighi and Vanderwende, 2009), information retrieval (Wei and Croft, 2006), image labelling (Feng and Lapata, 2010a) and visualisation of document collections (Chaney and Blei, 2012).

Topics are often represented by using the n terms with the highest marginal probabilities in the topic to generate a set of keywords. For example, *wine*, *bottle*, *grape*, *flavour*, *dry*. Interpreting such lists may not be straightforward, particularly since there may be no access to the source collection used to train the model. Therefore, researchers have recently begun developing automatic methods to generate meaningful and representative labels for topics. These techniques have focussed on the creation of textual labels (Mei et al., 2007; Lau et al., 2010; Lau et al., 2011).

An alternative approach is to represent a topic using an illustrative image (or set of images). Images have the advantage that they can be understood quickly and are language independent. This is particularly important for applications in which the topics are used to provide an overview of a collection with many topics being shown simultaneously (Chaney and Blei, 2012; Gretarsson et al., 2012; Hinneburg et al., 2012).

This paper explores the problem of selecting images to illustrate automatically generated topics. Our approach generates a set of candidate images for each topic by querying an image search engine with the top n topic terms. The most suitable image is selected using a graph-based method that makes use of both textual and visual information. Textual information is obtained from the metadata associated with each image while visual features are extracted from the images themselves. Our approach is evaluated using a data set created for this study that was annotated by crowdsourcing. Results of the evaluation show that the proposed method significantly outperforms three baselines.

The contributions of this paper are as follows: (1) introduces the problem of labelling topics using images; (2) describes an approach to this problem that makes use of multimodal information to select images from a set of candidates; (3) introduces a data set to evaluate image labelling; and (4) evaluates the proposed approach using this data set.

2 Related work

In early research on topic modelling, labels were manually assigned to topics for convenient presentation of research results (Mei and Zhai, 2005; Teh et al., 2006).

The first attempt at automatically assigning labels to topics is described by Mei et al. (2007). In their approach, a set of candidate labels are extracted from a reference collection using chunking and statistically important bigrams. Then, a relevance scoring function is defined which minimises the Kullback-Leibler divergence between word distribution in a topic and word distribution in candidate labels. Candidate labels are ranked according to their relevance and the top ranked label chosen to represent the topic.

Magatti et al. (2009) introduced an approach for labelling topics that relied on two hierarchical knowledge resources labelled by humans, the Google Directory and the OpenOffice English Thesaurus. A *topics tree* is a pre-existing hierarchical structure of labelled topics. The Automatic Labelling Of Topics algorithm computes the similarity between LDA inferred topics and topics in a *topics tree* by computing scores using six standard similarity measures. The label for the most similar topic in the *topic tree* is assigned to the LDA topic.

Lau et al. (2010) proposed selecting the most representative word from a topic as its label. A label is selected by computing the similarity between each word and all the others in the topic. Several sources of information are used to identify the best label including Pointwise Mutual Information scores, WordNet hypernymy relations and distributional similarity. These features are combined in a reranking model to achieve results above a baseline (the most probable word in the topic).

In more recent work, Lau et al. (2011) proposed a method for automatically labelling topics by making use of Wikipedia article titles as candidate labels. The candidate labels are ranked using information from word association measures, lexical features and an Information Retrieval technique. Results showed that this ranking method achieves better performance than a previous approach (Mei et al., 2007).

Mao et al. (2012) introduced a method for labelling hierarchical topics which makes use of sibling and parent-child relations of topics. Candidate labels are generated using a similar approach to the one used by Mei et al. (2007). Each candidate label is then assigned a score by creating a distribution based on the words it contains and measuring the Jensen-Shannon divergence between this and a reference corpus.

Hulpus et al. (2013) make use of the structured data in DBpedia[1] to label topics. Their approach maps topic words to DBpedia concepts. The best concepts are identified by applying graph centrality measures which assume that words that co-occurring in text are likely to refer to concepts that are close in the DBpedia graph.

Our own work differs from the approaches described above since, to our knowledge, it is the first to propose labelling topics with images rather than text.

Recent advances in computer vision has lead to the development of reliable techniques for exploiting information available in images (Datta et al., 2008; Szeliski, 2010) and these have been combined with NLP (Feng and Lapata, 2010a; Feng and Lapata, 2010b; Agrawal et al., 2011; Bruni et al., 2011). The closest work to our own is the text illustration techniques which have been proposed for story picturing (Joshi et al., 2006) and news articles illustration (Feng and Lapata, 2010b). The input to text illustration models is a textual document and a set of image candidates. The goal of the models is to associate the document with the correct image. Moreover, the problem of ranking images returned from a text query is related to, but different from, the one explored in our paper. Those approaches used queries that were much smaller (e.g. between one and three words) and more focussed than the ones

[1] http://dbpedia.org

we use (Jing and Baluja, 2008). In our work, the input is a topic and the aim is to associate it with an image, or images, denoting the main thematic subject.

3 Labelling Topics

In this section we propose an approach to identifying images to illustrate automatically generated topics. It is assumed that there are no candidate images available so the first step (Section 3.1) is to generate a set of candidate images. However, when a candidate set is available the first step can be skipped.

3.1 Selecting Candidate Images

For the experiments presented here we restrict ourselves to using images from Wikipedia available under the Creative Commons licence, since this allows us to make the data available. The top-5 terms from a topic are used to query Google using its Custom Search API[2]. The search is restricted to the English Wikipedia[3] with image search enabled. The top-20 images retrieved for each search are used as candidates for the topic.

3.2 Feature Extraction

Candidate images are represented by two modalities (textual and visual) and features extracted for each.

3.2.1 Textual Information

Each image's textual information consists of the metadata retrieved by the search. The assumption here is that image's metadata is indicative of the image's content and (at least to some extent) related to the topic. The textual information is formed by concatenating the *title* and the *link* fields of the search result. These represent, respectively, the web page title containing the image and the image file name. The textual information is preprocessed by tokenizing and removing stop words.

3.2.2 Visual Information

Visual information is extracted using low-level image keypoint descriptors, i.e. SIFT features (Lowe, 1999; Lowe, 2004) sensitive to colour information. SIFT features denote "interesting" areas in an image. Image features are extracted using dense sampling and described using Opponent colour SIFT descriptors provided by the *colordescriptor*[4] software. Opponent colour SIFT descriptors have been found to give the best performance in object scene and face recognition (Sande et al., 2008). The SIFT features are clustered to form a visual codebook of 1,000 visual words using K-Means such that each feature is mapped to a visual word. Each image is represented as a bag-of-visual words (BOVW).

[2] https://developers.google.com/apis-explorer/#s/customsearch/v1

[3] http://en.wikipedia.org

[4] http://koen.me/research/colordescriptors

3.3 Ranking Candidate Images

We rank images in the candidates set using graph-based algorithms. The graph is created by treating images as nodes and using similarity scores (textual or visual) between images to weight the edges.

3.3.1 PageRank

PageRank (Page et al., 1999) is a graph-based algorithm for identifying important nodes in a graph that was originally developed for assigning importance to web pages. It has been used for a range of NLP tasks including word sense disambiguation (Agirre and Soroa, 2009) and keyword extraction (Mihalcea and Tarau, 2004).

Let $G = (V, E)$ be a graph with a set of vertices, V, denoting image candidates and a set of edges, E, denoting similarity scores between two images. For example, $sim(V_i, V_j)$ indicates the similarity between images V_i and V_j. The PageRank score (Pr) over G for an image (V_i) can be computed by the following equation:

$$Pr(V_i) = d \cdot \sum_{V_j \in C(V_i)} \frac{sim(V_i, V_j)}{\sum_{V_k \in C(V_j)} sim(V_j, V_k)} Pr(V_j) + (1 - d)\mathbf{v} \quad (1)$$

where $C(V_i)$ denotes the set of vertices which are connected to the vertex V_i. d is the damping factor which is set to the default value of $d = 0.85$ (Page et al., 1999). In standard PageRank all elements of the vector $\mathbf{v}$ are the same, $\frac{1}{N}$ where N is the number of nodes in the graph.

3.3.2 Personalised PageRank

Personalised PageRank (PPR) (Haveliwala et al., 2003) is a variant of the PageRank algorithm in which extra importance is assigned to certain vertices in the graph. This is achieved by adjusting the values of the vector **v** in equation 1 to prefer certain nodes. Nodes that are assigned high values in **v** are more likely to also be assigned a high PPR score. We make use of PPR to prefer images with textual information that is similar to the terms in the topic.

3.3.3 Weighting Graph Edges

Three approaches were compared for computing the values of $sim(V_i, V_j)$ in equation 1 used to weight the edges of the graph. Two of these make use of the textual information associated with each image while the final one relies on visual features.

The first approach is **Pointwise Mutual Information** (PMI). The similarity between a pair of images (vertices in the graph) is computed as the average PMI between the terms in their metadata. PMI is computed using word co-occurrence counts over Wikipedia identified using a sliding window of length 20. We also experimented with other word association measures but these did not perform as well. The PageRank over the graph weighted using PMI is denoted as $\mathbf{PR_{PMI}}$.

The second approach, **Explicit Semantic Analysis** (ESA) (Gabrilovich and Markovitch, 2007), is a knowledge-based similarity measure. ESA transforms the text from the image metadata into vectors that consist of Wikipedia article titles weighted by their relevance. The similarity score between these vectors is computed as the cosine of the angle between them. This similarity measure is used to create the graph and its PageRank is denoted as $\mathbf{PR_{ESA}}$.

The final approach uses the **visual features** extracted from the images themselves. The visual words extracted from the images are used to form feature vectors and the similarity between a pair of images computed as the cosine of the angle between them. The PageRank of the graph created using this approach is $\mathbf{PR_{vis}}$ and it is similar to the approach proposed by Jing and Baluja (2008) for associating images to text queries.

3.3.4 Initialising the Personalisation Vector

The personalisation vector (see above) is weighted using the similarity scores computed between the topic and its image candidates. Similarity is computed using PMI and ESA (see above). When PMI and ESA are used to weight the personalisation vector they compute the similarity between the top 10 terms for a topic and the textual metadata associated with each image in the set of candidates. We refer to the personalisation vectors created using PMI and ESA as **Per(PMI)** and **Per(ESA)** respectively.

Using PPR allows information about the similarity between the images' metadata and the topics themselves to be considered when identifying a suitable image label. The situation is different when PageRank is used since this only considers the similarity between the images in the candidate set.

The personalisation vector used by PPR is employed in combination with a graph created using one of the approaches described above. For example, the graph may be weighted using visual features and the personalisation vector created using PMI scores. This approach is denoted as $\mathrm{PR_{vis}}$+Per(PMI).

4 Evaluation

This section discusses the experimental design for evaluating the proposed approaches to labelling topics with images. To our knowledge no data set for evaluating these approaches is currently available and consequently we developed one for this study[5]. Human judgements about the suitability of images are obtained through crowdsourcing.

4.1 Data

We created a data set of topics from two collections which cover a broad thematic range:

- **NYT** 47,229 New York Times news articles (included in the GigaWord corpus) that were published between May and December 2010.
- **WIKI** A set of Wikipedia categories randomly selected by browsing its hierarchy in a breadth-first-search manner starting from a few seed

[5]Data set can be downloaded from `http://staffwww.dcs.shef.ac.uk/people/N.Aletras/resources.html`.

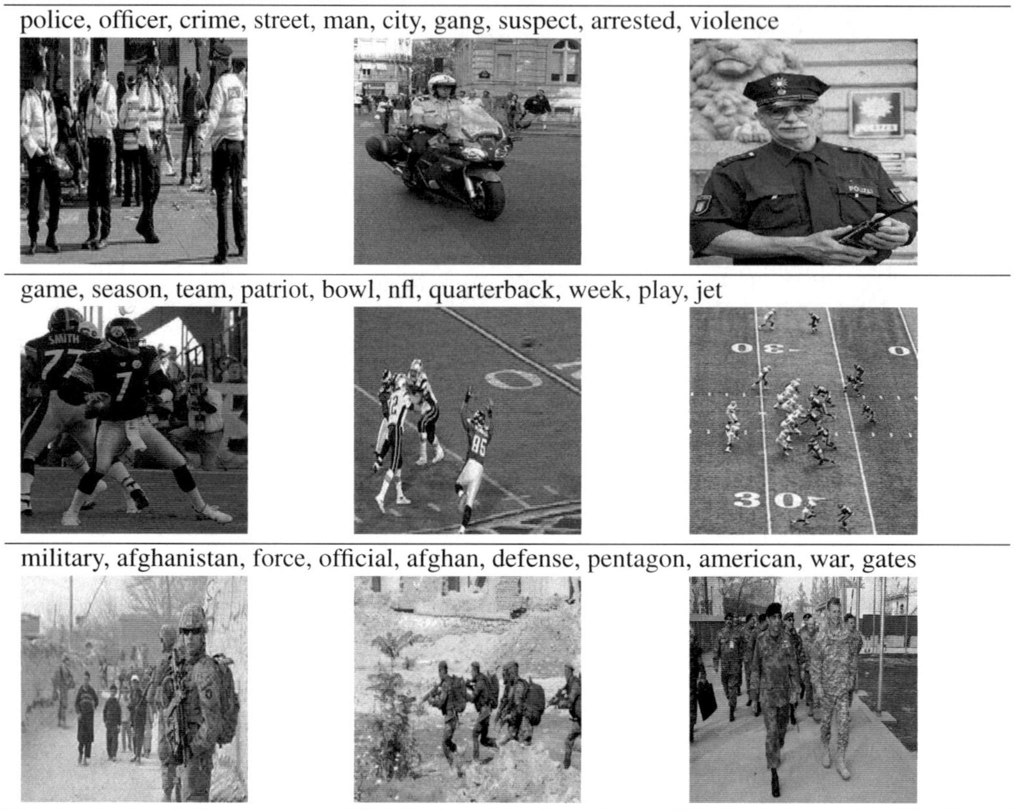

Figure 1: A sample of topics and their top-3 image candidates (i.e. with the highest average human annotations).

categories (e.g. SPORTS, POLITICS, COMPUTING). Categories that have more that 80 articles associated with them are considered. These articles are collected to produce a corpus of approximately 60,000 articles generated from 1,461 categories.

Documents in the two collections are tokenised and stop words removed. LDA was applied to learn 200 topics from NYT and 400 topics from WIKI. The *gensim* package[6] was used to implement and compute LDA. The hyperparameters (α, β) were set to $\frac{1}{num\_of\_topics}$. Incoherent topics are filtered out by applying the method proposed by Aletras and Stevenson (2013).

We randomly selected 100 topics from NYT and 200 topics from WIKI resulting in a data set of 300 topics. Candidate images for these topics were generated using the approach described in Section 3.1, producing a total of 6,000 candidate images (20 for each topic).

4.2 Human Judgements of Image Relevance

Human judgements of the suitability of each image were obtained using an online crowdsourcing platform, Crowdflower[7]. Annotators were provided with a topic (represented as a set of 10 keywords) and a candidate image. They were asked to judge how appropriate the image was as a representation of the main subject of the topic and provide a rating on a scale of 0 (completely unsuitable) to 3 (very suitable).

Quality control is important in crowdscourcing experiments to ensure reliability (Kazai, 2011). To avoid random answers, control questions with obvious answer were included in the survey. Annotations by participants that failed to answer these questions correctly or participants that gave the same rating for all pairs were removed.

[6] http://pypi.python.org/pypi/gensim

[7] http://crowdflower.com

The total number of filtered responses obtained was $62,221$ from 273 participants. Each topic-image pair was rated at least by 10 subjects. The average response for each pair was calculated in order to create the final similarity judgement for use as a gold-standard. The average variance across judges (excluding control questions) is 0.88.

Inter-Annotator agreement (IAA) is computed as the average Spearman's ρ between the ratings given by an annotator and the average ratings given by all other annotators. The average IAA across all topics was 0.50 which indicates the difficulty of the task, even for humans.

Figure 1 shows three example topics from the data set together with the images that received the highest average score from the annotators.

4.3 Evaluation Metrics

Evaluation of the topic labelling methods is carried out using a similar approach to the framework proposed by Lau et al. (2011) for labelling topics using textual labels.

Top-1 average rating is the average human rating assigned to the top-ranked label proposed by the system. This provides an indication of the overall quality of the image the system judges as the best one. The highest possible score averaged across all topics is 2.68, since for many topics the average score obtained from the human judgements is lower than 3.

The second evaluation measure is the normalized discounted cumulative gain (**nDCG**) (Järvelin and Kekäläinen, 2002; Croft et al., 2009) which compares the label ranking proposed by the system to the optimal ranking provided by humans. The discounted cumulative gain at position p (DCG_p) is computed using the following equation:

$$DCG_p = rel_1 + \sum_{i=2}^{p} \frac{rel_i}{log_2(i)} \quad (2)$$

where rel_i is the relevance of the label to the topic in position i. Then nDCG is computed as:

$$nDCG_p = \frac{DCG_p}{IDCG_p} \quad (3)$$

where $IDCG_p$ is the optimal ranking of the image labels, in our experiments this is the ranking provided by the scores in the human annotated data set. We follow Lau et al. (2011) in computing **nDCG-1**, **nDCG-3** and **nDCG-5** for the top 1, 3 and 5 ranked system image labels respectively.

4.4 Baselines

Since there are no previous methods for labelling topics using images, we compare our proposed models against three baselines.

The **Random** baseline randomly selects a label for the topic from the 20 image candidates. The process is repeated 10,000 times and the average score of the selected labels is computed for each topic.

The more informed **Word Overlap** baseline selects the image that is most similar to the topic terms by applying a Lesk-style algorithm (Lesk, 1986) to compare metadata for each image against the topic terms. It is defined as the number of common terms between a topic and image candidate normalised by the total number of terms in the topic and image's metadata.

We also compared our approach with the ranking returned by the **Google Image Search** for the top-20 images for a specific topic.

4.5 User Study

A user study was conducted to estimate human performance on the image selection task. Three annotators were recruited and asked to select the best image for each of the 300 topics in the data set. The annotators were provided with the topic (in the form of a set of keywords) and shown all candidate images for that topic before being asked to select exactly one. The Average Top-1 Rating was computed for each annotator and the mean of these values was 2.24.

5 Results

Table 1 presents the results obtained for each of the methods on the collection of 300 topics. Results are shown for both Top-1 Average rating and nDCG.

We begin by discussing the results obtained using the standard PageRank algorithm applied to graphs weighted using PMI, ESA and visual features (PR_{PMI}, PR_{ESA} and PR_{vis} respectively). Results using PMI consistently outperform all baselines and those obtained using ESA. This suggests that distributional word association measures are more suitable for identifying useful images than knowledge-based similarity measures. The best results using

Model	Top-1 Av. Rating	nDCG-1	nDCG-3	nDCG-5
Baselines				
Random	1.79	-	-	-
Word Overlap	1.85	0.69	0.72	0.74
Google Image Search	1.89	0.73	0.75	0.77
PageRank				
PR_{PMI}	1.87	0.70	0.73	0.75
PR_{ESA}	1.81	0.67	0.68	0.70
PR_{vis}	1.96	0.73	0.75	0.76
Personalised PageRank				
PR_{PMI}+Per(PMI)	1.98	0.74	0.76	0.77
PR_{PMI}+Per(ESA)	1.92	0.70	0.72	0.74
PR_{ESA}+Per(PMI)	1.91	0.70	0.72	0.73
PR_{ESA}+Per(ESA)	1.88	0.69	0.72	0.74
PR_{vis}+Per(PMI)	2.00	0.74	0.75	0.76
PR_{vis}+Per(ESA)	1.94	0.72	0.75	0.76
User Study	2.24	–	–	–

Table 1: Results for various approaches to topic labelling.

standard PageRank are obtained when the visual similarity measures are used to weight the graph, with performance that significantly outperforms the word overlap baseline (paired t-test, $p < 0.05$). This demonstrates that visual features are a useful source of information for deciding which images are suitable topic labels.

The Personalised version of PageRank produces consistently higher results compared to standard PageRank, demonstrating that the additional information provided by comparing the image metadata with the topics is useful for this task. The best results are obtained when the personalisation vector is weighted using PMI (i.e. Per(PMI)). The best overall result for the top-1 average rating (2.00) is obtained when the graph is weighted using visual features and the personalisation vector using the PMI scores (PR_{vis}+Per(PMI)) while the best results for the various DCG metrics are produced when both the graph and the personalisation vector are weighted using PMI scores (PR_{PMI}+Per(PMI)). In addition, these two methods, PR_{vis}+Per(PMI) and PR_{PMI}+Per(PMI), perform significantly better than the word overlap and the Google Image Search baselines ($p < 0.01$ and $p < 0.05$ respectively). Weighting the personalisation vector using ESA consistently produces lower performance compared to PMI. These results indicate that graph-based methods for ranking images are useful for illustrating topics.

6 Discussion

Figure 2 shows a sample of three topics together with the top-3 candidates (left-to-right) selected by applying the PR_{vis}+Per(PMI) approach. Reasonable labels have been selected for the first two topics. On the other hand, the images selected for the third topic do not seem to be as appropriate.

We observed that inappropriate labels can be generated for two reasons. Firstly, the topic may be abstract and difficult to illustrate. For example, one of the topics in our data set refers to the subject ALGEBRAIC NUMBER THEORY and contains the terms *number, ideal, group, field, theory, algebraic, class, ring, prime, theorem*. It is difficult to find a representative image for topics such as this one. Secondly, there are topics for which none of the candidate images returned by the search engine is relevant. An example of a topic like this in our data set is one that refers to PLANTS and contains the terms *family, sources, plants, familia, order, plant, species, taxonomy, classification, genera*. The images returned by the search engine include pictures of the Sagrada Familia cathedral in Barcelona, a car called "Familia"

Figure 2: A sample of topics and their top-3 images selected by applying the the PR_{vis}+Per(PMI) approach (left side) and the ones with the highest average human annotations (right side). The number under each image represents its average human annotations score.

and pictures of families but no pictures of plants.

7 Conclusions

This paper explores the use of images to represent automatically generated topics. An approach to selecting appropriate images was described. This begins by identifying a set of candidate images using a search engine and then attempts to select the most suitable. Images are ranked using a graph-based method that makes use of both textual and visual information. Evaluation is carried out on a data set created for this study. The results show that the visual features are a useful source of information for this task while the proposed graph-based method significantly outperforms several baselines.

This paper demonstrates that it is possible to identify images to illustrate topics. A possible application for this technique is to represent the contents of large document collections in a way that supports rapid interpretation and can be used to enable navigation (Chaney and Blei, 2012; Gretarsson et al., 2012; Hinneburg et al., 2012). We plan to explore this possibility in future work. Other possible extensions to this work include exploring alternative approaches to generating candidate images and developing techniques to automatically identify abstract topics for which suitable images are unlikely to be found, thereby avoiding the problem cases described in Section 6.

Acknowledgments

The research leading to these results was carried out as part of the PATHS project (`http://paths-project.eu`) funded by the European Community's Seventh Framework Programme (FP7/2007-2013) under grant agreement no. 270082.

References

Eneko Agirre and Aitor Soroa. 2009. Personalizing PageRank for word sense disambiguation. In *Proceedings of the 12th Conference of the European Chapter of the Association for Computational Linguistics (EACL '09)*, pages 33–41, Athens, Greece.

Rakesh Agrawal, Sreenivas Gollapudi, Anitha Kannan, and Krishnaram Kenthapadi. 2011. Enriching textbooks with images. In *Proceedings of the 20th ACM International Conference on Information and Knowledge Management (CIKM '11)*, pages 1847–1856, Glasgow, Scotland, UK.

Nikolaos Aletras and Mark Stevenson. 2013. Evaluating topic coherence using distributional semantics. In *Proceedings of the 10th International Conference on Computational Semantics (IWCS '13) – Long Papers*, pages 13–22, Potsdam, Germany.

David M. Blei, Andrew Y. Ng, and Michael I. Jordan. 2003. Latent Dirichlet Allocation. *Journal of Machine Learning Research*, 3:993–1022.

Jordan Boyd-Graber, David Blei, and Xiaojin Zhu. 2007. A topic model for word sense disambiguation. In *Proceedings of the 2007 Joint Conference on Empirical Methods in Natural Language Processing and Computational Natural Language Learning (EMNLP-CoNLL '07)*, pages 1024–1033, Prague, Czech Republic.

Elia Bruni, Giang Binh Tran, and Marco Baroni. 2011. Distributional semantics from text and images. In *Proceedings of the Workshop on GEometrical Models of Natural Language Semantics (GEMS '11)*, pages 22–32, Edinburgh, UK.

Allison June-Barlow Chaney and David M. Blei. 2012. Visualizing topic models. In *Proceedings of the Sixth International AAAI Conference on Weblogs and Social Media*, Dublin, Ireland.

Bruce W. Croft, Donald Metzler, and Trevor Strohman. 2009. *Search engines: Information retrieval in practice*. Addison-Wesley.

Ritendra Datta, Dhiraj Joshi, Jia Li, and James Z. Wang. 2008. Image Retrieval: Ideas, Influences, and Trends of the New Age. *ACM Computing Surveys*, 40(2):1–60.

Yansong Feng and Mirella Lapata. 2010a. How many words is a picture worth? Automatic caption generation for news images. In *Proceedings of the 48th Annual Meeting of the Association for Computational Linguistics*, pages 1239–1249, Uppsala, Sweden.

Yansong Feng and Mirella Lapata. 2010b. Topic Models for Image Annotation and Text Illustration. In *Proceedings of Human Language Technologies: The 2010 Annual Conference of the North American Chapter of the Association for Computational Linguistics*, pages 831–839, Los Angeles, California.

Evgeniy Gabrilovich and Shaul Markovitch. 2007. Computing semantic relatedness using Wikipedia-based explicit semantic analysis. In *Proceedings of the International Joint Conference on Artificial Intelligence (IJCAI '07)*, pages 1606–1611, Hyberabad, India.

Brynjar Gretarsson, John O'Donovan, Svetlin Bostandjiev, Tobias Höllerer, Arthur Asuncion, David Newman, and Padhraic Smyth. 2012. TopicNets: Visual analysis of large text corpora with topic modeling. *ACM Trans. Intell. Syst. Technol.*, 3(2):23:1–23:26.

Aria Haghighi and Lucy Vanderwende. 2009. Exploring content models for multi-document summarization. In *Proceedings of Human Language Technologies: The 2009 Annual Conference of the North American Chapter of the Association for Computational Linguistics*, pages 362–370, Boulder, Colorado.

Taher Haveliwala, Sepandar Kamvar, and Glen Jeh. 2003. An analytical comparison of approaches to personalizing PageRank. Technical Report 2003-35, Stanford InfoLab.

Alexander Hinneburg, Rico Preiss, and René Schröder. 2012. TopicExplorer: Exploring document collections with topic models. In Peter A. Flach, Tijl Bie, and Nello Cristianini, editors, *Machine Learning and Knowledge Discovery in Databases*, volume 7524 of *Lecture Notes in Computer Science*, pages 838–841. Springer Berlin Heidelberg.

Thomas Hofmann. 1999. Probabilistic latent semantic indexing. In *Proceedings of the 22nd Annual International ACM SIGIR Conference on Research and Development in Information Retrieval (SIGIR '99)*, pages 50–57, Berkeley, California, United States.

Ioana Hulpus, Conor Hayes, Marcel Karnstedt, and Derek Greene. 2013. Unsupervised graph-based topic labelling using DBpedia. In *Proceedings of the 6th ACM International Conference on Web Search and Data Mining (WSDM '13)*, pages 465–474, Rome, Italy.

Kalervo Järvelin and Jaana Kekäläinen. 2002. Cumulated gain-based evaluation of IR techniques. *ACM Trans. Inf. Syst.*, 20(4):422–446.

Yushi Jing and Shumeet Baluja. 2008. PageRank for product image search. In *Proceedings of the 17th International Conference on World Wide Web (WWW '08)*, pages 307–316, Beijing, China.

Dhiraj Joshi, James Z. Wang, and Jia Li. 2006. The Story Picturing Engine—A system for automatic text illustration. *ACM Trans. Multimedia Comput. Commun. Appl.*, 2(1):68–89.

Gabriella Kazai. 2011. In search of quality in crowdsourcing for search engine evaluation. *Advances in Information Retrieval*, pages 165–176.

Jey Han Lau, David Newman, Sarvnaz Karimi, and Timothy Baldwin. 2010. Best topic word selection for topic labelling. In *The 23rd International Conference on Computational Linguistics (COLING '10)*, pages 605–613, Beijing, China.

Jey Han Lau, Karl Grieser, David Newman, and Timothy Baldwin. 2011. Automatic labelling of topic models. In *Proceedings of the 49th Annual Meeting of the Association for Computational Linguistics: Human Language Technologies*, pages 1536–1545, Portland, Oregon, USA.

Michael Lesk. 1986. Automatic sense disambiguation using machine readable dictionaries: How to tell a pine cone from an ice cream cone. In *Proceedings of the 5th Annual International Conference on Systems Documentation (SIGDOC '86)*, pages 24–26, Toronto, Ontario, Canada.

David G. Lowe. 1999. Object Recognition from Local Scale-invariant Features. In *Proceedings of the Seventh IEEE International Conference on Computer Vision*, pages 1150–1157, Kerkyra, Greece.

David G. Lowe. 2004. Distinctive Image Features from Scale-Invariant Keypoints. *International Journal of Computer Vision*, 60(2):91–110.

Davide Magatti, Silvia Calegari, Davide Ciucci, and Fabio Stella. 2009. Automatic Labeling of Topics. In *Proceedings of the 9th International Conference on Intelligent Systems Design and Applications (ICSDA '09)*, pages 1227–1232, Pisa, Italy.

Xian-Li Mao, Zhao-Yan Ming, Zheng-Jun Zha, Tat-Seng Chua, Hongfei Yan, and Xiaoming Li. 2012. Automatic labeling hierarchical topics. In *Proceedings of the 21st ACM International Conference on Information and Knowledge Management (CIKM '12)*, Sheraton, Maui Hawai.

Qiaozhu Mei and ChengXiang Zhai. 2005. Discovering evolutionary theme patterns from text: an exploration of temporal text mining. In *Proceedings of the 11th ACM International Conference on Knowledge Discovery in Data Mining (SIGKDD '05)*, pages 198–207, Chicago, Illinois, USA.

Qiaozhu Mei, Xuehua Shen, and Cheng Xiang Zhai. 2007. Automatic Labeling of Multinomial Topic Models. In *Proceedings of the 13th ACM International Conference on Knowledge Discovery and Data Mining (SIGKDD '07)*, pages 490–499, San Jose, California.

Rada Mihalcea and Paul Tarau. 2004. TextRank: Bringing order into texts. In *Proceedings of International Conference on Empirical Methods in Natural Language Processing (EMNLP '04)*, pages 404–411, Barcelona, Spain.

Lawrence Page, Sergey Brin, Rajeev Motwani, and Terry Winograd. 1999. The PageRank citation ranking: Bringing order to the web. Technical Report 1999-66, Stanford InfoLab.

Koen E.A. Sande, Theo Gevers, and Cees G. M. Snoek. 2008. Evaluation of Color Descriptors for Object and Scene Recognition. In *Proceedings of the IEEE Computer Society Conference on Computer Vision and Pattern Recognition (CVPR '08)*, pages 1–8, Anchorage, Alaska, USA.

Richard Szeliski. 2010. *Computer Vision: Algorithms and Applications*. Springer-Verlag Inc.

Yee Whye Teh, Michael I. Jordan, Matthew J. Beal, and David M. Blei. 2006. Hierarchical dirichlet processes. *Journal of the American Statistical Association*, 101(476):1566–1581.

Xing Wei and W. Bruce Croft. 2006. LDA-based Document Models for Ad-hoc Retrieval. In *Proceedings of the 29th annual international ACM SIGIR conference on Research and Development in Information Retrieval (SIGIR '06)*, pages 178–185, Seattle, Washington, USA.

Drug Extraction from the Web: Summarizing Drug Experiences with Multi-Dimensional Topic Models

Michael J. Paul and **Mark Dredze**
Human Language Technology Center of Excellence
Center for Language and Speech Processing
Johns Hopkins University
Baltimore, MD 21218
{mpaul,mdredze}@cs.jhu.edu

Abstract

Multi-dimensional latent text models, such as *factorial LDA* (f-LDA), capture multiple factors of corpora, creating structured output for researchers to better understand the contents of a corpus. We consider such models for clinical research of new recreational drugs and trends, an important application for mining current information for healthcare workers. We use a "three-dimensional" f-LDA variant to jointly model combinations of drug (marijuana, salvia, etc.), aspect (effects, chemistry, etc.) and route of administration (smoking, oral, etc.) Since a purely unsupervised topic model is unlikely to discover these specific factors of interest, we develop a novel method of incorporating prior knowledge by leveraging user generated tags as priors in our model. We demonstrate that this model can be used as an exploratory tool for learning about these drugs from the Web by applying it to the task of extractive summarization. In addition to providing useful output for this important public health task, our prior-enriched model provides a framework for the application of f-LDA to other tasks.

1 Introduction

Topic models aid exploration of the main thematic elements of large text corpora by revealing latent structure and producing a high level semantic view (Blei et al., 2003). Topic models have been used for understanding the contents of a corpus and identifying interesting aspects of a collection for more in-depth analysis (Talley et al., 2011; Mimno, 2011). While standard topic models assume a flat semantic structure, there are potentially many dimensions of a corpus that contribute to word choice, such as sentiment, perspective and ideology (Mei et al., 2007; Paul and Girju, 2010; Eisenstein et al., 2011). Rather than studying these factors in isolation, **multi-dimensional** topic models can consider multiple factors jointly.

Paul and Dredze (2012b) introduced *factorial LDA* (f-LDA), a general framework for multi-dimensional text models that capture an arbitrary number of factors (explained in §3). While a standard topic model learns distributions over "topics" in documents, f-LDA learns distributions over combinations of multiple factors (e.g. topic, perspective) called tuples (e.g. (HEALTHCARE,LIBERAL)). While f-LDA can model factors without supervision, it has not been used in situations where the user has prior information about the factors.

In this paper we consider a setting where the user has prior knowledge about the end application: mining recreational drug trends from user forums, an important clinical research problem (§2). We show how to incorporate available information from these forums into f-LDA as a novel hierarchical prior over the model parameters, guiding the model toward the desired output (§3.1).

We then demonstrate the model's utility in exploring a corpus in a targeted manner by using it to automatically extract interesting sentences from the text, a simple form of extractive multi-document summarization (Goldstein et al., 2000). In the same way that topic models can be used for aspect-specific summarization (Titov and McDonald, 2008; Haghighi and Vanderwende, 2009), we use f-LDA to extract snippets corresponding to fine-grained information patterns. Our results demonstrate that our multi-dimensional modeling approach targets more informative text than a simpler model (§4).

2 Analyzing Drug Trends on the Web

Recreational drug use imposes a significant burden on the health infrastructure of the United States and other countries. Accurate information on drugs, usage profiles and side effects are necessary for supporting a range of healthcare activities, such as addiction treatment programs, toxin diagnosis, prevention and awareness campaigns, and public policy. These activities rely on up-to-date information on drug trends, but it is increasingly difficult to keep up with current drug information, as distribution and information-sharing of novel drugs is easier than ever via the web (Wax, 2002). For the third consecutive year, a record number of new drugs (49) were detected in Europe in 2011 (EMCDDA, 2012). About two-thirds of these new drugs were synthetic cannabinoids (used as legal marijuana substitutes), which led to 11,000 hospitalizations in the U.S. in 2010 (SAMHSA, 2012). Treatment is complicated by the fact that novel substances like these may have unknown side effects and other properties.

Accurate information on drug trends can be obtained by speaking directly with users, e.g. focus groups and interviews (Reyes et al., 2012; Hout and Bingham, 2012), but such studies are slow and costly, and can fail to identify the emergence of new drug classes, such as mephedrone (Dunn et al., 2011). More recently, researchers have begun to recognize clinical value in information obtained from the web (Corazza et al., 2011). By (manually) analyzing YouTube videos, Drugs-Forum (discussed below), and other social media websites and online communities, researchers have uncovered details about the use, effects, and popularity of a variety of new and emerging drugs (Morgan et al., 2010; Corazza et al., 2012; Gallagher et al., 2012), and comprehensive drug reviews now include nonstandard sources such as web forums in addition to standard sources (Hill and Thomas, 2011).

Organizing and understanding forums requires significant effort. We propose automated tools to aid in the exploration and analysis of these data. While topic models are a natural fit for corpus exploration (Eisenstein et al., 2012; Chaney and Blei, 2012), and have been used for similar public health applications (Paul and Dredze, 2011), online forums can be organized in many ways beyond topic. Guided by domain experts, we seek to model forums as a combination of drug type, route of intake (oral, injection, etc.) and aspect (cultural settings, drug chemistry, etc.) A multi-dimensional topic model can jointly capture these factors, providing a more informative understanding of the data, and can be used to produce fine-grained information such as the effects of taking a particular drug orally. Our hope is that models such as f-LDA can lead to exploratory tools that aide researchers in learning about new drugs.

Factor	Components
Drug	ALCOHOL AMPHETAMINES BETA-KETONES CANNABINOIDS CANNABIS COCAINE DMT DOWNERS DXM ECSTASY GHB HERBAL ECSTASY KETAMINE KRATOM LSA LSD NOOTROPICS OPIATES PEYOTE PHENETHYLAMINES SALVIA TOBACCO
Route	INJECTION ORAL SMOKING SNORTING
Aspect	CHEMISTRY (Pharmacology, TEK) CULTURE (Culture, Setting, Social, Spiritual) EFFECTS (Effects) HEALTH (Health, Overdose, Side effects) USAGE (Dose, Storing, Weight)

Table 1: The three factors of our model (details in §3.1). The forum tags shown in parentheses are grouped together to form aspects.

2.1 Corpus: Drugs-Forum

Our data set is taken from `drugs-forum.com`, a site active for more than 10 years with over 100,000 members and more than 1 million monthly readers. The site is an information hub where people can freely discuss recreational drugs with psychoactive effects, ranging from coffee to heroin, hosting information and discussions on specific drugs, as well as drug-related politics, law, news, recovery and addiction. With current information on a variety of drugs and an extensive archive, Drugs-Forum provides an ideal information source for public health researchers (Corazza et al., 2012).

Discussion threads are organized into numerous forums, including drugs, the law, addiction, etc. Since we are modeling drug use, we focus on the drug forums. Each thread is assigned to a specific forum or subforum (drug) and each thread has a user specified tag, which can indicate categories like "Effects" as well as routes of administration like "Oral." We organized the tags and subforum categorizations into factors and components, as shown in Table 1. We make use of these tags in §3.1.

3 Multi-Dimensional Text Models

Clinical researchers are interested in specific information about drug usage, including **drug** type, **route** of administration, and other **aspects** of drug use (e.g. dosage, side effects). Rather than considering these factors independently, we would like to model these in a way that can capture interesting interactions between all three factors, because the effects and other aspects of drugs can vary by route of administration. Oral consumption of drugs often produces longer lasting but milder effects than injection or smoking, for example. Many mephedrone users report nose bleeds and nasal pain as a health effect of snorting the drug: this could be modeled as the triple (MEPHEDRONE,SNORTING,HEALTH), a particular combination of all three factors.

To this end, we utilize the multi-dimensional text model **factorial LDA** (f-LDA) (Paul and Dredze, 2012b), which jointly models multiple semantic *factors* or dimensions. In this section we summarize f-LDA, then we describe an extension which incorporates user-generated metadata into the model (§3.1).

In a standard topic model such as LDA (Blei et al., 2003), each word token is associated with a latent "topic" variable. f-LDA is conceptually similar to LDA except that rather than a single topic variable, each token is associated with a K-dimensional **vector** of latent variables. In a three-dimensional f-LDA model, each token has three latent variables—drug, route, and aspect in this case.

In f-LDA, each document has a distribution over all possible K-tuples (rather than topics), and each K-tuple is associated with its own word distribution. Under this model, words are generated by first sampling a tuple from the document's tuple distribution, then sampling a word from that tuple's word distribution. In our three-dimensional model, we will consider **triples** such as (CANNABIS,SMOKING,EFFECTS).

Formally, each document has a distribution $\theta^{(d)}$ over triples, and each token is associated with a latent vector $\vec{z}$ of size K=3. (We'll describe the model in terms of the three factors we are modeling in this paper, but f-LDA generalizes to K dimensions.) The Cartesian product of the three factors forms a set of triples and the vector $\vec{z}$ references three discrete components to form a triple $\vec{t} = (t_1, t_2, t_3)$. The cardinality of each dimension (denoted Z_k) is the number of drugs, routes, and aspects, as shown in Table 1. Each triple has a corresponding word distribution $\phi_{\vec{t}}$. The graphical model is shown in Figure 1.

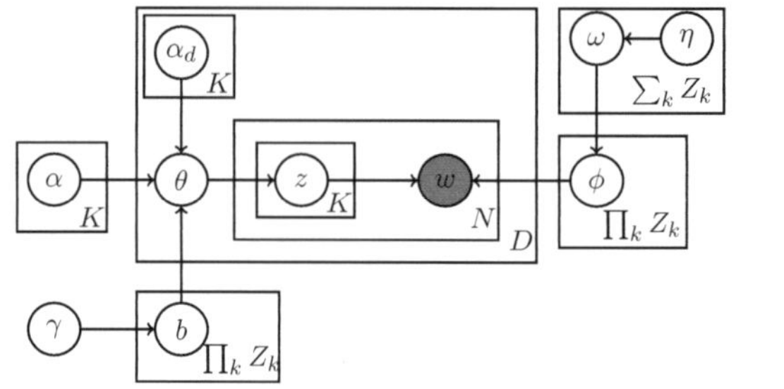

Figure 1: The graphical model for f-LDA augmented with priors η learned from labeled data (§3.1). In this work, $K = 3$.

One would expect that triples that have components in common should have similar word distributions: (CANNABIS,SMOKING,EFFECTS) is expected to have some commonalities with (CANNABIS,ORAL,EFFECTS). f-LDA models this intuition by sharing parameters across priors for triples which share components: all triples with CANNABIS as the drug include cannabis-specific parameters in the prior, and all triples with SMOKING as the route have smoking-specific parameters. Formally, $\phi_{\vec{t}}$ (the word distribution for tuple $\vec{t}$) has a Dirichlet($\hat{\omega}^{(\vec{t})}$) prior, where for each word w in the vector, $\hat{\omega}_w^{(\vec{t})}$ is a log-linear function:

$$\hat{\omega}_w^{(\vec{t})} \triangleq \exp\left(\omega^{(B)} + \omega_w^{(0)} + \omega_{t_1 w}^{(\text{drug})} + \omega_{t_2 w}^{(\text{route})} + \omega_{t_3 w}^{(\text{aspect})}\right) \tag{1}$$

where $\omega^{(B)}$ is a corpus-wide precision scalar (the bias), $\omega_w^{(0)}$ is a corpus-specific bias for word w, and $\omega_{t_k w}^{(k)}$ is a bias parameter for word w for component t_k of the kth factor. That is, each drug, route, and aspect has a weight vector over the vocabulary, and the prior for a particular triple is influenced by the weight vectors of each of the three factors. The ω parameters are all independent and normally distributed around 0 (effectively L2 regularization).

The prior over each document's distribution over triples has a similar log-linear prior, where weights for each factor are combined to influence the distribution. Under our model, $\theta^{(d)}$ is drawn from Dirichlet($\mathbf{B} \cdot \hat{\alpha}^{(d)}$), where $\cdot$ denotes an element-wise product between $\mathbf{B}$ (described below) and $\hat{\alpha}^{(d)}$, with

$\hat{\alpha}_{\vec{t}}^{(d)}$ for each triple $\vec{t}$ defined as:

$$\hat{\alpha}_{\vec{t}}^{(d)} \triangleq \exp\Big(\alpha^{(B)} + \alpha_{t_1}^{(\mathcal{D},\text{drug})} + \alpha_{t_1}^{(d,\text{drug})} + \alpha_{t_2}^{(\mathcal{D},\text{route})} + \alpha_{t_2}^{(d,\text{route})} + \alpha_{t_3}^{(\mathcal{D},\text{aspect})} + \alpha_{t_3}^{(d,\text{aspect})}\Big) \quad (2)$$

Similar to the ω formulation, $\alpha^{(B)}$ is a global bias parameter, while the $\alpha^{\mathcal{D}}$ vectors are corpus-wide weight vectors and α^{d} are document-specific weight vectors over the components of each factor. Structuring the prior in this way models the intuition that if a triple with a particular component has high probability, other triples containing that component are likely to also have high probability. For example, if a message discusses triples of the form (CANNABIS,*,EFFECTS), it is more likely to discuss (CANNABIS,*,HEALTH) than (COCAINE,*,HEALTH), because the message is about cannabis.

Finally, **B** is a 3-dimensional array that encodes a sparsity pattern over the space of possible triples. This is used to accommodate triples that can be generated by the model but are not supported by the data. For example, not all routes of administration may be applicable to certain drugs, or certain aspects of a drug may happen to not be discussed in the forum. Each element $b_{\vec{t}}$ of the array is a real-valued scalar in $(0, 1)$ which is multiplied with $\hat{\alpha}_{\vec{t}}^{(d)}$ to adjust the prior for that triple. If the b value is near 0 for a particular triple, then it will have very low prior probability. The b values have Beta(γ_0,γ_1) priors ($\gamma < 1$) which encourage them to be near 0 or 1, so that they function as binary variables.

Posterior inference and parameter estimation consist of a Monte Carlo EM algorithm that alternates between an iteration of collapsed Gibbs sampler on the $\vec{z}$ variables (E-step), and an iteration of gradient ascent on the α and ω hyperparameters (M-step). See Paul and Dredze (2012b) for more details.

3.1 Tags and Word Priors

In an unsupervised setting, there is no reason f-LDA would actually infer parameters corresponding to the three factors we have been describing. However, the forums include metadata that can help guide the model: the messages are organized into forums corresponding to drug type (factor 1), and some threads are tagged with labels corresponding to routes of administration and other aspects (factors 2 and 3). Tags for aspects are manually grouped into components: e.g. USAGE (tags: Dose, Storing, Weight). Table 1 shows the factors and components in our model.

One could simply use these tags as labels in a simple supervised model—this will be our experimental baseline (§4.1). However, this approach has limitations in that most documents are missing labels (less than a third of our corpus contains one of the labels in Table 1) and many messages discuss several components, not just the one implied by the tag. For example, a message tagged "Side effects" may talk about both side effects and dosage. While a supervised classifier may attribute all words to a single tag, f-LDA learns per-token assignments.

We will instead use the tags to inform the priors over our f-LDA word distribution parameters. We do this with a two-stage approach. First, we use the tags to train parameters of a related but simplified model. We then use the learned parameters as priors over the corresponding f-LDA parameters.

In particular, we will place priors on the ω vectors, the Dirichlet hyperparameters which influence the word distributions. Suppose that we are given a vector $\eta^{(0)}$ which is believed to contain desirable values for $\omega^{(0)}$, the weight vector over words in the corpus, and similarly we are given vectors $\eta_i^{(f)}$ over the vocabulary for the ith component of factor f, which are believed to be good values for $\omega_i^{(f)}$. One option

COCAINE	SNORTING	HEALTH
η (Prior over ω)		
coke	snort	kidney
cocaine	snorting	hcv
crack	snorted	pains
cola	nose	symptoms
blow	nasal	guidelines
lines	drip	diet
ω (Prior over ϕ)		
coke	snort	symptoms
cocaine	snorting	long-term
crack	snorted	depression
cola	passages	disorder
rocks	nostril	schizophrenia
coca	insufflating	severe

COCAINE SNORTING HEALTH
ϕ (Posterior)
nose
cocaine
coke
blood
water
pain

Figure 2: Example of parameters learned by f-LDA. The highest weight words in the ω and η vectors for three components are shown on the left. These are combined to form the prior for the word distribution ϕ. The tripling of (COCAINE,SNORTING,HEALTH) results in high probability words about nose bleeds and nasal damage.

is to fix ω as η, forcing the component weights to match the provided weights. However, in our case η will only be an approximation of the optimal component parameters since it is estimated from incomplete data (only some messages have tags) and the η vectors are learned using an approximate model (see below). Instead, these weight vectors will merely guide learning as prior knowledge over model parameters ω. While f-LDA assumes each ω is drawn from a 0-mean Gaussian, we alter the means of the appropriate ω parameters to use η.

$$\omega_w^{(0)} \sim \mathcal{N}(\eta_w^{(0)}, \sigma^2); \omega_{iw}^{(k)} \sim \mathcal{N}(\eta_{iw}^{(k)}, \sigma^2) \quad (3)$$

Recall that $\omega_w^{(0)}$ are corpus-wide bias parameters for each word and $\omega_{iw}^{(k)}$ are component-specific parameters for each word. This yields a hierarchical prior in which η parameterizes the prior over ω, while ω parameterizes the prior over ϕ (the word distributions). The resulting ω parameters can vary from the provided priors to adapt to the data. An example of learned parameters is shown in Figure 2, illustrating the hierarchical process behind this model.

Learning the Priors In various applications, priors can come from many different sources, such as labeled data (Jagarlamudi et al., 2012). We learn the prior means η from tagged messages. However, these parameters imply a latent division of responsibility for observed words: some are present because of the tag while others are general words in the corpus. As a result, they must be estimated.

We learn these parameters from the tagged messages using SAGE, which model words in a document as combinations of background and topic word distributions. Eisenstein et al. (2011) present SAGE models for Naive Bayes (one class per document), admixture models (one class per token), and admixture models where tokens come from multiple factors. We combine the first and third models, such that a document has multiple factors which are given as labels across the entire document—the drug type and the tag, which could correspond to a component of either the route or aspect factors. We posit the following model of text generation per document:

$$P(\text{word } w|\text{drug} = i, \text{factor} f = j) \quad (4)$$
$$= \frac{\exp(\eta_w^{(0)} + \eta_{iw}^{(\text{drug})} + \eta_{jw}^{(f)})}{\sum_{w'} \exp(\eta_{w'}^{(0)} + \eta_{iw'}^{(\text{drug})} + \eta_{jw'}^{(f)})}$$

This log-linear model has a similar form as Eq. 1, but with two factors instead of three, and it is a distribution rather than a Dirichlet vector. As in SAGE, we fix $\eta^{(\mathbf{0})}$ to be the observed vector of corpus log-frequencies over the vocabulary, which acts as an "overall" weight vector, while parameter estimation yields $\eta_i^{(f)}$, the logit parameters for the ith component of factor f.[1] These parameters are then used as the mean of the Gaussian priors over ω.

Standard optimization methods can be used to estimate these parameters. The partial derivative of the likelihood with respect to the parameter $\eta_{iw}^{(\text{drug})}$ is:

$$\frac{\partial}{\partial \eta_{iw}^{(\text{drug})}} = \sum_f \sum_{j \in f} c(i, j, w) - \pi(i, j, w) c(i, j, *) \quad (5)$$

where $c(i, j, w)$ is the number of times word w appears in documents labeled with i (drug) and j (tag), and $\pi(i, j, w)$ denotes the probability given by (4). The partial derivative of each $\eta_j^{(f)}$ is similar.

4 Experiments with Topic Modeling for Extractive Summarization

Our corpus consists of messages from `drugs-forum.com` (§2.1). The site categorizes threads into many forums and subforums, including some on specific drugs, which are categorized hierarchically. We treated higher-level categories with pharmacologically similar drugs as a single drug type (e.g. OPIOIDS, AMPHETAMINES); for others we took the finest-granularity subforum as the drug type. We selected 22 popular drugs and from these forums we crawled 410K messages. We selected a subset of tags to form components for the route and aspect factors. (Some tags were too general or infrequent to be useful.) A list of the tags and drugs used appears in Table 1. We also included a GENERAL component in the latter two factors to model word usage which does not pertain to a particular route or aspect; the prior parameters η for these components were simply set to $\mathbf{0}$.

We wish to demonstrate that our modified f-LDA model can be used to discover useful information in the text. One way to demonstrate this is by using the model to extract relevant snippets of text from the

[1] SAGE models sparsity on the weights via a Laplacian prior. Such sparsity is not modeled in f-LDA, so we ignore this here.

forums, which will form the basis of our evaluation experiments. Our goal is not to build a complete summarization system, but rather to use the model to direct researchers to interesting messages.

While we model all 22 drugs, our summarization experiments will focus on five drugs which have been studied only relatively recently: mephedrone and MDPV (β-ketones), Bromo-Dragonfly (synthetic phenethylamines), Spice/K2 (synthetic cannabinoids), and salvia divinorum. We will consider these drugs in particular because these are the five drugs for which technical reports were created by the EU Psychonaut Project (Schifano et al., 2006), an online database of novel and emerging drugs, whose information is collected by reading drug websites, including Drugs-Forum. Extensive technical reports were written about these five popular drugs, and we can use these reports to produce reference summaries for our experiments (§4.2).

Of these five drugs, only salvia has its own subforum; the others belong to subforums representing the broader categories shown in parentheses. We simply model the drug type as a proxy for the specific drug, as most of the drugs in each category have similar effects and properties. The first two drugs are both in the same subforum, so for the purpose of our model we treat mephedrone and MDPV as the single drug type, β-ketones. These two drugs are grouped together during summarization (§4.2), but the corresponding reference summaries incorporate excepts from the technical reports on both drugs.

4.1 Model Setup

Of the four drug types being considered for summarization, our data set contains 12K messages with one of the tags in Table 1 and 30K without. Of those without tags, we set aside 5K as development data. There are also over 300K messages (140K tagged) from the remaining 18 drug types: some of these messages are utilized when training f-LDA. Even though we only consider four drug types in our experiments, our intuition is that it can be beneficial to model other drugs as well, because this will help to learn parameters for the various aspects and routes of administration. Our model of the effects of mephedrone can be informed by also modeling the effects of other stimulants such as cocaine.

Each message was treated as a document, and we only used documents with at least five word tokens after stop words, low-frequency words, and punctuation were removed. The preprocessed data sets contained an average of 45 tokens per document.

Below, we describe two f-LDA variants as well as the baseline used in our experiments.

Baseline Our baseline model is a unigram language model trained on the subset of messages which are tagged. We treat the drug subforum as a label for the drug factor, and each message's tag is used as a label for either the route or aspect factor. For example, the word distribution for the pair (SALVIA,EFFECTS) is estimated as the empirical distribution from messages posted in the salvia forum and tagged with "Effects." We use add-λ smoothing where λ is chosen to optimize likelihood on the held-out development set.

This is a two-dimensional model, since we explicitly model pairs such as (MEPHEDRONE,SNORTING) or (SALVIA,EFFECTS). However, we also created word distributions for triples such as (SALVIA,ORAL,EFFECTS) by taking a mixture of the corresponding pairs: in this example, we estimate the unigram distribution from salvia documents tagged with either "Oral" or "Effects."

Factorial LDA Because f-LDA does not rely on tagged data (the tags are only used to create priors), we can run inference on larger sets of data. The drawback is that despite these priors, it is still mostly unsupervised and we want to be careful to ensure the model will learn the patterns we care about. We thus add some reasonable constraints to the parameter space to guide the model further.

First, we treat the drug type as an observed variable based on the subforum the message comes from, just as with the baseline. For example, only tuples of the form (SALVIA,$*$,$*$) can be assigned to tokens in the salvia forum. Second, we restrict the set of possible routes of administration that can be assigned to tokens in particular drug forums, since most drugs can be taken through only a subset of routes. For example, marijuana is typically smoked or eaten orally, but rarely injected. We therefore restrict each drug's allowable set of administration routes to those which are tagged (e.g. with "Oral" or "Snorting") in at least 1% of that drug's data. Similar ideas are used in Labeled LDA (Ramage et al.,

Reference Text	System Snippet
Mephedrone (β-ketones/Bath salts)	
It is recommended by users that Mephedrone be taken on an empty stomach. Doses usually vary between 100mg–1g.	• If it is SWIYs first time using Mephedrone SWIM recommends a 100mg oral dose on an empty stomach.
Reported negative side effects include: • Loss of appetite. • Dehydration and dry mouth • Tense jaw, mild muscle clenching, stiff neck, and bruxia (teeth grinding) • Anxiety and paranoia • Increase in mean body temperature (sweating/Mephedrone sweat and hot flushes) • Elevated heart rate (tachycardia) and blood pressure, and chest pains • Dermatitis like symptoms (Itch and rash)	• Neutral side effects: Lack of appetite, occasional loss of visual focus, [...] weight loss, possible diuretic. Negative side effects: Grinding teeth, "Cotton mouth", unable to acheive orgasm • Aside from his last session he has never experienced any negative symptoms at all, no raised heart beat, vasoconstriction , sweating, headaches, paranoia e.t.c nothing at all except sometimes cold hands the next day. • lot of people report that anxiety and paranoia are some of the side effects of taking mephedrone [...] is it also possible that alot of the chest pains people are experiencing is due to anxiety? • moisturize the affected areas of skin twice daily with E45 or a similar unperfumed dermatalogical lotion.
Salvia divinorum	
Sublingual ingestion of the leaf (quid): reduces intensity of effects and can taste disgusting. When Salvia is consumed as a smokeable formulation the duration of the trip lasts 30 minutes or less, whereas if Salvia is consumed sublingually the effects lasts for 1 hour or more.	• The taste of sublingual salvia is foul and it is easy to have a dud trip unless large amounts of it are used. • SWIM has heard from many other users that chewing the fresh leaves of the Salvia plant allow for a much longer and mellower trip. [...] SWIM has read that a trip this way can last anywhere from a half on hour or longer.
Dried leaves and/or salvia extract are smoked (using a butane lighter) either by pipe (considered to be the most effective but is considered to be quite painful) or water bong.	• 2. Use a water pipe. Its harsh and needs to be smoked hot so this should be self explanatory. 3. Use a torch style lighter [...] Salvinorin A has a VERY high boiling point (around 700 degrees F I believe) so a regular bic just wont do it
Salvia is appealing to recreational users because of intense, unique, hallucinatory effects. Brief hallucinations occur rapidly after administration and are typically very vivid. Users report weird thoughts, feelings of unreality, feelings of immersion in bizarre non-Euclidian dimensions/geometries, feelings of floating.	• He noticed very clear [closed eye visuals], which looked similar to patterns on a persian rug, or ethnic oriental design. SWIM felt as if he was moving around, that he had got up and run and fallen, and that falling had shattered the space around his body as if I'd fallen through many glass framed pictures [...] • I was aware of my body and my friends and my life below, but I was [...] standing outside of time and outside of space.

Figure 3: Example snippets generated by f-LDA along with the corresponding reference text. For space, the references and snippets shown have been shortened in some cases. "SWIM" and "SWIY" stand for "someone who isn't me/you" and are used to avoid self-incrimination on the web forum.

2009), in which tags are used to restrict the space of allowed topics in a document.

We use f-LDA as a three-dimensional model which explicitly models triples, but we also obtain distributions for pairs such as (SALVIA,EFFECTS) by marginalizing across all distributions of the form (SALVIA,$*$,EFFECTS). We trained f-LDA on two different data sets, yielding the following models:

- **f-LDA-1:** We use the 12K messages with tags and fill the set out with 13K messages with tags uniformly sampled from the 18 other drugs, for a total of 25K messages.
- **f-LDA-2:** We use all 37K messages (many without tags) and fill the set out with 63K messages with tags uniformly sampled from the 18 other drugs, for a total of 100K messages.

All f-LDA instances are run with 5000 iterations alternating between a sweep of Gibbs sampling followed by a step of gradient ascent on the hyperparameters. While we do not use the tags as strict labels during sampling, we initialize the Gibbs sampler so that each token in a document is assigned to its label given by the tag, when available. In the absence of tags (in f-LDA-2), we initialize tokens to the GENERAL components. We initialized ω to its prior mean (Eq. 3), while the variance σ^2 and the initialization of bias $\omega^{(B)}$ are chosen to optimize likelihood on the held-out development set.

We optimized the hyperparameters and sparsity array using gradient descent after each Gibbs sweep. We use a decreasing step size of $a/(t+1000)$, where t is the current iteration and a=10 for α and 1 for ω and the sparsity values. To learn priors η, we ran our version of SAGE for 100 iterations of gradient ascent (fixed step size of 0.1). See Paul and Dredze (2012a) for examples of parameters (the top words associated with various triples) learned by this model on this corpus.

4.2 Summary Generation

We created twelve reference summaries by editing together excerpts from the five Psychonaut Project reports ((Psychonaut), 2009). Each reference is matched to drug-specific pairs and triples. For example, a paragraph describing the differences in effects of salvia between smoking and oral routes was matched to distributions for (SALVIA,EFFECTS), (SALVIA,SMOKING,EFFECTS), (SALVIA,ORAL,EFFECTS). Descriptions of creating tinctures and blotters for oral consumption were matched to (SALVIA,ORAL,CHEMISTRY). We consider pairs in addition to triples because not all summaries correspond to particular routes or aspects.

For each tuple-specific word distribution (a pair or a triple), we create a "summary" by extracting a set of five text snippets which minimize KL-divergence to the target word distribution. We consider all overlapping text windows of widths {10,15,20} in the corpus as candidate snippets. Following Haghighi and Vanderwende (2009), we greedily add snippets one by one with the lowest KL-divergence at each step until we have added five.

We only considered candidate snippets within the subforum for the particular drug, and snippets are based on the preprocessed topic model input with no stop words. Before presenting snippets to users, we then map the snippets back to the raw text by taking all sentences which are at least partly spanned by the window of tokens. Because each reference may be matched to more than one tuple, there may be more than five snippets which correspond to a reference.

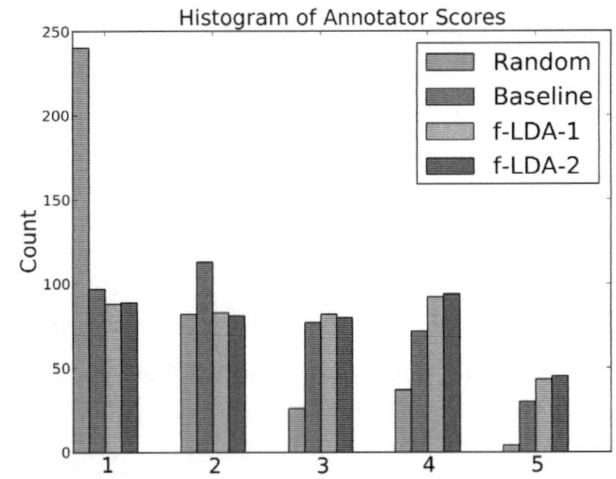

Figure 4: The distribution of annotator scores (§4.3.1). The "Random" counts have been scaled to fit the same range as the other systems, since fewer random snippets were shown to annotators.

4.3 Experimental Results

Recall that the reports used as reference summaries were themselves created by reading web forums. Our hypothesis is that f-LDA could be used as an exploratory tool to expedite the creation of these reports. Thus in our evaluation we want to measure how useful the extracted snippets would be in informing the writing of such reports. We performed both human and automatic evaluation on the summaries generated by f-LDA (variants 1 and 2) as well as our baseline. We also included randomly selected snippets as a control (five per reference).

Example output is shown in Figure 3.

4.3.1 Human Judgments of Quality

Three annotators were presented snippets pooled from all four systems we are evaluating alongside the corresponding reference text. Within each set corresponding to a reference summary, the snippets were shown in a random order. Annotators were asked to judge each snippet independently on a 5-point Likert scale as to how useful each snippet would be in writing the reference text.

The distribution of scores is shown in Figure 4 and summarized in Table 2. Annotators generally agreed on the relative quality of snippets: the average correlation of scores between each pair of annotators was 0.49. Snippets produced by f-LDA were given more high scores and fewer low scores than the baseline, while the two f-LDA variants were rated comparably. The breakdown is more interesting when we compare scores for snippets that were matched

	Rand.	Base.	f-LDA-1	f-LDA-2
	Annotator Scores			
Mean	1.67	2.55	2.79	**2.81**
Pairs only	n/a	2.58	**2.79**	2.72
Triples only	n/a	2.50	2.80	**2.95**
	ROUGE			
1-gram	.112	.326	**.355**	.327
2-gram	.023	.072	**.085**	.084

Table 2: Summary quality evaluation across four systems.

to word distributions for pairs versus word distributions for triples. The gap in scores between f-LDA and the baseline increases when we look at the scores for only triples: f-LDA beats the baseline by a margin of 0.45 for snippets matched to triples and 0.21 for pairs. This suggests that we produce better triples by modeling them jointly. For triples, f-LDA-2 (which uses more data) beats f-LDA-1 (which uses only tagged data), while the reverse is true for pairs.

While some of the randomly selected control snippets happened to be useful, the scores for these snippets were much lower than those extracted through model-based systems. This suggests that exploring the forums in a targeted way (e.g. through our topic model approach) would be more efficient than exploring the data in a non-targeted way (akin to the random approach).

Finally, we asked two expert annotators (faculty members in psychiatry and behavioral pharmacology, who have used drug forums in the past to study emerging drugs) to rate the snippets corresponding to mephedrone/MDPV. The best f-LDA system had an average score of 2.57 compared to a baseline score of 2.45 and random score of 1.63.

4.3.2 Automatic Evaluation of Recall

The human judgments effectively measured a form of precision, as the quality of snippets were judged by their correspondence to the reference text, without regard to how much of the reference text was covered by all snippets. We also used the automatic evaluation metric ROUGE (Lin, 2004) as a rough estimate of summary recall: this metric computes the percentage of n-grams in the reference text that appeared in the generated summaries.

We computed ROUGE for both 1-grams and 2-grams. When computing n-gram counts, we applied Porter's stemmer to all tokens. We excluded stop words from 1-gram counts but included them in 2-gram counts where we care about longer phrases.[2]

Results are shown in Table 2. We find that f-LDA-1 has the highest score for both 1- and 2-grams, suggesting that it is extracting a more diverse set of relevant snippets. When performing a paired t-test across the 12 reference summaries, we find that f-LDA is better than the baseline with p-values 0.14 and 0.10 for 1-gram and 2-gram recall, respectively. f-LDA's recall advantage may come from the fact that it learns from a larger amount of data and it may learn more diverse word distributions by directly modeling triples. f-LDA-1 had slightly better recall (under ROUGE), while f-LDA-2 was slightly better according to the human annotators.

5 Conclusion

We have proposed exploratory tools for the analysis of online drug communities. Such communities are an emerging source of drug research, but manually browsing through large corpora is impractical and important information could be missed. We have demonstrated that topic models are capable of modeling informative portions of text, and in particular multi-dimensional topic models can target desired structures such as the combination of aspect and route of administration for each drug. We have presented an extension to factorial LDA tailored to a particular application and data set which was demonstrated to induce desired properties. As a technical contribution, this study lays out practical guidelines for customizing and incorporating prior knowledge into multi-dimensional text models.

Acknowledgments

We are grateful to Dr. Margaret S. Chisolm and Dr. Ryan Vandrey from the Johns Hopkins School of Medicine for providing the mephedrone/MDPV annotations, and Alex Lamb and Hieu Tran for assisting with the full annotations. We also thank Dr. Matthew W. Johnson for additional advice, and the anonymous reviewers for helpful feedback and suggestions. This research was partly supported by an NSF Graduate Research Fellowship.

[2] In both cases, ROUGE scores were higher when stop words were included. f-LDA beats the baseline by similar margins regardless of whether we include stop words.

References

D. Blei, A. Ng, and M. Jordan. 2003. Latent Dirichlet allocation. *JMLR*.

A. Chaney and D. Blei. 2012. Visualizing topic models. In *ICWSM*.

O. Corazza, F. Schifano, M. Farre, P. Deluca, Z. Davey, C. Drummond, M. Torrens, Z. Demetrovics, L. Di Furia, L. Flesland, et al. 2011. Designer drugs on the Internet: a phenomenon out-of-control? The emergence of hallucinogenic drug Bromo-Dragonfly. *Current Clinical Pharmacology*, 6(2):125–129.

Ornella Corazza, Fabrizio Schifano, Pierluigi Simonato, Suzanne Fergus, Sulaf Assi, Jacqueline Stair, John Corkery, Giuseppina Trincas, Paolo Deluca, Zoe Davey, Ursula Blaszko, Zsolt Demetrovics, Jacek Moskalewicz, Aurora Enea, Giuditta di Melchiorre, Barbara Mervo, Lucia di Furia, Magi Farre, Liv Flesland, Manuela Pasinetti, Cinzia Pezzolesi, Agnieszka Pisarska, Harry Shapiro, Holger Siemann, Arvid Skutle, Aurora Enea, Giuditta di Melchiorre, Elias Sferrazza, Marta Torrens, Peer van der Kreeft, Daniela Zummo, and Norbert Scherbaum. 2012. Phenomenon of new drugs on the Internet: the case of ketamine derivative methoxetamine. *Human Psychopharmacology: Clinical and Experimental*, 27(2):145–149.

Matthew Dunn, Raimondo Bruno, Lucinda Burns, and Amanda Roxburgh. 2011. Effectiveness of and challenges faced by surveillance systems. *Drug Testing and Analysis*, 3(9):635–641.

J. Eisenstein, A. Ahmed, and E. P. Xing. 2011. Sparse additive generative models of text. In *ICML*.

Jacob Eisenstein, Duen Horng "Polo" Chau, Aniket Kittur, and Eric P. Xing. 2012. Topicviz: Semantic navigation of document collections. In *CHI Work-in-Progress Paper*.

EMCDDA. 2012. 2012 annual report on the state of the drugs problem in Europe. *European Monitoring Centre for Drugs and Drug Addiction, Lisbon*.

Cathal T. Gallagher, Sulaf Assi, Jacqueline L. Stair, Suzanne Fergus, Ornella Corazza, John M. Corkery, and Fabrizio Schifano. 2012. 5,6-methylenedioxy-2-aminoindane: from laboratory curiosity to 'legal high'. *Human Psychopharmacology: Clinical and Experimental*, 27(2):106–112.

Jade Goldstein, Vibhu Mittal, Jaime Carbonell, and Mark Kantrowitz. 2000. Multi-document summarization by sentence extraction. In *Proceedings of the 2000 NAACL-ANLP Workshop on Automatic summarization*, pages 40–48.

Aria Haghighi and Lucy Vanderwende. 2009. Exploring content models for multi-document summarization. In *NAACL '09: Proceedings of Human Language Technologies: The 2009 Annual Conference of the North American Chapter of the Association for Computational Linguistics*, pages 362–370.

Simon L. Hill and Simon H. L. Thomas. 2011. Clinical toxicology of newer recreational drugs. *Clinical Toxicology*, 49(8):705–719.

Marie Claire Van Hout and Tim Bingham. 2012. Costly turn on: Patterns of use and perceived consequences of mephedrone based head shop products amongst Irish injectors. *International Journal of Drug Policy*.

Jagadeesh Jagarlamudi, Hal Daumé III, and Raghavendra Udupa. 2012. Incorporating lexical priors into topic models. In *EACL*.

Chin-Yew Lin. 2004. Rouge: A package for automatic evaluation of summaries. In Stan Szpakowicz Marie-Francine Moens, editor, *Text Summarization Branches Out: Proceedings of the ACL-04 Workshop*, pages 74–81, Barcelona, Spain, July.

Q. Mei, X. Ling, M. Wondra, H. Su, and C. Zhai. 2007. Topic sentiment mixture: modeling facets and opinions in weblogs. In *WWW*.

David Mimno. 2011. Reconstructing Pompeian households. In *UAI*.

Elizabeth M. Morgan, Chareen Snelson, and Patt Elison-Bowers. 2010. Image and video disclosure of substance use on social media websites. *Computers in Human Behavior*, 26(6):1405–1411. Online Interactivity: Role of Technology in Behavior Change.

Michael J. Paul and Mark Dredze. 2011. You are what you Tweet: Analyzing Twitter for public health. In *5th International AAAI Conference on Weblogs and Social Media (ICWSM)*.

Michael J. Paul and Mark Dredze. 2012a. Experimenting with drugs (and topic models): Multi-dimensional exploration of recreational drug discussions. In *AAAI 2012 Fall Symposium on Information Retrieval and Knowledge Discovery in Biomedical Text*.

Michael J. Paul and Mark Dredze. 2012b. Factorial LDA: Sparse multi-dimensional text models. In *Neural Information Processing Systems (NIPS)*.

M. Paul and R. Girju. 2010. A two-dimensional topic-aspect model for discovering multi-faceted topics. In *AAAI*.

Psychonaut WebMapping Research Group (Psychonaut). 2009. Bromo-Dragonfly, MDPV, Spice, Mephodrone, and Salvia Divinorum reports. http://www.psychonautproject.eu/technical.php. Institute of Psychiatry, King's College London.

Daniel Ramage, David Hall, Ramesh Nallapati, and Christopher D. Manning. 2009. Labeled lda: a supervised topic model for credit attribution in multi-labeled corpora. In *EMNLP*, pages 248–256.

J. Reyes, J. Negrón, H. Colón, A. Padilla, M. Millán, T. Matos, and R. Robles. 2012. The emerging of xylazine as a new drug of abuse and its health consequences among drug users in Puerto Rico. *Journal of Urban Health*, pages 1–8.

SAMHSA. 2012. The DAWN report. http://www.samhsa.gov/data/2k12/DAWN105/SR105-synthetic-marijuana.pdf, December 4.

Fabrizio Schifano, Paolo Deluca, Alex Baldacchino, Teuvo Peltoniemi, Norbert Scherbaum, Marta Torrens, Magi Farrõ, Irene Flores, Mariangela Rossi, Dorte Eastwood, Claude Guionnet, Salman Rawaf, Lisa Agosti, Lucia Di Furia, Raffaella Brigada, Aino Majava, Holger Siemann, Mauro Leoni, Antonella Tomasin, Francesco Rovetto, and A. Hamid Ghodse. 2006. Drugs on the web: the Psychonaut 2002 EU project. *Progress in Neuro-Psychopharmacology and Biological Psychiatry*, 30(4):640 – 646.

Edmund Talley, David Newman, Bruce Herr II, Hanna Wallach, Gully Burns, Miriam Leenders, and Andrew McCallum. 2011. A database of National Institutes of Health (NIH) research using machine learned categories and graphically clustered grant awards. *Nature Methods*.

Ivan Titov and Ryan McDonald. 2008. Modeling online reviews with multi-grain topic models. In *International World Wide Web Conference (WWW)*, Beijing.

P.M. Wax. 2002. Just a click away: Recreational drug web sites on the Internet. *Pediatrics*, 109(6).

Towards Topic Labeling with Phrase Entailment and Aggregation

Yashar Mehdad **Giuseppe Carenini** **Raymond T. Ng** **Shafiq Joty**
Department of Computer Science, University of British Columbia
Vancouver, BC, V6T 1Z4, Canada
{mehdad, carenini, rng, rjoty}@cs.ubc.ca

Abstract

We propose a novel framework for topic labeling that assigns the most representative phrases for a given set of sentences covering the same topic. We build an entailment graph over phrases that are extracted from the sentences, and use the entailment relations to identify and select the most relevant phrases. We then aggregate those selected phrases by means of phrase generalization and merging. We motivate our approach by applying over conversational data, and show that our framework improves performance significantly over baseline algorithms.

1 Introduction

Given text segments about the same topic written in different ways (*i.e.*, language variability), topic labeling deals with the problem of automatically generating semantically meaningful labels for those text segments. The potential of integrating topic labeling as a prerequisite for higher-level analysis has been reported in several areas, such as summarization (Harabagiu and Lacatusu, 2010; Kleinbauer et al., 2007; Dias et al., 2007), information extraction (Allan, 2002) and conversation visualization (Liu et al., 2012). Moreover, the huge amount of textual data generated everyday specifically in conversations (*e.g.*, emails and blogs) calls for automated methods to analyze and re-organize them into meaningful coherent clusters.

Table 1 shows an example of two human written topic labels for a topic cluster collected from a blog[1],

Text: a: Where do you think the term "Horse laugh" comes from? b: And that rats also giggled when tickled. c: My hypothesis- if an animal can play, it can "laugh" or at least it is familiar with the concept of "laughing". Many animals play. There are various sorts of humour though. Some involve you laughing because your brain suddenly made a lots of unexpected connections.
Possible extracted phrases: animals play, rats have, laugh, Horse laugh, rats also giggle, rats
Human-authored topic labels: animals which laugh, animal laughter

Table 1: Topic labeling example.

and possible phrases that can be extracted from the topic cluster using different approaches. This example demonstrates that although most approaches (Mei et al., 2007; Lau et al., 2011; Branavan et al., 2007) advocate extracting phrase-level topic labels from the text segments, topically related text segments do not always contain one keyword or key phrase that can capture the meaning of the topic. As shown in this example, such labels do not exist in the original text and cannot be extracted using the existing probabilistic models (*e.g.*, (Mei et al., 2007)). The same problem can be observed with many other examples. This suggests the idea of aggregating and generating topic labels, instead of simply extracting them, as a challenging scenario for this field of research.

Moreover, to generate a label for a topic we have to be able to capture the overall meaning of a topic. However, most current methods disregard semantic relations, in favor of statistical models of word distributions and frequencies. This calls for the integra-

[1] http://slashdot.org

tion of semantic models for topic labeling.

Towards the solution of the mentioned problems, in this paper we focus on two novel contributions:

1. Phrase aggregation. We propose to generate topic labels using the extracted information by producing the most representative phrases for each text segment. We perform this task in two steps. First, we generalize some lexically diverse concepts in the extracted phrases. Second, we aggregate and generate new phrases that can semantically imply more than one original extracted phrase. For example, the phrase "*rats also giggle*" and "*horse laugh*" should be merged into a new phrase "*animals laugh*". Although our method is still relying on extracting phrases, we move beyond current extractive approaches, by generating new phrases through generalization and aggregation of the extracted ones.

2. Building a multidirectional entailment graph over the extracted phrases to identify and select the relevant information. We set such problem as an application-oriented variant of the Textual Entailment (TE) recognition task (Dagan and Glickman, 2004), to identify the information that are semantically equivalent, novel, or more informative with respect to the content of the others. In this way, we prune the redundant and less informative text portions (*e.g.*, phrases), and produce semantically informed phrases for the generation phase. In the case of the example in Table 1, we eliminate phrases such as "*rats have*", "*rats*" and "*laugh*" while keeping "*animal play*", "*Horse laugh*" and "*rats also giggle*".

The experimental results over conversational data sets show that, in all cases, our approach outperforms other models significantly. Although conversational data are known to be challenging (Carenini et al., 2011), we choose to test our method on conversations because this is a genre in which topic modeling is critically needed, as conversations lack the structure and organization of, for instance, edited monologues. The results indicate that our framework is sufficiently robust to deal with topic labeling in less structured, informal genres (when compared with edited monologues). As an additional result of our experiments, we show that the identification and selection phase using semantic relations (entailment graph) is a necessary step to perform the final step (*i.e.,* the phrase aggregation).

2 Topic Labeling Framework

Each topic cluster contains the sentences that can semantically represent a topic. The task of clustering the sentences into a set of coherent topic clusters is called topic segmentation (Joty et al., 2011), which is out of the scope of this paper. Our goal is to generate an understandable label (*i.e.*, a sequence of words) that could capture the semantic of the topic, and distinguish a topic from other topics (based on definition of a good topic label by (Mei et al., 2007)), given a set of topic clusters. Among possible choices of word sequences as topic labels, in order to balance the granularity, we set phrases as valid topic labels.

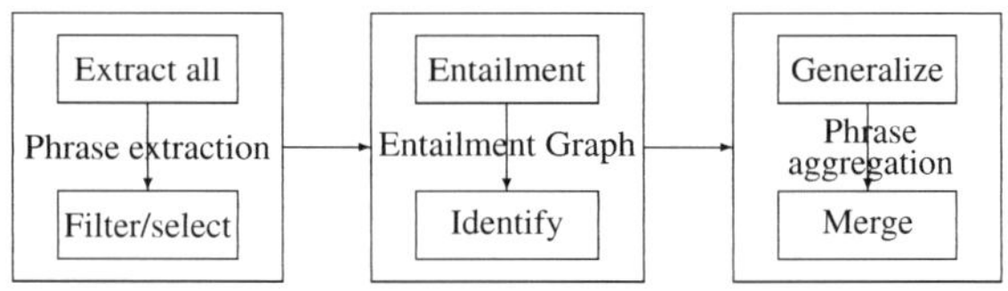

Figure 1: Topic labeling framework.

As shown in Figure 1, our framework consists of three main components that we describe in more details in the following sections.

2.1 Phrase extraction

We tokenize and preprocess each cluster in the collection of topic clusters with lemmas, stems, part-of-speech tags, sense tags and chunks. We also extract n-grams up to length 5 which do not start or end with a stop word. In this phase, we do not include any frequency count feature in our candidate extraction pipeline. Once we have built the candidates pool, the next step is to identify a subset containing the most significant of those candidates. Since most top systems in key phrase extraction use supervised approaches, we follow the same method (Kim et al., 2010b; Medelyan et al., 2008; Frank et al., 1999).

Initially, we consider a set of features used in the other systems to determine whether a phrase is likely to be a key phrase. However, since our dataset is conversational (more details in Section 3), and the text segments are not long, we aim for a classifier with high recall. Thus, we only use TFxIDF (Salton and McGill, 1986), position of the first occurrence (Frank et al., 1999) and phrase length as our features. We merge the training and test data released for SemEval-2010 Task #5 (Kim et al., 2010b), which consists of 244 scientific articles and 3705 key phrases, to train a Naive Bayes classifier in order to learn a supervised model. We then apply our model to extract the candidate phrases from the collected candidates pool.

As a further step, to increase the coverage (recall) of our extracted phrases and to reduce the number of very short phrases (frequent keywords), we choose the chunks containing any of the extracted keywords. We add those chunks to our extracted phrases and eliminate the associated keywords.

2.2 Entailment graph

So far, we have extracted a pool of key phrases from each topic cluster. Many such phrases include redundant information which are semantically equivalent but vary in lexical choices. By identifying the semantic relations between the phrases we can discover the information in one phrase that is semantically equivalent, novel, or more/less informative with respect to the content of the other phrase.

We set this problem as a variant of the Textual Entailment (TE) recognition task (Mehdad et al., 2010b; Adler et al., 2012; Berant et al., 2011). We build an entailment graph for each topic cluster, where nodes are the extracted phrases and edges are the entailment relations between nodes. Given two phrases (ph_1 and ph_2), we aim at identifying and handling the following cases:
i) ph_1 and ph_2 express the same meaning (*bidirectional* entailment). In such cases one of the phrases should be eliminated;
ii) ph_1 is more informative than ph_2 (*unidirectional* entailment). In such cases, the entailing phrase should replace or complement the entailed one;
iii) ph_1 contains facts that are not present in ph_2, and vice-versa (the "*unknown*" cases in TE parlance). In such cases, both phrases should remain.

Figure 2 shows how entailment relations can help in selecting the phrases by removing the redundant and less informative ones. For example, the phrase "*animals laugh*" entails "*rats giggle*", "*Horse laugh*" and "*Mice chuckle*",[2] but not "*Animals play*".

[2]Assuming that "animals laugh" is interpreted as "all animals laugh".

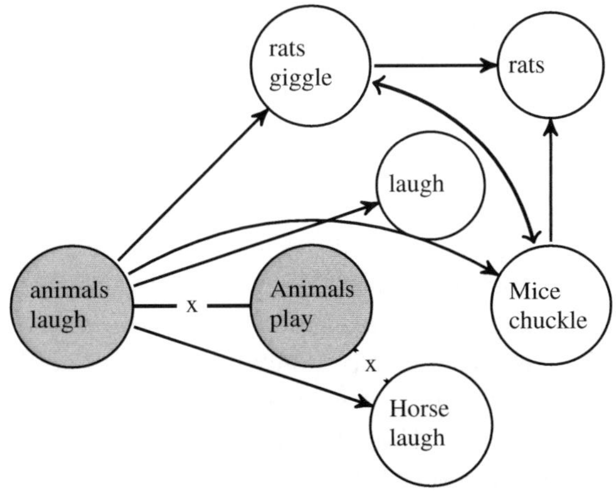

Figure 2: Building an entailment graph over phrases. Arrows and "x" represent the entailment direction and unknown cases respectively.

So we can keep "*animals laugh*" and "*Animals play*" and eliminate others. In this way, TE-based phrase identification method can be designed to distinguish meaning-preserving variations from true divergence, regardless of lexical choices and structures.

Similar to previous approaches in TE (*e.g.*, (Berant et al., 2011; Mehdad et al., 2010b; Mehdad et al., 2010a)), we use supervised method. To train and build the entailment graph, we perform the following three steps.

2.2.1 Training set collection

In the last few years, TE corpora have been created and distributed in the framework of several evaluation campaigns, including the Recognizing Textual Entailment (RTE) Challenge[3] and Cross-lingual textual entailment for content synchronization[4] (Negri et al., 2012). However, such datasets cannot directly support our application. Specifically, our entailment graph is built over the extracted phrases (with max. length of 5 tokens per phrase), while the RTE datasets are composed of longer sentences and paragraphs (Bentivogli et al., 2009; Negri et al., 2011).

In order to collect a dataset which is more similar to the goal of our entailment framework, we decide to select a subset of the sixth and seventh RTE challenge main task (*i.e.*, RTE within a Corpus). Our

[3]http://pascallin.ecs.soton.ac.uk/Challenges/RTE/
[4]http://www.cs.york.ac.uk/semeval-2013/task8/

dataset choice is based on the following reasons: *i)* the length of sentence pairs in RTE6 and RTE7 is shorter than the others, and *ii)* RTE6 and RTE7 main task datasets are originally created for summarization purpose which is closer to our work. We sort the RTE6 and RTE7 dataset pairs based on the sentence length and choose the first 2000 samples with a equal number of positive and negative examples. The average length of words in our training data is 6.7 words. There are certainly some differences between our training set and our phrases. However, the collected training samples was the closest available dataset to our purpose.

2.2.2 Feature representation and training

Working at the phrase level imposes another constraint. Phrases are short and in terms of syntactic structure, they are not as rich as sentences. This limits our features to the lexical level. Lexical models, on the other hand, are less computationally expensive and easier to implement and often deliver a strong performance for RTE (Sammons et al., 2011).

Our entailment decision criterion is based on similarity scores calculated with a phrase-to-phrase matching process. Each example pair of phrases (ph_1 and ph_2) is represented by a feature vector, where each feature is a specific similarity score estimating whether ph_1 entails ph_2.

We compute 18 similarity scores for each pair of phrases. In order to adapt the similarity scores to the entailment score, we normalize the similarity scores by the length of ph_2 (in terms of lexical items), when checking the entailment direction from ph_1 to ph_2. In this way, we can check the portion of information/facts in ph_2 which is covered by ph_1.

The first 5 scores are computed based on the exact lexical overlap between the phrases: word overlap, edit distance, ngram-overlap, longest common subsequence and Lesk (Lesk, 1986). The other scores were computed using lexical resources: WordNet (Fellbaum, 1998), VerbOcean (Chklovski and Pantel, 2004), paraphrases (Denkowski and Lavie, 2010) and phrase matching (Mehdad et al., 2011). We used WordNet to compute the word similarity as the least common subsumer between two words considering the synonymy-antonymy, hypernymy-hyponymy, and meronymy relations. Then, we calculated the sentence similarity as the sum of the similarity scores of the word pairs in Text and Hypothesis, normalized by the number of words in Hypothesis. We also use phrase matching features described in (Mehdad et al., 2011) which consists of phrasal matching at the level on ngrams (1 to 5 grams). The rationale behind using different entailment features is that combining various scores will yield a better model (Berant et al., 2011).

To combine the entailment scores and optimize their relative weights, we train a Support Vector Machine binary classifier, SVMlight (Joachims, 1999), over an equal number of positive and negative examples. This results in an entailment model with 95% accuracy over 2-fold and 5-fold cross-validation, which further proves the effectiveness of our feature set for this lexical entailment model. The reason that we gained a very high accuracy is because our selected sentences are a subset of RTE6 and RTE7 with a shorter length (less number of words) which makes the entailment recognition task much easier than recognizing entailment between paragraphs or complex long sentences.

2.2.3 Graph edge labeling

We set the edge labeling problem as a two-way classification task. Two-way classification casts multidirectional entailment as a unidirectional problem, where each pair is analyzed checking for entailment in both directions (Mehdad et al., 2012). In this condition, each original test example is correctly classified if both pairs originated from it are correctly judged ("*YES-YES*" for bidirectional,"*YES-NO*" and "*NO-YES*" for unidirectional entailment and "*NO-NO*" for unknown cases). Two-way classification represents an intuitive solution to capture multidimensional entailment relations. Moreover, since our training examples are labeled with binary judgments, we are not able to train a three-way classifier.

2.2.4 Identification and selection

Assigning all entailment relations between the extracted phrase pairs, we are aiming at identifying relevant phrases and eliminating the redundant (in terms of meaning) and less informative ones. In order to perform this task we follow a set of rules based on the graph edge labels. Note that since entailment

#	Merging patterns
1	merge ($cw1_{1(C_{POS=[N\mid V\mid J]})}..w1_n$, $cw2_{1(C_{POS=[N\mid V\mid J]})}..w2_n$) = $w1_1..w1_n$ and $w2_2..w2_n$
E.g.	merge (*challenging situation* , *challenging problem*) = *challenging situation and problem*
2	merge ($w1_1..cw1_{n(C_{POS=[N\mid V\mid J]})}$, $w2_1..cw2_{n(C_{POS=[N\mid V\mid J]})}$) = $w1_1..w1_{n-1}$ and $w2_1..w2_n$
E.g.	merge (*wet Mars* , *warm Mars*) = *wet and warm Mars*
3	merge ($w1_1..cw1_{n(C_{POS=[N\mid V\mid J]})}$, $cw2_{1(C_{POS=[N\mid V\mid J]})}..w2_n$) = $w1_1..w1_n$ $w2_2..w2_n$
E.g.	merge (*interesting story* , *story continues*) = *interesting story continues*
4	merge ($cw1_{1(C_{POS=[N\mid V\mid J]})}..w1_n$, $w2_1..cw2_{n(C_{POS=[N\mid V\mid J]})}$) = $w2_1..w2_n$ $w1_2..w1_n$
E.g.	merge (*LHC shutting down* , *details about LHC*) = *details about LHC shutting down*
5	merge ($w1_{1C_{pos}}$, $cw1_{2(C_{POS=[N\mid V\mid J]})}$, $w1_{3C_{pos}}$, $w2_{1C_{pos}}$, $cw2_{2(C_{POS=[N\mid V\mid J]})}$, $w2_{3C_{pos}}$) = $w1_1$ and $w2_1$ $w2_2$ $w2_3$ and $w1_3$
E.g.	merge (*technology grow fast* , *media grow exponentially*) = *technology and media grow exponentially and fast*

Table 2: Phrase merging patterns.

is a transitive relation, our entailment graph is transitive *i.e.*, if entail(ph_1,ph_2) and entail(ph_2,ph_3) then entail(ph_1,ph_3) (Berant et al., 2011).

Rule 1) If there is a chain of entailing nodes, we keep the one which is in the root of the chain and eliminate others (e.g. "*animals laugh*" in Figure 2);

Rule 2) Among the nodes that are connected with bidirectional entailment (semantically equivalent nodes) we keep only the one with more outgoing bidirectional and unidirectional entailment relations, respectively;

Rule 3) Among the nodes that are connected with unknown entailment (novel information with respect to others) we keep the ones with no incoming entailment relation (*e.g.*, "*Animals play*" in Figure 2).

Although deleting might be harsh, in our current framework, we only rely on the performance of an entailment model which gives us a yes/no entailment decision. In future, we are planning to improve our entailment graph by weighting the edges. In this way, we can take advantage of the weights to make a more conservative decision in pruning the entailment chains.

2.3 Phrase aggregation

Once we have identified and selected the informative phrases, the generation of topic labels can be done in two steps. First, we generalize the phrases containing the concepts that are lexically connected. Second, we merge the phrases with a set of hand written linguistically motivated patterns.

2.3.1 Phrase generalization

In this step, we generalize phrases that contain concepts which are lexically connected. For this purpose, we search in phrases for different words with the same part-of-speech and sense tag. Then, we find the link between those words in WordNet. If they are connected and the shortest path connecting them is less than 3 (estimated over the development set), we replace both by their common parent in the WordNet. In the case that they belong to the same synset, we can replace one by another. Note that we limit our search to nouns and verbs. For example, "*rat*" and "*horse*" can be replaced by "*animal*", or "*giggle*" and "*chuckle*" can be replaced by "*laugh*". The motivation behind the generalization step is to enrich the common terms between the phrases in favor of increasing the chance that they could merge to a single phrase. This also helps to move beyond the limitation of original lexical choices.

2.3.2 Phrase merging

The goal is to merge the phrases that are connected, and to generate a human readable phrase that contains more information than a single extracted phrase. Several approaches have been proposed to aggregate and merge sentences in Natural Language Generation (NLG) (*e.g.* (Barzilay and Lapata, 2006; Cheng and Mellish, 2000)), however most of them use syntactic structure of the sentences. To merge phrases at the lexical level, we set few common linguistically motivated aggregation patterns such as: simple conjunction, and conjunction via shared participants (Reiter and Dale, 2000).

Table 2 demonstrates the merging patterns, where wi_j is the jth word (or segment) in phrase i, cw is the common word (or segment) in both phrases and C_{POS} is the common part-of-speech tag of the corresponding word. To illustrate, pattern 1 looks for the first segment of each phrase (wi_1). If they are same (cwi_1) and share the same POS tag (C_{POS}), then we aggregate the first phrase ($w1_1..w1_n$) and the second phrase removing the first element ($w2_2..w2_n$) by using the connective "*and*". For instance, the aggregation of "*animals laugh*" and "*animals play*" results in "*animals laugh and play*". The rest of the patterns follow the same logic and for the sake of brevity we avoid illustrating each pattern. These patterns are among the most common domain and application independent methods by which two phrases/sentences can be aggregated, as described in the NLG literature (Reiter and Dale, 2000).

In our aggregation pipeline, we group the phrases based on their lexical overlap (number of common words). The merging process is conducted over each group in descending order (larger number of words in common), in order to increase the chance of merging rules application. Then, we perform the merging over the resulting generated phrases from each group. If our phrases cannot be merged (*i.e.*, do not match merging patterns), we select them as labels for the topic cluster.

3 Datasets and Evaluation Metrics

3.1 Datasets

To verify the effectiveness of our approach, we experiment with two different conversational datasets. Our interest in dealing with conversational texts derives from two reasons. First, the huge amount of textual data generated everyday in these conversations validates the need of text analysis frameworks to process such conversational texts effectively. Second, conversational texts pose challenges to the traditional techniques, including redundancies, disfluencies, higher language variabilities and ill-formed sentence structure (Liu et al., 2011).

Our conversational datasets are from two different asynchronous media: email and blog. For email, we use the dataset presented in (Joty et al., 2010), where three individuals annotated the publicly available BC3 email corpus (Ulrich et al., 2008) with topics. The corpus contains 40 email threads (or conversations) at an average of 5 emails per thread. On average it has 26.3 sentences and 2.5 topics per thread. A topic has an average length of 12.6 sentences. In total, the three annotators found 269 topics in a corpus of 1,024 sentences.

There are no publicly available blog corpora annotated with topics. For this study, we build our own blog corpus containing 20 blog conversations of various lengths from Slashdot, each annotated with topics by three human annotators.[5] The number of comments per conversation varies from 30 to 101 with an average of 60.3 and the number of sentences per conversation varies from 105 to 430 with an average of 220.6. The annotators first read a conversation and list the topics discussed in the conversation by a short description (e.g., Game contents or size, Bugs or faults) which provides a high-level overview of the topic. Then, they assign the most appropriate topic to each sentence in the conversation. The short high-level descriptions of the topics serve as reference (or gold) topic labels in our experiments. The target number of topics was not given in advance and the annotators were instructed to find as many topics as needed to convey the overall content structure of the conversation. The annotators found 5 to 23 topics per conversation with an average of 10.77. The number of sentences per topic varies from 11.7 to 61.2 with an average of 27.16. In total, the three annotators found 512 topics in our blog corpus containing 4,411 sentences overall.

Note that our annotators performed topic segmentation and labeling independently. In the email corpus, the three annotators found 100, 77 and 92 topics respectively (269 in total), and in the blog corpus, they found 251, 119 and 192 topics respectively (562 in total). For the evaluation, there is a single gold standard per topic written by each annotator. Table 1 shows a case in which two annotators selected the same topical cluster and so we have two labels for the same cluster.

3.2 Evaluation metrics

Traditionally, key phrase extraction is evaluated using precision, recall and f-measure based on exact matches on all the extracted key phrases with gold standards for a given text. However, as claimed by (Kim et al., 2010a), this approach is not flexible enough as it ignores the near-misses. Moreover, in the case of topic labeling, most of the human written

[5]The new blog corpus annotated with topics will be made publicly available for research purposes.

topic labels cannot be found in the text. Recently, (Kim et al., 2010a) evaluated the utility of different n-gram-based metrics for key phrase extraction and showed that the metric *R-precision* correlates most with human judgments. *R-precision* normalizes the approximate matching score by the maximum number of words in the reference and candidate phrases. Since this penalize our aggregation phase, where the phrases tend to be longer than original extracted phrase, we decide to use *R-f1* as our evaluation metric which considers length of both reference and candidate phrases.

$$R\text{−}precision = \frac{1}{k}\sum_{i=1}^{k}\frac{overlap(cand_i, ref)}{\#words(cand_i)}$$

$$R\text{−}recall = \frac{1}{k}\sum_{i=1}^{k}\frac{overlap(cand_i, ref)}{\#words(ref)}$$

$$R\text{−}f1 = \frac{2 * R\text{−}precision * R\text{−}recall}{(R\text{−}precision + R\text{−}recall)}$$

The metric described above only considers word overlap and ignores other semantic relations (e.g., synonymy, hypernymy) between words. However, annotators write labels of their own and may use words that are not directly from the conversation but are semantically related. Therefore, we propose to also use another variant of *R-f1* that incorporates semantic relation between words. To calculate the *Semantic R-f1*, we count the number of overlaps not only when they have the same form, but also when they are connected in WordNet with a synonymy, hypernymy, hyponymy and entailment relation.

Its worth noting that the generalizations phase and the evaluation method are completely independent. In the generalization step, we try to generalize the phrases which are automatically extracted from the text segments. While, in the evaluation, we compare the human written gold standards with the system output. Therefore, using WordNet in the generalization step does not bias the results in the evaluation.

4 Experiments and Results

4.1 Experimental settings

We conduct our experiments over the blog and email datasets described in Section 3.1, after eliminating the development set from the test datasets. In our experiments, the development set was used for the pattern extraction and the shortest path threshold connecting the words in Wordnet in the generalization phase. Our test dataset consists of 461 topics (*i.e.*, clusters and their associated topic labels) from 20 blog conversations and 242 topics from 40 email conversations.

For preprocessing our dataset we use OpenNLP[6] for tokenization, part-of-speech tagging and chuncking. For sense disambiguation, we use the extended gloss overlap measure with the window size of 5, developed by (Pedersen et al., 2005). We also apply Snowball algorithm (Porter, 2001) for stemming.

We compare our approach with two strong baselines. The first baseline Freq-BL ranks the words according to their frequencies and select the top 5 candidates applying Maximum Marginal Relevance algorithm (Carbonell and Goldstein, 1998) using the same pre- and post-processing as the work by (Mihalcea and Tarau, 2004). The second baseline Lead-BL, ranks the words based on their relevance to the leading sentences.[7] The ranking criteria is $log(tf_{w,L_t} + 1) \times log(tf_{w,t} + 1)$, where tf_{w,L_t} and $tf_{w,t}$ are the number of times word w appears in a set of leading sentences L_t and topic cluster t, respectively (Allan, 2002). The log expressions, as the ranking criterion, assign more weights to the words in the topic segment, that also appear in the leading sentences. This is because topics tend to be introduced in the first few sentences of a topical cluster. We also measure the performance of our framework at each step in order to compare the effectiveness of each phase independently or in combination.

4.2 Results

We evaluate the performance of different models using the metrics *R-f1* and *Semantic R-f1* (*Sem-R-f1*), described in Section 3.2. Table 4 shows the results in percentage for different models. The results show that our framework outperforms the baselines signif-

[6] http://opennlp.sourceforge.net/

[7] The key intuitions for this baseline is the leading sentences of a topic cluster carry the most informative clues for the topic labels. Based on our development set, when we consider the first three sentences, the coverage of content words that appear in human labeled topics are 39% and 49% for blog and email, respectively.

Blog		Email	
Human-authored	**system generated**	**Human-authored**	**system generated**
Shutting down the LHC	*story about the LHC shutting down* (#3)	*How it affects coding*	*it screws my coding*
typical shutdown and upgrade times	*typical and scheduled shutdown* (#2)	*Opinions and preferences of tools*	*opinion about what tools*
MARS was warm and wet 3B years ago	*Mars was warm and wet early history* (#3)	*white on black for disabled users*	*white text on black background* (#3)
Moon Treaty and outer space treaty	*Moon and Outer Space Treaty* (#2)	*Contact with Steven*	*email to Steven Pemberton* (#3)

Table 3: Successful examples of human-authored and system generated labels for blog and email datasets. The number near some examples refers to the aggregation patterns in Table 2.

	R-f1		Sem-R-f1	
Models	blog	email	blog	email
Lead-BL	13.5	14.0	34.5	30.1
Freq-BL	15.3	13.1	34.7	29.1
Extraction-BL	13.9	16.0	31.6	33.2
Entailment	12.2	15.6	30.8	33.3
Extraction+Aggregation	15.1	**18.5**	**35.5**	**37.6**
Extraction+Entailment+ Aggregation	**17.9**	**20.4**	**38.7**	**41.6**

Table 4: Results for candidate topic labels on blog and email corpora.

icantly[8] in both datasets.

On the blog corpus, our key phrase extraction method (*Extraction-BL*) fails to beat the other baselines (Lead-BL and Freq-BL) in majority of cases (except R-f1 for Lead-BL). However, in the email dataset, it improves the performance over both baselines in both evaluation metrics. This might be due to the shorter topic clusters (in terms of number of sentences) in email corpus which causes a smaller number of phrases to be extracted.

We also observe the effectiveness of the aggregation phase. In all cases, there is a significant improvement ($p < 0.05$) after applying the aggregation phase over the extracted phrases (*Extraction+Aggregation*).

Note that there is no improvement over the extraction phase after the entailment (*Entailment* row). This is mainly due to the fact that the entailment phase filters the equivalent phrases. This affects the results negatively when such filtered phrases share many common words with our human-authored phrases. However, the results improve more significantly ($p < 0.01$) when the aggregation is conducted after the entailment. This demonstrates that, the combination of these two steps are beneficial for topic labeling over conversational datasets.

In addition, the differences between the results using *R-f1* and *Sem-R-f1* metrics suggests the need for more flexible automatic evaluation methods for this task. Moreover, although the same trend of improvement is observed in blog and email corpora, the differences between their performance suggest the investigation of specialized methods for various conversational modalities.

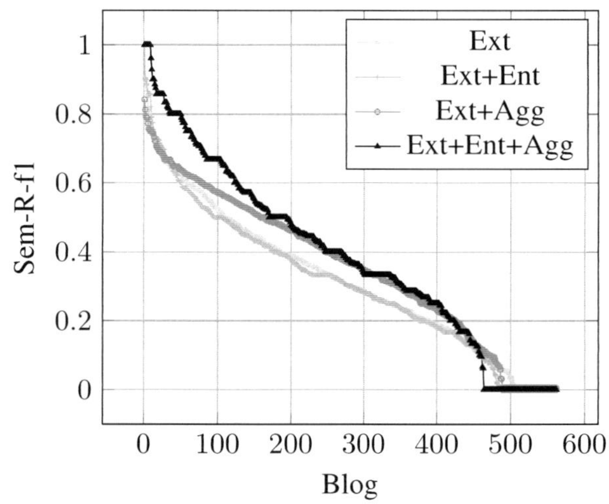

Figure 3: *Sem-R-f1* results distribution after each phase of our pipeline for blog corpus. The x-axis represents the examples sorted based on their *Sem-R-f1* score.

To further analyze the performance, in Figure 3, we show the *Sem-R-f1* results distribution for our blog dataset.[9] We can observe that the aggregation after the entailment phase (bold curve) clearly increase the number of correct labels, while such improvement can be only achieved when the entailment relations is used to identify the relevant phrases. This further highlights the need of semantics in this task. Comparing both datasets, this effect is more dominant in blogs. We believe that this is due to the length of topic clusters. Presumably, building an entailment graph over a greater pool of

[8] The statistical significance tests was calculated by approximate randomization described in (Yeh, 2000).

[9] For brevity's sake we do not show the email dataset graph.

original phrases is more effective to filter the redundant information and identify the relevant phrases.

5 Discussion

After analyzing the results and through manual verification of some cases, we observe that our approach led to some interestingly successful examples. Table 3 shows few generated labels and the human written topics for such cases.

In general, given that the results are expressed in percentage, it appears that the performance is still far from satisfactory level. This leaves an interesting challenge for the research community to tackle. However, this is not always due to the weakness of our proposed model. We have identified three different system independent sources of error:[10]

Type 1: Abstractive human-authored labels: the nature of our method is based on extraction (with the exception of our simple generalization phase) and in many cases the human-written labels cannot be extracted from the text and require more complex generalizations. In fact, only 9.81% of the labels in blog and 12.74% of the labels in email appear verbatim in their respective conversations. For example:

Human-authored label: *meeting schedule and location*

Generated phrases: *meeting, Boston area, mid October*

Type 2: Evaluation methods: in this work, we proposed a semantic method to evaluate our system. However, the current evaluation methods fail to capture the meaning. For example:

Human-authored label: *Food choices*

Generated phrase: *I would ask what people want to eat*

Type 3: Subjective topic labels: often is not easy for human to agree on one label for a topic cluster.[11] For example:

Human-authored label 1: *Member introduction*

Human-authored label 2: *Bio of Len*

Generated phrases: *own intro, Len Kasday, chair*

In light of this analysis, we conclude that a more comprehensive evaluation method (e.g., human evaluation) could better reveal the potential of our system in dealing with topic labeling, specially on conversational data.

[10]There are many examples of such cases, however for brevity we just mention one example for each type.

[11]The mean R-precision agreements computed based on one-to-one mappings of the topic clusters are 20.22 and 36.84 on blog and email data sets, respectively.

6 Conclusion

In this paper, we study the problem of automatic topic labeling, and propose a novel framework to label topic clusters with meaningful readable phrases. Within such framework, this paper makes two main contributions. First, in contrast with most current methods based on fully extractive models, we propose to aggregate topic labels by means of generalizing and merging techniques. Second, beyond current approaches which disregard semantic information, we integrate semantics by means of building textual entailment graphs over the topic clusters. To achieve our objectives, we successfully applied our framework over two challenging conversational datasets. Coherent results on both datasets demonstrate the potential of our approach in dealing with topic labeling task.

Future work will address both the improvement of our aggregation phase and ranking the output candidate phrases for each topic cluster. On one hand, we plan to accommodate more sophisticated NLG techniques for the aggregation and generation phase. Incorporating a better source of prior knowledge in the generalization phase (e.g., YAGO or DBpedia) is also an interesting research direction towards a better phrase aggregation step. On the other hand, we plan to apply a ranking strategy to select the top candidate phrases generated by our framework.

Acknowledgments

We would like to thank the anonymous reviewers and Frank Tompa for their valuable comments and suggestions to improve the paper, and the NSERC Business Intelligence Network for financial support. Yashar Mehdad also would like to acknowledge the early discussions on the related topics with Matteo Negri.

References

Meni Adler, Jonathan Berant, and Ido Dagan. 2012. Entailment-based text exploration with application to the health-care domain. In *Proceedings of the ACL 2012 System Demonstrations*, ACL '12, pages 79–84,

Stroudsburg, PA, USA. Association for Computational Linguistics.

James Allan. 2002. Topic detection and tracking: event-based information organization.

Regina Barzilay and Mirella Lapata. 2006. Aggregation via set partitioning for natural language generation. In *Proceedings of the main conference on Human Language Technology Conference of the North American Chapter of the Association of Computational Linguistics*, HLT-NAACL '06, pages 359–366, Stroudsburg, PA, USA. Association for Computational Linguistics.

Luisa Bentivogli, Ido Dagan, Hoa Trang Dang, Danilo Giampiccolo, and Bernardo Magnini. 2009. The fifth pascal recognizing textual entailment challenge. In *In Proc Text Analysis Conference (TAC09*.

Jonathan Berant, Ido Dagan, and Jacob Goldberger. 2011. Global learning of typed entailment rules. In *Proceedings of ACL*, Portland, OR.

SRK Branavan, Pawan Deshpande, and Regina Barzilay. 2007. Generating a table-of-contents. In *ACL*, volume 45, page 544.

Jaime Carbonell and Jade Goldstein. 1998. The use of mmr, diversity-based reranking for reordering documents and producing summaries. In *Proceedings of the 21st annual international ACM SIGIR conference on Research and development in information retrieval*, SIGIR '98, pages 335–336, New York, NY, USA. ACM.

Giuseppe Carenini, Gabriel Murray, and Raymond Ng. 2011. Methods for mining and summarizing text conversations.

Hua Cheng and Chris Mellish. 2000. Capturing the interaction between aggregation and text planning in two generation systems. In *In Proceedings of the 1st International Natural Language Generation Conference, 186193, Mitzpe*.

Timothy Chklovski and Patrick Pantel. 2004. Verbocean: Mining the web for fine-grained semantic verb relations. In Dekang Lin and Dekai Wu, editors, *Proceedings of EMNLP 2004*, pages 33–40, Barcelona, Spain, July. Association for Computational Linguistics.

I. Dagan and O. Glickman. 2004. Probabilistic textual entailment: Generic applied modeling of language variability.

Michael Denkowski and Alon Lavie. 2010. Meteor-next and the meteor paraphrase tables: improved evaluation support for five target languages. In *Proceedings of the Joint Fifth Workshop on Statistical Machine Translation and MetricsMATR*, WMT '10, pages 339–342, Stroudsburg, PA, USA. Association for Computational Linguistics.

Gaël Dias, Elsa Alves, and José Gabriel Pereira Lopes. 2007. Topic segmentation algorithms for text summarization and passage retrieval: an exhaustive evaluation. In *Proceedings of the 22nd national conference on Artificial intelligence - Volume 2*, AAAI'07, pages 1334–1339. AAAI Press.

Christiane Fellbaum. 1998. *WordNet: An Electronic Lexical Database*. Bradford Books.

Eibe Frank, Gordon W. Paynter, Ian H. Witten, Carl Gutwin, and Craig G. Nevill-Manning. 1999. Domain-specific keyphrase extraction. In *Proceedings of the Sixteenth International Joint Conference on Artificial Intelligence*, IJCAI '99, pages 668–673, San Francisco, CA, USA. Morgan Kaufmann Publishers Inc.

Sanda Harabagiu and Finley Lacatusu. 2010. Using topic themes for multi-document summarization. *ACM Trans. Inf. Syst.*, 28(3):13:1–13:47, July.

T. Joachims. 1999. Making large-scale svm learning practical. LS8-Report 24, Universität Dortmund, LS VIII-Report.

Shafiq Joty, Giuseppe Carenini, Gabriel Murray, and Raymond T. Ng. 2010. Exploiting conversation structure in unsupervised topic segmentation for emails. In *Proceedings of the 2010 Conference on Empirical Methods in Natural Language Processing*, EMNLP '10, Stroudsburg, PA, USA. Association for Computational Linguistics.

Shafiq Joty, Gabriel Murray, and Raymond T. Ng. 2011. Supervised topic segmentation of email conversations. In *In ICWSM11*. AAAI.

Su Nam Kim, Timothy Baldwin, and Min-Yen Kan. 2010a. Evaluating n-gram based evaluation metrics for automatic keyphrase extraction. In *Proceedings of the 23rd International Conference on Computational Linguistics*, COLING '10, pages 572–580, Stroudsburg, PA, USA. Association for Computational Linguistics.

Su Nam Kim, Olena Medelyan, Min-Yen Kan, and Timothy Baldwin. 2010b. Semeval-2010 task 5: Automatic keyphrase extraction from scientific articles. In *Proceedings of the 5th International Workshop on Semantic Evaluation*, SemEval '10, pages 21–26, Stroudsburg, PA, USA. Association for Computational Linguistics.

Thomas Kleinbauer, Stephanie Becker, and Tilman Becker. 2007. Combining multiple information layers for the automatic generation of indicative meeting abstracts. In *Proceedings of the Eleventh European Workshop on Natural Language Generation*, ENLG '07, pages 151–154, Stroudsburg, PA, USA. Association for Computational Linguistics.

Jey Han Lau, Karl Grieser, David Newman, and Timothy Baldwin. 2011. Automatic labelling of topic models. In *ACL*, pages 1536–1545.

Michael Lesk. 1986. Automatic sense disambiguation using machine readable dictionaries: how to tell a pine cone from an ice cream cone. In *Proceedings of the 5th annual international conference on Systems documentation*, SIGDOC '86, pages 24–26, New York, NY, USA. ACM.

F. Liu, Y. Liu, C. Busso, S. Harabagiu, and V. Ng. 2011. *Identifying the Gist of Conversational Text: Automatic Keyword Extraction and Summarization*. Ph.D. thesis, THE UNIVERSITY OF TEXAS AT DALLAS.

Shixia Liu, Michelle X. Zhou, Shimei Pan, Yangqiu Song, Weihong Qian, Weijia Cai, and Xiaoxiao Lian. 2012. Tiara: Interactive, topic-based visual text summarization and analysis. *ACM Trans. Intell. Syst. Technol.*, 3(2):25:1–25:28, February.

O. Medelyan, I.H. Witten, and D. Milne. 2008. Topic indexing with wikipedia. In *Proceedings of the AAAI WikiAI workshop*.

Y. Mehdad, A. Moschitti, and F.M. Zanzotto. 2010a. Syntactic semantic structures for textual entailment recognition. Association for Computational Linguistics.

Yashar Mehdad, Matteo Negri, and Marcello Federico. 2010b. Towards cross-lingual textual entailment. In *Human Language Technologies: The 2010 Annual Conference of the North American Chapter of the Association for Computational Linguistics*, HLT '10, pages 321–324, Stroudsburg, PA, USA. Association for Computational Linguistics.

Yashar Mehdad, Matteo Negri, and Marcello Federico. 2011. Using bilingual parallel corpora for cross-lingual textual entailment. In *Proceedings of the 49th Annual Meeting of the Association for Computational Linguistics: Human Language Technologies - Volume 1*, HLT '11, pages 1336–1345, Stroudsburg, PA, USA. Association for Computational Linguistics.

Yashar Mehdad, Matteo Negri, and Marcello Federico. 2012. Detecting semantic equivalence and information disparity in cross-lingual documents. In *Proceedings of the 50th Annual Meeting of the Association for Computational Linguistics: Short Papers - Volume 2*, ACL '12, pages 120–124, Stroudsburg, PA, USA. Association for Computational Linguistics.

Qiaozhu Mei, Xuehua Shen, and ChengXiang Zhai. 2007. Automatic labeling of multinomial topic models. In *Proceedings of the 13th ACM SIGKDD international conference on Knowledge discovery and data mining*, KDD '07, pages 490–499, New York, NY, USA. ACM.

R. Mihalcea and P. Tarau. 2004. TextRank: Bringing order into texts. In *Proceedings of EMNLP-04and the 2004 Conference on Empirical Methods in Natural Language Processing*, July.

Matteo Negri, Luisa Bentivogli, Yashar Mehdad, Danilo Giampiccolo, and Alessandro Marchetti. 2011. Divide and conquer: crowdsourcing the creation of cross-lingual textual entailment corpora. In *Proceedings of the Conference on Empirical Methods in Natural Language Processing*, EMNLP '11, pages 670–679, Stroudsburg, PA, USA. Association for Computational Linguistics.

Matteo Negri, Alessandro Marchetti, Yashar Mehdad, Luisa Bentivogli, and Danilo Giampiccolo. 2012. Semeval-2012 task 8: cross-lingual textual entailment for content synchronization. In *Proceedings of the First Joint Conference on Lexical and Computational Semantics - Volume 1: Proceedings of the main conference and the shared task, and Volume 2: Proceedings of the Sixth International Workshop on Semantic Evaluation*, SemEval '12, pages 399–407, Stroudsburg, PA, USA. Association for Computational Linguistics.

T. Pedersen, S. Banerjee, and S. Patwardhan. 2005. Maximizing Semantic Relatedness to Perform Word Sense Disambiguation. Research Report UMSI 2005/25, University of Minnesota Supercomputing Institute, March.

Martin F. Porter. 2001. Snowball: A language for stemming algorithms.

Ehud Reiter and Robert Dale. 2000. Building natural language generation systems.

Gerard Salton and Michael J. McGill. 1986. Introduction to modern information retrieval.

Mark Sammons, V.G.Vinod Vydiswaran, and Dan Roth. 2011. Recognizing Textual Entailment. In Daniel M. Bikel and Imed Zitouni, editors, *Multilingual Natural Language Applications: From Theory to Practice*. Prentice Hall, Jun.

Jan Ulrich, Gabriel Murray, and Giuseppe Carenini. 2008. A publicly available annotated corpus for supervised email summarization.

Alexander Yeh. 2000. More accurate tests for the statistical significance of result differences. In *Proceedings of the 18th conference on Computational linguistics - Volume 2*, COLING '00, pages 947–953, Stroudsburg, PA, USA. Association for Computational Linguistics.

Topic Segmentation with a Structured Topic Model

Lan Du
Department of Computing
Macquarie University
Sydney, Australia
lan.du@mq.edu.au

Wray Buntine
Canberra Research Lab
National ICT Australia
Canberra, Australia
wray.buntine@nicta.com.au

Mark Johnson
Department of Computing
Macquarie University
Sydney, Australia
mark.johnson@mq.edu.au

Abstract

We present a new hierarchical Bayesian model for unsupervised topic segmentation. This new model integrates a point-wise boundary sampling algorithm used in Bayesian segmentation into a structured topic model that can capture a simple hierarchical topic structure latent in documents. We develop an MCMC inference algorithm to split/merge segment(s). Experimental results show that our model outperforms previous unsupervised segmentation methods using only lexical information on Choi's datasets and two meeting transcripts and has performance comparable to those previous methods on two written datasets.

1 Introduction

Documents are usually comprised of topically coherent text segments, each of which contains some number of text passages (*e.g.*, sentences or paragraphs) (Salton et al., 1996). Within each topically coherent segment, one would expect that the word usage demonstrates more consistent lexical distributions (known as lexical cohesion (Eisenstein and Barzilay, 2008)) than that across segments. A linear partition of texts into topic segments may reveal information about, for example, themes of segments and the overall thematic structure of the text, and can subsequently be useful for text analysis tasks, such as information retrieval (*e.g.*, passage retrieval (Salton et al., 1996)), document summarisation and discourse analysis (Galley et al., 2003).

In this paper we consider how to automatically find a topic segmentation. It involves identifying the most prominent topic changes in a sequence of text passages, and splits those passages into a sequence of topically coherent segments (Hearst, 1997; Beeferman et al., 1999). This task can be cast as an unsupervised machine learning problem: placing topic boundaries in unannotated text.

Although a variety of cues in text can be used for topic segmentation, such as cue phases (Beeferman et al., 1999; Reynar, 1999; Eisenstein and Barzilay, 2008)) and discourse information (Galley et al., 2003), in this paper, we focus on lexical cohesion and use it as the primary cue in developing an unsupervised segmentation model. The effectiveness of lexical cohesion has been demonstrated by TextTiling (Hearst, 1997), c99 (Choi, 2000), MinCut (Malioutov and Barzilay, 2006), PLDA (Purver et al., 2006), Bayesseg (Eisenstein and Barzilay, 2008), TopicTiling (Riedl and Biemann, 2012), *etc.*

Our work uses recent progress in hierarchical topic modelling with non-parametric Bayesian methods (Du et al., 2010; Chen et al., 2011; Du et al., 2012a), and is based on Bayesian segmentation methods (Goldwater et al., 2009; Purver et al., 2006; Eisenstein and Barzilay, 2008) using topic models. This can also be viewed as a multi-topic extension of hierarchical Bayesian segmentation (Eisenstein, 2009), although our use of hierarchies is used to improve the performance of linear segmentation, rather than develop hierarchical segmentation.

Recently, topic models are increasingly used in various text analysis tasks including topic segmentation. Previous work (Purver et al., 2006; Misra et al., 2008; Sun et al., 2008; Misra et al., 2009; Riedl and Biemann, 2012) has shown that using topic assignments or topic distributions instead of word frequency can significantly improve segmentation performance. Here we consider more advanced topic models that model dependencies between (sub-)sections in a document, such as structured topic models (STMs) presented in (Du et al., 2010; Du et al., 2012b). STMs treat each text as a sequence of segments, each of which is a set of text passages (*e.g.*, a paragraph or sentence). Text passages in a segment share the same prior distribution on their topics. The topic distributions of segments in a single document are then encouraged to be similar via a hierarchical prior. This gives a substantial improvement in modelling accuracy. However, instead of explicitly learning the segmentation, STMs just leverage the existing structure of documents from the given segmentation.

Given a sequence of text passages, how can we automatically learn the segmentation? The word boundary sampling algorithm introduced in (Goldwater et al., 2009) uses point-wise sampling of word boundaries after phonemes in an utterance. Similarly, the segmentation method of PLDA (Purver et al., 2006) samples segment boundaries, but also jointly samples a topic model. This is different to other topic modelling approaches that run LDA as a precursor to a separate segmentation step (Misra et al., 2009; Riedl and Biemann, 2012). While conceptually similar to PLDA, our non-parametric approach built on STM required new methods to implement, but the resulting improvement by the standard segmentation scores is substantial.

This paper presents a new hierarchical Bayesian unsupervised topic segmentation model, integrating a point-wise boundary sampling algorithm with a structured topic model. This new model takes advantage of the high modelling accuracy of structured topic models (Du et al., 2010) to produce a topic segmentation based on the distribution of latent topics. We show that this model provides high quality segmentation performance on Choi's dataset, as well as two sets of meeting transcripts and written texts.

In the following sections we describe our topic segmentation model and an MCMC inference algorithm for the non-parametric split/merge process. The rest of the paper is organised as follows. In Section 2 we review recent related work in the topic segmentation literature. Section 3 presents the new topic segmentation model, followed by the derivation of a sampling algorithm in Section 4. We report the experimental results by comparing several related topic segmentation methods in Section 5. Section 6 concludes the paper.

2 Related Work

We are interested in unsupervised topic segmentation in either written or spoken language. There is a large body of work on unsupervised topic segmentation of text based on lexical cohesion. It can be characterised by how lexical cohesion is modelled.

One branch of this work represents the lexical cohesion in a vector space by exploring the word co-occurrence patterns, *e.g.*, TF or TF-IDF. Work following this line includes TextTiling (Hearst, 1997), which calculates the cosine similarity between two adjacent blocks of words purely based on the word frequency; C99 (Choi, 2000), an algorithm based on divisive clustering with a matrix-ranking scheme; LSeg (Galley et al., 2003), which uses a lexical chain to identify and weight word repetitions; U00 (Utiyama and Isahara, 2001), a probalistic approach using dynamic programming to find a segmentation with a minimum cost; MinCut (Malioutov and Barzilay, 2006), which casts segmentation as a graph cut problem, and APS (Kazantseva and Szpakowicz, 2011), which uses affinity propagation to learn clustering for segmentation.

The other branch of this work characterises the lexical cohesion using topic models, to which the model introduced in Section 3 belongs. Lexical cohesion in this line of research is modelled by a probabilistic generative process. PLDA presented by Purver *et al.* (2006) is an unsupervised topic modelling approach for segmentation. It chains a set of LDAs (Blei et al., 2003) by assuming a Markov structure on topic distributions. A binary topic shift variable is attached to each text passage (*i.e.*, an utterance in (Purver et al., 2006)). It is sampled to indicate whether the jth text passage shares the topic distribution with the $(j-1)^{th}$ passage.

Using a similar Markov structure, SITS (Nguyen et al., 2012) chains a set of HDP-LDAs (Teh et al., 2006). Unlike PLDA, SITS assumes each text passage is associated with a speaker identity that is attached to the topic shift variable as supervising information. SITS further assumes speakers have different topic change probabilities that work as priors on topic shift variables. Instead of assuming documents in a dataset share the same set of topics, Bayesseg (Eisenstein and Barzilay, 2008) treats words in a segment generated from a segment specific multinomial language model, *i.e.*, it assumes each segment is generated from one topic, and a later hierarchical extension (Eisenstein, 2009) assumes each segment is generated from one topic or its parents. Other methods using as input the output of topic models include (Sun et al., 2008), (Misra et al., 2009), and (Riedl and Biemann, 2012).

In this paper we take a generative approach lying between PLDA and SITS. In contrast to PLDA, which uses a flat topic model (*i.e.*, LDA), we assume each text has a latent topic structure that can reflect the topic coherence pattern, and the model adapts its parameters to the segments to further improve performance. Unlike SITS that targets analysing multiparty meeting transcripts, where speaker identities are available, we are interested in more general texts and assume each text has a specific topic change probability, since (1) the identity information is not always available for all kinds of texts (*e.g.*, continuous broadcast news transcripts (Allan et al., 1998)), (2) even for the same author, topic change probabilities for his/her different articles might be different.

3 Segmentation with Topic Models

In documents, topically coherent segments usually encapsulate a set of consecutive passages that are semantically related (Wang et al., 2011). However, the topic boundaries between segments are often unavailable *a priori*. Thus we treat all passage boundaries (*e.g.*, sentence boundaries, paragraph boundaries or pauses between utterances) as possible topic boundaries. To recover the topic boundaries we develop a structured topic segmentation model by integrating ideas from the segmented topic model (Du et al., 2010, STM) and Bayesian segmentation models.

The basic idea of our model is that each document consists of a set of segments where text passages in the same segment are generated from the same topic distribution, called segment level topic distribution. The segment level topic distribution is drawn from a topic distribution associated with the whole document, called document level topic distribution. The relationships between the levels is managed using Bayesian non-parametric methods and a significant change in segment level topic distribution indicates a segment change.

Our unsupervised topic segmentation model is based on the premise that using a hierarchical topic model like the STM with a point-wise segment sampling algorithm should allow better detection of topic boundaries. We believe that (1) segment change should be associated with significant change in the topic distribution, (2) topic cohesion can be reflected in document topic structure, (3) the log-likelihood of a topically coherent segment is typically higher than an incoherent segment (Misra et al., 2008).

Assume we have a corpus of D documents, each document d consists of a sequence of U_d text passages, and each passage u contains a set of $N_{d,u}$ words denoted by $\boldsymbol{w}_{d,u}$ that are from a vocabulary W. Our model consists of:

Modelling topic boundary: We assume each document has its own topic shift probability π_d, a Beta distributed random variable, *i.e.*, $\pi_d \sim Beta(\lambda_0, \lambda_1)$. Then, we associate a boundary indicator variable $\rho_{d,u}$ with u, like the topic shift variable in PLDA and SITS. $\rho_{d,u}$ is Bernoulli distributed with parameter π_d, *i.e.*, $\rho_{d,u} \sim Bernoulli(\pi_d)$. It indicates whether there is a topic boundary after text passage u or not. To sample $\rho_{d,u}$, we use a point-wise sampling algorithm. Consequently, a sequence of ρ's defines a set of segments, *i.e.*, a topic segmentation of d. For example, let a ρ vector $\boldsymbol{\rho} = (0, 0, 1, 0, 1, 0, 0, 1)$[1], it gives us three segments, which are $\{1, 2, 3\}$, $\{4, 5\}$ and $\{6, 7, 8\}$.

Modelling topic structure: Following the idea of the STM, we assume each document d is associated with a document level topic distribution $\boldsymbol{\mu}_d$, which is drawn from a Dirichlet distribution with parameter $\boldsymbol{\alpha}$; and text passages in topic segment s in d are generated from $\boldsymbol{\nu}_{d,s}$, a segment level topic distribution. The number of segments S_d can be computed as $S_d = 1 + \sum_{u=1}^{U_d - 1} \rho_{d,u}$. Then, a Pitman-Yor

[1] The last 1 in $\boldsymbol{\rho}$ is the document boundary that is know a priori. This means one does not need to sample it.

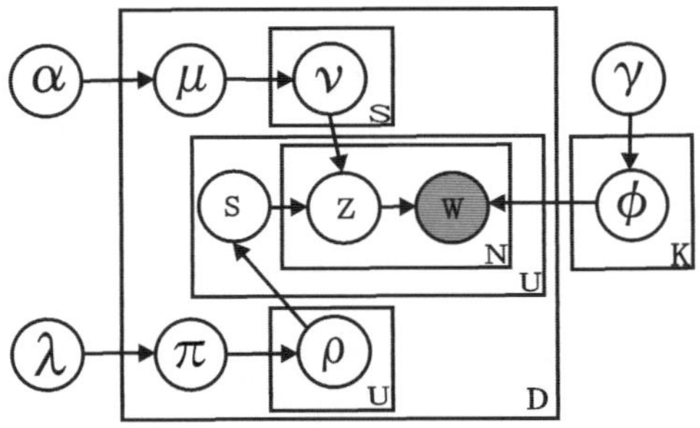

Figure 1: The topic segmentation model

process with a discount parameter a and a concentration parameter b is used to link $\boldsymbol{\mu}_d$ and $\boldsymbol{\nu}_{d,s}$ by $\boldsymbol{\nu}_{d,s} \sim \text{PYP}(a, b, \boldsymbol{\mu}_d)$, which forms a simple topic hierarchy. The idea here is that topics discussed in segments can be variants of topics of the whole document. Du *et al.* (2010) have shown that this topic structure can significantly improve the modelling accuracy, which should contribute to more accurate segmentation. This generative process is different from PLDA. PLDA does not assume the document level topic distribution and each time generates the segment level topic distribution directly from a Dirichlet distribution.

The complete probabilistic generative process, shown as a graph in Figure 1 is as follows:

1. For each topic $k \in \{1, \ldots, K\}$, draw a word distribution $\boldsymbol{\phi}_k \sim \text{Dirichlet}_W(\boldsymbol{\gamma})$.
2. For each document $d \in \{1, \ldots, D\}$,
   (a) Draw topic shift probability $\pi_d \sim \text{Beta}(\lambda_0, \lambda_1)$.
   (b) Draw $\boldsymbol{\mu}_d \sim \text{Dirichlet}_K(\boldsymbol{\alpha})$.
   (c) For each text passage (except last) $u \in \{1, \ldots, U_d - 1\}$, draw $\rho_{d,u} \sim \text{Bernoulli}(\pi_d)$.
   (d) Compute S_d the number of segments as $1 + \sum_{u=1}^{U_d-1} \rho_{d,u}$.
   (e) For each segment $s \in \{1, \ldots, S_d\}$, draw $\boldsymbol{\nu}_{d,s} \sim \text{PYP}(a, b, \boldsymbol{\mu}_d)$.
   (f) For each text passage $u \in \{1, \ldots, U_d\}$,
      i. Set segment $s_{d,u} = 1 + \sum_{v=1}^{u-1} \rho_{d,v}$.
      ii. For each word index $n \in \{1, \ldots, N_{d,u}\}$,
         A. Draw topic $z_{d,u,n} \sim \text{Discrete}_K\left(\boldsymbol{\nu}_{d,s_{d,u}}\right)$.
         B. Draw word $w_{d,u,n} \sim \text{Discrete}_K(\boldsymbol{\phi}_{z_{d,u,n}})$.

where $s_{d,u}$ indicates which segment text passage u belongs to. We assume the dimensionality of the Dirichlet distribution (*i.e.*, the number of topics) is known and fixed, and word probabilities are parameterized with a $K \times W$matrix $\boldsymbol{\Phi} = (\boldsymbol{\phi}_1, \ldots, \boldsymbol{\phi}_K)$. In future work we plan to investigate replace the Dirichlet prior $\boldsymbol{\alpha}$ on $\boldsymbol{\mu}$ with a Pitman-Yor prior (Pitman and Yor, 1997) to make the model fully nonparametric, like SITS.

Table 1: List of statistics

$M_{k,w}$	total number of words with topic k.
$\boldsymbol{M}_k$	a vector of $M_{k,w}$.
$n_{d,s,k}$	total number of words with topic k in segment s in document d.
$N_{d,s}$	total number of words in segment s.
$t_{d,s,k}$	table count of topic k in the CRP for segment s in document d.
$\boldsymbol{t}_{d,s}$	a vector of $t_{d,s,k}$ for segment s in d.
$T_{d,s}$	total table count in segment s.
$c_{d,1}$	total number of topic boundaries in d.
$c_{d,0}$	total number of non-topic boundaries in d.

4 Posterior Inference

In this section we develop a collapsed Gibbs sampling algorithm to do an approximate inference by integrating out some latent variables (*i.e.*, $\boldsymbol{\mu}$'s, $\boldsymbol{\nu}$'s and π_d's). The hierarchy in our model can be well explained with the Chinese restaurant franchise metaphor introduced in (Teh et al., 2006). For easier understanding, terminologies of the Chinese Restaurant Process (CRP) will be used throughout this section, *i.e.*, customers, dishes and restaurants, correspond to words, topics, and segments respectively. Statistics used are listed in Table 1.

To integrate out the $\boldsymbol{\nu}_{d,s}$'s generated from the PYP, we use the technique presented in (Chen et al., 2011), which computes the joint posterior for the PYP by summing out all the possible seating arrangements for a sequence of customers (Teh, 2006). In this technique an auxiliary binary variable, called *table indicator* ($\delta_{d,u,n}$), is introduced to facilitate computing table count $t_{d,s,k}$ for topic k. This method has two effects: (1) faster mixing of the sampler, and (2) elimination of the need for dynamic memory to store the populations/counts of each table in the CRP. In the CRP each word $w_{d,u,n}$ in topic k (*i.e.*, where $z_{d,u,n}{=}k$) contributes a count to $n_{d,s,k}$ for $u \in s$; and, if $w_{d,u,n}$, as a customer, also opens a new table to the CRP, it leads to increasing $t_{d,s,k}$ by one. In this case, $\delta_{d,u,n}{=}1$ indicates $w_{d,u,n}$ is the first customer on the table, called *table head*. Thus,

$$t_{d,s,k} = \sum_{u \in s} \sum_{n=1}^{N_{d,u}} \delta_{d,u,n} 1_{z_{d,u,n}=k} \,. \tag{1}$$

Note the two constraints on these two counts, *i.e.*,

$$n_{d,s,k} \geq t_{d,s,k} \geq 0 \text{ and } t_{d,s,k}{=}0 \textit{ iff } n_{d,s,k}{=}0 \tag{2}$$

can be replaced be a simpler constraint in the table indicator representation.

The sampler we develop is an MCMC sampler on the space $\boldsymbol{\theta} = \{\boldsymbol{z}, \boldsymbol{\delta}, \boldsymbol{\rho}\}$ where $\boldsymbol{z}$ defines the topic assignments of words, $\boldsymbol{\delta}$ maintains the needed CRP configuration (from which $\boldsymbol{t}$ is derived) and $\boldsymbol{\rho}$ defines the segmentation. Moreover, it is not a traditional Gibbs sampler changing one variable at a time, but is a block Gibbs sampler where two different kinds of blocks are used. The first block is $(z_{d,u,n}, \delta_{d,u,n})$ (for each word $w_{d,u,n}$), which can be sampled with a table indicator variant of a hierarchical topic sampler (Du et al., 2010), described in Section 4.1. This corresponds to Equation (6) in (Purver et al., 2006). The second kind of block is a boundary indicator $\rho_{d,u}$ together with a particular constrained set of table counts designed to handle splitting and merging, which corresponds to Equation (7) in (Purver et al., 2006). Sampling this second kind of block is harder in our non-parametric model requiring a potentially exponential summation, a problem we overcome using symmetric polynomials, shown in Section 4.2.

4.1 Sampling Topics

One step in our model is to sample the assignments of topics to words conditioned on all ρ's. As discussed in Section 3, given the sequence of $\rho_{d,u}$'s, $\boldsymbol{\rho}_d$, one can figure out which segment s text passage u belongs to. Thus, conditioned on a set of segments $\boldsymbol{s}$ given by $\boldsymbol{\rho}$, the joint posterior distribution of $\boldsymbol{w}$, $\boldsymbol{z}$ and $\boldsymbol{\delta}$ is computed as $p(\boldsymbol{z}, \boldsymbol{w}, \boldsymbol{\delta} \mid \boldsymbol{\rho}, \boldsymbol{\Phi}, a, b, \boldsymbol{\gamma})$

$$= \prod_d \frac{\text{Beta}_K(\boldsymbol{\alpha} + \sum_s \boldsymbol{t}_{d,s})}{\text{Beta}_K(\boldsymbol{\alpha})} \prod_k \frac{\text{Beta}_W(\boldsymbol{\gamma} + \boldsymbol{M}_k)}{\text{Beta}_W(\boldsymbol{\gamma})} \prod_d \prod_{s \in \boldsymbol{s}} \frac{(b|a)_{T_{d,s}}}{(b)_{N_{d,s}}} \prod_k \mathcal{S}^{n_{d,s,k}}_{t_{d,s,k},a} \binom{n_{d,s,k}}{t_{d,s,k}}^{-1}, \quad (3)$$

where $\text{Beta}_K(\cdot)$ is a K-dimension Beta function, $(x|y)_n$ the Pochhammer symbol[2], and $\mathcal{S}^n_{t,a}$ the generalised Stirling number of the second kind (Hsu and Shiue, 1998)[3] precomputed in a table so costing $O(1)$ to use (Buntine and Hutter, 2012).Eq (3) is an indicator variant of Eq (1) in (Du et al., 2010) with applying Theorem 1 in (Chen et al., 2011).

Given the current segmentation and topic assignments for all other words, using Bayes rule, we can derive the following two conditionals from Eq (3):

1. The joint probability of assigning topic k to word $w_{d,u,n}$ and $w_{d,u,n}$ being a *table head*, $p(z_{d,u,n} = k, \delta_{d,u,n} = 1 \mid \boldsymbol{\theta}')$

$$= \frac{\gamma_{w_{i,j,n}} + M_{k,w_{i,j,n}}}{\sum_w (\gamma_w + M_{k,w})} \frac{\alpha_k + \sum_s t_{d,s,k}}{\sum_k \alpha_k + \sum_{s,k} t_{d,s,k}} \frac{b + aT_{d,s}}{b + N_{d,s}} \frac{S^{n_{d,s,k}+1}_{t_{d,s,k}+1,a}}{S^{n_{d,s,k}}_{t_{d,s,k},a}} \frac{t_{d,s,k}+1}{n_{d,s,k}+1} \quad (4)$$

2. The joint probability of assigning k to $w_{d,u,n}$ and $w_{d,u,n}$ not being a *table head*, $p(z_{d,u,n} = k, \delta_{d,u,n} = 0 \mid \boldsymbol{\theta}')$

$$= \frac{\gamma_{w_{i,j,l}} + M_{k,w_{i,j,l}}}{\sum_w \gamma_w + M_{k,w}} \frac{1}{b + N_{d,s}} \frac{S^{n_{d,s,k}+1}_{t_{d,s,k},a}}{S^{n_{d,s,k}}_{t_{d,s,k},a}} \frac{n_{d,s,k} + 1 - t_{d,s,k}}{n_{d,s,k}+1} \quad (5)$$

where $\boldsymbol{\theta}' = \{\boldsymbol{z}^{-z_{d,u,n}}, \boldsymbol{w}, \boldsymbol{\delta}^{-\delta_{d,u,n}}, \boldsymbol{\rho}, \boldsymbol{\alpha}, a, b, \boldsymbol{\gamma}\}$. From the two conditionals, we develop a blocked Gibbs sampling algorithm for $(z_{d,u,n}, \delta_{d,u,n})$.

4.2 Sampling Segmentation Boundaries

In our model, each segment corresponds to a Chinese restaurant in the CRP. Sampling topic boundaries corresponds to splitting/merging restaurant(s). This is different from the split-merge process proposed by Jian and Neal (2004), where one actually splits/merges table(s). To our knowledge, there has been no method developed to split/merge restaurant(s). We tried different approximations, such as the minimum-path-assumption (Wallach, 2008), which in our case assumes one table for each topic k, and all words in k are placed in the same table. Although this simplifies the split-merge process, it yielded poor results. We instead developed a novel approximate block Gibbs sampling algorithm using symmetric polynomials. Its segmentation performance worked well in our development dataset.

For simplicity, we consider a passage u in document d, and assume: (1) If $\rho_{d,u}$=1, there are two segments, s_l and s_r; s_l ends at text passage u, and s_r starts at text passage u+1. (2) If $\rho_{d,u}$=0, there is one

[2] The Pochhammer symbol $(x|y)_n$ denotes the rising factorial with a specified increment, *i.e.*, y. It is defined as $(x|y)_n = x(x+y)...(x+(n-1)y)$.

[3] A Stirling number of the second kind is used to study the number of ways of partitioning a set of n objects into k nonempty subsets. The generalised version given by Hsu and Shiue (1998) has a linear recursion which in our case is $\mathcal{S}^{n+1}_{m,a} = \mathcal{S}^n_{m-1,a} + (n - ma)\mathcal{S}^n_{m,a}$.

segment, s_m, where u is is somewhere in the middle of s_m. The split-merge choice we sample is one to many, for a given split pair (s_l, s_r) we consider a set of merged states s_m (represented by different possible table counts). Then, to compute the Gibbs probability for splitting/merging restaurant(s), we consider the probability of the single split, the probability of the corresponding set of merges, and then if a merge is selected, we have to sample from the set of merges. These are as follows:

Splitting: split s_m into s_r and s_l by placing a boundary after u. Since passages have a fixed order in each document, all the words are put into s_r and s_l based on which passages they belong to. Then, given all the topic assignments, we first sample all table indicators $\delta_{d,u',n}$, for $n \in \{1, ..., N_{d,u'}\}$ and $u' \in s_m$ using Bernoulli sampling without replacement. It runs as follows: 1) sample $\delta_{d,u',n}$ according to probability $t_{d,s_m,k}/n_{d,s_m,k}$; 2) decrease $t_{d,s_m,k}$ if $\delta_{d,u',n} = 1$, otherwise, just decrease $n_{d,s_m,k}$. Using the sampled $\delta_{d,u',n}$'s we compute the inferred table counts $t_{d,s,k}$ (from Eq (1)) and customer counts $n_{d,s,k}$ respectively for segments $s{=}s_l$ and s_r and topics k. The computation may result in the following cases: for a given topic k,

(I) Both s_l and s_r have $n_{d,s,k}{>}0$ and $t_{d,s,k}{\geq}1$, which means both segments have words assigned to k and words being labelled with *table head*. According to constraints (2), after splitting, restaurants corresponding to s_l and s_r are valid. We do not make any change on table counts.

(II) Either s_l or s_r has $n_{d,s,k}{=}0$ and $t_{d,s,k}{=}0$. In this case, for example, all the words assigned to k in s_m are in s_l after splitting, and all those labelled with *table head* should also be in s_l. s_r has no words assigned to k. Thus, there is no need to change table counts.

(III) Either s_l or s_r has $n_{d,s,k}{>}0$ and $t_{d,s,k}{=}0$. Both segments have words assigned to k, but those labelled with *table head* only exist in one segment. For instance, if they only exist in s_l then s_r has no table head, which means the restaurant of s_r has customers eating a dish, but no tables serving that dish. Thus, we set $t_{d,s_r,k}{=}1$ to make the constraints (2) satisfied.

The Gibbs probability for splitting a segment is

$$p(\rho_{d,u} = 1 \,|\, \boldsymbol{\theta}'') \propto \frac{\lambda_1 + c_{d,1}}{\lambda_0 + \lambda_1 + c_{d,0} + c_{d,1}} \tag{6}$$

$$\mathrm{Beta}_K\Big(\boldsymbol{\alpha} + \sum_{s=1}^{S_d} \boldsymbol{t}_{d,s}\Big) \prod_{s \in \{s_l, s_r\}} \frac{(b|a)_{T_{d,s}}}{(b)_{N_{d,s}}} \prod_k S^{n_{d,s,k}}_{t_{d,s,k},a} \,,$$

where $\boldsymbol{\theta}'' = \{\boldsymbol{z}, \boldsymbol{w}, \boldsymbol{\delta}, \boldsymbol{\rho}^{-\rho_{d,u}}, \boldsymbol{\alpha}, a, b, \lambda_0, \lambda_1\}$.

Merging: remove the boundary after u, and merge s_r and s_l to one segment s_m. For this case, both s_r and s_l satisfy constraints (2) for all k's, and set $n_{d,s_m,k}{=}n_{d,s_r,k} + n_{d,s_l,k}$. The following cases are considered: for a topic k

(I) Both s_l and s_r have $n_{d,s,k}{>}0$ and $t_{d,s,k}{>}1$. We compute $t_{d,s_m,k}$ using Eq (7). Thus table counts before and after merging are equal.

(II) Either s_l or s_r has $n_{d,s,k}{=}0$ and $t_{d,s,k}{=}0$. Similar to the above case, we use Eq (7).

(III) Both s_l and s_r have $n_{d,s,k}{>}0$, and either of them has $t_{d,s,k}{=}1$ or both. We have to choose between Eq (7) and Eq (8), *i.e.*, to decide whether a table should be removed or not.

$$t_{d,s_m,k} = t_{d,s_l,k} + t_{d,s_r,k} \tag{7}$$

$$t_{d,s_m,k} = t_{d,s_l,k} + t_{d,s_r,k} - 1 \tag{8}$$

Note that choosing Eq (8) means we need to decrease the table count $t_{d,s_m,k}$ by one. The idea here is that we sample to decide whether the remove table was added due to splitting case (III) or not. Clearly, we have a one-to-many split-merge choice. To compute the probability of a set of possible merges, we use elementary symmetric polynomials as follows: let $\mathcal{KS}$ be a set of topic-segment combinations that satisfy the condition in merging case (III), for $(k, s) \in \mathcal{KS}$, we sample either Eq (7) or Eq (8). Let $\mathcal{T} = \{t_{d,s,k} : (k, s) \in \mathcal{KS}\}$ be the set of table counts affected by the changes of Eq (7) or Eq (8). The Gibbs probability for merging two segments is

$$p(\rho_{d,u} = 0 \,|\, \boldsymbol{\theta}''') = \sum_{\mathcal{T}} p(\rho_{d,u} = 0, \mathcal{T} \,|\, \boldsymbol{\theta}''') \tag{9}$$

$$\propto \sum_{\mathcal{T}} \Bigg(\frac{\lambda_0 + c_{d,0}}{\lambda_0 + \lambda_1 + c_{d,0} + c_{d,1}} \mathrm{Beta}_K\Big(\boldsymbol{\alpha} + \sum_{s=1}^{S_d} \boldsymbol{t}_{d,s}\Big) \frac{(b|a)_{T_{d,s_m}}}{(b)_{N_{d,s_m}}} \prod_k S^{n_{d,s_m,k}}_{t_{d,s_m,k},a} \Bigg) \,,$$

where $\boldsymbol{\theta}''' = \{\boldsymbol{z}, \boldsymbol{w}, \boldsymbol{t} - \mathcal{T}, \boldsymbol{\rho}^{-\rho_{d,u}}, \boldsymbol{\alpha}, a, b, \lambda_0, \lambda_1\}$. This is converted to a sum on $|\mathcal{T}|$ booleans with independent terms and evaluated recursively in $O(|\mathcal{T}|^2)$ by symmetric polynomials. If a merge is chosen, one then samples according to the terms in the sum using a similar recursion.

5 Experiments

To demonstrate the effectiveness of our model (denoted by TSM) in topic segmentation tasks, we evaluate it on three different kinds of corpora[4]: a set of synthetic documents, two meeting transcripts and two sets of text books (see Tables 2 and 3); and compare TSM with the following methods: two baselines (the Random algorithm that places topic boundaries uniformly at random, and the Even algorithm that places a boundary after every m^{th} text passage, where m is the average gold-standard segment length (Beeferman et al., 1999)), C99, MinCut, Bayesseg, APS (Kazantseva and Szpakowicz, 2011), and PLDA.

Metrics: We evaluated the segmentation performance with PK (Beeferman et al., 1999) and WindowDiff (WD^r) (Pevzner and Hearst, 2002), which are two common metrics used in topic segmentation. Both move a sliding window of fixed size k over the document, and compare the inferred segmentation with the gold-standard segmentation for each window. The window size is usually set to the half of the average gold-standard segment size (Pevzner and Hearst, 2002). In addition, we also used an extended WindowDiff proposed by Lamprier *et al.* (2007), denoted by WD^e. One problem of WD^r is that errors near the two ends of a text are penalised less than those in the middle. To solve the problem WD^e adds k fictive text passages at the beginning and the end of the text when computing the score. We evaluated all the methods with the same Java code for the three metrics.

Parameter Settings: In order to make all the methods comparable, we chose for each method the parameter settings that give the gold-standard number of segments[5]. Specifically, we used a 11×11 rank mask for C99, as suggested by Choi (2000), the configurations included in the code (`http://groups.csail.mit.edu/rbg/code`) for Bayesseg and manually tuned parameters for MinCut. For APS, a greedy approach was used to search parameter settings that can approximately give the gold-standard number of segments. For PLDA, two randomly initialised Gibbs chains were used. Each chain ran for 75,000 burn-in iterations, then 1000 samples were drawn at a lag of 25 from each chain. For TSM, 10 randomly initialised Gibbs chains were used. Each chain ran for 30,000 iterations with 25,000 for burn-in, then 200 samples were drawn. The concentration parameter b in TSM was sampled using the Adaptive-Reject sampling scheme introduced in (Du et al., 2012b), the discount parameter $a = 0.2$, and $\lambda_0 = \lambda_1 = 0.1$. To derive the final segmentation for PLDA and TSM, we first estimated the marginal probabilities of placing boundaries after text passages from the total of 2000 samples. These probabilities were then thresholded to give the gold-standard number of segments. Precisely, we apply a small amount of Gaussian smoothing to the marginal probabilities (except for Choi's dataset), like Puerver *et al.* (2006) does. Finally, we used a symmetric Dirichlet prior in PLDA and STM, the one on topic distributions is $\alpha = 0.1$, the other on word distributions $\gamma = 0.01$.

Table 2: The Choi's dataset

Range of n		3-11	3-5	6-8	9-11
#docs		400	100	100	100
DocLen	mean	69.7	39.3	69.6	98.6
	std	8.2	2.6	2.9	3.5
SegLen	mean	7	4	7	10
	std	2.57	0.84	0.87	1.03

Table 3: Real dataset statistics

		ICSI	Election	Fiction	Clinical
# doc		25	4	84	227
DocLen	mean	994.5	144.3	325.0	139.5
	std	354.5	16.4	230.1	110.4
SegLen	mean	188	7	22	35
	std	219.1	8.9	23.8	41.7

5.1 Evaluation on Choi's Dataset

Choi's dataset (Choi, 2000) is commonly used in evaluating topic segmentation methods. It consists of 700 documents, each being a concatenation of 10 segments. Each segment is the first n sentences of a randomly selected document from the Brown corpus, *s.t.* $3 \leq n \leq 11$. Those documents are divided into 4 subsets with different range of n, as shown in Table 2. We ran PLDA and STM with 50 topics. Results in Table 4 show that our model significantly outperforms all the other methods on the four subsets over all the metrics. Furthermore, comparing to other published results, this also outperforms (Misra et al., 2009) (see their table 2), and (Riedl and Biemann, 2012) (they report an average of 1.04 and 1.06 in Tables 1 and 2, whereas TSM averages 0.93). This gives TSM the best reported results to date.

[4] For preprocessing, we only removed stop words.

[5] The segments learnt by those methods will differ, but just the segment count will be the same as the gold-standard count.

Table 4: Comparison on Choi's datasets with WD and PK (%)

	3-11			3-5			6-8			9-11		
	WD^r	WD^e	PK	WD^r	WD^e	PK	WD^r	WD^e	PK	WD^r	WD^e	PK
Random	51.7	49.1	48.7	51.4	50.0	48.4	52.5	49.9	49.2	52.4	48.9	49.2
Even	49.1	46.7	49.0	46.3	45.8	46.3	38.8	37.3	38.8	30.0	28.6	30.0
MinCut	30.4	29.8	26.7	41.6	41.5	37.3	28.2	27.4	25.5	23.6	22.7	21.6
APS	40.7	38.8	38.4	32.0	30.6	31.8	34.4	32.6	32.7	34.5	32.2	33.2
C99	13.5	12.3	12.3	11.3	10.2	10.8	10.2	9.3	9.8	8.9	8.1	8.6
Bayesseg	11.6	10.9	10.9	11.8	11.5	11.1	7.7	7.2	7.3	6.1	5.7	5.7
PLDA	2.4	2.2	1.8	4.0	3.9	3.3	3.6	3.5	2.7	3.0	2.8	2.0
TSM	**0.8**	**0.8**	**0.6**	**1.3**	**1.3**	**1.0**	**1.4**	**1.4**	**0.9**	**1.9**	**1.8**	**1.2**

Table 5: Comparison on the meeting transcripts and written texts with WD and PK (%)

	ICSI			Election			Fiction			Clinical		
	WD^r	WD^e	PK	WD^r	WD^e	PK	WD^r	WD^e	PK	WD^r	WD^e	PK
Random	46.3	41.7	44.1	51.0	49.7	45.1	51.0	48.7	47.5	45.9	38.5	44.1
Even	48.3	43.0	46.4	56.0	55.1	51.2	48.1	45.9	46.3	49.2	42.0	48.8
C99	42.9	37.4	39.9	43.1	41.5	37.0	48.1	45.1	42.1	39.7	31.9	38.7
MinCut	40.6	36.9	36.9	43.6	43.3	39.0	40.5	39.7	37.1	38.2	36.2	36.8
APS	58.2	49.7	54.6	47.7	36.8	40.6	48.0	45.8	45.1	39.9	32.8	39.6
Bayesseg	32.4	29.7	26.7	41.1	41.3	34.1	**33.7**	**32.8**	**27.8**	35.0	**28.8**	34.0
PLDA	32.6	28.8	29.4	40.6	41.1	32.0	43.0	41.3	36.1	37.3	32.1	32.4
TSM	**30.2**	**26.8**	**25.8**	**38.1**	**38.9**	**31.3**	40.8	38.7	32.5	**34.5**	29.1	**30.6**

Note the lexical transitions in these concatenated documents are very sharp (Malioutov and Barzilay, 2006). The sharp transitions lead to significant change in segment level topic distributions, which further implies the variance of these distributions is large. In TSM, a large variance causes a small concentration parameter b. We observed that the sampled b's (about 0.1) are indeed small for the four subsets, which shows there is no topic sharing among segments. Therefore, TSM is able to recognise the segments are unrelated text.

5.2 Evaluation on Meeting Transcripts

We applied our model to segmenting the two meeting transcripts, which are the ICSI meeting transcripts (Janin et al., 2003) and the 2008 presidential election debates (Boydstun et al., 2011). The ICSI meeting has 75 transcripts, we used the 25 annotated transcripts provided by Galley *et al.* (2003) for evaluation. For the election debates, we used the four annotated debates used in (Nguyen et al., 2012). The statistics are shown in Table 3. PLDA and TSM were trained with 10 topics on the ICSI and 50 on the Election. In this set of experiments, we show that our model is robust to meeting transcripts.

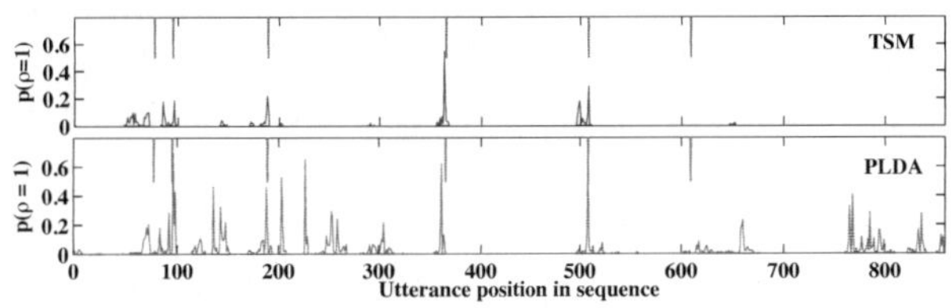

Figure 2: Probability of a topic boundary, compared with gold-standard segmentation (shown in red and at the top of each diagram) on one ICSI transcript.

As shown in Table 5, topic modelling based methods (*i.e.*, Bayesseg, PLDA and TSM) outperform those using either TF or TF-IDF, which is consistent with previously reported results (Misra et al., 2009; Riedl and Biemann, 2012). Among the topic model based methods, TSM achieves the best results on all the three metrics. On the ICSI transcripts, TSM performs 6.8%, 9.7% and 3.4% better than Bayesseg on the WD^r, WD^e and PK metrics respectively. Figure 2 shows an example of how the inferred topic boundary probabilities at utterances compare with the gold-standard boundaries on one ICSI meeting transcript. The gold-standard segmentation is {77, 95, 189, 365, 508, 609, 860}, TSM and PLDA infer {85, 96, 188, 363, 499, 508, 860} and {96, 136,

Table 6: Sampled concentration parameters

	Choi	ICSI	Election	Fiction	Clinical
b	0.1	5.2	5.4	18.4	4.8

203, 226, 361, 508, 860} respectively. Both models miss the boundary after the 609th utterance, but put a boundary after the 508th utterance. Note the boundaries placed by TSM are always within 10 utterances with respect to the gold standard.

Although TSM still performs the best on the debates, all the methods have relatively worse performance than on the ICSI meeting transcripts. Nguyen *et al.* (2012) pointed out that the ICSI meetings are characterised by pragmatic topic changes, in contrast, the debates are characterised by strategic topic changes with strong rewards for setting the agenda, dodging a question, *etc*. Thus, considering the properties of debates might further improve the segmentation performance.

5.3 Evaluation on Written Texts

We further tested TSM on two written text datasets, Clinical (Eisenstein and Barzilay, 2008) and Fiction (Kazantseva and Szpakowicz, 2011). The statistics are shown in Table 3. Each document in the Clinical dataset is a chapter of a medical textbook. Section breaks are selected to be the true topic boundaries. For the Fiction dataset, each document is a fiction downloaded from Project Gutenberg, the true topic boundaries are chapter breaks. We trained PLDA and TSM with 25 topics on the Fiction and 50 on the Clinical. Results are shown in Table 5. TSM compares favourably with Bayesseg and outperforms the other methods on the Clinical dataset, but it does not perform as well as Bayesseg on the Fiction dataset.

In fiction books, the topic boundaries between sections are usually blurred by the authors for reasons of continuity (Reynar, 1999). We observed that the sampled concentration (or inverse variance) parameter b in TSM is about 18.4 on Fiction, but 4.8 on Clinical, as shown in Table 6. This means the variance of segment level topic distributions $\boldsymbol{\nu}$ learnt by TSM is not large for the fiction, so chapter breaks may not necessarily indicate topic changes. For example, there is a document in the Fiction dataset where gold-standard topic boundaries are placed after each block of text. In contrast, Bayesseg assumes each segment has its own distribution over words, *i.e.*, one topic per segment, which means topics are not shared among segments. We hypothesize that for certain kinds of documents where the change in topic distribution is subtle, such as fiction, assuming one topic per segment can capture subtle changes in word usage. This is an area for future investigation.

6 Conclusion

In this paper, we have presented a hierarchical Bayesian model for unsupervised topic segmentation. This new model takes advances of both Bayesian segmentation and structured topic modelling. It uses a point-wise boundary sampling algorithm to sample a topic segmentation, while concurrently building a structured topic model. We have developed a novel approximation to compute the Gibbs probabilities of spliting/merging segment(s). Our model shows prominent segmentation performance on both written or spoken texts.

In future work, we would like to make the model fully nonparametric and investigate the effects of adding different cues in texts, such as cue phrases, pronoun usage, prosody, *etc*. Currently, our model uses marginal boundary probabilities to generate the final segmentation. Instead, we could develop a Metropolis-Hasting sampling algorithm to move one boundary at a time, given the gold-standard number of segments. To further study the effectiveness of our model, we would like to compare it with other methods, like SITS (Nguyen et al., 2012) and to run on more datasets, like email (Joty et al., 2010). For example, in order to compare with SITS, one can make an assumption that each document just has one speaker.

Acknowledgments

The authors would like to thank all the anonymous reviewers for their valuable comments. This research was supported under Australian Research Council's Discovery Projects funding scheme (project numbers DP110102506 and DP110102593). NICTA is funded by the Australian Government as represented by the Department of Broadband, Communications and the Digital Economy and the Australian Research Council through the ICT Centre of Excellence program.

References

J. Allan, J. Carbonell, G. Doddington, J. Yamron, and Y. Yang. 1998. Topic detection and tracking pilot study: Final report. In *Proceedings of the DARPA Broadcast News Transcription and Understanding Workshop*, pages 194–218.

Doug Beeferman, Adam Berger, and John Lafferty. 1999. Statistical models for text segmentation. *Mach. Learn.*, 34(1-3):177–210.

David M. Blei, Andrew Y. Ng, and Michael I. Jordan. 2003. Latent Dirichlet allocation. *J. Mach. Learn. Res.*, 3:993–1022.

A.E. Boydstun, C. Phillips, and R.A. Glazier. 2011. Its the economy again, stupid: Agenda control in the 2008 presidential debates.

W. Buntine and M. Hutter. 2012. A Bayesian review of the Poisson-Dirichlet process. Technical Report arXiv:1007.0296v2, *ArXiv*, Cornell.

Changyou Chen, Lan Du, and Wray Buntine. 2011. Sampling for the Poisson-Dirichlet process. In *European Conference on Machine Learning and Principles and Practice of Knowledge Discovery in Database*, pages 296–311.

Freddy Y. Y. Choi. 2000. Advances in domain independent linear text segmentation. In *Proceedings of the 1st North American chapter of the Association for Computational Linguistics conference*, NAACL 2000, pages 26–33.

Lan Du, Wray Buntine, and Huidong Jin. 2010. A segmented topic model based on the two-parameter Poisson-Dirichlet process. *Mach. Learn.*, 81(1):5–19.

Lan Du, Wray Buntine, and Huidong Jin. 2012a. Modelling sequential text with an adaptive topic model. In *Proceedings of the 2012 Joint Conference on Empirical Methods in Natural Language Processing and Computational Natural Language Learning*, pages 535–545.

Lan Du, Wray Buntine, Huidong Jin, and Changyou Chen. 2012b. Sequential latent Dirichlet allocation. *Knowledge and Information Systems*, 31(3):475–503.

Jacob Eisenstein and Regina Barzilay. 2008. Bayesian unsupervised topic segmentation. In *Proceedings of the Conference on Empirical Methods in Natural Language Processing*, EMNLP'08, pages 334–343.

Jacob Eisenstein. 2009. Hierarchical text segmentation from multi-scale lexical cohesion. In *Human Language Technologies: Conference of the North American Chapter of the Association of Computational Linguistics*, pages 353–361. The Association for Computational Linguistics.

Michel Galley, Kathleen R. McKeown, Eric Fosler-Lussier, and Hongyan Jing. 2003. Discourse segmentation of multi-party conversation. In *Proceedings of the 41st Annual Meeting of the Association for Computational Linguistics*, pages 562–569.

Sharon Goldwater, Thomas L. Griffiths, and Mark Johnson. 2009. A Bayesian framework for word segmentation: Exploring the effects of context. *Cognition*, 112(1):21–53.

Marti A. Hearst. 1997. TextTiling: segmenting text into multi-paragraph subtopic passages. *Comput. Linguist.*, 23(1):33–64.

Leetsch C. Hsu and Peter Jau-Shyong Shiue. 1998. A unified approach to generalized Stirling numbers. *Adv. Appl. Math.*, 20:366–384, April.

Sonia Jain and Radford Neal. 2004. A split-merge Markov chain Monte Carlo procedure for the Dirichlet process mixture model. *Journal of Computational and Graphical Statistics*, 13(1):158–182.

A. Janin, D. Baron, J. Edwards, D. Ellis, D. Gelbart, N. Morgan, B. Peskin, T. Pfau, E. Shriberg, A. Stolcke, and C. Wooters. 2003. The ICSI Meeting Corpus. In *Proceedings of 2003 IEEE International Conference on Acoustics, Speech, and Signal (ICASSP '03)*, pages 364–367.

Shafiq Joty, Giuseppe Carenini, Gabriel Murray, and Raymond T. Ng. 2010. Exploiting conversation structure in unsupervised topic segmentation for emails. In *Proceedings of the 2010 Conference on Empirical Methods in Natural Language Processing*, pages 388–398.

Anna Kazantseva and Stan Szpakowicz. 2011. Linear text segmentation using affinity propagation. In *Proceedings of the 2011 Conference on Empirical Methods in Natural Language Processing*, pages 284–293.

Sylvain Lamprier, Tassadit Amghar, Bernard Levrat, and Frederic Saubion. 2007. On evaluation methodologies for text segmentation algorithms. In *Proceedings of the 19th IEEE International Conference on Tools with Artificial Intelligence - Volume 02*, ICTAI '07, pages 19–26.

Igor Malioutov and Regina Barzilay. 2006. Minimum cut model for spoken lecture segmentation. In *Proceedings of the 21st International Conference on Computational Linguistics and the 44th annual meeting of the Association for Computational Linguistics*, ACL-44, pages 25–32.

Hemant Misra, Olivier Cappe, and Francois Yvon. 2008. Using LDA to detect semantically incoherent documents. In *Proceedings of CoNLL-08*, pages 41–48.

Hemant Misra, François Yvon, Joemon M. Jose, and Olivier Cappe. 2009. Text segmentation via topic modeling: an analytical study. In *Proceedings of the 18th ACM conference on Information and knowledge management*, CIKM '09, pages 1553–1556.

Viet-An Nguyen, Jordan Boyd-Graber, and Philip Resnik. 2012. SITS: A hierarchical nonparametric model using speaker identity for topic segmentation in multiparty conversations. In *Proceedings of the 50th Annual Meeting of the Association for Computational Linguistics (Volume 1: Long Papers)*, pages 78–87.

Lev Pevzner and Marti A. Hearst. 2002. A critique and improvement of an evaluation metric for text segmentation. *Comput. Linguist.*, 28(1):19–36.

J. Pitman and M. Yor. 1997. The two-parameter Poisson-Diriclet distribution derived from a stable subordinator. *Annals Probability*, 25:855–900.

Matthew Purver, Thomas L. Griffiths, Konrad P. Körding, and Joshua B. Tenenbaum. 2006. Unsupervised topic modelling for multi-party spoken discourse. In *Proceedings of the 21st International Conference on Computational Linguistics and the 44th annual meeting of the Association for Computational Linguistics*, ACL-44, pages 17–24.

Jeffrey C. Reynar. 1999. Statistical models for topic segmentation. In *Proceedings of the 37th Annual Meeting of the Association for Computational Linguistics*, pages 357–364.

Martin Riedl and Chris Biemann. 2012. How text segmentation algorithms gain from topic models. In *Proceedings of the 2012 Conference of the North American Chapter of the Association for Computational Linguistics: Human Language Technologies*.

Gerard Salton, Amit Singhal, Chris Buckley, and Mandar Mitra. 1996. Automatic text decomposition using text segments and text themes. In *Proceedings of the the seventh ACM conference on Hypertext*, pages 53–65.

Qi Sun, Runxin Li, Dingsheng Luo, and Xihong Wu. 2008. Text segmentation with LDA-based Fisher kernel. In *Proceedings of ACL-08: HLT, Short Papers*, pages 269–272.

Y. W. Teh, M. I. Jordan, M. J. Beal, and D. M. Blei. 2006. Hierarchical Dirichlet processes. *Journal of the American Statistical Association*, 101(476):1566–1581.

Y. W. Teh. 2006. A Bayesian interpretation of interpolated Kneser-Ney. Technical Report TRA2/06, School of Computing, National University of Singapore.

Masao Utiyama and Hitoshi Isahara. 2001. A statistical model for domain-independent text segmentation. In *Proceedings of 39th Annual Meeting of the Association for Computational Linguistics*, pages 499–506.

H.M. Wallach. 2008. Structured topic models for language. *doctoral dissertation, Univ. of Cambridge*.

Hongning Wang, Duo Zhang, and ChengXiang Zhai. 2011. Structural topic model for latent topical structure analysis. In *Proceedings of the 49th Annual Meeting of the Association for Computational Linguistics: Human Language Technologies*, pages 1526–1535.

Text Alignment for Real-Time Crowd Captioning

Iftekhar Naim, **Daniel Gildea**, **Walter Lasecki** and **Jeffrey P. Bigham**
Department of Computer Science
University of Rochester
Rochester, NY 14627

Abstract

The primary way of providing real-time captioning for deaf and hard of hearing people is to employ expensive professional stenographers who can type as fast as natural speaking rates. Recent work has shown that a feasible alternative is to combine the partial captions of ordinary typists, each of whom types part of what they hear. In this paper, we describe an improved method for combining partial captions into a final output based on weighted A* search and multiple sequence alignment (MSA). In contrast to prior work, our method allows the tradeoff between accuracy and speed to be tuned, and provides formal error bounds. Our method outperforms the current state-of-the-art on Word Error Rate (WER) (29.6%), BLEU Score (41.4%), and F-measure (36.9%). The end goal is for these captions to be used by people, and so we also compare how these metrics correlate with the judgments of 50 study participants, which may assist others looking to make further progress on this problem.

1 Introduction

Real-time captioning provides deaf or hard of hearing people access to speech in mainstream classrooms, at public events, and on live television. To maintain consistency between the captions being read and other visual cues, the latency between when a word was said and when it is displayed must be under five seconds. The most common approach to real-time captioning is to recruit a trained stenographer with a special purpose phonetic keyboard, who transcribes the speech to text within approximately 5 seconds. Unfortunately, professional captionists are quite expensive ($150 per hour), must be recruited in blocks of an hour or more, and are difficult to schedule on short notice. Automatic speech recognition (ASR) (Saraclar et al., 2002) attempts to solve this problem by converting speech to text completely automatically. However, the accuracy of ASR quickly plummets to below 30% when used on an untrained speaker's voice, in a new environment, or in the absence of a high quality microphone (Wald, 2006b).

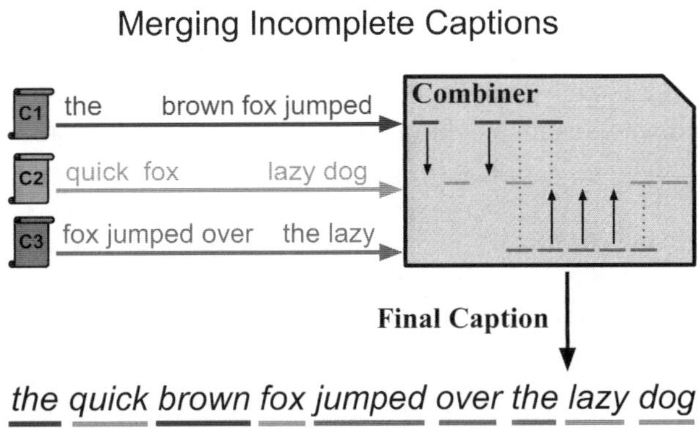

Figure 1: General layout of crowd captioning systems. Captionists (C1, C2, C3) submit partial captions that are automatically combined into a high-quality output.

An alternative approach is to combine the efforts of multiple non-expert captionists (anyone who can type) (Lasecki et al., 2012; Lasecki and Bigham, 2012; Lasecki et al., 2013). In this approach, multiple non-expert human workers transcribe an audio stream containing speech in real-time, and their partial input is combined to produce a final transcript (see Figure 1). This approach has been shown to dramatically outperform ASR in terms of both accuracy and Word Error Rate (WER), even when using captionists drawn from Amazon's Mechanical Turk. Furthermore, recall approached and even exceeded that of a trained expert stenographer with seven workers contributing, suggesting that the information is present to meet the performance of a stenographer. However, combining these captions involves real-time alignment of partial captions that may be incomplete and that often have spelling errors and inconsistent timestamps. In this paper, we present a more accurate combiner that leverages

Multiple Sequence Alignment (MSA) and Natural Language Processing to improve performance.

Gauging the quality of captions is not easy. Although word error rate (WER) is commonly used in speech recognition, it considers accuracy and completeness, not readability. As a result, a lower WER does not always result in better understanding (Wang et al., 2003). We compare WER with two other commonly used metrics: BLEU (Papineni et al., 2002) and F-measure (Melamed et al., 2003), and report their correlation with that of 50 human evaluators.

The key contributions of this paper are as follows:

- We have implemented an A*-search based Multiple Sequence Alignment algorithm (Lermen and Reinert, 2000) that can trade-off speed and accuracy by varying the heuristic weight and chunk-size parameters. We show that it outperforms previous approaches in terms of WER, BLEU score, and F-measure.
- We propose a beam-search based technique using the timing information of the captions that helps to restrict the search space and scales effectively to align longer sequences efficiently.
- We evaluate the correlation of WER, BLEU, and F-measure with 50 human ratings of caption readability, and found that WER was more highly correlated than BLEU score (Papineni et al., 2002), implying it may be a more useful metric overall when evaluating captions.

2 Related Work

Most of the previous research on real-time captioning has focused on Automated Speech Recognition (ASR) (Saraclar et al., 2002; Cooke et al., 2001; Pražák et al., 2012). However, experiments show that ASR systems are not robust enough to be applied for arbitrary speakers and in noisy environments (Wald, 2006b; Wald, 2006a; Bain et al., 2005; Bain et al., 2012; Cooke et al., 2001).

2.1 Crowd Captioning

To address these limitations of ASR-based techniques, the Scribe system collects partial captions from the crowd and then uses a graph-based incremental algorithm to combine them on the fly (Lasecki et al., 2012). The system incrementally builds a chain graph, where each node represents a set of equivalent words entered by the workers and the link between nodes are adjusted according to the order of the input words. A greedy search is performed to identify the path with the highest confidence, based on worker input and an n-gram language model. The algorithm is designed to be used online, and hence has high speed and low latency. However, due to the incremental nature of the algorithm and due to the lack of a principled objective function, it is not guaranteed to find the globally optimal alignment for the captions.

2.2 Multiple Sequence Alignment

The problem of aligning and combining multiple transcripts can be mapped to the well-studied Multiple Sequence Alignment (MSA) problem (Edgar and Batzoglou, 2006). MSA is an important problem in computational biology (Durbin et al., 1998). The goal is to find an optimal alignment from a given set of biological sequences. The pairwise alignment problem can be solved efficiently using dynamic programming in $O(N^2)$ time and space, where N is the sequence length. The complexity of the MSA problem grows exponentially as the number of sequences grows, and has been shown to be NP-complete (Wang and Jiang, 1994). Therefore, it is important to apply some heuristic to perform MSA in a reasonable amount of time.

Most MSA algorithms for biological sequences follow a progressive alignment strategy that first performs pairwise alignment among the sequences, and then builds a guide tree based on the pairwise similarity between these sequences (Edgar, 2004; Do et al., 2005; Thompson et al., 1994). Finally, the input sequences are aligned according to the order specified by the guide tree. While not commonly used for biological sequences, MSA with A*-style search has been applied to these problems by Horton (1997) and Lermen and Reinert (2000).

Lasecki et al. explored MSA in the context of merging partial captions by using the off-the-shelf MSA tool *MUSCLE* (Edgar, 2004), replacing the nucleotide characters by English characters (Lasecki et al., 2012). The substitution cost for nucleotides was replaced by the 'keyboard distance' between English characters, learned from the physical layout of a keyboard and based on common spelling errors. However, MUSCLE relies on a progressive alignment strategy and may result in suboptimal solutions. Moreover, it uses characters as atomic symbols instead of words. Our approach operates on a per-word basis and is able to arrive at a solution that is within a selectable error-bound of optimal.

3 Multiple Sequence Alignment

We start with an overview of the MSA problem using standard notations as described by Lermen and Reinert (2000). Let $S_1, \ldots, S_K, K \geq 2$, be the K sequences over an alphabet Σ, and having length $N_1, \ldots, N_K$. The special gap symbol is denoted by '$-$' and does not belong to Σ. Let $A = (a_{ij})$ be a $K \times N_f$ matrix, where $a_{ij} \in \Sigma \cup \{-\}$, and the ith row has exactly $(N_f - N_i)$ gaps and is identical to S_i if we ignore the gaps. Every column of A must have at least one non-gap symbol. Therefore, the jth column of A indicates an alignment state for the jth position, where the state can have one of the $2^K - 1$ possible combinations. Our goal is to find the optimum alignment matrix A_{OPT} that minimizes the sum of pairs (SOP) cost function:

$$c(A) = \sum_{1 \leq i \leq j \leq K} c(A_{ij}) \quad (1)$$

where $c(A_{ij})$ is the cost of the pairwise alignment between S_i and S_j according to A. Formally, $c(A_{ij}) = \sum_{l=1}^{N_f} \text{sub}(a_{il}, a_{jl})$, where $\text{sub}(a_{il}, a_{jl})$ denotes the cost of substituting a_{jl} for a_{il}. If a_{il} and a_{jl} are identical, the substitution cost is usually zero. For the caption alignment task, we treat each individual word as a symbol in our alphabet Σ. The substitution cost for two words is estimated based on the edit distance between two words. The exact solution to the SOP optimization problem is NP-Complete, but many methods solve it approximately. In this paper, we adapt weighted A* search for approximately solving the MSA problem.

3.1 A* Search for MSA

The problem of minimizing the SOP cost function for K sequences is equivalent to estimating the shortest path between a single source and single sink node in a K-dimensional lattice. The total number of nodes in the lattice is $(N_1 + 1) \times (N_2 + 1) \times \cdots \times (N_K + 1)$, each corresponding to a distinct position in K sequences. The source node is $[0, \ldots, 0]$ and the sink node is $[N_1, \ldots, N_K]$. The dynamic programming algorithm for estimating the shortest path from source to sink treats each node position $[n_1, \ldots, n_K]$ as a state and calculates a matrix that has one entry for each node. Assuming the sequences have roughly same length N, the size of the dynamic programming matrix is $O(N^K)$. At each vertex, we need to minimize the cost over all its $2^K - 1$ predecessor nodes, and, for each such transition, we need to estimate the SOP objective function that requires $O(K^2)$ operations. Therefore, the dynamic programming algorithm has time complexity of $O(K^2 2^K N^K)$ and space complexity of $O(N^K)$, which is infeasible for most practical problem instances. However, we can efficiently solve it via heuristic A* search (Lermen and Reinert, 2000).

Algorithm 1 MSA-A* Algorithm

Require: K input sequences $\mathcal{S} = \{S_1, \ldots, S_K\}$ having length $N_1, \ldots, N_K$, heuristic weight w, beam size b

$start \leftarrow 0^K$, $goal \leftarrow [N_1, \ldots, N_K]$
$g(start) \leftarrow 0$, $f(start) \leftarrow w \times h(start)$.
$Q \leftarrow \{start\}$
while $Q \neq \emptyset$ **do**
  $n \leftarrow$ EXTRACT-MIN(Q)
  for all $s \in \{0,1\}^K - \{0^K\}$ **do**
    $n_i \leftarrow n + s$
    if $n_i = goal$ **then**
      Return the alignment matrix for the reconstructed path from $start$ to n_i
    else if $n_i \notin Beam(b)$ **then**
      continue;
    else
      $g(n_i) \leftarrow g(n) + c(n, n_i)$
      $f(n_i) \leftarrow g(n_i) + w \times h(n_i)$
      INSERT-ITEM($Q, n_i, f(n_i)$)
    end if
  end for
end while

We use A* search based MSA (shown in Algorithm 1, illustrated in Figure 2) that uses a priority queue Q to store dynamic programming states corresponding to node positions in the K dimensional lattice. Let $n = [n_1, \ldots, n_K]$ be any node in the lattice, s be the source, and t be the sink. The A* search can find the shortest path using a greedy Best First Search according to an evaluation function $f(n)$, which is the summation of the cost func-

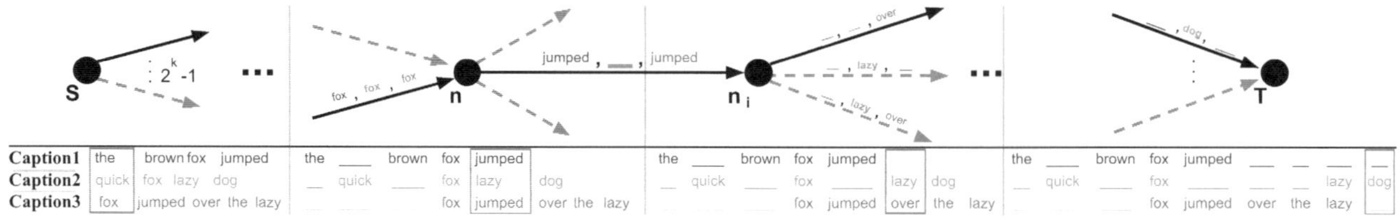

Figure 2: A^* MSA search algorithm. Each branch is one of $2^K - 1$ possible alignments for the current input. The branch with minimum sum of the current alignment cost and the expected heuristic value h_{pair} (precomputed).

tions $g(n)$ and the heuristic function $h(n)$ for node n. The cost function $g(n)$ denotes the cost of the shortest path from the source s to the current node n. The heuristic function $h(n)$ is the approximate estimated cost of the shortest path from n to the destination t. At each step of the A* search algorithm, we extract the node with the smallest $f(n)$ value from the priority queue Q and expand it by one edge. The heuristic function $h(n)$ is admissible if it never overestimates the cost of the cheapest solution from n to the destination. An admissible heuristic function guarantees that A* will explore the minimum number of nodes and will always find the optimal solution. One commonly used admissible heuristic function is $h_{pair}(n)$:

$$h_{pair}(n) = L(n \rightarrow t) = \sum_{1 \le i < j \le K} c(A_p^*(\sigma_i^n, \sigma_j^n)) \tag{2}$$

where $L(n \rightarrow t)$ denotes the lower bound on the cost of the shortest path from n to destination t, A_p^* is the optimal pairwise alignment, and σ_i^n is the suffix of node n in the i-th sequence. A* search using the pairwise heuristic function h_{pair} significantly reduces the search space and also guarantees finding the optimal solution. We must be able to estimate $h_{pair}(n)$ efficiently. It may appear that we need to estimate the optimal pairwise alignment for all the pairs of suffix sequences at every node. However, we can precompute the dynamic programming matrix over all the pair of sequences (S_i, S_j) once from the backward direction, and then reuse these values at each node. This simple trick significantly speeds up the computation of $h_{pair}(n)$.

Despite the significant reduction in the search space, the A* search may still need to explore a large number of nodes, and may become too slow for real-time captioning. However, we can further improve the speed by following the idea of *weighted A** search (Pohl, 1970). We modify the evaluation function $f(n) = g(n) + h_{pair}(n)$ to a weighted evaluation function $f'(n) = g(n) + wh_{pair}(n)$, where $w \ge 1$ is a weight parameter. By setting the value of w to be greater than 1, we increase the relative weight of the estimated cost to reach the destination. Therefore, the search prefers the nodes that are closer to the destination, and thus reaches the goal faster. Weighted A* search can significantly reduce the number of nodes to be examined, but it also loses the optimality guarantee of the admissible heuristic function. We can trade-off between accuracy and speed by tuning the weight parameter w.

3.2 Beam Search using Time-stamps

The computational cost of the A* search algorithm grows exponentially with increase in the number of sequences. However, in order to keep the crowd-sourced captioning system cost-effective, only a small number of workers are generally recruited at a time (typically $K \le 10$). We, therefore, are more concerned about the growth in computational cost as the sequence length increases.

In practice, we break down the sequences into smaller chunks by maintaining a window of a given time interval, and we apply MSA only to the smaller chunks of captions entered by the workers during that time window. As the window size increases, the accuracy of our MSA based combining system increases, but so does the computational cost and latency. Therefore, it is important to apply MSA with a relatively small window size for real-time captioning applications. Another interesting application can be the offline captioning, for example, captioning an entire lecture and uploading the captions later.

For the offline captioning problem, we can focus less on latency and more on accuracy by aligning longer sequences. To restrict the search space from exploding with sequence length (N), we apply a beam constraint on our search space using the time stamps of each captioned words. For example, if we

1.	so	now	what	i	want	to		do	is		introduce	some	of	the					
2.			what	i			wanna	do	is		introduce	some	of	the		aspects	of	the	class
3.	so	now	what	i	want	to		do	is	is	introduce	some	of	the		aspects	of	the	class
4.	so	now	what	i	want	to		do	is		introduce								
5.	so	now	what	i	want	to		do	is		introduce	some	of	the	operational		of	the	class
6.	so			i	want	to					introduce	some	of	the	operational	aspects	of	the	clas
C.	so	now	what	i	want	to		do	is		introduce	some	of	the	operational	aspects	of	the	class

Figure 3: An example of applying MSA-A* (threshold $t_v = 2$) to combine 6 partial captions (first 6 lines) by human workers to obtain the final output caption (C).

set the beam size to be 20 seconds, then we ignore any state in our search space that aligns two words having more than 20 seconds time lag. Given a fixed beam size b, we can restrict the number of priority queue removals by the A* algorithm to $O(Nb^K)$. The maximum size of the priority queue is $O(Nb^K)$. For each node in the priority queue, for each of the $O(2^K)$ successor states, the objective function and heuristic estimation requires $O(K^2)$ operations and each priority queue insertion requires $O(\log(Nb^K))$ i.e. $O(\log N + K \log b)$ operations. Therefore, the overall worst case computational complexity is $O\left(Nb^K 2^K (K^2 + \log N + K \log b)\right)$. Note that for fixed beam size b and number of sequences K, the computational cost grows as $O(N \log N)$ with the increase in N. However, in practice, weighted A* search explores much smaller number of states compared to this beam-restricted space.

3.3 Majority Voting after Alignment

After aligning the captions by multiple workers in a given chunk, we need to combine them to obtain the final caption. We do that via majority voting at each position of the alignment matrix containing a non-gap symbol. In case of tie, we apply the language model to choose the most likely word.

Often workers type in nonstandard symbols, abbreviations, or misspelled words that do not match with any other workers' input and end up as a single word aligned to gaps in all the other sequences. To filter out such spurious words, we apply a voting threshold (t_v) during majority voting and filter out words having less than t_v votes. Typically we set t_v = 2 (see the example in Figure 3). While applying the voting threshold improves the word error rate and readability, it runs the risk of loosing correct words if they are covered by only a single worker.

3.4 Incorporating an N-gram Language Model

We also experimented with a version of our system designed to incorporate the score from an n-gram language model into the search. For this purpose, we modified the alignment algorithm to produce a hypothesized output string as it moves through the input strings, as opposed to using voting to produce the final string as a post-processing step. The states for our dynamic programming are extended to include not only the current position in each input string, but also the last two words of the hypothesis string (i.e. $[n_1, \ldots, n_K, w_{i-1}, w_{i-2}]$) for use in computing the next trigram language model probability. We replace our sum-of-all-pairs objective function with the sum of the alignment cost of each input with the hypothesis string, to which we add the log of the language model probability and a feature for the total number of words in the hypothesis. Mathematically, we consider the hypothesis string to be the 0th row of the alignment matrix, making our objective function:

$$c(A) = \sum_{1 \le i \le K} c(A_{0,i}) + w_{len} \sum_{l=1}^{N_f} I(a_{0,l} \ne -) + w_{lm} \sum_{l=1}^{N_f} \log P(a_{0,l} | a_{0,l-2}, a_{0,l-1})$$

where w_{lm} and w_{len} are negative constants indicating the relative weights of the language model probability and the length penalty.

Extending states with two previous words results in a larger computational complexity. Given K sequences of length N each, we can have $O(NK)$ distinct words. Therefore, the number distinct states is $O(Nb^K(NK)^2)$ i.e. $O(N^3K^2b^K)$. Each state can have $O(K2^K)$ successors, giving an overall computational complexity of $O(N^3K^3b^K2^K(K^2 + \log N + \log K + K \log b))$. Alternatively, if the vocabulary size $|V|$ is smaller than NK, the number of distinct states is bounded by $O(Nb^K|V|^2)$.

3.5 Evaluation Metric for Speech to Text Captioning

Automated evaluation of speech to text captioning is known to be a challenging task (Wang et al., 2003). Word Error Rate (WER) is the most commonly used metric that finds the best pairwise alignment between the candidate caption and the ground truth reference sentence. WER is estimated as $\frac{S+I+D}{N}$, where S, I, and D is the number of incorrect word substitutions, insertions, and deletions required to match the candidate sentence with reference, and N is the total number of words in the reference. WER has several nice properties such as: 1) it is easy to estimate, and 2) it tries to preserve word ordering. However, WER does not account for the overall 'readability' of text and thus does not always correlate well with human evaluation (Wang et al., 2003; He et al., 2011).

The widely-used BLEU metric has been shown to agree well with human judgment for evaluating translation quality (Papineni et al., 2002). However, unlike WER, BLEU imposes no explicit constraints on the word ordering. BLEU has been criticized as an 'under-constrained' measure (Callison-Burch et al., 2006) for allowing too much variation in word ordering. Moreover, BLEU does not directly estimate recall, and instead relies on the brevity penalty. Melamed et al. (2003) suggest that a better approach is to explicitly measure both precision and recall and combine them via F-measure.

Our application is similar to automatic speech recognition in that there is a single correct output, as opposed to machine translation where many outputs can be equally correct. On the other hand, unlike with ASR, out-of-order output is frequently produced by our alignment system when there is not enough overlap between the partial captions to derive the correct ordering for all words. It may be the case that even such out-of-order output can be of value to the user, and should receive some sort of partial credit that is not possible using WER. For this reason, we wished to systematically compare BLEU, F-measure, and WER as metrics for our task.

We performed a study to evaluate the agreement of the three metrics with human judgment. We randomly extracted one-minute long audio clips from four MIT OpenCourseWare lectures. Each clip was transcribed by 7 human workers, and then aligned and combined using four different systems: the graph-based system, and three different versions of our weighted A* algorithm with different values of tuning parameters. Fifty people participated in the study and were split in two equal sized groups. Each group was assigned two of the four audio clips, and each person evaluated all four captions for both clips. Each participant assigned a score between 1 to 10 to these captions, based on two criteria: 1) the overall estimated agreement of the captions with the ground truth text, and 2) the readability and understandability of the captions.

Metric	Spearman Corr.	Pearson Corr.
1-WER	0.5258	0.6282
BLEU	0.3137	0.6181
F-measure	0.4389	0.6240

Table 1: The correlation of average human judgment with three automated metrics: 1-WER, BLEU, and F-measure.

Finally, we estimated the correlation coefficients (both Spearman and Pearson) for the three metrics discussed above with respect to the average score assigned by the human participants. The results are presented in Table 1. Among the three metrics, WER had the highest agreement with the human participants. This indicates that reconstructing the correct word order is in fact important to the users, and that, in this aspect, our task has more of the flavor of speech recognition than of machine translation.

4 Experimental Results

We experiment with the MSA-A* algorithm for captioning different audio clips, and compare the results with two existing techniques. Our experimental set up is similar to the experiments by Lasecki et al. (2012). Our dataset consists of four 5-minute long audio clips extracted from lectures available on MIT OpenCourseWare. The audio clips contain speech from electrical engineering and chemistry lectures. Each audio clip is transcribed by ten non-expert human workers in real-time. We then combine these inputs using our MSA-A* algorithm, and also compare with the existing graph-based system and mul-

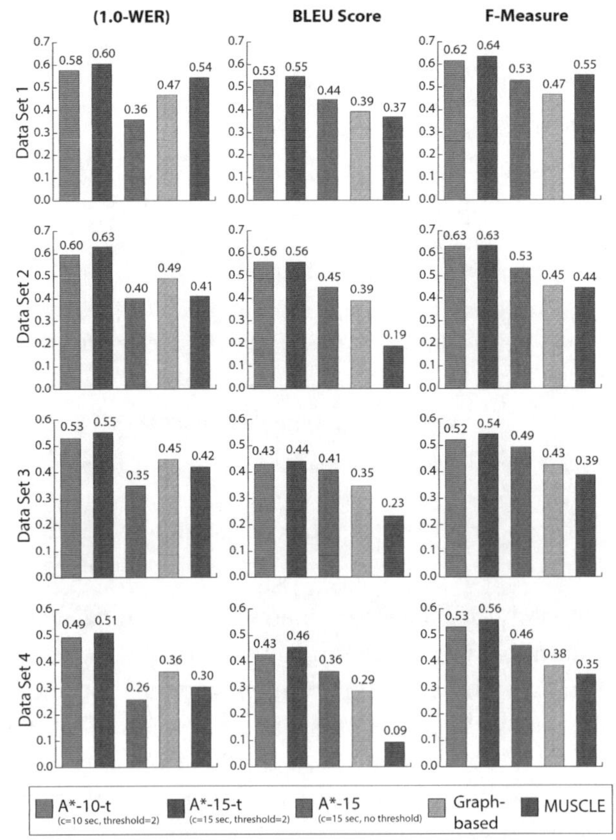

Figure 4: Evaluation of different systems on using three different automated metrics for measuring transcription quality: 1- Word Error Rate (WER), BLEU, and F-measure on the four audio clips.

tiple sequence alignment using MUSCLE.

As explained earlier, we vary the four key parameters of the algorithm: the chunk size (c), the heuristic weight (w), the voting threshold (t_v), and the beam size (b). The heuristic weight and chunk size parameters help us to trade-off between speed versus accuracy; the voting threshold t_v helps improve precision by pruning words having less than t_v votes, and beam size reduces the search space by restricting states to be inside a time window/beam. We use affine gap penalty (Edgar, 2004) with different gap opening and gap extension penalty. We set gap opening penalty to 0.125 and gap extension penalty to 0.05. We evaluate the performance using the three standard metrics: Word Error Rate (WER), BLEU, and F-measure. The performance in terms of these metrics using different systems is presented in Figure 4.

Out of the five systems in Figure 4, the first three are different versions of our A* search based MSA algorithm with different parameter settings: 1) A*-10-t system (c = 10 seconds, t_v = 2), 2) A*-15-t (c = 15 seconds, t_v = 2), and 3) A*-15 (c = 15 seconds, t_v = 1 i.e. no pruning while voting). For all three systems, the heuristic weight parameter w is set to 2.5 and beam size b = 20 seconds. The other two systems are the existing graph-based system and multiple sequence alignment using MUSCLE. Among the three A* based algorithms, both A*-15-t and A*-10-t produce better quality transcripts and outperform the existing algorithms. Both systems apply the voting threshold that improves precision. The system A*-15 applies no threshold and ends up producing many spurious words having poor agreement among the workers, and hence it scores worse in all the three metrics. The A*-15-t achieves 57.4% average accuracy in terms of (1-WER), providing 29.6% improvement with respect to the graph-based system (average accuracy 42.6%), and 35.4% improvement with respect to the MUSCLE-based MSA system (average accuracy 41.9%). On the same set of audio clips, Lasecki et al. (2012) reported 36.6% accuracy using ASR (Dragon Naturally Speaking, version 11.5 for Windows), which is worse than all the crowd-based based systems used in this experiment. To measure the statistical significance of this improvement, we performed a t-test at both the dataset level ($n = 4$ clips) and the word level ($n = 2862$ words). The improvement over the graph-based model was statistically significant with dataset level p-value 0.001 and word level p-value smaller than 0.0001. The average time to align each 15 second chunk with 10 input captions is ~400 milliseconds.

We have also experimented with a trigram language model, trained on the British National Corpus (Burnard, 1995) having ~122 million words. The language-model-integrated A* search provided a negligible 0.21% improvement in WER over the A*-15-t system on average. The task of combining captions does not require recognizing words; it only requires aligning them in the correct order. This could explain why language model did not improve accuracy, as it does for speech recognition. Since the standard MSA-A* algorithm (without language model) produced comparable accuracy and faster running time, we used that version in the rest of the

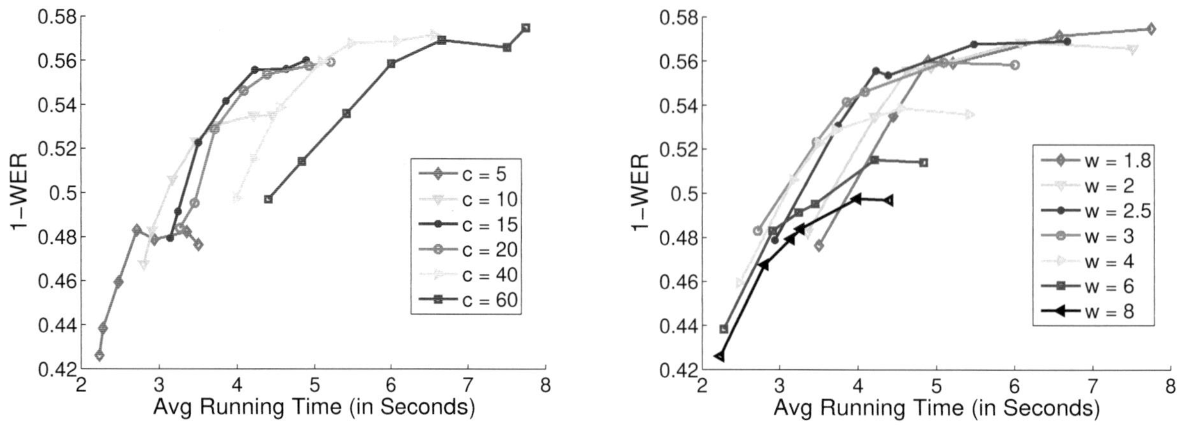

(a) Varying heuristic weights for fixed chunk sizes (c)

(b) Varying chunk size for fixed heuristic weight (w)

Figure 5: The trade-off between speed and accuracy for different heuristic weights and chunk size parameters.

experiments.

Next, we look at the critical speed versus accuracy trade-off for different values of the heuristic weight (w) and the chunk size (c) parameters. Since WER has been shown to correlate most with human judgment, we show the next results only with respect to WER. First, we fix the chunk size at different values, and then vary the heuristic weight parameter: w = 1.8, 2, 2.5, 3, 4, 6, and 8. The results are shown in Figure 5(a), where each curve represents how time and accuracy changed over the range of values of w and a fixed value of c. We observe that for smaller values of w, the algorithm is more accurate, but comparatively slower. As w increases, the search reaches the goal faster, but the quality of the solution degrades as well. Next, we fix w and vary chunk size $c = 5$, 10, 15, 20, 40, 60 second. We repeat this experiment for a range of values of w and the results are shown in Figure 5(b). We can see that the accuracy improves steeply up to $c = 20$ seconds, and does not improve much beyond $c = 40$ seconds. For all these benchmarks, we set the beam size (b) to 20 seconds and voting threshold (t_v) to 2.

In our tests, the beam size parameter (b) did not play a significant role in performance, and setting it to any reasonably large value (usually $\geq$ 15 seconds) resulted in similar accuracy and running time. This is because the A* search with h_{pair} heuristic already reduces the the search space significantly, and usually reaches the goal in a number of steps smaller than the state space size after the beam restriction.

Finally, we investigate how the accuracy of our algorithm varies with the number of inputs/workers. We start with a pool of 10 input captions for one of the audio clips. We vary the number of input captions (K) to the MSA-A* algorithm from 2 up to 10. The quality of input captions differs greatly among the workers. Therefore, for each value of K, we repeat the experiment $\min\left(20, \binom{10}{K}\right)$ times; each time we randomly select K input captions out of the total pool of 10. Figure 6 shows that accuracy steeply increases as the number of inputs increases to 7, and after that adding more workers does not provide much improvement in accuracy, but increases running time.

5 Discussion and Future Work

In this paper, we show that the A* search based MSA algorithm performs better than existing algorithms for combining multiple captions. The existing graph-based model has low latency, but it usually can not find a near optimal alignment because of its incremental alignment. Weighted A* search on the other hand performs joint multiple sequence alignment, and is guaranteed to produce a solution having cost no more than $(1 + \epsilon)$ times the cost of the optimal solution, given a heuristic weight of $(1 + \epsilon)$. Moreover, A* search allows for straightforward integration of an n-gram language model during the search.

Another key advantage of the proposed algorithm is the ease with which we can trade-off between

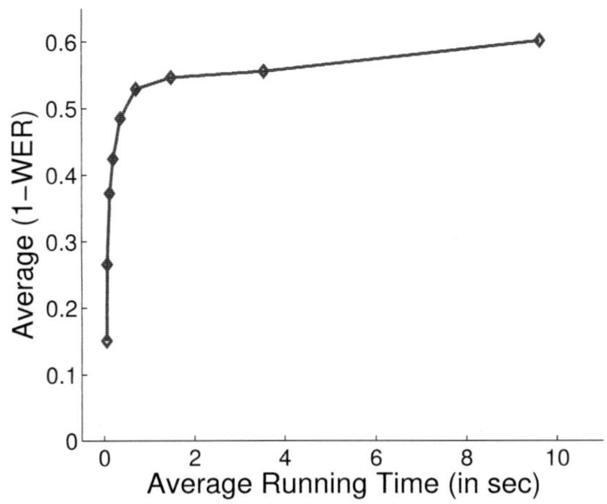

Figure 6: Experiments showing how the accuracy of the final caption by MSA-A* algorithm varies with the number of inputs from 2 to 10.

speed and accuracy. The algorithm can be tailored to real-time by using a larger heuristic weight. On the other hand, we can produce better transcripts for offline tasks by choosing a smaller weight.

It is interesting to compare our results with those achieved using the MUSCLE MSA tool of Edgar (2004). One difference is that our system takes a hierarchical approach in that it aligns at the word level, but also uses string edit distance at the letter level as a substitution cost for words. Thus, it is able to take advantage of the fact that individual transcriptions do not generally contain arbitrary fragments of words. More fundamentally, it is interesting to note that MUSCLE and most other commonly used MSA tools for biological sequences make use of a *guide tree* formed by a hierarchical clustering of the input sequences. The guide tree produced by the algorithms may or may not match the evolutionary tree of the organisms whose genomes are being aligned, but, nevertheless, in the biological application, such an underlying evolutionary tree generally exists. In aligning transcriptions, there is no particular reason to expect individual pairs of transcriptions to be especially similar to one another, which may make the guide tree approach less appropriate.

In order to get competitive results, the A* search based algorithm aligns sequences that are at least 7-10 seconds long. The delay for collecting the captions within a chunk can introduce latency, however, each alignment usually takes less than 300 milliseconds, allowing us to repeatedly align the stream of words, even before the window is filled. This provides less accurate but immediate response to users. Finally, when we have all the words entered in a chunk, we perform the final alignment and show the caption to users for the entire chunk.

After aligning the input sequences, we obtain the final transcript by majority voting at each alignment position, which treats each worker equally and does not take individual quality into account. Recently, some work has been done for automatically estimating individual worker's quality for crowd-based data labeling tasks (Karger et al., 2011; Liu et al., 2012). Extending these methods for crowd-based text captioning could be an interesting future direction.

6 Conclusion

In this paper, we have introduced a new A* search based MSA algorithm for aligning partial captions into a final output stream in real-time. This method has advantages over prior approaches both in formal guarantees of optimality and the ability to trade off speed and accuracy. Our experiments on real captioning data show that it outperforms prior approaches based on a dependency graph model and a standard MSA implementation (MUSCLE). An experiment with 50 participants explored whether exiting automatic metrics of quality matched human evaluations of readability, showing WER did best.

Acknowledgments Funded by NSF awards IIS-1218209 and IIS-0910611.

References

Keith Bain, Sara Basson, A Faisman, and D Kanevsky. 2005. Accessibility, transcription, and access everywhere. *IBM Systems Journal*, 44(3):589–603.

Keith Bain, Eunice Lund-Lucas, and Janice Stevens. 2012. 22. transcribe your class: Using speech recognition to improve access for at-risk students. *Collected Essays on Learning and Teaching*, 5.

Lou Burnard. 1995. Users Reference Guide British National Corpus Version 1.0.

Chris Callison-Burch, Miles Osborne, and Philipp Koehn. 2006. Re-evaluating the role of bleu in machine translation research. In *Proceedings of EACL*, volume 2006, pages 249–256.

Martin Cooke, Phil Green, Ljubomir Josifovski, and Ascension Vizinho. 2001. Robust automatic speech recognition with missing and unreliable acoustic data. *Speech Communication*, 34(3):267–285.

Chuong B Do, Mahathi SP Mahabhashyam, Michael Brudno, and Serafim Batzoglou. 2005. Probcons: Probabilistic consistency-based multiple sequence alignment. *Genome Research*, 15(2):330–340.

Richard Durbin, Sean R Eddy, Anders Krogh, and Graeme Mitchison. 1998. *Biological sequence analysis: probabilistic models of proteins and nucleic acids*. Cambridge university press.

Robert C Edgar and Serafim Batzoglou. 2006. Multiple sequence alignment. *Current opinion in structural biology*, 16(3):368–373.

Robert C Edgar. 2004. MUSCLE: multiple sequence alignment with high accuracy and high throughput. *Nucleic Acids Research*, 32(5):1792–1797.

Xiaodong He, Li Deng, and Alex Acero. 2011. Why word error rate is not a good metric for speech recognizer training for the speech translation task? In *IEEE International Conference on Acoustics, Speech and Signal Processing (ICASSP), 2011*, pages 5632–5635. IEEE.

Phillip B Horton. 1997. *Strings, algorithms, and machine learning applications for computational biology*. Ph.D. thesis, University of California, Berkeley.

David R Karger, Sewoong Oh, and Devavrat Shah. 2011. Iterative learning for reliable crowdsourcing systems. In *Proceedings of Advances in Neural Information Processing Systems (NIPS)*, volume 24, pages 1953–1961.

Walter Lasecki and Jeffrey Bigham. 2012. Online quality control for real-time crowd captioning. In *Proceedings of the 14th international ACM SIGACCESS conference on Computers and accessibility (ASSETS 2012)*, pages 143–150. ACM.

Walter Lasecki, Christopher Miller, Adam Sadilek, Andrew Abumoussa, Donato Borrello, Raja Kushalnagar, and Jeffrey Bigham. 2012. Real-time captioning by groups of non-experts. In *Proceedings of the 25rd annual ACM symposium on User interface software and technology, UIST '12*.

Walter Lasecki, Christopher Miller, and Jeffrey Bigham. 2013. Warping time for more effective real-time crowdsourcing. In *Proceedings of the ACM conference on Human Factors in Computing Systems*, CHI '13, page To Appear, New York, NY, USA. ACM.

Martin Lermen and Knut Reinert. 2000. The practical use of the A* algorithm for exact multiple sequence alignment. *Journal of Computational Biology*, 7(5):655–671.

Qiang Liu, Jian Peng, and Alex Ihler. 2012. Variational inference for crowdsourcing. In *Proceedings of Advances in Neural Information Processing Systems (NIPS)*, volume 25, pages 701–709.

Dan Melamed, Ryan Green, and Joseph P Turian. 2003. Precision and recall of machine translation. In *Proceedings HLT-NAACL 2003*, volume 2, pages 61–63. Association for Computational Linguistics.

Kishore Papineni, Salim Roukos, Todd Ward, and Wei-Jing Zhu. 2002. Bleu: a method for automatic evaluation of machine translation. In *Proceedings of the 40th annual meeting of Association for Computational Linguistics*, pages 311–318. Association for Computational Linguistics.

Ira Pohl. 1970. Heuristic search viewed as path finding in a graph. *Artificial Intelligence*, 1(3):193–204.

Aleš Pražák, Zdeněk Loose, Jan Trmal, Josef V Psutka, and Josef Psutka. 2012. Captioning of Live TV Programs through Speech Recognition and Respeaking. In *Text, Speech and Dialogue*, pages 513–519. Springer.

Murat Saraclar, Michael Riley, Enrico Bocchieri, and Vincent Goffin. 2002. Towards automatic closed captioning: Low latency real time broadcast news transcription. In *Proceedings of the International Conference on Spoken Language Processing (ICSLP)*, pages 1741–1744.

Julie D Thompson, Desmond G Higgins, and Toby J Gibson. 1994. Clustal w: improving the sensitivity of progressive multiple sequence alignment through sequence weighting, position-specific gap penalties and weight matrix choice. *Nucleic Acids Research*, 22(22):4673–4680.

Mike Wald. 2006a. Captioning for deaf and hard of hearing people by editing automatic speech recognition in real time. *Computers Helping People with Special Needs*, pages 683–690.

Mike Wald. 2006b. Creating accessible educational multimedia through editing automatic speech recognition captioning in real time. *Interactive Technology and Smart Education*, 3(2):131–141.

Lusheng Wang and Tao Jiang. 1994. On the complexity of multiple sequence alignment. *Journal of Computational Biology*, 1(4):337–348.

Ye-Yi Wang, Alex Acero, and Ciprian Chelba. 2003. Is word error rate a good indicator for spoken language understanding accuracy. In *IEEE Workshop on Automatic Speech Recognition and Understanding, 2003. ASRU'03. 2003*, pages 577–582. IEEE.

Discriminative Joint Modeling of Lexical Variation and Acoustic Confusion for Automated Narrative Retelling Assessment

Maider Lehr[†], **Izhak Shafran**[†], **Emily Prud'hommeaux**[°] **and Brian Roark**[†]
[†]Center for Spoken Language Understanding, Oregon Health & Science University
[°]Center for Language Sciences, University of Rochester
{maiderlehr,zakshafran,emilpx,roarkbr}@gmail.com

Abstract

Automatically assessing the fidelity of a retelling to the original narrative – a task of growing clinical importance – is challenging, given extensive paraphrasing during retelling along with cascading automatic speech recognition (ASR) errors. We present a word tagging approach using conditional random fields (CRFs) that allows a diversity of features to be considered during inference, including some capturing acoustic confusions encoded in word confusion networks. We evaluate the approach under several scenarios, including both supervised and unsupervised training, the latter achieved by training on the output of a baseline automatic word-alignment model. We also adapt the ASR models to the domain, and evaluate the impact of error rate on performance. We find strong robustness to ASR errors, even using just the 1-best system output. A hybrid approach making use of both automatic alignment and CRFs trained tagging models achieves the best performance, yielding strong improvements over using either approach alone.

1 Introduction

Narrative production tasks are an essential component of many standard neuropsychological test batteries. For example, narration of a wordless picture book is part of the Autism Diagnostic Observation Schedule (ADOS) (Lord et al., 2002) and retelling of previously narrated stories is part of both the Developmental Neuropsychological Assessment (NEPSY) (Korkman et al., 1998) and the Wechsler Logical Memory (WLM) test (Wechsler, 1997). Such tests also arise in reading comprehension, second language learning and other computer-based tutoring systems (Xie et al., 2012; Zhang et al., 2008).

The accuracy of automated scoring of a narrative retelling depends on correctly identifying which of the source narrative's propositions or events (what we will call 'story elements') have been included in the retelling. Speakers may choose to relate these elements using diverse words or phrases, and an automated method of identifying these elements needs to model the permissible variants and paraphrasings. In previous work (Lehr et al., 2012; Prud'hommeaux and Roark, 2012; Prud'hommeaux and Roark, 2011), we developed models based on automatic word-alignment methods, as described briefly in Section 3. Such alignments are learned in an unsupervised manner from a parallel corpus of manual or ASR transcripts of retellings and the original source narrative, much as in machine translation training.

Relying on manual transcripts to train the alignment models limits the ability of these methods to handle ASR errors. By instead training on ASR transcripts, these methods can automatically capture some regularities of lexical variants and their common realizations by the recognizer. Additionally, evidence of acoustic confusability is available in word lattice output from the recognizer, which can be exploited to yield more robust automatic scoring, particularly in high error-rate scenarios.

In this paper, we present and evaluate the use of word tagging models for this task, in contrast to just using automatic (unsupervised) word-alignment methods. The approach is general enough to allow tagging of word confusion networks derived from lattices, thus allowing us to explore the utility of such representations to achieve robustness. We present results under a range of experimental conditions, including: variously adapting the ASR models to the domain; using maximum entropy models rather than CRFs; differing tagsets (BIO versus IO); and with varying degrees of supervision. Finally, we demonstrate improved utility in terms of using the automatic scores to classify elderly individuals as having Mild Cognitive Impairment. Ultimately we find that hybrid approaches, making use of both word-alignment and tagging models, yield strong improvements over either used independently.

2 Wechsler Logical Memory (WLM) task

The Wechsler Logical Memory (WLM) task (Wechsler, 1997), a widely used subtest of a battery of neuropsychological tests used to assess memory function in adults, has been shown to be a good indicator of Mild Cognitive Impairment (MCI) (Storandt and Hill, 1989; Petersen et al., 1999; Wang and Zhou, 2002; Nordlund et al., 2005), the stage of cognitive decline that is often a precursor to dementia of the Alzheimer's type. In the WLM, the subject listens to the examiner read a brief narrative and then retells the narrative twice: immediately upon hearing it and after about 20 minutes. The examiner grades the subject's response by counting how many of the story elements the subject recalled.

An excerpt of the text read by the clinician while administering the WLM task is shown in Figure 1. The story elements in the text are delineated using slashes, 25 elements in all. An example retelling is shown in Figure 2 to illustrate how the retellings are scored. The clinical evaluation guidelines specify what lexical substitutions, if any, are allowed for each element. Some elements, such as *cafeteria* and *Thompson*, must be recalled verbatim. In other cases, subjects are given credit for variants, such as *Annie* for *Anna*, or paraphrasing of concepts such as *sympathetic* for *touched by the woman's story*. The example retelling received a score of 12, with one point for each of the recalled story elements: *Anna, Boston, employed, as a cook, and robbed of, she had four, small children, reported, station, touched by the woman's story, took up a collection* and *for her*.

> Anna / Thompson / of South / Boston / employed / as a cook / in a school / cafeteria / reported / at the police / station / that she had been held up / on State Street / the night before / and robbed / . . . / police / touched by the woman's story / took up a collection / for her.

Figure 1: Reference text and the set of story elements.

> <u>Ann</u> Taylor <u>worked</u> in <u>Boston</u> as a <u>cook</u>. And she was <u>robbed</u> of sixty-seven dollars. Is that right? And she had <u>four</u> <u>children</u> and <u>reported</u> at the some kind of <u>station</u>. The fellow <u>sympathetic</u> and <u>made a collection</u> <u>for her</u> so that she can feed the children.

Figure 2: An example retelling with 12 recalled story elements.

3 Unsupervised generative automated scoring with word alignment

In previous work (Lehr et al., 2012; Prud'hommeaux and Roark, 2012; Prud'hommeaux and Roark, 2011), we developed a pipeline for automatically scoring narrative retellings for the WLM task. The utterances corresponding to a retelling were recognized using an ASR system. The story elements were identified from the 1-best ASR transcript using word alignments produced by the Berkeley aligner (Liang et al., 2006), an EM-based word alignment package developed to align parallel texts for machine translation. The word alignment model was estimated in an unsupervised manner from a parallel corpus consisting of source narrative and manual transcripts of retellings from a small set of training subjects, and from a pairwise parallel corpus of manual retelling transcripts.

During inference or test, the ASR transcripts of the retellings were aligned using the estimated alignment model to the source narrative text. If a word in the retelling was mapped by the alignment model to a content word in the source narrative, the element associated with that content word was counted as correctly recalled in that retelling. Recall that the models were trained on unsupervised data so the aligned words may not always be permissible variants of the target elements. To alleviate such extraneous as well as unaligned words, the alignments below a threshold of posterior probability are discarded while decoding.

4 Supervised discriminative automated scoring with log-linear models

In this work, we frame the task of detecting story elements as a tagging task. Thus, our problem reduces to assigning a tag to each word position in the retelling, the tag indicating the story element that the word is associated with. In its simplest form, we have 26 tags: one for each of the 25 story elements indicating the word is 'in' that element (e.g., I15); and one for 'outside' of any story element ('O'). By tagging word positions, we are framing the problem in a general enough way to allow tagging of word confusion networks (Mangu et al., 2000), which encode word confusions that may provide additional robustness, particularly in high word-error rate scenarios. We make use of log-linear models, which have been used for tagging confusion networks (Kurata et al., 2012), and which allow very flexible feature vector definition and discriminative optimization.

The model allows us to experiment with three types of inputs as illustrated in the Figure 3 – the manual transcript, the 1-best ASR transcript, and the word confusion network. To create supervised training data, we force-align ASR transcripts to manual transcripts and transfer manually annotated story element tags from the reference transcripts to word positions in the confusion network or 1-best ASR output using the word-level time marks. Our unsupervised training scenario instead derives story element tags from a baseline word-alignment based model.

Figure 3: Feature vectors at each word position includes lexical variants and acoustic confusions.

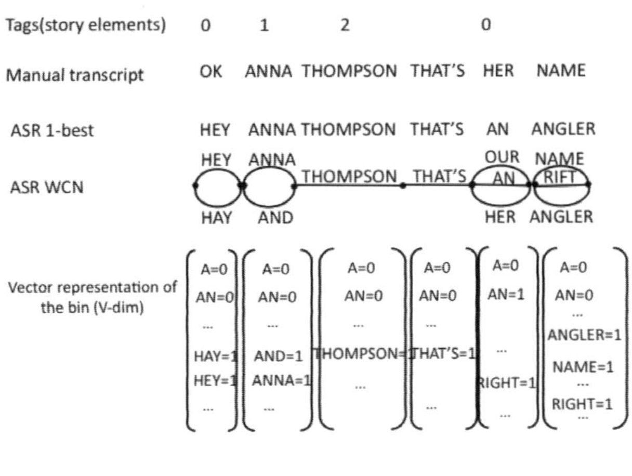

	Markov order 0 (MaxEnt)	Markov order 1 (CRF)
Context independent (CI)	y_i $y_i x_i$	$y_{i-1} y_i$ $y_{i-1} y_i x_i$
Context dependent (CD)	$y_i x_{i-1}$ $y_i x_{i+1}$	$y_{i-1} y_i x_{i-1}$ $y_{i-1} y_i x_{i+1}$

Table 1: Feature templates either using or not using neighboring tag y_{i-1} (MaxEnt vs. CRF); and for using or not using neighboring words x_{i-1}, x_{i+1} (CI vs. CD).

4.1 Features

Given a sequence of word positions $x = x_1 \ldots x_n$, the tagger assigns a sequence of labels $y = y_1 \ldots y_n$ from a tag lexicon. For each word x_i in the sequence, we can define features in the log-linear model based on word and tag identities. Table 1 presents several sets of features, defined over words and tags at various positions relative to the current word x_i and tag y_i and compound features are denoted as concatenated symbols.

Features that rely only on the current tag y_i are used in a Markov order 0 model, i.e., one for which each tag is labeled independently. A maximum entropy classifier (see Section 4.2) is used with these feature sets. Features that include prior tags encode dependencies between adjacent tags, and are used within conditional random fields models (see Section 4.3). To examine the utility of surrounding words x_{i-1} and x_{i+1}, we distinguish between models trained with context independent features (just x_i) and context dependent features. Note that models including context dependent feature sets also include the context independent features, and Markov order 1 models also include Markov order 0 features.

Two other details about our use of the feature templates are worth noting. First, when tagging confusion networks, each word in the network at position i results in a feature instance. Thus, if there are five confusable words at position i, then there will be five different x_i values being used to instantiate the features in Table 1. Second, following Kurata et al. (2012), we multiply the feature counts for the context dependent features by a weight to control their influence on the model. In this paper, the scaling weight of the context-dependent features was 0.3.

We investigate two different tagsets for this task, as presented in Table 2. The simpler tagset (IO) simply identifies words that are in a story element; the

Tagging	*anna*	*rent was due*
IO-tags	I1	I19 I19 I19
BIO-tags	B1	B19 I19 I19

Table 2: Two possible tagsets for labeling.

larger tagset (BIO) differentiates among positions in a story element chunk. The latter tagset is only of utility for models with Markov order greater than zero, and hence are only used with CRF models.

4.2 MaxEnt-based multiclass classifier

Our baseline model is a Maximum Entropy (MaxEnt) classifier where each position i from the retelling x gets assigned one of the IO output tags y_i corresponding to the set of 25 story elements and a null ('O') symbol. The output tag is modeled as the conditional probability $p(y_i \mid x_i)$ given the word x_i at position i in the retelling.

$$p(y_i \mid x_i) = \frac{exp\left(\sum_{k=1}^{d} \lambda_k \phi_k(x_i, y_i)\right)}{Z(x_i)}$$

where $Z(x_i)$ is a normalization factor. The feature functions $\phi(x_i, y_i)$ are the Markov order 0 features as defined as in the previous section. The parameters $\lambda \in \Re^d$ are estimated by optimizing the above conditional probability, with L2 regularization. We use the MALLET Toolkit (McCallum, 2002) with default regularization parameters.

4.3 CRF-based sequence labeling model

The MaxEnt models assign a tag to each position from the input retelling independently. However, there are a few reasons why reframing the task as a sequence modeling problem may improve tagging performance. First, some of the story elements are multiword sequences, such as *she had been held up* or *on State Street*. Second, even if a retelling orders recalled elements differently than the original narrative, there is a tendency for story elements to occur in certain orders.

The parameters of the CRF model, $\lambda \in \Re^d$ are estimated by optimizing the following conditional probability:

$$P(y \mid x) = \frac{\exp\left(\sum_{k=1}^{d} \lambda_k \phi_k(x, y)\right)}{Z(x)}$$

where $\Phi(x, y)$ aggregates features across the entire sequence, and $Z(x)$ is a global normalization constant over the sequence, rather than local for a particular position as with MaxEnt. Features for the CRF model are Markov order 1 features, and as with the MaxEnt training, we use default (L2) regularization parameters within the MALLET toolkit.

5 Combining tagging and alignment

This paper contrasts a discriminatively trained tagging approach with an unsupervised alignment-based approach, but there are several ways in which the two approaches can be combined. First, the alignment model is unsupervised and can provide its output as training data to the tagging approach, resulting in an unsupervised discriminative model. Second, the alignment model can provide features to the log-linear tagging model in the supervised condition. We explore both methods of combination here.

5.1 Unsupervised discriminative tagger

The tagging task based on log-linear models provides an appropriate framework to easily incorporate diverse features and discriminatively estimate the parameters of the model. However, this approach requires supervised tagged training data, in this case manual labels indicating the correspondence of phrases in the retellings with story elements in the original narrative. These manual annotations are used to derive sequences of story element tags labeling the words of the retelling. Manually labeling the retellings is costly, and the scoring (thus labeling) scheme is very specific to the test being analyzed. To avoid manual labeling and provide a general framework that can easily be adopted in any retelling based assessment task, we experiment here with an unsupervised discriminative approach.

In this unsupervised approach, the labeled training data required by the log-linear model is provided by the automatic word alignments trained without supervision. The resulting tag sequences replace the manual tag sequences used in the standard supervised approach.

5.2 Word-alignment derived features

When training discriminative models it is a common practice to incorporate into the feature space the output from a generative model, since it is a good estimator. Here we augment the feature space of the log-linear models with the tags generated by the automatic word alignments. In addition to the features defined in Section 4.1, we include new features that match predicted labels z_i from the word-alignment model with possible labels in the tagger y_i. Our features include the current tagger label with (1) the current predicted word-alignment label; (2) the previous predicted label; and (3) the next predicted label. Thus, the new features were $y_i z_i$, $y_i z_{i-1}$ and $y_i z_{i+1}$.

6 Experimental evaluations

Corpus: Our models were trained on immediate and delayed retellings from 144 subjects with a mean age of 85.4, of whom 36 were clinically diagnosed with MCI (training set). We evaluated our models on a set of retellings from 70 non-overlapping subjects with a mean age of 88.5, half of whom had received a diagnosis of MCI (test set). In contrast to the unsupervised word-alignment based method, the method outlined here required manual story element labels of the retellings. The training and test sets from this paper are therefore different from the sets used in previous work (Lehr et al., 2012; Prud'hommeaux and Roark, 2012; Prud'hommeaux and Roark, 2011), and the results are not directly comparable.

The recordings were sometimes made in an informal setting, such as the subject's home or a senior center. For this reason, there are often extraneous noises in the recordings such as music, footsteps, and clocks striking the hour. Although this presents a challenge for ASR, part of the goal of our work is to demonstrate the robustness of our methods to noisy audio.

6.1 Automatic transcription

The baseline ASR system used in the current work is a Broadcast News system which is modeled after Kingsbury et al. (2011). Briefly, the acoustics of speech are modeled by 4000 clustered allophone states defined over a pentaphone context, where states are represented by Gaussian mixture models with a total of 150K mixture components. The observation vectors consist of PLP features, stacked from 10 neighboring frames and projected to a 50-dimension space using linear discriminant analysis (LDA). The acoustic models were trained on 430 hours of transcribed speech from Broadcast News corpus (LDC97S44, LDC98S71). The language model is defined over an 84K vocabulary and consists of about 1.8M, 1M and and 331K bigrams, trigrams and 4-grams, estimated from standard Broadcast news corpus. The decoding is performed in several stages using successively refined acoustic models – a context-dependent model, a vocal-tract normalized model, a speaker-adapted maximum likelihood linear regression (MLLR) model, and finally a discriminatively trained model with the boosted MMI criteria (Povey et al., 2008). The system gives a word error rate of 13.1% on the 2004 Rich Transcription benchmark by NIST (Fiscus et al., 2007), which is comparable to state-of-the-art for equivalent amounts of acoustic training data. On the WLM corpus, the recognition word error rate was significantly higher at 47.2% due to a mismatch in domain and the skewed demographics (age) of the speakers.

System	1-best (%)	oracle WCN(%)	oracle lat(%)
Baseline	47.2	39.7	27.7
AM adaptation	38.2	35.5	21.2
LM adaptation	28.3	30.7	19.9
AM+LM adaptation	25.6	26.5	16.5

Table 3: Improvement in ASR word error-rate by adapting the Broadcast News models to the domain of narrative retelling.

We improved the performance of the above Broadcast News models by adapting to the domain of the WLM retellings. The acoustic models were adapted using standard MLLR, where linear transforms were estimated in an unsupervised manner to maximize the likelihood over the transcripts of the retellings. The transcripts were generated from the baseline system after the final stage of decoding with the discriminative model. The language models were adapted by interpolating the in-domain model (weight=0.7) with the out-of-domain model. The gains from these adaptations are reported in the Table 3. As expected, we find substantial gains from both acoustic model (AM) and language model (LM) adaptation. Furthermore, we find benefit in employing them simultaneously. We also include the oracle word error rate (WER) of the WCNs and lattices for each ASR configuration.

One thing to note is that the oracle WER of the WCNs is worse than the 1-best WER when adapting the language models. We speculate that this is due to bias introduced by the language model adapted to the story retellings, resulting in word candidates in the bins that are not truly acoustically confusable candidates. This is one potential reason for the lack of utility of WCNs in low WER conditions.

6.2 Evaluating retelling scoring

We analyzed the performance of the retelling scoring methods under five different input conditions for producing transcripts: (1) the out-of-domain Broadcast News recognizer with no adaptation; (2) domain adapted acoustic model; (3) domain adapted language model; (4) domain adapted acoustic and language models; and (5) manual (reference) transcripts. Each story element is automatically labeled by the systems as either having been recalled or not, and this is compared with manual scores to derive an F-score accuracy, by calculating precision and recall of recalled story elements. Derived word alignments or tag sequences are converted to binary story element indicators by simply setting the element to 1 if any open-class word is tagged for (or aligned to) that story element.

6.2.1 Word alignment based scoring

We evaluate the word alignment approach only on 1-best ASR transcripts and manual transcripts, not WCNs. The first row of Table 4 reports the story element F-scores for a range of ASR adaptation scenarios. The performance of the model improves significantly as the WER reduces with adaptation. With the fully adapted ASR the F-score improves more than 13%, and it is only 3.4% worse than with the manual transcripts. The alignments produced in each of these scenarios are used as training data in the unsupervised condition evaluated below.

6.2.2 Log-linear based automated scoring

Context-independent features Table 4 summarizes the performance of the log-linear models using context independent features (CI) in supervised (section 4), unsupervised (section 5.1) and hybrid (section 5.2) training scenarios for different inputs (reference transcript, ASR 1-best, and word confusion network ASR output) and four different ASR configurations.

The results show a few clear trends. Both in the supervised and unsupervised training scenarios the CRF model provides substantial improvements over the MaxEnt classifier. The F-scores obtained in the unsupervised training scenario are slightly worse than with supervision, though they are comparable to supervised results and an improvement over just using the word alignment approach, particularly in high WER scenarios. The hybrid training scenario – supervised learning with word alignment derived features – leads to reduced differences between MaxEnt and CRF training compared to the other two training scenarios. In fact, in high WER scenarios, the MaxEnt slightly outperforms the CRF.

As expected the best performance is obtained with manual transcripts and the worst with 1-best transcripts generated by the out-of-domain ASR with relatively high word error rate. For this ASR configuration, using WCNs provide some gain, though the gain is insignificant for the hybrid approach. In the hybrid approach, the output labels of the word alignment are already good indicators of the output tag and incorporating the confusable words from the

Table 4: Story element F-score achieved by baseline word-alignment model and log-linear models (MaxEnt and CRF) using **context independent** features (CI) under 3 different scenarios, with 3 different inputs (1-best ASR, word confusion network, and manual transcripts) and different ASR models (baseline out-of-domain, AM adapted, LM adapted and AM+LM adapted).

Training Scenario	Transcripts: / ASR:	1-best baseline	1-best AM	1-best LM	1-best AM+LM	WCN baseline	WCN AM	WCN LM	WCN AM+LM	manual N/A
Baseline word-alignment:		71.9	77.3	84.3	85.4	N/A				88.8
Supervised	MaxEnt-CI	76.0	81.7	84.6	85.6	78.9	83.4	84.0	84.7	86.4
	CRF-CI	80.3	87.3	89.7	91.4	83.7	88.8	88.2	90.8	94.4
Unsupervised	MaxEnt-CI	72.1	79.3	82.7	84.2	77.5	81.2	83.4	83.2	84.8
	CRF-CI	79.4	85.4	86.8	88.0	81.2	85.8	86.2	87.2	90.5
Hybrid	MaxEnt-CI	88.1	89.4	89.2	89.6	87.6	89.2	88.8	89.5	91.8
	CRF-CI	87.0	90.9	91.5	92.1	87.4	91.5	90.1	92.4	94.6

Training Scenario	Transcripts: ASR:	1-best baseline	1-best AM	1-best LM	1-best AM+LM	WCN baseline	WCN AM	WCN LM	WCN AM+LM	manual N/A
Supervised	MaxEnt-CD	80.1	87.3	90.0	91.1	83.5	88.6	88.2	90.3	93.3
	CRF-CD-IO	80.6	88.0	89.9	91.2	84.2	89.6	88.8	90.5	94.7
	CRF-CD-BIO	81.1	87.9	90.6	91.7	84.5	89.5	88.8	90.8	94.7
Un-supervised	MaxEnt-CD	77.1	83.1	86.5	89.0	80.2	85.0	86.2	87.6	90.7
	CRF-CD-IO	79.1	85.3	87.1	88.3	81.0	85.9	86.4	87.5	90.3
	CRF-CD-BIO	79.1	85.6	87.2	88.4	81.3	85.9	86.2	87.3	90.6
Hybrid	MaxEnt-CD	88.4	90.2	90.7	91.6	88.6	90.5	90.4	91.4	93.5
	CRF-CD-IO	87.9	91.3	91.6	92.5	88.3	91.7	90.7	92.1	94.8
	CRF-BIO	87.8	91.9	91.8	93.0	88.7	92.0	90.7	92.3	94.7

Table 5: Story element F-score achieved by log-linear models (MaxEnt and CRF) when adding **context dependent** features (CD) and **BIO tags** for the CRF models, under 3 different scenarios, with 3 different inputs (1-best ASR, word confusion network, and manual transcripts) and different ASR models (baseline out-of-domain, AM adapted, LM adapted and AM+LM adapted).

WCN into the feature vector apparently mainly adds noise.

When the transcripts are generated with the adapted models, the word confidence score of the 1-best is higher and the WCN bins have fewer acoustically confusable words. Still, the WCN input is helpful in the AM-adapted ASR system. When the transcripts are generated with LM adapted models, the performance is better with 1-best than with WCNs. As mentioned earlier, adapting the language models may introduce a bias due to the relatively low LM perplexity for this domain. In the lowest WER scenarios, the best performing systems achieve over 90% F-score, within two percent of the performance achieved with manual transcripts.

Context-dependent features Exercising the flexibility of log-linear models, we investigated the impact of using context-dependent (CD) features instead of the CI features used in the previous experiments. Our CD features take into account the two immediately neighboring word positions. As mentioned earlier, following Kurata et al. (2012), the counts from the neighboring word positions were weighted ($\alpha = 0.3$) to avoid data sparsity. This reduces the sensitivity of the model to time alignment errors between the tag and feature vector sequences without increasing the dimensions. In Table 5, we report the F-scores for the different ASR configurations, inputs, and log-linear models with context dependent features, using the standard IO tagset as in Table 4.

Although there are some exceptions, adding context information from the input features improves the performance of the models. In particular, the MaxEnt models benefit from incorporating this extra information. The MaxEnt models improve their performance substantially for all three training scenarios, while the gains for the CRF models are more modest, especially for the unsupervised approach where the performance degrades or does not change much, since some context information is already captured by the Markov order 1 features.

BIO tagset As detailed in Section 4.1, story elements sometimes span multiple words, so for the CRF models we investigated two different schemes for tagging, following typical practice in named entity extraction (Ratinov and Roth, 2009) and syntactic chunking (Sha and Pereira, 2003). The BIO tagging scheme makes the distinction between the tokens from the story elements that are in the beginning from the ones that are not. The O tag is assigned to the tokens that do not belong to any of the story elements. The IO tagging uses a single tag for the tokens that fall in the same story element, which is the approach we have followed so far. In addition to presenting results using context dependent features, Table 5 presents results with the BIO tagset.

For the supervised and hybrid approaches, the BIO tagging provides insignificant but consistent gains for most of the scenarios. The unsupervised approach provides mixed results. This may be due to the way in which the word alignment model scores the retellings. It tags only those words from the retelling that are aligned with a content word in the source narrative, which may result in the loss of the

Training Scenario	Transcripts: ASR:	1-best baseline	1-best AM	1-best LM	1-best AM+LM	WCN baseline	WCN AM	WCN LM	WCN AM+LM	manual N/A
Baseline word-alignment:		0.65	0.67	0.74	0.76	N/A				0.79
Supervised	MaxEnt-CD	0.65	0.73	0.76	0.77	0.70	0.73	0.77	0.77	0.81
	CRF-CD-BIO	0.69	0.76	0.77	0.76	0.73	0.76	0.77	0.78	0.82
Un-supervised	MaxEnt-CD	0.65	0.72	0.75	0.76	0.70	0.75	0.75	0.76	0.80
	CRF-CD-BIO	0.74	0.75	0.78	0.78	0.71	0.74	0.77	0.76	0.81
Hybrid	MaxEnt-CD	0.72	0.76	0.77	0.78	0.74	0.76	0.77	0.77	0.82
	CRF-CD-BIO	0.72	0.76	0.78	0.78	0.76	0.77	0.78	0.79	0.81

Table 6: Classification performance (AUC) for the baseline word-alignment model and the best performing log-linear models of both types (MaxEnt and CRF) under 3 different scenarios with 3 types of input and 4 types of ASR models.

structure of some multiwords story elements that we are trying to capture with the BIO scheme.

6.3 Evaluating MCI classification

Each of the individuals producing retellings in our corpus underwent a battery of neuropsychological tests, and were assigned a Clinical Dementia Rating (CDR) (Morris, 1993), which is a composite score derived from measures of cognitive function in six domains, including memory. Importantly, it is assigned independently of the Wechsler Logical Memory test we are analyzing in this paper, which allows us to evaluate the utility of our WLM analyses in an unbiased manner. MCI is defined as a CDR of 0.5 (Ritchie and Touchon, 2000), and subjects in this study have either a CDR of 0 (no impairment) or 0.5 (MCI).

In previous work, we found that the features extracted from the retellings are useful in distinguishing subjects with MCI from neurotypical age-matched controls (Lehr et al., 2012; Prud'hommeaux and Roark, 2012; Prud'hommeaux and Roark, 2011). From each retellings, we extract Boolean features for each story element, for a total of 50 features for classification. Each feature indicates whether the retelling contained that story element.

In this paper, we carry out similar classification experiments to investigate the impact of using log-linear models on the extraction of features for classification. We build a support vector machine (SVM) using the LibSVM (Chang and Lin, 2011) extension to the WEKA data mining Java API (Hall et al., 2009). This allows recollection of different elements to be weighted differently. This is unlike the manual scoring of WLM based on clinical guidelines where all elements are weighted equally irrespective of the difficulty. The SVM was trained on manually extracted story element feature vectors. We compared the performance of the MCI classification for three types of input and four ASR configurations under the supervised, unsupervised, and hybrid scenarios. For each scenario we chose the best scoring system from among the automated systems reported in Tables 4 and 5. Classification results, evaluated as area under the curve (AUC), are reported in Table 6, both for the log-linear trained tagging models and for the baseline word-alignment based method. For reference (not shown in the table), the SVM classifier performed at 0.83 when features values are manually populated.

The results show that the AUC improves steadily as the quality of the transcription is improved, going from the baseline system to the adapted models. This is consistent with the improvements seen in the F-score for detecting story elements. The different approaches for detecting the story elements from the transcriptions did not ultimately show significant differences in MCI classification results. Overall, the best classification values are given by the hybrid approach, which performs slightly better than the other two approaches. The best AUC in the hybrid scenario (0.79, very close to the AUC=0.81 achieved with manual transcripts) is obtained with a CRF trained with WCNs from the fully adapted ASR model and with context dependent features and BIO tags.

Comparing WCN versus 1-best as inputs, using WCN as input improves classification performance when the 1-best transcripts are poor, as in the case of out-of-domain ASR. The adapted recognizer improves the performance of the 1-best significantly making it unnecessary to resort to WCN as inputs.

Comparing the MaxEnt model with CRF model

for extracting story elements, we see that the average F-scores for the MaxEnt models trained on CD features are nearly as good as and sometimes slightly better than those produced using the CRF models. The CRF extracted story elements, however, tend to yield classifiers that perform slightly better, especially in the unsupervised approach with 1-best inputs.

7 Summary and discussion

This paper examines the task of automatically scoring narrative retellings in terms of their fidelity to the original narrative content, using discriminatively trained log-linear tagging models. Fully automatic scoring must account for both lexical variation and acoustic confusion from ASR errors. Lexical variation – due to extensive paraphrasing on the part of the individuals retelling the narrative – can be modeled effectively using word-alignment models such as those employed in machine translation systems (Lehr et al., 2012; Prud'hommeaux and Roark, 2011). This paper focuses on an alternative approach, where both lexical variation and ASR confusions are modeled using log-linear models. In addition to very flexible feature definitions, the log-linear models bring the advantage of a discriminative model to the task. We see improvements in story element F-score using these models over unsupervised word-alignment models. Further, the feature definition flexibility allows us to incorporate the unsupervised word-alignment labels into these models, resulting either in fully unsupervised approaches that perform competitively with the supervised models or in hybrid (supervised) approaches that provide the best performing systems in this study.

Our tagging models are able to process word confusion networks as inputs and thus improve performance over using 1-best ASR transcripts in scenarios where the speech recognition error rate is high. These improvements carry through to the MCI classification task, making use of features computed from the automatic scoring of narrative retelling.

One advantage of the word-alignment model is that such approaches do not require manual annotation of the story elements, which is more labor intensive than typical manual transcription of speech. Thus, the word-alignment model can exploit large numbers of retellings in an unsupervised manner when trained on ASR transcripts of the retellings. Controlled experiments here with relatively limited training sets demonstrate that semi-supervised approaches on larger untranscribed sets are likely to be successful.

Finally, experiments with different amounts of ASR adaptation show that both acoustic and language model adaptations in this domain are effective, yielding scenarios that are competitive with manual transcription both for detecting story elements as well as for subsequent classification. With full model adaptation to the domain, the 1-best transcripts improved significantly, and their performance was found to be at par with WCNs.

In future work, we would like to investigate two questions left open by these results. First, word-alignment models can be extended to process ASR lattices or word confusion networks as part of the unsupervised alignment learning algorithm, and incorporated into our approach. Second, the contextual features can be refined (e.g., concatenated features instead of smoothed features) when large amounts of training data is available.

It is noteworthy to mention that the lexical variants and paraphrasing learned from the data using automated method may be useful in refining the clinical guidelines for scoring (e.g., allowing additional lexical variants and paraphrasings, or assigning unequal credits for different story elements to reflect the difficulty of recollecting them) or to create the guidelines for new languages or stories.

Acknowledgments

This research was supported in part by NIH awards 5K25AG033723-02 and P30 AG024978-05 and NSF awards 1027834, 0958585, 0905095, 0964102 and 0826654. Any opinions, findings, conclusions or recommendations expressed in this publication are those of the authors and do not reflect the views of the NIH or NSF. We thank Brian Kingsbury and IBM for the use of their ASR software tools; Jeffrey Kaye and Diane Howeison for their valuable input; and the clinicians at the Oregon Center for Aging and Technology for their care in collecting the data.

References

Chih-Chung Chang and Chih-Jen Lin. 2011. LIBSVM: A library for support vector machines. *ACM Transactions on Intelligent Systems and Technology*, 2(27):1–27.

Jonathan Fiscus, John Garofolo, Audrey Le, Alvin Martin, greg Sanders, Mark Przybocki, and David Pallett. 2007. 2004 spring nist rich transcription (rt-04s) evaluation data. `http://www.ldc.upenn.edu/Catalog/catalogEntry.jsp?catalogId=LDC2007S12`.

Mark Hall, Eibe Frank, Geoffrey Holmes, Bernhard Pfahringer, Peter Reutemann, and Ian H. Witten. 2009. The WEKA data mining software: An update. *SIGKDD Explorations*, 11(1).

Brian Kingsbury, Hagen Soltau, George Saon, Stephen M. Chu, Hong-Kwang Kuo, Lidia Mangu, Suman V. Ravuri, Nelson Morgan, and Adam Janin. 2011. The IBM 2009 GALE Arabic speech transcription system. In *Proceedings of ICASSP*, pages 4672–4675.

Marit Korkman, Ursula Kirk, and Sally Kemp. 1998. *NEPSY: A developmental neuropsychological assessment*. The Psychological Corporation, San Antonio.

Gakuto Kurata, Nobuyasu Itoh, Masafumi Nishimura, Abhinav Sethy, and Bhuvana Ramabhadran. 2012. Leveraging word confusion networks for named entity modeling and detection from conversational telephone speech. *Speech Communication*, 54(3):491–502.

Maider Lehr, Emily Prud'hommeaux, Izhak Shafran, and Brian Roark. 2012. Fully automated neuropsychological assessment for detecting mild cognitive impairment. In *Interspeech*.

Percy Liang, Ben Taskar, and Dan Klein. 2006. Alignment by agreement. In *Proceedings of HLT-NAACL*.

Catherine Lord, Michael Rutter, Pamela DiLavore, and Susan Risi. 2002. *Autism Diagnostic Observation Schedule (ADOS)*. Western Psychological Services, Los Angeles.

Lidia Mangu, Eric Brill, and Andreas Stolcke. 2000. Finding consensus in speech recognition: Word error minimization and other applications of confusion networks. *Computer Speech and Language*, 14(4):373–400.

Andrew Kachites McCallum. 2002. Mallet: A machine learning for language toolkit. `http://mallet.cs.umass.edu`.

John Morris. 1993. The clinical dementia rating (CDR): Current version and scoring rules. *Neurology*, 43:2412–2414.

A. Nordlund, S. Rolstad, P. Hellstrom, M. Sjogren, S. Hansen, and A. Wallin. 2005. The Goteborg MCI study: Mild cognitive impairment is a heterogeneous condition. *Journal of Neurology, Neurosurgery and Psychiatry*, 76(11):1485–1490.

Ronald Petersen, Glenn Smith, Stephen Waring, Robert Ivnik, Eric Tangalos, and Emre Kokmen. 1999. Mild cognitive impairment: Clinical characterizations and outcomes. *Archives of Neurology*, 56:303–308.

Daniel Povey, Dimitri Kanevsky, Brian Kingsbury, Bhuvana Ramabhadran, George Saon, and Karthik Visweswariah. 2008. Boosted mmi for model and feature space discriminative training. In *Proceedings of ICASSP*.

Emily Prud'hommeaux and Brian Roark. 2011. Alignment of spoken narratives for automated neuropsychological assessment. In *Proceedings of ASRU*.

Emily Prud'hommeaux and Brian Roark. 2012. Graph-based alignment of narratives for automated neuropsychological assessment. In *Proceedings of the NAACL 2012 Workshop on Biomedical Natural Language Processing (BioNLP)*.

Lev Ratinov and Dan Roth. 2009. Design challenges and misconceptions in named entity recognition. In *EMNLP*.

Karen Ritchie and Jacques Touchon. 2000. Mild cognitive impairment: Conceptual basis and current nosological status. *Lancet*, 355:225–228.

Fei Sha and Fernando Pereira. 2003. Shallow parsing with conditional random fields. In *Proceedings of HLT-NAACL*.

Martha Storandt and Robert Hill. 1989. Very mild senile dementia of the Alzheimer's type: II Psychometric test performance. *Archives of Neurology*, 46:383–386.

Qing-Song Wang and Jiang-Ning Zhou. 2002. Retrieval and encoding of episodic memory in normal aging and patients with mild cognitive impairment. *Brain Research*, 924:113–115.

David Wechsler. 1997. *Wechsler Memory Scale - Third Edition*. The Psychological Corporation, San Antonio.

Shasha Xie, Keelan Evanini, and Klaus Zechner. 2012. Exploring content features for automated speech scoring. In *Proceedings of HLT-NAACL*.

Xiaonan Zhang, Xiaonan Zhang, Jack Mostow, Jack Mostow, Nell Duke, Christina Trotochaud, Joseph Valeri, and Al Corbett. 2008. Mining free-form spoken responses to tutor prompts. In *Proceedings of the First International Conference on Educational Data Mining*, pages 234–241.

Using Out-of-Domain Data for Lexical Addressee Detection in Human-Human-Computer Dialog

Heeyoung Lee[1*] **Andreas Stolcke**[2] **Elizabeth Shriberg**[2]
[1]Dept. of Electrical Engineering, Stanford University, Stanford, California, USA
[2]Microsoft Research, Mountain View, California, USA
heeyoung@stanford.edu, {anstolck,elshribe}@microsoft.com

Abstract

Addressee detection (AD) is an important problem for dialog systems in human-human-computer scenarios (contexts involving multiple people and a system) because system-directed speech must be distinguished from human-directed speech. Recent work on AD (Shriberg et al., 2012) showed good results using prosodic and lexical features trained on in-domain data. In-domain data, however, is expensive to collect for each new domain. In this study we focus on lexical models and investigate how well out-of-domain data (either outside the domain, or from single-user scenarios) can fill in for matched in-domain data. We find that human-addressed speech can be modeled using out-of-domain conversational speech transcripts, and that human-computer utterances can be modeled using single-user data: the resulting AD system outperforms a system trained only on matched in-domain data. Further gains (up to a 4% reduction in equal error rate) are obtained when in-domain and out-of-domain models are interpolated. Finally, we examine which parts of an utterance are most useful. We find that the first 1.5 seconds of an utterance contain most of the lexical information for AD, and analyze which lexical items convey this. Overall, we conclude that the H-H-C scenario can be approximated by combining data from H-C and H-H scenarios only.

*Work done while first author was an intern with Microsoft.

1 Introduction

Before a spoken dialog system can recognize and interpret a user's speech, it should ideally determine if speech was even meant to be interpreted by the system. We refer to this task as addressee detection (AD). AD is often overlooked, especially in traditional single-user scenarios, because with the exception of self-talk, side-talk or background speech, the majority of speech is usually system-directed. As dialog systems expand to more natural contexts and multiperson environments, however, AD can become a crucial part of the system's operational requirements. This is particularly true for systems in which explicit system addressing (e.g., push-to-talk or required keyword addressing) is undesirable.

Past research on addressee detection has focused on human-human (H-H) settings, such as meetings, sometimes with multimodal cues (op den Akker and Traum, 2009). Early systems relied primarily on rejection of H-H utterances either because they could not be interpreted (Paek et al., 2000), or because they yielded low speech recognition confidence (Dowding et al., 2006). Some systems combine gaze with lexical and syntactic cues to detect H-H speech (Katzenmaier et al., 2004). Others use relatively simple prosodic features based on pitch and energy in addition to those derived from automatic speech recognition (ASR) (Reich et al., 2011).

With some exceptions (Bohus and Horvitz, 2011; Shriberg et al., 2012), relatively little work has looked at the human-human-computer (H-H-C) scenario, i.e. at contexts involving two or more people who interact both with a system and with each other.

Shriberg et al. (2012) found that novel prosodic features were more accurate than lexical or semantic features based on speech recognition for the addressee task. The corpus, also used herein, is comprised of H-H-C dialog in which roughly half of the computer-addressed speech consisted of a small set of fixed commands. While the word-based features map directly to the commands, they had trouble distinguishing all other (noncommand) computer-directed speech from human-directed speech. This is because addressee detection in the H-H-C scenario becomes even more challenging when the system is designed for natural speech, i.e., utterances that are conversational in form and not limited to command phrases with restricted syntax. Furthermore, H-H utterances can be about the domain of the system (e.g., discussing the dialog task), making AD based on language content more difficult. The prosodic features were good at both types of distinctions—even improving performance significantly when combined with true-word (cheating) lexical features that have 100% accuracy on the commands. Nevertheless, the prior work showed that lexical n-grams are useful for addressee detection in the H-H-C scenario.

A problem with lexical features is that they are highly task- and domain-dependent. As with other language modeling tasks, one usually has to collect matched training data in significant quantities. Data collection is made more cumbersome and expensive by the multi-user aspect of the scenario. Thus, for practical reasons alone, it would be much better if the language models for AD could be trained on out-of-domain data, and if whatever in-domain data is needed could be limited to single-user interaction. We show in this paper that precisely this training scenario is feasible and achieves results that are comparable or better than using completely matched H-H-C training data.

In addition to studying the role of out-of-domain data for lexical AD models, we also examine which words are useful, and how soon in elapsed time they are available. Whereas most prior work in AD has looked at processing of entire utterances, we consider an online processing version where AD decisions are to be made as soon as possible after an utterance was initiated. We find that most of the addressee-relevant lexical information can be found

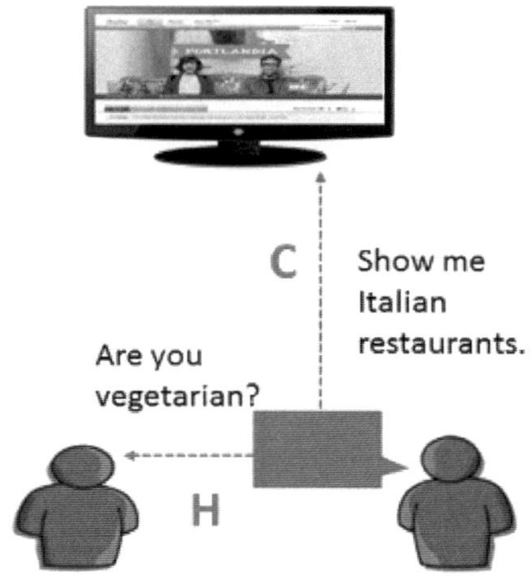

Figure 1: Conversational Browser dialog system environment with multi-human scenario

in the first 1.5 seconds, and analyze which words convey this information.

2 Data

We use in-domain and out-of-domain data from various sources. The corpora used in this work differ in size, domain, and scenario.

2.1 In-domain data

In-domain data is collected from interactions between two users and a "Conversational Browser" (CB) spoken dialog system. We used the same methodology as Shriberg et al. (2012), but using additional data. As depicted in Figure 1, the system shows a browser on a large TV screen and users are asked to use natural language for a variety of information-seeking tasks. For more details about the dialog system and language understanding approach, see Hakkani-Tür et al. (2011a; 2011b).

We split the in-domain data into training, development, and test sets, preserving sessions. Each session is about 5 to 40 minutes long. Even though the whole conversation is recorded, only the segments captured by the speech recognition system are used in our experiments. Each utterance segment belongs to one of four types: computer-command (C-command), comprising navigational commands to the system, computer-noncommand (C-noncommand), which are computer-directed utterances other than commands, human-directed (H), and mixed (M) utterances, which contain a combina-

Table 1: In-domain corpus

(a) Sizes, distribution, and ASR word error rates of in-domain utterance types

Data set	Train	Dev	Test	WER
Transcribed words	6,490	11,298	9,486	
ASR words	4,649	6,360	5,514	59.3%
H (%)	19.1	48.6	37.0	87.6%
C-noncomm. (%)	38.3	27.8	32.2	32.6%
C-command (%)	39.9	18.7	27.2	19.7%
M (%)	2.7	4.9	3.6	69.6%

(b) Example utterances by type

Type	Example
H	Do you want to watch a movie?
C-noncommand	How is the weather today?
C-command	Scroll down, Go back.
M	Show me sandwich shops. Oh, are you vegetarian?

tion of human- and computer-directed speech. The sizes and distribution of all utterance types, as well as sample utterances are shown in Table 1.

The ASR system used in the system was based on off-the-shelf acoustic models and had only the language model adapted to the domain, using very limited data. Consequently, as shown in the right-most column of Table 1(a), the word error rates (WERs) are quite high, especially for human-directed utterances. While these could be improved with targeted effort, we consider this a realistic application scenario, where in-domain training data is typically scarce, at least early in the development process. Therefore, any lexically based AD methods need to be robust to poor ASR accuracy.

2.2 Out-of-domain data

To replace the hard-to-obtain in-domain H-H-C data for training, we use the four out-of-domain corpora (two H-C and two H-H) shown in Table 2.

Single-user CB data comes from the same Conversational Browser system as the in-domain data, but with only one user present. This data can therefore be used for modeling H-C speech. Bing anchor text (Huang et al., 2010) is a large n-gram corpus of anchor text associated with links on web pages encountered by the Bing search engine. When users want to follow a link displayed on screen, they usually speak a variant of the anchor text for the link. We hypothesized that this corpus might aid the modeling of computer-noncommand type utterances in which such "verbal clicks" are frequent. Fisher telephone conversations and ICSI meetings are both corpora of human-directed speech. The Fisher corpus (Cieri et al., 2004) comprises two-person telephone conversations between strangers on prescribed topics. The ICSI meeting corpus (Janin et al., 2003) contains multiparty face-to-face technical discussions among colleagues.

Table 2: Out-of-domain corpora. "Single-user CB" is a corpus collected in same environment as the H-H-C in-domain data, except that only a single user was present.

Corpus	Addressee	Size
Single-user CB	H-C	21.9k words
Bing anchor text	H-C	1.3B bigrams
Fisher	H-H	21M words
ICSI meetings	H-H	0.7M words

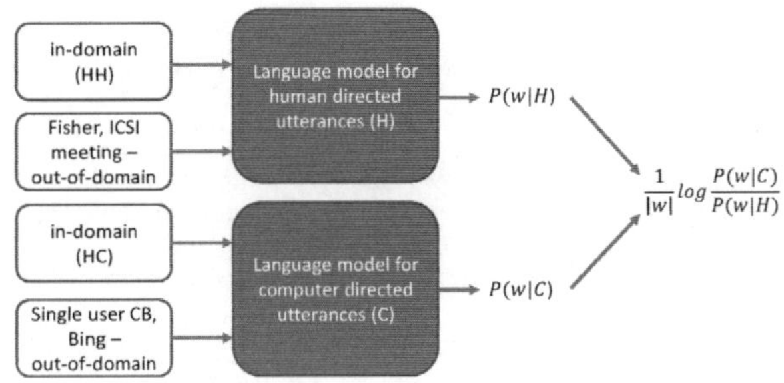

Figure 2: Language model-based score computation for addressee detection

3 Method

3.1 Language modeling for addressee detection

We use a lexical AD system that is based on modeling word n-grams in the two addressee-based utterance classes, H (for H-H) and C (for H-C utterances). This approach is similar to language model-based approaches to speaker and language recognition, and was shown to be quite effective for this task (Shriberg et al., 2012). Instead of making hard decisions, the system outputs a score that is the length-normalized likelihood ratio of the two classes:

$$\frac{1}{|w|}\log\frac{P(w|C)}{P(w|H)}, \tag{1}$$

where $|w|$ is the number of words in the recognition output w for an utterance. $P(w|C)$ and $P(w|H)$ are obtained from class-specific language models. Figure 2 gives a flow-chart of the score computation.

Class likelihoods are obtained from standard trigram backoff language models, using Witten-Bell discounting for smoothing (Witten and Bell, 1991). For combining various training data sources, we use language model adaptation by interpolation (Bellegarda, 2004). First, a separate model is trained from each source. The probability estimates from in-domain and out-of-domain models are then averaged in a weighted fashion:

$$P(w_k|h_k) = \lambda P_{in}(w_k|h_k) + (1-\lambda)P_{out}(w_k|h_k) \tag{2}$$

where w_k is the k-th word, h_k is the $(n-1)$-gram history for the word w_k. λ is the interpolation weight and is obtained by tuning a task-related metric on the development set. We investigated optimizing λ for either model perplexity or classification accuracy, as discussed below.

3.2 Part-of-speech-based modeling

So far we have only been modeling the lexical forms of words in utterances. If we encounter a word never before seen, it would appear as an out-of-vocabulary item in all class-specific language models, and not contribute much to the decision. More generally, if a word is rare, its n-gram statistics will be unreliable and poorly modeled by the system. (The sparseness issue is exacerbated by small amounts of training data as in our scenario.)

One common approach to deal with data sparseness in language modeling is to model n-grams over word classes rather than raw words (Brown et al., 1992). For example, if we have an utterance *How is the weather in Paris?*, the addressee probabilities are likely to be similar had we seen *London* instead of *Paris*. Therefore, replacing words with properly chosen word class labels can give better generalization from the observed training data. Among the many methods proposed to class words for language modeling purposes we chose part-of-speech (POS) tagging over other, purely data-derived classing algorithms (Brown et al., 1992), for two reasons. First, our goal here is not to minimize the perplexity of the data, but to enhance discrimination among utterance classes. Second, a data-driven class inference algorithm would suffer from the same sparseness issues when it comes to unseen and rare words (as no robust statistics are available to infer an unseen word's best class in the class induction step). A POS tagger, on the other hand, can do quite well on unseen words, using context and morphological cues.

A hidden Markov model tagger using POS-trigram statistics and context-independent class membership probabilities was used for tagging all LM training data. The tagger itself had been trained on the Switchboard (conversational telephone speech) transcripts of the Penn Treebank-3 corpus (Marcus et al., 1999), and used the 39 Treebank POS labels. To strike a compromise between generalization and discriminative power in the language model, we retained the top N most frequent word types from the in-domain training data as distinct tokens, and varied N as a metaparameter. Barzilay and Lee (2003) used a similar idea to generalize patterns by substituting words with slots. This strategy will tend to preserve words that are either generally frequent function and domain-independent words, capturing stylistic and syntactic patterns, or which are frequent domain-specific words, and can thus help characterize computer-directed utterances.

Here is a sample sentence and its transformed version:

> Original: *Let's find an Italian restaurant around this area.*
> POS-tagged: *Let's find an JJ NN around this area.*

The words except *Italian* and *restaurant* are unchanged because they are in the list of N most frequent words. We transformed all training and test data in this fashion and then modeled n-gram statistics as before. The one exception was the Bing anchor-text data, which was only available in the form of word n-grams (the sentence context required for accurate POS tagging was missing).

Table 3: Addressee detection performance (EER) with different training sets

	ASR	Transcript
Baseline (in-domain only)	31.1	17.3
Fisher+ICSI, Single-user CB+Bing (out-of-domain only)	27.8	14.2
Baseline + Fisher+ICSI, Single CB + Bing (both-all)	26.9	14.0
Baseline + ICSI, Single-user CB (both-small)	26.6	13.0

3.3 Evaluation metrics

Typically, an application-dependent threshold would be applied to the decision score to convert it into a binary decision. The optimal threshold is a function of prior class probabilities and error costs. As in Shriberg et al. (2012), we used equal error rate (EER) to compare systems, since we are interested in the discriminative power of the decision score independent of priors and costs. EER is the probability of false detections and misses at the operating point at which the two types of errors are equally probable. A prior-free metric such as EER is more meaningful than classification accuracy because the utterance type distribution is heavily skewed (Table 1), and because the rate of human- versus computer-directed speech can vary widely depending on the particular people, domain, and context. We also use classification accuracy (based on data priors) in one analysis below, because EERs are not comparable for different test data subdivisions.

3.4 Online model

The actual dialog system used in this work processes utterances after receiving an entire segment of speech from the recognition subsystem. However, we envision that a future version of the system would perform addressee detection in an online manner, making a decision as soon as enough evidence is gathered. This raises the question how soon the addressee can be detected once the user starts speaking. We simulate this processing mode using a windowed AD model.

As shown in Figure 3, we define windows starting at the beginning of the utterance and investigate how AD performance changes as a function of window size. We use only the words and n-grams falling completely within a given window. For example, the word *find* would be excluded from Window 1 in Figure 3.

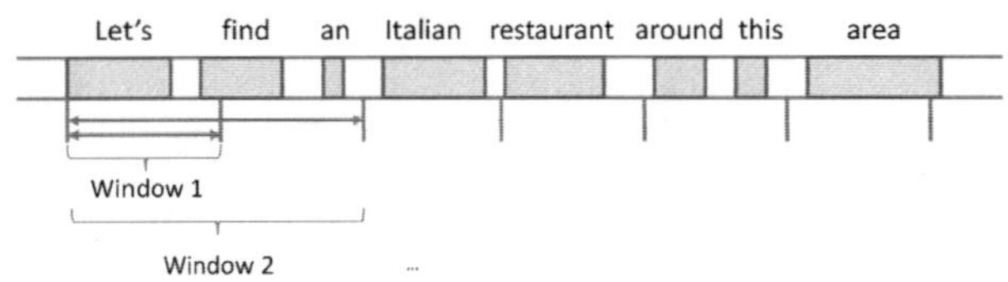

Figure 3: The window model

The benefit of early detection in this case is that once speech is classified as human-directed, it does not need to be sent to the speech recognizer and subsequent semantic processing. This saves processing time, especially if processing happens on a server. Based on the window model performance, we can assess the feasibility of an online AD model, which can be approached by shifting the detection window through time and finding addressee changes.

4 Results and Discussion

Table 3 compares the performance of our system using various training data sources. For diagnostic purposes we also compare performance based on recognized words (the realistic scenario) to that based on human transcripts (idealized, best-case word recognition).

Somewhat surprisingly, the system trained on out-of-domain data alone performs better by 3.3 EER points on ASR output and 3.1 points on transcripts compared to the in-domain baseline. Combining in-domain and out-of-domain data (both-all, both-small) gives about 1 point additional EER gain. Note that training on in-domain data plus the smaller-size out-of-domain corpora (both-small) is better than using all available data (both-all).

Figure 4 shows the detection error trade-off (DET) between false alarm and miss errors for the

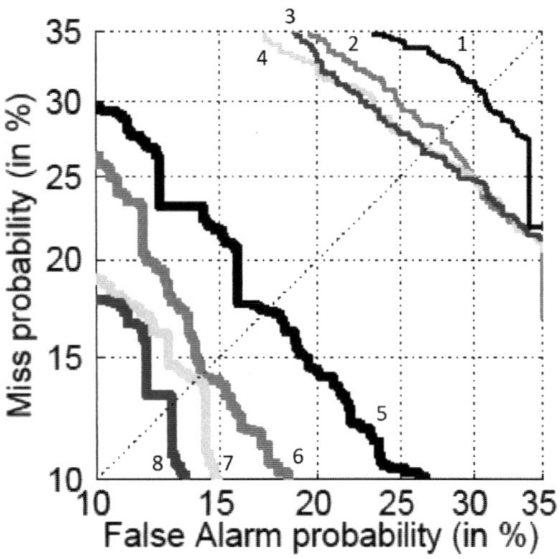

Figure 4: Detection error trade-off (DET) curves for the systems in Table 3. Thin lines at the top right corner use ASR output (1-4); thick lines at the bottom left corner use reference transcripts (5-8). Each line number represents one of the systems in Table 3: 1,5 = in-domain only, 2,6 = out-of-domain only, 4,7 = both-all, 3,8 = both-small.

systems in Table 3. The DET plot depicts performance not only at the EER operating point (which lies on the diagonal), but over the range of possible trade-offs between false alarm and miss error rates. As can be seen, replacing or combining in-domain data with out-of-domain data gives clear performance gains, regardless of operating point (score threshold), and for both reference and recognized words.

Figure 5 shows H-H vs. H-C classification accuracies on each of the four utterance subtypes listed in Table 1. It is clear that computer-command utterances are the easiest to classify; the accuracy is more than 90% using transcripts, and more than 85% using ASR output. This is not surprising, since commands are from a fixed small set of phrases. The biggest gain from use of out-of-domain data is found for computer-directed noncommand utterances. This is helpful, since in general it is the noncommand computer-directed utterances (rather than the commands) that are highly confusable with human-directed utterances: both use unconstrained natural language. We note that H-H utterance are very poorly recognized in the ASR condition when only out-of-domain data is used. This may be because the human-human corpora used in training consist of transcripts, whereas the ASR output for human-directed utterances is very errorful, creating a severe train-test mismatch.

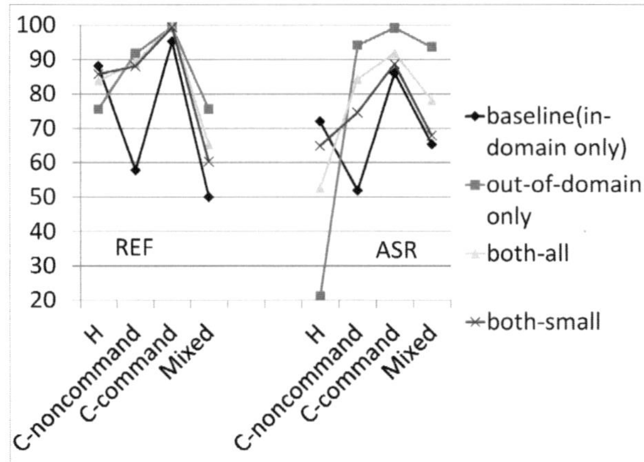

Figure 5: AD accuracies by utterance type

Table 4: Perplexities (computed on dev set ASR words) by utterance type, for different training corpora. Interpolation refers to the combination of the three models listed in each case.

	Test class	
Training set	H-C	H-H
In-domain H-C (ASR)	257	1856
Single-user CB	104	1237
Bing anchor text	356	789
Interpolation	58	370
In-domain H-H (ASR)	887	1483
Fisher	995	795
ICSI meeting	2007	1583
Interpolation	355	442

As for the optimization of the mixing weight λ, we found that minimizing perplexity on the development set of each class is effective. This is a standard optimization approach for interpolated language models, and can be carried out efficiently using an expectation maximization algorithm. We also tried search-based optimization using the classification metric (EER) as the criterion. While this approach could theoretically give better results (since perplexity is not a discriminative criterion) we found no significant improvement in our experiments.

Table 4 shows the perplexities by class of language models trained on different corpora. We can take these as an indication of training/test mismatch (lower perplexity indicating better match). We also find substantial perplexity reductions from interpolating models. In order to make perplexities comparable, we trained all models using the union of the vocabularies from the different sources.

In spite of perplexity being a good way to optimize the *weighting* of sources, it is not clear that it is a good criterion for *selecting* data sources. For example, we see that the Fisher model has a much lower perplexity on H-H utterances than the ICSI meeting model. However, as reflected in Table 3, the H language model that leaves out the Fisher data actually performed better. The most likely explanation is that the Fisher corpus is an order of magnitude larger than the ICSI corpus, and that sheer data size, not stylistic similarity, may account for the lower perplexity of the Fisher model. Further investigation is needed regarding good criteria for corpus selection for classification tasks such as AD.

Table 5 shows the EER performance of the POS-based model, for various sizes N of the most-frequent word list. We observe that the partial replacement of words with POS tags indeed improves over the baseline model performance, by 1.5 points on ASR output and by 1.1 points on transcripts. We also see that the gain over the corresponding word-only model is largest for the in-domain baseline model, and less or non-existent for the out-of-domain model. This is consistent with the notion that the in-domain model suffers the most from data sparseness, and therefore has the most to gain from better generalization.

Interpolating with out-of-domain data still helps here. The optimal N differs for ASR output versus transcripts. The POS-based model with $N = 300$ improves the EER by 0.5 points on ASR output, and $N = 1000$ improves the EER by 0.8 points on transcripts. Here we use relatively large amounts of training data, thus the performance gain is smaller, though still meaningful.

Figure 6 shows the performance of the system using time windows anchored at the beginnings of utterances. We incrementally increase the window width from 0.5 seconds to 3 seconds and compare results to using full utterances. The leveling off of

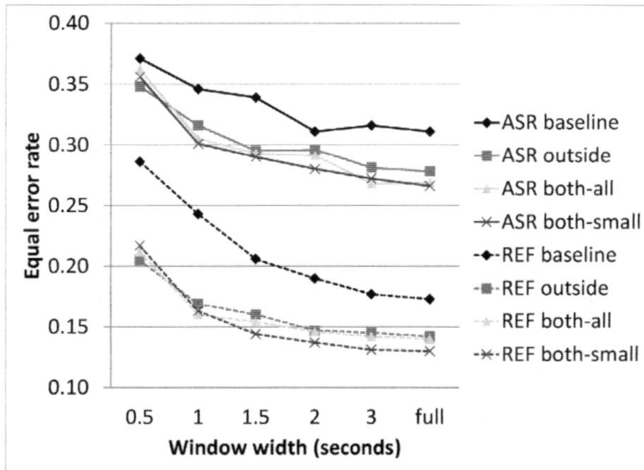

Figure 6: Simulated online performance on incremental windows

Table 6: The top 15 first words in utterances

ASR H-C	Transcript H-C	ASR H-H	Transcript H-H
go	go	play	I
scroll	scroll	go	ohh
start	start	is	so
show	stop	it	yeah
stop	show	what	it's
bing	find	this	you
search	Bing	show	uh
find	search	how	okay
play	pause	bing	what
pause	play	select	it
look	look	okay	and
what	uh	does	that's
select	what	start	is
how	how	so	no
the	ohh	I	we

the error plots indicates that most addressee information is contained in the first 1 to 1.5 seconds, although some additional information is found in the later part of utterances (the plots never level off completely). This pattern holds for both in-domain and out-of-domain training, as well as for combined models.

To give an intuitive understanding of where this early addressee-relevant information comes from, we tabulated the top 15 word unigrams in each utterance class, are shown in Table 6. Note that the substantial differences between the third and fourth columns in the table reflect the high ASR error rate for human-directed utterances, whereas

Table 5: Performance of POS-based model with various top-N word lists (EER)

	Training data	top100	top200	top300	top400	top500	top1000	top2000	Original
ASR	baseline	31.6	31.0	**29.6**	30.1	30.2	31.4	31.5	31.1
	out-of-domain only	36.5	37.0	37.2	36.9	36.8	36.6	37.3	**27.8**
	both-all	28.2	26.6	**26.1**	26.7	27.4	26.9	27.6	26.9
	both-small	28.0	26.5	**26.2**	26.6	26.4	26.3	26.5	26.6
REF	baseline	17.1	**16.2**	16.6	17.1	16.7	17.0	17.2	17.3
	out-of-domain only	17.6	17.6	17.5	17.2	17.1	17.2	18.1	**14.2**
	both-all	**12.5**	**12.5**	**12.5**	12.7	12.8	13.2	13.5	14.0
	both-small	13.0	13.2	12.8	13.2	12.8	**12.2**	12.7	13.0

for computer-directed utterances, the frequent first words are mostly recognized correctly.

In computer-directed utterances we see mostly command verbs, which, due to the imperative syntax of these commands occur in utterance-initial position. Human-directed utterances are characterized by subject pronouns such as *I* and *it*, or answer particles such as *yeah* and *okay*, which likewise occur in initial position. Based on word frequency and syntax alone it is thus clear why the beginnings of utterances contain strong lexical cues.

5 Conclusion

We explored the use of outside data for training lexical addressee detection systems for the human-human-computer scenario. Advantages include saving the time and expense of an in-domain data collection, as well as performance gains even when some in-domain data is available. We show that H-C training data can be obtained from a single-user H-C collection, and that H-H speech can be modeled using general conversational speech. Using the outside training data, we obtain results that are even better than results using matched (but smaller) H-H-C training data. Results can be improved considerably by adapting H-C and H-H language models with small amounts of matched H-H-C data, via interpolation. The main reason for the improvement is better detection of computer-directed noncommand utterances, which tend to be confusable with human-directed utterances. Another effective way to overcome scarce training data is to replace the less frequent words with part-of-speech labels. In both baseline and interpolated model, we found that POS-based models that keep an appropriate number of the top N most frequent word types can further improve the system's performance.

In a second study we found that the most salient phrases for lexical addressee detection occur within the first 1 to 1.5 seconds of speech in each utterance. It reflects a syntactic tendency of class-specific words to occur utterance-initially, which shows the feasibility of the online AD system.

Acknowledgments

We thank our Microsoft colleagues Madhu Chinthakunta, Dilek Hakkani-Tür, Larry Heck, Lisa Stiefelman, and Gokhan Tür for developing the dialog system used in this work, as well as for many valuable discussions. Ashley Fidler was in charge of much of the data collection and annotation required for this study. We also thank Dan Jurafsky for useful feedback.

References

Regina Barzilay and Lillian Lee. 2003. Learning to paraphrase: An unsupervised approach using multiple-sequence alignment. In *Proceedings HLT-NAACL 2003*, pages 16–23, Edmonton, Canada.

Jerome R. Bellegarda. 2004. Statistical language model adaptation: review and perspectives. *Speech Communication*, 42:93–108.

Dan Bohus and Eric Horvitz. 2011. Multiparty turn taking in situated dialog: Study, lessons, and directions. In *Proceedings ACL SIGDIAL*, pages 98–109, Portland, OR.

Peter F. Brown, Vincent J. Della Pietra, Peter V. deSouza, Jenifer C. Lai, and Robert L. Mercer. 1992. Class-based n-gram models of natural language. *Computational Linguistics*, 18(4):467–479.

Christopher Cieri, David Miller, and Kevin Walker. 2004. The Fisher corpus: a resource for the next generations of speech-to-text. In *Proceedings 4th International Conference on Language Resources and Evaluation*, pages 69–71, Lisbon.

John Dowding, Richard Alena, William J. Clancey, Maarten Sierhuis, and Jeffrey Graham. 2006. Are you talking to me? dialogue systems supporting mixed teams of humans and robots. In *Proccedings AAAI Fall Symposium: Aurally Informed Performance: Integrating Machine Listening and Auditory Presentation in Robotic Systems*, Washington, DC.

Dilek Hakkani-Tür, Gokhan Tur, and Larry Heck. 2011a. Research challenges and opportunities in mobile applications [dsp education]. *IEEE Signal Processing Magazine*, 28(4):108 –110.

Dilek Z. Hakkani-Tür, Gökhan Tür, Larry P. Heck, and Elizabeth Shriberg. 2011b. Bootstrapping domain detection using query click logs for new domains. In *Proceedings Interspeech*, pages 709–712.

Jian Huang, Jianfeng Gao, Jiangbo Miao, Xiaolong Li, Kuansang Wang, and Fritz Behr. 2010. Exploring web scale language models for search query processing. In *Proceedings 19th International Conference on World Wide Web*, pages 451–460, Raleigh, NC.

Adam Janin, Don Baron, Jane Edwards, Dan Ellis, David Gelbart, Nelson Morgan, Barbara Peskin, Thilo Pfau, Elizabeth Shriberg, Andreas Stolcke, and Chuck Wooters. 2003. The ICSI meeting corpus. In *Proceedings IEEE ICASSP*, volume 1, pages 364–367, Hong Kong.

Michael Katzenmaier, Rainer Stiefelhagen, and Tanja Schultz. 2004. Identifying the addressee in human-human-robot interactions based on head pose and speech. In *Proceedings 6th International Conference on Multimodal Interfaces*, ICMI, pages 144–151, New York, NY, USA. ACM.

Mitchell P. Marcus, Beatrice Santorini, Mary Ann Marcinkiewicz, and Ann Taylor. 1999. Treebank-3. Linguistic Data Consortium, catalog item LDC99T42.

Rieks op den Akker and David Traum. 2009. A comparison of addressee detection methods for multiparty conversations. In *Proceedings of Diaholmia*, pages 99–106.

Tim Paek, Eric Horvitz, and Eric Ringger. 2000. Continuous listening for unconstrained spoken dialog. In *Proceedings ICSLP*, volume 1, pages 138–141, Beijing.

Daniel Reich, Felix Putze, Dominic Heger, Joris Ijsselmuiden, Rainer Stiefelhagen, and Tanja Schultz. 2011. A real-time speech command detector for a smart control room. In *Proceedings Interspeech*, pages 2641–2644, Florence.

Elizabeth Shriberg, Andreas Stolcke, Dilek Hakkani-Tür, and Larry Heck. 2012. Learning when to listen: Detecting system-addressed speech in human-human-computer dialog. In *Proceedings Interspeech*, Portland, OR.

Ian H. Witten and Timothy C. Bell. 1991. The zero-frequency problem: Estimating the probabilities of novel events in adaptive text compression. *IEEE Transactions on Information Theory*, 37(4):1085–1094.

Segmentation Strategies for Streaming Speech Translation

Vivek Kumar Rangarajan Sridhar, John Chen, Srinivas Bangalore
Andrej Ljolje, Rathinavelu Chengalvarayan
AT&T Labs - Research
180 Park Avenue, Florham Park, NJ 07932
vkumar,jchen,srini,alj,rathi@research.att.com

Abstract

The study presented in this work is a first effort at real-time speech translation of TED talks, a compendium of public talks with different speakers addressing a variety of topics. We address the goal of achieving a system that balances translation accuracy and latency. In order to improve ASR performance for our diverse data set, adaptation techniques such as constrained model adaptation and vocal tract length normalization are found to be useful. In order to improve machine translation (MT) performance, techniques that could be employed in real-time such as monotonic and partial translation retention are found to be of use. We also experiment with inserting text segmenters of various types between ASR and MT in a series of real-time translation experiments. Among other results, our experiments demonstrate that a good segmentation is useful, and a novel conjunction-based segmentation strategy improves translation quality nearly as much as other strategies such as comma-based segmentation. It was also found to be important to synchronize various pipeline components in order to minimize latency.

1 Introduction

The quality of automatic speech-to-text and speech-to-speech (S2S) translation has improved so significantly over the last several decades that such systems are now widely deployed and used by an increasing number of consumers. Under the hood, the individual components such as automatic speech recognition (ASR), machine translation (MT) and text-to-speech synthesis (TTS) that constitute a S2S system are still loosely coupled and typically trained on disparate data and domains. Nevertheless, the models as well as the pipeline have been optimized in several ways to achieve tasks such as high quality offline speech translation (Cohen, 2007; Kingsbury et al., 2011; Federico et al., 2011), on-demand web based speech and text translation, low-latency real-time translation (Wahlster, 2000; Hamon et al., 2009; Bangalore et al., 2012), etc. The design of a S2S translation system is highly dependent on the nature of the audio stimuli. For example, talks, lectures and audio broadcasts are typically long and require appropriate segmentation strategies to chunk the input signal to ensure high quality translation. In contrast, single utterance translation in several consumer applications (apps) are typically short and can be processed without the need for additional chunking. Another key parameter in designing a S2S translation system for any task is latency. In offline scenarios where high latencies are permitted, several adaptation strategies (speaker, language model, translation model), denser data structures (N-best lists, word sausages, lattices) and rescoring procedures can be utilized to improve the quality of end-to-end translation. On the other hand, real-time speech-to-text or speech-to-speech translation demand the best possible accuracy at low latencies such that communication is not hindered due to potential delay in processing.

In this work, we focus on the speech translation of talks. We investigate the tradeoff between accuracy and latency for both offline and real-time translation of talks. In both these scenarios, appropriate segmentation of the audio signal as well as the ASR hypothesis that is fed into machine translation is critical for maximizing the overall translation quality of the talk. Ideally, one would like to train the models on entire talks. However, such corpora are not available in large amounts. Hence, it is necessary to conform to appropriately sized segments that are similar to the sentence units used in training the language and translation models. We propose several non-linguistic and linguistic segmentation strategies for the segmentation of text (reference or ASR hypotheses) for machine translation. We address the problem of latency in real-time translation as a function of the segmentation strategy; i.e., we ask the question "what is the segmentation strategy that maximizes the number of segments while still maximizing translation accuracy?".

2 Related Work

Speech translation of European Parliamentary speeches has been addressed as part of the TC-STAR project (Vilar et al., 2005; Fügen et al., 2006). The project focused primarily on offline translation of speeches. Simultaneous translation of lectures and speeches has been addressed in (Hamon et al., 2009; Fügen et al., 2007). However, the work focused on a single speaker in a limited domain. Offline speech translation of TED[1] talks has been addressed through the IWSLT 2011 and 2012 evaluation tracks. The talks are from a variety of speakers with varying dialects and cover a range of topics. The study presented in this work is the first effort on real-time speech translation of TED talks. In comparison with previous work, we also present a systematic study of the accuracy versus latency tradeoff for both offline and real-time translation on the same dataset.

Various utterance segmentation strategies for offline machine translation of text and ASR output have been presented in (Cettolo and Federico, 2006; Rao et al., 2007; Matusov et al., 2007). The work in (Fügen et al., 2007; Fügen and Kolss, 2007) also examines the impact of segmentation on offline speech translation of talks. However, the real-time analysis in that work is presented only for speech recognition. In contrast with previous work, we tackle the latency issue in simultaneous translation of talks as a function of segmentation strategy and present some new linguistic and non-linguistic methodologies. We investigate the accuracy versus latency tradeoff across translation of reference text, utterance segmented speech recognition output and partial speech recognition hypotheses.

[1]http://www.ted.com

3 Problem Formulation

The basic problem of text translation can be formulated as follows. Given a source (French) sentence $\mathbf{f} = f_1^J = f_1, \cdots, f_J$, we aim to translate it into target (English) sentence $\hat{\mathbf{e}} = \hat{e}_1^I = \hat{e}_1, \cdots, \hat{e}_I$.

$$\hat{\mathbf{e}}(\mathbf{f}) = \arg\max_{\mathbf{e}} \Pr(\mathbf{e}|\mathbf{f}) \quad (1)$$

If, as in talks, the source text (reference or ASR hypothesis) is very long, i.e., J is large, we attempt to break down the source string into shorter sequences, $\mathbf{S} = s_1 \cdots s_k \cdots s_{Q_s}$, where each sequence $s_k = [f_{j_k} f_{j_k+1} \cdots f_{j_{(k+1)}-1}]$, $j_1 = 1, j_{Q_s+1} = J+1$. Let the translation of each foreign sequence s_k be denoted by $t_k = [e_{i_k} e_{i_k+1} \cdots e_{i_{(k+1)}-1}]$, $i_1 = 1, i_{Q_s+1} = I' + 1$[2]. The segmented sequences can be translated using a variety of techniques such as independent chunk-wise translation or chunk-wise translation conditioned on history as shown in Eqs. 2 and 3, respectively. In Eq. 3, t_i^* denotes the best translation for source sequence s_i.

$$\hat{\hat{\mathbf{e}}}(\mathbf{f}) = \arg\max_{t_1} \Pr(t_1|s_1) \cdots \arg\max_{t_k} \Pr(t_k|s_k) \quad (2)$$

$$\hat{\hat{\mathbf{e}}}(\mathbf{f}) = \arg\max_{t_1} \Pr(t_1|s_1) \arg\max_{t_2} \Pr(t_2|s_2, s_1, t_1^*) \cdots \arg\max_{t_k} \Pr(t_k|s_1, \cdots, s_k, t_1^*, \cdots, t_{k-1}^*) \quad (3)$$

Typically, the hypothesis $\hat{\hat{e}}$ will be more accurate than $\hat{e}$ for long texts as the models approximating $\Pr(\mathbf{e}|\mathbf{f})$ are conventionally trained on short text segments. In Eqs. 2 and 3, the number of sequences Q_s is inversely proportional to the time it takes to generate partial target hypotheses. Our main focus in this work is to obtain a segmentation $\mathbf{S}$ such that the quality of translation is maximized with minimal latency. The above formulation for automatic speech recognition is very similar except that the foreign string $\check{\mathbf{f}} = \check{f}_1^J = \check{f}_1, \cdots, \check{f}_J$ is obtained by decoding the input speech signal.

[2]The segmented and unsegmented talk may not be equal in length, i.e., $I \neq I'$

	Model	Language	Vocabulary	#words	#sents	Corpora
ASR	Acoustic Model	en	46899	2611144	148460	1119 TED talks
	Language Model	en	378915	3398460155	151923101	Europarl, WMT11 Gigaword, WMT11 News crawl WMT11 News-commentary, WMT11 UN, IWSLT11 TED training
MT	Parallel text	en	503765	76886659	7464857	IWSLT11 TED training talks, Europarl, JRC-ACQUIS Opensubtitles, Web data
		es	519354	83717810	7464857	
	Language Model	es	519354	83717810	7464857	Spanish side of parallel text

Table 1: Statistics of the data used for training the speech translation models.

4 Data

In this work, we focus on the speech translation of TED talks, a compendium of public talks from several speakers covering a variety of topics. Over the past couple of years, the International Workshop on Spoken Language Translation (IWSLT) has been conducting the evaluation of speech translation on TED talks for English-French. We leverage the IWSLT TED campaign by using identical development (dev2010) and test data (tst2010). However, English-Spanish is our target language pair as our internal projects are cater mostly to this pair. As a result, we created parallel text for English-Spanish based on the reference English segments released as part of the evaluation (Cettolo et al., 2012).

We also harvested the audio data from the TED website for building an acoustic model. A total of 1308 talks in English were downloaded, out of which we used 1119 talks recorded prior to December 2011. We split the stereo audio file and duplicated the data to account for any variations in the channels. The data for the language models was also restricted to that permitted in the IWSLT 2011 evaluation. The parallel text for building the English-Spanish translation model was obtained from several corpora: Europarl (Koehn, 2005), JRC-Acquis corpus (Steinberger et al., 2006), Opensubtitle corpus (Tiedemann and Lars Nygaard, 2004), Web crawling (Rangarajan Sridhar et al., 2011) as well as human translation of proprietary data. Table 1 summarizes the data used in building the models. It is important to note that the IWSLT evaluation on TED talks is completely offline. In this work, we perform the first investigation into the real-time translation of these talks.

5 Speech Translation Models

In this section, we describe the acoustic, language and translation models used in our experiments.

5.1 Acoustic and Language Model

We use the AT&T WATSON^{SM} speech recognizer (Goffin et al., 2004). The speech recognition component consisted of a three-pass decoding approach utilizing two acoustic models. The models used three-state left-to-right HMMs representing just over 100 phonemes. The phonemes represented general English, spelled letters and head-body-tail representation for the eleven digits (with "zero" and "oh"). The pronunciation dictionary used the appropriate phoneme subset, depending on the type of the word. The models had 10.5k states and 27k HMMs, trained on just over 300k utterances, using both of the stereo channels. The baseline model training was initialized with several iterations of ML training, including two builds of context dependency trees, followed by three iterations of Minimum Phone Error (MPE) training.

The Vocal Tract Length Normalization (VTLN) was applied in two different ways. One was estimated on an utterance level, and the other at the talk level. No speaker clustering was attempted in training. The performance at test time was comparable for both approaches on the development set. Once the warps were estimated, after five iterations, the ML trained model was updated using MPE training. Constrained model adaptation (CMA) was applied to the warped features and the adapted features were recognized in the final pass with the VTLN model. All the passes used the same LM. For offline recognition the warps, and the CMA adaptation, are performed at the talk level. For the real-time speech translation experiments, we used the VTLN model.

The English language model was built using the permissible data in the IWSLT 2011 evaluation. The texts were normalized using a variety of cleanup, number and spelling normalization techniques and filtered by restricting the vocabulary to the top 375000 types; i.e., any sentence containing a token outside the vocabulary was discarded. First, we removed extraneous characters beyond the ASCII range followed by removal of punctuations. Subsequently, we normalized hyphenated words and removed words with more than 25 characters. The resultant text was normalized using a variety of number conversion routines and each corpus was filtered by restricting the vocabulary to the top 150000 types; i.e., any sentence containing a token outside the vocabulary was discarded. The vocabulary from all the corpora was then consolidated and another round of filtering to the top 375000 most frequent types was performed. The OOV rate on the TED dev2010 set is 1.1%. We used the AT&T FSM toolkit (Mohri et al., 1997) to train a trigram language model (LM) for each component (corpus). Finally, the component language models were interpolated by minimizing the perplexity on the dev2010 set. The results are shown in Table 2.

	Accuracy (%)	
Model	dev2010	test2010
Baseline MPE	75.5	73.8
VTLN	78.8	77.4
CMA	80.5	80.0

Table 2: ASR word accuracies on the IWSLT data sets.[3]

5.2 Translation Model

We used the Moses toolkit (Koehn et al., 2007) for performing statistical machine translation. Minimum error rate training (MERT) was performed on the development set (dev2010) to optimize the feature weights of the log-linear model used in translation. During decoding, the unknown words were preserved in the hypotheses. The data used to train the model is summarized in Table 1.

[3]We used the standard NIST scoring package as we did not have access to the IWSLT evaluation server that may normalize and score differently

We also used a finite-state implementation of translation without reordering. Reordering can pose a challenge in real-time S2S translation as the text-to-speech synthesis is monotonic and cannot retract already synthesized speech. While we do not address the text-to-speech synthesis of target text in this work, we perform this analysis as a precursor to future work. We represent the phrase translation table as a weighted finite state transducer (FST) and the language model as a finite state acceptor (FSA). The weight on the arcs of the FST is the dot product of the MERT weights with the translation scores. In addition, a word insertion penalty was also applied to each word to penalize short hypotheses. The decoding process consists of composing all possible segmentations of an input sentence with the phrase table FST and language model, followed by searching for the best path. Our FST-based translation is the equivalent of phrase-based translation in Moses without reordering. We present results using the independent chunk-wise strategy and chunk-wise translation conditioned on history in Table 3. The chunk-wise translation conditioned on history was performed using the *continue-partial-translation* option in Moses.

6 Segmentation Strategies

The output of ASR for talks is a long string of words with no punctuation, capitalization or segmentation markers. In most offline ASR systems, the talk is first segmented into short utterance-like audio segments before passing them to the decoder. Prior work has shown that additional segmentation of ASR hypotheses of these segments may be necessary to improve translation quality (Rao et al., 2007; Matusov et al., 2007). In a simultaneous speech translation system, one can neither find the optimal segmentation of the entire talk nor tolerate high latencies associated with long segments. Consequently, it is necessary to decode the incoming audio incrementally as well as segment the ASR hypotheses appropriately to maximize MT quality. We present a variety of linguistic and non-linguistic segmentation strategies for segmenting the source text input into MT. In our experiments, they are applied to different inputs including reference text, ASR 1-best hypothesis for manually segmented audio and incremental ASR hypotheses from entire talks.

6.1 Non-linguistic segmentation

The simplest method is to segment the incoming text according to length in number of words. Such a procedure can destroy semantic context but has little to no overhead in additional processing. We experiment with segmenting the text according to word window sizes of length 4, 8, 11, and 15 (denoted as data sets *win4*, *win8*, *win11*, *win15*, respectively in Table 3). We also experiment with concatenating all of the text from one TED talk into a single chunk (*complete talk*).

A novel hold-output model was also developed in order to segment the input text. Given a pair of parallel sentences, the model segments the source sentence into minimally sized chunks such that crossing links and links of one target word to many source words in an optimal GIZA++ alignment (Och and Ney, 2003) occur only within individual chunks. The motivation behind this model is that if a segment s_0 is input at time t_0 to an incremental MT system, it can be translated right away without waiting for a segment s_i that is input at a later time $t_i, t_i > 0$. The hold-output model detects these kinds of segments given a sequence of English words that are input from left to right. A kernel-based SVM was used to develop this model. It tags a token t in the input with either the label HOLD, meaning to chunk it with the next token, or the label OUTPUT, meaning to output the chunk constructed from the maximal consecutive sequence of tokens preceding t that were all tagged as HOLD. The model considers a five word and POS window around the target token t. Unigram, bigram, and trigram word and POS features based upon this window are used for classification. Training and development data for the model was derived from the English-Spanish TED data (see Table 1) after running it through GIZA++. Accuracy of the model on the development set was 66.62% F-measure for the HOLD label and 82.75% for the OUTPUT label.

6.2 Linguistic segmentation

Since MT models are trained on parallel text sentences, we investigate segmenting the source text into sentences. We also investigate segmenting the text further by predicting comma separated chunks within sentences. These tasks are performed by training a kernel-based SVM (Haffner et al., 2003) on a subset of English TED data. This dataset contained 1029 human-transcribed talks consisting of about 103,000 sentences containing about 1.6 million words. Punctuation in this dataset was normalized as follows. Different kinds of sentence ending punctuations were transformed into a uniform end of sentence marker. Double-hyphens were transformed into commas. Commas already existing in the input were kept while all other kinds of punctuation symbols were deleted. A part of speech (POS) tagger was applied to this input. For speed, a unigram POS tagger was implemented which was trained on the Penn Treebank (Marcus et al., 1993) and used orthographic features to predict the POS of unknown words. The SVM-based punctuation classifier relies on a five word and POS window in order to classify the target word. Specifically, token t_0 is classified given as input the window $t_{-2}t_{-1}t_o t_1 t_2$. Unigram, bigram, and trigram word and POS features based on this window were used for classification. Accuracy of the classifier on the development set was 60.51% F-measure for sentence end detection and 43.43% F-measure for comma detection. Subsequently, data sets *pred-sent* (sentences) and *pred-punct* (comma-separated chunks) were obtained. Corresponding to these, two other data sets *ref-sent* and *ref-punct* were obtained based upon gold-standard punctuations in the reference.

Besides investigating the use of comma-separated segments, we investigated other linguistically motivated segments. These included conjunction-word based segments. These segments are separated at either conjunction (e.g. "and," "or") or sentence-ending word boundaries. Conjunctions were identified using the unigram POS tagger. F-measure performance for detecting conjunctions by the tagger on the development set was quite high, 99.35%. As an alternative, text chunking was performed within each sentence, with each chunk corresponding to one segment. Text chunks are non-recursive syntactic phrases in the input text. We investigated segmenting the source into text chunks using TreeTagger, a decision-tree based text chunker (Schmid, 1994). Initial sets of text chunks were created by using either gold-standard sentence boundaries or boundaries detected using the punctuation classifier, yielding the data sets *chunk-ref-*

Segmentation type	Segmentation strategy	Reference text				ASR 1-best			
		BLEU			Mean #words per segment	BLEU			Mean #words per segment
		Independent chunk-wise		chunk-wise with history		Independent chunk-wise		chunk-wise with history	
		FST	Moses			FST	Moses		
Non-linguistic	win4	22.6	21.0	25.5	3.9±0.1	17.7	17.1	20.0	3.9±0.1
	win8	26.6	26.2	28.2	7.9±0.3	20.6	20.9	22.3	7.9±0.2
	win11	27.2	27.4	29.2	10.9 ± 0.3	21.5	21.8	23.1	10.9±0.4
	win15	28.5	28.5	29.4	14.9±0.6	22.3	22.8	23.3	14.9±0.7
	ref-hold	13.3	14.0	17.1	1.6±1.9	12.7	13.1	17.5	1.5±1.0
	pred-hold	15.9	15.7	16.3	2.2±1.9	12.6	12.9	17.4	1.5±1.0
	complete talk	23.8	23.9	–	2504	18.8	19.2	–	2515
Linguistic	ref-sent	30.6	31.5	30.5	16.7±11.8	24.3	25.1	24.4	17.0±11.6
	ref-punct	30.4	31.5	30.3	7.1±5.3	24.2	25.1	24.1	8.7±6.1
	pred-punct	30.6	31.5	30.4	8.7±8.8	24.1	25.0	24.0	8.8±6.8
	conj-ref-eos	30.5	31.5	30.2	11.2±7.5	24.1	24.9	24.0	11.5±7.7
	conj-pred-eos	30.3	31.2	30.3	10.9±7.9	24.0	24.8	24.0	11.4±8.5
	chunk-ref-punct	17.9	18.9	21.4	1.3±0.7	14.5	15.2	16.9	1.4±0.7
	lgchunk1-ref-punct	21.0	21.8	25.1	1.7±1.0	16.9	17.4	19.6	1.8±1.0
	lgchunk2-ref-punct	22.4	23.1	26.0	2.1±1.1	17.9	18.4	20.4	2.1±1.1
	lgchunk3-ref-punct	24.3	25.1	27.4	2.5±1.7	19.2	19.9	21.3	2.5±1.7
	chunk-pred-punct	17.9	18.9	21.4	1.3±0.7	14.5	15.1	16.9	1.4±0.7
	lgchunk1-pred-punct	21.2	21.9	25.2	1.8±1.0	16.7	17.2	19.7	1.8±1.0
	lgchunk2-pred-punct	22.6	23.1	26.0	2.1±1.2	17.7	18.3	20.5	2.1±1.2
	lgchunk3-pred-punct	24.5	25.3	27.4	2.6±1.8	19.1	20.0	21.3	2.5±1.7

Table 3: BLEU scores at the talk level for reference text and ASR 1-best for various segmentation strategies. The ASR 1-best was performed on manually segmented audio chunks provided in *tst2010* set.

punct and *chunk-pred-punct*. Chunk types included NC (noun chunk), VC (verb chunk), PRT (particle), and ADVC (adverbial chunk).

Because these chunks may not provide sufficient context for translation, we also experimented with concatenating neighboring chunks of certain types to form larger chunks. Data sets *lgchunk1* concatenate together neighboring chunk sequences of the form NC, VC or NC, ADVC, VC, intended to capture as single chunks instances of subject and verb. In addition to this, data sets *lgchunk2* capture chunks such as PC (prepositional phrase) and VC followed by VC (control and raising verbs). Finally, data sets *lgchunk3* capture as single chunks VC followed by NC and optionally followed by PRT (verb and its direct object).

Applying the conjunction segmenter after the aforementioned punctuation classifier in order to detect the ends of sentences yields the data set *conj-pred-eos*. Applying it on sentences derived from the gold-standard punctuations yields the data set *conj-ref-eos*. Finally, applying the hold-output model to sentences derived using the punctuation classifier produces the data set *pred-hold*. Obtaining English sentences tagged with HOLD and OUTPUT directly from the output of GIZA++ on English-Spanish sentences in the reference produces the data set *ref-hold*. The strategies containing the keyword *ref* for ASR simply means that the ASR hypotheses are used in place of the gold reference text.

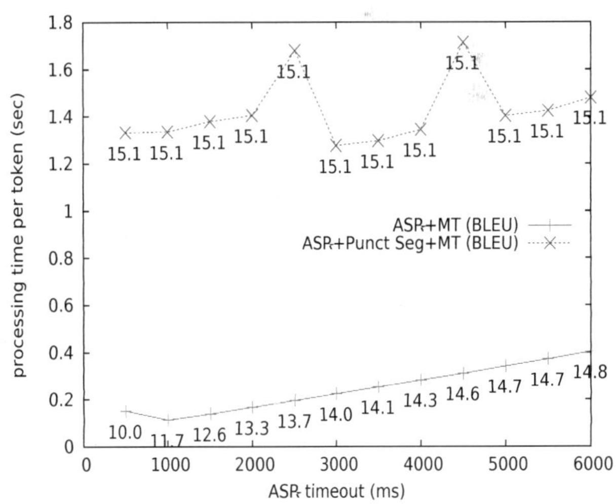

Figure 1: Latencies and BLEU scores for tst2010 set using incremental ASR decoding and translation

We also performed real-time speech translation by using incremental speech recognition, i.e., the decoder returns partial hypotheses that, independent of the pruning during search, will not change in the future. Figure 1 shows the plot for two scenarios: one in which the partial hypotheses are sent directly to machine translation and another where the best segmentation strategy *pred-punct* is used to segment the partial output before sending it to MT. The plot shows the BLEU scores as a function of ASR timeouts used to generate the partial hypotheses. Figure 1 also shows the average latency involved in incremental speech translation.

7 Discussion

The BLEU scores for the segmentation strategies over ASR hypotheses was computed at the talk level. Since the ASR hypotheses do not align with the reference source text, it is not feasible to evaluate the translation performance using the gold reference. While other studies have used an approximate edit distance algorithm for resegmentation of the hypotheses (Matusov et al., 2005), we simply concatenate all the segments and perform the evaluation at the talk level.

The *hold* segmentation strategy yields the poorest translation performance. The significant drop in BLEU score can be attributed to relatively short segments (2-4 words) that was generated by the model. The scheme oversegments the text and since the translation and language models are trained on sentence like chunks, the performance is poor. For example, the input text *the sea* should be translated as *el mar*, but instead the *hold* segmenter chunks it as *the·sea* which MT's chunk translation renders as *el·el mar*. It will be interesting to increase the span of the *hold* strategy to subsume more contiguous sequences and we plan to investigate this as part of future work.

The *chunk* segmentation strategy yields quite poor translation performance. In general, it does not make the same kinds of errors that the *hold* strategy makes; for example, the input text *the sea* will be treated as one NC chunk by the *chunk* segmentation strategy, leading MT to translate it correctly as *el mar*. The short chunk sizes of *chunk* lead to other kinds of errors. For example, the input text *we use* will be chunked into the NC *we* and the VC *use*, which will be translated incorrectly as *nosotros·usar*; the infinitive *usar* is selected rather than the properly conjugated form *usamos*. However, there is a marked improvement in translation accuracy with increasingly larger chunk sizes (*lgchunk1*, *lgchunk2*, and *lgchunk3*). Notably, *lgchunk3* yields performance that approaches that of *win8* with a chunk size that is one third of *win8*'s.

The *conj-pred-eos* and *pred-punct* strategies work the best, and it can be seen that the average segment length (8-12 words) generated in both these schemes is very similar to that used for training the models. It is also about the average latency (4-5 seconds) that can be tolerated in cross-lingual communication, also known as ear-voice span (Lederer, 1978). The non-linguistic segmentation using fixed word length windows also performs well, especially for the longer length windows. However, longer windows (*win15*) increase the latency and any fixed length window typically destroys the semantic context. It can also be seen from Table 3 that translating the complete talk is suboptimal in comparison with segmenting the text. This is primarily due to bias on sentence length distributions in the training data. Training models on complete talks is likely to resolve this issue. Contrasting the use of reference segments as input to MT (*ref-sent*, *ref-punct*, *conj-ref-eos*) versus the use of predicted segments (*pred-sent*, *pred-punct*, *conj-pred-eos*, respectively), it is interesting to note that the MT accuracies never differed greatly between the two, despite the noise in the set of predicted segments.

The performance of the real-time speech translation of TED talks is much lower than the offline scenario. First, we use only a VTLN model as performing CMA adaptation in a real-time scenario typically increases latency. Second, the ASR language model is trained on sentence-like units and decoding the entire talk with this LM is not optimal. A language model trained on complete talks will be more appropriate for such a framework and we are investigating this as part of current work.

Comparing the accuracies of different speech translation strategies, Table 3 shows that *pred-punct* performs the best. When embedded in an incremental MT speech recognition system, Figure 1 shows that it is more accurate than the system that sends partial ASR hypotheses directly to MT. This advantage decreases, however, when the ASR timeout parameter is increased to more than five or six seconds. In terms of latency, Figure 1 shows that the addition of the *pred-punct* segmenter into the incremental system introduces a significant delay. About one third of the increase in delay can be attributed to merely maintaining the two word lookahead window that the segmenter's classifier needs to make decisions. This is significant because this kind of window has been used quite frequently in previous work on simultaneous translation (cf. (Fügen et al., 2007)), and yet to our knowledge this penalty associated with this configuration was never mentioned. The remaining delay can be attributed to the long chunk sizes that the segmenter produces. An interesting aspect of the latency curve associated with the segmenter in Figure 1 is that there are two peaks at ASR timeouts of 2,500 and 4,500 ms, and that the lowest latency is achieved at 3,000 ms rather than at a smaller value. This may be attributed to the fact that the system is a pipeline consisting of ASR, segmenter, and MT, and that 3,000 ms is roughly the length of time to recite comma-separated chunks. Consequently, the two latency peaks appear to correspond with ASR producing segments that are most divergent with segments that the segmenter produces, leading to the most pipeline "stalls." Conversely, the lowest latency occurs when the timeout is set so that ASR's segments most resemble the segmenter's output to MT.

8 Conclusion

We investigated various approaches for incremental speech translation of TED talks, with the aim of producing a system with high MT accuracy and low latency. For acoustic modeling, we found that VTLN and CMA adaptation were useful for increasing the accuracy of ASR, leading to a word accuracy of 80% on TED talks used in the IWSLT evaluation track. In our offline MT experiments retention of partial translations was found useful for increasing MT accuracy, with the latter being slightly more helpful. We experimented with several linguistic and non-linguistic strategies for text segmentation before translation. Our experiments indicate that a novel segmentation into conjunction-separated sentence chunks resulted in accuracies almost as high and latencies almost as short as comma-separated sentence chunks. They also indicated that significant noise in the detection of sentences and punctuation did not seriously impact the resulting MT accuracy. Experiments on real-time simultaneous speech translation using partial recognition hypotheses demonstrate that introduction of a segmenter increases MT accuracy. They also showed that in order to reduce latency it is important for buffers in different pipeline components to be synchronized so as to minimize pipeline stalls. As part of future work, we plan to extend the framework presented in this work for performing speech-to-speech translation. We also plan to address the challenges involved in S2S translation across languages with very different word order.

Acknowledgments

We would like to thank Simon Byers for his help with organizing the TED talks data.

References

S. Bangalore, V. K. Rangarajan Sridhar, P. Kolan, L. Golipour, and A. Jimenez. 2012. Real-time incremental speech-to-speech translation of dialogs. In *Proceedings of NAACL:HLT*, June.

M. Cettolo and M. Federico. 2006. Text segmentation criteria for statistical machine translation. In *Proceedings of the 5th international conference on Advances in Natural Language Processing*.

M. Cettolo, C. Girardi, and M. Federico. 2012. WIT3: Web Inventory of Transcribed and Translated Talks. In *Proceedings of EAMT*.

J. Cohen. 2007. The GALE project: A description and an update. In *Proceedings of ASRU Workshop*.

M. Federico, L. Bentivogli, M. Paul, and S. Stüker. 2011. Overview of the IWSLT 2011 evaluation campaign. In *Proceedings of IWSLT*.

C. Fügen and M. Kolss. 2007. The influence of utterance chunking on machine translation performance. In *Proceedings of Interspeech*.

C. Fügen, M. Kolss, D. Bernreuther, M. Paulik, S. Stuker, S. Vogel, and A. Waibel. 2006. Open domain speech recognition & translation: Lectures and speeches. In *Proceedings of ICASSP*.

C. Fügen, A. Waibel, and M. Kolss. 2007. Simultaneous translation of lectures and speeches. *Machine Translation*, 21:209–252.

V. Goffin, C. Allauzen, E. Bocchieri, D. Hakkani-Tür, A. Ljolje, and S. Parthasarathy. 2004. The AT&T Watson Speech Recognizer. Technical report, September.

P. Haffner, G. Tür, and J. Wright. 2003. Optimizing svms for complex call classification. In *Proceedings of ICASSP'03*.

O. Hamon, C. Fügen, D. Mostefa, V. Arranz, M. Kolss, A. Waibel, and K. Choukri. 2009. End-to-end evaluation in simultaneous translation. In *Proceedings of the 12th Conference of the European Chapter of the ACL (EACL 2009)*, March.

B. Kingsbury, H. Soltau, G. Saon, S. Chu, Hong-Kwang Kuo, L. Mangu, S. Ravuri, N. Morgan, and A. Janin. 2011. The IBM 2009 GALE Arabic speech translation system. In *Proceedings of ICASSP*.

P. Koehn, H. Hoang, A. Birch, C. Callison-Burch, M. Federico, N. Bertoldi, B. Cowan, Shen W., C. Moran, R. Zens, C. J. Dyer, O. Bojar, A. Constantin, and E. Herbst. 2007. Moses: Open source toolkit for statistical machine translation. In *Proceedings of ACL*.

P. Koehn. 2005. Europarl: A parallel corpus for statistical machine translation. In *MT Summit*.

M. Lederer. 1978. Simultaneous interpretation: units of meaning and other features. In D. Gerver and H. W. Sinaiko, editors, *Language interpretation and communication*, pages 323–332. Plenum Press, New York.

M. Marcus, B. Santorini, and M. A. Marcinkiewicz. 1993. Building a large annotated corpus of English: the Penn treebank. *Computational Linguistics*, 19(2):313–330.

E. Matusov, G. Leusch, O. Bender, and H. Ney. 2005. Evaluating machine translation output with automatic sentence segmentation. In *Proceedings of IWSLT*.

E. Matusov, D. Hillard, M. Magimai-Doss, D. Hakkani-Tür, M. Ostendorf, and H. Ney. 2007. Improving speech translation with automatic boundary prediction. In *Proceedings of Interspeech*.

M. Mohri, F. Pereira, and M. Riley. 1997. At&t general-purpose finite-state machine software tools, http://www.research.att.com/sw/tools/fsm/.

F. J. Och and H. Ney. 2003. A systematic comparison of various statistical alignment models. *Computational Linguistics*, 29(1):19–51.

V. K. Rangarajan Sridhar, L. Barbosa, and S. Bangalore. 2011. A scalable approach to building a parallel corpus from the Web. In *Proceedings of Interspeech*.

S. Rao, I. Lane, and T. Schultz. 2007. Optimizing sentence segmentation for spoken language translation. In *Proceedings of Interspeech*.

H. Schmid. 1994. Probabilistic part-of-speech tagging using decision trees. In *Proceedings of the International Conference on New Methods in Language Processing*.

R. Steinberger, B. Pouliquen, A. Widiger, C. Ignat, T. Erjavec, and D. Tufis. 2006. The JRC-Acquis: A multilingual aligned parallel corpus with 20+ languages. In *Proceedings of LREC*.

J. Tiedemann and L. Lars Nygaard. 2004. The OPUS corpus - parallel & free. In *Proceedings of LREC*.

D. Vilar, E. Matusov, S. Hasan, R. Zens, and H. Ney. 2005. Statistical machine translation of European parliamentary speeches. In *Proceedings of MT Summit*.

W. Wahlster, editor. 2000. *Verbmobil: Foundations of Speech-to-Speech Translation*. Springer.

Enforcing Subcategorization Constraints in a Parser Using Sub-parses Recombining

Seyed Abolghasem Mirroshandel[†,⋆] **Alexis Nasr**[†] **Benoît Sagot**[◇]
[†]Laboratoire d'Informatique Fondamentale de Marseille- CNRS - UMR 7279
Université Aix-Marseille, Marseille, France
[◇]Alpage, INRIA & Université Paris-Diderot, Paris, France
[⋆]Computer Engineering Department, Faculty of Engineering,
University of Guilan, Rasht, Iran
(ghasem.mirroshandel@lif.univ-mrs.fr, alexis.nasr@lif.univ-mrs.fr,
benoit.sagot@inria.fr)

Abstract

Treebanks are not large enough to adequately model subcategorization frames of predicative lexemes, which is an important source of lexico-syntactic constraints for parsing. As a consequence, parsers trained on such treebanks usually make mistakes when selecting the arguments of predicative lexemes. In this paper, we propose an original way to correct subcategorization errors by combining sub-parses of a sentence S that appear in the list of the n-best parses of S. The subcategorization information comes from three different resources, the first one is extracted from a treebank, the second one is computed on a large corpora and the third one is an existing syntactic lexicon. Experiments on the French Treebank showed a 15.24% reduction of erroneous subcategorization frames (SF) selections for verbs as well as a relative decrease of the error rate of 4% Labeled Accuracy Score on the state of the art parser on this treebank.

1 Introduction

Automatic syntactic parsing of natural languages has witnessed many important changes in the last fifteen years. Among these changes, two have modified the nature of the task itself. The first one is the availability of treebanks such as the Penn Treebank (Marcus et al., 1993) or the French Treebank (Abeillé et al., 2003), which have been used in the parsing community to train stochastic parsers, such as (Collins, 1997; Petrov and Klein, 2008). Such work remained rooted in the classical language theoretic tradition of parsing, generally based on variants of generative context free grammars. The second change occurred with the use of discriminative machine learning techniques, first to rerank the output of a stochastic parser (Collins, 2000; Charniak and Johnson, 2005) and then in the parser itself (Ratnaparkhi, 1999; Nivre et al., 2007; McDonald et al., 2005a). Such parsers clearly depart from classical parsers in the sense that they do not rely anymore on a generative grammar: given a sentence S, all possible parses for S^1 are considered as possible parses of S. A parse tree is seen as a set of lexico-syntactic features which are associated to weights. The score of a parse is computed as the sum of the weights of its features.

This new generation of parsers allows to reach high accuracy but possess their own limitations. We will focus in this paper on one kind of weakness of such parser which is their inability to properly take into account subcategorization frames (SF) of predicative lexemes[2], an important source of lexico-syntactic constraints. The proper treatment of SF is actually confronted to two kinds of problems: (1) the acquisition of correct SF for verbs and (2) the integration of such constraints in the parser.

The first problem is a consequence of the use of treebanks for training parsers. Such treebanks are composed of a few thousands sentences and only a small subpart of acceptable SF for a verb actually

[1]Another important aspect of the new parsing paradigm is the use of dependency trees as a means to represent syntactic structure. In dependency syntax, the number of possible syntactic trees associated to a sentence is bounded, and only depends on the length of the sentence, which is not the case with syntagmatic derivation trees.

[2]We will concentrate in this paper on verbal SF.

occur in the treebank.

The second problem is a consequence of the parsing models. For algorithmic complexity as well as data sparseness reasons, the parser only considers lexico-syntactic configurations of limited domain of locality (in the parser used in the current work, this domain of locality is limited to configurations made of one or two dependencies). As described in more details in section 2, SF often exceed in scope such domains of locality and are therefore not easy to integrate in the parser. A popular method for introducing higher order constraints in a parser consist in reranking the n best output of a parser as in (Collins, 2000; Charniak and Johnson, 2005). The reranker search space is restricted by the output of the parser and high order features can be used. One drawback of the reranking approach is that correct SF for the predicates of a sentence can actually appear in different parse trees. Selecting complete trees can therefore lead to sub-optimal solutions. The method proposed in this paper merges parts of different trees that appear in an n best list in order to build a new parse.

Taking into account SF in a parser has been a major issue in the design of syntactic formalisms in the eighties and nineties. Unification grammars, such as Lexical Functional Grammars (Bresnan, 1982), Generalized Phrase Structure Grammars (Gazdar et al., 1985) and Head-driven Phrase Structure Grammars (Pollard and Sag, 1994), made SF part of the grammar. Tree Adjoining Grammars (Joshi et al., 1975) proposed to extend the domain of locality of Context Free Grammars partly in order to be able to represent SF in a generative grammar. More recently, (Collins, 1997) proposed a way to introduce SF in a probabilistic context free grammar and (Arun and Keller, 2005) used the same technique for French. (Carroll et al., 1998), used subcategorization probabilities for ranking trees generated by unification-based phrasal grammar and (Zeman, 2002) showed that using frame frequency in a dependency parser can lead to a significant improvement of the performance of the parser.

The main novelties of the work presented here is (1) the way a new parse is built by combining subparses that appear in the n best parse list and (2) the use of three very different resources that list the possible SF for verbs.

The organization of the paper is the following: in section 2, we will briefly describe the parsing model that we will be using for this work and give accuracy results on a French corpus. Section 3 will describe three different resources that we have been using to correct SF errors made by the parser and give coverage results for these resources on a development corpus. Section 4 will propose three different ways to take into account, in the parser, the resources described in section 3 and give accuracy results. Section 5 concludes the paper.

2 The Parser

The parser used in this work is the second order graph based parser (McDonald et al., 2005b) implementation of (Bohnet, 2010). The parser was trained on the French Treebank (Abeillé et al., 2003) which was transformed into dependency trees by (Candito et al., 2009). The size of the treebank and its decomposition into train, development and test sets are represented in table 1.

	nb of sentences	nb of tokens
TRAIN	9 881	278 083
DEV	1 239	36 508
TEST	1 235	36 340

Table 1: Size and decomposition of the French Treebank

The parser gave state of the art results for parsing of French, reported in table 2. Table 2 reports the standard Labeled Accuracy Score (LAS) and Unlabeled Accuracy Score (UAS) which is the ratio of correct labeled (for LAS) or unlabeled (for UAS) dependencies in a sentence. We also defined a more specific measure: the SF Accuracy Score (SAS) which is the ratio of verb occurrences that have been paired with the correct SF by the parser. We have introduced this quantity in order to measure more accurately the impact of the methods described in this paper on the selection of a SF for the verbs of a sentence.

	TEST	DEV
SAS	80.84	79.88
LAS	88.88	88.53
UAS	90.71	90.37

Table 2: Subcategorization Frame Accuracy, Labeled and Unlabeled Accuracy Score on TEST and DEV.

We have chosen a second order graph parser in this work for two reasons. The first is that it is the parsing model that obtained the best results on the French Treebank. The second is that it allows us to impose structural constraints in the solution of the parser, as described in (Mirroshandel and Nasr, 2011), a feature that will reveal itself precious when enforcing SF in the parser output.

3 The Resources

Three resources have been used in this work in order to correct SF errors. The first one has been extracted from a treebank, the second has been extracted from an automatically parsed corpus that is several order of magnitude bigger than the treebank. The third one has been extracted from an existing lexico-syntactic resource. The three resources are respectively described in sections 3.2, 3.3 and 3.4. Before describing the resources, we describe in details, in section 3.1 our definition of SF. In section 3.5, we evaluate the coverage of these resources on the DEV corpus. Coverage is an important characteristic of a resource: in case of an SF error made by the parser, if the correct SF that should be associated to a verb, in a sentence, does not appear in the resource, it will be impossible to correct the error.

3.1 Subcat Frames Description

In this work, a SF is defined as a couple (G, L) where G is the part of speech tag of the element that licenses the SF. This part of speech tag can either be a verb in infinitive form (VINF), a past participle (VPP), a finite tense verb (V) or a present participle (VPR). L is a set of couples (f, c) where f is a syntactic function tag chosen among a set $\mathcal{F}$ and c is a part of speech tag chosen among the set $\mathcal{C}$. Couple (f, c) indicates that function f can be realized as part of speech tag c. Sets $\mathcal{F}$ and $\mathcal{C}$ are respectively displayed in top and bottom tables of figure 1. An anchored SF (ASF) is a couple (v, S) where v is a verb lemma and S is a SF, as described above.

A resource is defined as a collection of ASF (v, S), each associated to a count c, to represent the fact that verb v has been seen with SF S c times. In the case of the resource extracted form an existing lexicon (section 3.4), the notion of count is not applicable and we will consider that it is always equal to one.

SUJ	subject
OBJ	object
A_OBJ	indirect object introduced by the preposition à
DE_OBJ	indirect object introduced by the preposition de
P_OBJ	indirect object introduced by another preposition
ATS	attribute of the subject
ATO	attribute of the direct object

ADJ	adjective
CS	subordinating conjunction
N	noun
V	verb finite tense
VINF	verb infinitive form
VPP	verb past participle
VPR	verb present participle

Figure 1: Syntactic functions of the arguments of the SF (top table). Part of speech tags of the arguments of the SF (bottom table)

Below is an example of three ASF for the french verb *donner* (*to give*). The first one is a transitive SF where both the subject and the object are realized as nouns as in *Jean donne un livre* (*Jean gives a book.*). The second one is ditransitive, it has both a direct object and an indirect one introduced by the preposition *à* as in *Jean donne un livre à Marie.* (*Jean gives a book to Marie*). The third one corresponds to a passive form as in *le livre est donné à Marie par Jean* (*The book is given to Marie by Jean*).

```
(donner, (V, (suj,N), (obj,N)))
(donner, (V, (suj,N), (obj,N), (a_obj,N)))
(donner, (VPP, (suj,N), (aux_pass,V),
                (a_obj,N), (p_obj,N)))
```

One can note that when an argument corresponds to an indirect dependent of the verb (introduced either by a preposition or a subordinating conjunction), we do not represent in the SF, the category of the element that introduces the argument, but the category of the argument itself, a noun or a verb.

Two important choices have to be made when defining SF. The first one concerns the dependents of the predicative element that are in the SF (argument/adjunct distinction) and the second is the level of abstraction at which SF are defined.

In our case, the first choice is constrained by the treebank annotation guidelines. The FTB distinguishes seven syntactic functions which can be considered as arguments of a verb. They are listed in the top table of figure 1. Most of them are straightforward and do not deserve an explanation. Something has to be said though on the syntactic function P_OBJ which is used to model arguments of the verb introduced by a preposition that is neither *à* nor *de*, such as the agent in passive form, which is introduced by the preposition *par*.

We have added in the SF two elements that do not correspond to arguments of the verb: the reflexive pronoun, and the passive auxiliary. The reason for adding these elements to the SF is that their presence influences the presence or absence of some arguments of the verb, and therefore the SF.

The second important choice that must be made when defining SF is the *level of abstraction*, or, in other words, how much the SF abstracts away from its realization in the sentence. In our case, we have used two ways to abstract away from the surface realization of the SF. The first one is factoring several part of speech tags. We have factored pronouns, common nouns and proper nouns into a single category N. We have not gathered verbs in different modes into one category since the mode of the verb influences its syntactic behavior and hence its SF. The second means of abstraction we have used is the absence of linear order between the arguments. Taking into account argument order increases the number of SF and, hence, data sparseness, without adding much information for selecting the correct SF, this is why we have decided to to ignore it. In our second example above, each of the three arguments can be realized as one out of eight parts of speech that correspond to the part of speech tag N and the 24 possible orderings are represented as one canonical ordering. This SF therefore corresponds to 12 288 possible realizations.

3.2 Treebank Extracted Subcat Frames

This resource has been extracted from the TRAIN corpus. At a first glance, it may seen strange to extract data from the corpus that have been used for training our parser. The reason is that, as seen in section 1, SF are not directly modeled by the parser, which only takes into account subtrees made of, at most, two dependencies.

The extraction procedure of SF from the treebank is straightforward : the tree of every sentence is visited and, for every verb of the sentence, its daughters are visited, and, depending whether they are considered as arguments of the verb (with respect to the conventions or section 3.1), they are added to the SF. The number of different verbs extracted, as well as the number of different SF and the average number of SF per verb are displayed in table 3. Column T (for Train) is the one that we are interested in here.

	T	L	A_0	A_5	A_{10}
nb of verbs	2058	7824	23915	4871	3923
nb of diff SF	666	1469	12122	2064	1355
avg. nb of SF	4.83	52.09	14.26	16.16	13.45

Table 3: Resources statistics

The extracted resource can directly be compared with the TREELEX resource (Kupsc and Abeillé, 2008), which has been extracted from the same treebank. The result that we obtain is different, due to the fact that (Kupsc and Abeillé, 2008) have a more abstract definition of SF. As a consequence, they define a smaller number of SF: 58 instead of 666 in our case. The smaller number of SF yields a smaller average number of SF per verb: 1.72 instead of 4.83 in our case.

3.3 Automatically computed Subcat Frames

The extraction procedure described above has been used to extract ASF from an automatically parsed corpus. The corpus is actually a collection of three corpora of slightly different genres. The first one is a collection of news reports of the French press agency *Agence France Presse*, the second is a collection of newspaper articles from a local French newspaper : *l'Est Républicain*. The third one is a collection of articles from the French Wikipedia. The size of the different corpora are detailed in table 4.

The corpus was first POS tagged with the MELT tagger (Denis and Sagot, 2010), lemmatized with the MACAON tool suite (Nasr et al., 2011) and parsed in order to get the best parse for every sentence. Then the ASF have been extracted.

The number of verbs, number of SF and average number of SF per verb are represented in table 3, in column A_0 (A stands for Automatic). As one can see, the number of verbs and SF are unrealistic. This is due to the fact that the data that we extract SF from is noisy: it consists of automatically produced syntactic trees which contain errors (recall

CORPUS	Sent. nb.	Tokens nb.
AFP	2 041 146	59 914 238
EST REP	2 998 261	53 913 288
WIKI	1 592 035	33 821 460
TOTAL	5 198 642	147 648 986

Table 4: sizes of the corpora used to collect SF

that the LAS on the DEV corpus is 88, 02%). There are two main sources of errors in the parsed data: the pre-processing chain (tokenization, part of speech tagging and lemmatization) which can consider as a verb a word that is not, and, of course, parsing errors, which tend to create crazy SF. In order to fight against noise, we have used a simple thresholding: we only collect ASF that occur more than a threshold i. The result of the thresholding appears in columns A_5 and A_{10} , where the subscript is the value of the threshold. As expected both the number of verbs and SF decrease sharply when increasing the value of the threshold.

Extracting SF for verbs from raw data has been an active direction of research for a long time, dating back at least to the work of (Brent, 1991) and (Manning, 1993). More recently (Messiant et al., 2008) proposed such a system for French verbs. The method we use for extracting SF is not novel with respect to such work. Our aim was not to devise new extraction techniques but merely to evaluate the resource produced by such techniques for statistical parsing.

3.4 Using an existing resource

The third resource that we have used is the Le*fff* (Lexique des formes fléchies du français — *Lexicon of French inflected form*), a large-coverage syntactic lexicon for French (Sagot, 2010). The Le*fff* was developed in a semi-automatic way: automatic tools were used together with manual work. The latest version of the Le*fff* contains 10,618 verbal entries for 7,835 distinct verbal lemmas (the Le*fff* covers all categories, but only verbal entries are used in this work).

A sub-categorization frame consists in a list of syntactic functions, using an inventory slightly more fine-grained than in the French Treebank, and for each of them a list of possible realizations (e.g., noun phrase, infinitive clause, or null-realization if the syntactic function is optional).

For each verbal lemma, we extracted all sub-categorization frames for each of the four verbal part-of-speech tags (V, VINF, VPR, VPP), thus creating an inventory of SFs in the same sense and format as described in Section 3.1. Note that such SFs do not contain alternatives concerning the way each syntactic argument is realized or not: this extraction process includes a de-factorization step. Its output, hereafter L, contains 801,246 distinct (lemma, SF) pairs.

3.5 Coverage

In order to be able to correct SF errors, the three resources described above must possess two important characteristics: high coverage and high accuracy. Coverage measures the presence, in the resource, of the correct SF of a verb, in a given sentence. Accuracy measures the ability of a resource to select the correct SF for a verb in a given context when several ones are possible.

We will give in this section coverage result, computed on the DEV corpus. Accuracy will be described and computed in section 4. The reason why the two measures are not described together is due to the fact that coverage can be computed on a reference corpus while accuracy must be computed on the output of a parser, since it is the parser that will propose different SF for a verb in a given context.

Given a reference corpus C and a resource R, two coverage measures have been computed, lexical coverage, which measures the ratio of verbs of C that appear in R and syntactic coverage, which measures the ratio of ASF of C that appear in R. Two variants of each measures are computed: on types and on occurrences. The values of these measures computed on the DEV corpus are summarized in table 5.

		T	L	A_0	A_5	A_{10}
Lex.	types	89.56	99.52	99.52	98.56	98.08
cov.	occ	96.98	99.85	99.85	99.62	99.50
Synt.	types	62.24	78.15	95.78	91.08	88.84
cov.	occ	73.54	80.35	97.13	93.96	92.39

Table 5: Lexical and syntactic coverage of the three resources on DEV

The figures of table 5 show that lexical coverage of the three resources is quite high, ranging from 89.56 to 99.52 when computed on types and from 96.98 to 99.85 when computed on occurrences. The lowest coverage is obtained by the T resource, which does not come as a surprise since it is computed on a rather small number of sentences. It is also interesting to note that lexical coverage of A does not decrease much when augmenting the threshold, while the size of the resource decreases dramatically (as shown in table 3). This validates the hypothesis that the resource is very noisy and that a simple threshold on the occurrences of ASF is a reasonable means to fight against noise.

Syntactic coverage is, as expected, lower than lexical coverage. The best results are obtained by A_0: 95.78 on types and 97.13 on occurrences. Thresholding on the occurrences of anchored SF has a bigger impact on syntactic coverage than it had on lexical coverage. A threshold of 10 yields a coverage of 88.84 on types and 92.39 on occurrences.

4 Integrating Subcat Frames in the Parser

As already mentioned in section 1, SF usually exceed the domain of locality of the structures that are directly modeled by the parser. It is therefore difficult to integrate directly SF in the model of the parser. In order to circumvent the problem, we have decided to work on the n-best output of the parser: we consider that a verb v, in a given sentence S, can be associated to any of the SF that v licenses in one of the n-best trees. The main weakness of this method is that an SF error can be corrected only if the right SF appears at least in one of the n-best parse trees.

In order to estimate an upper bound of the SAS that such methods can reach (how many SF errors can actually be corrected), we have computed the oracle SAS on the 100 best trees of the DEV corpus DEV (for how many verbs the correct SF appears in at least one of the n-best parse trees). The oracle score is equal to 95.16, which means that for 95.16% of the verb occurrences of the DEV, the correct SF appears somewhere in the 100-best trees. 95.16 is therefore the best SAS that we can reach. Recall that the baseline SAS is equal to 79.88% the room for progress is therefore equal to 15.28% absolute.

Three experiments are described below. In the first one, section 4.1, a simple technique, called Post Processing is used. Section 4.2 describes a second technique, called Double Parsing, which is a is a refinement of Post Processing. Both sections 4.1 and 4.2 are based on single resources. Section 4.3 proposes a simple way to combine the different resources.

4.1 Post Processing

The post processing method (PP) is the simplest one that we have tested. It takes as input the different ASF that occur in the n-best output of the parser as well as a resource R. Given a sentence, let's note $T_1 \ldots T_n$ the trees that appear in the n-best output of the parser, in decreasing order of their score. For every verb v of the sentence, we note $\mathcal{S}(v)$ the set of all the SF associated to v that appear in the trees $T_1 \ldots T_n$.

Given a verb v and a SF s, we define the following functions:

$\mathcal{C}(v, s)$ is the number of occurrences of the ASF (v, s) in the trees $T_1 \ldots T_n$.

$\mathcal{F}(v)$ is the SF associated to v in T_1

$\mathcal{C}_R(v, s)$ the number of occurrences of the ASF (v, s) in the resource R.

We define a selection function as a function that selects a SF for a given verb in a given sentence. A selection function has to take into account the information given by the resource (whether an SF is acceptable/frequent for a given verb) as well as the information given by the parser (whether the parser has a strong preference to associate a given SF to a given verb).

In our experiments, we have tested two simple selection functions. φ_R which selects the first SF $s \in \mathcal{S}(v)$, such that $\mathcal{C}_R(v, s) > 0$ when traversing the trees $T_1 \ldots T_n$ in the decreasing order of score (best tree first).

The second function, $\psi_R(v)$ compares the most frequent SF for v in the resource R with the SF of the first parse. If the ratio of the number of occurrences in the n-best of the former and the latter is above a threshold α, the former is selected. More formally:

$$\psi_R(v) = \begin{cases} \hat{s} = \arg\max_{s \in \mathcal{S}(v)} \mathcal{C}_R(v, s) \\ \qquad \text{if } \frac{\mathcal{C}(v, \hat{s})}{\mathcal{C}(v, \mathcal{F}(v))} > \alpha \\ \mathcal{F}(v) \\ \qquad \text{otherwise} \end{cases}$$

The coefficient α has been optimized on DEV corpus. Its value is equal to 2.5 for the Automatic resource, 2 for the Train resource and 1.5 for the Lefff.

The construction of the new solution proceeds as follows: for every verb v of the sentence, a SF is selected with the selection function. It is important to note, at this point, that the SF selected for different verbs of the sentence can pertain to different parse trees. The new solution is built based on tree T_1. For every verb v, its arguments are potentially modified in agreement with the SF selected by the selection function. There is no guarantee at this point that the solution is well formed. We will return to this problem in section 4.2.

We have evaluated the PP method with different selection functions on the TEST corpus. The results of applying function ψ_R were more successful. As a result we just report the results of this function in table 6. Different levels of thresholding for resource A gave almost the same results, we therefore used A_{10} which is the smallest one.

	B	T	L	A
SAS	80.84	83.11	82.14	82.17
LAS	88.88	89.14	89.03	89.03
UAS	90.71	90.91	90.81	90.82

Table 6: LAS and UAS on TEST using PP

The results of table 6 show two interesting facts. First, the SAS is improved, it jumps from 80.84 to 83.11. PP therefore corrects some SF errors made by the parser. It must be noted however that this improvement is much lower than the oracle score. The second interesting fact is the very moderate increase of both LAS and UAS. This is due to the fact that the number of dependencies modified is small with respect to the total number of dependencies. The impact on LAS and UAS is therefore weak.

The best results are obtained with resource T. Although the coverage of T is low, the resource is very close to the train data, this fact probably explains the good results obtained with this resource.

It is interesting, at this point, to compare our method with a reranking approach. In order to do so, we have compared the upper bound of the number of SF errors that can be corrected when using reranking and our approach. The results of the comparison computed on a list of 100 best trees is reported in table 7 which shows the ratio of subcat frame errors that could be corrected with a reranking approach and the ratio of errors sub-parse recombining could reach.

	DEV	TEST
reranking	53.9%	58.5%
sub-parse recombining	75.5%	76%

Table 7: Correction rate for subcat frames errors with different methods

Table 7 shows that combining sub-parses can, in theory, correct a much larger number of wrong SF assignments than reranking.

4.2 Double Parsing

The post processing method shows some improvement over the baseline. But it has an important drawback: it can create inconsistent parses. Recall that the parser we are using is based on a second order model. In other words, the score of a dependency depends on some neighboring dependencies. When building a new solution, the post processing method modifies some dependencies independently of their context, which may give birth to very unlikely configurations.

In order to compute a new optimal parse tree that preserves the modified dependencies, we have used a technique proposed in (Mirroshandel and Nasr, 2011) that modifies the scoring function of the parser in such a way that the dependencies that we want to keep in the parser output get better scores than all competing dependencies. The new solution is therefore the optimal solution that preserves the dependencies modified by the PP method.

The double parsing (DP) method is therefore a three stage method. First, sentence S is parsed, producing the n-best parses. Then, the post processing method is used, modifying the first best parse. Let's note $\mathcal{D}$ the set of dependencies that were changed in this process. In the last stage, a new parse is produced, that preserves $\mathcal{D}$.

	B	T	L	A
SAS	80.84	83.11	82.14	82.17
LAS	88.88	89.30	89.25	89.31
UAS	90.71	91.07	91.05	91.08

Table 8: LAS and UAS on TEST using DP

The results of DP on TEST are reported in table 8. SAS did not change with respect to PP, because DP keeps the SF selected by PP. As expected DP does increase LAS and UAS. Recomputing an optimal solution therefore increases the quality of the parses. Table 8 also shows that the three resources get almost the same LAS and UAS although SAS is better for resource T.

4.3 Combining Resources

Due to the different generation techniques of our three resources, another direction of research is combining them. We did different experiments concerning all possible combination of resources: A and L (AL), T and L (TL), T and A (TA), and all tree (TAL) resources. The results of these combinations for PP and DP methods are shown in tables 9 and 10, respectively.

The resource are combined in a back-off schema: we search for a candidate ASF in a first resource. If it is found, the search stops. Otherwise, the next resource(s) are probed. One question that arises is: which sequence is the optimal one for combining the resources. To answer this question, we did several experiments on DEV set. Our experiments have shown that it is better to search T resource, then A, and, eventually, L. The results of this combining method, using PP are reported in table 9. The best results are obtained for the TL combination. The SAS jumps from 83.11 to 83.76. As it was the case with single resources, the LAS and UAS increase is moderate.

	B	AL	TL	TA	TAL
SAS	80.84	82.12	83.76	83.50	83.50
LAS	88.88	89.03	89.22	89.19	89.19
UAS	90.71	90.79	90.98	90.95	90.95

Table 9: LAS and UAS on TEST using PP with resource combination

With DP (table 9), the order of resource combination is exactly the same as with PP. As was the case with single resources, DP has a positive, but moderate, impact on LAS and UAS.

The results of tables 9 and 10 do not show considerable improvement over single resources. This might be due to the large intersection between our resources. In other words, they do not have complementary information, and their combination will not introduce much information. Another possible reason for this result is the combination technique used. More sophisticated techniques might yield better results.

	B	AL	TL	TA	TAL
SAS	80.84	82.12	83.76	83.50	83.50
LAS	88.88	89.22	89.31	89.34	89.34
UAS	90.71	91.02	91.05	91.08	91.09

Table 10: LAS and UAS on TEST using DP with resource combination

5 Conclusions

Subcategorization frames for verbs constitute a rich source of lexico-syntactic information which is hard to integrate in graph based parsers. In this paper, we have used three different resources for subcategorization frames. These resources are from different origins with various characteristics. We have proposed two different methods to introduce the useful information from these resources in a second order model parser. We have conducted different experiments on French Treebank that showed a 15.24% reduction of erroneous SF selections for verbs. Although encouraging, there is still plenty of room for better results since the oracle score for 100 best parses is equal to 95.16% SAS and we reached 83.76%. Future work will concentrate on more elaborate selection functions as well as more sophisticated ways to combine the different resources.

Acknowledgments

This work has been funded by the French Agence Nationale pour la Recherche, through the project EDYLEX (ANR-08-CORD-009).

References

A. Abeillé, L. Clément, and F. Toussenel. 2003. Building a treebank for french. In Anne Abeillé, editor, *Treebanks*. Kluwer, Dordrecht.

A. Arun and F. Keller. 2005. Lexicalization in crosslinguistic probabilistic parsing: The case of french. In *Proceedings of the 43rd Annual Meeting on Association for Computational Linguistics*, pages 306–313. Association for Computational Linguistics.

B. Bohnet. 2010. Very high accuracy and fast dependency parsing is not a contradiction. In *Proceedings of ACL*, pages 89–97.

Michael Brent. 1991. Automatic acquisition of subcategorization frames from untagged text. In *Proceedings of ACL*.

Joan Bresnan, editor. 1982. *The Mental Representation of Grammatical Relations*. MIT Press.

M. Candito, B. Crabbé, P. Denis, and F. Guérin. 2009. Analyse syntaxique du français : des constituants aux dépendances. In *Proceedings of Traitement Automatique des Langues Naturelles*.

J. Carroll, G. Minnen, and T. Briscoe. 1998. Can subcategorisation probabilities help a statistical parser? *Arxiv preprint cmp-lg/9806013*.

Eugene Charniak and Mark Johnson. 2005. Coarse-to-Fine n-Best Parsing and MaxEnt Discriminative Reranking. In *Proceedings of ACL*.

Michael Collins. 1997. Three Generative, Lexicalised Models for Statistical Parsing. In *Proceedings of the 35th Annual Meeting of the ACL*.

Michael Collins. 2000. Discriminative Reranking for Natural Language Parsing. In *Proceedings of ICML*.

P. Denis and B. Sagot. 2010. Exploitation d'une ressource lexicale pour la construction d'un étiqueteur morphosyntaxique état-de-l'art du français. In *Proceedings of Traitement Automatique des Langues Naturelles*.

Gerald Gazdar, Ewan Klein, Geoffrey K. Pullum, and Ivan Sag. 1985. *Generalized Phrase Structure Grammar*. Harvard University Press.

Aravind Joshi, Leon Levy, and M Takahashi. 1975. Tree adjunct grammars. *Journal of Computer and System Sciences*, 10:136–163.

Anna Kupsc and Anne Abeillé. 2008. Treelex: A subcategorisation lexicon for french verbs. In *Proceedings of the First International Conference on Global Interoperability for Language Resources*.

Christopher Manning. 1993. Automatic acquisition of a large subcategorization dictionary from corpora. In *Proceedings of ACL*.

M.P. Marcus, M.A. Marcinkiewicz, and B. Santorini. 1993. Building a large annotated corpus of english: The penn treebank. *Computational linguistics*, 19(2):313–330.

R. McDonald, K. Crammer, and F. Pereira. 2005a. Online large-margin training of dependency parsers. In *Proceedings of the 43rd Annual Meeting of the Association for Computational Linguistics*, pages 91–98.

R. McDonald, F. Pereira, K. Ribarov, and J. Hajič. 2005b. Non-projective dependency parsing using spanning tree algorithms. In *Proceedings of HLT-EMNLP*, pages 523–530.

C. Messiant, A. Korhonen, T. Poibeau, et al. 2008. Lexschem: A large subcategorization lexicon for french verbs. In *Proceedings of the Language Resources and Evaluation Conference*.

S.A. Mirroshandel and A. Nasr. 2011. Active learning for dependency parsing using partially annotated sentences. In *Proceedings of International Conference on Parsing Technologies*.

A. Nasr, F. Béchet, J-F. Rey, B. Favre, and Le Roux J. 2011. MACAON: An NLP tool suite for processing word lattices. In *Proceedings of ACL*.

J. Nivre, J. Hall, J. Nilsson, A. Chanev, G. Eryigit, S. Kbler, S. Marinov, and E. Marsi. 2007. Maltparser: A language-independent system for data-driven dependency parsing. *Natural Language Engineering*, 13(2):95–135.

Slav Petrov and Dan Klein. 2008. Discriminative Log-Linear Grammars with Latent Variables. In J.C. Platt, D. Koller, Y. Singer, and S. Roweis, editors, *Advances in Neural Information Processing Systems 20 (NIPS)*, pages 1153–1160, Cambridge, MA. MIT Press.

Carl Pollard and Ivan Sag. 1994. *Head-driven Phrase Structure Grammmar*. CSLI Series. University of Chicago Press.

Adwait Ratnaparkhi. 1999. Learning to parse natural language with maximum entropy models. *Machine learning*, 34(1):151–175.

Benoît Sagot. 2010. The Le*fff*, a freely available and large-coverage morphological and syntactic lexicon for french. In *Proceedings of the Seventh conference on International Language Resources and Evaluation (LREC'10)*, pages 2744–2751, Valletta, Malta.

D. Zeman. 2002. Can subcategorization help a statistical dependency parser? In *Proceedings of the 19th international conference on Computational linguistics-Volume 1*, pages 1–7. Association for Computational Linguistics.

Large-Scale Discriminative Training for Statistical Machine Translation Using Held-Out Line Search

Jeffrey Flanigan **Chris Dyer** **Jaime Carbonell**
Language Technologies Institute
Carnegie Mellon University
Pittsburgh, PA 15213, USA
{jflanigan,cdyer,jgc}@cs.cmu.edu

Abstract

We introduce a new large-scale discriminative learning algorithm for machine translation that is capable of learning parameters in models with extremely sparse features. To ensure their reliable estimation and to prevent overfitting, we use a two-phase learning algorithm. First, the contribution of individual sparse features is estimated using large amounts of parallel data. Second, a small development corpus is used to determine the relative contributions of the sparse features and standard dense features. Not only does this two-phase learning approach prevent overfitting, the second pass optimizes corpus-level BLEU of the Viterbi translation of the decoder. We demonstrate significant improvements using sparse rule indicator features in three different translation tasks. To our knowledge, this is the first large-scale discriminative training algorithm capable of showing improvements over the MERT baseline with only rule indicator features in addition to the standard MERT features.

1 Introduction

This paper is about large scale discriminative training of machine translation systems. Like MERT (Och, 2003), our procedure directly optimizes the cost of the Viterbi output on corpus-level metrics, but does so while scaling to millions of features. The training procedure, which we call the **Held-Out Line Search** algorithm (HOLS), is a two-phase iterative batch optimization procedure consisting of (1) a gradient calculation on a differentiable approximation to the loss on a large amount of parallel training data and (2) a line search (using the standard MERT algorithm) to search in a subspace defined by the gradient for the weights that minimize the true cost.

While sparse features are successfully used in many NLP systems, such parameterizations pose a number of learning challenges. First, since any one feature is likely to occur infrequently, a large amount of training data is necessary to reliably estimate their weights. Therefore, we use the full parallel training data (rather than a small development set) to estimate the contribution of the sparse features in phase 1. Second, sparse features can lead to overfitting. To prevent this from hurting our model's ability to generalize to new data, we do two things. First, we use "grammar and language model folds" (translation grammars and language models built from other portions of the training data than are being used for discriminative training), and second, we run the phase 2 line search on a held-out development set. Finally, since our algorithm requires decoding the entire training corpus, it is desirable (on computational grounds) to only require one or two passes through the training data. To get the most out of these passes, we rescale features by their inverse frequency which improves the scaling of the optimization problem. In addition to learning with few passes through the training data, the HOLS algorithm has the advantage that it is easily parallelizable.

After reviewing related work in the next section, we analyze two obstacles to effective discriminative learning for machine translation: overfitting (since both rules and their weights must be learned, if they are learned together degenerate solutions that fail to generalize are possible) and poor scaling (since MT decoding is so expensive, it is not feasible to make many passes through large amounts of training data, so optimization must be efficient). We then present the details of our algorithm that addresses these issues, give results on three language pairs, and conclude.

2 Related Work

Discriminative training of machine translation systems has been a widely studied problem for the last ten years. The pattern of using small, high-quality development sets to tune a relatively small number of weights was established early (Och and Ney, 2002; Och, 2003). More recently, standard structured prediction algorithms that target linearly decomposable approximations of translation quality metrics have been thoroughly explored (Liang et al., 2006; Smith and Eisner, 2006; Watanabe et al., 2007; Rosti et al., 2010; Hopkins and May, 2011; Chiang, 2012; Gimpel and Smith, 2012; Cherry and Foster, 2012; Saluja et al., 2012). These have without exception used sentence-level approximations of BLEU to determine oracles and update weights using a variety of criteria and with a variety of different theoretical justifications.

Despite advancements in discriminative training for machine translation, large-scale discriminative training with rule indicator features has remained notoriously difficult. **Rule indicator features** are an extremely sparse and expressive parameterization of the translation model: every rule has a feature, each of which has its own separately tuned weight, which count how often a specific rule is used in a translation. Early experiments (Liang et al., 2006) used the structured perceptron to tune a phrase-based system on a large subset of the training data, showing improvements when using rule indicator features, word alignment features, and POS tag features. Another early attempt (Tillmann and Zhang, 2006) used phrase pair and word features in a block SMT system trained using stochastic gradient descent for a convex loss function, but did not compare to MERT. Problems of overfitting and degenerate derivations were tackled with a probabilistic latent variable model (Blunsom et al., 2008) which used rule indicator features yet failed to improve upon the MERT baseline for the standard Hiero features. Techniques for distributed learning and feature selection for the perceptron loss using rule indicator, rule shape, and source side-bigram features have recently been proposed (Simianer et al., 2012), but no comparison to MERT was made.

3 Difficulties in Large-Scale Training

Discriminative training for machine translation is complicated by several factors. First, both translation rules and feature weights are learned from parallel data. If the same data is used for both tasks, overfitting of the weights is very possible.[1] Second, the standard MT cost function, BLEU (Papineni et al., 2002), does not decompose additively over training instances (because of the "brevity penalty") and so approximations are used—these often have problems with the length (Nakov et al., 2012). Finally, state-of-the-art MT systems make extensive good use of "dense" features, such as the log probability of translation decisions under a simpler generative translation model. Our goal is to begin to use much sparser features without abandoning the proven dense features; however, extremely sparse features leads to problems of scaling in the optimization problem as we will show.

3.1 Training Data and Overfitting

One of the big questions in discriminative training of machine translation systems is why standard machine learning techniques can perform so poorly when applied to large-scale learning on the training data. Figure 1 shows a good example of this. The structured SVM (Tsochantaridis et al., 2004; Cherry and Foster, 2012) was used to learn the weights for a Chinese-English Hiero system (Chiang, 2005) with just eight features, using stochastic gradient descent (SGD) for online learning (Bottou, 1998; Bottou, 2010). The weights were initialized from MERT values tuned on a 2k-sentence dev set (MT06), and the figure shows the progress of the online method during a single pass through the 300k-sentence Chinese-English FBIS training set.

As the training progresses in Figure 1, BLEU scores on the training data go up, but scores on the

[1] Previous work has attempted to mitigate the risk of overfitting through careful regularization (Blunsom et al., 2008; Simianer et al., 2012).

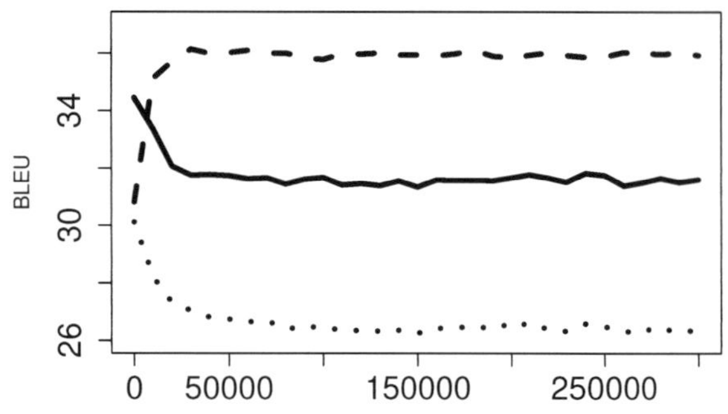

Figure 1: Progress of the online SVM training method after each training instance on FBIS dataset. The solid line is BLEU on the test set, training set is the dashed line, and the dev set is dotted.

dev and test sets go down. If we hope to apply discriminative training techniques for not eight but millions of features on the training data, we must find a way to prevent this overfitting.

We suggest that an important reason why overfitting occurs is that the training data is used not only to tune the system but also to extract the grammar, and the target side is included in the data used to build the language model. To test this hypothesis, we compare tuning using three different dev sets: 1000 sentences from the standard 4-reference MT06 dev set (Dev1000), a random selection of 1000 sentences that overlap with the corpus used to extract translation rules (In1000), and 1000 sentences that came from the training data but were then excluded from rule extraction (Out1000). We run MERT on each of these and evaluate. For evaluation we compare three different sets: a random 1000 sentences from the training corpus that was used to create the grammars but which do not overlap with In1000 (Train1000), the 1000 sentence dev set (Dev1000), and the standard 4-reference MT02-03 test set (Test). The entire experiment (including selection of the 1000 sentences) was replicated 5 times.

Table 1 shows the results, averaging over replications. Out1000 gives much higher scores on the testing data, validating our hypothesis that tuning on data used to build the LM and grammar can lead to overfitting. However, the results also show that tuning on the training data, even when it is held-out, can still lead to a small reduction in translation quality. One possible reason is that, unlike the training data which may come from various domains, the dev data is in the same domain as the test data and is typically of higher quality (e.g., it has multiple references).

Table 1: MERT on Zh-En FBIS

Tuning Set	Train1000	Dev1000	Test
Dev1000	32.2±1.1	30.2±.1	34.1±.3
In1000	37.0±1.2	25.7±.7	30.1±.6
Out1000	34.9±.8	29.0±.4	33.6±.5

3.2 Poor Scaling

When features occur with different frequencies, changing the weights of more frequent features has a larger effect than changing the weights of less frequent features.[2] An example of frequent features that have a large impact on the translation quality are the language model and translation model features. These features are non-zero for every sentence, and changing their weights slightly has a large impact on translation output. In contrast, changing the weight drastically for a feature that is non-zero for only one out of a million sentences has very little effect on translation metrics. The sensitivity of the translation output to some feature weights over others was also pointed out in a recent paper (Chiang, 2012).

When the objective function is more sensitive in some dimensions than others, the optimization problem is said to be **poorly scaled** (Nocedal and Wright, 2000), and can slow down the convergence rate for some optimizers. A typical fix is to rescale the dimensions, as we will do in Section 5.2.

To verify that BLEU is poorly scaled with respect to weights of rule indicator features, we look at the effect of changing the weights for individual rules. We vary the feature weights for four randomly chosen frequent rules and four randomly chosen infrequent rules on our FBIS dev set (Figure 2). One can think of this plot as a "cross-section" of the BLEU score in the direction of the feature weight. The dense features are set to MERT-tuned values which are normalized to one. All other rule indicator features are set to zero, except the rule feature weight that is varied. The frequent features

[2] By the "frequency of a feature" we mean this: given a set of input instances, how many input instances the feature is nonzero in the space of possible outputs for that input.

were selected randomly from the 20 most common rule indictor features in the n-best lists on the dev set, and the infrequent features were selected from the features that only occurred once in these n-best lists. The plots indicate that the BLEU score is poorly scaled for rule feature weights. Changing the weights for one of the common features changes the BLEU score by almost 2.5 BLEU points, while for the infrequent features the BLEU score changes by at most .02 BLEU points. We take this as a sign that gradient descent based optimizers for machine translation with rule features could be slow to converge due to poor scaling, and that rescaling will improve convergence.

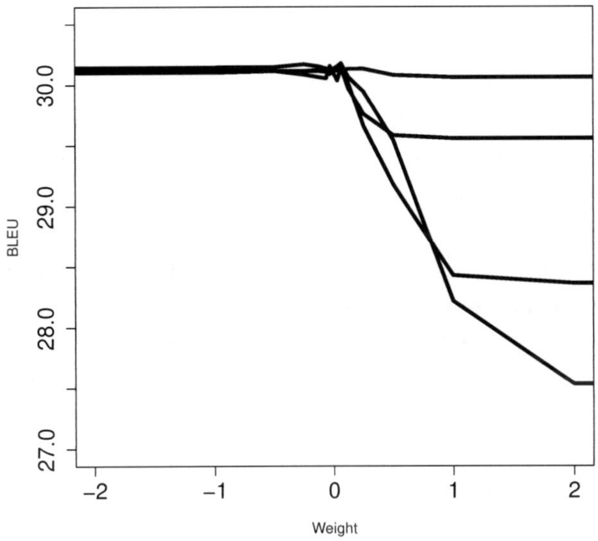

(a) Four representative *frequent* sparse features.

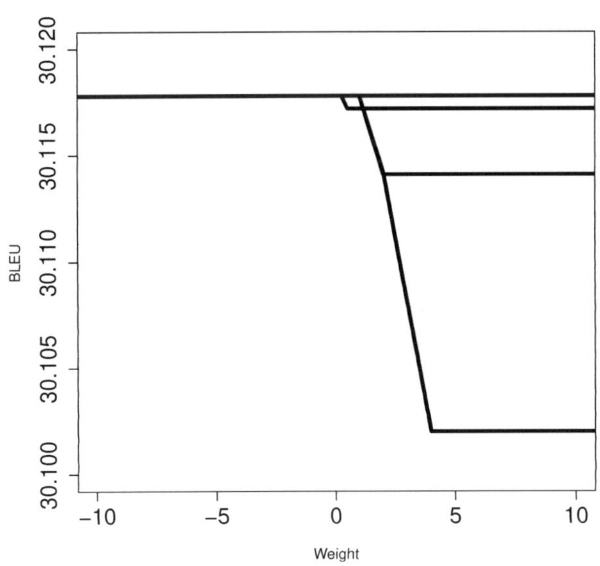

(b) Four representative *infrequent* sparse features

Figure 2: The effect of varying weights for rule indicator features on the BLEU score. Note the difference of scale on the y axis.

3.3 Sentence Level Approximations to BLEU

Finally, we note that discriminative training methods often use a sentence level approximation to BLEU. It has been shown that optimizing corpus level BLEU versus sentence level BLEU can lead to improvements of up to nearly .4 BLEU points on the test set (Nakov et al., 2012). Possible fixes to this problem include using a proper sentence level metric such a METEOR (Denkowski and Lavie, 2011) or a pseudo-corpus from the last few updates (Chiang et al., 2008). However, in light of the result from section 3.1 that tuning on the dev set is still better than tuning on a held-out portion of the training data, we observe that tuning a corpus level metric on a high-quality dev set from the same domain as the test set probably leads to the best translation quality. Attempts to improve upon this strong baseline lead us to the development of the HOLS algorithm which we describe next.

4 Held-Out Line Search Algorithm

In this section we give the details of the learning algorithm that we developed for use in large-scale discriminative training for machine translation, which we call the Held-Out Line Search algorithm (abbreviated HOLS). It optimizes millions of features using evidence from the full set of parallel training data to obtain optimal predictive performance on a secondary development set.

The learning algorithm is a batch optimizer where each iteration has two phases: a gradient calculation phase and a line search phase. In the gradient calculation phase, a surrogate loss function is used to compute a gradient for the feature weights. The gradient is computed over a subset of the training data. In the line search phase, a separate optimizer (MERT) is used to search along this gradient to optimize the evaluation score of the one-best prediction of a translation system on a secondary development set.[3] The secondary dev set is a crucial aspect of the algorithm that helps reduce overfitting (we will demonstrate this in the experiments section).

During the line search phase we allow some of the feature weights to be adjusted independently of the line search. We will call the features we optimize independently the dense features, and the features we include in the line search the sparse features.[4] The feature vector space V is the direct sum $V = V_d \oplus V_s$, where V_d is the vector space of the dense features and V_s is the vector space of the sparse features. The feature and weight vectors decompose as $\vec{f} = \vec{f}_d + \vec{f}_s$ and $\vec{w} = \vec{w}_d + \vec{w}_s$. $\vec{f}_d$ and $\vec{w}_d$ are in the dense vector space, and the $\vec{f}_s$ and $\vec{w}_s$ are in the sparse vector space.

In the gradient phase, we calculate a gradient of the surrogate loss function and project it onto the subspace of the sparse features. Let P_s be the projection operator onto V_s. Then the gradient projected onto the sparse feature space is

$$\vec{g} = \mathrm{P}_s \nabla_{\vec{w}} \tilde{L}(\vec{w}, \mathcal{D}_g)$$

where $\mathcal{D}_g$ is the subset of the training data used to calculate this gradient, and $\tilde{L}$ is the surrogate loss function. This just sets the dense components of the gradient of $\tilde{L}$ to zero.

In the line search phase, we use a separate optimizer to optimize the weights for the dense features and the stepsize α. Let L be the loss function we wish to minimize, then

$$(\vec{w}_d^*, \alpha^*) = \underset{\vec{w}_d, \alpha}{\arg\min}\, L(\vec{w}_d + \vec{w}_s + \alpha\vec{g}, \mathcal{D}_l)$$

Note $\vec{w}_s$ is held fixed from the previous iteration. $\mathcal{D}_l$ is the portion of the training data which is used in the line search phase, and must not overlap with $\mathcal{D}_g$ used in the gradient calculation phase.[5]

After the line search, the dense weights are updated to $\vec{w}_d^*$, and the sparse weights are updated with $\vec{w}_s \leftarrow \vec{w}_s + \alpha^*\vec{g}$. The process repeats for another iteration as desired (or until convergence).

[3] While we use BLEU any loss function whose sufficient statistics decompose over training instances could be used.

[4] The split over the features does not have to be done this way in practice.

[5] $L(\vec{w}_d^*, \alpha^*, \mathcal{D}_l)$ can be thought of as unbiased or more accurately less biased estimator of expected loss when $\mathcal{D}_l \cap \mathcal{D}_g = \emptyset$.

5 Procedure for Large-Scale Training

Now that we have described the HOLS algorithm in general, we next describe how to apply it to large-scale training of machine translation systems with millions of features. We find that it is necessary to use disjoint sets of training instances for grammar extraction and gradient estimation (§5.1) and to deal with the poor scaling of the optimization problem (§5.2).

5.1 Grammar and Language Model Folds

To address the problem of overfitting on the training data, we split the training data into n-folds, and extract grammars for each fold using the data from the other $n-1$ folds. Similarly, we build a language model for each fold using a target language monolingual corpus and the target side of the training data from the other $n-1$ folds. Whenever we decode a sentence from the training data, we use the grammar and language model for the appropriate fold. This ensures that a sentence is never decoded using a grammar or language model it helped build, thereby reducing the overfitting effect demonstrated in §3.1.

To perform the training, the HOLS algorithm is used on the training data. In our experiments, only 1-2 passes over the training data are necessary for significant gains. Data from one of the grammar folds is used for the line search, and the rest of the training data is used to calculate the gradient.

The procedure is iterative, first decoding training data to obtain a gradient, and then performing a line search with data from a held-out grammar fold. Instead of decoding the whole set of sentences used for the gradient updates at once, one can also decode a portion of the data, do a gradient update, and then continue the next iteration of HOLS on the remaining data before repeating.

The last line search of the HOLS algorithm is done using dev data, rather than training data. This is because the dev data is higher quality, and from Table 1 we can see that tuning on dev data produces better results than tuning on training data (even if the training data has been held out from the grammar process). The initial weights are obtained by running MERT on a subset of the one of the grammar folds.

If one has an existing implementation of an optimizer for the loss function used during the line search (in our case MERT), it can be used to perform the line search. This is done simply by calling MERT with two extra features in addition to the dense features and omitting the sparse features.

To see how, notice that the feature weights during the line search are decomposed as $\vec{w} = \vec{w}_{dense} + \vec{w}_{sparse} + \alpha\vec{g}$ where $\vec{g}$ is in the sparse feature subspace, so the model score decomposes as $score(x, y) = \vec{w}_d \cdot \vec{f_d}(x, y) + \vec{w}_s \cdot \vec{f_s}(x, y) + \alpha\vec{g} \cdot \vec{f_s}(x, y)$ where x is the input translation, y is the output translation and derivation. If we create two new features $f_1(x, y) = \vec{w}_s \cdot \vec{f_s}(x, y)$ and $f_2(x, y) = \vec{g} \cdot \vec{f_s}(x, y)$ then the score can be written

$$\begin{aligned} score(x, y) &= \vec{w}_d \cdot \vec{f_d}(x, y) \\ &\quad + f_1(x, y) + \alpha f_2(x, y) \\ &= (\vec{w}_d, 1, \alpha) \cdot (\vec{f_d}, f_1, f_2) \end{aligned}$$

Thus we can do the line search simply by calling MERT with the features $(\vec{f_d}, f_1, f_2)$. [6]

In summary our training algorithm is as follows: 1) split the training data into n-folds (we use $n = 5$), 2) initialize the dense weights to MERT values, 3) decode some or all the data in 4 of the 5 folds to get a gradient, 4) condition as in §5.2 (see below), 5) run MERT on a 10k subset of the remaining fold to do the line search, 6) repeat steps 3-4 until convergence or stop as desired, and 7) run MERT on the normal dev set as a final step. We only run MERT on a 10k subset of one of the folds so it does not require running MERT on an entire fold.

In the special case where just one iteration of HOLS is performed, the procedure is very simple: decode the training data to get a gradient, include the components of the gradient as an extra feature f_2 in addition to the dense features, and tune on a dev set using MERT.

5.2 Conditioning

To address the problem of poor scaling, we use a simple strategy of rescaling each component of the gradient based on how frequent the feature is. We call this process "conditioning." For each feature, we simply divide the corresponding dimension of the gradient by the number of n-best lists in which the feature was non-zero in.

The necessity for conditioning is evident when we run the HOLS algorithm as detailed so far on the training data without conditioning. On subsequent iterations, we observe that the features with the highest component of the gradient oscillate between iterations, but the rest of the feature gradients stay the same.

Based on our knowledge that the optimization problem was poorly scaled, we divided by the frequency of the feature. We can give the following heuristic justification for our method of conditioning. For the ith feature weight, we will take a step Δw_i. Assume that we want to take the step Δw_i proportional to the average gradient $\hat{g}_i$ calculated from n-best lists in which the feature is non-zero. In other words, we want $\Delta w_i = \alpha\hat{g}_i$. Let g_i be the total gradient calculated by adding the gradients over all n-best lists (i.e. summing over training examples in the corpus). For a feature that is nonzero in exactly n_i n-best lists, the gradient from each example will have been added up n_i times, so the total gradient $g_i = n_i\hat{g}_i$. Therefore we should take the step $\Delta w_i = \alpha g_i / n_i$. In other words, we rescale each component g_i of the gradient by $1/n_i$ before taking the gradient step.

We can relate this argument back to the oscillation we observed of the rule feature weights. For rules that are used a thousand times more often than the average rule, the corresponding component of the gradient is roughly a thousand times larger. But that does not indicate that the adjustment Δw_i to the rule weight should be a thousand times larger in each iteration.

6 Experiments

We evaluate and analyze the performance of our training method with three sets of experiments. The first set of experiments compares HOLS to other tuning algorithms used in machine translation in a medium-scale discriminative setting. The second set looks in detail at HOLS for large scale discriminative training for a Chinese-English task. The third set looks at two other languages.

All the experiments use a Hiero MT system with rule indicator features for the sparse features and the

[6] We could constrain the weight for f_1 to be 1, but this is not necessary since since MERT is invariant to the overall scale of the weights.

Table 2: Corpora

Language	Corpus	Sentences	Tokens	
			Source	Target
En	Gigaword	24M		594M
Ar-En	Train	1M	7M	31M
	Dev (MT06)	1797	13K	236K
	MT05	1,056	7K	144K
	MT08nw	813	5K	116K
	MT05wb	547	5K	89K
Mg-En	Train	89K	2.1M	1.7M
	Dev	1,359	34K	28K
	Test	1,133	29K	24K
Zh-En	Train (FBIS)	302K	1M	9.3M
	Dev (MT06)	1,664	4K	192K
	Test (MT02-03)	1,797	5K	223K
	MT08	1,357	4K	167K

following 8 dense features: LM, phrasal and lexical $p(e|f)$ and $p(f|e)$, phrase and word penalties, and glue rule. The total number of features is 2.2M (Mg-En), 28.8M (Ar-En), and 10.8M (Zh-En). The same features are used for all tuning methods, except MERT baseline which uses only dense features. Although we extract different grammars from various subsets of the training corpus, word alignments were done using the entire training corpus. We use GIZA++ for word alignments (Och and Ney, 2003), Thrax (Weese et al., 2011) to extract the grammars, our decoder is cdec (Dyer et al., 2010) which uses KenLM (Heafield, 2011), and we used a 4-gram LM built using SRILM (Stolcke, 2002). Our optimizer uses code implemented in the pycdec python interface to cdec (Chahuneau et al., 2012). To speed up decoding, for each source RHS we filtered the grammars to the top 15 rules ranked by $p(e \mid f)$. Statistics about the datasets we used are listed in Table 2.

We use the "soft ramp 3" loss function (Gimpel, 2012; Gimpel and Smith, 2012) as the surrogate loss function for calculating the gradient in HOLS. It is defined as

$$\tilde{L} = \sum_{i=1}^{n} \Big[-\log \sum_{y \in \text{Gen}(x_i)} e^{\vec{w}\cdot\vec{f}(x_i,y) - cost(y_i,y)} + \log \sum_{y \in \text{Gen}(x_i)} e^{\vec{w}\cdot\vec{f}(x_i,y) + cost(y_i,y)} \Big]$$

where the sum over i ranges over training examples, $\text{Gen}(x)$ is the space of possible outputs and derivations for the input x, and $cost(y_i, y)$ is add one smoothing sentence level BLEU.[7]

Except where noted, all experiments are repeated 5 times and results are averaged, initial weights for the dense features are drawn from a standard normal, and initial weights for the sparse features are set to zero. We evaluate using MultEval (Clark et al., 2011) and report standard deviations across optimizer runs and significance at $p = .05$ using MultEval's built-in permutation test. In the large-scale experiments for HOLS, we only run the full optimizer once, and report standard deviations using multiple runs of the last MERT run (i.e. the last line search on the dev data).

6.1 Comparison Experiments for ZH-EN

Our first set of experiments compares the performance of the proposed HOLS algorithm to learning algorithms popularly used in machine translation on a Chinese-English task. We also compare to a close relative of the HOLS algorithm: optimizing the soft ramp 3 loss directly with online stochastic gradient descent and with conditioning. As we will see, SGD SOFTRAMP3 performs significantly worse than HOLS, despite both algorithms optimizing similar loss functions.

In the experiments in this section, we do not use the full version of the training setup described in §5 since we wish to compare to algorithms that do not necessarily scale to large amounts of training data. We therefore use only one fifth of the training data for learning the weights for both the dense and sparse features.

In this section we refer to the subset of the training data used to learn the weights as the **tuning set** (Tune). The grammar and LM are built using the training data that is not in the tuning set (the LM also includes the English monolingual corpus), and the weights for the features are tuned using the tuning set. This is similar to the typical train-dev-test split commonly used to tune machine translation systems, except that the tuning set is much larger (60k sentence pairs versus the usual 1k-2k) and comes from a random subset of the training data rather than a

[7] We found this loss function to work well, but other "soft" loss functions (Gimpel, 2012; Gimpel and Smith, 2012) also work. $\text{Gen}(x)$ is restricted to a k-best size of 1000. Following (Gimpel, 2012) $cost(y_i, y)$ is multiplied by a factor of 20.

Table 3: Comparison Experiments for Zh-En

Algorithm	Tune	MT08	Runtime
MERT	22.1±.1	23.1±.1	**6 hours**
PRO	23.8±.05	**23.6**±.1	2 weeks
MIRA	21.7±.1	22.5±.1	19 hours
SOFTRAMP3	21.5±.3	22.3±.3	29 hours
HOLS	22.3±.1	23.4±.1	10 hours
HILS	**24.3**±.2	22.4±.1	10 hours

specialized development set.

We compare MERT, PRO (Hopkins and May, 2011), MIRA (Chiang, 2012), SOFTRAMP3, HOLS, and a variant of HOLS which we call HILS (discussed below). For HOLS, we used 10k of the 60k tuning set for the line search, and the rest of the tuning set was used for calculating the gradient. For HILS ("Held-In" Line Search), the full 60k tuning set was used to calculate the gradient, but the line search was on a 10k subset of that set. For MERT, we used a 10k subset of the tuning data because it takes a long time to run on large datasets, and it only has the eight dense features and so does not need the entire 60k tuning set. All the subsets are drawn randomly. Conditioning was performed only for HOLS, HILS, and SOFTRAMP3 because conditioning would affect the regularizer for PRO and require modifications to the MIRA algorithm. To do the conditioning for SOFTRAMP3 we used rule count during extraction of the grammar and not the frequency in the n-best lists because the online nature of SOFTRAMP3 prevents us from knowing how frequent a rule will be (and the dense features are conditioned using the corpus size). We chose MIRA's best learning rate ($\eta = .001$) from $\{.1, .01, .001\}$, used default settings for PRO in cdec, and for SOFTRAMP3 we used the same loss function as HOLS but included an L_2 regularizer of strength .001 and used a stepsize of 1 (which was scaled because of conditioning). To remedy problems of length bias for sentence level BLEU, we used brevity penalty smoothed and grounded BLEU+1 for sentence level scores (Nakov et al., 2012). Tuning was repeated four times with different initial weights, except for PRO which we only ran three times (due to training costs). The initial weights for MERT were drawn from a standard normal distribution, and final MERT weights were used as the initial weights for the dense features for the other algorithms. Initial weights for the sparse features were set to zero. For HOLS, and HILS, tuning set BLEU scores were evaluated on the set that the line search was run on. We also report run times for 8 threads on an Opteron 6220 processor.[8]

The results are shown in Table 3. PRO and HOLS are a statistically significant improvement upon the MERT baseline on the MT08 test data, but MIRA, SOFTRAMP3, and HILS are not.

HILS dramatically overfits the tuning set, while HOLS does not, justifying the use of a held-out dataset for the line search. SOFTRAMP3 performs significantly worse than HOLS on the test set. PRO is a promising training algorithm, but does not scale to the full FBIS corpus because it requires many iterations.

6.2 Full ZH-EN and Ablation Experiments

This set of experiments evaluates the performance of the full HOLS algorithm described in §5 for large-scale discriminative training on the full FBIS Chinese-English dataset. Since this is a relatively small and widely studied dataset, we also investigate what happens if different aspects of the procedure are omitted.

Table 4 gives the results. The number of updates is the number of times the HOLS line search optimizer is run (gradient updates). For 2 passes, 4 updates, a line search is performed after a half pass through the training data, which is repeated four times for a total of two passes.

Using just one pass through the training data and

[8]Standard MIRA and SGD SOFTRAMP3 are not parallelizable and only use a single thread. All of these algorithms were run for one iteration, except for MERT which ran for at least seven iterations, and PRO which we stopped after 20 iterations.

Table 4: Full-scale Chinese-English and Ablation Experiments

Configuration	Dev	Test
MERT Baseline	29.9±.3	34.0±.8
2 Pass, 4 updates	**31.1**±.2	**35.1**±.4
1 Pass, 1 update	30.7±.1	34.6±.5
−Folds	30.0±.2	34.0±.4
−Conditioning	30.1±.1	34.2±.2

Table 5: Arabic-English

System	Dev (MT06)	MT05	MT08(nw)	MT08(wb)
MERT Baseline	39.2±.4	50.3±.4	45.2±.2	29.4±.14
HOLS 1 Pass, 2 updates	**39.9**±.9	**51.2**±.4	**45.8**±.4	**30.0**±.4
ΔBLEU	+.7	+.9	+.6	+.6

Table 6: Malagasy-English

System	Dev	Test
MERT Baseline	19.8±.3	17.7±.2
HOLS 1 Pass, 1 update	**20.5**±.1	**18.4**±.2
ΔBLEU	+.7	+.7

one gradient update, HOLS improves upon the MERT baseline by .6 BLEU points, which is a statistically significant improvement. With 2 passes through the training data and 4 gradient updates, HOLS performs even better, obtaining a 1.1 BLEU point improvement over the baseline and is also statistically significant. With 16 threads, 1 pass, 1 update completed in 9 hours, and 2 pass, 4 updates, completed in 40 hours. The medium-scale PRO setup in §6.1 obtains a result of $34.4 \pm .1$ on this test set, which is a statistically significant improvement of .4 BLEU points over the MERT baseline but does not beat the large-scale HOLS results.

Is folding and conditioning necessary? We experiment with what happens if grammar and LM folds are not used and if conditioning is not done. −Folds denotes 1 pass 1 update without folds, and −Conditioning denotes 1 pass 1 update without conditioning. We can see that both these steps are important for the training procedure to work well.

The decrease in performance of the training procedure without folds or conditioning is dramatic but not too surprising. With just one gradient update, one would expect conditioning to be very important. And from the lessons learned in section 3.1, one would also expect the procedure to perform poorly or even worse than the MERT baseline without grammar or LM folds. But because HOLS runs MERT on the dev data for the last line search, it is almost impossible for HOLS to be worse than the MERT baseline. (This, in fact, was part of our motivation when we originally attempted the HOLS algorithm.)

6.3 Other Language Pairs

The last set of experiments looks at the performance of the learning algorithm for two other languages and data scenarios for one pass through the training data. Using the same setup for large-scale discriminative training as before, we apply the training procedure to a large data scenario Arabic-English task and a small data scenario Malagasy-English task (Tables 5 and 6). The training procedure gives statistically significant improvements over the baseline by .6 to .9 BLEU for Arabic, and a statistically significant improvement of .7 BLEU for Malagasy. With 16 threads, the runtime was 44 hours for Arabic and 5 hours for Malagasy.

7 Conclusion

We have explored the difficulties encountered in large-scale discriminative training for machine translation, and introduced a learning procedure designed to overcome them and scale to large corpora. We leave to future work to experiment with feature sets designed for the large-scale discriminative setting. In particular, we hope this framework will facilitate incorporation of richer linguistic knowledge into machine translation.

Acknowledgments

This work was sponsored by the U. S. Army Research Laboratory and the U. S. Army Research Office under contract/grant number W911NF-10-1-0533. Jeffrey Flanigan would like to thank his co-advisor Lori Levin for support and encouragement during this work.

References

Phil Blunsom, Trevor Cohn, and Miles Osborne. 2008. A discriminative latent variable model for statistical machine translation. In *Proc. ACL-HLT*.

Léon Bottou. 1998. Online algorithms and stochastic approximations. In David Saad, editor, *Online Learning and Neural Networks*. Cambridge University Press, Cambridge, UK. revised, oct 2012.

Léon Bottou. 2010. Large-scale machine learning with stochastic gradient descent. In Yves Lechevallier and Gilbert Saporta, editors, *Proceedings of the 19th International Conference on Computational Statistics (COMPSTAT'2010)*, pages 177–187, Paris, France, August. Springer.

V. Chahuneau, N. A. Smith, and C. Dyer. 2012. pycdec: A python interface to cdec. *The Prague Bulletin of Mathematical Linguistics*, 98:51–61.

Colin Cherry and George Foster. 2012. Batch tuning strategies for statistical machine translation. In *Proc. of NAACL*.

David Chiang, Yuval Marton, and Philip Resnik. 2008. Online large-margin training of syntactic and structural translation features. In *Proceedings of the Conference on Empirical Methods in Natural Language Processing*, EMNLP '08, pages 224–233, Stroudsburg, PA, USA. Association for Computational Linguistics.

David Chiang. 2005. A hierarchical phrase-based model for statistical machine translation. In *In ACL*, pages 263–270.

David Chiang. 2012. Hope and fear for discriminative training of statistical translation models. *Journal of Machine Learning Research*, pages 1159–1187.

Jonathan H. Clark, Chris Dyer, Alon Lavie, and Noah A. Smith. 2011. Better hypothesis testing for statistical machine translation: controlling for optimizer instability. In *Proceedings of the 49th Annual Meeting of the Association for Computational Linguistics: Human Language Technologies: short papers - Volume 2*, HLT '11, pages 176–181, Stroudsburg, PA, USA. Association for Computational Linguistics.

Michael Denkowski and Alon Lavie. 2011. Meteor 1.3: Automatic Metric for Reliable Optimization and Evaluation of Machine Translation Systems. In *Proceedings of the EMNLP 2011 Workshop on Statistical Machine Translation*.

Chris Dyer, Adam Lopez, Juri Ganitkevitch, Johnathan Weese, Ferhan Ture, Phil Blunsom, Hendra Setiawan, Vladimir Eidelman, and Philip Resnik. 2010. cdec: A decoder, alignment, and learning framework for finite-state and context-free translation models. In *Proceedings of ACL*.

Kevin Gimpel and Noah A. Smith. 2012. Structured ramp loss minimization for machine translation. In *Proc. of NAACL*.

K. Gimpel. 2012. *Discriminative Feature-Rich Modeling for Syntax-Based Machine Translation*. Ph.D. thesis, Carnegie Mellon University.

Kenneth Heafield. 2011. KenLM: Faster and smaller language model queries. In *Proceedings of the Sixth Workshop on Statistical Machine Translation*, Edinburgh, UK, July. Association for Computational Linguistics.

Mark Hopkins and Jonathan May. 2011. Tuning as ranking. In *Proc. of EMNLP*.

Percy Liang, Alexandre Bouchard-côté, Dan Klein, and Ben Taskar. 2006. An end-to-end discriminative approach to machine translation. In *In Proceedings of the Joint International Conference on Computational Linguistics and Association of Computational Linguistics (COLING/ACL*, pages 761–768.

Preslav Nakov, Francisco Guzmán, and Stephan Vogel. 2012. Optimizing for sentence-level bleu+1 yields short translations. In Martin Kay and Christian Boitet, editors, *COLING*, pages 1979–1994. Indian Institute of Technology Bombay.

Jorge Nocedal and Stephen J. Wright. 2000. *Numerical Optimization*. Springer.

Franz Josef Och and Hermann Ney. 2002. Discriminative training and maximum entropy models for statistical machine translation. In *Proc. of ACL*.

Franz Josef Och and Hermann Ney. 2003. A systematic comparison of various statistical alignment models. *Comput. Linguist.*, 29(1):19–51, March.

Franz Josef Och. 2003. Minimum error rate training in statistical machine translation. In *Proc. of ACL*.

Kishore Papineni, Salim Roukos, Todd Ward, and Wei-Jing Zhu. 2002. Bleu: a method for automatic evaluation of machine translation. In *Proceedings of the 40th Annual Meeting on Association for Computational Linguistics*, ACL '02, pages 311–318, Stroudsburg, PA, USA. Association for Computational Linguistics.

Antti-Veiko Rosti, Bing Zhang, Spyros Matsoukas, and Richard Schwartz. 2010. BBN system description for WMT10 system combination task. In *Proc. WMT*.

Avneesh Saluja, Ian Lane, and Joy Zhang. 2012. Machine Translation with Binary Feedback: a large-margin approach. In *Proceedings of The Tenth Biennial Conference of the Association for Machine Translation in the Americas*, San Diego, CA, July.

Patrick Simianer, Chris Dyer, and Stefan Riezler. 2012. Joint feature selection in distributed stochastic learning for large-scale discriminative training in SMT. In *Proc. ACL*.

David A. Smith and Jason Eisner. 2006. Minimum risk annealing for training log-linear models. In *Proc. of ACL*.

Andreas Stolcke. 2002. Srilm - an extensible language modeling toolkit. pages 901–904.

Christoph Tillmann and Tong Zhang. 2006. A discriminative global training algorithm for statistical mt. In *Proceedings of the 21st International Conference on*

Computational Linguistics and the 44th annual meeting of the Association for Computational Linguistics, ACL-44, pages 721–728, Stroudsburg, PA, USA. Association for Computational Linguistics.

Ioannis Tsochantaridis, Thomas Hofmann, Thorsten Joachims, and Yasemin Altun. 2004. Support vector machine learning for interdependent and structured output spaces. In *Proceedings of the twenty-first international conference on Machine learning*, ICML '04, pages 104–, New York, NY, USA. ACM.

Taro Watanabe, Jun Suzuki, Hajime Tsukada, and Hideki Isozaki. 2007. Online large-margin training for statistical machine translation. In *Proc. EMNLP-CoNLL*.

Jonathan Weese, Juri Ganitkevitch, Chris Callison-Burch, Matt Post, and Adam Lopez. 2011. Joshua 3.0: syntax-based machine translation with the thrax grammar extractor. In *Proceedings of the Sixth Workshop on Statistical Machine Translation*, WMT '11, pages 478–484, Stroudsburg, PA, USA. Association for Computational Linguistics.

Measuring Term Informativeness in Context

Zhaohui Wu
Computer Science and Engineering
The Pennsylvania State University
University Park, PA 16802, USA
zzw109@psu.edu

C. Lee Giles
Information Sciences and Technology
Computer Science and Engineering
The Pennsylvania State University
University Park, PA 16802, USA
giles@ist.psu.edu

Abstract

Measuring term informativeness is a fundamental NLP task. Existing methods, mostly based on statistical information in corpora, do not actually measure informativeness of a term with regard to its semantic context. This paper proposes a new lightweight feature-free approach to encode term informativeness in context by leveraging web knowledge. Given a term and its context, we model context-aware term informativeness based on semantic similarity between the context and the term's most featured context in a knowledge base, Wikipedia. We apply our method to three applications: core term extraction from snippets (text segment), scientific keywords extraction (paper), and back-of-the-book index generation (book). The performance is state-of-the-art or close to it for each application, demonstrating its effectiveness and generality.

1 Introduction

Computationally measuring importance of a word in text, or "term informativeness" (Kireyev, 2009; Rennie and Jaakkola, 2005), is fundamental to many NLP tasks such as keyword extraction, text categorization, clustering, and summarization, etc. Various features derived from statistical and linguistic information can be helpful in encoding term informativeness, whereas practical feature definition and selection are usually ad hoc, data-driven and application dependent. Statistical information based on term frequency (TF) and document frequency (DF) tend to be more effective in finding keywords in large corpora, but can have issues with small amounts of text or small corpora. Linguistic information such as POS tag patterns often require manual selection based on prior applications. We contend that few methods actually measure the informativeness of a term to the discourse unit it contains. For example, given a context such as *"A graph comprises nodes (also called vertices) connected by links (also known as edges or arcs)"*, it is difficult to measure the term informativeness of "graph", "nodes", or "links" based on any statistical or linguistic information.

This raises many issues. Is there a fundamental and less ad hoc way to measure the term informativeness of a word within a discourse unit? Can we actually find a general approach based on comprehensive and high-level "knowledge" and not have to nitpick over features? Can this new metric be effectively applied to real world applications? To answer these questions, we develop a new term informativeness metric, motivated by query-document relevance in information retrieval. The higher the relevance score a query-document pair is, the more informative the query is to the document. If a similar principle also exists between word and context and there is an effective search engine returning ranked contexts for a given word, then we contend that word is more informative in the higher rank contexts. To see the term informativeness of three words "graph", "nodes" and "links" in context, we manually check the search results from Wikipedia, Google, and Bing. We found that very similar contexts are among the top 5 ranked results of "graph" while no such contexts appear in that of the other two words. Thus, we define a context-aware term informativeness based on the semantic relatedness between the context and the term's featured contexts (or the top important contexts that cover most of a term's semantics).

We apply the context-aware term informativeness (CTI) to three typical NLP applications: core term extraction in snippets, keyword extraction and back-of-the-book index generation. Experiments show that the method is effective and efficient. Moreover, the metric can be easily combined with other methods, or as a feature for learning algorithms.

The remainder of this paper is organized as follows. Section 2 reviews the literature of term informativeness measurements. Section 3 proposes the formal definition of the context-aware term informativeness as well as its practical implementation using Web knowledge. Section 4 studies the three applications. Finally, we conclude with discussion and future work.

2 Related Work

Most known approaches to measure term informativeness fall into basically two categories: statistics-based and semantic-based.

Statistics-based methods, such as *TFIDF* (Salton and Buckley, 1988), *ResidualIDF(RIDF)*, *Variance*, *Burstiness* and *Gain*, are based on derivations from term frequency (TF) and document frequency (DF). Sprck Jones defines *IDF* or *inverse document frequency* as:

$$IDF(w) = -log_2(df_w/D) \quad (1)$$

where D is the size of the corpus (Jones, 1972; Jones, 1973). Based on a finding that informative words tend to have large deviation between *IDF* and collection frequency f_w(the total number of occurrence of a word), many other informativeness scores have been proposed. Bookstein and Swanson (Bookstein and Swanson, 1974) introduced the x^I as:

$$X^I = f_w - df_w$$

Church and Gale (1995) introduced

$$variance(w) = \frac{1}{D-1}\sum_{d=1}^{D}(t_{dw} - \bar{t_w}) \quad (2)$$

where t_{dw} denotes w's TF in d and $\bar{t_w} = f_w/D$ indicates its mean expected word rate. Another measure suggested by them is

$$burstiness(w) = \frac{f_w}{df_w} \quad (3)$$

which tends to compare collection frequency and document frequency directly. Informative words were found to have *IDF* scores that are larger than what would be expected according to the Poisson model; *residual IDF* (*RIDF*) was introduced to measure this deviation

$$RIDF(w) = IDF(w) - \widehat{IDF}(w) \quad (4)$$

where $\widehat{IDF}(w) = -log_2(1 - e^{-\bar{t_w}})$. In addition, Papineni (2001) introduced the notion of *gain* as

$$gain(w) = \frac{df_w}{D}\left(\frac{df_w}{D} - 1 - log(\frac{df_w}{D})\right) \quad (5)$$

More recently, Rennie and Jaakkola (2005) introduced an informativeness score based on the fit of a word's frequency to a mixture of 2 Unigram distribution and applied it to named entity detection. It is worth noting that term necessity, which measures the probability that a term occurs in documents relevant to a given query, has been well studied in Information Retrieval community (Zhao and Callan, 2010; Yang and Callan, 2010). Though our CIT is not designed for probabilistic retrieval models, we may apply it to measure the term necessity in a query by considering it as a context.

Despite extensive research on semantic analysis and understanding of word and text (Deerwester et al., 1990; Budanitsky and Hirst, 2006; Cilibrasi and Vitanyi, 2007; Gabrilovich and Markovitch, 2007; Agirre et al., 2009; Yazdani and Popescu-Belis, 2012), little work studied the measurement of the semantics of term informativeness. An exception is the $LSAspec$ from Kireyev (2009), based on latent semantic analysis (Deerwester et al., 1990), which is defined as the ratio of a term's LSA vector length to its document frequency and thus can be interpreted as the rate of vector length growth. However, latent semantic models such as LSA are notoriously hard to interpret since the "latent concepts" cannot be readily mapped to human knowledge (Gabrilovich and Markovitch, 2007). Our approach explicitly leverages the semantics of word and text using existing knowledge bases.

Previous methods, all corpus-based, might be effective in identifying informative words at the document or corpus level, but do not the ability to capture term informativeness in a particular context due to their absence of semantics and obliviousness of context. Our method measures the term informativeness within a context in a semantic-based approach, regardless of the absence of statistical information.

3 Context-aware Term Informativeness

3.1 Context

A context of a word or phrase may refer to a few words nearby (He et al., 2010), a sentence or paragraph (Soricut and Marcu, 2003), or even a set of documents containing it (Cilibrasi and Vitanyi, 2007). Here we define context as a syntactic unit of discourse such as a sentence or paragraph, for example, "PL/SQL is one of three key programming languages embedded in the Oracle Database", or "There are two types of functions in PL/SQL". The universal context set $U(t)$ of a word t is defined as all the contexts containing it in the web. Different contexts vary in their authority just like web pages vary. For the two examples, we could argue that the first context is much more "authoritative" than the second. This can be verified by their popularity on Google; (all results from actual search engines were at the time of this publication) the first retrieves approximately 302,000 exact matching results while the second retrieves only one. We consider this as the number of citations of a context, which, to some extent, indicates its "authority". We define the *source* of a context as the set of all documents citing it. Here "citing" instead of "containing" is used because some documents may not literally contain an exact copy of the context.

Given a term t, define its universal context set $U(t) = \{c_i\}$ and the source of c_i is $S(c_i) = \{d_{ij}\}$. Ideally, the authority of a context will be contributed by every document citing it. Therefore, we define the authority score of a context as

$$CA(c_i) = \sum_j DA(d_{ij}) \qquad (6)$$

where $DA(d_{ij})$ denotes the authority contributed by d_{ij}. It is very difficult to acquire the universal context set of a term. Considering that usually we only care about the top few results of a query returned by search engines and ignore a large faction of less important ones, it is reasonable to assume that a term's semantics will be well covered by a few important contexts. We therefore define the featured context set of term t, or $U_f(t)$, as the top k contexts with the highest authority scores, where k is an application dependent parameter. In our experiments, the default k for the Wikipedia based implementation is 20.

3.2 Term Informativeness

We now consider how to measure the term informativeness in context. Using the context "PL/SQL is one of three key programming languages embedded in the Oracle Database" (denoted by C_p) as an example, for its term "PL/SQL", the top three contexts returned by Google are

1. PL/SQL (Procedural Language/Structured Query Language) is Oracle Corporation's procedural extension language for SQL and the Oracle relational database.
2. PL/SQL is Oracle's procedural extension to industry-standard SQL. PL/SQL naturally, efficiently, and safely extends SQL.
3. This Oracle PL SQL tutorial teaches you the basics of programming in PL/SQL like cursors, stored procedures, PlSQL functions.

Those contexts, though being diverse in actual meaning, all have semantic relatedness to C_p. Even someone who does not completely understand them can gain some meaning by observing common words such as "Oracle", "database" and "programming". However, checking the Google results for "Oracle Database" or "programming languages", we will find little relatedness between them and C_p. This suggests that if term t_a in context c is more informative than t_b, then most likely the contexts from t_a's featured context set will be more related to c than will t_b. Thus, given a term t and its featured context set $U_f(t) = \{c_1, ..., c_k\}$, we define the term informativeness of t in context c_i as

$$I(t, c_i) = \sum_{c_j \in U_f(t)} \kappa(c_i, c_j) \cdot CA(c_j) \qquad (7)$$

where $\kappa(c_i, c_j)$ is the semantic relatedness of c_i and c_j, which can be computed by various semantic relatedness metrics such as Wikipedia based (Gabrilovich and Markovitch, 2007; Yazdani and Popescu-Belis, 2012), Wordnet based (Agirre et al., 2009; Budanitsky and Hirst, 2006), or simple cosine similarity and Jaccard similarity based (Zobel and Moffat, 1998).

The context-aware term informativeness (CTI) introduced above is a formal and general definition. As such the definition in Equation (7) includes several features such as context authority score, featured context set, semantic relatedness, and knowledge base, any or all of which could be flexible for different applications.

3.3 Implementation

Here, we present a simple practical implementation using Wikipedia as the knowledge base and the context authority estimated by the discounted rank of the Wikipedia document. Note that the problem is how to compute $CA(c_j)$ for each context in U_f. We rewrite Equation (6) as

$$CA(c_i) = DA(d_{i0}) + \sum_{j \neq 0} DA(d_{ij}) \tag{8}$$

where d_{i0} is the original document of c_i and all the others are further derivatives of "citing" c_i. For example, the Wikipedia page of "PL/SQL" will be considered as the original document of C_p while all other documents citing C_p are its derivatives. Intuitively, the authority of a context will mainly rely on the authority of its original document. Here, we simply assume that the context authority depends only on its original document, or

$$CA(c_i) \approx DA(d_{i0}) \tag{9}$$

We then take the top ranked document returned by the web knowledge base as the original document. We present a practical implementation of CTI in Algorithm 1. The discounted rank is used to represent the relative context authority score of each context in U_f. We use Wikipedia as our knowledge base to implement the metric since it is currently one of the largest and most readily available knowledge repositories and, more importantly, provides free, unlimited and fast query APIs[1]. Given any keyword, the Wikipedia query API will return the ranked Wikipedia entries along with the contexts containing the keyword. We set the default value 20 for k, or $len(U_f)$. Note that there could be other variations of this implementation. For example, we could rule out duplicate or very similar results in the U_f. Search engines such as Google and Bing are also potential sources since they return high quality web pages along with the contexts containing the query keyword.

In terms of scalability, the proposed method is inherently parallelizable, not only at the document level, but also a the context level, since computing CTI does not depend on any other context in the document. In addition, we do not need to issue the same query more than once. Our strategy is to locally cache the returned results of every seen query. For a new term seen in a previous query, we can directly access the local cached file. If we have built a large local pool, the queries will rarely go to a search engine or other source. Given a corpus size N (words in total), the number of actual issued queries will be at most the number of unique terms, which is far less than O(N). Of course, new terms never seen will have to be processed, but there will be fewer of these over time.

Algorithm 1: Wikipedia-based $I(t, c_i)$

Input: t, c_i
Output: $I(t, c_i)$
begin
    $I \longleftarrow 0$;
    $U_f \longleftarrow queryWikipedia(t)$;
    for $j \in range(len(U_f))$ **do**
        $s \longleftarrow \kappa(c_i, U_f[j])$;
        if $j > 0$ **then**
            $I \longleftarrow I + s/\log(j+1)$;
        else $I \longleftarrow I + s$
    return I;

4 Applications

4.1 Core Terms Extraction from Snippets

We first investigate CTI in a well defined setting. That is, if we have a collection of terms such that its most important context is a "definition," e.g. "*database*" and "*A database is a structured collection of data, which are typically organized to model relevant aspects of reality, in a way that supports*

[1] http://www.mediawiki.org/wiki/API:Query

Exemplary snippets of computer science terms	Top 5 terms ranked by CTI
Acrobat, a document exchange software from Adobe Systems, provides a platform-independent means of creating, viewing, and printing documents. Acrobat can convert a DOS, Windows, UNIX or Macintosh documents into a Portable Document Format (PDF) which can be displayed on any computer with an Acrobat reader. The Acrobat reader can be downloaded free from the Adobe website.	Acrobat:3.19 Acrobat reader:2.94 Portable Document Format:2.08 Adobe website:2.03 Adobe Systems:1.82
Data mining (DM), also known as Knowledge-Discovery in Databases (KDD) or Knowledge-Discovery and Data Mining (KDD), is the process of automatically searching large volumes of data for patterns. Data mining uses automated data analysis techniques to uncover previously undetected relationships among data items. Data mining often involves the analysis of data stored in a data warehouse. Three of the major data mining techniques are regression, classification and clustering.	data mining:3.77 data mining techniques:3.64 KDD:1.79 Knowledge-Discovery:1.66 data analysis techniques:1.20
Firefox, also known as Mozilla Firefox, is a free, open source, cross-platform, graphical web browser developed by the Mozilla Corporation and hundreds of volunteers. Firefox includes an integrated pop-up blocker, tabbed browsing, live bookmarks, support for open standards, and an extension mechanism for adding functionality. Although other browsers have some of these features, Firefox became the first such browser to include them all and achieve wide adoption.	Mozilla Firefox:3.89 firefox:3.13 web browser:2.44 browser:2.39 graphical web browser:2.35

Table 1: Term ranked by CTI from exemplary snippets

processes requiring this information", can CTI identify "database" as the most informative term in this context? To construct the term-context pairs, we could use the Wikipedia title and the top ranked context returned by searching the title using the Wikipedia API. Then we could test our metric based on other search engines such as Google or Bing. Testing manually, we found the results compare well to the search engine results, since both Google and Bing give top ranks to Wikipedia pages if the query keyword is a Wikipedia title. For further analysis, we need a collection of term-context pairs from other sources different from Wikipedia. Fortunately, we found a list of 1255 computer science terms with its definition snippets manually created by Web users [2]. The snippets are literally different from those contexts in Wikipedia and some of the terms are even not Wikipedia titles, e.g. bBlog, BetBug, etc. These can be part of an "initial" evaluation. The core term extraction algorithm works in the following steps for each term-context pair:

1. Extract all n-grams ($1 \leq n \leq 4$) in the context as candidates

2. For each candidate, calculate its CTI using Wikipedia based implementation

3. Return the top K highest CTI as core terms

We used the top 20 returned Wikipedia contexts as a featured context set U_f and apply the cosine similarity for κ. We show some exemplary snippets with its top 5 core terms and their CTI scores in Table 1. The overall performance is shown in Table 2, in terms of precision, recall and F1 scores based on the only one titled term of each snippet as the ground truth. CTI can correctly find the core term for 37.5% snippets. If we take the top 5 results, then the recall increase to 76.3%.

K	Precision (%)	Recall (%)	F1(%)
1	37.5	37.5	37.5
2	35.1	55.2	42.9
3	32.3	64.7	43.1
4	31.3	72.2	43.7
5	27.6	76.3	40.5
10	20.0	88.1	32.6

Table 2: Results on computer science term extraction from descriptive snippets

Though the algorithm can be easily parallelized, sequentially runtime on all snippets took only slightly more than a minute on a 2.35GHz Intel(R) Xeon(R) 4 processors, 23GB of RAM, and Red Hat Enterprise Linux Server(5.7) machine. However, the time could vary due to network conditions.

Though these results look promising, but it could be due to the high lexical similarity between this dataset and Wikipedia content. To test on a more general corpora, we explore more real world tasks.

4.2 Keyword Extraction

There is a rich literature on keyword extraction problem (Frank et al., 1999; Witten et al., 1999; Turney, 2000; Hulth et al., 2003; Tomokiyo and Hurst, 2003;

[2]http://www.labautopedia.org/mw/index.php/List_of_programming_and_computer_science_terms

	Wiki20			citeulike180		
Method	P	R	F	P	R	F
TFIDF	13.7	17.8	15.5	14.4	16.0	15.2
KEA	18.4	21.5	19.8	20.4	22.3	21.3
CTI	19.6	22.7	21.0	18.5	21.4	19.8

Table 3: Results on Wiki20 and citeulike180

Method	Precision (%)	Recall (%)	F1(%)
TFIDF	14.9	15.3	15.1
HUMB	27.2	27.8	27.5
CTI	19.3	20.1	19.7
CTI+	25.3	26.2	25.7

Table 4: Results on SemEval2010

Mihalcea and Tarau, 2004; Medelyan and Witten, 2008; Liu, 2010), most of which is treated as a classification or ranking problem with corresponding machine learning algorithms that use statistical and linguistic features in a corpus. Here, we consider the task as finding the most informative keywords in a document. Given a document $d = \{c_i\}$, our keyword extraction algorithm based on CTI works as follows.

1. For each context c_i in a document, compute the semantic relatedness $s(c_i, d)$ between c_i and d
2. For each n-gram ($1 \leq n \leq 4$) t in c_i, calculate $I(t, c_i)$ using Wikipedia based implementation
3. Select the top keywords with the highest $\sum_i I(t, c_i) * s(c_i, d)$

Note that for the last step keywords are selected based on a summarized weighted informativeness score over a document. Obviously, the pure cosine or Jaccard similarity is not a good choice to measure semantic relatedness between two text segments of very low lexical similarity. We thus use the Wikipedia based ESA (Gabrilovich and Markovitch, 2007) to compute the semantic relatedness $s(c_i, d)$ and $\kappa(c_i, c_j)$. To make the calculation more efficient, only the Wikipedia pages whose title is contained in the dataset are used to build the concept space. We ran the algorithm on several datasets including Wiki20 (Medelyan et al., 2008), citeulike180 (Medelyan et al., 2009) and SemEval2010 (Kim et al., 2010) [3].

Though keyword extraction as a research topic has a rich literature, to the best of our knowledge there is no large scale datasets publicly available. The Wiki20 dataset contains 20 computer science articles each with around 5 terms labeled by 15 different teams. Every term is a Wikipedia title. The citeulike180 contains a set of 180 papers each tagged with around three tags by 332 users. For each dataset, the collection of all labeled keywords by different taggers are considered as the gold standard for a document. We use the set of all keywords for evaluation; otherwise a more complicated evaluation metrics for each dataset will be needed. It would be better to investigate other weighting schemes. However, the datasets here are relatively small and the number of tags on which at least two annotators agreed is significantly small; weighting the keywords might not make too much difference. KEA [4] builds a Naive Bayes model using features TFIDF, first occurrence, length of a phrase, and node degree (number of candidates that are semantically related to this phrase) (Witten et al., 1999). First occurrence is computed as the percentage of the document preceding the first occurrence of the term in the document. We compute the node degree as the textrank (Mihalcea and Tarau, 2004) degree in a document by simply relating two candidate terms with each other if they are in the same context. KEA uses 5 fold cross validation. All precision P, recall R and F1 F results are over the top 10 candidate keywords and the micro-averaged results of the first two datasets are shown in Table 3. The CTI-based algorithm works better than KEA on Wiki20 but slightly worse on citeulike180. We argue that the reason might be two-fold. First, CTI does not use any inter-document or corpus information while KEA learns from the corpus. As such, CTI might not perform as well as supervised learning methods for a domain dependent large corpus. Second, the labeled keywords in Wiki20 are all Wikipedia titles while those in citeulike are general tags labeled by voluntary web users. CTI would give more preference to Wikipedia titles since their featured context set returned from Wikipedia is more semantically representative than other non-Wikipedia title words.

[3] http://code.google.com/p/maui-indexer/downloads/list

[4] http://www.nzdl.org/Kea/

Dataset	#Books	#Words	#Contexts	Main domains
Gutenberg	55	7,164,463	301,581	History, Art, Psychology, Philosophy, Literature, Zoology
Open Book	213	22,279,530	1,135,919	Computer Science, Engineering, Information Science

Table 5: Datasets for book index generation evaluation

The SemEval2010 dataset contains a set of 284 scientific papers with 15 keyphrases assigned by readers and authors. 144 of them are selected as training set while the other 100 are for testing. A comparison of CTI to the results from TFIDF and the best reported results HUMB (Lopez and Romary, 2010) is shown in Table 4. It achieves 19.8% by micro-averaged F1 score, ranking 11th out of the 19 systems submitted to the competition (Kim et al., 2010). However, by adding the structural features used by HUMB into CTI, we can improve the performance by around 6%, making our results close to that of HUMB. The structural information is encoded as weights for context that is located in title, abstract, section titles and general content. Each weight can be regarded as the prior probability that a keyword will appear in the corresponding location, whose value can be set according to the fraction of the number of keyword occurrences of this type of location with respect to the number of all keyword occurrences in the entire training set. Here they are set to be 0.3, 0.4, 0.25, and 0.05.

4.3 Back-of-the-book Index Generation

A back-of-the-book index (or book index) is a collection of words or phrases, often alphabetically arranged as an index, created to give readers important location of important information in a given book. Usually indexing is done by freelancers hired by authors or publishers, namely professional indexers [5]. Csomai and Mihalcea first evaluated the performance of different informativeness measurements for selecting book index terms (2007) and then investigated automatic book index generation in a supervised learning framework (2008) using syntactic features, linguistical features, encyclopedic features, etc., as a keyword extraction problem rather than building a actual book index.

A set of keywords is not a back-of-the-book index. What really matters for such an index is that an index term or phrase points to its proper location in the text. For example, in "pattern recognition and machine learning" by Bishop, "hidden Markov model" appears in more than 20 pages while the actual index entry has only 2 pages as its locators. Thus the actual problem is to identify a index term with its context. As such, learning a robust and efficient model for real book indexes is challenging. First, books from different domains vary in vocabulary composition and structure style, requiring various indexing specialties. There are different indexing guides for medicine (Wyman, 1999), psychology (Hornyak, 2002), and law (Kendrick and Zafran, 2001). Second, book indexing is a highly subjective work and indexes of different books are always created by different professional indexers who have their own preferences and background (Diodato and Gandt, 1991; Diodato, 1994). Third, the training set is extremely unbalanced. As we found in our dataset, the index size is only 0.42% of the length of book on average. All these motivate us to explore the automatic creation of index terms that are aware of the context at the term's locations (locators). To do so we propose the following efficient training-free and domain independent approach:

1. For each context c_i in a book, compute its weight w_i based on structural features
2. For each candidate term t in c_i, calculate $I(t, c_i)$ using Wikipedia based implementation
3. Select term-context pairs with the highest $w_i * I(t, c_i)$ as index entries

The weight in step 1 represents the relative importance of a context in a book. $w(c) = 1 - \frac{c_{id}(c) - c_{id}(title_c)}{N_{title_c}}$ measures the weight based on the normalized distance from the context to its direct chapter or sub-chapter title, where $c_{id}(c)$ denotes the id of context c, $title_c$ the title of context c and N_{title_c} the number of contexts under $title_c$. To select candidate terms, we first filter the improbable index terms

[5] http://www.asindexing.org/

based on POS patterns using the Standard POS Tagger (Toutanova et al., 2003). We then select multi-word keyphrases based on Pointwise Mutual Information (PMI) (Church and Hanks, 1990), which was shown to be the best metric to measure word associations (Terra and Clarke, 2003).

To evaluate our back-of-the-book index generation method, we conduct extensive experiments on books in various domains, from the Gutenberg dataset and the open book dataset described in Table 5. The first one was created by (Csomai and Mihalcea, 2006), containing 55 free books collected from Gutenburg[6]. Since the dataset does not provide the locators of index terms, we can only serve the evaluation as a keyword extraction task. The second dataset was collected from CiteSeer repository, most of which are in computer science and engineering. We extracted the paged body text and the back index using Pdfbox[7]. Having each index term associated with its locators (page numbers), we can perform an evaluation for different methods, not based solely on keyword extraction.

We first compare CTI with other metrics on both datasets for keywords extraction since all other metrics are context-oblivious. CTI selects index terms based on the sum of a term's CTI scores over all its contexts, the same as the algorithm used in Section 4.2. The results are shown in Table 6, where the index size = n indicates the number of output terms is n times of the true book index size for each book. The scores are the average recall over a dataset. The CTI outperforms all other 7 metrics in the two datasets as the output index size increases. Moreover, results show that TF and TFIDF are better than RIDF in identifying book index terms, which seems contradictory to previous findings (Church and Gale, 1995). A possible reason is that a book is much longer than a regular document thus enhancing TF as a better indicator of keywords but weakening the role of IDF. We believe this is why *Variance*, *Gain*, and *Burstiness*, which relies on DF, are less effective here. *Wikipedia keyphraseness* (Csomai and Mihalcea, 2008) can only find a small fraction of index terms because it emphasizes Wikipedia titles that have high in-degree in hyper-link network formed

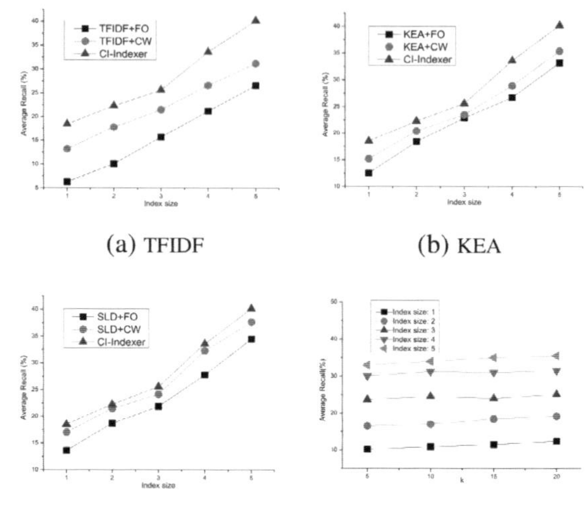

(a) TFIDF (b) KEA

(c) SLD (d) size of featured context set

Figure 1: Results for book index generation

by Wikipedia terms. However, a book index covers much broader terms not titled in Wikipedia.

We then compare with three baselines TFIDF, KEA, and SLD (supervised learning using decision tree in Csomai's (2008)) on the second dataset. For SLD, we use all the features except the discourse comprehension based ones which were too complicate to implement. We choose a decision tree because its training is much faster than the other two models while its performance is quite close to the best. We follow Csomai's setting to choose 90%(192) books for training and the other 10%(21) for test. We set two strategies to make the baselines context-aware. First, we select the page of a term's first occurrence as its locator, denoted by "+FO" in Figure 1. Second, we apply the context weight to them, denoted by "+CW". "CI-Indexer" denotes our method. The results are shown in Figure 1a, 1b and 1c respectively. For all the three baselines, adding context weight gives better performance than using the simple first occurrence guess, especially for TFIDF. KEA benefits least from the context weights, suggesting its first occurrence and node degree features play a similar role as the context weight features. SLD outperforms TFIDF and KEA under both strategies probably because of the new features of POS pattern and Wikipedia keyphraseness. "SLD+CW" is the closest to ours. Finally, we show in Figure 1d that increasing the size of featured context set for CTI from 5 to 20 can slightly improve

[6]www.gutenberg.org/

[7]pdfbox.apache.org/

Dataset	Open book dataset					Gutenberg dataset				
Index size	1	2	3	4	5	1	2	3	4	5
Variance	2.4	4.8	7.5	10.4	13.4	1.1	2.9	5.3	8.0	11.0
Gain	2.9	6.4	10.2	14.3	18.2	4.9	9.0	14	18.6	23.0
Wikipedia keyphraseness	5.3	9.5	13.5	16.4	20.5	9.2	14.1	18.5	21.4	24.3
Burstiness	6.0	11.4	16.6	21.4	25.8	10.0	15.8	20.2	23.1	26.2
RIDF	8.6	14.5	19.5	23.9	28.0	10.4	15.9	20.1	23.2	26.3
TF	9.8	16.9	23.3	29.0	31.7	10.4	17.6	23.5	28.1	30.7
TFIDF	10.3	17.3	23.8	29.3	33.6	11.8	19.9	24.7	28.9	32.9
CTI	**12.4**	**19.2**	**25.1**	**31.5**	**35.5**	**14.9**	**22.3**	**26.9**	**29.3**	**34.5**

Table 6: Average recall(%) comparisons as the output index size increases

performance in different index size settings.

4.4 Discussion

The three applications are (incrementally) designed for different goals. The first is a toy application to show the potential capability of this approach, regardless of syntactic or statistical information. Clearly, there are simple heuristics that can work very well for this task, e.g. the first term of the context. TF or TFIDF also performs quite well. We can rewrite each context (by reordering the terms, changing sentence structures, or substituting the core terms with pronouns) to make them ineffective. However, this will not effect our method, because what it essentially measures is a term's informativeness among a list of terms appearing in the same context. However, for keyword extraction, a topic with a rich literature, to the best of our knowledge, has no publicly available large scale datasets, which makes SemEval2010 the best available. We believe our application on back-of-the-book index generation showed how CTI can scale real world large corpora and will scale to millions of books since each book can be processed separately.

Based on the applications we explored, we can see that the practical utility of CTI used alone could be limited, especially for context-oblivious tasks. It seems reasonable that this method does not outperform supervised learning methods designed for keyword extraction. However, our method shows what simple but elegant methods can achieve without the overhead of machine learning, especially for context-aware scenarios such as finding book index terms.

5 Conclusion and Future Work

We developed a new web knowledge based method for encoding informativeness of terms within a unit of discourse. It is totally feature-free, corpus-free, easy to implement, and inherently parallelizable. Three typical applications on text snippets, scientific papers and non-fiction books show its effectiveness. The segmentation of context, the size of featured context set, the semantic relatedness metric κ, and the knowledge base might more or less affect the final performance of CTI in terms of accuracy or efficiency. For all applications, we treat a paragraph as an individual context, which is not necessary a complete discourse unit. However, it may not be fair to set the same number for all context terms. In addition, selection of semantic relatedness and knowledge bases need further investigation. The Wikipedia-based implementation might be a good choice for the definitional snippets, scientific articles and text books since they are all "educational" resources sharing a similar concept space. However, it is an open question as whether it works for corpora such as tweets, online reviews, and forum posts.

Based on the proposed methods and encouraging results, it would be interesting to build an online indexing tool which automatically finds informative terms in generic text and generates a back-of-the-book index for a sets of papers, books, theses and other collections.

6 Acknowledgments

We gratefully acknowledge partial support from the National Science Foundation and useful comments from referees.

References

E. Agirre, E. Alfonseca, K. Hall, J. Kravalova, M. Pasca, and A. Soroa. 2009. A study on similarity and relatedness using distributional and WordNet-based approaches. In *Proceedings of NAACL-HLT* 2009, pp. 19–27.

A. Bookstein and Don R. Swanson. 1974. Probabilistic models for automatic indexing. *Journal of the American Society for Information Science*, 25(5):312–316.

A. Budanitsky and G. Hirst. 2012. Evaluating WordNet-based measures of semantic distance. *Computational Linguistics* 32:13–47.

K. W. Church and W. A. Gale. 1995. Inverse document frequency(IDF): A measure of deviation from poisson. In *Proceedings of the Third Workshop on Very Large Corpora* 1995, pp. 121–130.

K. W. Church and P. Hanks. 1990. Word association norms, mutual information and lexicography. *Computational Linguistics*, 16:22–29.

Rudi L. Cilibrasi and Paul M.B. Vitanyi. 2007. The Google similarity distance. *IEEE Transaction on Knowledge and Data Engineering*, 19(3):370–383.

A. Csomai and R. Mihalcea. 2006. Creating a testbed for the evaluation of automatically generated back-of-the-book indexes. In *Proceedings of the 7th international conference on Computational Linguistics and Intelligent Text Processing* 2006, pp. 429–440.

A. Csomai and R. Mihalcea. 2007. Investigations in unsupervised back-of-the-book indexing. In *Proceedings of the Florida Artificial Intelligence Research Society* 2007, pp. 211–216.

A. Csomai and R. Mihalcea. 2008. Linguistically Motivated Features for Enhanced Back-of-the-Book Indexing. In *Proceedings of ACL* 2008, pp. 932–940.

S. Deerwester, S. T. Dumais, G. W. Furnas, T. K. Landauer, and R. Harshman. 1990. Indexing by Latent Semantic Analysis. *Journal of the American Society for Information Science* 41:391-407.

V. Diodato and G. Gandt. 1991. Back of book indexes and the characteristics of author and nonauthor indexing: Report of an exploratory study. *Journal of the American Society for Information Science*, 42:341–350.

V. Diodato. 1994. User preferences for features in back of book indexes. *Journal of the American Society for Information Science*, 45:529–536.

E. Frank, G. W. Paynter, I. H. Witten, and C. Gutwin. 1999 Domainspecic keyphrase extraction. In *Proceedings IJCAI* 1999, pp. 668-673.

E. Gabrilovich and S. Markovitch. 2007. Computing semantic relatedness using Wikipedia-based explicit semantic analysis. In *Proceedings of IJCAI* 2007, pp. 6–12.

Q. He, J. Pei, D. Kifer, P. Mitra, and C. L. Giles. 2010. Context-aware citation recommendation. In *Proceedings of WWW* 2010, pp. 421–430.

B. Hornyak. 2002. Indexing Specialties: Psychology. Medford, NJ : Information Today, Inc.

A. Hulth. 2003. Improved automatic keyword extraction given more linguistic knowledge. In *Proceedings of EMNLP* 2003, pp. 216-223.

Karen Sprck Jones. 1972. A statistical interpretation of term specificity and its application in retrieval. *Journal of Documentation*, 28(1):11–21.

Karen Sprck Jones. 1973. Index term weighting. *Information Storage and Retrieval*, 9(11):619–633.

P. Kendrick and E. L. Zafran. 2001. Indexing Specialties: Law. Medford, NJ : Information Today, Inc.

Su Nam Kim, Olena Medelyan, Min-Yen Kan, and Timothy Baldwin. 2010. Semeval-2010 task 5 : Automatic keyphrase extraction from scientic articles. In *Proceedings of the 5th SIGLEX Workshop on Semantic Evaluation.* 2010, pp. 21–26.

K. Kireyev. 2009. Semantic-based Estimation of Term Informativeness. In *Proceedings of NAACL-HLT* 2009, pp. 530–538.

Z. Liu, W. Huang, Y. Zheng, and M. Sun. 2010. Automatic keyphrase extraction via topic decomposition. In *Proceedings of EMNLP* 2010, pp. 366–376.

P. Lopez and L. Romary. 2010. HUMB: Automatic Key Term Extraction from Scientic Articles in GROBID. In *Proceedings of the 5th SIGLEX Workshop on Semantic Evaluation.* 2010, pp. 248-251.

O. Medelyan and I. H. Witten. 2008. Domain-independent automatic keyphrase indexing with small training sets. *J. Am. Soc. Inf. Sci. Technol.* 59:1026-1040.

O. Medelyan, I. H. Witten, and D. Milne. 2008. Topic indexing with Wikipedia. In *Proceedings of AAAI08 Workshop on Wikipedia and Artificial Intelligence: an Evolving Synergy* 2008, pp. 19–24.

O. Medelyan, E. Frank, and I. H. Witten. 2009. Human-competitive tagging using automatic keyphrase extraction. In *Proceedings of EMNLP* 2009, pp. 1318–1327.

R. Mihalcea and P. Tarau. 2004. TextRank: Bringing Order into Texts. In *Proceedings of EMNLP* 2004, pp. 404-411.

L. Page, S. Brin, R. Motwani, and T. Winograd. 1998. The PageRank Citation Ranking: Bringing Order to the Web. *Technical Report.* Stanford InfoLab.

K. Papineni. 2001. Why inverse document frequency? In *Proceedings of NAACL-HLT* 2001, pp. 1–8.

J. D. M. Rennie, and T. Jaakkola. 2005. Using Term Informativeness for Named Entity Detection. In *Proceedings of SIGIR* 2005, pp. 353–360.

G. Salton, and C. Buckley. 1988. Term-weighting approaches in automatic text retrieval. *Information Processing & Management* 24(5):513–523.

R. Soricut and D. Marcu. 2003. Sentence level discourse parsing using syntactic and lexical information. In *Proceedings of NAACL-HLT* 2003, pp. 149–156.

E. Terra and C. L. Clarke. 2003. Frequency estimates for statistical word similarity measures. In *Proceedings of NAACL-HLT* 2003, pp. 165–172.

T. Tomokiyo and M. Hurst. 2003. A language model approach to keyphrase extraction. In *Proceedings of the ACL 2003 workshop on Multiword expressions: analysis, acquisition and treatment*, 2003, pp. 3340.

K. Toutanova, D. Klein, C. Manning, and Y. Singer. 2003. Feature-Rich Part-of-Speech Tagging with a Cyclic Dependency Network. In *Proceedings of NAACL-HLT* 2003, pp. 252-259.

P. D. Turney. 2000. Learning Algorithms for Keyphrae Extraction. *Information Retrieval* 2:303-336.

I. H. Witten, G. W. Paynter, E. Frank, C. Gutwin, and C. G. Nevill-Manning. 1999. Kea: practical automatic keyphrase extraction. In *Proceedings of the fourth ACM conference on Digital libraries*, 1999, pp. 254–255.

L. P. Wyman. 1999. Indexing Specialities: Medicine. Medford, NJ : Information Today, Inc.

M. Yazdani and A. Popescu-Belis. 2012. Computing text semantic relatedness using the contents and links of a hypertext encyclopedia. *Artificial Intelligence* 194:176–202.

J. Zobel and A. Moffat. 1998. Exploring the similarity space. *ACM SIGIR Forum* 32(1):18–34.

Le Zhao and Jamie Callan. 2010. Term necessity prediction. In *Proceedings of the 19th ACM international conference on Information and knowledge management*, 2010, pp. 259–268.

Hui Yang and Jamie Callan. 2009. A metric-based framework for automatic taxonomy induction. In *Proceedings of the ACL*, 2009, pp. 271–279 .

Unsupervised Learning Summarization Templates from Concise Summaries

Horacio Saggion*
Universitat Pompeu Fabra
Department of Information and Communication Technologies
TALN Group
C/Tanger 122 - Campus de la Comunicación
Barcelona - 08018
Spain
http://www.dtic.upf.edu/~hsaggion/

Abstract

We here present and compare two unsupervised approaches for inducing the main conceptual information in rather stereotypical summaries in two different languages. We evaluate the two approaches in two different information extraction settings: monolingual and cross-lingual information extraction. The extraction systems are trained on auto-annotated summaries (containing the induced concepts) and evaluated on human-annotated documents. Extraction results are promising, being close in performance to those achieved when the system is trained on human-annotated summaries.

1 Introduction

Information Extraction (Piskorski and Yangarber, 2013) and Automatic Text Summarization (Saggion and Poibeau, 2013) are two Natural Language Processing tasks which require domain and language adaptation. For over two decades (Riloff, 1993; Riloff, 1996) the natural language processing community has been interested in automatic or semi-automatic methods which could be used to port systems from one domain or task to another, aiming at reducing at least in part the cost associated with the creation of human annotated datasets. Automatic system adaptation can take different forms: if high quality human annotated data is available, then rule-based or statistical systems can be trained on this data (Brill, 1994), reducing the efforts of writing rules and handcrafting dictionaries. If high quality human annotated data is unavailable, a large non-annotated corpus and a bootstrapping procedure can be used to produce annotated data (Ciravegna and Wilks, 2003; Yangarber, 2003). Here, we concentrate on developing and evaluating automatic procedures to learn the *main concepts of a domain* and at the same time *auto-annotate texts* so that they become available for training information extraction or text summarization applications. However, it would be naive to think that in the current state of the art we would be able to learn all knowledge from text automatically (Poon and Domingos, 2010; Biemann, 2005; Buitelaar and Magnini, 2005). We therefore here concentrate on learning template-like representations from concise event summaries which should contain the key information of an event.

18 de julio de 1994$_{DateOfAttack}$. Un atentado contra la **sede de la Asociación Mutual Israelita Argentina**$_{Target}$ de **Buenos Aires**$_{PlaceOfAttack}$ causa la muerte de **86**$_{NumberOfVictims}$ personas.
(18th July 1994. An attack against the headquarters of the Jewish Mutual Association in Buenos Aires, Argentina, kills 86 people.)

Figure 1: Sample of Human Annotated Summary in Spanish

An example of the summaries we want to learn from is presented in Figure 1. It is a summary in the terrorist attack domain in Spanish. It has been

*This work is partially supported by Ministerio de Economía y Competitividad, Secretaría de Estado de Investigación, Desarrollo e Innovación, Spain under project number TIN2012-38584-C06-03 and Advanced Research Fellowship RYC-2009-04291. We thank Biljana Drndarević for proofreading the paper.

manually annotated with concepts such as DateOfAttack, Target, PlaceOfAttack, and NumberOfVictims, which are key in the domain. Our task is to discover from this kind of summary what the concepts are and how to recognise them automatically. As will be shown in this paper and unlike current approaches (Chambers and Jurafsky, 2011; Leung et al., 2011), the methods to be presented here do not require parsing or semantic dictionaries to work or specification of the underlying number of concepts in the domain to be learn. The approach we take learns concepts in the set of domain summaries, relying on noun phrase contextual information. They are able to generate reasonable domain conceptualizations from relatively small datasets and in different languages.

The rest of the paper is structured as follows: In Section 2 we overview related work in the area of concept induction from text. Next, in Section 3 we describe the dataset used and how we have processed it while in Section 4 we outline the two unsupervised learning algorithms we compare in this paper for template induction from text. Then, in Section 5, we describe the experiments on template induction indicating how we have instantiated the algorithms and in Section 6 we explain how we have extrinsically evaluated the induction process. In Section 7 we discuss the obtained results and in Section 8 we summarize our findings and close the paper.

2 Related Work

A long standing issue in natural language processing is how to learn conceptualizations from text in automatic or semi-automatic ways. The availability of redundant data has been used, for example, to discover template-like representations (Barzilay and Lee, 2003) or sentence-level paraphrases which could be used for extraction or generation. Various approaches to concept learning use clustering techniques. (Leung et al., 2011) apply various clustering procedures to learn a small number of slots in three typical information extraction domains, using manually annotated data and fixing the number of concepts to be learnt. (Li et al., 2010) generate templates and extraction patterns for specific entity types (actors, companies, etc.). (Chambers and Jurafsky, 2011) learn the structure of MUC templates from raw data in English, an approach that needs both full parsing and semantic interpretation using WordNet (Fellbaum, 1998) in order to extract verb arguments and measure the similarity betweern verbs. In (Saggion, 2012) an iterative learning procedure is used to discover core domain conceptual information from short summaries in two languages. However, the obtained results were not assessed in a real information extraction scenario. There are approaches which do not need any human intervention or sophisticated text processing, but learn based on redundancy of the input dataset and some well grounded linguistic intuitions (Banko and Etzioni, 2008; Etzioni et al., 2004). Related to the work presented here are approaches that aim at generating short stereotypical summaries (DeJong, 1982; Paice and Jones, 1993; Ratnaparkhi, 2000; Saggion and Lapalme, 2002; Konstas and Lapata, 2012).

3 Dataset and Text Processing Steps

For the experiments reported here we rely on the CONCISUS corpus[1] (Saggion and Szasz, 2012) which is distributed free of charge. It is a corpus of Web summaries in Spanish and English in four different application domains: Aviation Accidents (32 English, 32 Spanish), Earthquakes (44 English, 56 Spanish), Train Accidents (36 English, 43 Spanish), and Terrorist Attacks (42 English, 53 Spanish). The dataset contains original and comparable summary pairs, automatic translations of Spanish summaries into English, automatic translation of English summaries into Spanish, and associated original full documents in Spanish and English for two of the domains (Aviation Accidents and Earthquakes). The dataset comes with human annotations representing the key information in each domain. In Table 1 we detail the concepts used in each of the domains. Note that not all concepts are represented in each of the summaries. Creation of such a dataset can take up to 500 hours for a human annotator, considering data collection, cleansing, and annotation proper. Only one human annotator and one curator were responsible for the annotation process.

[1] http://www.taln.upf.edu/pages/concisus/.

Aviation Accident	Airline, Cause, DateOfAccident, Destination, FlightNumber, NumberOfVictims, Origin, Passengers, Place, Survivors, Crew, TypeOfAccident, TypeOfAircraft, Year
Earthquake	City, Country, DateOfEarthquake, Depth, Duration, Epicentre, Fatalities, Homeless, Injured, Magnitude, OtherPlacesAffected, Province, Region, Survivors, TimeOfEarthquake
Terrorist Attack	City, Country, DateOfAccident, Fatalities, Injured, Target, Perpetrator, Place, NumberOfVictims, TypeOfAttack
Train Accident	Cause, DateOfAccident, Destination, NumberOfVictims, Origin, Passenger, Place, Survivors, TypeOfAccident, TypeOfTrain

Table 1: Conceptual Information in Summaries

3.1 Text Processing

In order to carry out experimentation we adopt the GATE infrastructure for document representation and annotation (Maynard et al., 2002). All documents in the dataset are processed with available natural language processors to compute shallow lingustic information. Documents in English are processed with the ANNIE system, a morphological analyzer, and a noun chunker, all three from GATE. The documents in Spanish are analyzed with TreeTagger (Schmid, 1995), a rule-base noun chunker, and an SVM-based named entity recognition and classification system.

4 Concept Induction Algorithms

Two algorithms are used to induce conceptual information in a domain from a set of textual summaries. The algorithms form concepts based on target strings (or chunks) in the set of summaries using token-level linguistic information. The chunks are represented with different features which are explained later in Section 5.1. One algorithm we use is based on *clustering*, while the other is based on *iterative learning*.

4.1 Clustering-based Induction

The procedure for learning conceptual information by clustering is straithforward: the chunks in the set of summaries are represented as instances considering both internal and sourrounding linguistic information. These instances are the input to a clustering procedure which returns a list of clusters each containing a set of chunks. We consider each cluster as a key concept in the set of domain summaries and the chunks in each cluster as the concept extension.

4.2 Iterative Induction

We use the iterative learning algorithm described in (Saggion, 2012) which learns from a set of summaries S, also annotated with target strings (e.g. chunks) and shallow linguistic information. In a nutshell the algorithm is as follows:

(1) Choose a document D from the set of summaries S and add it to a training set TRAIN. Set REST to S − TRAIN.

(2) Choose an available target concept T from D, i.e. a target concept not tried before by the algorithm.

(3) Train a classifier on TRAIN to learn instances of the target concept using the available linguistic features; the classifier uses the linguistic information provided.

(4) Apply the classifier to REST (all summaries minus those in TRAIN) to annotate all instances of the target concept T.

(5) Select a document BEST in REST, where there is an instance of the concept recognised with the highest probability in the REST set.

(6) Remove BEST from REST and add BEST to the training set, remove all identified instances of T from REST, and go to step 3.

The algorithm is executed a number of times (see Section 5.1 for parametrization of the algorithms) to learn all concepts in the set of summaries, and at each iteration a single concept is formed. There are two circumstances when a concept being formed is discarded and their associated initial target concept removed from the learning process: one case is when there are not enough occurrences of the concept across a set of summaries; another case is when too many identical strings are proposed as instances for the concept in the set of summaries. This latter restriction is only valid if we consider sets of non-redundant documents, which is the case to which we restrict our experiments.

4.3 Text Chunks

Given that the algorithms presented above try to induce a concept from the chunks in the summaries, we are interested in assessing how the type of chunk influences the learning process. Also, given that our objective is to test methods which learn with minimal human intervention, we are interested in investigating differences between the use of manual and automatic chunks. We therefore use the following chunk types in this work: *gold chunks (gold)* are the human produced annotations (as in Figure 1); *named entity chunks (ne)* are named entities computed by an off-the-shelf named entity recognizer; *noun chunks (nc)* are text chunks identified by rule-based off-the-shelf NP chunkers and finally, *wiki chunks (wiki)* are strings of text in the summaries which happen to be Wikipedia titles.

In order to automatically compute these chunk types, different levels of knowledge are needed. For example, NP chunks require syntactic information, while named entities and wiki chunks require some external form of knowledge, such as precompiled gazetteer lists or access to an encyclopædia or a semantic dictionary. Named entities and noun chunks are computed as described in Section 3, while wiki chunks are computed as follows: string n-grams $w_1 w_2 \ldots w_n$ are computed in each summary and strings $w_1\_w_2\_\ldots\_w_n$ are checked against the Wikipedia on-line encyclopædia, if a hit occurs (i.e. if for an English n-gram the page en.wikipedia.org/wiki/$w_1\ldots\_w_n$ exists or for a Spanish n-gram the page es.wikipedia.org/wiki/$w_1\ldots\_w_n$ exists), the n-gram is annotated in the summary as a wiki chunk. Wiki chunks are cached to speed up the automatic annotation process.

	P	R	F
Spanish			
Terrorist Attack	0.47	0.10	0.17
Aviation Accident	0.52	0.08	0.14
Earthquake	0.24	0.06	0.10
Train Accident	0.59	0.15	0.24
English			
Terrorist Attack	0.46	0.39	0.42
Aviation Accident	0.40	0.27	0.32
Earthquake	0.27	0.22	0.24
Train Accident	0.57	0.27	0.36

Table 2: Baseline Induction Performance

4.4 Mapping the Induced Concepts onto Human Concepts

For evaluation purposes, each induced concept is mapped onto one human concept applying the following procedure: let HC_i be the set of summary offsets where human concept i occurs, and let IC_i be the set of summary offsets where automatic concept i occurs, then the induced concept j is mapped onto concept k such that: $k = \arg\max_i(|\mathrm{HC}_i \cap \mathrm{IC}_j|)$, where $|X|$ is the size of set X. That is, the induced concept is mapped onto the label it gives it a best match. As an example, one induced concept in the terrorist attack domain containing the following string instances: *two bombs*, *car bomb*, *pair of bombs*, *10 coordinated shooting and bombing*, *two car bombs*, *suicide bomb*, *the attack*, *guerrilla warfare*, *the coca-growing regions*, etc. This induced concept is mapped onto the TypeOfAttack human concept in that domain.

4.5 Baseline Concept Induction

A baseline induction mechanism is designed for comparison with the two learning procedures proposed here. It is based on the mapping of named entity chunks onto concepts in a straightforward way: each named entity type is considered a different concept and therefore mapped onto human concepts as in Section 4.4. For example, in the terrorist attack domain, *Organization* named entity type is mapped by this procedure onto the human concept Target (i.e. churches, government buildings, etc., are common targets in terrorist attacks) while in the Aviation Accident domain the *Organization* named entity type is mapped onto TypeOfAircraft (i.e. Boeing, Airbus, etc. are names of organizations).

5 Experimental Setting and Results of the Induction Process

In this section we detail the different parameters used by the algorithms and report the performance of the induction process with different inputs.

5.1 Settings

The features used by the induction procedure are extracted from the text tokens. We extract the POS tag, root, and string of each token. The clustering-based algorithm uses a standard Expectation Maximization

	Spanish					
	Iterative			Clustering		
	P	R	F	P	R	F
Terrorist Attack	0.25	0.59	0.35	0.59	0.59	0.59†
Aviation Accident	0.50	0.62	0.55	0.66	0.66	0.66†
Earthquake	0.34	0.51	0.41	0.56	0.53	0.55†
Train Accident	0.41	0.69	0.52	0.58	0.58	0.58
	English					
	Iterative			Clustering		
	P	R	F	P	R	F
Terrorist Attack	0.23	0.39	0.29	0.50	0.50	0.50†
Aviation Accident	0.57	0.68	0.62	0.79	0.79	0.79†
Earthquake	0.26	0.53	0.34	0.39	0.39	0.39
Train Accident	0.50	0.59	0.54	0.61	0.61	0.61†

Table 3: Conceptual induction (Spanish and English) Using Gold Chunks for Learning

implementation from the Weka machine learning library (Witten and Frank, 1999). We instruct the algorithm to decide on the number of clusters based on the data, instead of setting the number of clusters by hand. The instances to cluster are representations of the input chunks; these representations contain the internal features of the chunks, as well as the information of 5 tokens to the left of the beginning of the chunk and 5 tokens to the right of the end of the chunk. The transformation from GATE documents into arff Weka files and the mapping from Weka onto the GATE documents, is carried out using specific programs. The classification algorithm used for the iterative learning process is an SVM classifier distributed with the GATE system and tuned to perform chunk learning using the same features as the clustering procedure (Li et al., 2004). This classifier outputs a probability which we use for selecting the best document at step (5) of the iterative procedure. The document selected to start the process is the one with more target strings, and the target string chosen is the next available in textual order. The iterative learning procedure is set to stop when the number of concepts induced reaches the average number of chunks in the corpus. Induced concepts not covering at least 10% of the number of documents are discarded, as are concepts with strings repeated at least 10% of the concept extension.

5.2 Experiments and Results

We carry out a number of experiments per domain where we run the algorithms using as input the summaries annotated with a different chunk type each time. After each experiment all concepts induced are

	Terrorist Attacks					
	Iterative			Clustering		
	P	R	F	P	R	F
nc	0.22	0.53	0.31†	0.15	0.51	0.23
ne	0.27	0.14	0.18	0.12	0.42	0.18
wiki	0.15	0.26	0.19	0.22	0.18	0.20
all	0.25	0.53	0.34†	0.12	0.51	0.20
	Aviation Accidents					
	Iterative			Clustering		
	P	R	F	P	R	F
nc	0.30	0.50	0.38†	0.21	0.51	0.30
ne	0.84	0.07	0.14	0.57	0.07	0.13
wiki	0.29	0.28	0.28†	0.27	0.17	0.21
all	0.39	0.62	0.48†	0.16	0.31	0.21
	Earthquakes					
	Iterative			Clustering		
	P	R	F	P	R	F
nc	0.29	0.42	0.34†	0.14	0.42	0.21
ne	0.20	0.19	0.20†	0.38	0.02	0.05
wiki	0.16	0.16	0.16	0.24	0.11	0.15
all	0.28	0.50	0.36†	0.12	0.46	0.19
	Train Accidents					
	Iterative			Clustering		
	P	R	F	P	R	F
nc	0.36	0.66	0.47†	0.23	0.51	0.32
ne	0.33	0.66	0.44†	0.65	0.12	0.20
wiki	0.25	0.25	0.25	0.51	0.13	0.21
all	0.33	0.62	0.44†	0.16	0.50	0.24

Table 4: Comparison of conceptual induction in Spanish

mapped onto the human concepts (see Section 4.4) producing auto-annotated summaries. The automatic annotations are then compared with the gold annotations, and precision, recall, and f-score figures are computed to observe the performance of the two algorithms, the baseline, and the effect of type of chunk on the learning process.

In Table 2 we report baseline performance on the entire dataset. As can be appreciated by the obtained numbers, directly mapping named entity types onto concepts does not provide a very good performance, especially for Spanish; we expected the learning procedures to produce better results. In Table 3 we present the results of inducing concepts from the gold chunks by the two algorithms. In almost all cases, using gold chunks improves over the baseline procedure, except for the Terrorist Attack domain in English, where the iterative learning procedure underperforms the baseline. In all tested domains, the clustering-based induction procedure has a very competitive performance. A t-test is run to verify differences in performance between the two systems in terms of f-score. In all tested domains in Spanish, except the Train Accident domain, there are sta-

	Terrorist Attacks					
	Iterative			Clustering		
	P	R	F	P	R	F
nc	0.43	0.50	0.46†	0.23	0.42	0.30
ne	0.28	0.44	0.34	0.42	0.29	0.34
wiki	0.24	0.33	0.28†	0.15	0.25	0.19
all	0.31	0.49	0.38†	0.09	0.39	0.15
	Aviation Accidents					
	Iterative			**Clustering**		
	P	R	F	P	R	F
nc	0.48	0.31	0.38	0.33	0.34	0.34
ne	0.53	0.38	0.44†	0.63	0.27	0.38
wiki	0.31	0.44	0.36†	0.28	0.37	0.32
all	0.50	0.67	0.58†	0.15	0.47	0.23
	Earthquakes					
	Iterative			**Clustering**		
	P	R	F	P	R	F
nc	0.29	0.48	0.36†	0.06	0.40	0.10
ne	0.28	0.34	0.30	0.30	0.25	0.28
wiki	0.21	0.30	0.25†	0.16	0.23	0.19
all	0.31	0.44	0.37†	0.08	0.40	0.13
	Train Accidents					
	Iterative			**Clustering**		
	P	R	F	P	R	F
nc	0.45	0.54	0.49†	0.32	0.50	0.39
ne	0.47	0.29	0.36	0.58	0.27	0.36
wiki	0.51	0.32	0.39†	0.30	0.29	0.29
all	0.50	0.58	0.53†	0.16	0.49	0.24

Table 5: Comparison of conceptual induction in English

	Spanish		
	P	R	F
Aviation Accident	0.83	0.60	0.70
Earthquake	0.61	0.48	0.53
Train Accident	0.77	0.54	0.64
	English		
	P	R	F
Aviation Accident	0.88	0.38	0.53
Earthquake	0.86	0.56	0.68
Train Accident	0.84	0.43	0.57

Table 6: Cross-lingual Information Extraction. System Trained with Gold Summaries.

	Aviation Accidents					
	Iterative			Clustering		
	P	R	F	P	R	F
gold	0.85	0.52	0.65†	0.84	0.41	0.55
all	0.88	0.49	0.63†	0.87	0.19	0.32
nc	0.87	0.46	0.60	0.88	0.46	0.60
	Earthquakes					
	Iterative			**Clustering**		
	P	R	F	P	R	F
gold	0.65	0.41	0.50†	0.66	0.31	0.43
all	0.64	0.36	0.46	0.62	0.40	0.49
nc	0.63	0.33	0.43	0.67	0.38	0.49
	Train Accidents					
	Iterative			**Clustering**		
	P	R	F	P	R	F
gold	0.81	0.54	0.65	0.82	0.52	0.64
all	0.81	0.52	0.64†	0.72	0.31	0.43
nc	0.79	0.54	0.64†	0.79	0.42	0.55

Table 7: Cross-lingual Information Extraction Results in Spanish Translations. System trained with auto-annotated summaries in Spanish.

	Aviation Accidents					
	Iterative			Clustering		
	P	R	F	P	R	F
gold	0.87	0.35	0.50	0.87	0.37	0.52
all	0.87	0.37	0.52†	0.82	0.18	0.29
nc	0.90	0.21	0.34†	0.90	0.17	0.29
	Earthquakes					
	Iterative			**Clustering**		
	P	R	F	P	R	F
gold	0.87	0.53	0.66†	0.87	0.36	0.51
all	0.88	0.51	0.64†	0.87	0.30	0.45
nc	0.88	0.51	0.65†	0.93	0.43	0.59
	Train Accidents					
	Iterative			**Clustering**		
	P	R	F	P	R	F
gold	0.82	0.30	0.44	0.87	0.32	0.47
all	0.84	0.39	0.53†	0.91	0.24	0.38
nc	0.89	0.36	0.51†	0.46	0.25	0.32

Table 8: Cross-lingual Information Extraction Results in English Translations. System trained with auto-annotated summaries in English.

tistically significant differences between the clustering procedure and the iterative learning procedure ($p = 0.01$). In all tested domains in English, except for the Earthquake domain, there are statistically significant differences between the performance of clustering and iterative learning ($p = 0.01$).

Now we turn to the results of both algorithms when automatic chunks are used, that is, when no human annotation is provided to the learners. Results are reported in Tables 4 (Spanish) and 5 (English). The results are presented by the chunk type used during the learning procedure. In addition to the chunk types specified above, we include a type **all**, which represents the use of all automatically computed chunks (i.e. **nc**, **ne**, **wiki**). We observe that, in general, when presented with automatic chuks, the iterative learning procedure is able to induce concepts with a better f-score than the clustering-based algorithm. A t-test is run to verify differences between the two induction procedures within each chunk condition (differences shown with a † in the tables). In 11 out of 16 cases in Spanish and in 12 out of 16 cases in English, statistically significant differences are observed. In three out of four domains the combination of automatic chunks outperforms the use of individual chunk types. Generally, named entity chunks and wiki chunks have the lowest performance. This is

	Spanish		
	P	R	F
Aviation Accident	0.56	0.47	0.51
Earthquake	0.64	0.41	0.50
	English		
	P	R	F
Aviation Accident	0.61	0.35	0.44
Earthquake	0.78	0.41	0.54

Table 9: Extraction from Full Documents. System Trained on Gold Summaries.

	Aviation Accidents					
	Iterative			Clustering		
	P	R	F	P	R	F
gold	0.55	0.37	0.44	0.54	0.31	0.39
all	0.55	0.36	0.43†	0.69	0.17	0.27
nc	0.45	0.22	0.30†	0.52	0.26	0.35
	Earthquake					
	Iterative			Clustering		
	P	R	F	P	R	F
gold	0.62	0.31	0.41†	0.63	0.22	0.33
all	0.61	0.26	0.37	0.63	0.31	0.41†
nc	0.60	0.24	0.35	0.70	0.28	0.40†

Table 10: Full-text Information Extraction Results in Spanish. System trained with auto-annotated summaries in Spanish.

not an unexpected result since named entities, for example, cover much fewer strings which may form part of a concept extension. Additionally, off-the-shelf entity recogizers only identify a limited number of entity types.

6 Information Extraction Evaluation Framework

The numbers above are interesting because they provide intrinsic evaluation of the concept induction procedure, but they do not tell us much about their usability. Therefore, and in order to better assess the value of the discovered concepts, we decided to carry out two extrinsic evaluations using an information extraction task. Once the conceps are induced and, as a result, the summaries are auto-annotated with domain specific concepts, we decide to train an off-the-shelf SVM token classification procedure and apply it to unseen human annotated documents. The SVM classifier uses the same linguistic information as the induction procedures: token level information and a window size of 5 around each token to be classified.

	Aviation Accidents					
	Iterative			Clustering		
	P	R	F	P	R	F
gold	0.60	0.28	0.39	0.62	0.31	0.41†
all	0.62	0.30	0.41†	0.54	0.14	0.23
nc	0.53	0.15	0.23†	0.46	0.10	0.16
	Earthquake					
	Iterative			Clustering		
	P	R	F	P	R	F
gold	0.70	0.35	0.47†	0.72	0.32	0.44
all	0.74	0.37	0.49	0.70	0.22	0.34
nc	0.73	0.36	0.48†	0.73	0.30	0.42

Table 11: Full-text Information Extraction Results in English. System trained with auto-annotated summaries in English.

6.1 Extraction from Automatic Translations

The first task we carry out is cross-lingual information extraction where the input documents are automatic translations of summaries in Spanish and English[2]. Note that the expriment is performed in three domains for which such translations are manually annotated. We first run an experiment to assess the extraction performance of the SVM when trained on human annotated data. Results of the experiment are reported in Table 6 and they should be taken as an upperbound of the performance of a system trained on auto-annotated summaries. We then train the SVM on the different auto-annotated datasets, but note that due to space restrictions, we here only report the three most revealing experiments per language: concepts induced with gold chunks, noun chunks, and all automatic chunks. Results are reported in Table 7 (Spanish) and in Table 8 (English). In most cases the SVM trained with auto-annotated summaries produced by the iterative learning procedure outperforms the clustering-based method with statistically significant differences († shown in the tables) ($p = 0.01$).

6.2 Extraction from Full Documents

The second and the last evaluation consists in the application of the SVM extraction system to full documents. In this case, the experiment can be run only in two domains for which full documents have been provided and manually annotated. We first test the performance of the system when trained on human annotated summaries and present the results in Table 9. Results of the experiments when the system is trained on auto-annotated datasets are shown in

[2]The translations were produced by Google translator.

Tables 10 (Spanish) and 11 (English). Results are lower than when training on clean human annotated summaries. It is unclear which approach is more competitive when training with auto-annotated summaries. What is clear is that the performance of the iterative learning algorithm when training with concepts induced from gold chunks is not statistically different (according to a t-test and $p = 0.01$) from the performance of the algorithm when training with concepts induced from automatically computed chunks. We consider this to be a positive outcome of the experiments.

7 Discussion

The two methods presented here are able to produce partial domain conceptualizations from a relatively small set of domain summaries[3]. We have found that the clustering-based procedure is very competitive when presented with gold chunks. On the other hand, the iterative learning procedure performs very well when presented with automatic chunks in all tested domains and the two languages. We have also found that the performance of the iterative induction system is not much affected by the use of automatically computed chunks. We have run a t-test to verify the differences in induction performance when learning with gold and automatic chunks (*all* condition) and have found statistically significant differences in only one domain out of four in Spanish (Terrorist Attack) and in two domains out of four in English (Aviation Accident and Train Accident) ($p = 0.01$). The applicability of the induction process, that is, if the auto-annotated data could be used for specific tasks, has been tested in two information extraction experiments. In a cross-lingual information extraction setting (Riloff et al., 2002; Saggion and Szasz, 2011) we have observed that a system trained on automatically computed chunks has a performance close to one trained on concepts induced from gold chunks. No statistically significant differences exist ($p = 0.01$) between the use of automatic chunks and gold chunks, except for the Train Accident domain in English, where the system trained on fully automatically annotated summaries has a better performance. In a full document information extraction task, although the best system trained on auto-annotated summaries in Spanish has a big difference with respect to a system trained on human-annotated summaries, in English the differences are slight. We belive that this is due to the differences in performance between the underlying text processing components. Our methods work by grouping together sets of chunks, unlike (Chambers and Jurafsky, 2011), whose approach is centered around verb arguments and clustering, and relies on the availability of considerable amounts of data. Ontology learning approaches such as OntoUSP (Poon and Domingos, 2010) are also clustering-based but focus on learning is-a relations only. Unlike (Leung et al., 2011) whose approach is based on gold-standard humman annotations, we here test the performance of the induction process using automatically computed candidate strings, and we additionally learn the number of concepts automatically.

[3]Depending on the language and domain, between 50% and 77% of all concepts are generated.

8 Conclusions and Future Work

In this paper we have concentrated on the problem of knowledge induction from text summaries. The approaches we have presented are fully unsupervised and are able to produce reasonable conceptualizations (close to human concepts) without relying on annotated data. Unlike previous work, our approach does not require full syntactic parsing or a semantic dictionary. In fact, it only requires a process of text chunking and named entity recognition, which we have carefully assessed here. We believe our work contributes with a viable methodology to induce conceptual information from texts, and at the same time with an auto-annotation mechanism which could be used to train information extraction systems. Since our procedure requires very little linguistic information, we believe it can be successfully applied to a number of languages. We also believe that there is much work to be carried out and that induction from summaries should be complemented with a process that explores full event reports, in order to reinforce some induced concepts, discard others, and discover additional ones.

References

Michele Banko and Oren Etzioni. 2008. The tradeoffs between open and traditional relation extraction. In

Proceedings of ACL-08, pages 28–36. Association for Computational Linguistics, June.

R. Barzilay and L. Lee. 2003. Learning to paraphrase: an unsupervised approach using multiple-sequence alignment. In *Proceedings of the 2003 Conference of the North American Chapter of the Association for Computational Linguistics on Human Language Technology - Volume 1*, NAACL '03, pages 16–23, Stroudsburg, PA, USA. Association for Computational Linguistics.

Chris Biemann. 2005. Ontology Learning from Text: A Survey of Methods. *LDV Forum*, 20(2):75–93.

E. Brill. 1994. Some Advances in Transformation-Based Part of Speech Tagging. In *Proceedings of the Twelfth National Conference on AI (AAAI-94)*, Seattle, Washington.

P. Buitelaar and B. Magnini. 2005. Ontology learning from text: An overview. In *In Paul Buitelaar, P., Cimiano, P., Magnini B. (Eds.), Ontology Learning from Text: Methods, Applications and Evaluation*, pages 3–12. IOS Press.

N. Chambers and D. Jurafsky. 2011. Template-Based Information Extraction without the Templates. In *ACL*, pages 976–986.

Fabio Ciravegna and Yorick Wilks. 2003. Designing adaptive information extraction for the semantic web in amilcare. In *Annotation for the Semantic Web, Frontiers in Artificial Intelligence and Applications. IOS*. Press.

Gerald DeJong. 1982. An Overview of the FRUMP System. In W.G. Lehnert and M.H. Ringle, editors, *Strategies for Natural Language Processing*, pages 149–176. Lawrence Erlbaum Associates, Publishers.

O. Etzioni, M. Cafarella, D. Downey, A. Popescu, T. Shaked, S. Soderland, D. S. Weld, and A. Yates. 2004. Methods for Domain-Indepedent Information Extraction from the Web: An Experimental Comparison. In *Proceedings of AAAI-2004*.

Christiane Fellbaum, editor. 1998. *WordNet - An Electronic Lexical Database*. MIT Press.

I. Konstas and M. Lapata. 2012. Concept-to-text generation via discriminative reranking. In *Proceedings of the 50th Annual Meeting of the Association for Computational Linguistics*, pages 369–378, Jeju Island, Korea, July. Association for Computational Linguistics.

Cane Wing-ki Leung, Jing Jiang, Kian Ming A. Chai, Hai Leong Chieu, and Loo-Nin Teow. 2011. Unsupervised information extraction with distributional prior knowledge. In *Proceedings of the 2011 Conference on Empirical Methods in Natural Language Processing*, pages 814–824, Edinburgh, Scotland, UK., July. Association for Computational Linguistics.

Y. Li, K. Bontcheva, and H. Cunningham. 2004. An SVM Based Learning Algorithm for Information Extraction. Machine Learning Workshop, Sheffield.

P. Li, J. Jiang, and Y. Wang. 2010. Generating Templates of Entity Summaries with an Entity-Aspect Model and Pattern Mining. In *Proceedings of ACL*, Uppsala. ACL.

D. Maynard, V. Tablan, H. Cunningham, C. Ursu, H. Saggion, K. Bontcheva, and Y. Wilks. 2002. Architectural Elements of Language Engineering Robustness. *Journal of Natural Language Engineering – Special Issue on Robust Methods in Analysis of Natural Language Data*, 8(2/3):257–274.

Chris D. Paice and Paul A. Jones. 1993. The Identification of Important Concepts in Highly Structured Technical Papers. In R. Korfhage, E. Rasmussen, and P. Willett, editors, *Proc. of the 16th ACM-SIGIR Conference*, pages 69–78.

J. Piskorski and R. Yangarber. 2013. Information extraction: Past, present and future. In Thierry Poibeau, Horacio Saggion, Jakub Piskorski, and Roman Yangarber, editors, *Multi-source, Multilingual Information Extraction and Summarization*, Theory and Applications of Natural Language Processing, pages 23–49. Springer Berlin Heidelberg.

H. Poon and P. Domingos. 2010. Unsupervised ontology induction from text. In *Proceedings of the 48th Annual Meeting of the Association for Computational Linguistics*, ACL '10, pages 296–305, Stroudsburg, PA, USA. Association for Computational Linguistics.

Adwait Ratnaparkhi. 2000. Trainable methods for surface natural language generation. In *Proceedings of the 1st North American chapter of the Association for Computational Linguistics conference*, NAACL 2000, pages 194–201, Stroudsburg, PA, USA. Association for Computational Linguistics.

E. Riloff, C. Schafer, and D. Yarowsky. 2002. Inducing information extraction systems for new languages via cross-language projection. In *Proceedings of the 19th international conference on Computational linguistics*, pages 1–7, Morristown, NJ, USA. Association for Computational Linguistics.

E. Riloff. 1993. Automatically constructing a dictionary for information extraction tasks. *Proceedings of the Eleventh Annual Conference on Artificial Intelligence*, pages 811–816.

E. Riloff. 1996. Automatically generating extraction patterns from untagged text. *Proceedings of the Thirteenth Annual Conference on Artificial Intelligence*, pages 1044–1049.

H. Saggion and G. Lapalme. 2002. Generating Indicative-Informative Summaries with SumUM. *Computational Linguistics*.

H. Saggion and T. Poibeau. 2013. Automatic text summarization: Past, present and future. In Thierry Poibeau, Horacio Saggion, Jakub Piskorski, and Roman Yangarber, editors, *Multi-source, Multilingual Information Extraction and Summarization*, Theory and Applications of Natural Language Processing, pages 3–21. Springer Berlin Heidelberg.

H. Saggion and S. Szasz. 2011. Multi-domain Cross-lingual Information Extraction from Clean and Noisy Texts. In *Proceedings of the 8th Brazilian Symposium in Information and Human Language Technology*, Cuiabá, Brazil. BCS.

H. Saggion and S. Szasz. 2012. The CONCISUS Corpus of Event Summaries. In *Proceedings of the 8th Language Resources and Evaluation Conference (LREC)*, Istanbul, Turkey. ELDA.

H. Saggion. 2012. Unsupervised content discovery from concise summaries. In *Proceedings of the Joint Workshop on Automatic Knowledge Base Construction and Web-scale Knowledge Extraction*, AKBC-WEKEX '12, pages 13–18, Stroudsburg, PA, USA. Association for Computational Linguistics.

H. Schmid. 1995. Improvements In Part-of-Speech Tagging With an Application To German. In *In Proceedings of the ACL SIGDAT-Workshop*, pages 47–50.

I. H. Witten and E. Frank. 1999. *Data Mining: Practical Machine Learning Tools and Techniques with Java Implementations*. Morgan Kaufmann.

R. Yangarber. 2003. Counter-Training in Discovery of Semantic Patterns. In *Proceedings of the 41st Annual Meeting of the Association for Computational Linguistics (ACL'03)*.

Classification of South African languages using text and acoustic based methods: A case of six selected languages

Peleira Nicholas Zulu
University of KwaZulu-Natal
Electrical, Electronic and
Computer Engineering
Durban, 4041, South Africa
zulup1@ukzn.ac.za

Abstract

Language variations are generally known to have a severe impact on the performance of Human Language Technology Systems. In order to predict or improve system performance, a thorough investigation into these variations, similarities and dissimilarities, is required. Distance measures have been used in several applications of speech processing to analyze different varying speech attributes. However, not much work has been done on language distance measures, and even less work has been done involving South African languages. This study explores two methods for measuring the linguistic distance of six South African languages. It concerns a text based method, (the Levenshtein Distance), and an acoustic approach using extracted mean pitch values. The Levenshtein distance uses parallel word transcriptions from all six languages with as little as 144 words, whereas the pitch method is text-independent and compares mean language pitch differences. Cluster analysis resulting from the distance matrices from both methods correlates closely with human perceptual distances and existing literature about the six languages.

1 Introduction

The development of objective metrics to assess the distances between different languages is of great theoretical and practical importance. Currently, subjective measures have generally been employed to assess the degree of similarity or dissimilarity between different languages (Gooskens & Heeringa, 2004; Van-Bezooijen & Heeringa, 2006; Van-Hout & Münstermann, 1981), and those subjective decisions are, for example, the basis for classifying separate languages, and certain groups of language variants as dialects of one another. It is well known that languages are complex; they differ in vocabulary, grammar, writing format, syntax and many other characteristics. This presents levels of difficulty in the construction of objective comparative measures between languages. Even if one intuitively knows, for example, that English is closer to French than it is to Chinese, what are the objective factors that allow one to assess the levels of distance?

This bears substantial similarities to the analogous questions that have been asked about the relationships between different species in the science of cladistics. As in cladistics, the most satisfactory answer would be a direct measure of the amount of time that has elapsed since the languages' first split from their most recent common ancestor. Also, as in cladistics, it is hard to measure this from the available evidence, and various approximate measures have to be employed instead. In the biological case, recent decades have seen tremendous improvements in the accuracy of biological measurements as it has become possible to measure differences between DNA sequences. In linguistics, the analogue of DNA measurements is historical information on the evolution of languages, and the more easily measured—though indirect measurements (akin to the biological phenotype)—are either the *textual* or *acoustic* representations of the languages in question.

In the current article, we focus on language distance measures derived from both text and acoustic formats; we apply two different techniques, namely Levenshtein distance between orthographic word transcriptions, and distances between language pitch means in order to obtain measures of dissimilarity amongst a set of languages. These methods are used to obtain language groupings which are represented graphically using multidimensional scaling and dendrograms—two standard statistical techniques. This allows us to visualize and assess the methods relative to known linguistic facts in order to judge their relative reliability(Zulu, Botha, & Barnard, 2008).

Our evaluation is based on six of the eleven official languages of South Africa.[1] The eleven official languages fall into two distinct groups, namely the Germanic group (represented by English and Afrikaans) and the South African Bantu languages, which belong to the South Eastern Bantu group. The South African Bantu languages can further be classified in terms of different sub-groupings: Nguni (consisting of Zulu, Xhosa, Ndebele and Swati), Sotho (consisting of Southern Sotho, Northern Sotho and Tswana), and a pair that falls outside these sub-families (Tsonga and Venda). The six languages chosen for our evaluation are English, Afrikaans, Zulu, Xhosa, Northern Sotho (also known as Sepedi) and Tswana, which equally represent the three groups; Germanic, Nguni and Sotho.

We believe that an understanding of these language distances is not only of inherent interest, but also of great practical importance. For purposes such as language learning, the selection of target languages for various resources and the development of Human Language Technologies, reliable knowledge of language distances would be of great value. Consider, for example, the common situation of an organization that wishes to publish information relevant to all languages in a particular multi-lingual community, but has insufficient funding to do so. Such an organization can be guided by knowledge of language distances and mutual intelligibility between languages to make an appropriate choice of publication languages.

The following sections describe the Levenshtein distance and pitch characteristics in detail. Thereafter, the paper will present an evaluation on the six languages of South Africa, highlighting language groupings and proximity patterns. In conclusion, the paper discusses the results.

[1] Data for all eleven languages is available on the Lwazi website: (http://www.meraka.org.za/lwazi/index.php).

2 Theoretical Background

Orthographic transcriptions are one of the most basic types of annotation used for speech transcription, and are particularly important in most fields of research concerned with spoken language. The orthography of a language refers to the set symbols used to write a language and includes its writing system. English, for example, has an alphabet of 26 letters which includes both consonants and vowels. However, each English letter may represent more than one phoneme, and each phoneme may be represented by more than one letter. In the current research, we investigate the use of Levenshtein distance on orthographic transcriptions for the assessment of language similarities.

On the other hand, speech has been and still very much is the most natural form of communication. Prosodic characteristics such as rhythm, stress and intonation in speech convey important information regarding the identity of a spoken language. Results of perception studies on spoken language identification confirm that prosodic information, specifically pitch and intensity—which represent intonation and stress respectively—are useful for language identification (Kometsu, Mori, Arai, & Murahara, 2001; Mori et al., 1999). This paper presents a preliminary investigation of pitch and its role in determining acoustic based language distances.

2.1 Levenshtein Distance

There are several ways in which phoneticians have tried to measure the distance between two linguistic entities, most of which are based on the description of sounds via various representations. This section introduces the Levenshtein Distance Measure, one of the more popular sequence-based distance measures. In 1995 Kessler introduced the use of the Levenshtein Distance as a tool for measuring linguistic distances between dialects (Kessler, 1995). The basic idea behind the Levenshtein Distance is to imagine that one is rewriting or transforming one string into another. Kessler successfully applied the Levenshtein Distance measure to the comparison of Irish dialects. In his work, the strings were transcriptions of word pronunciations. In general, rewriting is effected by basic operations, each of which is associated with a cost, as illustrated in Table 1 in the transformation of the string "*mošemane*" to the string "*umfana*", which are both orthographic translations of the word boy in Northern Sotho and Zulu respectively.

	Operation	Cost
mošemane	delete m	1
ošemane	delete š	1
oemane	delete e	1
omane	insert f	1
omfane	substitute o/u	2
umfane	substitute e/a	2
umfana		
	Total cost	8

Table 1. Levenshtein Distance between two strings.

The Levenshtein Distance between two strings can be defined as the least costly sum of costs needed to transform one string into another. In Table 1, the transformations shown are associated with costs derived from operations performed on the strings. The operations used are: (i) the deletion of a single symbol, (ii) the insertion of a single symbol, and (iii) the substitution of one symbol for another (Kruskal, 1999). The edit distance method was also taken up by (Nerbonne et al., 1996) who applied it to Dutch dialects. Whereas Kruskal (1999) and Nerbonne *et al.* (1996) applied this method to phonetic transcriptions in which the symbols represented sounds, here the symbols were associated with alphabetic letters.

Similarly, Gooskens and Heeringa (2004) calculated Levenshtein Distances between 15 Norwegian dialects and compared them to the distances as perceived by Norwegian listeners. This comparison showed a high correlation between the Levenshtein distances and the perceptual distances.

2.2 Language pitch distance

Speech is primarily intended to convey some message through a sequence of legal sound units in a language. However, speech cannot merely be characterized as a sequence of sound units. There are some characteristics that lend naturalness to speech, such as the variation of pitch, which provides some recognizable melodic properties to spoken language. This controlled modulation of pitch is referred to as *intonation*. The sound units are shortened or lengthened in accordance to some underlying pattern giving rhythmic properties to speech. The information attained from these rhythmic patterns increases the intelligibility of spoken languages, enabling the listener to segment continuous speech into phrases and words with ease (Shriberg, Stolcke, Hakkani-Tur, & Tur, 2000). The characteristics that make us perceive this and other information such as stress, accent and emotion are collectively referred to as prosody. Comparisons have shown that languages differ greatly in their prosodic features (Hirst & Cristo, 1998), therefore providing a basis for objective comparison between languages. Further, pitch is a perceptual attribute of sound, the physical correlate of which is fundamental frequency (F_0), which represents vibration of the vocal folds.

This paper extracts pitch contours from six different languages, and uses the mean fundamental frequency values for each language to calculate the differences in pitch amongst them. From this we derive a distance matrix of F_0 dissimilarities (differences) which in turn is used to obtain language groupings.

2.3 Language Clustering

In using the Levenshtein Distance measure, the distance between two languages is equal to the average of a sample of Levenshtein Distances of corresponding word pairs. With pitch, the distance between two languages is merely the difference between the mean fundamental frequencies of the two languages. When we have n languages, then these distances are calculated for each possible pair of languages. For n languages n x n distances can be calculated. The corresponding distances are arranged in an n x n matrix. The distance of each language with respect to itself is found in the distance matrix on the diagonal from the upper left to the lower right. As this is a dissimilarity matrix, these values are always zero and therefore give no real information, so that only n x (n - 1) distances are relevant. Furthermore, both the Levenshtein and pitch distances are symmetric, implying that the distance between language X and Y is equal to the distance between language Y and X. Therefore, the distance matrix is symmetric. We need to use only one half which contains (n x (n - 1))/2 distances. Given the distance matrix, groups of larger sizes are investigated. Hierarchical clustering methods are employed to classify the languages into related language groups using the distance matrix.

Data clustering is a common technique for statistical data analysis, which is used in many fields including machine learning, bioinformatics, image analysis, data mining and pattern recognition. Clustering is the classification of similar objects into different groups, or more precisely, the partitioning of a data set into subsets, so that the data in each subset share some common trait according to a defined distance measure. The result of this grouping is usually illustrated as a dendrogram; a tree diagram used to illustrate the arrangement of the groups produced by a clustering algorithm (Heeringa & Gooskens, 2003), whereas multidimensional scaling adds to illustrate the visualization of the language proximities in a 2-dimensional space.

3 Evaluation

This evaluation aims to present language groups of the six chosen languages of South Africa generated from dissimilarity matrices of the languages. These matrices are the results of Levenshtein distance and average pitch distance measurements. The diagrams provide visual representations of the pattern of similarities and dissimilarities between the languages.

3.1 Language grouping using Levenshtein distance

Levenshtein distances were calculated using existing parallel orthographic word transcriptions of 144 words from each of the six languages. The data was manually collected from various multilingual dictionaries and online resources. Initially, 200 common English words, mostly common nouns easily translated into the other five languages, were chosen. From this set, those words having unique translations into each of the other five languages were selected, resulting in 144 words that were used in the evaluations. Examples of four word translations in all six languages are shown in Table 2.

Eng	Afr	Xho	Zul	N.Sot	Tsw
fish	vis	intlanzi	inhlanzi	hlapi	tlhapi
house	huis	indlu	indlu	ntlo	ntlo
mother	ma	uma	umama	mma	mme
school	skool	isikolo	isikole	sekolo	sekole

Table 2. Example translations of four common words.

Distance matrix

Table 3 represents the distance matrix, containing the distances, taken pair-wise, between the different languages as calculated from the summed Levenshtein Distances between the 144 target words. The zero values along the diagonal axis of the matrix indicate no dissimilarity, making it clear that higher values reveal high levels of dissimilarity between the paired languages. The distance matrix contains n x $(n - 1)/2$ independent elements in light of the symmetry of the distance measure.

	Afr	Eng	Xho	Zul	N. Sot	Tsw
Afr	0	443	984	1014	829	887
Eng	443	0	981	1002	820	881
Xho	984	981	0	502	867	922
Zul	1014	1002	502	0	881	945
N. Sot	829	820	867	881	0	315
Tsw	887	881	922	945	315	0

Table 3. Distance matrices calculated from Levenshtein Distance between 144 words.

Graphical representation

The confusion matrices provide a clear indication of the ways the languages group into families. These relationships can be represented visually using graphical techniques. Multidimensional scaling (MDS) is a technique used in data visualization for exploring the properties of data in high-dimensional spaces. The algorithm uses a matrix of dissimilarities between items and then assigns each item a location in a low dimensional space to match those distances as closely as possible. The study used the dissimilarity matrix to serve as a measure between languages, and used the statistical package XLSTAT (XLSTAT, 2012). The dissimilarity matrix was input into the multidimensional scaling algorithm which mapped the language dissimilarities in a 2-dimensional space.

Figure 1 shows the mapping that was created using the dissimilarity matrix in Table 3; we can see that the languages from the same subfamilies group together. The mapping using just 144 words shows a definite grouping of the families. In the mapping the Sotho languages are more closely related internally than both the Nguni and Germanic languages as expected — from the historical record (Heine & Nurse, 2000), it is clear that a tighter internal grouping of the Sotho and Nguni languages is accurate.

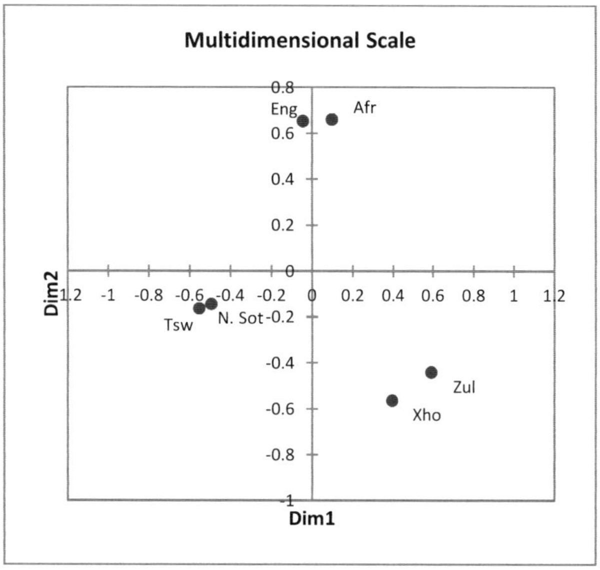

Figure 1. Multidimensional scale to represent dissimilarities between languages calculated from the dissimilarity matrix in Table 3.

In conjunction with multidimensional scaling, dendrograms also provide a visual representation of the pattern of similarities or dissimilarities among a set of objects. We again used the dissimilarity matrix in Table 3 with the statistical package XLSTAT.

Figure 2 illustrates the dendrogram derived from clustering the dissimilarities between the languages as depicted by the dissimilarity matrix in Table 3. The dendrogram shows three classes representing the previously defined language groupings, Nguni, Sotho and Germanic. This dendrogram closely relates to the language groupings described in (Heine & Nurse, 2000).

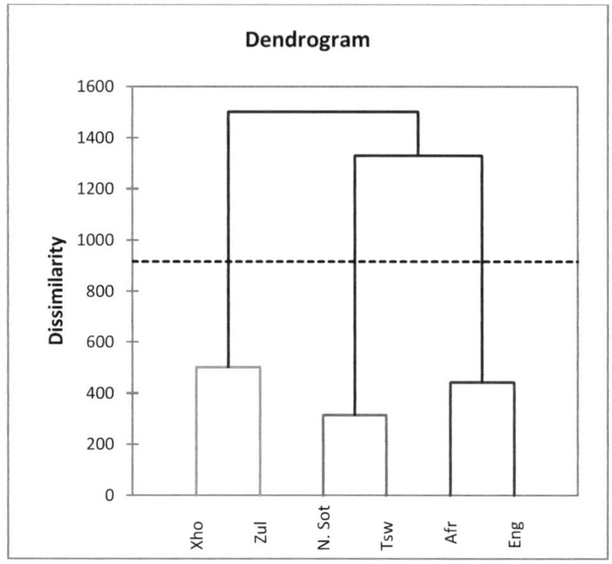

Figure 2. Dendrogram calculated from the dissimilarity matrix of Table 3.

3.2 Pitch Extraction and language grouping

The extraction of pitch contours was carried out with *Praat* (Boersma & Weenink, 2011), a free scientific software program for the analysis of speech and phonetics. The use of Praat is advantageous in that it is fairly easy to use, has high processing speed, is accurate and allows scripting, which is very useful in processing large numbers of files (in our case, speech recordings).

A Praat script was written specifying two main parameters; the expected minimum and maximum pitch values in Hertz, which were selected to be 75Hz and 600Hz respectively. The extraction of pitch contours is based on the detection of periodicities. The Praat command *To PointProcess (periodic, peaks)...* analyses the selected speech file and creates a sequence of points in time. The acoustic periodicity detection is performed on the basis of an accurate short-term analysis of the fundamental frequency and the harmonics-to-noise ratio working in the autocorrelation domain as described by Boersma (Boersma, 1993). This method was able to achieve more accurate and noise-resistant results when compared to combs or cepstrum based methods (Pokorny, 2011). The extracted acoustic periodicity contour is interpreted as being the frequency of an underlying sequence of glottal closures in vocal fold vibrations. For each speech file—for every voiced interval—a number of points representing glottal pulses are found and their points in time are saved, forming the pitch contour for that particular speech file (Pokorny, 2011). Pitch contours were extracted from 5000 speech files per language for each of the six languages, with each language having approximately 200 different speakers (25 recordings per speaker) with a relatively equal distribution of males and females, all aged between 18 and 65 years.

The extracted pitch frequency points for all 5000 files were collected and placed in a single array for each language. Each array represents the pitch distribution for the specific language, and the mean frequency for each language was used to model the respective language. The dissimilarity matrix was then derived from the differences of these means for each pair of languages. Figure 3 illustrates the distribution of pitch frequencies for the selected languages. It clearly shows the relative pitch content variations of the different languages, which is key to determining the dissimilarity amongst the languages. Also of note in Figure 3 are the peak positions representing approximate positions of male and female fundamental frequencies—in the range of 85 to 180Hz for males and 165 to 255 Hz for females.

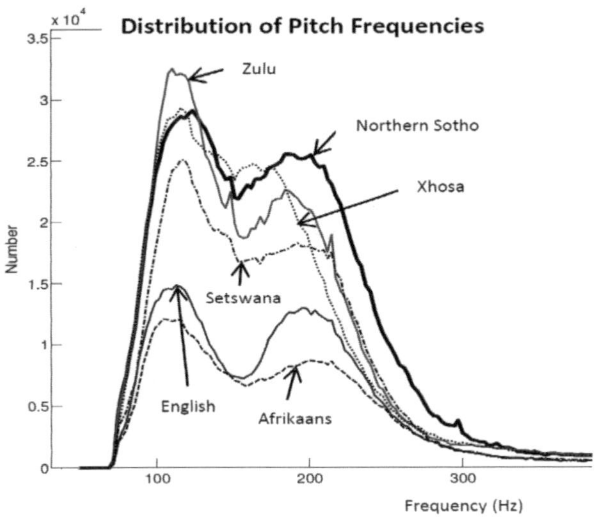

Figure 3. Distribution of pitch frequencies extracted from 6 South African languages.

Distance matrix

Table 4 represents the distance matrix—containing the distances taken pair-wise—between the different languages as calculated from the mean pitch frequencies of the six languages. Again, higher numbers in the matrix reflect high dissimilarity between the selected pair of languages.

	Afr	Eng	Xho	Zul	N. Sot	Tsw
Afr	0	5.1	16.09	17.11	9.66	12.61
Eng	5.1	0	10.99	12.01	4.56	7.51
Xho	16.09	10.99	0	1.02	6.43	3.48
Zul	17.11	12.01	1.02	0	7.45	4.5
N. Sot	9.66	4.56	6.43	7.45	0	2.95
Tsw	12.61	7.51	3.48	4.5	2.95	0

Table 4. Distance matrix calculated from mean pitch frequencies of six South African languages.

Graphical representation

As with the Levenshtein Distance, the relationships between the languages are represented visually in Figures 4 and 5 using graphical techniques and multidimensional scaling. The language dissimilarities are mapped on to a 2-dimensional space shown in Figure 4. Here also, the languages from the same sub-families are grouped together. The relative closeness within the three sub-families is not as clearly indicated in Figure 4 as in Figure 1, but the distinction is clearly visible.

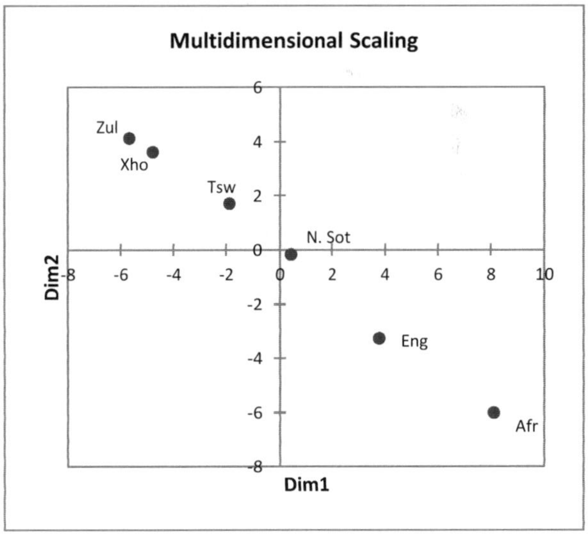

Figure 4. Multi-dimensional scale calculated from the pitch-based matrix of Table 4.

Figure 5 shows the dendrogram generated from the dissimilarities matrix of Table 4. As in Figure 2, the dendrogram shows three classes representing the previously defined language sub-families. Figure 5 differs from Figure 2 in the branching of the three sub-families, where Figure 2 shows the Germanic languages branching from the same parent as the Sotho sub-family. Figure 5 offers a more accurate account by separating the Germanic subgroup from the Bantu languages. Thus, Figure 5 depicts a more refined grouping of the languages than Figure 2.

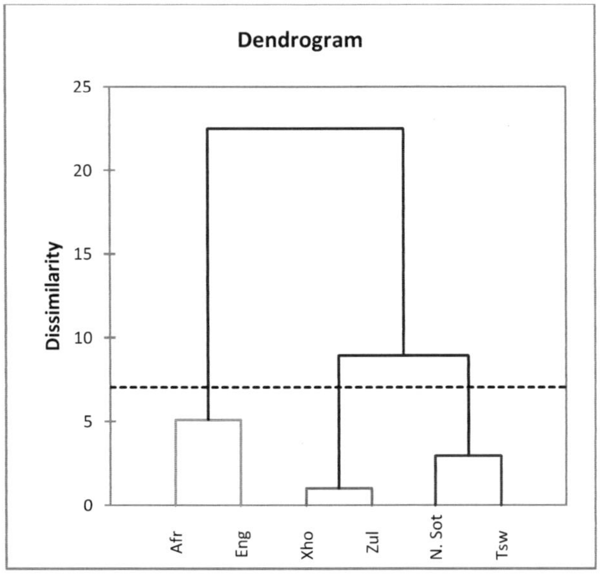

Figure 5. Dendrogram calculated from the pitch-based distance matrix of Table 4.

Conclusion

Both dissimilarity matrices resulting from the text-based Levenshtein Distance and the acoustic mean pitch frequency differences can effectively be combined with multidimensional scaling and dendrograms to epitomize language relationships. Both methods reflect the known family relationships between the languages being studied. The main conclusion of this research is therefore that statistical methods, used with both text-based and acoustic-based methods and data, are able to provide useful objective measures of language similarities or dissimilarities. It is clear that these methods can be refined further using other inputs such as phonetic transcriptions or further acoustic measurements; such refinements are likely to be important when, for example, fine distinctions between dialects are required.

However, each approach has its advantages and disadvantages. Levenshtein Distance measures do not require much data to perform a reasonable classification of the data. With as few as 50 words per language, reasonable classification is possible. Also, the process of generating the distance matrix is not computationally taxing. However, this method is less discriminating in assessing languages with different writing styles, for example Chinese and English. Using pitch bares the advantage of using language data in its most natural form, but has its disadvantages in being computationally taxing when dealing with large amounts of data—which is generally required in order to produce good results.

It would be most interesting to see whether closer agreement between these methods can be achieved by measuring Levenshtein Distances between larger text collections—perhaps even parallel corpora rather than translations of word lists. Comparing these distance measures with measures derived from different acoustic parameters, or a combination of parameters, is another pressing concern. Finally, it would be valuable to compare various distance measures against other criteria for language similarity (e.g. historical separation or mutual intelligibility) in a rigorous fashion.

References

Boersma, P. (1993). Accurate short-term analysis of the fundamental frequency and the harmonics-to-noise ratio of a sampled sound. *Institute of Phonetic Sciences, vol 17*, pp 97-110.

Boersma, P, & Weenink, D. (2011). Praat Version 5.3 2011. *http://www.fon.hum.uva.nl/praat/ Date of last access: 27 July. 2012*

Gooskens, C, & Heeringa, W. (2004). Perceptive evaluation of Levenshtein dialect distance measurements using Norwegian dialect data. *Language Variation and Change vol. 16*, pp. 189-207.

Heeringa, W, & Gooskens, C. (2003). Norwegian dialects examined perceptually and acoustically. *Computers and the Humanities, 37*, pp. 293-315.

Heine, B, & Nurse, D. (2000). African languages: An introduction. Cambridge University Press.

Hirst, D, & Cristo, A Di. (1998). Intonation systems: A survey of twenty languages. *Cambridge University Press, Cambridge.*

Kessler, B. (1995). Computational dialectology in Irish Gaelic. *The 7th Conference of the European Chapter of the Association for Computational Linguistics*, pp. 60-67.

Kometsu, M, Mori, K, Arai, T, & Murahara, Y. (2001). *Human language identification with reduced segmental information: comparison between Monolinguals and Bilinguals.* Paper presented at the EUROSPEECH, Scandanavia. pp 149-152.

Kruskal, J B. (1999). An overview of sequence comparison. Stanford. .

Mori, K, Toba, N, Harada, T, Arai, T, Kometsu, M, Aoyagi, M, & Murahara, Y. (1999). *Human language identification with reduced spectral information.* Paper presented at the EUROSPEECH, Budapest, Hungary. pp. 391-394.

Nerbonne, J, Heeringa, W, Hout, E Van den, Kooi, P Van der, Otten, S, & Vis, W Van de. (1996). Phonetic distance between Dutch dialects. *Sixth CLIN Meeting*, pp. 185-202.

Pokorny, F. (2011). Extraction of prosodic features from speech signals. Graz, Austria: Institute of Electronic Music and Acoustics, University of Music and Performing Arts.

Shriberg, E, Stolcke, A, Hakkani-Tur, D, & Tur, G. (2000). Prosody-based automatic segmentation of speech into sentences and topics. *Speech Communication. pp. 127-154*(32).

Van-Bezooijen, R, & Heeringa, W. (2006). Intuitions on linguistic distance: geographically or linguistically based? In: Tom Koole, Jacomine Northier and Bert Tahitu (eds). *Artikelen van de Vijfde sociolinguistiche conferentie*, pp. 77-87.

Van-Hout, R, & Münstermann, H. (1981). Linguistic distance, dialect and attitude. *Gramma 5*, pp. 101-123.

XLSTAT. (2012). XLSTAT. http://www.xlstat.com/en/download/. Date of access: 27 July. 2012

Zulu, P N, Botha, G, & Barnard, E. (2008). Orthographic measures of language distances between the official South African languages *Literator: Journal of Literary Criticism, Comparative Linguistics and Literaty Studies 29*(1), 185.

Improving Syntax-Augmented Machine Translation by Coarsening the Label Set

Greg Hanneman and **Alon Lavie**
Language Technologies Institute
Carnegie Mellon University
Pittsburgh, PA 15213 USA
{ghannema, alavie}@cs.cmu.edu

Abstract

We present a new variant of the Syntax-Augmented Machine Translation (SAMT) formalism with a category-coarsening algorithm originally developed for tree-to-tree grammars. We induce bilingual labels into the SAMT grammar, use them for category coarsening, then project back to monolingual labeling as in standard SAMT. The result is a "collapsed" grammar with the same expressive power and format as the original, but many fewer nonterminal labels. We show that the smaller label set provides improved translation scores by 1.14 BLEU on two Chinese–English test sets while reducing the occurrence of sparsity and ambiguity problems common to large label sets.

1 Introduction

The formulation of statistical machine translation in terms of synchronous parsing has become both theoretically and practically successful. In a parsing-based MT formalism, synchronous context-free grammar rules that match a source-language input can be hierarchically composed to produce a corresponding target-language output. SCFG translation grammars can be extracted automatically from data. While *formally* syntactic approaches with a single grammar nonterminal have often worked well (Chiang, 2007), the desire to exploit linguistic knowledge has motivated the use of translation grammars with richer, *linguistically* syntactic nonterminal inventories (Galley et al., 2004; Liu et al., 2006; Lavie et al., 2008; Liu et al., 2009).

Linguistically syntactic MT systems can derive their label sets, either monolingually or bilingually, from parallel corpora that have been annotated with source- and/or target-side parse trees provided by a statistical parser. The MT system may exactly adopt the parser's label set or modify it in some way. Larger label sets are able to represent more precise, fine-grained categories. On the other hand, they also exacerbate a number of computational and modeling problems by increasing grammar size, derivational ambiguity, and data sparsity.

In this paper, we focus on the Syntax-Augmented MT formalism (Zollmann and Venugopal, 2006), a monolingually labeled version of Hiero that can create up to 4000 "extended" category labels based on pairs of parse nodes. We take a standard SAMT grammar with target-side labels and extend its labeling to a bilingual format (Zollmann, 2011). We then coarsen the bilingual labels following the "label collapsing" algorithm of Hanneman and Lavie (2011). This represents a novel extension of the tree-to-tree collapsing algorithm to the SAMT formalism. After removing the source-side labels, we obtain a new SAMT grammar with coarser target-side labels than the original.

Coarsened grammars provide improvement of up to 1.14 BLEU points over the baseline SAMT results on two Chinese–English test sets; they also outperform a Hiero baseline by up to 0.60 BLEU on one of the sets. Aside from improved translation quality, in analysis we find significant reductions in derivational ambiguity and rule sparsity, two problems that make large nonterminal sets difficult to work with.

Section 2 provides a survey of large syntax-based

MT label sets, their associated problems of derivational ambiguity and rule sparsity, and previous attempts at addressing those problems. The section also summarizes the tree-to-tree label collapsing algorithm and the process of SAMT rule extraction. We then describe our method of label collapsing in SAMT grammars in Section 3. Experimental results are presented in Section 4 and analyzed in Section 5. Finally, Section 6 offers some conclusions and avenues for future work.

2 Background

2.1 Working with Large Label Sets

Aside from the SAMT method of grammar extraction, which we treat more fully in Section 2.3, several other lines of work have explored increasing the nonterminal set for syntax-based MT. Huang and Knight (2006), for example, augmented the standard Penn Treebank labels for English by adding lexicalization to certain types of nodes. Chiang (2010) and Zollmann (2011) worked with a bilingual extension of SAMT that used its notion of "extended categories" on both the source and target sides. Taking standard monolingual SAMT as a baseline, Baker et al. (2012) developed a tagger to augment syntactic labels with some semantically derived information. Ambati et al. (2009) extracted tree-to-tree rules with similar extensions for sibling nodes, resulting again in a large number of labels.

Extended categories allow for the extraction of a larger number of rules, increasing coverage and translation performance over systems that are limited to exact constituent matches only. However, the gains in coverage come with a corresponding increase in computational and modeling complexity due to the larger label set involved.

Derivational ambiguity — the condition of having multiple derivations for the same output string — is a particular problem for parsing-based MT systems. The same phrase pair may be represented with a large number of different syntactic labels. Further, new hierarchical rules are created by abstracting smaller phrase pairs out of larger ones; each of these substitutions must also be marked by a label of some kind. Keeping variantly labeled copies of the same rules fragments probabilities during grammar scoring and creates redundant hypotheses in the decoder at run time.

A complementary problem — when a desired rule application is impossible because its labels do not match — has been variously identified as "data sparsity," the "matching constraint," and "rule sparsity" in the grammar. It arises from the definition of SCFG rule application: in order to compose two rules, the left-hand-side label of the smaller rule must match a right-hand-side label in the larger rule it is being plugged in to. With large label sets, it becomes less likely that two arbitrarily chosen rules can compose, making the grammar less flexible for representing new sentences.

Previous research has attempted to address both of these problems in different ways. Preference grammars (Venugopal et al., 2009) are a technique for reducing derivational ambiguity by summing scores over labeled variants of the same derivation during decoding. Chiang (2010) addressed rule sparsity by introducing a soft matching constraint: the decoder may pay a learned label-pair-specific penalty for substituting a rule headed by one label into a substitution slot marked for another. Combining properties of both of the above methods, Huang et al. (2010) modeled monolingual labels as distributions over latent syntactic categories and calculated similarity scores between them for rule composition.

2.2 Label Collapsing in Tree-to-Tree Rules

Aiming to reduce both derivational ambiguity and rule sparsity, we previously presented a "label collapsing" algorithm for systems in which bilingual labels are used (Hanneman and Lavie, 2011). It coarsens the overall label set by clustering monolingual labels based on which labels they appear joined with in the other language.

The label collapsing algorithm takes as its input a set of SCFG rule instances extracted from a parallel corpus. Each time a tree-to-tree rule is extracted, its left-hand side is a label of the form $s{::}t$, where s is a label from the source-language category set S and t is a label from the target-language category set T. Operationally, the joint label means that a source-side subtree rooted at s was the translational equivalent of a target-side subtree rooted at t in a parallel sentence. Figure 1 shows several such subtrees, highlighted in grey and numbered. Joint left-hand-side labels for the collapsing algorithm,

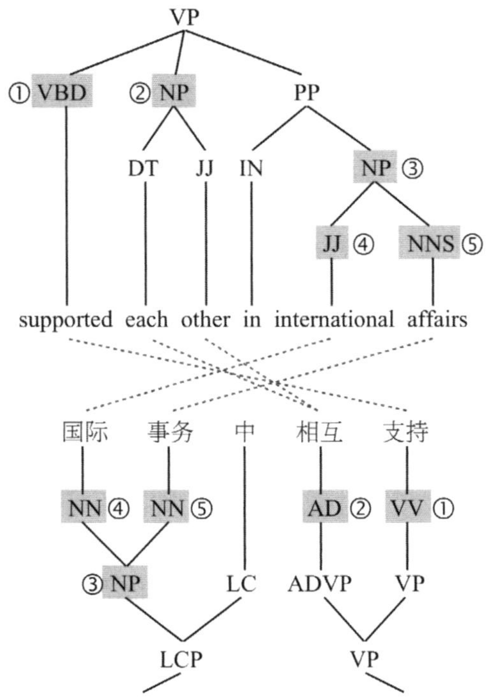

Figure 1: Sample extraction of bilingual nonterminals for label collapsing. Labels extracted from this tree pair include VBD::VV and NP::AD.

such as VBD::VV and NP::AD, can be assembled by matching co-numbered nodes.

From the counts of the extracted rules, it is thus straightforward to compute for all values of s and t the observed $P(s \mid t)$ and $P(t \mid s)$, the probability of one half of a joint nonterminal label appearing in the grammar given the other half. In the figure, for example, $P(\text{JJ} \mid \text{NN}) = 0.5$. The conditional probabilities accumulated over the whole grammar give rise to a simple L_1 distance metric over any pair of monolingual labels:

$$d(s_1, s_2) = \sum_{t \in T} |P(t \mid s_1) - P(t \mid s_2)| \qquad (1)$$

$$d(t_1, t_2) = \sum_{s \in S} |P(s \mid t_1) - P(s \mid t_2)| \qquad (2)$$

An agglomerative clustering algorithm then combines labels in a series of greedy iterations. At each step, the algorithm finds the pair of labels that is currently the closest together according to the distance metrics of Equations (1) and (2), combines those two labels into a new one, and updates the set of $P(s \mid t)$ and $P(t \mid s)$ values appropriately. The choice of label pair to collapse in each iteration can be expressed formally as

$$\underset{(s_i, s_j) \in S^2, (t_k, t_\ell) \in T^2}{\arg\min} \{d(s_i, s_j), d(t_k, t_\ell)\} \qquad (3)$$

That is, either a source label pair or a target label pair may be chosen by the algorithm in each iteration.

2.3 SAMT Rule Extraction

SAMT grammars pose a challenge to the label collapsing algorithm described above because their label sets are usually monolingual. The classic SAMT formulation (Zollmann and Venugopal, 2006) produces a grammar labeled on the target side only. Nonterminal instances that exactly match a target-language syntactic constituent in a parallel sentence are given labels of the form t. Labels of the form $t_1{+}t_2$ are assigned to nonterminals that span exactly two contiguous parse nodes. Categorial grammar labels such as t_1/t_2 and $t_1\backslash t_2$ are given to nonterminals that span an incomplete t_1 constituent missing a t_2 node to its right or left, respectively. Any nonterminal that cannot be labeled by one of the above three schemes is assigned the default label X.

Figure 2(a) shows the extraction of a VP-level SAMT grammar rule from part of a parallel sentence. At the word level, the smaller English phrase *supported each other* (and its Chinese equivalent) is being abstracted as a nonterminal within the larger phrase *supported each other in international affairs*. The larger phrase corresponds to a parsed VP node on the target side; this will become the label of the extracted rule's left-hand side. Since the abstracted sub-phrase does not correspond to a single constituent, the SAMT labeling conventions assign it the label VBD+NP. We can thus write the extracted rule as:

VP → [国际 事务 中 VBD+NP[1]]::
[VBD+NP[1] in international affairs] (4)

While the SAMT label formats can be trivially converted into joint labels X::t, X::$t_1{+}t_2$, X::t_1/t_2, X::$t_1\backslash t_2$, and X::X, they cannot be usefully fed into the label collapsing algorithm because the necessary conditional label probabilities are meaningless. To acquire meaningful source-side labels, we turn to a

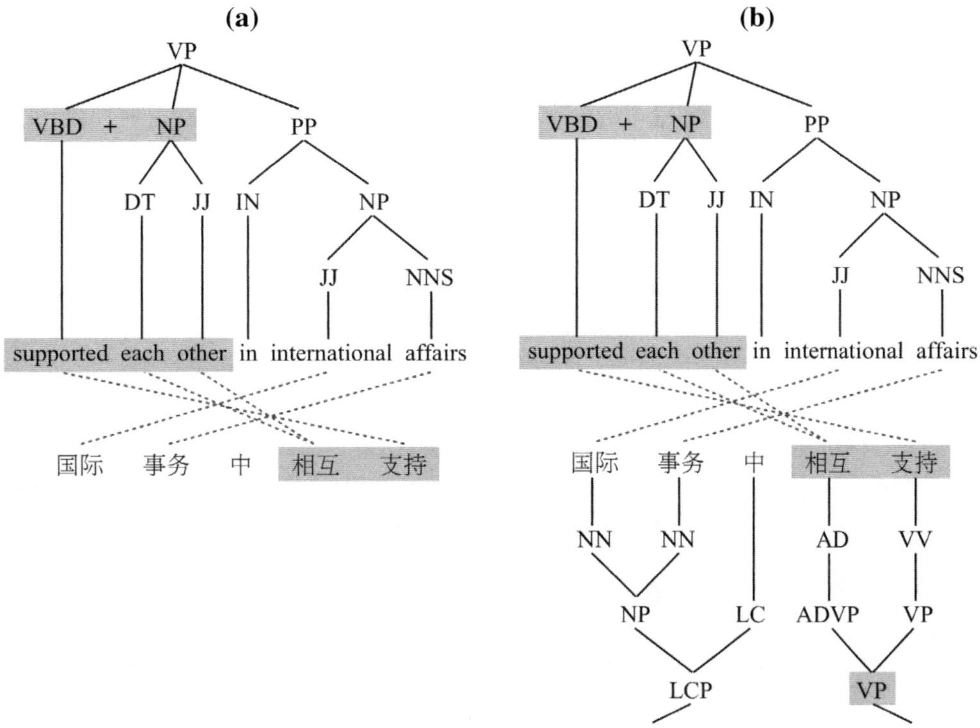

Figure 2: Sample extraction of an SAMT grammar rule: (a) with monolingual syntax and (b) with bilingual syntax.

bilingual SAMT extension used by Chiang (2010) and Zollmann (2011). Both a source- and a target-side parse tree are used to extract rules from a parallel sentence; two SAMT-style labels are worked out independently on each side for each nonterminal instance, then packed into a joint label. It is therefore possible for a nonterminal instance to be labeled s::t, $s_1\backslash s_2$::t, s_1+s_2::t_1/t_2, or various other combinations depending on what parse nodes the nonterminal spans in each tree.

Such a bilingually labeled rule is extracted in Figure 2(b). The target-side labels from Figure 2(a) are now paired with source-side labels extracted from an added Chinese parse tree. In this case, the abstracted sub-phrase *supported each other* is given the joint label VP::VBD+NP, while the rule's left-hand side becomes LCP+VP::VP.

We implement bilingual SAMT grammar extraction by modifying Thrax (Weese et al., 2011), an open-source, Hadoop-based framework for extracting standard SAMT grammars. By default, Thrax can produce grammars labeled either on the source or target side, but not both. It also outputs rules that are already scored according to a user-specified set of translation model features, meaning that the raw rule counts needed to compute the label conditional probabilities $P(s\,|\,t)$ and $P(t\,|\,s)$ are not directly available. We implement a new subclass of grammar extractor with logic for independently labeling both sides of an SAMT rule in order to get the necessary bilingual labels; an adaptation to the existing Thrax "rarity" feature provides the rule counts.

3 Label Collapsing in SAMT Rules

Our method of producing label-collapsed SAMT grammars is shown graphically in Figure 3.

We first obtain an SAMT grammar with bilingual labels, together with the frequency count for each rule, using the modified version of Thrax described in Section 2.3. The rules can be grouped according to the target-side label of their left-hand sides (Figure 3(a)).

The rule counts are then used to compute labeling probabilities $P(s\,|\,t)$ and $P(t\,|\,s)$ over left-hand-side usages of each source label s and each target label t. These are simple maximum-likelihood estimates: if $\#(s_i, t_j)$ represents the combined frequency counts of all rules with s_i::t_j on the left-hand

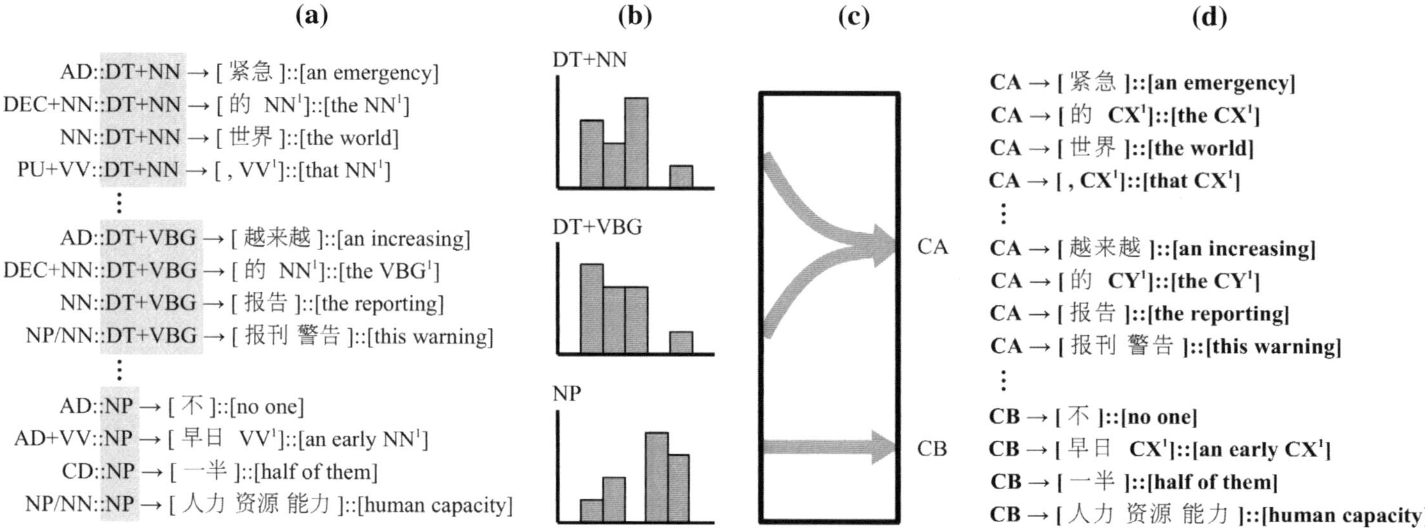

Figure 3: Stages of preparing label-collapsed rules for SAMT grammars. (a) SAMT rules with bilingual nonterminals are extracted and collected based on their target left-hand sides. (b) Probabiliites $P(t \mid s)$ and $P(s \mid s)$ are computed. (c) Nonterminals are clustered according to the label collapsing algorithm. (d) Source sides of nonterminals are removed to create a standard SAMT grammar.

side, the source-given-target labeling probability is:

$$P(s_i \mid t_j) = \frac{\#(s_i::t_j)}{\sum_{t \in T} \#(s_i::t)} \qquad (5)$$

The computation for target given source is analogous. Each monolingual label can thus be represented as a distribution over the labels it is aligned to in the opposite language (Figure 3(b)).

Such distributions over labels are the input to the label-collapsing algorithm, as described in Section 2.2. As shown in Figure 3(c), the algorithm results in the original target-side labels being combined into different groups, denoted in this case as new labels CA and CB. We run label collapsing for varying numbers of iterations to produce varying degrees of coarsened label sets.

Given a mapping from original target-side labels to collapsed groups, all nonterminals in the original SAMT grammar are overwritten accordingly. The source-side labels are dropped at this point: we use them only for the purpose of label collapsing, but not in assembling or scoring the final grammar. The resulting monolingual SAMT-style grammar with collapsed labels (Figure 3(d)) can now be scored and used for decoding in the usual way.

For constructing a baseline SAMT grammar without label collapsing, we merely extract a bilingual grammar as in the first step of Figure 3, immediately remove the source-side labels from it, and proceed to grammar scoring.

All grammars are scored according to a set of eight features. For an SCFG rule with left-hand-side label t, source right-hand side f, and target right-hand side e, they are:

- Standard maximum-likelihood phrasal translation probabilities $P(f \mid e)$ and $P(e \mid f)$
- Maximum-likelihood labeling probability $P(t \mid f, e)$
- Lexical translation probabilities $P_{lex}(f \mid e)$ and $P_{lex}(e \mid f)$, as calculated by Thrax
- Rarity score $\frac{\exp(\frac{1}{c})-1}{\exp(1)-1}$ for a rule with extracted count c
- Binary indicator features that mark phrase pair (as opposed to hierarchical) rules and glue rules

Scored grammars are filtered down to the sentence level, retaining only those rules whose source-side terminals match an individual tuning or testing sentence. In addition to losslessly filtering grammars in this way, we also carry out two types of lossy pruning in order to reduce overall grammar

System	Labels	Rules	Per Sent.
SAMT	4181	69,401,006	48,444
Collapse 1	913	64,596,618	35,004
Collapse 2	131	60,526,479	24,510
Collapse 3	72	58,483,310	20,445
Hiero	1	36,538,657	7,738

Table 1: Grammar statistics for different degrees of label collapsing: number of target-side labels, unique rules in the whole grammar, and average number of pruned rules after filtering to individual sentences.

size. One pruning pass keeps only the 80 most frequently observed target right-hand sides for each source right-hand side. A second pass globally removes hierarchical rules that were extracted fewer than six times in the training data.

4 Experiments

We conduct experiments on Chinese-to-English MT, using systems trained from the FBIS corpus of approximately 302,000 parallel sentence pairs. We parse both sides of the training data with the Berkeley parsers (Petrov and Klein, 2007) for Chinese and English. The English side is lowercased after parsing; the Chinese side is segmented beforehand. Unidirectional word alignments are obtained with GIZA++ (Och and Ney, 2003) and symmetrized, resulting in a parallel parsed corpus with Viterbi word alignments for each sentence pair. Our modified version of Thrax takes the parsed and aligned corpus as input and returns a list of rules, which can then be label-collapsed and scored as previously described.

In Thrax, we retain most of the default settings for Hiero- and SAMT-style grammars as specified in the extractor's configuration file. Inheriting from Hiero, we require the right-hand side of all rules to contain at least one pair of aligned terminals, no more than two nonterminals, and no more than five terminals and nonterminal elements combined. Nonterminals are not allowed to be adjacent on the source side, and they may not contain unaligned boundary words. Rules themselves are not extracted from any span in the training data longer than 10 tokens.

Our initial bilingual SAMT grammar uses 2699 unique source-side labels and 4181 unique target-side labels, leading to the appearance of 29,088 joint bilingual labels in the rule set. We provide the joint labels (along with their counts) to the label collapsing algorithm, while we strip out the source-side labels to create the baseline SAMT grammar with 4181 unique target-side labels. Table 1 summarizes how the number of target labels, unique extracted rules, and the average number of pruned rules available per sentence change as the initial grammar is label-collapsed to three progressively coarser degrees. Once the collapsing process has occurred exhaustively, the original SAMT grammar becomes a Hiero-format grammar with a single nonterminal.

Each of the five grammars in Table 1 is used to build an MT system. All systems are tuned and decoded with cdec (Dyer et al., 2010), an open-source decoder for SCFG-based MT with arbitrary rule formats and nonterminal labels. We tune the systems on the 1664-sentence NIST Open MT 2006 data set, optimizing towards the BLEU metric. Our test sets are the NIST 2003 data set of 919 sentences and the NIST 2008 data set of 1357 sentences. The tuning set and both test sets all have four English references.

We evaluate systems on BLEU (Papineni et al., 2002), METEOR (Denkowski and Lavie, 2011), and TER (Snover et al., 2006), as calculated in all three cases by MultEval version 0.5.0.[1] These scores for the MT '03 test set are shown in Table 2, and those for the MT '08 test set in Table 3, combined by MultEval over three optimization runs on the tuning set.

MultEval also implements statistical significance testing between systems based on multiple optimizer runs and approximate randomization. This process (Clark et al., 2011) randomly swaps outputs between systems and estimates the probability that the observed score difference arose by chance. We report these results in the tables as well for three MERT runs and a p-value of 0.05. Systems that were judged statistically different from the SAMT baseline have triangles in the appropriate "Sig. SAMT?" columns; systems judged different from the Hiero baseline have triangles under the "Sig. Hiero?" columns. An up-triangle (▲) indicates that the system was better, while a down-triangle (▽) means that the baseline was better.

[1] https://github.com/jhclark/multeval

System	Metric Scores BLEU	MET	TER	Sig. SAMT? B	M	T	Sig. Hiero? B	M	T
SAMT	31.18	30.64	61.02				▽	▽	▽
Collapse 1	31.42	31.31	60.95		▲		▽		▽
Collapse 2	31.90	31.73	60.98	▲	▲		▽	▲	▽
Collapse 3	32.32	31.75	60.54	▲	▲	▲		▲	▽
Hiero	32.30	31.42	60.10	▲	▲	▲			

Table 2: MT '03 test set results. The first section gives automatic metric scores; the remaining sections indicate whether each system is statistically significantly better (▲) or worse (▽) than the SAMT and Hiero baselines.

System	Metric Scores BLEU	MET	TER	Sig. SAMT? B	M	T	Sig. Hiero? B	M	T
SAMT	22.10	24.94	63.78				▽	▽	▽
Collapse 1	23.01	26.03	63.35	▲	▲	▲		▲	
Collapse 2	23.53	26.50	63.29	▲	▲	▲	▲	▲	
Collapse 3	23.61	26.37	63.07	▲	▲	▲	▲	▲	▲
Hiero	23.01	25.72	63.53	▲	▲	▲			

Table 3: MT '08 test set results. The first section gives automatic metric scores; the remaining sections indicate whether each system is statistically significantly better (▲) or worse (▽) than the SAMT and Hiero baselines.

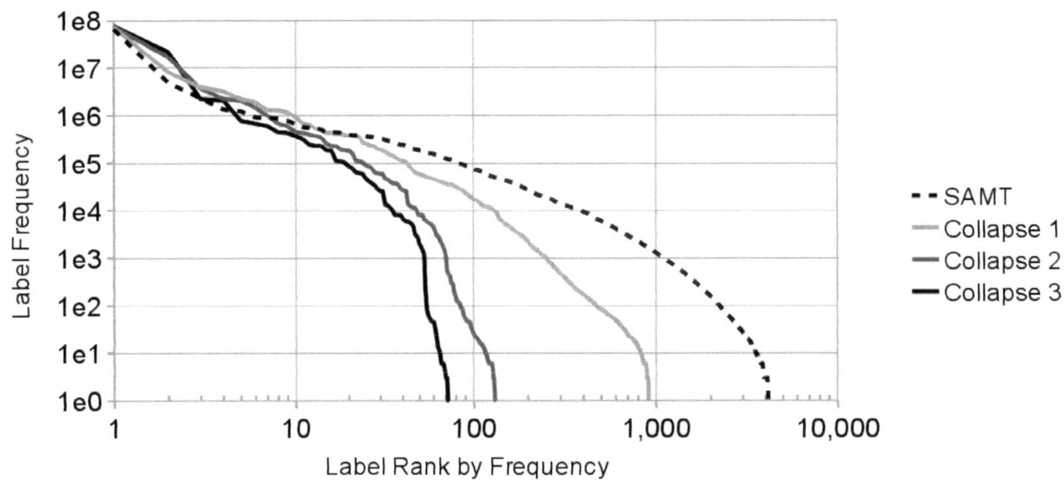

Figure 4: Extracted frequency of each target-side label, with labels arranged in order of decreasing frequency count. Note the log–log scale of the plot.

5 Analysis

Tables 2 and 3 show that the coarsened grammars significantly improve translation performance over the SAMT baseline. This is especially true for the "Collapse 3" setting of 72 labels, which scores 1.14 BLEU higher on MT '03 and 1.51 BLEU higher on MT '08 than the uncollapsed system.

On the easier MT '03 set, label-collapsed systems do not generally outperform Hiero, although Collapse 3 achieves a statistical tie according to BLEU (+0.02) and a statistical improvement over Hiero according to METEOR (+0.33). MT '08 appears as a significantly harder test set: metric scores for all systems are drastically lower, and we find approximately 7% to 8% fewer phrase pair matches per sentence. In this case the label-collapsed systems perform better, with all three of them achieving statistical significance over Hiero in at least one metric and statistical ties in the other. The coarsened systems' comparatively better performance on the harder test set suggests that the linguistic information encoded in multiple-nonterminal grammars helps the systems more accurately parse new types of input.

Table 1 already showed at a global scale the strong effect of label collapsing on reducing derivational ambiguity, as labeled variants of the same basic structural rule were progressively combined. Since category coarsening is purely a relabeling operation, any reordering pattern implemented in the original SAMT grammar still exists in the collapsed versions; therefore, any reduction in the size of the grammar is a reduction in variant labelings. Figure 4 shows this process in more detail for the baseline SAMT grammar and the three collapsed grammars. For each grammar, labels are arranged in decreasing order of extracted frequency, and the frequency count of each label is plotted. The long tail of rare categories in the SAMT grammar (1950 labels seen fewer than 100 times each) is combined into a progressively sharper distribution at each step. Not only are there fewer rare labels, but these hard-to-model categories consume a proportionally smaller fraction of the total label set: from 47% in the baseline grammar down to 26% in Collapse 3.

We find that label collapsing disproportionately affects frequently extracted and hierarchical rules over rarer rules and phrase pairs. The 15.7% reduction in total grammar size between the SAMT baseline and the Collapse 3 system affects 18.0% of the hierarchical rules, but only 1.6% of the phrase pairs. If rules are counted separately each time they match another source sentence, the average reduction in size of a sentence-filtered grammar is 57.8%.

Intuitively, hierarchical rules are more affected by label collapsing because phrase pairs do not have many variant left-hand-side labels to begin with, while the same hierarchical rule pattern may be instantiated in the grammar by a large number of variant labelings. We can see this situation in more detail by counting variants of a particular set of rules. Labeled forms of the Hiero-style rule

$$X \rightarrow [X^1 \text{ 的 } X^2] :: [\text{the } X^2 \text{ of } X^1] \qquad (6)$$

are among the most frequently used rules in all five of our systems. The way they are treated by label collapsing thus has a strong impact on the results of runtime decoding.

In the SAMT baseline, Rule (6) appears in the grammar with 221 different labels in the X^1 nonterminal slot, 53 labels for the X^2 slot, and 90 choices of left-hand side — a total of 1330 different labelings all together. More than three-fourths of these variants were extracted three times or fewer from the training data; even if they can be used in a test sentence, statistical features for such low-count rules are poorly estimated. During label collapsing, the number of labeled variations of Rule (6) drops from 1330 to 325, to 96, and finally to 63 in the Collapse 3 grammar. There, the pattern is instantiated with 14 possible X^1 labels, five X^2 labels, and three different left-hand sides.

It is difficult to measure rule sparsity directly (i.e. to count the number of rules that are missing during decoding), but a *reduction* in rule sparsity between systems should be manifested as an increased number of hierarchical rule applications. Figure 5 shows the average number of hierarchical rules applied per sentence, distinguishing syntactic rules from glue rules, on both test sets. The collapsed grammars allow for approximately one additional syntactic rule application per sentence compared to the SAMT baseline, or three additional applications compared to Hiero. This shows an implicit reduction in missing syntactic rules in the collapsed grammars. In the

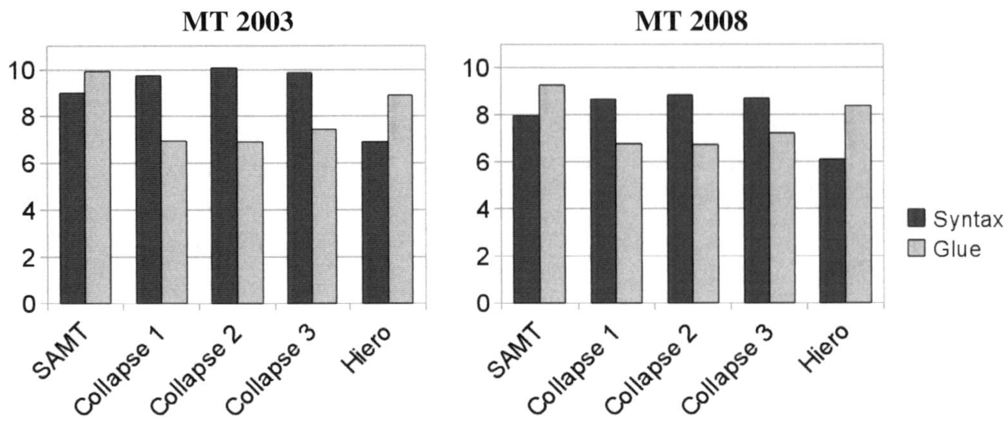

Figure 5: Average number of hierarchical rules (both syntactic and glue rules) applied per sentence on each test set.

glue rule columns, we note that label collapsing also promotes a shift away from generic glue rules, possibly via the creation of more permissive — but still meaningfully labeled — syntactic rules.

6 Conclusion

We demonstrated a viable technique for reducing the label set size in SAMT grammars by temporarily inducing bilingual syntax and using it in an existing tree-to-tree category coarsening algorithm. In collapsing SAMT category labels, we were able to significantly improve translation quality while using a grammar less than half the size of the original. We believe it is also more robust to test-set or domain variation than a single-nonterminal Hiero grammar. Collapsed grammars confer practical benefits during both model estimation and runtime decoding. We showed that, in particular, they suffer less from rule sparsity and derivational ambiguity problems that are common to larger label sets.

We can highlight two areas for potential improvements in future work. In our current implementation of label collapsing, we indiscriminately allow either source labels or target labels to be collapsed at each iteration of the algorithm (see Equation 3). This is an intuitively sensible setting when collapsing bilingual labels, but it is perhaps less obviously so for a monolingually labeled system such as SAMT. An alternative would be to collapse target-side labels only, leaving the source-side labels alone since they do not appear in the final grammar anyway. In this case, the target labels would be represented and clustered as distributions over a static set of latent categories.

A larger area of future concern is the stopping point of the collapsing algorithm. In our previous work (Hanneman and Lavie, 2011), we manually identified iterations in our run of the algorithm where the L_1 distance between the most recently collapsed label pair was markedly lower than the L_1 difference of the pair in the previous iteration. Such an approach is more feasible in our previous runs of 120 iterations than in ours here of nearly 2100, where it is not likely that three manually chosen stopping points represent the optimal collapsing results. In future work, we plan to work towards the development of an automatic stopping criterion, a more principled test for whether each successive iteration of label collapsing provides some useful benefit to the underlying grammar.

Acknowledgments

This research work was supported in part by computing resources provided by the NSF-sponsored XSEDE program under grant TG-CCR110017. Thanks to Chris Dyer for providing the word-aligned and preprocessed corpus we used in our experiments. We also thank the anonymous reviewers for helpful comments and suggestions for analysis.

References

Vamshi Ambati, Alon Lavie, and Jaime Carbonell. 2009. Extraction of syntactic translation models from parallel data using syntax from source and target languages.

In *Proceedings of the 12th Machine Translation Summit*, pages 190–197, Ottawa, Canada, August.

Kathryn Baker, Michael Bloodgood, Bonnie J. Dorr, Chris Callison-Burch, Nathaniel W. Filardo, Christine Piatko, Lori Levin, and Scott Miller. 2012. Use of modality and negation in semantically-informed syntactic MT. *Computational Linguistics*, 38(2):411–438.

David Chiang. 2007. Hierarchical phrase-based translation. *Computational Linguistics*, 33(2):201–228.

David Chiang. 2010. Learning to translate with source and target syntax. In *Proceedings of the 48th Annual Meeting of the Association for Computational Linguistics*, pages 1443–1452, Uppsala, Sweden, July.

Jonathan H. Clark, Chris Dyer, Alon Lavie, and Noah A. Smith. 2011. Better hypothesis testing for statistical machine translation: Crontrolling for optimizer instability. In *Proceedings of the 49th Annual Meeting of the Association for Computational Linguistics: Short Papers*, pages 176–181, Portland, OR, June.

Michael Denkowski and Alon Lavie. 2011. Meteor 1.3: Automatic metric for reliable optimization and evaluation of machine translation systems. In *Proceedings of the Sixth Workshop on Statistical Machine Translation*, pages 85–91, Edinburgh, United Kingdom, July.

Chris Dyer, Adam Lopez, Juri Ganitkevitch, Johnathan Weese, Ferhan Ture, Phil Blunsom, Hendra Setiawan, Vladimir Eidelman, and Philip Resnik. 2010. cdec: A decoder, alignment, and learning framework for finite-state and context-free translation models. In *Proceedings of the ACL 2010 System Demonstrations*, pages 7–12, Uppsala, Sweden, July.

Michel Galley, Mark Hopkins, Kevin Knight, and Daniel Marcu. 2004. What's in a translation rule? In *HLT-NAACL 2004: Main Proceedings*, pages 273–280, Boston, MA, May.

Greg Hanneman and Alon Lavie. 2011. Automatic category label coarsening for syntax-based machine translation. In *Proceedings of SSST-5: Fifth Workshop on Syntax, Semantics, and Structure in Statistical Translation*, pages 98–106, Portland, OR, June.

Bryant Huang and Kevin Knight. 2006. Relabeling syntax trees to improve syntax-based machine translation quality. In *Proceedings of the Human Language Technology Conference of the North American Chapter of the ACL*, pages 240–247, New York, NY, June.

Zhongqiang Huang, Martin Cmejrek, and Bowen Zhou. 2010. Soft syntactic constraints for hierarchical phrase-based translation using latent syntactic distributions. In *Proceedings of the 2010 Conference on Empirical Methods in Natural Language Processing*, pages 138–147, Cambridge, MA, October.

Alon Lavie, Alok Parlikar, and Vamshi Ambati. 2008. Syntax-driven learning of sub-sentential translation equivalents and translation rules from parsed parallel corpora. In *Proceedings of the Second ACL Workshop on Syntax and Structure in Statistical Translation*, pages 87–95, Columbus, OH, June.

Yang Liu, Qun Liu, and Shouxun Lin. 2006. Tree-to-string alignment template for statistical machine translation. In *Proceedings of the 21st International Conference on Computational Linguistics and 44th Annual Meeting of the ACL*, pages 609–616, Sydney, Australia, July.

Yang Liu, Yajuan Lü, and Qun Liu. 2009. Improving tree-to-tree translation with packed forests. In *Proceedings of the 47th Annual Meeting of the ACL and the Fourth IJCNLP of the AFNLP*, pages 558–566, Suntec, Singapore, August.

Franz Josef Och and Hermann Ney. 2003. A systematic comparison of various statistical alignment models. *Computational Linguistics*, 29(1):19–51.

Kishore Papineni, Salim Roukos, Todd Ward, and Wei-Jing Zhu. 2002. BLEU: A method for automatic evalution of machine translation. In *Proceedings of the 40th Annual Meeting of the Association for Computational Linguistics*, pages 311–318, Philadelphia, PA, July.

Slav Petrov and Dan Klein. 2007. Improved inference for unlexicalized parsing. In *Proceedings of NAACL HLT 2007*, pages 404–411, Rochester, NY, April.

Matthew Snover, Bonnie Dorr, Richard Schwartz, Linnea Micciulla, and John Makhoul. 2006. A study of translation edit rate with targeted human annotation. In *Proceedings of the Seventh Conference of the Association for Machine Translation in the Americas*, pages 223–231, Cambridge, MA, August.

Ashish Venugopal, Andreas Zollmann, Noah A. Smith, and Stephan Vogel. 2009. Preference grammars: Softening syntactic constraints to improve statistical machine translation. In *Human Language Technologies: The 2009 Annual Conference of the North American Chapter of the ACL*, pages 236–244, Boulder, CO, June.

Jonathan Weese, Juri Ganitkevitch, Chris Callison-Burch, Matt Post, and Adam Lopez. 2011. Joshua 3.0: Syntax-based machine translation with the Thrax grammar extractor. In *Proceedings of the Sixth Workshop on Statistical Machine Translation*, pages 478–484, Edinburgh, United Kingdom, July.

Andreas Zollmann and Ashish Venugopal. 2006. Syntax augmented machine translation via chart parsing. In *Proceedings of the Workshop on Statistical Machine Translation*, pages 138–141, New York, NY, June.

Andreas Zollmann. 2011. *Learning Multiple-Nonterminal Synchronous Grammars for Machine Translation*. Ph.D. thesis, Carnegie Mellon University.

Keyphrase Extraction for N-best Reranking in Multi-Sentence Compression

Florian Boudin and **Emmanuel Morin**
LINA - UMR CNRS 6241, Université de Nantes, France
{florian.boudin,emmanuel.morin}@univ-nantes.fr

Abstract

Multi-Sentence Compression (MSC) is the task of generating a short single sentence summary from a cluster of related sentences. This paper presents an N-best reranking method based on keyphrase extraction. Compression candidates generated by a word graph-based MSC approach are reranked according to the number and relevance of keyphrases they contain. Both manual and automatic evaluations were performed using a dataset made of clusters of newswire sentences. Results show that the proposed method significantly improves the informativity of the generated compressions.

1 Introduction

Multi-Sentence Compression (MSC) can be broadly described as the task of generating a short single sentence summary from a cluster of related sentences. It has recently attracted much attention, mostly because of its relevance to single or multi-document extractive summarization. A standard way to generate summaries consists in ranking sentences by importance, cluster them by similarity and select a sentence from the top ranked clusters (Wang et al., 2008). One difficulty is then to generate concise, non-redundant summaries. Selected sentences almost always contain additional information specific to the documents from which they came, leading to readability issues in the summary.

Sentence Compression (SC), i.e. the task of summarizing a sentence while retaining most of the informational content and remaining grammatical (Jing, 2000), is a straightforward solution to this problem. Another solution would be to create, for each cluster of related sentences, a concise and fluent fusion of information, reflecting facts common to all sentences. Originally defined as sentence fusion (Barzilay and McKeown, 2005), MSC is a text-to-text generation process in which a novel sentence is produced as a result of summarizing common information across a set of similar sentences.

Most of the previous MSC approaches rely on syntactic parsers for producing grammatical compressions, e.g. (Filippova and Strube, 2008; Elsner and Santhanam, 2011). Recently, (Filippova, 2010) proposed a word graph-based approach which only requires a Part-Of-Speech (POS) tagger and a list of stopwords. The key assumption behind her approach is that redundancy within the set of related sentences provides a reliable way of generating informative and grammatical sentences. Although this approach seemingly works well, 48% to 60% of the generated sentences are missing important information about the set of related sentences. In this study, we aim at producing more informative sentences by maximizing the range of topics they cover.

Keyphrases are words that capture the main topics of a document. Extracting keyphrases can benefit various Natural Language Processing tasks such as summarization, information retrieval and question-answering (Kim et al., 2010). In summarization, keyphrases provide semantic metadata that represent the content of a document. Sentences containing the most relevant keyphrases are used to generate the summary (D'Avanzo and Magnini, 2005). In the same way, we hypothesize that keyphrases can be used to better generate sentences that convey the gist of the set of related sentences.

In this paper, we present a reranking method of N-best multi-sentence compressions based on keyphrase extraction and describe a series of experiments conducted on a manually constructed evaluation corpus. More precisely, the main contributions of our work are as follows:

- We extend Filippova (2010)'s word graph-based MSC approach to produce well-punctuated and more informative compressions.
- We investigate the use of automatic Machine Translation (MT) and summarization evaluation metrics to evaluate MSC performance.
- We introduce a French evaluation dataset made of 40 sets of related sentences along with reference compressions composed by humans.

The rest of this paper is organized as follows. We first briefly review the previous work, followed by a description of the method we propose. Next, we give the details of the evaluation dataset we have constructed and present our experiments and results. Lastly, we conclude with a discussion and directions for further work.

2 Related work

2.1 Multi-sentence compression

MSC have received much attention recently and many different approaches have been proposed. The pioneering work of (Barzilay and McKeown, 2005) introduced the framework used by many subsequent works: input sentences are represented by dependency trees, some words are aligned to merge the trees into a lattice, and the lattice is linearized using tree traversal to produce fusion sentences. (Filippova and Strube, 2008) cast MSC as an integer linear program, and show promising results for German. Later, (Elsner and Santhanam, 2011) proposed a supervised approach trained on examples of manually fused sentences.

Previously described approaches require the use of a syntactic parser to control the grammaticality of the output. As an alternative, several word graph-based approaches that only require a POS tagger were proposed. The key assumption is that redundancy provides a reliable way of generating grammatical sentences. First, a directed word graph is constructed from the set of input sentences in which nodes represent unique words, defined as word and POS tuples, and edges express the original structure of sentences (i.e. word ordering). Sentence compressions are obtained by finding commonly used paths in the graph. Word graph-based MSC approaches were used in different tasks, such as guided microblog summarization (Sharifi et al., 2010), opinion summarization (Ganesan et al., 2010) and newswire summarization (Filippova, 2010).

2.2 Keyphrase extraction

Keyphrases are words that are representative of the main content of documents. Extracting keyphrases can benefit various Natural Language Processing tasks such as summarization, information retrieval and question-answering (Kim et al., 2010). Previous works fall into two categories: supervised and unsupervised methods. The idea behind supervised methods is to recast keyphrase extraction as a binary classification task. A model is trained using annotated data to determine whether a given phrase is a keyphrase or not (Frank et al., 1999; Turney, 2000).

Unsupervised approaches proposed so far have involved a number of techniques, including language modeling (Tomokiyo and Hurst, 2003), graph-based ranking (Mihalcea and Tarau, 2004; Wan and Xiao, 2008) and clustering (Liu et al., 2009). While supervised approaches have generally proven more successful, the need for training data and the bias towards the domain on which they are trained remain two critical issues.

3 Method

In this section, we first describe Filippova (2010)'s word graph-based MSC approach. Then, we present the keyphrase extraction approach we use and our method for reranking generated compressions.

3.1 Description of Filippova's approach

Let $G = (V, E)$ be a directed graph with the set of vertices (nodes) V and a set of directed edges E, where E is a subset of $V \times V$. Given a set of related sentences $S = \{s_1, s_2, ..., s_n\}$, a word graph is constructed by iteratively adding sentences to it.

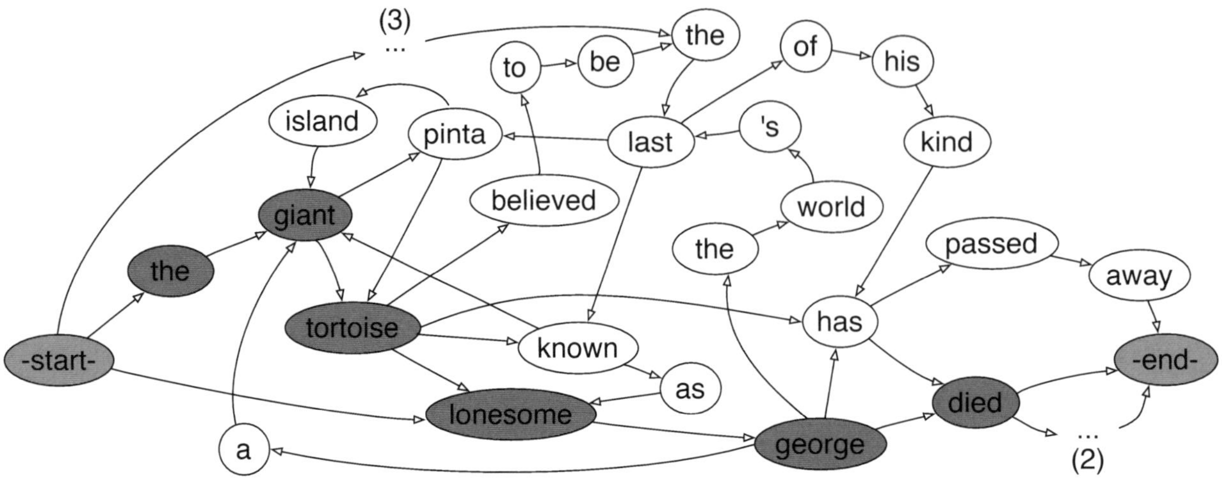

Figure 1: Word graph constructed from the set of related sentences, a possible compression path is also given.

Figure 1 is an illustration of the word graph constructed from the following sentences. For clarity, edge weights are omitted and italicized fragments from the sentences are replaced with dots.

1. Lonesome George, the world's last Pinta Island giant tortoise, has passed away.

2. The giant tortoise known as Lonesome George died *Sunday at the Galapagos National Park in Ecuador*.

3. *He was only about a hundred years old, but* the last known giant Pinta tortoise, Lonesome George, has passed away.

4. Lonesome George, a giant tortoise believed to be the last of his kind, has died.

At the first step, the graph simply represents one sentence plus the start and end symbols (–start– and –end– in Figure 1). A node is added to G for each word in the sentence, and words adjacent in the sentence are connected with directed edges. A word from the following sentences is mapped onto an existing node in the graph if they have the same lowercased word form and POS and that no word from this sentence has already been mapped onto this node. A new node is created if there is no suitable candidate in the graph.

Words are added to the graph in the following order:

i. non-stopwords for which no candidate exists in the graph or for which an unambiguous mapping is possible;

ii. non-stopwords for which there are either several possible candidates in the graph or which occur more than once in the sentence;

iii. stopwords.

For the last two groups of words where mapping is ambiguous (i.e. there are two or more nodes in the graph that refer to the same word/POS tuple), the immediate context (the preceding and following words in the sentence and the neighboring nodes in the graph) or the frequency (i.e. the node which has words mapped onto it) are used to select the candidate node. We use the stopword list included in nltk[1] extended with temporal nouns (e.g. monday, yesterday).

In Filippova's approach, punctuation marks are excluded. To generate well-punctuated compressions, we simply added a fourth step for adding punctuation marks in the graph. When mapping is ambiguous, we select the candidate which has the same immediate context.

Once the words from a sentence are added to the graph, words adjacent in the sentence are connected with directed edges. Edge weights are calculated using the weighting function defined in Equation 1.

[1] `http://nltk.org/`

$$w(i,j) = \frac{\text{cohesion}(i,j)}{\text{freq}(i) \times \text{freq}(j)} \quad (1)$$

$$\text{cohesion}(i,j) = \frac{\text{freq}(i) + \text{freq}(j)}{\sum_{s \in S} d(s,i,j)^{-1}} \quad (2)$$

where $\text{freq}(i)$ is the number of words mapped to the node i. The function $d(s,i,j)$ refers to the distance between the offset positions of words i and j in sentence s.

The purpose of this function is two fold: i. to generate a grammatical compression, links between words which appear often in this order are favored (see Equation 2); ii. to generate an informative compression, the weight of edges connecting salient nodes is decreased.

A K-shortest paths algorithm is then used to find the 50 shortest paths from start to end nodes in the graph. Paths shorter than eight words or that do not contain a verb are filtered. The remaining paths are reranked by normalizing the total path weight over its length. The path which has the lightest average edge weight is then considered as the best compression.

3.2 Reranking paths using keyphrases

The main difficulty of MSC is to generate sentences that are both informative and grammatically correct. Here, redundancy within the set of input sentences is used to identify important words and salient links between words. Although this approach seemingly works well, important information is missing in 48% to 60% of the generated sentences (Filippova, 2010). One of the reasons for this is that node salience is estimated only with the frequency measure. To tackle this issue, we propose to rerank the N-best list of compressions using keyphrases extracted from the set of related sentences. Intuitively, an informative sentence should contain the most relevant keyphrases. We propose to rerank generated compressions according to the number and relevance of keyphrases they contain.

An unsupervised method based on (Wan and Xiao, 2008) is used to extract keyphrases from each set of related sentences. This method is based on the assumption that a word recommends other co-occurring words, and the strength of the recommendation is recursively computed based on the importance of the words making the recommendation. Keyphrase extraction can be divided into two steps. First, a weighted graph is constructed from the set of related sentences, in which nodes represent words defined as word and POS tuples. Two nodes (words) are connected if their corresponding lexical units co-occur within a sentence. Edge weights are the number of times two words co-occur. TextRank (Mihalcea and Tarau, 2004), a graph-based ranking algorithm that takes into account edge weights, is applied for computing a salience score for each node. The score for node V_i is initialized with a default value and is computed in an iterative manner until convergence using this equation:

$$S(V_i) = (1-d) + d \times \sum_{V_j \in adj(V_i)} \frac{w_{ji}}{\sum_{V_k \in adj(V_i)} w_{jk}} S(V_i)$$

where $adj(V_i)$ denotes the neighbors of V_i and d is the damping factor set to 0.85.

The second step consists in generating and scoring keyphrase candidates. Sequences of adjacent words satisfying a specific syntactic pattern are collapsed into multi-word phrases. We use `(ADJ)*(NPP|NC)+(ADJ)*` for French, in which `ADJ` are adjectives, `NPP` are proper nouns and `NC` are common nouns.

The score of a candidate keyphrase k is computed by summing the salience scores of the words it contains normalized by its length + 1 to favor longer n-grams (see equation 3).

$$\text{score}(k) = \frac{\sum_{w \in k} \text{TextRank}(w)}{\text{length}(k) + 1} \quad (3)$$

The small vocabulary size as well as the high redundancy within the set of related sentences are two factors that make keyphrase extraction easier to achieve. On the other hand, a large number of the generated keyphrases are redundant. Some keyphrases may be contained within larger ones, e.g. *giant tortoise* and *Pinta Island giant tortoise*. To solve this problem, generated keyphrases are clustered using word overlap. For each cluster, we then select the keyphrase with the highest score. This filtering process enables the generation of a smaller subset of keyphrases while having a better coverage of the cluster content.

Reranking techniques can suffer from the limited scope of the N-best list, which may rule out many potentially good candidates. For this reason, we use a larger number of paths than the one in (Filippova, 2010). Accordingly, the K-shortest paths algorithm is used to find the 200 shortest paths. We rerank the paths by normalizing the total path weight over its length multiplied by the sum of keyphrase scores it contains. The score of a sentence compression c is given by:

$$\mathrm{score}(c) = \frac{\sum_{i,j \in \mathrm{path}(c)} w_{(i,j)}}{\mathrm{length}(c) \times \sum_{k \in c} \mathrm{score}(k)} \quad (4)$$

4 Experimental settings

4.1 Construction of the evaluation dataset

To our knowledge, there is no dataset available to evaluate MSC in an automatic way. The performance of the previously described approaches was assessed by human judges. In this work, we introduce a new evaluation dataset made of 40 sets of related sentences along with reference compressions composed by human assessors. The purpose of this dataset is to investigate the use of existing automatic evaluation metrics for the MSC task.

Similar to (Filippova, 2010), we collected news articles presented in clusters on the French edition of Google News[2] over a period of three months. Clusters composed of at least 20 news articles and containing one single prevailing event were manually selected. To obtain the sets of related sentences, we extracted the first sentences from each article in the cluster, removing duplicates. Leading sentences in news articles are known to provide a good summary of the article content and are used as a baseline in summarization (Dang, 2005).

The resulting dataset contains 618 sentences (33 tokens on average) spread over 40 clusters. The number of sentences within each cluster is on average 15, with a minimum of 7 and a maximum of 36. The word redundancy rate within the dataset, computed as the number of unique words over the number of words for each cluster, is 38.8%.

Three reference compressions were manually composed for each set of sentences. Human annotators, all native French speakers, were asked to carefully read the set of sentences, extract the most salient facts and generate a sentence (compression) that summarize the set of sentences. Annotators were also told to introduce as little new vocabulary as possible in their compressions. The purpose of this guideline is to reduce the number of possible mismatches, as existing evaluation metrics are based on n-gram comparison. Reference compressions have a compression rate of 60%.

4.2 Automatic evaluation

The use of automatic methods for evaluating machine-generated text has gradually become the mainstream in Computational Linguistics. Well known examples are the ROUGE (Lin, 2004) and BLEU (Papineni et al., 2002) evaluation metrics used in the summarization and MT communities. These metrics assess the quality of a system output by computing its similarity to one or more human-generated references.

Prior work in sentence compression use the F1 measure over grammatical relations to evaluate candidate compressions (Riezler et al., 2003). It was shown to correlate significantly with human judgments (Clarke and Lapata, 2006) and behave similarly to BLEU (Unno et al., 2006). However, this metric is not entirely reliable as it depends on parser accuracy and the type of dependency relations used (Napoles et al., 2011). In this work, the following evaluation measures are considered relevant: BLEU[3], ROUGE-1 (unigrams), ROUGE-2 (bigrams) and ROUGE-SU4 (bigrams with skip distance up to 4 words)[4]. ROUGE measures are computed using stopword removal and French stemming [5].

4.3 Manual evaluation

The quality of the generated compressions was assessed in an experiment with human raters. Two aspects were considered: grammaticality and informativity. Following previous work (Barzilay and McKeown, 2005), we asked raters to assess grammaticality on a 3-points scale: *perfect* (2 pts), if the compression is a complete grammatical sentence; *almost*

[2]http://news.google.fr

[3]ftp://jaguar.ncsl.nist.gov/mt/resources/mteval-v13a.pl

[4]We use the version 1.5.5 of the ROUGE package available from http://www.berouge.com

[5]http://snowball.tartarus.org/

(1 pt), if it requires minor editing, e.g. one mistake in articles, agreement or punctuation; *ungrammatical* (0 pts), if it is none of the above. Raters were explicitly asked to ignore lack of capitalization while evaluating grammaticality.

Informativity is evaluated according to the 3-points scale defined in (Filippova, 2010): *perfect* (2 pts), if the compression conveys the gist of the main event and is more or less like the summary the person would produce himself; *related* (1 pt), if it is related to the the main theme but misses something important; *unrelated* (0 pts), if the compression is not related to the main theme.

Three raters, all native French speakers, were hired to assess the generated compressions.

5 Results

To evaluate the effectiveness of our method, we compare the compressions generated with Filippova's approach (denoted as baseline) against the ones obtained by reranking paths using keyphrases (denoted as KeyRank). We evaluated the agreement between the three raters using Fleiss's kappa (Artstein and Poesio, 2008). The κ value is 0.56 which denotes a moderate agreement.

Table 1 presents the average grammaticality and informativity scores. Results achieved by the baseline are consistent with the ones presented in (Filippova, 2010). We observe a significant improvement in informativity for KeyRank. Grammaticality scores are, however, slightly decreased. One reason for that is the reranking we added to the shortest path method that outputs longer compressions. The average length for our method is nevertheless drastically shorter than the average length of the input sentences (19 vs. 33 tokens). This corresponds to a compression rate (58%) that is close to the one observed on reference compressions (60%).

Table 2 shows the distributions over the three scores for both grammaticality and informativity. We observe that 97.5% of the compressions generated with KeyRank are related to the main theme of the cluster, and 62.5% convey the very gist of it without missing any important information. This represents an absolute increase of 19.2% over the baseline. Although our reranking method has lower grammaticality scores, 65% of the generated sentences are perfectly grammatical.

Method	**Gram.**	**Info.**	**Length**		**CompR**
			Avg.	Std.Dev.	
Baseline	1.63	1.33	16.3	4.8	50%
KeyRank	1.53	$1.60^{\dagger}$	19	6.1	58%

Table 1: Average ratings over all clusters and raters along with average compression length (in tokens), standard deviation and corresponding compression rate († indicates significance at the 0.01 level using Student's t-test).

Method	**Gram.**			**Info.**		
	0	1	2	0	1	2
Baseline	9.2%	18.3%	72.5%	10.0%	46.7%	43.3%
KeyRank	11.7%	23.3%	65.0%	2.5%	35.0%	62.5%

Table 2: Distribution over possible manual ratings for grammaticality and informativity. Ratings are expressed on a scale of 0 to 2.

Table 3 shows the performance of the baseline and our reranking method in terms of ROUGE and BLEU scores. KeyRank significantly outperforms the baseline according to the different ROUGE metrics. This indicates an improvement in informativity for the compressions generated using our method. We observe a large but not significant increase in BLEU scores. The slightly decreased grammaticality scores could be a reason for this. BLEU is essentially a precision metric, and it measures how well a compression candidate overlaps with multiple references. Longer n-grams used by BLEU[6] tend to score for grammaticality rather than content.

Metric	**Baseline**	**KeyRank**
ROUGE-1	0.57441	$0.65677^{\ddagger}$
ROUGE-2	0.39212	$0.44140^{\dagger}$
ROUGE-SU4	0.37004	$0.43443^{\ddagger}$
BLEU	0.61560	0.65770

Table 3: Automatic evaluation scores († and ‡ indicate significance at the 0.01 and 0.001 levels respectively using Student's t-test)

To assess the effectiveness of automatic evalua-

[6] BLEU measures are computed using 4-grams.

tion metrics, we compute the Pearson's correlation coefficient between ROUGE and BLEU scores and averaged manual ratings. According to Table 4, results show medium to strong correlation between ROUGE scores and informativity ratings. On the other hand, BLEU scores better correlate with grammaticality ratings. Overall, automatic evaluation metrics are not highly correlated with manual ratings. One reason for that may be that the manual score assignments are arbitrary (i.e. 0, 1, 2), and that a score of one is in fact closer to two than to zero. Results suggest that automatic metrics do give an indication of the compression quality, but can not replace manual evaluation.

Metric	Gram.	Info.
ROUGE-1	0.402	0.591
ROUGE-2	0.432	0.494
ROUGE-SU4	0.386	0.542
BLEU	0.444	0.401

Table 4: Pearson correlation coefficients for automatic metrics vs. average human ratings.

6 Conclusion

This paper presented a multi-sentence compression approach that uses keyphrases to generate more informative compressions. We extended Filippova (2010)'s word graph-based MSC approach by adding a re-reranking step that favors compressions that contain the most relevant keyphrases of the input sentence set. An implementation of the proposed multi-sentence compression approach is available for download[7]. We constructed an evaluation dataset made of 40 sets of related sentences along with reference compressions composed by humans. This dataset is freely available for download[8]. We performed both manual and automatic evaluations and showed that our method significantly improves the informativity of the generated compressions. We also investigated the correlation between manual and automatic evaluation metrics and found that ROUGE and BLEU have a medium correlation with manual ratings.

In future work, we intend to examine how grammaticality of the generated compressions can be enhanced. Similar to the work of Hasan et al. (2006) in the Machine Translation field, we plan to experiment with high order POS language models reranking.

Acknowledgments

The authors would like to thank Sebastián Peña Saldarriaga and Ophélie Lacroix for helpful comments on this work. We thank the anonymous reviewers for their useful comments. This work was supported by the French Agence Nationale de la Recherche under grant ANR-12-CORD-0027 and by the French Region Pays de Loire in the context of the DEPART project (`http://www.projetdepart.org/`).

References

R. Artstein and M. Poesio. 2008. Inter-coder agreement for computational linguistics. *Computational Linguistics*, 34(4):555–596.

Regina Barzilay and Kathleen R. McKeown. 2005. Sentence fusion for multidocument news summarization. *Computational Linguistics*, 31(3):297–328.

James Clarke and Mirella Lapata. 2006. Models for sentence compression: A comparison across domains, training requirements and evaluation measures. In *Proceedings of the 21st International Conference on Computational Linguistics and 44th Annual Meeting of the Association for Computational Linguistics*, pages 377–384, Sydney, Australia, July. Association for Computational Linguistics.

Hoa Trang Dang. 2005. Overview of duc 2005. In *Proceedings of the Document Understanding Conference*.

Ernesto D'Avanzo and Bernardo Magnini. 2005. A keyphrase-based approach to summarization: the lake system at duc-2005. In *Proceedings of the Document Understanding Conference*.

Micha Elsner and Deepak Santhanam. 2011. Learning to fuse disparate sentences. In *Proceedings of the Workshop on Monolingual Text-To-Text Generation*, pages 54–63, Portland, Oregon, June. Association for Computational Linguistics.

Katja Filippova and Michael Strube. 2008. Sentence fusion via dependency graph compression. In *Proceedings of the 2008 Conference on Empirical Methods in Natural Language Processing*, pages 177–185, Honolulu, Hawaii, October. Association for Computational Linguistics.

Katja Filippova. 2010. Multi-Sentence Compression: Finding Shortest Paths in Word Graphs. In *Proceed-*

[7] `https://github.com/boudinfl/takahe`

[8] `https://github.com/boudinfl/lina-msc`

ings of the 23rd International Conference on Computational Linguistics (Coling 2010), pages 322–330, Beijing, China, August. Coling 2010 Organizing Committee.

Eibe Frank, Gordon W. Paynter, Ian H. Witten, Carl Gutwin, and Craig G. Nevill-Manning. 1999. Domain-specific keyphrase extraction.

Kavita Ganesan, ChengXiang Zhai, and Jiawei Han. 2010. Opinosis: A Graph Based Approach to Abstractive Summarization of Highly Redundant Opinions. In *Proceedings of the 23rd International Conference on Computational Linguistics (Coling 2010)*, pages 340–348, Beijing, China, August. Coling 2010 Organizing Committee.

S. Hasan, O. Bender, and H. Ney. 2006. Reranking translation hypotheses using structural properties. In *Proceedings of the EACL Workshop on Learning Structured Information in Natural Language Applications*, pages 41–48.

Hongyan Jing. 2000. Sentence reduction for automatic text summarization. In *Proceedings of the Sixth Conference on Applied Natural Language Processing*, pages 310–315, Seattle, Washington, USA, April. Association for Computational Linguistics.

Su Nam Kim, Olena Medelyan, Min-Yen Kan, and Timothy Baldwin. 2010. Semeval-2010 task 5 : Automatic keyphrase extraction from scientific articles. In *Proceedings of the 5th International Workshop on Semantic Evaluation*, pages 21–26, Uppsala, Sweden, July. Association for Computational Linguistics.

Chin-Yew Lin. 2004. Rouge: A package for automatic evaluation of summaries. In Stan Szpakowicz Marie-Francine Moens, editor, *Text Summarization Branches Out: Proceedings of the ACL-04 Workshop*, pages 74–81, Barcelona, Spain, July. Association for Computational Linguistics.

Zhiyuan Liu, Peng Li, Yabin Zheng, and Maosong Sun. 2009. Clustering to find exemplar terms for keyphrase extraction. In *Proceedings of the 2009 Conference on Empirical Methods in Natural Language Processing*, pages 257–266, Singapore, August. Association for Computational Linguistics.

Rada Mihalcea and Paul Tarau. 2004. Textrank: Bringing order into texts. In Dekang Lin and Dekai Wu, editors, *Proceedings of EMNLP 2004*, pages 404–411, Barcelona, Spain, July. Association for Computational Linguistics.

Courtney Napoles, Benjamin Van Durme, and Chris Callison-Burch. 2011. Evaluating sentence compression: Pitfalls and suggested remedies. In *Proceedings of the Workshop on Monolingual Text-To-Text Generation*, pages 91–97, Portland, Oregon, June. Association for Computational Linguistics.

Kishore Papineni, Salim Roukos, Todd Ward, and Wei-Jing Zhu. 2002. Bleu: a method for automatic evaluation of machine translation. In *Proceedings of 40th Annual Meeting of the Association for Computational Linguistics*, pages 311–318, Philadelphia, Pennsylvania, USA, July. Association for Computational Linguistics.

Stefan Riezler, Tracy H. King, Richard Crouch, and Annie Zaenen. 2003. Statistical sentence condensation using ambiguity packing and stochastic disambiguation methods for lexical-functional grammar. In *Proceedings of the 2003 Conference of the North American Chapter of the Association for Computational Linguistics on Human Language Technology-Volume 1*, pages 118–125. Association for Computational Linguistics.

Beaux Sharifi, Mark-Anthony Hutton, and Jugal Kalita. 2010. Summarizing Microblogs Automatically. In *Human Language Technologies: The 2010 Annual Conference of the North American Chapter of the Association for Computational Linguistics*, pages 685–688, Los Angeles, California, June. Association for Computational Linguistics.

Takashi Tomokiyo and Matthew Hurst. 2003. A language model approach to keyphrase extraction. In *Proceedings of the ACL 2003 Workshop on Multiword Expressions: Analysis, Acquisition and Treatment*, pages 33–40, Sapporo, Japan, July. Association for Computational Linguistics.

Peter D. Turney. 2000. Learning algorithms for keyphrase extraction. *Information Retrieval*, 2(4):303–336.

Yuya Unno, Takashi Ninomiya, Yusuke Miyao, and Jun'ichi Tsujii. 2006. Trimming cfg parse trees for sentence compression using machine learning approaches. In *Proceedings of the COLING/ACL 2006 Main Conference Poster Sessions*, pages 850–857, Sydney, Australia, July. Association for Computational Linguistics.

Xiaojun Wan and Jianguo Xiao. 2008. Collabrank: Towards a collaborative approach to single-document keyphrase extraction. In *Proceedings of the 22nd International Conference on Computational Linguistics (Coling 2008)*, pages 969–976, Manchester, UK, August. Coling 2008 Organizing Committee.

Dingding Wang, Tao Li, Shenghuo Zhu, and Chris Ding. 2008. Multi-document Summarization via Sentence-Level Semantic Analysis and Symmetric Matrix Factorization. In *Proceedings of the 31st annual international ACM SIGIR conference on Research and development in information retrieval*, SIGIR '08, pages 307–314, New York, NY, USA. ACM.

Development of a Persian Syntactic Dependency Treebank

Mohammad Sadegh Rasooli
Department of Computer Science
Columbia University
New York, NY
rasooli@cs.columbia.edu

Manouchehr Kouhestani
Department of Linguistics
Tarbiat Modares University
Tehran, Iran
m.kouhestani@modares.ac.ir

Amirsaeid Moloodi
Department of Linguistics
University of Tehran
Tehran, Iran
a.moloodi@ut.ac.ir

Abstract

This paper describes the annotation process and linguistic properties of the Persian syntactic dependency treebank. The treebank consists of approximately 30,000 sentences annotated with syntactic roles in addition to morpho-syntactic features. One of the unique features of this treebank is that there are almost 4800 distinct verb lemmas in its sentences making it a valuable resource for educational goals. The treebank is constructed with a bootstrapping approach by means of available tagging and parsing tools and manually correcting the annotations. The data is splitted into standard train, development and test set in the CoNLL dependency format and is freely available to researchers.

1 Introduction[1]

The process of manually annotating linguistic data from a huge amount of naturally occuring texts is a very expensive and time consuming task. Due to the recent success of machine learning methods and the rapid growth of available electronic texts, language processing tasks have been facilitated greatly. Considering the value of annotated data, a great deal of budget has been allotted to creating such data.

Among all linguistic datasets, treebanks play an important role in the natural language processing tasks especially in parsing because of its applications in tasks such as machine translation. Dependency treebanks are collections of sentences with their corresponding dependency trees. In the last decade, many dependency treebanks have been developed for a large number of languages. There are at least 29 languages for which at least one dependency treebank is available (Zeman et al., 2012). Dependency trees are much more similar to the human understanding of language and can easily represent the free word-order nature of syntactic roles in sentences (Kübler et al., 2009).

Persian is a language with about 110 million speakers all over the world (Windfuhr, 2009), yet in terms of the availability of teaching materials and annotated data for text processing, it is undoubtedly a low-resourced language. The need for more language teaching materials together with an ever-increasing need for Persian-language data processing has been the incentive for the inception of our project which has defined the development of the syntactic treebank of Persian as its ultimate aim. In this paper, we review the process of creating the Persian syntactic treebank based on dependency grammar. In this treebank, approximately 30,000 sentences from contemporary Persian-language texts are manually tokenized and annotated at morphological and syntactic levels. One valuable aspect of the treebank is its containment of near 5000 distinct verb lemmas in its sentences making it a good resource for educational goals. The dataset is developed after the creation of the syntactic valency lexicon of Persian verbs (Rasooli et al., 2011c). This treebank is developed with a bootstrapping approach by automatically building dependency trees based on the

[1]This research is done while working in Dadegan Research Group, Supreme Council of Information and Communications Technology (SCICT), Tehran, Iran. The project is fully funded by SCICT.

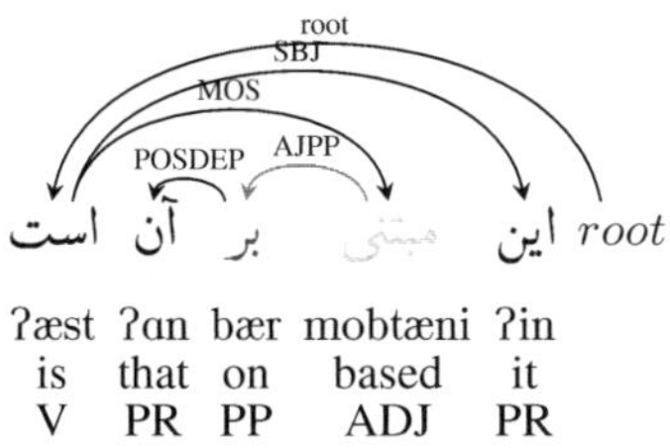

(a) A simple projective dependency tree for a Persian sentence: "It is based on that"'.

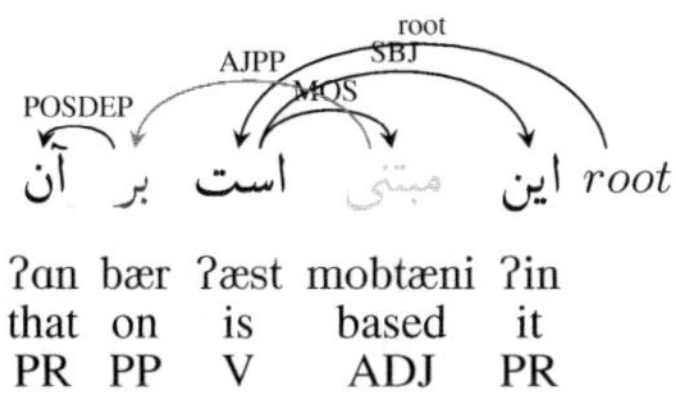

(b) A simple non-projective dependency tree for a Persian sentence: "It is based on that".

Figure 1: Examples of Persian sentences with the dependency-based syntactic trees. 1(a) and 1(b) are examples of a projective and a non-projective dependency tree, respectively. The first lines show the original words in Persian. The pronunciation and their meanings are shown in the second line and the third line respectively. In the fourth line, the part of speech (POS) tags of the words are presented. Note that the words are written from right to left (the direction of Perso-Arabic script). The dependency relations are described in Table 2. The relation is shown with an arc pointing from the head to the dependent.

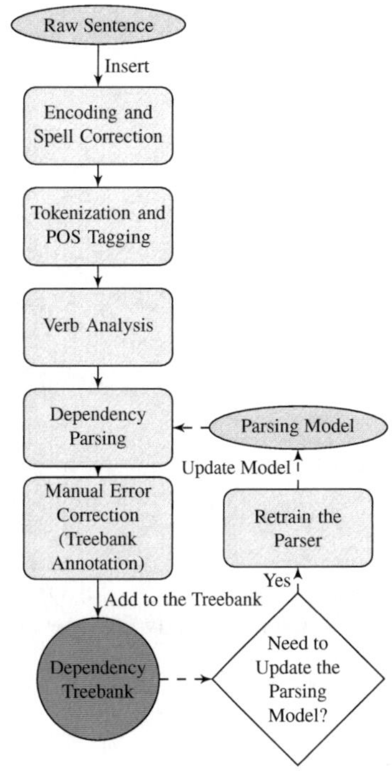

Figure 2: Diagram of bootstrapping approach in the development of the dependency treebank.

previous annotated trees. In the next step, automatic annotation is corrected manually.

The remainder of this paper is as follows. In Section 2, we briefly review the challenges in Persian language processing. In Sections 3 and 4, the details about the annotation process, linguistic and statistical information about the data and the annotator agreement are reported. In Section 5, the conclusion and suggestions for future research are presented.

2 Persian Language Processing Challenges

Persian is an Indo-European language that is written in Arabic script. There are lots of problems in its orthography such as encoding problems, hidden diacritics and writing standards (Kashefi et al., 2010). A number of challenges such as the free order of words, the existence of colloquial texts, the pro-drop nature of the Persian language and its complex inflections (Shamsfard, 2011) in addition to the lack of efficient annotated linguistic data have made the processing of Persian texts very difficult; e.g. there are more than 100 conjugates and 2800 declensions for some word forms in Persian (Rasooli et al., 2011b), some words in the Persian language do not have a clear word category (i.e. the lexical category "mismatch") (Karimi-Doostan, 2011a) and many compound verbs (complex predicates) can be separable (i.e. the non-verbal element may be separated from the verbal element by one or more other words) (Karimi-Doostan, 2011b).

After the development of the Bijankhan corpus (Bijankhan, 2004) with the annotation of word categories, other kinds of datasets have been created to address the need for Persian language processing. Among them, a Persian parser based on link grammar (Dehdari and Lonsdale, 2008), a computational grammar based on GPSG (Bahrani et al., 2011), syntactic treebank based on HPSG (Ghayoomi, 2012) and Uppsala dependency treebank (Seraji et al., 2012) are the efforts to satisfy the need for syntactic processing in the Persian language.

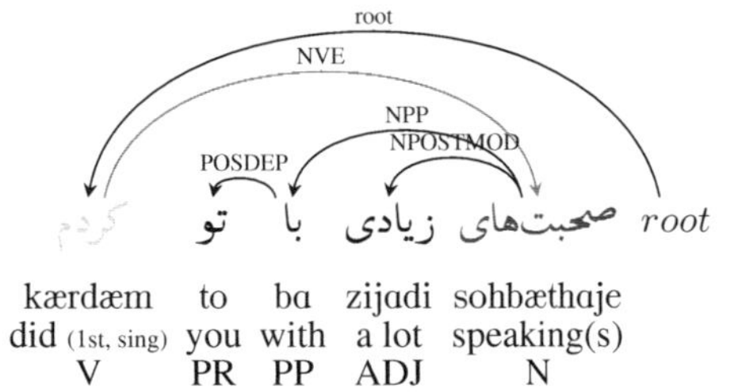

(a) A simple dependency tree with compound verb for a Persian sentence: "I spoke with you a lot". The *NVE* is a relation between a light verb and its nonverbal element. As shown in the tree, not only the nonverbal element is not near the light verb, but also it is inflected for plurality (i.e. speakings).

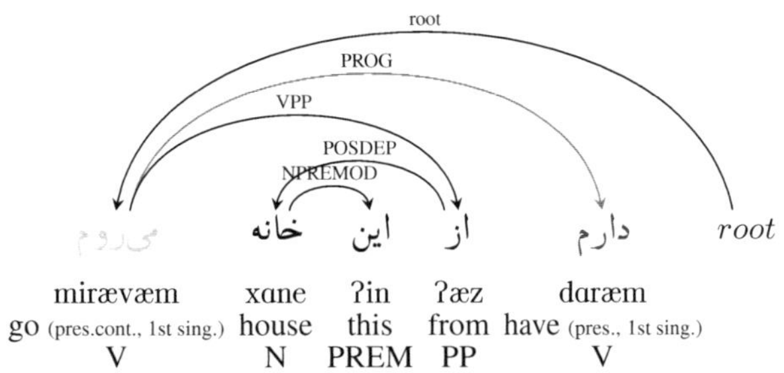

(b) A simple dependency tree for a Persian sentence with a progressive auxiliary: "I am going from this house". The *PROG* is a relation between a verb and its progressive auxiliary.

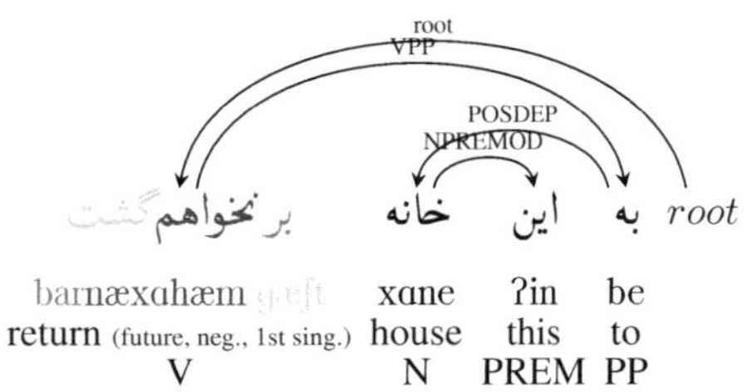

(c) A simple dependency tree for a Persian sentence with a an inflected form of a prefixed verb "I will not return to this house.". The word بر is the prefix, the word نخواهم is the auxiliary for the future and the word گشت is the main verb. Notice that the prefix is attached to the auxiliary without any space and the remaining part of the verb is separated by a space.

Figure 3: Examples of Persian sentences with the dependency-based syntactic trees. The format of the representation is the same as Figure 1.

3 Persian Dependency Treebank

3.1 Motivation

With the creation of the Virastyar spell checker software (Kashefi et al., 2010), many open-source libraries were released for Persian word processing such as POS tagging, encoding refinement, tokenization, etc. Regarding the need for syntactic analysis of Persian texts, we decided to prepare a valuable linguistic data infrastructure for Persian syntax. In the first step, there was a need for choosing from the existing theories of grammar that best suits Persian. Among grammatical theories, we decided to choose the dependency grammar. In dependency grammar, syntactic relations are shown with dependencies between the words. In computational dependency grammar, each word has one head and the head of the sentence is the dependent of an artificial root word (Kübler et al., 2009). A sample dependency tree is shown in Figure 1(a) for a Persian sentence. Note that Persian sentences are written from right to left.

There are several reasons for the preference of dependency grammar to grammars such as phrase-based structure grammars. Although in both of the representations, one can show the syntactic analysis of a sentence, dependency representation has the power to account for the free word order of many languages such as Turkish (Oflazer et al., 2003) and Czech (Hajic, 1998) and also Persian. As an example, a sample non-projective dependency tree for the Persian language is shown in Figure 1(b). The recent advances in very fast dependency parsing models (e.g. (Nivre, 2009; Bohnet and Nivre, 2012)), has made the syntactic processing task very popular in the recent decade.

In the Persian language, in addition to the abundance of crossings of the arcs, another problem occurs with compound verbs and verbs in the progressive aspect: compound and progressive verbs are multi-word expressions that may be separated depending on the context. Persian compound verbs consist of a light verb and a non-verbal element and the non-verbal element can be a noun, an adjective (in rare cases) or a sequence of a preposition and a noun (Dabir-Moghaddam, 1997). In addition, the nonverbal elements can also be inflected. The distance between the nonverbal element and the light verb on the one hand and the possibility of the nonverbal element being inflected on the other hand have made the task of compound verb identification very difficult. For example, in Bijankhan (Peykare) corpus (Bijankhan et al., 2011), approximately 9% of nonverbal elements of compound verbs are placed away from the light verb for the compound verbs with the light verb کردن /kærdæn/ (to do) (Rasooli et al., 2011a). A group of Persian progressive verbs are composed of two words, the first being the simple past or the simple present form derived from the infinitive داشتن /dɑʃtæn/ (to have) and the second being the past continuous or the present continuous form of the main verb. The first verb (an auxiliary) agrees with the second in number and person. The problem is that the progressive auxiliary can be away from the main verb. The sample trees with compound verbs and progressive auxiliary verbs are shown in Figures 3(a) and 3(b) respectively.

3.2 Representation and Dependency Relation

In this treebank, we followed the format of the CoNLL tab-separated format for dependency parsing (Buchholz and Marsi, 2006). In addition to the lemma, we annotated part of speech tags (both coarse and fine grained) and person, number and tense-mood-aspect (only for verbs) of words in sentences. The details of the part of speech tags and other morphosyntactic features and dependency relations are shown in Tables 1 and 2, respectively. The part of speech tag set in this treebank is not the same as that of Bijankhan (Peykare) corpus (Bijankhan et al., 2011) and it is essential to convert the tagset in Peykare corpus to the tagset in this treebank, in order to use both datasets[2]. We also tried to use the writing standard of the Academy of Persian Language and Literature except for the cases where for a word there were several standards all of which were used in Persian written texts (e.g. آنچه and آن‌چه /ʔɑntʃe/ (whatever)).

We also prepared two representations for objects accompanied by the accusative case marker. In the first representation (done manually), we assume the accusative case marker را /rɑ/ as the head of the two-

[2]It is important to note that the conversion between the coarse-grained POS tags is straightforward and does not need any special effort.

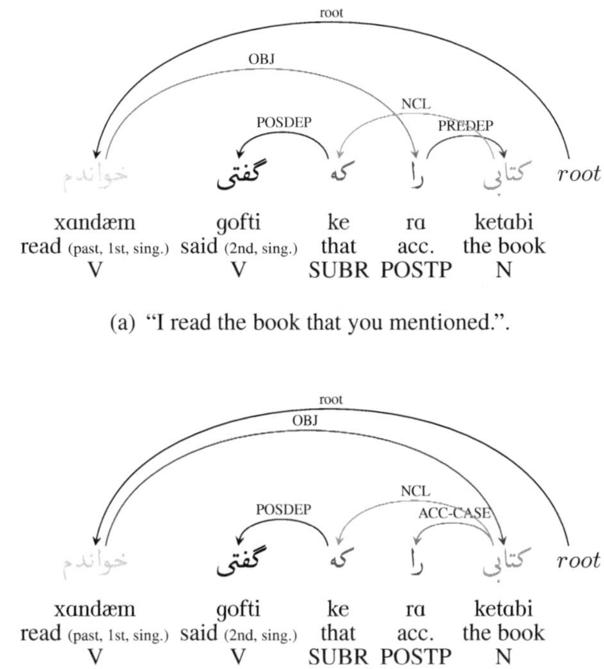

(a) "I read the book that you mentioned.".

(b) "I read the book that you mentioned."

Figure 4: A sample sentence with two kinds of representations of object-verb relation. The first one is done manually and the second automatically by converting the dependencies in the first representation.

word sequence object plus rɑ. The second representation, that is the automatic conversion of the first, is the reverse order of the first one in which the accusative case marker is the dependent of the direct object and the direct object is considered as the head of the aforementioned sequence. In the first representation, objects are much easier to find by the parser (because of the uniqueness of the accusative case marker in Persian and less distance of it from the verb as its head) but it may increase the number of non-projective arcs to the syntactic tree. We prepared both of the representations in two separate data packs. A sample comparison between the two structures is shown in Figure 4.

In the treebank, all words are single word forms (without spaces). There is only one exception for simple verb inflections where even multi-word tokens of simple verbs are shown as only one unit. The reason is that for many cases such as the case of inflections for prefixed verbs it is more straightforward to analyze the whole part instead of analyzing each

Morphosyntactic features in the Persian dependency treebank				
CPOS	**FPOS**	**Person**	**Number**	**TMA**
ADJ (adjective)	AJP (positive) AJCM (comparitive) AJSUP (superlative)			
ADR (address term)	PRADR (pre-noun) POSADR (post-noun)			
ADV (adverb)	SADV (genuine)			
CONJ (coordinating conjunction)	CONJ (conjunction)			
IDEN (title)	IDEN (title)			
N (noun)	ANM (animate) IANM (inanimate)		SING (singular) PLUR (plural)	
PART (particle)	PART (particle)			
POSNUM (post-noun modifier)	POSNUM (post-noun modifier)			
POSTP (postposition)	POSTP (postposition)			
PR (pronoun)	SEPER (separate personal) JOPER (enclitic personal) DEMON (demonstrative) INTG (interogative) CREFX (common reflexive) UCREFX (noncommon reflexive) RECPR (reciprocal)	1 2 3	SING (singular) PLUR (plural)	
PREM (pre-modifier)	EXAJ (exclamatory) QUAJ (interrogative) DEMAJ (demonstrative) AMBAJ (ambiguous)			
PRENUM (pre-noun numeral)	PRENUM (pre-noun numeral)			
PREP (preposition)	PREP (preposition)			
PSUS (pseudo-sentence)	PSUS (pseudo-sentence)			
PUNC (punctuation)	PUNC (punctuation)			
V (verb)	ACT (active) PAS (passive) MOD (modal)	1 2 3	SING (singular) PLUR (plural)	See Table 3
SUBR (subordinating clause)	SUBR (subordinating clause)			

Table 1: Morphosyntactic features in the Persian dependency treebank. Empty cells indicate that the mentioned feature is not present for the POS. *TMA* stands for *Tense/Mood/Aspect*, *CPOS* for *Coarse grained POS* and *FPOS* for *Fine grained POS*. There is also another feature for representing the typographical connectedness of words that are separated into two or more tokens with the values ISO (isolated word), NXT (attached to the next token) and PRV (attached to the previous token).

part separately[3]. In Table 3, possible types of the Persian verb inflections are shown. As seen in Table 3, 6 forms of 14 inflection types of Persian verbs are multi-word tokens and for passive verbs they may be composed of more words than their active counterparts (since for passive verbs an auxiliary form derived from the infinitive شدن /ʃodæn/ is used). In Figure 3(c), a sample tree with a multi-token prefixed verb is shown. As shown in the case of colored tokens, it seems more beneficial to put all morphemes of the word together before parsing. Furthermore, with the available Persian verb analyzer it is very easy to first preprocess the verbs[4].

[3]In (Seraji et al., 2012), multi-token verbs are considered as separate words.

[4]If it is needed to respect the exact format of CoNLL, spaces between the verb tokes should be replaced by a character such as underscore. Regarding the special fine-grained morphological tags for the verb such as tense-mood-aspect, it is also straightforward to separate all of the multi-word verbs and add new dependency relations between their words.

Abbreviation	Description	Abbreviation	Description
ACL	Complement Clause of Adjective	ADV	Adverb
ADVC	Adverbial Complement of Verb	AJCONJ	Conjunction of Adjective
AJPP	Prepositional Complement of Adjective	AJUCL	Adjunct Clause
APOSTMOD	Adjective Post-Modifer	APP	Apposition
APREMOD	Adjective Pre-Modifier	AVCONJ	Conjunction of Adverb
COMPPP	Comparative Preposition	ENC	Enclitic Non-Verbal Element
LVP	Light Verb Particle	MESU	Measure
MOS	Mosnad	MOZ	Ezafe Dependent
NADV	Adverb of Noun	NCL	Clause of Noun
NCONJ	Conjunction of Noun	NE	Non-Verbal Element of Infinitive
NEZ	Ezafe Complement of Adjective	NPOSTMOD	Post-Modifer of Noun
NPP	Preposition of Noun	NPREMOD	Pre-Modifier of Noun
NPRT	Particle of Infinitive	NVE	Non-Verbal Element
OBJ	Object	OBJ2	Second Object
PARCL	Participle Clause	PART	Interrogative Particle
PCONJ	Conjunction of Preposition	POSDEP	Post-Dependent
PRD	Predicate	PREDEP	Pre-Dependent
PROG	Progressive Auxiliary	PUNC	Punctuation Mark
ROOT	Sentence Root	SBJ	Subject
TAM	Tamiz	VCL	Complement Clause of Verb
VCONJ	Conjunction of Verb	VPP	Prepositional Complement of Verb
VPRT	Verb Particle	ACC-CASE	Accusative Case Marker (2nd. Rep.)

Table 2: Dependency relations in the Persian dependency treebank

Tense/Aspect/Mood	Abbreviation	Examples خوردن xordæn: to eat, 1st, sing.
Imperative	HA	بخور /boxor/
Indicative Future	AY	خواهم خورد /xɑhæm xord/
Indicative Imperfective Perfect	GNES	می‌خورده‌ام /mixorde?æm/
Indicative Imperfective Pluperfect	GBES	می‌خورده بودم /mixorde budæm/
Indicative Imperfective Preterite	GES	می‌خوردم /mixordæm/
Indicative Perfect	GN	خورده‌ام /xorde?æm/
Indicative Pluperfect	GB	خورده بودم /xorde budæm/
Indicative Present	H	می‌خورم /mixoræm /
Indicative Preterite	GS	خوردم /xordæm/
Subjunctive Imperfective Pluperfect	GBESE	می‌خورده بوده باشم /mixorde bude bɑʃæm/
Subjunctive Imperfective Preterite	GESEL	می‌خورده باشم /mixorde bɑʃæm/
Subjunctive Pluperfect	GBEL	خورده بوده باشم /xorde bude bɑʃæm/
Subjunctive Present	HEL	بخورم /boxoræm/
Subjunctive Preterite	GEL	خورده باشم /xorde bɑʃæm/

Table 3: Tense/Mood/Aspect Types in Persian verbs

3.3 Annotation Process

The annotation process consists of several consecutive steps. In Figure 2, a summary of the bootstrapping approach in the annotation process is shown. At first, a collection of independent sentences have been collected randomly from the web. For the first 5000 sentences, we crawled Persian news texts and randomly sampled the sentences. For the remaining sentences, we first listed the absent verb lemmas in the 5000 sentences based on the verb list extracted from the valency lexicon of Persian verbs (Rasooli et al., 2011c) and collected random sentences that included the absent verb lemmas in their words. We listed all possible inflections and per each verb lemma, sampled at most 8 sentences from the web. These sentences had to contain at least one present tense, one past tense, one passive voice and one future tense inflection unless we could not find them and were obliged to reduce the number. The sentences were not shortened and were kept with their original length and words. Finally, we manually removed sentences containing colloquial words. However, we did not remove loan words or cases of code-switching between latin-script words and Persian words in the sentences. The raw sentences were fed to the encoding and spell checking module. After spell correction, all sentences were tokenized and tagged with part of speech tags. All of the word processing steps were done using Virastyar library (Kashefi et al., 2010). After tokenization and POS tagging, the tokenized sentences were fed to the Persian verb analyzing tool (Rasooli et al., 2011a). In the next step, the preprocessed sentences were given to the dependency parser. We used MST parser (McDonald et al., 2005) for parsing the sentences.

In the final step, annotators corrected the errors of tokenization, POS tagging and parsing. In about every one to two weeks, the parser model was updated by training on the new version of the treebank. This process lasted 9 months and the number of annotators increased by time to speed up the process. In the first 6 months, we used 8 annotators and for the next 5 months, we hired 6 more annotators to speed up the process. The annotators and linguistic experts consisted of 1 PhD graduate (linguistics), 4 PhD candidates (linguistics), and 9 MA graduates or graduate students (7 linguistics, 1 Persian language and literature and 1 computational linguistics). All of the annotators were native Persian speakers.

After finalizing the annotation of all raw sentences, we applied a rule-based potential error finder to find the potentially erroneous sentences. The rules were gradually collected in the process of the annotation by the annotators. All the potentially erroneous sentences were given to the annotators to be checked for potential errors. In Section 4.1, the statistics about the changes after the correction is reported. One of the main reasons for the double checking phase in the process is that based on our manual investigations of the annotations, we found some inevitable mistakes by annotators that could be solved by manual rules. Mistakes such as scrolling the drop-down list unintentionally and changing the part of speech tag or dependency relation and mistakes caused by tiredness and lack of concentration in addition to some of the changes of the linguistic conventions in the annotation. Since all cases of dependency relations in this treebank may be usually either a left-branching relation or a right-branching one and most of the relations are restricted to certain types of parts of speech, it is easy to capture the potential errors in the annotations based on the rules mentioned and to keep track of the changes in the linguistic conventions by searching the cues for those conventions (most of the changed conventions were made to very rare relations in the syntactic structure).

In (Dligach and Palmer, 2011), it is concluded that although doubly annotated corpora are more reliable, annotating more sentences only once is more beneficial; i.e. annotating each sentence only once is less time-consuming and more cost-effective. We annotated all the sentences only once (with an additional checking phase) except for the 5% of the sentences in order to estimate the quality of our linguistic conventions and agreement among the annotators. The statistics about the annotators agreement is reported in Section 4.1.

4 Statistics of the Treebank

Finally, 29,982 sentences were manually annotated. The details about the statistics is shown in Table 4. It is worth mentioning that 39.24% of the words in the treebank are tagged as noun, 12.62% as verb, 11.64% as preposition and 7.39% as adjective. The most frequent dependency relations are post-dependent (15.08%) and Ezafeh construction (10.17%). As shown in Table 5, the number of non-projective arcs in the second representation is a little bit less than the first. As mentioned earlier, the main reason is the dependencies between the direct object and words after the accusative case marker such as the example in Figure 4. The change percentage after the correction of the potential errors is shown in Table 6. It seems that the rules for finding the poten-

Number of Sentences	29,982
Number of Words	498,081
Average Sentence Length	16.61
Number of Distinct Words	37,618
Number of Distinct Lemmas	22,064
Number of Verbs	60,579
Number of Verb Lemmas	4,782
Average Frequency of Verb Lemmas	12.67

Table 4: Statistics about the frequency of words in the Persian dependency treebank.

# Non-Projective	1st Rep.	2nd Rep.
Number of Arcs	9639	9091
Percent of Arcs	0.019	0.018
Number of Sentences	5540	5095
Percent of Sentences	1.85	1.70

Table 5: Statistics about non-projective relations in the Persian dependency treebank for both of the representations.

tial errors were useful for correcting the errors.

4.1 Annotators Agreement

The statistics about the agreement among the annotators is shown in Table 7. We can also use the Kappa (Cohen, 1960) to measure the quality of the annotation based on the agreement among the annotators (pr(a) in Eq. 1) and the expected agreement or probability of chance (pr(e) in Eq. 1). If we consider the accuracy of the parser on the raw text without gold POS tags (approximately 75% labeled and 80% unlabeled accuracy based on our experience during the bootstrapping) and the POS tagger that we used during the annotation process (approximately 94%) as the probability of chance, we see that for all of the tasks in Table 7, the quality of the annotaion is more than 0.81 and is considered as almost perfect according to (Landis and Koch, 1977).

$$k = \frac{pr(a) - pr(e)}{1 - pr(e)} \quad (1)$$

5 Conclusion

As mentioned earlier, Persian is a language with its own challenges. We tried to overcome some of those challenges by preparing valuable linguistic

Changes to Unlabeled Relations	4.91%
Changes to Labeled Relations	6.29%
Changes to POS Tags	4.23%

Table 6: Statistics about changes in the treebank after the manual correction of the potential errors.

Unlabeled Relations	97.06%
Labeled Relations	95.32%
POS Tags	98.93%

Table 7: Statistics about agreements among the annotators.

datasets[5]. In addition to the preparation of the treebank, we prepared some useful desktop and web-based tools for searching in the dataset, obtaining statistics and viewing syntactic structures graphically. We hope to report more details about the linguistic aspects and the findings of the project in addition to our detailed experiments on the parsing task in future publications. We believe that this treebank is just the very first step to satisfy the need for Persian language processing. Our future aim is to add a semantic level to the annotation.

Acknowledgments

The project is funded by Iran Supreme Council of Information and Communication Technology (SCICT). We really appreciate the linguists who helped us in annotating: Farzaneh Bakhtiary, Parinaz Dadras, Maryam Faal-Hamedanchi, Saeedeh Ghadrdoost-Nakhchi, Mostafa Mahdavi, Azadeh Mirzaei, Sahar Oulapoor, Neda Poormorteza-Khameneh, Morteza Rezaei-Sharifabadi, Sude Resalatpoo, Akram Shafie, and Salimeh Zamani; and the programmers who helped us in the process of the development of the treebank: Seyed Mahdi Hoseini, Alireza Noorian, Yasser Souri, and Mohsen Hossein-Alizadeh; and also our colleagues who helped us find linguistic sources from the web: Azadeh Abbasi Abyaneh, Shima Zamanpoor, Narmin Ghaderi, Houra Nouri and Seyedeh Maneli Hashemian; and other colleagues especially Mahdi Behniafar. We thank Nizar Habash for his support of this paper and Weiwei Guo and three anonymous reviewers for their useful comments on the paper.

[5]A comprehensive description of the syntactic relations and morphosyntactic features is reported in the treebank official report (Dadegan Research Group, 2012) in the treebank package both in Persian and English.

References

Mohammad Bahrani, Hossein Sameti, and Mehdi Hafezi Manshadi. 2011. A computational grammar for Persian based on GPSG. *Language Resources and Evaluation*, 45(4):387–408.

Mahmood Bijankhan, Javad Sheykhzadegan, Mohammad Bahrani, and Masood Ghayoomi. 2011. Lessons from building a persian written corpus: Peykare. *Language resources and evaluation*, 45(2):143–164.

Mahmood Bijankhan. 2004. The role of the corpus in writing a grammar: An introduction to a software. *Iranian Journal of Linguistics*, 19(2).

Bernd Bohnet and Joakim Nivre. 2012. A transition-based system for joint part-of-speech tagging and labeled non-projective dependency parsing. In *EMNLP-CoNLL*, pages 1455–1465.

Sabine Buchholz and Erwin Marsi. 2006. CoNLL-X shared task on multilingual dependency parsing. In *Proceeding of the Tenth Conforence on Computational Natural Language Learning (CoNLL).*

Jacob Cohen. 1960. A coefficient of agreement for nominal scales. *Educational and psychological measurement*, 20(1):37–46.

Mohammad Dabir-Moghaddam. 1997. Compound verbs in Persian. *Studies in the Linguistic Sciences*, 27(2):25–59.

Dadegan Research Group. 2012. *Persian Dependency Treebank, Annotation manual and user guide.* Supreme Council of Information and Communication Technology (SCICT), Tehran, Iran.

Jon Dehdari and Deryle Lonsdale. 2008. A link grammar parser for Persian. *Aspects of Iranian Linguistics*, 1.

Dmitriy Dligach and Martha Palmer. 2011. Reducing the need for double annotation. In *Proceedings of the 5th Linguistic Annotation Workshop*, pages 65–69.

Masood Ghayoomi. 2012. Bootstrapping the development of an HPSG-based treebank for Persian. *Linguistic Issues in Language Technology*, 7(1).

Jan Hajic. 1998. Building a syntactically annotated corpus: The Prague dependency treebank. *Issues of valency and meaning*, pages 106–132.

Gholamhossein Karimi-Doostan. 2011a. Lexical categories in Persian. *Lingua*, 121(2):207–220.

Gholamhossein Karimi-Doostan. 2011b. Separability of light verb constructions in Persian. *Studia Linguistica*, 65(1):70–95.

Omid Kashefi, Mitra Nasri, and Kamyar Kanani. 2010. *Automatic Spell Checking in Persian Language.* Supreme Council of Information and Communication Technology (SCICT), Tehran, Iran.

Sandra Kübler, Ryan McDonald, and Joakim Nivre. 2009. *Dependency Parsing.* Synthesis Lectures on Human Language Technologies. Morgan & Claypool Publishers.

J. Richard Landis and Gary G. Koch. 1977. The measurement of observer agreement for categorical data. *Biometrics*, pages 159–174.

Ryan McDonald, Koby Crammer, and Fernando Pereira. 2005. Online large-margin training of dependency parsers. In *Proceedings of the 43rd Annual Meeting on Association for Computational Linguistics (ACL)*, pages 91–98, Sydney, Australia.

Joakim Nivre. 2009. Non-projective dependency parsing in expected linear time. In *Proceedings of the Joint Conference of the 47th Annual Meeting of the ACL and the 4th International Joint Conference on Natural Language Processing*, pages 351–359.

Kemal Oflazer, Bilge Say, Dilek Zeynep Hakkani-Tür, and Gökhan Tür. 2003. Building a Turkish treebank. *Treebanks*, pages 261–277.

Mohammad Sadegh Rasooli, Heshaam Faili, and Behrouz Minaei-Bidgoli. 2011a. Unsupervised identification of Persian compound verbs. In *Proceedings of the Mexican international conference on artificial intelligence (MICAI)*, pages 394–406, Puebla, Mexico.

Mohammad Sadegh Rasooli, Omid Kashefi, and Behrouz Minaei-Bidgoli. 2011b. Effect of adaptive spell checking in Persian. In *7th International Conference on Natural Language Processing and Knowledge Engineering (NLP-KE)*, pages 161–164, Tokushima, Japan.

Mohammad Sadegh Rasooli, Amirsaeid Moloodi, Manouchehr Kouhestani, and Behrouz Minaei-Bidgoli. 2011c. A syntactic valency lexicon for Persian verbs: The first steps towards Persian dependency treebank. In *5th Language & Technology Conference (LTC): Human Language Technologies as a Challenge for Computer Science and Linguistics*, pages 227–231, Poznań, Poland.

Mojgan Seraji, Beáta Magyesi, and Joakim Nivre. 2012. Bootstrapping a Persian dependency treebank. *Linguistic Issues in Language Technology*, 7(1).

Mehrnoosh Shamsfard. 2011. Challenges and open problems in Persian text processing. In *5th Language & Technology Conference (LTC): Human Language Technologies as a Challenge for Computer Science and Linguistics*, pages 65–69, Poznań, Poland.

Gernot Windfuhr. 2009. *The Iranian Languages.* Routledge.

Daniel Zeman, David Mareček, Martin Popel, Loganathan Ramasamy, Jan Štěpánek, Zednéck Žabokrtský, and Jan Hajič. 2012. Hamledt: To parse or not to parse. In *Proceedings of the Eighth Conference on International Language Resources and Evaluation (LREC'12), Istanbul, Turkey.*

Improving reordering performance using higher order and structural features

Mitesh M. Khapra
IBM Research India
mikhapra@in.ibm.com

Ananthakrishnan Ramanathan
IBM Research India
anandr42@gmail.com

Karthik Visweswariah
IBM Research India
v-karthik@in.ibm.com

Abstract

Recent work has shown that word aligned data can be used to learn a model for reordering source sentences to match the target order. This model learns the cost of putting a word immediately before another word and finds the best reordering by solving an instance of the Traveling Salesman Problem (TSP). However, for efficiently solving the TSP, the model is restricted to pairwise features which examine only a pair of words and their neighborhood. In this work, we go beyond these pairwise features and learn a model to rerank the n-best reorderings produced by the TSP model using higher order and structural features which help in capturing longer range dependencies. In addition to using a more informative set of source side features, we also capture target side features indirectly by using the translation score assigned to a reordering. Our experiments, involving Urdu-English, show that the proposed approach outperforms a state-of-the-art PBSMT system which uses the TSP model for reordering by 1.3 BLEU points, and a publicly available state-of-the-art MT system, Hiero, by 3 BLEU points.

1 Introduction

Handling the differences in word orders between pairs of languages is crucial in producing good machine translation. This is especially true for language pairs such as Urdu-English which have significantly different sentence structures. For example, the typical word order in Urdu is Subject Object Verb whereas the typical word order in English is Subject Verb Object. Phrase based systems (Koehn et al., 2003) rely on a lexicalized distortion model (Al-Onaizan and Papineni, 2006; Tillman, 2004) and the target language model to produce output words in the correct order. This is known to be inadequate when the languages are very different in terms of word order (refer to Table 3 in Section 3).

Pre-ordering source sentences while training and testing has become a popular approach in overcoming the word ordering challenge. Most techniques for pre-ordering (Collins et al., 2005; Wang et al., 2007; Ramanathan et al., 2009) depend on a high quality source language parser, which means these methods work only if the source language has a parser (this rules out many languages). Recent work (Visweswariah et al., 2011) has shown that it is possible to learn a reordering model from a relatively small number of hand aligned sentences . This eliminates the need of a source or target parser.

In this work, we build upon the work of Visweswariah et al. (2011) which solves the reordering problem by treating it as an instance of the Traveling Salesman Problem (TSP). They learn a model which assigns costs to all pairs of words in a sentence, where the cost represents the penalty of putting a word immediately preceding another word. The best permutation is found via the chained Lin-Kernighan heuristic for solving a TSP. Since this model relies on solving a TSP efficiently, it cannot capture features other than pairwise features that examine the words and neighborhood for each pair of words in the source sentence. In the remainder of this paper we refer to this model as the TSP model.

Our aim is to go beyond this limitation of the TSP model and use a richer set of features instead of using pairwise features only. In particular, we are interested in features that allow us to examine triples of words/POS tags in the candidate reordering permutation (this is akin to going from bigram to trigram language models), and also structural features that allow us to examine the properties of the segmentation induced by the candidate permutation. To go beyond the set of features incorporated by the TSP model, we do not solve the search problem which would be NP-hard. Instead, we restrict ourselves to an n-best list produced by the base TSP model and then search in that list. Using a richer set of features, we learn a model to rerank these n-best reorderings. The parameters of the model are learned using the averaged perceptron algorithm. In addition to using a richer set of source side features we also indirectly capture target side features by interpolating the score assigned by our model with the score assigned by the decoder of a MT system.

To justify the use of these informative features, we point to the example in Table 1. Here, the head (*driver*) of the underlined English Noun Phrase (*The driver of the car*) appears to the left of the Noun Phrase whereas the head (*chaalak* {driver}) of the corresponding Urdu Noun Phrase (*gaadi* {*car*} *ka* {*of*} *chaalak* {*driver*}) appears to the right of the Noun Phrase. To produce the correct reordering of the source Urdu sentence the model has to make an unusual choice of putting *gaadi* {car} before *bola* {said}. We say this is an unusual choice because the model examines only pairwise features and it is unlikely that it would have seen sentences having the bigram "*car said*". If the exact segmentation of the source sentence was known, then the model could have used the information that the word *gaadi* {car} appears in a segment whose head is the noun *chaalak* {driver} and hence its not unusual to put *gaadi* {car} before *bola* {said} (because the construct "*NP said*" is not unusual). However, since the segmentation of the source sentence is not known in advance, we use a heuristic (explained later) to find the segmentation induced by a reordering. We then extract features (such as $first\_word\_current\_segment$, $end\_word\_current\_segment$) to approximate these long range dependencies.

Using this richer set of features with Urdu-English as the source language pair, our approach outperforms the following state of the art systems: (i) a PBSMT system which uses TSP model for reordering (by 1.3 BLEU points), (ii) a hierarchical PBSMT system (by 3 BLEU points). The overall gain is 6.3 BLEU points when compared to a standard PBSMT system which uses a lexicalized distortion model (Al-Onaizan and Papineni, 2006).

Input Urdu:	fir gaadi ka chaalak kuch bola
Gloss:	then car of driver said something
English:	Then the driver of the car said something.
Ref. reordering:	fir chaalak ka gaadi bola kuch

Table 1: Example motivating the use of structural features

The rest of this paper is organized as follows. In Section 2 we discuss our approach of re-ranking the n-best reorderings produced by the TSP model. This includes a discussion of the model used, the features used and the algorithm used for learning the parameters of the model. It also includes a discussion on the modification to the Chained Lin-Kernighan heuristic to produce n-best reorderings. Next, in Section 3 we describe our experimental setup and report the results of our experiments. In Section 4 we present some discussions based on our study. In section 5 we briefly describe some prior related work. Finally, in Section 6, we present some concluding remarks and highlight possible directions for future work.

2 Re-ranking using higher order and structural features

As mentioned earlier, the TSP model (Visweswariah et al., 2011) looks only at local features for a word pair (w_i, w_j). We believe that for better reordering it is essential to look at higher order and structural features (*i.e.*, features which look at the overall structure of a sentence). The primary reason why Visweswariah et al. (2011) consider only pairwise bigram features is that with higher order features the reordering problem can no longer be cast as a TSP and hence cannot be solved using existing efficient heuristic solvers. However, we do not have to deal with an NP-Hard search problem because instead of considering all possible reorderings we restrict our search space to only the n-best reorderings produced by the base TSP model. Formally, given a set of reorderings, $\Pi = [\pi_1, \pi_2, \pi_3, ..., \pi_n]$, for a source sentence s, we are interesting in assigning a score, $score(\pi)$, to each of these reorderings and pick the reordering which has the highest score. In this paper, we parametrize this score as:

$$score(\pi) = \theta^T \phi(\pi) \quad (1)$$

where, θ is the weight vector and $\phi(\pi)$ is a vector of features extracted from the reordering π. The aim then is to find,

$$\pi^* = \arg\max_{\pi \in \Pi} \; score(\pi) \tag{2}$$

In the following sub-sections, we first briefly describe our overall approach towards finding π^*. Next, we describe our modification to the Lin-Kernighan heuristic for producing n-best outputs for TSP instead of the 1-best output used by (Visweswariah et al., 2011). We then discuss the features used for re-ranking these n-best outputs, followed by a discussion on the learning algorithm used for estimating the parameters of the model. Finally, we describe how we interpolate the score assigned by our model with the score assigned by the decoder of a SMT engine to indirectly capture target side features.

2.1 Overall approach

The training stage of our approach involves two phases : (i) Training a TSP model which will be used to generate n-best reorderings and (ii) Training a re-ranking model using these n-best reorderings. For training both the models we need a collection of sentences where the desired reordering $\pi^*(x)$ for each input sentence x is known. These reference orderings are derived from word aligned source-target sentence pairs (see first 4 rows of Figure 1). We first divide this word aligned data into N parts and use A^{-i} to denote the alignments leaving out the i-th part. We then train a TSP model M^{-i} using reference reorderings derived from A^{-i} as described in (Visweswariah et al., 2011). Next, we produce n-best reorderings for the source sentences using the algorithm $getNBestReorderings(sentence)$ described later. Dividing the data into N parts is necessary to ensure that the re-ranking model is trained using a realistic n-best list rather than a very optimistic n-best list (which would be the case if part i is reordered using a model which has already seen part i during training).

Each of the n-best reorderings is then represented as a feature vector comprising of higher order and structural features. The weights of these features are then estimated using the averaged perceptron method. At test time, $getNBestReorderings(sentence)$ is used to generate the n-best reorderings for the test sentence using the trained TSP model. These reorderings are then represented using higher order and structural features and re-ranked using the weights learned earlier. We now describe the different stages of our algorithm.

2.2 Generating n-best reorderings for the TSP model

The first stage of our approach is to train a TSP model and generate n-best reorderings using it. The decoder used by Visweswariah et al. (2011) relies on the Chained Lin-Kernighan heuristic (Lin and Kernighan, 1973) to produce the 1-best permutation for the TSP problem. Since our algorithm aims at re-ranking an n-best list of permutations (reorderings), we made a modification to the Chained Lin-Kernighan heuristic to produce this n-best list as shown in Algorithm 1 .

Algorithm 1 $getNBestReorderings(sentence)$

```
NbestSet = φ
π* = Identity permutation
π* = linkernighan(π*)
insert(NbestSet, π*)
for i = 1 → nIter do
    π' = perturb(π*)
    π' = linkernighan(π')
    if C(π') < max_{π∈NbestSet} C(π) then
        InsertOrReplace(NbestSet, π')
    end if
    if C(π') < C(π*) then
        π* = π'
    end if
end for
```

In Algorithm 1 $perturb()$ is a four-edge perturbation described in (Applegate et al., 2003), and $linkernighan()$ is the Lin-Kernighan heuristic that applies a sequence of flips that potentially returns a lower cost permutation as described in (Lin and Kernighan, 1973). The cost $C(\pi)$ is calculated using a trained TSP model.

2.3 Features

We represent each of the n-best reorderings obtained above as a vector of features which can be divided into two sets : (i) higher order features and (ii) struc-

Segmentation Based Features (extracted for every segment in the induced segmentation)	Features fired for the segment [mere(PRP) ghar(NN)] in Figure1
$end\_lex\_current\_segment$	$ghar$
$end\_lex\_prev\_segment$	$Shyam$
$end\_pos\_current\_segment$	NN
$end\_pos\_prev\_segment$	NN
$length\_of\_current\_segment$	2
$first\_lex\_current\_segment$	$mere$
$first\_lex\_next\_segment$	$aaye$
$first\_pos\_current\_segment$	PRP
$first\_pos\_next\_segment$	VRB
Higher order features	**Features fired for the triplet Shyam(NN) the(Vaux) aaye(VRB) in Figure1**
$lex\_triplet\_jumps$	$lex\_triplet$ = *"Shyam the aaye" && jumps* $= [4, -1]$
$pos\_triplet\_jumps$	$pos\_triplet$ = *"NN Vaux VRB" && jumps* $= [4, -1]$

Table 2: Features used in our model.

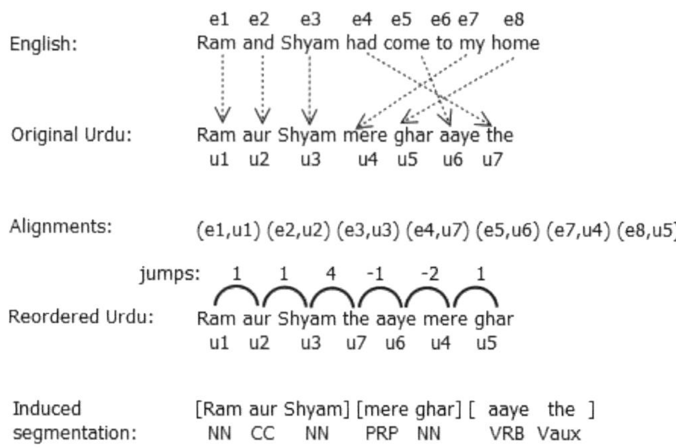

Figure 1: Segmentation induced on the Urdu sentence when it is reordered according to its English translation. Note that the words *Shyam* and *mere* are adjacent to each other in the original Urdu sentence but not in the reordered Urdu sentence. Hence, the word *mere* marks the beginning of a new segment.

tural features. The higher order features are essentially trigram lexical and pos features whereas the structural features are derived from the sentence structure induced by a reordering (explained later).

2.3.1 Higher Order Features

Since deriving a good reordering would essentially require analyzing the syntactic structure of the source sentence, the tasks of reordering and parsing are often considered to be related. The main motivation for using higher order features thus comes from a related work on parsing (Koo and Collins, 2010) where the performance of a state of the art parser was improved by considering higher order dependencies. In our model we use trigram features (see Table 2) of the following form:

$\phi(ru_i, ru_{i+1}, ru_{i+2}, J(ru_i, ru_{i+1}), J(ru_{i+1}, ru_{i+2}))$ where ru_i =*word at position* i *in the reordered source sentence* and $J(x, y)$ = *difference between the positions of* x *and* y *in the original source sentence.*

Figure 1 shows an example of jumps between different word pairs in an Urdu sentence. Since such higher order features will typically be sparse, we also use some back-off features. For example, instead of using the absolute values of jumps we divide the jumps into 3 buckets, *viz.*, high, low and medium and use these buckets in conjunction with the triplets as back-off features.

2.3.2 Structural Features

The second set of features is based on the hypothesis that any reordering of the source sentence induces a segmentation on the sentence. This segmentation is based on the following heuristic: if w_i and w_{i+1} appear next to each other in the original sentence but do not appear next to each other in the reordered sentence then w_i marks the end of a segment and w_{i+1} marks the beginning of the next segment. To understand this better please refer to Figure 1 which shows the correct reordering of an Urdu sentence based on its English translation and the corresponding segmentation induced on the Urdu sentence. If the correct segmentation of a sentence is known in advance then one could use a hierarchical model where the goal would be to reorder segments instead of reordering words individually (basically, instead of words, treat segments as units of reordering. In principle, this is similar to what is done by parser based reordering methods). Since the TSP model does not explicitly use segmentation based features it often produces wrong reorderings (refer to the motivating example in Section 1).

Reordering such sentences correctly requires some knowledge about the hierarchical structure of the sentence. To capture such hierarchical information, we use features which look at the elements (words, pos tags) of a segment and its neighboring segments. These features along with examples are listed in Table 2. These features should help us in selecting a reordering which induces a segmentation which is closest to the correct segmentation induced by the reference reordering. Note that every feature listed in Table 2 is a binary feature which takes on the value 1 if it fires for the given reordering and value 0 if it does not fire for the given reordering. In addition to the features listed in Table 2 we also use the score assigned by the TSP model as a feature.

2.4 Estimating model parameters

We use perceptron as the learning algorithm for estimating the parameters of our model described in Equation 1. To begin with, all parameters are initialized to 0 and the learning algorithm is run for N iterations. During each iteration the parameters are updated after every training instance is seen. For example, during the i-th iteration, after seeing the j-th training sentence, we update the k-th parameter θ_k using the following update rule:

$$\theta_k^{(i,j)} = \theta_k^{(i,j-1)} + \phi_k(\pi_j^{gold}) - \phi_k(\pi_j^*) \quad (3)$$

$$\begin{aligned} \textit{where, } \theta_k^{(i,j)} &= \textit{value of the } k\textit{-th parameter after} \\ &\quad \textit{seeing sentence } j \textit{ in iteration } i \\ \phi_k &= k\textit{-th feature} \\ \pi_j^{gold} &= \textit{gold reordering for the } j\textit{-th sentence} \\ \pi_j^* &= \arg\max_{\pi \in \Pi_j} \theta^{(i,j-1)^T} \phi(\pi) \end{aligned}$$

where Π_j is the set of n-best reorderings for the j-th sentence. π_j^* is thus the highest-scoring reordering for the j-th sentence under the current parameter vector. Since the averaged perceptron method is known to perform better than the perceptron method, we used the averaged values of the parameters at the end of N iterations, calculated as:

$$\theta_k^{avg} = \frac{1}{N \cdot t} \sum_{i=1}^{N} \sum_{j=1}^{t} \theta_k^{(i,j)} \quad (4)$$

$$\begin{aligned} \textit{where, } N &= \textit{Number of iterations} \\ t &= \textit{Number of training instances} \end{aligned}$$

We observed that in most cases the reference reordering in not a part of the n-best list produced by the TSP model. In such cases instead of using $\phi_k(\pi_j^{gold})$ for updating the weights in Equation 3 we use $\phi_k(\pi_j^{closest\_to\_gold})$ as this is known to be a better strategy for learning a re-ranking model (Arun and Koehn, 2007). $\pi_j^{closest\_to\_gold}$ is given by:

$$\arg\max_{\pi_j^i \in \Pi_j} \frac{\textit{\# of common bigram pairs in } \pi_j^i \textit{ and } \pi_j^{gold}}{len(\pi_j^{gold})}$$

$$\textit{where, } \Pi_j = \textit{set of } n\textit{-best reorderings for } j^{th} \textit{ sentence}$$

$\pi_j^{closest\_to\_gold}$ is thus the reordering which has the maximum overlap with π_j^{gold} in terms of the number of word pairs (w_m, w_n) where w_n is put next to w_m.

2.5 Interpolating with MT score

The approach described above aims at producing a better reordering by extracting richer features from the source sentence. Since the final aim is to improve the performance of an MT system, it would potentially be beneficial to interpolate the scores assigned by Equation 1 to a given reordering with the score assigned by the decoder of an MT system to the translation of the source sentence under this reordering. Intuitively, the MT score would allow us to capture features from the target sentence which are obviously not available to our model. With this motivation, we use the following interpolated score ($score_I$) to select the best translation.

$$score_I(t_i) = \lambda \cdot score_\theta(\pi_i) + (1 - \lambda) \cdot score_{MT}(t_i)$$

$$\begin{aligned} \textit{where, } t_i &= \textit{translation produced under the } i\textit{-th} \\ &\quad \textit{reordering of the source sentence} \\ score_\theta(\pi_i) &= \textit{score assigned by our model to the} \\ &\quad i\textit{-th reordering} \\ score_{MT}(t_i) &= \textit{score assigned by the MT system to } t_i \end{aligned}$$

The weight λ is used to ensure that $score_\theta(\pi_i)$ and $score_{MT}(\pi_i)$ are in the same range (it just serves as a normalization constant). We acknowledge that the above process is expensive because it requires the MT system to decode n reorderings for every source sentence. However, the aim of this work is to show that interpolating with the MT score which implicitly captures features from the target sentence helps in improving the performance. Ideally, this interpolation should (and can) be done at decode time without having to decode n reorderings for every source sentence (for example by expressing the n reorderings as a lattice), but, we leave this as future work.

3 Empirical evaluation

We evaluated our reordering approach on Urdu-English. We use two types of evaluation, one intrinsic and one extrinsic. For intrinsic evaluation, we compare the reordered source sentence in Urdu with a reference reordering obtained from the hand alignments using BLEU (referred to as monolingual BLEU or mBLEU by (Visweswariah et al., 2011)). Additionally, we evaluate the effect of reordering on MT performance using BLEU (extrinsic evaluation).

As mentioned earlier, our training process involves two phases : (i) Generating n-best reorderings for the training data and (ii) using these n-best reorderings to train a perceptron model. We use the same data for training the reordering model as well as our perceptron model. This data contains 180K words of manual alignments (part of the NIST MT-08 training data) and 3.9M words of automatically generated machine alignments (1.7M words from the NIST MT-08 training data[1] and 2.2M words extracted from sources on the web[2]). The machine alignments were generated using a supervised maximum entropy model (Ittycheriah and Roukos, 2005) and then corrected using an improved correction model (McCarley et al., 2011). We first divide the training data into 10 folds. The n-best reorderings for each fold are then generated using a model trained on the remaining 9 folds. This division into 10 folds is done for reasons explained earlier in Section 2.1. These n-best reorderings are then used to train the perceptron model as described in Section 2.4. Note that Visweswariah et al. (2011) used only manually aligned data for training the TSP model. However, we use machine aligned data in addition to manually aligned data for training the TSP model as it leads to better performance. We used this improvised TSP model as the state of the art baseline (rows 2 and 3 in Tables 3 and 4 respectively) for comparing with our approach.

We observed that the perceptron algorithm converges after 5 iterations beyond which there is very little ($<1\%$) improvement in the bigram precision on the training data itself (bigram precision is the fraction of word pairs which are correctly put next to each other). Hence, for all the numbers reported in this paper, we used 5 iterations of perceptron training. Similarly, while generating the n-best reorderings, we experimented with following values of n : 10, 25, 50, 100 and 200. We observed that, by restricting the search space to the top-50 reorderings we get the best reordering performance (mBLEU) on a development set. Hence, we used n=50 for our MT experiments.

For intrinsic evaluation we use a development set of 8017 Urdu tokens reordered manually. Table 3 compares the performance of the top-1 reordering output by our algorithm with the top-1 reordering generated by the improved TSP model in terms of mBLEU. We see a gain of 1.8 mBLEU points with our approach.

Next, we see the impact of the better reorderings produced by our system on the performance of a state-of-the-art MT system. For this, we used a standard phrase based system (Al-Onaizan and Papineni, 2006) with a lexicalized distortion model with a window size of +/-4 words (Tillmann and Ney, 2003). As mentioned earlier, our training data consisted of 3.9M words including the NIST MT-08 training data. We use HMM alignments along with higher quality alignments from a supervised aligner (McCarley et al., 2011). The Gigaword English corpus was used for building the English language model. We report results on the NIST MT-08 evaluation set, averaging BLEU scores from the News and Web conditions to provide a single BLEU score. Table 4 compares the MT performance obtained by reordering the training and test data using the following approaches:

1. No pre-ordering: A baseline system which does not use any source side reordering as a preprocessing step

2. HIERO : A state of the art hierarchical phrase based translation system (Chiang, 2007)

3. TSP: A system which uses the 1-best reordering produced by the TSP model

4. Higher order & structural features: A system

[1]http://www.ldc.upenn.edu

[2]http://centralasiaonline.com

Approach	mBLEU
Unreordered	31.2
TSP	56.6
Higher order & structural features	**58.4**

Table 3: mBLEU scores for Urdu to English reordering using different models.

Approach	BLEU
No pre-ordering	21.9
HIERO	25.2
TSP	26.9
Higher order & structural features	27.5
Interpolating with MT score	**28.2**

Table 4: MT performance for Urdu to English without reordering and with reordering using different approaches.

which reranks n-best reorderings produced by TSP using higher order and structural features

5. Interpolating with MT score : A system which interpolates the score assigned to a reordering by our model with the score assigned by a MT system

We used Joshua 4.0 (Ganitkevitch et al., 2012) which provides an open source implementation of HIERO. For training, tuning and testing HIERO we used the same experimental setup as described above. As seen in Table 4, we get an overall gain of 6.2 BLEU points with our approach as compared to a baseline system which does not use any reordering. More importantly, we outperform (i) a PBSMT system which uses the TSP model by 1.3 BLEU points and (ii) a state of the art hierarchical phrase based translation system by 3 points.

4 Discussions

We now discuss some error corrections and ablation tests.

4.1 Example of error correction

We first give an example where the proposed approach performed better than the TSP model. In the example below, I = input sentence, E= gold English translation, T = incorrect reordering produced by TSP and O = correct reordering produced by our approach. Note that the words *roman catholic aur protestant* in the input sentence get translated as a continuous phrase in English (*Roman Catholic and Protestant*) and hence should be treated as a single unit by the reordering model. The TSP model fails to keep this segment intact whereas our model (which uses segmentation based features) does so and matches the reference reordering.

Sentence length	mBLEU		
	Unreordered	TSP	Our approach
1-14 words (small)	29.7	58.7	57.8
15-22 words (med.)	28.2	56.8	59.2
23+ words (long)	33.4	55.8	58.2
All	31.2	56.6	58.4

Table 5: mBLEU improvements on sentences of different lengths

I: ab roman catholic aur protestant ke darmiyaan ikhtilafat khatam ho chuke hai

E: The differences between Roman Catholics and Protestants have now ended

T: ab roman ikhtilafat ke darmiyaan catholic aur protestant hai khatam ho chuke

O: ab ikhtilafat ke darmiyaan roman catholic aur protestant hai khatam ho chuke

4.2 Performance based on sentence length

We split the test data into roughly three equal parts based on length, and calculated the mBLEU improvements on each of these parts as reported in Table 5. These results show that the model works much better for medium-to-long sentences. In fact, we see a drop in performance for small sentences. A possible reason for this could be that the structural features that we use are derived through a heuristic that is error-prone, and in shorter sentences, where there would be fewer reordering problems, these errors hurt more than they help. While this needs to be analyzed further, we could meanwhile combine the two models fruitfully by using the base TSP model for small sentences and the new model for longer sentences.

Disabled feature	mBLEU
end_lex_current_segment	57.6
end_lex_prev_segment	57.6
end_pos_current_segment	57.8
end_pos_prev_segment	57.4
length	57.6
lex_triplet_jumps	58.0
pos_triplet_jumps	56.1
first_lex_current_segment	58.2
first_lex_next_segment	58.2
first_pos_current_segment	57.6
first_pos_next_segment	57.6
NONE	58.4

Table 6: Ablation test indicating the contribution of each feature to the reordering performance.

4.3 Ablation test

To study the contribution of each feature to the reordering performance, we did an ablation test wherein we disabled one feature at a time and measured the change in the mBLEU scores. Table 6 summarizes the results of our ablation test. The maximum drop in performance is obtained when the *pos_triplet_jumps* feature is disabled. This observation supports our claim that higher order features (more than bigrams) are essential for better reordering. The *lex_triplet_jumps* feature has the least impact on the performance mainly because it is a lexicalized feature and hence very sparse. Also note that there is a high correlation between the performances obtained by dropping one feature from each of the following pairs :
i) *first_lex_current_segment*, *first_lex_next_segment*
ii) *first_pos_current_segment*, *first_pos_next_segment*
iii) *end_lex_current_segment*, *end_lex_next_segment*.
This is because these pairs of features are highly dependent features. Note that similar to the *pos_triplet_jumps* feature we also tried a *pos_quadruplet_jumps* feature but it did not help (mainly due to overfitting and sparsity).

5 Related Work

There are several studies which have shown that reordering the source side sentence to match the target side order leads to improvements in Machine Translation. These approaches can be broadly classified into three types. First, approaches which reorder source sentences by applying rules to the source side parse; the rules are either hand-written (Collins et al., 2005; Wang et al., 2007; Ramanathan et al., 2009) or learned from data (Xia and McCord, 2004; Genzel, 2010; Visweswariah et al., 2010). These approaches require a source side parser which is not available for many languages. The second type of approaches treat machine translation decoding as a parsing problem by using source and/or target side syntax in a Context Free Grammar framework. These include Hierarchical models (Chiang, 2007) and syntax based models (Yamada and Knight, 2002; Galley et al., 2006; Liu et al., 2006; Zollmann and Venugopal, 2006). The third type of approaches, avoid the use of a parser (as required by syntax based models) and instead train a reordering model using reference reorderings derived from aligned data. These approaches (Tromble and Eisner, 2009; Visweswariah et al., 2011; DeNero and Uszkoreit, 2011; Neubig et al., 2012) have a low decode time complexity as reordering is done as a preprocessing step and not integrated with the decoder.

Our work falls under the third category, as it improves upon the work of (Visweswariah et al., 2011) which is closely related to the work of (Tromble and Eisner, 2009) but performs better. The focus of our work is to use higher order and structural features (based on segmentation of the source sentence) which are not captured by their model. Some other works have used collocation based segmentation (Henríquez Q. et al., 2010) and Multiword Expressions as segments (Bouamor et al., 2012) to improve the performance of SMT but without much success. The idea of improving performance by reranking a n-best list of outputs has been used recently for the related task of parsing (Katz-Brown et al., 2011) using targeted self-training for improving the performance of reordering. However, in contrast, in our work we directly aim at improving the performance of a reordering model.

6 Conclusion

In this work, we proposed a model for re-ranking the n-best reorderings produced by a state of the art reordering model (TSP model) which is limited to pair wise features. Our model uses a more informative set of features consisting of higher order features, structural features and target side features (captured indirectly using translation scores). The problem of intractability is solved by restricting the search space to the n-best reorderings produced by the TSP model. A detailed ablation test shows that of all the features used, the pos triplet features are most informative for reordering. A gain of 1.3 and 3 BLEU points over a state of the art phrase based and hierarchical machine translation system respectively provides good extrinsic validation of our claim that such long range features are useful.

As future work, we would like to evaluate our algorithm on other language pairs. We also plan to integrate the score assigned by our model into the decoder to avoid having to do n decodings for every source sentence. Also, it would be interesting to model the segmentation explicitly, where the aim would be to first segment the sentence and then use a two level hierarchical reordering model which first reorders these segments and then reorders the words within the segment.

References

Yaser Al-Onaizan and Kishore Papineni. 2006. Distortion models for statistical machine translation. In *Proceedings of ACL*, ACL-44, pages 529–536, Morristown, NJ, USA. Association for Computational Linguistics.

David Applegate, William Cook, and Andre Rohe. 2003. Chained lin-kernighan for large traveling salesman problems. In *INFORMS Journal On Computing*.

Abhishek Arun and Philipp Koehn. 2007. Online learning methods for discriminative training of phrase based statistical machine translation. In *In Proceedings of MT Summit*.

Dhouha Bouamor, Nasredine Semmar, and Pierre Zweigenbaum. 2012. Identifying bilingual multiword expressions for statistical machine translation. In Nicoletta Calzolari (Conference Chair), Khalid Choukri, Thierry Declerck, Mehmet Uur Doan, Bente Maegaard, Joseph Mariani, Jan Odijk, and Stelios Piperidis, editors, *Proceedings of the Eight International Conference on Language Resources and Evaluation (LREC'12)*, Istanbul, Turkey, may. European Language Resources Association (ELRA).

David Chiang. 2007. Hierarchical phrase-based translation. *Comput. Linguist.*, 33(2):201–228, June.

Michael Collins, Philipp Koehn, and Ivona Kučerová. 2005. Clause restructuring for statistical machine translation. In *Proceedings of ACL*, pages 531–540, Morristown, NJ, USA. Association for Computational Linguistics.

John DeNero and Jakob Uszkoreit. 2011. Inducing sentence structure from parallel corpora for reordering. In *Proceedings of the Conference on Empirical Methods in Natural Language Processing*, EMNLP '11, pages 193–203, Stroudsburg, PA, USA. Association for Computational Linguistics.

Michel Galley, Jonathan Graehl, Kevin Knight, Daniel Marcu, Steve DeNeefe, Wei Wang, and Ignacio Thayer. 2006. Scalable inference and training of context-rich syntactic translation models. In *Proceedings of the 21st International Conference on Computational Linguistics and the 44th annual meeting of the Association for Computational Linguistics*, ACL-44, pages 961–968, Stroudsburg, PA, USA. Association for Computational Linguistics.

Juri Ganitkevitch, Yuan Cao, Jonathan Weese, Matt Post, and Chris Callison-Burch. 2012. Joshua 4.0: Packing, pro, and paraphrases. In *Proceedings of the Seventh Workshop on Statistical Machine Translation*, pages 283–291, Montréal, Canada, June. Association for Computational Linguistics.

Dmitriy Genzel. 2010. Automatically learning source-side reordering rules for large scale machine translation. In *Proceedings of the 23rd International Conference on Computational Linguistics*, COLING '10, pages 376–384, Stroudsburg, PA, USA. Association for Computational Linguistics.

A. Carlos Henríquez Q., R. Marta Costa-jussà, Vidas Daudaravicius, E. Rafael Banchs, and B. José Mariño. 2010. Using collocation segmentation to augment the phrase table. In *Proceedings of the Joint Fifth Workshop on Statistical Machine Translation and MetricsMATR*, WMT '10, pages 98–102, Stroudsburg, PA, USA. Association for Computational Linguistics.

Abraham Ittycheriah and Salim Roukos. 2005. A maximum entropy word aligner for Arabic-English machine translation. In *Proceedings of HLT/EMNLP*, HLT '05, pages 89–96, Stroudsburg, PA, USA. Association for Computational Linguistics.

Jason Katz-Brown, Slav Petrov, Ryan McDonald, Franz Och, David Talbot, Hiroshi Ichikawa, Masakazu Seno, and Hideto Kazawa. 2011. Training a parser for machine translation reordering. In *Proceedings of the Conference on Empirical Methods in Natural Language Processing*, EMNLP '11, pages 183–192, Stroudsburg, PA, USA. Association for Computational Linguistics.

Philipp Koehn, Franz Josef Och, and Daniel Marcu. 2003. Statistical phrase-based translation. In *Proceedings of HLT-NAACL*.

Terry Koo and Michael Collins. 2010. Efficient third-order dependency parsers. In *Proceedings of the 48th*

Annual Meeting of the Association for Computational Linguistics, ACL '10, pages 1–11, Stroudsburg, PA, USA. Association for Computational Linguistics.

S. Lin and B. W. Kernighan. 1973. An effective heuristic algorithm for the travelling-salesman problem. *Operations Research*, pages 498–516.

Yang Liu, Qun Liu, and Shouxun Lin. 2006. Tree-to-string alignment template for statistical machine translation. In *Proceedings of the 21st International Conference on Computational Linguistics and the 44th annual meeting of the Association for Computational Linguistics*, ACL-44, pages 609–616, Stroudsburg, PA, USA. Association for Computational Linguistics.

J. Scott McCarley, Abraham Ittycheriah, Salim Roukos, Bing Xiang, and Jian-ming Xu. 2011. A correction model for word alignments. In *Proceedings of the Conference on Empirical Methods in Natural Language Processing*, EMNLP '11, pages 889–898, Stroudsburg, PA, USA. Association for Computational Linguistics.

Graham Neubig, Taro Watanabe, and Shinsuke Mori. 2012. Inducing a discriminative parser to optimize machine translation reordering. In *Proceedings of the 2012 Joint Conference on Empirical Methods in Natural Language Processing and Computational Natural Language Learning*, pages 843–853, Jeju Island, Korea, July. Association for Computational Linguistics.

Ananthakrishnan Ramanathan, Hansraj Choudhary, Avishek Ghosh, and Pushpak Bhattacharyya. 2009. Case markers and morphology: addressing the crux of the fluency problem in English-Hindi smt. In *Proceedings of ACL-IJCNLP*.

Christoph Tillman. 2004. A unigram orientation model for statistical machine translation. In *Proceedings of HLT-NAACL*.

Christoph Tillmann and Hermann Ney. 2003. Word reordering and a dynamic programming beam search algorithm for statistical machine translation. *Computational Linguistics*, 29(1):97–133.

Roy Tromble and Jason Eisner. 2009. Learning linear ordering problems for better translation. In *Proceedings of EMNLP*.

Karthik Visweswariah, Jiri Navratil, Jeffrey Sorensen, Vijil Chenthamarakshan, and Nandakishore Kambhatla. 2010. Syntax based reordering with automatically derived rules for improved statistical machine translation. In *Proceedings of the 23rd International Conference on Computational Linguistics*.

Karthik Visweswariah, Rajakrishnan Rajkumar, Ankur Gandhe, Ananthakrishnan Ramanathan, and Jiri Navratil. 2011. A word reordering model for improved machine translation. In *Proceedings of the Conference on Empirical Methods in Natural Language Processing*, EMNLP '11, pages 486–496, Stroudsburg, PA, USA. Association for Computational Linguistics.

Chao Wang, Michael Collins, and Philipp Koehn. 2007. Chinese syntactic reordering for statistical machine translation. In *Proceedings of EMNLP-CoNLL*.

Fei Xia and Michael McCord. 2004. Improving a statistical MT system with automatically learned rewrite patterns. In *COLING*.

Kenji Yamada and Kevin Knight. 2002. A decoder for syntax-based statistical mt. In *Proceedings of ACL*.

Andreas Zollmann and Ashish Venugopal. 2006. Syntax augmented machine translation via chart parsing. In *Proceedings on the Workshop on Statistical Machine Translation*.

Massively Parallel Suffix Array Queries and On-Demand Phrase Extraction for Statistical Machine Translation Using GPUs

Hua He
Dept. of Computer Science
University of Maryland
College Park, Maryland
huah@cs.umd.edu

Jimmy Lin
iSchool and UMIACS
University of Maryland
College Park, Maryland
jimmylin@umd.edu

Adam Lopez
HLTCOE
Johns Hopkins University
Baltimore, Maryland
alopez@cs.jhu.edu

Abstract

Translation models in statistical machine translation can be scaled to large corpora and arbitrarily-long phrases by looking up translations of source phrases "on the fly" in an indexed parallel corpus using suffix arrays. However, this can be slow because on-demand extraction of phrase tables is computationally expensive. We address this problem by developing novel algorithms for general purpose graphics processing units (GPUs), which enable suffix array queries for phrase lookup and phrase extraction to be massively parallelized. Compared to a highly-optimized, state-of-the-art serial CPU-based implementation, our techniques achieve at least an order of magnitude improvement in terms of throughput. This work demonstrates the promise of massively parallel architectures and the potential of GPUs for tackling computationally-demanding problems in statistical machine translation and language processing.

1 Introduction

Efficiently handling large translation models is a perennial problem in statistical machine translation. One particularly promising solution (§2) is to use the parallel text itself as an *implicit* representation of the translation model and extract translation units "on the fly" when they are needed to decode new input (Brown, 2004). This idea has been applied to phrase-based (Callison-Burch et al., 2005; Zhang and Vogel, 2005), hierarchical (Lopez, 2007; Lopez, 2008b; Lopez, 2008a), and syntax-based (Cromieres and Kurohashi, 2011) models. A benefit of this technique is that it scales to arbitrarily large models with very little pre-processing. For instance, Lopez (2008b) showed that a translation model trained on a large corpus with sparse word alignments and loose extraction heuristics substantially improved Chinese-English translation. An explicit representation of the model would have required nearly a terabyte of memory, but its implicit representation using the parallel text required only a few gigabytes.

Unfortunately, there is substantial computational cost in searching a parallel corpus for source phrases, extracting their translations, and scoring them on the fly. Since the number of possible translation units may be quite large (for example, all substrings of a source sentence) and their translations are numerous, both phrase lookup and extraction are performance bottlenecks. Despite considerable research and the use of efficient indexes like suffix arrays (Manber and Myers, 1990), this problem remains not fully solved.

We show how to exploit the massive parallelism offered by modern general purpose graphics processing units (GPUs) to eliminate the computational bottlenecks associated with "on the fly" phrase extraction. GPUs have previously been applied to DNA sequence matching using suffix trees (Schatz et al., 2007) and suffix arrays (Gharaibeh and Ripeanu, 2010). Building on this work, we present two novel contributions: First, we describe improved GPU algorithms for suffix array queries that achieve greater parallelism (§3). Second, we propose novel data structures and algorithms for phrase extraction (§4) and scoring (§5) that are amenable to GPU parallelization. The resulting implementation achieves at least an order of magnitude higher throughput than a state-of-the-art single-threaded CPU implementation (§6). Since our experiments verify that the GPU implementation produces *exactly* the same results as a CPU reference implementation on a full extraction, we can simply replace that component and reap significant performance advantages with no impact on translation quality. To the best of our knowledge, this is the first reported application of GPU acceleration techniques for statistical machine translation. We believe these results reveal a promising yet unexplored future direction in exploiting parallelism to tackle perennial performance bottlenecks in state-of-the-art translation models.

2 Phrase Extraction On Demand

Lopez (2008b) provides the following recipe for "translation by pattern matching", which we use as a guide for the remainder of this paper:

Algorithm 1 Translation by pattern matching

1: **for each** input sentence **do**
2:     **for each** possible phrase in the sentence **do**
3:         Find its occurrences in the source text
4:         **for** each occurrence **do**
5:             Extract its aligned target phrase (if any)
6:         **for** each extracted phrase pair **do**
7:             Compute feature values
8:     Decode as usual using the scored rules

The computational bottleneck occurs in lines 2–7: there are vast numbers of query phrases, matching occurrences, and extracted phrase pairs to process in the loops. In the next three sections, we attack each problem in turn.

3 Finding Every Phrase

First, we must find all occurrences of each source phrase in the input (line 3, Algorithm 1). This is a classic application of string pattern matching: given a short query pattern, the task is to find all occurrences in a much larger text. Solving the problem efficiently is crucial: for an input sentence F of length $|F|$, each of its $O(|F|^2)$ substrings is a potential query pattern.

3.1 Pattern Matching with Suffix Arrays

Although there are many algorithms for pattern matching, all of the examples that we are aware of for machine translation rely on *suffix arrays*. We briefly review the classic algorithms of Manber and Myers (1990) here since they form the basis of our techniques and analysis, but readers who are familiar with them can safely skip ahead to additional optimizations (§3.2).

A suffix array represents all suffixes of a corpus in lexicographical order. Formally, for a text T, the ith suffix of T is the substring of the text beginning at position i and continuing to the end of T. Each suffix can therefore be uniquely identified by the index i of its first word. A suffix array $S(T)$ of T is a permutation of these suffix identifiers $[1, |T|]$ arranged by the lexicographical order of the corresponding suffixes—in other words, the suffix array represents a sorted list of all suffixes in T. With both T and $S(T)$ in memory, we can find any query pattern Q in $O(|Q| \log |T|)$ time by comparing pattern Q against the first $|Q|$ characters of up to $\log |T|$ different suffixes using binary search.

An inefficiency in this solution is that each comparison in the binary search algorithm requires comparing all $|Q|$ characters of the query pattern against some suffix of text T. We can improve on this using an observation about the *longest common prefix* (LCP) of the query pattern and the suffix against which it is compared. Suppose we search for a query pattern Q in the span of the suffix array beginning at suffix L and ending at suffix R. For any suffix M which falls lexicographically between those at L and R, the LCP of Q and M will be at least as long as the LCP of Q and L or Q and R. Hence if we know the quantity $h = \text{MIN}(\text{LCP}(Q, L), \text{LCP}(Q, R))$ we can skip comparisons of the first h symbols between Q and the suffix M, since they must be the same.

The solution of Manber and Myers (1990) exploits this fact along with the observation that each comparison in binary search is carried out according to a fixed recursion scheme: a query is only ever compared against a specific suffix M for a single range of suffixes bounded by some fixed L and R. Hence if we know the longest common prefix between M and each of its corresponding L and R according to the fixed recursions in the algorithm, we can maintain a bound on h and reduce the aggregate number of symbol comparisons to $O(|Q| + \log |T|)$. To accomplish this, in addition to the suffix array, we pre-compute two other arrays of size $|T|$ for both left and right recursions (called the LCP arrays).

Memory use is an important consideration, since GPUs have less memory than CPUs. For the algorithms described here, we require four arrays: the original text T, the suffix array $S(T)$, and the two LCP arrays. We use a representation of T in which each word has been converted to a unique integer identifier; with 32-bit integers the total number of bytes is $16|T|$. As we will show, this turns out to be quite modest, even for large parallel corpora (§6).

3.2 Suffix Array Efficiency Tricks

Previous work on translation by pattern matching using suffix arrays on serial architectures has produced a number of efficiency optimizations:

1. Binary search bounds for longer substrings are initialized to the bounds of their longest prefix. Substrings are queried only if their longest prefix string was matched in the text.
2. In addition to conditioning on the longest prefix, Zhang and Vogel (2005) and Lopez (2007) condition on a successful query for the longest proper suffix.
3. Lopez (2007) queries each unique substring of a sentence exactly once, regardless of how many times it appears in an input sentence.
4. Lopez (2007) directly indexes one-word substrings with a small auxiliary array, so that their positions in the suffix array can be found in constant time. For longer substrings, this optimization reduces the $\log |T|$ term of query complexity to $\log(\text{count}(a))$, where a is the first word of the query string.

Although these efficiency tricks are important in the serial algorithms that serve as our baseline, not all of them are applicable to parallel architectures. In particular, optimizations (1), (2), and (3) introduce order dependencies between queries; they are disregarded in our GPU implementation so that we can fully exploit parallelization opportunities. We have not yet fully implemented (4), which is orthogonal to parallelization: this is left for future work.

3.3 Finding Every Phrase on a GPU

Recent work in computational biology has shown that suffix arrays are particularly amenable to GPU acceleration: the suffix-array-based DNA sequence matching system MummurGPU++ (Gharaibeh and Ripeanu, 2010) has been reported to outperform the already fast MummurGPU 2 (Trapnell and Schatz, 2009), based on suffix trees (an alternative indexing structure). Here, we apply the same ideas to machine translation, introducing some novel improvements to their algorithms in the process.

A natural approach to parallelism is to perform all substring queries in parallel (Gharaibeh and Ripeanu, 2010). There are no dependencies between iterations of the loop beginning on line 2 of Algorithm 1, so for input sentence F, we can parallelize by searching for all $O(|F|^2)$ substrings concurrently. We adopt this approach here.

However, naïve application of query-level parallelism leads to a large number of wasted threads, since most long substrings of an input sentence will not be found in the text. Therefore, we employ a novel two-pass strategy: in the first pass, we simply compute, for each position i in the input sentence, the length j of the longest substring in F that appears in T. These computations are carried out concurrently for every position i. During this pass, we also compute the suffix array bounds of the one-word substring $F[i]$, to be used as input to the second pass—a variant of optimizations (1) and (4) discussed in §3.2. On the second pass, we search for all substrings $F[i, k]$ for all $k \in [i + 1, i + j]$. These computations are carried out concurrently for all substrings longer than one word.

Even more parallelization is possible. As we saw in §3.1, each query in a suffix array actually requires two binary searches: one each for the first and last match in $S(T)$. The abundance of inexpensive threads on a GPU permits us to perform both queries concurrently on separate threads. By doing this in both passes we utilize more of the GPU's processing power and obtain further speedups.

As a simple example, consider an input sentence "The government puts more tax on its citizens", and suppose that substrings "The government", "government puts", and "puts more tax" are found in the training text, while none of the words in "on

Initial Word	Longest Match	Substrings	Threads	
			1st pass	2nd pass
The	2	*The, The government*	2	2
government	2	*government, government puts*	2	2
puts	3	*puts, puts more, puts more tax*	2	4
more	2	*more, more tax*	2	2
tax	1	*tax*	2	0
on	0	–	2	0
its	0	–	2	0
citizens	0	–	2	0
Total Threads:			16	10

Table 1: Example of how large numbers of suffix array queries can be factored across two highly parallel passes on a GPU with a total of 26 threads to perform all queries for this sample input sentence.

its citizens" are found. The number of threads spawned is shown in Table 1: all threads during a pass execute in parallel, and each thread performs a binary search which takes no more than $O(|Q| + \log|T|)$ time. While spawning so many threads may seem wasteful, this degree of parallelization still under-utilizes the GPU; the hardware we use (§6) can manage up to 21,504 concurrent threads in its resident occupancy. To fully take advantage of the processing power, we process multiple input sentences in parallel. Compared with previous algorithms, our two-pass approach and our strategy of thread assignment to increase the amount of parallelism represent novel contributions.

4 Extracting Aligned Target Phrases

The problem at line 5 of Algorithm 1 is to extract the target phrase aligned to each matching source phrase instance. Efficiency is crucial since some source phrases occur hundreds of thousands of times.

Phrase extraction from word alignments typically uses the consistency check of Och et al. (1999). A *consistent* phrase is one for which no words inside the phrase pair are aligned to words outside the phrase pair. Usually, consistent pairs are computed offline via dynamic programming over the alignment grid, from which we extract all consistent phrase pairs up to a heuristic bound on phrase length.

The online extraction algorithm of Lopez (2008a) checks for consistent phrases in a different manner. Rather than finding all consistent phrase pairs in a sentence, the algorithm asks: given a specific source phrase, is there a consistent phrase pair

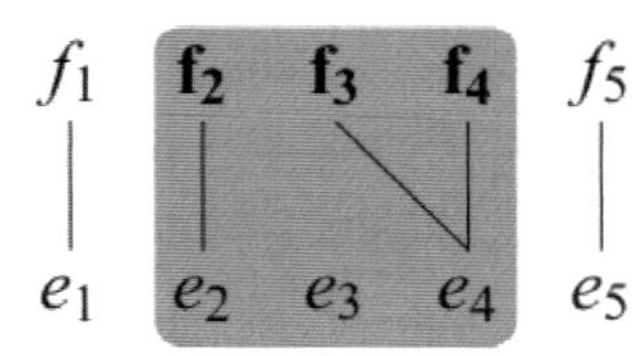

Figure 1: Source phrase $f_2f_3f_4$ and target phrase $e_2e_3e_4$ are extracted as a consistent pair, since the back-projection is contained within the original source span.

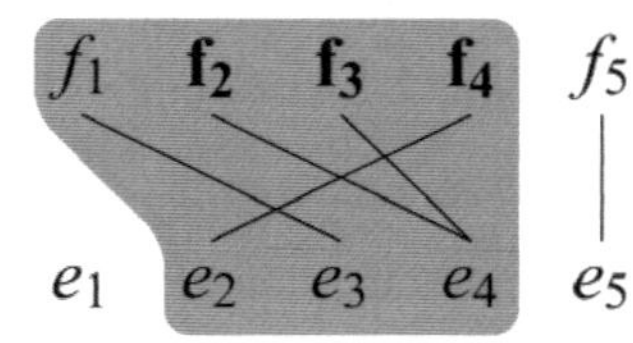

Figure 2: Source phrase $f_2f_3f_4$ and target phrase $e_2e_3e_4$ should not be extracted, since the back-projection is *not* contained within the original source span.

of which it is one side? To answer this, it first computes the projection of the source phrase in the target sentence: the minimum span containing all words that are aligned to any word of the source span. It then computes the projection of the target span back into the source; if this back-projection is contained within the original source span, the phrase pair is consistent, and the target span is extracted as the translation of the source. Figure 1 shows a "good" pair for source phrase $f_2f_3f_4$, since the back-projection is contained within the original source span, whereas Figure 2 shows a "bad" pair for source phrase $f_2f_3f_4$ since the back-projection is *not* contained within the original source span.

4.1 Sampling Consistent Phrases

Regardless of how efficient the extraction of a single target phrase is made, the fact remains that there are many phrases to extract. For example, in our Chinese Xinhua dataset (see §6), from 8,000 input query sentences, about 20 million source substrings can be extracted. The standard solution to this problem is to sample a set of occurrences of each source phrase, and only extract translations for those occurrences (Callison-Burch et al., 2005; Zhang and Vogel, 2005). As a practical matter, this can be done by sampling at uniform intervals from the matching span of a suffix array. Lopez (2008a) reports a sample size of 300; for phrases occurring fewer than 300 times, all translations are extracted.

4.2 GPU Implementation

We present novel data structures and an algorithm for efficient phrase extraction, which together are amenable to massive parallelization on GPUs. The basic insight is to pre-compute data structures for the source-to-target alignment projection and back-projection procedure described by Lopez (2008a) for checking consistent alignments.

Let us consider a single matching substring (from the output of the suffix array queries), span $[i, j]$ in the source text T. For each k, we need to know the leftmost and rightmost positions that it aligns to in the target T'. For this purpose we can define the target span $[i', j']$, along with leftmost and rightmost arrays L and R as follows:

$$i' := \min_{k \in [i,j]} L(k)$$
$$j' := \max_{k \in [i,j]} R(k)$$

The arrays L and R are each of length $|T|$, indexed by absolute corpus position. Each array element contains the leftmost and rightmost extents of the source-to-target alignments (in the target), respectively. Note that in order to save space, the values stored in the arrays are sentence-relative positions (e.g., token count from the beginning of each sentence), so that we only need one byte per array entry. Thus, i' and j' are sentence-relative positions (in the target).

Similarly, for the back-projection, we use two arrays L' and R' on the target side (length $|T'|$) to keep track of the leftmost and rightmost positions that k' in the target training text align to, as below:

$$i'' := \min_{k' \in [s'+i', s'+j']} L'(k')$$
$$j'' := \max_{k' \in [s'+i', s'+j']} R'(k')$$

The arrays L' and R' are indexed by absolute corpus positions, but their contents are sentence relative positions (on the source side). To index the arrays L' and R', we also need to obtain the corresponding target sentence start position s'. Note that the back-projected span $[i'', j'']$ may or may not be the same as the original span $[i, j]$. In fact, this is exactly what we must check for to ensure a consistent alignment.

The suffix array gives us i, which is an absolute corpus position, but we need to know the sentence-relative position, since the spans computed by R, L, R', L' are all sentence relative. To solve this, we introduce an array P (length $|T|$) that gives the relative sentence position of each source word.

We then pack the three source side arrays (R, L, and P) into a single RLP array of 32-bit integers (note that we are actually wasting one byte per array element). Finally, since the end-of-sentence special token is not used in any of R, L, or P, its position in RLP can be used to store an index to the start of the corresponding target sentence in the target array T'. Now, given a source phrase spanning $[i, j]$ (recall, these are absolute corpus positions), our phrase extraction algorithm is as follows:

Algorithm 2 Efficient Phrase Extraction Algorithm

```
for each source span [i, j] do
    Compute [i', j']
    s := i − P[i] − 1
    s' := RLP[s]
    i'' := min_{k'∈[s'+i', s'+j']} L'(k')
    j'' := max_{k'∈[s'+i', s'+j']} R'(k')
    If i − s = i'' and j − s = j'' then
        Extract T[i, j] with T'[s' + i', s' + j']
```

where s is the source sentence start position of a given source phrase and s' is the target sentence start position. If the back-projected spans match the original spans, the phrase pair $T[i, j]$ and $T'[s' + i', s' + j']$ is extracted.

In total, the data structures RLP, R', and L' require $4|T| + 2|T'|$ bytes. Not only is this phrase extraction algorithm fast—requiring only a few indirect array references—the space requirements for the auxiliary data structures are quite modest.

Given sufficient resources, we would ideally parallelize the phrase table creation process for each occurrence of the matched source substring. However, the typical number of source substring matches for an input sentence is even larger than the number of threads available on GPUs, so this strategy does not make sense due to context switching overhead. Instead, GPU thread blocks (groups of 512 threads) are used to process each source substring. This means that for substrings with large numbers of matches, one thread in the GPU block would process multiple occurrences. This strategy is widely used, and according to GPU programming best practices from NVIDIA, allocating more work to a single thread maintains high GPU utilization and reduces the cost of context switches.

5 Computing Every Feature

Finally, we arrive at line 7 in Algorithm 3, where we must compute feature values for each extracted phrase pair. Following the implementation of grammar extraction used in cdec (Lopez, 2008a), we compute several widely-used features:

1. Pair count feature, $c(e, f)$.
2. The joint probability of all target-to-source phrase translation probabilities, $p(e|f) = c(e, f)/c(f)$, where e is target phrase, f is the source phrase.
3. The logarithm of the target-to-source lexical weighting feature.
4. The logarithm of the source-to-target lexical weighting feature.
5. The coherence probability, defined as the ratio between the number of successful extractions of a source phrase to the total count of the source phrase in the suffix array.

The output of our phrase extraction is a large collection of phrase pairs. To extract the above features, aggregate statistics need to be computed over phrase pairs. To make the solution both compact and efficient, we first sort the unordered collection of phrases from the GPU into an array, then the aggregate statistics can be obtained in a single pass over the array, since identical phrase pairs are now grouped together.

6 Experimental Setup

We tested our GPU-based grammar extraction implementation under the conditions in which it would be used for a Chinese-to-English machine translation task, in particular, replicating the data conditions of Lopez (2008b). Experiments were performed on two data sets. First, we used the source (Chinese) side of news articles collected from the Xinhua Agency, with around 27 million words of Chinese in around one million sentences (totaling 137 MB). Second, we added source-side parallel text from the United Nations, with around 81 million words of Chinese in around four million sentences (totaling 561 MB). In a pre-processing phase, we mapped every word to a unique integer, with two special integers representing end-of-sentence and end-of-corpus, respectively.

Input query data consisted of all sentences from the NIST 2002–2006 translation campaigns, tokenized and integerized identically to the training data. On average, sentences contained around 29 words. In order to fully stress our GPU algorithms, we ran tests on batches of 2,000, 4,000, 6,000, 8,000, and 16,000 sentences. Since there are only around 8,000 test sentences in the NIST data, we simply duplicated the test data as necessary.

Our experiments used NVIDIA's Tesla C2050 GPU (Fermi Generation), which has 448 CUDA cores with a peak memory bandwidth 144 GB/s. Note that the GPU was released in early 2010 and represents previous generation technology. NVIDIA's current GPUs (Kepler) boasts raw processing power in the 1.3 TFlops (double precision) range, which is approximately three times the GPU we used. Our CPU is a 3.33 GHz Intel Xeon X5260 processor, which has two cores.

As a baseline, we compared against the publicly available implementation of the CPU-based algorithms described by Lopez (2008a) found in the pycdec (Chahuneau et al., 2012) extension of the cdec machine translation system (Dyer et al., 2010). Note that we only tested grammar extraction for continuous pairs of phrases, and we did not test the slower and more complex queries for hierarchical

Input Sentences		2,000	4,000	6,000	8,000	16,000
Number of Words		57,868	117,854	161,883	214,246	428,492
Xinhua						
With Sampling (s_{300})	GPU (words/second)	3811 (21.9)	4723 (20.4)	5496 (32.1)	6391 (29.7)	12405 (36.0)
	CPU (words/second)	200 (1.5)				
	Speedup	**19**×	**24**×	**27**×	**32**×	**62**×
No Sampling (s_∞)	GPU (words/second)	1917 (8.5)	2859 (11.1)	3496 (19.9)	4171 (23.2)	8186 (27.6)
	CPU (words/second)	1.13 (0.02)				
	Speedup	**1690**×	**2520**×	**3082**×	**3677**×	**7217**×
Xinhua + UN						
With Sampling (s_{300})	GPU (words/second)	2021 (5.3)	2558 (10.7)	2933 (13.9)	3439 (15.2)	6737 (29.0)
	CPU (words/second)	157 (1.8)				
	Speedup	**13**×	**16**×	**19**×	**22**×	**43**×
No Sampling (s_∞)	GPU (words/second)	500.5 (2.5)	770.1 (3.9)	984.6 (5.8)	1243.8 (5.4)	2472.3 (12.0)
	CPU (words/second)	0.23 (0.002)				
	Speedup	**2194**×	**3375**×	**4315**×	**5451**×	**10836**×

Table 2: Comparing the GPU and CPU implementations for phrase extraction on two different corpora. Throughput is measured in words per second under different test set sizes; the 95% confidence intervals across five trials are given in parentheses, along with relative speedups comparing the two implementations.

(gappy) patterns described by Lopez (2007). Both our implementation and the baseline are written primarily in C/C++.[1]

Our source corpora and test data are the same as that presented in Lopez (2008b), and using the CPU implementation as a reference enabled us to confirm that our extracted grammars and features are identical (modulo sampling). We timed our GPU implementation as follows: from the loading of query sentences, extractions of substrings and grammar rules, until all grammars for all sentences are generated in memory. Timing does not include offline preparations such as the construction of the suffix array on source texts and the I/O costs for writing the per-sentence grammar files to disk. This timing procedure is exactly the same for the CPU baseline. We are confident that our results represent a fair comparison between the GPU and CPU, and are not attributed to misconfigurations or other flaws in experimental procedures. Note that the CPU implementation runs in a single thread, on the same machine that hosts the GPU (described above).

7 Results

Table 2 shows performance results comparing our GPU implementation against the reference CPU implementation for phrase extraction. In one experimental condition, the sampling parameter for frequently-matching phrases is set to 300, per Lopez (2008a), denoted s_{300}. The experimental condition without sampling is denoted s_∞. Following standard settings, the maximum length of the source phrase is set to 5 and the maximum length of the target phrase is set to 15 (same for both GPU and CPU implementations). The table is divided into two sections: the top shows results on the Xinhua data, and the bottom on Xinhua + UN data. Columns report results for different numbers

[1]The Chahuneau et al. (2012) implementation is in Cython, a language for building Python applications with performance-critical components in C. In particular, all of the suffix array code that we instrumented for these experiments are compiled to C/C++. The implementation is a port of the original code written by Lopez (2008a) in Pyrex, a precursor to Cython. Much of the code is unchanged from the original version.

# Sent.	2000	4000	6000	8000	16000
Speedup	9.6×	14.3×	17.5×	20.9×	40.9×
Phrases	2.1×	1.8×	1.7×	1.6×	1.6×

Table 3: Comparing no sampling on the GPU with sampling on the CPU in terms of performance improvements (GPU over CPU) and increases in the number of phrase pairs extracted (GPU over CPU).

of input sentences. Performance is reported in terms of throughput: the number of processed words per second on average (i.e., total time divided by the batch size in words). The results are averaged over five trials, with 95% confidence intervals shown in parentheses. Note that as the batch size increases, we achieve higher throughput on the GPU since we are better saturating its full processing power. In contrast, performance is constant on the CPU regardless of the number of sentences processed.

The CPU throughput on the Xinhua data is 1.13 words per second without sampling and 200 words per second with sampling. On 16,000 test sentences, we have mostly saturated the GPU's processing power, and observe a 7217× speedup over the CPU implementation without sampling and 62× speedup with sampling. On the larger (Xinhua + UN) corpus, we observe 43× and 10836× speedup with sampling and no sampling, respectively.

Interestingly, a run without sampling on the GPU is still substantially faster than a run with sampling on the CPU. On the Xinhua corpus, we observe speedups ranging from nine times to forty times, as shown in Table 3. Without sampling, we are able to extract up to twice as many phrases.

In previous CPU implementations of on-the-fly phrase extraction, restrictions were placed on the maximum length of the source and target phrases due to computational constraints (in addition to sampling). Given the massive parallelism afforded by the GPU, might we be able to lift these restrictions and construct the complete phrase table? To answer this question, we performed an experiment without sampling and without any restrictions on the length of the extracted phrases. The complete phrase table contained about 0.5% more distinct pairs, with negligible impact on performance.

When considering these results, an astute reader might note that we are comparing performance of a single-threaded implementation with a fully-saturated GPU. To address this concern, we conducted an experiment using a multi-threaded version of the CPU reference implementation to take full advantage of multiple cores on the CPU (by specifying the `-j` option in cdec); we experimented with up to four threads to fully saturate the dual-core CPU. In terms of throughput, the CPU implementation scales linearly, i.e., running on four threads achieves roughly 4× throughput. Note that the CPU and GPU implementations take advantage of parallelism in completely different ways: cdec can be characterized as embarrassingly parallel, with different threads processing each complete sentence in isolation, whereas our GPU implementation achieves intra-sentential parallelism by exploiting many threads to concurrently process each sentence. In terms of absolute performance figures, even with the 4× throughput improvement from fully saturating the CPU, our GPU implementation remains faster by a wide margin. Note that neither our GPU nor CPU represents state-of-the-art hardware, and we would expect the performance advantage of GPUs to be even greater with latest generation hardware, since the number of available threads on a GPU is increasing faster than the number of threads available on a CPU.

Since phrase extraction is only one part of an end-to-end machine translation system, it makes sense to examine the overall performance of the entire translation pipeline. For this experiment, we used our GPU implementation for phrase extraction, serialized the grammar files to disk, and used cdec for decoding (on the CPU). The comparison condition used cdec for all three stages. We used standard phrase length constraints (5 on source side, 15 on target side) with sampling of frequent phrases. Finally, we replicated the data conditions in Lopez (2008a), where our source corpora was the Xinhua data set and our development/test sets were the NIST03/NIST05 data; the NIST05 test set contains 1,082 sentences.

Performance results for end-to-end translation are shown in Table 4, broken down in terms of total amount of time for each of the processing stages for the entire test set under different conditions. In the decoding stage, we varied the number of CPU threads (note here we do not observe linear

Phrase Extraction	I/O	Decoding	
GPU: 11.0	3.7	1 thread	55.7
		2 threads	35.3
CPU: 166.5		3 threads	31.5
		4 threads	26.2

Table 4: End-to-end machine translation performance: time to process the NIST05 test set in seconds, broken down in terms of the three processing stages.

speedup). In terms of end-to-end results, complete translation of the test set takes 41 seconds with the GPU for phrase extraction and CPU for decoding, compared to 196 seconds using the CPU for both (with four decoding threads in both cases). This represents a speedup of 4.8×, which suggests that even selective optimizations of individual components in the MT pipeline using GPUs can make a substantial difference in overall performance.

8 Future Work

There are a number of directions that we have identified for future work. For computational efficiency reasons, previous implementations of the "translation by pattern matching" approach have had to introduce approximations, e.g., sampling and constraints on phrase lengths. Our results show that the massive amounts of parallelism available in the GPU make these approximations unnecessary, but it is unclear to what extent they impact translation quality. For example, Table 3 shows that we extract up to twice as many phrase pairs without sampling, but do these pairs actually matter? We have begun to examine the impact of various settings on translation quality and have observed small improvements in some cases (which, note, come for "free"), but so far the results have not been conclusive.

The experiments in this paper focus primarily on throughput, but for large classes of applications latency is also important. One current limitation of our work is that large batch sizes are necessary to fully utilize the available processing power of the GPU. This and other properties of the GPU, such as the high latency involved in transferring data from main memory to GPU memory, make low-latency processing a challenge, which we hope to address.

Another broad future direction is to "GPU-ify" other machine translation models and other components in the machine translation pipeline. An obvious next step is to extend our work to the hierarchical phrase-based translation model (Chiang, 2007), which would involve extracting "gappy" phrases. Lopez (2008a) has tackled this problem on the CPU, but it is unclear to what extent the same types of algorithms he proposed can execute efficiently in the GPU environment. Beyond phrase extraction, it might be possible to perform decoding itself in the GPU—not only will this exploit massive amounts of parallelism, but also reduce costs in moving data to and from the GPU memory.

9 Conclusion

GPU parallelism offers many promises for practical and efficient implementations of language processing systems. This promise has been demonstrated for speech recognition (Chong et al., 2008; Chong et al., 2009) and parsing (Yi et al., 2011), and we have demonstrated here that it extends to machine translation as well. We believe that explorations of modern parallel hardware architectures is a fertile area of research: the field has only begun to examine the possibilities and there remain many more interesting questions to tackle. Parallelism is critical not only from the perspective of building real-world applications, but for overcoming fundamental computational bottlenecks associated with models that researchers are developing today.

Acknowledgments

This research was supported in part by the BOLT program of the Defense Advanced Research Projects Agency, Contract No. HR0011-12-C-0015; NSF under award IIS-1144034. Any opinions, findings, conclusions, or recommendations expressed in this paper are those of the authors and do not necessarily reflect views of the sponsors. The second author is grateful to Esther and Kiri for their loving support and dedicates this work to Joshua and Jacob. We would like to thank three anonymous reviewers for providing helpful suggestions and also acknowledge Benjamin Van Durme and CLIP labmates for useful discussions. We also thank UMIACS for providing hardware resources via the NVIDIA CUDA Center of Excellence, UMIACS IT staff, especially Joe Webster, for excellent support.

References

R. D. Brown. 2004. A modified Burrows-Wheeler Transform for highly-scalable example-based translation. In *Proceedings of the 6th Conference of the Association for Machine Translation in the Americas (AMTA 2004)*, pages 27–36.

C. Callison-Burch, C. Bannard, and J. Schroeder. 2005. Scaling phrase-based statistical machine translation to larger corpora and longer phrases. In *Proceedings of the 43rd Annual Meeting on Association for Computational Linguistics (ACL 2005)*, pages 255–262.

V. Chahuneau, N. A. Smith, and C. Dyer. 2012. pycdec: A Python interface to cdec. In *Proceedings of the 7th Machine Translation Marathon (MTM 2012)*.

D. Chiang. 2007. Hierarchical phrase-based translation. *Computational Linguistics*, 33(2):201–228.

J. Chong, Y. Yi, A. Faria, N. R. Satish, and K. Keutzer. 2008. Data-parallel large vocabulary continuous speech recognition on graphics processors. In *Proceedings of the Workshop on Emerging Applications and Manycore Architectures*.

J. Chong, E. Gonina, Y. Yi, and K. Keutzer. 2009. A fully data parallel WFST-based large vocabulary continuous speech recognition on a graphics processing unit. In *Proceedings of the 10th Annual Conference of the International Speech Communication Association (INTERSPEECH 2009)*, pages 1183–1186.

F. Cromieres and S. Kurohashi. 2011. Efficient retrieval of tree translation examples for syntax-based machine translation. In *Proceedings of the 2011 Conference on Empirical Methods in Natural Language Processing, EMNLP 2011*, pages 508–518.

C. Dyer, A. Lopez, J. Ganitkevitch, J. Weese, F. Ture, P. Blunsom, H. Setiawan, V. Eidelman, and P. Resnik. 2010. cdec: A decoder, alignment, and learning framework for finite-state and context-free translation models. In *Proceedings of the ACL 2010 System Demonstrations*, pages 7–12.

A. Gharaibeh and M. Ripeanu. 2010. Size matters: Space/time tradeoffs to improve GPGPU applications performance. In *Proceedings of the 2010 ACM/IEEE International Conference for High Performance Computing, Networking, Storage and Analysis (SC 2010)*, pages 1–12.

A. Lopez. 2007. Hierarchical phrase-based translation with suffix arrays. In *Proceedings of the 2007 Joint Conference on Empirical Methods in Natural Language Processing and Computational Natural Language Learning*, pages 976–985.

A. Lopez. 2008a. *Machine translation by pattern matching*. Ph.D. dissertation, University of Maryland, College Park, Maryland, USA.

A. Lopez. 2008b. Tera-scale translation models via pattern matching. In *Proceedings of the 22nd International Conference on Computational Linguistics (COLING 2008)*, pages 505–512.

U. Manber and G. Myers. 1990. Suffix arrays: a new method for on-line string searches. In *Proceedings of the First Annual ACM-SIAM Symposium on Discrete Algorithms (SODA '90)*, pages 319–327.

F. J. Och, C. Tillmann, and H. Ney. 1999. Improved alignment models for statistical machine translation. In *Proceedings of the 1999 Joint SIGDAT Conference on Empirical Methods in Natural Language Processing and Very Large Corpora*, pages 20–28.

M. Schatz, C. Trapnell, A. Delcher, and A. Varshney. 2007. High-throughput sequence alignment using graphics processing units. *BMC Bioinformatics*, 8(1):474.

C. Trapnell and M. C. Schatz. 2009. Optimizing data intensive GPGPU computations for DNA sequence alignment. *Parallel Computing*, 35(8-9):429–440.

Y. Yi, C.-Y. Lai, S. Petrov, and K. Keutzer. 2011. Efficient parallel CKY parsing on GPUs. In *Proceedings of the 12th International Conference on Parsing Technologies*, pages 175–185.

Y. Zhang and S. Vogel. 2005. An efficient phrase-to-phrase alignment model for arbitrarily long phrase and large corpora. In *Proceedings of the Tenth Conference of the European Association for Machine Translation (EAMT-05)*.

Discriminative Training of 150 Million Translation Parameters and Its Application to Pruning

Hendra Setiawan and Bowen Zhou
IBM T.J. Watson Research Center
Yorktown Heights, NY 10598, USA
{*hendras, zhou*}@*us.ibm.com*

Abstract

Until recently, the application of discriminative training to log linear-based statistical machine translation has been limited to tuning the weights of a limited number of features or training features with a limited number of parameters. In this paper, we propose to scale up discriminative training of (He and Deng, 2012) to train features with 150 million parameters, which is one order of magnitude higher than previously published effort, and to apply discriminative training to redistribute probability mass that is lost due to model pruning. The experimental results confirm the effectiveness of our proposals on NIST MT06 set over a strong baseline.

1 Introduction

State-of-the-art statistical machine translation systems based on a log-linear framework are parameterized by $\{\lambda, \Phi\}$, where the feature weights λ are discriminatively trained (Och and Ney, 2002; Chiang et al., 2008b; Simianer et al., 2012) by directly optimizing them against a translation-oriented metric such as BLEU. The feature parameters Φ can be roughly divided into two categories: dense feature that measures the plausibility of each translation rule from a particular aspect, e.g., the rule translation probabilities $p(f|e)$ and $p(e|f)$; and sparse feature that fires when certain phenomena is observed, e.g., when a frequent word pair co-occured in a rule. In contrast to λ, feature parameters in Φ are usually modeled by generative models for dense features, or by indicator functions for sparse ones. It is therefore desirable to train the dense features for each rule in a discriminative fashion to maximize some translation criterion. The maximum expected BLEU training of (He and Deng, 2012) is a recent effort towards this direction, and in this paper, we extend their work to a scaled-up task of discriminative training of the features of a strong hierarchical phrase-based model and confirm its effectiveness empirically.

In this work, we further consider the application of discriminative training to pruned model. Various pruning techniques (Johnson et al., 2007; Zens et al., 2012; Eck et al., 2007; Lee et al., 2012; Tomeh et al., 2011) have been proposed recently to filter translation rules. One common consequence of pruning is that the probability distribution of many surviving rules become deficient, i.e. $\sum_f p(f|e) < 1$. In practice, others have chosen either to leave the pruned rules as it-is, or simply to re-normalize the probability mass by distributing the pruned mass to surviving rules proportionally. We argue that both approaches are suboptimal, and propose a more principled method to re-distribute the probability mass, i.e. using discriminative training with some translation criterion. Our experimental results demonstrate that at various pruning levels, our approach improves performance consistently. Particularly at the level of 50% of rules being pruned, the discriminatively trained models performs better than the unpruned baseline grammar. This shows that discriminative training makes it possible to achieve smaller models that perform comparably or even better than the baseline model.

Our contributions in this paper are two-folded: First of all, we scale up the maximum expected BLEU training proposed in (He and Deng, 2012) in a number of ways including using 1) a hierarchical phrase-based model, 2) a richer feature set, and 3) a larger training set with a much larger parameter set, resulting in more than 150 million parameters in the model being updated, which is one order magnitude higher than the phrase-based model reported in (He and Deng, 2012). We are able to show a reasonable improvement over this strong baseline. Secondly, we combine discriminative training with pruning techniques to reestimate parameters of pruned grammar. Our approach is shown to alleviate the loss due to pruning, and sometimes can even outperform the baseline unpruned grammar.

2 Discriminative Training of Φ

Given the entire training data $\{F_n, E_n\}_{n=1}^N$, and current parameterization $\{\lambda, \Phi\}$, we decode the source side of training data F_n to produce hypothesis $\{\hat{E}_n\}_{n=1}^N$. Our goal is to update Φ towards Φ' that maximizes the expected BLEU scores of the entire training data given the current λ:

$$U(\Phi)=\sum_{\forall \hat{E}_1...\hat{E}_N} \tilde{P}_\Phi(\hat{E}_1..\hat{E}_N|F_1..F_N)B(\hat{E}_1..\hat{E}_N) \quad (1)$$

where $B(\hat{E}_1...\hat{E}_N)$ is the BLEU score of the concatenated hypothesis of the entire training data, following (He and Deng, 2012).

Eq. 1 summarizes over all possible combinations of $\hat{E}_1...\hat{E}_N$, which is intractable. Hence we make two simplifying approximations as follows. First, let the k-best hypotheses of the n-th sentence, $\hat{E}_n = \left\{\hat{E}_n^1, ..., \hat{E}_n^K\right\}$, approximate all its possible translation. In other words, we assume that $\sum_{k=1}^K \tilde{P}(\hat{E}_n^k|F_n) = 1, \forall n$. Second, let the sum of sentence-level BLEU approximate the corpus BLEU. We note that corpus BLEU is not strictly decomposable (Chiang et al., 2008a), however, as the training data's size N gets big as in our case, we expect them to become more positively correlated.

Under these assumptions and the fact that each sentence is decoded independently, Eq. 1 can be algebraically simplified into:

$$U(\Phi) = \sum_{n=1}^{N}\sum_{k=1}^{K} P_\Phi(\hat{E}_n^k|F_n)B(\hat{E}_n^k) \quad (2)$$

where $P_\Phi(\hat{E}_n^k|F_n)=\tilde{P}_\Phi(\hat{E}_n^k|F_n)/\sum_{\forall k}\tilde{P}_\Phi(\hat{E}_n^k|F_n)$. We detail the process in the Appendix.

To further simplify the problem and relate it with model pruning, we consider to update a subset of $\theta \subset \Phi$ while keeping other parameterization of Φ unchanged, where $\theta = \{\theta_{ij} = p(e_j|f_i)\}$ denotes our parameter set that satisfies $\sum_j \theta_{ij} = 1$ and $\theta_{ij} \geq 0$. In experiments, we also consider $\{\theta_{ji} = p(f_i|e_j)\}$.

To alleviate overfitting, we introduce KL-distance based reguralization as in (He and Deng, 2012). We thus arrive at the following objective function:

$$O(\theta) = \log(U(\theta)) - \tau \cdot KL(\theta||\theta^0)/N \quad (3)$$

where τ controls the regularization term's contribution, and θ^0 represents a prior parameter set, e.g., from the conventional maximum likelihood training.

The optimization algorithm is based on the Extended Baum Welch (EBW) (Gopalakrishnan et al., 1991) as derived by (He and Deng, 2012). The final update rule is as follow:

$$\theta'_{ij} = \frac{\sum_n\sum_k \gamma(n,k,i,j) + U(\theta)\tau\theta^0_{ij}/\lambda + D_i\theta_{ij}}{\sum_n\sum_k\sum_j \gamma(n,k,i,j) + U(\theta)\tau/\lambda + D_i} \quad (4)$$

where θ'_{ij} is the updated parameter, $\gamma(n,k,i,j) = P_\theta(\hat{E}_n^k|F_n)\{B(\hat{E}_n^k) - U_n(\theta)\}\sum_l 1(f_{n,k,l} = f_i, e_{n,k,l} = e_j)$; $U_n(\theta) = \sum_{k=1}^K P_\theta(\hat{E}_n^k|F_n)B(\hat{E}_n^k)$; $D_i = \sum_{n,k,j}\max(0, -\gamma(n,k,i,j))$ and λ is the current feature's weight.

3 DT is Beneficial for Pruning

Pruning is often a key part in deploying large-scale SMT systems for many reasons, such as for reducing runtime memory footprint and for efficiency. Many pruning techniques have been proposed to assess translation rules and filter rules out if they are less plausible than others. While different pruning techniques may use different criterion, they all assume that pruning does not affect the feature function values of the surviving rules. This assumption may be suboptimal for some feature functions that have probabilistic sense since pruning will remove a portion of the probability mass that is previously assigned to the pruned rules. To be concrete, for the rule translation probabilities θ_{ij} under consideration, the constraint $\sum_j \theta_{ij} = 1$ will not hold for all source rules i after pruning. Previous works typically left the probability mass as it-is, or simply renormalize the pruned mass, i.e. $\bar{\theta}_{ij} = \theta_{ij}/\sum_j \theta_{ij}$.

We argue that applying the DT techniques to a pruned grammar, as described in Sec. 2, provides a more principled method to redistribute the mass, i.e. by quantizing how each rule contributes to the expected BLEU score in comparison to other competing rules. To empirically verify this, we consider the significance test based pruning (Johnson et al., 2007), though our general idea can be appllied to any pruning techniques. For our experiments, we use the significance pruning tool that is available as part of Moses decoder package (Koehn et al., 2007).

4 Experiments

Our experiments are designed to serve two goals: 1) to show the performance of discriminative training of feature parameters θ in a large-scale task; and 2) to show the effectiveness of DT when applied to pruned grammar. Our baseline system is a state-of-the-art hierarchical phrase-based system as described in (Zhou et al., 2008), trained on six million parallel sentences corpora that are available to the DARPA BOLT Chinese-English task. The training corpora includes a mixed genre of news wire, broadcast news, web-blog and comes from various sources such as LDC, HK Hansard and UN data.

In total, there are 50 dense features in our translation system. In addition to the standard features which include the rule translation probabilities, we incorporate features that are found useful for developing a state-of-the-art baseline, e.g. provenance-based lexical features (Chiang et al., 2011). We use a large 6-gram language model, which we train on a 10 billion words monolingual corpus, including the English side of our parallel corpora plus other corpora such as Gigaword (LDC2011T07) and Google News. To prevent possible over-fitting, we only kept the rules that have at most three terminal words (plus up to two nonterminals) on the source side, resulting in a grammar with 167 million rules.

Our discriminative training procedure includes updating both λ and θ, and we follow (He and Deng, 2012) to optimize them in an alternate manner. That is, when we optimize θ via EBW, we keep λ fixed and when we optimize λ, we keep λ fixed. We use PRO (Hopkins and May, 2011) to tune λ.

For discriminative training of θ, we use a subset of 550 thousands of parallel sentences selected from the entire training data, mainly to allow for faster experimental cycle; they mainly come from news and web-blog domains. For each sentence of this subset, we generate 500-best of unique hypotheses using the baseline model. The 1-best and the oracle BLEU scores for this subset are 40.19 and 47.06 respectively. Following (He and Deng, 2012), we focus on discriminative training of $p(f|e)$ and $p(e|f)$, which in practice affects around 150 million of parameters; hence the title.

For the tuning and development sets, we set aside 1275 and 1239 sentences respectively from LDC2010E30 corpus. The tune set is used by PRO for tuning λ while the dev set is used to decide the best DT model. As for the blind test set, we report the performance on the NIST MT06 evaluation set, which consists of 1644 sentences from news and web-blog domains. Our baseline system's performance on MT06 is 39.91 which is among the best number ever published so far in the community.

Table 1 compares the key components of our baseline system with that of (He and Deng, 2012). As shown, we are working with a stronger system than (He and Deng, 2012), especially in terms of the number of parameters under consideration $|\theta|$.

	He&Deng(2012)	This paper
Model	phrase-based	hierarchical
n-gram lm	3-gram	6-gram
# features	10	50
Max terminal	4	3
$\lvert\theta\rvert$	9.2 M	150M
# training data	750K	6M
N for DT	750K	550K
max K-best	100	500

Table 1: Our system compares to He&Deng's (2012).

4.1 DT of 150 Million Parameters

To ensure the correctness of our implementation, we show in Fig 2, the first five EBW updates with $\tau = 0.10$. As shown, the utility function $\log(U(\theta))$ increases monotonically but is countered by the KL term, resulting in a smaller but consistent increase of the objective function $O(\theta)$. This monotonically-increasing trend of the objective function confirms the correctness of our implementation since EBW algorithm is a bound-based technique that ensures growth transformations between updates.

We then explore the optimal setting for τ which controls the contribution of the regularization term. Specifically, we perform grid search, exploring values of τ from 0.1 to 0.75. For each τ, we run several iterations of discriminative training where each iteration involves one simultaneous update of $p(f|e)$

and $p(e|f)$ according to Eq. 4, followed by one update of λ via PRO (as in (He and Deng, 2012)). In total, we run 10 such iterations for each τ.

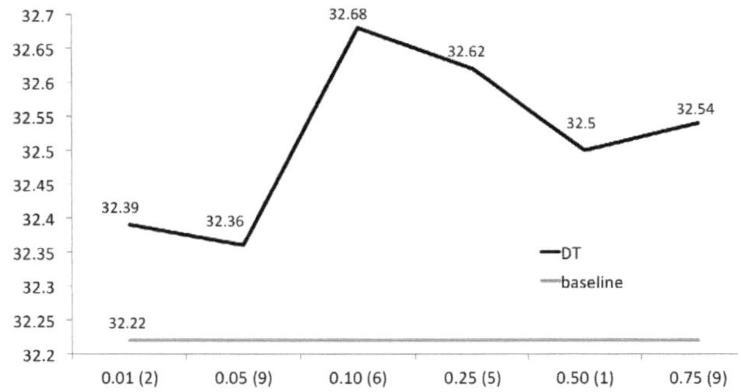

Figure 1: The dev set's BLEU score (y-axis) on different setting of τ (x-axis). The grey line indicates the baseline performance on dev set. The number in bracket on the x-axis indicates the iteration at which the score is obtained.

Across different τ, we find that the first iteration provides most of the gain while the subsequent iterations provide additional, smaller gain with occassional performance degradation; thus the translation performance is not always monotonically increasing over iteration. We report the best score of each τ in Fig. 1 and at which iteration that score is produced. As shown in Fig. 1, all settings of τ improve over the baseline and $\tau = 0.10$ gives the highest gain of 0.45 BLEU score. This improvement is in the same ballpark as in (He and Deng, 2012) though on a scaled-up task. We next decode the MT06 using the best model (i.e. $\tau = 0.10$ at 6-th iteration) observed on the dev set, and obtained 40.33 BLEU with an improvement of around 0.4 BLEU point. We see this result as confirming the effectiveness of discriminative training but on a larger-scale task, adding to what was reported by (He and Deng, 2012).

4.2 DT for Significance Pruning

Next, we show the contribution of discriminative training for model pruning. To do so, we prune the translation grammar so that its size becomes 50%, 25%, 10% of the original grammar. Respectively, we delete rules whose significance value below 15, 50 and 500. Table 2 compares the statistics of the pruned grammars and the unpruned one. In particular, columns 4 and 5 show the total averaged probability mass of the remaining rules. This statistics provides some indication of how deficient the features are after pruning. As shown, the total averaged probability mass after pruning is below 100% and even lower for the more aggressive pruning.

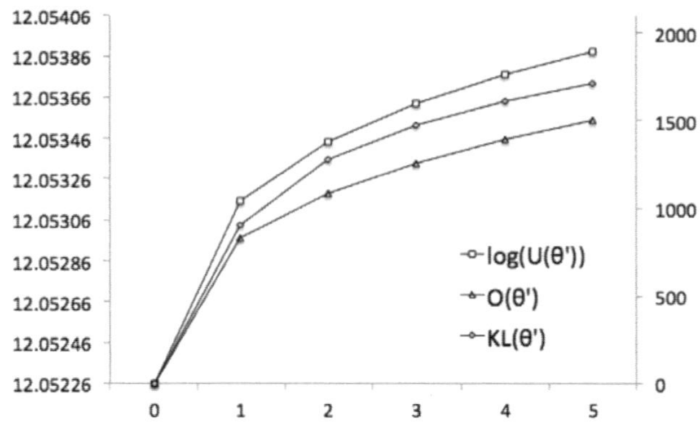

Figure 2: Objective function ($O(\theta')$), the regularization term ($KL(\theta')$) and the unregularized objective function ($\log(U(\theta'))$) for five EBW updates of updating $p(e_j|f_i)$

To show that the deficiency is suboptimal, we considers two baseline systems: models with/without mass renormalization. We tune a new λ for each model and use the new λ to decode the dev and test sets. The results are shown in columns 6 and 9 of Table 2 where we show the results for the unnormalized model in the brackets following the results for the re-normalized model. The results show that pruning degrades the performances and that naively re-normalizing the model provides no significant changes in performance. Subsequently, we will focus on the normalized models as the baseline as they represents the starting points of our EBW iteration.

Next, we run discriminative training that would reassign the probability mass to the surviving rules. First, we normalize $p(f|e)$ and $p(e|f)$, so that they satisfy the sum to one constraint required by the algorithm. Then, we run discriminative training on these pruned grammars using $\tau = 0.10$ (i.e. the setting that gives the best performance for the unpruned grammar as discussed in Section 4.1). We report the results in columns 7 and 9 for the dev and test sets respectively, as well as the gain over the baseline system in columns 8 and 10.

As shown in Table 2, DT provides a nice improvement over the baseline model of no mass reassignment. For all pruning levels, DT can compensate the loss associated with pruning. In particular, at 50% level of pruning, there is a loss about 0.4

size (%)	$\|f\|$ (M)	$\|e\|$ (M)	$p(*\|e)$	$p(*\|f)$	dev-set baseline (un)	dev-set DT (iter)	dev-set gain	test-set (MT06) baseline (un)	test-set (MT06) DT	test-set (MT06) gain
100	59	50	1.00	1.00	*32.22*(32.08)	**32.68** (6)	+0.44	*39.91* (39.71)	**40.33**	+0.42
50	38	35	0.92	0.94	31.84 (32.02)	**32.31** (6)	+0.57	39.61(39.72)	**40.08**	+0.47
25	14	14	0.87	0.91	31.39 (31.43)	31.68 (2)	+0.29	39.23 (39.17)	39.43	+0.20
10	4	3	0.77	0.84	27.27 (27.10)	27.82 (2)	+0.55	36.01 (36.04)	36.43	+0.42

Table 2: The statistics of grammars pruned at various level (column 1), including the number of unique source and target phrases (columns 2 & 3), total probability mass of the remaining rules for $p(f|e)$ and $p(e|f)$ (columns 4 & 5), the performance of the pruned model before and after discriminative training as well as the gain on the dev and the test sets (columns 6 to 11). The iteration at which DT gives the best dev set is indicated by the number enclosed by bracket in column 7. The baseline performance is in *italics*, followed by a number in the bracket which refers to the performance of using unnormalized model. The above-the-baseline performances are in **bold**.

BLEU point after pruning. With the DT on pruned model, all pruning losses are reclaimed and the new pruned model is even better than the unpruned original model. This empirical result shows that leaving probability mass unassigned after pruning is suboptimal and that discriminative training provides a principled way to redistribute the mass.

5 Conclusion

In this paper, we first extend the maximum expected BLEU training of (He and Deng, 2012) to train two features of a state-of-the-art hierarchical phrase-based system, namely: $p(f|e)$ and $p(e|f)$. Compared to (He and Deng, 2012), we apply the algorithm to a strong baseline that is trained on a bigger parallel corpora and comes with a richer feature set. The number of parameters under consideration amounts to 150 million. Our experiments show that discriminative training these two features (out of 50) gives around 0.40 BLEU point improvement, which is consistent with the conclusion of (He and Deng, 2012) but in a much larger-scale system.

Furthermore, we apply the algorithm to redistribute the probability mass of $p(f|e)$ and $p(e|f)$ that is commonly lost due to conventional model pruning. Previous techniques either leave the probability mass as it is or distribute it proportionally among the surviving rules. We show that our proposal of using discriminative training to redistribute the mass empirically performs better, demonstrating the effectiveness of our proposal.

Appendix

We describe the process to simplify Eq. 1 to Eq. 2, which is omitted in (He and Deng, 2012). For conciseness, we drop the conditions and write $P(\hat{E}_i|F_i)$ as $P(\hat{E}_i)$. We write Eq. 1 again below as Eq. 5 .

$$\sum_{\forall \hat{E}_1 ... \hat{E}_N} \prod_{i=1}^{N} P(\hat{E}_i|F_i) \cdot \sum_{i=1}^{N} B(\hat{E}_i) \tag{5}$$

We first focus on the first sentence E_1/F_1 and expand the related terms from the equation as follow:

$$\sum_{\forall \hat{E}_1} \sum_{\forall \hat{E}_2 ... \hat{E}_N} P(\hat{E}_1) \prod_{i=2}^{N} P(\hat{E}_i) . \left[B(\hat{E}_1) + \sum_{i=2}^{N} B(\hat{E}_i) \right]$$

Expanding the inner summation, we arrive at:

$$\sum_{\forall \hat{E}_1} P(\hat{E}_1) B(\hat{E}_1) \sum_{\forall \hat{E}_2 ... \hat{E}_N} \prod_{i=2}^{N} P(\hat{E}_i) +$$
$$\sum_{\forall \hat{E}_1} P(\hat{E}_1) \sum_{\forall \hat{E}_2 ... \hat{E}_N} \prod_{i=2}^{N} P(\hat{E}_i) \sum_{i=2}^{N} B(\hat{E}_i)$$

Due to the that $\sum_{k=1}^{K} \tilde{P}(\hat{E}_n^K|F_n) = 1$, we can equate $\sum_{\forall \hat{E}_2 ... \hat{E}_N} \prod_{i=2}^{N} P(\hat{E}_i)$ and $\sum_{\forall \hat{E}_1} P(\hat{E}_1)$ to 1. Thus, we arrive at:

$$\sum_{\forall \hat{E}_1} P(\hat{E}_1) B(\hat{E}_1) + \sum_{\forall \hat{E}_2 ... \hat{E}_N} \prod_{i=2}^{N} P(\hat{E}_i) \sum_{i=2}^{N} B(\hat{E}_i)$$

Notice that the second term has the same form as Eq. 5 except that the starting index starts from the second sentence. The same process can be performed and at the end, thus we can arrive at Eq. 2.

Acknowledgments

We thank Xiadong He for helpful discussions. We would like to acknowledge the support of DARPA under Grant HR0011-12-C-0015 for funding part of this work. The views, opinions, and/or findings contained in this article/presentation are those of the author/presenter and should not be interpreted as representing the official views or policies, either expressed or implied, of the DARPA.

References

David Chiang, Steve DeNeefe, Yee Seng Chan, and Hwee Tou Ng. 2008a. Decomposability of translation metrics for improved evaluation and efficient algorithms. In *Proceedings of the 2008 Conference on Empirical Methods in Natural Language Processing*, pages 610–619, Honolulu, Hawaii, October. Association for Computational Linguistics.

David Chiang, Yuval Marton, and Philip Resnik. 2008b. Online large-margin training of syntactic and structural translation features. In *Proceedings of the 2008 Conference on Empirical Methods in Natural Language Processing*, pages 224–233, Honolulu, Hawaii, October. Association for Computational Linguistics.

David Chiang, Steve DeNeefe, and Michael Pust. 2011. Two easy improvements to lexical weighting. In *Proceedings of the 49th Annual Meeting of the Association for Computational Linguistics: Human Language Technologies*, pages 455–460, Portland, Oregon, USA, June. Association for Computational Linguistics.

Matthias Eck, Stephan Vogel, and Alex Waibel. 2007. Translation model pruning via usage statistics for statistical machine translation. In *Human Language Technologies 2007: The Conference of the North American Chapter of the Association for Computational Linguistics; Companion Volume, Short Papers*, pages 21–24, Rochester, New York, April. Association for Computational Linguistics.

P. S. Gopalakrishnan, Dimitri Kanevsky, Arthur Nádas, and David Nahamoo. 1991. An inequality for rational functions with applications to some statistical estimation problems. *IEEE Transactions on Information Theory*, 37(1):107–113.

Xiaodong He and Li Deng. 2012. Maximum expected bleu training of phrase and lexicon translation models. In *Proceedings of the 50th Annual Meeting of the Association for Computational Linguistics (Volume 1: Long Papers)*, pages 292–301, Jeju Island, Korea, July. Association for Computational Linguistics.

Mark Hopkins and Jonathan May. 2011. Tuning as ranking. In *Proceedings of the 2011 Conference on Empirical Methods in Natural Language Processing*, pages 1352–1362, Edinburgh, Scotland, UK., July. Association for Computational Linguistics.

Howard Johnson, Joel Martin, George Foster, and Roland Kuhn. 2007. Improving translation quality by discarding most of the phrasetable. In *Proceedings of the 2007 Joint Conference on Empirical Methods in Natural Language Processing and Computational Natural Language Learning (EMNLP-CoNLL)*, pages 967–975, Prague, Czech Republic, June. Association for Computational Linguistics.

Philipp Koehn, Hieu Hoang, Alexandra Birch, Chris Callison-Burch, Marcello Federico, Nicola Bertoldi, Brooke Cowan, Wade Shen, Christine Moran, Richard Zens, Chris Dyer, Ondrej Bojar, Alexandra Constantin, and Evan Herbst. 2007. Moses: Open source toolkit for statistical machine translation. In *Proceedings of the 45th Annual Meeting of the Association for Computational Linguistics Companion Volume Proceedings of the Demo and Poster Sessions*, pages 177–180, Prague, Czech Republic, June. Association for Computational Linguistics.

Seung-Wook Lee, Dongdong Zhang, Mu Li, Ming Zhou, and Hae-Chang Rim. 2012. Translation model size reduction for hierarchical phrase-based statistical machine translation. In *Proceedings of the 50th Annual Meeting of the Association for Computational Linguistics (Volume 2: Short Papers)*, pages 291–295, Jeju Island, Korea, July. Association for Computational Linguistics.

Franz Josef Och and Hermann Ney. 2002. Discriminative training and maximum entropy models for statistical machine translation. In *Proceedings of 40th Annual Meeting of the Association for Computational Linguistics*, pages 295–302, Philadelphia, Pennsylvania, USA, July. Association for Computational Linguistics.

Patrick Simianer, Stefan Riezler, and Chris Dyer. 2012. Joint feature selection in distributed stochastic learning for large-scale discriminative training in smt. In *Proceedings of the 50th Annual Meeting of the Association for Computational Linguistics (Volume 1: Long Papers)*, pages 11–21, Jeju Island, Korea, July. Association for Computational Linguistics.

N. Tomeh, M. Turchi, G. Wisniewski, A. Allauzen, and F. Yvon. 2011. How good are your phrases? assessing phrase quality with single class classification. In *Proceedings of the International Workshop on Spoken Language Translation*, pages 261–268.

Richard Zens, Daisy Stanton, and Peng Xu. 2012. A systematic comparison of phrase table pruning techniques. In *Proceedings of the 2012 Joint Conference on Empirical Methods in Natural Language Processing and Computational Natural Language Learning*, pages 972–983, Jeju Island, Korea, July. Association for Computational Linguistics.

Bowen Zhou, Bing Xiang, Xiaodan Zhu, and Yuqing Gao. 2008. Prior derivation models for formally syntax-based translation using linguistically syntactic parsing and tree kernels. In *Proceedings of the ACL-08: HLT Second Workshop on Syntax and Structure in Statistical Translation (SSST-2)*, pages 19–27, Columbus, Ohio, June. Association for Computational Linguistics.

Applying Pairwise Ranked Optimisation to Improve the Interpolation of Translation Models

Barry Haddow
University of Edinburgh
Scotland
bhaddow@inf.ed.ac.uk

Abstract

In Statistical Machine Translation we often have to combine different sources of parallel training data to build a good system. One way of doing this is to build separate translation models from each data set and linearly interpolate them, and to date the main method for optimising the interpolation weights is to minimise the model perplexity on a heldout set. In this work, rather than optimising for this indirect measure, we directly optimise for BLEU on the tuning set and show improvements in average performance over two data sets and 8 language pairs.

1 Introduction

Statistical Machine Translation (SMT) requires large quantities of parallel training data in order to produce high quality translation systems. This training data, however, is often scarce and must be drawn from whatever sources are available. If these data sources differ systematically from each other, and/or from the test data, then the problem of combining these disparate data sets to create the best possible translation system is known as *domain adaptation*.

One approach to domain adaptation is to build separate models for each training domain, then weight them to create a system tuned to the test domain. In SMT, a successful approach to building domain specific language models is to build one from each corpus, then linearly interpolate them, choosing weights that minimise the perplexity on a suitable heldout set of in-domain data. This method has been applied by many authors (e.g. (Koehn and Schroeder, 2007)), and is implemented in popular language modelling tools like IRSTLM (Federico et al., 2008) and SRILM (Stolcke, 2002).

Similar interpolation techniques have been developed for translation model interpolation (Foster et al., 2010; Sennrich, 2012) for phrase-based systems but have not been as widely adopted, perhaps because the efficacy of the methods is not as clear-cut. In this previous work, the authors used standard phrase extraction heuristics to extract phrases from a heldout set of parallel sentences, then tuned the translation model (i.e. the phrase table) interpolation weights to minimise the perplexity of the interpolated model on this set of extracted phrases.

In this paper, we try to improve on this perplexity optimisation of phrase table interpolation weights by addressing two of its shortcomings. The first problem is that the perplexity is not well defined because of the differing coverage of the phrase tables, and their partial coverage of the phrases extracted from the heldout set. Secondly, perplexity may not correlate with the performance of the final SMT system.

So, instead of optimising the interpolation weights for the indirect goal of translation model perplexity, we optimise them directly for translation performance. We do this by incorporating these weights into SMT tuning using a modified version of Pairwise Ranked Optimisation (PRO) (Hopkins and May, 2011).

In experiments on two different domain adaptation problems and 8 language pairs, we show that our method achieves comparable or improved performance, when compared to the perplexity minimisation method. This is an encouraging result as it shows that PRO can be adapted to optimise translation parameters other than those in the standard linear model.

2 Optimising Phrase Table Interpolation Weights

2.1 Previous Approaches

In the work of Foster and Kuhn (2007), linear interpolation weights were derived from different measures of distance between the training corpora, but this was not found to be successful. Optimising the weights to minimise perplexity, as described in the introduction, was found by later authors to be more useful (Foster et al., 2010; Sennrich, 2012), generally showing small improvements over the default approach of concatenating all training data.

An alternative approach is to use log-linear interpolation, so that the interpolation weights can be easily optimised in tuning (Koehn and Schroeder, 2007; Bertoldi and Federico, 2009; Banerjee et al., 2011). However, this effectively multiplies the probabilities across phrase tables, which does not seem appropriate, especially for phrases absent from 1 table.

2.2 Tuning SMT Systems

The standard SMT model scores translation hypotheses as a linear combination of features. The model score of a hypothesis e is then defined to be $\mathbf{w} \cdot \mathbf{h}(e, f, a)$ where $\mathbf{w}$ is a weight vector, and $\mathbf{h}(e, f, a)$ a vector of feature functions defined over source sentences (f), hypotheses, and their alignments (a). The weights are normally optimised (*tuned*) to maximise BLEU on a heldout set (the *tuning* set).

The most popular algorithm for this weight optimisation is the line-search based MERT (Och, 2003), but recently other algorithms that support more features, such as PRO (Hopkins and May, 2011) or MIRA-based algorithms (Watanabe et al., 2007; Chiang et al., 2008; Cherry and Foster, 2012), have been introduced. All these algorithms assume that the model score is a linear function of the parameters $\mathbf{w}$. However since the phrase table probabilities enter the score function in log form, if these probabilities are a linear interpolation, then the model score is not a linear function of the interpolation weights. We will show that PRO can be used to simultaneously optimise such non-linear parameters.

2.3 Pairwise Ranked Optimisation

PRO is a *batch* tuning algorithm in the sense that there is an outer loop which repeatedly decodes a small (1000-2000 sentence) tuning set and passes the n-best lists from this tuning set to the core algorithm (also known as the *inner loop*). The core algorithm samples pairs of hypotheses from the n-best lists (according to a specific procedure), and uses these samples to optimise the weight vector $\mathbf{w}$.

The core algorithm in PRO will now be explained in more detail. Suppose that the N sampled hypothesis pairs (x_i^α, x_i^β) are indexed by i and have corresponding feature vectors pairs $(\mathbf{h}_i^\alpha, \mathbf{h}_i^\beta)$. If the gain of a given hypothesis (we use smoothed sentence BLEU) is given by the function $g(x)$, then we define y_i by

$$y_i \equiv \operatorname{sgn}(g(x_i^\alpha) - g(x_i^\beta)) \quad (1)$$

For weights $\mathbf{w}$, and hypothesis pair (x_i^α, x_i^β), the (model) score difference $\Delta s_i^{\mathbf{w}}$ is given by:

$$\Delta s_i^{\mathbf{w}} \equiv s^{\mathbf{w}}(x_i^\alpha) - s^{\mathbf{w}}(x_i^\beta) \equiv \mathbf{w} \cdot \left(\mathbf{h}_i^\alpha - \mathbf{h}_i^\beta\right) \quad (2)$$

Then the core PRO algorithm updates the weight vector to $\mathbf{w}^*$ by solving the following optimisation problem:

$$\mathbf{w}^* = \arg\max_{\mathbf{w}} \sum_{i=1}^{N} \log\left(\sigma\left(y_i \Delta s_i^{\mathbf{w}}\right)\right) \quad (3)$$

where $\sigma(x)$ is the standard sigmoid function. The derivative of the function can be computed easily, and the optimisation problem can be solved with standard numerical optimisation algorithms such as L-BFGS (Byrd et al., 1995). PRO is normally implemented by converting each sample to a training example for a 2 class maximum entropy classifier, with the feature values set to $\Delta \mathbf{h}_i$ and the responses set to the y_i, whereupon the log-likelihood is the objective given in Equation (3). As in maximum entropy modeling, it is usual to add a Gaussian prior to the objective (3) in PRO training.

2.4 Extending PRO for Mixture Models

We now show how to apply the PRO tuning algorithm of the previous subsection to simultaneously optimise the weights of the translation system, and the interpolation weights.

In the standard phrase-based model, some of the features are derived from logs of phrase translation probabilities. If the phrase table is actually a linear interpolation of two (or more) phrase tables, then we can consider these features as also being functions of the interpolation weights. The interpolation weights then enter the score differences $\{\Delta s_i^{\mathbf{w}}\}$ via the phrase features, and we can jointly optimise the objective in Equation (3) for translation model weights and interpolation weights.

To make this more concrete, suppose that the feature vector consists of m phrase table features and $n-m$ other features[1]

$$\mathbf{h} \equiv (\log(p^1), \ldots, \log(p^m), h^{m+1}, \ldots h^n) \quad (4)$$

where each p^j is an interpolation of two probability distributions p_A^j and p_B^j. So, $p^j \equiv \lambda^j p_A^j + (1-\lambda^j) p_B^j$ with $0 \leq \lambda^j \leq 1$. Defining $\boldsymbol{\lambda} \equiv (\lambda^1 \ldots \lambda^m)$, the optimisation problem is then:

$$(\mathbf{w}^*, \boldsymbol{\lambda}^*) = \arg\max_{(\mathbf{w},\boldsymbol{\lambda})} \sum_{i=1}^{N} \log\left(\sigma\left(y_i \Delta s_i^{(\mathbf{w},\boldsymbol{\lambda})}\right)\right) \quad (5)$$

where the sum is over the sampled hypothesis pairs and the Δ indicates the difference between the model scores of the two hypotheses in the pair, as before. The model score $s_i^{(\mathbf{w},\boldsymbol{\lambda})}$ is given by

$$\sum_{j=1}^{m} \left(w^j \cdot \log\left(\lambda^j p_{Ai}^j + (1-\lambda^j) p_{Bi}^j\right)\right) + \sum_{j=m+1}^{n} w^j h_i^j \quad (6)$$

where $\mathbf{w} \equiv (w^i \ldots w^n)$. A Gaussian regularisation term is added to the objective, as it was for PRO. By replacing the core algorithm of PRO with the optimisation above, the interpolation weights can be trained simultaneously with the other model weights.

Actually, the above explanation contains a simplification, in that it shows the phrase features interpolated at sentence level. In reality the phrase features are interpolated at the phrase level, then combined to give the sentence level feature value. This makes the definition of the objective more complex than that shown above, but still optimisable using bounded L-BFGS.

[1] Since the phrase penalty feature is a constant across phrase pairs it is not interpolated, and so is classed with the the "other" features. The lexical scores, although not actually probabilities, are interpolated.

3 Experiments

3.1 Corpus and Baselines

We ran experiments with data from the WMT shared tasks (Callison-Burch et al., 2007; Callison-Burch et al., 2012), as well as OpenSubtitles data[2] released by the OPUS project (Tiedemann, 2009).

The experiments targeted both the news-commentary (`nc`) and OpenSubtitles (`st`) domains, with `nc-devtest2007` and `nc-test2007` for tuning and testing in the `nc` domain, respectively, and corresponding 2000 sentence tuning and test sets selected from the `st` data. The news-commentary v7 corpus and a 200k sentence corpus selected from the remaining `st` data were used as in-domain training data for the respective domains, with europarl v7 (`ep`) used as out-of-domain training data in both cases. The language pairs we tested were the WMT language pairs for `nc` (English (en) to and from Spanish (es), German (de), French (fr) and Czech (cs)), with Dutch (nl) substituted for de in the `st` experiments.

To build phrase-based translation systems, we used the standard Moses (Koehn et al., 2007) training pipeline, in particular employing the usual 5 phrase features – forward and backward phrase probabilities, forward and backward lexical scores and a phrase penalty. The 5-gram Kneser-Ney smoothed language models were trained by SRILM (Stolcke, 2002), with KenLM (Heafield, 2011) used at runtime. The language model is always a linear interpolation of models estimated on the in- and out-of-domain corpora, with weights tuned by SRILM's perplexity minimisation[3]. All experiments were run three times with BLEU scores averaged, as recommended by Clark et al. (2011). Performance was evaluated using case-insensitive BLEU (Papineni et al., 2002), as implemented in Moses.

The baseline systems were tuned using the Moses version of PRO, a reimplementation of the original

[2] `www.opensubtitles.org`

[3] Our method could also be applied to language model interpolation but we chose to focus on phrase tables in this paper.

algorithm using the sampling scheme recommended by Hopkins and May. We ran 15 iterations of PRO, choosing the weights that maximised BLEU on the tuning set. For the PRO training of the interpolated models, we used the same sampling scheme, with optimisation of the model weights and interpolation weights implemented in Python using scipy[4]. The implementation is available in Moses, in the `contrib/promix` directory.

The phrase table interpolation and perplexity-based minimisation of interpolation weights used the code accompanying Sennrich (2012), also available in Moses.

3.2 Results

For each of the two test sets (`nc` and `st`), we compare four different translation systems (three baseline systems, and our new interpolation method):

in Phrase and reordering tables were built from just the in-domain data.

joint Phrase and reordering tables were built from the in- and out-of-domain data, concatenated.

perp Separate phrase tables built on in- and out-of-domain data, interpolated using perplexity minimisation. The reordering table is as for **joint**.

pro-mix As **perp**, but interpolation weights optimised using our modified PRO algorithm.

So the two interpolated models (**perp** and **pro-mix**) are the same as **joint** except that their 4 non-constant phrase features are interpolated across the two separate phrase tables. Note that the language models are the same across all four systems.

The results of this comparison over the 8 language pairs are shown in Figure 1, and summarised in Table 1, which shows the mean BLEU change relative to the **in** system. It can be seen that the **pro-mix** method presented here is out-performing the perplexity optimisation on the `nc` data set, and performing similarly on the `st` data set.

	joint	**perp**	**pro-mix**
nc	+0.18	+0.44	+0.91
st	-0.04	+0.55	+0.48

Table 1: Mean BLEU relative to **in** system for each data set. System names as in Figure 1

[4] `www.scipy.org`

4 Discussion and Conclusions

The results show that the **pro-mix** method is a viable way of tuning systems built with interpolated phrase tables, and performs better than the current perplexity minimisation method on one of two data sets used in experiments. On the other data set (`st`), the out-of-domain data makes much less difference to the system performance in general, most probably because the difference between the in and out-of-domain data sets in much larger (Haddow and Koehn, 2012). Whilst the differences between **pro-mix** and perplexity minimisation are not large on the `nc` test set (about +0.5 BLEU) the results have been demonstrated to apply across many language pairs.

The advantage of the **pro-mix** method over other approaches is that it directly optimises the measure that we are interested in, rather than optimising an intermediate measure and hoping that translation performance improves. In this work we optimise for BLEU, but the same method could easily be used to optimise for any sentence-level translation metric.

Acknowledgments

The research leading to these results has received funding from the European Union Seventh Framework Programme (FP7/2007-2013) under grant agreement 288769 (ACCEPT).

References

Pratyush Banerjee, Sudip K. Naskar, Johann Roturier, Andy Way, and Josef van Genabith. 2011. Domain Adaptation in Statistical Machine Translation of User-Forum Data using Component Level Mixture Modelling. In *Proceedings of MT Summit*.

Nicola Bertoldi and Marcello Federico. 2009. Domain Adaptation for Statistical Machine Translation from Monolingual Resources. In *Proceedings of WMT*.

R. H. Byrd, P. Lu, and J. Nocedal. 1995. A limited memory algorithm for bound constrained optimization. *SIAM Journal on Scientific and Statistical Computing*, 16(5):1190–1208.

Chris Callison-Burch, Cameron Fordyce, Philipp Koehn, Christof Monz, and Josh Schroeder. 2007. (meta-) evaluation of machine translation. In *Proceedings of the Second Workshop on Statistical Machine Translation*, pages 136–158, Prague, Czech Republic, June. Association for Computational Linguistics.

Chris Callison-Burch, Philipp Koehn, Christof Monz, Matt Post, Radu Soricut, and Lucia Specia. 2012.

Findings of the 2012 Workshop on Statistical Machine Translation. In *Proceedings of the Seventh Workshop on Statistical Machine Translation*, pages 10–51, Montréal, Canada, June. Association for Computational Linguistics.

Colin Cherry and George Foster. 2012. Batch Tuning Strategies for Statistical Machine Translation. In *Proceedings of NAACL*.

David Chiang, Yuval Marton, and Philip Resnik. 2008. Online Large-Margin Training of Syntactic and Structural Translation Features. In *Proceedings of EMNLP*.

Jonathan Clark, Chris Dyer, Alon Lavie, and Noah Smith. 2011. Better hypothesis testing for statistical machine translation: Controlling for optimizer instability. In *Proceedings of ACL*.

Marcello Federico, Nicola Bertoldi, and Mauro Cettolo. 2008. IRSTLM: an Open Source Toolkit for Handling Large Scale Language Models. In *Proceedings of Interspeech*, Brisbane, Australie.

George Foster and Roland Kuhn. 2007. Mixture-model adaptation for SMT. In *Proceedings of the Second Workshop on Statistical Machine Translation*, pages 128–135, Prague, Czech Republic, June. Association for Computational Linguistics.

George Foster, Cyril Goutte, and Roland Kuhn. 2010. Discriminative Instance Weighting for Domain Adaptation in Statistical Machine Translation. In *Proceedings of the 2010 Conference on Empirical Methods in Natural Language Processing*, pages 451–459, Cambridge, MA, October. Association for Computational Linguistics.

Barry Haddow and Philipp Koehn. 2012. Analysing the Effect of Out-of-Domain Data on SMT Systems. In *Proceedings of the Seventh Workshop on Statistical Machine Translation*, pages 422–432, Montréal, Canada, June. Association for Computational Linguistics.

Kenneth Heafield. 2011. KenLM: Faster and Smaller Language Model Queries. In *Proceedings of the Sixth Workshop on Statistical Machine Translation*, pages 187–197, Edinburgh, Scotland, July. Association for Computational Linguistics.

Mark Hopkins and Jonathan May. 2011. Tuning as Ranking. In *Proceedings of the 2011 Conference on Empirical Methods in Natural Language Processing*, pages 1352–1362, Edinburgh, Scotland, UK., July. Association for Computational Linguistics.

Philipp Koehn and Josh Schroeder. 2007. Experiments in Domain Adaptation for Statistical Machine Translation. In *Proceedings of the Second Workshop on Statistical Machine Translation*, pages 224–227, Prague, Czech Republic, June. Association for Computational Linguistics.

Philipp Koehn, Hieu Hoang, Alexandra Birch, Chris Callison-Burch, Marcello Federico, Nicola Bertoldi, Brooke Cowan, Wade Shen, Christine Moran, Richard Zens, Chris Dyer, Ondrej Bojar, Alexandra Constantin, and Evan Herbst. 2007. Moses: Open Source Toolkit for Statistical Machine Translation. In *Proceedings of the ACL Demo Sessions*, pages 177–180, Prague, Czech Republic, June. Association for Computational Linguistics.

Franz J. Och. 2003. Minimum Error Rate Training in Statistical Machine Translation. In *Proceedings of ACL*.

Kishore Papineni, Salim Roukos, Todd Ward, and Wei-Jing Zhu. 2002. Bleu: a Method for Automatic Evaluation of Machine Translation. In *Proceedings of 40th Annual Meeting of the Association for Computational Linguistics*, pages 311–318, Philadelphia, Pennsylvania, USA, July. Association for Computational Linguistics.

Rico Sennrich. 2012. Perplexity Minimization for Translation Model Domain Adaptation in Statistical Machine Translation. In *Proceedings of EACL*.

Andreas Stolcke. 2002. SRILM – An Extensible Language Modeling Toolkit. In *Proc. Intl. Conf. on Spoken Language Processing, vol. 2*, pages 901–904.

Jörg Tiedemann. 2009. News from OPUS - A Collection of Multilingual Parallel Corpora with Tools and Interfaces. In N. Nicolov, K. Bontcheva, G. Angelova, and R. Mitkov, editors, *Recent Advances in Natural Language Processing (vol V)*, pages 237–248. John Benjamins, Amsterdam/Philadelphia.

Taro Watanabe, Jun Suzuki, Hajime Tsukada, and Hideki Isozaki. 2007. Online Large-Margin Training for Statistical Machine Translation. In *Proceedings of the 2007 Joint Conference on Empirical Methods in Natural Language Processing and Computational Natural Language Learning (EMNLP-CoNLL)*, pages 764–773, Prague, Czech Republic, June. Association for Computational Linguistics.

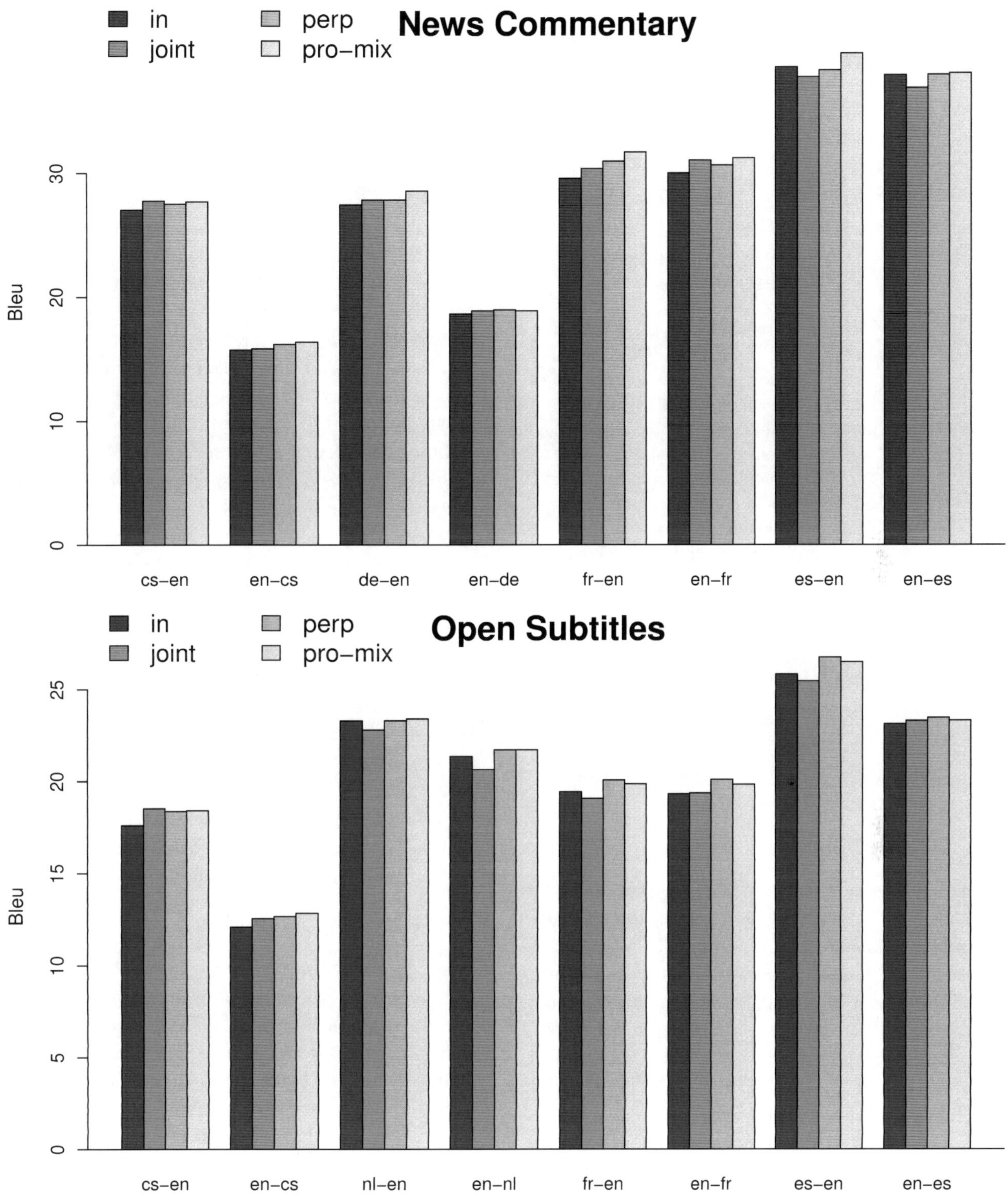

Figure 1: Comparison of the performance (BLEU) on in-domain data, of our **pro-mix** interpolation weight tuning method with three baselines: **in** using just in-domain parallel training data training; **joint** also using europarl data; and **perp** using perplexity minimisation to interpolate in-domain and europarl data.

Dialectal Arabic to English Machine Translation: Pivoting through Modern Standard Arabic

Wael Salloum and **Nizar Habash**
Center for Computational Learning Systems
Columbia University
{wael,habash}@ccls.columbia.edu

Abstract

Modern Standard Arabic (MSA) has a wealth of natural language processing (NLP) tools and resources. In comparison, resources for dialectal Arabic (DA), the unstandardized spoken varieties of Arabic, are still lacking. We present ELISSA, a machine translation (MT) system for DA to MSA. ELISSA employs a rule-based approach that relies on morphological analysis, transfer rules and dictionaries in addition to language models to produce MSA paraphrases of DA sentences. ELISSA can be employed as a general preprocessor for DA when using MSA NLP tools. A manual error analysis of ELISSA's output shows that it produces correct MSA translations over 93% of the time. Using ELISSA to produce MSA versions of DA sentences as part of an MSA-pivoting DA-to-English MT solution, improves BLEU scores on multiple blind test sets between 0.6% and 1.4%.

1 Introduction

Much work has been done on Modern Standard Arabic (MSA) natural language processing (NLP) and machine translation (MT), especially Statistical MT (SMT). MSA has a wealth of resources in terms of morphological analyzers, disambiguation systems, and parallel corpora. In comparison, research on dialectal Arabic (DA), the unstandardized spoken varieties of Arabic, is still lacking in NLP in general and MT in particular. In this paper we present ELISSA, our DA-to-MSA MT system, and show how it can help improve the translation of highly dialectal Arabic text into English by pivoting on MSA.

The ELISSA approach can be summarized as follows. First, ELISSA uses different techniques to identify dialectal words and multi-word constructions (phrases) in a source sentence. Then, ELISSA produces MSA paraphrases for the selected words and phrase using a rule-based component that depends on the existence of a dialectal morphological analyzer, a list of morphosyntactic transfer rules, and DA-MSA dictionaries. The resulting MSA is in a lattice form that we pass to a language model for n-best decoding. The output of ELISSA, whether a top-1 choice sentence or n-best sentences, is passed to an MSA-English SMT system to produce the English translation sentence. ELISSA-based MSA-pivoting for DA-to-English SMT improves BLEU scores (Papineni et al., 2002) on three blind test sets between 0.6% and 1.4%. A manual error analysis of translated words shows that ELISSA produces correct MSA translations over 93% of the time.

The rest of this paper is structured as follows: Section 2 motivates the use of ELISSA to improve DA-English SMT with an example. Section 3 discusses some of the challenges associated with processing Arabic and its dialects. Section 4 presents related work. Section 5 details ELISSA and its approach and Section 6 presents results evaluating ELISSA under a variety of conditions.

2 Motivating Example

Table 1 shows a motivating example of how pivoting on MSA can dramatically improve the translation quality of a statistical MT system that is trained on mostly MSA-to-English parallel corpora. In this example, we use Google Translate's online Arabic-English SMT system.[1] The table is divided into two parts. The top part shows a dialectal (Levantine) sentence, its reference translation to English, and its Google Translate translation. The Google Translate translation clearly struggles with most of the DA words, which were probably unseen in the training data (i.e., out-of-vocabulary – OOV) and were con-

[1]The system was used on February 21, 2013.

DA source	بهالحالة هاي ما حيكتبولو عحيط الصفحه الشخصية تبعو ولا بدن ياه يبعتلن كومينتات لأنو ماخبرهون ايمتا رح يروح عالبلد. *bhAlHAl¯hħAy mA Hyktbwlw ςHyT AlSfHh AlšxSy¯htbςw wlA bdn yAh ybςtln kwmyntAt lÂnw mAxbrhwn AymtA rH yrwH ςAlbld.*
Human Reference	In this case, they will not write on his profile wall and they do not want him to send them comments because he did not tell them when he will go to the country.
Google Translate	Bhalhalh Hi Hictpoulo Ahat Profile Tbau not hull Weah Abatln Comintat Anu Mabarhun Oamta welcomed calls them Aalbuld.
Human DA-to-MSA	في هذه الحالة لن يكتبوا له على حائط صفحته الشخصية ولا يريدونه أن يرسل لهم تعليقات لأنه لم يخبرهم متى سيذهب إلى البلد. *fy hðh AlHAl¯hn yktbwA lh ςlý HAŷT SfHth AlšxSy¯hwlA yrydwnh Ân yrsl lhm tςlyqAt lÂnh lm yxbrhm mtý syðhb Ǎlý Albld.*
Google Translate	In this case it would not write to him on the wall of his own and do not want to send their comments because he did not tell them when going to the country.

Table 1: A motivating example for DA-to-English MT by pivoting (bridging) on MSA. The top half of the table displays a DA sentence, its human reference translation and the output of Google Translate. The bottom half of the table shows the result of human translation into MSA of the DA sentence before sending it to Google Translate.

sidered proper nouns (transliterated and capitalized). The lack of DA-English parallel corpora suggests pivoting on MSA can improve the translation quality. In the bottom part of the table, we show a human MSA translation of the DA sentence above and its Google translation. We see that the results are quite promising. The goal of ELISSA is to model this DA-MSA translation automatically. In Section 5.4, we revisit this example to discuss ELISSA's performance on it. We show its output and its corresponding Google translation in Table 3.

3 Challenges for Processing Arabic and its Dialects

Contemporary Arabic is in fact a collection of varieties: MSA, the official language of the Arab World, which has a standard orthography and is used in formal settings; and DAs, the commonly used informal native varieties, which have no standard orthographies but have an increasing presence on the web. Arabic, in general, is a morphologically complex language which has rich inflectional morphology, expressed both templatically and affixationally, and several classes of attachable clitics. For example, the Arabic word وسيكتبونها *w+s+y-ktb-wn+hA*[2] 'and they will write it' has two proclitics (+و *w+* 'and' and +س *s+* 'will'), one prefix -ي *y-* '3rd person', one suffix ون- *-wn* 'masculine plural' and one pronominal enclitic ها+ *+hA* 'it/her'. DAs differ from MSA phonologically, morphologically and to a lesser degree syntactically. The morphological differences are most noticeably expressed in the use of clitics and affixes that do not exist in MSA. For instance, the Levantine Arabic equivalent of the MSA example above is وحيكتبوها *w+H+y-ktb-w+hA* 'and they will write it'. The optionality of vocalic diacritics helps hide some of the differences resulting from vowel changes; compare the diacritized forms: Levantine *wHayikitbuwhA* and MSA *wasayaktubuwnahA*.

All of the NLP challenges of MSA (e.g., optional diacritics and spelling inconsistency) are shared by DA. However, the lack of standard orthographies for the dialects and their numerous varieties pose new challenges. Additionally, DAs are rather impoverished in terms of available tools and resources compared to MSA, e.g., there is very little parallel DA-English corpora and almost no MSA-DA parallel corpora. The number and sophistication of morphological analysis and disambiguation tools in DA is very limited in comparison to MSA (Duh and Kirchhoff, 2005; Habash and Rambow, 2006; Abo Bakr et al., 2008; Habash, 2010; Salloum and Habash, 2011; Habash et al., 2012; Habash et al., 2013). MSA tools cannot be effectively used to handle DA, e.g., Habash and Rambow (2006) report that over one-third of Levantine verbs cannot be analyzed using an MSA morphological analyzer.

[2] Arabic transliteration throughout the paper is presented in the Habash-Soudi-Buckwalter scheme (Habash et al., 2007): (in alphabetical order) *AbtθjHxdðrzsšSDTĎςγfqklmnhwy* and the additional symbols: ' ء, Â أ, Ǎ إ, Ā آ, ŵ ؤ, ŷ ئ, ¯h ة, ý ى.

4 Related Work

Dialectal Arabic NLP. Several researchers have explored the idea of exploiting existing MSA rich resources to build tools for DA NLP (Chiang et al., 2006). Such approaches typically expect the presence of tools/resources to relate DA words to their MSA variants or translations. Given that DA and MSA do not have much in terms of parallel corpora, rule-based methods to translate DA-to-MSA or other methods to collect word-pair lists have been explored. For example, Abo Bakr et al. (2008) introduced a hybrid approach to transfer a sentence from Egyptian Arabic into MSA. This hybrid system consisted of a statistical system for tokenizing and tagging, and a rule-based system for constructing diacritized MSA sentences. Moreover, Al-Sabbagh and Girju (2010) described an approach of mining the web to build a DA-to-MSA lexicon. In the context of DA-to-English SMT, Riesa and Yarowsky (2006) presented a supervised algorithm for online morpheme segmentation on DA that cut the OOV words by half.

Machine Translation for Closely Related Languages. Using closely related languages has been shown to improve MT quality when resources are limited. Hajič et al. (2000) argued that for very close languages, e.g., Czech and Slovak, it is possible to obtain a better translation quality by using simple methods such as morphological disambiguation, transfer-based MT and word-for-word MT. Zhang (1998) introduced a Cantonese-Mandarin MT that uses transformational grammar rules. In the context of Arabic dialect translation, Sawaf (2010) built a hybrid MT system that uses both statistical and rule-based approaches for DA-to-English MT. In his approach, DA is normalized into MSA using a dialectal morphological analyzer. In previous work, we presented a rule-based DA-MSA system to improve DA-to-English MT (Salloum and Habash, 2011; Salloum and Habash, 2012). Our approach used a DA morphological analyzer (ADAM) and a list of hand-written morphosyntactic transfer rules. This use of "resource-rich" related languages is a specific variant of the more general approach of using pivot/bridge languages (Utiyama and Isahara, 2007; Kumar et al., 2007). In the case of MSA and DA variants, it is plausible to consider the MSA variants of a DA phrase as monolingual paraphrases (Callison-Burch et al., 2006; Du et al., 2010). Also related is the work by Nakov and Ng (2011), who use morphological knowledge to generate paraphrases for a morphologically rich language, Malay, to extend the phrase table in a Malay-to-English SMT system.

Pivoting on MSA or acquiring more DA-English data? Zbib et al. (2012) demonstrated an approach to cheaply obtaining DA-English data. They used Amazon's Mechanical Turk (MTurk) to create a DA-English parallel corpus of 1.5M words and added it to a 150M MSA-English parallel corpus to create the training corpus of their SMT system. They also used MTurk to translate their dialectal test set to MSA in order to compare the MSA-pivoting approach to the direct translation from DA to English approach. They showed that even though pivoting on MSA (produced by Human translators in an oracle experiment) can reduce OOV rate to 0.98% from 2.27% for direct translation (without pivoting), it improves by 4.91% BLEU while direct translation improves by 6.81% BLEU over their 12.29% BLEU baseline (direct translation using the 150M MSA system). They concluded that simple vocabulary coverage is not sufficient and the domain mismatch is a more important problem. The approach we take in this paper is orthogonal to such efforts to build parallel data. We plan to study interactions between the two types of solutions in the future.

Our work is most similar to Sawaf (2010)'s MSA-pivoting approach. In his approach, DA is normalized into MSA using character-based DA normalization rules, a DA morphological analyzer, a DA normalization decoder that relies on language models, and a lexicon. Similarly, we use some character normalization rules, a DA morphological analyzer, and DA-MSA dictionaries. In contrast, we use hand-written morphosyntactic transfer rules that focus on translating DA morphemes and lemmas to their MSA equivalents.

In our previous work (Salloum and Habash, 2011; Salloum and Habash, 2012), we applied our approach to tokenized Arabic and our DA-MSA transfer component used feature transfer rules only. We did not use a language model to pick the best path; instead we kept the ambiguity in the lattice and passed it to our SMT system. In contrast, in this paper, we run ELISSA on untokenized Arabic, we use feature, lemma, and surface form transfer rules, and we pick the best path of the generated MSA lattice through a language model.

Certain aspects of our approach are similar to Riesa and Yarowsky (2006)'s, in that we use morphological analysis for DA to help DA-English MT; but unlike them, we use a rule-based approach to model DA morphology.

5 ELISSA

ELISSA is a DA-to-MSA MT System. ELISSA uses a rule-based approach (with some statistical components) that relies on the existence of a DA morphological analyzer, a list of hand-written transfer rules, and DA-MSA dictionaries to create a mapping of DA to MSA words and construct a lattice of possible sentences. ELISSA uses a language model to rank and select the generated sentences.

ELISSA supports untokenized (raw) input only. ELISSA supports three types of output: top-1 choice, an n-best list or a map file that maps source words/phrases to target phrases. The top-1 and n-best lists are determined using an untokenized MSA language model to rank the paths in the MSA translation output lattice. This variety of output types makes it easy to plug ELISSA with other systems and to use it as a DA preprocessing tool for other MSA systems, e.g., MADA (Habash and Rambow, 2005) or AMIRA (Diab et al., 2007).

ELISSA's approach consists of three major steps preceded by a *preprocessing and normalization* step, that prepares the input text to be handled (e.g., UTF-8 cleaning, Alif/Ya normalization, word-lengthening normalization), and followed by a *post-processing* step, that produces the output in the desired form (e.g., encoding choice). The three major steps are **Selection**, **Translation**, and **Language Modeling**.

5.1 Selection

In the first step, ELISSA identifies which words or phrases to paraphrase and which words or phrases to leave as is. ELISSA provides different methods (techniques) for selection, and can be configured to use different subsets of them. In Section 6 we use the term "selection mode" to denote a subset of selection methods. Selection methods are classified into *Word-based selection* and *Phrase-based selection*.

Word-based selection. Methods of this type fall in the following categories:

a. User token-based selection: The user can mark specific words for selection using the tag '/DIA' (stands for 'dialect') after each word to select.

b. User type-based selection: The user can specify a list of words to select from, e.g., OOVs. Also the user can provide a list of words and their frequencies and specify a cut-off threshold to prevent selecting a frequent word.

c. Morphology-based word selection: ELISSA uses ADAM (Salloum and Habash, 2011) to select words that have DA analyses only (DIAONLY) or DA/MSA analyses (DIAMSA).

d. Dictionary-based selection: ELISSA selects words based on their existence in the DA side of our DA-MSA dictionaries.

e. All: ELISSA selects every word in an input sentence.

Phrase-based selection. This selection type uses hand-written rules to identify dialectal multi-word constructions that are mappable to single or multi-word MSA constructions. The current count of these rules is 25. Table 2 presents some rule categories and related examples.

In the current version of ELISSA, words can be selected using either the phrase-based selection method or a word-based selection method, but not both. Phrase-based selection has precedence. We evaluate different settings for selection step in Section 6.

5.2 Translation

In this step, ELISSA translates the selected words and phrases to their MSA equivalent paraphrases. The specific type of selection determines the type of the translation, e.g., phrase-based selected words are translated using phrase-based translation rules. The MSA paraphrases are then used to form an MSA lattice.

Word-based translation. This category has two types of translation techniques: *surface translation* that uses DA-to-MSA surface-to-surface (S2S) transfer rules (TRs) and *deep (morphological) translation* that uses the classic rule-based machine translation flow: analysis, transfer and generation. The

Rule Category	Selection Examples	Translation Examples
Dialectal Idafa	الجيش الوطني بتاعنا *Aljyš AlwTny btAςnA* 'the-army the-national ours'	جيشنا الوطني *jyšnA AlwTny* 'our-army the-national'
Verb + flipped direct and indirect objects	حضرلها ياهن *HDrlhA yAhn* 'he-prepared-for-her them'	حضرهم لها *HDrhm lhA* 'he-prepared-them for-her'
Special dialectal expressions	بدو اياها *bdw AyAhA* 'his-desire her'	يريدها *yrydhA* 'he-desires-her'
Negation + verb	وما حيكتبولو *wmA Hyktbwlw* 'and-not they-will-write-to-him'	ولن يكتبوا له *wln yktbwA lh* 'and-will-not they-write to-him'
Negation + agent noun	فمش لاقية *fmš lAqyħ* 'so-not finding'	فلا تجد *flA tjd* 'so-not she-finds'
Negation + closed-class words	ما عدكم *mA ςdkm* 'not with-you'	ليس لديكم *lys ldykm* 'not with-you'

Table 2: Examples of some types of phrase-based selection and translation rules.

DA Phrase	وما راحولا *wmA rAHwlA* 'And they did not go to her'				
Analysis	Word 1		Word 2		
	Proclitics	[Lemma & Features]	[Lemma & Features]	[Lemma & Features]	Enclitic
	w+ conj+ and+	mA [neg] not	rAHw [rAH PV subj:3MP] they go	+l +prep +to	+A +pron$_{3FS}$ +her
Transfer	Word 1		Word 2	Word 3	
	Proclitics	[Lemma & Features]	[Lemma & Features]	[Lemma & Features]	Enclitic
	conj+ and+	[lam] did not	[ðahab IV subj:3MP] they go	[Ǎlý] to	+pron$_{3FS}$ +her
Generation	w+	lm	yðhbwA	Ǎly	+hA
MSA Phrase	ولم يذهبوا إليها *wlm yðhbwA ǍlyhA* 'And they did not go to her'				

Figure 1: An example illustrating the analysis-transfer-generation steps to translate a dialectal multi-word expression into its MSA equivalent phrase.

dialectal morphological analysis step uses ADAM (Salloum and Habash, 2011) to get a list of dialectal analyses. The morphosyntactic transfer step uses lemma-to-lemma (L2L) and features-to-features (F2F) transfer rules to change lemmas, clitics or features, and even split up the dialectal word into multiple MSA word analyses (such as splitting negation words and indirect objects). The MSA morphological generation step uses the general tokenizer/generator TOKAN (Habash, 2007) to generate untokenized surface form words. For more details, see Salloum and Habash (2011).

Phrase-based translation. Unlike the word-based translation techniques which map single DA words to single or multi-word MSA sequences, this technique uses hand-written multi-word transfer rules that map multi-word DA constructions to single or multi-word MSA constructions. In the current system, there are 47 phrase-based transfer rules. Many of the word-based morphosyntactic transfer rules are re-used for phrase-based translation. Figure 1 shows an example of a phrase-based morphological translation of the two-word DA sequence وما راحولا *wmA rAHwlA* 'And they did not go to her'. If these two words were spelled as a single word, وماراحولا *wmArAHwlA*, we would still get the same result using the word-based translation technique only. Table 2 shows some rule categories along with selection and translation examples.

5.3 Language Modeling

The language model (LM) component uses the SRILM lattice-tool for weight assignment and n-best decoding (Stolcke, 2002). ELISSA comes with a default 5-gram LM file trained on ∼200M unto-

DA source	(بهالحالة هاي)[1] (ما حيكتبولو)[2] عحيط[3] (الصفحه الشخصية تبعو)[4] ولا (بدن ياه)[5] يبعتلن[6] كومينتات[7] لأنو[8] ماخبرهون[9] ايمتا[10] (رح يروح)[11] عالبلد[12]. *(bhAlHAl¯hhAy)[1] (mA Hyktbwlw)[2] ςHyT[3] (AlSfHh AlšxSy¯htbςw)[4] wlA (bdn yAh)[5] ybςtln[6] kwmyntAt[7] lÂnw[8] mAxbrhwn[9] AymtA[10] (rH yrwH)[11] ςAlbld[12].*
Human Reference	In this case, they will not write on his profile wall and they do not want him to send them comments because he did not tell them when he will go to the country.
Google Translate	Bhalhalh Hi Hictpoulo Ahat Profile Tbau not hull Weah Abatln Comintat Anu Mabarhun Oamta welcomed calls them Aalbuld.
ELISSA **DA-to-MSA**	(في هذه الحالة)[1] (لن يكتبوا له)[2] (علي حائط)[3] (صفحته الشخصية)[4] ولا (يريدونه ان)[5] (يرسل اليهم)[6] تعليقات[7] لانه[8] (لم يخبرهم)[9] متي[10] سيذهب[11] (الي البلد)[12]. *(fy hðh AlHAl¯ħ)[1] (ln yktbwA lh)[2] (ςly HAŷT)[3] (SfHth AlšxSy¯ħ)[4] wlA (yrydwnh An)[5] (yrsl Alyhm)[6] tςlyqAt[7] lAnh[8] (lm yxbrhm)[9] mty[10] syðhb[11] (Aly Albld)[12].*
Google Translate	In this case it would not write to him on the wall of his own and do not want to send them comments that he did not tell them when going to the country.

Table 3: Revisiting our motivating example, but with ELISSA-based DA-to-MSA middle step. ELISSA's output is Alif/Ya normalized. Parentheses are added for illustrative reasons to highlight how multi-word DA constructions are selected and translated. Superscript indices link the selected words and phrases with their MSA translations.

kenized Arabic words of Arabic Gigaword (Parker et al., 2009). Users can specify their own LM file and/or interpolate it with our default LM. This is useful for adapting ELISSA's output to the Arabic side of the training data.

5.4 Revisiting our Motivating Example

We revisit our motivating example in Section 2 and show automatic MSA-pivoting through ELISSA. Table 3 is divided into two parts. The first part is copied from Table 1 for convenience. The second part shows ELISSA's output on the dialectal sentence and its Google Translate translation. The produced MSA is not perfect, but is clearly an improvement over doing nothing as far as usability for MT into English.

6 Evaluation

In this section, we present two evaluations of ELISSA. The first is an extrinsic evaluation of ELISSA as part of MSA-pivoting for DA-to-English SMT. And the second is an intrinsic evaluation of the quality of ELISSA's MSA output.

6.1 DA-English MT Evaluation

6.1.1 Experimental Setup

We use the open-source Moses toolkit (Koehn et al., 2007) to build a phrase-based SMT system trained on mostly MSA data (64M words on the Arabic side) obtained from several LDC corpora including some limited DA data. Our system uses a standard phrase-based architecture. The parallel corpus is word-aligned using GIZA++ (Och and Ney, 2003). Phrase translations of up to 10 words are extracted in the Moses phrase table. The language model for our system is trained on the English side of the bitext augmented with English Gigaword (Graff and Cieri, 2003). We use a 5-gram language model with modified Kneser-Ney smoothing. Feature weights are tuned to maximize BLEU on the NIST MTEval 2006 test set using Minimum Error Rate Training (Och, 2003). This is only done on the baseline systems. The English data is tokenized using simple punctuation-based rules. The Arabic side is segmented according to the Arabic Treebank (ATB) tokenization scheme (Maamouri et al., 2004) using the MADA+TOKAN morphological analyzer and tokenizer v3.1 (Habash and Rambow, 2005; Roth et al., 2008). The Arabic text is also Alif/Ya normalized. MADA-produced Arabic lemmas are used for word alignment.

We use the same development (dev) and test sets used by Salloum and Habash (2011) (we will call them speech-dev and speech-test, respectively) and we compare to them in the next sections. We also evaluate on two web-crawled blind test sets: the Levantine test set presented in Zbib et al. (2012) (we will call it web-lev-test) and the Egyptian Dev-MT-v2 development data of the DARPA BOLT program (we will call it web-egy-test). The speech-dev set has 1,496 sentences with 32,047 untokenized Arabic words. The speech-test set has 1,568 sentences with

32,492 untokenized Arabic words. The web-lev-test set has 2,728 sentences with 21,179 untokenized Arabic words. The web-egy-test set has 1,553 sentences with 21,495 untokenized Arabic words. The two speech test sets contain multi-dialect (e.g., Iraqi, Levantine, Gulf, and Egyptian) broadcast conversational (BC) segments (with three reference translations), and broadcast news (BN) segments (with only one reference, replicated three times). The web-egy-test has two references while the web-lev-test has only one reference. Results are presented in terms of BLEU (Papineni et al., 2002). All evaluation results are case insensitive.

6.1.2 Results on the Development Set

We experimented with different method combinations in the selection and translation components in ELISSA. We use the term selection mode and translation mode to denote a certain combination of methods in selection or translation, respectively. Due to limited space, we only present the best selection mode variation experiments. Other selection modes were tried but they proved to be consistently lower than the rest. The 'F2F+L2L; S2S' word-based translation mode (using morphological transfer of features and lemmas along with surface form transfer) showed to be consistently better than other method combinations across all selection modes. In this paper we only use 'F2F+L2L; S2S' word-based translation mode. Phrase-based translation mode is used when phrase-based selection mode is used.

To rank paraphrases in the generated MSA lattice, we combine two 5-gram untokenized Arabic language models: one is trained on Arabic Gigaword data and the other is trained the Arabic side of our SMT training data. The use of the latter LM gave frequent dialectal phrases a higher chance to appear in ELISSA's output; thus, making the output "more dialectal" but adapting it to our SMT input. Experiments showed that using both LMs is better than using each one alone.

In all the experiments, we run the DA sentence through ELISSA to generate a top-1 MSA translation, which we then tokenize through MADA before sending to the MSA-English SMT system. Our baseline is to not run ELISSA at all; instead, we send the DA sentence through MADA before applying the MSA-English MT system.

Table 4 summarizes the experiments and results on the dev set. The rows of the table are the different systems (baseline and ELISSA's experiments). All differences in BLEU scores from the baseline are statistically significant above the 95% level. Statistical significance is computed using paired bootstrap re-sampling (Koehn, 2004). The name of the system in ELISSA's experiments denotes the combination of selection method. ELISSA's experiments are grouped into three groups: simple selection, frequency-based selection, and phrase-based selection. Simple selection group consists of five systems: OOV, ADAM, OOV U ADAM, DICT, and OOV U ADAM U DICT. The OOV selection mode identifies the untokenized OOV words. In the ADAM selection mode, or the morphological selection mode, we use ADAM to identify dialectal words. Experiments showed that ADAM's DI-AMSA mode (selecting words that have at least one dialectal analysis) is slightly better than ADAM's DIAONLY mode (selecting words that have only dialectal analyses and no MSA ones). The OOV U ADAM selection mode is the union of the OOVs and ADAM selection modes. In DICT selection mode, we select dialectal words that exist in our DA-MSA dictionaries. The OOV U ADAM U DICT selection mode is the union of the OOVs, ADAM, and DICT selection modes. The results show that combining the output of OOV selection method and ADAM selection method is the best. DICT selection method hurts the performance of the system when used because dictionaries usually have frequent dialectal words that the SMT system already knows how to handle.

In the frequency-based selection group, we exclude from word selection all words with number of occurrences in the training data that is above a certain threshold. This threshold was determined empirically to be 50. The string '- (Freq >= 50)' means that all words with frequencies of 50 or more should not be selected. The results show that excluding frequent dialectal words improves the best simple selection system. It also shows that using DICT selection improves the best system if frequent words are excluded.

In the last system group, phrase+word-based selection, phrase-based selection is used to select phrases and add them on top of the best performers of the previous two groups. Phrase-based trans-

Test Set	speech-dev	
	BLEU	Diff.
Baseline	37.20	0.00
Select: OOV	37.75	0.55
Select: ADAM	37.88	0.68
Select: OOV U ADAM	37.89	0.69
Select: DICT	37.06	-0.14
Select: OOV U ADAM U DICT	37.53	0.33
Select: (OOV U ADAM) - (Freq >= 50)	37.96	0.76
Select: (OOV U ADAM U DICT) - (Freq >= 50)	38.00	0.80
Select: Phrase; (OOV U ADAM)	37.99	0.79
Select: Phrase; ((OOV U ADAM) - (Freq >= 50))	38.05	0.85
Select: Phrase; ((OOV U ADAM U DICT) - (Freq >= 50))	**38.10**	**0.90**

Table 4: Results for the speech-dev set in terms of BLEU. The 'Diff.' column shows result differences from the baseline. The rows of the table are the different systems (baseline and ELISSA's experiments). The name of the system in ELISSA's experiments denotes the combination of selection method. In all ELISSA's experiments, all word-based translation methods are tried. Phrase-based translation methods are used when phrase-based selection is used (i.e., the last three rows). The best system is in bold.

lation is also added to word-based translation. Results show that selecting and translating phrases improve the three best performers of word-based selection. The best performer, shown in the last raw, suggests using phrase-based selection and restricted word-based selection. The restriction is to include OOV words and selected low frequency words that have at least one dialectal analysis or appear in our dialectal dictionaries. Comparing the best performer to the OOV selection mode system shows that translating low frequency in-vocabulary dialectal words and phrases to their MSA paraphrases can improve the English translation. This is a similar conclusion to our previous work in Salloum and Habash (2011).

6.1.3 Results on the Blind Test Sets

We run the system settings that performed best on the dev set along with the OOV selection mode system on the three blind test set. Results and their differences from the baseline are reported in Table 5. We see that OOV selection mode system always improves over the baseline for all test sets. Also, the best performer on the dev is the best performer for all test sets. The improvements of the best performer over the OOV selection mode system on all test sets confirm that translating low frequency in-vocabulary dialectal words and phrases to their MSA paraphrases can improve the English translation. Its improvements over the baseline for the three test sets are: 0.95% absolute BLEU (or 2.5% relative) for the speech-test, 1.41% absolute BLEU (or 15.4% relative) for the web-lev-test, and 0.61% absolute BLEU (or 3.2% relative) for the web-egy-test.

6.1.4 A Case Study

We next examine an example in some detail. Table 6 shows a dialectal sentence along with its ELISSA's translation, English references, the output of the baseline system and the output of our best system. The example shows a dialectal word هالمبلغ *hAlmblγ* 'this-amount/sum', which is not translated by the baseline (although it appears in the training data, but quite infrequently such that all of its phrase table occurrences have restricted contexts, making it effectively an OOV). The dialectal proclitic +هال *hAl+* 'this-' comes sometimes in the dialectal construction: 'hAl+NOUN DEM' (as in this example: هالمبلغ هذا *hAlmblγ hðA* 'this-amount/sum this'). ELISSA's selection component captures this multi-word expression and its translation component produces the following paraphrases: هذا المبلغ *hðA Almblγ* 'this amount/sum' (*hðA* is used with masculine singular nouns), هذه المبلغ *hðh Almblγ* 'this amount/sum' (*hðh* is used with feminine singular or irrational plural nouns), and هؤلاء المبلغ *hŵlA' Almblγ* 'these amount/sum' (*hŵlA'* is used with rational plural nouns). ELISSA's language modeling component picks the first MSA paraphrase, which perfectly fits the context and satisfies the gender/number/rationality agreement (note that the word *Almblγ* is an irrational masculine singular

Test Set	speech-test		web-lev-test		web-egy-test	
	BLEU	Diff.	BLEU	Diff.	BLEU	Diff.
Baseline	38.18	0.00	9.13	0.00	18.98	0.00
Select: OOV	38.76	0.58	9.65	0.62	19.19	0.21
Select: Phrase; ((OOV U ADAM U DICT) - (Freq >= 50))	**39.13**	**0.95**	**10.54**	**1.41**	**19.59**	**0.61**

Table 5: Results for the three blind test sets (table columns) in terms of BLEU. The 'Diff.' columns show result differences from the baselines. The rows of the table are the different systems (baselines and ELISSA's experiments). The best systems are in bold.

noun). For more on Arabic morpho-syntactic agreement patterns, see Alkuhlani and Habash (2011). Finally, the best system translation for the selected phrase is 'this sum'. We can see how both the accuracy and fluency of the sentence have improved.

DA sentence	fmA mA AtSwr **hAlmblγ hðA** yςny.
ELISSA's output	fmA mA AtSwr **hðA Almblγ** yςny.
References	I don't think **this amount** is I mean.
	So I do not I do not think **this cost** I mean.
	So I do not imagine **this sum** I mean
Baseline	So i don't think **hAlmblg this** means.
Best system	So i don't think **this sum** i mean.

Table 6: An example of handling dialectal words/phrases using ELISSA and its effect on the accuracy and fluency of the English translation. Words of interest are bolded.

6.2 DA-to-MSA Translation Quality

We conducted a manual error analysis comparing ELISSA's input (the original dev set) to its output using our best system settings from the experiments above. Out of 708 affected sentences, we randomly selected 300 sentences (42%). Out of the 482 handled tokens, 449 (93.15%) tokens have good MSA translations, and 33 (6.85%) tokens have wrong MSA translations. Most of the wrong translations are due to spelling errors, proper nouns, and weak input sentence fluency (especially due to speech effect). This analysis clearly validates ELISSA's MSA output. Of course, a correct MSA output can still be mistranslated by the MT system we used above if it is not in the vocabulary of the MT system.

7 Conclusion and Future Work

We presented ELISSA, a tool for DA-MSA translation. ELISSA employs a rule-based MT approach that relies on morphological analysis, transfer rules and dictionaries in addition to language models to produce MSA paraphrases of dialectal sentences. Using ELISSA to produce MSA versions of dialectal sentences as part of an MSA-pivoting DA-to-English MT solution, improves BLEU scores on three blind test sets by: 0.95% absolute BLEU (or 2.5% relative) for a speech multi-dialect (Iraqi, Levantine, Gulf, Egyptian) test set, 1.41% absolute BLEU (or 15.4% relative) for a web-crawled Levantine test set, and 0.61% absolute BLEU (or 3.2% relative) for a web-crawled Egyptian test set. A manual error analysis of translated selected words shows that our system produces correct MSA translations over 93% of the time.

In the future, we plan to extend ELISSA's coverage of phenomena in the handled dialects and to new dialects. We also plan to automatically learn additional rules from limited available data (DA-MSA or DA-English). We also would like to do additional MT experiments where we use ELISSA to preprocess the training data, comparable to experiments done by Sawaf (2010). We are interested in studying how our approach can be combined with solutions that simply add more dialectal training data since the two directions are complementary in that they address linguistic normalization and domain coverage. Finally, we look forward to experimenting with ELISSA as a preprocessing system for a variety of dialect NLP applications similar to Chiang et al. (2006)'s work on dialect parsing, for example.

ELISSA will be publicly available. Please contact the authors for more information.

Acknowledgment

This paper is based upon work supported by the Defense Advanced Research Projects Agency (DARPA) under Contract No. HR0011-12-C-0014. Any opinions, findings and conclusions or recommendations expressed in this paper are those of the authors and do not necessarily reflect the views of DARPA.

References

Hitham Abo Bakr, Khaled Shaalan, and Ibrahim Ziedan. 2008. A Hybrid Approach for Converting Written Egyptian Colloquial Dialect into Diacritized Arabic. In *The 6th International Conference on Informatics and Systems, INFOS2008*. Cairo University.

Rania Al-Sabbagh and Roxana Girju. 2010. Mining the Web for the Induction of a Dialectical Arabic Lexicon. In Nicoletta Calzolari, Khalid Choukri, Bente Maegaard, Joseph Mariani, Jan Odijk, Stelios Piperidis, Mike Rosner, and Daniel Tapias, editors, *LREC*. European Language Resources Association.

Sarah Alkuhlani and Nizar Habash. 2011. A Corpus for Modeling Morpho-Syntactic Agreement in Arabic: Gender, Number and Rationality. In *Proceedings of the 49th Annual Meeting of the Association for Computational Linguistics (ACL'11)*, Portland, Oregon, USA.

Chris Callison-Burch, Philipp Koehn, and Miles Osborne. 2006. Improved statistical machine translation using paraphrases. In *Proceedings of the Human Language Technology Conference of the NAACL, Main Conference*, pages 17–24.

David Chiang, Mona Diab, Nizar Habash, Owen Rambow, and Safiullah Shareef. 2006. Parsing Arabic Dialects. In *Proceedings of the European Chapter of ACL (EACL)*.

Mona Diab, Kadri Hacioglu, and Daniel Jurafsky. 2007. Automated Methods for Processing Arabic Text: From Tokenization to Base Phrase Chunking. In Antal van den Bosch and Abdelhadi Soudi, editors, *Arabic Computational Morphology: Knowledge-based and Empirical Methods*. Kluwer/Springer.

Jinhua Du, Jie Jiang, and Andy Way. 2010. Facilitating translation using source language paraphrase lattices. In *Proceedings of the 2010 Conference on Empirical Methods in Natural Language Processing*, EMNLP'10, pages 420–429, Cambridge, Massachusetts.

Kevin Duh and Katrin Kirchhoff. 2005. POS tagging of dialectal Arabic: a minimally supervised approach. In *Proceedings of the ACL Workshop on Computational Approaches to Semitic Languages*, Semitic '05, pages 55–62, Ann Arbor, Michigan.

David Graff and Christopher Cieri. 2003. English Gigaword, LDC Catalog No.: LDC2003T05. Linguistic Data Consortium, University of Pennsylvania.

Nizar Habash and Owen Rambow. 2005. Arabic Tokenization, Part-of-Speech Tagging and Morphological Disambiguation in One Fell Swoop. In *Proceedings of the 43rd Annual Meeting of the Association for Computational Linguistics (ACL'05)*, pages 573–580, Ann Arbor, Michigan.

Nizar Habash and Owen Rambow. 2006. MAGEAD: A Morphological Analyzer and Generator for the Arabic Dialects. In *Proceedings of the 21st International Conference on Computational Linguistics and 44th Annual Meeting of the Association for Computational Linguistics*, pages 681–688, Sydney, Australia.

Nizar Habash, Abdelhadi Soudi, and Tim Buckwalter. 2007. On Arabic Transliteration. In A. van den Bosch and A. Soudi, editors, *Arabic Computational Morphology: Knowledge-based and Empirical Methods*. Springer.

Nizar Habash, Ramy Eskander, and Abdelati Hawwari. 2012. A Morphological Analyzer for Egyptian Arabic. In *Proceedings of the Twelfth Meeting of the Special Interest Group on Computational Morphology and Phonology*, pages 1–9, Montréal, Canada.

Nizar Habash, Ryan Roth, Owen Rambow, Ramy Eskander, and Nadi Tomeh. 2013. Morphological Analysis and Disambiguation for Dialectal Arabic. In *Proceedings of the 2013 Conference of the North American Chapter of the Association for Computational Linguistics: Human Language Technologies (NAACL-HLT)*, Atlanta, GA.

Nizar Habash. 2007. Arabic Morphological Representations for Machine Translation. In A. van den Bosch and A. Soudi, editors, *Arabic Computational Morphology: Knowledge-based and Empirical Methods*. Springer.

Nizar Habash. 2010. *Introduction to Arabic Natural Language Processing*. Morgan & Claypool Publishers.

Jan Hajič, Jan Hric, and Vladislav Kubon. 2000. Machine Translation of Very Close Languages. In *Proceedings of the 6th Applied Natural Language Processing Conference (ANLP'2000)*, pages 7–12, Seattle.

Philipp Koehn, Hieu Hoang, Alexandra Birch, Christopher Callison-Burch, Marcello Federico, Nicola Bertoldi, Brooke Cowan, Wade Shen, Christine Moran, Richard Zens, Christopher Dyer, Ondrej Bojar, Alexandra Constantin, and Evan Herbst. 2007. Moses: open source toolkit for statistical machine translation. In *Proceedings of the 45th Annual Meeting of the Association for Computational Linguistics Companion Volume Proceedings of the Demo and Poster Sessions*, pages 177–180, Prague, Czech Republic.

Philipp Koehn. 2004. Statistical significance tests for machine translation evaluation. In *Proceedings of EMNLP 2004*, pages 388–395, Barcelona, Spain, July. Association for Computational Linguistics.

Shankar Kumar, Franz J. Och, and Wolfgang Macherey. 2007. Improving word alignment with bridge languages. In *Proceedings of the 2007 Joint Conference on Empirical Methods in Natural Language Processing and Computational Natural Language Learning (EMNLP-CoNLL)*, pages 42–50, Prague, Czech Republic.

Mohamed Maamouri, Ann Bies, Tim Buckwalter, and Wigdan Mekki. 2004. The Penn Arabic Treebank: Building a Large-Scale Annotated Arabic Corpus. In *NEMLAR Conference on Arabic Language Resources and Tools*, pages 102–109, Cairo, Egypt.

Preslav Nakov and Hwee Tou Ng. 2011. Translating from Morphologically Complex Languages: A Paraphrase-Based Approach. In *Proceedings of the Meeting of the Association for Computational Linguistics (ACL'2011)*, Portland, Oregon, USA.

F. J. Och and H. Ney. 2003. A systematic comparison of various statistical alignment models. *Computational Linguistics*, 29(1):19–51.

Franz Josef Och. 2003. Minimum Error Rate Training for Statistical Machine Translation. In *Proceedings of the 41st Annual Conference of the Association for Computational Linguistics*, pages 160–167, Sapporo, Japan.

Kishore Papineni, Salim Roukos, Todd Ward, and Wei-Jing Zhu. 2002. BLEU: a Method for Automatic Evaluation of Machine Translation. In *Proceedings of the 40th Annual Meeting of the Association for Computational Linguistics*, pages 311–318, Philadelphia, PA.

Robert Parker, David Graff, Ke Chen, Junbo Kong, and Kazuaki Maeda. 2009. Arabic Gigaword Fourth Edition. LDC catalog number No. LDC2009T30, ISBN 1-58563-532-4.

Jason Riesa and David Yarowsky. 2006. Minimally Supervised Morphological Segmentation with Applications to Machine Translation. In *Proceedings of the 7th Conference of the Association for Machine Translation in the Americas (AMTA06)*, pages 185–192, Cambridge,MA.

Ryan Roth, Owen Rambow, Nizar Habash, Mona Diab, and Cynthia Rudin. 2008. Arabic Morphological Tagging, Diacritization, and Lemmatization Using Lexeme Models and Feature Ranking. In *Proceedings of ACL-08: HLT, Short Papers*, pages 117–120, Columbus, Ohio.

Wael Salloum and Nizar Habash. 2011. Dialectal to Standard Arabic Paraphrasing to Improve Arabic-English Statistical Machine Translation. In *Proceedings of the First Workshop on Algorithms and Resources for Modelling of Dialects and Language Varieties*, pages 10–21, Edinburgh, Scotland.

Wael Salloum and Nizar Habash. 2012. Elissa: A Dialectal to Standard Arabic Machine Translation System. In *Proceedings of the 24th International Conference on Computational Linguistics (COLING 2012): Demonstration Papers*, pages 385–392, Mumbai, India.

Hassan Sawaf. 2010. Arabic dialect handling in hybrid machine translation. In *Proceedings of the Conference of the Association for Machine Translation in the Americas (AMTA)*, Denver, Colorado.

Andreas Stolcke. 2002. SRILM an Extensible Language Modeling Toolkit. In *Proceedings of the International Conference on Spoken Language Processing*.

Masao Utiyama and Hitoshi Isahara. 2007. A comparison of pivot methods for phrase-based statistical machine translation. In *HLT-NAACL*, pages 484–491.

Rabih Zbib, Erika Malchiodi, Jacob Devlin, David Stallard, Spyros Matsoukas, Richard Schwartz, John Makhoul, Omar F. Zaidan, and Chris Callison-Burch. 2012. Machine Translation of Arabic Dialects. In *Proceedings of the 2012 Conference of the North American Chapter of the Association for Computational Linguistics: Human Language Technologies*, pages 49–59, Montréal, Canada, June. Association for Computational Linguistics.

Xiaoheng Zhang. 1998. Dialect MT: a case study between Cantonese and Mandarin. In *Proceedings of the 36th Annual Meeting of the Association for Computational Linguistics and 17th International Conference on Computational Linguistics*, ACL '98, pages 1460–1464, Montreal, Canada.

What to do about bad language on the internet

Jacob Eisenstein
jacobe@gatech.edu
School of Interactive Computing
Georgia Institute of Technology

Abstract

The rise of social media has brought computational linguistics in ever-closer contact with *bad language*: text that defies our expectations about vocabulary, spelling, and syntax. This paper surveys the landscape of bad language, and offers a critical review of the NLP community's response, which has largely followed two paths: normalization and domain adaptation. Each approach is evaluated in the context of theoretical and empirical work on computer-mediated communication. In addition, the paper presents a quantitative analysis of the lexical diversity of social media text, and its relationship to other corpora.

1 Introduction

As social media becomes an increasingly important application domain for natural language processing, we encounter language that is substantially different from many benchmark corpora. The following examples are all from the social media service Twitter:

- *Work on farm Fri. Burning piles of brush WindyFire got out of control. Thank God for good naber He help get undr control Pants-BurnLegWound.* (Senator Charles Grassley)
- *Boom! Ya ur website suxx bro* (Sarah Silverman)
- *...dats why pluto is pluto it can neva b a star* (Shaquille O'Neil)
- *michelle obama great. job. and. whit all my. respect she. look. great. congrats. to. her.* (Ozzie Guillen)

These examples are selected from celebrities (for privacy reasons), but they contain linguistic challenges that are endemic to the medium, including non-standard punctuation, capitalization, spelling, vocabulary, and syntax. The consequences for language technology are dire: a series of papers has detailed how state-of-the-art natural language processing (NLP) systems perform significantly worse on social media text. In part-of-speech tagging, the accuracy of the Stanford tagger (Toutanova et al., 2003) falls from 97% on Wall Street Journal text to 85% accuracy on Twitter (Gimpel et al., 2011). In named entity recognition, the CoNLL-trained Stanford recognizer achieves 44% F-measure (Ritter et al., 2011), down from 86% on the CoNLL test set (Finkel et al., 2005). In parsing, Foster et al. (2011) report double-digit decreases in accuracy for four different state-of-the-art parsers when applied to social media text.

The application of language technology to social media is potentially transformative, leveraging the knowledge and perspectives of millions of people. But to deliver on this potential, the problems at the core of the NLP pipeline must be addressed. A growing thread of research takes up this challenge, including a shared task and workshop on "parsing the web," with new corpora which appear to sit somewhere between the Wall Street Journal and Twitter on the spectrum of bad language (Petrov and McDonald, 2012). But perhaps surprisingly, very little of this research has considered *why* social media language is so different. This review paper attempts to shed some light on this question, surveying a strong tradition of empirical and theoretical research on computer-mediated communication (CMC). I argue that the two main computational approaches to dealing with bad language — normalization and domain adaptation — are based on theories of social media language that are not descriptively accurate. I have worked and continue to work in both of these areas, so I make this argument not as a criticism of others, but in a spirit of self-reflection. It is hoped that a greater engagement with sociolinguistic and CMC research will lead to new, nuanced approaches to the challenge of bad language.

Why so much Twitter? Most of the examples in this paper will focus on Twitter, a microblogging service. Munro and Manning (2012) argue that Twitter has unfairly dominated recent research, at the expense of email and SMS text messages, which they found to be both linguistically distinct from Twitter and significantly more prevalent (in 2010). This matches earlier research arguing that email contained relatively little "neography," compared with text messages and chat (Anis, 2007).

A crucial advantage for Twitter is that it is public by default, while SMS and email are private. This makes Twitter data less problematic from a privacy standpoint,[1] far easier to obtain, and more amenable to target applications such as large-scale mining of events (Sakaki et al., 2010; Benson et al., 2011) and opinions (Sauper et al., 2011). Similar argument could be made on behalf of other public social media, such as blog comments (Ali-Hasan and Adamic, 2007), forums, and chatrooms (Paolillo, 2001). The main advantage of Twitter over these media is convenience in gathering large datasets through a single streaming interface. More comparative evaluation is needed to determine linguistic similarities and differences between Twitter and these other media; Section 4 presents an evaluation of the lexical similarity between Twitter and political blogs.

2 A tour of bad language

While many NLP researchers and engineers have wrestled with the difficulties imposed by bad language, there has been relatively little consideration of *why* language in social media is so different from our other corpora. A survey of laypeople found that more than half of the respondents agreed with the following partial explanations for non-standard spelling on the internet: "people are unsure of the correct spellings," "it's faster," "it's become the norm," and "people want to represent their own dialects and/or accents" (Jones, 2010). Let us now consider the evidence for these and other potential explanations.

2.1 Illiteracy

Some commentators have fixated on the proposal that the authors of non-standard language in social media are simply unaware or incapable of using more standard language (Thurlow, 2006). But empirical research suggests that many users of bad language are capable of using more traditional forms. Drouin and Davis (2009) find no significant differences in the literacy scores of individuals who do or do not use non-standard vocabulary in text messages. Tagliamonte and Denis (2008) review traces of instant messaging conversations among students, arguing that they "pick and choose ... from the entire stylistic repertoire of the language" in a way that would be impossible without skilled command of both formal and informal registers. While news text is usually more carefully composed and edited than much of the language in social media, there is little evidence that bad language results from an inability to speak anything else.

2.2 Length limits

In the case of Twitter, the limit of 140 characters for each message is frequently cited as an explanation for bad language (Finin et al., 2010). Does Twitter's character limit cause users to prefer shorter words, such as *u* instead of *you*? If so, one might expect shortening to be used most frequently in messages that are near the 140-character limit. Using a dataset of one million English-language tweets (Bamman et al., 2012), I have computed the average length of messages containing both standard words and their non-standard alternatives, focusing on the top five non-standard shortenings identified by the automatic method of Gouws et al. (2011a). The shortening *ur* can substitute for both *your* and *you're*. While *wit* and *bout* are also spellings for standard words, manual examination of one hundred randomly selected examples for each surface form revealed only one

[1] boyd and Crawford (2012) note that "public by default" data still raises important ethical considerations.

standard	length	alternative	length
your	85.1 ± 0.4	*ur*	81.9 ± 0.6
you're	90.0 ± 0.1		
with	87.9 ± 0.3	*wit*	78.8 ± 0.7
going	82.7 ± 0.5	*goin*	72.2 ± 1.0
know	86.1 ± 0.4	*kno*	78.4 ± 1.0
about	88.9 ± 0.4	*bout*	74.5 ± 0.7

Table 1: Average length of messages containing standard forms and their shortenings

case in which the standard meaning was intended for *wit*, and none for *bout*.

The average message lengths are shown in Table 1. In all five cases, the non-standard form tends to be used in shorter messages — not in long messages near the 140 character limit. Moreover, this difference is substantially greater than the saving of one or two characters offered by shortened form. This is not consistent with the explanation that Twitter's character limit is the primary factor driving the use of shortened forms. It is still possible that Twitter's length limitations might indirectly cause word shortenings: for example, by legitimizing shortened forms or causing authors to develop a habit of preferring them. But factors other than the length limit must be recruited to explain why such conventions or habits apply only to some messages and not others.

2.3 Text input affordances

Text input affordances — whether standard keyboards or predictive entry on mobile devices — play a role in computer-mediated communication that is perhaps under-appreciated. Gouws et al. (2011b) investigate orthographic variation on Twitter, and find differences across devices: for example, that messages from iPhones include more contractions than messages from Blackberries, and that tweets sent from the web browser are more likely to drop vowels. While each affordance facilitates some writing styles and inhibits others, the affordances themselves are unevenly distributed across users. For example, older people may prefer standard keyboards, and wealthier people may be more likely to own iPhones. Affordances are a moving target: new devices and software are constantly becoming available, the software itself may adapt to the user's input, and the user may adapt to the software and device.

2.4 Pragmatics

Emoticons are frequently thought of as introducing an expressive, non-verbal component into written language, mirroring the role played by facial expressions in speech (Walther and D'Addario, 2001), but they can also be seen as playing a pragmatic function: marking an utterance as facetious, or demonstrating a non-confrontational, less invested stance (Dresner and Herring, 2010). In many cases, **phrasal abbreviations** like *lol* (*laugh out loud*), *lmao* (*laughing my ass off*), *smh* (*shake my head*), and *ikr* (*i know, right?*) play a similar role: *yea she dnt like me lol*; *lmao I'm playin son*. A key difference from emoticons is that abbreviations can act as constituents, as in *smh at your ignorance*. Another form of non-standard language is **expressive lengthening** (e.g., *coooolllllll*), found by Brody and Diakopoulos (2011) to indicate subjectivity and sentiment. In running dialogues — such as in online multiplayer games — the symbols * and ^ can play an explicit pragmatic function (Collister, 2011; Collister, 2012).

2.5 Social variables

A series of papers has documented the interactions between social media text and social variables such as age (Burger and Henderson, 2006; Argamon et al., 2007; Rosenthal and McKeown, 2011), gender (Burger et al., 2011; Rao et al., 2010), race (Eisenstein et al., 2011), and location (Eisenstein et al., 2010; Wing and Baldridge, 2011). From this literature, it is clear that many of the features that characterize bad language have strong associations with specific social variables. In some cases, these associations mirror linguistic variables known from speech — such as geographically-associated lexical items like *hella*, or transcriptions of phonological variables like "g-dropping" (Eisenstein et al., 2010). But in other cases, apparently new lexical items, such as the abbreviations *ctfu*, *lls*, and *af*, acquire surprisingly strong associations with geographical areas and demographic groups (Eisenstein et al., 2011).

A robust finding from the sociolinguistics literature is that non-standard forms that mark social variables, such as regional dialects, are often inhibited in formal registers (Labov, 1972). For example, while the Pittsburgh spoken dialect sometimes features the address term *yinz* (Johnstone et al., 2006), one would not expect to find many examples in financial reports. Other investigators have found that much of the content in Twitter concerns social events and self presentation (Ramage et al., 2010), which may encourage the use of less formal registers in which socially-marketed language is uninhibited.

The use of non-standard language is often seen as a form of *identity work*, signaling authenticity, solidarity, or resistance to norms imposed from above (Bucholtz and Hall, 2005). In spoken language, many of the linguistic variables that perform identity work are phonological — for example, Eckert (2000) showed how the northern cities vowel shift was used by a subset of suburban teenagers to index affiliation with Detroit. The emergence of new linguistic variables in social media suggests that this identity work is as necessary in social media as it is in spoken language. Some of these new variables are transcriptions of existing spoken language variables: like *finna*, which transcribes *fixing to*. Others — abbreviations like *ctfu* and emoticons — seem to be linguistic inventions created to meet the needs of social communication in a new medium. In an early study of variation in social media, Paolillo (1999) notes that code-switching between English and Hindi also performs this type of identity work.

Finally, it is an uncomfortable fact that the text in many of our most frequently-used corpora was written and edited predominantly by working-age white men. The Penn Treebank is composed of professionally-written news text from 1989, when minorities comprised 7.5% of the print journalism workforce; the proportion of women in the journalism workforce was first recorded in 1999, when it was 37% (American Society of Newspaper Editors, 1999). In contrast, Twitter users in the USA contain an equal proportion of men and women, and a higher proportion of young adults and minorities than in the population as a whole (Smith and Brewer, 2012). Such demographic differences are very likely to lead to differences in language (Green, 2002; Labov, 2001; Eckert and McConnell-Ginet, 2003).

Overall, the reasons for language diversity in social media are manifold, though some of the most frequently cited explanations (illiteracy and length restrictions) do not hold up to scrutiny. The increasing prevalence of emoticons, phrasal abbreviations (*lol*, *ctfu*), and expressive lengthening may reflect the increasing use of written language for ephemeral social interaction, with the concomitant need for multiple channels through which to express multiple types of meaning. The fact many such neologisms are closely circumscribed in geography and demographics may reflect diffusion through social networks that are assortative on exactly these dimensions (Backstrom et al., 2010; Thelwall, 2009). But an additional consideration is that non-standard language is deliberately deployed in the performance of identity work and stancetaking. This seems a particularly salient explanation for the use of lexical variables that originate in spoken language (*jawn*, *hella*), and for the orthographic transcription of phonological variation (Eisenstein, 2013). Determining the role and relative importance of social network diffusion and identity work as factors in the diversification of social media language is an exciting direction for future research.

3 What can we do about it?

Having surveyed the landscape of bad language and its possible causes, let us now turn to the responses offered by the language technology research community.

3.1 Normalization

One approach to dealing with bad language is to turn it good: "normalizing" social media or SMS messages to better conform to the sort of language that our technology expects. Approaches to normalization include the noisy-channel model (Cook and Stevenson, 2009), string and distributional similarity (Han and Baldwin, 2011; Han et al., 2012), sequence labeling (Choudhury et al., 2007; Liu et al., 2011a), and machine translation (Aw et al., 2006). As this task has been the focus of substantial attention in recent years, labeled datasets have become available and accuracies have climbed.

That said, it is surprisingly difficult to find a precise definition of the normalization task. Writing before social media was a significant focus for NLP, Sproat et al. (2001) proposed to replace non-standard words with "the contextually appropriate word or sequence of words." In some cases, this seems clear enough: we can rewrite *dats why pluto is pluto* with *that's why...* But it is not difficult to find cases that are less clear, putting would-be normalizers in a difficult position. The labeled dataset of Han and Baldwin (2011) addresses a more tractable subset of the normalization problem, annotating only token-to-token normalizations. Thus, *imma* — a transcription of *I'm gonna*, which in turn transcribes *I'm going to* — is not normalized in this dataset. Abbreviations like *LOL* and *WTF* are also not normalized, even when they are used to abbreviate syntactic constituents, as in *wtf is the matter with you?* Nor are words like *hella* and *jawn* normalized, since they have no obvious one-word transcription in standard English. These decisions no doubt help to solidify the reliability of the annotations, but they provide an overly optimistic impression of the ability of string edit distance and related similarity-based techniques to normalize bad language. The resulting gold standard annotations seem little more amenable to automated parsing and information extraction than the original text.

But if we critique normalization for not going far enough, we must also ask whether it goes too far. The logic of normalization presupposes that the "norm" can be identified unambiguously, and that there is a direct mapping from non-standard words to the elements in this normal set. On closer examination, the norm reveals itself to be slippery. Whose norm are we targeting? Should we normalize *flvr* to *flavor* or *flavour*? Where does the normal end and the abnormal begin? For example, Han and Baldwin normalize *ain* to *ain't*, but not all the way to *isn't*. While *ain't* is certainly well-known to speakers of Standard American English, it does not appear in the Penn Treebank and probably could not be used in the Wall Street Journal, except in quotation.

Normalization is often impossible without changing the meaning of the text. Should we normalize the final word of *ya ur website suxx bro* to *brother*? At the very least, this adds semantic ambiguity where there was none before (is she talking to her biological brother? or possibly to a monk?). Language variation does not arise from passing standard text through a noisy channel; it often serves a pragmatic and/or stancetaking (Du Bois, 2007) function. Eliminating variation would strip those additional layers of meaning from whatever propositional content might survive the normalization process. Sarah Silverman's *ya ur website suxx bro* can only be understood as a critique from a caricatured persona — the type of person who ends sentences with *bro*. Similarly, we can assume that Shaquille O'Neil is capable of writing *that's why Pluto is Pluto*, but that to do so would convey an undesirably didactic and authoritative stance towards the audience and topic.

This is not to deny that there is great potential value in research aimed at understanding orthographic variation through a combination of local context, string similarity, and related finite-state machinery. Given the productivity of orthographic substitutions in social media text, it is clear that language technology must be made more robust. Normalization may point the way towards such robustness, even if we do not build an explicit normalization component directly into the language processing pipeline. Another potential benefit of this research is to better understand the underlying orthographic processes that lead to the diversity of language in social media, how these processes diffuse over social networks, and how they impact comprehensibility for both the target and non-target audiences.

3.2 Domain adaptation

Rather than adapting text to fit our tools, we may instead adapt our tools to fit the text. A series of papers has followed the mold of "NLP for Twitter," including part-of-speech tagging (Gimpel et al., 2011; Owoputi et al., 2013), named entity recognition (Finin et al., 2010; Ritter et al., 2011; Liu et al., 2011b), parsing (Foster et al., 2011), dialogue modeling (Ritter et al., 2010) and summarization (Sharifi et al., 2010). These papers adapt various parts of the natural language processing pipeline for social media text, and make use of a range of techniques:

- **preprocessing** to normalize expressive lengthening, and eliminate or group all hashtags, usernames, and URLs (Gimpel et al., 2011; Foster et al., 2011)
- **new labeled data**, enabling the application of semi-supervised learning (Finin et al., 2010; Gimpel et al., 2011; Ritter et al., 2011)

- **new annotation schemes** specifically customized for social media text (Gimpel et al., 2011)
- **self-training** on unlabeled social media text (Foster et al., 2011)
- **distributional features** to address the sparsity of bag-of-words features (Gimpel et al., 2011; Owoputi et al., 2013; Ritter et al., 2011)
- **joint normalization**, incorporated directly into downstream application (Liu et al., 2012)
- **distant supervision**, using named entity ontologies and topic models (Ritter et al., 2011)

Only a few of these techniques (normalization and new annotation systems) are specific to social media; the rest can found in other domain adaptation settings. Is domain adaptation appropriate for social media? Darling et al. (2012) argue that social media is not a coherent domain at all, and that a POS tagger for Twitter will not necessarily generalize to other social media. One can go further: Twitter itself is not a unified genre, it is composed of many different styles and registers, with widely varying expectations for the degree of standardness and dimensions of variation (Androutsopoulos, 2011). I am the co-author on a paper entitled "Part-of-speech tagging for Twitter," but if we take this title literally, it is impossible on a trivial level: Twitter contains text in dozens or hundreds of languages, including many for which no POS tagger exists. Even within a single language — setting aside issues of code-switching (Paolillo, 1996) — Twitter and other social media can contain registers ranging from hashtag wordplay (Naaman et al., 2011) to the official pronouncements of the British Monarchy. And even if all good language is alike, bad language can be bad in many different ways — as Androutsopoulos (2011) notes when contrasting the types of variation encountered when "visiting a gamer forum" versus "joining the Twitter profile of a rap star."

4 The lexical coherence of social media

The internal coherence of social media — and its relationship to other types of text — can be quantified in terms of the similarity of distributions over bigrams. While there are many techniques for comparing word distributions, I apply the relatively simple method of counting out-of-vocabulary (OOV) bigrams. The relationship between OOV rate and domain adaptation has been explored by McClosky et al. (2010), who use it as a feature to predict how well a parser will perform when applied across domains.[2]

Specifically, the datasets A and B are compared by counting the number of bigram tokens in A that are unseen in B. The following corpora are compared:

- **Twitter-month**: randomly selected tweets from each month between January 2010 to October 2012 (Eisenstein et al., 2012).
- **Twitter-hour**: randomly selected tweets from each hour of the day, randomly sampled during the period from January 2010 to October 2012.
- **Twitter-#**: tweets in which the first token is a hashtag. The hashtag itself is not included in the bigram counts; see below for more details on which bigrams are included.
- **Twitter-@**: tweets in which the first token is a username. The username itself is not included in the bigram counts.
- **Penn Treebank**: sections 2-21
- **Infinite Jest**: the text of the 1996 novel by David Foster Wallace (Wallace, 2012). Consists of only 482,558 tokens.
- **Blog articles**: A randomly-sampled subset of the American political blog posts gathered by Yano et al. (2009).
- **Blog comments**: A randomly-selected subset of comments associated with the blog posts described above.

In all corpora, only fully alphabetic tokens are counted; thus, all hashtags and usernames are discarded. The Twitter text is tokenized using Tweet-

[2]A very recent study compares Twitter with other corpora, using a number of alternative metrics, such as the use of high and low frequency words, pronouns, and intensifiers (Hu et al., 2013). This is complementary to the present study, which focuses on the degree of difference in the lexical distributions of corpora gathered from various media.

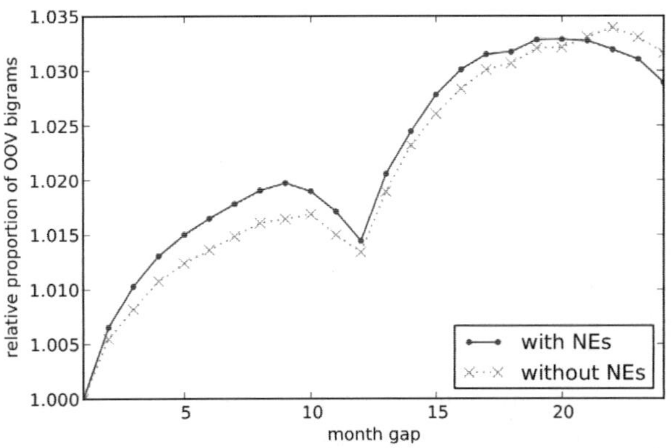

Figure 1: Lexical mismatch increases over time, as social media language evolves.

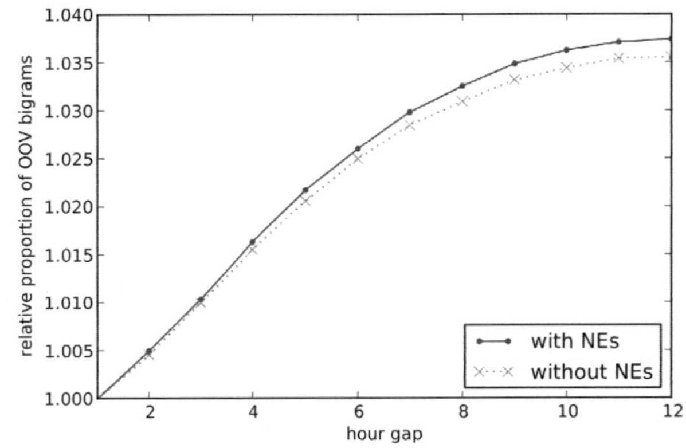

Figure 2: Different times of day have unique lexical signatures, reflecting differing topics and authors.

motif;[3] the Penn Treebank data uses the gold standard tokenization; Infinite Jest and the blog data are tokenized using NLTK (Bird et al., 2009). All tokens are downcased, and sequences of three or more consecutive identical characters are reduced to three characters (e.g., *coooool* → *coool*). All Twitter corpora are subject to the following filters: messages must be from the United States and should be written in English,[4] they may not include hyperlinks (eliminating most marketing messages), they may not be retweets, and the author must not have more than 1,000 followers or follow more than 1,000 people. These criteria serve to eliminate text from celebrities, businesses, or automated bots.

Twitter over time Figure 1 shows how the proportion of out-of-vocabulary bigrams increases over time. It is possible that the core features of language are constant but the set of named entities that are mentioned changes over time. To control for this, the CMU Twitter Part-of-Speech tagger (Owoputi et al., 2013) was used to identify named entity mentions, and they were replaced with a special token. The OOV rate is standardized with respect to a one-month time gap, where it is 24.4% when named entities are included, and 21.3% when they are not. These rates reach maxima at 25.2% and 22.0% respectively, with dips at 12 and 24 months indicating cyclic yearly effects. While the proportion of OOV tokens is smaller when named entities are not included, the rate of growth is similar in each case. The steadily increasingly rate of OOV bigrams suggests that we cannot annotate our way out of the bad language problem. An NLP system trained from data gathered in January 2010 will be increasingly outdated as time passes and social media language continues to evolve.

One need not wait months to see language change on Twitter: marked changes can be observed over the course of a single day (Golder and Macy, 2011). A quantitative comparison is shown in Figure 2. Here the OOV rate is standardized with respect to a one-hour gap, where it is 24.2% when named entities are included, and 21.1% when they are not. These rates rise monotonically as the time gap increases, peaking at 25.1% and 21.9% respectively. Such diurnal changes may reflect the diverse language of the different types of authors who post throughout the day.

Types of usage The **Twitter-#** and **Twitter-@** corpora are designed to capture the diversity of ways in which social media is used to communicate. **Twitter-#** contains tweets that begin with hashtags, and are thus more likely to be part of running jokes

[3] https://github.com/brendano/tweetmotif

[4] Approximate language detection was performed as follows. We first identify the 1000 most common words, then sort all *authors* by the proportion of these types that they used, and eliminate the bottom 10%. This filtering mechanism eliminates individuals who never write in English, but a small amount of foreign language still enters the dataset via code-switching authors. The effect of more advanced language detection methods (Bergsma et al., 2012) on these results may be considered in future work.

or trending topics (Naaman et al., 2011). **Twitter-@** contains tweets that begin with usernames — an addressing mechanism that is used to maintain dialogue threads on the site. These datasets are compared with a set of randomly selected tweets from June 2011, and with several other corpora: Penn Treebank, the novel Infinite Jest, and text and comments from political blogs. There was no attempt to remove named entities from any of these corpora, as such a comparison would merely reflect the different accuracy levels of NER in each corpus.

The results are shown in Table 2. A few observations stand out. First, the Penn Treebank is the clear outlier: a PTB dictionary has by far the most OOV tokens for all three Twitter domains and Infinite Jest, although it is a better match for the blog corpora than Infinite Jest is. Second, the social media are fairly internally coherent: the Twitter datasets better match each other than any other corpus, with a maximum OOV rate of 33.4 for **Twitter-#** against **Twitter-@**, though this is significantly higher than the OOV rate of 27.8 between two separate generic Twitter samples drawn from the same month. Finally, the OOV rate increase between Twitter and blogs — also social media — is substantial. Contrary to expectations, the **Blog-body** corpus was no closer to the **PTB** standard than **Blog-comment**.

These results suggest that the Penn Treebank corpus is so distant from social media that there are indeed substantial gains to be reaped by adapting from news text towards generic Twitter or Blog target domains. The internal differences within these social media — at least as measured by the distinctions drawn in Table 2 — are much smaller than the differences between these corpora and the PTB standard. However, in the long run, the effectiveness of this approach will be limited, as it is clear from Figure 1 that social media is a moving target. Any static system that we build today, whether by manual annotation or automated adaptation, will see its performance decay over time.

5 What to do next

Language is shaped by a constant negotiation between processes that encourage change and linguistic diversity, and countervailing processes that enforce existing norms. The decision of the NLP community to focus so much effort on news text is eminently justified on practical grounds, but has unintended consequences not just for technology but for language itself. By developing software that works best for standard linguistic forms, we throw the weight of language technology behind those forms, and against variants that are preferred by disempowered groups. By adopting a model of "normalization," we declare one version of language to be the norm, and all others to be outside that norm. By adopting a model of "domain adaptation," we confuse a medium with a coherent domain. Adapting language technology towards the median Tweet can improve accuracy on average, but it is certain to leave many forms of language out.

Much of the current research on the relationship between social media language and metadata has the goal of using language to predict the metadata — *revealing* who is a woman or a man, who is from Oklahoma or New Jersey, and so on. This perspective on social variables and personal identity ignores the *local categories* that are often more linguistically salient (Eckert, 2008); worse, it strips individuals of any agency in using language as a resource to create and shape their identity (Coupland, 2007), and conceals the role that language plays in creating and perpetuating categories like gender (Bucholtz and Hall, 2005). An alternative possibility is to reverse the relationship between language and metadata, using metadata to achieve a more flexible and heterogeneous domain adaptation that is sensitive to the social factors that shape variation. Such a reversal would help language technology to move beyond false dichotomies between normal and abnormal text, source and target domains, and good and bad language.

Acknowledgments

This paper benefitted from discussions with David Bamman, Natalia Cecire, Micha Elsner, Sharon Goldwater, Scott Kiesling, Brendan O'Connor, Tyler Schnoebelen, and Yi Yang. Many thanks to Brendan O'Connor and David Bamman for providing Twitter datasets, Tae Yano for the blog comment dataset, and Byron Wallace for the *Infinite Jest* dataset. Thanks also to the anonymous reviewers for their helpful feedback.

	Tw-June	Tw-@	Tw-#	Blog-body	Blog-comment	Infinite-Jest	PTB
Tw-June		28.7	29.3	47.1	48.6	54.0	63.9
Tw-@	25.9		29.7	47.8	49.9	56.3	66.4
Tw-#	29.8	33.4		49.6	51.0	54.7	66.2
Blog-body	41.9	44.1	43.8		27.2	49.1	48.0
Blog-comment	47.4	49.6	49.2	30.2		53.0	48.4
Infinite-Jest	49.4	51.1	49.9	48.3	47.4		55.5
PTB	72.2	73.1	72.7	64.5	61.9	71.9	

Table 2: Percent OOV bigram tokens across corpora. Rows are the dataset providing the tokens, columns are the dataset providing the dictionary.

References

Noor Ali-Hasan and Lada Adamic. 2007. Expressing social relationships on the blog through links and comments. In *Proceedings of ICWSM*.

American Society of Newspaper Editors. 1999. *1999 Newsroom Census: Minority Employment Inches up in Daily Newspapers*. American Society of Newspaper Editors, Reston, VA.

Jannis Androutsopoulos. 2011. Language change and digital media: a review of conceptions and evidence. In Nikolas Coupland and Tore Kristiansen, editors, *Standard Languages and Language Standards in a Changing Europe*. Novus, Oslo.

Jacques Anis. 2007. Neography: Unconventional spelling in French SMS text messages. In Brenda Danet and Susan C. Herring, editors, *The multilingual internet: Language, culture, and communication online*, pages 87 – 115. Oxford University Press.

Shlomo Argamon, Moshe Koppel, James W. Pennebaker, and Jonathan Schler. 2007. Mining the blogosphere: age, gender, and the varieties of self-expression. *First Monday*, 12(9).

AiTi Aw, Min Zhang, Juan Xiao, and Jian Su. 2006. A phrase-based statistical model for SMS text normalization. In *Proceedings of ACL*, pages 33–40.

Lars Backstrom, Eric Sun, and Cameron Marlow. 2010. Find me if you can: improving geographical prediction with social and spatial proximity. In *Proceedings of WWW*, pages 61–70.

David Bamman, Jacob Eisenstein, and Tyler Schnoebelen. 2012. Gender in twitter: Styles, stances, and social networks. Technical Report 1210.4567, arXiv, October.

Edward Benson, Aria Haghighi, and Regina Barzilay. 2011. Event discovery in social media feeds. In *Proceedings of ACL*.

Shane Bergsma, Paul McNamee, Mossaab Bagdouri, Clayton Fink, and Theresa Wilson. 2012. Language identification for creating language-specific twitter collections. In *Proceedings of the Second Workshop on Language in Social Media*, pages 65–74, June.

Steven Bird, Ewan Klein, and Edward Loper. 2009. *Natural language processing with Python*. O'Reilly Media, Incorporated.

danah boyd and Kate Crawford. 2012. Critical questions for big data. *Information, Communication & Society*, 15(5):662–679, May.

Samuel Brody and Nicholas Diakopoulos. 2011. Cooooooooooooooollllllllllll!!!!!!!!!!!!!!: using word lengthening to detect sentiment in microblogs. In *Proceedings of EMNLP*.

Mary Bucholtz and Kira Hall. 2005. Identity and interaction: A sociocultural linguistic approach. *Discourse studies*, 7(4-5):585–614.

John D. Burger and John C. Henderson. 2006. An exploration of observable features related to blogger age. In *AAAI Spring Symposium: Computational Approaches to Analyzing Weblogs*.

John D. Burger, John C. Henderson, George Kim, and Guido Zarrella. 2011. Discriminating gender on twitter. In *Proceedings of the Conference on Empirical Methods in Natural Language Processing*.

Monojit Choudhury, Rahul Saraf, Vijit Jain, Animesh Mukherjee, Sudeshna Sarkar, and Anupam Basu. 2007. Investigation and modeling of the structure of texting language. *International Journal on Document Analysis and Recognition*, 10(3):157–174.

Lauren B. Collister. 2011. *-repair in online discourse. *Journal of Pragmatics*, 43(3):918–921, February.

Lauren B. Collister. 2012. The discourse deictics ^ and <-- in a world of warcraft community. *Discourse, Context & Media*, 1(1):9–19, March.

Paul Cook and Suzanne Stevenson. 2009. An unsupervised model for text message normalization. In *Proceedings of the NAACL-HLT Workshop on Computational Approaches to Linguistic Creativity*, pages 71–78.

Nikolas Coupland. 2007. *Style (Key Topics in Sociolinguistics)*. Cambridge University Press, July.

William M. Darling, Michael J. Paul, and Fei Song. 2012. Unsupervised part-of-speech tagging in noisy and esoteric domains with a syntactic-semantic bayesian hmm. In *Proceedings of EACL Workshop on Semantic Analysis in Social Media*.

Eli Dresner and Susan C. Herring. 2010. Functions of the non-verbal in cmc: Emoticons and illocutionary force. *Communication Theory*, 20(3):249–268.

Michelle Drouin and Claire Davis. 2009. R u txting? is the use of text speak hurting your literacy? *Journal of Literacy Research*, 41(1):46–67.

John W. Du Bois. 2007. The stance triangle. In Robert Engelbretson, editor, *Stancetaking in discourse*, pages 139–182. John Benjamins Publishing Company, Amsterdam/Philadelphia.

Penelope Eckert and Sally McConnell-Ginet. 2003. *Language and Gender*. Cambridge University Press, New York.

Penelope Eckert. 2000. *Linguistic variation as social practice*. Blackwell.

Penelope Eckert. 2008. Variation and the indexical field. *Journal of Sociolinguistics*, 12(4):453–476.

Jacob Eisenstein, Brendan O'Connor, Noah A. Smith, and Eric P. Xing. 2010. A latent variable model for geographic lexical variation. In *Proceedings of EMNLP*.

Jacob Eisenstein, Noah A. Smith, and Eric P. Xing. 2011. Discovering sociolinguistic associations with structured sparsity. In *Proceedings of ACL*.

Jacob Eisenstein, Brendan O'Connor, Noah A. Smith, and Eric P. Xing. 2012. Mapping the geographical diffusion of new words. Technical Report 1210.5268, arXiv.

Jacob Eisenstein. 2013. Phonological factors in social media writing. In *Proceedings of the NAACL Workshop on Language Analysis in Social Media*.

Tim Finin, Will Murnane, Anand Karandikar, Nicholas Keller, Justin Martineau, and Mark Dredze. 2010. Annotating named entities in twitter data with crowdsourcing. In *Proceedings of the NAACL HLT Workshop on Creating Speech and Language Data with Amazon's Mechanical Turk*.

Jenny R. Finkel, Trond Grenager, and Christopher Manning. 2005. Incorporating non-local information into information extraction systems by gibbs sampling. In *Proceedings of ACL*, pages 363–370.

Jennifer Foster, Ozlem Cetinoglu, Joachim Wagner, Joseph Le Roux, Joakim Nivre, Deirdre Hogan, and Josef van Genabith. 2011. From news to comment: Resources and benchmarks for parsing the language of web 2.0. In *Proceedings of IJCNLP*.

Kevin Gimpel, Nathan Schneider, Brendan O'Connor, Dipanjan Das, Daniel Mills, Jacob Eisenstein, Michael Heilman, Dani Yogatama, Jeffrey Flanigan, and Noah A. Smith. 2011. Part-of-speech tagging for twitter: annotation, features, and experiments. In *Proceedings of ACL*.

Scott A. Golder and Michael W. Macy. 2011. Diurnal and seasonal mood vary with work, sleep, and daylength across diverse cultures. *Science*, 333(6051):1878–1881, September.

Stephan Gouws, Dirk Hovy, and Donald Metzler. 2011a. Unsupervised mining of lexical variants from noisy text. In *Proceedings of the First workshop on Unsupervised Learning in NLP*, pages 82–90, July.

Stephan Gouws, Donald Metzler, Congxing Cai, and Eduard Hovy. 2011b. Contextual bearing on linguistic variation in social media. In *Proceedings of the ACL Workshop on Language in Social Media*.

Lisa Green. 2002. *African American English*. Cambridge University Press.

Bo Han and Timothy Baldwin. 2011. Lexical normalisation of short text messages: Makn sens a# twitter. In *Proceedings of ACL*, volume 1.

Bo Han, Paul Cook, and Timothy Baldwin. 2012. Automatically constructing a normalisation dictionary for microblogs. In *Proceedings of EMNLP*.

Yuheng Hu, Kartik Talamadupula, and Subbarao Kambhampati. 2013. Dude, srsly?: The surprisingly formal nature of twitter's language. In *Proceedings of ICWSM*.

Barbara Johnstone, Jennifer Andrus, and Andrew E Danielson. 2006. Mobility, indexicality, and the enregisterment of pittsburghese. *Journal of English Linguistics*, 34(2):77–104.

Lucy Jones. 2010. The changing face of spelling on the internet. Technical report, The English Spelling Society.

William Labov. 1972. *Sociolinguistic patterns*. Philadelphia: University of Pennsylvania Press.

William Labov. 2001. *Principles of linguistic change. Vol.2 : Social factors*. Blackwell Publishers, Oxford.

Fei Liu, Fuliang Weng, Bingqing Wang, and Yang Liu. 2011a. Insertion, deletion, or substitution? normalizing text messages without pre-categorization nor supervision. In *Proceedings of ACL*, pages 71–76.

Xiaohua Liu, Shaodian Zhang, Furu Wei, and Ming Zhou. 2011b. Recognizing named entities in tweets. In *Proceedings of ACL*.

Xiaohua Liu, Ming Zhou, Xiangyang Zhou, Zhongyang Fu, and Furu Wei. 2012. Joint inference of named entity recognition and normalization for tweets. In *Proceedings of ACL*.

David McClosky, Eugene Charniak, and Mark Johnson. 2010. Automatic domain adaptation for parsing. In *Proceedings of NAACL*, pages 28–36, June.

Robert Munro and Christopher D. Manning. 2012. Short message communications: users, topics, and in-language processing. In *Proceedings of the 2nd ACM Symposium on Computing for Development*.

Mor Naaman, Hila Becker, and Luis Gravano. 2011. Hip and trendy: Characterizing emerging trends on twitter. *Journal of the American Society for Information Science and Technology*, 62(5):902–918.

Olutobi Owoputi, Brendan O'Connor, Chris Dyer, Kevin Gimpel, Nathan Schneider, and Noah A. Smith. 2013. Improved part-of-speech tagging for online conversational text with word clusters. In *Proceedings of NAACL*.

John C. Paolillo. 1996. Language choice on soc.culture.punjab. *Electronic Journal of Communication/La Revue Electronique de Communication*, 6(3).

John C. Paolillo. 1999. The virtual speech community: Social network and language variation on irc. *Journal of Computer-Mediated Communication*, 4(4):0.

John C. Paolillo. 2001. Language variation on internet relay chat: A social network approach. *Journal of Sociolinguistics*, 5(2):180–213.

Slav Petrov and Ryan McDonald. 2012. Overview of the 2012 shared task on parsing the web. In *Notes of the First Workshop on Syntactic Analysis of Non-Canonical Language (SANCL)*.

Daniel Ramage, Sue Dumais, and D. Liebling. 2010. Characterizing microblogs with topic models. In *Proceedings of ICWSM*.

Delip Rao, David Yarowsky, Abhishek Shreevats, and Manaswi Gupta. 2010. Classifying latent user attributes in twitter. In *Proceedings of Workshop on Search and mining user-generated contents*.

Alan Ritter, Colin Cherry, and Bill Dolan. 2010. Unsupervised modeling of twitter conversations. In *Proceedings of NAACL*.

Alan Ritter, Sam Clark, Mausam, and Oren Etzioni. 2011. Named entity recognition in tweets: an experimental study. In *Proceedings of EMNLP*.

Sara Rosenthal and Kathleen McKeown. 2011. Age prediction in blogs: A study of style, content, and online behavior in pre- and Post-Social media generations. In *Proceedings of ACL*.

Takeshi Sakaki, Makoto Okazaki, and Yutaka Matsuo. 2010. Earthquake shakes twitter users: real-time event detection by social sensors. In *Proceedings of WWW*, pages 851–860.

Christina Sauper, Aria Haghighi, and Regina Barzilay. 2011. Content models with attitude. In *Proceedings of ACL*.

Beaux Sharifi, Mark-Anthony Hutton, and Jugal Kalita. 2010. Summarizing microblogs automatically. In *Proceedings of NAACL*.

Aaron Smith and Joanna Brewer. 2012. Twitter use 2012. Technical report, Pew Research Center, May.

Richard Sproat, Alan W Black, Stanley Chen, Shankar Kumar, Mari Ostendorf, and Christopher Richards. 2001. Normalization of non-standard words. *Computer Speech & Language*, 15(3):287–333.

Sali A. Tagliamonte and Derek Denis. 2008. Linguistic ruin? lol! instant messaging and teen language. *American Speech*, 83(1):3–34, March.

Mike Thelwall. 2009. Homophily in MySpace. *J. Am. Soc. Inf. Sci.*, 60(2):219–231.

Crispin Thurlow. 2006. From statistical panic to moral panic: The metadiscursive construction and popular exaggeration of new media language in the print media. *J. Computer-Mediated Communication*, pages 667–701.

Kristina Toutanova, Dan Klein, Christopher D. Manning, and Yoram Singer. 2003. Feature-rich part-of-speech tagging with a cyclic dependency network. In *Proceedings of NAACL*.

Byron Wallace. 2012. Multiple narrative disentanglement: Unraveling infinite jest. In *Proceedings of NAACL*.

Joseph B. Walther and Kyle P. D'Addario. 2001. The impacts of emoticons on message interpretation in computer-mediated communication. *Social Science Computer Review*, 19(3):324–347.

Benjamin Wing and Jason Baldridge. 2011. Simple supervised document geolocation with geodesic grids. In *Proceedings of ACL*.

Tae Yano, William W. Cohen, and Noah A. Smith. 2009. Predicting response to political blog posts with topic models. In *Proceedings of NAACL*.

Minibatch and Parallelization for Online Large Margin Structured Learning

Kai Zhao[1]
[1]Computer Science Program, Graduate Center
City University of New York
kzhao@gc.cuny.edu

Liang Huang[2,1]
[2]Computer Science Dept, Queens College
City University of New York
huang@cs.qc.cuny.edu

Abstract

Online learning algorithms such as perceptron and MIRA have become popular for many NLP tasks thanks to their simpler architecture and faster convergence over batch learning methods. However, while batch learning such as CRF is easily parallelizable, online learning is much harder to parallelize: previous efforts often witness a decrease in the converged accuracy, and the speedup is typically very small ($\sim$3) even with many (10+) processors. We instead present a much simpler architecture based on "mini-batches", which is trivially parallelizable. We show that, unlike previous methods, minibatch learning (in serial mode) actually *improves* the converged accuracy for both perceptron and MIRA learning, and when combined with simple parallelization, minibatch leads to very significant speedups (up to 9x on 12 processors) on state-of-the-art parsing and tagging systems.

1 Introduction

Online structured learning algorithms such as the structured perceptron (Collins, 2002) and k-best MIRA (McDonald et al., 2005) have become more and more popular for many NLP tasks such as dependency parsing and part-of-speech tagging. This is because, compared to their batch learning counterparts, online learning methods offer faster convergence rates and better scalability to large datasets, while using much less memory and a much simpler architecture which only needs 1-best or k-best decoding. However, online learning for NLP typically involves expensive inference on each example for 10 or more passes over millions of examples, which often makes training too slow in practice; for example systems such as the popular (2nd-order) MST parser (McDonald and Pereira, 2006) usually require the order of days to train on the Treebank on a commodity machine (McDonald et al., 2010).

There are mainly two ways to address this scalability problem. On one hand, researchers have been developing modified learning algorithms that allow inexact search (Collins and Roark, 2004; Huang et al., 2012). However, the learner still needs to loop over the whole training data (on the order of millions of sentences) many times. For example the best-performing method in Huang et al. (2012) still requires 5-6 hours to train a very fast parser.

On the other hand, with the increasing popularity of multicore and cluster computers, there is a growing interest in speeding up training via parallelization. While batch learning such as CRF (Lafferty et al., 2001) is often trivially parallelizable (Chu et al., 2007) since each update is a batch-aggregate of the update from each (independent) example, online learning is much harder to parallelize due to the dependency between examples, i.e., the update on the first example should in principle influence the decoding of all remaining examples. Thus if we decode and update the first and the 1000th examples in parallel, we lose their interactions which is one of the reasons for online learners' fast convergence. This explains why previous work such as the iterative parameter mixing (IPM) method of McDonald et al. (2010) witnesses a decrease in the accuracies of parallelly-learned models, and the speedup is typically very small (about 3 in their experiments) even with 10+ processors.

We instead explore the idea of "minibatch" for online large-margin structured learning such as perceptron and MIRA. We argue that minibatch is advantageous in *both* serial and parallel settings.

First, for minibatch perceptron in the serial setting, our intuition is that, although decoding is done independently within one minibatch, updates are done by averaging update vectors in batch, providing a "mixing effect" similar to "averaged parameters" of Collins (2002) which is also found in IPM (McDonald et al., 2010), and online EM (Liang and Klein, 2009).

Secondly, minibatch MIRA in the serial setting has an advantage that, different from previous methods such as SGD which simply sum up the updates from all examples in a minibatch, a minibatch MIRA update tries to simultaneously satisfy an aggregated set of constraints that are collected from multiple examples in the minibatch. Thus each minibatch MIRA update involves an optimization over many more constraints than in pure online MIRA, which could potentially lead to a better margin. In other words we can view MIRA as an online version or stepwise approximation of SVM, and minibatch MIRA can be seen as a better approximation as well as a middleground between pure MIRA and SVM.[1]

More interestingly, the minibatch architecture is trivially parallelizable since the examples within each minibatch could be decoded in parallel on multiple processors (while the update is still done in serial). This is known as "synchronous minibatch" and has been explored by many researchers (Gimpel et al., 2010; Finkel et al., 2008), but all previous works focus on probabilistic models along with SGD or EM learning methods while our work is the first effort on large-margin methods.

We make the following contributions:

- Theoretically, we present a serial minibatch framework (Section 3) for online large-margin learning and prove the convergence theorems for minibatch perceptron and minibatch MIRA.
- Empirically, we show that serial minibatch could speed up convergence and improve the converged accuracy for both MIRA and perceptron on state-of-the-art dependency parsing and part-of-speech tagging systems.
- In addition, when combined with simple (synchronous) parallelization, minibatch MIRA leads to very significant speedups (up to 9x on 12 processors) that are much higher than that of IPM (McDonald et al., 2010) on state-of-the-art parsing and tagging systems.

[1] This is similar to Pegasos (Shalev-Shwartz et al., 2007) that applies subgradient descent over a minibatch. Pegasos becomes pure online when the minibatch size is 1.

Algorithm 1 Generic Online Learning.

Input: data $D = \{(x^{(t)}, y^{(t)})\}_{t=1}^{n}$ and feature map $\mathbf{\Phi}$
Output: weight vector $\mathbf{w}$
repeat
  for each example (x, y) **in** D **do**
    $C \leftarrow$ FINDCONSTRAINTS$(x, y, \mathbf{w})$ ▷ decoding
    if $C \neq \emptyset$ **then** UPDATE$(\mathbf{w}, C)$
until converged

2 Online Learning: Perceptron and MIRA

We first present a unified framework for online large-margin learning, where perceptron and MIRA are two special cases. Shown in Algorithm 1, the online learner considers each input example (x, y) sequentially and performs two steps:

1. find the set C of violating constraints, and
2. update the weight vector $\mathbf{w}$ according to C.

Here a triple $\langle x, y, z\rangle$ is said to be a "violating constraint" with respect to model $\mathbf{w}$ if the incorrect label z scores higher than (or equal to) the correct label y in $\mathbf{w}$, i.e., $\mathbf{w} \cdot \Delta\mathbf{\Phi}(\langle x, y, z\rangle) \leq 0$, where $\Delta\mathbf{\Phi}(\langle x, y, z\rangle)$ is a short-hand notation for the update vector $\mathbf{\Phi}(x, y) - \mathbf{\Phi}(x, z)$ and $\mathbf{\Phi}$ is the feature map (see Huang et al. (2012) for details). The subroutines FINDCONSTRAINTS and UPDATE are analogous to "APIs", to be specified by specific instances of this online learning framework. For example, the structured perceptron algorithm of Collins (2002) is implemented in Algorithm 2 where FINDCONSTRAINTS returns a singleton constraint if the 1-best decoding result z (the highest scoring label according to the current model) is different from the true label y. Note that in the UPDATE function, C is always a singleton constraint for the perceptron, but we make it more general (as a set) to handle the batch update in the minibatch version in Section 3.

On the other hand, Algorith 3 presents the k-best MIRA Algorithm of McDonald et al. (2005) which generalizes multiclass MIRA (Crammer and Singer, 2003) for structured prediction. The decoder now

Algorithm 2 Perceptron (Collins, 2002).

function FINDCONSTRAINTS$(x, y, \mathbf{w})$
  $z \leftarrow \mathbf{argmax}_{s \in \mathcal{Y}(x)}\, \mathbf{w} \cdot \boldsymbol{\Phi}(x, s)$ ▷ decoding
  if $z \neq y$ **then return** $\{\langle x, y, z\rangle\}$
  else return $\emptyset$
procedure UPDATE$(\mathbf{w}, C)$
  $\mathbf{w} \leftarrow \mathbf{w} + \frac{1}{|C|} \sum_{c \in C} \Delta\boldsymbol{\Phi}(c)$ ▷ (batch) update

Algorithm 3 k-best MIRA (McDonald et al., 2005).

function FINDCONSTRAINTS$(x, y, \mathbf{w})$
  $Z \leftarrow k\text{-best}_{z \in \mathcal{Y}(x)} \mathbf{w} \cdot \boldsymbol{\Phi}(x, z)$
  $Z \leftarrow \{z \in Z \mid z \neq y, \mathbf{w} \cdot \Delta\boldsymbol{\Phi}(\langle x, y, z\rangle) \leq 0\}$
  return $\{(\langle x, y, z\rangle, \ell(y, z)) \mid z \in Z\}$
procedure UPDATE$(\mathbf{w}, C)$
  $\mathbf{w} \leftarrow \mathop{\mathbf{argmin}}_{\mathbf{w}' : \forall (c, \ell) \in C,\ \mathbf{w}' \cdot \Delta\boldsymbol{\Phi}(c) \geq \ell} \|\mathbf{w}' - \mathbf{w}\|^2$

finds the k-best solutions Z first, and returns a set of violating constraints in Z, The update in MIRA is more interesting: it searches for the new model $\mathbf{w}'$ with minimum change from the current model $\mathbf{w}$ so that $\mathbf{w}'$ corrects each violating constraint by a margin at least as large as the loss $\ell(y, z)$ of the incorrect label z.

Although not mentioned in the pseudocode, we also employ "averaged parameters" (Collins, 2002) for both perceptron and MIRA in all experiments.

3 Serial Minibatch

The idea of serial minibatch learning is extremely simple: divide the data into $\lceil n/m \rceil$ minibatches of size m, and do batch updates after decoding each minibatch (see Algorithm 4). The FIND-CONSTRAINTS and UPDATE subroutines remain unchanged for both perceptron and MIRA, although it is important to note that a perceptron batch update uses the average of update vectors, not the sum, which simplifies the proof. This architecture is often called "synchronous minibatch" in the literature (Gimpel et al., 2010; Liang and Klein, 2009; Finkel et al., 2008). It could be viewed as a middleground between pure online learning and batch learning.

3.1 Convergence of Minibatch Perceptron

We denote $C(D)$ to be the set of all possible violating constraints in data D (cf. Huang et al. (2012)):

$$C(D) = \{\langle x, y, z\rangle \mid (x, y) \in D, z \in \mathcal{Y}(x) - \{y\}\}.$$

Algorithm 4 Serial Minibatch Online Learning.

Input: data D, feature map $\boldsymbol{\Phi}$, and minibatch size m
Output: weight vector $\mathbf{w}$
Split D into $\lceil n/m \rceil$ minibatches $D_1 \ldots D_{\lceil n/m \rceil}$
repeat
  for $i \leftarrow 1 \ldots \lceil n/m \rceil$ **do** ▷ for each minibatch
    $C \leftarrow \cup_{(x,y) \in D_i}$ FINDCONSTRAINTS$(x, y, \mathbf{w})$
    if $C \neq \emptyset$ **then** UPDATE$(\mathbf{w}, C)$ ▷ batch update
until converged

A training set D is **separable** by feature map $\boldsymbol{\Phi}$ with **margin** $\delta > 0$ if there exists a unit oracle vector $\mathbf{u}$ with $\|\mathbf{u}\| = 1$ such that $\mathbf{u} \cdot \Delta\boldsymbol{\Phi}(\langle x, y, z\rangle) \geq \delta$, for all $\langle x, y, z\rangle \in C(D)$. Furthermore, let radius $R \geq \|\Delta\boldsymbol{\Phi}(\langle x, y, z\rangle)\|$ for all $\langle x, y, z\rangle \in C(D)$.

Theorem 1. *For a separable dataset D with margin δ and radius R, the minibatch perceptron algorithm (Algorithms 4 and 2) will terminate after t minibatch updates where $t \leq R^2/\delta^2$.*

Proof. Let $\mathbf{w}^t$ be the weight vector **before** the tth update; $\mathbf{w}^0 = \mathbf{0}$. Suppose the tth update happens on the constraint set $C_t = \{c_1, c_2, \ldots, c_a\}$ where $a = |C_t|$, and each $c_i = \langle x_i, y_i, z_i\rangle$. We convert them to the set of update vectors $\mathbf{v}_i = \Delta\boldsymbol{\Phi}(c_i) = \Delta\boldsymbol{\Phi}(\langle x_i, y_i, z_i\rangle)$ for all i. We know that:

1. $\mathbf{u} \cdot \mathbf{v}_i \geq \delta$ (margin on unit oracle vector)
2. $\mathbf{w}^t \cdot \mathbf{v}_i \leq 0$ (violation: z_i dominates y_i)
3. $\|\mathbf{v}_i\|^2 \leq R^2$ (radius)

Now the update looks like

$$\mathbf{w}^{t+1} = \mathbf{w}^t + \frac{1}{|C_t|} \sum_{c \in C_t} \Delta\boldsymbol{\Phi}(c) = \mathbf{w}^t + \frac{1}{a} \textstyle\sum_i \mathbf{v}_i. \tag{1}$$

We will bound $\|\mathbf{w}^{t+1}\|$ from two directions:

1. Dot product both sides of the update equation (1) with the unit oracle vector $\mathbf{u}$, we have

$$\begin{aligned} \mathbf{u} \cdot \mathbf{w}^{t+1} &= \mathbf{u} \cdot \mathbf{w}^t + \frac{1}{a} \textstyle\sum_i \mathbf{u} \cdot \mathbf{v}_i \\ &\geq \mathbf{u} \cdot \mathbf{w}^t + \frac{1}{a} \textstyle\sum_i \delta && \text{(margin)} \\ &= \mathbf{u} \cdot \mathbf{w}^t + \delta && (\textstyle\sum_i = a) \\ &\geq t\delta && \text{(by induction)} \end{aligned}$$

Since for any two vectors $\mathbf{a}$ and $\mathbf{b}$ we have $\|\mathbf{a}\|\|\mathbf{b}\| \geq \mathbf{a}\cdot\mathbf{b}$, thus $\|\mathbf{u}\|\|\mathbf{w}^{t+1}\| \geq \mathbf{u}\cdot\mathbf{w}^{t+1} \geq t\delta$. As $\mathbf{u}$ is a unit vector, we have $\|\mathbf{w}^{t+1}\| \geq t\delta$.

2. On the other hand, take the norm of both sides of Eq. (1):

$$\begin{aligned}
\|\mathbf{w}^{t+1}\|^2 &= \|\mathbf{w}^t + \frac{1}{a}\textstyle\sum_i \mathbf{v}_i\|^2 \\
=&\|\mathbf{w}^t\|^2 + \|\textstyle\sum_i \frac{1}{a}\mathbf{v}_i\|^2 + \frac{2}{a}\,\mathbf{w}^t\cdot\textstyle\sum_i \mathbf{v}_i \\
\leq&\|\mathbf{w}^t\|^2 + \|\textstyle\sum_i \frac{1}{a}\mathbf{v}_i\|^2 + 0 && \text{(violation)} \\
\leq&\|\mathbf{w}^t\|^2 + \textstyle\sum_i \frac{1}{a}\|\mathbf{v}_i\|^2 && \text{(Jensen's)} \\
\leq&\|\mathbf{w}^t\|^2 + \textstyle\sum_i \frac{1}{a}R^2 && \text{(radius)} \\
=&\|\mathbf{w}^t\|^2 + R^2 && (\textstyle\sum_i = a) \\
\leq& tR^2 && \text{(by induction)}
\end{aligned}$$

Combining the two bounds, we have

$$t^2\delta^2 \leq \|\mathbf{w}^{t+1}\|^2 \leq tR^2$$

thus the number of minibatch updates $t \leq R^2/\delta^2$. □

Note that this bound is identical to that of pure online perceptron (Collins, 2002, Theorem 1) and is irrelevant to minibatch size m. The use of Jensen's inequality is inspired by McDonald et al. (2010).

3.2 Convergence of Minibatch MIRA

We also give a proof of convergence for MIRA with relaxation.[2] We present the optimization problem in the UPDATE function of Algorithm 3 as a quadratic program (QP) with slack variable ξ:

$$\begin{aligned}
\mathbf{w}^{t+1} \leftarrow & \underset{\mathbf{w}^{t+1}}{\mathbf{argmin}} \|\mathbf{w}^{t+1} - \mathbf{w}^t\|^2 + \xi \\
& \text{s.t. } \mathbf{w}^{t+1}\cdot\mathbf{v}_i \geq \ell_i - \xi, \text{ for all}(c_i, \ell_i) \in C_t
\end{aligned}$$

where $\mathbf{v}_i = \Delta\mathbf{\Phi}(c_i)$ is the update vector for constraint c_i. Consider the Lagrangian:

$$\begin{aligned}
\mathcal{L} =& \|\mathbf{w}^{t+1} - \mathbf{w}^t\|^2 + \xi + \sum_{i=1}^{|C_t|} \eta_i(\ell_i - \mathbf{w}'\cdot\mathbf{v}_i - \xi) \\
& \eta_i \geq 0, \text{ for } 1 \leq i \leq |C_t|.
\end{aligned}$$

[2]Actually this relaxation is *not* necessary for the convergence proof. We employ it here solely to make the proof shorter. It is *not* used in the experiments either.

Set the partial derivatives to 0 with respect to $\mathbf{w}'$ and ξ we have:

$$\mathbf{w}' = \mathbf{w} + \textstyle\sum_i \eta_i \mathbf{v}_i \tag{2}$$

$$\textstyle\sum_i \eta_i = 1 \tag{3}$$

This result suggests that the weight change can always be represnted by a linear combination of the update vectors (i.e. normal vectors of the constraint hyperplanes), with the linear coefficencies sum to 1.

Theorem 2 (convergence of minibatch MIRA)**.** *For a separable dataset D with margin δ and radius R, the minibatch MIRA algorithm (Algorithm 4 and 3) will make t updates where $t \leq R^2/\delta^2$.*

Proof. 1. Dot product both sides of Equation 2 with unit oracle vector $\mathbf{u}$:

$$\begin{aligned}
\mathbf{u}\cdot\mathbf{w}^{t+1} &= \mathbf{u}\cdot\mathbf{w}^t + \textstyle\sum_i \eta_i \mathbf{u}\cdot\mathbf{v}_i \\
\geq& \mathbf{u}\cdot\mathbf{w}^t + \textstyle\sum_i \eta_i\delta && \text{(margin)} \\
=& \mathbf{u}\cdot\mathbf{w}^t + \delta && \text{(Eq. 3)} \\
=& t\delta && \text{(by induction)}
\end{aligned}$$

2. On the other hand

$$\begin{aligned}
\|\mathbf{w}^{t+1}\|^2 &= \|\mathbf{w}^t + \textstyle\sum_i \eta_i\mathbf{v}_i\|^2 \\
=&\|\mathbf{w}^t\|^2 + \|\textstyle\sum_i \eta_i\mathbf{v}_i\|^2 + 2\,\mathbf{w}^t\cdot\textstyle\sum_i \eta_i\mathbf{v}_i \\
\leq&\|\mathbf{w}^t\|^2 + \|\textstyle\sum_i \eta_i\mathbf{v}_i\|^2 + 0 && \text{(violation)} \\
\leq&\|\mathbf{w}^t\|^2 + \textstyle\sum_i \eta_i\mathbf{v}_i^2 && \text{(Jensen's)} \\
\leq&\|\mathbf{w}^t\|^2 + \textstyle\sum_i \eta_i R^2 && \text{(radius)} \\
=&\|\mathbf{w}^t\|^2 + R^2 && \text{(Eq. 3)} \\
\leq& tR^2 && \text{(by induction)}
\end{aligned}$$

From the two bounds we have:

$$t^2\delta^2 \leq \|\mathbf{w}^{t+1}\|^2 \leq tR^2$$

thus within at most $t \leq R^2/\delta^2$ minibatch updates MIRA will converge.

□

4 Parallelized Minibatch

The key insight into parallelization is that the calculation of constraints (i.e. decoding) for each example within a minibatch is completely independent of

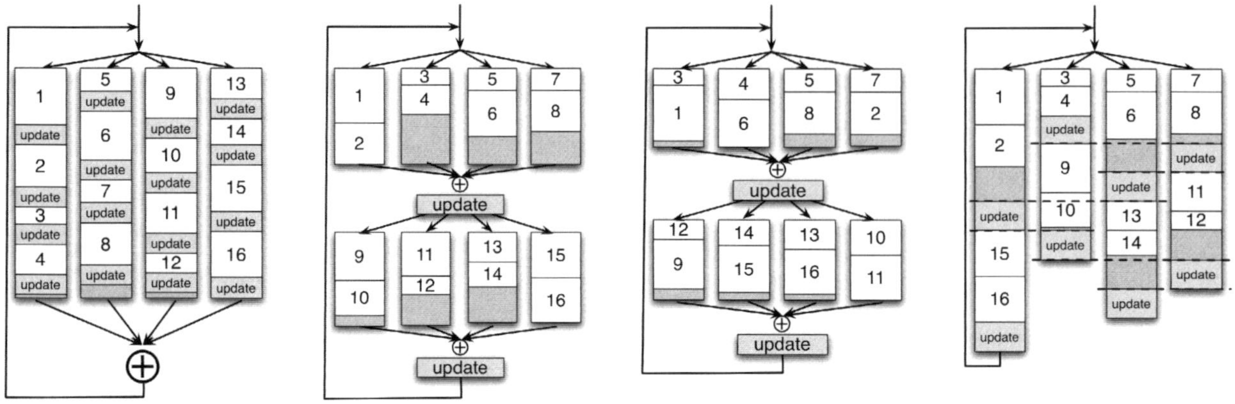

(a) IPM (b) unbalanced (c) balanced (d) asynchronous

Figure 1: Comparison of various methods for parallelizing online learning (number of processors $p = 4$). (a) iterative parameter mixing (McDonald et al., 2010). (b) unbalanced minibatch parallelization (minibatch size $m = 8$). (c) minibatch parallelization after load-balancing (within each minibatch). (d) asynchronous minibatch parallelization (Gimpel et al., 2010) (not implemented here). Each numbered box denotes the decoding of one example, and $\oplus$ denotes an aggregate operation, i.e., the merging of constraints after each minibatch or the mixing of weights after each iteration in IPM. Each gray shaded box denotes time wasted due to synchronization in (a)-(c) or blocking in (d). Note that in (d) at most one update can happen concurrently, making it substantially harder to implement than (a)-(c).

Algorithm 5 Parallized Minibatch Online Learning.

Input: D, $\mathbf{\Phi}$, minibatch size m, and # of processors p
Output: weight vector $\mathbf{w}$
Split D into $\lceil n/m \rceil$ minibatches $D_1 \ldots D_{\lceil n/m \rceil}$
Split each D_i into m/p groups $D_{i,1} \ldots D_{i,m/p}$
repeat
  for $i \leftarrow 1 \ldots \lceil n/m \rceil$ **do** ▷ for each minibatch
    for $j \leftarrow 1 \ldots m/p$ **in parallel do**
      $C_j \leftarrow \cup_{(x,y)\in D_{i,j}} \textsc{FindConstraints}(x, y, \mathbf{w})$
    $C \leftarrow \cup_j C_j$ ▷ in serial
    if $C \neq \emptyset$ **then** $\textsc{Update}(\mathbf{w}, C)$ ▷ in serial
until converged

other examples in the same batch. Thus we can easily distribute decoding for different examples in the same minibatch to different processors.

Shown in Algorithm 5, for each minibatch D_i, we split D_i into groups of equal size, and assign each group to a processor to decode. After all processors finish, we collect all constraints and do an update based on the union of all constraints. Figure 1 (b) illustrates minibatch parallelization, with comparison to iterative parameter mixing (IPM) of McDonald et al. (2010) (see Figure 1 (a)).

This synchronous parallelization framework should provide significant speedups over the serial mode. However, in each minibatch, inevitably, some processors will end up waiting for others to finish, especially when the lengths of sentences vary substantially (see the shaded area in Figure 1 (b)).

To alleviate this problem, we propose "**per-minibatch load-balancing**", which rearranges the sentences within each minibatch based on their lengths (which correlate with their decoding times) so that the total workload on each processor is balanced (Figure 1c). It is important to note that this shuffling does **not** affect learning at all thanks to the independence of each example within a minibatch. Basically, we put the shortest and longest sentences into the first thread, the second shortest and second longest into the second thread, etc. Although this is not necessary optimal scheduling, it works well in practice. As long as decoding time is linear in the length of sentence (as in incremental parsing or tagging), we expect a much smaller variance in processing time on each processor in one minibatch, which is confirmed in the experiments (see Figure 8).[3]

[3]In IPM, however, the waiting time is negligible, since the workload on each processor is almost balanced, analogous to a huge minibatch (Fig. 1a). Furthermore, shuffling *does* affect learning here since each thread in IPM is a pure online learner. So our IPM implementation does *not* use load-balancing.

5 Experiments

We conduct experiments on two typical structured prediction problems: incremental dependency parsing and part-of-speech tagging; both are done on state-of-the-art baseline. We also compare our parallelized minibatch algorithm with the iterative parameter mixing (IPM) method of McDonald et al. (2010). We perform our experiments on a commodity 64-bit Dell Precision T7600 workstation with two 3.1GHz 8-core CPUs (16 processors in total) and 64GB RAM. We use Python 2.7's `multiprocessing` module in all experiments.[4]

5.1 Dependency Parsing with MIRA

We base our experiments on our dynamic programming incremental dependency parser (Huang and Sagae, 2010).[5] Following Huang et al. (2012), we use max-violation update and beam size $b = 8$. We evaluate on the standard Penn Treebank (PTB) using the standard split: Sections 02-21 for training, and Section 22 as the held-out set (which is indeed the test-set in this setting, following McDonald et al. (2010) and Gimpel et al. (2010)). We then extend it to employ 1-best MIRA learning. As stated in Section 2, MIRA separates the gold label y from the incorrect label z with a margin at least as large as the loss $\ell(y, z)$. Here in incremental dependency parsing we define the loss function between a gold tree y and an incorrect *partial* tree z as the number of incorrect edges in z, plus the number of correct edges in y which are already ruled out by z. This MIRA extension results in slightly higher accuracy of 92.36, which we will use as the pure online learning baseline in the comparisons below.

5.1.1 Serial Minibatch

We first run minibatch in the serial mode with varying minibatch size of 4, 16, 24, 32, and 48 (see Figure 2). We can make the following observations. First, except for the largest minibatch size of 48, minibatch learning generally improves the accuracy

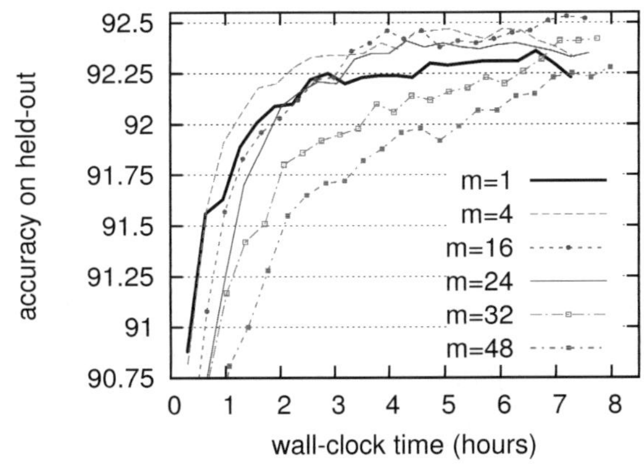

Figure 2: Minibatch with various minibatch sizes ($m = 4, 16, 24, 32, 48$) for parsing with MIRA, compared to pure MIRA ($m = 1$). All curves are on a single CPU.

of the converged model, which is explained by our intuition that optimization with a larger constraint set could improve the margin. In particular, $m = 16$ achieves the highest accuracy of 92.53, which is a 0.27 improvement over the baseline.

Secondly, minibatch learning can reach high levels of accuracy faster than the baseline can. For example, minibatch of size 4 can reach 92.35 in 3.5 hours, and minibatch of size 24 in 3.7 hours, while the pure online baseline needs 6.9 hours. In other words, just minibatch alone in serial mode can already speed up learning. This is also explained by the intuition of better optimization above, and contributes significantly to the final speedup of parallelized minibatch.

Lastly, larger minibatch sizes slow down the convergence, with $m = 4$ converging the fastest and $m = 48$ the slowest. This can be explained by the trade-off between the relative strengths from online learning and batch update: with larger batch sizes, we lose the dependencies between examples within the same minibatch.

Although larger minibatches slow down convergence, they actually offer better potential for parallelization since the number of processors p has to be smaller than minibatch size m (in fact, p should divide m). For example, $m = 24$ can work with 2, 3, 4, 6, 8, or 12 processors while $m = 4$ can only work with 2 or 4 and the speed up of 12 processors could easily make up for the slightly slower convergence

[4] We **turn off garbage-collection** in worker processes otherwise their running times will be highly unbalanced. We also admit that Python is not the best choice for parallelization, e.g., asychronous minibatch (Gimpel et al., 2010) requires "shared memory" not found in the current Python (see also Sec. 6).

[5] Available at `http://acl.cs.qc.edu/`. The version with minibatch parallelization will be available there soon.

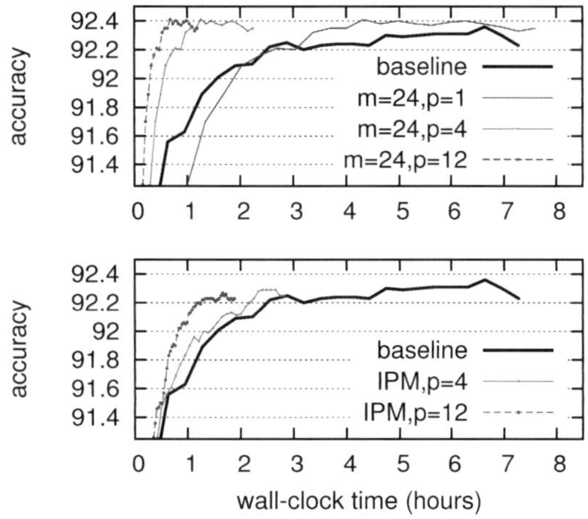

Figure 3: Parallelized minibatch is much faster than iterative parameter mixing. Top: minibatch of size 24 using 4 and 12 processors offers significant speedups over the serial minibatch and pure online baselines. Bottom: IPM with the same processors offers very small speedups.

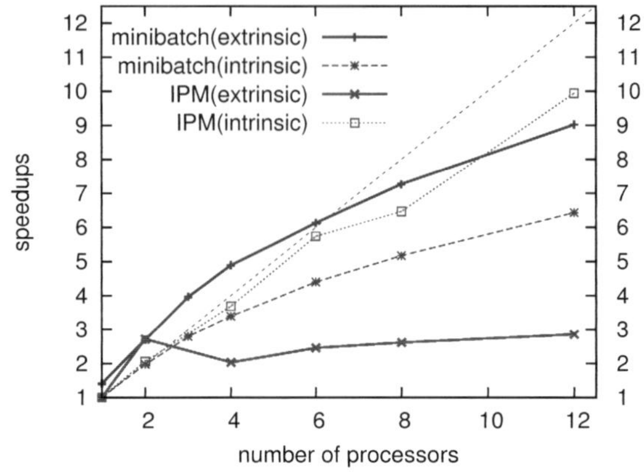

Figure 4: Speedups of minibatch parallelization vs. IPM on 1 to 12 processors (parsing with MIRA). Extrinsic comparisons use "the time to reach an accuracy of 92.27" for speed calculations, 92.27 being the converged accuracy of IPM using 12 processors. Intrinsic comparisons use average time per iteration regardless of accuracy.

rate. So there seems to be a "sweetspot" of minibatch sizes, similar to the tipping point observed in McDonald et al. (2010) when adding more processors starts to hurt convergence.

5.1.2 Parallelized Minibatch vs. IPM

In the following experiments we use minibatch size of $m = 24$ and run it in parallel mode on various numbers of processors ($p = 2 \sim 12$). Figure 3 (top) shows that 4 and 12 processors lead to very significant speedups over the serial minibatch and pure online baselines. For example, it takes the 12 processors only 0.66 hours to reach an accuracy of 92.35, which takes the pure online MIRA 6.9 hours, amounting to an impressive speedup of 10.5.

We compare our minibatch parallelization with the iterative parameter mixing (IPM) of McDonald et al. (2010). Figure 3 (bottom) shows that IPM not only offers much smaller speedups, but also converges lower, and this drop in accuracy worsens with more processors.

Figure 4 gives a detailed analysis of speedups. Here we perform both extrinsic and intrinsic comparisons. In the former, we care about the time to reach a given accuracy; in this plot we use 92.27 which is the converged accuracy of IPM on 12 processors. We choose it since it is the lowest accuracy among all converged models; choosing a higher accuracy would reveal even larger speedups for our methods. This figure shows that our method offers superlinear speedups with small number of processors (1 to 6), and almost linear speedups with large number of processors (8 and 12). Note that even $p = 1$ offers a speedup of 1.5 thanks to serial minibatch's faster convergence; in other words, within the 9 fold speed-up at $p = 12$, parallelization contributes about 6 and minibatch about 1.5. By contrast, IPM only offers an almost constant speedup of around 3, which is consistent with the findings of McDonald et al. (2010) (both of their experiments show a speedup of around 3).

We also try to understand where the speedup comes from. For that purpose we study **intrinsic speedup**, which is about the speed regardless of accuracy (see Figure 4). For our minibatch method, intrinsic speedup is the average time per iteration of a parallel run over the serial minibatch baseline. This answers the questions such as "how CPU-efficient is our parallelization" or "how much CPU time is wasted". We can see that with small number of processors (2 to 4), the **efficiency**, defined as S_p/p where S_p is the intrinsic speedup for p processors, is almost 100% (ideal linear speedup), but with more processors it decreases to around 50% with $p = 12$, meaning about half of CPU time is

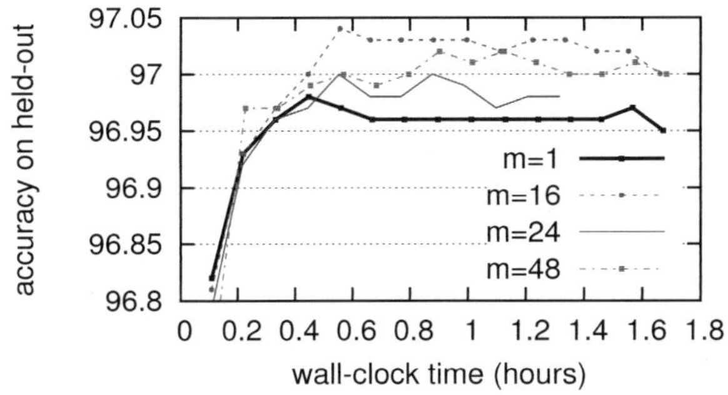

Figure 5: Minibatch learning for tagging with perceptron ($m = 16, 24, 32$) compared with baseline ($m = 1$) for tagging with perceptron. All curves are on single CPU.

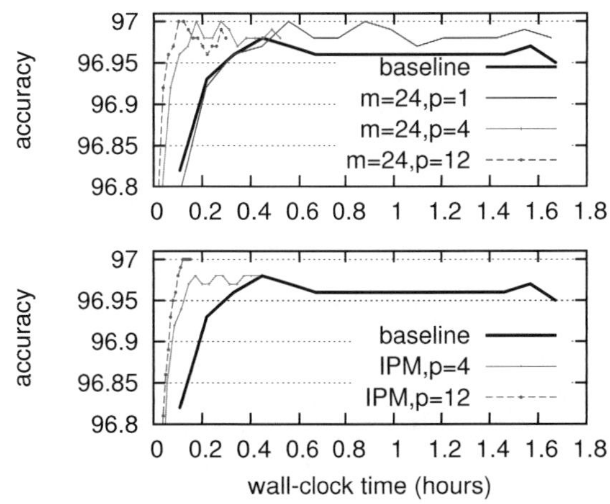

Figure 6: Parallelized minibatch is faster than iterative parameter mixing (on tagging with perceptron). Top: minibatch of size 24 using 4 and 12 processors offers significant speedups over the baselines. Bottom: IPM with the same 4 and 12 processors offers slightly smaller speedups. Note that IPM with 4 processors converges lower than other parallelization curves.

wasted. This wasting is due to two sources: first, the load-balancing problem worsens with more processors, and secondly, the update procedure still runs in serial mode with $p - 1$ processors sleeping.

5.2 Part-of-Speech Tagging with Perceptron

Part-of-speech tagging is usually considered as a simpler task compared to dependency parsing. Here we show that using minibatch can also bring better accuracies and speedups for part-of-speech tagging.

We implement a part-of-speech tagger with averaged perceptron. Following the standard splitting of Penn Treebank (Collins, 2002), we use Sections 00-18 for training and Sections 19-21 as held-out. Our implementation provides an accuracy of 96.98 with beam size 8.

First we run the tagger on a single processor with minibatch sizes 8, 16, 24, and 32. As in Figure 5, we observe similar convergence acceleration and higher accuracies with minibatch. In particular, minibatch of size $m = 16$ provides the highest accuracy of 97.04, giving an improvement of 0.06. This improvement is smaller than what we observe in MIRA learning for dependency parsing experiments, which can be partly explained by the fast convergence of the tagger, and that perceptron does not involve optimization in the updates.

Then we choose minibatch of size 24 to investigate the parallelization performance. As Figure 6 (top) shows, with 12 processors our method takes only 0.10 hours to converge to an accuracy of 97.00, compared to the baseline of 96.98 with 0.45 hours. We also compare our method with IPM as in Figure 6 (bottom). Again, our method converges faster and better than IPM, but this time the differences are much smaller than those in parsing.

Figure 7 uses 96.97 as a criteria to evaluate the extrinsic speedups given by our method and IPM. Again we choose this number because it is the lowest accuracy all learners can reach. As the figure suggests, although our method does not have a higher pure parallelization speedup (intrinsic speedup), it still outperforms IPM.

We are interested in the reason why tagging benefits less from minibatch and parallelization compared to parsing. Further investigation reveals that in tagging the working load of different processors are more unbalanced than in parsing. Figure 8 shows that, when p is small, waiting time is negligible, but when $p = 12$, tagging wastes about 40% of CPU cycles and parser about 30%. By contrast, there is almost no waiting time in IPM and the intrinsic speedup for IPM is almost linear. The communication overhead is not included in this figure, but by comparing it to the speedups (Figures 4 and 7), we conclude that the communication overhead is about 10% for both parsing and tagging at $p = 12$.

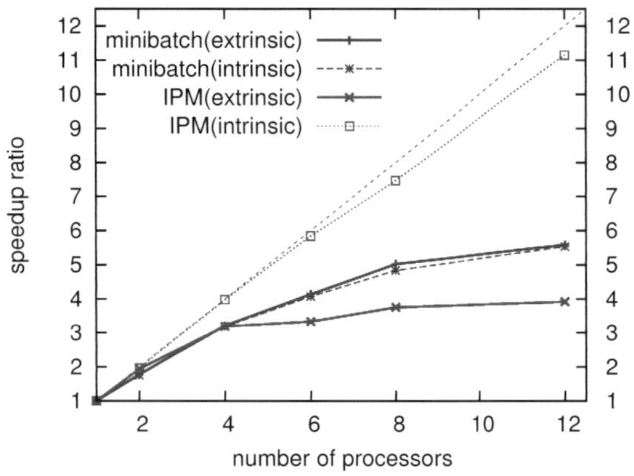

Figure 7: Speedups of minibatch parallelization and IPM on 1 to 12 processors (tagging with perceptron). Extrinsic speedup uses "the time to reach an accuracy of 96.97" as the criterion to measure speed. Intrinsic speedup measures the pure parallelization speedup. IPM has an almost linear intrinsic speedup but a near constant extrinsic speedup of about 3 to 4.

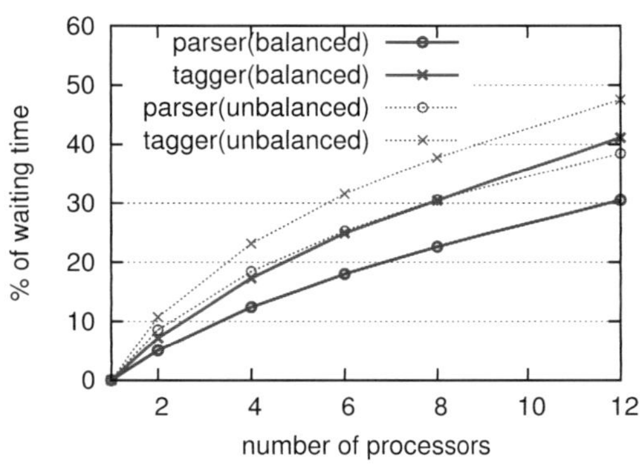

Figure 8: Percentage of time wasted due to synchronization (waiting for other processors to finish) (minibatch $m = 24$), which corresponds to the gray blocks in Figure 1 (b-c). The number of sentences assigned to each processor decreases with more processors, which worsens the unbalance. Our load-balancing strategy (Figure 1 (c)) alleviates this problem effectively. The communication overhead and update time are **not** included.

6 Related Work and Discussions

Besides synchronous minibatch and iterative parameter mixing (IPM) discussed above, there is another method of asychronous minibatch parallelization (Zinkevich et al., 2009; Gimpel et al., 2010; Chiang, 2012), as in Figure 1. The key advantage of asynchronous over synchronous minibatch is that the former allows processors to remain near-constant use, while the latter wastes a significant amount of time when some processors finish earlier than others in a minibatch, as found in our experiments. Gimpel et al. (2010) show significant speedups of asychronous parallelization over synchronous minibatch on SGD and EM methods, and Chiang (2012) finds asynchronous parallelization to be much faster than IPM on MIRA for machine translation. However, asynchronous is significantly more complicated to implement, which involves locking when one processor makes an update (see Fig. 1 (d)), and (in languages like Python) message-passing to other processors after update. Whether this added complexity is worthwhile on large-margin learning is an open question.

7 Conclusions and Future Work

We have presented a simple minibatch parallelization paradigm to speed up large-margin structured learning algorithms such as (averaged) perceptron and MIRA. Minibatch has an advantage in both serial and parallel settings, and our experiments confirmed that a minibatch size of around 16 or 24 leads to a significant speedups over the pure online baseline, and when combined with parallelization, leads to almost linear speedups for MIRA, and very significant speedups for perceptron. These speedups are significantly higher than those of iterative parameter mixing of McDonald et al. (2010) which were almost constant (3$\sim$4) in both our and their own experiments regardless of the number of processors.

One of the limitations of this work is that although decoding is done in parallel, update is still done in serial and in MIRA the quadratic optimization step (Hildreth algorithm (Hildreth, 1957)) scales superlinearly with the number of constraints. This prevents us from using very large minibatches. For future work, we would like to explore parallelized quadratic optimization and larger minibatch sizes, and eventually apply it to machine translation.

Acknowledgement

We thank Ryan McDonald, Yoav Goldberg, and Hal Daumé, III for helpful discussions, and the anonymous reviewers for suggestions. This work was partially supported by DARPA FA8750-13-2-0041 "Deep Exploration and Filtering of Text" (DEFT) Program and by Queens College for equipment.

References

David Chiang. 2012. Hope and fear for discriminative training of statistical translation models. *J. Machine Learning Research (JMLR)*, 13:1159–1187.

C.-T. Chu, S.-K. Kim, Y.-A. Lin, Y.-Y. Yu, G. Bradski, A. Ng, and K. Olukotun. 2007. Map-reduce for machine learning on multicore. In *Advances in Neural Information Processing Systems 19*.

Michael Collins and Brian Roark. 2004. Incremental parsing with the perceptron algorithm. In *Proceedings of ACL*.

Michael Collins. 2002. Discriminative training methods for hidden markov models: Theory and experiments with perceptron algorithms. In *Proceedings of EMNLP*.

Koby Crammer and Yoram Singer. 2003. Ultraconservative online algorithms for multiclass problems. *J. Mach. Learn. Res.*, 3:951–991, March.

Jenny Rose Finkel, Alex Kleeman, and Christopher D. Manning. 2008. Efficient, feature-based, conditional random field parsing. In *Proceedings of ACL*.

Kevin Gimpel, Dipanjan Das, and Noah Smith. 2010. Distributed asynchronous online learning for natural language processing. In *Proceedings of CoNLL*.

Clifford Hildreth. 1957. A quadratic programming procedure. *Naval Research Logistics Quarterly*, 4(1):79–85.

Liang Huang and Kenji Sagae. 2010. Dynamic programming for linear-time incremental parsing. In *Proceedings of ACL 2010*.

Liang Huang, Suphan Fayong, and Yang Guo. 2012. Structured perceptron with inexact search. In *Proceedings of NAACL*.

John Lafferty, Andrew McCallum, and Fernando Pereira. 2001. Conditional random fields: Probabilistic models for segmenting and labeling sequence data. In *Proceedings of ICML*.

Percy Liang and Dan Klein. 2009. Online em for unsupervised models. In *Proceedings of NAACL*.

Ryan McDonald and Fernando Pereira. 2006. Online learning of approximate dependency parsing algorithms. In *Proceedings of EACL*.

Ryan McDonald, Koby Crammer, and Fernando Pereira. 2005. Online large-margin training of dependency parsers. In *Proceedings of the 43rd ACL*.

Ryan McDonald, Keith Hall, and Gideon Mann. 2010. Distributed training strategies for the structured perceptron. In *Proceedings of NAACL*, June.

Shai Shalev-Shwartz, Yoram Singer, and Nathan Srebro. 2007. Pegasos: Primal estimated sub-gradient solver for svm. In *Proceedings of ICML*.

M. Zinkevich, A. J. Smola, and J. Langford. 2009. Slow learners are fast. In *Advances in Neural Information Processing Systems 22*.

Improved Part-of-Speech Tagging for Online Conversational Text with Word Clusters

Olutobi Owoputi* **Brendan O'Connor*** **Chris Dyer***
Kevin Gimpel† **Nathan Schneider*** **Noah A. Smith***
*School of Computer Science, Carnegie Mellon University, Pittsburgh, PA 15213, USA
†Toyota Technological Institute at Chicago, Chicago, IL 60637, USA
Corresponding author: `brenocon@cs.cmu.edu`

Abstract

We consider the problem of part-of-speech tagging for informal, online conversational text. We systematically evaluate the use of large-scale unsupervised word clustering and new lexical features to improve tagging accuracy. With these features, our system achieves state-of-the-art tagging results on both Twitter and IRC POS tagging tasks; Twitter tagging is improved from 90% to 93% accuracy (more than 3% absolute). Qualitative analysis of these word clusters yields insights about NLP and linguistic phenomena in this genre. Additionally, we contribute the first POS annotation guidelines for such text and release a new dataset of English language tweets annotated using these guidelines. Tagging software, annotation guidelines, and large-scale word clusters are available at: **`http://www.ark.cs.cmu.edu/TweetNLP`** This paper describes release 0.3 of the "CMU Twitter Part-of-Speech Tagger" and annotated data.

ikr	smh	he	asked	fir	yo	last
!	G	O	V	P	D	A
name	so	he	can	add	u	on
N	P	O	V	V	O	P
fb	lololol					
^	!					

Figure 1: Automatically tagged tweet showing nonstandard orthography, capitalization, and abbreviation. Ignoring the interjections and abbreviations, it glosses as *He asked for your last name so he can add you on Facebook.* The tagset is defined in Appendix A. Refer to Fig. 2 for word clusters corresponding to some of these words.

1 Introduction

Online conversational text, typified by microblogs, chat, and text messages,[1] is a challenge for natural language processing. Unlike the highly edited genres that conventional NLP tools have been developed for, conversational text contains many nonstandard lexical items and syntactic patterns. These are the result of unintentional errors, dialectal variation, conversational ellipsis, topic diversity, and creative use of language and orthography (Eisenstein, 2013). An example is shown in Fig. 1. As a result of this widespread variation, standard modeling assumptions that depend on lexical, syntactic, and orthographic regularity are inappropriate. There is preliminary work on social media part-of-speech (POS) tagging (Gimpel et al., 2011), named entity recognition (Ritter et al., 2011; Liu et al., 2011), and parsing (Foster et al., 2011), but accuracy rates are still significantly lower than traditional well-edited genres like newswire. Even web text parsing, which is a comparatively easier genre than social media, lags behind newspaper text (Petrov and McDonald, 2012), as does speech transcript parsing (McClosky et al., 2010).

To tackle the challenge of novel words and constructions, we create a new Twitter part-of-speech tagger—building on previous work by Gimpel et al. (2011)—that includes new large-scale distributional features. This leads to state-of-the-art results in POS tagging for both Twitter and Internet Relay Chat (IRC) text. We also annotated a new dataset of tweets with POS tags, improved the annotations in the previous dataset from Gimpel et al., and developed annotation guidelines for manual POS tagging of tweets. We release all of these resources to the research community:

- an open-source part-of-speech tagger for online conversational text (§2);
- unsupervised Twitter word clusters (§3);
- an improved emoticon detector for conversational text (§4);

[1] Also referred to as *computer-mediated communication*.

- POS annotation guidelines (§5.1); and
- a new dataset of 547 manually POS-annotated tweets (§5).

2 MEMM Tagger

Our tagging model is a first-order maximum entropy Markov model (MEMM), a discriminative sequence model for which training and decoding are extremely efficient (Ratnaparkhi, 1996; McCallum et al., 2000).[2] The probability of a tag y_t is conditioned on the input sequence $\boldsymbol{x}$ and the tag to its left y_{t-1}, and is parameterized by a multiclass logistic regression:

$$p(y_t = k \mid y_{t-1}, \boldsymbol{x}, t; \boldsymbol{\beta}) \propto \exp\left(\beta^{(trans)}_{y_{t-1},k} + \sum_j \beta^{(obs)}_{j,k} f_j(\boldsymbol{x}, t)\right)$$

We use transition features for every pair of labels, and extract base observation features from token t and neighboring tokens, and conjoin them against all $K = 25$ possible outputs in our coarse tagset (Appendix A). Our feature sets will be discussed below in detail.

Decoding. For experiments reported in this paper, we use the $O(|\boldsymbol{x}|K^2)$ Viterbi algorithm for prediction; K is the number of tags. This exactly maximizes $p(\boldsymbol{y} \mid \boldsymbol{x})$, but the MEMM also naturally allows a faster $O(|\boldsymbol{x}|K)$ left-to-right greedy decoding:

for $t = 1 \ldots |\boldsymbol{x}|$:
$\quad \hat{y}_t \leftarrow \arg\max_k p(y_t = k \mid \hat{y}_{t-1}, \boldsymbol{x}, t; \boldsymbol{\beta})$

which we find is 3 times faster and yields similar accuracy as Viterbi (an insignificant accuracy decrease of less than 0.1% absolute on the DAILY547 test set discussed below). Speed is paramount for social media analysis applications—which often require the processing of millions to billions of messages—so we make greedy decoding the default in the released software.

This greedy tagger runs at 800 tweets/sec. (10,000 tokens/sec.) on a single CPU core, about 40 times faster than Gimpel et al.'s system. The tokenizer by itself (§4) runs at 3,500 tweets/sec.[3]

Training and regularization. During training, the MEMM log-likelihood for a tagged tweet $\langle \boldsymbol{x}, \boldsymbol{y} \rangle$ is the sum over the observed token tags y_t, each conditional on the tweet being tagged and the observed previous tag (with a start symbol before the first token in $\boldsymbol{x}$),

$$\ell(\boldsymbol{x}, \boldsymbol{y}, \boldsymbol{\beta}) = \sum_{t=1}^{|\boldsymbol{x}|} \log p(y_t \mid y_{t-1}, \boldsymbol{x}, t; \boldsymbol{\beta}).$$

We optimize the parameters $\boldsymbol{\beta}$ with OWL-QN, an L_1-capable variant of L-BFGS (Andrew and Gao, 2007; Liu and Nocedal, 1989) to minimize the regularized objective

$$\arg\min_{\boldsymbol{\beta}} \; -\tfrac{1}{N} \sum_{\langle \boldsymbol{x}, \boldsymbol{y} \rangle} \ell(\boldsymbol{x}, \boldsymbol{y}, \boldsymbol{\beta}) + R(\boldsymbol{\beta})$$

where N is the number of tokens in the corpus and the sum ranges over all tagged tweets $\langle \boldsymbol{x}, \boldsymbol{y} \rangle$ in the training data. We use elastic net regularization (Zou and Hastie, 2005), which is a linear combination of L_1 and L_2 penalties; here j indexes over all features:

$$R(\boldsymbol{\beta}) = \lambda_1 \sum_j |\beta_j| + \tfrac{1}{2}\lambda_2 \sum_j \beta_j^2$$

Using even a very small L_1 penalty eliminates many irrelevant or noisy features.

3 Unsupervised Word Clusters

Our POS tagger can make use of any number of possibly overlapping features. While we have only a small amount of hand-labeled data for training, we also have access to billions of tokens of *unlabeled* conversational text from the web. Previous work has shown that unlabeled text can be used to induce unsupervised word clusters which can improve the performance of many supervised NLP tasks (Koo et al., 2008; Turian et al., 2010; Täckström et al., 2012, *inter alia*). We use a similar approach here to improve tagging performance for online conversational text. We also make our induced clusters publicly available in the hope that they will be useful for other NLP tasks in this genre.

[2] Although when compared to CRFs, MEMMs theoretically suffer from the "label bias" problem (Lafferty et al., 2001), our system substantially outperforms the CRF-based taggers of previous work; and when comparing to Gimpel et al. system with similar feature sets, we observed little difference in accuracy. This is consistent with conventional wisdom that the quality of lexical features is much more important than the parametric form of the sequence model, at least in our setting: part-of-speech tagging with a small labeled training set.

[3] Runtimes observed on an Intel Core i5 2.4 GHz laptop.

<table>
<tr><th></th><th>Binary path</th><th>Top words (by frequency)</th></tr>
<tr><td>A1</td><td>111010100010</td><td>lmao lmfao lmaoo lmaooo hahahahaha lool ctfu rofl loool lmfaoo lmfaooo lmaoooo lmbo lololol</td></tr>
<tr><td>A2</td><td>111010100011</td><td>haha hahaha hehe hahahaha hahah aha hehehe ahaha hah hahahah kk hahaa ahah</td></tr>
<tr><td>A3</td><td>111010100100</td><td>yes yep yup nope yess yesss yessss ofcourse yeap likewise yepp yesh yw yuup yus</td></tr>
<tr><td>A4</td><td>111010100101</td><td>yeah yea nah naw yeahh nooo yeh noo noooo yeaa ikr nvm yeahhh nahh nooooo</td></tr>
<tr><td>A5</td><td>11101011011100</td><td>smh jk #fail #random #fact smfh #smh #winning #realtalk smdh #dead #justsaying</td></tr>
<tr><td>B</td><td>011101011</td><td>u yu yuh yhu uu yuu yew y0u yuhh youh yhuu iget yoy yooh yuo [illegible] yue juu Ʊ dya youz yyou</td></tr>
<tr><td>C</td><td>11100101111001</td><td>w fo fa fr fro ov fer fir whit abou aft serie fore fah fuh w/her w/that fron isn agains</td></tr>
<tr><td>D</td><td>111101011000</td><td>facebook fb itunes myspace skype ebay tumblr bbm flickr aim msn netflix pandora</td></tr>
<tr><td>E1</td><td>0011001</td><td>tryna gon finna bouta trynna boutta gne fina gonn tryina fenna qone trynaa qon</td></tr>
<tr><td>E2</td><td>0011000</td><td>gonna gunna gona gna guna gnna ganna qonna gonnna gana qunna gonne goona</td></tr>
<tr><td>F</td><td>0110110111</td><td>soo sooo soooo sooooo soooooo sooooooo soooooooo sooooooooo soooooooooo</td></tr>
<tr><td>G1</td><td>11101011001010</td><td>;) :p :-) xd ;-) ;d (; :3 ;p =p :-p =)) ;] xdd #gno xddd >:) ;-p >:d 8-) ;-d</td></tr>
<tr><td>G2</td><td>11101011001011</td><td>:) (: =) :)) :] ☺ :') =] ^_^ :))) ^.^ [: ;)) 😁 ((: ^__^ (= ^-^ :))))</td></tr>
<tr><td>G3</td><td>1110101100111</td><td>:(:/ -_- -.- :-(:'(d: :| :s -__- =(=/ >.< -___- :-/ </3 :\ -____- ;(/: :((>_< =[:[#fml</td></tr>
<tr><td>G4</td><td>111010110001</td><td><3 ♥ xoxo <33 xo <333 ❤ ♡ #love s2 <URL-twitition.com> #neversaynever <3333</td></tr>
</table>

Figure 2: Example word clusters (HMM classes): we list the most probable words, starting with the most probable, in descending order. Boldfaced words appear in the example tweet (Figure 1). The binary strings are root-to-leaf paths through the binary cluster tree. For example usage, see e.g. `search.twitter.com`, `bing.com/social` and `urbandictionary.com`.

3.1 Clustering Method

We obtained hierarchical word clusters via Brown clustering (Brown et al., 1992) on a large set of unlabeled tweets.[4] The algorithm partitions words into a base set of 1,000 clusters, and induces a hierarchy among those 1,000 clusters with a series of greedy agglomerative merges that heuristically optimize the likelihood of a hidden Markov model with a one-class-per-lexical-type constraint. Not only does Brown clustering produce effective features for discriminative models, but its variants are better unsupervised POS taggers than some models developed nearly 20 years later; see comparisons in Blunsom and Cohn (2011). The algorithm is attractive for our purposes since it scales to large amounts of data.

When training on tweets drawn from a single day, we observed time-specific biases (e.g., numerical dates appearing in the same cluster as the word *tonight*), so we assembled our unlabeled data from a random sample of 100,000 tweets per day from September 10, 2008 to August 14, 2012, and filtered out non-English tweets (about 60% of the sample) using `langid.py` (Lui and Baldwin, 2012).[5] Each tweet was processed with our tokenizer and lowercased. We normalized all at-mentions to $\langle$*@MENTION*$\rangle$ and URLs/email addresses to their domains (e.g. `http://bit.ly/dP8rR8` $\Rightarrow$ $\langle$*URL-bit.ly*$\rangle$). In an effort to reduce spam, we removed duplicated tweet texts (this also removes retweets) before word clustering. This normalization and cleaning resulted in 56 million unique tweets (847 million tokens). We set the clustering software's count threshold to only cluster words appearing 40 or more times, yielding 216,856 word types, which took 42 hours to cluster on a single CPU.

3.2 Cluster Examples

Fig. 2 shows example clusters. Some of the challenging words in the example tweet (Fig. 1) are highlighted. The term *lololol* (an extension of *lol* for "laughing out loud") is grouped with a large number of laughter acronyms (A1: "laughing my (fucking) ass off," "cracking the fuck up"). Since expressions of laughter are so prevalent on Twitter, the algorithm creates another laughter cluster (A1's sibling A2), that tends to have onomatopoeic, non-acronym variants (e.g., *haha*). The acronym *ikr* ("I know, right?") is grouped with expressive variations of "yes" and "no" (A4). Note that A1–A4 are grouped in a fairly specific subtree; and indeed, in this message *ikr* and

[4]As implemented by Liang (2005), v. 1.3: `https://github.com/percyliang/brown-cluster`

[5]`https://github.com/saffsd/langid.py`

lololol are both tagged as interjections.

smh ("shaking my head," indicating disapproval) seems related, though is always tagged in the annotated data as a miscellaneous abbreviation (G); the difference between acronyms that are interjections versus other acronyms may be complicated. Here, *smh* is in a related but distinct subtree from the above expressions (A5); its usage in this example is slightly different from its more common usage, which it shares with the other words in its cluster: message-ending expressions of commentary or emotional reaction, sometimes as a metacomment on the author's message; e.g., *Maybe you could get a guy to date you if you actually respected yourself #smh* or *There is really NO reason why other girls should send my boyfriend a goodmorning text #justsaying*.

We observe many variants of categories traditionally considered closed-class, including pronouns (B: *u* = "you") and prepositions (C: *fir* = "for").

There is also evidence of grammatical categories specific to conversational genres of English; clusters E1–E2 demonstrate variations of single-word contractions for "going to" and "trying to," some of which have more complicated semantics.[6]

Finally, the HMM learns about orthographic variants, even though it treats all words as opaque symbols; cluster F consists almost entirely of variants of "so," their frequencies monotonically decreasing in the number of vowel repetitions—a phenomenon called "expressive lengthening" or "affective lengthening" (Brody and Diakopoulos, 2011; Schnoebelen, 2012). This suggests a future direction to jointly model class sequence and orthographic information (Clark, 2003; Smith and Eisner, 2005; Blunsom and Cohn, 2011).

We have built an HTML viewer to browse these and numerous other interesting examples.[7]

3.3 Emoticons and Emoji

We use the term *emoticon* to mean a face or icon constructed with traditional alphabetic or punctuation symbols, and *emoji* to mean symbols rendered in software as small pictures, in line with the text.

Since our tokenizer is careful to preserve emoticons and other symbols (see §4), they are clustered just like other words. Similar emoticons are clustered together (G1–G4), including separate clusters of happy [[*:) =)* ^_^]], sad/disappointed [[*:/ :(-_- </3*]], love [[□*xoxo* □□]] and winking [[*;) (^_-)*]] emoticons. The clusters are not perfectly aligned with our POS annotation guidelines; for example, the "sad" emoticon cluster included emotion-bearing terms that our guidelines define as non-emoticons, such as *#ugh*, *#tear*, and *#fml* ("fuck my life"), though these seem potentially useful for sentiment analysis.

One difficult task is classifying different types of symbols in tweets: our annotation guidelines differentiate between emoticons, punctuation, and garbage (apparently non-meaningful symbols or tokenization errors). Several Unicode character ranges are reserved for emoji-style symbols (including the three Unicode hearts in G4); however, depending on the user's software, characters in these ranges might be rendered differently or not at all. We have found instances where the clustering algorithm groups proprietary iOS emoji symbols along with normal emoticons; for example, the character U+E056, which is interpreted on iOS as a smiling face, is in the same G2 cluster as smiley face emoticons. The symbol U+E12F, which represents a picture of a bag of money, is grouped with the words *cash* and *money*.

3.4 Cluster-Based Features

Since Brown clusters are hierarchical in a binary tree, each word is associated with a tree path represented as a bitstring with length ≤ 16; we use prefixes of the bitstring as features (for all prefix lengths $\in \{2, 4, 6, \ldots, 16\}$). This allows sharing of statistical strength between similar clusters. Using prefix features of hierarchical clusters in this way was similarly found to be effective for named-entity recognition (Turian et al., 2010) and Twitter POS tagging (Ritter et al., 2011).

When checking to see if a word is associated with a cluster, the tagger first normalizes the word using the same techniques as described in §3.1, then creates a priority list of fuzzy match transformations

[6]One coauthor, a native speaker of the Texan English dialect, notes "finna" (short for "fixing to", cluster E1) may be an immediate future auxiliary, indicating an immediate future tense that is present in many languages (though not in standard English). To illustrate: "She finna go" approximately means "She will go," but sooner, in the sense of "She is about to go."

[7]`http://www.ark.cs.cmu.edu/TweetNLP/cluster_viewer.html`

of the word by removing repeated punctuation and repeated characters. If the normalized word is not in a cluster, the tagger considers the fuzzy matches. Although only about 3% of the tokens in the development set (§6) did not appear in a clustering, this method resulted in a relative error decrease of 18% among such word tokens.

3.5 Other Lexical Features

Besides unsupervised word clusters, there are two other sets of features that contain generalized lexical class information. We use the tag dictionary feature from Gimpel et al., which adds a feature for a word's most frequent part-of-speech tag.[8] This can be viewed as a feature-based domain adaptation method, since it gives lexical type-level information for standard English words, which the model learns to map between PTB tags to the desired output tags. Second, since the lack of consistent capitalization conventions on Twitter makes it especially difficult to recognize names—Gimpel et al. and Foster et al. (2011) found relatively low accuracy on proper nouns—we added a token-level name list feature, which fires on (non-function) words from names from several sources: Freebase lists of celebrities and video games (Google, 2012), the Moby Words list of US Locations,[9] and lists of male, female, family, and proper names from Mark Kantrowitz's name corpus.[10]

4 Tokenization and Emoticon Detection

Word segmentation on Twitter is challenging due to the lack of orthographic conventions; in particular, punctuation, emoticons, URLs, and other symbols may have no whitespace separation from textual words (e.g. *no:-d,yes* should parse as four tokens), and internally may contain alphanumeric symbols that could be mistaken for words: a naive *split(/[^a-zA-Z0-9]+/)* tokenizer thinks the words "p" and "d" are among the top 100 most common words on Twitter, due to misanalysis of *:p* and *:d*. Traditional Penn Treebank–style tokenizers are hardly better, often breaking a string of punctuation characters into a single token per character.

We rewrote `twokenize` (O'Connor et al., 2010), a rule-based tokenizer, emoticon, and URL detector, for use in the tagger. Emoticons are especially challenging, since they are open-class and productive. We revise O'Connor et al.'s regular expression grammar that describes possible emoticons, adding a grammar of horizontal emoticons (e.g. -_-), known as "Eastern-style,"[11] though we observe high usage in English-speaking Twitter (Fig. 2, G2–G3). We also add a number of other improvements to the patterns. Because this system was used as preprocessing for the word clustering experiment in §3, we were able to infer the emoticon clusters in Fig. 2. Furthermore, whether a token matches the emoticon pattern is also used as a feature in the tagger (§2).

URL recognition is also difficult, since the *http://* is often dropped, resulting in protocol-less URLs like *about.me*. We add recognition patterns for these by using a list of top-level and country domains.

5 Annotated Dataset

Gimpel et al. (2011) provided a dataset of POS-tagged tweets consisting almost entirely of tweets sampled from one particular day (October 27, 2010). We were concerned about overfitting to time-specific phenomena; for example, a substantial fraction of the messages are about a basketball game happening that day.

We created a new test set of 547 tweets for evaluation. The test set consists of one random English tweet from every day between January 1, 2011 and June 30, 2012. In order for a tweet to be considered English, it had to contain at least one English word other than a URL, emoticon, or at-mention. We noticed biases in the outputs of `langid.py`, so we instead selected these messages completely manu-

[8] Frequencies came from the *Wall Street Journal* and Brown corpus sections of the Penn Treebank. If a word has multiple PTB tags, each tag is a feature with value for the frequency rank; e.g. for three different tags in the PTB, this feature gives a value of 1 for the most frequent tag, 2/3 for the second, etc. Coarse versions of the PTB tags are used (Petrov et al., 2011). While 88% of words in the dictionary have only one tag, using rank information seemed to give a small but consistent gain over only using the most common tag, or using binary features conjoined with rank as in Gimpel et al.

[9] `http://icon.shef.ac.uk/Moby/mwords.html`

[10] `http://www.cs.cmu.edu/afs/cs/project/ai-repository/ai/areas/nlp/corpora/names/0.html`

[11] `http://en.wikipedia.org/wiki/List_of_emoticons`

ally (going through a random sample of one day's messages until an English message was found).

5.1 Annotation Methodology

Gimpel et al. provided a tagset for Twitter (shown in Appendix A), which we used unmodified. The original annotation guidelines were not published, but in this work we recorded the rules governing tagging decisions and made further revisions while annotating the new data.[12] Some of our guidelines reiterate or modify rules made by Penn Treebank annotators, while others treat specific phenomena found on Twitter (refer to the next section).

Our tweets were annotated by two annotators who attempted to match the choices made in Gimpel et al.'s dataset. The annotators also consulted the POS annotations in the Penn Treebank (Marcus et al., 1993) as an additional reference. Differences were reconciled by a third annotator in discussion with all annotators.[13] During this process, an inconsistency was found in Gimpel et al.'s data, which we corrected (concerning the tagging of *this/that*, a change to 100 labels, 0.4%). The new version of Gimpel et al.'s data (called OCT27), as well as the newer messages (called DAILY547), are both included in our data release.

5.2 Compounds in Penn Treebank vs. Twitter

Ritter et al. (2011) annotated tweets using an augmented version of the PTB tagset and presumably followed the PTB annotation guidelines. We wrote new guidelines because the PTB conventions are inappropriate for Twitter in several ways, as shown in the design of Gimpel et al.'s tagset. Importantly, "compound" tags (e.g., nominal+verbal and nominal+possessive) are used because tokenization is difficult or seemingly impossible for the nonstandard word forms that are commonplace in conversational text.

For example, the PTB tokenization splits contractions containing apostrophes: *I'm* $\Rightarrow$ *I*/PRP *'m*/VBP. But conversational text often contains variants that resist a single PTB tag (like *im*), or even challenge traditional English grammatical categories (like *imma* or *umma*, which both mean "I am going to"). One strategy would be to analyze these forms into a PTB-style tokenization, as discussed in Forsyth (2007), who proposes to analyze *doncha* as *do*/VBP *ncha*/PRP, but notes it would be difficult. We think this is impossible to handle in the rule-based framework used by English tokenizers, given the huge (and possibly growing) number of large compounds like *imma*, *gonna*, *w/that*, etc. These are not rare: the word clustering algorithm discovers hundreds of such words as statistically coherent classes (e.g. clusters E1 and E2 in Fig. 2); and the word *imma* is the 962nd most common word in our unlabeled corpus, more frequent than *cat* or *near*.

We do not attempt to do Twitter "normalization" into traditional written English (Han and Baldwin, 2011), which we view as a lossy translation task. In fact, many of Twitter's unique linguistic phenomena are due not only to its informal nature, but also a set of authors that heavily skews towards younger ages and minorities, with heavy usage of dialects that are different than the standard American English most often seen in NLP datasets (Eisenstein, 2013; Eisenstein et al., 2011). For example, we suspect that *imma* may implicate tense and aspect markers from African-American Vernacular English.[14] Trying to impose PTB-style tokenization on Twitter is linguistically inappropriate: should the lexico-syntactic behavior of casual conversational chatter by young minorities be straightjacketed into the stylistic conventions of the 1980s *Wall Street Journal*? Instead, we would like to directly analyze the syntax of online conversational text on its own terms.

Thus, we choose to leave these word forms untokenized and use compound tags, viewing compositional multiword analysis as challenging future work.[15] We believe that our strategy is sufficient for many applications, such as chunking or named entity recognition; many applications such as sentiment analysis (Turney, 2002; Pang and Lee, 2008, §4.2.3), open information extraction (Carlson et al., 2010; Fader et al., 2011), and information retrieval (Allan and Raghavan, 2002) use POS

[12] The annotation guidelines are available online at `http://www.ark.cs.cmu.edu/TweetNLP/`

[13] Annotators are coauthors of this paper.

[14] See "Tense and aspect" examples in `http://en.wikipedia.org/wiki/African_American_Vernacular_English`

[15] For example, *wtf* has compositional behavior in "Wtf just happened??", but only debatably so in "Huh wtf".

	#Msg.	#Tok.	Tagset	Dates
OCT27	1,827	26,594	App. A	Oct 27-28, 2010
DAILY547	547	7,707	App. A	Jan 2011–Jun 2012
NPSCHAT	10,578	44,997	PTB-like	Oct–Nov 2006
(w/o sys. msg.)	7,935	37,081		
RITTERTW	789	15,185	PTB-like	unknown

Table 1: Annotated datasets: number of messages, tokens, tagset, and date range. More information in §5, §6.3, and §6.2.

patterns that seem quite compatible with our approach. More complex downstream processing like parsing is an interesting challenge, since contraction parsing on traditional text is probably a benefit to current parsers. We believe that any PTB-trained tool requires substantial retraining and adaptation for Twitter due to the huge genre and stylistic differences (Foster et al., 2011); thus tokenization conventions are a relatively minor concern. Our simple-to-annotate conventions make it easier to produce new training data.

6 Experiments

We are primarily concerned with performance on our annotated datasets described in §5 (OCT27, DAILY547), though for comparison to previous work we also test on other corpora (RITTERTW in §6.2, NPSCHAT in §6.3). The annotated datasets are listed in Table 1.

6.1 Main Experiments

We use OCT27 to refer to the entire dataset described in Gimpel et al.; it is split into training, development, and test portions (OCT27TRAIN, OCT27DEV, OCT27TEST). We use DAILY547 as an additional test set. Neither OCT27TEST nor DAILY547 were extensively evaluated against until final ablation testing when writing this paper.

The total number of features is 3.7 million, all of which are used under pure L_2 regularization; but only 60,000 are selected by elastic net regularization with $(\lambda_1, \lambda_2) = (0.25, 2)$, which achieves nearly the same (but no better) accuracy as pure L_2,[16] and we use it for all experiments. We observed that it was

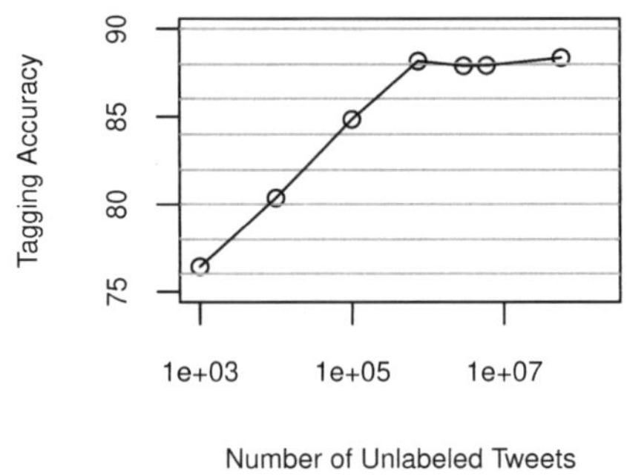

Figure 3: OCT27 development set accuracy using only clusters as features.

Model	In dict.	Out of dict.
Full	93.4	85.0
No clusters	92.0 (−1.4)	79.3 (−5.7)
Total tokens	*4,808*	*1,394*

Table 3: DAILY547 accuracies (%) for tokens in and out of a traditional dictionary, for models reported in rows 1 and 3 of Table 2.

possible to get radically smaller models with only a slight degradation in performance: $(4, 0.06)$ has 0.5% worse accuracy but uses only 1,632 features, a small enough number to browse through manually.

First, we evaluate on the new test set, training on all of OCT27. Due to DAILY547's statistical representativeness, we believe this gives the best view of the tagger's accuracy on English Twitter text. The full tagger attains **93.2%** accuracy (final row of Table 2).

To facilitate comparisons with previous work, we ran a series of experiments training only on OCT27's training and development sets, then report test results on both OCT27TEST and all of DAILY547, shown in Table 2. Our tagger achieves substantially higher accuracy than Gimpel et al. (2011).[17]

Feature ablation. A number of ablation tests indicate the word clusters are a very strong source of lexical knowledge. When dropping the tag dictionaries and name lists, the word clusters maintain most of the accuracy (row 2). If we drop the clusters and rely only on tag dictionaries and namelists, accuracy decreases significantly (row 3). In fact, we can remove *all* observation features except for word clusters—no word features, orthographic fea-

[16] We conducted a grid search for the regularizer values on part of DAILY547, and many regularizer values give the best or nearly the best results. We suspect a different setup would have yielded similar results.

[17] These numbers differ slightly from those reported by Gimpel et al., due to the corrections we made to the OCT27 data, noted in Section 5.1. We retrained and evaluated their tagger (version 0.2) on our corrected dataset.

Feature set	Oct27Test	Daily547	NPSChatTest	
All features	91.60	92.80	91.19	1
with clusters; without tagdicts, namelists	91.15	92.38	90.66	2
without clusters; with tagdicts, namelists	89.81	90.81	90.00	3
only clusters (and transitions)	89.50	90.54	89.55	4
without clusters, tagdicts, namelists	86.86	88.30	88.26	5
Gimpel et al. (2011) version 0.2	88.89	89.17		6
Inter-annotator agreement (Gimpel et al., 2011)	92.2			7
Model trained on all Oct27		93.2		8

Table 2: Tagging accuracies (%) in ablation experiments. Oct27Test and Daily547 95% confidence intervals are roughly ±0.7%. Our final tagger uses all features and also trains on Oct27Test, achieving 93.2% on Daily547.

tures, affix n-grams, capitalization, emoticon patterns, etc.—and the accuracy is in fact still better than the previous work (row 4).[18]

We also wanted to know whether to keep the tag dictionary and name list features, but the splits reported in Fig. 2 did not show statistically significant differences; so to better discriminate between ablations, we created a lopsided train/test split of all data with a much larger test portion (26,974 tokens), having greater statistical power (tighter confidence intervals of ± 0.3%).[19] The full system got 90.8% while the no–tag dictionary, no-namelists ablation had 90.0%, a statistically significant difference. Therefore we retain these features.

Compared to the tagger in Gimpel et al., most of our feature changes are in the new lexical features described in §3.5.[20] We do not reuse the other lexical features from the previous work, including a phonetic normalizer (Metaphone), a name list consisting of words that are frequently capitalized, and distributional features trained on a much smaller unlabeled corpus; they are all worse than our new lexical features described here. (We did include, however, a variant of the tag dictionary feature that uses phonetic normalization for lookup; it seemed to yield a small improvement.)

[18]Furthermore, when evaluating the clusters as *unsupervised* (hard) POS tags, we obtain a many-to-one accuracy of 89.2% on Daily547. Before computing this, we lowercased the text to match the clusters and removed tokens tagged as URLs and at-mentions.

[19]Reported confidence intervals in this paper are 95% binomial normal approximation intervals for the proportion of correctly tagged tokens: $\pm 1.96\sqrt{p(1-p)/n_{tokens}} \lesssim 1/\sqrt{n}$.

[20]Details on the exact feature set are available in a technical report (Owoputi et al., 2012), also available on the website.

Non-traditional words. The word clusters are especially helpful with words that do not appear in traditional dictionaries. We constructed a dictionary by lowercasing the union of the *ispell* 'American', 'British', and 'English' dictionaries, plus the standard Unix *words* file from Webster's Second International dictionary, totalling 260,985 word types. After excluding tokens defined by the gold standard as punctuation, URLs, at-mentions, or emoticons,[21] 22% of Daily547's tokens do not appear in this dictionary. Without clusters, they are very difficult to classify (only 79.2% accuracy), but adding clusters generates a 5.7 point improvement—much larger than the effect on in-dictionary tokens (Table 3).

Varying the amount of unlabeled data. A tagger that only uses word clusters achieves an accuracy of 88.6% on the Oct27 development set.[22] We created several clusterings with different numbers of unlabeled tweets, keeping the number of clusters constant at 800. As shown in Fig. 3, there was initially a logarithmic relationship between number of tweets and accuracy, but accuracy (and lexical coverage) levels out after 750,000 tweets. We use the largest clustering (56 million tweets and 1,000 clusters) as the default for the released tagger.

6.2 Evaluation on RitterTw

Ritter et al. (2011) annotated a corpus of 787 tweets[23] with a single annotator, using the PTB

[21]We retain hashtags since by our guidelines a #-prefixed token is ambiguous between a hashtag and a normal word, e.g. *#1* or *going #home*.

[22]The only observation features are the word clusters of a token and its immediate neighbors.

[23]`https://github.com/aritter/twitter_nlp/blob/master/data/annotated/pos.txt`

Tagger	Accuracy
This work	90.0 ± 0.5
Ritter et al. (2011), basic CRF tagger	85.3
Ritter et al. (2011), trained on more data	88.3

Table 4: Accuracy comparison on Ritter et al.'s Twitter POS corpus (§6.2).

Tagger	Accuracy
This work	93.4 ± 0.3
Forsyth (2007)	90.8

Table 5: Accuracy comparison on Forsyth's NPSCHAT IRC POS corpus (§6.3).

tagset plus several Twitter-specific tags, referred to in Table 1 as RITTERTW. Linguistic concerns notwithstanding (§5.2), for a controlled comparison, we train and test our system on this data with the same 4-fold cross-validation setup they used, attaining 90.0% (±0.5%) accuracy. Ritter et al.'s CRF-based tagger had 85.3% accuracy, and their best tagger, trained on a concatenation of PTB, IRC, and Twitter, achieved 88.3% (Table 4).

6.3 IRC: Evaluation on NPSCHAT

IRC is another medium of online conversational text, with similar emoticons, misspellings, abbreviations and acronyms as Twitter data. We evaluate our tagger on the NPS Chat Corpus (Forsyth and Martell, 2007),[24] a PTB-part-of-speech annotated dataset of Internet Relay Chat (IRC) room messages from 2006.

First, we compare to a tagger in the same setup as experiments on this data in Forsyth (2007), training on 90% of the data and testing on 10%; we average results across 10-fold cross-validation.[25] The full tagger model achieved 93.4% (±0.3%) accuracy, significantly improving over the best result they report, 90.8% accuracy with a tagger trained on a mix of several POS-annotated corpora.

We also perform the ablation experiments on this corpus, with a slightly different experimental setup: we first filter out system messages then split data into 5,067 training and 2,868 test messages. Results show a similar pattern as the Twitter data (see final column of Table 2). Thus the Twitter word clusters are also useful for language in the medium of text chat rooms; we suspect these clusters will be applicable for deeper syntactic and semantic analysis in other online conversational text mediums, such as text messages and instant messages.

[24] Release 1.0: `http://faculty.nps.edu/cmartell/NPSChat.htm`

[25] Forsyth actually used 30 different 90/10 random splits; we prefer cross-validation because the same test data is never repeated, thus allowing straightforward confidence estimation of accuracy from the number of tokens (via binomial sample variance, footnote 19). In all cases, the models are trained on the same amount of data (90%).

7 Conclusion

We have constructed a state-of-the-art part-of-speech tagger for the online conversational text genres of Twitter and IRC, and have publicly released our new evaluation data, annotation guidelines, open-source tagger, and word clusters at `http://www.ark.cs.cmu.edu/TweetNLP`.

Acknowledgements

This research was supported in part by the National Science Foundation (IIS-0915187 and IIS-1054319).

A Part-of-Speech Tagset

N	common noun
O	pronoun (personal/WH; not possessive)
^	proper noun
S	nominal + possessive
Z	proper noun + possessive
V	verb including copula, auxiliaries
L	nominal + verbal (e.g. *i'm*), verbal + nominal (*let's*)
M	proper noun + verbal
A	adjective
R	adverb
!	interjection
D	determiner
P	pre- or postposition, or subordinating conjunction
&	coordinating conjunction
T	verb particle
X	existential *there*, predeterminers
Y	X + verbal
#	hashtag (indicates topic/category for tweet)
@	at-mention (indicates a user as a recipient of a tweet)
~	discourse marker, indications of continuation across multiple tweets
U	URL or email address
E	emoticon
$	numeral
,	punctuation
G	other abbreviations, foreign words, possessive endings, symbols, garbage

Table 6: POS tagset from Gimpel et al. (2011) used in this paper, and described further in the released annotation guidelines.

References

J. Allan and H. Raghavan. 2002. Using part-of-speech patterns to reduce query ambiguity. In *Proc. of SIGIR*.

G. Andrew and J. Gao. 2007. Scalable training of L_1-regularized log-linear models. In *Proc. of ICML*.

P. Blunsom and T. Cohn. 2011. A hierarchical Pitman-Yor process HMM for unsupervised part of speech induction. In *Proc. of ACL*.

S. Brody and N. Diakopoulos. 2011. Cooooooooooooooollllllllllllll!!!!!!!!!!!!!!: using word lengthening to detect sentiment in microblogs. In *Proc. of EMNLP*.

P. F. Brown, P. V. de Souza, R. L. Mercer, V. J. Della Pietra, and J. C. Lai. 1992. Class-based n-gram models of natural language. *Computational Linguistics*, 18(4).

A. Carlson, J. Betteridge, B. Kisiel, B. Settles, E. R. Hruschka Jr, and T. M. Mitchell. 2010. Toward an architecture for never-ending language learning. In *Proc. of AAAI*.

A. Clark. 2003. Combining distributional and morphological information for part of speech induction. In *Proc. of EACL*.

J. Eisenstein, N. A. Smith, and E. P. Xing. 2011. Discovering sociolinguistic associations with structured sparsity. In *Proc. of ACL*.

J. Eisenstein. 2013. What to do about bad language on the internet. In *Proc. of NAACL*.

A. Fader, S. Soderland, and O. Etzioni. 2011. Identifying relations for open information extraction. In *Proc. of EMNLP*.

E. N. Forsyth and C. H. Martell. 2007. Lexical and discourse analysis of online chat dialog. In *Proc. of ICSC*.

E. N. Forsyth. 2007. Improving automated lexical and discourse analysis of online chat dialog. Master's thesis, Naval Postgraduate School.

J. Foster, O. Cetinoglu, J. Wagner, J. L. Roux, S. Hogan, J. Nivre, D. Hogan, and J. van Genabith. 2011. #hardtoparse: POS tagging and parsing the Twitterverse. In *Proc. of AAAI-11 Workshop on Analysing Microtext*.

K. Gimpel, N. Schneider, B. O'Connor, D. Das, D. Mills, J. Eisenstein, M. Heilman, D. Yogatama, J. Flanigan, and N. A. Smith. 2011. Part-of-speech tagging for Twitter: Annotation, features, and experiments. In *Proc. of ACL*.

Google. 2012. Freebase data dumps. `http://download.freebase.com/datadumps/`.

B. Han and T. Baldwin. 2011. Lexical normalisation of short text messages: Makn sens a #twitter. In *Proc. of ACL*.

T. Koo, X. Carreras, and M. Collins. 2008. Simple semi-supervised dependency parsing. In *Proc. of ACL*.

J. Lafferty, A. McCallum, and F. Pereira. 2001. Conditional random fields: Probabilistic models for segmenting and labeling sequence data. In *Proc. of ICML*.

P. Liang. 2005. Semi-supervised learning for natural language. Master's thesis, Massachusetts Institute of Technology.

D. C. Liu and J. Nocedal. 1989. On the limited memory BFGS method for large scale optimization. *Mathematical programming*, 45(1).

X. Liu, S. Zhang, F. Wei, and M. Zhou. 2011. Recognizing named entities in tweets. In *Proc. of ACL*.

M. Lui and T. Baldwin. 2012. langid.py: An off-the-shelf language identification tool. In *Proc. of ACL*.

M. P. Marcus, B. Santorini, and M. A. Marcinkiewicz. 1993. Building a large annotated corpus of English: The Penn Treebank. *Computational Linguistics*, 19(2).

A. McCallum, D. Freitag, and F. Pereira. 2000. Maximum entropy Markov models for information extraction and segmentation. In *Proc. of ICML*.

D. McClosky, E. Charniak, and M. Johnson. 2010. Automatic domain adaptation for parsing. In *Proc. of NAACL*.

B. O'Connor, M. Krieger, and D. Ahn. 2010. TweetMotif: exploratory search and topic summarization for Twitter. In *Proc. of AAAI Conference on Weblogs and Social Media*.

O. Owoputi, B. O'Connor, C. Dyer, K. Gimpel, and N. Schneider. 2012. Part-of-speech tagging for Twitter: Word clusters and other advances. Technical Report CMU-ML-12-107, Carnegie Mellon University.

B. Pang and L. Lee. 2008. *Opinion mining and sentiment analysis*. Now Publishers.

S. Petrov and R. McDonald. 2012. Overview of the 2012 shared task on parsing the web. Notes of the First Workshop on Syntactic Analysis of Non-Canonical Language (SANCL).

S. Petrov, D. Das, and R. McDonald. 2011. A universal part-of-speech tagset. *arXiv preprint arXiv:1104.2086*.

A. Ratnaparkhi. 1996. A maximum entropy model for part-of-speech tagging. In *Proc. of EMNLP*.

A. Ritter, S. Clark, Mausam, and O. Etzioni. 2011. Named entity recognition in tweets: An experimental study. In *Proc. of EMNLP*.

T. Schnoebelen. 2012. Do you smile with your nose? Stylistic variation in Twitter emoticons. *University of Pennsylvania Working Papers in Linguistics*, 18(2):14.

N. A. Smith and J. Eisner. 2005. Contrastive estimation: Training log-linear models on unlabeled data. In *Proc. of ACL*.

O. Täckström, R. McDonald, and J. Uszkoreit. 2012. Cross-lingual word clusters for direct transfer of linguistic structure. In *Proc. of NAACL*.

J. Turian, L. Ratinov, and Y. Bengio. 2010. Word representations: A simple and general method for semi-supervised learning. In *Proc. of ACL.*

P. D. Turney. 2002. Thumbs up or thumbs down?: semantic orientation applied to unsupervised classification of reviews. In *Proc. of ACL.*

H. Zou and T. Hastie. 2005. Regularization and variable selection via the elastic net. *Journal of the Royal Statistical Society: Series B (Statistical Methodology)*, 67(2):301–320.

Parser lexicalisation through self-learning

Marek Rei
Computer Labratory
University of Cambridge
United Kingdom
Marek.Rei@cl.cam.ac.uk

Ted Briscoe
Computer Laboratory
University of Cambridge
United Kingdom
Ted.Briscoe@cl.cam.ac.uk

Abstract

We describe a new self-learning framework for parser lexicalisation that requires only a plain-text corpus of in-domain text. The method first creates augmented versions of dependency graphs by applying a series of modifications designed to directly capture higher-order lexical path dependencies. Scores are assigned to each edge in the graph using statistics from an automatically parsed background corpus. As bilexical dependencies are sparse, a novel directed distributional word similarity measure is used to smooth edge score estimates. Edge scores are then combined into graph scores and used for reranking the top-n analyses found by the unlexicalised parser. The approach achieves significant improvements on WSJ and biomedical text over the unlexicalised baseline parser, which is originally trained on a subset of the Brown corpus.

1 Introduction

Most parsers exploit supervised machine learning methods and a syntactically annotated dataset (i.e. treebank), incorporating a wide range of features in the training process to deliver competitive performance. The use of lexically-conditioned features, such as relations between lemmas or word forms, is often critical when choosing the correct syntactic analysis in ambiguous contexts. However, utilising such features leads the parser to learn information that is often specific to the domain and/or genre of the training data. Several experiments have demonstrated that many lexical features learnt in one domain provide little if any benefit when parsing text from different domains and genres (Sekine, 1997; Gildea, 2001). Furthermore, manual creation of in-domain treebanks is an expensive and time-consuming process, which can only be performed by experts with sufficient linguistic and domain knowledge.

In contrast, unlexicalised parsers avoid using lexical information and select a syntactic analysis using only more general features, such as POS tags. While they cannot be expected to achieve optimal performance when trained and tested in a single domain, unlexicalised parsers can be surprisingly competitive with their lexicalised counterparts (Klein and Manning, 2003; Petrov et al., 2006). In this work, instead of trying to adapt a lexicalised parser to new domains, we explore how bilexical features can be integrated effectively with any unlexicalised parser. As our novel self-learning framework requires only a large unannotated corpus, lexical features can be easily tuned to a specific domain or genre by selecting a suitable dataset. In addition, we describe a graph expansion process that captures selected bilexical relations which improve performance but would otherwise require sparse higher-order dependency path feature types in most approaches to dependency parsing. As many bilexical features will still be sparse, we also develop an approach to estimating confidence scores for dependency relations using a directional distributional word similarity measure. The final framework integrates easily with any unlexicalised (and therefore potentially less domain/genre-biased) parser capable of returning ranked dependency analyses.

2 Background

We hypothesise that a large corpus will often contain examples of dependency relations in non-ambiguous contexts, and these will mostly be correctly parsed by an unlexicalised parser. Lexical statistics derived from the corpus can then be used to select the correct parse in a more difficult context. For example, consider the following sentences:

(1) a. Government projects interest researchers

b. Government raises interest rates

c. Government projects receive funding

d. Interest rates are increasing

Noun-verb ambiguities over *projects* and *interest* might erroneously result in the unlexicalised parser returning similar dependency graphs for both *a* and *b*. However, sentences *c* and *d* contain less ambiguous instances of the same phrases and can provide clues to correctly parsing the first two examples. In a large in-domain corpus we are likely to find more cases of *researchers* being the object for *interest* and fewer cases where it is the object of *project*. In contrast, *rates* is more likely to have *interest* as a modifier than as a head in an object relation. Exploiting this lexical information, we can assign the correct derivation to each of the more ambiguous sentences.

Similar intuitions have been used to motivate the acquisition of bilexical features from background corpora for improving parser accuracy. However, previous work has focused on including these statistics as auxiliary features during supervised training. For example, van Noord (2007) incorporated bilexical preferences as features via self-training to improve the Alpino parser for Dutch. Plank and van Noord (2008) investigated the application of auxiliary distributions for domain adaptation. They incorporated information from both in-domain and out-of-domain sources into their maximum entropy model and found that the out-of-domain auxiliary distributions did not contribute to parsing accuracy in the target domain. Zhou et al. (2011) extracted n-gram counts from Google queries and a large corpus to improve the MSTParser. In contrast to previous work, we refer to our approach as self-learning because it differs from self-training by utilising statistics found using an initial parse ranking model to create a *separate* unsupervised reranking component, without retraining the baseline unlexicalised model.

We formulate our self-learning framework as a reranking process that assigns new scores to the top-n ranked analyses found by the original parser. Parse reranking has been successfully used in previous work as a method of including a wider range of features to rescore a smaller selection of highly-ranked candidate parses. Collins (2000) was one of the first to propose supervised reranking as an additional step to increase parser accuracy and achieved 1.55% accuracy improvement for his parser. Charniak and Johnson (2005) utilise a discriminative reranker and show a 1.3% improvement for the Charniak parser. McClosky et al. (2006) extend their work by adding new features and further increase the performance by 0.3%. Ng et al. (2010) implemented a discriminative maximum entropy reranker for the C&C parser and showed a 0.23% improvement over the baseline. Bansal and Klein (2011) discriminatively rerank derivations from the Berkeley unlexicalised parser (Petrov et al., 2006) demonstrating that lexical features derived from the Google n-gram corpus improve accuracy even when used in conjunction with other reranking features. They have all treated reranking as a supervised task and trained a discriminative classifier using parse tree features and annotated in-domain data. In contrast, our reranker only uses statistics from an unlabelled source and requires no manual annotation or training of the reranking component. As we utilise an unlexicalised parser, our baseline performance on WSJ text is lower compared to some fully-lexicalised parsers. However, an unlexicalised parser is also likely to be less biased to domains or genres manifested in the text used to train its original ranking model. This may allow the reranker to adapt it to a new domain and/or genre more effectively.

3 Reordering dependency graphs

For our experiments, we make use of the unlexicalised RASP parser (Briscoe et al., 2006) as the baseline system. For every sentence s the parser returns a list of dependency graphs G_s, ranked by the log probability of the associated derivation in the structural ranking model. Our goal is to reorder this list to improve ranking accuracy and, most importantly, to improve the quality of the highest-ranked dependency graph. This is done by assigning a confidence score to every graph $g_{s,r} \in G_s$ where r is the rank of g_s for sentence s. The method treats each sentence independently, therefore we can omit the sentence identifiers and refer to $g_{s,r}$ as g_r.

We first calculate confidence scores for all the individual edges and then combine them into an overall score for the dependency graph. In the following sections, we describe a series of graph modifications that incorporates selected higher-order dependency path relations, without introducing unwanted noise or complexity into the reranker. Next, we outline different approaches for calculating and smoothing the confidence scores for bilexical relations. Finally, we describe methods for combining together these scores and calculating an overall score for a dependency graph. We make publically available all the code developed for performing these steps in the parse reranking system.[1]

3.1 Graph modifications

For every dependency graph g_r the graph expansion procedure creates a modified representation g'_r which contains a wider range of bilexical relations. The motivation for this graph expansion step is similar to that motivating the move from first-order to higher-order dependency path feature types (e.g., Carreras (2007)). However, compared to using all nth-order paths, these rules are chosen to maximise the utility and minimise the sparsity of the resulting bilexical features. In addition, the cascading nature of the expansion steps means in some cases the expansion captures useful 3rd and 4th order dependencies. Similar approaches to graph modifications have been successfully used for several NLP tasks (van Noord, 2007; Arora et al., 2010).

For any edge e we also use notation (rel, w_1, w_2), referring to an edge from w_1 to w_2 with the label rel. We perform the following modifications on every dependency graph:

1. **Normalising lemmas.** All lemmas are converted to lowercase. Numerical lemmas are replaced with more generic tags to reduce sparsity.

2. **Bypassing conjunctions.** For every edge pair (rel_1, w_1, w_2) and (rel_2, w_2, w_3) where w_2 is tagged as a conjunction, we create an additional edge (rel_1, w_1, w_3). This bypasses the conjunction node and creates direct edges between the head and dependents of the conjunctive lemma.

3. **Bypassing prepositions.** For every edge pair (rel_1, w_1, w_2) and (rel_2, w_2, w_3) where w_2 is tagged as a preposition, we create an additional edge (rel_3, w_1, w_3). $rel_3 = rel_1$ +'_prep', where '_prep' is added as a marker to indicate that the relation originally contained a preposition.

4. **Bypassing verbs.** For every edge pair (rel_1, w_1, w_2) and (rel_2, w_1, w_3) where w_1 is tagged as a verb, w_2 and w_3 are both tagged as open-class lemmas, rel_1 starts with a subject relation, and rel_2 starts with an object relation, we create an additional edge (rel_3, w_2, w_3) where $rel_3 = rel_1$ + '-' + rel_2. This creates an additional edge between the subject and the object, with the new edge label containing both of the original labels.

5. **Duplicating nodes.** For every existing node in the graph, containing the lemma and POS for each token (*lemma_pos*), we create a parallel node without the POS information (*lemma*). Then, for each existing edge, we create three corresponding edges, interconnecting the parallel nodes to each other and the original graph. This allows the reranker to exploit both specific and more generic instantiations of each lemma.

Figure 1 illustrates the graph modification process. It is important to note that each of these modifications gets applied in the order that they are described above. For example, when creating edges for bypassing verbs, the new edges for prepositions and conjunctions have already been created and also participate in this step. We performed ablation tests on the development data and verified that each of these modifications contributes positively to the final performance.

3.2 Edge scoring methods

We start the scoring process by assigning individual confidence scores to every bilexical relation in the

[1]www.marekrei.com/projects/lexicalisation

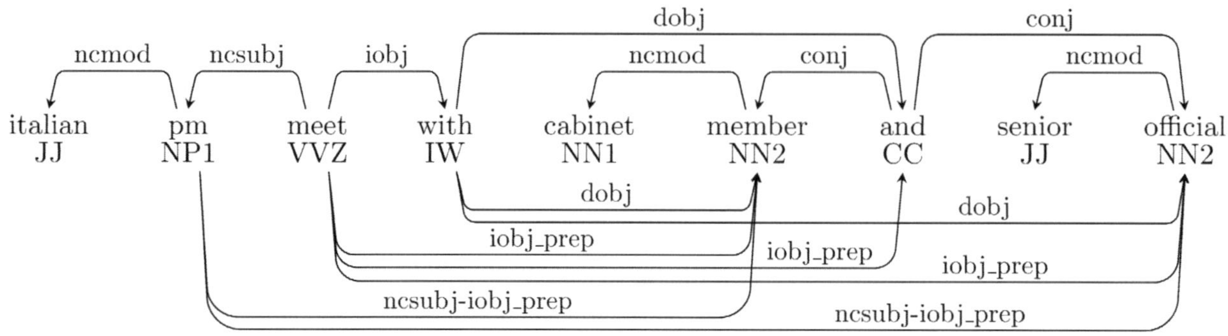

Figure 1: Modified graph for the sentence *'Italian PM meets with Cabinet members and senior officials'* after steps 1-4. Edges above the text are created by the parser, edges below the text are automatically created using the operations described in Section 3.1. The 5th step will create 9 new nodes and 45 additional edges (not shown).

modified graph. In this section we give an overview of some possible strategies for performing this task.

The parser returns a ranked list of graphs and this can be used to derive an edge score without requiring any additional information. We estimate that the likelihood of a parse being the best possible parse for a given sentence is roughly inversely proportional to the rank that it is assigned by the parser. These values can be summed for all graphs that contain a specific edge, normalised to approximate a probability. We then calculate the score for edge e as the Reciprocal Edge Score (RES) – the probability of e belonging to the best possible parse:

$$\text{RES}(e) = \frac{\sum_{r=1}^{R}[\frac{1}{r} \times \text{contains}(g'_r, e)]}{\sum_{r=1}^{R} \frac{1}{r}}$$

where R is the total number of parses for a sentence, and $\text{contains}(g'_r, e)$ returns 1 if graph g'_r contains edge e, and 0 otherwise. The value is normalised, so that an edge which is found in all parses will have a score of 1.0, but occurrences at higher ranks will have a considerably larger contribution.

The score of an edge can also be assigned by estimating the probability of that edge using a parsed reference corpus. van Noord (2007) improved overall parsing performance in a supervised self-training framework using feature weights based on pointwise mutual information:

$$\text{I}(e) = \log \frac{\text{P}(rel, w_1, w_2)}{\text{P}(rel, w_1, *) \times \text{P}(*, *, w_2)}$$

where $\text{P}(rel, w_1, w_2)$ is the probability of seeing an edge from w_1 to w_2 with label rel, $\text{P}(rel, w_1, *)$ is the probability of seeing an edge from w_1 to any node with label rel, and $\text{P}(*, *, w_2)$ is the probability of seeing any type of edge linking to w_2. Plank and van Noord (2008) used the same approach for semi-supervised domain adaptation but were not able to achieve similar performance benefits. In our implementation we omit the logarithm in the equation, as this improves performance and avoids problems with $\log(0)$ for unseen edges.

$\text{I}(e)$ compares the probability of the complete edge to the probabilities of partially specified edges, but it assumes that w_2 will have an incoming relation, and that w_1 will have an outgoing relation of type rel to some unknown node. These assumptions may or may not be true – given the input sentence, we have observed w_1 and w_2 but do not know what relations they are involved in. Therefore, we create a more general version of the measure that compares the probability of the complete edge to the individual probabilities of the two lemmas – the Conditional Edge Score (CES_1):

$$\text{CES}_1(e) = \frac{\text{P}(rel, w_1, w_2)}{\text{P}(w_1) \times \text{P}(w_2)}$$

where $\text{P}(w_1)$ is the probability of seeing w_1 in text, estimated from a background corpus using maximum likelihood.

Finally, we know that w_1 and w_2 are in a sentence together but cannot assume that there is a dependency relation between them. However, we can choose to think of each sentence as a fully connected graph, with an edge going from every lemma to every other lemma in the same sentence. If there exists

$$\text{ECES}_1(rel, w_1, w_2) = \frac{1}{2} \times \left(\frac{\sum_{c_1 \in C_1} \text{sim}(c_1, w_1) \times \frac{\text{P}(rel, c_1, w_2)}{\text{P}(c_1) \times \text{P}(w_2)}}{\sum_{c_1 \in C_1} \text{sim}(c_1, w_1)} + \frac{\sum_{c_2 \in C_2} \text{sim}(c_2, w_2) \times \frac{\text{P}(rel, w_1, c_2)}{\text{P}(w_1) \times \text{P}(c_2)}}{\sum_{c_2 \in C_2} \text{sim}(c_2, w_2)}\right)$$

$$\text{ECES}_2(rel, w_1, w_2) = \frac{1}{2} \times \left(\frac{\sum_{c_1 \in C_1} \text{sim}(c_1, w_1) \times \frac{\text{P}(rel, c_1, w_2)}{\text{P}(*, c_1, w_2)}}{\sum_{c_1 \in C_1} \text{sim}(c_1, w_1)} + \frac{\sum_{c_2 \in C_2} \text{sim}(c_2, w_2) \times \frac{\text{P}(rel, w_1, c_2)}{\text{P}(*, w_1, c_2)}}{\sum_{c_2 \in C_2} \text{sim}(c_2, w_2)}\right)$$

Figure 2: Expanded edge score calculation methods using the list of distributionally similar lemmas

no genuine relation between the lemmas, the edge is simply considered a *null* edge. We can then find the conditional probability of the relation type given the two lemmas:

$$\text{CES}_2(e) = \frac{\text{P}(rel, w_1, w_2)}{\text{P}(*, w_1, w_2)}$$

where $\text{P}(rel, w_1, w_2)$ is the probability of the fully-specified relation, and $\text{P}(*, w_1, w_2)$ is the probability of there being an edge of any type from w_1 to w_2, including a *null* edge. Using fully connected graphs, the latter is equivalent to the probability of w_1 and w_2 appearing in a sentence together, which again can be calculated from the background corpus.

3.3 Smoothing edge scores

Apart from RES, all the scoring methods from the previous section rely on correctly estimating the probability of the fully-specified edge, $\text{P}(rel, w_1, w_2)$. Even in a large background corpus these triples will be very sparse, and it can be useful to find approximate methods for estimating the edge scores.

Using smoothing techniques derived from work on language modelling, we could back-off to a more general version of the relation. For example, if *(dobj, read, publication)* is not frequent enough, the value could be approximated using the probabilities of *(dobj, read, *)* and *(dobj, *, publication)*. However, this can lead to unexpected results due to compositionality – while *(dobj, read, *)* and *(dobj, *, rugby)* can be fairly common, *(dobj, read, rugby)* is an unlikely relation.

Instead, we can consider looking at other lemmas which are similar to the rare lemmas in the relation. If *(dobj, read, publication)* is infrequent in the data, the system might predict that *book* is a reasonable substitute for *publication* and use *(dobj, read, book)* to estimate the original probability.

Given that we have a reliable way of finding likely substitutes for a given lemma, we can create expanded versions of CES_1 and CES_2, as shown in Figure 2. C_1 is the list of substitute lemmas for w_1, and $\text{sim}(c_1, w_1)$ is a measure showing how similar c_1 is to w_1. The methods iterate over the list of substitutes and calculate the CES score for each of the modified relations. The values are then combined by using the similarity score as a weight – more similar lemmas will have a higher contribution to the final result. This is done for both the head and the dependent in the original relation, and the scores are then normalised and averaged.

Experiments with a wide variety of distributional word similarity measures revealed that *WeightedCosine* (Rei, 2013), a directional similarity measure designed to better capture hyponymy relations, performed best. Hyponyms are more specific versions of a word and normally include the general properties of the hypernym, making them well-suited for lexical substitution. The *WeightedCosine* measure incorporates an additional directional weight into the standard cosine similarity, assigning different importance to individual features for the hyponymy relation. We retain the 10 most distributionally similar putative hyponyms for each lemma and substitute them in the relation. The original lemma is also included with similarity 1.0, thereby assigning it the highest weight. The lemma vectors are built from the same vector space model that is used for calculating edge probabilities, which includes all the graph modifications described in Section 3.1.

3.4 Combining edge scores

While the CES and ECES measures calculate confidence scores for bilexical relations using statistics from a large background corpus, they do not include any knowledge about grammar, syntax, or the con-

$$\text{CMB}_1(e) = \sqrt[3]{\text{RES}(e) * \text{CES}_1(e) * \text{CES}_2(e)} \qquad \text{CMB}_2(e) = \sqrt[3]{\text{RES}(e) * \text{ECES}_1(e) * \text{ECES}_2(e)}$$

Figure 3: Edge score combination methods

text in a specific sentence. In contrast, the RES score implicitly includes some of this information, as it is calculated based on the original parser ranking. In order to take advantage of both information sources, we combine these scores into CMB_1 and CMB_2, as shown in Figure 3.

3.5 Graph scoring

Every edge in graph g'_r is assigned a score indicating the reranker's confidence in that edge belonging to the best parse. We investigated different strategies for combining these values together into a confidence score for the whole graph. The simplest solution is to sum together individual edge scores, but this would lead to always preferring graphs that have a larger number of edges. Interestingly, averaging the edge scores does not produce good results either because it is biased towards smaller graph fragments containing only highly-confident edges.

We created a new scoring method which prefers graphs that cover all the nodes, but does not create bias for a higher number of edges. For every node in the graph, it finds the average score of all edges which have that node as a dependent. These scores are then averaged again over all nodes:

$$\text{NScore}(n) = \frac{\sum_{e \in E_g} \text{EdgeScore}(e) \times \text{isDep}(e, n)}{\sum_{e \in E_g} \text{isDep}(e, n)}$$

$$\text{GraphScore}(g) = \frac{\sum_{n \in N_g} \text{NScore}(n)}{|N_g|}$$

where g is the graph being scored, $n \in N_g$ is a node in graph g, $e \in E_g$ is an edge in graph g, $\text{isDep}(e, n)$ is a function returning 1.0 if n is the dependent in edge e, and 0.0 otherwise. $\text{NScore}(n)$ is set to 0 if the node does not appear as a dependent in any edges. We found this metric performs well, as it prefers graphs that connect together many nodes without simply rewarding a larger number of edges.

While the score calculation is done using the modified graph g'_r, the resulting score is directly assigned to the corresponding original graph g_r, and the reordering of the original dependency graphs is used for evaluation.

4 Experiments

4.1 Evaluation methods

In order to evaluate how much the reranker improves the highest-ranked dependency graph, we calculate the microaveraged precision, recall and F-score over all dependencies from the top-ranking parses for the test set. Following the official RASP evaluation (Briscoe et al., 2006) we employ the hierarchical edge matching scheme which aggregates counts up the dependency relation subsumption hierarchy and thus rewards the parser for making more fine-grained distinctions.[2] Statistical significance of the change in F-score is calculated by using the Approximate Randomisation Test (Noreen, 1989; Cohen, 1995) with 10^6 iterations.

We also wish to measure how well the reranker does at the overall task of ordering dependency graphs. For this we make use of an oracle that creates the perfect ranking for a set of graphs by calculating their individual F-scores; this ideal ranking is then compared to the output of our system. Spearman's rank correlation coefficient between the two rankings is calculated for each sentence and then averaged over all sentences. If the scores for all of the returned analyses are equal, this coefficient cannot be calculated and is set to 0.

4.2 DepBank

We evaluated our self-learning framework using the DepBank/GR reannotation (Briscoe and Carroll, 2006) of the PARC 700 Dependency Bank (King et al., 2003). The dataset is provided with the open-source RASP distribution[3] and has been used for evaluating different parsers, including RASP (Briscoe and Carroll, 2006; Watson et al., 2007) and

[2] Slight changes in the performance of the baseline parser compared to previous publications are due to using a more recent version of the parser and minor corrections to the gold standard annotation.

[3] ilexir.co.uk/2012/open-source-rasp-3-1/

C&C (Clark and Curran, 2007). It contains 700 sentences, randomly chosen from section 23 of the WSJ Penn Treebank (Marcus et al., 1993), divided into development (140 sentences) and test data (560 sentences). We made use of the development data to experiment with a wider selection of edge and graph scoring methods, and report the final results on the test data.

For reranking we collect up to 1000 top-ranked analyses for each sentence. The actual number of analyses that the RASP parser outputs depends on the sentence and can be smaller. As the parser first constructs parse trees and converts them to dependency graphs, several parse trees may result in identical graphs; we remove any duplicates to obtain a ranking of unique dependency graphs.

Our approach relies on a large unannotated corpus of in-domain text, and for this we used the BLLIP corpus containing 50M words of in-domain WSJ articles. Our version of this corpus excludes texts that are found in the Penn Treebank, thereby also excluding the section that we use for evaluation.

The baseline system is the unlexicalised RASP parser with default settings. In order to construct the upper bound, we use an oracle to calculate the F-score for each dependency graph individually, and then create the best possible ranking using these scores.

Table 1 contains evaluation results on the DepBank/GR test set. The baseline system achieves 76.41% F-score on the test data, with 32.70% average correlation. I and RES scoring methods give comparable results, with RES improving correlation by 9.56%. The CES and ECES scores all make use of corpus-based statistics and all significantly improve over the baseline system, with absolute increases in F-score of more than 2% for the fully-connected edge score variants.

Finally, we combine the RES score with the corpus-based methods and the fully-connected CMB_2 variant again delivers the best overall results. The final F-score is 79.21%, an absolute improvement of 2.8%, corresponding to 33.65% relative error reduction with respect to the upper bound. Correlation is also increased by 16.32%; this means the methods not only improve the chances of finding the best dependency graph, but also manage to create a better overall ranking. The F-scores for all the corpus-based scoring methods are statistically significant when compared to the baseline ($p < 0.05$).

By using our self-learning framework, we were able to significantly improve the original unlexicalised parser. To put the overall result in a wider perspective, Clark and Curran (2007) achieve an F-score of 81.86% on the DepBank/GR test sentences using the C&C lexicalised parser, trained on 40,000 manually-treebanked sentences from the WSJ. The unlexicalised RASP parser, using a manually-developed grammar and a parse ranking component trained on 4,000 partially-bracketed unlabelled sentences from a domain/genre balanced subset of Brown (Watson et al., 2007), achieves an F-score of 76.41% on the same test set. The method introduced here improves this to 79.21% F-score without using any further manually-annotated data, closing more than half of the gap between the performance of a fully-supervised in-domain parser and a more weakly-supervised more domain-neutral one.

We also performed an additional detailed analysis of the results and found that, with the exception of the auxiliary dependency relation, the reranking process was able to improve the F-score of all other individual dependency types. Complements and modifiers are attached with much higher accuracy, resulting in 3.34% and 3.15% increase in the corresponding F-scores. The non-clausal modifier relation (*ncmod*), which is the most frequent label in the dataset, increases by 3.16%.

4.3 Genia

One advantage of our reranking framework is that it does not rely on any domain-dependent manually annotated resources. Therefore, we are interested in seeing how it performs on text from a completely different domain and genre.

The GENIA-GR dataset (Tateisi et al., 2008) is a collection of 492 sentences taken from biomedical research papers in the GENIA corpus (Kim et al., 2003). The sentences have been manually annotated with dependency-based grammatical relations identical to those output by the RASP parser. However, it does not contain dependencies for all tokens and many multi-word phrases are treated as single units. For example, the tokens *'intracellular redox status'* are annotated as one node with label *intracellular_redox_status*. We retain this annotation and

	DepBank/GR				GENIA-GR			
	Prec	**Rec**	**F**	ρ	**Prec**	**Rec**	**F**	ρ
Baseline	77.91	74.97	76.41	32.70	79.91	78.86	79.38	36.54
Upper Bound	86.74	82.82	84.73	75.36	86.33	84.71	85.51	78.66
I	77.77	75.00	76.36	33.32	77.18	76.21	76.69	30.23
RES	78.13	74.94	76.50	42.26	80.06	78.89	79.47	**47.52**
CES$_1$	79.68	76.40	<u>78.01</u>	41.95	78.64	77.50	78.07	36.06
CES$_2$	80.48	77.28	<u>78.85</u>	48.43	79.92	78.92	79.42	43.09
ECES$_1$	79.96	76.68	<u>78.29</u>	42.41	79.09	78.11	78.60	38.02
ECES$_2$	80.71	77.52	<u>79.08</u>	**49.05**	79.84	78.95	79.39	43.64
CMB$_1$	80.64	77.31	<u>78.94</u>	48.25	80.60	79.51	80.05	44.96
CMB$_2$	**80.88**	**77.60**	**<u>79.21</u>**	49.02	**80.69**	**79.64**	**<u>80.16</u>**	46.24

Table 1: Performance of different edge scoring methods on the test data. For each measure we report precision, recall, F-score, and average Spearman's correlation (ρ). The highest results for each measure are marked in bold. The underlined F-scores are significantly better compared to the baseline.

allow the unlexicalised parser to treat these nodes as atomic unseen words during POS tagging and parsing. However, we use the last lemma in each multiword phrase for calculating the edge score statistics.

In order to initialise our parse reranking framework, we also need a background corpus that closely matches the evaluation domain. The annotated sentences in GENIA-GR were chosen from abstracts that are labelled with the MeSH term *'NF-kappa B'*. Following this method, we created our background corpus by extracting 7,100 full-text articles (1.6M sentences) from the PubMed Central Open Access collection, containing any of the following terms with any capitalisation: *'nf-kappa b'*, *'nf-kappab'*, *'nf kappa b'*, *'nf-kappa_b'*, *'nf-kb'*, *'nf-κb'*. Since we retain all texts from matching documents, this keyword search acts as a broad indicator that the sentences contain topics which correspond to the evaluation dataset. This focussed corpus was then parsed with the unlexicalised parser and used to create a statistical model for the reranking system, following the same methods as described in Sections 3 and 4.2.

Table 1 also contains the results for experiments in the biomedical domain. The first thing to notice is that while the upper bound for the unlexicalised parser is similar to that for the DepBank experiments in Section 4.2, the baseline results are considerably higher. This is largely due to the nature of the dataset – since many complicated multi-word phrases are treated as single nodes, the parser is not evaluated on edges within these nodes. In addition, treating these nodes as unseen words eliminates many incorrect derivations that would otherwise split the phrases. This results in a naturally higher baseline of 79.38%, and also makes it more difficult to further improve the performance.

The edge scoring methods I, CES$_1$ and ECES$_1$ deliver F-scores lower than the baseline in this experiment. RES, CES$_2$ and ECES$_2$ yield a modest improvement in both F-score and Spearman's correlation. Finally, the combination methods again give the best performance, with CMB$_2$ delivering an F-score of 80.16%, an absolute increase of 0.78%, which is statistically significant ($p < 0.05$). The experiment shows that our self-learning framework works on very different domains, and it can be used to significantly increase the accuracy of an unlexicalised parser without requiring any annotated data.

5 Conclusion

We developed a new self-learning framework for dependency graph reranking that requires only a plaintext corpus from a suitable domain. We automatically parse this corpus and use the highest ranked analyses to estimate maximum likelihood probabilities for bilexical relations. Every dependency graph is first modified to incorporate additional edges that model selected higher-order dependency path relationships. Each edge in the graph is then assigned a confidence score based on statistics from the background corpus and ranking preferences from the unlexicalised parser. We also described a novel method for smoothing these scores using directional distributional similarity measures. Finally, the edge scores are combined into an overall graph score by first averaging them over individual nodes.

As the method requires no annotated data, it can be easily adapted to different domains and genres. Our experiments showed that the reranking process significantly improved performance on both WSJ and biomedical data.

References

Shilpa Arora, Elijah Mayfield, Carolyn Penstein-Rosé, and Eric Nyberg. 2010. Sentiment Classification using Automatically Extracted Subgraph Features. In *Proceedings of the NAACL HLT 2010 Workshop on Computational Approaches to Analysis and Generation of Emotion in Text.*

Mohit Bansal and Dan Klein. 2011. Web-scale features for full-scale parsing. In *Proceedings of the 49th Annual Meeting of the Association for Computational Linguistics*, pages 693–702.

Ted Briscoe and John Carroll. 2006. Evaluating the accuracy of an unlexicalized statistical parser on the PARC DepBank. In *Proceedings of the COLING/ACL on Main conference poster sessions*, number July, pages 41–48, Morristown, NJ, USA. Association for Computational Linguistics.

Ted Briscoe, John Carroll, and Rebecca Watson. 2006. The second release of the RASP system. In *Proceedings of the COLING/ACL 2006 Interactive Presentation Sessions*, number July, pages 77–80, Sydney, Australia. Association for Computational Linguistics.

Xavier Carreras. 2007. Experiments with a higher-order projective dependency parser. In *Proceedings of the CoNLL Shared Task Session of EMNLP-CoNLL*, volume 7, pages 957–961.

Eugene Charniak and Mark Johnson. 2005. Coarse-to-fine n-best parsing and MaxEnt discriminative reranking. *Proceedings of the 43rd Annual Meeting on Association for Computational Linguistics - ACL '05*, 1(June):173–180.

Stephen Clark and James R. Curran. 2007. Formalism-independent parser evaluation with CCG and DepBank. In *Proceedings of the 45th Annual Meeting of the Association of Computational Linguistics*, volume 45, pages 248–255.

Paul R Cohen. 1995. *Empirical Methods for Artificial Intelligence*. The MIT Press, Cambridge, MA.

Michael Collins. 2000. Discriminative reranking for natural language parsing. In *The 17th International Conference on Machine Learning (ICML)*.

Daniel Gildea. 2001. Corpus variation and parser performance. In *Proceedings of the 2001 Conference on Empirical Methods in Natural Language Processing*, pages 167–202.

Jin-Dong Kim, Tomoko Ohta, Yuka Tateisi, and Jun'ichi Tsujii. 2003. GENIA corpus - a semantically annotated corpus for bio-textmining. *Bioinformatics*, 19(1):180–182.

Tracy H. King, Richard Crouch, Stefan Riezler, Mary Dalrymple, and Ronald M. Kaplan. 2003. The PARC 700 dependency bank. In *Proceedings of the EACL03: 4th International Workshop on Linguistically Interpreted Corpora (LINC-03)*, pages 1–8.

Dan Klein and Christopher D. Manning. 2003. Accurate unlexicalized parsing. In *Proceedings of the 41st Annual Meeting on Association for Computational Linguistics*, number July, pages 423–430. Association for Computational Linguistics Morristown, NJ, USA.

Mitchell P. Marcus, Beatrice Santorini, and Mary Ann Marcinkiewicz. 1993. Building a large annotated corpus of English: The Penn Treebank. *Computational linguistics*, pages 1–22.

David McClosky, Eugene Charniak, and Mark Johnson. 2006. Effective self-training for parsing. In *Proceedings of the Human Language Technology Conference of the North American Chapter of the Association of Computational Linguistics*, number June, pages 152–159, Morristown, NJ, USA. Association for Computational Linguistics.

Dominick Ng, Matthew Honnibal, and James R. Curran. 2010. Reranking a wide-coverage CCG parser. In *Australasian Language Technology Association Workshop 2010*, page 90.

Eric W. Noreen. 1989. *Computer Intensive Methods for Testing Hypotheses: An Introduction*. Wiley, New York.

Slav Petrov, Leon Barrett, Romain Thibaux, and Dan Klein. 2006. Learning accurate, compact, and interpretable tree annotation. In *Proceedings of the 21st International Conference on Computational Linguistics and the 44th annual meeting of the ACL (ACL '06)*, pages 433–440, Morristown, NJ, USA. Association for Computational Linguistics.

Barbara Plank and Gertjan van Noord. 2008. Exploring an auxiliary distribution based approach to domain adaptation of a syntactic disambiguation model. In *Coling 2008: Proceedings of the Workshop on Cross-Framework and Cross- Domain Parser Evaluation*, pages 9–16, Manchester, UK. Association for Computational Linguistics.

Marek Rei. 2013. *Minimally supervised dependency-based methods for natural language processing*. Ph.D. thesis, University of Cambridge.

Satoshi Sekine. 1997. The domain dependence of parsing. In *Proceedings of the fifth conference on Applied natural language processing*, volume 1, pages 96–102, Morristown, NJ, USA. Association for Computational Linguistics.

Yuka Tateisi, Yusuke Miyao, Kenji Sagae, and Jun'ichi Tsujii. 2008. GENIA-GR: a Grammatical Relation Corpus for Parser Evaluation in the Biomedical Domain. In *Proceedings of LREC*, pages 1942–1948.

Gertjan van Noord. 2007. Using self-trained bilexical preferences to improve disambiguation accuracy. In *Proceedings of the 10th International Conference on Parsing Technologies*, number June, pages 1–10, Morristown, NJ, USA. Association for Computational Linguistics.

Rebecca Watson, Ted Briscoe, and John Carroll. 2007. Semi-supervised training of a statistical parser from unlabeled partially-bracketed data. *Proceedings of the 10th International Conference on Parsing Technologies - IWPT '07*, (June):23–32.

Guangyou Zhou, Jun Zhao, Kang Liu, and Li Cai. 2011. Exploiting Web-Derived Selectional Preference to Improve Statistical Dependency Parsing. In *49th Annual Meeting of the Association for Computational Linguistics*, pages 1556–1565.

Mining User Relations from Online Discussions using Sentiment Analysis and Probabilistic Matrix Factorization

Minghui Qiu[†], **Liu Yang**[†,‡], **Jing Jiang**[†]
[†] School of Information Systems, Singapore Management University, Singapore
[‡] School of Software and Microelectronics, Peking University, China
{minghui.qiu.2010, jingjiang}@smu.edu.sg, yang.liu@pku.edu.cn

Abstract

Advances in sentiment analysis have enabled extraction of user relations implied in online textual exchanges such as forum posts. However, recent studies in this direction only consider direct relation extraction from text. As user interactions can be sparse in online discussions, we propose to apply collaborative filtering through probabilistic matrix factorization to generalize and improve the opinion matrices extracted from forum posts. Experiments with two tasks show that the learned latent factor representation can give good performance on a relation polarity prediction task and improve the performance of a subgroup detection task.

1 Introduction

The fast growth of the social Web has led to a large amount of interest in online social network analysis. Most existing work on social network analysis relies on explicit links among users such as undirected friendship relations (Liben-Nowell and Kleinberg, 2003), directed following relations (Hopcroft et al., 2011) and trust/distrust relations (Leskovec et al., 2010). However, besides these explicit social relations, the various kinds of interactions between online users often suggest other implicit relations. In particular, in online discussion forums, users interact through textual posts and these exchanged texts often reveal whether two users are friends or foes, or whether two users share the same viewpoint towards a given issue.

To uncover such implicit relations requires text analysis and particularly sentiment analysis. Recently, Hassan et al. (2012) studied predicting the polarity of user interactions in online discussions based on textual exchanges. They found that the automatically predicted signed relations had an accuracy above 80%. The extracted signed network was further used to detect ideological subgroups. This is a piece of pioneering work that extracts online social relations based on text analysis.

In this paper, we further extend the idea of mining social relations from online forum posts by incorporating collaborative filtering. Our work is motivated by the observation that direct textual exchanges between users are sparse. For example, in the data set we use, only around 13% of user-user pairs have direct interactions. Collaborative filtering is a commonly used technique in recommender systems to predict missing ratings. The key assumption is that if two people have the same opinion on an item A, they are likely to also have the same opinion on a different item B. In online discussion forums, users express their opinions about each other as well as the various aspects of the topic under discussion, but not every user comments on every aspect or every other user. Collaborative filtering allows us to identify users with the same opinion even if they have not directly interacted with each other or commented on any common aspect.

Our method starts with extracting opinions on users and topic aspects from online posts using sentiment analysis. The results are two matrices indicating the sentiment polarity scores between pairs of users and pairs of a user and an aspect. To incorporate collaborative filtering, we choose probabilistic matrix factorization (PMF) (Salakhutdinov and Mnih, 2008), a technique that has been successfully applied for collaborative filtering-based recommendation problems. PMF automatically discovers a low-rank representation for both users and items based on observed rating data. In our problem, the predicted sentiment polarity scores are treated as rating data, and the results of PMF are low-rank vectors representing each user in online discussions.

We evaluate our method on two tasks. The first is to predict the polarity of interactions between two users not from their own textual exchanges but from their interactions with other users or comments on topic aspects. The second is to use the latent vectors to group users based on viewpoints. We find that the latent factor representation can produce good prediction results for the first task and improve the clustering results of the second task compared with a number of baselines, showing the effectiveness of collaborative filtering for mining social relations from online discussions.

2 Related Work

Our work is closely related to recent studies on detecting subgroups from online discussions (Abu-Jbara et al., 2012; Dasigi et al., 2012; Hassan et al., 2012). Abu-Jbara et al. (2012) proposed to build discussant attitude profiles (DAP) from online posts and use these profiles to cluster users into subgroups. A DAP is a vector that contains the attitudes of a discussant towards other discussants and a set of opinion targets. We also extract opinions of users towards other users and opinion targets from posts, which are similar to DAPs. The difference is that we further apply probabilistic matrix factorization to derive a low-rank representation from the raw opinion scores. Our comparison with DAP-based clustering shows that probabilistic matrix factorization can improve subgroup detection. Hassan et al. (2012) proposed to predict the polarity of interactions between users based on their textual exchanges. They defined a set of interaction features using sentiment analysis and applied supervised learning for polarity prediction. In comparison, our work is unsupervised, that is, we do not use any ground truth of interaction polarity for training.

Probabilistic matrix factorization was proposed by Salakhutdinov and Mnih (2008) as a collaborative filtering method for recommender systems. It has attracted much attention and been extended by Ma et al. (2008) and Wang and Blei (2011). In particular, Ma et al. (2008) proposed a SocRec model that combines social network information with rating data using the PMF framework to perform social recommendation. Our model bears similarity to SocRec in that we also consider two types of interactions, i.e. user-user interactions and user-aspect interactions. However, different from Ma et al. (2008), we predict both the user-user and user-aspect scores from textual posts using sentiment analysis, and the user-user opinion polarity scores are symmetric.

Part of our method uses sentiment analysis to extract opinions from text. This is built on top of a large body of existing work on opinion extraction, e.g. Choi et al. (2006) and Wu et al. (2009). As the sentiment analysis component is not our main contribution, we do not review existing work along this direction in detail here. Interested readers can refer to Pang and Lee (2008).

The idea of incorporating sentiment analysis into collaborative filtering algorithms has been explored by Kawamae (2011), Moshfeghi et al. (2011) and Leung et al. (2011). While their work also combines sentiment analysis with collaborative filtering, the purpose is to improve the accuracy of item recommendation. In contrast, we borrow the idea and technique of collaborative filtering to improve user relation mining from online text.

3 Method Overview

In this section, we provide an overview of our method. We first introduce some concepts.

User: We use *user* to refer to a discussant in an online discussion. Each user has an online ID, which can be used by other users to refer to him/her in a post. Users are both opinion holders and opinion targets. For example, User 1 below expresses a negative opinion towards another user in the following snippet.

User 1: Actually, I have to disagree with ***you****.*

Aspect: We use *topic aspect* or *aspect* to refer to an opinion target that is related to the topic under discussion. For example, when debating about whether one should vote for Obama, people may express opinions on targets such as "President Obama" and "Republican party," as shown in the following snippets. These aspects are all related to Obama's presidential campaign. As we will explain later, the aspects we consider are named entities and frequent noun phrases.

User 2: Americans should vote for ***President Obama*** *because he picks good corporations as winners.*

User 3: I simply point out how absolutely terrible the ***Republican party*** *is.*

Polarity Score: A sentiment polarity score is a real number between 0 and 1, where 0 indicates a completely negative opinion and 1 indicates a completely positive opinion.

User-User Opinion Matrix: The opinions extracted from posts between users are represented by a user-user opinion matrix S, where entry $s_{i,j}$ is a polarity score between the i-th user and the j-th user. We assume that the polarity scores are symmetric.

User-Aspect Opinion Matrix: The opinions held by different users on the various topic aspects are represented by a user-aspect opinion matrix R, where entry $r_{i,k}$ is a polarity score indicating the i-th user's opinion towards the k-th aspect.

Given the matrices S and R, we perform probabilistic matrix factorization to derive a low-rank vector representation for users and aspects such that if the polarity score between two users or a user and an aspect is high, the dot product between the corresponding two vectors is also high.

In Section 4, we will explain in detail how we identify topic aspects from a discussion thread and how we obtain polarity scores from posts. In Section 5, we will present the details of our probabilistic matrix factorization model.

4 Construction of Opinion Matrices

The opinion matrices are constructed from a single forum thread discussing some controversial topic.

4.1 Aspect Identification

As we have pointed out, there are two kinds of opinion targets, namely users and aspects. Users are clearly defined and can often be identified in posts by their IDs or second person pronouns. For aspects, however, there is not a pre-defined set. We observe that these topic aspects are usually named entities or noun phrases frequently mentioned. We therefore use the OpenNLP toolkit[1] to perform chunking and obtain noun phrases and the Standford NER tagger[2] to identify named entities from the posts.

Some of the candidate aspect phrases identified above actually refer to the same actual aspect, e.g. "Obama voter," "Obama voters" and "the Obama voter." We remove stop words from each candidate phrase and use the WordNet by Miller (1995) to obtain the lemma of each word such that we can normalize the candidate aspect phases to some extent.

Finally, to select salient aspects for a given discussion topic, we count the number of times each candidate aspect has been expressed a positive or negative opinion on by all users, and select those candidate aspects which have opinion expressions from at least M users. We set M to 2 in our experiments. Figure 1 shows the top salient aspects for the thread on "Will you vote for Obama?" We acknowledge there are still duplicate aspects in the results like "Republican Party" and "GOP". To normalize these aspects, some additional information such as Wikipedia entries and Google snippets may be considered. We will study this problem in our future work.

4.2 Opinion Expression Identification

Our next step is to identify candidate opinion expressions. This problem has been studied in Hu and Liu (2004), Popescu and Etzioni (2005), and Hassan and Radev (2010). Based on previous work, we do the following. We first combine three popular sentiment lexicons to form a single sentiment lexicon: the lexicon used in Hu and Liu (2004), MPQA Subjectivity Lexicon by Wilson et al. (2005) and SentiWordNet by Baccianella et al. (2010). Our final sentiment lexicon contains 15,322 negative expressions and 10,144 positive expressions. We then identify candidate opinion expressions by searching for occurrences of words in this lexicon in the posts.

4.3 Opinion Relation Extraction

Given a post that contains an aspect and an opinion expression, we still need to determine whether the opinion expression is used to describe the aspect. This is a relation extraction problem. We use a supervised learning approach based on dependency

[1] http://opennlp.apache.org/

[2] http://nlp.stanford.edu/ner/index.shtml

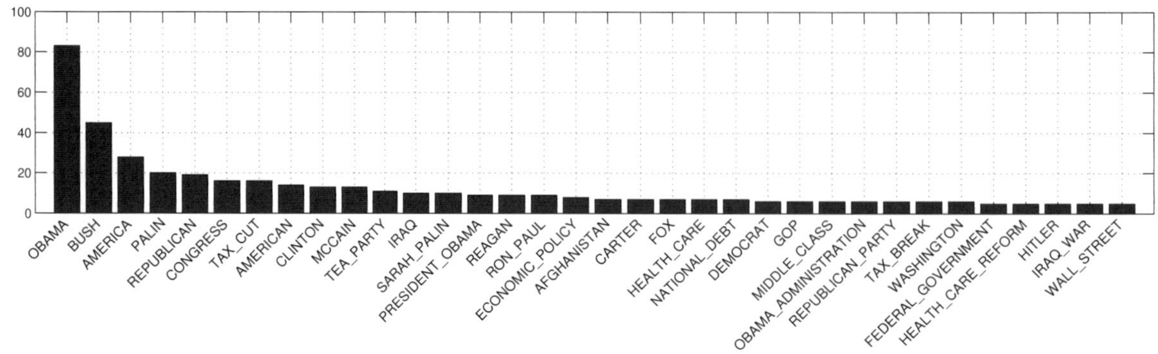

Figure 1: Salient aspects and number of users who express opinions on them in the thread "Will you vote for Obama?"

ID	Dependency path rule	Example
R1	$ADJ_{OP} \leftarrow amod \leftarrow N_{TR}$	I simply point out how *terrible* REPUBLICAN PARTY is.
R2	$ADJ_{OP} \rightarrow nsubj \rightarrow N_{TR}$	BUSH is even more *reasonable* for tax hike than Obama.
R3	$V_{OP} \rightarrow dobj \rightarrow N_{TR}$	I would never *support* OBAMA.
R4	$V_{OP} \rightarrow prep\_* \rightarrow N_{TR}$	I'll *vote* for OBAMA.
R5	$V_{OP} \rightarrow nsubjpass \rightarrow N_{TR}$	DEMOCRATIC PARTY are ultimately *corrupted* by love of money.
R6	$N_{OP} \leftarrow dobj \leftarrow V \rightarrow nsubj \rightarrow N_{TR}$	PAKISTAN is increasing terrorist *threat*.
R7	$ADJ_{OP} \leftarrow amod \leftarrow N \rightarrow nsubj \rightarrow N_{TR}$	OBAMA was a *top* scorer for occidental college.
R8	$ADV_{OP} \leftarrow advmod \leftarrow V \rightarrow nsubj \rightarrow N_{TR}$	OBAMA is *smarter* than people.

Table 1: Examples of frequent dependency path rules in our training data. OP and TR refer to the opinion and the target. The opinion words are in italic and the aspect words are in uppercase.

paths. Previous work by Mintz et al. (2009), and Qiu et al. (2009) has shown that the shortest path between a candidate opinion aspect and a candidate opinion expression in the dependency parse tree can be effective in extracting opinion relations. We use the Stanford Parser from Klein and Manning (2003) to obtain the dependency parse trees for each sentence in the posts and then get the dependency paths between each pair of candidate aspect and opinion expression. We use dependency relations and POS tags of nodes along the path to represent a dependency path. Given a set of training sentences (we use the one from Wu et al. (2009)), we can get a set of dependency path rules based on their frequencies in the training data. Table 1 shows the frequent dependency path rules in our training data.

When a pair of aspect and opinion expression is identified to be related, we use the polarity of the opinion expression to label the relation. Finally, given a pair of users, we use the percentage of positive interactions between them over all subjective interactions (i.e. interactions with either positive or negative opinions) as extracted from their exchanged posts as the sentiment polarity score between the two users, regardless of the reply-to direction of the posts. Similarly, given a user and an aspect, we also use the percentage of positive opinion relations extracted as the sentiment polarity score between them. Thus the user-user opinion matrix and the user-aspect opinion matrix are constructed. If there is no subjective interaction detected between two users or between a user and an aspect, the corresponding entry in the matrix is left empty. We will see later that empty entries in the matrices are not used in the probabilistic matrix factorization step.

5 Probabilistic Matrix Factorization

As we have pointed out earlier, a problem with the matrices extracted as described in Section 4 is that the matrices are sparse, i.e. many entries are empty. For the data set we use, we find that around 87% of entries in the user-user opinion matrix and around 90% of entries in the user-aspect opinion matrix are empty. In this section, we describe how we use Probabilistic Matrix Factorization (PMF) to represent users and aspects in a latent factor space and thus generalize the user preferences.

Our model is almost a direct application of probabilistic matrix factorization from Salakhutdinov and Mnih (2008), originally proposed for recommender systems. The main difference is that the user-user opinion polarity scores are symmetric. Our model is also similar to the one used by Ma et al. (2008). We describe our model as follows.

We assume that there are K latent factors with which both users and aspects can be represented. Let $u_i \in \mathbb{R}^K$ denote the vector in the latent factor space for the i-th user, and a_k the vector for the k-th aspect.

Recall that the opinions extracted from posts between users are represented by a user-user opinion matrix S, and the opinions held by different users on the various topic aspects are represented by a user-aspect opinion matrix R. We assume that the polarity scores $s_{i,j}$ between the i-th and the j-th users and $r_{i,k}$ between the i-th user and the k-th aspect in the two matrices S and R are generated in the following way:

$$\begin{aligned} p(s_{i,j}|u_i, u_j, \sigma_1^2) &= \mathcal{N}(s_{i,j}|g(u_i^T u_j), \sigma_1^2), \\ p(r_{i,k}|u_i, a_k, \sigma_2^2) &= \mathcal{N}(r_{i,k}|g(u_i^T a_k), \sigma_2^2), \end{aligned}$$

where σ_1^2 and σ_2^2 are variance parameters, $g(\cdot)$ the logistic function, and $\mathcal{N}(\cdot|\mu, \sigma^2)$ is the normal distribution with mean μ and variance σ^2.

We can see that with this generative assumption, if two users are similar in terms of their dot product in the latent factor space, then they are more likely to have positive interactions as extracted from their textual exchanges. Similarly, if a user and an aspect are similar, then the user is more likely to express a positive opinion on the aspect in his/her posts. The latent factors can therefore encode user preferences and similarity between two users in the latent factor space reflects whether they share similar viewpoints.

We also place the following prior over u_i and a_k:

$$\begin{aligned} p(u_i|\sigma_U^2) &= \mathcal{N}(u_i|\vec{0}, \sigma_U^2\mathbf{I}), \\ p(a_k|\sigma_A^2) &= \mathcal{N}(a_k|\vec{0}, \sigma_A^2\mathbf{I}), \end{aligned}$$

where σ_U^2 and σ_A^2 are two variance parameters for users and aspects, respectively, and $\mathbf{I}$ is the identify matrix.

Figure 2 shows the plate notation for the generative model.

Let $\mathcal{U}$ be a $K \times U$ matrix containing the vectors u_i for all U users, and $\mathcal{A}$ be an $K \times A$ matrix containing the vectors a_k for all A aspects. To automatically learn $\mathcal{U}$ and $\mathcal{A}$, we minimize the following objective function:

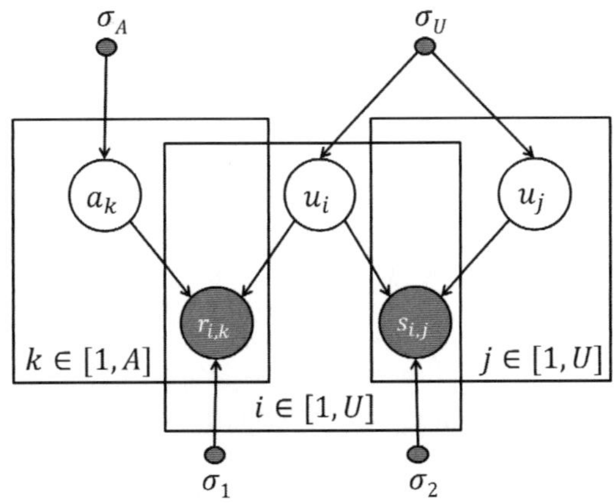

Figure 2: Probabilistic matrix factorization model on opinion matrices.

$$\begin{aligned} &\mathcal{L}(\mathcal{U}, \mathcal{A}, \mathcal{S}, \mathcal{R}) \\ = \;& \frac{1}{2}\sum_{i=1}^{U}\sum_{k=1}^{A}\mathbb{I}(r_{i,k})(r_{i,k} - g(u_i^T a_k))^2 \\ + \;& \frac{\lambda_1}{2}\sum_{i=1}^{U}\sum_{j=1}^{U}\mathbb{I}(s_{i,j})(s_{i,j} - g(u_i^T u_j))^2 \\ + \;& \frac{\lambda_U}{2}||\mathcal{U}||_F^2 + \frac{\lambda_A}{2}||\mathcal{A}||_F^2, \qquad (1) \end{aligned}$$

where $\lambda = \frac{\sigma_1^2}{\sigma_2^2}$, $\lambda_U = \frac{\sigma_1^2}{\sigma_U^2}$, and $\lambda_A = \frac{\sigma_1^2}{\sigma_A^2}$, $\mathbb{I}(s)$ is an indicator function which equals 1 when s is not empty and otherwise 0.

To optimize the objective function above, we can perform gradient descent on $\mathcal{U}$ and $\mathcal{A}$ to find a local optimum point. The derivation is similar to Ma et al. (2008).

Degenerate Versions of the Model

We refer to the complete model described above as PMF-UOM (PMF model based on User Opinion Matrices). PMF-UOM has the following two degenerate versions by considering either only the user-user opinion matrix or only the user-aspect opinion matrix.

PMF-UU: In this degenerate version of the model, we use only the user-user opinion matrix to learn the latent factor representation. Specifically, the objective function is modified such that we drop the sum of the square errors involving R and the regularizer on $\mathcal{A}$.

PMF-UA: In this degenerate version of the model, we use only the user-aspect opinion matrix to learn the latent factor representation. Specifically, the objective function is modified such that we drop the sum of the square errors involving S.

6 Experiments

In this section, we present our experiments that evaluate our model.

6.1 Data Set and Experiment Settings

The data set we use comes from Abu-Jbara et al. (2012) and Hassan et al. (2012). The data set contains a set of discussion threads collected from two political forums (Createdebate[3] and Politicalforum[4]) and one Wikipedia discussion session. We randomly select 6 threads from the original data set to evaluate our model. Some details of the data we use are listed in Table 2.

ID	topic	#sides	#sentences	#users
DS1	Vote for Obama	2	12492	197
DS2	Abortion Banned	6	3844	70
DS3	Profile Muslims	4	2167	69
DS4	England and USA	6	2030	62
DS5	Tax Cuts	2	1193	26
DS6	Political Spectrum	7	1130	50

Table 2: Some statistics of the data sets.

In our experiments, for the PMF-based methods, we set the number of latent factors to be 10 as we do not observe big difference when vary the latent factor size from 10 to 50. For the other parameters, we select the optimal setting for each thread based on the average of 50 runs. λ_U is chosen from $\{0.1, 0.01\}$, λ_A from $\{0.01, 0.001\}$ and λ from $\{1, 0.1\}$.

6.2 Relation Polarity Prediction

The first task we use to evaluate our model is to predict the polarity of interactions between two users. Different from Hassan et al. (2012), however, we are not using this task to evaluate the accuracy of sentiment analysis from text. Our experimental setting is completely different in that we do not make use of the text exchanges between the two users but instead use their interactions with other users or aspects. The purpose is to test the effectiveness of collaborative filtering.

Experimental Setting: The experiments are set up in the following way. Given a pair of users i and j who have directly exchanged posts, i.e. $s_{i,j}$ is not empty, we first hide the value of $s_{i,j}$ in the matrix S. Let the altered matrix be $S_{\neg(i,j)}$. We then use $S_{\neg(i,j)}$ instead of S in the learning process as described in Section 5 to learn the latent factor representation. Let $\hat{u}_i$ and $\hat{u}_j$ denote the learned latent vectors for user i and user j. We predict the polarity of relation between i and j as follows:

$$\hat{s}_{i,j} = \begin{cases} 1 & \text{if } g(\hat{u}_i^T \hat{u}_j) > 0.5, \\ 0 & \text{otherwise,} \end{cases}$$

where $g(\cdot)$ is the logistic function to convert the dot product into a value between 0 and 1.

To judge the quality of the predicted polarity $\hat{s}_{i,j}$, we could compare it with $s_{i,j}$. But since $s_{i,j}$ itself is predicted from the textual exchanges between i and j, it is not the ground truth. Instead, we ask two human annotators to assign the true polarity label for user i and user j by reading the textual exchanges between them and judging whether they are friends or foes in the discussion thread. The annotators are asked to assign a score of 0 (indicating a negative relation), 0.5 (indicating a neutral relation) or 1 (indicating a positive relation). The lowest agreement score based on Cohen's kappa coefficient among the 6 threads we use is 0.56, showing fair to good agreement. As ground truth, we set the final polarity score to 1 if the average score of the two annotators is larger than 0.5 and 0 otherwise.

We compare the PMF-based methods with two majority baselines: MBL-0 always predicts negative relations for all the user pairs (assuming most relations are negative) and MBL-1 always predicts positive relations (assuming most relations are positive).

We use *MAE* (mean absolute error) and *RMSE* (root mean square error) as defined below as performance metrics:

$$\mathit{MAE} = \frac{\sum_{i,j} |\hat{s}_{i,j} - l_{i,j}|}{N},$$

$$\mathit{RMSE} = \sqrt{\frac{\sum_{i,j} (\hat{s}_{i,j} - l_{i,j})^2}{N}},$$

[3] www.createdebate.com

[4] www.politicalforum.com

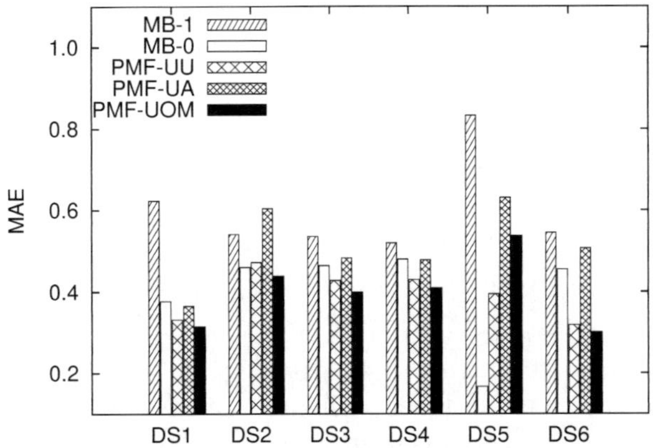

Figure 3: Comparing all the methods in terms of MAE.

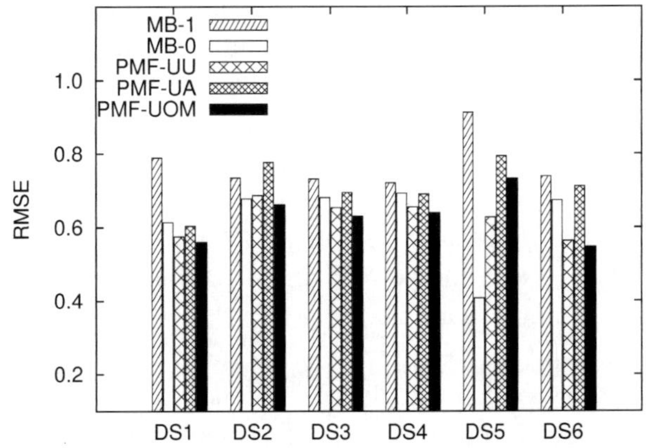

Figure 4: Comparing all the methods in terms of RMSE.

where N is the total number of user pairs we test, and $l_{i,j}$ is the ground truth polarity score between user i and user j.

Results: We show the results of our model and of PMF-UU and PMF-UA in terms of MAE in Figure 3 and RMSE in Figure 4. The *MAE* values range between 0.31 and 0.44 except for DS5, which has a higher error rate of 0.53. The results show that even without knowing the textual exchanges between two users, from their interactions with other users and/or with topic aspects, we can still infer the polarity of their relation with decent accuracy most of the time.

The results also show the comparison between our model and the competing methods. We can see that overall the complete model (PMF-UOM) performs better than the two degenerate models (PMF-UU and PMF-UA). The differences are statistically significant at the 5% level without considering DS5, as indicated by a 2-tailed paired t-test. Comparing to the majority baselines, our model significantly outperforms MBL-1 at 1% significance level while outperforms MBL-0 on all the data sets except DS5. A close examinations shows DS5 has very unbalanced relations (around 83% of relations are negative). Except for the unbalanced data set, our model has reasonably good performance.

6.3 Subgroup Detection

The second task we study is the problem of detecting ideological subgroups from discussion threads. The original data set has been labeled with the ground truth for this problem, that is, for each thread the number of viewpoints is known and the viewpoint held by each user is labeled. A subgroup is defined as a set of users holding the same viewpoint.

Experimental Setting: Through this second experiment, we would like to verify the hypothesis that using the learned latent factor representation $\mathcal{U}$ for users, we can better detect subgroups than directly using the opinion matrices S and R. For all the methods we compare, we first construct a feature vector representation for each user. We then apply K-means clustering to group users. The number of clusters is set to be the true number of viewpoints for each thread. The different methods are described below:

- PMF-based methods: We simply use the learned latent vectors $\hat{u}_i$ after optimizing the objective function as the feature vectors to represent each user.
- BL-1: This is our own implementation to simulate the method by Abu-Jbara et al. (2012). Here each user is represented by a $(3 \times (U + A))$-dimensional vector, where U is the number of users and A is the number of aspects, i.e. $(U + A)$ is the total number of opinion targets. For each opinion target, there are 3 dimensions in the feature vector, corresponding to the number of positive, neutral and negative opinion expressions towards the target from the online posts.
- BL-2: BL-2 is similar to BL-1 except that we only use a $(U+A)$-dimensional vector to repre-

sent each user. Here for each opinion target, we directly use the corresponding sentiment polarity score $s_{i,j}$ or $r_{i,j}$ from the matrix S or R. For empty entries in S and R, we use a score of 0.5.

We use *Purity* (the higher the better), *Entropy* (the lower the better) and *Rand Index* (the higher the better) to evaluate the performance of subgroup detection (Manning et al., 2008). We further use *Accuracy* obtained by choosing the best alignment of clusters with the ground truth class labels and computing the percentage of users that are "classified" correctly.

Results: We first give an overview of the performance of all the methods on the task. We show the average performance of the methods on all the data sets in Figure 5. Overall, our model has a better performance than all the competing methods.

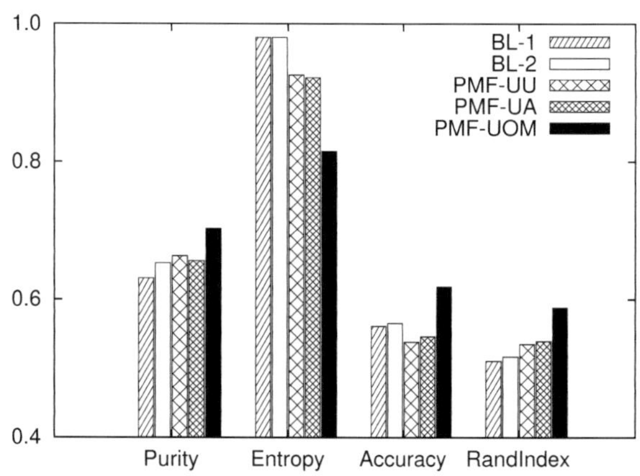

Figure 5: An overview of the average performance of all the methods on the 6 threads.

We present all the results in Table 3. We perform 2-tailed paired t-test on the results. We find that PMF-UOM outperforms all the other methods in terms of RandIndex at 5% significance level and outperforms other methods in terms of Purity and Entropy at 10% significance level. Furthermore, the PMF-UOM model outperforms its degenerative models PMF-UU and PMF-UA at 10% significance level in terms of all the measures.

We observe that PMF-UOM achieves the best performance in terms of all the measures for almost all threads. In particular, comparison with BL-1 and BL-2 shows that collaborative filtering can generalize the user preferences and help better group the users based on their viewpoints. The fact that PMF-UOM outperforms both PMF-UU and PMF-UA shows that it is important to consider both user-user interactions and user-aspect interactions.

The Effects of Cluster Size: To test the effect of the number of clusters on the experiment result, we vary the number of clusters from 2 to 10 in all methods. We find that all methods tend to achieve better results when the number of clusters equals the ground truth cluster size. Overall, our method PMF-UOM shows a better performance than the other four methods when the number of clusters changes, which indicates the robustness of our method.

		BL-1	BL-2	PMF-UU	PMF-UA	PMF-UOM
DS1	*P*	0.61	0.61	0.61	0.61	**0.62**
	E	0.96	0.96	**0.94**	0.95	**0.94**
	A	0.59	0.59	0.55	0.57	**0.60**
	R	0.51	0.51	0.50	0.51	**0.52**
DS2	*P*	0.53	0.63	0.64	0.61	**0.68**
	E	1.17	1.22	1.14	1.09	**0.99**
	A	0.47	0.53	0.48	0.47	**0.50**
	R	0.50	0.50	0.56	0.56	**0.58**
DS3	*P*	0.66	**0.68**	0.62	0.60	**0.68**
	E	1.05	1.01	1.06	1.07	**0.94**
	A	0.61	**0.63**	0.48	0.47	0.58
	R	0.50	0.52	0.53	0.53	**0.57**
DS4	*P*	0.64	0.64	0.66	0.65	**0.70**
	E	0.92	0.94	0.90	0.91	**0.85**
	A	0.59	0.64	0.62	0.62	**0.68**
	R	0.49	0.52	0.52	0.51	**0.56**
DS5	*P*	0.86	0.86	0.86	0.86	0.86
	E	0.56	0.56	0.49	0.48	**0.38**
	A	0.70	0.70	0.57	0.60	**0.71**
	R	0.52	0.52	0.43	0.45	**0.56**
DS6	*P*	0.50	0.50	0.60	0.60	**0.68**
	E	1.35	1.35	1.03	1.04	**0.79**
	A	0.40	0.30	0.53	0.54	**0.64**
	R	0.53	0.53	0.68	0.68	**0.74**

Table 3: Results on subgroup detection on all the 6 threads. *P*, *E*, *A* and *R* refer to *Purity*, *Entropy*, *Accuracy* and *RandIndex*, respectively.

7 Conclusions

In this paper, we studied how to use probabilistic matrix factorization, a common technique for collaborative filtering, to improve relation mining from online discussion forums. We first applied sentiment analysis to extract user-user opinions and user-aspect opinions from forum posts. The extracted opinions form two opinion matrices. We then applied probabilistic matrix factorization using these two matrices to discover a low-rank latent factor space which aims to better generalize the users' underlying preferences and indicate user similarities based on their viewpoints. Using a data set with 6 discussion threads, we showed that the learned latent vectors can be used to predict the polarity of user relations well without using the users' direct interaction data, demonstrating the effectiveness of collaborative filtering. We further found that for the task of subgroup detection, the latent vectors gave better performance than using the directly extracted opinion data, again showing that collaborative filtering through probabilistic matrix factorization can help address the sparseness problem in the extracted opinion matrices and help improve relation mining.

Our current work mainly focuses on the user opinion matrices. As future work, we would like to explore how to incorporate textual contents without opinionated expressions. One possible way is to consider the combination of matrix factorization and topic modeling as studied by Wang and Blei (2011) where we can use topic modeling to study textual contents.

Acknowledgments

We thank the reviewers for their valuable comments on this work.

References

Amjad Abu-Jbara, Pradeep Dasigi, Mona Diab, and Dragomir R. Radev. 2012. Subgroup detection in ideological discussions. In *Proceedings of the 50th Annual Meeting of the Association for Computational Linguistics*, pages 399–409.

Stefano Baccianella, Andrea Esuli, and Fabrizio Sebastiani. 2010. Sentiwordnet 3.0: An enhanced lexical resource for sentiment analysis and opinion mining. In *LREC*.

Yejin Choi, Eric Breck, and Claire Cardie. 2006. Joint extraction of entities and relations for opinion recognition. In *Proceedings of the 2006 Conference on Empirical Methods in Natural Language Processing*, EMNLP '06, pages 431–439, Stroudsburg, PA, USA. Association for Computational Linguistics.

Pradeep Dasigi, Weiwei Guo, and Mona T. Diab. 2012. Genre independent subgroup detection in online discussion threads: A study of implicit attitude using textual latent semantics. In *Proceedings of the 50th Annual Meeting of the Association for Computational Linguistics*, pages 65–69.

Ahmed Hassan and Dragomir Radev. 2010. Identifying text polarity using random walks. In *Proceedings of the 48th Annual Meeting of the Association for Computational Linguistics*, ACL '10, pages 395–403, Stroudsburg, PA, USA. Association for Computational Linguistics.

Ahmed Hassan, Amjad Abu-Jbara, and Dragomir Radev. 2012. Detecting subgroups in online discussions by modeling positive and negative relations among participants. In *Proceedings of the 2012 EMNLP*, pages 59–70.

John Hopcroft, Tiancheng Lou, and Jie Tang. 2011. Who will follow you back?: reciprocal relationship prediction. In *Proceedings of the 20th ACM international conference on Information and knowledge management*, pages 1137–1146.

Minqing Hu and Bing Liu. 2004. Mining and summarizing customer reviews. In *Proceedings of the 10th ACM SIGKDD international conference on Knowledge discovery and data mining*, pages 168–177.

Noriaki Kawamae. 2011. Predicting future reviews: sentiment analysis models for collaborative filtering. In *Proceedings of the fourth ACM international conference on Web search and data mining*, WSDM '11, pages 605–614.

Dan Klein and Christopher D. Manning. 2003. Accurate unlexicalized parsing. In *Proceedings of the 41st Annual Meeting on Association for Computational Linguistics - Volume 1*, ACL '03, pages 423–430, Stroudsburg, PA, USA. Association for Computational Linguistics.

Jure Leskovec, Daniel Huttenlocher, and Jon Kleinberg. 2010. Predicting positive and negative links in online social networks. In *Proceedings of the 19th international conference on World wide web*, pages 641–650.

Cane Wing-Ki Leung, Stephen Chi-Fai Chan, Fu-Lai Chung, and Grace Ngai. 2011. A probabilistic rating inference framework for mining user preferences from reviews. *World Wide Web*, 14(2):187–215.

David Liben-Nowell and Jon Kleinberg. 2003. The link prediction problem for social networks. In *Proceedings of the twelfth international conference on Information and knowledge management*.

Hao Ma, Haixuan Yang, Michael R. Lyu, and Irwin King. 2008. Sorec: Social recommendation using probabilistic matrix factorization. In *Proc. of ACM international conference on Information and knowledge management*.

Christopher D. Manning, Prabhakar Raghavan, and Hinrich Schtze. 2008. *Introduction to Information Retrieval*. Cambridge University Press, July.

George A. Miller. 1995. Wordnet: A lexical database for english. *Communications of the ACM*, Vol. 38, No. 11:39–41.

Mike Mintz, Steven Bills, Rion Snow, and Dan Jurafsky. 2009. Distant supervision for relation extraction without labeled data. In *Proceedings of the Joint Conference of the 47th Annual Meeting of the ACL and the 4th International Joint Conference on Natural Language Processing of the AFNLP: Volume 2 - Volume 2*, ACL '09, pages 1003–1011, Stroudsburg, PA, USA. Association for Computational Linguistics.

Yashar Moshfeghi, Benjamin Piwowarski, and Joemon M. Jose. 2011. Handling data sparsity in collaborative filtering using emotion and semantic based features. In *Proceedings of the 34th international ACM SIGIR conference on Research and development in Information Retrieval*, SIGIR '11, pages 625–634.

Bo Pang and Lillian Lee. 2008. Opinion mining and sentiment analysis. *Found. Trends Inf. Retr.*, 2(1-2):1–135, January.

Ana-Maria Popescu and Oren Etzioni. 2005. Extracting product features and opinions from reviews. In *Proceedings of the conference on Human Language Technology and Empirical Methods in Natural Language Processing*, HLT '05, pages 339–346, Stroudsburg, PA, USA. Association for Computational Linguistics.

Guang Qiu, Bing Liu, Jiajun Bu, and Chun Chen. 2009. Expanding domain sentiment lexicon through double propagation. In *Proceedings of the 21st international jont conference on Artifical intelligence*, IJCAI'09, pages 1199–1204, San Francisco, CA, USA. Morgan Kaufmann Publishers Inc.

Ruslan Salakhutdinov and Andriy Mnih. 2008. Probabilistic matrix factorization. In *Advances in Neural Information Processing Systems*, volume 20.

Chong Wang and David M. Blei. 2011. Collaborative topic modeling for recommending scientific articles. In *Proceedings of the 17th ACM SIGKDD international conference on Knowledge discovery and data mining*, pages 448–456.

Theresa Wilson, Janyce Wiebe, and Paul Hoffmann. 2005. Recognizing contextual polarity in phrase-level sentiment analysis. In *HLT/EMNLP*.

Yuanbin Wu, Qi Zhang, Xuanjing Huang, and Lide Wu. 2009. Phrase dependency parsing for opinion mining. In *Proceedings of the 2009 Conference on Empirical Methods in Natural Language Processing: Volume 3 - Volume 3*, EMNLP '09, pages 1533–1541, Stroudsburg, PA, USA. Association for Computational Linguistics.

Focused training sets to reduce noise in NER feature models

Amber McKenzie
Computer Science and Engineering Department
University of South Carolina
mckenzie.amber@gmail.com

Abstract

Feature and context aggregation play a large role in current NER systems, allowing significant opportunities for research into optimizing these features to cater to different domains. This work strives to reduce the noise introduced into aggregated features from disparate and generic training data in order to allow for contextual features that more closely model the entities in the target data. The proposed approach trains models based on only a part of the training set that is more similar to the target domain. To this end, models are trained for an existing NER system using the top documents from the training set that are similar to the target document in order to demonstrate that this technique can be applied to improve any pre-built NER system. Initial results show an improvement over the University of Illinois NE tagger with a weighted average F1 score of 91.67 compared to the Illinois tagger's score of 91.32. This research serves as a proof-of-concept for future planned work to cluster the training documents to produce a number of more focused models from a given training set, thereby reducing noise and extracting a more representative feature set.

1 Introduction

Though research in the area of named entity recognition (NER) is fairly extensive, current state-of-the-art solutions are generic, succeeding only for domains similar to their training data, and still fail to adequately provide functionality that is adaptable to a broad range of domains (Tkachenko and Simanovsky, 2012). This leaves room for improvement in designing a system that can more easily adapt to previously unseen data. In particular, the increasingly popular feature set produced by feature and context aggregation provides many opportunities for different types of optimization given the strong correlation between the training input and the feature values that are produced. This is due to the fact that aggregation looks at features at a document or corpus level, rather than at the token level, and therefore will be sensitive to changes in the training set. This research looks to exploit this aspect of feature and context aggregation by identifying portions of a training set that are more similar to the target data and will thus provide feature values that are likely more representative of the entities within that data.

Rather than train a model with a full training set, this approach extracts portions of the training data that are most similar to the target data and trains a model using only those documents. This initial work tailors a model to a given target document to demonstrate that less, but more appropriate, training data is preferable to a full generic training set.

Similar to that of Dalton et al. (2011), in which they use passage retrieval to expand their feature set, cosine similarity is used to retrieve documents containing similar entity instances in an effort to achieve a more relevant feature set that will result in more likely output label predictions. However, the proposed approach conducts document similarity above the tagger level, without modifying the underlying tagging system. This allows for domain adaptation improvements using any available NER tagger. This approach is able to be implemented with any pre-existing NER tagger in order to improve the performance of the tagger for out-of-domain data. Initial results show an improvement over the standard NE tagger from the University of Illinois at Urbana-Champaign using a smaller training set and no additional external data sources.

2 Related work

Feature aggregation refers to collecting feature information from across a document or document set, rather than simply taking the information from a particular word instance. With feature aggregation, researchers strive to expand the context used to predict the classification of a given token. Much of the recent work on features for NER has been related to aggregation of some sort in an effort to widen model coverage, decrease human interaction in the feature generation process, and increase detection and classification accuracy. Many systems incorporating feature aggregation have seen performance improvements over other nearly state-of-the-art systems.

The global features discussed by Chieu and Ng (2003) represent context aggregation in that they extract features about the word in multiple instances within a document. Krishnan and Manning (2006) introduce a two-stage approach to feature aggregation layering two CRFs in which the second uses the output of the first as features, aggregated over both documents and the entire corpus.

Ratinov and Roth (2009) use a similar implementation for their work, substituting relative frequencies of tags within a 1000 token window for the majority tags used by Krishnan and Manning. They refer to the information gathered from aggregation as non-local features and categorize the different approaches as context aggregation, two-stage prediction aggregation and extended prediction history. In an effort not to treat all tokens in a text similarly, which they assert is the case with context aggregation and two-stage prediction, Ratinov and Roth developed an approach for non-local feature generation based on extended prediction history. Their approach is based on the idea that named entities are easier to spot at the beginning of texts where they are first introduced. They keep track of all label assignments for the token in the last 1000 words and use that probability information as a prediction history feature for the token.

Huang and Yates (2009) present their feature aggregation approaches in the form of smoothing of the dataset. Their goal for smoothing is the same as for aggregation in that they strive to extend the usefulness of the model by sharing information about multiple contexts for a token in order to provide more information about words that are rarely, or never, seen in training. In experimentation, the authors found that their smoothing approach improved performance on rare words, out-of-domain text, and smaller training sets.

Dalton et al. (2011) take an external knowledge approach to context aggregation. Using an information retrieval method called Pseudo-Relevance Feedback (PRF), they query for relevant passages in an external data set using the context for the target token. Given that they searched for the context that the entity occurs in, it is assumed that the top returned passages all contain instances of the entity with the same label. They then aggregate the features for this token across a number of the top retrieved documents and induce features based on this information. Their approach is compared with the Stanford and Illinois NER systems and found that their aggregated features improved performance over those systems.

Apart from the body of work attempting to incorporate external data sources, such as Wikipedia, to augment training data, approaches for domain adaptation for NER focus on either adapting features to fit the domain or searching for more abstract features that can span multiple domains (Zhang and Johnson, 2003; Huang and Yates, 2009; Lin and Wu, 2009). This is largely due to the assumption that a domain-specific, tagged training set will not be available for most target domains.

This research expands on previous work by providing a more informative training set that is a closer representation of the features contained in the target documents. Further, the proposed system does not require external knowledge sources or additional tagged data to augment the utilized training set. The modifications that are made are implemented above the tagger level allowing for any existing tagger to be used without need to alter the underlying source code.

3 NER approach

Feature aggregation has become an integral part of building an NER prediction model. Because aggregating the context of every named entity across an entire training set can be fairly computationally expensive and introduces significant noise into the features due to the many contexts in which an entity may occur, many researchers have chosen instead to conduct local aggregation, such as across a document, or with a certain window of tokens that may span several documents. The NER tagger produced by the University of Illinois at Urbana-Champaign, one of the best performing systems on the CoNLL 2003 data set, uses a 1000 token window across which to take their global context aggregation (Ratinov and Roth, 2009). By choosing 1000 tokens, the researchers hope to be able to capture a large enough example set to provide a robust feature value while maintaining a reasonable computation time. However, this method leaves the choice of context to chance: determined by how the documents are organized within the training set. A better option would be to choose the context that best represents the entities to be tagged. To that end, this work serves to provide a more useful and informative training set from which to pull context information.

The hypothesis explored in this work is that the context aggregation feature would prove more useful if the training data were more specific to the target entities. For this research, documents from the training set were compiled based on their similarity to the target document. These documents were then used to train a model for the Illinois NE tagger. In this way we strive to reduce the noise present in the context aggregation feature as a result of the generic contexts found in a large, often heterogeneous, training set and produce feature values that are more representative of the target entities, thus producing more reliable output labels.

3.1 Methodology

For an initial proof-of-concept test, vectors were created for all test (not the development set) and training documents in the CoNLL-2003 shared task data. This corpus was chosen due to the previous NER research using this corpus and the results available using the LBJ tagger. Also, it has been noted that the test and training sets within the corpus are not as similar in nature as are the development and training sets (Ratinov and Roth, 2009). The training set contains 946 documents, while the test set contains 231. For each test document, a specified number of the top documents from the training set most similar to that test document was collected. For this initial work, a simple cosine similarity measure was used. These top similar documents were used as a training set for the LBJ tagger, and the test document was then tagged using the resultant model. The system was tested by pulling the top 20, 50, 100, and 300 similar training documents to train the models. The performance of this customized model is compared to that of the standard, two-phase LBJ tagger trained on the full CoNLL '03 training set.

3.2 Results

For this research, because each test document is tagged using a different model, we chose to measure our performance on a per-document basis, rather than the standard overall measure for the entire test set.[1] This performance is compared to that achieved by the standard LBJ tagger on the same document. Figure 1 shows how many documents were tagged more accurately using the proposed system compared to the LBJ tagger.

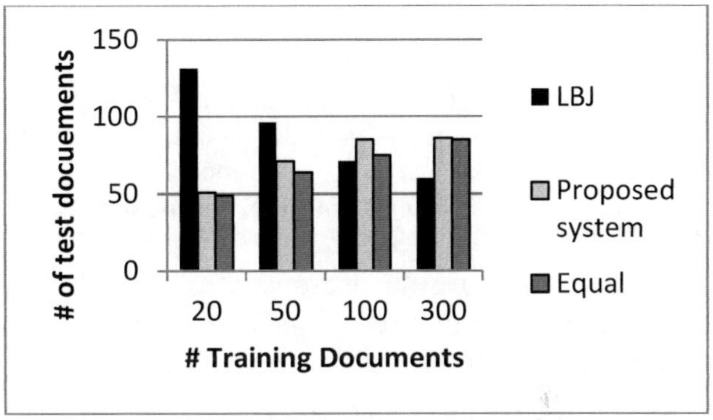

Figure 1 – Results showing the number of documents for which each system performed better or for which they had equal F1 scores.

Further, Figure 2 displays the average percentage better and worse in terms of F1 score for each training document size. In contrast to Figure 1, Figure 2 demonstrates the average difference in F1 scores between the LBJ tagger trained on the entire training set and the proposed system trained on varying numbers of training documents. These numbers indicate that there exists an optimal balance that can achieve the dual advantages of having a smaller, more relevant training set while also maintaining enough data to ensure enough features to accurately predict NER labels.

The overall aggregated difference is also provided as a more global view of performance achievements. This measurement is calculated by multiplying the F1 score of a given document by the number of entity tokens contained in that document, summing these calculations, and then dividing by the total number of entity tokens across the test dataset. These results reveal an improvement over the Illinois tagger for the 300 document train-

[1] The Illinois NE tagger only provides performance information in the form of percentages and does not give enough information to calculate an overall F1 score for the test set using the CoNLL eval script.

ing set with a weighted average F1 score of 91.67 compared to the Illinois score of 91.32.

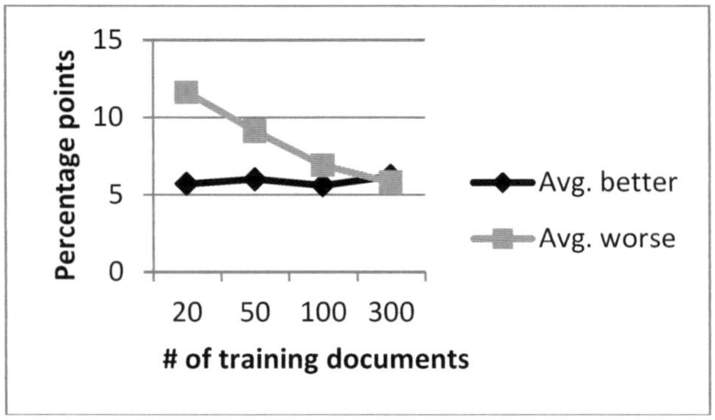

Figure 2 – Average percentage points better and worse in the F1 score that the proposed system achieved compared to the standard LBJ tagger for models trained with the top 20, 50, 100, and 300 similar documents.

These initial results demonstrate that an available training set can be easily tailored to better serve the needs of a target data set that differs from the training set and showed improvements on an existing competitive NER system by modifying the training data set used to build the prediction model. By identifying a smaller, relevant training set, the sequence tagging model is better equipped to accurately predict output labels for target data that does not closely align with the training documents.

4 Future work

Given the computational expense of training a model for each individual document to be tagged, improvements must be made to the approach to transform it into a viable long-term NER solution. The next logical step in this research will be to cluster the training documents and train models based on those clusters. Subsequently, the test documents can be clustered to the training set clusters and be tagged using the appropriate model for that cluster set. Alternatively, the test set could be initially clustered, with the training set then fit to those clusters. Tests must be conducted to determine which option produces the best prediction accuracy levels. Once a viable clustering methodology has been developed, further testing will be conducted to compare it with some of the best current techniques (e.g. the work of Dalton et. al 2011) to provide a more comprehensive evaluation.

The results presented here were achieved using baseline document representation and document similarity techniques. Significant work remains for experimentation to determine which alternative methodologies will result in the optimal NER performance. Not only could different clustering algorithms be employed, but an investigation into which type of clustering, in particular linear or hierarchical, is better suited for NER would be prudent. Also, further work will test the validity of this approach for successful domain adaptation by demonstrating that it is extensible to other data sets.

5 Summary

This research has implications in the NER domain adaptation space as it demonstrates that fewer training documents are required as long as they are sufficiently similar to the targeted test set. This methodology could potentially allow for better utilization of existing, freely-available (possibly generic) training sets by extracting portions of the training set that are more similar to the target data. It also allows for existing NER systems to be better adapted to domain-specific data without modification for feature augmentation or the inclusion of additional external data sources. The opportunities for continuing this tread of research are numerous, and initial results illustrate significant promise given the relative simplicity of the execution compared with its achievement.

6 Acknowledgements

This document was prepared by Oak Ridge National Laboratory, P.O. Box 2008, Oak Ridge, Tennessee 37831-6285; managed by UT-Battelle, LLC, for the US Department of Energy under contract number DE-AC05-00OR22725.

This manuscript has been authored by UT-Battelle, LLC, under contract DE-AC05-00OR22725 with the U.S. Department of Energy. The United States Government retains and the publisher, by accepting the article for publication, acknowledges that the United States Government retains a non-exclusive, paid-up, irrevocable, world-wide license to publish or reproduce the published form of this manuscript, or allow others to do so, for United States Government purposes.

References

Dan Wu, Wee Sun Lee, and Hai Leong Chieu. 2009. Domain adaptive bootstrapping for named entity recognition. In *EMNLP*, pp. 142 - 147.

Fei Hueng, and Alexander Yates. 2009. Distributional representations for handling sparsity in supervised sequence-labeling. *Proceedings of the Joint Conference of the 47th Annual Meeting of the ACL and the 4th International Joint Conference on Natural Language Processing of the AFNLP. 1*, pp. 495-503. Suntec, Singapore: ACL.

Hai Leong Chieu, and Hwee Tou Ng. 2003. Named entity recognition with a maximum entropy approach. *Proceedings CoNLL 2003*, (pp. 160-163). Edmonton, Canada.

Jeffrey Dalton, James Allan, and David A. Smith. 2011. Passage retrieval for incorporating global evidence in sequence labeling. *Proceedings of the 20th ACM International Conference on Information and Knowledge Management* (pp. 355-364). Glasgow, UK: ACM.

Lev Ratinov, and Dan Roth. 2009. Design challenges and misconceptions in named entity recognition. *CoNLL '09 Proceedings of the Thirteenth Conference on Computational Natural Language Learning* (pp. 147-155). Boulder, CO: Association for Computational Linguistics.

Maksim Tkachenko and Andrey Simanovsky. 2012. Named entity recognition: exploiting features. *Proceedings of KONVENS 2012*. Vienna, Austria.

Terry Koo, Xavier Carreras, and Michael John Collins. 2008. Simple semi-supervised dependency parsing. *Proceedings of ACL*, (pp. 595-603).

Vijay Krishnan, and Christopher D. Manning. 2006. An effective two-stage model for exploiting non-local dependencies in named entity recognition. *Proceedings of the 21st International Conference on Computational Linguistics and 44th Annual Meeting of the ACL*, (pp. 1121-1128). Sydney, Australia.

Xiaohua Liu, Shaodian Zhang, Furu Wei, and Ming Zhou. 2011. Recognizing named entities in tweets. *Proceedings of the 49th Annual Meeting of the Association for Computational Linguistics: Human Language Technologies. 1*, pp. 359-367. Portland, OR: Association for Computational Linguistics.

Learning to Relate Literal and Sentimental Descriptions of Visual Properties

Mark Yatskar
Computer Science & Engineering
University of Washington
Seattle, WA
my89@cs.washington.edu

Svitlana Volkova
Center for Language and Speech Processing
Johns Hopkins University
Baltimore, MD
svitlana@jhu.edu

Asli Celikyilmaz
Conversational Understanding Sciences
Microsoft
Mountain View, CA
asli@ieee.org

Bill Dolan
NLP Group
Microsoft Research
Redmond, WA
billdol@microsoft.edu

Luke Zettlemoyer
Computer Science & Engineering
University of Washington
Seattle, WA
lsz@cs.washington.edu

Abstract

Language can describe our visual world at many levels, including not only what is literally there but also the sentiment that it invokes. In this paper, we study visual language, both literal and sentimental, that describes the overall appearance and style of virtual characters. Sentimental properties, including labels such as "youthful" or "country western," must be inferred from descriptions of the more literal properties, such as facial features and clothing selection. We present a new dataset, collected to describe Xbox avatars, as well as models for learning the relationships between these avatars and their literal and sentimental descriptions. In a series of experiments, we demonstrate that such learned models can be used for a range of tasks, including predicting sentimental words and using them to rank and build avatars. Together, these results demonstrate that sentimental language provides a concise (though noisy) means of specifying low-level visual properties.

This is a light tan young man with short and trim haircut. He has straight eyebrows and large brown eyes. He has a neat and trim appearance.

State of mind: angry, upset, determined. Likes: country western, rodeo. Occupation: cowboy, wrangler, horse trainer. Overall: youthful, cowboy.

Figure 1: (A) Literal avatar descriptions and (B) sentimental descriptions of four avatar properties, including possible occupations and interests.

1 Introduction

Language can describe varied aspects of our visual world, including not only what is literally there but also the social, cultural, and emotional sentiment it invokes. Recently, there has been a growing effort to study *literal* language that describes directly observable properties, such as object color, shape, or category (Farhadi et al., 2009; Mitchell et al., 2010; Matuszek et al., 2012). Here, we add a focus on *sentimental* visual language, which compactly describes more subjective properties such as if a person looks determined, if a resume looks professional, or if a restaurant looks romantic. Such models enable many new applications, such as text editors that automatically select properties including font, color, or text alignment to best match high level descriptions such as "professional" or "artistic."

In this paper, we study visual language, both literal and sentimental, that describes the overall appearance and style of virtual characters, like those in Figure 1. We use literal language as feature norms, a tool used for studying semantic information in cognitive science (Mcrae et al., 2005). Literal words, such "black" or "hat," are annotated for objects to indicate how people perceive visual properties. Such feature norms provide our gold-standard visual detectors, and allow us to focus on learning to model sentimental language, such as "youthful" or "goth."

We introduce a new corpus of descriptions of Xbox avatars created by actual gamers. Each avatar is specified by 19 attributes, including clothing and body type, allowing for more than 10^{20} possibilities. Using Amazon Mechanical Turk,[1] we collected literal and sentimental descriptions of complete avatars and many of their component parts, such as the cowboy hat in Figure 1(B). In all, there are over 100K descriptions. To demonstrate potential for learning, we also report an A/B test which shows that native speakers can use sentimental descriptions to distinguish the labeled avatars from random distractors. This new data will enable study of the relationships between the co-occurring literal and sentimental text in a rich visual setting.[2]

We describe models for three tasks: (i) classifying when words match avatars, (ii) ranking avatars given a description, and (iii) constructing avatars to match a description. Each model includes literal part descriptions as feature norms, enabling us to learn which literal and sentinel word pairs best predict complete avatars.

Experiments demonstrate the potential for jointly modeling literal and sentimental visual descriptions on our new dataset. The approach outperforms several baselines and learns varied relationships between the sentimental and literal descriptions. For example, in one experiment "nerdy student" is predictive of an avatar with features indicating its shirt is "plaid" and glasses are "large" and faces that are not "bearded." We also show that individual sentimental words can be predicted but that multiple avatars can match a single sentimental description. Finally, we use our model to build complete avatars and show that we can accurately predict the sentimental terms annotators ascribe to them.

[1] www.mturk.com

[2] Data available at http://homes.cs.washington.edu/~my89/avatar.

2 Related Work

To the best of our knowledge, our focus on learning to understand visual sentiment descriptions is novel. However, visual sentiment has been studied from other perspectives. Jrgensen (1998) provides examples which show that visual descriptions communicate social status and story information in addition to literal object and properties. Tousch et al. (2012) draw the distinction between "of-ness" (objective and concrete) and "about-ness" (subjective and abstract) in image retrieval, and observe that many image queries are abstract (for example, images about freedom). Finally, in descriptions of people undergoing emotional distress, Fussell and Moss (1998) show that literal descriptions co-occur frequently with sentimental ones.

There has been significant work on more literal aspects of grounded language understanding, both visual and non-visual. The Words-Eye project (Coyne and Sproat, 2001) generates 3D scenes from literal paragraph-length descriptions. Generating literal textual descriptions of visual scenes has also been studied, including both captions (Kulkarni et al., 2011; Yang et al., 2011; Feng and Lapata, 2010) and descriptions (Farhadi et al., 2010). Furthermore, Chen and Dolan (2011) collected literal descriptions of videos with the goal of learning paraphrases while Zitnick and Parikh (2013) describe a corpus of descriptions for clip art that supports the discovery of semantic elements of visual scenes.

There has also been significant recent work on automatically recovering visual attributes, both absolute (Farhadi et al., 2009) and relative (Kovashka et al., 2012), a challenge that we avoid having to solve with our use of feature norms (Mcrae et al., 2005).

Grounded language understanding has also received significant attention, where the goal is to learn to understand situated non-visual language use. For example, there has been work on learning to execute instructions (Branavan et al., 2009; Chen and Mooney, 2011; Artzi and Zettlemoyer, 2013), provide sports commentary (Chen et al., 2010), understand high level strategy guides to improve game

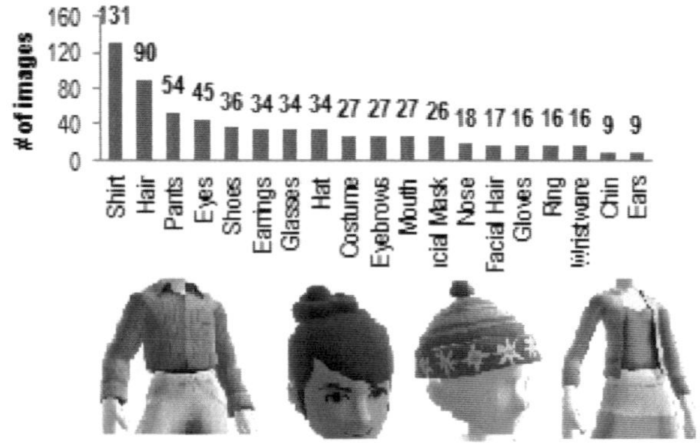

Figure 2: The number of assets per category and example images from the *hair, shirt* and *hat* categories.

play (Branavan et al., 2011; Eisenstein et al., 2009), and understand referring expression (Matuszek et al., 2012).

Finally, our work is similar in spirit to sentiment analysis (Pang et al., 2002), emotion detection from images and speech (Zeng et al., 2009), and metaphor understanding (Shutova, 2010a; Shutova, 2010b). However, we focus on more general visual context.

3 Data Collection

We gathered a large number of natural language descriptions from Mechanical Turk (MTurk). They include: (1) literal descriptions of specific facial features, clothing or accessories and (2) high level subjective descriptions of human-generated avatars.[3]

Literal Descriptions We showed annotators a single image of clothing, a facial feature or an accessory and asked them to produce short descriptions. Figure 2 shows the distribution over object types. We restricted descriptions to be between 3 and 15 words. In all, we collected 33.2K descriptions and had on average 7 words per descriptions. The example annotations with highlighted overlapping patterns are in Table 1.

Sentimental Descriptions We also collected 1913 gamer-created avatars from the web. The avatars were filtered to contain only items from the set of 665 for which we gathered literal descriptions. The gender distribution is 95% male.

[3](2) also has phrases describing emotional reactions. We also collected (3) multilingual literal, (4) relative literal and (5) comprehensive full-body descriptions. We do not use this data, but it will be included in the public release.

LITERAL DESCRIPTIONS
full-sleeved executive blue shirt
blue, long-sleeved button-up shirt
mens blue button dress shirt with dark blue stripes
multi-blue striped long-sleeve button-up dress shirt with cuffs and breast pocket

Table 1: Literal descriptions of shirt in Figure 2.

To gather high level sentimental descriptions, annotators were presented with an image of an avatar and asked to list phrases in response to the follow different aspects:

- State of mind of the avatar.
- Things the avatar might care about.
- What the avatar might do for a living.
- Overall appearance of the avatar.

6144 unique vocabulary items occurred in these descriptions, but only 1179 occurred more than 10 times. Figure 1 (B) shows an avatar and its corresponding sentimental descriptions.

Quality Control All annotations in our dataset are produced by non-expert annotators. We relied on manual spot checks to limit poor annotations. Over time, we developed a trusted crowd of annotators who produced only high quality annotations during the earliest stage of data collection.

4 Feasibility

Our hypothesis is that sentimental language does not uniquely identify an avatar, but instead summarizes or otherwise describes its overall look. In general, there is a trade off between concise and precise descriptions. For example, given a single word you might be able to generally describe the overall look of an avatar, but a long, detailed, literal description would be required to completely specify their appearance.

To demonstrate that the sentimental descriptions we collected are precise enough to be predictive of appearance, we conducted an experiment that prompts people to judge when avatars match descriptions. We created an A/B test where we show English speakers two avatars and one sentimental description. They were asked to select which avatar is better matched by the description and how difficult they felt, on a scale from 1 to 4, it was to judge. For 100 randomly selected descriptions, we

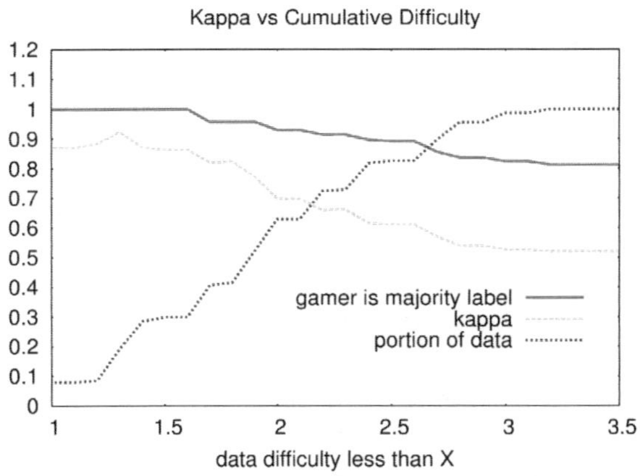

Figure 3: Judged task difficulty versus agreement, gamer avatar preference, and percentage of data covered. The difficulty axis is cumulative.

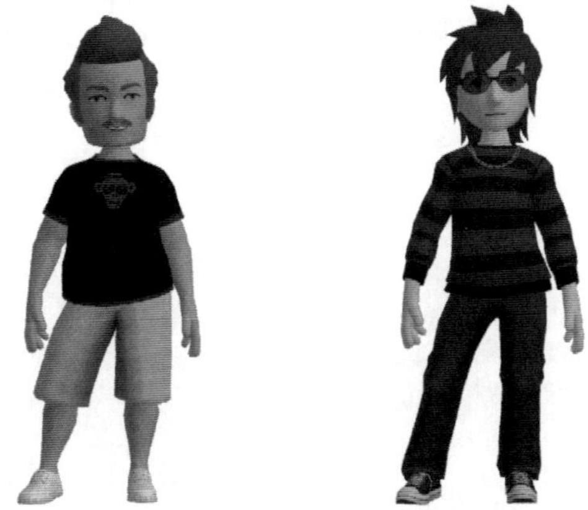

State of mind: playful, happy; Likes: sex Occupation: hobo Overall: dumb	State of mind: content, humble, satisfied, peaceful, relaxed, calm. Likes: fashion, friends, money, cars, music, education. Occupation: teacher, singer, actor, performer, dancer, computer engineer. Overall: nerdy, cool, smart, comfy, easygoing, reserved

Figure 4: Avatars rated as difficult.

asked 5 raters to compare the gamer avatars to randomly generated ones (where each asset is selected independently according to a uniform distribution). Figure 3 shows a plot of Kappa and the percent of the time a majority of the raters selected the gamer avatar. The easiest 20% of the data pairs had the strongest agreement, with kappa=.92, and two thirds of the data has kappa = .70. While agreement falls off to .52 for the full data set, the gamer avatar remains the majority judgment 81% of the time.

The fact that random avatars are sometimes preferred indicates that it can be difficult to judge sentimental descriptions. Consider the avatars in Figure 4. Neither conforms to a clear sentimental description based on the questions we asked. The right one is described with conflicting words and the words describing the left one are very general (like "dumb"). This corresponds to our intuition that while many avatars can be succinctly summarized with our questions, some would be more easily described using literal language.

5 Tasks and Evaluation

We formulate three tasks to study the feasibility of learning the relationship between sentimental and literal descriptions. In this section, we first define the space of possible avatars, followed by the tasks.

Avatars Figure 5 summarizes the notation we will develop to describe the data. An avatar is defined by a 19 dimensional vector $\vec{a}$ where each position is an index into a list of possible items $\vec{i}$. Each dimension represents a position on the avatar, for example, *hat* or *nose*. Each possible item is called an asset and is associated with a set of positions it can fill. Most assets take up exactly one position, while there are a few cases where assets take multiple positions.[4] An avatar $\vec{a}$ is valid if all of its mandatory positions are filled, and no two assets conflict on a position. Mandatory positions include hair, eyes, ears, eyebrows, nose, mouth, chin, shirt, pants, and shoes. All other positions are optional. We refer to this set of valid $\vec{a}$ as A. Practically speaking, if an avatar is not valid, it cannot be reliably rendered graphically.

Each item i is associated with the literal descriptions $\vec{d_i} \in D$ where D is the set of literal descriptions. Furthermore, every avatar $\vec{a}$ is associated a list of sentimental query words $\vec{q}$, describing subjective aspects of an avatar.[5]

Sentimental Word Prediction We first study individual words. The word prediction task is to decide whether a given avatar can be described with a

[4]For example, long sleeve shirts cover up watches, so they take up both shirt and wristwear positions. Costumes tend to span many more positions, for example there a suit that takes up shirt, pants, wristwear and shoes positions.

[5]We do not distinguish which prompt (e.g., "state of mind" or "occupation") a word in $\vec{q}$ came from, although the vocabularies are relatively disjoint.

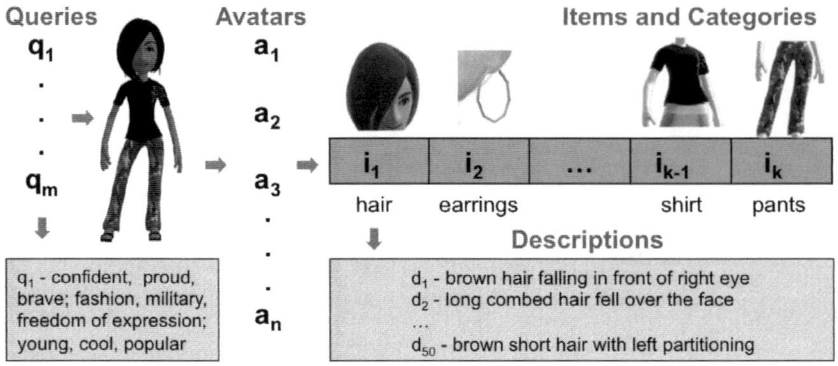

Figure 5: Avatars, queries, items, literal descriptions.

particular sentimental word q^*. We evaluate performance with F-score.

Avatar Ranking We also consider an avatar retrieval task, where the goal is to rank the set of avatars in our data, $\cup_{j=1...n}\vec{a_j}$, according to which one best matches a sentimental description, $\vec{q_i}$. As an automated evaluation, we report the average percentile position assigned to the true $\vec{a_i}$ for each example. However, in general, many different avatars can match each $\vec{q_i}$, an interesting phenomena we will further study with human evaluation.

Avatar Generation Finally, we consider the problem of generating novel, previously unseen avatars, by selecting a set of items that best embody some sentimental description. As with ranking, we aim to construct the avatar $\vec{a_i}$ that matches each sentimental description $\vec{q_i}$. We evaluate by considering the item overlap between $\vec{a_i}$ and the output avatar $\vec{a^*}$, discounting for empty positions:[6]

$$f = \frac{\sum_{j=1}^{|\vec{a^*}|} I(\vec{a_j^*} = \vec{a}_{ij})}{\max(numparts(\vec{a^*}), numparts(\vec{a_i}))}, \quad (1)$$

where $numparts$ returns the number of non-empty avatar positions. The score is a conservative measure because some items are significantly more visually salient than others. For instance, shirts and pants occupy a large portion of the physical realization of the avatar, while rings are small and virtually unnoticeable. We additionally perform a human evaluation in Section 8 to better understand these challenges.

[6]Optional items are infrequently used. Therefore not predicting them at all offers a strong baseline. Yet doing this demonstrates nothing about an algorithm's ability to predict items which contribute to the sentimental qualities of an avatar.

6 Methods

We present two different models: one that considers words in isolation and another that jointly models the query words. This section defines the models and how we learn them.

6.1 Independent Sentimental Word Model

The independent word model (S-Independent) assumes that each word independently describes the avatar. We construct a separate linear model for each word in the vocabulary.

To train these model, we transform the data to form a binary classification problem for each word, where the positive data includes all avatars the word was seen with, $(q, \vec{a_i}, 1)$ for all i and $q \in \vec{q_i}$, and the rest are negative, $(q, \vec{a_i}, 0)$ for all i and $q \notin \vec{q_i}$.

We use the following features:

- an indicator feature for the cross product of a sentiment query word q, a literal description word $w \in D$, and the avatar position index j (for example, $q =$ "angry" with $w =$ "pointy" and $j =$ eyebrows):

$$I(q \in \vec{q_i}, w \in \vec{d_{a_{ij}}}, j)$$

- a bias feature for keeping a position empty:

$$I(q \in \vec{q_i}, a_{ij} = empty, j)$$

These features will allow the model to capture correlations between our feature norms which provide descriptions of visual attributes, like black, and sentimental words, like gothic.

S-Independent is used for both word prediction and ranking. For prediction, we train a linear model using averaged binary perceptron. For ranking, we try to rank all positive instances above negative instances. We use an averaged structured perceptron to train the ranker (Collins, 2002). To rank with respect to an entire query $\vec{q_i}$, we sum the scores of each word $q \in \vec{q_i}$.

6.2 Joint Sentimental Model

The second approach (S-Joint) jointly models the query words to learn the relationships between literal and sentimental words with score s:

$$s(\vec{a}|\vec{q}, D) = \sum_{i=1}^{|\vec{a}|} \sum_{j=1}^{|\vec{q}|} \theta^T f(\vec{a_i}, \vec{q_j}, \vec{d_{a_i}})$$

Where every word in the query has a separate factor and every position is treated independently subject to the constraint that $\vec{a}$ is valid. The feature function f uses the same features as the word independent model above.

This model is used for ranking and generation. For ranking, we try to rank the avatar a_i for query q_i above all other avatars in the candidate set. For generation, we try to score a_i above all other valid avatars given the query q_i. In both cases, we train with averaged structured perceptron (Collins, 2002) on the original data, containing query, avatar pairs $(\vec{q_i}, \vec{a_i})$.

7 Experimental Setup

Random Baseline For the ranking and avatar generation tasks, we report random baselines. For ranking, we randomly order the avatars. In the generation case, we select an item randomly for every position. This baseline does not generate optional assets because they are rare in the real data.

Sentimental-Literal Overlap (SL-Overlap) We also report a baseline that measures the overlap between words in the sentiment query $\vec{q_i}$ and words in the literal asset descriptions D. In generation, for each position in the avatar, $\vec{a_i}$, SL-Overlap selects the item whose literal description has the most words in common with $\vec{q_i}$. If no item had overlap with the query, we backoff to a random choice. In the case of ranking, it orders avatars by the sum over every position of the number of words in common between the literal description and the query, $\vec{q_i}$. This baseline tests the degree to which literal and sentimental descriptions overlap lexically.

Word	F-Score	Precision	Recall	N
happi	0.84	0.89	0.78	149
student	0.78	0.82	0.74	129
friend	0.76	0.84	0.70	153
music	0.74	0.89	0.63	148
confid	0.74	0.82	0.76	157
sport	0.69	0.62	0.76	76
casual	0.63	0.6	0.67	84
youth	0.6	0.57	0.64	88
waitress	0.59	0.42	1	5
smart	0.57	0.54	0.6	88
fashion	0.54	0.54	0.54	70
monei	0.54	0.52	0.56	76
cool	0.54	0.52	0.56	84
relax	0.53	0.52	0.56	90
game	0.51	0.44	0.62	61
musician	0.51	0.44	0.61	66
parti	0.51	0.43	0.62	58
content	0.5	0.47	0.53	75
friendli	0.49	0.42	0.6	56
smooth	0.49	0.4	0.63	57

Table 2: Top 20 words (stemmed) for classification. N is the number of occurances in the test set.

Feature Generation For all models that use lexical features, we limited the number of words. 6144 unique vocabulary items occur in the query set, and 3524 in the literal description set. There are over 400 million entries in the full set of features that include the cross product of these sets with all possible avatar positions, as described in Section 6. Since this would present a challenge for learning, we prune in two ways. We stem all words with a Porter stemmer. We also filter out all features which do not occur at least 10 times in our training set. The final model has approximately 700k features.

8 Results

We present results for the tasks described in Section 5 with the appropriate models from Section 6.

8.1 Word Prediction Results

The goal of our first experiment is to study when individual sentiment words can be accurately predicted. We computed sentimental word classification accuracy for 1179 word classes with 10 or more

Algorithm	Percentile Rank
S-joint	77.3
S-independant	73.5
SL-overlap	60.4
Random	48.8

Table 3: Automatic evaluation of ranking. The average percentile that a test avatar was ranked given its sentimental description.

mentions. Table 2 shows the top 20 words ordered by F-score.[7] Many common words can be predicted with relatively high accuracy. Words with strong individual cues like happy (a smiling mouth), and confidence (wide eyes) and nerdi (particular glasses) can be predicted well.

The average F-score among all words was .085. 33.2% of words have an F-score of zero. These zeros include words like: unusual, bland, sarcastic, trust, prepared, limber, healthy and poetry. Some of these words indicate broad classes of avatars (e.g., unusual avatars) and others indicate subtle modifications to looks that without other words are not specific (e.g., a prepared surfer vs. a prepared business man). Furthermore, evaluation was done assuming that when a word is not mentioned, it is should be predicted as negative. This fails to account for the fact that people do not mention everything that's true, but instead make choices about what to mention based on the most relevant qualities. Despite these difficulties, the classification performance shows that we can accurately capture usage patterns for many words.

8.2 Ranking Results

Ranking allows us to test the hypothesis that multiple avatars are valid for a high level description. Furthermore, we consider the differences between S-Joint and S-Independent, showing that jointly modelings all words improves ranking performance.

Automatic Evaluation The results are shown in Table 3. Both S-Independent and S-Joint outperform the SL-overlap baseline. SL-Overlap's poor performance can be attributed to low direct overlap between sentimental words and literal words. S-Joint also outperforms the S-Independent.

[7]Accuracy numbers are inappropriate in this case because the number of negative instances, in most cases, is far larger than the number of positive ones.

Inspection of the parameters shows that S-Joint does better than S-Independent in modeling words that only relate to a subset of body positions. For example, in one case we found that for the word "puzzled" nearly 50% of the weights were on features that related to eyebrows and eyes. This type of specialization was far more pronounced for S-Joint. The joint nature of the learning allows the features for individual words to specialize for specific positions. In contrast, S-Independent must independently predict all parts for every word.

Human Evaluation We report human relevancy judgments for the top-5 returned results from S-Joint. On average, 56.2% were marked to be relevant. This shows that S-Joint is performing better than automatic numbers would indicate, confirming our intuition that there is a one-to-many relationship between a sentimental description and avatars. Sentimental descriptions, while having significant signal, are not exact. These results also indicate that relying on automatic measures of accuracy that assume a single reference avatar underestimates performance. Figure 6 shows the top ranked results returned by S-Joint for a sentimental description where the model performs well.

8.3 Generation Results

Finally we evaluate three models for avatar generation: Random, SL-Overlap and S-Joint using automatic measures and human evaluation.

Automatic Evaluation Table 4 presents results for automatic evaluation. The Random baseline performs badly, on average assigning items correctly to less than 1 position in the generated avatar. The SL-Overlap baseline improves, but still performs quite poorly. The S-Joint model performs significantly better, correctly guessing 2-3 items for each output avatar. However, as we will see in the manual evaluation, many of the non-matching parts it produces are still a good fit for the query.

Human Evaluation As before, there are many reasonable avatars that could match as well as the reference avatars. Therefore, we also evaluated generation with A/B tests, much like in Section 4. Annotators were asked to judge which of two avatars better matched a sentimental description. They

pensive,confrontational; music,socializing; musician,bar tending,club owner; smart,cool.

Figure 6: A sentimental description paired with the highest ranked avatars found by S-Joint.

Model	Overlap
Random	0.041
SL-Overlap	0.049
S-Joint	0.126

Table 4: Automatic generation evaluation results. The item overlap metric is defined in Section 5.

	Kappa	Majority	Random	Sys.
SL-Overlap	0.20	0.25	0.34	0.32
S-Joint	0.52	0.90	0.07	0.81
Gamer	0.52	0.81	0.08	0.77

Table 5: Human evaluation of automatically generated avatars. Majority represents the percentage of time the system output is preferred by a majority of raters. Random and System (Sys.) indicate the percentage of time each was preferred.

could rate System A or System B as better, or report that they were equal or that neither matched the description. We consider two comparisons: SL-Overlap vs. Random and S-Joint vs Random. Five annotators performed each condition, rating 100 examples with randomly ordered avatars.

We report the results for human evaluation including kappa, majority judgments, and a distribution over judgments in Table 5. The SL-Overlap baseline is indistinguishable from a random avatar. This contrasts with the ranking case, where this simple baseline showed improvement, indicating that generation is a much harder problem. Furthermore, agreement is low; people felt the need to make a choice but were not consistent.

We also see in Table 5 that people prefer the S-Joint model outputs to random avatars as often as they prefer gamer to random. While this does not necessarily imply that S-Joint creates gamer-quality avatars, it indicates substantial progress by learning a mapping between literal and sentimental words.

Qualitative Results Table 6 presents the highest and lowest weighted features for different sentimental query words. Figure 7 shows four descriptions that were assigned high quality avatars.

In general, many of the weaker avatars had aspects of the descriptions but lacked such distinctive overall looks. This was especially true when the descriptions contained seemingly contradictory information. For example, one avatar was described as being both nerdy and popular. We generated a look that had aspects of both of these descriptions, including a head that contained both conservative elements (like glasses) and less conservative elements (like crazy hair and earrings). However, the combination would not be described as nerdy or popular, because of difficult to predict global interactions between the co-occurring words and items. This is an important area for future work.

9 Conclusions

We explored how visual language, both literal and sentimental, maps to the overall physical appearance and style of virtual characters. While this paper focused on avatar design, our approach has implications for a broad class of natural language-driven

Ambition; business, fashion, success; salesman; smooth, professional.

Capable, confident, firm; heavy metal, extreme sports, motorcycles; engineer, mechanic, machinist; aggressive, strong, protective.

Stressed, bored, discontent; emo music; works at a record store; goth, dark, drab.

Happy, content, confident, home, career, family, secretary,student, classy,clean,casual

Figure 7: Avatars automatically generated with the S-Joint model.

Sentiment	positive features	negative features
happi	mouth:thick, mouth:smilei, mouth:make, mouth:open	mouth:tight, mouth:emotionless, mouth:brownish, mouth:attract
gothic	shoes:brown, shirt:black, pants:hot, shirt:band	shirt:half, shirt:tight, pants:sexi, hair:brownish
retro	eyebrows:men, eyebrows:large, hair:round, pants:light	eyebrows:beauti, pants:side; eyebrows:trim, pants:cut
beach	pants:yello, pants:half, nose:narrow, pants:white	shirt:brown, shirt:side; shoes:long, pants:jean

Table 6: Most positive and negative features for a word stem. A feature is [position]:[literal word].

dialog scenarios. In many situations, a user may be perfectly able to formulate a high-level description of their intent ("Make my resume look cleaner" "Buy me clothes for a summer wedding," or "Play something more danceable") while having little or no understanding of the complex parameter space that the underlying software must manipulate in order to achieve this result.

We demonstrated that these high-level sentimental specifications can have a strong relationship to literal aspects of a problem space and showed that sentimental language is a concise, yet noisy, way of specifying high level characteristics. Sentimental language is an unexplored avenue for improving natural language systems that operate in situated settings. It has the potential to bridge the gap between lay and expert understandings of a problem domain.

Acknowledgments

This work is partially supported by the DARPA CSSG (N11AP20020) and the NSF (IIS-1115966). The authors would like to thank Chris Brockett, Noelle Sophy, Rico Malvar for helping with collecting and processing the data. We would also like to thank Tom Kwiatkowski and Nicholas FitzGerald and the anonymous reviewers for their helpful comments.

References

Yoav Artzi and Luke Zettlemoyer. 2013. Weakly supervised learning of semantic parsers for mapping instructions to actions. *Transactions of the Association for Computational Linguistics*, 1(1):49–62.

SRK Branavan, H. Chen, L.S. Zettlemoyer, and R. Barzilay. 2009. Reinforcement learning for mapping instructions to actions. In *Proceedings of the Joint Conference of the 47th Annual Meeting of the ACL and the 4th International Joint Conference on Natural Language Processing of the AFNLP*, pages 82–90.

SRK Branavan, David Silver, and Regina Barzilay. 2011. Learning to win by reading manuals in a monte-carlo framework. In *Proceedings of the 49th Annual Meeting of the Association for Computational Linguistics: Human Language Technologies-Volume 1*, pages 268–277.

David L. Chen and William B. Dolan. 2011. Collecting highly parallel data for paraphrase evaluation. In *Proceedings of the 49th Annual Meeting of the Association for Computational Linguistics*, pages 190–200.

D.L. Chen and R.J. Mooney. 2011. Learning to interpret natural language navigation instructions from observations. In *Proceedings of the 25th AAAI Conference on Artificial Intelligence (AAAI-2011)*, pages 859–865.

David L. Chen, Joohyun Kim, and Raymond J. Mooney. 2010. Training a multilingual sportscaster: Using perceptual context to learn language. *Journal of Artificial Intelligence Research*, 37:397–435.

Michael Collins. 2002. Discriminative training methods for hidden markov models: theory and experiments with perceptron algorithms. In *Proceedings of the ACL-02 conference on Empirical methods in natural language processing*, pages 1–8.

B. Coyne and R. Sproat. 2001. Wordseye: an automatic text-to-scene conversion system. In *Proceedings of the 28th annual conference on Computer graphics and interactive techniques*, pages 487–496.

J. Eisenstein, J. Clarke, D. Goldwasser, and D. Roth. 2009. Reading to learn: Constructing features from semantic abstracts. In *Proceedings of the 2009 Conference on Empirical Methods in Natural Language Processing*, pages 958–967.

Ali Farhadi, Ian Endres, Derek Hoiem, and David Forsyth. 2009. Describing objects by their attributes. In *Proceedings of the IEEE Computer Society Conference on Computer Vision and Pattern Recognition*.

Ali Farhadi, Mohsen Hejrati, Mohammad Amin Sadeghi, Peter Young, Cyrus Rashtchian, Julia Hockenmaier, and David Forsyth. 2010. Every picture tells a story: generating sentences from images. In *Proceedings of the 11th European conference on Computer Vision*, ECCV'10, pages 15–29.

Yansong Feng and Mirella Lapata. 2010. Topic models for image annotation and text illustration. In *Human Language Technologies: The 2010 Annual Conference of the North American Chapter of the Association for Computational Linguistics*, pages 831–839.

Susan R Fussell and Mallie M Moss. 1998. Figurative language in emotional communication. *Social and cognitive approaches to interpersonal communication*, page 113.

Corinne Jrgensen. 1998. Attributes of images in describing tasks. *Information Processing & Management*, 34(23):161 – 174.

Adriana Kovashka, Devi Parikh, and Kristen Grauman. 2012. Whittlesearch: Image search with relative attribute feedback. In *Computer Vision and Pattern Recognition (CVPR)*, pages 2973–2980.

G. Kulkarni, V. Premraj, S. Dhar, S. Li, Y. Choi, A.C. Berg, and T.L. Berg. 2011. Baby talk: Understanding and generating simple image descriptions. In *Computer Vision and Pattern Recognition (CVPR)*, pages 1601–1608.

Cynthia Matuszek, Nicholas FitzGerald, Luke Zettlemoyer, Liefeng Bo, and Dieter Fox. 2012. A Joint Model of Language and Perception for Grounded Attribute Learning. In *Proc. of the 2012 International Conference on Machine Learning*.

Ken Mcrae, George S. Cree, Mark S. Seidenberg, and Chris Mcnorgan. 2005. Semantic feature production norms for a large set of living and nonliving things. *Behavior Research Methods*, 37(4):547–559.

Margaret Mitchell, Kees van Deemter, and Ehud Reiter. 2010. Natural reference to objects in a visual domain. In *Proceedings of the 6th International Natural Language Generation Conference*, INLG '10, pages 95–104.

B. Pang, L. Lee, and S. Vaithyanathan. 2002. Thumbs up?: sentiment classification using machine learning techniques. In *Proceedings of the ACL-02 conference on Empirical methods in natural language processing*, pages 79–86.

Ekaterina Shutova. 2010a. Automatic metaphor interpretation as a paraphrasing task. In *Human Language Technologies: The 2010 Annual Conference of the North American Chapter of the Association for Computational Linguistics*, HLT '10, pages 1029–1037.

Ekaterina Shutova. 2010b. Models of metaphor in nlp. In *Proceedings of the 48th Annual Meeting of the Association for Computational Linguistics*, ACL '10, pages 688–697.

Anne-Marie Tousch, Stphane Herbin, and Jean-Yves Audibert. 2012. Semantic hierarchies for image annotation: A survey. *Pattern Recognition*, 45(1):333 – 345.

Yezhou Yang, Ching Lik Teo, Hal Daumé III, and Yiannis Aloimonos. 2011. Corpus-guided sentence generation of natural images. In *Empirical Methods in Natural Language Processing*.

Z. Zeng, M. Pantic, G.I. Roisman, and T.S. Huang. 2009. A survey of affect recognition methods: Audio, visual, and spontaneous expressions. *Pattern Analysis and Machine Intelligence, IEEE Transactions on*, 31(1):39–58.

C Lawrence Zitnick and Devi Parikh. 2013. Bringing semantics into focus using visual abstraction. In *Computer Vision and Pattern Recognition (To Appear)*.

Morphological Analysis and Disambiguation for Dialectal Arabic

Nizar Habash, Ryan Roth, Owen Rambow, Ramy Eskander, and Nadi Tomeh
Center for Computational Learning Systems
Columbia University
{habash,ryanr,rambow,reskander,nadi}@ccls.columbia.edu

Abstract

The many differences between Dialectal Arabic and Modern Standard Arabic (MSA) pose a challenge to the majority of Arabic natural language processing tools, which are designed for MSA. In this paper, we retarget an existing state-of-the-art MSA morphological tagger to Egyptian Arabic (ARZ). Our evaluation demonstrates that our ARZ morphology tagger outperforms its MSA variant on ARZ input in terms of accuracy in part-of-speech tagging, diacritization, lemmatization and tokenization; and in terms of utility for ARZ-to-English statistical machine translation.

1 Introduction

Dialectal Arabic (DA) refers to the day-to-day native vernaculars spoken in the Arab World. DA is used side by side with Modern Standard Arabic (MSA), the official language of the media and education (Holes, 2004). Although DAs are historically related to MSA, there are many phonological, morphological and lexical differences between them. Unlike MSA, DAs have no standard orthographies or language academies. Furthermore, different DAs, such as Egyptian Arabic (henceforth, ARZ), Levantine Arabic or Moroccan Arabic have important differences among them, similar to those seen among Romance languages (Holes, 2004; Abdel-Massih et al., 1979). Most tools and resources developed for natural language processing (NLP) of Arabic are designed for MSA. Such resources are quite limited when it comes to processing DA, e.g., a state-of-the-art MSA morphological analyzer only has 60% coverage of Levantine Arabic verb forms (Habash and Rambow, 2006).

In this paper, we describe the process of retargeting an existing state-of-the-art tool for modeling MSA morphology disambiguation to ARZ, the most commonly spoken DA. The MSA tool we extend is MADA – Morphological Analysis and Disambiguation of Arabic (Habash and Rambow, 2005). The approach used in MADA, which was inspired by earlier work by Hajič (2000), disambiguates in context for every aspect of Arabic morphology, thus solving all tasks in "one fell swoop". The disadvantage of the MADA approach is its dependence on two complex resources: a morphological analyzer for the language and a large collection of manually annotated words for all morphological features in the same representation used by the analyzer. For ARZ, such resources have recently become available, with the development of the CALIMA ARZ morphological analyzer (Habash et al., 2012b) and the release by the Linguistic Data Consortium (LDC) of a large ARZ corpus annotated morphologically in a manner compatible with CALIMA (Maamouri et al., 2012a). In the work presented here, we utilize these new resources within the paradigm of MADA, transforming MADA into MADA-ARZ. The elegance of the MADA solution makes this conceptually a simple extension.

Our evaluation demonstrates that our Egyptian DA version of MADA, henceforth MADA-ARZ, outperforms MADA for MSA on ARZ morphological tagging and improves the quality of ARZ to English statistical machine translation (MT).

The rest of this paper is structured as follows: Section 2 discusses related work. Section 3 presents the challenges of processing Arabic dialects. Section 4 outlines our approach. And Section 5 presents and discusses our evaluation results.

2 Related Work

There has been a considerable amount of work on MSA morphological analysis, disambiguation, part-of-speech (POS) tagging, tokenization, lemmatization and diacritization; for an overview, see (Habash, 2010). Most solutions target specific problems, such as diacritization (Zitouni et al., 2006), tokenization or POS tagging (Diab et al., 2007). In contrast, MADA provides a solution to all of these problems together (Habash and Rambow, 2005).

Previous work on DA morphological tagging focused on creating resources, using noisy or incomplete annotations, and using unsupervised/semi-supervised methods. Duh and Kirchhoff (2005) adopt a minimally supervised approach that only requires raw text data from several DAs, as well as a MSA morphological analyzer. They report a POS accuracy of 70.9% on a rather coarse-grained POS tagset (17 tags).

Al-Sabbagh and Girju (2012) describe a supervised tagger for Egyptian Arabic social networking corpora trained using transformation-based learning (Brill, 1995). They report 94.5% F-measure on tokenization and 87.6% on POS tagging. Their tokenization and POS tagsets are comparable to the set used by the Arabic Treebank (ATB). We do not compare to them since their data sets are not public.

Stallard et al. (2012) show that unsupervised methods for learning DA tokenization can outperform MSA tokenizers on MT from Levantine Arabic to English. We do not compare to them directly since our work is on ARZ. However, we carry a similar MT experiment in Section 5.

Mohamed et al. (2012) annotated a small corpus of Egyptian Arabic for morphological segmentation and learned segmentation models using memory-based learning (Daelemans and van den Bosch, 2005). Their best system achieves a 91.90% accuracy on the task of morpheme-segmentation. We compare to their work and report on their test set in Section 5.

There are some other morphological analyzers for DA. Kilany et al. (2002) worked on ARZ, but the analyzer has very limited coverage. Their lexicon was used as part of the development of CALIMA (Habash et al., 2012b). Other efforts are not about ARZ (Habash and Rambow, 2006; Salloum and Habash, 2011).

Given the similarity between MSA and DA, there has been some work on mapping DA to MSA to exploit rich MSA resources (Chiang et al., 2006; Abo Bakr et al., 2008; Salloum and Habash, 2011; Salloum and Habash, 2013). Other researchers have studied the value of simply combining DA and MSA data, such as Zbib et al. (2012) for DA to English MT. In our approach, we target DA directly, and we evaluate the use of additional MSA annotated resources to our training in Section 5.

3 Arabic Dialect Challenges

General Arabic Challenges Arabic, as MSA or DA, poses many challenges for NLP. Arabic is a morphologically complex language which includes rich inflectional morphology and a number of clitics. For example, the MSA word وسيكتبونها *wsyktbwnhA (wa+sa+ya-ktub-uwna+hA)*[1] 'and they will write it [lit. and+will+they-write-they+it]' has two proclitics, one circumfix and one pronominal enclitic. Additionally, Arabic has a high degree of ambiguity resulting from its diacritic-optional writing system and common deviation from spelling standards (e.g., Alif and Ya variants) (Buckwalter, 2007). The Standard Arabic Morphological Analyzer for (SAMA) (Graff et al., 2009) produces 12 analyses per MSA word on average.

Differences between ARZ **and** MSA As mentioned above, most tools developed for MSA cannot be expected to perform well on ARZ. This is due to the numerous differences between the two variants. Lexically, the number of differences is quite significant. For example, ARZ طربيزة *Trbyz¯ħ*table' corresponds to MSA طاولة *TAwl¯h* Phonologically, there are many important differences which relate to orthography in DA, e.g., the MSA consonant ث /θ/ is pronounced as /t/ in ARZ (or /s/ in more recent borrowings from MSA); for a fuller discussion, see (Habash, 2010; Habash et al., 2012a). Examples of morphological differences include changes in the

[1]Arabic transliteration is presented in the Habash-Soudi-Buckwalter scheme (Habash et al., 2007): (in alphabetical order) *AbtθjHxdðrzsšSDTĎςγfqklmnhwy* and the additional symbols: ' ء, Â أ, Ǎ إ, Ā آ, ŵ ؤ , ŷ ئ , ¯*h*ة, ý ى.

morpheme form, e.g., the MSA future proclitic +س *sa+* appears in ARZ as +ه *ha+*. There are some morphemes in ARZ that do not exist in MSA such as the negation circum-clitic ش+ ...+ما *mA+ ... +š*. And there are MSA features that are absent from ARZ, most notably case and mood.

Since there are no orthographic standards, ARZ words may be written in a variety of ways reflecting different writing rules, e.g., phonologically or etymologically. A conventional orthography for Dialectal Arabic (CODA) has been proposed and used for writing ARZ in the context of NLP applications (Habash et al., 2012a; Al-Sabbagh and Girju, 2012; Eskander et al., 2013). Finally, MSA and ARZ coexist and are often used interchangeably, especially in more formal settings. The CALIMA morphological analyzer we use addresses several of these issues by modeling both ARZ and MSA together, including a limited set of inter-dialect morphology phenomena, and by mapping ARZ words into CODA orthography internally while accepting a wide range of spelling variants.

4 Approach

4.1 The MADA Approach

MADA is a method for Arabic morphological analysis and disambiguation (Habash and Rambow, 2005; Roth et al., 2008). MADA uses a morphological analyzer to produce, for each input word, a list of analyses specifying every possible morphological interpretation of that word, covering all morphological features of the word (diacritization, POS, lemma, and 13 inflectional and clitic features). MADA then applies a set of models (support vector machines and N-gram language models) to produce a prediction, per word in-context, for different morphological features, such as POS, lemma, gender, number or person. A ranking component scores the analyses produced by the morphological analyzer using a tuned weighted sum of matches with the predicted features. The top-scoring analysis is chosen as the predicted interpretation for that word in context.

4.2 Extending MADA into MADA-ARZ

Adjusting MADA to handle DA requires a number of modifications. The most significant change is replacing the MSA analyzer SAMA with the ARZ analyzer CALIMA to address the differences outlined in Section 3. In addition, new feature prediction models are needed; these are trained using ARZ data sets annotated by the LDC (Maamouri et al., 2006; Maamouri et al., 2012b). The data sets were not usable as released due to numerous annotation inconsistencies and differences from CALIMA, as well due to gaps in CALIMA. We synchronized the annotations with the latest version of CALIMA following a technique described by Habash and Rambow (2005). The result of this synchronization step is the data we use in this study (for training, development and testing). Our synchronized annotations fully match the LDC annotations in 90% of the words (in full morphological tag). We performed a manual analysis on randomly chosen 100 words that did not fully match. The choice we made is correct or acceptable in 55% of the cases of mismatch with the LDC annotation, which means that the our choice is accurate in over 95% of all cases.

Some of the original MADA features (which were needed for MSA) are not used in ARZ and so are dropped in MADA-ARZ; these features are case, mood, the question-marking proclitic, state and voice. Additional ARZ feature values have been added, e.g., to handle the progressive particle and future marker, among others. These are provided by CALIMA and are classified and selected by MADA-ARZ. In our current implementation, ARZ features that are not present in MSA, such as the negation and indirect-object enclitics, are not classified by MADA-ARZ classifiers, but since they are provided by CALIMA they can be selected by the whole MADA-ARZ system.

5 Evaluation

We evaluate MADA-ARZ intrinsically — in terms of performance on morphological disambiguation — and extrinsically in the context of MT.

5.1 POS Tagging, Diacritization, Lemmatization and Segmentation

Experimental Settings We use two sets of annotated data from the LDC: ATB-123, which includes parts 1, 2 and 3 of the MSA Penn Arabic Treebank

Train Data	Development MADA MSA	MADA-ARZ ARZ	MADA-ARZ ALL	Test MADA MSA	MADA-ARZ ARZ	MADA-ARZ ALL
Morph Tag	35.8	**84.0**	77.3	35.7	**84.5**	75.5
Penn POS	77.5	89.6	**90.2**	79.0	90.0	**90.1**
MADA POS	80.7	90.8	**91.3**	82.1	91.1	**91.4**
Diacritic	31.3	**82.6**	72.9	32.2	**83.2**	72.2
Lemma	64.0	**85.2**	81.6	67.1	**86.3**	82.8
Full	26.2	**74.3**	65.4	27.0	**75.4**	64.7
ATB Segmentation	90.6	97.4	**97.6**	90.5	97.4	**97.5**

Table 1: Evaluation metrics on the ATB-ARZ development and test sets. The best results are **bolded**. We compare MADA and MADA-ARZ with different training data conditions. Definitions of metrics are in Section 5.1. MSA training data is ATB-123. ARZ training data is ATB-ARZ. ALL training data is ATB-123 plus ATB-ARZ.

(Maamouri et al., 2004); and ATB-ARZ, the Egyptian Arabic Treebank (parts 1-5) (Maamouri et al., 2012a). For ATB-123 training, we use all of parts 1 and 2 plus the training portion of ATB-3 (as defined by Zitouni et al. (2006)); for development and test, we split Zitouni et al. (2006)'s devtest set into two. We sub-divide ATB-ARZ into development, training, and test sets (roughly a 10/80/10 split). The ATB-ARZ training data has 134K words, and the ATB-123 training data has 711K words.

We evaluate two systems. We used the latest release of MADA for MSA (v3.2), trained on ATB-123 (MSA), as our baseline. For MADA-ARZ, we compare two training settings: using ATB-ARZ (ARZ) and combining ATB-ARZ with ATB-123 (ALL). We present our results on the ATB-ARZ development and blind test sets (21.1K words and 20.4K words). Tuning for MADA-ARZ was done using a random 10% of the ATB-ARZ training data, which was later integrated back into the training set.

Metrics We use several evaluation metrics to measure the effectiveness of MADA-ARZ. **Morph Tag** refers to the accuracy of correctly predicting the full CALIMA morphological tag (i.e., not the diacritics or the lemma). **Penn POS** and MADA **POS** are also tag accuracy metrics. **Penn POS**, also known as the *Reduced Tag Set*, is a tag set reduction of the full Arabic morphological tag set, which was proposed for MSA (Kulick et al., 2006; Diab, 2007; Habash, 2010); since it retains no MSA-specific morphological features, it also makes sense for ARZ. MADA **POS** is the small POS tag set (36 tags) MADA uses internally. **Diacritic** and **Lemma** are the accuracies of the choice of diacritized form and Lemma, respectively. **Full** is the harshest metric, requiring that every morphological feature of the chosen analysis be correct. Finally, **ATB Segmentation** is the percentage of words with correct ATB segmentation (splitting off all clitics except for the determiner +ال *Al+*).

Results The results are shown in Table 1. MADA-ARZ performs much better than the MADA baselines in all evaluation metrics. Comparing the two MADA-ARZ systems, it is evident that adding MSA data (ATB123) results in slightly better performance only for the Penn POS, MADA POS, and ATB Segmentation metrics. Including the MSA data results in accuracy reductions for the other metrics, but the resulting system still outperforms the MADA MSA baseline in all cases. The results are consistent for development and blind test.

The CMUQ-ECA Test Set Mohamed et al. (2012) reported on the task of ARZ raw orthography morph segmentation (determining the morphs in the raw word). The CMUQ-ECA test data comprised 36 ARZ political comments and jokes from the Egyptian web site `www.masrawy.com`. The set contains 2,445 words including punctuation. Their best system gets a 91.9% word-level accuracy. Since MADA-ARZ modifies the spelling

Tokenization	OOV	BLEU	METEOR	TER
Punct	9.2	22.1	27.2	63.2
MADA ATB	5.8	24.4	29.6	60.5
MADA-ARZ ATB	4.9	**25.2**	**29.9**	**59.4**

Table 2: Machine translation results on the test set. "Punct" refers to the baseline which only tokenizes at punctuation.

of the word when it maps into CODA, we needed a manual analysis where no exact match with the gold occurs (11.8% of the time). We determined MADA-ARZ's accuracy on their test set for morph-segmentation to be 93.2%.

5.2 Egyptian Arabic to English MT

MT Experimental Settings We use the open-source Moses toolkit (Koehn et al., 2007) to build a phrase-based SMT system. We use MGIZA++ for word alignment (Gao and Vogel, 2008). Phrase translations of up to 8 words are extracted in the phrase table. We use SRILM (Stolcke, 2002) with modified Kneser-Ney smoothing to build two 4-gram language models. The first model is trained on the English side of the bitext, while the other is trained on the English Gigaword data. Feature weights are tuned to maximize BLEU (Papineni et al., 2002) on a development set using Minimum Error Rate Training (Och, 2003). We perform case-insensitive evaluation in terms of BLEU , METEOR (Banerjee and Lavie, 2005) and TER (Snover et al., 2006) metrics.

Data We trained on DA-English parallel data (Egyptian and Levantine) obtained from several LDC corpora. The training data amounts to 3.8M untokenized words on the Arabic side. The dev set, used for tuning the parameters of the MT system, has 15,585 untokenized Arabic words. The test set has 12,116 untokenized Arabic words. Both dev and test data contain two sets of reference translations. The English data is lower-cased and tokenized using simple punctuation-based rules.

Systems We build three translation systems which vary in tokenization of the Arabic text. The first system applies only simple punctuation-based rules. The second and third systems use MADA and MADA-ARZ, respectively, to tokenize the Arabic text in the ATB tokenization scheme (Habash and Sadat, 2006). The Arabic text is also Alif/Ya normalized.

Results The MT results are in Table 2, which also shows the percentage of out-of-vocabulary (OOV) words – test words not in the training data. MADA-ARZ delivers the best translation performance according to all metrics. All MADA-ARZ improvements over MADA are statistically significant at the .01 level (except in the case of METEOR). All improvements over Punct by MADA and MADA-ARZ are also statistically significant. For BLEU scores, we observe 3.1% absolute improvement to Punct (14% relative), and 0.8% absolute improvement to MADA (3.3% relative). In addition to better morphological disambiguation, MADA-ARZ reduces the OOV ratio (16% relative to MADA), which we suspect contributes to the observed improvements in MT quality.

6 Conclusion and Future Work

We have presented MADA-ARZ, a system for morphological tagging of ARZ. We have shown that it outperforms an state-of-the-art MSA tagger (MADA) on ARZ text, and that it helps ARZ-to-English machine translation more than MADA.

In the future, we intend to perform further feature engineering to improve the results of MADA-ARZ, and extend the system to handle other DAs.

Acknowledgments

This paper is based upon work supported by the Defense Advanced Research Projects Agency (DARPA) under Contract No. HR0011-12-C-0014. Any opinions, findings and conclusions or recommendations expressed in this paper are those of the authors and do not necessarily reflect the views of DARPA.

References

Ernest T. Abdel-Massih, Zaki N. Abdel-Malek, and El-Said M. Badawi. 1979. *A Reference Grammar of Egyptian Arabic*. Georgetown University Press.

Hitham Abo Bakr, Khaled Shaalan, and Ibrahim Ziedan. 2008. A Hybrid Approach for Converting Written Egyptian Colloquial Dialect into Diacritized Arabic. In *The 6th International Conference on Informatics and Systems, INFOS2008*. Cairo University.

Rania Al-Sabbagh and Roxana Girju. 2012. A supervised POS tagger for written Arabic social networking corpora. In Jeremy Jancsary, editor, *Proceedings of KONVENS 2012*, pages 39–52. ÖGAI, September. Main track: oral presentations.

Satanjeev Banerjee and Alon Lavie. 2005. METEOR: An Automatic Metric for MT Evaluation with Improved Correlation with Human Judgments. In *Proceedings of the ACL Workshop on Intrinsic and Extrinsic Evaluation Measures for Machine Translation and/or Summarization*, pages 65–72, Ann Arbor, Michigan.

Eric Brill. 1995. Transformation-Based Error-Driven Learning and Natural Language Processing: A Case Study in Part-of-Speech Tagging. *Computational Linguistics*, 21(4):543–565.

Tim Buckwalter. 2007. Issues in Arabic Morphological Analysis. In A. van den Bosch and A. Soudi, editors, *Arabic Computational Morphology: Knowledge-based and Empirical Methods*. Springer.

David Chiang, Mona Diab, Nizar Habash, Owen Rambow, and Safiullah Shareef. 2006. Parsing Arabic Dialects. In *Proceedings of the European Chapter of ACL (EACL)*.

Walter Daelemans and Antal van den Bosch. 2005. *Memory-Based Language Processing*. Studies in Natural Language Processing. Cambridge University Press, Cambridge, UK.

Mona Diab, Kadri Hacioglu, and Daniel Jurafsky. 2007. Automated methods for processing arabic text: From tokenization to base phrase chunking. In Antal van den Bosch and Abdelhadi Soudi, editors, *Arabic Computational Morphology: Knowledge-based and Empirical Methods*. Kluwer/Springer.

Mona Diab. 2007. Improved Arabic Base Phrase Chunking with a New Enriched POS Tag Set. In *Proceedings of the 2007 Workshop on Computational Approaches to Semitic Languages: Common Issues and Resources*, pages 89–96, Prague, Czech Republic, June.

Kevin Duh and Katrin Kirchhoff. 2005. POS tagging of dialectal Arabic: a minimally supervised approach. In *Proceedings of the ACL Workshop on Computational Approaches to Semitic Languages*, Semitic '05, pages 55–62, Ann Arbor, Michigan.

Ramy Eskander, Nizar Habash, Owen Rambow, and Nadi Tomeh. 2013. Processing Spontaneous Orthography. In *Proceedings of the 2013 Conference of the North American Chapter of the Association for Computational Linguistics: Human Language Technologies (NAACL-HLT)*, Atlanta, GA.

Qin Gao and Stephan Vogel. 2008. Parallel implementations of word alignment tool. In *Software Engineering, Testing, and Quality Assurance for Natural Language Processing*, SETQA-NLP '08, pages 49–57, Stroudsburg, PA, USA. Association for Computational Linguistics.

David Graff, Mohamed Maamouri, Basma Bouziri, Sondos Krouna, Seth Kulick, and Tim Buckwalter. 2009. Standard Arabic Morphological Analyzer (SAMA) Version 3.1. Linguistic Data Consortium LDC2009E73.

Nizar Habash and Owen Rambow. 2005. Arabic Tokenization, Part-of-Speech Tagging and Morphological Disambiguation in One Fell Swoop. In *Proceedings of the 43rd Annual Meeting of the Association for Computational Linguistics (ACL'05)*, pages 573–580, Ann Arbor, Michigan.

Nizar Habash and Owen Rambow. 2006. MAGEAD: A Morphological Analyzer and Generator for the Arabic Dialects. In *Proceedings of the 21st International Conference on Computational Linguistics and 44th Annual Meeting of the Association for Computational Linguistics*, pages 681–688, Sydney, Australia.

Nizar Habash and Fatiha Sadat. 2006. Arabic Preprocessing Schemes for Statistical Machine Translation. In *Proceedings of the 7th Meeting of the North American Chapter of the Association for Computational Linguistics/Human Language Technologies Conference (HLT-NAACL06)*, pages 49–52, New York, NY.

Nizar Habash, Abdelhadi Soudi, and Tim Buckwalter. 2007. On Arabic Transliteration. In A. van den Bosch and A. Soudi, editors, *Arabic Computational Morphology: Knowledge-based and Empirical Methods*. Springer.

Nizar Habash, Mona Diab, and Owen Rabmow. 2012a. Conventional Orthography for Dialectal Arabic. In *Proceedings of the Language Resources and Evaluation Conference (LREC)*, Istanbul.

Nizar Habash, Ramy Eskander, and Abdelati Hawwari. 2012b. A Morphological Analyzer for Egyptian Arabic. In *NAACL-HLT 2012 Workshop on Computational Morphology and Phonology (SIGMORPHON2012)*, pages 1–9.

Nizar Habash. 2010. *Introduction to Arabic Natural Language Processing*. Morgan & Claypool Publishers.

Jan Hajič. 2000. Morphological tagging: Data vs. dictionaries. In *Proceedings of the 1st Meeting of the*

North American Chapter of the Association for Computational Linguistics (NAACL'00), Seattle, WA.

Clive Holes. 2004. *Modern Arabic: Structures, Functions, and Varieties*. Georgetown Classics in Arabic Language and Linguistics. Georgetown University Press.

H. Kilany, H. Gadalla, H. Arram, A. Yacoub, A. El-Habashi, and C. McLemore. 2002. Egyptian Colloquial Arabic Lexicon. LDC catalog number LDC99L22.

Philipp Koehn, Hieu Hoang, Alexandra Birch, Christopher Callison-Burch, Marcello Federico, Nicola Bertoldi, Brooke Cowan, Wade Shen, Christine Moran, Richard Zens, Christopher Dyer, Ondrej Bojar, Alexandra Constantin, and Evan Herbst. 2007. Moses: open source toolkit for statistical machine translation. In *Proceedings of the 45th Annual Meeting of the Association for Computational Linguistics Companion Volume Proceedings of the Demo and Poster Sessions*, pages 177–180, Prague, Czech Republic.

Seth Kulick, Ryan Gabbard, and Mitch Marcus. 2006. Parsing the Arabic Treebank: Analysis and Improvements. In *Proceedings of the Treebanks and Linguistic Theories Conference*, pages 31–42, Prague, Czech Republic.

Mohamed Maamouri, Ann Bies, Tim Buckwalter, and Wigdan Mekki. 2004. The Penn Arabic Treebank : Building a Large-Scale Annotated Arabic Corpus. In *NEMLAR Conference on Arabic Language Resources and Tools*, pages 102–109, Cairo, Egypt.

Mohamed Maamouri, Ann Bies, Tim Buckwalter, Mona Diab, Nizar Habash, Owen Rambow, and Dalila Tabessi. 2006. Developing and Using a Pilot Dialectal Arabic Treebank. In *The fifth international conference on Language Resources and Evaluation (LREC)*, pages 443–448, Genoa, Italy.

Mohamed Maamouri, Ann Bies, Seth Kulick, Dalila Tabessi, and Sondos Krouna. 2012a. Egyptian Arabic Treebank Pilot.

Mohamed Maamouri, Sondos Krouna, Dalila Tabessi, Nadia Hamrouni, and Nizar Habash. 2012b. Egyptian Arabic Morphological Annotation Guidelines.

Emad Mohamed, Behrang Mohit, and Kemal Oflazer. 2012. Annotating and Learning Morphological Segmentation of Egyptian Colloquial Arabic. In *Proceedings of the Language Resources and Evaluation Conference (LREC)*, Istanbul.

Franz Josef Och. 2003. Minimum Error Rate Training for Statistical Machine Translation. In *Proceedings of the 41st Annual Conference of the Association for Computational Linguistics*, pages 160–167, Sapporo, Japan.

Kishore Papineni, Salim Roukos, Todd Ward, and Wei-Jing Zhu. 2002. BLEU: a Method for Automatic Evaluation of Machine Translation. In *Proceedings of the 40th Annual Meeting of the Association for Computational Linguistics*, pages 311–318, Philadelphia, PA.

Ryan Roth, Owen Rambow, Nizar Habash, Mona Diab, and Cynthia Rudin. 2008. Arabic morphological tagging, diacritization, and lemmatization using lexeme models and feature ranking. In *ACL 2008: The Conference of the Association for Computational Linguistics; Companion Volume, Short Papers*, Columbus, Ohio.

Wael Salloum and Nizar Habash. 2011. Dialectal to Standard Arabic Paraphrasing to Improve Arabic-English Statistical Machine Translation. In *Proceedings of the First Workshop on Algorithms and Resources for Modelling of Dialects and Language Varieties*, pages 10–21, Edinburgh, Scotland.

Wael Salloum and Nizar Habash. 2013. Dialectal Arabic to English Machine Translation: Pivoting through Modern Standard Arabic. In *Proceedings of the 2013 Conference of the North American Chapter of the Association for Computational Linguistics: Human Language Technologies (NAACL-HLT)*, Atlanta, GA.

Matt Snover, Bonnie J. Dorr, Richard Schwartz, Linnea Micciulla, and John Makhoul. 2006. A Study of Translation Error Rate with Targeted Human Annotation. In *Proceedings of the Association for Machine Transaltion in the Americas (AMTA 2006)*, Cambridge, Massachusetts.

David Stallard, Jacob Devlin, Michael Kayser, Yoong Keok Lee, and Regina Barzilay. 2012. Unsupervised Morphology Rivals Supervised Morphology for Arabic MT. In *Proceedings of the 50th Annual Meeting of the Association for Computational Linguistics*, pages 322–327, Jeju Island, Korea.

Andreas Stolcke. 2002. SRILM - an Extensible Language Modeling Toolkit. In *Proceedings of the International Conference on Spoken Language Processing (ICSLP)*, volume 2, pages 901–904, Denver, CO.

Rabih Zbib, Erika Malchiodi, Jacob Devlin, David Stallard, Spyros Matsoukas, Richard Schwartz, John Makhoul, Omar F. Zaidan, and Chris Callison-Burch. 2012. Machine translation of arabic dialects. In *Proceedings of the 2012 Conference of the North American Chapter of the Association for Computational Linguistics: Human Language Technologies*, pages 49–59, Montréal, Canada.

Imed Zitouni, Jeffrey S. Sorensen, and Ruhi Sarikaya. 2006. Maximum entropy based restoration of arabic diacritics. In *Proceedings of the 21st International Conference on Computational Linguistics and 44th Annual Meeting of the Association for Computational Linguistics*, pages 577–584, Sydney, Australia.

Using a Supertagged Dependency Language Model to Select a Good Translation in System Combination

Wei-Yun Ma
Department of Computer Science
Columbia University
New York, NY 10027, USA
ma@cs.columbia.edu

Kathleen McKeown
Department of Computer Science
Columbia University
New York, NY 10027, USA
kathy@cs.columbia.edu

Abstract

We present a novel, structured language model - Supertagged Dependency Language Model to model the syntactic dependencies between words. The goal is to identify ungrammatical hypotheses from a set of candidate translations in a MT system combination framework and help select the best translation candidates using a variety of sentence-level features. We use a two-step mechanism based on constituent parsing and elementary tree extraction to obtain supertags and their dependency relations. Our experiments show that the structured language model provides significant improvement in the framework of sentence-level system combination.

1 Introduction

In recent years, there has been a burgeoning interest in incorporating syntactic structure into Statistical machine translation (SMT) models (e..g, Galley et al., 2006; DeNeefe and Knight 2009; Quirk et al., 2005). In addition to modeling syntactic structure in the decoding process, a methodology for candidate translation selection has also emerged. This methodology first generates multiple candidate translations followed by rescoring using global sentence-level syntactic features to select the final translation. The advantage of this methodology is that it allows for easy integration of complex syntactic features that would be too expensive to use during the decoding process. The methodology is usually applied in two scenarios: one is as part of an n-best reranking (Och et al., 2004; Hasan et al., 2006), where n-best candidate translations are generated through a decoding process. The other is translation selection or reranking (Hildebrand and Vogel 2008; Callison-Burch et al., 2012), where candidate translations are generated by different decoding processes or different decoders.

This paper belongs to the latter; the goal is to identify ungrammatical hypotheses from given candidate translations using grammatical knowledge in the target language that expresses syntactic dependencies between words. To achieve that, we propose a novel Structured Language Model (SLM) - Supertagged Dependency Language Model (SDLM) to model the syntactic dependencies between words. Supertag (Bangalore and Joshi, 1999) is an elementary syntactic structure based on Lexicalized Tree Adjoining Grammar (LTAG). Traditional supertagged n-gram LM predicts the next supertag based on the immediate words to the left with supertags, so it can not explicitly model long-distance dependency relations. In contrast, SDLM predicts the next supertag using the words with supertags on which it syntactically depend, and these words could be anywhere and arbitrarily far apart in a sentence. A candidate translation's grammatical degree or "fluency" can be measured by simply calculating the SDLM likelihood of the supertagged dependency structure that spans the entire sentence.

To obtain the supertagged dependency structure, the most intuitive way is through a LTAG parser (Schabes et al., 1988). However, this could be very slow as it has time complexity of $O(n^6)$. Instead we propose an alternative mechanism in this paper: first we use a constituent parser[1] of $O(n^3)$ ~ $O(n^5)$ to obtain the parse of a sentence, and then we extract elementary trees with dependencies from the parse in linear time. Aside from the consideration of time complexity, another motivation of this two-step mechanism is that compared with LTAG parsing, the mechanism is more flexible for defining syntactic structures of elementary trees for our needs. Because those structures are defined only within the elementary tree extractor, we can easily adjust the definition of those structures within the extractor and avoid redesigning or retraining our constituent parser.

We experiment with sentence-level translation combination of five different translation systems; the goal is for the system to select the best translation for each input source sentence among the translations provided by the five systems. The results show a significant improvement of 1.45 Bleu score over the best single MT system and 0.72 Bleu score over a baseline sentence-level combination system of using consensus and n-gram LM.

2 Related Work

Och et al., (2004) investigated various syntactic feature functions to rerank the n-best candidate translations. Most features are syntactically motivated and based on alignment information between the source sentence and the target translation. The results are rather disappointing. Only the non-syntactic IBM model 1 yielded significant improvement. All other tree-based feature functions had only a very small effect on the performance.

In contrast to (Och et al., 2004)'s bilingual syntax features, Hasan et al., (2006) focused on monolingual syntax features in n-best reranking. They also investigated the effect of directly using the log-likelihood of the output of a HMM-based supertagger, and found it did not improve performance significantly. It is worth noticing that this log-likelihood is based on supertagged n-gram LM, which is one type of class-based n-gram LM, so it does not model explicit syntactic dependencies between words in contrast to the work we describe in this paper. Hardmeier et al., (2012) use tree kernels over constituency and dependency parse trees for either the input or output sentences to identify constructions that are difficult to translate in the source language, and doubtful syntactic structures in the output language. The tree fragments extracted by their tree kernels are similar to our elementary trees but they only regard them as the individual inputs of support vector machine regression while binary relations of our elementary trees are considered in a formulation of a structural language model.

Outside the field of candidate translation selection, Hassan et al., (2007) proposed a phrase-based SMT model that integrates supertags into the target side of the translation model and the target n-gram LM. Two kinds of supertags are employed: those from LTAG and Combinatory Categorial Grannar (CCG), and both yield similar improvements. They found that using both or either of the supertag-based translation model and supertagged LM can achieve significant improvement. Again, the supertagged LM is a class-based n-gram LM and does not model explicit syntactic dependencies during decoding.

In the field of MT system combination, word-level confusion network decoding is one of the most successful approaches (Matusov et al., 2006; Rosti et al., 2007; He et al. 2008; Karakos et al. 2008; Sim et al. 2007; Xu et al. 2011). It is capable of generating brand new translations but it is difficult to consider more complex syntax such as dependency LM during decoding since it adds one word at a time while a dependency based LM must parse a complete sentence. Typically, a confusion network approach selects one translation as the best and uses this as the backbone for the confusion network. The work we present here could provide a more sophisticated mechanism for selecting the backbone. Alternatively, one can enhance confusion network models by collaborating with a sentence-level combination model which uses complex syntax to re-rank n-best outputs of a confusion network model. This kind of collaboration is one of our future works.

[1] Stanford parser (http://nlp.stanford.edu/software/lex-parser.shtml). We use its PCFG version of $O(n^3)$ for SDLM training of part of Gigaword in addition to Treebank and use its factor version of $O(n^5)$ to calculate the SDLM likelihood of translations.

3 LTAG and Supertag

LTAG (Joshi et al., 1975; Schabes et al., 1988) is a formal tree rewriting formalism, which consists of a set of elementary trees, corresponding to minimal linguistic structures that localize dependencies, including long-distance dependencies, such as predicate-argument structure. Each elementary tree is associated with at least one lexical item on its frontier. The lexical item associated with an elementary tree is called the anchor in that tree; an elementary tree thus serves as a description of syntactic constraints of the anchor. The elementary syntactic structures of elementary trees are called supertags (Bangalore and Joshi, 1999), in order to distinguish them from the standard part-of-speech tags. Some examples are provided in figure 1 (b).

Elementary trees are divided into initial and auxiliary trees. Initial trees are those for which all non-terminal nodes on the frontier are substitutable. Auxiliary trees are defined as initial trees, except that exactly one frontier, non-terminal node must be a foot node, with the same label as the root node. Two operations - substitution and adjunction - are provided in LTAG to combine elementary trees into a derived tree.

4 SDLM

Our goal is to use SDLM to calculate the grammaticality of translated sentences. We do this by calculating the likelihood of the supertagged dependency structure that spans the entire sentence using SDLM. To obtain the supertagged dependency linkage, the most intuitive way is through a LTAG parser (Schabes et al., 1988). However, this could be very slow as it has time complexity of $O(n^6)$. Another possibility is to follow the procedure in (Joshi and Srinivas 1994, Bangalore and Joshi, 1999): use a HMM-based supertagger to assign words with supertags, followed by derivation of a shallow parse in linear time based on only the supertags to obtain the dependencies. But since this approach uses only the local context, in (Joshi and Srinivas 1994), they also proposed another greedy algorithm based on supertagged dependency probabilities to gradually select the path with the maximum path probability to extend to the remaining directions in the dependency list.

In contrast to the LTAG parsing and supertagging-based approaches, we propose an alternative mechanism: first we use a state-of-the-art constituent parser to obtain the parse of a sentence, and then we extract elementary trees with dependencies from the parse to assign each word with an elementary tree. The second step is similar to the approach used in extracting elementary trees from the TreeBank (Xia, 1999; Chen and Vijay-Shanker, 2000).

4.1 Elementary Tree Extraction

We use an elementary tree extractor, a modification of (Chen and Vijay-Shanker, 2000), to serve our purpose. Heuristic rules were used to distinguish arguments from adjuncts, and the extraction process can be regarded as a process that gradually decomposes a constituent parse to multiple elementary trees and records substitutions and adjunctions. From elementary trees, we can obtain supertags by only considering syntactic structure and ignoring anchor words. Take the sentence – "The hungry boys ate dinner" as an example; the constituent parse and extracted supertags are shown in Figure 1.

In Figure 1 (b), dotted lines represent the operations of substitution and adjunction. Note that each word in a translated sentence would be assigned exactly one elementary syntactic structure which is associated with a unique supertag id for the whole corpus. Different anchor words could own the same elementary syntactic structure and would be assigned the same supertag id, such as "$\alpha 1$" for "boys" and "dinner". For our corpus, around 1700 different elementary syntactic structures (1700 supertag ids) are extracted.

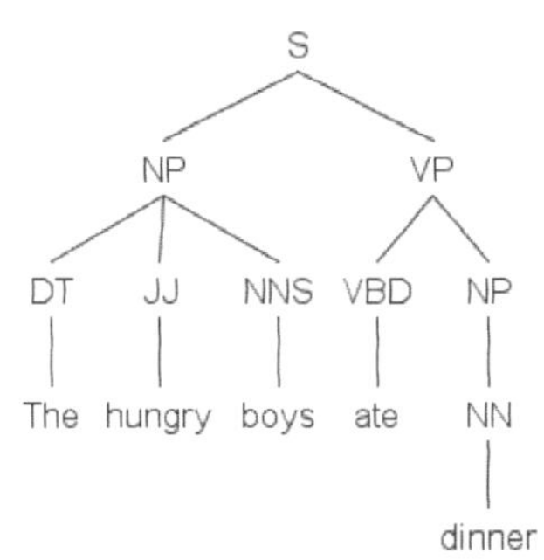

Figure 1. (a) Parse of "The hungry boys ate dinner"

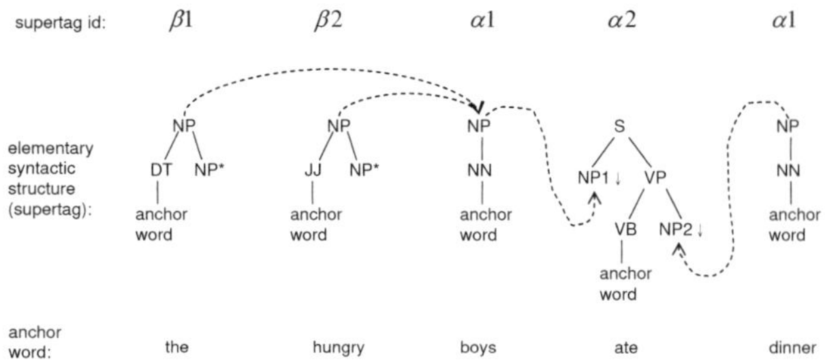

Figure 1. (b) Extracted elementary trees

4.2 Model

Bangalore and Joshi (1999) gave a concise description for dependencies between supertags: "A supertag is dependent on another supertag if the former substitutes or adjoins into the latter". Following this description, for the example in Figure 1 (b), supertags of "the" and "hungry" are dependent on the supertag of "boys", and supertags of "boys" and "dinner" are dependent on the supertag of "ate". These dependencies between supertags also provide the dependencies between anchor words.

Since the syntactic constraints for each word in its context are decided and described through its supertag, the likelihood of SDLM for a sentence could also be regarded as the degree of violations of the syntactic constraints on all words in the sentence. Consider a sentence $S = w_1\ w_2 \ldots w_n$ with corresponding supertags $T = t_1\ t_2 \ldots t_n$. We use $d_i = j$ to represent the dependency relations for words or supertags. For example, $d_3 = 5$ means that w_3 depends on w_5 or t_3 depends on t_5. We propose five different bigram SDLM as follows and evaluate their effects in section 5.

$$\prod_i P(w_i t_i \mid w_{d_i} t_{d_i}) \qquad \text{SDLM model(1)}$$

$$\prod_i P(w_i t_i \mid w_{d_i} t_{d_i}) \approx \prod_i P(t_i \mid t_{d_i}) P(w_i \mid t_i) \qquad \text{SDLM model(2)}$$

$$\prod_i P(t_i \mid t_{d_i}) \qquad \text{SDLM model(3)}$$

$$\prod_i P(w_i \mid t_i) \qquad \text{SDLM model(4)}$$

$$\prod_i P(w_i \mid w_{d_i}) \qquad \text{SDLM model(5)}$$

SDLM model (2) is the approximation form of model (1); model (3) and (4) are individual terms of model (2); model (5) models word dependencies based on elementary tree dependencies. The estimation of the probabilities is done using maximum likelihood estimations with Laplace smoothing. Take Figure 1 (b) as an example; if using model (1), the SDLM likelihood of "The hungry boys ate dinner" is

$$P(the, \beta 1 \mid boys, \alpha 1) * P(hungry, \beta 2 \mid boys, \alpha 1) * P(boys, \alpha 1 \mid ate, \alpha 2) * P(dinner, \alpha 1 \mid ate, \alpha 2) * P(ate, \alpha 2 \mid root)$$

In our experiment on sentence-level translation combination, we use a log-linear model to integrate all features including SDLM models. The corresponding weights are trained discriminatively for Bleu score using Minimum Error Rate Training (MERT).

5 Experiment

Our experiments are conducted and reported on the Chinese-English dataset from NIST 2008 (LDC2010T01). It consists of four human reference translations and corresponding machine translations for the NIST Open MT08 test set, which consists of newswire and web data. The test set contains 105 documents with 1312 sentences and output from 23 machine translation systems. Each system provides the top one translation hypothesis for every sentence. We further divide the NIST Open MT08 test set into the tuning set and test set for our experiment of sentence-level translation combination. We divided the 1312 sentences into tuning data of 524 sentences and the test set of 788 sentences. Out of 23 MT systems, we manually select the top five MT systems as our MT systems for our combination experiment.

In terms of SDLM training, since the size of TreeBank-extracted elementary trees is much smaller compared to most practical n-gram LMs trained from the Gigaword corpus, we also extract elementary trees from automatically-generated parses of part of the Gigaword corpus (around one-year newswire of "afp_eng" in Gigaword 4) in addition to TreeBank-extracted elementary trees.

5.1 Feature Functions

For the baseline combination system, we use the following feature functions in the log-linear model to calculate the score of a system translation.

- Sentence consensus based on Translation Edit Ratio (TER)
- Gigaword-trained 3-gram LM and word penalty

For testing SDLM, in additional to all features that the baseline combination system uses, we add single or multiple SDLM models in the log-linear model, and each SDLM model has its own weight.

5.2 Result

From table 1, we can see that the combination of SDLM model 3, 4 and 5 yields the best performance, which is better than the best MT system by Bleu of 1.45, TER of 0.67 and METEOR of 1.25, and also better than the baseline combination system by Bleu of 0.72, TER of 0.25 and METEOR of 0.44. Compared with SDLM model 5, which represents a type of word dependency LM without labels, the results show that adding appropriate syntactic "labels" (here, they are "supertags") on word dependencies brings benefits.

	Bleu	TER	METEOR
Best MT system	30.16	55.45	54.43
baseline	30.89	55.03	55.24
baseline+ model 1	31.29	54.99	55.63
baseline+ model 2	31.25	55.23	55.37
baseline+ model 3	31.25	55.06	55.40
baseline+ model 4	31.44	54.70	55.54
baseline+ model 5	31.39	55.15	55.68
baseline+ model 3+ model 4+ model 5	31.61	54.78	55.68

Table 1. Result of Sentence-level Translation Combination

6 Conclusion

In this paper we presented Supertagged Dependency Language Model for explicitly modeling syntactic dependencies of the words of translated sentences. Our goal is to select the most grammatical translation from candidate translations. To obtain the supertagged dependency structure of a translation candidate, a two-step mechanism based on constituent parsing and elementary tree extraction is also proposed. SDLM shows its effectiveness in the scenario of translation selection.

There are several avenues for future work: we have focused on bigram dependencies in our models; extension to more than two dependent elementary trees is straightforward. It would also be worth investigating the performance of using our sentence-level model to re-rank n-best outputs of a confusion network model. And in terms of applications, SDLM can be directly applied to many other NLP tasks, such as speech recognition and natural language generation.

Acknowledgments

We would like to thank Owen Rambow for providing the elementary tree extractor and also thank the anonymous reviewers for their helpful comments. This work is supported by the National Science Foundation via Grant No. 0910778 entitled "Richer Representations for Machine Translation". All views expressed in this paper are those of the authors and do not necessarily represent the view of the National Science Foundation.

References

Srinivas Bangalore and Aravind K. Joshi. 1999. Supertagging: An approach to almost parsing. *Computational Linguistics*, 25(2):237–265.

John Chen and K. Vijay-Shanker. 2000. Automated extraction of TAGs from the Penn treebank. *In Proceedings of the Sixth International Workshop on Parsing Technologies*

Chris Callison-Burch, Philipp Koehn, Christof Monz, Matt Post, Radu Soricut and Lucia Specia. 2012. Findings of the 2012 Workshop on Statistical Machine Translation. *In Proceedings of WMT12.*

Steve DeNeefe and Kevin Knight. 2009 Synchronous Tree Adjoining Machine Translation. *In Proceedings of EMNLP*

Michel Galley, Jonathan Graehl, Kevin Knight, Daniel Marcu, Steve DeNeefe, Wei Wang, Ignacio Thayer. 2006. Scalable Inference and Training of Context-Rich Syntactic Translation Models. *In Proceedings of the Annual Meeting of the Association for Computational Linguistics*

Christian Hardmeier, Joakim Nivre and Jörg Tiedemann. 2012. Tree Kernels for Machine Translation Quality Estimation. *In Proceedings of WMT12*

S. Hasan, O. Bender, and H. Ney. 2006. Reranking translation hypotheses using structural properties. *In Proceedings of the EACL'06 Workshop on Learning Structured Information in Natural Language Applications*

Hany Hassan , Khalil Sima'an and Andy Way. 2007. Supertagged Phrase-Based Statistical Machine Translation. *In Proceedings of the Annual Meeting of the Association for Computational Linguistics*

Xiaodong He, Mei Yang, Jianfeng Gao, Patrick Nguyen, and Robert Moore. 2008. Indirect-hmm-based hypothesis alignment for computing outputs from machine translation systems. *In Proceedings of EMNLP*

Almut Silja Hildebrand and Stephan Vogel. 2008. Combination of machine translation systems via hypothesis selection from combined n-best lists. *In Proceedings of the Eighth Conference of the Association for Machine Translation in the Americas*

Aravind K. Joshi and B. Srinivas. 1994. Disambiguation of super parts of speech (or supertags): Almost parsing. *In Proceedings of the 15th International Conference on Computational Linguistics*

Aravind K. Joshi, Leon S. Levy, and Masako Takahashi. 1975. Tree Adjunct Grammars. *Journal of Computer and System Science*, 10:136–163.

Evgeny Matusov, Nicola Ueffing, and Hermann Ney 2006. Computing consensus translation from multiple machine translation systems using enhanced hypotheses alignment. *In Proceedings of EACL*

Franz Josef Och, Daniel Gildea, Sanjeev Khudanpur, Anoop Sarkar, Kenji Yamada, Alex Fraser, Shankar Kumar, Libin Shen, David Smith, Katherine Eng, Viren Jain, Zhen Jin, and Dragomir Radev. 2004 A smorgasbord of features for statistical machine translation. *In Proceedings of the Meeting of the North American chapter of the Association for Computational Linguistics*

Damianos Karakos, Jason Eisner, Sanjeev Khudanpur, and Markus Dreyer. 2008. Machine translation system combination using ITG-based alignments. *In Proceedings of ACL-HLT*

Chris Quirk, Arul Menezes, and Colin Cherry. 2005. Dependency Treelet Translation: Syntactically Informed Phrasal SMT, *In Proceedings of the Association for Computational Linguistics*

Antti-Veikko I. Rosti, Spyros Matsoukas, and Richard Schwartz. 2007. Improved word-level system combination for machine translation. *In Proceedings of ACL*

Yves Schabes, Anne Abeille and Aravind K. Joshi. 1988. Parsing strategies with 'lexicalized' grammars: Application to Tree Adjoining Grammars. *In Proceedings of the 12th International Conference on Computational Linguistics*

K.C. Sim, W.J. Byrne, M.J.F. Gales, H. Sahbi and P.C. Woodland .2007. Consensus Network Decoding for Statistical Machine Translation System Combination. *In Proceedings of ICASSP*

Fei Xia. 1999. Extracting Tree Adjoining Grammars from Bracketed Corpora. *In Proceedings of the 5th Natural Language Processing Pacific Rim Symposium (NLPRS-1999)*

Daguang Xu, Yuan Cao, Damianos Karakos. 2011. Description of the JHU System Combination Scheme for WMT 2011. *In Proceedings of the Sixth Workshop on Statistical Machine Translation*

Dudley North visits North London: Learning When to Transliterate to Arabic

Mahmoud Azab **Houda Bouamor** **Behrang Mohit** **Kemal Oflazer**
Carnegie Mellon University
P.O. Box 24866, Doha, Qatar
{mazab, hbouamor, behrang, ko}@qatar.cmu.edu

Abstract

We report the results of our work on automating the transliteration decision of named entities for English to Arabic machine translation. We construct a classification-based framework to automate this decision, evaluate our classifier both in the limited news and the diverse Wikipedia domains, and achieve promising accuracy. Moreover, we demonstrate a reduction of translation error and an improvement in the performance of an English-to-Arabic machine translation system.

1 Introduction

Translation of named entities (NEs) is important for NLP applications such as Machine Translation (MT) and Cross-lingual Information Retrieval. For MT, NEs are major subset of the out-of-vocabulary terms (OOVs). Due to their diversity, they cannot always be found in parallel corpora, dictionaries or gazetteers. Thus, state-of-the-art of MT needs to handle NEs in specific ways. For instance, in the English-Arabic automatic translation example given in Figure 1, the noun "North" has been erroneously translated to "الشمالية /Al$mAlyp " (indicating the north direction in English) instead of being transliterated to "نورث / nwrv".

As shown in Figure 1, direct translation of in-vocabulary terms could degrade translation quality. Also blind transliteration of OOVs does not necessarily contribute to translation adequacy and may actually create noisy contexts for the language model and the decoder.

English Input:	Dudley **North** was an English merchant.
SMT output:	كان دودلي **الشمالية** تاجر الإنجليزية. kAn dwdly **Al$mAlyp** tAjr AlInjlyzyp.
Correct Translation:	كان دودلي **نورث** تاجر إنجليزي. kAn dwdly **nwrv** tAjr Injlyzy.

Figure 1: Example of a NE translation error.

An intelligent decision between translation and transliteration should use semantic and contextual information such as the type of the named-entity and the surrounding terms. In this paper, we construct and evaluate a classification-based framework to automate the translation vs. transliteration decision. We evaluate our classifier both in the limited news and diverse Wikipedia domains, and achieve promising accuracy. Moreover, we conduct an extrinsic evaluation of the classifier within an English to Arabic MT system. In an in-domain (news) MT task, the classifier contributes to a modest (yet significant) improvement in MT quality. Moreover, for a Wikipedia translation task, we demonstrate that our classifier can reduce the erroneous translation of 60.5% of the named entities.

In summary our contributions are: (a) We automatically construct a bilingual lexicon of NEs paired with the transliteration/translation decisions in two domains.[1] (b) We build a binary classifier for transliteration and translation decision with a promising accuracy (c) We demonstrate its utility

[1]The dataset can be found at http://www.qatar.cmu.edu/~behrang/NETLexicon .

within an MT framework.

2 Learning when to transliterate

We model the decision as a binary classification at the token level. A token (within a named-entity) gets translation or transliteration label. In "*Dudley North*" and "*North London*", our classifier is expected to choose transliteration of "North" in the former case, as opposed to translation in the latter. The binary decision needs to use a rich set of local and contextual features. We use the Support Vector Machines as a robust framework for binary classification using a set of interdependent features.[2] We build two classifiers: (a) **Classifier $\mathbf{C}_{news}$**, trained on a large set of distinct NEs extracted from news-related parallel corpora; and (b) **Classifier $\mathbf{C}_{diverse}$**, trained on a combination of the news related NEs and a smaller set of diverse-topic NEs extracted from Wikipedia titles. We evaluate the two classifiers in both news and the diverse domains to observe the effects of noise and domain change.

2.1 Preparing the labeled data

Our classifier requires a set of NEs with token-level gold labels. We compile such data from two resources: We heuristically extract and label parallel NEs from a large word aligned parallel corpus and we use a lexicon of bilingual NEs collected from Arabic and Wikipedia titles. Starting with a word aligned parallel corpus, we use the UIUC NE tagger (Ratinov and Roth, 2009) to tag the English sentences with four classes of NEs: Person (PER), Location (LOC), Organization (ORG) and Miscellaneous (MISC). Furthermore, we use the word alignments to project and collect the span of the associated Arabic named-entities. To reduce the noisy nature of word alignments, we designed a procedure to clean up the noisy Arabic NE spans by POS verification, and heuristically filtering impossible items (e.g. verbs). This results in a bilingual lexicon of about 57K named-entity pairs. The distribution of NEs categories is reported in Table 1.

	PER	LOC	ORG	MISC
News$_{/57K}$	43.0%	10.0%	40.0%	7.0%
Wiki$_{/4K}$	73.0%	19.0%	2.5%	5.5%

Table 1: Distribution of the four NE categories used in 57K News and 4K Wiki datasets.

To train and evaluate the $\mathbf{C}_{diverse}$ classifier, we expand our labeled data with Wikipedia NEs using the cross-lingual hyperlinks. Wikipedia article titles often correspond to NEs (Kazama and Torisawa, 2007) and have been already used in different works for NEs recognition (Nothman et al., 2013) and disambiguation (Cucerzan, 2007). We improve the Arabic-English Wikipedia title lexicon of Mohit et al. (2012) and build a Wikipedia exclusive lexicon with 4K bilingual entities. In order to test the domain effects, our lexicon includes only NEs which are not present in the parallel corpus. The statistics given in Table 1 demonstrate different nature of the labeled datasets. The two datasets were labeled semi-automatically using the transliteration similarity measure (Fr_{score}) proposed by Freeman et al. (2006), a variant of edit distance measuring the similarity between an English word and its Arabic transliteration. In our experiments, English tokens having an $\text{Fr}_{score} > 0.6$ are considered as transliteration, others having $\text{Fr}_{score} < 0.5$ as translation. These thresholds were determined after tuning with a held out development set. For tokens having Fr_{score} between 0.5 and 0.6, the decision is not obvious. To label these instances (around 5K unique tokens), we manually transliterate them using Microsoft Maren tool.[3] We again compute the Fr_{score} between the obtained transliteration, in its Buckwalter form and the corresponding English token and use the same threshold to distinguish between the two classes. Some examples of NEs and their appropriate classes are presented in Table 2.

Transliteration	Translation
Minnesota ↔ مينيسوتا/mynyswta : 0.77	Agency ↔ وكالة/wkAlp : 0.33
Fluke ↔ فلوك/flwk : 0.57	Islamic ↔ الاسلامية/AlAslAmyp : 0.55

Table 2: Examples of NEs labeled using Freeman Score.

2.2 Classification Features

We use a total of 32 features selected from the following classes:

Token-based features: These consist of several features based on the token string and indicate

[2] We use the LIBSVM package (Chang and Lin, 2011).

[3] `http://afkar.microsoft.com/en/maren`

whether the token is capital initial, composed entirely of capital letters, ends with a period (such as Mr.), contains a digit or a Latin number (e.g. Muhammad II) or contains punctuation marks. The string of the token is also added as a feature. We also add the POS tag, which could be a good indicator for proper nouns that should mainly be transliterated. We also check if the token is a regular noun in the WORDNET (Fellbaum, 1998) which increases its chance of being translated as opposed to transliterated.

Semantic features: These features mainly indicate the NE category obtained using an NE tagger. We also define a number of markers of person (such as Doctor, Engineer, etc.) and organization (such as Corp.) names. We used the list of markers available at: `http://drupal.org/node/1439292`, that we extended manually.

Contextual features: These features are related to the token's local *context within the NE*. These include information about the current token's surrounding tokens, its relative position in the NE (beginning, middle or end). Another feature represents the length of the NE in number of tokens.

2.3 Experiments

We train two classifiers and tune their parameters using a held out development set of 500 NEs drawn randomly from the news parallel corpus. We use 55k NEs from the same corpus to train the $\mathbf{C}_{news}$ classifier. Furthermore, we train the $\mathbf{C}_{diverse}$ classifier cumulatively with the 55K news NEs and another 4600 NEs from Wikipedia titles.

The classifiers are evaluated on three different datasets: $\mathbf{Test}_{News}$ which consists of 2K of NEs selected randomly from the news corpus, $\mathbf{Test}_{Wiki}$ consisting of 1K NEs extracted from the Wikipedia and $\mathbf{Test}_{Combination}$, an aggregation of the two previous sets. We manually reviewed the labels of these test sets and fixed any incorrect labels. Table 3 compares the accuracy of the two classifiers under different training and test data settings. Starting with a majority class baseline, our classifiers achieve a promising performance in most settings. The majority class for both classifiers is the *translation* which performs as a baseline approach with an accuracy equal to the distribution of the two classes. We also

	$\mathbf{Test}_{News}$	$\mathbf{Test}_{Wiki}$	$\mathbf{Test}_{Combination}$
Baseline	56.70	57.09	56.89
$\mathbf{C}_{news}$	90.40	84.10	88.64
$\mathbf{C}_{diverse}$	**90.42**	86.00	89.18

Table 3: Accuracy results for the two classifiers and the baseline on the three test datasets

observe that the addition of a small diverse training set in $\mathbf{C}_{diverse}$ provides a relatively large improvement (about 2%) when tested on Wikipedia. Finally, Figure 2 illustrates the contribution of different classes of features on our diverse classifier (evaluated on $\mathbf{Test}_{Wiki}$). We observe a fairly linear relationship between the size of the training data and the accuracy. Furthermore, *we observe that the features describing the category of the NE are more important than the token's local context.* For example, in the case of "Dudley North" and "North London", the most effective feature for the decision is the category of the named entities.

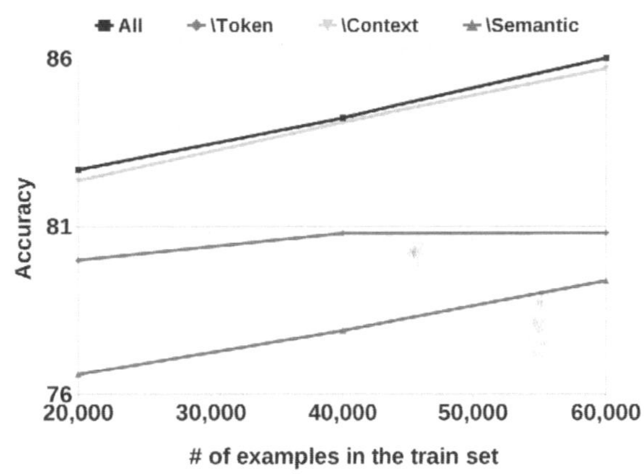

Figure 2: Learning curves obtained on Wiki dataset by removing features individually.

3 Extrinsic MT evaluation

We evaluate the effects of the classifier on an English to Arabic statistical MT system. Our first evaluation focuses on the utility of our classifier in preventing erroneous translation of NEs which need to be transliterated. In the following experiments we use $\mathbf{C}_{news}$ classifier. In order to experiment with a diverse set of NEs, we conducted a study on a small corpus (98,197 terms) of Wikipedia articles from a diverse set of topics. We use 10 Wikipedia articles describing: Anarchism, Artemis, Buddhism, Isfahan, Shawn Michaels, Turkey, etc. We first use our classifier to locate the subset of NEs which should be transliterated. An annotator validates the decision and examines the phrase table on the default MT decision on those NEs. We observe that out of 1031 NE tokens, 624 tokens (60.5%) which would have been translated incorrectly, are directed to the transliteration module.

Finally, we deploy the transliteration classifier as a pre-translation component to the MT system.[4] Our MT test set is the MEDAR corpus (Maegaard et al., 2010). The MEDAR corpus consists of about 10,000 words English texts on news related to the climate change with four Arabic reference translations. Due to the lack of non-news English-Arabic corpus, we have to limit this experiment only to the news domain. However, we expect that many of the NEs may already exist in the training corpus and the effects of the classifier is more limited than using a diverse domain like Wikipedia. We automatically locate the NEs in the source language sentences and use the classifier to find those which should be transliterated. For such terms, we offer the transliterated form as an option to the decoder aiming to improve the decoding process. For that a human annotator selected the transliterations from the suggested list that is provided by the automatic transliterator (Maren) without any knowledge of the reference transliterations.

Table 4 shows the impact of adding the classifier to the SMT pipeline with a modest improvement. Moreover, a bilingual annotator examined the automatically tagged NEs in the MT test set and labeled them with the translation vs. transliteration decisions. Having such gold standard decisions, we evaluated the classifier against the MT test set. The classifier's accuracy was 89% which is as strong as the earlier intrinsic evaluation. The false positives are 5% which represents around 12.6% of the total errors.

	MT Baseline	MT Baseline + Classifier
BLEU	16.63	**16.91**

Table 4: Results of the extrinsic usage of the classifier in SMT

The following example shows how our classifier prevents the MT to choose a wrong decoding for the NE *Python* (being transliterated rather than translated). Moreover, the MT system transliterates the term *Monty* that is unknown to the underlying system. Such entities tend to be unseen in the standard news corpora and consequently unknown (UNK) to the MT systems. Using our classifier in such conditions is expected to reduce the domain gap and improve the translation quality.

English Input: The British comedy troupe **Monty Python**.

Baseline MT: الفرقة الكوميدية البريطانية **UNK افعي**.
Alfrqp Alkwmydyp AlbryTAnyp **UNK AfEY**

MT+Classifier: الفرقة الكوميدية البريطانية **مونتي بايثون** .
Alfrqp Alkwmydyp AlbryTAnyp **mwnty bAyvwn**.

4 Related work

A number of efforts have been made to undertake the NE translation problem for different language pairs. Among them some use sequence of phonetic-based probabilistic models to convert names written in Arabic into the English script (Glover-Stalls and Knight, 1998) for transliteration of names and technical terms that occurs in Arabic texts and originate in English. Others rely on spelling-based model that directly maps an English letter sequence into an Arabic one (Al-Onaizan and Knight, 2002a). In a related work, Al-Onaizan and Knight (2002b) describe a combination of a phonetic-based model and a spelling-based one to build a transliteration model to generate Arabic to English name translations. In the same direction, Hassan et al. (2007) extracted NE translation pairs from both comparable and parallel corpora and evaluate their quality in a NE translation system. More recently, Ling et al. (2011) propose a Web-based method that translates Chinese NEs into English. Our work is similar in its general objectives and framework to the work pre-

[4]The baseline MT system is the MOSES phrase-based decoder (Koehn et al., 2007) trained on a standard English-Arabic parallel corpus. The 18 million parallel corpus consists of the non-UN parts of the NIST corpus distributed by the Linguistic Data Consortium. We perform the standard preprocessing and tokenization on the English side. We also use MADA+TOKAN (Habash et al., 2009) to preprocess and tokenize the Arabic side of the corpus. We use the standard setting of GIZA++ and the grow-diagonal-final heuristic of MOSES to get the word alignments. We use a set of 500 sentences to tune the decoder parameters using the MERT (Och, 2003). We use El Kholy and Habash (2010) detokenization framework for the Arabic decoding. We evaluate the MT system with the BLEU metric (Papineni et al., 2002).

sented by Hermjakob et al. (2008), which describes an approach for identifying NEs that should be transliterated from Arabic into English during translation. Their method seeks to find a corresponding English word for each Arabic word in a parallel corpus, and tag the Arabic words as either NEs or non-NEs based on a matching algorithm. In contrast, we tackle this problem in the reverse direction (translating/transliterating English NEs into Arabic). We also present a novel binary classifier for identifying NEs that should be translated and those that should be transliterated.

5 Conclusion and future work

We reported our recent progress on building a classifier which decides if an MT system should translate or transliterate a given named entity. The classifier shows a promising performance in both intrinsic and extrinsic evaluations. We believe that our framework can be expanded to new languages if the required data resources and tools (mainly parallel corpus, Named Entity tagger and transliteration engine) are available. We plan to expand the features and apply the classifier to new languages and conduct MT experiments in domains other than news.

6 Acknowledgements

We thank Nizar Habash and colleagues for the MADA, Arabic detokenization and the transliteration similarity software and also their valuable suggestions. We thank anonymous reviewers for their valuable comments and suggestions. This publication was made possible by grants YSREP-1-018-1-004 and NPRP-09-1140-1-177 from the Qatar National Research Fund (a member of the Qatar Foundation). The statements made herein are solely the responsibility of the authors.

References

Yaser Al-Onaizan and Kevin Knight. 2002a. Named-Entity translation. In *Proceedings of HLT*, San Francisco, USA.

Yaser Al-Onaizan and Kevin Knight. 2002b. Translating Named Entities Using Monolingual and Bilingual Resources. In *Proceedings of ACL*, Philadelphia, USA.

Chih-Chung Chang and Chih-Jen Lin. 2011. LIBSVM: A Library for Support Vector Machines. *ACM Transactions on Intelligent Systems and Technology*, 2:27:1–27:27. Software available at `http://www.csie.ntu.edu.tw/~cjlin/libsvm`.

Silviu Cucerzan. 2007. Large-Scale Named-Entity Disambiguation Based on Wikipedia Data. In *Proceedings of EMNLP-CoNLL*, Prague, Czech Republic.

Ahmed El Kholy and Nizar Habash. 2010. Techniques for Arabic Morphological Detokenization and Orthographic Denormalization. In *Proceedings of LREC*, Valletta, Malta.

Christiane Fellbaum. 1998. WordNet: An Electronic Lexical Database. *The MIT Press*.

Andrew Freeman, Sherri Condon, and Christopher Ackerman. 2006. Cross Linguistic Name Matching in English and Arabic. In *Proceedings of NAACL*, New York City, USA.

Bonnie Glover-Stalls and Kevin Knight. 1998. Translating Named and Technical Terms in Arabic Text. In *Proceeding of the COLING/ACL Workshop on Computational Approaches to Semitic Languages*, Montreal, Canada.

Nizar Habash, Owen Rambow, and Ryan Roth. 2009. Mada+Tokan: A Toolkit for Arabic Tokenization, Diacritization, Morphological Disambiguation, POS Tagging, Stemming and Lemmatization. In *Proceedings of the Second International Conference on Arabic Language Resources and Tools (MEDAR)*, Cairo, Egypt.

Ahmed Hassan, Haytham Fahmy, and Hany Hassan. 2007. Improving Named Entity Translation by Exploiting Comparable and Parallel Corpora. In *Proceedings of RANLP*, Borovets, Bulgaria.

Ulf Hermjakob, Kevin Knight, and Hal Daumé III. 2008. Name Translation in Statistical Machine Translation - Learning When to Transliterate. In *Proceedings of ACL-HLT*, Columbus, Ohio.

Jun'ichi Kazama and Kentaro Torisawa. 2007. Exploiting Wikipedia as External Knowledge for Named-Entity Recognition. In *Proceedings of EMNLP-CoNLL*, Prague, Czech Republic.

Philipp Koehn, Hieu Hoang, Alexandra Birch, Chris Callison-Burch, Marcello Federico, Nicola Bertoldi, Brooke Cowan, Wade Shen, Christine Moran, Richard Zens, Chris Dyer, Ondrej Bojar, Alexandra Constantin, and Evan Herbst. 2007. Moses: Open Source Toolkit for Statistical Machine Translation. In *Proceedings of ACL: Demo session*, Prague, Czech Republic.

Wang Ling, Pavel Calado, Bruno Martins, Isabel Trancoso, and Alan Black. 2011. Named-Entity Translation using Anchor Texts. In *Proceedings of IWSLT*, San Francisco, USA.

Bente Maegaard, Mohamed Attia, Khalid Choukri, Olivier Hamon, Steven Krauwer, and Mustafa Yaseen. 2010. Cooperation for Arabic Language Resources and Tools–The MEDAR Project. In *Proceedings of LREC*, Valetta, Malta.

Behrang Mohit, Nathan Schneider, Rishav Bhowmick, Kemal Oflazer, and Noah A. Smith. 2012. Recall-

Oriented Learning of Named Entities in Arabic Wikipedia. In *Proceedings of EACL*, Avignon, France.

Joel Nothman, Nicky Ringland, Will Radford, Tara Murphy, and James R. Curran. 2013. Learning Multilingual Named Entity Recognition from Wikipedia. *Artificial Intelligence*, 194(0):151 – 175.

Franz Josef Och. 2003. Minimum Error Rate Training in Statistical Machine Translation. In *Proceedings of ACL*, Sapporo, Japan.

Kishore Papineni, Salim Roukos, Todd Ward, and Wei-Jing Zhu. 2002. BLEU: a Method for Automatic Evaluation of Machine Translation. In *Proceedings of ACL*, Philadelphia, USA.

Lev Ratinov and Dan Roth. 2009. Design Challenges and Misconceptions in Named Entity Recognition. In *Proceedings of CONLL*, Boulder, USA.

Better Twitter Summaries?

Joel Judd & Jugal Kalita
Department of Computer Science
University of Colorado
Colorado Springs, Colorado
Email: {jjudd2,jkalita}@uccs.edu

Abstract

This paper describes an approach to improve summaries for a collection of Twitter posts created using the Phrase Reinforcement (PR) Algorithm (Sharifi et al., 2010a). The PR algorithm often generates summaries with excess text and noisy speech. We parse these summaries using a dependency parser and use the dependencies to eliminate some of the excess text and build better-formed summaries. We compare the results to those obtained using the PR Algorithm.

1 Introduction

Millions of people use the Web to express themselves and share ideas. Twitter is a very popular micro blogging site. According to a recent study approximately 340 million Tweets are sent out every day[1]. People mostly upload daily routines, fun activities and other words of wisdom for readers. There is also plenty of serious information beyond the personal; according to a study approximately 4% of posts on Twitter have relevant news data[2]. Topics that may be covered by reputable new sources like CNN (Cable News Network) were considered relevant. A topic is simply a keyword or key phrase that one may use to search for Twitter posts containing it. It is possible to gather large amounts of posts from Twitter on many different topics in short amounts of time. Obviously, processing all this information by human hands is impossible. One way to extract information from Twitter posts on a certain topic is to automatically summarize them. (Sharifi et al., 2010a; Sharifi et al., 2010b; Sharifi et al., 2010c) present an algorithm called the Phrase Reinforcement Algorithm to produces summaries of a set of Twitter posts on a certain topic. The PR algorithm produces good summaries for many topics, but for sets of posts on certain topics, the summaries become syntactically malformed or too wordy. This is because the PR Algorithm does not pay much attention to syntactic well-formedness as it constructs a summary sentence from phrases that occur frequently in the posts it summarizes. In this paper, we attempt to improve Twitter summaries produced by the PR algorithm.

[1] `http://blog.twitter.com/2012/03/twitter-turns-six.htm`

[2] `http://www.pearanalytics.com/blog/wp-content/uploads/2010/05/Twitter-Study-August-2009.pdf`

2 The PR Algorithm Revisited

Given a number of Twitter posts on a certain topic, the PR algorithm starts construction of what is called a word graph with a root node containing the topic phrase. It builds a graph showing how words occur before and after the phrase in the root node, considering all the posts on the topic. It builds a subgraph to the left of the topic phrase and another subgraph to its right in a similar manner. To construct the left graph, the algorithm starts with the root node and obtains the set of words that occur immediately before the current node's phrase. For each of these unique words, the algorithm adds them to the graph as nodes with their associated counts to the left of the current node. The algorithm continues this process recursively for each node added to the graph until all the potential words have been added to the left-hand side of the graph. The algorithm repeats these steps symmetrically to construct the right subgraph. Once the full graph is there, the algorithm weights individual nodes. The weights are initialized to the same values as their frequency counts. Then, to account for the fact that some phrases are naturally longer than others, they penalize nodes that occur farther from the root node by an amount that is proportional to their distance. To generate a summary, the algorithm looks for the most overlapping phrases within the graph. Since the nodes' weights are proportional to their overlap, the algorithm searches for the path within the graph with the highest cumulative weight. The sequence of words in this path becomes the summary.

3 Problem Description

We start by making some observations on the phrase-reinforcement algorithm. Certain topics do not produce well-formed summaries, while others yield very good summaries. For the posts that have a well-centered topic without a huge amount of variation among the posts, the algorithm works well and creates good summaries. Here is an example summary produced by the PR algorithm.

> *Phillies defeat Dodgers to take the National League Championship series.*

(Sharifi et al., 2010a; Sharifi et al., 2010b; Sharifi et al., 2010c) provide additional examples. The PR algorithm limits the length of the summary to approximately 140 characters, the maximum length of a Twitter post. However, often the summary sentence produced has extraneous parts that appear due to the fact that they appear frequently in the posts being summarized, but these parts make the summary malformed or too wordy. An example with some wordiness is given below.

> *today is day for vote obama this election day*

Some "raw" PR summaries are a lot more wordy than the one above. The goal we address in this paper is to create grammatically better formed summaries by processing the "raw" summaries formed by the PR Algorithm. We drop this excess text and the phrases or extract pieces of text which make sense grammatically to form the final summary. This usually produces a summary with more grammatical accuracy and less noise in between the words. This gets the main point of the summary across better.

4 Approach

The idea behind creating the desired summary is to parse the "raw" summary and build dependencies between the dependent and governor words in each summary. We perform parts of speech tagging and obtain lists of governing and dependent words. This data forms the basis for creating a valid summary. For example given the Twitter post, *today is day for vote obama this election day*, a dependency parser produces the governor-dependent relationships as given in Table 1. Figure 1 also shows the same grammatical dependencies between words in the phrases.

We believe that a word which governs many words is key to the phrase as a whole, and dependent words

Table 1: Governor and Dependent Words for *today is day*^{1} *for vote obama this election day*^{2}

Governor	Dependent
day^1	today
	is
	for
	day^2
obama	vote
for	obama
day^2	this
	election

Algorithm 1 Algorithm to Fix "Raw" PRA Summaries

I. For each word, check grammatical compatibility with words before and after the word being checked.
II. If a word has no dependencies immediately before or after it, drop the word.
III. After each word has been checked, check for the words that form a grammatical phrase.
IV. Write out the summary without the dropped words and without phrases with only two words.
V. If needed, go back to step III, because there shouldn't be any more single words with no dependencies to check, and repeat as many times as necessary.

which are closely related, or in other words, lay close to each other in the phrase should be left in the order they appear. Conceptually, our approach works as follows: look at every word and see if it makes sense with the word before and after it. This builds dependencies between the word in question with the words around it. If a word before or after the word being analyzed does not make sense grammatically, it can be removed from that grammatically correct phrase. Dependent words that are not close to each other may not be as important as words that lay close to each other and have more dependencies, and thus may be thrown out of the summaries. Through this process grammatically correct phrases can be formed.

The dependencies are built by tagging each word as a part of speech and seeing if it relates to other words. For example, it checks whether or not the conjunction "and" is serving its purpose of combining a set of words or ideas, in other words, if those dependencies exist. If dependencies exist with the nearby words, that given collection of words can be set aside as a grammatically correct phrase until it reaches words with no dependencies, and the process

Figure 1: Dependency Parse for *today is day[1] for vote obama this election day[2]*

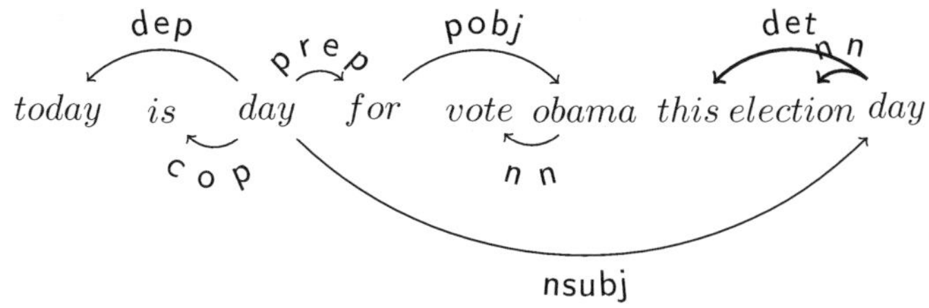

can continue. The phrases with few words can be dropped, as well as single words. These new phrases can be checked for grammatical accuracy in the same way as the previous phrases, and if they pass, can remain combined forming a longer summary that should be grammatically correct. The main steps are given in Algorithm 1.

Now, take the example summary produced by the PR Algorithm for the election Twitter posts. Looking at this summary, we, as humans, may make changes and make the summary grammatically correct. Two potential ideal summaries would be the following.

today is the day to vote for obama

vote for obama this election day

The actual process used in the making of the grammatical summaries is as follows. Two main lists are created from lists of governor and dependent words, one with the governor words and another with the dependent words. The governor words are checked to see how many dependent words are linked to them. The governing words with the highest number of dependent words are kept for later. For example using the above phrase about the elections, the word "day" was the governing word with the highest amount of dependent words and was thus kept for the final summary. The superscripts on the word "day" differentiate its two occurrences. The dependent words are kept in groups of closely linked dependent words. Using the same example about the election, an intermediate list of closely related dependent words is "today," "is," "for," "vote," "obama," "this," "election," and "day." And the final list of closely related dependent words is "for," "vote," "obama," "this," "election" and "day." After these two lists are in the final stages the lists are merged placing the words in proper order.

5 Experiments and Results

To begin, the Twitter posts were collected manually and stored in text files. The topics we chose to focus on important current events and some pop culture. Approximately 100 posts were collected on ten different topics. These topics are "The Avengers," "Avril Lavigne," "Christmas," "the election," "Election Day," "Iron Man 3," "president 2012," "Hurricane Sandy," "Thanksgiving," and "vote."

Table 2: ROUGE-L without Stopwords, Before

Task	Recall	Precision	F-score
Task 1	0.667	0.343	0.453
Task 2	1.000	0.227	0.370
Task 3	0.353	0.240	0.286
Task 4	0.800	0.154	0.258
Task 5	1.000	0.185	0.313
Task 6	0.667	0.150	0.245
Task 7	0.889	0.125	0.219
Task 8	0.636	0.125	0.209
Task 9	0.500	0.300	0.375
Task 10	0.455	0.100	0.164
Average	0.696	0.195	0.289

The collections of posts were passed on to three volunteers to produce short accurate summaries that capture the main idea from the posts. The collections of posts were also first run through the PR Algorithm and then through the process described in this paper to try and refine the summaries output by the PR Algorithm. The Stanford CoreNLP parser[3] was used to build the lists of governor and dependent words.

We use ROUGE evaluation metrics (Lin 2004) just like (Sharifi et al., 2010a; Sharifi et al., 2010b; Sharifi et al., 2010c), who evaluated summaries obtained with the PR Algorithm. Specifically, we use ROUGE-L, which uses the longest common subsequence (LCS) to compare summaries. As the LCS of the two summaries in comparison increases in length, so does the similarity of the two summaries.

We now discuss results using ROUGE-L on the summaries we produce. Tables 2 through 5 show the results of four different ROUGE-L evaluations, comparing them to the results found using the PR

[3]`http://nlp.stanford.edu/software/corenlp.shtml`

Table 3: ROUGE-L without Stopwords, After

Task	Recall	Precision	F-score
Task 1	0.667	0.480	0.558
Task 2	0.400	0.500	0.444
Task 3	0.000	0.000	0.000
Task 4	0.400	0.333	0.363
Task 5	0.900	0.600	0.720
Task 6	0.389	0.350	0.368
Task 7	0.556	0.250	0.345
Task 8	0.545	0.500	0.522
Task 9	0.417	0.417	0.417
Task 10	0.363	0.200	0.258
Average	0.464	0.363	0.400

Algorithm, and Table 6 shows the comparisons of the averaged scores to the scores (Sharifi et al., 2010a) obtained using the PR Algorithm. Table 2 shows the regular ROUGE-L scores, meaning the recall, precision and F-scores for each task and the average overall scores, for the collection of posts before using the dependency parser to refine the summaries. Table 3 displays the results after using the dependency parser on the summaries formed by the PR Algorithm. One of the options in ROUGE is to show the "best" result, for each task. Table 4 has this result for the PR Algorithm results. Table 5 shows the results of the "best" scores, after running it through the dependency parser. Table 6 shows the averages from Tables 3 and 5, using the dependency parser, compared to Sharifi et al.'s results using the PR Algorithm. Stopwords were not removed in our experiments.

Table 4: ROUGE-L Best without Stopwords, Before

	Recall	Precision	F-score
Task 1	1.000	0.429	0.600
Task 2	1.000	0.227	0.370
Task 3	0.500	0.200	0.286
Task 4	1.000	0.154	0.267
Task 5	1.000	0.167	0.286
Task 6	1.000	0.200	0.333
Task 7	1.000	0.125	0.222
Task 8	1.000	0.071	0.133
Task 9	1.000	0.400	0.571
Task 10	1.000	0.100	0.182
Average	0.950	0.207	0.325

As one can see, the use of our algorithm on the summaries produced by the PR Algorithm improves the F-score values, at least in the example cases we tried. In almost every case, there is substantial rise in the F-score. As previously mentioned, some collections of Tweets do not produce good summaries. Task 3 had some poor scores in all cases, so one can deduce that the posts on that topic (Christmas) were widely spread, or they did not have a central theme.

Table 5: ROUGE-L Best without Stopwords, After

	Recall	Precision	F-score
Task 1	1.000	0.600	0.750
Task 2	0.400	0.500	0.444
Task 3	0.000	0.000	0.000
Task 4	0.500	0.333	0.400
Task 5	1.000	0.600	0.750
Task 6	0.600	0.600	0.600
Task 7	0.667	0.400	0.500
Task 8	1.000	0.333	0.500
Task 9	1.000	0.667	0.800
Task 10	1.000	0.250	0.400
Average	0.718	0.428	0.515

Table 6: ROUGE-L Averages after applying our algorithm vs. Sharifi et al.

	Recall	Precision	F-score
Sharifi (PRA)	0.31	0.34	0.33
Rouge-L after reconstruction	0.46	0.36	0.40
Rouge-L best after reconstruction	0.72	0.43	0.52

6 Conclusion

The PR Algorithm is not a pure extractive algorithm. It creates summaries of Twitter posts by piecing together the most commonly occurring words and phrases in the entire set of tweets, but keeping the order of constituents as close to the order in which they occur in the posts, collectively speaking. As we noted in this paper, the heuristic method using which the PR Algorithm composes a summary sentence out of the phrases sometimes leads to ungrammatical sentences or wordy sentences. This paper shows that the "raw" summaries produced by the PR Algorithm can be improved by taking into account governor-dependency relationships among the constituents. There is nothing in this clean-up algorithm that says that it works only with summaries of tweets. The same approach can potentially be used to improve grammaticality of sentences written by humans in a sloppy manner. In addition, given several sentences with overlapping content (from multiple sources), the same process can potentially be used to construct a grammatical sentence out of all the input sentences. This problem often arises in general multi-document summarization. We believe that a corrective approach like ours can be used together with a sentence compression approach, such as (Knight and Marcu 2002), to produce even better summaries in conjunction with the PR or other summarization algorithms that work with socially-generated texts which are often malformed and short.

We have shown in this paper that simply focusing on grammatical dependency tends to make the final summaries more grammatical and readable compared to the raw summaries. However, we believe that more complex restructuring of the words and constituents would be necessary to improve the quality of the raw summaries, in general.

References

Knight, K. and Marcu, D. 2004. Summarization beyond sentence extraction: A probabilistic approach to sentence compression, Artificial Intelligence, Vol. 139, No. 1, pp. 91–107.

Lin, C.Y. 2004. Rouge: A package for automatic evaluation of summaries, Text Summarization Branches Out: Proceedings of the ACL-04 Workshop, pp. 74–81.

Sharifi, Beaux, Mark-Anthony Hutton, and Jugal Kalita. 2010. Summarizing Microblogs Automatically, Annual Conference of the National Association for Advancement of Computational Linguistics-Human Language Technology (NAACL-HLT), pp. 685-688, Los Angeles.

Sharifi, Beaux, Mark-Anthony Hutton, and Jugal Kalita. 2010. Experiments in Microblog Summarization, Second IEEE International Conference on Social Computing (SocialCom 2010), pp. 49-56, Minneapolis.

Sharifi, Beaux, Mark-Anthony Hutton and Jugal Kalita. 2010. Automatic Summarization of Twitter Topics, National Workshop on Design and Analysis of Algorithms, NWDAA 10, Tezpur University, Assam, India.

Training MRF-Based Phrase Translation Models using Gradient Ascent

Jianfeng Gao
Microsoft Research
Redmond, WA, USA
jfgao@microsoft.com

Xiaodong He
Microsoft Research
Redmond, WA, USA
xiaohe@microsoft.com

Abstract

This paper presents a general, statistical framework for modeling phrase translation via Markov random fields. The model allows for arbituary features extracted from a phrase pair to be incorporated as evidence. The parameters of the model are estimated using a large-scale discriminative training approach that is based on stochastic gradient ascent and an N-best list based expected BLEU as the objective function. The model is easy to be incoporated into a standard phrase-based statistical machine translation system, requiring no code change in the runtime engine. Evaluation is performed on two Europarl translation tasks, German-English and French-English. Results show that incoporating the Markov random field model significantly improves the performance of a state-of-the-art phrase-based machine translation system, leading to a gain of 0.8-1.3 BLEU points.

1 Introduction

The phrase translation model, also known as the *phrase table*, is one of the core components of a phrase-based statistical machine translation (SMT) system. The most common method of constructing the phrase table takes a two-phase approach. First, the bilingual phrase pairs are extracted heuristically from an automatically word-aligned training data. The second phase is parameter estimation, where each phrase pair is assigned with some scores that are estimated based on counting of words or phrases on the same word-aligned training data.

There has been a lot of research on improving the quality of the phrase table using more principled methods for phrase extraction (e.g., Lamber and Banchs 2005), parameter estimation (e.g., Wuebker et al. 2010; He and Deng 2012), or both (e.g., Marcu and Wong 2002; Denero et al. 2006). The focus of this paper is on the parameter estimation phase. We revisit the problem of scoring a phrase translation pair by developing a new phrase translation model based on Markov random fields (MRFs) and large-scale discriminative training. We strive to address the following three primary concerns.

First of all, instead of parameterizing a phrase translation pair using a set of scoring functions that are learned independently (e.g., phrase translation probabilities and lexical weights) we use a general, statistical framework in which arbitrary features extracted from a phrase pair can be incorporated to model the translation in a unified way. To this end, we propose the use of a MRF model.

Second, because the phrase model has to work with other component models in an SMT system in order to produce good translations and the quality of translation is measured via BLEU score, it is desirable to optimize the parameters of the phrase model jointly with other component models with respect to an objective function that is closely related to the evaluation metric under consideration, i.e., BLEU in this paper. To this end, we resort to a large-scale discriminative training approach, following the pioneering work of Liang et al. (2006). Although there are established methods of tuning a handful of features on small training sets, such as the MERT method (Och 2003), the development of discriminative training methods for millions of features on millions of sentence pairs is still an ongoing area of research. A recent survey is due to Koehn (2010). In this paper we show that by using stochastic gradient ascent and an N-best list based expected BLEU as the objective function, large-scale discriminative training can lead to significant improvements.

The third primary concern is the ease of adoption of the proposed method. To this end, we use a simple and well-established learning method, ensuring that the results can be easily reproduced. We also develop the features for the MRF model in such a way that the resulting model is of the same format as that of a traditional phrase table. Thus, the model can be easily incorporated into a standard phrase-based SMT system, requiring no code change in the runtime engine.

In the rest of the paper, Section 2 presents the MRF model for phrase translation. Section 3 describes the way the model parameters are estimated. Section 4 presents the experimental results on two Europarl translation tasks. Section 5 reviews previous work that lays the foundation of this study. Section 6 concludes the paper.

2 Model

The traditional translation models are directional models that are based on conditional probabilities. As suggested by the noisy-channel model for SMT (Brown et al. 1993):

$$E^* = \operatorname*{argmax}_E P(E|F) = \operatorname*{argmax}_E P(E)P(F|E \quad (1)$$

The Bayes rule leads us to invert the conditioning of translation probability from a foreign (source) sentence F to an English (target) translation E.

However, in practice, the implementation of state-of-the-art phrase-based SMT systems uses a weighted log-linear combination of several models $h(F,E,A)$ including the logarithm of the phrase probability (and the lexical weight) in source-to-target and target-to-source directions (Och and Ney 2004)

$$E^* = \operatorname{argmax}_E \textstyle\sum_{m=1}^{M} \lambda_m h_m(F,E,A) \quad (2)$$
$$= \operatorname*{argmax}_E Score_\lambda(F,E)$$

where A in $h(F,E,A)$ is a hidden structure that best derives E from F, called the *Viterbi derivation* afterwards. In phrase-based SMT, A consists of (1) the segmentation of the source sentence into phrases, (2) the segmentation of the target sentence into phrases, and (3) an alignment between the source and target phrases.

In this paper we use Markov random fields (MRFs) to model the joint distribution $P_\mathbf{w}(\mathbf{f},\mathbf{e})$ over a source-target translation phrase pair $(\mathbf{f},\mathbf{e})$, parameterized by $\mathbf{w}$. Different from the directional translation models, as in Equation (1), the MRF model is undirected, which we believe upholds the spirit of the use of bi-directional translation probabilities under the log-linear framework. That is, the agreement or the *compatibility* of a phrase pair is more effective to score translation quality than a directional translation probability which is modeled based on an imagined generative story does.

2.1 MRF

MRFs, also known as undirected graphical models, are widely used in modeling joint distributions of spatial or contextual dependencies of physical phenomena (Bishop 2006). A Markov random field is constructed from a graph G. The nodes of the graph represent random variables, and edges define the independence semantics between the random variables. An MRF satisfies the Markov property, which states that a node is independent of all of its non-neighbors, defined by the clique configurations of G. In modeling a phrase translation pair, we define two types of nodes, (1) two phrase nodes and (2) a set of word nodes, each for a word in these phrases, such as the graph in Figure 1. Let us denote a clique by c and the set of variables in that clique by $(\mathbf{f},\mathbf{e})_c$. Then, the joint distribution over the random variables in G is defined as

$$P_\mathbf{w}(\mathbf{f},\mathbf{e}) = \frac{1}{Z}\prod_{c\epsilon C(G)} \varphi_c((\mathbf{f},\mathbf{e})_c;\mathbf{w}), \quad (3)$$

where $\mathbf{e} = e_1,\dots,e_{|\mathbf{e}|}$, $\mathbf{f} = f_1,\dots,f_{|\mathbf{f}|}$ and $C(G)$ is the set of cliques in G, and each $\varphi_c((\mathbf{f},\mathbf{e})_c;\mathbf{w})$ is a non-negative potential function defined over a clique c that measures the *compatibility* of the variables in c, $\mathbf{w}$ is a set of parameters that are used within the potential function. Z in Equation (3), sometimes called the *partition function*, is a normalization constant and is given by

$$Z = \textstyle\sum_\mathbf{f}\sum_\mathbf{e}\prod_{c\epsilon C(G)} \varphi_c((\mathbf{f},\mathbf{e})_c;\mathbf{w}) \quad (4)$$
$$= \textstyle\sum_\mathbf{f}\sum_\mathbf{e} Score(\mathbf{f},\mathbf{e}),$$

which ensures that the distribution $P_\mathbf{w}(\mathbf{f},\mathbf{e})$ given by Equation (3) is correctly normalized. The pres-

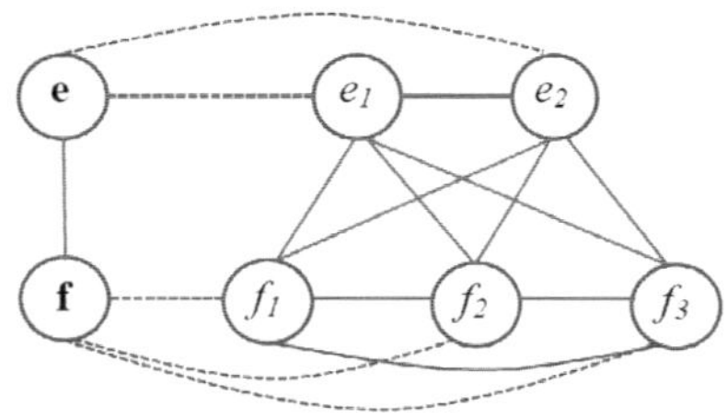

Figure 1: A Markov random field model for phrase translation of $\mathbf{e} = e_1, e_2$ and $\mathbf{f} = f_1, f_2, f_3$.

ence of Z is one of the major limitations of MRFs because it is generally not feasible to compute due to the exponential number of terms in the summation. However, we notice that Z is a global constant which is independent of **e** and **f**. Therefore, in ranking phrase translation hypotheses, as performed by the decoder in SMT systems, we can drop Z and simply rank each hypothesis by its unnormalized joint probability. In our implementation, we only store in the phrase table for each translation pair $(\mathbf{f}, \mathbf{e})$ its unnormalized probability, i.e., $Score(\mathbf{f}, \mathbf{e})$ as defined in Equation (4).

It is common to define MRF potential functions of the exponential form as $\varphi_c((\mathbf{f}, \mathbf{e})_c; \mathbf{w}) = \exp(w_c \phi(c))$, where $\phi(c)$ is a real-valued feature function over clique c and w_c is the weight of the feature function. In phrase-based SMT systems, the sentence-level translation probability from F to E is decomposed as the product of a set of phrase translation probabilities. By dropping the phrase segmentation and distortion model components, we have

$$P(E|F) \approx \max_A P(E|A, F) \quad (5)$$

$$P(E|A, F) = \prod_{(\mathbf{f},\mathbf{e}) \in A} P(\mathbf{e}|\mathbf{f}),$$

where A is the Viterbi derivation. Similarly, the joint probability $P(F, E)$ can be decomposed as

$$P(F, E) \approx \max_A P(F, A, E) \quad (6)$$

$$P(F, A, E) = \prod_{(\mathbf{f},\mathbf{e}) \in A} P_{\mathbf{w}}(\mathbf{f}, \mathbf{e})$$

$$\propto \sum_{(\mathbf{f},\mathbf{e}) \in A} \log P_{\mathbf{w}}(\mathbf{f}, \mathbf{e})$$

$$\propto \sum_{(\mathbf{f},\mathbf{e}) \in A} \sum_{c \in C(G_{(\mathbf{f},\mathbf{e})})} w_c \phi(c)$$

$$= \sum_{(\mathbf{f},\mathbf{e}) \in A} \mathbf{w} \cdot \boldsymbol{\phi}(\mathbf{f}, \mathbf{e})$$

which is essentially proportional to a weighted linear combination of a set of features.

To instantiate an MRF model, one needs to define a graph structure representing the translation dependencies between source and target phrases, and a set of potential functions over the cliques of this graph.

2.2 Cliques and Potential Functions

The MRF model studied in this paper is constructed from the graph G in Figure 1. It contains two types of nodes, including two phrase nodes for the source and target phrases respectively and word nodes, each for a word in these phrases. The cliques and their corresponding potential functions (or features) attempt to abstract the idea behind those translation models that have been proved effective for machine translation in previous work. In this study we focus on three types of cliques.

First, we consider cliques that contain two phrase nodes. A potential function over such a clique captures phrase-to-phrase translation dependencies similar to the use the bi-directional translation models in phrase-based SMT systems. The potential is defined as $\varphi_p(\mathbf{f}, \mathbf{e}) = w_p \phi_p(\mathbf{f}, \mathbf{e})$, where the feature $\phi_p(\mathbf{f}, \mathbf{e})$, called the *phrase-pair feature*, is an indicator function whose value is 1 if **e** is target phrase and **f** is source phrase, and 0 otherwise. While the conditional probabilities in a directional translation model are estimated using relative frequencies of phrase pairs extracted from word-aligned parallel sentences, the parameter of the phrase-pair function w_p is learned discriminatively, as we will describe in Section 3.

Second, we consider cliques that contain two word nodes, one in source phrase and the other in target phrase. A potential over such a clique captures word-to-word translation dependencies similar to the use the IBM Model 1 for lexical weighting in phrase-based SMT systems (Koehn et al. 2003). The potential function is defined as $\varphi_t(f, e) = w_t \phi_t(f, e)$, where the feature $\phi_t(f, e)$, called the *word-pair feature*, is an indicator function whose value is 1 if e is a word in target phrase **e** and f is a word in source phrase **f**, and 0 otherwise.

The third type of cliques contains three word nodes. Two of them are in one language and the third in the other language. A potential over such a clique is intended to capture inter-word dependencies for selecting word translations. The potential function is inspired by the triplet lexicon model (Hasan et al. 2008) which is based on lexicalized triplets (e, f, f'). It can be understood as two source (or target) words triggering one target (or source) word. The potential function is defined as $\varphi_{tp}(f, f', e) = w_{tp}\phi_{tp}(f, f', e)$, where the feature $\phi_{tp}(f, f', e)$, called the *triplet feature*, is an indicator function whose value is 1 if e is a word in target phrase $\mathbf{e}$ and f and f' are two different words in source phrase $\mathbf{f}$, and 0 otherwise.

For any clique c that contains nodes in only one language we assume that $\varphi(c) = 1$ for all setting of the clique, which has no impact on scoring a phrase pair. One may wish to define a potential over cliques containing a phrase node and word nodes in target language, which could act as a form of target language model. One may also add edges in the graph so as to define potentials that capture more sophisticated translation dependencies. The optimal potential set could vary among different language pairs and depend to a large degree upon the amount and quality of training data. We leave a comprehensive study of features to future work.

3 Training

This section describes the way the parameters of the MRF model are estimated. Although MRFs are by nature generative models, it is not always appropriate to train the parameters using conventional likelihood based approaches mainly for two reasons. The first is due to the difficulty in computing the partition function in Equation (4), especially in a task of our scale. The second is due to the metric divergence problem (Morgan et al. 2004). That is, the maximum likelihood estimation is unlikely to be optimal for the evaluation metric under consideration, as demonstrated on a variety of tasks including machine translation (Och 2003) and information retrieval (Metzler and Croft 2005; Gao et al. 2005). Therefore, we propose a large-scale discriminative training approach that uses stochastic gradient ascent and an N-best list based expected BLEU as the objective function.

We cast machine translation as a structured classification task (Liang et al. 2006). It maps an input source sentence F to an output pair (E, A) where E is the output target sentence and A the Viterbi derivation of E. A is assumed to be constructed during the translation process. In phrase-based SMT, A consists of a segmentation of the source and target sentences into phrases and an alignment between source and target phrases.

We also assume that translations are modeled using a linear model parameterized by a vector $\boldsymbol{\theta}$. Given a vector $\mathbf{h}(F, E, A)$ of feature functions on (F, E, A), and assuming $\boldsymbol{\theta}$ contains a component for each feature, the output pair (E, A) for a given input F are selected using the argmax decision rule

$$(E^*, A^*) = \underset{(E,A)}{\operatorname{argmax}}\, \boldsymbol{\theta}^T \mathbf{h}(F, E, A) \quad (7)$$

In phrase-based SMT, computing the argmax exactly is intractable, so it is performed approximately by beam decoding.

In a phrase-based SMT system equipped by a MRF-based phrase translation model, the parameters we need to learn are $\boldsymbol{\theta} = (\boldsymbol{\lambda}, \mathbf{w})$, where $\boldsymbol{\lambda}$ is a vector of a handful parameters used in the log-linear model of Equation (2), with one weight for each component model; and $\mathbf{w}$ is a vector containing millions of weights, each for one feature function in the MRF model of Equation (3). Our method takes three steps to learn $\boldsymbol{\theta}$:

1. Given a baseline phrase-based SMT system and a pre-set $\boldsymbol{\lambda}$, we generate for each source sentence in training data an N-best list of translation hypotheses.
2. We fix $\boldsymbol{\lambda}$, and optimize $\mathbf{w}$ with respect to an objective function on training data.
3. We fix $\mathbf{w}$, and optimize $\boldsymbol{\lambda}$ using MERT (Och 2003) to maximize the BLEU score on development data.

Now, we describe Steps 1 and 2 in detail.

3.1 N-Best Generation

Given a set of source-target sentence pairs as training data $(F_n, E_n^r), n = 1 \ldots N$, we use the baseline phrase-based SMT system to generate for each source sentence F a list of 100-best candidate translations, each translation E coupled with its Viterbi derivation A, according to Equation (7). We denote the 100-best set by $\text{GEN}(F)$. Then, each output pair (E, A) is labeled by a sentence-level BLEU score, denoted by sBLEU, which is computed according to Equation (8) (He and Deng 2012),

$$\text{sBLEU}(E, E^r) = BP \times \tfrac{1}{4}\textstyle\sum_{n=1}^{4} \log p_n, \quad (8)$$

where E^r is the reference translation, and $p_n, n = 1 \ldots 4$, are precisions of n-grams. While precisions of lower order n-grams, i.e., p_1 and p_2, are computed directly without any smoothing, matching counts for higher order n-grams could be sparse at the sentence level and need to be smoothed as

$$p_n = \frac{\#(matched\ ngram) + \alpha p_n^0}{\#(ngram) + \alpha}, \text{for } n = 3{,}4$$

where α is a smoothing parameter and is set to 5, and p_n^0 is the prior value of p_n, whose value is computed as $p_n^0 = (p_{n-1})^2 / p_{n-2}$ for $n = 3$ and 4. BP in Equation (8) is the sentence-level *brevity penalty*, computed as $BP = \exp\left(1 - \beta \frac{r}{c}\right)$, which differs from its corpus-level counterpart (Papineni et al. 2002) in two ways. First, we use a non-clipped BP, which leads to a better approximation to the corpus-level BLEU computation because the per-sentence BP might effectively exceed unity in corpus-level BLEU computation, as discussed in Chiang et al. (2008). Second, the ratio between the length of reference sentence r and the length of translation hypothesis c is scaled by a factor β such that the total length of the references on training data equals that of the 1-best translation hypotheses produced by the baseline SMT system. In our experiments, the value of β is computed, on the N-best training data, as the ratio between the total length of the references and that of the 1-best translation hypotheses

In our experiments we find that using sBLEU defined above leads to a small but consistent improvement over other variations of sentence-level BLEU proposed previously (e.g., Liang et al. 2006). In particular, the use of the scaling factor β in computing BP makes BP of the baseline's 1-best output close to perfect on training data, and has an effect of forcing the discriminative training to improve BLEU by improving n-gram precisions rather than by improving brevity penalty.

3.2 Parameter Estimation

We use an N-best list based expected BLEU, a variant of that in Rosti et al. (2011), as the objective function for parameter optimization. Given the current model $\boldsymbol{\theta}$, the expected BLEU, denoted by $\text{xBLEU}(\boldsymbol{\theta})$, over one training sample i.e., a labeled N-best list $\text{GEN}(F)$ generated from a pair of source and target sentences (F, E^r), is defined as

---

Initialize $\mathbf{w}$, assuming $\boldsymbol{\lambda}$ is fixed during training
For $t = 1 \ldots T$ (T = the total number of iterations)
  For each training sample (labeled 100-best list)
    Compute $P_{\boldsymbol{\theta}}(E|F)$ for each translation hypothesis E based on the current model $\boldsymbol{\theta} = (\boldsymbol{\lambda}, \mathbf{w})$
    Update the model via $\mathbf{w} = \mathbf{w} + \eta \cdot \mathbf{g}(\mathbf{w})$, where η is the learning rate and $\mathbf{g}$ the gradient computed according to Equations (12) and (13)

Figure 2: The algorithm of training a MRF-based phrase translation model.

$$\text{xBLEU}(\boldsymbol{\theta}) = \textstyle\sum_{E \in \text{GEN}(F)} P_{\boldsymbol{\theta}}(E|F) \text{sBLEU}(E, E^r), \quad (9)$$

where sBLEU is the sentence-level BLEU, defined in Equation (8), and $P_{\boldsymbol{\theta}}(E|F)$ is a normalized translation probability from F to E computed using *softmax* as

$$P_{\boldsymbol{\theta}}(E|F) = \frac{\exp(Score_{\boldsymbol{\theta}}(F,E))}{\sum_{E'} \exp(Score_{\boldsymbol{\theta}}(F,E'))}, \quad (10)$$

where $Score(.)$ is the translation score according to the current model $\boldsymbol{\theta}$

$$Score_{\boldsymbol{\theta}}(F,E) = \boldsymbol{\lambda} \cdot \mathbf{h}(F,E,A) + \textstyle\sum_{(\mathbf{f},\mathbf{e}) \in A} \mathbf{w} \cdot \boldsymbol{\phi}(\mathbf{f},\mathbf{e}). \quad (11)$$

The right hand side of (11) contains two terms. The first term is the score produced by the baseline system, which is fixed during phrase model training. The second term is the translation score produced by the MRF model, which is updated after each training sample during training. Comparing Equations (2) and (11), we can view the MRF model yet another component model under the log linear model framework with its λ being set to 1.

Given the objective function, the parameters of the MRF model are optimized using stochastic gradient ascent. As shown in Figure 2, we go through the training set T times, each time is considered an *epoch*. For each training sample, we update the model parameters as

$$\mathbf{w}^{new} = \mathbf{w}^{old} + \eta \cdot \mathbf{g}(\mathbf{w}^{old}) \quad (12)$$

where η is the learning rate, and the gradient $\mathbf{g}$ is computed as

$$\mathbf{g}(\mathbf{w}) = \frac{\partial \text{xBLEU}(\mathbf{w})}{\partial \mathbf{w}} \quad (13)$$

$$= \sum_{(E,A)} \mathrm{U}(\boldsymbol{\theta}, E) P_{\boldsymbol{\theta}}(E|F) \phi(F, E, A),$$

where $\mathrm{U}(\boldsymbol{\theta}, E) = \mathrm{sBLEU}(E, E^r) - \mathrm{xBLEU}(\boldsymbol{\theta})$.

Two considerations regarding the development of the training method in Figure 2 are worth mentioning. They significantly simplify the training procedure without sacrificing much the quality of the trained model. First, we do not include a regularization term in the objective function because we find early stopping and cross valuation more effective and simpler to implement. In experiments we produce a MRF model after each epoch, and test its quality on a development set by first combining the MRF model with other baseline component models via MERT and then examining BLEU score on the development set. We performed training for T epochs ($T = 100$ in our experiments) and then pick the model with the best BLEU score on the development set. Second, we do not use the leave-one-out method to generate the N-best lists (Wuebker et al. 2010). Instead, the models used in the baseline SMT system are trained on the same parallel data on which the N-best lists are generated. One may argue that this could lead to over-fitting. For example, comparing to the translations on unseen test data, the generated translation hypotheses on the training set are of artificially high quality with the derivations containing artificially long phrase pairs. The discrepancy between the translations on training and test sets could hurt the training performance. However, we found in our experiments that the impact of over-fitting on the quality of the trained MRF models is negligible[1].

4 Experiments

We conducted our experiments on two Europarl translation tasks, German-to-English (DE-EN) and French-to-English (FR-EN). The data sets are published for the shared task in NAACL 2006 Workshop on Statistical Machine Translation (WMT06) (Koehn and Monz 2006).

For DE-EN, the training set contains 751K sentence pairs, with 21 words per sentence on average. The official development set used for the shared task contains 2000 sentences. In our experiments, we used the first 1000 sentences as a development set for MERT training and optimizing parameters for discriminative training, such as learning rate and the number of iterations. We used the rest 1000 sentences as the first test set (TEST1). We used the WMT06 test data as the second test set (TEST2), which contains 2000 sentences.

Systems	DE-EN (TEST2)	FR-EN (TEST2)
Rank-1 system	27.3	30.8
Rank-2 system	26.0	30.7
Rank-3 system	25.6	30.5
Our baseline	26.0	31.4

Table 1: Baseline results in BLEU. The results of top ranked systems are reported in Koehn and Monz (2006)[2].

For FR-EN, the training set contains 688K sentence pairs, with 21 words per sentence on average. The development set contains 2000 sentences. We used 2000 sentences from the WMT05 shared task as TEST1, and the 2000 sentences from the WMT06 shared task as TEST2.

Two baseline phrase-based SMT systems, each for one language pair, are developed as follows. These baseline systems are used in our experiments both for comparison purpose and for generating N-best lists for discriminative training. First, we performed word alignment on the training set using a hidden Markov model with lexicalized distortion (He 2007), then extracted the phrase table from the word aligned bilingual texts (Koehn et al. 2003). The maximum phrase length is set to four. Other models used in a baseline system include a lexicalized reordering model, word count and phrase count, and a trigram language model trained on the English training data provided by the WMT06 shared task. A fast beam-search phrase-based decoder (Moore and Quirk 2007) is used and the distortion limit is set to four. The decoder is modified so as to output the Viterbi derivation for each translation hypothesis.

The metric used for evaluation is case insensitive BLEU score (Papineni et al. 2002). We also performed a significance test using the paired t-test. Differences are considered statistically significant when the p-value is less than 0.05. Table 1

[1] As pointed out by one of the reviewers, the fact that our training works fine without leave-one-out is probably due to the small phrase length limit (i.e., 4) we used. If a longer phrase limit (e.g., 7) is used the result might be different. We leave it to future work.

[2] The official results are accessible at http://www.statmt.org/wmt06/shared-task/results.html

#	Systems	DE-EN		FR-EN	
		TEST1	TEST2	TEST1	TEST2
1	**Baseline**	26.0	26.0	31.3	31.4
2	$\mathbf{MRF}_{p+t+tp}$	**27.3** $^{\alpha}$	**27.1** $^{\alpha}$	**32.4** $^{\alpha}$	**32.2** $^{\alpha}$
3	$\mathbf{MRF}_{p+t}$	27.2 $^{\alpha}$	26.9 $^{\alpha}$	32.3 $^{\alpha}$	32.0 $^{\alpha}$
4	$\mathbf{MRF}_{p}$	26.8 $^{\alpha\beta}$	26.7 $^{\alpha\beta}$	32.2 $^{\alpha}$	31.8 $^{\alpha\beta}$
5	$\mathbf{MRF}_{t}$	26.8 $^{\alpha\beta}$	26.8 $^{\alpha}$	32.1 $^{\alpha}$	31.9 $^{\alpha\beta}$

Table 2: Main results (BLEU scores) of MRF-based phrase translation models with different feature classes. The superscripts α and β indicate statistically significant difference ($p < 0.05$) from **Baseline** and $\mathbf{MRF}_{p+t+tp}$, respectively.

Feature classes	# of features (weights)	
	DE-EN	FR-EN
phrase-pair features (*p*)	2.5M	2.3M
word-pair features (*t*)	12.2M	9.7M
triplet features (*tp*)	13.4M	13.8M

Table 3: Statistics of the features used in building MRF-based phrase translation models.

presents the baseline results. The performance of our phrase-based SMT systems compares favorably to the top-ranked systems, thus providing a fair baseline for our research.

4.1 Results

Table 2 shows the main results measured in BLEU evaluated on TEST1 and TEST2.

Row 1 is the baseline system. Rows 2 to 5 are the systems enhanced by integrating different versions of the MRF-based phrase translation model. These versions, labeled as $\mathbf{MRF}_f$, are trained using the method described in Section 3, and differ in the feature classes (which are specified by the subscript f) incorporated in the MRF-based model. In this study we focused on three classes of features, as described in Section 2, phrase-pair features (p), word-pair features (t) and triplet features (tp). The statistics for these features are given in Table 3.

Table 2 shows that all the MRF models lead to a substantial improvement over the baseline system across all test sets, with a statistically significant margin from 0.8 to 1.3 BLEU points. As expected, the best phrase model incorporates all of the three classes of features ($\mathbf{MRF}_{p+t+tp}$ in Row 2). We also find that both $\mathbf{MRF}_p$ and $\mathbf{MRF}_t$, although using only one class of features, perform quite well. In TEST2 of DE-EN and TEST1 of FR-EN, they are in a near statistical tie with $\mathbf{MRF}_{p+t}$ and $\mathbf{MRF}_{p+t+tp}$.

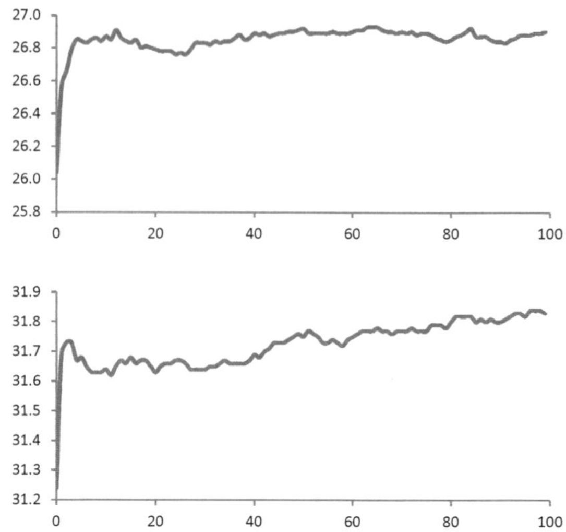

Figure 3: BLEU score on development data (y axis) for DE-EN (top) and FR-EN (bottom) as a function of the number of epochs (x axis).

The result suggests that while the MRF models are very effective in modeling phrase translations, the features we used in this study may not fully realize the potential of the modeling technology.

We also measured the sensitivity of the discriminative training method to different initializations and training parameters. Results show that our method is very robust. All the MRF models in Table 2 are trained by setting the initial feature vector to zero, and the learning rate η=0.01. Figure 3 plots the BLEU score on development sets as a function of the number of epochs t. The BLEU score improves quickly in the first 5 epochs, and then either remains flat, as on the DE-EN data, or keeps increasing but in a much slower pace, as on the FR-EN data.

4.2 Comparing Objective Functions

This section compares different objective functions for discriminative training. As shown in Table 4, xBLEU is compared to three widely used convex loss functions, i.e., hinge loss, logistic loss, and log loss. The hinge loss and logistic loss take into account only two hypotheses among an N-best list GEN: the one with the best sentence-level BLEU score with respect to its reference translation, denoted by (E^*, A^*), called the *oracle* candidate henceforth, and the highest scored *incorrect* candidate according to the current model, denoted by (E', A'), defined as

#	Objective functions	DE-EN		FR-EN	
		TEST 1	TEST2	TEST1	TEST2
1	**xBLEU**	27.2	26.9	32.3	32.0
2	**hinge loss**	26.4^{α}	26.2^{α}	31.8^{α}	31.5^{α}
3	**logistic loss**	26.3^{α}	26.2^{α}	31.7^{α}	31.5^{α}
4	**log loss**	26.5^{α}	26.2^{α}	32.1	31.7^{α}

Table 4: BLEU scores of MRF-based phrase translation models trained using different objective functions. The MRF models use phrase-pair and word-pair features. The superscript α indicates statistically significant difference ($p < 0.05$) from **xBLUE**.

$$(E', A') = \operatorname{argmax}_{(E,A)\in \mathrm{GEN}(F)\setminus\{(E^*,A^*)\}} Score_\theta(F, E, A),$$

where $Score_\theta(.)$ is defined in Equation (11). Let $\mathbf{x} = \mathbf{h}(F, E^*, A^*) - \mathbf{h}(F, E', A')$. The hinge loss under the N-best re-ranking framework is defined as $\max(0, 1 - \boldsymbol{\theta}^T\mathbf{x})$. It is easy to verify that to train a model using this version of hinge loss, the update rule of Equation (12) can be rewritten as

$$\mathbf{w}^{new} = \begin{cases} \mathbf{w}^{old}, & \text{if } \hat{E} = E^* \\ \mathbf{w}^{old} + \eta\mathbf{x}, & otherwise \end{cases} \quad (14)$$

where $\hat{E}$ is the highest scored candidate in GEN. Following Shalev-Shwartz (2012), by setting $\eta = 1$, we reach the Perceptron-based training algorithm that has been widely used in previous studies of discriminative training for SMT (e.g., Liang et al. 2006; Simianer et al. 2012).

The logistic loss $\log(1 + \exp(-\boldsymbol{\theta}^T\mathbf{x}))$ leads to an update rule similar to that of hinge loss

$$\mathbf{w}^{new} = \begin{cases} \mathbf{w}^{old}, & \text{if } \hat{E} = E^* \\ \mathbf{w}^{old} + \eta P_{\boldsymbol{\theta}}(\mathbf{x})\mathbf{x}, & otherwise \end{cases} \quad (15)$$

where $P_{\boldsymbol{\theta}}(\mathbf{x}) = 1/(1 + \exp(\boldsymbol{\theta}^T\mathbf{x}))$.

The log loss is widely used when a probabilistic interpretation of the trained model is desired, as in conditional random fields (CRFs) (Lafferty et al. 2001). Given a training sample, log loss is defined as $\log P_{\boldsymbol{\theta}}(E^*|F)$, where E^* is the oracle translation hypothesis with respect to its reference translation. $P_{\boldsymbol{\theta}}(E^*|F)$ is computed as Equation (10). So, unlike hinge loss and logistic loss, log loss takes into account the distribution over all hypotheses in an N-best list.

The results in Table 4 suggest that the objective functions that take into account the distribution over all hypotheses in an N-best list (i.e., xBLEU and log loss) are more effective than the ones that do not. xBLEU, although it is a non-concave function, significantly outperforms the others because it is more closely coupled with the evaluation metric under consideration (i.e., BLEU).

5 Related Work

Among the attempts to learning phrase translation probabilities that go beyond pure counting of phrases on word-aligned corpora, Wuebker et al. (2010) and He and Deng (2012) are most related to our work. The former find phrase alignment directly on training data and update the translation probabilities based on this alignment. The latter learn phrase translation probabilities discriminatively, which is similar to our approach. But He and Deng's method involves multiple stages, and is not straightforward to implement[3]. Our method differs from previous work in its use of a MRF model that is simple and easy to understand, and a stochastic gradient ascent based training method that is efficient and easy to implement.

A large portion of previous studies on discriminative training for SMT either use a handful of features or use small training sets of a few thousand sentences (e.g., Och 2003; Shen et al. 2004; Watanabe et al. 2007; Duh and Kirchhoff 2008; Chiang et al. 2008; Chiang et al. 2009). Although there is growing interest in large-scale discriminative training (e.g., Liang et al. 2006; Tillmann and Zhang 2006; Blunsom et al. 2008; Hopkins and May 2011; Zhang et al. 2011), only recently does some improvement start to be observed (e.g., Simianer et al. 2012; He and Deng 2012). It still remains uncertain if the improvement is attributed to new features, new training algorithms, objective functions, or simply large amounts of training data. We show empirically the importance of objective functions. Gimple and Smith (2012) also analyze objective functions, but more from a theoretical viewpoint.

The proposed MRF-based translation model is inspired by previous work of applying MRFs for information retrieval (Metzler and Croft 2005), query expansion (Metzler et al. 2007; Gao et al. 2012) and POS tagging (Haghighi and Klein 2006).

[3] For comparison, the method of He and Deng (2012) also achieved very similar results to ours using the same experimental setting, as described in Section 4.

Another undirected graphical model that has been more widely used for NLP is a CRF (Lafferty et al. 2001). An MRF differs from a CRF in that its partition function is no longer observation dependent. As a result, learning an MRF is harder than learning a CRF using maximum likelihood estimation (Haghighi and Klein 2006). Our work provides an alternative learning method that is based on discriminative training.

6 Conclusions

The contributions of this paper are two-fold. First, we present a general, statistical framework for modeling phrase translations via MRFs, where different features can be incorporated in a unified manner. Second, we demonstrate empirically that the parameters of the MRF model can be learned effectively using a large-scale discriminative training approach which is based on stochastic gradient ascent and an N-best list based expected BLEU as the objective function.

In future work we strive to fully realize the potential of the MRF model by developing features that can capture more sophisticated translation dependencies that those used in this study. We will also explore the use of MRF-based translation models for translation systems that go beyond simple phrases, such as hierarchical phrase based systems (Chiang 2005) and syntax-based systems (Galley et al. 2004).

References

Bishop, C. M. 2006. *Patten recognition and machine learning*. Springer.

Blunsom, P., Cohn, T., and Osborne, M. 2008. A discriminative latent variable models for statistical machine translation. In *ACL-HLT*.

Brown, P. F., Della Pietra, S. A., Della Pietra, V. J., and Mercer, R. L. 1993. The mathematics of statistical machine translation: parameter estimation. *Computational Linguistics*, 19(2): 263-311.

Chiang, D. 2005. A hierarchical phrase-based model for statistical machine translation. In *ACL*, pp. 263-270.

Chiang, D., Knight, K., and Wang, W. 2009. 11,001 new features for statistical machine translation. In *NAACL-HLT*.

Chiang, D., Marton, Y., and Resnik, P. 2008. Online large-margin training of syntactic and structural translation features. In *EMNLP*.

DeNero, J., Gillick, D., Zhang, J., and Klein, D. 2006. Why generative phrase models underperform surface heuristics. In *Workshop on Statistical Machine Translation*, pp. 31-38.

Duh, K., and Kirchhoff, K. 2008. Beyond log-linear models: boosted minimum error rate training for n-best ranking. In *ACL*.

Galley, M., Hopkins, M., Knight, K., Marcu, D. 2004. What's in a translation rule? In *HLT-NAACL*, pp. 273-280.

Gao, J., Xie, S., He, X., and Ali, A. 2012. Learning lexicon models from search logs for query expansion. In *EMNLP-CoNLL*, pp. 666-676.

Gao, J., Qi, H., Xia, X., and Nie, J-Y. 2005. Linear discriminant model for information retrieval. In *SIGIR*, pp. 290-297.

Gimpel, K., and Smith, N. A. 2012. Structured ramp loss minimization for machine translation. In *NAACL-HLT*.

Haghighi, A., and Klein, D. 2006. Prototype-driven learning for sequence models. In *NAACL*.

Hasan, S., Ganitkevitch, J., Ney, H., and Andres-Fnerre, J. 2008. Triplet lexicon models for statistical machine translation. In *EMNLP*, pp. 372-381.

He, X. 2007. Using word-dependent transition models in HMM based word alignment for statistical machine translation. In *Proc. of the Second ACL Workshop on Statistical Machine Translation*.

He, X., and Deng, L. 2012. Maximum expected bleu training of phrase and lexicon translation models. In *ACL*, pp. 292-301.

Hopkins, H., and May, J. 2011. Tuning as ranking. In *EMNLP*.

Koehn, P. 2010. *Statistical machine translation. Cambridge University Press.*

Koehn, P., and Monz, C. 2006. Manual and automatic evaluation of machine translation between European languages. In *Workshop on Statistical Machine Translation*, pp. 102-121.

Koehn, P., Och, F., and Marcu, D. 2003. Statistical phrase-based translation. In *HLT-NAACL*, pp. 127-133.

Lafferty, J., McCallum, A., and Pereira, F. 2001. Conditional random fields: probablistic models for segmenting and labeling sequence data. In *ICML*.

Lambert, P., and Banchs, R.E. 2005. Data inferred multi-word expressions for statistical machine translation. In *MT Summit X*, Phuket, Thailand.

Liang, P., Bouchard-Cote, A. Klein, D., and Taskar, B. 2006. An end-to-end discriminative approach to machine translation. In *COLING-ACL*.

Marcu, D., and Wong, W. 2002. A phrase-based, joint probability model for statistical machine translation. In *EMNLP*.

Metzler, D., and Croft, B. 2005. A markov random field model for term dependencies. In *SIGIR*, pp. 472-479.

Metzler, D., and Croft, B. 2007. Latent concept expansion using markov random fields. In *SIGIR*, pp. 311-318.

Morgan, W., Greiff, W., and Henderson, J. 2004. *Direct maximization of average precision by hill-climbing with a comparison to a maximum entropy approach.* Technical report. MITRE.

Moore, R., and Quirk, C. 2007. Faster beam-search decoding for phrasal statistical machine translation. In *MT Summit XI*.

Och, F., and Ney, H. 2004. The alignment template approach to statistical machine translation. *Computational Linguistics*, 29(1): 19-51.

Och, F. 2003. Minimum error rate training in statistical machine translation. In *ACL*, pp. 160-167.

Papinein, K., Roukos, S., Ward, T., and Zhu W-J. 2002. BLEU: a method for automatic evaluation of machine translation. In *ACL*.

Rosti, A-V., Hang, B., Matsoukas, S., and Schwartz, R. S. 2011. Expected BLEU training for graphs: bbn system description for WMT system combination task. In *Workshop on Statistical Machine Translation*.

Shalev-Shwartz, Shai. 2012. Online learning and online convex optimization. *Foundations and Trends in Machine Learning*, 4(2):107-194.

Shen, L., Sarkar, A., and Och, F. 2004. Discriminative reranking for machine translation. In *HLT/NAACL*.

Simianer, P., Riezler, S., and Dyer, C. 2012. Joint feature selection in distributed stochasic learning for large-scale discriminative training in SMT. In *ACL*, pp. 11-21.

Tillmann, C., and Zhang, T. 2006. A discriminative global training algorithm for statistical MT. In *COLING-ACL*.

Watanabe, T., Suzuki, J., Tsukada, H., and Isozaki, H. 2007. Online large-margin training for statistical machine translation. In *EMNLP*.

Wuebker, J., Mauser, A., and Ney, H. 2010. Training phrase translation models with leaving-one-out. In *ACL*, pp. 475-484.

Zhang, Y., Deng, L., He, X., and Acero, A., 2011. A Novel decision function and the associated decision-feedback learning for speech translation, in *ICASSP*.

Automatic Morphological Enrichment of a Morphologically Underspecified Treebank

Sarah Alkuhlani, Nizar Habash and Ryan Roth
Center for Computational Learning Systems
Columbia University
{salkuhlani,habash,ryanr}@ccls.columbia.edu

Abstract

In this paper, we study the problem of automatic enrichment of a morphologically underspecified treebank for Arabic, a morphologically rich language. We show that we can map from a tagset of size six to one with 485 tags at an accuracy rate of 94%-95%. We can also identify the unspecified lemmas in the treebank with an accuracy over 97%. Furthermore, we demonstrate that using our automatic annotations improves the performance of a state-of-the-art Arabic morphological tagger. Our approach combines a variety of techniques from corpus-based statistical models to linguistic rules that target specific phenomena. These results suggest that the cost of treebanking can be reduced by designing underspecified treebanks that can be subsequently enriched automatically.

1 Introduction

Collections of manually-annotated morphological and syntactic analyses of sentences, or treebanks, are an important resource for building statistical parsing models or for syntax-aware approaches to applications such as machine translation. Rich treebank annotations have also been used for a variety of natural language processing (NLP) applications such as tokenization, diacritization, part-of-speech (POS) tagging, morphological disambiguation, base phrase chunking, and semantic role labeling.

The development of a treebank with rich annotations is demanding in time and money, especially for morphologically complex languages. Consequently, the richer the annotation, the slower the annotation process and the smaller the size of the treebank. As such, a tradeoff is usually made between the size of the treebank and the richness of its annotations.

In this paper, we investigate the possibility of automatically enriching the morphologically underspecified Columbia Arabic Treebank (CATiB) (Habash and Roth, 2009; Habash et al., 2009) with the more complex POS tags and lemmas used in the Penn Arabic Treebank (PATB) (Maamouri et al., 2004). We employ a variety of techniques that range from corpus-based statistical models to handwritten rules based on linguistic observations. Our best method reaches accuracy rates of 94%-95% on full POS tag identification. We can also identify the unspecified lemmas in CATiB with an accuracy over 97%. 37% of our POS tag errors are due to gold tree or gold POS errors. A learning curve experiment to evaluate the dependence of our method on annotated data shows that while the quality of some components may reduce sharply with less data (12% absolute reduction in accuracy when using $\frac{1}{32}$ of the data or some 10K annotated words), the overall effect is a lot smaller (2% absolute drop). These results suggest that the cost of treebanking can be reduced by designing underspecified treebanks that can be subsequently enriched automatically.

The rest of this paper is structured as follows: Section 2 presents related work; Section 3 details various language background facts about Arabic and its treebanking; Section 4 explains our approach; and Section 5 presents and discusses our results.

2 Related Work

Arabic Treebanking There has been a lot work on building treebanks for different languages. In the case of Modern Standard Arabic (MSA), there are three efforts that vary in terms of richness and representation choice. The Penn Arabic Treebank (PATB) (Maamouri et al., 2004; Maamouri et al., 2009b; Maamouri et al., 2009a), the Prague Arabic Dependency Treebank (PADT) (Smrž and Hajič, 2006; Smrž et al., 2008) and the Columbia Arabic Treebank (CATiB) (Habash and Roth, 2009; Habash et al., 2009) . The PATB uses phrase structure representation, while the other two use two different dependency representations. The PATB and PADT representations are quite detailed. The PATB not only provides tokenization, complex POS tags (485 tags in our data set), and syntactic structure; it also provides empty categories, diacritization, lemma choices, glosses and some semantic tags. In comparison CATiB only provides tokenization, six POS tags and eight dependency relations. The tradeoff is speed: CATiB's complete POS and syntax annotation rate is 540 tokens/hour (and annotator training takes two months), a much higher speed than reported for complete (POS and syntax) annotation in PATB (around 250-300 tokens/hour and 6-12 months for annotator training) and PADT (around 75 tokens/hour) (Habash and Roth, 2009). An important recent addition to the family of Arabic treebanks is the Quran Treebank, which targets the Classical Arabic language of the Quran, not MSA (Dukes and Buckwalter, 2010).

Treebank Enrichment There has been a number of efforts on developing treebanks with rich representations and on treebank enrichment for many languages, such Danish, English, German, Italian and Spanish (Oepen et al., 2002; Hinrichs et al., 2004; Müller, 2010). Additionally, there has been some work on Arabic treebank enrichment that built on the PATB by manually extending its already rich annotations or automatically converting them to new formalisms. The Arabic Propbank (Propositional Bank) (Palmer et al., 2008) and the OntoNotes project (Hovy et al., 2006) both annotate for Arabic semantic information. Alkuhlani and Habash (2011) add annotations marking functional gender and number, and rationality; and Abdul-Mageed and Diab (2012) annotate the sentence level with sentiment labels. Tounsi et al. (2009) automatically converted the PATB to a lexical functional grammar (LFG) representation. Similarly, Habash and Roth (2009) used a similar technique to build an initial version of CATiB. We use this CATiB version of PATB to evaluate our approach in this paper. Also related to this is the work on automatic enrichment of specific features, e.g., Habash et al. (2007a) demonstrated that nominal case, can be determined for gold syntactic analyses at high accuracy. We replicate their results and improve upon them. And unlike them, we handle all the morphological features in the PATB, not just case.

Morphological Disambiguation There has been a lot of work on Arabic POS tagging and morphological disambiguation (Diab et al., 2004; Habash and Rambow, 2005; Smith et al., 2005; Hajič et al., 2005; Roth et al., 2008; Habash et al., 2013). These approaches are intended to apply to raw text and determine the appropriate in-context morphological reading for each word. In contrast, in this paper, we are starting from a partially disambiguated and relatively rich representation: we have tokenization, general POS tags and syntactic dependency information.

Finally, morphological information (beyond tokenization) has been shown to be useful for many NLP applications. Marton et al. (2011) demonstrated that morphology helps Arabic parsing. Using morphological features such as case has also improved parsing for Russian, Turkish and Hindi (Nivre et al., 2008; Eryigit et al., 2008; Nivre, 2009). Other work has shown value for morphology in the context of Arabic named entity recognition (Benajiba et al., 2009). These results support the value of our goal of enriching resources with morphological information, which then can be used to improve different NLP applications.

3 Linguistic Background

In this section, we present some relevant general linguistic facts about Arabic and then discuss the specifics of the tagsets we work with in this paper.

Arabic Linguistic Facts The Arabic language poses many challenges for NLP. Arabic is a morphologically complex language which includes rich inflectional and cliticizational morphology, e.g., the word وسيكتبونها *w+s+y-ktb-wn+hA*[1] 'and they will write it' has two proclitics, one prefix, one suffix and one pronominal enclitic. Additionally, Arabic has a high degree of ambigiouty due to the absence of the diacritics and inconsistent spelling of letters such as Alif, أ Â and Ya ي *y*. The Buckwalter Arabic Morphological Analyzer (BAMA) (Buckwalter, 2004), which is used in the PATB, produces an average of 12 analyses per word.

In this paper, we work with gold tokenized Arabic as it appears in the PATB and CATiB treebanks.

[1]Arabic transliteration is presented in the Habash-Soudi-Buckwalter scheme (Habash et al., 2007b): (in alphabetical order) *AbtθjHxdðrzssšSDTĎςγfqklmnhwy* and the additional symbols: ' ء, Â أ, Ǎ إ, Ā آ, ŵ ؤ , ŷ ئ , ¯h ة, ý ى.

As such, the words are partially disambiguated with regards to possible tokenizable clitics and Alif/Ya spelling forms. That said, there is still a lot of ambiguity remaining especially because diacritics are not marked. Words in the treebank may be ambiguous in terms of their POS, lemmas and inflectional features. The inflectional features include gender, number, person, case, state, mood, voice, aspect and the presence of the determiner +ال *Al+* 'the', which is not tokenized off in the treebanks.

Arabic has a well known discrepancy in form and function that appears most commonly in the form of irregular plurals, called Broken Plurals, which although functionally are plural, have singular suffixes. We will not discuss form and function discrepancy in this paper except as needed. For more on this see Habash (2010).

The Buckwalter Tagset The Buckwalter POS tagset is perhaps one of the most commonly used tagsets for Arabic NLP research. The tagset's popularity is in part due to its use in the PATB. Buckwalter tags can be used for tokenized and untokenized text. The untokenized tags are produced by BAMA (Buckwalter, 2004) and consist of 485 tags. The tokenized tags, which are used in the PATB, are derived from the untokenized tags and can reach thousands of tags. Both variants use the same basic 70 or so sub-tag symbols (such as DET 'determiner', NSUFF 'nominal suffix', ADJ 'adjective' and ACC 'accusative') (Maamouri et al., 2009a). These sub-tags are combined to form around 170 morpheme tags such as NSUFF_FEM_SG 'feminine singular nominal suffix' and CASE_DEF_ACC 'accusative definite'. The word tags are constructed out of one or more morpheme tags, e.g. DET+NOUN_PROP+CASE_DEF_NOM for the word الصين *Al+Siyn+u* 'China'.

CATiB Trees and POS Tags CATiB uses the same basic tokenization scheme used by PATB and PADT. However, the CATiB POS tagset is much smaller. Whereas in practice PATB uses 485 Buckwalter tags specifying every aspect of Arabic word morphology such as definiteness, gender, number, person, mood, voice and case, CATiB uses 6 POS tags: **NOM** (non-proper nominals including nouns, pronouns, adjectives and adverbs), **PROP** (proper nouns), **VRB** (verbs), **VRB-PASS** (passive-voice verbs), **PRT** (particles such as prepositions or con-

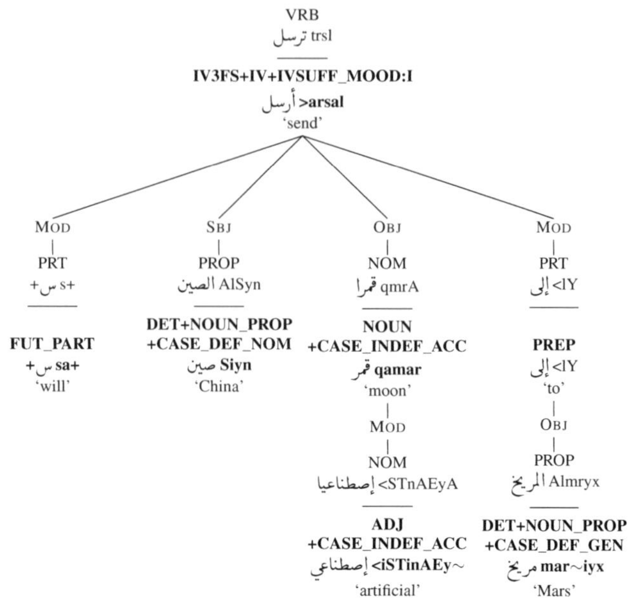

Figure 1: An example dependency tree for the sentence ستُرسل الصين قمرا إصطناعيا إلى المريخ *s+trsl AlSyn qmrA ǍSTnAςyA Ǎlý Almryx* 'China will send a satellite to Mars'. In every tree node, the terms above the line are part of the CATiB annotations: the word, POS (VRB, PRT, PROP, NOM) and relation (MOD, SBJ, OBJ). The terms under the line are the Buckwalter POS tag, the lemma and the gloss, respectively.

junctions) and **PNX** (punctuation). CATiB uses a dependency representation that models predicate-argument structure (subject, object, etc.) and Arabic nominal structure (idafa, tamyiz, modification). The eight CATiB relation labels are: **SBJ** (subject of verb or topic of simple nominal sentence), **OBJ** (object of verb, preposition, or deverbal noun), **TPC** (topic in complex nominal sentences containing an explicit pronominal referent), **PRD** (predicate marking the complement in some copular constructions), **IDF** (relation between the possessor [dependent] and the possessed [head] in the idafa/possessive nominal construction), **TMZ** (relation of the specifier [dependent] to the specified [head] in the tamyiz/specification nominal constructions), **MOD** (general modifier of verbs or nouns), and — (marking *flatness* inside constructions such as first-last proper name sequences). This relation label set is much smaller than the twenty or so dash-tags used in PATB to mark syntactic and semantic functions. Furthermore, no empty categories, coreference, or semantic relations (e.g., TMP or LOC) are provided (Habash and Roth, 2009). A detailed discussion of CATiB guidelines and further comparison with PATB appears in (Habash et al., 2009).

In this paper, we target the enrichment of CATiB with the morphological information used in the PATB: Buckwalter POS tags and lemmas. We do not address other kinds of rich information. Figure 1 presents an example of a CATiB tree with the extensions we predict automatically for each word.

4 Approach

We define our task as assigning a Buckwalter POS tag and lemma to each word in a CATiB syntactic tree, i.e., disambiguating the CATiB POS tag in terms of the finer grained Buckwalter tag in context. Our approach utilizes a variety of corpus-based and rule-based techniques. We use corpus-based techniques that exploit available training data in the form of portions of the PATB that are automatically converted to CATiB style trees. We also use rule-based solutions that allow us to apply linguistic knowledge and insights. An important tool that we use is a morphological analyzer which generates for every word all possible out-of-context analyses. We use these analyses as a constraint on the space from which we will select the appropriate in-context tag. The approach is quite similar to how MADA (Morphological Analysis and Disambiguation for Arabic) (Habash and Rambow, 2005) works except that we are using the CATiB tree as the context in which we disambiguate. Given the degree of richness of the tree, we expect to outperform basic disambiguation on text.

In the rest of this section, we discuss our general strategy, followed by a detailed presentation of our approach: morphological disambiguation and morphological filtering.

4.1 From CATiB to Buckwalter: Devising a Strategy

In CATiB trees, different pieces of information can be relevant to different disambiguation tasks. We analyzed a sample of the data we have and obtained the following observations which we use to devise our strategy for how to address different types of ambiguity:

- Words in the CATiB treebank are tokenized. This resolves many ambiguous cases: analyses involving cliticized prepositions or conjunctions are dismissed. Further more, separated clitics are marked, which restricts their reading. The ambiguity in terms of the number of lemmas per word reduces from 2.7 for untokenized words to just 1.1 for tokenized words.
- The CATiB POS tagset, although two orders of magnitude smaller than the Buckwalter tagset, provides a lot of information. It resolves ambiguity amongst verbs (active or passive), nominals, particles, proper nouns and punctuation.
- The CATiB tags NOM and PRT are the most ambiguous. They are challenging because there are both lexical and morphosyntactic features at play. We rely on our training data to learn models of how to disambiguate them. The CATiB treebank annotation does not deterministically allow us to identify the finer grained tag using the POS and relations alone: e.g., the NOM child of an NOM parent (with the relation MOD) can be an ADJ (67% probability) or a NOUN (21%).
- Case, state, mood and to a lesser degree aspect are syntactically dependent features, for which we use the CATiB tree and linguistic rules to disambiguate the correct value in context.
- Gender, number and person are expressed using affixes that highly limit the feature-value possibilities, e.g., the suffix ة+ +$\bar{h}$deterministically selects for +NSUFF_FEM_SG suffix tag.

4.2 Morphological Analysis & Disambiguation

We use the morphological analyzer BAMA to get a list of all possible analyses for a word. BAMA returns unranked analyses for untokenized text only. Since we know that the input is already tokenized, we built an extension to BAMA that handles clitics and accepts analyses that are consistent with the tokenization of the input, discarding all other analyses.

We use both the morphological analyzer BAMA and a training set from the PATB to predict the Buckwalter tag for a given word. We use BAMA to get a list of all possible Buckwalter tag and lemma pairs for each word. We then rank these choices using one of the following two methods: a maximum likelihood estimate model (MLE) conditioned on specific features in the CATiB tree or a MADA-like suite of classifiers that select for specific POS tag features such as gender or number.

4.2.1 Maximum Likelihood Model

The MLE model ranks the set of choices from BAMA returning the most probable analysis. We consider two models:

- **MLE Baseline 1** selects the Buckwalter tag with the highest unconditioned probability in the training data, P(BW), among the set of BAMA choices for the word whose tag we want to determine.
- **MLE Baseline 2** selects the Buckwalter tag with the highest probability conditioned on the word and CATiB tag: P(BW|word,CATiB). This model backs off to the Buckwalter tag with the highest probability conditioned on the CATiB tag, i.e., P(BW|CATiB), and then backs off to MLE Baseline 1.

4.2.2 Analysis and Disambiguation of Tokenized Arabic

We retrained the MADA system (Habash and Rambow, 2005) using a tokenized version of the PATB. We call the new version TADA: Tokenized Analysis and Disambiguation of Arabic. TADA takes tokenized text, and returns a ranked list of analyses for each tokenized word and clitic. Just like MADA, TADA uses BAMA to identify possible analyses of the word. It then uses a suite of classifiers to predict inflectional and lexical features that are used to rank the possible analyses.

As expected, TADA outperforms the simple MLE models described earlier; however, its performance is not high enough since it makes no use of tree features. The results are presented in Section 5. However, we will present here a preliminary error analysis of TADA's output to motivate the morphological filters presented next (Section 4.3).

TADA Preliminary Error Analysis We considered the first 100 errors in the Buckwalter tags in our development set. About half of the errors involved a problem in case (42%), state (13%) or mood (3%). Case and state errors had many overlaps. All of these errors are syntactically determinable using the tree representation in a manner similar to Habash et al. (2007a). In 17% of the cases, a POS error can be resolved using the CATiB tag, (e.g., proper noun vs adjective or verb). In 2% of the cases, the error involved an orthographic normalization (Alif-form) that led to an undesirable solution (e.g., ألسنة Âlsn¯*h*'tongues' vs السنة Alsn¯*h*'the-year'). These cases should be resolved by enforcing the CATiB tree word form. Ambiguity in CATiB tags was a problem for nominal forms 15% of the time (e.g., NOUN vs ADJ), particles 10% of the time (e.g., +و w+ 'and' can be CONJ or SUB_CONJ), and pronouns 5% of the time (e.g., هم+ +hm 'them' can be IVSUFF_DO:3MP or PVSUFF_DO:3MP [attached to an imperfective or perfective verb]).[2] In 1% of the cases, there was an error involving ambiguity in number (dual/plural). And finally, in 3% of the cases, we determined that the gold POS tag was actually incorrect. Within the same set of sentences studied, we found 18 lemma choice errors. Almost all, except for three cases, involve a nominal form ambiguity resulting from diacrtic absence, e.g., مهدد *muhad∼id* 'threatening' or *muhad∼ad* 'threatened'. Eight of the 18 cases (or 44%) happened without an accompanying POS error. Overall, the accuracy of lemma choice is highly dependent on the correctness of the chosen core Buckwalter tag; lemma accuracy when the tag is correct is 97.9%, but it drops to 71.3% when the tag is wrong.

4.3 Morphological Filters

We implemented a set of filters that take the list of ranked analyses produced by TADA and discard any analyses that are inconsistent with the filters' decisions in the tree context. TADA ranking is preserved among the remaining analyses.

4.3.1 CATiB Filter

TADA returns all analyses for word, including different forms of the word (i.e., different Alif/Ya forms as part of BAMA's back-off mode). For example, when given the word على *ςlý*, TADA returns analyses for both the words على *ςlý* 'on' and علي *ςly* 'Ali'. Since the input to our system is the gold word form from CATiB trees, the CATiB filter will discard analyses that do not match the given word form.

The CATiB filter also resolves some POS ambiguity given information in the CATiB POS tag. For example, the CATiB POS tags NOM or VRB can easily decide whether the ambiguous word كاتب *kAtb* is a noun (*kAtib* 'writer') or a verb (*kAtab* 'to correspond').

[2]This is a peculiarity of the tagset used in PATB. The distinction does not seem to be necessary to our knowledge, but we still consider it the gold goal.

4.3.2 Pronominal Filter

The pronominal filter (PRON) selects the pronouns that are consistent with the verbs they are attached to. A pronoun attached to a verb could either be IVSUFF_DO, PVSUFF_DO or CVSUFF_DO depending on whether the verb is imperfective (IV), perfective (PV), or imperative (CV).

4.3.3 Noun/Adjective Filter

The noun/adjective (NOUN/ADJ) filter is applied to words with the CATiB tag NOM. It uses a nominal classifier, which classifies CATiB NOM words into one of the following Buckwalter noun/adjective classes: NOUN, NOUN.VN, NOUN_QUANT, NOUN_NUM, ADJ, ADJ.VN, ADV_COMP, ADV_NUM. The NA (not-applicable) tag is assigned to all other words. For example, the classifier will decide whether كبيرة *kbyr¯h* is a noun 'abomination' or an adjective 'great [feminine singular]' based on the context.

To build the nominal classifier, we use Yamcha (Kudo and Matsumoto, 2003), a support-vector-machine-based sequence tagger trained on our PATB training data. We use the following set of features: the word form, CATiB POS tag, parent features (word form, CATiB POS tag), dependency relation, order of appearance (the word comes before or after its parent), the distance between the word and its parent, and different types of relation-child POS (REL-CTB) features. The REL-CTB features state whether a word has a child with a CATiB POS (CTB) under a dependency relation (REL). A word can have 0 or more children. We have six CATiB POS tags and eight dependency relations and thus up to 48 different REL-CTB binary learning features. An example of this feature is a PRT that has a child NOM under a dependency relation OBJ. In this case, the value of the feature OBJ-NOM is 1. We also add a window of two words before and two words after the word being tagged as static features, and the tag of the previous two words as dynamic features. The nominal classifier predicts the correct nominal class with an accuracy of 97.70%.

4.3.4 Particle Filter

The particle filter (PRT) selects the specific Buckwalter POS for a particle. For example, the particle ما *mA* can be the negative particle 'not', the relative pronoun 'that' or the interrogative pronoun 'what?'. The PRT filter uses a particle classifier that uses the same learning features and training data as the nominal classifier. The particle classifier predicts the correct particle class with an accuracy of 99.54%.

4.3.5 Verbal Mood and Aspect Filter

The Buckwalter POS tags for verbs have three markers for aspect: imperfective (IV), perfective (PV), and imperative (CV); and three markers for mood: jussive (J), subjunctive (S) and indicative (I). We apply our rule-based mood-and-aspect filter (MOOD/ASPECT) to words that have the CATiB tag VRB or VRB-PASS.

If the verb is preceded by a jussive, subjunctive or future particle then it is imperfective in aspect and its mood is determined by the particle. The mood is indicative if the verb is preceded by a future particle such as سوف *swf* 'will'; it is jussive if the verb is preceded by a jussive particle such as لم *lm* 'not+past', +ل *l+* 'for'; and it is subjunctive if the verb is preceded by a subjunctive particle such as أن *Ân* 'that', لن *ln* 'not+future', كي *ky* 'so as to', and حتى *Htý* 'until'. This is also valid when a negating لا *lA* intervenes between the subjunctive particle and the verb. If the verb is proceeded with the particle لقد *lqd* 'already', then the verb is perfective. Otherwise, the verb could be either imperfective (with an indicative mood), perfective or imperative (all allowed through the filter).

4.3.6 Nominal State Filter

The Buckwalter POS tags have three nominal state markers: INDEF, DEF and POSS.[3] The nominal state filter (STATE) applies the following rules: If the word is head of an idafa (IDF), then we exclude the INDEF analyses. Otherwise, we exclude the POSS and the non-Al/DET determined DEF analysis (which are only used for IDF heads).

4.3.7 Nominal Case Filter

The nominal case filter (CASE) assigns the values *nom* (nominative), *acc* (accusative) or *gen* (genitive) to each NOM/PROP word primarily based on the CATiB dependency relation label that describes the type of relation between the word and its parent. The nominal case filter extends the case predictor in Habash et al. (2007a). The following four rules are applied in sequence.

[3]These values do not exactly match the functional values for state in Arabic (Smrž, 2007).

- RULE 1: Assign *acc* to all NOM/PROP words as a default.

- RULE 2: Assign *nom* to NOM/PROP words that (a) head the tree, (b) have the label TPC, (c) have the label SBJ but are not headed by a particle from the closed class of *Inna and its sisters* (Habash et al., 2007a), or (d) have the label PRD but is not headed by a verb or deverbal noun. Exempt words in the closed class of adverb-like nouns such as فوق *fwq* 'over', قبل *qbl* 'before', and حول *Hwl* 'around'.

- RULE 3: Assign *gen* to NOM/PROP words that have the label OBJ under a preposition, or that have the label IDF.

- RULE 4: All children of NOM/PROP parents whose label is MOD, and NOM/PROP children of conjunctions whose label is OBJ, copy the case of their parent. Conjunctions carry the case temporarily to pass on agreement.

4.3.8 MLE Override

We added an MLE-based component to override answers that are provided by our final system. We used a no-BAMA version of the MLE Baseline 2. The difference between the MLE override component and MLE Baseline 2 is that it takes into account all possible Buckwalter POS tags that appear in the training set for a specific word regardless of whether they are provided by BAMA or not. This MLE override component is trained on the same training set and returns the most common Buckwalter tag and lemma pair for a given word form and CATiB POS tag pair. BAMA is not used here since the reason behind this additional step is to overcome any limitation caused by using BAMA to start with. These limitations include primarily cases of BAMA failure to produce analyses (OOV) or minor version differences between BAMA and the PATB. If a Buckwalter tag and lemma pair appear above a threshold of n times and always with the same word-lemma pair, then we override our answer with the new answer from the MLE. When we override, we only override the core part of the Buckwalter tag. We do not override the state, case, and mood features since they are syntactic features. We tried different values for the threshold and got the best results when $n = 4$.

4.4 Putting it All Together

TADA provides an initial list of ranked analyses. Then, the morphological filters discard analyses that are not consistent with the CATiB tree information. The analysis with the highest TADA rank among the remaining analyses is selected as the answer.

We apply our filters in the following order. We first apply the CATiB filter. After that, we apply the pronominal, noun/adjective and particle filters. These three filters can be applied in any order since they are applied on disjoint sets of words. The next filter is the mood/aspect filter which has to be applied after the particle filter since it depends on the particle choice in predicting the mood of the following verb. At this point, we freeze the lemma choice for the word. The next two filters, state and case, look at syntactic features and should not affect the choice of the lemma.

We use two back-off mechanisms. The first one is with the application of each filter. If the effect of applying a filter results in an empty set (no match found) then we undo the effect of the filter and pass the list of analyses as is to the next filter. The second mechanism is using the MLE override at the end of the pipeline. TADA, the noun/adjective and particle filters, and the MLE override use corpus-based components while all other filters are rule-based.

5 Evaluation

5.1 Experimental Settings

We use a CATiB version of the PATB part 3v3.1 and part 2v3.0 released by the Linguistic Data Consortium (LDC) (Maamouri et al., 2004). We use the train/development/test (80/10/10) splits of Marton et al. (2010) for PATB part 3v3.1 (16.6K sentences; 400K tokens): we use their train as our training data, their development as the tuning data for TADA and their test as our development set. For our blind test, we use the first 1000 sentences in PATB part 2v3.0 (38K tokens).

We report all results in terms of token accuracy on the full Buckwalter tag, reduced Buckwalter tag and the lemma. The reduced Buckwalter tag is the Buckwalter tag without case, state, and mood. The number of tags is reduced to 220 tags (compared to 485 tags for the full Buckwalter tagset).

In cases of gold full Buckwalter tags that are underspecified for case, state or mood, we do not penalize our systems if our more specific predicted

	Full BW	Reduced BW	Diff	Lemma
MLE Baseline 1	57.19	73.44	16.25	90.87
MLE Baseline 2	77.69	93.27	15.58	94.31
TADA	86.15	94.04	7.89	96.97
++ CATiB	87.33	95.50	8.17	97.72
++ PRON	88.16	96.32	8.16	97.72
++ NOUN/ADJ	88.93	97.26	8.33	97.72
++ PRT	89.24	97.57	8.33	97.72
++ MOOD/ASPECT	89.46	97.60	8.14	97.74
++ STATE	89.92	97.61	7.69	97.74
++ CASE	94.90	97.61	2.71	97.74
++ MLE override	**95.27**	**98.00**	**2.73**	**97.81**

Table 1: Accuracy of enriching CATiB trees with Buckwalter (BW) tags and lemmas on the **development** set. Reduced Buckwalter is similar to Buckwalter, but ignores case, mood and state. The **Diff**erence between the two metrics highlights the errors from case, mood and state.

tag otherwise matches the gold tag. Words whose lemmas are unknown (nolemma, TBupdate) or has the lemma DEFAULT (including digits and punctuation) are excluded from the evaluation, but not training: in the development set, 4,498 out of 25,446 words were excluded (~18%).

5.2 Results

Table 1 shows the results of our experiments on the development set. Considering the baseline systems, we see that using both the CATiB POS tag and the word form in MLE Baseline 2 gives us a 20.5% absolute increase above MLE Baseline 1. Using TADA improves the performance significantly (adding 8.46% absolute over MLE Baseline 2). Every additional morphological filter has a positive impact and the improvement of the accuracy for full Buckwalter with each new filter ranged between 0.22% and 1.18% absolute except for the case filter, which adds almost 5%. Adding the MLE override has a positive impact on the accuracy of the full and reduced Buckwalter tags and the lemma.

We apply our baselines, TADA, TADA+filters and TADA+filters+MLE to the blind test set (see Table 2). The test set is a bit harder than the development set, but the results are consistent with those seen for the development set.

5.3 Error Analysis

We conducted an analysis of the errors in the output of the final system TADA+filters+MLE on the development set. We considered 100 randomly selected error cases and examined them in the CATiB trees to assess the source of the error. About 37% of all errors are due to gold treebank errors: 21% are gold tree structure/relation errors and 16% are gold POS errors. The rest of the errors result from failures in our system. The most common error is in NOM disambiguation: NOUN/NOUN_NUM, NOUN/ADJ, NOUN/NOUN_QUANT, etc. The NOM errors accounted for 33% of all errors. Case comes second with 12% errors, then PRT and gender-number-person errors with 5% each. State errors contribute to 3% of total errors.

	Full BW	Reduced BW	Diff	Lemma
MLE Baseline 1	55.96	71.88	15.92	90.77
MLE Baseline 2	77.15	92.88	15.73	94.03
TADA	86.49	94.42	7.93	96.63
++ All filters	93.44	97.25	3.81	97.13
++ MLE override	**93.61**	**97.43**	**3.82**	**97.17**

Table 2: Accuracy of enriching CATiB trees with Buckwalter (BW) tags and lemmas on the **blind test** set.

5.4 Learning Curve Study

The non-rule-based components of our approach, namely TADA, NOUN/ADJ and PRT filters, and MLE override depend on the existence of an annotated treebank in rich format. To understand the degree of dependence, we ran a series of experiments on different sizes of the training data: $\frac{1}{2}$, $\frac{1}{4}$, $\frac{1}{8}$, $\frac{1}{16}$, and $\frac{1}{32}$ of the full training set (341.1K words). These data sets were used to train new versions of TADA, the NOUN/ADJ and PRT filters, and the MLE override. The results of running TADA and the final system on the development set using the different data sets are summarized in Tables 3 and 4, respectively. As expected, when the training data size goes down the accuracy goes down. Our final system, which adds filters on top of TADA, had a significant effect on the performance as shown in Table 4. Using only 10.6K of annotated words, the quality of TADA reduces sharply (12.12% absolute reduction in accuracy) while the overall effect on our full system is a lot smaller (2.03% absolute drop). Similarly, the performance of the nominal and particle classifiers degrade when trained on less data. When we use $\frac{1}{32}$ of the training data, the correct nominal class is predicted at an accuracy of 90.49% (7.21% absolute drop), while the correct particle class is predicted at an accuracy of 96.59% (2.95% absolute drop). We used the MLE override threshold determined based

	Size	Full BW	Reduced BW	Diff	Lemma
1/32	10.6K	74.03	88.78	14.75	93.41
1/16	21.3K	77.16	90.30	13.14	94.37
1/8	42.6K	79.76	91.63	11.87	95.56
1/4	85.3K	81.91	92.80	10.89	96.22
1/2	170.7K	84.12	93.62	9.50	96.74
1	341.1K	86.15	94.04	7.89	96.97

Table 3: Accuracy of enriching CATiB trees with Buckwalter (BW) tags and lemmas using TADA only for different training sizes on the development set.

	Size	Full BW	Reduced BW	Diff	Lemma
1/32	10.6K	93.24	95.81	2.57	95.68
1/16	21.3K	93.67	96.28	2.61	96.27
1/8	42.6K	94.14	96.79	2.65	96.94
1/4	85.3K	94.56	97.26	2.70	97.22
1/2	170.7K	94.96	97.66	2.70	97.61
1	341.1K	95.27	98.00	2.73	97.81

Table 4: Accuracy of enriching CATiB trees with Buckwalter (BW) tags and lemmas using our best performing system for different training sizes on the development set.

on the full training data, which may not be optimal for smaller data sets.

The contribution of our full system over TADA when using $\frac{1}{32}$ of the full training data is over 19% absolute (on full Buckwalter tag determination) compared to 9% when using the full training data. The morph analysis (out of context) is the same for all experiments and that this provides a lot of stability to the results. The high lemma accuracy overall is a result of disambiguating tokenized words, where the average numbers of lemmas per word is only 1.1 as mentioned above. These results suggest that our approach is usable even in the early stages of developing new richly annotated treebanks.

5.5 Extrinsic Evaluation

We applied our automatic enrichment to the underspecified CATiB treebank (as opposed to the parts of PATB, which we used throughout the paper to simulate CATiB). We evaluate the added value of these annotations by using them to extend the training data for the morphological tagger MADA (Habash and Rambow, 2005), which is used on untokenized text. We train a new set of MADA classifier models using a combination of the original MADA (v 3.2) training data (578K words taken from PATBs 1, 2 and 3) and the enriched CATiB data (218K words). We apply the new MADA system to our development set and evaluate on several metrics. As a baseline, we process the same development set using MADA (v 3.2). Other than the training data used to construct the classifier models, there are no differences between the two systems. The CATiB-enriched system results in a Buckwalter POS tag accuracy of 85.6% (a 2.2% error reduction over the baseline). When evaluating on the set of 14 MADA morphological features, the new system results in a 85.7% accuracy (2.4% error reduction). The new system also improves PATB segmentation accuracy (99.2%, a 5.4% error reduction). In the future, we will evaluate the contribution of the additional annotations in the context of other applications, such as syntactic parsing.

6 Conclusion and Future Work

We have demonstrated that an underspecified version of an Arabic treebank can be fully specified for Arabic's rich morphology automatically at an accuracy rate of 94%-95% for POS tags and 97% for lemmas. Our approach combines a variety of techniques from corpus-based statistical models (which require some rich annotations) to linguistic rules that target specific phenomena. Since the underspecified treebank is much faster to manually annotate than its fully specified version, these results suggest that the cost of treebanking can be reduced by designing underspecified treebanks that can be subsequently enriched automatically.

In the future, we plan to extend the automatic enrichment effort to include more complex features such as empty nodes and semantic labels. We also plan to take the insights from this effort and apply them to treebanks of other languages. A small portion of a treebank that is fully annotated in rich format will of course be needed before we can apply these insights to other languages.

Acknowledgments

The first author was funded by a scholarship from the Saudi Arabian Ministry of Higher Education. The rest of the work was funded under DARPA projects number HR0011-08-C-0004 and HR0011-12-C-0014. Any opinions, findings and conclusions or recommendations expressed in this paper are those of the authors and do not necessarily reflect the views of DARPA.

References

M. Abdul-Mageed and M. Diab. 2012. AWATIF: A Multi-Genre Corpus for Modern Standard Arabic Subjectivity and Sentiment Analysis. *The 8th International Conference on Language Resources and Evaluation (LREC2012)*.

Sarah Alkuhlani and Nizar Habash. 2011. A Corpus for Modeling Morpho-Syntactic Agreement in Arabic: Gender, Number and Rationality. In *Proceedings of the 49th Annual Meeting of the Association for Computational Linguistics (ACL'11)*, Portland, Oregon, USA.

Yassine Benajiba, Mona Diab, and Paolo Rosso. 2009. Arabic Named Entity Recognition: A Feature-driven Study. *IEEE Transactions on Audio, Speech & Language Processing*, 17(5):926–934.

Tim Buckwalter. 2004. Buckwalter Arabic Morphological Analyzer Version 2.0. LDC catalog number LDC2004L02, ISBN 1-58563-324-0.

Mona Diab, Kadri Hacioglu, and Daniel Jurafsky. 2004. Automatic tagging of Arabic text: From raw text to base phrase chunks. In *Proceedings of the 5th Meeting of the North American Chapter of the Association for Computational Linguistics/Human Language Technologies Conference (HLT-NAACL04)*, Boston, MA.

Kais Dukes and Tim Buckwalter. 2010. A Dependency Treebank of the Quran using Traditional Arabic Grammar. In *Proceedings of the 7th international conference on Informatics and Systems (INFOS 2010)*, Cairo, Egypt.

Gülsen Eryigit, Joakim Nivre, and Kemal Oflazer. 2008. Dependency Parsing of Turkish. *Computational Linguistics*, 34(3):357–389.

Nizar Habash and Owen Rambow. 2005. Arabic Tokenization, Part-of-Speech Tagging and Morphological Disambiguation in One Fell Swoop. In *Proceedings of the 43rd Annual Meeting of the Association for Computational Linguistics (ACL'05)*, pages 573–580, Ann Arbor, Michigan.

Nizar Habash and Ryan Roth. 2009. CATiB: The Columbia Arabic Treebank. In *Proceedings of the ACL-IJCNLP 2009 Conference Short Papers*, pages 221–224, Suntec, Singapore.

Nizar Habash, Ryan Gabbard, Owen Rambow, Seth Kulick, and Mitch Marcus. 2007a. Determining Case in Arabic: Learning Complex Linguistic Behavior Requires Complex Linguistic Features. In *Proceedings of the 2007 Joint Conference on Empirical Methods in Natural Language Processing and Computational Natural Language Learning (EMNLP-CoNLL)*, pages 1084–1092.

Nizar Habash, Abdelhadi Soudi, and Tim Buckwalter. 2007b. On Arabic Transliteration. In A. van den Bosch and A. Soudi, editors, *Arabic Computational Morphology: Knowledge-based and Empirical Methods*. Springer.

Nizar Habash, Reem Faraj, and Ryan Roth. 2009. Syntactic Annotation in the Columbia Arabic Treebank. In *Proceedings of MEDAR International Conference on Arabic Language Resources and Tools*, Cairo, Egypt.

Nizar Habash, Ryan Roth, Owen Rambow, Ramy Eskander, and Nadi Tomeh. 2013. Morphological Analysis and Disambiguation for Dialectal Arabic. In *Proceedings of the 2013 Conference of the North American Chapter of the Association for Computational Linguistics: Human Language Technologies (NAACL-HLT)*, Atlanta, GA.

Nizar Habash. 2010. *Introduction to Arabic Natural Language Processing*. Morgan & Claypool Publishers.

Jan Hajič, Otakar Smrž, Tim Buckwalter, and Hubert Jin. 2005. Feature-based tagger of approximations of functional Arabic morphology. In *Proceedings of the Workshop on Treebanks and Linguistic Theories (TLT)*, Barcelona, Spain.

Erhard Hinrichs, Sandra Kübler, Karin Naumann, Heike Telljohann, and Julia Trushkina. 2004. Recent Developments in Linguistic Annotations of the TüBa-D/Z Treebank. In *Proceedings of the Third Workshop on Treebanks and Linguistic Theories*.

Eduard Hovy, Mitchell Marcus, Martha Palmer, Lance Ramshaw, and Ralph Weischedel. 2006. OntoNotes: The 90% Solution. In *NAACL '06: Proceedings of the Human Language Technology Conference of the NAACL, Companion Volume: Short Papers on XX*, pages 57–60, Morristown, NJ, USA.

Taku Kudo and Yuji Matsumoto. 2003. Fast Methods for Kernel-Based Text Analysis. In Erhard Hinrichs and Dan Roth, editors, *Proceedings of ACL*, pages 24–31.

Mohamed Maamouri, Ann Bies, Tim Buckwalter, and Wigdan Mekki. 2004. The Penn Arabic Treebank : Building a Large-Scale Annotated Arabic Corpus.

Mohamed Maamouri, Ann Bies, Sondos Krouna, Fatma Gaddeche, and Basma Bouziri, 2009a. *Penn Arabic Treebank Guidelines*. Linguistic Data Consortium.

Mohamed Maamouri, Ann Bies, and Seth Kulick. 2009b. Creating a Methodology for Large-Scale Correction of Treebank Annotation: The Case of the Arabic Treebank. In *Proceedings of MEDAR International Conference on Arabic Language Resources and Tools*, Cairo, Egypt.

Yuval Marton, Nizar Habash, and Owen Rambow. 2010. Improving Arabic Dependency Parsing with Lexical and Inflectional Morphological Features. In *Proceedings of the NAACL HLT 2010 First Workshop on Statistical Parsing of Morphologically-Rich Languages*, pages 13–21, Los Angeles, CA, USA, June.

Yuval Marton, Nizar Habash, and Owen Rambow. 2011. Improving Arabic Dependency Parsing with Form-based and Functional Morphological Features. In *Proceedings of the 49th Annual Meeting of the Association for Computational Linguistics (ACL'11)*, Portland, Oregon, USA.

Henrik Müller. 2010. Annotation of Morphology and NP Structure in the Copenhagen Dependency Treebanks (CDT). In *Proceedings of the Ninth International Workshop on Treebanks and Linguistic Theories*, pages 151–162.

Joakim Nivre, Igor M. Boguslavsky, and Leonid L. Iomdin. 2008. Parsing the SynTagRus Treebank of Russian. In *COLING '08: Proceedings of the 22nd International Conference on Computational Linguistics*, pages 641–648, Stroudsburg, PA, USA. Association for Computational Linguistics.

Joakim Nivre. 2009. Parsing Indian Languages with MaltParser. *Proceedings of the ICON09 NLP Tools Contest: Indian Language Dependency Parsing*, pages 12–18.

Stephan Oepen, Dan Flickinger, Kristina Toutanova, and Christoper D. Manning. 2002. LinGO Redwoods - A Rich and Dynamic Treebank for HPSG. In *LREC workshop on parsing evaluation*, Las Palmas, Spain.

Martha Palmer, Olga Babko-Malaya, Ann Bies, Mona Diab, Mohamed Maamouri, Aous Mansouri, and Wajdi Zaghouani. 2008. A Pilot Arabic Propbank. In *Proceedings of LREC*, Marrakech, Morocco, May.

Ryan Roth, Owen Rambow, Nizar Habash, Mona Diab, and Cynthia Rudin. 2008. Arabic Morphological Tagging, Diacritization, and Lemmatization Using Lexeme Models and Feature Ranking. In *Proceedings of ACL-08: HLT, Short Papers*, pages 117–120, Columbus, Ohio.

Noah Smith, David Smith, and Roy Tromble. 2005. Context-Based Morphological Disambiguation with Random Fields. In *Proceedings of the 2005 Conference on Empirical Methods in Natural Language Processing (EMNLP05)*, pages 475–482, Vancouver, Canada.

Otakar Smrž and Jan Hajič. 2006. The Other Arabic Treebank: Prague Dependencies and Functions. In Ali Farghaly, editor, *Arabic Computational Linguistics: Current Implementations*. CSLI Publications.

Otakar Smrž, Viktor Bielický, Iveta Kouřilová, Jakub Kráčmar, Jan Hajič, and Petr Zemánek. 2008. Prague Arabic Dependency Treebank: A Word on the Million Words. In *Proceedings of the Workshop on Arabic and Local Languages (LREC 2008)*, pages 16–23, Marrakech, Morocco.

Otakar Smrž. 2007. *Functional Arabic Morphology. Formal System and Implementation*. Ph.D. thesis, Charles University in Prague, Prague, Czech Republic.

Lamia Tounsi, Mohammed Attia, and Josef van Genabith. 2009. Automatic Treebank-Based Acquisition of Arabic LFG Dependency Structures. In *Proceedings of the EACL 2009 Workshop on Computational Approaches to Semitic Languages*, pages 45–52, Athens, Greece.

A Beam-Search Decoder for Normalization of Social Media Text with Application to Machine Translation

Pidong Wang
Department of Computer Science
National University of Singapore
13 Computing Drive
Singapore 117417
wangpd@comp.nus.edu.sg

Hwee Tou Ng
Department of Computer Science
National University of Singapore
13 Computing Drive
Singapore 117417
nght@comp.nus.edu.sg

Abstract

Social media texts are written in an informal style, which hinders other natural language processing (NLP) applications such as machine translation. Text normalization is thus important for processing of social media text. Previous work mostly focused on normalizing words by replacing an informal word with its formal form. In this paper, to further improve other downstream NLP applications, we argue that other normalization operations should also be performed, e.g., missing word recovery and punctuation correction. A novel beam-search decoder is proposed to effectively integrate various normalization operations. Empirical results show that our system obtains statistically significant improvements over two strong baselines in both normalization and translation tasks, for both Chinese and English.

1 Introduction

Social media texts include SMS (Short Message Service) messages, Twitter messages, Facebook updates, etc. They are different from formal texts due to their significant informal characteristics, so they always pose difficulties for applications such as machine translation (MT) (Aw et al., 2005) and named entity recognition (Liu et al., 2011), because of a lack of training data containing informal texts. Thus, the applications always suffer from a substantial performance drop when evaluated on social media texts. For example, Ritter et al. (2011) reported a drop from 90% to 76% on part-of-speech tagging, and Foster et al. (2011) found a drop of 20% in dependency parsing.

Creating training data of social media texts specifically for a text processing task is time-consuming. For example, to create parallel Chinese-English training texts for translation of social media texts, it takes three minutes on average to translate an informally written social media text of eleven words from Chinese into English. On the other hand, it takes thirty seconds to normalize the same message, a six-fold increase in speed. After training a text normalization system to normalize social media texts, we can use an existing statistical machine translation (SMT) system trained on normal texts (non-social media texts) to carry out translation. So we argue that normalization followed by regular translation is a more practical approach. Thus, text normalization is important for social media text processing.

Most previous work on normalization of social media text focused on word substitution (Beaufort et al., 2010; Gouws et al., 2011; Han and Baldwin, 2011; Liu et al., 2012). However, we argue that some other normalization operations besides word substitution are also critical for subsequent natural language processing (NLP) applications, such as missing word recovery (e.g., zero pronouns) and punctuation correction.

In this paper, we propose a *novel* beam-search decoder for normalization of social media text for MT. Our decoder can effectively integrate different normalization operations together. In contrast to previous work, some of our normalization operations are specifically designed for MT, e.g., missing word recovery based on conditional random fields

(CRF) (Lafferty et al., 2001) and punctuation correction based on dynamic conditional random fields (DCRF) (Sutton et al., 2004).

To the best of our knowledge, our work is the first to perform missing word recovery and punctuation correction for normalization of social media text, and also the first to perform message-level normalization of Chinese social media text. We investigate the effects on translating social media text after addressing various characteristics of informal social media text through normalization. To show the applicability of our normalization approach for different languages, we experiment with two languages, Chinese and English. We achieved statistically significant improvements over two strong baselines: an improvement of 9.98%/7.35% in BLEU scores for normalization of Chinese/English social media text, and an improvement of 1.38%/1.35% in BLEU scores for translation of Chinese/English social media text. We created two corpora: a Chinese corpus containing 1,000 Weibo[1] messages with their normalizations and English translations; and another similar English corpus containing 2,000 SMS messages from the NUS SMS corpus (How and Kan, 2005). As far as we know, our corpora are the first publicly available Chinese/English corpora for normalization and translation of social media text[2].

2 Related Work

Zhu et al. (2007) performed text normalization of informally written email messages using CRF (Lafferty et al., 2001). Due to its importance, normalization of social media text has been extensively studied recently. Aw et al. (2005) proposed a noisy channel model consisting of different operations: substitution of non-standard acronyms, deletion of flavor words, and insertion of auxiliary verbs and subject pronouns. Choudhury et al. (2007) used hidden Markov model to perform word-level normalization. Kobus et al. (2008) combined MT and automatic speech recognition (ASR) to better normalize French SMS message. Cook and Stevenson (2009) used an unsupervised noisy channel model considering different word formation processes. Han and Baldwin (2011) normalized informal words using morphophonemic similarity. Pennell and Liu (2011) only dealt with SMS abbreviations. Xue et al. (2011) normalized social media texts incorporating orthographic, phonetic, contextual, and acronym factors. Liu et al. (2012) designed a system combining different human perspectives to perform word-level normalization. Oliva et al. (2013) normalized Spanish SMS messages using a normalization and a phonetic dictionary. For normalization of Chinese social media text, Xia et al. (2005) investigated informal phrase detection, and Li and Yarowsky (2008) mined informal-formal phrase pairs from Web corpora.

All the above work focused on normalizing words. In contrast, our work also performs other normalization operations such as missing word recovery and punctuation correction, to further improve machine translation. Previously, Aw et al. (2006) adopted phrase-based MT to perform SMS normalization, and required a relatively large number of manually normalized SMS messages. In contrast, our approach performs beam search at the sentence level, and does not require large training data.

We evaluate the success of social media text normalization in the context of machine translation, so research on machine translation of social media text is relevant to our work. However, there is not much comparative evaluation of social media text translation other than the Haitian Creole to English SMS translation task in the 2011 Workshop on Statistical Machine Translation (WMT 2011) (Callison-Burch et al., 2011). However, the setup of the WMT 2011 task is different from ours, in that the task provided parallel training data of SMS texts and their translations. As such, text normalization is not necessary in that task. For example, the best reported system in that task (Costa-jussà and Banchs, 2011) did not perform SMS message normalization.

In speech to speech translation (Paul, 2009; Nakov et al., 2009), the input texts contain wrongly transcribed words due to errors in automatic speech recognition, whereas social media texts contain abbreviations, new words, etc. Although the input texts in both cases deviate from normal texts, the exact deviations are different.

[1]A Chinese version of Twitter at www.weibo.com

[2]Available at www.comp.nus.edu.sg/~nlp/corpora.html

Category	Freq.	Example
Punctuation	81	你好*[hi]* ～(你好 。*[hi .]*);
Pronunciation	47	表*[watch]*(不要*[don't]*); 酱紫(这样子*[this]*);
New word	43	萌*[bud]*(可爱*[cute]*);
Interjection	27	好的*[ok]* 哦*[oh]*(好的*[ok]*);
Pronoun	23	想要*[want]*(我*[i]* 想要*[want]*);
Segmentation	14	表酱紫(不要*[don't]* 这样子*[this]*);
Pronunciation	288	*4(for); oredi(already)*;
Abbreviation	98	*slp(sleep); whr(where)*;
Prefix	74	*lect(lecture); doin(doing)*;
Punctuation	69	*where r u(where r u ?)*;
Interjection	68	*ok lor .(ok .)*;
Quotation	24	*im sure(i 'm sure); dont go(don 't go)*;
Be	24	*i coming; you free?*;
Tokenization	19	*ok.why ?(ok . why ?)*;
Time	2	*end at 730(end at 7:30); 1130 am(11:30 am)*;

Table 1: Occurrence frequency of various informal characteristics in 200 Chinese/English social media texts.

3 Challenges in Normalization of Social Media Text

To better understand the informal characteristics of social media texts, we first analyzed a small sample of such texts in Chinese and English. We crawled 200 Chinese messages from Weibo. The informal characteristics of these messages are shown in the first half of Table 1. The manually normalized form is shown in round brackets, and the English gloss is shown in square brackets. Omitted, extraneous, and misused punctuation symbols occur frequently. On average, each Chinese message contains only less than one informal word, and many informal words are either new words or existing words with new meaning. The messages also contain redundant interjections like "哦*[oh]*". Pronouns are often omitted in Chinese messages, especially for "我*[I]*". Chinese informal words can be wrongly segmented due to lack of word segmentation training data containing informal words.

Similarly, 200 English SMS messages were randomly selected from the NUS SMS corpus (How and Kan, 2005). The informal characteristics of these messages are shown in the second half of Table 1. We found that our English messages contain more informal words than Chinese messages. English words are shortened in three ways: (1) using a shorter word form with similar pronunciation; (2) abbreviating a formal word; and (3) using only a prefix of a formal word. Other informal characteristics include: (1) informal punctuation conventions including omitted and misused punctuation; (2) redundant interjections; (3) quotation-related problems, e.g., omitted quotation marks; (4) "*be*" omission; (5) tokenization problems; and (6) informally written time expressions.

4 Methods

As can be seen in Section 3, social media texts of different languages exhibit different informal characteristics. For example, English messages have more informal words than Chinese messages, while punctuation problems are more prevalent for Chinese messages. Also, fixing different types of informal characteristics often depends on each other. For example, to be able to correct punctuation, it helps that the surrounding words are already correctly normalized. On the other hand, with punctuation already corrected, it will be easier to normalize the surrounding words.

In this section, we first present our punctuation correction method based on a DCRF model, and then present missing word recovery based on a CRF model. Next, we present a novel beam-search decoder for normalization of social media text, which can effectively integrate different normalization operations, including statistical and rule-based normalization. Finally, details of text normalization for Chinese and English are presented.

4.1 Punctuation Correction

In normalization of social media text, punctuation correction is also important besides word normalization, as the subsequent NLP applications are typically trained on formal texts with correct punctuation. We define punctuation correction as correcting punctuation in sentences which may have no or unreliable punctuation. The task performs three punctuation operations: insertion, deletion, and substitution.

To our knowledge, no previous work has been done on punctuation correction for normalization of social media text. In ASR, punctuation prediction only inserts punctuation symbols into ASR output that has no punctuation (Kim and Woodland, 2001; Huang and Zweig, 2002), but without punctuation deletion or substitution. Lu and Ng (2010) argued that punctuation prediction should be jointly performed with sentence boundary detection, so they modeled punctuation prediction using a two-layer DCRF model (Sutton et al., 2004).

We also believe that punctuation correction is closely related to sentence boundary detection. Thus, we propose a two-layer DCRF model for punctuation correction. Layer 1 gives the actual punctuation tags *None*, *Comma*, *Period*, *Question-Mark*, and *Exclamatory-Mark*. Layer 2 gives the sentence boundary, including tags *Declarative-Begin*, *Declarative-In*, *Question-Begin*, *Question-In*, *Exclamatory-Begin*, and *Exclamatory-In*, indicating whether the current word is at the beginning of (or inside) a declarative, question, or exclamatory sentence.

We use word n-grams ($n = 1, 2, 3$) and punctuation symbols within 5 words before and after the current word as binary features in the DCRF model. As an example, Table 2 shows the tags and features for the word "*where*" in the message "*where*| .|? *i*| *can*| *not*| *see*| *you*| !|!", where the punctuation symbols after the vertical bars are the corrected symbols.

Tags	**Content**
Layer 1	*Question-Mark*
Layer 2	*Question-Begin*
Features	**Content**
unigram	<s>@-1 where@0 i@1 can@2 not@3 see@4 you@5
bigram	<s>+where@-1 where+i@0 i+can@1 can+not@2 not+see@3 see+you@4 you+</s>@5
trigram	<s>+where+i@-1 where+i+can@0 i+can+not@1 can+not+see@2 not+see+you@3 see+you+</s>@4
punctuation	.@0 !@5

Table 2: An example of tags and features used in punctuation correction.

Due to the lack of informal training texts with corrected punctuation, we train our punctuation correction model on formal texts with synthetically created punctuation errors. We randomly add, delete, and substitute punctuation symbols in formal texts with equal probabilities. Specifically, for $s \in \{,.?!\}$, $P(none|s) = P(,|s) = P(.|s) = P(?|s) = P(!|s) = 0.2$ denotes the probability of replacing a punctuation symbol s (replacing s by $none$ denotes deletion); and for a real word (not a punctuation symbol) w, $P(none|w) = P(,|w) = P(.|w) = P(?|w) = P(!|w) = 0.2$ denotes the probability of inserting a punctuation symbol after w (inserting $none$ after w denotes no insertion).

4.2 Missing Word Recovery

As shown in Section 3, some words are often omitted in social media texts, e.g., the pronoun "我*[I]*" in Chinese and *be* in English. To fix this problem, we propose a CRF model to recover such missing words. We explain the CRF model using *be* in English. The CRF model has five tags: *None*, *BE*, *IS*, *ARE*, and *AM*. In an input sentence, every token (including words, punctuation symbols, and a special start-of-sentence placeholder) will be assigned a tag, denoting the insertion of the form of *be* after the token. We use the same n-gram features as our punctuation correction model, but exclude the punctuation features. The model is trained on synthetically created training texts in which *be* has been randomly deleted with probability 0.5.

4.3 A Decoder for Text Normalization

When designing our text normalization system, we aim for a general framework that can be applied to text normalization across different languages with minimal effort. This is a challenging task, since social media texts in different languages exhibit different informal characteristics, as illustrated in Section 3. Motivated by the beam-search decoders for SMT (Koehn et al., 2007), ASR (Young et al., 2002), and grammatical error correction (Dahlmeier and Ng, 2012), we propose a novel beam-search decoder for normalization of social media text.

Given an input message, the normalization decoder searches for its best normalization, i.e., the best hypothesis, by iteratively performing two subtasks: (1) producing new sentence-level hypotheses from hypotheses in the current stack, carried out by *hypothesis producers*; and (2) evaluating the new hypotheses to retain good ones, carried out by *feature functions*. Each hypothesis is the result of applying successive normalization operations on the initial input message, where each normalization operation is carried out by one hypothesis producer that deals with one aspect of the informal characteristics of social media text. The hypotheses are grouped into stacks, where stack i stores all hypotheses obtained by applying i hypothesis producers on the input message. The beam-search algorithm is shown

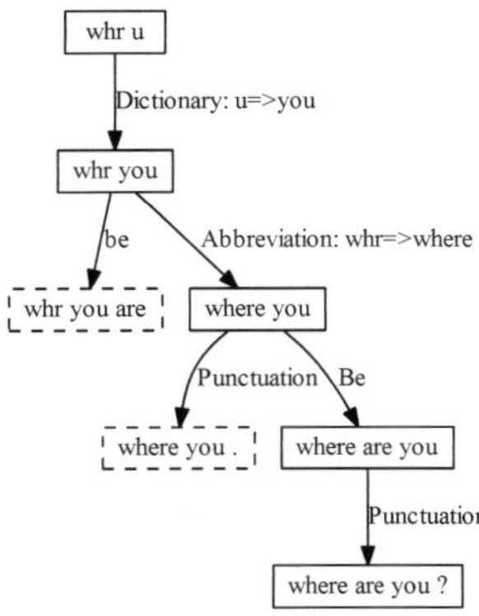

Figure 1: An example search tree when normalizing "*whr u*". The solid (dashed) boxes represent good (bad) hypotheses. The hypothesis producers are indicated on the edges.

in Algorithm 1, and Figure 1 shows an example search tree for an English message.

Algorithm 1 The beam-search decoder

INPUT: a raw message **M** whose length is **N**
RETURN: the best normalization for **M**

```
initialize hypothesisStacks[N+1] and hypothesisProducers;
add the initial hypothesis M to stack hypothesisStacks[0];
for i ← 0 to N-1 do
    for each hypo in hypothesisStacks[i] do
        for each producer in hypothesisProducers do
            for each newHypo produced by producer from hypo do
                add newHypo to hypothesisStacks[i+1];
                prune hypothesisStacks[i+1];
return the best hypothesis in hypothesisStacks[0...N];
```

We give the details of the hypothesis producers for Chinese and English social media texts in the next two subsections. A number of the hypothesis producers detect and deal with informal words w present in a hypothesis by relying on bigram counts of w in a large corpus of formal texts. Specifically, a word w in a hypothesis $\ldots w_{-1}ww_1\ldots$ is considered an informal word if both bigrams $w_{-1}w$ and ww_1 occur infrequently (≤ 5) in the formal corpus.

Given a hypothesis message h, the feature functions include a language model score (the normalized sentence probability of h), an informal word count penalty (the number of informal words detected in h), and count feature functions. Each count feature function gives the count of the modifications made by a hypothesis producer. The feature functions are used by the decoder to distinguish good hypotheses from bad ones. All feature functions are combined using a linear model to obtain the score for a hypothesis h:

$$score(h) = \sum_i \lambda_i f_i(h), \qquad (1)$$

where f_i is the i-th feature function with weight λ_i. The weights of the feature functions are tuned using the pairwise ranking optimization algorithm (Hopkins and May, 2011) on the development set.

4.4 Text Normalization for Chinese

Taking into account the informal characteristics of Chinese social media text in Section 3, we design the following **hypothesis producers** for Chinese text normalization:

Dictionary: We have manually assembled a dictionary of 703 informal-formal word pairs from the Internet. The word pairs are used to produce new hypotheses. For example, given a hypothesis "神马*[magical horse]* 时候*[time]*", if the dictionary contains the word pair "(神马,什么*[what]*)", the Dictionary hypothesis producer generates a new hypothesis "什么*[what]* 时候*[time]*".

Punctuation: A punctuation correction model (Section 4.1) is adopted to correct punctuation in the current hypothesis, e.g., it may normalize "什么*[what]* 时候*[time]*" into "什么 时候？".

Pronunciation: We use Chinese Pinyin to model the pronunciation similarity of words. To accomplish this, we pair some Pinyin initials that sound similar into a group. The groups of paired Pinyin initials are *(c, ch)*, *(s, sh)*, and *(z, zh)*. For example, given the hypothesis "北京*[Beijing]* 筒子*[tube]* 来了*[come]*", the Pinyin of the informal word "筒子" is "*t ong z i*". The Pinyin of the formal word "同志*[comrade]*" is "*t ong zh i*". Since the similar sounding Pinyin initials *z* and *zh* are paired in a group, a new hypothesis "北京*[Beijing]* 同志*[comrade]* 来了*[come]*" can be produced.

In practice, this hypothesis producer can propose many spurious candidates w' for an informal word w. As such, after we replace w by w' in the hypothesis, we require that some 4-gram containing w' and its surrounding words in the hypothesis appears in a formal corpus. We call this filtering process *contextual filtering*.

Pronoun: With the method of Section 4.2, a CRF model is trained to recover the missing pronoun "我*[I]*".

Interjection: If a word w in a pre-defined list of frequent redundant interjections appears at the end of a sentence, we produce a new hypothesis by removing w, e.g., from "好的*[ok]* 哦*[oh]*" to "好的*[ok]*".

Resegmentation: This hypothesis producer fixes word segmentation problems. If an informal word is a concatenation of two constituent informal words w_1 and w_2 in our normalization dictionary, the informal word will be segmented into two words w_1 and w_2. As a result, the Dictionary hypothesis producer can subsequently normalize w_1 and w_2.

4.5 Text Normalization for English

Similar to Chinese text normalization, we also create the Dictionary, Punctuation, and Interjection hypothesis producers for English text normalization. We also add the following English-specific hypothesis producers:

Pronunciation: This hypothesis producer uses pronunciation similarity to find formal candidates for a given informal word. It considers a word as a sequence of letters and convert it into a sequence of phones using phrase-based SMT trained on the CMU pronouncing dictionary (Weide, 1998). Similar sounding phones are paired together in a group: *(ah, ao)*, *(ow, uw)*, and *(s, z)*. To illustrate, in the hypothesis "*wat is it*", the informal word "*wat*" maps to the phone sequence "*w ao t*". Since the formal word "*what*" maps to the phone sequence "*w ah t*" and the phones *ah* and *ao* are paired in a group, the new hypothesis "*what is it*" is generated.

Be: We train a CRF model to recover missing words *be*, as described in Section 4.2.

Retokenization: This hypothesis producer fixes tokenization problems. More precisely, given an informal word which is not a URL or email address and contains a period, it splits the informal word at the period. For example, "*how r u.where r u*" is normalized to "*how r u . where r u*".

Prefix: This hypothesis producer generates a formal word w' for an informal word w if w is a prefix of w'. To avoid spurious candidates, we only generate w' if $|w| \geq 3$ and $|w'| - |w| \leq 4$.

Quotation: If an informal word ends with a letter in *(m, s, t)* and if the word produced by inserting a quotation mark before the letter is a formal word, a new hypothesis with the quotation mark inserted is produced. This hypothesis producer thus generates "*i'm*" from "*im*", "*she's*" from "*shes*", "*isn't*" from "*isnt*", etc.

Abbreviation: Letters denoting the vowels in a formal word are often deleted to form an informal word. This hypothesis producer generates a formal word w' from an informal word w if w' can be obtained from w by adding missing vowels. To avoid spurious candidates, we only consider w where $|w| \geq 2$.

Time: If a number can be a potential time expression and appears after "*at*" or before "*am*" or "*pm*", a new hypothesis is produced by changing the number into a time expression, e.g., "*1130 am*" is normalized to "*11 : 30 am*".

Since the Pronunciation, Prefix, and Abbreviation hypothesis producers can propose spurious candidates for an informal word, we also use contextual filtering to further filter the candidates for these hypothesis producers.

5 Experiments

5.1 Evaluation Corpora

As previous work (Choudhury et al., 2007; Han and Baldwin, 2011; Liu et al., 2012) mostly focused on word normalization, no data is available with corrected punctuation and recovered missing words. We thus create the following two corpora (Table 3):

Chinese-English corpus We crawled 1,000 messages from Weibo which were first normalized into formal Chinese and then translated into formal English. The first half of the corpus serves as our development set to tune our text normalization decoder for Chinese, while the second half serves as the test set to evaluate text normalization for Chinese and Chinese-English MT.

English-Chinese corpus From the NUS English SMS corpus (How and Kan, 2005), we randomly selected 2,000 messages. The messages were first normalized into formal English and then translated into formal Chinese. Similar to the Chinese-English corpus, the first half of the corpus serves as our development set while the second half serves as the test set.

Corpus	# messages	# tokens (EN/CN/NCN)
CN2EN-dev	500	6.95K/5.45K/5.70K
CN2EN-test	500	7.14K/5.64K/5.82K
Corpus	**# messages**	**# tokens (EN/CN/NEN)**
EN2CN-dev	1,000	16.63K/18.14K/18.21K
EN2CN-test	1,000	16.14K/17.69K/17.76K

Table 3: Statistics of the corpora. *CN2EN-dev*/*CN2EN-test* is the development/test set in our Chinese-English experiments. *EN2CN-dev*/*EN2CN-test* is the development/test set in our English-Chinese experiments. *NEN*/*NCN* denotes manually normalized English/Chinese texts.

The formal corpus used (as described in Section 4) is the concatenation of two Chinese-English spoken parallel corpora: the IWSLT 2009 corpus (Paul, 2009) and another spoken text corpus collected at the Harbin Institute of Technology[3]. The language model used for Chinese (English) text normalization is the Chinese (English) side of the formal corpus and the LDC Chinese (English) Gigaword corpus.

To evaluate the effect of text normalization on MT, we build phrase-based MT systems using Moses (Koehn et al., 2007), with word alignments generated by GIZA++ (Och and Ney, 2003). The MT training data contains the above formal corpus and some LDC[4] parallel corpora (LDC2000T46, LDC2002E18, LDC2003E14, LDC2004E12, LDC2005T06, LDC2005T10, LDC2007T23, LDC2008T06, LDC2008T08, LDC2008T18, LDC2009T02, LDC2009T06, LDC2009T15, LDC2010T03). In total, 214M/192M English/Chinese tokens are used to train our MT systems. The language model of the Chinese-English (English-Chinese) MT system is the English (Chinese) side of the FBIS corpus (LDC2003E14) and the English (Chinese) Gigaword corpus. Our MT systems are tuned on the manually normalized messages of our development sets.

Following (Aw et al., 2006; Oliva et al., 2013), we use BLEU scores (Papineni et al., 2002) to evaluate text normalization. We also use BLEU scores to evaluate MT quality. We use the sign test to determine statistical significance, for both text normalization and translation.

[3]`http://mitlab.hit.edu.cn/`

[4]`http://www.ldc.upenn.edu/Catalog/`

5.2 Baselines

We compare our text normalization decoder against three baseline methods for performing text normalization. We then send the respective normalized texts to the same MT system to evaluate the effect of text normalization on MT.

The simplest baseline for text normalization is one that does no text normalization. The raw text (un-normalized) is simply passed on to the MT system for translation. We call this baseline ORIGINAL.

The second baseline, LATTICE, is to use a lattice to normalize text. For each input message, a lattice is generated in which each informal word is augmented with its formal candidates taken from the same normalization dictionary (downloaded from Internet) used in our text normalization decoder. The lattice is then decoded by the same language model used in our text normalization decoder to generate the normalized text (Stolcke, 2002). Another possible way of using lattice is to directly feed the lattice to the MT system (Eidelman et al., 2011), but since in this paper, we assume that the MT system can only translate plain text, we leave this as future work.

The third baseline, PBMT, is a competitive baseline that performs text normalization via phrase-based MT, as proposed in Aw et al. (2006). Moses (Koehn et al., 2007) is used to perform text normalization, by "translating" un-normalized text to normalized text. The training data used is the same development set used in our text normalization decoder. The normalized text is then sent to our MT system for translation. This method was also used in the SMS translation task of WMT 2011 by (Stymne, 2011).

In the tables showing experimental results, normalization and translation BLEU scores that are significantly higher than ($p < 0.01$) the LATTICE or PBMT baseline are **in bold** or <u>underlined</u>, respectively.

5.3 Chinese-English Experimental Results

The Chinese-English normalization and translation results are shown in Table 4. The first group of experiments is the three baselines, and the second group is an oracle experiment using manually normalized messages as the output of text normaliza-

System	BLEU scores (%) Normalization	MT
ORIGINAL baseline	61.01	9.06
LATTICE baseline	74.52	11.50
PBMT baseline	76.77	12.65
ORACLE	100.00	15.04
Dictionary	**77.80**	12.35
Punctuation	65.95	9.63
Pronunciation	61.30	9.13
Pronoun	61.11	9.01
Interjection	61.05	9.14
Resegmentation	60.98	9.03
Dictionary	**77.80**	12.35
+Punctuation	**84.69**	**13.37**
+Pronunciation	**84.69**	**13.40**
+Pronoun	**84.96**	**13.50**
+Interjection	**85.33**	**13.68**
+Resegmentation	**86.75**	**14.03**

Table 4: Chinese-English experimental results.

tion which indicates the theoretical upper bounds of perfect normalization. In the normalization experiments, the ORIGINAL baseline gets a BLEU score of 61.01%, and the LATTICE baseline greatly improves the ORIGINAL baseline by 13.51%, which shows that the dictionary collected from the Internet is highly effective in text normalization. The PBMT baseline further improves the BLEU score by 2.25%. In the corresponding MT experiments, as the normalization BLEU scores increase, the MT BLEU scores also increase.

The third group is the isolated experiments, i.e., each experiment only uses one hypothesis producer. As expected, the individual hypothesis producers alone do not work well except the Dictionary hypothesis producer. One interesting discovery is that the Dictionary hypothesis producer outperforms the LATTICE baseline, which shows that our normalization decoder can utilize the dictionary more effectively, probably because of the additional features used in our normalization decoder such as the informal word penalty. The Resegmentation hypothesis producer alone worsens the BLEU scores, since it can only split informal words, and is designed to work together with other hypothesis producers to normalize words.

The last group is the combined experiments. We add each hypothesis producer in the order of its normalization effectiveness in the isolated experiments. Adding the Punctuation hypothesis producer greatly improves the BLEU scores of both normalization and translation, which confirms the importance of punctuation correction. The Pronoun and Interjection hypothesis producers also contribute some improvements. Finally, Resegmentation significantly improves the normalization/translation BLEU scores by 1.42%/0.35%. Compared with the isolated experiments, the combined experiments show that our normalization decoder can effectively integrate different hypothesis producers to achieve better performance for both text normalization and translation.

Overall, in the Chinese text normalization experiments, our normalization decoder outperforms the best baseline PBMT by 9.98% in BLEU score. In the Chinese-English MT experiments, the normalized texts output by our normalization decoder lead to improved translation quality compared to normalization by the PBMT baseline, by 1.38% in BLEU score.

5.4 English-Chinese Experimental Results

The English-Chinese normalization and translation results are shown in Table 5, with the same experimental setup as in the Chinese-English experiments.

The text normalization BLEU score of the ORIGINAL baseline is much lower in English compared to Chinese, since the English texts contain more informal words. Again, the individual hypothesis producers alone do not work well, except the Dictionary hypothesis producer. The Retokenization hypothesis producer greatly improves the normalization/translation BLEU scores by 2.37%/0.86%. The Punctuation hypothesis producer helps less for English compared to Chinese, suggesting that our Chinese texts contain noisier punctuation.

Overall, we achieved similar improvements in English text normalization and English-Chinese translation, and the improvements in BLEU scores are 7.35% and 1.35% respectively.

5.5 Further Analysis

The effect of contextual filtering. To measure the effect of contextual filtering proposed in Section 4.4, we ran our normalization decoder without contextual filtering. We obtained BLEU scores of 65.05%/22.38% in the English-Chinese experiments, which were lower than 66.54%/22.81% ob-

System	BLEU scores (%) Normalization	MT
ORIGINAL baseline	37.38	13.63
LATTICE baseline	56.98	20.56
PBMT baseline	59.19	21.46
ORACLE	100.00	28.48
Dictionary	**59.90**	**20.84**
Retokenization	38.79	14.06
Prefix	38.68	13.90
Interjection	38.37	13.92
Quotation	38.04	13.65
Abbreviation	37.94	13.74
Time	37.65	13.66
Pronunciation	37.62	13.80
Punctuation	37.62	13.79
Be	37.47	13.59
Dictionary	**59.90**	**20.84**
+Retokenization	**62.27**	**21.70**
+Prefix	**63.22**	**21.88**
+Interjection	**64.85**	**22.30**
+Quotation	**65.24**	**22.31**
+Abbreviation	**65.35**	**22.34**
+Time	**65.59**	**22.38**
+Pronunciation	**65.64**	**22.38**
+Punctuation	**66.38**	**22.74**
+Be	**66.54**	**22.81**

Table 5: English-Chinese experimental results.

tained with contextual filtering. This shows the beneficial effect of contextual filtering.

Decoding speed. The decoding speed of our text normalization decoder was 0.2 seconds per message on our test sets, using a 2.27 GHz Intel Xeon CPU with 32 GB memory.

The effect of text normalization decoder on MT. We manually analyzed the effect of our text normalization decoder on MT. For example, given the un-normalized English test message "*yeah must sign up , im in lt25*", our English-Chinese MT system translated it into "对*[yeah]* 必须*[must]* 签署*[sign up]* ， im 在*[in]* lt25" On the other hand, our normalization decoder normalized it into "*yeah must sign up , i 'm in lt25 .*" which was then translated into "对 必须 签署 , 我 在 lt25 。" by our MT system. This example shows that our text normalization decoder uses word normalization and punctuation correction to improve translation.

6 Conclusion

This paper presents a novel beam-search decoder for normalization of social media text. Our decoder for text normalization effectively integrates multiple normalization operations. In our experiments, we achieved statistically significant improvements over two strong baselines: an improvement of 9.98%/7.35% in BLEU scores for normalization of Chinese/English social media text, and an improvement of 1.38%/1.35% in BLEU scores for translation of Chinese/English social media text. Future work can investigate how to more tightly integrate our beam-search decoder for text normalization with a standard MT decoder, e.g., by using a lattice or an n-best list.

Acknowledgments

We thank all the anonymous reviewers for their comments which have helped us improve this paper. This research is supported by the Singapore National Research Foundation under its International Research Centre @ Singapore Funding Initiative and administered by the IDM Programme Office.

References

AiTi Aw, Min Zhang, PohKhim Yeo, ZhenZhen Fan, and Jian Su. 2005. Input normalization for an English-to-Chinese SMS translation system. In *Proceedings of the Tenth MT Summit.*

AiTi Aw, Min Zhang, Juan Xiao, and Jian Su. 2006. A phrase-based statistical model for SMS text normalization. In *Proceedings of ACL-COLING.*

Richard Beaufort, Sophie Roekhaut, Louise-Amélie Cougnon, and Cédrick Fairon. 2010. A hybrid rule/model-based finite-state framework for normalizing SMS messages. In *Proceedings of ACL.*

Chris Callison-Burch, Philipp Koehn, Christof Monz, and Omar Zaidan. 2011. Findings of the 2011 workshop on statistical machine translation. In *Proceedings of WMT.*

Monojit Choudhury, Rahul Saraf, Vijit Jain, Animesh Mukherjee, Sudeshna Sarkar, and Anupam Basu. 2007. Investigation and modeling of the structure of texting language. *International Journal on Document Analysis and Recognition*, 10(3-4):157–174.

Paul Cook and Suzanne Stevenson. 2009. An unsupervised model for text message normalization. In *Proceedings of the Workshop on Computational Approaches to Linguistic Creativity.*

Marta R. Costa-jussà and Rafael E. Banchs. 2011. The BM-I2R Haitian-Créole-to-English translation system description for the WMT 2011 evaluation campaign. In *Proceedings of WMT.*

Daniel Dahlmeier and Hwee Tou Ng. 2012. A beam-search decoder for grammatical error correction. In *Proceedings of EMNLP-CoNLL.*

Vladimir Eidelman, Kristy Hollingshead, and Philip Resnik. 2011. Noisy SMS machine translation in low-density languages. In *Proceedings of WMT*.

Jennifer Foster, Özlem Çetinoglu, Joachim Wagner, Joseph Le Roux, Stephen Hogan, Joakim Nivre, Deirdre Hogan, and Josef Van Genabith. 2011. # hardtoparse: POS tagging and parsing the twitterverse. In *Proceedings of the AAAI Workshop On Analyzing Microtext*.

Stephan Gouws, Dirk Hovy, and Donald Metzler. 2011. Unsupervised mining of lexical variants from noisy text. In *Proceedings of the First Workshop on Unsupervised Learning in NLP*.

Bo Han and Timothy Baldwin. 2011. Lexical normalisation of short text messages: Makn sens a #twitter. In *Proceedings of ACL-HLT*.

Mark Hopkins and Jonathan May. 2011. Tuning as ranking. In *Proceedings of EMNLP*.

Yijue How and Min-Yen Kan. 2005. Optimizing predictive text entry for short message service on mobile phones. In *Proceedings of Human Computer Interfaces International*.

Jing Huang and Geoffrey Zweig. 2002. Maximum entropy model for punctuation annotation from speech. In *Proceedings of ICSLP*.

Ji Hwan Kim and P. C. Woodland. 2001. The use of prosody in a combined system for punctuation generation and speech recognition. In *Proceedings of Eurospeech*.

Catherine Kobus, François Yvon, and Géraldine Damnati. 2008. Normalizing SMS: are two metaphors better than one? In *Proceedings of COLING*.

Philipp Koehn, Hieu Hoang, Alexandra Birch, Chris Callison-Burch, Marcello Federico, Nicola Bertoldi, Brooke Cowan, Wade Shen, Christine Moran, Richard Zens, Chris Dyer, Ondrej Bojar, Alexandra Constantin, and Evan Herbst. 2007. Moses: Open source toolkit for statistical machine translation. In *Proceedings of ACL Demo and Poster Sessions*.

John D. Lafferty, Andrew McCallum, and Fernando C. N. Pereira. 2001. Conditional random fields: Probabilistic models for segmenting and labeling sequence data. In *Proceedings of the Eighteenth International Conference on Machine Learning*.

Zhifei Li and David Yarowsky. 2008. Mining and modeling relations between formal and informal Chinese phrases from web corpora. In *Proceedings of EMNLP*.

Xiaohua Liu, Shaodian Zhang, Furu Wei, and Ming Zhou. 2011. Recognizing named entities in tweets. In *Proceedings of ACL-HLT*.

Fei Liu, Fuliang Weng, and Xiao Jiang. 2012. A broad-coverage normalization system for social media language. In *Proceedings of ACL*.

Wei Lu and Hwee Tou Ng. 2010. Better punctuation prediction with dynamic conditional random fields. In *Proceedings of EMNLP*.

Preslav Nakov, Chang Liu, Wei Lu, and Hwee Tou Ng. 2009. The NUS statistical machine translation system for IWSLT 2009. In *Proceedings of the International Workshop on Spoken Language Translation*.

Franz Josef Och and Hermann Ney. 2003. A systematic comparison of various statistical alignment models. *Computational Linguistics*, 29(1):19–51.

J. Oliva, J. I. Serrano, M. D. Del Castillo, and Á. Igesias. 2013. A SMS normalization system integrating multiple grammatical resources. *Natural Language Engineering*, 19(1):121–141.

Kishore Papineni, Salim Roukos, Todd Ward, and Wei-Jing Zhu. 2002. BLEU: a method for automatic evaluation of machine translation. In *Proceedings of ACL*.

Michael Paul. 2009. Overview of the IWSLT 2009 evaluation campaign. In *Proceedings of the International Workshop on Spoken Language Translation*.

Deana L. Pennell and Yang Liu. 2011. A character-level machine translation approach for normalization of SMS abbreviations. In *Proceedings of IJCNLP*.

Alan Ritter, Sam Clark, Mausam, and Oren Etzioni. 2011. Named entity recognition in tweets: An experimental study. In *Proceedings of EMNLP*.

Andreas Stolcke. 2002. SRILM – An extensible language modeling toolkit. In *Proceedings of the International Conference on Spoken Language Processing*.

Sara Stymne. 2011. Spell checking techniques for replacement of unknown words and data cleaning for Haitian Creole SMS translation. In *Proceedings of WMT*.

Charles Sutton, Khashayar Rohanimanesh, and Andrew McCallum. 2004. Dynamic conditional random fields: Factorized probabilistic models for labeling and segmenting sequence data. In *Proceedings of the 21st International Conference on Machine Learning*.

Robert L. Weide. 1998. The CMU pronouncing dictionary. *URL: http://www.speech.cs.cmu.edu/cgi-bin/cmudict*.

Yunqing Xia, Kam-Fai Wong, and Wei Gao. 2005. NIL is not nothing: Recognition of Chinese network informal language expressions. In *4th SIGHAN Workshop on Chinese Language Processing*.

Zhenzhen Xue, Dawei Yin, and Brian D. Davison. 2011. Normalizing microtext. In *Proceedings of the AAAI Workshop on Analyzing Microtext*.

Steve Young, Gunnar Evermann, Dan Kershaw, Gareth Moore, Julian Odell, Dave Ollason, Valtcho Valtchev, and Phil Woodland. 2002. The HTK book. *Cambridge University Engineering Department*.

Conghui Zhu, Jie Tang, Hang Li, Hwee Tou Ng, and Tie-Jun Zhao. 2007. A unified tagging approach to text normalization. In *Proceedings of ACL*.

Parameter Estimation for LDA-Frames

Jiří Materna
Centre for Natural Language Processing
Faculty of Informatics, Masaryk University
Botanická 68a, 602 00, Brno, Czech Republic
xmaterna@fi.muni.cz

Abstract

LDA-frames is an unsupervised approach for identifying semantic frames from semantically unlabeled text corpora, and seems to be a useful competitor for manually created databases of selectional preferences. The most limiting property of the algorithm is such that the number of frames and roles must be predefined. In this paper we present a modification of the LDA-frames algorithm allowing the number of frames and roles to be determined automatically, based on the character and size of training data.

1 Introduction

Semantic frames and valency lexicons are useful lexical sources capturing semantic roles valid for a set of lexical units. The structures of linked semantic roles are called semantic frames. Linguists are using them for their ability to describe an interface between syntax and semantics. In practical natural language processing applications, they can be used, for instance, for the word sense disambiguation task or in order to resolve ambiguities in syntactic analysis of natural languages.

The lexicons of semantic frames or verb valencies are mainly created manually or semi-automatically by highly trained linguists. Manually created lexicons involve, for instance, a well-known lexicon of semantic frames FrameNet (Ruppenhofer et al., 2006) or a lexicon of verb valencies VerbNet (Schuler, 2006). These and other similar lexical resources have many promising applications, but suffer from several disadvantages:

- Creation of them requires manual work of trained linguists which is very time-consuming and expensive.
- Coverage of the resources is usually small or limited to some specific domain.
- Most of the resources do not provide any information about relative frequency of usage in corpora. For instance, both patterns `[Person]` *acquire* `[Physical_object]` and `[Person]` *acquire* `[Disease]` reflect correct usage of verb *acquire*, but the former is much more frequent in English.
- Notion of semantic classes and frames is subjectively biased when the frames are created manually without corpus evidence.

In order to avoid those problems we proposed a method for creating probabilistic semantic frames called LDA-frames (Materna, 2012). The main idea of LDA-frames is to generate the set of semantic frames and roles automatically by maximizing posterior probability of a probabilistic model on a syntactically annotated training corpus. A semantic role is represented as probability distribution over all its realizations in the corpus, a semantic frame as a tuple of semantic roles, each of them connected with some grammatical relation. For every lexical unit (a verb in case of computing verb valencies), a probability distribution over all semantic frames is generated, where the probability of a frame corresponds to the relative frequency of usage in the corpus for a given lexical unit. An example of LDA-frames computed on the British National Corpus is available at the LDA-frames website[1].

The original LDA-frames algorithm has two parameters that must be predefined – number of frames and number of roles – which is the most limiting property of the algorithm. A simple cross-validation approach can be used in case of very small data. However, real data is much bigger and it is not recommended to use such techniques. For example, the inference on the British National Corpus using a single core 2.4 GHz CPU takes several days to compute one reasonable combination of parameters.

In this paper we present a non-parametric modification of the LDA-frames algorithm allowing to determine the parameters automatically, based on the character and size of training data.

2 LDA-Frames

LDA-frames (Materna, 2012) is an unsupervised approach for identifying semantic frames from semantically unlabeled text corpora. In the LDA-frames, a frame is represented as a tuple of semantic roles, each of them connected with a grammatical relation i.e. subject, object, modifier, etc. These frames are related to a lexical unit via probability distribution. Every semantic role is represented as probability distribution over its realizations.

The method of automatic identification of semantic frames is based on probabilistic generative process. Training data for the algorithm consists of tuples of grammatical relation realizations acquired using a dependency parser from the training corpus for every lexical unit. For example, suppose that the goal is to generate semantic frames of verbs from a corpus for grammatical relations *subject* and *object*. The training data for lexical unit *eat* may look like {`(peter, cake)`, `(man, breakfast)`, `(dog, meat)`, ...}, where the first component of the tuples corresponds to *subject* and the second to *object*.

In the generative process, each grammatical relation realization is treated as being generated from a given semantic frame according to the realization distribution of the corresponding semantic role. Supposing the number of frames is given by parameter F, the number of semantic roles by R, the number of slots (grammatical relations) by S and the size of vocabulary is V. The realizations are generated as follows.

For each lexical unit $u \in \{1, 2, \ldots, U\}$:

1. Choose a frame distribution φ_u from $\text{Dir}(\alpha)$.
2. For each lexical unit realization $t \in \{1, 2, \ldots, T_u\}$ choose a frame $f_{u,t}$ from $\text{Multinomial}(\varphi_u)$, where $f_{u,t} \in \{1, 2, \ldots, F\}$.
3. For each slot $s \in \{1, 2, \ldots, S\}$ of frame $f_{u,t}$, generate a grammatical relation realization $w_{u,t,s}$ from $\text{Multinomial}(\theta_{r_{f_{u,t},s}})$, where $r_{f,s}$ is a projection $(f, s) \mapsto r$, which assigns a semantic role for each slot s in frame f. The multinomial distribution of realizations, symbolized by θ_r, for semantic role r is generated from $\text{Dir}(\beta)$.

The graphical model for LDA-Frames is shown in figure 1. It is parametrized by hyperparameters of prior distributions α and β, usually set by hand to a value between 0.01 – 0.1.

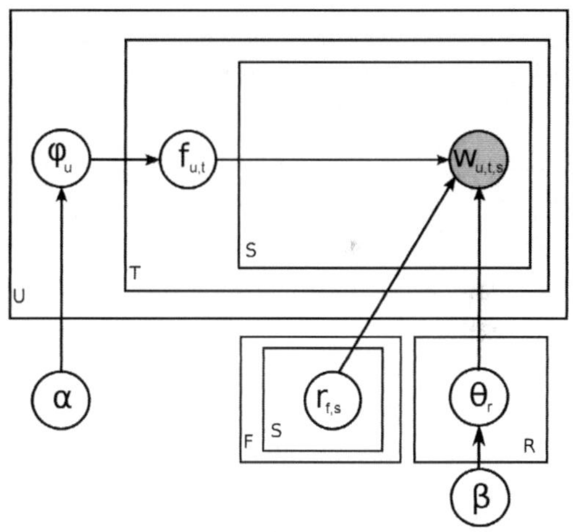

Figure 1: Graphical model for LDA-frames.

The inference is performed using the Collapsed Gibbs sampling (Neal, 2000), where the θ and φ distributions are marginalized out of the equations. In each iteration, latent variables $f_{u,t}$ and $r_{f,s}$ are sampled as follows

$$P(f_{u,t}|\mathbf{f}^{-(u,t)}, \mathbf{r}, \mathbf{w}, \alpha, \beta) \propto$$
$$(fc^{-(u,t)}_{f_{u,t},u} + \alpha) \prod_{s=1}^{S} \frac{wc^{-(u,t,s)}_{w_{u,t,s},r_{f_{u,t},s}} + \beta}{wc^{-(u,t,s)}_{*,r_{f_{u,t},s}} + V\beta} \quad (1)$$

[1] http://nlp.fi.muni.cz/projekty/lda-frames/

$$P(r_{f,s}|\mathbf{f},\mathbf{r}^{-(f,s)},\mathbf{w},\alpha,\beta) \propto \prod_{v=1}^{V} \left(\frac{wc_{v,r_{f,s}}^{-(f,s)} + \beta}{wc_{*,r_{f,s}}^{-(f,s)} + V\beta} \right)^{wc_{f,s,v}}, \tag{2}$$

where $fc_{f,u}^{-(u,t)}$ is the number of times frame f is assigned to lexical unit u excluding (u,t), $wc_{v,r}^{-(u,t,s)}$ is the number of times word v is assigned to role r excluding (u,t,s), and $wc_{f,s,v}$ is the number of times word v is assigned to slot s in frame f. The asterisk sign * stands for any value in its position.

After having all latent variables $\mathbf{f}$ and $\mathbf{r}$ inferred, one can proceed to compute the lexical unit–frame distribution and the semantic role–word distribution using the following formulas:

$$\varphi_u = \frac{fc_{f,u} + \alpha}{\sum_f fc_{f,u} + F\alpha} \tag{3}$$

$$\theta_r = \frac{wc_{v,r} + \beta}{\sum_v wc_{v,r} + V\beta}. \tag{4}$$

3 Parameter Estimation

As one can see from the LDA-frames model, the requirement is to define the number of frames and roles in advance. It is not clear, however, how to select the best values that depend on several factors. First of all, the number of frames and roles usually increase with the growing size of training corpus. If the training data is small and covers just a small proportion of lexical unit usage patterns, the number of semantic frames should be small as well. The parameters are also affected by the granularity of roles and frames. One way to estimate the parameters automatically is to select those that maximize posterior probability of the model given training data.

LDA-frames algorithm generates frames from the Dirichlet distribution (DD) which requires a fixed number of components. Similarly, the latent variables $r_{f,s}$ are chosen from a fixed set of semantic roles. In order to be able to update the number of frames and roles during the inference process, we propose to add the Chinese restaurant process (CRP) (Aldous, 1985) prior for the $r_{f,s}$ variables, and to replace the Dirichlet distribution the semantic frames are generated from with the Dirichlet process (Ferguson, 1973).

3.1 Number of Semantic Roles

In the original version of the LDA-frames model, the latent variables $r_{f,s}$, representing semantic role assignment for slot s in frame f, are chosen from a fixed set of semantic roles without any prior distribution. We propose to generate $r_{f,s}$ from the CRP, which is a single parameter distribution over partitions of integers. The generative process can be described by using an analogy with a Chinese restaurant. Consider a restaurant with an infinite number of tables, each of them associated with some dish, and N customers choosing a table. The first customer sits at the first table. The nth customer sits at table t drawn from the following distribution

$$\begin{aligned} P(t = \text{occupied table } i) &= \frac{n_i}{\gamma + n - 1} \\ P(t = \text{next unoccupied table}) &= \frac{\gamma}{\gamma + n - 1}, \end{aligned} \tag{5}$$

where n_i is the number of customers sitting at the table i and $\gamma > 0$ is a concentration parameter which controls how often a customer chooses a new table. The seating plan makes a partition of the customers (Aldous, 1985).

In the proposed modification of the LDA-frames model, the dishes are replaced with the semantic role numbers and customers with slots of frames. In the model we use prior distribution ω corresponding to the CRP with concentration parameter γ. The latent variables $r_{f,s}$ are then sampled as follows

$$P(r_{f,s}|\mathbf{f},\mathbf{r}^{-(f,s)},\mathbf{w},\alpha,\beta,\gamma) \propto (rc_{r_{f,s}}^{-(f,s)} + \gamma) \prod_{v=1}^{V} \left(\frac{wc_{v,r_{f,s}}^{-(f,s)} + \beta}{wc_{*,r_{f,s}}^{-(f,s)} + V\beta} \right)^{wc_{f,s,v}}, \tag{6}$$

where $rc_r^{-(f,s)}$ is the number of times role r is used in any frame and slot excluding slot s in frame f. Notice that the sampling space has $R+1$ dimensions with the probability of the last unseen component proportional to

$$\gamma \prod_{v=1}^{V} \frac{1}{V^{wc_{f,s,v}}}. \tag{7}$$

3.2 Number of Semantic Frames

Estimating the number of frames is a little bit more complicated than the case of semantic roles. The idea is to replace DD φ_u with the Dirichlet process.

The Dirichlet process $DP(\alpha_0, G_0)$ is a stochastic process that generates discrete probability distributions. It has two parameters, a base distribution G_0 and a concentration parameter $\alpha_0 > 0$. A sample from the Dirichlet process (DP) is then

$$G = \sum_{k=1}^{\infty} \beta_k \delta_{\phi_k}, \tag{8}$$

where ϕ_k are independent random variables distributed according to G_0, δ_{ϕ_k} is an atom at ϕ_k, and weights β_k are also random and dependent on the parameter α_0 (Teh et al., 2006). Simply, DP is a distribution over some infinite and discrete distributions. It is the reason why DP is often used instead of DD in order to avoid using a fixed number of components.

The question, however, is how to make the sampled frames shared between different lexical units. We propose to generate base distributions of the DPs from GEM distribution (Pitman, 2002) τ with concentration parameter δ. The idea is inspired by the Hierarchical Dirichlet Process (Teh et al., 2006) used for topic modeling. The graphical model of the non-parametric LDA-frames is shown in figure 2.

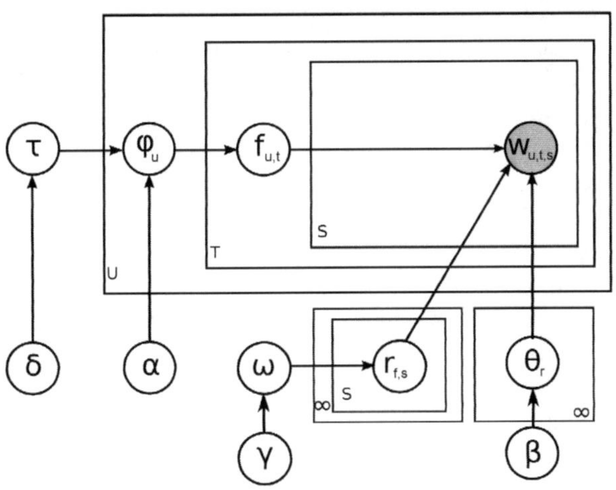

Figure 2: Graphical model for non-parametric LDA-frames.

Since it is hard to integrate out the DP with base distribution generated from GEM in this model, we proceeded to sample τ separately (Porteous, 2010). The base distribution proportions can be sampled by simulating how new components are created for $fc_{f,u}$ draws from DP with the concentration parameter $\alpha\tau_f$, which is a sequence of Bernoulli trials for each u and f (Heinrich, 2011):

$$\begin{aligned} P(u_{f,u,r} = 1) &= \frac{\alpha\tau_f}{\alpha\tau_f + r - 1} \forall r \in [1, fc_{f,u}] \\ \tau &\sim \mathrm{Dir}(\{u_f\}_f, \delta) \text{ with } u_f = \sum_u \sum_r u_{f,u,r}. \end{aligned} \tag{9}$$

Finally, the latent variables $f_{u,t}$ are sampled as follows

$$\begin{aligned} &P(f_{u,t} | \mathbf{f}^{-(u,t)}, \mathbf{r}, \mathbf{w}, \alpha, \beta, \tau) \propto \\ &(fc^{-(u,t)}_{f_{u,t},u} + \alpha\tau_f) \prod_{s=1}^{S} \frac{wc^{-(u,t,s)}_{w_{u,t,s}, r_{f_{u,t},s}} + \beta}{wc^{-(u,t,s)}_{*, r_{f_{u,t},s}} + V\beta}. \end{aligned} \tag{10}$$

4 Evaluation

The non-parametric algorithm was evaluated by an experiment on a synthetic data set consisting of 155 *subject-object* tuples. The training data was generated randomly from a predefined set of 7 frames and 4 roles for 16 verbs using the following algorithm. For every lexical unit u:

1. Choose a number of corpus realizations $N_u \in \{5, \dots, 15\}$ from the uniform distribution.

2. For each realization $n_u \in \{1, \dots, N_u\}$, among all permitted frames for lexical unit u, choose a semantic frame f_{n_u} from the uniform distribution.

3. For each frame f_{n_u}, generate a realization of all its roles from the uniform distribution.

Each semantic role had 6 possible realizations on average, some of them assigned to more than one semantic role to reflect the character of real languages. Since the data was generated artificially, we knew the number of frames and roles, how the frames were defined, and which frame and which role was responsible for generating each realization in the data.

We ran the non-parametric algorithm with hyperparameters $\alpha = 5, \beta = \gamma = 0.1, \delta = 1.5$. It has been shown that the selection of hyperparameters has little impact on the resulting frames when they are in some reasonable range, thus, the hyperparameters were chosen empirically by hand. The experiment led to correct assignments of $f_{u,t}$ and $r_{f,s}$ after 56 iterations on average (based on 10 independent runs of the algorithm).

In order to compare the non-parametric algorithm with the original, we ran the original algorithm with the same data that had the number of frames and roles set to $R \in \{1 \dots 10\}$, $F \in \{1 \dots 20\}$, and measured the perplexity of the data given to the model after convergence. The perplexities for all settings are shown in figure 3. The lowest perplexity was reached with $F = 7$, $R = 4$ and had the same value as the case of the non-parametric algorithm. The $f_{u,t}$ and $r_{f,s}$ assignments were correct as well.

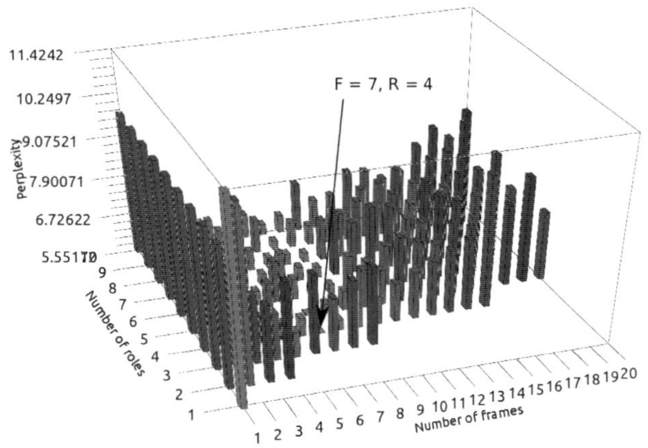

Figure 3: Perplexities for different values of F and R.

We also ran the non-parametric algorithm with the same hyperparameters on real data (1.4 millions of *subject-object* tuples) acquired from the British National Corpus[2] using the Stanford Parser (de Marneffe et al., 2006). The algorithm reached the optimal perplexity with 427 frames and 144 roles. This experiment has been performed only for illustrating the algorithm on real data. Because of long running time of the algorithm on such huge data set, we did not perform the same experiments as with the case of the small synthetic data.

5 Conclusion

In this paper we presented a method for estimating the number of frames and roles for the LDA-frames model. The idea is based on using the Chinese Restaurant Process and the Dirichlet Process instead of the Dirichlet Distributions and selecting such parameters that maximize the posterior probability of the model for given training data. An experiment showed that the non-parametric algorithm infers correct values of both the number of frames and roles on a synthetic data set.

Acknowledgments

This work has been partly supported by the Ministry of Education of the Czech Republic under the project LINDAT-Clarin LM2010013.

References

Aldous, D. J. (1985). Exchangeability and Related Topics. *École d'Été de Probabilités de Saint-Flour XIII – 1983*, 1117:1 – 198.

de Marneffe, M.-C., MacCartney, B., and Manning, C. D. (2006). Generating Typed Dependency Parses from Phrase Structure Parses. In *The International Conference on Language Resources and Evaluation (LREC) 2006*.

Ferguson, T. S. (1973). A Bayesian Analysis of Some Nonparametric Problems. *The Annals of Statistics*, 1:209 – 230.

Heinrich, G. (2011). "Infinite LDA" – Implementing the HDP with Minimum Code complexity. Technical report.

Materna, J. (2012). LDA-Frames: An Unsupervised Approach to Generating Semantic Frames. In Gelbukh, A., editor, *Proceedings of the 13th International Conference CICLing 2012, Part I*, pages 376–387, New Delhi, India. Springer Berlin / Heidelberg.

Neal, R. M. (2000). Markov Chain Sampling Methods for Dirichlet Process Mixture Models. *Journal of computational and graphical statistics*, 9(2):249–265.

Pitman, J. (2002). Combinatorial Stochastic Processes. *Lecture Notes for St. Flour Summer School*.

Porteous, I. (2010). *Networks of mixture blocks for non parametric bayesian models with applications*. PhD thesis, University of California.

Ruppenhofer, J., Ellsworth, M., Petruck, M. R. L., Johnson, C. R., and Scheffczyk, J. (2006). FrameNet II: Extended Theory and Practice. http://www.icsi.berkeley.edu/framenet.

Schuler, K. K. (2006). *VerbNet: A Broad-Coverage, Comprehensive Verb Lexicon*. PhD thesis, University of Pennsylvania.

Teh, Y. W., Jordan, M. I., Beal, M. J., and Blei, D. M. (2006). Hierarchical Dirichlet processes . *Journal of the American Statistical Association*, 101:1566 – 1581.

[2] http://www.natcorp.ox.ac.uk

Approximate PCFG Parsing Using Tensor Decomposition

Shay B. Cohen
Department of Computer Science
Columbia University, USA
scohen@cs.columbia.edu

Giorgio Satta
Department of Information Engineering
University of Padua, Italy
satta@dei.unipd.it

Michael Collins
Department of Computer Science
Columbia University, USA
mcollins@cs.columbia.edu

Abstract

We provide an approximation algorithm for PCFG parsing, which asymptotically improves time complexity with respect to the input grammar size, and prove upper bounds on the approximation quality. We test our algorithm on two treebanks, and get significant improvements in parsing speed.

1 Introduction

The problem of speeding-up parsing algorithms based on probabilistic context-free grammars (PCFGs) has received considerable attention in recent years. Several strategies have been proposed, including beam-search, best-first and A*. In this paper we focus on the standard approach of approximating the source PCFG in such a way that parsing accuracy is traded for efficiency.

Nederhof (2000) gives a thorough presentation of old and novel ideas for approximating non-probabilistic CFGs by means of finite automata, on the basis of specialized preprocessing of self-embedding structures. In the probabilistic domain, approximation by means of regular grammars is also exploited by Eisner and Smith (2005), who filter long-distance dependencies on-the-fly.

Beyond finite automata approximation, Charniak et al. (2006) propose a coarse-to-fine approach in which an approximated (not necessarily regular) PCFG is used to construct a parse forest for the input sentence. Some statistical parameters are then computed on such a structure, and exploited to filter parsing with the non-approximated grammar. The approach can also be iterated at several levels. In the non-probabilistic setting, a similar filtering approach was also proposed by Boullier (2003), called "guided parsing."

In this paper we rely on an algebraic formulation of the inside-outside algorithm for PCFGs, based on a tensor formulation developed for latent-variable PCFGs in Cohen et al. (2012). We combine the method with known techniques for tensor decomposition to approximate the source PCFG, and develop a novel algorithm for approximate PCFG parsing. We obtain improved time upper bounds with respect to the input grammar size for PCFG parsing, and provide error upper bounds on the PCFG approximation, in contrast with existing heuristic methods.

2 Preliminaries

This section introduces the special representation for probabilistic context-free grammars that we adopt in this paper, along with the decoding algorithm that we investigate. For an integer $i \geq 1$, we let $[i] = \{1, 2, \ldots, i\}$.

2.1 Probabilistic Context-Free Grammars

We consider context-free grammars (CFGs) in Chomsky normal form, and denote them as $(\mathcal{N}, \mathcal{L}, \mathcal{R})$ where:

- $\mathcal{N}$ is the finite set of nonterminal symbols, with $m = |\mathcal{N}|$, and $\mathcal{L}$ is the finite set of words (lexical tokens), with $\mathcal{L} \cap \mathcal{N} = \emptyset$ and with $n = |\mathcal{L}|$.
- $\mathcal{R}$ is a set of rules having the form $a \to b\ c$, $a, b, c \in \mathcal{N}$, or the form $a \to x$, $a \in \mathcal{N}$ and $x \in \mathcal{L}$.

A probabilistic CFG (PCFG) is a CFG associated with a set of parameters defined as follows:

- For each $(a \to b\ c) \in \mathcal{R}$, we have a parameter $p(a \to b\ c \mid a)$.

- For each $(a \rightarrow x) \in \mathcal{R}$, we have a parameter $p(a \rightarrow x \mid a)$.

- For each $a \in \mathcal{N}$, we have a parameter π_a, which is the probability of a being the root symbol of a derivation.

The parameters above satisfy the following normalization conditions:

$$\sum_{(a \rightarrow b\ c) \in \mathcal{R}} p(a \rightarrow b\ c \mid a) + \sum_{(a \rightarrow x) \in \mathcal{R}} p(a \rightarrow x \mid a) = 1,$$

for each $a \in \mathcal{N}$, and $\sum_{a \in \mathcal{N}} \pi_a = 1$.

The probability of a tree τ deriving a sentence in the language, written $p(\tau)$, is calculated as the product of the probabilities of all rule occurrences in τ, times the parameter π_a where a is the symbol at the root of τ.

2.2 Tensor Form of PCFGs

A three-dimensional **tensor** $C \in \mathbb{R}^{(m \times m \times m)}$ is a set of m^3 parameters $C_{i,j,k}$ for $i, j, k \in [m]$. In what follows, we associate with each tensor three functions, each mapping a pair of vectors in $\mathbb{R}^m$ into a vector in $\mathbb{R}^m$.

Definition 1 *Let $C \in \mathbb{R}^{(m \times m \times m)}$ be a tensor. Given two vectors $y^1, y^2 \in \mathbb{R}^m$, we let $C(y^1, y^2)$ be the m-dimensional row vector with components:*

$$[C(y^1, y^2)]_i = \sum_{j \in [m], k \in [m]} C_{i,j,k} y^1_j y^2_k .$$

We also let $C_{(1,2)}(y^1, y^2)$ be the m-dimensional column vector with components:

$$[C_{(1,2)}(y^1, y^2)]_k = \sum_{i \in [m], j \in [m]} C_{i,j,k} y^1_i y^2_j .$$

Finally, we let $C_{(1,3)}(y^1, y^2)$ be the m-dimensional column vector with components:

$$[C_{(1,3)}(y^1, y^2)]_j = \sum_{i \in [m], k \in [m]} C_{i,j,k} y^1_i y^2_k .$$

For two vectors $x, y \in \mathbb{R}^m$ we denote by $x \odot y \in \mathbb{R}^m$ the Hadamard product of x and y, i.e., $[x \odot y]_i = x_i y_i$. Finally, for vectors $x, y, z \in \mathbb{R}^m$, $xy^\top z^\top$ is the tensor $D \in \mathbb{R}^{m \times m \times m}$ where $D_{i,j,k} = x_i y_j z_k$ (this is analogous to the outer product: $[xy^\top]_{i,j} = x_i y_j$).

We extend the parameter set of our PCFG such that $p(a \rightarrow b\ c \mid a) = 0$ for all $a \rightarrow b\ c$ not in $\mathcal{R}$, and $p(a \rightarrow x \mid a) = 0$ for all $a \rightarrow x$ not in $\mathcal{R}$. We also represent each $a \in \mathcal{N}$ by a unique index in $[m]$, and we represent each $x \in \mathcal{L}$ by a unique index in $[n]$: it will always be clear from the context whether these indices refer to a nonterminal in $\mathcal{N}$ or else to a word in $\mathcal{L}$.

In this paper we assume a tensor representation for the parameters $p(a \rightarrow b\ c \mid a)$, and we denote by $T \in \mathbb{R}^{m \times m \times m}$ a tensor such that:

$$T_{a,b,c} \triangleq p(a \rightarrow b\ c \mid a).$$

Similarly, we denote by $Q \in \mathbb{R}^{m \times n}$ a matrix such that:

$$Q_{a,x} \triangleq p(a \rightarrow x \mid a).$$

The root probabilities are denoted using a vector $\pi \in \mathbb{R}^{m \times 1}$ such that π_a is defined as before.

2.3 Minimum Bayes-Risk Decoding

Let $z = x_1 \cdots x_N$ be some input sentence; we write $\mathcal{T}(z)$ to denote the set of all possible trees for z. It is often the case that parsing aims to find the highest scoring tree τ^* for z according to the underlying PCFG, also called the "Viterbi parse:"

$$\tau^* = \operatorname*{argmax}_{\tau \in \mathcal{T}(z)} p(\tau)$$

Goodman (1996) noted that Viterbi parsers do not optimize the same metric that is usually used for parsing evaluation (Black et al., 1991). He suggested an alternative algorithm, which he called the "Labelled Recall Algorithm," which aims to fix this issue.

Goodman's algorithm has two phases. In the first phase it computes, for each $a \in \mathcal{N}$ and for each substring $x_i \cdots x_j$ of z, the marginal $\mu(a, i, j)$ defined as:

$$\mu(a, i, j) = \sum_{\tau \in \mathcal{T}(z) \colon (a,i,j) \in \tau} p(\tau).$$

Here we write $(a, i, j) \in \tau$ if nonterminal a spans words $x_i \cdots x_j$ in the parse tree τ.

Inputs: Sentence $x_1 \cdots x_N$, PCFG $(\mathcal{N}, \mathcal{L}, \mathcal{R})$, parameters $T \in \mathbb{R}^{(m \times m \times m)}$, $Q \in \mathbb{R}^{(m \times n)}$, $\pi \in \mathbb{R}^{(m \times 1)}$.

Data structures:

- Each $\mu(a, i, j) \in \mathbb{R}$ for $a \in \mathcal{N}$, $i, j \in [N]$, $i \leq j$, is a marginal probability.
- Each $\gamma^{i,j} \in \mathbb{R}$ for $i, j \in [N]$, $i \leq j$, is the highest score for a tree spanning substring $x_i \cdots x_j$.

Algorithm:

(Marginals) $\forall a \in \mathcal{N}, \forall i, j \in [N], i \leq j$, compute the marginals $\mu(a, i, j)$ using the inside-outside algorithm.

(Base case) $\forall i \in [N]$,

$$\gamma^{i,i} = \max_{(a \rightarrow x_i) \in \mathcal{R}} \mu(a, i, i)$$

(Maximize Labelled Recall) $\forall i, j \in [N], i < j$,

$$\gamma^{i,j} = \max_{a \in \mathcal{N}} \mu(a, i, j) + \max_{i \leq k < j} \left(\gamma^{i,k} + \gamma^{k+1,j} \right)$$

Figure 1: The labelled recall algorithm from Goodman (1996). The algorithm in this figure finds the highest score for a tree which maximizes labelled recall. The actual parsing algorithm would use backtrack pointers in the score computation to return a tree. These are omitted for simplicity.

The second phase includes a dynamic programming algorithm which finds the tree τ^* that maximizes the sum over marginals in that tree:

$$\tau^* = \operatorname*{argmax}_{\tau \in \mathcal{T}(z)} \sum_{(a,i,j) \in \tau} \mu(a, i, j).$$

Goodman's algorithm is described in Figure 1.

As Goodman notes, the complexity of the second phase ("Maximize Labelled Recall," which is also referred to as "minimum Bayes risk decoding") is $\mathcal{O}(N^3 + mN^2)$. There are two nested outer loops, each of order N, and inside these, there are two separate loops, one of order m and one of order N, yielding this computational complexity. The reason for the linear dependence on the number of nonterminals is the lack of dependence on the actual grammar rules, once the marginals are computed.

In its original form, Goodman's algorithm does not enforce that the output parse trees are included in the tree language of the PCFG, that is, certain combinations of children and parent nonterminals may violate the rules in the grammar. In our experiments we departed from this, and changed Goodman's algorithm by incorporating the grammar into the dynamic programming algorithm in Figure 1. The reason this is important for our experiments is that we *binarize* the grammar prior to parsing, and we need to enforce the links between the split nonterminals (in the binarized grammar) that refer to the same syntactic category. See Matsuzaki et al. (2005) for more details about the binarization scheme we used. This step changes the dynamic programming equation of Goodman to be linear in the size of the grammar (figure 1). However, empirically, it is the inside-outside algorithm which takes most of the time to compute with Goodman's algorithm. In this paper we aim to asymptotically reduce the time complexity of the calculation of the inside-outside probabilities using an approximation algorithm.

3 Tensor Formulation of the Inside-Outside Algorithm

At the core of our approach lies the observation that there is a (multi)linear algebraic formulation of the inside-outside algorithm. It can be represented as a series of tensor, matrix and vector products. A similar observation has been made for latent-variable PCFGs (Cohen et al., 2012) and hidden Markov models, where only matrix multiplication is required (Jaeger, 2000). Cohen and Collins (2012) use this observation together with tensor decomposition to improve the speed of latent-variable PCFG parsing.

The representation of the inside-outside algorithm in tensor form is given in Figure 2. For example, if we consider the recursive equation for the inside probabilities (where $\alpha^{i,j}$ is a vector varying over the nonterminals in the grammar, describing the inside probability for each nonterminal spanning words i to j):

$$\alpha^{i,j} = \sum_{k=i}^{j-1} T(\alpha^{i,k}, \alpha^{k+1,j})$$

Inputs: Sentence $x_1 \cdots x_N$, PCFG $(\mathcal{N}, \mathcal{L}, \mathcal{R})$, parameters $T \in \mathbb{R}^{(m \times m \times m)}$, $Q \in \mathbb{R}^{(m \times n)}$, $\pi \in \mathbb{R}^{(m \times 1)}$.

Data structures:

- Each $\alpha^{i,j} \in \mathbb{R}^{1 \times m}$, $i, j \in [N]$, $i \leq j$, is a row vector of inside terms ranging over $a \in \mathcal{N}$.
- Each $\beta^{i,j} \in \mathbb{R}^{m \times 1}$, $i, j \in [N]$, $i \leq j$, is a column vector of outside terms ranging over $a \in \mathcal{N}$.
- Each $\mu(a, i, j) \in \mathbb{R}$ for $a \in \mathcal{N}$, $i, j \in [N]$, $i \leq j$, is a marginal probability.

Algorithm:

(Inside base case) $\forall i \in [N], \forall (a \to x_i) \in \mathcal{R}$,

$$[\alpha^{i,i}]_a = Q_{a,x}$$

(Inside recursion) $\forall i, j \in [N], i < j$,

$$\alpha^{i,j} = \sum_{k=i}^{j-1} T(\alpha^{i,k}, \alpha^{k+1,j})$$

(Outside base case) $\forall a \in \mathcal{N}$,

$$[\beta^{1,N}]_a = \pi_a$$

(Outside recursion) $\forall i, j \in [N], i \leq j$,

$$\beta^{i,j} = \sum_{k=1}^{i-1} T_{(1,2)}(\beta^{k,j}, \alpha^{k,i-1}) + \sum_{k=j+1}^{N} T_{(1,3)}(\beta^{i,k}, \alpha^{j+1,k})$$

(Marginals) $\forall a \in \mathcal{N}, \forall i, j \in [N], i \leq j$,

$$\mu(a, i, j) = [\alpha^{i,j}]_a \cdot [\beta^{i,j}]_a$$

Figure 2: The tensor form of the inside-outside algorithm, for calculation of marginal terms $\mu(a, i, j)$.

and then apply the tensor product from Definition 1 to this equation, we get that coordinate a in $\alpha^{i,j}$ is defined recursively as follows:

$$\begin{aligned}[\alpha^{i,j}]_a &= \sum_{k=i}^{j-1} \sum_{b,c} T_{a,b,c} \times \alpha_b^{i,k} \times \alpha_c^{k+1,j} \\ &= \sum_{k=i}^{j-1} \sum_{b,c} p(a \to b\ c \mid a) \times \alpha_b^{i,k} \times \alpha_c^{k+1,j},\end{aligned}$$

which is exactly the recursive definition of the inside algorithm. The correctness of the outside recursive equations follows very similarly.

The time complexity of the algorithm in this case is $\mathcal{O}(m^3 N^3)$. To see this, observe that each tensor application takes time $\mathcal{O}(m^3)$. Furthermore, the tensor T is applied $\mathcal{O}(N)$ times in the computation of each vector $\alpha^{i,j}$ and $\beta^{i,j}$. Finally, we need to compute a total of $\mathcal{O}(N^2)$ inside and outside vectors, one for each substring of the input sentence.

4 Tensor Decomposition for the Inside-Outside Algorithm

In this section, we detail our approach to approximate parsing using tensor decomposition.

4.1 Tensor Decomposition

In the formulation of the inside-outside algorithm based on tensor T, each vector $\alpha^{i,j}$ and $\beta^{i,j}$ consists of m elements, where computation of each element requires time $\mathcal{O}(m^2)$. Therefore, the algorithm has a $\mathcal{O}(m^3)$ multiplicative factor in its time complexity, which we aim to reduce by means of an approximate algorithm.

Our approximate method relies on a simple observation. Given an integer $r \geq 1$, assume that the tensor T has the following special form, called "Kruskal form:"

$$T = \sum_{i=1}^{r} \lambda_i u_i v_i^\top w_i^\top . \quad (1)$$

In words, T is the sum of r tensors, where each tensor is obtained as the product of three vectors u_i, v_i and w_i, together with a scalar λ_i. Exact Kruskal decomposition of a tensor is not necessarily unique. See Kolda and Bader (2009) for discussion of uniqueness of tensor decomposition.

Consider now two vectors $y^1, y^2 \in \mathbb{R}^m$, associated with the inside probabilities for the left (y^1) and right child (y^2) of a given node in a parse tree. Let us introduce auxiliary arrays $U, V, W \in \mathbb{R}^{r \times m}$, with the i-th row being u_i, v_i and w_i, respectively. Let also $\lambda = (\lambda_1, \dots, \lambda_r)$. Using the decomposition in Eq. (1) within Definition 1 we can express the array $T(y^1, y^2)$ as:

$$T(y^1, y^2) = \left[\sum_{i=1}^{r} \lambda_i u_i v_i^\top w_i^\top \right] (y^1, y^2) = \sum_{i=1}^{r} \lambda_i u_i (v_i^\top y^1)(w_i^\top y^2) = \left(U^\top (\lambda \odot V y^1 \odot W y^2) \right) . \quad (2)$$

The total complexity of the computation in Eq. (2) is now $\mathcal{O}(rm)$. It is well-known that an exact tensor decomposition for T can be achieved with $r = m^2$ (Kruskal, 1989). In this case, there is no computational gain in using Eq. (2) for the inside calculation. The minimal r required for an exact tensor decomposition can be smaller than m^2. However, identifying that minimal r is NP-hard (Høastad, 1990).

In this section we focused on the computation of the inside probabilities through vectors $T(\alpha^{i,k}, \alpha^{k+1,j})$. Nonetheless, the steps above can be easily adapted for the computation of the outside probabilities through vectors $T_{(1,2)}(\beta^{k,j}, \alpha^{k,i-1})$ and $T_{(1,3)}(\beta^{i,k}, \alpha^{j+1,k})$.

4.2 Approximate Tensor Decomposition

The PCFG tensor T will not necessarily have the exact decomposed form in Eq. (1). We suggest to *approximate* the tensor T by finding the closest tensor according to some norm over $\mathbb{R}^{m \times m \times m}$.

An example of such an approximate decomposition is the canonical polyadic decomposition (CPD), also known as CANDECOMP/PARAFAC decomposition (Carroll and Chang, 1970; Harshman, 1970; Kolda and Bader, 2009). Given an integer r, *least squares* CPD aims to find the nearest tensor in Kruskal form, minimizing squared error.

More formally, for a given tensor $D \in \mathbb{R}^{m \times m \times m}$, let $\|D\|_F = \sqrt{\sum_{i,j,k} D^2_{i,j,k}}$. Let the set of tensors in Kruskal form $\mathcal{C}_r$ be:

$$\mathcal{C}_r = \{ C \in \mathbb{R}^{m \times m \times m} \mid C = \sum_{i=1}^{r} \lambda_i u_i v_i^\top w_i^\top \\ \text{s.t. } \lambda_i \in \mathbb{R}, u_i, v_i, w_i \in \mathbb{R}^m, \\ \|u_i\|_2 = \|v_i\|_2 = \|w_i\|_2 = 1 \}.$$

The least squares CPD of C is a tensor $\hat{C}$ such that $\hat{C} \in \operatorname{argmin}_{\hat{C} \in \mathcal{C}_r} \|C - \hat{C}\|_F$. Here, we treat the argmin as a set because there could be multiple solutions which achieve the same accuracy.

There are various algorithms to perform CPD, such as alternating least squares, direct linear decomposition, alternating trilinear decomposition and pseudo alternating least squares (Faber et al., 2003) and even algorithms designed for sparse tensors (Chi and Kolda, 2011). Most of these algorithms treat the problem of identifying the approximate tensor as an optimization problem. Generally speaking, these optimization problems are hard to solve, but they work quite well in practice.

4.3 Parsing with Decomposed Tensors

Equipped with the notion of tensor decomposition, we can now proceed with approximate tensor parsing in two steps. The first is approximating the tensor using a CPD algorithm, and the second is applying the algorithms in Figure 1 and Figure 2 to do parsing, while substituting all tensor product computations with the approximate $\mathcal{O}(rm)$ operation of tensor product.

This is not sufficient to get a significant speed-up in parsing time. Re-visiting Eq. (2) shows that there are additional ways to speed-up the tensor application T in the context of the inside-outside algorithm.

The first thing to note is that the projections Vy^1 and Wy^2 in Eq. (2) can be cached, and do not have to be re-calculated every time the tensor is applied. Here, y^1 and y^2 will always refer to an outside or an inside probability vector over the nonterminals in the grammar. Caching these projections means that after each computation of an inside or outside probability, we can immediately project it to the necessary r-dimensional space, and then re-use this computation in subsequent application of the tensor.

The second thing to note is that the U projection in T can be delayed, because of rule of distributivity. For example, the step in Figure 2 that computes the inside probability $\alpha^{i,j}$ can be re-formulated as follows (assuming an exact decomposition of T):

$$\alpha^{i,j} = \sum_{k=i}^{j-1} T(\alpha^{i,k}, \alpha^{k+1,j})$$
$$= \sum_{k=1}^{j-1} U^\top (\lambda \odot V\alpha^{i,k} \odot W\alpha^{k+1,j})$$
$$= U^\top \left(\sum_{k=1}^{j-1} (\lambda \odot V\alpha^{i,k} \odot W\alpha^{k+1,j}) \right). \quad (3)$$

This means that projection through U can be done outside of the loop over splitting points in the sentence. Similar reliance on distributivity can be used to speed-up the outside calculations as well.

The caching speed-up and the delayed projection speed-up make the approximate inside-outside computation asymptotically faster. While naïve application of the tensor yields an inside algorithm which runs in time $\mathcal{O}(rmN^3)$, the improved algorithm runs in time $\mathcal{O}(rN^3 + rmN^2)$.

5 Quality of Approximate Tensor Parsing

In this section, we give the main approximation result, that shows that the probability distribution induced by the approximate tensor is close to the original probability distribution, if the distance between the approximate tensor and the rule probabilities is not too large.

Denote by $\mathcal{T}(N)$ the set of trees in the tree language of the PCFG with N words (any nonterminal can be the root of the tree). Let $\overline{\mathcal{T}}(N)$ be the set of pairs of trees $\overline{\tau} = (\tau_1, \tau_2)$ such that the total number of binary rules combined in τ_1 and τ_2 is $N-2$ (this means that the total number of words combined is N). Let $\hat{T}$ be the approximate tensor for T. Denote the probability distribution induced by $\hat{T}$ by $\hat{p}$.[1] Define the vector $\xi(\overline{\tau})$ such that $[\xi(\overline{\tau})]_a = T_{a,b,c} \cdot p(\tau_1 \mid b) \cdot p(\tau_2 \mid c)$ where the root τ_1 is nonterminal b and the root of τ_2 is c. Similarly, define $[\hat{\xi}(\overline{\tau})]_a = \hat{T}_{a,b,c} \cdot \hat{p}(\tau_1 \mid b) \cdot \hat{p}(\tau_2 \mid c)$.

Define $Z(a,N) = \sum_{\overline{\tau} \in \overline{\mathcal{T}}(N)} [\hat{\xi}(\overline{\tau})]_a$. In addition, define $D(a,N) = \sum_{\overline{\tau} \in \overline{\mathcal{T}}(N)} |[\hat{\xi}(\overline{\tau})]_a - [\xi(\overline{\tau})]_a|$ and define $F(a,N) = D(a,N)/Z(a,N)$. Define $\Delta = \|\hat{T} - T\|_F$. Last, define $\nu = \min_{(a\to b\ c)\in\mathcal{R}} p(a \to b\ c \mid a)$. Then, the following lemma holds:

[1] Here, $\hat{p}$ does not have to be a distribution, because $\hat{T}$ could have negative values, in principle, and its slices do not have to normalize to 1. However, we just treat $\hat{p}$ as a function that maps trees to products of values according to $\hat{T}$.

Lemma 1 *For any a and any N, it holds:*

$$D(a,N) \leq Z(a,N) \left((1 + \Delta/\nu)^N - 1 \right)$$

Proof sketch: The proof is by induction on N. Assuming that $1 + F(b,k) \leq (1+\Delta/\nu)^k$ and $1 + F(c, N-k-1) \leq (1+\Delta/\nu)^{N-k-1}$ for F defined as above (this is the induction hypothesis), it can be shown that the lemma holds. ■

Lemma 2 *The following holds for any N:*

$$\sum_{\tau\in\mathcal{T}(N)} |\hat{p}(\tau) - p(\tau)| \leq m \left((1+\Delta/\nu)^N - 1 \right)$$

Proof sketch: Using Hölder's inequality and Lemma 1 and the fact that $Z(a,N) \leq 1$, it follows that:

$$\sum_{\tau\in\mathcal{T}(N)} |\hat{p}(\tau) - p(\tau)| \leq \sum_{\overline{\tau}\in\overline{\mathcal{T}}(N), a} |[\xi(\overline{\tau})]_a - [\hat{\xi}(\overline{\tau})]_a|$$
$$\leq \left(\sum_a Z(a,N) \right) \left((1+\Delta/\nu)^N - 1 \right)$$
$$\leq m \left((1+\Delta/\nu)^N - 1 \right)$$

■

Then, the following is a result that explains how accuracy changes as a function of the quality of the tensor approximation:

Theorem 1 *For any N, and $\epsilon < 1/4$, it holds that if $\Delta \leq \dfrac{\epsilon\nu}{2Nm}$, then:*

$$\sum_{\tau\in\mathcal{T}(N)} |\hat{p}(\tau) - p(\tau)| \leq \epsilon$$

Proof sketch: This is the result of applying Lemma 2 together with the inequality $(1+y/t)^t - 1 \leq 2y$ for any $t > 0$ and $y \leq 1/2$. ■

We note that Theorem 1 also implicitly bounds the difference between a marginal $\mu(a, i, j)$ and its approximate version. A marginal corresponds to a sum over a subset of summands in Eq. (1).

A question that remains at this point is to decide whether for a given grammar, the optimal ν that can be achieved is large or small. We define:

$$\Delta_r^* = \min_{\hat{T} \in \mathcal{C}_r} \|T - \hat{T}\|_F \quad (4)$$

The following theorem gives an upper bound on the value of Δ_r^* based on intrinsic property of the grammar, or more specifically T. It relies on the fact that for three-dimensional tensors, where each dimension is of length m, there exists an exact decomposition of T using m^2 components.

Theorem 2 *Let:*

$$T = \sum_{i=1}^{m^2} \lambda_i^* u_i^* (v_i^*)^\top (w_i^*)^\top$$

be an exact Kruskal decomposition of T such that $\|u_i^*\|_2 = \|v_i^*\|_2 = \|w_i^*\| = 1$ and $\lambda_i^* \geq \lambda_{i+1}^*$ for $i \in [m^2 - 1]$. Then, for a given r, it holds:

$$\Delta_r^* \leq \sum_{i=r+1}^{m^2} |\lambda_i^*|$$

Proof: Let $\hat{T}$ be a tensor that achieves the minimum in Eq. (4). Define:

$$T_r' = \sum_{i=1}^{r} \lambda_i^* u_i^* (v_i^*)^\top (w_i^*)^\top$$

Then, noting that Δ_r^* is a minimizer of the norm difference between T and $\hat{T}$ and then applying the triangle inequality and then Cauchy-Schwartz inequality leads to the following chain of inequalities:

$$\begin{aligned}\Delta_r^* &= \|T - \hat{T}\|_F \leq \|T - T_r'\|_F \\ &= \|\sum_{i=r+1}^{m^2} \lambda_i^* u_i^* (v_i^*)^\top (w_i^*)^\top \|_F \\ &\leq \sum_{i=r+1}^{m^2} |\lambda_i^*| \cdot \|u_i^* (v_i^*)^\top (w_i^*)^\top \|_F \quad = \sum_{i=r+1}^{m^2} |\lambda_i^*|\end{aligned}$$

as required. ■

6 Experiments

In this section, we describe experiments that demonstrate the trade-off between the accuracy of the tensor approximation (and as a consequence, the accuracy of the approximate parsing algorithm) and parsing time.

Experimental Setting We compare the tensor approximation parsing algorithm versus the vanilla Goodman algorithm. Both algorithms were implemented in Java, and the code for both is almost identical, except for the set of instructions which computes the dynamic programming equation for propagating the beliefs up in the tree. This makes the clocktime comparison reliable for drawing conclusions about the speed of the algorithms. Our implementation of the vanilla parsing algorithm is linear in the size of the grammar (and not cubic in the number of nonterminals, which would give a worse running time).

In our experiments, we use the method described in Chi and Kolda (2011) for tensor decomposition.[2] This method is fast, even for large tensors, as long as they are sparse. Such is the case with the tensors for our grammars.

We use two treebanks for our comparison: the Penn treebank (Marcus et al., 1993) and the Arabic treebank (Maamouri et al., 2004). With the Penn treebank, we use sections 2–21 for training a maximum likelihood model and section 22 for parsing, while for the Arabic treebank we divide the data into two sets, of size 80% and 20%, one is used for training a maximum likelihood model and the other is used for parsing.

The number of binary rules in the treebank grammar is 7,240. The number of nonterminals is 112 and the number of preterminals is 259[3]Unary rules are removed by collapsing non-terminal chains. This increased the number of preterminals. The number of binary rules in the Arabic treebank is significantly smaller and consists of 232 rules. We run all parsing experiments on sentences of length ≤ 40. The number of nonterminals is 48 and the number of preter-

[2]We use the implementation given in Sandia's Matlab Tensor Toolbox, which can be downloaded at `http://www.sandia.gov/~tgkolda/TensorToolbox/index-2.5.html`.

[3].

	rank (r)	baseline	20	60	100	140	180	220	260	300	340
Arabic	speed	0.57	0.04	0.06	0.1	0.12	0.16	0.19	0.22	0.26	0.28
	F_1	63.78	51.80	58.39	63.63	63.77	63.88	63.82	63.84	63.80	63.88
English	speed	3.89	0.15	0.21	0.30	0.37	0.44	0.52	0.60	0.70	0.79
	F_1	71.07	57.83	61.67	68.28	69.63	70.30	70.82	71.42	71.28	71.13

Table 1: Results for the Arabic and English treebank of parsing using a vanilla PCFG with and without tensor decomposition. Speed is given in seconds per sentence.

minals is 81.

Results Table 1 describes the results of comparing the tensor decomposition algorithm to the vanilla PCFG parsing algorithm.

The first thing to note is that the running time of the parsing algorithm is linear in r. This indeed validates the asymptotic complexity of the inside-outside component in Goodman's algorithm with the approximate tensors. It also shows that most of the time during parsing is spent on the inside-outside algorithm, and not on the dynamic programming algorithm which follows it.

In addition, compared to the baseline which uses a vanilla CKY algorithm (linear in the number of rules), we get a speed up of a factor of 4.75 for Arabic ($r = 140$) and 6.5 for English ($r = 260$) while retaining similar performance. Perhaps more surprising is that using the tensor approximation actually *improves* performance in several cases. We hypothesize that the cause of this is that the tensor decomposition requires less parameters to express the rule probabilities in the grammar, and therefore leads to better generalization than a vanilla maximum likelihood estimate.

We include results for a more complex model for Arabic, which uses horizontal Markovization of order 1 and vertical Markovization of order 2 (Klein and Manning, 2003). This grammar includes 2,188 binary rules. Parsing exhaustively using this grammar takes 1.30 seconds per sentence (on average) with an F_1 measure of 64.43. Parsing with tensor decomposition for $r = 280$ takes 0.62 seconds per sentence (on average) with an F_1 measure of 64.05.

7 Discussion

In this section, we briefly touch on several other topics related to tensor approximation.

7.1 Approximating the Probability of a String

The probability of a sentence z under a PCFG is defined as $p(z) = \sum_{\tau \in \mathcal{T}(z)} p(\tau)$, and can be approximated using the algorithm in Section 4.3, running in time $\mathcal{O}(rN^3 + rmN^2)$. Of theoretical interest, we discuss here a time $\mathcal{O}(rN^3 + r^2N^2)$ algorithm, which is more convenient when $r < m$.

Observe that in Eq. (3) vector $\alpha^{i,j}$ always appears within one of the two terms $V\alpha^{i,j}$ and $W\alpha^{i,j}$ in $\mathbb{R}^{r\times 1}$, whose dimensions are independent of m. We can therefore use Eq. (3) to compute $V\alpha^{i,j}$ as $V\alpha^{i,j} = VU^\top \left(\sum_{k=1}^{j-1}(\lambda \odot V\alpha^{i,k} \odot W\alpha^{k+1,j})\right)$, where $VU^\top$ is a $\mathbb{R}^{r\times r}$ matrix that can be computed off-line, i.e., independently of z. A symmetrical relation can be used to compute $W\alpha^{i,j}$. Finally, we can write $p(z) = \pi^\top U \left(\sum_{k=1}^{N-1}(\lambda \odot V\alpha^{1,k} \odot W\alpha^{k+1,N})\right)$, where $\pi^\top U$ is a $\mathbb{R}^{1\times r}$ vector that can again be computed off-line. This algorithm then runs in time $\mathcal{O}(rN^3 + r^2N^2)$.

7.2 Applications to Dynamic Programming

The approximation method presented in this paper is not limited to PCFG parsing. A similar approximation method has been used for latent-variable PCFGs (Cohen and Collins, 2012), and in general, tensor approximation can be used to speed-up inside-outside algorithms for general dynamic programming algorithms or weighted logic programs (Eisner et al., 2004; Cohen et al., 2011). In the general case, the dimension of the tensors will not be necessarily just three (corresponding to binary rules), but can be of a higher dimension, and therefore the speed gain can be even greater. In addition, tensor approximation can be used for computing marginals of latent variables in graphical models.

For example, the complexity of the forward-backward algorithm for HMMs can be reduced to be linear in the number of states (as opposed to quadratic) and linear in the rank used in an approximate singular-value decomposition (instead of tensor decomposition) of the transition and emission matrices.

7.3 Tighter (but Slower) Approximation Using Singular Value Decomposition

The accuracy of the algorithm depends on the ability of the tensor decomposition algorithm to decompose the tensor with a small reconstruction error. The decomposition algorithm is performed on the tensor T which includes all rules in the grammar.

Instead, one can approach the approximation by doing a decomposition for each *slice* of T separately using singular value decomposition. This will lead to a more accurate approximation, but will also lead to an extra factor of m during parsing. This factor is added because now there is not a single U, V and W, but instead there are such matrices for each nonterminal in the grammar.

8 Conclusion

We described an approximation algorithm for probabilistic context-free parsing. The approximation algorithm is based on tensor decomposition performed on the underlying rule table of the CFG grammar. The approximation algorithm leads to significant speed-up in PCFG parsing, with minimal loss in performance.

References

E. Black, S. Abney, D. Flickenger, C. Gdaniec, R. Grishman, P Harrison, D. Hindle, R. Ingria, F. Jelinek, J. Klavans, M. Liberman, M. Marcus, S. Roukos, B. Santorini, and T. Strzalkowski. 1991. A procedure for quantitatively comparing the syntactic coverage of English grammars. In *Proceedings of DARPA Workshop on Speech and Natural Language*.

P. Boullier. 2003. Guided earley parsing. In *8th International Workshop on Parsing Technologies*, pages 43–54.

J. D. Carroll and J. J. Chang. 1970. Analysis of individual differences in multidimensional scaling via an N-way generalization of Eckart-Young decomposition. *Psychometrika*, 35:283–319.

E. Charniak, M. Johnson, M. Elsner, J. Austerweil, D. Ellis, I. Haxton, C. Hill, R. Shrivaths, J. Moore, M. Pozar, and T. Vu. 2006. Multilevel coarse-to-fine pcfg parsing. In *Proceedings of HLT-NAACL*.

E. C. Chi and T. G. Kolda. 2011. On tensors, sparsity, and nonnegative factorizations. arXiv:1112.2414 [math.NA], December.

S. B. Cohen and M. Collins. 2012. Tensor decomposition for fast latent-variable PCFG parsing. In *Proceedings of NIPS*.

S. B. Cohen, R. J. Simmons, and N. A. Smith. 2011. Products of weighted logic programs. *Theory and Practice of Logic Programming*, 11(2–3):263–296.

S. B. Cohen, K. Stratos, M. Collins, D. F. Foster, and L. Ungar. 2012. Spectral learning of latent-variable PCFGs. In *Proceedings of ACL*.

J. Eisner and N. A. Smith. 2005. Parsing with soft and hard constraints on dependency length. In *Proceedings of IWPT*, Parsing '05.

J. Eisner, E. Goldlust, and N. A. Smith. 2004. Dyna: A declarative language for implementing dynamic programs. In *Proc. of ACL* (companion volume).

N. M. Faber, R. Bro, and P. Hopke. 2003. Recent developments in CANDECOMP/PARAFAC algorithms: a critical review. *Chemometrics and Intelligent Laboratory Systems*, 65(1):119–137.

J. Goodman. 1996. Parsing algorithms and metrics. In *Proceedings of ACL*.

R. A. Harshman. 1970. Foundations of the PARAFAC procedure: Models and conditions for an "explanatory" multi-modal factor analysis. *UCLA working papers in phoentics*, 16:1–84.

J. Høastad. 1990. Tensor rank is NP-complete. *Algorithms*, 11:644–654.

H. Jaeger. 2000. Observable operator models for discrete stochastic time series. *Neural Computation*, 12(6):1371–1398.

D. Klein and C. D. Manning. 2003. Accurate unlexicalized parsing. In *Proceedings of ACL*.

T. G. Kolda and B. W. Bader. 2009. Tensor decompositions and applications. *SIAM Rev.*, 51:455–500.

J. B. Kruskal. 1989. Rank, decomposition, and uniqueness for 3-way and N-way arrays. In R. Coppi and S. Bolasco, editors, *Multiway Data Analysis*, pages 7–18.

M. Maamouri, A. Bies, T. Buckwalter, and W. Mekki. 2004. The Penn Arabic Treebank: Building a large-scale annotated Arabic corpus. In *Proceedings NEMLAR*.

M. P. Marcus, B. Santorini, and M. A. Marcinkiewicz. 1993. Building a large annotated corpus of English: The Penn treebank. *Computational Linguistics*, 19(2):313–330.

T. Matsuzaki, Y. Miyao, and J. Tsujii. 2005. Probabilistic CFG with latent annotations. In *Proceedings of ACL*.

M.-J. Nederhof. 2000. Practical experiments with regular approximation of context-free languages. *Computational Linguistics*, 26(1):17–44.

Negative Deceptive Opinion Spam

Myle Ott **Claire Cardie**
Department of Computer Science
Cornell University
Ithaca, NY 14853
{myleott,cardie}@cs.cornell.edu

Jeffrey T. Hancock
Department of Communication
Cornell University
Ithaca, NY 14853
jeff.hancock@cornell.edu

Abstract

The rising influence of user-generated online reviews (Cone, 2011) has led to growing incentive for businesses to solicit and manufacture DECEPTIVE OPINION SPAM—fictitious reviews that have been deliberately written to sound authentic and deceive the reader. Recently, Ott et al. (2011) have introduced an opinion spam dataset containing gold standard deceptive *positive* hotel reviews. However, the complementary problem of *negative* deceptive opinion spam, intended to slander competitive offerings, remains largely unstudied. Following an approach similar to Ott et al. (2011), in this work we create and study the first dataset of deceptive opinion spam with *negative* sentiment reviews. Based on this dataset, we find that standard n-gram text categorization techniques can detect negative deceptive opinion spam with performance far surpassing that of human judges. Finally, in conjunction with the aforementioned *positive* review dataset, we consider the possible interactions between sentiment and deception, and present initial results that encourage further exploration of this relationship.

1 Introduction

Consumer's purchase decisions are increasingly influenced by user-generated online reviews of products and services (Cone, 2011). Accordingly, there is a growing incentive for businesses to solicit and manufacture DECEPTIVE OPINION SPAM—fictitious reviews that have been deliberately written to sound authentic and deceive the reader (Ott et al., 2011). For example, Ott et al. (2012) has estimated that between 1% and 6% of *positive* hotel reviews appear to be deceptive, suggesting that some hotels may be posting fake positive reviews in order to hype their own offerings.

In this work we distinguish between two kinds of deceptive opinion spam, depending on the sentiment expressed in the review. In particular, reviews intended to promote or hype an offering, and which therefore express a positive sentiment towards the offering, are called *positive* deceptive opinion spam. In contrast, reviews intended to disparage or slander competitive offerings, and which therefore express a negative sentiment towards the offering, are called *negative* deceptive opinion spam. While previous related work (Ott et al., 2011; Ott et al., 2012) has explored characteristics of *positive* deceptive opinion spam, the complementary problem of *negative* deceptive opinion spam remains largely unstudied.

Following the framework of Ott et al. (2011), we use Amazon's Mechanical Turk service to produce the first publicly available[1] dataset of *negative* deceptive opinion spam, containing 400 gold standard deceptive negative reviews of 20 popular Chicago hotels. To validate the credibility of our deceptive reviews, we show that human deception detection performance on the negative reviews is low, in agreement with decades of traditional deception detection research (Bond and DePaulo, 2006). We then show that standard n-gram text categorization techniques can be used to detect negative deceptive opinion spam with approximately 86% accuracy — far

[1]Dataset available at: http://www.cs.cornell.edu/~myleott/op_spam.

surpassing that of the human judges.

In conjunction with Ott et al. (2011)'s *positive* deceptive opinion spam dataset, we then explore the interaction between sentiment and deception with respect to three types of language features: (1) changes in first-person singular use, often attributed to psychological distancing (Newman et al., 2003), (2) decreased spatial awareness and more narrative form, consistent with theories of reality monitoring (Johnson and Raye, 1981) and imaginative writing (Biber et al., 1999; Rayson et al., 2001), and (3) increased negative emotion terms, often attributed to leakage cues (Ekman and Friesen, 1969), but perhaps better explained in our case as an exaggeration of the underlying review sentiment.

2 Dataset

One of the biggest challenges facing studies of deception is obtaining labeled data. Recently, Ott et al. (2011) have proposed an approach for generating *positive* deceptive opinion spam using Amazon's popular Mechanical Turk crowdsourcing service. In this section we discuss our efforts to extend Ott et al. (2011)'s dataset to additionally include *negative* deceptive opinion spam.

2.1 Deceptive Reviews from Mechanical Turk

Deceptive negative reviews are gathered from Mechanical Turk using the same procedure as Ott et al. (2011). In particular, we create and divide 400 HITs evenly across the 20 most popular hotels in Chicago, such that we obtain 20 reviews for each hotel. We allow workers to complete only a single HIT each, so that each review is written by a unique worker.[2] We further require workers to be located in the United States and to have an average past approval rating of at least 90%. We allow a maximum of 30 minutes to complete the HIT, and reward accepted submissions with one US dollar ($1).

Each HIT instructs a worker to imagine that they work for the marketing department of a hotel, and that their manager has asked them to write a fake negative review of a competitor's hotel to be posted online. Accompanying each HIT is the name and URL of the hotel for which the fake negative review is to be written, and instructions that: (1) workers should not complete more than one similar HIT, (2) submissions must be of sufficient quality, i.e., written for the correct hotel, legible, reasonable in length,[3] and not plagiarized,[4] and, (3) the HIT is for academic research purposes.

Submissions are manually inspected to ensure that they are written for the correct hotel and to ensure that they convey a generally negative sentiment.[5] The average accepted review length was 178 words, higher than for the positive reviews gathered by Ott et al. (2011), who report an average review length of 116 words.

2.2 Truthful Reviews from the Web

Negative (1- or 2-star) truthful reviews are mined from six popular online review communities: Expedia, Hotels.com, Orbitz, Priceline, TripAdvisor, and Yelp. While reviews mined from these communities cannot be considered *gold standard* truthful, recent work (Mayzlin et al., 2012; Ott et al., 2012) suggests that deception rates among travel review portals is reasonably small.

Following Ott et al. (2011), we sample a subset of the available truthful reviews so that we retain an equal number of truthful and deceptive reviews (20 each) for each hotel. However, because the truthful reviews are on average longer than our deceptive reviews, we sample the truthful reviews according to a log-normal distribution fit to the lengths of our deceptive reviews, similarly to Ott et al. (2011).[6]

3 Deception Detection Performance

In this section we report the deception detection performance of three human judges (Section 3.1) and supervised n-gram Support Vector Machine (SVM) classifiers (Section 3.2).

[2]While Mechanical Turk does not provide a convenient mechanism for ensuring the uniqueness of workers, this constraint can be enforced with Javascript. The script is available at: `http://uniqueturker.myleott.com`.

[3]We define "reasonable length" to be ≥ 150 characters.

[4]We use `http://plagiarisma.net` to determine whether or not a review is plagiarized.

[5]We discarded and replaced approximately 2% of the submissions, where it was clear that the worker had misread the instructions and instead written a deceptive *positive* review.

[6]We use the R package GAMLSS (Rigby and Stasinopoulos, 2005) to fit a log-normal distribution (left truncated at 150 characters) to the lengths of the deceptive reviews.

			TRUTHFUL			DECEPTIVE		
		Accuracy	**P**	**R**	**F**	**P**	**R**	**F**
HUMAN	JUDGE 1	65.0%	65.0	65.0	65.0	65.0	65.0	65.0
	JUDGE 2	61.9%	63.0	57.5	60.1	60.9	66.3	63.5
	JUDGE 3	57.5%	57.3	58.8	58.0	57.7	56.3	57.0
META	MAJORITY	**69.4%**	70.1	**67.5**	**68.8**	**68.7**	71.3	**69.9**
	SKEPTIC	58.1%	**78.3**	22.5	35.0	54.7	**93.8**	69.1

Table 1: Deception detection performance, incl. (P)recision, (R)ecall, and (F)1-score, for three human judges and two meta-judges on a set of 160 *negative* reviews. The largest value in each column is indicated with boldface.

3.1 Human Performance

Recent large-scale meta-analyses have shown human deception detection performance is low, with accuracies often not much better than chance (Bond and DePaulo, 2006). Indeed, Ott et al. (2011) found that two out of three human judges were unable to perform statistically significantly better than chance (at the $p < 0.05$ level) at detecting *positive* deceptive opinion spam. Nevertheless, it is important to subject our reviews to human judgments to validate their convincingness. In particular, if human detection performance is found to be very high, then it would cast doubt on the usefulness of the Mechanical Turk approach for soliciting gold standard deceptive opinion spam.

Following Ott et al. (2011), we asked three volunteer undergraduate university students to read and make assessments on a subset of the negative review dataset described in Section 2. Specifically, we randomized all 40 deceptive and truthful reviews from each of four hotels (160 reviews total). We then asked the volunteers to read each review and mark whether they believed it to be truthful or deceptive.

Performance for the three human judges appears in Table 1. We additionally show the deception detection performance of two meta-judges that aggregate the assessments of the individual human judges: (1) the MAJORITY meta-judge predicts *deceptive* when at least two out of three human judges predict *deceptive* (and *truthful* otherwise), and (2) the SKEPTIC meta-judge predicts *deceptive* when at least one out of three human judges predicts *deceptive* (and *truthful* otherwise).

A two-tailed binomial test suggests that JUDGE 1 and JUDGE 2 both perform better than chance ($p = 0.0002, 0.003$, respectively), while JUDGE 3 fails to reject the null hypothesis of performing at-chance ($p = 0.07$). However, while the best human judge is accurate 65% of the time, inter-annotator agreement computed using Fleiss' kappa is only *slight* at 0.07 (Landis and Koch, 1977). Furthermore, based on Cohen's kappa, the highest pairwise inter-annotator agreement is only 0.26, between JUDGE 1 and JUDGE 2. These low agreements suggest that while the judges may perform statistically better than chance, they are identifying different reviews as deceptive, i.e., few reviews are consistently identified as deceptive.

3.2 Automated Classifier Performance

Standard n-gram–based text categorization techniques have been shown to be effective at detecting deception in text (Jindal and Liu, 2008; Mihalcea and Strapparava, 2009; Ott et al., 2011; Feng et al., 2012). Following Ott et al. (2011), we evaluate the performance of linear Support Vector Machine (SVM) classifiers trained with unigram and bigram term-frequency features on our novel *negative* deceptive opinion spam dataset. We employ the same 5-fold stratified cross-validation (CV) procedure as Ott et al. (2011), whereby for each cross-validation iteration we train our model on all reviews for 16 hotels, and test our model on all reviews for the remaining 4 hotels. The SVM cost parameter, C, is tuned by nested cross-validation on the training data.

Results appear in Table 2. Each row lists the sentiment of the train and test reviews, where "Cross Val." corresponds to the cross-validation procedure described above, and "Held Out" corresponds to classifiers trained on reviews of one sentiment and tested on the other. The results suggest that n-gram–based SVM classifiers can detect *negative* deceptive opinion spam in a balanced dataset with performance far surpassing that of untrained human judges (see Section 3.1). Furthermore, our results show that

			TRUTHFUL			DECEPTIVE		
Train Sentiment	**Test Sentiment**	**Accuracy**	**P**	**R**	**F**	**P**	**R**	**F**
POSITIVE (800 reviews)	POSITIVE (800 reviews, Cross Val.)	89.3%	89.6	88.8	89.2	88.9	89.8	89.3
	NEGATIVE (800 reviews, Held Out)	75.1%	69.0	91.3	78.6	87.1	59.0	70.3
NEGATIVE (800 reviews)	POSITIVE (800 reviews, Held Out)	81.4%	76.3	91.0	83.0	88.9	71.8	79.4
	NEGATIVE (800 reviews, Cross Val.)	86.0%	86.4	85.5	85.9	85.6	86.5	86.1
COMBINED (1600 reviews)	POSITIVE (800 reviews, Cross Val.)	88.4%	87.7	89.3	88.5	89.1	87.5	88.3
	NEGATIVE (800 reviews, Cross Val.)	86.0%	85.3	87.0	86.1	86.7	85.0	85.9

Table 2: Automated classifier performance for different train and test sets, incl. (P)recision, (R)ecall and (F)1-score.

classifiers trained and tested on reviews of different sentiments perform worse, despite having more training data,[7] than classifiers trained and tested on reviews of the same sentiment. This suggests that cues to deception differ depending on the sentiment of the text (see Section 4).

Interestingly, we find that training on the combined sentiment dataset results in performance that is comparable to that of the "same sentiment" classifiers (88.4% vs. 89.3% accuracy for positive reviews and 86.0% vs. 86.0% accuracy for negative reviews). This is explainable in part by the increased training set size (1,280 vs. 640 reviews per 4 training folds).

4 Interaction of Sentiment and Deception

An important question is how language features operate in our fake negative reviews compared with the fake positive reviews of Ott et al. (2011). For example, fake positive reviews included less spatial language (e.g., floor, small, location, etc.) because individuals who had not actually experienced the hotel simply had less spatial detail available for their review (Johnson and Raye, 1981). This was also the case for our negative reviews, with less spatial language observed for fake negative reviews relative to truthful. Likewise, our fake negative reviews had more verbs relative to nouns than truthful, suggesting a more narrative style that is indicative of imaginative writing (Biber et al., 1999; Rayson et al., 2001), a pattern also observed by Ott et al. (2011).

There were, however, several important differences in the deceptive language of fake negative relative to fake positive reviews. First, as might be expected, negative emotion terms were more frequent, according to LIWC (Pennebaker et al., 2007), in our fake negative reviews than in the fake positive reviews. But, importantly, the fake negative reviewers over-produced negative emotion terms (e.g., terrible, disappointed) relative to the truthful reviews in the same way that fake positive reviewers over-produced positive emotion terms (e.g., elegant, luxurious). Combined, these data suggest that the more frequent negative emotion terms in the present dataset are not the result of "leakage cues" that reveal the emotional distress of lying (Ekman and Friesen, 1969). Instead, the differences suggest that fake hotel reviewers exaggerate the sentiment they are trying to convey relative to similarly-valenced truthful reviews.

Second, the effect of deception on the pattern of pronoun frequency was not the same across positive and negative reviews. In particular, while first person singular pronouns were produced more frequently in fake reviews than truthful, consistent with the case for positive reviews, the increase was diminished in the negative reviews examined here. In the positive reviews reported by Ott et al. (2011), the rate of first person singular in fake reviews (M=4.36%, SD=2.96%) was twice the rate observed in truthful reviews (M=2.18%, SD=2.04%). In contrast, the rate of first person singular in the deceptive negative reviews (M=4.47%, SD=2.83%) was only 57% greater than for truthful reviews (M=2.85%, SD=2.23%). These results suggest that the emphasis on the self, perhaps as a strategy of convincing the reader that the author had actually been to the hotel, is not as evident in the fake negative reviews, perhaps because the negative tone of the reviews caused the reviewers to psychologically distance themselves from their negative statements, a phenomenon observed in several other deception studies, e.g., Hancock et al. (2008).

[7] "Cross Val." classifiers are effectively trained on 80% of the data and tested on the remaining 20%, whereas "Held Out" classifiers are trained and tested on 100% of each data.

5 Conclusion

We have created the first publicly-available corpus of gold standard *negative* deceptive opinion spam, containing 400 reviews of 20 Chicago hotels, which we have used to compare the deception detection capabilities of untrained human judges and standard n-gram–based Support Vector Machine classifiers. Our results demonstrate that while human deception detection performance is greater for *negative* rather than *positive* deceptive opinion spam, the best detection performance is still achieved through automated classifiers, with approximately 86% accuracy.

We have additionally explored, albeit briefly, the relationship between sentiment and deception by utilizing Ott et al. (2011)'s positive deceptive opinion spam dataset in conjunction with our own. In particular, we have identified several features of language that seem to remain consistent across sentiment, such as decreased awareness of spatial details and exaggerated language. We have also identified other features that vary with the sentiment, such as first person singular use, although further work is required to determine if these differences may be exploited to improve deception detection performance. Indeed, future work may wish to jointly model sentiment and deception in order to better determine the effect each has on language use.

Acknowledgments

This work was supported in part by NSF Grant BCS-0904822, a DARPA Deft grant, the Jack Kent Cooke Foundation, and by a gift from Google. We also thank the three Cornell undergraduate volunteer judges, as well as the NAACL reviewers for their insightful comments, suggestions and advice on various aspects of this work.

References

D. Biber, S. Johansson, G. Leech, S. Conrad, E. Finegan, and R. Quirk. 1999. *Longman grammar of spoken and written English*, volume 2. MIT Press.

C.F. Bond and B.M. DePaulo. 2006. Accuracy of deception judgments. *Personality and Social Psychology Review*, 10(3):214.

Cone. 2011. 2011 Online Influence Trend Tracker. Online: `http://www.coneinc.com/negative-reviews-online-reverse-purchase-decisions`, August.

P. Ekman and W.V. Friesen. 1969. Nonverbal leakage and clues to deception. *Psychiatry*, 32(1):88.

Song Feng, Ritwik Banerjee, and Yejin Choi. 2012. Syntactic stylometry for deception detection. In *Proceedings of the 50th Annual Meeting of the Association for Computational Linguistics: Short Papers-Volume 2*, pages 171–175. Association for Computational Linguistics.

J.T. Hancock, L.E. Curry, S. Goorha, and M. Woodworth. 2008. On lying and being lied to: A linguistic analysis of deception in computer-mediated communication. *Discourse Processes*, 45(1):1–23.

N. Jindal and B. Liu. 2008. Opinion spam and analysis. In *Proceedings of the international conference on Web search and web data mining*, pages 219–230. ACM.

M.K. Johnson and C.L. Raye. 1981. Reality monitoring. *Psychological Review*, 88(1):67–85.

J.R. Landis and G.G. Koch. 1977. The measurement of observer agreement for categorical data. *Biometrics*, 33(1):159.

Dina Mayzlin, Yaniv Dover, and Judith A Chevalier. 2012. Promotional reviews: An empirical investigation of online review manipulation. Technical report, National Bureau of Economic Research.

R. Mihalcea and C. Strapparava. 2009. The lie detector: Explorations in the automatic recognition of deceptive language. In *Proceedings of the ACL-IJCNLP 2009 Conference Short Papers*, pages 309–312. Association for Computational Linguistics.

M.L. Newman, J.W. Pennebaker, D.S. Berry, and J.M. Richards. 2003. Lying words: Predicting deception from linguistic styles. *Personality and Social Psychology Bulletin*, 29(5):665.

M. Ott, Y. Choi, C. Cardie, and J.T. Hancock. 2011. Finding deceptive opinion spam by any stretch of the imagination. In *Proceedings of the 49th Annual Meeting of the Association for Computational Linguistics: Human Language Technologies-Volume 1*, pages 309–319. Association for Computational Linguistics.

Myle Ott, Claire Cardie, and Jeff Hancock. 2012. Estimating the prevalence of deception in online review communities. In *Proceedings of the 21st international conference on World Wide Web*, pages 201–210. ACM.

J.W. Pennebaker, C.K. Chung, M. Ireland, A. Gonzales, and R.J. Booth. 2007. The development and psychometric properties of LIWC2007. *Austin, TX: LIWC (www.liwc.net)*.

P. Rayson, A. Wilson, and G. Leech. 2001. Grammatical word class variation within the British National Corpus sampler. *Language and Computers*, 36(1):295–306.

R. A. Rigby and D. M. Stasinopoulos. 2005. Generalized additive models for location, scale and shape,(with discussion). *Applied Statistics*, 54:507–554.

Improving speech synthesis quality by reducing pitch peaks in the source recordings

Luisina Violante, **Pablo Rodríguez Zivic** and **Agustín Gravano**
Departamento de Computación, FCEyN
Universidad de Buenos Aires, Argentina
{lviolante,prodriguez,gravano}@dc.uba.ar

Abstract

We present a method for improving the perceived naturalness of corpus-based speech synthesizers. It consists in removing pronounced pitch peaks in the original recordings, which typically lead to noticeable discontinuities in the synthesized speech. We perceptually evaluated this method using two concatenative and two HMM-based synthesis systems, and found that using it on the source recordings managed to improve the naturalness of the synthesizers and had no effect on their intelligibility.

1 Introduction

By definition, corpus-based speech synthesizers, such as concatenative and HMM-based systems, rely heavily on the quality of the speech corpus used for building the systems. Creating speech corpora for this purpose is expensive and time consuming, so when the synthesized speech obtained is not as good as expected, it may be desirable to modify or correct the corpus rather than record a new one. Common corrections are limited to discarding mispronounced words or noisy units. In this work we describe a simple method for attenuating pronounced pitch peaks, a frequent problem in recordings made by professional speakers, and evaluate it using four different corpus-based systems. Sections 2 and 3 describe the speech synthesis systems and corpus employed in this work. In Section 4 we present the method for reducing pitch peaks. In Section 5 we describe how we evaluated the effect of our method on intelligibility and naturalness of the synthesizers.

2 Synthesis systems

Festival[1] is a general framework for building speech synthesis systems, written in C++ and developed by the Center of Speech Technology Research at the University of Edinburgh (Black et al., 2001). It provides an implementation of concatenative speech synthesis as well as synthesis based on Hidden Markov Models (HMM). In this work we used a Festival module called *Clunits unit selection engine* to build concatenative synthesizers. The unit size is the *phone*, although since a percentage of the previous unit is included in the acoustic distance measure, the unit size is rather "phone plus previous phone", thus similar to a *diphone* (Black and Lenzo, 2007). Additionally, we used a second Festival module called *Clustergen parametric synthesis engine* for building HMM-based speech synthesizers.

MARY TTS[2] is an open-source synthesis platform written in Java, originally jointly developed by the Language Technology Lab at the German Research Center for Artificial Intelligence (DFKI) and the Institute of Phonetics at Saarland University, and currently maintained by DFKI. Like Festival, MARY provides toolkits for building unit selection and HMM-based synthesis voices (Schröder and Trouvain, 2003).

3 Corpus

For building our systems we used the SECYT corpus, created by the Laboratorio de Investigaciones Sensoriales (Universidad de Buenos Aires) for

[1] http://festvox.org/festival

[2] http://mary.dfki.de

studying the prosody of Argentine Spanish (Torres and Gurlekian, 2004). It consists of 741 declarative sentences recorded by a female professional speaker (pitch range: 130-380Hz). On average, sentences are 7 words and 3.9 seconds long. The entire corpus has manual phonetic transcriptions and time alignments, following a version of the *Speech Assessment Methods Phonetic Alphabet* (SAMPA) adapted for Argentine Spanish (Gurlekian et al., 2001).

A priori, this corpus is a very good candidate for building a synthesis system – its 741 sentences are phonetically balanced, the audio quality is excellent, and it has precise time-aligned phonetic transcriptions. We thus built two concatenation systems using this corpus: Festival's diphone-like and MARY's diphone systems. The results were not satisfactory. The new voices presented clearly noticeable discontinuities, both in intensity and pitch, which affected their naturalness – as judged impressionistically by the authors and non-expert colleagues.

In an attempt to attenuate these problems, we leveled the intensity of all recordings to a mean of 72dB using linear interpolation. Specifically, each sound was multiplied by a number such that its new average RMS intensity was 72dB; so that all sentences in the corpus ended up with the same average intensity. After this conversion, we rebuilt the systems. The resulting voices sounded somewhat better, but their most noticeable problem, severe pitch discontinuities, persisted.

Further analysis of the corpus recordings revealed that this issue was likely due to the speaking style employed by the professional speaker. It contains frequent pronounced pitch peaks, a verbal stylistic device acquired by the speaker as part of her professional training. These events produced units with very different pitch levels and slopes, thus leading to the discontinuities mentioned above.

4 Reduction of pitch peaks

We searched for ways to reduce the magnitude of these pitch peaks by manipulating the pitch track of the recordings using the *Time-Domain Pitch-Synchronous OverLap-and-Add* (TD-PSOLA) signal processing technique (Moulines and Charpentier, 1990). We used the implementation of TD-PSOLA included in the Praat toolkit (Boersma and Weenink, 2012).

We tried several formulas for TD-PSOLA and ended up choosing the one that appeared to yield the best results, evaluated perceptually by the authors:

$$f(x) = \begin{cases} (x - T) * s + T & \text{if } x > T \\ x & \text{otherwise.} \end{cases}$$

This formula linearly scales the pitch track by a scaling factor s above a threshold T, and leaves it intact below T. When $0 < s < 1$, the pitch track gets compressed above the threshold. We experimented with several values for the two constants, and selected $T = 200\text{Hz}$ and $s = 0.4$ as the ones producing the best results. Figure 1 illustrates the pitch peak reduction method. The black solid line corresponds to the pitch track of the original audio; the red dotted line, to the pitch track of the modified audio. Note that the modified pitch track is scaled down above 200Hz, but identical to the original below it.

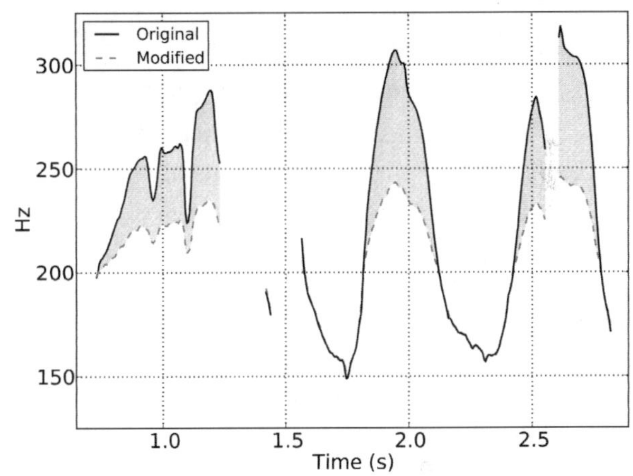

Figure 1: Reduction of pitch peaks. The original pitch track (in black) is scaled down 40% above 200Hz.

5 Evaluation of the method

Next we proceeded to evaluate the effect on synthesizer quality of reducing pitch peaks in the training corpus. For this purpose we prepared two versions of the SECYT corpus – with and without applying our pitch-peak reduction technique. We refer to these two as the *original* and *modified* recordings, respectively. In both cases, the intensity level of all audios was first leveled to a mean of 72dB using linear interpolation, to compensate for differences across recordings.

Subsequently, we built 8 speech synthesizers, consisting in all combinations of: Festival and MARY frameworks, concatenative and HMM-based synthesis, and original and modified recordings. We refer to these systems using the following notation: {fest, mary}_{conc, hmm}_{orig, mod}; e.g., mary_conc_mod is a concatenative system built using the MARY framework with the modified corpus.

We evaluated these systems along two dimensions: intelligibility and naturalness. Our goal was to compare four system pairs: systems built using the original recordings vs. those built using the modified recordings. The null hypothesis was that there was no difference between 'orig' and 'mod' systems; and the alternative hypothesis was that 'mod' systems were better than 'orig' ones.

5.1 Intelligibility

To evaluate intelligibility we used the *Semantically Unpredictable Sentences* (SUS) method (Nye and Gaitenby, 1974), which consists in asking participants to listen to and transcribe sentences with correct syntax but no semantic sense, for later measuring and comparing the number of transcription errors. We used a set of 50 such sentences, each 6-10 words long, created by Gurlekian et al. (2012) for evaluating Spanish speech synthesizers. A sample sentence is, *El viento dulce armó un libro de panqueques* (The sweet wind made a book of pancakes).

For each participant, 40 sentences were selected at random and synthesized with the 8 systems (5 sentences per system, with no repetitions). Participants were given the following instructions,

> *La primera tarea consiste en escuchar varios audios, y transcribir para cada audio la oración que escuches. Prestá atención, porque podés escuchar cada audio una sola vez.*
> (The first task consists in listening to several audios, and transcribing for each audio the sentence you hear. Pay attention, because you can only listen to each audio once.)

5.2 Naturalness

To evaluate naturalness we used the *Mean Opinion Score* (MOS) method, in which participants are asked to rate the overall quality of synthesized speech on a 10-point scale (Viswanathan and Viswanathan, 2005).

We used a set of 20 sentences, each 5-20 words long, created by Gurlekian et al. (2012), plus 20 additional sentences created for this study. A sample sentence is, *El sector de informática es el nuevo generador de empleo del país* (The information technology sector is the country's new job creator).

Again, for each participant, 40 sentences were selected at random and synthesized with the 8 systems (5 sentences per system). Participants were given the following instructions,

> *La segunda (y última) tarea consiste en escuchar otros audios, y puntuar la naturalidad de cada uno. Usar una escala de 1 a 10, donde 1 significa "no suena natural en lo absoluto" y 10 significa "suena completamente natural". En este caso, podés escuchar cada audio una o más veces.*
> (The second (and last) task consists in listening to other audios, and score the naturalness of each. Use a scale from 1 to 10, where 1 means "it does not sound natural at all" and 10 means "it sounds completely natural". In this case, you may listen to each audio one or more times.)

5.3 Results

SUS and MOS tests were administered on a computer interface in a silent laboratory using regular headphones. 14 graduate and undergraduate students (11 male, 3 female; mean age: 27.6) completed both tests – first SUS, followed by MOS.

The transcriptions of the SUS tests were manually corrected for obvious typos and spelling errors that did not form a valid Spanish word. Suspected typos and spelling errors that formed a valid word were not corrected. For example, *peliculas* was corrected to *películas*, and *precion* to *presión*; but *canto* was not corrected to *cantó*, since it is a valid word. Subsequently, we computed the Levenshtein distance between each transcription and the corresponding sentence. Figure 2 shows the distribution of Levenshtein distances for each of our eight systems. We observe that all systems had a low error count, with a median of 0 or 1 errors per sentence. Two-tail Wilcoxon signed-rank tests revealed no significant differences between the systems built with the original and modified recordings ($p = 0.70$ for fest_conc, $p = 0.40$ for fest_hmm, $p = 0.69$ for mary_conc, $p = 0.40$ for mary_hmm, and $p = 0.41$ for all systems together). These results indicate that the intelligibility of all four system types was not affected by the

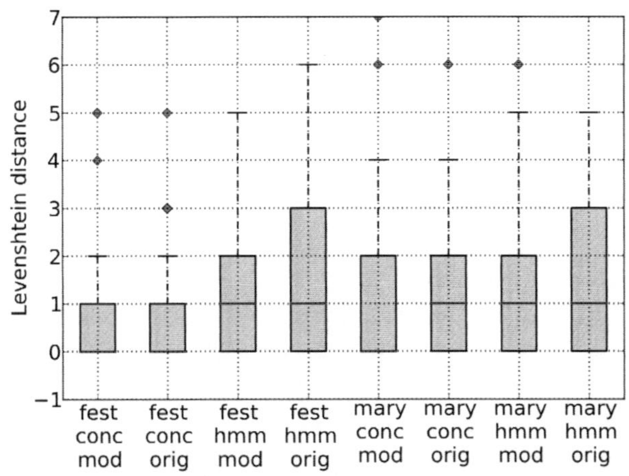

Figure 2: Intelligibility (SUS) results.

modifications performed on the corpus for reducing pitch peaks.

To account for the different interpretations of the 10-point scale, we normalized all MOS test scores by participant using z-scores.[3] Figure 3 shows the distribution of values for each system.

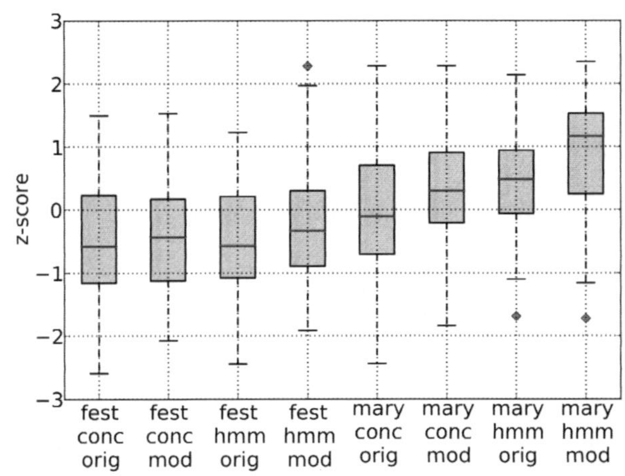

Figure 3: Naturalness (MOS) results.

We performed a series of Wilcoxon signed-rank tests to assess the statistical significance of the observed differences. The null hypothesis was that there was no difference between 'orig' and 'mod' systems; and the alternative hypothesis was that 'mod' systems were perceived as more natural than 'orig' ones. Table 5.3 summarizes these results.

For mary_conc and mary_hmm (concatenative and HMM-based systems built using the MARY

[3] $z = (x - \overline{x})/s$, where $\overline{x}$ and s are estimates of the participant's mean and standard deviation, respectively.

	W	p-value
fest_conc	2485	0.559
fest_hmm	2175	0.126
mary_conc	1933	0.016
mary_hmm	1680.5	0.001
All systems	34064.5	0.004

Table 1: Results of Wilcoxon tests comparing systems using the original and modified audios.

framework) the perceived naturalness was significantly higher for systems built using the modified recordings (i.e., after reducing pitch peaks) than for systems built with the original recordings. For fest_conc (concatenative system built with Festival) we found no evidence of such differences. Finally, for fest_hmm (Festival HMM-based) the difference approaches significance at 0.126.

6 Conclusions

In this paper we presented a method for improving the perceived naturalness of corpus-based speech synthesizers. It consists in removing pronounced pitch peaks in the original recordings, which typically produce discontinuities in the synthesized speech. We evaluated this method using two common technologies (concatenative and HMM-based synthesis) and two different implementations (Festival and MARY), aiming at a good coverage of state-of-the-art speech synthesizers, and obtained clear results. First, its utilization on the source recordings had no effect (negative or positive) on the intelligibility of any of the systems. Second, the naturalness of the concatenative and HMM-based systems built with the MARY framework improved significantly; the HMM-based system built with Festival showed an improved naturalness at a level approaching significance; and the Festival concatenative system showed no improvement. In summary, the presented method did not harm the intelligibility of the systems, and in some cases managed to improve their naturalness. Therefore, since the impact of the proposed modifications on all four systems was positive to neutral, developers may find this methodology beneficial.

Acknowledgments

This work was funded in part by CONICET, ANPCYT PICT 2009-0026, and UBACYT 20020090300087. The authors thank Jorge A. Gurlekian, Humberto M. Torres and Christian G. Cossio-Mercado from LIS (INIGEM, CONICET-UBA) for kindly sharing the SECYT corpus and other materials for the present study, as well as for valuable suggestions and comments.

References

Alan W. Black and Kevin A. Lenzo. 2007. *Building Synthetic Voices*. Language Technologies Institute, Carnegie Mellon University, http://festvox.org/bsv.

A. Black, P. Taylor, R. Caley, R. Clark, K. Richmond, S. King, V. Strom, and H. Zen. 2001. The festival speech synthesis system.

Paul Boersma and David Weenink. 2012. Praat: doing phonetics by computer. *http://www.praat.org/*.

J. Gurlekian, L. Colantoni, and H. Torres. 2001. El alfabeto fonético SAMPA y el diseño de corpora fonéticamente balanceados. *Fonoaudiológica*, 47:58–69.

J. A. Gurlekian, C. Cossio-Mercado, H. Torres, and M. E. Vaccari. 2012. Subjective evaluation of a high quality text-to-speech system for Argentine Spanish. In *Proceedings of Iberspeech*, Madrid, Spain.

E. Moulines and F. Charpentier. 1990. Pitch-synchronous waveform processing techniques for text-to-speech synthesis using diphones. *Speech communication*, 9(5):453–467.

P. W. Nye and J. H. Gaitenby. 1974. The intelligibility of synthetic monosyllabic words in short, syntactically normal sentences. *Haskins Laboratories Status Report on Speech Research*, 37(38):169–190.

M. Schröder and J. Trouvain. 2003. The German text-to-speech synthesis system MARY: A tool for research, development and teaching. *International Journal of Speech Technology*, 6(4):365–377.

H. M. Torres and J. A. Gurlekian. 2004. Automatic determination of phrase breaks for Argentine Spanish. In *Speech Prosody 2004, International Conference*.

Mahesh Viswanathan and Madhubalan Viswanathan. 2005. Measuring speech quality for text-to-speech systems: Development and assessment of a modified mean opinion score (MOS) scale. *Computer Speech & Language*, 19(1):55–83.

Robust Systems for Preposition Error Correction Using Wikipedia Revisions

Aoife Cahill*, **Nitin Madnani***, **Joel Tetreault**[†] **and Diane Napolitano***

* Educational Testing Service, 660 Rosedale Road, Princeton, NJ 08541, USA
{acahill, nmadnani, dnapolitano}@ets.org
[†] Nuance Communications, Inc., 1198 E. Arques Ave, Sunnyvale, CA 94085, USA
Joel.Tetreault@nuance.com

Abstract

We show that existing methods for training preposition error correction systems, whether using well-edited text or error-annotated corpora, do not generalize across very different test sets. We present a new, large error-annotated corpus and use it to train systems that generalize across three different test sets, each from a different domain and with different error characteristics. This new corpus is automatically extracted from Wikipedia revisions and contains over one million instances of preposition corrections.

1 Introduction

One of the main themes that has defined the field of automatic grammatical error correction has been the availability of error-annotated learner data to train and test a system. Some errors, such as determiner-noun number agreement, are easily corrected using rules and regular expressions (Leacock et al., 2010). On the other hand, errors involving the usage of prepositions and articles are influenced by several factors including the local context, the prior discourse and semantics. These errors are better handled by statistical models which potentially require millions of training examples.

Most statistical approaches to grammatical error correction have used one of the following training paradigms: 1) training solely on examples of correct usage (Han et al., 2006); 2) training on examples of correct usage and artificially generated errors (Rozovskaya and Roth, 2010); and 3) training on examples of correct usage and real learner errors (Dahlmeier and Ng, 2011; Dale et al., 2012). The latter two methods require annotated corpora of errors, and while they have shown great promise, manually annotating grammatical errors in a large enough corpus of learner writing is often a costly and time-consuming endeavor.

In order to efficiently and automatically acquire a very large corpus of annotated learner errors, we investigate the use of error corrections extracted from Wikipedia revision history. While Wikipedia revision history has shown promise for other NLP tasks including paraphrase generation (Max and Wisniewski, 2010; Nelken and Yamangil, 2008) and spelling correction (Zesch, 2012), this resource has not been used for the task of grammatical error correction.

To evaluate the usefulness of Wikipedia revision history for grammatical error correction, we address the task of correcting errors in preposition selection (i.e., where the context licenses the use of a preposition, but the writer selects the wrong one). We first train a model directly on instances of correct and incorrect preposition usage extracted from the Wikipedia revision data. We also generate artificial errors using the confusion distributions derived from this data. We compare both of these approaches to models trained on well-edited text and evaluate each on three test sets with a range of different characteristics. Each training paradigm is applied to multiple data sources for comparison. With these multiple evaluations, we address the following research questions:

1. Across multiple test sets, which data source

is more useful for correcting preposition errors: a large amount of well-edited text, a large amount of potentially noisy error-annotated data (either artificially generated or automatically extracted) or a smaller amount of higher quality error-annotated data?

2. Given error-annotated data, is it better to train on the corrections directly or to use the confusion distributions derived from these corrections for generating artificial errors in well-edited text?

3. What is the impact of having a mismatch in the error distributions of the training and test sets?

2 Related Work

In this section, we only review work in preposition error correction in terms of the three training paradigms and refer the reader to Leacock et al. (2010) for a more comprehensive review of the field.

2.1 Training on Well-Edited Text

Early approaches to error detection and correction did not have access to large amounts of error-annotated data to train statistical models and thus, systems were trained on millions of well-edited examples from news text instead (Gamon et al., 2008; Tetreault and Chodorow, 2008; De Felice and Pulman, 2009). Feature sets usually consisted of n-grams around the preposition, POS sequences, syntactic features and semantic information. Since the model only had knowledge of correct usage, an error was flagged if the system's prediction for a particular preposition context differed from the preposition the writer used.

2.2 Artificial Errors

The issue with training solely on correct usage was that the systems had no knowledge of typical learner errors. Ideally, a system would be trained on examples of correct and incorrect usage, however, for many years, such error-annotated corpora were not available. Instead, several researchers generated artificial errors based on the error distributions derived from the error-annotated learner corpora available at the time. Izumi et al. (2003) was the first to evaluate a model trained on incorrect usage as well as artificial errors for the task of correcting several different error types, including prepositions. However, with limited training data, system performance was quite poor. Rozovskaya and Roth (2010) evaluated different ways of generating artificial errors and found that a system trained on artificial errors could outperform the more traditional training paradigm of using only well-edited texts. Most recently, Imamura et al. (2012) showed that performance could be improved by training a model on artificial errors and addressing domain adaptation for the task of Japanese particle correction.

2.3 Error-Annotated Learner Corpora

Recently, error-annotated learner data has become more readily and publicly available allowing models to be trained on both examples of correct usage as well typical learner errors. Han et al. (2010) showed that a preposition error detection and correction system trained on 100,000 annotated preposition errors from the Chungdahm Corpus of Korean Learner English (in addition to 1 million examples of correct usage) outperformed a model trained only on 5 million examples of correct usage. Gamon (2010) and Dahlmeier and Ng (2011) showed that combining models trained separately on examples of correct and incorrect usage could also improve the performance of a preposition error correction system.

3 Mining Wikipedia Revisions for Grammatical Error Corrections

3.1 Related Work

Many NLP researchers have taken advantage of the wealth of information available in Wikipedia revisions. Dutrey et al. (2011) define a typology of modifications found in the French Wikipedia (WiCoPaCo). They show that the kinds of edits made range from specific lexical changes to more general rewrite edits. Similar types of edits are found in the English Wikipedia. The data extracted from Wikipedia revisions has been used for a wide variety of tasks including spelling correction (Max and Wisniewski, 2010; Zesch, 2012), lexical error detection (Nelken and Yamangil, 2008), sentence compression (Yamangil and Nelken, 2008), paraphrase generation (Max and Wisniewski, 2010; Nelken and Yamangil, 2008), lexical simplification (Yatskar et al., 2010) and entailment (Zanzotto and Pennacchiotti, 2010;

(1) [Wiki clean] In addition, sometimes it is also left to stand overnight (*at* → *in*) the refrigerator.

(2) [Wiki clean] Also none of the witnesses present (*of* → *on*) those dates supports Ranneft's claims.

(3) [Wiki dirty] ... cirque has a permanent production (*to* → *at*) the Mirage, love.

(4) [Wiki dirty] In the late 19th century Vasilli Andreyev a salon violinist took up the balalaika in his performances for French tourists (*in* → *to*) Petersburg.

Figure 1: Example sentences with preposition errors extracted from Wikipedia revisions. The second preposition is assumed to be the correction.

Cabrio et al., 2012). To our knowledge, no one has previously extracted data for training a grammatical error detection system from Wikipedia revisions.

3.2 Extracting Preposition Correction Data from Wikipedia Revisions

As the source of our Wikipedia revisions, we used an XML snapshot of Wikipedia generated in July 2011 containing 8,735,890 articles and 288,583,063 revisions.[1] We then used the following process to extract preposition errors and their corresponding corrections from this snapshot:

Step 1: Extract the plain text versions of all revisions of all articles using the Java Wikipedia Library (Ferschke et al., 2011).

Step 2: For each Wikipedia article, compare each revision with the revision immediately preceding it using an efficient *diff* algorithm.[2]

Step 3: Compute all 1-word **edit chains** for the article, i.e., sequences of related edits derived from all revisions of the same article. For example, say revision 10 of an article inserts the preposition *of* into a sentence and revision 12 changes that preposition to *on*. Assuming that no other revisions change this sentence, the corresponding edit chain would contain the following 3 elements: $\epsilon \rightarrow of \rightarrow on$. The extracted chains contain the full context on either side of the 1-word edit, up to the automatically detected sentence boundaries.

Step 4: (a) Ignore any *circular* chains, i.e., where the first element in the edit chain is the same as the last element. (b) Collapse all *non-circular* chains, i.e., only retain the first and the last elements in a chain. Both these decisions are motivated by the assumption that the intermediate links in the chain are unreliable for training an error correction system since a Wikipedia contributor modified them.

Step 5 : From all remaining 2-element chains, find those where a preposition is replaced with another preposition. If the preposition edit is the only edit in the sentence, we convert the chain into a sentence pair and label it *clean*. If there are other 1-word edits but not within 5 words of the preposition edit on either side, we label the sentence *somewhat clean*. Otherwise, we label it *dirty*. The motivation is that the presence of other nearby edits make the preposition correction less reliable when used in isolation, due to the possible dependencies between corrections.

All extracted sentences were part-of-speech tagged using the Stanford Tagger (Toutanova et al., 2003). Using the above process, we are able to extract approximately 2 million sentences containing prepositions errors and their corrections. Some examples of the sentences we extracted are given in Figure 1. Example (4) shows an example of a bad correction.

4 Corpora

We use several corpora for training and testing our preposition error correction system. The properties of each are outlined in Table 1, organized by paradigm. For each corpus we report the total number of prepositions used for training, as well as the number and percentage of preposition corrections.

4.1 Well-edited Text

We train our system on two well-edited corpora. The first is the same corpus used by Tetreault and

[1] http://dumps.wikimedia.org/enwiki/

[2] http://code.google.com/p/google-diff-match-patch/

	Corpus	Total # Preps	# Corrected Preps	
Well-edited Text	Wikipedia Snapshot (10m sents)	26,069,860	0	(0%)
	Lexile/SJM	6,719,077	0	(0%)
Artificially Generated Errors	Wikipedia Snapshot	26,127,464	2,844,227	(10.9%)
	Lexile/SJM	6,723,206	792,195	(11.8%)
Naturally Occurring Errors	Wikipedia Revisions All	7,125,317	1,027,643	(20.6%)
	Wikipedia Revisions ~Clean	3,001,900	381,644	(12.7%)
	Wikipedia Revisions Clean	1,978,802	266,275	(14.4%)
	Lang-8	129,987	53,493	(41.2%)
	NUCLE Train	72,741	922	(1.3%)
Test Corpora	NUCLE Test	9,366	125	(1.3%)
	FCE	33,243	2,900	(8.7%)
	HOO 2011 Test	1,703	81	(4.8%)

Table 1: Corpora characteristics

Chodorow (2008), comprising roughly 1.8 million sentences from the San Jose Mercury News Corpus[3] and roughly 1.8 million sentences from grades 11 and 12 of the MetaMetrics Lexile Corpus. Our second corpus is a random sample of 10 million sentences containing at least one preposition from the June 2012 snapshot of English Wikipedia Articles.[4]

4.2 Artificially Generated Errors

Similar to Foster and Andersen (2009) and Rozovskaya and Roth (2010), we artificially introduce preposition errors into well-edited corpora (the two described above). We do this based on a distribution of possible confusions and train a model that is aware of the corrections. The two sets of confusion distributions we used were derived based on the errors extracted from Wikipedia revisions and Lang-8 respectively (discussed in Section 4.3). For each corrected preposition p_i in the revision data, we calculated $P(p_i|p_j)$, where p_j is each of the possible original prepositions that were confused with p_i. Then, for each sentence in the well-edited text, all prepositions are extracted. A preposition is randomly selected (without replacement) and changed based on the distribution of possible confusions (note that the original preposition is also included in the distribution, usually with a high probability, meaning that there is a strong preference not to change the preposition). If a preposition is changed to something other than the original preposition, all remaining prepositions in the sentence are left unchanged.

[3]The San Jose Mercury News is available from the Linguistic Data Consortium (catalog number LDC93T3A).

[4]We used a newer version of the Wikipedia text for the well-edited text, since we assume that more recent versions of the text will be most grammatical, and therefore closer to well-edited.

4.3 Naturally Occurring Errors

We have a number of corpora that contain annotated preposition errors. Note that we are only considering incorrectly selected prepositions, we do not consider missing or extraneous.

NUCLE The NUS Corpus of Learner English (NUCLE)[5] contains one million words of learner essay text, manually annotated with error tags and corrections. We use the same training, dev and test splits as Dahlmeier and Ng (2011).

FCE The CLC FCE Dataset[6] is a collection of 1,244 exam scripts written by learners of English as part of the Cambridge ESOL First Certificate in English (Yannakoudakis et al., 2011). It includes demographic metadata about the candidate, a grade for each essay and manually-annotated error corrections.

Wikipedia We use three versions of the preposition errors extracted from the Wikipedia revisions as described in Section 3.2. The first includes corrections where the preposition was the only word corrected in the entire sentence

[5]http://bit.ly/nuclecorpus

[6]http://ilexir.co.uk/applications/clc-fce-dataset/

(*clean*). The second contains all *clean* corrections, as well as all corrections where there were no other edits within a five-word span on either side of the preposition ($\sim$*clean*). The third contains all corrections regardless of any other changes in the surrounding context (*all*).

Lang-8 The Lang-8 website contains journals written by language learners, where native speakers highlight and correct errors on a sentence-by-sentence basis. As a result, it contains typical grammatical mistakes made by language learners, which can be easily downloaded. We automatically extract 75,622 sentences with preposition errors and corrections from the first million journal entries.[7]

HOO 2011 We take the test set from the HOO 2011 shared task (Dale and Kilgarriff, 2011) and extract all examples of preposition selection errors. The texts are fragments of ACL papers that have been manually annotated for grammatical errors.[8]

It is important to note that the three test sets we use are from entirely different domains: exam scripts from non-native English speakers (FCE), essays by highly proficient college students in Singapore (NUCLE) and ACL papers (HOO). In addition, they have a different number of total prepositions as well as erroneous prepositions.

5 Preposition Error Correction Experiments

We use the preposition error correction model described in Tetreault and Chodorow (2008)[9] to evaluate the many ways of using Wikipedia error corrections as described in the Section 4. We use this system since it has been recreated for other work (Dahlmeier and Ng, 2011; Tetreault et al., 2010) and is similar in methodology to Gamon et al. (2008) and De Felice and Pulman (2009). In short, the method models the problem of preposition error correction (for replacement errors) as a 36-way classification problem using a multinomial logistic regression model.[10] The system uses 25 lexical, syntactic and n-gram features derived from the contexts of each preposition training instance.

We modified the training paradigm of Tetreault and Chodorow (2008) so that a model could be trained on examples of correct usage as well as actual errors. We did this by adding a new feature specifying the writer's original preposition (as in Han et al. (2010) and Dahlmeier and Ng (2011)).

5.1 Results

We train a preposition correction system using each of the three data paradigms and test on the FCE, NUCLE and HOO 2011 test corpora. For each preposition in the test corpus, we record whether the system predicted that it should be changed, and if so, what it should be changed to. We then compare the prediction to the annotation in the test corpus. We report results in terms of f-score, where precision and recall are calculated as follows:[11]

$$\text{Precision} = \frac{\text{Number of correct preposition corrections}}{\text{Total number of corrections suggested}}$$

$$\text{Recall} = \frac{\text{Number of correct preposition corrections}}{\text{Total number of corrections in test set}}$$

Note that due to the high volume of unchanged prepositions in the test corpus, we obtain very high accuracies, which are not indicative of true performance, and are not included in our results.

The results of our experiments are presented in Table 2.[12] The first part of the table shows the f-scores of preposition error correction systems that

[7] Tajiri et al. (2012) extract a corpus of English verb phrases corrected for tense/aspect errors from Lang-8. They kindly provided us with their scripts to carry out the scraping of Lang-8.

[8] The results of the HOO 2011 shared task were not reported at level of preposition selection error, therefore it is not possible to compare the results presented in this paper with those results.

[9] Note that in that work, the model was evaluated in terms of preposition error *detection* rather than correction, however the model itself does not change.

[10] We use liblinear (Fan et al., 2008) with the L1-regularized logistic regression solver and default parameters.

[11] As Chodorow et al. (2012) note, it is not clear how to handle cases where the system predicts a preposition that is neither the same as the writer preposition nor the correct preposition. We count these cases as false positives.

[12] No thresholds were used in the systems that were trained on well-edited text. Traditionally, thresholds are applied so as to only predict a correction when the system is highly confident. This has the effect of increasing precision at the cost of recall, and sometimes leads to an overall improved f-score. Here we take the prediction of the system, regardless of the confidence, reflecting a lower-bound of this method.

	Data Source	Paradigm	CLC-FCE N=33,243	NUCLE N=9,366	HOO2011 N=1,703
Without Wikipedia Revisions (**nonWikiRev**)	Wikipedia Snapshot	Well-edited Text	24.43*	5.02*	12.36*
	Lexile/SJM	Well-edited Text	24.73*	4.29*	9.73*
	Wikipedia Snapshot	Artificial Errors (Lang-8)	42.15*	19.91*	28.75
	Lexile/SJM	Artificial Errors (Lang-8)	**45.36**	18.00*	25.15
	Lang-8	Error-annotated Text	38.22*	8.18*	24.00
	NUCLE train	Error-annotated Text	5.38*	20.14	4.82*
With Wikipedia Revisions (**WikiRev**)	Wikipedia Snapshot	Artificial Errors (Wiki)	31.17*	24.52	28.30
	Lexile/SJM	Artificial Errors (Wiki)	34.35*	23.38	32.76
	Wikipedia Revisions All	Error-annotated Text	33.59*	**26.39**	**36.84**
	Wikipedia Revisions ∼Clean	Error-annotated Text	29.68*	22.13	36.04
	Wikipedia Revisions Clean	Error-annotated Text	28.09*	21.74	28.30

Table 2: Preposition selection error correction results (f-score). The systems with scores in bold are statistically significantly better than all systems marked with an asterisk ($p < 0.01$). Confidence intervals were obtained using bootstrap resampling with 50,000 replicates.

one might be able to train with publicly available data excluding the Wikipedia revisions that we have extracted. We refer to these systems as **nonWikiRev** systems. The second part of the table shows the f-scores of systems trained on the Wikipedia revisions data – either directly on the annotated errors or on the artificial errors produced using the confusion distributions derived from these annotated errors. We refer to this second set of systems as **WikiRev** systems. The **nonWikiRev** systems perform inconsistently, heavily dependent on the characteristics of the test set in question. On the other hand, it is obvious that the **WikiRev** systems — while not always outperforming the best **nonWikiRev** systems — generalize much better across the three test sets. In fact, for the NUCLE test set, the best **WikiRev** system performs as well as the **nonWikiRev** system trained on data from the *same* domain and with *identical* error characteristics as the test set. The distributions of errors in the three test sets are not similar, and therefore, the stability in performance of the **WikiRev** systems cannot be attributed to the hypothesis that the **WikiRev** training data error distributions are more similar to the test data than any of the other training corpora. Therefore, we claim that if a preposition error correction system is to be deployed on data for which the error characteristics are not known in advance, i.e. most real-world scenarios, training the system using Wikipedia revisions is likely to be the most robust option.

6 Discussion

We examine the results of our experiments in light of the research questions we posed in Section 1.

6.1 Which Data Source is More Useful?

We wanted to know whether it was better to have a smaller corpus of carefully annotated corrections, or a much larger (but automatically generated, and therefore noisier) error-annotated corpus. We also wanted to compare this scenario to training on large amounts of well-edited text. From our experiments, it is clear that the composition of the test set plays a major role in answering this question. On a test set with few corrections (NUCLE), training on well-edited text (and without using thresholds) performs particularly poorly. On the other hand, when evaluating on the FCE test set which contains far more errors, training on well-edited text performs reasonably well (though statistically significantly worse than training on all of the Wikipedia errors). Similarly, training on the smaller, high-quality NUCLE corpus and evaluating on the NUCLE test set achieves good results, however training on NUCLE and testing on FCE achieves the lowest f-score of all our systems on that test set.

Figure 2 shows the learning curves obtained by increasing the size of the training data for two of the test sets.[13] Although one might assume

[13]For space reasons, the graph for HOO2011 is omitted. Also note that the results in Table 2 may not appear in the graph,

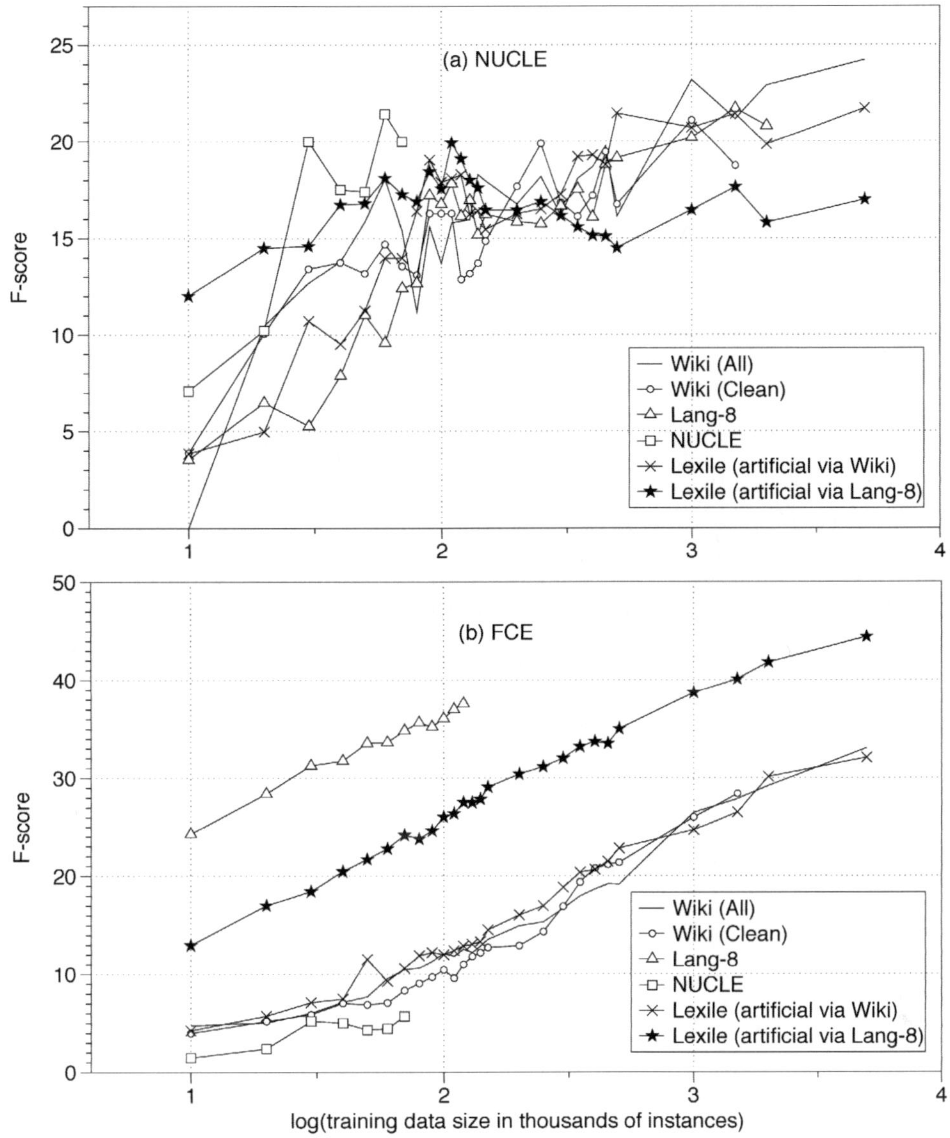

Figure 2: The effect of varying the size of the training corpus

that Wikipedia-*clean* would be more reliable than Wikipedia-*all*, the *cleanness* of the Wikipedia data seems to make very little difference, probably because the data extracted in the *dirty* contexts is not as noisy as we expected. Interestingly, it also seems that additional data would lead to further improvements for models trained on artificial errors in Lexile data and for those trained on all of the automatically extracted Wikipedia errors.

Another interesting aspect of Figure 2 is that training on the Lang-8 data shows a very steep rising trend. This suggests that automatically-scraped data that is highly targeted towards language learners is very useful in correcting preposition errors in texts where they are reasonably frequent.

6.2 Natural or Artificially Generated Errors?

Table 2 shows that training on artificially generated errors via Wikipedia revisions performs fairly consistently across test corpora. While using Lang-8 for artificial error generation is also quite promising for FCE, it does not generalize across test sets.

since we were sampling at specific data points which did not correspond exactly to the total sizes of the training corpora.

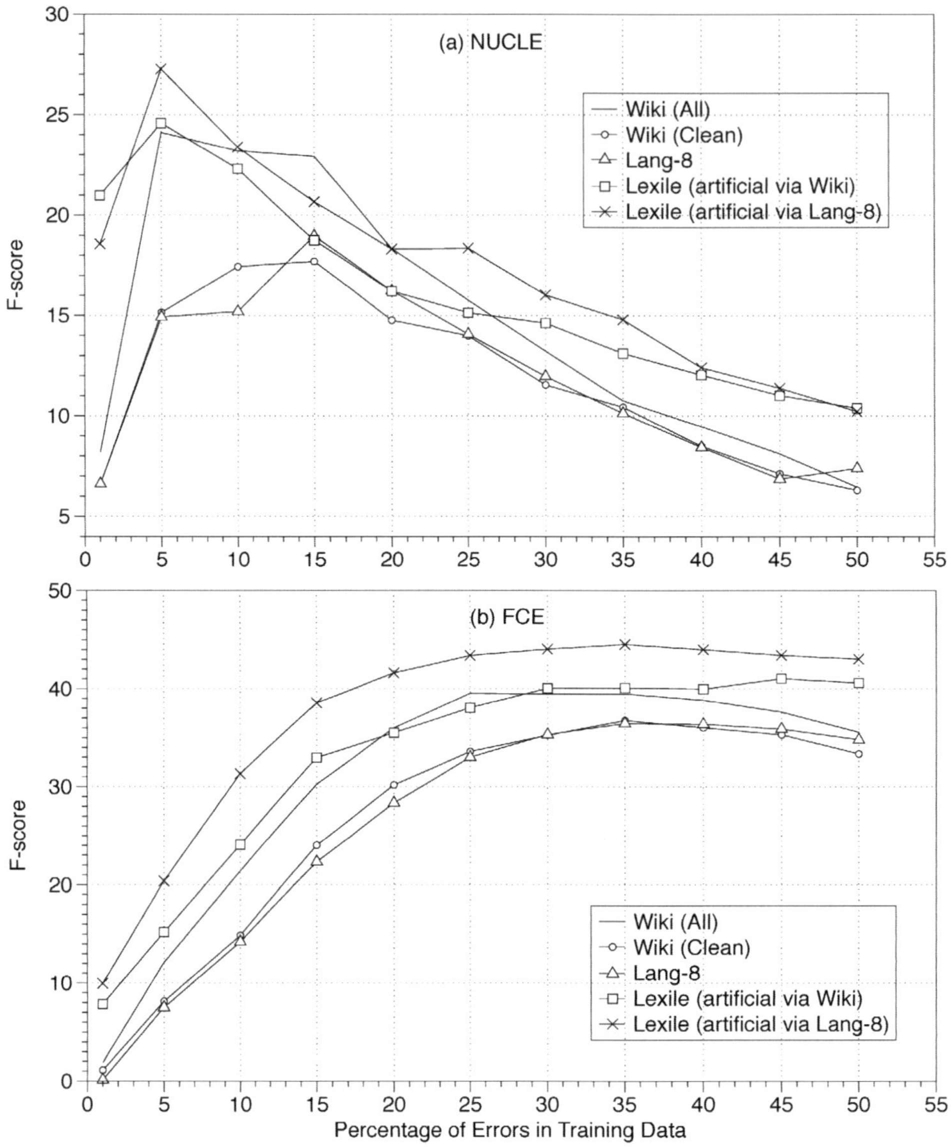

Figure 3: The effect of varying the percentage of errors in the training corpus

On FCE it achieves the highest results, on NUCLE it performs statistically significantly worse than the best system, and on HOO 2011 it achieves a lower (though not statistically significant) result than the best system. This highlights that extracting errors from Wikipedia is useful in two ways: (1) training a system on the errors alone works well and (2) generating artificial errors in well-edited corpora of different domains and training a system on that also works well. It also indicates that if the system were to be applied to a specific domain, applying the confusion distributions to a domain specific corpus – if available – would likely yield the best results.

6.3 Mismatching Distributions

The proportion of errors in the training and test data plays an important role in the performance of any preposition error correction system. This is clearly evident by comparing system performances across the three test sets which have fairly different compositions. FCE contains a much higher proportion of errors than NUCLE, and HOO falls somewhere in between. Interestingly, the system trained on Lang-8 data (which contains the highest proportion of errors among all training corpora) performs best on the FCE data. On the other hand, the same system performs poorly on NUCLE test which contains far fewer errors. In this instance, the system learns to predict an incorrect preposition too often. We see a similar pattern with the system trained on the NUCLE training data. It performs poorly on FCE which contains many errors, but well on NUCLE test which contains a similar proportion of errors.

In order to better understand the relationship between the percentage of errors in the training data and system performance, we vary the percentage of errors in each training corpus from 1-50% and test on the unchanged FCE and NUCLE test corpora. For each training corpus, we reduce the size to be twice the size of the total number of errors.[14] Keeping this size constant, we then artificially change the percentage of errors. Note that because the total size of the corpus has changed, the results in Table 2 may not appear in the graph. Figure 3 shows the effect on f-score when the data composition is changed. For both test sets, there is a peak after which increasing the proportion of errors in the training corpus is detrimental. For NUCLE test with its low number of preposition errors, this peak is very pronounced. For FCE, it is more of a gentle degradation in performance, but the pattern is clear. Also noteworthy is the fact that the degradation for models trained on artificial errors is less steep suggesting that they may be more stable across test sets.

In general, these results indicate that when building a preposition error detection using error-annotated data, the characteristics of the data to which the system will be applied should play a vital role in how the system is to be trained. Our results show that the **WikiRev** systems are robust across test sets, however if the exact distribution of errors in the data is known in advance, other models may perform better.

7 Conclusion

Although previous approaches to preposition error correction using either well-edited text or small hand-annotated corrections performed well on some specific test set, they did not generalize well across very different test sets. In this paper, we present work that automatically extracts preposition error corrections from Wikipedia Revisions and uses it to build *robust* error correction systems. We show that this data is useful for two purposes. Firstly, a model trained directly on the corrections performs well across test sets. Secondly, models trained on artificial errors generated from the distribution of confusions in the Wikipedia data perform equally well. The distribution of confusions can also be applied to other well-edited corpora in different domains, providing a very powerful method of automatically generating error corpora. The results of our experiments also highlight the importance of the distribution of expected errors in the test set. Models that perform well on one kind of distribution may not necessarily work on a completely different one, as evident in the performances of the systems trained on either Lang-8 or NUCLE. In general, the **WikiRev** models perform well across distributions. We also conducted some preliminary system combination experiments and found that while they yielded promising results, further investigation is necessary. We have also made the Wikipedia preposition correction corpus available for download.[15]

In future work, we will examine whether the results we obtain for English generalize to other Wikipedia languages. We also plan to extract multi-word corrections for other types of errors and to examine the usefulness of including error contexts in our confusion distributions (e.g., preposition confusions following verbs versus those following nouns).

Acknowledgments

The authors would like to thank Daniel Dahlmeier, Torsten Zesch, Mamoru Komachi, Tajiri Toshikazu, Tomoya Mizumoto and Yuji Matsumoto for providing scripts and data that enabled us to carry out this research. We would also like to thank Martin Chodorow and the anonymous reviewers for their helpful suggestions and comments.

References

Elena Cabrio, Bernardo Magnini, and Angelina Ivanova. 2012. Extracting Context-Rich Entailment Rules from

[14] We omit the NUCLE train corpus from this comparison, because it contains too few errors to obtain a meaningful result.

[15] http://bit.ly/etsprepdata

Wikipedia Revision History. In *Proceedings of the 3rd Workshop on the People's Web Meets NLP: Collaboratively Constructed Semantic Resources and their Applications to NLP*, pages 34–43, Jeju, Republic of Korea, July. Association for Computational Linguistics.

Martin Chodorow, Markus Dickinson, Ross Israel, and Joel Tetreault. 2012. Problems in Evaluating Grammatical Error Detection Systems. In *Proceedings of COLING 2012*, pages 611–628, Mumbai, India, December. The COLING 2012 Organizing Committee.

Daniel Dahlmeier and Hwee Tou Ng. 2011. Grammatical Error Correction with Alternating Structure Optimization. In *Proceedings of the 49th Annual Meeting of the Association for Computational Linguistics: Human Language Technologies*, pages 915–923, Portland, Oregon, USA, June. Association for Computational Linguistics.

Robert Dale and Adam Kilgarriff. 2011. Helping Our Own: The HOO 2011 Pilot Shared Task. In *Proceedings of the Generation Challenges Session at the 13th European Workshop on Natural Language Generation*, pages 242–249, Nancy, France, September. Association for Computational Linguistics.

Robert Dale, Ilya Anisimoff, and George Narroway. 2012. HOO 2012: A Report on the Preposition and Determiner Error Correction Shared Task. In *Proceedings of the Seventh Workshop on Building Educational Applications Using NLP*, pages 54–62, Montréal, Canada, June. Association for Computational Linguistics.

Rachele De Felice and Stephen G. Pulman. 2009. Automatic detection of preposition errors in learner writing. *CALICO Journal*, 26(3):512–528.

Camille Dutrey, Houda Bouamor, Delphine Bernhard, and Aurélien Max. 2011. Local modifications and paraphrases in Wikipedias revision history. *SEPLN journal(Revista de Procesamiento del Lenguaje Natural)*, 46:51–58.

Rong-En Fan, Kai-Wei Chang, Cho-Jui Hsieh, Xiang-Rui Wang, and Chih-Jen Lin. 2008. LIBLINEAR: A library for large linear classification. *Journal of Machine Learning Research*, 9:1871–1874.

Oliver Ferschke, Torsten Zesch, and Iryna Gurevych. 2011. Wikipedia Revision Toolkit: Efficiently Accessing Wikipedia's Edit History. In *Proceedings of the 49th Annual Meeting of the Association for Computational Linguistics: Human Language Technologies. System Demonstrations.*

Jennifer Foster and Oistein Andersen. 2009. GenERRate: Generating Errors for Use in Grammatical Error Detection. In *Proceedings of the Fourth Workshop on Innovative Use of NLP for Building Educational Applications*, pages 82–90, Boulder, Colorado, June. Association for Computational Linguistics.

Michael Gamon, Jianfeng Gao, Chris Brockett, Alex Klementiev, William B. Dolan, Dmitriy Belenko, and Lucy Vanderwende. 2008. Using Contextual Speller Techniques and Language Modeling for ESL Error Correction. In *Proceedings of the International Joint Conference on Natural Language Processing (IJCNLP)*, pages 449–456, Hyderabad, India.

Michael Gamon. 2010. Using Mostly Native Data to Correct Errors in Learners' Writing. In *Human Language Technologies: The 2010 Annual Conference of the North American Chapter of the Association for Computational Linguistics*, pages 163–171, Los Angeles, California, June. Association for Computational Linguistics.

Na-Rae Han, Martin Chodorow, and Claudia Leacock. 2006. Detecting errors in English article usage by non-native speakers. *Natural Language Engineering*, 12(2):115–129.

Na-Rae Han, Joel Tetreault, Soo-Hwa Lee, and Jin-Young Ha. 2010. Using Error-Annotated ESL Data to Develop an ESL Error Correction System. In *Proceedings of the Seventh International Conference on Language Resources and Evaluation (LREC)*, Malta.

Kenji Imamura, Kuniko Saito, Kugatsu Sadamitsu, and Hitoshi Nishikawa. 2012. Grammar Error Correction Using Pseudo-Error Sentences and Domain Adaptation. In *Proceedings of the 50th Annual Meeting of the Association for Computational Linguistics (Volume 2: Short Papers)*, pages 388–392, Jeju Island, Korea, July. Association for Computational Linguistics.

Emi Izumi, Kiyotaka Uchimoto, Toyomi Saiga, Thepchai Supnithi, and Hitoshi Isahara. 2003. Automatic Error Detection in the Japanese Learners' English Spoken Data. In *The Companion Volume to the Proceedings of 41st Annual Meeting of the Association for Computational Linguistics*, pages 145–148, Sapporo, Japan, July. Association for Computational Linguistics.

Claudia Leacock, Martin Chodorow, Michael Gamon, and Joel Tetreault. 2010. *Automated Grammatical Error Detection for Language Learners*. Synthesis Lectures on Human Language Technologies. Morgan Claypool.

Aurélien Max and Guillaume Wisniewski. 2010. Mining Naturally-occurring Corrections and Paraphrases from Wikipedia's Revision History. In Nicoletta Calzolari (Conference Chair), Khalid Choukri, Bente Maegaard, Joseph Mariani, Jan Odijk, Stelios Piperidis, Mike Rosner, and Daniel Tapias, editors, *Proceedings of the Seventh conference on International Language Resources and Evaluation (LREC'10)*, Valletta, Malta, may. European Language Resources Association (ELRA).

Rami Nelken and Elif Yamangil. 2008. Mining Wikipedias Article Revision History for Training

Computational Linguistics Algorithms. In *Proceedings of the 1st AAAI Workshop on Wikipedia and Artificial Intelligence*, pages 31–36, Chicago, IL.

Alla Rozovskaya and Dan Roth. 2010. Generating Confusion Sets for Context-Sensitive Error Correction. In *Proceedings of the 2010 Conference on Empirical Methods in Natural Language Processing*, pages 961–970, Cambridge, MA, October. Association for Computational Linguistics.

Toshikazu Tajiri, Mamoru Komachi, and Yuji Matsumoto. 2012. Tense and Aspect Error Correction for ESL Learners Using Global Context. In *Proceedings of the 50th Annual Meeting of the Association for Computational Linguistics (ACL), Short Papers*, pages 198–202, Jeju Island, Korea.

Joel R. Tetreault and Martin Chodorow. 2008. The Ups and Downs of Preposition Error Detection in ESL Writing. In *Proceedings of the 22nd International Conference on Computational Linguistics (Coling 2008)*, pages 865–872, Manchester, UK.

Joel Tetreault, Jennifer Foster, and Martin Chodorow. 2010. Using Parse Features for Preposition Selection and Error Detection. In *Proceedings of the ACL 2010 Conference Short Papers*, pages 353–358, Uppsala, Sweden, July. Association for Computational Linguistics.

Kristina Toutanova, Dan Klein, Christopher D. Manning, and Yoram Singer. 2003. Feature-rich Part-of-speech Tagging with a Cyclic Dependency Network. In *Proceedings of NAACL*, pages 173–180.

Elif Yamangil and Rani Nelken. 2008. Mining Wikipedia Revision Histories for Improving Sentence Compression. In *Proceedings of ACL-08: HLT, Short Papers*, pages 137–140, Columbus, Ohio, June. Association for Computational Linguistics.

Helen Yannakoudakis, Ted Briscoe, and Ben Medlock. 2011. A New Dataset and Method for Automatically Grading ESOL Texts. In *Proceedings of the 49th Annual Meeting of the Association for Computational Linguistics: Human Language Technologies*, pages 180–189, Portland, Oregon, USA, June. Association for Computational Linguistics.

Mark Yatskar, Bo Pang, Cristian Danescu-Niculescu-Mizil, and Lillian Lee. 2010. For the sake of simplicity: Unsupervised extraction of lexical simplifications from Wikipedia. In *Human Language Technologies: The 2010 Annual Conference of the North American Chapter of the Association for Computational Linguistics*, pages 365–368, Los Angeles, California, June. Association for Computational Linguistics.

Fabio Massimo Zanzotto and Marco Pennacchiotti. 2010. Expanding textual entailment corpora from Wikipedia using co-training. In *Proceedings of the 2nd Workshop on The People's Web Meets NLP: Collaboratively Constructed Semantic Resources*, pages 28–36, Beijing, China, August. Coling 2010 Organizing Committee.

Torsten Zesch. 2012. Measuring Contextual Fitness Using Error Contexts Extracted from the Wikipedia Revision History. In *Proceedings of the 13th Conference of the European Chapter of the Association for Computational Linguistics*, pages 529–538, Avignon, France, April. Association for Computational Linguistics.

Supervised Bilingual Lexicon Induction with Multiple Monolingual Signals

Ann Irvine
Center for Language and Speech Processing
Johns Hopkins University

Chris Callison-Burch*
Computer and Information Science Dept.
University of Pennsylvania

Abstract

Prior research into learning translations from source and target language monolingual texts has treated the task as an unsupervised learning problem. Although many techniques take advantage of a seed bilingual lexicon, this work is the first to use that data for supervised learning to combine a diverse set of signals derived from a pair of monolingual corpora into a single discriminative model. Even in a low resource machine translation setting, where induced translations have the potential to improve performance substantially, it is reasonable to assume access to some amount of data to perform this kind of optimization. Our work shows that only a few hundred translation pairs are needed to achieve strong performance on the bilingual lexicon induction task, and our approach yields an average relative gain in accuracy of nearly 50% over an unsupervised baseline. Large gains in accuracy hold for all 22 languages (low and high resource) that we investigate.

1 Introduction

Bilingual lexicon induction is the task of identifying word translation pairs using source and target monolingual corpora, which are often comparable. Most approaches to the task are based on the idea that words that are translations of one another have similar distributional properties across languages. Prior research has shown that contextual similarity (Rapp, 1995), temporal similarity (Schafer and Yarowsky, 2002), and topical information (Mimno et al., 2009) are all good signals for learning translations from monolingual texts.

Most prior work either makes use of only one or two monolingual signals or uses unsupervised methods (like rank combination) to aggregate orthogonal signals (Schafer and Yarowsky, 2002; Klementiev and Roth, 2006). Surprisingly, no past research has employed *supervised* approaches to combine diverse monolingually-derived signals for bilingual lexicon induction. The field of machine learning has shown decisively that supervised models dramatically outperform unsupervised models, including for closely related problems like statistical machine translation (Och and Ney, 2002).

For the bilingual lexicon induction task, a supervised approach is natural, particularly because computing contextual similarity typically requires a seed bilingual dictionary (Rapp, 1995), and that same dictionary may be used for estimating the parameters of a model to combine monolingual signals. Alternatively, in a low resource machine translation (MT) setting, it is reasonable to assume a small amount of parallel data from which a bilingual dictionary can be extracted for supervision. In this setting, bilingual lexicon induction is critical for translating source words which do not appear in the parallel data or dictionary.

We frame bilingual lexicon induction as a binary classification problem; for a pair of source and target language words, we predict whether the two are translations of one another or not. For a given source language word, we score all target language candidates separately and then rerank them. We use a variety of signals derived from source and target

*Performed while faculty at Johns Hopkins University

monolingual corpora as features and use supervision to estimate the strength of each. In this work we:

- Use the following similarity metrics derived from monolingual corpora to score word pairs: contextual, temporal, topical, orthographic, and frequency.
- For the first time, explore using supervision to combine monolingual signals and learn a discriminative model for predicting translations.
- Present results for 22 low and high resource languages paired with English and show large accuracy gains over an unsupervised baseline.

2 Previous Work

Prior work suggests that a wide variety of monolingual signals, including distributional, temporal, topic, and string similarity, may inform bilingual lexicon induction (Rapp, 1995; Fung and Yee, 1998; Rapp, 1999; Schafer and Yarowsky, 2002; Schafer, 2006; Klementiev and Roth, 2006; Koehn and Knight, 2002; Haghighi et al., 2008; Mimno et al., 2009; Mausam et al., 2010). Klementiev et al. (2012) use many of those signals to score an existing phrase table for end-to-end MT but do not learn any new translations. Schafer and Yarowsky (2002) use an unsupervised rank-combination method for combining orthographic, contextual, temporal, and frequency similarities into a single ranking.

Recently, Ravi and Knight (2011), Dou and Knight (2012), and Nuhn et al. (2012) have worked toward learning a phrase-based translation model from monolingual corpora, relying on decipherment techniques. In contrast to that work, we use a seed bilingual lexicon for supervision and multiple monolingual signals proposed in prior work.

Haghighi et al. (2008) and Daumé and Jagarlamudi (2011) use some supervision to learn how to project contextual and orthographic features into a low-dimensional space, with the goal of representing words which are translations of one another as vectors which are close together in that space. However, both of those approaches focus on only two signals, high resource languages, and frequent words (frequent nouns, in the case of Haghighi et al. (2008)). In our classification framework, we can incorporate any number of monolingual signals, including contextual and string similarity, and directly learn how to combine them.

Language	#Words	Language	#Words
Nepali	0.4	Somali	0.5
Uzbek	1.4	Azeri	2.6
Tamil	3.7	Albanian	6.5
Bengali	6.6	Welsh	7.5
Bosnian	12.9	Latvian	40.2
Indonesian	21.8	Romanian	24.1
Serbian	25.8	Turkish	31.2
Ukrainian	37.6	Hindi	47.4
Bulgarian	49.5	Polish	104.5
Slovak	124.3	Urdu	287.2
Farsi	710.3	Spanish	972

Table 1: Millions of monolingual web crawl and Wikipedia word tokens

3 Monolingual Data and Signals

3.1 Data

Throughout our experiments, we seek to learn how to translate words in a given source language into English. Table 1 lists our languages of interest, along with the total amount of monolingual data that we use for each. We use web crawled time-stamped news articles to estimate temporal similarity, Wikipedia pages which are inter-lingually linked to English pages to estimate topic similarity, and both datasets to estimate frequency and contextual similarity. Following Irvine et al. (2010), we use pairs of Wikipedia page titles to train a simple transliterator for languages written in a non-Roman script, which allows us to compute orthographic similarity for pairs of words in different scripts.

3.2 Signals

Our definitions of orthographic, topic, temporal, and contextual similarity are taken from Klementiev et al. (2012), and the details of each may be found there. Here, we give briefly describe them and give our definition of a novel, frequency-based signal.

Orthographic We measure orthographic similarity between a pair of words as the normalized[1] edit distance between the two words. For non-Roman script languages, we transliterate words into the Roman script before measuring orthographic similarity.

Topic We use monolingual Wikipedia pages to estimate topical signatures for each source and target

[1]Normalized by the average of the lengths of the two words

language word. Signature vectors are the length of the number of inter-lingually linked source and English Wikipedia pages and contain counts of how many times the word appears on each page. We use cosine similarity to compare pairs of signatures.

Temporal We use time-stamped web crawl data to estimate temporal signatures, which, for a given word, are the length of the number of time-stamps (dates) and contain counts of how many times the word appears in news articles with the given date. We use a sliding window of three days and use cosine similarity to compare signatures. We expect that source and target language words which are translations of one another will appear with similar frequencies over time in monolingual data.

Contextual We score monolingual contextual similarity by first collecting context vectors for each source and target language word. The context vector for a given word contains counts of how many times words appear in its context. We use bag of words contexts in a window of size two. We gather both source and target language contextual vectors from our web crawl data and Wikipedia data (separately).

Frequency Words that are translations of one another are likely to have similar relative frequencies in monolingual corpora. We measure the frequency similarity of two words as the absolute value of the difference between the logs of their relative monolingual corpus frequencies.

4 Supervised Bilingual Lexicon Induction

4.1 Baseline

Our unsupervised baseline method is based on ranked lists derived from each of the signals listed above. For each source word, we generate ranked lists of English candidates using the following six signals: Crawls Context, Crawls Time, Wikipedia Context, Wikipedia Topic, Edit distance, and Log Frequency Difference. Then, for each English candidate we compute its mean reciprocal rank[2] (MRR) based on the six ranked lists. The baseline ranks English candidates according to the MRR scores. For evaluation, we use the same test sets, accuracy metric, and correct translations described below.

[2]The MRR of the jth English word, e_j, is $\frac{1}{N}\sum_{i=1}^{N}\frac{1}{rank_{ij}}$, where N is the number of signals and $rank_{ij}$ is e_j's rank according to signal i.

4.2 Supervised Approach

In addition to the monolingual resources described in Section 3.1, we have a bilingual dictionary for each language, which we use to project context vectors and for supervision and evaluation. For each language, we choose up to $8,000$ source language words among those that occur in the monolingual data at least three times and that have at least one translation in our dictionary. We randomly divide the source language words into three equally sized sets for training, development, and testing. We use the training data to train a classifier, the development data to choose the best classification settings and feature set, and the test set for evaluation.

For all experiments, we use a linear classifier trained by stochastic gradient descent to minimize squared error[3] and perform 100 passes over the training data.[4] The binary classifiers predict whether a pair of words are translations of one another or not. The translations in our training data serve as positive supervision, and the source language words in the training data paired with random English words[5] serve as negative supervision. We used our development data to tune the number of negative examples to three for each positive example. At test time, after scoring all source language words in the test set paired with all English words in our candidate set,[6] we rank the English candidates by their classification scores and evaluate accuracy in the top-k translations.

4.3 Features

Our monolingual features are listed below and are based on raw similarity scores as well as ranks:

- Crawls Context: Web crawl context similarity score
- Crawls Context RR: reciprocal rank of crawls context

[3]We tried using logistic rather than linear regression, but performance differences on our development set were very small and not statistically significant.

[4]We use `http://hunch.net/~vw/` version 6.1.4, and run it with the following arguments that affect how updates are made in learning: –exact adaptive norm –power t 0.5

[5]Among those that appear at least five times in our monolingual data, consistent with our candidate set.

[6]All English words appearing at least five times in our monolingual data. In practice, we further limit the set to those that occur in the top-1000 ranked list according to at least one of our signals.

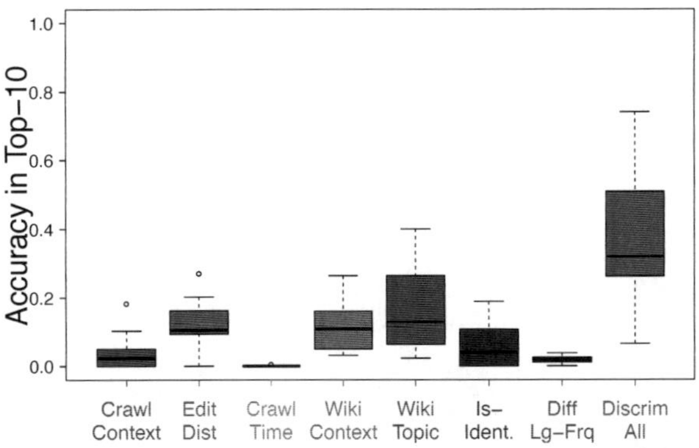

Figure 1: Each box-and-whisker plot summarizes performance on the development set using the given feature(s) across all 22 languages. For each source word in our development sets, we rank all English target words according to the monolingual similarity metric(s) listed. All but the last plot show the performance of individual features. *Discrim-All* uses supervised data to train classifiers for each language based on all of the features.

- Crawls Time: Web crawl temporal similarity score
- Crawls Time RR: reciprocal rank of crawls time
- Edit distance: normalized (by average length of source and target word) edit distance
- Edit distance RR: reciprocal rank of edit distance
- Wiki Context: Wikipedia context similarity score
- Wiki Context RR: recip. rank of wiki context
- Wiki Topic: Wikipedia topic similarity score
- Wiki Topic RR: recip. rank of wiki topic
- Is-Identical: source and target words are the same
- Difference in log frequencies: Difference between the logs of the source and target word monolingual frequencies
- Log Freqs Diff RR: reciprocal rank of difference in log frequencies

We train classifiers separately for each source language, and the learned weights vary based on, for example, corpora size and the relatedness of the source language and English (e.g. edit distance is informative if there are many cognates). In order to use the trained classifiers to make top-k translation predictions for a given source word, we rank candidates by their classification scores.

4.4 Feature Evaluation and Selection

After training initial classifiers, we use our development data to choose the most informative subset of features. Figure 1 shows the top-10 accuracy on the development data when we use individual features to predict translations. Top-10 accuracy refers to the percent of source language words for which a correct English translation appears in the top-10 ranked English candidates. Each box-and-whisker plot summarizes performance over the 22 languages. We don't display reciprocal rank features, as their performance is very similar to that of the corresponding raw similarity score. It's easy to see that features based on the Wikipedia topic signal are the most informative. It is also clear that training a supervised model to combine all of the features (the last plot) yields performance that is dramatically higher than using any individual feature alone.

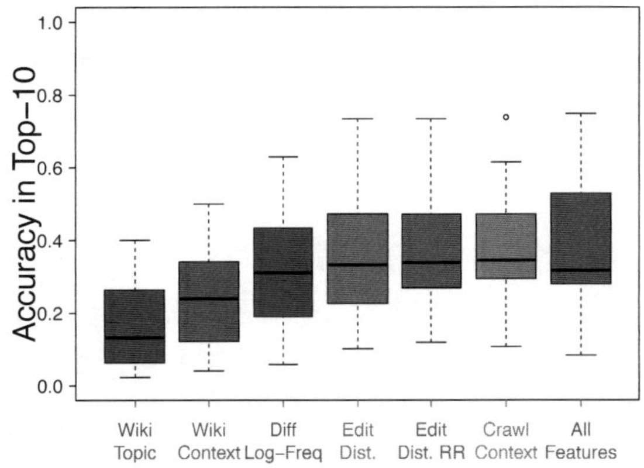

Figure 2: Performance on the development set goes up as features are greedily added to the feature space. Mean performance is slightly higher using this subset of six features (second to last bar) than using all features (last bar).

Figure 2, from left to right, shows a greedy search for the best subset of features among those listed above. Again, the Wikipedia topic score is the most informative stand-alone feature, and the Wikipedia context score is the most informative second feature. Adding features to the model beyond the six shown in the figure does not yield additional performance gains over our set of languages.

4.5 Learning Curve Analysis

Figure 3 shows learning curves over the number of positive training instances. In all cases, the number of randomly generated negative training instances is three times the number of positive. For all languages, performance is stable after about 300 correct translations are used for training. This shows that our supervised method for combining signals requires only a small training dictionary.

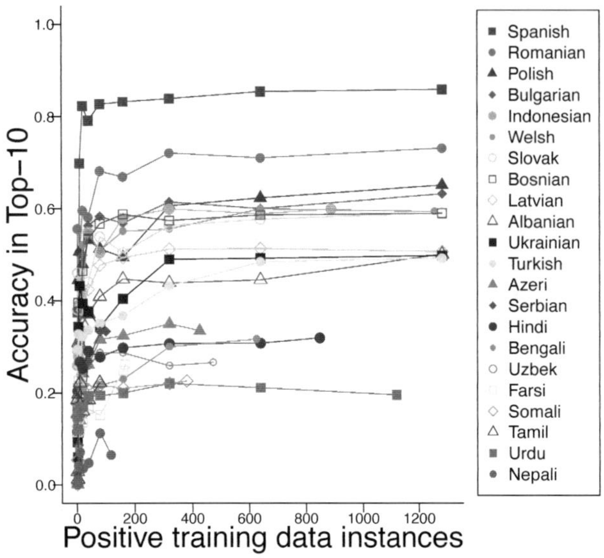

Figure 3: Learning curves over number of positive training instances, up to 1250. For some languages, 1250 positive training instances are not available. In all cases, evaluation is on the development data and the number of negative training instances is three times the number of positive. For all languages, performance is fairly stable after about 300 positive training instances.

5 Results

We use a model based on the six features shown in Figure 2 to score and rank English translation candidates for the test set words in each language. Table 2 gives the result for each language for the MRR baseline and our supervised technique. Across languages, the average top-10 accuracy using the MRR baseline is 30.4, and the average using our technique is 43.9, a relative improvement of about 44%. We did not attempt a comparison with more sophisticated unsupervised rank aggregation methods. However, we believe the improvements we observe drastically outweigh the expected performance differences between different rank aggregation methods. Figure 4 plots the accuracies yielded by our supervised technique versus the total amount of monolingual data for each language. An increase in monolingual data tends to improve accuracy. The correlation isn't perfect, however. For example, performance on Urdu and Farsi is relatively poor, despite the large amounts of monolingual data available for each. This may be due to the fact that we have large web crawls for those languages, but their Wikipedia datasets, which tend to provide a strong topic signal, are relatively small.

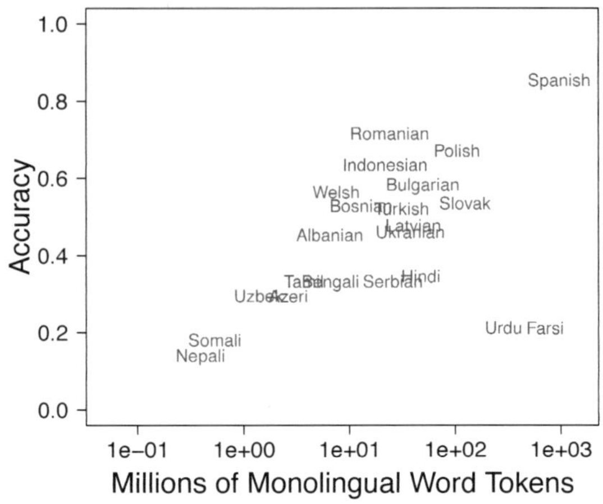

Figure 4: Millions of monolingual word tokens vs. Lexicon Induction Top-10 Accuracy

Lang	MRR	Supv.	Lang	MRR	Supv.
Nepali	11.2	13.6	Somali	16.7	18.1
Uzbek	23.2	29.6	Azeri	16.1	29.4
Tamil	28.4	33.3	Albanian	32.0	45.3
Bengali	19.3	32.8	Welsh	36.1	56.4
Bosnian	32.6	52.8	Latvian	29.6	47.7
Indonesian	41.5	63.5	Romanian	53.3	71.6
Serbian	29.0	33.3	Turkish	31.4	52.1
Ukrainian	29.7	46.0	Hindi	18.2	34.6
Bulgarian	40.2	57.9	Polish	47.4	67.1
Slovak	34.6	53.5	Urdu	13.2	21.2
Farsi	10.5	21.1	Spanish	74.8	85.0

Table 2: Top-10 Accuracy on test set. Performance increases for all languages moving from the baseline (*MRR*) to discriminative training (*Supv*).

6 Conclusions

On average, we observe relative gains of more than 44% over an unsupervised rank-combination baseline by using a seed bilingual dictionary and a diverse set of monolingual signals to train a supervised classifier. Using supervision for bilingual lexicon induction makes sense. In some cases a dictionary is already assumed for computing contextual similarity, and, in the remaining cases, one could be compiled easy, either automatically, e.g. Haghighi et al. (2008), or through crowdsourcing, e.g. Irvine and Klementiev (2010) and Callison-Burch and Dredze (2010). We have shown that only a few hundred translation pairs are needed to achieve good performance. Our framework has the additional advantage that any new monolingually-derived similarity metrics can easily be added as new features.

7 Acknowledgements

This material is based on research sponsored by DARPA under contract HR0011-09-1-0044 and by the Johns Hopkins University Human Language Technology Center of Excellence. The views and conclusions contained in this publication are those of the authors and should not be interpreted as representing official policies or endorsements of DARPA or the U.S. Government.

References

Chris Callison-Burch and Mark Dredze. 2010. Creating speech and language data with Amazon's Mechanical Turk. In *Proceedings of the NAACL Workshop on Creating Speech and Language Data with Amazon's Mechanical Turk*.

Hal Daumé, III and Jagadeesh Jagarlamudi. 2011. Domain adaptation for machine translation by mining unseen words. In *Proceedings of the Conference of the Association for Computational Linguistics (ACL)*.

Qing Dou and Kevin Knight. 2012. Large scale decipherment for out-of-domain machine translation. In *Proceedings of the Joint Conference on Empirical Methods in Natural Language Processing and Computational Natural Language Learning*.

Pascale Fung and Lo Yuen Yee. 1998. An IR approach for translating new words from nonparallel, comparable texts. In *Proceedings of the Conference of the Association for Computational Linguistics (ACL)*.

Aria Haghighi, Percy Liang, Taylor Berg-Kirkpatrick, and Dan Klein. 2008. Learning bilingual lexicons from monolingual corpora. In *Proceedings of the Conference of the Association for Computational Linguistics (ACL)*.

Ann Irvine and Alexandre Klementiev. 2010. Using mechanical turk to annotate lexicons for less commonly used languages. In *Proceedings of the NAACL Workshop on Creating Speech and Language Data with Amazon's Mechanical Turk*.

Ann Irvine, Chris Callison-Burch, and Alexandre Klementiev. 2010. Transliterating from all languages. In *Proceedings of the Conference of the Association for Machine Translation in the Americas (AMTA)*.

Alexandre Klementiev and Dan Roth. 2006. Weakly supervised named entity transliteration and discovery from multilingual comparable corpora. In *Proceedings of the Conference of the Association for Computational Linguistics (ACL)*.

Alex Klementiev, Ann Irvine, Chris Callison-Burch, and David Yarowsky. 2012. Toward statistical machine translation without parallel corpora. In *Proceedings of the Conference of the European Association for Computational Linguistics (EACL)*.

Philipp Koehn and Kevin Knight. 2002. Learning a translation lexicon from monolingual corpora. In *ACL Workshop on Unsupervised Lexical Acquisition*.

Mausam, Stephen Soderland, Oren Etzioni, Daniel S. Weld, Kobi Reiter, Michael Skinner, Marcus Sammer, and Jeff Bilmes. 2010. Panlingual lexical translation via probabilistic inference. *Artificial Intelligence*, 174:619–637, June.

David Mimno, Hanna Wallach, Jason Naradowsky, David Smith, and Andrew McCallum. 2009. Polylingual topic models. In *Proceedings of the Conference on Empirical Methods in Natural Language Processing (EMNLP)*.

Malte Nuhn, Arne Mauser, and Hermann Ney. 2012. Deciphering foreign language by combining language models and context vectors. In *Proceedings of the Conference of the Association for Computational Linguistics (ACL)*.

Franz Josef Och and Hermann Ney. 2002. Discriminative training and maximum entropy models for statistical machine translation. In *Proceedings of the Conference of the Association for Computational Linguistics (ACL)*.

Reinhard Rapp. 1995. Identifying word translations in non-parallel texts. In *Proceedings of the Conference of the Association for Computational Linguistics (ACL)*.

Reinhard Rapp. 1999. Automatic identification of word translations from unrelated English and German corpora. In *Proceedings of the Conference of the Association for Computational Linguistics (ACL)*.

Sujith Ravi and Kevin Knight. 2011. Deciphering foreign language. In *Proceedings of the Conference of the Association for Computational Linguistics (ACL)*.

Charles Schafer and David Yarowsky. 2002. Inducing translation lexicons via diverse similarity measures and bridge languages. In *Proceedings of the Conference on Natural Language Learning (CoNLL)*.

Charles Schafer. 2006. *Translation Discovery Using Diverse Similarity Measures*. Ph.D. thesis, Johns Hopkins University.

Creating Reverse Bilingual Dictionaries

Khang Nhut Lam
Department of Computer Science
University of Colorado
Colorado Springs, USA
klam2@uccs.edu

Jugal Kalita
Department of Computer Science
University of Colorado
Colorado Springs, USA
jkalita@uccs.edu

Abstract

Bilingual dictionaries are expensive resources and not many are available when one of the languages is resource-poor. In this paper, we propose algorithms for creation of new reverse bilingual dictionaries from existing bilingual dictionaries in which English is one of the two languages. Our algorithms exploit the similarity between word-concept pairs using the English Wordnet to produce reverse dictionary entries. Since our algorithms rely on available bilingual dictionaries, they are applicable to any bilingual dictionary as long as one of the two languages has Wordnet type lexical ontology.

1 Introduction

The Ethnologue organization[1] lists 6,809 distinct languages in the world, most of which are resource-poor. Most existing online bilingual dictionaries are between two resource-rich languages (e.g., English, Spanish, French or German) or between a resource-rich language and a resource-poor language. There are languages for which we are lucky to find a single bilingual dictionary online. For example, the University of Chicago hosts bilingual dictionaries from 29 Southeast Asian languages[2], but many of these languages have only one bilingual dictionary online.

Existing algorithms for creating new bilingual dictionaries use intermediate languages or intermediate dictionaries to find chains of words with the same meaning. For example, (Gollins and Sanderson, 2001) use lexical triangulation to translate in parallel across multiple intermediate languages and fuse the results. They query several existing dictionaries and then merge results to maximize accuracy. They use four pivot languages, German, Spanish, Dutch and Italian, as intermediate languages. Another existing approach for creating bilingual dictionaries is using probabilistic inference (Mausam et al., 2010). They organize dictionaries in a graph topology and use random walks and probabilistic graph sampling. (Shaw et al., 2011) propose a set of algorithms to create a reverse dictionary in the context of single language by using converse mapping. In particular, given an English-English dictionary, they attempt to find the original words or terms given a synonymous word or phrase describing the meaning of a word.

The goal of this research is to study the feasibility of creating a reverse dictionary by using only one existing dictionary and Wordnet lexical ontology. For example, given a Karbi[3]-English dictionary, we will construct an ENG-AJZ dictionary. The remainder of this paper is organized as follows. In Section 2, we discuss the nature of bilingual dictionaries. Section 3 describes the algorithms we propose to create new bilingual dictionaries from existing dictionaries. Results of our experiments are presented in Section 4. Section 5 concludes the paper.

2 Existing Online Bilingual Dictionaries

Powerful online translators developed by Google and Bing provide pairwise translations (including for individual words) for 65 and 40 languages, respectively. Wiktionary, a dictionary created by volunteers, supports over 170 languages. We find a

[1] http://www.ethnologue.com/

[2] http://dsal.uchicago.edu/dictionaries/list.html

[3] Karbi is an endangered language spoken by 492,000 people (2007 Ethnologue data) in Northeast India, ISO 639-3 code AJZ. ISO 693-3 code for English is ENG.

large number of bilingual dictionaries at PanLex[4] including an ENG-Hindi[5] and a Vietnamese[6]-ENG dictionary. The University of Chicago has a number of bilingual dictionaries for South Asian languages. Xobdo[7] has a number of dictionaries, focused on Northeast India.

We classify the many freely available dictionaries into three main kinds.

- Word to word dictionaries: These are dictionaries that translate one word in one language to one word or a phrase in another language. An example is an ENG-HIN dictionary at Panlex.
- Definition dictionaries: One word in one language has one or more meanings in the second language. It also may have pronunciation, parts of speech, synonyms and examples. An example is the VIE-ENG dictionary, also at Panlex.
- One language dictionaries: A dictionary of this kind is found at dictionary.com.

We have examined several hundred online dictionaries and found that they occur in many different formats. Extracting information from these dictionaries is arduous. We have experimented with five existing bilingual dictionaries: VIE-ENG, ENG-HIN, and a dictionary supported by Xobdo with 4 languages: Assamese[8], ENG, AJZ, and Dimasa[9]. We consider the last one to be a collection of 3 bilingual dictionaries: ASM-ENG, AJZ-ENG, and DIS-ENG. We choose these languages since one of our goals is to work with resource-poor languages to enhance the quantity and quality of resources available.

3 Proposed Solution Approach

A dictionary entry, called *LexicalEntry*, is a 2-tuple *<LexicalUnit, Definition>*. A *LexicalUnit* is a word or a phrase being defined, also called *definiendum* (Landau, 1984). A list of entries sorted by the LexicalUnit is called a *lexicon* or a *dictionary*. Given a *LexicalUnit*, the *Definition* associated with it usually contains its class and pronunciation, its *meaning*, and possibly additional information. The meaning associated with it can have several *Senses*. A *Sense* is a discrete representation of a single aspect of the meaning of a word. Thus, a dictionary entry is of the form *<LexicalUnit*, $Sense_1$, $Sense_2, \cdots$>.

In this section, we propose a series of algorithms, each one of which automatically creates a reverse dictionary, or $ReverseDictionary$, from a dictionary that translates a word in language L_1 to a word or phrase in language L_2. We require that at least one of two these languages has a Wordnet type lexical ontology (Miller, 1995). Our algorithms are used to create reverse dictionaries from them at various levels of accuracy and sophistication.

3.1 Direct Reversal (DR)

The existing dictionary has alphabetically sorted *LexicalUnits* in L_1 and each of them has one or more *Senses* in L_2. To create *ReverseDictionary*, we simply take every pair <$LexicalUnit, Sense$> in *SourceDictionary* and swap the positions of the two.

Algorithm 1 DR Algorithm

$ReverseDictionary := \phi$
for all $LexicalEntry_i \in SourceDictionary$ **do**
  for all $Sense_j \in LexicalEntry_i$ **do**
    Add tuple <$Sense_j$, $LexicalEntry_i.LexicalUnit$> to $ReverseDictionary$
  end for
end for

This is a baseline algorithm so that we can compare improvements as we create new algorithms. If in our input dictionary, the sense definitions are mostly single words, and occasionally a simple phrase, even such a simple algorithm gives fairly good results. In case there are long or complex phrases in senses, we skip them. The approach is easy to implement, and produces a high-accuracy $ReverseDictionary$. However, the number of entries in the created dictionaries are limited because this algorithm just swaps the positions of *LexicalUnit* and *Sense* of each entry in the $SourceDictionary$ and does not have any method to find the additional words having the same meanings.

[4]http://panlex.org/
[5]ISO 693-3 code HIN
[6]ISO 693-3 code VIE
[7]http://www.xobdo.org/
[8]Assamese is an Indo-European language spoken by about 30 million people, but it is resource-poor, ISO 693-3 code ASM.
[9]Dimasa is another endangered language from Northeast India, spoken by about 115,000 people, ISO 693-3 code DIS.

3.2 Direct Reversal with Distance (DRwD)

To increase the number of entries in the output dictionary, we compute the distance between words in the Wordnet hierarchy. For example, the words "hasta-lipi" and "likhavat" in HIN have the meanings "handwriting" and "script", respectively. The distance between "handwriting" and "script" in Wordnet hierarchy is 0.0, so that "handwriting" and "script" likely have the same meaning. Thus, each of "hasta-lipi" and "likhavat" should have both meanings "handwriting" and "script". This approach helps us find additional words having the same meanings and possibly increase the number of lexical entries in the reverse dictionaries.

To create a *ReverseDictionary*, for every $LexicalEntry_i$ in the existing dictionary, we find all $LexicalEntry_j, i \neq j$ with distance to $LexicalEntry_i$ equal to or smaller than a threshold α. As results, we have new pairs of entries <$LexicalEntry_i.LexicalUnit$, $LexicalEntry_j.Sense$> ; then we swap positions in the two-tuples, and add them into the *ReverseDictionary*. The value of α affects the number of entries and the quality of created dictionaries. The greater the value of α, the larger the number of lexical *entries*, but the smaller the accuracy of the *ReverseDictionary*.

The distance between the two *LexicalEntrys* is the distance between the two $LexicalUnit$s if the *LexicalUnits* occur in Wordnet ontology; otherwise, it is the distance between the two $Sense$s. The distance between each phrase pair is the average of the total distances between every word pair in the phrases (Wu and Palmer, 1994). If the distance between two words or phrases is 1.00, there is no similarity between these words or phrases, but if they have the same meaning, the distance is 0.00.

We find that a $ReverseDictionary$ created using the value 0.0 for α has the highest accuracy. This approach significantly increases the number of entries in the *ReverseDictionary*. However, there is an issue in this approach. For instance, the word "tuhbi" in DIS means "crowded", "compact", "dense", or "packed". Because the distance between the English words "slow" and "dense" in Wordnet is 0.0, this algorithm concludes that "slow" has the meaning "tuhbi" also, which is wrong.

Algorithm 2 DRwD Algorithm

$ReverseDictionary := \phi$
for all $LexicalEntry_i \in SourceDictionary$ **do**
  for all $Sense_j \in LexicalEntry_i$ **do**
    for all $LexicalEntry_u \in SourceDictionary$ **do**
      for all $Sense_v \in LexicalEntry_u$ **do**
        if $distance($<$LexicalEntry_i.LexicalUnit, Sense_j$> ,<$LexicalEntry_u.LexicalUnit, Sense_v$> $) \leqslant \alpha$ **then**
          Add tuple <$Sense_j$, $LexicalEntry_u.LexicalUnit$> to $ReverseDictionary$
        end if
      end for
    end for
  end for
end for

3.3 Direct Reversal with Similarly (DRwS)

The DRwD approach computes simply the distance between two senses, but does not look at the meanings of the senses in any depth. The DRwS approach represents a concept in terms of its Wordnet synset[10], synonyms, hyponyms and hypernyms. This approach is like the DRwD approach, but instead of computing the distance between lexical entries in each pair, we calculate the similarity, called *simValue*. If the *simValue* of a <$LexicalEntry_i, LexicalEntry_j$>, $i \neq j$ pair is equal or larger than β, we conclude that the $LexicalEntry_i$ has the same meaning as $LexicalEntry_j$.

To calculate *simValue* between two phrases, we obtain the *ExpansionSet* for every word in each phrase from the WordNet database. An *ExpansionSet* of a phrase is a union of synset, and/or synonym, and/or hyponym, and/or hypernym of every word in it. We compare the similarity between the *ExpansionSets*. The value of β and the kinds of *ExpansionSets* are changed to create different *ReverseDictionarys*. Based on experiments, we find that the best value of β is 0.9, and the best *ExpansionSet* is the union of synset, synonyms, hyponyms, and hypernyms. The algorithm for computing the *simValue* of entries is shown in Algorithm 3.

[10]Synset is a set of cognitive synonyms.

Algorithm 3 simValue($LexicalEntry_i$, $LexicalEntry_j$)

$simWords := \phi$
if $LexicalEntry_i.LexicalUnit$ & $LexicalEntry_j.LexicalUnit$ have a Wordnet lexical ontology **then**
  for all $(LexicalUnit_u \in LexicalEntry_i)$ & $(LexicalUnit_v \in LexicalEntry_j)$ **do**
    Find $ExpansionSet$ of every $LexicalEntry$ based on $LexicalUnit$
  end for
else
  for all $(Sense_u \in LexicalEntry_i)$ & $(Sense_v \in LexicalEntry_j)$ **do**
    Find $ExpansionSet$ of every $LexicalEntry$ based on $Sense$
  end for
end if
simWords $\leftarrow$ ExpansionSet ($LexicalEntry_i$) $\cap$ ExpansionSet($LexicalEntry_j$)
n $\leftarrow$ExpansionSet($LexicalEntry_i$).length
m $\leftarrow$ExpansionSet($LexicalEntry_j$).length
simValue$\leftarrow$min$\{\frac{simWords.length}{n}, \frac{simWords.length}{m}\}$

4 Experimental results

The goals of our study are to create the high-precision reverse dictionaries, and to increase the numbers of lexical entries in the created dictionaries. Evaluations were performed by volunteers who are fluent in both source and destination languages. To achieve reliable judgment, we use the same set of 100 non-stop word ENG words, randomly chosen from a list of the most common words[11]. We pick randomly 50 words from each created $ReverseDictionary$ for evaluation. Each volunteer was requested to evaluate using a 5-point scale, 5: excellent, 4: good, 3: average, 2: fair, and 1: bad. The average scores of entries in the *ReverseDictionarys* is presented in Figure 1. The DRwS dictionaries are the best in each case. The percentage of agreements between raters is in all cases is around 70%.

The dictionaries we work with frequently have several meanings for a word. Some of these meanings are unusual, rare or very infrequently used. The DR algorithm creates entries for the rare or unusual meanings by direct reversal. We noticed that our evaluators do not like such entries in the reversed dictionaries and mark them low. This results in lower average scores in the DR algorithm comparing to averages cores in the DRwS algorithm. The DRwS algorithm seems to have removed a number of such unusual or rare meanings (and entries similar to the rare meanings, recursively) improving the average score

Our proposed approaches do not work well for dictionaries containing an abundance of complex phrases. The original dictionaries, except the VIE-ENG dictionary, do not contain many long phrases or complex words. In Vietnamese, most words we find in the dictionary can be considered compound words composed of simpler words put together. However, the component words are separated by space. For example, "bái thần giáo" means "idolatry". The component words are "bái" meaning "bow low"; "thần" meaning "deity"; and "giáo" meaning "lance", "spear", "to teach", or "to educate". The presence of a large number of compound words written in this manner causes problems with the ENG-VIE dictionary. If we look closely at Figure 1, all language pairs, except ENG-VIE show substantial improvement in score when we compare the DR algorithm with DRwS algorithm.

Figure 1: Average entry score in $ReverseDictionary$

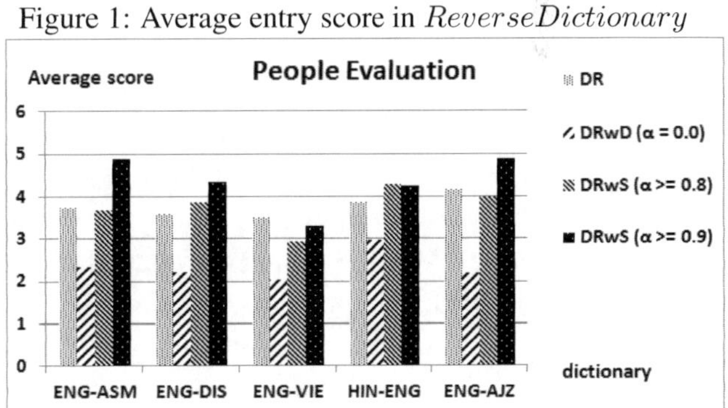

The DRwD approach significantly increases the number of entries, but the accuracy of the created dictionaries is much lower. The DRwS approach using a union of synset, synonyms, hyponyms, and hypernyms of words, and $\beta \geq 0.9$ produces the best reverse dictionaries for each language pair. The DRwS approach increases the number of entries in the created dictionaries compared to the DR algorithm as

[11]http://www.world-english.org/english500.htm

shown in Figure 2.

Figure 2: Number of lexical entries in $ReverseDictionary$s generated from 100 common words

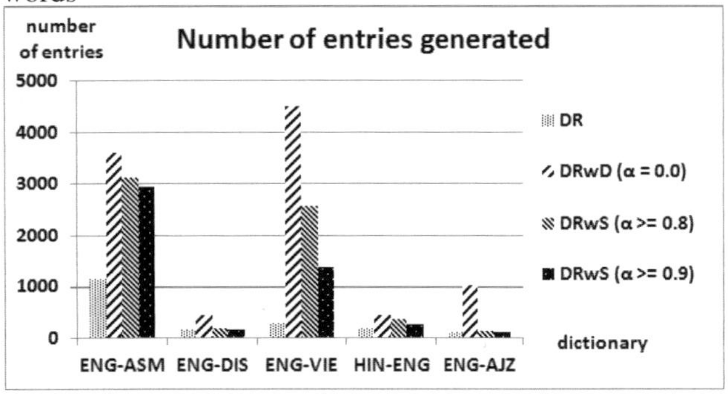

We also create the entire reverse dictionary for the AJZ-ENG dictionary. The total number of entries in the ENG-AJZ dictionaries created by using the DR algorithm and DRwS algorithm are 4677 and 5941, respectively. Then, we pick 100 random words from the ENG-AJZ created by using the DRwS algorithm for evaluation. The average score of every entry in this created dictionary is 4.07. Some of the reversal bilingual dictionaries can be downloaded at http://cs.uccs.edu/ linclab/creatingBilingualLexicalResource.html.

5 Conclusion

We proposed approaches to create a reverse dictionary from an existing bilingual dictionary using Wordnet. We show that a high precision reverse dictionary can be created without using any other intermediate dictionaries or languages. Using the Wordnet hierarchy increases the number of entries in the created dictionaries. We perform experiments with several resource-poor languages including two that are in the UNESCO's list of endangered languages.

Acknowledgements

We would like to thank the volunteers evaluating the dictionaries we create: Morningkeey Phangcho, Dharamsing Teron, Navanath Saharia, Arnab Phonglosa, Abhijit Bendale, and Lalit Prithviraj Jain. We also thank all friends in the Xobdo project who provided us with the ASM-ENG-DIS-AJZ dictionaries.

References

Mausam, S. Soderlan, O. Etzioni, D.S. Weld, K. Reiter, M. Skinner, M. Sammer, and J. Bilmers 2010. *Panlingual lexical translation via probabilistic inference*, Artificial Intelligence, 174:619–637.

R. Shaw, A. Datta, D. VanderMeer, and K. Datta 2011. *Building a scalable database - Driven Reverse Dictionary*, IEEE Transactions on Knowledge and Data Engineering, volume 99.

T. Gollins and M. Sanderson. 2001. *Improving cross language information retrieval with triangulated translation*, SIGIR '01 Proceedings of the 24th annual international ACM SIGIR conference on Research and development in information retrieval, New York, 90–95.

S.I. Landau. 1984. *Dictionaries*, Cambridge Univ Press.

G.A. Miller. 1995. *Wordnet: a lexical database for English*, Communications of the ACM, volume 38(11):39–41.

Z. Wu and P. Palmer. 1994. *Verbs semantics and lexical selection*, In proceeding of the 32nd annual meeting on Association for computaional linguistics, Stroudsburg, 133–138.

Identification of Temporal Event Relationships in Biographical Accounts

Lucian Silcox
University of Texas PanAm
1201 W. University Dr.
Edinburg, Tx 78539
lucian.silcox@gmail.com

Emmett Tomai
University of Texas PanAm
1201 W. University Dr.
Edinburg, Tx 78539
tomaie@utpa.edu

Abstract

This paper examines the efficacy of the application of a pre-existing technique in the area of event-event temporal relationship identification. We attempt to both reproduce the results of said technique, as well as extend the previous work with application to a newly-created domain of biographical data. We find that initially the simpler feature sets perform as expected, but that the final improvement to the feature set underperforms. In response, we provide an analysis of the individual features and identify differences existing between two corpora.

1 Introduction

As natural language systems continue to grow, so too does the importance of extracting temporal information from text. Narratives often contain a wealth of temporal information, linking specific events to each other and to individual named entities of importance, but such information is often implicitly conveyed, rather than explicitly stated. The continued interest in Question Answering and other data extraction systems has emphasized the need to better understand these relations to move past superficial understanding to a level of deeper comprehension. For native speakers, the temporal clues hidden in the text are relatively simple to comprehend. However, even for human annotators, the task of identifying and classifying the specific relationship between two events can be problematic. This complexity, of course, only exacerbates the problem of trying to automate the process for any information extraction system.

The creation of the TimeBank Corpus (Pustejovsky et al, 2003a), a fully-annotated newswire domain, opened up the possibility of applying machine learning techniques to the task of automatically extracting temporal relations. We look to the standards of the TimeBank Corpus to create a corpus of biographical accounts, and apply techniques that have been shown to work on TimeBank to the new domain.

2 Related Work

Domain-independent approaches have often focused on events that can be bound to a global timeline (Mani et al, 2003). This includes dates and times, but often neglects phrases that indicate events occurring in relative time (e.g. "during school," "before the crash," or "recently"). Research conducted on news articles attempted to identify the specific temporal relationships between two events, as seen in (Mani et al, 2006). Further work in that domain extended this start by identifying additional features that better predicted those temporal relations. (Lapata & Lascarides 2007; Chambers et al, 2007).

In this work, we are primarily interested in applying event ordering techniques to documents less structured than news articles, specifically biographies. It is the intention of our work to validate the efficacy of previous techniques in a different domain, and thus we attempt to extend the work completed by Chambers et al through application to a newly created corpus of biographical data. In the previous work, Chambers reports best results of 59.43% accuracy with gold standard features on TimeBank. We attempt to reproduce these results, and also adopt the policy of including incremental results against features selected based on the work of Mani et al (2006), and Lapata & Lascarides (2007).

3 Data

For purposes of validation of our implementation, we adopt the use of the TimeBank corpus (v1.1), which consists of 186 newswire documents and 3,406 identified event pairs with temporal relationships. The number of identified event pairs differs slightly from the previous work, which reports only 3,345. We cannot account for this discrepancy.

Furthermore, we oversee the creation of the Bio Corpus, consisting of 17 biographical accounts and annotated with 1,594 event pairs. Despite the small size of the corpus, we feel that the greatly increased event relationship density of our samples compared to a similar number of TimeBank documents offsets the disadvantage of the small document count.

The accounts are drawn from those available at Biography.com, and describe multiple aspects of the subject's life. Because the style of the biographies tends to explore one aspect of life fully, before moving on to another, we frequently see references to events contained in previous sections. These relations, which are not only across sentence boundaries but often in entirely different paragraphs, are one of the most striking differences between TimeBank documents and those of the new corpus.

To prepare the corpus, each document was automatically event tagged through the adoption of EVITA, the Events in Text Analyzer (Sauri et al, 2005). EVITA was previously found to perform with 80.12% accuracy, a result comparable to the accuracy of graduate student annotators with basic training. The temporal relations between event pairs were then hand-annotated according to the TimeML standard (Pustejovsky et al, 2003b).

4 Methodology

In an attempt to reproduce the event relationship classification techniques of the previous work, we first implement the approach and test it on our version of the TimeBank corpus. We then demonstrate that the validated techniques are applicable to the biographical domain, and that where discrepancies do occur, the specific feature set can be modified to elicit improvements not seen in the TimeBank data. In all possible cases we utilize the same techniques and tools as the earlier work, except where sufficient information is lacking, such as in the specific implementation of the machine learning techniques. In such situations, assumptions are made as deemed necessary.

Chambers' work attempts to identify the relationships between event pairs according to a previously defined set consisting of *Before, iBefore, Includes, Begins, Ends*, and *Simultaneous*. The set of event pairs are pre-selected and chosen for preexisting relationships, so a classification of *No Relation* is not required. In order to achieve classification, a support vector machine (SVM) is implemented via the Library for Support Vector Machines (Chang & Lin, 2011) and is trained on an extensive set of thirty-five features, as detailed below.

(1) Mani	Tense, Aspect, Class, Tense_Agree, Aspect_Agree, Event Words
(2) Lapata	Subord., Before, Synsets, Lemmas
(3) Chambers	POS, Class_Agree, Temporal Bigrams, Dominance, Prepositions, Same_Sentence

Table 1. Features of classification at each stage.

The feature set was incrementally built by a number of previous experiments, as detailed in Table 1, above. Initially, five temporal attributes originally identified by TimeML as having temporal significance, are adopted. These include the tense, aspect, and class of each event, as well as the modality and polarity of each. However, per the previous work, which demonstrated modality and polarity performing with high majority baselines, we exclude them from consideration. While Chambers et al include the task of automating the identification of these features, we report results versus the gold standards taken from TimeBank.

Mani et al (2006) added features indicating an agreement between the two events in the case of tense and aspect, and Chambers extends this to include a class agreement variable. In addition to simple agreement, bigrams of tense, aspect, and class are first included by Chambers to more fully represent the relationship between the event attributes (e.g. "Past Present," "Perfect Prog").

Next to be included are the event strings themselves, extracted verbatim, and the corresponding

	Baseline	Mani	Lapata	Chambers
TimeBank – Chambers	37.22	50.97	52.29	60.45
TimeBank – New	37.11	51.97	53.79	58.22
Bio Corpus	45.67	53.14	52.89	56.65

Table 2: Accuracy of SVM classification for Temporal Relationships.

	Baseline – (Lapata)	Part-of-Speech	Prepositional Head	Class Agreement	Temporal Bigrams
TimeBank	53.79	55.99	56.48	55.02	54.84
Bio Corpus	55.40	54.77	57.34	55.71	55.49

Table 3: Accuracy of feature subset analysis. Includes all features attributed to Mani and Lapata.

Wordnet (Fellbaum, 1998) synsets and lemmas. Also included are the parts-of-speech for both event words, the two words immediately preceding each event, and that of the token immediately following the events. Bigrams for part-of-speech from each event and its preceding token are also included, as well as a bigram for the part-of-speech of the two events as related to each other.

Lapata and Lascarides (2006) first added a feature indicating whether or not two events were in a subordinate relationship, which Chambers' includes, and extends it with the addition of one indicating a dominating relationship. This information is extracted by considering the parse tree as defined by an intermediate stage of the Stanford Parser. Similar to these two linguistic ordering features, we include another feature indicating the textual ordering of the two events (true if Event 1 is before Event 2, and false if not), and one indicating whether the two events are intra- or inter- sentential (same sentence or different sentences). Finally, we adopt Chambers' use of a feature for identifying whether or not each event is a part of a prepositional phrase.

All of these features are extracted from the text via regular expressions and application of the aforementioned third-party tools (such as WordNet and the Stanford Parser). With the features extracted, the first experiment on TimeBank uses only those features identified by Mani et al. Experiments two and three incrementally grow the feature set with those identified by Lapata & Lascarides and Chambers, respectively. The feature sets can be seen in Table 1, above. Results of this reproduction of the previous work are used as a point of comparison to the results of classification on our own Bio Corpus, using the same incremental growth classification scheme as before.

Furthermore, we provide independent feature analysis of a selection of the new features added by Chambers over the Mani+Lapata set, leveraging the results to draw some conclusions as to the linguistic differences existing between the two corpora.

5 Results

We first perform classification on TimeBank with the feature set attributed to Mani, the results of which can be seen in Table 2. Our system returns an accuracy of 51.97%, outperforming Chambers' reported result by one full point. This over-performance is extended to the Lapata feature set in a 1.82 point increase over our results for Mani's features, versus the 1.32 increase seen in Chambers' reported results, which at least maintains a similar magnitude of improvement.

With the full set of features, including Chambers' additions, our system exhibits a reversal in the previous trend of over-performance. As seen in Table 2, when Chambers' reported results of 60.45%, our own system returns results of only 58.22%. Not only does this leave a void of over two percent between the expected and actual accuracies, but it represents a much smaller increase in performance between Lapata's and Chambers' feature sets on Bio. In an effort to identify an under-performing feature, although without point of comparison from previous work, we explore an independent analysis of the new features, and found all features to be performing with at least some measure of improvement, as can be seen in Table 3.

Mani's feature set, when applied to the Bio Corpus, returns similar results as on TimeBank, with slightly higher accuracy at 53.14%. This translates to a smaller improvement over the baseline than we see in the newswire domain, but maintains approximately the same level of accuracy. Also following the same trend that is exhibited on TimeBank, the new features attributed to Lapata yield results with a small degree of improvement over the expected values at 55.4% versus TimeBank's 53.79%.

The application of the full feature set returns the expected reversal of trend, but underperforms by an even greater degree at 56.65%, leading us to suspect linguistic differences between the two corpora. In an effort to confirm this, we perform the same independent feature analysis as we performed on TimeBank. Notable results of re-classification (seen in Table 3) came from the part-of-speech features, as well as from the prepositional phrase heads. Part-of-speech was found to degrade performance and drop accuracy from 55.40% to 54.77%. Omission of the part-of-speech from a full feature set classification does not, however, improve performance over the initial classification. The prepositional phrase feature, on the other hand, returned the opposite result from part-of-speech – an improvement over the full feature set accuracy at 57.34%, strongly suggesting the importance of prepositional phrases in classification in the Bio Corpus.

6 Discussion

On TimeBank, results of temporal relationship classification return results similar to what was expected. In the simpler feature sets of Mani and Lapata, our own experiments over-perform by a small margin in each case, maintaining a similar magnitude of improvement at each step. This small but interesting variation is likely the result of the 61 additional event pairs in our version of the TimeBank corpus. Given our lack of justification for the difference, this claim is merely speculative. On the final feature set, with the inclusion of all features set out by Chambers, we still see a small improvement over the prior feature sets, but a small magnitude of change, coming in at a high of 58.22% compared to Chambers' 60.45%. While still reasonable, a sudden underperformance compared to the previous slight over-performances is unusual. Justification for this discrepancy could be attributed to the differences in the data set, but there is also a possibility that ambiguity in the description of the features led to improper extraction techniques. Our analysis of the individual feature fails to return what we can identify as an underperforming feature, however.

In the case of the Bio Corpus, we initially see a similar trend in performance, with the feature sets attributed to Mani and Lapata performing as expected, while the full Chambers set returns a less than impressive result. Additional analysis of the individual improvements from Chambers' new features, however, identifies two outliers to performance on Bio. The underperformance of part-of-speech, and the surprising improvement based solely on the prepositional phrase feature, would suggest different linguistic trends between the two corpora.

In future explorations of this topic, we would like to expand the size of the biographical corpus and reaffirm its correctness through the use of cross-validation between multiple annotators. This would help to ensure that no unintentional biases have skewed our results. In addition, we would like to further investigate feature selection to find a best-case subset for performance on the Bio corpus. While we initially began such an analysis, the sheer number of potential combinations rendered it outside of the scope of this work.

References

Chang, C., Lin, C. (2001). LIBSVM : a library for support vector machines. Software available <http://www.csie.ntu.edu.tw/~cjlin/libsvm>.

Chambers, N., Wang, S., Jurafsky, D. (2007). Classifying Temporal Relations Between Events. ACL-07, Prague.

Fellbaum, C. (1998, ed.). WordNet: An Electronic Lexical Database. Cambridge, MA: MIT Press.

Lapata, M., Lascarides, A. 2006. Learning sentence-internal temporal relations. In Journal of AI Research, volume 27, pages 85–117.

Mani, I., Verhagen, M., Wellner, B., Lee, C. M., Pustejovsky, J. (2006). Machine Learning of Temporal Relations. Proceedings of the 21st International Conference on Computational Linguistics and 44th Annual Meeting of the ACL (2006): 753-60. TimeML Publications.

Pustejovsky, J., Hanks, P., Saurí, R., See, A., Gaizauskas, R., Setzer, A., Radev, D., Sundheim, B., Day, D., Ferrom L., Lazo, M. (2003). The TIMEBANK Corpus. Proceedings of Corpus Linguistics 2003: 647-656.

Pustejovsky, J., Castaño, J., Ingria, R., Saurí, R., Gaizauskas, R., Setzer, A., Katz, G. (2003). TimeML: Robust Specification of Event and Temporal Expressions in Text. IWCS-5, Fifth International Workshop on Computational Semantics.

Saurí, R., Knippen, R., Verhagen, M., Pustejovsky, J. (2005). Evita: A Robust Event Recognizer for QA Systems. Proceedings of HLT/EMNLP 2005: 700-707.

Predicative Adjectives: An Unsupervised Criterion to Extract Subjective Adjectives

Michael Wiegand
Spoken Language Systems
Saarland University
michael.wiegand@lsv.uni-saarland.de

Josef Ruppenhofer
Dept. of Information Science
and Language Technology
Hildesheim University
ruppenho@uni-hildesheim.de

Dietrich Klakow
Spoken Language Systems
Saarland University
dietrich.klakow@lsv.uni-saarland.de

Abstract

We examine predicative adjectives as an unsupervised criterion to extract subjective adjectives. We do not only compare this criterion with a weakly supervised extraction method but also with gradable adjectives, i.e. another highly subjective subset of adjectives that can be extracted in an unsupervised fashion. In order to prove the robustness of this extraction method, we will evaluate the extraction with the help of two different state-of-the-art sentiment lexicons (as a gold standard).

1 Introduction

Since the early work on sentiment analysis, it has been established that the part of speech with the highest proportion of subjective words are adjectives (Wiebe et al., 2004) (see Sentence (1)). However, not all adjectives are subjective (2).

(1) A *grumpy* guest made some *impolite* remarks to the *insecure* and *inexperienced* waitress.
(2) The *old* man wearing a *yellow* pullover sat on a *plastic* chair.

This justifies the exploration of criteria to automatically separate the subjective adjectives from the non-subjective adjectives.

In this work, we are interested in an out-of-context assessment of adjectives and therefore evaluate them with the help of sentiment lexicons. We examine the property of being a *predicative* adjective as an extraction criterion. Predicative adjectives are adjectives that do not modify the head of a noun phrase, but which predicate a property of the referent of a noun phrase to which they are linked via a copula or a control predicate (3).

We show that adjectives that frequently occur as predicative adjectives are more likely to convey subjectivity (in general) than adjectives that occur non-predicatively, such as the pre-nominal (attributive) adjectives (4). A subjective adjective may occur both as a predicative (3) and a non-predicative (5) adjective and also convey subjectivity in both contexts. However, a large fraction of non-subjective adjectives do not occur as predicative adjectives (6).

(3) Her idea was *brilliant*.
(4) This is a *financial* problem.
(5) She came up with a *brilliant* idea.
(6) ?The problem is *financial*.

2 Related Work

The extraction of subjective adjectives has already attracted some considerable attention in previous research. Hatzivassiloglou and McKeown (1997) extract polar adjectives by a weakly supervised method in which subjective adjectives are found by searching for adjectives that are conjuncts of a pre-defined set of polar seed adjectives. Wiebe (2000) induces subjective adjectives with the help of distributional similarity. Hatzivassiloglou and Wiebe (2000) examine the properties of dynamic, gradable and polar adjectives as a means to detect subjectivity. Vegnaduzzo (2004) presents another bootstrapping method of extracting subjective adjectives with the help of head nouns of the subjective candidates and distributional similarity. Baroni and Vegnaduzzo

(2004) employ Web-based Mutual information for this task and largely outperform the results produced by Vegnaduzzo (2004).

3 Method

In the following, we present different features with the help of which subjective adjectives can be extracted. For all resulting lists, the adjectives will be ranked according to their frequency of co-occurring with a particular feature.

3.1 Extracting Predicative Adjectives (PRD)

For the extraction of predicative adjectives, we exclusively rely on the output of a dependency parser. Predicative adjectives are usually connected to the subject of the sentence via the dependency label `nsubj` (Example (7) would correspond to Sentence (3)).

(7) `nsubj(brilliant, idea)`

3.2 Extracting Gradable Adjectives (GRD)

As an alternative extraction method, we consider morpho-syntactically *gradable adjectives*. Gradable adjectives, such as *nice* or *small*, are adjectives "that can be inflected to specify the degree or grade of something" (Wiktionary[1]). It has been stated in previous work that if some adjective can build a comparative (e.g. *nicer*) or a superlative (e.g. *nicest*), then this adjective tends to be subjective (Hatzivassiloglou and Wiebe, 2000).

We employ the property of gradability, since, firstly, it is very predictive towards subjectivity and, secondly, it is the only other unsupervised criterion currently known to extract subjective adjectives. For the extraction of gradable adjectives, we rely, on the one hand, on the part-of-speech labels `JJR` (comparative) and `JJS` (superlative). On the other hand, we also consider adjectives being modified by either *more* or *most*. For the former case, we need to normalize the comparative (e.g. *nicer*) or superlative (e.g. *nicest*) word form to the canonical positive word form (e.g. *nice*) that is commonly used in sentiment lexicons.

[1] `http://en.wiktionary.org/wiki/gradable`

3.3 Weakly-Supervised Extraction (WKS)

We also consider a weakly supervised extraction method in this paper, even though it is not strictly fair to compare such a method with our two previous extraction methods which are completely unsupervised. WKS considers an adjective subjective, if it co-occurs as a conjunct of a previously defined highly subjective (seed) adjective (8). In order to detect such conjunctions, we employ the dependency relation `conj`. By just relying on surface patterns, we would not be able to exclude spurious conjunctions in which other constituents than the two adjectives are coordinated, such as Sentence (10).

(8) This approach is *ill-conceived* and *ineffective*.

(9) `conj(ill-conceived, ineffective)`

(10) [Evil witches are stereotypically dressed in *black*] and [*good* fairies in white].

We also experimented with other related weakly-supervised extraction methods, such as *mutual information* of two adjectives at the sentence level (or even smaller window sizes). However, using conjunctions largely outperformed these alternative approaches so we only pursue conjunctions here.

4 Experiments

As a large unlabeled (training) corpus, we chose the North American News Text Corpus (LDC95T21) comprising approximately 350 million words of news text. For syntactic analysis we use the Stanford Parser (Finkel et al., 2005). In order to decide whether an extracted adjective is subjective or not, we employ two sentiment lexicons, namely the *Subjectivity Lexicon (**SUB**)* (Wilson et al., 2005) and *SO-CAL (**SOC**)* (Taboada et al., 2011). According to the recent in-depth evaluation presented in Taboada et al. (2011), these two sentiment lexicons are the most effective resources for English sentiment analysis. By taking into account two different lexicons, which have also been built independently of each other, we want to provide evidence that our proposed criterion to extract subjective adjectives is not sensitive towards a particular gold standard (which would challenge the general validity of the proposed method).

ALL	other new last many first such next political federal own several few good* former same economic public major recent American second big* foreign high small local military financial little* national
PRD	able* likely available clear* difficult* important* ready* willing* hard* good* due possible* sure* interested unlikely necessary* high responsible* easy* strong* unable* different enough open aware happy impossible* right* wrong* confident*

Table 2: The 30 most frequent adjectives (ALL) and predicative adjectives (PRD); * marks matches with both sentiment lexicons SUB and SOC.

In order to produce the subjective seed adjectives for the weakly supervised extraction, we collect from the sentiment lexicon that we evaluate the n most frequent subjective adjectives according to our corpus. In order to further improve the quality of the seed set, we only consider *strong subjective* expressions from SUB and expressions with the intensity strength ± 5 from SOC.

Table 1 lists the size of the different sentiment lexicons and the rankings produced by the different extraction methods. Of course, the list of all adjectives from the corpus **(ALL)** is the largest list[2] while PRD is the second largest and GRD the third largest. The rankings produced by WKS are fairly sparse, in particular the ones induced with the help of SOC; apparently there are more frequently occurring strong subjective adjectives in SUB than there are high intensity adjectives in SOC.

4.1 Frequent Adjectives vs. Frequent Predicative Adjectives

Table 2 compares the 30 most frequent adjectives (ALL) and predicative adjectives (PRD). Not only does this table show that the proportion of subjective adjectives is much larger among the predicative adjectives but we may also gain some insight into what non-subjective adjectives are excluded. Among the high frequent adjectives are many quantifiers (*many*, *few* and *several*) and ordinal expressions (*first*, *next* and *last*). In principle, most of these expressions are not subjective. One may argue that these adjectives behave like function words. Since they occur very frequently, one might exclude some of them by just ignoring the most frequent adjectives. However, there are also other types of adjectives, especially pertainyms (*political*, *federal*, *economic*, *public*, *American*, *foreign*, *local*, *military*, *financial* and *national*) that appear on this list which could not be excluded by that heuristic. We found that these non-subjective content adjectives are present throughout the entire ranking and they are fairly frequent (on the ranking). On the list of predicative adjectives all these previous types of adjectives are much less frequent. Many of them only occur on lower ranks (and we assume that several of them only got on the list due to parsing errors).

[2]It will also contain many words erroneously tagged as adjectives, however, this is unlikely to affect our experiments since we only focus on the highly ranked (i.e. most frequent) words. The misclassifications rather concern infrequent words.

4.2 Comparison of the Different Extraction Methods

Table 3 compares the precision of the different extraction methods at different cut-off values. It is interesting to see that for ALL in particular the higher ranks are worse than the lower ranks (e.g. rank 1000). We assume that this is due to the high-frequency adjectives which are similar to function words (see Section 4.1). At all cut-off values, however, this baseline is beaten by every other method, including our proposed method PRD. The two unsupervised methods PRD and GRD perform on a par with each other. On SUB, PRD even mostly outperforms GRD. The precision achieved by WKS is quite good. However, the coverage of this method is low. It would require more seed expressions to increase it, however, this would also mean considerably more manual guidance.

Table 3 also shows that the precision of all extraction methods largely drops on the lower ranks. However, one should not conclude from that the extraction methods proposed only work well for highly frequent words. The drop can be mostly explained by the fact that the two sentiment lexicons we use for evaluation are finite (i.e. SUB: 4396 words/SOC: 2827 words (Table 1)), and that neither of these lexicons (nor their union) represents the complete set of all English subjective adjectives. Both lexicons will have a bias towards frequently occurring subjective expressions.

Inspecting the ranks 3001-3020 produced by PRD as displayed in Table 4, for example, actually reveals that there are still many more subjective adjectives

Lexicons		Extraction Methods										
					WKS-5		WKS-10		WKS-25		WKS-50	
SUB	SOC	ALL	PRD	GRD	SUB	SOC	SUB	SOC	SUB	SOC	SUB	SOC
4396	2827	212287	20793	7942	292	81	440	131	772	319	1035	385

Table 1: Statistics regarding the size (i.e. number of adjectives) of the different sentiment lexicons and rankings.

artistic* appealable airtight adjustable* activist* accommodating acclimated well-meaning weakest upsetting* unsurpassed unsatisfying* unopposed unobtrusive* unobjectionable unemployable understanding* uncharacteristic submerged speechless

Table 4: A set of entries PRD produces on lower ranks (ranks 3001-3020); * marks matches with either of the sentiment lexicons SUB or SOC.

than the matches with our sentiment lexicons suggest (e.g. *appealable*, *accomodating*, *well-meaning*, *weakest*, *unsurpassed*, *unopposed*, *unobjectionable*, *unemployable*, *uncharacteristic* or *speechless*). In other words, these are less frequent words; many of them are actually subjective even though they are not listed in the sentiment lexicons. Moreover, irrespective of the drop in precision on the lower ranks, PRD and GRD still outperform ALL on both sentiment lexicons (Table 3). Despite the sparseness of our two gold standards on the lower ranks, we thus have some indication that PRD and GRD are more effective than ALL.

The problem of the evaluation of less-frequent words could not be solved by an extrinsic evaluation, either, e.g. by using the extracted lists for some text classification task (at the sentence/document level). The evaluation on contextual classification on corpora would also be biased towards high-frequency words (as the word distribution is typically Zipfian). For instance, on the MPQA-corpus (Wiebe et al., 2005), i.e. the standard dataset for (fine-grained) sentiment analysis, there is not a single mention of the subjective words *appealable*, *accommodating*, *unsurpassed*, *unopposed*, *unobtrusive* or *speechless*, which were found among the lower ranks 3001-3020.

4.3 How Different Are Gradable and Predicative Adjectives?

Since in the previous experiments the proportion of subjective adjectives was similar among the gradable adjectives and the predicative adjectives, we may wonder whether these two extraction methods produce the same adjectives. In principle, the set of gradable adjectives extracted is much smaller than the list of extracted predicative adjectives (see Table 1). We found that the gradable adjectives are a proper subset of predicative adjectives, which is in line with the observation by (Bolinger, 1972, 21) that gradable adjectives (which he calls degree words) readily occur predicatively whereas non-gradable ones tend not to.

However, while gradability implies compatibility with predicative use, the reverse is not true. Accordingly, we found adjectives that are definitely not gradable among the predicative adjectives that are subjective, for instance *endless*, *insolvent*, *nonexistent*, *stagnant*, *unavailable* or *untrue*. This means that with the criterion of predicative adjectives one is able to extract relevant subjective adjectives that cannot be caught by the gradability criterion alone, namely *complementary* adjectives that refer to a simple binary opposition (Cruse, 1986, 198-99).

4.4 Intersecting the Different Unsupervised Criteria

In this section, we want to find out whether we can increase the precision by considering intersections of the two different unsupervised extraction criteria. (Due to the sparsity of WKS, it does not make sense to include that method in this experiment.) In our previous experiments it turned out that as far as precision is concerned, our new proposed extraction criterion was similar to the gradability criterion. If, however, the intersection of these two criteria produces better results, then we have provided some further proof of the effectiveness of our proposed criterion (even though we may sacrifice some exclusive subjective adjectives in PRD as pointed out in Section 4.3). It would mean that this criterion is also beneficial in the presence of the gradability criterion.

Figure 1 shows the corresponding results. We computed the intersection of PRD and GRD at var-

	ALL		PRD		GRD		WKS-5		WKS-10		WKS-25		WKS-50	
Rank n	**SUB**	**SOC**	**SUB**	**SOC**	**SUB**	**SOC**	**SUB**	**SOC**	**SUB**	**SOC**	**SUB**	**SOC**	**SUB**	**SOC**
10	10.00	30.00	90.00	90.00	80.00	60.00	80.00	90.00	80.00	90.00	90.00	70.00	90.00	70.00
25	20.00	32.00	88.00	60.00	64.00	60.00	92.00	80.00	91.00	80.00	92.00	80.00	92.00	84.00
50	30.00	34.00	88.00	64.00	70.00	68.00	82.00	78.00	92.00	78.00	92.00	84.00	90.00	86.00
100	37.00	38.00	81.00	68.00	79.00	75.00	80.00	*N/A*	82.00	72.00	89.00	78.00	92.00	77.00
250	45.60	43.20	79.60	75.60	84.80	76.00	70.80	*N/A*	74.40	*N/A*	80.40	67.50	82.04	67.20
500	48.00	49.20	77.20	70.00	82.20	74.00	*N/A*	*N/A*	*N/A*	*N/A*	72.60	*N/A*	75.20	*N/A*
1000	48.70	48.10	75.50	65.60	72.60	65.00	*N/A*	*N/A*	*N/A*	*N/A*	*N/A*	*N/A*	64.30	*N/A*
1500	49.07	46.53	68.60	59.07	66.27	58.60	*N/A*	*N/A*	*N/A*	*N/A*	*N/A*	*N/A*	*N/A*	*N/A*
2000	48.00	43.85	64.55	55.40	61.55	54.25	*N/A*	*N/A*	*N/A*	*N/A*	*N/A*	*N/A*	*N/A*	*N/A*
2500	46.08	40.96	59.52	51.28	56.36	50.00	*N/A*	*N/A*	*N/A*	*N/A*	*N/A*	*N/A*	*N/A*	*N/A*
3000	44.20	39.17	54.63	47.13	51.47	46.03	*N/A*	*N/A*	*N/A*	*N/A*	*N/A*	*N/A*	*N/A*	*N/A*

Table 3: Precision at rank n of the different extraction methods; *WKS-m* denotes that for the extraction the m most frequent subjective adjectives from the respective sentiment lexicon were considered as seed expressions.

ious cut-off values of n. The resulting intersection comprises m ranks with $m < n$. The precision of the intersection was consequently compared against the precision of PRD and GRD at rank m. The figure shows that with the exception of the higher ranks on SUB (< 200) there is indeed a systematic increase in precision when the intersection of PRD and GRD is considered.

5 Conclusion

We examined predicative adjectives as a criterion to extract subjective adjectives. As this extraction method is completely unsupervised, it is preferable to weakly supervised extraction methods since we are not dependent on a manually designed high quality seed set and we obtain a much larger set of adjectives. This extraction method is competitive if not slightly better than gradable adjectives. In addition, combining these two unsupervised methods by assessing their intersection results mostly in an increase in precision.

Acknowledgements

This work was performed in the context of the Software-Cluster project EMERGENT. Michael Wiegand was funded by the German Federal Ministry of Education and Research (BMBF) under grant no. "01IC10S01". The authors would like to thank Maite Taboada for providing her sentiment lexicon (SO-CAL) to be used for the experiments presented in this paper.

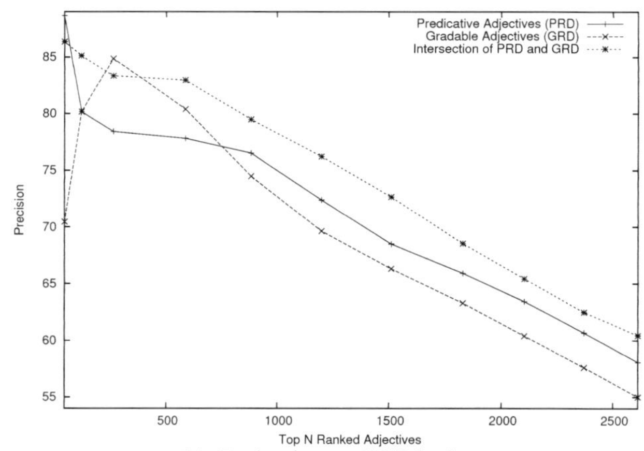

(a) Evaluation on SUB lexicon

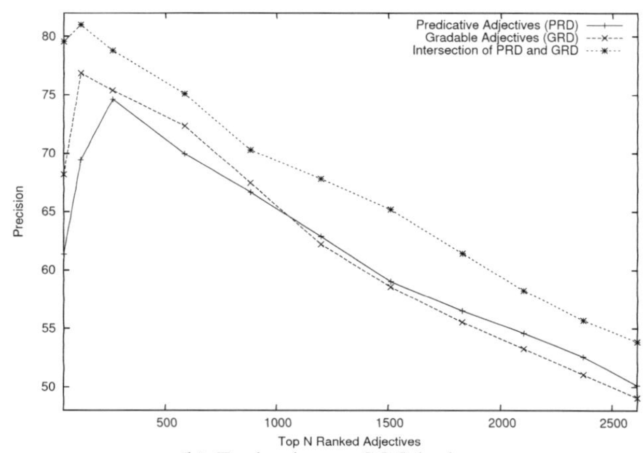

(b) Evaluation on SOC lexicon

Figure 1: Comparison of the individual rankings of GRD and PRD with their intersection.

References

Marco Baroni and Stefano Vegnaduzzo. 2004. Identifying Subjective Adjectives through Web-based Mutual Information. In *Proceedings of KONVENS*, pages 17–24, Vienna, Austria.

Dwight Bolinger. 1972. *Degree words*. Mouton, The Hague.

David Alan Cruse. 1986. *Lexical Semantics*. Cambridge University Press, Cambridge, UK.

Jenny Rose Finkel, Trond Grenager, and Christopher Manning. 2005. Incorporating Non-local Information into Information Extraction Systems by Gibbs Sampling. In *Proceedings of the Annual Meeting of the Association for Computational Linguistics (ACL)*, pages 363–370, Ann Arbor, MI, USA.

Vasileios Hatzivassiloglou and Kathleen R. McKeown. 1997. Predicting the Semantic Orientation of Adjectives. In *Proceedings of the Conference on European Chapter of the Association for Computational Linguistics (EACL)*, pages 174–181, Madrid, Spain.

Vasileios Hatzivassiloglou and Janyce Wiebe. 2000. Effects of Adjective Orientation and Gradability on Sentence Subjectivity. In *Proceedings of the International Conference on Computational Linguistics (COLING)*, pages 299–305, Saarbrücken, Germany.

Maite Taboada, Julian Brooke, Milan Tofiloski, Kimberly Voll, and Manfred Stede. 2011. Lexicon-Based Methods for Sentiment Analysis. *Computational Linguistics*, 37(2):267 – 307.

Stefano Vegnaduzzo. 2004. Acquisition of Subjective Adjectives with Limited Resources. In *Proceedings of the AAAI Spring Symposium on Exploring Attitude and Affect in Text: Theories and Applications*, Stanford, CA, USA.

Janyce Wiebe, Theresa Wilson, Rebecca Bruce, Matthew Bell, and Melanie Martin. 2004. Learning Subjective Language. *Computational Linguistics*, 30(3).

Janyce Wiebe, Theresa Wilson, and Claire Cardie. 2005. Annotating Expressions of Opinions and Emotions in Language. *Language Resources and Evaluation*, 39(2/3):164–210.

Janyce M. Wiebe. 2000. Learning Subjective Adjectives from Corpora. In *Proceedings of the National Conference on Artificial Intelligence (AAAI)*, pages 735–740, Austin, TX, USA.

Theresa Wilson, Janyce Wiebe, and Paul Hoffmann. 2005. Recognizing Contextual Polarity in Phrase-level Sentiment Analysis. In *Proceedings of the Conference on Human Language Technology and Empirical Methods in Natural Language Processing (HLT/EMNLP)*, pages 347–354, Vancouver, BC, Canada.

Modeling Syntactic and Semantic Structures in Hierarchical Phrase-based Translation

Junhui Li
University of Maryland
College Park, USA
lijunhui@umiacs.umd.edu

Philip Resnik
University of Maryland
College Park, USA
resnik@umd.edu

Hal Daumé III
University of Maryland
College Park, USA
hal@umiacs.umd.edu

Abstract

Incorporating semantic structure into a linguistics-free translation model is challenging, since semantic structures are closely tied to syntax. In this paper, we propose a two-level approach to exploiting predicate-argument structure reordering in a hierarchical phrase-based translation model. First, we introduce linguistically motivated constraints into a hierarchical model, guiding translation phrase choices in favor of those that respect syntactic boundaries. Second, based on such translation phrases, we propose a predicate-argument structure reordering model that predicts reordering not only between an argument and its predicate, but also between two arguments. Experiments on Chinese-to-English translation demonstrate that both advances significantly improve translation accuracy.

1 Introduction

Hierarchical phrase-based (HPB) translation models (Chiang, 2005; Chiang, 2007) that utilize synchronous context free grammars (SCFG) have been widely adopted in statistical machine translation (SMT). Although formally syntactic, such models rarely respect linguistically-motivated syntax, and have no formal notion of semantics. As a result, they tend to produce translations containing both grammatical errors and semantic role confusions. Our goal is to take advantage of syntactic and semantic parsing to improve translation quality of HPB translation models. Rather than introducing semantic structure into the HPB model directly, we construct an improved translation model by incorporating linguistically motivated *syntactic constraints* into a standard HPB model. Once the translation phrases are linguistically constrained, we are able to propose a *predicate-argument reordering model*. This reordering model aims to solve two problems: ensure that arguments are ordered properly after translation, and to ensure that the proper argument structures even *exist*, for instance in the case of PRO-drop languages. Experimental results on Chinese-to-English translation show that both the hard syntactic constraints and the predicate-argument reordering model obtain significant improvements over the syntactically and semantically uninformed baseline.

In principle, semantic frames (or, more specifically, predicate-argument structures: PAS) seem to be a promising avenue for translational modeling. While languages might diverge syntactically, they are less likely to diverge semantically. This has previously been recognized by Fung et al. (2006), who report that approximately 84% of semantic role mappings remained consistent across translations between English and Chinese. Subsequently, Zhuang and Zong (2010) took advantage of this consistency to jointly model semantic frames on Chinese/English bitexts, yielding improved frame recognition accuracy on both languages.

While there has been some encouraging work on integrating syntactic knowledge into Chiang's HPB model, modeling semantic structure in a linguistically naive translation model is a challenge, because the semantic structures themselves are syntactically motivated. In previous work, Liu and Gildea (2010) model the reordering/deletion of source-side semantic roles in a tree-to-string translation model. While it is natural to include semantic structures in a tree-based translation model, the effect of semantic structures is presumably limited, since tree templates themselves have already encoded semantics to some extent. For example, template *(VP (VBG giving) NP#1 NP#2)* entails *NP#1* as *receiver* and *NP#2* as *thing given*. Xiong et al. (2012) model the reordering between predicates and their arguments by assuming arguments are translated as a unit. However, they only considered the reordering between arguments and their predicates.

2 Syntactic Constraints for HPB Translation Model

In this section, we briefly review the HPB model, then present our approach to incorporating syntactic constraints into it.

2.1 HPB Translation Model

In HPB models, synchronous rules take the form $X \rightarrow \langle \gamma, \alpha, \sim \rangle$, where X is the non-terminal symbol, γ and α are strings of lexical items and non-terminals in the source and target side, respectively, and $\sim$ indicates the one-to-one correspondence between non-terminals in γ and α. Each such rule is associated with a set of translation model features $\{\phi_i\}$, including phrase translation probability $p(\alpha \mid \gamma)$ and its inverse $p(\gamma \mid \alpha)$, the lexical translation probability $p_{lex}(\alpha \mid \gamma)$ and its inverse $p_{lex}(\gamma \mid \alpha)$, and a rule penalty that affects preference for longer or shorter derivations. Two other widely used features are a target language model feature and a target word penalty.

Given a derivation d, its translation probability is estimated as:

$$P(d) \propto \prod_i \phi_i(d)^{\lambda_i} \quad (1)$$

where λ_i is the corresponding weight of feature ϕ_i. See (Chiang, 2007) for more details.

2.2 Syntactic Constraints

Translation rules in an HPB model are extracted from *initial phrase* pairs, which must include at least one word inside one phrase aligned to a word inside the other, such that no word inside one phrase can be aligned to a word outside the other phrase. It is not surprising to observe that initial phrases frequently are non-intuitive and inconsistent with linguistic constituents, because they are based only on statistical word alignments. Nothing in the framework actually requires linguistic knowledge.

Koehn et al. (2003) conjectured that such non-intuitive phrases do not help in translation. They tested this conjecture by restricting phrases to syntactically motivated constituents on both the source and target side: only those initial phrase pairs are subtrees in the derivations produced by the model. However, their phrase-based translation experiments (on Europarl data) showed the restriction to syntactic constituents is actually harmful, because too many phrases are eliminated. The idea of hard syntactic constraints then seems essentially to have been abandoned: it doesn't appear in later work.

On the face of it, there are many possible reasons Koehn et al. (2003)'s hard constraints did not work, including, for example, tight restrictions that unavoidably exclude useful phrases, and practical issues like the quality of parse trees. Although ensuing work moved in the direction of *soft* syntactic constraints (see Section 6), our ultimate goal of capturing predicate-argument structure requires linguistically valid syntactic constituents, and therefore we revisit the idea of hard constraints, avoiding problems with their strictness by relaxing them in three ways.

First, requiring source phrases to be subtrees in a linguistically informed syntactic parse eliminates many reasonable phrases. Consider the English-Chinese phrase pair ⟨*the red car, hongse de qiche*⟩.[1] It is easily to get a translation entry for the whole phrase pair. By contrast, the phrase pair ⟨*the red, hongse de*⟩ is typically excluded because it does not correspond to a complete subtree on the source side. Yet translating *the red* is likely to be more useful than translating *the red car*, since it is more general: it can be followed by any other noun translation. To this end, we relax the syntactic constraints by allowing phrases on the source side corresponding to either *one subtree* or *sibling subtrees* with a common parent node in the syntactic parse. For example, *the red* in Figure 1(a) is allowed since it spans two subtrees that have a common parent node *NP*.

Second, we might still exclude useful phrases because the syntactic parses of some languages, like Chinese, prefer deep trees, resulting in a head and its modifiers being distributed across multiple structural levels. Consider the English sentence *I still*

[1] We use English as source language for better readability.

like the red car very much and its syntactic structure as shown in Figure 1(a). Phrases *I still*, *still like*, *I still like* are not allowed, since they don't map to either a subtree or sibling subtrees. Logically, however, it might make sense not just to include phrases mapping to (sibling) subtrees, but to include phrases mapping to subtrees with the same head. To this end, we flatten the syntactic parse so that a head and all its modifiers appear at the same level. Another advantage of this flattened structure is that flattened trees are more reliable than unflattened ones, in the sense that some bracketing errors in unflattened trees can be eliminated during tree flattening. Figure 1(b) illustrates flattening a syntactic parse by moving the head (*like*) and all its modifiers (*I*, *still*, *the red car*, and *very much*) to the same level.

Third, initial phrase pair extraction in Chiang's HPB generates a very large number of rules, which makes training and decoding very slow. To avoid this, a widely used strategy is to limit initial phrases to a reasonable length on either side during rule extraction (e.g., 10 in Chiang (2007)). A corresponding constraint to speed up decoding prohibits any X from spanning a substring longer than a fixed length, often the same as the maximum phrase length in rule extraction. Although the initial phrase length limitation mainly keeps non-intuitive phrases out, it also closes the door on some useful phrases. For example, a translation rule $\langle$*I still like X, wo rengran xihuan X*$\rangle$ will be prohibited if the non-terminal X covers 8 or more words. In contrast, our hard constraints have already filtered out dominating non-intuitive phrases; thus there is more room to include additional useful phrases. As a result, we can switch off the constraints on initial phrase length in both training and decoding.

2.3 Reorderable Glue Rules

In decoding, if no good rule (e.g., a rule whose left-hand side is X) can be applied or the length of the potential source span is larger than a pre-defined length, a glue rule (either $S \rightarrow \langle X_1, X_1\rangle$ or $S \rightarrow \langle S_1X_2, S_1X_2\rangle$) will be used to simply stitch two consequent translated phrases together in monotonic way. This will obviously prevent some reasonable translation derivations because in certain cases, the order of phrases may be inverted on the target side. Moreover, even that the syntactic constraints discussed above make translation node Xs are syntactically informed, stitching translated phrases from left to right will unavoidably generate non-syntactically informed node Ss. For example, the combination of X $(like)$ and X (the) does not make much sense in linguistic perspective.

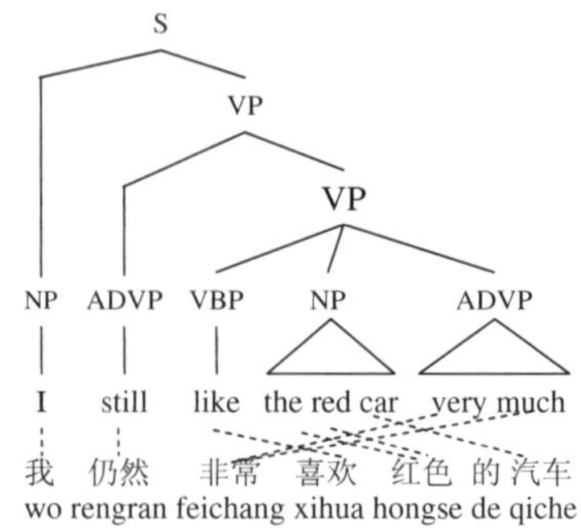

a. Word alignment for an English-Chinese sentence pair with the parse tree for the English sentence

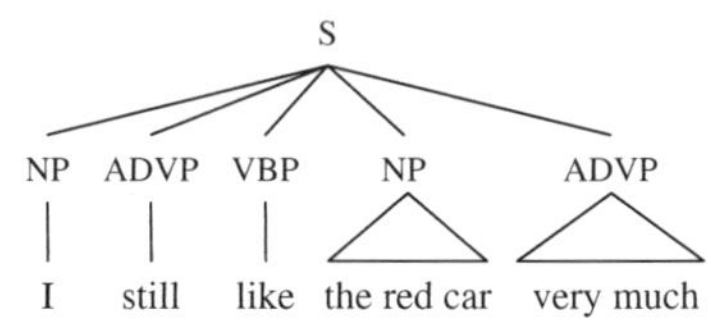

b. Flattened parse tree for the English sentence

Figure 1: Example of flattening parse tree.

Alternatively, we replace glue rules of HPB with reorderable ones:

- $T \rightarrow \langle X_1, X_1\rangle$
- $T \rightarrow \langle T_1T_2, T_1T_2\rangle$
- $T \rightarrow \langle T_1T_2, T_2T_1\rangle$

where the second (third) rule combines two translated phrases in a monotonic (inverted) way. Specifically, we set the translation probability of the first translation rule as 1 while estimating the probabilities of the other two rules from training data. In both training and decoding, we require the phrases covered by T to satisfy our syntactic constraints. Therefore, all translation nodes (both Xs and Ts) in derivations are syntactically informed, providing room to explore PAS reordering in HPB model.

3 PAS Reordering Model

Ideally, we aim to model PAS reordering based on the true semantic roles of both the source and target side, as to better cater not only consistence but

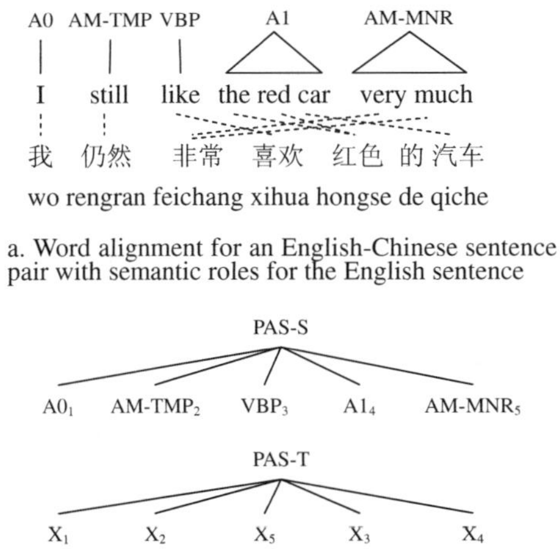

a. Word alignment for an English-Chinese sentence pair with semantic roles for the English sentence

b. PAS-S and PAS-T for predicate *like*

Figure 2: Example of PAS on both the source and target side. Items are aligned by indices.

divergence between semantic frames of the source and target language. However, considering there is no efficient way of jointly performing MT and SRL, accurate SRL on target side can only be done after translation. Similar to related work (Liu and Gildea, 2010; Xiong et al., 2012), we obtain the PAS of the source language (PAS-S) via a shallow semantic parser and project the PAS of the target language (PAS-T) using the word alignment derived from the translation process. Specifically, we use PropBank standard (Palmer et al., 2005; Xue, 2008) which defines a set of numbered core arguments (i.e., A0-A5) and adjunct-like arguments (e.g., AM-TMP for temporal, AM-MNR for manner). Figure 2(b) shows an example of PAS projection from source language to target language.[2] The PAS reordering model describes the probability of reordering *PAS-S* into *PAS-T*. Given a predicate p, it takes the following form:

$$P\,(\text{PAS-T} \mid \text{PAS-S, PRE=}p) \tag{2}$$

Note that cases for *untranslated roles* can be naturally reflected in our PAS reordering model. For example, if the argument I_{A0} is untranslated in Figure 2, its PAS-T will be $X_2X_5X_3X_4$.

[2]In PAS-S, we use parts-of-speech (POS) of predicates to distinguish different types of verbs since the semantic structures of Chinese adjective verbs are different from those of others.

3.1 Probability Estimation

While it is hard and unnecessary to translate a predicate and all its associated arguments with one rule, especially if the sentence is long, a practicable way, as most decoders do, is to translate them in multiple level rules. In addition, some adjunct-like arguments are optional, or structurally dispensable part of a sentence, which may result in data sparsity issue. Based on these observations, we decompose Formula 2 into two parts: *predicate-argument reordering* and *argument-argument reordering*.

Predicate-Argument Reordering estimates the reordering probability between a predicate and one of its arguments. Taking predicate *like* and its argument A1 *the red car* in Figure 2(a) as an example, the predicate-argument pattern on the source side (PA-S) is $VBP_1\ A1_2$ while the predicate-argument pattern on the target side (PA-T) is X_1X_2. The reordering probability is estimated as:

$$P_{\text{P-A}}\,(\text{PA-T=X}_1\,\text{X}_2 \mid \text{PA-S=VBP}_1\,\text{A1}_2,\ \text{PRE=like}) = \frac{Count\,(\text{PA-T=X}_1\,\text{X}_2,\ \text{PA-S=VBP}_1\,\text{A1}_2,\ \text{PRE=like})}{\sum_{\mathcal{T}\in\Phi(\text{PA-S})} Count\,(\text{PA-T=}\mathcal{T},\ \text{PA-S=VBP}_1\,\text{A1}_2,\ \text{PRE=like})} \tag{3}$$

where $\Phi\,(PA\text{-}S)$ enumerates all possible reorderings on the target side. Moreover, we take the predicate lexicon of predicate into account. To avoid data sparsity, we set a threshold (e.g., 100) to retain frequent predicates. For infrequent predicates, their probabilities are smoothed by replacing predicate lexicon with its POS. Finally, if source side patterns are infrequent (e.g., less than 10) for frequent predicates, their probabilities are smoothed as well with the same way.

Argument-Argument Reordering estimates the reordering probability between two arguments, i.e., argument-argument pattern on the source side (AA-S) and its counterpart on the target side (AA-T). However, due to that arguments are driven and pivoted by their predicates, we also include predicate in patterns of AA-S and AA-T. Let's revisit Figure 2(a). A1 *the red car* and AM-MNR *very much* are inverted on the target side, whose probability is estimated as:

$$P_{\text{A-A}}\,(\text{AA-T=X}_3\,\text{X}_1\,\text{X}_2 \mid \text{AA-S=VBP}_1\,\text{A1}_2\,\text{AM-MNR}_3,\ \text{PRE=like}) \tag{4}$$

Similarly we smooth the probabilities by distinguishing frequent predicates from infrequent ones, as well as frequent patterns from infrequent ones.

3.2 Integrating the PAS Reordering Model into the HPB Model

We integrate the PAS reordering model into the HPB SMT by adding a new feature into the log-linear translation model. Unlike the conventional phrase and lexical translation features whose values are phrase pair-determined and thus can be calculated offline, the value of the PAS reordering model can only be obtained with being aware of the predicate-argument structures a hypothesis may cover. Before we present the algorithm of integrating the PAS reordering model, we define a few functions by assuming p for a predicate, a for an argument, and H for a hypothesis:

- $\mathcal{A}(i, j, p)$: returns arguments of p which are fully located within the span from word i to j on the source side. For example, in Figure 2, $\mathcal{A}(4, 8, like) = \{A1, AM\text{-}MRN\}$.[3]
- $\mathcal{B}(i, j, p)$: returns *true* if p is located within $[i, j]$; otherwise returns *false*.
- $\mathcal{C}(a, p)$: returns *true* if predicate-argument reordering for a and p has not calculated yet; otherwise returns *false*.
- $\mathcal{D}(a_1, a_2, p)$: returns *true* if argument-argument reordering for p's arguments a_1 and a_2 has not calculated yet; otherwise returns *false*.
- $\mathcal{P}_{P\text{-}A}(H, a, p)$: according to Eq. 3, returns the probability of predicate-argument reordering of a and p, given a and p are covered by H. The positional relation of a and p on the target side can be detected according to translation derivation of H.
- $\mathcal{P}_{A\text{-}A}(H, a_1, a_2, p)$: according to Eq. 4, returns the probability of argument-argument reordering of p's arguments a_1 and a_2, given a_1, a_2 and p are covered by H.

Algorithm 1 integrates the PAS reordering model into a CKY-style decoder whenever a new hypothesis is generated. Given a hypothesis H, it first looks for predicates and their arguments which are covered

---

Algorithm 1: Integrating the PAS reordering model into a CKY-style decoder

---

Input: Sentence f in the source language
Predicate-Argument Structures of f
Hypothesis H spanning from word i to j
Output: Log-Probability of the PAS reordering model
1. set $prob = 0.0$
2. **for** predicate p in f, such that $\mathcal{B}(i, j, p)$ is $true$
3. $\quad ARG = \mathcal{A}(i, j, p)$
4. $\quad$ **for** $a \in ARG$ such that $\mathcal{C}(a, p)$ is $true$
5. $\quad\quad prob \mathrel{+}= \log \mathcal{P}_{P\text{-}A}(H, a, p)$
6. $\quad$ **for** $a_1, a_2 \in ARG$ such that $a_1 \neq a_2$ and $\mathcal{D}(a_1, a_2, p)$ is $true$
7. $\quad\quad prob \mathrel{+}= \log \mathcal{P}_{A\text{-}A}(H, a_1, a_2, p)$
8. **return** $prob$

---

by H (line 2-3). Then it respectively calculates the probabilities of predicate-argument reordering and argument-argument reordering(line 4-7).

4 Experiments

We have presented our two-level approach to incorporating syntactic and semantic structures in a HPB system. In this section, we test the effect of such structural information on a Chinese-to-English translation task. The baseline system is a reproduction of Chiang's (2007) HPB system. The bilingual training data contains 1.5M sentence pairs with 39.4M Chinese words and 46.6M English words.[4] We obtain the word alignments by running GIZA++ (Och and Ney, 2000) on the corpus in both directions and applying "grow-diag-final-and" refinement (Koehn et al., 2003). We use the SRI language modeling toolkit to train a 5-gram language model on the Xinhua portion of the Gigaword corpus and standard MERT (Och, 2003) to tune the feature weights on the development data.

To obtain syntactic parse trees for instantiating syntactic constraints and predicate-argument structures for integrating the PAS reordering model, we first parse the source sentences with the Berkeley Parser (Petrov and Klein, 2007) trained on Chinese TreeBank 6.0 and then ran the Chinese semantic role

[3] The hard constraints make sure a valid source text span would never fully cover some roles while partially cover other roles. For example, phrases *like the red, the read car very* in Figure 1 are invalid.

[4] This dataset includes LDC2002E18, LDC2003E07, LDC2003E14, Hansards portion of LDC2004T07, LDC2004T08 and LDC2005T06

	System	MT 02	MT 04	MT 05	Ave.
	base HPB	40.00	35.33	32.97	36.10
max-phrase-length=10 max-char-span=10	+ basic constraints + unflattened tree	33.90	32.00	29.83	31.91
	+ our constraints + unflattened tree	38.47	34.51	32.15	35.04
	+ our constraints + flattened tree	38.55	35.38	32.44	35.46
max-phrase-length=∞ max-char-span=∞	+ basic constraints + unflattened tree	35.38	32.89	30.42	32.90
	+ our constraints + unflattened tree	39.41	36.02	33.21	36.21
	+ our constraints + flattened tree	**40.01**	**36.24**	**33.65**	**36.71**

Table 1: Effects of hard constraints. Here max-phrase-length is for maximum initial phrase length in training and max-char-span for maximum phrase length can be covered by non-terminal *X* in decoding.

labeler (Li et al., 2010) on all source parse trees to annotate semantic roles for all verbal predicates.

We use the 2003 NIST MT evaluation test data (919 sentence pairs) as the development data, and the 2002, 2004 and 2005 NIST MT evaluation test data (878, 1788 and 1082 sentence pairs, respectively) as the test data. For evaluation, the NIST BLEU script (version 11b) is used to calculate the NIST BLEU scores, which measures case-insensitive matching of n-grams with n up to 4. To test whether a performance difference is statistically significant, we conduct significance tests following the paired bootstrapping approach (Koehn, 2004).

4.1 Effects of Syntactic Constraints

We have also tested syntactic constraints that simply require phrases on the source side to map to a subtree (called basic constraints). Similar to requiring initial phrases on the source side to satisfy the constraints in training process, we only perform chart parsing on text spans which satisfy the constraints in decoding process. Table 1 shows the results of applying syntactic constraints with different experimental settings. From the table, we have the following observations.

- Consistent with the conclusion in Koehn et al. (2003), using the basic constraints is harmful to HPB. Fortunately, our constraints consistently work better than the basic constraints.

- Relaxing maximum phrase length in training and maximum char span length in decoding, we obtain an average improvement of about 1.0~1.2 BLEU points for systems with both basic constraints and our constraints. It is worth noting that after relaxing the lengths, the system with our constraints performs on a par with the base HPB system (e.g., 36.21 *vs.* 36.10).

System	MT 02	MT 04	MT 05	Ave.
base HPB	40.00	35.33	32.97	36.10
+our constraints	40.01	36.24^{++}	33.65^{+}	36.71
with reorderable glue rules	$\mathbf{40.70}^{+}$	36.00^{+}	33.67^{+}	36.79
+PAS model	40.41^{+}	$\mathbf{36.73}^{++**}$	$\mathbf{34.24}^{++*}$	**37.13**

Table 2: Effects of reorderable glue rules and the PAS reordering model. +/++: significant over base HPB at 0.05/0.01; */**: significant over the system with reorderable glue rules at 0.05/0.01.

- Flattening parse trees further improves 0.4~0.5 BLEU points on average for systems with our syntactic constraints. Our final system with constraints outperforms the base HPB system with an average of 0.6 BLEU points improvement (36.71 *vs.* 36.10).

Another advantage of applying syntactic constraints is efficiency. By comparing the base HPB system and the system with our syntactic constraints (i.e., the last row in Table 1), it is not surprising to observe that the size of rules extracted from training data drops sharply from 193M in base HPB system to 60M in the other. Moreover, the system with constraints needs less decoding time than base HPB does. Observation on 2002 NIST MT test data (26 words per sentence on average) shows that basic HPB system needs to fill 239 cells per sentence on average in chart parsing while the other only needs to fill 108 cells.

4.2 Effects of Reorderable Glue Rules

Based on the system with our syntactic constraints and relaxed phrase lengths in training and decoding, we replace traditional glue rules with reorderable glue rules. Table 2 shows the results, from which we find that the effect of reorderable glue rules is elusive: surprisingly, it achieves 0.7 BLEU points

sentence length	1-10	11-20	21-30	31-40	41+	all
sentence count	337	1001	1052	768	590	3748
base HPB	**32.21**	37.51	36.71	34.96	35.00	35.73
+our constraints	31.70	**37.57**	**37.10**	**36.20**$^{++}$	**35.78**$^{++}$	**36.39**$^{++}$

Table 3: Experimental results over different sentence length on the three test sets. +/++: significant over base HPB at 0.05/0.01.

improvement on NIST MT 2002 test set while having negligible or even slightly negative impact on the other two test sets. The reason of reorderable glue rules having limited influence on translation results over monotonic only glue rules may be due to that the monotonic reordering overwhelms the inverted one: estimated from training data, the probability of the monotonic glue rule is 95.5%.

4.3 Effects of the PAS Reordering Model

Based on the system with reorderable glue rules, we examine whether the PAS reordering model is capable of improving translation performance. The last row in Table 2 presents the results . It shows the system with the PAS reordering model obtains an average of 0.34 BLEU points over the system without it (e.g., 37.13 *vs.* 36.79). It is interesting to note that it achieves significant improvement on NIST MT 2004 and 2005 test sets ($p < 0.05$) while slightly lowering performance on NIST MT 2002 test set ($p > 0.05$): the surprising improvement of applying reorderable glue rules on NIST MT 2002 test set leaves less room for further improvement. Finally, it shows we obtain an average improvement of 1.03 BLEU points on the three test sets over the base HPB system.

5 Discussion and Future Work

The results in Table 1 demonstrate that significant and sometimes substantial gains over baseline can be obtained by incorporating hard syntactic constraints into the HPB model. Due to the capability of translation phrases of arbitrary length, we conjecture that the improvement of our system over the baseline HPB system mostly comes from long sentences. To test the conjecture, we combine all test sentences in the three test sets and group them in terms of sentence length. Table 3 presents the sentence distribution and BLEU scores over different length. The results validate our assumption that the system with constraints outperforms the base systems on long sentences (e.g., sentences with 20+ words).

Figure 3 displays a translation example which shows the difference between the base HPB system and the system with constraints. The inappropriate translation of the base HPB system can be mainly blamed on the rule $\langle X_{[2,5]} \rightarrow$ 的$_2$ 发展$_3$ $X_{[4,5]}$, $X_{[4,5]}$ *the development of*$\rangle$, where 的$_2$ 发展$_3$, a part of the subtree $[0,3]$ spanning from word 0 to 3, is translated immediately to the right of $X_{[2,5]}$, making a direct impact that subtree $[0,3]$ is translated discontinuously on the target side. On the contrary, we can see that our constraints are able to help select appropriate phrase segments with respect to its syntactic structure.

Although our syntactic constraints apply on the source side, they are completely ignorant of syntax on the target side, which might result in excluding some useful translation rules. Let's revisit the sentence in Figure 3, where we can see that a transition rule spanning from word 0 to 5, say $\langle X_{[0,5]} \rightarrow X_{[0,3]}$ 是$_4$ 取决于$_5$, $X_{[0,3]}$ *depends on*$\rangle$ is intuitive: the syntactic structure on the target side satisfies the constraints, although that of the source side doesn't. One natural extension of this work, therefore, would be to relax the constraints by including translation rules whose syntactic structure of either the source side or the target side satisfies the constraints.

To illustrate how the PAS reordering model impacts translation output, Figure 4 displays two translation examples of systems with or without it. The predicate 传递*/convey* in the first example has three core arguments, i.e., A0, A2, and A1. The difference between the two outputs is the reordering of A1 and A2 while the PAS reordering model gives priority to pattern *VV A1 A2*. In the second example, we clearly observe two serious translation errors in the system without PAS reordering model: 他们/them$_{A1}$ is untranslated; 中国/china$_{A0}$ is moved to the immediate right of predicate 允许*/allow* and plays as direct object.

Including the PAS reordering model improves the BLEU scores. One further direction to refine the approach is to alleviate verb sparsity via verb classes. Another direction is to include useful context in estimating reordering probability. For example, the content of a temporal argument AM-TMP can be a

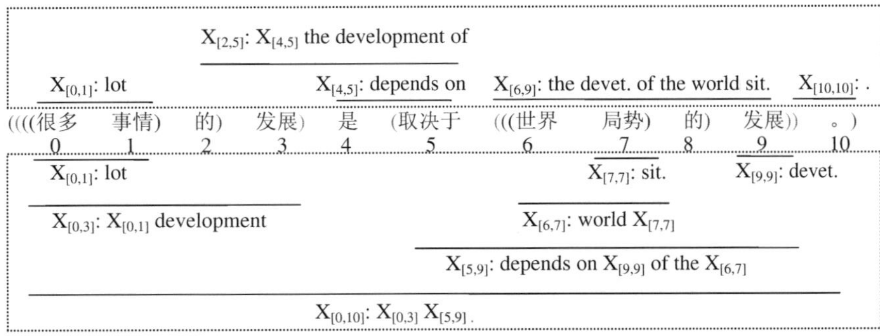

Figure 3: A translation example of the base HPB system (above) and the system with constraints (below).

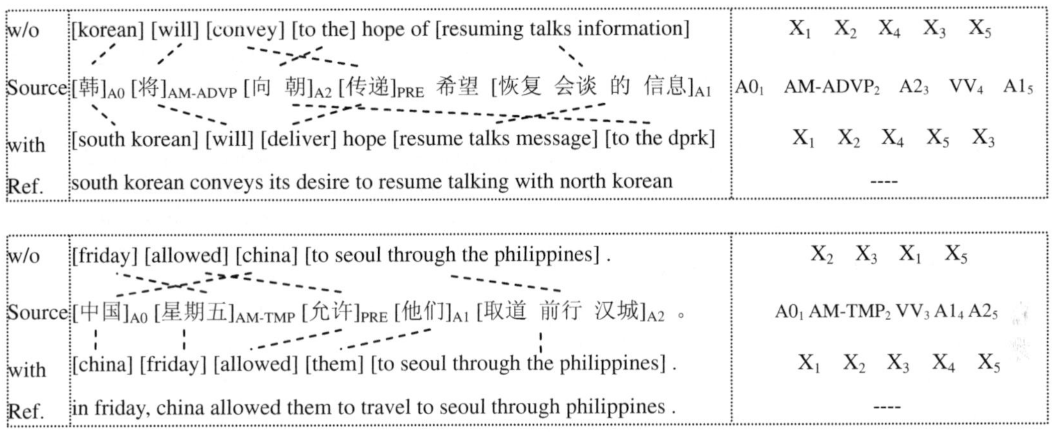

Figure 4: Two translation examples of the system with/without PAS reordering model

short/simple phrase (e.g., *friday*) or a long/complex one (e.g., *when I was 20 years old*), which has impact on its reordering in translation.

6 Related Work

While there has been substantial work on linguistically motivated SMT, we limit ourselves here to several approaches that leverage syntactic constraints yet still allow cross-constituent translations. In terms of tree-based SMT with cross-constituent translations, Cowan et al. (2006) allowed non-constituent sub phrases on the source side and adopted phrase-based translation model for modifiers in clauses. Marcu (2006) and Galley et al. (2006) inserted artificial constituent nodes in parsing tree as to capture useful but non-constituent phrases. The parse tree binarization approach (Wang et al., 2007; Marcu, 2007) and the forest-based approach (Mi et al., 2008) would also cover non-constituent phrases to some extent. Shen et al. (2010) defined well-formed dependency structure to cover uncompleted dependency structure in translation rules. In addition to the fact that the constraints of Shen et al. (2010) and this paper are based on different syntactic perspectives (i.e., dependency structure vs. constituency structure), the major difference is that in this work we don't limit the length of phrases to a fixed maximum size (e.g., 10 in Hiero). Consequently, we obtain some translation rules that are not found in Hiero systems constrained by the length. In terms of (hierarchical) phrase-based SMT with syntactic constraints, particular related to constituent boundaries, Koehn et al. (2003) tested constraints allowing constituent matched phrases only. Chiang (2005) and Cherry (2008) used a soft constraint to award or penalize hypotheses which respect or violate syntactic boundaries. Marton and Resnik (2008) further explored the idea of soft constraints by distinguishing among constituent types. Xiong et al. (2009; 2010) presented models that learn phrase boundaries from aligned dataset.

On the other hand, semantics motivated SMT has also seen an increase in activity recently. Wu and

Fung (2009) re-ordered arguments on the target side translation output, seeking to maximize the cross-lingual match of the semantic frames of the re-ordered translation to that of the source sentence. Liu and Gildea (2010) added two types of semantic role features into a tree-to-string translation model. Although Xiong et al. (2012) and our work are both focusing on source side PAS reordering, our model differs from theirs in two main aspects: 1) we consider reordering not only between an argument and its predicate, but also between two arguments; and 2) our reordering model can naturally model cases of untranslated arguments or predicates.

7 Conclusion

In this paper, we have presented an approach to incorporating syntactic and semantic structures for the HPB translation model. To accommodate the close tie of semantic structures to syntax, we first revisited the idea of hard syntactic constraints, and we demonstrated that hard constraints can, in fact, lead to significant improvement in translation quality when applied to Chiang's HPB framework. Then our PAS reordering model, thanks to the constraints which guided translation phrases in favor of syntactic boundaries, made further improvements by predicting reordering not only between an argument and its predicate, but also between two arguments. In the future work, we will extend the PAS reordering model to include useful context, e.g., the head words and the syntactic categories of arguments.

Acknowledgments

This research was supported in part by the BOLT program of the Defense Advanced Research Projects Agency, Contract No. HR0011-12-C-0015. Any opinions, findings, conclusions or recommendations expressed in this paper are those of the authors and do not necessarily reflect the view of DARPA. The authors would like to thank three anonymous reviewers for providing helpful suggestions, and also acknowledge Ke Wu and other CLIP labmates in MT group for useful discussions. We also thank creators of the valuable off-the-shelf NLP packages, such as GIZA++ and Berkeley Parser.

References

Colin Cherry. 2008. Cohesive phrase-based decoding for statistical machine translation. In *Proceedings of ACL-HLT 2008*, pages 72–80.

David Chiang. 2005. A hierarchical phrase-based model for statistical machine translation. In *Proceedings of ACL 2005*, pages 263–270.

David Chiang. 2007. Hierarchical phrase-based translation. *Computational Linguistics*, 33(2):201–228.

Brooke Cowan, Ivona Kučerová, and Michael Collins. 2006. A discriminative model for tree-to-tree translation. In *Proceedings of EMNLP 2006*, pages 232–241.

Pascale Fung, Zhaojun Wu, Yongsheng Yang, and Dekai Wu. 2006. Automatic learning of Chinese-English semantic structure mapping. In *Proceedings of SLT 2006*, pages 230–233.

Michel Galley, Jonathan Graehl, Kevin Knight, Daniel Marcu, Steve DeNeefe, Wei Wang, and Ignacio Thayer. 2006. Scalable inference and training of context-rich syntactic translation models. In *Proceedings of ACL-COLING 2006*, pages 961–968.

Philipp Koehn, Franz J. Och, and Daniel Marcu. 2003. Statistical phrase-based translation. In *Proceedings of NAACL 2003*, pages 48–54.

Philipp Koehn. 2004. Statistical significance tests for machine translation evaluation. In *Proceedings of EMNLP 2004*, pages 388–395.

Junhui Li, Guodong Zhou, and Hwee Tou Ng. 2010. Joint syntactic and semantic parsing of Chinese. In *Proceedings of ACL 2010*, pages 1108–1117.

Ding Liu and Daniel Gildea. 2010. Semantic role features for machine translation. In *Proceedings of COLING 2010*, pages 716–724.

Daniel Marcu, Wei Wang, Abdessamad Echihabi, and Kevin Knight. 2006. SPMT: Statistical machine translation with syntactified target language phrases. In *Proceedings of EMNLP 2006*, pages 44–52.

Steve DeNeefe; Kevin Knight; Wei Wang; Daniel Marcu. 2007. What can syntax-based mt learn from phrase-based mt? In *Proceedings of EMNLP-CoNLL 2007*, pages 755–763.

Yuval Marton and Philip Resnik. 2008. Soft syntactic constraints for hierarchical phrased-based translation. In *Proceedings of ACL-HLT 2008*, pages 1003–1011.

Haitao Mi, Liang Huang, and Qun Liu. 2008. Forest-based translation. In *Proceedings of ACL-HLT 2008*, pages 192–199.

Franz Josef Och and Hermann Ney. 2000. Improved statistical alignment models. In *Proceedings of ACL 2000*, pages 440–447.

Franz Josef Och. 2003. Minimum error rate training in statistical machine translation. In *Proceedings of ACL 2003*, pages 160–167.

Martha Palmer, Daniel Gildea, and Paul Kingsbury. 2005. The Proposition Bank: An annotated corpus of semantic roles. *Computational Linguistics*, 31(1):71–106.

Slav Petrov and Dan Klein. 2007. Improved inference for unlexicalized parsing. In *Proceedings of NAACL-HLT 2007*, pages 404–411.

Libin Shen, Jinxi Xu, and Ralph Weischedel. 2010. String-to-dependency statistical machine translation. *Computational Linguistics*, 36(4):649–671.

Wei Wang, Kevin Knight, and Daniel Marcu. 2007. Binarizing syntax trees to improve syntax-based machine translation accuracy. In *Proceedings of EMNLP-CoNLL 2007*, pages 746–754.

Dekai Wu and Pascale Fung. 2009. Semantic roles for smt: A hybrid two-pass model. In *Proceedings of NAACL-HLT 2009*, pages 13–16.

Deyi Xiong, Min Zhang, Aiti Aw, and Haizhou Li. 2009. A syntax-driven bracketing model for phrase-based translation. In *Proceedings of ACL-IJCNLP 2009*, pages 315–323.

Deyi Xiong, Min Zhang, and Haizhou Li. 2010. Learning translation boundaries for phrase-based decoding. In *Proceedings of NAACL-HLT 2010*, pages 136–144.

Deyi Xiong, Min Zhang, and Haizhou Li. 2012. Modeling the translation of predicate-argument structure for smt. In *Proceedings of ACL 2012*, pages 902–911.

Nianwen Xue. 2008. Automatic labeling of semantic roles. *Computational Linguistics*, 34(4):225–255.

Tao Zhuang and Chengqing Zong. 2010. Joint inference for bilingual semantic role labeling. In *Proceedings of EMNLP 2010*, pages 304–314.

Using Derivation Trees for Informative Treebank Inter-Annotator Agreement Evaluation

Seth Kulick and Ann Bies and Justin Mott and Mohamed Maamouri
Linguistic Data Consortium
University of Pennsylvania
{skulick,bies,jmott,maamouri}@ldc.upenn.edu

Beatrice Santorini and Anthony Kroch
Department of Linguistics
University of Pennsylvania
{beatrice,kroch}@ling.upenn.edu

Abstract

This paper discusses the extension of a system developed for automatic discovery of treebank annotation inconsistencies over an entire corpus to the particular case of evaluation of inter-annotator agreement. This system makes for a more informative IAA evaluation than other systems because it pinpoints the inconsistencies and groups them by their structural types. We evaluate the system on two corpora - (1) a corpus of English web text, and (2) a corpus of Modern British English.

1 Introduction

This paper discusses the extension of a system developed for automatic discovery of treebank annotation inconsistencies over an entire corpus to the particular case of evaluation of inter-annotator agreement (IAA). In IAA, two or more annotators annotate the same sentences, and a comparison identifies areas in which the annotators might need more training, or the annotation guidelines some refinement. Unlike other IAA evaluation systems, this system application results in a precise pinpointing of inconsistencies and the grouping of inconsistencies by their structural types, making for a more informative IAA evaluation.

Treebank annotation, consisting of syntactic structure with words as the terminals, is by its nature more complex and therefore more prone to error than many other annotation tasks. However, high annotation consistency is crucial to providing reliable training and testing data for parsers and linguistic research. Error detection is therefore an important area of research, and the importance of work such as Dickinson and Meurers (2003) is that errors and annotation inconsistencies might be automatically discovered, and once discovered, be targeted for subsequent quality control.

A recent approach to this problem (Kulick et al., 2011; Kulick et al., 2012) (which we will call the KBM system) improves upon Dickinson and Meurers (2003) by decomposing the full syntactic tree into smaller units, using ideas from Tree Adjoining Grammar (TAG) (Joshi and Schabes, 1997). This allows the comparison to be based on small syntactic units instead of string n-grams, improving the detection of inconsistent annotation.

The KBM system, like that of Dickinson and Meurers (2003) before it, is based on the notion of comparing identical strings. In the general case, this is a problematic assumption, since annotation inconsistencies are missed because of superficial word differences between strings which one would want to compare.[1] However, this limitation is not present for IAA evaluation, since the strings to compare are, by definition, identical.[2] The same is also true of parser evaluation, since the parser output and the gold standard are based on the same sentences.

We therefore take the logical step of applying the KBM system developed for automatic discovery of annotation inconsistency to the special case of IAA.[3]

[1] Boyd et al. (2007) and other current work tackles this problem. However, that is not the focus of this paper.

[2] Aside from possible tokenization differences by annotators.

[3] In this paper, we do not yet apply the system to parser evaluation, although it is conceptually the same problem as IAA evaluation. We wanted to first refine the system using annotator input for the IAA application before applying it to parser

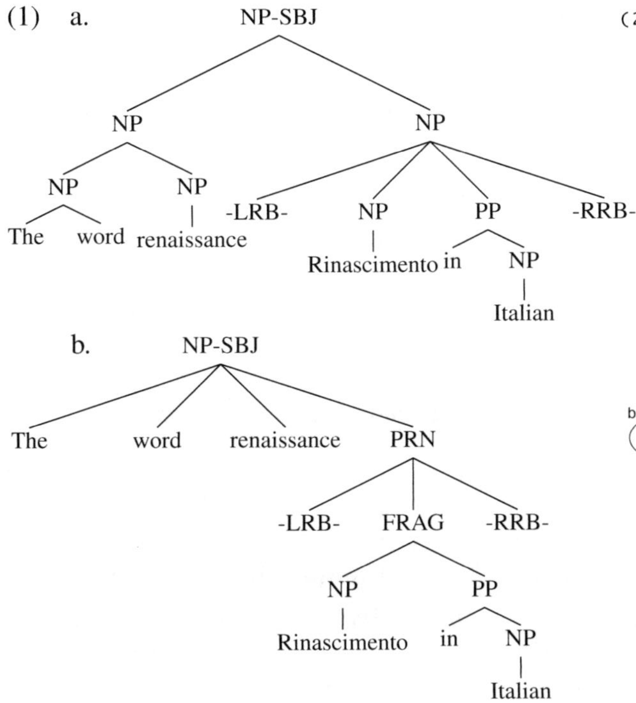

Figure 1: Two example trees showing a difference in IAA

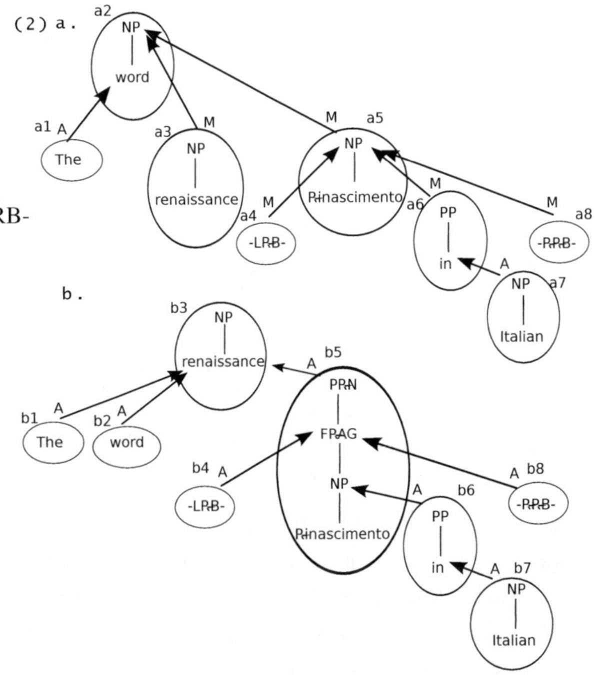

Figure 2: E-trees and derivation trees corresponding to (1ab)

To our knowledge, this work is the first to utilize such a general system for this special case.

The advantages of the KBM system play out somewhat differently in the context of IAA evaluation than in the more general case. In this context, the comparison of word sequences based on syntactic units allows for a precise pinpointing of differences. The system also retains the ability to group inconsistencies together by their structural type, which we have found to be useful for the more general case. Together, these two properties make for a useful and informative system for IAA evaluation.

In Section 2 we describe the basic working of our system. In Section 3 we discuss in more detail the advantages of this approach. In Section 4 we evaluate the system on two treebanks, a corpus of English web text and a corpus of Modern British English. Section 5 discusses future work.

2 System Overview

The basic idea of the KBM system is to detect word sequences that are annotated in inconsistent ways by comparing local syntactic units. Following Dickinson and Meurers (2003), we refer to sequences examined for inconsistent annotation as nuclei. The sentence excerpts (1ab) in Figure 1, from the test corpora used in this work, illustrate an inconsistency in the annotation of corresponding strings. We focus here on the difference in the annotation of the nucleus *The word renaissance*, which in (1a) is annotated as an appositive structure, while in (1b) it is flat.

Following the TAG approach, KBM decomposes the full phrase structure into smaller chunks called elementary trees (henceforth, e-trees). The relationship of the e-trees underlying a full phrase structure to each other is recorded in a derivation tree, in which each node is an e-tree, related to its parent node by a composition operation, as shown in (2ab).[4]

KBM uses two composition operations, each with left and right variants, shown in Figure 3: (1) ad-

evaluation.

[4]The decomposition is based on head-finding heuristics, with the result here that *word* is the head of (1a), while *renaissance* is the head of (1b), as reflected in their respective derivation trees (2a) and (2b). We omit the POS tags in (1ab) and (2ab) to avoid clutter.

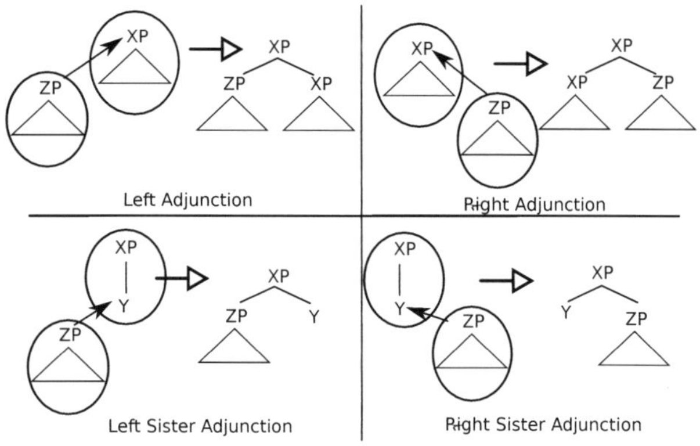

Figure 3: Composition operations (left and right)

junction, which attaches one tree to a target node in another tree by creating a copy of the target node, and (2) sister adjunction, which attaches one tree as a sister to a target node in another tree. Each arc in Figure 2 is labeled by an "M" for adjunction and "A" for sister-adjunction. [5]

The system uses the tree decomposition and resulting derivation tree for the comparison of different instances of the same nucleus. The full derivation tree for a sentence is not used, but rather only that slice of it having e-trees with words that are in the nucleus being examined, which we call a derivation tree fragment. That is, for a given nucleus with a set of instances, we compare the derivation fragments for each instance.

For example, for the nucleus *The word renaissance*, the derivation tree fragment for the instance in (1a) consists of the e-trees a1, a2, a3 (and their arcs) in (2a), and likewise the derivation tree from the instance in (1b) consists of the e-trees b1, b2, b3 in (2b). These derivation fragments have a different structure, and so the two instances of *The word renaissance* are recognized as inconsistent.

Two important aspects of the overall system require mention here: (1) Nuclei are identified by using sequences that occur as a constituent anywhere in the corpus, even if other instances of the same sequence are not constituents. Both instances of *The word renaissance* are compared, because the sequence occurs at least once as a constituent. (2) We partition each comparison of the instances of a nucleus by the lowest nonterminal in the derivation tree fragment that covers the sequence. The two instances of *The word renaissance* are compared because the lowest nonterminal is an NP in both instances.

3 Advantages of this approach

As Kulick et al. (2012) stressed, using derivation tree fragments allows the comparison to abstract away from interference by irrelevant modifiers, an issue with Dickinson and Meurers (2003). However, in the context of IAA, this advantage of KBM plays out in a different way, in that it allows for a precise pinpointing of the inconsistencies. For IAA, the concern is not whether an inconsistent annotation will be reported, since at some level higher in the tree every difference will be found, even if the context is the entire tree. KBM, however, will find the inconsistencies in a more informative way, for example reporting just *The word renaissance*, not some larger unit. Likewise, it reports *Rinascimento in Italian* as an inconsistently annotated sequence.[6]

A critical desirable property of KBM that carries over from the more general case is that it allows for different nuclei to be grouped together in the system's output if they have the same annotation inconsistency type. As in Kulick et al. (2011), each nucleus found to be inconsistent is categorized by an inconsistency type, which is simply the collection of different derivation tree fragments used for the comparison of its instances, including POS tags but not the words. For example, the inconsistency type of the nucleus *The word renaissance* in (1ab) is the pair of derivation tree fragments (a1,a2,a3) and (b1,b2,b3) from (2ab), with the POS tags. This nu-

[5] KBM is based on a variant of Spinal TAG (Shen et al., 2008), and uses sister adjunction without substitution. Space prohibits full discussion, but multiple adjunction to a single node (e.g., a4, a6, a8 to a5 in (2a)) does not create multiple levels of recursion, while a special specification handles the extra NP recursion for the apposition with a2, a3, and a5. For reasons of space, we also leave aside a precise comparison to Tree Insertion Grammar (Chiang, 2003) and Spinal TAG (Shen et al., 2008).

[6] Note however that it does *not* report *-LRB- Rinascimento in Italian -RRB-* which is also a constituent, and so might be expected to be compared. The lowest nonterminal above this substring in the two derivation trees in Figure 2 is the NP in a5 and the FRAG in b5, thus exempting them from comparison. It is exactly this sort of case that motivated the "external check" discussed in Kulick et al. (2012), which we have not yet implemented for IAA.

Inconsistency type	# Found	# Accurate
Function tags only	53	53
POS tags only	18	13
Structural	129	122

Table 1: Inconsistency types found for system evaluation

cleus is then reported together with other nuclei that use the same derivation fragments. In this case, it therefore also reports the nucleus *The term renaissance*, which appears elsewhere in the corpus with the two annotations from the different annotators as in (3):

(3)
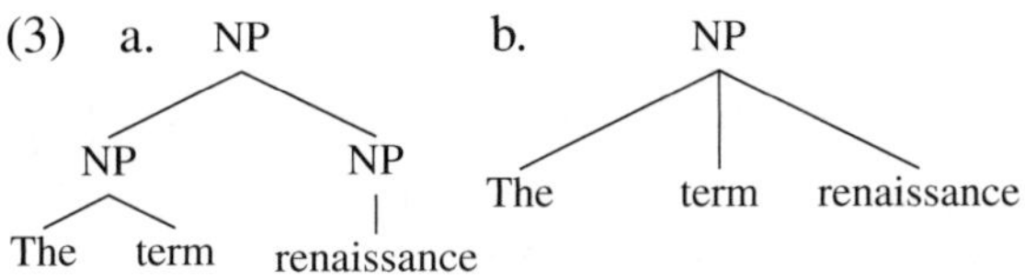

KBM reports *The word renaissance* and *The term renaissance* together because they are inconsistently annotated in exactly the same way, in spite of the difference in words. This grouping together of inconsistencies based on structural characteristics of the inconsistency is critically important for understanding the nature of the annotation inconsistencies.

It is the combination of these two characteristics - (1) pinpointing of errors and (2) grouping by structure - that makes the system so useful for IAA. This is an improvement over alternatives such as using evalb (Sekine and Collins, 2008) for IAA. No other system to our knowledge groups inconsistencies by structural type, as KBM does. The use of the derivation tree fragments greatly lessens the multiple reporting of a single annotation difference, which is a difficulty for using evalb (Manning and Schuetze, 1999, p. 436) or Dickinson and Meurers (2003).

4 Evaluation

4.1 English web text

We applied our approach to pre-release subset of (Bies et al., 2012), dually annotated and used for annotator training, from which the examples in Sections 2 and 3 are taken. It is a small section of the corpus, with 4,270 words dually annotated.

For this work, we also took the further step of characterizing the inconsistency types themselves, allowing for an even higher-level view of the inconsistencies found. In addition to grouping together different strings as having the same inconsistent annotation, the types can also be grouped together for comparison at a higher level. For this IAA sample, we separated the inconsistency types into the three groups in Table 1, with the derivation tree fragments differing (1) only on function tags, (2) only on POS tags[7], and (3) on structural differences. We manually examined each inconsistency group to determine if it was an actual inconsistency found, or a spurious false positive. As shown in Table 1, the precision of the reported inconsistencies is very high. It is in fact even higher than it appears, because the seven (out of 129) instances incorrectly listed as structural problems were actually either POS or function tag inconsistencies, that were discovered by the system only by a difference in the derivation tree fragment, and so were categorized as structural problems instead of POS or function tag inconsistencies. [8]

Because of the small size of the corpus, there are relatively few nuclei grouped into inconsistency types. The 129 structural inconsistency types include 130 nuclei, with the only inconsistency type with more than one nucleus being the type with *The word renaissance* and *The term renaissance*, as discussed above. There is more grouping together in the "POS tags only" case (37 nuclei included in the 18 inconsistency types), and the "function tags only" case (56 nuclei included in the 53 inconsistency types).

4.2 Modern British English corpus

We also applied our approach to a supplemental section (Kroch and Santorini, in preparation) to a corpus of modern British English (Kroch et al., 2010), part of a series of corpora used for research into language change. The annotation style is similar to that of the Penn Treebank, although with some differences. In this case, because neither the function tags nor part-of-speech tags were part of the IAA work,

[7]As mentioned in footnote 4, although POS tags were left out of Figure 2 for readability, they are included in the actual e-trees. This allows POS differences in a similar syntactic context to be naturally captured within the overall KBM framework.

[8]A small percentage of inconsistencies are the result of linguistic ambiguities and not an error by one of the annotators.

we do not separate out the inconsistency types, as done in Section 4.1.

The supplement section consisted of 82,701 words dually annotated. The larger size, as compared with the corpus in Section 4.1, results in some differences in the system output. Because of the larger size, there are more substantial cases of different nuclei grouped together as the same inconsistency type than in Section 4.1. The first inconsistency type (sorted by number of nuclei) has 88 nuclei, and the second has 37 nuclei. In total, there are 1,532 inconsistency types found, consisting of 2,194 nuclei in total. We manually examined the first 20 inconsistency types (sorted by number of nuclei), consisting in total of 375 nuclei. All were found to be true instances of inconsistent annotation.

(4)
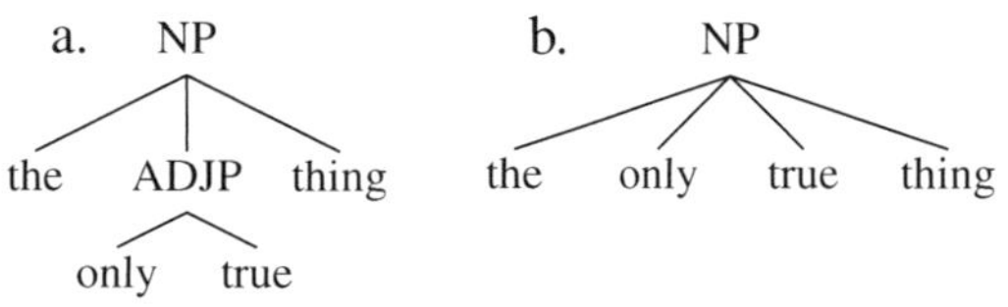

(5)
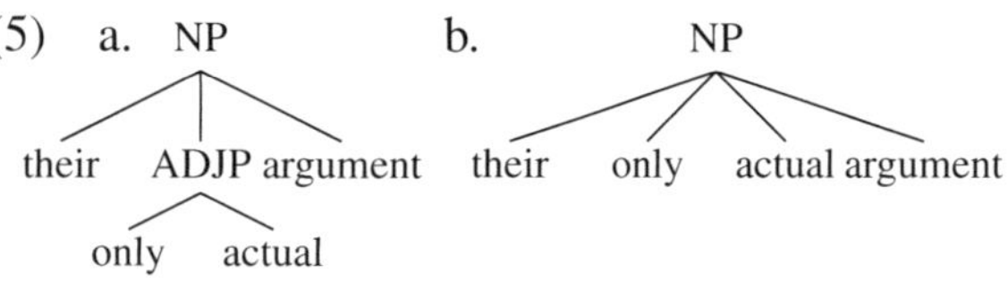

The trees in (4) and (5) show two of the 88 nuclei grouped into the first inconsistency type. As with *The word renaissance* and *The term renaissance* in the English web corpus, nuclei with similar (although not identical) words are often grouped into the same inconsistency type. To repeat the point, this is not because of any search for similarity of the words in the nuclei. It arises from the fact that the nuclei are annotated inconstantly in the same way. Of course not all nuclei in an inconsistency type have the same words. Nuclei found in this inconsistency type include *only true* and *only actual* as shown above, and also nuclei such as *new English*, *greatest possible*, *thin square*, *only necessary*. Taken together, they clearly indicate an issue with the annotation of multi-word adjective phrases.[9]

[9]Note that the inconsistencies discussed throughout this paper are not taken from the the published corpora. These results are only from internal annotator training files.

5 Future work

There are several ways in which we plan to improve the current approach. As mentioned above, there is a certain class of inconsistencies which KBM will not pinpoint precisely, which requires adopting the "external check" from Kulick et al. (2012). The abstraction on inconsistency types described in Section 4 can also be taken further. For example, one might want to examine in particular inconsistency types that arise from PP attachment or that have to do with the PRN function tag.

One main area for future work is the application of this work to parser evaluation as well as IAA. For this area, there is some connection to the work of Goldberg and Elhadad (2010) and Dickinson (2010), which are both concerned with examining dependency structures of more than one edge. The connection is that those works are focused on dependency representations, and ithe KBM system does phrase structure analysis using a TAG-like derivation tree, which strongly resembles a dependency tree (Rambow and Joshi, 1997). There is much in this area of common concern that is worth examining further.

Acknowledgments

This material is based upon work supported by the Defense Advanced Research Projects Agency (DARPA) under Contract No. HR0011-11-C-0145. The content does not necessarily reflect the position or the policy of the Government, and no official endorsement should be inferred. This applies to the first four authors. The first, fifth, and sixth authors were supported in part by National Science Foundation Grant # BCS-114749. We would also like to thank Colin Warner, Aravind Joshi, Mitch Marcus, and the computational linguistics group at the University of Pennsylvania for helpful conversations and feedback.

References

Ann Bies, Justin Mott, Colin Warner, and Seth Kulick. 2012. English Web Treebank. LDC2012T13. Linguistic Data Consortium.

Adriane Boyd, Markus Dickinson, and Detmar Meurers. 2007. Increasing the recall of corpus annotation error detection. In *Proceedings of the Sixth Workshop on Treebanks and Linguistic Theories (TLT 2007)*, Bergen, Norway.

David Chiang. 2003. Statistical parsing with an automatically extracted Tree Adjoining Grammar. In *Data Oriented Parsing*. CSLI.

Markus Dickinson and Detmar Meurers. 2003. Detecting inconsistencies in treebanks. In *Proceedings of the Second Workshop on Treebanks and Linguistic Theories (TLT 2003)*, Sweden. Treebanks and Linguistic Theories.

Markus Dickinson. 2010. Detecting errors in automatically-parsed dependency relations. In *Proceedings of the 48th Annual Meeting of the Association for Computational Linguistics*, pages 729–738, Uppsala, Sweden, July. Association for Computational Linguistics.

Yoav Goldberg and Michael Elhadad. 2010. Inspecting the structural biases of dependency parsing algorithms. In *Proceedings of the Fourteenth Conference on Computational Natural Language Learning*, pages 234–242, Uppsala, Sweden, July. Association for Computational Linguistics.

A.K. Joshi and Y. Schabes. 1997. Tree-adjoining grammars. In G. Rozenberg and A. Salomaa, editors, *Handbook of Formal Languages, Volume 3: Beyond Words*, pages 69–124. Springer, New York.

Anthony Kroch and Beatrice Santorini. in preparation. Supplement to the Penn Parsed Corpus of Modern British English.

Anthony Kroch, Beatrice Santorini, and Ariel Diertani. 2010. Penn Parsed Corpus of Modern British English. http://www.ling.upenn.edu/hist-corpora/PPCMBE-RELEASE-1/index.html.

Seth Kulick, Ann Bies, and Justin Mott. 2011. Using derivation trees for treebank error detection. In *Proceedings of the 49th Annual Meeting of the Association for Computational Linguistics: Human Language Technologies*, pages 693–698, Portland, Oregon, USA, June. Association for Computational Linguistics.

Seth Kulick, Ann Bies, and Justin Mott. 2012. Further developments in treebank error detection using derivation trees. In *LREC 2012: 8th International Conference on Language Resources and Evaluation*, Istanbul.

Christopher Manning and Hinrich Schuetze. 1999. *Foundations of Statistical Natural Language Processing*. MIT Press.

Owen Rambow and Aravind Joshi. 1997. A formal look at dependency grammars and phrase-structure grammars, with special consideration of word-order phenomena. In L. Wanner, editor, *Recent Trends in Meaning-Text Theory*, pages 167–190. John Benjamins, Amsterdam and Philadelphia.

Satoshi Sekine and Michael Collins. 2008. Evalb. http://nlp.cs.nyu.edu/evalb/.

Libin Shen, Lucas Champollion, and Aravind Joshi. 2008. LTAG-spinal and the Treebank: A new resource for incremental, dependency and semantic parsing. *Language Resources and Evaluation*, 42(1):1–19.

Embracing Ambiguity: A Comparison of Annotation Methodologies for Crowdsourcing Word Sense Labels

David Jurgens
Department of Computer Science
University of California, Los Angeles
jurgens@cs.ucla.edu

Abstract

Word sense disambiguation aims to identify which meaning of a word is present in a given usage. Gathering word sense annotations is a laborious and difficult task. Several methods have been proposed to gather sense annotations using large numbers of untrained annotators, with mixed results. We propose three new annotation methodologies for gathering word senses where untrained annotators are allowed to use multiple labels and weight the senses. Our findings show that given the appropriate annotation task, untrained workers can obtain at least as high agreement as annotators in a controlled setting, and in aggregate generate equally as good of a sense labeling.

1 Introduction

Word sense annotation is regarded as one of the most difficult annotation tasks (Artstein and Poesio, 2008) and building manually-annotated corpora with high-quality sense labels is often a time- and resource-consuming task. As a result, nearly all sense-tagged corpora in wide-spread use are created using trained annotators (Hovy et al., 2006; Passonneau et al., 2010), which results in a knowledge acquisition bottleneck for training systems that require sense labels (Gale et al., 1992). In other NLP areas, this bottleneck has been addressed through gathering annotations using many untrained workers on platforms such as Amazon Mechanical Turk (MTurk), a task commonly referred to as crowdsourcing. Recently, several works have proposed gathering sense annotations using crowdsourcing (Snow et al., 2008; Biemann and Nygaard, 2010; Passonneau et al., 2012b; Rumshisky et al., 2012). However, these methods produce sense labels that are different from the commonly used sense inventories such as WordNet (Fellbaum, 1998) or OntoNotes (Hovy et al., 2006). Furthermore, while Passonneau et al. (2012b) did use WordNet sense labels, they found the quality was well below that of trained experts.

We revisit the task of crowdsourcing word sense annotations, focusing on two key aspects: (1) the annotation methodology itself, and (2) the restriction to single sense assignment. First, the choice in sense inventory plays an important role in gathering high-quality annotations; fine-grained inventories such as WordNet often contain several related senses for polysemous words, which untrained annotators find difficult to correctly apply in a given context (Chugur et al., 2002; McCarthy, 2006; Palmer et al., 2007; Rumshisky and Batiukova, 2008; Brown et al., 2010). However, many agreement studies have restricted annotators to using a single sense, which can significantly lower inter-annotator agreement (IAA) in the presence of ambiguous or polysemous usages; indeed, multiple studies have shown that when allowed, annotators readily assign multiple senses to a single usage (Véronis, 1998; Murray and Green, 2004; Erk et al., 2009; Passonneau et al., 2012b). Therefore, we focus on annotation methodologies that enable workers to use as many labels as they feel appropriate, asking the question: if allowed to make labeling ambiguity explicit, will annotators agree? Furthermore, we adopt the goal of Erk et al. (2009), which enabled annotators to weight each sense by its applicability to the given context, thereby quantifying the ambiguity.

This paper provides the following contributions. First, we demonstrate that the choice in annotation setup can significantly improve IAA and that the labels of untrained workers follow consistent patterns that enable creating high quality labeling from their aggregate. Second, we find that the sense labeling from crowdsourcing matches performance with annotators in a controlled setting.

2 Related Work

Given the potential utility of a sense-labeled corpus, multiple studies have examined how to efficiently gather high quality sense annotations. Snow et al. (2008) had MTurk workers, referred to as Turkers, disambiguate uses of "president." While they reported extremely high IAA (0.952), their analysis was only performed on a single word.

Biemann and Nygaard (2010) and Biemann (2012) construct a sense-labeled corpus by concurrently constructing the sense inventory itself. Turkers used a lexical substitution task to identify valid substitutions of a target word. The contexts for the resulting substitutions were clustered based on their word overlap and the resulting clusters were labeled as senses. Biemann and Nygaard (2010) showed that the number of sense definitions for a word in their inventory was correlated with the number in WordNet, often with their inventory having fewer senses by combining related meanings and omitting rare meanings.

Hong and Baker (2011) evaluated multiple annotation strategies for gathering FrameNet sense annotations, ultimately yielding high (>90%) accuracy for most terms after filtering. They highlight ambiguous and polysemous usages as a notable source of errors, which the present work directly addresses.

In the most related work, Passonneau et al. (2012b) had Turkers annotate contexts using one or more senses, with the requirement that a worker labels all contexts. While they found that agreement between all workers was low, their annotations could be combined using the GLAD model (Whitehill et al., 2000) to obtain good performance, though not as good as trained annotators.

3 Annotation Methodologies

We consider three methodologies for gathering sense labels: (1) the methodology of Erk et al. (2009) for gathering weighted labels, (2) a multi-stage strategy that uses both binary and Likert ratings, and (3) MaxDiff, a paired choice format.

Likert Ratings Likert rating scales provide the most direct way of gathering weighted sense labels; Turkers are presented with all senses of a word and then asked to rate each on a numeric scale. We adopt the annotation guidelines of Erk et al. (2009) which used a five-point scale, ranging from 1 to 5, indicating the sense does not apply or that it matches the contextual usage exactly, respectively.

Select and Rate Recent efforts in crowdsourcing have proposed multi-stage processes for accomplishing complex tasks, where efforts by one group of workers are used to create new subtasks for other workers to complete (Bernstein et al., 2010; Kittur et al., 2011; Kulkarni et al., 2012). We propose a two-stage strategy that aims to reduce the complexity of the annotation task, referred to as Select and Rate (S+R). First, Turkers are presented with all the senses and asked to make a binary choice of which senses apply. Second, a Likert rating task is created for only those senses whose selection frequency is above a threshold, thereby concentrating worker focus on a potentially smaller set of senses.

Our motivation for S+R is two-fold. First, the sense definitions of certain words may be unclear or misinterpreted by a minority of the Turkers, who then systematically rate inapplicable senses as applicable. The Select task can potentially remove such noise and therefore improve both IAA and rating quality in the subsequent Rate task. Second, while the present study analyzes words with 4–8 senses, we are ultimately interested in annotating highly polysemous words with tens of senses, which could present a significant cognitive burden for an annotator to rate concurrently. Here, the Select stage can potentially reduce the number of senses presented, leading to less cognitive burden in the Rate stage. Furthermore, as a pragmatic benefit, removing inapplicable senses reduces the visual space required for displaying the questions on the MTurk platform, which can improve annotation throughput.

MaxDiff MaxDiff is an alternative to scale-based ratings in which Turkers are presented with a only subset of all of a word's senses and then asked to select (1) the sense option that *best* matches the mean-

	add.v	ask.v	win.v	argument.n	interest.n	paper.n	different.a	important.a
Erk et al. (2009) IAA	0.470	0.354	0.072	0.497	0.320	0.403	0.212	0.466
MTurk Likert IAA	0.336	0.212	0.129	0.250	0.209	0.522	0.030	0.240
MTurk Select	0.309	0.127	0.179	0.192	0.164	0.449	0.024	0.111
MTurk Rate	0.204	0.076	0.026	0.005	0.081	0.108	0.005	0.116
MTurk MaxDiff	0.493	0.353	0.295	-	0.349	0.391	0.220	0.511
Likert Mode	0.500	0.369	0.083	0.445	0.388	0.518	0.124	0.516
S+R Median	0.473	0.394	0.149	0.497	0.390	0.497	0.103	0.416
MTurk MaxDiff	0.508	0.412	0.184	-	0.408	0.496	0.115	0.501
Sampled Baseline	0.238	0.178	0.042	0.254	0.162	0.205	0.100	0.221
Random Baseline	0.239	0.186	0.045	0.249	0.269	0.200	0.110	0.269

Table 1: IAA per word (top) and IAA between aggregate labelings and the GWS annotators (bottom)

ing in the example context and (2) the sense option that *least* matches (Louviere, 1991). In our setting, we presented three options at a time for words with fewer than seven senses, and four options for those with seven senses. For a single context, multiple subsets of the senses are presented and then their relative ranking is used to produce the numeric rating. The final applicability ratings were produced using a modification of the counting procedure of Orme (2009). First, all sense ratings are computed as the number of times the sense was rated *best* minus the number of times rated *least*. Second, all negatively-rated senses are assigned score of 1, and all positively ratings are normalized to be $(1, 5]$.

4 Experiments

For measuring the difference in methodologies, we propose three experiments based on different analyses of comparing Turker and non-Turker annotations on the same dataset, the latter of which we refer to as the reference labeling. First, we measure the ability of the Turkers individually by evaluating their IAA with the reference labeling. Second, many studies using crowdsourcing combine the results into a single answer, thereby leveraging the wisdom of the crowds (Surowiecki, 2005) to smooth over inconsistencies in the data. Therefore, in the second experiment, we evaluate different methods of combining Turker responses into a single sense labeling, referred to as an *aggregate* labeling, and comparing that with the reference labeling. Third, we measure the replicability of the Turker annotations (Kilgarriff, 1999) using a sampling methodology. Two equally-sized sets of Turker annotations are created by randomly sampling without replacement from the full set of annotations for each item. IAA is calculated between the aggregate labelings computed from each set. This sampling is repeated 50 times and we report the mean IAA as a measure of the expected degree of replicability when annotating using different groups of Turkers.

For the reference sense labeling, we use a subset of the GWS dataset of Erk et al. (2009), where three annotators rated 50 instances each for eight words. For clarity, we refer to these individuals as the GWS annotators. Given a word usage in a sentence, GWS annotators rated the applicability of all WordNet 3.0 senses using the same Likert scale as described in Section 3. Contexts were drawn evenly from the SemCor (Miller et al., 1993) and SENSEVAL-3 lexical substitution (Mihalcea et al., 2004) corpora. GWS annotators were apt to use multiple senses, with nearly all instances having multiple labels.

For each annotation task, Turkers were presented with an identical set of annotation guidelines, followed by methodology-specific instructions.[1] To increase the familiarity with the task, four instances were shown per task, with all instances using the same target word. Unlike Passonneau et al. (2012b), we did not require a Turker to annotate all contexts for a single word; however many Turkers did complete the majority of instances. Both the Likert, Select, and Rate tasks used ten Turkers each. Senses were passed from Select to Rate if they received at

[1]Full guidelines are available at `http://cs.ucla.edu/~jurgens/sense-annotation/`

least three votes. For MaxDiff, we gathered at least $3n$ annotations per context where n is the number of senses of the target word, ensuring that each sense appeared at least once. Due to resource limitations, we omitted the evaluation of *argument.n* for MaxDiff. Following the recommendation of Kosinski et al. (2012), Turkers were paid $0.05USD for each Likert, Select, and Rate task. For MaxDiff, due to their shorter nature and comparably high volume, Turkers were paid $0.03USD per task.

To ensure fluency in English as well as reduce the potential for low-quality results, we prefaced each task with a simple test question that asked the Turker to pick out a definition of the target word from a list of four options. The incorrect options were selected so that they would be nonsensical for anyone familiar with the target word. Additionally, we rejected all Turker responses where more than one option was missing a rating. In the case of missing ratings, we infer a rating of 1. Approximately 20-30% of the submissions were rejected by these criteria, underscoring the importance of filtering.

For measuring IAA, we selected Krippendorff's α (Krippendorff, 1980; Artstein and Poesio, 2008), which is an agreement coefficient that handles missing data, as well as different levels of measurement, e.g., nominal data (Select and MaxDiff) and interval data (Likert and Rate).[2] Krippendorff's α adjusts for chance, ranging between $[-1, 1]$ for nominal data and $(-1, 1]$ for interval data, where 1 indicates perfect agreement and -1 indicates systematic disagreement; random labels would have an expected α of zero. We treat each sense and instance combination as a separate item to rate.

5 Results

The results of the first experiment appear in the top of Table 1. Two important aspects emerge. First, the word itself plays a significant role in IAA. Though Erk et al. (2009) reported a pair-wise IAA of the GWS annotators between 0.466 and 0.506 using Spearman's ρ, the IAA varies considerably between words for both Turkers and GWS annotators when measured using Krippendorff's α.

Second, the choice of annotation methodology significantly impacts IAA. While both the Likert and S+R tasks have lower IAA than the GWS annotators do, the MaxDiff annotators achieve higher IAA for almost all words. We hypothesize that comparing senses for applicability is an easier task for the untrained worker, rather than having to construct a mental scale of what constitutes the applicability of each sense. Surprisingly, the binary Select task has a lower IAA than the more complex the Likert task. An analysis of the duration of median task completion times for the Likert and Select tasks showed little difference (with the exception of *paper.n*, which was on average 50 second faster for Likert ratings), suggesting that both tasks are equally as cognitively demanding. In addition, the Rate task has the lowest IAA, despite its similarity to the Likert task. An inspection of the annotations shows that the full rating scale was used, so the low value is not due to Turkers always using the same rating, which would yield an IAA near chance.

In the second experiment, we created a aggregate sense labeling and compared its IAA with the GWS annotators, shown in Table 1 (bottom). For scale-based ratings, we considered three arithmetic operations for selecting the final rating: mode, median, and mean. We found that the mode yielded the highest average IAA for the Likert ratings and median for S+R; however, the differences in IAA using each operation were often small. We compare the IAA with GWS annotators against two baselines: one generated by sampling from the GWS annotators' rating distribution, and a second generated by uniformly sampling in $[1, 5]$. By comparison, the aggregate labelings have a much larger IAA than the baselines, which is often at least as high as the IAA amongst the GWS annotators themselves, indicating that the Turkers in aggregate are capable of producing equivalent ratings. Of the three annotation methodologies, MaxDiff provides the highest IAA both within its annotators and with its aggregate key. Surprisingly, neither the Likert or S+R aggregate labeling appears better than the other.

Based on the second experiment, we measured the average IAA across all words between the aggregate Likert and MaxDiff solutions, which was 0.472. However, this IAA is significantly affected by the annotations for *win.v* and *different.a*, which had the lowest IAA among Turkers (Table 1) and there-

[2] We note that although the ratings are technically given on an ordinal scale (ranks), we use the interval scale to allow comparison with rational ratings from the aggregate solutions.

Corpus	Sense Inventory	IAA	Measurement
SensEval-1 (Kilgarriff and Rosenzweig, 2000)	HECTOR	0.950	Replicability experiment (Kilgarriff, 1999)
OntoNotes (Hovy et al., 2006)	OntoNotes	$\geq 0.90^{\dagger}$	Pair-wise agreement
SALSA (Burchardt et al., 2006)	FrameNet	0.86	Percentage agreement
SensEval-2 Lexical Sample (Kilgarriff, 2002)	WordNet 1.7	0.853, 0.710, $0.673^{\ddagger}$	Adjudicated Agreement
GWS with MaxDiff Replicability$^{\diamond}$	WordNet 3.0	0.815	Krippendorff's α
SemCor (Fellbaum et al., 1998)	WordNet 1.6	0.786, $0.57^{\star}$	Percentage agreement
SensEval-3 (Snyder and Palmer, 2004)	WordNet 1.7	0.725	Percentage agreement
MASC (Passonneau et al., 2012a)	WordNet 3.1	-0.02 to $0.88^{\triangleleft}$	Krippendorff's α with MASI (Passonneau et al., 2006)
MASC, single phase reported in Passonneau et al. (2010)	WordNet 3.1	0.515	Krippendorff's α
GWS with Likert Replicability	WordNet 3.0	0.409	Krippendorff's α
GWS with Erk et al. (2009) annotators	WordNet 3.0	0.349	Krippendorff's α

† Not all words achieved this agreement.
‡ Kilgarriff (2002) uses a multi-stage agreement procedure where two annotators rate each item, and in the case of disagreement, a third annotator is added. If the third annotator agrees with either of the first two, the instance is marked as a case of agreement. However, the unadjudicated agreement for the dataset was 67.3 measured using pair-wise agreement. A re-annotation by Palmer et al. (2004) produced a similar pair-wise agreement of 71.0.
* Tou et al. (1999) perform a re-annotation test of the same data using student annotators, finding substantially lower agreement
$^{\diamond}$ Excludes agreement for *argument.n*, which was not annotated
$^{\triangleleft}$ IAA ranges for 37 words; no corpus-wide IAA is provided.

Table 2: IAA for sense-annotated corpora

fore produce noisy aggregate solutions. When *win.v* and *different.a* are excluded, the agreement between aggregate Likert and MaxDiff solutions is 0.649. While this IAA is still moderate, it suggests that Turkers can still produce similar annotations even when using different annotation methodologies.

For the third experiment, replicability is reported as the average IAA between the sampled aggregate labelings for all annotated words. Table 2 shows this IAA for Likert and MaxDiff methodologies in comparison to other sense annotation studies. Krippendorff (2004) recommends that an α of 0.8 is necessary to claim high-quality agreement, which is achieved by the MaxDiff methodology. In contrast, the average IAA between sampled Likert ratings is significantly lower, though the methodology does achieve an α of 0.812 for *paper.n*. However, when the two words with the lowest IAA, *win.v* and *different.a*, are excluded, the average α increases to 0.880 for MaxDiff and 0.649 for Likert. Overall, these results suggest that MaxDiff can generate highly replicable annotations with agreement on par with that of other high-quality sense-labeled corpora. Furthermore, the Likert methodology may in aggregate still produce moderately replicable annotations in some cases.

6 Conclusion and Future Work

Word sense disambiguation is a difficult task, both for humans and algorithms, with an important bottleneck in acquiring large sense annotated corpora. As a potential solution, we proposed three annotation methodologies for crowdsourcing sense labels. Importantly, we relax the single sense assignment restriction in order to let annotators explicitly note ambiguity through weighted sense ratings. Our findings reveal that moderate IAA can be obtained using MaxDiff ratings, with IAA surpassing that of annotators in a controlled setting. Furthermore, our findings showed marked differences in rating difficulty per word, even in the weighted rating setting. In future work, we will investigate what factors influence annotation difficulty in order to improve IAA to what is considered expert levels, drawing from existing work analyzing difficulty in the single label setting (Murray and Green, 2004; Passonneau et al., 2009; Cinková et al., 2012).

References

R. Artstein and M. Poesio. 2008. Inter-coder agreement for computational linguistics. *Computational Linguistics*, 34(4):555–596.

Michael S. Bernstein, Ggreg Little, Robert C. Miller, Bjön Hartmann, Mark S. Ackerman, David R. Karger, David Crowell, and Katrina Panovich. 2010. Soylent: a word processor with a crowd inside. In *Proceedings of UIST*, pages 313–322. ACM.

Chris Biemann and Valerie Nygaard. 2010. Crowdsourcing WordNet. In *The 5th International Conference of the Global WordNet Association (GWC-2010)*.

Chris Biemann. 2012. Turk Bootstrap Word Sense Inventory 2.0: A Large-Scale Resource for Lexical Substitution. In *Proceedings of LREC*.

Susan Windisch Brown, Travis Rood, and Martha Palmer. 2010. Number or nuance: Which factors restrict reliable word sense annotation? In *Proceedings of LREC*.

Aljoscha Burchardt, Katrin Erk, Anette Frank, Andrea Kowalski, Sebastian Padó, and Manfred Pinkal. 2006. The SALSA corpus: a German corpus resource for lexical semantics. In *Proceedings of LREC*.

Irina Chugur, Julio Gonzalo, and Felisa Verdejo. 2002. Polysemy and sense proximity in the senseval-2 test suite. In *Proceedings of the SIGLEX/SENSEVAL Workshop on Word Sense Disambiguation: Recent Successes and Future Directions*, pages 32–39. ACL.

Silvie Cinková, Martin Holub, and Vincent Krí. 2012. Managing uncertainty in semantic tagging. In *Proceedings of EACL*, pages 840–850. ACL.

Katrin Erk, Diana McCarthy, and Nicholas Gaylord. 2009. Investigations on word senses and word usages. In *Proceedings of ACL*, pages 10–18. ACL.

Christiane Fellbaum, Jaochim Grabowski, and Shari Landes. 1998. Performance and confidence in a semantic annotation task. *WordNet: An electronic lexical database*, pages 217–237.

Christine Fellbaum, editor. 1998. *WordNet: An Electronic Lexical Database*. The MIT Press.

William A. Gale, Kenneth W. Church, and David Yarowsky. 1992. A method for disambiguating word senses in a large corpus. *Computers and the Humanities*, 26(5):415–439.

J. Hong and C.F. Baker. 2011. How Good is the Crowd at "real" WSD? In *Proceedings of the Fifth Linguistic Annotation Workshop (LAW V)*, pages 30–37. ACL.

Eduard Hovy, Mitchell Marcus, Martha Palmer, Lance Ramshaw, and Ralph Weischedel. 2006. OntoNotes: the 90% solution. In *Proceedings of NAACL*, pages 57–60. ACL.

A. Kilgarriff and J. Rosenzweig. 2000. Framework and results for english senseval. *Computers and the Humanities*, 34(1):15–48.

Adam Kilgarriff. 1999. 95% replicability for manual word sense tagging. In *Proceedings of EACL*, pages 277–278. ACL.

Adam Kilgarriff. 2002. English lexical sample task description. In *Senseval-2: Proceedings of the 2nd International Workshop on Evaluating Word Sense Disambiguation Systems*.

A. Kittur, B. Smus, S. Khamkar, and R.E. Kraut. 2011. Crowdforge: Crowdsourcing complex work. In *Proceedings of UIST*, pages 43–52. ACM.

M. Kosinski, Y. Bachrach, G. Kasneci, J. Van-Gael, and T. Graepel. 2012. Crowd IQ: Measuring the intelligence of crowdsourcing platforms. In *ACM Web Sciences*. ACM.

Klaus Krippendorff. 1980. *Content Analysis: An Introduction to Its Methodology*. Sage, Beverly Hills, CA.

Klaus Krippendorff. 2004. *Content Analysis: An Introduction to Its Methodology*. Sage, Thousand Oaks, CA, second edition.

A. Kulkarni, M. Can, and B. Hartmann. 2012. Collaboratively crowdsourcing workflows with turkomatic. In *Proceedings of CSCW*, pages 1003–1012. ACM.

J. J. Louviere. 1991. Best-Worst Scaling: A Model for the Largest Difference Judgments. Technical report, University of Alberta. Working Paper.

Diana McCarthy. 2006. Relating WordNet senses for word sense disambiguation. In *Proceedings of the ACL Workshop on Making Sense of Sense: Bringing Psycholinguistics and Computational Linguistics Together*, pages 17–24.

Rada Mihalcea, Timothy Chklovski, and Adam Kilgarriff. 2004. The Senseval-3 English lexical sample task. In *Senseval-3: Third International Workshop on the Evaluation of Systems for the Semantic Analysis of Text*, pages 25–28. ACL.

George A. Miller, Claudia Leacock, Randee Tengi, and Ross T. Bunker. 1993. A semantic concordance. In *Proceedings of HLT*, pages 303–308. ACL.

G. Craig Murray and Rebecca Green. 2004. Lexical knowledge and human disagreement on a WSD task. *Computer Speech & Language*, 18(3):209–222.

Bryan Orme. 2009. MaxDiff Analysis: Simple Counting, Individual-Level Logit, and HB. Sawtooth Software.

Martha Palmer, Olga Babko-Malaya, and Hoa Trang Dang. 2004. Different sense granularities for different applications. In *Proceedings of the Second Workshop on Scalable Natural Language Understanding Systems*. ACL.

Martha Palmer, Hoa Trang Dang, and Christiane Fellbaum. 2007. Making fine-grained and coarse-grained sense distinctions, both manually and automatically. *Natural Language Engineering*, 13(02):137–163.

Rebecca Passonneau, Nizar Habash, and Owen Rambow. 2006. Inter-annotator agreement on a multilingual semantic annotation task. In *Proceedings of LREC*, pages 1951–1956.

Rebecca J. Passonneau, Ansaf Salleb-Aouissi, and Nancy Ide. 2009. Making sense of word sense variation. In *Proceedings of the NAACL HLT Workshop on Semantic Evaluations: Recent Achievements and Future Directions*.

Rebecca J. Passonneau, Ansaf Salleb-Aoussi, Vikas Bhardwaj, and Nancy Ide. 2010. Word sense annotation of polysemous words by multiple annotators. In *Proceedings of LREC*.

Rebecca J Passonneau, Collin Baker, Christiane Fellbaum, and Nancy Ide. 2012a. The MASC word sense sentence corpus. In *Proceedings of LREC*.

Rebecca J. Passonneau, Vikas Bhardwaj, Ansaf Salleb-Aouissi, and Nancy Ide. 2012b. Multiplicity and word sense: evaluating and learning from multiply labeled word sense annotations. *Language Resources and Evaluation*, 46(2):209–252.

Anna Rumshisky and Olga Batiukova. 2008. Polysemy in verbs: systematic relations between senses and their effect on annotation. In *Proceedings of the Workshop on Human Judgements in Computational Linguistics*, pages 33–41. ACL.

Anna Rumshisky, Nick Botchan, Sophie Kushkuley, and James Pustejovsky. 2012. Word Sense Inventories by Non-experts. In *Procoeedings of LREC*.

Rion Snow, Brendan O'Connor, Dan Jurafsky, and Andrew Y. Ng. 2008. Cheap and fastbut is it good?: Evaluating non-expert annotations for natural language tasks. In *Proceedings of EMNLP*, pages 254–263. ACL.

Benjamin Snyder and Martha Palmer. 2004. The english all-words task. In *Senseval-3: Third International Workshop on the Evaluation of Systems for the Semantic Analysis of Text*, pages 41–43.

James Surowiecki. 2005. *The wisdom of crowds*. Anchor.

Ng Hwee Tou, Chung Yong Lim, and Shou King Foo. 1999. A Case Study on Inter-Annotator Agreement for Word Sense Disambiguation. In *Proceedings of the ACL SIGLEX Workshop on Standardizing Lexical Resources*.

Jean Véronis. 1998. A study of polysemy judgments and inter-annotator agreement. In *Program and advanced papers of the Senseval workshop*, pages 2–4.

Jacob Whitehill, Paul Ruvolo, Tingfan Wu, Jacob Bergsma, and Javier Movellan. 2000. Whose vote should count more: Optimal integration of labels from labelers of unknown expertise. In *Proceedings of NIPS*.

Compound Embedding Features for Semi-supervised Learning

Mo Yu[1], Tiejun Zhao[1], Daxiang Dong[2], Hao Tian[2] and Dianhai Yu[2]
Harbin Institute of Technology, Harbin, China
Baidu Inc., Beijing, China
{yumo,tjzhao}@mtlab.hit.edu.cn
{dongdaxiang,tianhao,yudianhai}@baidu.com

Abstract

To solve data sparsity problem, recently there has been a trend in discriminative methods of NLP to use representations of lexical items learned from unlabeled data as features. In this paper, we investigated the usage of word representations learned by neural language models, i.e. word embeddings. The direct usage has disadvantages such as large amount of computation, inadequacy with dealing word ambiguity and rare-words, and the problem of linear non-separability. To overcome these problems, we instead built compound features from continuous word embeddings based on clustering. Experiments showed that the compound features not only improved the performances on several NLP tasks, but also ran faster, suggesting the potential of embeddings.

1 Introduction

Supervised learning methods have achieved great successes in the field of ***Natural Language Processing (NLP)***. However, in practice most methods are usually limited by the problem of data sparsity, since it is impossible to obtain sufficient labeled data for all NLP tasks. In these situations semi-supervised learning can help to make use of both labeled data and easy-to-obtain unlabeled data.

The semi-supervised framework that is widely applied to NLP is to first learn word representations, which are feature vectors of lexical items, from unlabeled data and then plug them into a supervised system. These methods are very effective in utilizing large-scale unlabeled data and have successfully improved performances of state-of-the-art supervised systems on a variety of tasks (Koo et al., 2008; Huang and Yates, 2009; Täckström et al., 2012).

With the development of ***neural language models (NLM)*** (Bengio et al., 2003; Mnih and Hinton, 2009), recently researchers become interested in word representations (also called **word embeddings**) learned by these models. Word embeddings are dense low dimensional real-valued vectors. They are composed of some latent features, which are expected to capture useful syntactic and semantic properties. Word embeddings are usually served as the first layer in deep learning systems for NLP (Collobert and Weston, 2008; Socher et al., 2011a, 2011b) and help these systems perform comparably with the state-of-the-art models based on hand-crafted features. They also have been directly added as features to the state-of-the-art models of chunking and NER, and have achieved significant improvements (Turian et al. 2010).

Although the direct usage of continuous embeddings has been proved to be an effective method for enhancing the state-of-the-art supervised models, it has some disadvantages, which made them be out-performed by simpler Brown cluster features (Turian et al, 2010) and made them computationally complicated. Firstly, embeddings of rare words are insufficiently trained since they are only updated few times and are close to their random initial values. As shown in (Turian et al, 2010), this is the main reason that models with embedding features made more errors than those with Brown cluster features. Secondly, in NLMs, each word has its unique representation, so it is difficult to represent different senses for ambiguous words. Thirdly, word embeddings are unsuitable for linear models in some tasks as will be proved in Section

4.2. This is possibly because in these tasks, either the target labels are correlated with combinations of different dimensions of word embeddings, or discriminative information may be coded in different intervals in the same dimension. So treating embeddings directly as inputs to a linear model could not fully utilize them. Moreover, since embeddings are dense vectors, it will introduce large amount of computations when they are directly used as inputs, making the method impractical.

In this paper, we first introduced the idea of clustering embeddings to overcome the last two disadvantages discussed above. The high-dimensional cluster features make samples from different classes better separated by linear models. And models with these features can still run fast because the clusters are sparse and discrete.

Second, we proposed the compound features based on clustering. Compound features, which are conjunctive features of neighboring words, have been widely used in NLP models for improving the performances because they are more discriminative. Compound features of embeddings can also help a model to better predict labels associated with rare-words and ambiguous words, because compound features composed of embeddings of nearby words can help to better describe the property of these words. Compound features are difficult to build on dense embeddings. However they are easy to induce from the sparse embedding clusters proposed in this paper.

Experiments on chunking and NER showed that based on the same embeddings, the compound features managed to achieve better performances. Moreover, we proposed analyses to reveal the reasons for the improvements of embedding-clusters and compound features. They suggest that these features can better deal with rare-words and word ambiguity, and are more suitable for linear models.

In addition, although Brown clustering was considered better in (Turian et al 2010), our experiment results and comparisons showed that our compound features from embedding clustering is at least comparable with those from Brown clustering. Since embeddings can greatly benefit from the improvement and developing of deep learning in the future, we believe that our proposed method has a large space of performance growth and will benefit more applications in NLP.

In the rest of the paper, Section 2 introduces how compound embedding features were obtained. Section 3 gives experimental results. In Section 4, we give analysis about the advantages of compound features. Section 5 gives the conclusions.

2 Clustering of Word Embeddings

2.1 Learning Word Embeddings

Word embeddings in this paper were trained by NLMs (Bengio et al., 2003). The model predicts the scores of probabilities of words given their context information in the sentences. It first converts the current word and its context words (e.g. n-1 words before it as in n-gram models) into embeddings. Then these embeddings are put together and propagate forward on the network to compute the score of current word. After minimizing the loss on training data, embeddings are learned and can be further used as smoothing representations for words.

2.2 Clustering of embeddings

In order to get compound features of embeddings, we first induce discrete clusters from the embeddings. Concretely, the k-means clustering algorithm is used. Each word is treated as a single sample. A cluster is represented as the mean of the embeddings of words assigned to it. Similarities between words and clusters are measured by Euclidean distance. As discussed and experimented later, different numbers of ks contain information of different granularity. So we combine clustering results achieved by different ks as features to better utilize the embeddings.

2.3 Compound features

Based on embedding clusters, more powerful compound features can be built. Compound features are conjunctions between basic features of words and their contexts, which are widely used in NLP. Koo et al. (2008) also observed that compound features of Brown clusters achieved more improvements on parsing.

It is also necessary to build compound embedding features since they can better deal with rare-words and ambiguous words. For example, although embedding of a rare-word is not fully trained and hence inaccurate, embeddings of its context words can still be accurate as long as they are not rare and are fully trained. So we could utilize the combination of embeddings before and after the word to predict its tag correctly. We conducted analysis to verify our theory in Section4.

We combined the compound features together with other state-of-the-art human-craft features in supervised models. Examples of the resulted feature templates in chunking and NER are shown in Table 1 & 2. The feature $y_{-1}/y_0/c_{-1}/c_1$ in the last row is an example of compound feature made up of the embedding clusters of words before and after current word. Compound feature extraction can similarly be applied to form compound features of Brown clusters. For example, Brown clusters can replace embedding clusters in 3th row of Table 1.

Words	$w_{i,i\in\{-2:2\}}, w_{i-1}/w_{i,i\in\{0,1\}}$
POS	$p_{i,i\in\{-2:2\}}, p_{i-1}/p_{i,i\in\{-1,2\}}$
Cluster	$c_{i,i\in\{-2:2\}}, c_{i-1}/c_{i,i\in\{0,1\}}, c_{-1}/c_1$
Transition	$y_{-1}/y_0/\{w_0, p_0, c_0, c_{-1}/c_1\}$

Table 1: Chunking features. Cluster features are suitable for both Brown clusters and embedding clusters. Symbol y_i is the tag predicted on word w_i.

Words	$w_{i,i\in\{-2:2\}}, w_{i-1}/w_{i,i\in\{0,1\}}$
Pre/suffix	$w^{1:i}_{0,i\in\{2:4\}}, w^{-i:-1}_{0,i\in\{1:4\}}$
Orthography	$Hyp(w_0), Cap(w_0)$
POS	$p_{i,i\in\{-2:2\}}, p_{i-1}/p_{i,i\in\{-1,2\}}$
Chunking	$b_{i,i\in\{-2:2\}}, b_{i-1}/b_{i,i\in\{-1,2\}}$
Cluster	$c_{i,i\in\{-2:2\}}, c_{i-1}/c_{i,i\in\{0,1\}}, c_{-1}/c_1$
Transition	$y_{-1}/y_0/\{w_0, p_0, c_0, c_{-1}/c_1\}$

Table 2: NER features. Hyp indicates if word contains hyphen and Cap indicates if first letter is capitalized.

3 Experiments

3.1 Experimental settings

We tested our compound features on the same chunking (CoNLL2000) and NER (CoNLL2003) tasks in (Turian et al., 2010). The Brown cluster features were used for comparison, which shared the same feature template used by clusters of embeddings. To compare with the work of (Turian et al, 2010), which aimed to solve the same problem but using embedding directly, we used the same word embeddings (CW 50) and Brown clusters (1000 clusters) they provided. The embeddings in (Turian et al, 2010) are trained on RCV corpus, while the CoNLL2000 data is a part of the WSJ corpus. Since we believe that word representations trained on similar domain may better help to improve the results, we also used embeddings and Brown clusters trained on unlabeled WSJ data from (Nivre et al, 2007) for comparison.

Moreover, we wish to find out whether our method extends well to languages other than English. So we conducted experiments on Chinese NER, where large amount of training data exists, which makes improving accuracies more difficult. We used data from People's Daily (Jan.-Jun. 1998) and converted them following the style of Penn CTB (Xue et al, 2005). Data from April was chosen as test set (1,309,616 words in 55,177 sentences), others for training (6,119,063 words in 255,951 sentences). The Chinese word representations were trained on Chinese Wikipedia until March 2011. The features used in Chinese NER are similar to those in English, except for the orthography, pre/suffixes, and chunking features.

We did little pre-processing work for the training of word representations on WSJ data. The datasets were tokenized and capital words were kept. For training of Chinese Wikipedia, we retained the bodies of all articles and replaced words with frequencies lower than 10 as an "UK_WORD" token. On each dataset, we induced embeddings with 64 dimensions based on 7-gram models and 1000 Brown clusters. The method in (Schwenk, 2007) was used to accelerate the training processes of NLMs. All the NLMs were trained for 5 epochs.

For clustering of embeddings we choose k=500 and 2500 since such combination performed best on development set as shown in the next section. We chose the Sofia-ml toolkit (Sculley 2010) for clustering of embeddings in order to save time.

In the experiments CRF models were used and were optimized by ASGD (implemented by Léon Bottou). For comparison we re-implemented the direct usage of embeddings in (Turian et al, 2010) with CRFsuite (Okazaki, 2007) since their features contain continuous values.

3.2 Performances

Table 3 shows the chunking results. The results reported in (Turian et al. 2010) were denoted as "**direct**". Based on the same word representations, our compound features got better performances in all cases. The embedding features trained on unlabeled WSJ data yield further improvements, showing that word representations from similar domains can better help the supervised tasks.

System	Direct	Compound
Baseline	93.75	
+Embedding (RCV)	94.10	94.19
+Brown (RCV)	94.11	94.24
+Brown&Emb (RCV)	94.35	**94.42**
+Embedding (WSJ)	94.20	94.37
+Brown (WSJ)	94.25	94.36
+Brown&Emb (WSJ)	94.43	**94.58**

Table 3: F1-scores of chunking

In the experiments of NER, first we evaluated how the numbers of clusters *k* will affect the performances on development set (Figure 1). The results showed that both the cluster features (excluding all compound embedding features) and compound features could achieve better results than direct usage of the same embeddings. It also showed that the performances did not vary much when *k* was between 500 and 3000. When *k*=2500, the result was a little higher than others. We finally chose combination of *k*=500 and 2500, which achieved best results on development set.

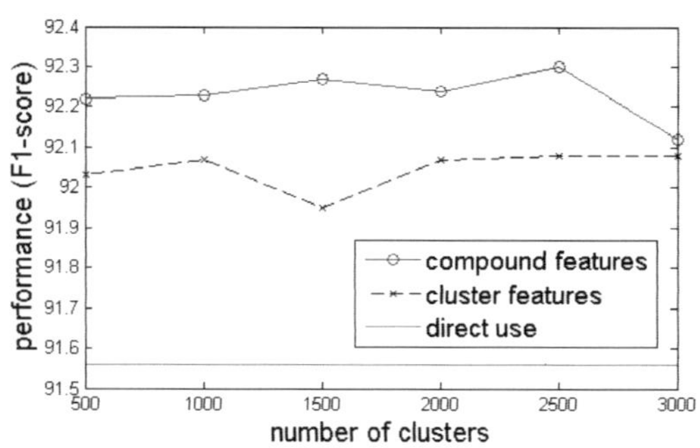

Figure 1: Relation between numbers of clusters k and performances on development set.

The performances of NER on test set are shown in Table 4. Our baseline is slightly lower than that in (Turian et al, 2010), because the first-order CRF cannot utilize context information of NE tags. Despite of this, same conclusions with chunking held.

System	Direct	Compound
Baseline	83.78	
+Embedding	87.38	88.46
+Brown	88.14	88.23
+Brown&Embedding	88.85	89.06

Table 4: F1-scores of English NER on test data

Performances on Chinese NER are shown in Table 5. Similar results were observed as in English NER, showing that our method extends to other languages as well.

System	Direct	Compound
Baseline	88.24	
+Embedding	89.98	90.37
+Brown	90.24	90.55
+Brown&Embedding	90.66	**90.96**

Table 5: F1-scores of Chinese NER on test data

Above results gave evidences that although clustering embeddings may lose some information, the derived compound features did have better performances. The compound features can also improve the performances of Brown clusters, but not as much as they did on embeddings. And the combination of embedding-clusters and Brown-clusters could further improve the performances, since they made use of different type of context information.

The compound features also reduced the time cost of using embedding features. For example, the time for tagging one sentence in English NER was reduced from 5.6 ms to 1.6 ms, shown in Table 6.

Embedding	Time (ms)
Baseline	1.2
Embeddings (direct)	5.6
Embeddings (compound)	1.6

Table 6: Running time of different features

4 Analysis

Our compound embedding features greatly outperformed the direct usage of same embeddings on English NER. In this section we conducted analyses to show the reasons for the improvements.

4.1 Rare-words and ambiguous words

To show the compound features have stronger abilities to handle rare words, we counted the numbers of errors made on words with different frequencies on unlabeled data. Here the word frequencies are from the results of Brown clustering provided by (Turian et al. 2010). We compared our compound embedding features with direct usage of embeddings as well as Brown clusters, which is believed to work better on rare words. Figure 2(a) shows that the compound features indeed resulted in fewer errors than the two baseline methods in most cases. Errors of embeddings occurred on words with frequencies lower than 2K and those in the range of 16 to 256 were reduced by 10.55% and 24.44%, respectively.

Our compound features also reduced the errors caused by ambiguous words, as shown in Figure

2(b), where the numbers of senses for a word are measured by the numbers of different POS tags it has in Penn Treebank. 12.1% of the errors on ambiguous words were reduced, comparing to 8.4% of the errors on unambiguous ones.

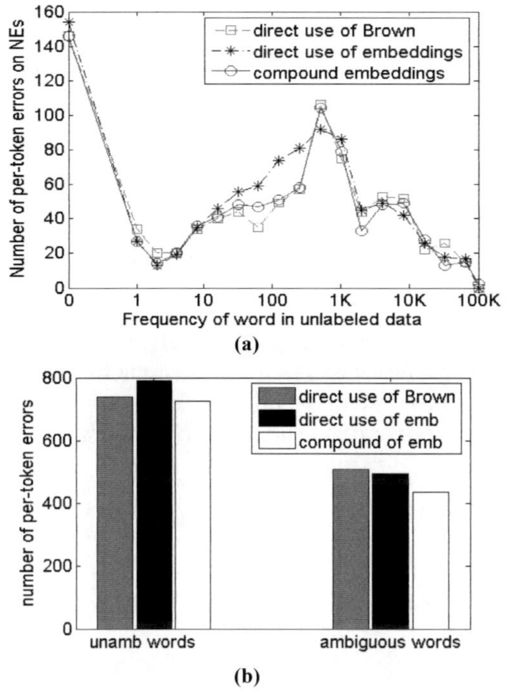

Figure 2: Errors incurred on words with different frequencies (a) and ambiguous words (b) in NER.

4.2 Linear separability of embeddings

Another reason for the good performances of compound features on NER is that they made linear models better separate ***named entities (NEs)*** and ***non-NEs***, which are more difficult to be linearly separated when embeddings are directly used as features. Here we designed an experiment to prove this. Based on training data of CoNLL2003, a classification task was built to tell whether a word belongs to NE or not. Linear SVM and a non-linear model ***Multilayer Perceptron (MLP)*** were used to build the classifiers. As shown in Table 7, when embeddings were directly used as features, MLP performed much better than linear SVM. And the linear model was under-fitting on this task since it had similar accuracies on both training set and development set. Above observations showed that linear models could not separate NEs and non-NEs well in the space of embeddings.

When clusters of embeddings were used as features, the accuracies of linear models increased even when there were only one or two non-zero features for each sample. At the same time the performances of MLP decreased because of the loss of information during clustering. The gaps between accuracies of linear models and non-linear ones decreased in the spaces of clusters, showing that cluster features are more suitable for linear models. At last, the compound features made the linear model out-perform all non-linear ones, since extra context information could be utilized.

Embeddings	Models	Accuracy
direct	linear	94.38
direct	MLP	96.87
cluster 1000	linear	95.31
cluster 1000	MLP	95.32
cluster 500+2500	linear	96.10
cluster 500+2500	MLP	96.02
compound	linear	**97.30**

Table 7: Performances of linear and non-linear models on development set with different embedding features.

5 Conclusion and perspectives

In this paper, we first introduced the idea of clustering embeddings and then proposed the compound features based on clustering, in order to overcome the disadvantages of the direct usage of continuous embeddings. Experiments showed that the compound features built on the same original word representation features (either embeddings or Brown clusters) achieve better performances on the same tasks. Further analyses showed that the compound features reduced errors on rare-words and ambiguous words and could be better utilized by linear models.

The usage of word embeddings also has some limitations, e.g. they are weak in capturing structural information of languages, which is necessary in NLP. In the future, we will research on task-specific representations for sub-structures, such as phrases and sub-trees based on word embeddings and documents representations (Xu et al., 2012).

Acknowledgments

We would like to thank Dr. Hua Wu, Haifeng Wang, Jie Zhou and Rui Zhang for many discussions and thank the anonymous reviewers for their valuable suggestions. This work was supported by National Natural Science Foundation of China (61173073), and the Key Project of the National High Technology Research and Development Program of China (2011AA01A207).

References

Bengio, Y., Ducharme, R., Vincent, P., and Jauvin, C. (2003). A neural probabilistic language models. The *Journal of Machine Learning Research*, 3:1137–1155.

Collobert, R. and Weston, J. (2008). A unified architecture for natural language processing: Deep neural networks with multitask learning. In *Proceedings of the 25th international conference on Machine learning*, pages 160–167. ACM.

Finkel, J., Grenager, T., and Manning, C. (2005). Incorporating non-local information into information extraction systems by gibbs sampling. In *Proceedings of the 43rd Annual Meeting on Association for Computational Linguistics*, pages 363–370. Association for Computational Linguistics.

Huang, F. and Yates, A. (2009). Distributional representations for handling sparsity in supervised sequence labeling. In *Proceedings of the Joint Conference of the 47th Annual Meeting of the ACL and the 4th International Joint Conference on Natural Language Processing of the AFNLP*: Volume 1-Volume 1, pages 495–503. Association for Computational Linguistics.

Koo, T., Carreras, X., and Collins, M. (2008). Simple semi-supervised dependency parsing. In *Proceedings of Association for Computational Linguistics*, pages 595–603. Association for Computational Linguistics.

Mnih, A. and Hinton, G. E. (2009). A scalable hierarchical distributed language model. *Advances in neural information processing systems*, 21:1081–1088.

Nivre, J., Hall, J., Kübler, S., McDonald, R., Nilsson, J., Riedel, S., and Yuret, D. (2007). The CoNLL 2007 shared task on dependency parsing. In *Proceedings of the CoNLL Shared Task Session of EMNLP-CoNLL*, pages 915–932.

Okazaki, N. (2007). Crfsuite: a fast implementation of conditional random fields (crfs). URL http://www.chokkan.org/software/crfsuite.

Schwenk, H. (2007). Continuous space language models. *Computer Speech & Language*, 21(3):492–518.

Sculley, D. (2010). Web-scale k-means clustering. In *Proceedings of the 19th international conference on World Wide Web*, pages 1177–1178. ACM.

Socher, R., Huang, E., Pennington, J., Ng, A., and Manning, C. (2011a). Dynamic pooling and unfolding recursive auto-encoders for paraphrase detection. *Advances in Neural Information Processing Systems*, 24:801–809.

Socher, R., Pennington, J., Huang, E., Ng, A., and Manning, C. (2011b). Semi-supervised recursive auto-encoders for predicting sentiment distributions. In *Proceedings of the Conference on Empirical Methods in Natural Language Processing*, pages 151–161. Association for Computational Linguistics.

Täckström, O., McDonald, R., and Uszkoreit, J. (2012). Cross-lingual word clusters for direct transfer of linguistic structure. In *Proceedings of the North American Chapter of the Association for Computational Linguistics: Human Language Technologies*, pages 477–487, Montréal, Canada, June 3-8, 2012.

Turian, J., Ratinov, L., and Bengio, Y. (2010). Word representations: a simple and general method for semi-supervised learning. In *Annual Meeting-Association For Computational Linguistics*. Urbana, 51:61801.

Xu, Z., Chen, M., Weinberger, K., and Sha, F. An alternative text representation to TF-IDF and Bag-of-Words. In *Proceedings of 21st ACM Conf. of Information and Knowledge Management (CIKM)*, Hawaii, 2012.

Xue, N., Xia, F., Chiou, F., and Palmer, M. (2005). The penn chinese treebank: Phrase structure annotation of a large corpus. Natural Language Engineering, 11(2):207.

On Quality Ratings for Spoken Dialogue Systems – Experts vs. Users

Stefan Ultes, Alexander Schmitt, and Wolfgang Minker
Ulm University
Albert-Einstein-Allee 43
89073 Ulm, Germany
{stefan.ultes,alexander.schmitt,wolfgang.minker}@uni-ulm.de

Abstract

In the field of Intelligent User Interfaces, Spoken Dialogue Systems (SDSs) play a key role as speech represents a true intuitive means of human communication. Deriving information about its quality can help rendering SDSs more user-adaptive. Work on automatic estimation of subjective quality usually relies on statistical models. To create those, manual data annotation is required, which may be performed by actual users or by experts. Here, both variants have their advantages and drawbacks. In this paper, we analyze the relationship between user and expert ratings by investigating models which combine the advantages of both types of ratings. We explore two novel approaches using statistical classification methods and evaluate those with a pre-existing corpus providing user and expert ratings. After analyzing the results, we eventually recommend to use expert ratings instead of user ratings in general.

1 Introduction and Motivation

In human-machine interaction it is important that user interfaces can adapt to the specific requirements of its users. Handicapped persons or angry users, for example, have specific needs and should be treated differently than regular users.

Speech is a major component of modern user interfaces as it is the natural means of human communication. Therefore, it seems logical to use Spoken Dialogue Systems (SDS) as part of Intelligent User Interfaces enabling speech communication of different complexity reaching from simple spoken commands up to complex dialogues. Besides the spoken words, the speech signal also may be used to acquire information about the user state, e.g., about their emotional state (cf., e.g., (Polzehl et al., 2011))). By additional analysis of the human-computer-dialogues, even more abstract information may be derived, e.g., the quality of the system (cf., e.g., (Engelbrecht and Möller, 2010)). System quality information may be used to adapt the system's behavior online during the ongoing dialogue (cf. (Ultes et al., 2012)).

For determining the quality of Spoken Dialogue Systems, several aspects are of interest. Möller et al. (2009) presented a taxonomy of quality criteria. They describe quality as a bipartite issue consisting of Quality of Service (QoS) and Quality of Experience (QoE). Quality of Service describes objective criteria like dialogue duration or number of turns. While these are well-defined items that can be determined easily, Quality of Experience, which describes the user experience with subjective criteria, is more vague and without a sound definition, e.g., User Satisfaction (US).

Subjective aspects like US are either determined by using questionnaires like SASSI (Hone and Graham, 2000) or the ITU-standard augmented framework for questionnaires (Möller, 2003), or by using single-valued ratings, i.e., a rater only applies one single score. In general, two major categories of work on determining single-valued User Satisfaction exist. The satisfaction ratings are applied either

- by **users** during or right after the dialogue or
- by **experts** by listening to recorded dialogues.

In this work, users or *user raters* are people who actually perform a dialogue with the system and apply ratings while doing so. There is no constraint about their expertise in the field of Human Computer Interaction or Spoken Dialogue Systems: They may be novices or have a high expertise. With experts or *expert raters*, we refer to people who are not participating in the dialogue thus constituting a completely different set of people. Expert raters listen to recorded dialogues after the interactions and rate them by assuming the point of view of the actual person performing the dialogue. These experts are supposed to have some experience with dialogue systems. In this work, expert raters were "advanced students of computer science and engineering" (Schmitt et al., 2011a).

For *User* Satisfaction, ratings applied by the users seem to be clearly the better choice over ratings applied by third persons. However, determining true User Satisfaction is only possible by asking real users interacting with the system. Ideally, the ratings are applied by users talking to a system employed in the field, e.g., commercial systems, as these users have real concerns.

For such Spoken Dialogue Systems, though, it is not easy to get users to apply quality ratings to the dialogue – especially for each system-user-exchange. The users would have to rate either by pressing a button on the phone or by speech, which would significantly influence the performance of the dialogue. Longer dialogues imply longer call durations which cost money. Further, most callers only want to quickly get some information from the system. Therefore, it may be assumed that most users do not want to engage in dialogues which are artificially made longer. This also inhabits the risk that users who participated in long dialogues do not want to call again. Therefore, collecting ratings applied by users are considered to be expensive. One possible way of overcoming the problem of rating input would be to use some special installation which enables the users to provide ratings more easily (cf. (Schmitt et al., 2011b)). However, this is also expensive and the system's usability would be very restricted. Further, this setup could most likely only be used in a lab situation.

Expert raters, on the other hand, are able to simply listen to the recorded dialogues and to apply ratings, e.g., by using a specialized rating software. This process is much easier and does not require the same amount of effort needed for acquiring user ratings. Further, as already pointed out, we refer to experts as people who have some basic understanding of dialogue systems but are not required to be high-level experts in the field. That is why we believe that these people can be found easily.

As both categories of ratings have their advantages and disadvantages, this contribution aims at learning about the differences and similarities of user and expert ratings with the ultimate goal of either being able to predict user ratings more efficiently or of advocating for replacing the use of user ratings by using only expert ratings in general.

Therefore, this work analyzes the relation between quality ratings applied by user and expert raters by analyzing approaches which take advantage of both categories: Using the less expensive rating process with expert raters and still predicting *real* User Satisfaction ratings. Moreover, this works' goal is to shed light on the question whether information about one rating (in this case the less expensive expert ratings) may be used to predict the other rating (the more expensive user ratings). For this, we present two approaches applying two different statistical classification methods for a showcase corpus. Results of both methods are compared to a given baseline.

The remainder of this paper is organized as follows. First, we give a brief overview of work done in both categories (user ratings vs. expert ratings) in Section 2 and present our choice of data the analysis in this paper is based on in Section 3. Further, evaluation metrics are illustrated in Section 4 and approaches on facilitating prediction of user rater scores by expert rater information are presented in Section 5 followed by an evaluation and discussion of the results in Section 6.

2 Significant Related Work

Predicting User Satisfaction for SDSs has been in the focus of research for many years, most famously the PARADISE framework by Walker et al. (1997). The authors assume a linear dependency between quantitative parameters derived from the dialogue and US, modeling this dependency using linear regression. Unfortunately, for generating the regression model, weighting factors have to be computed for each system anew. This generates high costs as dialogues have to be performed with real users where each user further has to complete a questionnaire after completing the dialogue. Moreover, in the PARADISE framework, only quality measurement for the whole dialogue (or system) is allowed. However, this is not suitable for using quality information for online adaption of the dialogue (cf. (Ultes et al., 2012)). Furthermore, PARADISE relies on questionnaires while we focus on work using single-valued ratings.

Numerous work on predicting User Satisfaction as a single-valued rating task for each system-user-exchange has been performed in both categories. This work is briefly presented in the following.

2.1 Expert Ratings

Higashinaka et al. (2010a) proposed a model to predict turn-wise ratings for human-human dialogues (transcribed conversation) and human-machine dialogues (text from chat system). Ratings ranging from 1-7 were applied by two expert raters labeling "Smoothness", "Closeness", and "Willingness" not achieving a Match Rate per Rating (MR/R)[1] of more than 0.2-0.24. This results are only slightly above the random baseline of 0.14. Further work by Higashinaka et al. (2010b) uses ratings for overall dialogues to predict ratings for each system-user-exchange. Again, evaluating in three user satisfaction categories "Smoothness", "Closeness", and "Willingness" with ratings ranging from 1-7 achieved best performance of 0.19 MR/R.

Interaction Quality (IQ) has been introduced by Schmitt et al. (2011a) as an alternative performance measure to User Satisfaction. In their terminology, US ratings are only applied by users. As their presented measure uses ratings applied by expert raters, a different term is used. Each system-user exchange was annotated by three different raters using strict guidelines. The ratings ranging from 1-5 are used as target variable for statistical classifiers using a set of automatically derivable interaction parameters as input. They achieve a MR/R of 0.58.

[1]MR/R is equal to Unweighted Average Recall (UAR) which is explained in Section 4.

2.2 User Ratings

An approach presented by Engelbrecht et al. (2009) uses Hidden Markov Models (HMMs) to model the SDS as a process evolving over time. User Satisfaction was predicted at any point within the dialogue on a 5 point scale. Evaluation was performed based on labels the users applied themselves during the dialogue.

Hara et al. (2010) derived turn level ratings from an overall score applied by the users after the dialogue. Using n-gram models reflecting the dialogue history, the achieved results for recognizing User Satisfaction on a 5 point scale showed to be hardly above chance.

Work by Schmitt et al. (2011b) deals with determining User Satisfaction from ratings applied by the users themselves during the dialogues. A statistical classification model was trained using automatically derived interaction parameter to predict User Satisfaction for each system-user-exchange on a 5-point scale achieving an MR/R of 0.49.

3 Corpus

The corpus used by Schmitt et al. (2011b) not only contains user ratings but also expert ratings which makes it a perfect candidate for our research presented in this paper. Adopting the terminology by Schmitt et al., user ratings are described as User Satisfaction (US) whereas expert ratings are referred to with the term Interaction Quality (IQ) (cf. (Schmitt et al., 2011a)). The data used for all experiments of this work was collected by Schmitt et al. (2011b) during a lab user study with 38 users in the domain of the "Let's Go Bus Information" system (Raux et al., 2006) of the Carnegie Mellon University in Pittsburgh. 128 calls were collected consisting of a total of 2,897 system-user exchanges. Both ratings, IQ and US, are at a scale from 1 to 5 where 1 stands for "extremely unsatisfied" and 5 for "satisfied". Each dialogue starts with a rating of 5 as the user is expected to be satisfied in the beginning because nothing unsatisfying has happened yet.

Further, the corpus also provides interaction parameters which may be used as input variables for the IQ and US recognition models. These parameters have been derived automatically from three dialogue modules: Automatic Speech Recog-

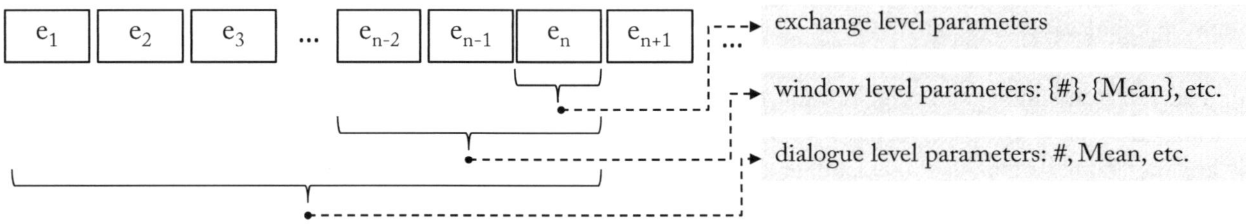

Figure 1: *The three different modeling levels representing the interaction at exchange e_n: The most detailed exchange level, comprising parameters of the current exchange; the window level, capturing important parameters from the previous n dialog steps (here $n = 3$); the dialog level, measuring overall performance values from the entire previous interaction.*

nition, Spoken Language Understanding, and Dialogue Management. Furthermore, the parameters are modeled on three different levels (see Figure 1):

- *Exchange level* parameters can be derived directly from the respective dialogue modules, e.g., `ASRConfidence`.
- *Dialogue level* parameters consist of counts (#), means (Mean), etc. of the exchange level parameters calculated from all exchanges of the whole dialogue up to the current exchange, e.g., `MeanASRConfidence`.
- *Window level* parameters consist of counts ({#}), means ({Mean}), etc. of the exchange level parameters calculated from the last three exchanges, e.g., `{Mean}ASRConfidence`.

4 Evaluation metrics

For measuring the performance of the classification algorithms, we rely on *Unweighted Average Recall (UAR)*, *Cohen's Kappa* and *Spearman's Rho*. The latter two also represent a measure for similarity of paired data. All measures will be briefly described in the following:

Unweighted Average Recall The Unweighted Average Recall (UAR) is defined as the sum of all class-wise recalls r_c divided by the number of classes $|C|$:

$$UAR = \frac{1}{|C|} \sum_{c \in C} r_c \; . \tag{1}$$

Recall r_c for class c is defined as

$$r_c = \frac{1}{|R_c|} \sum_{i=1}^{|R_c|} \delta_{h_i r_i} \; , \tag{2}$$

where δ is the Kronecker-delta, h_i and r_i represent the corresponding hypothesis-reference-pair of rating i, and $|R_c|$ the total number of all ratings of class c. In other words, UAR for multi-class classification problems is the accuracy corrected by the effects of unbalanced data.

Cohen's Kappa To measure the relative agreement between two corresponding sets of ratings, the number of label agreements corrected by the chance level of agreement divided by the maximum proportion of times the labelers could agree is computed. κ is defined as

$$\kappa = \frac{p_0 - p_c}{1 - p_c} \; , \tag{3}$$

where p_0 is the rate of agreement and p_c is the chance agreement (Cohen, 1960). As US and IQ are on an ordinal scale, a weighting factor w is introduced reducing the discount of disagreements the smaller the difference is between two ratings (Cohen, 1968):

$$w = \frac{|r_1 - r_2|}{|r_{max} - r_{min}|} \; . \tag{4}$$

Here, r_1 and r_2 denote the rating pair and r_{max} and r_{min} the maximal and minimal rating. This results in $w = 0$ for agreement and $w = 1$ if the ratings have maximal difference.

Spearman's Rho The correlation of two variables describes the degree by that one variable can be expressed by the other. *Spearman's Rank Correlation Coefficient* is a non-parametric method assuming a monotonic function between the two variables (Spearman, 1904). It is defined by

$$\rho = \frac{\sum_i (x_i - \bar{x})(y_i - \bar{y})}{\sqrt{\sum_i (x_i - \bar{x})^2 \sum_i (y_i - \bar{y})^2}}, \quad (5)$$

where x_i and y_i are corresponding ranked ratings and $\bar{x}$ and $\bar{y}$ the mean ranks. Thus, two sets of ratings can have total correlation even if they never agree. This would happen if all ratings are shifted by the same value, for example.

5 Recognition of US Using IQ Information

As discussed in Section 1, automatic recognition of ratings applied by users as performed by Schmitt et al. (2011b) for User Satisfaction is time-consuming and expensive. Therefore, approaches are presented which facilitate expert ratings, i.e., Interaction Quality, with the hope of making US recognition more feasible. IQ an US are strongly related as both metrics represent the same quantity applied by different rater groups. Results of the Mann-Whitney U test, which is used to test for significant difference between Interaction Quality and User Satisfaction, show their difference ($p < 0.05$) but values for Cohen's Kappa (Cohen, 1960) and Spearman's Rank Correlation Coefficient (Spearman, 1904) emphasize the that IQ and US are quite similar. Achieving $\kappa = 0.5$ can be considered as a *moderate* agreement according to Landis and Koch's Kappa Benchmark Scale (Landis and Koch, 1977). Furthermore, a correlation of $\rho = 0.66$ ($p < 0.01$) indicates a *strong* relationship between IQ and US (Cohen, 1988).

While it has been shown that user and expert ratings are similar, it is desirable nonetheless to being able to predict real user ratings. These ratings are the desired kind of ratings when it comes to subjective dialogue system assessment. Only users can give a rating about their satisfaction level, i.e., how they like the system and the interaction with the system. However, user ratings are expensive as elaborated in Section 1. Therefore, we investigate approaches to recognize US which rely on means of IQ recognition.

5.1 Belief-Based Sequential Recognition

Methods used for IQ and US recognition by Schmitt et al. (2011b; 2011a) suffer from the fact that the sequential character of the data is modeled inadequately as they assume statistical independence between the single exchanges (recognition of IQ and US does *not* depend on the respective value of the previous exchange). Hence, we present a Markovian approach overcoming these issues. A probability distribution over all US states, called *belief state*, is updated after each system-user-exchange taking also into account the *belief state* of the previous exchange. This belief update[2] is equivalent to the Forward Algorithm known from Hidden Markov Models (cf. (Rabiner, 1989)). In doing so, the new US probabilities also depend on the US values of the previous exchange. Moreover, a latent variable is introduced in order to decouple the target variable US with the variable the observation probability depends on IQ. This results in an indirect approach for recognizing User Satisfaction that is based on the more affordable recognition of Interaction Quality assuming that a universal mapping between IQ and US exists.

Thus, to determine the probability $b(US)$ of having the true User Satisfaction label US after the current system-user-exchange, we rely on Interaction Quality recognition, whose observation probability is depicted as $P(o|IQ)$. Furthermore, for coupling both quantities, we introduce a coherence probability $P(IQ|US)$. Belief update for estimating the new values for $b'(US')$ is as follows:

$$b'(US') = \alpha \cdot \sum_{IQ'} P(o'|IQ') \cdot P(IQ'|US') \cdot \sum_{US} P(US'|US)b(US) \quad (6)$$

The observation probability $P(o'|IQ')$ is modeled using confidence scores of classifiers applied for IQ recognition. Further, we compute the sum over all previous US beliefs $b(US)$ weighted by the transition probability $P(US'|US)$. Both, transition and coherence probability have been computed by taking the frequency of their occurrences in the training data. The α factor is used for normalization only.

Since we are aiming at generating an estimate $\hat{US}$

[2]Terminology is taken from Partially Observable Markov Decision Processes, cf. (Kaelbling et al., 1998)

at each exchange, it is calculated by

$$\hat{US} = \arg\max_{US'} b'(US') \tag{7}$$

generating a sequence of estimates for each dialogue.

As the action of the system a can be expected to influence the satisfaction level of the user, action-dependency is added to Equation 6 resulting in

$$b'(US') = \alpha \cdot \sum_{IQ'} P(o'|IQ') \cdot P(IQ'|US', a) \cdot \sum_{US} P(US'|US, a) b(US). \tag{8}$$

Hence, each system action a influences coherence and transition probabilities. It should be noted that action-dependency can only be introduced as in a SDS each turn a system action is selected and executed by the dialogue manager.

5.2 Model Exchange

While in *Belief-Based Sequential Recognition*, probability models are used for coupling expert and user ratings explicitly, a simpler approach has also been examined. A statistical classifier trained on the target variable IQ is used to evaluate classification of the target variable US. This seems to be reasonable as the set of scores and meaning of the scores of both metrics are equivalent. Furthermore, necessary prerequisites are fulfilled: the sample corpus contains both labels, the labels for US and IQ correspond, and both recognition approaches are based on the same feature set.

6 Experiments and Results

For evaluating *Belief-Based Sequential Recognition*, not only the absolute performance is of interest but also how this performance is influenced by the characteristics of the observation probability, i.e., the performance of the applied statistical classification approach and the variance of their confidence scores. In order to obtain different confidence characteristics, multiple classification algorithms, or algorithm variants respectively, are needed. Hence, five statistical classifiers have been chosen arbitrarily to produce the observation probabilities for *Belief-Based Sequential Recognition*:

- SVM[3] with cubic kernel
- SVM with RBF-kernel
- Naive Bayes
- Naive Bayes with kernel
- Rule Induction

In contrast to Schmitt et al. (2011b; 2011a), a reduced feature set was used consisting of 43 parameters as some textual parameters were removed which are very specific and take many different values, e.g., UTTERANCE (the system utterance) or INTERPRETATION (the interpretation of the speech input).

The resulting feature set consists of the following parameters (parameter names are in accordance with the parameter names of the LEGO corpus (Schmitt et al., 2012)):

Exchange Level ACTIVITY, ACTIVITYTYPE, UTD, BARGED-IN?, ASRCONFIDENCE, MEANASRCONFIDENCE, TURNNUMBER, MODALITY, LOOPNAME, ASRRECOGNITIONSTATUS, ROLEINDEX, ROLENAME, NOISE?, HELPREQUEST?, REPROMPT?, WPST, WPUT

Dialogue Level #BARGEINS #ASRSUCCESS, #HELPREQUESTS, #TIMEOUTS, #TIMEOUTS_ASRREJECTIONS, #ASRREJECTIONS, #REPROMPTS, #SYSTEMQUESTIONS, #SYSTEMTURNS, #USERTURNS, %BARGEINS, %ASRSUCCESS, %HELPREQUESTS, %TIMEOUTS, %TIMEOUTS_ASRREJECTIONS, %ASRREJECTIONS, %REPROMPTS

Window Level {#}TIMEOUTS_ASRREJCTIONS, {#}HELPREQUESTS, {#}ASRREJECTIONS, {MEAN}ASRCONFIDENCE, {#}TIMEOUTS, {#}REPROMPTS, {#}SYSTEMQUESTIONS, {#}ASRSUCCESS, {#}BARGEINS

All results are evaluated with respect to the reference experiment of direct US recognition (US recognition using models trained on US). This is performed in accordance to Schmitt et al. (2011b) using the statistical classification algorithms stated

[3]Support Vector Machine, cf. (Vapnik, 1995)

Table 1: *Results (UAR, Cohen's Kappa, and Spearman's Rho) of 10-fold cross-validation for US recognition of US recognition using models trained on US*

Classifier	UAR	κ	ρ
SVM (cubic Kernel)	0.39	0.33	0.48
SVM (RBF-Kernel)	0.39	0.42	0.55
Naive Bayes	0.36	0.40	0.55
Naive Bayes (Kernel)	0.42	0.44	0.59
Rule Induction	0.50	0.51	0.61

Table 2: *Results (UAR, Cohen's Kappa, and Spearman's Rho) of 10-fold cross-validation for US recognition of the Model Exchange approach (trained on IQ, evaluated on US)*

Classifier	UAR	κ	ρ
SVM (cubic Kernel)	0.34	0.42	0.55
SVM (RBF-Kernel)	0.34	0.42	0.58
Naive Bayes	0.35	0.40	0.57
Naive Bayes (Kernel)	0.34	0.37	0.60
Rule Induction	0.34	0.42	0.59

above. The performance of the reference experiment is shown in Table 1.

Using the same feature set, these classification algorithms are also applied for the evaluation of the *Model Exchange* approach using 10-fold cross validation. Note that the parameters of the classifiers also remained the same. The data was partitioned randomly on exchange level, i.e., without regarding their belonging to a specific dialogue. The measured results of the *Model Exchange* approach for the five classification methods can be seen in Table 2.

While the results are significantly above chance[4], comparing them to the reference experiment reveals that in terms of UAR the reference experiment outperforms *Model Exchange* for all five classifiers. The achieved κ and ρ values show similar scores for both the reference experiment and the *Model Exchange* approach. However, in the data used for the experiments, the amount of occurrences of the ratings was not balanced (equal for all classes) which has been identified as the most likely reason for this effect.

Experiments for *Belief-Based Sequential Recognition* have also been performed using 10-fold cross validation. As complete dialogues and the order

[4]UAR of 0.2 for five classes

Table 3: *Results (UAR, Cohen's Kappa, and Spearman's Rho) of 10-fold cross-validation for US recognition of action-independent Belief-Based Sequential Recognition*

Classifier	UAR	κ	ρ
SVM (cubic Kernel)	0.28	0.36	0.48
SVM (RBF-Kernel)	0.30	0.40	0.54
Naive Bayes	0.32	0.39	0.54
Naive Bayes (Kernel)	0.33	0.45	0.61
Rule Induction	0.33	0.47	0.63

Table 4: *Results (UAR, Cohen's Kappa, and Spearman's Rho) of 10-fold cross-validation for US recognition of action-dependent Belief-Based Sequential Recognition*

Classifier	UAR	κ	ρ
SVM (cubic Kernel)	0.28	0.35	0.48
SVM (RBF-Kernel)	0.29	0.40	0.54
Naive Bayes	0.32	0.40	0.55
Naive Bayes (Kernel)	0.34	0.44	0.60
Rule Induction	0.35	0.47	0.62

of exchanges within the dialogues are important for this approach, the data was partitioned randomly on the dialogue level. As previously explained, for the probability distributions of the observation probability model, classification results of IQ recognition with 10-fold cross validation has been used in order to get good estimates for the whole data set. Results for the action-independent version can be seen in Table 3.

For the action-dependent version, four different basic actions ANNOUNCEMENT, CONFIRMATION, QUESTION, and WAIT have been used, generating results presented in Table 4. The results illustrate that neither action-independent nor action-dependent *Belief-Based Sequential Recognition* can outperform the reference experiment (cf. Table 1). Still, both variants achieve results clearly above chance. Again, the unbalanced data causes κ and ρ to be similar to the reference experiment.

A comparison of the action-independent with the action-dependent approach shows almost no differences in their performances. Only a slight tendency towards better UARs for action-dependency can be spotted.

Figure 2 displays the performances of both variants of *Belief-Based Sequential Recognition* along with performance of IQ recognition and the variance σ^2 of the corresponding confidence distribu-

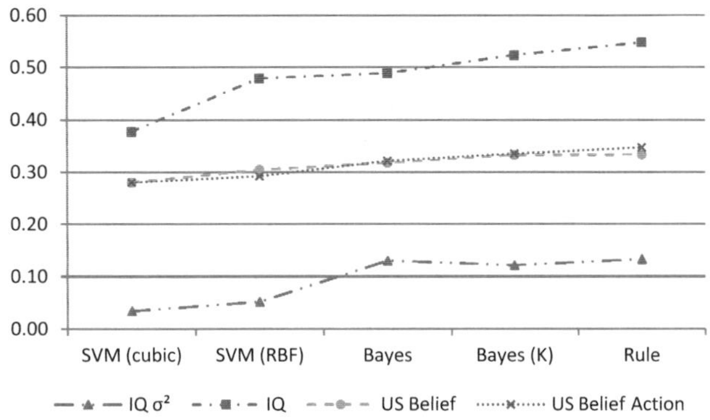

Figure 2: *UAR of IQ recognition and Belief-Based Sequential Recognition along with σ^2 of confidence distributions of IQ recognition*

Table 5: *Recognition performance and variance of confidence distributions for IQ recognition*

Classifier	σ^2	UAR	κ	ρ
SVM (cubic Kernel)	0.03	0.38	0.54	0.69
SVM (RBF-Kernel)	0.05	0.48	0.65	0.77
Naive Bayes	0.13	0.49	0.57	0.71
Naive Bayes (Kernel)	0.12	0.52	0.59	0.73
Rule Induction	0.13	0.55	0.68	0.79

tion (cf. Table 5). It can easily be seen that with rising UAR for IQ recognition, σ^2 also rises. This directly transfers to the performance of the *Belief-Based Sequential Recognition*. The more accurate the observation performance, the more accurate the belief prediction. Furthermore, when comparing the action-dependent to the action-independent variant of *Belief-Based Sequential Recognition*, better IQ performance and therefore a higher variance also causes slightly better results for the action-dependent variant. These differences, however, are only marginally. Therefore, they do not allow for drawing a conclusion.

7 Conclusions

For estimating User Satisfaction-like ratings, two categories exist: work relying on user ratings and work relying on expert ratings. To learn something about their differences and similarities, we explored the possibility of using the information encoded in the expert ratings to predict user ratings with the hope to get acceptable user rating prediction results. Therefore, we investigated if it is possible to determine the preferred true User Satisfaction value based on less expensive expert ratings. For this, a corpus containing both kinds of ratings was chosen, i.e., User Satisfaction (US) and Interaction Quality (IQ) ratings. Furthermore, interaction parameters were used to create statistical recognition models for predicting IQ and US, respectively. Two approaches have been investigated: *Belief-Based Sequential Recognition*, which is based on an HMM-like structure with IQ as an additional latent variable, and *Model Exchange*, which uses statistical models trained on IQ to recognize US. Unfortunately, neither *Belief-Based Sequential Recognition* nor *Model Exchange* achieved results with an acceptable UAR.

The high correlation between expert and user ratings, depicted by high values for Cohen's κ and Spearman's ρ, already allow the conclusion that expert ratings can be used as a good replacement for user ratings. Moreover, the presented recognition results of the *Model Exchange* approach being clearly above chance underpin the strong similarity of IQ and US. Furthermore, IQ recognition is much more reliable and accurate than US recognition (shown by higher UAR, κ and ρ values).

While the experiments disproved the hope of getting acceptable user rating prediction results, the obtained results confirmed the similarity between both kinds of ratings. And as it is not necessary to use user ratings for most applications, e.g., for using the quality information to automatically improve the interaction (cf. (Ultes et al., 2012)), we believe that it suffices to use expert ratings as those can be acquired easier and less expensively and are similar enough to user ratings. Prompting the user to apply quality ratings in everyday situations with real-life systems will always be annoying to the user while recording of such interactions are always much easier to rate.

By providing a study for determining quality ratings of dialogues, we hope to encourage other researchers to look into this research for other parameters, e.g., emotion recognition.

References

Jacob Cohen. 1960. A coefficient of agreement for nominal scales. In *Educational and Psychological Measurement*, volume 20, pages 37–46, April.

Jacob Cohen. 1968. Weighted kappa: Nominal scale

agreement provision for scaled disagreement or partial credit. *Psychological bulletin*, 70(4):213.

Jacob Cohen. 1988. *Statistical power analysis for the behavioral sciences.* New Jersey: Lawrence Erlbaum Associates, July.

Klaus-Peter Engelbrecht and Sebastian Möller. 2010. A User Model to Predict User Satisfaction with Spoken Dialog Systems. In Gary Geunbae Lee, Joseph Mariani, Wolfgang Minker, and Satoshi Nakamura, editors, *Spoken Dialogue Systems for Ambient Environments. 2nd Int. Workshop on Spoken Dialogue Systems Technology*, Lecture Notes in Artificial Intelligence, pages 150–155. Springer, October.

Klaus-Peter Engelbrecht, Florian Gödde, Felix Hartard, Hamed Ketabdar, and Sebastian Möller. 2009. Modeling user satisfaction with hidden markov model. In *SIGDIAL '09: Proceedings of the SIGDIAL 2009 Conference*, pages 170–177, Morristown, NJ, USA. Association for Computational Linguistics.

Sunao Hara, Norihide Kitaoka, and Kazuya Takeda. 2010. Estimation method of user satisfaction using n-gram-based dialog history model for spoken dialog system. In Nicoletta Calzolari (Conference Chair), Khalid Choukri, Bente Maegaard, Joseph Mariani, Jan Odijk, Stelios Piperidis, Mike Rosner, and Daniel Tapias, editors, *Proceedings of the Seventh conference on International Language Resources and Evaluation (LREC'10)*, Valletta, Malta, May. European Language Resources Association (ELRA).

Ryuichiro Higashinaka, Yasuhiro Minami, Kohji Dohsaka, and Toyomi Meguro. 2010a. Issues in predicting user satisfaction transitions in dialogues: Individual differences, evaluation criteria, and prediction models. In Gary Lee, Joseph Mariani, Wolfgang Minker, and Satoshi Nakamura, editors, *Spoken Dialogue Systems for Ambient Environments*, volume 6392 of *Lecture Notes in Computer Science*, pages 48–60. Springer Berlin / Heidelberg.

Ryuichiro Higashinaka, Yasuhiro Minami, Kohji Dohsaka, and Toyomi Meguro. 2010b. Modeling user satisfaction transitions in dialogues from overall ratings. In *Proceedings of the SIGDIAL 2010 Conference*, pages 18–27, Tokyo, Japan, September. Association for Computational Linguistics.

Kate S. Hone and Robert Graham. 2000. Towards a tool for the subjective assessment of speech system interfaces (sassi). *Nat. Lang. Eng.*, 6(3-4):287–303.

L. P. Kaelbling, M. L. Littman, and A. R. Cassandra. 1998. Planning and acting in partially observable stochastic domains. *Artificial Intelligence*, 101(1-2):99–134.

J. R. Landis and G. G. Koch. 1977. The measurement of observer agreement for categorical data. *Biometrics*, 33(1):159–174, March.

Sebastian Möller, Klaus-Peter Engelbrecht, C. Kühnel, I. Wechsung, and B. Weiss. 2009. A taxonomy of quality of service and quality of experience of multimodal human-machine interaction. In *Quality of Multimedia Experience, 2009. QoMEx 2009. International Workshop on*, pages 7–12, July.

Sebastian Möller. 2003. Subjective Quality Evaluation of Telephone Services Based on Spoken Dialogue Systems. ITU-T Recommendation P.851, International Telecommunication Union, Geneva, Switzerland, November. Based on ITU-T Contr. COM 12-59 (2003).

Tim Polzehl, Alexander Schmitt, and Florian Metze. 2011. Salient features for anger recognition in german and english ivr portals. In Wolfgang Minker, Gary Geunbae Lee, Satoshi Nakamura, and Joseph Mariani, editors, *Spoken Dialogue Systems Technology and Design*, pages 83–105. Springer New York. 10.1007/978-1-4419-7934-6_4.

Lawrence R. Rabiner. 1989. *A tutorial on hidden Markov models and selected applications in speech recognition.* Morgan Kaufmann Publishers Inc., San Francisco, CA, USA.

Antoine Raux, Dan Bohus, Brian Langner, Alan W. Black, and Maxine Eskenazi. 2006. Doing research on a deployed spoken dialogue system: One year of lets go! experience. In *Proc. of the International Conference on Speech and Language Processing (ICSLP)*, September.

Alexander Schmitt, Benjamin Schatz, and Wolfgang Minker. 2011a. Modeling and predicting quality in spoken human-computer interaction. In *Proceedings of the SIGDIAL 2011 Conference*, Portland, Oregon, USA, June. Association for Computational Linguistics.

Alexander Schmitt, Benjamin Schatz, and Wolfgang Minker. 2011b. A statistical approach for estimating user satisfaction in spoken human-machine interaction. In *Proceedings of the IEEE Jordan Conference on Applied Electrical Engineering and Computing Technologies (AEECT)*, Amman, Jordan, December. IEEE.

Alexander Schmitt, Stefan Ultes, and Wolfgang Minker. 2012. A parameterized and annotated corpus of the cmu let's go bus information system. In *International Conference on Language Resources and Evaluation (LREC)*.

C. Spearman. 1904. The proof and measurement of association between two things. *American Journal of Psychology*, 15:88–103.

Stefan Ultes, Alexander Schmitt, and Wolfgang Minker. 2012. Towards quality-adaptive spoken dialogue management. In *NAACL-HLT Workshop on Future directions and needs in the Spoken Dialog Commu-*

nity: Tools and Data (SDCTD 2012), pages 49–52, Montréal, Canada, June. Association for Computational Linguistics.

Vladimir N. Vapnik. 1995. *The nature of statistical learning theory*. Springer-Verlag New York, Inc., New York, NY, USA.

Marilyn Walker, Diane Litman, Candace A. Kamm, and Alicia Abella. 1997. Paradise: a framework for evaluating spoken dialogue agents. In *Proceedings of the eighth conference on European chapter of the Association for Computational Linguistics*, pages 271–280, Morristown, NJ, USA. Association for Computational Linguistics.

Overcoming the Memory Bottleneck in Distributed Training of Latent Variable Models of Text

Yi Yang
Northwestern University
Evanston, IL
yiyang@eecs.northwestern.edu

Alexander Yates
Temple University
Philadelphia, PA
yates@temple.edu

Doug Downey
Northwestern University
Evanston, IL
ddowney@eecs.northwestern.edu

Abstract

Large unsupervised latent variable models (LVMs) of text, such as Latent Dirichlet Allocation models or Hidden Markov Models (HMMs), are constructed using parallel training algorithms on computational clusters. The memory required to hold LVM parameters forms a bottleneck in training more powerful models. In this paper, we show how the memory required for parallel LVM training can be reduced by partitioning the training corpus to minimize the number of unique words on any computational node. We present a greedy document partitioning technique for the task. For large corpora, our approach reduces memory consumption by over 50%, and trains the same models up to three times faster, when compared with existing approaches for parallel LVM training.

1 Introduction

Unsupervised latent variable models (LVMs) of text are utilized extensively in natural language processing (Griffiths and Steyvers, 2004; Ritter et al., 2010; Downey et al., 2007; Huang and Yates, 2009; Li and McCallum, 2005). LVM techniques include Latent Dirichlet Allocation (LDA) (Blei et al., 2003), Hidden Markov Models (HMMs) (Rabiner, 1989), and Probabilistic Latent Semantic Analysis (Hofmann, 1999), among others.

LVMs become more predictive as they are trained on more text. However, training LVMs on massive corpora introduces computational challenges, in terms of both time and space complexity. The time complexity of LVM training has been addressed through parallel training algorithms (Wolfe et al., 2008; Chu et al., 2006; Das et al., 2007; Newman et al., 2009; Ahmed et al., 2012; Asuncion et al., 2011), which reduce LVM training time through the use of large computational clusters.

However, the memory cost for training LVMs remains a bottleneck. While LVM training makes sequential scans of the corpus (which can be stored on disk), it requires consistent random access to model parameters. Thus, the model parameters must be stored in memory on each node. Because LVMs include a multinomial distribution over words for each latent variable value, the model parameter space increases with the number of latent variable values times the vocabulary size. For large models (i.e., with many latent variable values) and large corpora (with large vocabularies), the memory required for training can exceed the limits of the commodity servers comprising modern computational clusters. Because model accuracy tends to increase with both corpus size and model size (Ahuja and Downey, 2010; Huang and Yates, 2010), training accurate language models requires that we overcome the memory bottleneck.

We present a simple technique for mitigating the memory bottleneck in parallel LVM training. Existing parallelization schemes begin by partitioning the training corpus *arbitrarily* across computational nodes. In this paper, we show how to reduce memory footprint by instead partitioning the corpus to *minimize the number of unique words* on each node (and thereby minimize the number of parameters the node must store). Because corpus partitioning is a pre-processing step in parallel LVM training, our technique can be applied to reduce the memory footprint of essentially any existing LVM or training approach. The accuracy of LVM training for a *fixed* model size and corpus remains unchanged, but intelligent corpus partitioning allows us to train larger and typically more accurate models using the same memory capacity.

While the general minimization problem we encounter is NP-hard, we develop greedy approximations that work well. In experiments with both HMM and LDA models, we show that our technique offers large advantages over existing approaches in terms of both memory footprint and execution time. On a large corpus using 50 nodes in parallel, our best partitioning method can reduce the memory required per node to less than 1/10th that when training without corpus partitioning, and to half that of a random partitioning. Further, our approach reduces the training time of an existing parallel HMM codebase by 3x. Our work includes the release of our partitioning codebase, and an associated codebase for the parallel training of HMMs.[1]

2 Problem Formulation

In a distributed LVM system, a training corpus $D = \{d_1, d_2, \ldots, d_N\}$ of documents is distributed across T computational nodes. We first formalize the memory footprint on each node n_t, where $t = \{1, ..., T\}$. Let $D_t \subset D$ denote the document collection on node n_t, and V_t be the number of word types (i.e., the number of unique words) in D_t. Let K be the number of latent variable values in the LVM.

With these quantities, we can express how many parameters must be held in memory on each computational node for training LVMs in a distributed environment. In practice, the LVM parameter space is dominated by an *observation model*: a conditional distribution over words given the latent variable value. Thus, the observation model includes $K(V_t - 1)$ parameters. Different LVMs include various other parameters to specify the complete model. For example, a first-order **HMM** includes additional distributions for the initial latent variable and latent variable transitions, for a total of $K(V_t - 1) + K^2$ parameters. **LDA**, on the other hand, includes just a single multinomial over the latent variables, making a total of $K(V_t - 1) + K - 1$ parameters.

[1] https://code.google.com/p/corpus-partition/

The LVM parameters comprise almost all of the memory footprint for LVM training. Further, as the examples above illustrate, the number of parameters on each node tends to vary almost linearly with V_t (in practice, V_t is typically larger than K by an order of magnitude or more). Thus, in this paper we attempt to minimize memory footprint by limiting V_t on each computational node. We assume the typical case in a distributed environment where nodes are homogeneous, and thus our goal is to partition the corpus such that the *maximum* vocabulary size $V_{max} = max_{t=1}^{T} V_t$ on any single node is minimized. We define this task formally as follows.

Definition $\mathcal{CORPUSPART}$: Given a corpus of N documents $D = \{d_1, d_2, \ldots, d_N\}$, and T nodes, partition D into T subsets $D_1, D_2, \ldots, D_T$, such that V_{max} is minimized.

For illustration, consider the following small example. Let corpus C contain three short documents $\{c_1$="I live in Chicago", c_2="I am studying physics", c_3="Chicago is a city in Illinois"$\}$, and consider partitioning C into 2 non-empty subsets, i.e., $T = 2$. There are a total of three possibilities:

- $\{\{c_1, c_2\}, \{c_3\}\}$. $V_{max} = 7$
- $\{\{c_1, c_3\}, \{c_2\}\}$. $V_{max} = 8$
- $\{\{c_2, c_3\}, \{c_1\}\}$. $V_{max} = 10$

The decision problem version of $\mathcal{CORPUSPART}$ is NP-Complete, by a reduction from independent task scheduling (Zhu and Ibarra, 1999). In this paper, we develop greedy algorithms for the task that are effective in practice.

We note that $\mathcal{CORPUSPART}$ has a *submodular* problem structure, where greedy algorithms are often effective. Specifically, let $|S|$ denote the vocabulary size of a set of documents S, and let $S' \subseteq S$. Then for any document c the following inequality holds.

$$|S' \cup c| - |S'| \geq |S \cup c| - |S|$$

That is, adding a document c to the subset S' increases vocabulary size at least as much as adding c to S; the vocabulary size function is submodular. The $\mathcal{CORPUSPART}$ task thus seeks a partition of the data that minimizes the maximum of a set of submodular functions. While formal approximation guarantees exist for similar problems, to our knowledge none apply directly in our case. For example, (Krause et al., 2007) considers maximizing the minimum over a set of monotonic submodular functions, which is the opposite of our problem. The distinct task of minimizing a single submodular function has been investigated in e.g. (Iwata et al., 2001).

It is important to emphasize that data partitioning is a *pre-processing* step, after which we can employ precisely the same Expectation-Maximization (EM), sampling, or variational parameter learning techniques as utilized in previous work. In fact, for popular learning techniques including EM for HMMs (Rabiner, 1989) and variational EM for LDA (Wolfe et al., 2008), it can be shown that the parameter updates are *independent* of how the corpus is partitioned. Thus, for those approaches our partitioning is guaranteed to produce the same models as any other partitioning method; i.e., model accuracy is unchanged.

Lastly, we note that we target *synchronized* LVM training, in which all nodes must finish each training iteration before any node can proceed to the next iteration. Thus, we desire balanced partitions to help ensure iterations have similar durations across nodes. We achieve this in practice by constraining each node to hold at most 3% more than Z/T tokens, where Z is the corpus size in tokens.

3 Corpus Partitioning Methods

Our high-level greedy partitioning framework is given in Algorithm 1. The algorithm requires answering two key questions: How do we select which document to allocate next? And, given a document, on which node should it be placed? We present alternative approaches to each question below.

Algorithm 1 Greedy Partitioning Framework

INPUT: $\{D, T\}$
OUTPUT: $\{D_1, \dots, D_T\}$
Objective: Minimize V_{max}
Initialize each subset $D_t = \emptyset$ for T nodes
repeat
  document selection:Select document d from D
  node selection: Select node n_t, and add d to D_t
  Remove d from D
until all documents are allocated

A **baseline** partitioning method commonly used in practice simply distributes documents across nodes randomly. As our experiments show, this baseline approach can be improved significantly.

In the following, set operations are interpreted as applying to the set of unique words in a document. For example, $|d \cup D_t|$ indicates the number of unique word types in node n_t after document d is added to its document collection D_t.

3.1 Document Selection

For document selection, previous work (Zhu and Ibarra, 1999) proposed a heuristic **DISSIMILARITY** method that selects the document d that is *least similar* to *any* of the node document collections D_t, where the similarity of d and D_t is calculated as: $Sim(d, D_T) = |d \cap D_t|$. The intuition behind the heuristic is that dissimilar documents are more likely to impact future node selection decisions. Assigning the dissimilar documents earlier helps ensure that more greedy node selections are informed by these impactful assignments.

However, DISSIMILARITY has a prohibitive time complexity of $\mathcal{O}(TN^2)$, because we must compare T nodes to an order of N documents for a total of N iterations. To scale to large corpora, we propose a novel BATCH DISSIMILARITY method. In BATCH DISSIMILARITY, we select the top L most dissimilar documents in each iteration, instead of just the most dissimilar. Importantly, L is altered dynamically: we begin with $L = 1$, and then increase L by one for iteration $i+1$ *iff* using a batch size of $L+1$ in iteration i would not have altered the algorithm's ultimate selections (that is, if the most dissimilar document in iteration $i+1$ is in fact the $L+1$st most dissimilar in iteration i). In the ideal case where L is incremented each iteration, BATCH DISSIMILAR will have a reduced time complexity of $O(TN^{3/2})$.

Our experiments revealed two key findings regarding document selection. First, BATCH DISSIMILARITY provides a memory reduction within 0.1% of that of DISSIMILARITY (on small corpora where running DISSIMILARITY is tractable), but partitions an estimated 2,600 times faster on our largest evaluation corpus. Second, we found that document selection has *relatively minor* impact on memory footprint, providing a roughly 5% incremental benefit over random document selection. Thus, although we utilize BATCH DISSIMILARITY in the final system we evaluate, simple random document selection may be preferable in some practical settings.

3.2 Node Selection

Given a selected document d, the **MINIMUM** method proposed in previous work selects node n_t having the minimum number of word types after allocation of d to n_t (Zhu and Ibarra, 1999). That is, MINIMUM minimizes $|d \cup D_t|$. Here, we introduce an alternative node selection method **JACCARD** that selects node n_t maximizing the Jaccard index, defined here as $|d \cap D_t|/|d \cup D_t|$.

Our experiments showed that our JACCARD node selection method outperforms the MINIMUM selection method. In fact, for the largest corpora used in our experiments, JACCARD offered an 12.9% larger reduction in V_{max} than MINIMUM. Our proposed system, referred to as BJAC, utilizes our best-performing strategies for document selection (BATCH DISSIMILARITY) and node selection (JACCARD).

4 Evaluation of Partitioning Methods

We evaluate our partitioning method against the baseline and **Z&I**, the best performing scalable method from previous work, which uses random document selection and MINIMUM node selection (Zhu and Ibarra, 1999). We evaluate on three corpora (Table 1): the *Brown* corpus of newswire text (Kucera and Francis, 1967), the Reuters Corpus Volume1 (*RCV1*) (Lewis et al., 2004), and a larger *Web-Sent* corpus of sentences gathered from the Web (Downey et al., 2007).

Corpus	N	V	Z
Brown	57339	56058	1161183
RCV1	804414	288062	99702278
Web-Sent	2747282	214588	58666983

Table 1: Characteristics of the three corpora. N = # of documents, V = # of word types, Z = # of tokens. We treat each sentence as a document in the Brown and Web-Sent corpora.

Table 2 shows how the maximum word type size V_{max} varies for each method and corpus, for $T = 50$ nodes. BJAC significantly decreases V_{max} over the random partitioning baseline typically employed in practice. Furthermore, the advantage of BJAC over the baseline is maintained as more computational nodes are utilized, as illustrated in Figure 1. BJac reduces V_{max} by a larger factor over the baseline as more computational nodes are employed.

Corpus	baseline	Z&I	BJAC
Brown	6368	5714	4369
RCV1	49344	32136	24923
Web-Sent	72626	45989	34754

Table 2: Maximum word type size V_{max} for each partitioning method, for each corpus. For the larger corpora, BJAC reduces V_{max} by over 50% compared to the baseline, and by 23% compared to Z&I.

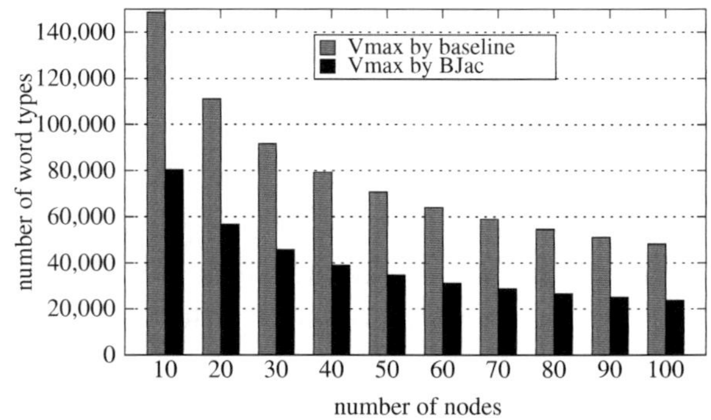

Figure 1: Effects of partitioning as the number of computational nodes increases (Web-Sent corpus). With 100 nodes, BJac's V_{max} is half that of the baseline, and 1/10th of the full corpus vocabulary size.

5 Evaluation in Parallel LVM Systems

We now turn to an evaluation of our corpus partitioning within parallel LVM training systems.

Table 3 shows the memory footprint required for HMM and LDA training for three different partitioning methods. We compare BJAC with the random partitioning baseline, Zhu's method, and with *all-words*, the straightforward approach of simply storing parameters for the entire corpus vocabulary on every node (Ahuja and Downey, 2010; Asuncion et al., 2011). All-words has the same memory footprint as when training on a single node.

For large corpora, BJAC reduces memory size per node by approximately a factor of two over the random baseline, and by a factor of 8-11 over all-

LVM	Corpus	all-words	baseline	BJAC
HMM	Brown	435.3	56.2	40.9
	RCV1	2205.4	384.1	197.8
	Web-Sent	1644.8	561.7	269.7
LDA	Brown	427.7	48.6	33.3
	RCV1	2197.7	376.5	190.1
	Web-Sent	1637.2	554.1	262.1

Table 3: Memory footprint of computational nodes in megabytes(MB), using 50 computational nodes. Both models utilize 1000 latent variable values.

T	all-words	baseline	BJAC
25	4510	1295	1289
50	2248	740	735
100	1104	365	364
200	394	196	192

Table 4: Average iteration time(sec) for training an HMM with 50 hidden states on Web-Sent. Partitioning with BJAC outperforms all-words, which stores parameters for all word types on each node.

words. The results demonstrate that in addition to the well-known savings in computation time offered by parallel LVM training, distributed computation *also* significantly reduces the memory footprint on each node. In fact, for the RCV1 corpus, BJAC reduces memory footprint to less than 1/10th that of training with all words on each computational node.

We next evaluate the *execution time* for an iteration of model training. Here, we use a parallel implementation of HMMs, and measure iteration time for training on the Web-sent corpus with 50 hidden states as the number of computational nodes varies. We compare against the random baseline and against the all-words approach utilized in an existing parallel HMM codebase (Ahuja and Downey, 2010). The results are shown in Table 4. Moving beyond the all-words method to exploit corpus partitioning reduces training iteration time, by a factor of two to three. However, differences in partitioning methods have only small effects in iteration time: BJAC has essentially the same iteration time as the random baseline in this experiment.

It is also important to consider the additional time required to execute the partitioning methods themselves. However, in practice this additional time is negligible. For example, BJAC can partition the Web-sent corpus in 368 seconds, using a single computational node. By contrast, training a 200-state HMM on the same corpus requires over a hundred CPU-days. Thus, BJAC's time to partition has a negligible impact on total training time.

6 Related Work

The $\mathcal{CORPUSPART}$ task has some similarities to the graph partitioning task investigated in other parallelization research (Hendrickson and Kolda, 2000). However, our LVM training task differs significantly from those in which graph partitioning is typically employed. Specifically, graph partitioning tends to be used for scientific computing applications where communication is the bottleneck. The graph algorithms focus on creating balanced partitions that minimize the cut edge weight, because edge weights represent communication costs to be minimized. By contrast, in our LVM training task, memory consumption is the bottleneck and communication costs are less significant.

Zhu & Ibarra (1999) present theoretical results and propose techniques for the general partitioning task we address. In contrast to that work, we focus on the case where the data to be partitioned is a large corpus of text. In this setting, we show that our heuristics partition faster and provide smaller memory footprint than those of (Zhu and Ibarra, 1999).

7 Conclusion

We presented a general corpus partitioning technique which can be exploited in LVM training to reduce memory footprint and training time. We evaluated the partitioning method's performance, and showed that for large corpora, our approach reduces memory consumption by over 50% and learns models up to three times faster when compared with existing implementations for parallel LVM training.

Acknowledgments

This work was supported in part by NSF Grants IIS-101675 and IIS-1065397, and DARPA contract D11AP00268.

References

Amr Ahmed, Moahmed Aly, Joseph Gonzalez, Shravan Narayanamurthy, and Alexander J. Smola. 2012. Scalable inference in latent variable models. In *Proceedings of the fifth ACM international conference on Web search and data mining*, WSDM '12, pages 123–132, New York, NY, USA. ACM.

Arun Ahuja and Doug Downey. 2010. Improved extraction assessment through better language models. In *Human Language Technologies: Annual Conference of the North American Chapter of the Association for Computational Linguistics (NAACL HLT)*.

Arthur U. Asuncion, Padhraic Smyth, and Max Welling. 2011. Asynchronous distributed estimation of topic models for document analysis. *Statistical Methodology*, 8(1):3 – 17. Advances in Data Mining and Statistical Learning.

David M. Blei, Andrew Y. Ng, and Michael I. Jordan. 2003. Latent dirichlet allocation. *J. Mach. Learn. Res.*, 3:993–1022, March.

Cheng T. Chu, Sang K. Kim, Yi A. Lin, Yuanyuan Yu, Gary R. Bradski, Andrew Y. Ng, and Kunle Olukotun. 2006. Map-Reduce for machine learning on multicore. In Bernhard Schölkopf, John C. Platt, and Thomas Hoffman, editors, *NIPS*, pages 281–288. MIT Press.

Abhinandan S. Das, Mayur Datar, Ashutosh Garg, and Shyam Rajaram. 2007. Google news personalization: scalable online collaborative filtering. In *Proceedings of the 16th international conference on World Wide Web*, WWW '07, pages 271–280, New York, NY, USA. ACM.

D. Downey, S. Schoenmackers, and O. Etzioni. 2007. Sparse information extraction: Unsupervised language models to the rescue. In *Proc. of ACL*.

T. L. Griffiths and M. Steyvers. 2004. Finding scientific topics. *Proceedings of the National Academy of Sciences*, 101(Suppl. 1):5228–5235, April.

Bruce Hendrickson and Tamara G Kolda. 2000. Graph partitioning models for parallel computing. *Parallel computing*, 26(12):1519–1534.

Thomas Hofmann. 1999. Probabilistic latent semantic indexing. In *Proceedings of the 22nd annual international ACM SIGIR conference on Research and development in information retrieval*, SIGIR '99, pages 50–57, New York, NY, USA. ACM.

Fei Huang and Alexander Yates. 2009. Distributional representations for handling sparsity in supervised sequence labeling. In *Proceedings of the Annual Meeting of the Association for Computational Linguistics (ACL)*.

Fei Huang and Alexander Yates. 2010. Exploring representation-learning approaches to domain adaptation. In *Proceedings of the ACL 2010 Workshop on Domain Adaptation for Natural Language Processing (DANLP)*.

Satoru Iwata, Lisa Fleischer, and Satoru Fujishige. 2001. A combinatorial strongly polynomial algorithm for minimizing submodular functions. *J. ACM*, 48:761–777.

Andreas Krause, H. Brendan Mcmahan, Google Inc, Carlos Guestrin, and Anupam Gupta. 2007. Selecting observations against adversarial objectives. Technical report, In NIPS, 2007a.

H. Kucera and W. N. Francis. 1967. *Computational analysis of present-day American English*. Brown University Press, Providence, RI.

David D. Lewis, Yiming Yang, Tony G. Rose, Fan Li, G. Dietterich, and Fan Li. 2004. Rcv1: A new benchmark collection for text categorization research. *Journal of Machine Learning Research*, 5:361–397.

Wei Li and Andrew McCallum. 2005. Semi-supervised sequence modeling with syntactic topic models. In *Proceedings of the 20th national conference on Artificial intelligence - Volume 2*, AAAI'05, pages 813–818. AAAI Press.

David Newman, Arthur Asuncion, Padhraic Smyth, and Max Welling. 2009. Distributed algorithms for topic models. *Journal of Machine Learning Research*, 10:1801–1828.

L. R. Rabiner. 1989. A tutorial on Hidden Markov Models and selected applications in speech recognition. *Proceedings of the IEEE*, 77(2):257–286.

Alan Ritter, Colin Cherry, and Bill Dolan. 2010. Unsupervised modeling of twitter conversations. In *Human Language Technologies: The 2010 Annual Conference of the North American Chapter of the Association for Computational Linguistics*, HLT '10, pages 172–180, Stroudsburg, PA, USA. Association for Computational Linguistics.

Jason Wolfe, Aria Haghighi, and Dan Klein. 2008. Fully distributed EM for very large datasets. In *Proceedings of the 25th international conference on Machine learning*, ICML '08, pages 1184–1191, New York, NY, USA. ACM.

Huican Zhu and Oscar H. Ibarra. 1999. On some approximation algorithms for the set partition problem. In *Proceedings of the 15th Triennial Conf. of Int. Federation of Operations Research Society*.

Processing Spontaneous Orthography

Ramy Eskander, Nizar Habash, Owen Rambow, and Nadi Tomeh
Center for Computational Learning Systems
Columbia University
{reskander,habash,rambow,nadi}@ccls.columbia.edu

Abstract

In cases in which there is no standard orthography for a language or language variant, written texts will display a variety of orthographic choices. This is problematic for natural language processing (NLP) because it creates spurious data sparseness. We study the transformation of spontaneously spelled Egyptian Arabic into a conventionalized orthography which we have previously proposed for NLP purposes. We show that a two-stage process can reduce divergences from this standard by 69%, making subsequent processing of Egyptian Arabic easier.

1 Introduction

In areas with **diglossia**, vernacular spoken variants ("low") of a language family co-exist with a largely written variant ("high"), which is often not spoken as a native language. Traditionally, the low variants have not been written: written language is reserved for formal occasions and in those formal occasions only the high variant is used. Prototypical examples of diglossia are the German speaking parts of Switzerland, and the Arab world. The advent of the internet has changed linguistic behavior: it is now common to find written informal conversations, in the form of email exchanges, text messages, Twitter exchanges, and interactions on blogs and in web forums. These written conversations are typically written in the low variants (or in a mixture of low and high), since conversations in the high variant seem unnatural to the discourse participants. For natural language processing (NLP), this poses many challenges, one of which is the fact that the low variants have not been written much in the past and do not have a standard orthography which is generally agreed on by the linguistic community (and perhaps sanctioned by an authoritative institution). Instead, each discourse participant devises a **spontaneous orthography**, in which she chooses among conventions from the high variant to render the spoken language. We are thus faced with a large number of ways to spell the same word, none of which can be assumed as "standard" since there is no standard. As a result, the increased data sparseness adds to the challenges of NLP tasks such as machine translation, compared to languages for which orthography is standardized.

In this paper, we work on Egyptian Arabic (EGY). We follow the conventions which we have previously proposed for the normalized orthography for EGY (Habash et al., 2012), called CODA (Conventional Orthography for Dialectal Arabic). In this paper, we investigate how easy it is to convert spontaneous orthography of EGY written in Arabic script into CODA orthography automatically. We will refer to this process as "normalization" or "codafication". We present a freely available system called CODAFY, which we propose as a preprocessor for NLP modules for EGY. We show that a "do nothing" baseline achieves a normalization performance of 75.5%, and CODAFY achieves a normalization performance of 92.4%, an error reduction of 69.2% over this baseline on an unseen test set.

The paper is structured as follows. We first review relevant linguistic facts in Section 2 and then present the conventionalized orthography we use in this paper. After reviewing related work in Section 4, we present our data (Section 5), our approach (Section 6), and our results (Section 7). We conclude with a discussion of future work.

2 Linguistic Facts

2.1 Writing without a Standard Orthography

An **orthography** is a specification of how the words of a language are mapped to and from a particular script (in our case, the Arabic script). In cases when a standard orthography is absent, writers make decisions about spontaneous orthography based on various criteria. Most prominent among them is **phonology**: how can my pronunciation of the word be rendered in the chosen writing system, given some (language-specific) assumptions about grapheme-to-phoneme mapping? Often, these assumptions come from the "high" variant of the language, or some related language. Another criterion for choosing orthography is a cognate in a related language or language variant (Modern Standard Arabic or MSA, the high variant for EGY), where a cognate pair is a pair of words (or morphemes) in two languages or language variants which are related by **etymology** (in some unspecified manner) and which have roughly the same meaning. Finally, the chosen spontaneous orthography can be altered to reflect **speech effects**, notably the lengthening of syllables to represent emphasis or other effects (such as كتييير *ktyyyyr*[1] 'very').

It is important to distinguish typos from spontaneous orthography. We define **spontaneous orthography** to be an intentional choice of graphemes to render the words in a language or language variant. We define a **typographical error (typo)** to be an unintended sequence of graphemes. For example, كدا *kdA* and كده *kdh* can be intended spellings for EGY /kida/ 'like this', while كرا *krA* is not a plausible intentional spelling since it neither relates /kida/ to an MSA cognate, nor does the sequence of graphemes represent the phonology of EGY using standard assumptions. Instead, we can explain the spelling by assuming that the writer accidentally substituted the grapheme ر for the grapheme د, which look somewhat alike and are near each other on some Arabic keyboard layouts. Of course, when we encounter a specific spelling in a corpus, it can be, in certain cases, difficult to determine whether it is a conscious choice or a typo.

[1]Arabic transliteration is presented in the Habash-Soudi-Buckwalter scheme (Habash et al., 2007): (in alphabetical order) *AbtθjHxdðrzsšSDTĎςγfqklmnhwy* and the additional symbols: ' ء, Â أ, Ǎ إ, Ā آ, ŵ ؤ , ŷ ئ , ¯h ة, ý ى.

2.2 Relevant Differences between EGY and MSA

Lexical Variations Lexically, the number of differences is quite significant. For example, EGY مرات *mrAt* 'wife [of]' corresponds to MSA زوجة *zwj¯h*In such cases of lexical difference, no cognate spelling is available.

Phonological Variations There is an extensive literature on the phonology of Arabic dialects (Watson, 2002; Holes, 2004; Habash, 2010). Several phonological differences exist between EGY and MSA which relate to orthography. Here, we discuss one representative difference. The MSA consonant ث /θ/ is pronounced as /t/ in EGY (or /s/ in more recent borrowings from MSA). For example, MSA يكثر *ykθr* 'increase (imperfective)' is pronounced /yakθur/ in MSA versus /yiktar/ in EGY, giving rise to the EGY phonological spelling يكتر *yktr*.

Morphological Variations There are a lot of morphological differences between MSA and EGY. For orthography, two differences are most relevant. The MSA future proclitic /sa/+ (spelled +س *s*+) appears in EGY as /ha/+ or /Ha/+. The two forms appear in free variation, and we have not been able to find a variable that predicts which form is used when. This variation is not a general phonological variation between /h/ and /H/, we find it only in this morpheme. Predictably, this leads to two spellings in EGY: +ح *H*+ and +هـ *h*+. Negation in EGY is realized as the circum-clitic /mā/+ ... +/š/. The principal orthographic question is whether the prefix is a separate word or is part of the main word; both variants are found.

3 CODA

CODA is a conventionalized orthography for Arabic dialects (Habash et al., 2012). In this section, we summarize CODA so that the reader can understand the goals of this paper. CODA has five key properties.

1. CODA is an internally consistent and coherent convention for writing DA: every word has a

single orthographic rendering.

2. CODA is created for computational purposes.
3. CODA uses the Arabic script as used for MSA, with no extra symbols from, for example, Persian or Urdu.
4. CODA is intended as a unified framework for writing all dialects. In this paper, we only discuss the instantiation of CODA for EGY.
5. CODA aims to maintain a level of dialectal uniqueness while using conventions based on similarities between MSA and the dialects.

We list some features of CODA relevant to this paper.

Phonological Spelling CODA generally uses phonological spelling for EGY (as MSA spelling does for MSA).

Etymologically Spelled Consonants A limited number of consonants may be spelled differently from their phonology if the following two conditions are met: (1) the consonant must be an EGY root radical and (2) the EGY root must have a cognate MSA root. If the conditions are met, then we spell the consonant using the corresponding radical from the cognate MSA root of the dialectal word's root. One such example is the spelling of the EGY verb pronounced /kitir/ as كثر *kθr* ' it increased'.

Morphologically Faithful CODA preserves dialectal morphology and spells the dialectal morphemes (clitics and inflections) phonologically. For example, for the attachable future marker clitic, the variant ح+ is chosen, not the MSA س+, so that EGY /Hatiktar/ (and its variant /hatiktar/) are both spelled حتكثر *Htkθr*. The negation prefix and indirect object pronoun (*l+pronoun*) suffixes are separated, e.g., ما قلت لهاش *mA qlt lhAš* /ma'ultilhāš/ 'I did not tell her'.

Alif-Maqsura The letter ى *ý* is often used in Egypt to write word-final ي *y* and *vice versa* (even when writing MSA). In CODA, all rules for using Alif-Maqsura are the same as MSA. For example, EGY /maSrī/ 'Egyptian' can be seen in spontaneous orthography as مصرى *mSrý*, but in CODA it is مصري *mSry*.

Ta-Marbuta As in MSA, the Ta-Marbuta (ة ~~h~~) is used morphemically in CODA. The Ta-Marbuta is always written as ة ~~h~~ in CODA, e.g., /'arbaςa/ 'four' is أربعة *Ârbς~~h~~* in CODA, though it can be found as أربعه *Ârbςh* (or اربعه *Arbςh*) in spontaneous orthography.

Lexical Exceptions EGY CODA guidelines include a word list specifying ad hoc spellings of EGY words that may be inconsistent with the default mapping outlined above. An example is /kida/ 'like this', which we find as both كدا *kdA* and كده *kdh* in spontaneous orthography; the CODA spelling is كده *kdh*.

4 Related Work

To our knowledge, this paper is the first to discuss the task of automatically providing a conventionalized spelling for a written Arabic dialect text. While there is no direct precedent, we discuss here some related research.

Our proposed work has some similarity to **automatic spelling correction** (ASC) and related tasks such as post editing for optical character recognition (OCR). Our task is different from ASC since ASC work assumes a standard orthography that the writer is also assumed to aim for. Both supervised and unsupervised approaches to this task have been explored. Unsupervised approaches rely on improving the fluency of the text and reducing the percentage of out-of-vocabulary words using NLP tools, resources, and heuristics, e.g., morphological analyzers, language models, and edit-distance measure, respectively (Kukich, 1992; Oflazer, 1996; Ben Othmane Zribi and Ben Ahmed, 2003; Shaalan et al., 2003; Haddad and Yaseen, 2007; Hassan et al., 2008; Shaalan et al., 2010; Alkanhal et al., 2012). Supervised approaches learn models of correction by training on paired examples of errors and their corrections. This data is hard to come by naturally, though for applications such as OCR corpora can be created from the application itself (Kolak and Resnik, 2002; Magdy and Darwish, 2006; Abuhakema et al., 2008; Habash and Roth, 2011).

There has been some work on **conversion** of dialectal Arabic to MSA. Al-Gaphari and Al-Yadoumi (2010) introduced a rule-based method to convert Sanaani dialect to MSA, and Shaalan et al. (2007) used a rule-based lexical transfer approach to transform from EGY to MSA. Similarly, both Sawaf

(2010) and Salloum and Habash (2011) showed that translating dialectal Arabic to MSA can improve dialectal Arabic machine translation into English by pivoting on MSA. A common feature across these conversion efforts is the use of morphological analysis and morphosyntactic transformation rules (for example, Al-Gaphari and Al-Yadoumi (2010)). While all this work is similar to ours in that dialectal input is processed, our output is still dialectal, while the work on conversion aims for a transformation into MSA.

The work most closely related to ours is that of Dasigi and Diab (2011). They identify the spelling variants in a given document and normalize them. However, they do not present a system that converts spontaneous spelling to a pre-existing convention such as CODA, and thus their results cannot be directly related to ours. Furthermore, their technique is different. First, similarity metrics based on string difference are used to identify if two strings are similar. Also, a contextual string similarity is used based on the fact that if two words are orthographic variants of each other, then they are bound to appear in similar contexts. After identifying the similar strings, the strings of interest are modeled in a vector space and clustered according to the similarity of their vectors.

5 Data

In this work, we use a manually annotated EGY Arabic corpus, developed by the Linguistic Data Consortium (LDC), and labeled as "ARZ" (Maamouri et al., 2012), parts 1, 2, 3, 4 and 5. The corpus consists of about 160K words (excluding numbers and punctuations), and follows the part-of-speech (POS) guidelines used by the LDC for Egyptian Arabic. The corpus contains a full analysis of Egyptian Arabic text in spontaneous orthography. The analysis includes the correct CODA orthography of the raw text, in addition to the full morphological/POS annotations.

Data Preparation We divide the ARZ corpus into three parts: training, development and test, which are of about 122K, 19K and 19K words, respectively. We only consider the orthographic information in the ARZ corpus: for every word in the corpus, we retain the spontaneous orthographic form and its CODA-compliant form.

We manually checked the CODA-compliant annotations for about 500 words in the development corpus. We found that the accuracy of the gold annotations in this subset is about 93%. We performed next an error analysis for the erroneous gold annotations. About one half of the gold errors are CODA phonological and orthographical errors. Examples of the CODA phonological errors include wrong additions and deletions of ا *A* and ي *y*, in addition to the ت/ث *t/θ* transformations, and the transformations that correspond to the different phonological forms of pronouncing the letter ه *h*. The CODA orthographical errors are those errors where a word orthography looks the same as its pronunciation, while it should not be, such as the ه/ة *h/¯ h*transformations. One fifth of the gold errors are annotation typos, such as writing قطورات *qTwrAt* instead of قطارات *qTArAt* 'trains'. Moreover, 9% of the gold errors are wrong merges for the negation particle ما *mA* and the indirect object pronouns (*l+pronouns*). Since we use the gold in our study, and given the error analysis for the gold, we expect a qualitatively better gold standard to yield better results.

Transformation Statistics We observe two types of transformations when converting from spontaneous orthography to CODA: character substitutions that do not affect the word length, and character additions/deletions that change the word length. Tables 1 and 2 show the most common character substitution and addition/deletion transformations, respectively, as they appear in the training corpus, associated with their frequencies relative to the occurrence of transformations. The character substitutions are dominant, and constitute about 84% of all the transformations in the training corpus. While the classification of the character substitutions is automatically generated, the classification of the character additions/deletions is done manually using a random sample of 400 additions/deletions in the training corpus. This is because many additions/deletions are ambiguous.

6 Approach

We describe next the various approaches for spontaneous orthography codafication. Our codafication techniques fall into two main categories: contex-

Transformation	Frequency %
ا/أ/إ/آ A/Â/Ǎ/Ā ⇔ ا/أ/إ/آ A/Â/Ǎ/Ā	38.5
ي y ⇔ ى ý	29.7
ه h ⇔ ة ħ	16.9
ه h ⇔ ح H	2.5
ث θ ⇔ ت/س t/s	1.0
ا A ⇔ ه h	0.7
ق q ⇔ ا/أ/إ/آ/ء/ؤ/ئ A/Â/Ǎ/Ā/'/ŵ/ŷ	0.4
و w ⇔ ه h	0.3
ذ ð ⇔ د/ز d/z	0.3
ة ħ ⇔ ت t	0.3
ا A ⇔ ة ħ	0.2
ض D ⇔ د/ز/ظ d/z/Ď	0.2

Table 1: Spontaneous to CODA character substitution transformations

Transformation	Frequency %
Errors in closed class words	22.0
Missing space after ما/لا/يا *mA/lA/yA*	19.0
ا *A* **additions & deletions**	16.8
Gold errors	10.3
Speech effects	8.5
Missing space before ل *l* **(+pron)**	8.5
وا/ه/و *w/h/wA* ⇔ وا/ه/و *w/h/wA*	8.3
ي *y* **additions & deletions**	3.0

Table 2: Spontaneous to CODA character addition/deletion transformations

tual and non-contextual, where the non-contextual approaches are a lot faster than the contextual ones.

6.1 Speech Effect Handling

Before applying any codafication techniques, we perform a special preprocessing step for speech effects, which represent redundant repetitions of some letter in sequence. Sometimes people intend these repetitions to show affirmation or intensification. This is simply handled by removing the repetitions when a letter is repeated more than twice in a row, except for some letters whose repetitions for more than once indicates a speech effect; these letters are ا *A*, آ *Ā*, ء *'*, ئ *ŷ*, ى *ý* and ة *ħ* Handling speech effects on its own corrects about 2% of the non-CODA spontaneous orthography to its CODA-compliant form, without introducing any new errors. In all experiments we report in this paper, we have initially processed speech effects.

6.2 Character Edit Classification (CEC)

In this approach, a set of transformations is applied on a character level, where a character may receive a change or not. As a result, a word changes if one or more of its characters is changed. The output of these transformations is what constitutes the CODA orthography. This is a surface modeling technique that does not depend on the word context (though it does depend on character context inside the word).

First, we train classifiers for the most frequent transformations from EGY spontaneous orthography to the corresponding CODA, listed in Tables 1 and 2 in Section 5. Second, we apply the trained classifiers to generate the CODA output.

Training the classifiers For each transformation listed in the data section, we train a separate classifier. The classifiers are trained on our training corpus using the k-nearest neighbor algorithm (k-NN) (Wang et al., 2000), which is a method for classifying objects based on the closest training examples in the feature space. We did experiments using the other classification methods included in the WEKA machine learning tool (Hall et al., 2009), including SVMs, Naïve Bayes, and decision trees. However, k-NN gives the best results for our problem.

In the training process, a set of nine static features is applied, which are the character that is queried for the transformation with its preceding and following two characters (a special token indicates a character position that does not exist because it is beyond the word boundary), along with the first two and the last two characters in the underlying word.

In this model, each data point is a character, where a classifier determines whether a character should receive a substitution, deletion, or addition of another character. The effect of each classifier is examined separately on the development set. We then determine for each classification whether it helps or weakens the process by comparing its effect to the baseline which is doing nothing, i.e., no change to a word occurs. Those classifiers that on their own perform worse than the baseline are eliminated. For eliminating the classifiers, we examine them in a descending order according to the frequencies of their corresponding transformations. We now discuss the seven classifiers we retain in our system:

1. The different ا *A* form (ا/أ/إ/آ *A/Â/Ǎ/Ā*) classifier. The classifier can change any ا *A* form into any other ا *A* form. The arbitrary selection of the different ا *A* forms represents the most frequent divergence from CODA in Arabic spontaneous orthography.
2. The ي/ى *y/ý* classifier. The classifier handles transformations between ي *y* and ى *ý* in both directions, as their selection is mostly arbitrary in EGY spontaneous orthography.
3. The ه/ة/و *h/ħ/w* classifier. The classifier handles transformations between ه *h*, ة *ħ* and و *w* in both directions. These transformations are likely to happen at word endings, since they represent common misspellings in writing ه *h*, ة *ħ* and و *w*, where ه *h* is often substituted for the graphically similar ة *ħ* and ه *h* and و *w* can both be used to represent the 3rd person masculine singular accusative or genitive clitic. (Note that in Table 1, we list transformations between ه *h* and ة *ħ* as well as between ه *h* and و *w*; the remaining transformations are not frequent.)
4. The ه/ح *h/H* classifier. The transformation from ه *h* to ح *H* is likely to happen at word beginnings, since it represents a common deviation in writing the ح *H* future particle.
5. The ا *A* deletion classifier. The classifier handles the deletion of extra ا *A* at some positions, which is a common deviation in EGY spontaneous orthography, where the CODA orthography requires only short vowels instead.
6. The ا *A* addition classifier. The classifier handles the addition of ا *A* in some positions, where it is mostly omitted in EGY spontaneous orthography, such as adding ا *A* after the ح *H* future particle and the ب *b* progressive particle (when used with the 1st person singular imperfective), as well as the و *w* plural pronoun at word endings. When training this classifier, we target the letter after which the ا *A* should be added.
7. The space addition classifier. The classifier handles the addition of spaces in the middle of words, i.e., splitting a word into two words. This is required to add spaces after ما/لا/يا *mA/lA/yA* for negation and vocation, and before the indirect object *l+pronoun*, so that the text becomes CODA-compliant.

Generating CODA Orthography Next, we apply the trained classifiers on the spontaneous-orthography text. Each classifier determines a set of character corrections, where the characters may receive transformations corresponding to those on which the classifier is trained. The classifiers are independent of one another, so their order of application is irrelevant.

By way of example, we apply the classifiers on the word اربعه *Arbςh*, 'four'. The first classifier, corresponding to the different ا *A* forms, determines the transformation of ا *A* to أ *Â*, while the ه/ة *h/ħ* classifier determines the correction of ه *h* to ة *ħ* The other classifiers are either not involved since they do not work on any of the word characters, or they determine that no character transformation should happen for this word. Thus applying the CEC technique in this case changes the word اربعه *Arbςh* to أربعة *Ârbςħ* which is the correct CODA form.

6.3 Maximum Likelihood Estimate (MLE)

Another surface modeling approach for spontaneous orthography codafication is to use a maximum likelihood model that operates on the word level. In this approach, we build a unigram model that replaces every word in the spontaneous orthography with its most likely CODA form as seen in the training data. This assumes that the underlying word exists in the training corpus. For unseen words, the technique keeps them with no change.

The MLE approach chooses the correct CODA form for most of the words seen in training, making this approach highly dependent on the training data. It is efficient at correcting common misspellings in frequent words, especially those that are from closed classes.

6.4 Morphological Tagger

In addition to the approaches discussed above, we use a morphological tagger, MADA_{ARZ} (Morphological Analysis and Disambiguation for Egyptian Arabic) (Habash et al., 2013). Although $MADA_{ARZ}$ is originally developed to work as a morphological tagger, it still can help the codafication process, since the choice of a full morphological analysis for a word in context determines its CODA spelling. Therefore, $MADA_{ARZ}$ is able to correct many word misspellings that are common in spontaneous orthography. These corrections include (ا/أ/إ/آ *A/Â/Ǎ/Ā*), ي/ى *y/ý* and ه/ة *h/ħ*transformations. However, $MADA_{ARZ}$, as a codafication technique, uses the context of the word, which makes it a contextual modeling approach unlike CEC and MLE. It is much slower than they are.

6.5 Combined Techniques

The CEC and MLE techniques can be applied alone, or they can be applied together in a pipeline in either order. This gives a total of four possible combinations. Next, we conducted experiments with $MADA_{ARZ}$, running alone and as a pre- or postprocessor for a combination of CEC and/or MLE. In all cases, when we first apply one module and then another on the output of the first, we train the second module on the training corpus which has been passed through the first module. The results of running the different codafication approaches are discussed next.

7 Evaluation

7.1 Accuracy Evaluation

The different codafication approaches, discussed in the previous section, are tested against the development set, which was not used as part of our training. The evaluation metric we use is a word accuracy metric, i.e., we evaluate how well we can correctly predict the CODA form of the input spontaneous orthography.

Table 3 lists the effects of using the different codafication approaches. For each approach, two numbers are reported; exact and normalized. In the exact evaluation, the output of the codafication approach is exactly matched against the correct CODA orthography, while in the normalized evaluation, the match is relaxed for the (ا/أ/إ/آ *A/Â/Ǎ/Ā*) and ي/ى *y/ý* alternations, i.e., these differences do not count as errors. In many NLP applications (such as machine translation), the input is normalized for these two phenomena, so that the normalized evaluation gives a sense of the relevance of codafication to downstream processes which normalize.

In this evaluation we compare our different codafication techniques, CEC, MLE, CEC+MLE and MLE+CEC, against the baseline. We also show the effect of using $MADA_{ARZ}$ as a codafication system. We see that MLE on its own outperforms CEC. Running CEC first and then MLE gives us our best result using surface techniques, namely 91.5%, for an error reduction of 63.4% against the baseline. This configuration also gives the highest normalized accuracy of 95.2%, for an error reduction of 49.5% against the baseline.

We now turn to deep modeling techniques. The performance of $MADA_{ARZ}$ on its own as a codafication system is close to the performance of CEC+MLE, by which it is outperformed in the exact-match accuracy by 0.4%.

The best deep modeling (and the best overall) performance is achieved when running $MADA_{ARZ}$ on top of MLE. This gives the highest accuracy of 92.6% (exact) and 95.8% (normalized), for error reductions of 68.1% (exact) and 55.8% (normalized) against the baseline, respectively. Note that the non-contextual modeling techniques CEC (5,584 words/sec) and MLE (6,698 words/sec) are a lot faster than the deep modeling technique $MADA_{ARZ}$ (53 words/sec), while their combination CEC+MLE+$MADA_{ARZ}$ is the slowest among all the approaches, operating at a rate of 52 words/sec. Thus, a small drop in accuracy results in a large increase in speed.

We also evaluated using $MADA_{MSA}$ (v 3.2) (Morphological Analysis and Disambiguation for MSA) (Habash and Rambow, 2005; Habash et al., 2010). $MADA_{MSA}$ is able to do some codafication, but it performs far worse than our codafication approaches.

Table 4 lists the results of the best performing codafication surface approach, CEC+MLE, and deep approach, MLE+$MADA_{ARZ}$, when applied on the test set, which was not used as part of our training or development, i.e., a completely blind test. We see that on the test set, the addition of $MADA_{ARZ}$ improves results relatively more as compared to the development set.

Approach	Exact Match		Norm Match		w/s
	Acc%	ER%	Acc%	ER%	
Baseline	76.8	___	90.5	___	___
MADA_{MSA}	83.6	29.3	91.7	12.6	70
CEC	90.0	56.9	93.9	35.8	5,584
MLE	90.5	59.1	94.6	43.2	6,698
CEC+MLE	91.5	63.4	95.2	49.5	4,284
MLE+CEC	90.7	59.9	94.7	44.2	4,284
MADA_{ARZ}	91.1	61.6	95.2	49.5	53
MADA_{ARZ}+CEC	91.5	63.4	95.4	51.6	53
MADA_{ARZ}+MLE	91.9	65.1	95.8	55.8	53
CEC+MADA_{ARZ}	92.2	66.4	95.6	53.7	53
MLE+MADA_{ARZ}	**92.6**	**68.1**	**95.8**	**55.8**	**53**
MADA_{ARZ}+CEC+MLE	91.8	64.7	95.6	53.7	52
CEC+MLE+MADA_{ARZ}	92.0	65.5	95.8	55.8	52

Table 3: Comparison of the performance of the different codafication approaches on the development corpus. *Acc* stands for Accuracy; *ER* is error reduction against the Baseline. w/s is speed (words/sec).

Approach	Exact Match		Norm Match	
	Acc%	ER%	Acc%	ER%
Baseline	75.5	___	89.7	___
CEC+MLE	91.3	64.5	94.8	49.5
MLE+MADA_{ARZ}	**92.9**	**71.0**	**95.5**	**56.3**

Table 4: Comparison of the performance of the different codafication approaches on the test corpus. *Acc* stands for Accuracy; *ER* is error reduction against the Baseline.

7.2 Extrinsic Evaluation

Morphological Analysis We tested the effect of codafication on morphological tagging, specifically full POS and lemma determination in context by the morphological tagger MADA_{ARZ}. Here, we are evaluating MADA_{ARZ} not on its conversion to CODA (as above), but on its core functionality, namely morphological tagging. We compare the performance of MADA_{ARZ} against running CEC+MLE+MADA_{ARZ}. When tested on the development set, the initial CEC+MLE codafication step helps MADA_{ARZ} improve the identification of the complete Arabic (Buckwalter) POS tag from 84% to 85.3%, for an error reduction of 8.1%, while the correct lemma choice increases from 85.2% to 85.7%, for an error reduction of 3.4%. When tested on the test set, we get improvements on the choice of the complete Buckwalter POS tag and lemma from 84.5% to 85.4% (5.8% error reduction) and from 86.3% to 86.7% (2.9% error reduction), respectively.

Arabic to English MT The goal of this experiment is to test the effect of codafication on machine translation from dialectal Arabic to English. We use the open-source Moses toolkit (Koehn et al., 2007) to build a phrase-based SMT system. We use MGIZA++ for word alignment (Gao and Vogel, 2008). Phrase translations of up to 8 words are extracted in the phrase table. We use SRILM (Stolcke, 2002) with modified Kneser-Ney smoothing to build two 4-gram language models. The first model is trained on the English side of the bitext, while the other is trained on the English Gigaword data. Feature weights are tuned to maximize BLEU (Papineni et al., 2002) on a development set using MERT (Och, 2003). We perform case-insensitive evaluation in terms of the BLEU metric.

We train the system on dialectal Arabic-English parallel data, obtained from several LDC corpora, which amounts to ~500k sentences with 3.8M untokenized words on the Arabic side. The development set, used for tuning the parameters of the MT system, has 1,547 sentences with 15,585 untokenized Arabic words. The test set has 1,065 sentences with

12,116 untokenized Arabic words. Both development and test sets have two reference translations each. The English data is lower-cased and tokenized using simple punctuation-based rules.

We build two systems which vary in preprocessing of the Arabic text. The baseline system applies only simple punctuation-based rules. The second system applies our codafication in addition to punctuation separation. The Arabic text is Alif/Ya normalized and is kept untokenized in both settings. The baseline system achieves a BLEU score of 22.1%. The system using codafication obtains a BLEU score of 22.6%, and outperforms the baseline by 0.5% absolute BLEU points. This result shows that improvements observed in intrinsic evaluation of codafication carry on to the extrinsic task of machine translation.

7.3 Error Analysis

We conducted an error analysis for the best performing codafication approach on the development set. The most frequent error types are listed in Table 5. About two thirds of the errors are CODA phonological and orthographical errors, denoted by CODA-Phon and CODA-Orth, respectively. The wrong additions and deletions of ا *A* and ي *y* and the ت/ث *t/θ* transformations are examples of CODA phonological errors. The CODA orthographic errors include cases such as the ي/ى *y/ý* transformations. 21% of the errors are not real errors in the codafication output, but result from gold errors. Finally, about 13% of the errors are wrong merges and splits for the the negation particle ما *mA*, the vocative particle يا *yA* and the indirect-object *l+pronouns*.

8 Conclusion and Future Work

We have presented the problem of transforming spontaneous orthography of the Egyptian Arabic dialect into a conventionalized form, CODA. Our best technique involves a combination of character transformations, whole-word transformations, and the use of a full morphological tagger. The tagger can be omitted for a small decrease in performance and a large increase in speed.[2] In future work, we plan to extend our approach to other Arabic dialects. We will also investigate incorporating the unsupervised work of Dasigi and Diab (2011) into our algorithm, as well as other unsupervised techniques.

[2]Our system will be freely available. Please contact the authors for more information.

Error Type	Description	Percentage
Gold Error	*Annotation Error*	21.0
CODA-**Orth**	ه *h* ⇔ ة *ħ*	13.7
CODA-**Phon**	ا *A* → ϵ	8.7
Merge	ما *mA*/NEG_PART	7.3
CODA-**Phon**	ϵ → ي *y*	6.8
CODA-**Phon**	ϵ → ا *A*	5.9
CODA-**Orth**	ي *y* ⇔ ى *ý*	4.1
Merge	يا *yA*/VOC_PART	3.7
CODA-**Phon**	ه *h* ⇔ ح *H*	3.2
CODA-**Phon**	ي *y* ⇔ ى *ý*	3.2

Table 5: System Error Analysis: the most frequent error types.

Acknowledgment

This paper is based upon work supported by the Defense Advanced Research Projects Agency (DARPA) under Contract No. HR0011-12-C-0014. Any opinions, findings and conclusions or recommendations expressed in this paper are those of the authors and do not necessarily reflect the views of DARPA. We thank three anonymous reviewers for helpful comments, and Ryan Roth for help with running MADA.

References

G. Abuhakema, R. Faraj, A. Feldman, and E. Fitzpatrick. 2008. Annotating an Arabic Learner Corpus for Error. *Proceedings of the Sixth International Language Resources and Evaluation (LREC'08).*

G Al-Gaphari and M Al-Yadoumi. 2010. A method to convert Sana'ani accent to Modern Standard Arabic. *International Journal of Information Science and Management*, pages 39–49.

Mohamed I. Alkanhal, Mohammed A. Al-Badrashiny, Mansour M. Alghamdi, and Abdulaziz O. Al-Qabbany. 2012. Automatic Stochastic Arabic Spelling Correction With Emphasis on Space Insertions and Deletions. *IEEE Transactions on Audio, Speech & Language Processing*, 20:2111–2122.

Chiraz Ben Othmane Zribi and Mohammed Ben Ahmed. 2003. Efficient Automatic Correction of Misspelled Arabic Words Based on Contextual Information. In *Proceedings of the Knowledge-Based Intelligent Information and Engineering Systems Conference*, Oxford, UK.

Pradeep Dasigi and Mona Diab. 2011. CODACT: TowardsIdentifying Orthographic Variants in Dialectal Arabic. In *Proceedings of the 5th International Joint Conference on Natural Language Processing*, pages 318–326, Chaing Mai, Thailand.

Qin Gao and Stephan Vogel. 2008. Parallel implementations of word alignment tool. In *Software Engineering, Testing, and Quality Assurance for Natural Language Processing*, SETQA-NLP '08, pages 49–57, Stroudsburg, PA, USA. Association for Computational Linguistics.

Nizar Habash and Owen Rambow. 2005. Arabic Tokenization, Part-of-Speech Tagging and Morphological Disambiguation in One Fell Swoop. In *Proceedings of the 43rd Annual Meeting of the Association for Computational Linguistics (ACL'05)*, pages 573–580, Ann Arbor, Michigan.

Nizar Habash and Ryan Roth. 2011. Using deep morphology to improve automatic error detection in arabic handwriting recognition. In *Proceedings of the 49th Annual Meeting of the Association for Computational Linguistics: Human Language Technologies*, pages 875–884, Portland, Oregon, USA, June. Association for Computational Linguistics.

Nizar Habash, Abdelhadi Soudi, and Tim Buckwalter. 2007. On Arabic Transliteration. In A. van den Bosch and A. Soudi, editors, *Arabic Computational Morphology: Knowledge-based and Empirical Methods*. Springer.

Nizar Habash, Owen Rambow, and Ryan Roth. 2010. MADA+TOKAN Manual. Technical Report CCLS-10-01, Center for Computational Learning Systems (CCLS), Columbia University.

Nizar Habash, Mona Diab, and Owen Rabmow. 2012. Conventional Orthography for Dialectal Arabic. In *Proceedings of the Language Resources and Evaluation Conference (LREC)*, Istanbul.

Nizar Habash, Ryan Roth, Owen Rambow, Ramy Eskander, and Nadi Tomeh. 2013. Morphological Analysis and Disambiguation for Dialectal Arabic. In *Proceedings of the 2013 Conference of the North American Chapter of the Association for Computational Linguistics: Human Language Technologies (NAACL-HLT)*, Atlanta, GA.

Nizar Habash. 2010. *Introduction to Arabic Natural Language Processing*. Morgan & Claypool Publishers.

Bassam Haddad and Mustafa Yaseen. 2007. Detection and Correction of Non-Words in Arabic: A Hybrid Approach. *International Journal of Computer Processing Of Languages (IJCPOL).*

Mark Hall, Eibe Frank, Geoffrey Holmes, Bernhard Pfahringer, Peter Reutemann, and Ian H. Witten. 2009. The weka data mining software: an update. *SIGKDD Explor. Newsl.*, 11(1):10–18.

Ahmed Hassan, Sara Noeman, and Hany Hassan. 2008. Language Independent Text Correction using Finite State Automata. In *Proceedings of the International Joint Conference on Natural Language Processing (IJCNLP 2008).*

Clive Holes. 2004. *Modern Arabic: Structures, Functions, and Varieties*. Georgetown Classics in Arabic Language and Linguistics. Georgetown University Press.

Philipp Koehn, Hieu Hoang, Alexandra Birch, Christopher Callison-Burch, Marcello Federico, Nicola Bertoldi, Brooke Cowan, Wade Shen, Christine Moran, Richard Zens, Christopher Dyer, Ondrej Bojar, Alexandra Constantin, and Evan Herbst. 2007. Moses: open source toolkit for statistical machine translation. In *Proceedings of the 45th Annual Meeting of the Association for Computational Linguistics Companion Volume Proceedings of the Demo and Poster Sessions*, pages 177–180, Prague, Czech Republic.

Okan Kolak and Philip Resnik. 2002. OCR error correction using a noisy channel model. In *Proceedings of the second international conference on Human Language Technology Research.*

Karen Kukich. 1992. Techniques for Automatically Correcting Words in Text. *ACM Computing Surveys*, 24(4).

Mohamed Maamouri, Ann Bies, Seth Kulick, Dalila Tabessi, and Sondos Krouna. 2012. Egyptian Arabic Treebank Pilot.

Walid Magdy and Kareem Darwish. 2006. Arabic OCR Error Correction Using Character Segment Correction,

Language Modeling, and Shallow Morphology. In *Proceedings of 2006 Conference on Empirical Methods in Natural Language Processing (EMNLP 2006)*, pages 408–414, Sydney, Austrailia.

Franz Josef Och. 2003. Minimum Error Rate Training for Statistical Machine Translation. In *Proceedings of the 41st Annual Conference of the Association for Computational Linguistics*, pages 160–167, Sapporo, Japan.

Kemal Oflazer. 1996. Error-tolerant finite-state recognition with applications to morphological analysis and spelling correction. *Computational Linguistics*, 22:73–90.

Kishore Papineni, Salim Roukos, Todd Ward, and Wei-Jing Zhu. 2002. BLEU: a Method for Automatic Evaluation of Machine Translation. In *Proceedings of the 40th Annual Meeting of the Association for Computational Linguistics*, pages 311–318, Philadelphia, PA.

Wael Salloum and Nizar Habash. 2011. Dialectal to Standard Arabic Paraphrasing to Improve Arabic-English Statistical Machine Translation. In *Proceedings of the First Workshop on Algorithms and Resources for Modelling of Dialects and Language Varieties*, pages 10–21, Edinburgh, Scotland.

Hassan Sawaf. 2010. Arabic dialect handling in hybrid machine translation. In *Proceedings of the Conference of the Association for Machine Translation in the Americas (AMTA)*, Denver, Colorado.

Khaled Shaalan, Amin Allam, and Abdallah Gomah. 2003. Towards Automatic Spell Checking for Arabic. In *Conference on Language Engineering, ELSE*, Cairo, Egypt.

K. Shaalan, Abo Bakr, and I. H. Ziedan. 2007. Transferring Egyptian Colloquial into Modern Standard Arabic. In *International Conference on Recent Advances in Natural Language Processing (RANLP)*, Borovets, Bulgaria.

K. Shaalan, R. Aref, and A. Fahmy. 2010. An approach for analyzing and correcting spelling errors for non-native Arabic learners. *Proceedings of Informatics and Systems (INFOS)*.

Andreas Stolcke. 2002. SRILM - an Extensible Language Modeling Toolkit. In *Proceedings of the International Conference on Spoken Language Processing (ICSLP)*, volume 2, pages 901–904, Denver, CO.

Jun Wang, Zucker, and Jean-Daniel. 2000. Solving multiple-instance problem: A lazy learning approach. In Pat Langley, editor, *17th International Conference on Machine Learning*, pages 1119–1125.

Janet C. E. Watson. 2002. *The Phonology and Morphology of Arabic*. Oxford University Press.

Purpose and Polarity of Citation: Towards NLP-based Bibliometrics

Amjad Abu-Jbara
Department of EECS
University of Michigan
Ann Arbor, MI, USA
amjbara@umich.edu

Jefferson Ezra
Department of EECS
University of Michigan
Ann Arbor, MI, USA
jezra@umich.edu

Dragomir Radev
Department of EECS
and School of Information
University of Michigan
Ann Arbor, MI, USA
radev@umich.edu

Abstract

Bibliometric measures are commonly used to estimate the popularity and the impact of published research. Existing bibliometric measures provide "quantitative" indicators of how good a published paper is. This does not necessarily reflect the "quality" of the work presented in the paper. For example, when *h-index* is computed for a researcher, all incoming citations are treated equally, ignoring the fact that some of these citations might be negative. In this paper, we propose using NLP to add a "qualitative" aspect to biblometrics. We analyze the text that accompanies citations in scientific articles (which we term *citation context*). We propose supervised methods for identifying citation text and analyzing it to determine the purpose (i.e. author intention) and the polarity (i.e. author sentiment) of citation.

1 Introduction

An objective and fair evaluation of the impact of published research requires both quantitative and qualitative assessment. Existing bibliometric measures such as *H-Index* (Hirsch, 2005; Hirsch, 2010), *G-index* (Egghe, 2006), and *Impact Factor* (Garfield, 1994) focus on the quantitative aspect of this evaluation which dose not always correlate with the qualitative aspect.

For example, the number of papers published by a researcher only tells how productive she or he is. It does not say anything about the quality or the impact of the work. Similarly, the number of citations that a paper receives should not be used to gauge the quality of the work as it really only measures the popularity of the work and the interest of other researchers in it (Garfield, 1979). Controversial papers or those based on fabricated data or experiments may receive a large number of citations. A popular example of fraudulent research that deceived many researchers and caught media attention was the case of a South Korean research scientist, Hwang Woo-suk, who was found to have faked his research results in the area of human stem cell cloning. His research was published in *Science* and received close to 200 citations after the fraud was discovered. The vast majority of those citations were negative.

This suggests that the *purpose* of citation should be taken into consideration when biblometric measures are computed. Negative citations should be weighted less than positive or neutral citations. This motivates the need to automatically distinguish between positive, negative, and neutral citations and to identify the purpose of a citation; i.e. the author's intention behind choosing a published article and citing it.

This analysis of citation purpose and polarity can be useful for many applications. For example, it can be used to build systems that help funding agencies and hiring committees at universities and research institutions evaluate researchers' work more accurately. It can also be used as a preprocessing step in systems that process scholarly data. For example, citation-based summarization systems (Qazvinian and Radev, 2008; Qazvinian et al., 2010; Abu-Jbara and Radev, 2011) and survey generation systems (Mohammad et al., 2009; Qazvinian et al., 2013) can benefit from citation purpose and polarity analysis to improve paper and content selection.

In this paper, we investigate the use of linguistic analysis techniques to automatically identify the purpose of citing a paper and the polarity of this citation. We first present a sequence labeling method for extracting the text that cites a given target reference; i.e. the text that appears in a scientific article and refers to another article and comments on it. We use the term *citation context* to refer to this text. Next, we use supervised classification techniques to analyze this text and identify the purpose and polarity of citation.

The rest of this paper is organized as follows. Section 2 reviews the related work. We present our approach in Section 3. We then describe the data and experiments in Section 4. Finally, Section 5 concludes the paper and suggests directions for future work.

2 Related Work

Our work is related to a large body of research on citations. Studying citation patterns and referencing practices has interested researchers for many years (Hodges, 1972; Garfield et al., 1984). White (2004) provides a good survey of the different research directions that study or use citations. In the following subsections, we review three lines of research that are closely related to our work.

2.1 Citation Context Identification

The first line of related research addresses the problem of identifying citation context. The context of a citation that cites a given target paper can be a set of sentences, one sentence, or a fragment of a sentence.

Nanba and Okumura (1999) use the term *citing area* to refer to the same concept. They define the citing area as the succession of sentences that appear around the location of a given reference in a scientific paper and have connection to it. Their algorithm starts by adding the sentence that contains the target reference as the first member sentence in the citing area. Then, they use a set of cue words and hand-crafted rules to determine whether the surrounding sentences should be added to the citing area or not. In (Nanba et al., 2000), they use their algorithm to improve citation type classification and automatic survey generation.

Qazvinian and Radev (2010) addressed a similar problem. They proposed a method based on probabilistic inference to extract non-explicit citing sentences; i.e., sentences that appear around the sentence that contains the target reference and are related to it. They showed experimentally that citation-based survey generation produces better results when using both explicit and non-explicit citing sentences rather than using the explicit ones alone.

In previous work, we addressed the issue of identifying the scope of a given target reference in citing sentences that contain multiple references (2012). Our definition of *reference scope* was limited to fragments of the explicit citing sentence (i.e. the sentence in which actual citation appears). That method does not identify related text in surrounding sentences.

In this work, we propose a supervised sequence labeling method for identifying the citation context of given reference which includes the explicit citing sentence and the related surrounding sentences.

2.2 Citation Purpose Classification

Several research efforts have focused on studying the different purposes for citing a paper (Garfield, 1964; Weinstock, 1971; Moravcsik and Murugesan, 1975; and Moitra, 1975; Bonzi, 1982). Bonzi (1982) studied the characteristics of citing and cited works that may aid in determining the relatedness between them. Garfield (1964) enumerated several reasons why authors cite other publications, including "alerting researchers to forthcoming work", paying homage to the leading scholars in the area, and citations which provide pointers to background readings. Weinstock (1971) adopted the same scheme that Garfield proposed in her study of citations.

Spiegel-Rosing (1977) proposed 13 categories for citation purpose based on her analysis of the first four volumes of Science Studies. Some of them are: Cited source is the specific point of departure for the research question investigated, Cited source contains the concepts, definitions, interpretations used, Cited source contains the data used by the citing paper. Nanba and Okumura (1999) came up with a simple schema composed of only three categories: *Basis*, *Comparison*, and other *Other*. They proposed a rule-based method that uses a set of statistically selected cue words to determine the category of a citation. They used this classification as a first step for scientific paper summarization. Teufel et al. (2006), in their work on citation function classification, adopted 12 categories from Spiegel-Rosing's taxonomy. They trained an SVM classifier and used it to label each citing sentence with exactly one category. Further, they mapped the twelve categories to four top level categories namely: weakness, contrast

(4 categories), positive (6 categories) and neutral.

The taxonomy that we use in this work is based on previous work. We adopt a scheme that contains six categories. We selected the six categories after studying all the previously used citation taxonomies. We included the ones we believed are important for improving bibliometric measures and for the applications that we are planning to pursue in the future (Section 5).

2.3 Citation Polarity Classification

The polarity (or sentiment) of a citation has also been studied previously. Previous work showed that positive and negative citations are common, although negative citations might be expressed indirectly or in an implicit way (Ziman, 1968; MacRoberts and MacRoberts, 1984; THOMPSON and YIYUN, 1991). Athar (2011) addressed the problem of identifying sentiment in citing sentences. He used a set of structure-based features to train a machine learning classifier using annotated data. This work uses the citing sentence only to predict sentiment. Context sentences were ignored. Athar and Teufel (2012a) observed that taking the context into consideration when judging sentiment in citations increases the number of negative citations by a factor of 3. They proposed two methods for utilizing the context. In the first method, they treat the citing sentence and a fixed context (a window of four sentences around the citing sentence) as if they were a single sentence. They extract features from the merged text and train a classifier similar to what they did in their 2011 paper. In the second method, they use a four-class annotation scheme. Each sentence in a window of four sentences around the citation is labeled as positive, negative, neutral, or excluded (unrelated to the cited work). There experiments surprisingly gave negative results and showed that classifying sentiment *without* considering the context achieves better results. They attributed this to the small size of their training data and to the noise that including the context text introduces to the data. In (Athar and Teufel, 2012b), the authors present a method for automatically identifying all the mentions of the cited paper in the citing paper. They show that considering all the mentions improves the performance of detecting sentiment in citations.

In our work, we propose a sequence labeling method for identifying the citation context first, and then use a supervised approach to determine the polarity of a given citation.

3 Approach

In this section, we describe our approach to three tasks: citation context identification, citation purpose classification, and citation polarity identification. We also describe a preprocessing stage that is applied to the citation text before performing any of the three tasks.

3.1 Preprocessing

The goal of the preprocessing stage is to clean and prepare the citation text for part-of-speech tagging and parsing. The available POS taggers and parsers are not trained on citation text. Citation text is different from normal text in that it contains references written in a special format (e.g., author names and publication year written in parentheses; or reference indices written in square brackets). Many citing sentences contain multiple references, some of which might be grouped together in a pair of parentheses and separated by a comma or a semi-colons. These references are usually not syntactic nor semantic constituents of the sentences they appear in. This results in many POS tagging and parsing errors. We address this issue in the pre-processing stage to improve the performance of the feature extraction component. We perform three pre-processing steps:

a. Reference Tagging: In the first step, we find and tag all the references that appear in the text. We use a regular expression to find references and replace each reference with a placeholder. The reference to the target paper is replaced by the placeholder *TREF*. Each other reference is replaced by *REF*.

b. Reference Grouping: In this step, we identify grouped references (i.e. multiple references listed between one pair of parentheses separated by semicolons). Each such group is replaced by a placeholder, *GREF*. If the target reference is a member of the group, we use a different placeholder: *GTREF*.

c. Non-syntactic Reference Removal: A reference or a group of references could either be a syntactic constituent and has a semantic role in the sentence or not (Whidby, 2012; Abu Jbara and Radev, 2012). If the reference is not a syntactic compo-

Feature	Description
Demonstrative determiners	Takes a value of 1 if the current sentence contains contains a *demonstrative determiner* (this, these, etc.), and 0 otherwise.
Conjunctive adverbs	Takes a value of 1 if the current sentence starts with a *conjunctive adverb* (However, Furthermore, Accordingly, etc.), and 0 otherwise.
Position	Position of the current sentence with respect to the citing sentence. This feature takes one of four values: -1, 0, 1, and 2.
Contains Closest Noun Phrase	Takes a value of 1 if the current sentence contains closest noun phrase (if any) immediately before the reference position in the citing sentence, and 0 otherwise. This noun phrase often is the name of a method, a tool, or corpus originating from the cited reference.
2-3 grams	The first bigram and trigram in the sentence (*This approach*, *One problem with*, etc.).
Contains Other references	Takes a value of 1 if the current sentence contains references other than the target, and 0 otherwise.
Contains a Mention of target reference	Takes a value of 1 if the current sentence contains a mention (explicit or anaphoric) of the target reference, and 0 otherwise.
Multiple references	Takes a value of 1 if the citing sentence contains multiple references, and 0 otherwise. If the citing sentence contains multiple references, it becomes less likely that the surrounding sentences are related.

Table 1: Features used for citation context identification

nent in the sentence, we remove it to reduce parsing errors. Following our previous work (Abu Jbara and Radev, 2012), we use a rule-based algorithm to determine whether a reference should be removed from the sentence or kept. The algorithm uses stylistic and linguistic features such as the style of the reference, the position of the reference, and the surrounding words to make the decision. When a reference is removed, the head of the closest noun phrase (NP) immediately before the position of the removed reference is used as a representative of the reference. This is needed for feature extraction as shown later in the paper.

3.2 Citation Context Identification

The task of identifying the citation context of a given target reference can be formally defined as follows. Given a scientific article A that cites another article B, find a set of sentences in A that talk about the work done in B such that at least one of these sentences contains an explicit reference to B.

We treat this problem as a sequence labeling problem. The goal is to find the globally best sequence of labels for all the sentences that appear within a window around the *citing sentence*. The *citing sentence* is the one that contains an explicit reference to the cited paper. Each sentence within the window is labeled as *INCLUDED* or *EXCLUDED* from the citation context of the given target paper. To determine the size of the window, we examined a development set of 300 sentences. We noticed that the related context almost always falls within a window of four sentences. The window includes the citing sentence, one sentence before the citing sentence, and two sentences after the citing sentence.

We use Conditional Random Fields (CRFs) for sequence labeling. In particular, we use a first-order chain-structured CRF. The chain consists of two sets of nodes: 1) a set of hidden nodes **Y** which represent the context labels of sentences (INCLUDED or EXCLUDED), and 2) a set of observed nodes **X** which represent the features extracted from the sentences. The task is to estimate the probability of a sequence of labels Y given the sequence of observed features X: $P(\mathbf{Y}|\mathbf{X})$

Lafferty et al. (2001) define this probability to be a normalized product of potential functions ψ:

$$P(\mathbf{y}|\mathbf{x}) = \prod_t \psi_k(y_t, y_{t-1}, \mathbf{x}) \quad (1)$$

Where $\psi_k(y_t, y_{t-1}, \mathbf{x})$ is defined as

$$\psi_k(y_t, y_{t-1}, \mathbf{x}) = exp(\sum_k \lambda_k f(y_t, y_{t-1}, \mathbf{x})) \quad (2)$$

where $f(y_t, y_{t-1}, \mathbf{x})$ is a transition feature function of the label at positions $i-1$ and i and the observation sequence $\mathbf{x}$; and λ_j is a parameter that the algorithm estimates from training data.

The features we use to train the CRF model include structural and lexical features that attempt to capture indicators of relatedness to the given target reference. The features that we used and their descriptions are listed in table 1.

Category	Description	Example
Criticizing	Criticism can be positive or negative. A citing sentence is classified as "criticizing" when it mentions the weakness/strengths of the cited approach, negatively/positively criticizes the cited approach, negatively/positively evaluates the cited source.	Chiang (2005) introduced a constituent feature to reward phrases that match a syntactic tree but did not yield significant improvement.
Comparison	A citing sentence is classified as "comparison" when it compares or contrasts the work in the cited paper to the author's work. It overlaps with the first category when the citing sentence says one approach is not as good as the other approach. In this case we use the first category.	Our approach permits an alternative to minimum error-rate training (MERT; Och, 2003);
Use	A citing sentence is classified as "use" when the citing paper uses the method, idea or tool of the cited paper.	We perform the MERT training (Och, 2003) to tune the optimal feature weights on the development set.
Substantiating	A citing sentence is classified as "substantiating" when the results, claims of the citing work substantiate, verify the cited paper and support each other.	It was found to produce automated scores, which strongly correlate with human judgements about translation fluency (Papineni et al. , 2002).
Basis	A citing sentence is classified as "basis" when the author uses the cited work as starting point or motivation and extends on the cited work.	Our model is derived from the hidden-markov model for word alignment (Vogel et al., 1996; Och and Ney, 2000).
Neutral (Other)	A citing sentence is classified as "neutral" when it is a neutral description of the cited work or if it doesn't come under any of the above categories.	The solutions of these problems depend heavily on the quality of the word alignment (Och and Ney, 2000).

Table 2: Annotation scheme for citation purpose. Motivated by the work of (Spiegel-Rösing, 1977) and (Teufel et al., 2006)

3.3 Citation Purpose Classification

In this section, we describe the citation purpose classification task. Given a target paper B and its citation context (extracted using the method described above) in a given article A, we want to determine the purpose of citing B by A. The purpose is defined as intention behind selecting B and citing it by the author of A (Garfield, 1964).

We use a taxonomy that consists of six categories. We designed this taxonomy based on our study of similar taxonomies proposed in previous work. We selected the categories that we believe are more important and useful from a bibliometric point of view, and the ones that can be detected through citation text analysis. We also tried to limit the number of categories by grouping similar categories proposed in previous work under one category. The six categories, their descriptions, and an example for each category are listed in Table 2.

We use a supervised approach whereby a classification model is trained on a number of lexical and structural features extracted from a set of labeled citation contexts. Some of the features that we use to train the classifier are listed in table 3.

3.4 Citation Polarity Identification

In this section, we describe the citation polarity identification task. Given a target paper B and its citation context in a given article A, we want to determine the polarity of the citation text with respect to B. The polarity can be: *positive*, *negative*, or *neutral (objective)*. Positive, negative, and neutral in this context are defined in a slightly different way than their usual sense. A citation is marked positive if it either explicitly states a strength of the target paper or indicates that the work done in the target paper has been used either by the author or a third-party. It is also marked as positive if it is compared to another paper (possibly by the same authors) and deemed better in some way. A citation is marked negative if it explicitly points to a weakness of the target paper. It is also marked as negative if it is compared to another paper and deemed worse in some way. A citation is marked as neutral if it is only descriptive.

Similar to citation purpose classification, we use a supervised approach for this problem. We train a classification model using the same features listed in Table 3. Due to the high skewness in the data (more than half of the citations are neutral), we use two setups for binary classification. In the first setup, the citation is classified as *Polarized (Subjective)* or *(Neutral) Objective*. In the second one, *Subjective* citations are classified as *Positive* or *Negative*. We find that this method gives more intuitive results than using a 3-way classifier.

Feature	Description
Reference count	The number of references that appear in the citation context.
Is Separate	Whether the target reference appears within a group of references or separate (i.e. single reference).
Closest Verb / Adjective / Adverb	The lemmatized form of the closest verb/adjective/adverb to the target reference or its representative or any mention of it. Distance is measure based on the shortest path in the dependency tree.
Self Citation	Whether the citation from the source paper to the target reference is a self citation.
Contains 1st/3rd PP	Whether the citation context contains a first/third person pronoun.
Negation	Whether the citation context contains a negation cue. The list of negation cues is taken from the training data of the *SEM 2012 negation detection shared task (Morante and Blanco, 2012).
Speculation	Whether the citation context contains a speculation cue. The list is taken from Quirk et al. (1985)
Closest Subjectivity Cue	The closest subjectivity cue to the target reference or its representative or any anaphoric mention of it. The list of cues is taken from OpinionFinder (Wilson et al., 2005)
Contrary Expressions	Whether the citation context contains a contrary expression. The list is taken from Biber (1988)
Section	The headline of the section in which the citation appears. We identify five title categorizes: 1) *Introduction, Motivation, etc.* 2) *Background, Prior Work, Previous Work, etc.* 3) *Experiments, Data, Results, Evaluation, etc.* 4) *Discussion, Conclusion, Future work, etc.*. 5) All other section headlines. Headlines are identified using regular expressions.
Dependency Relations	All the dependency relations that appear in the citation context. For example, $nsubj(outperform, algorithm)$ is one of the relations extracted from "This algorithm outperforms the one proposed by...". The arguments of the dependency relation are replaced by their lemmatized forms. This type of features has been shown to give good results in similar tasks (Athar and Teufel, 2012a).

Table 3: The features used for citation purpose and polarity classification

4 Evaluation

In this section, we describe the data that we used for evaluation and the experiments that we conducted.

4.1 Data

We use the ACL Anthology Network corpus (AAN) (Radev et al., 2009; Radev et al., 2013) in our evaluation. AAN is a publicly available collection of more than 19,000 NLP papers. It includes a manually curated citation network of its papers as well as the full text of the papers and the citing sentences associated with each edge in the citation network. From this set, we selected 30 papers that have different numbers of incoming citations and that were consistently cited since they were published. These 30 papers received a total of about 3,500 citations from within AAN (average = 115 citation/paper, Min = 30, and Max = 338). These citations come from 1,493 unique papers. For each of these citations, we extracted a window of 4 sentences around the reference position. This brings the number of sentences in our dataset to a total of roughly 14,000 sentences. We refer to this dataset as *training/testing dataset*.

In addition to this dataset, we created another dataset that contains 300 citations that cite 5 papers from AAN. We refer to this dataset as the *development* dataset. This dataset was used to determine the size of the citation context window, and to develop the feature sets used in the three tasks described in Section 3 above.

4.2 Annotation

In this section, we describe the annotation process. We asked graduate students with good background in NLP (the topic of the annotated sentences) to provide three annotations for each citation example (a window of 4 sentences around the reference anchor) in the *training/testing dataset*. We asked them to mark the sentences that are related to a given target reference. In addition, we asked them to determine the purpose of citing the target reference by choosing from the six purpose categories that we described earlier. We also asked them to determine whether the citation is negative, positive, or neutral.

To estimate the inter-annotator agreement, we picked 400 sentences from the *training/testing dataset* and assigned them to two different annotators. We use the Kappa coefficient (Cohen, 1968) to measure the agreement. The Kappa coefficient is defined as follows:

$$K = \frac{P(A) - P(E)}{1 - P(E)} \quad (3)$$

where P(A) is the relative observed agreement among annotators and P(E) is the hypothetical probability of chance agreement. The agreement between the two annotators on the context identification task was $K = 0.89$. On Landis and Kochs (Landis and Koch, 1977) scale, this value indicates *almost perfect* agreement. The agreement on the purpose and the polarity classification task were $K = 0.61$ and $K = 0.66$, respectively; which indicates *substantial agreement* on the same scale.

The annotation shows that in 22% of the citation examples, the citation context consists of 2 or more sentences. The distribution of the purpose categories in the data was: 14.7% criticism, 8.5% comparison, 17.7% use, 7% substantiation, 5% basis, and 47% other. The distribution of the polarity categories was: 30% positive, 12% negative, and 58% neutral.

4.3 Experimental Setup

We use the CRF++[1] toolkit for CRF training and testing. We use the Stanford parser to parse the citation text and generate the dependency parse trees of sentences. We use Weka for classification experiments. We experimented with several classifiers including: SVM, Logistic Regression (LR), and Naive Bayes. All the experiments that we conducted used the *training/testing dataset* in a 10-fold cross validation mode. All the results have been tested for statistical significance using a 2-tailed paired t-test.

4.4 Evaluation of Citation Context Identification

We compare the CRF approach to three baselines. The first baseline (ALL) labels all the sentences in the citation window of size 4 as *INCLUDED* in the citation context. The second baseline (CS-ONLY) labels the citing sentence only as *INCLUDED* in the citation context. In the third baseline, we use a supervised classification method instead of sequence labeling. We use Support Vector Machines (SVM) to train a model using the same set of features as in the CRF approach.

Table 4 shows the precision, recall, and F1 score of the CRF approach and the baselines. The results show that our CRF approach outperforms all the baselines. It also asserts our expectation that addressing this problem as a sequence labeling problem leads to better performance than individual sentence classification, which is also clear from the nature of the task.

	Precision	Recall	F1
CRFs	**98.5%**	**82.0%**	**89.5%**
ALL	30.7%	100.0%	46.9%
CS-ONLY	88.0%	74.0%	80.4%
SVM	92.0%	76.4%	83.5%

Table 4: Results of citation context identification

Feature Analysis: We evaluated the importance of the features listed in Table 1 by computing the chi-squared statistic for every feature with respect to the class. We found that the lexical features (such as determiners and conjunction adverbs) are generally more important than the structural features (such as position and reference count). The features shown in Table 1 are listed in the order of their importance based on this analysis.

4.5 Evaluation of Citation Purpose Classification

Our experiments with several classification algorithms showed that the SVM classifier outperforms Logistic Regression and Naive Bayes classifiers. Due to space limitations, we only show the results for SVM. Table 5 shows the precision, recall, and F1 for each of the six categories. It also shows the overall accuracy and the Macro-F measure.

Feature Analysis: The chi-squared evaluation of the features listed in Table 3 shows that both lexical and structural features are important. It also shows that among lexical features, the ones that are limited to the existence of a direct relation to the target reference (such as *closest* verb, adjective, adverb, subjective cue, etc.) are most useful. This can be explained by the fact that the restricting the features to having direct dependency relation introduces much less noise than other features (such as *Dependency Triplets*). Among the structural features, the number of references in the citation context showed to be more useful.

4.6 Evaluation of Citation Polarity Identification

Similar to the case of citation purpose classification, our experiments showed that the SVM classifier outperforms the other classifiers that we experimented with. Table 6 shows the precision, recall, and F1 for

[1]http://crfpp.googlecode.com/svn/trunk/doc/index.html

	Criticism	Comparison	Use	Substantiating	Basis	Other
Precision	53.0%	55.2%	60.0%	50.1%	47.3%	64.0%
Recall	77.4%	43.1%	73.0%	57.3%	39.1%	85.1%
F1	63.0%	48.4%	66.0%	53.5%	42.1%	73.1%
Accuracy: 70.5%						
Macro-F: 58.0%						

Table 5: Summary of Citation Purpose Classification Results (10-fold cross validation, SVM: Linear Kernel, c = 1.0)

each of the three categories. It also shows the overall accuracy and the Macro-F measure. The analysis of the features used to train this classifier using chi-squared analysis leads to the same conclusions about the relative importance of the features as described in the previous subsection. However, we noticed that features that are related to subjectivity (*Subjectivity Cues*, *Negation*, *Speculation*) are ranked higher which makes sense in the case of polarity classification.

	Negative %	Positive %	Neutral %
Precision	68.7 (66.4) [69.8]	54.9 (52.1) [55.4]	83.6 (82.8) [84.2]
Recall	79.2 (71.1) [81.1]	48.1 (45.6) [46.3]	95.5 (95.1) [95.3]
F1	73.6 (68.7) [75.0]	51.3 (48.6) [50.4]	89.1 (88.5) [89.4]
Accuracy: 81.4 (74.2) [84.2] %			
Macro-F: 71.3 (62.1) [74.2] %			

Table 6: Summary of Citation Polarity Classification Results (10-fold cross validation, SVM: Linear Kernel, c = 1.0). Numbers between rounded parentheses are when only the explicit citing sentence is used (i.e. no context). Numbers in square brackets are when the gold standard context is used.

4.7 Impact of Context on Classification Accuracy

To study the impact of using citation context in addition to the citing sentence on classification performance, we ran two polarity classification experiments. In the first experiment, we used the citing sentence only to extract the features that are used to train the classifiers. In the second experiment, we used the gold context sentences (the ones labeled *INCLUDED* by human annotators). Table 6 shows the results of the first experiment between rounded parentheses and the results of the second experiments in square brackets. The results show that adding citation context improves the classification accuracy especially in the *subjective* categories, specially in the negative category if we want to be more specific. This supports our intuition about polarized citations that authors start their review of the cited work with an objective (neutral) sentence and then follow it with their criticism if they have any. We also reached to similar conclusions with purpose classification, but we are not showing the numbers due to space limitations.

4.8 Other Experiments

4.8.1 Can We Do Better?

In this section, we investigate whether it is possible to improve the performance in the two classification tasks. One factor that we believe could have an impact on the result is the size of the training data. To examine this hypothesis, we ran the experiment on different sizes of data. Figure 1 shows the learning curve of the two classifiers for different sizes of training data. The accuracy increases as more training data is available so we can expect that with even more data, we can do even better.

4.8.2 Relation Between Citation Purpose/Polarity and Citation Count

The main motivation of this work is our hypothetical assumption that using NLP for analyzing citations gives a clearer picture of the impact of the cited work. As a way to check the validity of this assumption, we study the correlation between the counts of the different purpose and polarity categories. We also study the correlation between these categories and the total number of citations that a paper received since it was published. We use the *training/testing dataset* and the gold annotations for this study.

We compute the Pearson correlation coefficient between the counts of citations from the different categories that a paper received per year since its publication. We found that, on average, the correlation between positive and negative citations is negative (AVG P = -0.194) and that the correlation be-

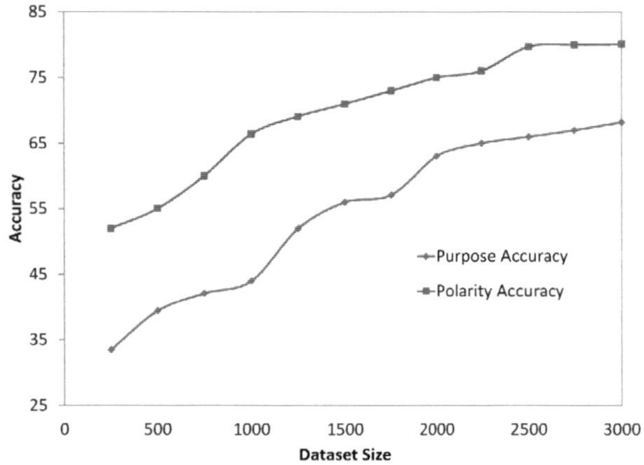

Figure 1: The effect of size of the data set size on the classifiers accuracy.

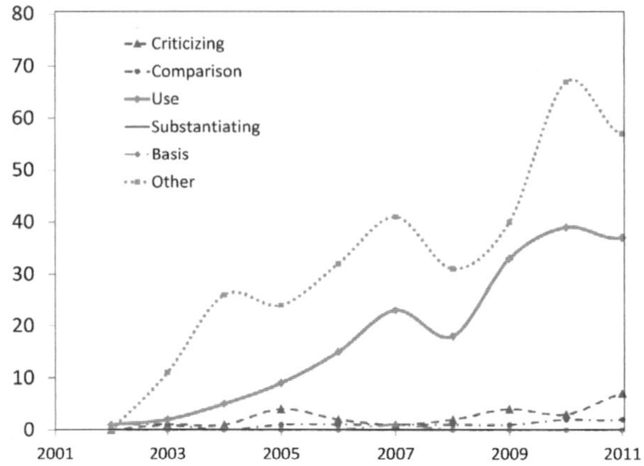

Figure 2: Change in the purpose of the citations to Papineni et al. (2002)

tween the count of positive citations and the total number of citations is higher than the correlation between negative citations and total citations (AVG P = 0.531 for positive vs. AVG P = 0.054 for negative).

Similarly, we noticed that there is a higher positive correlation between *Use* citations and total citations than in the case of both *Substantiation* and *Basis*. This can be explained by the intuition that publications that present new algorithms, tools, or corpora that are used by the research community become more and more popular with time and thus receive more and more citations.

Figure 2 shows the result of running our purpose classifier on all the citations to Papineni et al.'s (2002) paper about Bleu, an automatic metric for evaluating Machine Translation (MT) systems. The figure shows that this paper receives a high number of *Use* citations. This makes sense for a paper that describes an evaluation metric that has been widely used in the MT area. The figure also shows that in the recent years, this metric started to receive some *Criticizing* citations that resulted in a slight decrease in the number of *Use* citations. Such a temporal analysis of citation purpose and polarity is useful for studying the dynamics of research. It can also be used to detect the emergence or de-emergence of research techniques.

5 Conclusion

In this paper, we presented methods for three tasks: citation context identification, citation purpose classification, and citation polarity classification. This work is motivated by the need for more accurate bibliometric measures that evaluates the impact of research both qualitatively and quantitatively. Our experiments showed that we can classify the purpose and polarity of citation with a good accuracy. It also showed that using the citation context improves the classification accuracy and increases the number of polarized citations detected. For future work, we plan to use the output of this research in several applications such as predicting future prominence of publications, studying the dynamics of research, and designing more accurate bibliometric measures.

Acknowledgement

This research is supported by the Intelligence Advanced Research Projects Activity (IARPA) via Department of Interior National Business Center (DoI/NBC) contract number D11PC20153. The U.S. Government is authorized to reproduce and distribute reprints for Governmental purposes notwithstanding any copyright annotation thereon. Disclaimer: The views and conclusions contained herein are those of the authors and should not be interpreted as necessarily representing the official policies or endorsements, either expressed or implied, of IARPA, DoI/NBC, or the U.S. Government.

References

Daryl E. and Soumyo D. Moitra. 1975. Content analysis of references: Adjunct or alternative to citation counting? *Social Studies of Science*, 5(4):pp. 423–441.

Amjad Abu-Jbara and Dragomir Radev. 2011. Coherent citation-based summarization of scientific papers. In *Proceedings of the 49th Annual Meeting of the Association for Computational Linguistics: Human Language Technologies*, pages 500–509, Portland, Oregon, USA, June. Association for Computational Linguistics.

Amjad Abu Jbara and Dragomir Radev. 2012. Reference scope identification in citing sentences. In *Proceedings of the 2012 Conference of the North American Chapter of the Association for Computational Linguistics: Human Language Technologies*, pages 80–90, Montréal, Canada, June. Association for Computational Linguistics.

Awais Athar and Simone Teufel. 2012a. Context-enhanced citation sentiment detection. In *Proceedings of the 2012 Conference of the North American Chapter of the Association for Computational Linguistics: Human Language Technologies*, pages 597–601, Montréal, Canada, June. Association for Computational Linguistics.

Awais Athar and Simone Teufel. 2012b. Detection of implicit citations for sentiment detection. In *Proceedings of the Workshop on Detecting Structure in Scholarly Discourse*, pages 18–26, Jeju Island, Korea, July. Association for Computational Linguistics.

Awais Athar. 2011. Sentiment analysis of citations using sentence structure-based features. In *Proceedings of the ACL 2011 Student Session*, pages 81–87, Portland, OR, USA, June. Association for Computational Linguistics.

Douglas Biber. 1988. *Variation across speech and writing*. Cambridge University Press, Cambridge.

Susan Bonzi. 1982. Characteristics of a literature as predictors of relatedness between cited and citing works. *Journal of the American Society for Information Science*, 33(4):208–216.

J. Cohen. 1968. Weighted kappa: Nominal scale agreement with provision for scaled disagreement or partial credit. *Psychological Bulletin*, 70:213–220.

Leo Egghe. 2006. Theory and practise of the g-index. *Scientometrics*, 69:131–152.

E. Garfield, Irving H. Sher, and R. J. Torpie. 1984. *The Use of Citation Data in Writing the History of Science*. Institute for Scientific Information Inc., Philadelphia, Pennsylvania, USA.

Eugene Garfield. 1964. Can citation indexing be automated?

E. Garfield. 1979. Is citation analysis a legitimate evaluation tool? *Scientometrics*, 1(4):359–375.

Eugene Garfield. 1994. The thomson reuters impact factor.

J. E. Hirsch. 2005. An index to quantify an individual's scientific research output. *Proceedings of the National Academy of Sciences*, 102(46):16569–16572, November.

J. E. Hirsch. 2010. An index to quantify an individual's scientific research output that takes into account the effect of multiple coauthorship. *Scientometrics*, 85(3):741–754, December.

T. L. Hodges. 1972. Citation indexing-its theory and application in science, technology, and humanities. *Ph.D. thesis, University of California at Berkeley.Ph.D. thesis, University of California at Berkeley.*

John D. Lafferty, Andrew McCallum, and Fernando C. N. Pereira. 2001. Conditional random fields: Probabilistic models for segmenting and labeling sequence data. In *Proceedings of the Eighteenth International Conference on Machine Learning*, ICML '01, pages 282–289, San Francisco, CA, USA. Morgan Kaufmann Publishers Inc.

J. Richard Landis and Gary G. Koch. 1977. The Measurement of Observer Agreement for Categorical Data. *Biometrics*, 33(1):159–174, March.

Michael H. MacRoberts and Barbara R. MacRoberts. 1984. The negational reference: Or the art of dissembling. *Social Studies of Science*, 14(1):pp. 91–94.

Saif Mohammad, Bonnie Dorr, Melissa Egan, Ahmed Hassan, Pradeep Muthukrishan, Vahed Qazvinian, Dragomir Radev, and David Zajic. 2009. Using citations to generate surveys of scientific paradigms. In *Proceedings of Human Language Technologies: The 2009 Annual Conference of the North American Chapter of the Association for Computational Linguistics*, pages 584–592, Boulder, Colorado, June. Association for Computational Linguistics.

Roser Morante and Eduardo Blanco. 2012. *sem 2012 shared task: resolving the scope and focus of negation. In *Proceedings of the First Joint Conference on Lexical and Computational Semantics - Volume 1: Proceedings of the main conference and the shared task, and Volume 2: Proceedings of the Sixth International Workshop on Semantic Evaluation*, SemEval '12, pages 265–274, Stroudsburg, PA, USA. Association for Computational Linguistics.

M. J. Moravcsik and P. Murugesan. 1975. Some results on the function and quality of citations. *Social Studies of Science*, 5:86–92.

Hidetsugu Nanba and Manabu Okumura. 1999. Towards multi-paper summarization using reference information. In *IJCAI '99: Proceedings of the Six-*

teenth International Joint Conference on Artificial Intelligence, pages 926–931, San Francisco, CA, USA. Morgan Kaufmann Publishers Inc.

Hidetsugu Nanba, Noriko Kando, Manabu Okumura, and Of Information Science. 2000. Classification of research papers using citation links and citation types: Towards automatic review article generation.

Kishore Papineni, Salim Roukos, Todd Ward, and Wei-Jing Zhu. 2002. Bleu: a method for automatic evaluation of machine translation. In *Proceedings of 40th Annual Meeting of the Association for Computational Linguistics*, pages 311–318, Philadelphia, Pennsylvania, USA, July. Association for Computational Linguistics.

Vahed Qazvinian and Dragomir R. Radev. 2008. Scientific paper summarization using citation summary networks. In *Proceedings of the 22nd International Conference on Computational Linguistics (Coling 2008)*, pages 689–696, Manchester, UK, August. Coling 2008 Organizing Committee.

Vahed Qazvinian and Dragomir R. Radev. 2010. Identifying non-explicit citing sentences for citation-based summarization. In *Proceedings of the 48th Annual Meeting of the Association for Computational Linguistics*, pages 555–564, Uppsala, Sweden, July. Association for Computational Linguistics.

Vahed Qazvinian, Dragomir R. Radev, and Arzucan Ozgur. 2010. Citation summarization through keyphrase extraction. In *Proceedings of the 23rd International Conference on Computational Linguistics (Coling 2010)*, pages 895–903, Beijing, China, August. Coling 2010 Organizing Committee.

Vahed Qazvinian, Dragomir R. Radev, Saif Mohammad, Bonnie Dorr, David Zajic, Michael Whidby, and Taesun Moon. 2013. Generating extractive summaries of scientific paradigms. *Journal of Artificial Intelligence Research.*

Randolph Quirk, Sidney Greenbaum, Geoffrey Leech, and Jan Svartvik. 1985. *A Comprehensive Grammar of the English Language*. Longman, London.

Dragomir R. Radev, Pradeep Muthukrishnan, and Vahed Qazvinian. 2009. The acl anthology network corpus. In *NLPIR4DL '09: Proceedings of the 2009 Workshop on Text and Citation Analysis for Scholarly Digital Libraries*, pages 54–61, Morristown, NJ, USA. Association for Computational Linguistics.

Dragomir R. Radev, Pradeep Muthukrishnan, Vahed Qazvinian, and Amjad Abu-Jbara. 2013. The acl anthology network corpus. *Language Resources and Evaluation*, pages 1–26.

Ina Spiegel-Rösing. 1977. Science Studies: Bibliometric and Content Analysis. *Social Studies of Science*, 7(1):97–113, February.

Simone Teufel, Advaith Siddharthan, and Dan Tidhar. 2006. Automatic classification of citation function. In *In Proc. of EMNLP-06.*

GEOFF THOMPSON and YE YIYUN. 1991. Evaluation in the reporting verbs used in academic papers. *Applied Linguistics*, 12(4):365–382.

Melvin Weinstock. 1971. *Citation Indexes.* Encyclopedia of Library and Information Science.

Michael Alan Whidby. 2012. Citation handling: Processing citation text in scientific documents. In *Master Thesis.*

Howard D. White. 2004. Citation analysis and discourse analysis revisited. *Applied Linguistics*, 25(1):89–116.

Theresa Wilson, Paul Hoffmann, Swapna Somasundaran, Jason Kessler, Janyce Wiebe, Yejin Choi, Claire Cardie, Ellen Riloff, and Siddharth Patwardhan. 2005. Opinionfinder: a system for subjectivity analysis. In *Proceedings of HLT/EMNLP on Interactive Demonstrations*, HLT-Demo '05, pages 34–35, Stroudsburg, PA, USA. Association for Computational Linguistics.

J. M. Ziman. 1968. *Public knowledge: An essay concerning the social dimension of science.* Cambridge U.P., London.

Author Index

Association for Computational Linguistics
209 N. Eighth Street
Stroudsburg, Pennsylvania 18360

CURRAN ASSOCIATES INC
proceedings
.com

2013 Conference of the North American Chapter of the Association for Computational Linguistics: Human Language Technologies

(NAACL HLT 2013)

Atlanta, Georgia, USA
9-14 June 2013

Volume 2 of 2

ISBN: 978-1-62748-838-9

Printed from e-media with permission by:

Curran Associates, Inc.
57 Morehouse Lane
Red Hook, NY 12571

Some format issues inherent in the e-media version may also appear in this print version.

Printed by Curran Associates, Inc. (2013)

For permission requests, please contact the Association for Computational Linguistics at the address below.

Association for Computational Linguistics
209 N. Eighth Street
Stroudsburg, Pennsylvania 18360

Phone: 1-570-476-8006
Fax: 1-570-476-0860

acl@aclweb.org

Additional copies of this publication are available from:

Curran Associates, Inc.
57 Morehouse Lane
Red Hook, NY 12571 USA
Phone: 845-758-0400
Fax: 845-758-2634
Email: curran@proceedings.com
Web: www.proceedings.com

NAACL HLT 2013

The 2013 Conference of the North American Chapter of the Association for Computational Linguistics: Human Language Technologies

Proceedings of the Main Conference

9–14 June 2013
Westin Peachtree Plaza Hotel
Atlanta, Georgia

Sponsors

NAACL HLT 2013 gratefully acknowledges the following sponsors for their support.

Gold Level

Google

Microsoft® Research

Bronze Level

ETS® Listening. Learning. Leading.®

Rakuten

Appen ButlerHill

Student Best Paper Award and Student Lunch Sponsor

IBM Research

Student Volunteer Sponsor

AI @ ISI

Conference Bags

SDL Research

General Chair Preface

Welcome everyone!

It is my pleasure to welcome you all to Atlanta, Georgia, for the 2013 NAACL Human Language Technologies conference. This is a great opportunity to reconnect with old friends and make new acquaintances, learn the latest in your own field and become curious about new areas, and also to experience Atlanta's warm southern hospitality. That hospitality starts with Priscilla Rasmussen! Priscilla thinks about everything that we all take for granted: the registration that just took place, the rooms in which we sit, the refreshments that keep us energized, and the social events that make this conference so fun, and many other details that you would miss if they weren't there. Please introduce yourself and say hi. Priscilla is the backbone of the NAACL organization. Thank you!

This conference started a year ago, when Hal Daumé III and Katrin Kirchhoff graciously agreed to be program co-chairs. It is no exaggeration to say how much their dedication has shaped this conference and how grateful I am for their initiative and hard work. Thank you Hal and Katrin, especially for all the fun discussion that made the work light and the year go by fast! This conference could not have happened with you.

Thanks go to the entire organizing committee. As I am writing this to be included in the proceedings, I am grateful for the fantastic detailed and proactive work by Colin Cherry and Matt Post, the publications chairs. The tutorials chairs, Katrin Erk and Jimmy Lin, selected, and solicited, 6 tutorials to present in depth material on some of the diverse topics represented in our community. Chris Dyer and Derrick Higgins considered which projects shine best when shown as a demonstration. The workshops chairs for NAACL, Sujith Ravi and Luke Zettlemoyer, worked jointly with ACL and EMNLP to select the workshops to be held at NAACL. They also worked with ICML 2013 to co-host workshops that bridge the two communities, in addition to the Joint NAACL/ICML symposium.

Posters from the student research workshop are part of the poster and demonstrations session on Monday night. This is a great opportunity for the students to be recognized in the community and to benefit from lively discussion of their presentations (attendees take note!) Annie Louis and Richard Socher are the student research workshop chairs, and Julia Hockenmaier and Eric Ringger generously share their wisdom as the faculty advisors. The student research workshop itself will be held on the first day of workshops. There are so many people who contribute their time to the behind-the-scenes organization of the conference, without which the conference cannot take place. Asking for money is probably not a natural fit for anyone, but Chris Brew worked on local sponsorship, and Dan Bikel and Patrick Pantel worked to obtain sponsorship across the ACL conferences this year - thank you! Jacob Eisenstein had the more fun role of distributing money as the student volunteer coordinator, and we thank all of the student volunteers who will be helping to run a smooth conference. Kristy Boyer kept the communication "short and tweet" using a variety of social media (and old-fashioned media too). An important part of the behind-the-scenes efforts that enable a conference like NAACL to come together are the sponsors. We thank all of the sponsors for the contributions to the conference , both for the general funding made available as well as the specific programs that are funded through sponsorship. You can read more about these sponsors in our conference handbook.

This year there are several initiatives, and if successful, we hope they'll be part of NAACL conferences in the future. One is to make the proceedings available prior to the conference; we hope you will benefit from the extra time to read the papers beforehand. Another is for tutorials and all oral presentations to be recorded on video and made available post-conference. We are also delighted to host presentations, in both oral and poster formats, from the new Transactions of the ACL journal, to enhance the impact these will already have as journal publications. Finally, Matt Post is creating a new digital form of conference handbook to go with our digital age; thanks also go to Alex Clemmer who has prepared the paper copy that you may be reading right now. We hope you use the #NAACL2013 tag when you are tweeting about the conference or papers at the conference; together, we'll be creating a new social media corpus to explore.

Once again, we are pleased to be co-located with *SEM conference, and the SemEval workshop. We are lucky to have ICML 2013 organized so close in time and place. Several researchers who span the two communities have reconvened the Joint NAACL/ICML symposium on June 15, 2013. In addition, two workshops that address areas of interest to both NAACL and ICML members have been organized on June 16th, as part of the ICML conference.

NAACL 2013 has given me a great appreciation for the volunteering that is part of our culture. Besides the organizing committee itself, we are guided by the NAACL executive board, who think about questions with a multi-year perspective. I also want to recognize the members who first initiated and now maintain the ACL Anthology, where all of our published work will be available to all in perpetuity, a fabulous contribution and one that distinguishes our academic community.

Have a fun conference!

Lucy Vanderwende, Microsoft Research
NAACL HLT 2013 General Chair

Program Chair Preface

Welcome to NAACL HLT 2013 in Atlanta, Georgia. We have an exciting program consisting of six tutorials, 24 sessions of talks (both for long and short papers), an insane poster madness session that includes posters from the newly revamped student research workshop, ten workshops and two additional cross-pollination workshops held jointly with ICML (occurring immediately after NAACL HLT, just one block away). There are a few innovations in the conference this year, the most noticeable of which is the twitter channel #naacl2013 and the fact that we are the first conference to host papers published in the Transactions of the ACL journal – there are six such papers in our program, marked as [TACL]. We are very excited about our two invited talks, one on Monday morning and one Wednesday morning. The first is by Gina Kuperberg, who will talk about "Predicting Meaning: What the Brain tells us about the Architecture of Language Comprehension." The second presenter is our own Kathleen KcKeown, who will talk about "Natural Language Applications from Fact to Fiction."

The morning session on Tuesday includes the presentation of best paper awards to two worthy recipients. The award for Best Short Paper goes to Marta Recasens, Marie-Catherine de Marneffe and Christopher Potts for their paper "The Life and Death of Discourse Entities: Identifying Singleton Mentions" The award for Best Student Paper goes to the long paper "Automatic Generation of English Respellings" by Bradley Hauer and Greg Kondrak. We gratefully acknowledge IBM's support for the Student Best Paper Award. Finally, many thanks to the Best Paper Committee for selecting these excellent papers!

The complete program includes 95 long papers (of which six represent presentations from the journal Transactions of the ACL, a first for any ACL conference!) and 51 short papers. We are excited that the conference is able to present such a dynamic array of papers, and would like to thank the authors for their great work. We worked hard to keep the conference to three parallel sessions at any one time to hopefully maximize a participant's ability to see everything she wants! This represents an acceptance rate of 30% for long papers and 37% for short papers. More details about the distribution across areas and other statistics will be made available in the NAACL HLT Program Chair report on the ACL wiki: `http://aclweb.org/adminwiki/index.php?title=Reports`

The review process for the conference was double-blind, and included an author response period for clarifying reviewers' questions. We were very pleased to have the assistance of 350 reviewers, each of whom reviewed an average of 3.7 papers, in deciding the program. We are especially thankful for the reviewers who spent time reading the author responses and engaging other reviewers in the discussion board. Assigning reviewers would not have been possible without the hard work of Mark Dredze and his miracle assignment scripts. Furthermore, constructing the program would not have been possible without 22 excellent area chairs forming the Senior Program Committee: Eugene Agichtein, Srinivas Bangalore, David Bean, Phil Blunsom, Jordan Boyd-Graber, Marine Carpuat, Joyce Chai, Vera Demberg, Bill Dolan, Doug Downey, Mark Dredze, Markus Dreyer, Sanda Harabagiu, James Henderson, Guy Lapalme, Alon Lavie, Percy Liang, Johanna Moore, Ani Nenkova, Joakim Nivre, Bo Pang, Zak Shafran, David Traum, Peter Turney, and Theresa Wilson. Area chairs were responsible for managing paper assignments, collating reviewer responses, handling papers for other area chairs or program chairs who had conflicts of interest, making recommendations for paper acceptance or rejection, and nominating best papers from their areas. We are very grateful for the time and energy that they have put into the program.

There are a number of other people that we interacted with who deserve a hearty thanks for the success of the program. Rich Gerber and the START team at Softconf have been invaluable for helping us with the mechanics of the reviewing process. Matt Post and Colin Cherry, as publications co-chairs, have been very helpful in assembling the final program and coordinating the publications of the workshop proceedings. There are several crucial parts of the overall program that were the responsibility of various contributors, including Annie Louis, Richard Socher, Julia Hockenmaier and Eric Ringger (Student Research Workshop chairs, who did an amazing job revamping the SRW); Jimmy Lin and Katrin Erk (Tutorial Chairs); Luke Zettlemoyer and Sujith Ravi (Workshop Chairs); Chris Dyer and Derrick Higgins (Demo Chairs); Jacob Eisenstein (Student Volunteer Coordinator); Chris Brew (Local Sponsorship Chair); Patrick Pantel and Dan Bikel (Sponsorship Chairs); and the new-founded Publicity chair who handled #naacl2013 tweeting among other things, Kristy Boyer.

We would also like to thank Chris Callison-Burch and the NAACL Executive Board for guidance during the process. Michael Collins was amazingly helpful in getting the inaugural TACL papers into the NAACL HLT conference. Priscilla Rasmussen deserves, as always, special mention and warmest thanks as the local arrangements chair and general business manager. Priscilla is amazing and everyone who sees her at the conference should thank her.

Finally, we would like to thank our General Chair, Lucy Vanderwende, for both her trust and guidance during this process. She helped turn the less-than-wonderful parts of this job to roses, and her ability to organize an incredibly complex event is awe inspiring. None of this would have happened without her.

We hope that you enjoy the conference!

Hal Daumé III, University of Maryland
Katrin Kirchhoff, University of Washington

Organizing Committee

General Conference Chair

Lucy Vanderwende, Microsoft Research

Program Committee Chairs

Hal Daumé III, University of Maryland
Katrin Kirchhoff, University of Washington

Local Arrangements

Priscilla Rassmussen

Workshop Chairs

Luke Zettlemoyer, University of Washington
Sujith Ravi, Google

Tutorial Chairs

Jimmy Lin, University of Maryland
Katrin Erk, University of Texas at Austin

Student Research Workshop

Chairs:
  Annie Louis, University of Pennsylvania
  Richard Socher, Stanford University
Faculty Advisors:
  Julia Hockenmaier, University of Illinois at Urbana-Champaign
  Eric Ringger, Brigham Young University

Student Volunteer Coordinator

Jacob Eisenstein, School of Interactive Computing, Georgia Tech

Demonstrations Chairs

Chris Dyer, Carnegie Mellon University
Derrick Higgins, Educational Testing Service

Local Sponsorship Chair

Chris Brew, Educational Testing Service

NAACL Sponsorship Chairs

Patrick Pantel, Microsoft Research
Dan Bikel, Google

Publications Chairs

Matt Post, Johns Hopkins University
Colin Cherry, National Research Council, Canada

Publicity Chair

Kristy Boyer, North Carolina State University

Program Committee

Program Committee Chairs

Hal Daumé III, University of Maryland
Katrin Kirchhoff, University of Washington

Area Chairs

Phonology and Morphology, Word Segmentation
Markus Dreyer (SDL Language Weaver)
Syntax, Tagging, Chunking and Parsing
Joakim Nivre (Uppsala University)
James Henderson (Université de Genève)
Semantics
Percy Liang (Stanford University)
Peter Turney (National Research Council of Canada)
Multimodal NLP
Srinivas Bangalore (AT&T)
Discourse, Dialogue, Pragmatics
David Traum (Institute for Creative Technologies)
Joyce Chai (Michigan State University)
Linguistic Aspects of CL
Vera Demberg (Saarland University)
Summarization
Guy Lapalme (Université de Montréal)
Generation
Johanna Moore (University of Edinburgh)
ML for Language Processing
Phil Blunsom (University of Oxford)
Mark Dredze (Johns Hopkins University)

Machine Translation
Alon Lavie (Carnegie Mellon University)
Marine Carpuat (National Research Council of Canada)
Information Retrieval and QA
Eugene Agichtein (Emory University)
Information Extraction
Doug Downey (Northwestern University)
Sanda Harabagiu (University of Texas at Dallas)
Spoken Language Processing
Zak Shafran (Oregon Health and Science University)
Sentiment Analysis and Opinion Mining
Bo Pang (Cornell University)
Theresa Wilson (Johns Hopkins University)
NLP-enabled Technology
David Bean (TDW)
Document Categorization and Topic Clustering
Jordan Boyd-Graber (University of Maryland)
Social Media Analysis and Processing
Bill Dolan (Microsoft Research)
Language Resources and Evaluation Methods
Ani Nenkova (University of Pennsylvania)

Primary Reviewers

Ahmed Abbasi
Mikhail Ageev
Eneko Agirre
Gregory Aist
Jan Alexandersson
Nicholas Andrews
David Andrzejewski
Gabor Angeli
Yoav Artzi
Michael Auli
Michiel Bacchiani
Anton Bakalov
Kirk Baker
Tyler Baldwin
Marco Baroni
Roberto Basili
Beata Beigman Klebanov
Kedar Bellare
Patrice Bellot
Emily M. Bender
Jonathan Berant
Justin Betteridge
Chandra Bhagavatula
Arianna Bisazza
Nathan Bodenstab
Danushka Bollegala
Alexandre Bouchard
Jordan Boyd-Graber
S.R.K. Branavan
Thorsten Brants
Chris Brew
Wray Buntine
David Burkett
Jill Burstein
Aoife Cahill
Chris Callison-Burch
Nicoletta Calzolari
Nicola Cancedda
Sandra Carberry
Claire Cardie
Xavier Carreras
Daniel Cer
Nate Chambers
Ming-Wei Chang
Boxing Chen
Chen Chen
David Chen
Colin Cherry
David Chiang
Yejin Choi
Jennifer Chu-Carroll
Stephen Clark
James Clarke
Martin Cmejrek
Shay Cohen
Trevor Cohn
Kevyn Collins-Thompson
John Conroy
Aron Culotta
James Cussens
Lyne Da Sylva
Ido Dagan
Robert Daland
Bhavana Dalvi
William Darling
Dipanjan Das

Pradipto Das
Eric De La Clergerie
Steve DeNeefe
John DeNero
David DeVault
Michael Denkowski
Jacob Devlin
Laura Dietz
Gregory Druck
Lan Du
Chris Dyer
Koji Eguchi
Vladimir Eidelman
Jacob Eisenstein
Jason Eisner
Ahmad Emami
Andrea Esuli
Anthony Fader
Atefeh Farzindar
Anna Feldman
Radu Florian
George Foster
Jennifer Foster
Mary Ellen Foster
Bob Frank
Dayne Freitag
Michel Galley
Michael Gamon
Sudeep Gandhe
Kavita Ganesan
Claire Gardent
Matt Gardner
Niyu Ge
Matthew Gerber
George Giannakopoulos
Daniel Gildea
Daniel Gillick
Kevin Gimpel
Filip Ginter
Yoav Goldberg
Dan Goldwasser
Sharon Goldwater
Dave Golland
Kyle Gorman
Cyril Goutte
Amit Goyal
Joao Graca
Brigitte Grau
Edward Grefenstette
Justin Grimmer
Carlos Gómez-Rodríguez
Nizar Habash
Barry Haddow
Eva Hajicova
John Hale
David Hall
Keith Hall
Greg Hanneman
Claudia Hauff
Xiaodong He
Kenneth Heafield
James Henderson
John Henderson
Ulf Hermjakob
Derrick Higgins
Graeme Hirst
Anna Hjalmarsson
Hieu Hoang
Julia Hockenmaier
Matthew Hoffman
Kristy Hollingshead
Yuening Hu
Fei Huang
Liang Huang
Minlie Huang
Zhongqiang Huang
Rebecca Hwa
Diana Inkpen
Ann Irvine
Abe Ittycheriah
Jagadeesh Jagarlamudi
Jiarong Jiang
Howard Johnson
Michael Johnston
David Jurgens
Alexander Kain
Pallika Kanani
Anna Kazantseva
Alistair Kennedy
Tracy Holloway King
Brian Kingsbury
Alexandre Klementiev
Philipp Koehn
Rob Koeling
Moshe Koppel
Alexander Kotov
Jayant Krishnamurthy
Sandra Kuebler
Marco Kuhlmann
Jonas Kuhn
Roland Kuhn
Seth Kulick
Shankar Kumar
Oren Kurland
Tom Kwiatkowski
Yoong Keok Lee
Maider Lehr
Alessandro Lenci
Gregor Leusch
Rivka Levitan
Fangtao Li
Mu Li
Shoushan Li
Percy Liang
Jimmy Lin
Xiao Ling
Diane Litman
Ding Liu
Qun Liu
Yang Liu
Adam Lopez
Annie Louis
Xiaofei Lu
Yue Lu
Michael Lucas
Xiaoqiang Luo
Klaus Macherey
Wolfgang Macherey
Nitin Madnani
Suresh Manandhar
Gideon Mann
Lluis Marquez
Erwin Marsi
Andre Martins
Yuval Marton

Sameer Maskey
Yuji Matsumoto
Evgeny Matusov
Arne Mauser
Diana McCarthy
David McClosky
Arul Menezes
Florian Metze
Donald Metzler
Haitao Mi
Rada Mihalcea
Minel Minel
Margaret Mitchell
Yusuke Miyao
Saif Mohammad
Taesun Moon
Robert Moore
Roser Morante
Louis-Philippe Morency
Preslav Nakov
Nava Nava
Roberto Navigli
Mark-Jan Nederhof
Hwee Tou Ng
Vincent Ng
Patrick Nguyen
Viet-An Nguyen
Joakim Nivre
Brendan O'Connor
Stephan Oepen
Miles Osborne
Myle Ott
Karolina Owczarzak
Martha Palmer
Sinno J. Pan
Bo Pang
Rebecca J. Passonneau
Siddharth Patwardhan
Michael Paul
Lisa Pearl
Ted Pedersen
Gerald Penn
Slav Petrov
Thierry Poibeau
Heather Pon-Barry
Hoifung Poon
Andrei Popescu-Belis
Matthew Purver
Chris Quirk
Reinhard Rapp
Roi Reichart
Ehud Reiter
Jason Riesa
Stefan Riezler
Ellen Riloff
Eric Ringger
Alan Ritter
Brian Roark
Antonio Roque
Carolyn Rose
Andrew Rosenberg
Markus Saers
Alicia Sagae
Kenji Sagae
Horacio Saggion
Saurav Sahay
Mark Sammons
Murat Saraclar
Anoop Sarkar
Giorgio Satta
Roser Saurí
Asad Sayeed
David Schlangen
Judith Schlesinger
Lane Schwartz
Holger Schwenk
Hendra Setiawan
Zak Shafran
Libin Shen
Wade Shen
Michel Simard
Sameer Singh
Jason Smith
Nathaniel Smith
Noah A. Smith
Swapna Somasundaran
Lucia Specia
Valentin Spitkovsky
Caroline Sporleder
Vivek Srikumar
Keith Stevens
Mark Stevenson
Matthew Stone
Veselin Stoyanov
Fabian Suchanek
Ang Sun
Mihai Surdeanu
Jun Suzuki
Stan Szpakowicz
Partha Talukdar
Christoph Tillmann
Ivan Titov
Kristina Toutanova
Reut Tsarfaty
Oren Tsur
Benjamin Van Durme
Josef van Genabith
Vincent Vanhoucke
Enrique Vidal
Karthik Visweswariah
Adam Vogel
Stephan Vogel
Xiaojun Wan
Haifeng Wang
Taro Watanabe
Bonnie Webber
David Weir
Michael White
Jan Wiebe
Shuly Wintner
Kristian Woodsend
Bing Xiang
Peng Xu
Hui Yang
Muyun Yang
Yi Yang
Tae Yano
Limin Yao
Mahsa Yarmohammadi
Alexander Yates
Wen-tau Yih
Yisong Yue
Rabih Zbib
Richard Zens
Luke Zettlemoyer

Ke Zhai
Congle Zhang
Lei Zhang
Min Zhang
Shiqi Zhao
Tiejun Zhao
Bowen Zhou
Jun Zhu
Xiaodan Zhu
Chengqing Zong
Geoffrey Zweig

Secondary Reviewers

JH
Karteek Addanki
Neil Ashton
Daniel Blanchard
Hailong Cao
Dave Carter
Glen Coppersmith
Daniel Dahlmeier
David Etter
Paul Felt
Francisco Guzman
Robbie Haertel
Khairun Nisa Hassanali
Kriste Krstovski
Jun Lang
Wang Ling
Hito Matsushita
Hans Moen
Kevin Seppi
Jun Sun
Xavier Tannier
Svitlana Volkova
Haochang Wang
Xinglong Wang
Mo Yu
Feifei Zhai
Bo Zhao
Kai Zhao
Xiaoning Zhu

Table of Contents

Conference Program

Monday, June 10, 2013

8:45–9:00 Welcome to NAACL 2013!

9:00–10:10 Invited talk by Gina Kuperberg – Predicting Meaning: What the Brain tells us about the Architecture of Language Comprehension

10:10–10:40 Break

M1a: Machine Translation

10:40-11:05 *Model With Minimal Translation Units, But Decode With Phrases*
Nadir Durrani, Alexander Fraser and Helmut Schmid

11:05-11:30 *Beyond Left-to-Right: Multiple Decomposition Structures for SMT*
Hui Zhang, Kristina Toutanova, Chris Quirk and Jianfeng Gao

11:30-11:55 *Improved Reordering for Phrase-Based Translation using Sparse Features*
Colin Cherry

11:55-12:20 *Simultaneous Word-Morpheme Alignment for Statistical Machine Translation*
Elif Eyigöz, Daniel Gildea and Kemal Oflazer

M1b: Information Extraction

10:40-11:05 *Multi-faceted Event Recognition with Bootstrapped Dictionaries*
Ruihong Huang and Ellen Riloff

11:05-11:30 *Named Entity Recognition with Bilingual Constraints*
Wanxiang Che, Mengqiu Wang, Christopher D. Manning and Ting Liu

11:30-11:55 *Minimally Supervised Method for Multilingual Paraphrase Extraction from Definition Sentences on the Web*
Yulan Yan, Chikara Hashimoto, Kentaro Torisawa, Takao Kawai, Jun'ichi Kazama and Stijn De Saeger

11:55-12:20 *Relation Extraction with Matrix Factorization and Universal Schemas*
Sebastian Riedel, Limin Yao, Andrew McCallum and Benjamin M. Marlin

Monday, June 10, 2013 (continued)

M1c: Cognitive and Psycholinguistics

10:40-11:05 *Extracting the Native Language Signal for Second Language Acquisition*
Ben Swanson and Eugene Charniak

11:05-11:30 *An Analysis of Frequency- and Memory-Based Processing Costs*
Marten van Schijndel and William Schuler

11:30-11:55 *Cross-Lingual Semantic Similarity of Words as the Similarity of Their Semantic Word Responses*
Ivan Vulić and Marie-Francine Moens

11:55-12:20 *Combining multiple information types in Bayesian word segmentation*
Gabriel Doyle and Roger Levy

12:20–2:00 Lunch

M2a: Parsing and Syntax

2:00-2:25 *Training Parsers on Incompatible Treebanks*
Richard Johansson

2:25-2:50 *Learning a Part-of-Speech Tagger from Two Hours of Annotation*
Dan Garrette and Jason Baldridge

2:50-3:15 *Experiments with Spectral Learning of Latent-Variable PCFGs*
Shay B. Cohen, Karl Stratos, Michael Collins, Dean P. Foster and Lyle Ungar

Monday, June 10, 2013 (continued)

M2b: Topic Modeling and Text Mining

M2c: Spoken Language Processing

Monday, June 10, 2013 (continued)

Measuring Term Informativeness in Context
Zhaohui Wu and C. Lee Giles

Unsupervised Learning Summarization Templates from Concise Summaries
Horacio Saggion

Classification of South African languages using text and acoustic based methods: A case of six selected languages
Peleira Nicholas Zulu

Improving Syntax-Augmented Machine Translation by Coarsening the Label Set
Greg Hanneman and Alon Lavie

Keyphrase Extraction for N-best Reranking in Multi-Sentence Compression
Florian Boudin and Emmanuel Morin

Development of a Persian Syntactic Dependency Treebank
Mohammad Sadegh Rasooli, Manouchehr Kouhestani and Amirsaeid Moloodi

Improving reordering performance using higher order and structural features
Mitesh M. Khapra, Ananthakrishnan Ramanathan and Karthik Visweswariah

Massively Parallel Suffix Array Queries and On-Demand Phrase Extraction for Statistical Machine Translation Using GPUs
Hua He, Jimmy Lin and Adam Lopez

Discriminative Training of 150 Million Translation Parameters and Its Application to Pruning
Hendra Setiawan and Bowen Zhou

Applying Pairwise Ranked Optimisation to Improve the Interpolation of Translation Models
Barry Haddow

Dialectal Arabic to English Machine Translation: Pivoting through Modern Standard Arabic
Wael Salloum and Nizar Habash

What to do about bad language on the internet
Jacob Eisenstein

Monday, June 10, 2013 (continued)

Embracing Ambiguity: A Comparison of Annotation Methodologies for Crowdsourcing Word Sense Labels
David Jurgens

Compound Embedding Features for Semi-supervised Learning
Mo Yu, Tiejun Zhao, Daxiang Dong, Hao Tian and Dianhai Yu

On Quality Ratings for Spoken Dialogue Systems – Experts vs. Users
Stefan Ultes, Alexander Schmitt and Wolfgang Minker

Overcoming the Memory Bottleneck in Distributed Training of Latent Variable Models of Text
Yi Yang, Alexander Yates and Doug Downey

Processing Spontaneous Orthography
Ramy Eskander, Nizar Habash, Owen Rambow and Nadi Tomeh

Purpose and Polarity of Citation: Towards NLP-based Bibliometrics
Amjad Abu-Jbara, Jefferson Ezra and Dragomir Radev

Estimating effect size across datasets
Anders Søgaard

Systematic Comparison of Professional and Crowdsourced Reference Translations for Machine Translation
Rabih Zbib, Gretchen Markiewicz, Spyros Matsoukas, Richard Schwartz and John Makhoul

Down-stream effects of tree-to-dependency conversions
Jakob Elming, Anders Johannsen, Sigrid Klerke, Emanuele Lapponi, Hector Martinez Alonso and Anders Søgaard

6:00–6:30 Break

6:30–8:30 Poster and Demonstrations Session

Tuesday, June 11, 2013

9:15–9:25	Best paper awards
	Best Short Paper
9:25–9:45	*The Life and Death of Discourse Entities: Identifying Singleton Mentions* Marta Recasens, Marie-Catherine de Marneffe and Christopher Potts
	IBM Best Student Paper
9:45–10:15	*Automatic Generation of English Respellings* Bradley Hauer and Grzegorz Kondrak
10:15–10:45	Break
	T1a: Machine Translation and Multilinguality
10:45-11:00	*A Simple, Fast, and Effective Reparameterization of IBM Model 2* Chris Dyer, Victor Chahuneau and Noah A. Smith
11:00-11:15	*Phrase Training Based Adaptation for Statistical Machine Translation* Saab Mansour and Hermann Ney
11:15-11:30	*Translation Acquisition Using Synonym Sets* Daniel Andrade, Masaki Tsuchida, Takashi Onishi and Kai Ishikawa
11:30-11:45	*Supersense Tagging for Arabic: the MT-in-the-Middle Attack* Nathan Schneider, Behrang Mohit, Chris Dyer, Kemal Oflazer and Noah A. Smith
11:45-12:00	*Zipfian corruptions for robust POS tagging* Anders Søgaard

Tuesday, June 11, 2013 (continued)

T1b: Sentiment Analysis and Topic Modeling

10:45-11:00 *A Multi-Dimensional Bayesian Approach to Lexical Style*
Julian Brooke and Graeme Hirst

11:00-11:15 *Unsupervised Domain Tuning to Improve Word Sense Disambiguation*
Judita Preiss and Mark Stevenson

11:15-11:30 *What's in a Domain? Multi-Domain Learning for Multi-Attribute Data*
Mahesh Joshi, Mark Dredze, William W. Cohen and Carolyn P. Rosé

11:30-11:45 *An opinion about opinions about opinions: subjectivity and the aggregate reader*
Asad Sayeed

11:45-12:00 *An Examination of Regret in Bullying Tweets*
Jun-Ming Xu, Benjamin Burchfiel, Xiaojin Zhu and Amy Bellmore

T1c: Spoken Language Processing

10:45-11:00 *A Cross-language Study on Automatic Speech Disfluency Detection*
Wen Wang, Andreas Stolcke, Jiahong Yuan and Mark Liberman

11:00-11:15 *Distributional semantic models for the evaluation of disordered language*
Masoud Rouhizadeh, Emily Prud'hommeaux, Brian Roark and Jan van Santen

11:15-11:30 *Atypical Prosodic Structure as an Indicator of Reading Level and Text Difficulty*
Julie Medero and Mari Ostendorf

11:30-11:45 *Using Document Summarization Techniques for Speech Data Subset Selection*
Kai Wei, Yuzong Liu, Katrin Kirchhoff and Jeff Bilmes

11:45-12:00 *Semi-Supervised Discriminative Language Modeling with Out-of-Domain Text Data*
Arda Çelebi and Murat Saraçlar

12:00–2:00 Lunch (and Business Meeting 1-2)

Tuesday, June 11, 2013 (continued)

T2c: Discourse and Dialog

2:00-2:15 *Differences in User Responses to a Wizard-of-Oz versus Automated System*
Jesse Thomason and Diane Litman

2:15-2:30 *Improving the Quality of Minority Class Identification in Dialog Act Tagging*
Adinoyi Omuya, Vinodkumar Prabhakaran and Owen Rambow

2:30-2:45 *Discourse Connectors for Latent Subjectivity in Sentiment Analysis*
Rakshit Trivedi and Jacob Eisenstein

2:45-3:00 *Coherence Modeling for the Automated Assessment of Spontaneous Spoken Responses*
Xinhao Wang, Keelan Evanini and Klaus Zechner

3:00-3:15 *Disfluency Detection Using Multi-step Stacked Learning*
Xian Qian and Yang Liu

3:15–3:45 Break

T3a: Semantics

4:10-4:35 *Using Semantic Unification to Generate Regular Expressions from Natural Language*
Nate Kushman and Regina Barzilay

4:35-5:00 *Probabilistic Frame Induction*
Jackie Chi Kit Cheung, Hoifung Poon and Lucy Vanderwende

5:00–5:25 *A Quantum-Theoretic Approach to Distributional Semantics*
William Blacoe, Elham Kashefi and Mirella Lapata

T3b: Information Extraction

3:45-4:10 *Answer Extraction as Sequence Tagging with Tree Edit Distance*
Xuchen Yao, Benjamin Van Durme, Chris Callison-Burch and Peter Clark

4:10-4:35 *Open Information Extraction with Tree Kernels*
Ying Xu, Mi-Young Kim, Kevin Quinn, Randy Goebel and Denilson Barbosa

4:35-5:00 *Finding What Matters in Questions*
Xiaoqiang Luo, Hema Raghavan, Vittorio Castelli, Sameer Maskey and Radu Florian

5:00-5:25 *A Just-In-Time Keyword Extraction from Meeting Transcripts*
Hyun-Je Song, Junho Go, Seong-Bae Park and Se-Young Park

T3c: Discourse

3:45-4:10 *Same Referent, Different Words: Unsupervised Mining of Opaque Coreferent Mentions*
Marta Recasens, Matthew Can and Daniel Jurafsky

4:10-4:35 *Global Inference for Bridging Anaphora Resolution*
Yufang Hou, Katja Markert and Michael Strube

4:35-5:00 *Classifying Temporal Relations with Rich Linguistic Knowledge*
Jennifer D'Souza and Vincent Ng

5:00-5:25 *Improved Information Structure Analysis of Scientific Documents Through Discourse and Lexical Constraints*
Yufan Guo, Roi Reichart and Anna Korhonen

7:00–9:30 Banquet

Wednesday, June 12, 2013

9:00–10:10 Invited talk by Kathleen McKeown – Natural Language Applications from Fact to Fiction

10:10–10:40 Break

W1a: Machine Translation

W1b: Semantics

Wednesday, June 12, 2013 (continued)

W1c: Social Media Processing

10:40-11:05 *Broadly Improving User Classification via Communication-Based Name and Location Clustering on Twitter*
Shane Bergsma, Mark Dredze, Benjamin Van Durme, Theresa Wilson and David Yarowsky

11:05-11:30 *To Link or Not to Link? A Study on End-to-End Tweet Entity Linking*
Stephen Guo, Ming-Wei Chang and Emre Kiciman

11:30-11:55 *A Latent Variable Model for Viewpoint Discovery from Threaded Forum Posts*
Minghui Qiu and Jing Jiang

11:55-12:20 *Identifying Intention Posts in Discussion Forums*
Zhiyuan Chen, Bing Liu, Meichun Hsu, Malu Castellanos and Riddhiman Ghosh

12:20–2:00 Lunch

W2a: Parsing and Syntax

2:25-2:50 *Dependency-based empty category detection via phrase structure trees*
Nianwen Xue and Yaqin Yang

2:50-3:15 *Target Language Adaptation of Discriminative Transfer Parsers*
Oscar Täckström, Ryan McDonald and Joakim Nivre

W2b: Dialog

2:00-2:25 *Emergence of Gricean Maxims from Multi-Agent Decision Theory*
Adam Vogel, Max Bodoia, Christopher Potts and Daniel Jurafsky

2:25-2:50 *Open Dialogue Management for Relational Databases*
Ben Hixon and Rebecca J. Passonneau

2:50-3:15 *A method for the approximation of incremental understanding of explicit utterance meaning using predictive models in finite domains*
David DeVault and David Traum

Wednesday, June 12, 2013 (continued)

W2c: Annotation and Language Resources

2:00-2:25 *Paving the Way to a Large-scale Pseudosense-annotated Dataset*
Mohammad Taher Pilehvar and Roberto Navigli

2:25-2:50 *Labeling the Languages of Words in Mixed-Language Documents using Weakly Supervised Methods*
Ben King and Steven Abney

2:50-3:15 *Learning Whom to Trust with MACE*
Dirk Hovy, Taylor Berg-Kirkpatrick, Ashish Vaswani and Eduard Hovy

3:15–3:45 Break

W3a: Semantics and Syntax

3:45-4:10 *Supervised All-Words Lexical Substitution using Delexicalized Features*
György Szarvas, Chris Biemann and Iryna Gurevych

4:10-4:35 *A Tensor-based Factorization Model of Semantic Compositionality*
Tim Van de Cruys, Thierry Poibeau and Anna Korhonen

W3b: Summarization and Generation

3:45-4:10 *A Participant-based Approach for Event Summarization Using Twitter Streams*
Chao Shen, Fei Liu, Fuliang Weng and Tao Li

4:10-4:35 *Towards Coherent Multi-Document Summarization*
Janara Christensen, Mausam, Stephen Soderland and Oren Etzioni

4:35-5:00 *Generating Expressions that Refer to Visible Objects*
Margaret Mitchell, Kees van Deemter and Ehud Reiter

Estimating effect size across datasets

Anders Søgaard
Center for Language Technology
University of Copenhagen
soegaard@hum.ku.dk

Abstract

Most NLP tools are applied to text that is different from the kind of text they were evaluated on. Common evaluation practice prescribes significance testing across data points in available test data, but typically we only have a single test sample. This short paper argues that in order to assess the robustness of NLP tools we need to evaluate them on diverse samples, and we consider the problem of finding the most appropriate way to estimate the true effect size across datasets of our systems over their baselines. We apply *meta-analysis* and show experimentally – by comparing estimated error reduction over observed error reduction on held-out datasets – that this method is significantly more predictive of success than the usual practice of using macro- or micro-averages. Finally, we present a new parametric meta-analysis based on non-standard assumptions that seems superior to standard parametric meta-analysis.

1 Introduction

NLP tools and online services such as the Stanford Parser or Google Translate are used for a wide variety of purposes and therefore also on very different kinds of data. Some use the Stanford Parser to parse literature (van Cranenburgh, 2012), while others use it for processing social media content (Brown, 2011). The parser, however, was not necessarily evaluated on literature or social media content during development. Still, users typically expect reasonable performance on any natural language input. This paper asks what we as developers can do to estimate the effect of a change to our system – not on the labeled test data that happens to be available to us, but on future, still unseen datasets provided by our end users.

The usual practice in NLP is to evaluate a system on a small sample of held-out labeled data. The observed effect size on this sample is then validated by significance testing across data points, testing whether the observed difference in performance means is likely to be due to mere chance. The preferred significance test is probably the non-parametric paired bootstrap (Efron and Tibshirani, 1993; Berg-Kirkpatrick et al., 2012), but many researchers also resort to Student's t-test for dependent means relying on the assumption that their metric scores are normally distributed.

Such significance tests tell us nothing about how likely our change to our system is to lead to improvements on new datasets. The significance tests all rely on the assumption that our datapoints are sampled i.i.d. at random. The significance tests only tell us how likely it is that the observed difference in performance means would change if we sampled a bigger test sample the same way we sampled the one we have available to us right now.

In standard machine learning papers a similar situation arises. If we are developing a new perceptron learning algorithm, for example, we are interested in how likely the new learning algorithm is to perform better than other perceptron learning algorithms *across* datasets, and we may for that reason evaluate it on a large set of repository datasets.

Demsar (2006) presents motivation for using non-parametric methods such as the Wilcoxon signed rank test to estimate significance across datasets. The t-test is based on means, and typically results across datasets are not commensurable. The t-test is also extremely sentitive to outliers. Notice also that typically we do not have enough datasets to do paired bootstrapping (van den Noortgate and Onghena, 2005).

In this paper we will assume that the Wilcoxon signed rank test provides a reasonable estimate of the significance of an observed difference in performance means across datasets, or of the significance of observed error reductions, but note that this still depends on the assumption that datasets are sampled i.i.d. at random. More importantly, a non-parametric test across data sets does not provide an actual estimate of the effect size. Estimating effect size is important, e.g. when there is a trade-off between performance gains and computational efficiency.

In evaluations across datasets in NLP we typically use the macro-average as an estimate of effect size, but in other fields such as psychology or medicine it is more common to use a weighted mean obtained using what is known as the **fixed effects model** or the **random effects model** for meta-analysis.

The experiments reported on in this paper focus on estimating error reduction and show that meta-analysis is generally superior to macro- and micro-average in terms of predicting future error reductions. Parametric meta-analysis, however, overparameterizes the distribution of error reductions, leading to some instability. While meta-analysis is generally superior to macro-average, it is sometimes off by a large margin. We therefore introduce a new parametric meta-analysis that seems better suited to predicting error reductions. In our experiments test set sizes are balanced, so micro-averages will be near-identical to macro-averages.

2 Meta-analysis

Meta-analysis is the statistical analysis of the effect sizes of several studies and is very popular in fields such as psychology or medicine. Meta-analysis has not been applied very often to NLP. In NLP most people work on applying *new* methods to *old* datasets, and meta-analysis is designed to analyze series of studies applying *old* methods to *new* datasets, e.g. running the same experiments on new subjects. However, meta-analysis *is* applicable to experiments with multiple datasets.

In psychology or medicine you often see studies running similar experiments on different samples with very different results. Meta-analysis stems from the observation that if we want to estimate an effect from a large set of studies, the average effect across all the studies will put too much weight on results obtained on small datasets in which you typically see more variance. The most popular approaches to meta-analysis are the fixed effects and the random effects model. The fixed effects model is applicable when you assume a true effect size (estimated by the individual studies). If you cannot make that assumption because the studies may differ in various aspects, leading the within-study estimates to be estimates of slightly different effect sizes, you need to use the random effects model. Both approaches to meta-analysis are parametric and rely on the effect sizes to be normally distributed.

2.1 Fixed effects model

In the fixed effects model we weight the effect sizes $T_1, \ldots, T_M$ – or error reductions, in our case – by the inverse of the variance v_i in the study, i.e. $w_i = \frac{1}{v_i}$. The combined effect size T is then:

$$\hat{T} = \frac{\sum_{i\geq 1}^{M} w_i T_i}{\sum_{i\geq 1}^{M} w_i}$$

The variance of the combined effect is now:

$$v = \frac{1}{\sum_{i\geq 1}^{M} w_i}$$

and the 95% confidence interval is then $\hat{T} \pm 1.96\sqrt{v}$.

2.2 Random effects model

In the random effects model we replace the variance v_i with the variance plus between-studies variance τ^2:

$$\tau^2 = \frac{\sum_{i\geq 1}^{k} w_i T_i^2 - \frac{(\sum_{i\geq 1}^{k} w_i T_i)^2}{\sum_{i\geq 1}^{k} w_i} - df}{\sum_{i\geq 1}^{k} w_i - \frac{\sum_{i\geq 1}^{k} w_i^2}{\sum_{i\geq 1}^{k} w_i}} \quad (1)$$

with $df = N - 1$, except all negative values are replaced by 0.

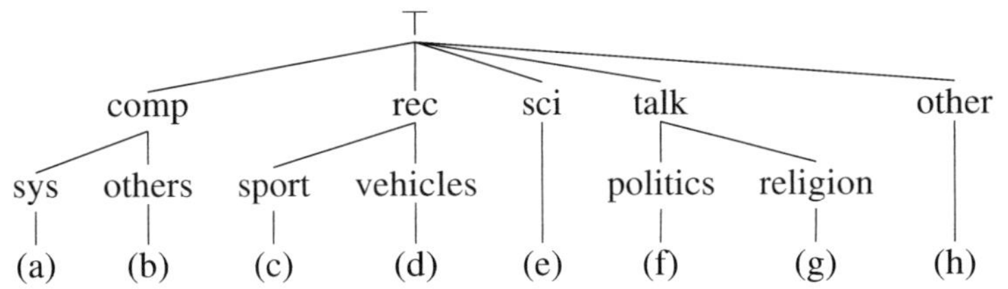

Figure 1: Hierarchical structure of 20 Newsgroups. (a) IBM, MAC, (b) GRAPHICS, MS-WINDOWS, X-WINDOWS, (c) BASEBALL, HOCKEY, (d) AUTOS, MOTORCYCLES, (e) CRYPTOGRAPHY, ELECTRONICS, MEDICINE, SPACE, (f) GUNS, MIDEAST, MISCELLANEOUS, (g) ATHEISM, CHRISTIANITY, MISCELLANEOUS, (h) FORSALE

	macro-av	fixed	random	gumbel
$k = 5$				
err.	-0.1656	**-0.0350**	-0.0428	-0.0400
p-value	-	< 0.001	< 0.001	< 0.001
$k = 10$				
err.	-0.1402	**-0.0329**	-0.0413	-0.0359
p-value	-	< 0.001	< 0.001	< 0.001
$k = 15$				
err.	-0.0809	-0.0799	-0.0804	**-0.0704**
p-value	-	< 0.001	< 0.001	< 0.001

Figure 2: Using macro-average and meta-analysis to predict error reductions on document classification datasets based on k observations. The scores are averages across 20 experiments. The p-values were computed using Wilcoxon signed rank tests.

The random effects model is obviously more conservative in its confidence intervals, and often we will not be able to obtain significance across datasets using a random effects model. If, for example, we apply a fixed effects model to test whether Bernoulli naive Bayes (NB) fairs better than a perceptron (P) model on 25 randomly extracted cross-domain document classification problem instances from the 20 Newsgroups dataset (see Sect. 4), the 95% confidence interval is $[3.9\%, 5.2\%]$. The weighted mean is 4.6% (macro-average 3.9%). Using a random effects model on the same 25 datasets, the 95% confidence interval becomes $[-6.5\%, 6.6\%]$. The weighted mean estimate is also slighly different from that of a fixed effects model. The first question we ask is which of these models provides the best estimate of effect size as observed on future datasets?

2.3 The error reductions distribution

Both the fixed effects and the random effects model assume that effect sizes are normally distributed. We can apply Darling-Anderson tests to test whether error reductions in 20 Newsgroups are in fact normally distributed. Even a small sample of ten 20 Newsgroups datasets provides enough evidence to reject the hypothesis that error reductions (of NB over P) are normally distributed. The Darling-Anderson tests consistently tell us that the chance that our sample distribtutions of error reductions are normally distributed is below 1%. The over-paramaterization means that the estimates we get are unstable. While both models are superior to macro-average estimates, they may provide 'far-off' estimates.

Using Darling-Anderson tests we could also reject the hypothesis that error reductions were logistically distributed, but we did not find evidence for rejecting the hypothesis that error reductions are Gumbel-distributed.[1] Gumbel distributions are used to model error distributions in the latent variable formulation of multinomial logit regression. A parametric meta-analysis model based on the assumption that error reductions are Gumbel distributed is an interesting alternative to non-parametric meta-analysis (Hedges and Olkin, 1984; van den Noortgate and Onghena, 2005), since there seems to be little consensus in the literature about the best way to approach non-parametric meta-analysis.

Gumbel distributions take the following form:

$$\frac{1}{\beta}e^{z-e^{-z}}$$

where $z = \frac{x-\alpha}{\beta}$ with α the location, and β the scale. We fit a Gumbel distribution to our weighted error reductions ($w_i T_i$) and compute the combined

[1] Abidin et al. (2012) has shown that Darling-Anderson is superior to other goodness-of-fit tests for Gumbel distributions.

	macro-av	fixed	random	gumbel
$k = 5$				
err.	0.0531	0.0525	0.0526	**0.0489**
p-value	-	~ 0.98	~ 0.98	~ 0.79
$k = 7$				
err.	0.0928	**0.0852**	**0.0852**	0.0858
p-value	-	< 0.001	< 0.001	< 0.001
$k = 9$				
err.	0.0587	0.05743	0.05743	**0.0532**
p-value	-	~ 0.68	~ 0.68	~ 0.13

Figure 3: Using macro-average and meta-analysis to predict error reductions in cross-lingual dependency parsing. See text for details.

effect

$$\hat{T} = \frac{\alpha + 0.57721\beta}{\frac{1}{M}\sum_{i\geq 1}^{M} w_i}$$

where 0.57721 is the Euler-Mascheroni constant, and the variance of the combined effect $v = \frac{\pi^2}{6}\beta^2$.

3 Experiments in document classification and dependency parsing

Our first experiment makes use of the 20 Newsgroups document classification dataset.[2] The topics in 20 Newsgroups are hierarchically structured, which enables us to extract a large set of binary classification problems with considerable bias between source and target data (Chen et al., 2009; Sun et al., 2011). See the hierarchy in Figure 1. We extract 20 high-level binary classification problems by considering all pairs of top-level categories, e.g. COMPUTERS-RECREATIVE (comp-rec). For each of these 20 problems, we have different possible datasets, e.g. IBM-BASEBALL, MAC-MOTORCYCLES, etc. A *problem instance* takes training and test data from two *different* datasets belong to the same high-level problem. For example a problem instance could be learning to distinguish articles about Macintosh and motorcycles MAC-MOTORCYCLES (evaluated on the 20 Newsgroups test section) using labeled data from IBM-BASEBALL (the training section). In total we have 288 available problem instances in the 20 Newsgroups dataset.

In our first experiment we are interested in predicting the error reductions of a naive Bayes learner over a perceptron model. We use publicly available implementations with default parameters.[3] In each experiment we randomly select k datasets and estimate the true effect size using macro-average, a fixed effects model, a random effects model, and a corrected random effects model. In order to estimate the within-study variance we take 50 paired bootstrap samples of the system outputs. We evaluate our estimates against the observed average effect across 5 new randomly extracted datasets. For each k we repeat the experiment 20 times and report average error. We vary k to see how many observations are needed for our estimates to be reliable.

The results are presented in Figure 2. We note that meta-analysis provides much better estimates than macro-averages across the board. Our parametric meta-analysis based on the assumption that error reductions are Gumbel distributed performs best with more observations.

Our second experiment repeats the same procedure using available data from cross-lingual dependency parsing. We use the submitted results by participants in the CoNLL-X shared task (Buchholz and Marsi, 2006) and try to predict the error reduction of one system over another given k many observations. Given that we only have 12 submissions per system we use $k \in \{5, 7, 9\}$ randomly extracted datasets for observations and test on another five randomly extracted datasets. While results (Figure 3) are only statistically significant with $k = 7$, we see that meta-analysis estimates effect size across data sets better than macro-average in all cases.

4 Conclusions

We have argued that evaluation across datasets is important for developing robust NLP tools, and that meta-analysis can provide better estimates of effect size across datasets than macro-average. We also noted that parametric meta-analysis over-parameterizes error reduction distributions and suggested a new parametric method for estimating effect size across datasets.

Acknowledgements

Anders Søgaard is funded by the ERC Starting Grant LOWLANDS No. 313695.

[2] http://people.csail.mit.edu/jrennie/20Newsgroups/

[3] http://scikit-learn.org/stable/

References

Nahdiya Abidin, Mohd Adam, and Habshah Midi. 2012. The goodness-of-fit test for Gumbel distribution: a comparative study. *MATEMATIKA*, 28(1):35–48.

Taylor Berg-Kirkpatrick, David Burkett, and Dan Klein. 2012. An empirical investigation of statistical significance in nlp. In *EMNLP*.

Gregory Brown. 2011. An error analysis of relation extraction in social media documents. In *ACL*.

Sabine Buchholz and Erwin Marsi. 2006. CoNLL-X Shared Task on Multilingual Dependency Parsing. In *CoNLL*.

Bo Chen, Wai Lam, Ivor Tsang, and Tak-Lam Wong. 2009. Extracting discriminative concepts for domain adaptation in text mining. In *KDD*.

Janez Demsar. 2006. Statistical comparisons of classifiers over multiple data sets. *Journal of Machine Learning Research*, 7:1–30.

Bradley Efron and Robert Tibshirani. 1993. *An introduction to the bootstrap*. Chapman & Hall, Boca Raton, FL.

Larry Hedges and Ingram Olkin. 1984. Nonparametric estimators of effect size in meta-analysis. *Psychological Bulletin*, 96:573–580.

Qian Sun, Rita Chattopadhyay, Sethuraman Panchanathan, and Jieping Ye. 2011. Two-stage weighting framework for multi-source domain adaptation. In *NIPS*.

Andreas van Cranenburgh. 2012. Literary authorship attribution with phrase-structure fragments. In *Workshop on Computational Linguistics for Literature, NAACL*.

Wim van den Noortgate and Patrick Onghena. 2005. Parametric and nonparametric bootstrap methods for meta-analysis. *Behavior Research Methods*, 37:11–22.

Systematic Comparison of Professional and Crowdsourced Reference Translations for Machine Translation

Rabih Zbib, Gretchen Markiewicz, Spyros Matsoukas, Richard Schwartz, John Makhoul
Raytheon BBN Technologies
Cambridge, MA 02138, USA
{rzbib,gmarkiew,smatsouk,schwartz,makhoul}@bbn.com

Abstract

We present a systematic study of the effect of crowdsourced translations on Machine Translation performance. We compare Machine Translation systems trained on the same data but with translations obtained using Amazon's Mechanical Turk vs. professional translations, and show that the same performance is obtained from Mechanical Turk translations at 1/5th the cost. We also show that adding a Mechanical Turk reference translation of the development set improves parameter tuning and output evaluation.

1 Introduction

Online crowdsourcing services have been shown to be a cheap and effective data annotation resource for various Natural Language Processing (NLP) tasks (Callison-Burch and Dredze, 2010; Zaidan and Callison-Burch, 2011a; Zaidan and Callison-Burch, 2011b). The resulting quality of annotations is high enough to be used for training statistical NLP models, with a saving in cost and time of up to an order of magnitude. Statistical Machine Translation (SMT) is one of the NLP tasks that can benefit from crowdsourced annotations. With appropriate quality control mechanisms, reference translations collected by crowdsourcing have been successfully used for training and evaluating SMT systems (Zbib et al., 2012; Zaidan and Callison-Burch, 2011b).

In this work, we used Amazon's Mechanical Turk (MTurk) to obtain alternative reference translations of four Arabic-English parallel corpora previously released by the Linguistic Data Consortium (LDC) for the DARPA BOLT program. This data, totaling over 500K Arabic tokens, was originally collected from web discussion forums and translated professionally to English. We used alternative MTurk translations of the same data to train and evaluation MT systems; and conducted the first systematic study that quantifies the effect of the reference translation process on MT output. We found that:

- Mechanical Turk can be used to translate enough data for training an MT system at 1/10th the price of professional translation, and at a much faster rate.
- Training MT systems on MTurk reference translations gives the same performance as training with professional translations at 20% of the cost.
- A second translation of the development set obtained via MTurk improves parameter tuning and output evaluation.

2 Previous Work

There have been several publications on crowdsourcing data annotation for NLP. Callison-Burch and Dredze (2010) give an overview of the NAACL-2010 Workshop on using Mechanical Turk for data annotation. They describe tasks for which MTurk can be used, and summarize a set of best practices. They also include references to the workshop contributions.

Zaidan and Callison-Burch (2011a) created a monolingual Arabic data set rich in dialectal content from user commentaries on newspaper websites. They hired native Arabic speakers on MTurk to identify the dialect level and used the collected labels to train automatic dialect identification systems. They did not translate the collected data, however. Zaidan and Callison-Burch (2011b) obtained multiple translations of the NIST 2009 Urdu-English evaluation set using MTurk. They trained a statistical model on a set of features to select among the multiple translations. They showed that the MTurk translations selected by their model approached the range of quality of professional translations, and that the selected MTurk translations can be used reliably to score the outputs of different MT systems submitted to the NIST evaluation. Unlike our work, they did not investigate the use of crowdsourced translations for training or parameter tuning. Zbib et al. (2012) trained a Dialectal Arabic to English MT system using Mechanical Turk translations. But the data they translated on MTurk does not have professional translations to conduct the systematic comparison we do in this paper.

It is well known that scoring MT output against multiple references improves MT scores such as BLEU significantly, since it increases the chance of matching *n-grams* between the MT output and the references. Tuning system parameter with multiple references also improves machine translation for the same reason Madnani et al. (2007) and Madnani et al. (2008) showed that tuning on additional references obtained by automatic paraphrasing helps when only few tuning references are available.

3 Data Translation

The data we used are Arabic-English parallel corpora released by the LDC for the DARPA BOLT Phase 1 program[1]. The data was collected from Egyptian online discussion forums, and consists of separate discussion threads, each composed of an initial user posting and multiple reply postings. The data tends to be bimodal: the first posting in the thread is often formal and expressed in Modern Standard Arabic, while the subsequent threads use a less formal style, and contain colloquial Egyptian dialect. The data was manually segmented into sentence units, and translated professionally.

We used non-professional translators hired on MTurk to get second translations. We used several measures to control the quality of translations and detect cheaters. Those include the rendering of Arabic sentences as images, comparing the output to Google Translate and Bing Translator, and other automatic checks. The quality of individual worker's translations was quantified by asking a native Arabic speaker judge to score a sample of the Turker's translations. The translation task unit (aka Human Intelligence Task or HIT) consisted of a sequence of contiguous sentences from a discussion thread amounting to between 40 and 60 words. The instructions were simply to translate the Arabic source fully and accurately, and to take surrounding sentence segments into account to help resolve ambiguities. The HIT rewards were set to 2.5¢ per word.

At the end of the effort, we had 26 different workers translate 567K Arabic tokens in 4 weeks. The resulting translations were less fluent than their professional counterparts, and 10% shorter on average. The following section presents results of MT experiments using the MTurk translations.

4 MT Experiments

The MT system used is based on a string-to-dependency-tree hierarchical model of Shen et al. (2008). Sentence alignment was done using GIZA++ (Och and Ney, 2003). Decoder features include translation probabilities, smoothed lexical probabilities, and a dependency tree language model. Additionally, we used 50,000 sparse, binary-valued source and target features based on Chiang et al. (2009). The English language model was trained on 7 billion words from the LDC Gigaword corpus and from a web crawl. We used expected BLEU maximization (Devlin, 2009) to tune feature weights.

We defined a tuning set (3581 segments, 43.3K tokens) and a test set (4166 segments, 47.7K tokens) using LDC2012E30, the corpus designated as a development set by the LDC, augmented with around 50K Words held out from LDC2012E15 and LDC2012E19, to make a development set large enough to tune the large number of feature weights[2]. The remaining data was used for training. We defined three nested training sets containing 100K, 200K and 400K Arabic tokens respectively, with

[1]Corpora: LDC2012E15, LDC2012E19, LDC2012E55

[2]Only full forum threads were held out

Training	Web-forum Only			Newswire(10MW)+Web-forum			
	100KW	**200KW**	**400KW**	**0KW**	**100KW**	**200KW**	**400KW**
Prof. refs	17.71	20.23	22.61	22.82	24.05	24.85	25.19
MTurk refs	16.41	18.43	20.08	22.82	23.79	24.20	24.51
Two Training refs	19.03	21.19	23.06	22.82	24.26	25.19	25.38
Add'l Training data	-	19.80	21.53	22.82	-	24.31	25.16

Table 1: Comparison of the effect of web forum training data when using professional and MTurk reference translations. All results use professional references for the tuning and test sets.

two versions of each set: one with the professional reference translations for the target, and the other with the same source data, but the MTurk translations. We defined two versions of the test and tuning sets similarly. We report translation results in terms of lower-case BLEU scores (Papineni et al., 2002).

4.1 Training Data References

We first study the effect of training data references, varying the amount of training data and type of translations, while using the same professional translation references for tuning and scoring. The first set of baseline experiments were trained on web forum data only, using professional translations. The first line of Table 1 shows that doubling of the training data adds 2.5 then 2.3 BLEU points. We repeated the experiments, but with MTurk training references, and saw that the scores are lower by 1.3-2.5 BLEU points, depending on the size of training data, and that the gain obtained from doubling the training data decreases to 2.0 and 1.6 BLEU points.

The lower MT scores and slower learning curve of the MTurk systems are both due to the lower quality of the translations, and to the mismatch with the professional development set translations (we discuss this issue further in §4.3). However, by interpolation of the MT scores, we find that the same MT performance can be obtained by using twice the amount of MTurk translated data as professional data. Considering that the MTurk translations is 10 times cheaper than professional translations (2.5¢ versus 25-30¢), this constitutes a cost ratio of 5x.

We repeated the above experiments, but this time added 10 million words of parallel data from the NIST MT 2012 corpora (mostly news) for training. We weighted the web forum part of the training data by a factor of 5. Note from the results in the right half of Table 1 that the newswire data improves the BLEU score by 2.5 to 6.3 BLEU points, depending on the size of the web forum data. This significant improvement is because some of the web forum user postings are formal and written in MSA (§3). More relevant to our aims is the comparison when we vary the web forum training references in the presence of the newswire training. The difference between the MTurk translation systems and the professional translation drops to 0.26-0.68 points. We conclude that in a domain adaptation scenario, where out-of-domain training data (i.e. newswire) already exists, crowdsourced translations for the in-domain (i.e. web forum) training data can be used with little to no loss in MT performance.

4.2 More Data vs. Multiple Translations

To our knowledge no previous work has compared using multiple reference translations for training data versus using additional training data of the same size. We studied this question by using both translations on the target side of the training data. Using the MTurk translations in addition to the professional translations in training gave a gain of 0.4 to 1.3 BLEU points (bottom half of Table 1). The gain was smaller in the presence of the GALE newswire data. When we compared with using the same amount of different training data instead of multiple references, we saw that training on new data with crowdsourced translations is better: training on two translations of 100KW gives 19.03, compared to 19.80 when training on a single translation of 200KW. The advantage of different-source data drops to 0.34 points when we start with 200KW. With a larger initial corpus, the additional source coverage of new data is not as critical, and the advantage of more variety on the target-side of the extracted translation rules becomes more competitive. This coverage is even less critical in the presence of the news data, where the ad-

Training	**Tuning**	**Test**	**Training Data Size**			
			100KW	**200KW**	**400KW**	**400KW(no_lex)**
Prof.	**Prof.**	**Prof.**	17.71	20.23	22.61	20.01
Prof.	**Prof.**	**Prof.+MTurk**	22.53	25.75	28.38	25.42
Prof.	**Prof. (len=0.95)**	**Prof.+MTurk**	23.63	26.84	**29.54**	26.17
Prof.	**Prof.+MTurk**	**Prof.+MTurk**	25.26	28.44	**30.94**	27.22
MTurk	**MTurk**	**MTurk**	16.66	18.47	20.35	17.75
MTurk	**MTurk**	**Prof.+MTurk**	23.83	26.45	28.66	25.44
MTurk	**MTurk (len=1.05)**	**Prof.+MTurk**	23.73	26.19	**28.74**	25.87
MTurk	**Prof.+MTurk**	**Prof.+MTurk**	24.91	27.66	**29.78**	26.45

Table 2: Effect of Tuning and Scoring References on MT.

vantage of new web forum source data disappears (lower-right quadrant of Table 1).

4.3 Development Data References

So far, we have focused on varying training data conditions, and kept the tuning and evaluation conditions fixed. But since we have re-translated the tuning and test sets on MTurk as well, we can study the effect of their reference translations on MT. As Table 2 shows, scoring the MT output using both reference translations, the BLEU scores increase by over 5 points (and more for the MTurk-trained system). This increase by itself is not remarkable. What is important to note is that the gain obtained by doubling the amount of training data is larger when measured using the multiple reference test set. We also ran experiments with 400KW training data, but with the lexical smoothing features (Koehn et al., 2003; Devlin, 2009) turned off. The bigger gains show that improvements in the MT output (from additional training or new features) can be better measured using a second MTurk reference of the test set.

Finally, we study the effect of tuning the system parameters using both translation references. Looking at the system trained on the professional translations, we see a gain of 2.5 to 2.7 BLEU points from adding the MTurk references to the tuning set. But as we mentioned earlier, the MTurk translations are shorter than the professional translations by around 10% on average. Tuning on both references, therefore, shortens the system output by around 5%. To neutralize the effect of length mismatch, we compared to a fairer baseline tuned on the professional references only, but we tuned the output-to-reference length ratio to be 0.95 (thus producing a shorter output). In this case, we see a gain of 1.4 points from adding the MTurk references to the tuning set.

We also used the multiple-reference tuning set to retune the systems trained on MTurk translations. Comparing that to a baseline that is tuned and scored using MTurk references only, we see a gain of around 1%. Note, however, that in this case the length mismach is reversed, and the output of the multiple-reference system is around 5% longer than that of the baseline. If we compare with a baseline that is tuned with a length ratio of 1.05 (to produce a longer output), we see the gain shrink only slightly.

To sum up this section, a second set of reference translations obtained via MTurk makes measurements of improvement on the test set more reliable. Also, a second set of references for tuning improves the output of the MT systems trained on either professional or MTurk references.

5 Conclusion

We compared professional and crowdsourced translations of the same data for training, tuning and scoring Arabic-English SMT systems. We showed that the crowdsourced translations yield the same MT performance as professional translations for as little as 20% of the cost. We also showed that a second crowsourced reference translation of the development set allows for a more accurate evaluation of MT output.

Acknowledgments

This work was supported in part by DARPA/IPTO Contract No. HR0011-12-C-0014 under the BOLT

Program. The views expressed are those of the authors and do not reflect the official policy or position of the Department of Defense or the U.S. Government. Distribution Statement A (Approved for Public Release, Distribution Unlimited).

References

Chris Callison-Burch and Mark Dredze. 2010. Creating speech and language data with Amazon's Mechanical Turk. In *Proceedings of the NAACL HLT 2010 Workshop on Creating Speech and Language Data with Amazon's Mechanical Turk*, pages 1–12, Los Angeles, June.

David Chiang, Kevin Knight, and Wei Wang. 2009. 11,001 new features for statistical machine translation. In *NAACL '09: Proceedings of the 2009 Human Language Technology Conference of the North American Chapter of the Association for Computational Linguistics*, Boulder, Colorado.

Jacob Devlin. 2009. Lexical features for statistical machine translation. Master's thesis, University of Maryland, December.

P. Koehn, F. J. Och, and D. Marcu. 2003. Statistical phrase-based translation. In *Proceedings of the 2003 Human Language Technology Conference of the North American Chapter of the Association for Computational Linguistics*, pages 48–54, Edmonton, Canada.

Nitin Madnani, Necip Fazil, Ayan, Philip Resnik, and Bonnie Dorr. 2007. Using paraphrases for parameter tuning in statistical machine translation. In *Proceedings of the Second Workshop on Statistical Machine Translation*, pages 120–127, Prague, Czech Republic. Association for Computational Linguistics.

Nitin Madnani, Philip Resnik, Bonnie Dorr, and Richard Schwartz. 2008. Are multiple reference translations necessary? investigating the value of paraphrased reference translations in parameter optimization. In *Proceedings of the 8th Conf. of the Association for Machine Translation in the Americas (AMTA 2008)*, Waikiki, Hawaii, USA.

Franz Josef Och and Hermann Ney. 2003. A systematic comparison of various statistical alignment models. *Computational Linguistics*, 29(1):19–51.

Kishore Papineni, Salim Roukos, Todd Ward, and Wei-Jing Zhu. 2002. Bleu: a method for automatic evaluation of machine translation. In *Proceedings of the 40th Annual Meeting of the Association for Computational Linguistics (ACL)*, Philadelphia, PA.

Libin Shen, Jinxi Xu, and Ralph Weischedel. 2008. A new string-to-dependency machine translation algorithm with a target dependency language model. In *Proceedings of the 46th Annual Meeting of the Association for Computational Linguistics (ACL)*, pages 577–585, Columbus, Ohio.

Omar F. Zaidan and Chris Callison-Burch. 2011a. The Arabic online commentary dataset: an annotated dataset of informal Arabic with high dialectal content. In *Proceedings of the 49th Annual Meeting of the Association for Computational Linguistics: Human Language Technologies*, pages 37–41, Portland, Oregon, June.

Omar F. Zaidan and Chris Callison-Burch. 2011b. Crowdsourcing translation: Professional quality from non-professionals. In *Proceedings of the 49th Annual Meeting of the Association for Computational Linguistics: Human Language Technologies*, pages 1220–1229, Portland, Oregon, June.

Rabih Zbib, Erika Malchiodi, Jacob Devlin, David Stallard, Spyros Matsoukas, Richard Schwartz, John Makhoul, Omar F. Zaidan, and Chris Callison-Burch. 2012. Machine translation of arabic dialects. In *The 2012 Conference of the North American Chapter of the Association for Computational Linguistics*, Montreal, June. Association for Computational Linguistics.

Down-stream effects of tree-to-dependency conversions

Jakob Elming, Anders Johannsen, Sigrid Klerke, Emanuele Lapponi[†],
Hector Martinez, Anders Søgaard
Center for Language Technology, University of Copenhagen
[†]Institute for Informatics, University of Oslo

Abstract

Dependency analysis relies on morphosyntactic evidence, as well as semantic evidence. In some cases, however, morphosyntactic evidence seems to be in conflict with semantic evidence. For this reason dependency grammar theories, annotation guidelines and tree-to-dependency conversion schemes often differ in how they analyze various syntactic constructions. Most experiments for which constituent-based treebanks such as the Penn Treebank are converted into dependency treebanks rely blindly on one of four-five widely used tree-to-dependency conversion schemes. This paper evaluates the down-stream effect of choice of conversion scheme, showing that it has dramatic impact on end results.

1 Introduction

Annotation guidelines used in modern dependency treebanks and tree-to-dependency conversion schemes for converting constituent-based treebanks into dependency treebanks are typically based on a specific dependency grammar theory, such as the Prague School's Functional Generative Description, Meaning-Text Theory, or Hudson's Word Grammar. In practice most parsers constrain dependency structures to be tree-like structures such that each word has a single syntactic head, limiting diversity between annotation a bit; but while many dependency treebanks taking this format agree on how to analyze many syntactic constructions, there are still many constructions these treebanks analyze differently. See Figure 1 for a standard overview of clear and more difficult cases.

The difficult cases in Figure 1 are difficult for the following reason. In the easy cases morphosyntactic and semantic evidence cohere. Verbs govern subjects morpho-syntactically and seem semantically more important. In the difficult cases, however, morpho-syntactic evidence is *in conflict* with the semantic evidence. While auxiliary verbs have the same distribution as finite verbs in head position and share morpho-syntactic properties with them, and govern the infinite main verbs, main verbs seem semantically superior, expressing the main predicate. There may be distributional evidence that complementizers head verbs syntactically, but the verbs seem more important from a semantic point of view.

Tree-to-dependency conversion schemes used to convert constituent-based treebanks into dependency-based ones also take different stands on the difficult cases. In this paper we consider four different conversion schemes: the Yamada-Matsumoto conversion scheme **yamada**,[1] the CoNLL 2007 format **conll07**,[2] the conversion scheme **ewt** used in the English Web Treebank (Petrov and McDonald, 2012),[3] and the **lth** conversion scheme (Johansson

[1]The Yamada-Matsumoto scheme can be replicated by running penn2malt.jar available at http://w3.msi.vxu.se/~nivre/research/Penn2Malt.html. We used Malt dependency labels (see website). The Yamada-Matsumoto scheme is an elaboration of the Collins scheme (Collins, 1999), which is not included in our experiments.

[2]The CoNLL 2007 conversion scheme can be obtained by running pennconverter.jar available at http://nlp.cs.lth.se/software/treebank_converter/with the 'conll07' flag set.

[3]The EWT conversion scheme can be replicated using the Stanford converter available at http://nlp.stanford.edu/software/stanford-dependencies.shtml

Clear cases		Difficult cases	
Head	Dependent	?	?
Verb	Subject	Auxiliary	Main verb
Verb	Object	Complementizer	Verb
Noun	Attribute	Coordinator	Conjuncts
Verb	Adverbial	Preposition	Nominal
			Punctuation

Figure 1: Clear and difficult cases in dependency annotation.

and Nugues, 2007).[4] We list the differences in Figure 2. An example of differences in analysis is presented in Figure 3.

In order to access the impact of these conversion schemes on down-stream performance, we need extrinsic rather than intrinsic evaluation. In general it is important to remember that while researchers developing learning algorithms for part-of-speech (POS) tagging and dependency parsing seem obsessed with accuracies, POS sequences or dependency structures have no interest on their own. The accuracies reported in the literature are only interesting insofar they correlate with the usefulness of the structures predicted by our systems. Fortunately, POS sequences and dependency structures *are* useful in many applications. When we consider tree-to-dependency conversion schemes, down-stream evaluation becomes particularly important since some schemes are more fine-grained than others, leading to lower performance as measured by intrinsic evaluation metrics.

Approach in this work

In our experiments below we apply a state-of-the-art parser to five different natural language processing (NLP) tasks where syntactic features are known to be effective: negation resolution, semantic role labeling (SRL), statistical machine translation (SMT), sentence compression and perspective classification. In all five tasks we use the four tree-to-dependency conversion schemes mentioned above and evaluate them in terms of down-stream performance. We also compare our systems to baseline systems not relying on syntactic features, when possible, and to results in the literature, when comparable results exist. Note that negation resolution and SRL are not end applications. It is not easy to generalize across five very different tasks, but the tasks will serve to show that the choice of conversion scheme has significant impact on down-stream performance.

We used the most recent release of the Mate parser first described in Bohnet (2010),[5] trained on Sections 2–21 of the Wall Street Journal section of the English Treebank (Marcus et al., 1993). The graph-based parser is similar to, except much faster, and performs slightly better than the MSTParser (McDonald et al., 2005), which is known to perform well on long-distance dependencies often important for down-stream applications (McDonald and Nivre, 2007; Galley and Manning, 2009; Bender et al., 2011). This choice may of course have an effect on what conversion schemes seem superior (Johansson and Nugues, 2007). Sentence splitting was done using splitta,[6], and the sentences were then tokenized using PTB-style tokenization[7] and tagged using the in-built Mate POS tagger.

Previous work

There has been considerable work on down-stream evaluation of syntactic parsers in the literature, but most previous work has focused on evaluating parsing models rather than linguistic theories. No one has, to the best of our knowledge, compared the impact of choice of tree-to-dependency conversion scheme across several NLP tasks.

Johansson and Nugues (2007) compare the impact of **yamada** and **lth** on semantic role labeling

[4]The LTH conversion scheme can be obtained by running pennconverter.jar available at http://nlp.cs.lth.se/software/treebank_converter/ with the 'oldLTH' flag set.

[5]http://code.google.com/p/mate-tools/

[6]http://code.google.com/p/splitta/

[7]http://www.cis.upenn.edu/~treebank/tokenizer.sed

FORM$_1$	FORM$_2$	**yamada**	**conll07**	**ewt**	**lth**
Auxiliary	Main verb	1	1	2	2
Complementizer	Verb	1	2	2	2
Coordinator	Conjuncts	2	1	2	2
Preposition	Nominal	1	1	1	2

Figure 2: Head decisions in conversions. Note: yamada also differ from CoNLL 2007 in proper names.

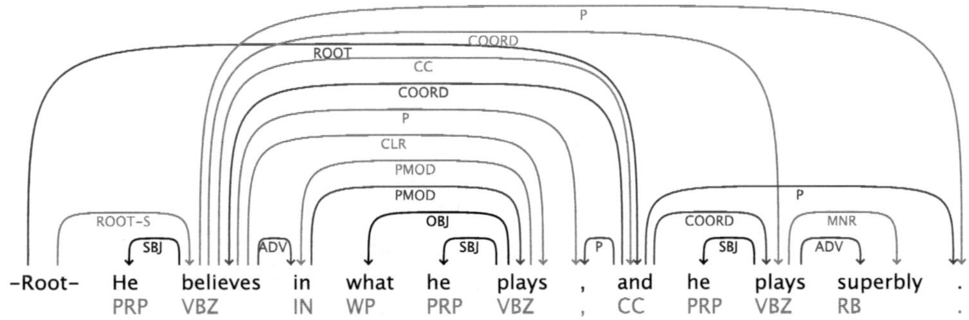

Figure 3: CoNLL 2007 (blue) and LTH (red) dependency conversions.

performance, showing that **lth** leads to superior performance.

Miyao et al. (2008) measure the impact of syntactic parsers in an information extraction system identifying protein-protein interactions in biomedical research articles. They evaluate dependency parsers, constituent-based parsers and deep parsers.

Miwa et al. (2010) evaluate down-stream performance of linguistic representations and parsing models in biomedical event extraction, but do not evaluate linguistic representations directly, evaluating representations and models jointly.

Bender et al. (2011) compare several parsers across linguistic representations on a carefully designed evaluation set of hard, but relatively frequent syntactic constructions. They compare dependency parsers, constituent-based parsers and deep parsers. The authors argue in favor of evaluating parsers on diverse and richly annotated data. Others have discussed various ways of evaluating across annotation guidelines or translating structures to a common format (Schwartz et al., 2011; Tsarfaty et al., 2012).

Hall et al. (2011) discuss optimizing parsers for specific down-stream applications, but consider only a single annotation scheme.

Yuret et al. (2012) present an overview of the SemEval-2010 Evaluation Exercises on Semantic Evaluation track on recognition textual entailment using dependency parsing. They also compare several parsers using the heuristics of the winning system for inference. While the shared task is an example of down-stream evaluation of dependency parsers, the evaluation examples only cover a subset of the textual entailments relevant for practical applications, and the heuristics used in the experiments assume a fixed set of dependency labels (**ewt** labels).

Finally, Schwartz et al. (2012) compare the above conversion schemes and several combinations thereof in terms of learnability. This is very different from what is done here. While learnability may be a theoretically motivated parameter, our results indicate that learnability and downstream performance do not correlate well.

2 Applications

Dependency parsing has proven useful for a wide range of NLP applications, including statistical machine translation (Galley and Manning, 2009; Xu et al., 2009; Elming and Haulrich, 2011) and sentiment analysis (Joshi and Penstein-Rose, 2009; Johansson and Moschitti, 2010). This section describes the applications and experimental set-ups included in this study.

In the five applications considered below we

use syntactic features in slightly different ways. While our statistical machine translation and sentence compression systems use dependency relations as additional information about words and *on a par* with POS, our negation resolution system uses dependency paths, conditioning decisions on both dependency arcs and labels. In perspective classification, we use dependency triples (e.g. SUBJ(John, snore)) as features, while the semantic role labeling system conditions on a lot of information, including the word form of the head, the dependent and the argument candidates, the concatenation of the dependency labels of the predicate, and the labeled dependency relations between predicate and its head, its arguments, dependents or siblings.

2.1 Negation resolution

Negation resolution (NR) is the task of finding negation cues, e.g. the word *not*, and determining their *scope*, i.e. the tokens they affect. NR has recently seen considerable interest in the NLP community (Morante and Sporleder, 2012; Velldal et al., 2012) and was the topic of the 2012 *SEM shared task (Morante and Blanco, 2012).

The data set used in this work, the Conan Doyle corpus (CD),[8] was released in conjunction with the *SEM shared task. The annotations in CD extend on cues and scopes by introducing annotations for in-scope events that are negated in factual contexts. The following is an example from the corpus showing the annotations for cues (bold), scopes (underlined) and negated events (italicized):

(1) Since we have been so **un***fortunate* as to miss him [. . .]

CD-style scopes can be discontinuous and overlapping. Events are a portion of the scope that is semantically negated, with its truth value reversed by the negation cue.

The NR system used in this work (Lapponi et al., 2012), one of the best performing systems in the *SEM shared task, is a CRF model for scope resolution that relies heavily on features extracted from dependency graphs. The feature model contains token distance, direction, n-grams of word forms, lemmas, POS and combinations thereof, as well as the syntactic features presented in Figure 4. The results in our

[8]http://www.clips.ua.ac.be/sem2012-st-neg/data.html

Syntactic	constituent dependency relation parent head POS grand parent head POS word form+dependency relation POS+dependency relation
Cue-dependent	directed dependency distance bidirectional dependency distance dependency path lexicalized dependency path

Figure 4: Features used to train the conditional random field models

experiments are obtained from configurations that differ only in terms of tree-to-dependency conversions, and are trained on the training set and tested on the development set of CD. Since the negation cue classification component of the system does not rely on dependency features at all, the models are tested using gold cues.

Table 1 shows F_1 scores for scopes, events and full negations, where a true positive correctly assigns both scope tokens and events to the rightful cue. The scores are produced using the evaluation script provided by the *SEM organizers.

2.2 Semantic role labeling

Semantic role labeling (SRL) is the attempt to determine semantic predicates in running text and label their arguments with semantic roles. In our experiments we have reproduced the second best-performing system in the CoNLL 2008 shared task in syntactic and semantic parsing (Johansson and Nugues, 2008).[9]

The English training data for the CoNLL 2008 shared task were obtained from PropBank and NomBank. For licensing reasons, we used OntoNotes 4.0, which includes PropBank, but not NomBank. This means that our system is only trained to classify verbal predicates. We used the Clearparser conversion tool[10] to convert the OntoNotes 4.0 and subsequently supplied syntactic dependency trees using our different conversion schemes. We rely on gold standard argument identification and focus solely on the performance metric semantic labeled F1.

[9]http://nlp.cs.lth.se/software/semantic_parsing:_propbank_nombank_frames

[10]http://code.google.com/p/clearparser/

2.3 Statistical machine translation

The effect of the different conversion schemes was also evaluated on SMT. We used the *reordering by parsing* framework described by Elming and Haulrich (2011). This approach integrates a syntactically informed reordering model into a phrase-based SMT system. The model learns to predict the word order of the translation based on source sentence information such as syntactic dependency relations. Syntax-informed SMT is known to be useful for translating between languages with different word orders (Galley and Manning, 2009; Xu et al., 2009), e.g. English and German.

The baseline SMT system is created as described in the guidelines from the original shared task.[11] Only modifications are that we use truecasing instead of lowercasing and recasing, and allow training sentences of up to 80 words. We used data from the English-German restricted task: ∼3M parallel words of news, ∼46M parallel words of Europarl, and ∼309M words of monolingual Europarl and news. We use newstest2008 for tuning, newstest2009 for development, and newstest2010 for testing. Distortion limit was set to 10, which is also where the baseline system performed best. The phrase table and the lexical reordering model is trained on the union of all parallel data with a max phrase length of 7, and the 5-gram language model is trained on the entire monolingual data set.

We test four different experimental systems that only differ with the baseline in the addition of a syntactically informed reordering model. The baseline system was one of the tied best performing system in the WMT 2011 shared task on this dataset. The four experimental systems have reordering models that are trained on the first 25,000 sentences of the parallel news data that have been parsed with each of the tree-to-dependency conversion schemes. The reordering models condition reordering on the word forms, POS, and syntactic dependency relations of the words to be reordered, as described in Elming and Haulrich (2011). The paper shows that while reordering by parsing leads to significant improvements in standard metrics such as BLEU (Papineni et al., 2002) and METEOR (Lavie and Agarwal, 2007), improvements are more spelled out with human judgements. All SMT results reported below are averages based on 5 MERT runs following Clark et al. (2011).

2.4 Sentence compression

Sentence compression is a restricted form of sentence simplification with numerous usages, including text simplification, summarization and recognizing textual entailment. The most commonly used dataset in the literature is the Ziff-Davis corpus.[12] A widely used baseline for sentence compression experiments is Knight and Marcu (2002), who introduce two models: the noisy-channel model and a decision tree-based model. Both are tree-based methods that find the most likely compressed syntactic tree and outputs the yield of this tree. McDonald et al. (2006) instead use syntactic features to directly find the most likely compressed sentence.

Here we learn a discriminative HMM model (Collins, 2002) of sentence compression using MIRA (Crammer and Singer, 2003), comparable to previously explored models of noun phrase chunking. Our model is thus neither tree-based nor sentence-based. Instead we think of sentence compression as a sequence labeling problem. We compare a model informed by word forms and predicted POS with models also informed by predicted dependency labels. The baseline feature model conditions emission probabilities on word forms and POS using a ± 2 window and combinations thereoff. The augmented syntactic feature model simply adds dependency labels within the same window.

2.5 Perspective classification

Finally, we include a document classification dataset from Lin and Hauptmann (2006).[13] The dataset consists of blog posts posted at bitterlemons.org by Israelis and Palestinians. The bitterlemons.org website is set up to "contribute to mutual understanding through the open exchange of ideas." In the dataset, each blog post is labeled as either Israeli or Palestinian. Our baseline model is just a standard bag-of-words model, and the system adds dependency triplets to the bag-of-words model in a way similar to Joshi and Penstein-Rose (2009). We do not remove stop words, since perspective classification is

[11] http://www.statmt.org/wmt11/translation-task.html

[12] LDC Catalog No.: LDC93T3A.

[13] https://sites.google.com/site/weihaolinatcmu/data

	bl	yamada	conll07	ewt	lth
DEPRELS	-	12	21	47	41
PTB-23 (LAS)	-	**88.99**	88.52	81.36*	87.52
PTB-23 (UAS)	-	90.21	90.12	84.22*	**90.29**
Neg: scope F_1	-	**81.27**	80.43	78.70	79.57
Neg: event F_1	-	76.19	72.90	73.15	**76.24**
Neg: full negation F_1	-	**67.94**	63.24	61.60	64.31
SentComp F_1	68.47	**72.07**	64.29	71.56	71.56
SMT-dev-Meteor	35.80	36.06	36.06	**36.16**	36.08
SMT-test-Meteor	37.25	37.48	37.50	**37.58**	37.51
SMT-dev-BLEU	13.66	**14.14**	14.09	14.04	14.06
SMT-test-BLEU	14.67	15.04	15.04	14.96	**15.11**
SRL-22-gold	-	81.35	83.22	**84.72**	84.01
SRL-23-gold	-	79.09	80.85	80.39	**82.01**
SRL-22-pred	-	74.41	76.22	**78.29**	66.32
SRL-23-pred	-	73.42	74.34	**75.80**	64.06
bitterlemons.org	96.08	**97.06**	95.58	96.08	96.57

Table 1: Results. *: Low parsing results on PTB-23 using **ewt** are explained by changes between the PTB-III and the Ontonotes 4.0 release of the English Treebank.

similar to authorship attribution, where stop words are known to be informative. We evaluate performance doing cross-validation over the official training data, setting the parameters of our learning algorithm for each fold doing cross-validation over the actual training data. We used soft-margin support vector machine learning (Cortes and Vapnik, 1995), tuning the kernel (linear or polynomial with degree 3) and $C = \{0.1, 1, 5, 10\}$.

3 Results and discussion

Our results are presented in Table 1. The parsing results are obtained relying on predicted POS rather than, as often done in the dependency parsing literature, relying on gold-standard POS. Note that they comply with the result in Schwartz et al. (2012) that Yamada-Matsumoto-style annotation is more easily learnable.

The **negation resolution** results are significantly better using syntactic features in **yamada** annotation. It is not surprising that a syntactically oriented conversion scheme performs well in this task. Since Lapponi et al. (2012) used Maltparser (Nivre et al., 2007) with the freely available pre-trained parsing model for English,[14] we decided to also run that parser with the gold-standard cues, in addition to Mate. The pre-trained model was trained on Sections 2–21 of the Wall Street Journal section of the English Treebank (Marcus et al., 1993), augmented with 4000 sentences from the QuestionBank,[15] which was converted using the Stanford converter and thus similar to the **ewt** annotations used here. The results were better than using **ewt** with Mate trained on Sections 2–21 alone, but worse than the results obtained here with **yamada** conversion scheme. F_1 score on full negation was 66.92%.

The case-sensitive BLEU evaluation of the **SMT** systems indicates that choice of conversion scheme has no significant impact on overall performance. The difference to the baseline system is significant ($p < 0.01$), showing that the reordering model leads to improvement using any of the schemes. However, the conversion schemes lead to very different translations. This can be seen, for example, by the fact that the relative tree edit distance between translations of different syntactically informed SMT systems is 12% higher than within each system (across different MERT optimizations).

The reordering approach puts a lot of weight on the syntactic dependency relations. As a consequence, the number of relation types used in the conversion schemes proves important. Consider the

[14]http://www.maltparser.org/mco/english_parser/engmalt.html

[15]http://www.computing.dcu.ie/~jjudge/qtreebank/

REFERENCE:	Zum Glück kam ich beim Strassenbahnfahren an die richtige Stelle .
SOURCE:	Luckily , on the way to the tram , I found the right place .
yamada:	Glücklicherweise hat auf dem Weg zur S-Bahn , stellte ich fest , dass der richtige Ort .
conll07:	Glücklicherweise hat auf dem Weg zur S-Bahn , stellte ich fest , dass der richtige Ort .
ewt:	Zum Glück fand ich auf dem Weg zur S-Bahn , am richtigen Platz .
lth:	Zum Glück fand ich auf dem Weg zur S-Bahn , am richtigen Platz .
BASELINE:	Zum Glück hat auf dem Weg zur S-Bahn , ich fand den richtigen Platz .

Figure 5: Examples of SMT output.

ORIGINAL:	* 68000 sweden ab of uppsala , sweden , introduced the teleserve , an integrated answering machine and voice-message handler that links a macintosh to touch-tone phones .
BASELINE:	68000 sweden ab introduced the teleserve an integrated answering machine and voice-message handler .
yamada	68000 sweden ab introduced the teleserve integrated answering machine and voice-message handler .
conll07	68000 sweden ab **sweden** introduced the teleserve integrated answering machine and voice-message handler .
ewt	68000 sweden ab introduced the teleserve integrated answering machine and voice-message handler .
lth	68000 sweden ab introduced the teleserve **an** integrated answering machine and voice-message handler .
HUMAN:	68000 sweden ab introduced the teleserve integrated answering machine and voice-message handler .

Figure 6: Examples of sentence compression output.

example in Figure 5. German requires the verb in second position, which is obeyed in the much better translations produced by the **ewt** and **lth** systems. Interestingly, the four schemes produce virtually identical structures for the source sentence, but they differ in their labeling. Where **conll07** and **yamada** use the same relation for the first two constituents (ADV and vMOD, respectively), **ewt** and **lth** distinguish between them (ADVMOD/PREP and ADV/LOC). This distinction may be what enables the better translation, since the model may learn to move the verb after the sentence adverbial. In the other schemes, sentence adverbials are not distinguished from locational adverbials. Generally, **ewt** and **lth** have more than twice as many relation types as the other schemes.

The schemes **ewt** and **lth** lead to better **SRL** performance than **conll07** and **yamada** when relying on gold-standard syntactic dependency trees. This supports the claims put forward in Johansson and Nugues (2007). These annotations also happen to use a larger set of dependency labels, however, and syntactic structures may be harder to reconstruct, as reflected by labeled attachment scores (LAS) in syntactic parsing. The biggest drop in SRL performance going from gold-standard to predicted syntactic trees is clearly for the **lth** scheme, at an average 17.8% absolute loss (**yamada** 5.8%; **conll07** 6.8%; **ewt** 5.5%; **lth** 17.8%).

The **ewt** scheme resembles **lth** in most respects, but in preposition-noun dependencies it marks the preposition as the head rather than the noun. This is an important difference for SRL, because semantic arguments are often nouns embedded in prepositional phrases, like agents in passive constructions. It may also be that the difference in performance is simply explained by the syntactic analysis of prepositional phrases being easier to reconstruct.

The **sentence compression** results are generally much better than the models proposed in Knight and Marcu (2002). Their noisy channel model obtains an F_1 compression score of 14.58%, whereas the decision tree-based model obtains an F_1 compression score of 31.71%. While F_1 scores should be complemented by human judgements, as there are typically many good sentence compressions of any source sentence, we believe that error reductions of more than 50% indicate that the models used here

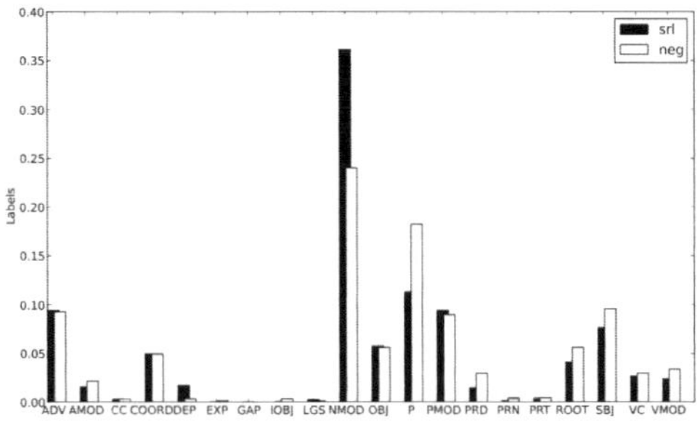

Figure 7: Distributions of dependency labels in the Yamada-Matsumoto scheme

(though previously unexplored in the literature) are fully competitive with state-of-the-art models.

We also see that the models using syntactic features perform better than our baseline model, except for the model using **conll07** dependency annotation. This may be surprising to some, since distributional information is often considered important in sentence compression (Knight and Marcu, 2002). Some output examples are presented in Figure 6. Unsurprisingly, it is seen that the baseline model produces grammatically incorrect output, and that most of our syntactic models correct the error leading to ungrammaticality. The model using **ewt** annotation is an exception. We also see that **conll07** introduces another error. We believe that this is due to the way the **conll07** tree-to-dependency conversion scheme handles coordination. While the word *Sweden* is not coordinated, it occurs in a context, surrounded by commas, that is very similar to coordinated items.

In **perspective classification** we see that syntactic features based on **yamada** and **lth** annotations lead to improvements, with **yamada** leading to slightly better results than **lth**. The fact that a syntactically oriented conversion scheme leads to the best results may reflect that perspective classification, like authorship attribution, is less about content than stylistics.

While **lth** seems to lead to the overall best results, we stress the fact that the five tasks considered here are incommensurable. What is more interesting is that, task to task, results are so different. The semantically oriented conversion schemes, **ewt** and **lth**, lead to the best results in SRL, but with a significant drop for **lth** when relying on predicted parses, while the **yamada** scheme is competitive in the other four tasks. This may be because distributional information is more important in these tasks than in SRL.

The distribution of dependency labels seems relatively stable across applications, but differences in data may of course also affect the usefulness of different annotations. Note that **conll07** leads to very good results for negation resolution, but bad results for SRL. See Figure 7 for the distribution of labels in the **conll07** conversion scheme on the SRL and negation scope resolution data. Many differences relate to differences in sentence length. The negation resolution data is literary text with shorter sentences, which therefore uses more punctuation and has more root dependencies than newspaper articles. On the other hand we do see very few predicate dependencies in the SRL data. This may affect down-stream results when classifying verbal predicates in SRL. We also note that the number of dependency labels have less impact on results in general than we would have expected. The number of dependency labels and the lack of support for some of them may explain the drop with predicted syntactic parses in our SRL results, but generally we obtain our best results with **yamada** and **lth** annotations, which have 12 and 41 dependency labels, respectively.

4 Conclusions

We evaluated four different tree-to-dependency conversion schemes, putting more or less emphasis on syntactic or semantic evidence, in five down-stream applications, including SMT and negation resolution. Our results show why it is important to be precise about exactly what tree-to-dependency conversion scheme is used. Tools like pennconverter.jar gives us a wide range of options when converting constituent-based treebanks, and even small differences may have significant impact on down-stream performance. The small differences are also important for more linguistic comparisons that also tend to gloss over exactly what conversion scheme is used, e.g. Ivanova et al. (2012).

Acknowledgements

Hector Martinez is funded by the ERC grant CLARA No. 238405, and Anders Søgaard is funded by the ERC Starting Grant LOWLANDS No. 313695.

References

Emily Bender, Dan Flickinger, Stephan Oepen, and Yi Zhang. 2011. Parser evaluation over local and non-local dependencies in a large corpus. In *EMNLP*.

Bernd Bohnet. 2010. Top accuracy and fast dependency parsing is not a contradiction. In *COLING*.

Jonathan H. Clark, Chris Dyer, Alon Lavie, and Noah A. Smith. 2011. Better hypothesis testing for statistical machine translation: controlling for optimizer instability. In *ACL*.

Mike Collins. 1999. *Head-driven statistical models for natural language parsing*. Ph.D. thesis, University of Pennsylvania.

Michael Collins. 2002. Discriminative training methods for Hidden Markov Models. In *EMNLP*.

Corinna Cortes and Vladimir Vapnik. 1995. Support-vector networks. *Machine Learning*, 20(3):273–297.

Koby Crammer and Yoram Singer. 2003. Ultraconservative algorithms for multiclass problems. In *JMLR*.

Jakob Elming and Martin Haulrich. 2011. Reordering by parsing. In *Proceedings of International Workshop on Using Linguistic Information for Hybrid Machine Translation (LIHMT-2011)*.

Michel Galley and Christopher Manning. 2009. Quadratic-time dependency parsing for machine translation. In *ACL*.

Keith Hall, Ryan McDonald, Jason Katz-Brown, and Michael Ringgaard. 2011. Training dependency parsers by jointly optimizing multiple objectives. In *EMNLP*.

Angelina Ivanova, Stephan Oepen, Lilja Øvrelid, and Dan Flickinger. 2012. Who did what to whom? a contrastive study of syntactico-semantic dependencies. In *LAW*.

Richard Johansson and Alessandro Moschitti. 2010. Syntactic and semantic structure for opinion expression detection. In *CoNLL*.

Richard Johansson and Pierre Nugues. 2007. Extended constituent-to-dependency conversion for English. In *NODALIDA*.

Richard Johansson and Pierre Nugues. 2008. Dependency-based syntactic-semantic analysis with propbank and nombank. In *CoNLL*.

Mahesh Joshi and Carolyn Penstein-Rose. 2009. Generalizing dependency features for opinion mining. In *ACL*.

Kevin Knight and Daniel Marcu. 2002. Summarization beyond sentence extraction: a probabilistic approach to sentence compression. *Artificial Intelligence*, 139:91–107.

Emanuele Lapponi, Erik Velldal, Lilja Øvrelid, and Jonathon Read. 2012. UiO2: Sequence-labeling negation using dependency features. In **SEM*.

Alon Lavie and Abhaya Agarwal. 2007. Meteor: an automatic metric for mt evaluation with high levels of correlation with human judgments. In *WMT*.

Wei-Hao Lin and Alexander Hauptmann. 2006. Are these documents written from different perspectives? In *COLING-ACL*.

Mitchell Marcus, Mary Marcinkiewicz, and Beatrice Santorini. 1993. Building a large annotated corpus of English: the Penn Treebank. *Computational Linguistics*, 19(2):313–330.

Ryan McDonald and Joakim Nivre. 2007. Characterizing the errors of data-driven dependency parsers. In *EMNLP-CoNLL*.

Ryan McDonald, Fernando Pereira, Kiril Ribarov, and Jan Hajič. 2005. Non-projective dependency parsing using spanning tree algorithms. In *Proceedings of the Conference on Human Language Technology and Empirical Methods in Natural Language Processing 2005*, pages 523–530, Vancouver, British Columbia.

Ryan McDonald. 2006. Discriminative sentence compression with soft syntactic evidence. In *EACL*.

Makoto Miwa, Sampo Pyysalo, Tadayoshi Hara, and Jun'ichi Tsujii. 2010. Evaluating dependency representation for event extraction. In *COLING*.

Yusuke Miyao, Rune Sæ tre, Kenji Sagae, Takuya Matsuzaki, and Jun'ichi Tsujii. 2008. Task-oriented evaluation of syntactic parsers and their representations. In *ACL*.

Roser Morante and Eduardo Blanco. 2012. *sem 2012 shared task: Resolving the scope and focus of negation. In **SEM*.

Roser Morante and Caroline Sporleder. 2012. Modality and negation: An introduction to the special issue. *Computational linguistics*, 38(2):223–260.

Joakim Nivre, Johan Hall, Jens Nilsson, Atanas Chanev, Gülsen Eryigit, Sandra Kübler, Svetoslav Marinov, and Erwin Marsi. 2007. MaltParser: a language-independent system for data-driven dependency parsing. *Natural Language Engineering*, 13(2):95–135.

Kishore Papineni, Salim Roukos, Todd Ward, and Wei-Jing Zhu. 2002. Bleu: a method for automatic evaluation of machine translation. In *ACL*.

Slav Petrov and Ryan McDonald. 2012. Overview of the 2012 Shared Task on Parsing the Web. In *Notes of the First Workshop on Syntactic Analysis of Non-Canonical Language (SANCL)*.

Roy Schwartz, and Omri Abend, Roi Reichart, and Ari Rappoport. 2011. Neutralizing linguistically problematic annotations in unsupervised dependency parsing evaluation. In *ACL*.

Roy Schwartz, Omri Abend, and Ari Rappoport. 2012. Learnability-based syntactic annotation design. In *COLING*.

Reut Tsarfaty, Joakim Nivre, and Evelina Andersson. 2012. Cross-framework evaluation for statistical parsing. In *EACL*.

Erik Velldal, Lilja Øvrelid, Jonathon Read, and Stephan Oepen. 2012. Speculation and negation: Rules, rankers, and the role of synta. *Computational linguistics*, 38(2):369–410.

Peng Xu, Jaeho Kang, Michael Ringgaard, and Franz Och. 2009. Using a dependency parser to improve SMT for subject-object-verb languages. In *NAACL-HLT*, Boulder, Colorado.

Deniz Yuret, Laura Rimell, and Aydin Han. 2012. Parser evaluation using textual entailments. *Language Resources and Evaluation*, Published online 31 October 2012.

The Life and Death of Discourse Entities: Identifying Singleton Mentions

Marta Recasens
Linguistics Department
Stanford University
Stanford, CA 94305
recasens@google.com

Marie-Catherine de Marneffe
Linguistics Department
The Ohio State University
Columbus, OH 43210
mcdm@ling.osu.edu

Christopher Potts
Linguistics Department
Stanford University
Stanford, CA 94305
cgpotts@stanford.edu

Abstract

A discourse typically involves numerous entities, but few are mentioned more than once. Distinguishing discourse entities that die out after just one mention (singletons) from those that lead longer lives (coreferent) would benefit NLP applications such as coreference resolution, protagonist identification, topic modeling, and discourse coherence. We build a logistic regression model for predicting the singleton/coreferent distinction, drawing on linguistic insights about how discourse entity lifespans are affected by syntactic and semantic features. The model is effective in its own right (78% accuracy), and incorporating it into a state-of-the-art coreference resolution system yields a significant improvement.

1 Introduction

Not all discourse entities are created equal. Some lead long lives and appear in a variety of discourse contexts (**coreferent**), whereas others never escape their birthplaces, dying out after just one mention (**singletons**). The ability to make this distinction based on properties of the NPs used to identify these referents (mentions) would benefit not only coreference resolution, but also topic analysis, textual entailment, and discourse coherence.

The existing literature provides numerous generalizations relevant to answering the question of whether a given discourse entity will be singleton or coreferent. These involve the internal syntax and morphology of the target NP (Prince, 1981a; Prince, 1981b; Wang et al., 2006), the grammatical function and discourse role of that NP (Chafe, 1976; Hobbs, 1979; Walker et al., 1997; Beaver, 2004), and the interaction of all of those features with semantic operators like negation, modals, and attitude predicates (Karttunen, 1973; Karttunen, 1976; Kamp, 1981; Heim, 1982; Heim, 1992; Roberts, 1990; Groenendijk and Stokhof, 1991; Bittner, 2001).

The first step in our analysis is to bring these insights together into a single logistic regression model — the *lifespan model* — and assess their predictive power on real data. We show that the features generally behave as the existing literature leads us to expect, and that the model itself is highly effective at predicting whether a given mention is singleton or coreferent. We then provide an initial assessment of the engineering value of making the singleton/coreferent distinction by incorporating our lifespan model into the Stanford coreference resolution system (Lee et al., 2011). This addition results in a significant improvement on the CoNLL-2012 Shared Task data, across the MUC, B^3, CEAF, and CoNLL scoring algorithms.

2 Data

All the data used throughout the paper come from the CoNLL-2012 Shared Task (Pradhan et al., 2012), which included the 1.6M English words from OntoNotes v5.0 (Hovy et al., 2006) that have been annotated with different layers of annotation (coreference, parse trees, etc.). We used the training, development (dev), and test splits as defined in the shared task (Table 1). Since the OntoNotes coreference annotations do not contain singleton mentions, we automatically marked as singletons all the NPs

			Mentions	
Dataset	Docs	Tokens	Coreferent	Singletons
Training	2,802	1.3M	152,828	192,248
Dev	343	160K	18,815	24,170
Test	348	170K	19,392	24,921

Table 1: CoNLL-2012 Shared Task data statistics. We added singletons (NPs not annotated as coreferent).

not annotated as coreferent. Thus, our singletons include non-referential NPs but not verbal mentions.

3 Predicting lifespans

Our lifespan model makes a binary distinction between discourse referents that are not part of a coreference chain (singletons) and items that are part of one (coreferent). The distribution of lifespans in our data (Figure 1) suggests that this is a natural division. The propensity of singletons also highlights the relevance of detecting singletons for a coreference system. We fit a binary logistic regression model in R (R Core Team, 2012) on the training data, coding singletons as "0" and coreferent mentions as "1". Throughout the following tables of coefficient estimates, positive values favor coreferents and negative ones favor singletons. We turn now to describing and motivating the features of this model.

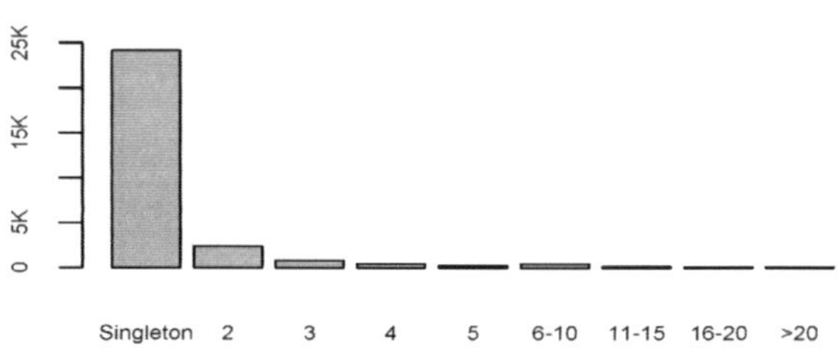

Figure 1: Distribution of lifespans in the dev set. Singletons account for 56% of the data.

Internal morphosyntax of the mention Table 2 summarizes the features from our model that concern the internal morphology and syntactic structure of the mention. Many are common in coreference systems (Recasens and Hovy, 2009), but our model highlights their influence on lifespans. The picture is expected on the taxonomy of given and new defined by Prince (1981b) and assumed throughout dynamic semantics (Kamp, 1981; Heim, 1982): pronouns depend on anaphoric connections to previous mentions for disambiguation and thus are very likely to be coreferent. This is corroborated by the positive coefficient estimate for 'Type = pronoun' in Table 2. Few quantified phrases easily participate in discourse anaphora (Partee, 1987; Wang et al., 2006), accounting for the association between quantifiers and singletons (negative coefficient estimate for 'Quantifier = quantified' in Table 2). The one surprise is the negative coefficient for indefinites. In theories stretching back to Karttunen (1976), indefinites function primarily to establish new discourse entities, and should be able to participate in coreference chains, but here the association with such chains is negative. However, interactions explain this fact (see Table 4 and our discussion of it).

The person, number, and animacy values suggest that singular animates are excellent coreferent NPs, a previous finding of Centering Theory (Grosz et al., 1995; Walker et al., 1998) and of cross-linguistic work on obviative case-marking (Aissen, 1997).

Our model also includes named-entity features for all of the eighteen OntoNotes entity-types (omitted from Table 2 for space and clarity reasons). As a rule, they behave like 'Type = proper noun' in associating with coreferents. The exceptions are ORDINAL, PERCENT, and QUANTITY, which seem intuitively unlikely to participate in coreference chains.

	Estimate	P-value
Type = pronoun	1.21	< 0.001
Type = proper noun	1.88	< 0.001
Animacy = inanimate	−1.36	< 0.001
Animacy = unknown	−0.38	< 0.001
Person = 1	1.05	< 0.001
Person = 2	0.13	< 0.001
Person = 3	1.62	< 0.001
Number = singular	0.61	< 0.001
Number = unknown	0.17	< 0.001
Quantifier = indefinite	−1.49	< 0.001
Quantifier = quantified	−1.23	< 0.001
Number of modifiers	−0.39	< 0.001

Table 2: Internal morphosyntactic features.

Grammatical role of the mention Synthesizing much work in Centering Theory and information structuring, we conclude that coreferent mentions are likely to appear as core verbal arguments and will favor sentence-initial (topic-tracking) positions (Ward and Birner, 2004). The coefficient estimates

	Estimate	P-value
Sentence Position = end	−0.22	< 0.001
Sentence Position = first	0.04	0.07
Sentence Position = last	−0.31	< 0.001
Sentence Position = middle	−0.11	< 0.001
Relation = noun argument	0.56	< 0.001
Relation = other	−0.67	< 0.001
Relation = root	−0.61	< 0.001
Relation = subject	0.65	< 0.001
Relation = verb argument	0.32	< 0.001
In coordination	−0.48	< 0.001

Table 3: Grammatical role features.

in Table 3 corroborate these conclusions. To define the 'Relation' and 'In coordination' features, we used the Stanford dependencies (de Marneffe et al., 2006) on the gold constituents.

Semantic environment of the mention Table 4 highlights the complex interactions between discourse anaphora and semantic operators. These interactions have been a focus of logical semantics since Karttunen (1976), whose guiding observation is semantic: an indefinite interpreted inside the scope of a negation, modal, or attitude predicate is generally unavailable for anaphoric reference outside of the scope of that operator, as in *Kim didn't understand [an exam question]$_i$. #It$_i$ was too hard.* Of course, such discourses cohere if the indefinite is interpreted as taking wide scope ('there is a question Kim didn't understand'). Such readings are often disfavored, but they become more salient when modifiers like *certain* are included (Schwarzschild, 2002) or when the determiner is sensitive to the polarity or intensionality of its environment (Baker, 1970; Ladusaw, 1980; van der Wouden, 1997; Israel, 1996; Israel, 2001; Giannakidou, 1999). Subsequent research identified many other factors that further extend or restrict the anaphoric potential of an indefinite (Roberts, 1996).

We do not have direct access to semantic scope, but we expect syntactic scope to correlate strongly with semantic scope, so we used dependency representations to define features capturing syntactic scope for negation, modal auxiliaries, and a broad range of attitude predicates. These features tend to bias in favor of singletons because they so radically restrict the possibilities for intersentential anaphora. Interacting these features with those for the internal syntax of mentions is also informative. Since proper names and pronouns are not scope-taking, they are largely unaffected by the environment features, whereas indefinites emerge as even more restricted, just as Karttunen and others would predict.

Attitude predicates seem initially anomalous, though. They share the relevant semantic properties with negation and modals, and yet they seem to facilitate coreference. Here, the findings of de Marneffe et al. (2012) seem informative. Those authors find that, in texts of the sort we are studying, attitude predicates are used predominantly to mark the source of information that is effectively asserted despite being embedded (Rooryck, 2001; Simons, 2007). That is, though *X said p* does not semantically entail *p*, it is often interpreted as a commitment to *p*, which correspondingly elevates mentions in *p* to main-clause status (Harris and Potts, 2009).

	Estimate	P-value
Presence of negation	−0.18	< 0.001
Presence of modality	−0.22	< 0.001
Under an attitude verb	0.03	0.01
AttitudeVerb * (Type = pronoun)	0.29	< 0.001
AttitudeVerb * (Type = proper noun)	0.14	< 0.001
Modal * (Type = pronoun)	0.12	0.04
Modal * (Type = proper noun)	0.35	< 0.001
Negation * (Type = pronoun)	1.07	< 0.001
Negation * (Type = proper noun)	0.30	< 0.001
Negation * (Quantifier = indefinite)	−0.37	< 0.001
Negation * (Quantifier = quantified)	−0.36	0.23
Negation * (Number of modifiers)	0.11	< 0.001

Table 4: Semantic environment features and interactions.

Results The model successfully learns to tease singletons and coreferent mentions apart. Table 5 summarizes its performance on the dev set. The STANDARD model uses 0.5 as the decision boundary, with 78% accuracy. The CONFIDENT model predicts singleton if Pr < .2 and coreferent if Pr > .8, which increases precision (P) at a cost to recall (R).

	STANDARD			CONFIDENT		
Prediction	R	P	F1	R	P	F1
Singleton	82.3	79.2	80.7	50.5	89.6	64.6
Coreferent	72.2	76.1	74.1	41.3	86.8	55.9

Table 5: Recall, precision, and F1 for the lifespan model.

System	MUC R	MUC P	MUC F1	B^3 R	B^3 P	B^3 F1	CEAF-ϕ_3 R / P / F1	CEAF-ϕ_4 R	CEAF-ϕ_4 P	CEAF-ϕ_4 F1	CoNLL F1
Baseline	**66.64***	64.72	65.67	**68.05***	71.58	**69.77***	58.31	45.49	**47.55***	46.50	60.65
w/ Lifespan	66.08	**67.33***	**66.70***	66.40	**73.14***	69.61	**58.83***	**47.77***	46.38	**47.07***	**61.13***

Table 6: Performance on the test set according to the official CoNLL-2012 scorer. Scores are on automatically predicted mentions. Stars indicate a statistically significant difference (paired Mann-Whitney U-test, $p < 0.05$).

System	B^3 R	B^3 P	B^3 F1	CEAF-ϕ_3 R	CEAF-ϕ_3 P	CEAF-ϕ_3 F1	CoNLL F1
Baseline	**58.53***	71.58	64.40	**63.71***	58.31	60.89	58.86
w/ Lifespan	58.14	**73.14***	**64.78***	63.38	**58.83***	**61.02**	**59.52***

Table 7: B^3, CEAF-ϕ_3 and CoNLL measures on the test set according to a modified CoNLL-2012 scorer that follows Cai and Strube (2010). Scores are on automatically predicted mentions.

4 Application to coreference resolution

To assess the usefulness of the lifespan model in an NLP application, we incorporate it into the Stanford coreference resolution system (Lee et al., 2011), which we take as our baseline. This was the highest-scoring system in the CoNLL-2011 Shared Task, and was also part of the highest-scoring system in the CoNLL-2012 Shared Task (Fernandes et al., 2012). It is a rule-based system that includes a total of ten rules (or "sieves") for entity coreference, such as exact string match and pronominal resolution. The sieves are applied from highest to lowest precision, each rule adding coreference links.

Incorporating the lifespan model The lifespan model can improve coreference resolution in two different ways: (i) mentions classified as singletons should not be considered as either antecedents or coreferent, and (ii) mentions classified as coreferent should be linked with another mention(s). By successfully predicting singletons (i), we can enhance the system's precision; by successfully predicting coreferent mentions (ii), we can improve the system's recall. Here we focus on (i) and use the lifespan model for detecting singletons. This decision is motivated by two factors. First, given the large number of singletons (Figure 1), we are more likely to see a gain in performance from discarding singletons. Second, the multi-sieve nature of the Stanford coreference system does not make it straightforward to decide which antecedent a mention should be linked to even if we know that it is coreferent. We leave the incorporation of coreferent predictions for future work.

To integrate the singleton model into the Stanford coreference system, we let a sieve consider whether a pair of mentions is coreferent only if neither of the two mentions are classified as singletons by our CONFIDENT model. Experiments on the dev set showed that the model often made wrong predictions for NEs. We do not trust the model for NE mentions. Performance on coreference (on the dev set) was higher with the CONFIDENT model than with the STANDARD model.

Results and discussion To evaluate the coreference system with and without the lifespan model, we used the English dev and test sets from the CoNLL-2012 Shared Task, presented in Section 2. Although the CoNLL shared task evaluated systems on only multi-mention (i.e., non-singleton) entities, by stopping singletons from being linked to multi-mention entities, we expected the lifespan model to increase the system's precision. Our evaluation uses five of the measures given by the CoNLL-2012 scorer: MUC (Vilain et al., 1995), B^3 (Bagga and Baldwin, 1998), CEAF-ϕ_3 and CEAF-ϕ_4 (Luo, 2005), and the CoNLL official score (Denis and Baldridge, 2009). We do not include BLANC (Recasens and Hovy, 2011) because it assumes gold mentions and so is not suited for the scenario considered in this paper, which uses automatically predicted mentions.

Table 6 summarizes the test set performance. All the scores are on automatically predicted mentions. We use gold POS, parse trees, and NEs. The baseline is the Stanford system, and 'w/ Lifespan' is the same system extended with our lifespan model to discard singletons, as explained above.

As expected, the lifespan model increases precision but decreases recall. Overall, however, we obtain a significant improvement of 0.5–1 points in the F1 score of MUC, CEAF-ϕ_3, CEAF-ϕ_4 and CoNLL. The drop in B^3 traces to a bug in the CoNLL scorer's implementation of Cai and Strube (2010)'s algorithm for aligning gold and automatically predicted mentions, which affects the computation of B^3 and CEAF-ϕ_3.[1] Table 7 presents the results after modifying the CoNLL-2012 scorer to compute B^3 and CEAF-ϕ_3 according to Cai and Strube (2010).[2] We do see an improvement in the precision and F1 scores of B^3, and the overall CoNLL score remains significant. The CEAF-ϕ_3 F1 score is no longer significant, but is still in the expected direction.

5 Conclusion

We built a model to predict the lifespan of discourse referents, teasing apart singletons from coreferent mentions. The model validates existing linguistic insights and performs well in its own right. This alone has ramifications for tracking topics, identifying protagonists, and modeling coreference and discourse coherence. We applied the lifespan model to coreference resolution, showing how to incorporate it effectively into a state-of-the-art rule-based coreference system. We expect similar improvements with machine-learning-based coreference systems, where incorporating all the power of the lifespan model would be easier.

Our lifespan model has been integrated into the latest version of the Stanford coreference resolution system.[3]

[1]At present, if the system links two mentions that do not exist in the gold standard, the scorer adds two singletons to the gold standard. This results in a higher B^3 F1 score (when it should be lower) because recall increases instead of staying the same (precision goes up).

[2]In the modified scorer, twinless predicted mentions are added to the gold standard to compute precision but not to compute recall.

[3]`http://nlp.stanford.edu/software/dcoref.shtml`

Acknowledgments

We thank Emili Sapena for modifying the CoNLL-2012 scorer to follow Cai and Strube (2010).

This research was supported in part by ONR grant No. N00014-10-1-0109 and ARO grant No. W911NF-07-1-0216. The first author was supported by a Beatriu de Pinós postdoctoral scholarship (2010 BP-A 00149) from Generalitat de Catalunya.

References

Judith Aissen. 1997. On the syntax of obviation. *Language*, 73(4):705–750.

Amit Bagga and Breck Baldwin. 1998. Algorithms for scoring coreference chains. In *Proceedings of the LREC 1998 Workshop on Linguistic Coreference*, pages 563–566.

C. L. Baker. 1970. Double negatives. *Linguistic Inquiry*, 1(2):169–186.

David Beaver. 2004. The optimization of discourse anaphora. *Linguistics and Philosophy*, 27(1):3–56.

Maria Bittner. 2001. Surface composition as bridging. *Journal of Semantics*, 18(2):127–177.

Jie Cai and Michael Strube. 2010. Evaluation metrics for end-to-end coreference resolution systems. In *Proceedings of SIGDIAL 2010*, pages 28–36.

Wallace L. Chafe. 1976. Givenness, Contrastiveness, Definiteness, Subjects, Topics, and Point of View. In Charles N. Li, editor, *Subject and Topic*, pages 25–55. Academic Press, New York.

Marie-Catherine de Marneffe, Bill MacCartney, and Christopher D. Manning. 2006. Generating typed dependency parses from phrase structure parses. In *Proceedings of LREC 2006*.

Marie-Catherine de Marneffe, Christopher D. Manning, and Christopher Potts. 2012. Did it happen? The pragmatic complexity of veridicality assessment. *Computational Linguistics*, 38(2):301–333.

Pascal Denis and Jason Baldridge. 2009. Global joint models for coreference resolution and named entity classification. *Procesamiento del Lenguaje Natural*, 42:87–96.

Eraldo Fernandes, Cícero dos Santos, and Ruy Milidiú. 2012. Latent structure perceptron with feature induction for unrestricted coreference resolution. In *Proceedings of CoNLL-2012: Shared Task*, pages 41–48.

Anastasia Giannakidou. 1999. Affective dependencies. *Linguistics and Philosophy*, 22(4):367–421.

Jeroen Groenendijk and Martin Stokhof. 1991. Dynamic predicate logic. *Linguistics and Philosophy*, 14(1):39–100.

Barbara J. Grosz, Aravind K. Joshi, and Scott Weinstein. 1995. Centering: A framework for modeling the local coherence of discourse. *Computational Linguistics*, 21(2):203–225.

Jesse A. Harris and Christopher Potts. 2009. Perspective-shifting with appositives and expressives. *Linguistics and Philosophy*, 32(6):523–552.

Irene Heim. 1982. *The Semantics of Definite and Indefinite Noun Phrases*. Ph.D. thesis, UMass Amherst.

Irene Heim. 1992. Presupposition projection and the semantics of attitude verbs. *Journal of Semantics*, 9(2):183–221.

Jerry R. Hobbs. 1979. Coherence and coreference. *Cognitive Science*, 3(1):67–90.

Eduard Hovy, Mitchell Marcus, Martha Palmer, Lance Ramshaw, and Ralph Weischedel. 2006. OntoNotes: The 90% solution. In *Proceedings of HLT-NAACL 2006*, pages 57–60.

Michael Israel. 1996. Polarity sensitivity as lexical semantics. *Linguistics and Philosophy*, 19(6):619–666.

Michael Israel. 2001. Minimizers, maximizers, and the rhetoric of scalar reasoning. *Journal of Semantics*, 18(4):297–331.

Hans Kamp. 1981. A theory of truth and discourse representation. In Jeroen Groenendijk, Theo M. V. Janssen, and Martin Stockhof, editors, *Formal Methods in the Study of Language*, pages 277–322. Mathematical Centre, Amsterdam.

Lauri Karttunen. 1973. Presuppositions and compound sentences. *Linguistic Inquiry*, 4(2):169–193.

Lauri Karttunen. 1976. Discourse referents. In James D. McCawley, editor, *Syntax and Semantics*, volume 7: Notes from the Linguistic Underground, pages 363–385. Academic Press, New York.

William A. Ladusaw. 1980. On the notion 'affective' in the analysis of negative polarity items. *Journal of Linguistic Research*, 1(1):1–16.

Heeyoung Lee, Yves Peirsman, Angel Chang, Nathanael Chambers, Mihai Surdeanu, and Dan Jurafsky. 2011. Stanford's multi-pass sieve coreference resolution system at the CoNLL-2011 Shared Task. In *Proceedings of CoNLL-2011: Shared Task*, pages 28–34.

Xiaoqiang Luo. 2005. On coreference resolution performance metrics. In *Proceedings of HLT-EMNLP 2005*, pages 25–32.

Barbara H. Partee. 1987. Noun phrase interpretation and type-shifting principles. In Jeroen Groenendijk, Dick de Jong, and Martin Stokhof, editors, *Studies in Discourse Representation Theory and the Theory of Generalized Quantifiers*, pages 115–143. Foris Publications, Dordrecht.

Sameer Pradhan, Alessandro Moschitti, Nianwen Xue, Olga Uryupina, and Yuchen Zhang. 2012. CoNLL-2012 Shared Task: Modeling multilingual unrestricted coreference in OntoNotes. In *Proceedings of EMNLP and CoNLL-2012: Shared Task*, pages 1–40.

Ellen Prince. 1981a. On the inferencing of indefinite 'this' NPs. In Bonnie Lynn Webber, Ivan Sag, and Aravind Joshi, editors, *Elements of Discourse Understanding*, pages 231–250. Cambridge University Press, Cambridge.

Ellen F. Prince. 1981b. Toward a taxonomy of given–new information. In Peter Cole, editor, *Radical Pragmatics*, pages 223–255. Academic Press, New York.

R Core Team, 2012. *R: A Language and Environment for Statistical Computing*. R Foundation for Statistical Computing, Vienna, Austria.

Marta Recasens and Eduard Hovy. 2009. A deeper look into features for coreference resolution. In Sobha Lalitha Devi, António Branco, and Ruslan Mitkov, editors, *Anaphora Processing and Applications*, volume 5847 of *Lecture Notes in Computer Science*, pages 29–42. Springer.

Marta Recasens and Eduard Hovy. 2011. BLANC: Implementing the Rand index for coreference evaluation. *Natural Language Engineering*, 17(4):485–510.

Craige Roberts. 1990. *Modal Subordination, Anaphora, and Distributivity*. Garland, New York.

Craige Roberts. 1996. Anaphora in intensional contexts. In Shalom Lappin, editor, *The Handbook of Contemporary Semantic Theory*, pages 215–246. Blackwell Publishers, Oxford.

Johan Rooryck. 2001. Evidentiality, Part II. *Glot International*, 5(5):161–168.

Roger Schwarzschild. 2002. Singleton indefinites. *Journal of Semantics*, 19(3):289–314.

Mandy Simons. 2007. Observations on embedding verbs, evidentiality, and presupposition. *Lingua*, 117(6):1034–1056.

Ton van der Wouden. 1997. *Negative Contexts: Collocation, Polarity and Multiple Negation*. Routledge, London and New York.

Marc Vilain, John Burger, John Aberdeen, Dennis Connolly, and Lynette Hirschman. 1995. A model-theoretic coreference scoring scheme. In *Proceedings of MUC-6*, pages 45–52.

Marilyn A. Walker, Aravind K. Joshi, and Ellen F. Prince, editors. 1997. *Centering in Discourse*. Oxford University Press.

Marilyn A. Walker, Aravind K. Joshi, and Ellen F. Prince. 1998. Centering in naturally-occurring discourse: An overview. In Marilyn A. Walker, Aravind K. Joshi, and Ellen F. Prince, editors, *Centering Theory in Discourse*, pages 1–28, Oxford. Clarendon Press.

Linton Wang, Eric McCready, and Nicholas Asher. 2006. Information dependency in quantificational subordination. In Klaus von Heusinger and Ken Turner, editors,

Where Semantics Meets Pragmatics, pages 267–304. Elsevier Science, Amsterdam.

Gregory Ward and Betty Birner. 2004. Information structure and non-canonical syntax. In Laurence R. Horn and Gregory Ward, editors, *The Handbook of Pragmatics*, pages 153–174. Blackwell, Oxford.

Automatic Generation of English Respellings

Bradley Hauer and Grzegorz Kondrak
Department of Computing Science
University of Alberta
Edmonton, Alberta, Canada, T6G 2E8
{bmhauer,gkondrak}@ualberta.ca

Abstract

A *respelling* is an alternative spelling of a word in the same writing system, intended to clarify pronunciation. We introduce the task of automatic generation of a respelling from the word's phonemic representation. Our approach combines machine learning with linguistic constraints and electronic resources. We evaluate our system both intrinsically through a human judgment experiment, and extrinsically by passing its output to a letter-to-phoneme converter. The results show that the respellings generated by our system are better on average than those found on the Web, and approach the quality of respellings designed by an expert.

1 Introduction

Respellings are a widely employed method of conveying the pronunciation of English and foreign words, both in print and on the Web. For example, *Huatulco*, the name of a Mexican resort, is respelled as *'wah-tool-koh'* in a travel guide (Noble, 2012). The advantage of using respellings lies in removing the need for a separately defined phonetic transcription system. Since they contain only the letters of the Latin alphabet, their phonetic interpretation relies exclusively on orthographic intuitions of readers. For this reason, respellings are widely used in travel phrase books, medical compendia, and drug name pronunciation guides, among others.

Despite their utility, good respellings are not easy to create. Respellings found on the Web often contain errors or ambiguities. For example, *Henoch-Schoenlein purpura*, a skin disease, is respelled both as *'heh-nok shoon-line purr-puh-ruh'* and *'hen-awk sher-line purr-purr-ah'*. Does *'heh'* rhyme with *eh* [e] or with *Nineveh* [ə], or is it the same vowel as in *hen* [ɛ]? Clearly, if both respellings refer to the same pronunciation, at least one of them must be wrong. In addition, converting the pronunciation of a foreign name to English phonemes is in itself a non-trivial task.

In this paper, we focus on the task of generating respellings from the intended pronunciation given as a sequence of phonemes. We develop a stand-alone system that combines linguistic knowledge and resources with machine learning models trained on data mined from the Web and electronic dictionaries. One of our ultimate objectives is to aid writers by evaluating their respellings, improving them, or generating new candidates. Accordingly, we endeavour to maintain the generation and the evaluation stages as separate modules in our system.

The evaluation of respellings is a challenging problem. Since English spelling conventions are notoriously inconsistent, there is no algorithm for accurately predicting the pronunciation of an out-of-vocabulary word. The current state-of-the-art letter-to-phoneme (L2P) converters are typically reported with 10-30% error rates on dictionary words (Bisani and Ney, 2008). On the other hand, human readers often disagree on the details of the pronunciation implied by a respelling. In this paper, we conduct two kinds of evaluations: an automated verification with an independent L2P system, and an experiment with human participants that pass judgments on different respellings of the same word. We interpret the results as evidence that the output of our system compares favourably with typical respellings found on the Web.

2 Definitions and Conventions

Although Chomsky and Halle (1968) characterize English orthography as close to optimal, Kominek and Black (2006) estimate that it is about 3 times more complex than German, and 40 times more complex than Spanish. This is confirmed by lower accuracy of letter-to-phoneme systems on English (Bisani and Ney, 2008). A survey of English spelling (Carney, 1994) devotes 120 pages to describe phoneme-to-letter correspondences, and lists 226 letter-to-phoneme rules, almost all of which admit exceptions.

There is no consensus on how to best convey the pronunciation of an uncommon word in English. Most dictionaries employ either the International Phonetic Alphabet (IPA), or their own transcription schemes that incorporate special symbols and diacritics. Unfortunately, many readers are unfamiliar with phonetic transcription. Instead, respellings are often preferred by writers in the news and on the Web. In this section, we define the respelling task in detail.

2.1 Form of Respellings

A *respelling* is a non-standard spelling of a word, that is intended to better convey its pronunciation. We assume that the pronunciation is defined as a sequence of English phonemes, and that the respelling contains only the 26 letters of the alphabet, with optional hyphenation. Some transcription schemes combine respellings with special symbols for representing certain phonemes. For example, an otherwise purely alphabetic Wikipedia scheme employs the symbol ə for the vowel *schwa*. In our opinion, such devices destroy the main advantage of respellings, which is their universality, without attaining the precision of a true phonetic transcription. In fact, Fraser (1997) identifies the *schwa* symbol as the cause of many pronunciation errors.

In our system, we consistently use hyphens to segment multi-syllable respellings. Each syllable-size segment contains the representation of exactly one vowel phoneme, so that the number of segments matches the number of syllables.[1] However, the hyphenation need not correspond exactly to the actual syllable breaks. This approach has several advantages. First, individual syllables are easier to pronounce than an entire unfamiliar word. Second, hyphens limit the context that affects the pronunciation of a given letter (e.g. *th* in *Beethoven 'bayt-hoe-ven'*). Finally, hyphens indicate whether adjacent vowel letters, such as *oe* in *'hoe'*, represent one vowel phoneme or two.

Some respellings explicitly indicate the stressed syllable by expressing it in a different font. This is potentially helpful because unstressed vowels tend to be reduced, which changes their pronunciation. However, since the vowel reduction phenomenon is by no means universal, the readers may be unsure whether to apply it to, e.g. the final *o* in *'KWAT-ro'*. In this paper, we make no distinction between stressed and unstressed syllables; instead, we follow the principle that each syllable is to be pronounced as if it was a separate word. Nonetheless, it would be straightforward to project the stress indicators onto the appropriate syllables in the respellings generated by our system.

2.2 Quality of Respellings

There is no clear-cut distinction between good and bad respellings. The quality of a respelling is more of a subjective opinion rather than a verifiable fact. We propose to evaluate it according to the following three criteria: ambiguity, correctness, and preference.

A respelling is *ambiguous* if it is perceived as compatible with more than one pronunciation. Because most of the rules of English spelling have exceptions, it is rarely possible to demonstrate that a respelling is completely unambiguous. However, some respellings are clearly more ambiguous than others. For example, the digraph *ee* almost always represents the vowel [i], whereas the letter sequence *ough* can represent several different phonemes.[2] Respellings that contain highly ambiguous letter-phoneme mappings can be expected to be ambiguous themselves. Ambiguity is a property of a respelling itself, regardless of the intended pronunciation.

A respelling is *correct* if it accurately conveys the intended pronunciation to the reader. Unlike the am-

[1] Henceforth, we refer to "syllable-size segments" simply as "syllables".

[2] Compare *bough, cough, dough, tough, lough, through.*

biguity, correctness can be verified objectively for a particular reader, by comparing the intended pronunciation with the pronunciation inferred by the reader. A respelling that is judged correct with respect to one pronunciation cannot be judged correct with respect to a different pronunciation. Nevertheless, it is entirely possible that different readers will derive different pronunciations from the same respelling.

A respelling can be classified as unambiguous and yet incorrect by a given reader, but it cannot be judged as simultaneously ambiguous and correct. Indeed, an ambiguous respelling is compatible with at least two pronunciations, only one of which can be the intended pronunciation. Therefore, for a given reader, unambiguity is a necessary but not sufficient condition for correctness.

Given two unambiguous and correct respellings, a reader may prefer one over the other, perhaps because of the ease of inferring the intended pronunciation. For example, *'rode-ease-yew'* may be preferred to *'roh-dee-zyoo'* because the former is entirely composed of actual English words with unique pronunciation, whereas the latter contains an unusual consonant cluster *zy*. Preference is also expressed implicitly if only one of the alternative respellings is judged as unambiguous (or correct),

3 Related Work

Fraser (1997) describes an experiment in which 15 human subjects were asked to pronounce uncommon words after being shown a representation of their pronunciation. The respellings designed by the author were much more effective for that purpose than either the IPA phonetic transcription or phonemic respelling (Section 4.3). However, the creation of respellings was described as labour-intensive, and at least one of them was found to be sub-optimal during the experiment.

Williams and Jones (2008) propose respellings as a way of extending pronunciation lexicons by informants who lack linguistic training. Galescu (2009) reports that the addition of respellings of medical terms from an on-line dictionary improves the accuracy of an L2P system. The author identifies an automatic pronunciation-to-respelling system as future work.

Ghoshal et al. (2009) extract a large number of respellings from the Web, and show that they can be exploited to improve the accuracy of the L2P conversion by supplementing the data in pronunciation dictionaries. Can et al. (2009) further analyze the effect of using respellings on the accuracy of spoken-term detection (STD) systems.

4 Direct Methods

In this section, we discuss three direct methods of generating respellings: manual design, dictionary lookup, and phonemic respelling.

4.1 Manual Design

Respellings found on the Web and in news articles are usually ad-hoc creations of the authors of those texts. Respellings designed by different writers for the same word are rarely identical.[3] The quality of Web respellings vary.

The respellings found in specialized lexicons are more likely to be designed by experts, and are often guided by a set of respelling rules. Nevertheless, such respelling guides may also be ambiguous.[4] Regardless of the source, since respellings are often used for names and foreign words, no lexicon can be expected to provide a complete coverage.

4.2 Dictionary Lookup

Pronunciation dictionaries can be helpful in generating respellings. Assuming that we have a method of dividing pronunciations into syllables, a complete respelling of an out-of-dictionary word can in some cases be automatically derived from the list of syllable pronunciations. For example, *hyphy* can be respelled as *'high-fee'* by following such a procedure. If each of the syllables has a unique pronunciation, such respellings are arguably both unambiguous and correct.

Unfortunately, only a subset of potential phonemic syllables actually occur in a lexicon. Considering only the syllables of the CVC type (consonant-vowel-consonant), there are over ten thousand distinct possibilities (e.g., [bɛb], [bɛʃ], etc.), of which

[3]For example, the word *capoeira* is represented by 99 different respellings in the corpus of Ghoshal et al. (2009).

[4]For an example of a confusing respelling guide see `http://www.ama-assn.org/go/usan`.

fewer than three thousand can be found in the Combilex pronunciation dictionary (Richmond et al., 2009). While the dictionary lookup may produce attractive respellings, it is not sufficient for a stand-alone use.

4.3 Phonemic Respelling

A simple method that can produce a respelling for any word is to directly map each phoneme to a particular letter or a letter sequence that is frequently used to represent that phoneme. Phonemes such as [m], [d] and [f] are indeed closely associated with individual letters. This is not surprising since the Roman letters were originally created to represent single phonemes in Latin, and some of those phonemes also exist in English. However, many phonemes, especially vowels, have no obvious orthographic representation. One solution is to use digraphs such as *ee* and *aw*, but a number of phonemes, such as [aʊ] as in *loud*, have no mappings that work in all contexts.

The principal weakness of a phonemic respelling is its inflexibility, which often results in counter-intuitive respellings. For example, many readers are baffled by respelling such as *'gee'* for *ghee* or *'john'* for *Joan*. Phonemic respelling tends to fail in cases where it generates a sequence of letters that is inherently ambiguous, or which pronunciation changes because of the context. On the other hand, mappings such as *uu* for [ʊ] and *ahy* for [aɪ], which never occur in real English words, are difficult to interpret for some readers.

In this paper, we adopt a context-free phonemic respelling scheme as the baseline, with the mappings from the online dictionary *Dictionary.com*, which differs from the system used in Wikipedia only in a few details.

5 Candidate Generation

In this section, we present our syllabification approach, as well as two generation modules: a trained phoneme-to-letter (P2L) model and a rule-based respeller.

5.1 Syllabification

Our respelling generation process is for the most part performed on the level of individual syllables.

	VOWEL	ONSET	LAX	CODA
nt	*			
ndən		*		
bæ			*	
dənm				*
bæn				

Table 1: Examples of syllables that violate phonotactic constraints.

Correct syllabification is by itself a non-trivial problem, but even if it was provided by an oracle, it might not correspond to the optimal segmentation of a respelling. For example, the word *trigonal* [trɪgənəl] is usually syllabified as *tri-go-nal*, but a better segmentation for the purposes of respelling is *trig-on-al*. We adopt an overgenerate-and-rank approach, whereby instead of committing to a specific word segmentation at the start of the process, we process multiple syllabification alternatives in parallel, one of which is ultimately selected at the respelling evaluation stage.

Ideally, syllabification should conform to the phonotactic constraints of English, so that the resulting respellings are easy to pronounce. The consonant sonority should be rising in onsets, and falling in codas (Kenstowicz, 1994). We verify that syllables follow the sonority principle by following the formulation of Bartlett et al. (2009). The sonority constraints are not tested at the boundaries of the word, which are independent of the syllabification choice. We also incorporate another important principle of English phonotactics that asserts that lax vowels do not occur in open syllables (Rogers, 2000).

In our implementation, each candidate syllable is tested with respect to the following sequence of four violable constraints, ordered from the strongest to the weakest: (1) the syllable contains exactly one *vowel* phoneme; (2) the *onset* satisfies the sonority principle; (3) if the nucleus contains a *lax* vowel (except ə), the coda is non-empty; (4) the *coda* satisfies the sonority principle. For a syllabification to be accepted, all its syllables must satisfy the four constraints. However, if this results in rejection of all possible syllabifications, the constraints are gradually relaxed starting from the weakest.

As an example, consider the word *abandonment* [əbændənmənt], which has 18 different syllabifications satisfying the VOWEL constraint (Table 1). 8 of the 18 satisfy the ONSET constraint as well, but only two syllabifications satisfy all four constraints: [əb-æn-dən-mənt] and [ə-bæn-dən-mənt].

5.2 P2L Generator

The respelling problem can be viewed as a string transduction problem, with the transduction occurring between phonemes and letters. As such, it is directly related to the well-studied letter-to-phoneme conversion task. The difference is that the letters may not conform to the standard orthography of English. If we had a sufficiently large training set of pronunciation-respelling pairs, we could train a machine learning algorithm to directly generate respellings for any strings of English phonemes. However, such a training set is not readily available. The respellings in the corpus collected by Ghoshal et al. (2009) are not easily matched to the phonetic transcriptions, and few of them can be found in electronic pronunciation dictionaries. In addition, the quality of Web respellings vary greatly.

In place of a direct pronunciation-to-respelling model, we aim to model the orthographic intuitions of readers by deriving a phoneme-to-letter (P2L) transduction model from an English pronunciation dictionary. A possible criticism of such an approach is that our model may create ambiguous respellings, which abound in English orthography. However, we rely on a separate evaluation module to identify and filter ambiguous respellings at a later stage.

Our systems utilizes the DIRECTL+ program (Jiampojamarn et al., 2008), which was originally designed for L2P conversion. Since our basic unit is the syllable, rather than the word, we train our P2L model on a set of of 4215 pairs of monosyllabic words and their pronunciations extracted from the Combilex dictionary. We exclude syllables in multisyllabic words from training because their pronunciation is often affected by context. This is consistent with our expectation that the reader will pronounce each hyphen-delimited segment of the respelling as if it was an individual word.

Since the P2L training data consists of a relatively small set of syllables, we ensure that the phoneme-letter alignment is highly accurate. As a preprocessing step, we replace the letter x with *ks*, and we convert digraphs, such as *ch* and *th*, to single symbols. The alignment is performed by M2M-ALIGNER (Jiampojamarn et al., 2007), under the restriction that each phoneme is matched to either one or two letter symbols.

5.3 Context-Sensitive Respeller

A hand-crafted context-sensitive respeller is intended to complement the trained P2L model described in the previous section. It is similar to to the phonemic respelling approach described in Section 4.3 in that it converts each phoneme to a letter sequence. However, the mappings depend on adjacent phonemes, as well as on the CV pattern of the current syllable. In addition, more than one mapping for a phoneme can be proposed. We designed the mappings by analyzing their frequency and consistency in pronunciation dictionaries.

The process of candidate generation involves establishing the pattern of consonants in the input syllable. The consonant mappings are the same as in the baseline, except for [g] and [θ], while the vowels yield up to three different letter sequences. For example, [o] is mapped to *oh* as a default, but also to *o* if both onset and coda are empty, or to *o* followed by a consonant and a silent *e* if the coda is composed of a single consonant. So, given the syllable [tok] as input, the respeller produces two candidates: *tohk* and *toke*.

We make no claims about the completeness or optimality of the mappings, but in our development experiments we observed that the context-sensitive respeller contributes to the robustness of our system, and in some cases produces more attractive respellings that the P2L model.

6 Candidate Selection

We aim at developing a stand-alone method for the assessment of respellings that could be applied regardless of their origin. We consider two criteria: correctness, which is evaluated against the intended pronunciation, and ambiguity, which is a property of the respelling itself. As was the case in the generation stage, the evaluation is performed at the level of syllables.

6.1 L2P Correctness Filter

The principal method of verifying the correctness of a respelling involves the application of a letter-to-phoneme (L2P) model trained on the word-pronunciation pairs extracted from an English dictionary. The generated pronunciation of each syllable is compared against its intended pronunciation; if any of the syllables fail the test, the entire respelling is rejected.

The L2P model is derived using the DIRECTL+ system. The main difference between the L2P model described in this section and the P2L model from Section 5.2 is that the input and output data are reversed. However, the L2P model is not simply a mirror image of the P2L model. Often the phonemic output of the composition of the two models is different from the initial phonemic input; e.g., [ro] → *row* → [raʊ]. This is because the intermediate orthographic string may be ambiguous. Furthermore, the L2P model is also intended to test the correctness of respellings that were generated with other methods.

Other differences between the two models pertain to the preprocessing of the training data, and the letter-to-phoneme alignment. As with the P2L model, the training data consists of a set of monosyllabic words from the Combilex dictionary. However, in order to make our correctness filter more conservative, we also remove all words that contain diacritics (e.g., *crêpe*), non-English phonemes (e.g., *avant*), or silent consonants (e.g., *limn*). The alignment is restricted to matching each letter symbol to at most one phoneme, and is derived with the ALINE phonetic aligner (Kondrak, 2000), which has been shown to outperform other 1-1 alignment methods (Jiampojamarn and Kondrak, 2010).

6.2 Vowel Counter

Syllables that contain multiple vowel groups may be confusing to readers even if they correctly represent the intended pronunciation. For example, readers might be unsure whether *takess* represents one or two syllables. A simple vowel counter is provided to filter out such syllables. The vowel filter accepts a syllable only if (a) it contains exactly one vowel group (e.g., *moe*), or (b) the second vowel group consists of a single *e* at the end of the syllable (e.g., *zake*).

6.3 SVM Ambiguity Classifier

This module is designed to compute a score that reflects the ambiguity of an orthographic syllable. The ambiguity score of a respelling is defined as the average of scores assigned to each of its syllables. The score can then be used to select the best respelling from a number of candidates generated by our system, or to rate a respelling from another source.

Since we have no explicit ambiguity annotations for respellings, we attempt instead to exploit ambiguity judgments that are implicitly made when respellings are created by human authors. We approach ambiguity as a binary classification task. For any given syllable, we wish to determine whether it is ambiguous (a negative instance), or unambiguous (a positive instance). Our assumption is that a syllable will not be respelled unless it is necessary due to ambiguity. For each observed word-respelling pair, we take all syllables from the respelling as positive instances, and all syllables in the original word that are not preserved in the respelling as negative instances. For example, the pair consisting of the word *cec-il-y* respelled as *'sehs-il-ee'* provides three positive instances: *sehs, il* and *ee*; and two negative instances: *cec* and *y*.

We extracted word-respelling pairs from the Web-derived corpora of Ghoshal et al. (2009). The syllable breaks in the respellings were mapped onto the original words using ALINE. In order to improve the quality of the data, we applied a letter-to-phoneme model to both the original words and their respellings, and removed pairs with divergent pronunciations (computed as normalized edit distance $\leq$ 0.8). After the filtering, we were left a set of 25067 word-respelling pairs containing 78411 training syllables, which yielded 47270 positive and 31141 negative instances.

For the classification task we utilize the SVM-light software package (Joachims, 1999). Each instance is represented by a set of binary indicator features. The features correspond to character n-grams (including syllable boundary markers) with the values of n ranging from 1 to 5. For example, the syllable *-il-* turns on the following features: *i, l, -i, il, l-, -il, il-, -il-*. The model learns which n-grams are characteristic of ambiguous or unambiguous syllables. For example, it classifies both *le* and *li* as ambiguous, and *lee* as unambiguous. Apart from the binary classification, the classifier also provides a real-valued score for each syllable.

6.4 Lexical Reviser

Since the use of familiar English letter sequences makes the respellings easier to interpret (Fraser, 1997), we incorporate dictionary lookup (Section 4.2) into our system. When the pronunciation of a syllable happens to correspond to the pronunciation an actual dictionary word, the syllable may be respelled using that word. This is done as the final step in the generation process because dictionary words often receive poor scores from the SVM classifier on the account of their n-gram composition. The lexical reviser is restricted to optionally improving the top-ranked word respelling candidate as determined by the SVM classifier without altering its syllabification. For example, the respelling *'surr-sin-uss'* of *circinus* is modified to *'sir-sin-us'*. If more than one word can be used, we let the SVM classifier select the least ambiguous one.

7 System Overview

Our respelling generation system is a multi-stage process. The input is a sequence of phonemes representing the pronunciation of the word. We start by identifying acceptable syllabifications of phonemes as described in Section 5.1. For each syllable, we take up to five respelling candidates produced by the P2L model (Section 5.2), and between one and three candidates proposed by the context-sensitive respeller (Section 5.3). The next stage involves filtering the candidate respellings with the L2P model (Section 6.1), and the vowel counter (Section 6.2). If all candidates happen to be rejected, we retain the first output of the context-sensitive respeller as the default. The candidate respellings are then scored by the SVM model (Section 6.3). At this point the syllables are combined into word respellings, which are ranked according to their syllable score average. Finally, the lexical reviser described in Section 6.4 is applied to the top candidate in an attempt to further improve the result.

8 Evaluation

In this section, after describing our test sets, we present the results of two evaluation experiments: direct human judgment, and indirect validation with an L2P system.

8.1 Test Sets

Our two test sets were defined after the development of our system had been completed. There is no overlap between the test sets and any of our training sets. The first test set consists of 27 out of 30 words compiled by Fraser (1997) — 3 words from the original set were excluded because the corresponding respellings assume a non-rhotic variety of English. We refer to Fraser's respellings as *expert*, and consider them as the upper bound in terms of quality.

The second test set of 231 words (henceforth referred to as the *Web set*) was extracted from the corpus of Ghoshal et al. (2009) after performing additional data clean-up described in Section 6.3. We identified a subset of words for which we could find phonetic transcriptions composed of English phonemes on Wikipedia. In order to ensure that the respellings and the corresponding transcriptions reflect the same pronunciation, we adapted the Soundex algorithm to apply to phonetic transcriptions, and retained only the respelling/transcription pairs that yielded identical Soundex codes. We removed words that are found in the Combilex dictionary as those could be familiar to human judges. Since longer words are more challenging to respell, and more likely to exhibit variation in respellings from different sources, we retained only words containing at least eight phonemes.

8.2 Human Judgment

We conducted an experiment with human evaluators using a specially developed graphical annotation program with synthesized word pronunciations. The evaluators were students enrolled in an introductory linguistic course, who were not involved in our project. 13 out of 20 evaluators declared themselves as native speakers of English.

The evaluation process involves 40 randomly selected words: 10 from Fraser's set, and 30 from the Web set. For each word, the program displays in a random sequence three respellings, which are from

Source	Web set		Fraser's set	
	U	U&C	U	U&C
Baseline	43.0	25.5	41.0	20.0
Web	68.0	32.6	—	
Expert	—		72.0	46.0
Our system	70.0	41.3	67.0	38.5

Table 2: Human judgments on respellings in %: U - unambiguous; U&C - unambiguous & correct.

the following sources: (1) the Baseline approach described in Section 4.3, (2) our system, and (3) either expert design (for Fraser's set) or the Web (for the Web set). In order to reduce bias, the original spelling of the word is not shown. Each respelling is judged separately with regards to ambiguity, and those that are judged ambiguous are removed from further consideration. Next, an audio clip synthesized from the phonemic sequence representing the intended pronunciation is played through headphones. For each of the remaining respellings, the evaluators decide whether it is correct with respect to the recorded pronunciation. Finally, if more than one respelling have been judged both unambiguous and correct, the evaluators are asked to identify the one that they prefer.

The results of the experiment are shown in Table 2. Our system significantly outperforms both Web respellings and the Baseline approach in terms of unambiguity and correctness. In addition, the respellings produced by our system are more likely to be preferred over the Web respellings, and more than twice as likely to be preferred over the baseline respellings than vice versa. The results on the small Fraser's set are less conclusive, but suggest that in terms of overall quality our system is much closer to the upper bound than to the baseline.

8.3 Automated Appraisal

Human evaluation is expensive and limited in terms of the number of variant respellings. Moreover, human judgements may be biased by previously seen respellings or by the familiarity with the standard spelling of a word. An automated evaluation is much less constrained, and facilitates an ablation study to determine the relative importance of various components of our system.

Source	Web set		Fraser's set	
	WA	PA	WA	PA
No respelling	13.0	76.2	14.8	76.3
Baseline	8.2	78.9	7.4	71.0
Web	14.3	77.9	—	
Expert	—		37.0	85.6
Our system	58.0	93.0	70.4	95.6

Table 4: Word accuracy (WA) and phoneme accuracy (PA) of *eSpeak* on respellings.

Source	Web set	
	WA	PA
Full system	58.0	93.0
w/o lexical reviser	57.6	93.1
w/o context-sensitive respeller	56.7	92.8
w/o P2L generator	51.9	92.1
w/o L2P correctness filter	33.8	88.0
w/o syllable breaks	20.8	83.9

Table 5: Accuracy of *eSpeak* on respellings produced by variants of our system.

eSpeak is a publicly available speech synthesizer[5] that can also convert text into phonemic sequences. The letter-to-phoneme component for English utilizes about five thousand rules, and a dictionary of about three thousand words, names, and abbreviations. In our evaluation, we treat *eSpeak* as a "black box" which translates a respelling into its most likely pronunciation. By determining if there is a match between the output of *eSpeak* and the intended pronunciation, we directly test the correctness of the respelling, and indirectly also its ambiguity.

The results of the automated evaluation are shown in Table 4. The accuracy on the original orthography is low, which is unsurprising since the test sets contain mostly rare, unusually spelled words. Neither the baseline nor the Web respellings are significantly easier for *eSpeak* than the original words. On the other hand, respellings generated by our system make a massive difference, boosting phoneme accuracy to well over 90% on both sets. They are also significantly more effective than the expert respellings.

Table 5 shows the results of our system on the

[5] `http://espeak.sourceforge.net`

No.	Spelling	IPA	Web/HF respelling	Score	System respelling	Score
1	*Incirlik*	[inʤirlik]	*injirlik*	1/6	*een-jeer-leek*	4/6
2	*Captopril*	[kæptəprɪl]	*kap-toh-pril*	1/6	*cap-tuh-prill*	4/6
3	*Coquitlam*	[kokwɪtləm]	*ko-kwit-lam*	1/6	*koh-quit-lumb*	4/6
4	*Karolina*	[kɑrɔlinɑ]	*karo-leena*	4/6	*car-awl-ee-nah*	1/6
5	*subluxation*	[səbləkseʃən]	*sub-luck-say-shun*	3/5	*suh-bluck-say-shun*	1/5
6	*swingle*	[swɪŋgəl]	*swing-gl*	0/5	*swing-gull*	2/5
7	*cockatrice*	[kɑkətraɪs]	*kok-a-trice*	0/7	*cock-uh-trice*	4/7
8	*recalesce*	[rikəlɛs]	*ree-ka-less*	1/5	*re-cull-ess*	3/5
9	*jongleur*	[ʒɑŋglər]	*jong-gler*	7/9	*zhahng-gler*	0/9
10	*ylang-ylang*	[ilæŋilæŋ]	*ee-lang-ee-lang*	5/5	*eel-ang-eel-ang*	1/5

Table 3: Examples of respellings.

Web set with various modules disabled, which provides an estimate of their importance. Neither the context-sensitive respeller nor dictionary lookup seem to contribute much to *eSpeak*'s performance. On the other hand, disabling the P2L generator produces a significant drop in word accuracy, while removing the L2P correctness filter almost doubles the phoneme error rate. Interestingly, removing syllable breaks from the output of the full system has an even greater negative impact.

8.4 Analysis

Each of 20 evaluators judged 3 variant respellings of 40 different words. The average number of judgments per word was 7.4 for the 27 words in Fraser's set, and 2.8 for the 212 words in the Web set (due to random selection, 19 words from the Web set were not judged). Table 3 shows examples of respellings that were judged by at least five evaluators. The score columns indicate the proportion of the evaluators that judged a particular respellings as unambiguous and correct. The baseline respellings are not included as their scores were rarely higher than the scores of the other respellings for a given word. An interesting exception is *palimpsest*, for which the baseline respelling is identical to the actual spelling of the word.

Examples 1-5 in Table 3 come from the Web set, while examples 6-10 are from Fraser's set. The low scores of the first three Web respellings can be attributed to specific letter-to-phoneme mappings: [i]→*i*, [ə]→*oh*, and [ə]→*a*. Each of the examples 3-5 indicate the evaluators' acceptance of a particular respelling device: silent letters, multi-syllable units, and dictionary words. In examples 6-8, the syllables immediately after the first hyphen in Helen Fraser's respellings seem to be problematic. The expert respelling of *jongleur* is considered correct even though the initial *j* suggests [ʤ], not [ʒ]. Finally, the last example demonstrates that the hyphenation choice can result in very different judgments.

9 Conclusion

In this paper, we introduced the task of automatically generating respellings from the given pronunciation. We investigated the characteristics of good respellings, and discussed three direct methods of their creation. We proposed a system that combines supervised and unsupervised learning with phonetic and orthographic principles. The evaluation experiment involving human participants indicates that the respellings produced by our system are better on average than those found on the Web. The automated verification demonstrates that they are also much easier to interpret for a rule-based text-to-speech converter. In the future we plan to address the related tasks of improving existing respellings, and assisting writers in creating respellings without direct access to the phonemic representations.

Acknowledgements

We thank Aditya Bhargava and Clarke Chomyc for their contribution to the creation of data sets, and Ben Tucker for advice on the complexities of the human evaluation experiment. This research was partially funded by the Natural Sciences and Engineering Research Council of Canada.

References

Susan Bartlett, Grzegorz Kondrak, and Colin Cherry. 2009. On the syllabification of phonemes. In *Proc. of HLT-NAACL*, pages 308–316.

Maximilian Bisani and Hermann Ney. 2008. Joint-sequence models for grapheme-to-phoneme conversion. *Speech Communication*, 50(5):434–451.

Doğan Can, Erica Cooper, Arnab Ghoshal, Martin Jansche, Sanjeev Khudanpur, Bhuvana Ramabhadran, Michael Riley, Murat Saraçlar, Abhinav Sethy, Morgan Ulinski, and Christopher White. 2009. Web derived pronunciations for spoken term detection. In *Proc. of ACM SIGIR*, pages 83–90.

Edward Carney. 1994. *A Survey of English Spelling*. Routledge.

Noam Chomsky and Morris Halle. 1968. *The Sound Pattern of English*. New York: Harper & Row.

Helen Fraser. 1997. Dictionary pronunciation guides for English. *International Journal of Lexicography*, 10(3):181–208.

Lucian Galescu. 2009. Extending pronunciation lexicons via non-phonemic respellings. In *Proc. of HLT-NAACL: Short Papers*, pages 129–132.

Arnab Ghoshal, Martin Jansche, Sanjeev Khudanpur, Michael Riley, and Morgan Ulinski. 2009. Web-derived pronunciations. In *Proc. of ICASSP*, pages 4289–4292.

Sittichai Jiampojamarn and Grzegorz Kondrak. 2010. Letter-phoneme alignment: An exploration. In *Proc. of ACL*, pages 780–788.

Sittichai Jiampojamarn, Grzegorz Kondrak, and Tarek Sherif. 2007. Applying many-to-many alignments and hidden Markov models to letter-to-phoneme conversion. In *Proc. of HLT-NAACL*, pages 372–379.

Sittichai Jiampojamarn, Colin Cherry, and Grzegorz Kondrak. 2008. Joint processing and discriminative training for letter-to-phoneme conversion. In *Proc. of ACL*, pages 905–913.

Thorsten Joachims. 1999. Making large-scale SVM learning practical. In B. Schalkopf, C. Burges, and A. Smola, editors, *Advances in Kernel Methods - Support Vector Learning*. MIT Press.

Michael Kenstowicz. 1994. *Phonology in Generative Grammar*. Blackwell.

John Kominek and Alan W Black. 2006. Learning pronunciation dictionaries: Language complexity and word selection strategies. In *Proc. of HLT-NAACL*, pages 232–239.

Grzegorz Kondrak. 2000. A new algorithm for the alignment of phonetic sequences. In *Proc. of NAACL*, pages 288–295.

John Noble. 2012. *Mexico*. Lonely Planet, 13th edition.

Korin Richmond, Robert Clark, and Sue Fitt. 2009. Robust LTS rules with the Combilex speech technology lexicon. In *Proc. of Interspeech*, pages 1295–1298.

Henry Rogers. 2000. *The Sounds of Language*. Pearson.

Briony Williams and Rhys James Jones. 2008. Acquiring pronunciation data for a placenames lexicon in a less-resourced language. In *Proc. of LREC*.

A Simple, Fast, and Effective Reparameterization of IBM Model 2

Chris Dyer **Victor Chahuneau** **Noah A. Smith**
Language Technologies Institute
Carnegie Mellon University
Pittsburgh, PA 15213, USA
{cdyer,vchahune,nasmith}@cs.cmu.edu

Abstract

We present a simple log-linear reparameterization of IBM Model 2 that overcomes problems arising from Model 1's strong assumptions and Model 2's overparameterization. Efficient inference, likelihood evaluation, and parameter estimation algorithms are provided. Training the model is consistently ten times faster than Model 4. On three large-scale translation tasks, systems built using our alignment model outperform IBM Model 4.

An open-source implementation of the alignment model described in this paper is available from **http://github.com/clab/fast_align** .

1 Introduction

Word alignment is a fundamental problem in statistical machine translation. While the search for more sophisticated models that provide more nuanced explanations of parallel corpora is a key research activity, simple and effective models that scale well are also important. These play a crucial role in many scenarios such as parallel data mining and rapid large scale experimentation, and as subcomponents of other models or training and inference algorithms. For these reasons, IBM Models 1 and 2, which support exact inference in time $\Theta(|\mathbf{f}| \cdot |\mathbf{e}|)$, continue to be widely used.

This paper argues that both of these models are suboptimal, even in the space of models that permit such computationally cheap inference. Model 1 assumes all alignment structures are uniformly likely (a problematic assumption, particularly for frequent word types), and Model 2 is vastly overparameterized, making it prone to degenerate behavior on account of overfitting.[1] We present a simple log-linear reparameterization of Model 2 that avoids both problems (§2). While inference in log-linear models is generally computationally more expensive than in their multinomial counterparts, we show how the quantities needed for alignment inference, likelihood evaluation, and parameter estimation using EM and related methods can be computed using two simple algebraic identities (§3), thereby defusing this objection. We provide results showing our model is an order of magnitude faster to train than Model 4, that it requires no staged initialization, and that it produces alignments that lead to significantly better translation quality on downstream translation tasks (§4).

2 Model

Our model is a variation of the lexical translation models proposed by Brown et al. (1993). Lexical translation works as follows. Given a source sentence $\mathbf{f}$ with length n, first generate the length of the target sentence, m. Next, generate an *alignment*, $\mathbf{a} = \langle a_1, a_2, \ldots, a_m \rangle$, that indicates which source word (or null token) each target word will be a translation of. Last, generate the m output words, where each e_i depends only on f_{a_i}.

The model of alignment configurations we propose is a log-linear reparameterization of Model 2.

[1]Model 2 has independent parameters for every alignment position, conditioned on the source length, target length, and current target index.

$$\text{Given}: \mathbf{f},\ n = |\mathbf{f}|,\ m = |\mathbf{e}|,\ p_0,\ \lambda,\ \boldsymbol{\theta}$$

$$h(i,j,m,n) = -\left|\frac{i}{m} - \frac{j}{n}\right|$$

$$\delta(a_i = j \mid i,m,n) = \begin{cases} p_0 & j = 0 \\ (1-p_0) \times \frac{e^{\lambda h(i,j,m,n)}}{Z_\lambda(i,m,n)} & 0 < j \leq n \\ 0 & \text{otherwise} \end{cases}$$

$$a_i \mid i,m,n \sim \delta(\cdot \mid i,m,n) \qquad 1 \leq i \leq m$$

$$e_i \mid a_i, f_{a_i} \sim \theta(\cdot \mid f_{a_i}) \qquad 1 \leq i \leq m$$

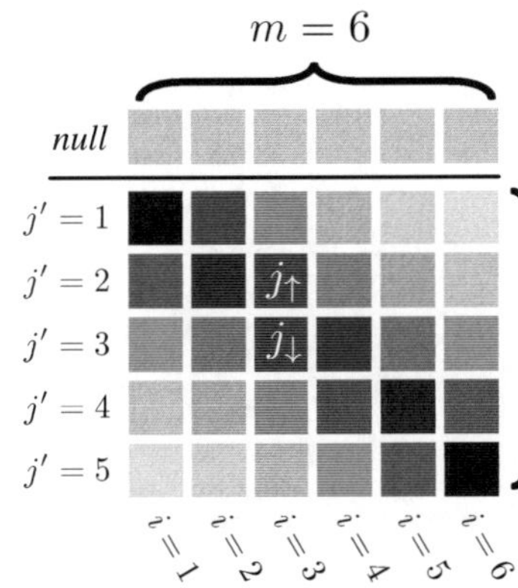

Figure 1: Our proposed generative process yielding a translation **e** and its alignment **a** to a source sentence **f**, given the source sentence **f**, alignment parameters p_0 and λ, and lexical translation probabilities $\boldsymbol{\theta}$ (left); an example visualization of the distribution of alignment probability mass under this model (right).

Our formulation, which we write as $\delta(a_i = j \mid i,m,n)$, is shown in Fig. 1.[2] The distribution over alignments is parameterized by a null alignment probability p_0 and a precision $\lambda \geq 0$ which controls how strongly the model favors alignment points close to the diagonal. In the limiting case as $\lambda \to 0$, the distribution approaches that of Model 1, and, as it gets larger, the model is less and less likely to deviate from a perfectly diagonal alignment. The right side of Fig. 1 shows a graphical illustration of the alignment distribution in which darker squares indicate higher probability.

3 Inference

We now discuss two inference problems and give efficient techniques for solving them. First, given a sentence pair and parameters, compute the marginal likelihood and the marginal alignment probabilities. Second, given a corpus of training data, estimate likelihood maximizing model parameters using EM.

3.1 Marginals

Under our model, the marginal likelihood of a sentence pair $\langle \mathbf{f}, \mathbf{e} \rangle$ can be computed exactly in time $\Theta(|\mathbf{f}| \cdot |\mathbf{e}|)$. This can be seen as follows. For each position in the sentence being generated, $i \in [1, 2, \ldots, m]$, the alignment to the source and its translation is independent of all other translation and alignment decisions. Thus, the probability that the ith word of **e** is e_i can be computed as:

$$p(e_i, a_i \mid \mathbf{f}, m, n) = \delta(a_i \mid i, m, n) \times \theta(e_i \mid f_{a_i})$$
$$p(e_i \mid \mathbf{f}, m, n) = \sum_{j=0}^{n} p(e_i, a_i = j \mid \mathbf{f}, m, n).$$

We can also compute the posterior probability over alignments using the above probabilities,

$$p(a_i \mid e_i, \mathbf{f}, m, n) = \frac{p(e_i, a_i \mid \mathbf{f}, m, n)}{p(e_i \mid \mathbf{f}, m, n)}. \qquad (1)$$

Finally, since all words in **e** (and their alignments) are conditionally independent,[3]

$$p(\mathbf{e} \mid \mathbf{f}) = \prod_{i=1}^{m} p(e_i \mid \mathbf{f}, m, n)$$
$$= \prod_{i=1}^{m} \sum_{j=0}^{n} \delta(a_i \mid i, m, n) \times \theta(e_i \mid f_{a_i}).$$

[2] Vogel et al. (1996) hint at a similar reparameterization of Model 2; however, its likelihood and its gradient are not efficient to evaluate, making it impractical to train and use. Och and Ney (2003) likewise remark on the overparameterization issue, removing a single variable of the original conditioning context, which only slightly improves matters.

[3] We note here that Brown et al. (1993) derive their variant of this expression by starting with the joint probability of an alignment and translation, marginalizing, and then reorganizing common terms. While identical in implication, we find the direct probabilistic argument far more intuitive.

3.2 Efficient Partition Function Evaluation

Evaluating and maximizing the data likelihood under log-linear models can be computationally expensive since this requires evaluation of normalizing partition functions. In our case,

$$Z_\lambda(i,m,n) = \sum_{j'=1}^{n} \exp \lambda h(i,j',m,n).$$

While computing this sum is obviously possible in $\Theta(|\mathbf{f}|)$ operations, our formulation permits exact computation in $\Theta(1)$, meaning our model can be applied even in applications where computational efficiency is paramount (e.g., MCMC simulations). The key insight is that the partition function is the (partial) sum of two geometric series of unnormalized probabilities that extend up and down from the probability-maximizing diagonal. The closest point on or above the diagonal $j_\uparrow$, and the next point down $j_\downarrow$ (see the right side of Fig. 1 for an illustration), is computed as follows:

$$j_\uparrow = \left\lfloor \frac{i \times n}{m} \right\rfloor, \qquad j_\downarrow = j_\uparrow + 1.$$

Starting at $j_\uparrow$ and moving up the alignment column, as well as starting at $j_\downarrow$ and moving down, the unnormalized probabilities decrease by a factor of $r = \exp \frac{-\lambda}{n}$ per step.

To compute the value of the partition, we only need to evaluate the unnormalized probabilities at $j_\uparrow$ and $j_\downarrow$ and then use the following identity, which gives the sum of the first ℓ terms of a geometric series (Courant and Robbins, 1996):

$$s_\ell(g_1, r) = \sum_{k=1}^{\ell} g_1 r^{k-1} = g_1 \frac{1-r^\ell}{1-r}.$$

Using this identity, $Z_\lambda(i,m,n)$ can be computed as

$$s_{j_\uparrow}(e^{\lambda h(i,j_\uparrow,m,n)}, r) + s_{n-j_\downarrow}(e^{\lambda h(i,j_\downarrow,m,n)}, r).$$

3.3 Parameter Optimization

To optimize the likelihood of a sample of parallel data under our model, one can use EM. In the E-step, the posterior probabilities over alignments are computed using Eq. 1. In the M-step, the lexical translation probabilities are updated by aggregating these as counts and normalizing (Brown et al., 1993). In the experiments reported in this paper, we make the further assumption that $\theta_f \sim \text{Dirichlet}(\boldsymbol{\mu})$ where $\mu_i = 0.01$ and approximate the posterior distribution over the θ_f's using a mean-field approximation (Riley and Gildea, 2012).[4]

During the M-step, the λ parameter must also be updated to make the E-step posterior distribution over alignment points maximally probable under $\delta(\cdot \mid i,m,n)$. This maximizing value cannot be computed analytically, but a gradient-based optimization can be used, where the first derivative (here, for a single target word) is:

$$\nabla_\lambda \mathcal{L} = \mathbb{E}_{p(a_i|e_i,\mathbf{f},m,n)} \left[h(i,a_i,m,n)\right] - \mathbb{E}_{\delta(j'|i,m,n)} \left[h(i,j',m,n)\right] \quad (2)$$

The first term in this expression (the expected value of h under the E-step posterior) is fixed for the duration of each M-step, but the second term's value (the derivative of the log-partition function) changes many times as λ is optimized.

3.4 Efficient Gradient Evaluation

Fortunately, like the partition function, the derivative of the log-partition function (i.e., the second term in Eq. 2) can be computed in constant time using an algebraic identity. To derive this, we observe that the values of $h(i,j',m,n)$ form an arithmetic sequence about the diagonal, with common difference $d = -1/n$. Thus, the quantity we seek is the sum of a series whose elements are the products of terms from an arithmetic sequence and those of the geometric sequence above, divided by the partition function value. This construction is referred to as an arithmetico-geometric series, and its sum may be computed as follows (Fernandez et al., 2006):

$$\begin{aligned} t_\ell(g_1,a_1,r,d) &= \sum_{k=1}^{\ell} \left[a_1 + d(k-1)\right] g_1 r^{k-1} \\ &= \frac{a_\ell g_{\ell+1} - a_1 g_1}{1-r} + \frac{d\,(g_{\ell+1} - g_1 r)}{(1-r)^2}. \end{aligned}$$

In this expression r, the g_1's and the ℓ's have the same values as above, $d = -1/n$ and the a_1's are

[4]The μ_i value was fixed at the beginning of experimentation by minimizing the AER on the 10k sentence French-English corpus discussed below.

equal to the value of h evaluated at the starting indices, $j_\uparrow$ and $j_\downarrow$; thus, the derivative we seek at each optimization iteration inside the M-step is:

$$\nabla_\lambda \mathcal{L} = \mathbb{E}_{p(a_i|e_i,\mathbf{f},m,n)} [h(i, a_i, m, n)] - \frac{1}{Z_\lambda}(t_{j_\uparrow}(e^{\lambda h(i,j_\uparrow,m,n)}, h(i, j_\uparrow, m, n), r, d) + t_{n-j_\downarrow}(e^{\lambda h(i,j_\downarrow,m,n)}, h(i, j_\uparrow, m, n), r, d)).$$

4 Experiments

In this section we evaluate the performance of our proposed model empirically. Experiments are conducted on three datasets representing different language typologies and dataset sizes: the FBIS Chinese-English corpus (LDC2003E14); a French-English corpus consisting of version 7 of the Europarl and news-commentary corpora;[5] and a large Arabic-English corpus consisting of all parallel data made available for the NIST 2012 Open MT evaluation. Table 1 gives token counts.

We begin with several preliminary results. First, we quantify the benefit of using the geometric series trick (§3.2) for computing the partition function relative to naïve summation. Our method requires only 0.62 seconds to compute all partition function values for $0 < i, m, n < 150$, whereas the naïve algorithm requires 6.49 seconds for the same.[6]

Second, using a 10k sample of the French-English data set (only 0.5% of the corpus), we determined 1) whether p_0 should be optimized; 2) what the optimal Dirichlet parameters μ_i are; and 3) whether the commonly used "staged initialization" procedure (in which Model 1 parameters are used to initialize Model 2, etc.) is necessary for our model. First, like Och and Ney (2003) who explored this issue for training Model 3, we found that EM tended to find poor values for p_0, producing alignments that were overly sparse. By fixing the value at $p_0 = 0.08$, we obtained minimal AER. Second, like Riley and Gildea (2012), we found that small values of α improved the alignment error rate, although the impact was not particularly strong over large ranges of α. Finally, we (perhaps surprisingly) found that the standard staged initialization procedure was *less effective* in terms of AER than simply initializing our model with uniform translation probabilities and a small value of λ and running EM. Based on these observations, we fixed $p_0 = 0.08$, $\mu_i = 0.01$, and set the initial value of λ to 4 for the remaining experiments.[7]

We next compare the alignments produced by our model to the Giza++ implementation of the standard IBM models using the default training procedure and parameters reported in Och and Ney (2003). Our model is trained for 5 iterations using the procedure described above (§3.3). The algorithms are

Table 1: CPU time (hours) required to train alignment models in one direction.

Language Pair	Tokens	Model 4	Log-linear
Chinese-English	17.6M	2.7	**0.2**
French-English	117M	17.2	**1.7**
Arabic-English	368M	63.2	**6.0**

Table 2: Alignment quality (AER) on the WMT 2012 French-English and FBIS Chinese-English. Rows with EM use expectation maximization to estimate the θ_f, and ~Dir use variational Bayes.

Model	Estimator	FR-EN	ZH-EN
Model 1	EM	29.0	56.2
Model 1	~Dir	26.6	53.6
Model 2	EM	21.4	53.3
Log-linear	EM	18.5	46.5
Log-linear	~Dir	16.6	**44.1**
Model 4	EM	**10.4**	45.8

Table 3: Translation quality (BLEU) as a function of alignment type.

Language Pair	Model 4	Log-linear
Chinese-English	34.1	**34.7**
French-English	27.4	**27.7**
Arabic-English	54.5	**55.7**

[5] http://www.statmt.org/wmt12

[6] While this computational effort is a small relative to the total cost in EM training, in algorithms where λ changes more rapidly, for example in Bayesian posterior inference with Monte Carlo methods (Chahuneau et al., 2013), this savings can have substantial value.

[7] As an anonymous reviewer pointed out, it is a near certainty that tuning of these hyperparameters for each alignment task would improve results; however, optimizing hyperparameters of alignment models is quite expensive. Our intention is to show that it is possible to obtain reasonable (if not optimal) results *without* careful tuning.

compared in terms of (1) time required for training; (2) alignment error rate (AER, lower is better);[8] and (3) translation quality (BLEU, higher is better) of hierarchical phrase-based translation system that used the alignments (Chiang, 2007). Table 1 shows the CPU time in hours required for training (one direction, English is generated). Our model is at least 10× faster to train than Model 4. Table 3 reports the differences in BLEU on a held-out test set. Our model's alignments lead to consistently better scores than Model 4's do.[9]

5 Conclusion

We have presented a fast and effective reparameterization of IBM Model 2 that is a compelling replacement for for the standard Model 4. Although the alignment quality results measured in terms of AER are mixed, the alignments were shown to work exceptionally well in downstream translation systems on a variety of language pairs.

Acknowledgments

This work was sponsored by the U. S. Army Research Laboratory and the U. S. Army Research Office under contract/grant number W911NF-10-1-0533.

References

P. F. Brown, V. J. Della Pietra, S. A. Della Pietra, and R. L. Mercer. 1993. The mathematics of statistical machine translation: parameter estimation. *Computational Linguistics*, 19(2):263–311.

V. Chahuneau, N. A. Smith, and C. Dyer. 2013. Knowledge-rich morphological priors for Bayesian language models. In *Proc. NAACL*.

D. Chiang. 2007. Hierarchical phrase-based translation. *Computational Linguistics*, 33(2):201–228.

R. Courant and H. Robbins. 1996. The geometric progression. In *What Is Mathematics?: An Elementary Approach to Ideas and Methods*, pages 13–14. Oxford University Press.

[8]Our Arabic training data was preprocessed using a segmentation scheme optimized for translation (Habash and Sadat, 2006). Unfortunately the existing Arabic manual alignments are preprocessed quite differently, so we did not evaluate AER.

[9]The alignments produced by our model were generally sparser than the corresponding Model 4 alignments; however, the extracted grammar sizes were sometimes smaller and sometimes larger, depending on the language pair.

P. A. Fernandez, T. Foregger, and J. Pahikkala. 2006. Arithmetic-geometric series. PlanetMath.org.

N. Habash and F. Sadat. 2006. Arabic preprocessing schemes for statistical machine translation. In *Proc. of NAACL*.

F. Och and H. Ney. 2003. A systematic comparison of various statistical alignment models. *Computational Linguistics*, 29(1):19–51.

D. Riley and D. Gildea. 2012. Improving the IBM alignment models using Variational Bayes. In *Proc. of ACL*.

S. Vogel, H. Ney, and C. Tillmann. 1996. HMM-based word alignment in statistical translation. In *Proc. of COLING*.

Phrase Training Based Adaptation for Statistical Machine Translation

Saab Mansour and **Hermann Ney**
Human Language Technology and Pattern Recognition
Computer Science Department
RWTH Aachen University, Aachen, Germany
{mansour,ney}@cs.rwth-aachen.de

Abstract

We present a novel approach for translation model (TM) adaptation using phrase training. The proposed adaptation procedure is initialized with a standard general-domain TM, which is then used to perform phrase training on a smaller in-domain set. This way, we bias the probabilities of the general TM towards the in-domain distribution. Experimental results on two different lectures translation tasks show significant improvements of the adapted systems over the general ones. Additionally, we compare our results to mixture modeling, where we report gains when using the suggested phrase training adaptation method.

1 Introduction

The task of domain-adaptation attempts to exploit data mainly drawn from one domain (e.g. news, parliamentary discussion) to maximize the performance on the test domain (e.g. lectures, web forums). In this work, we focus on translation model (TM) adaptation. A prominent approach in recent work is weighting at different levels of granularity. Foster and Kuhn (2007) perform weighting at the corpus level, where different corpora receive different weights and are then combined using mixture modeling. A finer grained weighting is that of Matsoukas et al. (2009), who weight each sentence in the bitexts using features of meta-information and optimize a mapping from the feature vectors to weights using a translation quality measure.

In this work, we propose to perform TM adaptation using phrase training. We start from a general-domain phrase table and adapt the probabilities by training on an in-domain data. Thus, we achieve direct phrase probabilities adaptation as opposed to weighting. Foster et al. (2010) perform weighting at the phrase level, assigning each phrase pair a weight according to its relevance to the test domain. They compare phrase weighting to a "flat" model, where the weight directly approximates the phrase probability. In their experiments, the weighting method performs better than the flat model, therefore, they conclude that retaining the original relative frequency probabilities of the TM is important for good performance. The "flat" model of Foster et al. (2010) is similar to our work. We differ in the following points: *(i)* we use the same procedure to perform the phrase training based adaptation and the search thus avoiding inconsistencies between the two; *(ii)* we do not directly interpolate the original statistics with the new ones, but use a training procedure to manipulate the original statistics. We perform experiments on the publicly available IWSLT TED task, on both Arabic-to-English and German-to-English lectures translation tracks. We compare our suggested phrase training adaptation method to a variety of baselines and show its effectiveness. Finally, we experiment with mixture modeling based adaptation. We compare mixture modeling to our adaptation method, and apply our method within a mixture modeling framework.

In Section 2, we present the phrase training method and explain how it is utilized for adaptation. Experimental setup including corpora statistics and the SMT system are described in Section 3. Section 4 summarizes the phrase training adaptation results ending with a comparison to mixture modeling.

2 Phrase Training

The standard phrase extraction procedure in SMT consists of two phases: *(i)* word-alignment training (e.g., IBM alignment models), *(ii)* heuristic phrase extraction and relative frequency based phrase translation probability estimation. In this work, we utilize phrase training for the task of adaptation. We use the forced alignment (FA) method (Wuebker et al., 2010) to perform the phrase alignment training and probability estimation. We perform phrase training by running a normal SMT decoder on the training data and constrain the translation to the given target instance. Using n-best possible phrase segmentation for each training instance, the phrase probabilities are re-estimated over the output. Leaving-one-out is used during the forced alignment procedure phase to avoid over-fitting (Wuebker et al., 2010).

In the standard phrase training procedure, we are given a training set y, from which an initial heuristics-based phrase table p_y^0 is generated. FA training is then done over the training set y using the phrases and probabilities in p_y^0 (possibly updated by the leaving-one-out method). Finally, re-estimation of the phrase probabilities is done over the decoder output, generating the FA phrase table p^1. We explain next how to utilize FA training for adaptation.

2.1 Adaptation

In this work, we utilize phrase training for the task of adaptation. The main idea is to generate the initial phrase table required for FA using a general-domain training data y', thus resulting in $p_{y'}^0$, and perform the FA training over y_{IN}, the in-domain training data (instead of y' in the standard procedure). This way, we bias the probabilities of $p_{y'}^0$ towards the in-domain distribution. We denote this new procedure by Y'-FA-IN. This differs from the standard IN-FA-IN by that we have more phrase pairs to use for FA. Thus, we obtain phrase pairs relevant to IN in addition to "general" phrase pairs which were not extracted from IN, perhaps due to faulty word alignments. The probabilities of the general phrase table will be tailored towards IN. In practice, we usually have in-domain IN and other-domain OD data. We denote by ALL the concatenation of IN and OD. To adapt the ALL phrase table, we perform the FA procedure ALL-FA-IN. We also utilize leaving-one-out to avoid over-fitting.

Another procedure we experimented with is adapting the OD phrase table using FA over IN, without leaving-one-out. We denote it by OD-FA$_0$-IN. In this FA scenario, we do not use leaving-one-out as IN is not contained in OD, therefore, over-fitting will not occur. By this procedure, we train phrases from OD that are relevant for both OD and IN, while the probabilities will be tailored to IN. In this case, we do not expect improvements over the IN based phrase table, but, improvements over OD and reduction in the phrase table size.

We compare our suggested FA based adaptation to the standard FA procedure.

3 Experimental Setup

3.1 Training Corpora

To evaluate the introduced methods experimentally, we use the IWSLT 2011 TED Arabic-to-English and German-to-English translation tasks. The IWSLT 2011 evaluation campaign focuses on the translation of TED talks, a collection of lectures on a variety of topics ranging from science to culture. For Arabic-to-English, the bilingual data consists of roughly 100K sentences of in-domain TED talks data and 8M sentences of "other"-domain United Nations (UN) data. For the German-to-English task, the data consists of 130K TED sentences and 2.1M sentences of "other"-domain data assembled from the news-commentary and the europarl corpora. For language model training purposes, we use an additional 1.4 billion words (supplied as part of the campaign monolingual training data).

The bilingual training and test data for the Arabic-to-English and German-to-English tasks are summarized in Table 1[1]. The English data was tokenized and lowercased while the Arabic data was tokenized and segmented using MADA v3.1 (Roth et al., 2008) with the ATB scheme. The German source is decompounded (Koehn and Knight, 2003) and part-of-speech-based long-range verb reordering rules (Popović and Ney, 2006) are applied.

From Table 1, we note that using the general data considerably reduces the number of out-of-

[1] For a list of the IWSLT TED 2011 training corpora, see http://www.iwslt2011.org/doku.php?id=06_evaluation

Set	Sen	Tok	OOV/IN	OOV/ALL
German-to-English				
IN	130K	2.5M		
OD	2.1M	55M		
dev	883	20K	398 (2.0%)	215 (1.1%)
test	1565	32K	483 (1.5%)	227 (0.7%)
eval	1436	27K	490 (1.8%)	271 (1.0%)
Arabic-to-English				
IN	90K	1.6M		
OD	7.9M	228M		
dev	934	19K	408 (2.2%)	184 (1.0%)
test	1664	31K	495 (1.6%)	228 (0.8%)
eval	1450	27K	513 (1.9%)	163 (0.6%)

Table 1: IWSLT 2011 TED bilingual corpora statistics: the number of tokens is given for the source side. OOV/X denotes the number of OOV words in relation to corpus X (the percentage is given in parentheses). *IN* is the TED in-domain data, *OD* denotes other-domain data, *ALL* denotes the concatenation of *IN* and *OD*.

vocabulary (OOV) words. This comes with the price of increasing the size of the training data by a factor of more than 20. A simple concatenation of the corpora might mask the phrase probabilities obtained from the in-domain corpus, causing a deterioration in performance. One way to avoid this contamination is by filtering the general corpus, but this discards phrase translations completely from the phrase model. A more principled way is by adapting the phrase probabilities of the full system to the domain being tackled. We perform this by phrase training the full phrase table over the in-domain training set.

3.2 Translation System

The baseline system is built using the open-source SMT toolkit Jane 2.0, which provides a state-of-the-art phrase-based SMT system (Wuebker et al., 2012a). In addition to the phrase based decoder, Jane 2.0 implements the forced alignment procedure used in this work for the purpose of adaptation. We use the standard set of models with phrase translation probabilities for source-to-target and target-to-source directions, smoothing with lexical weights, a word and phrase penalty, distance-based reordering and an n-gram target language model. The SMT systems are tuned on the *dev* (dev2010) development set with minimum error rate training (Och, 2003) using BLEU (Papineni et al., 2002) accuracy measure as the optimization criterion. We test the performance of our system on the *test* (tst2010) and *eval* (tst2011) sets using the BLEU and translation edit rate (TER) (Snover et al., 2006) measures. We use TER as an additional measure to verify the consistency of our improvements and avoid over-tuning. The Arabic-English results are case sensitive while the German-English results are case insensitive.

4 Results

For TM training, we define three different sets: in-domain (IN) which is the TED corpus, other-domain (OD) which consists of the UN corpus for Arabic-English and a concatenation of news-commentary and europarl for German-English, and ALL which consists of the concatenation of IN and OD. We experiment with the following extraction methods:

- Heuristics: standard phrase extraction using word-alignment training and heuristic phrase extraction over the word alignment. The extraction is performed for the three different training data, IN, OD and ALL.

- FA standard: standard FA phrase training where the same training set is used for initial phrase table generation as well as the FA procedure. We perform the training on the three different training sets and denote the resulting systems by IN-FA, OD-FA and ALL-FA.

- FA adaptation: FA based adaptation phrase training, where the initial table is generated from some general data and the FA training is performed on the IN data to achieve adaptation. We perform two experiments, OD-FA_0-IN without leaving-one-out and ALL-FA-IN with leaving-one-out.

The results of the various experiments over both Arabic-English and German-English tasks are summarized in Table 2. The usefulness of the OD data differs between the Arabic-to-English and the German-to-English translation tasks. For Arabic-to-English, the *OD* system is 2.5%-4.3% BLEU worse than the *IN* system, whereas for the German-to-English task the differences between *IN* and *OD* are smaller and range from 0.9% to 1.6% BLEU. The

Phrase training method	System	Rules number	dev BLEU	dev TER	test BLEU	test TER	eval BLEU	eval TER
Arabic-to-English								
Heuristics	IN	1.1M	27.2	54.1	25.3	57.1	24.3	59.9
	OD	36.3M	24.7	57.7	21.2	62.6	21.0	64.7
	ALL	36.9M	27.1	54.8	24.4	58.6	23.8	61.1
FA standard	IN-FA	1.0M	27.0	54.4	25.0	57.5	23.8	60.3
	OD-FA	1.8M	24.5	57.7	21.0	62.4	21.2	64.3
	ALL-FA	2.0M	27.2	54.2	24.5	58.1	23.8	60.6
FA adaptation	OD-FA$_0$-IN	0.3M	25.8	55.8	23.6	59.4	22.7	61.7
	ALL-FA-IN	0.5M	27.7	53.7	25.3	56.9	24.7	59.3
German-to-English								
Heuristics	IN	1.3M	31.0	48.9	29.3	51.0	32.7	46.8
	OD	7.3M	29.8	49.2	27.7	51.5	31.8	47.5
	ALL	7.8M	31.2	48.3	29.5	50.5	33.6	46.1
FA standard	IN-FA	0.5M	31.6	48.2	29.7	50.5	33.3	46.4
	OD-FA	3.0M	29.1	51.0	27.6	53.0	30.7	49.6
	ALL-FA	3.2M	31.4	48.3	29.4	50.8	33.6	46.2
FA adaptation	OD-FA$_0$-IN	0.9M	31.2	48.7	29.1	50.9	32.7	46.9
	ALL-FA-IN	0.9M	31.8	47.4	29.7	49.7	33.6	45.5

Table 2: TED 2011 translation results. BLEU and TER are given in percentages. *IN* denotes the TED lectures in-domain corpus, *OD* denotes the other-domain corpus, *ALL* is the concatenation of *IN* and *OD*. *FA*$_0$ denotes forced alignment training without leaving-one-out (otherwise, leaving-one-out is used).

inferior performance of the *OD* system can be related to noisy data or bigger discrepancy between the OD data domain distribution and the IN distribution. The *ALL* system performs according to the usefulness of the OD training set, where for Arabic-to-English we observe deterioration in performance for all test sets and up-to -0.9% BLEU on the *test* set. On the other hand, for German-to-English, the *ALL* system is improving over *IN* where the biggest improvement is observed on the *eval* set with +0.9% BLEU improvement.

The standard FA procedure achieves mixed results, where *IN-FA* deteriorates the results over the *IN* counterpart for Arabic-English, while improving for German-English. *ALL-FA* performs comparably to the *ALL* system on both tasks, while reducing the phrase table size considerably. The *OD-FA* system deteriorates the results in comparison to the *OD* system in most cases, which is expected as training over the OD set fits the phrase model on the OD domain, making it perform worse on IN. (Wuebker et al., 2012b) also report mixed results with FA training.

The FA adaptation results are summarized in the last block of the experiments. The *OD-FA*$_0$*-IN* improves over the *OD* system, which means that the training procedure was able to modify the OD probabilities to perform well on the IN data. On the German-to-English task, the *OD-FA*$_0$*-IN* performs comparably to the IN system, whereas for Arabic-to-English *OD-FA*$_0$*-IN* was able to close around half of the gap between OD and IN.

The FA adapted ALL system (*ALL-FA-IN*) performs best in our experiments, improving on both BLEU and TER measures. In comparison to the best heuristics system (*IN* for Arabic-English and *ALL* for German-English), +0.4% BLEU and -0.6% TER improvements are observed on the *eval* set for Arabic-English. For German-English, the biggest improvements are observed on TER with -0.8% on *test* and -0.5% on *eval*. The results suggest that *ALL-FA-IN* is able to learn more useful phrases than the *IN* system and adjust the *ALL* phrase probabilities towards the in-domain distribution.

System	dev		test	
	BLEU	TER	BLEU	TER
Arabic-to-English				
$\text{Heuristics}_{\text{best}}$	27.2	54.1	25.3	57.1
IN,OD	28.2	53.1	25.5	56.8
IN,OD-FA_0-IN	28.4	52.9	25.7	56.5
German-to-English				
$\text{Heuristics}_{\text{best}}$	31.2	48.3	29.5	50.5
IN,OD	31.6	48.2	29.9	50.5
IN,OD-FA_0-IN	31.8	47.8	30.0	50.0

Table 3: TED 2011 mixture modeling results. $\text{Heuristics}_{\text{best}}$ is the best heuristics based system, *IN* for Arabic-English and *ALL* for German-English. *X,Y* denotes linear interpolation between X and Y phrase tables.

4.1 Mixture Modeling

In this section, we compare our method to mixture modeling based adaptation, in addition to applying mixture modeling on top of our method. We focus on linear interpolation (Foster and Kuhn, 2007) of the in-domain (IN) and other-domain phrase tables, where we vary the latter between the heuristically extracted phrase table (*OD*) and the FA adapted one (*OD-FA_0-IN*). The interpolation weight is uniform for the interpolated phrase tables (0.5). The results of mixture modeling are summarized in Table 3. In this table, we include the best heuristics based system ($\text{Heuristics}_{\text{best}}$) from Table 2 as a reference system. The results on the *eval* set are omitted as they show similar tendencies to the *test* set results.

Linear interpolation of *IN* and *OD* (*IN,OD*) is performing well in our experiments, with big improvements over the *dev* set, +1.0% BLEU for Arabic-to-English and +0.4% BLEU for German-to-English. On the *test* set, we observe smaller improvements. Interpolating *IN* with the phrase training adapted system *OD-FA_0-IN* (*IN,OD-FA_0-IN*) achieves additional gains over the *IN,OD* system, the biggest are observed on TER for German-to-English, with -0.4% and -0.5% improvements on the *dev* and *test* sets correspondingly.

Comparing heuristics based interpolation (*IN,OD*) to our best phrase training adapted system (*ALL-FA-IN*) shows mixed results. For Arabic-to-English, the systems are comparable, while for the German-to-English *test* set, *IN,OD* is +0.2% BLEU better and +0.8% TER worse than *ALL-FA-IN*. We hypothesize that for Arabic-to-English interpolation is important due to the larger size of the OD data, where it could reduce the masking of the IN training data by the much larger OD data. Nevertheless, as mentioned previously, using phrase training adapted phrase table in a mixture setup consistently improves over using heuristically extracted tables.

5 Conclusions

In this work, we propose a phrase training procedure for adaptation. The phrase training is implemented using the FA method. First, we extract a standard phrase table using the whole available training data. Using this table, we initialize the FA procedure and perform training on the in-domain set.

Experiments are done on the Arabic-to-English and German-to-English TED lectures translation tasks. We show that the suggested procedure is improving over unadapted baselines. On the Arabic-to-English task, the FA adapted system is +0.9% BLEU better than the full unadapted counterpart on both test sets. Unlike the Arabic-to-English setup, the German-to-English OD data is helpful and produces a strong unadapted baseline in concatenation with IN. In this case, the FA adapted system achieves BLEU improvements mainly on the development set with +0.6% BLEU, on the *test* and *eval* sets, improvements of -0.8% and -0.6% TER are observed correspondingly. As a side effect of the FA training process, the size of the adapted phrase table is less than 10% of the size of the full table.

Finally, we experimented with mixture modeling where improvements are observed over the unadapted baselines. The results show that using our phrase training adapted OD table yields better performance than using the heuristically extracted OD in a mixture framework.

Acknowledgments

This material is based upon work supported by the DARPA BOLT project under Contract No. HR0011-12-C-0015. Any opinions, findings and conclusions or recommendations expressed in this material are those of the authors and do not necessarily reflect the views of DARPA.

References

George Foster and Roland Kuhn. 2007. Mixture-model adaptation for SMT. In *Proceedings of the Second Workshop on Statistical Machine Translation*, pages 128–135, Prague, Czech Republic, June. Association for Computational Linguistics.

George Foster, Cyril Goutte, and Roland Kuhn. 2010. Discriminative instance weighting for domain adaptation in statistical machine translation. In *Proceedings of the 2010 Conference on Empirical Methods in Natural Language Processing*, pages 451–459, Cambridge, MA, October. Association for Computational Linguistics.

Philipp Koehn and Kevin Knight. 2003. Empirical Methods for Compound Splitting. In *Proc. 10th Conf. of the Europ. Chapter of the Assoc. for Computational Linguistics (EACL)*, pages 347–354, Budapest, Hungary, April.

Spyros Matsoukas, Antti-Veikko I. Rosti, and Bing Zhang. 2009. Discriminative corpus weight estimation for machine translation. In *Proceedings of the 2009 Conference on Empirical Methods in Natural Language Processing*, pages 708–717, Singapore, August. Association for Computational Linguistics.

Franz J. Och. 2003. Minimum Error Rate Training in Statistical Machine Translation. In *Proceedings of the 41th Annual Meeting of the Association for Computational Linguistics*, pages 160–167, Sapporo, Japan, July.

Kishore Papineni, Salim Roukos, Todd Ward, and Wei-Jing Zhu. 2002. Bleu: a Method for Automatic Evaluation of Machine Translation. In *Proceedings of the 41st Annual Meeting of the Association for Computational Linguistics*, pages 311–318, Philadelphia, Pennsylvania, USA, July.

M. Popović and H. Ney. 2006. POS-based Word Reorderings for Statistical Machine Translation. In *International Conference on Language Resources and Evaluation*, pages 1278–1283.

Ryan Roth, Owen Rambow, Nizar Habash, Mona Diab, and Cynthia Rudin. 2008. Arabic morphological tagging, diacritization, and lemmatization using lexeme models and feature ranking. In *Proceedings of ACL-08: HLT, Short Papers*, pages 117–120, Columbus, Ohio, June. Association for Computational Linguistics.

Matthew Snover, Bonnie Dorr, Richard Schwartz, Linnea Micciulla, and John Makhoul. 2006. A Study of Translation Edit Rate with Targeted Human Annotation. In *Proceedings of the 7th Conference of the Association for Machine Translation in the Americas*, pages 223–231, Cambridge, Massachusetts, USA, August.

Joern Wuebker, Arne Mauser, and Hermann Ney. 2010. Training phrase translation models with leaving-one-out. In *Proceedings of the 48th Annual Meeting of the Assoc. for Computational Linguistics*, pages 475–484, Uppsala, Sweden, July.

Joern Wuebker, Matthias Huck, Stephan Peitz, Malte Nuhn, Markus Freitag, Jan-Thorsten Peter, Saab Mansour, and Hermann Ney. 2012a. Jane 2: Open source phrase-based and hierarchical statistical machine translation. In *International Conference on Computational Linguistics*, Mumbai, India, December.

Joern Wuebker, Mei-Yuh Hwang, and Chris Quirk. 2012b. Leave-one-out phrase model training for large-scale deployment. In *NAACL 2012 Seventh Workshop on Statistical Machine Translation*, pages 460–467, Montreal, Canada, June. Association for Computational Linguistics.

Translation Acquisition Using Synonym Sets

Daniel Andrade **Masaaki Tsuchida** **Takashi Onishi** **Kai Ishikawa**
Knowledge Discovery Research Laboratories, NEC Corporation, Nara, Japan
{s-andrade@cj, m-tsuchida@cq,
t-onishi@bq, k-ishikawa@dq}.jp.nec.com

Abstract

We propose a new method for translation acquisition which uses a set of synonyms to acquire translations from comparable corpora. The motivation is that, given a certain query term, it is often possible for a user to specify one or more synonyms. Using the resulting set of query terms has the advantage that we can overcome the problem that a single query term's context vector does not always reliably represent a terms meaning due to the context vector's sparsity. Our proposed method uses a weighted average of the synonyms' context vectors, that is derived by inferring the mean vector of the von Mises-Fisher distribution. We evaluate our method, using the synsets from the cross-lingually aligned Japanese and English WordNet. The experiments show that our proposed method significantly improves translation accuracy when compared to a previous method for smoothing context vectors.

1 Introduction

Automatic translation acquisition is an important task for various applications. For example, finding term translations can be used to automatically update existing bilingual dictionaries, which are an indispensable resource for tasks such as cross-lingual information retrieval and text mining.

Various previous research like (Rapp, 1999; Fung, 1998) has shown that it is possible to acquire word translations from comparable corpora.

We suggest here an extension of this approach which uses several query terms instead of a single query term. A user who searches a translation for a query term that is not listed in an existing bilingual dictionary, might first try to find a synonym of that term. For example, the user might look up a synonym in a thesaurus[1] or might use methods for automatic synonym acquisition like described in (Grefenstette, 1994). If the synonym is listed in the bilingual dictionary, we can consider the synonym's translations as the translations of the query term. Otherwise, if the synonym is not listed in the dictionary either, we use the synonym together with the original query term to find a translation.

We claim that using a set of synonymous query terms to find a translation is better than using a single query term. The reason is that a single query term's context vector is, in general, unreliable due to sparsity. For example, a low frequent query term tends to have many zero entries in its context vector. To mitigate this problem it has been proposed to smooth a query's context vector by its nearest neighbors (Pekar et al., 2006). However, nearest neighbors, which context vectors are close the query's context vector, can have different meanings and therefore might introduce noise.

The contributions of this paper are two-fold. First, we confirm experimentally that smoothing a query's context vector with its synonyms leads in deed to higher translation accuracy, compared to smoothing with nearest neighbors. Second, we propose a simple method to combine a set of context vectors that performs in this setting better than a method previously proposed by (Pekar et al., 2006).

Our approach to combine a set of context vec-

[1]Monolingual thesauri are, arguably, easier to construct than bilingual dictionaries.

tors is derived by learning the mean vector of a von Mises-Fisher distribution. The combined context vector is a weighted-average of the original context-vectors, where the weights are determined by the word occurrence frequencies.

In the following section we briefly show the relation to other previous work. In Section 3, we explain our method in detail, followed by an empirical evaluation in Section 4. We summarize our results in Section 6.

2 Related Work

There are several previous works on extracting translations from comparable corpora ranging from (Rapp, 1999; Fung, 1998), and more recently (Haghighi et al., 2008; Laroche and Langlais, 2010), among others. Essentially, all these methods calculate the similarity of a query term's context vector with each translation candidate's context vector. The context vectors are extracted from the comparable corpora, and mapped to a common vector space with the help of an existing bilingual dictionary.

The work in (Déjean et al., 2002) uses cross-lingually aligned classes in a multilingual thesaurus to improve the translation accuracy. Their method uses the probability that the query term and a translation candidate are assigned to the same class. In contrast, our method does not need cross-lingually aligned classes.

Ismail and Manandhar (2010) proposes a method that tries to improve a query's context vector by using in-domain terms. In-domain terms are the terms that are highly associated to the query, as well as highly associated to one of the query's highly associated terms. Their method makes it necessary that the query term has enough highly associated context terms.[2] However, a low-frequent query term might not have enough highly associated terms.

In general if a query term has a low-frequency in the corpus, then its context vector is sparse. In that case, the chance of finding a correct translation is reduced (Pekar et al., 2006). Therefore, Pekar et al. (2006) suggest to use distance-based averaging to smooth the context vector of a low-frequent query term. Their smoothing strategy is dependent on the occurrence frequency of a query term and its close neighbors. Let us denote $\boldsymbol{q}$ the context vector of the query word, and K be the set of its close neighbors. The smoothed context vector $\boldsymbol{q}'$ is then derived by using:

$$\boldsymbol{q}' = \gamma \cdot \boldsymbol{q} + (1-\gamma) \cdot \sum_{\boldsymbol{x} \in K} w_x \cdot \boldsymbol{x}\,, \qquad (1)$$

where w_x is the weight of neighbor x, and all weights sum to one. The context vectors $\boldsymbol{q}$ and $\boldsymbol{x}$ are interpreted as probability vectors and therefore L1-normalized. The weight w_x is a function of the distance between neighbor x and query q. The parameter γ determines the degree of smoothing, and is a function of the frequency of the query term and its neighbors:

$$\gamma = \frac{\log f(q)}{\log \max_{x \in K \cup \{q\}} f(x)} \qquad (2)$$

where $f(x)$ is the frequency of term x. Their method forms the baseline for our proposed method.

3 Proposed Method

Our goal is to combine the context vectors to one context vector which is less sparse and more reliable than the original context vector of query word q. We assume that for each occurrence of a word, its corresponding context vector was generated by a probabilistic model. Furthermore, we assume that synonyms are generated by the same probability distribution. Finally we use the mean vector of that distribution to represent the combined context vector. By using the assumption that *each* occurrence of a word corresponds to one sample of the probability distribution, our model places more weight on synonyms that are highly-frequent than synonyms that occur infrequently. This is motivated by the assumption that context vectors of synonyms that occur with high frequency in the corpus, are more reliable than the ones of low-frequency synonyms.

When comparing context vectors, work like Laroche and Langlais (2010) observed that often the cosine similarity performs superior to other distance-measures, like, for example, the euclidean distance. This suggests that context vectors tend to lie in the spherical vector space,

[2] In their experiments, they require that a query word has at least 100 associated terms.

and therefore the von Mises-Fisher distribution is a natural choice for our probabilistic model. The von Mises-Fisher distribution was also successfully used in the work of (Basu et al., 2004) to cluster text data.

The von Mises-Fisher distribution with location parameter $\boldsymbol{\mu}$, and concentration parameter κ is defined as:

$$p(\boldsymbol{x}|\boldsymbol{\mu},\kappa) = c(\kappa)\cdot e^{\kappa\cdot\boldsymbol{x}\cdot\boldsymbol{\mu}^T},$$

where $c(\kappa)$ is a normalization constant, and $||\boldsymbol{x}|| = ||\boldsymbol{\mu}|| = 1$, and $\kappa \geq 0$. $||$ denotes here the L2-norm. The cosine-similarity measures the angle between two vectors, and the von Mises distribution defines a probability distribution over the possible angles. The parameter $\boldsymbol{\mu}$ of the von Mises distribution is estimated as follows (Jammalamadaka and Sengupta, 2001): Given the words $x_1, ..., x_n$, we denote the corresponding context vectors as $\mathbf{x}_1, ..., \mathbf{x}_n$, and assume that each context vector is L2-normalized. Then, the mean vector $\boldsymbol{\mu}$ is calculated as:

$$\boldsymbol{\mu} = \frac{1}{Z}\sum_{i=1}^{n}\frac{\mathbf{x}_i}{n}$$

where Z ensures that the resulting context vector is L2-normalized, i.e. Z is $||\sum_{i=1}^{n}\frac{\mathbf{x}_i}{n}||$. For our purpose, κ is irrelevant and is assumed to be any fixed positive constant.

Since we assume that each occurrence of a word x in the corpus corresponds to one observation of the corresponding word's context vector $\mathbf{x}$, we get the following formula:

$$\boldsymbol{\mu} = \frac{1}{Z'}\cdot\sum_{i=1}^{n}\frac{f(x_i)}{\sum_{j=1}^{n}f(x_j)}\cdot\mathbf{x}_i$$

where Z' is now $||\sum_{i=1}^{n}\frac{f(x_i)}{\sum_{j=1}^{n}f(x_j)}\cdot\mathbf{x}_i||$. We then use the vector $\boldsymbol{\mu}$ as the combined vector of the words' context vectors $\mathbf{x}_i$.

Our proposed procedure to combine the context vector of query word q and its synonyms can be summarized as follows:

1. Denote the context vectors of q and its synonyms as $\mathbf{x}_1, ..., \mathbf{x}_n$, and L2-normalize each context vector.

2. Calculate the weighted average of the vectors $\mathbf{x}_1, ..., \mathbf{x}_n$, whereas the weights correspond to the frequencies of each word x_i.

3. L2-normalize the weighted average.

4 Experiments

As source and target language corpora we use a corpus extracted from a collection of complaints concerning automobiles compiled by the Japanese Ministry of Land, Infrastructure, Transport and Tourism (MLIT)[3] and the USA National Highway Traffic Safety Administration (NHTSA)[4], respectively. The Japanese corpus contains 24090 sentences that were POS tagged using MeCab (Kudo et al., 2004). The English corpus contains 47613 sentences, that were POS tagged using Stepp Tagger (Tsuruoka et al., 2005), and use the Lemmatizer (Okazaki et al., 2008) to extract and stem content words (nouns, verbs, adjectives, adverbs).

For creating the context vectors, we calculate the association between two content words occurring in the same sentence, using the log-odds-ratio (Evert, 2004). It was shown in (Laroche and Langlais, 2010) that the log-odds-ratio in combination with the cosine-similarity performs superior to several other methods like PMI[5] and LLR[6]. For comparing two context vectors we use the cosine similarity.

To transform the Japanese and English context vectors into the same vector space, we use a bilingual dictionary with around 1.6 million entries.[7] To express all context vectors in the same vector space, we map the context vectors in English to context vectors in Japanese.[8] First, for all the words which are listed in the bilingual dictionary we calculate word translation probabilities. These translation probabilities are calculated using the EM-algorithm described in (Koehn and Knight, 2000). We then create a translation matrix T which contains in each

[3]http://www.mlit.go.jp/jidosha/carinf/rcl/defects.html

[4]http://www-odi.nhtsa.dot.gov/downloads/index.cfm

[5]point-wise mutual information

[6]log-likelihood ratio

[7]The bilingual dictionary was developed in the course of our Japanese language processing efforts described in (Sato et al., 2003).

[8]Alternatively, we could, for example, use canonical correlation analysis to match the vectors to a common latent vector space, like described in (Haghighi et al., 2008).

column the translation probabilities for a word in English into any word in Japanese. Each context vector in English is then mapped into Japanese using the linear transformation described by the translation matrix T. For word x with context vector $\mathbf{x}$ in English, let $\mathbf{x}'$ be its context vector after transformation into Japanese, i.e. $\mathbf{x}' = T \cdot \mathbf{x}$.

The gold-standard was created by considering all nouns in the Japanese and English WordNet where synsets are aligned cross-lingually. This way we were able to create a gold-standard with 215 Japanese nouns, and their respective English translations that occur in our comparable corpora.[9] Note that the cross-lingual alignment is needed only for evaluation. For evaluation, we consider only the translations that occur in the corresponding English synset as correct.

Because all methods return a ranked list of translation candidates, the accuracy is measured using the rank of the translation listed in the gold-standard. The inverse rank is the sum of the inverse ranks of each translation in the gold-standard.

In Table 1, the first row shows the results when using no smoothing. Next, we smooth the query's context vector by using Equation (1) and (2). The set of neighbors K is defined as the k-terms in the source language that are closest to the query word, with respect to the cosine similarity (sim). The weight w_x for a neighbor x is set to $w_x = 10^{0.13 \cdot sim(x,q)}$ in accordance to (Pekar et al., 2006). For k we tried values between 1 and 100, and got the best inverse rank when using k=19. The resulting method (Top-k Smoothing) performs consistently better than the method using no smoothing, see Table 1, second row. Next, instead of smoothing the query word with its nearest neighbors, we use as the set K the set of synonyms of the query word (Syn Smoothing). Table 1 shows a clear improvement over the method that uses nearest neighbor-smoothing. This confirms our claim that using synonyms for smoothing can lead to better translation accuracy than using nearest neighbors. In the last row of Table 1, we compare our proposed method to combine context vectors of synonyms (Syn Mises-Combination), with the previous method (Syn Smoothing). A pair-wise comparison of our proposed method with Syn Smoothing shows a statistically significant improvement ($p < 0.01$).[10]

Finally, we also show the result when simply adding each synonym vector to the query's context vector to form a new combined context vector (Syn Sum).[11] Even though, this approach does not use the frequency information of a word, it performs better than Syn Smoothing. We suppose that this is due to the fact that it actually indirectly uses frequency information, since the log-odds-ratio tends to be higher for words which occur with high frequency in the corpus.

Method	**Top1**	**Top5**	**Top10**	**MIR**
No Smoothing	0.14	0.30	0.36	0.23
Top-k Smoothing	0.16	0.33	0.43	0.26
Syn Smoothing	0.18	0.35	0.46	0.28
Syn Sum	0.23	0.46	0.57	0.35
Syn Mises-Combination	0.31	0.46	0.55	0.40

Table 1: Shows Top-n accuracy and mean inverse rank (MIR) for baseline methods which use no synonyms (No Smoothing, Top-k Smoothing), the proposed method (Syn Mises-Combination) which uses synonyms, and alternative methods that also use synonyms (Syn Smoothing, Syn Sum).

5 Discussion

We first discuss an example where the query terms are クルーズ (cruise) and 巡航 (cruise). Both words can have the same meaning. The resulting translation candidates suggested by the baseline methods and the proposed method is shown in Table 2. Using no smoothing, the baseline method outputs the correct translation for クルーズ (cruise) and 巡航 (cruise) at rank 10 and 15, respectively. When combining both queries to form one context vector our proposed method (Syn Mises-Combination) retrieves the correct translation at rank 2. Note that we considered all nouns that occur three or more times as possible translation candidates. As can be seen in Table 2, this also includes spelling mistakes like "sevice" and "infromation".

[9] The resulting synsets in Japanese and English, contain in average 2.2 and 2.8 words, respectively. The ambiguity of a query term in our gold-standard is low, since, in average, a query term belongs to only 1.2 different synsets.

[10] We use the sign-test (Wilcox, 2009) to test the hypothesis that the proposed method ranks higher than the baseline.

[11] No normalization is performed before adding the context vectors.

Method	Query	Output	Rank
No Smoothing	クルーズ	..., affinity, delco, **cruise**, sevice, sentrum,...	10
No Smoothing	巡航	..., denali, attendant, **cruise**, abs, tactic,...	15
Top-k Smoothing	クルーズ	pillar, multi, **cruise**, star, affinity,...	3
Top-k Smoothing	巡航	..., burnout, dipstick, **cruise**, infromation, speed, ...	8
Syn Smoothing	クルーズ smoothed with 巡航	..., affinity, delco, **cruise**, sevice, sentrum,...	10
Syn Smoothing	巡航 smoothed with クルーズ	..., alldata, mode, **cruise**, expectancy, mph,...	8
Syn Sum	クルーズ, 巡航	assumption, level, **cruise**, reimbursment, infromation,...	3
Syn Mises-Combination	クルーズ, 巡航	pillar, **cruise**, assumption, level, speed,...	2

Table 2: Shows the results for クルーズ and 巡航 which both have the same meaning "cruise". The third column shows part of the ranked translation candidates separated by comma. The last column shows the rank of the correct translation "cruise". Syn Smoothing uses Equation (1) with $\mathbf{q}$ corresponding to the context vector of the query word, and K contains only the context vector of the term that is used for smoothing.

Finally, we note that some terms in our test set are ambiguous, and the ambiguity is not resolved by using the synonyms of only one synset. For example, the term 操舵 (steering, guidance) belongs to the synset "steering, guidance" which includes the terms 舵取り (steering, guidance) and ガイド (guidance), 案内 (guidance). Despite this conflation of senses in one synset, our proposed method can improve the finding of (one) correct translation. The baseline system using only 操舵 (steering, guidance) outputs the correct translation "steering" at rank 4, whereas our method using all four terms outputs it at rank 2.

6 Conclusions

We proposed a new method for translation acquisition which uses a set of synonyms to acquire translations. Our approach combines the query term's context vector with all the context vectors of its synonyms. In order to combine the vectors we use a weighted average of each context vector, where the weights are determined by a term's occurrence frequency.

Our experiments, using the Japanese and English WordNet (Bond et al., 2009; Fellbaum, 1998), show that our proposed method can increase the translation accuracy, when compared to using only a single query term, or smoothing with nearest neighbours. Our results suggest that instead of directly searching for a translation, it is worth first looking for synonyms, for example by considering spelling variations or monolingual resources.

References

S. Basu, M. Bilenko, and R.J. Mooney. 2004. A probabilistic framework for semi-supervised clustering. In *Proceedings of the ACM SIGKDD International Conference on Knowledge Discovery and Data Mining*, pages 59–68.

F. Bond, H. Isahara, S. Fujita, K. Uchimoto, T. Kuribayashi, and K. Kanzaki. 2009. Enhancing the japanese wordnet. In *Proceedings of the 7th Workshop on Asian Language Resources*, pages 1–8. Association for Computational Linguistics.

H. Déjean, É. Gaussier, and F. Sadat. 2002. An approach based on multilingual thesauri and model combination for bilingual lexicon extraction. In *Proceedings of the International Conference on Computational Linguistics*, pages 1–7. International Committee on Computational Linguistics.

S. Evert. 2004. The statistics of word cooccurrences: word pairs and collocations. *Doctoral dissertation, Institut für maschinelle Sprachverarbeitung, Universität Stuttgart.*

C. Fellbaum. 1998. Wordnet: an electronic lexical database. *Cambrige, MIT Press, Language, Speech, and Communication.*

P. Fung. 1998. A statistical view on bilingual lexicon extraction: from parallel corpora to non-parallel corpora. *Lecture Notes in Computer Science*, 1529:1–17.

G. Grefenstette. 1994. *Explorations in automatic thesaurus discovery.* Springer.

A. Haghighi, P. Liang, T. Berg-Kirkpatrick, and D. Klein. 2008. Learning bilingual lexicons from monolingual corpora. In *Proceedings of the Annual Meeting of the Association for Computational Linguistics*, pages 771–779. Association for Computational Linguistics.

A. Ismail and S. Manandhar. 2010. Bilingual lexicon extraction from comparable corpora using in-domain terms. In *Proceedings of the International Conference on Computational Linguistics*, pages 481 – 489.

S.R. Jammalamadaka and A. Sengupta. 2001. *Topics in circular statistics*, volume 5. World Scientific Pub Co Inc.

P. Koehn and K. Knight. 2000. Estimating word translation probabilities from unrelated monolingual corpora using the em algorithm. In *Proceedings of the National Conference on Artificial Intelligence*, pages 711–715. Association for the Advancement of Artificial Intelligence.

T. Kudo, K. Yamamoto, and Y. Matsumoto. 2004. Applying conditional random fields to Japanese morphological analysis. In *Proceedings of the Conference on Empirical Methods in Natural Language Processing*, pages 230–237. Association for Computational Linguistics.

A. Laroche and P. Langlais. 2010. Revisiting context-based projection methods for term-translation spotting in comparable corpora. In *Proceedings of the International Conference on Computational Linguistics*, pages 617 – 625.

N. Okazaki, Y. Tsuruoka, S. Ananiadou, and J. Tsujii. 2008. A discriminative candidate generator for string transformations. In *Proceedings of the Conference on Empirical Methods in Natural Language Processing*, pages 447–456. Association for Computational Linguistics.

V. Pekar, R. Mitkov, D. Blagoev, and A. Mulloni. 2006. Finding translations for low-frequency words in comparable corpora. *Machine Translation*, 20(4):247–266.

R. Rapp. 1999. Automatic identification of word translations from unrelated English and German corpora. In *Proceedings of the Annual Meeting of the Association for Computational Linguistics*, pages 519–526. Association for Computational Linguistics.

K. Sato, T. Ikeda, T. Nakata, and S. Osada. 2003. Introduction of a Japanese language processing middleware used for CRM. In *Annual Meeting of the Japanese Association for Natural Language Processing (in Japanese)*, pages 109–112.

Y. Tsuruoka, Y. Tateishi, J. Kim, T. Ohta, J. McNaught, S. Ananiadou, and J. Tsujii. 2005. Developing a robust part-of-speech tagger for biomedical text. *Lecture Notes in Computer Science*, 3746:382–392.

R.R. Wilcox. 2009. *Basic Statistics: Understanding Conventional Methods and Modern Insights*. Oxford University Press.

Supersense Tagging for Arabic: the MT-in-the-Middle Attack

Nathan Schneider* **Behrang Mohit**† **Chris Dyer*** **Kemal Oflazer**† **Noah A. Smith***
School of Computer Science
Carnegie Mellon University
*Pittsburgh, PA 15213, USA
†Doha, Qatar
{nschneid@cs.,behrang@,cdyer@cs.,ko@cs.,nasmith@cs.}cmu.edu

Abstract

We consider the task of tagging Arabic nouns with WordNet supersenses. Three approaches are evaluated. The first uses an expert-crafted but limited-coverage lexicon, Arabic WordNet, and heuristics. The second uses unsupervised sequence modeling. The third and most successful approach uses machine translation to translate the Arabic into English, which is automatically tagged with English supersenses, the results of which are then projected back into Arabic. Analysis shows gains and remaining obstacles in four Wikipedia topical domains.

يتحكم مدير النوافذ في وضع وشكل نوافذ التطبيقات .

Ann-A	Gloss	Ann-B
	controls	
	manager the-windows	
	in	
	configuration	
	and-layout	
	windows the-applications	

'The window manager controls the configuration and layout of application windows.'

Figure 1: A sentence from the "X Window System" article with supersense taggings from two annotators and post hoc English glosses and translation.

1 Introduction

A taxonomic view of lexical semantics groups word senses/usages into categories of varying granularities. WordNet *supersense tags* denote coarse semantic classes, including and (for nouns) and and (for verbs); these categories can be taken as the top level of a taxonomy. Nominal *supersense tagging* (Ciaramita and Johnson, 2003) is the task of identifying lexical chunks in the sentence for common as well as proper nouns, and labeling each with one of the 25 nominal supersense categories. Figure 1 illustrates two such labelings of an Arabic sentence. Like the narrower problem of named entity recognition, supersense tagging of text holds attraction as a way of inferring representations that move toward language independence. Here we consider the problem of nominal supersense tagging for Arabic, a language with ca. 300 million speakers and moderate linguistic resources, including a WordNet (Elkateb et al., 2006), annotated datasets (Maamouri et al., 2004; Hovy et al., 2006), monolingual corpora, and large amounts of Arabic-English parallel data.

The supervised learning approach that is used in state-of-the-art English supersense taggers (Ciaramita and Altun, 2006) is problematic for Arabic, since there are supersense annotations for only a small amount of Arabic text (65,000 words by Schneider et al., 2012, versus the 360,000 words that are annotated for English). Here, we reserve that corpus for development and evaluation, not training.

We explore several approaches in this paper, the most effective of which is to (1) translate the Arabic sentence into English, returning the alignment structure between the source and target, (2) apply English supersense tagging to the target sentence, and (3) heuristically project the tags back to the Arabic sentence across these alignments. This "**MT-in-the-middle**" approach has also been successfully used for mention detection (Zitouni and Florian, 2008) and coreference resolution (Rahman and Ng, 2012).

We first discuss the task and relevant resources (§2), then the approaches we explored (§3), and finally present experimental results and analysis in §4.

2 Task and Resources

A gold standard corpus of sentences annotated with nominal supersenses (as in figure 1) facilitates automatic evaluation of supersense taggers. For development and evaluation we use the AQMAR Arabic Wikipedia Supersense Corpus[1] (Schneider et al., 2012), which augmented a named entity corpus (Mohit et al., 2012) with nominal supersense tags. The corpus consists of 28 articles selected from four topical areas: **history** (e.g., "Islamic Golden Age"), **science** ("Atom"), **sports** ("Real Madrid"), and **technology** ("Linux"). Schneider et al. (2012) found the distributions of supersense categories in these four topical domains to be markedly different; e.g., most instances of (which includes kinds of software) occurred in the technology domain, whereas most s were found in the science domain.

The 18 test articles have 1,393 sentences (39,916 tokens) annotated at least once.[2] As the corpus was released with two annotators' (partially overlapping) taggings, rather than a single gold standard, we treat the output of each annotator as a separate test set. Both annotated some of every article; the first (**Ann-A**) annotated 759 sentences, the second (**Ann-B**) 811 sentences.

Lexicon. What became known as "supersense tags" arose from a high-level partitioning of synsets in the original English WordNet (Fellbaum, 1998) into *lexicographer files*. Arabic WordNet (AWN) (Elkateb et al., 2006) allows us to recover supersense categories for some 10,500 Arabic nominal types, since many of the synsets in AWN are cross-referenced to English WordNet, and can therefore be associated with supersense categories. Further, OntoNotes contains named entity annotations for Arabic (Hovy et al., 2006).

From these, we construct an Arabic supersense lexicon, mapping Arabic noun lemmas to supersense tags. This lexicon contains 23,000 types, of which 11,000 are multiword units. Token coverage of the test set is 18% (see table 1). Lexical units encountered in the test data were up to 9-ways supersense-ambiguous; the average ambiguity of in-vocabulary tokens was 2.0 supersenses.

Unlabeled Arabic text. For unsupervised learning we collected 100,000 words of Arabic Wikipedia text, not constrained by topic. The articles in this sample were subject to a minimum length threshold and are all cross-linked to corresponding articles in English, Chinese, and German.

Arabic→English machine translation. We used two independently developed Arabic-English MT systems. One (**QCRI**) is a phrase-based system (Koehn et al., 2003), similar to Moses (Koehn et al., 2007); the other (**cdec**) is a hierarchical phrase-based system (Chiang, 2007), as implemented in cdec (Dyer et al., 2010). Both were trained on about 370M tokens of parallel data provided by the LDC (by volume, mostly newswire and UN data). Each system includes preprocessing for Arabic morphological segmentation and orthographic normalization.[3] The **QCRI** system used a 5-gram modified Kneser-Ney language model that generated full-cased forms (Chen and Goodman, 1999). **cdec** used a 4-gram KN language model over lowercase forms and was recased in a post-processing step. Both language models were trained using the Gigaword v. 4 corpus. Both systems were tuned to optimize BLEU on a held-out development set (Papineni et al., 2002).

English supersense tagger. For English supersense tagging, an open-source reimplementation of the approach of Ciaramita and Altun (2006) was released by Michael Heilman.[4] This tagger was trained on the SemCor corpus (Miller et al., 1993) and achieves 77% F_1 in-domain.

3 Methods

We explored 3 approaches to the supersense tagging of Arabic: heuristic tagging with a lexicon, unsupervised sequence tagging, and MT-in-the-middle.

3.1 Heuristic Tagging with a Lexicon

Using the lexicon built from AWN and OntoNotes (see §2), our heuristic approach works as follows:

1. Stem and vocalize; we used MADA (Habash and Rambow, 2005; Roth et al., 2008).
2. Greedily detect word sequences matching lexicon entries from left to right.
3. If a lexicon entry has more than one associated supersense, Arabic WordNet synsets are

[1] `http://www.ark.cs.cmu.edu/ArabicSST`

[2] Our development/test split of the data follows Mohit et al. (2012), but we exclude two test set documents—"Light" and "Ibn Tolun Mosque"—due to preprocessing issues.

[3] **QCRI** accomplishes this using MADA (Habash and Rambow, 2005; Roth et al., 2008). **cdec** includes a custom CRF-based segmenter and standard normalization rules.

[4] `http://www.ark.cs.cmu.edu/mheilman/questions`

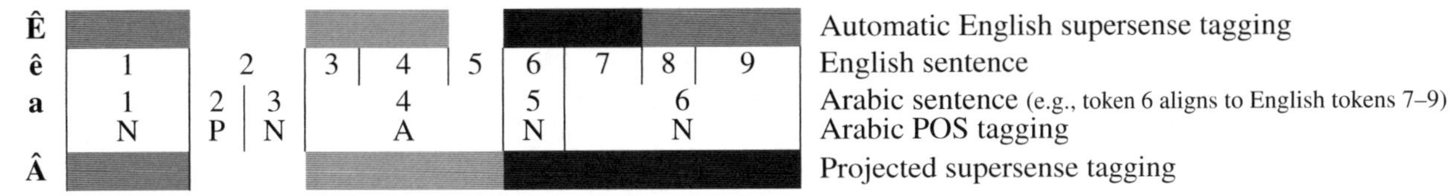

Figure 2: A hypothetical aligned sentence pair of 9 English words (with their supersense tags) and 6 Arabic words (with their POS tags). Step 4 of the projection procedure constructs the Arabic-to-English mapping $\{1\rightarrow\ {}^{1}_{1}, 4\rightarrow\ {}^{4}_{3}, \{5,6\}\rightarrow\ {}^{7}_{6}\}$, resulting in the tagging shown in the bottom row.

weighted to favor earlier senses (presumed by lexicographers to be more frequent) and then the supersense with the greatest aggregate weight is selected. Formally: Let *senses*(w) be the ordered list of AWN senses of lemma w. Let $senses(w, s) \subseteq senses(w)$ be those senses that map to a given supersense s. We choose $\arg\max_s(|senses(w, s)|/ \min_{i:senses(w)_i \in senses(w,s)} i)$.

3.2 Unsupervised Sequence Models

Unsupervised sequence labeling is our second approach (Merialdo, 1994). Although it was largely developed for part-of-speech tagging, the hope is to use in-domain Arabic data (the unannotated Wikipedia corpus discussed in §2) to infer clusters that correlate well with supersense groupings. We applied the generative, feature-based model of Berg-Kirkpatrick et al. (2010), replicating a feature-set used previously for NER (Mohit et al., 2012)—including context tokens, character n-grams, and POS—and adding the vocalized stem and several stem shape features: 1) **ContainsDigit?**; 2) digits replaced by #; 3) digit sequences replaced by # (for stems mixing digits with other characters); 4) **YearLike?**—true for 4-digit numerals starting with `19` or `20`; 5) **LatinWord?**, per the morphological analysis; 6) the shape feature of Ciaramita and Altun (2006) (Latin words only). We used 50 iterations of learning (tuned on dev data). For evaluation, a many-to-one mapping from unsupervised clusters to supersense tags is greedily induced to maximize their correspondence on evaluation data.

3.3 MT-in-the-Middle

A standard approach to using supervised linguistic resources in a second language is **cross-lingual projection** (Yarowsky and Ngai, 2001; Yarowsky et al., 2001; Smith and Smith, 2004; Hwa et al., 2005; Mihalcea et al., 2007; Burkett and Klein, 2008; Burkett et al., 2010; Das and Petrov, 2011; Kim et al., 2012, who use parallel sentences extracted from Wikipedia for NER). The simplest such approach starts with an aligned parallel corpus, applies supersense tagging to the English side, and projects the labels through the word alignments. A supervised monolingual tagger is then trained on the projected labels. Preliminary experiments, however, showed that this underperformed even the simple heuristic baseline above (likely due to domain mismatch), so it was abandoned in favor of a technique that we call **MT-in-the-middle** projection.

This approach does not depend on having parallel data in the training domain, but rather on an Arabic→English machine translation system that can be applied to the sentences we wish to tag. The approach is inspired by token-level pseudo-parallel data methods of previous work (Zitouni and Florian, 2008; Rahman and Ng, 2012). MT output for this language pair is far from perfect—especially for Wikipedia text, which is distant from the domain of the translation system's training data—but, in the spirit of Church and Hovy (1993), we conjecture that it may still be useful. The method is as follows:

1. Preprocess the input Arabic sentence **a** to match the decoder's model of Arabic.
2. Translate the sentence, recovering not just the English output **ê** but also the derivation/alignment structure **z** relating words and/or phrases of the English output to words and/or phrases of the Arabic input.
3. Apply the English supersense tagger to the English translation, discarding any verbal supersense tags. Call the tagger output **Ê**.
4. Project the supersense tags back to the Arabic sentence, yielding **Â**: Each Arabic token $a \in \mathbf{a}$ that is (a) a noun, or (b) an adjective following 0 or more adjectives following a noun is mapped to the first English supersense mention in **Ê** containing some word aligned to a. Then, for each English supersense men-

		Coverage			Ann-A			Ann-B		
		Nouns	All Tokens	Mentions	P	R	F_1	P	R	F_1
Lexicon heuristics (§3.1)		8,058 33%	8,465 18%	8,407	32 55	16 29	21.6 37.9	29 53	15 27	19.4 35.6
Unsupervised (§3.2)					20 59	16 48	17.5 52.6	14 56	10 39	11.6 45.9
MT-in-the-middle (§3.3)	**QCRI**	14,401 59%	16,461 35%	12,861	34 65	27 50	29.9 56.4	36 64	28 51	31.6 56.6
	cdec	14,270 58%	15,542 33%	13,704	**37 69**	**31 57**	**33.8 62.4**	**38 67**	**32 56**	**34.6 61.0**
MTitM + Lex.	**cdec**	16,798 68%	18,461 40%	16,623	**35 64**	**36 65**	**35.5 64.6**	**36 63**	**36 63**	**36.0 63.2**

Table 1: Supersense tagging results on the test set: coverage measures[5] and gold-standard evaluation—exact labeled/unlabeled[6] mention precision, recall, and F-score against each annotator. The last row is a hybrid: MT-in-the-middle followed by lexicon heuristics to improve recall. Best single-technique and best hybrid results are bolded.

tion, all its mapped Arabic words are grouped into a single mention and the supersense category for that mention is projected. Figure 2 illustrates this procedure. The **cdec** system provides word alignments for its translations derived from the training data; whereas **QCRI** only produces phrase-level alignments, so for every aligned phrase pair $\langle \bar{a}, \bar{e} \rangle \in \mathbf{z}$, we consider every word in $\bar{a}$ as aligned to every word in $\bar{e}$ (introducing noise when English supersense mention boundaries do not line up with phrase boundaries).

4 Experiments and Analysis

Table 1 compares the techniques (§3) for full Arabic supersense tagging.[7] The number of nouns, tokens, and mentions covered by the automatic tagging is reported, as is the mention-level evaluation against human annotations. The evaluation is reported separately for the two annotators in the dataset.

With heuristic lexicon lookup, 18% of the tokens are marked as part of a nominal supersense mention. Both labeled and unlabeled mention recall with this method are below 30%; labeled precision is about 30%, and unlabeled mention precision is above 50%. From this we conclude that the biggest problems are (a) out-of-vocabulary items and (b) poor semantic disambiguation of in-vocabulary items.

The unsupervised sequence tagger does even worse on the labeled evaluation. It has some success at *detecting* supersense mentions—unlabeled recall is substantially improved, and unlabeled precision is slightly improved. But it seems to be much worse at assigning semantic categories; the number of labeled true positive mentions is actually *lower* than with the lexicon-based approach.

MT-in-the-middle is by far the most successful single approach: both systems outperform the lexicon-only baseline by about 10 F_1 points, despite many errors in the automatic translation, English tagging, and projection, as well as underlying linguistic differences between English and Arabic. The baseline's unlabeled recall is doubled, indicating substantially more nominal expressions are detected, in addition to the improved labeled scores.

We further tested simple **hybrids** combining the lexicon-based and MT-based approaches. Applying MT-in-the-middle first, then expanding token coverage with the lexicon improves recall at a small cost to precision (table 1, last row). Combining the techniques in the reverse order is slightly worse than MT-based projection without consulting the lexicon.

MT-in-the middle improves upon the lexicon-only baseline, yet performance is still dwarfed by the supervised English tagger (at least in the SemCor evaluation; see §2), and also well below the 70% inter-annotator F_1 reported by Schneider et al. (2012). We therefore examine the weaknesses of our approach for Arabic.

4.1 MT for Projection

In analyzing our projection framework, we performed a small-scale MT evaluation with the Wikipedia data. Reference English translations for 140 Arabic Wikipedia sentences—5 per article in the corpus—were elicited from a bilingual linguist. Table 2 compares the two systems under three standard metrics of overall sentence translation quality.[8]

[5] The unsupervised evaluation greedily maps clusters to tags, separately for each version of the test set; coverage numbers thus differ and are not shown here.

[6] Unlabeled tagging refers to noun chunk *detection* only.

[7] It was produced in part using the `chunkeval.py` script: see `https://github.com/nschneid/pyutil`

[8] BLEU (Papineni et al., 2002); METEOR (Banerjee and Lavie, 2005; Lavie and Denkowski, 2009), with default options;

تتكون الذرة من سحابة من الشحنات السالبة (الإلكترونات) تحوم حول نواة موجبة الشحنة صغيرة جدا في الوسط .

QCRI: corn consists of a negative shipments (electron hovering around the nucleus of the shipment) are very small in the center . (3/6)
cdec: The corn is composed of negative shipments (electronics) cloud hovering over the nucleus of a very small positive shipment in the center . (2/6)

تأهلت البرتغال للنهائيات بمنتهى السهولة ، فالبرتغال لم تهزم طوال مشوار التصفيات .

QCRI: Portugal qualified for the finals very easily , Portugal defeated throughout the mission liquidations . (3/5)
cdec: Portugal qualified easily for the finals , Portugal unbeaten throughout the journey . (3/4)

Figure 3: Example Arabic inputs and the outputs of the two MT systems, with lexical projection precision ratios.

While the resulting number of sentences with references is far from ideal and there is only one reference translation for each, all three measures favor **QCRI**.

	BLEU	METEOR	TER	Lex. Prec.
QCRI	**32.86**	**32.10**	**0.46**	**91.9%**
cdec	28.84	31.38	0.49	90.0%

Table 2: MT quality measures comparing the two systems over 140 sentences. The first three are automatic measures with 1 reference translation. For the fourth, a bilingual judged the translation acceptability of phrases that were identified as supersense mentions by the English tagger (**lexical projection precision**).

For a targeted measure of *lexical* translation quality of noun expressions, we elicited acceptability judgments from a bilingual annotator for translated and supersense-projected phrases. Given each MT system output (for the same 140 sentences) in which mentions predicted by the English supervised tagger were highlighted, along with the Arabic source sentence, the judge was asked for each English mention whether it was a valid translation.[9] We call this **lexical projection precision**. Figure 3 shows examples, and the last column of table 2 gives overall statistics. Upwards of 90% of the lexical translations were accepted; as with the automatic MT measures, **QCRI** slightly outperforms **cdec** (especially in the technology and sports domains[10]). Of the problematic lexical translations, some are almost certainly domain effects: e.g., *corn* or *maize* instead of *atom*. Others are more nuanced, e.g., *shipments* for *charges* and *electronics* for *electrons*. Transliteration errors included *IMAX* in place of *EMACS* and *genoa lynx* for *GNU Linux*. However, lexical projection precision seems to be a relatively small part of the problem, especially considering that not all translation errors lead to supersense tagging errors.

Lexical projection *recall* was not measured, but noun token coverage (see table 1) is instructive. Most noun tokens ought to be tagged; 77% is the noun coverage rate in the gold standard. In table 1, noun coverage gains track overall improvements.

If **QCRI** produces better translations, why is **cdec** more useful for supersense tagging? As noted in §3.3, **cdec** gives word-level alignments (even when the decoder uses large phrasal units for translation), allowing for more precise projections.[11] We suspect this is especially important in light of findings that larger phrase sizes are indicative of better translations (Gamon et al., 2005), so these are exactly the cases where we expect the translations to be valuable.

5 Conclusion

To our knowledge, this is the first study of automatic Arabic supersense tagging. We have shown empirically that an MT-in-the-middle technique is most effective of several approaches that do not require labeled training data. Analysis sheds light on several challenges that would need to be overcome for better Arabic lexical semantic tagging.

Acknowledgments

We thank Wajdi Zaghouani for the translation of the Arabic Wikipedia MT set, Francisco Guzman and Preslav Nakov for the output of QCRI's MT system, and Waleed Ammar and anonymous reviewers for their comments. This publication was made possible by grant NPRP-08-485-1-083 from the Qatar National Research Fund (a member of the Qatar Foundation). The statements made herein are solely the responsibility of the authors.

and translation edit rate (TER) (Snover et al., 2006)

[9] The judge did not see alignments or supersense categories.

[10] For technology articles, the differences in F_1 scores between the two systems were 6.1 and 4.2 for **Ann-A** and **Ann-B**, respectively. For sports the respective differences were 4.3 and 4.4. In the other domains the differences never exceeded 3.3. Interestingly, this is the only generalization about topical domain performance we were able to find that holds across annotators and systems, in contrast with the stark topical effects observed by Mohit et al. (2012) for NER.

[11] Our experiments use **QCRI** as an off-the-shelf system. As a reviewer notes, it could be retrained to produce word-level alignments, which would likely improve the accuracy of supersense tag projection.

References

Satanjeev Banerjee and Alon Lavie. 2005. METEOR: an automatic metric for MT evaluation with improved correlation with human judgments. In *Proceedings of the ACL Workshop on Intrinsic and Extrinsic Evaluation Measures for Machine Translation and/or Summarization*, pages 65–72, Ann Arbor, Michigan, June. Association for Computational Linguistics.

Taylor Berg-Kirkpatrick, Alexandre Bouchard-Côté, John DeNero, and Dan Klein. 2010. Painless unsupervised learning with features. In *Human Language Technologies: The 2010 Annual Conference of the North American Chapter of the Association for Computational Linguistics (NAACL-HLT 2010)*, pages 582–590, Los Angeles, California, June. Association for Computational Linguistics.

David Burkett and Dan Klein. 2008. Two languages are better than one (for syntactic parsing). In *Proceedings of the 2008 Conference on Empirical Methods in Natural Language Processing (EMNLP 2008)*, pages 877–886, Honolulu, Hawaii, October. Association for Computational Linguistics.

David Burkett, Slav Petrov, John Blitzer, and Dan Klein. 2010. Learning better monolingual models with unannotated bilingual text. In *Proceedings of the Fourteenth Conference on Computational Natural Language Learning (CoNLL 2010)*, pages 46–54, Uppsala, Sweden, July. Association for Computational Linguistics.

Stanley F. Chen and Joshua Goodman. 1999. An empirical study of smoothing techniques for language modeling. *Computer Speech & Language*, 13(4):359–393, October.

David Chiang. 2007. Hierarchical phrase-based translation. *Computational Linguistics*, 33(2):201–228, June.

Kenneth W. Church and Eduard H. Hovy. 1993. Good applications for crummy machine translation. *Machine Translation*, 8(4):239–258, December.

Massimiliano Ciaramita and Yasemin Altun. 2006. Broad-coverage sense disambiguation and information extraction with a supersense sequence tagger. In *Proceedings of the 2006 Conference on Empirical Methods in Natural Language Processing*, pages 594–602, Sydney, Australia, July. Association for Computational Linguistics.

Massimiliano Ciaramita and Mark Johnson. 2003. Supersense tagging of unknown nouns in WordNet. In *Proceedings of the 2003 Conference on Empirical Methods in Natural Language Processing*, pages 168–175, Sapporo, Japan, July.

Dipanjan Das and Slav Petrov. 2011. Unsupervised part-of-speech tagging with bilingual graph-based projections. In *Proceedings of the 49th Annual Meeting of the Association for Computational Linguistics: Human Language Technologies (ACL-HLT 2011)*, pages 600–609, Portland, Oregon, USA, June. Association for Computational Linguistics.

Chris Dyer, Adam Lopez, Juri Ganitkevitch, Jonathan Weese, Ferhan Ture, Phil Blunsom, Hendra Setiawan, Vladimir Eidelman, and Philip Resnik. 2010. cdec: A decoder, alignment, and learning framework for finite-state and context-free translation models. In *Proceedings of the ACL 2010 System Demonstrations*, pages 7–12, Uppsala, Sweden, July. Association for Computational Linguistics.

Sabri Elkateb, William Black, Horacio Rodríguez, Musa Alkhalifa, Piek Vossen, Adam Pease, and Christiane Fellbaum. 2006. Building a WordNet for Arabic. In *Proceedings of the Fifth International Conference on Language Resources and Evaluation (LREC 2006)*, pages 29–34, Genoa, Italy, May.

Christiane Fellbaum, editor. 1998. *WordNet: an electronic lexical database*. MIT Press, Cambridge, MA.

Michael Gamon, Anthony Aue, and Martine Smets. 2005. Sentence-level MT evaluation without reference translations: Beyond language modeling. In *Proceedings of the 10th European Association for Machine Translation Conference (EAMT 2005)*, pages 103–111, Budapest, May.

Nizar Habash and Owen Rambow. 2005. Arabic tokenization, part-of-speech tagging and morphological disambiguation in one fell swoop. In *Proceedings of the 43rd Annual Meeting of the Association for Computational Linguistics (ACL'05)*, pages 573–580, Ann Arbor, Michigan, June. Association for Computational Linguistics.

Eduard Hovy, Mitchell Marcus, Martha Palmer, Lance Ramshaw, and Ralph Weischedel. 2006. OntoNotes: the 90% solution. In *Proceedings of the Human Language Technology Conference of the NAACL (HLT-NAACL 2006)*, pages 57–60, New York City, USA, June. Association for Computational Linguistics.

Rebecca Hwa, Philip Resnik, Amy Weinberg, Clara Cabezas, and Okan Kolak. 2005. Bootstrapping parsers via syntactic projection across parallel texts. *Natural Language Engineering*, 11(3):311–325, September.

Sungchul Kim, Kristina Toutanova, and Hwanjo Yu. 2012. Multilingual named entity recognition using parallel data and metadata from Wikipedia. In *Proceedings of the 50th Annual Meeting of the Association for Computational Linguistics (ACL 2012)*, pages 694–702, Jeju Island, Korea, July. Association for Computational Linguistics.

Philipp Koehn, Franz Josef Och, and Daniel Marcu. 2003. Statistical phrase-based translation. In *Proceed-*

ings of the 2003 Conference of the North American Chapter of the Association for Computational Linguistics on Human Language Technology (HLT-NAACL 2003), pages 48–54, Edmonton, Canada. Association for Computational Linguistics.

Philipp Koehn, Hieu Hoang, Alexandra Birch, Chris Callison-Burch, Marcello Federico, Nicola Bertoldi, Brooke Cowan, Wade Shen, Christine Moran, Richard Zens, Chris Dyer, Ondřej Bojar, Alexandra Constantin, and Evan Herbst. 2007. Moses: Open source toolkit for statistical machine translation. In *Proceedings of the 45th Annual Meeting of the Association for Computational Linguistics Demo and Poster Sessions*, pages 177–180, Prague, Czech Republic, June. Association for Computational Linguistics.

Alon Lavie and Michael J. Denkowski. 2009. The METEOR metric for automatic evaluation of machine translation. *Machine Translation*, 23(2–3):105–115, September.

Mohamed Maamouri, Ann Bies, Tim Buckwalter, and Wigdan Mekki. 2004. The Penn Arabic Treebank: building a large-scale annotated Arabic corpus. In *NEMLAR Conference on Arabic Language Resources and Tools*, pages 102–109.

Bernard Merialdo. 1994. Tagging English text with a probabilistic model. *Computational Linguistics*, 20(2):155–171.

Rada Mihalcea, Carmen Banea, and Janyce Wiebe. 2007. Learning multilingual subjective language via cross-lingual projections. In *Proceedings of the 45th Annual Meeting of the Association of Computational Linguistics (ACL 2007)*, pages 976–983, Prague, Czech Republic, June. Association for Computational Linguistics.

George A. Miller, Claudia Leacock, Randee Tengi, and Ross T. Bunker. 1993. A semantic concordance. In *Proceedings of the Workshop on Human Language Technology (HLT '93)*, pages 303–308, Plainsboro, NJ, USA, March. Association for Computational Linguistics.

Behrang Mohit, Nathan Schneider, Rishav Bhowmick, Kemal Oflazer, and Noah A. Smith. 2012. Recall-oriented learning of named entities in Arabic Wikipedia. In *Proceedings of the 13th Conference of the European Chapter of the Association for Computational Linguistics (EACL 2012)*, pages 162–173, Avignon, France, April. Association for Computational Linguistics.

Kishore Papineni, Salim Roukos, Todd Ward, and Wei-Jing Zhu. 2002. BLEU: a method for automatic evaluation of machine translation. In *Proceedings of 40th Annual Meeting of the Association for Computational Linguistics (ACL 2002)*, pages 311–318, Philadelphia, Pennsylvania, USA, July. Association for Computational Linguistics.

Altaf Rahman and Vincent Ng. 2012. Translation-based projection for multilingual coreference resolution. In *Proceedings of the 2012 Conference of the North American Chapter of the Association for Computational Linguistics: Human Language Technologies (NAACL-HLT 2012)*, pages 720–730, Montréal, Canada, June. Association for Computational Linguistics.

Ryan Roth, Owen Rambow, Nizar Habash, Mona Diab, and Cynthia Rudin. 2008. Arabic morphological tagging, diacritization, and lemmatization using lexeme models and feature ranking. In *Proceedings of ACL-08: HLT*, pages 117–120, Columbus, Ohio, June. Association for Computational Linguistics.

Nathan Schneider, Behrang Mohit, Kemal Oflazer, and Noah A. Smith. 2012. Coarse lexical semantic annotation with supersenses: an Arabic case study. In *Proceedings of the 50th Annual Meeting of the Association for Computational Linguistics (ACL 2012)*, pages 253–258, Jeju Island, Korea, July. Association for Computational Linguistics.

David A. Smith and Noah A. Smith. 2004. Bilingual parsing with factored estimation: using English to parse Korean. In *Proceedings of the 2004 Conference on Empirical Methods in Natural Language Processing (EMNLP'04)*, pages 49–56, Barcelona, Spain.

Matthew Snover, Bonnie Dorr, Richard Schwartz, Linnea Micciulla, and John Makhoul. 2006. A study of translation edit rate with targeted human annotation. In *Proceedings of the 7th Conference of the Association for Machine Translation in the Americas (AMTA 2006)*, pages 223–231, Cambridge, Massachusetts, USA, August.

David Yarowsky and Grace Ngai. 2001. Inducing multilingual POS taggers and NP bracketers via robust projection across aligned corpora. In *Proceedings of the Second Meeting of the North American Chapter of the Association for Computational Linguistics (NAACL'01)*, Pittsburgh, Pennsylvania, USA, June.

David Yarowsky, Grace Ngai, and Richard Wicentowski. 2001. Inducing multilingual text analysis tools via robust projection across aligned corpora. In *Proceedings of the First International Conference on Human Language Technology Research (HLT'01)*, San Diego, California, USA, March.

Imed Zitouni and Radu Florian. 2008. Mention detection crossing the language barrier. In *Proceedings of the 2008 Conference on Empirical Methods in Natural Language Processing (EMNLP 2008)*, pages 600–609, Honolulu, Hawaii, October. Association for Computational Linguistics.

Zipfian corruptions for robust POS tagging

Anders Søgaard
Center for Language Technology
University of Copenhagen
soegaard@hum.ku.dk

Abstract

Inspired by robust generalization and adversarial learning we describe a novel approach to learning structured perceptrons for part-of-speech (POS) tagging that is less sensitive to domain shifts. The objective of our method is to minimize average loss under random distribution shifts. We restrict the possible target distributions to mixtures of the source distribution and random Zipfian distributions. Our algorithm is used for POS tagging and evaluated on the English Web Treebank and the Danish Dependency Treebank with an average 4.4% error reduction in tagging accuracy.

1 Introduction

Supervised learning approaches have advanced the state of the art on a variety of tasks in natural language processing, often resulting in systems approaching the level of inter-annotator agreement on in-domain data, e.g. in POS tagging, where Shen et al. (2007) report a tagging accuracy of 97.3%. However, performance of state-of-the-art supervised systems is known to drop considerably on out-of-domain data. State-of-the-art POS taggers trained on the Penn Treebank (Marcus et al., 1993) mapped to Google's universal tag set (Petrov et al., 2011) achieve tagging accuracies in the range of 89–91% on Web 2.0 data (Petrov and McDonald, 2012) .

To bridge this gap we may consider using semi-supervised or transfer learning methods to adjust to new target domains (Blitzer et al., 2006; Daume III, 2007), pooling unlabeled data from those domains. However, in many applications this is not possible. If we want to provide an online service or design a piece of software with many potential users covering a wide range of use cases, we do not know the target domain in advance. This is the usual problem of *robust* learning, but in this paper we describe a novel learning algorithm that goes beyond robust learning by making various assumptions about the difference between the source domain and the (unknown) target domain. Under these assumptions we can minimize average loss under (all possible or a representative sample of) domain shifts. We evaluate our approach on two recently introduced cross-domain POS tagging datasets.

Our approach is inspired by work in robust generalization (Ben-Tal and Nemirovski, 1998; Trafalis and Gilbert, 2007) and adversarial learning (Globerson and Roweis, 2006; Dekel and Shamir, 2008; Søgaard and Johannsen, 2012). Our approach also bears similarities to feature bagging (Sutton et al., 2006). Sutton et al. (2006) noted that in learning of linear models useful features are often swamped by correlating, but more indicative features. If the more indicative features are absent in the target domain due to out-of-vocabulary (OOV) effects, we are left with the swamped features which were not updated properly. This is, indirectly, the problem solved in adversarial learning with corrupted data points. Adversarial learning can also be seen as a way of averaging exponentially many models (Hinton et al., 2012).

Adversarial learning techniques have been developed for security-related learning tasks, e.g. where systems need to be robust to failing sensors. We also show how we can do better than straight-forward application of adversarial learning techniques by making a second assumption about our data, namely that domains are mixtures of Zipfian distributions over our features. Similar assumptions have been made before in computational linguistics, e.g. by Goldberg and Elhadad (2008).

2 Approach overview

In this paper we consider the structured perceptron (Collins, 2002) – with POS tagging as our practical application. The structured perceptron is prone to feature swamping (Sutton et al., 2006), and we want to prevent that using a technique inspired by adversarial learning (Globerson and Roweis, 2006; Dekel and Shamir, 2008). The modification presented here to the structured perceptron only affects a single line of code in a publicly available implementation (see below), but the consequences are significant.

Online adversarial learning (Søgaard and Johannsen, 2012), briefly, works by sampling random corruptions of our data, or random feature deletions, in the learning phase. A discriminative learner seeing corrupted data points with missing features will not update part of the model and will thus try to find a decision boundary classifying the training data correctly relying on the remaining features. This decision boundary may be very different from the decision boundary found otherwise by the discriminative learner. If we sample enough corruptions, the model learned from the corrupted data will converge on the model minimizing average loss over all corruptions (Dekel and Shamir, 2008).

Example Consider the plot in Figure 1. The solid line with no stars (2d-fit) is the SVM fit in two dimensions, while the dashed line is what that fit amounts to if the feature x is missing in the target. The solid line with stars (1d-fit) is our fit if we could predict the missing feature, training an SVM only with the y feature. The 1d-fit decision boundary only misclassifies a single data point compared to the original fit which misclassifies more than 15 negatives with the x feature missing.

The plot thus shows that the best fit in m dimensions is often not the best in $< m$ dimensions. Consequently, if we think there is a risk that features will be missing in the target, finding the best fit in m dimensions is not necessarily the best we can do. Of

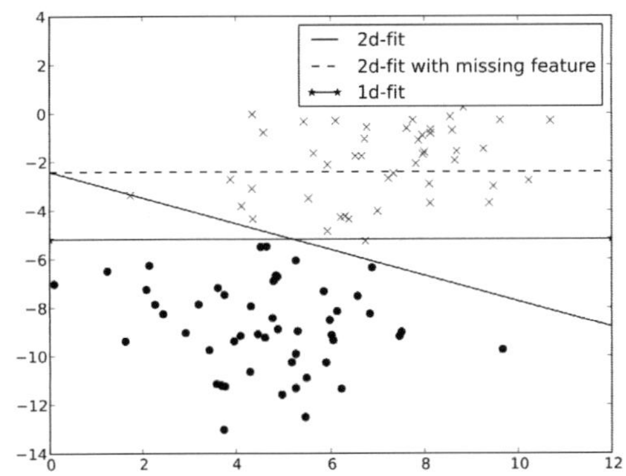

Figure 1: The best fit in m dimensions is often not the best in $< m$ dimensions.

course we do not know what features will be missing in advance. The intuition in adversarial learning is that we may obtain more robust decision boundaries by minimizing loss over a set of possible feature deletions. We extend this idea below, modeling not only OOV effects, but a broader class of distributional shifts.

3 Structured perceptron

The structured perceptron (Collins, 2002) models sequences as Markov chains of unobserved variables (POS), each emitting an observed variable (a word form). The structured perceptron is similar to the averaged perceptron (Freund and Schapire, 1999), except data points are sequences of vectors rather than just vectors. Consequently, the structured perceptron does not predict a class label but a sequence of labels (using Viterbi decoding). In learning we update the features at the positions where the predicted labels are different from the true labels. We do this by adding weight to features present in the correct solution and subtracting weight from features only present in the predicted solution. The generic averaged perceptron learning algorithm is presented in Figure 2. A publicly available and easy-to-modify Python reimplementation of the structured perceptron can be found in the LXMLS toolkit.[1] We use the LXMLS toolkit as our baseline with the default feature model, but use the PTB tagset rather than the Google tagset (Petrov et al., 2011) used by default in the LXMLS toolkit.

[1] https://github.com/gracaninja/lxmls-toolkit

```
X = {⟨y_i, x_i⟩}_{i=1}^N
w^0 = 0, v = 0, i = 0
for k ∈ K do
    for n ∈ N do
        if sign(w · x) ≠ y_n then
            w^{i+1} ← update(w^i)
            i ← i + 1
        end if
        v ← v + w^i
    end for
end for
return w = v/(N × K)
```

Figure 2: Generic averaged perceptron

```
X = {⟨y_i, x_i⟩}_{i=1}^N
w^0 = 0, v = 0, i = 0
for k ∈ K do
    for n ∈ N do
        ξ ← random.zipf(3, M)
        if sign(w · x ∘ ξ) ≠ y_n then
            w^{i+1} ← update(w^i)
            i ← i + 1
        end if
        v ← v + w^i
    end for
end for
return w = v/(N × K)
```

Figure 3: Z_3SP

4 Minimizing loss under OOV effects

We will think of domain shifts as data point corruptions. Søgaard and Johannsen (2012) model domain shifts using binary vectors of length m where m is the size of of our feature representation. Each vector then represents an expected OOV effect by encoding what features are (predicted to be) missing in the target data, i.e. the ith feature will be missing if the ith element of the binary vector is 0. However, since we are minimizing average loss under OOV effects it makes sense to restrict the class of vectors to encode OOV effects that we are likely to observe. This could, for example, involve fixing an expected rate of missing features or bounding it by some interval, or it could involve distinguishing between features that are likely to be missing in the target and features that are not. Here is what we do in this paper:

Rather than thinking of domain shifts as something that deletes features, we propose to see domain shifts as something making certain features less likely to occur in our data. We will in other words simulate *soft* OOV effects, rather than hard OOV effects. One way to think of this is as an importance weighting of our features. This section provides some intuition for using inverse Zipfian distributions as weight functions.

Say we are interested in making a model $\theta_{\mathcal{D}_1}$ learned from a known distribution $\mathcal{D}_1$ robust against the distributional differences between $\mathcal{D}_1$ and an unknown distribution $\mathcal{D}_2$. These two distributions are somehow related to a distribution $\mathcal{D}_0$ (the underlying language distribution from which the domain distributions are sampled).

It is common to assume that linguistic distributions follow power laws (Zipf, 1935; Goldberg and Elhadad, 2008). We will assume that $\mathcal{D}_1 = \mathcal{D}_0 \times \mathcal{Z}_1$ where $\mathcal{Z}_1$ is some Zipfian distribution. Say $\mathcal{D}_0 \sim \mathcal{Z}_0$ is the master Zipfian distribution of language $\mathcal{L}_0$. If we assume that (otherwise independent) domains $\mathcal{L}_1$ and $\mathcal{L}_2$ follow products of Zipfians $\mathcal{Z}_0 \times \mathcal{Z}_1$ and $\mathcal{Z}_0 \times \mathcal{Z}_2$, we derive the following:

Say $\mathbf{w} = \theta_{\mathcal{Z}_0 \times \mathcal{Z}_1}$ is the model learned from the source data. The ideal model is $\mathbf{w}' = \theta_{\mathcal{Z}_0 \times \mathcal{Z}_2}$, but both Zipfians $\mathcal{Z}_1$ and $\mathcal{Z}_2$ are unknown. Since $\mathcal{Z}_2$ is unknown (and in many applications, we want to model several $\mathcal{Z}_i$), the overall best model we can hope for is $\mathbf{w}' = \theta_{\mathcal{Z}_0}$. $\mathcal{Z}_0$ is also unknown, but we can observe a finite sample $\mathcal{Z}_0 \times \mathcal{Z}_1$. Since the density of $\mathcal{Z}_1$ is directly related to the weights in $\mathbf{w}$, a crude estimate of $\theta_{\mathcal{Z}_0}$ would be $\mathbf{w}' \sim \mathbf{w}\frac{1}{\mathcal{Z}_1}$. Since we cannot observe $\mathcal{Z}_1$, we instead try to minimize average loss under all hypotheses about $\mathcal{Z}_1$.

In practice, we implement the idea of reweighting by random inverse Zipfian distributitons (instead of binary vectors) in the following way: Passing through the data in averaged perceptron learning (Figure 2), we consider one data point at a time. In order to minize loss in all possible domains, we need to consider all possible inverse Zipfian reweightings. This would be possible if we provided a convex formulation of the minimization problem along the lines of Dekel and Shamir (2008), but instead we randomly sample from a Zipfian and factor its inverse into our dataset. The parameter of the Zipfians is set (to 3) on development data (the EWT-email development data). The modified learning algorithm, Z_3SP, is presented in Figure 3.

5 POS tagging

POS tagging is the problem of assigning syntactic categories or POS to tokenized word forms in running text. Most approaches to POS tagging use supervised learning to learn sequence labeling models from annotated ressources. The major ressource for English is the Wall Street Journal (WSJ) sections of the English Treebank (Marcus et al., 1993). POS taggers are usually trained on Sect. 0–18 and evaluated on Sect. 22–24. In this paper we are not interested in in-domain performance on WSJ data, but rather in developing a robust POS tagger that is less sensitive to domain shifts than current state-of-the-art POS taggers and use the splits from a recent parsing shared task rather than the standard POS tagging ones.

6 Experiments

We train our tagger on Sections 2–21 of the WSJ sections of the English Treebank, in the Ontotes 4.0 release. This was also the training data used in the experiments in the Parsing the Web (PTW) shared task at NAACL 2012.[2] In the shared task they used the coarse-grained Google tagset (Petrov et al., 2011). We believe this tagset is too coarse-grained for most purposes (Manning, 2011) and do experiments with the original PTB tagset instead.

Our evaluation data comes from the English Web Treebank (EWT),[3] which was also used in the PTW shared task. The EWT contains development and evaluation data for five domains: answers (from Yahoo!), emails (from the Enron corpus), BBC newsgroups, Amazon reviews, and weblogs. In order not to optimize on in-domain data, we tune on the Email development data and evaluate on the remaining domains (the test sections).

The Web 2.0 data used for evaluation contains a lot of non-canonical language use. An example is the sentence *you r retarded.* from the Email section. The POS tagger finds no support for *r* as a verb in the training data, but needs to infer this from the context.

We also include experiments on the Danish Dependency Treebank (DDT) (Buch-Kromann, 2003), which comes with meta-data enabling us to single out four domains: newspaper, law, literature and magazines. We train our tagger on the newspaper data and evaluate on the remaining three sections.

[2]https://sites.google.com/site/sancl2012/home/shared-task

[3]LDC Catalog No.: LDC2012T13.

	SP	BSP	Z_3SP
EWT-answers	85.22	85.45	**85.59**
EWT-newsgroups	86.82	86.94	**87.42**
EWT-reviews	84.92	85.14	85.67
EWT-weblogs	87.00	87.06	**87.39**
DDT-law	92.38	92.80	**93.35**
DDT-lit	93.61	93.80	**93.85**
DDT-mag	**94.71**	94.44	94.68

Table 1: Results. BSP samples binary vectors with probabilities $\{0 : 0.1, 1 : 0.9\}$

6.1 Results

The results are presented in Table 1. We first note that improvements over the structured perceptron are statistically significant with $p < 0.01$ across all domains, except DDT-mag. We also note that using inverse Zipfian reweightings is better than using binary vectors in almost all cases. We believe that these are strong results given that we are assuming *no* knowledge of the target domain, and our modification of the learning algorithm does not affect computational efficiency at training or test time. The average error reduction of Z_3SP over the structured perceptron (SP) is 8%. Since using inverse Zipfian reweightings seems more motivated for node potentials than for edge potentials, we also tried using BSP for edge potentials and Z_3SP for node potentials. This mixed model acchieved 93.70, 93.91 and 94.35 on the DDT data, which on average is slightly better than Z_3SP.

7 Conclusions

Inspired by robust generalization and adversarial learning we introduced a novel approach to learning structured perceptrons for sequential labeling, which is less sensitive to OOV effects. We evaluated our approach on POS tagging data from the EWT and the DDT with an average 4.4% error reduction over the structured perceptron.

Acknowledgements

Anders Søgaard is funded by the ERC Starting Grant LOWLANDS No. 313695.

References

Aharon Ben-Tal and Arkadi Nemirovski. 1998. Robust convex optimization. *Mathematics of Operations Research*, 23(4).

John Blitzer, Ryan McDonald, and Fernando Pereira. 2006. Domain adaptation with structural correspondence learning. In *EMNLP*.

Matthias Buch-Kromann. 2003. The Danish Dependency Treebank and the DTAG Treebank Tool. In *TLT*.

Michael Collins. 2002. Discriminative training methods for Hidden Markov Models. In *EMNLP*.

Hal Daume III. 2007. Frustratingly easy domain adaptation. In *ACL*.

Ofer Dekel and Ohad Shamir. 2008. Learning to classify with missing and corrupted features. In *ICML*.

Yoav Freund and Robert Schapire. 1999. Large margin classification using the perceptron algorithm. *Machine Learning*, 37:277–296.

Amir Globerson and Sam Roweis. 2006. Nightmare at test time: robust learning by feature deletion. In *ICML*.

Yoav Goldberg and Michael Elhadad. 2008. splitSVM: fast, space-efficient, non-heuristic, polynomial kernel computation for NLP applications. In *ACL*.

Geoffrey Hinton, N. Srivastava, A. Krizhevsky, I. Sutskever, and R. Salakhutdinov. 2012. Improving neural networks by preventing co-adaptation of feature detectors. http://arxiv.org/abs/1207.0580.

Chris Manning. 2011. Part-of-speech tagging from 97%˜to 100%: Is it time for some linguistics? In *CICLing*.

Mitchell Marcus, Mary Marcinkiewicz, and Beatrice Santorini. 1993. Building a large annotated corpus of English: the Penn Treebank. *Computational Linguistics*, 19(2):313–330.

Slav Petrov and Ryan McDonald. 2012. Overview of the 2012 Shared Task on Parsing the Web. In *Notes of the First Workshop on Syntactic Analysis of Non-Canonical Language (SANCL)*.

Slav Petrov, Dipanjan Das, and Ryan McDonald. 2011. A universal part-of-speech tagset. CoRR abs/1104.2086.

Libin Shen, Giorgio Satta, and Aravind Joshi. 2007. Guided learning for bidirectional sequence classification. In *ACL*.

Anders Søgaard and Anders Johannsen. 2012. Robust learning in random subspaces: equipping NLP against OOV effects. In *COLING*.

Charles Sutton, Michael Sindelar, and Andrew McCallum. 2006. Reducing weight undertraining in structured discriminative learning. In *NAACL*.

T Trafalis and R Gilbert. 2007. Robust support vector machines for classification and computational issues. *Optimization Methods and Software*, 22:187–198.

George Zipf. 1935. *The psycho-biology of language*. Houghton Mifflin.

A Multi-Dimensional Bayesian Approach to Lexical Style

Julian Brooke
Department of Computer Science
University of Toronto
jbrooke@cs.toronto.edu

Graeme Hirst
Department of Computer Science
University of Toronto
gh@cs.toronto.edu

Abstract

We adapt the popular LDA topic model (Blei et al., 2003) to the representation of stylistic lexical information, evaluating our model on the basis of human-interpretability at the word and text level. We show, in particular, that this model can be applied to the task of inducing stylistic lexicons, and that a multi-dimensional approach is warranted given the correlations among stylistic dimensions.

1 Introduction

In language, stylistic variation is a reflection of various contextual factors, including the backgrounds of and relationship between the parties involved. Although in the context of prescriptive linguistics (Strunk and White, 1979), style is often assumed to be a matter of aesthetics, the stylistic intuitions of language users are inextricably linked to the conventions of register and genre (Biber and Conrad, 2009). Intentional or not, stylistic differences play a role in numerous NLP tasks. Examples include genre classification (Kessler et al., 1997), author profiling (Garera and Yarowsky, 2009; Rosenthal and McKeown, 2011), social relationship classification (Peterson et al., 2011), sentiment analysis (Wilson et al., 2005), readability classification (Collins-Thompson and Callan, 2005), and text generation (Hovy, 1990; Inkpen and Hirst, 2006). Following the classic work of Biber (1988), computational modeling of style has often focused on textual statistics and the frequency of function words and syntactic categories. When content words are considered, they are often limited to manually-constructed lists (Argamon et al., 2007), or used as individual features for supervised classification, which can be confounded by topic (Petrenz and Webber, 2011) or fail in the face of lexical variety. Our interest is models that offer broad lexical coverage of human-identifiable stylistic variation.

Research most similar to ours has focused on classifying the lexicon in terms of individual aspects relevant to style (e.g. formality, specificity, readability) (Brooke et al., 2010; Pan and Yang, 2010; Kidwell et al., 2009) and a large body of research on the induction of polarity lexicons, in particular from large corpora (Turney, 2002; Kaji and Kitsuregawa, 2007; Velikovich et al., 2010). Our work is the first to represent multiple dimensions of style in a single statistical model, adapting latent Dirichlet allocation (Blei et al., 2003), a Bayesian 'topic' model, to our stylistic purposes; as such, our approach also follows on recent interest in the interpretability of topic-model topics (Chang et al., 2009; Newman et al., 2011). We show that our model can be used for acquisition of stylistic lexicons, and we also evaluate the model relative to theories of register variation and the expected stylistic character of particular genres.

2 Model

2.1 Linguistic foundations

In English manuals of style and other prescriptivist texts (Fowler and Fowler, 1906; Gunning, 1952; Follett, 1966; Strunk and White, 1979; Kane, 1983; Hayakawa, 1994), writers are urged to pay attention to various aspects of lexical style, including elements such as clarity, familiarity, readability, formality, fanciness, colloquialness, specificity, concreteness, objectivity, and naturalness; these stylistic categories reflect common aesthetic judgments about language. In descriptive studies of register, some researchers have posited a few fixed styles (Joos, 1961) or a small, discrete set of situational constraints which determine style and register (Crystal and Davy, 1969; Halliday and Hasan, 1976); by contrast, the applied approach of Biber (1988) and theoretical framework of Leckie-Tarry (1995) offer a more continuous interpretation of register variation.

In Biber's approach, functional dimensions such as *Involved vs. Informational*, *Argumentative vs. Non-argumentative*, and *Abstract vs. non-Abstract* are derived in an unsupervised manner from a mixed-genre corpus, with the labels assigned depending on where features (a small set of known indicators of register) and genres fall on each spectrum. The theory of Leckie-Tarry posits a single main cline of register with one pole (the oral pole) reflecting a full reliance on the context of the linguistic situation, and the other (the literate pole) reflecting a reliance on cultural knowledge. The more specific elements of register are represented as subclines which are strongly influenced by this main cline, creating probabilistic relationships between related dimensions (Birch, 1995).

For the present study, we have chosen 3 dimensions (6 styles) which are clearly represented in the lexicon, which are discussed often in the relevant literature, and which fit well into the Leckie-Tarry conception of related subclines: colloquial vs. literary, concrete vs. abstract, and subjective vs. objective. In addition to a negative correlation between opposing styles, we also expect a positive correlation between stylistic aspects that tend toward the same main pole, situational (i.e. colloquial, concrete, subjective) or cultural (i.e. literary, abstract, objective). These correlations can potentially interfere with accurate lexical acquisition.

2.2 Implementation

Our main model is an adaption of the popular latent Dirichlet allocation topic model (Blei et al., 2003), with each of the 6 styles corresponding to a topic. Briefly, latent Dirichlet allocation (LDA) is a generative Bayesian model: for each document d, a distribution of topics θ_d is drawn from a Dirichlet prior (with parameter α). For each topic z, there is a probability distribution β_z[1] corresponding to the probability of that topic generating any given word in the vocabulary. Words in document d are generated by first selecting a topic z randomly according to θ_d, and then randomly selecting a word w according to β_z. An extension of LDA, the correlated topic model (CTM) (Blei and Lafferty, 2007), supposes a more complex representation of topics: given a matrix Σ representing the covariance between topics and μ representing the means, for each document a topic distribution η (analogous to θ) is drawn from the logistic normal distribution. Given a corpus, good estimates for the relevant parameters can be derived using Bayesian inference.

For both LDA and CTM we use the original variational Bayes implementation of Blei. Variational Bayes (VB) works by approximating the true posterior with a simpler distribution, minimizing the Kullback-Leibler divergence between the two through iterative updates of specially-introduced free variables. The mathematical and algorithmic details are omitted here; see Blei et al. (2003; 2007). Our early investigations used an online, batch version of LDA (Hoffman et al., 2010), which is more appropriate for large corpora because it requires only a single iteration over the dataset. We discovered, however, that batch models were markedly inferior to more traditional models for our purposes because the influence of the initial model diminishes too quickly; here, we need particular topics in the model to correspond to particular styles, and we accomplish this by seeding the model with known instances of each style (see Section 3). Specifically, our initial β consists of distributions where the entire probability mass is divided amongst the seeds for each corresponding topic, and a full iteration over the corpus occurs before β is updated. Typically, LDA iterates over the corpus until a convergence requirement is met, but in this case this is neither practical (due to the size of our corpus) nor necessarily desirable; the diminishing effects of the initial seeding means that the model may not stabilize, in terms of its likelihood, until after it has shifted away from our desired stylistic dimensions towards some other

[1]Some versions of LDA smooth this distribution using a Dirichlet prior; here, though, we use the original formulation from Blei (2003), which does not.

variation in the data. Therefore, we treat the optimal number of iterations as a variable to investigate.

The model is trained on a 1 million text portion of the 2009 version of the ICWSM Spinn3r dataset (Burton et al., 2009), a corpus of blogs we have previously used for formality lexicon induction (Brooke et al., 2010). Since our method relies on co-occurrence, we followed our earlier work in using only texts with at least 100 different word types. All words were tokenized and converted to lower-case, with no further lemmatization. Following Hoffman et al. (2010), we initialized the α of our models to $1/k$ where k is the number of topics. Otherwise we used the default settings; when they overlap they were identical for the LDA and CTM models.

3 Lexicon Induction

Our primary evaluation is based on the stylistic induction of held-out seed words. The words were collected from various sources by the first author and further reviewed by the second; we are both native speakers of English with significant experience in English linguistics. Included words had to be clear, extreme members of their stylistic category, with little or no ambiguity with respect to their style. The colloquial seeds consist of English slang terms and acronyms, e.g. *cuz*, *gig*, *asshole*, *lol*. The literary seeds were primarily drawn from web sites which explain difficult language in texts such as the Bible and *Lord of the Rings*; examples include *behold*, *resplendent*, *amiss*, and *thine*. The concrete seeds all denote objects and actions strongly rooted in the physical world, e.g. *shove* and *lamppost*, while the abstract seeds all involve concepts which require significant human psychological or cultural knowledge to grasp, for instance *patriotism* and *nonchalant*. For our subjective seeds, we used an edited list of strongly positive and negative terms from a manually-constructed sentiment lexicon (Taboada et al., 2011), e.g. *gorgeous* and *depraved*, and for our objective set we selected words from sets of near-synonyms where one was clearly an emotionally-distant alternative, e.g. *residence* (for *home*), *jocular* (for *funny*) and *communicable* (for *contagious*). We filtered initial lists to 150 of each type, removing words which did not appear in the corpus or which occurred in multiple lists. For evaluation we used stratified 3-fold crossvalidation, averaged over 5 different (3-way) splits of the seeds, with the same splits used for all evaluated conditions.

Given two sets of opposing seeds, we follow our earlier work in evaluating our performance in terms of the number of pairings of seeds from each set which have the expected stylistic relationship relative to each other (the guessing baseline is 0.5). Given a word w and two opposing styles (topics) p and n, we place w on the PN dimension according to the β of our trained model as follows:

$$PN_w = \frac{\beta_{pw} - \beta_{nw}}{\beta_{pw} + \beta_{nw}}$$

The normalization is important because otherwise more-common words would tend to have higher PN's, when in fact the opposite is true (rare words tend to be more stylistically prominent). We then calculate pairwise accuracy as the percentage of pairs $\langle w_p, w_n \rangle$ ($w_p \in P_{seeds}$ and $w_n \in N_{seeds}$) where $PN_{w_p} > PN_{w_n}$. However, this metric does not address the case where the degree of a word in one stylistic dimension is overestimated because of its status on a parallel dimension. Two more-holistic alternatives are total accuracy, the percentage of seeds for which the highest β_{tw} is the topic t for which w is a seed (guessing baseline is 0.17), and the average rank of the correct t as ordered by β_{tw} (in the range 1–6, guessing baseline is 3.5); the latter is more forgiving of near misses.

We tested a few options which involved straightforward modifications to model training. Standard LDA produces all tokens in the document, but when dealing with style rather than topic, the number of times a word appears is much less relevant (Brooke et al., 2010). Our binary model assumes an LDA that generates types, not tokens.[2] A key comparison

[2] At the theoretical level, this move is admittedly problematic, since our LDA model is thus being trained under the assumption that texts with multiple instances of the same type can be generated, when of course such texts cannot by definition exist. We might address this by moving to Bayesian models with very different generative assumptions, e.g. the spherical topic model (Reisinger et al., 2010), but these methods involve a significant increase of computational complexity and we believe that on a practical level there are no real negatives associated with directly using a binary representation as input to LDA; in fact, we are avoiding what appears to be a much more serious problem, burstiness (Doyle and Elkan, 2009), i.e. the fact that

Model	Pairwise Accuracy (%)				Total Acc. (%)	Avg. Rank
	Lit/Col	Abs/Con	Obj/Sub	All		
guessing baseline	50.0	50.0	50.0	50.0	16.6.	3.50
basic LDA (iter 2)	94.3	98.8	93.0	95.4	55.0	1.79
binary LDA (iter 2)	**96.2**	98.9	**93.5**	**96.2**	**57.7**	**1.74**
combo binary LDA (iter 1)	95.4	**99.2**	93.3	96.0	53.1	1.86
binary CTM (iter 1)	96.3	99.0	89.6	95.0	53.0	1.87

Table 1: Model performance in lexical induction of seeds. Bold indicates best in column.

here is with a combined LDA model (*combo*), an amalgamation of three independently trained 2-topic models, one for each dimension; this tests our key hypothesis that training dimensions of style together is beneficial. Finally, we test against the correlated topic model (CTM), which offers an explicit representation of style correlation, but which has done poorly with respect to interpretability, despite offering better perplexity (Chang et al., 2009).

The results of the lexicon induction evaluation are in Table 1. Since the number of optimal iterations varies, we report the result from the best of the first five iterations, as measured by total accuracy; the best iteration is shown in parenthesis. In general, all the results are high enough—we are reliably above 90% for the pairwise task, and above 50% for the 6-way task—for us to conclude with some confidence that our model is capturing a significant amount of stylistic variation. As predicted, using words as boolean features had a net positive gain, consistent across all of our metrics, though this effect was not as marked as we have seen previously. The model with independent training of each dimension (*combo*) did noticeably worse, supporting our conclusion that a multidimensional approach is warranted here. Particularly striking is the much larger drop in overall accuracy as compared to pairwise accuracy, which suggests that the combo model is capturing the general trends but not distinguishing correlated styles as well. However, the most complex model, the CTM, actually does slightly worse than the combo, which was contrary to our expectations but nonetheless consistent with previous work on the interpretability of topic models. The performance of the full LDA models benefited from a second iteration, but this was not true of combo LDA or CTM, and the performance of all models dropped after the second iteration.

An analysis of individual errors reveals, unsurprisingly, that most of the errors occur across styles on the same pole; by far the largest single common misclassification is objective words to abstract. Of the words that consistently show this misclassification across the runs, many of them, e.g. *animate*, *aperture*, *encircle*, and *constrain* are clearly errors (if anything, these words tend towards concreteness), but in other cases the word in question is arguably also fairly abstract, e.g. *categorize* and *predominant*, and might not be labeled an error at all. Other signs that our model might be doing better than our total accuracy metric gives it credit for: many of the subjective words that are consistently mislabeled as literary have an exaggerated, literary feel, e.g. *jubilant*, *grievous*, and *malevolent*.

4 Text-level Analysis

Our secondary analysis involved evaluating the θ's of our best configuration (based on average pairwise and total accuracy) on other texts. After training, we carried out inference on the BNC corpus, averaging the resulting θ's to see which styles are associated with which genres. Appearances of the seed terms for each model were disregarded during this process; only the induced part of the lexicon was used. The average differences relative to the mean across the various stylistic dimensions (as measured by the probabilities in θ) are given for a selection of genres in Table 2.

The most obvious pattern in table 2 is the dominance of the medium: all written genres are positive for our styles on the 'cultural' pole and negative for styles on the 'situational' pole and the opposite is

traditional LDA is influenced too much by multiple instances of the same word.

Genre	Styles					
	Literary	**Abstract**	**Objective**	**Colloquial**	**Concrete**	**Subjective**
News	+0.67	+0.50	+0.43	−0.31	−0.72	−0.57
Religious texts	+0.38	+0.38	+0.28	−0.27	−0.44	−0.32
Academic	+0.18	+0.29	+0.26	−0.20	−0.36	−0.18
Fiction	+0.31	+0.09	+0.02	−0.05	−0.12	−0.25
Meeting	−0.61	−0.54	−0.42	+0.35	+0.69	+0.55
Courtroom	−0.63	−0.53	−0.41	+0.32	+0.69	+0.57
Conversation	−0.56	−0.63	−0.54	+0.43	+0.80	+0.50

Table 2: Average differences from corpus mean of LDA-derived stylistic dimension probabilities for various genres in the BNC, in hundredths.

true for spoken genres. The magnitude of this effect is more difficult to interpret: though it is clear why fiction should sit on the boundary (since it contains spoken dialogue), the appearance of news at the written extreme is odd, though it might be due to the fact that news blogs are the most prevalent formal genre in the training corpus.

However, if we ignore magnitude and focus on the relative ratios of the stylistic differences for styles on the same pole, we can identify some individual stylistic effects among genres within the same medium. Relative to the other written genres, for instance, fiction is, sensibly, more literary and much less objective, while academic texts are much more abstract and objective; for the other two written genres, the spread is more even, though relative to religious texts, news is more objective. At the situational pole, fiction also stands out, being much more colloquial and concrete than other written genres. Predictably, if we consider again the ratios across styles, conversation is the most colloquial genre here, though the difference is subtle.

We carried out a correlation analysis of the LDA-reduced styles of all texts in the BNC and, consistent with the genre results in Table 2, found a strong positive correlation for all styles on the same main pole, averaging 0.83. The average negative correlation between opposing poles is even higher, −0.88. This supports the Leckie-Tarry formulation. The independence assumptions of the LDA model did not prevent strong correlations from forming between these distinct yet clearly interrelated dimensions; if anything, the correlations are stronger than we would have predicted.

5 Conclusion

We have introduced a Bayesian model of stylistic variation. Topic models like LDA are often evaluated using information-theoretic measures, but our emphasis has been on interpretibility: at the word level we can use the model to induce stylistic lexicons which correspond to human judgement, and at the text level we can use it distinguish genres in expected ways. Another theme has been to offer evidence that indeed a multi-dimensional approach is strongly warranted: importantly, our results indicate that separate unidimensional models of style are inferior for identifying the core stylistic character of each word, and in our secondary analysis we found strong correlations among styles attributable to the situational/cultural dichotomy. However, an off-the-shelf model that integrates correlation among topics did not outperform basic LDA.

One advantage of a Bayesian approach is in the flexibility of the model: there are any number of other interesting possible extensions at both the θ and β levels of the model, including alternative approaches to correlation (Li and McCallum, 2006). Beyond Bayesian models, vector space and graphical approaches should be compared. More work is clearly needed to improve evaluation: some of our seeds could fall into multiple stylistic categories, so a more detailed annotation would be useful.

Acknowledgements

This work was financially supported by the Natural Sciences and Engineering Research Council of Canada.

References

Shlomo Argamon, Casey Whitelaw, Paul Chase, Sobhan Raj Hota, Navendu Garg, and Shlomo Levitan. 2007. Stylistic text classification using functional lexical features. *Journal of the American Society for Information Science and Technology*, 7:91–109.

Douglas Biber and Susan Conrad. 2009. *Register, Genre, and Style*. Cambridge University Press.

Douglas Biber. 1988. *Variation Across Speech and Writing*. Cambridge University Press.

David Birch. 1995. Introduction. In Helen Leckie-Tarry, editor, *Language and Context: A Functional Linguistic Theory of Register*. Pinter.

David M. Blei and John D. Lafferty. 2007. Correlated topic models. *Annals of Applied Statistics*, 1(1):17–35.

David M. Blei, Andrew Y. Ng, Michael I. Jordan, and John Lafferty. 2003. Latent Dirichlet allocation. *Journal of Machine Learning Research*, 3:993–1022.

Julian Brooke, Tong Wang, and Graeme Hirst. 2010. Automatic acquisition of lexical formality. In *Proceedings of the 23rd International Conference on Computational Linguistics (COLING '10)*, Beijing.

Kevin Burton, Akshay Java, and Ian Soboroff. 2009. The ICWSM 2009 Spinn3r Dataset. In *Proceedings of the Third Annual Conference on Weblogs and Social Media (ICWSM 2009)*, San Jose, CA.

Jonathan Chang, Jordan Boyd-Graber, Sean Gerrish, Chong Wang, and David Blei. 2009. Reading tea leaves: How humans interpret topic models. In *Proceedings of Neural Information Processing Systems (NIPS '09)*.

Kevyn Collins-Thompson and Jamie Callan. 2005. Predicting reading difficulty with statistical language models. *Journal of the American Society for Information Science Technology*, 56(13):1448–1462.

David Crystal and Derek Davy. 1969. *Investigating English Style*. Indiana University Press.

Gabriel Doyle and Charles Elkan. 2009. Accounting for burstiness in topic models. In *International Conference on Machine Learning (ICML '09)*.

Wilson Follett. 1966. *Modern American Usage*. Hill & Wang, New York.

H. W. Fowler and F. G. Fowler. 1906. *The King's English*. Clarendon Press, Oxford, 2nd edition.

Nikesh Garera and David Yarowsky. 2009. Modeling latent biographic attributes in conversational genres. In *Proceedings of the Joint Conference of the 47th Annual Meeting of the ACL and the 4th International Joint Conference on Natural Language Processing of the AFNLP (ACL-IJCNLP '09)*, pages 710–718, Singapore.

Robert Gunning. 1952. *The Technique of Clear Writing*. McGraw-Hill, New York.

M.A.K. Halliday and Ruqaiya Hasan. 1976. *Cohesion in English*. Longman, London.

S.I. Hayakawa, editor. 1994. *Choose the Right Word*. HarperCollins Publishers, second edition. Revised by Eugene Ehrlich.

Matthew D. Hoffman, David M. Blei, and Francis R. Bach. 2010. Online learning for latent Dirichlet allocation. In *Neural Information Processing Systems (NIPS '10)*, pages 856–864.

Eduard H. Hovy. 1990. Pragmatics and natural language generation. *Artificial Intelligence*, 43:153–197.

Diana Inkpen and Graeme Hirst. 2006. Building and using a lexical knowledge base of near-synonym differences. *Computational Linguistics*, 32(2):223–262.

Martin Joos. 1961. *The Five Clocks*. Harcourt, Brace and World, New York.

Nobuhiro Kaji and Masaru Kitsuregawa. 2007. Building lexicon for sentiment analysis from massive collection of HTML documents. In *Proceedings of the 2007 Joint Conference on Empirical Methods in Natural Language Processing and Computational Natural Language Learning (EMNLP-CoNLL '07)*.

Thomas S. Kane. 1983. *The Oxford Guide to Writing*. Oxford Univeristy Press.

Brett Kessler, Geoffrey Nunberg, and Hinrich Schütze. 1997. Automatic detection of text genre. In *Proceedings of the 35th Annual Meeting of the Association for Computational Linguistics (ACL '97)*, pages 32–38, Madrid, Spain.

Paul Kidwell, Guy Lebanon, and Kevyn Collins-Thompson. 2009. Statistical estimation of word acquisition with application to readability prediction. In *Proceedings of the 2009 Conference on Empirical Methods in Natural Language Processing (EMNLP'09)*, pages 900–909, Singapore.

Helen Leckie-Tarry. 1995. *Language and Context: A Functional Linguistic Theory of Register*. Pinter.

Wei Li and Andrew McCallum. 2006. Pachinko allocation: DAG-structured mixture models of topic correlations. In *Proceedings of the 23rd International Conference on Machine Learning*, ICML '06, pages 577–584.

David Newman, Edwin V. Bonilla, and Wray Buntine. 2011. Improving topic coherence with regularized topic models. In *Proceedings of Advances in Neural Information Processing Systems (NIPS '11)*.

Sinno Jialin Pan and Qiang Yang. 2010. A survey on transfer learning. *IEEE Transactions on Knowledge and Data Engineering*, 22(10).

Kelly Peterson, Matt Hohensee, and Fei Xia. 2011. Email formality in the workplace: A case study on the Enron corpus. In *Proceedings of the 49th Annual Meeting of the Association for Computational Linguistics (ACL '11)*, Portland, Oregon.

Philipp Petrenz and Bonnie Webber. 2011. Stable classification of text genres. *Computational Linguistics*, 37(2):385–393, June.

J. Reisinger, A. Waters, B. Silverthorn, and R. Mooney. 2010. Spherical topic models. In *International Conference on Machine Learning (ICML '10)*.

Sara Rosenthal and Kathleen McKeown. 2011. Age prediction in blogs: A study of style, content, and online behavior in pre- and post-social media generations. In *Proceedings of the 49th Annual Meeting of the Association for Computational Linguistics (ACL '11)*, Portland, Oregon.

William Strunk and E.B. White. 1979. *The Elements of Style*. Macmillan, 3rd edition.

Maite Taboada, Julian Brooke, Milan Tofiloski, Kimberly Voll, and Manfred Stede. 2011. Lexicon-based methods for sentiment analysis. *Computational Linguistics*, 37(2):267–307.

Peter D. Turney. 2002. Thumbs up or thumbs down?: semantic orientation applied to unsupervised classification of reviews. In *Proceedings of the 40th Annual Meeting on Association for Computational Linguistics*, ACL '02, pages 417–424, Philadelphia, Pennsylvania.

Leonid Velikovich, Sasha Blair-Goldensohn, Kerry Hannan, and Ryan McDonald. 2010. The viability of web-derived polarity lexicons. In *Human Language Technologies: The 2010 Annual Conference of the North American Chapter of the Association for Computational Linguistics*, HLT '10, pages 777–785, Los Angeles, California.

Theresa Wilson, Janyce Wiebe, and Paul Hoffmann. 2005. Recognizing contextual polarity in phrase-level sentiment analysis. In *Proceedings of the conference on Human Language Technology and Empirical Methods in Natural Language Processing*, HLT/EMNLP '05, pages 347–354.

Unsupervised Domain Tuning to Improve Word Sense Disambiguation

Judita Preiss and **Mark Stevenson**
j.preiss@sheffield.ac.uk and m.stevenson@dcs.shef.ac.uk
Department of Computer Science, University of Sheffield
211 Portobello, Sheffield, S1 4DP, UK

Abstract

The topic of a document can prove to be useful information for Word Sense Disambiguation (WSD) since certain meanings tend to be associated with particular topics. This paper presents an LDA-based approach for WSD, which is trained using any available WSD system to establish a sense per (Latent Dirichlet allocation based) topic. The technique is tested using three unsupervised and one supervised WSD algorithms within the SPORT and FINANCE domains giving a performance increase each time, suggesting that the technique may be useful to improve the performance of any available WSD system.

1 Introduction

Assigning each word its most frequent sense (MFS) is commonly used as a baseline in Word Sense Disambiguation (WSD). This baseline can be difficult to beat, particularly for unsupervised systems which do not have access to the annotated training data used to determine the MFS. However, it has also been shown that unsupervised methods can be used to identify the most likely sense for each ambiguous word type and this approach can be effective for disambiguation (McCarthy et al., 2004).

Knowledge of the domain of a document has been shown to be useful information for WSD. For example, Khapra et al. (2010) improve the performance of a graph-based WSD system using a small number of hand-tagged examples, but further examples would be required for each new domain. Agirre et al. (2009) automatically construct a thesaurus from texts in a domain which they use for WSD. Unfortunately, performance drops when the thesaurus is combined with information from local context. Stevenson et al. (2011) showed that performance of an unsupervised WSD algorithm can be improved by supplementing the context with domain information. Cai et al. (2007) use LDA to create an additional feature for a supervised WSD algorithm, by inferring topics for labeled training data. Boyd-Graber et al. (2007) integrate a topic model with WordNet and use it to carry out disambiguation and learn topics simultaneously. Li et al. (2010) use sense paraphrases to estimate probabilities of senses and carry out WSD. Koeling et al. (2005) showed that automatically acquiring the predominant sense of a word from a corpus from the same domain increases performance (over using a predominant sense acquired from a balanced corpus), but their work requires a separate thesaurus to be built for each domain under investigation. Navigli et al. (2011) extracted relevant terms from texts in a domain and used them to initialize a random walk over the WordNet graph.

Our approaches rely on a one sense per topic hypothesis (Gale et al., 1992), making use of topics induced using LDA – we present three novel techniques for exploiting domain information that are employable with any WSD algorithm (unsupervised or supervised). Using any WSD algorithm, we create a sense per topic distribution for each LDA topic, and the classification of a new document into a topic determines the sense distribution of the words within. Once a sense per topic distribution is obtained, no further WSD annotation of new texts is required. Instead of fixing domains, our technique allows these to be dynamically created (using LDA) and we using four existing publicly available WSD algorithms (three unsupervised and one supervised) to show that our technique increases their performance with no changes to the original algorithm.

Section 2 briefly introduces LDA, while Section 3 describes our three techniques for adding domain information to a WSD algorithm. The WSD algorithms employed in the evaluation of our techniques are described in Section 4 with experiments and results in Section 5. Section 6 draws our conclusions and presents avenues for future work.

2 Latent Dirichlet allocation

LDA (Blei et al., 2003) is a widely used topic model, which views the underlying document distribution as having a Dirichlet prior. We employ a publicly available implementation of LDA[1] which has two main execution methods: parameter estimation (model building) and inference for new data (classification of a new document). Both invocation methods produce θ distributions (the topic-document distributions, i.e., $p(t_i|d)$ for t_i topics and d document), and ϕ distributions (word-topic distributions, i.e., $p(w_j|t_i)$ for words w_j). The parameter estimation phase also creates a list of n words most likely to be associated with each topic.

3 Using LDA for WSD

The underlying idea of our approach lies in deriving a document invariant sense distribution for each topic, $p(w, s|t)$. Once this word sense distribution is obtained, the underlying WSD algorithm is never needed again. We make the assumption that while the WSD algorithm may not be able to select the correct sense within an individual text due to insufficient domain information, the topic specific sense will be selected with a greater frequency over all documents pertaining to a topic, and thus the probability distributions over senses generated in this fashion should be more accurate.

Only the distribution $p(w, s|t)$ is dependent on an underlying WSD algorithm – once this distribution is obtained, it can be combined with the LDA derived θ distribution, $p(t|d_{new})$, to compute the desired word sense distribution within the new document d_{new}:

$$p(w, s|d_{new}) = \sum_t p(w, s|t)p(t|d_{new})$$

Sections 3.1, 3.2 and 3.3 describe three different methods for deriving $p(w, s|t)$, and we investigate the performance changes with different WSD algorithms: two versions of Personalized PageRank, described in Section 4.1, a similarity based WSD system outlined in Section 4.2, and a supervised graph based algorithm (Section 4.3).

3.1 Sense-based topic model (SBTM)

In its usual form, the ϕ distribution generated by LDA merely provides a word-topic distribution $(p(w|t))$. However, we modify the approach to directly output $p(w, s|t)$, but we remain able to classify (non WSD annotated) new text. The topic model is built from documents annotated with word senses using the chosen WSD algorithm.[2] The topic model created from this data is based on word-sense combinations and thus ϕ represents $p(w, s|t)$.

To classify new (non sense disambiguated) documents, the model is transformed to a word (rather than word-sense) based for: i.e., the $p(w, s|t)$ probabilities are summed over all senses of w to give resulting probabilities for the wordform. A new document, d_{new}, classified using this system gives rise to a number of distributions, including the probability of a topic given a document distribution $(p(t|d_{new}))$.

3.2 Linear equations (LinEq)

If the topic model is created directly from wordforms, we can use the known probabilities $p(s|w, d)$ (obtained from the WSD algorithm), and $p(t|d)$ (from the LDA classifier) to yield an overdetermined system of linear equations of the form

$$p(s|w, d) = \sum_t p(s|w, t)p(t|d)$$

We use an existing implementation of linear least squares to find a solution (i.e. $p(s|w, t)$ for each t)

[1] http://jgibblda.sourceforge.net/.

[2] It is not crucial to word sense disambiguate all words in the text – a word can be passed to LDA in either its word-sense, disambiguated, form or in its raw form. While we do not attempt this in our work, it would be possible to build a model specifically for noun senses of a word, by including noun senses of the word and leaving the raw form for any non-noun occurrences.

by minimizing the sum of squared differences between the data values and their corresponding modeled values, i.e., minimizing:

$$\sum_d \left(p(s|w,d) - \sum_t p(s|w,t)p(t|d) \right)^2$$

3.3 Topic words (TopicWord)

The techniques presented in Sections 3.1 and 3.2 both require the WSD algorithm to annotate a reasonably high proportion of the data used to build the topic model. For systems which do not rely on word order, an alternative based on the most likely words per topic is possible: the LDA algorithm generates ϕ, a word-topic distribution. It is therefore possible to extract the most likely words per topic.

To acquire a sense-topic distribution for a topic t, each target word w is included in a bag of words which includes the most likely words for t and the unsupervised WSD algorithm is executed (w is added to the list if t does not already contain it). This technique is not applicable to non bag-of-words WSD algorithms, as structure is absent.

4 Word Sense Disambiguation

Only the topic model documents need to be automatically annotated with the chosen WSD system, after this, the WSD system is never applied again (an LDA classification determines the sense distribution) – this is particularly useful for supervised system which frequently have a long execution time. We explore three different types of WSD system: two versions of a knowledge base based system (Section 4.1), an unsupervised system (Section 4.2) and a supervised system (Section 4.3).

4.1 Personalized PageRank (ppr and w2w)

We use the freely available[3] Personalized PageRank algorithm (Agirre and Soroa, 2009) with WordNet 3.0. In Section 5 we present results from two options of the Personalized PageRank algorithm: *ppr*, which performs one PageRank calculation for a whole content, and *w2w*, which performs one PageRank calculation for every word in the context to be disambiguated.

[3] Available from http://ixa2.si.ehu.es/ukb/

4.2 WordNet similarity (sim)

We also evaluated another unsupervised approach, the Perl package WordNet::SenseRelate::AllWords (Pedersen and Kolhatkar, 2009), which finds senses of each word in a text based on senses of the surrounding words. The algorithm is invoked with Lesk similarity (Banerjee and Pedersen, 2002).

4.3 Vector space model (vsm)

An existing vector space model (VSM) based state-of-the-art supervised WSD system with features derived from the text surrounding the ambiguous word (Stevenson et al., 2008) is trained on Semcor (Miller et al., 1993).[4]

5 Experiments

5.1 Data

The approach is evaluated using a domain-specific WSD corpus (Koeling et al., 2005) which includes articles from the FINANCE and SPORTS domains taken from the Reuters corpus (Rose et al., 2002). This corpus contains 100 manually annotated instances (from each domain) for 41 words.[5]

The word-sense LDA topic models are created from 80,128 documents randomly selected from the Reuters corpus (this corresponds to a tenth of the entire Reuters corpus). LDA can abstract a model from a relatively small corpus and a tenth of the Reuters corpus is much more manageable in terms of memory and time requirements, particularly given the need to word sense disambiguate (some part of) each document in this dataset.[6]

[4] A version of Semcor automatically transformed to WordNet 3.0 available from http://www.cse.unt.edu/~rada/downloads.html#semcor was used in this work.

[5] Unfortunately, the entire domain-specific sense disambiguated corpus could not be used in the evaluation of our system, as the released corpus does not link each annotated sentence to its source document, and it is not always possible to recover these; approximately 87% of the data could be used. This dataset is available at http://staffwww.dcs.shef.ac.uk/people/J.Preiss/downloads/source_texts.tgz

[6] In this work, all 80,128 documents were word sense disambiguated. However, it would be possible to restrict this set to a smaller number, as long as a reliable distribution of word senses per topic could be obtained.

	ppr	w2w	sim	vsm
Baseline	36	41	23	27
SBTM model	39	43	30	31
LinEq	41	44	–	33
TopicWord	38	41	–	–

Table 1: Summary of results based on 150 topics

5.2 Results

Table 1 presents the performance results for the four WSD algorithms based on 150 topics. A range of topic values was explored, and 150 topics yielded highest performance, though the variance between the performance based on different topics (ranging from 50 to 250) was very small (0.4% difference to the average performance with 250 topics, and 3% with 50). The performance shown indicates the precision (number correct / number attempted). Recall is 100% in all cases.

The similarity algorithm (sim) fails on certain documents and therefore the linear equations technique could not be applied. The topic word technique (TopicWord) could not be evaluated using the similarity algorithm, due to the high sensitivity to word order within the test paragraph. In addition, the topic words technique is not applicable to supervised systems, due to its reliance on structured sentences. The best results with this technique were obtained with including all likely words with probabilities exceeding 0.001 and smoothing of 0.1 of the topic document distribution.

Using a Wilcoxon signed-rank test, the results were found to be significantly better over the original algorithms in every case (apart from TopicWords). Both the WordNet similarity (sim) and the VSM approach (vsm) have a lower performance than the two PPR based WSD algorithms (ppt and w2w). For example, sim assigns the same (usually incorrect) sense to all occurrences of the word *tie*, while both PPR based algorithms detect an obvious domain change. The vsm approach suffers from a lack of training data (only a small number of examples of each word appear in Semcor), while sim does not get enough information from the context.

As an interesting aside, the topic models based on word-sense combinations, as opposed to wordforms only, are more informative with less overlap. Examining the word *stake* annotated with the *w2w* WSD algorithm: only topic 1 contains *stake* among the top 12 terms associated with a topic in the word-sense model, while 10 topics are found in the wordform topic model. Table 2 shows the top 12 terms associated with topics containing the word *stake*.

Topic	Word-based model
39	say, will, company, share, deal, european, buy, agreement, **stake**, new, hungary, oil
63	say, share, united, market, offer, stock, union, percent, **stake**, will, point, new
90	say, will, fund, price, london, sell, **stake**, indonesia, court, investment, share, buy
91	say, market, bond, russia, press, party, **stake**, russian, country, indonesia, new, election
97	say, million, bank, uk, percent, share, **stake**, world, will, year, central, british
113	say, will, percent, week, billion, last, italy, plan, **stake**, year, budget, czech
134	say, china, percent, hong, kong, official, **stake**, billion, report, buy, group, year
142	say, percent, market, first, bank, rate, year, dealer, million, money, close, **stake**
145	say, will, new, brazil, dollar, group, percent, **stake**, year, one, make, do
147	say, yen, forecast, million, parent, market, share, will, profit, percent, **stake**, group
	Sense-based model
1	**stake*13286801-n**, share*13285176-n, sell*02242464-v, buy*02207206-v, have*02204692-v, group*00031264-n, company*08058098-n, percent*13817526-n, hold*02203362-v, deal*01110274-n, shareholder, interest*13286801-n

Table 2: The presence of *stake* within the word- and sense-based topic models

6 Conclusion

We present three unsupervised techniques based on acquiring LDA topics which can be used to improve the performance of a number of WSD algorithms. All approaches make use of topic information obtained using LDA and do not require any modification of the underlying WSD system. While the technique is dependent on the accuracy of the WSD algorithm, it consistently outperforms the baselines for all four different algorithms.

Acknowledgments

This research was supported by a Google Research Award. Our thanks also go to the two anonymous reviewers whose comments have made this paper much clearer.

References

Agirre, E., de Lacalle, O. L., and Soroa, A. (2009). Knowledge-based WSD on specific domains: performing better than generic supervised WSD. In *Proceedings of the 21st International Joint Conference on Artificial Intelligence*, pages 1501–1506.

Agirre, E. and Soroa, A. (2009). Personalizing pagerank for word sense disambiguation. In *Proceedings of EACL*.

Banerjee, S. and Pedersen, T. (2002). An adapted lesk algorithm for word sense disambiguation using wordnet. In *Proceedings of the Third International Conference on Intelligent Text Processing and Computational Linguistics*, pages 135–145.

Blei, D. M., Ng, A. Y., and Jordan, M. I. (2003). Latent Dirichlet allocation. *Journal of Machine Learning Research*, 3:993–1022.

Boyd-Graber, J., Blei, D., and Zhu, X. (2007). A topic model for word sense disambiguation. In *Proceedings of the EMNLP-CoNLL*, pages 1024–1033.

Cai, J. F., Lee, W. S., and Teh, Y. W. (2007). Nus-ml: Improving word sense disambiguation using topic features. In *Proceedings of SEMEVAL*.

Gale, W. A., Church, K. W., and Yarowsky, D. (1992). One sense per discourse. In *Proceedings of the 4th DARPA Speech and Natural Language Workshop*, pages 233–237.

Khapra, M., Kulkarni, A., Sohoney, S., and Bhattacharyya, P. (2010). All words domain adapted WSD: Finding a middle ground between supervision and unsupervision. In *Proceedings of ACL 2010*, pages 1532–1541, Uppsala, Sweden.

Koeling, R., Mccarthy, D., and Carroll, J. (2005). Domain specific sense distributions and predominant sense acquisition. In *Proceedings of Joint HLT-EMNLP05*, pages 419–426.

Li, L., Roth, B., and Sporleder, C. (2010). Topic models for word sense disambiguation and token-based idiom detection. In *Proceedings of the 48th Annual Meeting of the Association for Computational Linguistics*, pages 1138–1147.

McCarthy, D., Koeling, R., Weeds, J., and Carroll, J. (2004). Finding predominant senses in untagged text. In *Proceedings of the 42nd Annual Meeting of the Association for Computational Linguistics*, pages 280–287.

Miller, G. A., Leacock, C., Tengi, R., and Bunker, R. T. (1993). A semantic concordance. In *Proceedings of the ARPA Workshop on Human Language Technology*, pages 303–308.

Navigli, R., Faralli, S., Soroa, A., de Lacalle, O. L., and Agirre, E. (2011). Two birds with one stone: learning semantic models for text categorization and word sense disambiguation. In *CIKM*, pages 2317–2320.

Pedersen, T. and Kolhatkar, V. (2009). Wordnet::senserelate::allwords - a broad coverageword sense tagger that maximizes semantic relatedness (demonstration system). In *Proceedings of the North American Chapter of the Association for Computational Linguistics - Human Language Technologies Conference*, pages 17–20.

Rose, T. G., Stevenson, M., and Whitehead, M. (2002). The Reuters corpus volume 1 - from yesterday's news to tomorrow's language resources. In *Proceedings of the Third International Conference on Language Resources and Evaluation*, pages 827–832.

Stevenson, M., Agirre, E., and Soroa, A. (2012). Exploiting domain information for word sense disambiguation of medical documents. *Journal of the American Medical Informatics Association*, 19(2):235–240.

Stevenson, M., Guo, Y., Gaizauskas, R., and Martinez, D. (2008). Knowledge sources for word sense disambiguation of biomedical text. In *Proceedings of the Workshop on Current Trends in Biomedical Natural Language Processing at ACL*, pages 80–87.

What's in a Domain? Multi-Domain Learning for Multi-Attribute Data

Mahesh Joshi[⋆] **Mark Dredze**[†] **William W. Cohen**[⋆] **Carolyn P. Rosé**[⋆]
[⋆] School of Computer Science, Carnegie Mellon University
Pittsburgh, PA, 15213, USA
[†] Human Language Technology Center of Excellence, Johns Hopkins University
Baltimore, MD, 21211, USA
maheshj@cs.cmu.edu, mdredze@cs.jhu.edu
wcohen@cs.cmu.edu, cprose@cs.cmu.edu

Abstract

Multi-Domain learning assumes that a single metadata attribute is used in order to divide the data into so-called domains. However, real-world datasets often have multiple metadata attributes that can divide the data into domains. It is not always apparent which single attribute will lead to the best domains, and more than one attribute might impact classification. We propose extensions to two multi-domain learning techniques for our *multi-attribute* setting, enabling them to simultaneously learn from several metadata attributes. Experimentally, they outperform the multi-domain learning baseline, even when it selects the single "best" attribute.

1 Introduction

Multi-Domain Learning (Evgeniou and Pontil, 2004; Daumé III, 2007; Dredze and Crammer, 2008; Finkel and Manning, 2009; Zhang and Yeung, 2010; Saha et al., 2011) algorithms learn when training instances are spread across many domains, which impact model parameters. These algorithms use examples from each domain to learn a general model that is also sensitive to individual domain differences.

However, many data sets include a host of metadata attributes, many of which can potentially define the domains to use. Consider the case of restaurant reviews, which can be categorized into domains corresponding to the cuisine, location, price range, or several other factors. For multi-domain learning, we should use the metadata attribute most likely to characterize a domain: a change in vocabulary (i.e. features) that most impacts the classification decision (Ben-David et al., 2009). This choice is not easy. First, we may not know which metadata attribute is most likely to fit this role. Perhaps the location most impacts the review language, but it could easily be the price of the meal. Second, multiple metadata attributes could impact the classification decision, and picking a single one might reduce classification accuracy. Therefore, we seek multi-domain learning algorithms which can simultaneously learn from many types of domains (metadata attributes).

We introduce the *multi-attribute multi-domain* (MAMD) learning problem, in which each learning instance is associated with multiple metadata attributes, each of which may impact feature behavior. We present extensions to two popular multi-domain learning algorithms, FEDA (Daumé III, 2007) and MDR (Dredze et al., 2009). Rather than selecting a single domain division, our algorithms consider all attributes as possible distinctions and discover changes in features across attributes. We evaluate our algorithms using two different data sets – a data set of restaurant reviews (Chahuneau et al., 2012), and a dataset of transcribed speech segments from floor debates in the United States Congress (Thomas et al., 2006). We demonstrate that multi-attribute algorithms improve over their multi-domain counterparts, which can learn distinctions from only a single attribute.

2 MAMD Learning

In multi-domain learning, each instance $\mathbf{x}$ is drawn from a domain d with distribution $\mathbf{x} \sim \mathcal{D}_d$ over a vectors space $\mathbb{R}^D$ and labeled with a domain specific function f_d with label $y \in \{-1, +1\}$ (for binary classification). In multi-attribute multi-domain

(MAMD) learning, we have M metadata attributes in a data set, where the mth metadata attribute has K_m possible unique values which represent the domains induced by that metadata attribute. Each instance $\mathbf{x}_i$ is drawn from a distribution $\mathbf{x}_i \sim \mathcal{D}_a$ specific to a *set* of attribute values $\mathcal{A}_i$ associated with each instance. Additionally, each unique set of attributes indexes a function $f_{\mathcal{A}}$.[1] $\mathcal{A}_i$ could contain a value for each attribute, or no values for any attribute (which would index a domain-agnostic "background" distribution and labeling function). Just as a domain can change a feature's probability and behavior, so can each metadata attribute.

Examples of data for MAMD learning abound. The commonly used Amazon product reviews data set (Blitzer et al., 2007) only includes product types, but the original reviews can be attributed with author, product price, brand, and so on. Additional examples include congressional floor debate records (e.g. political party, speaker, bill) (Joshi et al., 2012). In this paper, we use restaurant reviews (Chahuneau et al., 2012), which have upto 20 metadata attributes that define domains, and congressional floor debates, with two attributes that define domains.

It is difficult to apply multi-domain learning algorithms when it is unclear which metadata attribute to choose for defining the "domains". It is possible that there is a single "best" attribute to use for defining domains, one that when used in multi-domain learning will yield the best classifier. To find this attribute, one must rely on one's intuition about the problem,[2] or perform an exhaustive empirical search over all attributes using some validation set. Both these strategies can be brittle, because as the nature of data changes over time so may the "best" domain distinction. Additionally, multi-domain learning was not designed to benefit from multiple helpful attributes.

We note here that Eisenstein et al. (2011), as well as Wang et al. (2012), worked with a "multifaceted topic model" using the framework of sparse additive generative models (SAGE). Both those models capture interactions between topics and multiple aspects, and can be adapted to the case of MAMD. While our problem formulation has significant conceptual overlap with the SAGE–like multifaceted topic models framework, our proposed methods are motivated from a fast online learning perspective.

A naive approach for MAMD would be to treat every unique set of attributes as a domain, including unique proper subsets of different attributes to account for the case of missing attributes in some instances.[3] However, introducing an exponential number of domains requires a similar increase in training data, clearly an infeasible requirement. Instead, we develop multi-attribute extensions for two multi-domain learning algorithms, such that the increase in parameters is linear in the number of metadata attributes, and no special handling is required for the case where some metadata attributes might be missing from an instance.

Multi-Attribute `FEDA` The key idea behind FEDA (Daumé III, 2007) is to encode each domain using its own parameters, one per feature. FEDA maps a feature vector $\mathbf{x}$ in $\mathbb{R}^D$ to $\mathbb{R}^{D(K+1)}$. This provides a separate parameter sub-space for every domain $k \in 1 \ldots K$, and also maintains a domain-agnostic shared sub-space. Essentially, each feature is duplicated for every instance in the appropriate sub-space of $\mathbb{R}^{D(K+1)}$ that corresponds to the instance's domain. We extend this idea to the MAMD setting by using one parameter per attribute value. The original instance $\mathbf{x} \in \mathbb{R}^D$ is now mapped into $\mathbb{R}^{D(1+\sum_m K_m)}$; a separate parameter for each attribute value and a shared set of parameters. In effect, for every metadata attribute $a \in \mathcal{A}_i$, the original features are copied into the appropriate sub-space. This grows linearly with the number of metadata attribute values, as opposed to exponentially in our naive solution. While this is still substantial growth, each instance retains the same feature sparsity as in the original input space. In this new setup, FEDA allows an instance to contribute towards learning the shared parameters, and the attribute-specific parameters for all the attributes present on an instance. Just like multi-domain FEDA, any supervised learning algorithm can be applied to the transformed representation.

[1] Distributions and functions that share attributes could share parameters.

[2] Intuition is often critical for learning and in some cases can help, such as in the Amazon product reviews data set, where product type clearly corresponds to domain. However, for other data sets the choice may be less clear.

[3] While we used a similar setup for formulating our problem, we did not rule out the potential for factoring the distributions.

Multi-Attribute MDR We make a similar change to MDR (Dredze et al., 2009) to extend it for the MAMD setting. In the original formulation, Dredze et al. used confidence-weighted (CW) learning (Dredze et al., 2008) for learning shared and domain-specific classifiers, which are combined based on the confidence scores associated with the feature weights. For training the MDR approaches in a multi-domain learning setup, they found that computing updates for the combined classifier and then equally distributing them to the shared and domain-specific classifiers was the best strategy, although it approximated the true objective that they aimed to optimize. In our multi-attribute setup confidence-weighted (CW) classifiers are learned for each of the $\sum_m K_m$ attribute values in addition to a shared CW classifier. At classification time, a combined classifier is computed for every instance. However, instead of combining the shared classifier and a *single* domain-specific classifier, we combine the shared CW classifier and $|\mathcal{A}_i|$ different attribute value-specific CW classifiers associated with $\mathbf{x}_i$. The combined classifier is found by minimizing the KL-divergence of the combined classifier with respect to each of the underlying classifiers.[4]

When learning the shared and domain-specific classifiers, we follow the best result in Dredze et al. and use the "averaged update" strategy (§7.3 in Dredze et al.), where updates are computed for the combined classifier, and are then distributed to the shared and domain-specific classifiers. MDR-U will indicate that the updates to the combined classifiers are *uniformly* distributed to the underlying shared and domain-specific classifiers.

Dredze et al. also used another scheme called "variance" to distribute the combined update to the underlying classifiers (§4, last paragraph in Dredze et al.) Their idea was to give a lower portion of the update to the underlying classifier that has higher variance (or in their terminology, "less confidence") since it contributed less to the combined classifier. We refer to this as MDR-V. However, this conflicts with the original CW intuition that features with higher variance (lower confidence) should receive higher updates; since they are more in need of change. Therefore, we implemented a modified "variance" scheme, where the updates are distributed to the underlying classifiers such that higher variance features receive the larger updates. We refer to this as MDR-NV. We observed significant improvements with this modified scheme.

[4]We also tried the l_2 distance method of Dredze et al. (2009) but it gave consistently worse results.

3 Experiments

To evaluate our multi-attribute algorithms we consider two datasets. First, we use two subsets of the restaurant reviews dataset (1,180,308 reviews) introduced by Chahuneau et al. (2012) with the goal of labeling reviews as positive or negative. The first subset (50K-RND) randomly selects 50,000 reviews while the second (50K-BAL) is a class-balanced sample. Following the approach of Blitzer et al. (2007), scores above and below 3-stars indicated positive and negative reviews, while 3-star reviews were discarded. Second, we use the transcribed segments of speech from the United States Congress floor debates (Convote), introduced by Thomas et al. (2006). The binary classification task on this dataset is that of predicting whether a given speech segment supports or opposes a bill under discussion in the floor debate.

In the WordSalad datasets, each restaurant review can have many metadata attributes, including a unique identifier, name (which may not be unique), address (we extract the zipcode), and type (Italian, Chinese, etc.). We select the 20 most common metadata attributes (excluding latitude, longitude, and the average rating). [5] In the Convote dataset, each speech segment is associated with the political party affiliation of the speaker (democrat, independent, or republican) and the speaker identifier (we use bill identifiers for creating folds in our 10-fold cross-validation setup).

In addition to our new algorithms, we evaluate several baselines. All methods use confidence-weighted (CW) learning (Crammer et al., 2012).

BASE A single classifier trained on all the data, and which ignores metadata attributes and uses unigram features. For CW, we use the best-performing setting from Dredze et al. (2008) — the "variance" algorithm, which computes approximate but closed–form updates, which also lead to faster learning. Parameters are tuned over a validation set within each training fold.

[5]Our method requires categorical metadata attributes, although real-valued attributes can be discretized.

	metadata	1-META	FEDA	MDR-U	MDR-V	MDR-NV
50K-RND	NONE (BASE)	92.29 (±0.14)				
	ALL (META)	† 92.69 (±0.10)				
	CATEGORY	† 92.48 (±0.11)	92.47 (±0.10)	†‡ 92.99 (±0.12)	91.16 (±0.16)	†‡ **93.24 (±0.13)**
	ZIPCODE	92.40 (±0.09)	† 92.73 (±0.09)	†‡ 92.99 (±0.12)	91.19 (±0.20)	†‡ **93.22 (±0.11)**
	NEIGHBORHOOD	92.42 (±0.11)	† 92.65 (±0.13)	†‡ 93.02 (±0.13)	91.17 (±0.21)	†‡ **93.21 (±0.12)**
50K-BAL	NONE (BASE)	89.95 (±0.10)				
	ALL (META)	† 90.39 (±0.09)				
	CATEGORY	90.09 (±0.11)	† 90.50 (±0.11)	† 90.60 (±0.11)	87.89 (±0.13)	†‡ **91.33 (±0.08)**
	ZIPCODE	89.97 (±0.12)	† 90.42 (±0.13)	† 90.56 (±0.09)	87.78 (±0.16)	†‡ **91.30 (±0.10)**
	ID	† 90.42 (±0.11)	†‡ 90.64 (±0.11)	† 90.50 (±0.11)	87.78 (±0.25)	†‡ **91.27 (±0.09)**

Table 1: Average accuracy (± standard error) for the best three metadata attributes, when using a single attribute at a time. Results that are *numerically the best* within a row are in **bold**. Results significantly better than BASE are marked with †, and better than META are marked with ‡. Significance is measured using a two-tailed paired t-test with $\alpha = 0.05$.

	#attributes	FEDA	MDR-U	MDR-V	MDR-NV
50K-RND	MAMD	†‡ 93.07 (±0.19)	†‡ 93.12 (±0.11)	87.08 (±1.72)	†‡ **93.19 (±0.12)**
	1-ORCL	†‡ 93.06 (±0.11)	†‡ 93.17 (±0.11)	92.37 (±0.11)	†‡ **93.39 (±0.12)**
	1-TUNE	† 92.64 (±0.12)	† 92.81 (±0.16)	92.15 (±0.17)	†‡ **93.07 (±0.14)**
	1-MEAN	† **92.61 (±0.09)**	† 92.59 (±0.10)	91.41 (±0.12)	† 92.58 (±0.10)
50K-BAL	MAMD	†‡ **91.42 (±0.09)**	†‡ 91.06 (±0.04)	81.43 (±2.79)	†‡ 91.40 (±0.08)
	1-ORCL	†‡ 90.89 (±0.10)	†‡ 90.87 (±0.11)	89.33 (±0.13)	†‡ **91.45 (±0.07)**
	1-TUNE	† 90.33 (±0.10)	†‡ 90.70 (±0.14)	89.13 (±0.16)	†‡ **91.26 (±0.08)**
	1-MEAN	† **90.30 (±0.06)**	89.92 (±0.07)	88.25 (±0.07)	90.06 (±0.08)

Table 2: Average accuracy (± standard error) using 10-fold cross-validation for methods that use all attributes, either directly (our proposed methods) or for selecting the "best" single attribute using one of the strategies described earlier. Formatting and significance symbols are the same as in Table 1.

META Identical to BASE with a unique bias feature added for each attribute value (Joshi et al., 2012).

1-META A special case of META where a unique bias feature is added *only for a single attribute*.

To use multi-domain learning directly, we could select a single attribute as the domain. We consider several strategies for picking this attribute and evaluate both FEDA and MDR in this setting.

1-MEAN Choose an attribute randomly, equivalent to the expected (mean) error over all attributes.

1-TUNE Select the best performing attribute on a validation set.

1-ORCL Select the best performing attribute on the *test* set. Though impossible in practice, this gives the oracle upper bound on multi-domain learning.

All experiments use ten-fold cross-validation. We report the mean accuracy, along with standard error.

4 Results

Table 1 shows the results of single-attribute multi-domain learning methods for the WordSalad datasets. The table shows the three best-performing metadata attributes (as decided by the highest accuracy among all the methods across all 20 metadata attributes). Clearly, several of the attributes can provide meaningful domains, which demonstrates that methods that can select multiple attributes at once are desirable. We also see that our modification to MDR (MDR-NV) works the best.

Table 3 shows the results of single-attribute multi-domain learning methods for the Convote dataset. The first observation to be made on this dataset is that neither the PARTY, nor the SPEAKER attribute individually achieve significant improvement over the META baseline, which uses both these attributes as features. This is in contrast with the results on the WordSalad dataset, where some attributes by themselves showed an improvement over the META baseline. Thus, this dataset represents a more challenging setup for our multi–attribute multi–domain learning methods — they need to exploit the two weak attributes simultaneously.

We next demonstrate multi-attribute improvements over the multi-domain baselines (Tables 2 and 4). For WordSalad datasets, our extensions that can use all metadata attributes simultaneously are consistently better than both the 1-MEAN and the 1-TUNE strategies (except for the case of the old variance scheme used by (Dredze et al., 2009)). For the skewed subset

metadata	1-META	FEDA	MDR-U	MDR-V	MDR-NV
NONE (BASE)	67.08 ($\pm$1.74)				
ALL (META)	† 82.60 ($\pm$1.95)				
PARTY	† 78.81 ($\pm$1.47)	† **84.19** ($\pm$**2.44**)	† 83.23 ($\pm$2.48)	† 81.38 ($\pm$2.22)	† 83.92 ($\pm$2.31)
SPEAKER	† 77.49 ($\pm$1.75)	† **82.88** ($\pm$**2.43**)	† 78.32 ($\pm$1.91)	62.43 ($\pm$2.20)	† 72.26 ($\pm$1.37)

Table 3: Convote: Average accuracy ($\pm$ standard error) when using a single attribute at a time. Results that are *numerically the best* within a row are in **bold**. Results significantly better than BASE are marked with †, and better than META are marked with ‡. Significance is measured using a two-tailed paired t-test with $\alpha = 0.05$.

#attributes	FEDA	MDR-U	MDR-V	MDR-NV
MAMD	†‡ 85.71 ($\pm$2.74)	† 84.12 ($\pm$2.56)	50.44 ($\pm$1.78)	†‡ **86.19** ($\pm$**2.49**)
1-ORCL	† **84.77** ($\pm$**2.47**)	† 83.88 ($\pm$2.27)	† 81.38 ($\pm$2.22)	† 83.92 ($\pm$2.31)
1-TUNE	† **84.19** ($\pm$**2.44**)	† 83.23 ($\pm$2.48)	† 81.38 ($\pm$2.22)	† 83.92 ($\pm$2.31)
1-MEAN	† **83.53** ($\pm$**2.40**)	† 80.77 ($\pm$1.92)	† 71.91 ($\pm$1.82)	† 78.09 ($\pm$1.69)

Table 4: Convote: Average accuracy ($\pm$ standard error) using 10-fold cross-validation for methods that use all attributes, either directly (our proposed methods) or for selecting the "best" single attribute using one of the strategies described earlier. Formatting and significance symbols are the same as in Table 3.

50K-RND, MAMD+FEDA is significantly better than 1-TUNE+FEDA; MAMD+MDR-U is significantly better than 1-TUNE+MDR-U; MAMD+MDR-NV is not significantly different from 1-TUNE+MDR-U. For the balanced subset 50K-BAL, a similar pattern holds, except that MAMD+MDR-NV is significantly better than 1-TUNE+MDR-NV. Clearly, our multi-attribute algorithms provide a benefit over existing approaches. Even with oracle knowledge of the test performance using multi-domain learning, we can still obtain improvements (FEDA and MDR-U in the 50K-BAL set, and all the Convote results, except MDR-V).

Although MAMD+MDR-NV is not significantly better than 1-TUNE+MDR-NV on the 50K-RND set, we found that in every single fold in our ten-fold cross-validation experiments, the "best" single metadata attribute decided using a validation set did not match the best-performing single metadata attribute on the corresponding test set. This shows the potential instability of choosing a single best attribute. Also, note that MDR-NV is a variant that we have proposed in the current work, and in fact for the earlier variant of MDR (MDR-U), as well as for FEDA, we do see significant improvements when using all metadata attributes. Furthermore, the computational cost of evaluating every metadata attribute independently to tune the single best metadata attribute can be high and often impractical. Our approach requires no such tuning. Finally, observe that for FEDA, the 1-TUNE strategy is not significantly different from 1-MEAN, which just randomly picks a single best metadata attribute. For MDR-U, 1-TUNE is significantly better than 1-MEAN on the balanced subset 50K-BAL, but not on the skewed subset 50K-RND.

As mentioned earlier, the Convote dataset is a challenging setting for our methods due to the fact that no single attribute is strong enough to yield improvements over the META baseline. In this setting, both MAMD+FEDA and MAMD+MDR-NV achieve a significant improvement over the META baseline, with MDR-NV being the best (though not significantly better than FEDA). Additionally, both of them are significantly better than their corresponding 1-TUNE strategies. This result further supports our claim that using multiple attributes in combination for defining domains (even when any single one of them is not particularly beneficial for multi–domain learning) is important.

5 Conclusions

We propose multi-attribute multi-domain learning methods that can utilize multiple metadata attributes simultaneously for defining domains. Using these methods, the definition of "domains" does not have to be restricted to a single metadata attribute. Our methods achieve a better performance on two multi-attribute datasets as compared to traditional multi-domain learning methods that are tuned to use a single "best" attribute.

Acknowledgments

This research is supported by the Office of Naval Research grant number N000141110221.

References

Shai Ben-David, John Blitzer, Koby Crammer, Alex Kulesza, Fernando Pereira, and Jennifer Wortman Vaughan. 2009. A theory of learning from different domains. *Machine Learning*.

John Blitzer, Mark Dredze, and Fernando Pereira. 2007. Biographies, Bollywood, Boom-boxes and Blenders: Domain Adaptation for Sentiment Classification. In *Proceedings of the 45th Annual Meeting of the Association of Computational Linguistics*, pages 440–447. Association for Computational Linguistics.

Victor Chahuneau, Kevin Gimpel, Bryan R. Routledge, Lily Scherlis, and Noah A. Smith. 2012. Word Salad: Relating Food Prices and Descriptions. In *Proceedings of the Conference on Empirical Methods in Natural Language Processing and Natural Language Learning (EMNLP 2012)*.

Koby Crammer, Mark Dredze, and Fernando Pereira. 2012. Confidence-weighted linear classification for text categorization. *Journal of Machine Learning Research (JMLR)*.

Hal Daumé III. 2007. Frustratingly Easy Domain Adaptation. In *Proceedings of the 45th Annual Meeting of the Association of Computational Linguistics*, pages 256–263. Association for Computational Linguistics.

Mark Dredze and Koby Crammer. 2008. Online methods for multi-domain learning and adaptation. *Proceedings of the Conference on Empirical Methods in Natural Language Processing - EMNLP '08*.

Mark Dredze, Koby Crammer, and Fernando Pereira. 2008. Confidence-weighted linear classification. *Proceedings of the 25th international conference on Machine learning - ICML '08*.

Mark Dredze, Alex Kulesza, and Koby Crammer. 2009. Multi-domain learning by confidence-weighted parameter combination. *Machine Learning*, 79(1–2):123–149.

Jacob Eisenstein, Amr Ahmed, and Eric P. Xing. 2011. Sparse Additive Generative Models of Text. In *Proceedings of the 28th International Conference on Machine Learning (ICML)*.

Theodoros Evgeniou and Massimiliano Pontil. 2004. Regularized multi–task learning. In *Proceedings of the 2004 ACM SIGKDD international conference on Knowledge discovery and data mining - KDD '04*.

Jenny R Finkel and Christopher D Manning. 2009. Hierarchical Bayesian Domain Adaptation. In *Proceedings of Human Language Technologies: The 2009 Annual Conference of the North American Chapter of the Association for Computational Linguistics*, pages 602–610. Association for Computational Linguistics.

Mahesh Joshi, Mark Dredze, William W. Cohen, and Carolyn P. Rosé. 2012. Multi-domain learning: When do domains matter? In *Proceedings of EMNLP-CoNLL 2012*, pages 1302–1312.

Avishek Saha, Piyush Rai, Hal Daumé III, and Suresh Venkatasubramanian. 2011. Online learning of multiple tasks and their relationships. In *Proceedings of AISTATS 2011*.

Matt Thomas, Bo Pang, and Lillian Lee. 2006. Get out the vote: Determining support or opposition from Congressional floor-debate transcripts. In *Proceedings of EMNLP*, pages 327–335.

William Yang Wang, Elijah Mayfield, Suresh Naidu, and Jeremiah Dittmar. 2012. Historical Analysis of Legal Opinions with a Sparse Mixed-Effects Latent Variable Model. In *Proceedings of the 50th Annual Meeting of the Association for Computational Linguistics (ACL 2012)*.

Yu Zhang and Dit-Yan Yeung. 2010. A Convex Formulation for Learning Task Relationships in Multi-Task Learning. In *Proceedings of the Proceedings of the Twenty-Sixth Conference Annual Conference on Uncertainty in Artificial Intelligence (UAI-10)*.

An opinion about opinions about opinions: subjectivity and the aggregate reader

Asad Sayeed
Computational Linguistics and Phonetics / M[2]CI Cluster of Excellence
Saarland University
66123 Saarbrücken, Germany
asayeed@coli.uni-saarland.de

Abstract

This opinion piece proposes that recent advances in opinion detection are limited in the extent to which they can detect important categories of opinion because they are not designed to capture some of the pragmatic aspects of opinion. A component of these is the perspective of the user of an opinion-mining system as to what an opinion really is, which is in itself a matter of opinion (metasubjectivity). We propose a way to define this component of opinion and describe the challenges it poses for corpus development and sentence-level detection technologies. Finally, we suggest that investment in techniques to handle metasubjectivity will likely bear costs but bring benefits in the longer term.

1 Introduction

Opinion mining, also known as sentiment analysis (Pang and Lee, 2008), is a relatively recent area of research in natural language processing. It has grown very quickly as a research area, developing around a small number of basic approaches. However, these approaches are based on particular definitions of opinion, assumptions about opinion expressions, and evaluation practices that we believe need to be expanded in order for sentiment analysis to reach new domains and applications.

We are not the first to express concern over the direction of sentiment analysis as a field. This paper seeks to further expand upon the views expressed in Alm (2011) that prevailing evaluation concepts in sentiment analysis limit the kinds of models we can build, particularly through the encouragement of a focus on "high-performing" systems.

The central thread that connects our view of the field is the idea that the basis of standard techniques and evaluation in information retrieval and extraction that underlie existing approaches needs to be rethought for applications that are inherently subjective and that the field needs to return to more theoretical groundwork. This will entail sacrificing some of the performance gains made in recent times, as well as potentially reducing the capacity for easily comparable research that has been gained by the rapid adoption of corpora that are very easily produced, shared, and used.

This problem is particularly relevant in the expansion of sentiment analysis techniques to areas such as market prediction (Bollen et al., 2010) and social science. In these areas, it is not enough to detect opinions in predefined areas of text or even to mine for the locations of opinions in large corpora, but it is necessary to be able to connect opinions across documents and to reconstruct the social networks that underlie social trends. Furthermore, it must be possible to do this in text that can have an arbitrary number of opinions intertwined in ways that go beyond the base case of product review text. This requires both additional consideration of the perspective of the user and attention to the finer-grained details of sentiment expression.

Do existing resources and techniques really reflect the ultimate goals and end-uses of fine-grained opinion-mining, particularly focusing on the sentential and sub-sentential levels? Consider an "ideal case" of a marketing director or a political campaign manager requesting a forecast of how a product or concept will unfold in the media and market. How do the present conceptions of opinion mining relate to this among other real-world problems of affect?

In the remainder of this position paper, we briefly describe three closely related issues in sentiment analysis that pertain to expanding beyond the current limits of the field.

2 Challenges

2.1 Metasubjectivity and pragmatic opinion

Recent efforts in opinion mining (Ruppenhofer et al., 2008) technology have often tended to take the position that opinion is an internal characteristic of the speaker, a "private state", and that the overall aim of the opinion mining field is to discover techniques that allow us to infer the that latent state from the evidence presented in text. But this may not always be appropriate to all circumstances.

A very simple boundary example comes from Somasundaran and Wiebe (2009): *The blackberry is something like $150 and the iPhone is $500.* This comes from a corpus of opinions on cell phone preference, and this sentence is intended to be a negative opinion about the iPhone. According to Somasundaran and Wiebe, this kind of opinion-expression requires a model of world-knowledge that is either not practical under current technologies, or it requires the development of techniques that can recruit a larger context in the text in order to make the correct inference. They refer to this phenomenon as "pragmatic opinion".

One crucial piece of world-knowledge that provides an opinion its polarity is that of the perspective of the reader or listener to the opinion; we can minimally represent this as the "application" to which the opinion will be put. We refer to variation in the application-specific interpretation of the concept of opinion as "metasubjectivity." Metasubjectivity is a serious problem in extending sentiment analysis work to other domains, particularly for reasons that we describe in the next section.

Metasubjectivity is closely related to the underlying relative nature of veridicality assessment. The veridicality of an utterance is the level to which the listener may judge it as a factual statement about the world. de Marneffe et al. (2012) note that this requires, in some cases, extensive pragmatic knowledge. They present this sentence as an example: *FBI agents alleged in court documents today that Zazi had admitted receiving weapons and explosives training from al-Qaeda operatives in Pakistan last year.* There is an interplay between the trustworthiness of the source of the sentence, the mentioned entities, and the veridicality of words *alleged* and *admitted*, all of which are mediated by the perspective of the reader. For example, if the reader is strongly inclined to trust the FBI, then there may be a high level of veridicality in "alleged" than otherwise. But it could also be the case that the reader believes that Zazi is misleading the FBI.

These distinctions operate directly in the context of determining polarity in opinion mining. Consider the following example sentence from a major information technology (IT) business journal: *Lloyd Hession, chief security officer at BT Radianz in New York, said that virtualization also opens up a slew of potential network access control issues.*

This sentence can be taken to represent an opinion or merely a factual statement. A casual reader without experience in the domain of IT might be convinced that this sentence is simply a neutral statement of fact. But from the perspective of an interested reader such as an investor, this may actually represent a mildly negative statement about virtualization, or it may represent a negative statement about network access control. From the perspective of the manager of an IT support department, it may well be very negative. But from the perspective of Lloyd Hession, we have no idea outside of the pragmatic context. Mr. Hession could be a developer of IT solutions, in which case he would view this as a positive development for the market in new network access control technologies, or, for that matter, he may be invested in a set of technological approaches that compete with virtualization.

This extends to the vocabulary used to express opinions. The use of the word "slew", in this case, has negative connotations, but only if the whole statement is construed by the perspective of the reader to represent an opinion. However, if Lloyd Hession is a provider of new network access control solutions, then the use of "open" may convert this negative context into a positive context.

This is not merely a matter of the perspectives of individual users and participants. It is a matter of how providers of sentiment analysis applications choose to represent these choices to the user, which is in turn reflected in the way in which they create resources, models, and algorithms. If, for example, our goal is to provide sentiment analysis for domain-specific market prediction or social science, then we need to model the reactions not of the private state of Mr. Hession or of the writer of the article, but of an "aggregate reader" with a presumed interest in the text. Here is a definition of this external state aggregate reader model that might apply to the IT business domain:

> Opinion source A expresses opinion about opinion target B if an interested third party C's actions towards B may be affected by A's textually recorded actions, in a context where actions have positive or negative weight.

This accounts for the cases in which the opinion of interest in the IT example happens to be held by an investor or a IT support manager or other interested readers, and it can be generalized to apply to other domains in which the world's opinion matters.

It is once again within the area of veridicality assessment that we suggest that a possible form of solution exists. de Marneffe et al. (2012) present a model in which the uncertainty in veridicality is represented as a distribution rather than a discrete labelling problem.

In the case of veridicality, there is generally an ultimate ground truth in verifiable facts about the world, apart from the relative veridical nature of a statement. For sentiment, however, there is no such foundation: opinion presence and opinion polarity exist entirely relative to the perspective of the aggregate reader. This requires a different process of annotation, the challenges of which we describe in the next section.

2.2 Corpus development and evaluation

Considering the prevalence of machine learning techniques in opinion mining research, addressing the issue of metasubjectivity must mean addressing the matter of the corpus development.

Existing evaluation techniques depend on a notion of "gold standard data" that are produced by expert judges or crowdsourced annotators (Wilson, 2007; Kessler et al., 2010; Hsueh et al., 2009). There are NLP areas in which popular notions of objectivity may partly apply, such as query relevance; due, among other things, to metasubjectivity, opinion mining is not entirely one of these. However, gold standard data for opinion mining is typically produced using procedures that are standard for information retrieval research, and the quality measures that are generally used happen to assume the presence of an underlying objective truth.

This assumption can be coerced to fit particular cases. For example, a large proportion of opinion mining research is invested in predicting the ratings of product reviews and then aggregating results into a single ratings summary, sometimes based on a lower-level breakdown of product features (de Albornoz et al., 2011). Implicit in this type of work is the assumption of the existence of an ideal rater who uses language in a roughly predictable way to express his or her feelings about the text.

The users of these types of systems can be assumed, to some degree of safety, to share some of the expectations of the builders of these systems, particularly since groups of users as product raters are often the source of the information itself.

But in environments where the users of the system may have various different perspectives on the nature of sentiment, it does not make sense to assume that there would ever be significant agreement among annotators, particularly for market-relevant applications where prediction of reader reaction is central to the task. We attempted to annotate IT business press articles for sentence-level reader-perspective opinion occurrences and found that multiple trained annotators had very low inter-rater agreement by Cohen's κ. Multiple attempts at further annotator training and error analysis revealed that the annotators simply found it very difficult to agree on what the definition of an opinion was. Originally, we had two trained student annotators for this task, with repeated training and joint practice annotations in order to achieve consensus as to what counts as an opinion mention instance and what does not. Other groups of annotators and annotation designs had no better success.

However, we observed that this appears to be primarily a problem of conservativity where annotators differed in the quantity of sentences that they considered to be opinionated, and had a large amount of overlap in those that they did consider to be opinionated. Further discussion with the annotators found that some simply had a much lower threshold at which they would consider a sentence to contain an opinion. In other words, this form of annotation is more affected by metasubjectivity than opinion annotation focused on opinion source perspective. It should be noted that this is a different task from finding opinion sources and labelling the textual evidence of their private states; we were attempting to model the "ideal case" we identified in section 1.

We suggest that the answer to this problem is to deploy the concept of the aggregate reader mentioned in the previous section and to pose the annotation question indirectly. The former requires the collection of data from a larger number of people and can be provided by existing crowdsourcing techniques (Snow et al., 2008). The latter, however, requires designing the annotation in such a way that it avoids letting the annotator consider the question: "What is an opinion?" This is most likely done by a user interface that simulates the behaviour of the intended aggregate reader (Sayeed et al., 2011).

2.3 Grammatical expression

There are a number of types of features with which one can construct and train supervised sentence-level sentiment detection models. Most recent techniques (Kim and Hovy, 2006; Choi et al., 2006; Jakob and Gurevych, 2010) take into account the syntactic context of the sentence but limit the amount of syntactic context thus used. These restrictions reduce the presence or absence of particular structures to binary features in the model. We argue that we need techniques that take into account more syntactic context, particularly without making use of predefined structures.

The latest techniques make use of larger syntactic contexts with potentially unlimited scope. One example is Nakagawa et al. (2010), who use factor graphs (McCallum et al., 2009) to learn a model that traces paths through the dependency trees of opinion-relevant sentences (de Marneffe and Manning, 2008). However, this is in the service of polarity classification, as it assumes that the appropriate sentences have already been identified; then it is a matter of correctly processing negations and other polarity-changing items. The challenge of metasubjectivity is a barrier to opinion sentence detection itself, well before polarity classification.

Another example is Qiu et al. (2011). They are more directly focused on detecting opinion-relevant language. However, they make use of a system of hard-coded heuristics to find opinion words in dependency parses. While these types of heuristics support longer-distance syntactic relations, they tend to focus on cases where some form of semantic compositionality holds. However, consider this sentence from the IT business press: *The contract is consistent with the desktop computing* ***Outsourcing*** *deals Citibank awarded EDS and Digital Equipment in 1996...* In this case, an interested aggregate reader might note that "awarded" is a word that puts "outsourcing" in a positive light. However, the syntactic relationship between these two words does not directly imply or permit any semantic compositionality, In order to find these relationships, we would need to invest in techniques that can learn from arbitrary non-compositional structure, thereby potentially capturing patterns in grammar that actually reflect some aspects of external pragmatic knowledge.

3 Conclusions

This paper has proposed a challenge for opinion mining, the challenge of metasubjectivity: where the answer to the question "What is an opinion?" is in itself an opinion and an intrinsic part of the task. We first established the context of metasubjectivity relative to existing characterizations of the opinion mining task, establishing the notion of an external aggregate reader as a way to extend from existing notions of sentiment as an internal state. Then we described how this affects the annotation process, given the as-yet-continuing dependence on supervised corpus-based detection techniques. Finally, we described how this affects sentence-level fine-grained opinion detection at the level of syntactic analysis.

One of the risks for the field in proceeding to investigations of how to deal with the question of metasubjectivity is one familiar in natural language processing as a whole: there is a strong risk that these techniques will—initially and for a non-trivial quantity of time—cause the incremental performance gains in existing research to be lost or damaged. It will also require the creation of new training corpora and related resources, temporarily threatening comparability. Nevertheless, we believe that these risks need to be accepted in order to make progress in sentiment analysis.

References

Alm, C. O. (2011). Subjective natural language problems: Motivations, applications, characterizations, and implications. In *ACL (Short Papers)*.

Bollen, J., Mao, H., and Zeng, X.-J. (2010). Twitter mood predicts the stock market. *CoRR*, abs/1010.3003.

Choi, Y., Breck, E., and Cardie, C. (2006). Joint extraction of entities and relations for opinion recognition. In *Proceedings of the Conference on Empirical Methods in Natural Language Processing (EMNLP)*.

de Albornoz, J., Plaza, L., Gervás, P., and Díaz, A. (2011). A joint model of feature mining and sentiment analysis for product review rating. In Clough, P., Foley, C., Gurrin, C., Jones, G., Kraaij, W., Lee, H., and Mudoch, V., editors, *Advances in information retrieval*, volume 6611 of *Lecture Notes in Computer Science*, pages 55–66. Springer Berlin / Heidelberg.

de Marneffe, M.-C. and Manning, C. D. (2008). The stanford typed dependencies representation. In *CrossParser '08: Coling 2008: Proceedings of the workshop on Cross-Framework and Cross-Domain Parser Evaluation*, Morristown, NJ, USA. Association for Computational Linguistics.

de Marneffe, M.-C., Manning, C. D., and Potts, C. (2012). Did it happen? the pragmatic complexity of veridicality assessment. *Computational linguistics*, 35(1).

Hsueh, P.-Y., Melville, P., and Sindhwani, V. (2009). Data quality from crowdsourcing: a study of annotation selection criteria. In *Proceedings of the NAACL HLT 2009 Workshop on Active Learning for Natural Language Processing*, HLT '09, Stroudsburg, PA, USA. Association for Computational Linguistics.

Jakob, N. and Gurevych, I. (2010). Extracting opinion targets in a single and cross-domain setting with conditional random fields. In *EMNLP*.

Kessler, J. S., Eckert, M., Clark, L., and Nicolov, N. (2010). The 2010 ICWSM JDPA sentment corpus for the automotive domain. In *4th Int'l AAAI Conference on Weblogs and Social Media Data Workshop Challenge (ICWSM-DWC 2010)*.

Kim, S.-M. and Hovy, E. (2006). Extracting opinions, opinion holders, and topics expressed in online news media text. In *SST '06: Proceedings of the Workshop on Sentiment and Subjectivity in Text*, pages 1–8, Morristown, NJ, USA. Association for Computational Linguistics.

McCallum, A., Schultz, K., and Singh, S. (2009). Factorie: Probabilistic programming via imperatively defined factor graphs. In *Neural Information Processing Systems (NIPS)*.

Nakagawa, T., Inui, K., and Kurohashi, S. (2010). Dependency tree-based sentiment classification using crfs with hidden variables. In *HLT-NAACL*.

Pang, B. and Lee, L. (2008). Opinion mining and sentiment analysis. *Found. Trends Inf. Retr.*, 2(1-2).

Qiu, G., Liu, B., Bu, J., and Chen, C. (2011). Opinion word expansion and target extraction through double propagation. *Computational linguistics*, 37(1):9—27.

Ruppenhofer, J., Somasundaran, S., and Wiebe, J. (2008). Finding the sources and targets of subjective expressions. In Calzolari, N., Choukri, K., Maegaard, B., Mariani, J., Odjik, J., Piperidis, S., and Tapias, D., editors, *Proceedings of the Sixth International Language Resources and Evaluation (LREC'08)*, Marrakech, Morocco. European Language Resources Association (ELRA).

Sayeed, A. B., Rusk, B., Petrov, M., Nguyen, H. C., Meyer, T. J., and Weinberg, A. (2011). Crowdsourcing syntactic relatedness judgements for opinion mining in the study of information technology adoption. In *Proceedings of the Association for Computational Linguistics 2011 workshop on Language Technology for Cultural Heritage, Social Sciences, and the Humanities (LaTeCH)*. Association for Computational Linguistics.

Snow, R., O'Connor, B., Jurafsky, D., and Ng, A. Y. (2008). Cheap and fast—but is it good?: evaluating non-expert annotations for natural language tasks. In *EMNLP 2008*.

Somasundaran, S. and Wiebe, J. (2009). Recognizing stances in online debates. In *Proceedings of the Joint Conference of the 47th Annual Meeting of the ACL and the 4th International Joint Conference on Natural Language Processing of the AFNLP: Volume 1*, ACL '09.

Wilson, T. (2007). *Fine-grained Subjectivity and Sentiment Analysis: Recognizing the Intensity, Polarity, and Attitudes of private states*. PhD thesis, Intelligent Systems Program, University of Pittsburgh.

An Examination of Regret in Bullying Tweets

Jun-Ming Xu, Benjamin Burchfiel, Xiaojin Zhu
Department of Computer Sciences
University of Wisconsin-Madison
Madison, WI 53706, USA
{xujm,burchfie,jerryzhu}@cs.wisc.edu

Amy Bellmore
Department of Educational Psychology
University of Wisconsin-Madison
Madison, WI 53706, USA
abellmore@wisc.edu

Abstract

Social media users who post bullying related tweets may later experience regret, potentially causing them to delete their posts. In this paper, we construct a corpus of bullying tweets and periodically check the existence of each tweet in order to infer if and when it becomes deleted. We then conduct exploratory analysis in order to isolate factors associated with deleted posts. Finally, we propose the construction of a regrettable posts predictor to warn users if a tweet might cause regret.

1 Introduction

A large body of literature suggests that participants in bullying events, including victims, bullies, and witnesses, are likely to report psychological adjustment problems (Jimerson, Swearer, and Espelage, 2010). One potential source of therapy for these issues can be self-disclosure of the experience to an adult or friend (Mishna and Alaggia, 2005); existing research suggests that victims who seek advice and help from others report less maladjustment than victims who do not (Shelley and Craig, 2010).

Disclosure of bullying experiences through social media may be a particularly effective mechanism for participants seeking support because social media has the potential to reach large audiences and because participants may feel less inhibition when sharing private information in an online setting (Walther, 1996). Furthermore, there is evidence that online communication stimulates self-disclosure, which leads to higher quality social relationships and increased well-being (Valkenburg and Peter, 2009).

Online disclosure may also present risks for those involved in bullying however, such as re-victimization, embarrassment, and social ostracization. Evidence exists that some individuals may react to these risks retroactively, by deleting their social media posts (Child et al., 2011; Christofides, Muise, and Desmarais, 2009). Several relevant motives have been found to be associated with deleting posted information, including conflict management, safety, fear of retribution, impression management, and emotional regulation (Child, Haridakis, and Petronio, 2012).

Our previous work (Xu et al., 2012) demonstrates that social media can be a valuable data source when studying bullying, and proposes a text categorization method to recognize social media posts describing bullying episodes, *bullying traces*. To better understand, and possibly prevent, user regret after posting bullying related tweets, we collect bullying traces using the same method and perform regular status checks to determine if and when tweets become inaccessible. While a tweet becoming inaccessible does not guarantee it has been deleted, we attempt to leverage http response codes to rule out other common causes of inaccessibility. Speculating that regret may be a major cause of deletion, we first conduct exploratory analysis on this corpus and then report the results of an off-the-shelf regret predictor.

2 Data Collection

We adopt the procedure used in (Xu et al., 2012) to obtain bullying traces; each identified trace contains at least one bullying related keyword and passes a bullying-or-not text classifier.

Our data was collected in realtime using the Twitter streaming API; once a tweet is collected, we query its url (`https://twitter.com/USERID/status/TWEETID`) at regular intervals and infer its status from the resulting http response code. We interpret an HTTP 200 response as an indication a tweet still exists and an HTTP 404 response, which indicates the tweet is unavailable, as indicating deletion. A user changing their privacy settings can also result in an HTTP 403 response; we do not consider this to be a deletion. Other response codes, which appear quite rarely, are treated as anomalies and ignored. All non HTTP 200 responses are retried twice to ensure they are not transient oddities.

To determine when a tweet is deleted, we attempted to access each tweet at time points $T_i = 5 \times 4^i$ minutes for $i = 0, 1 \ldots 7$ after the creation time. These roughly correspond to periods of 5 minutes, 20 minutes, 1.5 hours, 6 hours, 1 day, 4 days, 2 weeks, and 2 months. While we assume that user deletion is the main cause of a tweet becoming unavailable, other causes are possible such as the censorship of illegal contents by Twitter (Twitter, 2012).

Our sample data was collected from July 31 through October 31, 2012 and contains 522,984 bullying traces. Because of intermittent network and computer issues, several multiple day data gaps exist in the data. To combat this, we filter our data to include only tweets of unambiguous status. If any check within the 20480 minutes (about two weeks) interval returns an HTTP 404 code, the tweet is no longer accessible and we consider it *deleted.* If the 20480 minute or 81920 minute check returns an HTTP 200 response, that tweet is still accessible and we consider it *surviving*. The union of the surviving and deleted groups formed our cleaned dataset, containing 311,237 tweets in total.

3 Exploratory Data Analysis

A user's decision to delete a bullying trace may be the result of many factors which we would like to isolate and understand. In this section we will examine several such possible factors.

3.1 Word Usage

Our dataset contains 331,070 distinct words and we are interested in isolating those with a significantly higher presence among either deleted or surviving tweets. We define the odds ratio of a word w

$$r(w) = \frac{P(w \mid \text{deleted})}{P(w \mid \text{surviving})},$$

where $P(w \mid \text{deleted})$ is the probability of word w occurring in a deleted tweet, and $P(w \mid \text{surviving})$ is the probability of w appearing in a surviving tweet. In order to ensure stability in the probability estimation, we only considered words appearing at least 50 times in either the surviving or deleted corpora.

Following (Bamman, OConnor, and Smith, 2012), we qualitatively analyzed words with extreme values of $r(w)$, and found some interesting trends. There was a significant tendency for "joking" words to occur with $r(w) < 0.5$; examples include "xd," "haha," and "hahaha." Joking words occur less frequently in deleted tweets than surviving ones. On the other end of the spectrum, there were no joking words with $r(w) > 2$. What we found instead were words such as "rip," "fat," "kill," and "suicide." While it is relatively clear that joking is less likely to occur in deleted tweets, there was less of a trend among words appearing more frequently in deleted tweets.

3.2 Surviving Time

Let N be the total number of tweets in our corpus, and $D(T_i)$ be the number of tweets that were first detected as deleted at minute T_i after creation. Note that $D(T_i)$ is not cumulative over time: it includes only deletions that occurred in the time interval $(T_{i-1}, T_i]$. Then we may define the deletion rate at time T_i as

$$R_T(T_i) = \frac{D(T_i)}{N(T_i - T_{i-1})}.$$

In other words, $R_T(t)$ is the fraction of tweets that are deleted during the one minute period $(t, t+1)$.

We plot R_T vs. t using logarithmic scales on both axes in Figure 1 and the result is a quite strong linear trend. Fitting the plot with a linear regression, we derive an inverse relationship between R_T and t of the form

$$R_T(t) \propto 1/t.$$

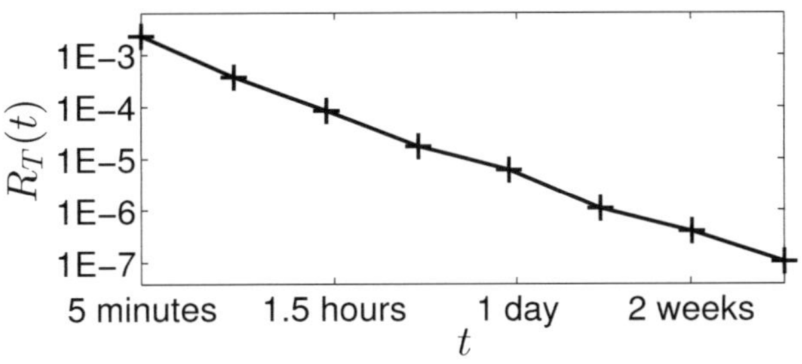

Figure 1: Deletion rate decays over time.

This result makes sense; the social effects of a particular bullying tweet may decay over time, making regret less of a factor. Furthermore, the author may assume an older tweet has already been seen, rendering deletion ineffective. Additionally, because the drop off in deletion rate is so extreme, we are able to safely exclude deletions occurring after two weeks from our filtered dataset without introducing a significant amount of noise. Finally, $\sum_{t=0}^{\infty} R_T(t)$ gives the overall fraction of deletion, which in our case is around 4%.

3.3 Location and Hour of Creations

Some bullying traces contain location meta-data in the form of GPS coordinates or a user-created profile string. We employed a reverse geocoding database (`http://www.datasciencetoolkit.org`) and a rule-based string matching method to map these tweets to their origins (at the state level; only for tweets within the USA). This also allowed us to convert creation timestamps from UTC to local time by mapping user location to timezone. Because many users don't share their location, we were only able to successfully map 85,465 bullying traces to a US state s, and local hour of day h. Among these traces, 3,484 were deleted which translates to an overall deletion rate of about 4%.

Let $N(s, h)$ be the count of bullying traces created in state s and hour h. Aggregating these counts temporally yields $N_S(s) = \sum_h N(s, h)$, while aggregating spatially produces $N_H(h) = \sum_s N(s, h)$. Similarly, we can define $D(s, h)$, $D_S(s)$ and $D_H(h)$ as the corresponding counts of deleted traces. We can now compute the deletion rate

$$R_H(h) = \frac{D_H(h)}{N_H(h)}, \text{ and } R_S(s) = \frac{D_S(s)}{N_S(s)}.$$

The top row of Figure 2 shows $N_H(h)$, $D_H(h)$, and $R_H(h)$. We find that $N_H(h)$ and $D_H(h)$ peak in the evening, indicating social media users are generally more active at that time. The peak of $R_H(h)$ appears at late night and, while there are multiple potential causes for this, we hypothesize that users may fail to fully evaluate the consequences of their posts when tired. The bottom row of Figure 2 shows $N_S(s)$, $D_S(S)$, and $R_S(s)$. The plot of $N_S(s)$ shows that bullying traces are more likely to originate in California, Texas or New York which is the result of a population effect. Importantly however, the deletion rate $R_S(s)$ is not affected by population bias and we see, as expected, that spatial differences in $R_S(s)$ are small. We performed χ^2-test to see if a state's deletion rate is significantly different from the national average. We chose the significance level at 0.05 and used Bonferroni correction for multiple testing. Only four states have significantly different deletion rates from the average: Arizona (6.3%, $p = 5.9 \times 10^{-5}$), California (5.2%, $p = 2.7 \times 10^{-7}$), Maryland (1.9%, $p = 2.3 \times 10^{-5}$), and Oklahoma (7.1%, $p = 3.5 \times 10^{-5}$).

3.4 Author's Role

Participants in a bullying episode assume well-defined roles which dramatically affect the viewpoint of the author describing the event. We trained a text classifier to determine author role (Xu et al., 2012), and used it to label each bullying trace in the cleaned corpus by author role: *Accuser*, *Bully*, *Reporter*, *Victim* or *Other*.

Table 1 shows that compared to tweets produced by bullies, victims create more bullying traces, possibly due to an increased need for social support on the part of the victim. More importantly, $P(\text{deleted} \mid \text{victim})$ is higher than $P(\text{deleted} \mid \text{bully})$, a statistically significant difference in a two-proportion z-test. Possibly, victims are more sensitive to their audience's reaction than bullies.

3.5 Teasing

Many bullying traces are written jokingly. We built a text classifier to identify teasing bullying traces (Xu et al., 2012) and applied it to the cleaned corpus.

Table 2 shows that $P(\text{deletion} \mid \text{Teasing})$ is much lower than $P(\text{deletion} \mid \text{Not Teasing})$ and the difference is statistically significant in a two-proportion z-

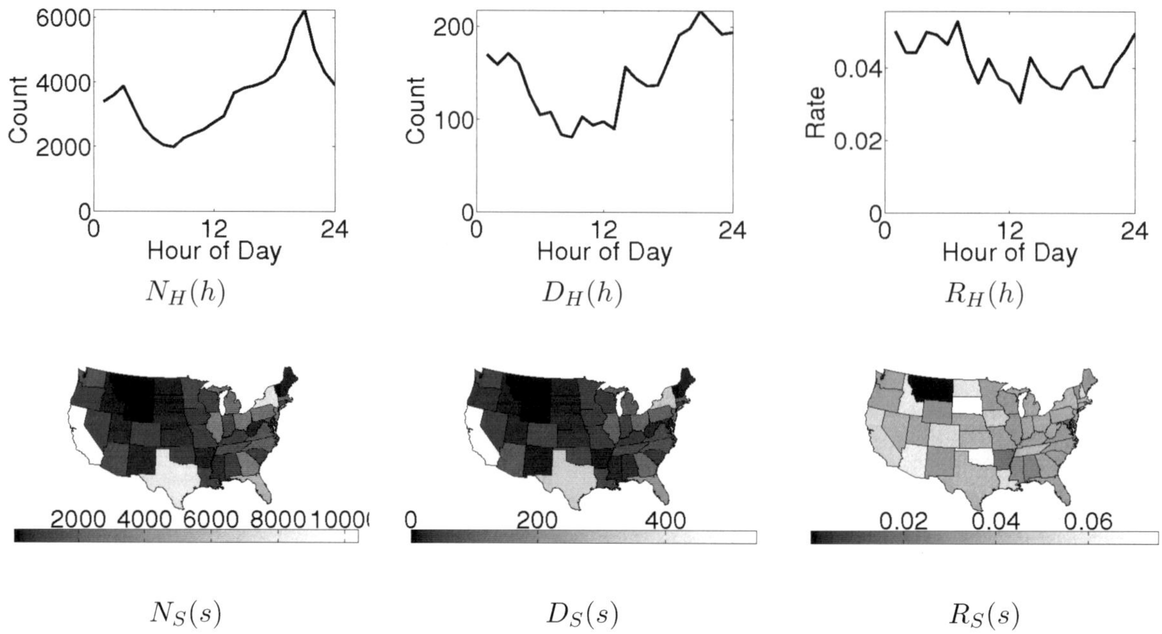

Figure 2: Counts and deletion rates of geo-tagged bullying traces.

	Deleted	Total	$P(\text{deleted} \mid \text{Role})$
Accuser	2541	50088	5.07%
Bully	1792	30123	5.95%
Reporter	11370	147164	7.73%
Victim	6497	83412	7.79%
Other	41	450	9.11%

Table 1: Counts and deletion rate for different roles.

	Deleted	Total	$P(\text{deleted} \mid \text{Teasing?})$
Yes	858	22876	3.75%
Not	21383	288361	7.42%

Table 2: Counts and deletion rate for teasing or not.

test. It seems plausible that authors are less likely to regret teasing posts because they are less controversial and have less potential to generate negative audience reactions. This also corroborates our findings in word usage that joking words are less frequent in deleted tweets.

4 Predicting Regrettable Tweets

Once a bullying tweet is published and seen by others, the ensuing effects are often impossible to undo. Since ill-thought-out posts may cause unexpectedly negative consequences to an author's reputation, relationship, and career (Wang et al., 2011), it would be helpful if a system could warn users before a potentially regrettable tweet is posted. One straightforward approach is to formulate the task as a binary text categorization problem.

We use the cleaned dataset, in which each tweet is known to be surviving or deleted after 20480 minutes (about two weeks). Since this dataset contains 22,241 deleted tweets, we randomly sub-sampled the surviving tweets down to 22,241 to force our deleted and surviving datasets to be of equal size. Consequentially, the baseline accuracy of the classifier is 0.5. While this does make the problem artificially easier, our initial goal was to test for the presence of a signal in the data.

We then followed the preprocessing procedure in (Xu et al., 2012), performing case-folding, anonymization, and tokenization, treating URLs, emoticons and hashtags specially. We also chose the unigrams+bigrams feature representation, only keeping tokens appearing at least 15 times in the corpus.

We chose to employ a linear SVM implemented in LIBLINEAR (Fan et al., 2008) due to its efficiency on this large sparse text categorization task and a 10-fold cross validation was conducted to evaluate its performance. Within the first fold, we use an inner 5-fold cross validation on the training portion to tune the regularization parameter on the grid $\{2^{-10}, 2^{-9}, \ldots, 1\}$; the selected parameter is then fixed for all the remaining folds.

The resulting cross validation accuracy was 0.607 with a standard deviation of 0.012. While it is statistically significantly better than the random-guessing baseline accuracy of 0.5 with a p-value of 5.15×10^{-10}, this accuracy is nevertheless too low to be useful in a practical system. One possibility is that the tweet text contains very limited information for predicting inaccessibility; a user's decision to delete a tweet potentially depends on many other factors, such as the conversation context and the characteristics of the author and audience.

In the spirit of exploring additional informative features for deletion prediction, we also used the teasing and author role classifiers in (Xu et al., 2012), and appended the predicted teasing, and author role labels to our feature vector. This augmented feature representation achieved a cross validation accuracy of 0.606, with standard deviation 0.007; not statistically significantly different from the text-only feature representation. While it seems that a signal does exist, leveraging it usefully in real world scenarios may prove challenging due to the highly-skewed nature of the data.

5 Discussion

There have been several recent works examining causes of deletion in social media. Wang *et al.* (2011) qualitatively investigated regret associated with users' posts on social networking sites and identified several possible causes of regret. Bamman *et al.* (2012) focused on censorship-related deletion of social media posts, identifying a set of sensitive terms related to message deletion through a statistical analysis and spatial variation of deletion rate.

Assuming that deletion in social media is indicative of regret, we studied regret in a bullying context by analyzing deletion trends in bullying related tweets. Through our analysis, we were able to isolate several factors related to deletion, including word usage, surviving time, and author role. We used these factors to build a regret predictor which achieved statistically significant results on this very noisy data. In the future, we plan to explore more factors to better understand deletion behavior and regret, including users' recent posts, historical behavior, and other statistics related to their specific social network.

Acknowledgments

We thank Kwang-Sung Jun, Angie Calvin, and Charles Dyer for helpful discussions. This work is supported by National Science Foundation grants IIS-1216758 and IIS-1148012.

References

Bamman, David, Brendan OConnor, and Noah Smith. 2012. Censorship and deletion practices in chinese social media. *First Monday*, 17(3-5).

Child, Jeffrey T., Paul M. Haridakis, and Sandra Petronio. 2012. Blogging privacy rule orientations, privacy management, and content deletion practices: The variability of online privacy management activity at different stages of social media use. *Computers in Human Behavior*, 28(5):1859 – 1872.

Child, Jeffrey T, Sandra Petronio, Esther A Agyeman-Budu, and David A Westermann. 2011. Blog scrubbing: Exploring triggers that change privacy rules. *Computers in Human Behavior*, 27(5):2017–2027.

Christofides, Emily, Amy Muise, and Serge Desmarais. 2009. Information disclosure and control on facebook: are they two sides of the same coin or two different processes? *CyberPsychology & Behavior*, 12(3):341–345.

Fan, Rong-En, Kai-Wei Chang, Cho-Jui Hsieh, Xiang-Rui Wang, and Chih-Jen Lin. 2008. Liblinear: A library for large linear classification. *The Journal of Machine Learning Research*, 9:1871–1874.

Jimerson, Shane R., Susan M. Swearer, and Dorothy L. Espelage. 2010. *Handbook of Bullying in Schools: An international perspective*. Routledge/Taylor & Francis Group, New York, NY.

Mishna, Faye and Ramona Alaggia. 2005. Weighing the risks: A child's decision to disclose peer victimization. *Children & Schools*, 27(4):217–226.

Shelley, Danielle and Wendy M Craig. 2010. Attributions and coping styles in reducing victimization. *Canadian Journal of School Psychology*, 25(1):84–100.

Twitter. 2012. The twitter rules. `http://support.twitter.com/articles/18311-the-twitter-rules`.

Valkenburg, Patti M and Jochen Peter. 2009. Social consequences of the internet for adolescents a decade of research. *Current Directions in Psychological Science*, 18(1):1–5.

Walther, Joseph B. 1996. Computer-mediated communication impersonal, interpersonal, and hyperpersonal interaction. *Communication research*, 23(1):3–43.

Wang, Yang, Gregory Norcie, Saranga Komanduri, Alessandro Acquisti, Pedro Giovanni Leon, and Lorrie Faith Cranor. 2011. "I regretted the minute I pressed share": a qualitative study of regrets on facebook. In *Proceedings of the Seventh Symposium on Usable Privacy and Security*, SOUPS '11, pages 10:1–10:16. ACM.

Xu, Jun-Ming, Kwang-Sung Jun, Xiaojin Zhu, and Amy Bellmore. 2012. Learning from bullying traces in social media. In *Proceedings of the 2012 Conference of the North American Chapter of the Association for Computational Linguistics: Human Language Technologies*, pages 656–666, Montréal, Canada, June. Association for Computational Linguistics.

A Cross-language Study on Automatic Speech Disfluency Detection

Wen Wang
SRI International
Menlo Park, CA
wwang@speech.sri.com

Andreas Stolcke
Microsoft Research
Mountain View, CA
anstolck@microsoft.com

Jiahong Yuan, Mark Liberman
University of Pennsylvania
Philadelphia, PA
jiahong.yuan@gmail.com
markyliberman@gmail.com

Abstract

We investigate two systems for automatic disfluency detection on English and Mandarin conversational speech data. The first system combines various lexical and prosodic features in a Conditional Random Field model for detecting edit disfluencies. The second system combines acoustic and language model scores for detecting filled pauses through constrained speech recognition. We compare the contributions of different knowledge sources to detection performance between these two languages.

1 Introduction

Speech disfluencies are common phenomena in spontaneous speech. They consist of spoken words and phrases that represent self-correction, hesitation, and floor-grabbing behaviors, but do not add semantic information; removing them yields the intended, fluent utterance. The presence of disfluencies in conversational speech data can cause problems for both downstream processing (parsing and other natural language processing tasks) and human readability of speech transcripts. There has been much research effort on automatic disfluency detection in recent years (Shriberg and Stolcke, 1997; Snover et al., 2004; Liu et al., 2006; Lin and Lee, 2009; Schuler et al., 2010; Georgila et al., 2010; Zwarts and Johnson, 2011), particularly from the DARPA EARS (Effective, Affordable, Reusable Speech-to-Text) MDE (MetaData Extraction) (DARPA Information Processing Technology Office, 2003) program, which focused on the automatic transcription of sizable amounts of speech data and rendering such transcripts in readable form, for both conversational telephone speech (CTS) and broadcast news (BN).

However, the EARS MDE effort was focused on English only, and there hasn't been much research on the effectiveness of similar automatic disfluency detection approaches for multiple languages. This paper presents three main innovations. First, we extend the EARS MDE-style disfluency detection approach combining lexical and prosodic features using a Conditional Random Field (CRF) model, which was employed for detecting disfluency on English conversational speech data (Liu et al., 2005), to Mandarin conversational speech, as presented in Section 2. Second, we implement an automatic filled pause detection approach through constrained speech recognition, as presented in Section 3. Third, for both disfluency detection systems, we compare side-by-side contributions of different knowledge sources to detection performance for two languages, English and Mandarin, as presented in Section 4. Conclusions appear in Section 5.

2 EARS MDE Style Automatic Disfluency Detection

We focus on two types of disfluencies, *Fillers* and *Edit disfluencies*, following the EARS MDE disfluency types modeled in (Liu et al., 2006). Fillers include filled pauses (FP), discourse markers (DM), and explicit editing terms (ET). FPs are words used by the speakers as floor holders to maintain control of a conversation. They can also indicate hesitations of the speaker. In this work, English FPs comprise *uh* and *um*, based on English CTS corpora. For Mandarin, Zhao and Jurafsky found that Mandarin speakers intensively used both demonstratives *zhege (literally 'this')* and *nage (literally 'that')* and *uh/mm* as FPs based on a large speech corpus of Mandarin telephone conversation (Zhao and Jurafsky, 2005). We study the same set of Chinese FPs in this study. DMs are words or phrases related to the structure of the discourse and help taking or keeping a turn, or serving as acknowledgment, for example, *I mean, you know*. An explicit ET is an editing term in an edit disfluency that is not an FP or a DM. For example, *we have two action items* $*$ *sorry three action items from the meeting*, where *sorry* is an explicit ET.

Edit disfluencies involve syntactically relevant content that is either repeated, revised, or abandoned. The basic pattern for edit disfluencies has the form **(reparandum)** $*$ **<editing term> correction**. The reparandum is the portion of the utterance that is corrected or abandoned entirely (in the case of restarts). An interruption point (IP), marked with '$*$' in the pattern, is the point at which the speaker breaks off the original utterance and then repeats, revises, or restarts the utterance. The editing term is optional and consists of one or more filler words. The correction is the portion of the utterance that corrects the original reparandum. Revisions denote the cases when a speaker modifies the original utterance with a similar syntactic structure, e.g., *we have two action items* $*$ *sorry three action items from the meeting*. Restarts denote the cases when a speaker abandons an utterance or a constituent and restarts all over again, e.g., *He* $*$ *I like this idea*.

We used a CRF model to combine lexical features, shallow syntactic features, and prosodic features for joint detection of edit words and IP words. A CRF defines a global log-linear distribution of the state (or label) sequence E conditioned on an observation sequence, in our case including the word sequence W and the features F, and optimized globally over the entire sequence considering the context event information for making decisions at each point. We used the Mallet package (McCallum, 2002) to implement the CRF model. We used a first-order model that includes only two sequential events in the feature set. The CRF model is trained to maximize the conditional log-likelihood of a given training set $P(E|W,F)$. During testing, the most likely sequence E is found using the Viterbi algorithm. To avoid over-fitting, a zero-mean Gaussian prior (McCallum and Li, 2003) was applied to the parameters, where the variance of the prior was optimized on the development test set. Each word is associated with a class label, representing whether it is an edit word or not. We included IP in the target classes and used five states, as *outside edit* (O), *begin edit with an IP* (B-E+IP), *begin edit* (B-E), *inside edit with an IP* (I-E+IP), and *inside edit* (I-E) (Liu et al., 2006). State transitions are also the same as in (Liu et al., 2006). We built a Hidden Markov Model (HMM) based part-of-speech (POS) taggers for English conversational speech and Mandarin broadcast conversation data. After employing the co-training approach described in (Wang et al., 2007), we achieved 94% POS tagging accuracy for both data sets. The features for CRF modeling include: n-grams from words and automatically generated POS tags, speaker turns, whether there is a repeated word sequence ending at a word boundary, whether a word is a fragment, whether there is a predefined filler phrase after the word boundary, and the prosody model posterior probabilities from a decision tree model (Shriberg and Stolcke, 1997) and discretized by cumulative binning (Liu et al., 2006). The prosodic features were computed for each interword boundary from words and phonetic alignments of the manual transcriptions. We extracted the same set of prosodic features for English and Mandarin data, based on duration, fundamental frequency (f0), energy, and pause information, and nonprosodic information such as speaker gender and speaker change, for training and applying the decision-tree-based prosody model (Liu et al., 2006).

We implemented a rule-based system for filler word detection. We defined a list of possible Chinese and English filler words, including filled pauses and discourse markers. The rules also explore POS tags assigned by our Chinese and English POS taggers.

3 Constrained Speech Recognition for Filled Pause Detection

We also propose an alternative approach for automatic detection of FPs given speech transcripts that omit FPs but are otherwise accurate. This approach is motivated by situations where only an edited, "cleaned-up" transcript is available, but where an accurate verbatim transcript is to be recovered automatically. We treat this task as a constrained speech recognition problem, and investigate how effectively it is solved by a state-of-the-art large vocabulary continuous speech recognition (LVCSR) system. Hence, this approach can be considered as combining LVCSR acoustic model (AM) and language model (LM) knowledge sources in a search framework for FP detection. Compared to the FP detection component in the disfluency detection systems described in Section 2, this alternative approach explores different knowledge sources. In particular, the AMs explore different front-end features compared to the lexical and prosodic features explored in those disfluency detection systems presented in Section 2. Details of the front-end features are illustrated below.

We evaluated this approach on both English and Mandarin conversational speech. For detecting FPs in English conversational speech, we used a modified and simplified form of the recognition system developed for the 2004 NIST Rich Transcription Conversational Telephone Speech (CTS) evaluations, described in (Stolcke et al., 2006). The first pass of the recognizer uses a within-word MFCC+MLP model (i.e, trained on Mel-frequency cepstral coefficient (MFCC) features augmented with Multi-Layer Perceptron (MLP) based phone-posterior features), while the second pass uses a cross-word model trained on Perceptual Linear Prediction (PLP) features adapted (by speaker) to the output of the first pass. For purposes of FP detection, the recognition is constrained to a word lattice formed by the manually transcribed non-FP reference words, with optional FP words inserted between any two words and at the beginning and end of each utterance. Both first and second pass decoding was constrained by the optional-FP lattices. In the second pass, HTK lattices were generated with bigram LM probabilities and rescored with a 4-gram LM. The consensus decoding output from the rescored lattices was used for scoring FP detection. The system thus evaluates the posterior probability of an FP at every word boundary using both acoustic model (AM) and language model (LM) evidence. The acoustic model for the English recognition system was trained on about 2300 hours of CTS data. The language models (which models FP like any other word) are bigram and 4-gram statistical word n-gram LMs estimated from the same data plus additional non-CTS data and web data.

For detecting FPs in Mandarin broadcast conversation speech, we used a modified form of the recognition system developed for the 2008 DARPA GALE (Global Autonomous Language Exploitation) Speech-to-Text evaluation, described in (Lei et al., 2009). The system conducted a constrained decoding on the optional-FP lattices, using a speaker-independent within-word triphone MPE-trained MFCC+pitch+MLP model and a pruned trigram LM. For the Mandarin ASR system, the MFCC+MLP front-end features were augmented with 3-dimension smoothed pitch features (Lei et al., 2006). HTK lattices were generated with probabilities from the pruned trigram LM and rescored by the full trigram LM. The consensus decoding output from the rescored lattices was used for scoring FP detection. The AMs for this system were trained on 1642 hours of Mandarin broadcast news and conversation speech data and the LMs were trained on 1.4 billion words comprising a variety of resources. Details of training data and system development were illustrated in (Lei et al., 2009).

This procedure is similar to forced aligning the word lattices to the audio data (Finke and Waibel, 1997). Both Finke et al.'s approach (Finke and Waibel, 1997) and our approach built a lattice from each transcription sentence (in our approach, optional filled pauses are inserted between any two words and at the beginning and end of each utterance). Then Finke et al. force-aligned the lattice with utterance; whereas, we used multi-pass constrained decoding with within-word and cross-word models, MLLR adaptation of the acoustic models, and rescoring with a higher-order n-gram LM, so the performance will be better than just flexible alignment to the lattices. Note that when constructing the word lattices with optional FP words, for English, the optional FP words are a choice between *uh* and *um*. For Mandarin, the optional FP words are a choice between *uh*, *mm*, *zhege*, and *nage*. We assigned equal weights to FP words.

4 Experimental Results

Scoring of EARS MDE-style automatic disfluency detection output is done using the NIST tools [1], computing the error rate as the average number of misclassified words per reference event word. For English, the training and evaluation data were from the 40 hours CTS data in the NIST RT-04F MDE training data including speech, their transcriptions and disfluency annotations by LDC. We randomly held out two 3-hour subsets from this training data set for evaluation and parameter tuning respectively, and used the remaining data for training. Note that for Mandarin, there is no LDC released Mandarin MDE training data. We adapted the English MDE annotation guidelines for Mandarin and manually annotated the manual transcripts of 92 Mandarin broadcast conversation (BC) shows released by LDC under the DARPA GALE program, for edit disfluencies and filler words. We randomly held out two 3-hour subsets from the 92 shows for evaluation and parameter tuning respectively, and manually corrected disfluency annotation errors on the evaluation set.

Table 1 shows the results in NIST error rate (%) for edit word, IP, and filler word detection. We observe that adding POS features improves edit word, edit IP, and filler word detection for both languages, and adding a prosody model produced further improvement (note that filler word detection systems did not employ prosodic features). The gains from combining the word, POS, and prosody model over the word n-gram baseline are statistically significant for both languages (confidence level $p < 0.05$ using matched pair test). Also, adding the prosody model over word+POS yielded a larger relative gain in edit word+IP detection performance for Mandarin than for English data. A preliminary study of these results has shown that the prosody model contributes differently for different types of disfluencies for English and Mandarin conversational speech and we will continue this study in future work. We also plan to investigate the prosodic features considering the special characteristics of edited disfluencies in Mandarin studied in (Lin and Lee, 2009).

Table 1: NIST error rate (%) for edit word, IP, and filler word detection on the English and Mandarin test set, using word n-gram features, POS n-gram features, and prosody model.

Feature	NIST Error Rate (%)		
	Edit Word	Edit IP	Filler Word
	English		
Word	53.0	38.7	31.2
+POS	52.6	38.2	29.8
++Prosody	52.3	38.0	29.8
	Mandarin		
Word	58.5	42.8	33.4
+POS	57.7	42.1	32.9
++Prosody	56.9	41.5	32.9

For evaluating constrained speech recognition for FP detection, the English test set of conversational speech data and word transcripts is derived from the CTS subset of the NIST 2002 Rich Transcription evaluation. The waveforms were segmented according to utterance boundaries given by the human-generated transcripts, resulting in 6554 utterance segments with a total duration of 6.8 hours. We then excluded turns that have fewer than five tokens or have two or more FPs in a row (such as 'uh um' and 'uh, uh'), resulting in 3359 segments. This yields the test set from which we computed English FP detection scores. The transcripts of this test set contain 54511 non-FP words and 1394 FPs, transcribed as either *uh* or *um*. When evaluating FP detection performance, these two orthographical forms were mapped to a single token type, so recognizing one form as the other is not penalized. The Mandarin test set is the DARPA GALE 2008 Mandarin speech-to-text development test set of 1 hour duration. The transcripts of this test set contain 9820 non-FP words and 370 FP words, transcribed as *uh*, *mm*, *zhege*, and *nage*. We collapsed them to a single token type for FP scoring. We evaluated FP detection performance in terms of both false alarm (incorrect detection) and miss (failed detection) rates, shown in Table 2. We observed that adding pronunciation scores didn't change the P_{fa} and P_{miss}. On the English

[1] www.itl.nist.gov/iad/mig/tests/rt/2004-fall/index.html

test set, adding LM scores degraded P_{miss} but improved P_{fa}. However, on the Mandarin test set, increasing LM weight improved both P_{miss} and P_{fa}, suggesting that for the Mandarin LVCSR system in this study, the LM could provide complementary information to the AM to discriminate FP and non-FP words.

Table 2: Probabilities of false alarms (FAs) and misses in FP detection on the English and Mandarin test set w.r.t. acoustic model weight w_a, language model weight w_g, and pronunciation score weight w_p.

$\{w_a, w_g, w_p\}$	**FAs (%)**	**Misses (%)**
	English	
{1,0,8}	1.76	3.23
{1,8,8}	1.18	4.73
	Mandarin	
{1,0,8}	1.19	19.68
{1,8,8}	0.76	16.76

5 Conclusion

In conclusion, we have presented two automatic disfluency detection systems, one combining various lexical and prosodic features, and the other combining LVCSR acoustic and language model knowledge sources. We observed significant improvements in combining lexical and prosodic features over just employing word n-gram features, for both languages. When combining AM and LM knowledge sources for FP detection in constrained speech recognition, we found increasing LM weight improved both false alarm and miss rates for Mandarin but degraded the miss rate for English.

Acknowledgments

The authors thank all the anonymous reviewers of this paper for valuable suggestions. This work is supported in part by NSF grant IIS-0964556.

References

DARPA Information Processing Technology Office. 2003. Effective,affordable, reusable speech-to-text (EARS). http://www.darpa.mil/ipto/programs/ears.

Michael Finke and Alex Waibel. 1997. Flexible transcription alignment. In *IEEE Workshop on Speech Recognition and Understanding*, pages 34–40.

K. Georgila, N. Wang, and J. Gratch. 2010. Cross-domain speech disfluency detection. In *Proceedings of SIGDIAL*, pages 237–240, Tokyo.

X. Lei, M. Siu, M.Y. Hwang, M. Ostendorf, and T. Lee. 2006. Improved tone modeling for Mandarin broadcast news speech recognition. In *Proceedings of Interspeech*.

X. Lei, W. Wu, W. Wang, A. Mandal, and A. Stolcke. 2009. Development of the 2008 SRI Mandarin speech-to-text system for broadcast news and conversation. In *Proceedings of Interspeech*, Brighton, UK.

C. K. Lin and L. S. Lee. 2009. Improved features and models for detecting edit disfluencies in transcribing spontaneous mandarin speech. *IEEE Transactions on Audio, Speech, and Language Processing*, 17(7):1263–1278, September.

Yang Liu, Elizabeth Shriberg, Andreas Stolcke, and Mary Harper. 2005. Comparing HMM, maximum entropy, and conditional random fields for disfluency detection. In *Proc. Interspeech*, pages 3313–3316, Lisbon, September.

Yang Liu, Elizabeth Shriberg, Andreas Stolcke, Dustin Hillard, Mari Ostendorf, and Mary Harper. 2006. Enriching speech recognition with automatic detection of sentence boundaries and disfluencies. *IEEE Transactions on Audio, Speech, and Language Processing*, 14(5):1526–1540, September. Special Issue on Progress in Rich Transcription.

A. McCallum and W. Li. 2003. Early results for named entity recognition with conditional random fields. In *Proceedings of the CoNLL*.

Andrew McCallum. 2002. Mallet: A machine learning for language toolkit. http://mallet.cs.umass.edu.

W. Schuler, S. AbdelRahman, T. Miller, and L. Schwartz. 2010. Broad-coverage incremental parsing using human-like memory constraints. *Computational Linguistics*, 36(1).

E. Shriberg and A. Stolcke. 1997. A prosody-only decision-tree model for disfluency detection. In *Proceedings of Eurospeech*, pages 2383–2386.

M. Snover, B. Dorr, and R. Schwartz. 2004. A lexically-driven algorithm for disfluency detection. In Susan Dumais, Daniel Marcu, and Salim Roukos, editors, *Proc. HLT-NAACL*, Boston, May. Association for Computational Linguistics.

Andreas Stolcke, Barry Chen, Horacio Franco, Venkata Ramana Rao Gadde, Martin Graciarena, Mei-Yuh Hwang, Katrin Kirchhoff, Arindam Mandal, Nelson Morgan, Xin Lin, Tim Ng, Mari Ostendorf, Kemal Sönmez, Anand Venkataraman, Dimitra Vergyri, Wen Wang, Jing Zheng, and Qifeng Zhu. 2006. Recent innovations in speech-to-text transcription at SRI-ICSI-UW. *IEEE Trans. Audio, Speech, and Lang. Pro-*

cess., 14(5):1729–1744, September. Special Issue on Progress in Rich Transcription.

W. Wang, Z. Huang, and M. P. Harper. 2007. Semi-supervised learning for part-of-speech tagging of Mandarin transcribed speech. In *Proceedings of ICASSP*, pages 137–140.

Y. Zhao and D. Jurafsky. 2005. A preliminary study of mandarin filled pause. In *Proceedings of DISS*, pages 179–182, Aix-en-Provence.

S. Zwarts and M. Johnson. 2011. The impact of language models and loss functions on repair disfluency detection. In *Proceedings of ACL/HLT*, pages 703–711, Portland.

Distributional semantic models for the evaluation of disordered language

Masoud Rouhizadeh[†], **Emily Prud'hommeaux**[°], **Brian Roark**[†], **Jan van Santen**[†]
[†]Center for Spoken Language Understanding, Oregon Health & Science University
[°]Center for Language Sciences, University of Rochester
{rouhizad,vansantj}@ohsu.edu, {emilypx,roarkbr}@gmail.com

Abstract

Atypical semantic and pragmatic expression is frequently reported in the language of children with autism. Although this atypicality often manifests itself in the use of unusual or unexpected words and phrases, the rate of use of such unexpected words is rarely directly measured or quantified. In this paper, we use distributional semantic models to automatically identify unexpected words in narrative retellings by children with autism. The classification of unexpected words is sufficiently accurate to distinguish the retellings of children with autism from those with typical development. These techniques demonstrate the potential of applying automated language analysis techniques to clinically elicited language data for diagnostic purposes.

1 Introduction

Autism spectrum disorder (ASD) is a neurodevelopmental disorder characterized by impaired communication and social behavior. Although the symptoms of ASD are numerous and varied, atypical and idiosyncratic language has been one of the core symptoms observed in verbal individuals with autism since Kanner first assigned a name to the disorder (Kanner, 1943). Atypical language currently serves as a diagnostic criterion in many of the most widely used diagnostic instruments for ASD (Lord et al., 2002; Rutter et al., 2003), and the phenomenon is especially marked in the areas of semantics and pragmatics (Tager-Flusberg, 2001; Volden and Lord, 1991).

Because structured language assessment tools are not always sensitive to the particular atypical semantic and pragmatic expression associated with ASD, measures of atypical language are often drawn from spontaneous language samples. Expert manual annotation and analysis of spontaneous language in young people with ASD has revealed that children and young adults with autism include significantly more bizarre and irrelevant content (Loveland et al., 1990; Losh and Capps, 2003) in their narratives and more abrupt topic changes (Lam et al., 2012) in their conversations than their language-matched typically developing peers. Most normed clinical instruments for analyzing children's spontaneous language, however, focus on syntactic measures and developmental milestones related to the acquisition of vocabulary and syntactic structures. Measures of semantic and pragmatic atypicality in spontaneous language are rarely directly measured. Instead, the degree of language atypicality is often determined via subjective parental reports (e.g., asking a parent whether their child has ever used odd phrases (Rutter et al., 2003)) or general impressions during clinical examination (e.g., rating the child's degree of "stereotyped or idiosyncratic use of words or phrases" on a four-point scale (Lord et al., 2002)). This has led to a lack of reliable and objective information about the frequency of atypical language use and its precise nature in ASD.

In this study, we attempt to automatically detect instances of contextually atypical language in spontaneous speech at the lexical level in order to quantify its prevalence in the ASD population. We first determine manually the off-topic, surprising, or inappropriate words in a set of narrative retellings elicited in a clinical setting from children with ASD and typical development. We then apply word ranking methods and distributional semantic modeling to these narrative retellings in order to automatically identify these unexpected words. The results indicate not only that children with ASD do in fact produce more semantically unexpected and inappropriate words in their narratives than typically developing children but also that our automated methods for identifying these words are accurate enough to serve as an adequate substitute for manual annotation. Although unexpected off-topic word use is just one example of the atypical language observed in ASD, the work presented here highlights the potential of computational language evaluation and analysis methods for improving our understanding of the linguistic deficits associated with ASD.

2 Data

Participants in this study included 37 children with typical development (TD) and 21 children with autism spectrum disorder (ASD). ASD was diagnosed via clinical consensus according to the DSM-IV-TR criteria (American Psychiatric Association, 2000) and the established threshold scores on two diagnostic instruments: the Autism Diagnostic Observation Schedule (ADOS) (Lord et al., 2002), a semi-structured series of activities designed to allow an examiner to observe behaviors associated with autism; and the Social Communication Questionnaire (SCQ) (Rutter et al., 2003), a parental questionnaire. None of the children in this study met the criteria for a language impairment, and there were no significant between-group differences in age (mean=6.4) or full-scale IQ (mean=114).

The narrative retelling task analyzed here is the Narrative Memory subtest of the NEPSY (Korkman et al., 1998), a large and comprehensive battery of tasks that test neurocognitive functioning in children. The NEPSY Narrative Memory (NNM) subtest is a narrative retelling test in which the subject listens to a brief narrative, excerpts of which are shown in Figure 1, and then must retell the narrative to the examiner. The NNM was administered to each participant in the study, and each participant's retelling was recorded and transcribed. Using Amazon's Mechanical Turk, we also collected a large corpus of retellings from neurotypical adults, who listened to a recording of the story and provided written retellings. We describe how this corpus was used in Section 3, below.

Two annotators, blind to the diagnosis of the experimental subjects, identified every word in each retelling transcript that was unexpected or inappropriate given the larger context of the story. For instance, in the sentence *T-rex could smell things*, both *T-rex* and *smell* were marked as unexpected, since there is no mention of either concept in the story. In a seemingly more appropriate sentence, *the boy sat up off the bridge*, the word *bridge* is considered unexpected since the boy is trapped up in a tree rather than on a bridge.

3 Methods

We start with the expectation that different retellings of the same source narrative will share a common vocabulary and semantic space. The presence of words outside of this vocabulary or semantic space in a retelling may indicate that the speaker has strayed from the topic of the story. Our approach for automatically identifying these unexpected words relies on the ranking of words according to the strength of their association with the target topic of the corpus. The word association scores used in the

Figure 1: Excerpts from the NNM narrative.

Jim was a boy whose best friend was Pepper. Pepper was a big black dog. [...] Near Jim's house was a very tall oak tree with branches so high that he couldn't reach them. Jim always wanted to climb that tree, so one day he took a ladder from home and carried it to the oak tree. He climbed up [...] When he started to get down, his foot slipped, his shoe fell off, and the ladder fell to the ground. [...] Pepper sat below the tree and barked. Suddenly Pepper took Jim's shoe in his mouth and ran away. [...] Pepper took the shoe to Anna, Jim's sister. He barked and barked. Finally, Anna understood that Jim was in trouble. She followed Pepper to the tree where Jim was stuck. Anna put the ladder up and rescued Jim.

ranking are informed by the frequency of a word in the child's retelling relative to the frequency of that word in other retellings in the larger corpus of retellings. These association measures are similar to those developed for the information retrieval task of topic modeling, in which the goal is to identify topic-specific words – i.e., words that appear frequently in only a subset of documents – in order to cluster together documents about a similar topic. Details about how these scores are calculated and interpreted are provided in the following sections.

The pipeline for determining the set of unusual words in each retelling begins by calculating word association scores, described below, for each word in each retelling and ranking the words according to these scores. A threshold over these scores is determined for each child using leave-one-out cross validation in order to select a set of potentially unexpected words. This set of potential unexpected words is then filtered using two external resources that allow us to eliminate words that were not used in other retellings but are likely to be semantically related to topic of the narrative. This final set of words is evaluated against the set of manually identified words in order determine the accuracy of our unexpected word classification.

3.1 Word association measures

Before calculating the word association measures, we tokenize, downcase, and stem (Porter, 1980) the transcripts and remove all punctuation. We then use two association measures to score each word in each child's retelling: *tf-idf*, the term frequency-inverse document frequency measure (Salton and Buckley, 1988), and the log odds ratio (van Rijsbergen et al., 1981). We use the following formulation to calculate *tf-idf* for each child's retelling i and each word in that retelling j, where c_{ij} is the count of word j in retelling i; f_j is the number of retellings from the full corpus of child and adult retellings containing that word j; and D is the total number of retellings in the full corpus (Manning et al., 2008):

$$\textit{tf-idf}_{ij} = \begin{cases} (1 + \log c_{ij}) \log \frac{D}{f_j} & \text{if } c_{ij} \geq 1 \\ 0 & \text{otherwise} \end{cases}$$

The log odds ratio, another association measure used in information retrieval and extraction tasks, is the ratio between the odds of a particular word, j, appearing in a child's retelling, i, as estimated using its relative frequency in that retelling, and the odds of that word appearing in all other retellings, again estimated using its relative frequency in all other retellings. Letting the probability of a word appearing in a retelling be p_1 and the probability of that word appearing in all other retellings be p_2, we can express the odds ratio as follows:

$$\text{odds ratio} = \frac{\text{odds}(p_1)}{\text{odds}(p_2)} = \frac{p_1/(1-p_1)}{p_2/(1-p_2)}$$

A large *tf-idf* or log odds score indicates that the word j is very specific to the retelling i, which in turn suggests that the word might be unexpected or inappropriate in the larger context of the NNM narrative. Thus we expect that the words with higher association measure scores are likely to be the words that were manually identified as unexpected in the context of the NNM narrative.

3.2 Application of word association measures

As previously mentioned, both of these word association measures are used in information retrieval (IR) to cluster together documents about a similar target topic. In IR, words that appear only in a subset of documents from a large and varied corpus of documents will have high word association scores, and the documents containing those words will likely be focused on the same topic. In our task, however, we have a single cluster of documents focused on a single topic: the NNM narrative. Topic-specific words ought to occur much more frequently than other words. As a result, words with high *tf-idf* and log odds scores are likely to be those *unrelated* to the topic of the NNM story. If a child veers away from the topic of the NNM story and uses words that do not occur frequently in the retellings produced by neurotypical speakers, his retellings will contain more words with high word association scores. We predict that this set of high-scoring words is likely to overlap significantly with the set of words identified by the manual annotators as unexpected or off-topic.

Applying these word association scoring approaches to each word in each child's retelling yields a list of words from each retelling ranked in order of decreasing *tf-idf* or log odds score. We use cross-validation to determine, for each measure, the operating point that maximizes the unexpected word identification accuracy in terms of F-measure. For each child, the threshold is found using the data from all of the other children. This threshold is then applied to the ranked word list of the held-out child. All words above this threshold are potential unexpected words, while all words below this threshold are considered to be expected and appropriate in the context of the NNM narrative. Table 1 shows the recall, precision, and F-measure using the two word association measures discussed here. We see that these two techniques result in high recall at the expense of precision. The next stage in the pipeline is therefore to use external resources to eliminate any semantically appropriate words from the set of potentially unexpected or inappropriate words generated via thresholding on the *tf-idf* or log odds score.

3.3 Filtering with external resources

Recall that the corpus of retellings used to generate the word association measures described above, is very small. It is therefore quite possible that a child may have used an entirely appropriate word that by chance was never used by another child or one of the neurotypical adults. One way of increasing the lexical coverage of the corpus of retellings is through semantic expansion using an external resource. For each word in the set of potential unexpected words, we located the WordNet synset for that word (Fellbaum, 1998). If any of the WordNet synonyms of the potentially unexpected word was present in the source narrative or in one of the adult retellings, that word was removed from the set of unexpected words.

In the final step, we used the CHILDES corpus of transcripts of children's conversational speech (MacWhinney, 2000) to generate topic estimates for each remaining potentially unexpected word. For each of these words, we located every utterance in the CHILDES corpus containing that potentially unexpected word. We then measured the association of that word with every other open-class word that appeared in an utterance with that word using the log likelihood ratio (Dunning, 1993). The 20 words from the CHILDES corpus with the highest log likelihood ratio (i.e., the words most strongly associated with the potentially unexpected word), were assumed to collectively represent a particular topic. If more than two of the words in the vector of words representing this topic were also present in the NNM source narrative or the adult retellings, the word that generated that topic was eliminated from the set of unexpected words.

We note that the optimized threshold described in Section 3.2, above, is determined after filtering. There is therefore potentially a different threshold for each condition tested, and hence we do not necessarily expect precision to increase and recall to decrease after filtering. Rather, since the threshold is selected in order to optimize F-measure, we expect that if the filtering is effective, F-measure will increase with each additional filtering condition applied.

4 Results

We evaluated the performance of our two word ranking techniques, both individually and combined by taking either the maximum of the two measures or the sum, against the set of manually annotations described in Section 2. In addition, we report the results of applying these word ranking techniques in combination with the two filtering techniques. We compare these results with a simple baseline method in which every word used in a retelling that is never used in another retelling is considered to be unexpected. Table 1 shows the precision, accuracy, and F-measure of these approaches. We see that all of the more sophisticated unexpected word identification approaches outperform the baseline by a wide margin, and that *tf-idf* and log odds perform comparably under the condition without filtering and both filtering conditions. Filtering improves F-measure under both word ranking schemes, and combining the two measures results in further improvements under both filtering conditions. Although applying topic-estimate filtering yields the highest precision, the simple WordNet-based approach results in the highest F-measure and a reasonable balance between precision and recall.

Recall that the purpose of identifying these unexpected words was to determine whether children with ASD produce unexpected and inappropriate words at a higher rate than children with typical development. This appears to be true in our manually annotated data. On average, 7.5% of the words

Unexpected word identification method	P	R	F1
Baseline	46.3	74.0	57.0
TF-IDF	72.1	79.5	75.6
Log-odds	70.5	79.5	74.7
Sum(TF-IDF, Log-odds)	72.2	83.3	77.4
Max(TF-IDF, Log-odds)	69.9	83.3	76.0
TF-IDF+WordNet	83.8	80.5	82.1
Log-odds+WordNet	82.1	83.1	82.6
Sum(TF-IDF, Log-odds)+WordNet	84.2	83.1	83.7
Max(TF-IDF, Log-odds)+WordNet	83.3	84.4	83.9
TF-IDF+WordNet+topic	85.7	77.9	81.7
Log-odds+WordNet+topic	83.8	80.5	82.1
Sum(TF-IDF, Log-odds)+WordNet+topic	86.1	80.5	83.2
Max(TF-IDF, Log-odds)+WordNet+topic	85.1	81.8	83.4

Table 1: Accuracy of unexpected word identification.

types produced by children with ASD were marked as unexpected, while only 2.5% of words produced by children with TD were marked as unexpected, a significant difference ($p < 0.01$, using a one-tailed t-test). This significant between-group difference in rate of unexpected word use holds even when using the automated methods of unexpected word identification, with the best performing unexpected word identification method estimating a mean of 6.6% in the ASD group and 2.5% in the TD group ($p < 0.01$).

5 Conclusions and future work

The automated methods presented here for ranking and filtering words according to their distributions in different corpora, which are adapted from techniques originally developed for topic modeling in the context of information retrieval and extraction tasks, demonstrate the utility of automated approaches for the analysis of semantics and pragmatics. We were able to use these methods to identify unexpected or inappropriate words with high enough accuracy to replicate the patterns of unexpected word use manually observed in our two diagnostic groups. This work underscores the potential of automated techniques for improving our understanding of the prevalence and diagnostic utility of linguistic features associated with ASD and other communication and language disorders.

In future work, we plan to use a development set to determine the optimal number of topical words to select during the topic estimate filtering stage of the pipeline in order to maintain improvements in precision without a loss in recall. We would also like to investigate using part-of-speech, word sense, and parse information to improve our approaches for both semantic expansion and topic estimation. Although the rate of unexpected word use alone is unlikely to provide sufficient power to classify the two diagnostic groups investigated here, we expect that it can serve as one feature in an array of features that capture the broad range of semantic and pragmatic atypicalities observed in the spoken language of children with autism. Finally, we plan to apply these same methods to identify the confabulations and topic shifts often observed in the narrative retellings of the elderly with neurodegenerative conditions.

Acknowledgments

This work was supported in part by NSF Grant #BCS-0826654, and NIH NIDCD grant #1R01DC012033-01. Any opinions, findings, conclusions or recommendations expressed in this publication are those of the authors and do not necessarily reflect the views of the NSF or the NIH.

References

American Psychiatric Association. 2000. *DSM-IV-TR: Diagnostic and Statistical Manual of Mental Disorders*. American Psychiatric Publishing, Washington, DC.

Ted Dunning. 1993. Accurate methods for the statistics of surprise and coincidence. *Computational linguistics*, 19(1):61–74.

Christian Fellbaum. 1998. *WordNet: An Electronic Lexical Database*. MIT Press, Cambridge, MA.

Leo Kanner. 1943. Autistic disturbances of affective content. *Nervous Child*, 2:217–250.

Marit Korkman, Ursula Kirk, and Sally Kemp. 1998. *NEPSY: A developmental neuropsychological assessment*. The Psychological Corporation, San Antonio.

Yan Grace Lam, Siu Sze, and Susanna Yeung. 2012. Towards a convergent account of pragmatic language deficits in children with high-functioning autism: Depicting the phenotype using the pragmatic rating scale. *Research in Autism Spectrum Disorders*, 6:792797.

Catherine Lord, Michael Rutter, Pamela DiLavore, and Susan Risi. 2002. *Autism Diagnostic Observation Schedule (ADOS)*. Western Psychological Services, Los Angeles.

Molly Losh and Lisa Capps. 2003. Narrative ability in high-functioning children with autism or asperger's syndrome. *Journal of Autism and Developmental Disorders*, 33(3):239–251.

Katherine Loveland, Robin McEvoy, and Belgin Tunali. 1990. Narrative story telling in autism and down's syndrome. *British Journal of Developmental Psychology*, 8(1):9–23.

Brian MacWhinney. 2000. *The CHILDES project: Tools for analyzing talk*. Lawrence Erlbaum Associates, Mahwah, NJ.

Christopher D. Manning, Prabhakar Raghavan, and Hinrich Schütze. 2008. *Introduction to information retrieval*. Cambridge University Press.

M.F. Porter. 1980. An algorithm for suffix stripping. *Program*, 14(3):130–137.

Michael Rutter, Anthony Bailey, and Catherine Lord. 2003. *Social Communication Questionnaire (SCQ)*. Western Psychological Services, Los Angeles.

Gerard Salton and Christopher Buckley. 1988. Term-weighting approaches in automatic text retrieval. *Information Processing and Management*, 24(5):513–523.

Helen Tager-Flusberg. 2001. Understanding the language and communicative impairments in autism. *International Review of Research in Mental Retardation*, 23:185–205.

C.J. van Rijsbergen, D.J. Harper, and M.F. Porter. 1981. The selection of good search terms. *Information Processing and Management*, 17(2):77–91.

Joanne Volden and Catherine Lord. 1991. Neologisms and idiosyncratic language in autistic speakers. *Journal of Autism and Developmental Disorders*, 21:109–130.

Atypical Prosodic Structure as an Indicator of Reading Level and Text Difficulty

Julie Medero and Mari Ostendorf
Electrical Engineering Department
University of Washington
Seattle, WA 98195 USA
{jmedero,ostendor}@uw.edu

Abstract

Automatic assessment of reading ability builds on applying speech recognition tools to oral reading, measuring words correct per minute. This work looks at more fine-grained analysis that accounts for effects of prosodic context using a large corpus of read speech from a literacy study. Experiments show that lower-level readers tend to produce relatively more lengthening on words that are not likely to be final in a prosodic phrase, i.e. in less appropriate locations. The results have implications for automatic assessment of text difficulty in that locations of atypical prosodic lengthening are indicative of difficult lexical items and syntactic constructions.

1 Introduction

Fluent reading is known to be a good indicator of reading comprehension, especially for early readers (Rasinski, 2006), so oral reading is often used to evaluate a student's reading level. One method that can be automated with speech recognition technology is the number of words that a student can read correctly of a normed passage, or Words Correct Per Minute (WCPM) (Downey et al., 2011). Since WCPM depends on speaking rate as well as literacy, we are interested in identifying new measures that can be automatically computed for use in combination with WCPM to provide a better assessment of reading level. In particular, we investigate fine-grained measures that, if useful in identifying points of difficulty for readers, can lead to new approaches for assessing text difficulty.

The WCPM is reduced when a person repeats or incorrectly reads a word, but also when they introduce pauses and articulate words more slowly. Pauses and lengthened articulation can be an indicator of uncertainty for a low-level reader, but these phenomena are also used by skilled readers to mark prosodic phrase structure, facilitating comprehension in listeners. Since prosodic phrase boundaries tend to occur in locations that coincide with certain syntactic constituent boundaries, it is possible to automatically predict prosodic phrase boundary locations from part-of-speech labels and syntactic structure with fairly high reliability for read news stories (Ananthakrishnan and Narayanan, 2008). Thus, we hypothesize that we can more effectively leverage word-level articulation and pause information by focusing on words that are less likely to be associated with prosodic phrase boundaries. By comparing average statistics of articulation rate and pausing for words at boundary vs. non-boundary locations, we hope to obtain a measure that could augment reading rate for evaluating reading ability. We also hypothesize that the specific locations of hesitation phenomena (word lengthening and pausing) observed for multiple readers will be indicative of particular points of difficulty in a text, either because a word is difficult or because a syntactic construction is difficult. Detecting these regions and analyzing the associated lexical and syntactic correlates is potentially useful for automatically characterizing text difficulty.

Our study of hesitation phenomena involves empirical analysis of the oral reading data from the Fluency Addition to the National Assessment of Adult

Literacy (FAN), which collected oral readings from roughly 12,000 adults, reading short (150-200 word) fourth- and eighth grade passages (Baer et al., 2009). The participants in that study were chosen to reflect the demographics of adults in the United States; thus, speakers of varying reading levels and non-native speakers were included. For our study, we had access to time alignments of automatic transcriptions, but not the original audio files.

2 Related Work

For low-level readers, reading rate and fluency are good indicators of reading comprehension (Miller and Schwanenflugel, 2006; Spear-Swerling, 2006). Zhang and colleagues found that features of children's oral readings, along with their interactions with an automated tutor, could predict a single student's comprehension question performance over the course of a document (2007). Using oral readings is appealing because it avoids the difficulty of separating question difficulty from passage difficulty (Ozuru et al., 2008) and of questions that can be answered through world knowledge (Keenan and Betjemann, 2006).

WCPM is generally used as a tool for assessing reading level by averaging across one or more passages. It is more noisy when comparing the readability of different texts, especially when the reading level is measured at a fine-grained (e.g. word) level. If longer words take longer to read orally, it may be merely a consequence of having more phonemes, and not of additional reading difficulty. Further, for communication reasons, pauses and slow average articulation rates tend to coincide with major phrase boundaries. In our work, we would like to account for prosodic context in using articulation rate to identify difficult words and constructions.

Much of the previous work on using automatic speech recognition (ASR) output for reading level or readability analysis has focused on assessing the reading level of children (Downey et al., 2011; Duchateau et al., 2007). Similar success has been seen in predicting fluency scores in oral reading tests for L2 learners of English (Balogh et al., 2012; Bernstein et al., 2011). Project LISTEN has a reading tutor for children that gives real-time feedback, and has used orthographic and phonemic features of individual words to predict the likelihood of real word subsitutions (Mostow et al., 2002).

3 FAN Literacy Scores

To examine the utility of word-level pause and articulation rate features for predicting reading level when controlled for prosodic context, we use the Basic Reading Skills (BRS) score available for each reader in the FAN data. The BRS score measures an individual's average reading rate in WCPM. Each participant read three word lists, three pseudo-word lists, one easy text passage, and one harder text passage, and the BRS is the average WCPM over the eight different readings. Specifically, the WCPM for each case is computed automatically using Ordinate's VersaReader system to transcribe the speech given the target text (Balogh et al., 2005). The system output is then automatically aligned to the target texts using the track-the-reader method of Rasmussen et al. (2011), which defines weights for regressions and skipped words and then identifies a least-cost alignment between the ASR output and a text. Automatic calculation of WCPM has high correlation (.96-1.0) with human judgment of WCPM (Balogh et al., 2012), so it has the advantage of being easy to automate.

Word Error Rate (WER) for the the ASR component in Ordinate's prototype reading tracker (Balogh et al., 2012) may be estimated to be between 6% and 10%. In a sample of 960 passage readings, where various sets of two passages were read by each of 480 adults (160 native Spanish speakers, 160 native English-speaking African Americans, and 160 other native English speakers), the Ordinate ASR system exhibited a 6.9% WER on the 595 passages that contained no spoken material that was unintelligible to human transcribers. On the complete set of 960 passages, the system exhibited a 9.9% WER, with each unintelligible length of speech contributing one or more errors to the word error count.

The greatest problem with speech recognition errors is for very low-level readers (Balogh et al., 2012). In order to have more reliable time alignments and BRS scores, approximately 15% of the FAN participants were excluded from the current analysis. This 15% were those participants whose BRS score was labeled "Below Basic" in the NAAL reading scale. Additional participants were eliminated because of missing or incomplete (less than a few seconds) recordings. With these exclusions, the number of speakers in our study was 7587.

4 Prosodic Boundary Prediction

We trained a regression tree[1] on hand-annotated data from the Boston University Radio News Corpus (Ostendorf et al., 1995) to predict the locations where we expect to see prosodic boundaries. Each word in the Radio News Corpus is labeled with a prosodic boundary score from 0 (clitic, no boundary) to 6 (sentence boundary). For each word, we use features based on parse depth and structure and POS bigrams to predict the prosodic boundary value.

For evaluation, the break labels are grouped into: 0-2 (no intonational boundary marker), 3 (intermediate phrase), and 4-6 (intonational phrase boundary). Words with 0-2 breaks are considered non-boundary words; 4-6 are boundary words. We expect that, for fluent readers, lengthening and possibly pausing will be observed after boundary words but not after non-boundary words. Since the intermediate boundaries are the most difficult to classify, and may be candidates for both boundaries and non-boundaries for fluent readers, we omit them in our analyses. Our model achieves 87% accuracy in predicting $\pm$ intonational phrase boundaries and 83% accuracy in predicting $\pm$ no intonational boundary, treating intermediate phrase boundaries as negative instances in both cases.

Note that our 3-way prosodic boundary prediction is aimed at identifying locations where fluent readers are likely to place boundaries (or not), i.e., reliable locations for feature extraction, vs. acceptable locations for text-to-speech synthesis. Because of this goal and because work on prosodic boundary prediction labels varies in its treatment of intermediate phrase boundaries, our results are not directly comparable to prior studies. However, performance is in the range reported in recent studies predicting prosodic breaks from text features only. Treating intermediate phrase boundaries as positive examples, Ananthakrishnan and Narayanan (2008) achieve 88% accuracy. Treating them as negative examples, Margolis and Ostendorf (2010) achieve similar results. Both report results on a single held-out test set, while our results are based on 10-fold cross validation.

[1]Our approach differs slightly from previous work in the use of a regression (vs. classification) model; this gave a small performance gain.

5 Experiments with Prosodic Context

5.1 Word-level Rate Features

We looked at two acoustic cues related to hesitation or uncertainty: pause duration and word lengthening. While pause duration is straightforward to extract (and not typically normalized), various methods have been used for word lengthening. We explore two measures of word lengthening: i) the longest normalized vowel, and ii) the average normalized length of word-final phones (the last vowel and all following consonants). Word-final lengthening is known to be a correlate of fluent prosodic phrase boundaries (Wightman et al., 1992), and we hypothesized that the longest normalized vowel might be useful for hesitations though it can also indicate prosodic prominence.

For word-level measures of lengthening, it is standard to normalize to account for inherent phoneme durations. We use a z-score: measured duration minus phone mean divided by phone standard deviation. In addition, Wightman et al. (1992) found it useful to account for speaking rate in normalizing phone duration. We adopt the same model, which assumes that phone durations can be characterized by a Gamma distribution and that speaker variability is characterized by a linear scaling of the phone-dependent mean parameters, where the scaling term is shared by all phones. The linear scale factor α for a speaker is estimated as:

$$\alpha = \frac{1}{N} \sum_{i=1}^{N} \frac{d_i}{\mu_{p(i)}} \tag{1}$$

where d_i is the duration of the i-th phone which has label $p(i)$ and where μ_p is the speaker-independent mean of phone p. Here, we use a speaker-independent phone mean computed from the TIMIT Corpus,[2] which has hand-marked phonetic labels and times. We make use of the speaking rate model

[2]Available from the Linguistic Data Consortium.

to adjust the speaker-independent TIMIT phone durations to the speakers in the FAN corpus by calculating the linear scale factor α for each speaker. Thus, the phone mean and standard deviation used in the z-score normalization is $\alpha\mu_{p_i}$ and $\alpha\sigma_{p_i}$, respectively.

From the many readings of the eight passages, we identified roughly 777K spoken word instances at predicted phrase boundaries and 2.0M spoken words at predicted non-boundaries. For each uttered word, we calculated three features: the length of the following pause, the length of the longest normalized vowel, and the averaged normed length of all phones from the last vowel to the end of the word, as described above. The word-level features can be averaged across instances from a speaker for assessing reading level or across instances of a particular word in a text uttered by many speakers to assess local text difficulty.

The phone and pause durations are based on recognizer output, so they will be somewhat noisy. The fact that the recognizer is biased towards the intended word sequence and the omission of the lowest-level readers from this study together contribute to reducing the error rate ($< 10\%$) and increasing the reliability of the features. In addition, noise is reduced by averaging over multiple words or multiple speakers.

5.2 Reading Level Analysis

To assess the potential for prosodic context to improve the utility of word-level features for assessing reading difficulty, we looked at duration lengthening and pauses at boundary and non-boundary locations, where the boundary labels are predicted using the text-based algorithm and 3-class grouping described in section 4.

First, for each speaker, we averaged each feature across all boundary words read by that person and across all non-boundary words read by that person. We hypothesized that skilled readers would have shorter averages for all three features at non-boundary words compared to at boundary words, while the differences for lower-level readers would be smaller because of lengthening due to uncertainty at non-boundary words. The difference between the boundary and non-boudnary word averages for normalized duration of end-of-word phones is plotted in

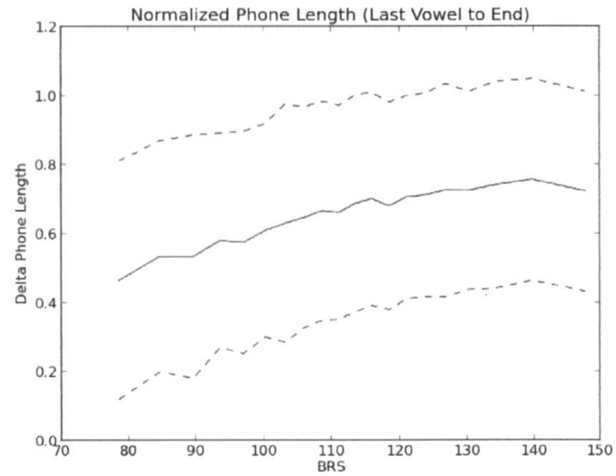

Figure 1: Mean end-of-word normalized phone duration (+/- standard deviation) as a function of BRS score

Figure 1 as a function of reading level. As expected, the difference increases with reading skill, as measured by BRS. A similar trend is observed for the longest normalized vowel in the word.

We also looked at pause duration, finding that the average pause duration decreases as reading skill increases for both boundary and non-boundary words. Since pauses are not always present at intonational phrase boundaries, but are more likely at sentence boundaries, we investigated dividing the cases by punctuation rather than prosodic context. Table 1 shows that for both the top 20% of readers and the bottom 20% of readers, sentence boundaries had much longer pauses on average, followed by comma boundaries, and unpunctuated word boundaries. The drop in both pause frequency and average pause duration is much greater for the more skilled readers.

Looking at all speakers, the unpunctuated words had an average pause duration that scaled with the speaking rate estimate for that passage, with high correlation (0.94). The correlation was much lower for sentence boundaries (0.44). Thus, we conclude that the length of pauses at non-boundary locations is related to the speaker's reading ability.

5.3 Identifying Difficult Texts

Instead of averaging over multiple words in a passage, we can average over multiple readings of a particular word. We identified difficult regions in texts by sorting all tokens by the average normalized length of their end-of-word phones for the lowest

	Top 20%		Bottom 20%	
	Pause Rate	Avg. Pause Duration	Pause Rate	Avg. Pause Duration
Sentence-final	81.0%	177 ms	84.7%	283 ms
Comma	26.1%	94 ms	47.0%	168 ms
No punctuation	4.6%	77 ms	16.6%	139 ms

Table 1: Frequency of occurrence and average duration of pauses at sentence boundaries, comma boundaries, and unpunctuated word boundaries for the top and bottom 20% of all readers, as sorted by BRS score

20% of readers. The examples suggest that lengthening may coincide with reading difficulty caused by syntactic ambiguity. Two sentences, with the lengthened word in bold, illustrate representative ambiguities:

- She was there for **me** the whole time my grandfather was in the hospital.
- Since dogs are **gentler** when raised by a family the dogs are given to children when the dogs are about fourteen months old.

In the first example, "me" could be the end of the sentence, while in the second example, readers may expect "gentler" to be the end of the subordinate clause started by "since". The lengthening on these words is much smaller for the top 20% of readers, suggesting that the extra lengthening is associated with points of difficulty for the less skilled readers.

Similarly, we identified sentences with non-boundary locations where readers commonly paused, with the word after the pause in bold:

- We have always been able to share our **escapades** and humor with our friends.
- Check with your doctor first if you are a man over forty or a woman over fifty **and** you plan to do vigorous activity instead of moderate activity.

We observe a wider variety of potential difficulties here. Some are associated with difficult words, as in the first example, while others involve syntactic ambiguities similar to the ones seen in the lengthening cases.

6 Summary

We have shown that duration lengthening and pause cues align with expected prosodic structure (predicted from syntactic features) more for skilled readers than for low-level readers, which we hope may lead to a richer assessment of individual reading difficulties. In addition, we have proposed a method of characterizing text difficulty at a fine grain based on these features using multiple oral readings. In order to better understand the information provided by the different features, we are conducting eye tracking experiments on these passages, and future work will include an analysis of readers' gaze during reading of these constructions that have been categorized in terms of their likely prosodic context.

In this work, where the original recordings were not available, the study was restricted to duration features. However, other work has suggested that other prosodic cues, particularly pitch and energy features, are useful for detecting speaker uncertainty (Litman et al., 2009; Litman et al., 2012; Pon-Barry and Shieber, 2011). Incorporating these cues may increase the reliability of detecting points of reading difficulty and/or offer complementary information for characterizing text difficulties.

Acknowledgments

We are grateful to the anonymous reviewers for their feedback, and to our colleagues at Pearson Knowledge Technologies for their insights and data processing assistance. This material is based upon work supported by the National Science Foundation Graduate Research Fellowship under Grant No. DGE-0718124 and by the National Science Foundation under Grant No. IIS-0916951. Any opinions, findings, and conclusions or recommendations expressed in this material are those of the authors and do not necessarily reflect the views of the National Science Foundation.

References

S. Ananthakrishnan and S.S. Narayanan. 2008. Automatic Prosodic Event Detection Using Acoustic, Lexical, and Syntactic Evidence. *IEEE Trans. Audio, Speech, and Language Processing*, 16(1):216–228.

J. Baer, M. Kutner, J. Sabatini, and S. White. 2009. Basic Reading Skills and the Literacy of Americas Least Literate Adults: Results from the 2003 National Assessment of Adult Literacy (NAAL) Supplemental Studies. Technical report, NCES.

J. Balogh, J. Bernstein, J. Cheng, and B. Townshend. 2005. Final Report Ordinates Scoring of FAN NAAL Phase III: Accuracy Analysis. Technical report, Ordinate.

J. Balogh, J. Bernstein, J. Cheng, A. Van Moere, B. Townshend, and M. Suzuki. 2012. Validation of Automated Scoring of Oral Reading. *Educational and Psychological Measurement*, 72:435–452.

J. Bernstein, J. Cheng, and M. Suzuki. 2011. Fluency Changes with General Progress in L2 Proficiency. In *Proc. Interspeech*, number August, pages 877–880.

R. Downey, D. Rubin, J. Cheng, and J. Bernstein. 2011. Performance of Automated Scoring for Children's Oral Reading. *Proc. Workshop on Innovative Use of NLP for Building Educational Applications*, (June):46–55, June.

J. Duchateau, L. Cleuren, H. Van, and P. Ghesqui. 2007. Automatic Assessment of Childrens Reading Level. *Proc. Interspeech*, pages 1210–1213.

J.M. Keenan and R. Betjemann. 2006. Comprehending the Gray Oral Reading Test Without Reading It: Why Comprehension Tests Should Not Include Passage-Independent Items. *Scientific Studies of Reading*, 10(4):363–380.

D. Litman, M. Rotaru, and G. Nicholas. 2009. Classifying turn-level uncertainty using word-level prosody. In *Proc. Interspeech*.

D. Litman, H. Friedberg, and K. Forbes-Riley. 2012. Prosodic cues to disengagement and uncertainty in physics tutorial dialogues. In *Proc. Interspeech*.

A. Margolis, M. Ostendorf, and K. Livescu. 2010. Cross-genre training for automatic prosody classification. In *Proc. Speech Prosody Conference*.

J. Miller and P.J. Schwanenflugel. 2006. Prosody of Syntactically Complex Sentences in the Oral Reading of Young Children. *Journal of Educational Psychology*, 98(4):839–843.

J. Mostow, J. Beck, S. Winter, S. Wang, and B. Tobin. 2002. Predicting Oral Reading Miscues. In *Proc. ICSLP*.

M. Ostendorf, P.J. Price, and S. Shattuck-Hufnagel. 1995. The Boston University Radio News Corpus. Technical report, Boston University, March.

Y. Ozuru, M. Rowe, T. O'Reilly, and D.S. McNamara. 2008. Where's the difficulty in standardized reading tests: the passage or the question? *Behavior Research Methods*, 40(4):1001–1015.

H. Pon-Barry and S.M. Shieber. 2011. Recognizing uncertainty in speech. *CoRR*, abs/1103.1898.

T. Rasinski. 2006. Reading fluency instruction: Moving beyond accuracy, automaticity, and prosody. *The Reading Teacher*, 59(7):704–706, April.

M.H. Rasmussen, J. Mostow, Z. Tan, B. Lindberg, and Y. Li. 2011. Evaluating Tracking Accuracy of an Automatic Reading Tutor. In *Proc. Speech and Language Technology in Education Workshop*.

L. Spear-Swerling. 2006. Childrens Reading Comprehension and Oral Reading Fluency in Easy Text. *Reading and Writing*, 19(2):199–220.

C.W. Wightman, S. Shattuck-Hufnagel, M. Ostendorf, and P.J. Price. 1992. Segmental durations in the vicinity of prosodic phrase boundaries. *The Journal of the Acoustical Society of America*, 91(3):1707—-1717.

X.N. Zhang, J. Mostow, and J.E. Beck. 2007. Can a Computer Listen for Fluctuations in Reading Comprehension? *Artificial Intelligence in Education*, 158:495–502.

Using Document Summarization Techniques for Speech Data Subset Selection

Kai Wei*, **Yuzong Liu***, **Katrin Kirchhoff**, **Jeff Bilmes**
Department of Eletrical Engineering
University of Washington
Seattle, WA 98195, USA
{kaiwei,yzliu,katrin,bilmes}@ee.washington.edu

Abstract

In this paper we leverage methods from submodular function optimization developed for document summarization and apply them to the problem of subselecting acoustic data. We evaluate our results on data subset selection for a phone recognition task. Our framework shows significant improvements over random selection and previously proposed methods using a similar amount of resources.

1 Introduction

Present-day applications in spoken language technology (speech recognizers, keyword spotters, etc.) can draw on an unprecedented amount of training data. However, larger data sets come with increased demands on computational resources; moreover, they tend to include redundant information as their size increases. Therefore, the performance gain curves of large-scale systems with respect to the amount of training data often show "diminishing returns": new data is often less valuable (in terms of performance gain) when added to a larger pre-existing data set than when added to a smaller pre-existing set (e.g.,(Moore, 2003)). Therefore it is of prime importance to develop methods for data subset selection. We distinguish two data subselection scenarios: (a) a priori selection of a data set before (re-)training a system; in this case the goal is to subselect the existing data set as well as possible, eliminating redundant information; (b) selection for adaptation, where the goal is to tune a system to a known development or test set. While many studies have addressed the second scenario, this paper investigates the first: our goal is to select a smaller subset of the data that fits a given 'budget' (e.g. maximum number of hours of data) but provides, to the extent possible, as much information as the complete data set. Additionally, our selection method should be a low-resource method that does not require an already-trained complex system such as an existing word recognizer.

This problem is akin to unsupervised data 'summarization'. In (Lin and Bilmes, 2009) a novel class of summarization techniques based on submodular function optimization were proposed for extractive document summarization. Interestingly, these methods can also be applied to speech data 'summarization' with only small modifications. In the following sections we develop a submodular framework for speech data summarization and evaluate it on a proof-of-concept phone recognition task.

2 Related Work

Most approaches to data subset selection in speech have relied on "rank-and-select" approaches that determine the utility of each sample in the data set, rank all samples according to their utility scores, and then select the top N samples. In weakly supervised approaches (e.g.,(Kemp and Waibel, 1998; Lamel et al., 2002; Hakkani-Tur et al., 2002), utility is related to the confidence of an existing word recognizer on new data samples: untranscribed training data is automatically transcribed using an existing baseline speech recognizer, and individual utterances are selected as additional training data if they have low

*These authors are joint first authors with equal contributions.

confidence. These are active learning approaches suitable for a scenario where a well-trained speech recognizer is already available and additional data for retraining needs to be selected. However, we would like to reduce available training data ahead of time with a low-resource approach. In (Chen et al., 2009) individual samples are selected for the purpose of discriminative training by considering phone accuracy and the frame-level entropy of the Gaussian posteriors. (Itoh et al., 2012) use a utility function consisting of the entropy of word hypothesis N-best lists and the representativeness of the sample using a phone-based TF-IDF measure. The latter is comparable to methods used in this paper, though the first term in their objective function still requires a word recognizer. In (Wu et al., 2007) acoustic training data associated with transcriptions is subselected to maximize the entropy of the distribution over linguistic units (phones or words). Most importantly, all these methods select samples in a greedy fashion without optimality guarantees. As we will explain in the next section, greedy selection is near-optimal only when applied to monotone submodular functions.

3 Submodular Functions

Submodular functions (Edmonds, 1970) have been widely studied in mathematics, economics, and operations research and have recently attracted interest in machine learning (Krause and Guestrin, 2011). A submodular function is defined as follows: Given a finite ground set of objects (samples) $V = \{v_1, ..., v_n\}$ and a function $f : 2^V \rightarrow \mathbb{R}^+$ that returns a real value for any subset $S \subseteq V$, f is submodular if $\forall A \subseteq B$, and $v \notin B$, $f(A+v) - f(A) \geq f(B+v) - f(B)$. That is, the incremental "value" of v decreases when the set in which v is considered grows from A to B. Powerful optimization guarantees exist for certain subtypes of submodular functions. If, for example, the function is *monotone submodular*, i.e. $\forall A \subseteq B, f(A) \leq f(B)$, then it can be maximized, under a cardinality constraint, by a greedy algorithm that scales to extremely large data sets, and finds a solution guaranteed to approximate the optimal solution to within a constant factor $1 - 1/e$ (Nemhauser et al., 1978). Submodular functions can be considered the discrete analog of convexity.

3.1 Submodular Document Summarization

In (Lin and Bilmes, 2011) submodular functions were recently applied to extractive document summarization. The problem was formulated as a monotone submodular function that had to be maximized subject to cardinality or knapsack constraints:

$$\text{argmax}_{S \subseteq V} \{f(S) : c(S) \leq K\} \qquad (1)$$

where V is the set of sentences to be summarized, K is the maximum number of sentences to be selected, and $c(\cdot) \geq 0$ is sentence cost. $f(S)$ was instantiated by a form of **saturated coverage**:

$$f_{SC}(S) = \sum_{i \in V} \min\{C_i(S), \alpha C_i(V)\} \qquad (2)$$

where $C_i(S) = \sum_{j \in S} w_{ij}$, and where $w_{ij} \geq 0$ indicates the similarity between sentences i and j — $C_i : 2^V \rightarrow \mathbb{R}$ is itself monotone submodular (modular in fact) and $0 \leq \alpha \leq 1$ is a saturation coefficient. $f_{SC}(S)$ is monotone submodular and therefore has the previously mentioned performance guarantees. The weighting function w was implemented as the cosine similarity between TF-IDF weighted n-gram count vectors for the sentences in the dataset.

3.2 Submodular Speech Summarization

Similar to the procedure described above we can treat the task of subselecting an acoustic data set as an extractive summarization problem. For our *a priori* data selection scenario we would like to extract those training samples that jointly are representative of the total data set. Initial explorations of submodular functions for speech data can be found in (Lin and Bilmes, 2009), where submodular functions were used in combination with a purely acoustic similarity measure (Fisher kernel). In addition Equation 2 the **facility location** function was used:

$$f_{fac}(S) = \sum_{i \in V} \max_{j \in S} w_{ij} \qquad (3)$$

Here our focus is on utilizing methods that move beyond purely acoustic similarity measures and consider kernels derived from discrete representations of the acoustic signal. To this end we first run a tokenizer over the acoustic signal that converts it into a sequence of discrete labels. In our case we use a simple bottom-up monophone recognizer (without higher-level constraints such as a phone language model) that produces phone labels. We then use the hypothesized sequence of phonetic labels to compute two different sentence similarity measures: (a) cosine similarity using TF-IDF weighted phone n-gram counts, and (b) string kernels. We compare their performance to that of the Fisher kernel as a purely acoustic similarity measure.

TF-IDF weighted cosine similarity

The cosine similarity between phone sequences s_i and s_j is computed as

$$\text{sim}_{ij} = \frac{\sum_{w \in s_i} \text{tf}_{w,s_i} \times \text{tf}_{w,s_j} \times \text{idf}_w^2}{\sqrt{\sum_{w \in s_i} \text{tf}_{w,s_i}^2 \, \text{idf}_w^2} \sqrt{\sum_{w \in s_j} \text{tf}_{w,s_j}^2 \, \text{idf}_w^2}} \tag{4}$$

where tf_{w,s_i} is the count of n-gram w in s_i and idf_w is the inverse document count of w (each sentence is a "document"). We use $n = 1, 2, 3$.

String kernel

The particular string kernel we use is a gapped, weighted subsequence kernel of the type described in (Rousu and Shawe-Taylor, 2005). Formally, we define a sentence s as a concatenation of symbols from a finite alphabet Σ (here the inventory of phones) and an embedding function from strings to feature vectors, $\phi : \Sigma^* \rightarrow \mathcal{H}$. The string kernel function $\mathcal{K}(s,t)$ computes the distance between the resulting vectors for two sentences s_i and s_j. The embedding function is defined as

$$\phi_u^k(s) := \sum_{\mathbf{i}:u=s(\mathbf{i})} \lambda^{|i|} \quad u \in \Sigma^k \tag{5}$$

where k is the maximum length of subsequences, $|i|$ is the length of i, and λ is a penalty parameter for each gap encountered in the subsequence. $\mathcal{K}$ is defined as

$$\mathcal{K}(s_i, s_j) = \sum_u \langle \phi_u(s_i), \phi_u(s_j) \rangle w_u \tag{6}$$

where w is a weight dependent on the length of u, $l(u)$. Finally, the kernel score is normalized by $\sqrt{\mathcal{K}(s_i,s_i) \cdot \mathcal{K}(s_j,s_j)}$ to discourage long sentences from being favored.

Fisher kernel

The Fisher kernel is based on the vector of derivatives U_X of the log-likelihood of the acoustic data (X) with respect to the parameters in the phone HMMs $\theta_1, ..., \theta_m$ for m models, having similarity score:

$$\text{sim}_{ij} = (\max_{i',j'} d_{i'j'}) - d_{ij}, \text{ where } d_{ij} = ||U_i' - U_j'||_1,$$

$$U_X^\theta = \nabla_\theta \log P(X|\theta), \text{ and } U_X' = U_X^{\theta_1} \circ U_x^{\theta_2}, ..., \circ U_X^{\theta_m}.$$

4 Data and Systems

We evaluate our approach on subselecting training data from the TIMIT corpus for training a phone recognizer. Although this not a large-scale data task, it is an appropriate proof-of-concept task for rapidly testing different combinations of submodular functions and similarity measures. Our goal is to focus on acoustic modeling only; we thus look at phone recognition performance and do not have to take into account potential interactions with a language model. We also chose a simple acoustic model, a monophone HMM recognizer, rather than a more powerful but computationally complex model in order to ensure quick experimental turnaround time. Note that the goal of this study is not to obtain the highest phone accuracy possible; what is important is the relative performance of the different subset selection methods, especially on small data subsets.

The sizes of the training, development and test data are 4620, 200 and 192 utterances, respectively. Preprocessing was done by extracting 39-dimensional MFCC feature vectors every 10 ms, with a window of 25.6ms. Speaker mean and variance normalization was applied. A 16-component Gaussian mixture monophone HMM system was trained on the full data set to generate parameters for the Fisher kernel and phone sequences for the string kernel and TF-IDF based similarity measures.

Following the selection of subsets (2.5%, 5%, 10%, 20%, 30%, 40%, 50%, 60%, 70% and 80% of the data, measured as percentage of non-silence speech frames), we train a 3-state HMM monophone recognizer for all 48 TIMIT phone classes on the resulting sets and evaluate the performance on the core test set of 192 utterances, collapsing the 48 classes into 39 in line with standard practice (Lee and Hon, 1989). The HMM state output distributions are modeled by diagonal-covariance Gaussian mixtures with the number of Gaussians ranging between 4 and 64, depending on the data size.

As a baseline we perform 100 random draws of the specified subset sizes and average the results.

The second baseline consists of the method in (Wu et al., 2007), where utterances are selected to maximize the entropy of the distribution over phones in the selected subset.

5 Experiments

We tested the three different similarity measures described above in combination with the submodular functions in Equations 2 and 3. The parameters of the gapped string kernel (i.e. the kernel order (k), the gap penalty (λ), and the contiguous substring length l) were optimized on the development set. The best values were $\lambda = 0.1, k = 4, l = 3$. We found that facility location was superior to saturated cover function across the board.

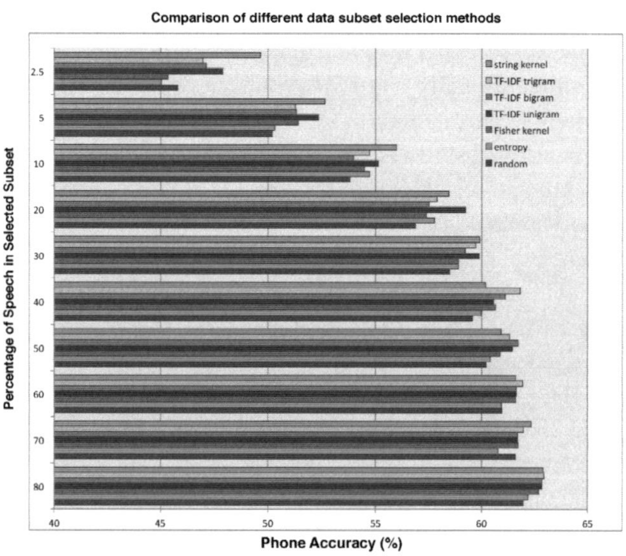

Figure 1: Phone accuracy for different subset sizes; each block of bars lists, from bottom to top: random baseline, entropy baseline, Fisher kernel, TF-IDF (unigram), TF-IDF (bigram), TF-IDF (trigram), string kernel.

Figure 1 shows the performance of the random and entropy-based baselines as well as the performance of the facility location function with different similarity measures. The entropy-based baseline beats the random baseline for most percentage cases but is otherwise the lowest-performing method overall. Note that this baseline uses the true transcriptions in line with (Wu et al., 2007) rather than the hypothesized phone labels output by our recognizer. The low performance and the fact that it is even outperformed by the random baseline in the 2.5% and 70% cases

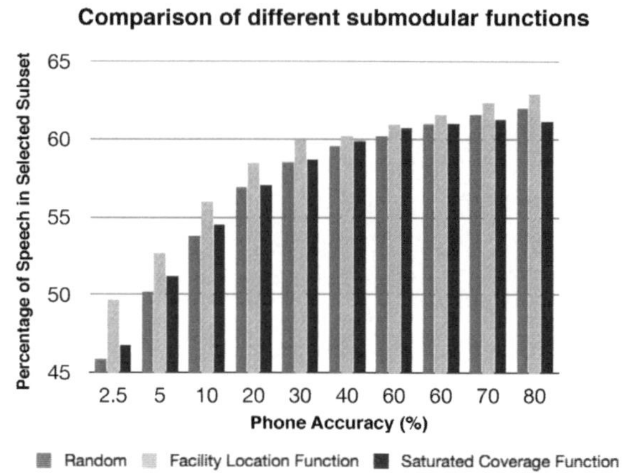

Figure 2: Phone accuracy obtained by random selection, facility location function, and saturated coverage function (string kernel similarity measure).

may be because the selection method encourages highly diverse but not very representative subsets. Furthermore, the entropy-based baseline utilizes a non-submodular objective function with a heuristic greedy search method. No theoretical guarantee of optimality can be made for the subset found by this method.

Among the different similarity measures the Fisher kernel outperforms the baseline methods but has lower performance than the TF-IDF kernel and the string kernel. The best performance is obtained with the string kernel, especially when using small training data sets (2.5%-10%). The submodular selection methods yield significant improvements ($p < 0.05$) over both the random baseline and over the entropy-based method.

We also investigated using different submodular functions, i.e. the facility location function and the saturated coverage function. Figure 2 shows the performance of the facility location (f_{fac}) and saturated coverage (f_{SC}) functions in combination with the string kernel similarity measure. The reason f_{fac} outperforms f_{SC} is that f_{SC} primarily controls for over-coverage of any element not in the subset via the α saturation hyper-parameter. However, it does not ensure that every non-selected element has good representation in the subset. f_{SC} measures the quality of the subset by how well each individual element outside the subset has a surrogate within the subset (via

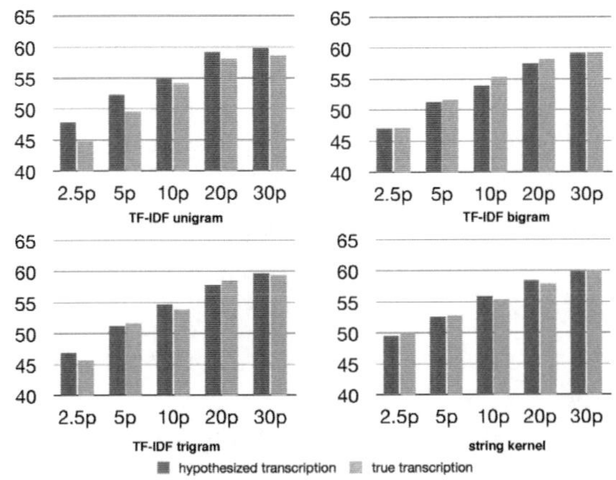

Figure 3: Phone accuracy for true vs. hypothesized phone labels, for string-based similarity measures.

the max function) and hence tends to model complete coverage better, leading to better results.

Finally we examined whether using hypothesized phone sequences vs. the true transcriptions has negative effects. Figure 3 shows that this is not the case: interestingly, the hypothesized labels even result in slightly better results. This may be because the recognized phone sequences are a function of both the underlying phonetic sequences that were spoken and the acoustic signal characteristics, such as the speaker and channel. The true transcriptions, on the other hand, are able to provide information only about phonetic as opposed to acoustic characteristics.

6 Discussion

We have presented a low-resource framework for acoustic data subset selection based on submodular function optimization, which was previously developed for document summarization. Evaluation on a proof-of-concept task has shown that the method is successful at selecting data subsets that outperform subsets selected randomly or by a previously proposed low-resource method. We note that the best selection strategies for the experimental conditions tested here involve similarity measures based on a discrete tokenization of the speech signal rather than direct acoustic similarity measures.

Acknowledgments
This material is based on research sponsored by Intelligence Advanced Research Projects Activity (IARPA) under agreement number FA8650-12-2-7263. The U.S. Government is authorized to reproduce and distribute reprints for Governmental purposes notwithstanding any copyright notation thereon. The views and conclusions contained herein are those of the authors and should not be interpreted as necessarily representing the official policies or endorsements, either expressed or implied, of Intelligence Advanced Research Projects Activity (IARPA) or the U.S. Government.

References

B. Chen, S.H Liu, and F.H. Chu. 2009. Training data selection for improving discriminative training of acoustic models. *Pattern Recognition Letters*, 30:1228–1235.

J. Edmonds, 1970. *Combinatorial Structures and their Applications*, chapter Submodular functions, matroids and certain polyhedra, pages 69–87. Gordon and Breach.

G. Hakkani-Tur, G. Riccardi, and A. Gorin. 2002. Active learning for automatic speech recognition. In *Proc. of ICASSP*, pages 3904–3907.

N. Itoh, T.N. Sainath, D.N. Jiang, J. Zhou, and B. Ramabhadran. 2012. N-best entropy based data selection for acoustic modeling. In *Proceedings of ICASSP*.

Thomas Kemp and Alex Waibel. 1998. Unsupervised training of a speech recognizer using TV broadcasts. In *in Proceedings of the International Conference on Spoken Language Processing (ICSLP-98)*, pages 2207–2210.

A. Krause and C. Guestrin. 2011. Submodularity and its applications in optimized information gathering. *ACM Transactions on Intelligent Systems and Technology*, 2(4).

L. Lamel, J.L. Gauvain, and G. Adda. 2002. Lightly supervised and unsupervised acoustic model training. *Computer, Speech and Language*, 16:116 – 125.

K.F. Lee and H.W. Hon. 1989. Speaker-independent phone recognition using Hidden Markov Models. *IEEE Trans. ASSP*, 37:1641–1648.

Hui Lin and Jeff A. Bilmes. 2009. How to select a good training-data subset for transcription: Submodular active selection for sequences. In *Proc. Annual Conference of the International Speech Communication Association (INTERSPEECH)*, Brighton, UK, September.

H. Lin and J. Bilmes. 2011. A class of submodular functions for document summarization. In *Proceedings of ACL*.

R.K. Moore. 2003. A comparison of the data requirements of automatic speech recognition systems and human listeners. In *Proceedings of Eurospeech*, pages 2581–2584.

G. L. Nemhauser, L. A. Wolsey, and M. L. Fisher. 1978. An analysis of approximations for maximizing submodular functions-I. *Math. Program.*, 14:265–294.

J. Rousu and J. Shawe-Taylor. 2005. Efficien computation of of gapped substring kernels for large alphabets. *Journal of Machine Leaning Research*, 6:13231344.

Y. Wu, R. Zhang, and A. Rudnicky. 2007. Data selection for speech recognition. In *Proceedings of ASRU*.

Semi-Supervised Discriminative Language Modeling with Out-of-Domain Text Data

Arda Çelebi[1] and Murat Saraçlar[2]
[1]Department of Computer Engineering
[2]Department of Electrical and Electronics Engineering
Boğaziçi University, Istanbul, Turkey
{arda.celebi, murat.saraclar}@boun.edu.tr

Abstract

One way to improve the accuracy of automatic speech recognition (ASR) is to use discriminative language modeling (DLM), which enhances discrimination by learning where the ASR hypotheses deviate from the uttered sentences. However, DLM requires large amounts of ASR output to train. Instead, we can simulate the output of an ASR system, in which case the training becomes semi-supervised. The advantage of using simulated hypotheses is that we can generate as many hypotheses as we want provided that we have enough text material. In typical scenarios, transcribed in-domain data is limited but large amounts of out-of-domain (OOD) data is available. In this study, we investigate how semi-supervised training performs with OOD data. We find out that OOD data can yield improvements comparable to in-domain data.

1 Introduction

Discriminative language modeling (DLM) helps ASR systems to discriminate between acoustically similar word sequences in the process of choosing the most accurate transcription of an utterance. DLM characterizes and learns from ASR errors by comparing the reference transcription of the utterance and the candidate hypotheses generated by the ASR system. Although previous studies based on this supervised setting have been successful (Roark et al., 2007; Arısoy et al., 2009; Arısoy et al., 2012; Sak et al., 2012), they require large amounts of transcribed speech data and a well-trained in-domain ASR system, both of which are hard to obtain. To overcome this difficulty, instead of training with the real ASR output, we can use simulated output, in which case the training becomes semi-supervised.

Semi-supervised training for discriminative language modeling has been shown to achieve as good word error rate (WER) reduction as the training done with real ASR output (Sagae et al., 2012; Çelebi et al., 2012). In this approach, first a confusion model (CM) is estimated from supervised data. This CM contains all seen confusions and their occurrence probabilities in hypotheses generated by an ASR system. Then, the CM is used to generate a number of alternative-but-incorrect hypotheses, or simulated hypotheses, for a given sentence. Since the CM characterizes the errors that the ASR system makes, simulated hypotheses carry these characteristics. At the end, the DLM is trained on the reference sentences and their simulated hypotheses. Although being able to simulate the output of the ASR system allows us to generate as much output as we need for the DLM training, there is not always enough text data that is in the same domain as the ASR system. Yet, it is easier to find large amounts of out-of-domain (OOD) text data. In this study, we extend the previous studies where in-domain text data was used for hypothesis simulation. Instead of using limited in-domain data, we experiment with larger amounts of OOD data for hypothesis simulation.

The rest of the paper is organized as follows. In Section 2, we summarize the related work. In Section 3, we explain the methods to simulate the hypotheses and to train the DLM. We give the experimental results in Section 4 before concluding with Section 5.

2 Related Work

The earliest work on hypothesis simulation for DLM was done by Kurata et al. (2009; 2012). They generate the probable n-best lists that an ASR system may output for a hypothetical input utterance given a word sequence. In another study, Tan et al. (2010) propose a system for channel modeling of ASR for simulating the ASR corruption using a phrase-based machine translation system trained between the reference and output phoneme sequences from a phoneme recognizer. Jyothi and Fosler-Lussier (2010) also model the phonetic confusions using a confusion matrix that takes into account word-based phone confusion log likelihoods and distances between the phonetic acoustic models. This model is then used to generate confusable word graphs for training a DLM using the perceptron algorithm. Xu et al. (2009) propose the concept of cohorts and report significant WER improvement for self-supervised DLM. Similarly, Sagae et al. (2012) use phrasal cohorts to simulate ASR output and the perceptron algorithm for training. They observe half of the WER reduction that the fully supervised methods achieve. In another parallel study, Çelebi et al. (2012) work on a Turkish ASR system and consider various confusion models at four different granularities (word, morph, syllable, and phone) and different sampling methods to choose from a large list of simulated hypotheses. They observe that the strategy that matches the word error (WE) distribution of the simulated hypotheses to the WE distribution of the ASR outputs yields the best WER reduction.

While the previous studies use in-domain data sets for simulation, it is quite common to collect large amounts of OOD text data from the web. However, given the nature of web data, some kind of selection mechanism is needed to ensure quality. Bulyko et al. (2007) use perplexity-based filtering to select a relevant subset from vast amounts of web data in order to increase the training data of the generative LM used by the ASR system. There are also studies that use a relative-entropy based selection mechanism in order to match the n-gram distribution of the selected data against the in-domain data by Sethy et al. (2006; 2009). In this study, we consider the perplexity-based selection method for a start.

3 Method

3.1 Sentence Selection from OOD Data

In order to select sentences from the OOD data, we use three methods in addition to random selection. We calculate the perplexity of each sentence with SRILM toolkit, which gives normalized scores with respect to the length of the sentence. Then, we order sentences based on their perplexity scores in increasing order. Perplexity is calculated by a LM trained on in-domain data. After ordering, the top of the list contains those sentences that resemble the in-domain data the most whereas the sentences at the bottom resemble the in-domain data the least. We apply the three methods on this ordered list of sentences. The first two methods, TOP-N and BOTTOM-N, simply get the top and bottom N sentences, respectively. The third method, RC-NxM, picks uniformly separated N clusters of M consecutive sentences, while making sure that top and bottom M sentences are among the selected ones.

3.2 Hypothesis Simulation

Semi-supervised DLM training uses artificially generated hypotheses which mimic the ASR system output. To generate the hypotheses, we follow the three-step finite state transducer based pipeline given in Çelebi et al. (2012) and summarized by the following composition sequence:

$$\mathrm{sample}(N\text{-best}(\mathrm{prune}(\mathcal{W}\circ\mathcal{L}_{\mathcal{W}}\circ\mathcal{CM})\circ{\mathcal{L}_{\mathcal{M}}}^{-1}\circ\mathcal{G}_{\mathcal{M}}))$$

In the first step of the pipeline, we use the confusion model transducer ($\mathcal{CM}$) to generate all possible confusions that the ASR system can make for a given reference sentence $\mathcal{W}$. We consider syllable, morph and word based confusion models, and convert $\mathcal{W}$ to these units using the lexicon $\mathcal{L}_{\mathcal{W}}$. The generated alternatives are pruned for efficiency reasons.

As the output of the first step may include many implausible sequences, the second step converts them to morphs using ${\mathcal{L}_{\mathcal{M}}}^{-1}$ and reweights them with a morph-based language model $\mathcal{G}_{\mathcal{M}}$ to favor the meaningful sequences. For this, we use three approaches. The first approach is to use the LM that is used by the ASR system, called GEN-LM. The second LM called ASR-LM is trained from the output of the ASR system, whereas the third approach is not to use any language model, denoted by NO-LM, in which case we just use the scores coming from the confusion model in the first step. A large list of of N-best ($N = 1000$) hypotheses are produced at this stage.

The third step, called sampling, involves picking a subset of the hypotheses from a larger set with broad variety. This step is done in order to pick samples so as to make sure that they include error variety instead of just high scoring hypotheses. As done by Çelebi et al. (2012), we use four sampling methods to pick 50 hypotheses out of the highest scoring 1000 hypotheses. The simplest of them is Top50, where we select the highest scoring 50 hypotheses. Another method is Uniform Sampling (US) which selects instances from the WER-ordered list in uniform intervals. Third method, called RC5x10, forms 5 clusters separated uniformly, each containing 10 hypotheses. Lastly, ASRdist-50 selects 50 hypotheses in such a way that the WE distribution of selected hypotheses resembles the WE distribution of the real ASR output as much as it can. We accomplish this by filling the WE bins with the hypotheses having required number of WEs.

3.3 DLM Estimation

The training of the DLM involves representing the training data as feature vectors and processing via a discriminative learning algorithm. We represent the simulated N-best lists using unigram features as described by Dikici et al. (2012). As the learning algorithm, we apply the WER-sensitive perceptron algorithm proposed by Sak et al. (2011b), which has been shown to perform better for reranking ASR hypotheses as it minimizes an objective function based on the WER rather than the number of misclassifications.

4 Experiments

4.1 Experimental Setup

We employ DLM on a Turkish broadcast news transcription data set (Arısoy et al., 2009), which comprises disjoint training (105356 sentences), held-out (1947 sentences) and test (1784 sentences) subsets consisting of ASR outputs represented as N-best lists. We use Morfessor (Creutz and Lagus, 2005) to obtain the morph level word segmentations from which we build the LMs. For semi-supervised experiments, we use the first half of the training subset (t_1: 53992 sentences, 965K morphs) to learn the confusion models, and the reference transcriptions of the second half (t_2: 51364 sentences, 935K morphs) to generate in-domain simulated n-best lists to be compared against OOD simulated ones. For this setup, the generative baseline WER and oracle WER on the held-out set are 22.9% and 14.2% and on the test set are 22.4% and 13.9%, respectively. When we use ASR 50-best from t_1 for DLM training, WERs drop to 22.2% and 21.8% on the held-out and the test sets, respectively.

For OOD data, we use a data set of 10.8M sentences (140M morphs) from newspaper articles downloaded from the Internet (Sak et al., 2011a). To calculate the perplexity of OOD sentences for selection, we use a language model trained over the reference transcripts and 50-best lists of t_1 and t_2.

4.2 Results on Out-of-Domain Data

We start our experiments with 500K randomly selected OOD sentences, or RAND-500K. We run the simulation pipeline with four sampling methods, three confusion and three language models, giving 36 experiments in total. We choose among the proposed sampling approaches and confusion models using a rank-based comparison as done by Dikici et al. (2012).

We look at which sampling method performs the best by first dividing experiments into 9 groups, each having 4 results from all sampling methods. Within each group, we rank the sampling methods based on the WER they achieve in increasing order and take the average of assigned ranks. ASRdist-50 gets the lowest average rank of 1.8, while RC5x10, US-50, and TOP-50 come after with the averages of 2.1, 2.4, and 3.4, respectively. This shows that ASRdist-50 gives the best WER reduction on OOD data, which is also true for in-domain data (Çelebi et al., 2012).

Doing the same rank-based comparison for the CMs this time, we observe that the syllable and morph-based models have the same average rank of 1.5, whereas the word-based model has 2.8. However, a closer look reveals that the syllable-based CM paired with NO-LM is an outlier because NO-LM approach allows variety at the output but when the unit of the confusion model is as small as syllables, it produces too much variety that deteriorates the discriminative model. If we don't consider the ranks coming from NO-LM, the average rank of syllable- and morph-based models become 1.1 and 1.8, respectively. Thus, we use syllable-based models over the others for the rest of the experiments.

Knowing that the ASRdist-50 sampling method and syllable-based CM together give the best results for RAND-500K, we experiment with three more sentence selection methods described in Section 3.1. Table 1 shows all the results obtained from four 500K OOD data sets.

OOD Data sets	GEN-LM	ASR-LM	NO-LM
TOP-500K	22.6	22.6	22.6
BOTTOM-500K	22.4	**22.2**	22.5
RAND-500K	**22.2**	22.5	22.6
RC-5x100K	22.4	22.6	22.5

Table 1: WER (%) on held-out set obtained with syllable-based CMs and ASRdist-50 sampling method

According to Table 1, the highest WER reduction is achieved with BOTTOM-500K+ASR-LM and RAND-500K+GEN-LM combinations. While ASR-LM exceeds the other two LMs only in the case of BOTTOM-500K, for other three OOD data sets GEN-LM gives the best results. More interestingly, using OOD sentences resembling in-domain data (or TOP-500K) is outperformed in all cases, especially by BOTTOM-500K. To understand this, we look at the number of morphs in each data set given in Table 2. Even though each OOD data set has 500K sentences, BOTTOM-500K has the highest number of morphs (~6.5M) and TOP-500K had the lowest (~3.5M), while the other two have around 5.5M morphs. We also look at the morph unigram distribution (M) of all four data sets and calculating the KL divergence KL(M || U)[1] of each M to uniform distribution (U). We observe that the unigram morph distribution of the TOP-500K data set is the least uniform with KL distance of 6.6, whereas BOTTOM-500K has KL distance of 2.7 and the other two have KL distances of around 4.3. In other words, this shows that TOP-500K has the lowest content variation, especially when compared to BOTTOM-500K. Note also the slightly high value of KL distance for t_2, which can be attributed to the relatively low number of unique morphs (types).

[1] KL(M || U) = $\sum_i p_i log(\frac{p_i}{1/V}) = log(V) - H(p)$, where $V = 61294$ and $H(p)$ is the entropy of p.

Data set	KLD	Types	Tokens
t_2 (50K)	4.65	22,107	935,137
TOP-500K	6.63	20,689	3,519,012
BOTTOM-500K	2.71	54,458	6,474,385
RAND-500K	4.36	50,422	5,559,763
RC-5x100K	4.35	50,561	5,343,342

Table 2: KL distance, KL(M || U), between uniform distribution (U) and unigram morph distribution (M); number of unique morphs and tokens.

4.3 Out-of-Domain vs In-Domain Data

In this section, we compare the results for in-domain data with the results for four OOD data sets in Table 3. In order to see how the size of OOD data set affects the WER reduction, we start with 50K sentences and increase the size gradually up to 500K. The first row of Table 3 shows the WER obtained with the in-domain data t_2, containing approximately 50K sentences.

Data	50K	100K	200K	500K
t_2	22.4	-	-	-
TOP	22.8	22.7	22.7	22.6
BOTTOM	22.6	22.4	22.3	22.2
RAND	22.5	22.3	22.3	22.2
RC-5	22.5	22.5	22.3	22.4

Table 3: WER (%) on held-out set for in-domain (Syllable+ASR-LM+ASRdist-50) and four OOD data sets in increasing sizes

According to Table 3, even though 50K OOD sentences yield worse results than the same amount of in-domain sentences, as the size of OOD data set increases, the amount of WER reduction increases and surpasses the level obtained by using in-domain data. What is more interesting is that RAND outperforms in-domain data starting from 100K, whereas BOTTOM starts at a higher WER but drops relatively fast, leveling with RAND starting at 200K. Note that the best WER achieved with the simulated data matches the supervised DLM performance using ASR 50-best from t_1, reported in Section 4.1.

Then we go one step further and expand the BOTTOM data set to 1M sentences and we observe WER of 22.1% on the held-out set. This further supports the observation that the more OOD data we use, the lower WER we can achieve.

As a side observation, when we calculate the WER of five 100K-blocks from the RAND-500K set, we find that the standard deviation of WER is 0.06%, which gives and idea about the significance level of the WER differences.

4.4 Merging Real and Simulated Hypotheses

We also evaluate whether merging simulated hypotheses with real ASR hypotheses yields further WER reductions. The result of merging the real hypotheses from t_1 with the simulated ones from in-domain and OOD data are shown in Table 4. The first row shows the WER of the combination with the simulated hypotheses from in-domain data t_2.

Real	Simulated	WER (%)
t_1	t_2 (50K)	22.0
t_1	TOP-500K	22.3
t_1	BOTTOM-500K	22.1
t_1	RAND-500K	22.0
t_1	RC-5x100K	22.1
t_1	BOTTOM-1M	21.9

Table 4: WER (%) on held-out set obtained by merging real and simulated hypotheses

When combined with the real hypotheses from t_1, RAND500K achieves the same level of WER reduction as the simulated hypotheses from t_2 on the heldout set. The results on the test set are also similar. On the test set, the combination of the real hypotheses from t_1 and the simulated hypotheses from t_2 achieve 21.5% WER, whereas the WER is 21.6% when the simulated hypotheses from t_2 are replaced by those from RAND500K. This indicates that enough OOD data can replace the in-domain data and yield similar performance, even in combination with in-domain real data.

Moreover, we further expand the OOD data to 1M for BOTTOM, however even though it reduces the WER on the heldout set, it achieves slightly higher WER on the test set (21.7%).

Next, we combine the in-domain real hypotheses from t_1, simulated hypotheses from t_2 and simulated ones from the OOD data sets. However, compared to the combination of t_1 and t_2, adding extra 500K OOD hypotheses on top of those two gives similar WERs on the held-out set while WERs on the test set increases slightly. From another point of view, adding in-domain simulated hypotheses from t_2 on top of real ones from t_1 and 500K OOD data (rows 2-5 in Table 4) provides slight WER improvement on the held-out set but not on the test set.

5 Conclusion

In this study, we investigate whether we can achieve the same level of WER reduction for semi-supervised DLM with the large amounts of OOD data instead of in-domain data. We observe that ASRdist-50 sampling method and syllable-based CMs yield the best results with the OOD data. Moreover, selecting OOD sentences randomly rather than using perplexity-based methods is enough to achieve the best WER reduction. We also observe that simulated hypotheses from the OOD data is almost as good as in-domain simulated hypotheses or even real ones. As a future work, we will increase the size of the OOD data and examine other methods like relative entropy based OOD selection.

Acknowledgments

This research is supported in part by TÜBİTAK under the project number 109E142.

References

Ebru Arısoy, Doğan Can, Sıddıka Parlak, Haşim Sak, and Murat Saraçlar. 2009. Turkish broadcast news transcription and retrieval. *IEEE Transactions on Audio, Speech, and Language Processing*, 17(5):874–883, July.

Ebru Arısoy, Murat Saraçlar, Brian Roark, and Izhak Shafran. 2012. Discriminative language modeling with linguistic and statistically derived features. *IEEE Transactions on Audio, Speech, and Language Processing*, 20(2):540–550, February.

Ivan Bulyko, Mari Ostendorf, Man-Hung Siu, Tim Ng, Andreas Stolcke, and Özgür Çetin. 2007. Web resources for language modeling in conversational speech recognition. *ACM Transactions on Speech and Language Processing*, 5(1):1–25, December.

Arda Çelebi, Haşim Sak, Erinç Dikici, Murat Saraçlar, Maider Lehr, Emily T. Prud'hommeaux, Puyang Xu, Nathan Glenn, Damianos Karakos, Sanjeev Khudanpur, Brian Roark, Kenji Sagae, Izhak Shafran, Daniel Bikel, Chris Callison-Burch, Yuan Cao, Keith Hall,

Eva Hasler, Philipp Koehn, Adam Lopez, Matt Post, and Darcey Riley. 2012. Semi-supervised discriminative language modeling for Turkish ASR. In *Proc. ICASSP*, pages 5025–5028.

Mathias Creutz and Krista Lagus. 2005. Unsupervised morpheme segmentation and morphology induction from text corpora using morfessor 1.0. Technical report, Helsinki University of Technology. Publications in Computer and Information Science Report A81.

Erinç Dikici, Arda Çelebi, and Murat Saraçlar. 2012. Performance comparison of training algorithms for semi-supervised discriminative language modeling. In *Proc. Interspeech*, Oregon, Portland, September.

Preethi Jyothi and Eric Fosler-Lussier. 2010. Discriminative language modeling using simulated ASR errors. In *Proc. Interspeech*, pages 1049–1052.

Gakuto Kurata, Nobuyasu Itoh, and Masafumi Nishimura. 2009. Acoustically discriminative training for language models. In *Proc. ICASSP*, pages 4717–4720.

Gakuto Kurata, Abhinav Sethy, Bhuvana Ramabhadran, Ariya Rastrow, Nobuyasu Itoh, and Masafumi Nishimura. 2012. Acoustically discriminative language model training with pseudo-hypothesis. *Speech Communication*, 54(2):219–228.

Brian Roark, Murat Saraçlar, and Michael Collins. 2007. Discriminative n-gram language modeling. *Computer Speech and Language*, 21(2):373–392, April.

Kenji Sagae, Maider Lehr, Emily T. Prud'hommeaux, Puyang Xu, Nathan Glenn, Damianos Karakos, Sanjeev Khudanpur, Brian Roark, Murat Saraçlar, Izhak Shafran, Daniel Bikel, Chris Callison-Burch, Yuan Cao, Keith Hall, Eva Hasler, Philipp Koehn, Adam Lopez, Matt Post, and Darcey Riley. 2012. Hallucinated n-best lists for discriminative language modeling. In *Proc. ICASSP*.

Haşim Sak, Tunga Güngör, and Murat Saraçlar. 2011a. Resources for turkish morphological processing. *Language Resources and Evaluation*, 45(2):249–261.

Haşim Sak, Murat Saraçlar, and Tunga Güngör. 2011b. Discriminative reranking of ASR hypotheses with morpholexical and n-best-list features. In *Proc. ASRU*, pages 202–207.

Haşim Sak, Murat Saraçlar, and Tunga Güngör. 2012. Morpholexical and discriminative language models for Turkish automatic speech recognition. *IEEE Transactions on Audio, Speech, and Language Processing*, 20(8):2341–2351, October.

Abhinav Sethy, Panayiotis G. Georgiou, and Shrikanth Narayanan. 2006. Text data acquisition for domain-specific language models. In *EMNLP '06 Proceedings of the 2006 Conference on Empirical Methods in Natural Language Processing*, pages 382–389.

Abhinav Sethy, Panayiotis G. Georgiou, Bhuvana Ramabhadran, and Shrikanth Narayanan. 2009. An iterative relative entropy minimization-based data selection approach for n-gram model adaptation. *IEEE Transactions on Audio, Speech and Language Processing*, 17(1):13–23, January.

Qun Feng Tan, Kartik Audhkhasi, Panayiotis G. Georgiou, Emil Ettelaie, and Shrikanth Narayanan. 2010. Automatic speech recognition system channel modeling. In *Proc. Interspeech*, pages 2442–2445.

Puyang Xu, Damianos Karakos, and Sanjeev Khudanpur. 2009. Self-supervised discriminative training of statistical language models. In *Proc. ASRU*, pages 317–322.

More than meets the eye: Study of Human Cognition in Sense Annotation

Salil Joshi
IBM Research India
Bangalore, India
saljoshi@in.ibm.com

Diptesh Kanojia
Gautam Buddha Technical University
Lucknow, India
dipteshkanojia@gmail.com

Pushpak Bhattacharyya
Computer Science and Engineering Department
Indian Institute of Technology, Bombay
Mumbai, India
pb@cse.iitb.ac.in

Abstract

Word Sense Disambiguation (WSD) approaches have reported good accuracies in recent years. However, these approaches can be classified as weak AI systems. According to the classical definition, a strong AI based WSD system should perform the task of sense disambiguation in the same manner and with similar accuracy as human beings. In order to accomplish this, a detailed understanding of the human techniques employed for sense disambiguation is necessary. Instead of building yet another WSD system that uses contextual evidence for sense disambiguation, as has been done before, we have taken a step back - we have endeavored to discover the cognitive faculties that lie at the very core of the human sense disambiguation technique.

In this paper, we present a hypothesis regarding the cognitive sub-processes involved in the task of WSD. We support our hypothesis using the experiments conducted through the means of an eye-tracking device. We also strive to find the levels of difficulties in annotating various classes of words, with senses. We believe, once such an in-depth analysis is performed, numerous insights can be gained to develop a robust WSD system that conforms to the principle of strong AI.

1 Introduction

Word Sense Disambiguation (WSD) is formally defined as the task of computationally identifying senses of a word *in a context*. The phrase 'in a context' is not defined explicitly in the literature. NLP researchers define it according to their convenience. In our current work, we strive to unravel the appropriate meaning of contextual evidence used for the human annotation process. Chatterjee et al. (2012) showed that the contextual evidence is the predominant parameter for the human sense annotation process. They also state that WSD is successful as a *weak AI* system, and further analysis into human cognitive activities lying at the heart of sense annotation can aid in development of a WSD system built upon the principles of strong AI.

Knowledge based approaches, which can be considered to be closest form of WSD conforming to the principles of strong AI, typically achieve low accuracy. Recent developments in domain-specific knowledge based approaches have reported higher accuracies. A domain-specific approach due to Agirre et al. (2009) beats supervised WSD done in generic domains. Ponzetto and Navigli (2010) present a knowledge based approach which rivals the supervised approaches by using the semantic relations automatically extracted from Wikipedia. They reported approximately 7% gain over the closet supervised approach.

In this paper, we delve deep into the cognitive roles associated with sense disambiguation through the means of an eye-tracking device capturing the gaze patterns of lexicographers, during the annotation process. In-depth discussions with trained lexicographers indicate that there are multiple cognitive sub-processes driving the sense disambiguation task. The eye movement paths available from the screen recordings done during sense annotation conform to this theory.

Khapra et al. (2011) points out that the accuracy of various WSD algorithms is poor on certain

Part-of-speech (POS) categories, particularly, verbs. It is also a general observation for lexicographers involved in sense annotation that there are different levels of difficulties associated with various classes of words. This fact is also reflected in our analysis on sense annotation. The data available after the eye-tracking experiments gave us the fixation times and saccades pertaining to different classes of words. From the analysis of this data we draw conclusive remarks regarding the reasons behind this phenomenon. In our case, we classified words based on their POS categories.

In this paper, we establish that contextual evidence is the prime parameter for the human annotation. Further, we probe into the implication of context used as a clue for sense disambiguation, and the manner of its usage. In this work, we address the following questions:

- *What are the cognitive sub-processes associated with the human sense annotation task?*
- *Which classes of words are more difficult to disambiguate and why?*

By providing relevant answers to these questions we intend to present a comprehensive understanding of sense annotation as a complex cognitive process and the factors involved in it. The remainder of this paper is organized as follows. Section 2 contains related work. In section 3 we present the experimental setup. Section 4 displays the results. We summarize our findings in section 5. Finally, we conclude the paper in section 6 presenting the future work.

2 Related Work

As mentioned earlier, we used the eye-tracking device to ascertain the fact that contextual evidence is the prime parameter for human sense annotation as quoted by Chatterjee et al. (2012) who used different annotation scenarios to compare human and machine annotation processes. An eye movement experiment was conducted by Vainio et al. (2009) to examine effects of local lexical predictability on fixation durations and fixation locations during sentence reading. Their study indicates that local lexical predictability influences in decisions but not where the initial fixation lands in a word. In another work based on word grouping hypothesis and eye movements during reading by Drieghe et al. (2008), the distribution of landing positions and durations of first fixations in a region containing a noun preceded by either an article or a high-frequency three-letter word were compared.

Recently, some work is done on the study of sense annotation. A study of sense annotations done on 10 polysemous words was conducted by Passonneau et al. (2010). They opined that the word meanings, contexts of use, and individual differences among annotators gives rise to inter-annotation variations. De Melo et al. (2012) present a study with a focus on MASC (Manually-Annotated SubCorpus) project, involving annotations done using WordNet sense identifiers as well as FrameNet lexical units.

In our current work we use eye-tracking as a tool to make findings regarding the cognitive processes connected to the human sense disambiguation procedure, and to gain a better understanding of "contextual evidence" which is of paramount importance for human annotation. Unfortunately, our work seems to be a first of its kind, and to the best of our knowledge we do not know of any such work done before in the literature.

3 Experimental Setup

We used a generic domain (*viz.*, News) corpus in Hindi language for experimental purposes. To identify the levels of difficulties associated with human annotation, across various POS categories, we conducted experiments on around 2000 words (including function words and stop words). The analysis was done only for open class words. The statistics pertaining to the our experiment are illustrated in table 1. For statistical significance of our experiments, we collected the data with the help of 3 skilled lexicographers and 3 unskilled lexicographers.

POS	Noun	Verb	Adjective	Adverb
#(senses)	2.423	3.814	2.602	3.723
#(tokens)	452	206	96	177

Table 1: Number of words (tokens) and average degree of corpus polysemy (senses) of words per POS category (taken from Hindi News domain) used for experiments

For our experiments we used a Sense Annotation

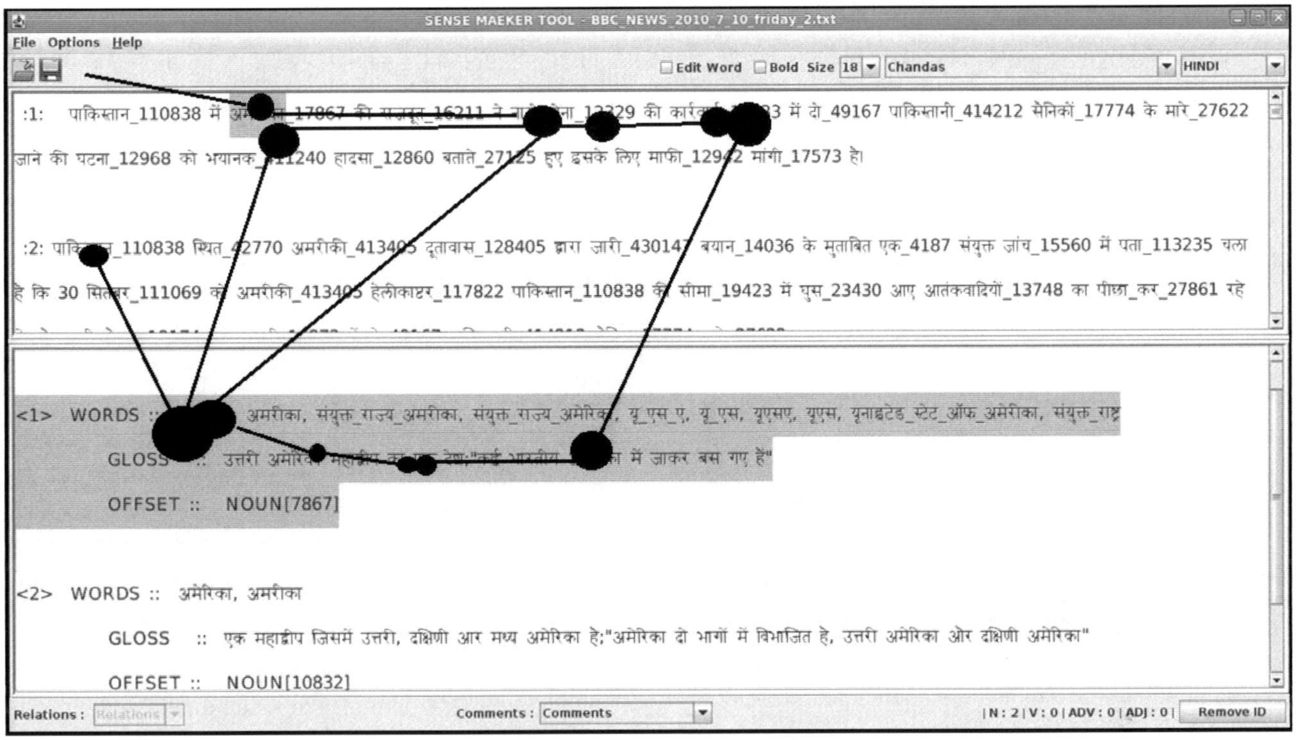

Figure 1: Sense marker tool showing an example Hindi sentence in the *Context Window* and the wordnet synsets of the highlighted word in the *Synset Window* with the black dots and lines indicating the scan path

Tool, designed at IIT Bombay and an eye-tracking device. The details of the tools and their purposes are explained below:

3.1 The Sense Marker Tool

A word may have a number of senses, and the task of identifying and marking which particular sense has been used in the given context, is known as *sense marking*.

The Sense Marker tool[1] is a Graphical User Interface based tool developed using Java, which facilitates the task of manual sense marking. This tool displays the senses of the word as available in the Marathi, Hindi and Princeton (English) WordNets and allows the user to select the correct sense of the word from the candidate senses.

3.2 Eye-Tracking device

An eye tracker is a device for measuring eye positions and eye movement. A *saccade* denotes movement to another position. The resulting series of fixations and saccades is called a *scan path*. Figure 1 shows a sample scan path. In our experiments, we have used an eye tracking device manufactured by SensoMotoric Instruments[2]. We recorded saccades, fixations, length of each fixation and scan paths on the stimulus monitor during the annotation process. A remote eye-tracking device (RED) measures gaze hotspots on a stimulus monitor.

4 Results

In our experiments, each lexicographer performed sense annotation on the stimulus monitor of the eye tracking device. Fixation times, saccades and scan paths were recorded during the sense annotation process. We analyzed this data and the corresponding observations are enumerated below.

Figure 2 shows the annotation time taken by different lexicographers across POS categories. It can be observed that the time taken for disambiguating the verbs is significantly higher than the remaining POS

[1] http://www.cse.iitb.ac.in/šalilj/resources /SenseMarker/SenseMarkerTool.zip

[2] http://www.smivision.com/

Word	Degree of polysemy	Unskilled Lexicographer (Seconds)				Skilled Lexicographer (Seconds)			
		T_{hypo}	T_{clue}	T_{gloss}	T_{total}	T_{hypo}	T_{clue}	T_{gloss}	T_{total}
लाना (laanaa - to bring)	4	0.63	0.80	5.20	6.63	0.31	1.20	1.82	3.30
करना (karanaa - to do)	22	0.90	1.42	2.20	4.53	0.50	0.64	1.14	2.24
जताना (jataanaa - to express)	4	0.70	2.45	5.93	9.09	0.25	0.39	0.62	1.19

Table 2: Comparison of time taken across different cognitive stages of sense annotation by lexicographers for verbs

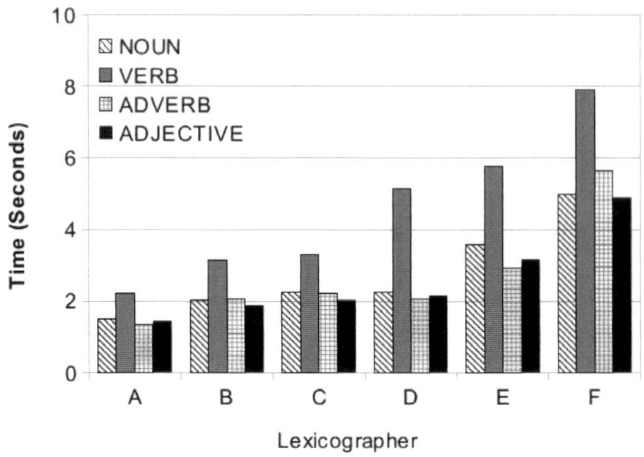

Figure 2: Histogram showing time taken (in seconds) by each lexicographer across POS categories for sense annotation

categories. This behavior can be consistently seen in the timings recorded for all the six lexicographers.

Table 2 presents the comparison of time taken across different cognitive stages of sense annotation by lexicographers for some of the most frequently occurring verbs.

To know if the results gathered from all the lexicographers are consistent, we present the correlation between each pair of lexicographers in table 3. The table also shows the value of the t-test statistic generated for each pair of lexicographers.

5 Discussion

The data obtained from the eye-tracking device and corresponding analysis of the fixation times, saccades and scan paths of the lexicographers' eyes reveal that sense annotation is a complex cognitive process. From the videos of the scan paths obtained from the eye-tracking device and from detailed discussion with lexicographers it can be inferred that this cognitive process can be broken down into 3 stages:

1. When a lexicographer sees a word, he/she makes a hypothesis about the domain and consequently about the correct sense of the word, mentally. In cases of highly polysemous words, the hypothesis may narrow down to multiple senses. We denote the time required for this phase as T_{hypo}.

2. Next the lexicographer searches for clues to support this hypothesis and in some cases to eliminate false hypotheses, when the word is polysemous. These clues are available in the form of neighboring words around the target word. We denote the time required for this activity as T_{clue}.

3. The clue words aid the lexicographer to decide which one of the initial hypotheses was true. To narrow down the candidate synsets, the lexicographers use synonyms of the words in a synset to check if the sentence retains its meaning.

From the scan paths and fixation times obtained from the eye-tracking experiment, it is evident that stages 1, 2 and 3 are chronological stages in the human cognitive process associated with sense disambiguation. In cases of highly polysemous words and instances where senses are fine-grained, stages 2 and 3 get interleaved. It is also clear that each stage takes up separate proportions of the sense disambiguation time for humans. Hence time taken to disambiguate a word using the Sense Marker Tool (as explained in Section 3.1) can be factored as follows:

$$T_{total} = T_{hypo} + T_{clue} + T_{gloss}$$

Where:
T_{total} = Total time for sense disambiguation

	Correlation value					T-test statistic				
Lexicographer	**B**	**C**	**D**	**E**	**F**	**B**	**C**	**D**	**E**	**F**
A	0.933	0.976	0.996	0.996	0.769	0.007	0.123	0.185	0.036	0.006
B		0.987	0.960	0.915	0.945		0.009	0.028	0.084	0.026
C			0.989	0.968	0.879			0.483	0.088	0.067
D				0.988	0.820				0.367	0.709
E					0.734					0.418

Table 3: Pairwise correlation between annotation time taken by lexicographers

T_{hypo} = Time for hypothesis building
T_{clue} = Clue word searching time
T_{gloss} = Gloss Matching time and winner sense selection time.

The results in table 2 reveal the different ratios of time invested during each of the above stages. T_{hypo} takes the minimum amount of time among the different sub-processes. $T_{gloss} > T_{clue}$ in all cases.

- *For unskilled lexicographers*: $T_{gloss} >> T_{clue}$ because of errors in the initial hypothesis.
- *For skilled lexicographers*: $T_{gloss} \sim T_{clue}$, as they can identify the POS category of the word and their hypothesis thus formed is pruned. Hence during selection of the winner sense, they do not browse through other POS categories, which unskilled lexicographers do.

The results shown in figure 2 reveal that verbs take the maximum disambiguation time. In fact the average time taken by verbs is around 75% more than the time taken by other POS categories. This supports the fact that verbs are the most difficult to disambiguate.

The analysis of the scan paths and fixation times available from the eye-tracking experiments in case of verbs show that the T_{gloss} covers around 66% of T_{total}, as shown in table 2. This means that the lexicographer takes more time in selecting a winner sense from the list of wordnet senses. This happens chiefly because of following reasons:

1. Higher degree of polysemy of verbs compared to other POS categories (as shown in tables 1 and 2).
2. In several cases the senses are fine-grained.
3. Sometimes the hypothesis of the lexicographers may not match any of the wordnet senses. The lexicographer then selects the wordnet sense closest to their hypothesis.

Adverbs and adjectives show higher degree of polysemy than nouns (as shown in table 1), but take similar disambiguation time as nouns (as shown in figure 2). In case of adverbs and adjectives, the lexicographer is helped by their position around a verb or noun respectively. So, T_{clue} only involves searching for the nearby verbs or nouns, as the case may be, hence reducing total disambiguation time T_{total}.

6 Conclusion and Future Work

In this paper we examined the cognitive process that enables the human sense disambiguation task. We have also laid down our findings regarding the varying levels of difficulty in sense annotation across different POS categories. These experiments are just a stepping stone for going deeper into finding the meaning and manner of usage of contextual evidence which is fundamental to the human sense annotation process.

In the future we aim to perform an in-depth analysis of clue words that aid humans in sense disambiguation. The distance of clue words from the target word and their and pattern of occurrence could give us significant insights into building a 'Discrimination Net'.

References

E. Agirre, O.L. De Lacalle, A. Soroa, and I. Fakultatea. 2009. Knowledge-based wsd on specific domains: performing better than generic supervised wsd. *Proceedigns of IJCAI*, pages 1501–1506.

Arindam Chatterjee, Salil Joshi, Pushpak Bhattacharyya, Diptesh Kanojia, and Akhlesh Meena. 2012. A study of the sense annotation process: Man v/s machine. In *Proceedings of 6th International Conference on Global Wordnets*, January.

G. De Melo, C.F. Baker, N. Ide, R.J. Passonneau, and C. Fellbaum. 2012. Empirical comparisons of masc word sense annotations. In *Proceedings of the 8th international conference on language resources and evaluation (LREC12). Istanbul: European Language Resources Association (ELRA).*

D. Drieghe, A. Pollatsek, A. Staub, and K. Rayner. 2008. The word grouping hypothesis and eye movements during reading. *Journal of Experimental Psychology: Learning, Memory, and Cognition*, 34(6):1552.

Mitesh M. Khapra, Salil Joshi, and Pushpak Bhattacharyya. 2011. It takes two to tango: A bilingual unsupervised approach for estimating sense distributions using expectation maximization. In *Proceedings of 5th International Joint Conference on Natural Language Processing*, pages 695–704, Chiang Mai, Thailand, November. Asian Federation of Natural Language Processing.

R.J. Passonneau, A. Salleb-Aouissi, V. Bhardwaj, and N. Ide. 2010. Word sense annotation of polysemous words by multiple annotators. *Proceedings of LREC-7, Valleta, Malta.*

S.P. Ponzetto and R. Navigli. 2010. Knowledge-rich word sense disambiguation rivaling supervised systems. In *Proceedings of the 48th annual meeting of the association for computational linguistics*, pages 1522–1531. Association for Computational Linguistics.

S. Vainio, J. Hyönä, and A. Pajunen. 2009. Lexical predictability exerts robust effects on fixation duration, but not on initial landing position during reading. *Experimental psychology*, 56(1):66.

Improving Lexical Semantics for Sentential Semantics: Modeling Selectional Preference and Similar Words in a Latent Variable Model

Weiwei Guo
Department of Computer Science
Columbia University
weiwei@cs.columbia.edu

Mona Diab
Department of Computer Science
George Washington University
mtdiab@gwu.edu

Abstract

Sentence Similarity [SS] computes a similarity score between two sentences. The SS task differs from document level semantics tasks in that it features the sparsity of words in a data unit, i.e. a sentence. Accordingly it is crucial to robustly model each word in a sentence to capture the complete semantic picture of the sentence. In this paper, we hypothesize that by better modeling lexical semantics we can obtain better sentential semantics. We incorporate both corpus-based (selectional preference information) and knowledge-based (similar words extracted in a dictionary) lexical semantics into a latent variable model. The experiments show state-of-the-art performance among unsupervised systems on two SS datasets.

1 Introduction

Sentence Similarity [SS] is emerging as a crucial step in many NLP tasks that focus on sentence level semantics such as word sense disambiguation (Guo and Diab, 2010; Guo and Diab, 2012a), summarization (Zhou et al., 2006), text coherence (Lapata and Barzilay, 2005), tweet clustering (Sankaranarayanan et al., 2009; Jin et al., 2011), etc. SS operates in a very small context, on average 11 words per sentence in Semeval-2012 dataset (Agirre et al., 2012), resulting in inadequate evidence to generalize to robust sentential semantics.

Weighted Textual Matrix Factorization [WTMF] (Guo and Diab, 2012b) is a latent variable model that outperforms Latent Semantic Analysis [LSA] (Deerwester et al., 1990) and Latent Dirichelet Allocation [LDA] (Blei et al., 2003) models by a large margin in the SS task, yielding state-of-the-art performance on the LI06 (Li et al., 2006) SS dataset. However, all of these models make harsh simplifying assumptions on how a token is generated: (1) in LSA/WTMF, a token is generated by the inner product of the word latent vector and the document latent vector; (2) in LDA, all the tokens in a document are sampled from the same document level topic distribution. Under this framework, they ignore rich linguistic phenomena such as inter-word dependency, semantic scope of words, etc. This is a result of simply using document IDs as features to represent a word.

Modeling quality lexical semantics in latent variable models does not draw enough attention in the community, since people usually apply dimension reduction techniques for documents, which have abundant words for extracting the document level semantics. However, in the SS setting, it is crucial to make good use of each word, given the limited number of words in a sentence. We believe a reasonable word generation story will avoid introducing noise in sentential semantics, encouraging robust lexical semantics which can further boost the sentential semantics. In this paper, we explicitly encode lexical semantics, both corpus-based and knowledge-based information, in the WTMF model, by which we are able to achieve even better results in SS task.

The additional corpus-based information we exploit is selectional preference semantics (Resnik, 1997), a feature already existing in the data yet ignored by most latent variable models. Selectional preference focuses on the admissible arguments for a word, thus capturing more nuanced semantics than the sentence IDs (when applied to a corpus of sentences as opposed to documents). Consider the following example:

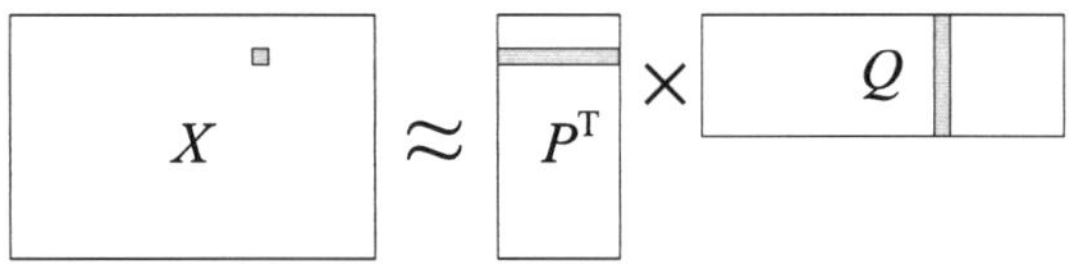

Figure 1: matrix factorization

Many analysts say the global Brent crude oil benchmark price, currently around $111 a barrel ...

In WTMF/LSA/LDA, a word will receive semantics from all the other words in a sentence, hence, the word *oil*, in the above example, will be assigned the incorrect *finance* topic that reflects the sentence level semantics. Moreover, the problem worsens for adjectives, adverbs and verbs, which have a much narrower semantic scope than the whole sentence. For example, the verb *say* should only be associated with *analyst* (only receiving semantics from *analyst*), as it is not related to other words in the sentence. In contrast, *oil*, according to its selectional preference, should be associated with *crude* indicating the *resource* topic. We believe modeling selectional preference capturing local evidence completes the semantic picture for words, hence further rendering better sentential semantics. To our best knowledge, this is the first work to model selectional preference for sentence/document semantics.

We also integrate knowledge-based semantics in the WTMF framework. Knowledge-based semantics, a human-annotated clean resource, is an important complement to corpus-based noisy co-occurrence information. We extract similar word pairs from Wordnet (Fellbaum, 1998). Leveraging these pairs, an infrequent word such as *purchase* can exploit robust latent vectors from its synonyms such as *buy*. Similar words pairs can be seamlessly modeled in WTMF, since in the matrix factorization framework a latent vector profile is explicitly created for each word, while in LDA all the data structures are designed for documents/sentences. We construct a graph to connect words according to the extracted similar word pairs, to encourage similar words to share similar latent vector profiles. We will refer to our proposed novel model as WTMF+PK.

2 Weighted Textual Matrix Factorization

Our previous work (Guo and Diab, 2012b) models the sentences in the weighted matrix factorization framework (Figure 1). The corpus is stored in an $M \times N$ matrix X, with each cell containing the TF-IDF values of words. The rows of X are M distinct words and columns are N sentences. As in Figure 1, X is approximated by the product of a $K \times M$ matrix P and a $K \times N$ matrix Q. Accordingly, each sentence s_j is represented by a K dimensional latent vector $Q_{\cdot,j}$. Similarly a word w_i is generalized by $P_{\cdot,i}$. P and Q is optimized by minimize the objective function:

$$\sum_i \sum_j W_{ij} \left(P_{\cdot,i} \cdot Q_{\cdot,j} - X_{ij}\right)^2 + \lambda ||P||_2^2 + \lambda ||Q||_2^2 \qquad (1)$$
$$W_{i,j} = \begin{cases} 1, & \text{if } X_{ij} \neq 0 \\ w_m, & \text{if } X_{ij} = 0 \end{cases}$$

where λ is a regularization term. Missing tokens are modeled by assigning a different weight w_m for each 0 cell in the matrix X. We can see the inner product of a word vector $P_{\cdot,i}$ and a sentence vector $Q_{\cdot,j}$ is used to approximate the cell X_{ij}.

The graphical model of WTMF is illustrated in Figure 2a. A w_i/s_j node is a latent vector $P_{\cdot,i}/Q_{\cdot,j}$, corresponding to a word/sentence, respectively. A shaded node is a non-zero cell in X, representing an observed token in a sentence. For simplicity, the missing tokens and weights are not shown in the graph.

3 Corpus-based Semantics: Selectional Preference

In this paper, we focus on selectional preference that reflects the association of two words: if two words form a bigram, then the two words should share similar latent dimensions. In the previous example, *crude* and *oil* form a bigram, and they share the *resource* topic. In our framework, this is implemented by adding extra columns in X, so that each additional column corresponds to a bigram, treating each bigram as a *pseudo-sentence* for the two words. The graphical model is illustrated in Figure 2b. Therefore, *oil* will receive more *resource* topic from *crude* through the bigram *crude oil*, instead of only *finance* topic from the sentence as a whole.

Each non-zero cell in the new columns of X, i.e. an observed token in a bigram (pseudo-sentence), is given a different weight:

$$W_{i,j} = \begin{cases} 1, & \text{if } X_{ij} \neq 0 \text{ and j is a sentence index} \\ \gamma \cdot freq(j), & \text{if } X_{ij} \neq 0 \text{ and j is a bigram index} \\ w_m, & \text{if } X_{ij} = 0 \end{cases}$$

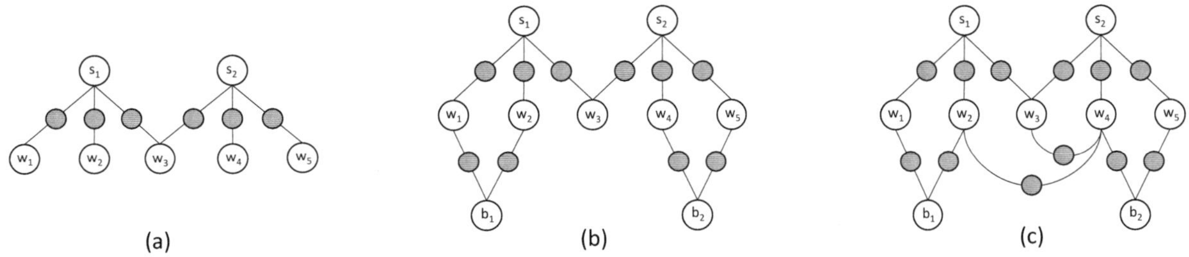

Figure 2: WTMF+PK model (WTMF + corpus-based Selectional [P]references semantics + [K]nowledge-based semantics): a *w*/*s*/*b* node represents a word/sentence/bigram, respectively

$freq(j)$ denotes the frequency of bigram j appearing in the corpus, hence the strength of association is differentiated such that higher weights are assigned on the more probable bigrams. The coefficient γ is the importance of selectional preference. A larger γ indicates that we trust the selectional preference over the global sentential semantics.

4 Knowledge-based Semantics: Similar Word Pairs

We first extract synonym pairs from WordNet, which are words associated with the same sense, synset. We further expand the set by exploiting the relations defined in WordNet. For the extracted words, we consider the first sense of each word, and if it is connected to other senses by any of the WordNet defined relations (*hypernym, similar words*, etc.), then we treat the words associated with the other senses as similar words. In total, we are able to discover $80K$ pairs of similar words for the $46K$ distinct words in our corpus.

Given a pair of similar words w_{i_1}/w_{i_2}, we want the two corresponding latent vectors $P_{\cdot,i_1}/P_{\cdot,i_2}$ to be as close as possible, namely the cosine similarity to be close to 1. Accordingly, a term is added in equation 1 for each similar word pair w_{i_1}/w_{i_2}:

$$\delta \cdot (P_{\cdot,i_1} \cdot P_{\cdot,i_2} - |P_{\cdot,i_1}||P_{\cdot,i_2}|)^2 \qquad (2)$$

$|P_{\cdot,i}|$ denotes the length of the vector $P_{\cdot,i}$. The coefficient δ, analogous to γ, denotes the importance of the knowledge-based evidence. The Figure 2c shows the final WTMF+PK model.

5 Inference

In (Guo and Diab, 2012b) we use Alternating Least Square [ALS] for inference, which is to set the derivative of equation 1 for P/Q to 0 and iteratively compute P/Q by fixing the other matrix (Srebro and Jaakkola, 2003). However, it is no longer applicable with the new term (equation 2) involving the length of word vectors $|P_{\cdot,i}|$. Therefore we approximate the objective function by treating the vector length $|P_{\cdot,i}|$ as fixed values during the ALS iterations:

$$\begin{aligned} Q_{\cdot,j} &= \left(P\tilde{W}^{(j)}P^\top + \lambda I\right)^{-1} P\tilde{W}^{(j)}X_{\cdot,j} \\ P_{\cdot,i} &= \left(Q\tilde{W}^{(i)}Q^\top + \lambda I + \delta P_{\cdot,s(i)}P_{\cdot,s(i)}^\top\right)^{-1} \\ &\quad \left(Q\tilde{W}^{(i)}X_{i,\cdot}^\top + \delta L_i P_{\cdot,s(i)} L_{s(i)}\right) \end{aligned} \qquad (3)$$

where $P_{\cdot,s(i)}$ are the latent vectors of similar words of word i; the length of these vectors in the current iteration are stored in $L_{s(i)}$ (similarly L_i is the current length of $P_{\cdot,i}$) (*cf.* (Steck, 2010; Guo and Diab, 2012b) for optimization details).

6 Experimental Setting

We build the model WTMF+PK on the same **corpora** as used in our previous work (Guo and Diab, 2012b), comprising the following: Brown corpus (each sentence is treated as a document), sense definitions from Wiktionary and Wordnet (only definitions without target words and usage examples). We follow the preprocessing steps in (Guo and Diab, 2012c): tokenization, pos-tagging, lemmatization and further merge lemmas. The corpus is used for building matrix X.

The **evaluation datasets** are LI06 dataset and Semeval-2012 STS [STS12] (Agirre et al., 2012) dataset. LI06 consists of 30 sentence pairs (dictionary definitions). For STS12,[1] the training data (2000 pairs) are used as the tuning set for setting the

[1] A detailed description of the data sets is provided in (Agirre et al., 2012).

parameters of our models. This data comprises msr-par, msr-vid, smt-eur. Once the models are tuned, we evaluate them on the STS12 test data that comprises 3150 sentence pairs from msr-par, msr-vid, smt-eur, smt-news, On-WN. It is worth noting that smt-news and On-WN are not part of the tuning data. We use cosine similarity to measure the similarity scores between two sentences. Pearson correlation between the system's answer and gold standard similarity scores is used as the evaluation metric.

We include three **baselines** LSA, LDA and WTMF using the setting described in (Guo and Diab, 2012b). We run Gibbs Sampling based LDA for 2000 iterations and average the model over the last 10 iterations. For WTMF, we run 20 iterations and fix the missing words weight at $w_m = 0.01$ with a regularization coefficient set at $\lambda = 20$, which is the best condition found in (Guo and Diab, 2012b).

7 Experiments

Table 1 summarizes the results at dimension $K = 100$ (the dimension of latent vectors). To remove randomness, each reported number is the averaged results of 10 runs. Based on the STS tuning set, we experiment with different values for the selectional preference weight ($\gamma = \{0, 1, 2\}$), and likewise for the similar word pairs weight varying the δ value as follows $\delta = \{0, 0.1, 0.3, 0.5, 0.7\}$. The performance on STS12 tuning and test dataset as well as on the LI06 dataset are illustrated in Figures 3a, 3b and 3d. The parameters of model 6 in Table 1 ($\gamma = 2, \delta = 0.3$) are the chosen values based on tuning set performance.

7.1 Evaluation on the STS12 datasets

Table 1 shows WTMF is already a very strong baseline: it outperforms LSA and LDA by a large margin. Same as in (Guo and Diab, 2012b), LSA performance degrades dramatically when trained on a corpus of sentence sized documents, yielding results worse than the surface words baseline 31% (Agirre et al., 2012). Using corpus-based selectional preference semantics **alone** (model 4 WTMF+P in Table 1) boosts the performance of WTMF by $+1.17\%$ on the test set, while using knowledge-based semantics **alone** (model 5 WTMF+K) improves the over the WTMF results by an absolute $+2.31\%$. Combining them (model 6 WTMF+PK) yields the best results, with an absolute increase of $+3.39\%$, which suggests that the two sources of semantic evidence are useful, but more importantly, they are complementary for each other.

Table 1 also presents the performance on each individual dataset. The gain on each individual source is not as much as the overall gain, which suggests part of the overall gain comes from the correct ranking of intra-source pairs. Note that WTMF+PK improves all individual datasets except smt-eur. This may be caused by too many overlapping words in the sentence pairs in smt-eur, while our approach focuses on extracting similarity between different words.

Observing the performance using different values of weights in figure 3a and 3b, we can conclude that the selectional preference and similar word pairs yield very promising results. The trends hold in different parameter conditions with a consistent improvement. Figure 3c illustrates the impact of dimension $K = \{50, 75, 100, 125, 150\}$ on WTMF and WTMF+PK. Generally a larger K leads to a higher Pearson correlation, but the improvement is tiny when $K \geq 100$ (0.1% increase).

Compared to all the unsupervised systems that participated in Semeval STS 2012 task, WTMF+PK yields state-of-the-art performance (70.70%).[2] In (Guo and Diab, 2012c) we also apply WTMF ($K = 100$) on STS12, achieving a correlation of 69.5%. However, additional data is incorporated in the training corpora: (1) STS12 tuning set; (2) for WordNet and Wiktionary data, the target words are also included in the definitions (hence synonym pairs were used); (3) the usage examples of target words were also appended to the definitions.[3] While trained with this experimental setting, our model WTMF+PK ($\gamma = 2, \delta = 0.3, K = 100$) is able to reach an even higher correlation of 72.0%.

[2]WTMF+PK is an unsupervised system, since the gold standard similarly scores are never used in the objective function. Moreover, even without a tuning set, a non-zero value of γ or δ will always improve the baseline WTMF according to figure 3a and 3b.

[3]We do not adopt this corpora schema, since some definitions are test set sentences in On-WN, thereby adding target words and usage examples introduces additional information for some of the test set sentences

Models	Parameters	STS12 tune	STS12 test	msr-par	msr-vid	On-WN	smt-eur	smt-news	LI06
1. LSA	-	21.67%	24.41%	27.18%	9.91%	50.93%	27.86%	19.73%	63.77%
2. LDA	$\alpha = 0.05, \beta = 0.05$	71.10%	63.18%	29.15%	76.73%	62.81%	47.81%	27.2%	83.71%
3. WTMF	-	71.41%	67.31%	44.00%	82.59%	70.78%	**50.89%**	37.77%	89.81%
4. WTMF+P	$\gamma = 2, \delta = 0$	72.94%	68.48%	46.21%	83.29%	70.61%	49.54%	39.50%	90.16%
5. WTMF+K	$\gamma = 0, \delta = 0.3$	73.84%	69.64%	45.04%	83.04%	70.40%	49.88%	**41.66%**	90.11%
6. WTMF+PK	$\gamma = 2, \delta = 0.3$	**75.29%**	**70.70%**	**46.77%**	**83.90%**	**71.03%**	49.77%	40.48%	**90.17%**

Table 1: Evaluation Results using Pearson Correlation on STS12 and LI06

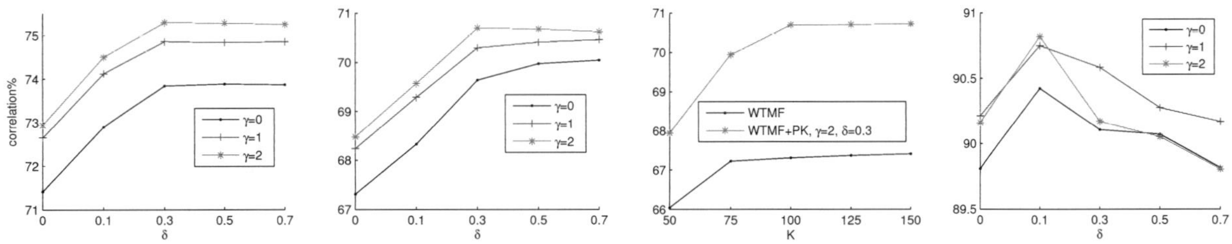

(a) STS12 tuning set ($K = 100$) (b) STS12 test set ($K = 100$) (c) STS12 test set (d) LI06 ($K = 100$)

Figure 3: Pearson correlation at different parameter settings

7.2 Evaluation on the LI06 dataset

Figure 3d presents the results obtained on the LI06 data set at different weight values for the corpus-based selectional preference semantics γ and for the knowledge-based semantics δ. Our previous experiments (Guo and Diab, 2012b) show that WTMF is the state-of-the-art model on LI06. With lexical semantics explicitly modeled, WTMF+PK yields better results than WTMF (see Table 1). It should be noted that LI06 prefers a smaller similar word pair weight (a $\delta = 0.1$ yields the best performance around of 90.75%), yet in almost all conditions WTMF+PK outperforms WTMF as shown in Figure 3d.

8 Related Work

SS has progressed immensely in recent years, especially with the establishment of the Semantic Textual Similarity task in SEMEVAL 2012. Early work in SS focused on word pair similarity in the high dimensional space (Li et al., 2006; Liu et al., 2007; Islam and Inkpen, 2008; Tsatsaronis et al., 2010; Ho et al., 2010), where co-occurrence information was not efficiently exploited. Researchers (O'Shea et al., 2008) find LSA does not yield good performance. In (Guo and Diab, 2012b; Guo and Diab, 2012c), we show the superiority of the latent space approach in WTMF. In this paper, we improve the WTMF model and achieve state-of-the-art Pearson correlation on two standard SS datasets.

There are latent variable models designed for lexical semantics, such as word senses (Boyd-Graber et al., 2007; Guo and Diab, 2011), function words (Griffiths et al., 2005), selectional preference (Ritter et al., 2010), synonyms and antonyms (Yih et al., 2012), etc. However little improvement is shown on document/sentence level semantics: (Ritter et al., 2010) and (Yih et al., 2012) focus on selectional preference and antonym identification, respectively; in (Griffiths et al., 2005) the LDA performance degrades in the text categorization task including the modeling of function words. Rather, we concentrate on nuanced lexical semantics phenomena that could benefit sentential semantics.

9 Conclusion

We incorporate corpus-based (selectional preference) and knowledge-based (similar word pairs) lexical semantics into a latent variable model. Our system yields state-of-the-art unsupervised performance on two most popular and standard SS datasets.

10 Acknowledgment

This work is supported by the IARPA SCIL program.

References

Eneko Agirre, Daniel Cer, Mona Diab, and Aitor Gonzalez-Agirre. 2012. Semeval-2012 task 6: A pilot on semantic textual similarity. In *First Joint Conference on Lexical and Computational Semantics (*SEM)*.

David M. Blei, Andrew Y. Ng, and Michael I. Jordan. 2003. Latent dirichlet allocation. *Journal of Machine Learning Research*, 3.

Jordan Boyd-Graber, David Blei, and Xiaojin Zhu. 2007. A topic model for word sense disambiguation. In *Proceedings of the 2007 Joint Conference on Empirical Methods in Natural Language Processing and Computational Natural Language Learning*.

Scott Deerwester, Susan T Dumais, George W Furnas, Thomas K Landauer, and Richard Harshman. 1990. Indexing by latent semantic analysis. *Journal of the American Society for Information Science*.

Christiane Fellbaum. 1998. *WordNet: An Electronic Lexical Database*. MIT Press.

Thomas L. Griffiths, Mark Steyvers, David M. Blei, and Joshua B. Tenenbaum. 2005. Integrating topics and syntax. In *Advances in Neural Information Processing Systems*.

Weiwei Guo and Mona Diab. 2010. Combining orthogonal monolingual and multilingual sources of evidence for all words wsd. In *Proceedings of the 48th Annual Meeting of the Association for Computational Linguistics*.

Weiwei Guo and Mona Diab. 2011. Semantic topic models: Combining word distributional statistics and dictionary definitions. In *Proceedings of the 2011 Conference on Empirical Methods in Natural Language Processing*.

Weiwei Guo and Mona Diab. 2012a. Learning the latent semantics of a concept by its definition. In *Proceedings of the 50th Annual Meeting of the Association for Computational Linguistics*.

Weiwei Guo and Mona Diab. 2012b. Modeling sentences in the latent space. In *Proceedings of the 50th Annual Meeting of the Association for Computational Linguistics*.

Weiwei Guo and Mona Diab. 2012c. Weiwei: A simple unsupervised latent semantics based approach for sentence similarity. In *First Joint Conference on Lexical and Computational Semantics (*SEM)*.

Chukfong Ho, Masrah Azrifah Azmi Murad, Rabiah Abdul Kadir, and Shyamala C. Doraisamy. 2010. Word sense disambiguation-based sentence similarity. In *Proceedings of the 23rd International Conference on Computational Linguistics*.

Aminul Islam and Diana Inkpen. 2008. Semantic text similarity using corpus-based word similarity and string similarity. *ACM Transactions on Knowledge Discovery from Data*, 2.

Ou Jin, Nathan N. Liu, Kai Zhao, Yong Yu, and Qiang Yang. 2011. Transferring topical knowledge from auxiliary long texts for short text clustering. In *Proceedings of the 20th ACM international conference on Information and knowledge management*.

Mirella Lapata and Regina Barzilay. 2005. Automatic evaluation of text coherence: Models and representations. In *Proceedings of the 19th International Joint Conference on Artificial Intelligence*.

Yuhua Li, Davi d McLean, Zuhair A. Bandar, James D. O'Shea, and Keeley Crockett. 2006. Sentence similarity based on semantic nets and corpus statistics. *IEEE Transaction on Knowledge and Data Engineering*, 18.

Xiao-Ying Liu, Yi-Ming Zhou, and Ruo-Shi Zheng. 2007. Sentence similarity based on dynamic time warping. In *The International Conference on Semantic Computing*.

James O'Shea, Zuhair Bandar, Keeley Crockett, and David McLean. 2008. A comparative study of two short text semantic similarity measures. In *Proceedings of the Agent and Multi-Agent Systems: Technologies and Applications, Second KES International Symposium (KES-AMSTA)*.

Philip Resnik. 1997. Selectional preference and sense disambiguation. In *Proceedings of the ACL SIGLEX Workshop on Tagging Text with Lexical Semantics: Why, What, and How?*

Alan Ritter, Mausam, and Oren Etzioni. 2010. A latent dirichlet allocation method for selectional preferences. In *Proceedings of the 48th Annual Meeting of the Association for Computational Linguistics*.

Jagan Sankaranarayanan, Hanan Samet, Benjamin E. Teitler, Michael D. Lieberman, and Jon Sperling. 2009. Twitterstand: news in tweets. In *Proceedings of the 17th ACM SIGSPATIAL International Conference on Advances in Geographic Information Systems*.

Nathan Srebro and Tommi Jaakkola. 2003. Weighted low-rank approximations. In *Proceedings of the Twentieth International Conference on Machine Learning*.

Harald Steck. 2010. Training and testing of recommender systems on data missing not at random. In *Proceedings of the 16th ACM SIGKDD International Conference on Knowledge Discovery and Data Mining*.

George Tsatsaronis, Iraklis Varlamis, and Michalis Vazirgiannis. 2010. Text relatedness based on a word thesaurus. *Journal of Articial Intelligence Research*, 37.

Wentau Yih, Geoffrey Zweig, and John C. Platt. 2012. Polarity inducing latent semantic analysis. In *Proceedings of the 2012 Joint Conference on Empirical Methods in Natural Language Processing and Computational Natural Language Learning*.

Liang Zhou, Chin-Yew Lin, Dragos Stefan Munteanu, and Eduard Hovy. 2006. Paraeval: Using paraphrases to evaluate summaries automatically. In *Proceedings of Human Language Technology Conference of the North American Chapter of the ACL,*.

Linguistic Regularities in Continuous Space Word Representations

Tomas Mikolov*, Wen-tau Yih, Geoffrey Zweig
Microsoft Research
Redmond, WA 98052

Abstract

Continuous space language models have recently demonstrated outstanding results across a variety of tasks. In this paper, we examine the vector-space word representations that are implicitly learned by the input-layer weights. We find that these representations are surprisingly good at capturing syntactic and semantic regularities in language, and that each relationship is characterized by a relation-specific vector offset. This allows vector-oriented reasoning based on the offsets between words. For example, the male/female relationship is automatically learned, and with the induced vector representations, "King - Man + Woman" results in a vector very close to "Queen." We demonstrate that the word vectors capture syntactic regularities by means of syntactic analogy questions (provided with this paper), and are able to correctly answer almost 40% of the questions. We demonstrate that the word vectors capture semantic regularities by using the vector offset method to answer SemEval-2012 Task 2 questions. Remarkably, this method outperforms the best previous systems.

1 Introduction

A defining feature of neural network language models is their representation of words as high dimensional real valued vectors. In these models (Bengio et al., 2003; Schwenk, 2007; Mikolov et al., 2010), words are converted via a learned lookup-table into real valued vectors which are used as the inputs to a neural network. As pointed out by the original proposers, one of the main advantages of these models is that the distributed representation achieves a level of generalization that is not possible with classical n-gram language models; whereas a n-gram model works in terms of discrete units that have no inherent relationship to one another, a continuous space model works in terms of word vectors where similar words are likely to have similar vectors. Thus, when the model parameters are adjusted in response to a particular word or word-sequence, the improvements will carry over to occurrences of similar words and sequences.

By training a neural network language model, one obtains not just the model itself, but also the learned word representations, which may be used for other, potentially unrelated, tasks. This has been used to good effect, for example in (Collobert and Weston, 2008; Turian et al., 2010) where induced word representations are used with sophisticated classifiers to improve performance in many NLP tasks.

In this work, we find that the learned word representations in fact capture meaningful syntactic and semantic regularities in a very simple way. Specifically, the regularities are observed as constant vector offsets between pairs of words sharing a particular relationship. For example, if we denote the vector for word i as x_i, and focus on the singular/plural relation, we observe that $x_{apple} - x_{apples} \approx x_{car} - x_{cars}$, $x_{family} - x_{families} \approx x_{car} - x_{cars}$, and so on. Perhaps more surprisingly, we find that this is also the case for a variety of semantic relations, as measured by the SemEval 2012 task of measuring relation similarity.

*Currently at Google, Inc.

The remainder of this paper is organized as follows. In Section 2, we discuss related work; Section 3 describes the recurrent neural network language model we used to obtain word vectors; Section 4 discusses the test sets; Section 5 describes our proposed vector offset method; Section 6 summarizes our experiments, and we conclude in Section 7.

2 Related Work

Distributed word representations have a long history, with early proposals including (Hinton, 1986; Pollack, 1990; Elman, 1991; Deerwester et al., 1990). More recently, neural network language models have been proposed for the classical language modeling task of predicting a probability distribution over the "next" word, given some preceding words. These models were first studied in the context of feed-forward networks (Bengio et al., 2003; Bengio et al., 2006), and later in the context of recurrent neural network models (Mikolov et al., 2010; Mikolov et al., 2011b). This early work demonstrated outstanding performance in terms of word-prediction, but also the need for more computationally efficient models. This has been addressed by subsequent work using hierarchical prediction (Morin and Bengio, 2005; Mnih and Hinton, 2009; Le et al., 2011; Mikolov et al., 2011b; Mikolov et al., 2011a). Also of note, the use of distributed topic representations has been studied in (Hinton and Salakhutdinov, 2006; Hinton and Salakhutdinov, 2010), and (Bordes et al., 2012) presents a semantically driven method for obtaining word representations.

3 Recurrent Neural Network Model

The word representations we study are learned by a recurrent neural network language model (Mikolov et al., 2010), as illustrated in Figure 1. This architecture consists of an input layer, a hidden layer with recurrent connections, plus the corresponding weight matrices. The input vector $\mathbf{w}(t)$ represents input word at time t encoded using 1-of-N coding, and the output layer $\mathbf{y}(t)$ produces a probability distribution over words. The hidden layer $\mathbf{s}(t)$ maintains a representation of the sentence history. The input vector $\mathbf{w}(t)$ and the output vector $\mathbf{y}(t)$ have dimensionality of the vocabulary. The values in the hidden and

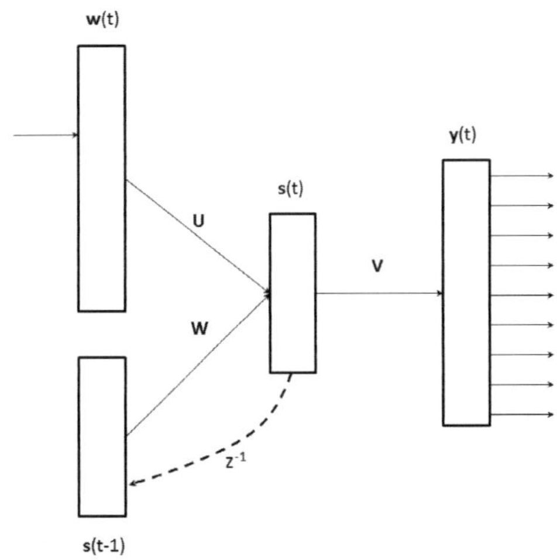

Figure 1: Recurrent Neural Network Language Model.

output layers are computed as follows:

$$\mathbf{s}(t) = f\left(\mathbf{U}\mathbf{w}(t) + \mathbf{W}\mathbf{s}(t-1)\right) \quad (1)$$

$$\mathbf{y}(t) = g\left(\mathbf{V}\mathbf{s}(t)\right), \quad (2)$$

where

$$f(z) = \frac{1}{1+e^{-z}}, \quad g(z_m) = \frac{e^{z_m}}{\sum_k e^{z_k}}. \quad (3)$$

In this framework, the word representations are found in the columns of $\mathbf{U}$, with each column representing a word. The RNN is trained with backpropagation to maximize the data log-likelihood under the model. The model itself has no knowledge of syntax or morphology or semantics. Remarkably, training such a purely lexical model to maximize likelihood will induce word representations with striking syntactic and semantic properties.

4 Measuring Linguistic Regularity

4.1 A Syntactic Test Set

To understand better the syntactic regularities which are inherent in the learned representation, we created a test set of analogy questions of the form "a is to b as c is to ___" testing base/comparative/superlative forms of adjectives; singular/plural forms of common nouns; possessive/non-possessive forms of common nouns; and base, past and 3rd person present tense forms of verbs. More precisely, we tagged 267M words of newspaper text with Penn

Category	Relation	Patterns Tested	# Questions	Example
Adjectives	Base/Comparative	JJ/JJR, JJR/JJ	1000	good:better rough:___
Adjectives	Base/Superlative	JJ/JJS, JJS/JJ	1000	good:best rough:___
Adjectives	Comparative/ Superlative	JJS/JJR, JJR/JJS	1000	better:best rougher:___
Nouns	Singular/Plural	NN/NNS, NNS/NN	1000	year:years law:___
Nouns	Non-possessive/ Possessive	NN/NN_POS, NN_POS/NN	1000	city:city's bank:___
Verbs	Base/Past	VB/VBD, VBD/VB	1000	see:saw return:___
Verbs	Base/3rd Person Singular Present	VB/VBZ, VBZ/VB	1000	see:sees return:___
Verbs	Past/3rd Person Singular Present	VBD/VBZ, VBZ/VBD	1000	saw:sees returned:___

Table 1: Test set patterns. For a given pattern and word-pair, both orderings occur in the test set. For example, if "see:saw return:___" occurs, so will "saw:see returned:___".

Treebank POS tags (Marcus et al., 1993). We then selected 100 of the most frequent comparative adjectives (words labeled JJR); 100 of the most frequent plural nouns (NNS); 100 of the most frequent possessive nouns (NN_POS); and 100 of the most frequent base form verbs (VB). We then systematically generated analogy questions by randomly matching each of the 100 words with 5 other words from the same category, and creating variants as indicated in Table 1. The total test set size is 8000. The test set is available online. [1]

4.2 A Semantic Test Set

In addition to syntactic analogy questions, we used the SemEval-2012 Task 2, *Measuring Relation Similarity* (Jurgens et al., 2012), to estimate the extent to which RNNLM word vectors contain semantic information. The dataset contains 79 fine-grained word relations, where 10 are used for training and 69 testing. Each relation is exemplified by 3 or 4 gold word pairs. Given a group of word pairs that supposedly have the same relation, the task is to order the target pairs according to the *degree* to which this relation holds. This can be viewed as another analogy problem. For example, take the *Class-Inclusion:Singular_Collective* relation with the prototypical word pair *clothing:shirt*. To measure the degree that a target word pair *dish:bowl* has the same relation, we form the analogy "*clothing* is to *shirt* as *dish* is to *bowl*," and ask how valid it is.

5 The Vector Offset Method

As we have seen, both the syntactic and semantic tasks have been formulated as analogy questions. We have found that a simple vector offset method based on cosine distance is remarkably effective in solving these questions. In this method, we assume relationships are present as vector offsets, so that in the embedding space, all pairs of words sharing a particular relation are related by the same constant offset. This is illustrated in Figure 2.

In this model, to answer the analogy question *a:b c:d* where *d* is unknown, we find the embedding vectors x_a, x_b, x_c (all normalized to unit norm), and compute $y = x_b - x_a + x_c$. y is the continuous space representation of the word we expect to be the best answer. Of course, no word might exist at that exact position, so we then search for the word whose embedding vector has the greatest cosine similarity to y and output it:

$$w^* = argmax_w \frac{x_w y}{\|x_w\| \|y\|}$$

When d is given, as in our semantic test set, we simply use $\cos(x_b - x_a + x_c, x_d)$ for the words

[1] http://research.microsoft.com/en-us/projects/rnn/default.aspx

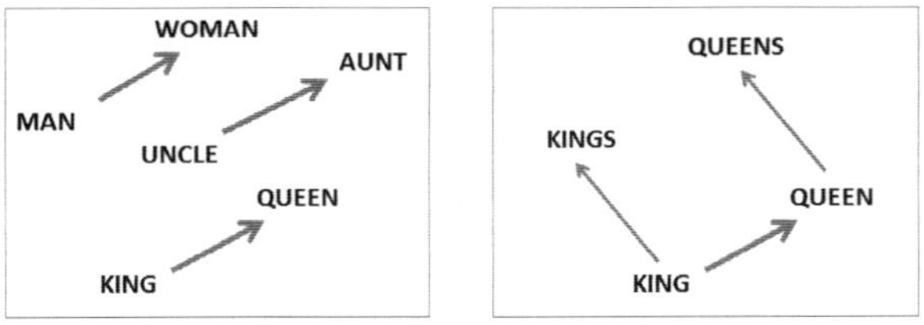

Figure 2: Left panel shows vector offsets for three word pairs illustrating the gender relation. Right panel shows a different projection, and the singular/plural relation for two words. In high-dimensional space, multiple relations can be embedded for a single word.

provided. We have explored several related methods and found that the proposed method performs well for both syntactic and semantic relations. We note that this measure is qualitatively similar to relational similarity model of (Turney, 2012), which predicts similarity between members of the word pairs (x_b, x_d), (x_c, x_d) and dis-similarity for (x_a, x_d).

6 Experimental Results

To evaluate the vector offset method, we used vectors generated by the RNN toolkit of Mikolov (2012). Vectors of dimensionality 80, 320, and 640 were generated, along with a composite of several systems, with total dimensionality 1600. The systems were trained with 320M words of Broadcast News data as described in (Mikolov et al., 2011a), and had an 82k vocabulary. Table 2 shows results for both RNNLM and LSA vectors on the syntactic task. LSA was trained on the same data as the RNN. We see that the RNN vectors capture significantly more syntactic regularity than the LSA vectors, and do remarkably well in an absolute sense, answering more than one in three questions correctly. [2]

In Table 3 we compare the RNN vectors with those based on the methods of Collobert and Weston (2008) and Mnih and Hinton (2009), as implemented by (Turian et al., 2010) and available online [3] Since different words are present in these datasets, we computed the intersection of the vocabularies of the RNN vectors and the new vectors, and restricted the test set and word vectors to those. This resulted in a 36k word vocabulary, and a test set with 6632

[2]Guessing gets a small fraction of a percent.

[3]http://metaoptimize.com/projects/wordreprs/

Method	Adjectives	Nouns	Verbs	All
LSA-80	9.2	11.1	17.4	12.8
LSA-320	11.3	18.1	20.7	16.5
LSA-640	9.6	10.1	13.8	11.3
RNN-80	9.3	5.2	30.4	16.2
RNN-320	18.2	19.0	45.0	28.5
RNN-640	21.0	25.2	54.8	34.7
RNN-1600	**23.9**	**29.2**	**62.2**	**39.6**

Table 2: Results for identifying syntactic regularities for different word representations. Percent correct.

Method	Adjectives	Nouns	Verbs	All
RNN-80	**10.1**	8.1	**30.4**	**19.0**
CW-50	1.1	2.4	8.1	4.5
CW-100	1.3	4.1	8.6	5.0
HLBL-50	4.4	5.4	23.1	13.0
HLBL-100	7.6	**13.2**	30.2	18.7

Table 3: Comparison of RNN vectors with Turian's Collobert and Weston based vectors and the Hierarchical Log-Bilinear model of Mnih and Hinton. Percent correct.

questions. Turian's Collobert and Weston based vectors do poorly on this task, whereas the Hierarchical Log-Bilinear Model vectors of (Mnih and Hinton, 2009) do essentially as well as the RNN vectors. These representations were trained on 37M words of data and this may indicate a greater robustness of the HLBL method.

We conducted similar experiments with the semantic test set. For each target word pair in a relation category, the model measures its relational similarity to each of the prototypical word pairs, and then uses the average as the final score. The results are evaluated using the two standard metrics defined in the task, Spearman's rank correlation coefficient ρ and MaxDiff accuracy. In both cases, larger values are better. To compare to previous systems, we report the average over all 69 relations in the test set.

From Table 4, we see that as with the syntactic regularity study, the RNN-based representations perform best. In this case, however, Turian's CW vectors are comparable in performance to the HLBL vectors. With the RNN vectors, the performance improves as the number of dimensions increases. Surprisingly, we found that even though the RNN vec-

Method	Spearman's ρ	MaxDiff Acc.
LSA-640	0.149	0.364
RNN-80	0.211	0.389
RNN-320	0.259	0.408
RNN-640	0.270	0.416
RNN-1600	**0.275**	**0.418**
CW-50	0.159	0.363
CW-100	0.154	0.363
HLBL-50	0.149	0.363
HLBL-100	0.146	0.362
UTD-NB	0.230	0.395

Table 4: Results in measuring relation similarity

tors are not trained or tuned specifically for this task, the model achieves better results (RNN-320, RNN-640 & RNN-1600) than the previously best performing system, UTD-NB (Rink and Harabagiu, 2012).

7 Conclusion

We have presented a generally applicable vector offset method for identifying linguistic regularities in continuous space word representations. We have shown that the word representations learned by a RNNLM do an especially good job in capturing these regularities. We present a new dataset for measuring syntactic performance, and achieve almost 40% correct. We also evaluate semantic generalization on the SemEval 2012 task, and outperform the previous state-of-the-art. Surprisingly, both results are the byproducts of an unsupervised maximum likelihood training criterion that simply operates on a large amount of text data.

References

Y. Bengio, R. Ducharme, Vincent, P., and C. Jauvin. 2003. A neural probabilistic language model. *Journal of Machine Learning Reseach*, 3(6).

Y. Bengio, H. Schwenk, J.S. Senécal, F. Morin, and J.L. Gauvain. 2006. Neural probabilistic language models. *Innovations in Machine Learning*, pages 137–186.

A. Bordes, X. Glorot, J. Weston, and Y. Bengio. 2012. Joint learning of words and meaning representations for open-text semantic parsing. In *Proceedings of 15th International Conference on Artificial Intelligence and Statistics*.

R. Collobert and J. Weston. 2008. A unified architecture for natural language processing: Deep neural networks with multitask learning. In *Proceedings of the 25th international conference on Machine learning*, pages 160–167. ACM.

S. Deerwester, S.T. Dumais, G.W. Furnas, T.K. Landauer, and R. Harshman. 1990. Indexing by latent semantic analysis. *Journal of the American Society for Information Science*, 41(96).

J.L. Elman. 1991. Distributed representations, simple recurrent networks, and grammatical structure. *Machine learning*, 7(2):195–225.

G.E. Hinton and R.R. Salakhutdinov. 2006. Reducing the dimensionality of data with neural networks. *Science*, 313(5786):504–507.

G. Hinton and R. Salakhutdinov. 2010. Discovering binary codes for documents by learning deep generative models. *Topics in Cognitive Science*, 3(1):74–91.

G.E. Hinton. 1986. Learning distributed representations of concepts. In *Proceedings of the eighth annual conference of the cognitive science society*, pages 1–12. Amherst, MA.

David Jurgens, Saif Mohammad, Peter Turney, and Keith Holyoak. 2012. Semeval-2012 task 2: Measuring degrees of relational similarity. In **SEM 2012: The First Joint Conference on Lexical and Computational Semantics (SemEval 2012)*, pages 356–364. Association for Computational Linguistics.

Hai-Son Le, I. Oparin, A. Allauzen, J.-L. Gauvain, and F. Yvon. 2011. Structured output layer neural network language model. In *Proceedings of ICASSP 2011*.

Mitchell P. Marcus, Mary Ann Marcinkiewicz, and Beatrice Santorini. 1993. Building a large annotated corpus of english: the penn treebank. *Computational Linguistics*, 19(2):313–330.

Tomas Mikolov, Martin Karafiat, Jan Cernocky, and Sanjeev Khudanpur. 2010. Recurrent neural network based language model. In *Proceedings of Interspeech 2010*.

Tomas Mikolov, Anoop Deoras, Daniel Povey, Lukas Burget, and Jan Cernocky. 2011a. Strategies for Training Large Scale Neural Network Language Models. In *Proceedings of ASRU 2011*.

Tomas Mikolov, Stefan Kombrink, Lukas Burget, Jan Cernocky, and Sanjeev Khudanpur. 2011b. Extensions of recurrent neural network based language model. In *Proceedings of ICASSP 2011*.

Tomas Mikolov. 2012. RNN toolkit.

A. Mnih and G.E. Hinton. 2009. A scalable hierarchical distributed language model. *Advances in neural information processing systems*, 21:1081–1088.

F. Morin and Y. Bengio. 2005. Hierarchical probabilistic neural network language model. In *Proceedings of the international workshop on artificial intelligence and statistics*, pages 246–252.

J.B. Pollack. 1990. Recursive distributed representations. *Artificial Intelligence*, 46(1):77–105.

Bryan Rink and Sanda Harabagiu. 2012. UTD: Determining relational similarity using lexical patterns. In **SEM 2012: The First Joint Conference on Lexical and Computational Semantics (SemEval 2012)*, pages 413–418. Association for Computational Linguistics.

Holger Schwenk. 2007. Continuous space language models. *Computer Speech and Language*, 21(3):492 – 518.

J. Turian, L. Ratinov, and Y. Bengio. 2010. Word representations: a simple and general method for semi-supervised learning. In *Proceedings of Association for Computational Linguistics (ACL 2010)*.

P.D. Turney. 2012. Domain and function: A dual-space model of semantic relations and compositions. *Journal of Artificial Intelligence Research*, 44:533–585.

TruthTeller: Annotating Predicate Truth

Amnon Lotan
Department of Linguistics
Tel Aviv University
amnonlot@post.tau.ac.il

Asher Stern and **Ido Dagan**
Department of Computer Science
Bar Ilan University
astern7@gmail.com dagan@cs.biu.ac.il

Abstract

We propose a novel semantic annotation type of assigning truth values to predicate occurrences, and present TRUTHTELLER, a standalone publicly-available tool that produces such annotations. TRUTHTELLER integrates a range of semantic phenomena, such as negation, modality, presupposition, implicativity, and more, which were dealt only partly in previous works. Empirical evaluations against human annotations show satisfactory results and suggest the usefulness of this new type of tool for NLP.

1 Introduction

In a text, the action or relation denoted by every predicate can be seen as being either positively or negatively inferred from its sentence, or otherwise having an unknown truth status. Only in (3) below can we infer that Gal sold her shop, hence the positive *truth value* of the predicate *sell*, while according to (2) and (4) Gal did not sell it, hence the negative truth values, and in (1) we do not know if she sold it or not (the notations PT+, PT- and PT? denote truth states, defined in Subsection 2.3). Identifying these predicate truth values is an important subtask within many semantic processing scenarios, including various applications such as Question Answering (QA), Information Extraction (IE), paraphrasing and summarization. The following examples illustrate the phenomenon:

(1) *Gal made an attempt* $^{pt+}$ *to sell* $^{pt?}$ *her shop.*

(2) *Gal did* ***not*** *try* $^{pt-}$ *to sell* $^{pt-}$ *her shop* ***after*** *hearing* $^{pt+}$ *the offers.*

(3) ***Maybe*** *Gal wasn't smart* $^{pt?}$ *to sell* $^{pt+}$ *her shop.*

(4) *Gal wasn't smart* $^{pt-}$ ***enough*** *to sell* $^{pt-}$ *the shop* ***that*** *she had bought* $^{pt+}$*.*

Previous works addressed specific aspects of the truth detection problem: Nairn et al. (2006), and later MacCartney & Manning (2007; 2009), were the first to build paraphrasing and inference systems that combine negation (see *try* in (2)), modality (*smart* in (3)) and "natural logic", a recursive truth value calculus (*sell* in (1-3)); recently, Mausam et al. (2012) built an open IE system that identifies granulated variants of modality and conditions on predicates (*smart* in (3)); and Kiparsky & Kiparsky (1970) and Karttunen (1971; 2012) laid the ground work for factive and implicative entailment calculus (*sell* in (1-4)), as well as many generic constructions of *presupposition* (*hearing* in (2) is presupposed because it heads an adverbial clause and *bought* in (4) heads a finite relative clause), which, to our knowledge, have not yet been implemented computationally. Notice in the examples that presuppositions persist under negation, in questions and if-clauses, while entailments do not. In addition, there is a growing research line of negation and modality detection. See, for example, Morante & Daelemans (2012).

We present TRUTHTELLER[1], a novel algorithm and system that identifies the truth value of each predicate in a given sentence. It annotates nodes in the text's dependency parse-tree via a combination of pattern-based annotation rules and a recursive algorithm based on natural logic. In the course of computing truth value, it also computes the implicativity/factivity signature of predicates, and their negation and modality to a basic degree, both of which are made available in the system output. It addresses and combines the aforementioned phenomena (see Section 2), many of which weren't dealt in previous systems.

TRUTHTELLER is an open source and publicly available annotation tool, offers a relatively simple algebra for truth value computation, and is accompanied by a publicly available lexicon of over 1,700 implicative and factive predicates. Also, we provide an intuitive GUI for viewing and modifying the algorithm's annotation rules.

2 Annotation Types and Algorithm

This section summarizes the annotation algorithm (a detailed report is available with the system release). We perform the annotations over dependency parse trees, generated according to the Stanford Dependencies standard (de Marneffe and Manning, 2008). For all verbs, nouns and adjectives in a sentence's parse tree, we produce the following 4 annotation types, given in the order they are calculated, as described in the following subsections:

1. Predicate Implication Signature (*sig*) - describes the pattern by which the predicate entails or presupposes its complements, e.g., the verb *refuse* entails the negative of its complements: *Ed refused to pay* entails that *Ed didn't pay*.

2. Negation and Uncertainty (NU) - indicates whether the predicate is modified by an uncertainty modifier like *might, probably*, etc., or whether it's negated by *no, never* etc.

3. Clause-Truth (CT) - indicates whether the entire clause headed by the predicate is entailed by the complete sentence

4. Predicate Truth (PT) - indicates whether the predicate itself is entailed by the sentence, as defined below

Before presenting the detailed definitions and descriptions below, we give a high-level description of TRUTHTELLER's algorithm, where each step relies on the results of its predecessor: a) every predicate in the parse tree is annotated with a predicate implication signature, identified by lexicon lookup; b) NU annotations are added, according to the presence of uncertainty modifiers (*maybe, might, etc.*) and negation modifies (*not, never, etc.*); c) predicates in certain presupposition constructions (e.g., adverbial clauses, WH arguments) are annotated with positive CT values; d) the parse tree is depth-first scanned, in order to compute both CT and PT annotations by the recursive effects of factives and implicatives; e) in conjunction with the previous step, relative clause constructions are identified and annotated with CT and PT.

Except for steps a) and d), all of the procedure is implemented as an ordered sequence of *annotation rule* applications. An annotation rule is a dependency parse tree template, possibly including variables, which assigns certain annotations to any parse tree node that matches against it. Step a) is implemented with signature lexicon lookups, and step d) is an algorithm implemented in code.

To illustrate this entire process, Figure 1 presents the annotation process of a simple sentence, step by step, resulting in TRUTHTELLER's complete output, fully specified below. Most other examples in this paper show only partial annotations for brevity.

2.1 Predicate Implication Signature

Our system marks the signature of each predicate, as defined in Table 1. There, each signature has a left sign and a right sign. The *left* sign determines the *clause truth value* of the predicate's complements, when the predicate is in *positive* contexts (e.g., not negated), while the *right* sign applies in *negative* contexts (clause

[1]http://cs.biu.ac.il/~nlp/downloads/TruthTeller

#	Sig	Positive context example	Negative context example
1	+/-	Ed *managed* to escape ⇒ Ed escaped	Ed didn't *manage* to escape ⇒ Ed didn't escape
2	+/?	Ed was *forced* to sell ⇒ Ed sold	Ed wasn't *forced* to sell ⇒ *no entailments*
3	?/-	Ed was *allowed* to go ⇒ *no entailments*	Ed wasn't *allowed* to go ⇒ Ed didn't go
4	-/+	Ed *forgot* to pay ⇒ Ed didn't pay	Ed didn't *forget* to pay ⇒ Ed paid
5	-/?	Ed *refused* to fight ⇒ Ed didn't fight	Ed didn't *refuse* to fight ⇒ *no entailments*
6	?/+	Ed *hesitated* to ask ⇒ *no entailments*	Ed didn't *hesitate* to ask ⇒ Ed asked
7	+/+	Ed was *glad* to come ⇒ Ed came	Ed wasn't *glad* to come ⇒ Ed came
8	-/-	Ed *pretended* to pay ⇒ Ed didn't pay	Ed didn't *pretend* to pay ⇒ Ed didn't pay
9	?/?	Ed *wanted* to fly ⇒ *no entailments*	Ed didn't *want* to fly ⇒ *no entailments*

Table 1: Implication signatures, based on MacCartney & Manning (2009) and Karttunen (2012). The first six signatures are named implicatives, and the last three factive, counter factive and regular, respectively.

a) Annotate signatures via lexicons lookup

Gal wasn't allowed$^{?/-}$ *to come*$^{?/?}$

b) Annotate NU

Gal wasn't allowed$^{?/-,nu-}$ *to come*$^{?/?,nu+}$

c) Annotate CT to presupposition constructions

Gal wasn't allowed$^{?/-,nu-,ct+}$ *to come*$^{?/?,nu+,ct+}$

d) Recursive CT and PT annotation

Gal wasn't allowed$^{?/-,nu-,ct+,pt-}$ *to come*$^{?/?,nu+,ct-,pt-}$

e) Annotate CT and PT of relative clauses (has no effect on this example)

Gal wasn't allowed$^{?/-,nu-,ct+,pt-}$ *to come*$^{?/?,nu+,ct-,pt-}$

Figure 1: An illustration of the annotation process

truth is defined in Subsection 2.3). See examples for both context types in the table. Each sign can be either + (positive), - (negative) or ? (unknown). The unknown sign signifies that the predicate does not entail its complements in any way.

Signatures are identified via lookup, using two lexicons, one for single-word predicates and the other for *verb+noun* phrasal verbs, e.g., *take the time to X*. Our single-word lexicon is similar to those used in (Nairn et al., 2006) and (Bar-Haim et al., 2007), but is far greater, holding over 1,700 entries, while each of the previous two has, to the best of our knowledge, less than 300 entries. It was built semi automatically, out of a kernel of 320 manually inspected predicates, which was then expanded with WordNet synonyms (Fellbaum, 1998). The second lexicon is the implicative phrasal verb lexicon of Karttunen (2012), adapted into our framework. The +/? implicative serves as the default signature for all unlisted predicates.

Signature is also sensitive to the type of the complement. Consider:

(6) *Ed forgot*$^{-/+}$ *to call*$^{pt-}$ *Joe*

(7) *Ed forgot*$^{+/+}$ *that he called*$^{pt+}$ *Joe*

Therefore, signatures are specified separately for finite and non finite complements of each predicate.

After the initial signature lookup, two annotation rules correct the signatures of +/+ factives modified by *enough* and *too*, into +/- and -/+, correspondingly, see Kiparsky & Kiparsky (1970). Compare:

(8) *Ed was mad*$^{+/+}$ *to go* ⇒ *Ed went*

(9) *Ed was* ***too*** *mad*$^{-/+}$ *to go* ⇒ *Ed didn't go*

In addition, we observed, like Karttunen (2012), that most verbs that have passive voice and the *into* preposition become +/? implicatives, e.g.,

(10) *Workers* ***were pushed / maddened / managed***$^{+/?}$ ***into*** *signing* ⇒ *They signed*

(11) *Workers* ***weren't pushed / maddened / managed***$^{+/?}$ ***into*** *signing* ⇒ *It is unknown whether they signed*

so we captured this construction in another rule.

2.2 Negation and Uncertainty (NU)

NU takes the values {NU+, NU-, NU?}, standing for non-negated certain actions, negated certain actions, and uncertain actions. The first NU rules match against a closed set of negation modifiers around the predicate, like *not, never, neither* etc. (see (2)), while later rules detect uncertainty modifiers, like *maybe, probably*, etc. Therefore, NU? takes precedence over NU-.

Many constructions of subject-negation, object-negation and "double negation" are accounted for in our rules, as in:

(12) ***Nobody*** *was seen*$^{nu-}$ *at the site*

(13) ***Almost nobody*** *was seen*$^{nu+}$ *at the site*

2.3 Clause Truth and Predicate Truth

Clause Truth (CT, denoted as *ct(p)*) corresponds to POLARITY of Nairn et al. (2006). It represents whether the clause headed by a predicate p is entailed by the sentence, contradicted or unknown, and thus takes three values {CT+, CT-, CT?}.

Predicate Truth (PT) (denoted as *pt(p)*) represents whether we can infer from the sentence that the action described by the predicate happened (or that its relation holds). It is defined as the binary product of NU and CT:

Definition 1. $PT = NU \cdot CT$

and takes analogous values: {PT+, PT-, PT?}. Intuitively, the product of two identical positive/negative values yields PT+, a positive and a negative yield PT-, and NU? or CT? always yield PT?. To illustrate these definitions, consider:

(14) *Meg* ***may*** *have slept*$^{ct+,pt?}$ ***after*** *eating*$^{ct+,pt+}$ *the meal Ed cooked*$^{ct+,pt+}$, ***while no*** *one was there*$^{ct+,pt-}$

After signatures and NU are annotated, CT and PT are calculated. At first, we apply a set of rules that annotate generic presupposition constructions with CT+. These include adverbial clauses opening with {*while, before, after, where, how come, because, since, owing to, though, despite, yet, therefore...*}, WH arguments (*who, which, whom, what*), and

$$ct(p) = \begin{cases} \text{CT+}: & p \text{ was already annotated by a presupposition rule} \\ ct(gov(p)): & p \text{ heads a relative clause} \\ compCT(p): & \text{otherwise, and } p \text{ is a complement} \\ \text{CT?}: & \text{otherwise (default)} \end{cases}$$

Figure 2: Formula of *ct(p)*, for any predicate p. $ct(gov(p))$ is the CT of p's governing predicate.

parataxis[2]. See for example the effects of *after* and *while* in (14).

Then, we apply the following recursive sequential procedure. The tree root always gets CT+ (see *slept* in (14)). The tree is then scanned downwards, predicate by predicate. At each one, we compute CT by the formula in Figure 2, as follows. First, we check if one of the aforementioned presupposition rules already matched the node. Second, if none matched, we apply to the node's entire subtree another set of rules that annotate each relative clause with the CT of its governing noun[3], $ct(gov(p))$ (see *failed* in (15)). Third, if no previous rule matched, and p is a complement of another predicate $gov(p)$, then *compCT(p)* is calculated, by the following logic: when $pt(gov(p))$ is PT+ or PT-, the corresponding left or right sign of $sig(gov(p))$ is copied. Otherwise, if $pt(gov(p))$ = PT?, CT? is returned, except when the signature of $gov(p)$ is +/+ (or -/-) factive, which always yields CT+ (or CT-).

Third, if nothing applied to p, CT? is returned by default. Finally, PT is set, according to Definition 1.

To illustrate, consider these annotations:

(15) *Gal managed*$^{+/-,ct+,pt+}$ *a building*$^{+/?,ct+,pt+}$, *which Ginger failed*$^{-/+,ct+,pt+}$ *to sell*$^{+/?,ct-,pt-}$

First, *managed* gets CT+ as the tree root. Then, we get $compCT(building)$ = CT+, as the complement of *managed*$^{+/-,pt+}$. Next, a relative clause rule copies CT+ from *building* to *failed.*

[2]The placing of clauses or phrases one after another, without words to indicate coordination, as in "veni, vidi, vici" in contrast to "veni, vidi *and* vici".

[3]We also annotate nouns and adjectives as predicates in copular constructions, and in instances where nouns have complements.

Finally, $compCT(sell)$ = CT- is calculated, as the complement of $failed^{-/+,pt+}$.

3 Evaluation

To evaluate TRUTHTELLER's accuracy, we sampled 25 sentences from each of the RTE5 and RTE6 Test datasets (Bentivogli et al., 2009; Bentivogli et al., 2010), widely used for textual inference benchmarks. In these 50 sentences, we manually annotated each predicate, 153 in total, forming a gold standard. As baseline, we report the most frequent value for each annotation. The results, in Table 2, show high accuracy for all types, reducing the baseline CT and PT errors by half. Furthermore, most of the remaining errors were due to parser errors, according to a manual error analysis we conducted.

The baseline for NU annotations shows that negations are scarce in these RTE datasets, which was also the case for CT- and PT- annotations. Thus, Table 2 mostly indicates TruthTeller's performance in distinguishing positive CT and PT annotations from unknown ones, the latter constituting ∽20% of the gold standard. To further assess CT- and PT- annotations we performed two targeted measurements. Precision for CT- and PT- was measured by manually judging the correctness of such annotations by TRUTHTELLER, on a sample from RTE6 Test including 50 CT- and 124 PT- annotations. This test yielded 78% and 83% precision, respectively. PT- is more frequent as it is typically triggered by CT-, as well as by other constructions involving negation. Recall was estimated by employing a human annotator to go through the dataset and look for CT- and PT- gold standard annotations. The annotator identified 40 "CT-"s and 50 "PT-"s, out of which TRUTHTELLER found 47.5% of the "CT-"s and 74% of the "PT-"s. In summary, TRUTHTELLER's performance on our target PT annotations is quite satisfactory with 89% accuracy overall, having 83% precision and 74% recall estimates specifically for PT-.

Annotation	TruthTeller	Baseline
Signature	89.5%	81% (+/?)
NU	98%	97.3% (NU+)
CT	90.8%	78.4% (CT+)
PT	89%	77% (PT+)

Table 2: The accuracy measures for TRUTHTELLER's 4 annotations. The right column gives the accuracy for the corresponding most-frequent baseline: {+/?, NU+, CT+, PT+}.

4 Conclusions and Future Work

We have presented TRUTHTELLER, a novel algorithm and system that identifies truth values of predicates, the first such system to a) address or combine a wide variety of relevant grammatical constructions; b) be an open source annotation tool; c) address the truth value annotation task as an independent tool, which makes it possible for client systems to use its output, while previous works only embedded annotations in their task-specific systems; and d) annotate *unknown* truth values extensively and explicitly.

TRUTHTELLER may be used for several purposes, such as inferring parts of a sentence from the whole and improving textual entailment (and contradiction) detection. It includes a novel, large and accurate, lexicon of predicate implication signatures.

While in this paper we evaluated the correctness of TRUTHTELLER as an individual component, in the future we propose integrating it in a state-of-the-art RTE system and report its impact. One challenge in this scenario is having other system components interact with TRUTHTELLER's decisions, possibly masking its effects. In addition, we plan to incorporate monotonicity calculations in the annotation process, like in MacCartney and Manning (2009).

5 Acknowledgements

This work was partially supported by the Israel Science Foundation grant 1112/08 and the European Community's Seventh Framework Programme (FP7/2007-2013) under grant agreement no. 287923 (EXCITEMENT).

We thank Roni Katzir and Fred Landman for useful discussions.

References

Roy Bar-Haim, Ido Dagan, Iddo Greental, and Eyal Shnarch. 2007. Semantic inference at the lexical-syntactic level. In *Proceedings of AAAI*, pages 871–876.

Luisa Bentivogli, Bernardo Magnini, Ido Dagan, Hoa Trang Dang, and Danilo Giampiccolo. 2009. The fifth pascal recognizing textual entailment challenge. In *Preproceedings of the Text Analysis Conference (TAC)*.

Luisa Bentivogli, Peter Clark, Ido Dagan, Hoa T. Dang, and Danilo Giampiccolo. 2010. The sixth PASCAL recognizing textual entailment challenge. In *The Text Analysis Conference (TAC 2010)*.

Marie-Catherine de Marneffe and Christopher D. Manning. 2008. The stanford typed dependencies representation. In *COLING Workshop on Cross-framework and Cross-domain Parser Evaluation*.

Christiane Fellbaum, editor. 1998. *WordNet: An Electronic Lexical Database (Language, Speech, and Communication)*. MIT Press.

Lauri Karttunen. 1971. Implicative verbs. *Language*, 47:340–358.

Lauri Karttunen. 2012. Simple and phrasal implicatives. In **SEM 2012*, pages 124–131.

P. Kiparsky and C. Kiparsky. 1970. Fact. In *Progress in Linguistics*, pages 143–173. The Hague: Mouton de Gruyter.

Bill MacCartney and Christopher D. Manning. 2007. Natural logic for textual inference. In *Proceedings of ACL workshop on textual entailment and paraphrasing*.

Bill MacCartney and Christopher D. Manning. 2009. An extended model of natural logic. In *Proceedings of the Eighth International Conference on Computational Semantics (IWCS-8)*.

Mausam, Michael Schmitz, Stephen Soderland, Robert Bart, and Oren Etzioni. 2012. Open language learning for information extraction. In *Proceedings of the 2012 Joint Conference on Empirical Methods in Natural Language Processing and Computational Natural Language Learning*, pages 523–534.

Roser Morante and Walter Daelemans. 2012. Annotating modality and negation for a machine reading evaluation. In *CLEF (Online Working Notes/Labs/Workshop)*.

Rowan Nairn, Cleo Condoravdi, and Lauri Karttunen. 2006. Computing relative polarity for textual inference. In *In Proceedings of ICoS-5 (Inference in Computational Semantics)*.

PPDB: The Paraphrase Database

Juri Ganitkevitch[1] **Benjamin Van Durme**[1,2] **Chris Callison-Burch**[2,3]
[1]Center for Language and Speech Processing, Johns Hopkins University
[2]Human Language Technology Center of Excellence, Johns Hopkins University
[3]Computer and Information Science Department, University of Pennsylvania

Abstract

We present the 1.0 release of our paraphrase database, PPDB. Its English portion, PPDB:Eng, contains over 220 million paraphrase pairs, consisting of 73 million phrasal and 8 million lexical paraphrases, as well as 140 million paraphrase patterns, which capture many meaning-preserving syntactic transformations. The paraphrases are extracted from bilingual parallel corpora totaling over 100 million sentence pairs and over 2 billion English words. We also release PPDB:Spa, a collection of 196 million Spanish paraphrases. Each paraphrase pair in PPDB contains a set of associated scores, including paraphrase probabilities derived from the bitext data and a variety of monolingual distributional similarity scores computed from the Google n-grams and the Annotated Gigaword corpus. Our release includes pruning tools that allow users to determine their own precision/recall tradeoff.

1 Introduction

Paraphrases, i.e. differing textual realizations of the same meaning, have proven useful for a wide variety of natural language processing applications. Past paraphrase collections include automatically derived resources like DIRT (Lin and Pantel, 2001), the MSR paraphrase corpus and phrase table (Dolan et al., 2004; Quirk et al., 2004), among others. Although several groups have independently extracted paraphrases using Bannard and Callison-Burch (2005)'s bilingual pivoting technique (see Zhou et al. (2006), Riezler et al. (2007), Snover et al. (2010), among others), there has never been an official release of this resource.

In this work, we release version 1.0 of the *ParaPhrase DataBase* PPDB,[1] a collection of ranked English and Spanish paraphrases derived by:

- Extracting lexical, phrasal, and syntactic paraphrases from large bilingual parallel corpora (with associated paraphrase probabilities).
- Computing distributional similarity scores for each of the paraphrases using the Google n-grams and the Annotated Gigaword corpus.

In addition to the paraphrase collection itself, we provide tools to filter PPDB to only retain high precision paraphrases, scripts to limit the collection to phrasal or lexical paraphrases (synonyms), and software that enables users to extract paraphrases for languages other than English.

2 Extracting Paraphrases from Bitexts

To extract paraphrases we follow Bannard and Callison-Burch (2005)'s bilingual pivoting method. The intuition is that two English strings e_1 and e_2 that translate to the same foreign string f can be assumed to have the same meaning. We can thus *pivot* over f and extract $\langle e_1, e_2 \rangle$ as a pair of paraphrases, as illustrated in Figure 1. The method extracts a diverse set of paraphrases. For *thrown into jail*, it extracts *arrested, detained, imprisoned, incarcerated, jailed, locked up, taken into custody*, and *thrown into prison*, along with a set of incorrect/noisy paraphrases that have different syntactic types or that are due to misalignments.

For PPDB, we formulate our paraphrase collection as a weighted *synchronous context-free grammar* (SCFG) (Aho and Ullman, 1972; Chiang, 2005)

[1]Freely available at `http://paraphrase.org`.

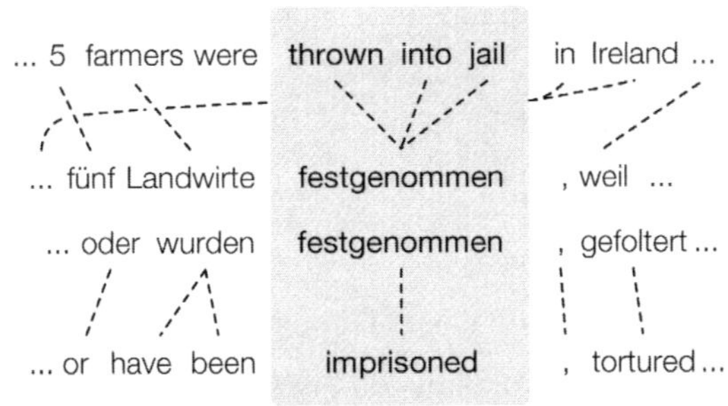

Figure 1: Phrasal paraphrases are extracted via bilingual pivoting.

with syntactic nonterminal labels, similar to Cohn and Lapata (2008) and Ganitkevitch et al. (2011). An SCFG rule has the form:

$$\mathbf{r} \stackrel{\text{def}}{=} C \rightarrow \langle f, e, \sim, \vec{\varphi} \rangle,$$

where the left-hand side of the rule, C, is a nonterminal and the right-hand sides f and e are strings of terminal and nonterminal symbols. There is a one-to-one correspondence, $\sim$, between the nonterminals in f and e: each nonterminal symbol in f has to also appear in e. Following Zhao et al. (2008), each rule $\mathbf{r}$ is annotated with a vector of feature functions $\vec{\varphi} = \{\varphi_1 ... \varphi_N\}$ which are combined in a log-linear model (with weights $\vec{\lambda}$) to compute the *cost* of applying $\mathbf{r}$:

$$cost(\mathbf{r}) = -\sum_{i=1}^{N} \lambda_i \log \varphi_i. \quad (1)$$

To create a syntactic paraphrase grammar we first extract a foreign-to-English translation grammar from a bilingual parallel corpus, using techniques from syntactic machine translation (Koehn, 2010). Then, for each pair of translation rules where the left-hand side C and foreign string f match:

$$\mathbf{r}_1 \stackrel{\text{def}}{=} C \rightarrow \langle f, e_1, \sim_1, \vec{\varphi}_1 \rangle$$
$$\mathbf{r}_2 \stackrel{\text{def}}{=} C \rightarrow \langle f, e_2, \sim_2, \vec{\varphi}_2 \rangle,$$

we *pivot* over f to create a paraphrase rule $\mathbf{r}_p$:

$$\mathbf{r}_p \stackrel{\text{def}}{=} C \rightarrow \langle e_1, e_2, \sim_p, \vec{\varphi}_p \rangle,$$

with a combined nonterminal correspondency function $\sim_p$. Note that the common source side f implies that e_1 and e_2 share the same set of nonterminal symbols.

The paraphrase rules obtained using this method are capable of making well-formed generalizations of meaning-preserving rewrites in English. For instance, we extract the following example paraphrase, capturing the English possessive rule:

$$NP \rightarrow \text{the } NP_1 \text{ of } NNS_2 \mid \text{the } NNS_2 \text{ 's } NP_1.$$

The paraphrase feature vector $\vec{\varphi}_p$ is computed from the translation feature vectors $\vec{\varphi}_1$ and $\vec{\varphi}_2$ by following the pivoting idea. For instance, we estimate the conditional paraphrase probability $p(e_2|e_1)$ by marginalizing over all shared foreign-language translations f:

$$p(e_2|e_1) \approx \sum_f p(e_2|f)p(f|e_1). \quad (2)$$

3 Scoring Paraphrases Using Monolingual Distributional Similarity

The bilingual pivoting approach anchors paraphrases that share an interpretation because of a shared foreign phrase. Paraphrasing methods based on monolingual text corpora, like DIRT (Lin and Pantel, 2001), measure the similarity of phrases based on distributional similarity. This results in a range of different types of phrases, including paraphrases, inference rules and antonyms. For instance, for *thrown into prison* DIRT extracts good paraphrases like *arrested, detained,* and *jailed.* However, it also extracts phrases that are temporarily or causally related like *began the trial of, cracked down on, interrogated, prosecuted* and *ordered the execution of,* because they have similar distributional properties. Since bilingual pivoting rarely extracts these non-paraphrases, we can use monolingual distributional similarity to re-rank paraphrases extracted from bitexts (following Chan et al. (2011)) or incorporate a set of distributional similarity scores as features in our log-linear model.

Each similarity score relies on precomputed distributional signatures that describe the contexts that a phrase occurs in. To describe a phrase e, we gather counts for a set of contextual features for each occurrence of e in a corpus. Writing the context vector for the i-th occurrence of e as $\vec{s}_{e,i}$, we can aggregate over all occurrences of e, resulting in a *distributional* signature for e, $\vec{s}_e = \sum_i \vec{s}_{e,i}$. Following the intuition that phrases with similar meanings occur in

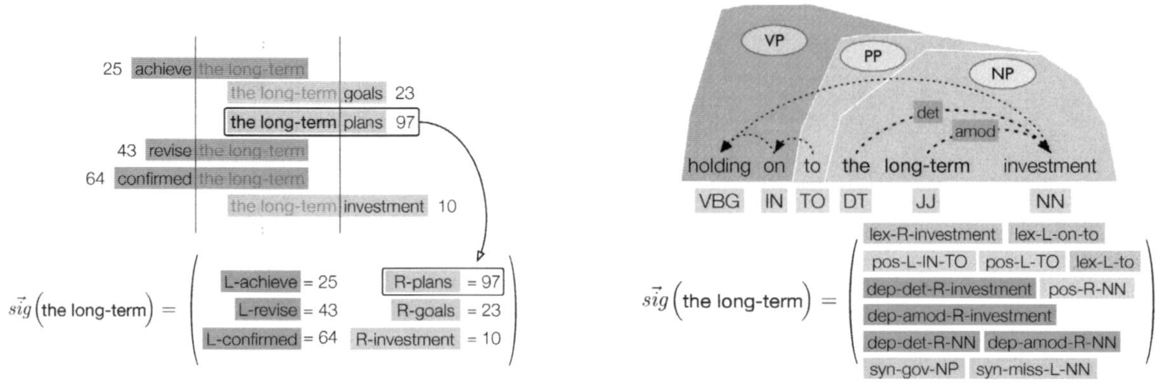

(a) The n-gram corpus records *the long-term* as preceded by *revise* (43 times), and followed by *plans* (97 times). We add corresponding features to the phrase's distributional signature retaining the counts of the original n-grams.

(b) Here, position-aware lexical and part-of-speech n-gram features, labeled dependency links , and features reflecting the phrase's CCG-style label NP/NN are included in the context vector.

Figure 2: Features extracted for the phrase *the long term* from the n-gram corpus (2a) and Annotated Gigaword (2b).

similar contexts, we can then quantify the goodness of e' as a paraphrase of e by computing the cosine similarity between their distributional signatures:

$$sim(e, e') = \frac{\vec{s}_e \cdot \vec{s}_{e'}}{|\vec{s}_e||\vec{s}_{e'}|}.$$

A wide variety of features have been used to describe the distributional context of a phrase. Rich, linguistically informed feature-sets that rely on dependency and constituency parses, part-of-speech tags, or lemmatization have been proposed in work such as by Church and Hanks (1991) and Lin and Pantel (2001). For instance, a phrase is described by the various syntactic relations such as: "what verbs have this phrase as the subject?", or "what adjectives modify this phrase?". Other work has used simpler n-gram features, e.g. "what words or bigrams have we seen to the left of this phrase?". A substantial body of work has focussed on using this type of feature-set for a variety of purposes in NLP (Lapata and Keller, 2005; Bhagat and Ravichandran, 2008; Lin et al., 2010; Van Durme and Lall, 2010).

For PPDB, we compute n-gram-based context signatures for the 200 million most frequent phrases in the Google n-gram corpus (Brants and Franz, 2006; Lin et al., 2010), and richer linguistic signatures for 175 million phrases in the Annotated Gigaword corpus (Napoles et al., 2012). Our features extend beyond those previously used in the work by Ganitkevitch et al. (2012). They are:

- n-gram based features for words seen to the left and right of a phrase.
- Position-aware lexical, lemma-based, part-of-speech, and named entity class unigram and bigram features, drawn from a three-word window to the right and left of the phrase.
- Incoming and outgoing (wrt. the phrase) dependency link features, labeled with the corresponding lexical item, lemmata and POS.
- Syntactic features for any constituents governing the phrase, as well as for CCG-style slashed constituent labels for the phrase.

Figure 2 illustrates the feature extraction for an example phrase.

4 English Paraphrases – PPDB:Eng

We combine several English-to-foreign bitext corpora to extract PPDB:Eng: Europarl v7 (Koehn, 2005), consisting of bitexts for the 19 European languages, the 10^9 French-English corpus (Callison-Burch et al., 2009), the Czech, German, Spanish and French portions of the News Commentary data (Koehn and Schroeder, 2007), the United Nations French- and Spanish-English parallel corpora (Eisele and Chen, 2010), the JRC Acquis corpus (Steinberger et al., 2006), Chinese and Arabic

	Identity	Paraphrases	Total
Lexical	0.6M	7.6M	8.1M
Phrasal	4.9M	68.4M	73.2M
Syntactic	46.5M	93.6M	140.1M
All	52.0M	169.6M	221.4M

Table 1: A breakdown of PPDB:Eng size by paraphrase type. We distinguish lexical (i.e. one-word) paraphrases, phrasal paraphrases and syntactically labeled paraphrase patterns.

	Identity	Paraphrases	Total
Lexical	1.0M	33.1M	34.1M
Phrasal	4.3M	73.2M	77.5M
Syntactic	29.4M	55.3M	84.7M
All	34.7M	161.6M	196.3M

Table 2: An overview of PPDB:Spa. Again, we partition the resource into lexical (i.e. one-word) paraphrases, phrasal paraphrases and syntactically labeled paraphrase patterns.

newswire corpora used for the GALE machine translation campaign,[2] parallel Urdu-English data from the NIST translation task,[3] the French portion of the OpenSubtitles corpus (Tiedemann, 2009), and a collection of Spanish-English translation memories provided by TAUS.[4]

The resulting composite parallel corpus has more than 106 million sentence pairs, over 2 billion English words, and spans 22 pivot languages. To apply the pivoting technique to this multilingual data, we treat the various pivot languages as a joint *Non-English* language. This simplifying assumption allows us to share statistics across the different languages and apply Equation 2 unaltered.

Table 1 presents a breakdown of PPDB:Eng by paraphrase type. We distinguish *lexical* (a single word), *phrasal* (a continuous string of words), and *syntactic* paraphrases (expressions that may contain both words and nonterminals), and separate out identity paraphrases. While we list lexical and phrasal paraphrases separately, it is possible that a single word paraphrases as a multi-word phrase and vice versa – so long they share the same syntactic label.

5 Spanish Paraphrases – PPDB:Spa

We also release a collection of Spanish paraphrases: PPDB:Spa is extracted analogously to its English counterpart and leverages the Spanish portions of the bitext data available to us, totaling almost 355 million Spanish words, in nearly 15 million sentence pairs. The paraphrase pairs in PPDB:Spa are annotated with distributional similarity scores based on lexical features collected from the Spanish portion of the multilingual release of the Google n-gram corpus (Brants and Franz, 2009), and the Spanish Gigaword corpus (Mendonca et al., 2009). Table 2 gives a breakdown of PPDB:Spa.

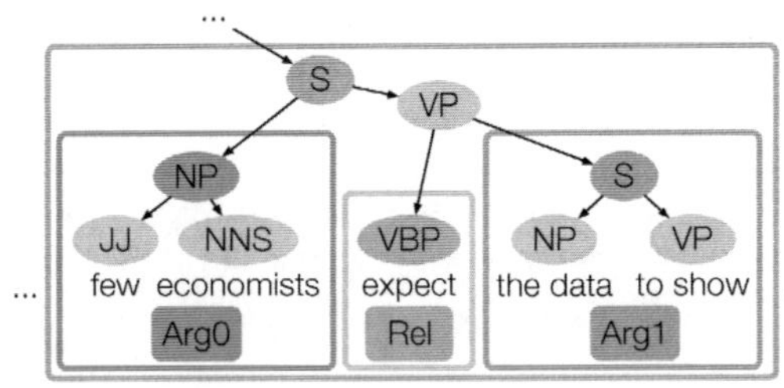

Figure 3: To inspect our coverage, we use the Penn Treebank's parses to map from Propbank annotations to PPDB's syntactic patterns. For the above annotation predicate, we extract $VBP \rightarrow$ expect, which is matched by paraphrase rules like $VBP \rightarrow$ expect | anticipate and $VBP \rightarrow$ expect | hypothesize. To search for the entire relation, we replace the argument spans with syntactic nonterminals. Here, we obtain $S \rightarrow$ *NP* expect S, for which PPDB has matching rules like $S \rightarrow$ *NP* expect S | *NP* would hope S, and $S \rightarrow$ *NP* expect S | *NP* trust S. This allows us to apply sophisticated paraphrases to the predicate while capturing its arguments in a generalized fashion.

6 Analysis

To estimate the usefulness of PPDB as a resource for tasks like semantic role labeling or parsing, we analyze its coverage of Propbank predicates and predicate-argument tuples (Kingsbury and Palmer, 2002). We use the Penn Treebank (Marcus et al., 1993) to map Propbank annotations to patterns which allow us to search PPDB:Eng for paraphrases that match the annotated predicate. Figure 3 illus-

[2] http://projects.ldc.upenn.edu/gale/data/Catalog.html

[3] LDC Catalog No. LDC2010T23

[4] http://www.translationautomation.com/

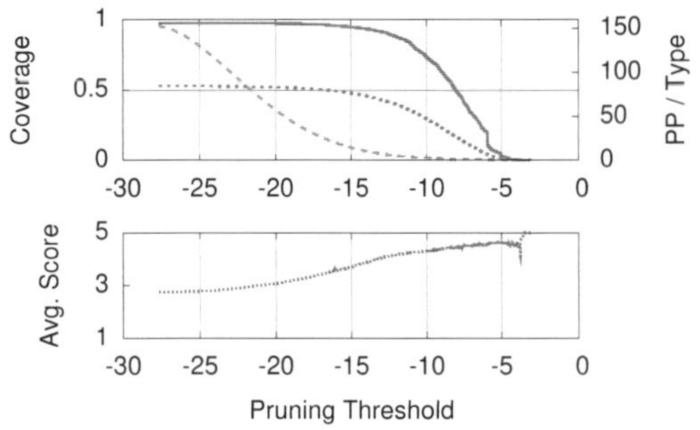

(a) PPDB:Eng coverage of Propbank predicates (top), and average human judgment score (bottom) for varying pruning thresholds.

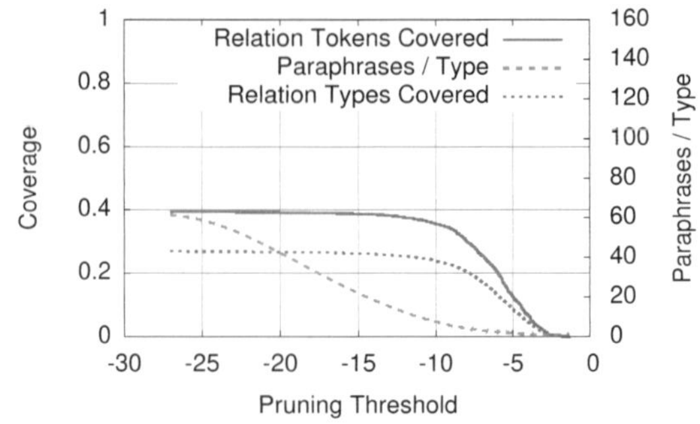

(b) PPDB:Eng's coverage of Propbank predicates with up to two arguments. Here we consider rules that paraphrase the full predicate-argument expression.

Figure 4: An illustration of PPDB's coverage of the manually annotated Propbank predicate phrases (4a) and binary relations with argument non-terminals (4b). The curves indicate the coverage on tokens (solid) and types (dotted), as well as the average number of paraphrases per covered type (dashed) at the given pruning level.

trates this mapping.

In order to quantify PPDB's precision-recall tradeoff in this context, we perform a sweep over our collection, beginning with the full set of paraphrase pairs and incrementally discarding the lowest-scoring ones. We choose a simple estimate for each paraphrase pair's score by uniformly combining its paraphrase probability features in Eq. 1.

The top graph in Figure 4a shows PPDB's coverage of predicates (e.g. $VBP \rightarrow$ expect) at the type level (i.e. counting distinct predicates), as well as the token level (i.e. counting predicate occurrences in the corpus). We also keep track of average number of paraphrases per covered predicate type for varying pruning levels. We find that PPDB has a predicate type recall of up to 52% (accounting for 97.5% of tokens). Extending the experiment to full predicate-argument relations with up to two arguments (e.g. $S \rightarrow NNS$ expect S), we obtain a 27% type coverage rate that accounts for 40% of tokens (Figure 4b). Both rates hold even as we prune the database down to only contain high precision paraphrases. Our pruning method here is based on a simple uniform combination of paraphrase probabilities and similarity scores.

To gauge the quality of our paraphrases, the authors judged 1900 randomly sampled predicate paraphrases on a scale of 1 to 5, 5 being the best. The bottom graph in Figure 4a plots the resulting human score average against the sweep used in the coverage experiment. It is clear that even with a simple weighing approach, the PPDB scores show a clear correlation with human judgements. Therefore they can be used to bias the collection towards greater recall or higher precision.

7 Conclusion and Future Work

We present the 1.0 release of PPDB:Eng and PPDB:Spa, two large-scale collections of paraphrases in English and Spanish. We illustrate the resource's utility with an analysis of its coverage of Propbank predicates. Our results suggest that PPDB will be useful in a variety of NLP applications.

Future releases of PPDB will focus on expanding the paraphrase collection's coverage with regard to both data size and languages supported. Furthermore, we intend to improve paraphrase scoring by incorporating additional sources of information, as well as by better utilizing information present in the data, like domain or topic. We will also address points of refinement such as handling of phrase ambiguity, and effects specific to individual pivot languages. Our aim is for PPDB to be a continuously updated and improving resource.

Finally, we will explore extensions to PPDB to include aspects of related large-scale resources such as lexical-semantic hierarchies (Snow et al., 2006), textual inference rules (Berant et al., 2011), relational patterns (Nakashole et al., 2012), and (lexical) conceptual networks (Navigli and Ponzetto, 2012).

Acknowledgements

We would like to thank Frank Ferraro for his Propbank processing tools. This material is based on research sponsored by the NSF under grant IIS-1249516 and DARPA under agreement number FA8750-13-2-0017 (the DEFT program). The U.S. Government is authorized to reproduce and distribute reprints for Governmental purposes. The views and conclusions contained in this publication are those of the authors and should not be interpreted as representing official policies or endorsements of DARPA or the U.S. Government.

References

Alfred V. Aho and Jeffrey D. Ullman. 1972. *The Theory of Parsing, Translation, and Compiling*. Prentice Hall.

Colin Bannard and Chris Callison-Burch. 2005. Paraphrasing with bilingual parallel corpora. In *Proceedings of ACL*.

Jonathan Berant, Jacob Goldberger, and Ido Dagan. 2011. Global learning of typed entailment rules. In *Proceedings of ACL*.

Rahul Bhagat and Deepak Ravichandran. 2008. Large scale acquisition of paraphrases for learning surface patterns. In *Proceedings of ACL/HLT*.

Thorsten Brants and Alex Franz. 2006. Web 1T 5-gram version 1.

Thorsten Brants and Alex Franz. 2009. Web 1T 5-gram, 10 european languages version 1. *Linguistic Data Consortium, Philadelphia*.

Chris Callison-Burch, Philipp Koehn, Christof Monz, and Josh Schroeder. 2009. Findings of the 2009 Workshop on Statistical Machine Translation. In *Proceedings of WMT*, pages 1–28, Athens, Greece, March.

Tsz Ping Chan, Chris Callison-Burch, and Benjamin Van Durme. 2011. Reranking bilingually extracted paraphrases using monolingual distributional similarity. In *EMNLP Workshop on GEMS*.

David Chiang. 2005. A hierarchical phrase-based model for statistical machine translation. In *Proceedings of ACL*.

Kenneth Church and Patrick Hanks. 1991. Word association norms, mutual information and lexicography. *Computational Linguistics*, 6(1):22–29.

Trevor Cohn and Mirella Lapata. 2008. Sentence compression beyond word deletion. In *Proceedings of the COLING*.

Bill Dolan, Chris Quirk, and Chris Brockett. 2004. Unsupervised construction of large paraphrase corpora: Exploiting massively parallel news sources. In *Proceedings of the COLING*.

Andreas Eisele and Yu Chen. 2010. MultiUN: A multilingual corpus from united nation documents. In *Proceedings of LREC*, Valletta, Malta.

Juri Ganitkevitch, Chris Callison-Burch, Courtney Napoles, and Benjamin Van Durme. 2011. Learning sentential paraphrases from bilingual parallel corpora for text-to-text generation. In *Proceedings of EMNLP*.

Juri Ganitkevitch, Benjamin Van Durme, and Chris Callison-Burch. 2012. Monolingual distributional similarity for text-to-text generation. In *Proceedings of *SEM*. Association for Computational Linguistics.

Paul Kingsbury and Martha Palmer. 2002. From treebank to propbank. In *Proceedings of LREC*.

Philipp Koehn and Josh Schroeder. 2007. Experiments in domain adaptation for statistical machine translation. In *Proceedings of WMT*, Prague, Czech Republic, June. Association for Computational Linguistics.

Philipp Koehn. 2005. Europarl: A parallel corpus for statistical machine translation. In *MT summit*, volume 5.

Philipp Koehn. 2010. *Statistical Machine Translation*. Cambridge University Press.

Mirella Lapata and Frank Keller. 2005. Web-based models for natural language processing. *ACM Transactions on Speech and Language Processing*, 2(1).

Dekang Lin and Patrick Pantel. 2001. Discovery of inference rules from text. *Natural Language Engineering*.

Dekang Lin, Kenneth Church, Heng Ji, Satoshi Sekine, David Yarowsky, Shane Bergsma, Kailash Patil, Emily Pitler, Rachel Lathbury, Vikram Rao, Kapil Dalwani, and Sushant Narsale. 2010. New tools for web-scale n-grams. In *Proceedings of LREC*.

Mitchell P. Marcus, Mary Ann Marcinkiewicz, and Beatrice Santorini. 1993. Building a large annotated corpus of english: the Penn Treebank. *Computational Linguistics*, 19(2).

Angelo Mendonca, David Andrew Graff, and Denise DiPersio. 2009. *Spanish Gigaword Second Edition*. Linguistic Data Consortium.

Ndapandula Nakashole, Gerhard Weikum, and Fabian Suchanek. 2012. PATTY: a taxonomy of relational patterns with semantic types. In *Proceedings of EMNLP*.

Courtney Napoles, Matt Gormley, and Benjamin Van Durme. 2012. Annotated gigaword. In *Proceedings of AKBC-WEKEX 2012*.

Roberto Navigli and Simone Paolo Ponzetto. 2012. BabelNet: The automatic construction, evaluation and application of a wide-coverage multilingual semantic network. *Artificial Intelligence*, 193.

Chris Quirk, Chris Brockett, and William Dolan. 2004. Monolingual machine translation for paraphrase generation. In *Proceedings of EMNLP*.

Stefan Riezler, Alexander Vasserman, Ioannis Tsochantaridis, Vibhu Mittal, and Yi Liu. 2007. Statistical machine translation for query expansion in answer retrieval. In *Proceedings of the 45th Annual Meeting of the ACL*.

Matthew Snover, Nitin Madnani, Bonnie Dorr, and Richard Schwartz. 2010. Ter-plus: paraphrase, semantic, and alignment enhancements to translation edit rate. *Machine Translation*, 23(2-3):117–127.

Rion Snow, Daniel Jurafsky, and Andrew Y. Ng. 2006. Semantic taxonomy induction from heterogenous evidence. In *Proceedings of the ACL/Coling*.

Ralf Steinberger, Bruno Pouliquen, Anna Widiger, Camelia Ignat, Tomaz Erjavec, Dan Tufis, and Dániel Varga. 2006. The JRC-Acquis: A multilingual aligned parallel corpus with 20+ languages. In *Proceedings of LREC*, Genoa, Italy.

Jörg Tiedemann. 2009. News from OPUS: A collection of multilingual parallel corpora with tools and interfaces. In *Recent Advances in Natural Language Processing*, volume 5.

Benjamin Van Durme and Ashwin Lall. 2010. Online generation of locality sensitive hash signatures. In *Proceedings of ACL, Short Papers*.

Shiqi Zhao, Cheng Niu, Ming Zhou, Ting Liu, and Sheng Li. 2008. Combining multiple resources to improve SMT-based paraphrasing model. In *Proceedings of ACL/HLT*.

Liang Zhou, Chin-Yew Lin, Dragos Stefan Munteanu, and Eduard Hovy. 2006. Paraeval: Using paraphrases to evaluate summaries automatically. In *Proceedings of HLT/NAACL*.

Exploiting the Scope of Negations and Heterogeneous Features for Relation Extraction: A Case Study for Drug-Drug Interaction Extraction

Md. Faisal Mahbub Chowdhury [†‡] **and Alberto Lavelli** [‡]
[‡] Fondazione Bruno Kessler (FBK-irst), Italy
[†] University of Trento, Italy
fmchowdhury@gmail.com, lavelli@fbk.eu

Abstract

This paper presents an approach that exploits the scope of negation cues for relation extraction (RE) without the need of using any specifically annotated dataset for building a separate negation scope detection classifier. New features are proposed which are used in two different stages. These also include non-target entity specific features. The proposed RE approach outperforms the previous state of the art for drug-drug interaction (DDI) extraction.

1 Introduction

Negation is a linguistic phenomenon where a *negation cue* (e.g. *not*) can alter the meaning of a particular text segment or of a fact. This text segment (or fact) is said to be inside the *scope of that negation (cue)*. In the context of RE, there is not much work that aims to exploit the scope of negations.[1] The only work on RE that we are aware of is Sanchez-Graillet and Poesio (2007) where they used various heuristics to extract negative protein interaction.

Despite the recent interest on automatically detecting the scope of negation[2] till now there seems to be no empirical evidence supporting its exploitation for the purpose of RE. Even if we could manage to obtain highly accurate automatically detected negation scopes, it is not clear how to feed this information inside the RE approach. Simply considering whether a pair of candidate mentions falls under the scope of a negation cue might not be helpful.

In this paper, we propose that the scope of negations can be exploited at two different levels. Firstly, the system would check whether all the target entity[3] mentions inside a sentence along with possible relation clues (or trigger words), if any, fall (directly or indirectly) under the scope of a negation cue. If such a sentence is found, then it should be discarded (i.e. candidate mention pairs[4] inside that sentence would not be considered). Secondly, for each of the remaining pairs of candidate mentions, the system should exploit features related to the scope of negation (rather than simply adding a feature for negation cue, approach adopted in various RE systems) that can provide indication (if any such evidence exists) that the corresponding relation of interest actually does not hold in that particular context.

In the subsequent sections, we describe our approach. The RE task considered is drug-drug interaction (DDI) extraction. The task has significant importance for public health safety.[5] We used

[1]In the context of event extraction (a closely related task of RE), there have been efforts in BioNLP shared tasks of 2009 and 2011 for (non-mandatory sub-task of) event negation detection (3 participants in 2009; 2 in 2011) (Kim et al., 2009; Kim et al., 2011). The participants approached the sub-task using either pre-defined patterns or some heuristics.

[2]This task is popularized by various recently held shared tasks (Farkas et al., 2010; Morante and Blanco, 2012).

[3]The target entities, for example, for *DDI* extraction and for *EMP-ORG* relation extraction would be {*DRUG*} and {*PER, GPE, ORG*} respectively. Any entity other than the target entities (w.r.t. the particular RE task) belongs to non-target entities.

[4]Candidate mention pairs for RE are taken from target entity mentions.

[5]After the death of pop star Michael Jackson, allegedly due to DDI, it was reported that about 2.2 million people in USA, age 57 to 85, were taking potentially dangerous combinations of drugs (Landau, 2009). An earlier report mentioned that deaths from accidental drug interactions rose 68 percent between 1999 and 2004 (Payne, 2007).

the DDIExtraction-2011 challenge corpus (Segura-Bedmar et al., 2011). The official training and test data of the corpus contain 4,267 and 1,539 sentences, and 2,402 and 755 DDI annotations respectively.

2 Proposed Approach

2.1 Stage 1: Exploiting scope of negation to filter out sentences

We propose a two stage RE approach. In the first stage, our goal is to exploit the scope of negations to reduce the number of candidate mention pairs by discarding sentences. For this purpose, we propose the following features to train a binary classifier:

- *has2TM:* If the sentence has exactly 2 target entity mentions (i.e. drug mentions for DDI extraction).
- *has3OrMoreTM:* Whether the sentence has more than 2 target entity mentions.
- *allTMonRight:* Whether all target entity mentions inside the sentence appear after the negation cue.
- *neitherAllTMonLeftOrRight:* Whether some but not all target entity mentions appear after the negation cue.
- *negCue:* The negation cue itself.
- *immediateGovernor:* The word on which the cue is directly syntactically dependent.
- *nearestVerbGovernor:* The nearest verb in the dependency graph on which the cue is syntactically dependent.
- *isVerbGovernorRoot:* Whether the *nearestVerbGovernor* is root of the dependency graph of the sentence.
- *allTMdependentOnNVG:* Whether all target entity mentions are syntactically dependent (directly/indirectly) on the *nearestVerbGovernor*.
- *allButOneTMdependentOnNVG:* Whether all but one target entity mentions are syntactically dependent on the *nearestVerbGovernor*.
- *although*PrecedeCue:* Whether the syntactic clause containing the negation cue begins with "although / though / despite / in spite".
- *commaBeforeNextTM:* Whether there is a comma in the text between the negation cue and the next target entity mention after the cue.
- *commaAfterPrevTM:* Whether there is a comma in the text between the previous target entity mention before the negation cue and the cue itself.
- *sentHasBut:* Whether the sentence contains the word *"but"*.

The objective of the classifier is to decide whether all of the target entity mentions (i.e. drugs) as well as any possible evidence of the relation of interest (for which we assume the immediate and the nearest verb governors of the negation cue would be good candidates) inside the corresponding sentence fall under the scope of a negation cue in such a way that the sentence is unlikely to contain a DDI.

At present, we limit our focus only on the first occurrence of the following negation cues: *"no"*, *"n't"* or *"not"*.[6] In the Stage 1, any sentence that contains at least one DDI is considered by the classifier as a positive (training/test) instance. Other sentences are considered as negative instances. We rule out any sentence (i.e. we do not consider as training/test instance for the classifier that filters less informative sentences) during both training and testing if any of the following conditions holds:

- The sentence contains less than two target entity mentions (such sentence would not contain the relation of interest anyway).
- It has any of the following phrases – *"not recommended"*, *"should not be"* or *"must not be"*.[7]
- There is no *"no"*, *"n't"* or *"not"* in the sentence.
- No target entity mention appears in the sentence after *"no"*, *"n't"* or *"not"*.

To assess the effectiveness of the proposed Stage 1 classifier, we defined a ***baseline*** classifier that filters any sentence that contains *"no"*, *"n't"* or *"not"*.

2.2 Stage 2

Once the sentences which are likely to have no DDI are identified and removed, the next step is to apply a state-of-the-art RE approach on the remaining sentences. In this section, we propose a new hybrid kernel, K_{Hybrid}, for this purpose. It is defined as follows:

$$K_{Hybrid}(R_1, R_2) = K_{HF}(R_1, R_2) + K_{SL}(R_1, R_2) + w * K_{PET}(R_1, R_2)$$

[6]These cues usually occur more frequently and generally have larger negation scope than other negation cues.

[7]These expressions often provide clues that one of the bio-entity mentions negatively influences the level of activity of the other.

Here, K_{HF} stands for a new feature based kernel (proposed in this paper) that uses a heterogeneous set of features. K_{SL} stands for the Shallow Linguistic (SL) kernel proposed by Giuliano et al. (2006). K_{PET} stands for the Path-enclosed Tree (PET) kernel (Moschitti, 2004). w is a multiplicative constant used for the PET kernel. It allows the hybrid kernel to assign more (or less) weight to the information obtained using tree structures depending on the corpus.

The proposed kernel composition is valid according to the closure properties of kernels. We exploit the SVM-Light-TK toolkit (Moschitti, 2006; Joachims, 1999) for kernel computation. In Stage 2, each candidate drug mention pair represents an instance.

2.2.1 Proposed K_{HF} kernel

As mentioned earlier, this proposed kernel uses heterogeneous features. The first version of the heterogeneous feature set (henceforth, *HF v1*) combines features proposed by two previous RE works. The former is Zhou et al. (2005), which uses 51 different features. We select the following 27 of their features for our feature set:

> *WBNULL, WBFL, WBF, WBL, WBO, BM1F, BM1L, AM2F, AM2L, #MB, #WB, CPHBNULL, CPHBFL, CPHBF, CPHBL, CPHBO, CPHBM1F, CPHBM1L, CPHAM2F, CPHAM2F, CPP, CPPH, ET12SameNP, ET12SamePP, ET12SameVP, PTP, PTPH*

The latter is the TPWF kernel (Chowdhury and Lavelli, 2012a) from which we use following features:

> *HasTriggerWord, Trigger-X, DepPattern-i, e-walk, v-walk*

The TPWF kernel extracts the *HasTriggerWord, Trigger-X* and *DepPattern-i* features from a sub-graph called *reduced graph*. We also follow this approach with one minor difference. Unlike Chowdhury and Lavelli (2012a), we look for trigger words in the whole reduced graph instead of using only the root of the sub-graph.

Due to space limitation we refer the readers to the corresponding papers for the description of the above mentioned features and the definition of *reduced graph*.

In addition, *HF v1* also includes surrounding tokens within the window of {-2,+2} for each candidate mention. We are unaware of any available list of trigger words for drug-drug interaction. So, we created such a list.[8]

We extend the heterogeneous feature set by adding features related to the scope of negation (henceforth, *HF v2*). We use a list of 13 negation cues[9] to search inside the reduced graph of a candidate pair. If the reduced graph contains any of the negation cues or their morphological variants then we add the following features:

- *negCue:* The corresponding negation cue.
- *immediateNegatedWord:* If the word following the negation cue is neither a preposition nor a "*be* verb", then that word, otherwise the word after the next word.[10]

Furthermore, if the corresponding matched negation cue is either *"no"*, *"n't"* or *"not"*, then we add additional features related to negation scope:

- *bothEntDependOnImmediateGovernor:* Whether the immediate governor (if any) of the negation cue is also governor of a dependency sub-tree (of the dependency graph of the corresponding sentence) that includes both of the candidate mentions.
- *immediateGovernorIsVerbGovernor:* Whether the immediate governor of the negation cue is a verb.
- *nearestVerbGovernor:* The closest verb governor (i.e. parent or grandparent inside the dependency graph), if any, of the negation cue.

We further extend the heterogeneous feature set by adding features related to relevant non-target entities (with respect to the relation of interest; henceforth, *HF v3*). For the purpose of DDI extraction, we deem the presence of *DISEASE* mentions (which might result as a consequence of a DDI) can provide some clues. So, we use a publicly available state-of-the-art disease NER system called BioEnEx (Chowdhury and Lavelli, 2010) to annotate the DDIExtraction-2011 challenge corpus. For

[8]The RE system developed for this work and the created list of trigger words for DDI can be downloaded from https://github.com/fmchowdhury/HyREX .

[9]No, not, neither, without, lack, fail, unable, abrogate, absence, prevent, unlikely, unchanged, rarely.

[10]For example, "interested" from "... not interested ...", and "confused" from "... not to be confused ...".

each candidate (drug) mention pair, we add the following features in *HF v3*:

- *NTEMinsideSentence:* Whether the corresponding sentence contains important non-target entity mention(s) (e.g. disease for DDI).
- *immediateGovernorIsVerbGovernorOfNTEM:* The immediate governor (if any) of the non-target entity mention, only if such governor is also governing a dependency sub-tree that includes both of the target candidate entity mentions.
- *nearestVerbGovernorOfNTEM:* The closest verb governor (if any) of the non-target entity mention, only if it also governs the candidate entity mentions.
- *immediateGovernorIsVerbGovernorOfNTEM:* Whether the immediate governor is a verb.

3 Results and Discussion

We train a linear SVM classifier in Stage 1 and tune the hyper-parameters (by doing 5-fold cross-validation) for obtaining maximum possible recall. In this way we minimize the number of false negatives (i.e. sentences that contain DDIs but are wrongly identified as not having any).

During the cross-validation experiments on the training data, 334 sentences (7.83% of the total sentences) containing at least 2 drug mentions were identified by our proposed classifier (in Section 2.1) as unlikely to have any DDI and hence are candidates for discarding. Only 19 of these sentences were incorrectly identified. When we trained on the training data and tested on the official test data of DDIExtraction-2011 challenge corpus, 121 sentences (7.86% of the total test sentences) were identified by the classifier as candidates for discarding. Only 5 of them were incorrectly identified.

Unlike Stage 1, in Stage 2 where we train the hybrid kernel based RE classifier and use it for RE (i.e. DDI extraction) from the test data, sentences are not the RE training/test instances. Instead, a RE instance corresponds to a candidate mention pair.

All the DDIs (i.e. positive RE instances) of the incorrectly identified sentences in Stage 1 (i.e. the sentences which are incorrectly labelled as not having any DDI and filtered) are automatically considered as false negatives during the calculation of DDI extraction results in Stage 2.

To verify whether our proposed hybrid kernel achieves state-of-the-art results without taking benefits of the output of Stage 1, we did some experiments without discarding any sentence. These experiments are done using Zhou et al. (2005), TPWF kernel, SL kernel, different versions of proposed K_{HF} kernel and K_{Hybrid} kernel. Table 1 shows the results of 5-fold cross-validation experiments (hyper-parameters are tuned for obtaining maximum F-score). As the results show, there is a gain +0.9 points in F-score (mainly due to the boost in recall) after the addition of features related to negation scope. There is also some minor improvement due to the proposed non-target entity specific features.

We also performed (5-fold cross validation) experiments by combining the Stage 1 classifier with each of the Zhou et al. (2005), TPWF kernel, SL kernel, PET kernel, K_{HF} kernel and K_{Hybrid} kernel separately (only the results of K_{Hybrid} are reported in Table 1 due to space limitation). In each case, there were improvements in precision, recall and F-score. The gain in F-score ranged from *1.0* to *1.4* points.

	P / R / F-score
Using SL kernel (Giuliano et al., 2006)	51.3 / 64.7 / 57.3
Using (Zhou et al., 2005)	58.7 / 37.1 / 45.5
Using PET kernel (Moschitti, 2004)	46.8 / 602 / 52.7
TPWF (Chowdhury and Lavelli, 2012a)	43.7 / 60.7 / 50.8
Proposed approaches	
Proposed $K_{HF\ v1}$	53.4 / 51.5 / 52.4
$K_{HF\ v2}$ (i.e. + neg scope feat.)	53.9 / 52.6 / 53.3 (+0.9)
$K_{HF\ v3}$ (i.e. + non-target entity feat.)	53.6 / 53.5 / 53.6 (+0.3)
Proposed K_{Hybrid}	56.3 / 68.5 / 61.8
Proposed K_{Hybrid} with Stage 1	57.3 / 69.4 / 62.8 (+1.0)

Table 1: 5-fold cross-validation results on training data.

Table 2 reports the results of the previously published studies that used the same corpus. Our proposed K_{Hybrid} kernel obtains an F-score that is higher than that of the previous state of the art.

When the Stage 1 classifier (based on negation scope features) is exploited before using the K_{Hybrid} kernel, the F-score reaches up to 67.4. This is +1.0 points higher than without exploiting the Stage 1 classifier and +1.7 higher than previous state of the art. We did separate experiments (also reported in Table 2) to assess the performance improvement when the output of Stage 1 is used to filter sentences from either training or test data only. The results remain the same when only training sentences are filtered; while there are some improvements when only test sentences are filtered. Filtering both training and test sentences provides the larger gain which is statistically significant.

Usually, the number of negative instances in a corpus is much higher than that of the positive instances. In a recent work, Chowdhury and Lavelli (2012b) showed that by removing less informative (negative) instances (henceforth, *LIIs*), not only the skewness in instance distribution could be reduced but it also leads to a better result. The proposed Stage 1 classifier, presented in this work, also reduces skewness in instance distribution. This is because we are only removing those sentences that are unlikely to contain any positive instance. So, in principle, the Stage 1 classifier is focused on removing only negative instances (although the classifier mistakenly discards few positive instances, too).

We wanted to study how the Stage 1 classifier would contribute if we use it on top of the techniques that were proposed in Chowdhury and Lavelli (2012b) to remove LIIs. As Table 2 shows, by using the Stage 1 classifier along with LLI filtering, we could further improve the results (+3.2 points difference in F-score with the previous state of the art).

4 Conclusion

A major flexibility in the proposed approach is that it does not require a separate dataset (which needs to match the genre of the text to be used for RE) annotated with negation scopes. Instead, the proposed Stage 1 classifier uses the RE training data (which do not have negation scope annotations) to self-supervise itself. Various new features have been exploited (both in stages 1 and 2) that can provide strong indications of the scope of negation cues with respect to the relation to be extracted. The only thing needed is the list of possible negation cues (Morante (2010) includes such a comprehensive list).

Our proposed kernel, which has a component that exploits a heterogeneous set of features including negation scope and presence of non-target entities, already obtains better results than previous studies.

	P	R	F-score
(Thomas et al., 2011)	60.5	71.9	65.7
(Chowdhury et al., 2011)	58.6	70.5	64.0
(Chowdhury and Lavelli, 2011)	58.4	70.1	63.7
(Bjorne et al., 2011)	58.0	68.9	63.0
Proposed K_{Hybrid}	60.0	74.3	66.4
K_{Hybrid} + Stage 1 baseline	61.8	68.9	65.1
K_{Hybrid} + proposed Stage 1 (only training sentences are filtered)	60.0	74.2	66.4
K_{Hybrid} + proposed Stage 1 (only test sentences are filtered)	61.4	73.8	67.0
K_{Hybrid} + proposed Stage 1 (both training and test sentences are filtered)	62.1	73.8	67.4 stat. sig.
Proposed K_{Hybrid} + LII filtering	61.1	75.1	67.4 stat. sig.
Proposed K_{Hybrid} + LII filtering + proposed Stage 1	63.5	75.2	68.9 stat. sig.

Table 2: Results obtained on the official test set of the 2011 DDI Extraction challenge. LII filtering refers to the techniques proposed in Chowdhury and Lavelli (2012b) for reducing skewness in RE data distribution. stat. sig. indicates that the improvement of F-score, due to usage of Stage 1 classifier, is statistically significant (verified using *Approximate Randomization Procedure* (Noreen, 1989); number of iterations = 1,000, confidence level = 0.01).

The results considerably improve when possible irrelevant sentences from both training and test data are filtered by exploiting features related to the scope of negations.

In future, we would like to exploit the scope of more negation cues, apart from the three cues that are used in this study. We believe our approach would help to improve RE in other genres of text (such as newspaper) as well.

Acknowledgement

This work was carried out in the context of the project "eOnco - Pervasive knowledge and data management in cancer care".

References

J Bjorne, A Airola, T Pahikkala, and T Salakoski. 2011. Drug-drug interaction extraction with RLS and SVM classifiers. In *Proceedings of the 1st Challenge task on Drug-Drug Interaction Extraction (DDIExtraction 2011)*, pages 35–42, Huelva, Spain, September.

MFM Chowdhury and A Lavelli. 2010. Disease mention recognition with specific features. In *Proceedings of the 2010 Workshop on Biomedical Natural Language Processing*, pages 83–90, Uppsala, Sweden, July. Association for Computational Linguistics.

MFM Chowdhury and A Lavelli. 2011. Drug-drug interaction extraction using composite kernels. In *Proceedings of the 1st Challenge task on Drug-Drug Interaction Extraction (DDIExtraction 2011)*, pages 27–33, Huelva, Spain, September.

MFM Chowdhury and A Lavelli. 2012a. Combining tree structures, flat features and patterns for biomedical relation extraction. In *Proceedings of the 13th Conference of the European Chapter of the Association for Computational Linguistics (EACL 2012)*, pages 420–429, Avignon, France, April. Association for Computational Linguistics.

MFM Chowdhury and A Lavelli. 2012b. Impact of Less Skewed Distributions on Efficiency and Effectiveness of Biomedical Relation Extraction. In *Proceedings of the 24th International Conference on Computational Linguistics (COLING 2012) : Posters*, pages 205–216, Mumbai, India, December.

MFM Chowdhury, AB Abacha, A Lavelli, and P Zweigenbaum. 2011. Two different machine learning techniques for drug-drug interaction extraction. In *Proceedings of the 1st Challenge task on Drug-Drug Interaction Extraction (DDIExtraction 2011)*, pages 19–26, Huelva, Spain, September.

R Farkas, V Vincze, G Móra, J Csirik, and G Szarvas. 2010. The CoNLL-2010 shared task: Learning to detect hedges and their scope in natural language text. In *Proceedings of the Fourteenth Conference on Computational Natural Language Learning*, pages 1–12, Uppsala, Sweden, July. Association for Computational Linguistics.

C Giuliano, A Lavelli, and L Romano. 2006. Exploiting shallow linguistic information for relation extraction from biomedical literature. In *Proceedings of the 11th Conference of the European Chapter of the Association for Computational Linguistics (EACL 2006)*, pages 401–408.

T Joachims. 1999. Making large-scale support vector machine learning practical. In *Advances in kernel methods: support vector learning*, pages 169–184. MIT Press, Cambridge, MA, USA.

JD Kim, T Ohta, S Pyysalo, Y Kano, and J Tsujii. 2009. Overview of BioNLP'09 shared task on event extraction. In *Proceedings of the BioNLP 2009 Workshop Companion Volume for Shared Task*, pages 1–9, Boulder, Colorado, June. Association for Computational Linguistics.

JD Kim, Y Wang, T Takagi, and A Yonezawa. 2011. Overview of Genia event task in BioNLP shared task 2011. In *Proceedings of BioNLP Shared Task 2011 Workshop*, pages 7–15, Portland, Oregon, USA, June. Association for Computational Linguistics.

E Landau. 2009. Jackson's death raises questions about drug interactions [Published in CNN; June 26, 2009]. `http://articles.cnn.com/2009-06-26/health/jackson.drug.interaction.caution_1_drug-interactions-heart-rhythms-antidepressants?_s=PM:HEALTH`.

R Morante and E Blanco. 2012. *SEM 2012 shared task: Resolving the scope and focus of negation. In **SEM 2012: The First Joint Conference on Lexical and Computational Semantics – Volume 1: Proceedings of the main conference and the shared task, and Volume 2: Proceedings of the Sixth International Workshop on Semantic Evaluation (SemEval 2012)*, pages 265–274, Montréal, Canada, 7-8 June. Association for Computational Linguistics.

R Morante. 2010. Descriptive Analysis of Negation Cue in Biomedical Texts. In *Proceedings of the 7th International Conference on Language Resources and Evaluation (LREC 2010)*, Malta.

A Moschitti. 2004. A study on convolution kernels for shallow semantic parsing. In *Proceedings of the 42nd Annual Meeting of the Association for Computational Linguistics (ACL 2004)*, Barcelona, Spain.

A Moschitti. 2006. Making Tree Kernels Practical for Natural Language Learning. In *Proceedings of 11th Conference of the European Chapter of the Association for computational Linguistics (EACL 2006)*, Trento, Italy.

EW Noreen. 1989. *Computer-Intensive Methods for Testing Hypotheses : An Introduction*. Wiley-Interscience, April.

JW Payne. 2007. A Dangerous Mix [Published in The Washington Post; February 27, 2007]. `http://www.washingtonpost.com/wp-dyn/content/article/2007/02/23/AR2007022301780.html`.

O Sanchez-Graillet and M Poesio. 2007. Negation of protein-protein interactions: analysis and extraction. *Bioinformatics*, 23(13):i424–i432.

I Segura-Bedmar, P Martínez, and CD Pablo-Sánchez. 2011. The 1st DDIExtraction-2011 challenge task: Extraction of Drug-Drug Interactions from biomedical texts. In *Proceedings of the 1st Challenge task on Drug-Drug Interaction Extraction (DDIExtraction 2011)*, pages 1–9, Huelva, Spain, September.

P Thomas, M Neves, I Solt, D Tikk, and U Leser. 2011. Relation extraction for drug-drug interactions using ensemble learning. In *Proceedings of the 1st Challenge task on Drug-Drug Interaction Extraction*

(DDIExtraction 2011), pages 11–18, Huelva, Spain, September.

GD Zhou, J Su, J Zhang, and M Zhang. 2005. Exploring various knowledge in relation extraction. In *Proceedings of the 43rd Annual Meeting on Association for Computational Linguistics (ACL 2005)*, pages 427–434, Ann Arbor, Michigan, USA.

Graph-Based Seed Set Expansion for Relation Extraction Using Random Walk Hitting Times

Joel Lang
University of Geneva
7 Route de Drize
1227 Carouge, Switzerland
joel.lang@unige.ch

James Henderson
Xerox Research Centre Europe
6 Chemin de Maupertuis
38240 Meylan, France
james.henderson@xrce.xerox.com

Abstract

Iterative bootstrapping methods are widely employed for relation extraction, especially because they require only a small amount of human supervision. Unfortunately, a phenomenon known as *semantic drift* can affect the accuracy of iterative bootstrapping and lead to poor extractions. This paper proposes an alternative bootstrapping method, which ranks relation tuples by measuring their distance to the seed tuples in a bipartite tuple-pattern graph. In contrast to previous bootstrapping methods, our method is not susceptible to semantic drift, and it empirically results in better extractions than iterative methods.

1 Introduction

The goal of relation extraction is to extract tuples of a particular relation from a corpus of natural language text. A widely employed approach to relation extraction is based on iterative bootstrapping (Brin, 1998; Agichtein and Gravano, 2000; Pasca et al., 2006; Pantel and Pennacchiotti, 2006), which can be applied with only small amounts of supervision and which scales well to very large datasets.

A well-known problem with iterative bootstrapping is a phenomenon known as *semantic drift* (Curran et al., 2007): as bootstrapping proceeds it is likely that unreliable patterns will lead to false extractions. These extraction errors are amplified in the following iterations and the extracted relation will drift away from the intended target. Semantic drift often results in low precision extractions and therefore poses a major limitation of iterative bootstrapping algorithms. Previous work on iterative bootstrapping has addressed the issue of reducing semantic drift for example by bagging the results of various runs employing differing seed tuples, constructing filters which identify false tuples or patterns and adding further constraints to the bootstrapping process (T. McIntosh, 2010; McIntosh and Curran, 2009; Curran et al., 2007).

However, the analysis of Komachi et al. (2008) has shown that semantic drift is an inherent property of iterative bootstrapping algorithms and therefore poses a fundamental problem. They have shown that iterative bootstrapping without pruning corresponds to an eigenvector computation and thus as the number of iterations increases the resulting ranking will always converge towards the same static ranking of tuples, *regardless of the particular choice of seed instances*.

In this paper, we describe an alternative method, that is not susceptible to semantic drift. We represent our data as a bipartite graph, whose vertices correspond to patterns and tuples respectively and whose edges capture cooccurrences and then measure the distance of a tuple to the seed set in terms of random walk hitting times. Experimental results confirm that semantic drift is avoided by our method and show that substantial improvements over iterative forms of bootstrapping are possible.

2 Scoring with Hitting Times

From a given corpus, we extract a dataset consisting of *tuples* and *patterns*. Tuples are pairs of co-occurring strings in the corpus, such as *(Bill Gates, Microsoft)*, which potentially belong to a particular relation of interest. In our case, patterns are simply the sequence of tokens occurring between tuple elements, e.g. *"is the founder of"*. We represent all the tuple types[1] X and all the extraction pattern types Y contained in a given corpus through an undirected, weighted, bipartite graph $G = (V, E)$ with vertices $V = X \cup Y$ and edges $E \subset X \times Y$, where an edge $(x, y) \in E$ indicates that tuple x occurs with pattern y somewhere in the corpus. Edge weights are defined through a weight matrix W which holds the weight $W_{i,j} = w(v_i, v_j)$ for edges $(v_i, v_j) \in E$. Specifically, we use the count of how many times a tuple occurs with a pattern in the corpus and weights for unconnected vertices are zero.

Our goal is to compute a score vector σ holding a score $\sigma_i = \sigma(x_i)$ for each tuple $x_i \in X$, which quantifies how well the tuple matches the seed tuples. Higher scores indicate that the tuple is more likely to belong to the relation defined through the seeds and thus the score vector effectively provides a ranking of the tuples.

We define scores of tuples based on their *distance*[2] to the seed tuples in the graph. The distance of some tuple x to the seed set S can be naturally formalized in terms of the average time it takes until a random walk starting in S reaches x, the *hitting time*. The random walk is defined through the probability distribution over start vertices and through a matrix of transition probabilities. Edge weights are constrained to be non-negative, which allows us to define the transition matrix P with $P_{i,j} = p(v_j|v_i) = \frac{1}{d_{v_i}} w(v_i, v_j)$, where $d_v = \sum_{v_k \in V} w(v, v_k)$ is the degree of a vertex $v \in V$.

The distance of two vertices is measured in terms of the average time of a random walk between the two. Specifically, we adopt the notion of *T-truncated hitting time* (Sarkar and Moore, 2007) defined as the expected number of steps it takes until a random walk of at most T steps starting at v_i reaches v_j for the first time:

$$h^T(v_j|v_i) = \begin{cases} 0 & \text{iff. } v_j = v_i \text{ or T=0} \\ 1 + \sum_{v_k \in V} p(v_k|v_i) h^{T-1}(v_j|v_k) \end{cases}$$

The truncated hitting time $h^T(v_j|v_i)$ can be approximately computed by sampling M independent random walks starting at v_i of length T and computing

$$\hat{h}^T(v_j|v_i) = \frac{1}{M} \sum_{k=1}^{m} t_k + \left(1 - \frac{m}{M}\right) T \qquad (1)$$

where $\{t_1 \dots t_m\}$ are the sampled first-hit times of random walks which reach v_j within T steps (Sarkar et al., 2008).

The score $\sigma_{HT}(v)$ of a vertex $v \notin S$ to the seed set S is then defined as the inverse of the average T-truncated hitting time of random walks starting at a randomly chosen vertex $s \in S$:

$$\frac{1}{\sigma_{HT}(v)} = h^T(v|S) = \frac{1}{|S|} \sum_{s \in S} h^T(v|s) \qquad (2)$$

3 Experiments

We extracted tuples and patterns from the fifth edition of the Gigaword corpus (Parker et al., 2011), by running a named entity tagger and extracting all pairs of named entities and extracting occurring within the same sentence which do not have another named entity standing between them. Gold standard seed and test tuples for a set of relations were obtained from YAGO (Suchanek et al., 2007). Specifically, we took all relations for which there are at least 300 tuples, each of which occurs at least once in the corpus. This resulted in the set of relations shown in Table 1, plus the development relation *hasWonPrize*.

For evaluation, we use the *percentile rank of the median test set element* (PRM, see Francois et al. 2007), which reflects the quality of the

[1]Note that we are using tuple and pattern *types* rather than particular mentions in the corpus.

[2]The term is used informally. In particular, hitting times are not a *distance metric*, since they can be asymmetric.

full produced ranking, not just the top N elements and is furthermore computable with only a small set of labeled test tuples [3].

We compare our proposed method based on hitting times (HT) with two variants of iterative bootstrapping. The first one (IB1) does not employ pruning and corresponds to the algorithm described in Komachi et al. (2008). The second one (IB2) corresponds to a standard bootstrapping algorithm which employs pruning after each step in order to reduce semantic drift. Specifically, scores are pruned after projecting from X onto Y and from Y onto X, retaining only the top $N^{(t)} = N_0 t$ scores at iteration t and setting all other scores to zero.

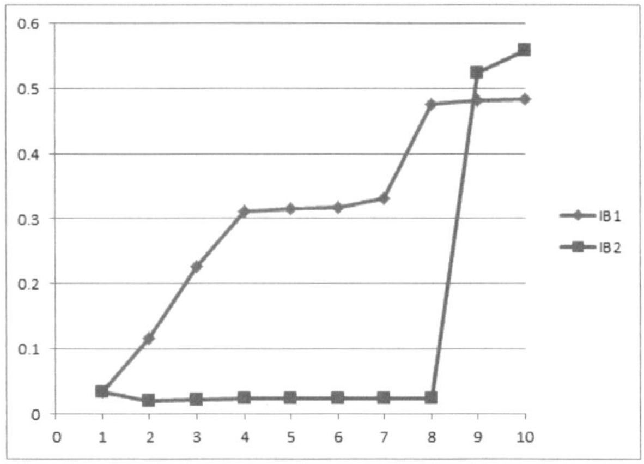

Figure 1: PRM for iterative bootstrapping without pruning (IB1) and with pruning (IB2). A lower PRM is better.

3.1 Parametrizations

The experiments in this section were conducted on the held out development relation *hasWonPrize*. The ranking produced by both forms of iterative bootstrapping IB1 and IB2 depend on the number of iterations, as shown in Figure 1. IB1 achieves an optimal ranking after just one iteration and thereafter scores get worse due to semantic drift. In contrast, pruning helps avoid semantic drift for IB2, which attains an optimal score after 2 iterations and achieves relatively constant scores for several iterations. However, during iteration 9 an incorrect pattern is kept and this at once leads to a drastic loss in accuracy, showing that semantic drift is only deferred and not completely eliminated.

Our method HT has parameter T, corresponding to the truncation time, i.e., maximal number of steps of a random walk. Figure 2 shows the PRM of our method for different values of T. Performance gets better as T increases and is optimal for $T = 12$, whereas for larger values, the performance gets slightly worse again. The figure shows that, if T is large enough (> 5), the PRM is relatively constant and there is no phenomenon comparable to semantic drift, which causes instability in the produced rankings.

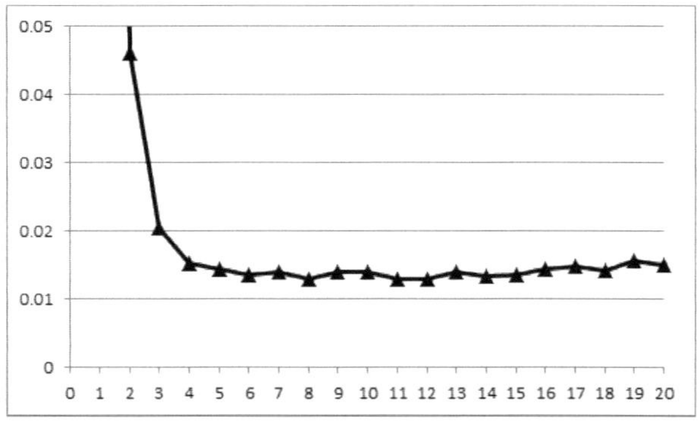

Figure 2: PRM for our method based on hitting times, for different values of the truncation time parameter T.

3.2 Method Comparison

To evaluate the methods, firstly the parameters for each method were set to the optimal values as determined in the previous section. For the experiments here, we again use 200 randomly chosen tuples as the seeds for each relation. All the remaining gold standard tuples are used for testing.

Table 1 shows the PRM for the three methods. For a majority of the relations (12/16) HT attains the best, i.e. lowest, PRM, which confirms that hitting times constitute an accurate way of measuring the distance of tuples to the seed set. IB1 and IB2 each perform best on 2/16 of the relations. A sign test on these results yields that

[3] other common metrics do not satisfy these conditions.

Relation	IB1	IB2	HT
created	1.82	1.71	**0.803**
dealsWith	**0.0262**	0.107	0.0481
diedIn	30.5	**18.4**	20.4
directed	0.171	0.238	**0.166**
hasChild	7.66	32.2	**4.26**
influences	5.93	**5.48**	6.60
isAffiliatedTo	1.54	2.01	**1.30**
isCitizenOf	1.74	1.87	**1.68**
isLeaderOf	1.37	1.91	**0.401**
isMarriedTo	4.69	4.14	**1.27**
isPoliticianOf	**0.0117**	0.110	0.0409
livesIn	3.17	2.48	**1.70**
owns	11.0	2.10	**2.07**
produced	1.55	0.967	**0.240**
wasBornIn	11.3	9.37	**8.42**
worksAt	1.52	2.21	**0.193**

Table 1: PRM in percent for all relations, for all three models. A lower PRM corresponds to a better model, with the best score indicated in bold.

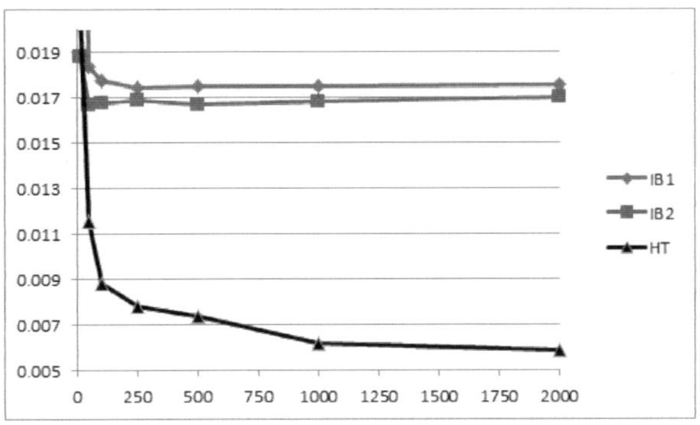

Figure 3: PRM for the three methods, as a function of the size of the seed set for the relation created.

HT is better than both IB1 and IB2 at significance level $\alpha < 0.01$.

Moreover, the ranking produced by HT is stable and not affected by semantic drift, given that even where results are worse than for IB1 or IB2, they are still close to the best performing method. In contrast, when semantic drift occurs, the performance of IB1 and IB2 can deteriorate drastically, e.g. for the *worksAt* relation, where both IB1 and IB2 produce rankings that are a lot worse than the one produced by HT.

3.3 Sensitivity to Seed Set Size

Figure 3 shows the PRM for each of the three methods as a function of the size of the seed set for the relation *created*. For small seed sets, the performance of the iterative methods can be increased by adding more seeds. However, from a seed set size of 50 onwards, performance remains relatively constant. In other words, iterative bootstrapping is not benefitting from the information provided by the additional labeled data, and thus has a poor learning performance. In contrast, for our method based on hitting times, the performance continually improves as the seed set size is increased. Thus, also in terms of learning performance, our method is more sound than iterative bootstrapping.

4 Conclusions

The paper has presented a graph-based method for seed set expansion which is not susceptible to semantic drift and on most relations outperforms iterative bootstrapping. The method measures distance between vertices through random walk hitting times. One property which makes hitting times an appropriate distance measure is their ability to reflect the overall connectivity structure of the graph, in contrast to measures such as the shortest path between two vertices. The hitting time will decrease when the number of paths from the start vertex to the target vertex increases, when the length of paths decreases or when the likelihood (weights) of paths increases. These properties are particularly important when the observed graph edges must be assumed to be merely a sample of all plausible edges, possibly perturbated by noise. This has also been asserted by previous work, which has shown that hitting times successfully capture the notion of similarity for other natural language processing problems such as learning paraphrases (Kok and Brockett, 2010) and related problems such as query suggestion (Mei et al., 2008). Future work will be aimed towards employing our hitting time based method in combination with a richer feature set.

References

Agichtein, E. and Gravano, L. (2000). Snowball: Extracting Relations from Large Plaintext Collections. In *Proceedings of the Fifth ACM Conference on Digital Libraries*.

Brin, S. (1998). Extracting Patterns and Relations from the World-Wide Web. In *Proceedings of the 1998 International Workshop on the Web and Databases*.

Curran, J., Murphy, T., and Scholz, B. (2007). Minimising Semantic Drift with Mutual Exclusion Bootstrapping. In *Proceedings of the 10th Conference of the Pacific Association for Computational Linguistics*.

Francois, F., Pirotte, A., Renders, J., and Saerens, M. (2007). Random-Walk Computation of Similarities between Nodes of a Graph with Application to Collaborative Recommendation. *IEEE Transactions on Knowledge and Data Engineering*, 19(3):355 –369.

Kok, S. and Brockett, C. (2010). Hitting the Right Paraphrases in Good Time. In *Proceedings of the Annual Conference of the North American Chapter of the Association for Computational Linguistics*.

Komachi, M., Kudo, T., Shimbo, M., and Matsumoto, Y. (2008). Graph-based Analysis of Semantic Drift in Espresso-like Bootstrapping Algorithms. In *Proceedings of the Conference on Empirical Methods in Natural Language Processing*.

McIntosh, T. and Curran, J. (2009). Reducing Semantic Drift with Bagging and Distributional Similarity. In *Proceedings of the Joint Conference of the 47th Annual Meeting of the ACL*.

Mei, Q., Zhou, D., and Church, K. (2008). Query Suggestion Using Hitting Time. In *Proceedings of the 17th ACM Conference on Information and Knowledge Management*.

Pantel, P. and Pennacchiotti, M. (2006). Espresso: Leveraging Generic Patterns for Automatically Harvesting Semantic Relations. In *Proceedings of the 21st International Conference on Computational Linguistics and the 44th Annual Meeting of the Association for Computational Linguistics*.

Parker, R., Graff, D., Kong, J., Chen, K., and Maeda, K. (2011). English Gigaword Fifth Edition. Technical report, Linguistic Data Consortium.

Pasca, M., Lin, D., Bigham, J., Lifchits, A., and Jain, A. (2006). Organizing and Searching the World Wide Web of Facts – Step One: the One-million Fact Extraction Challenge. In *Proceedings of the 21st National Conference on Artificial Intelligence (AAAI)*.

Sarkar, P. and Moore, A. (2007). A Tractable Approach to Finding Closest Truncated-commute-time Neighbors in Large Graphs. In *Proceedings of the 23rd Conference on Uncertainty in Artificial Intelligence*.

Sarkar, P., Moore, A., and Prakash, A. (2008). Fast Incremental Proximity Search in Large Graphs. In *Proceedings of the 25th International Conference on Machine Learning*.

Suchanek, F., Kasneci, G., and Weikum, G. (2007). Yago: A Core of Semantic Knowledge. In *Proceedings of the International World Wide Web Conference (WWW)*.

T. McIntosh (2010). Unsupervised Discovery of Negative Categories in Lexicon Bootstrapping. In *Proceedings of the 2010 Conference on Empirical Methods in Natural Language Processing*.

Distant Supervision for Relation Extraction with an Incomplete Knowledge Base

Bonan Min, Ralph Grishman, Li Wan
New York University
New York, NY 10003
{min,grishman,wanli}
@cs.nyu.edu

Chang Wang, David Gondek
IBM T. J. Watson Research Center
Yorktown Heights, NY 10598
{wangchan,dgondek}
@us.ibm.com

Abstract

Distant supervision, heuristically labeling a corpus using a knowledge base, has emerged as a popular choice for training relation extractors. In this paper, we show that a significant number of "*negative*" examples generated by the labeling process are *false negatives* because the knowledge base is incomplete. Therefore the heuristic for generating negative examples has a serious flaw. Building on a state-of-the-art distantly-supervised extraction algorithm, we proposed an algorithm that learns from only *positive* and *unlabeled* labels at the pair-of-entity level. Experimental results demonstrate its advantage over existing algorithms.

1 Introduction

Relation Extraction is a well-studied problem (Miller et al., 2000; Zhou et al., 2005; Kambhatla, 2004; Min et al., 2012a). Recently, Distant Supervision (DS) (Craven and Kumlien, 1999; Mintz et al., 2009) has emerged to be a popular choice for training relation extractors without using manually labeled data. It automatically generates training examples by labeling relation mentions[1] in the source corpus according to whether the argument pair is listed in the target relational tables in a knowledge base (KB). This method significantly reduces human efforts for relation extraction.

The labeling heuristic has a serious flaw. Knowledge bases are usually highly incomplete. For example, 93.8% of *persons* from Freebase[2] have no *place of birth*, and 78.5% have no *nationality* (section 3). Previous work typically assumes that if the argument entity pair is not listed in the KB as having a relation, all the corresponding relation mentions are considered *negative* examples.[3] This crude assumption labeled many entity pairs as *negative* when in fact some of their mentions express a relation. The number of such *false negative matches* even exceeds the number of *positive* pairs, by 3 to 10 times, leading to a significant problem for training. Previous approaches (Riedel et al., 2010; Hoffmann et al., 2011; Surdeanu et al., 2012) bypassed this problem by heavily under-sampling the "*negative*" class.

We instead deal with a learning scenario where we only have entity-pair level labels that are either *positive* or *unlabeled*. We proposed an extension to Surdeanu et al. (2012) that can train on this dataset. Our contribution also includes an analysis on the incompleteness of Freebase and the *false negative match* rate in two datasets of labeled examples generated by DS. Experimental results on a realistic and challenging dataset demonstrate the advantage of the algorithm over existing solutions.

2 Related Work

Distant supervision was first proposed by Craven and Kumlien (1999) in the biomedical domain.

[1] An occurrence of a pair of entities with the source sentence.

[2] Freebase is a large collaboratively-edited KB. It is available at http://www.freebase.com.

[3] There are variants of labeling heuristics. For example, Surdeanu et al. (2011) and Sun et al. (2011) use a pair $< e, v >$ as a negative example, when it is not listed in Freebase, but e is listed with a different v'. These assumptions are also problematic in cases where the relation is not functional.

Since then, it has gain popularity (Mintz et al., 2009; Bunescu and Mooney, 2007; Wu and Weld, 2007; Riedel et al., 2010; Hoffmann et al., 2011; Surdeanu et al., 2012; Nguyen and Moschitti, 2011). To tolerate noisy labels in positive examples, Riedel et al. (2010) use Multiple Instance Learning (MIL), which assumes only at-least-one of the relation mentions in each "bag" of mentions sharing a pair of argument entities which bears a relation, indeed expresses the target relation. MultiR (Hoffmann et al., 2011) and Multi-Instance Multi-Label (MIML) learning (Surdeanu et al., 2012) further improve it to support multiple relations expressed by different sentences in a bag. Takamatsu et al. (2012) models the probabilities of a pattern showing relations, estimated from the heuristically labeled dataset. Their algorithm removes mentions that match low-probability patterns. Sun et al. (2011) and Min et al. (2012b) also estimate the probablities of patterns showing relations, but instead use them to relabel examples to their most likely classes. Their approach can correct highly-confident false negative matches.

3 Problem Definition

Distant Supervision: Given a KB $\mathcal{D}$ (a collection of relational tables $r(e_1, e_2)$, in which $r \epsilon R$ (R is the set of relation labels), and $< e_1, e_2 >$ is a pair of entities that is known to have relation r) and a corpus C, the key idea of distant supervision is that we align $\mathcal{D}$ to C, label each *bag*[4] of relation mentions that share argument pair $< e_1, e_2 >$ with r, otherwise *OTHER*. This generates a dataset that has labels on entity-pair (bag) level. Then a relation extractor is trained with single-instance learning (by assuming all mentions have the same label as the bag), or Multiple-Instance Learning (by assuming at-least-one of the mentions expresses the bag-level label), or Multi-Instance Multi-Label learning (further assuming a bag can have multiple labels) algorithms. All of these works treat the *OTHER* class as examples that are labeled as *negative*.

The incomplete KB problem: KBs are usually incomplete because they are manually constructed, and it is not possible to cover all human knowledge nor stay current. We took frequent relations, which involve an entity of type PERSON, from Freebase for analysis. We define the incompleteness $\partial(r)$ of a relation r as follows:

$$\partial(r) = \frac{|\{e\}| - |\{e | \exists e', s.t. r(e,e') \epsilon \mathcal{D}\}|}{|\{e\}|}$$

$\partial(r)$ is the percentage of all *persons* $\{e\}$ that do not have an attribute e' (with which $r(e, e')$ holds). Table 1 shows that 93.8% of *persons* have no *place of birth*, and 78.5% of them have no *nationality*. These are must-have attributes for a person. This shows that Freebase is highly incomplete.

Freebase relation types	Incompleteness
/people/person/education	0.792
/people/person/employment_history	0.923
/people/person/nationality*	0.785
/people/person/parents*	0.988
/people/person/place_of_birth*	0.938
/people/person/places_lived*	0.966

Table 1: The incompleteness of Freebase (* are must-have attributes for a person).

We further investigate the rate of *false negative matches*, as the percentage of entity-pairs that are not listed in Freebase but one of its mentions generated by DS does express a relation in the target set of types. We randomly picked 200 *unlabeled* bags[5] from each of the two datasets (Riedel et al., 2010; Surdeanu et al., 2012) generated by DS, and we manually annotate all relation mentions in these bags. The result is shown in Table 2, along with a few examples that indicate a relation holds in the set of false negative matches (bag-level). Both datasets have around 10% false negative matches in the *unlabeled* set of bags. Taking into consideration that the number of *positive* bags and *unlabeled* bags are highly imbalanced (1:134 and 1:37 in the *Riedel* and *KBP* dataset respectively, before under-sampling the *unlabeled* class), the number of false negative matches are 11 and 4 times the number of *positive* bags in *Reidel* and *KBP* dataset, respectively. Such a large ratio shows false negatives do have a significant impact on the learning process.

4 A semi-supervised MIML algorithm

Our goal is to model the bag-level label noise, caused by the incomplete KB problem, in addition

[4]A bag is defined as a set of relation mentions sharing the same entity pair as relation arguments. We will use the terms *bag* and *entity pair* interchangeably in this paper.

[5]85% and 95.7% of the bags in the Riedel and KBP datasets have only one relation mention.

Dataset (training)	# positive bags	# positive : # unlabeled	% are false negatives	# positive : # false negative	has human assessment	Examples of false negative mentions
Riedel	4,700	1:134(BD*)	8.5%	1:11.4	no	(/location/location/contains)... in **Brooklyn** 's **Williamsburg**.
						(/people/person/place_lived) **Cheryl Rogowski** , a farmer from **Orange County** ...
KBP	183,062	1:37(BD*)	11.5%	1:4	yes	(per:city_of_birth) **Juan Martn Maldacena** (born September 10, 1968) is a theoretical physicist born in **Buenos Aires**
						(per:employee_of)**Dave Matthews**, from the **ABC News**, ...

Table 2: False negative matches on the *Riedel* (Riedel et al., 2010) and *KBP* dataset (Surdeanu et al., 2012). All numbers are on bag (pairs of entities) level. *BD** are the numbers before downsampling the *negative* set to 10% and 5% in *Riedel* and *KBP* dataset, respectively.

to modeling the instance-level noise using a 3-layer MIL or MIML model (e.g., Surdeanu et al. (2012)). We propose a 4-layer model as shown in Figure 1.

The input to the model is a list of n bags with a vector of binary labels, either *Positive (P)*, or *Unlabled (U)* for each relation r. Our model can be viewed as a semi-supervised[6] framework that extends a state-of-the-art Multi-Instance Multi-Label (MIML) model (Surdeanu et al., 2012). Since the input to previous MIML models are bags with per-relation binary labels of either *Positive (P)* or *Negative (N)*, we add a set of latent variables ℓ which models the true bag-level labels, to bridge the observed bag labels $\mathbf{y}$ and the MIML layers. We consider this as our main contribution to the model. Our hierarchical model is shown in Figure 1.

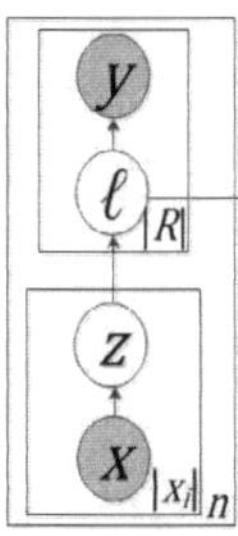

Figure 1: Plate diagram of our model.

Let i, j be the index in the bag and mention level, respectively. Following Surdeanu et al. (2012), we model mention-level extraction $p(z_{ij}^r|\mathbf{x}_{ij};\mathbf{w}_z)$ and multi-instance multi-label aggregation $p(\ell_i^r|\mathbf{z}_i;\mathbf{w}_\ell^r)$ in the bottom 3 layers. We define:

- r is a relation label. $r \epsilon R \cup \{OTHER\}$, in which *OTHER* denotes no relation expressed.
- $y_i^r \epsilon \{P, U\}$: r holds for ith bag or the bag is unlabeled.
- $\ell_i^r \epsilon \{P, N\}$: a hidden variable that denotes whether r holds for the ith bag.
- θ is an observed constant controlling the total number of bags whose latent label is *positive*.

We define the following conditional probabilities:

- $p(y_i^r|\ell_i^r) = \begin{cases} 1/2 & \text{if } y_i^r = P \wedge \ell_i^r = P; \\ 1/2 & \text{if } y_i^r = U \wedge \ell_i^r = P; \\ 1 & \text{if } y_i^r = U \wedge \ell_i^r = N; \\ 0 & \text{otherwise ;} \end{cases}$

  It encodes the constraints between true bag-level labels and the entity pair labels in the KB.
- $p(\theta|\ell) \sim \mathcal{N}(\frac{\sum_{i=1}^n \sum_{r \epsilon R} \delta(\ell_i^r, P)}{n}, \frac{1}{k})$ where $\delta(x, y) = 1$ if $x = y$, 0 otherwise. k is a large number. θ is the fraction of the bags that are positive. It is an observed parameter that depends on both the source corpus and the KB used.

Similar to Surdeanu et al. (2012), we also define the following parameters and conditional probabilities (details are in Surdeanu et al. (2012)):

- $z_{ij} \epsilon R \cup \{OTHER\}$: a latent variable that denotes the relation type of the jth mention in the ith bag.
- $\mathbf{x}_{ij}$ is the feature representation of the jth relation mention in the ith bag. We use the set of features in Surdeanu et al. (2012).
- $\mathbf{w}_z$ is the weight vector for the multi-class relation mention-level classifier.
- $\mathbf{w}_\ell^r$ is the weight vector for the rth binary top-level aggregation classifier (from mention labels to bag-level prediction). We use $\mathbf{w}_\ell$ to represent $\mathbf{w}_\ell^1, \mathbf{w}_\ell^2, ...\mathbf{w}_\ell^{|R|}$.
- $p(\ell_i^r|\mathbf{z}_i;\mathbf{w}_\ell^r) \sim Bern(f_\ell(\mathbf{w}_\ell^r, \mathbf{z}_i))$ where f_ℓ is probability produced by the rth top-level classifier, from the mention-label level to the bag-label level.
- $p(z_{ij}^r|\mathbf{x}_{ij};\mathbf{w}_z) \sim Multi(f_z(\mathbf{w}_z, \mathbf{x}_{ij}))$ where f_z

[6]We use the term *semi-supervised* because the algorithm uses *unlabeled* bags but existing solutions requires bags to be labeled either *positive* or *negative*.

is probability produced by the mention-level classifier, from the mentions to the mention-label level.[7]

4.1 Training

We use hard Expectation-Maximization (EM) algorithm for training the model. Our objective function is to maximize log-likelihood:

$$L(\mathbf{w}_z, \mathbf{w}_\ell) = logp(\mathbf{y}, \theta | \mathbf{x}; \mathbf{w}_z, \mathbf{w}_\ell)$$
$$= log \sum_{\ell} p(\mathbf{y}, \theta, \ell | \mathbf{x}; \mathbf{w}_z, \mathbf{w}_\ell)$$

Since solving it exactly involves exploring an exponential assignment space for ℓ, we approximate and iteratively set $\ell^* = \arg_\ell \max p(\ell | \mathbf{y}, \theta, \mathbf{x}; \mathbf{w}_z, \mathbf{w}_\ell)$

$$p(\ell | \mathbf{y}, \theta, \mathbf{x}; \mathbf{w}_z, \mathbf{w}_\ell) \propto p(\mathbf{y}, \theta, \ell | \mathbf{x}; \mathbf{w}_z, \mathbf{w}_\ell)$$
$$= p(\mathbf{y}, \theta | \ell, \mathbf{x}) p(\ell | \mathbf{x}; \mathbf{w}_z, \mathbf{w}_\ell)$$
$$= p(\mathbf{y} | \ell) p(\theta | \ell) p(\ell | \mathbf{x}; \mathbf{w}_z, \mathbf{w}_\ell)$$

Rewriting in log form:

$$logp(\ell | \mathbf{y}, \theta, \mathbf{x}; \mathbf{w}_z, \mathbf{w}_\ell)$$
$$= logp(\mathbf{y} | \ell) + logp(\theta | \ell) + logp(\ell | \mathbf{x}; \mathbf{w}_z, \mathbf{w}_\ell)$$
$$= \sum_{i=1}^{n} \sum_{r \epsilon R} logp(y_i^r | \ell_i^r) - k\left(\frac{\sum_{i=1}^{n} \sum_{r \epsilon R} \delta(\ell_i^r, P)}{n} - \theta\right)^2$$
$$+ \sum_{i=1}^{n} \sum_{r \epsilon R} logp(\ell_i^r | \mathbf{x}_i; \mathbf{w}_z, \mathbf{w}_\ell) + const$$

Algorithm 1 Training (**E-step**:2-11; **M-step**:12-15)

1: **for** $i = 1, 2$ to T **do**
2: $\quad \ell_i^r \leftarrow N$ for all $y_i^r = U$ and $r \epsilon R$
3: $\quad \ell_i^r \leftarrow P$ for all $y_i^r = P$ and $r \epsilon R$
4: $\quad I = \{< i, r > | \ell_i^r = N\}; I' = \{< i, r > | \ell_i^r = P\}$
5: $\quad$ **for** $k = 0, 1$ to $\theta n - |I'|$ **do**
6: $\quad\quad < i', r' >= \arg\max_{<i,r> \epsilon I} p(\ell_i^r | \mathbf{x}_i; \mathbf{w}_z, \mathbf{w}_\ell)$
7: $\quad\quad \ell_{i'}^{r'} \leftarrow P; I = I \backslash \{< i', r' >\}$
8: $\quad$ **end for**
9: $\quad$ **for** $i = 1, 2$ to n **do**
10: $\quad\quad \mathbf{z}_i^* = \arg\max_{\mathbf{z}_i} p(\mathbf{z}_i | \ell_i, \mathbf{x}_i; \mathbf{w}_z, \mathbf{w}_\ell)$
11: $\quad$ **end for**
12: $\quad \mathbf{w}_z^* = \arg\max_{\mathbf{w}_z} \sum_{i=1}^{n} \sum_{j=1}^{|\mathbf{x}_i|} logp(z_{ij} | \mathbf{x}_{ij}, \mathbf{w}_z)$
13: $\quad$ **for all** $r \epsilon R$ **do**
14: $\quad\quad \mathbf{w}_\ell^{r(*)} = \arg\max_{w_\ell^r} \sum_{i=1}^{n} p(\ell_i^r | \mathbf{z}_i, \mathbf{w}_\ell^r)$
15: $\quad$ **end for**
16: **end for**
17: **return** $\mathbf{w}_\mathbf{z}, \mathbf{w}_\ell$

In the E-step, we do a greedy search (steps 5-8 in algorithm 1) in all $p(\ell_i^r | \mathbf{x}_i; \mathbf{w}_z, \mathbf{w}_\ell)$ and update ℓ_i^r until the second term is maximized. $\mathbf{w}_z$, $\mathbf{w}_\ell$ are the model weights learned from the previous iteration.

After fixed ℓ, we seek to maximize:

$$logp(\ell | \mathbf{x}_i; \mathbf{w}_z, \mathbf{w}_\ell) = \sum_{i=1}^{n} logp(\ell_i | \mathbf{x}_i; \mathbf{w}_z, \mathbf{w}_\ell)$$
$$= \sum_{i=1}^{n} log \sum_{z_i} p(\ell_i, \mathbf{z}_i | \mathbf{x}_i; \mathbf{w}_z, \mathbf{w}_\ell)$$

which can be solved with an approximate solution in Surdeanu et al. (2012) (step 9-11): update $\mathbf{z}_i$ independently with: $\mathbf{z}_i^* = \arg\max_{\mathbf{z}_i} p(\mathbf{z}_i | \ell_i, \mathbf{x}_i; \mathbf{w}_z, \mathbf{w}_\ell)$. More details can be found in Surdeanu et al. (2012).

In the M-step, we retrain both of the mention-level and the aggregation level classifiers.

The full EM algorithm is shown in algorithm 1.

4.2 Inference

Inference on a bag $\mathbf{x}_i$ is trivial. For each mention:

$$z_{ij}^* = \arg_{z_{ij} \epsilon R \cup \{OTHER\}} \max p(z_{ij} | x_{ij}, \mathbf{w}_z)$$

Followed by the aggregation (directly with $\mathbf{w}_\ell$):

$$y_i^{r(*)} = \arg_{y_i^r \epsilon \{P,N\}} \max p(y_i^r | \mathbf{z}_i; \mathbf{w}_\ell^r)$$

4.3 Implementation details

We implement our model on top of the MIML(Surdeanu et al., 2012) code base.[8] We use the same mention-level and aggregate-level feature sets as Surdeanu et al. (2012). We adopt the same idea of using cross validation for the E and M steps to avoid overfitting. We initialize our algorithm by sampling 5% *unlabeled* examples as *negative*, in essence using 1 epoch of MIML to initialize. Empirically it performs well.

5 Experiments

Data set: We use the KBP (Ji et al., 2011) dataset[9] prepared and publicly released by Surdeanu et al. (2012) for our experiment since it is 1) large and realistic, 2) publicly available, 3) most importantly, it is the only dataset that has associated human-labeled ground truth. Any KB held-out evaluation without manual assessment will be significantly affected by KB incompleteness. In KBP

[7] All classifiers are implemented with L2-regularized logistic regression with Stanford CoreNLP package.

[8] Available at http://nlp.stanford.edu/software/mimlre.shtml

[9] Available from Linguistic Data Consortium (LDC). http://projects.ldc.upenn.edu/kbp/data/

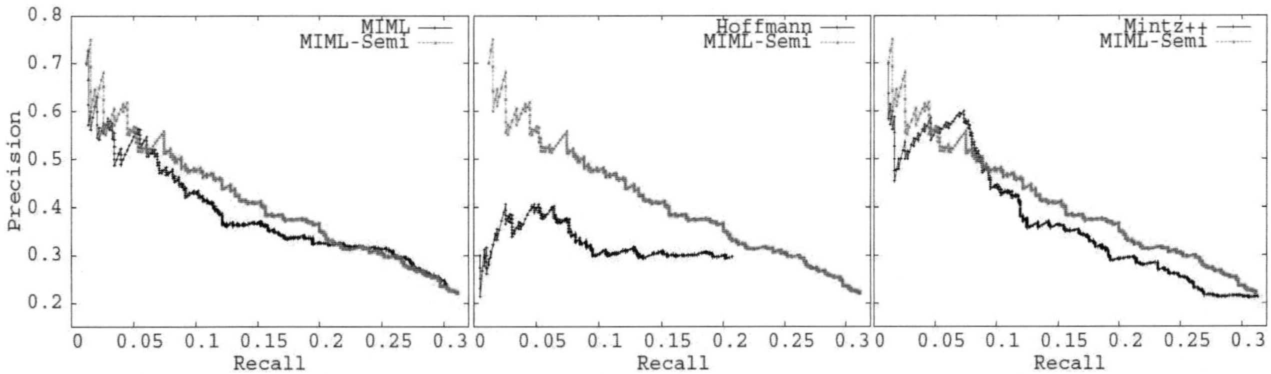

Figure 2: Performance on the KBP dataset. The figures on the left, middle and right show *MIML*, *Hoffmann*, and *Mintz++* compared to the same *MIML-Semi* curve, respectively. *MIML-Semi* is shown in red curves (lighter curves in black and white) while other algorithms are shown in black curves (darker curves in black and white).

dataset, the training bags are generated by mapping Wikipedia (http://en.wikipedia.org) infoboxes (after merging similar types following the KBP 2011 task definition) into a large unlabeled corpus (consisting of 1.5M documents from the KBP source corpus and a complete snapshot of Wikipedia). The KBP shared task provided 200 query named entities with their associated slot values (in total several thousand pairs). We use 40 queries as development dataset (*dev*), and the rest (160 queries) as evaluation dataset. We set $\theta = 0.25$ by tuning on the *dev* set and use it in the experiments. For a fair comparison, we follow Surdeanu et al. (2012) and begin by downsampling the "negative" class to 5%. We also set T=8 and use the following noisy-or (for ith bag) of mention-level probability to rank predicted types (r) of pairs and plot the precision-recall curves for all experiments.

$$Prob_i(r) = 1 - \prod_j (1 - p(z_{ij} = r|\mathbf{x}_{ij}; \mathbf{w}_z))$$

Evaluation: We compare our algorithm (*MIML-semi*) to three algorithms: 1) *MIML* (Surdeanu et al., 2012), the Multiple-Instance Multiple Label algorithm which labels the bags directly with the KB ($y = \ell$). 2) *MultiR* (denoted as *Hoffmann*) (Hoffmann et al., 2011), a Multiple-Instance algorithm that supports overlapping relations. It also imposes $y = \ell$. 3) *Mintz++* (Surdeanu et al., 2012), a variant of the single-instance learning algorithm (section 3). The first two are stat-of-the-art Multi-Instance Multi-Label algorithms. *Mintz++* is a strong baseline (Surdeanu et al., 2012) and an improved version of Mintz et al. (2009). Figure 2 shows that our algorithm consistently outperforms all three algorithms at almost all recall levels (with the exception of a very small region in the PR-curve). This demonstrates that by treating unla-beled data set differently and leveraging the missing positive bags, *MIML-semi* is able to learn a more accurate model for extraction. Although the proposed solution is a specific algorithm, we believe the idea of treating unlabeled data differently can be incorporated into any of these algorithms that only use unlabeled data as negative examples.

6 Conclusion

We show that the distant-supervision labeling process generates a significant number of false negatives because the knowledge base is incomplete. We proposed an algorithm that learns from only positive and unlabeled bags. Experimental results demonstrate its advantage over existing algorithms.

Acknowledgments

Supported in part by the Intelligence Advanced Research Projects Activity (IARPA) via Department of Interior National Business Center contract number D11PC20154. The U.S. Government is authorized to reproduce and distribute reprints for Governmental purposes notwithstanding any copyright annotation thereon. The views and conclusions contained herein are those of the authors and should not be interpreted as necessarily representing the official policies or endorsements, either expressed or implied, of IARPA, DoI/NBC, or the U.S. Government.

References

Razvan Bunescu and Raymond Mooney. 2007. Learning to extract relations from the web using minimal supervision. In *Proceedings of the 45th Annual Meeting of the Association for Computational Linguistics*.

Mark Craven and Johan Kumlien. 1999. Constructing biological knowledge bases by extracting information from text sources. In *Proceedings of the Seventh International Conference on Intelligent Systems for Molecular Biology*.

Raphael Hoffmann, Congle Zhang, Xiao Ling, Luke Zettlemoyer, and Daniel S. Weld. 2011. Knowledge-based weak supervision for information extraction of overlapping relations. In *Proceedings of the Annual Meeting of the Association for Computational Linguistics*.

Heng Ji, Ralph Grishman, and Hoa T. Dang. 2011. Overview of the TAC 2011 knowledge base population track. In *Proceedings of the Text Analytics Conference*.

Jing Jiang and ChengXiang Zhai. 2007. A systematic exploration of the feature space for relation extraction. In *Proceedings of HLT-NAACL-2007*.

Nanda Kambhatla. 2004. Combining lexical, syntactic, and semantic features with maximum entropy models for information extraction. In *Proceedings of ACL-2004*.

Scott Miller, Heidi Fox, Lance Ramshaw, and Ralph Weischedel. 2000. A novel use of statistical parsing to extract information from text. In *Proceedings of NAACL-2000*.

Bonan Min, Shuming Shi, Ralph Grishman and Chin-Yew Lin. 2012a. Ensemble Semantics for Large-scale Unsupervised Relation Extraction. In *Proceedings of EMNLP-CoNLL 2012*.

Bonan Min, Xiang Li, Ralph Grishman and Ang Sun. 2012b. New York University 2012 System for KBP Slot Filling. In *Proceedings of the Text Analysis Conference (TAC)* 2012.

Mike Mintz, Steven Bills, Rion Snow, and Daniel Jurafsky. 2009. Distant supervision for relation extraction without labeled data. In *Proceedings of the 47th Annual Meeting of the Association for Computational Linguistics*.

Truc Vien T. Nguyen and Alessandro Moschitti. 2011. End-to-end relation extraction using distant supervision from external semantic repositories. In *Proceedings of the 49th Annual Meeting of the Association for Computational Linguistics: Human Language Technologies*.

Sebastian Riedel, Limin Yao, and Andrew McCallum. 2010. Modeling relations and their mentions without labeled text. In *Proceedings of the European Conference on Machine Learning and Knowledge Discovery in Databases (ECML PKDD 10)*.

Ang Sun, Ralph Grishman, Wei Xu, and Bonan Min. 2011. New York University 2011 system for KBP slot filling. In *Proceedings of the Text Analytics Conference*.

Mihai Surdeanu, Sonal Gupta, John Bauer, David McClosky, Angel X. Chang, Valentin I. Spitkovsky, and Christopher D. Manning. 2011. Stanfords distantly-supervised slot-filling system. In *Proceedings of the Text Analytics Conference*.

Mihai Surdeanu, Julie Tibshirani, Ramesh Nallapati, Christopher D. Manning. 2012. Multi-instance Multi-label Learning for Relation Extraction. In *Proceedings of the 2012 Conference on Empirical Methods in Natural Language Processing and Natural Language Learning*.

TAC KBP 2011 task definition. 2011. http://nlp.cs.qc.cuny.edu/kbp/2011/KBP2011_TaskDefinition.pdf

Shingo Takamatsu, Issei Sato, Hiroshi Nakagawa. 2012. Reducing Wrong Labels in Distant Supervision for Relation Extraction. In *Proceedings of 50th Annual Meeting of the Association for Computational Linguistics*.

Fei Wu and Daniel S. Weld. 2007. Autonomously semantifying wikipedia. In *Proceedings of the International Conference on Information and Knowledge Management (CIKM-2007)*.

Guodong Zhou, Jian Su, Jie Zhang and Min Zhang. 2005. Exploring various knowledge in relation extraction. In *Proceedings of ACL-2005*.

Measuring the Structural Importance through Rhetorical Structure Index

Narine Kokhlikyan[†], **Alex Waibel**[† ‡], **Yuqi Zhang**[†], **Joy Ying Zhang**[‡]
[†]Karlsruhe Institute of Technology
Adenauerring 2
76131 Karlsruhe, Germany
[‡] Carnegie Mellon University
NASA Research Park, Bldg. 23
Moffett Field, CA 94035
narine.kokhlikyan@student.kit.edu, waibel@cs.cmu.edu,
yuqi.zhang@kit.edu, joy.zhang@sv.cmu.edu

Abstract

In this paper, we propose a novel Rhetorical Structure Index (RSI) to measure the structural importance of a word or a phrase. Unlike TF-IDF and other content-driven measurements, RSI identifies words or phrases that are structural cues in an unstructured document. We show structurally motivated features with high RSI values are more useful than content-driven features for applications such as segmenting unstructured lecture transcripts into meaningful segments. Experiments show that using RSI significantly improves the segmentation accuracy compared to TF-IDF, a traditional content-based feature weighting scheme.

1 Introduction

Online learning, a new trend in distance learning, provides numerous lectures to students all over the world. More than 19,000 colleges offer thousands of free online lectures[1]. Starting from video recordings of lectures which sometimes also come with the presentation material, a set of processes can be applied to extract information from the unstructured data to assist students in browsing, searching and understanding the content of the lecture. These processes include *automatic speech recognition (ASR)* which converts the audio to text, *lecture segmentation* which inserts paragraph boundaries and adds section titles to the lecture transcriptions, *automatic summarization* that generates a short summary from the full lecture, and *lecture translation* that translates the lecture from the original language to the native language of the student.

The transcription of a lecture generated by the ASR system is a sequence of words which does not contain any *structural* information such as paragraph, section boundaries and section titles. Zhang et al. (2007; 2008; 2010) used acoustic and linguistic features for rhetorical structure detection and summarization. They showed that linguistic features such as TF-IDF are the most influential in segmentation and summarization and that knowing the structure of a lecture can significantly improve the performance of lecture summarization. Our experiments with a real-time lecture translation system also show that displaying the rolling translation results of a live lecture with proper paragraphing and inserted section titles makes it easier for students to grasp the key points during a lecture.

In this paper, we apply existing algorithms, namely the Hidden Markov Model (HMM) (Gales and Young, 2007) to unstructured lecture transcription to infer the underlying structure for better lecture segmentation and summarization. HMM has been successfully applied in early works (van Mulbregt et al., 1998; Sherman and Liu, 2008) for text segmentation, event tracking and boundary detection. The focus of this work is to identify cue words and phrases that are good indicators of lecture structure. Intuitively, words and phrases such as "last week we talked about", "this is an outline of my talk", "now I am going to talk about", "in conclusion", and "any questions" should be important features to recognize lecture structure.

[1]`http://www.thebestcolleges.org/free-online-classes-and-course-lectures/`

These words/phrases, however, may not be so important content-wise. Thus, content-driven metrics such as the TF-IDF score usually do not assign higher weights to these structurally important words/phrases. We propose a novel metric called Rhetorical Structural Index (RSI) to weigh words/phrases based on their structural importance.

2 Rhetorical Structural Index

RSI incorporates both frequency of occurrences and, more importantly, the position distribution of occurrences of a word/phrase. The intuition is that if a term is a structural marker, it usually occurs at a certain *position* in a lecture. Because the term is mainly about the structure rather than the content of a lecture, it can appear with high *frequency* in lectures that are of different topics. For example, "today we" occurs at the beginning of a lecture and "thank you" usually appears towards the end (Figure 1) no matter whether the lecture is about history or computer science.

We define the RSI of a word w as:

$$\mathrm{RSI}(w) = \frac{1}{\lambda \mathrm{Var}(L_w) + (1-\lambda)\mathrm{idf}(w, D)} \quad (1)$$

where L_w is the random variable of "normalized positions" of a word w in a lecture. For each occurrence of w in a particular lecture d, we divide its position by the length of the lecture $|d|$ to estimate its "normalized position". L_w takes a value between [0, 1]. A value close to 0 indicates this word occurs at the beginning and close to 1 means w is close to the end of the lecture. $\mathrm{Var}(L_w)$ is the variance of the normalized position of a word w. A small $\mathrm{Var}(L_w)$ indicates that w always occurs at certain positions of a typical lecture (e.g., "bye") while a large value means w can occur at any position (e.g., function words "of" and "the").

The second part of RSI is the *inverse document frequency* (idf), or effectively the document frequency since RSI is proportional to the 1/idf term. Lectures, such as different research talks, can vary in content but usually have a very similar structure and share some common structural cues. A good structural cue word should be common to many lectures. idf has been widely used in information retrieval research to assign higher weights to words that occur in just a few documents as compared to

Table 1: Examples of n-grams with high RSI values which are likely to be structural cues.

n-gram	$\mathrm{Var}(L_w)$	idf	RSI
now	0.0004	0.60	1.04
here	0.0004	0.62	1.03
class	0.0001	2.12	0.90
week	0.0001	2.23	0.89
goodbye	0.0001	3.62	0.80
thank you	0.0003	1.53	0.95
talk about	0.0003	1.90	0.92
dealing with	0.0002	2.00	0.91
today we	0.0003	2.51	0.87
see how	0.0009	2.69	0.85
ladies and gentlemen	0.0008	1.35	0.96
last time we	0.0004	2.22	0.89
here we have	0.0005	2.35	0.88
next time we	0.0002	2.51	0.86

common words that occur in all documents. Define the idf of a word w given a collection of lectures D as:

$$\mathrm{idf}(w, D) = \log \frac{|D|}{|\{d \in D | w \in d\}|} \quad (2)$$

$|D|$ is the number of all lectures in the collection and $|\{d \in D | w \in d\}|$ is the number of lectures where w appears. A low idf (w, D) value indicates that word w occurs in many documents and thus is more likely to be a common structural cue.

Combining the variance of normalized position and idf by scaling factor λ, we define RSI as in equation 1. We found 0.9 as an optimal value of λ according our experiments over all data sets. A word w with high RSI value is more likely to be structurally important. Similarly, we can calculate the RSI values for phrases (n-grams) such as "I would like to talk about", "I will switch gear to" and "thank you for your attention".

Table 1 shows examples of n-grams and the calculated variance, idf-scores and RSI values from a collection of lectures.

3 Incorporating RSI in Lecture Segmentation

Several algorithms have been developed for text segmentation including the Naive Bayes classifier for keyword extraction (Balagopalan et al., 2012), the

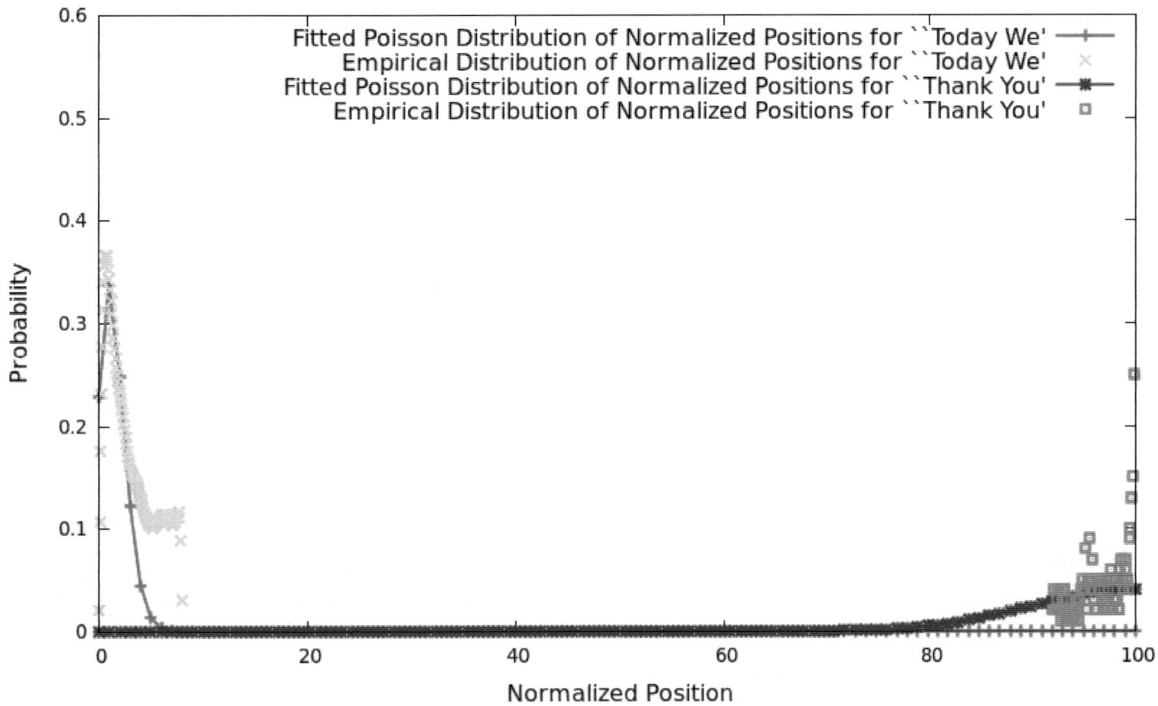

Figure 1: *Fitted Poisson-distribution of normalized positions in lectures for the bigrams "today we" and "thank you". "today we" appears more frequently at the beginning of a lecture, whereas "thank you" more in the concluding part of a lecture. The x-axis is the normalized word position in a lecture and y-axis is the probability of seeing the word at a position.*

Hidden Markov Model (Gales and Young, 2007), the Maximum entropy Markov model (McCallum et al., 2000), the Conditional Random Field (Lafferty et al., 2001) and the Latent Content Analysis (Ponte and Croft, 1997). In this paper, we evaluate the effectiveness of the proposed RSI feature on lecture segmentation using an HMM.

We represent each segment in a lecture as a state in the Markov model and use the EM algorithm to learn HMM parameters from unlabeled lecture data. We use a fully connected HMM with five states. Typical state labels for lecture are: "Introduction", "Background", "Main Topic", "Questions" and "Conclusion" as shown in Figure 2. HMM states emit word tokens. Instead of considering the full vocabulary as the possible emission alphabet, which usually leads to model over-fitting, we only consider terms with high RSI values and high TF-IDF* scores for comparison. For a word w, define its TF-IDF* score as:

$$\text{TF-IDF*}(w) = \max_{d} \text{TF-IDF}(w, d), \quad (3)$$

which is the highest TF-IDF score of a word in any document in the collection. Our experiments try to answer the question that "*if HMM is meant to capture the underlying structure of lectures no matter which topic the lecture is about, what kind of features should be emitted from each state to reflect such structural patterns among lectures*?"

The learned HMM model is then applied to unseen lecture data to label each sentence to be "Introduction", "Background", "Main Topic", "Questions" or "Conclusion" and, based on the label, we segment the lecture to different sections for evaluation. Segment boundaries are defined in the positions where sentence labels change.

3.0.1 Bootstrap HMM from K-Means Clustering Segmentation

Initial HMM parameters are bootstrapped using results from K-means clustering where we cluster a sequence of sentences to form a "segment". K corresponds to the number of desired segments of a lecture. Similarities are computed based on the content similarity (using n-gram matches) and the relative sentence position defined as:

$$Sim(S_i, C_j) = \alpha M(S_i, C_j) + (1 - \alpha)P(S_i, C_j), \quad (4)$$

where S_i is the i-th sentence, C_j is the centroid of the j-th cluster. M(S_i, C_j) is the content similarity between sentence S_i and centroid C_j and P(S_i, C_j) is the position similarity (distance). α is a scaling factor (set to optimal value 0.2 based on all data sets in our experiments).

Content similarity is based on the number of common words between two sentences, or between a sentence and the centroid vector of a cluster. Denote the binary word frequency vector (bag of words) in sentence S_i as $\vec{S_i}$ and similarly $\vec{C_j}$ for cluster centroid C_j, define:

$$M(S_i, C_j) = \frac{\vec{S_i} \cdot \vec{C_j}}{\parallel \vec{S_i} \parallel \parallel \vec{C_j} \parallel}. \quad (5)$$

P(S_i, C_j) measures the position similarity of two sentences. Position similarity is based on the relative position distance between the sentence and the cluster:Define

$$P(S_i, C_j) = \frac{L}{|\text{Pos}(S_i) - \text{Pos}(C_j)| + \epsilon}, \quad (6)$$

where S_i is the i-th sentence, C_j is the j-th cluster. Pos(S_i) is the position of sentence S_i. Pos(C_j) is the average sentence position of all members belong to cluster C_j and L is the total number of sentences in a lecture. ϵ is a small constant to avoid division by zeros.

4 Experiments and Evaluation

We evaluated segmentation on three different data sets: college lectures recorded by Karlsruhe Institute of Technology (KIT), Microsoft research (MSR) lectures[2] and scientific papers[3]. Both college and Microsoft research lectures are manually transcribed. The reason why we do not include experiments on ASR output is that current ASR quality of lecture data is still quite poor. Word-Error-Rates (WER) of ASR output range from 24.37 to 30.80 for KIT lectures. Roughly speaking, every one out of 3 or 4 words is mis-recognized.

[2]http://research.microsoft.com/apps/catalog/

[3]http://aclweb.org/anthology-new/

For evaluation, human annotators annotated a few lectures to create test/reference sets. The test data from KIT is annotated by one human annotator and MSR lectures are annotated by four annotators. The segmentation gold standard is created based on the agreed annotations. Since the number of annotated lectures is small and human annotation is subjective, we also used ACL papers as an additional data set. ACL papers are in a way "lectures in written form" and have titles for section and subsections which can be used to identify the segments and annotate the data set automatically. The statistics of each data set are listed in Table 2.

Table 2: Statistics of three data sets used in the experiments: our own lecture data (KIT), Microsoft research talks (MSR) and conference proceedings from ACL anthology archive. We removed equations, short titles such as "Abstract" and "Conclusion", when extracting text from PDF files from the ACL anthology, which results in a relatively small number of words per paper. Words are simply tokenized without case normalization or stemming, which results in relatively large vocabulary sizes.

Properties	KIT	MSR	ACL
Num.	74	1,182	3,583
Avg. Num. of Sent.	484	655	212
Avg. Num. of Words	10,078	10,225	3,896
Avg. Duration (Min.)	43.57	39.15	-
Vocabulary Size	1.3K	22K	24K

First, we calculate the RSI and TF-IDF* scores for each word in the dataset and choose the top N words as the HMM emission vocabulary. To avoid over-fitting, we choose N that is much smaller than the full vocabulary size of the data set. In our experiments, we set N=300 for KIT, N=5000 for MSR and N=5400 for ACL. The top 5 words with the highest TF-IDF* scores from the MSR data set are: "RFID", "Cherokee", "tree-to-string", "GPU", and "data-triggered", whereas the top 5 words selected by RSI are "today", "work", "question", "now", and "thank", which are more structurally informative.

To estimate the accuracy of the segmentation module, we used Recall, Precision, F-Measure and P_k (Beeferman et al., 1999) as evaluation metric. We used an error window of length 6 to calculate Precision, Recall and F-Measure and a sliding window with a length equal to half of the average seg-

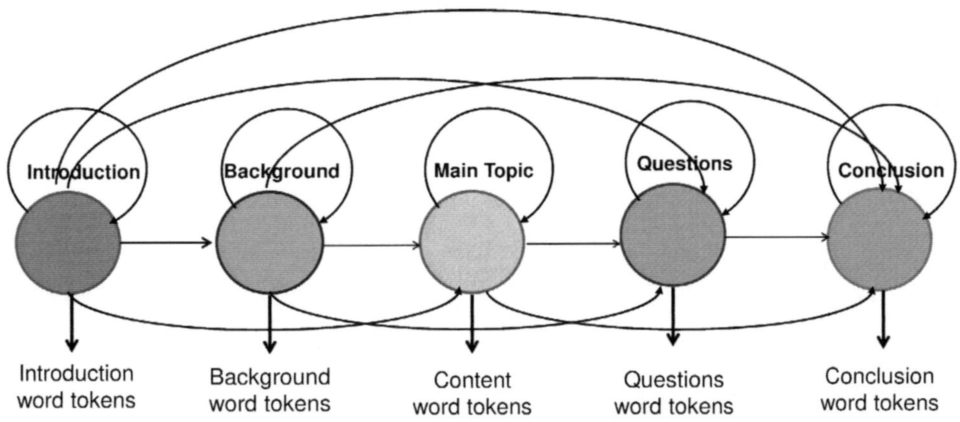

Figure 2: Fully connected 5-state HMM representing *Introduction, Background, Main Topic, Questions, Conclusion* in a typical lecture.

ment length to estimate the P_k score. With error window we mean that hypothesis boundaries do not have to be exactly the same as the reference segment boundaries. Hypothesis boundaries are acceptable if they are close enough to reference boundaries in that window. The P_k score indicates the probability of segmentation inconsistency. Therefore, the lower the P_k score the better the segmentation is.

Table 3: Segmentation results measured by P_k (the smaller the better), Precision, Recall and F-Measure scores (the higher the better) for three data sets comparing HMM using TF-IDF*-filtered word tokens as emission and RSI-filtered words as emissions.

Evaluation Score	KIT	MSR	ACL
P_k			
HMM + TF-IDF*	0.06	0.06	0.05
HMM + RSI	0.01	0.02	0.01
Precision			
HMM + TF-IDF*	32.01	30.47	32.85
HMM + RSI	41.10	41.01	42.70
Recall			
HMM + TF-IDF*	39.32	36.09	38.08
HMM + RSI	47.38	46.39	48.95
F-Measure			
HMM + TF-IDF*	35.29	33.04	35.27
HMM + RSI	44.01	43.53	45.61

The evaluation results on all data sets listed in Table 3 show that according F-Measure and P_k scores, considering words with high RSI values as HMM emission significantly improve over the baseline method of choosing word tokens with high TF-IDF* scores.

5 Conclusions

In this work we propose the Rhetorical Structure Index (RSI), a method to identify structurally important terms in lectures. Experiments show that terms with high RSI values are better candidates than those with high TF-IDF values when used by an HMM-based segmenter as state emissions. In other words, terms with high RSI values are more likely to be structural cues in lectures independent of the lecture topic. In the future we will run experiments on ASR output and incorporate other prosodic features such as pitch, intensity, duration into the RSI to improve this metric for structural analysis of lectures and apply the RSI to other structure discovery applications such as dialogue segmentation.

Acknowledgments

The authors gratefully acknowledge the support by an interACT student exchange scholarship. The research leading to these results has received funding from the European Union Seventh Framework Programme (FP7/2007-2013) under grant agreement no 287658.

We would like to thank Jan Niehues and Teresa Herrmann for their suggestions and help.

References

A. Balagopalan, L.L. Balasubramanian, V. Balasubramanian, N. Chandrasekharan, and A. Damodar. 2012. Automatic keyphrase extraction and segmentation of video lectures. In *Technology Enhanced Education (ICTEE), 2012 IEEE International Conference on*, pages 1–10.

Doug Beeferman, Adam Berger, and John Lafferty. 1999. Statistical models for text segmentation. *Mach. Learn.*, 34(1-3):177–210, February.

Mark J. F. Gales and Steve J. Young. 2007. The application of hidden markov models in speech recognition. *Foundations and Trends in Signal Processing*, 1(3):195–304.

John D. Lafferty, Andrew McCallum, and Fernando C. N. Pereira. 2001. Conditional random fields: Probabilistic models for segmenting and labeling sequence data. In *ICML*, pages 282–289.

Andrew McCallum, Dayne Freitag, and Fernando C. N. Pereira. 2000. Maximum entropy markov models for information extraction and segmentation. In *Proceedings of the Seventeenth International Conference on Machine Learning*, ICML '00, pages 591–598, San Francisco, CA, USA. Morgan Kaufmann Publishers Inc.

Jay M. Ponte and W. Bruce Croft. 1997. Text segmentation by topic. In *ECDL*, pages 113–125.

Melissa Sherman and Yang Liu. 2008. Using hidden markov models for topic segmentation of meeting transcripts. In *SLT*, pages 185–188.

Paul van Mulbregt, Ira Carp, Lawrence Gillick, Steve Lowe, and Jon Yamron. 1998. Text segmentation and topic tracking on broadcast news via a hidden markov model approach. In *ICSLP*.

Justin Jian Zhang, Ricky Ho Yin Chan, and Pascale Fung. 2007. Improving lecture speech summarization using rhetorical information. In *ASRU*, pages 195–200.

Justin Jian Zhang, Shilei Huang, and Pascale Fung. 2008. Rshmm++ for extractive lecture speech summarization. In *SLT*, pages 161–164.

Justin Jian Zhang, Ricky Ho Yin Chan, and Pascale Fung. 2010. Extractive speech summarization using shallow rhetorical structure modeling. *IEEE Transactions on Audio, Speech & Language Processing*, 18(6):1147–1157.

Separating Fact from Fear: Tracking Flu Infections on Twitter

Alex Lamb, Michael J. Paul, Mark Dredze
Human Language Technology Center of Excellence
Department of Computer Science
Johns Hopkins University
Baltimore, MD 21218
{alamb3,mpaul19,mdredze}@jhu.edu

Abstract

Twitter has been shown to be a fast and reliable method for disease surveillance of common illnesses like influenza. However, previous work has relied on simple content analysis, which conflates flu tweets that report infection with those that express concerned awareness of the flu. By discriminating these categories, as well as tweets about the authors versus about others, we demonstrate significant improvements on influenza surveillance using Twitter.

1 Introduction

Twitter is a fantastic data resource for many tasks: measuring political (O'Connor et al., 2010; Tumasjan et al., 2010), and general sentiment (Bollen et al., 2011), studying linguistic variation (Eisenstein et al., 2010) and detecting earthquakes (Sakaki et al., 2010). Similarly, Twitter has proven useful for public health applications (Dredze, 2012), primarily disease surveillance (Collier, 2012; Signorini et al., 2011), whereby public health officials track infection rates of common diseases. Standard government data sources take weeks while Twitter provides an immediate population measure.

Strategies for Twitter influenza surveillance include supervised classification (Culotta, 2010b; Culotta, 2010a; Eiji Aramaki and Morita, 2011), unsupervised models for disease discovery (Paul and Dredze, 2011), keyword counting[1], tracking geographic illness propagation (Sadilek et al., 2012b), and combining tweet contents with the social network (Sadilek et al., 2012a) and location information (Asta and Shalizi, 2012). All of these methods rely on a relatively simple NLP approach to analyzing the tweet content, i.e. n-gram models for classifying related or not related to the flu. Yet examining flu tweets yields a more complex picture:

- going over to a friends house to check on her son. he has the flu and i am worried about him
- Starting to get worried about swine flu...

Both are related to the flu and express worry, but tell a different story. The first reports an infection of another person, while the second expresses the author's concerned awareness. While infection tweets indicate a rise in infection rate, awareness tweets may not. Automatically making these distinctions may improve influenza surveillance, yet requires more than keywords.

We present an approach for differentiating between flu infection and concerned awareness tweets, as well as self vs other, by relying on a deeper analysis of the tweet. We present our features and demonstrate improvements in influenza surveillance.

1.1 Related Work

Much of the early work on web-based influenza surveillance relied on query logs and click-through data from search engines (Eysenbach, 2006), most famously Google's Flu Trends service (Ginsberg et al., 2008; Cook et al., 2011). Other sources of information include articles from the news media and online mailing lists (Brownstein et al., 2010).

2 Capturing Nuanced Trends

Previous work has classified messages as being related or not related to influenza, with promising surveillance results, but has ignored nuanced differences between flu tweets. Tweets that are related to

[1]The DHHS competition relied solely on keyword counting. http://www.nowtrendingchallenge.com/

flu but do not report an infection can corrupt infection tracking.

Concerned Awareness vs. Infection (A/I) Many flu tweets express a concerned awareness as opposed to infection, including fear of getting the flu, an awareness of increased infections, beliefs related to flu infection, and preventative flu measures (e.g. flu shots.) Critically, these people do not seem to have the flu, whereas infection tweets report having the flu. This distinction is similar to modality (Prabhakaran et al., 2012a). Conflating these tweets can hurt surveillance, as around half of our annotated flu messages were awareness. Identifying awareness tweets may be of use in-and-of itself, such as for characterizing fear of illness (Epstein et al., 2008; Epstein, 2009), public perception, and discerning sentiment (e.g. flu is negative, flu shots may be positive.) We focus on surveillance improvements.[2]

Self vs. Other (S/O) Tweets for both awareness and infection can describe the author (self) or others. It may be that self infection reporting is more informative. We test this hypothesis by classifying tweets as self vs. other.

Finding Flu Related Tweets (R/U) We must first identify messages that are flu related. We construct a classifier for flu related vs. unrelated.

3 Features

Token sequences (n-grams) are an insufficient feature set, since our classes share common vocabularies. Consider,

- A little worried about the swine flu epidemic!
- Robbie might have swine flu. I'm worried.

Both tweets mention flu and worried, which distinguish them as flu related but not specifically awareness or infection, nor self or other. Motivated by Bergsma et al. (2012), we complement 3-grams with additional features that capture longer spans of text and generalize using part of speech tags. We begin by processing each tweet using the ARK POS tagger (Gimpel et al., 2011) and find phrase segmentations using punctuation tags.[3] Most phrases were two (31.2%) or three (26.6%) tokens long.

[2]While tweets can both show awareness and report an infection, we formulate a binary task for simplicity since only a small percentage of tweets were so labeled.

[3]We used whitespace for tokenization, which did about the same as Jerboa (Van Durme, 2012).

Class Name	Words in Class
Infection	getting, got, recovered, have, having, had, has, catching, catch, cured, infected
Possession	bird, the flu, flu, sick, epidemic
Concern	afraid, worried, scared, fear, worry, nervous, dread, dreaded, terrified
Vaccination	vaccine, vaccines, shot, shots, mist, tamiflu, jab, nasal spray
Past Tense	was, did, had, got, were, or verb with the suffix "ed"
Present Tense	is, am, are, have, has, or verb with the suffix "ing"
Self	I, I've, I'd, I'm, im, my
Others	your, everyone, you, it, its, u, her, he, she, he's, she's, she, they, you're, she'll, he'll, husband, wife, brother, sister, your, people, kid, kids, children, son, daughter

Table 1: Our manually created set of word class features.

Word Classes For our task, many word types can behave similarly with regard to the label. We create word lists for possessive words, flu related words, fear related words, "self" words, "other" words, and fear words (Table 1). A word's presence triggers a count-based feature corresponding to each list.

Stylometry We include Twitter-specific style features. A feature is included for retweet, hashtags, and mentions of other users. We include a feature for emoticons (based on the emoticon part-of-speech tag). We include a more specific feature for positive emoticons (:) :D :)). We also include a feature for negative emoticons (:(:/). Additionally, we include a feature for links to URLs.

Part of Speech Templates We include features based on a number of templates matching specific sequences of words, word classes, and part of speech tags. Where any word included in the template matches a word in one of the word classes, an additional feature is included indicating that the word class was included in that template.

- Tuples of (subject,verb,object) and pairs of (subject, verb), (subject, object), and (verb, object). We use a simple rule to construct these tuples: the first noun or pronoun is taken as the subject, and the first verb appearing after the subject is taken as the verb. The object is taken as any noun or pronoun that appears before a verb or at the end of a phrase.

• A pairing of the first pronoun with last noun. These are useful for S/O, e.g. *I am worried that my son has the flu* to recognize the difference between the author (I) and someone else.
• Phrases that begin with a verb (pro-drop). This is helpful for S/O, e.g. *getting the flu!* which can indicate self even without a self-related pronoun. An additional feature is included if this verb is past-tense.
• Numeric references. These often indicate awareness (number of people with the flu) and are generally not detected by an n-gram model. We add a separate feature if the word following has the root "died", e.g. *So many people dying from the flu, I'm scared!*
• Pair of first pronoun/noun with last verb in a phrase. Many phrases have multiple verbs, but the last verb is critical, e.g. *I had feared the flu.* Additional features are added if the noun/pronoun is in the "self" or "other" word class, and if the verb is in the "possessive" word class.
• Flu appears as a noun before first verb in a phrase. This indicates when flu is a subject, which is more likely to be about awareness.
• Pair of verb and following noun. This indicates the verbs object, which can change the focus of A/I, e.g., *I am getting a serious case of the flu* vs. *I am getting a flu shot.* Additional features are added if the verb is past tense (based on word list and suffix "-ed".)
• Whether a flu related word appears as a noun or an adjective. When flu is used as an adjective, it may indicate a more general discussion of the flu, as opposed to an actual infection *I hate this flu* vs. *I hate this flu hype.*
• If a proper noun is followed by a possessive verb. This may indicate others for the S/O task *Looks like Denmark has the flu.* An additional feature fires for any verb that follows a proper noun and any past tense verb that follows a proper noun.
• Pair each noun with "?". While infection tweets are often statements and awareness questions, the subject matters, e.g. *Do you think that swine flu is coming to America?* as awareness. An equivalent feature is included for phrases ending with "!".

While many of our features can be extracted using a syntactic parser (Foster et al., 2011), tweets are very short, so our simple rules and over-generating features captures the desired effects without parsing.

	Self	Other	Total
Awareness	23.15%	24.07%	47.22%
Infection	37.21%	15.57%	52.78%
Total	60.36%	39.64%	

Table 2: The distribution over labels of the data set. Infection tweets are more likely to be about the author (self) than those expressing awareness.

3.1 Learning

We used a log-linear model from Mallet (McCallum, 2002) with L_2 regularization. For each task, we first labeled tweets as related/not-related and then classified the related tweets as awareness/infection and self/others. We found this two phase approach worked better than multi-class.

4 Data Collection

We used two Twitter data sets: a collection of 2 billion tweets from May 2009 and October 2010 (O'Connor et al., 2010)[4] and 1.8 billion tweets collected from August 2011 to November 2012. To obtain labeled data, we first filtered the data sets for messages containing words related to concern and influenza,[5] and used Amazon Mechanical Turk (Callison-Burch and Dredze, 2010) to label tweets as concerned awareness, infection, media and unrelated. We allowed multiple categories per tweet. Annotators also labeled awareness/infection tweets as self, other or both. We included tweets we annotated to measure Turker quality and obtained three annotations per tweet. More details can be found in Lamb et al. (2012).

To construct a labeled data set we removed low quality annotators (below 80% accuracy on gold tweets.) This seemed like a difficult task for annotators as a fifth of the data had no annotations after this step. We used the majority label as truth and ties were broken using the remaining low quality annotators. We then hand-corrected all tweets, changing 13.5% of the labels. The resulting data set contained 11,990 tweets (Table 2), 5,990 from 2011-2012 for training and the remaining from 2009-2010 as test.[6]

[4]This coincided with the second and larger H1N1 (swine flu) outbreak of 2009; swine flu is mentioned in 39.6% of the annotated awareness or infection tweets.

[5]e.g. "flu", "worried", "worry", "scared", "scare", etc.

[6]All development was done using cross-validation on training data, reserving test data for the final experiments.

Feature Removed	A/I	S/O
n-grams	0.6701	0.8440
Word Classes	**0.7735**	0.8549
Stylometry	0.8011	**0.8522**
Pronoun/Last Noun	0.7976	0.8534
Pro-Drop	0.7989	0.8523
Numeric Reference	0.7988	0.8530
Pronoun/Verb	0.7987	0.8530
Flu Noun Before Verb	0.7987	0.8526
Noun in Question	0.8004	0.8534
Subject,Object,Verb	0.8005	0.8541

Table 3: F1 scores after feature ablation.

5 Experiments

We begin by evaluating the accuracy on the binary classification tasks and then measure the results from the classifiers for influenza surveillance. We created precision recall curves on the test data (Figure 1), and measured the highest F1, for the three binary classifiers. For `A/I` and `S/O`, our additional features improved over the n-gram baselines. We performed feature ablation experiments (Table 3) and found that for `A/I`, the word class features helped the most by a large margin, while for `S/O` the stylometry and pro-drop features were the most important after n-grams. Interestingly, `S/O` does equally well removing just n-gram features, suggesting that the `S/O` task depends on a few words captured by our features.

Since live data will have classifiers run in stages – to filter out not-related tweets – we evaluated the performance of two-staged classification. F1 dropped to 0.7250 for `A/I` and `S/O` dropped to 0.8028.

5.1 Influenza surveillance using Twitter

We demonstrate how our classifiers can improve influenza surveillance using Twitter. Our hypothesis is that by isolating infection tweets we can improve correlations against government influenza data. We include several baseline methods:

Google Flu Trends: Trends from search queries.[7]

Keywords: Tweets that contained keywords from the DHHS Twitter surveillance competition.

ATAM: We obtained 1.6 million tweets that were automatically labeled as influenza/other by ATAM (Paul and Dredze, 2011). We trained a binary classifier with n-grams and marked tweets as flu infection.

We evaluated three trends using our three binary classifiers trained with a reduced feature set close to the n-gram features:[8]

All Flu: Tweets marked as flu by Keywords or ATAM were then classified as related/unrelated.[9] This trend used all flu-related tweets.

Infection: Related tweets were classified as either awareness or infection. This used infection tweets.

Infection+Self: Infection were then labeled as self or other. This trend used self tweets.

All five of these trends were correlated against data from the Centers for Disease Control and Prevention (CDC) weekly estimates of influenza-like illness (ILI) in the U.S., with Pearson correlations computed separately for 2009 and 2011 (Table 4).[10] Previous work has shown high correlations for 2009 data, but since swine flu had so dominated social media, we expect weaker correlations for 2011.

Data	System	2009	2011
Google	Flu Trends	0.9929	0.8829
Twitter	ATAM	0.9698	0.5131
	Keywords	0.9771	0.6597
	All Flu	0.9833	0.7247
	Infection	**0.9897**	**0.7987**
	Infection+Self	0.9752	0.6662

Table 4: Correlations against CDC ILI data: Aug 2009-Aug 2010, Dec 2011 to Aug 2012.

Results are show in Table 4 and Figure 2 shows two classifiers against the CDC ILI data. We see that in 2009 the Infection curve fits the CDC curve very closely, while the All Flu curve appears to substantially overestimate the flu rate at the peak. While 2009 is clearly easier, and all trends have similar correlations, our Infection classifier beats the other Twitter methods. All trends do much worse in

[7] http://www.google.org/flutrends/

[8] Classifiers trained on 2011 data and thresholds selected to maximize F1 on held out 2009 data.

[9] Since our data set to train related or unrelated focused on tweets that appeared to mention the flu, we first filtered out obvious non-flu tweets by running ATAM and Keywords.

[10] While the 2009 data is a 10% sample of Twitter, we used a different approach for 2011. To increase the amount of data, we collected Tweets mentioning health keywords and then normalized by the public stream counts. For our analysis, we excluded days that were missing data. Additionally, we used a geolocator based on user provided locations to exclude non-US messages. See (Dredze et al., 2013) for details and code for the geolocator.

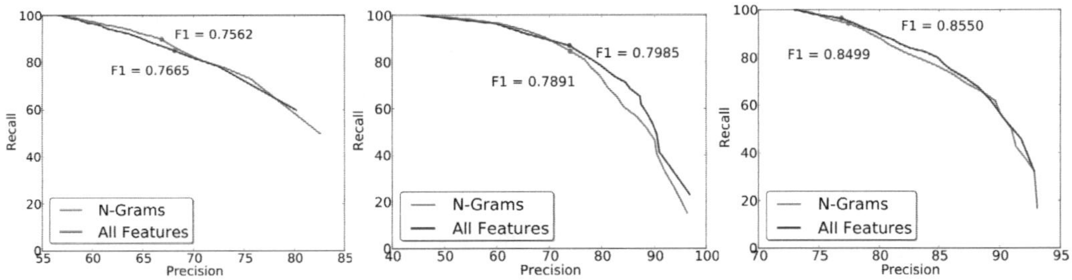

Figure 1: Left to right: Precision-recall curves for related vs. not related, awareness vs. infection and self vs. others.

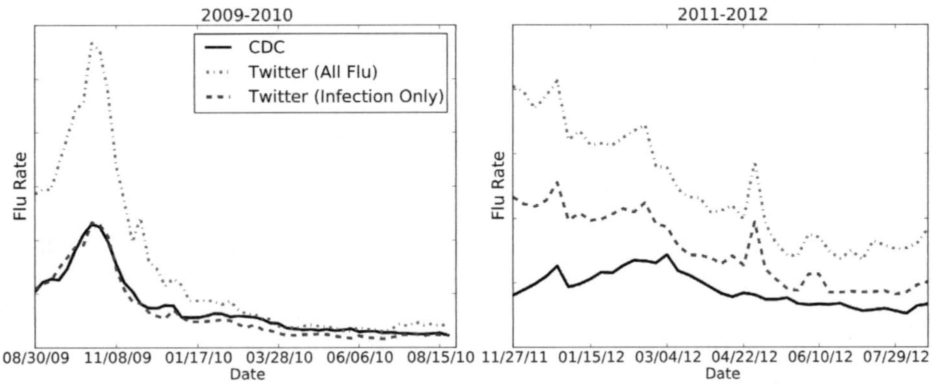

Figure 2: The Twitter flu rate for two years alongside the ILI rates provided by the CDC. The y-axes are not comparable between the two years due to differences in data collection, but we note that the 2011-12 season was much milder.

the 2011 season, which was much milder and thus harder to detect. Of the Twitter methods, those using our system were dramatically higher, with the Infection curve doing the best by a significant margin. Separating out infection from awareness (`A/I`) led to significant improvements, while the `S/O` classifier did not, for unknown reasons.

The best result using Twitter reported to date has been by Doan et al. (2012), whose best system had a correlation of 0.9846 during the weeks beginning 8/30/09–05/02/10. Our Infection system had a correlation of 0.9887 during the same period. While Google does better than any of the Twitter systems, we note that Google has access to much more (proprietary) data, and their system is trained to predict CDC trends, whereas our Twitter system is intrinsically trained only on the tweets themselves.

Finally, we are also interested in daily trends in addition to weekly, but there is no available evaluation data on this scale. Instead, we computed the stability of each curve, by measuring the day-to-day changes. In the 2009 season, the relative increase or decrease from the previous day had a variance of 3.0% under the Infection curve, compared to 4.1% under ATAM and 6.7% under Keywords.

6 Discussion

Previous papers have implicitly assumed that flu-related tweets mimick the infection rate. While this was plausible on 2009 data that focused on the swine flu epidemic, it is clearly false for more typical flu seasons. Our results show that by differentiating between types of flu tweets to isolate reports of infection, we can recover reasonable surveillance. This result delivers a promising message for the NLP community: deeper content analysis of tweets matters. We believe this conclusion is applicable to numerous Twitter trend tasks, and we encourage others to investigate richer content analyses for these tasks. In particular, the community interested in modeling author beliefs and influence (Diab et al., 2009; Prabhakaran et al., 2012b; Biran and Rambow, 2011) may find our task and data of interest. Finally, beyond surveillance, our methods can be used to study disease awareness and sentiment, which has implications for how public health officials respond to outbreaks. We conclude with an example of this distinction. On June 11th, 2009, the World Health Organization declared that the swine flu had become a global flu pandemic. On that day, flu awareness increased 282%, while infections increased only 53%.

References

Dena Asta and Cosma Shalizi. 2012. Identifying influenza trends via Twitter. In *NIPS Workshop on Social Network and Social Media Analysis: Methods, Models and Applications*.

Shane Bergsma, Matt Post, and David Yarowsky. 2012. Stylometric analysis of scientific articles. In *Proc. NAACL-HLT*, pages 327–337.

O. Biran and O. Rambow. 2011. Identifying justifications in written dialogs. In *Semantic Computing (ICSC), 2011 Fifth IEEE International Conference on*, pages 162–168. IEEE.

J. Bollen, A. Pepe, and H. Mao. 2011. Modeling public mood and emotion: Twitter sentiment and socio-economic phenomena. In *Proceedings of the Fifth International AAAI Conference on Weblogs and Social Media*, pages 450–453.

John S. Brownstein, Clark C. Freifeld, Emily H. Chan, Mikaela Keller, Amy L. Sonricker, Sumiko R. Mekaru, and David L. Buckeridge. 2010. Information technology and global surveillance of cases of 2009 h1n1 influenza. *New England Journal of Medicine*, 362(18):1731–1735.

Chris Callison-Burch and Mark Dredze. 2010. Creating speech and language data with Amazon's Mechanical Turk. In *NAACL Workshop on Creating Speech and Language Data With Mechanical Turk*.

N. Collier. 2012. Uncovering text mining: A survey of current work on web-based epidemic intelligence. *Global Public Health*, 7(7):731–749.

Samantha Cook, Corrie Conrad, Ashley L. Fowlkes, and Matthew H. Mohebbi. 2011. Assessing google flu trends performance in the united states during the 2009 influenza virus a (h1n1) pandemic. *PLOS ONE*, 6(8):e23610.

A. Culotta. 2010a. Towards detecting influenza epidemics by analyzing Twitter messages. In *ACM Workshop on Soc.Med. Analytics*.

Aron Culotta. 2010b. Detecting influenza epidemics by analyzing Twitter messages. arXiv:1007.4748v1 [cs.IR], July.

Mona T. Diab, Lori Levin, Teruko Mitamura, Owen Rambow, Vinodkumar Prabhakaran, and Weiwei Guo. 2009. Committed belief annotation and tagging. In *ACL Third Linguistic Annotation Workshop*.

S. Doan, L. Ohno-Machado, and N. Collier. 2012. Enhancing Twitter data analysis with simple semantic filtering: Example in tracking influenza-like illnesses. *arXiv preprint arXiv:1210.0848*.

Mark Dredze, Michael J. Paul, Shane Bergsma, and Hieu Tran. 2013. A Twitter geolocation system with applications to public health. Working paper.

Mark Dredze. 2012. How social media will change public health. *IEEE Intelligent Systems*, 27(4):81–84.

Sachiko Maskawa Eiji Aramaki and Mizuki Morita. 2011. Twitter catches the flu: Detecting influenza epidemics using Twitter. In *Empirical Natural Language Processing Conference (EMNLP)*.

Jacob Eisenstein, Brendan O'Connor, Noah A. Smith, and Eric P. Xing. 2010. A latent variable model for geographic lexical variation. In *Empirical Natural Language Processing Conference (EMNLP)*.

Joshua Epstein, Jon Parker, Derek Cummings, and Ross Hammond. 2008. Coupled contagion dynamics of fear and disease: Mathematical and computational explorations. *PLoS ONE*, 3(12).

J.M. Epstein. 2009. Modelling to contain pandemics. *Nature*, 460(7256):687–687.

G. Eysenbach. 2006. Infodemiology: tracking flu-related searches on the web for syndromic surveillance. In *AMIA Annual Symposium*, pages 244–248. AMIA.

J. Foster, Ö. Çetinoglu, J. Wagner, J. Le Roux, S. Hogan, J. Nivre, D. Hogan, J. Van Genabith, et al. 2011. # hardtoparse: Pos tagging and parsing the Twitterverse. In *proceedings of the Workshop On Analyzing Microtext (AAAI 2011)*, pages 20–25.

Kevin Gimpel, Nathan Schneider, Brendan O'Connor, Dipanjan Das, Daniel Mills, Jacob Eisenstein, Michael Heilman, Dani Yogatama, Jeffrey Flanigan, and Noah A. Smith. 2011. Part-of-speech tagging for Twitter: Annotation, features, and experiments. In *Association for Computational Linguistics (ACL)*.

J. Ginsberg, M.H. Mohebbi, R.S. Patel, L. Brammer, M.S. Smolinski, and L. Brilliant. 2008. Detecting influenza epidemics using search engine query data. *Nature*, 457(7232):1012–1014.

Alex Lamb, Michael J. Paul, and Mark Dredze. 2012. Investigating Twitter as a source for studying behavioral responses to epidemics. In *AAAI Fall Symposium on Information Retrieval and Knowledge Discovery in Biomedical Text*.

A.K. McCallum. 2002. MALLET: A machine learning for language toolkit.

Brendan O'Connor, Ramnath Balasubramanyan, Bryan R. Routledge, and Noah A. Smith. 2010. From Tweets to polls: Linking text sentiment to public opinion time series. In *ICWSM*.

Michael J. Paul and Mark Dredze. 2011. You are what you Tweet: Analyzing Twitter for public health. In *ICWSM*.

Vinodkumar Prabhakaran, Michael Bloodgood, Mona Diab, Bonnie Dorr, Lori Levin, Christine D. Piatko, Owen Rambow, and Benjamin Van Durme. 2012a.

Statistical modality tagging from rule-based annotations and crowdsourcing. In *Extra-Propositional Aspects of Meaning in Computational Linguistics (ExProM 2012)*.

Vinodkumar Prabhakaran, Owen Rambow, and Mona Diab. 2012b. Predicting overt display of power in written dialogs. In *North American Chapter of the Association for Computational Linguistics (NAACL)*.

Adam Sadilek, Henry Kautz, and Vincent Silenzio. 2012a. Modeling spread of disease from social interactions. In *Sixth AAAI International Conference on Weblogs and Social Media (ICWSM)*.

Adam Sadilek, Henry Kautz, and Vincent Silenzio. 2012b. Predicting disease transmission from geotagged micro-blog data. In *Twenty-Sixth AAAI Conference on Artificial Intelligence*.

Takeshi Sakaki, Makoto Okazaki, and Yutaka Matsuo. 2010. Earthquake shakes Twitter users: real-time event detection by social sensors. In *WWW*, New York, NY, USA.

A. Signorini, A.M. Segre, and P.M. Polgreen. 2011. The use of Twitter to track levels of disease activity and public concern in the US during the influenza a H1N1 pandemic. *PLoS One*, 6(5):e19467.

A. Tumasjan, T.O. Sprenger, P.G. Sandner, and I.M. Welpe. 2010. Predicting elections with twitter: What 140 characters reveal about political sentiment. In *Proceedings of the fourth international aaai conference on weblogs and social media*, pages 178–185.

B. Van Durme. 2012. Jerboa: A toolkit for randomized and streaming algorithms. Technical report, Technical Report 7, Human Language Technology Center of Excellence, Johns Hopkins University.

Differences in User Responses to a Wizard-of-Oz versus Automated System

Jesse Thomason
University of Pittsburgh
Pittsburgh, PA 15260, USA
jdt34@pitt.edu

Diane Litman
University of Pittsburgh
Pittsburgh, PA 15260, USA
litman@cs.pitt.edu

Abstract

Wizard-of-Oz experimental setup in a dialogue system is commonly used to gather data for informing an automated version of that system. Previous work has exposed dependencies between user behavior towards systems and user belief about whether the system is automated or human-controlled. This work examines whether user behavior changes when user belief is held constant and the system's operator is varied. We perform a post-hoc experiment using generalizable prosodic and lexical features of user responses to a dialogue system backed with and without a human wizard. Our results suggest that user responses are different when communicating with a wizarded and an automated system, indicating that wizard data may be less reliable for informing automated systems than generally assumed.

1 Introduction

In a Wizard-of-Oz (WOZ) experimental setup, some or all of the automated portions of a dialogue system are replaced with a hidden, human evaluator. This setup is often used to gather data from users who believe they are interacting with an automated system (Wolska et al., 2004; Andrews et al., 2008; Becker et al., 2011). This data can inform a downstream, real automated system. A WOZ experimental protocol calls for holding "all other input and output ... constant so that the only unknown variable is who does the internal processing" (Paek, 2001). Thus, hiding the human wizard's input by layers of system interface can render that system believably automated.

An assumption of this WOZ data-gathering strategy is that user behavior will not vary substantially between the WOZ and automated (AUT) experimental setups. However, it was shown in a dialogue system that training with a small set of data from an automated system gave rise to better performance than training with a large set of data from an analogous wizarded system (Drummond and Litman, 2011). There, it was suggested that differences in system automation may be responsible for the performance gap. It is possible that user responses to these dialogue systems differed substantially.

This paper aims to investigate this possibility by comparing data between a wizarded and automated version of a tutoring dialogue system. We hypothesize that what users say and how they say it will differ when the only change is whether the system's speech recognition and correctness evaluation components are wizarded or automated.

2 Dialogue System

The data for this study is provided by the baseline conditions (one wizarded (WOZ) and one automated (AUT)) of two prior experiments with a spoken tutorial dialogue system. Users of this system were students recruited at our university, and each was a native speaker of American English. Users were novices and were tutored in basic Newtonian physics by the system. Each was engaged by a set of dialogues that illustrated one or more basic physics concepts. Those dialogues included remedial subdialogues that were accessed when the users pro-

Tutor: So what are the forces acting on the packet after it's dropped from the plane?
Student: um gravity then well air resistance is negligible just gravity
Tutor: Fine. So what's the direction of the force of gravity on the packet?
Student: vertically down

Figure 1: Tutor text is shown on a screen and read aloud via text-to-speech. The user responds verbally to the tutor's queries.

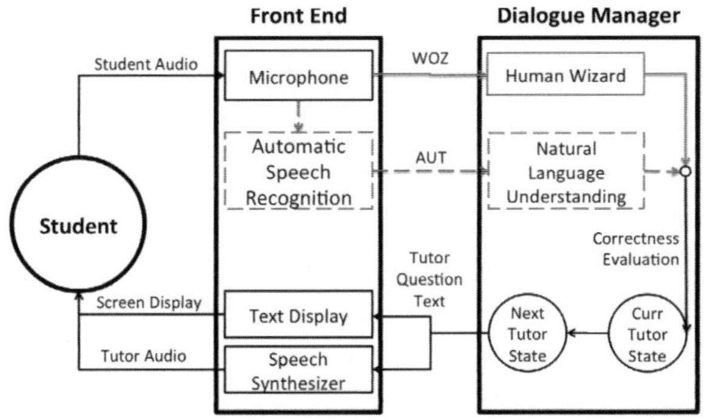

Figure 2: The workflow of the tutoring dialogue system with the WOZ setup component shown in solid, blue and the AUT setup component shown in dashed, red.

System	#Users	#Qu	#Turns
WOZ	21	111	1542
AUT	25	111	2034

Table 1: Counts for users, unique questions, and user turns in each data set.

vided incorrect or off-topic answers. These prior experiments were examining the effects of system adaptation in response to detected student uncertainty (Forbes-Riley and Litman(a), 2011; Forbes-Riley and Litman(b), 2011). However, in this study we consider only the baseline, non-adaptive conditions of those experiments. Figure 1 shows a sample dialogue excerpt between the student and tutor.

In the baseline conditions of the WOZ and AUT system past experiments, as shown in Figure 2, the setups varied only by the system component responsible for understanding and evaluating a user's verbal response. Each student participated in only one of the two setups, and students were not informed when the system was wizarded. In the WOZ setup a human wizard marked student responses to prompts as correct or incorrect. In the AUT setup, automatic speech recognition was performed on student responses[1], and (in)correctness of answers was determined using natural language understanding models trained from the WOZ experiment's data.

3 Post-Hoc Experiment

Using both lexical and prosodic features, we aimed to determine whether there exist significant differences in users' turn-level responses to the WOZ and AUT systems.

It was suspected that the imperfect accuracy[2] (87%) of the AUT system's evaluations of the (in)correctness of user responses may have led to remedial sub-dialogues being accessed by the AUT system more often, since false-negatives accounted for 72% of inaccurate evaluations. To correct for this imbalance, rather than comparing user responses to all questions, we compared the features of user responses (turns) to each question individually. We omitted questions which were presented in only one setup[3] as well as turns for which a human transcriber found no user speech. Table 1 gives the numbers of users, number of unique questions asked, and total number of user responses contained in the remaining data and used in our investigations.

For prosodic features, we considered duration, pitch, and energy (RMS), each extracted using openSMILE (Eyben et al., 2010). From pitch and energy, which contain many samples during a single turn, we extracted features for maximum, minimum, mean, and standard deviation of these readings. We also considered speech duration and the length of the pause before speech began. This gave us a total of 10 prosodic features. To account for any differences in recording environment and users' voices, we normalized each prosodic feature by dividing its value on each turn by its value in the first turn of the current problem dialogue for that user. This normal-

[1]The average word-error rate for these AUT responses was 19%.

[2]Agreement of $\kappa = 0.7$ between the system and human.

[3]There were 3 such questions containing 6 user responses; each question was a remedial sub-dialogue accessed in the AUT but not WOZ setup.

ization scheme was chosen for our analysis because it is used in the live system, though we note that alternative methods considering more user responses could be explored in the future.

For lexical features, we used the *Linguistic Inquiry and Word Count* (LIWC). LIWC (Pennebaker et al., 2001), a word-count dictionary, provides features representing the percentage of words in an utterance falling under particular categories. Though still a counting strategy, these categories capture higher-level concepts than would simple unigrams. For example, one category is *Tentative(T)*, which includes words such as "maybe", "perhaps", and "guess". Less abstract categories, such as *Prepositions(P)*, with words such as "to", "with", and "above", are also generated by LIWC. Using these example categories, the utterance "Maybe above" would receive feature vector:

$$\langle 0,\ldots,0,T=50,0,\ldots,0,P=50,0,\ldots,0\rangle \quad (1)$$

Human transcriptions of users' speech were made available post-hoc for both system versions. We extracted 69 LIWC categories as lexical features from these human transcriptions of each user turn.

Between the WOZ and AUT setups, we looked for user response feature differences in two ways. First, a Welch's two-tailed t-test was used to compare the distributions of each feature's values between WOZ and AUT user responses per question. We noted the features found to be significantly different. Second, we built classification models to distinguish between user responses per question from the WOZ and AUT experiments. For each question, a J48[4] decision tree model was trained and tested using 10-fold cross validation via the Weka[5] toolkit. Only questions with at least 10 responses between both setups were considered. Each model was compared against majority-class baseline for its respective question by checking for statistically significant differences in the model's accuracy.

[4]We tried Logistic Regression and Support Vector classifiers but these were consistently outperformed by J48.

[5]http://www.cs.waikato.ac.nz/ml/weka

4 Results

4.1 Statistical Comparison of Features

The number of questions for which at least one feature differed statistically significantly was calculated. Since distinct sets of students were involved in the WOZ and AUT setups, it is possible that some of these differences are inherent between the students and not resulting from the presence or absence of a human wizard. To control for this possibility, we assigned students randomly into two new groups (preserving the original class distribution in each new group) and tested for feature differences between these new groups. Table 2 summarizes the differences found by each feature set. We report only questions for which at least one feature differed between WOZ and AUT but not between these two random groups[6]. Table 2 also shows the percentage of turns that those questions comprised in the corpus. Prosodic and lexical features each differ for a substantial portion of the corpus of turns, and when both sets are considered about 67% of the corpus is captured.

Feature set	#Qu	% Corpus by Turns
Prosodic	42	46.22%
Lexical	33	35.46%
Either	61	66.86%

Table 2: Number of questions for which at least one feature from the feature set was found to differ with significance $p < 0.05$ between WOZ and AUT responses and the percentage the corpus represented by those questions, weighted by the speech turns they comprise.

After controlling for possible between-student differences, all 10 prosodic features and 29 out of 69 lexical features differed significantly ($p < 0.05$) for at least one question. Table 3 gives the features which were able to differentiate at least 10% of the corpus by turns.

These t-tests show there exist features which differ for a substantial number of questions between the two experimental setups. Examination of Table

[6]We repeated this random split procedure 10 times and found, after omitting features found significant in any of the 10 splits, that 58.08% of the corpus was still captured. Less than 2% of the turns belonged to questions with at least one feature different through all 10 splits.

Feature	% CbT	#Qu	#W>A
Duration	22.15%	19	1
RMS Min	16.86%	15	14
Dictionary Words	15.13%	13	11
pronoun	12.56%	10	10
social	11.35%	9	8
funct	10.99%	9	9
Six Letter Words	10.91%	9	0

Table 3: Features shown to differ with significance $p < 0.05$ between WOZ and AUT responses in questions comprising at least 10% of the corpus by turns (CbT). The numbers of questions these turns comprised and of questions with greater (W)OZ than (A)UT mean are also given.

Tutor: So how do these two forces' directions compare?
Top two most common responses:
WOZ(9),AUT(2): they are opposite
WOZ(3),AUT(8): opposite
Longest responses per tutor setup:
WOZ Student: the relationship between the two forces' directions are towards each other since the sun is pulling the gravitational force of the earth
AUT Student: they are opposite directions

Figure 3: The tutor question and select user responses to a question for which the *Dictionary Words* feature was greater for WOZ responses.

3 in addition suggests that users used more words with the wizarded system. For example, the fourth row shows that all of the questions showing differences for the LIWC category *pronoun* (the words "they", "he", and "it" are popular in this corpus) exposed higher percentage of pronouns in the WOZ utterances. The usual dominance of the third row, *Dictionary Words*, by the WOZ utterances also reflects this trend. Figure 3 gives common and characteristic student responses for each setup on a question for which *Dictionary Words* differed significantly. We next applied machine learning to classify the experiment-of-origin of responses based on these features.

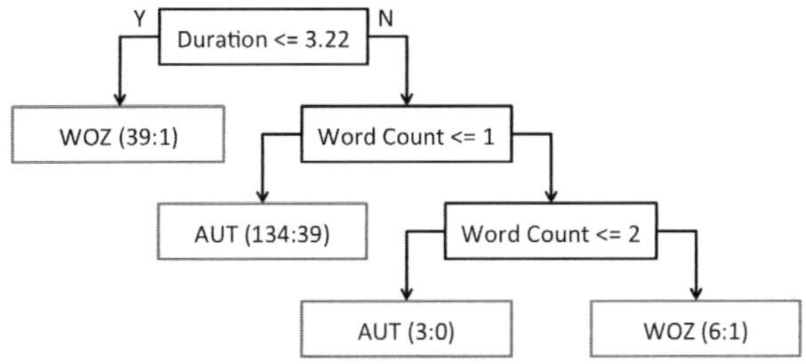

Figure 4: The J48 tree for the question "Would you like to do another problem?". Classification nodes are marked in blue and red for WOZ and AUT, respectively, and specify (#Instances:#Incorrect).

4.2 Response Classification Experiments

After removing questions with less than 10 responses between the two setups, there remained 97 questions totaling 2980 turns. Of the J48 models built and tested on each question, 21 of 97 outperformed the majority-class baseline accuracies for those questions with significance $p < 0.05$. These 21 questions represented 32.79% of the corpus by turns. We present in detail the two of these 21 questions with the most turns.

The question "Would you like to do another problem?" represented 6.11% of the corpus by turns and the J48 model built for it, shown in Figure 4, outperformed the baseline accuracy with $p < 0.001$. While the *Duration* feature was the root node, a bigger decision was made by *Word Count* ≤ 1, for which most responses were from AUT data. This result is consistent with literature (Schechtman and Horowitz, 2003; Rosé and Torrey, 2005) that suggests that users interacting with automated systems will be more curt.

The question "Now let's find the forces exerted on the car in the vertical direction during the collision. First, what vertical force is always exerted on an object near the surface of the earth?" represented 1.54% of the corpus by turns and the J48 model built for it, shown in Figure 5, outperformed the baseline accuracy with $p < 0.01$. Again, *Duration* emerged as the tree root, but here the biggest decision fell to *RMS mean*. Student responses approximately louder than the initial response to the tutor in this question dialogue were marked, almost entirely accurately, as AUT.

Since both trees were rooted at *Duration*, we sam-

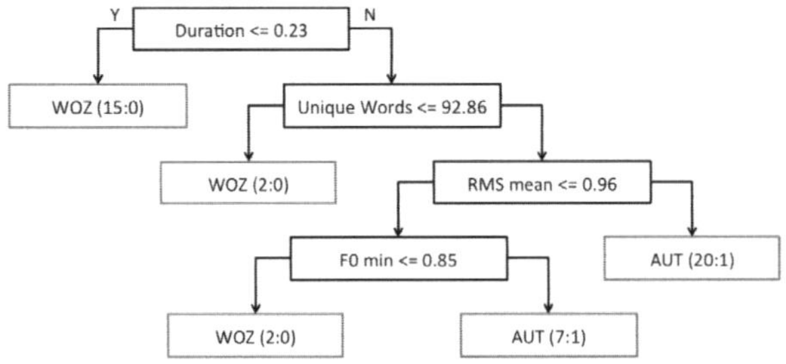

Figure 5: The J48 tree for the question "Now let's find the forces exerted on the car in the vertical direction during the collision. First, what vertical force is always exerted on an object near the surface of the earth?". Classification nodes are marked in blue and red for WOZ and AUT, respectively, and specify (#Instances:#Incorrect).

pled common responses from each experiment for both problems. We noticed that hyper-articulation (speaking slowly, loudly, and enunciating each syllable) was more common in the AUT responses. For example, one user answering "Would you like to do another problem?" took almost 4 seconds to clearly and slowly pronounce the word "yes". We suspect that these hyper-articulations may have contributed to the classifiers' ability to detect WOZ responses based on their brevity.

The performance of the per-question J48 models shows, for a non-trivial portion of the turns, that the experiment-of-origin can be classified based on generalizable prosodic and lexical features alone. The two trees discussed above demonstrate the simplicity of the models needed to perform this separation.

5 Discussion and Future Work

We demonstrate that there exist significant differences between user responses to a wizarded and an automatic dialogue system's questions, even when the contribution of the wizard is as atomic as speech recognition and correctness evaluation. Our generalizable features are derived exclusively from the recordings of the users' responses and human transcriptions of their speech.

Because the role of the wizard in the WOZ setup was limited to evaluating users' spoken response to a prompt, our results suggest that user speech changes as a result of user confidence in the system's accuracy. For example, Figure 3 demonstrates that users in the WOZ setup used complete sentences and gave long responses, where AUT users, possibly anticipating system error, used shorter (sometimes one word) responses. This relationship between user confidence and user speech may be analogous to observed differences like users' longer speech and typed responses to systems when told those systems are human-operated (Schechtman and Horowitz, 2003; Rosé and Torrey, 2005). Our results suggest ways in which raw wizarded data may fall short of ideal for training an automated system.

Having established that differences exist, our future work will focus on deeper exploration of the nature of these differences in users' responses. We suspect users become less confident in the automated system over time, so one direction of study will be to measure how the observed differences change over the course of the dialogue. We expect that they are minimal early on and become more pronounced in the automated setup as users' confidence is shaken. Additionally, some technical aspects of our methodology may impact these and future results: using different methods of normalization for user speech values than the one from this paper may affect visibility of observed differences between the setups.

Future work may also attempt to address these differences directly. Intentional wizard error could be introduced to frustrate the user into responding as she would to a less accurate system, analogous to intentional errors produced in user simulation in spoken dialogue systems (Lee and Eskenazi, 2012). This strategy would be further informed by studies of the relationship between the system's evaluation accuracy and student responses' deviation from wizarded responses. Alternatively, post-hoc domain adaptation could be used to adjust the WOZ data. Generalizable statistical classification domain adaptation (Daumé and Marcu, 2006) and adaptation demonstrated to work well in NLP-specific domains (Jiang and Zhai, 2007) both have the potential to adjust WOZ data to better match that seen by automated systems.

Acknowledgments

This work is funded by NSF award 0914615. We thank Scott Silliman for his support and Pamela Jordan, Wenting Xiong, and the anonymous reviewers for their helpful suggestions and commentary.

References

Pierre Andrews, Suresh Manandhar, and Marco De Boni. 2008. Argumentative Human Computer Dialogue for Automated Persuasion. *Proceedings of the 9th SIGDIAL Workshop on Discourse and Dialogue*, pages 138-147, Columbus, June 2008. Association for Computational Linguistics.

Lee Becker, Wayne Ward, Sarel van Vuuren, Martha Palmer. 2011. DISCUSS: A dialogue move taxonomy layered over semantic representations. *International Workshop on Computational Semantics (IWCS)*, Main Conference. Association for Computational Linguistics.

Hal Daumé III and Daniel Marcu. 2006. Domain Adaptation for Statistical Classifiers. *Journal of Artificial Intelligence Research*, 26:101-126. AI Access Foundation.

Joanna Drummond and Diane Litman. 2011. Examining the Impacts of Dialogue Content and System Automation on Affect Models in a Spoken Tutorial Dialogue System. *Proceedings of the SIGDIAL 2011 Conference*, Portland, Oregon, June. Association for Computational Linguistics.

Florian Eyben, Martin Wöllmer, and Björn Schuller. 2010. Opensmile: The Munich Versatile and Fast Open-Source Audio Feature Extractor. *MM '10 Proceedings of the International Conference on Multimedia*, 1459-1462.

Kate Forbes-Riley and Diane Litman. 2011. Designing and Evaluating a Wizarded Uncertainty-Adaptive Spoken Dialogue Tutoring System. *Computer Speech and Language*, 25(1): 105-126.

Kate Forbes-Riley and Diane Litman. 2011. Benefits and Challenges of Real-Time Uncertainty Detection and Adaptation in a Spoken Dialogue Computer Tutor. *Speech Communication 2011*, 53(9-10): 1115-1136.

Jing Jiang and ChengXiang Zhai. 2007. Instance Weighting for Domain Adaptation in NLP. *Proceedings of the 45th Annual Meeting of the Association of Computational Linguistics*, pages 264-271, Prague, Czech Republic, June 2007.

Sungjin Lee and Maxine Eskenazi. 2012. An Unsupervised Approach to User Simulation: toward Self-Improving Dialog Systems. *Proceedings of the 13th Annual Meeting of the Special Interest Group on Discourse and Dialogue (SIGDIAL)*, pages 50-59, Seoul, South Korea, 5-6 July 2012. Association for Computational Linguistics.

Tim Paek. 2001. Empirical Methods for Evaluating Dialog Systems. *SIGDIAL '01 Proceedings of the Second SIGdial Workshop on Discourse and Dialogue*, 16:1-9.

James Pennebaker, Martha Francis, and Roger Booth. 2001. Linguistic Inquiry and Word Count (LIWC): LIWC2001. Lawrence Erlbaum Associates, Mahwah, NJ.

Carolyn P. Rosé and Cristen Torrey. 2005. Interactivity and Expectation: Eliciting Learning Oriented Behavior with Tutorial Dialogue Systems. *Human-Computer Interaction-INTERACT 2005*, 323-336. Springer Berlin/Heidelberg.

Nicole Schechtman and Leonard M. Horowitz. 2003. Media Inequality in Conversation: How People Behave Differently When Interacting with Computers and People. *CHI '03 Proceedings of the SIGCHI conference on Human factors in computing systems*, 281-288.

Magdalena Wolska, Ivana Kruijff-Korbayová, Helmut Horacek. 2004. Lexical-Semantic Interpretation of Language Input in Mathematical Dialogs. *Proceedings of the ACL 2nd Workshop on Text Meaning and Interpretation*, 81-88.

Improving the Quality of Minority Class Identification in Dialog Act Tagging

Adinoyi Omuya
10gen
New York, NY, USA
wisdom@10gen.com

Vinodkumar Prabhakaran
CS, Columbia University
New York, NY, USA
vinod@cs.columbia.edu

Owen Rambow
CCLS, Columbia University
New York, NY, USA
rambow@ccls.columbia.edu

Abstract

We present a method of improving the performance of dialog act tagging in identifying minority classes by using per-class feature optimization and a method of choosing the class based not on confidence, but on a cascade of classifiers. We show that it gives a minority class F-measure error reduction of 22.8%, while also reducing the error for other classes and the overall error by about 10%.

1 Introduction

In this paper, we discuss **dialog act tagging**, the task of assigning a dialog act to an utterance, where a **dialog act** (DA) is a high-level categorization of the pragmatic meaning of the utterance. Our data is email. Our starting point is the tagger described in (Hu et al., 2009), which uses a standard multi-class classifier based on support vector machines (SVMs). While the performance of this system is pretty good as measured by accuracy, it performs badly on the DA REQUEST-ACTION, which is a rare class. Multi-class SVMs are typically implemented as a set of SVMs, one per class, with the overall choice of class being determined by the SVM with the highest confidence ("one-against-all"). Multi-class SVMs are typically packaged as a single system, whose inner workings are ignored by the NLP researcher. In this paper we show that, for our problem of DA classification, we can boost the performance of the rare classes (while maintaining the overall performance) by performing feature optimization separately for each individual classifier. But we also show that we can achieve an all-around error reduction by altering the method by which the multi-class classifier combines the individual SVMs. This new method of combination is a simple cascade: we run the individual classifiers in ascending order of frequency of the classes in the training corpus; the first classifier to classify the data point positively determines the choice of the overall classifier. If no classifier classifies the data point positively, we use the usual confidence-based method. This new method obtains a 22.8% error reduction for the minority class, and around 10% error reduction for the other classes and for the overall classifier.

This paper is structured as follows. We start out by discussing related work (Section 2). We then present our data in Section 3, and in Section 4 we present the experiments with our systems and the results. We report the results of an extrinsic evaluation in Section 5, and conclude.

2 Related Work

Dialog act (DA) annotations and tagging, inspired by the speech act theory of Austin (1975) and Searle (1976), have been used in the NLP community to understand and model dialog. Initial work was done on spoken interactions (see for example (Stolcke et al., 2000)). Recently, studies have explored dialog act tagging in written interactions such as emails (Cohen et al., 2004), forums (Kim et al., 2006; Kim et al., 2010b), instant messaging (Kim et al., 2010a) and Twitter (Zhang et al., 2012). Most DA tagging systems for written interactions use a message/post level tagging scheme, and allow multiple tags for each message/post. In such a tagging scheme, individual binary classifiers for each tag are independent of one another. However, recent studies have found merit in segmenting each message into functional units and assigning a single DA to each segment (Hu et al., 2009). Our work falls in this paradigm (we choose a single DA for smaller textual units). We build on the work by (Hu et al., 2009); we improve their dialog act predicting performance on minority classes using per-class feature optimization.

3 Data

In this study, we use the email corpus presented in (Hu et al., 2009), which is manually annotated for DA tags. The corpus contains 122 email threads with a total of 360 messages and 20,740 word tokens. This set of email threads is chosen from a version of the Enron email corpus with some missing messages restored from other emails in which they were quoted (Yeh and Harnly, 2006; Agarwal et al., 2012). Most emails are concerned with exchanging information, scheduling meetings, or solving problems, but there are also purely social emails.

Dialog Act Tag	Count (%)
REQUEST-ACTION (R-A)	35 (2.5%)
REQUEST-INFORMATION (R-I)	151 (10.7%)
CONVENTIONAL (CONV)	357 (25.4%)
INFORM (INF)	853 (60.7%)
Total # of DFUs	1406

Table 1: Annotation statistics

Each message in the thread is segmented into Dialog Functional Units (DFUs). A DFU is a contiguous span within an email message which has a coherent communicative intention. Each DFU is assigned a single DA label which is one of the following: REQUEST-ACTION (R-A), REQUEST-INFORMATION (R-I), CONVENTIONAL (CONV) and INFORM (INF). There are three other DA labels — INFORM-OFFLINE, COMMIT, and NODA for no dialog act — which occurred 5 or fewer times in the corpus. We ignore these DA labels in this paper. The corpus also contains links between the DFUs, but we do not use those annotations in this study. Table 1 presents the distribution of DA labels in our corpus. We now describe each of the DAs we consider in our experiments.

In a REQUEST-ACTION, the writer signals her desire that the reader perform some non-communicative act, i.e., an act that cannot in itself be part of the dialogue. For example, a writer can ask the reader to write a report or make coffee.

In a REQUEST-INFORMATION, the writer signals her desire that the reader perform a specific communicative act, namely that he provide information (either facts or opinion).

In an INFORM, the writer conveys information, or more precisely, the writer signals that her desire that the reader adopt a certain belief. It covers many different types of information that can be conveyed including answers to questions, beliefs (committed or not), attitudes, and elaborations on prior DAs.

A CONVENTIONAL dialog act does not signal any specific communicative intention on the part of the writer, but rather it helps structure and thus facilitate the communication. Examples include greetings, introductions, expressions of gratitude, etc.

4 System

We developed four systems for our experiments: a baseline (BAS) system which is close to the system described in (Hu et al., 2009), and three variants of our novel divide and conquer (DAC) system. Features used in both systems are extracted as explained in Section 4.2. Section 4.3 describes the baseline system, the basic DAC system, and two variations of the DAC system.

4.1 Experimental Framework

In all our experiments, we use linear kernel Support Vector Machines (SVM). However, across the systems, there are differences in how we use them. Our framework was built with the ClearTK toolkit (Ogren et al., 2008) with its wrapper for SVMLight (Joachims, 1999). The ClearTK wrapper internally shifts the prediction threshold based on posterior probabilistic scores calculated using the algorithm of Lin et al. (2007). We report results from 5-fold cross validation performed on the entire corpus.

4.2 Feature Engineering

In developing our system, we classified our features into three categories: lexical, verbal and message-level. Lexical features consists of n-grams of words, n-grams of POS tags, mixed n-grams of closed class words and POS tags (Prabhakaran et al., 2012), as well as a small set of specialized features — StartPOS/Lemma (POS tag and lemma of the first word), LastPOS/Lemma (POS tag and lemma of the last word), MDCount (number of modal verbs in the DFU) and QuestionMark (is there a question mark in the DFU). We used the POS tags produced by the OpenNLP POS tagger. Verbal features capture the position and identity of the first verb in the DFU. Finally, message-level features capture aspects of the location of the DFU in the message and of the message in the thread (relative position and size). In optimizing each system, we first performed an exhaustive search across all combinations of features within each category. For the lexical n-gram features we varied the n-gram window from 1 to 5. This step gave us the best performing feature combination within each category. In a second step, we found the best combination of categories, using the previously determined features for each category. In this paper, we do not report best performing feature sets for each configuration, due to lack of space.

4.3 Experiments

Baseline (BAS) System This system uses the ClearTK built-in one-versus-all multiclass SVM in prediction. Internally, the multi-class SVM builds a set of binary classifiers, one for each dialog act. For a given test instance, the classifier that obtains the highest probability score determines the overall prediction. We performed feature optimization on the whole multiclass classifier (as described in Section 4.2), i.e., the same set of features was available to all component classifiers. We optimized for system accuracy. Table 2 shows results using this system. In this and all tables, we give the performance of the system on the four DAs, using precision, recall, and F-measure. The DAs are listed in ascending order of frequency in the corpus (least frequent DA first). We also give an overall accuracy evaluation. As we can see, detecting REQUEST-ACTION is much harder than detecting the other DAs.

	Prec.	**Rec.**	**F-meas.**
R-A	57.9	31.4	40.7
R-I	91.5	78.2	84.3
CONV	92.0	95.8	93.8
INF	91.6	95.1	93.3
Accuracy		91.3	

Table 2: Results for baseline (BAS) system (standard multiclass SVM)

Basic Divide and Conquer (DAC) System Like the BAS system, the DAC system also builds a binary classifier for each dialog act separately, and the component classifier with highest probability score determines the overall prediction. The crucial difference in the DAC system is that the feature optimization is performed for each component classifier separately. Each component classifier is optimized for F-measure. Table 3 shows results using this system.

	Prec.	**Recall**	**F-meas.**	**ER**
R-A	66.7	40.0	50.0	15.6
R-I	91.5	78.2	84.3	0.0
CONV	93.9	94.1	94.0	2.6
INF	91.4	96.1	93.7	5.7
Accuracy		91.7		4.9

Table 3: Results for basic DAC system (per-class feature optimization followed by maximum confidence based choice); "ER" refers to error reduction in percent over standard multiclass SVM (Table 2)

Minority Preference (DAC_{MP}) System This system is exactly the same as the basic DAC system except for one crucial difference: overall classification is biased towards a specified minority class. If the minority class binary classifier predicts true, this system chooses the minority class as the predicted class. In cases where the minority class classifier predicts false, it backs off to the basic DAC system after removing the minority class classifier from the confidence tally. Table 4 shows our results using REQUEST-ACTION as the minority class.

Cascading Minority Preference (DAC_{CMP}) System This system is similar to the Minority Preference System; however, instead of a single supplied minority class, the system accepts an ordered list of classes. The classifier then works, in order, through this list; whenever any classifier in the list predicts

	Prec.	Recall	F-meas.	ER
R-A	66.7	45.7	54.2	22.8
R-I	91.5	78.2	84.3	0.0
CONV	93.9	94.1	94.0	2.6
INF	91.6	96.0	93.8	6.5
Accuracy		91.8		5.7

Table 4: Results for minority-preference DAC system — DAC_{MP} (first consult REQUEST-ACTION tagger, then default to choice by maximum confidence); "ER" refers to error reduction in percent over standard multiclass SVM (Table 2)

true, for a given instance, it then assigns this class as the predicted class. The subsequent classifiers in the list are not run. If all classifiers predict false, we back off to the basic DAC system, i.e., the component classifier with highest probability score determines the overall prediction. We ordered the list of classes in the ascending order of their frequencies in the training data. This ordering is driven by the observation that the less frequent classes are also hard to predict correctly. Table 5 shows our results using the ordered list: (REQUEST-ACTION, REQUEST-INFORMATION, CONVENTIONAL, INFORM).

	Prec.	Recall	F-meas.	ER
R-A	66.7	45.7	54.2	22.8
R-I	91.0	80.8	85.6	8.4
CONV	93.7	95.3	94.5	10.1
INF	92.4	95.8	94.0	10.0
Accuracy		92.2		10.6

Table 5: Results for cascading minority-preference DAC system — DAC_{CMP} (consult classifiers in reverse order of frequency of class); "ER" refers to error reduction in percent over standard multiclass SVM (Table 2)

4.4 Discussion

As shown in Table 3, the basic DAC system obtained a 15.6% F-measure error reduction for the minority class REQUEST-ACTION over the BAS system. It also improves performance of two other classes — CONVENTIONAL and INFORM, and obtaines a 4.9% error reduction on overall accuracy. Recall here that the only difference between the DAC system and the BAS system is the per-class feature optimization and therefore this must be the reason for this boost in performance. When we turn to DAC_{MP}, we see that the performance on the minority class REQUEST-ACTION is further enhanced, with an F-measure error reduction of 22.8%; the overall accuracy improves slightly with an error reduction of 5.7%. Finally, DAC_{CMP} further improves the performance. Since the method of choosing the minority class REQUEST-ACTION does not change over DAC_{MP}, the F-measure error reduction remains the same. However, now all three other classes also improve their performance, and we obtain a 10.6% error reduction on overall accuracy over the baseline system.

Following (Guyon et al., 2002), we performed a post-hoc analysis by inspecting the feature weights of the best performing models created for each individual classifier in the DAC system. Table 6 lists some interesting features chosen during feature optimization for the individual SVMs. We selected them from the top 25 features in terms of absolute value of feature weights.

Some features help distinguish different DA categories. For example, the feature *QuestionMark* is the feature with the highest negative weight for INFORM, but has the highest positive weight for REQUEST-INFORMATION. Features like *fyi* and *period (.)* have high positive weights for INFORM and high negative weights for CONVENTIONAL. Some other features are important only for certain classes. For e.g., *please* and *VB_NN* are important for REQUEST-ACTION, but not so for other classes. Overall, the most discriminating features for both INFORM and CONVENTIONAL are mostly word ngrams, while those for REQUEST-ACTION and REQUEST-INFORMATION are mostly POS ngrams. This shows why our approach of per-class feature optimization is important to boost the classification performance.

Another interesting observation is that the least frequent category, REQUEST-ACTION, has the least strong indicators (as measured by feature weights). Presumably this is because there is much less training data for this class. This explains why our cascading classifiers approach giving priority to the least frequent categories worked better than a simple confidence based approach, since the simple approach drowns out the less confident classifiers.

Request-Action	Request-Information	Conventional	Inform
please (0.9)	QuestionMark (6.6)	StartPOS_NNP (2.7)	QuestionMark (-3.0)
VB_NN (0.7)	_BOS_PRP (-1.2)	thanks (2.3)	thanks (-2.2)
you_VB (0.3)	WRB (1.0)	. (-2.0)	. (2.2)
PRP (-0.3)	PRP_VBP (-0.9)	fyi (-2.0)	fyi (1.9)
MD_PRP_VB (0.3)	_BOS_MD (0.8)	, (0.9)	you (-1.0)
will (-0.2)	_BOS_DT (-0.7)	QuestionMark (-0.8)	can_you (-0.9)

Table 6: Post-hoc analysis on the models built by the DAC system: some of the top features with corresponding feature weights in parentheses, for each individual tagger. (POS tags are capitalized; _BOS_ stands for Beginning Of Sentence)

5 Extrinsic Evaluation

In this section, we perform an extrinsic evaluation for the dialog act tagger presented in Section 4 by applying it to the task of identifying Overt Displays of Power (ODP) in emails, proposed by Prabhakaran et al. (2012). The task is to identify utterances where the linguistic form introduces additional constraints on its responses, beyond those introduced by the general dialog act. The dialog act features were found to be useful and the best performing system obtained an F-measure of 65.8 using gold dialog act tags. For our extrinsic evaluation, we retrained the ODP tagger using dialog act tags predicted by our BAS and DAC_{CMP} systems instead of gold dialog acts. ODP tagger uses the same dataset as ours for training. In the cross validation step, we made sure that the test folds for ODP were excluded from training the taggers to obtain DA tags. At each ODP cross validation step, we trained a BAS or DAC_{CMP} tagger using ODP's training folds for that step and used tags produced by that tagger for both training and testing the ODP tagger for that step. Table 7 lists the results obtained.

	Prec.	Rec.	F-meas.
No-DA	55.7	45.4	50.0
Gold-DA	75.8	58.1	65.8
BAS-DA	60.6	46.5	52.6
DAC_{CMP}-DA	67.2	45.4	54.2

Table 7: Results for ODP system using various sources of DA tags

Using BAS tagged DA, the F-measure of ODP system reduced by 13.2 points to 52.6 from using gold dialog acts (F=65.8). Using DAC_{CMP}, the F-measure improved over BAS by 1.6 points to 54.2. This constitutes an error reduction of 12.1%, taking the system using gold DA tags as the reference. This improvement is noteworthy, given the fact that the overall error reduction obtained by DAC_{CMP} over BAS in the DA tagging was around 10.6%. Also, the DAC_{CMP}-based ODP system obtained an error reduction of about 26.6% over a system that does not use the DA features at all (F=50.0).

6 Conclusion

We presented a method of improving the performance of dialog act tagging in identifying minority classes by using per-class feature optimization and choosing the class based on a cascade of classifiers. We showed that it gives a minority class F-measure error reduction of 22.8% while also reducing the error on other classes and the overall error by around 10%. We also presented an extrinsic evaluation of this technique on detecting Overt Displays of Power in dialog, where we achieve an error reduction of 12.1% over using the standard multiclass SVM to generate dialog act tags.

Acknowledgements

This work is supported, in part, by the Johns Hopkins Human Language Technology Center of Excellence. Any opinions, findings, and conclusions or recommendations expressed in this material are those of the authors and do not necessarily reflect the views of the sponsor. While working on this project, the first author Adinoyi Omuya was affiliated with the Center for Computational Learning Systems at Columbia University. We thank several anonymous reviewers for their constructive feedback.

References

Apoorv Agarwal, Adinoyi Omuya, Aaron Harnly, and Owen Rambow. 2012. A Comprehensive Gold Standard for the Enron Organizational Hierarchy. In *Proceedings of the 50th Annual Meeting of the Association for Computational Linguistics (Volume 2: Short Papers)*, pages 161–165, Jeju Island, Korea, July. Association for Computational Linguistics.

J. L. Austin. 1975. *How to Do Things with Words*. Harvard University Press, Cambridge, Mass.

William W. Cohen, Vitor R. Carvalho, and Tom M. Mitchell. 2004. Learning to Classify Email into "Speech Acts" . In Dekang Lin and Dekai Wu, editors, *Proceedings of EMNLP 2004*, pages 309–316, Barcelona, Spain, July. Association for Computational Linguistics.

Isabelle Guyon, Jason Weston, Stephen Barnhill, and Vladimir Vapnik. 2002. Gene Selection for Cancer Classification using Support Vector Machines. *Mach. Learn.*, 46:389–422, March.

Jun Hu, Rebecca Passonneau, and Owen Rambow. 2009. Contrasting the Interaction Structure of an Email and a Telephone Corpus: A Machine Learning Approach to Annotation of Dialogue Function Units. In *Proceedings of the SIGDIAL 2009 Conference*, London, UK, September. Association for Computational Linguistics.

Thorsten Joachims. 1999. Making Large-Scale SVM Learning Practical. In Bernhard Schölkopf, Christopher J.C. Burges, and A. Smola, editors, *Advances in Kernel Methods - Support Vector Learning*, Cambridge, MA, USA. MIT Press.

J. Kim, G. Chern, D. Feng, E. Shaw, and E. Hovy. 2006. Mining and Assessing Discussions on the Web Through Speech Act Analysis. In *Proceedings of the Workshop on Web Content Mining with Human Language Technologies at the 5th International Semantic Web Conference*.

S.N. Kim, L. Cavedon, and T. Baldwin. 2010a. Classifying Dialogue Acts in One-on-one Live Chats. In *Proceedings of the 2010 Conference on Empirical Methods in Natural Language Processing*, pages 862–871. Association for Computational Linguistics.

S.N. Kim, L. Wang, and T. Baldwin. 2010b. Tagging and Linking Web Forum Posts. In *Proceedings of the Fourteenth Conference on Computational Natural Language Learning*, pages 192–202. Association for Computational Linguistics.

Hsuan-Tien Lin, Chih-Jen Lin, and Ruby C. Weng. 2007. A Note on Platt's Probabilistic Outputs for Support Vector Machines. *Mach. Learn.*, 68:267–276, October.

Philip V. Ogren, Philipp G. Wetzler, and Steven Bethard. 2008. ClearTK: A UIMA toolkit for statistical natural language processing. In *Towards Enhanced Interoperability for Large HLT Systems: UIMA for NLP workshop at Language Resources and Evaluation Conference (LREC)*.

Vinodkumar Prabhakaran, Owen Rambow, and Mona Diab. 2012. Predicting Overt Display of Power in Written Dialogs. In *Human Language Technologies: The 2012 Annual Conference of the North American Chapter of the Association for Computational Linguistics*, Montreal, Canada, June. Association for Computational Linguistics.

J.R. Searle. 1976. A Classification of Illocutionary Acts. *Language in society*, 5(01):1–23.

A. Stolcke, K. Ries, N. Coccaro, E. Shriberg, R. Bates, D. Jurafsky, P. Taylor, R. Martin, C.V. Ess-Dykema, and M. Meteer. 2000. Dialogue Act Modeling for Automatic Tagging and Recognition of Conversational Speech. *Computational linguistics*, 26(3):339–373.

J.Y. Yeh and A. Harnly. 2006. Email Thread Reassembly Using Similarity Matching. In *Third Conference on Email and Anti-Spam (CEAS)*, pages 27–28.

R. Zhang, D. Gao, and W. Li. 2012. Towards Scalable Speech Act Recognition in Twitter: Tackling Insufficient Training Data. *EACL 2012*, page 18.

Discourse Connectors for Latent Subjectivity in Sentiment Analysis

Rakshit Trivedi
College of Computing
Georgia Institute of Technology
Atlanta, GA 30308, USA
rtrivedi6@gatech.edu

Jacob Eisenstein
School of Interactive Computing
Georgia Institute of Technology
Atlanta, GA 30308, USA
jacobe@gatech.edu

Abstract

Document-level sentiment analysis can benefit from fine-grained subjectivity, so that sentiment polarity judgments are based on the relevant parts of the document. While fine-grained subjectivity annotations are rarely available, encouraging results have been obtained by modeling subjectivity as a latent variable. However, latent variable models fail to capitalize on our linguistic knowledge about discourse structure. We present a new method for injecting linguistic knowledge into latent variable subjectivity modeling, using discourse connectors. *Connector-augmented transition features* allow the latent variable model to learn the relevance of discourse connectors for subjectivity transitions, without subjectivity annotations. This yields significantly improved performance on document-level sentiment analysis in English and Spanish. We also describe a simple heuristic for automatically identifying connectors when no predefined list is available.

1 Introduction

Document-level sentiment analysis can benefit from consideration of discourse structure. Voll and Taboada (2007) show that adjective-based sentiment classification is improved by examining topicality (whether each sentence is central to the overall point); Yessenalina et al. (2010b) show that bag-of-ngrams sentiment classification is improved by examining subjectivity (whether a sentence expresses a subjective opinion or objective fact). However, it is unclear how best to obtain the appropriate discourse analyses. Voll and Taboada (2007) find that domain-independent discourse parsing (Soricut and Marcu, 2003) offers little improvement for sentiment analysis, so they resort to training a domain-specific model for identifying topic sentences in reviews. But this requires a labeled dataset of topic sentences, imposing a substantial additional cost.

Yessenalina et al. (2010b) treat sentence level subjectivity as a *latent variable*, automatically inducing the "annotator rationale" (Zaidan et al., 2007; Yessenalina et al., 2010a) for each training sentence so as to focus sentiment learning on the subjective parts of the document. This yields significant improvements over bag-of-ngrams supervised sentiment classification. Latent variable subjectivity analysis is attractive because it requires neither subjectivity annotations nor an accurate domain-independent discourse parser. But while the "knowledge-free" nature of this approach is appealing, it is unsatisfying that it fails to exploit decades of research on discourse structure.

In this paper, we explore a lightweight approach to injecting linguistic knowledge into latent variable models of subjectivity. The entry point is a set of *discourse connectors*: words and phrases that signal a shift or continuation in the discourse structure. Such connectors have been the subject of extensive study in the creation of the Penn Discourse Treebank (PDTB: Prasad et al. 2008). The role of discourse connectors in sentiment analysis can be clearly seen in examples, such as "*It's hard to imagine the studios hiring another manic German maverick to helm a cop thriller.* ***But*** *that's exactly why the movie is unmissable.*" (Huddleston, 2010)

We present a new approach to incorporate discourse connectors in a latent subjectivity model (Yessenalina et al., 2010b). This approach requires no manually-specified information about the meaning of the connectors, just the connectors themselves. Our approach builds on proximity features, which give the latent variable model a way to prefer or disprefer subjectivity and sentiment transitions, usually with the goal of encouraging smoothness across the document. By taking the cross-product of these features with a set of discourse connectors, we obtain a new set of *connector-augmented transition features*, which capture the way discourse connectors are used to indicate subjectivity and sentiment transitions. The model is thus able to learn that subjectivity shifts are likely to be accompanied by connectors such as *however* or *nonetheless*.

We present experiments in both English and Spanish showing that this method of incorporating discourse connectors yields significant improvements in document-level sentiment analysis. In case no list of connectors is available, we describe a simple heuristic for automatically identifying candidate connector words. The automatically identified connectors do not perform as well as the expert-defined lists, but they still outperform a baseline method that ignores discourse connectors (in English). This demonstrates both the robustness of the approach and the value of linguistic knowledge.

2 Model

Given accurate labels of the subjectivity of each sentence, a document-level sentiment analyzer could safely ignore the sentences marked as non-subjective.[1] This would be beneficial for training as well as prediction, because the learning algorithm would not be confused by sentences that contradict the document label. But in general we cannot rely on having access to sentence-level subjectivity annotations. Instead, we treat subjectivity as a *latent variable*, and ask the learner to impute its value. Given document-level sentiment annotations and an initial model, the learner can mark as non-subjective those sentences whose analysis disagrees with the document label.

[1]Discourse parsing often focuses on sub-sentence *elementary discourse units* (Mann and Thompson, 1988). For simplicity, we consider units at the sentence level only, and leave finer-grained analysis for future work.

More formally, each document has a label $y \in \{-1, 1\}$, a set of sentences $\mathbf{x}$, and a set of per-sentence subjectivity judgments $\mathbf{h} \in \{0, 1\}^S$, where S is the number of sentences. We compute a set of features on these variables, and score each instance by a weighted combination of the features, $\mathbf{w}^\mathsf{T}\mathbf{f}(y, \mathbf{x}, \mathbf{h})$. At prediction time, we seek a label y which achieves a high score given the observed $\mathbf{x}$ and the ideal $\mathbf{h}$.

$$\hat{y} = \arg\max_{y} \left(\max_{\mathbf{h}} \mathbf{w}^\mathsf{T}\mathbf{f}(y, \mathbf{x}, \mathbf{h}) \right). \quad (1)$$

At training time, we seek weights w which achieve a high score given all training examples $\{\mathbf{x}, y\}_t$,

$$\hat{w} = \arg\max_{w} \sum_{t} \max_{\mathbf{h}} \mathbf{w}^\mathsf{T}\mathbf{f}(y_t, \mathbf{x}_t, \mathbf{h}). \quad (2)$$

We can decompose the feature vector into two parts: polarity features $\mathbf{f}_{\text{pol}}(y, \mathbf{x}, \mathbf{h})$, and subjectivity features $\mathbf{f}_{\text{subj}}(\mathbf{x}, \mathbf{h})$. The basic feature set decomposes across sentences, though the polarity features involve the document-level polarity. For sentence i, we have $\mathbf{f}_{\text{pol}}(y, \mathbf{x}_i, h_i) = y h_i \mathbf{x}_i$: the bag-of-words features for sentence i are multiplied by the document polarity $y \in \{-1, 1\}$ and the sentence subjectivity $h_i \in \{0, 1\}$. The weights $\mathbf{w}_{\text{pol}}$ capture the sentiment polarity of each possible word. As for the subjectivity features, we simply have $\mathbf{f}_{\text{subj}}(\mathbf{x}_i, h_i) = h_i \mathbf{x}_i$. The weights $\mathbf{w}_{\text{subj}}$ capture the subjectivity of each word, with large values indicate positive subjectivity.

However, these features do not capture transitions between the subjectivity and sentiment of adjacent sentences. For this reason, Yessenalina et al. (2010b) introduce an additional set of *proximity* features, $\mathbf{f}_{\text{prox}}(h_i, h_{i-1})$, which are parametrized by the subjectivity of both the current sentence i and the previous sentence $i-1$. The effect of these features will be to learn a preference for consistency in the subjectivity of adjacent sentences.

By augmenting the transition features with the text $\mathbf{x}_i$, we allow this preference for consistency to be modulated by discourse connectors. We design the *transition* feature vector $\mathbf{f}_{\text{trans}}(\mathbf{x}_i, h_i, h_{i-1})$

to contain two elements for every discourse connector, one for $h_i = h_{i-1}$, and one for $h_i \neq h_{i-1}$. For example, the feature $\langle$*moreover*, CONTINUE$\rangle$ fires when sentence i starts with *moreover* and $h_{i-1} = h_{i,i}$. We would expect to learn a positive weight for this feature, and negative weights for features such as $\langle$*moreover*, SHIFT$\rangle$ and $\langle$*however*, CONTINUE$\rangle$.

3 Experiments

To evaluate the utility of adding discourse connectors to latent subjectivity sentiment analysis, we compare several models on movie review datasets in English and Spanish.

3.1 Data

We use two movie review datasets:

- 50,000 English-language movie reviews (Maas et al., 2011). Each review has a rating from 1-10; we marked ratings of 5 or greater as positive. Half the dataset is used for test and half for training. Parameter tuning is performed by cross-validation.
- 5,000 Spanish-language movie reviews (Cruz et al., 2008). Each review has a rating from 1-5; we marked 3-5 as positive. We randomly created a 60/20/20 split for training, validation, and test.

3.2 Connectors

We first consider single-word discourse connectors: in English, we use a list of all 57 one-word connectors from the Penn Discourse Tree Bank (Prasad et al., 2008); in Spanish, we selected 25 one-word connectors from a Spanish language education website.[2] We also consider multi-word connectors. Using the same sources, this expands the English set to 93 connectors, and Spanish set to 80 connectors.

In case no list of discourse connectors is available, we propose a simple technique for automatically identifying potential connectors. We use a χ^2 test to select words which are especially likely to initiate sentences. The top K words (with the lowest p values) were added as potential connectors, where K is equal to the number of "true" connectors provided by the gold-standard resource.

[2] `russell.famaf.unc.edu.ar/~laura/shallowdisc4summ/discmar/`

Finally, we consider a model with connector-augmented transition features for all words in the vocabulary. Thus, there are four connector sets:

- true-unigram-connectors: unigram connectors from the Penn Discourse Treebank and the Spanish language education website
- true-multiword-connectors: unigram and multiword connectors from these same resources
- auto-unigram-connectors: automatically-selected connectors using the χ^2 test
- all-unigram-connectors: all words are potential connectors

3.3 Systems

The connector-augmented transition features are incorporated into a latent variable support vector machine (SVM). We also consider two baselines:

- no-connectors: the same latent variable SVM, but without the connector features. This is identical to the prior work of Yessenalina et al. (2010b).
- SVM: a standard SVM binary classifier

The latent variable models require an initial guess for the subjectivity of each sentence. Yessenalina et al. (2010b) compare several initializations and find the best results using OpinionFinder (Wilson et al., 2005). For the Spanish data, we performed initial subjectivity analysis by matching against a publicly-available full-strength Spanish lexicon set (Rosas et al., 2012).

3.4 Implementation details

Both our implementation and the baselines are built on the latent structural SVM (Yu and Joachims, 2009; `http://www.cs.cornell.edu/~cnyu/latentssvm/`), which is in turn built on the SVM-Light distribution (`http://svmlight.joachims.org/`). The regularization parameter C was chosen by cross-validation.

4 Results

Table 1 shows the sentiment analysis accuracy with each system and feature set. The best overall results in both language are given by the models with

system	English	Spanish
true-multiword-connectors	91.25	**79.80**
true-unigram-connectors	**91.36**	77.50
auto-connectors	90.22	76.90
all-unigram-connectors	87.60	74.30
No-connectors	88.21	76.42
SVM	84.79	69.44

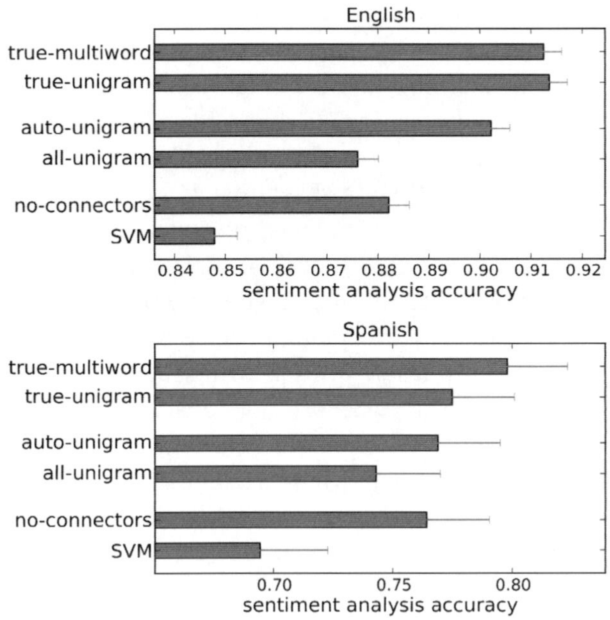

Figure 1: Document-level sentiment analysis accuracy. The 95% confidence intervals are estimated from the cumulative density function of the binomial distribution.

connector-augmented transition features. In English, the multiword and unigram connectors perform equally well, and significantly outperform all alternatives at $p < .05$. The connector-based features reduce the error rate of the latent subjectivity SVM by 25%. In Spanish, the picture is less clear because the smaller test set yields larger confidence intervals, so that only the comparison with the SVM classifier is significant at $p < .05$. Nonetheless, the connector-augmented transition features give the best accuracy, with an especially large improvement obtained by the multiword connectors.

Next, we investigated the quality of the automatically-induced discourse connectors. The χ^2 heuristic for selecting candidate connectors gave results that were significantly better than the no-connector baseline in English, though the

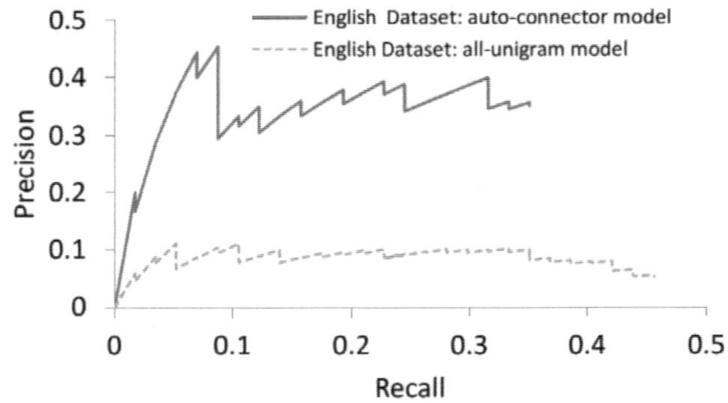

Figure 2: Precision-Recall curve for top-K discovered connectors when compared with PDTB connector set

difference in Spanish was minimal. However, when every word is included as a potential connectors, the performance suffers, dropping below the accuracy of the no-connector baseline. This shows that the improvement in accuracy offered by the connector features is not simply due to the increased flexibility of the model, but depends on identifying a small set of likely discourse connectors.

For a qualitative evalatuation, we ranked all English-language unigram connectors by their feature weights, and list the top ten for each subjectivity transition:

- SHIFT: *however; though; but; if; unlike; although; while; overall; nevertheless; still*
- CONTINUATION: *as; there; now; even; in; after; once; almost; because; so*

Overall these word lists cohere with our intuitions, particularly the words associated with SHIFT transitions: *however, but*, and *nevertheless*. As one of the reviewers noted, some of the words associated with CONTINUATION transitions are better seen as discourse **cues** rather than connectors, such as *now*. Other words seem to connect two **subsequent** clauses, e.g., ***if** Nicholas Cage had played every role, the film might have reached its potential.* Incorporating such connectors must be left for future work.

Finally, in learning weights for each connector feature, our model can be seen as *discovering* discourse connectors. We compare the highly weighted discovered connectors from the all-unigram and auto-unigram settings with the one-word connectors from the Penn Discourse Tree Bank. The results of this comparison are shown in Figure 2, which traces a precision-recall curve by taking the top K connectors for various values of K. The auto-unigram model is able to identify many true connectors from the Penn Discourse Treebank, while the all-unigram model achieves low precision. This graph helps to explain the large performance gap between the auto-unigram and all-unigram feature sets; the all-unigram set includes too many weak features, and the learning algorithm is not able to distinguish the true discourse connectors. The Spanish discourse connectors identified by this approach were extremely poor, possibly because so many more of the Spanish connectors include multiple words.

5 Related Work

Polanyi and Zaenen (2006) noted the importance of accounting for *valence shifters* in sentiment analysis, identifying relevant connectors at the sentence and discourse levels. They propose a heuristic approach to use shifters to modify the contributions of sentiment words. There have been several subsequent efforts to model within-sentence valence shifts, including compositional grammar (Moilanen and Pulman, 2007), matrix-vector products across the sentence (Yessenalina and Cardie, 2011), and methods that reason about polarity shifters within the parse tree (Socher et al., 2012; Sayeed et al., 2012). The value of discourse structure towards predicting opinion polarity has also demonstrated in the context of multi-party dialogues (Somasundaran et al., 2009). Our approach functions at the discourse level within single-author documents, so it is complementary to this prior work.

Voll and Taboada (2007) investigate various techniques for focusing sentiment analysis on sentences that are central to the main topic. They obtain negative results with the general-purpose SPADE discourse parser (Soricut and Marcu, 2003), but find that training a decision tree classifier to identify topic-central sentences yields positive results. Wiebe (1994) argues that in coherent narratives, objectivity and subjectivity are usually consistent between adjacent sentences, an insight exploited by Pang and Lee (2004) in a supervised system for subjectivity analysis. Later work employed structured graphical models to model the flow of subjectivity and sentiment over the course of the document (Mao and Lebanon, 2006; McDonald et al., 2007). All of these approaches depend on labeled training examples of subjective and objective sentences, but Yessenalina et al. (2010b) show that subjectivity can be modeled as a *latent variable*, using a latent variable version of the structured support vector machine (Yu and Joachims, 2009).

Our work can be seen as a combination of the machine learning approach of Yessenalina et al. (2010b) with the insight of Polanyi and Zaenen (2006) that connectors play a key role in transitions between subjectivity and sentiment. Eisenstein and Barzilay (2008) incorporated discourse connectors into an unsupervised model of topic segmentation, but this work only considered the role of such markers to differentiate adjoining segments of text, and not to identify their roles with respect to one another. That work was also not capable of learning from supervised annotations in a downstream task. In contrast, our approach uses document-level sentiment annotations to learn about the role of discourse connectors in sentence-level subjectivity.

6 Conclusion

Latent variable machine learning is a powerful tool for inducing linguistic structure directly from data. However, adding a small amount of linguistic knowledge can substantially improve performance. We have presented a simple technique for combining a latent variable support vector machine with a list of discourse connectors, by creating an augmented feature set that combines the connectors with pairwise subjectivity transition features. This improves accuracy, even with a noisy list of connectors that has been identified automatically. Possible directions for future work include richer representations of discourse structure, and the combination of discourse-level and sentence-level valence and subjectivity shifters.

Acknowledgments

Thanks to the anonymous reviewers for their helpful feedback. This work was supported by a Google Faculty Research Award.

References

Fermin L. Cruz, Jose A. Troyano, Fernando Enriquez, and Javier Ortega. 2008. Clasificación de documentos basada en la opinión: experimentos con un corpus de crıticas de cine en espanol. *Procesamiento de Lenguaje Natural*, 41.

Jacob Eisenstein and Regina Barzilay. 2008. Bayesian unsupervised topic segmentation. In *Proceedings of EMNLP*.

Tom Huddleston. 2010. Review of The Bad Lieutenant: Port of Call New Orleans. *Time Out*, May 18.

Andrew L. Maas, Raymond E. Daly, Peter T. Pham, Dan Huang, Andrew Y. Ng, and Christopher Potts. 2011. Learning word vectors for sentiment analysis. In *Proceedings of ACL*.

William C Mann and Sandra A Thompson. 1988. Rhetorical structure theory: Toward a functional theory of text organization. *Text*, 8(3).

Yi Mao and Guy Lebanon. 2006. Isotonic conditional random fields and local sentiment flow. In B. Schölkopf, J. Platt, and T. Hoffman, editors, *Advances in Neural Information Processing Systems 19*.

Ryan McDonald, Kerry Hannan, Tyler Neylon, Mike Wells, and Jeff Reynar. 2007. Structured models for fine-to-coarse sentiment analysis. In *Proceedings of ACL*.

Karo Moilanen and Stephen Pulman. 2007. Sentiment composition. In *Proceedings of RANLP*.

Bo Pang and Lillian Lee. 2004. A sentimental education: Sentiment analysis using subjectivity summarization based on minimum cuts. In *Proceedings of ACL*.

Livia Polanyi and Annie Zaenen. 2006. Contextual valence shifters. *Computing attitude and affect in text: Theory and applications*.

Rashmi Prasad, Nikhil Dinesh, Alan Lee, Eleni Miltsakaki, Livio Robaldo, Aravind Joshi, and Bonnie Webber. 2008. The penn discourse treebank 2.0. In *Proceedings of LREC*.

Veronica Perez Rosas, Carmen Banea, and Rada Mihalcea. 2012. Learning sentiment lexicons in spanish. In *Proceedings of LREC*.

Asad B. Sayeed, Jordan Boyd-Graber, Bryan Rusk, and Amy Weinberg. 2012. Grammatical structures for word-level sentiment detection. In *Proceedings of NAACL*.

Richard Socher, Brody Huval, Christopher D. Manning, and Andrew Y. Ng. 2012. Semantic compositionality through recursive matrix-vector spaces. In *Proceedings of EMNLP-CoNLL*.

Swapna Somasundaran, Galileo Namata, Janyce Wiebe, and Lise Getoor. 2009. Supervised and unsupervised methods in employing discourse relations for improving opinion polarity classification. In *Proceedings of EMNLP*.

Radu Soricut and Daniel Marcu. 2003. Sentence level discourse parsing using syntactic and lexical information. In *Proceedings of NAACL*.

Kimberly Voll and Maite Taboada. 2007. Not all words are created equal: Extracting semantic orientation as a function of adjective relevance. In *Proceedings of Australian Conference on Artificial Intelligence*.

Janyce M. Wiebe. 1994. Tracking point of view in narrative. *Computational Linguistics*, 20(2).

Theresa Wilson, Paul Hoffmann, Swapna Somasundaran, Jason Kessler, Janyce Wiebe, Yejin Choi, Claire Cardie, Ellen Riloff, and Siddharth Patwardhan. 2005. Opinionfinder: A system for subjectivity analysis. In *Proceedings of HLT-EMNLP: Interactive Demonstrations*.

Ainur Yessenalina and Claire Cardie. 2011. Compositional matrix-space models for sentiment analysis. In *Proceedings of EMNLP*.

Ainur Yessenalina, Yejin Choi, and Claire Cardie. 2010a. Automatically generating annotator rationales to improve sentiment classification. In *Proceedings of ACL: Short Papers*.

Ainur Yessenalina, Yisong Yue, and Claire Cardie. 2010b. Multi-Level structured models for Document-Level sentiment classification. In *Proceedings of EMNLP*.

Chun-Nam John Yu and Thorsten Joachims. 2009. Learning structural svms with latent variables. In *Proceedings of ICML*.

Omar F. Zaidan, Jason Eisner, and Christine Piatko. 2007. Using "annotator rationales" to improve machine learning for text categorization. In *Proceedings of HLT-NAACL*.

Coherence Modeling for the Automated Assessment of Spontaneous Spoken Responses

Xinhao Wang, Keelan Evanini, Klaus Zechner
Educational Testing Service
660 Rosedale Road
Princeton, NJ 08541, USA
xwang002,kevanini,kzechner@ets.org

Abstract

This study focuses on modeling discourse coherence in the context of automated assessment of spontaneous speech from non-native speakers. Discourse coherence has always been used as a key metric in human scoring rubrics for various assessments of spoken language. However, very little research has been done to assess a speaker's coherence in automated speech scoring systems. To address this, we present a corpus of spoken responses that has been annotated for discourse coherence quality. Then, we investigate the use of several features originally developed for essays to model coherence in spoken responses. An analysis on the annotated corpus shows that the prediction accuracy for human holistic scores of an automated speech scoring system can be improved by around 10% relative after the addition of the coherence features. Further experiments indicate that a weighted F-Measure of 73% can be achieved for the automated prediction of the coherence scores.

1 Introduction

In recent years, much research has been conducted into developing automated assessment systems to automatically score spontaneous speech from non-native speakers with the goals of reducing the burden on human raters, improving reliability, and generating feedback that can be used by language learners. Various features related to different aspects of speaking proficiency have been exploited, such as delivery features for pronunciation, prosody, and fluency (Strik and Cucchiarini, 1999; Chen et al., 2009; Cheng, 2011; Higgins et al., 2011), as well as language use features for vocabulary and grammar, and content features (Chen and Zechner, 2011; Xie et al., 2012). However, discourse-level features related to topic development have rarely been investigated in the context of automated speech scoring. This is despite the fact that an important criterion in the human scoring rubrics for speaking assessments is the evaluation of coherence, which refers to the conceptual relations between different units within a response.

Methods for automatically assessing discourse coherence in text documents have been widely studied in the context of applications such as natural language generation, document summarization, and assessment of text readability. For example, Foltz et al. (1998) measured the overall coherence of a text by utilizing Latent Semantic Analysis (LSA) to calculate the semantic relatedness between adjacent sentences. Barzilay and Lee (2004) introduced an HMM-based model for the document-level analysis of topics and topic transitions. Barzilay and Lapata (2005; 2008) presented an approach to coherence modeling which focused on the entities in the text and their grammatical transitions between adjacent sentences, and calculated the entity transition probabilities on the document level. Pitler et al. (2010) provided a summary of the performance of several different types of features for automated coherence evaluation, such as cohesive devices, adjacent sentence similarity, Coh-Metrix (Graesser et al., 2004), word co-occurrence patterns, and entity-grid.

In addition to studies on well-formed text, researchers have also addressed coherence modeling on text produced by language learners, which may contain many spelling and grammar errors. Utilizing LSA and Random Indexing methods, Higgins et al. (2004) measured the global coherence of students' essays by calculating the semantic relatedness between sentences and the corresponding prompts. In addition, Burstein et. al (2010) combined entity-grid features with writing quality features produced by an automated assessment system of essays to predict the coherence scores of student essays. Recently, Yannakoudakis and Briscoe (2012) systematically analyzed a variety of coherence modeling methods within the framework of an automated assessment system for non-native free text responses and indicated that features based on Incremental Semantic Analysis (ISA), local histograms of words, the part-of-speech IBM model, and word length were the most effective.

In contrast to these previous studies involving well-formed text or learner text containing errors, this paper focuses on modeling coherence in spontaneous spoken responses as well as investigating discourse features in an attempt to extend the construct coverage of an automated speech scoring system. In a related study, Hassanali et al. (2012) investigated coherence modeling for spoken language in the context of a story retelling task for the automated diagnosis of children with language impairment. They annotated transcriptions of children's narratives with coherence scores as well as markers of narrative structure and narrative quality; furthermore they built models to predict the coherence scores based on Coh-Metrix features and the manually annotated narrative features. The current study differs from this one in that it deals with free spontaneous spoken responses provided by students at a university level; these responses therefore contain more varied and more complicated information than the child narratives.

The main contributions of this paper can be summarized as follows: First, we obtained coherence annotations on a corpus of spontaneous spoken responses drawn from a university-level English language proficiency assessment, and demonstrated an improvement of around 10% relative in the accuracy of the automated prediction of human holistic scores with the addition of the coherence annotations. Second, we applied the entity-grid features and writing quality features from an automated essay scoring system to predict the coherence scores; the experimental results have shown promising correlations between some of these features and the coherence scores.

2 Data and Annotation

2.1 Data

For this study, we collected 600 spoken responses from the international TOEFL® iBT assessment of English proficiency for non-native speakers. 100 responses were drawn from each of 6 different test questions comprising two different speaking tasks: 1) providing an opinion based on personal experience (N = 200) and 2) summarizing or discussing material provided in a reading and/or listening passage (N = 400). The spoken responses were all transcribed by humans with punctuation and capitalization. The average number of words contained in the responses was 104.4 (st. dev. = 34.4) and the average number of sentences was 5.5 (st. dev. = 2.1).

The spoken responses were all provided with holistic English proficiency scores on a scale of 1 - 4 by expert human raters in the context of operational, high-stakes scoring for the spoken language assessment. The scoring rubrics address the following three main aspects of speaking proficiency: delivery (pronunciation, fluency, prosody), language use (grammar and lexical choice), and topic development (content and coherence). In order to ensure a sufficient quantity of responses from each proficiency level for training and evaluating the coherence prediction features, the spoken responses selected for this study were balanced based on the human scores as follows: 25 responses were selected randomly from each of the 4 score points (1 - 4) for each of the 6 test questions. In some cases, more than one response was selected from a given test-taker; in total, 471 distinct test-takers are represented in the data set.

2.2 Annotation and Analysis

The coherence annotation guidelines used for the spoken responses in this study were modified based on the annotation guidelines developed for written essays described in Burstein et al. (2010). According to these guidelines, expert annotators provided each response with a score on a scale of 1 - 3. The three score points were defined as follows: 3 = highly coherent (contains no instances of confusing arguments or examples), 2 = somewhat coherent (contains some awkward points in which the speaker's line of argument is unclear), 1 = barely coherent (the entire response was confusing and hard to follow; it was intuitively incoherent as a whole and the annotators had difficulties in identifying specific weak points). For responses receiving a coherence score of 2, the annotators were required to highlight the specific awkward points in the response. In addition, the annotators were specifically required to ignore disfluencies and grammatical errors as much as possible; thus, they were instructed to not label sentences or clauses as awkward points solely because of the presence of disfluent or ungrammatical speech.

Two annotators (not drawn from the pool of expert human raters who provided the holistic scores) made independent coherence annotations for all 600 spoken responses. The distribution of annotations across the three score points is presented in Table 1. The two annotators achieved a moderate inter-annotator agreement (Landis and Koch, 1977) of $\kappa = 0.68$ on the 3-point scale. The average of the two coherence scores provided by the two annotators correlates with the holistic speaking proficiency scores at $r = 0.66$, indicating that the overall proficiency scores of spoken responses can benefit from the discourse coherence annotations.

	1	2	3
# 1	160 (27%)	278 (46%)	162 (27%)
# 2	125 (21%)	251 (42%)	224 (37%)

Table 1. Distribution of coherence annotations from two annotators

Furthermore, coherence features based on the human annotations were examined within the context of an automated spoken language assessment system, SpeechRater[SM] (Zechner et al., 2007; 2009). We extracted 96 features related to pronunciation, prosody, fluency, language use, and content development using SpeechRater. These features were either extracted directly from the speech signal or were based on the output of an automatic speech recognition system (with a word error rate of around 28%[1]). By utilizing a decision tree classifier (the J48 implementation from Weka (Hall et al., 2009)), 4-fold cross validation was conducted on the 600 responses to train and evaluate a scoring model for predicting the holistic proficiency scores. The resulting correlation between the predicted scores (based on the 96 baseline SpeechRater features) and the human holistic proficiency scores was $r = 0.667$.

In order to model a spoken response's coherence, three different features were extracted from the human annotations. Firstly, the average of the two annotators' coherence scores was directly used as a feature with a 5-point scale (henceforth Coh_5). Secondly, following the work in Burstein et al. (2010), we collapsed the average coherence scores into a 2-point scale to deal with the difficulty in distinguishing somewhat and highly coherent responses. For this second feature (henceforth Coh_2), scores 1 and 1.5 were mapped to score 1, and scores 2, 2.5, and 3 were mapped to score 2. Finally, the number of awkward points was also counted as a feature (henceforth Awk). As shown in Table 2, when these three coherence features were combined separately with the SpeechRater features, the correlations could be improved from $r = 0.667$ to $r > 0.7$. Meanwhile, the accuracy (i.e., the percentage of correctly predicted holistic scores) could be improved from 0.487 to a range between 0.535 and 0.543.

Features	r	Accuracy
SpeechRater	0.667	0.487
SpeechRater+Coh_5	0.714	0.540
SpeechRater+Coh_2	0.705	0.543
SpeechRater+Awk	0.702	0.535
SpeechRater+Coh_5+Awk	0.703	0.537
SpeechRater+Coh_2+Awk	0.701	0.542

Table 2. Improvement to an automated speech scoring system after the addition of human-assigned coherence scores and measures, showing both Pearson r correlations and the ratio of correctly matched holistic scores between the system and human experts

These experimental results demonstrate that the automatic scoring system can benefit from coherence modeling either by directly using a human-assigned coherence score or the identified awkward points. However, the use of both kinds of annotations does not provide further improvement. When collapsing the average scores into a 2-point scale, there was a 0.009 correlation drop (not statistically significant), but the accuracy was slightly improved. In addition, due to the relatively small

[1] Both the training and evaluation sets used to develop the speech recognizer consist of similar spoken responses drawn from the same assessment. However, there is no response overlap between these sets and the corpus used for discourse coherence annotation in this study.

size of the set of available coherence annotations, we adopted the collapsed 2-point scale instead of the 5-point scale for the coherence prediction experiments in the next section.

2.3 Experimental Design

As demonstrated in Section 2.2, the collapsed average coherence score can be used to improve the performance of an automated speech scoring system. Therefore, this study treats coherence prediction as a binary classification task: low-coherent vs. high-coherent, where the low-coherent responses are those with average scores 1 and 1.5, and the high-coherent responses are those with average scores 2, 2.5, and 3.

For coherence modeling, we again use the J48 decision tree from the Weka machine learning toolkit (Hall et al., 2009) and run 4-fold cross-validation on the 600 annotated responses. The correlation coefficient (r) and the weighted average F-Measure[2] are used as evaluation metrics.

In this experiment, we examine the performance of the entity-grid features and a set of features produced by the e-rater® system (an automated writing assessment system for learner essays) (Attali and Burstein, 2006) to predict the coherence scores of the spontaneous spoken responses, where all the features are extracted from human transcriptions of the responses.

2.4 Entity Grid and e-rater Features

First, we applied the algorithm from Barzilay and Lapata (2008) to extract entity-grid features, which calculated the vector of entity transition probabilities across adjacent sentences. Several different methods of representing the entities can be used before generating the entity-grid. First, all the entities can be described by their syntactic roles including S (Subject), O (Object), and X (Other). Alternatively, these roles can also be reduced to P (Present) or N (Absent). Furthermore, entities can be defined as salient, when they appear two or more times, otherwise as non-salient. In this study, we generated there basic entity grids: EG_SOX (entity grid with the syntactic roles S, O, and X), EG_REDUCED (entity grid with the reduced representations P and N), and EG_SALIENT (entity grid with salient and non-salient entities). In addition to these entity-grid features, we also used 130 writing quality features related to grammar, usage, mechanics, and style from e-rater to model the coherence.

A baseline system for this task would simply assign the majority class (high-coherent) to all of the responses; this baseline achieves an F-Measure of 0.587. Table 3 shows that the EG_REDUCED and e-rater features can obtain F-Measures of 0.677 and 0.726 as well as correlations with human scores of 0.20 and 0.33, respectively. However, the combination of the two sets of features only brings a very small improvement (from 0.33 to 0.34). In addition, our experiments show that by introducing the component of co-reference resolution for entity grid building, we can only get a very slight improvement on EG_SALIENT, but no improvement on EG_SOX and EG_REDUCED. That may be because it is generally more difficult to parse the transcriptions of spoken language than well-formed text, and more errors are introduced during the process of co-reference resolution.

	r	F-Measure
Baseline	0.0	0.587
EG_SOX	0.16	0.664
EG_REDUCED	**0.2**	**0.677**
EG_SALIENT	0.2	0.678
e-rater	**0.33**	**0.726**
EG_SOX +e-rater	0.30	0.714
EG_REDUCED +e-rater	**0.34**	**0.73**
EG_SALIENT + e-rater	0.26	0.695

Table 3. Performance of entity grid and e-rater features on the coherence modeling task

2.5 Discussion and Future Work

In order to further analyze these features, the correlation coefficients between various features and the average coherence scores (on a five-point scale) were calculated; Figure 1 shows the histogram of these correlation values. As the figure shows, there are a total of approximately 50 features with correlations larger than 0.1. Four of the entity-grid features have correlations between 0.15 and 0.29. As for the writing quality features, some

[2] The data distribution in the experimental corpus is unbalanced: 71% of the responses are high-coherent and 29% are low-coherent. Therefore, we adopt the weighted average F-Measure to evaluate the performance of coherence prediction: first, the F1-Measure of each category is calculated, and then the percentages of responses in each category are used as weights to obtain the final weighted average F-Measure.

of them show high correlations with the average coherence scores, despite the fact that they are not explicitly related to discourse coherence, such as the number of good lexical collocations.

Based on the above analysis, we plan to investigate additional superficial features explicitly related to discourse coherence, such as the distribution of conjunctions, pronouns, and discourse connectives. Moreover, based on the research on well-formed texts and learner essays, we will attempt to examine more effective features and models to better cover the discourse aspects of spontaneous speech. For example, local semantic features related to inter-sentential coherence and the ISA feature will be investigated on spoken responses. In addition, we will apply the features and build coherence models using the output of automatic speech recognition in addition to human transcriptions. Finally, various coherence features or models will be integrated into a practical automated scoring system, and further experiments will be performed to measure their effect on the performance of automated assessment of spontaneous spoken responses.

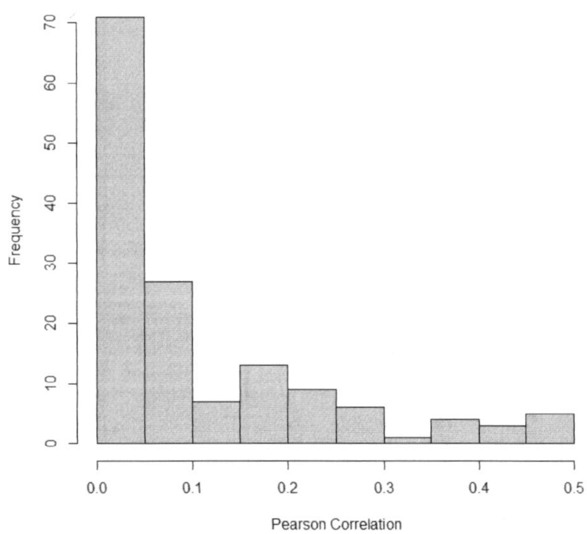

Figure1. Histogram of entity-grid and writing quality features based on their correlations with coherence scores

3 Conclusion

In this paper, we present a corpus of coherence annotations for spontaneous spoken responses provided in the context of an English speaking proficiency assessment. Entity-grid features and features from an automated essay scoring system were examined for coherence modeling of spoken responses. The analysis on the annotated corpus showed promising results for improving the performance of an automated scoring system by means of modeling the coherence of spoken responses.

Acknowledgments

The authors wish to express our thanks to the discourse annotators Melissa Lopez and Matt Mulholland for their dedicated work and our colleagues Jill Burstein and Slava Andreyev for their support in generating entity-grid features.

References

Yigal Attali and Jill Burstein. 2006. Automated essay scoring with e-rater® V.2.0. *Journal of Technology, Learning, and Assessment*. 4(3): 159-174.

Regina Barzilay and Lillian Lee. 2004. Catching the drift: Probabilistic content models, with applications to generation and summarization. *Proceedings of NAACL-HLT*, 113-120.

Regina Barzilay and Mirella Lapata. 2005. Modeling local coherence: An entity-based approach. *Proceedings of ACL*, 141-148.

Regina Barzilay and Mirella Lapata. 2008. Modeling local coherence: An entity-based approach. *Computational Linguistics, 34*(1):1-34.

Jill Burstein, Joel Tetreault and Slava Andreyev. 2010. Using entity-based features to model coherence in student essays. *Proceedings of NAACL-HLT*, 681-684. Los Angeles, California.

Lei Chen, Klaus Zechner and Xiaoming Xi. 2009. Improved pronunciation features for construct-driven assessment of non-native spontaneous speech. *Proceedings of NAACL-HLT*, 442-449.

Miao Chen and Klaus Zechner. 2011. Computing and evaluating syntactic complexity features for automated scoring of spontaneous non-native speech. *Proceedings of ACL*, 722-731.

Jian Cheng. 2011. Automatic assessment of prosody in high-stakes English tests. *Proceedings of Interspeech* , 27-31.

Peter W. Foltz, Walter Kintsch and Thomas K. Landauer. 1998. The measurement of textual coherence with Latent Semantic Analysis. *Discourse Processes*, 25(2&3):285-307.

Arthur C. Graesser, Danielle S. McNamara, Max M. Louwerse and Zhiqiang Cai. 2004. Coh-Metrix: Analysis of text on cohesion and language. *Behavior*

Research Methods, Instruments, & Computers, 36(2):193-202.

Mark Hall, Eibe Frank, Geoffrey Holmes, Bernhard Pfahringer, Peter Reutemann and Ian H. Witten. 2009. The WEKA data mining software: An update. *SIGKDD Explorations, 11*(1):10-18.

Khairun-nisa Hassanali, Yang Liu and Thamar Solorio. 2012. Coherence in child language narratives: A case study of annotation and automatic prediction of coherence. *Proceedings of the Interspeech Workshop on Child, Computer and Interaction.*

Derrick Higgins, Jill Burstein, Daniel Marcu and Claudia Gentile. 2004. Evaluating multiple aspects of coherence in student essays. *Proceedings of NAACL-HLT*, 185-192.

Derrick Higgins, Xiaoming Xi, Klaus Zechner and David Williamson. 2011. A three-stage approach to the automated scoring of spontaneous. *Computer Speech and Language*, 25:282-306.

J. Richard Landis and Gary G. Koch. 1977. The measurement of observer agreement for categorical data. *Biometrics, 33*(1):159-174.

Emily Pitler, Annie Louis and Ani Nenkova. 2010. Automatic evaluation of linguistic quality in multi-document summarization. *Proceedings of ACL.* 544–554. Uppsala.

Helmer Strik and Catia Cucchiarini. 1999. Automatic assessment of second language learners' fluency. *Proceedings of the 14th International Congress of Phonetic Sciences*, 759-762. Berkeley, CA.

Shasha Xie, Keelan Evanini and Klaus Zechner. 2012. Exploring content features for automated speech scoring. *Proceedings of NAACL-HLT*, 103-111.

Helen Yannakoudakis and Ted Briscoe. 2012. Modeling coherence in ESOL learner texts. *Proceedings of the 7th Workshop on the Innovative Use of NLP for Building Educational Applications*, 33-43. Montreal.

Klaus Zechner, Derrick Higgins and Xiaoming Xi. 2007. SpeechRater^{SM}: A construct-driven approach to scoring spontaneous non-native speech. *Proceedings of the International Speech Communication Association Special Interest Group on Speech and Language Technology in Education*, 128-131.

Klaus Zechner, Derrick Higgins, Xiaoming Xi and David M. Williamson. 2009. Automatic scoring of non-native spontaneous speech in tests of spoken English. *Speech Communication*, 51(10):883-895.

Disfluency Detection Using Multi-step Stacked Learning

Xian Qian and **Yang Liu**
Computer Science Department
The University of Texas at Dallas
{qx,yangl}@hlt.utdallas.edu

Abstract

In this paper, we propose a multi-step stacked learning model for disfluency detection. Our method incorporates refined n-gram features step by step from different word sequences. First, we detect filler words. Second, edited words are detected using n-gram features extracted from both the original text and filler filtered text. In the third step, additional n-gram features are extracted from edit removed texts together with our newly induced in-between features to improve edited word detection. We use Max-Margin Markov Networks (M^3Ns) as the classifier with the weighted hamming loss to balance precision and recall. Experiments on the Switchboard corpus show that the refined n-gram features from multiple steps and M^3Ns with weighted hamming loss can significantly improve the performance. Our method for disfluency detection achieves the best reported F-score 0.841 without the use of additional resources.[1]

1 Introduction

Detecting disfluencies in spontaneous speech can be used to clean up speech transcripts, which helps improve readability of the transcripts and make it easy for downstream language processing modules. There are two types of disfluencies: filler words including filled pauses (e.g., 'uh', 'um') and discourse markers (e.g., 'I mean', 'you know'), and edited words that are repeated, discarded, or corrected by the following words. An example is shown below that includes edited words and filler words.

$$\text{I want a flight } \underbrace{\textit{to Boston}}_{\text{edited}} \; \underbrace{\textit{uh I mean}}_{\text{filler}} \text{ to Denver}$$

Automatic filler word detection is much more accurate than edit detection as they are often fixed phrases (e.g., "uh", "you know", "I mean"), hence our work focuses on edited word detection.

Many models have been evaluated for this task. Liu et al. (2006) used Conditional Random Fields (CRFs) for sentence boundary and edited word detection. They showed that CRFs significantly outperformed Maximum Entropy models and HMMs. Johnson and Charniak (2004) proposed a TAG-based noisy channel model which showed great improvement over boosting based classifier (Charniak and Johnson, 2001). Zwarts and Johnson (2011) extended this model using minimal expected F-loss oriented n-best reranking. They obtained the best reported F-score of 83.8% on the Switchboard corpus. Georgila (2009) presented a post-processing method during testing based on Integer Linear Programming (ILP) to incorporate local and global constraints.

From the view of features, in addition to textual information, prosodic features extracted from speech have been incorporated to detect edited words in some previous work (Kahn et al., 2005; Zhang et al., 2006; Liu et al., 2006). Zwarts and Johnson (2011) trained an extra language model on additional corpora, and used output log probabilities of language models as features in the reranking stage. They reported that the language model gained about absolute 3% F-score for edited word detection on the Switchboard development dataset.

[1] Our source code is available at http://code.google.com/p/disfluency-detection/downloads/list

In this paper, we propose a multi-step stacked learning approach for disfluency detection. In our method, we first perform filler word detection, then edited word detection. In every step, we generate new refined n-gram features based on the processed text (remove the detected filler or edited words from the previous step), and use these in the next step. We also include a new type of features, called in-between features, and incorporate them into the last step. For edited word detection, we use Max-Margin Markov Networks (M^3Ns) with weighted hamming loss as the classifier, as it can well balance the precision and recall to achieve high performance. On the commonly used Switchboard corpus, we demonstrate that our proposed method outperforms other state-of-the-art systems for edit disfluency detection.

2 Balancing Precision and Recall Using Weighted M^3Ns

We use a sequence labeling model for edit detection. Each word is assigned one of the five labels: *BE* (beginning of the multi-word edited region), *IE* (in the edited region), *EE* (end of the edited region), *SE* (single word edited region), *O* (other). For example, the previous sentence is represented as:

I/*O* want/*O* a/*O* flight/*O* to/*BE* Boston/*EE* uh/*O* I/*O* mean/*O* to/*O* Denver/*O*

We use the F-score as the evaluation metrics (Zwarts and Johnson, 2011; Johnson and Charniak, 2004), which is defined as the harmonic mean of the precision and recall of the edited words:

$$P = \frac{\#\text{correctly predicted edited words}}{\#\text{predicted edited words}}$$
$$R = \frac{\#\text{correctly predicted edited words}}{\#\text{gold standard edited words}}$$
$$F = \frac{2 \times P \times R}{P + R}$$

There are many methods to train the sequence model, such as CRFs (Lafferty et al., 2001), averaged structured perceptrons (Collins, 2002), structured SVM (Altun et al., 2003), online passive aggressive learning (Crammer et al., 2006). Previous work has shown that minimizing F-loss is more effective than minimizing log-loss (Zwarts and Johnson, 2011), because edited words are much fewer than normal words.

In this paper, we use Max-margin Markov Networks (Taskar et al., 2004) because our preliminary results showed that they outperform other classifiers, and using weighted hamming loss is simple in this approach (whereas for perceptron or CRFs, the modification of the objective function is not straightforward).

The learning task for M^3Ns can be represented as follows:

$$\begin{aligned} \min_{\alpha} \quad & \frac{1}{2}C\|\sum_{x,y}\alpha_{x,y}\Delta f(x,y)\|_2^2 + \sum_{x,y}\alpha_{x,y}L(x,y) \\ s.t. \quad & \sum_{y}\alpha_{x,y} = 1 \qquad \forall x \\ & \alpha_{x,y} \geq 0, \qquad \forall x, y \end{aligned}$$

The above shows the dual form for training M^3Ns, where x is the observation of a training sample, $y \in \mathcal{Y}$ is a label. α is the parameter needed to be optimized, $C > 0$ is the regularization parameter. $\Delta f(x,y)$ is the residual feature vector: $f(x,\tilde{y}) - f(x,y)$, where $\tilde{y}$ is the true label of x. $L(x,y)$ is the loss function. Taskar et al. (2004) used un-weighted hamming loss, which is the number of incorrect components: $L(x,y) = \sum_t \delta(y_t,\tilde{y}_t)$, where $\delta(a,b)$ is the binary indicator function (it is 0 if $a = b$). In our work, we use the weighted hamming loss:

$$L(x,y) = \sum_t v(y_t,\tilde{y}_t)\delta(y_t,\tilde{y}_t)$$

where $v(y_t,\tilde{y}_t)$ is the weighted loss for the error when $\tilde{y}_t$ is mislabeled as y_t. Such a weighted loss function allows us to balance the model's precision and recall rates. For example, if we assign a large value to $v(O,\cdot E)$ ($\cdot E$ denotes SE, BE, IE, EE), then the classifier is more sensitive to false negative errors (edited word misclassified as non-edited word), thus we can improve the recall rate. In our work, we tune the weight matrix v using the development dataset.

3 Multi-step Stacked Learning for Edit Disfluency Detection

Rather than just using the above M^3Ns with some features, in this paper we propose to use stacked learning to incorporate gradually refined n-gram features. Stacked learning is a meta-learning approach (Cohen and de Carvalho, 2005). Its idea is to use two (or more) levels of predictors, where the outputs of the low level predictors are incorporated as features into the next level predictors. It has the advantage of incorporating non-local features as well as non-linear classifiers. In our task, we do not just use the classifier's output (a word is an edited word or not) as a feature, rather we use such output to remove the disfluencies and extract new n-gram features for the subsequent stacked classifiers. We use 10 fold cross validation to train the low level predictors. The following describes the three steps in our approach.

3.1 Step 1: Filler Word Detection

In the first step, we automatically detect filler words. Since filler words often occur immediately after edited words (before the corrected words), we expect that removing them will make rough copy detection easy. For example, in the previous example shown in Section 1, if "uh I mean" is removed, then the reparandum "to Boston" and repair "to Denver" will be adjacent and we can use word/POS based n-gram features to detect that disfluency. Otherwise, the classifier needs to skip possible filler words to find the rough copy of the reparandum.

For filler word detection, similar to edited word detection, we define 5 labels: BP, IP, EP, SP, O. We use un-weighted hamming loss to learn M^{3}Ns for this task. Since for filler word detection, our performance metric is not F-measure, but just the overall accuracy in order to generate cleaned text for subsequent n-gram features, we did not use the weighted hamming hoss for this. The features we used are listed in Table 1. All n-grams are extracted from the original text.

unigrams	$w_0, w_{-1}, w_1, w_{-2}, w_2$ $p_0, p_{-1}, p_1, p_{-2}, p_2, w_0p_0$
bigrams	$w_{-1}w_0, w_0w_1, p_{-1}p_0, p_0p_1$
trigrams	$p_{-2}p_{-1}p_0, p_{-1}p_0p_1, p_0p_1p_2$
logic unigrams	$I(w_i, w_0), I(p_i, p_0), \quad -4 \leq i \leq 4$
logic bigrams	$I(w_{i-1}w_i, w_{-1}, w_0)$ $I(p_{i-1}p_i, p_{-1}p_0)$ $I(w_iw_{i+1}, w_0w_1)$ $I(p_ip_{i+1}, p_0p_1), \quad -4 \leq i \leq 4$
transitions	$y_{-1}y_0$

Table 1: Feature templates for filler word detection. w_0, p_0 denote the current word and POS tag respectively. w_{-i} denotes the ith word to the left, w_i denotes the ith word to the right. The logic function $I(a, b)$ indicates whether a and b are identical (eigher unigrams or bigrams).

All templates in Table 1	
unigrams	w'_1, w'_2, w'_3, w'_4
bigrams	$p_0p'_1, p_0p'_2, p_0p'_3, p_0p'_4$ $w_0p'_1, w_0p'_2, w_0p'_3, w_0p'_4$ $w_0p_1, w_0p_2, w_0p_3, w_0p_4$
logic unigrams	$I(w_0, w'_i), \quad 1 \leq i \leq 4$
transitions	$p_0y_{-1}y_0$

Table 2: Feature templates for edit detection (step 2). w'_i, p'_i denote the ith word/POS tag to the right in the filler words removed text. If current word w_0 is removed in step 1, we use its original n-gram features rather than the refined n-gram features.

3.2 Step 2: Edited Word Detection

In the second step, edited words are detected using M^{3}Ns with the weighted-hamming loss. The features we used are listed in Table 2. All n-grams in the first step are also used here. Besides that, word n-grams, POS n-grams and logic n-grams extracted from filler word removed text are included. Feature templates $I(w_0, w'_i)$ is to generate features detecting rough copies separated by filler words.

3.3 Step 3: Refined Edited Word Detection

In this step, we use n-gram features extracted from the text after removing edit disfluencies based on the previous step. According to our analysis of the errors produced by step 2, we observed that many errors occurred at the boundaries of the disfluencies, and the word bigrams after removing the edited words are unnatural. The following is an example:

- **Ref:** *The new type is prettier than what their/SE they used to look like.*
- **Sys:** *The new type is prettier than what/BE their/EE they used to look like.*

Using the system's prediction, we would have bigram *than they*, which is odd. Usually, the pronoun following *than* is accusative case. We expect adding n-gram features derived from the cleaned-up sentences would allow the new classifier to fix such hypothesis. This kind of n-gram features is similar to the language models used in (Zwarts and Johnson,

2011). They have the benefit of measuring the fluency of the cleaned text.

Another common error we noticed is caused by the ambiguities of coordinates, because the coordinates have similar patterns as rough copies. For example,

- **Coordinates:** *they ca n't decide which are the good aspects and which are the bad aspects*
- **Rough Copies:** *it/BE 's/IE a/IE pleasure/IE to/EE it s good to get outside*

To distinguish the rough copies and the coordinate examples shown above, we analyze the training data statistically. We extract all the pieces lying between identical word bigrams *AB* ... *AB*. The observation is that coordinates are often longer than edited sequences. Hence we introduce the in-between features for each word. If a word lies between identical word bigrams, then its in-between feature is the log length of the subsequence lying between the two bigrams; otherwise, it is zero (we use log length to avoid sparsity). We also used other patterns such as *A* ... *A* and *ABC* ... *ABC*, but they are too noisy or infrequent and do not yield much performance gain.

Table 3 lists the feature templates used in this last step.

All templates in Table 1, Table 2	
word n-grams	$w_1'', w_0 w_1''$
in-between	$L_{AB}, w_0 b_{AB}, b_{AB}$

Table 3: Feature templates for refined edit detection (step 3). w_i'' denotes the ith word tag to the right in the edited word removed text. L_{AB} denotes the log length of the sub-sequence in the pattern *AB*...*AB*, b_{AB} indicates whether the current word lies between two identical bigrams.

4 Experiments

4.1 Experimental Setup

We use the Switchboard corpus in our experiment, with the same train/develop/test split as the previous work (Johnson and Charniak, 2004). We also remove the partial words and punctuation from the training and test data for the reason to simulate the situation when speech recognizers are used and such kind of information is not available (Johnson and Charniak, 2004).

We tuned the weight matrix for hamming loss on the development dataset using simple grid search. The diagonal elements are fixed at 0; for false positive errors, $O \rightarrow \cdot E$ (non-edited word mis-labeled as edited word), their weights are fixed at 1; for false negative errors, $\cdot E \rightarrow O$, we tried the weight from 1 to 3, and increased the weight 0.5 each time. The optimal weight matrix is shown in Table 4. Note that we use five labels in the sequence labeling task; however, for edited word detection evaluation, it is only a binary task, that is, all of the words labeled with $\cdot E$ will be mapped to the class of edited words.

truth \ predict	*BE*	*IE*	*EE*	*SE*	*O*
BE	0	1	1	1	2
IE	1	0	1	1	2
EE	1	1	0	1	2
SE	1	1	1	0	2
O	1	1	1	1	0

Table 4: Weighted hamming loss for M^{3}Ns.

4.2 Results

We compare several sequence labeling models: CRFs, structured averaged perceptron (AP), M^{3}Ns with un-weighted/weighted loss, and online passive-aggressive (PA) learning. For each model, we tuned the parameters on the development data: Gaussian prior for CRFs is 1.0, iteration number for AP is 10, iteration number and regularization penalty for PA are 10 and 1. For M^{3}Ns, we use Structured Sequential Minimal Optimization (Taskar, 2004) for model training. Regularization penalty is $C = 0.1$ and iteration number is 30.

Table 5 shows the results using different models and features. The baseline models use only the n-grams features extracted from the original text. We can see that M^{3}Ns with the weighted hamming loss achieve the best performance, outperforming all the other models. Regarding the features, the gradually added n-gram features have consistent improvement for all models. Using the weighted hamming loss in M^{3}Ns, we observe a gain of 2.2% after deleting filler words, and 1.8% after deleting edited words. In our analysis, we also noticed that the in-between fea-

	CRF	AP	PA	M^3N	w. M^3N
Baseline	78.8	79.0	78.9	79.4	80.1
Step 2	81.0	81.1	81.1	81.5	82.3
Step 3	82.9	83.0	82.8	83.3	**84.1**

Table 5: Effect of training strategy and recovered features for stacked learning. F scores are reported. AP = Averaged Perceptron, PA = online Passive Aggresive, M^3N = un-weighted M^3Ns, w. M^3N = weighted M^3Ns.

tures yield about 1% improvement in F-score for all models (the gain of step 3 over step 2 is because of the in-between features and the new n-gram features extracted from the text after removing previously detected edited words). We performed McNemar's test to evaluate the significance of the difference among various methods, and found that when using the same features, weighted M^3Ns significantly outperforms all the other models (p value < 0.001). There are no significant differences among CRFs, AP and PA. Using recovered n-gram features and in-between features significantly improves all sequence labeling models (p value < 0.001).

We also list the state-of-the-art systems evaluated on the same dataset, as shown in Table 6. We achieved the best F-score. The most competitive system is (Zwarts and Johnson, 2011), which uses extra resources to train language models.

System	F score
(Johnson and Charniak, 2004)	79.7
(Kahn et al., 2005)	78.2
(Zhang et al., 2006)†	81.2
(Georgila, 2009)*	80.1
(Zwarts and Johnson, 2011)$^+$	83.8
This paper	**84.1**

Table 6: Comparison with other systems. † they used the re-segmented Switchboard corpus, which is not exactly the same as ours. * they reported the F-score of *BE* tag (beginning of the edited sequences). $^+$ they used language model learned from 3 additional corpora.

5 Conclusion

In this paper, we proposed multi-step stacked learning to extract n-gram features step by step. The first level removes the filler words providing new ngrams for the second level to remove edited words. The third level uses the n-grams from the original text and the cleaned text generated by the previous two steps for accurate edit detection. To minimize the F-loss approximately, we modified the hamming loss in M^3Ns. Experimental results show that our method is effective, and achieved the best reported performance on the Switchboard corpus without the use of any additional resources.

Acknowledgments

We thank three anonymous reviewers for their valuable comments. This work is partly supported by DARPA under Contract No. HR0011-12-C-0016 and FA8750-13-2-0041. Any opinions expressed in this material are those of the authors and do not necessarily reflect the views of DARPA.

References

Yasemin Altun, Ioannis Tsochantaridis, and Thomas Hofmann. 2003. Hidden markov support vector machines. In *Proc. of ICML.*

Eugene Charniak and Mark Johnson. 2001. Edit detection and parsing for transcribed speech. In *Proc. of NAACL.*

William W. Cohen and Vitor Rocha de Carvalho. 2005. Stacked sequential learning. In *Proc. of IJCAI.*

Michael Collins. 2002. Discriminative training methods for hidden markov models: Theory and experiments with perceptron algorithms. In *Proc. of EMNLP.*

Koby Crammer, Ofer Dekel, Joseph Keshet, Shai Shalev-Shwartz, Yoram Singer, and Yoram Singer. 2006. Online passive-aggressive algorithms. *Journal of Machine Learning Research.*

Kallirroi Georgila. 2009. Using integer linear programming for detecting speech disfluencies. In *Proc. of NAACL.*

Mark Johnson and Eugene Charniak. 2004. A TAG-based noisy-channel model of speech repairs. In *Proc. of ACL.*

Jeremy G. Kahn, Matthew Lease, Eugene Charniak, Mark Johnson, and Mari Ostendorf. 2005. Effective use of prosody in parsing conversational speech. In *Proc. of HLT-EMNLP.*

John D. Lafferty, Andrew McCallum, and Fernando C. N. Pereira. 2001. Conditional random fields: Probabilistic models for segmenting and labeling sequence data. In *Proc. of ICML.*

Yang Liu, E. Shriberg, A. Stolcke, D. Hillard, M. Ostendorf, and M. Harper. 2006. Enriching speech recognition with automatic detection of sentence boundaries and disfluencies. *IEEE Transactions on Audio, Speech, and Language Processing*, 14(5).

Ben Taskar, Carlos Guestrin, and Daphne Koller. 2004. Max-margin markov networks. In *Proc. of NIPS*.

Ben Taskar. 2004. *Learning Structured Prediction Models: A Large Margin Approach*. Ph.D. thesis, Stanford University.

Qi Zhang, Fuliang Weng, and Zhe Feng. 2006. A progressive feature selection algorithm for ultra large feature spaces. In *Proc. of ACL*.

Simon Zwarts and Mark Johnson. 2011. The impact of language models and loss functions on repair disfluency detection. In *Proc. of ACL-HLT*.

Using Semantic Unification to Generate Regular Expressions from Natural Language

Nate Kushman Regina Barzilay
Computer Science and Artificial Intelligence Laboratory
Massachusetts Institute of Technology
{nkushman, regina}@csail.mit.edu

Abstract

We consider the problem of translating natural language text queries into regular expressions which represent their meaning. The mismatch in the level of abstraction between the natural language representation and the regular expression representation make this a novel and challenging problem. However, a given regular expression can be written in many semantically equivalent forms, and we exploit this flexibility to facilitate translation by finding a form which more directly corresponds to the natural language. We evaluate our technique on a set of natural language queries and their associated regular expressions which we gathered from Amazon Mechanical Turk. Our model substantially outperforms a state-of-the-art semantic parsing baseline, yielding a 29% absolute improvement in accuracy.[1]

1 Introduction

Regular expressions (regexps) have proven themselves to be an extremely powerful and versatile formalism that has made its way into everything from spreadsheets to databases. However, despite their usefulness and wide availability, they are still considered a dark art that even many programmers do not fully understand (Friedl, 2006). Thus, the ability to automatically generate regular expressions from natural language would be useful in many contexts.

Our goal is to learn to generate regexps from natural language, using a training set of natural language and regular expression pairs such as the one in Figure 1. We do not assume that the data includes an alignment between fragments of the natural language and fragments of the regular expression. Inducing such an alignment during learning is particularly challenging because oftentimes even humans are unable to perform a *fragment-by-fragment* alignment.

Text Description	Regular Expression
three letter word starting with 'X'	`\bX[A-Za-z]{2}\b`

Figure 1: An example text description and its associated regular expression.[3]

We can think of this task as an instance of grounded semantic parsing, similar to the work done in the domain of database queries (Kate and Mooney, 2006; Zettlemoyer and Collins, 2005; Kwiatkowski et al., 2010). However, the current success in semantic parsing relies on two important properties of the data. First, while the past work did not assume the alignment was given, they did assume that finding a fine grained fragment-by-fragment alignment was possible. Secondly, the semantic domains considered in the past were strongly typed. This typing provides constraints which significantly reduce the space of possible parses, thereby greatly reducing the ambiguity.

However, in many interesting domains these two properties may not hold. In our domain, the alignment between the natural language and the regular expressions often happens at the level of the whole phrase, making fragment-by-fragment alignment impossible. For example, in Figure 1 no fragment of the regexp maps clearly to the phrase "three letter". Instead, the regexp explicitly represents the fact that there is only two characters after X, which is not stated explicitly by the text description and must be inferred. Furthermore, regular expressions have

[1]The dataset used in this work is available at http://groups.csail.mit.edu/rbg/code/regexp/

[3]Our regular expression syntax supports Perl regular expression shorthand which utilizes `\b` to represent a break (i.e. a space or the start or end of the line). Our regular expression syntax also supports intersection (&) and complement(~).

([A-Za-z]{3})&(\b[A-Za-z]+\b)&(X.*)

(a)

three letter	[A-Za-z]{3}
word	\b[A-Za-z]+\b
starting with 'X'	X.*

(b)

Figure 2: (a) shows a regexp which is semantically equivalent to that in Figure 1, yet admits a fragment-by-fragment mapping to the natural language. (b) shows this mapping.

relatively few type constraints.

The key idea of our work is to utilize semantic unification in the logical domain to disambiguate the meaning of the natural language. Semantic unification utilizes an inference engine to determine the semantic equality of two syntactically divergent expressions. This is a departure from past work on semantic parsing which has largely focused on the *syntactic* interface between the natural language and the logical form, and on example-based semantic equality, neither of which utilize the inference power inherent in many symbolic domains.

To see how we can take advantage of semantic unification, consider the regular expression in Figure 2(a). This regular expression is semantically equivalent to the regular expression in Figure 1. Furthermore, it admits a fragment-by-fragment mapping as can be seen in Figure 2(b). In contrast, as we noted earlier, the regexp in Figure 1 does not admit such a mapping. In fact, learning can be quite difficult if our training data contains only the regexp in Figure 1. We can, nonetheless, use the regexp in Figure 2 as a stepping-stone for learning *if* we can use semantic inference to determine the equivalence between the two regular expressions. More generally, whenever the regexp in the training data does not factorize in a way that facilitates a direct mapping to the natural language description, we must find a regexp *which does factorize* and be able to compute its equivalence to the regexp we see in the training data. We compute this equivalence by converting each regexp to a minimal deterministic finite automaton (DFA) and leveraging the fact that minimal DFAs are guaranteed to be the same for semantically equivalent regexps (Hopcroft et al., 1979).

We handle the additional ambiguity stemming from the weak typing in our domain through the use of a more effective parsing algorithm. The state of the art semantic parsers (Kwiatkowski et al., 2011; Liang et al., 2011) utilize a pruned chart parsing algorithm which fails to represent many of the top parses and is prohibitively slow in the face of weak typing. In contrast, we use an n-best parser which always represents the most likely parses, and can be made very efficient through the use of the parsing algorithm from Jimenez and Marzal (2000).

Our approach works by inducing a combinatory categorial grammar (CCG) (Steedman, 2001). This grammar consists of a lexicon which pairs words or phrases with regular expression functions. The learning process initializes the lexicon by pairing each sentence in the training data with the full regular expression associated with it. These lexical entries are iteratively refined by considering all possible ways to split the regular expression and all possible ways to split the phrase. At each iteration we find the n-best parses with the current lexicon, and find the subset of these parses which are correct using DFA equivalence. We update the weights of a log-linear model based on these parses and the calculated DFA equivalence.

We evaluate our technique using a dataset of sentence/regular expression pairs which we generated using Amazon Mechanical Turk (Turk, 2013). We find that our model generates the correct regexp for 66% of sentences, while the state-of-the-art semantic parsing technique from Kwiatkowski et al. (2010) generates correct regexps for only 37% of sentences. The results confirm our hypothesis that leveraging the inference capabilities of the semantic domain can help disambiguate natural language meaning.

2 Related Work

Generating Regular Expressions Past work has looked at generating regular expressions from natural language using rule based techniques (Ranta, 1998), and also at automatically generating regular expressions from examples (Angluin, 1987). To the best of our knowledge, however, our work is the first to use training data to learn to automatically generate regular expressions from natural language.

Language Grounding There is a large body of research mapping natural language to some form of meaning representation (Kate and Mooney, 2006; Kate et al., 2005; Raymond and Mooney, 2006; Thompson and Mooney, 2003; Wong and Mooney,

2006; Wong and Mooney, 2007; Zelle and Mooney, 1996; Branavan et al., 2009; Mihalcea et al., 2006; Poon and Domingos, 2009). In some of the considered domains the issue of semantic equivalence does not arise because of the way the data is generated. The most directly related work in these domains, is that by Kwiatkowski et al. (2010 and 2011) which is an extension of earlier work on CCG-based semantic parsing by Zettlemoyer and Collins (2005). Similar to our work, Kwiatkowski et al. utilize unification to find possible ways to decompose the logical form. However, they perform only *syntactic unification*. Syntactic unification determines equality using only variable substitutions and does not take advantage of the inference capabilities available in many semantic domains. Thus, syntactic unification is unable to determine the equivalence of two logical expressions which use different lexical items, such as "`.*`" and "`.*.*`". In contrast, our DFA based technique can determine the equivalence of such expressions. It does this by leveraging the equational inference capabilities of the regular expression domain, making it a form of *semantic unification*. Thus, the contribution of our work is to show that using semantic unification to find a deeper level of equivalence helps to disambiguate language meanings.

In many other domains of interest, determining semantic equivalence is important to the learning process. Previous work on such domains has focused on either heuristic or example-driven measures of semantic equivalence. For example, Artzi and Zettlemoyer (2011) estimate semantic equivalence using a heuristic loss function. Other past work has executed the logical form on an example world or in a situated context and then compared the outputs. This provides a very weak form of semantic equivalence valid only in that world/context (Clarke et al., 2010; Liang et al., 2009; Liang et al., 2011; Chen and Mooney, 2011; Artzi and Zettlemoyer, 2013). In contrast, our work uses an exact, theoretically sound measure of semantic equivalence that determines whether two logical representations are equivalent in *any* context, i.e. on any input string.

3 Background

3.1 Finding Regexp Equivalence Using DFAs

Regular expressions can be equivalently represented as minimal DFAs, which are guaranteed to be equal for the same regular language (Hopcroft et al., 1979). The DFA representation of a regular expression may be exponentially larger than the the original regular expression. However, past work has shown that most regular expressions do not exhibit this exponential behavior (Tabakov and Vardi, 2005; Moreira and Reis, 2012), and the conversion process is renowned for its good performance in practice (Moreira and Reis, 2012). Hence, we compare the equivalence of two regular expressions by converting them to minimal DFAs and comparing the DFAs. We do this using a modified version of Møller (2010).[4]

function sig.	regexp	function signature	regexp
cons(R,R,...)	`ab`	rep*(R)	`a*`
and(R,R,...)	`[a-b]&[b-c]`	repminmax(I,I,R)	`a{3,5}`
or(R,R,...)	`a|b`	repmin(I,R)	`a{3,}`
not(R)	`~(a)`	repexact(I,R)	`a{3}`

Figure 3: This shows the signatures of all functions in our lambda calculus along with their regexp syntax.

3.2 Lambda Calculus Representation

To take advantage of the inherent structure of regular expressions, we deterministically convert them from a flat string representation into simply typed lambda calculus expressions. The full set of functions available in our lambda calculus can be seen in Figure 3. As can be seen from the figures, our lambda calculus is very weakly typed. It has only two primitive types, integer (I) and regexp (R), with most arguments being of type R.

3.3 Parsing

Our parsing model is based on a Combinatory Categorial Grammar. In CCG parsing most of the grammar complexity is contained in the lexicon, Λ, while the parser itself contains only a few simple rewrite rules called combinators.

Lexicon The lexicon, Λ, consists of a set of lexical entries that couple natural language with a lambda calculus expression. Our lexical entries contain words or phrases, each of which is associated with a function from the lambda calculus we described in §3.2. For example:

[4]We set a timeout on this process to catch any cases where the resulting DFA might be prohibitively large. We use a one second timeout in our experiments, which results in timeouts on less than 0.25% of the regular expressions.

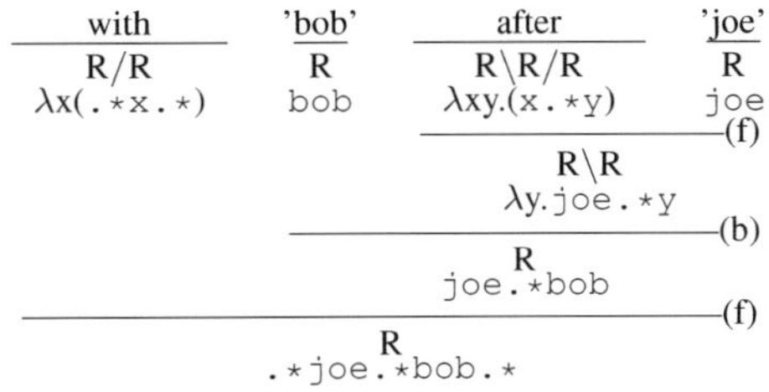

Figure 4: This shows an example parse.

⟨ after, R\R/R:λxy.(x.*y) ⟩
⟨ at least, R/I/R:λxy.((x){y,}) ⟩

Note that the lambda expressions contain type information indicating the number of arguments and the type of those arguments as described in §3.2. However, this information is augmented with a (/) or a (\) for each argument indicating whether that argument comes from the left or the right, in sentence order. Thus R\R/R can be read as a function which first takes an argument of type R on the right then takes another argument of type R on the left, and returns an expression of type R.

Combinators Parses are built by combining lexical entries through the use of a set of combinators. Our parser uses only the two most basic combinators, forward function application and backward function application.[5] These combinators work as follows:

R/R:f	R:g	→	R:f(g)	(forward)
R:f	R\R:g	→	R:g(f)	(backward)

The forward combinator applies a function to an argument on its right when the type of the argument matches the type of the function's first argument. The backward combinator works analogously. Figure 4 shows an example parse.

4 Parsing Model

For a given lexicon, Λ, and sentence, $\vec{w}$, there will in general be many valid parse trees, $t \in T(\vec{w}; \Lambda)$. We assign probabilities to these parses using a standard log-linear parsing model with parameters θ:

$$p(t|\vec{w}; \theta, \Lambda) = \frac{e^{\theta \cdot \phi(t, \vec{w})}}{\sum_{t'} e^{\theta \cdot \phi(t', \vec{w})}}$$

Our training data, however, includes only the correct regular expression, r, and not the correct parse, t. The training objective used by the past work in such circumstances, is to maximize the probability of the correct regular expression by marginalizing over all parses which generate that exact regular expression. Such an objective is limited, however, because it does not allow parses that generate semantically correct regexps which are not syntactically equivalent to r, such as those in Figure 2. The main departure of our work is to use an objective which allows such parses through the use of the DFA-EQUAL procedure. DFA-EQUAL uses the process described in §3.1 to determine whether parse t evaluates to a regexp which is semantically equivalent to r, leading to the following objective:

$$O = \sum_i \log \sum_{t|\text{DFA-EQUAL}(t, r_i)} p(t|\vec{w}_i; \theta, \Lambda) \quad (1)$$

At testing time, for efficiency reasons, we calculate only the top parse. Specifically, if $r = eval(t)$ is the regexp which results from evaluating parse t, then we generate $t^* = \arg\max_{t \in T(\vec{w})} p(t|\vec{w}; \theta, \Lambda)$, and return $r^* = eval(t^*)$.

5 Learning

Our learning algorithm starts by generating a single lexical entry for each training sample which pairs the full sentence, $\vec{w}_i$, with the associated regular expression, r_i. Formally, we initialize the lexicon as $\Lambda = \{\langle \vec{w}_i, R : r_i \rangle | i = 1 \ldots n\}$. We then run an iterative process where in each iteration we update both Λ and θ for each training sample. Our initial Λ will perfectly parse the training data. However it won't generalize at all to the test data since the lexical entries contain only full sentences. Hence, in each iteration we refine the lexicon by splitting existing lexical entries to generate more granular lexical entries which will generalize better. The candidates for splitting are all lexical entries used by parses which generate the correct regular expression, r_i, for the current training sample. We consider all possible ways to factorize each lexical entry, and we add to Λ a new lexical entry for each possible factorization, as discussed in §5.2. Finally, we update θ by performing a single stochastic gradient ascent update step for each training sample, as discussed in §5.1. See Algorithm 1 for details.

This learning approach follows the structure of the previous work on CCG based semantic parsers (Zettlemoyer and Collins, 2005;

[5]Technically, this choice of combinators makes our model just a Categorial Grammar instead of a CCG.

Inputs: Training set of sentence regular expression pairs.
$\{\langle \vec{w}_i, r_i \rangle | i = 1 \dots n\}$

Functions:

- $\texttt{N-BEST}(\vec{w}; \theta, \Lambda)$ n-best parse trees for $\vec{w}$ using the algorithm from §5.1
- $\texttt{DFA-EQUAL}(t, r)$ calculates the equality of the regexp from parse t and regexp r using the algorithm from §3.1
- $\texttt{SPLIT-LEX}(T)$ splits all lexical entries used by any parse tree in set T, using the process described in §5.2

Initialization: $\Lambda = \{\langle \vec{w}_i, R : r_i \rangle | i = 1 \dots n\}$

For $k = 1 \dots K, i = 1 \dots n$

Update Lexicon: Λ
- $T = \texttt{N-BEST}(\vec{w}_i; \theta, \Lambda)$
- $C = \{t | t \in T \wedge \texttt{DFA-EQUAL}(t, r_i)\}$
- $\Lambda = \Lambda \cup \texttt{SPLIT-LEX}(C)$

Update Parameters: θ
- $T = \texttt{N-BEST}(\vec{w}_i; \theta, \Lambda)$
- $C = \{t | t \in T \wedge \texttt{DFA-EQUAL}(t, r_i)\}$
- $\Delta = E_{p(t|t \in C)}[\phi(t, \vec{w})] - E_{p(t|t \in T)}[\phi(t, \vec{w})]$
- $\theta = \theta + \alpha\Delta$

Output: The lexicon and the parameters, $\langle \Lambda, \theta \rangle$

Algorithm 1: The full learning algorithm.

Kwiatkowski et al., 2010). However, our domain has distinct properties that led to three important departures from this past work.

First, we use the DFA based semantic unification process described in §3.1 to determine the set of correct parses when performing parameter updates. This is in contrast to the *syntactic* unification technique, used by Kwiatkowski et al. (2010), and the example based unification used by other semantic parsers, e.g. Artzi and Zettlemoyer (2011). Using semantic unification allows us to handle training data which does not admit a fragment-by-fragment mapping between the natural language and the regular expression, such as the example in Figure 2.

Second, our parser is based on the efficient n-best parsing algorithm of Jimenez and Marzal (2000) instead of the pruned chart parsing algorithm used by the past work (Zettlemoyer and Collins, 2005; Kwiatkowski et al., 2010). As we show in §8.2, this results in a parser which more effectively represents the most likely parses. This allows our parser to better handle the large number of potential parses that exist in our domain due to the weak typing.

Third, we consider splitting lexical entries used in *any* correct parse, while the past work (Zettlemoyer and Collins, 2005; Kwiatkowski et al., 2010) considers splitting only those used in the *best* parse. We must utilize a less constrictive splitting policy since our domain does not admit the feature weight initialization technique used in the domains of the past work. We discuss this in §5.2.1. In the remainder of this section we discuss the process for learning θ and for generating the lexicon, Λ.

5.1 Estimating Theta

To estimate θ we will use stochastic gradient ascent, updating the parameters based on one training example at a time. Hence, we can differentiate the objective from equation 1 to get the gradient of parameter θ_j for training example i, as follows:

$$\frac{\partial O_i}{\partial \theta_j} = E_{p(t|\texttt{DFA-EQUAL}(t,r_i),\cdot)}[\phi_j(t, \vec{w}_i)] - E_{p(t|\cdot)}[\phi_j(t, \vec{w}_i)] \quad (2)$$

This gives us the standard log-linear gradient, which requires calculating expected feature counts. We define the features in our model over individual parse productions, admitting the use of dynamic programming to efficiently calculate the unconditioned expected counts. However, when we condition on generating the correct regular expression, as in the first term in (2), the calculation no longer factorizes, rendering exact algorithms computationally infeasible.

To handle this, we use an approximate gradient calculation based on the n-best parses. Our n-best parser uses an efficient algorithm developed originally by (Jimenez and Marzal, 2000), and subsequently improved by (Huang and Chiang, 2005). This algorithm utilizes the fact that the first best parse, t_1, makes the optimal choice at each decision point, and the 2nd best parse, t_2 must make the same optimal choice at every decision point, *except for one*. To execute on this intuition, the algorithm first calculates t_1 by generating an unpruned CKY-style parse forest which includes a priority queue of possible subparses for each constituent. The set of possible 2nd best parses T are those that choose the 2nd best subparse for exactly one constituent of t_1 but are otherwise identical to t_1. The algorithm chooses $t_2 = \arg\max_{t \in T} p(t)$. More generally, T is maintained as a priority queue of possible nth best parses. At each iteration, i, the algorithm sets $t_i = \arg\max_{t \in T} p(t)$ and augments T by all parses which both differ from t_i at exactly one constituent c_i and choose the next best possible subparse for c_i.

We use the n-best parses to calculate an approximate version of the gradient. Specifically, T_i is the set of n-best parses for training sample i, and C_i includes all parses t in T_i such that DFA-EQUAL(t, r_i). We calculate the approximate gradient as:

$$\Delta = E_{p(t|t \in C_i;\theta,\Lambda)}[\phi(t, \vec{w_i})] - E_{p(t|t \in T_i;\theta,\Lambda)}[\phi(t, \vec{w_i})] \quad (3)$$

In contrast to our n-best technique, the past work has calculated equation (2) using a beam search approximation of the full inside-outside algorithm (Zettlemoyer and Collins, 2005; Kwiatkowski et al., 2010; Liang et al., 2011). Specifically, since the conditional probability of t given r does not factorize, a standard chart parser would need to maintain the full logical form (i.e. regular expression) for each subparse, and there may be an exponential number of such subparses at each chart cell. Thus, they approximate this full computation using beam search, maintaining only the m-best logical forms at each chart cell.

Qualitatively, our n-best approximation always represents the most likely parses in the approximation, but the number of represented parses scales only linearly with n. In contrast, the number of parses represented by the beam search algorithm of the past work can potentially scale exponentially with the beam size, m, due to its use of dynamic programming. However, since the beam search prunes myopically at each chart cell, it often prunes out the highest probability parses. In fact, we find that the single most likely parse is pruned out almost 20% of the time. Furthermore, our results in §8 show that the beam search's inability to represent the likely parses significantly impacts the overall performance. It is also important to note that the runtime of the n-best algorithm scales much better. Specifically, as n increases, the n-best runtime increases as $O(n|\vec{w}|\log(|\vec{w}||P| + n)$, where P is the set of possible parse productions. In contrast, as m is increased, the beam search runtime scales as $O(|\vec{w}|^5 m^2)$, where the $|\vec{w}|^5$ factor comes from our use of headwords, as discussed in §6. In practice, we find that even with n set to $10,000$ and m set to 200, our algorithm still runs almost 20 times faster.

5.2 Lexical Entry Splitting

Each lexical entry consists of a sequence of n words aligned to a typed regular expression function, $\langle w_{0:l}, T : r\rangle$. Our splitting algorithm considers all possible ways to split a lexical entry into two new

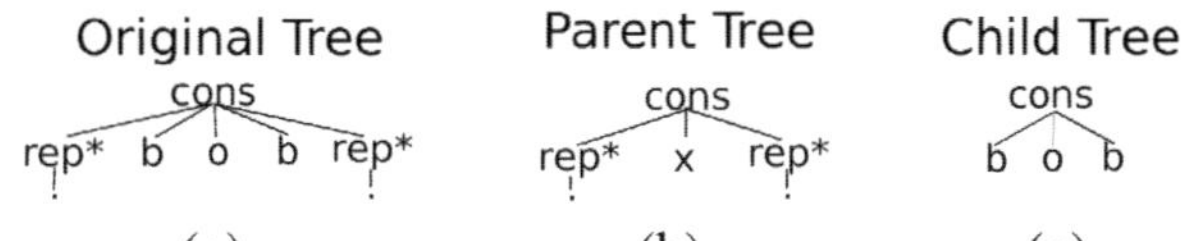

(a) (b) (c)

Figure 5: The tree in (a) represents the lambda expression from the lexical entry ⟨with bob, R:.*bob.*⟩. One possible split of this lexical entry generates the parent lexical entry ⟨with, R/R:λx.(.*x.*)⟩ and the child lexical entry, ⟨bob, R:bob⟩, whose lambda expressions are represented by (b) and (c), respectively.

lexical entries such that they can be recombined via function application to obtain the original lexical entry. This process is analogous to the syntactic unification process done by Kwiatkowski et al. (2010).

We first consider all possible ways to split the lambda expression r. The splitting process is most easily explained using a tree representation for r, as shown in Figure 5(a). This tree format is simply a convenient visual representation of a lambda calculus function, with each node representing one of the function type constants from Figure 3. Each split, $s \in S(r)$, generates a child expression s_c and a parent expression s_p such that $r = s_p(s_c)$. For each node, n, in r besides the root node, we generate a split where s_c is the subtree rooted at node n. For such splits, s_p is the lambda expression r with the sub-expression s_c replaced with a bound variable, say x. In addition to these simple splits, we also consider a set of more complicated splits at each node whose associated function type constant can take any number of arguments, i.e. or, and, or cons. If $C(n)$ are the children of node n, then we generate a split for each possible subset, $\{V | V \subset C(n)\}$. Note that for cons nodes V must be contiguous. In §6 we discuss additional restrictions placed on the splitting process to avoid generating an exponential number of splits. For the split with subset V, the child tree, s_c, is a version of the tree rooted at node n pruned to contain only the children in V. Additionally, the parent tree, s_p, is generated from r by replacing all the children in V with a single bound variable, say x. Figure 5 shows an example of such a split. We only consider splits in which s_c does not have any bound variables, so its type, T_c, is always either R or I. The type of s_p is then type of the original expression, T augmented by an additional argument of the child type, i.e. either T/T_c or $T\backslash T_c$.

Each split s generates two pairs of lexical entries,

one for forward application, and one for backward application. The set of such pairs of pairs is:

$$\{(\langle w_{0:j}, T/T_c : s_p\rangle, \langle w_{j:l}, T_c : s_c\rangle), \\ (\langle w_{0:j}, T_c : s_c\rangle, \langle w_{j:l}, T\backslash T_c : s_p\rangle) | \\ (0 \le j \le l) \wedge (s \in S(r))\}$$

5.2.1 Adding New Lexical Entries

Our model splits all lexical entries used in parses which generate correct regular expressions, i.e. those in C_i, and adds *all* of the generated lexical entries to Λ. In contrast, the previous work (Zettlemoyer and Collins, 2005; Kwiatkowski et al., 2010) has a very conservative process for adding new lexical entries. This process relies on a good initialization of the feature weights associated with a new lexical entry. They perform this initialization using a Giza++ alignment of the words in the training sentences with the names of functions in the associated lambda calculus expression. Such an initialization is ineffective in our domain since it has very few primitive functions and most of the training examples use more than half of these functions. Instead, we add new lexical entries more aggressively, and rely on the n-best parser to effectively ignore any lexicon entries which do not generate high probability parses.

6 Applying the Model

Features To allow inclusion of head words in our features, our chart cells are indexed by start word, end word, and head word. Thus for each parse production we have a set of features that combine the head word and CCG type, of the two children and the newly generated parent. Additionally, for each lexical entry $\langle \vec{w}_i, R : r_i\rangle \in \Lambda$, we have four types of features: (1) a feature for $\langle \vec{w}_i, R : r_i\rangle$, (2) a feature for $\vec{w}_i$, (3) a feature for $R : r_i$, and (4) a set of features indicating whether $\vec{w}_i$ contains a string literal and whether the leaves of r_i contain any exact character matches (rather than character range matches).

Initialization In addition to the sentence level initialization discussed in §5 we also initialize the lexicon, Λ, with two other sets of lexical entries. The first set is all of the quoted string literals in the natural language phrases from the training set. Thus for the phrase, "lines with 'bob' twice" we would add the lexical entry ⟨ 'bob', R:`bob` ⟩. We also add lexical entries for both numeric and word representations of numbers, such as ⟨ 1, R:`1`⟩ and ⟨ one, R:`1`⟩. We add these last two types of lexical entries because learning them from the data is almost impossible due to data sparsity. Lastly, for every individual word in our training set vocabulary, we add an identity lexical entry whose lambda expression is just a function which takes one argument and returns that argument. This allows our parser to learn to skip semantically unimportant words in the natural language description, and ensures that it generates at least one parse for every example in the dataset. At test time we also add both identity lexical entries for every word in the test set vocabulary as well as lexical entries for every quoted string literal seen in the test queries. Note that the addition of these lexical entries requires only access to the test queries and does not make use of the regular expressions (i.e. labels) in the test data in any way.

Parameters We initialize the weight of all lexical entry features except the identity features to a default value of 1 and initialize all other features to a default weight of 0. We regularize our log-linear model using the L^2-norm and a λ value of 0.001. We use a learning rate of $\alpha = 1.0$, set $n = 10,000$ in our n-best parser, and run each experiment with 5 random restarts and $K = 50$ iterations. We report results using the pocket algorithm technique originated by Gallant (1990).

Constraints on Lexical Entry Splitting To prevent the generation of an exponential number of splits, we constrain the lexical entry splitting process as follows:

- We only consider splits at nodes which are at most a depth of 2 from the root of the original tree.
- We limit lambda expressions to 2 arguments.
- In unordered node splits (`and` and `or`) the resulting child can contain at most 4 of the arguments.

These restrictions ensure the number of splits is at most an M-degree polynomial of the regexp size. The unification process used by Kwiatowski et al. (2010) bounded the number of splits similarly.

7 Experimental Setup

Dataset Our dataset consists of 824 natural language and regular expression pairs gathered using Amazon Mechanical Turk (Turk, 2013) and oDesk (oDesk, 2013).[6] On Mechanical Turk we asked workers to

[6]This is similar to the size of the datasets used by past work.

generate their own original natural language queries to capture a subset of the lines in a file (similar to UNIX `grep`). In order to compare to example based techniques we also ask the Mechanical Turk workers to generate 5 positive and 5 negative examples for each query. On oDesk we hired a set of programmers to generate regular expressions for each of these natural language queries. We split our data into 3 sets of 275 queries each and tested using 3-fold cross validation. We tuned our parameters separately on each development set but ended up with the same values in each case.

Evaluation Metrics We evaluate by comparing the generated regular expression for each sentence with the correct regular expression using our DFA equivalence technique. As discussed in §3.1 this metric is exact, indicating whether the generated regular expression is semantically equivalent to the correct regular expression. Additionally, as discussed in §6, our identity lexical entries ensure we generate a valid parse for every sentence, so we report only accuracy instead of precision and recall.

Baselines We compared against six different baselines. The *UBL* baseline uses the published code from Kwiatkowski et al. (2010) after configuring it to handle the lambda calculus format of our regular expressions.[7] The other baselines are ablated and/or modified versions of our model. The *BeamParse* baselines replace the `N-BEST` procedure from Algorithm 1 with the beam search algorithm used for parsing by past CCG parsers (Zettlemoyer and Collins, 2005; Kwiatkowski et al., 2010).[8] The *StringUnify* baseline replaces the `DFA-EQUAL` procedure from Algorithm 1 with exact regular expression string equality. The *HeuristicUnify* baselines strengthen this by replacing `DFA-EQUAL` with a smart heuristic form of semantic unification. Our heuristic unification procedure first flattens the regexp trees by merging all children into the parent node if they are both of the same type and of type `or`, `and`, or `cons`. It then sorts all children of the `and` and `or` operators. Finally, it converts both regexps back to a flat string and compares these strings for equivalence. This process should more effective than any form of syntactic unification and any simpler heuristics. The *ExampleUnify* baseline represents the performance of the example based semantic unification techniques. It replaces `DFA-EQUAL` with a procedure that evaluates the regexp on all the positive and negative examples associated with the given query and returns true if all 10 are correctly classified. Finally, *BeamParse-HeuristicUnify-TopParse* uses the same algorithm as that for *BeamParse-HeuristicUnify* except that it only generates lexical entries from the top parse instead of all parses. This more closely resembles the conservative lexical entry splitting algorithm used by Kwiatkowski et al.

[7]This was done in consultation with the original authors.

[8]we set the beam size to 200, which is equivalent to the past work. With this setting, the slow runtime of this algorithm allowed us to run only two random restarts.

Model	Percent Correct
UBL	36.5%
BeamParse-HeuristicUnify	9.4%
BeamParse-HeuristicUnify-TopParse	22.1%
NBestParse-StringUnify	31.1%
NBestParse-ExampleUnify	52.3%
NBestParse-HeuristicUnify	56.8%
Our Full Model	**65.5%**

Table 1: Accuracy of our model and the baselines.

8 Results

Our model outperforms all of the baselines, as shown in Table 1. The first three baselines – *UBL*, *BeamParse-HeuristicUnify*, and *BeamParse-HeuristicUnify-TopParse*– represent the algorithm used by Kwiatkowski et al. Our model outperforms the best of these by over 30% in absolute terms and 180% in relative terms.

The improvement in performance of our model over the *NBestParse-StringUnify*, *NBestParse-ExampleUnify* and *NBestParse-HeuristicUnify* baselines highlights the importance of our DFA based semantic unification technique. Specifically, our model outperforms exact string based unification by over 30%, example based semantic unification by over 13% and our smart heuristic unification procedure by 9%. These improvements confirm that leveraging exact semantic unification during the learning process helps to disambiguate language meanings.

8.1 Effect of Additional Training Data

Table 2 shows the change in performance as we increase the amount of training data. We see that our model provides particularly large gains when there

%age of Data	15%	30%	50%	75%
NBestParse-HeuristicUnify	12.4%	26.4%	39.0%	45.4%
Our Model	29.0%	50.3%	58.7%	65.2%
Relative Gain	**2.34x**	**1.91x**	**1.51x**	**1.43x**

Table 2: Results for varying amounts of training data.

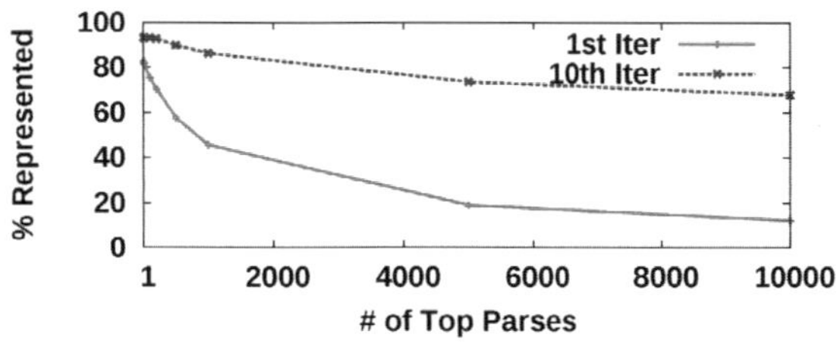

Figure 6: This graph compares the set of parses represented by the n-best algorithm used in our model to the set of parses represented by the beam search algorithm used by the past work. Note that our n-best algorithm represents 100% of the top 10000 parses.

is a small amount of training data. These gains decrease as the amount of training data increases because the additional data allows the baseline to learn new lexical entries for every special case. This reduces the need for the fine grained lexicon decomposition which is enabled by our DFA based unification. For example, our DFA based model will learn separate lexical entries for "line", "word", "starting with", and "ending with". The baseline instead will just learn separate lexical entries for every possible combination such as "line starting with", "word ending with", etc. Our model's ability to decompose, however, allows it to provide equivalent accuracy to even the best baseline with less than half the amount of training data. Furthermore, we would expect this gain to be even larger for domains with more complex mappings and a larger number of different combinations.

8.2 Beam Search vs. N-Best

A critical step in the training process is calculating the expected feature counts over all parses that generate the correct regular expression. In §4 we discussed the trade-off between approximating this calculation using the n-best parses, as our model does, verses the beam search model used by the past work. The effect of this trade-off can be seen clearly in Figure 6. The n-best parser always represents the n-best parses, which is set to 10,000 in our experiments. In contrast, on the first iteration, the beam search algorithm fails to represent the top parse almost 20% of the time and represents less than 15% of the 10,000 most likely parses. Even after 10 iterations it still only represents 70% of the top parses and fails to represent the top parse almost 10% of the time. This difference in representation ability is what provides the more than 30% difference in accuracy between the *BeamParse-HeuristicUnify* version of our model and the *NBestParse-HeuristicUnify* version of our model.

9 Conclusions and Future Work

In this paper, we present a technique for learning a probabilistic CCG which can parse a natural language text search into the regular expression that performs that search. The key idea behind our approach is to use a DFA based form of semantic unification to disambiguate the meaning of the natural language descriptions. Experiments on a dataset of natural language regular expression pairs show that our model significantly outperforms baselines based on a state-of-the-art model.

We performed our work on the domain of regular expressions, for which semantic unification is tractable. In more general domains, semantic unification is undecidable. Nevertheless, we believe our work motivates the use of semantic inference techniques for language grounding in more general domains, potentially through the use of some form of approximation or by restricting those domains in some way. For example, SAT and SMT solvers have seen significant success in performing semantic inference for program induction and hardware verification despite the computational intractability of these problems in the general case.

10 Acknowledgments

The authors acknowledge the support of Battelle Memorial Institute (PO#300662) and NSF (grant IIS-0835652). We thank Luke Zettlemoyer, Tom Kwiatkowski, Yoav Artzi, Mirella Lapata, the MIT NLP group, and the ACL reviewers for their suggestions and comments. Any opinions, findings, conclusions, or recommendations expressed in this paper are those of the authors, and do not necessarily reflect the views of the funding organizations.

References

Dana Angluin. 1987. Learning regular sets from queries and counterexamples. *Information and computation*, 75(2):87–106.

Yoav Artzi and Luke Zettlemoyer. 2011. Bootstrapping semantic parsers from conversations. In *Proceedings of the Conference on Empirical Methods in Natural Language Processing*, pages 421–432. Association for Computational Linguistics.

Yoav Artzi and Luke Zettlemoyer. 2013. Weakly supervised learning of semantic parsers for mapping instructions to actions. *Transactions of the Association for Computational Linguistics*.

S.R.K Branavan, Harr Chen, Luke Zettlemoyer, and Regina Barzilay. 2009. Reinforcement learning for mapping instructions to actions. In *Proceedings of ACL*, pages 82–90.

David L Chen and Raymond J Mooney. 2011. Learning to interpret natural language navigation instructions from observations. In *Proceedings of the 25th AAAI Conference on Artificial Intelligence (AAAI-2011)*, pages 859–865.

J. Clarke, D. Goldwasser, M.W. Chang, and D. Roth. 2010. Driving semantic parsing from the world's response. In *Proceedings of the Fourteenth Conference on Computational Natural Language Learning*, pages 18–27. Association for Computational Linguistics.

Jeffrey Friedl. 2006. *Mastering Regular Expressions*. OReilly.

Steven I Gallant. 1990. Perceptron-based learning algorithms. *Neural Networks, IEEE Transactions on*, 1(2):179–191.

J.E. Hopcroft, R. Motwani, and J.D. Ullman. 1979. *Introduction to automata theory, languages, and computation*, volume 2. Addison-wesley Reading, MA.

Liang Huang and David Chiang. 2005. Better k-best parsing. In *Proceedings of the Ninth International Workshop on Parsing Technology*, pages 53–64. Association for Computational Linguistics.

Victor M. Jimenez and Andres Marzal. 2000. Computation of the n best parse trees for weighted and stochastic context-free grammars. *Advances in Pattern Recognition*, pages 183–192.

R.J. Kate and R.J. Mooney. 2006. Using string-kernels for learning semantic parsers. In *ASSOCIATION FOR COMPUTATIONAL LINGUISTICS*, volume 44, page 913.

R.J. Kate, Y.W. Wong, and R.J. Mooney. 2005. Learning to transform natural to formal languages. In *Proceedings of the National Conference on Artificial Intelligence*, volume 20, page 1062. Menlo Park, CA; Cambridge, MA; London; AAAI Press; MIT Press; 1999.

Tom Kwiatkowski, Luke Zettlemoyer, Sharon Goldwater, and Mark Steedman. 2010. Inducing probabilistic ccg grammars from logical form with higher-order unification. In *Proceedings of EMNLP*.

T. Kwiatkowski, L. Zettlemoyer, S. Goldwater, and M. Steedman. 2011. Lexical generalization in ccg grammar induction for semantic parsing. In *Proceedings of the Conference on Empirical Methods in Natural Language Processing*, pages 1512–1523. Association for Computational Linguistics.

Percy Liang, Michael I. Jordan, and Dan Klein. 2009. Learning semantic correspondences with less supervision. In *Proceedings of ACL*, pages 91–99.

P. Liang, M.I. Jordan, and D. Klein. 2011. Learning dependency-based compositional semantics. *Computational Linguistics*, pages 1–94.

R. Mihalcea, H. Liu, and H. Lieberman. 2006. Nlp (natural language processing) for nlp (natural language programming). *Computational Linguistics and Intelligent Text Processing*, pages 319–330.

Anders Møller. 2010. dk.brics.automaton – finite-state automata and regular expressions for Java. `http://www.brics.dk/automaton/`.

N. Moreira and R. Reis. 2012. Implementation and application of automata.

oDesk. 2013. `http://odesk.com/`.

H. Poon and P. Domingos. 2009. Unsupervised semantic parsing. In *Proceedings of the 2009 Conference on Empirical Methods in Natural Language Processing: Volume 1-Volume 1*, pages 1–10. Association for Computational Linguistics.

Aarne Ranta. 1998. A multilingual natural-language interface to regular expressions. In *Proceedings of the International Workshop on Finite State Methods in Natural Language Processing*, pages 79–90. Association for Computational Linguistics.

R.G. Raymond and J. Mooney. 2006. Discriminative reranking for semantic parsing. In *Proceedings of the COLING/ACL on Main conference poster sessions*, pages 263–270. Association for Computational Linguistics.

M. Steedman. 2001. *The syntactic process*. MIT press.

D. Tabakov and M. Vardi. 2005. Experimental evaluation of classical automata constructions. In *Logic for Programming, Artificial Intelligence, and Reasoning*, pages 396–411. Springer.

C.A. Thompson and R.J. Mooney. 2003. Acquiring word-meaning mappings for natural language interfaces. *Journal of Artificial Intelligence Research*, 18(1):1–44.

Mechanical Turk. 2013. `http://mturk.com/`.

Y.W. Wong and R.J. Mooney. 2006. Learning for semantic parsing with statistical machine translation. In

Proceedings of the main conference on Human Language Technology Conference of the North American Chapter of the Association of Computational Linguistics, pages 439–446. Association for Computational Linguistics.

Y.W. Wong and R. Mooney. 2007. Learning synchronous grammars for semantic parsing with lambda calculus. In *ANNUAL MEETING-ASSOCIATION FOR COMPUTATIONAL LINGUISTICS*, volume 45, page 960.

J.M. Zelle and R.J. Mooney. 1996. Learning to parse database queries using inductive logic programming. In *Proceedings of the National Conference on Artificial Intelligence*, pages 1050–1055.

L.S. Zettlemoyer and M. Collins. 2005. Learning to map sentences to logical form: Structured classification with probabilistic categorial grammars.

L.S. Zettlemoyer and M. Collins. 2007. Online learning of relaxed ccg grammars for parsing to logical form. In *In Proceedings of the 2007 Joint Conference on Empirical Methods in Natural Language Processing and Computational Natural Language Learning (EMNLP-CoNLL-2007*. Citeseer.

L.S. Zettlemoyer and M. Collins. 2009. Learning context-dependent mappings from sentences to logical form. In *Proceedings of the Joint Conference of the 47th Annual Meeting of the ACL and the 4th International Joint Conference on Natural Language Processing of the AFNLP: Volume 2-Volume 2*, pages 976–984. Association for Computational Linguistics.

Probabilistic Frame Induction

Jackie Chi Kit Cheung*
Department of Computer Science
University of Toronto
Toronto, ON, M5S 3G4, Canada
jcheung@cs.toronto.edu

Hoifung Poon
One Microsoft Way
Microsoft Research
Redmond, WA 98052, USA
hoifung@microsoft.com

Lucy Vanderwende
One Microsoft Way
Microsoft Research
Redmond, WA 98052, USA
lucyv@microsoft.com

Abstract

In natural-language discourse, related events tend to appear near each other to describe a larger scenario. Such structures can be formalized by the notion of a *frame* (a.k.a. template), which comprises a set of related events and prototypical participants and event transitions. Identifying frames is a prerequisite for information extraction and natural language generation, and is usually done manually. Methods for inducing frames have been proposed recently, but they typically use ad hoc procedures and are difficult to diagnose or extend. In this paper, we propose the first probabilistic approach to frame induction, which incorporates frames, events, and participants as latent topics and learns those frame and event transitions that best explain the text. The number of frame components is inferred by a novel application of a split-merge method from syntactic parsing. In end-to-end evaluations from text to induced frames and extracted facts, our method produces state-of-the-art results while substantially reducing engineering effort.

1 Introduction

Events with causal or temporal relations tend to occur near each other in text. For example, a BOMBING scenario in an article on terrorism might begin with a DETONATION event, in which terrorists set off a bomb. Then, a DAMAGE event might ensue to describe the resulting destruction and any casualties, followed by an INVESTIGATION event covering subsequent police investigations. Afterwards, the BOMBING scenario may transition into a CRIMINAL-PROCESSING scenario, which begins with police catching the terrorists, and proceeds to a trial, sentencing, etc. A common set of participants serves as the event arguments; e.g., the agent (or subject) of DETONATION is often the same as the theme (or object) of INVESTIGATION and corresponds to a PERPETRATOR.

Such structures can be formally captured by the notion of a *frame* (a.k.a. template, scenario), which consists of a set of *events* with prototypical transitions, as well as a set of *slots* representing the common participants. Identifying frames is an explicit or implicit prerequisite for many NLP tasks. Information extraction, for example, stipulates the types of events and slots that are extracted for a frame or template. Online applications such as dialogue systems and personal-assistant applications also model users' goals and subgoals using frame-like representations. In natural-language generation, frames are often used to represent contents to be expressed as well as to support surface realization.

Until recently, frames and related representations have been manually constructed, which has limited their applicability to a relatively small number of domains and a few slots within a domain. Furthermore, additional manual effort is needed after the frames are defined in order to extract frame components from text (e.g., in annotating examples and designing features to train a supervised learning model). This paradigm makes generalizing across tasks difficult, and might suffer from annotator bias.

Recently, there has been increasing interest in au-

*This research was undertaken during the author's internship at Microsoft Research.

tomatically inducing frames from text. A notable example is Chambers and Jurafsky (2011), which first clusters related verbs to form frames, and then clusters the verbs' syntactic arguments to identify slots. While Chambers and Jurafsky (2011) represents a major step forward in frame induction, it is also limited in several aspects. The clustering used ad hoc steps and customized similarity metrics, as well as an additional retrieval step from a large external text corpus for slot generation. This makes it hard to replicate their approach or adapt it to new domains. Lacking a coherent model, it is also difficult to incorporate additional linguistic insights and prior knowledge.

In this paper, we present PROFINDER (PRObabilistic Frame INDucER), the first probabilistic approach to frame induction. PROFINDER defines a joint distribution over the words in a document and their frame assignments by modeling frame and event transitions, correlations among events and slots, and their surface realizations. Given a set of documents, PROFINDER outputs a set of induced frames with learned parameters, as well as the most probable frame assignments that can be used for event and entity extraction. The numbers of events and slots are dynamically determined by a novel application of the split-merge approach from syntactic parsing (Petrov et al., 2006). In end-to-end evaluations from text to entity extraction using standard MUC and TAC datasets, PROFINDER achieved state-of-the-art results while significantly reducing engineering effort and requiring no external data.

2 Related Work

In information extraction and other semantic processing tasks, the dominant paradigm requires two stages of manual effort. First, the target representation is defined manually by domain experts. Then, manual effort is required to construct an extractor or to annotate examples to train a machine-learning system. Recently, there has been a burgeoning body of work in reducing such manual effort. For example, a popular approach to reduce annotation effort is bootstrapping from seed examples (Patwardhan and Riloff, 2007; Huang and Riloff, 2012). However, this still requires prespecified frames or templates, and selecting seed words is often a challenging task (Curran et al., 2007). Filatova et al. (2006) construct simple domain templates by mining verbs and the named entity type of verbal arguments that are topical, whereas Shinyama and Sekine (2006) identify query-focused slots by clustering common named entities and their syntactic contexts. Open IE (Banko and Etzioni, 2008) limits the manual effort to designing a few domain-independent relation patterns, which can then be applied to extract relational triples from text. While extremely scalable, this approach can only extract atomic factoids within a sentence, and the resulting triples are noisy, non-canonicalized text fragments.

More relevant to our approach is the recent work in unsupervised semantic induction, such as unsupervised semantic parsing (Poon and Domingos, 2009), unsupervised semantical role labeling (Swier and Stevenson, 2004) and induction (Lang and Lapata, 2011, e.g.), and slot induction from web search logs (Cheung and Li, 2012). As in PROFINDER, they model distributional contexts for slots and roles. However, these approaches focus on the semantics of independent sentences or queries, and do not capture discourse-level dependencies.

The modeling of frame and event transitions in PROFINDER is similar to a sequential topic model (Gruber et al., 2007), and is inspired by the successful applications of such topic models in summarization (Barzilay and Lee, 2004; Daumé III and Marcu, 2006; Haghighi and Vanderwende, 2009, inter alia). There are, however, two main differences. First, PROFINDER contains not a single sequential topic model, but two (for frames and events, respectively). In addition, it also models the interdependencies among events, slots, and surface text, which is analogous to the USP model (Poon and Domingos, 2009). PROFINDER can thus be viewed as a novel combination of state-of-the-art models in unsupervised semantics and discourse modeling.

In terms of aim and capability, PROFINDER is most similar to Chambers and Jurafsky (2011), which culminated from a series of work for identifying correlated events and arguments in narratives (Chambers and Jurafsky, 2008; Chambers and Jurafsky, 2009). By adopting a probabilistic approach, PROFINDER has a sound theoretical underpinning, and is easy to modify or extend. For example, in Section 3, we show how PROFINDER can easily be augmented with additional linguistically-motivated features. Likewise, PROFINDER can easily be used as a semi-supervised system if some slot designations and labeled examples are available.

The idea of representing and capturing stereotypical knowledge has a long history in artificial intelligence and psychology, and has assumed various names such as *frames* (Minsky, 1974), *schemata* (Rumelhart, 1975), and *scripts* (Schank and Abelson, 1977). In the linguistics and computational linguistics communities, frame semantics (Fillmore, 1982) uses frames as the central representation of word meaning, culminating in the development of FrameNet (Baker et al., 1998), which contains over 1000 manually annotated frames. A similarly rich lexical resource is the MindNet project (Richardson et al., 1998). Our notion of frame is related to these representations, but there are also subtle differences. For example, Minsky's frame emphasizes *inheritance*, which we do not model in this paper[1]. As in semantic role labeling, FrameNet focuses on semantic roles and does not model event or frame transitions, so the scope of its frames is often no more than an event in our model. Perhaps the most similar to our frame is Roger Schank's scripts, which capture prototypical events and participants in a scenario such as restaurant dining. In their approach, however, scripts are manually defined, making it hard to generalize. In this regard, our work may be viewed as an attempt to revive a long tradition in AI and linguistics, by leveraging the recent advances in computational power, NLP, and machine learning.

3 Probabilistic Frame Induction

In this section, we present PROFINDER, a probabilistic model for frame induction. Let $\mathcal{F}$ be a set of frames, where each frame $F = (E_F, S_F)$ comprises a unique set of events E_F and slots S_F. Given a document D and a word w in D, $Z_w = (f, e)$ represents an assignment of w to frame $f \in \mathcal{F}$ and frame element $e \in E_f \cup S_f$. At the heart of PROFINDER is a generative model $P_\theta(D, Z)$ that defines a joint distribution over document D and the frame assignment to its words Z. Given a set of documents $\mathcal{D}$, frame induction in PROFINDER amounts to determining the number of events and slots in each frame, as well as learning the parameters θ by summing out the latent assignments Z to maximize the likelihood of the document set

$$\prod_{D \in \mathcal{D}} P_\theta(D).$$

The induced frames identify the key event structures in the document set. Additionally, PROFINDER can conduct event and entity extraction by computing the most probable frame assignment Z. In the remainder of the section, we first present the base model for PROFINDER. We then introduce several linguistically motivated refinements, as well as efficient algorithms for learning and inference in PROFINDER.

3.1 Base Model

The probabilistic formulation of PROFINDER makes it extremely flexible for incorporating linguistic intuition and prior knowledge. In this paper, we design our PROFINDER model to capture three types of dependencies.

Frame transitions between clauses A sentence contains one or more clauses, each of which is a minimal unit expressing a proposition. A clause is unlikely to straddle different frames, so we stipulate that the words in a clause be assigned to the same frame. On the other hand, frame transitions can happen between clauses, and we adopt the common Markov assumption that the frame of a clause only depends on the previous clause in the document. Clauses are automatically extracted from the dependency parse and further decomposed into an *event head* and its syntactic arguments.

Event transitions within a frame Events tend to transition into related events in the same frame, as determined by their causal or temporal relations. Each clause is assigned an event compatible with its frame assignment (i.e., the event is in the given frame). Like frame transitions, we assume that the event assignment of a clause depends only on the event of the previous clause.

Emission of event heads and slot words Similar to topics in topic models, each event determines

[1] This should be a straightforward extension — using the split-and-merge approach, PROFINDER already produces a hierarchy of events and slots in learning, although currently it makes no use of the intermediate levels.

a multinomial from which the event head is generated; e.g., a DETONATION event might use verbs such as *detonate, set off* or nouns such as *denotation, bombing* as its event head. Additionally, as in USP (Poon and Domingos, 2009), an event also contains a multinomial of slots for each of its argument types[2]; e.g., the agent argument of a DETONATION event is generally the PERPETRATOR slot of the BOMBING frame. Finally, each slot has its own multinomials for generating the argument head and dependency label, regardless of the event.

Formally, let D be a document and $C_1, \cdots, C_l$ be its clauses, the PROFINDER model is defined by

$$P_\theta(D, Z) = P_{\texttt{F-INIT}}(F_1) \times \prod_i P_{\texttt{F-TRAN}}(F_{i+1}|F_i)$$
$$\times P_{\texttt{E-INIT}}(E_1|F_1)$$
$$\times \prod_i P_{\texttt{E-TRAN}}(E_{i+1}|E_i, F_{i+1}, F_i)$$
$$\times \prod_i P_{\texttt{E-HEAD}}(e_i|E_i)$$
$$\times \prod_{i,j} P_{\texttt{SLOT}}(S_{i,j}|E_{i,j}, A_{i,j})$$
$$\times \prod_{i,j} P_{\texttt{A-HEAD}}(a_{i,j}|S_{i,j})$$
$$\times \prod_{i,j} P_{\texttt{A-DEP}}(dep_{i,j}|S_{i,j})$$

Here, F_i, E_i denote the frame and event assignment to clause C_i, respectively, and e_i denotes the event head. For the j-th argument of clause i, $S_{i,j}$ denotes the slot assignment, $A_{i,j}$ the argument type, $a_{i,j}$ the head word, and $dep_{i,j}$ the dependency from the event head. $P_{\texttt{E-TRAN}}(E_{i+1}|E_i, F_{i+1}, F_i) = P_{\texttt{E-INIT}}(E_{i+1}|F_{i+1})$ if $F_{i+1} \neq F_i$.

Essentially, PROFINDER combines a frame HMM with an event HMM, where the first models frame transition and emits events, and the second models event transition within a frame and emits argument slots.

3.2 Model refinements

The base model captures the main dependencies in event narrative, but it can be easily extended to leverage additional linguistic intuition. PROFINDER incorporates three such refinements.

Background frame Event narratives often contain interjections of general content common to all frames. For example, in newswire articles, ATTRIBUTION is commonplace to describe who said or reported a particular quote or fact. To avoid contaminating frames with generic content, we introduce a background frame with its own events, slots, and emission distributions, and a binary switch variable $B_i \in \{BKG, CNT\}$ that determines whether clause i is generated from the actual content frame F_i (CNT) or background (BKG). We also stipulate that if BKG is chosen, the nominal frame stays the same as the previous clause.

Stickiness in frame and event transitions Prior work has demonstrated that promoting topic coherence in natural-language discourse helps discourse modeling (Barzilay and Lee, 2004). We extend PROFINDER to leverage this intuition by incorporating a "stickiness" prior (Haghighi and Vanderwende, 2009) to encourage neighboring clauses to stay in the same frame. Specifically, along with introducing the background frame, the frame transition component now becomes

$$P_{\texttt{F-TRAN}}(F_{i+1}|F_i, B_{i+1}) = \quad (1)$$
$$\begin{cases} \mathbf{1}(F_{i+1} = F_i), & \text{if } B_{i+1} = BKG \\ \beta \mathbf{1}(F_{i+1} = F_i) + \\ (1-\beta) P_{\texttt{F-TRAN}}(F_{i+1}|F_i), & \text{if } B_{i+1} = CNT \end{cases}$$

where β is the stickiness parameter, and the event transition component correspondingly becomes

$$P_{\texttt{E-TRAN}}(E_{i+1}|E_i, F_{i+1}, F_i, B_{i+1}) = \quad (2)$$
$$\begin{cases} \mathbf{1}(E_{i+1} = E_i), & \text{if } B_{i+1} = BKG \\ P_{\texttt{E-TRAN}}(E_{i+1}|E_i), & \text{if } B_{i+1} = CNT, F_i = F_{i+1} \\ P_{\texttt{E-INIT}}(E_{i+1}), & \text{if } B_{i+1} = CNT, F_i \neq F_{i+1} \end{cases}$$

Argument dependencies as caseframes As noticed in previous work such as Chambers and Jurafsky (2011), the combination of an event head and a dependency relation often gives a strong signal of the slot that is indicated. For example, *bomb* > *nsubj* (subject argument of *bomb*) often indicates a PERPETRATOR. Thus, rather than simply emitting

[2]USP generates the argument types along with events from clustering. For simplicity, in PROFINDER we simply classify a syntactic argument into subject, object, and prepositional object, according to its Stanford dependency to the event head.

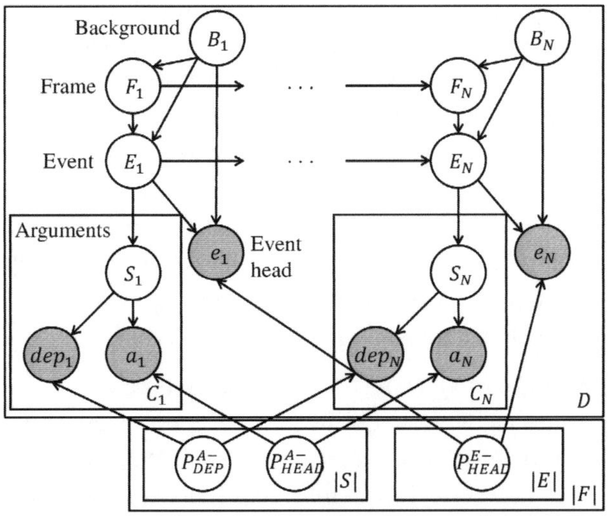

Figure 1: Graphical representation of our model. Hyperparameters, the stickiness factor, and the frame and event initial and transition distributions are not shown for clarity.

the dependency from the event head to an event argument $dep_{i,j}$, our model instead emits the pair of event head and dependency relation, which we call a *caseframe* following Bean and Riloff (2004).

3.3 Full generative story

To summarize, the distributions that are learned by our model are the default distributions $P_{\texttt{BKG}}(B)$, $P_{\texttt{F-INIT}}(F)$, $P_{\texttt{E-INIT}}(E)$; the transition distributions $P_{\texttt{F-TRAN}}(F_{i+1}|F_i)$, $P_{\texttt{E-TRAN}}(E_{i+1}|E_i)$; and the emission distributions $P_{\texttt{SLOT}}(S|E, A, B)$, $P_{\texttt{E-HEAD}}(e|E, B)$, $P_{\texttt{A-HEAD}}(a|S)$, $P_{\texttt{A-DEP}}(dep|S)$. We used additive smoothing with uniform Dirichlet priors for all the multinomials. The overall generative story of our model is as follows:

1. Draw a Bernoulli distribution for $P_{\texttt{BKG}}(B)$
2. Draw the frame, event, and slot distributions
3. Draw an event head emission distribution $P_{\texttt{E-HEAD}}(e|E, B)$ for each frame including the background frame
4. Draw event argument lemma and caseframe emission distributions for each slot in each frame including the background frame
5. For each clause in each document, generate the clause-internal structure.

The clause-internal structure at clause i is generated by the following steps:

1. Generate whether this clause is background ($B_i \in \{CNT, BKG\} \sim P_{\texttt{BKG}}(B)$)
2. Generate the frame F_i and event E_i from $P_{\texttt{F-INIT}}(F)$, $P_{\texttt{E-INIT}}(E)$, or according to equations 1 and 2
3. Generate the observed event head e_i from $P_{\texttt{E-HEAD}}(e_i|E_i)$.
4. For each event argument:
   (a) Generate the slot $S_{i,j}$ from $P_{\texttt{SLOT}}(S|E, A, B)$.
   (b) Generate the dependency/caseframe emission $dep_{i,j} \sim P_{\texttt{A-DEP}}(dep|S)$ and the lemma of the head word of the event argument $a_{i,j} \sim P_{\texttt{A-HEAD}}(a|S)$.

3.4 Learning and Inference

Our generative model admits efficient inference by dynamic programming. In particular, after collapsing the latent assignment of frame, event, and background into a single hidden variable for each clause, the expectation and most probable assignment can be computed using standard forward-backward and Viterbi algorithms on fixed tree structures.

Parameter learning can be done using EM by alternating the computation of expected counts and the maximization of multinomial parameters. In particular, PROFINDER uses incremental EM, which has been shown to have better and faster convergence properties than standard EM (Liang and Klein, 2009).

Determining the optimal number of events and slots is challenging. One solution is to adopt a non-parametric Bayesian method by incorporating a hierarchical prior over the parameters (e.g., a Dirichlet process). However, this approach can impose unrealistic restrictions on the model choice and result in intractability which requires sampling or approximate inference to overcome. Additionally, EM learning can suffer from local optima due to its non-convex learning objective, especially when dealing with a large number hidden states without a good initialization.

To address these issues, we adopt a novel application of the split-merge method previously used in syntactic parsing for inferring refined latent syntactic categories (Petrov et al., 2006). First, the model is initialized with a number of frames, which is a hyperparameter, and each frame is associated with one event and two slots. Starting from this minimal structure, EM training begins. After a number of iterations, each event and slot state is "split" in two; that is, each original state now becomes two new states. Each of the new states is generated with half of the probability of the original, and contains a duplicate of the associated emission distributions. Some perturbation is then added to the probabilities to break symmetry. After splitting, we merge back a portion of the newly split events and slots that result in the least improvement in the likelihood of the training data. For more details on split-merge, see Petrov et al. (2006)

By adjusting the number of split-merge cycles and the merge parameters, our model learns the number of events and slots in a dynamical fashion that is tailored to the data. Moreover, our model starts with a small number of frame elements, which reduces the number of local optima and facilitates initial learning. After each split, the subsequent learning starts with (a perturbed version of) the previously learned parameters, which makes a good initialization that is crucial for EM. Finally, it is also compatible with the hierarchical nature of events and slots. For example, slots can first be coarsely split into persons versus locations, and later refined into subcategories such as perpetrators and victims.

4 MUC-4 Entity Extraction Experiments

We first evaluate our model on a standard entity extraction task, using the evaluation settings from Chambers and Jurafsky (2011) (henceforth, C&J) to enable a head-to-head comparison. Specifically, we use the MUC-4 data set (1992) , which contains 1300 training and development documents on terrorism in South America, with 200 additional documents for testing. MUC-4 contains four templates: ATTACK, KIDNAPPING, BOMBING, and ARSON.[3] All templates share the same set of predefined slots, with the evaluation focusing on the following four: PERPETRATOR, PHYSICAL TARGET, HUMAN TARGET, and INSTRUMENT.

For each slot in a MUC template, the system first identifies an induced slot that best maps to it by F_1 on the development set. As in C&J, template is ignored in final evaluation, so all the clusters that belong to the same slot are then merged across the templates; e.g., the PERPETRATOR clusters for KIDNAPPING and BOMBING are merged. The final precision, recall, and F_1 are computed based on these merged clusters. Correctness is determined by matching head words, and slots marked as optional in MUC are ignored when computing recall. All hyperparameters are tuned on the development set (see Appendix A for their values).

Named entity type Named entity type is a useful feature to filter out entities for particular slots; e.g. a location cannot be an INSTRUMENT. We thus divide each induced cluster into four clusters by named entity type before performing the mapping, following C&J's heuristic and using a named entity recognizer and word lists derived from WordNet: PERSON/ORGANIZATION, PHYSICAL OBJECT, LOCATION, and OTHER.

Document classification The MUC-4 dataset contains many documents that have words related to MUC slots (e.g., *plane* and *aviation*), but are not about terrorism. To reduce precision errors, C&J first filtered irrelevant documents based on the specificity of event heads to learned frames. To estimate the specificity, they used additional data retrieved from a large external corpus. In PROFINDER, however, specificity can be easily estimated using the probability distributions learned during training. In particular, we define the probability of an event head in a frame j as:

$$P_F(w) = \sum_{E_F \in F} P_{\texttt{E-HEAD}}(w|E)/|F|, \tag{3}$$

and the probability of a frame given an event head as:

$$P(F|w) = P_F(w) / \sum_{F' \in \mathcal{F}} P_{F'}(w). \tag{4}$$

We then follow the rest of C&J's procedure to score each learned frame with each MUC document. Specifically, a document is mapped to a frame if the average $P_F(w)$ in the document is above a threshold and the document contains at least one *trigger word* w' with $P(F|w') > 0.2$. The threshold and the induced frame were determined on the development set, and were used to filter irrelevant documents in the test set.

[3] Two other templates have negligible counts and are ignored as in C&J.

Unsupervised methods	P	R	F_1
ProFinder (This work)	32	**37**	**34**
Chambers and Jurafsky (2011)	**48**	25	33
With additional information			
ProFinder +doc. classification	41	**44**	**43**
C&J 2011 +granularity	**44**	36	40

Table 1: Results on MUC-4 entity extraction. C&J 2011 +granularity refers to their experiment in which they mapped one of their templates to five learned clusters rather than one.

Event: Attack	**Event: Discussion**
report, participate, kidnap, kill, release	*hold, meeting, talk, discuss, investigate*
Slot: Perpetrator	**Slot: Victim**
PERSON/ORG	PERSON/ORG
Words: *guerrilla, police, source, person, group*	**Words:** *people, priest, leader, member, judge*
Caseframes: *report>nsubj, kidnap>nsubj, kill>nsubj, participate>nsubj, release>nsubj*	**Caseframes:** *kill>dobj, murder>dobj, release>dobj, report>dobj, kidnap>dobj*

Figure 2: A partial frame learned by ProFinder from the MUC-4 data set, with the most probable emissions for each event and slot. Labels are assigned by the authors for readability.

Results Compared to C&J, ProFinder is conceptually much simpler, using a single probabilistic model and standard learning and inference algorithms, and not requiring multiple processing steps or customized similarity metrics. It only used the data in MUC-4, whereas C&J required additional text to be retrieved from a large external corpus (Gigaword (Graff et al., 2005)) for each event cluster. It currently does not make use of coreference information, whereas C&J did. Remarkably, despite all these, ProFinder was still able to outperform C&J on entity extraction, as shown in Table 1. We also evaluated ProFinder's performance assuming perfect document classification (+doc. classification). This led to a substantially higher precision, suggesting that further improvement is possible from better document classification.

Figure 2 shows part of a frame learned by ProFinder, which includes some slots and events annotated in MUC. ProFinder is also able to identify events and slots not annotated in MUC, a desirable characteristic of unsupervised methods. For example, it found a DISCUSSION event, an ARREST event (*call, arrest, express, meet, charge*), a PEACE AGREEMENT slot (*agreement, rights, law, proposal*), and an AUTHORITIES slot (*police, government, force, command*). The background frame was able to capture many verbs related to attribution, such as *say, continue, add, believe*, although it missed *report*.

5 Evaluating Frame Induction Using Guided Summarization Templates

The MUC-4 dataset was originally designed for information extraction and focuses on a limited number of template and slot types. To evaluate ProFinder's capabilities in generalizing to a greater variety of text, we designed and conducted a novel evaluation based on the TAC guided-summarization dataset. This evaluation was inspired by the connection between summarization and information extraction (White et al., 2001), and reflects a conceptualization of summarization as inducing and extracting structured information from source text. Essentially, we adapted the TAC summarization annotation to create gold-standard slots, and used them to evaluate entity extraction as in MUC-4.

Dataset We used the TAC 2010 guided-summarization dataset in our experiments (Owczarzak and Dang, 2010). This data set consists of text from five domains (termed *categories* in TAC), each with a template defined by TAC organizers. In total, there are 46 document clusters (termed *topics* in TAC), each of which contains 20 documents and has eight human-written summaries. Each summary was manually segmented using the Pyramid method (Nenkova and Passonneau, 2004) and each segment was annotated with a slot (termed *aspect* in TAC) from the corresponding template. Figure 3 shows an example and the full set of templates is available at `http://www.nist.gov/tac/2010/Summarization/Guided-Summ.2010.guidelines.html`. In

(a) **Accidents and Natural Disasters:**
WHAT: what happened
WHEN: date, time, other temporal markers
WHERE: physical location
WHY: reasons for accident/disaster
WHO_AFFECTED: casualties...
DAMAGES: ... caused by the disaster
COUNTERMEASURES: rescue efforts...

(b) *(*WHEN *During the night of July 17,)* *(*WHAT *a 23-foot* <WHAT *tsunami) hit the north coast of Papua New Guinea (PNG)*>, *(*WHY *triggered by a 7.0 undersea earthquake in the area).*

(c) WHEN: *night* WHAT: *tsunami, coast*
WHY: *earthquake*

Figure 3: (a) A frame from the TAC Guided Summarization task with abbreviated slot descriptions. (b) A TAC text span, segmented into several contributors with slot labels. Note that the two WHAT contributors overlap, and are demarcated by different bracket types. (c) The entities that are extracted for evaluation.

TAC, each annotated segment (Figure 3b) is called a *contributor*.

Evaluation Method We converted the contributors into a form that is more similar to the previous MUC evaluation, so that we can fairly compare against previous work such as C&J that were designed to extract information into that form. Specifically, we extracted the head lemma from all the maximal noun phrases found in the contributor (Figure 3c) and treated them as gold-standard entity slots to extract. While this conversion may not be ideal in some cases, it simplifies the TAC slots and enables automatic evaluation. We leave the refinement of this conversion to future work, and believe it could be done by crowdsourcing.

For each TAC slot in a TAC category, we extract entities from the summaries that belong to the given TAC category. A system-induced entity is considered a match to a TAC-derived entity from the same document if the head lemma in the former matches one in the latter. Based on this matching criterion, the system-induced slots are mapped to the TAC slots in a way that achieves the best F_1 for each TAC slot. We allow a system slot to map to multiple TAC slots, due to potential overlaps in entities among TAC slots. For example, in a document about a tsunami, *earthquake* may appear both in the WHAT slot as a disaster itself, and in the CAUSE slot as a cause for the tsunami.

	1-best			*5-best*		
Systems	P	R	F_1	P	R	F_1
PROFINDER	24	**25**	**24**	21	**38**	**27**
C&J	**58**	6.1	11	**50**	12	20

Table 2: Results on TAC 2010 entity extraction with N-best mapping for $N = 1$ and $N = 5$. Intermediate values of N produce intermediate results, and are not shown for brevity.

One salient difference between TAC and MUC slots is that TAC slots are often more general than MUC slots. For example, TAC slots such as WHY and COUNTERMEASURES likely correspond to multiple slots at the granularity of MUC. As a result, we also consider mapping the N-best system-induced slots to each TAC slot, for N up to 5.

Experiments We trained PROFINDER and a reimplementation of C&J on the 920 full source texts of TAC 2010, and tested them on the 368 model summaries. We did not provide C&J's model with access to external data, in order to enable fair comparison with our model. Since all of the summary sentences are expected to be relevant, we did not conduct document or sentence relevance classification in C&J or PROFINDER. We tuned all parameters by two-fold cross validation on the summaries. We computed the overall precision, recall, and F_1 by taking a micro-average over the results for each TAC slot.

Results The results are shown in Table 2. PROFINDER substantially outperformed C&J in F_1, in both 1-best and N-best cases. As in MUC-4, the precision of C&J is higher, partly because C&J often did not do much in clustering and produced many small clusters. For example, in the 1-best setting, the average number of entities mapped to each TAC slot by C&J is 21, whereas it is 208 for PROFINDER. For both systems, the results are generally lower compared to that in MUC-4, which is expected since this task is harder given the greater diversity in frames and slots to be induced.

6 Conclusion

We have presented ProFinder, the first probabilistic approach to frame induction and shown that it achieves state-of-the-art results on end-to-end entity extraction in standard MUC and TAC data sets. Our model is inspired by recent advances in unsupervised semantic induction and content modeling in summarization. Our probabilistic approach makes it easy to extend the model with additional linguistic insights and prior knowledge. While we have made a case for unsupervised methods and the importance of robustness across domains, our method is also amenable to semi-supervised or supervised learning if annotated data is available. In future work, we would like to further investigate frame induction evaluation, particularly in evaluating event clustering.

Acknowledgments

We would like to thank Nate Chambers for answering questions about his system. We would also like to thank Chris Quirk for help with preprocessing the MUC corpus, and the members of the NLP group at Microsoft Research for useful discussions.

Appendix A. Hyperparameter Settings

We document below the hyperparameter settings for ProFinder that were used to generate the results in the paper.

Hyperparameter	**MUC**	**TAC**
Number of frames, $\|\mathcal{F}\|$	9	8
Frame stickiness, β	0.125	0.5
Smoothing (frames, events, slots)	0.5	2
Smoothing (emissions)	0.05	0.2
Number of split-merge cycles	4	2
Iterations per cycle	10	10

References

Collin F. Baker, Charles J. Fillmore, and John B. Lowe. 1998. The Berkeley FrameNet project. In *Proceedings of the 17th International Conference on Computational linguistics*.

Michele Banko and Oren Etzioni. 2008. The tradeoffs between open and traditional relation extraction. *Proceedings of ACL-08: HLT*, pages 28–36.

Regina Barzilay and Lillian Lee. 2004. Catching the drift: Probabilistic content models, with applications to generation and summarization. In *Proceedings of the Human Language Technology Conference of the North American Chapter of the Association for Computational Linguistics: HLT-NAACL 2004*.

David Bean and Ellen Riloff. 2004. Unsupervised learning of contextual role knowledge for coreference resolution. In *Proceedings of the Human Language Technology Conference of the North American Chapter of the Association for Computational Linguistics: HLT-NAACL 2004*.

Nathanael Chambers and Dan Jurafsky. 2008. Unsupervised learning of narrative event chains. In *Proceedings of ACL-08: HLT*, pages 789–797, Columbus, Ohio, June. Association for Computational Linguistics.

Nathanael Chambers and Dan Jurafsky. 2009. Unsupervised learning of narrative schemas and their participants. In *Proceedings of the Joint Conference of the 47th Annual Meeting of the ACL and the 4th International Joint Conference on Natural Language Processing of the AFNLP*. Association for Computational Linguistics.

Nathanael Chambers and Dan Jurafsky. 2011. Template-based information extraction without the templates. In *Proceedings of the 49th Annual Meeting of the Association for Computational Linguistics: Human Language Technologies*, pages 976–986, Portland, Oregon, USA, June. Association for Computational Linguistics.

Jackie C. K. Cheung and Xiao Li. 2012. Sequence clustering and labeling for unsupervised query intent discovery. In *Proceedings of the 5th ACM International Conference on Web Search and Data Mining*, pages 383–392.

James R. Curran, Tara Murphy, and Bernhard Scholz. 2007. Minimising semantic drift with mutual exclusion bootstrapping. In *Proceedings of the 10th Conference of the Pacific Association for Computational Linguistics*.

Hal Daumé III and Daniel Marcu. 2006. Bayesian Query-Focused summarization. In *Proceedings of the 21st International Conference on Computational Linguistics and 44th Annual Meeting of the Association for Computational Linguistics*, pages 305–312, Sydney, Australia, July. Association for Computational Linguistics.

Elena Filatova, Vasileios Hatzivassiloglou, and Kathleen McKeown. 2006. Automatic creation of domain templates. In *Proceedings of the COLING/ACL 2006 Main Conference Poster Sessions*, pages 207–214, Sydney, Australia, July. Association for Computational Linguistics.

Charles J. Fillmore. 1982. Frame semantics. *Linguistics in the Morning Calm*, pages 111–137.

David Graff, Junbo Kong, Ke Chen, and Kazuaki Maeda. 2005. English gigaword second edition. *Linguistic Data Consortium, Philadelphia.*

Amit Gruber, Michael Rosen-Zvi, and Yair Weiss. 2007. Hidden topic markov models. *Artificial Intelligence and Statistics (AISTATS).*

Aria Haghighi and Lucy Vanderwende. 2009. Exploring content models for multi-document summarization. In *Proceedings of Human Language Technologies: The 2009 Annual Conference of the North American Chapter of the Association for Computational Linguistics*, pages 362–370, Boulder, Colorado, June. Association for Computational Linguistics.

Ruihong Huang and Ellen Riloff. 2012. Bootstrapped training of event extraction classifiers. In *Proceedings of the 13th Conference of the European Chapter of the Association for Computational Linguistics*, pages 286–295, Avignon, France, April. Association for Computational Linguistics.

Joel Lang and Mirella Lapata. 2011. Unsupervised semantic role induction via split-merge clustering. In *Proceedings of the 49th Annual Meeting of the Association for Computational Linguistics: Human Language Technologies*, pages 1117–1126, Portland, Oregon, USA, June. Association for Computational Linguistics.

Percy Liang and Dan Klein. 2009. Online EM for unsupervised models. In *Proceedings of Human Language Technologies: The 2009 Annual Conference of the North American Chapter of the Association for Computational Linguistics*, pages 611–619, Boulder, Colorado, June. Association for Computational Linguistics.

Marvin Minsky. 1974. A framework for representing knowledge. Technical report, Cambridge, MA, USA.

1992. *Proceedings of the Fourth Message Understanding Conference (MUC-4).* Morgan Kaufmann.

Ani Nenkova and Rebecca Passonneau. 2004. Evaluating content selection in summarization: The pyramid method. In *Proceedings of the Human Language Technology Conference of the North American Chapter of the Association for Computational Linguistics: HLT-NAACL 2004*, volume 2004, pages 145–152.

Karolina Owczarzak and Hoa T. Dang. 2010. TAC 2010 guided summarization task guidelines.

Siddharth Patwardhan and Ellen Riloff. 2007. Effective information extraction with semantic affinity patterns and relevant regions. In *Proceedings of the 2007 Joint Conference on Empirical Methods in Natural Language Processing and Computational Natural Language Learning (EMNLP-CoNLL)*, pages 717–727, Prague, Czech Republic, June. Association for Computational Linguistics.

Slav Petrov, Leon Barrett, Romain Thibaux, and Dan Klein. 2006. Learning accurate, compact, and interpretable tree annotation. In *Proceedings of the 21st International Conference on Computational Linguistics and 44th Annual Meeting of the Association for Computational Linguistics.*

Hoifung Poon and Pedro Domingos. 2009. Unsupervised semantic parsing. In *Proceedings of the 2009 Conference on Empirical Methods in Natural Language Processing*, pages 1–10.

Stephen D. Richardson, William B. Dolan, and Lucy Vanderwende. 1998. MindNet: Acquiring and structuring semantic information from text. In *Proceedings of the 36th Annual Meeting of the Association for Computational Linguistics and 17th International Conference on Computational Linguistics, Volume 2*, pages 1098–1102, Montreal, Quebec, Canada, August. Association for Computational Linguistics.

David Rumelhart, 1975. *Notes on a schema for stories*, pages 211–236. Academic Press, Inc.

Roger C. Schank and Robert P. Abelson. 1977. *Scripts, Plans, Goals, and Understanding: An Inquiry Into Human Knowledge Structures.* Lawrence Erlbaum, July.

Yusuke Shinyama and Satoshi Sekine. 2006. Preemptive information extraction using unrestricted relation discovery. In *Proceedings of the Human Language Technology Conference of the NAACL, Main Conference*, New York City, USA, June. Association for Computational Linguistics.

Robert S. Swier and Suzanne Stevenson. 2004. Unsupervised semantic role labelling. In Dekang Lin and Dekai Wu, editors, *Proceedings of EMNLP 2004*, pages 95–102, Barcelona, Spain, July. Association for Computational Linguistics.

Michael White, Tanya Korelsky, Claire Cardie, Vincent Ng, David Pierce, and Kiri Wagstaff. 2001. Multidocument summarization via information extraction. In *Proceedings of the First International Conference on Human Language Technology Research.* Association for Computational Linguistics.

A Quantum-Theoretic Approach to Distributional Semantics

William Blacoe[1], **Elham Kashefi**[2], **Mirella Lapata**[1]
[1]Institute for Language, Cognition and Computation,
[2]Laboratory for Foundations of Computer Science
School of Informatics, University of Edinburgh, 10 Crichton Street, Edinburgh EH8 9AB
w.b.blacoe@sms.ed.ac.uk, ekashefi@inf.ed.ac.uk, mlap@inf.ed.ac.uk

Abstract

In this paper we explore the potential of quantum theory as a formal framework for capturing lexical meaning. We present a novel semantic space model that is syntactically aware, takes word order into account, and features key quantum aspects such as superposition and entanglement. We define a dependency-based Hilbert space and show how to represent the meaning of words by density matrices that encode dependency neighborhoods. Experiments on word similarity and association reveal that our model achieves results competitive with a variety of classical models.

1 Introduction

The fields of cognitive science and natural language processing have recently produced an ensemble of semantic models which have an impressive track record of replicating human behavior and enabling real-world applications. Examples include simulations of word association (Denhière and Lemaire, 2004; Griffiths et al., 2007), semantic priming (Lund and Burgess, 1996; Landauer and Dumais, 1997; Griffiths et al., 2007), categorization (Laham, 2000), numerous studies of lexicon acquisition (Grefenstette, 1994; Lin, 1998), word sense discrimination (Schütze, 1998), and paraphrase recognition (Socher et al., 2011). The term "semantic" derives from the intuition that words seen in the context of a given word contribute to its meaning (Firth, 1957). Although the specific details of the individual models differ, they all process a corpus of text as input and represent words (or concepts) in a (reduced) high-dimensional space.

In this paper, we explore the potential of quantum theory as a formal framework for capturing lexical meaning and modeling semantic processes such as word similarity and association (see Section 6 for an overview of related research in this area). We use the term *quantum theory* to refer to the abstract mathematical foundation of quantum mechanics which is not specifically tied to physics (Hughes, 1989; Isham, 1989). Quantum theory is in principle applicable in any discipline where there is a need to formalize uncertainty. Indeed, researchers have been pursuing applications in areas as diverse as economics (Baaquie, 2004), information theory (Nielsen and Chuang, 2010), psychology (Khrennikov, 2010; Pothos and Busemeyer, 2012), and cognitive science (Busemeyer and Bruza, 2012; Aerts, 2009; Bruza et al., 2008). But what are the features of quantum theory which make it a promising framework for modeling meaning?

Superposition, entanglement, incompatibility, and interference are all related aspects of quantum theory, which endow it with a unique character.[1] *Superposition* is a way of modeling uncertainty, more so than in classical probability theory. It contains information about the potentialities of a system's state. An electron whose location in an atom is uncertain can be modeled as being in a superposition of locations. Analogously, words in natural language can have multiple meanings. In isolation, the word *pen* may refer to a writing implement, an enclosure for confining livestock, a playpen, a penitentiary or a female swan. However, when observed in the context of the word *ink* the ambiguity resolves into the sense of the word dealing with writing. The meanings of words in a semantic space are superposed in a way which is intuitively similar to the atom's electron.

Entanglement concerns the relationship between

[1]It is outside the scope of the current paper to give a detailed introduction on the history of quantum mechanics. We refer the interested reader to Vedral (2006) and Kleppner and Jackiw (2000) for comprehensive overviews.

systems for which it is impossible to specify a joint probability distribution from the probability distributions of their constituent parts. With regard to word meanings, entanglement encodes (hidden) relationships between concepts. The different senses of a word "exist in parallel" until it is observed in some context. This reduction of ambiguity has effects on other concepts connected via entanglement. The notion of *incompatibility* is fundamental to quantum systems. In classical systems, it is assumed by default that measurements are compatible, that is, independent, and as a result the order in which these take place does not matter. By contrast in quantum theory, measurements may share (hidden) order-sensitive inter-dependencies and the outcome of the first measurement can change the outcome of the second measurement.

Interference is a feature of quantum probability that can cause classical assumptions such as the law of total probability to be violated. When concepts interact their joint representation can exhibit non-classical behavior, e.g., with regard to conjunction and disjunction (Aerts, 2009). An often cited example is the "guppy effect". Although *guppy* is an example of a *pet-fish* it is neither a very typical *pet* nor *fish* (Osherson and Smith, 1981).

In the following we use the rich mathematical framework of quantum theory to model semantic information. Specifically, we show how word meanings can be expressed as quantum states. A word brings with it its own subspace which is spanned by vectors representing its potential usages. We present a specific implementation of a semantic space that is syntactically aware, takes word order into account, and features key aspects of quantum theory. We empirically evaluate our model on word similarity and association and show that it achieves results competitive with a variety of classical models. We begin by introducing some of the mathematical background needed for describing our approach (Section 2). Next, we present our semantic space model (Section 3) and our evaluation experiments (Sections 4 and 5). We conclude by discussing related work (Section 6).

2 Preliminaries

Let $c = re^{i\theta}$ be a complex number, expressed in polar form, with absolute value $r = |c|$ and phase θ. Its complex conjugate $c^* = re^{-i\theta}$ has the inverse phase. Thus, their product $cc^* = (re^{i\theta})(re^{-i\theta}) = r^2$ is real.

2.1 Vectors

We are interested in finite-dimensional, complex-valued vector spaces $\mathbb{C}^n$ with an inner product, otherwise known as Hilbert space. A column vector $\overrightarrow{\psi} \in \mathbb{C}^n$ can be written as an ordered vertical array of its n complex-valued components, or alternatively as a weighted sum of base vectors:

$$\overrightarrow{\psi} = \begin{pmatrix} \psi_1 \\ \psi_2 \\ \vdots \\ \psi_n \end{pmatrix} = \psi_1 \begin{pmatrix} 1 \\ 0 \\ \vdots \\ 0 \end{pmatrix} + \ldots + \psi_n \begin{pmatrix} 0 \\ \vdots \\ 0 \\ 1 \end{pmatrix} \quad (1)$$

Whereas Equation (1) uses base vectors from the standard base $\mathcal{B}_{std} = \{\overrightarrow{b_1}, ..., \overrightarrow{b_n}\}$, any other set of n orthonormal vectors serves just as well as a base for the same space. Dirac (1939) introduced the so-called bra-ket notation which is equally expressive but notationally more convenient. A column vector becomes a ket:

$$\overrightarrow{\psi} \equiv |\psi\rangle = \psi_1|b_1\rangle + \psi_2|b_2\rangle + \ldots + \psi_n|b_n\rangle \quad (2)$$

and a row vector becomes a bra $\langle\psi|$. Transposing a complex-valued vector or matrix (via the superscript "†") involves complex-conjugating all components:

$$|\psi\rangle^\dagger = \langle\psi| = \psi_1^*\langle b_1| + \psi_2^*\langle b_2| + \ldots + \psi_n^*\langle b_n| \quad (3)$$

The Dirac notation for the inner product $\langle\cdot|\cdot\rangle$ illustrates the origin of the terminology "bra-ket". Since $\mathcal{B}_{std}$'s elements are normalised and pairwise orthogonal their inner product is:

$$\langle b_i|b_j\rangle = \begin{cases} 1, & \text{if } i = j \\ 0, & \text{otherwise} \end{cases} \quad (4)$$

The inner product is also applicable to pairs of non-base kets:

$$\begin{aligned} &(\psi_1^* \, \psi_2^* \cdots \psi_n^*) \begin{pmatrix} \phi_1 \\ \phi_2 \\ \vdots \\ \phi_n \end{pmatrix} \equiv \langle\psi|\phi\rangle \\ &= \left(\Sigma_i \psi_i^* \langle b_i|\right)\left(\Sigma_j \phi_j |b_j\rangle\right) \\ &= \Sigma_{i,j} \psi_i^* \phi_j \langle b_i|b_j\rangle = \Sigma_i \psi_i^* \phi_i \langle b_i|b_i\rangle \\ &= \Sigma_i \psi_i^* \phi_i \end{aligned} \quad (5)$$

Reversing the order of an inner product complex-conjugates it:

$$(\langle\psi|\phi\rangle)^* = \langle\phi|\psi\rangle \tag{6}$$

2.2 Matrices

Matrices are sums of outer products $|\cdot\rangle\langle\cdot|$. For example, the matrix $(M_{i,j})_{i,j}$ can be thought of as the weighted sum of "base-matrices" $B_{i,j} \equiv |b_i\rangle\langle b_j|$, whose components are all 0 except for a 1 in the i-th row and j-th column. The outer product extends linearly to non-base kets in the following manor:

$$\begin{aligned} |\psi\rangle\langle\phi| &= (\textstyle\sum_i \psi_i|b_i\rangle)\left(\textstyle\sum_j \phi_j^*\langle b_j|\right) \\ &= \textstyle\sum_{i,j} \psi_i\phi_j^*|b_i\rangle\langle b_j| \end{aligned} \tag{7}$$

This is analogous to the conventional multiplication:

$$\begin{pmatrix} \psi_1 \\ \vdots \\ \psi_n \end{pmatrix} (\phi_1^* \cdots \phi_n^*) = \begin{pmatrix} \psi_1\phi_1^* & \cdots & \psi_1\phi_n^* \\ \vdots & \ddots & \vdots \\ \psi_n\phi_1^* & \cdots & \psi_n\phi_n^* \end{pmatrix} \tag{8}$$

We will also make use of the tensor product. Its application to kets, bras and outer products is linear:

$$\begin{aligned} &(|a\rangle + |b\rangle) \otimes |c\rangle = |a\rangle \otimes |c\rangle + |b\rangle \otimes |c\rangle \\ &(\langle a| + \langle b|) \otimes \langle c| = \langle a| \otimes \langle c| + \langle b| \otimes \langle c| \\ &(|a\rangle\langle b| + |c\rangle\langle d|) \otimes |e\rangle\langle f| = \\ &(|a\rangle \otimes |e\rangle)(\langle b| \otimes \langle f|) + (|c\rangle \otimes |e\rangle)(\langle d| \otimes \langle f|) \end{aligned} \tag{9}$$

For convenience we omit "$\otimes$" where no confusion arises, e.g., $|a\rangle \otimes |b\rangle = |a\rangle|b\rangle$. When applied to Hilbert spaces, the tensor product creates the composed Hilbert space $\mathcal{H} = \mathcal{H}_1 \otimes \ldots \otimes \mathcal{H}_n$ whose base kets are simply induced by the tensor product of its subspaces' base kets:

$$\begin{aligned} &base(\mathcal{H}_1 \otimes \ldots \otimes \mathcal{H}_n) = \\ &\left\{ \bigotimes_{i=1}^{n} |b\rangle_i \ : \ |b\rangle_i \in base(\mathcal{H}_i),\ 1 \leq i \leq n \right\} \end{aligned} \tag{10}$$

Whereas the order of composed kets $|a\rangle|b\rangle|c\rangle$ usually suffices to identify which subket lives in which subspace, we make this explicit by giving subkets the same subscript as the corresponding subspace. Thus, the order no longer matters, as in the following inner product of composed kets:

$$(\langle a|_1\langle b|_2\langle c|_3)(|e\rangle_3|d\rangle_1|f\rangle_2) = \langle a|d\rangle\langle b|f\rangle\langle c|e\rangle \tag{11}$$

Definition 1. *Self-adjoint Matrix*

A matrix M is self-adjoint iff $M_{i,j} = M_{j,i}^*$ for all i, j. Consequently, all diagonal elements are real-valued, and $M = M^\dagger$ is its own transpose conjugate.

Definition 2. *Density Matrix*

A self-adjoint matrix M is a density matrix iff it is positive semi-definite, i.e., $\langle\phi|M|\phi\rangle \geq 0$ for all $|\phi\rangle \in \mathbb{C}^n$, and it has unit trace, i.e., $Tr(M) = \sum_{|b\rangle\in\mathcal{B}} \langle b|M|b\rangle = 1$.

The term "density matrix" is synonymous with "density operator". Any density matrix ρ can be decomposed arbitrarily as $\rho = \sum_i p_i|s_i\rangle\langle s_i|$, the weighted sum of sub-matrices $|s_i\rangle\langle s_i|$ with $p_i \in \mathbb{R}_{>0}$ and $\langle s_i|s_i\rangle = 1$. The p_i need not sum to 1. In fact the decomposition where the p_i sum to 1 and the $|s_i\rangle$ are mutually orthogonal is unique and is called the eigen decomposition. Consequently $\mathcal{B}_{eig} = \{|s_i\rangle\}_i$ constitutes an orthonormal base, ρ's so-called eigen base. Density operators are used in quantum theory to describe the state of some system. If the system's state ρ is certain we call it a pure state and write $\rho = |s\rangle\langle s|$ for some unit ket $|s\rangle$. Systems whose state is uncertain are described by a mixed state $\rho = \sum_i p_i|s_i\rangle\langle s_i|$ which represents an ensemble of substates or pure states $\{(p_i, s_i)\}_i$ where the system is in substate s_i with probability p_i. Hence, the term "density" as in probability density.

It is possible to normalize a density matrix without committing to any particular decomposition. Only the trace function is required, because $norm(\rho) = \rho/Tr(\rho)$. Definition 2 mentions what the trace function does. However, notice that the same result is produced for any orthonormal base $\mathcal{B}$, including ρ's eigen base $\mathcal{B}_{eig} = \{|e_i\rangle\}_i$. Even though we do not know the content of $\mathcal{B}_{eig}$, we know that it exists. So we use it to show that dividing ρ by:

$$
\begin{aligned}
Tr(\rho) &= Tr(\sum_i p_i |e_i\rangle\langle e_i|) \\
&= \sum_j \langle e_j|(\sum_i p_i |e_i\rangle\langle e_i|)|e_j\rangle \\
&= \sum_{i,j} p_i \langle e_j|e_i\rangle\langle e_i|e_j\rangle \\
&= \sum_i p_i \langle e_i|e_i\rangle\langle e_i|e_i\rangle = \sum_i p_i
\end{aligned}
\tag{12}
$$

normalizes its probability distribution over eigen kets:

$$
\begin{aligned}
\frac{\rho}{Tr(\rho)} = \frac{\sum_i p_i |e_i\rangle\langle e_i|}{\sum_j p_j} = \\
\sum_i \frac{p_i}{\sum_j p_j} |e_i\rangle\langle e_i|
\end{aligned}
\tag{13}
$$

3 Semantic Space Model

We represent the meaning of words by density matrices. Specifically, a lexical item w is modeled as an ensemble $U_w = \{(p_i, u_i)\}_i$ of usages u_i and the corresponding probabilities p_i that w gets used "in the i-th manor". A word's usage is comprised of distributional information about its syntactic and semantic preferences, in the form of a ket $|u_i\rangle$. The density matrix $\rho_w = \sum_i p_i |u_i\rangle\langle u_i|$ represents the ensemble U_w. This section explains our method of extracting lexical density matrices from a dependency-parsed corpus. Once density matrices have been learned, we can predict the expected usage similarity of two words as a simple function of their density matrices. Our explication will be formally precise, but at the same time illustrate each principle through a toy example.

3.1 Dependency Hilbert Space

Our model learns the meaning of words from a dependency-parsed corpus. Our experiments have used the Stanford parser (de Marneffe and Manning, 2008), however any other dependency parser with broadly similar output could be used instead. A word's usage is learned from the type of dependency relations it has with its immediate neighbors in dependency graphs. Its semantic content is thus approximated by its "neighborhood", i.e., its co-occurrence frequency with neighboring words.

Neighborhoods are defined by a vocabulary $V = \{w_1, ..., w_{n_V}\}$ of the n_V most frequent (non-stop) words in the corpus. Let $Rel = \{\texttt{sub}^{-1}, \texttt{dobj}^{-1}, \texttt{amod}, \texttt{num}, \texttt{poss}, ...\}$ denote

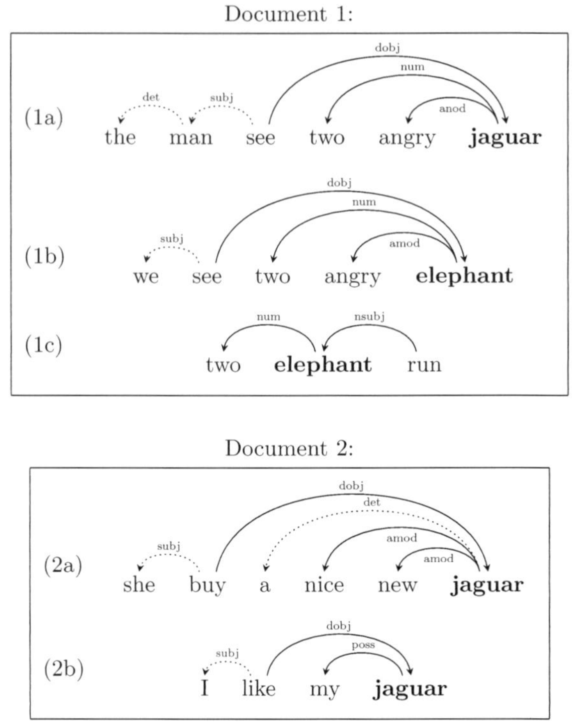

Figure 1: Example dependency trees in a toy corpus. Dotted arcs are ignored because they are either not connected to the target words *jaguar* and *elephant* or because their relation is not taken into account in constructing the semantic space. Words are shown as lemmas.

a subset of all dependency relations provided by the parser and their inverses. The choice of *Rel* is a model parameter. We considered only the most frequently occuring relations above a certain threshold, which turned out to be about half of the full inventory. Relation symbols with the superscript "$^{-1}$" indicate the inversion of the dependency direction (dependent to head). All other relation symbols have the conventional direction (head to dependent). Hence, $w \xrightarrow{\texttt{xyz}} v$ is equivalent to $v \xrightarrow{\texttt{xyz}^{-1}} w$. We then partition *Rel* into disjoint clusters of syntactically similar relations $Part = \{RC_1, ..., RC_{n_{Part}}\}$. For example, we consider syntactically similar relations which connect target words with neighbors with the same part of speech. Each relation cluster RC_k is assigned a Hilbert space $\mathcal{H}_k$ whose base kets $\{|w_j^{(k)}\rangle\}_j$ correspond to the words in $V = \{w_j\}_j$.

Figure 1 shows the dependency parses for a toy corpus consisting of two documents and five sentences. To create a density matrix for the target words *jaguar* and *elephant*, let us assume that we will consider the following relation clusters: $RC_1 = \{\texttt{dobj}^{-1}, \texttt{iobj}^{-1}, \texttt{agent}^{-1}, \texttt{nsubj}^{-1}, ...\}$, $RC_2 = \{\texttt{advmod}, \texttt{amod}, \texttt{tmod}, ...\}$ and $RC_3 = \{\texttt{nn}, \texttt{appos}, \texttt{num}, \texttt{poss}, ...\}$.

3.2 Mapping from Dependency Graphs to Kets

Next, we create kets which encode syntactic and semantic relations as follows. For each occurrence of the target word w in a dependency graph, we only consider the subtree made up of w and the immediate neighbors connected to it via a relation in Rel. In Figure 1, arcs from the dependency parse that we ignore are shown as dotted. Let the subtree of interest be $st = \{(RC_1, v_1), ..., (RC_{n_{Part}}, v_{n_{Part}})\}$, that is, w is connected to v_k via some relation in RC_k, for $k \in \{1, ..., n_{Part}\}$. For any relation cluster RC_k that does not feature in the subtree, let RC_k be paired with the abstract symbol $w_\emptyset$ in st. This symbol represents uncertainty about a potential RC_k-neighbor.

We convert all subtrees st in the corpus for the target word w into kets $|\psi_{st}\rangle \in \mathcal{H}_1 \otimes ... \otimes \mathcal{H}_{n_{Part}}$. These in turn make up the word's density matrix ρ_w. Before we do so, we assign each relation cluster RC_k a complex value $\alpha_k = e^{i\theta_k}$. The idea behind these values is to control for how much each subtree contributes to the overall density matrix. This becomes more apparent after we formulate our method of inducing usage kets and density matrices.

$$|\psi_{st}\rangle = \alpha_{st} \bigotimes_{(RC_k, v) \in st} |v\rangle_k, \qquad (14)$$

where $\alpha_{st} = \sum_{(RC_k, v) \in st, v \neq w_\emptyset} \alpha_k$. Every RC_k paired with some neighbor $v \in V$ induces a basic subket $|v\rangle_k \in base(\mathcal{H}_k)$, i.e., a base ket of the k-th subspace or subsystem. All other subkets $|w_\emptyset\rangle_k = \sum_{v \in V} |V|^{-\frac{1}{2}} |v\rangle_k$ are in a uniformly weighted superposition of all base kets. The factor $|V|^{-\frac{1}{2}}$ ensures that $\langle w_\emptyset | w_\emptyset \rangle = 1$. The composed ket for the subtree st is again weighted by the complex-valued α_{st}.

α_{st} is the sum of complex values $\alpha_k = e^{i\theta_k}$, each with absolute value 1. Therefore, its own absolute value depends highly on the relative orientation θ_k among its summands: equal phases reinforce absolute value, but the more phases are opposed (i.e., their difference approaches π), the more they cancel out the sum's absolute value. Only those α_k contribute to this sum whose relation cluster is not paired with $w_\emptyset$. The choice of the parameters θ_k allows us to put more weight on some combinations of dependency relations than others.

(a)

	$\langle\psi_{st_1}\vert$	$\langle\psi_{st_2}\vert$	$\langle\psi_{st_3}\vert$
$\vert\psi_{st_1}\rangle$	$\neq 0$	$\neq 0$	$\neq 0$
$\vert\psi_{st_2}\rangle$	$\neq 0$	$\neq 0$	$\neq 0$
$\vert\psi_{st_3}\rangle$	$\neq 0$	$\neq 0$	$\neq 0$

(b)

	$\langle\psi_{st_1}\vert$	$\langle\psi_{st_2}\vert$	$\langle\psi_{st_3}\vert$
$\vert\psi_{st_1}\rangle$	$\neq 0$	0	0
$\vert\psi_{st_2}\rangle$	0	$\neq 0$	0
$\vert\psi_{st_3}\rangle$	0	0	$\neq 0$

Figure 2: Excerpts of density matrices that result from the dependency subtrees st_1, st_2, st_3. Element $m_{i,j}$ in row i and column j is $m_{i,j}|\psi_{st_i}\rangle\langle\psi_{st_j}|$ in Dirac notation. (a) All three subtrees are in the same document. Thus their kets contribute to diagonal and off-diagonal matrix elements. (b) Each subtree is in a separate document. Therefore their kets do not group, affecting only diagonal matrix elements.

Arbitrarily choosing $\theta_1 = \frac{\pi}{4}$, $\theta_2 = \frac{7\pi}{4}$, and $\theta_3 = \frac{3\pi}{4}$ renders the subtrees in Figure 1 as $|\psi_{st_{1a}}\rangle = e^{i\pi/4}|see\rangle_1|angry\rangle_2|two\rangle_3$, $|\psi_{st_{2a}}\rangle = \sqrt{2}|buy\rangle_1(|nice\rangle_2 + |new\rangle_2)|w_\emptyset\rangle_3$, $|\psi_{st_{2b}}\rangle = \sqrt{2}e^{i\pi/2}|like\rangle_1|w_\emptyset\rangle_2|my\rangle_3$, which are relevant for *jaguar*, and $|\psi_{st_{1b}}\rangle = e^{i\pi/4}|see\rangle_1|angry\rangle_2|two\rangle_3$, $|\psi_{st_{1c}}\rangle = \sqrt{2}e^{i\pi/2}|run\rangle_1|w_\emptyset\rangle_2|two\rangle_3$, which are relevant for *elephant*. The subscripts outside of the subkets correspond to those of the relation clusters RC_1, RC_2, RC_3 chosen in Section 3.1.

In sentence 2a, *jaguar* has two neighbors under RC_2. Therefore the subket from $\mathcal{H}_2$ is a superposition of the base kets $|nice\rangle_2$ and $|new\rangle_2$. This is a more intuitive formulation of the equivalent approach which first splits the subtree for *buy nice new jaguar* into two similar subtrees for *buy nice jaguar* and for *buy new jaguar*, and then processes them as seperate subtrees within the same document.

3.3 Creating Lexical Density Matrices

We assume that a word's usage is uniform throughout the same document. In our toy corpus in Figure 1, *jaguar* is always the direct object of the main verb. However, in Document 1 it is used in the animal sense, whereas in Document 2 it is used in the car sense. Even though the usage of *jaguar* in sentence (2b) is ambiguous, we group it with that of sentence (2a).

These considerations can all be comfortably en-

$$\rho_{jaguar} = (|\psi_{st_{1a}}\rangle\langle\psi_{st_{1a}}| + (|\psi_{st_{2a}}\rangle + |\psi_{st_{2b}}\rangle)(\langle\psi_{st_{2a}}| + \langle\psi_{st_{2b}}|))/7 =$$
$$0.14|see\rangle_1|angry\rangle_2|two\rangle_3\langle see|_1\langle angry|_2\langle two|_3 + 0.29|buy\rangle_1|nice\rangle_2|w_\emptyset\rangle_3\langle buy|_1\langle nice|_2\langle w_\emptyset|_3 +$$
$$0.29|buy\rangle_1|nice\rangle_2|w_\emptyset\rangle_3\langle buy|_1\langle new|_2\langle w_\emptyset|_3 + 0.29|buy\rangle_1|new\rangle_2|w_\emptyset\rangle_3\langle buy|_1\langle nice|_2\langle w_\emptyset|_3 +$$
$$0.29|buy\rangle_1|new\rangle_2|w_\emptyset\rangle_3\langle buy|_1\langle new|_2\langle w_\emptyset|_3 + 0.29e^{\pi/2}|like\rangle_1|w_\emptyset\rangle_2|my\rangle_3\langle buy|_1\langle nice|_2\langle w_\emptyset|_3 +$$
$$0.29e^{\pi/2}|like\rangle_1|w_\emptyset\rangle_2|my\rangle_3\langle buy|_1\langle new|_2\langle w_\emptyset|_3 + 0.29e^{-\pi/2}|buy\rangle_1|nice\rangle_2|w_\emptyset\rangle_3\langle like|_1\langle w_\emptyset|_2\langle my|_3 +$$
$$0.29e^{-\pi/2}|buy\rangle_1|new\rangle_2|w_\emptyset\rangle_3\langle like|_1\langle w_\emptyset|_2\langle my|_3 + 0.29|like\rangle_1|w_\emptyset\rangle_2|my\rangle_3\langle like|_1\langle w_\emptyset|_2\langle my|_3$$

$$\rho_{elephant} = ((|\psi_{st_{1b}}\rangle + |\psi_{st_{1c}}\rangle)(\langle\psi_{st_{1b}}| + \langle\psi_{st_{1c}}|))/3 =$$
$$0.33|see\rangle_1|angry\rangle_2|two\rangle_3\langle see|_1\langle angry|_2\langle two|_3 + 0.47e^{\pi/4}|run\rangle_1|w_\emptyset\rangle_2|two\rangle_3\langle see|_1\langle angry|_2\langle two|_3 +$$
$$0.47e^{-\pi/4}|see\rangle_1|angry\rangle_2|two\rangle_3\langle run|_1\langle w_\emptyset|_2\langle two|_3 + 0.67|run\rangle_1|w_\emptyset\rangle_2|two\rangle_3\langle run|_1\langle w_\emptyset|_2\langle two|_3$$

$$Tr(\rho_{jaguar}\rho_{elephant}) = Tr(0.05|\psi_{st_{1a}}\rangle\langle\psi_{st_{1b}}| + 0.05e^{i\pi/4}|\psi_{st_{1a}}\rangle\langle\psi_{st_{1c}}|) = Tr(0.05|see\rangle_1|angry\rangle_2|two\rangle_3\langle see|_1\langle angry|_2\langle two|_3 +$$
$$0.07e^{-\pi/4}|see\rangle_1|angry\rangle_2|two\rangle_3\langle run|_1\langle w_\emptyset|_2\langle two|_3) = \sum_{|b\rangle\in base(\mathcal{H}_1\otimes\mathcal{H}_2\otimes\mathcal{H}_3)} \langle b|(0.05|see\rangle_1|angry\rangle_2|two\rangle_3\langle see|_1\langle angry|_2\langle two|_3 +$$
$$0.07e^{-\pi/4}|see\rangle_1|angry\rangle_2|two\rangle_3\langle run|_1\langle w_\emptyset|_2\langle two|_3)|b\rangle = 0.05$$

Figure 3: Lexical density matrices for the words *jaguar* and *elephant* and their similarity.

coded in a density matrix. This is simply generated via the outer product of our subtree kets $|\psi_{st}\rangle$. For example, $\rho_{D_1,jaguar} = |\psi_{st_{1a}}\rangle\langle\psi_{st_{1a}}|$ represents the contribution that document D_1 makes to ρ_{jaguar}. Document D_2, however, has more than one ket relevant to ρ_{jaguar}. Due to our assumption of document-internal uniformity of word usage, we group D_2's subtree-kets additively: $\rho_{D_2,jaguar} = (|\psi_{st_{2a}}\rangle + |\psi_{st_{2b}}\rangle)(\langle\psi_{st_{2a}}| + \langle\psi_{st_{2b}}|)$. The target word's density matrix ρ_w is the normalized sum of all density matrices $\rho_{D,w}$ obtained from each D:

$$\rho_{D,w} = \left(\sum_{st\in ST_{D,w}} |\psi_{st}\rangle\right)\left(\sum_{st\in ST_{D,w}} \langle\psi_{st}|\right) \quad (15)$$

where $ST_{D,w}$ is the set of all subtrees for target word w in document D. To illustrate the difference that this grouping makes, consider the density matrices in Figure 2. Whereas in (a) the subtrees st_1, st_2, st_3 share a document, in (b) they are from distinct documents. This grouping causes them to not only contribute to diagonal matrix elements, e.g., $|\psi_{st_2}\rangle\langle\psi_{st_2}|$, as in (b), but also to off diagonal ones, e.g., $|\psi_{st_2}\rangle\langle\psi_{st_1}|$, as in (a).

Over the course of many documents the summation of all contributions, no matter how small or large the groups are, causes "clusters of weight" to form, which hopefully coincide with word usages. As mentioned in Section 3.2, adding complex-valued matrix elements increases or decreases the sum's absolute value depending on relative phase orientation. This makes it possible for interference to occur. Since the same word appears in varying contexts, the corresponding complex-valued outer products interact upon summation. Finally, the density matrix gets normalized, i.e., divided by its trace. This leaves the distributional information intact and merely normalizes the probabilities. Figure 3 illustrates the estimation of the density matrices for the words *jaguar* and *elephant* from the toy corpus in Figure 1.

3.4 Usage Similarity

Decomposing the density matrix of the target word w, $\rho_w = \sum_i p_i|u_i\rangle\langle u_i|$ recovers the usage ensemble $U_w = \{(p_i, u_i)\}_i$. However, in general there are infinitely many possible ensembles which ρ_w might represent. This subsection explains our metric for estimating the usage similarity of two words. The math involved shows that we can avoid the question of how to best decompose ρ_w.

We compute the usage similarity of two words w and v by comparing each usage of w with each usage of v and weighting these similarity values with the corresponding usage probabilities. Let $\rho_w = \sum_i p_i^{(w)}|u_i^{(w)}\rangle\langle u_i^{(w)}|$ and $\rho_v = \sum_i p_i^{(v)}|u_i^{(v)}\rangle\langle u_i^{(v)}|$. The similarity of some usage kets $|u_i^{(w)}\rangle$ and $|u_j^{(v)}\rangle$ is obtained, as is common in the literature, by their inner product $\langle u_i^{(w)}|u_j^{(v)}\rangle$. However, as this is a complex value, we multiply it with its complex conjugate, rendering the real value $\langle u_j^{(v)}|u_i^{(w)}\rangle\langle u_i^{(w)}|u_j^{(v)}\rangle = |\langle u_i^{(w)}|u_j^{(v)}\rangle|^2$. Therefore, in total the expected similarity of w and v is:

$$sim(w,v) = \sum_{i,j} p_i^{(w)} p_j^{(v)} \langle u_j^{(v)} | u_i^{(w)} \rangle \langle u_i^{(w)} | u_j^{(v)} \rangle \quad (16)$$

$$= Tr\left(\sum_{i,j} p_i^{(w)} p_j^{(v)} |u_i^{(w)}\rangle \langle u_i^{(w)} | u_j^{(v)} \rangle \langle u_j^{(v)}| \right) =$$

$$Tr\left((\sum_i p_i^{(w)} |u_i^{(w)}\rangle \langle u_i^{(w)}|)(\sum_j p_j^{(v)} |u_j^{(v)}\rangle \langle u_j^{(v)}|) \right)$$

$$= Tr(\rho_w \rho_v)$$

We see that the similarity function simply reduces to multiplying ρ_w with ρ_v and applying the trace function. The so-called cyclic property of the trace function (i.e., $Tr(M_1M_2) = Tr(M_2M_1)$ for any two matrices M_1, M_2) gives us the corollary that this particular similarity function is symmetric.

Figure 3 (bottom) shows how to calculate the similarity of *jaguar* and *elephant*. Only the coefficient of the first outer product survives the tracing process because its ket and bra are equal modulo transpose conjugate. As for the second outer product, $0.05e^{i\pi/4}\langle b|\psi_{st_{1a}}\rangle\langle\psi_{st_{1c}}|b\rangle$ is 0 for all base kets $|b\rangle$.

3.5 What Does This Achieve?

We represent word meanings as described above for several reasons. The density matrix decomposes into usages each of which are a superposition of combinations of dependents. Internally, these usages are established automatically by way of "clustering".

Our model is parameterized with regard to the phases of sub-systems (i.e., clusters of syntactic relations) which allows us to make optimal use of interference, as this plays a large role in the overall quality of representation. It is possible for a combination of (groups of) dependents to get entangled if they repeatedly appear together under the same word, and only in that combination. If the co-occurence of (groups of) dependents is uncorrelated, though, they remain unentangled. Quantum entanglement gives our semantic structures the potential for long-distance effects, once quantum measurement becomes involved. This is in analogy to the nonlocal correlation between properties of subatomic particles, such as the magnetic spin of electrons or the polarization of photons. Such an extension to our implementation will also uncover which sets of measurements are order-sensitive, i.e., incompatible.

Our similarity metric allows two words to "select" each other's usages via their pairwise inner products. Usage pairs with a high distributional similarity roughly "align" and then get weighted by the probabilities of those usages. Two words are similar if they are substitutable, that is, if they can be used in the same syntactic environment and have the same meaning. Hopefully, this leads to more accurate estimation of distributional similarity and can be used to compute word meaning in context.

4 Experimental Setup

Data All our experiments used a dependency parsed and lemmatized version of the British National Corpus (BNC). As mentioned in Section 3, we obtained dependencies from the output of the Stanford parser (de Marneffe and Manning, 2008). The BNC comprises 4,049 texts totalling approximately 100 million words.

Evaluation Tasks We evaluated our model on word similarity and association. Both tasks are employed routinely to assess how well semantic models predict human judgments of word relatedness. We used the WordSim353 test collection (Finkelstein et al., 2002) which consists of similarity judgments for word pairs. Participants gave each pair a similarity rating using a 0 to 10 scale (e.g., *tiger–cat* are very similar, whereas *delay–racism* are not). The average rating for each pair represents an estimate of the perceived similarity of the two words. The collection contains ratings for 437 unique words (353 pairs) all of which appeared in our corpus. Word association is a slightly different task: Participants are given a cue word (e.g., *rice*) and asked to name an associate in response (e.g., *Chinese, wedding, food, white*). We used the norms collected by Nelson et al. (1998). We estimated the strength of association between a cue and its associate, as the relative frequency with which it was named. The norms contain 9,968 unique words (70,739 pairs) out of which 9,862 were found in our corpus, excluding multiword expressions.

For both tasks, we used correlation analysis to examine the degree of linear relationship between human ratings and model similarity values. We report correlation coefficients using Spearman's rank correlation coefficient.

Quantum Model Parameters The quantum framework presented in Section 3 is quite flexible. Depending on the choice of dependency relations *Rel*, dependency clusters RC_j, and complex values $\alpha_j = e^{i\theta_j}$, different classes of models can be derived. To explore these parameters, we partitioned the WordSim353 dataset and Nelson et al.'s (1998) norms into a development and test set following a 70–30 split. We tested 9 different intuitively chosen relation partitions $\{RC_1, ..., RC_{n_{Part}}\}$, creating models that considered only neighboring heads, models that considered only neighboring dependents, and models that considered both. For the latter two we experimented with partitions of one, two or three clusters. In addition to these more coarse grained clusters, for models that included both heads and dependents we explored a partition with twelve clusters broadly corresponding to objects, subjects, modifiers, auxiliaries, determiners and so on. In all cases stopwords were not taken into account in the construction of the semantic space.

For each model variant we performed a grid search over the possible phases $\theta_j = k\pi$ with range $k = \frac{0}{4}, \frac{1}{4}, ..., \frac{7}{4}$ for the complex-valued α_j assigned to the respective relation cluster RC_j (see Section 3.2 for details). In general, we observed that the choice of dependency relations and their clustering as well as the phases assigned to each cluster greatly influenced the semantic space. On both tasks, the best performing model had the relation partition described in Section 3.1. Section 5 reports our results on the test set using this model.

Comparison Models We compared our quantum space against three classical distributional models. These include a simple semantic space, where a word's meaning is a vector of co-occurrences with neighboring words (Mitchell and Lapata, 2010), a syntax-aware space based on weighted distributional triples that encode typed co-occurrence relations among words (Baroni and Lenci, 2010) and word embeddings computed with a neural language model (Bengio, 2001; Collobert and Weston, 2008) For all three models we used parameters that have been reported in the literature as optimal.

Specifically, for the simple co-occurrence-based space we follow the settings of Mitchell and Lapata (2010): a context window of five words on either side of the target word and 2,000 vector dimensions (i.e., the 2000 most common context words in the BNC). Vector components were set to the ratio of the probability of the context word given the target word to the probability of the context word overall. For the neural language model, we adopted the best performing parameters from our earlier comparison of different vector sources for distributional semantics (Blacoe and Lapata, 2012) where we also used the BNC for training. There we obtained best results with 50 dimensions, a context window of size 4, and an embedding learning rate of 10^{-9}. Our third comparison model uses Baroni and Lenci's (2010) third-order tensor[2] which they obtained from a very large dependency-parsed corpus containing approximately 2.3 billion words. Their tensor assigns a mutual information score to instances of word pairs w, v and a linking word l. We obtained vectors $\overrightarrow{w}$ from the tensor following the methodology proposed in Blacoe and Lapata (2012) using 100 (l, v) contexts as dimensions.

Models	WordSim353	Nelson Norms
SDS	0.433	0.151
DM	0.318	0.123
NLM	0.196	0.091
QM	**0.535**	**0.185**

Table 1: Performance of distributional models on WordSim353 dataset and Nelson et al.'s (1998) norms (test set). Correlation coefficients are all statistically significant ($p < 0.01$).

5 Results

Our results are summarized in Table 1. As can be seen, the quantum model (QM) obtains performance superior to other better-known models such as Mitchell and Lapata's (2010) simple semantic space (SDS), Baroni and Lenci's (2010) distributional memory tensor (DM), and Collobert and Weston's (2008) neural language model (NLM). Our results on the association norms are comparable to the state of the art (Silberer and Lapata, 2012; Griffiths et al., 2007). With regard to WordSim353, Huang et al. (2012) report correlations in the range of 0.713–0.769, however they use Wikipedia as a training corpus and a more sophisticated version of the NLM presented here, that takes into account global context and performs word sense discrimination. In the future, we also plan to evaluate our model on larger Wikipedia-scale corpora. We would also like to model semantic composition as our approach can do this easily by taking advantage of the notion of quantum measurement. Specifically, we

[2] Available at http://clic.cimec.unitn.it/dm/.

Models	bar	order
SDS	pub, snack, restaurant, grill, coctail	form, direct, procedure, plan, request
DM	counter, rack, strip, pipe, code	court, demand, form, law, list
NLM	room, pole, drink, rail, coctail	direct, command, plan, court, demand
QM	prison, liquor, beer, club, graph	organization, food, law, structure, regulation
HS	drink, beer, stool, alcohol, grill	food, form, law, heat, court

Table 2: Associates for *bar* and *order* ranked according to similarity. Underlined associates overlap with the human responses (HS).

can work out the meaning of a dependency tree by measuring the meaning of its heads in the context of their dependents.

Table 2 shows the five most similar associates (ordered from high to low) for the cues *bar* and *order* for the quantum model and the comparison models. We also show the human responses (HS) according to Nelson et al.'s (1998) norms. The associates generated by the quantum model correspond to several different meanings correlated with the target. For example, *prison* refers to the "behind bars" sense of *bar*, *liquor* and *beer* refer to what is consumed or served in bars, *club* refers to the entertainment function of bars, whereas *graph* refers to how data is displayed in a chart.

6 Related Work

Within cognitive science the formal apparatus of quantum theory has been used to formulate models of cognition that are superior to those based on traditional probability theory. For example, conjunction fallacies[3] (Tversky and Kahneman, 1983) have been explained by making reference to quantum theory's context dependence of the probability assessment. Violations of the sure-thing principle[4] (Tversky and Shafir, 1992) have been modeled in terms of a quantum interference effect. And the asymmetry of similarity relations has been explained by postulating that different concepts correspond to subspaces of different dimensionality (Pothos and Busemeyer, 2012). Several approaches have drawn on quantum theory in order to model semantic phenomena such as concept combination (Bruza and Cole, 2005), the emergence of new concepts (Aerts and Gabora, 2005), and the human mental lexicon (Bruza et al., 2009). Chen (2002) captures syllogisms in a quantum theoretic framework; the model takes statements like *All whales are mammals and all mammals are animals* as input and outputs conclusions like *All whales are animals*.

The first attempts to connect the mathematical basis of semantic space models with quantum theory are due to Aerts and Czachor (2004) and Bruza and Cole (2005). They respectively demonstrate that Latent Semantic Analysis (Landauer and Dumais, 1997) and the Hyperspace Analog to Language model (Lund and Burgess, 1996) are essentially Hilbert space formalisms, without, however, providing concrete ways of building these models beyond a few hand-picked examples. Interestingly, Bruza and Cole (2005) show how lexical operators may be contrived from corpus co-occurrence counts, albeit admitting to the fact that their operators do not provide sensical eigenkets, most likely because of the simplified method of populating the matrix from corpus statistics. Grefenstette et al. (2011) present a model for capturing semantic composition in a quantum theoretical context, although it appears to be reducible to the classical probabilistic paradigm. It does not make use of the unique aspects of quantum theory (e.g., entanglement, interference, or quantum collapse).

Our own work follows Aerts and Czachor (2004) and Bruza and Cole (2005) in formulating a model that exhibits important aspects of quantum theory. Contrary to them, we present a fully-fledged semantic space rather than a proof-of-concept. We obtain quantum states (i.e., lexical representations) for each word by taking its *syntactic* context into account. Quantum states are expressed as density operators rather than kets. While a ket can only capture one pure state of a system, a density operator contains an ensemble of pure states which we argue is advantageous from a modeling perspective. Within this framework, not only can we compute the meaning of individual words but also phrases or sentences, without postulating any additional operations. Compositional meaning reduces to quantum measurement at each inner node of the (dependency) parse of the structure in question.

[3] A conjunction fallacy occurs when it is assumed that specific conditions are more probable than a single general one.

[4] The principle is the expectation that human behavior ought to conform to the law of total probability

References

Diederik Aerts and Marek Czachor. 2004. Quantum aspects of semantic analysis and symbolic artificial intelligence. *Journal of PhysicsA: Mathematical and General*, 37:123–132.

Diederik Aerts and Liane Gabora. 2005. A state-context-property model of concepts and their combinations ii: A hilbert space representation. *Kybernetes*, 1-2(34):192–221.

Diederik Aerts. 2009. Quantum structure in cognition. *Journal of Mathematical Psychology*, 53:314–348.

Belal E. Baaquie. 2004. *Quantum Finance: Path Integrals and Hamiltonians for Oprions and Interest Rates*. Cambridge University Press, Cambridge.

Marco Baroni and Alessandro Lenci. 2010. Distributional memory: A general framework for corpus-based semantics. *Computational Linguistics*, 36(4):673–721.

Yoshua Bengio. 2001. Neural net language models. *Scholarpedia*, 3(1):3881.

William Blacoe and Mirella Lapata. 2012. A comparison of vector-based representations for semantic composition. In *Proceedings of the 2012 Joint Conference on Empirical Methods in Natural Language Processing and Computational Natural Language Learning*, pages 546–556, Jeju Island, Korea, July. Association for Computational Linguistics.

Peter D. Bruza and Richard J. Cole. 2005. Quantum logic of semantic space: An exploratory investigation of context effects in practical reasoning. In S. Artemov, H. Barringer, S. A. d'Avila Garcez, L. C. Lamb, and J. Woods, editors, *We Will Show Them: Essays in Honour of Dov Gabbay*, volume 1, pages 339–361. London: College Publications.

Peter D. Bruza, Kirsty Kitto, Douglas McEnvoy, and Cathy McEnvoy. 2008. Entangling words and meaning. In *Second Quantum Interaction Symposium*. Oxford University.

Peter D. Bruza, Kirsty Kitto, Douglas Nelson, and Cathy McEvoy. 2009. Is there something quantum-like in the human mental lexicon? *Journal of Mathematical Psychology*, 53(5):362–377.

Jerome R. Busemeyer and Peter D. Bruza. 2012. *Quantum Models of Cognition and Decision*. Cambridge University Press, Cambridge.

Joseph C. H. Chen. 2002. *Quantum computation and natural language processing*. Ph.D. thesis, Universität Hamburg.

Ronan Collobert and Jason Weston. 2008. A unified architecture for natural language processing: deep neural networks with multita sk learning. In *Proceedings of the 25th International Conference on Machine Learning*, pages 160–167, New York, NY. ACM.

Marie-Catherine de Marneffe and Christopher D. Manning. 2008. The Stanford typed dependencies representation. In *Coling 2008: Proceedings of the workshop on Cross-Framework and Cross-Domain Parser Evaluation*, pages 1–8, Manchester, UK.

Guy Denhière and Benoît Lemaire. 2004. A computational model of children's semantic memory. In *Proceedings of the 26th Annual Meeting of the Cognitive Science Society*, pages 297–302, Mahwah, NJ. Lawrence Erlbaum Associates.

Paul A. M. Dirac. 1939. A new notation for quantum mechanics. *Mathematical Proceedings of the Cambridge Philosophical Society*, 35:416–418.

Lev Finkelstein, Evgeniy Gabrilovich, Yossi Matias, Ehud Rivlin, Zach Solan, Gadi Wolfman, and Eytan Ruppin. 2002. Placing Search in Context: The Concept Revisited. *ACM Transactions on Information Systems*, 20(1):116–131, January.

John R. Firth. 1957. A synopsis of linguistic theory 1930-1955. In *Studies in Linguistic Analysis*, pages 1–32. Philological Society, Oxford.

Edward Grefenstette, Mehrnoosh Sadrzadeh, Stephen Clark, Bob Coecke, and Stephen Pulman. 2011. Concrete sentence spaces for compositional distributional models of meaning. *Proceedings of the 9th International Conference on Computational Semantics (IWCS11)*, pages 125–134.

Gregory Grefenstette. 1994. *Explorations in Automatic Thesaurus Discovery*. Kluwer Academic Publishers.

Thomas L. Griffiths, Mark Steyvers, and Joshua B. Tenenbaum. 2007. Topics in semantic representation. *Psychological Review*, 114(2):211–244.

Eric Huang, Richard Socher, Christopher Manning, and Andrew Ng. 2012. Improving word representations via global context and multiple word prototypes. In *Proceedings of the 50th Annual Meeting of the Association for Computational Linguistics (Volume 1: Long Papers)*, pages 873–882, Jeju Island, Korea, July. Association for Computational Linguistics.

R. I. G. Hughes. 1989. *The Structure and Interpretation of Quantum Mechnics*. Harvard University Press, Cambridge, MA.

Chris J. Isham. 1989. *Lectures on Quantum Theory*. Singapore: World Scientific.

Andrei Y. Khrennikov. 2010. *Ubiquitous Quantum Structure: From Psychology to Finance*. Springer.

Daniel Kleppner and Roman Jackiw. 2000. One hundred years of quantum physics. *Science*, 289(5481):893–898.

Darrell R. Laham. 2000. *Automated Content Assessment of Text Using Latent Semantic Analysis to Simulate Human Cognition*. Ph.D. thesis, University of Colorado at Boulder.

Thomas K. Landauer and Susan T. Dumais. 1997. A solution to Plato's problem: the latent semantic analysis theory of acquisition, induction and representation of knowledge. *Psychological Review*, 104(2):211–240.

Dekang Lin. 1998. Automatic retrieval and clustering of similar words. In *Proceedings of the joint Annual Meeting of the Association for Computational Linguistics and International Conference on Computational Linguistics*, pages 768–774, Montréal, Canada.

Kevin Lund and Curt Burgess. 1996. Producing high-dimensional semantic spaces from lexical co-occurrence. *Behavior Research Methods, Instruments & Computers*, 28:203–208.

Jeff Mitchell and Mirella Lapata. 2010. Composition in distributional models of semantics. *Cognitive Science*, 38(8):1388–1429.

Douglas L. Nelson, Cathy L. McEvoy, and Thomas A. Schreiber. 1998. The University of South Florida Word Association, Rhyme, and Word Fragment Norms.

Michael A. Nielsen and Isaac L. Chuang. 2010. *Quantum Computation and Information Theory*. Cambridge University Press, Cambridge.

Daniel Osherson and Edward E. Smith. 1981. On the adequacy of prototype theory as a theory of concepts. *Cognition*, 9:35–38.

Emmanuel M. Pothos and Jerome R. Busemeyer. 2012. Can quantum probability provide a new direction for cognitive modeling? *Behavioral and Brain Sciences*. to appear.

Hinrich Schütze. 1998. Automatic word sense discrimination. *Computational Linguistics*, 24(1):97–124.

Carina Silberer and Mirella Lapata. 2012. Grounded models of semantic representation. In *Proceedings of the 2012 Joint Conference on Empirical Methods in Natural Language Processing and Computational Natural Language Learning*, pages 1423–1433, Jeju Island, Korea. Association for Computational Linguistics.

Richard Socher, Eric H. Huang, Jeffrey Pennin, Andrew Y. Ng, and Christopher D. Manning. 2011. Dynamic pooling and unfolding recursive autoencoders for paraphrase detection. In J. Shawe-Taylor, R.S. Zemel, P. Bartlett, F.C.N. Pereira, and K.Q. Weinberger, editors, *Advances in Neural Information Processing Systems 24*, pages 801–809.

Amos Tversky and Daniel Kahneman. 1983. Extensional versus intuitive reasoning: The conjuctive fallacy in probability judgment. *Psychological Review*, 4(90):293–315.

Amos Tversky and Eldar Shafir. 1992. The disjunction effect in choice under uncertainty. *Psychological Science*, 3(5):305–309.

Vlatko Vedral. 2006. *Introduction to Quantum Information Science*. Oxford University Press, New York.

Answer Extraction as Sequence Tagging with Tree Edit Distance

Xuchen Yao and **Benjamin Van Durme**
Johns Hopkins University
Baltimore, MD, USA

Chris Callison-Burch*
University of Pennsylvania
Philadelphia, PA, USA

Peter Clark
Vulcan Inc.
Seattle, WA, USA

Abstract

Our goal is to extract answers from pre-retrieved sentences for Question Answering (QA). We construct a linear-chain Conditional Random Field based on pairs of questions and their possible answer sentences, learning the association between questions and answer types. This casts answer extraction as an answer sequence tagging problem for the first time, where knowledge of shared structure between question and source sentence is incorporated through features based on Tree Edit Distance (TED). Our model is free of manually created question and answer templates, fast to run (processing 200 QA pairs per second excluding parsing time), and yields an F1 of 63.3% on a new public dataset based on prior TREC QA evaluations. The developed system is open-source, and includes an implementation of the TED model that is state of the art in the task of ranking QA pairs.

1 Introduction

The success of IBM's Watson system for Question Answering (QA) (Ferrucci et al., 2010) has illustrated a continued public interest in this topic. Watson is a sophisticated piece of software engineering consisting of many components tied together in a large parallel architecture. It took many researchers working full time for years to construct. Such resources are not available to individual academic researchers. If they are interested in evaluating new ideas on some aspect of QA, they must either construct a full system, or create a focused subtask paired with a representative dataset. We follow the latter approach and focus on the task of answer extraction, i.e., producing the exact answer strings for a question.

We propose the use of a linear-chain Conditional Random Field (CRF) (Lafferty et al., 2001) in order to cast the problem as one of *sequence tagging* by labeling each token in a candidate sentence as either Beginning, Inside or Outside (BIO) of an answer. This is to our knowledge the first time a CRF has been used to extract answers.[1] We utilize not only traditional contextual features based on POS tagging, dependency parsing and Named Entity Recognition (NER), but most importantly, features extracted from a Tree Edit Distance (TED) model for aligning an answer sentence tree with the question tree. The linear-chain CRF, when trained to learn the associations between question and answer types, is a robust approach against error propagation introduced in the NLP pipeline. For instance, given an NER tool that always (i.e., in both training and test data) recognizes the pesticide DDT as an ORG, our model realizes, when a question is asked about the type of chemicals, the correct answer might be *incorrectly but consistently* recognized as ORG by NER. This helps reduce errors introduced by wrong answer types, which were estimated as the most significant contributer (36.4%) of errors in the then state-of-the-art QA system of Moldovan et al. (2003).

The features based on TED allow us to draw the

*Performed while faculty at Johns Hopkins University.

[1] CRFs have been used in judging answer-bearing sentences (Shima et al., 2008; Ding et al., 2008; Wang and Manning, 2010), but not extracting exact answers from these sentences.

connection between the question and answer sentences *before* answer extraction, whereas traditionally the exercise of *answer validation* (Magnini et al., 2002; Penas et al., 2008; Rodrigo et al., 2009) has been performed *after* as a remedy to ensure the answer is really "about" the question.

Motivated by a desire for a fast runtime,[2] we base our TED implementation on the dynamic-programming approach of Zhang and Shasha (1989), which helps our final system process 200 QA pairs per second on standard desktop hardware, when input is syntactically pre-parsed.

In the following we first provide background on the TED model, going on to evaluate our implementation against prior work in the context of question answer sentence ranking (QASR), achieving state of the art in that task. We then describe how we couple TED features to a linear-chain CRF for answer extraction, providing the set of features used, and finally experimental results on an extraction dataset we make public (together with the software) to the community.[3] Related prior work is interspersed throughout the paper.

2 Tree Edit Distance Model

Tree Edit Distance (§2.1) models have been shown effective in a variety of applications, including textual entailment, paraphrase identification, answer ranking and information retrieval (Reis et al., 2004; Kouylekov and Magnini, 2005; Heilman and Smith, 2010; Augsten et al., 2010). We chose the variant proposed by Heilman and Smith (2010), inspired by its simplicity, generality, and effectiveness. Our approach differs from those authors in their reliance on a greedy search routine to make use of a complex tree kernel. With speed a consideration, we opted for the dynamic-programming solution of Zhang and Shasha (1989) (§2.1). We added new lexical-semantic features §(2.2) to the model and then evaluated our implementation on the QASR task, showing strong results §(2.3).

Feature	Description
distance	tree edit distance from answer sentence to question
renNoun renVerb renOther	# edits changing POS from or to noun, verb, or other types
insN, insV, insPunc, insDet, insOtherPos	# edits inserting a noun, verb, punctuation mark, determiner or other POS types
delN, delV, ...	deletion mirror of above
ins{N,V,P}Mod insSub, insObj insOtherRel	# edits inserting a modifier for {noun, verb, preposition}, subject, object or other relations
delNMod, ...	deletion mirror of above
renNMod, ...	rename mirror of above
XEdits	# basic edits plus sum of ins/del/ren edits
alignNodes, alignNum, alignN, alignV, alignProper	# aligned nodes, and those that are numbers, nouns, verbs, or proper nouns

Table 1: Features for ranking QA pairs.

2.1 Cost Design and Edit Search

Following Bille (2005), we define an *edit script* between trees T_1, T_2 as the edit sequence transforming T_1 to T_2 according to a *cost function*, with the total summed cost known as the *tree edit distance*. *Basic edit* operations include: *insert*, *delete* and *rename*.

With T a dependency tree, we represent each node by three fields: lemma, POS and the type of dependency relation to the node's parent (DEP). For instance, Mary/nnp/sub is the proper noun *Mary* in subject position.

Basic edits are refined into 9 types, where the first six (INS_LEAF, INS_SUBTREE, INS, DEL_LEAF, DEL_SUBTREE, DEL) insert or delete a leaf node, a whole subtree, or a node that is neither a leaf nor part of a whole inserted subtree. The last three (REN_POS, REN_DEP, REN_POS_DEP) serve to rename a POS tag, dependency relation, or both.

[2]For instance, Watson was designed under the constraint of a 3 second response time, arising from its intended live use in the television gameshow, `Jeopardy!`.

[3]`http://code.google.com/p/jacana/`

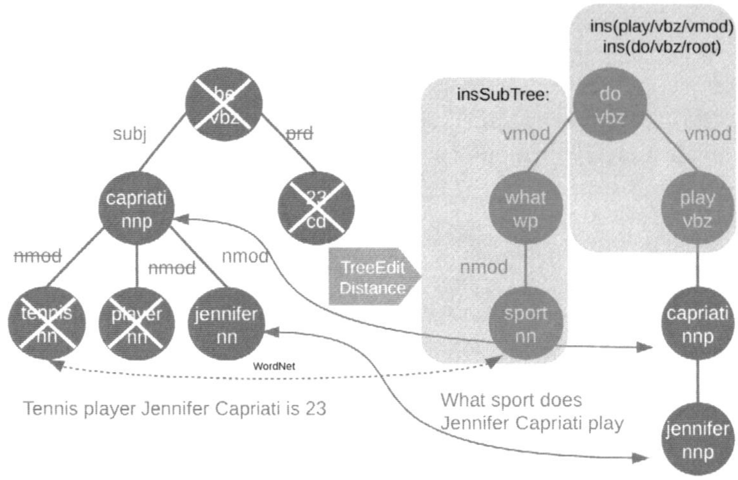

Figure 1: Edits transforming a source sentence (left) to a question (right). Each node consists of: lemma, POS tag and dependency relation, with root nodes and punctuation not shown. Shown includes deletion (× and ~~strikethrough~~ on the left), alignment (arrows) and insertion (shaded area). Order of operations is not displayed. The standard TED model does not capture the alignment between *tennis* and *sport* (see Section 2.2).

We begin by uniformly assigning basic edits a cost of 1.0,[4] which brings the cost of a full node insertion or deletion to 3 (all the three fields inserted or deleted). We allow renaming of POS and/or relation type iff the lemmas of source and target nodes are identical.[5] When two nodes are identical and thus do not appear in the edit script, or when two nodes are renamed due to the same lemma, we say they are *aligned* by the tree edit model (see Figure 1).

We used Zhang and Shasha (1989)'s dynamic programming algorithm to produce an optimal edit script with the lowest tree edit distance. The approach explores both trees in a bottom-up, post-order manner, running in time:

$$O(|T_1|\,|T_2|\min(D_1, L_1)\min(D_2, L_2))$$

where $|T_i|$ is the number of nodes, D_i is the depth, and L_i is the number of leaves, with respect to tree T_i.

Additionally, we fix the cost of stopword renaming to 2.5, even in the case of identity, regardless of whether two stopwords have the same POS tags or relations. Stopwords tend to have fixed POS tags and dependency relations, which often leads to less expensive alignments as compared to renaming content terms. In practice this gave stopwords "too much say" in guiding the overall edit sequence.

The resultant system is fast in practice, processing 10,000 pre-parsed tree pairs per second on a contemporary machine.[6]

2.2 TED for Sentence Ranking

The task of Question Answer Sentence Ranking (QASR) takes a question and a set of source sentences, returning a list sorted by the probability likelihood that each sentence contains an appropriate answer. Prior work in this includes that of: Punyakanok et al. (2004), based on mapping syntactic dependency trees; Wang et al. (2007) utilizing Quasi-Synchronous Grammar (Smith and Eisner, 2006); Heilman and Smith (2010) using TED; and Shima et al. (2008), Ding et al. (2008) and Wang and Manning (2010), who each employed a CRF in various ways. Wang et al. (2007) made their dataset public, which we use here for system validation. To date, models based on TED have shown the best performance for this task.

Our implementation follows Heilman and Smith (2010), with the addition of 15 new features beyond their original 33 (see Table 1). Based on results

[4]This applies separately to each element of the tripartite structure; e.g., deleting a POS entry, inserting a lemma, etc.

[5]This is aimed at minimizing node variations introduced by morphology differences, tagging or parsing errors.

[6]In later tasks, feature extraction and decoding will slow down the system, but the final system was still able to process 200 pairs per second.

set	source	#ques.	#pairs	%pos.	len.
TRAIN-ALL	TREC8-12	1229	53417	12.0	any
TRAIN	TREC8-12	94	4718	7.4	≤ 40
DEV	TREC13	82	1148	19.3	≤ 40
TEST	TREC13	89	1517	18.7	≤ 40

Table 2: Distribution of data, with imbalance towards negative examples (sentences without an answer).

System	MAP	MRR
Wang et al. (2007)	0.6029	0.6852
Heilman and Smith (2010)	0.6091	0.6917
Wang and Manning (2010)	0.5951	0.6951
this paper (48 features)	0.6319	0.7270
+WNsearch	**0.6371**	0.7301
+WNfeature (11 more feat.)	0.6307	**0.7477**

Table 3: Results on the QA Sentence Ranking task.

in DEV, we extract edits in the direction from the source sentence to the question.

In addition to syntactic features, we incorporated the following lexical-semantic relations from WordNet: *hypernym* and *synonym* (nouns and verbs); *entailment* and *causing* (verbs); and *membersOf*, *substancesOf*, *partsOf*, *haveMember*, *haveSubstance*, *havePart* (nouns). Such relations have been used in prior approaches to this task (Wang et al., 2007; Wang and Manning, 2010), but not in conjunction with the model of Heilman and Smith (2010).

These were made into features in two ways: **WNsearch** loosens renaming and alignment within the TED model from requiring strict lemma equality to allowing lemmas that shared any of the above relations, leading to renaming operations such as REN_...(country, china) and REN_...(sport, tennis); **WNfeature** counts how many words between the sentence and answer sentence have each of the above relations, separately as 10 independent features, plus an aggregate count for a total of 11 new features beyond the earlier 48.

These features were then used to train a logistic regression model using Weka (Hall et al., 2009).

2.3 QA Sentence Ranking Experiment

We trained and tested on the dataset from Wang et al. (2007), which spans QA pairs from TREC QA 8-13 (see Table 2). Per question, sentences with non-stopword overlap were first retrieved from the task collection, which were then compared against the TREC answer pattern (in the form of Perl regular expressions). If a sentence matched, then it was deemed a (noisy) positive example. Finally, TRAIN, DEV and TEST were manually corrected for errors. Those authors decided to limit candidate source sentences to be no longer than 40 words.[7] Keeping with prior work, those questions with only positive or negative examples were removed, leaving 94 of the original 100 questions for evaluation.

The data was processed by Wang et al. (2007) with the following tool chain: POS tags via MXPOST (Ratnaparkhi, 1996); parse trees via MSTParser (McDonald et al., 2005) with 12 coarse-grained dependency relation labels; and named entities via Identifinder (Bikel et al., 1999). Mean Average Precision (MAP) and Mean Reciprocal Rank (MRR) are reported in Table 3. Our implementation gives state of the art performance, and is furthered improved by our inclusion of semantic features drawn from WordNet.[8]

3 CRF with TED for Answer Extraction

In this section we move from *ranking* source sentences, to the next QA stage: *answer extraction*. Given our competitive TED-based alignment model, the most obvious solution to extraction would be to report those spans aligned from a source sentence to a question's *wh-* terms. However, we show that this approach is better formulated as a (strongly indicative) feature of a larger set of answer extraction signals.

3.1 Sequence Model

Figure 2 illustrates the task of tagging each token in a candidate sentence with one of the following la-

[7] TRAIN-ALL is not used in QASR, but later for answer extraction; TRAIN comes from the first 100 questions of TRAIN-ALL.

[8] As the test set is of limited size (94 questions), then while our MAP/MRR scores are $2.8\% \sim 5.6\%$ higher than prior work, this is not statistically significant according to the Paired Randomization Test (Smucker et al., 2007), and thus should be considered *on par* with the current state of the art.

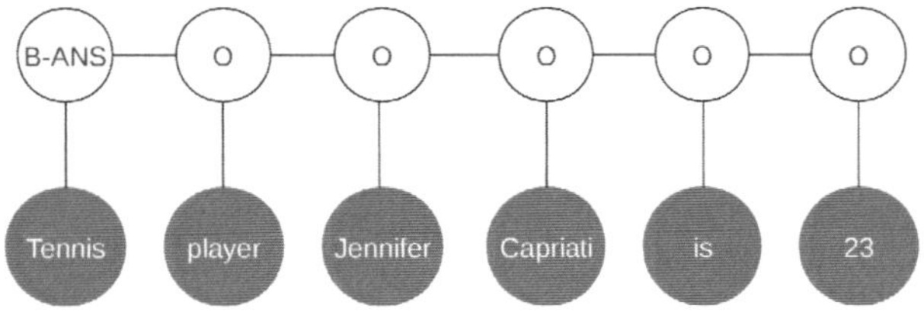

Figure 2: An example of linear-chain CRF for answer sequence tagging.

bels: B-ANSWER (beginning of answer), I-ANSWER (inside of answer), O (outside of answer).

Besides local POS/NER/DEP features, at each token we need to inspect the entire input to connect the answer sentence with the question sentence through tree edits, drawing features from the question and the edit script, motivating the use of a linear-chain CRF model (Lafferty et al., 2001) over HMMs. To the best of our knowledge this is the first time a CRF has been used to label answer fragments, despite success in other sequence tagging tasks.

3.2 Feature Design

In this subsection we describe the local and global features used by the CRF.

Chunking We use the POS/NER/DEP tags directly just as one would in a chunking task. Specifically, suppose t represents the current token position and $pos[t]$ its POS tag, we extract unigram, bigram and trigram features over the local context, e.g., $pos[t-2], pos[t-2] : pos[t-1]$, and $pos[t-2] : pos[t-1] : pos[t]$. Similar features are extracted for named entity types ($ner[t]$), and dependency relation labels ($dep[t]$).

Our intuition is these chunking features should allow for learning which types of words tend to be answers. For instance, we expect adverbs to be assigned lower feature weights as they are rarely a part of answer, while prepositions may have different feature weights depending on their context. For instance, *of* in *kind of silly* has an adjective on the right, and is unlikely to be the Beginning of an answer to a TREC-style question, as compared to *in* when paired with a question on time, such as seen in an answer *in 90 days*, where the preposition is followed by a number then a noun.

Feature	Description
edit=X	type of edit feature. X: DEL, DEL_SUBTREE, DEL_LEAF, REN_POS, REN_DEP, REN_POS_DEP or ALIGN.
X_pos=? X_ner=? X_dep=?	Delete features. X is either DEL, DEL_SUBTREE or DEL_LEAF. ? represents the corresponding POS/NER/DEP of the current token.
Xpos_from=$?_f$ Xpos_to=$?_t$ Xpos_f_t=$?_f$_$?_t$ Xner_from=$?_f$ Xner_to=$?_t$ Xner_f_t=$?_f$_$?_t$ Xdep_from=$?_f$ Xdep_to=$?_t$ Xdep_f_t=$?_f$_$?_t$	Rename features. X is either REN_POS, REN_DEP or REN_POS_DEP. Suppose word f in answer is renamed to word t in question, then $?_f$ and $?_t$ represent corresponding POS/NER/DEP of f and t.
align_pos=? align_ner=? align_dep=?	Align features. ? represents the corresponding POS/NER/DEP of the current token.

Table 4: Features based on edit script for answer sequence tagging.

Question-type Chunking features do not capture the connection between question word and answer types. Thus they have to be combined with question types. For instance, how many questions are usually associated with numeric answer types. We encode each major question-type: who, whom, when, where, how many, how much, how long, and then for each token, we combine the question term with its chunking features described in (most tokens have different features because they have different POS/NER/DEP types). One feature example of the QA pair how_much/100_dollars for the word 100 would be: qword=how_much|pos[t]=CD|pos[t+1]=NNS. We expect high weight for this feature since it is a good pattern for matching question type and answer type. Similar features also apply to what, which, why and how questions, even though they do not indicate an answer type as clearly as how much does.

Some extra features are designed for what/which questions per required answer types. The question dependency tree is analyzed and the Lexical Answer Type (LAT) is extracted. The following are some examples of LAT for what questions:

- color: what is Crips' gang color?
- animal: what kind of animal is an agouti?

The extra LAT=? feature is also used with chunking features for what/which questions.

There is significant prior work in building specialized templates or classifiers for labeling question types (Hermjakob, 2001; Li and Roth, 2002; Zhang and Lee, 2003; Hacioglu and Ward, 2003; Metzler and Croft, 2005; Blunsom et al., 2006; Moschitti et al., 2007). We designed our shallow question type features based on the intuitions of these prior work, with the goal of having a relatively compact approach that still extracts useful predictive signal. One possible drawback, however, is that if an LAT is not observed during training but shows up in testing, the sequence tagger would not know which answer type to associate with the question. In this case it falls back to the more general qword=? feature and will most likely pick the type of answers that are mostly associated with what questions in training.

Edit script Our TED module produces an edit trace for each word in a candidate sentence: the word is either deleted, renamed (if there is a word of the same lemma in the question tree) or strictly aligned (if there is an identical node in the question tree). A word in the deleted edit sequence is a cue that it could be the answer. A word being aligned suggests it is less likely to be an answer. Thus for each word we extract features based on its edit type, shown in Table 4.

These features are also appended with the token's POS/NER/DEP information. For instance, a deleted noun usually carries higher edit feature weights than an aligned adjective.

Alignment distance We observed that a candidate answer often appears close to an aligned word (i.e., answer tokens tend to be located "nearby" portions of text that align across the pair), especially in compound noun constructions, restrictive clauses, preposition phrases, etc. For instance, in the following pair, the answer Limp Bizkit comes from the leading compound noun:

- What is the name of Durst 's group?
- Limp Bizkit lead singer Fred Durst did a lot ...

Past work has designed large numbers of specific templates aimed at these constructions (Soubbotin, 2001; Ravichandran et al., 2003; Clark et al., 2003; Sneiders, 2002). Here we use a single general feature that we expect to pick up much of this signal, without the significant feature engineering.

Thus we incorporated a simple feature to *roughly* model this phenomenon. It is defined as the distance to the nearest aligned nonstop word in the original word order. In the above example, the only aligned nonstop word is Durst. Then this nearest alignment distance feature for the word Limp is:

nearest_dist_to_align(Limp):5

This is the only integer-valued feature. All other features are binary-valued. Note this feature does not specify answer types: an adverb close to an aligned word can also be wrongly taken as a strong candidate. Thus we also include a version of the POS/NER/DEP based feature for each token:

- nearest_dist_pos(Limp)=NNP
- nearest_dist_dep(Limp)=NMOD
- nearest_dist_ner(Limp)=B-PERSON

3.3 Overproduce-and-vote

We make an assumption that each sentence produces a candidate answer and then vote among all answer candidates to select the most-voted as the answer to the original question. Specifically, this overproduce-and-vote strategy applies voting in two places:

1. If there are overlaps between two answer candidates, a partial vote is performed. For instance, for a when question, if one answer candidate is April , 1994 and the other is 1994, then besides the base vote of 1, both candidates have an extra partial vote of $\#\text{overlap}/\#\text{total words} = 1/4$. We call this *adjusted vote*.

2. If the CRF fails to find an answer, we still try to "force" an answer out of the tagged sequence, O's). thus *forced vote*. Due to its lower credibility (the sequence tagger does not think it is an answer), we manually downweight the prediction score by a factor of 0.1 (divide by 10).

```
During what war did Nimitz serve ?
O        O:0.921060    Conant
O        O:0.991168    had
O        O:0.997307    been
O        O:0.998570    a
O        O:0.998608    photographer
O        O:0.999005    for
O        O:0.877619    Adm
O        O:0.988293    .
O        O:0.874101    Chester
O        O:0.924568    Nimitz
O        O:0.970045    during
B-ANS    O:0.464799    World
I-ANS    O:0.493715    War
I-ANS    O:0.449017    II
O        O:0.915448    .
```

Figure 3: A sample sequence tagging output that fails to predict an answer. From line 2 on, the first column is the reference output and the second column is the model output with the marginal probability for predicated labels. Note that World War II has much lower probabilities as an O than others.

The modified score for an answer candidate is thus: total vote = adjusted vote + $0.1 \times$ forced vote. To compute forced vote, we make the following observation. Sometimes the sequence tagger does not tag an answer in a candidate sentence at all, if there is not enough probability mass accumulated for B-ANS. However, a possible answer can still be caught if it has an "outlier" marginal probability. Figure 3 shows an example. The answer candidate World War II has a much lower marginal probability as an "O" but still not low enough to be part of B-ANS/I-ANS.

To catch such an outlier, we use Median Absolute Deviation (MAD), which is the median of the absolute deviation from the median of a data sequence. Given a data sequence $\mathbf{x}$, MAD is defined as:

$$\text{MAD}(\mathbf{x}) = \text{median}(|\ \mathbf{x} - \text{median}(\mathbf{x})\ |)$$

Compared to mean value and standard deviation, MAD is more robust against the influence of outliers since it does not directly depend on them. We select those words whose marginal probability is 50 times of MAD away from the median of the whole sequence as answer candidates. They contribute to the forced vote. Downweight ratio (0.1) and MAD ratio (50) were hand-tuned on DEV.[9]

System	Train	Prec.%	Rec.%	F1%
CRF	TRAIN	55.7	43.8	49.1
	TRAIN-ALL	**67.2**	50.6	57.7
CRF +WNsearch	TRAIN	58.6	46.1	51.6
	TRAIN-ALL	66.7	49.4	56.8
CRF forced	TRAIN	54.5	53.9	54.2
	TRAIN-ALL	60.9	59.6	60.2
CRF forced +WNsearch	TRAIN	55.2	53.9	54.5
	TRAIN-ALL	63.6	**62.9**	**63.3**

Table 5: Performance on TEST. "CRF" only takes votes from candidates tagged by the sequence tagger. "CRF forced" (described in §3.3) further collects answer candidates from sentences that CRF does not tag an answer by detecting outliers.

4 Experiments

4.1 QA Results

The dataset listed in Table 2 was not designed to include an answer for each positive answer sentence, but only a binary indicator on whether a sentence contains an answer. We used the answer pattern files (in Perl regular expressions) released along with TREC8-13 to pinpoint the exact answer fragments. Then we manually checked TRAIN, DEV, and TEST for errors. TRAIN-ALL already came as a noisy dataset so we did not manually clean it, also due to its large size.

We trained on only the positive examples of TRAIN and TRAIN-ALL separately with CRFsuite (Okazaki, 2007). The reason for training solely with positive examples is that they only constitute 10% of all training data and if trained on all, the CRF tagger was very biased on negative examples and reluctant to give an answer for most of the questions. The CRF tagger attempted an answer for about 2/3 of all questions when training on just positive examples.

DEV was used to help design features. A practical benefit of our compact approach is that an entire round of feature extraction, training on TRAIN and testing on DEV took less than one minute. Table 5

[9]One might further improve this by leveraging the probability of a sentence containing an answer from the QA pair ranker described in Section 2 or via the conditional probability of the sequence labels, $p(\mathbf{y} \mid \mathbf{x})$, under the CRF.

reports F1 scores on both the positive and negative examples of TEST.

Our baseline model, which aligns the question word with some content word in the answer sentence,[10] achieves 31.4% in F1. This model does not require any training. "CRF" only takes votes from those sentences with an identified answer. It has the best precision among all models. "CRF forced" also detects outliers from sentences not tagged with an answer. Large amount of training data, even noisy, is helpful. In general TRAIN-ALL is able to boost the F1 value by $7 \sim 8\%$. Also, the overgenerate-and-vote strategy, used by the "forced" approach, greatly increased recall and achieved the best F1 value.

We also experimented with the two methods utilizing WordNet in Section 2.2 , i.e., WNsearch and WNfeature. In general, WNsearch helps F1 and yields the best score (63.3%) for this task. For WNfeature[11] we observed that the CRF model converged to a larger objective likelihood with these features. However, it did not make a difference in F1 after overgenerate-and-vote.

Finally, we found it difficult to do a head-to-head comparison with other QA systems on this task.[12] Thus we contribute this dataset to the community, hoping to solicit direct comparisons in the future. Also, we believe our chunking and question-type features capture many intuitions most current QA systems rely on, while our novel features are based on TED. We further conduct an ablation test to compare traditional and new QA features.

4.2 Ablation Test

We did an ablation test for each of the four types of features. Note that the question type features are used in combination with chunking features (e.g., qword=how_much|pos[t]=CD|pos[t+1]=NN), while the chunking feature is defined over POS/NER/DEP separately. We tested the CRF model with deletion of one of the following features each time:

- POS, NER or DEP. These features are all combined with question types.
- The three of the above. Deletion of these features also deletes question type feature implicitly.
- EDIT. Features extracted from edit script.
- ALIGN. Alignment distance features.
- The two of the above, based on the TED model.

Table 6 shows the F1 scores of ablation test when trained on TRAIN. NER and EDIT are the two single most significant features. NER is important because it closely relates question types with answer entity types (e.g., qword=who|ner[t]=PERSON). EDIT is also important because it captures the syntactic association between question tree and answer tree. Taking out all three POS/NER/DEP features means the chunking and question type features do not fire anymore. This has the biggest impact on F1. Note the feature redundancy here: the question type features are combined with all three POS/NER/DEP features

	CRF	Forced		CRF	Forced
All	49.1	54.2	-above 3	19.4	25.3
-POS	44.7	48.9	-EDIT	44.3	47.5
-NER	44.0	50.8	-ALIGN	47.4	51.1
-DEP	49.4	54.5	-above 2	40.5	42.0

Table 6: F1 based on feature ablation tests.

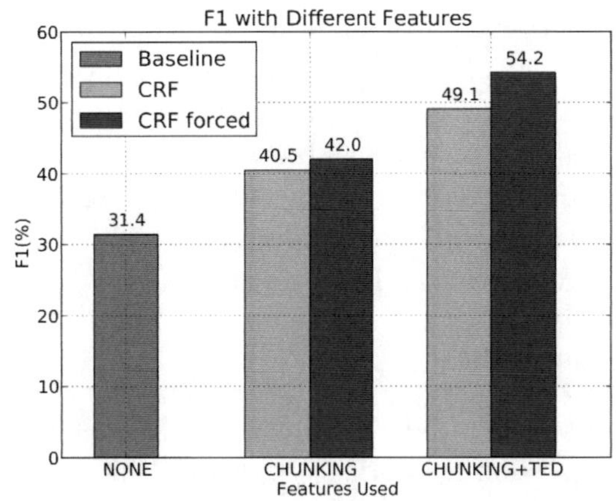

Figure 4: Impact of adding features based on chunking and question-type (CHUNKING) and tree edits (TED), e.g., EDIT and ALIGN.

[10] This only requires minimal modification to the original TED algorithm: the question word is aligned with a certain word in the answer tree instead of being inserted. Then the whole subtree headed by the aligned word counts as the answer.

[11] These are binary features indicating whether an answer candidate has a WordNet relation (c.f. §2.2) with the LAT. For instance, tennis is a hyponym of the LAT word sport in the what sport question in Figure 1.

[12] Reasons include: most available QA systems either retrieve sentences from the web, have different preprocessing steps, or even include templates learned from our test set.

thus taking out a single one does not decrease performance much. However, since TED related features do not combine question type features, taking out all three POS/NER/DEP features decreases F1 by 30%. Without TED related features (both EDIT and ALIGN) F1 also drops more than 10%.

Figure 4 is a bar chart showing how much improvement each feature brings. While having a baseline model with 31.4% in F1, traditional features based on POS/DEP/NER and question types brings a 10% increase with a simple sequence tagging model (second bar labeled "CHUNKING" in the figure). Furthermore, adding TED based features to the model boosted F1 by another 10%.

5 Conclusion

Answer extraction is an essential task for any text-based question-answering system to perform. In this paper, we have cast answer extraction as a sequence tagging problem by deploying a fast and compact CRF model with simple features that capture many of the intuitions in prior "deep pipeline" approaches. We introduced novel features based on TED that boosted F1 score by 10% compared with the use of more standard features. Besides answer extraction, our modified design of the TED model is the state of the art in the task of ranking QA pairs. Finally, to improve the community's ability to evaluate QA components without requiring increasingly impractical end-to-end implementations, we have proposed answer extraction as a subtask worth evaluating in its own right, and contributed a dataset that could become a potential standard for this purpose. We believe all these developments will contribute to the continuing improvement of QA systems in the future.

Acknowledgement We thank Vulcan Inc. for funding this work. We also thank Michael Heilman and Mengqiu Wang for helpful discussion and dataset, and the three anonymous reviewers for insightful comments.

References

Nikolaus Augsten, Denilson Barbosa, Michael Böhlen, and Themis Palpanas. 2010. TASM: Top-k Approximate Subtree Matching. In *Proceedings of the International Conference on Data Engineering (ICDE-10)*, pages 353–364, Long Beach, California, USA, March. IEEE Computer Society.

D.M. Bikel, R. Schwartz, and R.M. Weischedel. 1999. An algorithm that learns what's in a name. *Machine learning*, 34(1):211–231.

P. Bille. 2005. A survey on tree edit distance and related problems. *Theoretical Computer Science*, 337(1):217–239.

P. Blunsom, K. Kocik, and J.R. Curran. 2006. Question classification with log-linear models. In *Proceedings of the 29th annual international ACM SIGIR conference on Research and development in information retrieval*, pages 615–616. ACM.

Peter Clark, Vinay Chaudhri, Sunil Mishra, Jérôme Thoméré, Ken Barker, and Bruce Porter. 2003. Enabling domain experts to convey questions to a machine: a modified, template-based approach. In *Proceedings of the 2nd international conference on Knowledge Capture*, pages 13–19, New York, NY, USA. ACM.

Shilin Ding, Gao Cong, Chin yew Lin, and Xiaoyan Zhu. 2008. Using conditional random fields to extract contexts and answers of questions from online forums. In *In Proceedings of ACL-08: HLT*.

D. Ferrucci, E. Brown, J. Chu-Carroll, J. Fan, D. Gondek, A.A. Kalyanpur, A. Lally, J.W. Murdock, E. Nyberg, J. Prager, et al. 2010. Building Watson: An overview of the DeepQA project. *AI Magazine*, 31(3):59–79.

K. Hacioglu and W. Ward. 2003. Question classification with support vector machines and error correcting codes. In *Proceedings of NAACL 2003, short papers*, pages 28–30.

M. Hall, E. Frank, G. Holmes, B. Pfahringer, P. Reutemann, and I.H. Witten. 2009. The WEKA data mining software: an update. *ACM SIGKDD Explorations Newsletter*, 11(1):10–18.

Michael Heilman and Noah A. Smith. 2010. Tree edit models for recognizing textual entailments, paraphrases, and answers to questions. In *Proceedings of NAACL 2010*, pages 1011–1019, Los Angeles, California.

U. Hermjakob. 2001. Parsing and question classification for question answering. In *Proceedings of the workshop on Open-domain question answering-Volume 12*, pages 1–6.

Milen Kouylekov and Bernardo Magnini. 2005. Recognizing textual entailment with tree edit distance algorithms. In *PASCAL Challenges on RTE*, pages 17–20.

John D. Lafferty, Andrew McCallum, and Fernando C. N. Pereira. 2001. Conditional random fields: Probabilistic models for segmenting and labeling sequence data.

In *Proceedings of the Eighteenth International Conference on Machine Learning*, pages 282–289, San Francisco, CA, USA. Morgan Kaufmann Publishers Inc.

X. Li and D. Roth. 2002. Learning question classifiers. In *Proceedings of ACL 2002*, pages 1–7.

B. Magnini, M. Negri, R. Prevete, and H. Tanev. 2002. Is it the right answer?: exploiting web redundancy for answer validation. In *Proceedings of ACL 2002*, pages 425–432.

R. McDonald, K. Crammer, and F. Pereira. 2005. Online large-margin training of dependency parsers. In *Proceedings of ACL 2005*, pages 91–98.

D. Metzler and W.B. Croft. 2005. Analysis of statistical question classification for fact-based questions. *Information Retrieval*, 8(3):481–504.

D. Moldovan, M. Paşca, S. Harabagiu, and M. Surdeanu. 2003. Performance issues and error analysis in an open-domain question answering system. *ACM Transactions on Information Systems (TOIS)*, 21(2):133–154.

A. Moschitti, S. Quarteroni, R. Basili, and S. Manandhar. 2007. Exploiting syntactic and shallow semantic kernels for question answer classification. In *Proceedings of ACL 2007*, volume 45, page 776.

Naoaki Okazaki. 2007. CRFsuite: a fast implementation of Conditional Random Fields (CRFs).

A. Penas, A. Rodrigo, V. Sama, and F. Verdejo. 2008. Testing the reasoning for question answering validation. *Journal of Logic and Computation*, 18(3):459–474.

Vasin Punyakanok, Dan Roth, and Wen T. Yih. 2004. Mapping Dependencies Trees: An Application to Question Answering. In *Proceedings of the 8th International Symposium on Artificial Intelligence and Mathematics*, Fort Lauderdale, Florida.

A. Ratnaparkhi. 1996. A maximum entropy model for part-of-speech tagging. In *Proceedings of EMNLP 1996*, volume 1, pages 133–142.

Deepak Ravichandran, Abraham Ittycheriah, and Salim Roukos. 2003. Automatic derivation of surface text patterns for a maximum entropy based question answering system. In *Proceedings of NAACL 2003, short papers*, pages 85–87, Stroudsburg, PA, USA.

D. C. Reis, P. B. Golgher, A. S. Silva, and A. F. Laender. 2004. Automatic web news extraction using tree edit distance. In *Proceedings of the 13th international conference on World Wide Web*, pages 502–511, New York, NY, USA. ACM.

Á. Rodrigo, A. Peñas, and F. Verdejo. 2009. Overview of the answer validation exercise 2008. *Evaluating Systems for Multilingual and Multimodal Information Access*, pages 296–313.

H. Shima, N. Lao, E. Nyberg, and T. Mitamura. 2008. Complex cross-lingual question answering as sequential classification and multi-document summarization task. In *Proceedings of NTICIR-7 Workshop, Japan*.

David A. Smith and Jason Eisner. 2006. Quasi-synchronous grammars: Alignment by soft projection of syntactic dependencies. In *Proceedings of the HLT-NAACL Workshop on Statistical Machine Translation*, pages 23–30, New York, June.

Mark D. Smucker, James Allan, and Ben Carterette. 2007. A comparison of statistical significance tests for information retrieval evaluation. In *CIKM '07: Proceedings of the sixteenth ACM conference on Conference on information and knowledge management*, pages 623–632, New York, NY, USA. ACM.

E. Sneiders. 2002. *Automated question answering: template-based approach*. Ph.D. thesis, KTH.

Martin M. Soubbotin. 2001. Patterns of potential answer expressions as clues to the right answers. In *Proceedings of the Tenth Text REtrieval Conference (TREC 2001)*.

Mengqiu Wang and Christopher D. Manning. 2010. Probabilistic tree-edit models with structured latent variables for textual entailment and question answering. In *Proceedings of ACL 2010*, pages 1164–1172, Stroudsburg, PA, USA.

Mengqiu Wang, Noah A. Smith, and Teruko Mitamura. 2007. What is the Jeopardy model? a quasi-synchronous grammar for QA. In *Proceedings of the 2007 Joint Conference on Empirical Methods in Natural Language Processing and Computational Natural Language Learning (EMNLP-CoNLL)*, pages 22–32, Prague, Czech Republic, June.

D. Zhang and W.S. Lee. 2003. Question classification using support vector machines. In *Proceedings of the 26th annual international ACM SIGIR conference on Research and development in informaion retrieval*, pages 26–32. ACM.

K. Zhang and D. Shasha. 1989. Simple fast algorithms for the editing distance between trees and related problems. *SIAM J. Comput.*, 18(6):1245–1262, December.

Open Information Extraction with Tree Kernels

Ying Xu, Mi-Young Kim, Kevin Quinn, Randy Goebel and **Denilson Barbosa**
Department of Computing Science
University of Alberta
{yx2,miyoung2,kfjquinn,goebel,denilson}@cs.ualberta.ca

Abstract

Traditional relation extraction seeks to identify pre-specified semantic relations within natural language text, while open Information Extraction (Open IE) takes a more general approach, and looks for a variety of relations without restriction to a fixed relation set. With this generalization comes the question, what is a relation? For example, should the more general task be restricted to relations mediated by verbs, nouns, or both? To help answer this question, we propose two levels of subtasks for Open IE. One task is to determine if a sentence potentially contains a relation between two entities? The other task looks to confirm explicit relation words for two entities. We propose multiple SVM models with dependency tree kernels for both tasks. For explicit relation extraction, our system can extract both noun and verb relations. Our results on three datasets show that our system is superior when compared to state-of-the-art systems like REVERB and OLLIE for both tasks. For example, in some experiments our system achieves 33% improvement on nominal relation extraction over OLLIE. In addition we propose an unsupervised rule-based approach which can serve as a strong baseline for Open IE systems.

1 Introduction

Relation Extraction (RE) systems are designed to discover various semantic relations (e.g. <Obama, president, the United States>) from natural language text. Traditional RE systems extract specific relations for prespecified name-entity types (Bunescu and Mooney, 2005; Chan and Dan, 2011; Zhou and Zhu, 2011). To train such systems, every relation needs manually annotated training examples, which supports limited scope and is difficult to extend. For this reason, Banko et al. (2007) proposed Open Information Extraction (Open IE), whose goal is to extract general relations for two entities. The idea is to avoid the need for specific training examples, and to extract a diverse range of relations. This generalized form has received significant attention, e.g., (Banko et al., 2007; Akbik, 2009; Wu and Weld, 2010; Fader et al., 2011; Mausam et al., 2012).

Because Open IE is not guided by or not restricted to a prespecified list of relations, the immediate challenge is determining about what counts as a relation? Most recent Open IE systems have targeted verbal relations (Banko et al., 2007; Mausam et al., 2012), claiming that these are the majority. However, Chan and Dan (2011) show that only 20% of relations in the ACE programs Relation Detection and Characterization (RDC) are verbal. Our manually extracted relation triple set from the Penn Treebank shows that there are more nominal relations than verbal ones, 3 to 2. This difference arises because of the ambiguity of what constitutes a relation in Open IE. It is often difficult even for humans to agree on what constitutes a relation, and which words in the sentence establish a relation between a pair of entities. For example, in the sentence "Olivetti broke Cocom rules" is there a relation between *Olivetti* and *Cocom*? This ambiguity in the problem definition leads to significant challenges and confusion when evaluating and comparing the performance of different methods and systems. An example are the results in Fader et al. (2011) and Mausam et al. (2012). In Fader et al. (2011), REVERB "is reported" as superior to WOE^{parse}, a system proposed in Wu and Weld (2010); while in Mausam et al. (2012), it is reported the opposite.

To better answer the question, what counts as a relation? we propose two tasks for Open IE. The first task seeks to determine whether there is a relation between two entities (called "Binary task"). The other is to confirm whether the relation words extracted for the two entities are appropriate (the "Triple task"). The Binary task does not restrict relation word forms, whether they are mediated by nouns, verbs, prepositions, or even implicit relations. The Triple task requires an abstract representation of relation word forms, which we develop here. We assume that relation words are nouns or verbs; in our data, these two types comprise 71% of explicit relations.

We adapt an SVM dependency tree kernel model (Moschitti, 2006) for both tasks. The input to our tasks is a dependency parse, created by Stanford Parser. Selecting relevant features from a parse tree for semantic tasks is difficult. SVM tree kernels avoid extracting explicit features from parse trees by calculating the inner product of the two trees. For the Binary task, our dependency path is the path between two entities. For the Triple task, the path is among entities and relation words (i.e. relation triples). Tree kernels have been used in traditional RE and have helped achieve state of the art performance (Culotta and Sorensen, 2004; Bunescu and Mooney, 2005; Wang, 2008; Nguyen et al., 2009; Zhou and Zhu, 2011). But one challenge of using tree kernels on Open IE is that the lexicon of relations is much larger than those of traditional RE, making it difficult to include the lexical information as features. Here we proposed an unlexicalized tree structure for Open IE. As far as we know, this is the first time an SVM tree kernel has been applied in Open IE. Experimental results on multiple datasets show our system outperforms state-of-the-art systems REVERB and OLLIE. Typically an Open IE system is tested on one dataset. However, because the definition of relation is ambiguous, we believe that is necessary to test with multiple datasets.

In addition to the supervised model, we also propose an unsupervised model which relies on several heuristic rules. Results with this approach show that this simple unsupervised model provides a robust strong baseline for other approaches.

In summary, our main contributions are:

- Use SVM tree kernels for Open IE. Our system is robust comparing with other Open IE systems, achieving superior scores in two test sets and comparative scores in another set.
- Extend beyond verbal relations, which are prevalent in current systems. Analyze implicit relation problem in Open IE, which is ignored by other work.
- Propose an unsupervised model for Open IE, which can be a strong baseline for other approaches.

The rest of this paper is organized as follows. Section 2 provides the problem description and system structure, before summarizing previous work in Section 3. Section 4 defines our representation of relation word patterns crucial to our task two, and Section 5 describes tree kernels for SVM. Section 6 describes the unsupervised model, and Section 7 explains our experiment design and results. Section 8 concludes with a summary, and anticipation of future work.

2 Problem Definition and System Structure

The common definition of the Open IE task is a function from a sentence, s, to a set of triples, $\{< E1, R, E2 >\}$, where $E1$ and $E2$ are entities (noun phrases) and R is a textual fragment indicating a semantic relation between the two entities. Our "Triple task" is within this definition. However it is often difficult to determine which textual fragments to extract. In addition, semantic relations can be implicit, e.g., consider the *located in* relation in the sentence fragment "Washington, US." To illustrate how much information is lost when restricting the relation forms, we add another task (the "Binary task"), determining if there is a relation between the two entities. It is a function from s, to a set of binary relations over entities, $\{< E1, E2 >\}$. This binary task is designed to overcome the disadvantage of current Open IE systems, which suffer because of restricting the relation form, e.g., to only verbs, or only nouns. The two tasks are independent to each other.

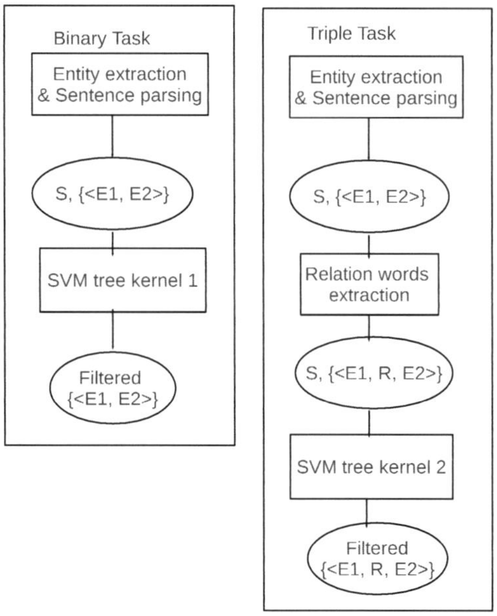

Figure 1: Our Open IE system structure.

Figure 1 presents our Open IE system structure. Both tasks need pre-processing with the Stanford NLP tools [1]. Entities and pairs within a certain distance are extracted[2], and sentences are parsed. We employ the typed collapsed dependency parse (De Marneffe et al., 2006), which is computed from the constituent parsing and has proved to be useful for semantic tasks (MacCartney et al., 2006). For the Binary task, an SVM model is employed to filter out the extracted entity pair candidates, and output pairs which have certain relations. For the Triple task, we identify relation word candidates of the pairs, based on regular expression patterns. Then another SVM model is employed to decide if the relation triples are correct or not.

3 Related Work

In traditional relation extraction, SVM tree kernel models are the basis for the current state of the art (Culotta and Sorensen, 2004; Bunescu and Mooney, 2005; Wang, 2008; Nguyen et al., 2009; Zhou and Zhu, 2011). But there is more recent work on Open IE (Banko et al., 2007; Akbik, 2009; Wu and Weld, 2010; Christensen et al., 2011; Fader et al., 2011; Mausam et al., 2012).

[1]Other equivalent tools such as Open NLP could be used.
[2]Here distance means number of tokens in between

Pattern = *RelW* E1 *RelW* E2 *RelW*
st. at least one *RelW* has *N* or *V*

RelW= *V* | *V P* | *V W* P* | *N* | *N P* | *P*
V = verb particle? adv?
W = (noun | adj | adv | pron | det)
P = (prep | particle | inf.marker)
N = (adj | noun) * noun

Figure 2: Relation Pattern Form (*RelW* represents *relation words*, E1 and E2 are two entities.)

Fader et al. (2011) have developed REVERB, which solves the problem of incoherent extractions and uninformative extractions of two previous systems. Instead of extracting entities first, they extract verbal relation sequences based on a set of POS patterns. Then entities are identified around the relation sequence, so their system only extracts relation tokens between two entities tokens, e.g. relations such as <he, live in, city> in "Living in this city, he loves the city." are ignored. Finally, relation triple candidate noise is filtered by a supervised model which is based on lexical and POS features.

Mausam et al. (2012) present an improved system called OLLIE, which relaxes the previous systems' constraints that relation words are mediated by verbs, or relation words that appear between two entities. OLLIE creates a training set which includes millions of relations extracted by REVERB with high confidence. Then OLLIE learns relation patterns composed of dependency path and lexicon information. Relations matching the patterns can then be extracted.

Both REVERB and OLLIE output a confidence value for every relation triples, instead of classifying them as true or false.

4 Relation Candidate Extraction

For the Triple task, we extract textual fragments which matches certain POS patterns in an entity pair's context as relation candidates for that pair. In our experiments, the fragments are n-grams with $n < 5$ and between the pairs or in a window size of 10 before the first entity or after the second entity, which is experimentally a good choice to minimize noise while attaining maximum number of relations.

Our representation of POS regular expression pattern sets expands that of Fader et al. (2011). The patterns are composed of verb and noun phrases (see Figure 2). A relation candidate can consist of words before, between, or after the pair, or the combination of two consecutive positions. Instead of extracting only verbal relations (e.g. *give birth to*), our patterns also extract relations specified through noun phrases. In the sentence "Obama, the president of the United States, made a speech" the relation "president" matches the relational form "RelW=N, N=noun". Our method can also extract relation words interspersed between the two entities: e.g., ORG *has* NUM *employees*, which matches the pattern "E1 RelW E2 RelW"; the first RelW matches V, with V=verb, and the second RelW matches N, with N=noun. We choose not to use the dependency path for relation word extraction because of the reason mentioned in (Fader et al., 2011). The dependency method will create incoherent relations. For example, in the sentence "They recalled that Nungesser began his career as a precinct leader." *recall began* will be extracted as a relation because the two words are linked. Although this pattern based method has limitations, finding further improvements remains future work.

5 Tree Kernels

Many methods recognize the value of leveraging parsing information in support of semantic tasks. But selecting relevant features from a parse tree is a difficult task. With kernel-based SVMs, both learning and classification relies on the inner-product between instances. SVM tree kernels avoid extracting explicit features from parse trees by calculating the inner product of the two trees, so the tree kernel value depends on the common substructure of two trees. A tree kernel function over Tree T_1 and T_1 is

$K(T_1, T_2) = \sum_{n1 \in N_{T_1}} \sum_{n2 \in N_{T_2}} \Delta(n_1, n_2)$, N_{T_1} and N_{T_2} are the set of trees' nodes (Collins and Duffy, 2001). The Δ function provides the basis for identifying subtrees of nodes, which is the essential distinction between different tree kernel functions. Here we adapt the partial tree kernel (PTK) proposed by Moschitti (2006)[3], which can be used with both constituent and dependency parse trees. The com-

[3]Thanks to Prof. Moschitti for his PTK package.

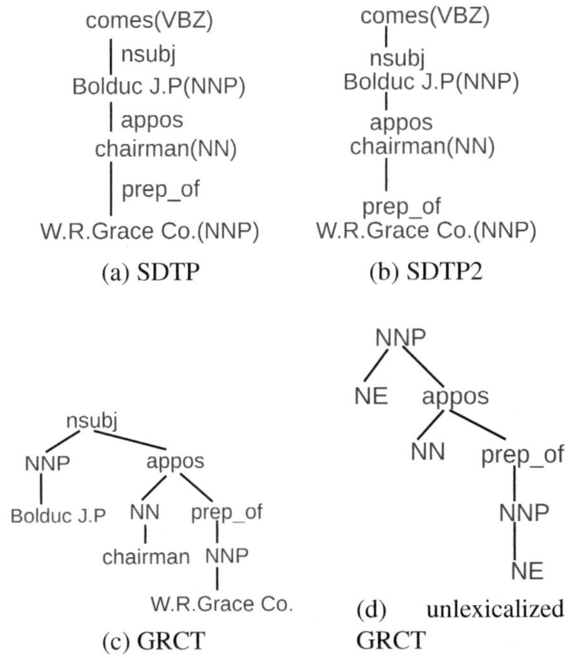

Figure 3: Example trees for shortest dependency path between *J.P. Bolduc* and *W.R.Grace Co.* in sentence "J.P. Bolduc, vice chairman of W.R.Grace Co., comes here." Figure (a) is the shortest dependency tree path (SDTP), (b) is the collapsed form, (c) is the GRCT, (d) is an unlexicalized GRCT with "NE".

putation of Δ function of PTK is

$$\Big(\sum_{J_1, J_2, l(J_1)=l(J_2)} \lambda^{d(J_1)+d(J_2)} \prod_{i=1}^{l(J_1)} \Delta(c_{n_1}(J_{1i}), c_{n_2}(J_{2i})) + \lambda^2 \Big)\mu \quad (1)$$

when the node labels of n_1 and n_2 are the same, $\Delta = 0$ when they are different. c_{n_1} and c_{n_2} are child sequences of nodes n_1 and n_2 respectively, $J_1 =< J_{11}, J_{12}, J_{13}... >$ and $J_2 =< J_{21}, J_{22}, J_{23}... >$ are index sequences of the two child sequences, J_{1i} and J_{2i} are the i-th children of the two sequences. $l()$ means the sequence length, $d(J_1) = J_{1l(J_1)} - J_{11}$ and $d(J_2) = J_{2l(J_2)} - J_{21}$. μ and λ are two decay factors for the height of the tree and the length of the child sequences respectively, which we choose the default setting in the experiments. For a more detailed description of PTK, please refer to (Moschitti, 2006).

Now we present our unlexicalized dependency

tree structures for the tree kernel. One question arising in the conversion dependency structures (e.g., Figure 3a) for the tree kernel is how should we add POS tags and dependency link labels? The kernel cannot process labels on the arcs; they must be associated with tree nodes. Our conversion is similar to the idea of a Grammatical Relation Centered Tree (GRCT) of Croce et al. (2011). First we order the nodes of dependency trees so that the *dominant*, i.e. the parent of the dependency link is on the top, the *dependent*, i.e. the child at the bottom. At this stage, the link label is with the corresponding *dependent* POS-tag and the word (Figure 3b). If a dominant has more than one child, the children will be ordered according to their position in the sentence, from left to right. Next, every node is expanded such that the *dependent* POS-tags are the children of the link labels and parent of their words. For example, in Figure 3c, *NN* is the child of *appos*, parent of *chairman*. It is on the left of *prep_of* because *chairman* is on the left of *W.R.Grace Co.* in the sentence. As customary in Open IE, we do not add content words, while function words are optional. The unlexicalized GRCT is shown in Figure 3d. Note that for the root node, the link label is replaced by the POS-tag of the fist node in the path.

Recall that we have two tasks: detecting whether there is a relation between two entities (the Binary task), and whether the relation triple <*E1, relation, E2*> is correct (the Triplet task). We define two expanded versions of unlexicalized GRCT for the two tasks. The two versions contain different fragments of a dependency tree of a sentence.

For the Binary task, the shortest path between two entities' heads[4] is extracted and represented as a GRCT. The root node is the POS-tag of the fist node in the path. "NE" is used to represent the position of two entities while relation words are not specified. Figure 3d shows the example final outcome of our tree structure. It is used to decide if there is a relation between the entities *Bolduc J.P.* and *W.R.Grace Co.*

For the Triple task, we first extract relation words based on regular expression patterns as indicated in Section 4. If any relation word is between the shortest path of the two entities, the path is chosen as the input for SVM. Otherwise, two shortest paths between two entities and relation words will be extracted separately. The shortest one will be attached to the path between two entities. In our representation, relation words are tagged by having "R" as the child. Figure 4a shows the path form of the previous example. Figure 4b shows another example where "R" is not in the shortest path of the pair. The triple is <United States, president, Obama> for the sentence "United States President Barack Obama says so." The figure on the left is the dependency path. The figure on the right is the final tree for the triple task. The root is the POS-tag for *Obama*.

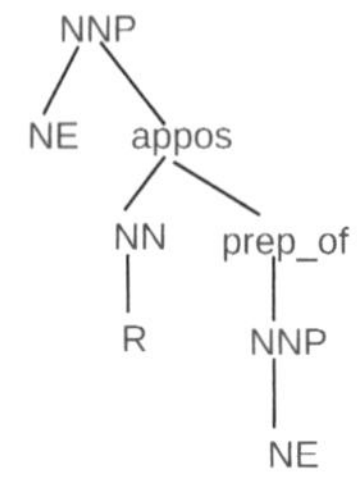

(a) Example 1.

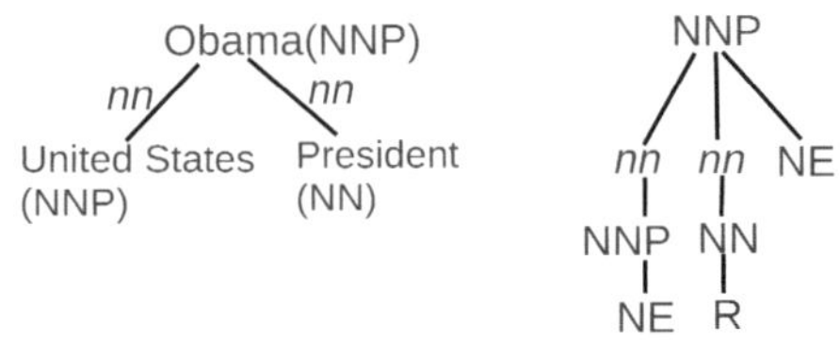

(b) Example 2.

Figure 4: Tree structure with "R" added. Figure (a) is the example 1, which has R in the SDTP of the entity pair. Figure (b) is the example 2, with R not in the SDTP of the entity pair.

For the Triple task we combine the tree kernel with a polynomial kernel (Moschitti, 2005) applied to a feature vector. The feature set is in Table 1. F3 tries to preserve the semantic link between two discontinuous relation word segments. F6 constrains relation words to include only necessary prepositions. For verbal relations, if there is a preposition at the end of the relation word sequence, then there must be a preposition link between the relation and any of the two entities, and vice versa. For instance, in the sentence "Bob teaches at the Univer-

[4]The head words of phrases are words which do not depend on any words in the phrases.

sity" <Bob, *teach at*, University> is correct while <Bob, *teach*, University> is wrong. For nominal relations, inclusion of the head word is necessary. Prepositions can be ignored, but if they exist, they must match with the dependency link. We concentrate on verb prepositions because prepositions are more attached to noun phrases than verb phrases. Verb relations have more preposition choices, and different choices have different semantic impact, for example, the subject or object. But noun relations' preposition are more fixed, such as "president of". The last two features F7 and F8 are added according to the observation of experiment results in a development set: we note that one problem is the apposition or conjunction structure between entities [5].

6 Unsupervised Method

We also propose the use of an unsupervised method based on heuristic rules to produce a relation word noise filter, as an alternative to using SVM in the Triple task. The heuristic rules are also based on the Stanford collapsed dependency parsing. There are two parts in the noise filter: one is that the relation words should have necessary links with two entities and the other is that relation words should be consistent.

We first mention the heuristic rules for necessary dependency links. The intuition is from Chan and Dan (2011), they classified relations into 5 different syntactic structures; premodifier, possessive, preposition, formulaic, and verbal. They proposed heuristic POS patterns covering the first four patterns with the exception of the verbal structure.

We present heuristic rules based on dependency paths instead of POS for the structures, except the category formulaic, which are implicit relations. In a premodifier structure one entity and the relation are modifiers of the other entity, (e.g., US. *President* Obama). In a possessive structure one entity is in a possessive case (e.g., Microsoft's *CEO* Steve Ballmer). In a preposition structure, relation words are related with one entity by a preposition (e.g., Steve Ballmer, *CEO* of Microsoft). In a verbal structure relations are verb phrases.

The heuristic rules are presented in Figure 5. The

[5]But adding the two features seems does not solve the problem.

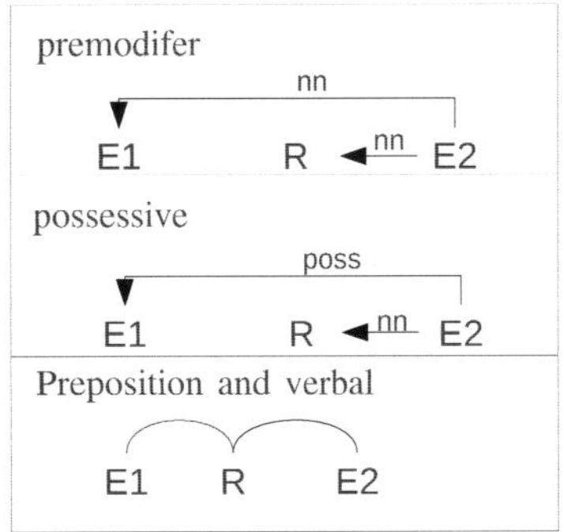

Figure 5: Dependent link heuristics for relation detection.

premodifier and possessive relation words are not in the Stanford collapsed form of the dependency path between two entities. When there is a direct dependency link between two entities that is labelled *nn* or *poss*, there should be an *nn* link between the second entity and the relation candidate (in Figure 5's top two rows). Otherwise, there should be links between the two entities and the relation, respectively (in Figure 5's last row). In this case, link types and directions are not constrained. For example, both *E1* ←(nsubj) *R* →(dobj) *E2* for the triple <Obama, visit, Canada> in "*Obama* visited *Canada*." and *E1* →(appos) *R* →(prep_of) *E2* for the triple <Obama, president, United States> in "*Obama*, the president of the *United States*, visited Canada." belong to that structure. To refine the verbal pattern, the link between the relation words and entities cannot be a conjunction.

Next, we need to check the consistency of relation words. Two separated sequences of relation words should have a dependency link between each other to confirm that they are semantically related. Relation sequences should include only necessary prepositions.

7 Experiments

We compared the unsupervised heuristic rule method and the supervised SVM method discussed above against REVERB (Fader et al., 2011) and OLLIE (Mausam et al., 2012), using three datasets. One dataset consists of sentences from the Penn Treebank, and the other two are the experiment datasets of each of the two systems being compared.

E feature	F1	the dependency link label between two entities, *null* if none.
R features	F2	whether relation is a noun phrase or a verb phrase
	F3	whether there is a link between the two segments (if there are two discontinuous segments)
between E and R	F4	whether there is a link between entities and the relation
	F5	the shortest dependency path distance between entities and the relation (1,2,3,4, or >4)
	F6	the preposition link and the last preposition word of relation (if there is such a link or word)
	F7	whether there is a conjunction link in the shortest path between entities and the relation
	F8	whether there is a apposition link in the shortest path between entities and the relation

Table 1: Noise filter feature vector.

7.1 Treebank Set

7.1.1 Preparing Data

Within the research community, it is difficult to find Open IE test data which includes all kinds of relations. So we have created our own data from the Penn Treebank for evaluation[6]. We assess the drop in performance introduced by using a tool to parse sentences compared to using "ideal" parse trees provided in the Penn Treebank. Named entities are tagged for every sentence using the Stanford NLP tool. Candidate NE pairs are extracted within a certain distance[7]. We randomly selected 756 sentences from WSJ Sections 2-21 as our training set, 100 each from Section 22 and Section 23-24 as the development and the test set, respectively. This is also the setting for most parsers.

We manually annotated whether there is a relation between two entities in a sentence (for evaluation of the Binary task). If there is a relation between two entities, the annotator needs to indicate which words are relation words (for evaluation of the Triple task). There is no restriction of relation forms for the annotator in this task.

We manually analyzed 417 relation instances from our training set. 28% are implicit relations, i.e., relations without words or with prepositions. Less than 1% are with adjectives, while 71% are noun or verb phrases. In the 71%, 60% are noun relations and 40% are verbal. The relation pattern in Section 4 can extract 80% of them. Our data contains more verbal relations than the ACE's RDC, less than corpora in other Open IE papers.

We compare every system by recall, precision, and F-score. The evaluation of the Binary task is based on entity pairs and is straightforward. The evaluation of the Triple task is based on relation triples. We need to manually compare the triples extracted by each system and the gold standard to avoid double-counting. For instance, if both *vice president* and *president* are extracted, it is counted as one[8]. Several entity pairs have multiple relations, such as "A is CEO and founder of B." Any relation which can not be represented by a verb or noun is counted as one miss in the Triple task.

To compare with the REVERB system, NE pairs are labelled as two noun phrase chunks for the system input. It is difficult to compare with OLLIE, as the system is a black box with integrated entity extraction and parsing. We compared manually the pairs extracted by OLLIE and the tagged data. Only results of intersection entity pairs are considered. The threshold of OLLIE and REVERB confidence is set to achieve the best F-score in the development set.

7.1.2 Results

The Binary task results on the test set are shown in Table 2. Each system decides whether there is a relation between two entities. The heuristic rule (DP rules) method, REVERB, and OLLIE each tag pairs containing a relation if any relation candidates are identified. As indicated, the SVM method performs the best with DP rules ranking second. Note that OLLIE uses MaltParser, so it's better to compare with the coupling of SVM with Stanford Parser, but that comparison doesn't change the result.

The Triple task results are shown in Table 3. Each system extracts relation triples from sentences. The SVM features include both tree (Figure 4) and vector features (Table 1). *All relations* in the table include nominal, verbal, and implicit relations. To scrutinize

[6]The data can be downloaded from http://cs.ualberta.ca/~yx2/

[7]Here we set the distance as 20, determined by empirical evidence, a majority of the relations are within this distance.

[8]It is difficult to decide if *president* in this case is wrong. This is related to multi-word expression and will be future work.

	P	R	F-score
Treebank parsing + DP rules	0.833	0.549	0.662
Treebank parsing + SVM	0.896	0.767	0.826
Stanford parsing + DP rules	0.783	0.522	0.627
Stanford parsing + SVM	0.744	0.711	0.727
REVERB (no parsing)	0.333	0.1	0.153
OLLIE (MaltParser)	0.583	0.389	0.467

Table 2: Relation extraction results on Treebank set (Binary)

All relations	P	R	F-score
Treebank parsing + DP rules	0.741	0.467	0.573
Treebank parsing + SVM	0.824	0.462	**0.592**
Stanford parsing + SVM	0.75	0.433	**0.549**
OLLIE (MaltParser)	0.583	0.389	0.467
Noun relations	P	R	F-score
Treebank parsing + DP rules	0.75	0.735	0.742
Treebank parsing + SVM	0.829	0.708	**0.764**
Stanford parsing + SVM	0.756	0. 689	**0.721**
OLLIE (MaltParser)	0.8	0.408	0.54
Verb relations	P	R	F-score
Treebank parsing + DP rules	0.7	0.368	0.483
Treebank parsing + SVM	0.727	0.381	0.5
Stanford parsing + SVM	0.727	0.32	0.444
REVERB (no parsing)	0.286	0.381	0.327
OLLIE (MaltParser)	0.429	0.714	**0.536**

Table 3: Relation extraction results on Treebank set (Triple)

the result, we also show the results on noun and verb relations separately. The SVM model achieves best performance, 33% improvement on nominal relation extractions over OLLIE.

The loss of recall for systems (except SVM) in the Binary task can be explained by the fact that nearly 20% of relations are implicit.

In both the Binary and Triple tasks, one source of failure arose from conjunction and apposition structures. For example, in the sentence "...industry executives analyzed the appointment of the new chief executive, Robert Louis-Dreyfus, who joins Saatchi ..." the method can detect the relation *<chief executive, joins, Saatchi>*, but not *<Robert Louis-Dreyfus, joins, Saatchi>*. We attempted to address this problem by adding features into SVM linear kernel (Table 1), but this has not worked in our tests.

One cause of recall loss in the Triple task for REVERB and our two approaches is that verbal relation words can be non-consecutive. For instance, the preposition might be far away from the related verb in one sentence, in which case both our methods and REVERB can not confirm that extraction. OLLIE has better results on verb relations mainly because they use dependency link patterns to extract relation words, which alleviate the problem. On the other side, one drawback of OLLIE is that it failed to extract a few premodifer structure relations, e.g. "U.S. President Obama." That may happen because they do not have an independent step for named entity extraction, which is crucial for that type of relations.

	P	R	F-score
Stanford parsing + DP rules	0.711	0.811	0.756
Stanford parsing + SVM	0.718	0.859	**0.781**
REVERB	0.577	0.95	0.716

Table 4: Relation extraction results on REVERB set (Triple).

7.2 REVERB Set

The authors of the REVERB method provide 1000 tagged training sentences and 500 test sentences. They also provide REVERB's extracted relations and instances' confidence for the 500 test sentences. The 500 test sentences are segmented into 5 folds for a significance t-test. At each iteration, the remaining 400 sentences are used as a development set to set the threshold of REVERB confidence.

To compare with REVERB, we use as input the sentences parsed by the Stanford parser and relation triples extracted by REVERB for both training and testing. The output of our system is true or false for every triple by using the tree kernel[9]. The SVM system is trained on the 1000 training sentences. The results are shown in Table 4. Only SVM is statistically significant better than REVERB (with $\alpha = 0.05$)[10].

7.3 OLLIE set

The authors of the OLLIE system provide a test set which has 300 sentences and OLLIE extracted 900 triples. Experiment setting is similar to that of REVERB set. The SVM tree kernel model is trained on OLLIE's leave one out dataset. The results in Table

[9]The polynomial kernel is not used for REVERB and OLLIE data as the their relation word form is simpler than ours.

[10]Note that the results here seem better than the results shown on (Fader et al., 2011). It is because our evaluation is based on the set REVERB extracted, as we only want to compare noise filters not with entity extraction, while the results in (Fader et al., 2011) is based on the union relation set of several systems.

	P	R	F-score
Stanford parsing + SVM	0.685	0.941	**0.793**
OLLIE	0.667	0.961	0.787

Table 5: Relation extraction results on OLLIE set (Triple).

5 show our method achieves slightly better performance, although not statistically significant.

Besides errors caused by parsing, one main cause of loss of precision is that our system is unable to detect entities that are wrong as we only concern the head of the entity. For instance, "Bogan 's Birmingham Busters , before moving to Los Angeles , California" is one entity in one OLLIE relation, where only "Bogan 's Birmingham Busters" is the correct entity.

8 Conclusion

We have described some of the limits of current Open IE systems, which concentrate on identifying explicit relations, i.e., relations which are mediated by open class words. This strategy ignores what we describe as implicit relations, e.g., *locate* relations in "Washington, U.S." We propose two subtasks for Open IE: first confirming whether there is a relation between two entities, and then whether a relation thus extracted is correct. The first task include both implicit and explicit relations; the second task is common in the previous Open IE which deals with explicit relations. In our case we have developed an Open IE system which uses SVM tree kernels applied to dependency parses for both tasks. Our system achieves superior results on several datasets. We also propose an unsupervised method which is based on heuristic rules from dependency parse links, and compared that with our SVM tree kernel methods. Our experiments show it is a strong baseline for Open IE.

For further work, we intend to improve Open IE by tackling the conjunction and apposition structure problem. Another direction will be to extract relation words for implicit relations. Relation words such as *locate* for "Washington, U.S." will be considered.

Acknowledgments

We would like to acknowledge Prof. Grzegorz Kondrak 's valuable advice. We also want to thank the anonymous reviewers for their helpful suggestions. This work was funded in part by the NSERC Business Intelligence Network, Alberta Innovates Center for Machine Learning (AICML) and Alberta Innovates Technology Futures (AITF).

References

Alan Akbik. 2009. Wanderlust : Extracting semantic relations from natural language text using dependency grammar patterns. In *WWW 2009 Workshop on Semantic Search*, volume 137, pages 279–290.

Michele Banko, Michael J Cafarella, Stephen Soderl, Matt Broadhead, and Oren Etzioni. 2007. Open information extraction from the web. In *In International Joint Conference on Artificial Intelligence*, pages 2670–2676.

Razvan C. Bunescu and Raymond J. Mooney. 2005. A shortest path dependency kernel for relation extraction. In *Proceedings of the conference on Human Language Technology and Empirical Methods in Natural Language Processing*, HLT '05, pages 724–731, Stroudsburg, PA, USA. Association for Computational Linguistics.

Yee Seng Chan and Roth Dan. 2011. Exploiting syntactico-semantic structures for relation extraction. In *Proceedings of the 49th Annual Meeting of the Association for Computational Linguistics: Human Language Technologies - Volume 1*, HLT '11, pages 551–560, Stroudsburg, PA, USA. Association for Computational Linguistics.

Janara Christensen, Mausam, Stephen Soderland, and Oren Etzioni. 2011. An analysis of open information extraction based on semantic role labeling. In *Proceedings of the sixth international conference on Knowledge capture*, K-CAP '11, pages 113–120, New York, NY, USA. ACM.

Michael Collins and Nigel Duffy. 2001. Convolution kernels for natural language. In *Advances in Neural Information Processing Systems 14*, pages 625–632. MIT Press.

Danilo Croce, Alessandro Moschitti, and Roberto Basili. 2011. Structured lexical similarity via convolution kernels on dependency trees. In *Proceedings of the Conference on Empirical Methods in Natural Language Processing*, EMNLP '11, pages 1034–1046, Stroudsburg, PA, USA. Association for Computational Linguistics.

Aron Culotta and Jeffrey Sorensen. 2004. Dependency tree kernels for relation extraction. In *Proceedings of the 42nd Annual Meeting on Association for Computational Linguistics*, ACL '04, Stroudsburg, PA, USA. Association for Computational Linguistics.

M.C. De Marneffe, B. MacCartney, and C.D. Manning. 2006. Generating typed dependency parses from phrase structure parses. In *Proceedings of LREC*, volume 6, pages 449–454.

Anthony Fader, Stephen Soderland, and Oren Etzioni. 2011. Identifying relations for open information extraction. In *Proceedings of the Conference on Empirical Methods in Natural Language Processing*, EMNLP '11, pages 1535–1545, Stroudsburg, PA, USA. Association for Computational Linguistics.

Bill MacCartney, Trond Grenager, Marie-Catherine de Marneffe, Daniel Cer, and Christopher D. Manning. 2006. Learning to recognize features of valid textual entailments. In *Proceedings of the main conference on Human Language Technology Conference of the North American Chapter of the Association of Computational Linguistics*, HLT-NAACL '06, pages 41–48. Association for Computational Linguistics.

Mausam, Michael Schmitz, Robert Bart, Stephen Soderland, and Oren Etzioni. 2012. Open language learning for information extraction. In *Proceedings of the 2012 Joint Conference on Empirical Methods in Natural Language Processing and Computational Natural Language Learning*, pages 523–534. Association for Computational Linguistics.

Alessandro Moschitti. 2005. *Automatic text categorization: from information retrieval to support vector learning*. Aracne.

Alessandro Moschitti. 2006. Efficient convolution kernels for dependency and constituent syntactic trees. In *Proceedings of the 17th European conference on Machine Learning*, ECML'06, pages 318–329, Berlin, Heidelberg. Springer-Verlag.

Truc-Vien T. Nguyen, Alessandro Moschitti, and Giuseppe Riccardi. 2009. Convolution kernels on constituent, dependency and sequential structures for relation extraction. In *Proceedings of the 2009 Conference on Empirical Methods in Natural Language Processing: Volume 3 - Volume 3*, EMNLP '09, pages 1378–1387, Stroudsburg, PA, USA. Association for Computational Linguistics.

Mengqui Wang. 2008. A re-examination of dependency path kernels for relation extraction. In *Proceedings of the Third International Joint Conference on Natural Language Processing*, pages 841–846, Hyderabad, India. Asian Federation of Natural Language Processing, Association for Computational Linguistics.

Fei Wu and Daniel S. Weld. 2010. Open information extraction using wikipedia. In *Proceedings of the 48th Annual Meeting of the Association for Computational Linguistics*, ACL '10, pages 118–127, Stroudsburg, PA, USA. Association for Computational Linguistics.

Guo-Dong Zhou and Qiao-Ming Zhu. 2011. Kernel-based semantic relation detection and classification via enriched parse tree structure. *J. Comput. Sci. Technol.*, 26(1):45–56, January.

Finding What Matters in Questions

Xiaoqiang Luo, Hema Raghavan, Vittorio Castelli, Sameer Maskey and Radu Florian
IBM T.J. Watson Research Center
1101 Kitchawan Road, Yorktown Heights, NY 10598
{xiaoluo,hraghav,vittorio,smaskey,raduf}@us.ibm.com

Abstract

In natural language question answering (QA) systems, questions often contain terms and phrases that are critically important for retrieving or finding answers from documents. We present a learnable system that can extract and rank these terms and phrases (dubbed *mandatory matching phrases* or MMPs), and demonstrate their utility in a QA system on Internet discussion forum data sets. The system relies on deep syntactic and semantic analysis of questions only and is independent of relevant documents. Our proposed model can predict MMPs with high accuracy. When used in a QA system features derived from the MMP model improve performance significantly over a state-of-the-art baseline. The final QA system was the best performing system in the DARPA BOLT-IR evaluation.

1 Introduction

In most question answering (QA) systems and search engines term-weights are assigned in a context independent fashion using simple TF-IDF like models (Robertson and Walker, 1994; Ponte and Croft, 1998). Even the more recent advances in information retrieval techniques for query term weighting (Bendersky et al., 2010; Bendersky, 2011) typically rely on bag-of-words models and corpus statistics, such as inverse-document-frequency (IDF), to assign weights to terms in questions. While such solutions may work for keyword queries of the type common on search engines such as Google, they do not exploit syntactic and semantic information when it comes to well formed natural language questions. In this paper we propose a new model that identifies important terms and phrases in a natural language question, providing better query analysis that ultimately leads to significant improvements in a QA system.

To motivate the work presented here, consider the query "How does one apply for a New York day care license?". A bag-of-words model would likely assign a high score to "**New licenses** for **day care** centers in **York** county, PA" because of high word overlap, but it does not answer the question, and also the state is wrong. A matching component that uses the phrases "New York," "day care," and "license" is likely to do better. However, a better matching component will understand that *in the context of this query* all three phrases "New York," "day care" and "license" are important, and that "New York" needs to modify "day care." A snippet that does not *contain*[1] these important phrases, is unlikely an answer. We call these important phrases *mandatory matching phrases* (MMPs).

In this paper, we explore deep syntactic and semantic analyses of questions to determine and rank MMPs. Unlike existing work (Zhao and Callan, 2010; Bendersky et al., 2010; Bendersky, 2011), where term/concept weights are learned from a set of questions and judged documents based on *corpus-based statistics*, we annotate *questions* and build a trainable system to select and score MMPs. This model relies heavily on existing syntactic parsers and semantic-oriented named-entity recognizers, but does not need question answer pairs. This is espe-

[1]"contain" here means semantic equivalence or entailment, not necessarily the exact words or phrases.

cially attractive at the initial system-building stage when no or little answer data is available.

The main contributions of this paper are: firstly, we propose a framework to select and rank important question phrases (MMPs) for question answering in Section 3. This framework seamlessly incorporates lexical, syntactic and semantic information, resulting in an MMP prediction F-measure as high as 88.6%. Secondly, we show that features derived from identified MMPs improve significantly a relevance classification model, in Section 4.2. Thirdly, we show that using the improved relevance model into our QA system results in a statistically significant 5 point improvement in F-measure, in Section 5. This finding is further corroborated by the results on the official 2012 BOLT IR (IR, 2012) task where the combined system yielded the best performance in the evaluation.

2 Related Work

Popular information retrieval systems like BM25 (Robertson and Walker, 1994) and language models (Ponte and Croft, 1998) use unsupervised techniques based on corpus statistics for term weighting. Many of these techniques are variants of the one proposed by (Luhn, 1958). Recently, several researchers have studied approaches for term weighting using supervised learning techniques. However, much of this research has focused on information retrieval task rather than on question answering problems of the nature addressed in this paper. (Bendersky and Croft, 2008) restricted themselves to predicting key noun phrases, which is perhaps sufficient for a retrieval task. However, for questions like "Find comments about how American hedge funds legally avoid taxes," the verb "avoid" is perhaps as important as the noun phrase "American hedge funds" and "taxes". Works like that of (Lease et al., 2009) and (Zhao and Callan, 2010) predict importance at the word level. While word level importance is perhaps sufficient for an IR task, predicting the importance of phrases, especially those derived from a parse tree, gives a much richer representation that might also be useful for better question understanding and thus generate more relevant answers. Both (Lease et al., 2009; Zhao and Callan, 2010) propose supervised methods that learn from a large set of queries and relevance judgments on their answers. While this is possible in a TREC Ad-hoc-retrieval-like task, such a large training corpus of question-answer pairs is unavailable for most scenarios. (Monz, 2007) learns term weights for the IR component of a question answering task. His work unlike ours does not aim to find the answers to the questions.

Most QA systems in the literature have dealt with answering factoid questions, where the answer is a noun phrase in response to questions of the form "Who," "Where," "When." Most systems have a question analysis component that represents the question as syntactic relations in a parse or as deep semantic relations in a handcrafted ontology (Hermjakob et al., 2000; Chu-carroll et al., 2003; Moldovan et al., 2003). In addition certain systems (Bunescu and Huang, 2010) aim to find the "focus" of the question, that is, the noun-phrases in the question that would co-refer with answers. Additionally, much past work has focused on finding the lexical answer type (Pinchak, 2006; Li and Roth, 2002). Since these papers considered a small number of answer types, rules over the detected relations and answer types could be applied to find the relevant answer. However, since our system answers non-factoid questions that can have answer of arbitrary types, we want to use as few rules as possible. The MMPs therefore become a critical component of our system, both for question analysis and for relevance detection.

3 Question Data and MMP Model

To train the MMP model, we first create a set of questions and label their MMPs. The labeled data is then used to train a statistical model to predict MMPs for new questions as discussed next.

3.1 Question Corpus

We use a subset of the DARPA BOLT corpus (see Section 5.1) containing forum postings in English. Four annotators use a search tool to explore this document collection. They can perform keyword searches and retrieve forum threads from which they generate questions. The program participants decided a basic set of question types that are out-of-scope of the current research agenda. Accordingly, annotators cannot generate questions (1) that require reasoning or calculation over the data to compute the answers; (2) that are vague or ambiguous; (3) that can be broken into multiple disjoint questions; (4) that are multiple choice questions; (5) that are factoid questions—the kinds that have already been well studied in TREC (Voorhees, 2004). Any other kind of question is allowed. Two other annotators, who have neither browsed the corpus nor generated the questions, mark selected spans of the questions into one of two categories—*MMP-Must* and *MMP-maybe*. The annotation tool allows arbitrary spans to be highlighted and the annotators are instructed to select spans corresponding to the smallest semantic units. The phrases that are very likely to appear contiguously in a relevant answer are marked as *MMP-Must*. Annotators can mark multiple spans per question, but not overlapping spans. We generated 201 annotated questions using this process.

Figure 1 contains an example, where "American," "hedge fund," and "legally avoid taxes" are required elements to find answers and are thus marked as *MMP-Must*s (signified by enclosing rectangles). We purposely annotate MMPs at the word level and not in the parse tree, because this requires minimal linguistic knowledge. We do, however, employ an automatic procedure to attach MMPs to parse tree nodes when generating MMP training instances.

3.2 MMP Training

Questions annotated in Section 3.1 are first processed by an information extraction (IE) pipeline consisting of syntactic parsing, mention detection and coreference resolution (Florian et al., 2004; Luo et al., 2004; Luo and Zitouni, 2005). After IE, we have access to the syntactic structure represented by a parse tree and semantic information represented by coreferenced mentions (including those of named entities).

To take advantage of the availability of the syntactic and semantic information, we first attach the MMP annotations to parse tree nodes of a question, and, if necessary, we augment the parse tree.

There are several reasons why we want to embed the MMPs into a parse tree. First, many constituents in parse trees correspond to important phrases we want to capture, especially proper names. Second, after an MMP is attached to a tree node, the problem

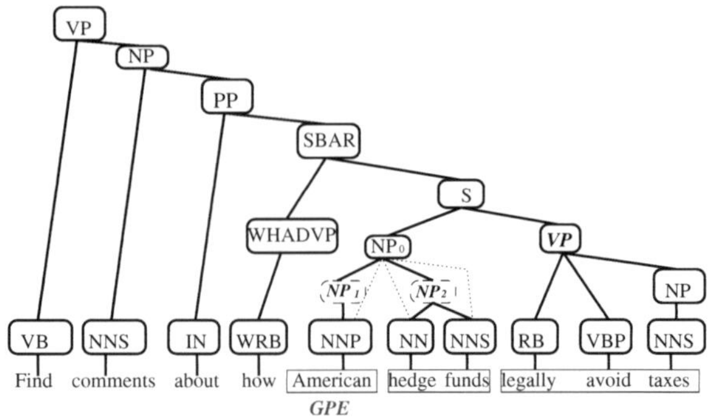

Figure 1: MMPs are aligned with tree nodes: MMPs are shown in rectangular boxes along with their aligned nodes (with slanted labels); augmented parse tree nodes (i.e., NP1, NP2) in dashed nodes. Dotted edges under NP0 are the structure before the tree is augmented.

of predicting MMPs reduces to classifying parse tree nodes, and syntactic information can be naturally built into the MMP classifier. Lastly, and more importantly, associating MMPs with tree nodes opens the door to explore features derived from the syntactic parse tree. For instance, it is easy to read bilexical dependencies from a parse tree (provided that head information is propagated); with MMPs aligned with the parse tree, bilexical dependencies can be ranked by examining whether or not an MMP phrase is a head or a dependent. This way, not only are the dependencies in a question captured, but MMP scores or ranks can be propagated to dependencies as well. We will discuss more how MMP features are computed in Section 4.2.2.

Annotators can mark MMPs that are not perfectly aligned with a tree node. Hence, care has to be taken when generating MMP training instances. As an example, In Figure 1, "American" and "hedge funds" are marked as two separate MMPs, but the Penn-Tree-style parse tree has a flat "NP0" constituent spanning directly on "American hedge fund," illustrated in Figure 1 as dotted edges.

To anchor MMPs in the parse tree, we *augment* it by combining the IE output and the MMP annotation. In the aforementioned example, "American" is a named mention with the entity type GPE (geo-political entity) and there is no non-terminal node spanning it: so, a new node "NP1" is created; "hedge funds" is marked as an MMP: so, a second node ("NP2") is created to anchor it.

A training instance for building the MMP model is defined as a span along with an MMP label. For instance, "hedge funds" in Figure 1 will generate a positive training instance as $\langle$`(5,6), +1`$\rangle$, where `(5,6)` is the span of "hedge funds" in the question sentence, and `+1` signifies that it is a positive training instance. For the purpose of this paper we use only binary labels, mapping all MMP-Must to $+1$ and MMP-Skip and MMP-Maybe to -1.

Formally, we use the following procedure to generate training instances:

Algorithm 1 Pseudo code to generate MMP training instances.

Input: An input question tree with detected mentions and marked MMPs
Output: A list of MMP training instances
1: Foreach mention m in the question
2: if no node spans m, and m does not cross bracket
3: Find lowest node N dominating m
4: Insert a child node of N that spans exactly m
5: Foreach mention p in marked MMPs
6: Find lowest non-terminal N_p dominating p
7: Generate a positive training example for N_p
8: Mark N_p as visited
9: Recursively generate instances for N_p's children
10: Generate a negative training instance for all unvisited nodes in Step 5-9

Steps 1 to 4 augment the question tree by creating a node for each named mention, provided that no existing node spans exactly the mention and the mention does not cross-bracket tree constituents. Steps 5 to 8 generate positive training instances for marked MMPs; step 9 recursively generates positive training instances [2] for tree nodes dominated by N_p, where N_p is the lowest non-terminal node dominating the marked MMP p.

After MMP training instances are generated we design and compute features for each instance, and use them to train a classifier.

3.3 MMP Features and Classifier

We compute four types of features that will be used in a statistical classifier. These features are designed to characterize a phrase from the lexical, syntactic, semantic and corpus-level aspect. The weights associated with these features are automatically learned from training data.

We will use "(NP1 American)" in Figure 1 as the running example below.

Lexical Features: Lexical features are motivated by the observation that spellings in English sometimes offer important cues about word significance. For example, an all-capitalized word often signifies an acronym; an all-digit word in a question is likely a year, etc. We compute the following lexical features for a candidate MMP:

CaseFeatures: is the first word of an MMP upper-case? Is it all capital letters? Does it contain numeric letters? For "(NP American)" in Figure 1, the upper-case feature fires.

CommonQWord: Does the MMP contain question words, including "What," "When," "Who," etc.

Syntactic Features: The second group of features are computed from syntactic parse trees after annotated MMPs are aligned with question parse-trees as described previously.

PhraseLabel: this feature returns the phrasal label of the MMP. For "(NP American)" in Figure 1, the feature value is "NP." This captures that an NP is more likely an MMP than, say, an ADVP.

NPUnique: this Boolean feature fires if a phrase is the only NP in a question, indicating that this constituent probably should be matched. For "(NP American)," the feature value would be false.

PosOfPTN: these features characterize the position of the parse tree node to which an MMP is anchored. They compute: (1) the position of the left-most word of the node; (2) whether the left-most word is the beginning of the question; (3) the depth of the anchoring node, defined as the length of the path to the root node. For "(NP American)" in Figure 1, the features state that it is the 5th word in the sentence; it is not the first word of the sentence; and the depth of the node is 6 (where root has depth 0).

PhrLenToQLenRatio: This feature computes the number of words in an MMP, and its relative ratio to the sentence length. This feature controls the length of MMPs at decoding time, since most of MMPs are short.

Semantic Features (NETypes): The third group of features are computed from named entities and aim to capture semantic information. The feature tests if

[2]One exception to this step is that if a node spans a single stop word, then a negative training instance is generated.

a phrase is or contains a named entity, and, if this is the case, the value is the entity type. For "(NP American)" in Figure 1, the feature value would be "GPE."

Corpus-based Features (AvgCorpusIDF): This group of features computes the average of the IDFs of the words in this phrase. From the corpus IDF, we also compute the ratio between the number of stop words and the total number of words in the MMP, and use it as another feature.

3.4 MMP Classification Results

We now show that we can reliably predict MMPs of questions. We split our set of 201 annotated questions into a training set consisting of 174 questions and a test set with the remaining 27 questions. We use the procedure and features described in Section 3 to train a logistic regression binary classifier using WEKA. Then, the trained MMP classifier is applied to the test set question trees. Since the class bias is quite skewed (only 16% of the phrases are marked as MMP-Must) we also use re-sampling at training time to balance the prior probability of the two classes. At testing time, a parser and a mention detection algorithm (Florian et al., 2004; Luo et al., 2004; Luo and Zitouni, 2005) are run on each question. The detected mentions are then used to augment the question parse trees. The MMP classifier achieves an 88.6% F-measure (cf. Table 1, with 91.6% precision). This is a respectable number, considering the limited amount of training data. We experimented with decision trees and bagging as well but found logistic regression to work the best.

Feature	P	R	F1
AvgCorpusIDF	0.849	0.634	0.725
+NPUnique	0.868	0.634	0.732
+NETypes	0.867	0.662	0.750
+PhraseLabel	0.890	0.705	0.783
+CaseFeatures	0.829	0.820	0.824
+PosOfPTN	0.911	0.852	0.880
+PhrLenToQLenRatio	0.915	0.855	0.883
+commonQWord	0.916	0.858	0.886

Table 1: The performances of the MMP classifier while incrementally adding features.

The examples in Table 2 illustrate the top three MMPs produced by the model on two questions. These results are encouraging: in the first example the word AIDS is clearly the most "important" word, but IDF alone is not adequate to place it in the top since AIDS is also a common verb (words are lower-cased before IDF look-up). Similarly, in the third example, the phrase "the causes" has a much higher MMP score than the phrase "the concerns" (MMP score of 0.109), even though the words "concerns" has a slightly higher IDF, 2.80, than the word "causes"(2.68). However, in this question, understanding that the word "causes" is critical to the meaning of the question is critical and is captured by the MMP model.

We analyzed feature importance for MMP classification by incrementally adding each feature group to the model. The result is tabulated in Table 1. Not surprisingly, syntactical (i.e., "NPUnique," "PhraseLabel" and "PosOfPTN") and semantic features (i.e., "NETypes") are complementary to the corpus-based statistics features (i.e., average IDF). Lexical features also improve recall: the addition of "CaseFeatures" boosts the F-measure by 4 points. At first sight, it is surprising that the feature group "PosOfPTN," which characterize the position of a candidate MMP relative to the sentence and relative to the parse tree, has such a large impact—it improves the F-measure by 5.6 points. However, a cursory browsing of the training questions reveals that most MMPs are short and concentrate towards the end of the sentence. So this feature group helps by directing the model to predict MMPs at the end of the sentence and to prefer short phrases versus long ones.

4 Relevance Model with MMPs

We now validate our second hypothesis that MMPs are effective for open domain question answering. We demonstrate this through the improvement in performance on relevance prediction. More specifically, given a natural language question, the task is one of finding relevant sentences in posts on online forums. The relevance prediction component is critical for question answering as has been seen in TREC(Ittycheriah and Roukos, 2001) and more recently in the Jeopardy challenge(Gondek et al., 2012). The improved relevance model further improves our question answering system as seen in Section 5.

Question	Top 3 MMPs	MMP-score	Top words by IDF
List statistics about changes in the demographics of AIDS.	1: AIDS 2: changes 3: the demographics	0.955 0.525 0.349	demographics AIDS statistics
What are the concerns about the causes of autism?	1: autism 2: the causes 3: the causes of autism	0.989 0.422 0.362	autism concerns causes

Table 2: Example questions and the top-3 phrases ranked by the MMP model.

4.1 Data for Relevance Model

The data to train and test the relevance model is obtained as follows. First, a rudimentary version (i.e., key word search) of a QA system using Lucene is built. The Lucene index comprised of a large number of threads in online forums released to the participants of the BOLT-IR task(IR, 2012) for development of our systems. The corpus is described in more detail in Sec. 5. Top snippets returned by the search engine are judged for relevancy by our annotators. The initial (small) batch of data is used to train a relevance model which is deployed in the system. The new model is in turn used to create more answers for new questions. When more data is collected, the relevance model is retrained and redeployed to collect more data. The process is iterated for several months, and at the end of this process, a total of 390 training questions are created and about 28,915 snippets are judged by human annotators, out of which about 6,528 are relevant answers. These question-answers pairs are used to train the final relevance model used in our question-answering system. A separate held-out test set of 59 questions is created and its system output is also judged by humans. This data set is our test set.

4.2 Relevance Prediction

A key component in our question-answering system is the snippet relevance model, which is used to compute the probability that a snippet is relevant to a question. The relevance model is a conditional distribution $P(r|q, s; D)$, where r is a binary random variable indicating if the candidate snippet s is relevant to the question q. D is the document where the snippet s is found.

In our question answering system, MMPs extracted from questions are used to compute the features for the relevance model. To test their effectiveness, we conduct a controlled experiment by comparing the system with MMP features with 2 baselines: (1) a system without MMP features; (2) a baseline with each word as an MMP and the word's IDF as the MMP score.

4.2.1 Baseline Features

We list the features used in our baseline system, where no MMP feature is used. The features can be categorized into the following types. **(1) Text Match Features**: One set of features are the cosine scores between different representations of the query and the snippet. In one version the query and snippet words are used as is; in another version the query and snippet are stemmed using porter stemmer; in yet another the words are morphed to their roots by a table extracted from WordNet. We also compute the inclusion scores (the proportion of query words found in the snippet) and other word overlap features. **(2) Answer Type Features:** The top 3 predictions of a statistical classifier trained to predict answer categories were used as features. **(3) Mention Match Features** compute whether a named entity in the query occurs in the snippet. The matching takes into consideration the results from within and cross document coreference resolution components for nominal and pronominal mentions. **(4) Event match features** use several hand-crafted dictionaries containing terms exclusive to various types of events like "violence", "legal", "election". Accordingly a set of features that take a value of "1" if both the query and snippet contain the same event type were designed. **(5) Snippet Statistics:** Several features based on snippet length, the position of the snippet in the post etc were created.

4.2.2 Features Derived from MMP

The MMPs extracted from questions are used to compute features in the following ways.

As MMPs are aligned with a question's syntactic tree, they can be used to find answers by matching a question constituent with that of a candidate snippet. The MMP model also returns a score for each phrase, which can be used to compute the degree to which a question matches a candidate snippet.

In this section, we use $s = w_1^n$ to denote a snippet with words $w_1, w_2, \cdots, w_n$, and m to denote a phrase from the MMP model along with a score $M(m)$. The features are listed below:

HardMatch: Let $I(m \in s)$ be a 1 or 0 function indicating if a snippet contains the MMP m, then the hard match score is computed as:

$$HM(q,s) = \frac{\sum_{m \in q} M(m) I(m \in s)}{\sum_{m \in q} M(m)}.$$

SoftLMMatch: The SoftLMMatch score is a language-model (LM) based score, similar to that used in (Bendersky and Croft, 2008), except that MMPs play the role of concepts. The snippet-side language model score $LM(v|s)$ is computed as:

$$LM(v|s) = \frac{\sum_{i=1}^{n} I(w_i = v) + 0.05}{n + 0.05|V|},$$

where w_i is the ith in snippet s; $I(w_i = v)$ is an indicator function, taking value 1 if w_i is v and 0 otherwise; $|V|$ is the vocabulary size.

The soft match score between a question q and a snippet s is then:

$$SM(q,s) = \frac{\sum_{m \in q} \left(M(m) \prod_{w \in m} LM(w|s) \right)}{\sum_{m \in q} M(m)},$$

where $m \in q$ denotes all MMPs in question q, and similarly, $w \in m$ signifying words in m.

MMPInclScore: An MMP m's inclusion score is:

$$IS(m,s) = \frac{\sum_{w \in m} I(l(w,s) > \delta) IDF(w)}{\sum_{w \in m} IDF(w)},$$

where $w \in m$ are the words in m; $I(\cdot)$ is the indicator function taking value 1 when the argument is true and 0 otherwise; δ is a constant threshold; $IDF(w)$ is the IDF of word w. $l(w,s)$ is the similarity of word w to the snippet s as: $l(w,s) = max_{v \in s} JW(w,v)$, where $JW(w,v)$ is the Jaro Winkler similarity score between words w and v.

The MMP weighted inclusion score between the question q and snippet s is computed as:

$$IS(q,s) = \frac{\sum_{m \in q} M(m) IS(m,s)}{\sum_{m \in q} M(m)}$$

MMPRankDep: This feature, $RD(q,s)$ first tests if there exists a matched bilexcial dependency between q and s; if yes, it further tests if the head or dependent in the matched dependency is the head of any MMP.

Let $m_{(i)}$ be the ith ranked MMP; let $\langle w_h, w_d | q \rangle$ and $\langle u_h, u_d | s \rangle$ be bilexical dependencies from q and s, respectively, where w_h and u_h are the heads and w_d and u_d are the dependents; let $EQ(w,u)$ be a function testing if the question word w and snippet word u are a match. In our implementation, $EQ(w,u)$ is true if either w and u are exactly the same, or their morphs are the same, or they head the same entity, or their synset in WordNet overlap. With these notations, $RD(q,s)$ is true if and only if

$$EQ(w_h, u_h) \wedge EQ(w_d, u_d) \wedge w_h \in m_{(i)} \wedge w_d \in m_{(j)}$$

is true for some $\langle w_h, w_d | q \rangle$, for some $\langle u_h, u_d | s \rangle$ and for some i and j.

$EQ(w_h, u_h) \wedge EQ(w_d, u_d)$ requires that the question dependency $\langle w_h, w_d | q \rangle$ and the snippet dependency $\langle u_h, u_d | s \rangle$ match; $w_h \in m_{(i)} \wedge w_d \in m_{(j)}$ requires that the head word and dependent word are in the ith-rank and j^{th} rank MMP, respectively. Therefore, $RD(q,s)$ is a dependency feature enhanced with MMPs.

To test the effectiveness of the MMP features, we trained 3 snippet classifiers on the data described in Section 4.1: one baseline system without MMP features (henceforth "no-MMP"); a second baseline with words as MMPs and their IDFs as the scores in the MMP model(henceforth "IDF-as-MMP"); the third system uses the MMPs generated by the model from Section 3 and all MMP features described in this section. We used two types of classifiers: decision tree (DTree) and logistic regression (Logit).

The classification results on a set of 59 questions disjoint from the training set are shown in Table 3. The numbers in the table are F-measure on answer snippets (or positive snippets). Within a machine

Model	Learner DTree	Logit
noMMP	0.426	0.458
IDF-as-MMP	0.413	0.455
MMP	0.451	**0.470**

Table 3: F-measure for Relevance Prediction.

learning method, the model with MMP features is always the best. Between the two classifiers, the logistic regression models are consistently better than the decision tree ones. The results show that MMP features are very helpful to the relevance model.

5 End-to-End System Results

The question-answering system is used in the 2012 BOLT IR evaluation (IR, 2012). The task is to answer questions against a corpus of posts collected from Internet discussion forums in 3 languages: Arabic, Chinese and English. There are 499K, 449K and 262K threads in each of these languages. The Arabic and Chinese posts were first translated into English before being processed. We now describe our experiments on the set of 59 questions developed internally and demonstrate the effectiveness of an MMP based relevance model in the end-to-end system. In the next subsection we discuss our performance in the BOLT-IR evaluation done by NIST for DARPA.

We now briefly describe the question-answering system we developed for the DARPA BOLT IR task, where we applied the MMP classifier and its features. Users submit questions to the system in natural language; the BOLT program mandates that these questions comply with the restrictions described in Section 3.1. Questions are analyzed by a query preprocessing stage that includes our MMP extraction classifier. The preprocessed queries are converted to search queries. These are sent to an Indri-based search engine (Strohman et al., 2005), which returns candidate passages, typically spanning numerous sentences. Each sentence of the retrieved passages is analyzed by a relevance detection module, consisting of a statistical classifier that uses, among others, features computed from the MMPs extracted from the questions. Sentences or spans that are deemed relevant to the question by the relevance detection module are further grouped into equivalence classes that provide different information about the answers. The system generates a single answer for each equivalence class, since elements of the same class are redundant with respect to each other. The elements of each equivalence class are converted into citations that support the corresponding answer.

The ultimate goal of the MMP model is to improve the performance of our question-answering system. To test the effectiveness of the MMP model, we contrast the model trained in Section3 with an IDF baseline, where each non-stop word in a question is an MMP and its score is the corpus IDF. The IDF baseline is what a typical question answering system would do in absence of deep question analysis. To have a fair comparison, the two systems are tested on the same set of 59 questions as the relevance model.

The results of the IDF baseline and MMP system are tabulated in Table 4. Note that the recalls are less than 1.0 because (1) annotated snippets come from both systems; (2) the annotation is done for all snippets in a window surrounding system snippets.

As can be seen from Table 4, the MMP system is about 5 points better than the baseline system. The precision is notably better by 2 points, and the recall is far better (by 7.7%) than that of the baseline. We also compute the question-level F-measures and conduct a Wilcoxon signed-rank test for paired samples. The test indicates that the MMP system is better than the baseline system at $p < 0.00066$. Therefore, the MMP system has a clear advantage over the baseline system.

System	Prec	Recall	F1
baseline	.4228	.3679	.3935
MMP	.4425	.4452	.4438

Table 4: End-to-End system result on 59 questions.

5.1 BOLT Evaluation Results

The BOLT evaluation consists of 146 questions, mostly event- or topic- related, e.g., "What are people saying about the ending of NASA's space shuttle program?". A system answer, if correct, is mapped manually to a facet, which is one semantic unit that answers the question. For each question, facets are collected across all participants' submission. A facet-based F-measure is computed for each participating site. The recall from which the official F-measure is computed is weighted by snippet citations (a citation is a reference to the original document that supports the correct facet). In other words, a snippet with more citations leads to a higher recall than one with less citations. The performances of 4 participating sites are listed in Table 5. Note that the F-measure is weighted and is not necessarily a number between the precision and the recall.

	Facet Metric		
Site	Precision	Recall	(Weighted) F
SITE 1	0.2713	0.1595	0.1713
SITE 2	0.1500	0.1316	0.1109
SITE 3	0.1935	0.2481	0.1734
Ours	0.2729	0.2195	0.2046

Table 5: Official BOLT 2012 IR evaluation results.

Among 4 participating sites, our system has the highest performance. SITE 1 has about the same level of precision, with lower recall, while SITE 3 has the best recall, but lower precision. The results validate that the MMP question analysis technique presented in this paper is quite effective.

6 Conclusions

We propose a framework to select and rank mandatory matching phrases (MMP) for question answering. The framework makes full use of the lexical, syntactic and semantic information in a question and does not require answer data.

The proposed MMP framework is tested at 3 levels in a full QA system and is shown to be very effective to improve its performance: first, we show that it is possible to reliably predict MMPs from questions alone: the MMP classifier can achieve an F-measure as high as 88.6%; second, phrases proposed by the MMP model are incorporated into a snippet relevance model and we show that it improves its performance; third, the MMP framework is used in an question answering system which achieved the best performance in the official 2012 BOLT IR (IR, 2012) evaluation.

Acknowledgments

This work was partially supported by the Defense Advanced Research Projects Agency under contract No. HR0011-12-C-0015. The views and findings contained in this material are those of the authors and do not necessarily reflect the position or policy of the U.S. government and no official endorsement should be inferred.

References

Michael Bendersky and W. Bruce Croft. 2008. Discovering key concepts in verbose queries. *Proceedings of the 31st annual international ACM SIGIR conference on research and development in information retrieval - SIGIR '08*, page 491.

Michael Bendersky, Donald Metzler, and W. Bruce Croft. 2010. Learning concept importance using a weighted dependence model. *Proceedings of the third ACM international conference on Web search and data mining - WSDM '10*, page 31.

Michael Bendersky. 2011. Parameterized concept weighting in verbose queries. *Proceedings of the 34th annual international ACM SIGIR conference on research and development in information retrieval.*

Razvan Bunescu and Yunfeng Huang. 2010. Towards a general model of answer typing: Question focus identification. In *Proceedings of the 11th International Conference on Intelligent Text Processing and Computational Linguistics (CICLing).*

Jennifer Chu-carroll, John Prager, Christopher Welty, Krzysztof Czuba, and David Ferrucci. 2003. A multi-strategy and multi-source approach to question answering. In *In Proceedings of Text REtrieval Conference.*

R Florian, H Hassan, A Ittycheriah, H Jing, N Kambhatla, X Luo, N Nicolov, and S Roukos. 2004. A statistical model for multilingual entity detection and tracking. In Daniel Marcu Susan Dumais and Salim Roukos, editors, *HLT-NAACL 2004: Main Proceedings*, pages 1–8, Boston, Massachusetts, USA, May 2 - May 7. Association for Computational Linguistics.

D. C. Gondek, A. Lally, A. Kalyanpur, J. W. Murdock, P. A. Duboue, L. Zhang, Y. Pan, Z. M. Qiu, and C. Welty. 2012. A framework for merging and ranking of answers in DeepQA. *IBM Journal of Research and Development*, 56(3.4):14:1 –14:12, may-june.

Ulf Hermjakob, Eduard H. Hovy, and Chin yew Lin. 2000. Knowledge-based question answering. In *In Proceedings of the 6th World Multiconference on Systems, Cybernetics and Informatics (SCI-2002*, pages 772–781.

BOLT IR. 2012. Broad operational language translation (BOLT). www.darpa.mil/Our_Work/I2O/Programs/Broad_Operational_Language_Translat%ion_(BOLT).aspx. [Online; accessed 10-Dec-2012].

Abraham Ittycheriah and Salim Roukos. 2001. IBM's statistical question answering system - TREC-11. In *Proceedings of the Text REtrieval Conference*.

Matthew Lease, James Allan, and W. Bruce Croft. 2009. *Advances in Information Retrieval*, volume 5478 of *Lecture Notes in Computer Science*. Springer Berlin Heidelberg, Berlin, Heidelberg, April.

Xin Li and Dan Roth. 2002. Learning question classifiers. In *Proceedings of the 19th international conference on Computational linguistics - Volume 1*, COLING '02, pages 1–7, Stroudsburg, PA, USA. Association for Computational Linguistics.

H. P. Luhn. 1958. A business intelligence system. *IBM J. Res. Dev.*, 2(4):314–319, October.

Xiaoqiang Luo and Imed Zitouni. 2005. Multilingual coreference resolution with syntactic features. In *Proc. of Human Language Technology (HLT)/Empirical Methods in Natural Language Processing (EMNLP)*.

Xiaoqiang Luo, Abe Ittycheriah, Hongyan Jing, Nanda Kambhatla, and Salim Roukos. 2004. A mention-synchronous coreference resolution algorithm based on the bell tree. In *Proc. of ACL*.

Dan Moldovan, Christine Clark, Sanda Harabagiu, and Steve Maiorano. 2003. Cogex: a logic prover for question answering. In *Proceedings of the 2003 Conference of the North American Chapter of the Association for Computational Linguistics on Human Language Technology - Volume 1*, NAACL '03, pages 87–93.

Christof Monz. 2007. Model tree learning for query term weighting in question answering. In *Proceedings of the 29th European conference on IR research*, ECIR'07, pages 589–596, Berlin, Heidelberg. Springer-Verlag.

Christopher Pinchak. 2006. A probabilistic answer type model. In *In EACL*, pages 393–400.

Jay M. Ponte and W. Bruce Croft. 1998. A language modeling approach to information retrieval. In *Proceedings of the 21st annual international ACM SIGIR conference on research and development in information retrieval*, SIGIR '98, pages 275–281, New York, NY, USA. ACM.

S. E. Robertson and S. Walker. 1994. Some simple effective approximations to the 2-poisson model for probabilistic weighted retrieval. In *Proceedings of the 17th annual international ACM SIGIR conference on research and development in information retrieval*, SIGIR '94, pages 232–241, New York, NY, USA. Springer-Verlag New York, Inc.

Trevor Strohman, Donald Metzler, Howard Turtle, and W. Bruce Croft. 2005. Indri: a language-model based search engine for complex queries. Technical report, in Proceedings of the International Conference on Intelligent Analysis.

Ellen M. Voorhees. 2004. Overview of the TREC 2004 question answering track. In *TREC*.

Le Zhao and Jamie Callan. 2010. Term necessity prediction. *Proceedings of the 19th ACM international conference on Information and knowledge management - CIKM '10*, page 259.

A Just-In-Time Keyword Extraction from Meeting Transcripts

Hyun-Je Song **Junho Go** **Seong-Bae Park** **Se-Young Park**
School of Computer Science and Engineering
Kyungpook National University
Daegu, Korea
{hjsong,jhgo,sbpark,sypark}@sejong.knu.ac.kr

Abstract

In a meeting, it is often desirable to extract keywords from each utterance as soon as it is spoken. Thus, this paper proposes a just-in-time keyword extraction from meeting transcripts. The proposed method considers two major factors that make it different from keyword extraction from normal texts. The first factor is the temporal history of preceding utterances that grants higher importance to recent utterances than old ones, and the second is topic relevance that forces only the preceding utterances relevant to the current utterance to be considered in keyword extraction. Our experiments on two data sets in English and Korean show that the consideration of the factors results in performance improvement in keyword extraction from meeting transcripts.

1 Introduction

A meeting is generally accomplished by a number of participants and a wide range of subjects are discussed. Therefore, it would be helpful to meeting participants to provide them with some additional information related to the current subject. For instance, assume that a participant is discussing a specific topic with other participants at a meeting. The summary of previous meetings on the topic is then one of the most important resources for her discussion.

In order to provide information on a topic to participants, keywords should be first generated for the topic since keywords are often representatives of a topic. A number of techniques have been proposed for automatic keyword extraction (Frank et al., 1999; Turney, 2000; Mihalcea and Tarau, 2004; Wan et al., 2007), and they are designed to extract keywords from a written document. However, they are not suitable for meeting transcripts. In a meeting, it is often desirable to extract keywords at the time at which a new utterance is made for just-in-time service of additional information. Otherwise, the extracted keywords become just the important words at the end of the meeting.

Two key factors for just-in-time keyword extraction from meeting transcripts are time of preceding utterances and topic of current utterance. First, current utterance is affected by temporal history of preceding utterances. That is, when a new utterance is made it is likely to be related more closely with latest utterances than old ones. Second, the preceding utterances which carry similar topics to current utterance are more important than irrelevant utterances. Since a meeting consists of several topics, the utterances that have nothing to do with current utterance are inappropriate as a history of the current utterance.

This paper proposes a graph-based keyword extraction to reflect these factors. The proposed method represents an utterance as a graph of which nodes are candidate keywords. The preceding utterances are also expressed as a history graph in which the weight of an edge is the temporal importance of the keywords connected by the edge. To reflect the temporal history of utterances, *forgetting curve* (Wozniak, 1999) is adopted in updating the weights of edges in the history graph. It expresses effectively not only the reciprocal relation between memory retention and time, but also active recall that makes frequent words more consequential in keyword extraction. Then, a subgraph that is relevant to the current utterance is derived from the history graph, and used as an actual history of the current utterance. The keywords of the current utterance are extracted by TextRank (Mihalcea and Tarau, 2004) from the merged graph of the current utterance and the history graphs.

The proposed method is evaluated with two kinds of data sets: the National Assembly transcripts in Korean and the ICSI meeting corpus (Janin et al., 2003) in English. The experimental results show that it outperforms both the TFIDF framework (Frank et al., 1999; Liu et al., 2009) and the PageRank-based graph model (Wan et al., 2007). One thing to note is that the proposed method improves even the supervised methods that do not reflect utterance time and topic relevance for the ICSI corpus. This proves that it is critical to consider time and content of utterances simultaneously in keyword extraction from meeting transcripts.

The rest of the paper is organized as follows. Section 2 reviews the related studies on keyword extraction. Section 3 explains the overall process of the proposed method, and Section 4 addresses its detailed description how to reflect meeting characteristics. Experimental results are presented in Section 5. Finally, Section 6 draws some conclusions.

2 Related Work

Keyword extraction has been of interest for a long time in various fields such as information retrieval, document clustering, summarization, and so on. Thus, there have been many studies on automatic keyword extraction. The frequency-based keyword extraction with TFIDF weighting (Frank et al., 1999) and the graph-based keyword extraction (Mihalcea and Tarau, 2004) are two base models for this task. Many studies recently tried to extend them by incorporating specific information such as linguistic knowledge (Hulth, 2003), web-based resource (Turney, 2003), and semantic knowledge (Chen et al., 2010). As a result, they show good performance on written text. However, it is difficult to use them directly for spoken genres, since spoken genres have significantly different characteristics from written text.

There have been a few studies focused on keyword extraction from spoken genres. Among them, the extraction from meetings has attracted more concern, since the need for grasping important points of a meeting or an opinion of each participant has increased. The studies on meetings focused on the exterior features of meeting dialogues such as unstructured and ill-formed sentences. Liu et al. (2009) used some knowledge sources such as Part-of-Speech (POS) filtering, word clustering, and sentence salience to reflect dialogue features, and they found out that a simple TFIDF-based keyword extraction using these knowledge sources works reasonably well. They also extended their work by adopting various features such as decision making sentence features, speech-related features, and summary features that reflect meeting transcripts better (Liu et al., 2011). Chen et al. (2010) extracted keywords from spoken course lectures. In this study, they considered prosodic information from HKT forced alignment and topics in a lecture generated by Probabilistic Latent Semantic Analysis (pLSA). These studies focused on the exterior characteristics of spoken genres, since they assumed that entire scripts are given in advance and then they extracted keywords that best describe the scripts. However, to the best of our knowledge, there is no previous study considered time of utterances which is an intrinsic element of spoken genres.

The relevance between current utterance and preceding utterances is also a critical feature in keyword extraction from meeting transcripts. The study that considers this relevance explicitly is *CollabRank* proposed by Wan and Xiao (2008). This is collaborative approach to extract keywords in a document. In this study, it is assumed that a few neighbor documents close to a current document can help extract keywords. Therefore, they applied a clustering algorithm to a document set and then extracted words that are reinforced by the documents within a cluster. However, this method also does not consider the utterance time, since it is designed to extract keywords from normal documents. As a result, if it is applied to meeting transcripts, all preceding utterances would affect the current utterance uniformly, which leads to a poor performance.

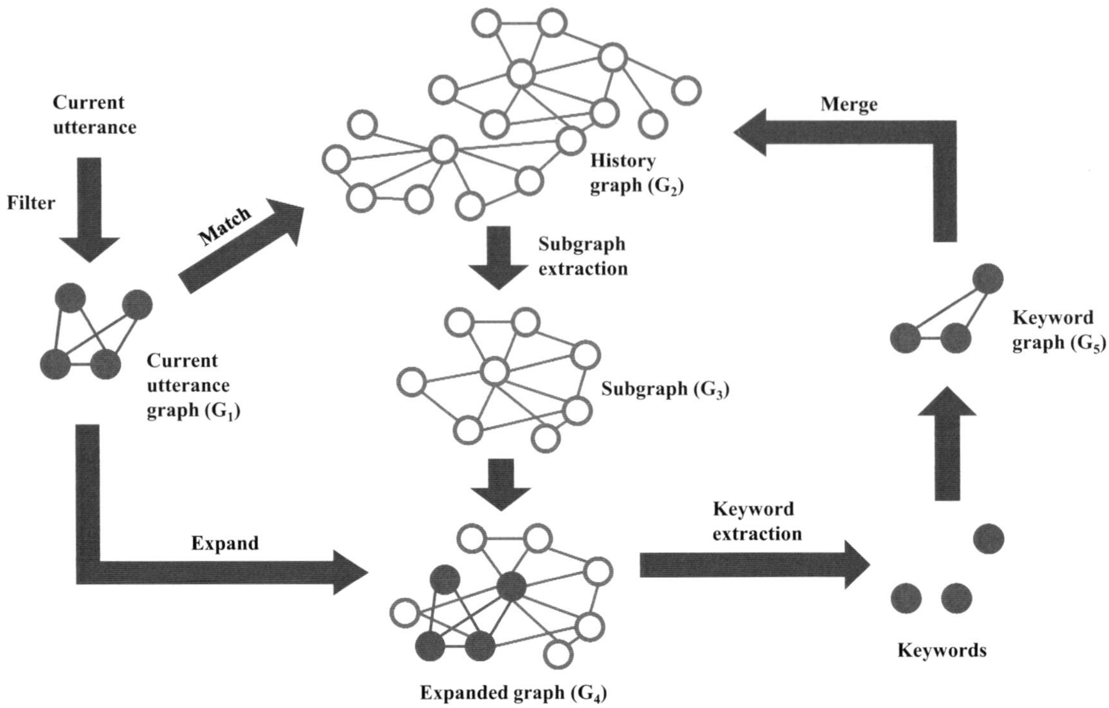

Figure 1: The overall process of the just-in-time keyword extraction from meeting transcripts.

3 Just-In-Time Keyword Extraction for a Meeting

Figure 1 depicts the overall process of extracting keywords from an utterance as soon as it is spoken. We represent all the components in a meeting as graphs. This is because graphs are effective to express the relationship between words, and the graph operations that are required for keyword extraction are also efficiently performed. That is, whenever an utterance is spoken, it is represented as a graph (G_1) of which nodes are the potential keywords in the utterance. This graph is named as *current utterance graph*.

The summary of all preceding utterances is also represented as a *history graph* (G_2). We assume that only the preceding utterances that are directly related with the current utterance are important for extracting keywords from the current utterance. Therefore, a subgraph of G_2 that maximally covers the current utterance graph (G_1) is extracted. This subgraph is labeled as G_3 in Figure 1. Then, the current utterance graph G_1 is expanded by merging it and G_3. This expanded graph (G_4) is a combined representation of the current and preceding utterances, and then the keywords of the current utterance is extracted from this graph. The keywords are so-called hub nodes of G_4.

After keywords are extracted from the current utterance, the current utterance becomes a part of the history graph for the next utterance. For this, the extracted keywords are also represented as a graph (G_5), and it is merged into the current history G_2. This merged graph becomes a new history graph for the next utterance. In merging two graphs, the weight of each edge in G_2 is updated to reflect the temporal history. If an edge is connecting two nouns from an old utterance, its weight becomes small. In the same way, the weights for the edges from recent utterances get large. The weights of the edges from G_5 are 1, the largest possible value.

4 Graph Representation and Weight Update

4.1 Current Utterance Graph and History Graph

Current utterance graph is a graph-representation of the current utterance. When current utterance consists of m words, we first extract the potential keywords from the current utterance. Since all words within the current utterance are not keywords, some words are filtered out. For this filtering out, we follow the POS filtering approach proposed by Liu et al. (2009). This approach filters out non-keywords using a stop-word list and POS tags of the words. Assume that n words remain after the filtering out, where $n \leq m$. These n words become the vertices of the current utterance graph.

Formally, the *current utterance graph* $G_1 = (V_1, E_1)$ is an undirected graph, where $|V_1| = n$. E_1 is a set of edges and each edge implies that the nouns connected by the edge co-occur within a window sized W. For each $e^1_{ij} \in E_1$ that connects nodes v^1_i and v^1_j, its weight is given by

$$w^1_{ij} = \begin{cases} 1 & \text{if } v^1_i \& v^1_j \text{ cooccur within the window,} \\ 0 & \text{otherwise.} \end{cases} \quad (1)$$

In a meeting, preceding utterances affect the current utterance. We assume that only the keywords of preceding utterances are effective. Therefore, the *history graph* $G_2 = (V_2, E_2)$ is an undirected graph of keywords in the preceding utterances. That is, all vertices in V_2 are keywords extracted from one or more previous utterances, and the edge between two keywords implies that they co-occurred at least once. Every edge in E_2 has a weight that represents its temporal importance.

The history graph is updated whenever keywords are extracted from a new utterance. This is because the current utterance becomes a part of the history graph for the next utterance. As a history, old utterances are less important than recent ones. Thus, the temporal importance should decrease gradually according to the passage of time. In addition, the keywords which occur frequently at a meeting are more important than those mentioned just once or twice. Since the frequently-mentioned keywords are normally major topics of the meeting, their influence should last for a long time.

To model these characteristics, the *forgetting curve* (Wozniak, 1999) is adopted in updating the history graph. It models the decline of memory retention in time. Figure 2 shows a typical representation of the forgetting curve. The X-axis of this figure is time and the Y-axis is memory retention. As shown in this figure, memory retention of new

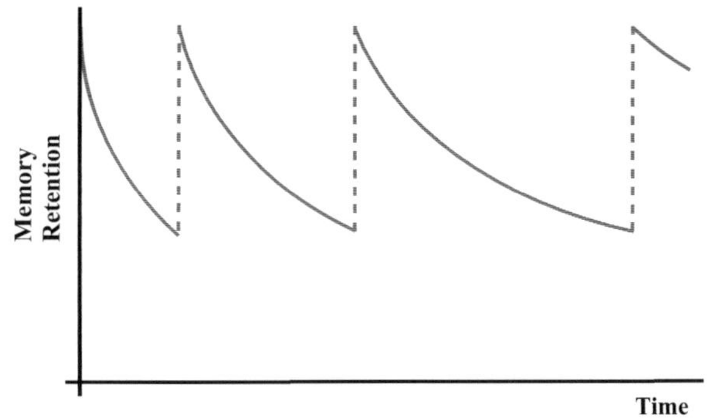

Figure 2: Memory retention according to time.

information decreases gradually by the exponential nature of forgetting. However, whenever the information is repeated, it is recalled longer. This is formulated as

$$R = e^{-\frac{t}{S}},$$

where R is memory retention, t is time, and S is the relative strength of memory.

Based on the forgetting curve, the weight of each edge $e^2_{ij} \in E_2$ between keywords v^2_i and v^2_j is set as

$$w^2_{ij} = \exp^{-\frac{t}{f(v_i, v_j)}}, \quad (2)$$

where t is the elapse of utterance time and $f(v_i, v_j)$ is the frequency that v_i and v_j co-occur from the beginning of the meeting to now. According to this equation, the temporal importance between keywords decreases gradually as time passes by, but the keyword relations repeated during the meeting are remembered for a long time in the history graph.

4.2 Keyword Extraction by Merging Current Utterance and History Graphs

All words within the history graph are not equally important in extracting keywords from the current utterance. In general, many participants discuss a wide range of topics in a meeting. Therefore, some preceding utterances that shares topics with the current utterance are more significant. We assume that the preceding utterances that contain the nouns in the current utterance share topics with the current utterance. Thus, only a subgraph of G_2 that contain words in G_1 is relevant for keyword extraction from G_1.

Given the current utterance graph $G_1 = (V_1, E_1)$ and the history graph $G_2 = (V_2, E_2)$, the relevant graph $G_3 = (V_3, E_3)$ is a subgraph of G_2. Here, $V_3 = (V_1 \cap V_2) \cup adjacency(V_1)$ and $adjacency(V_1)$ is a set of vertices from G_2 which are directly connected to the words in V_1. That is, V_3 contains the words of G_1 and their direct neighbor words in G_2. E_3 is a subset of E_2. Only the edges that appear in E_2 are included in E_3. The weight w_{ij}^3 of each $e_{ij}^3 \in E_3$ is also borrowed from G_2. That is, $w_{ij}^3 = w_{ij}^2$. Therefore, G_3 is a 1-walk subgraph[1] of G_2 in which words in G_1 and their neighbor words appear.

The keywords of the current utterance should reflect the relevant history as well as the current utterance itself. For this purpose, G_1 is expanded with respect to G_3. The expanded graph $G_4 = (V_4, E_4)$ of G_1 is defined as

$$V_4 = V_1 \cup V_3,$$
$$E_4 = E_1 \cup E_3.$$

For each edge $e_{ij}^4 \in E_4$, its weight w_{ij}^4 is determined to be the larger value between w_{ij}^1 and w_{ij}^3 if it appears in both G_1 and G_3. When it appears in only one of the graphs, w_{ij}^4 is set to be the weight of its corresponding graph. That is,

$$w_{ij}^4 = \begin{cases} \max(w_{ij}^1, w_{ij}^3) & \text{if } e_{ij}^4 \in E_1 \text{ and } e_{ij}^4 \in E_3, \\ w_{ij}^1 & \text{if } e_{ij}^4 \in E_1 \text{ and } e_{ij}^4 \notin E_3, \\ w_{ij}^3 & \text{otherwise.} \end{cases}$$

From this expanded graph G_4, the keywords are extracted by TextRank (Mihalcea and Tarau, 2004). TextRank is an unsupervised graph-based method for keyword extraction. It singles out the key vertices of a graph by providing a ranking mechanism. In order to rank the vertices, it computes the score of each vertex $v_i^4 \in V_4$ by

$$S(v_i^4) = (1-d) + d \cdot \sum_{v_j^4 \in adj(v_i^4)} \frac{w_{ji}^4}{\sum_{v_k^4 \in adj(v_j^4)} w_{jk}^4} S(v_j^4), \quad (3)$$

[1]If a m-walk subgraph ($m > 1$) is used, more affluent history is used. However, this graph contains some words irrelevant to the current utterance. According to our experiments, 1-walk subgraph outperforms other m-walk subgraphs where $m > 1$. In addition, extracting G_3 becomes expensive for large m.

where $0 \leq d \leq 1$ is a damping factor and $adj(v_i)$ denotes v_i's neighbors. Finally, the words whose score is larger than a specific threshold θ are chosen as keywords. Especially when the current utterance is the first utterance of a meeting, the history graph does not exist. In this case, the current utterance graph becomes the expanded graph ($G_4 = G_1$), and keywords are extracted from the current utterance graph.

The proposed method extracts keywords whenever an utterance is spoken. Thus, it tries to extract keywords even if the current utterance is not related to the topics of a meeting or is too short. However, if the current utterance is irrelevant to the meeting, it has just a few connections with other previous utterances, and thus the potential keywords in this utterance are apt to have a low score. The proposed method, however, does not select the words whose score is smaller than the threshold θ as keywords. As a result, it extracts only the relevant keywords during the meeting.

Since the keywords for the current utterance should be the history for the next utterance, they have to be reflected into the history graph. Therefore, a *keyword graph* $G_5 = (V_5, E_5)$ is constructed from the keywords. Here, V_5 is a set of keywords extracted from G_4, and E_5 is a subset of E_4 that corresponds to V_5. The weights of edges in E_5 are same with those in E_4. That is, $w_{ij}^5 = w_{ij}^4$. The keyword graph G_5 is then merged into the history graph G_2 in the same way that G_1 and G_3 are merged. As stated above, the weights of the edges in the history graph G_2 are updated by Equation (2). Therefore, before merging G_5 and G_2, all weights of G_2 are updated by increasing t as $t + 1$ to reflect temporal importance of preceding utterances.

5 Experiments

The proposed method is evaluated with two kinds of data sets: the *National Assembly transcripts* in Korean and the *ICSI meeting corpus* in English. Both data sets are the records of meetings that are manually dictated by human transcribers.

Table 1: Simple statistics of the National Assembly transcripts

	the first meeting	the second meeting
No. of utterances	1,280	573
Average No. of words per utterance	7.22	10.17

5.1 National Assembly Transcripts in Korean

The first corpus used to evaluate our method is the National Assembly transcripts[2]. This corpus is obtained from the Knowledge Management System of the National Assembly of KoreaIt is transcribed from the 305th assembly record of the Knowledge Economy Committee in 2012. Table 1 summarizes simple statistics of the National Assembly transcripts. The 305th assembly record actually consists of two meetings. The first meeting contains 1,280 utterances and the second has 573 utterances. The average number of words per utterance in the first meeting is 7.22 while the second meeting contains 10.17 words per utterance on average. The second meeting transcript is used as a development data set to determine window size W of Equation (1), the damping factor d of Equation (3), and the threshold θ. For all experiments below, d is set 0.85, W is 10, and θ is 0.28. The remaining first meeting transcript is used as a data set to extract keywords since this transcript contains more utterances. Only nouns are considered as potential keywords. That is, only the words whose POS tag is NNG (common noun) or NNP (proper noun) can be a keyword.

Three annotators are engaged to extract keywords manually for each utterance in the first meeting transcript, since the Knowledge Management System does not provide the keywords[3]. The average number of keywords per utterance is 2.58. To see the inter-judge agreement among the annotators, the Kappa coefficient (Carletta, 1996) was investigated. The kappa agreement of the National Assembly transcript is 0.31 that falls under the category of 'Fair'. Even though all congressmen in the transcript belong to the same committee, they discussed various topics at the meeting. As a result, the keywords are difficult to be agreed unanimously by all three annotators. Therefore, in this paper the words that are recommended by more than two annotators are chosen as keywords.

The evaluation is done with two metics: F-measure and the weighted relative score (WRS). Since the previous work by Liu et al. (2009) reported only F-measure and WRS, F-measure instead of precision/recall are used for the comparison with their method. The weighted relative score is derived from *Pyramid* metric (Nenkova and Passonneau, 2004). When a keyword extraction system generates keywords which many annotators agree, a higher score is given to it. On the other hand, a lower score is given if fewer annotators agree.

The proposed method is compared with two baseline models to see its relative performance. One is the frequency-based keyword extraction with TFIDF weighting (Frank et al., 1999) and the other is TextRank in which the weight of edges is mutual information between vertices (Wan et al., 2007). In TFIDF, each utterance is considered as a *document*, and thus all utterances including the current one are regarded as *whole documents*. The frequency-based TFIDF chooses top-K words according to their TFIDF value from the set of words appearing in the meeting transcript. Since the human annotators are restricted to extract up to five keywords, the keyword extraction systems including our method are also requested to select top-5 keywords when more than five keywords are produced.

In order to see the effect of preceding utterances in baseline models, the performances are measured according to the number of preceding utterances used. Figure 3 shows the results. The X-axis of this figure is the number of preceding utterances and the Y-axis represents F-measures. As shown in this figure, the performance of the baseline models improves monotonically at first as the number of preceding utterances increases. However, the performance improvement stops when many preceding utterances are involved, and the performance begins to drop

[2]The data set is available: `http://ml.knu.ac.kr/dataset/keywordextraction.html`

[3]A guideline was given to the annotators that keywords must be a single word and the maximum number of keywords per utterance is five.

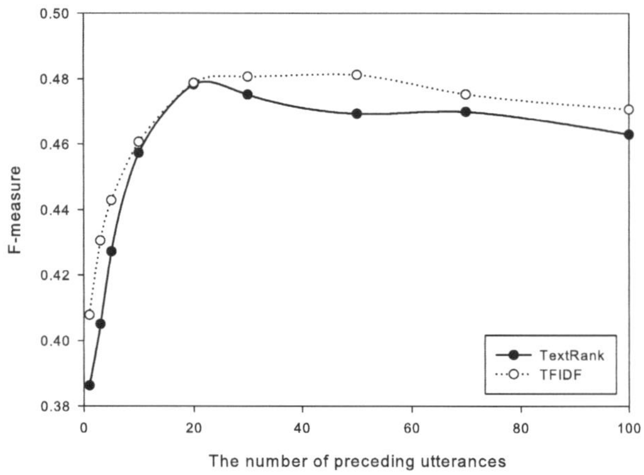

Figure 3: The performance of baseline models according to the number of preceding utterances

Table 2: The experimental results on the National Assembly transcripts

Methods	F-measure	WRS
TextRank	0.478	0.387
TFIDF	0.481	0.394
Proposed method	**0.533**	**0.421**

when too many utterances are considered. The performance of TextRank model drops from 20 preceding utterances, while that of TFIDF model begins to drops at 50 utterances. When too many preceding utterances are taken into account, it is highly possible that some of their topics are irrelevant to the current utterance, which leads to performance drop.

Table 2 compares our method with the baseline models on the National Assembly transcripts. The performances of baseline models are obtained when they show the best performance for various number of preceding utterances. TextRank model achieves F-measure of 0.478 and weighted relative score of 0.387, while TFIDF reports its best F-measure of 0.481 and weighted relative score of 0.394. Thus, the difference between TFIDF and TextRank is not significant. However, F-measure and weighted relative score of the proposed method are 0.533 and 0.421 respectively, and they are much higher than those of baseline models. In addition, our method achieves precision of 0.543 and recall of 0.523 and

Table 3: The importance of temporal history

	F-measure	WRS
With Temporal History	0.533	0.421
Without Temporal History	0.518	0.413

this is much higher performance than TextRank whose precision is just 0.510. Since the proposed method uses, as history, the preceding utterances relevant to the current utterance, its performance is kept high even if whole utterances are used. Therefore, it could be inferred that it is important to adopt only the relevant history in keyword extraction from meeting transcripts.

One of the key factors of our method is the temporal history. Its importance is given in Table 3. As explained above, the temporal history is achieved by Equation (2). Thus, the proposed model does not reflect the temporal importance of preceding utterances if $w_{ij}^2 = 1$ always. That is, under $w_{ij}^2 = 1$, old utterances are regarded as important as recent utterances. Without temporal history, F-measure and weighted relative score are just 0.518 and 0.413 respectively. These poor performances prove the importance of the temporal history in keyword extraction from meeting transcripts.

5.2 ICSI Meeting Corpus in English

The proposed method is also evaluated on the ICSI meeting corpus (Janin et al., 2003) which consists of naturally occurring meetings recordings. This corpus is widely used for summarizing and extracting keywords of meetings. We followed all the experimental settings proposed by Liu et al. (2009) for this corpus. Among 26 meeting transcripts chosen by Liu et al. from 161 transcripts of the ICSI meeting corpus, 6 transcripts are used as development data and the remaining transcripts are used as data to extract keywords. The parameters for the ICSI meeting corpus are set to be $d = 0.85, W = 10$, and $\theta = 0.20$. Each meeting of the corpus consists of several topic segments, and every topic segment contains three sets of keywords that are annotated by three annotators. Up to five keywords are annotated for a topic segment.

Table 4 shows simple statistics of the ICSI meeting data. Total number of topic segments in the 26 meetings is originally 201, but some of them do not

Table 4: Simple statistics of the ICSI meeting data

Information	Value
# of meetings	26
# of topic segments	201
# of topic segments used actually	140
Average # of utterances per topic segment	260
Average # of words per utterance	7.22

Table 5: The experimental results on the ICSI corpus

Methods	F-measure	WRS
TFIDF-Liu	0.290	0.404
TextRank-Liu	0.277	0.380
ME model	0.312	0.401
Proposed method	**0.334**	**0.533**

have keywords. Such segments are discarded, and the remaining 140 topic segments are actually used. The average number of utterances in a topic segment is 260 and the average number of words per utterance is 7.22.

Unlike the National Assembly transcripts, the keywords of the ICSI meeting corpus are annotated at the topic segment level, not the utterance level. Therefore, the proposed method which extracts keywords at the utterance level can not be applied directly to this corpus. In order to obtain keywords for a topic segment with the proposed method, the keywords are first extracted from each utterance in the segment by the proposed method and then they are all accumulated. The proposed method extracts keywords for a topic segment from these accumulated utterance-level keywords as follows. Assume that a topic segment consists of l utterances. Since our method can extract up to 5 keywords for each utterance, the number of keywords for the segment can reach to $5 \cdot l$. From these keywords, we select top-5 keywords ranked by Equation (3).

The proposed method is compared with three previous studies. The first two are the methods proposed by Liu et al. (2009) One is the frequency-based method of TFIDF weighting with the features such as POS filtering, word clustering, and sentence salience score, and the other is the graph-based method with POS filtering. The last method is a maximum entropy model applied to this task (Liu et al., 2008). Note that the maximum entropy is a supervised learning model.

Table 6: The effect of considering topic relevance

Methods	F-measure	WRS
With topic relevance	0.334	0.533
Without topic relevance	0.291	0.458

Table 5 summarizes the comparison results. As shown in this table, the proposed method outperforms all previous methods. Our method achieves precision of 0.311 and recall of 0.361, and thus the F-score is 0.334. The weight relative score of the proposed method is 0.533. This is the improvement of up to 0.044 in F-measure and 0.129 in weighted relative score over other unsupervised methods (TFIDF-Liu and TextRank-Liu). It should be also noted that the proposed method outperforms even the supervised method (ME model). The difference between our method and the maximum entropy model in weighted relative score is 0.132.

One possible variant of the proposed method for the ICSI corpus is to simply merge the current utterance graph (G_1) with the history graph (G_2) rather than to extract keywords from each utterance. After the current utterance graph of the last utterance in a topic segment is merged into the history graph, the keywords for the segment are extracted from the history graph. This variant and the proposed method both rely on the temporal history, but the difference is that the history graph of the variant accumulates all information within the topic segment. Thus, the keywords extracted from the history graph by this variant are those without consideration of topic relevance.

Table 6 compares the proposed method with the variant. The performance of the variant is higher than those of TFIDF-Liu and TextRank-Liu. This proves the importance of the temporal history in keyword extraction from meeting transcripts. However, the proposed method still outperforms the variant, and it demonstrates the importance of topic relevance. Therefore, it can be concluded that the consideration of temporal history and topic relevance is critical in keyword extraction from meeting transcripts.

6 Conclusion

In this paper, we have proposed a just-in-time keyword extraction from meeting transcripts. Whenever an utterance is spoken, the proposed method extracts keywords from the utterance that best describe the utterance. Based on the graph representation of all components in a meeting, the proposed method extracts keywords by TextRank with some graph operations.

Temporal history and topic of the current utterance are two major factors especially in keyword extraction from meeting transcripts. This is because recent utterances are more important than old ones and only the preceding utterances of which topic is relevant to the current utterance are important. To model the temporal importance of the preceding utterances, the concept of forgetting curve is used in updating the history graph of preceding utterances. In addition, the subgraph of the history graph that shares words appearing in the current utterance graph is used to extract keywords rather than whole history graph. The proposed method was evaluated with the National Assembly transcripts and the ICSI meeting corpus. According to our experimental results on these data sets, the performance of keyword extraction is improved when we consider temporal history and topic relevance.

Acknowledgments

This research was supported by the Converging Research Center Program funded by the Ministry of Education, Science and Technology (2012K001342)

References

Jean Carletta. 1996. Assessing agreement on classification tasks: The kappa statistic. *Computational Linguistics*, 22(2):249–254.

Yun-Nung Chen, Yu Huang, Sheng-Yi Kong, , and Lin-Shan Lee. 2010. Automatic key term extraction from spoken course lectures using branching entropy and prosodic/semantic features. In *Proceedings of IEEE Workshop on Spoken Language Technology*, pages 265–270.

Eibe Frank, Gordon W. Paynter, Ian H. Witten, Carl Gutwin, and Craig G. Nevill-Manning. 1999. Domain-specific keyphrase extraction. In *Proceedings of the 18th International Joint Conference on Artificial intelligence*, pages 668–671.

Anette Hulth. 2003. Improved automatic keyword extraction given more linguistic knowledge. In *Proceedings of International Conference on Empirical Methods in Natural Language Processing*, pages 216–223.

Adam Janin, Don Baron, Jane Edwards, Dan Ellis, David Gelbart, Nelson Morgan, Barbara Peskin, Thilo Pfau, Elizabeth Shriberg, Andreas Stolcke, and Chuck Wooters. 2003. The icsi meeting corpus. In *Proceedings of International Conference on Acoustics, Speech, and Signal Processing*, pages 364–367.

Fei Liu, Feifan Liu, and Yang Liu. 2008. Automatic keyword extraction for the meeting corpus using supervised approach and bigram expansion. In *Proceedings of IEEE Spoken Language Technology*, pages 181–184.

Feifan Liu, Deana Pennell, Fei Liu, and Yang Liu. 2009. Unsupervised approaches for automatic keyword extraction using meeting transcripts. In *Proceedings of Annual Conference of the North American Chapter of the ACL*, pages 620–628.

Fei Liu, Feifan Liu, and Yang Liu. 2011. A supervised framework for keyword extraction from meeting transcripts. *IEEE Transactions on Audio, Speech, and Language Processing*, 19(3):538–548.

Rada Mihalcea and Paul Tarau. 2004. Textrank: Bringing order into texts. In *Proceedings of International Conference on Empirical Methods in Natural Language Processing*, pages 404–411.

Ani Nenkova and Rebecca Passonneau. 2004. Evaluating content selection in summarization: The pyramid method. In *Proceedings of Annual Conference of the North American Chapter of the ACL*, pages 145–152.

Peter D. Turney. 2000. Learning algorithms for keyphrase extraction. *Information Retrieval*, 2:303–336.

Peter D. Turney. 2003. Coherent keyphrase extraction via web mining. In *Proceedings of the 18th International Joint Conference on Artificial intelligence*, pages 434–439.

Xiaojun Wan and Jianguo Xiao. 2008. Collabrank: Towards a collaborative approach to single-document keyphrase extraction. In *Proceedings of International Conference on Computational Linguistics*, pages 969–976.

Xiaojun Wan, Jianwu Yang, and Jianguo Xiao. 2007. Towards an iterative reinforcement approach for simultaneous document summarization and keyword extraction. In *Proceedings of the 45th Annual Meeting of the Association of Computational Linguistics*, pages 552–559.

Robert H. Wozniak. 1999. *Classics in Psychology, 1855–1914: Historical Essays*. Thoemmes Press.

Same Referent, Different Words: Unsupervised Mining of Opaque Coreferent Mentions

Marta Recasens[*], **Matthew Can**[†], **and Dan Jurafsky**[*]
[*]Linguistics Department, Stanford University, Stanford, CA 94305
[†]Computer Science Department, Stanford University, Stanford, CA 94305
recasens@google.com, {mattcan, jurafsky}@stanford.edu

Abstract

Coreference resolution systems rely heavily on string overlap (e.g., *Google Inc.* and *Google*), performing badly on mentions with very different words (**opaque** mentions) like *Google* and *the search giant*. Yet prior attempts to resolve opaque pairs using ontologies or distributional semantics hurt precision more than improved recall. We present a new unsupervised method for mining opaque pairs. Our intuition is to *restrict* distributional semantics to articles about the same event, thus promoting referential match. Using an English comparable corpus of tech news, we built a dictionary of opaque coreferent mentions (only 3% are in WordNet). Our dictionary can be integrated into any coreference system (it increases the performance of a state-of-the-art system by 1% F1 on all measures) and is easily extendable by using news aggregators.

1 Introduction

Repetition is one of the most common coreferential devices in written text, making string-match features important to all coreference resolution systems. In fact, the scores achieved by just head match and a rudimentary form of pronominal resolution[1] are not far from that of state-of-the-art systems (Recasens and Hovy, 2010). This suggests that **opaque** mentions (i.e., lexically different) such as *iPad* and *the Cupertino slate* are a serious problem for modern systems: they comprise 65% of the non-pronominal errors made by the Stanford system on the CoNLL-2011 data. Solving this problem is critical for overcoming the recall gap of state-of-the-art systems (Haghighi and Klein, 2010; Stoyanov et al., 2009).

Previous systems have turned either to ontologies (Ponzetto and Strube, 2006; Uryupina et al., 2011; Rahman and Ng, 2011) or distributional semantics (Yang and Su, 2007; Kobdani et al., 2011; Bansal and Klein, 2012) to help solve these errors. But neither semantic similarity nor hypernymy are the same as coreference: *Microsoft* and *Google* are distributionally similar but not coreferent; *people* is a hypernym of both *voters* and *scientists*, but *the people* can corefer with *the voters*, but is less likely to corefer with *the scientists*. Thus ontologies lead to precision problems, and to recall problems like missing NE descriptions (e.g., *Apple* and *the iPhone maker*) and metonymies (e.g., *agreement* and *wording*), while distributional systems lead to precision problems like coreferring *Microsoft* and *the Mountain View giant* because of their similar vector representation (*release*, *software*, *update*).

We increase precision by drawing on the intuition that referents that are *both* similar *and* participate in the same event are likely to corefer. We restrict distributional similarity to collections of articles that discuss the same event. In the following two documents on the Nexus One from different sources, we take the subjects of the identical verb *release*—*Google* and *the Mountain View giant*—as coreferent.

Document 1: Google **has released** a software update.

Document 2: The Mountain View giant **released** an update.

Based on this idea, we introduce a new unsupervised method that uses verbs in comparable corpora

[1]Closest NP with the same gender and number.

as pivots for extracting the hard cases of coreference resolution, and build a dictionary of opaque coreferent mentions (i.e., the dictionary entries are pairs of mentions). This dictionary is then integrated into the Stanford coreference system (Lee et al., 2011), resulting in an average 1% improvement in the F1 score of all the evaluation measures.

Our work points out the importance of context to decide whether a specific mention pair is coreferent. On the one hand, we need to know what semantic relations are potentially coreferent (e.g., *content* and *video*). On the other, we need to distinguish contexts that are compatible for coreference—(1) and (2-a)—from those that are not—(1) and (2-b).

(1) Elemental helps those big media entities process content across a full slate of mobile devices.

(2) a. Elemental provides the picks and shovels to make video work across multiple devices.
b. Elemental is powering **the video** for HBO Go.

Our dictionary of opaque coreferent pairs is our solution to the first problem, and we report on some preliminary work on context compatibility to address the second problem.

2 Building a Dictionary for Coreference

To build a dictionary of semantic relations that are appropriate for coreference we will use a cluster of documents about the same news event, which we call a **story**. Consider as an example the story *Sprint blocks out vacation days for employees*. We determine using tf-idf the representative verbs for this story, the main actions and events of the story (e.g., *block out*). Since these verbs are representative of the story, different instances across documents in the cluster are likely to refer to the same events (*Sprint blocks out*... and *the carrier blocks out*...). By the same logic, the subjects and objects of the verbs are also likely to be coreferent (*Sprint* and *the carrier*).

2.1 Comparable corpus

To build our dictionary, we require a monolingual **comparable corpus**, containing clusters of documents from different sources that discuss the same story. To ensure likely coreference, the story must be the very same; documents that are merely clustered by (general) topic do not suffice. The corpus does not need to be parallel in the sense that documents in the same cluster do not need to be sentence aligned.

We used Techmeme,[2] a news aggregator for technology news, to construct a comparable corpus. Its website lists the major tech stories, each with links to several articles from different sources. We used the Readability API[3] to download and extract the article text for each document. We scraped two years worth of data from Techmeme and only took stories containing at least 5 documents. Our corpus contains approximately 160 million words, 25k stories, and 375k documents. Using a corpus from Techmeme means that our current coreference dictionary is focused on the technological domain. Our method can be easily extended to other domains, however, since getting comparable corpora is relatively simple from the many similar news aggregator sites.

2.2 Extraction

After building our corpus, we used Stanford's CoreNLP tools[4] to tokenize the text and annotate it with POS tags and named entity types. We parsed the text using the MaltParser 1.7, a linear time dependency parser (Nivre et al., 2004).[5]

We then extracted the representative verbs of each story by ranking the verbs in each story according to their tf-idf scores. We took the top ten to be the representative set. For each of these verbs, we clustered together its subjects and objects (separately) across instances of the verb in the document cluster, excluding pronouns and NPs headed by the same noun. For example, suppose that *crawl* is a representative verb and that in one document we have *Google crawls web pages* and *The search giant crawls sites* in another document. We will create the clusters {*Google, the search giant*} and {*web pages, sites*}.

When detecting representative verbs, we kept phrasal verbs as a unit (e.g., *give up*) and excluded auxiliary and copular verbs,[6] light verbs,[7] and report

[2]http://www.techmeme.com

[3]http://www.readability.com/developers/api

[4]http://nlp.stanford.edu/software/corenlp.shtml

[5]http://www.maltparser.org

[6]Auxiliary and copular verbs include *appear, be, become, do, have, seem*.

[7]Light verbs include *do, get, give, go, have, keep, make, put, set, take*.

verbs,[8] as they are rarely representative of a story and tend to add noise to our dictionary. To increase recall, we also considered the synonyms from WordNet and nominalizations from NomBank of the representative verbs, thus clustering together the subjects and objects of any synonym as well as the arguments of nominalizations.[9] We used syntactic relations instead of semantic roles because the MaltParser is faster than any SRL system, but we checked for frequent syntactic structures in which the agent and patient are inverted, such as passive and ergative constructions.[10]

From each cluster of subject or object mentions, we generated all pairs of mentions. This forms the initial version of our dictionary. The next sections describe how we filter and generalize these pairs.

2.3 Filtering

We manually analyzed 200 random pairs and classified them into coreference and spurious relations. The spurious relations were caused by errors due to the parser, the text extraction, and violations of our algorithm assumption (i.e., the representative verb does not refer to a unique event). We employed a filtering strategy to improve the precision of the dictionary. We used a total of thirteen simple rules, which are shown in Table 1. For instance, we sometimes get the same verb with non-coreferent arguments, especially in tech news that compare companies or products. In these cases, NEs are often used, and so we can get rid of a large number of errors by automatically removing pairs in which both mentions are NEs (e.g., *Google* and *Samsung*).

Before filtering, 53% of all relations were good coreference relations versus 47% spurious ones. Of the relations that remained after filtering, 74% were coreferent and only 26% were spurious. In total, about half of the dictionary relations were removed in the filtering process, resulting in a total of 128,492 coreferent pairs.

Both mentions are NEs
Both mentions appear in the same document
Object of a negated verb
Enumeration or list environment
Sentence is ill-formed
Number NE
Temporal NE
Quantifying noun
Coordinated
Verb is preceded by a determiner or an adjective
Head is not nominal
Sentence length $\geq$ 100
Mention length $\geq$ 70% of sentence length

Table 1: Filters to improve the dictionary precision. Unless otherwise noted, the filter was applied if either mention in the relation satisfied the condition.

2.4 Generalization

The final step of generating our dictionary is to process the opaque mention pairs so that they generalize better. We strip mentions of any determiners, relative clauses, and -ing and -ed clauses. However, we retain adjectives and prepositional modifiers because they are sometimes necessary for coreference to hold (e.g., ***online*** *piracy* and *distribution* ***of pirated material***). We also generalize NEs to their types so that our dictionary entries can function as templates (e.g., *Cook's departure* becomes *<person>'s departure*), but we keep NE tokens that are in the head position as these are pairs containing world knowledge (e.g., *iPad* and *slate*). Finally, we replace all tokens with their lemmas. Table 2 shows a snapshot of the dictionary.

2.5 Semantics of coreference

From manually classifying a sample of 200 dictionary pairs (e.g., Table 2), we find that our dictionary includes many synonymy (e.g., *IPO* and *offering*) and hypernymy relations (e.g., *phone* and *device*), which are the relations that are typically extracted from ontologies for coreference resolution. However, not all synonyms and hypernyms are valid for coreference (recall the *voters-people* vs. *scientists-people* example in the introduction), so our dic-

[8] Report verbs include *argue, claim, say, suggest, tell*, etc.

[9] As a general rule, we extract possessive phrases as subjects (e.g. ***Samsung****'s plan*) and *of*-phrases as objects (e.g. *development of* ***the new logo***).

[10] We can easily detect passive subjects (i-b) as they have their own dependency label, and ergative subjects (ii-b) using a list of ergative verbs extracted from Levin (1993).

(i) a. Developers hacked **the device**.
b. **The device** was hacked.

(ii) a. Police scattered **the crowds**.
b. **The crowds** scattered.

Mention 1	Mention 2
offering	IPO
user	consumer
phone	device
Apple	company
hardware key	digital lock
iPad	slate
content	photo
bug	issue
password	login information
Google	search giant
site	company
filing	complaint
company	government
TouchPad	tablet
medical record	medical file
version	handset
information	credit card
government	chairman
app	software
Android	platform
the leadership change	<person>'s departure
change	update

Table 2: Coreference relations in our dictionary.

tionary only includes the ones that are relevant for coreference (e.g., *update* and *change*). Furthermore, only 3% of our 128,492 opaque pairs are related in WordNet, confirming that our method is introducing a large number of new semantic relations.

We also discover other semantic relations that are relevant for coreference, such as various metonymy relations like mentioning the part for the whole. Again though, we can use some part-whole relations coreferentially (e.g., *car* and *engine*) but not others (e.g., *car* and *window*). Our dictionary includes part-whole relations that have been observed as coreferent at least once (e.g., *company* and *site*). We also extract world-knowledge descriptions for NEs (e.g., *Google* and *the Internet giant*).

3 Integration into a Coreference System

We next integrated our dictionary into an existing coreference resolution system to see if it improves resolution.

3.1 Stanford coreference resolution system

Our baseline is the Stanford coreference resolution system (Lee et al., 2011) which was the highest-scoring system in the CoNLL-2011 Shared Task, and was also part of the highest-scoring system in the CoNLL-2012 Shared Task (Fernandes et al., 2012). It is a rule-based system that includes a total of ten rules (or "sieves") for entity coreference, shown in Table 3. The sieves are applied from highest to lowest precision, each rule extending entities (i.e., mention clusters) built by the previous tiers, but never modifying links previously made. The majority of the sieves rely on string overlap.[11]

Sieve number	Sieve name
1	Discourse processing
2	Exact string match
3	Relaxed string match
4	Precise constructs
5–7	Strict head match
8	Proper head noun match
9	Relaxed head match
10	Pronoun match

Table 3: Rules of the baseline system.

The highly modular architecture made it easy for us to integrate additional sieves using our dictionary to increase recall.

3.2 Dictionary sieves

We propose four new sieves, each one using a different granularity level from our dictionary, with each consecutive sieve using higher precision relations than the previous one. The Dict 1 sieve uses only the heads of mentions in each relation (e.g., *devices*). Dict 2 uses the heads and one premodifier, if it exists (e.g., *iOS devices*). Dict 3 uses the heads and up to two premodifiers (e.g., *new iOS devices*). Dict 4 uses the full mentions, including any postmodifiers (e.g., *new iOS devices for businesses*).

We take advantage of frequency counts to get rid of low-precision coreference pairs and only keep (i) pairs that have been seen more than 75 times (Dict 1) or 15 times (Dict 2, Dict 3, Dict 4); and (ii) pairs with a frequency count larger than 8 (Dict 1) or 2 (Dict 2, Dict 3, Dict 4) and a normalized PMI score larger than 0.18. We use the normalized PMI score (Bouma, 2009) as a measure of association between the mentions m_i and m_j of a

[11]Exceptions: sieve 1 links first-person pronouns inside a quotation with the speaker; sieve 4 links mention pairs that appear in an appositive, copular, acronym, etc., construction; sieve 10 implements generic pronominal coreference resolution.

dictionary pair, computed as

$$(\ln \frac{p(m_i,m_j)}{p(m_i)p(m_j)}) \; / - \ln p(m_i, m_j)$$

These thresholds were set on the development set.

Since the different coreference rules in the Stanford system are arranged in decreasing order of precision, we start by applying the sieve that uses the highest-precision relations in the dictionary (Dict 4), followed by Dict 3, Dict 2, and Dict 1. We add these new sieves right before the last sieve, as the pronominal sieve can perform better if opaque mentions have been successfully linked. The current sieves only use the dictionary for linking singular mentions, as the experiments on the dev showed that plural mentions brought too much noise.

For any mention pair under analysis, each sieve checks whether it is supported by the dictionary as well as whether basic constraints are satisfied, such as number, animacy and NE-type agreement, and NE–common noun order (not the opposite).

4 Experiments

4.1 Data

Although our dictionary creation technology can apply across domains, our current coreference dictionary is focused on the technical domain, so we created a coreference labeled corpus in this domain for evaluation. We extracted new data from Techmeme (different from that used to extract the dictionary) to create a development and a test set. It is important to note that we do not need comparable data at this stage. A massive comparable corpus is only needed for mining the coreference dictionary (Section 2); once it is built, it can be used for solving coreference within and across documents.

The annotation was performed by two experts, using the Callisto annotation tool. The development and test sets were annotated with coreference relations following the OntoNotes guidelines (Pradhan et al., 2007). We annotated full NPs (with all modifiers), excluding appositive phrases and predicate nominals. Only premodifiers that were proper nouns or possessive phrases were annotated. We extended the OntoNotes guidelines by also annotating singletons. Table 4 shows the dataset statistics.

Dataset	Stories	Docs	Tokens	Entities	Mentions
Dev	4	27	7837	1360	2279
Test	24	24	8547	1341	2452

Table 4: Dataset statistics: development (dev) and test.

4.2 Evaluation measures

We evaluated using six coreference measures, as they sometimes provide different results and there is no agreement on a standard. We used the scorer of the CoNLL-2011 Shared Task (Pradhan et al., 2011).

- MUC (Vilain et al., 1995). Link-based metric that measures how many links the true and system partitions have in common.
- B^3 (Bagga and Baldwin, 1998). Mention-based metric that measures the proportion of mention overlap between gold and predicted entities.
- CEAF-ϕ_3 (Luo, 2005). Mention-based metric that, unlike B^3, enforces a one-to-one alignment between gold and predicted entities.
- CEAF-ϕ_4 (Luo, 2005). The entity-based version of the above metric.
- BLANC (Recasens and Hovy, 2011). Link-based metric that considers both coreference and non-coreference links.
- CoNLL (Denis and Baldridge, 2009). Average of MUC, B^3 and CEAF-ϕ_4. It was the official metric of the CoNLL-2011 Shared Task.

4.3 Results

We always start from the baseline, which corresponds to the Stanford system with the sieves listed in Table 3. This is the set of sieves that won the CoNLL-2011 Shared Task (Pradhan et al., 2011), and they exclude WordNet.

Table 5 shows the incremental scores, on the development set, for the four sieves that use the dictionary, corresponding to the different granularity levels, from the highest precision one (Dict 4) to the lowest one (Dict 1). The largest improvement is achieved by Dict 4 and Dict 3, as they improve recall (R) without hurting precision (P). R is equivalent to P for CEAF-ϕ_4, and vice versa. The other two sieves increase R further, especially Dict 1, but also decrease P, although the trade-off for the F-score (F1) is still positive. It is the best score, with the exception of B^3.

System	MUC R	MUC P	MUC F1	B^3 R	B^3 P	B^3 F1	CEAF-ϕ_3 R / P / F1	CEAF-ϕ_4 R	CEAF-ϕ_4 P	CEAF-ϕ_4 F1	BLANC R	BLANC P	BLANC B	CoNLL F1
Baseline	55.9	**72.8**	63.3	74.1	**89.8**	81.2	74.6	**85.2**	73.6	79.0	66.6	87.1	72.6	74.5
+Dict 4	57.0	**72.8**	63.9	75.1	89.4	81.6	75.3	**85.2**	74.3	79.4	68.2	**87.3**	74.2	75.0
+Dict 3	57.6	**72.8**	64.3	75.4	89.3	**81.7**	**75.5**	85.1	74.6	79.5	68.4	87.2	**74.4**	**75.2**
+Dict 2	57.6	72.5	64.2	75.4	89.1	**81.7**	75.4	85.0	74.6	79.5	68.4	87.0	74.3	75.1
+Dict 1	**58.4**	71.9	**64.5**	**75.7**	88.5	81.6	**75.5**	84.6	**75.1**	**79.6**	**68.6**	86.6	**74.4**	**75.2**

Table 5: Incremental results for the four sieves using our dictionary on the development set. Baseline is the Stanford system without the WordNet sieves. Scores are on gold mentions.

System	MUC R	MUC P	MUC F1	B^3 R	B^3 P	B^3 F1	CEAF-ϕ_3 R / P / F1	CEAF-ϕ_4 R	CEAF-ϕ_4 P	CEAF-ϕ_4 F1	BLANC R	BLANC P	BLANC B	CoNLL F1
Baseline	62.4	**78.2**	69.4	73.7	**89.5**	80.8	75.1	**86.2**	73.8	79.5	71.4	88.6	77.3	76.6
w/ WN	63.5	75.3	68.9	74.2	87.5	80.3	74.1	83.7	74.1	78.6	71.8	87.3	77.3	75.9
w/ Dict	64.7*	77.6*	70.6*	**75.7***	88.5*	81.6*	**76.5***	85.3*	75.0*	79.9*	**74.6***	88.6	**79.9***	77.3*
w/ Dict + Context	**64.8***	77.8*	**70.7***	**75.7***	88.6*	**81.7***	**76.5***	85.5*	**75.1***	**80.0***	**74.6***	**88.7**	**79.9***	**77.5***

Table 6: Performance on the test set. Scores are on gold mentions. Stars indicate a statistically significant difference with respect to the baseline.

Table 6 reports the scores on the test set and compares the scores obtained by adding the WordNet sieves to the baseline (w/ WN) with those obtained by adding the dictionary sieves (w/ Dict). Whereas adding WordNet only brings a small improvement in R that is much lower than the loss in P, the dictionary sieves succeed in increasing R by a larger amount and at a smaller cost to P, resulting in a significant improvement in F1: 1.2 points according to MUC, 0.8 points according to B^3, 1.4 points according to CEAF-ϕ_3, 0.4 points according to CEAF-ϕ_4, 2.6 points according to BLANC, and 0.7 points according to CoNLL. Section 5.2 presents the last line (w/ Dict + Context).

5 Discussion

5.1 Error analysis

Thanks to the dictionary, the coreference system improves the baseline by establishing coreference links between the bolded mentions in (3) and (4).

(3) With **Groupon Inc.**'s stock down by half from its IPO price and **the company** heading into its first earnings report since an accounting blowup [...] outlining opportunity ahead and the promise of new products for **the daily-deals company**.

(4) Thompson revealed the diagnosis as evidence arose that seemed to contradict his story about why he was not responsible for a degree listed on his resume that he does not have, the newspaper reports, citing anonymous sources familiar with **the situation** [...] a Yahoo board committee appointed to investigate **the matter**.

The first case requires world knowledge and the second case, semantic knowledge.

We manually analyzed 40 false positive errors caused by the dictionary sieves. Only a small number of them were due to noise in the dictionary. The majority of errors were due to the discourse context: the two mentions could be coreferent, but not in the given context. For example, *Apple* and *company* are potentially coreferent—which is successfully captured by our dictionary—and while they are coreferent in (5), they are not in (6).[12]

(5) It will only get better as **Apple** will be updating it with iOS6, an operating system that **the company** will likely be showing off this summer.

(6) Since *Apple* reinvented the segment, **Microsoft** is the latest entrant into the tablet market, banking on its Windows 8 products to bridge the gap between PCs and tablets. [...] **The company** showed off Windows 8 last September.

[12]Examples in this section show gold coreference relations in bold and incorrectly predicted coreferent mentions in italics.

In these cases it does not suffice to check whether the opaque mention pair is included in the coreference dictionary, but we need a method for taking the surrounding context into account. In the next section we present our preliminary work in this direction.

5.2 Context fit

To help the coreference system choose the right antecedent in examples like (6), we exploit the fact that *the company* is closely followed by *Windows 8*, which is a clue for selecting *Microsoft* instead of *Apple* as the antecedent. We devise a contextual constraint that rules out a mention pair if the contexts are incompatible. To check for context compatibility, we borrow the idea of topic signatures from Lin and Hovy (2000) and that Agirre et al. (2001) used for Word Sense Disambiguation. Instead of identifying the keywords of a topic, we find the NEs that tend to co-occur with another NE. For example, the signature for *Apple* should include terms like *iPhone*, *MacBook*, *iOS*, *Steve Jobs*, etc. This is what we call the **NE signature** for *Apple*.

To construct NE signatures, we first compute the log-likelihood ratio (LLR) statistic between NEs in our corpus (the same one used to build the dictionary). Then, the signature for a NE, w, is the list of k other NEs that have the highest LLR with w. The LLR between two NEs, w_1 and w_2, is $-2 \ln \frac{L(H_1)}{L(H_2)}$, where H_1 is the hypothesis that
$P(w_1 \in sent | w_2 \in sent) = P(w_1 \in sent | w_2 \notin sent)$,
H_2 is the hypothesis that
$P(w_1 \in sent | w_2 \in sent) \neq P(w_1 \in sent | w_2 \notin sent)$,
and $L(\cdot)$ is the likelihood. We assume a binomial distribution for the likelihood.

Once we have NE signatures, we determine the context fit as follows. When the system compares a NE antecedent with a (non-NE) anaphor, we check whether any NEs in the anaphor's sentence are in the antecedent's signature. We also check whether the antecedent is in the signature list of any NE's in the anaphor's sentence. If neither of these is true, we do not allow the system to link the antecedent and the anaphor. In (6), *Apple* is not linked with *the company* because it is not in Windows' signature, and *Windows* is not in Apple's signature either (but *Microsoft* is in Windows' signature).

The last two lines in Table 6 compare the scores without using this contextual feature (w/ Dict) with those using context (w/ Dict + Context). Our feature for context compatibility leads to a small but positive improvement, taking the final improvement of the dictionary sieves to be about 1 percentage point above the baseline according to all six evaluation measures. We leave as future work to test this idea on a larger test set and refine it further so as to address more challenging cases where comparing NEs is not enough, like in (7).

(7) **Snapchat** will notify users [...] The program is available for free in *Apple*'s App Store [...] While **the company** "attempts to delete image data as soon as possible after the message is transmitted," it cannot guarantee messages will always be deleted.

To resolve (7), it would be helpful to know that Snapchat is a picture messaging platform, as the context mentions *image data* and *messages*.

6 Related Work

Existing ontologies are not optimal for solving opaque coreferent mentions because of both a precision and a recall problem (Lee et al., 2011; Uryupina et al., 2011). On the other hand, using data-driven methods such as distributional semantics for coreference resolution suffers especially from a precision problem (Ng, 2007). Our work combines ideas from distributional semantics and paraphrase acquisition methods in order to efficiently use contextual information to extract coreference relations.

The main idea that we borrow from paraphrase acquisition is the use of monolingual (non-parallel) comparable corpora, which have been exploited to extract both sentence-level (Barzilay and McKeown, 2001) and sub-sentential-level paraphrases (Shinyama and Sekine, 2003; Wang and Callison-Burch, 2011). To ensure that the NPs are coreferent, we limit the meaning of *comparable corpora* to collections of documents that report on the very same story, as opposed to collections of documents that are about the same (general) topic. However, the distinguishing factor is that while most paraphrasing studies, including Lin and Pantel (2001), use NEs—or nouns in general—as pivots to learn paraphrases of their surrounding context, we use verbs as pivots to learn coreference relations at the NP level.

There are many similarities between paraphrase and coreference, and our work is most similar to that by Wang and Callison-Burch (2011). However, some paraphrases that might not be considered to be valid (e.g., *under $200* and *around $200*) can be acceptable coreference relations. Unlike Wang and Callison-Burch (2011), we do not work on document pairs but on sets of at least five (comparable) documents, and we do not require sentence alignment, but just verb alignment.

Another source of inspiration is the work by Bean and Riloff (2004). They use contextual roles (i.e., the role that an NP plays in an event) for extracting patterns that can be used in coreference resolution, showing the relevance of verbs in deciding on coreference between their arguments. However, they use a very small corpus (two domains) and do not aim to build a dictionary. The idea of creating a repository of extracted concept-instance relations appears in Fleischman et al. (2003), but restricted to person-role pairs, e.g. *Yasser Arafat* and *leader*. Although it was originally designed for answering who-is questions, Daumé III and Marcu (2005) successfully used it for coreference resolution.

The coreference relations that we extract might overlap but go beyond those detected by Bansal and Klein (2012)'s Web-based features. First, they focus on NP headwords, while we extract full NPs, including multi-word mentions. Second, the fact that they use the Google *n*-gram corpus means that the two headwords must appear at most four words apart, thus ruling out coreferent mentions that can only appear far from each other. Finally, while their extraction patterns focus on synonymy and hypernymy relations, we discover other types of semantic relations that are relevant for coreference (Section 2.5).

7 Conclusions

We have pointed out an important problem with current coreference resolution systems: their heavy reliance on string overlap. Pronouns aside, opaque mentions account for 65% of the errors made by state-of-the-art systems. To improve coreference scores beyond 60-70%, we therefore need to make better use of semantic and world knowledge to deal with non-identical-string coreference. But, as we have also shown, coreference is not the same as semantic similarity or hypernymy. Only certain semantic relations in certain contexts are good cues for coreference. We therefore need semantic resources specifically targeted at coreference.

We proposed a new solution for detecting opaque mention pairs: restricting distributional similarity to a comparable corpus of articles about the very same story, thus ensuring that similar mentions will also likely be coreferent. We used this corpus to build a dictionary focused on coreference, and successfully extracted the specific semantic and world knowledge relevant for coreference. The resulting dictionary can be added on top of any coreference system to increase recall at a minimum cost to precision. Integrated into the Stanford coreference resolution system, which won the CoNLL-2011 shared task, the F-score increases about 1 percentage point according to all of the six evaluation measures. The dictionary and NE signatures are available on the Web.[13]

We showed that apart from the need for extracting coreference-specific semantic and world knowledge, we need to take into account the context surrounding the mentions. The results from our preliminary work for identifying incompatible contexts is promising.

Our unsupervised method for extracting opaque coreference relations can be easily extended to other domains by using online news aggregators, and trained on more data to build a more comprehensive dictionary that can increase recall even further. We integrated the dictionary into a rule-based coreference system, but it remains for future work to integrate it into a learning-based architecture, where the system can combine the dictionary features with other features. This can also make it easier to include contextual features that take into account how well a dictionary pair fits in a specific context.

Acknowledgments

We would like to thank the members of the Stanford NLP Group, Valentin Spitkovsky, and Ed Hovy for valuable comments at various stages of the project.

The first author was supported by a Beatriu de Pinós postdoctoral scholarship (2010 BP-A 00149) from Generalitat de Catalunya. We also gratefully acknowledge the support of Defense Advanced Research Projects Agency (DARPA) Machine Reading Program under Air Force Research Laboratory (AFRL) prime contract no. FA8750-09-C-0181.

[13]http://nlp.stanford.edu/pubs/coref-dictionary.zip

References

Eneko Agirre, Olatz Ansa, David Martinez, and Eduard Hovy. 2001. Enriching wordnet concepts with topic signatures. In *Proceedings of the NAACL Workshop on WordNet and Other Lexical Resources: Applications, Extensions and Customizations*, pages 23–28.

Amit Bagga and Breck Baldwin. 1998. Algorithms for scoring coreference chains. In *Proceedings of the LREC 1998 Workshop on Linguistic Coreference*, pages 563–566.

Mohit Bansal and Dan Klein. 2012. Coreference semantics from web features. In *Proceedings of ACL*, pages 389–398.

Regina Barzilay and Kathleen McKeown. 2001. Extracting paraphrases from a parallel corpus. In *Proceedings of ACL*, pages 50–57.

David Bean and Ellen Riloff. 2004. Unsupervised learning of contextual role knowledge for coreference resolution. In *Proceedings of NAACL-HTL*.

Geolof Bouma. 2009. Normalized (pointwise) mutual information in collocation extraction. In *Proceedings of the Biennial GSCL Conference*, pages 31–40.

Hal Daumé III and Daniel Marcu. 2005. A large-scale exploration of effective global features for a joint entity detection and tracking model. In *Proceedings of HLT-EMNLP*, pages 97–104.

Pascal Denis and Jason Baldridge. 2009. Global joint models for coreference resolution and named entity classification. *Procesamiento del Lenguaje Natural*, 42:87–96.

Eraldo Fernandes, Cícero dos Santos, and Ruy Milidiú. 2012. Latent structure perceptron with feature induction for unrestricted coreference resolution. In *Proceedings of CoNLL - Shared Task*, pages 41–48.

Michael Fleischman, Eduard Hovy, and Abdessamad Echihabi. 2003. Offline strategies for online question answering: answering questions before they are asked. In *Proceedings of ACL*, pages 1–7.

Aria Haghighi and Dan Klein. 2010. Coreference resolution in a modular, entity-centered model. In *Proceedings of HLT-NAACL*, pages 385–393.

Hamidreza Kobdani, Hinrich Schütze, Michael Schiehlen, and Hans Kamp. 2011. Bootstrapping coreference resolution using word associations. In *Proceedings of ACL*, pages 783–792.

Heeyoung Lee, Yves Peirsman, Angel Chang, Nathanael Chambers, Mihai Surdeanu, and Dan Jurafsky. 2011. Stanford's multi-pass sieve coreference resolution system at the CoNLL-2011 Shared Task. In *Proceedings of CoNLL - Shared Task*, pages 28–34.

Beth Levin. 1993. *English Verb Class and Alternations: A Preliminary Investigation.* University of Chicago Press, Chicago.

Chin-Yew Lin and Eduard Hovy. 2000. The automated acquisition of topic signatures for text summarization. In *Proceedings of COLING*, pages 495–501.

Dekang Lin and Patrick Pantel. 2001. DIRT - Discovery of inference rules from text. In *Proceedings of the ACM SIGKDD*, pages 323–328.

Xiaoqiang Luo. 2005. On coreference resolution performance metrics. In *Proceedings of HLT-EMNLP*, pages 25–32.

Vincent Ng. 2007. Shallow semantics for coreference resolution. In *Proceedings of IJCAI*, pages 1689–1694.

Joakim Nivre, Johan Hall, and Jens Nilsson. 2004. Memory-based dependency parsing. In *Proceedings of CoNLL*, pages 49–56.

Simone Paolo Ponzetto and Michael Strube. 2006. Exploiting semantic role labeling, WordNet and Wikipedia for coreference resolution. In *Proceedings of HLT-NAACL*, pages 192–199.

Sameer S. Pradhan, Lance Ramshaw, Ralph Weischedel, Jessica MacBride, and Linnea Micciulla. 2007. Unrestricted coreference: Identifying entities and events in OntoNotes. In *Proceedings of ICSC*, pages 446–453.

Sameer Pradhan, Lance Ramshaw, Mitchell Marcus, Martha Palmer, Ralph Weischedel, and Nianwen Xue. 2011. CoNLL-2011 Shared Task: Modeling unrestricted coreference in OntoNotes. In *Proceedings of CoNLL - Shared Task*, pages 1–27.

Altaf Rahman and Vincent Ng. 2011. Coreference resolution with world knowledge. In *Proceedings of ACL*, pages 814–824.

Marta Recasens and Eduard Hovy. 2010. Coreference resolution across corpora: Languages, coding schemes, and preprocessing information. In *Proceedings of ACL*, pages 1423–1432.

Marta Recasens and Eduard Hovy. 2011. BLANC: Implementing the Rand index for coreference evaluation. *Natural Language Engineering*, 17(4):485–510.

Yusuke Shinyama and Satoshi Sekine. 2003. Paraphrase acquisition for information extraction. In *Proceedings of ACL*, pages 65–71.

Veselin Stoyanov, Nathan Gilbert, Claire Cardie, and Ellen Riloff. 2009. Conundrums in noun phrase coreference resolution: Making sense of the state-of-the-art. In *Proceedings of ACL-IJCNLP*, pages 656–664.

Olga Uryupina, Massimo Poesio, Claudio Giuliano, and Kateryna Tymoshenko. 2011. Disambiguation and filtering methods in using web knowledge for coreference resolution. In *Proceedings of FLAIRS*, pages 317–322.

Marc Vilain, John Burger, John Aberdeen, Dennis Connolly, and Lynette Hirschman. 1995. A model-theoretic coreference scoring scheme. In *Proceedings of MUC-6*, pages 45–52.

Rui Wang and Chris Callison-Burch. 2011. Paraphrase fragment extraction from monolingual comparable corpora. In *Proceedings of the 4th ACL Workshop on Building and Using Comparable Corpora*, pages 52–60.

Xiaofeng Yang and Jian Su. 2007. Coreference resolution using semantic relatedness information from automatically discovered patterns. In *Proceedings of ACL*, pages 528–535.

Global Inference for Bridging Anaphora Resolution

Yufang Hou[1], **Katja Markert**[2], **Michael Strube**[1]
[1] Heidelberg Institute for Theoretical Studies gGmbH, Heidelberg, Germany
(yufang.hou|michael.strube)@h-its.org
[2]School of Computing, University of Leeds, UK
scskm@leeds.ac.uk

Abstract

We present the first work on antecedent selection for bridging resolution without restrictions on anaphor or relation types. Our model integrates global constraints on top of a rich local feature set in the framework of Markov logic networks. The global model improves over the local one and both strongly outperform a reimplementation of prior work.

1 Introduction

Identity coreference is a relatively well understood and well-studied instance of entity coherence. However, entity coherence can rely on more complex, lexico-semantic, frame or encyclopedic relations than identity. Anaphora linking distinct entities or events this way are called *bridging* or *associative anaphora* and have been widely discussed in the linguistic literature (Clark, 1975; Prince, 1981; Gundel et al., 1993).[1] In Example 1, the phrases *the windows, the carpets* and *walls* can be felicitously used because they are semantically related via a part-of relation to their antecedent *the Polish center*.[2]

(1) ...as much as possible of *the Polish center* will be made from aluminum, steel and glass recycled from Warsaw's abundant rubble. ...**The windows** will open. **The carpets** won't be glued down and **walls** will be coated with non-toxic finishes.

Bridging is frequent amounting to between 5% (Gardent and Manuélian, 2005) and 20% (Caselli and Prodanof, 2006) of definite descriptions (both studies limited to NPs starting with *the* or non-English equivalents). Bridging resolution is needed to fill gaps in entity grids based on coreference only (Barzilay and Lapata, 2008). Example 1 does not exhibit any coreferential entity coherence. Coherence can only be established when the bridging anaphora are resolved. Bridging resolution may also be important for textual entailment (Mirkin et al., 2010).

Bridging resolution can be divided into two tasks, recognizing that a bridging anaphor is present and finding the correct antecedent among a list of candidates. These two tasks have frequently been handled in a pipeline with most research concentrating on antecedent selection only. We also handle only the task of antecedent selection.

Previous work on antecedent selection for bridging anaphora is restricted. It makes strong untested assumptions about bridging anaphora types or relations, limiting it to definite NPs (Poesio and Vieira, 1998; Poesio et al., 2004; Lassalle and Denis, 2011) or to part-of relations between anaphor and antecedent (Poesio et al., 2004; Markert et al., 2003; Lassalle and Denis, 2011). We break new ground by considering all relations and anaphora/antecedent types and show that the variety of bridging anaphora is much higher than reported previously.

Following work on coreference resolution, we apply a *local* pairwise model (Soon et al., 2001) for antecedent selection. We then develop novel semantic, syntactic and salience features for this task, showing strong improvements over one of the best known

[1]Poesio and Vieira (1998) include cases where antecedent and anaphor are coreferent but do not share the same head noun. We restrict *bridging* to non-coreferential cases. We also exclude *comparative anaphora* (Modjeska et al., 2003)

[2]Examples are from OntoNotes (Weischedel et al., 2011). Bridging anaphora are typed in boldface; antecedents in italics.

prior models (Poesio et al., 2004).

However, this local model classifies each anaphor-antecedent candidate pair in isolation. Thus, it neglects that bridging anaphora referring to a single antecedent often occur in clusters (see Example 1). It also neglects that once an entity is an antecedent for a bridging anaphor it is more likely to be used again as antecedent. In addition, such local models construct the list of possible antecedent candidates normally relying on a window size constraint to restrict the set of candidates: is the window too small, we miss too many correct antecedents; is it too large, we include so many incorrect antecedents as to lead to severe data imbalance in learning.

To remedy these flaws we change to a *global* Markov logic model that allows us to:

- model constraints that certain anaphora are likely to share the same antecedent;
- model the global semantic connectivity of a salient potential antecedent to all anaphora in a text;
- consider the union of potential antecedents for all anaphora instead of a static window-sized constraint.

We show that this global model with the same local features but enhanced with global constraints improves significantly over the local model.

2 Related Work

Prior corpus-linguistic studies on bridging are beset by three main problems. First, reliability is not measured or low (Fraurud, 1990; Poesio, 2003; Gardent and Manuélian, 2005; Riester et al., 2010).[3] Second, annotated corpora are small (Poesio et al., 2004; Korzen and Buch-Kromann, 2011). Third, they are often based on strong untested assumptions about bridging anaphora types, antecedent types or relations, such as limiting it to definite NP anaphora (Poesio and Vieira, 1998; Poesio et al., 2004; Gardent and Manuélian, 2005; Caselli and Prodanof, 2006; Riester et al., 2010; Lassalle and Denis, 2011), to NP antecedents (all prior work) or to part-of relations between anaphor and antecedent (Markert et al., 2003; Poesio et al., 2004). In our own work (Markert et al., 2012) we established a corpus that circumvents these problems, i.e. human bridging recognition was reliable, it contains a medium number of bridging cases that allows generalisable statistics and we did not limit bridging anaphora or antecedents according to their syntactic type or relations between them. However, we only discussed human agreement on bridging recognition in Markert et al. (2012), disregarding antecedent annotation. We also did not discuss the different types of bridging in the corpus. We will remedy this in Section 3.

Automatic work on bridging distinguishes between recognition (Vieira and Poesio, 2000; Rahman and Ng, 2012; Cahill and Riester, 2012; Markert et al., 2012) and antecedent selection. Work on antecedent selection suffers from focusing on subproblems, e.g. only part-of bridging (Poesio et al., 2004; Markert et al., 2003) or definite NP anaphora (Lassalle and Denis, 2011). Most relevant for us is Lassalle and Denis (2011) who restrict anaphora to definite descriptions but have no other restrictions on relations or antecedent NPs (in a French corpus) with an accuracy of 23%. Also the evaluation setup is sometimes not clear: The high results in Poesio et al. (2004) cannot be used for comparison as they test unrealistically: they distinguish only between the correct antecedent and *one* or *three* false candidates (baseline of 50% for the former). They also restrict the phenomenon to part-of relations.

There is a partial overlap between bridging and implicit noun roles (Ruppenhofer et al., 2010). However, work on implicit noun roles is mostly focused on few predicates (e.g. Gerber and Chai (2012)). We consider all bridging anaphors in running text. The closest work to ours interpreting implicit role filling as anaphora resolution is Silberer and Frank (2012).

3 Corpus for Bridging: An Overview

We use the dataset we created in Markert et al. (2012) with almost 11,000 NPs annotated for information status including 663 bridging NPs and their antecedents in 50 texts taken from the WSJ portion of the OntoNotes corpus (Weischedel et al., 2011). Bridging anaphora can be any noun phrase. They

[3] Although the overall information status scheme in Riester et al. (2010) achieved high agreement, their confusion matrix shows that the anaphoric bridging category (BRI) is frequently confused with other categories so that the two annotators agreed on only less than a third of bridging anaphors.

are not limited to definite NPs as in previous work. In contrast to Nissim et al. (2004), antecedents are annotated and can be noun phrases, verb phrases or even clauses. Our bridging annotation is also not limited with regards to semantic relations between anaphor and antecedent.

In Markert et al. (2012) we achieved high agreement for the overall information status annotation scheme between three annotators (κ between 75 and 80, dependent on annotator pairs) as well as for all subcategories, including bridging (κ over 60 for all annotator pairings, over 70 for two expert annotators). Here, we add the following new results:

- Agreement for selecting bridging antecedents was around 80% for all annotator pairings.
- Surprisingly, only 255 of the 663 (38%) bridging anaphors are definite NPs, which calls into question the strategy of prior approaches to limit themselves to these types of bridging.
- NPs are the most frequent antecedents by far with only 42 of 663 (6%) bridging anaphora having a non-NP antecedent (mostly verb phrases).
- Bridging is a relatively local phenomenon with 71% of NP antecedents occurring in the same or up to 2 sentences prior to the anaphor. However, farther away antecedents are common when the antecedent is the global focus of a document.
- The semantic relations between anaphor and antecedent are extremely diverse with only 92 of 663 (14%) anaphors having a part-of/attribute-of antecedent (see Example 1) and only 45 (7%) anaphors standing in a set relationship to the antecedent (see Example 2). This contrasts with Gardent and Manuélian's (2005) finding that 52% of bridging cases had meronymic relations. We find many different types of relations in our corpus, including encyclopedic relations such as *restaurant — the waiter* as well as, frequently, relational person nouns as bridging anaphors such as *friend, husband, president*.
- There are only a few cases of bridging where surface cues may indicate the antecedent. First, some bridging anaphors are modified by a small number of adjectives that have more than one role filler, with the bridging relation often being temporal or spatial sequence between two entities of the same semantic type as in Example 3 (see also Lassalle and Denis (2011) for a discussion of such cases). Second, some anaphors are compounds where the nominal premodifier matches the antecedent head as in Example 4.

(2) Still *employees* do occasionally try to smuggle out a gem or two. **One man** wrapped several diamonds in the knot of his tie. **Another** poked a hole in the heel of his shoe. **None** made it past the body searches ...

(3) *His truck* is parked across the field ... The farmer at **the next truck** shouts ...

(4) ... it doesn't make *the equipment needed to produce those chips*. And IBM worries that the Japanese will take over **that equipment market**.

4 Models for Bridging Resolution

4.1 Pairwise mention-entity model

The pairwise model is widely used in coreference resolution (Soon et al., 2001). We adapt it for bridging resolution[4]: Given an anaphor mention m and the set of antecedent candidate entities E_m which appear before m, we create a pairwise instance (m, e) for every $e \in E_m$. A binary decision whether m is bridged to e is made for each instance (m, e) separately. A post-processing step to choose one antecedent is necessary (closest first or best first are common strategies). This model causes three problems for bridging resolution: First, the ratio between positive and negative instances is 1 to 17 even if only antecedent candidates from the current and the immediately preceding two sentences are considered. The ratio will be even worse with a larger window size. Therefore, usually a fixed window size is used restricting the set of candidates. This, however, causes a second problem: antecedents which are beyond the window cannot be found. In our data, only 81% of NP antecedents appear within the previous 5 sentences, and only 71% of NP antecedents appear within the previous 2 sentences. The third problem is a shortcoming of the pairwise model itself: decisions are made for each instance separately, ignoring

[4]Different from coreference, we treat an anaphor as a mention and an antecedent as an entity. The anaphor is the first mention of the corresponding entity in the document.

relations between instances. We resolve these problems by employing a global model based on Markov logic networks.

4.2 Markov Logic Networks

Bridging can be considered a document global phenomenon, where globally salient entities are preferred as antecedents and two or more anaphors having the same antecedent should be related or similar. Motivated by this observation, we explore Markov logic networks (Domingos and Lowd, 2009, MLNs) to model bridging resolution on the global discourse level.

MLNs are a powerful representation for joint inference with uncertainty. An MLN consists of a set of pairs (F_i, w_i), where F_i is a formula in first-order logic and w_i is its associated real numbered weight. It can be viewed as a template for constructing Markov networks. Given different sets of constants, an MLN will produce different ground Markov networks which may vary in size but have the same structure and parameters. For a ground Markov network, the probability distribution over possible worlds x is given by

$$P(X = x) = \frac{1}{Z} \exp\left(\sum_i w_i n_i(x)\right) \qquad (1)$$

where $n_i(x)$ is the number of true groundings of F_i in x. The normalization factor Z is the partition function.

MLNs have been applied to many NLP tasks and achieved good performance by leveraging rich relations among objects (Poon and Domingos, 2008; Meza-Ruiz and Riedel, 2009; Fahrni and Strube, 2012, inter alia). We use *thebeast*[5] to learn weights for the formulas and to perform inference. *thebeast* employs cutting plane inference (Riedel, 2008) to improve the accuracy and efficiency of MAP inference for Markov logic.

With MLNs, we model bridging resolution globally on the discourse level: given the set M of all anaphors and sets of local antecedent candidates E_m for each anaphor $m \in M$, we select antecedents for all anaphors from $E = \bigcup_{m \in M} E_m$ at the same time. Table 1 shows the hidden predicates and formulas used. Each formula is associated with a weight. The polarity of the weights is indicated by the leading $+$ or $-$. The weight value (except for hard constraints) is learned from training data. For some formulas the final weight consists of a learned weight w multiplied by a score d (e.g. inverse distance between antecedent and anaphor). In these cases the final weight for a formula in a ground Markov network does not just depend on the respective formula, but also on the specific constants. We indicate such combined weights by the term $w \cdot d$.

We tackle the previously mentioned problems of the pairwise model: (1) We construct hard constraints to specify that each anaphor has at most one antecedent entity (Table 1: f1) and that the antecedent must precede the anaphor (f2). This eliminates the need for the post-processing step in the pairwise model. (2) We select the antecedent entity for each anaphor from the antecedent candidate entities pool E which alleviates the missing true antecedent problem in the pairwise model. Based on (1) and (2), MLNs allow us to express relations between anaphor-anaphor and anaphor-antecedent pairs ((m,n) or (m,e)) on the global discourse level improving accuracy by performing joint inference.

5 Features

5.1 Local features

5.1.1 Poesio et al.'s feature set

Table 2 shows the feature set proposed by Poesio et al. (2004) for part-of bridging. Google distance is the inverse value of Google hit counts for the *ofPattern* query (e.g. *the windows of the center*). WordNet distance is the inverse value of the shortest path length between an anaphor and an antecedent candidate among all synset combinations. These features are supposed to capture the meronymy relation between anaphor and antecedent. The other ones measure the salience of the antecedent candidate.

Group	Feature	Value
lexical	Google distance	numeric
	WordNet distance	numeric
salience	utterance distance	numeric
	local first mention	boolean
	global first mention	boolean

Table 2: Poesio et al.'s feature set

[5] `http://code.google.com/p/thebeast`

Hidden predicates			
p1	$isBridging(m, e)$		
p2	$hasSameAntecedent(m, n)$		
Formulas			
Hard constraints			
f1	$\forall m \in M: \ \lvert e \in E: isBridging(m, e) \rvert \leq 1$		
f2	$\forall m \in M \forall e \in E: \ hasPairDistance(e, m, d) \wedge d < 0 \rightarrow \neg isBridging(m, e)$		
f3	$\forall m, n \in M: \ m \neq n \wedge hasSameAntecedent(m, n) \rightarrow hasSameAntecedent(n, m)$		
f4	$\forall m, n, l \in M: \ m \neq n \wedge m \neq l \wedge n \neq l \wedge hasSameAntecedent(m, n) \wedge hasSameAntecedent(n, l) \rightarrow hasSameAntecedent(m, l)$		
f5	$\forall m, n \in M \forall e \in E: \ m \neq n \wedge hasSameAntecedent(m, n) \wedge isBridging(m, e) \rightarrow isBridging(n, e)$		
f6	$\forall m, n \in M \forall e \in E: \ m \neq n \wedge isBridging(m, e) \wedge isBridging(n, e) \rightarrow hasSameAntecedent(m, n)$		
Discourse level formulas			
f7	$+$	(w)	$\forall m \in M \forall e \in E: \ predictedGlobalAnte(e) \wedge hasPairDistance(e, m, d) \wedge d > 0 \rightarrow isBridging(m, e)$
f8	$+$	(w)	$\forall m, n \in M \ conjunction(m, n) \rightarrow hasSameAntecedent(m, n)$
f9	$+$	(w)	$\forall m, n \in M \ sameHead(m, n) \rightarrow hasSameAntecedent(m, n)$
f10	$+$	(w)	$\forall m, n \in M \ similarTo(m, n) \rightarrow hasSameAntecedent(m, n)$
f11	$+$	(w)	$\forall m \in M \forall e \in E: \ hasSemanticClass(m, "rolePerson") \wedge hasSemanticClass(e, "org\lvert gpe") \wedge hasPairDistance(e, m, d) \wedge d > 0 \rightarrow isBridging(m, e)$
f12	$+$	$(w \cdot d)$	$\forall m \in M \forall e \in E: \ hasSemanticClass(m, "relativePerson") \wedge hasSemanticClass(e, "otherPerson") \wedge hasPairDistanceInverse(e, m, d) \rightarrow isBridging(m, e)$
f13	$+$	$(w \cdot d)$	$\forall m \in M \forall e \in E: \ hasSemanticClass(m, "date") \wedge hasSemanticClass(e, "date") \wedge hasPairDistanceInverse(e, m, d) \rightarrow isBridging(m, e)$
Local formulas			
f14	$+$	(w)	$\forall m \in M \ \forall e \in E_m: \ isTopRelativeRankPrepPattern(m, e) \rightarrow isBridging(m, e)$
f15	$+$	(w)	$\forall m \in M \ \forall e \in E_m: \ isTopRelativeRankVerbPattern(m, e) \rightarrow isBridging(m, e)$
f16	$+$	$(w \cdot d)$	$\forall m \in M \ \forall e \in E_m: \ isPartOf(m, e) \wedge hasPairDistanceInverse(e, m, d) \rightarrow isBridging(m, e)$
f17	$+$	(w)	$\forall m \in M \ \forall e \in E_m: \ isTopRelativeRankDocSpan(m, e) \rightarrow isBridging(m, e)$
f18	$-$	(w)	$\forall m \in M \ \forall e \in E_m: \ isSameHead(m, e) \rightarrow isBridging(m, e)$
f19	$+$	(w)	$\forall m \in M \ \forall e \in E_m: \ isPremodOverlap(m, e) \rightarrow isBridging(m, e)$
f20	$-$	(w)	$\forall m \in M \ \forall e \in E_m: \ isCoArgument(m, e) \rightarrow isBridging(m, e)$

Table 1: Hidden predicates and formulas used for bridging resolution (m, n, l represent mentions, M the set of bridging anaphora mentions in the whole document, e the antecedent candidate entity, E_m the set of local antecedent candidate entities for m, and $E = \bigcup_{m \in M} E_m$)

5.1.2 Other features

Since Poesio et al. (2004) deal exclusively with meronymy bridging, we have to extend the feature set to capture more diverse relations between anaphor and antecedent. All numeric features in Table 3 are normalized among all antecedent candidates of one anaphor. For anaphor m_i and its antecedent candidates E_{m_i} ($e_{ij} \in E_{m_i}$), the numeric score for pair $\{m_i, e_{ik}\}$ is S_{ik}. Then the value $NormS_{ik}$ for this pair is normalized (set to values between 0 and 1) as below:

$$NormS_{ik} = \frac{S_{ik} - \min_j S_{ij}}{\max_j S_{ij} - \min_j S_{ij}} \quad (2)$$

A second variant of numeric features tells whether the score of an anaphor-antecedent candidate pair is the highest among all pairs for this anaphor.

Group	Feature	Value
semantic	$feat1$ preposition pattern	numeric
	$feat2$ verb pattern	numeric
	$feat3$ WordNet partOf	boolean
	$feat4$ semantic class	nominal
salience	$feat5$ document span	numeric
surface	$feat6$ isSameHead	boolean
	$feat7$ isPremodOverlap	boolean
syntactic	$feat8$ isCoArgument	boolean

Table 3: Local features we developed

Preposition pattern ($feat1$). The *ofPattern* proposed by Poesio et al. (2004) is useful for part-of and attribute-of relations but cannot cover all bridging relations (such as *sanctions against a country*). We extend the *ofPattern* to a generalised *preposition pattern* by using the Gigaword (Parker et al., 2011) and the Tipster (Harman and Liberman, 1993) corpora (both automatically POS tagged and NP chunked for improving query match precision).

First, we extract the three most highly associated prepositions for each anaphor. Then for each anaphor-antecedent candidate pair, we use their head words to create the query *"anaphor preposition antecedent"*. To improve recall, we take lowercase, uppercase, singular and plural forms of the head word into account, and replace proper names by fine-grained named entity types (using a gazetteer). All raw hit counts are converted into the Dunning Root Loglikelihood association measure,[6] then normalized using Formula 2 within all antecedent candidates of one anaphor.

Verb pattern ($feat2$). A set-membership relation between anaphor and antecedent is often hard to capture by the *preposition pattern* because the anaphor often has no common noun head (see Example 2 in Section 3). Hence, we measure the compatibility of the antecedent candidates with the verb the anaphor depends on.

First, we hypothesise that anaphors whose lexical head is a pronoun or a number are potential set bridging cases and then extract the verb the anaphor depends on. In example 2, for the set anaphor **Another**, *poked* is the verb. Then for each antecedent candidate, subject-verb or verb-object queries are applied to the Web 1T 5-gram corpus (Brants and Franz, 2006). In this case, *employees poked* and *diamonds poked* are example queries. The hit counts are transformed into PMI and all pairs for one anaphor are normalized as described in Formula 2.

WordNet partOf relation ($feat3$). To capture part-of bridging, we extract whether the anaphor is part of the antecedent candidate in WordNet. To improve recall, we use hyponym information of the antecedent. If an antecedent e is a hypernym of x and an anaphor m is a meronym of x, then m is a meronym of e.

Semantic class ($feat4$). The anaphor and the antecedent candidate are assigned one of 16 coarse-grained semantic classes, e.g. location, organization, GPE, roleperson, relativePerson, otherPerson[7], product, language, NORP (nationalities, religious or political groups) and several classes for numbers (such as date, money or percent).

Salience feature ($feat5$). Salient entities are preferred as antecedents. We capture salience superficially by computing the *"antecedent document span"* of an antecedent candidate. We compute the

[6] `http://tdunning.blogspot.de/2008/03/surprise-and-coincidence.html`

[7] We use WordNet to extract lists for *rolePerson* (persons like *president* or *teacher* playing a role in an organization) and *relativePerson* (persons like *father* or *son* indicating that they have a relation with another person). Persons not in these two lists are counted as *otherPerson*.

span of text (measured in sentences) in which the antecedent candidate entity is mentioned. This is divided by the number of sentences in the whole document. This score is normalized using Formula 2 for all antecedent candidates of one anaphor.

Surface features ($feat6$-$feat7$). *isSameHead* ($feat6$) checks whether antecedent candidates have the same head as the anaphor: this is rarely the case in bridging anaphora (except in some cases of set bridging and spatial/temporal sequence, see Example 3) and can therefore be used to exclude antecedent candidates. *isPremodOverlap* ($feat7$) determines the antecedent for compound noun anaphors whose head is prenominally modified by the antecedent head (see Example 4).

Syntactic feature ($feat8$) The *isCoArgument* feature is based on the intuition that the subject cannot be the bridging antecedent of the object in the same clause. This feature excludes (some) close antecedent candidates. In Example 4, the antecedent candidate *the Japanese* isCoArgument with the anaphor **that equipment market**.

5.2 Global features for MLNs

$f1$-$f13$ in Table 1 are discourse level constraints. All antecedent candidates come from the antecedent candidates pool E in the whole document.

Global salience (Table 1: $f3$-$f10$). The salience feature in the pairwise model only measures the salience for candidates within the local window. However, globally salient antecedents are preferred even if they are far away from the anaphor. We model this from two perspectives:

$f7$ models the preference for globally salient antecedents, which we derive for each document. For $m \in M$ and $e \in E$, let $score(m, e)$ be the preposition pattern score for pair (m,e). Calculate pattern semantic salience score e_{sal} for each $e \in E$ as

$$e_{sal} = \sum_{m \in M} score(m, e) \tag{3}$$

If e appears in the title and also has the highest pattern semantic salience score e_{sal} among all e in E, then e is the predicted globally salient antecedent for this document. Note that global salience here is based on semantic connectivity to all anaphors in the document and that not every document has a globally salient antecedent.

$f3$-$f6$ and $f8$-$f10$ model that similar or related anaphors in one document are likely to have the same antecedent. To make the ground Markov network more sparse for more efficient inference, we add the hidden predicate ($p2$) and hard constraints ($f3$-$f6$) specifying relations among similar/related anaphors m, n and l (reflexivity and transitivity). Formulas $f8$-$f10$ explore three different ways (syntactic and semantic) to compute the similarity between two anaphors. In $f10$, we use SVM^{light} (similarity scores from WordNet plus sentence distance as features) to predict whether two anaphors not sharing the same head are similar or not.

Frequent bridging relations (Table 1: $f11$-$f13$). Three common bridging relations are restricted by semantic class of anaphor and antecedent (see also Section 3). It is worth noting that in formula $f11$ (modeling that a role person mention like *president* or *chairman* prefers organization or GPE antecedents), we do not penalize the antecedents far away from the anaphor. In formula $f12$ (modeling that a relativePerson mention such as *mother* or *husband* prefers close person antecedents) and $f13$, we prefer close antecedents by including the distance between antecedent and anaphor into the weights.

MLN formulation of local features (Table 1: $f14$-$f20$). Corresponding to features of the pairwise model (Table 3) – we exclude only semantic class as this is modelled globally via features $f11$-$f13$. These local features are only used for an anaphor m and its local antecedent candidate e from E_m.

6 Experiments and Results

6.1 Experimental setup

We perform experiments on our gold standard corpus via 10-fold cross-validation on documents. We use gold standard mentions, true coreference information, and the OntoNotes named entity and syntactic annotation layers for feature extraction.

6.2 Improved baseline

We reimplement the algorithm from Poesio et al. (2004) as baseline. Since they did not explain whether they used the mention-mention or mention-entity model, we assume they treated antecedents as entities and use a 2 and 5 sentence window for candidates[8]. Since the GoogleAPI is not available any more, we use the Web 1T 5-gram corpus (Brants and Franz, 2006) to extract the Google distance feature. We improve it by taking all information about entities via coreference into account as well as by replacing proper names. All other features (Table 2 in Section 5.1.1) are extracted as Poesio et al. did. A Naive Bayes classifier with standard settings in WEKA (Witten and Frank, 2005) is used. In order to evaluate their model in the more realistic setting of our experiment, we apply the *best first* strategy to select the antecedent for each anaphor.

6.3 Pairwise models

Pairwise model I: We use the *preposition pattern* feature ($feat1$) plus Poesio et al.'s salience features (Table 2). We use a 2 sentence window as it performed on a par with the 5 sentence window in the baseline. We replace Naive Bayes with SVM^{light} because it can deal better with imbalanced data[9].

Pairwise model II: Based on *Pairwise model I*. Local features $feat2$-$feat8$ from Table 2 are added.

Pairwise model III: Based on *Pairwise model II*. We apply a more advanced antecedent candidate selection strategy, which allows to include 77% of NP antecedents compared to 71% in *Pairwise model II*. For each anaphor, we add the top k salient entities measured through the length of the coreference chains (k is set to 10%) as additional antecedent candidates. For potential set anaphors (as automatically determined by pronoun or number heads), singular antecedent candidates are filtered out. We compiled a small set of adjectives (using FrameNet and thesauri) that indicate spatial or temporal sequences (see Example 3). For anaphors modified by such adjectives we consider only antecedent candidates that have the same semantic class as the anaphor.

[8] They use a 5 sentence window, because all antecedents in their corpus are within the previous 5 sentences.

[9] The SVM^{light} parameter is set according to the ratio between positive and negative instances in the training set.

6.4 MLN models

MLN model I: MLN system using local formulas $f1$-$f2$ and $f14$-$f20$. The same strategy as in *Pairwise model III* is used to select local antecedent candidates E_m for each anaphor m.

MLN model II: Based on *MLN model I*, all formulas in Table 1 are used.

6.5 Results

Table 4 shows the comparison of our models to baselines. Significance tests are conducted using McNemar's test on overall accuracy at the level of 1%.

		acc
improved baseline	*2 sent. + NB*	18.85
	5 sent. + NB	18.40
pairwise model	*pairwise model I*	29.11
	pairwise model II	33.94
	pairwise model III	36.35
MLN model	*MLN model I*	35.60
	MLN model II	**41.32**

Table 4: Results for MLN models compared to pairwise models and baselines.

MLN model II, which is inspired by the linguistic observation that globally salient entities are preferred as antecedents, performs significantly better than all other systems. The gains come from three aspects. First, by selecting the antecedent for each anaphor from the antecedent candidate pool E in the whole document 91% of NP antecedents are accessible compared to 77% in *pairwise model III*. Second, we leverage semantics and salience by using local formulas and discourse level formulas. Local formulas are used to capture semantic relations for bridging pairs as well as surface and syntactic constraints. Global formulas resolve several bridging anaphors together, often to a globally salient antecedent beyond the local window. Third, the model allows us to express specific relations among bridging anaphors and their antecedents ($f11$-$f13$).

However, our *pairwise model I* already outperforms *improved baselines* by about 10%, which suggests that our *preposition pattern* feature can capture more diverse semantic relations. The continuous improvements shown in *pairwise model II* and *pairwise model III* verify the contribution of our other features and advanced antecedent candidate selection strategy. *pairwise model III* would become too complex if we tried to integrate discourse level formulas $f7$, $f11$-$f13$ into antecedent candidate selection. *MLN model II* solves this task elegantly.

6.6 Discussion and error analysis

We analyse our best model (*MLN model II*) and compare it to the best local one (*pairwise model III*).

Anaphors with long distance antecedents are harder to resolve. Table 5 shows the comparison of correctly resolved anaphors with regard to anaphor-antecedent distance. We can see that the global model is equal or better to the local model for all anaphor types but that the difference is especially large for anaphora with antecedents that are 3 or more sentences away due to the use of global salience and accessibility of possible antecedents beyond a fixed window-size.

	# pairs	*MLN II*	*pairwise III*
sent. distance			
0	175	48.57	45.14
1	260	34.62	35
2	90	47.78	43.33
≥3	158	**35.44**	16.46

Table 5: Comparison of the percentage of correctly resolved anaphors with regard to anaphor-antecedent distance. Significance tests are conducted using McNemar's test at the level of 1%.

We now distinguish between "sibling anaphors" (anaphors that share an antecedent with other bridging anaphors) and "non-siblings" (anaphors that do not share an antecedent with any other anaphor). The performance of our *MLN model II* is 54% on sibling anaphors but only 24% on non-sibling anaphors. This shows that our use of global salience and links between related anaphors does indeed help to capture the behaviour of sibling anaphors.

However, our global model is good at predicting the right antecedent for sibling anaphors where the antecedent is globally salient but not as good for sibling anaphors where the (shared) antecedent is a locally salient subtopic. Thus, in the future we need to model equivalent constraints for local salience of antecedents, taking into account topic segmentation/shifts to improve over the 54% for sibling anaphors.

The semantic knowledge we employ is still insufficient. Typical cases where we have problems are: (i) cases with very context-specific bridging relations. For example, in one text about the stealing of Sago Palms in California we found *the thieves* as a bridging anaphor with the antecedent *palms*, which is not a very usual semantic link. (ii) more frequently, we have cases where several good antecedents from a semantic perspective can be found. For example, two laws are discussed and a later anaphor *the veto* could be the veto of either bills. Integration of the wider context apart from the two NPs is necessary in these cases. This includes the semantics of modification, whereas we currently consider only head noun knowledge. An example is that the anaphor *the local council* would preferably be interpreted as *the council of a village* instead of *the council of a state* due to the occurrence of *local*.

Finally, 6% of the anaphors in our corpus have a non-NP antecedent. These cases are not correctly resolved in our current model as we only extract NP phrases as potential candidate antecedents.

7 Conclusions

We provide the first reasonably sized and reliably annotated English corpus for bridging resolution. It covers a diverse set of relations between anaphor and antecedent as well as all anaphor/antecedent types. We developed novel semantic, syntactic and salience features based on linguistic intuition. Inspired by the observation that salient entities are preferred as antecedents, we implemented a global model for antecedent selection within the framework of Markov logic networks. We show that our global model significantly outperforms other local models and baselines. This work is – to our knowledge – the first bridging resolution algorithm that tackles the unrestricted phenomenon in a real setting.

Acknowledgements. Yufang Hou is funded by a PhD scholarship from the Research Training Group *Coherence in Language Processing* at Heidelberg University. Katja Markert receives a Fellowship for Experienced Researchers by the Alexander-von-Humboldt Foundation. We thank HITS gGmbH for hosting Katja Markert and funding the annotation. We thank our colleague Angela Fahrni for advice on using Markov logic networks.

References

Regina Barzilay and Mirella Lapata. 2008. Modeling local coherence: An entity-based approach. *Computational Linguistics*, 34(1):1–34.

Thorsten Brants and Alex Franz. 2006. Web 1t 5-gram version 1. LDC2006T13, Philadelphia, Penn.: Linguistic Data Consortium.

Aoife Cahill and Arndt Riester. 2012. Automatically acquiring fine-grained information status distinctions in German. In *Proceedings of the SIGdial 2012 Conference: The 13th Annual Meeting of the Special Interest Group on Discourse and Dialogue,* Seoul, Korea, 5–6 July 2012, pages 232–236.

Tommaso Caselli and Irina Prodanof. 2006. Annotating bridging anaphors in Italian: In search of reliability. In *Proceedings of the 5th International Conference on Language Resources and Evaluation,* Genoa, Italy, 22–28 May 2006.

Herbert H. Clark. 1975. Bridging. In *Proceedings of the Conference on Theoretical Issues in Natural Language Processing,* Cambridge, Mass., June 1975, pages 169–174.

Pedro Domingos and Daniel Lowd. 2009. *Markov Logic: An Interface Layer for Artificial Intelligence.* Morgan Claypool Publishers.

Angela Fahrni and Michael Strube. 2012. Jointly disambiguating and clustering concepts and entities with Markov logic. In *Proceedings of the 24th International Conference on Computational Linguistics,* Mumbai, India, 8–15 December 2012, pages 815–832.

Kari Fraurud. 1990. Definiteness and the processing of noun phrases in natural discourse. *Journal of Semantics*, 7:395–433.

Claire Gardent and Hélène Manuélian. 2005. Création d'un corpus annoté pour le traitement des descriptions définies. *Traitement Automatique des Langues*, 46(1):115–140.

Matthew Gerber and Joyce Chai. 2012. Semantic role labeling of implicit arguments for nominal predicates. *Computational Linguistics*, 38(4):756–798.

Jeanette K. Gundel, Nancy Hedberg, and Ron Zacharski. 1993. Cognitive status and the form of referring expressions in discourse. *Language*, 69:274–307.

Donna Harman and Mark Liberman. 1993. TIPSTER Complete. LDC93T3A, Philadelphia, Penn.: Linguistic Data Consortium.

Iorn Korzen and Matthias Buch-Kromann. 2011. Anaphoric relations in the Copenhagen dependency treebanks. In S. Dipper and H. Zinsmeister, editors, *Corpus-based Investigations of Pragmatic and Discourse Phenomena*, volume 3 of *Bochumer Linguistische Arbeitsberichte*, pages 83–98. University of Bochum, Bochum, Germany.

Emmanuel Lassalle and Pascal Denis. 2011. Leveraging different meronym discovery methods for bridging resolution in French. In *Proceedings of the 8th Discourse Anaphora and Anaphor Resolution Colloquium (DAARC 2011),* Faro, Algarve, Portugal, 6–7 October 2011, pages 35–46.

Katja Markert, Malvina Nissim, and Natalia N. Modjeska. 2003. Using the web for nominal anaphora resolution. In *Proceedings of the EACL Workshop on the Computational Treatment of Anaphora.* Budapest, Hungary, 14 April 2003, pages 39–46.

Katja Markert, Yufang Hou, and Michael Strube. 2012. Collective classification for fine-grained information status. In *Proceedings of the 50th Annual Meeting of the Association for Computational Linguistics,* Jeju Island, Korea, 8–14 July 2012, pages 795–804.

Ivan Meza-Ruiz and Sebastian Riedel. 2009. Jointly identifying predicates, arguments and senses using Markov logic. In *Proceedings of Human Language Technologies 2009: The Conference of the North American Chapter of the Association for Computational Linguistics,* Boulder, Col., 31 May – 5 June 2009, pages 155–163.

Shachar Mirkin, Ido Dagan, and Sebastian Padó. 2010. Assessing the role of discourse references in entailment inference. In *Proceedings of the 48th Annual Meeting of the Association for Computational Linguistics,* Uppsala, Sweden, 11–16 July 2010, pages 1209–1219.

Natalia M. Modjeska, Katja Markert, and Malvina Nissim. 2003. Using the web in machine learning for other-anaphora resolution. In *Proceedings of the 2003 Conference on Empirical Methods in Natural Language Processing,* Sapporo, Japan, 11–12 July 2003, pages 176–183.

Malvina Nissim, Shipara Dingare, Jean Carletta, and Mark Steedman. 2004. An annotation scheme for information status in dialogue. In *Proceedings of the 4th International Conference on Language Resources and Evaluation,* Lisbon, Portugal, 26–28 May 2004, pages 1023–1026.

Robert Parker, David Graff, Junbo Kong, Ke Chen, and Kazuaki Maeda. 2011. English Gigaword Fifth Edition. LDC2011T07.

Massimo Poesio and Renata Vieira. 1998. A corpus-based investigation of definite description use. *Computational Linguistics*, 24(2):183–216.

Massimo Poesio, Rahul Mehta, Axel Maroudas, and Janet Hitzeman. 2004. Learning to resolve bridging references. In *Proceedings of the 42nd Annual Meeting of the Association for Computational Linguistics,* Barcelona, Spain, 21–26 July 2004, pages 143–150.

Massimo Poesio. 2003. Associate descriptions and salience: A preliminary investigation. In *Proceedings of the EACL Workshop on the Computational Treatment of Anaphora.* Budapest, Hungary, 14 April 2003, pages 31–38.

Hoifung Poon and Pedro Domingos. 2008. Joint unsupervised coreference resolution with Markov Logic. In *Proceedings of the 2008 Conference on Empirical Methods in Natural Language Processing,* Waikiki, Honolulu, Hawaii, 25–27 October 2008, pages 650–659.

Ellen F. Prince. 1981. Towards a taxonomy of given-new information. In P. Cole, editor, *Radical Pragmatics,* pages 223–255. Academic Press, New York, N.Y.

Altaf Rahman and Vincent Ng. 2012. Learning the fine-grained information status of discourse entities. In *Proceedings of the 13th Conference of the European Chapter of the Association for Computational Linguistics,* Avignon, France, 23–27 April 2012, pages 798–807.

Sebastian Riedel. 2008. Improving the accuracy and efficiency of MAP inference for Markov logic. In *Proceedings of the 24th Conference on Uncertainty in Artificial Intelligence,* Helsinki, Finland, 9–12 July 2008, pages 468–475.

Arndt Riester, David Lorenz, and Nina Seemann. 2010. A recursive annotation scheme for referential information status. In *Proceedings of the 7th International Conference on Language Resources and Evaluation,* La Valetta, Malta, 17–23 May 2010, pages 717–722.

Josef Ruppenhofer, Caroline Sporleder, Roser Morante, Collin Baker, and Martha Palmer. 2010. SemEval-2010 Task 10: Linking events and their participants in discourse. In *Proceedings of the 5th International Workshop on Semantic Evaluations (SemEval-2),* Uppsala, Sweden, 15–16 July 2010, pages 45–50.

Carina Silberer and Anette Frank. 2012. Casting implicit role linking as an anaphora resolution task. In *Proceedings of STARSEM 2012: The First Joint Conference on Lexical and Computational Semantics,* Montréal, Québec, Canada, 7–8 June 2012, pages 1–10.

Wee Meng Soon, Hwee Tou Ng, and Daniel Chung Yong Lim. 2001. A machine learning approach to coreference resolution of noun phrases. *Computational Linguistics,* 27(4):521–544.

Renata Vieira and Massimo Poesio. 2000. An empirically-based system for processing definite descriptions. *Computational Linguistics,* 26(4):539–593.

Ralph Weischedel, Martha Palmer, Mitchell Marcus, Eduard Hovy, Sameer Pradhan, Lance Ramshaw, Nianwen Xue, Ann Taylor, Jeff Kaufman, Michelle Franchini, Mohammed El-Bachouti, Robert Belvin, and Ann Houston. 2011. OntoNotes release 4.0. LDC2011T03, Philadelphia, Penn.: Linguistic Data Consortium.

Ian H. Witten and Eibe Frank. 2005. *Data Mining: Practical Machine Learning Tools and Techniques.* Morgan Kaufmann, San Francisco, Cal., 2nd edition.

Classifying Temporal Relations with Rich Linguistic Knowledge

Jennifer D'Souza and **Vincent Ng**
Human Language Technology Research Institute
University of Texas at Dallas
Richardson, TX 75083-0688
{jld082000,vince}@hlt.utdallas.edu

Abstract

We examine the task of temporal relation classification. Unlike existing approaches to this task, we (1) classify an event-event or event-time pair as one of the 14 temporal relations defined in the TimeBank corpus, rather than as one of the six relations collapsed from the original 14; (2) employ sophisticated linguistic knowledge derived from a variety of semantic and discourse relations, rather than focusing on morpho-syntactic knowledge; and (3) leverage a novel combination of rule-based and learning-based approaches, rather than relying solely on one or the other. Experiments with the TimeBank corpus demonstrate that our knowledge-rich, hybrid approach yields a 15–16% relative reduction in error over a state-of-the-art learning-based baseline system.

1 Introduction

Recent years have seen a surge of interest in temporal information extraction (IE). Temporal relation classification, one of the most important temporal IE tasks, involves classifying a given event-event pair or event-time pair as one of a set of predefined temporal relations. The creation of the TimeBank corpus (Pustejovsky et al., 2003) and the organization of the TempEval-1 (Verhagen et al., 2007) and TempEval-2 (Verhagen et al., 2010) evaluation exercises have facilitated the development and evaluation of temporal relation classification systems.

Our goal in this paper is to advance the state of the art in temporal relation classification. Our work differs from existing work with respect to both the *complexity* of the task we are addressing and the *approach* we adopt. Regarding task complexity, rather than focus on six temporal relations as is typically done in previous work (see Section 2 for more information), we address an arguably more challenging version of the task where we consider all the 14 relations originally defined in the TimeBank corpus.

Our approach to temporal relation classification can be distinguished from existing approaches in two respects. The first involves a large-scale expansion of the linguistic features made available to the classification system. Recall that existing approaches have relied primarily on morpho-syntactic features as well as a few semantic features extracted from WordNet synsets and VerbOcean's (Chklovski and Pantel, 2004) semantic relations. On the other hand, we propose not only novel lexical and grammatical features, but also sophisticated features involving semantics and discourse. Most notably, we propose (1) semantic features encoding a variety of semantic relations, including PropBank-style predicate-argument relations as well as those extracted from the Merriam-Webster dictionary, and (2) discourse features encoding automatically computed Penn Discourse TreeBank (PDTB) style (Prasad et al., 2008) discourse relations.

Second, while the vast majority of existing approaches to temporal relation classification are learning-based, we propose a system architecture in which we combine a learning-based approach and a rule-based approach. Our motivation behind adopting a hybrid approach stems from two hypotheses. First, a rule-based method could better handle the skewed class distribution underlying the dataset for our 14-class classification problem. Second, better decision rules could be formed by leveraging human insights to combine the available linguistic features than by using fully automatic machine learning methods. Note that while rule-based approaches have been shown to underperform learning-based approaches on this task (Mani et al., 2006), to our knowledge they have not been used in combination with learning-based approaches. Moreover, while the rules employed in previous work are created based on intuition (e.g., Mani et al. (2006), Puşcaşu (2007)), our rules are created in a *data-driven* manner via a manual inspection of the annotated temporal relations in the TimeBank corpus.

Experiments on the TimeBank corpus demonstrate the effectiveness of our knowledge-rich, hybrid approach to temporal relation classification: it yields a 15–16% relative reduction in error over a state-of-the-art learning-based baseline system.

To our knowledge, we are the first to (1) report results for the 14-class temporal relation classification task on the TimeBank (v1.2) corpus; (2) successfully employ automatically computed PDTB-style discourse relations to improve performance on this task; and (3) show that a hybrid approach to this task can yield better results than either a rule-based or learning-based approach. Note that hybrid approaches in this spirit were popular in the natural language processing community back in the mid-90s (Klavans and Resnik, 1994). We believe that they are among the most competitive approaches to language processing tasks that require complex reasoning and should be given more attention in the community. We release the complete set of rules that we mined from the TimeBank corpus and used in our rule-based approach in hopes that our insights into how features can be combined as decision rules can benefit researchers interested in this task.

The rest of the paper is organized as follows. Section 2 provides an overview of the TimeBank corpus. Sections 3 and 4 describe the baseline system and our approach, respectively. We present evaluation results in Section 5 and conclude in Section 6.

2 Corpus

For evaluation, we use the TimeBank (v1.2) corpus, which consists of 183 newswire articles. In each article, the *events*, *times*, and their *temporal relations* are marked up. An event, which can be a tensed verb, adjective, or nominal, contains various attributes, including the *class* of event, *tense*, *aspect*, *polarity*, and *modality*. A time expression has a *class* attribute, which specifies whether it is a date, time, duration, or set, and its value is normalized based on TIMEX3. A temporal relation can be an *order* relation, which orders two events (as in sentence (1)), or an *anchor* relation, which anchors an event to a time expression (as in sentence (2)).

(1) A steep *rise* in world oil prices followed the Kuwait *invasion*.

(2) We are there to *stay* for a long *period*.

Each temporal relation has a *type*. For example, the relation defined on *rise* and *invasion* in (1) has type **After**, whereas the relation defined on *stay* and *period* in (2) has type **During**. Note that a temporal relation is defined on an *ordered* pair. For example, in (1), the pair (*rise*, *invasion*) has type **After**, whereas the pair (*invasion*, *rise*) has type **Before**).

14 relation types are defined and used to annotate the temporal relations in the TimeBank corpus. Table 1 provides a brief description of these relation types and the relevant statistics.

In our experiments, we assume that our temporal relation classification system is given an event-event or event-time pair that is known to belong to one of the 14 relation types defined in TimeBank and aims to determine its relation type. Following previous evaluations of the temporal relation classification task on the TimeBank corpus (e.g., Mani et al. (2006), Chambers et al. (2007)) and in TempEval-1/2, we assume as input gold events and time expressions.

Unlike Mani et al. (2006) and Chambers et al. (2007), who focus on six relation types (**Simultaneous**, **Before**, **IBefore**, **Begins**, **Ends**, and **Includes**), we report results on 14 relation types. Note that the aforementioned six relation types are chosen by (1) discarding **During**, **During_Inv**, and **Identity**, and (2) combining the two relation types in each of the five pairs, namely (**Before**, **After**), (**IBefore**, **IAfter**), (**Includes**, **Is_Included**), (**Begins**, **Begun_By**), and (**Ends**, **Ended_By**), into a single type because they are inverses of each other. In other words, if a relation instance (e_1, e_2) is anno-

Id	Relation	Description	Total %	E-E	E-T
1	**Simultaneous**	e_1 and e_2 happen at the same time or are temporally distinguishable	660 (13.3)	599	61
2	**Identity**	e_1 and e_2 are coreferent	702 (14.1)	696	6
3	**Before**	e_1 happens before e_2 in time	689 (13.9)	639	50
4	**After**	e_1 happens after e_2 in time	744 (15)	681	63
5	**IBefore**	e_1 happens immediately before e_2 in time	39 (0.8)	38	1
6	**IAfter**	e_1 happens immediately after e_2 in time	28 (0.6)	25	3
7	**Includes**	As in *Ed arrived in Seoul last Sunday* (e_1=*last Sunday*; e_2=*arrived*)	758 (15.3)	318	440
8	**Is_Included**	As in *Ed arrived in Seoul last Sunday* (e_1=*arrived*; e_2=*last Sunday*)	762 (15.3)	201	561
9	**During**	e_1 persists throughout duration e_2	102 (2.1)	19	83
10	**During_Inv**	e_2 persists throughout duration e_1	124 (2.5)	44	80
11	**Begins**	e_1 marks the beginning of e_2	66 (1.3)	44	22
12	**Begun_By**	e_2 marks the beginning of e_1	61 (1.2)	32	29
13	**Ends**	e_1 marks the end of e_2	66 (1.3)	21	45
14	**Ended_By**	e_2 marks the end of e_1	170 (3.42)	93	77

Table 1: The 14 temporal relations and their frequency of occurrences in TimeBank (v1.2). Each relation is defined on an ordered event-event or event-time pair (e_1,e_2). The "Total" and "%" columns show the number and percentage of instances annotated with the corresponding relation in the corpus, respectively, and the "E-E" and "E-T" columns show the breakdown by the number of event-event pairs and event-time pairs.

tated as **After**, it is replaced with the instance (e_2, e_1) with class **Before**, and subsequently a relation classifier is presented with (e_2, e_1) but not (e_1, e_2). On the other hand, our 14-class task is arguably more challenging since our system has to further distinguish a relation type from its inverse given an instance in which the two elements are in arbitrary order.

3 Baseline Temporal Relation Classifier

Since the currently best-performing systems for temporal relation classification are learning-based, we will employ a learning-based system as our baseline. Below we describe how we train this baseline.

Without loss of generality, assume that (e_1,e_2) is an event-event/event-time pair such that (1) e_1 precedes e_2 in the associated text and (2) (e_1,e_2) belongs to one of the 14 TimeBank temporal relation types. We create one training instance for each event-event/event-time pair in a training document that satisfies the two conditions above, labeling it with the relation type that exists between e_1 and e_2.

To build a strong baseline, we represent each instance using 68 linguistic features modeled after the top-performing temporal relation classification systems on TimeBank (e.g., Mani et al. (2006), Chambers et al. (2007)) and in the TempEval shared tasks (e.g., Min et al. (2007), Puşcaşu (2007), Ha et al. (2010), Llorens et al. (2010), Mirroshandel and Ghassem-Sani (2011)).[1] These features can be divided into six categories, as described below.

Lexical (5). The strings of e_1 and e_2, the head words of e_1 and e_2, and a binary feature indicating whether e_1 and e_2 have the same string.

Grammatical (33). The POS tags of the head words of e_1 and e_2, the POS tags of the five tokens preceding and following e_1 and e_2, the POS bigram formed from the head word of e_1 and its preceding token, the POS bigram formed from the head word of e_2 and its preceding token, the POS tag pair formed from the head words of e_1 and e_2, the prepositional lexeme of the prepositional phrase (PP) if e_1 is headed by a PP (Chambers et al., 2007), the prepositional lexeme of the PP if e_2 is headed by a PP, the prepositional lexeme of the PP if e_1 is governed by a PP (Mirroshandel and Ghassem-Sani, 2011), the prepositional lexeme of the PP if e_2 is governed by a PP, the POS of the head of the verb phrase (VP) if e_1 is governed by a VP, the POS of the head of the VP if e_2 is governed by a VP, whether e_1 syntactically dominates e_2 (Chambers et al., 2007), and the shortest path from e_1 to e_2 in the associated syntactic parse tree. We obtain parse trees and POS tags using the Stanford CoreNLP tool.[2]

[1] Note, however, that these features were designed for the arguably simpler 6-class temporal relation classification tasks.

[2] `http://nlp.stanford.edu/software/corenlp.shtml`

Entity attributes (13). The tense, aspect, modality, polarity, and event type of e_1 and e_2 if they are events (if one of them is a time expression, then the class attribute will be set to its class and the rest of them will have the value NULL), pairwise features formed by pairing up the tense values, the aspect values, and the class values of e_1 and e_2.

Semantic (7). The subordinating temporal role token of e_1 if it appears within a temporal semantic role argument (Llorens et al., 2010), the subordinating temporal role token of e_2 if it appears within a temporal semantic role argument, the first WordNet synset to which e_1 belongs, the first WordNet synset to which e_2 belongs, and whether e_1 and e_2 are in the *happens-before*, *happens-after*, and *similar* relation according to VerbOcean.[3]

Distance (1). Are e_1 and e_2 in the same sentence?

DCT related (3). The temporal relation type between e_1 and the document creation time (DCT) [its value can be one of the 14 relation types, or NULL if no relation exists], the temporal relation type between e_2 and the DCT, and whether e_1 and e_2 have different relation types with the DCT.

After creating the training instances, we train a 14-class classifier on them using SVM^{multiclass} (Tsochantaridis et al., 2004).[4] We then use it to make predictions on the test instances, which are generated in the same way as the training instances.

4 Our Hybrid Approach

In this section, we describe our hybrid learning-based and rule-based approach to temporal relation classification. Section 4.1 describes our novel features, which will be used to augment the baseline feature set (see Section 3) to train a temporal relation classifier. Section 4.2 outlines our manual rule creation process. Section 4.3 discusses how we combine our hand-crafted rules and the learned classifier to make predictions in our hybrid approach.

[3] *happens-after* is not a relation in VerbOcean: we create this relation simply by inverting the *happens-before* relation.

[4] For all the experiments involving SVM^{multiclass}, we set C, the regularization parameter, to 10,000, since preliminary experiments indicate that preferring generalization to overfitting (by setting C to a small value) tends to yield poorer classification performance. The remaining learning parameters are set to their default values.

4.1 Six Types of New Features

4.1.1 Pairwise Features

Recall that some of the features in the baseline feature set are computed based on either e_1 or e_2 but not both. Since our task is to predict the *relation* between them, we hypothesize that *pairwise* features, which are computed based on both elements, could better capture the relationship between them.

Specifically, we introduce pairwise versions of the head word feature and the two prepositional lexeme-based features in the baseline. In addition, we create two quadruple-wise features, one by pairing up the tense and class attribute values of e_1 with those of e_2, and the other by pairing up their tense and aspect values. Next, we create two *trace* features, one based on prepositions and the other on verbs, since prepositions and verb tenses have been shown to play an important role in temporal relation classification The *preposition trace* feature is computed by (1) collecting the list of prepositions along the path from e_1/e_2 to the root of its syntactic parse trees, and (2) concatenating the resulting lists computed from e_1 and e_2. The *verb trace* feature is computed in a similar manner, except that we collect the POS tags of the verbs appearing in the corresponding paths.

4.1.2 Dependency Relations

We introduce features computed based on dependency parse trees obtained via the Stanford CoreNLP tool, motivated by our observation that some dependency relation types are more closely associated with certain temporal relation types than with others. Let us illustrate with an example:

(3) Ed *changed* his plans as the mood *took* him.

In (3), there is a adverbial clause modifier dependency between *changed* and *took*, because *took* appears in an adverbial clause (headed by *as*) modifying *changed*. Intuitively, if the two events participate in this type of dependency relation and the adverbial clause is headed by *as* and there is a temporal relation between them, then it is likely that this temporal relation is **Simultaneous**. While the temporal relation type is dependent on the connective heading the adverbial clause, in general an adverbial clause modifier dependency between two events implies that their temporal relation is likely to be **Si-**

multaneous, **Before**, or **After**.

Given the potential usefulness of dependency relations for temporal relation classification, we create dependency-based features as follows. For each of the 25 dependency relation types produced by the Stanford parser, we create four binary features: whether e_1/e_2 is the governing entity in the relation, and whether e_1/e_2 is the dependent in the relation.

4.1.3 Webster Relations

Some events are not connected by a dependency relation but by a *lexical* relation. We hypothesize that some of these lexical relations could be useful for temporal relation classification. Consider the following example.

(4) The phony war has *finished* and the real referendum campaign has *begun*.

In this sentence, the two events, *finished* and *begun*, are connected by an antonym relation. Statistically speaking, if (1) two events are in two clauses connected by a coordinating conjunction (e.g., *and*), (2) one is an antonym of the other, and (3) there is a temporal relation between them, then the temporal relation is likely to be **Simultaneous**.

Given the potential usefulness of lexical relations for temporal relation classification, we create features based on four types of lexical relations present in Webster's online thesaurus[5], namely synonyms, related-words, near-antonyms, and antonyms. Specifically, for each event e appearing in TimeBank, we first use the head word of e to retrieve four lists, which are the lists corresponding to the synonyms, related words, near-antonyms, and antonyms of e. Then, given a training/test instance involving e_1 and e_2, we create eight binary features: whether e_1 appears in e_2's list of synonyms/related words/near-antonyms/antonyms, and whether e_2 appears in e_1's list of synonyms/related words/near-antonyms/antonyms.

4.1.4 WordNet Relations

Previous uses of WordNet for temporal relation classification are limited to synsets (e.g., Llorens et al. (2010)). We hypothesize that other WordNet lexical relations could also be useful for the task. Specifically, we employ four types of WordNet relations, namely hypernyms, hyponyms, troponyms, and similar, to create eight binary features for temporal relation classification. These eight features are created from the four WordNet relations in the same way as the eight features were created from the four Webster relations in the previous subsection.

4.1.5 Predicate-Argument Relations

So far we have exploited lexical and dependency relations for temporal relation classification. We hypothesize that semantic relations, in particular predicate-argument relations, could be useful for the task. Consider the following example.

(5) "What sector is *stepping forward* to pick up the slack?" he asked.

Using SENNA (Collobert et al., 2011), a PropBank-style semantic role labeler, we know that *forward* is in the directional argument of the predicate *stepping*. This enables us to infer that an **Includes** relation exists between *stepping* and *forward* since intuitively an action includes a direction.

As another example, consider another PropBank-style predicate-argument relation, *cause*. Assuming that e_2 is in e_1's cause argument, we can infer that e_2 occurs **Before** e_1 since intuitively the cause of an action precedes the action.

Consequently, we create features for temporal relation classification based on four types of PropBank-style predicate-argument relations, namely directional, manner, temporal, and cause. Specifically, using SENNA's output, we create four binary features that encode whether argument e_2 is related to predicate e_1 through the four types of relations, and we create another four binary features that encode whether argument e_1 is related to predicate e_2 through the four types of relations.

4.1.6 Discourse Relations

Rhetorical relations such as causation, elaboration and enablement could aid in tracking the temporal progression of the discourse (Hitzeman et al., 1995). Hence, unlike syntactic dependencies and predicate-argument relations through which we can identify *intra-sentential* temporal relations, discourse relations can potentially be exploited to discover both *inter-sentential* and *intra-sentential* temporal relations. However, no recent work has attempted to use discourse relations for temporal relation clas-

[5] http://www.merriam-webster.com/

(6)	{_Arg1 Hewlett-Packard Co. *said* it raised its stake in Octel Communications Corp. to 8.5% of the common shares outstanding. _Arg1} {_Arg2_RESTATEMENT In a Securities and Exchange Commission *filing*, Hewlett-Packard said it now holds 1,384,119 Octel common shares _Arg2}.
(7)	{_Arg1 Reports *said* that Saudi Arabia told U.S. oil companies of a 15–20 percent cutback in its oil supply in September. _Arg1} {_Conn SYNCHRONY Meanwhile _Conn} {_Arg2 Egypt's Middle East Agency said *Thursday* that Saddam was the target of an assassination attempt. _Arg2}

Table 2: Examples illustrating the usefulness of discourse relations for temporal relation classification.

sification. In this subsection, we examine whether we can improve a temporal relation identifier via *explicit* and *implicit* PDTB-style discourse relations automatically extracted by Lin et al.'s (2013) end-to-end discourse parser.

Let us first review PDTB-style discourse relations. Each relation is represented by a triple (*Arg1*, *sense*, *Arg2*), where *Arg1* and *Arg2* are the two arguments of the relation and *sense* is the sense/type of the relation. A discourse relation can be explicit or implicit. An explicit relation is triggered by a discourse connective. On the other hand, an implicit relation is not triggered by a discourse connective, and may exist only between two consecutive sentences. Generally, implicit relations are much harder to identify than their explicit counterparts.

Next, to motivate why discourse relations can be useful for temporal relation classification, we use two examples (see Table 2), one involving an implicit relation (Example (6)) and the other an explicit relation (Example (7)). For convenience, both sentences are also annotated using Lin et al.'s (2013) discourse parser, which marks up the two arguments with the _Arg1 and _Arg2 tags and outputs the relation sense next to the beginning of Arg2.

In (6), we aim to determine the order relation between the reporting event *said* and the occurrence event *filing*. The parser determines that a RESTATEMENT implicit relation exists between the two sentences. Intuitively, if no asynchronous relations can be found among the events in two discourse units connected by the RESTATEMENT relation, then the temporal relation between two temporally linked events within these units is likely to be either **Identity** or **Simultaneous**. In this case, we can rule out **Identity**: since *said* and *filing* belong to different event classes, they are not coreferent.

In (7), we aim to determine the anchor relation between the reporting event *said* and the date *Thursday*. The parser determines that a SYNCHRONY explicit relation triggered by *Meanwhile* exists between the two sentences. Intuitively, if a temporally related reporting event and date occur within different discourse units connected by the SYNCHRONY relation, then it is likely that the event **Is_Included** in the date. Note that without this discourse relation, it could be difficult for a machine to confidently associate a reporting event with a date occurring in a different discourse segment.

Given the potential usefulness of discourse relations for temporal relation classification, we create four features based on discourse relations. In the first feature, if e_1 is in Arg1, e_2 is in Arg2, and Arg1 and Arg2 possess an explicit relation with sense s, then its feature value is s; otherwise its value is NULL. In the second feature, if e_2 is in Arg1, e_1 is in Arg2, and Arg1 and Arg2 possess a explicit relation with sense s, then its feature value is s; otherwise its value is NULL. The third and fourth features are computed in the same way as the first two features, except that they are computed over implicit rather than explicit relations.

4.2 Manual Rule Creation

As noted before, we adopt a hybrid learning-based and rule-based approach to temporal relation classification. Hence, in addition to training a temporal relation classifier, we also manually design a set of rules in which each rule returns a temporal relation type for a given test instance. We hypothesize that a rule-based approach can complement a purely learning-based approach, since a human could combine the available linguistic features into rules using commonsense knowledge that may not be accessible to a learning algorithm.

The design of the rules is partly based on intuition and partly data-driven: we first use our intuition to come up with a rule and then manually refine it based on the observations we made on the TimeBank data. For this purpose, we partition the TimeBank documents into five folds of roughly the same size, reserving three folds for developing our rules and using the remaining two folds for evaluating final system performance. We order these rules in decreasing order of accuracy, where the accuracy of a rule is defined as the number of times the rule yields the correct temporal relation type divided by the number of times it is applied, as measured on the three development folds. A new instance is classified using the first applicable rule in the ruleset.

Some of these rules were shown in the previous subsection when we motivated each feature type with examples. The complete set of rules can be accessed via our website.[6]

4.3 Combining Rules and Machine Learning

We investigate three ways to combine the hand-crafted rules and the machine-learned classifier.

In the first method, we employ all of the rules as additional features for training the classifier. The value of each such feature is the temporal relation type predicted by the corresponding rule.

The second method can be viewed as an extension of the first one. Given a test instance, we first apply to it the ruleset composed only of rules that are at least 80% accurate. If none of the rules is applicable, we classify it using the classifier employed in the first method.[7]

The third method is essentially the same as the second, except we do not employ the rules as features when training the classifier.

5 Evaluation

5.1 Experimental Setup

Dataset. As mentioned before, we partition the 183 documents in the TimeBank (v1.2) corpus into five folds of roughly the same size, reserving three folds (say Folds 1–3) for manual rule development and using the remaining two folds (say Folds 4–5) for testing. We perform two-fold cross-validation experiments using the two test folds. In the first fold experiment, we train a temporal relation classifier on Folds 1–4 and test on Fold 5; and in the second fold experiment, we train the classifier on all but Fold 4 and test on Fold 4. The results reported in the rest of the paper are averaged over the two test folds.

Evaluation metrics. We employ *accuracy* (Acc) and *macro F-score* (F^{ma}). Accuracy is the percentage of correctly classified test instances, and is the standard evaluation metric for temporal relation classification. Since each test instance belongs to one of the 14 temporal relation types, accuracy is the same as micro F-score. On the other hand, macro F-score is rarely used to evaluate this task. We chose it because it could provide insights into how well our approach performs on the minority classes.

5.2 Results and Discussion

Table 3 shows the two-fold cross-validation results for our 14-class temporal relation classification task. The six columns of the table correspond to six different system architectures. The "Feature" column corresponds to a purely learning-based architecture where the results are obtained simply by training a temporal relation classifier using the available features. The next two columns correspond to two purely rule-based architectures, differing by whether all rules are used regardless of their accuracy or whether only high-accuracy rules (i.e., those that are at least 80% accurate) are used. The rightmost three columns correspond to the three ways of combining rules and machine learning described in Section 4.3.

On the other hand, the rows of the table differ in terms of what features are available to a system. In row 1, only the baseline features are available. In the subsequent rows, the six types of features discussed in Section 4 are added incrementally to the baseline feature set. This means that the last row corresponds to the case where all feature types are used.

A point merits clarification. It may not be immediately clear how to interpret the results under, for instance, the "All Rules" column. In other words, it may not be clear what it means to add the six types of features incrementally to a rule-based system. Recall that one of our goals is to compare a purely learning-based system with a purely rule-

[6] http://www.hlt.utdallas.edu/~jld082000/temporal-relations/

[7] Although this classifier is applied to only those test instances that the rules cannot handle, we did not retrain it on only those training instances that the rules cannot handle.

		Features		All Rules		All Rules with accuracy ≥ 0.8		Features + Rules as Features		Rules + Features		Rules + Features + Rules as Features	
	Feature Type	Acc	F^{ma}	Acc	F^{ma}	Acc	F^{ma}	Acc	F^{ma}	Acc	F^{ma}	Acc	F^{ma}
1	Baseline	45.3	24.9	–	–	–	–	–	–	–	–	–	–
2	+ Pairwise	46.5	25.8	37.6	26.5	5.1	13.9	46.7	26.5	48.0	31.9	48.2	32.1
3	+ Dependencies	47.0	25.9	39.0	27.8	6.9	15.7	47.2	26.7	49.2	32.3	49.2	32.6
4	+ WordNet	46.9	26.0	43.5	30.4	6.9	15.7	47.5	26.8	49.2	32.3	49.5	32.8
5	+ Webster	46.9	25.8	43.3	29.9	6.9	15.7	48.1	26.8	49.2	32.0	50.1	33.1
6	+ PropBank	47.2	26.0	44.3	30.5	8.1	16.6	48.0	26.8	49.5	32.2	50.0	33.0
7	+ Discourse	48.1	26.6	47.5	35.1	12.8	23.3	48.9	27.5	53.0	36.0	**53.4**	**36.6**

Table 3: Two-fold cross-validation accuracies and macro F-scores as features are added incrementally to the baseline.

based system, since we hypothesized that humans may be better at combining the available features to form rules than a learning algorithm would be. To facilitate this comparison, all and only those features that are available to a learning-based system in a given row can be used in hand-crafting the rules of the rule-based system in the same row. The other columns involving the use of rules can be interpreted in a similar manner.

The highest accuracy and macro F-score are achieved when all types of features are used in combination with the "Rules + Features + Rules as Features" architecture. Specifically, this system achieves an accuracy of 53.4% and a macro F-score of 36.6% on the 2000-instance test set. This translates to a relative error reduction of 15–16% in comparison to the baseline result shown in row 1. A closer examination of these results reveals that the hand-crafted rules used by the system correctly classify 239 of the 305 test instances to which they are applicable. In other words, the rules achieve a precision of 78.3% and a recall of 15.3% on the test data.

Our results suggest that the rules are effective at improving performance when they are used to make classification decisions prior to the application of the classifier, as the performance of the "Rules + Features + Rules as Features" architecture is significantly better than that of the "Features + Rules as Features" architecture.[8] On the other hand, the "Rules + Features + Rules as Features" architecture does not benefit from the use of rules as features, as its performance is statistically indistinguishable from that of the "Rules + Features" architecture. Nevertheless, both "Rules + Features + Rules as Features" and "Rules + Features" are significantly better than the remaining four architectures. This suggests that the best-performing approach for our 14-class temporal relation classification task is the hybrid approach where high-accuracy rules are first applied and then the learned classifier is used to classify those cases that cannot be handled by the rules.

Among the remaining four architectures, "All Rules with accuracy ≥ 0.8", the version of the rule-based architecture where only the high-accuracy rules are used, performs significantly worse than the others, presumably because the coverage of the ruleset is low. The results of the two feature-based architectures, "Features" and "Features + Rules as Features", are statistically indistinguishable from each other at the $p < 0.01$ level. At the $p < 0.05$ level, however, their results are mixed: "Features + Rules as Features" is better than "Features" according to accuracy, whereas the reverse is true according to macro F-score. Combining these results with those we discussed above concerning the "Rules + Features" and "Rules + Features + Rules as Features" architectures, we can conclude that the features encoding the hand-crafted rules are (mildly) useful only when used in combination with a weak-performing system. Finally, comparing the "Features" architecture and the "All Rules" architecture, we also see mixed results: "Features" is better than "All Rules" according to accuracy, whereas the reverse is true according to macro F-score. These results confirm our earlier hypothesis that the rule-based system is indeed better at identifying instances of minority relation types.

Next, to determine whether the addition of a particular type of features to the feature set is useful, we apply the paired t-test to each pair of adjacent rows in Table 3. We found that adding pairwise features, dependency relations, and most

[8]Unless otherwise stated, all statistical significance tests are paired t-tests, with $p < 0.05$.

	Feature Type	Event-Event Acc	Event-Event F^{ma}	Event-Time Acc	Event-Time F^{ma}
1	Baseline	36.7	15.6	63.3	19.2
2	+ Pairwise	40.4	25.4	64.7	24.2
3	+ Dependencies	42.4	28.4	64.9	25.4
4	+ WordNet	42.6	28.1	64.7	25.3
5	+ Webster	43.0	29.7	64.6	25.3
6	+ PropBank	43.2	28.6	64.3	25.1
7	+ Discourse	46.8	36.3	65.4	26.4

Table 4: Event-event and event-time classification results of our best system (Rules + Features+ Rules as features).

importantly, discourse relations significantly improves both accuracy and macro F-score ($p < 0.05$). Adding the Webster relations improves accuracy at a slightly lower significance level ($p < 0.07$) but does not significantly improve macro F-score. Somewhat counter-intuitively, the WordNet and predicate-argument relations are not useful. We speculate that their failure to improve performance could be attributed to the fact that these relations are extracted by imperfect analyzers. Additional experiments involving the use of gold-standard quality features are needed to precisely determine the reason.

Recall that the results shown in Table 3 were computed over both the order (i.e., event-event) and anchor (i.e., event-time) temporal relations. To gain additional insights into our best-performing system, we show in Table 4 its performance on classifying event-event and event-time relations separately. In comparison to the baseline, both accuracy and macro F-score increase significantly when our system is used in combination with all feature types. In particular, our system yields a relative error reduction of 16–25% for event-event classification and 6–9% for event-time classification over the baseline. The pairwise features, as well as dependency relations and discourse relations, contribute significantly to the classification of both event-event and event-time relations.

Finally, we show in Table 5 the per-class results of the baseline system and our best-performing system. As we can see, our system performs significantly better than the baseline on all relation types, owing to a simultaneous rise in recall and precision.

6 Conclusions

We have investigated a knowledge-rich, hybrid approach to the 14-class temporal relation classification task. Results on the TimeBank corpus show that our approach achieves a relative error reduction of 15–16% over a learning-based baseline that employs a state-of-the-art feature set. Our results suggest that (1) the pairwise features, dependency relations, and discourse relations are useful for temporal relation classification; and (2) hand-crafted rules can better handle the skewed class distribution underlying our dataset via improving minority class prediction. To our knowledge, we are the first to (1) report results for the 14-class temporal relation classification task on TimeBank; (2) successfully employ PDTB-style discourse relations to improve this task; and (3) show that a hybrid approach to this task can yield better results than either a rule-based or learning-based approach. To stimulate research on this task, we make our complete set of hand-crafted rules available to other researchers. We believe that hybrid rule-based and learning-based approaches are promising approaches to language processing tasks that require complex reasoning and hope that they will be given more attention in the community.

Relation	Baseline R	Baseline P	Baseline F	Our System R	Our System P	Our System F
Simultaneous	22.5	30.5	25.9	29.5	39.5	33.8
Identity	56.5	51.5	53.9	59.0	57.5	58.2
Before	39.5	38.5	39.0	50.5	50.5	50.5
After	50.5	35.0	41.4	59.5	44.5	50.9
IBefore	0.0	0.0	0.0	32.5	85.5	47.1
IAfter	0.0	0.0	0.0	5.5	50.0	9.9
Includes	54.5	50.5	52.4	61.0	55.5	58.1
Is_Included	71.5	64.5	67.8	74.5	65.0	69.4
During	11.0	31.0	16.2	19.0	34.5	24.5
During_Inv	14.0	20.0	16.5	19.5	40.5	26.3
Begins	4.5	10.0	6.2	37.0	43.5	40.0
Begun_By	6.5	14.5	9.0	35.0	44.0	39.0
Ends	6.5	10.0	7.9	23.5	70.0	35.2
Ended_By	9.0	10.0	9.5	29.0	26.5	27.7

Table 5: Per-class results of the baseline system and our best system (Rules + Features+ Rules as features).

Acknowledgments

We thank the three anonymous reviewers for their detailed and insightful comments on an earlier draft of the paper. This work was supported in part by NSF Grants IIS-1147644 and IIS-1219142. Any opinions, findings, or conclusions expressed in this paper are those of the authors and do not necessarily reflect the views or official policies of NSF.

References

Nathanael Chambers, Shan Wang, and Dan Jurafsky. 2007. Classifying temporal relations between events. In *Proceedings of the 45th Annual Meeting of the Association for Computational Linguistics Companion Volume: Proceedings of the Demo and Poster Sessions*, pages 173–176.

Timothy Chklovski and Patrick Pantel. 2004. Verbocean: Mining the web for fine-grained semantic verb relations. In *Proceedings of the 2004 Conference on Empirical Methods in Natural Language Processing*, pages 33–40.

Ronan Collobert, Jason Weston, Léon Bottou, Michael Karlen, Koray Kavukcuoglu, and Pavel P. Kuksa. 2011. Natural language processing (almost) from scratch. *Journal of Machine Learning Research*, 12:2493–2537.

Eun Young Ha, Alok Baikadi, Carlyle Licata, and James Lester. 2010. NCSU: Modeling temporal relations with markov logic and lexical ontology. In *Proceedings of the 5th International Workshop on Semantic Evaluation*, pages 341–344.

Janet Hitzeman, Marc Moens, and Claire Grover. 1995. Algorithms for analysing the temporal structure of discourse. In *Proceedings of the 7th Conference of the European Chapter of the Association for Computational Linguistics*, pages 253–260.

Judith Klavans and Philip Resnik, editors. 1994. *The Balancing Act: Combining Symbolic and Statistical Approaches to Language*. Association for Computational Linguistics.

Ziheng Lin, Hwee Tou Ng, and Min-Yen Kan. 2013. A PDTB-styled end-to-end discourse parser. *Natural Language Engineering (to appear)*.

Hector Llorens, Estela Saquete, and Borja Navarro. 2010. TIPSem (English and Spanish): Evaluating CRFs and semantic roles in TempEval-2. In *Proceedings of the 5th International Workshop on Semantic Evaluation*, pages 284–291.

Inderjeet Mani, Marc Verhagen, Ben Wellner, Chong Min Lee, and James Pustejovsky. 2006. Machine learning of temporal relations. In *Proceedings of the 21st International Conference on Computational Linguistics and 44th Annual Meeting of the Association for Computational Linguistics*, pages 753–760.

Congmin Min, Munirathnam Srikanth, and Abraham Fowler. 2007. LCC-TE: A hybrid approach to temporal relation identification in news text. In *Proceedings of the Fourth International Workshop on Semantic Evaluations (SemEval-2007)*, pages 219–222.

Seyed Abolghasem Mirroshandel and Gholamreza Ghassem-Sani. 2011. Temporal relation extraction using expectation maximization. In *Proceedings of the International Conference Recent Advances in Natural Language Processing 2011*, pages 218–225.

Rashmi Prasad, Nikhil Dinesh, Alan Lee, Eleni Miltsakaki, Livio Robaldo, Aravind Joshi, and Bonnie Webber. 2008. The penn discourse treebank 2.0. In *Proceedings of the 6th International Conference on Language Resources and Evaluation*.

Georgiana Puşcaşu. 2007. WVALI: Temporal relation identification by syntactico-semantic analysis. In *Proceedings of the Fourth International Workshop on Semantic Evaluations (SemEval-2007)*, pages 484–487.

James Pustejovsky, Patrick Hanks, Roser Sauri, Andrew See, David Day, Lisa Ferro, Robert Gaizauskas, Marcia Lazo, Andrea Setzer, and Beth Sundheim. 2003. The TimeBank corpus. In *Corpus Linguistics*, pages 647–656.

Ioannis Tsochantaridis, Thomas Hofmann, Thorsten Joachims, and Yasemin Altun. 2004. Support vector machine learning for interdependent and structured output spaces. In *Proceedings of the 21st International Conference on Machine Learning*, pages 104–112.

Marc Verhagen, Robert Gaizauskas, Frank Schilder, Mark Hepple, Graham Katz, and James Pustejovsky. 2007. SemEval-2007 Task 15: TempEval temporal relation identification. In *Proceedings of the Fourth International Workshop on Semantic Evaluations (SemEval-2007)*, pages 75–80.

Marc Verhagen, Roser Sauri, Tommaso Caselli, and James Pustejovsky. 2010. SemEval-2010 Task 13: TempEval-2. In *Proceedings of the 5th International Workshop on Semantic Evaluation*, pages 57–62.

Improved Information Structure Analysis of Scientific Documents Through Discourse and Lexical Constraints

Yufan Guo
University of Cambridge, UK
yg244@cam.ac.uk

Roi Reichart
University of Cambridge, UK
rr439@cam.ac.uk

Anna Korhonen
University of Cambridge, UK
alk23@cam.ac.uk

Abstract

Inferring the information structure of scientific documents is useful for many downstream applications. Existing feature-based machine learning approaches to this task require substantial training data and suffer from limited performance. Our idea is to guide feature-based models with declarative domain knowledge encoded as posterior distribution constraints. We explore a rich set of discourse and lexical constraints which we incorporate through the Generalized Expectation (GE) criterion. Our constrained model improves the performance of existing fully and lightly supervised models. Even a fully unsupervised version of this model outperforms lightly supervised feature-based models, showing that our approach can be useful even when no labeled data is available.

1 Introduction

Techniques that enable automatic analysis of the information structure of scientific articles can help scientists identify information of interest in the growing volume of scientific literature. For example, classification of sentences according to argumentative zones (AZ) – an information structure scheme that is applicable across scientific domains (Teufel et al., 2009) – can support information retrieval, information extraction and summarization (Teufel and Moens, 2002; Tbahriti et al., 2006; Ruch et al., 2007; Liakata et al., 2012; Contractor et al., 2012).

Previous work on sentence-based classification of scientific literature according to categories of information structure has mostly used feature-based machine learning, such as Support Vector Machines (SVM) and Conditional Random Fields (CRF) (e.g. (Teufel and Moens, 2002; Lin et al., 2006; Hirohata et al., 2008; Shatkay et al., 2008; Guo et al., 2010; Liakata et al., 2012)). Unfortunately, the performance of these methods is rather limited, as indicated e.g. by the relatively low numbers reported by Liakata et al. (2012) in biochemistry and chemistry with per-class F-scores ranging from .18 to .76.

We propose a novel approach to this task in which traditional feature-based models are augmented with explicit declarative expert and domain knowledge, and apply it to sentence-based AZ. We explore two sources of declarative knowledge for our task - *discourse* and *lexical*. One way to utilize discourse knowledge is to guide the model predictions by encoding a desired predicted class (i.e. information category) distribution in a given position in the document. Consider, for example, sentence (1) from the first paragraph of the *Discussion* section in a paper:

(1) *In time, this will prove to be most suitable for detailed analysis of the role of these hormones in mammary cancer development.*

Although the future tense and cue phrases such as "*in time*" can indicate that authors are discussing future work (i.e. the "Future work" class in the AZ scheme), in this case they refer to their own contribution (i.e. the "Conclusion" class in AZ). As most authors discuss their own contribution in the beginning of the *Discussion* section and future directions in the end, encoding the desired class distribution as a function of the position in this section can guide the model to the right decision.

Likewise, lexical knowledge can guide the model

through predicted class distributions for sentences that contain specific vocabulary. Consider, for example, sentence (2):

(2) *The values calculated for lungs include the presumed DNA adduct of BA and might thus be slightly overestimated.*

The verb "*calculated*" usually indicates the "Method" class, but, when accompanied by the modal verb "*might*", it is more likely to imply that authors are interpreting their own results (i.e. the "Conclusion" class in AZ). This can be explicitly encoded in the model through a target distribution for sentences containing certain modal verbs.

Recent work has shown that explicit declaration of domain and expert knowledge can be highly useful for structured NLP tasks such as parsing, POS tagging and information extraction (Chang et al., 2007; Mann and McCallum, 2008; Ganchev et al., 2010). These works have encoded expert knowledge through constraints, with different frameworks differing in the type of constraints and the inference and learning algorithms used. We build on the Generalized Expectation (GE) framework (Mann and McCallum, 2007) which encodes expert knowledge through a preference (i.e. soft) constraints for parameter settings for which the predicted label distribution matches a target distribution.

In order to integrate domain knowledge with a features-based model, we develop a simple taxonomy of constraints (i.e. desired class distributions) and employ a top-down classification algorithm on top of a Maximum Entropy Model augmented with GE constraints. This algorithm enables us to break the multi-class prediction into a pipeline of consecutive, simpler predictions which can be better assisted by the encoded knowledge.

We experiment in the biological domain with the eight-category AZ scheme (Table 1) adapted from (Mizuta et al., 2006) and described in (Contractor et al., 2012). The results show that our constrained model substantially outperforms a baseline unconstrained Maximum Entropy Model. While this type of constrained models have previously improved the feature-based model performance mostly in the weakly supervised and domain adaptation scenarios (e.g. (Mann and McCallum, 2007; Mann and McCallum, 2008; Ganchev et al., 2010)), we demonstrate substantial gains both when the Maximum Entropy Model is fully trained and when its training data is sparse. This demonstrates the importance of expert knowledge for our task and supports our modeling decision that combines feature-based methods with domain knowledge encoded via constraints.

Table 1: The AZ categories included in the categorization scheme of this paper.

Zone	Definition
Background (BKG)	the background of the study
Problem (PROB)	the research problem
Method (METH)	the methods used
Result (RES)	the results achieved
Conclusion (CON)	the authors' conclusions
Connection (CN)	work consistent with the current work
Difference (DIFF)	work inconsistent with the current work
Future work (FUT)	the potential future direction of the research

2 Previous work

Information structure analysis The information structure of scientific documents (e.g. journal articles, abstracts, essays) can be analyzed in terms of patterns of topics, functions or relations observed in multi-sentence scientific text. Computational approaches have mainly focused on analysis based on argumentative zones (Teufel and Moens, 2002; Mizuta et al., 2006; Hachey and Grover, 2006; Teufel et al., 2009), discourse structure (Burstein et al., 2003; Webber et al., 2011), qualitative dimensions (Shatkay et al., 2008), scientific claims (Blake, 2009), scientific concepts (Liakata et al., 2010) and information status (Markert et al., 2012).

Most existing methods for analyzing scientific text according to information structure use full supervision in the form of thousands of manually annotated sentences (Teufel and Moens, 2002; Burstein et al., 2003; Mizuta et al., 2006; Shatkay et al., 2008; Guo et al., 2010; Liakata et al., 2012; Markert et al., 2012). Because manual annotation is prohibitively expensive, approaches based on light supervision are now emerging for the task, including those based on active learning and self-training (Guo et al., 2011) and unsupervised methods (Varga et al., 2012; Reichart and Korhonen, 2012). Unfortunately, these approaches do not reach the performance level of fully supervised models, let alone exceed it. Our novel method addresses this problem.

Declarative knowledge and constraints Previous work has shown that incorporating declarative constraints into feature-based machine learning models works well in many NLP tasks (Chang et al., 2007; Mann and McCallum, 2008; Druck et al., 2008; Bellare et al., 2009; Ganchev et al., 2010). Such constraints can be used in a semi-supervised or unsupervised fashion. For example, (Mann and McCallum, 2008) shows that using CRF in conjunction with auxiliary constraints on unlabeled data significantly outperforms traditional CRF in information extraction, and (Druck et al., 2008) shows that using declarative constraints alone for unsupervised learning achieves good results in text classification. We show that declarative constraints can be highly useful for the identification of information structure of scientific documents. In contrast with most previous works, we show that such constraints can improve the performance of a fully supervised model. The constraints are particularly helpful for identifying low-frequency information categories, but still yield high performance on high-frequency categories.

3 Maximum-Entropy Estimation and Generalized Expectation (GE)

In this section we describe the Generalized Expectation method for declarative knowledge encoding.

Maximum Entropy (ME) The idea of Generalized Expectation (Dudík, 2007; Mann and McCallum, 2008; Druck et al., 2008) stems from the principle of maximum entropy (Jaynes, 1957; Pietra and Pietra, 1993) which raises the following constrained optimization problem:

$$\begin{aligned} \max_{p} \quad & H(\cdot) \\ \text{subject to} \quad & E_p[\mathbf{f}(\cdot)] = E_{\tilde{p}}[\mathbf{f}(\cdot)] \\ & p(\cdot) \geq 0 \\ & \sum p(\cdot) = 1, \end{aligned} \tag{1}$$

where $\tilde{p}(\cdot)$ is the empirical distribution, $p(\cdot)$ is a probability distribution in the model and $H(\cdot)$ is the corresponding information entropy, $\mathbf{f}(\cdot)$ is a collection of feature functions, and $E_p[\mathbf{f}(\cdot)]$ and $E_{\tilde{p}}[\mathbf{f}(\cdot)]$ are the expectations of $\mathbf{f}$ with respect to $p(\cdot)$ and $\tilde{p}(\cdot)$. An example of $p(\cdot)$ could be a conditional probability distribution $p(y|x)$, and $H(\cdot)$ could be a conditional entropy $H(y|x)$. The optimal $p(y|x)$ will take on an exponential form:

$$p_\lambda(y|x) = \frac{1}{Z_\lambda} exp(\lambda \cdot \mathbf{f}(x, y)), \tag{2}$$

where λ is the Lagrange multipliers in the corresponding unconstrained objective function, and Z_λ is the partition function. The dual problem becomes maximizing the conditional log-likelihood of labeled data $\mathcal{L}$ (Berger et al., 1996):

$$\max_{\lambda} \sum_{(x_i, y_i) \in \mathcal{L}} log(p_\lambda(y_i|x_i)), \tag{3}$$

which is usually known as a Log-linear or Maximum Entropy Model (MaxEnt).

ME with Generalized Expectation The objective function and the constraints on **expectations** in (1) can be **generalized** to:

$$\begin{aligned} \max_{\lambda} & - \sum_{x} \tilde{p}(x) D(p_\lambda(y|x) || p_0(y|x)) \\ & - g(E_{\tilde{p}(x)}[E_{p_\lambda(y|x)}[\mathbf{f}(x, y)|x]]), \end{aligned} \tag{4}$$

where $D(p_\lambda||p_0)$ is the divergence from p_λ to a base distribution p_0, and $g(\cdot)$ is a constraint/penalty function that takes empirical evidence $E_{\tilde{p}(x,y)}[\mathbf{f}(x, y)]$ as a reference point (Pietra and Pietra, 1993; Chen et al., 2000; Dudík, 2007). Note that a special case of this is MaxEnt where p_0 is set to be a uniform distribution, $D(\cdot)$ to be the KL divergence, and $g(\cdot)$ to be an equality constraint.

The constraint $g(\cdot)$ can be set in a relaxed manner:

$$\sum_k \frac{1}{2\rho_k^2} (E_{\tilde{p}(x)}[E_{p_\lambda(y|x)}[f_k(x, y)|x]] - E_{\tilde{p}(x,y)}[f_k(x, y)])^2,$$

which is the logarithm of a Gaussian distribution centered at the reference values with a diagonal covariance matrix (Pietra and Pietra, 1993), and the dual problem will become a regularized MaxEnt with a Gaussian prior ($\mu_k = 0$, $\sigma_k^2 = \frac{1}{\rho_k^2}$) over the parameters:

$$\max_{\lambda} \sum_{(x_i, y_i) \in \mathcal{L}} log(p_\lambda(y_i|x_i)) - \sum_k \frac{\lambda_k^2}{2\sigma_k^2} \tag{5}$$

Such a model can be further extended to include expert knowledge or auxiliary constraints on unlabeled data $\mathcal{U}$ (Mann and McCallum, 2008; Druck et al., 2008; Bellare et al., 2009):

$$\begin{aligned} \max_{\lambda} & \sum_{(x_i, y_i) \in \mathcal{L}} log(p_\lambda(y_i|x_i)) - \sum_k \frac{\lambda_k^2}{2\sigma_k^2} \\ & - \gamma g^*(E_{p_\lambda(y|x)}[\mathbf{f}^*(x, y)]) \end{aligned} \tag{6}$$

where $\mathbf{f}^*(\cdot)$ is a collection of auxiliary feature functions on $\mathcal{U}$, $g^*(\cdot)$ is a constraint function that takes expert/declarative knowledge $E_{p^*(y|x)}[\mathbf{f}^*(x, y)]$ as a reference point, and γ is the weight of the auxiliary GE term.

The auxiliary constraint $g^*(\cdot)$ can take on many forms and the one we used in this work is an L^2 penalty function (Dudík, 2007). We trained the model with L-BFGS (Nocedal, 1980) in supervised, semi-supervised and unsupervised fashions on labeled and/or unlabeled data, using the Mallet software (McCallum, 2002).

4 Incorporating Expert Knowledge into GE constraints

We defined the auxiliary feature functions – the expert knowledge on unlabeled data as[1]:

$$f_k^*(x, y) = \mathbb{1}_{(x_k, y_k)}(x, y), \quad \text{such that } E_{p^*(y|x)}[f_k(x, y)] = p^*(y_k|x_k), \tag{7}$$

where $\mathbb{1}_{(x_k, y_k)}(x, y)$ is an indicator function, and $p^*(y_k|x_k)$ is a conditional probability specified in the form of

$$p^*(y_k|x_k) \in [a_k, b_k] \tag{8}$$

by experts. In particular, we took

$$p^*(y_k|x_k) = \begin{cases} a_k & \text{if } p_\lambda(y_k|x_k) < a \\ b_k & \text{if } p_\lambda(y_k|x_k) > b \\ p_\lambda(y_k|x_k) & \text{if } a \le p_\lambda(y_k|x_k) \le b \end{cases} \tag{9}$$

as the reference point when calculating $g^*(\cdot)$.

We defined two types of constraints: those based on *discourse* properties such as the location of a sentence in a particular section or paragraph, and those based on *lexical* properties such as citations, references to tables and figures, word lists, tenses, and so on. Note that the word lists actually contain both lexical and semantic information.

To make an efficient use of the declarative knowledge we build a taxonomy of information structure categories centered around the distinction between categories that describe the authors' OWN work and those that describe OTHER work (see Section 5). In practice, our model labels every sentence with an AZ category augmented by one of the two categories, OWN or OTHER. In evaluation we consider only the standard AZ categories which are part of the annotation scheme of (Contractor et al., 2012).

[1]Accordingly, $E_{p_\lambda(y|x)}[f_k(x, y)] = p_\lambda(y_k|x_k)$

Table 2: Discourse and lexical constraints for identifying information categories at different levels of the information structure taxonomy.

(a) OWN / OTHER

OWN	**Discourse** (1) Target(last part of paragraph) = 1 (2) Target(last part of section) = 1 **Lexical** (3) Target(tables/figures) $\geq$ 1 (4) $\exists$x $\in$ {w|w$\sim$*we*} Target(x) = 1 $\wedge$ $\forall$y $\in$ {w|w$\sim$*previous*} Target(y) = 0 (5) $\exists$x $\in$ {w|w$\sim$*thus*} Target(x) = 1
OTHER	**Lexical** (6) Target(cite) = 1 (7) Target(cite) > 1 (8) Backward(cite) = 1 $\wedge$ $\exists$x $\in$ {w|w$\sim$*in_addition*} Target(x) = 1

(b) PROB / METH / RES / CON / FUT

PROB	**Discourse** (1) Target(last part in section) = 1 **Lexical** (2) $\exists$x $\in$ {w|w$\sim$*aim*} Target(x) = 1 (3) $\exists$x $\in$ {w|w$\sim$*question*} Target(x) = 1 (4) $\exists$x $\in$ {w|w$\sim$*investigate*} Target(x) = 1
METH	**Lexical** (5) $\exists$x $\in$ {w|w$\sim${*use,method*}} Target(x) = 1
RES	**Lexical** (6) Target(*tables/figures*) $\geq$ 1 (7) $\exists$x $\in$ {w|w$\sim$*observe*} Target(x) = 1
CON	**Lexical** (8) Target(*cite*) $\geq$ 1 (9) $\exists$x $\in$ {w|w$\sim$*conclude*} Target(x) = 1 (10) $\exists$x $\in$ {w|w$\sim${*suggest, thus, because, likely*}} Target(x) = 1
FUT	**Discourse** (11) Target(first part in section) = 1 (12) Target(last part in section) = 1 $\wedge$ $\exists$x $\in$ {w|w$\sim${*will,need,future*}} Target(x) = 1 **Lexical** (13) $\exists$x {w|w$\sim$*will,future*} Target(x) = 1 (14) Target(present continuous tense) = 1

(c) BKG / CN / DIFF

BKG	**Discourse** (1) Target(first part in paragraph) = 1 (2) Target(first part in section) = 1 **Lexical** (3) $\exists$x $\in$ {w|w$\sim$*we*} Target(x) = 1 $\wedge$ $\forall$y $\in$ {w|w$\sim$*previous*} Target(y) = 0 (4) Forward(*cite*) = 1 $\wedge$ $\forall$x $\in$ {w|w$\sim${*consistent,inconsistent,than*}} (Target(x) = 0 $\wedge$ Forward(x) = 0)
CN	**Lexical** (5) $\exists$x $\in$ {w|w$\sim$*consistent*} Target(x) = 1 (6) $\exists$x $\in$ {w|w$\sim$*consistent*} Forward(x) = 1
DIFF	**Lexical** (7) $\exists$x $\in$ {w|w$\sim$*inconsistent*} Target(x) = 1 (8) $\exists$x $\in$ {w|w$\sim$*inconsistent*} Forward(x) = 1 (9) $\exists$x $\in$ {w|w$\sim${*inconsistent,than,however*}} Forward(x) = 1 $\wedge$ $\exists$y $\in$ {w|w$\sim$*we*} Forward(y) = 1 $\wedge$ $\forall$z $\in$ {w|w$\sim$*previous*}} Forward(z) = 0

Table 3: The lexical sets used as properties in the constraints.

Cue	Synonyms
we	our, present_study
previous	previously, recent, recently
thus	therefore
aim	objective, goal, purpose
question	hypothesis, ?
investigate	explore, study, test, examine, evaluate, assess, determine, characterize, analyze, report, present
use	employ
method	algorithm, assay
observe	see, find, show
conclude	conclusion, summarize, summary
suggest	illustrate, demonstrate, imply, indicate, confirm, reflect, support, prove, reveal
because	result_from, attribute_to
likely	probable, probably, possible, possibly, may, could
need	remain
future	further
consistent	match, agree, support, in_line, in_agreement, similar, same, analogous
inconsistent	conflicting, conflict, contrast, contrary, differ, different, difference
than	compare
however	other_hand, although, though, but

The constraints in Table 2(a) refer to the top level of this taxonomy: distinction between the authors' own work and the work of others, and the constraints in Tables 2(b)-(c) refer to the bottom level of the taxonomy: distinction between AZ categories related to the authors' own work (Table 2(b)) and other's work (Table 2(c)).

The first and second columns in each table refer to the y and x variables in Equation (8), respectively. The functions Target($\cdot$), Forward($\cdot$) and Backward($\cdot$) refer to the property value for the target, next and preceding sentence, respectively. If their value is 1 then the property holds for the respective sentence, if it is 0, the property does not hold. In some cases the value of such functions can be greater than 1, meaning that the property appears multiple times in the sentence. Terms of the form $\{\mathrm{w}|\mathrm{w}{\sim}\{w_i\}\}$ refer to any word/bi-grams that have the same sense as w_i, where the actual word set we use with every example word in Table 2 is described in Table 3.

For example, take constraints (1) and (4) in Table 2(a). The former is a standard discourse constraint that refers to the probability that the target sentence describes the authors' own work given that it appears in the last of the ten parts in the paragraph. The latter is a standard lexical constraint that refers to the probability that a sentence presents other people's work given that it contains any words in {*we, our, present_study*} and that it doesn't contain any words

Figure 1: The constraint taxonomy for top-down modeling.

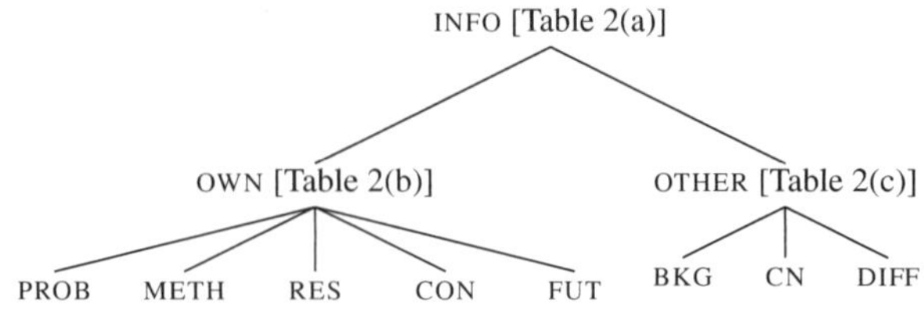

in {*previous, previously, recent, recently*}. Our constraint set further includes constraints that combine both types of information. For example, constraint (12) in Table 2(b) refers to the probability that a sentence discusses future work given that it appears in the last of the ten parts of the section (discourse) and that it contains at least one word in {*will, future, further, need, remain*} (lexical).

5 Top-Down Model

An interesting property of our task and domain is that the available expert knowledge does not directly support the distinctions between AZ categories, but it does provide valuable indirect guidance. For example, the number of citations in a sentence is only useful for separating the authors' work from other people's work, but not for further fine grained distinctions between zone categories. Moreover, those constraints that are useful for making fine grained distinctions between AZ categories are usually useful only for a particular subset of the categories only. For example, all the constraints in Table 2(b) are conditioned on the assumption that the sentence describes the authors' own work.

To make the best use of the domain knowledge, we developed a simple constraint taxonomy, and apply a top-down classification approach which utilizes it. The taxonomy is presented in Figure 1. For classification we trained three MaxEnt models augmented with GE constraints: one for distinguishing between OWN and OTHER[2], one for distinguishing between the AZ categories under the OWN auxiliary category and one for distinguishing between the AZ categories under the OTHER auxiliary category. At test time we first apply the first classifier and based on its prediction we apply either the classifier that distinguishes between OWN categories or the one that distinguishes between OTHER categories.

[2]For the training of this model, each training data AZ category is mapped to its respective auxiliary class.

6 Experiments

Data We used the full paper corpus used by Contractor et al. (2012) which contains 8171 sentences from 50 biomedical journal articles. The corpus is annotated according to the AZ scheme described in Table 1. AZ describes the logical structure, scientific argumentation and intellectual attribution of a scientific paper. It was originally introduced by Teufel and Moens (2002) and applied to computational linguistics papers, and later adapted to other domains such as biology (Mizuta et al., 2006) – which we used in this work – and chemistry (Teufel et al., 2009).

Table 4 shows the AZ class distribution in full articles as well as in individual sections. Since section names vary across scientific articles, we grouped similar sections before calculating the statistics (e.g. *Discussion* and *Conclusions* sections were grouped under *Discussion*). We can see that although there is a major category in each section (e.g. CON in *Discussion*), up to 36.5% of the sentences in each section still belong to other categories.

Features We extracted the following features from each sentence and used them in the feature-based classifiers: (1) Discourse features: location in the article/section/paragraph. For this feature each text batch was divided to ten equal size parts and the corresponding feature value identifies the relevant part; (2) Lexical features: number of citations and references to tables and figures (0, 1, or more), word, bi-gram, verb, and verb class (obtained by spectral clustering (Sun and Korhonen, 2009)); (3) Syntactic features: tense and voice (POS tags of main and auxiliary verbs), grammatical relation, subject and object. The lexical and the syntactic features were extracted for the represented sentence as well as for its surrounding sentences. We used the C&C POS tagger and parser (Curran et al., 2007) for extracting the lexical and the syntactic features. Note that all the information encoded into our constraints is also encoded in the features and is thus available to the feature-based model. This enables us to properly evaluate the impact of our modeling decision which augments a feature-based model with constraints.

Baselines We compared our model against four baselines, two with full supervision: Support Vector Machines (SVM) and Maximum Entropy Models (MaxEnt), and two with light supervision: Transductive SVM (TSVM) and semi-supervised MaxEnt based on Entropy Regularization (ER) (Vapnik, 1998; Jiao et al., 2006). SVM and MaxEnt have proved successful in information structure analysis (e.g. (Merity et al., 2009; Guo et al., 2011)) but, to the best of our knowledge, their semi-supervised versions have not been used for AZ of full articles.

Table 4: Class distribution (shown in percentages) in articles and their individual sections in the AZ-annotated corpus.

	BKG	PROB	METH	RES	CON	CN	DIFF	FUT
Article	16.9	2.8	34.8	17.9	22.3	4.3	0.8	0.2
Introduction	74.8	13.2	5.4	0.6	5.9	0.1	-	-
Methods	0.5	0.2	97.5	1.4	0.2	0.2	0.1	-
Results	4.0	2.1	11.7	68.9	12.1	1.1	0.1	-
Discussion	16.9	1.1	0.7	1.5	63.5	13.3	2.4	0.7

Table 5: Performance of baselines on the *Discussion* section.

	BKG	PROB	METH	RES	CON	CN	DIFF	FUT
Full supervision								
SVM	.56	0	0	0	.84	.35	0	0
MaxEnt	.55	.08	0	0	.84	.38	0	0
Light supervision with 150 labeled sentence								
SVM	.26	0	0	0	.80	.05	0	0
TSVM	.25	.04	.04	.03	.33	14	.06	.02
MaxEnt	.25	0	0	0	.80	.10	0	0
MaxEnt+ER	.23	0	0	0	.80	.07	0	0

Parameter tuning The boundaries of the reference probabilities (a_k and b_k in Equation (8)) were defined and optimized on the development data which consists of one third of the corpus. We considered six types of boundaries: Fairly High for 1, High for [0.9,1), Medium High for [0.5,0.9), Medium Low for [0.1,0.5), Low for [0,0.1), and Fairly Low for 0.

Evaluation We evaluated the precision, recall and F-score for each category, using a standard ten-fold cross-validation scheme. The models were tested on each of the ten folds and trained on the rest of them, and the results were averaged across the ten folds.

7 Results

We report results at two levels of granularity. We first provide detailed results for the *Discussion* section which should be, as is clearly evident from Table 4, the most difficult section for AZ prediction as only 63.5% of its sentences take its most dominant class (CON). As we show below, this is also where our constrained model is most effective. We then show the advantages of our model for other sections.

Results for the *Discussion* section To get a bet-

Table 6: *Discussion* section performance of MaxEnt, MaxEnt+GE and a MaxEnt+GE model that does not include our top-down classification scheme. Results are presented for different amounts of labeled training data. The MaxEnt+GE (Top-down) model outperforms the MaxEnt in 44 out of 48 cases, and MaxEnt+GE (Flat) in 39 out of 48 cases.

	MaxEnt						**MaxEnt + GE (Top-down)**						**MaxEnt + GE (Flat)**					
	50	100	150	500	1000	Full	50	100	150	500	1000	Full	50	100	150	500	1000	Full
BKG	.10	.26	.25	.44	.48	.55	.49	.49	.48	.52	.55	.57	.35	.37	.37	.46	.51	.53
PROB	0	0	0	0	0	0	.38	.16	.29	.13	.30	.41	.38	.23	.19	.39	.38	.33
METH	0	0	0	0	0	0	.17	.22	.37	.35	.50	.39	.16	.17	.21	.24	.32	.29
RES	0	0	0	0	0	0	.18	.24	.58	0	0	.46	.13	.05	.21	.31	.25	.34
CON	.79	.80	.80	.83	.83	.84	.77	.78	.82	.83	.84	.84	.63	.66	.68	.74	.78	.78
CN	.02	.04	.10	.24	.34	.38	.29	.31	.33	.35	.40	.39	.21	.21	.24	.26	.30	.32
DIFF	0	0	0	0	0	0	.26	.25	.25	.19	.24	.21	.14	.16	.15	.14	.18	.17
FUT	0	0	0	0	0	0	.35	.38	.31	.25	.35	.31	.36	.36	.39	.33	.25	.37

Figure 2: Performance of the MaxEnt and MaxEnt+GE models on the *Introduction* (left), *Methods* (middle) and *Results* (right) sections. The MaxEnt+GE model is superior.

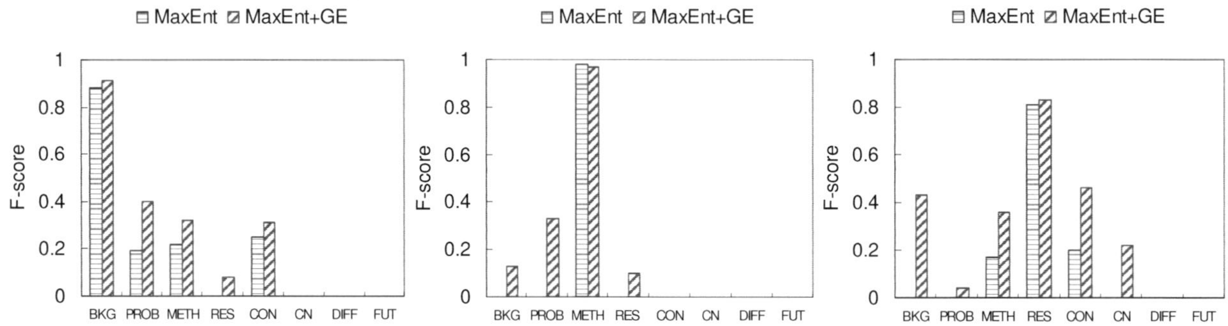

Table 7: *Discussion* section performance of the MaxEnt, MaxEnt+GE and unsupervised GE models when the former two are trained with 150 labeled sentences. Unsupervised GE outperforms the standard MaxEnt model for all categories except for CON – the major category of the section. The result pattern for the other sections are very similar.

	MaxEnt			**MaxEnt + GE**			**Unsup GE**		
	P	R	F	P	R	F	P	R	F
BKG	.38	.19	.25	.49	.48	**.48**	.49	.44	.46
PROB	0	0	0	.38	.23	.29	.28	.38	**.32**
METH	0	0	0	.29	.50	**.37**	.08	.56	.14
RES	0	0	0	.68	.51	**.58**	.08	.51	.14
CON	.69	.96	.80	.81	.84	**.82**	.74	.69	.71
CN	.35	.06	.10	.39	.29	**.33**	.40	.13	.20
DIFF	0	0	0	.21	.30	**.25**	.12	.13	.12
FUT	0	0	0	.24	.44	.31	.26	.61	**.36**

Table 8: Analysis of the impact of the different constraint types for the lightly supervised and the fully supervised cases. Results are presented for the *Discussion* section. Using only the lexical constraints is generally preferable in the fully supervised case. Combining the different constraint types is preferable for the lightly supervised case.

	Discourse		**Lexical**		**Discourse+Lexical**	
	150	Full	150	Full	150	Full
BKG	.29	.55	.46	**.58**	**.48**	.57
PROB	0	0	**.37**	.40	.29	**.41**
METH	0	.11	.29	.35	**.37**	**.39**
RES	0	.06	.32	**.47**	**.58**	.46
CON	.81	.84	.80	**.84**	**.82**	**.84**
CN	.12	.34	**.35**	**.42**	.33	.39
DIFF	0	0	.21	**.21**	**.25**	**.21**
FUT	0	0	0	.29	**.31**	**.31**

ter understanding of the nature of the challenge we face, Table 5 shows the F-scores of fully- and semi-supervised SVM and MaxEnt on the *Discussion* section. The dominant zone category CON, which accounts for 63.5% of the section sentences, has the highest F-scores for all methods and scenarios. Most of the methods also identify the second and the third most frequent zones BKG and CN, but with relatively lower F-scores. Other low-frequency categories can hardly be identified by any of the methods regardless of the amount of labeled data available for training. Note that the compared models perform quite similarly. We therefore use the MaxEnt model, which is most naturally augmented with GE constraints, as the baseline unconstrained model.

When adding the GE constraints we observe a substantial performance gain, in both the fully and the lightly supervised cases, especially for the low-frequency categories. Table 6 presents the F-scores of MaxEnt with and without GE constraints ("MaxEnt+GE (Top-down)" and "MaxEnt") in the light and full supervision scenarios. Incorporating GE into MaxEnt results in a substantial F-score improvement for all AZ categories except for the major category CON for which the performance is kept very similar. In total, MaxEnt+GE (Top-down) is better in 44 out of the 48 cases presented in the table. Importantly, the constrained model provides substantial improvements for both the relatively high-frequency classes (BKG and CN which together label 30.2% of the sentences) and for the low-frequency classes (which together label 6.4% of the sentences).

The table also clearly demonstrates the impact of our tree-based top-down classification scheme, by comparing the Top-down version of MaxEnt+GE to the standard "Flat" version. In 39 out of 48 cases, the Top-down model performs better. In some cases, especially for high-frequency categories and when the amount of training data increases, unconstrained MaxEnt even outperforms the flat MaxEnt+GE model. The results presented in the rest of the paper for the MaxEnt+GE model therefore refer to its Top-down version.

All sections We next turn to the performance of our model on the three other sections. Our experiments show that augmenting the MaxEnt model with domain knowledge constraints improves performance for all the categories (either low or high frequency), except the major section category, and keep the performance for the latter on the same level. Figure 2 demonstrates this pattern for the lightly supervised case with 150 training sentences but the same pattern applies to all other amounts of training data, including the fully supervised case. Naturally, we cannot demonstrate all these cases due to space limitations. The result patterns are very similar to those presented above for the *Discussion* section.

Unsupervised GE We next explore the quality of the domain knowledge constraints when used in isolation from a feature-based model. The objective function of this model is identical to Equation (6) except that the first (likelihood) term is omitted. Our experiments reveal that this unsupervised GE model outperforms standard MaxEnt for all the categories except the major category of the section, when up to 150 training sentences are used. Table 7 demonstrates this for the *Discussion* section. This pattern holds for the other scientific article sections. Even when more than 150 labeled sentences are used, the unsupervised model better detects the low frequency categories (i.e. those that label less than 10% of the sentences) for all sections. These results provide strong evidence for the usefulness of our constraints even when they are used with no labeled data.

Model component analysis We finally analyze the impact of the different types of constraints on the performance of our model. Table 8 presents the *Discussion* section performance of the constrained model with only one or the full set of constraints. Interestingly, when the feature-based model is fully trained the application of the lexical constraints alone results in a very similar performance to the application of the full set of lexical and discourse constraints. It is only in the lightly supervised case where the full set of constraints is required and results in the best performing model.

8 Conclusions and Future Work

We have explored the application of posterior discourse and lexical constraints for the analysis of the information structure of scientific documents. Our results are strong. Our constrained model outperforms standard feature-based models by a large margin in both the fully and the lightly supervised cases. Even an unsupervised model based on these constraints provides substantial gains over feature-based models for most AZ categories.

We provide a detailed analysis of the results which reveals a number of interesting properties of our model which may be useful for future research. First, the constrained model significantly outperforms its unconstrained counterpart for low-medium frequency categories while keeping the performance on the major section category very similar to that of the baseline model. Improved modeling of the major category is one direction for future research. Second, our full constraint set is most beneficial in the lightly supervised case while the lexical constraints alone yield equally good performance in the fully supervised case. This calls for better understanding of the role of discourse constraints for our task as well as for the design of additional constraints that can enhance the model performance either in combination with the existing constraints or when separately applied to the task. Finally, we demonstrated that our top-down tree classification scheme provides a substantial portion of our model's impact. A clear direction for future research is the design of more fine-grained constraint taxonomies which can enable efficient usage of other constraint types and can result in further improvements in performance.

References

Kedar Bellare, Gregory Druck, and Andrew McCallum. 2009. Alternating projections for learning with expectation constraints. In *Proceedings of the Twenty-Fifth Conference on Uncertainty in Artificial Intelligence*, UAI '09, pages 43–50, Arlington, Virginia, United States. AUAI Press.

Adam L. Berger, Vincent J. Della Pietra, and Stephen A. Della Pietra. 1996. A maximum entropy approach to natural language processing. *Comput. Linguist.*, 22(1):39–71.

Catherine Blake. 2009. Beyond genes, proteins, and abstracts: Identifying scientific claims from full-text biomedical articles. *J Biomed Inform*, 43(2):173–89.

Jill Burstein, Daniel Marcu, and Kevin Knight. 2003. Finding the write stuff: Automatic identification of discourse structure in student essays. *IEEE Intelligent Systems*, 18(1):32–39.

M.W. Chang, L. Ratinovc, and D. Roth. 2007. Guiding semi-supervision with constraint-driven learning. In *ACL*.

Stanley F. Chen, Ronald Rosenfeld, and Associate Member. 2000. A survey of smoothing techniques for me models. *IEEE Transactions on Speech and Audio Processing*, 8:37–50.

Danish Contractor, Yufan Guo, and Anna Korhonen. 2012. Using argumentative zones for extractive summarization of scientific articles. In *COLING*.

J. R. Curran, S. Clark, and J. Bos. 2007. Linguistically motivated large-scale nlp with c&c and boxer. In *Proceedings of the ACL 2007 Demonstrations Session*, pages 33–36.

Gregory Druck, Gideon Mann, and Andrew McCallum. 2008. Learning from labeled features using generalized expectation criteria. In *Proceedings of the 31st annual international ACM SIGIR conference on Research and development in information retrieval*, pages 595–602.

Miroslav Dudík. 2007. *Maximum entropy density estimation and modeling geographic distributions of species*. Ph.D. thesis.

K. Ganchev, J. Graca, J. Gillenwater, and B. Taskar. 2010. Posterior regularization for structured latent variable models. *Journal of Machine Learning Research*.

Yufan Guo, Anna Korhonen, Maria Liakata, Ilona Silins Karolinska, Lin Sun, and Ulla Stenius. 2010. Identifying the information structure of scientific abstracts: an investigation of three different schemes. In *Proceedings of BioNLP*, pages 99–107.

Yufan Guo, Anna Korhonen, and Thierry Poibeau. 2011. A weakly-supervised approach to argumentative zoning of scientific documents. In *Proceedings of the 2011 Conference on Empirical Methods in Natural Language Processing*, pages 273–283.

Ben Hachey and Claire Grover. 2006. Extractive summarisation of legal texts. *Artif. Intell. Law*, 14:305–345.

K. Hirohata, N. Okazaki, S. Ananiadou, and M. Ishizuka. 2008. Identifying sections in scientific abstracts using conditional random fields. In *Proceedings of 3rd International Joint Conference on Natural Language Processing*, pages 381–388.

E. T. Jaynes. 1957. Information Theory and Statistical Mechanics. *Physical Review Online Archive (Prola)*, 106(4):620–630.

F. Jiao, S. Wang, C. Lee, R. Greiner, and D. Schuurmans. 2006. Semi-supervised conditional random fields for improved sequence segmentation and labeling. In *COLING/ACL*, pages 209–216.

M. Liakata, S. Teufel, A. Siddharthan, and C. Batchelor. 2010. Corpora for the conceptualisation and zoning of scientific papers. In *Proceedings of LREC'10*.

Maria Liakata, Shyamasree Saha, Simon Dobnik, Colin Batchelor, and Dietrich Rebholz-Schuhmann. 2012. Automatic recognition of conceptualisation zones in scientific articles and two life science applications. *Bioinformatics*, 28:991–1000.

J. Lin, D. Karakos, D. Demner-Fushman, and S. Khudanpur. 2006. Generative content models for structural analysis of medical abstracts. In *Proceedings of BioNLP-06*, pages 65–72.

G. Mann and A. McCallum. 2007. Simple, robust, scalable semi-supervised learning via expectation regularization. In *ICML*.

G. Mann and A. McCallum. 2008. Generalized expectation criteria for semi-supervised learning of conditional random fields. In *ACL*.

Katja Markert, Yufang Hou, and Michael Strube. 2012. Collective classification for fine-grained information status. In *Proceedings of ACL 2012*, pages 795–804.

A. K. McCallum. 2002. Mallet: A machine learning for language toolkit. http://mallet.cs.umass.edu.

S. Merity, T. Murphy, and J. R. Curran. 2009. Accurate argumentative zoning with maximum entropy models. In *Proceedings of the 2009 Workshop on Text and Citation Analysis for Scholarly Digital Libraries*, pages 19–26.

Y. Mizuta, A. Korhonen, T. Mullen, and N. Collier. 2006. Zone analysis in biology articles as a basis for information extraction. *International Journal of Medical Informatics on Natural Language Processing in Biomedicine and Its Applications*, 75(6):468–487.

Jorge Nocedal. 1980. Updating Quasi-Newton Matrices with Limited Storage. *Mathematics of Computation*, 35(151):773–782.

S. Della Pietra and V. Della Pietra. 1993. Statistical modeling by me. Technical report, IBM.

Roi Reichart and Anna Korhonen. 2012. Document and corpus level inference for unsupervised and transductive learning of information structure of scientic documents. In *Proceedings of COLING 2012*.

P. Ruch, C. Boyer, C. Chichester, I. Tbahriti, A. Geissbuhler, P. Fabry, J. Gobeill, V. Pillet, D. Rebholz-Schuhmann, C. Lovis, and A. L. Veuthey. 2007. Using argumentation to extract key sentences from biomedical abstracts. *Int J Med Inform*, 76(2-3):195–200.

H. Shatkay, F. Pan, A. Rzhetsky, and W. J. Wilbur. 2008. Multi-dimensional classification of biomedical text: Toward automated, practical provision of high-utility text to diverse users. *Bioinformatics*, 24(18):2086–2093.

L. Sun and A. Korhonen. 2009. Improving verb clustering with automatically acquired selectional preference. In *Proceedings of EMNLP*, pages 638–647.

I. Tbahriti, C. Chichester, Frederique Lisacek, and P. Ruch. 2006. Using argumentation to retrieve articles with similar citations. *Int J Med Inform*, 75(6):488–495.

S. Teufel and M. Moens. 2002. Summarizing scientific articles: Experiments with relevance and rhetorical status. *Computational Linguistics*, 28:409–445.

S. Teufel, A. Siddharthan, and C. Batchelor. 2009. Towards discipline-independent argumentative zoning: Evidence from chemistry and computational linguistics. In *EMNLP*.

V. N. Vapnik. 1998. *Statistical learning theory*. Wiley, New York.

Andrea Varga, Daniel Preotiuc-Pietro, and Fabio Ciravegna. 2012. Unsupervised document zone identification using probabilistic graphical models. In *Proceedings of the Eight International Conference on Language Resources and Evaluation (LREC'12)*.

B. Webber, M. Egg, and V. Kordoni. 2011. Discourse structure and language technology. *Natural Language Engineering*, 18:437–490.

Adaptation of Reordering Models for Statistical Machine Translation

Boxing Chen, George Foster and Roland Kuhn
National Research Council Canada
first.last@nrc-cnrc.gc.ca

Abstract

Previous research on domain adaptation (DA) for statistical machine translation (SMT) has mainly focused on the translation model (TM) and the language model (LM). To the best of our knowledge, there is no previous work on reordering model (RM) adaptation for phrase-based SMT. In this paper, we demonstrate that mixture model adaptation of a lexicalized RM can significantly improve SMT performance, even when the system already contains a domain-adapted TM and LM. We find that, surprisingly, different training corpora can vary widely in their reordering characteristics for particular phrase pairs. Furthermore, particular training corpora may be highly suitable for training the TM or the LM, but unsuitable for training the RM, or vice versa, so mixture weights for these models should be estimated separately. An additional contribution of the paper is to propose two improvements to mixture model adaptation: smoothing the in-domain sample, and weighting instances by document frequency. Applied to mixture RMs in our experiments, these techniques (especially smoothing) yield significant performance improvements.

1 Introduction

A phrase-based statistical machine translation (SMT) system typically has three main components: a translation model (TM) that contains information about how to translate word sequences (phrases) from the source language to the target language, a language model (LM) that contains information about probable word sequences in the target language, and a reordering model (RM) that indicates how the order of words in the source sentence is likely to influence the order of words in the target sentence. The TM and the RM are trained on parallel data, and the LM is trained on target-language data. Usage of language and therefore the best translation practice differs widely across genres, topics, and dialects, and even depends on a particular author's or publication's style; the word "domain" is often used to indicate a particular combination of all these factors. Unless there is a perfect match between the training data domain and the (test) domain in which the SMT system will be used, one can often get better performance by adapting the system to the test domain.

In offline domain adaptation, the system is provided with a sample of translated sentences from the test domain prior to deployment. In a popular variant of offline adaptation, linear mixture model adaptation, each training corpus is used to generate a separate model component that forms part of a linear combination, and the sample is used to assign a weight to each component (Foster and Kuhn, 2007). If the sample resembles some of the corpora more than others, those corpora will receive higher weights in the combination.

Previous research on domain adaptation for SMT has focused on the TM and the LM. Such research is easily motivated: translations across domains are unreliable. For example, the Chinese translation of the English word "mouse" would most likely be "laoshu 老鼠" if the topic is the animal; if the topic is computer hardware, its translation would most likely be "shubiao 鼠标". However, when the translation is for people in Taiwan, even when the topic is computer hardware, its translation would more likely be "huashu 滑鼠". It is intuitively obvious why TM and LM adaptation would be helpful here.

By contrast, it is not at all obvious that RM model adaptation will improve SMT performace. One would expect reordering behaviour to be characteristic of a particular language pair, but not of particular domains. At most, one might think that reordering is lexicalized—perhaps, (for instance) in translating from Chinese to English, or from Arabic to English, there are certain words whose English translations tend to undergo long-distance movement from their original positions, while others stay close to their original positions. However, one would not expect a particular Chinese adverb or a particular Arabic noun to undergo long-distance movement when being translated into English in one domain, but not in others. Nevertheless, that is what we observe: see section 5 below.

This paper shows that RM adaptation improves the performance of our phrase-based SMT system. In our implementation, the RM is adapted by means of a linear mixture model, but it is likely that other forms of RM adaptation would also work. We obtain even more effective RM adaptation by smoothing the in-domain sample and by weighting orientation counts by the document frequency of the phrase pair. Both improvements could be applied to the TM or the LM as well, though we have not done so.

Finally, the paper analyzes reordering to see why RM adaptation works. There seem to be two factors at work. First, the reordering behaviour of words and phrases often differs dramatically from one bilingual corpus to another. Second, there are corpora (for instance, comparable corpora and bilingual lexicons) which may contain very valuable information for the TM, but which are poor sources of RM information; RM adaptation downweights information from these corpora significantly, and thus improves the overall quality of the RM.

2 Reordering Model

In early SMT systems, such as (Koehn, 2004), changes in word order when a sentence is translated were modeled by means of a penalty that is incurred when the decoder chooses, as the next source phrase to be translated, a phrase that does not immediately follow the previously translated source sentence. Thus, the system penalizes deviations from monotone order, with the magnitude of the penalty being proportional to distance in the source sentence between the end of the previously translated source phrase and the start of the newly chosen source phrase.

Many SMT systems, including our own, still use this distance-based penalty as a feature. However, starting with (Tillmann and Zhang, 2005; Koehn et al., 2005), a more sophisticated type of reordering model has often been adopted as well, and has yielded consistent performance gains. This type of RM typically identifies three possible orientations for a newly chosen source phrase: monotone (M), swap (S), and discontinuous (D). The M orientation occurs when the newly chosen phrase is immediately to the right of the previously translated phrase in the source sentence, the S orientation occurs when the new phrase is immediately to the left of the previous phrase, and the D orientation covers all other cases.[1] This type of RM is lexicalized: the estimated probabilities of M, S and D depend on the source-language and target-language words in both the previous phrase pair and the newly chosen one.

Galley and Manning (2008) proposed a "hierarchical" lexicalized RM in which the orientation (M, S, or D) is determined not by individual phrase pairs, but by blocks. A block is the largest contiguous sequence of phrase pairs that satisfies the phrase pair consistency requirement of having no external links. Thus, classification of the orientation of a newly chosen phrase as M, S, or D is carried out as if the decoder always chose the longest possible source phrase in the past, and will choose the longest possible source phrase in the future.

The RM used in this paper is hierarchical and lexicalized. For a given phrase pair (f, e), we estimate the probabilities that it will be in an M, S, or D orientation o with respect to the previous phrase pair and the following phrase pair (two separate distributions). Orientation counts $c(o, f, e)$ are obtained from a word-aligned corpus using the method de-

[1]Some researchers have distinguished between left and right versions of the D orientation, but this 4-orientation scheme has not yielded significant gains over the 3-orientation one.

scribed in (Cherry et al., 2012), and corresponding probabilities $p(o|f,e)$ are estimated using recursive MAP smoothing:

$$p(o|f,e) = \frac{c(o,f,e) + \alpha_f\, p(o|f) + \alpha_e\, p(o|e)}{c(f,e) + \alpha_f + \alpha_e}$$

$$p(o|f) = \frac{c(o,f) + \alpha_g\, p(o)}{c(f) + \alpha_g}$$

$$p(o) = \frac{c(o) + \alpha_u/3}{c(\cdot) + \alpha_u}, \qquad (1)$$

where $p(o|e)$ is defined analogously to $p(o|f)$, and the four smoothing parameters α_e, α_f, α_g, and α_u are set to values that minimize the perplexity of the resulting model on held-out data.

During decoding, orientations with respect to the previous context are obtained from a shift-reduce parser, and orientations with respect to following context are approximated using the coverage vector (Cherry et al., 2012).

3 RM Adaptation

3.1 Linear mixture model

Following previous work (Foster and Kuhn, 2007; Foster et al., 2010), we adopt the linear mixture model technique for RM adaptation. This technique trains separate models for each training corpus, then learns weights for each of the models and combines the weighted component models into a single model.

If we have N sub-corpora, the global reordering model probabilities $p(o|f,e)$ are computed as in (2):

$$p(o|f,e) = \sum_{i=1}^{N} \alpha_i\, p_i(o|f,e) \qquad (2)$$

where $p_i(o|f,e)$ is the reordering model trained on sub-corpus i, and α_i is its weight.

Following (Foster et al., 2010), we use the EM algorithm to learn the weights that maximize the probability of phrase-pair orientations in the development set (in-domain data):

$$\hat{\alpha} = \operatorname*{argmax}_{\alpha} \sum_{o,f,e} \tilde{p}(o,f,e) \log \sum_{i=1}^{N} \alpha_i\, p_i(o|f,e) \qquad (3)$$

where $\tilde{p}(o,f,e)$ is the empirical distribution of counts in the dev set (proportional to $c(o,f,e)$). Two separate sets of mixing weights are learned: one for the distribution with respect to the previous phrase pair, and one for the next phrase pair.

3.2 Development set smoothing

In Equation 3, $\tilde{p}(o,f,e)$ is extracted from the in-domain development set. Since dev sets for SMT systems are typically small (1,000-3,000 sentences), we apply smoothing to this RM. We first obtain a smoothed conditional distribution $p(o|f,e)$ using the MAP technique described above, then multiply by the empirical marginal $\tilde{p}(e,f)$ to obtain a final smoothed joint distribution $p(o,f,e)$.

There is nothing about this idea that limits it to the RM: smoothing could be applied to the statistics in the dev that are used to estimate a mixture TM or LM, in order to mitigate over-fitting. However, we note that, compared to the TM, the over-fitting problem is likely to be more acute for the RM, since it splits counts for each phrase pair into three categories.

3.3 Document-frequency weighting

Mixture models, like the RM in this paper, depend on the existence of multiple training corpora, with each sub-corpus nominally representing a domain. A recent paper suggests that some phrase pairs belong to general language, while others are domain-specific (Foster et al., 2010). If a phrase pair exists in all training corpora, it probably belongs to general language; on the other hand, if it appears in only one or two training corpora, it is more likely to be domain-specific.

We were interested in seeing whether information about domain-specificity could improve the estimation of mixture RM weights. The intuition is that phrase pairs that belong to general language should contribute more to determining sub-corpus weights, since they are the ones whose reordering behaviour is most likely to shift with domain. To capture this intuition, we multiplied the empirical distribution in (3) by the following factor, inspired by the standard document-frequency formula:

$$D(f,e) = \log(DF(f,e) + K), \qquad (4)$$

where $DF(f,e)$ is the number of sub-corpora that (f,e) appears in, and K is an empirically-determined smoothing term.

corpus	# segs	# en tok	%	genres
fbis	250K	10.5M	3.7	nw
financial	90K	2.5M	0.9	financial
gale_bc	79K	1.3M	0.5	bc
gale_bn	75K	1.8M	0.6	bn ng
gale_nw	25K	696K	0.2	nw
gale_wl	24K	596K	0.2	wl
hkh	1.3M	39.5M	14.0	Hansard
hkl	400K	9.3M	3.3	legal
hkn	702K	16.6M	5.9	nw
isi	558K	18.0M	6.4	nw
lex&ne	1.3M	2.0M	0.7	lexicon
others_nw	146K	5.2M	1.8	nw
sinorama	282K	10.0M	3.5	nw
un	5.0M	164M	58.2	un
TOTAL	10.1M	283M	100.0	(all)
devtest				
tune	1,506	161K		nw wl
NIST06	1,664	189K		nw bn ng
NIST08	1,357	164K		nw wl

Table 1: NIST Chinese-English data. In the *genres* column: nw=newswire, bc=broadcast conversation, bn=broadcast news, wl=weblog, ng=newsgroup, un=United Nations proceedings.

4 Experiments

4.1 Data setting

We carried out experiments in two different settings, both involving data from NIST Open MT 2012.[2] The first setting uses data from the Chinese to English constrained track, comprising 283M English tokens. We manually identified 14 sub-corpora on the basis of genres and origins. Table 1 summarizes the statistics and genres of all the training corpora and the development and test sets; for the training corpora, we show their size in number of words as a percentage of all training data. Most training corpora consist of parallel sentence pairs. The *isi* and *lex&ne* corpora are exceptions: the former is extracted from comparable data, while the latter is a lexicon that includes many named entities. The development set (*tune*) was taken from the NIST 2005 evaluation set, augmented with some web-genre material reserved from other NIST corpora.

[2]http://www.nist.gov/itl/iad/mig/openmt12.cfm

corpus	# segs	# en toks	%	genres
gale_bc	57K	1.6M	3.3	bc
gale_bn	45K	1.2M	2.5	bn
gale_ng	21K	491K	1.0	ng
gale_nw	17K	659K	1.4	nw
gale_wl	24K	590K	1.2	wl
isi	1,124K	34.7M	72.6	nw
other_nw	224K	8.7M	18.2	nw
TOTAL	1,512K	47.8M	100.0	(all)
devtest				
NIST06	1,664	202K		nw wl
NIST08	1,360	205K		nw wl
NIST09	1,313	187K		nw wl

Table 2: NIST Arabic-English data. In the *genres* column: nw=newswire, bc=broadcast conversation, bn=broadcase news, ng=newsgroup, wl=weblog.

The second setting uses NIST 2012 Arabic to English data, but excluding the UN data. There are about 47.8 million English running words in these training data. We manually grouped the training data into 7 groups according to genre and origin. Table 2 summarizes the statistics and genres of all the training corpora and the development and test sets. Note that for this language pair, the comparable isi data represent a large proportion of the training data: 72% of the English words. We use the evaluation sets from NIST 2006, 2008, and 2009 as our development set and two test sets, respectively.

4.2 System

Experiments were carried out with an in-house phrase-based system similar to Moses (Koehn et al., 2007). The corpus was word-aligned using IBM2, HMM, and IBM4 models, and the phrase table was the union of phrase pairs extracted from these separate alignments, with a length limit of 7. The translation model was smoothed in both directions with KN smoothing (Chen et al., 2011). The DF smoothing term K in equation 4 was set to 0.1 using held-out optimization. We use the hierarchical lexicalized RM described above, with a distortion limit of 7. Other features include lexical weighting in both directions, word count, a distance-based RM, a 4-gram LM trained on the target side of the parallel data, and a 6-gram English *Gigaword* LM. The sys-

system	Chinese	Arabic
baseline	31.7	46.8
baseline+loglin	29.6	45.9
RMA	31.8	47.7**
RMA+DF	32.2*	47.9**
RMA+dev smoothing	32.3*	**48.3****
RMA+dev smoothing+DF	**32.8****	48.2**

Table 3: Results for variants of RM adaptation.

system	Chinese	Arabic
LM+TM adaptation	33.2	47.7
+RMA+dev-smoothing+DF	33.5	48.4**

Table 4: RM adaptation improves over a baseline containing adapted LMs and TMs.

tem was tuned with batch lattice MIRA (Cherry and Foster, 2012).

4.3 Results

For our main baseline, we simply concatenate all training data. We also tried augmenting this with separate log-linear features corresponding to sub-corpus-specific RMs. Our metric is case-insensitvie IBM BLEU-4 (Papineni et al., 2002); we report BLEU scores averaged across both test sets. Following (Koehn, 2004), we use the bootstrap-resampling test to do significance testing. In tables 3 to 5, * and ** denote significant gains over the baseline at $p < 0.05$ and $p < 0.01$ levels, respectively.

Table 3 shows that reordering model adaptation helps in both data settings. Adding either document-frequency weighting (equation 4) or dev-set smoothing makes the improvement significant in both settings. Using both techniques together yields highly significant improvements.

Our second experiment measures the improvement from RM adaptation over a baseline that includes adapted LMs and TMs. We use the same technique—linear mixtures with EM-tuned weights—to adapt these models. Table 4 shows that adapting the RM gives gains over this strong baseline for both language pairs; improvements are significant in the case of Arabic to English.

The third experiment breaks down the gains in the last line of table 4 by individual adapted model. As shown in table 5, RM adaptation yielded the largest improvement on Arabic, while TM adaptation did best on Chinese. Surprisingly, both methods significantly outperformed LM adaptation, which only achieved significant gains over the baseline for Chinese.

system	Chinese	Arabic
baseline	31.7	46.8
LM adaptation	32.1*	47.0
TM adaptation	33.0**	47.5**
RM adaptation	32.8**	48.2**

Table 5: Comparison of LM, TM, and RM adaptation.

5 Analysis

Why does RM adaptation work? Intuitively, one would think that reordering behaviour for a given phrase pair should not be much affected by domain, making RM adaptation pointless. That is probably why (as far as we know) no-one has tried it before. In this section, we describe three factors that account for at least part of the observed gains.

5.1 Weighting by corpus quality

One answer to the above question is that some corpora are better for training RMs than others. Furthermore, corpora that are good for training the LM or TM are not necessarily good for training the RM, and vice versa. Tables 6 and 7 illustrate this. These list the weights assigned to various sub-corpora for LM, TM, and RM mixture models.

The weights assigned to the *isi* sub-corpus in particular exhibit a striking pattern. These are high in the LM mixtures, moderate in the TM mixtures, and very low in the RM mixtures. When one considers that isi contains 72.6% of the English words in the Arabic training data (see table 2), its weight of 0.01 in the RM mixture is remarkable.

On reflection, it makes sense that EM would assign weights in the order it does. The *isi* corpus consists of comparable data: sentence pairs whose source- and target-language sides are similar, but often not mutual translations. These are a valuable source of in-domain n-grams for the LM; a somewhat noisy source of in-domain phrase pairs for the TM; and an unreliable source of re-ordering patterns for the RM. Figure 1 shows this. Although the two

LM	TM	RM
isi (0.23)	un (0.29)	un (0.21)
gale_nw (0.11)	fbis (0.15)	gale_nw (0.13)
un (0.11)	hkh (0.10)	lex&ne (0.12)
sino. (0.09)	gale_nw (0.09)	hkh (0.08)
fbis (0.08)	gale_bn (0.07)	fbis (0.08)
fin. (0.07)	oth_nw (0.06)	gale_bn (0.08)
oth_nw (0.07)	sino. (0.06)	gale_wl (0.06)
gale_bn (0.07)	isi (0.05)	gale_bc (0.06)
gale_wl (0.06)	hkn (0.04)	hkn (0.04)
hkh (0.06)	fin. (0.04)	fin. (0.04)
hkn (0.03)	gale_bc (0.03)	oth_nw (0.03)
gale_bc (0.02)	gale_wl (0.02)	hkl (0.03)
lex&ne (0.00)	lex&ne (0.00)	isi (0.01)
hkl (0.00)	hkl (0.00)	sino. (0.01)

Table 6: Chinese-English sub-corpora for LM, TM, and RM mixture models, ordered by mixture weight.

LM	TM	RM
isi (0.41)	isi (0.35)	gale_bc (0.21)
oth_nw (0.19)	oth_nw (0.29)	gale_ng (0.20)
gale_ng (0.15)	gale_bc (0.10)	gale_nw (0.20)
gale_wl (0.09)	gale_ng (0.08)	oth_nw (0.13)
gale_nw (0.07)	gale_bn (0.07)	gale_ng (0.12)
gale_bc (0.05)	gale_nw (0.07)	gale_wb (0.11)
gale_bn (0.02)	gale_wl (0.05)	isi (0.01)

Table 7: Arabic-English sub-corpora for LM, TM, and RM mixture models, ordered by mixture weight.

sides of the comparable data are similar, they give the misleading impression that the phrases labeled 1, 2, 3 in the Chinese source should be reordered as 2, 3, 1 in English. We show a reference translation of the Chinese source (not found in the comparable data) that reorders the phrases as 1, 3, 2.

Thus, RM adaptation allows the RM to learn that certain corpora whose reordering information is of lower quality corpora should have lower weights. The optimal weights for corpora inside an RM may be different from the optimal weights inside a TM or LM.

5.2 Weighting by domain match

So is this all that RM adaptation does: downweight poor-quality data? We believe there is more to RM adaptation than that. Specifically, even if one considers only high-quality data for training RMs (ignoring comparable data, etc.) one sees differences in reordering behaviour between different domains. This isn't just because of differences in word frequencies between domains, because we observe domain-dependent differences in reordering for the same phrase pair. Two examples are given below: one Chinese-English, one Arabic-English.

Table 8 shows reordering data for the phrase pair "立即 immediately" in various corpora. Notice the strong difference in behaviour between the three Hong Kong corpora—*hkh, hkl* and *hkn*—and some of the other corpora, for instance *fbis*. In the

REF: The American list of goods that would incur tariffs in retaliation would certainly not be accepted by the Chinese government.

SRC: 美国(1) 的 报复 清单是 中国(2) 政府 绝对 不 接受 的(3)。

TGT: And the Chinese(2) side would certainly not accept(3) the unreasonable demands put forward by the Americans(1) concerning the protection of intellectual property rights .

Figure 1: Example of sentence pair from comparable data; underlined words with the same number are translations of each other

Corpus	M	S	D	Count
fbis	0.50	0.07	0.43	685
financial	0.32	0.28	0.41	65
gale_bc	0.60	0.10	0.31	50
gale_bn	0.47	0.15	0.37	109
gale_nw	0.51	0.05	0.44	326
gale_wl	0.42	0.26	0.32	52
hkh	0.29	0.23	0.48	130
hkl	0.28	0.16	0.56	263
hkn	0.30	0.27	0.43	241
isi	0.24	0.16	0.60	240
lex&ne	0.94	0.03	0.02	1
others_nw	0.29	0.16	0.55	23
sinorama	0.44	0.07	0.49	110
un	0.37	0.10	0.53	15
dev	0.46	0.24	0.31	11

Table 8: Orientation frequencies for the phrase pair "立即 immediately", with respect to the previous phrase.

Corpus	M	S	D	Count
gale_bc	0.50	0.27	0.22	233
gale_bn	0.56	0.21	0.23	226
gale_ng	0.51	0.13	0.37	295
gale_nw	0.47	0.20	0.33	167
gale_wl	0.56	0.18	0.26	127
isi	0.50	0.06	0.44	5502
other_nw	0.50	0.16	0.34	1450
dev	0.75	0.12	0.13	52

Table 9: Orientation frequencies for the phrase pair "work AlEml" with respect to the previous phrase.

Hong Kong corpora, *immediately* is much less likely (probability of around 0.3) to be associated with a monotone (M) orientation than it is in *fbis* (probability of 0.5). This phrase pair is relatively frequent in both corpora, so this disparity seems too great to be due to chance.

Table 9 shows reordering behaviour for the phrase pair "work AlEml"[3] across different sub-corpora. As in the Chinese example, there appear to be significant differences in reordering patterns for certain corpora. For instance, *gale_bc* swaps this well-attested phrase pair twice as often (probability of 0.27) as *gale_ng* (probability of 0.13).

For Chinese, it is possible that dialect plays a role in reordering behaviour. In theory, Mandarin Chinese is a single language which is quite different, especially in spoken form, from other languages of China such as Cantonese, Hokkien, Shanghainese, and so on. In practice, many speakers of Mandarin may be unconsciously influenced by other languages that they speak, or by other languages that they don't speak but that have an influence over people they interact with frequently. Word order can be affected by this: the Mandarin of Mainland China, Hong Kong and Taiwan sometimes has slightly different word order. Hong Kong Mandarin can be somewhat influenced by Cantonese, and Taiwan Mandarin by Hokkien. For instance, if a verb is modified by an adverb in Mandarin, the standard word order is "adverb verb". However, since in Cantonese, "verb adverb" is a more common word order, speakers and writers of Mandarin in Hong Kong may adopt the

Figure 2: An example of different word ordering in Mandarin from different area.

"verb adverb" order in that language as well. Figure 2 shows how a different word order in the Mandarin source affects reordering when translating into English. Perhaps in situations where different training corpora represent different dialects, RM adaptation involves an element of dialect adaptation. We are eager to test this hypothesis for Arabic—different dialects of Arabic are much more different from each other than dialects of Mandarin, and reordering is often one of the differences—but we do not have access to Arabic training, dev, and test data in which the dialects are clearly separated.

It is possible that RM adaptation also has an element of genre adaptation. We have not yet been able to confirm or refute this hypothesis. However, whatever is causing the corpus-dependent reordering patterns for particular phrase pairs shown in the two tables above, it is clear that they may explain the performance improvements we observe for RM adaptation in our experiments.

5.3 Penalizing highly-specific phrase pairs

In section 3.3 we described our strategy for giving general (high document-frequency) phrase pairs that occur in the dev set more influence in determining mixing weights. An artifact of our implementation applies a similar strategy to the probability estimates for *all* phrase pairs in the model. This is that 0 probabilities are assigned to all orientations whenever a phrase pair is absent from a particular sub-corpus.

Thus, for example, a pair (f, e) that occurs only in sub-corpus i will receive a probability $p(o|f, e) = \alpha_i p_i(o|f, e)$ in the mixture model (equation 2). Since $\alpha_i \leq 1$, this amounts to a penalty on pairs that occur in few sub-corpora, especially ones with low mixture weights.

The resulting mixture model is deficient (non-

[3]We represent the Arabic word *AlEml* in its Buckwalter transliteration.

normalized), but easy to fix by backing off to a global distribution such as $p(o)$ in equation 1. However, we found that this "fix" caused large drops in performance, for instance from the Arabic BLEU score of 48.3 reported in table 3 to 46.0. We therefore retained the original strategy, which can be seen as a form of instance weighting. Moreover, it is one that is particularly effective in the RM, since, compared to a similar strategy in the TM (which we also employ), it applies to whole phrase pairs and results in much larger penalties.

6 Related work

Domain adaptation is an active topic in the NLP research community. Its application to SMT systems has recently received considerable attention. Previous work on SMT adaptation has mainly focused on translation model (TM) and language model (LM) adaptation. Approaches that have been tried for SMT model adaptation include mixture models, transductive learning, data selection, data weighting, and phrase sense disambiguation.

Research on mixture models has considered both linear and log-linear mixtures. Both were studied in (Foster and Kuhn, 2007), which concluded that the best approach was to combine sub-models of the same type (for instance, several different TMs or several different LMs) linearly, while combining models of different types (for instance, a mixture TM with a mixture LM) log-linearly. (Koehn and Schroeder, 2007), instead, opted for combining the sub-models directly in the SMT log-linear framework.

In transductive learning, an MT system trained on general domain data is used to translate in-domain monolingual data. The resulting bilingual sentence pairs are then used as additional training data (Ueffing et al., 2007; Chen et al., 2008; Schwenk, 2008; Bertoldi and Federico, 2009).

Data selection approaches (Zhao et al., 2004; Lü et al., 2007; Moore and Lewis, 2010; Axelrod et al., 2011) search for bilingual sentence pairs that are similar to the in-domain "dev" data, then add them to the training data. The selection criteria are typically related to the TM, though the newly found data will be used for training not only the TM but also the LM and RM.

Data weighting approaches (Matsoukas et al., 2009; Foster et al., 2010; Huang and Xiang, 2010; Phillips and Brown, 2011; Sennrich, 2012) use a rich feature set to decide on weights for the training data, at the sentence or phrase pair level. For instance, a sentence from a corpus whose domain is far from that of the dev set would typically receive a low weight, but sentences in this corpus that appear to be of a general nature might receive higher weights.

The 2012 JHU workshop on Domain Adaptation for MT [4] proposed phrase sense disambiguation (PSD) for translation model adaptation. In this approach, the context of a phrase helps the system to find the appropriate translation.

All of the above work focuses on either TM or LM domain adaptation.

7 Conclusions

In this paper, we adapt the lexicalized reordering model (RM) of an SMT system to the domain in which the system will operate using a mixture model approach. Domain adaptation of translation models (TMs) and language models (LMs) has become common for SMT systems, but to our knowledge this is the first attempt in the literature to adapt the RM. Our experiments demonstrate that RM adaptation can significantly improve translation quality, even when the system already has TM and LM adaptation. We also experimented with two modifications to linear mixture model adaptation: dev set smoothing and weighting orientation counts with document frequency of phrase pairs. Both ideas are potentially applicable to TM and LM adaptation. Dev set smoothing, in particular, seems to improve the performance of RM adaptation significantly. Finally, we investigate why RM adaptation helps SMT performance. Three factors seem to be important: downweighting information from corpora that are less suitable for modeling reordering (such as comparable corpora), dialect/genre effects, and implicit instance weighting.

[4] http://www.clsp.jhu.edu/workshops/archive/ws-12/groups/dasmt

References

Amittai Axelrod, Xiaodong He, and Jianfeng Gao. 2011. Domain adaptation via pseudo in-domain data selection. In *EMNLP 2011*.

Nicola Bertoldi and Marcello Federico. 2009. Domain adaptation for statistical machine translation with monolingual resources. In *Proceedings of the 4th Workshop on Statistical Machine Translation*, Athens, March. WMT.

Boxing Chen, Min Zhang, Aiti Aw, and Haizhou Li. 2008. Exploiting n-best hypotheses for smt self-enhancement. In *ACL 2008*.

Boxing Chen, Roland Kuhn, George Foster, and Howard Johnson. 2011. Unpacking and transforming feature functions: New ways to smooth phrase tables. In *MT Summit 2011*.

Colin Cherry and George Foster. 2012. Batch tuning strategies for statistical machine translation. In *NAACL 2012*.

Colin Cherry, Robert C. Moore, and Chris Quirk. 2012. On hierarchical re-ordering and permutation parsing for phrase-based decoding. In *WMT 2012*.

George Foster and Roland Kuhn. 2007. Mixture-model adaptation for SMT. In *Proceedings of the ACL Workshop on Statistical Machine Translation*, Prague, June. WMT.

George Foster, Cyril Goutte, and Roland Kuhn. 2010. Discriminative instance weighting for domain adaptation in statistical machine translation. In *Proceedings of the 2010 Conference on Empirical Methods in Natural Language Processing (EMNLP)*, Boston.

Michel Galley and C. D. Manning. 2008. A simple and effective hierarchical phrase reordering model. In *EMNLP 2008*, pages 848–856, Hawaii, October.

Fei Huang and Bing Xiang. 2010. Feature-rich discriminative phrase rescoring for SMT. In *COLING 2010*.

Philipp Koehn and Josh Schroeder. 2007. Experiments in domain adaptation for statistical machine translation. In *Proceedings of the Second Workshop on Statistical Machine Translation*, pages 224–227, Prague, Czech Republic, June. Association for Computational Linguistics.

P. Koehn, A. Axelrod, A. B. Mayne, C. Callison-Burch, M. Osborne, D. Talbot, and M. White. 2005. Edinburgh system description for the 2005 NIST MT evaluation. In *Proceedings of Machine Translation Evaluation Workshop*.

P. Koehn, H. Hoang, A. Birch, C. Callison-Burch, M. Federico, N. Bertoldi, B. Cowan, W. Shen, C. Moran, R. Zens, C. Dyer, O. Bojar, A. Constantin, and E. Herbst. 2007. Moses: Open source toolkit for statistical machine translation. In *ACL 2007, Demonstration Session*.

Philipp Koehn. 2004. Pharaoh: a beam search decoder for phrase-based statistical machine translation models. In *Proceedings of the 6th Conference of the Association for Machine Translation in the Americas*, Georgetown University, Washington D.C., October. Springer-Verlag.

Yajuan Lü, Jin Huang, and Qun Liu. 2007. Improving Statistical Machine Translation Performance by Training Data Selection and Optimization. In *Proceedings of the 2007 Conference on Empirical Methods in Natural Language Processing (EMNLP)*, Prague, Czech Republic.

Spyros Matsoukas, Antti-Veikko I. Rosti, and Bing Zhang. 2009. Discriminative corpus weight estimation for machine translation. In *Proceedings of the 2009 Conference on Empirical Methods in Natural Language Processing (EMNLP)*, Singapore.

Robert C. Moore and William Lewis. 2010. Intelligent selection of language model training data. In *ACL 2010*.

Kishore Papineni, Salim Roukos, Todd Ward, and Wei-Jing Zhu. 2002. BLEU: A method for automatic evaluation of Machine Translation. In *Proceedings of the 40th Annual Meeting of the Association for Computational Linguistics (ACL)*, pages 311–318, Philadelphia, July. ACL.

Aaron B. Phillips and Ralf D. Brown. 2011. Training machine translation with a second-order taylor approximation of weighted translation instances. In *MT Summit 2011*.

Holger Schwenk. 2008. Investigations on large-scale lightly-supervised training for statistical machine translation. In *IWSLT 2008*.

Rico Sennrich. 2012. Mixture-modeling with unsupervised clusters for domain adaptation in statistical machine translation. In *EACL 2012*.

Christoph Tillmann and Tong Zhang. 2005. A localized prediction model for statistical machine translation. In *Proceedings of the 43th Annual Meeting of the Association for Computational Linguistics (ACL)*, Ann Arbor, Michigan, July. ACL.

Nicola Ueffing, Gholamreza Haffari, and Anoop Sarkar. 2007. Transductive learning for statistical machine translation. In *Proceedings of the 45th Annual Meeting of the Association for Computational Linguistics (ACL)*, Prague, Czech Republic, June. ACL.

Bing Zhao, Matthias Eck, and Stephan Vogel. 2004. Language model adaptation for statistical machine translation with structured query models. In *Proceedings of the International Conference on Computational Linguistics (COLING) 2004*, Geneva, August.

Multi-Metric Optimization Using Ensemble Tuning

Baskaran Sankaran, Anoop Sarkar
Simon Fraser University
Burnaby BC. CANADA
{baskaran,anoop}@cs.sfu.ca

Kevin Duh
Nara Institute of Science & Technology
Ikoma, Nara. JAPAN
kevinduh@is.naist.jp

Abstract

This paper examines tuning for statistical machine translation (SMT) with respect to multiple evaluation metrics. We propose several novel methods for tuning towards multiple objectives, including some based on *ensemble decoding* methods. Pareto-optimality is a natural way to think about multi-metric optimization (MMO) and our methods can effectively combine several Pareto-optimal solutions, obviating the need to choose one. Our best performing *ensemble tuning* method is a new algorithm for multi-metric optimization that searches for Pareto-optimal ensemble models. We study the effectiveness of our methods through experiments on multiple as well as single reference(s) datasets. Our experiments show simultaneous gains across several metrics (BLEU, RIBES), without any significant reduction in other metrics. This contrasts the traditional tuning where gains are usually limited to a single metric. Our human evaluation results confirm that in order to produce better MT output, optimizing multiple metrics is better than optimizing only one.

1 Introduction

Tuning algorithms are used to find the weights for a statistical machine translation (MT) model by minimizing error with respect to a single MT evaluation metric. The tuning process improves the performance of an SMT system as measured by this metric; with BLEU (Papineni et al., 2002) being the most popular choice. Minimum error-rate training (MERT) (Och, 2003) was the first approach in MT to directly optimize an evaluation metric. Several alternatives now exist: MIRA (Watanabe et al., 2007; Chiang et al., 2008), PRO (Hopkins and May, 2011), linear regression (Bazrafshan et al., 2012) and ORO (Watanabe, 2012) among others.

However these approaches optimize towards the best score as reported by a single evaluation metric. MT system developers typically use BLEU and ignore all the other metrics. This is done despite the fact that other metrics model wide-ranging aspects of translation: from measuring the translation edit rate (TER) in matching a translation output to a human reference (Snover et al., 2006), to capturing lexical choices in translation as in METEOR (Lavie and Denkowski, 2009) to modelling semantic similarity through textual entailment (Padó et al., 2009) to RIBES, an evaluation metric that pays attention to long-distance reordering (Isozaki et al., 2010). While some of these metrics such as TER, METEOR are gaining prominence, BLEU enjoys the status of being the *de facto* standard tuning metric as it is often claimed and sometimes observed that optimizing with BLEU produces better translations than other metrics (Callison-Burch et al., 2011).

The gains obtained by the MT system tuned on a particular metric do not improve performance as measured under other metrics (Cer et al., 2010), suggesting that over-fitting to a specific metric might happen without improvements in translation quality. In this paper we propose a new tuning framework for jointly optimizing multiple evaluation metrics.

Pareto-optimality is a natural way to think about multi-metric optimization and multi-metric optimization (MMO) was recently explored using the notion of Pareto optimality in the Pareto-based Multi-objective Optimization (PMO) approach (Duh et al., 2012). PMO provides several equivalent solutions (parameter weights) having different trade-offs between the different MT metrics. In (Duh et al., 2012) the choice of which option to use rests with the MT system developer and in that sense their approach is an *a posteriori* method to specify the preference (Marler and Arora, 2004).

In contrast to this, our tuning framework provides a principled way of using the Pareto optimal options using *ensemble* decoding (Razmara et al., 2012). We also introduce a novel method of *ensemble tuning* for jointly tuning multiple MT evaluation metrics and further combine this with the PMO approach (Duh et al., 2012). We also introduce three other approaches for multi-metric tuning and compare their performance to the ensemble tuning. Our experiments yield the highest metric scores across many different metrics (that are being optimized), something that has not been possible until now.

Our ensemble tuning method over multiple metrics produced superior translations than single metric tuning as measured by a post-editing task. HTER (Snover et al., 2006) scores in our human evaluation confirm that multi-metric optimization can lead to better MT output.

2 Related Work

In grammar induction and parsing (Spitkovsky et al., 2011; Hall et al., 2011; Auli and Lopez, 2011) have proposed multi-objective methods based on round-robin iteration of single objective optimizations.

Research in SMT parameter tuning has seen a surge of interest recently, including online/batch learning (Watanabe, 2012; Cherry and Foster, 2012), large-scale training (Simianer et al., 2012; He and Deng, 2012), and new discriminative objectives (Gimpel and Smith, 2012; Zheng et al., 2012; Bazrafshan et al., 2012). However, few works have investigated the multi-metric tuning problem in depth. Linear combination of BLEU and TER is reported in (Zaidan, 2009; Dyer et al., 2009; Servan and Schwenk, 2011); an alternative is to optimize on BLEU with MERT while enforcing that TER does not degrade per iteration (He and Way, 2009). Studies on metric tunability (Liu et al., 2011; Callison-Burch et al., 2011; Chen et al., 2012) have found that the metric used for evaluation may not be the best metric used for tuning. For instance, (Mauser et al., 2008; Cer et al., 2010) report that tuning on linear combinations of BLEU-TER is more robust than a single metric like WER.

The approach in (Devlin and Matsoukas, 2012) modifies the optimization function to include traits such as output length so that the hypotheses produced by the decoder have maximal score according to one metric (BLEU) but are subject to an output length constraint, e.g. that the output is 5% shorter. This is done by rescoring an N-best list (forest) for the metric combined with each trait condition and then the different trait hypothesis are combined using a system combination step. The traits are independent of the reference (while tuning). In contrast, our method is able to combine multiple metrics (each of which compares to the reference) during the tuning step and we do not depend on N-best list (or forest) rescoring or system combination.

Duh et. al. (2012) proposed a Pareto-based approach to SMT multi-metric tuning, where the linear combination weights do not need to be known in advance. This is advantageous because the optimal weighting may not be known in advance. However, the notion of Pareto optimality implies that multiple "best" solutions may exist, so the MT system developer may be forced to make a choice after tuning.

These approaches require the MT system developer to make a choice either before tuning (e.g. in terms of linear combination weights) or afterwards (e.g. the Pareto approach). Our method here is different in that we do not require any choice. We use *ensemble decoding* (Razmara et al., 2012) (see sec 3) to combine the different solutions resulting from the multi-metric optimization, providing an elegant solution for deployment. We extend this idea further and introduce *ensemble tuning*, where the metrics have separate set of weights. The tuning process alternates between ensemble decoding and the update step where the weights for each metric are optimized separately followed by joint update of metric (meta) weights.

3 Ensemble Decoding

We now briefly review ensemble decoding (Razmara et al., 2012) which is used as a component in the algorithms we present. The prevalent model of statistical MT is a log-linear framework using a vector of feature functions ϕ:

$$p(e|f) \propto \exp\Big(w \cdot \phi\Big) \quad (1)$$

The idea of ensemble decoding is to combine several models dynamically at decode time. Given multiple models, the scores are combined for each partial hypothesis across the different models during decoding using a user-defined mixture operation $\otimes$.

$$p(e|f) \propto \exp\Big(w_1 \cdot \phi_1 \otimes w_2 \cdot \phi_2 \otimes \dots\Big) \quad (2)$$

(Razmara et al., 2012) propose several mixture operations, such as *log-wsum* (simple linear mixture), *wsum* (log-linear mixture) and *max* (choose locally best model) among others. The different mixture operations allows the user to encode the beliefs about the relative strengths of the models. It has been applied successfully for domain adaptation setting and shown to perform better approaches that pre-compute linear mixtures of different models.

4 Multi-Metric Optimization

In statistical MT, the multi-metric optimization problem can be expressed as:

$$w^* = \arg\max_{w} g\Big([M_1(H), \ldots, M_k(H)] \Big) \quad (3)$$
$$\text{where } H = \mathcal{N}(\mathbf{f}; w)$$

where $\mathcal{N}(\mathbf{f}; w)$ is the decoding function generating a set of candidate hypotheses H based on the model parameters w, for the source sentences $\mathbf{f}$. For each source sentence $f_i \in \mathbf{f}$ there is a set of candidate hypotheses $\{h_i\} \in H$. The goal of the optimization is to find the weights that maximize the function $g(.)$ parameterized by different evaluation metrics $M_1, \ldots, M_k$.

For the Pareto-optimal based approach such as PMO (Duh et al., 2012), we can replace $g(\cdot)$ above with $g_{\text{PMO}}(\cdot)$ which returns the points in the Pareto frontier. Alternately a weighted averaging function $g_{\text{wavg}}(\cdot)$ would result in a linear combination of the metrics being considered, where the tuning method would maximize the joint metric. This is similar to the (TER-BLEU)/2 optimization (Cer et al., 2010; Servan and Schwenk, 2011).

We introduce four methods based on the above formulation and each method uses a different type of $g(\cdot)$ function for combining different metrics and we compare experimentally with existing methods.

4.1 PMO Ensemble

PMO (Duh et al., 2012) seeks to maximize the number of points in the Pareto frontier of the metrics considered. The inner routine of the PMO-PRO tuning is described in Algorithm 1. This routine is contained within an outer loop that iterates for a fixed number iterations of decoding the tuning set and optimizing the weights.

The tuning process with PMO-PRO is independently repeated with different set of weights for metrics[1] yielding a set of equivalent solutions

Algorithm 1 PMO-PRO (*Inner routine for tuning*)

Input: Hypotheses H = $\mathcal{N}(\mathbf{f}; w)$; Weights w
Initialize $\mathcal{T} = \{\}$
for each f in tuning set **f** **do**
  $\{h\} = H(f)$
  $\{M(\{h\})\}$ = ComputeMetricScore($\{h\}, \hat{e}$)
  $\{\mathcal{F}\}$ = FindParetoFrontier($\{M(\{h\})\}$)
  for each h in $\{h\}$ **do**
    if $h \in \mathcal{F}$ **then** add $(1, h)$ to $\mathcal{T}$
    else add (ℓ, h) to $\mathcal{T}$ (see footnote 1)
$w^p \leftarrow$ PRO($\mathcal{T}$) (optimize using PRO)
Output: Pareto-optimal weights w^p

$\{p_{s_1}, \ldots, p_{s_n}\}$ which are points on the Pareto frontier. The user then chooses one solution by making a trade-off between the performance gains across different metrics. However, as noted earlier this *a posteriori* choice ignores other solutions that are indistinguishable from the chosen one.

We alleviate this by complementing PMO with ensemble decoding, which we call *PMO ensemble*, in which each point in the Pareto solution is a distinct component in the ensemble decoder. This idea can also be used in other MMO approaches such as linear combination of metrics ($g_{\text{wavg}}(.)$) mentioned above. In this view, PMO ensemble is a special case of *ensemble combination*, where the decoding is performed by an ensemble of optimal solutions.

The ensemble combination model introduces new hyperparameters β that are the weights of the ensemble components (meta weights). These ensemble weights could set to be uniform in a naïve implementation. Or the user can encode her beliefs or expectations about the individual solutions $\{p_{s_1}, \ldots, p_{s_n}\}$ to set the ensemble weights (based on the relative importance of the components). Finally, one could also include a meta-level tuning step to set the weights β.

The PMO ensemble approach is graphically illustrated in Figure 1; we will also refer to this figure while discussing other methods.[2] The orig-

[1]For example Duh et al. (2012) use five different weight settings for metrics (M_1, M_2), viz. $(0.0, 1.0)$, $(0.3, 0.7)$, $(0.5, 0.5)$, $(0.7, 0.3)$ and $(1.0, 0.0)$. They combine the metric weights q_i with the sentence-level metric scores M_i as $\ell = \left(\sum_k q_k M_k\right) / k$ where ℓ is the target value for negative examples (the *else* line in Alg 1) in the optimization step.

[2]The illustration is based on two metrics, metric-1 and metric-2, but could be applied to any number of metrics. Without loss of generality we assume accuracy metrics, i.e. higher

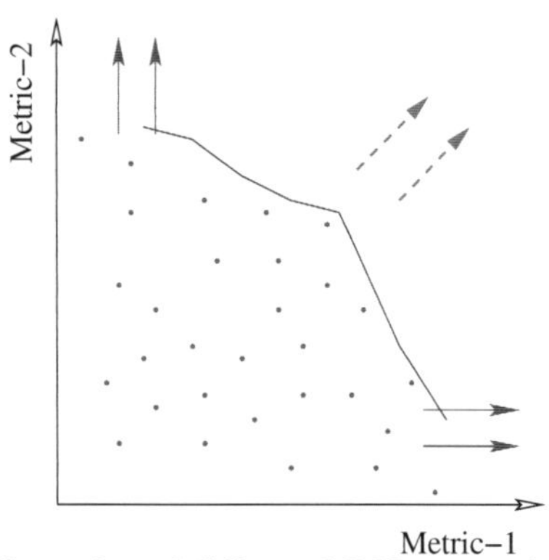

Figure 1: Illustration of different MMO approaches involving two metrics. Solid (red) arrows indicate optimizing two metrics independently and the dashed (green) arrow optimize them jointly. The Pareto frontier is indicated by the curve.

inal PMO-PRO seeks to maximize the points on the Pareto frontier (blue curve in the figure) leading to Pareto-optimal solutions. On the other hand, the PMO ensemble combines the different Pareto-optimal solutions and potentially moving in the direction of dashed (green) arrows to some point that has higher score in either or both dimensions.

4.2 Lateen MMO

Lateen EM has been proposed as a way of jointly optimizing multiple objectives in the context of dependency parsing (Spitkovsky et al., 2011). It uses a secondary hard EM objective to move away, when the primary soft EM objective gets stuck in a local optima. The course correction could be performed under different conditions leading to variations that are based on when and how often to shift from one objective function to another during optimization.

The lateen technique can be applied to the multi-metric optimization in SMT by treating the different metrics as different objective functions. While the several lateen variants are also applicable for our task, our objective here is to improve performance across the different metrics (being optimized). Thus, we restrict ourselves to the style where the search alternates between the metrics (in round-robin fashion) at each iteration. Since the notion of convergence is unclear in lateen setting, we stop after a fixed number of iterations optimizing the tuning set. In terms of Figure 1, lateen MMO corresponds to alternately maximizing the metrics along two dimensions as depicted by the solid arrows.

By the very nature of lateen-alternation, the weights obtained at each iteration are likely to be best for the metric that was optimized in that iteration. Thus, one could use weights from the last k iterations (for lateen-tuning with as many metrics) and then decode the test set with an ensemble of these weights as in PMO ensemble. However in practice we find the weights to converge and we simply use the weights from the final iteration to decode the test set in our lateen experiments.

metric score is better.

4.3 Union of Metrics

At each iteration lateen MMO excludes all but one metric for optimization. An alternative would be to consider all the metrics at each iteration so that the optimizer could try to optimize them jointly. This has been the general motivation for considering the linear combination of metrics (Cer et al., 2010; Servan and Schwenk, 2011) resulting in a joint metric, which is then optimized.

However due to the scaling differences between the scores of different metrics, the linear combination might completely suppress the metric having scores in the lower-range. As an example, the RIBES scores that are typically in the high 0.7-0.8 range, dominate the BLEU scores that is typically around 0.3. While the weighted linear combination tries to address this imbalance, they introduce additional parameters that are manually fixed and not separately tuned.

We avoid this linear combination pitfall by taking the union of the metrics under which we consider the union of training examples from all metrics and optimize them jointly. Mathematically,

$$w^* = \arg\max_{w} \; g(M_1(H)) \cup \ldots \cup g(M_k(H)) \quad (4)$$

Most of the optimization approaches involve two phases: i) select positive and negative examples and ii) optimize parameters to favour positive examples while penalizing negative ones. In the *union* approach, we independently generate positive and negative sets of examples for all the metrics and take their union. The optimizer now seeks to move towards positive examples from all metrics, while penalizing others.

This is similar to the PMO-PRO approach except that here the optimizer tries to simultaneously maximize the number of high scoring points across all metrics. Thus, instead of the entire Pareto frontier curve in Figure 1, the union approach optimizes the two dimensions simultaneously in each iteration.

5 Ensemble Tuning

These methods, even though novel, under utilize the power of ensembles as they combine the solution only at the end of the tuning process. We would prefer to tightly integrate the idea of ensembles into the tuning. We thus extend the ensemble decoding to *ensemble tuning*. The feature weights are replicated separately for each evaluation metric, which are treated as components in the ensemble decoding and tuned independently in the optimization step. Initially the ensemble decoder decodes a devset using a weighted ensemble to produce a single N-best list. For the optimization, we employ a two-step approach of optimizing the feature weights (of each ensemble component) followed by a step for tuning the meta (component) weights. The optimized weights are then used for decoding the devset in the next iteration and the process is repeated for a fixed number of iterations.

Modifying the MMO representation in Equation 3, we formulate *ensemble tuning* as:

$$H_{ens} = \mathcal{N}_{ens}\Big(\mathbf{f}; \{w_M\}; \otimes; \boldsymbol{\lambda}\Big) \quad (5)$$

$$\mathbf{w}^* = \Big\{ \arg\max_{w_{M_i}} H_{ens} \mid {}_{1 \le i \le k} \Big\} \quad (6)$$

$$\boldsymbol{\lambda} = \arg\max_{\lambda} g\left(\{M_i(H_{ens})|_{1 \le i \le k}\}; \mathbf{w}^*\right) \quad (7)$$

Here the ensemble decoder function $\mathcal{N}_{ens}(.)$ is parameterized by an ensemble of weights $w_{M_1}, \ldots, w_{M_k}$ (denoted as $\{w_M\}$ in Eq 5) for each metric and a mixture operation ($\otimes$). $\boldsymbol{\lambda}$ represents the weights of the ensemble components.

Pseudo-code for ensemble tuning is shown in Algorithm 2. In the beginning of each iteration (line 2), the tuning process ensemble decodes (line 4) the tuning set using the weights obtained from the previous iteration. Equation 5 gives the detailed expression for the ensemble decoding, where H_{ens} denotes the N-best list generated by the ensemble decoder.

The method now uses a dual tuning strategy involving two phases to optimize the weights. In the first step it optimizes each of the k metrics independently (lines 6-7) along its respective dimension in

Algorithm 2 Ensemble Tuning Algorithm

1: **Input:** Tuning set $\mathbf{f}$,
  Metrics $M_1, \ldots, M_k$ (ensemble components)
  Initial weights $\{w_M\} \leftarrow w_{M_1}, \ldots w_{M_k}$ and
  Component (meta) weights $\boldsymbol{\lambda}$
2: **for** $j = 1, \ldots$ **do**
3:   $\{w_M^{(j)}\} \leftarrow \{w_M\}$
4:   *Ensemble* decode the tuning set
    $H_{ens} = \mathcal{N}_{ens}(\mathbf{f}; \{w_M^{(j)}\}; \otimes; \boldsymbol{\lambda})$
5:   $\{w_M\} = \{\}$
6:   **for** each metric $M_i \in \{M\}$ **do**
7:     $w^*_{M_i} \leftarrow$ PRO(H_{ens}, w_{M_i})   (use PRO)
8:     Add $w^*_{M_i}$ to $\{w_M\}$
9:   $\boldsymbol{\lambda} \leftarrow$ PMO-PRO($H_{ens}, \{w_M\}$)   (Alg 1)
10: **Output:** Optimal weights $\{w^M\}$ and $\boldsymbol{\lambda}$

the multi-metric space (as shown by the solid arrows along the two axes in Figure 1). This yields a new set of weights $\mathbf{w}^*$ for the features in each metric.

The second tuning step (line 9) then optimizes the meta weights ($\boldsymbol{\lambda}$) so as to maximize the multi-metric objective along the joint k-dimensional space as shown in Equation 7. This is illustrated by the dashed arrows in the Figure 1. While $g(.)$ could be any function that combines multiple metrics, we use the PMO-PRO algorithm (Alg. 1) for this step.

The main difference between *ensemble tuning* and *PMO ensemble* is that the former is an ensemble model over metrics and the latter is an ensemble model over Pareto solutions. Additionally, PMO ensemble uses the notion of ensembles only for the final decoding after tuning has completed.

5.1 Implementation Notes

All the proposed methods fit naturally within the usual SMT tuning framework. However, some changes are required in the decoder to support ensemble decoding and in the tuning scripts for optimizing with multiple metrics. For ensemble decoding, the decoder should be able to use multiple weight vectors and dynamically combine them according to some desired mixture operation. Note that, unlike Razmara et al. (2012), our approach uses just one model but has different weight vectors for each metric and the required decoder modifications are simpler than full ensemble decoding.

While any of the mixture operations proposed by Razmara et al. (2012) could be used, in this paper we use *log-wsum* – the linear combination of the ensemble components and *log-wmax* – the combination that prefers the locally best component. These are simpler to implement and also performed competitively in their domain adaptation experiments. Unless explicitly noted otherwise, the results presented in Section 6 are based on linear mixture operation log-wsum, which empirically performed better than the log-wmax for ensemble tuning.

6 Experiments

We evaluate the different methods on Arabic-English translation in single as well as multiple references scenario. Corpus statistics are shown in Table 1. For all the experiments in this paper, we use Kriya, our in-house Hierarchical phrase-based (Chiang, 2007) (Hiero) system, and integrated the required changes for ensemble decoding. Kriya performs comparably to the state of the art in phrase-based and hierarchical phrase-based translation over a wide variety of language pairs and data sets (Sankaran et al., 2012).

We use PRO (Hopkins and May, 2011) for optimizing the feature weights and PMO-PRO (Duh et al., 2012) for optimizing meta weights, wherever applicable. In both cases, we use SVM-Rank (Joachims, 2006) as the optimizer.

We used the default parameter settings for different MT tuning metrics. For METEOR, we tried both METEOR-tune and METEOR-hter settings and found the latter to perform better in BLEU and TER scores, even though the former was marginally better in METEOR[3] and RIBES scores. We observed the margin of loss in BLEU and TER to outweigh the gains in METEOR and RIBES and we chose METEOR-hter setting for both optimization and evaluation of all our experiments.

6.1 Evaluation on Tuning Set

Unlike conventional tuning methods, PMO (Duh et al., 2012) was originally evaluated on the tuning set to avoid potential mismatch with the test set. In order to ensure robustness of evaluation, they re-decode the devset using the optimal weights from the last tuning iteration and report the scores on 1-best candidates.

Corpus	Training size	Tuning/ test set
ISI corpus	1.1 M	1664/ 1313 (MTA)
		1982/ 987 (ISI)

Table 1: Corpus Statistics (# of sentences) for Arabic-English. MTA (4-refs) and ISI (1-ref).

We follow the same strategy and compare our PMO-ensemble approach with PMO-PRO (denoted P) and a linear combination[4] (denoted L) baseline. Similar to Duh et al. (2012), we use five different BLEU:RIBES weight settings, viz. $(0.0, 1.0)$, $(0.3, 0.7)$, $(0.5, 0.5)$, $(0.7, 0.3)$ and $(1.0, 0.0)$, marked L1 through L5 or P1 through P5. The Pareto frontier is then computed from 80 points (5 runs and 15 iterations per run) on the devset.

Figure 2(a) shows the Pareto frontier of L and P baselines using BLEU and RIBES as two metrics. The frontier of the P dominates that of L for most part showing that the PMO approach benefits from picking Pareto points during the optimization.

We use the PMO-ensemble approach to combine the optimized weights from the 5 tuning runs and re-decode the devset employing ensemble decoding. This yields the points *LEns* and *PEns* in the plot, which obtain better scores than most of the individual runs of L and P. This ensemble approach of combining the final weights also generalizes to the unseen test set as we show later.

Figure 2(b) plots the change in BLEU during tuning in the multiple references and the single reference scenarios. We show for each baseline method L and P, plots for two different weight settings that obtain high BLEU and RIBES scores. In both datasets, our ensemble tuning approach dominates the curves of the (L and P) baselines. In summary, these results confirm that the ensemble approach achieves results that are competitive with previous MMO methods on the devset Pareto curve. We now provide a more comprehensive evaluation on the test set.

6.2 Evaluation on Test Set

This section contains multi-metric optimization results on the unseen test sets, one test set has multiple references and the other has a single-reference.

[3]This behaviour was also noted by Denkowski and Lavie (2011) in their analysis of Urdu-English system for *tunable metrics* task in WMT11.

[4]Linear combination is a generalized version of the combined (TER-BLEU)/2 metric and its variants.

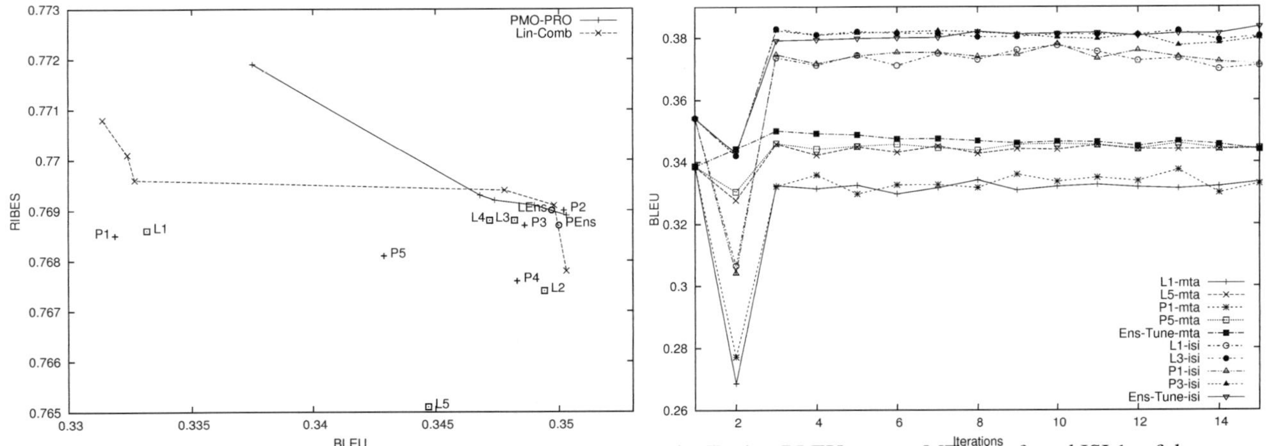

(a) Pareto frontier and BLEU-RIBES scores: MTA 4-refs devset (b) Tuning BLEU scores: MTA 4-refs and ISI 1-ref devsets

Figure 2: Devset (redecode): Comparison of Lin-comb (L) and PMO-PRO (P) with Ensemble decoding (Lens and PEns) and Ensemble tuning (Ens-Tune)

We plot BLEU scores against other metrics (RIBES, METEOR and TER) and this allows us to compare the performance of each metric relative to the de-facto standard BLEU metric.

Baseline points are identified by single letters B for BLEU, T for TER, etc. and the baseline (single-metric optimized) score for each metric is indicated by a dashed line on the corresponding axis. MMO points use a series of single letters referring to the metrics used, e.g. BT for BLEU-TER. The union of metrics method is identified with the suffix 'J' and lateen method with suffix 'L' (thus BT-L refers to the *lateen* tuning with BLEU-TER). MMO points without any suffix use the ensemble tuning approach.

Figures 3 and 4(a) plot the scores for the MTA test set with 4-references. We see noticeable and some statistically significant improvements in BLEU and RIBES (see Table 2 for BLEU improvements). All our MMO approaches, except for the union method, show gains on both BLEU and RIBES axes. Figures 3(b) and 4(a) show that none of the proposed methods managed to improve the baseline scores for METEOR and TER. However, several of our ensemble tuning combinations work well for both METEOR (BR, BMRTB3, etc.) and TER (BMRT and BRT) in that they improved or were close to the baseline scores in either dimension. We again see in these figures that the MMO approaches can improve the BLEU-only tuning by 0.3 BLEU points, without much drop in other metrics. This is in tune with the finding that BLEU could be tuned easily (Callison-Burch et al., 2011) and also explains why it remains a popular choice for optimizing SMT systems.

Approach and Tuning Metric(s)	BLEU	
	MTA	ISI
Single Objective Baselines		
BLEU	36.06	37.20
METEOR	35.05	36.91
RIBES	33.35	36.60
TER	33.92	35.85
Ensemble Tuning: 2 Metrics		
B-M	36.02	***37.26***
B-R	**36.15**	***37.37***
B-T	35.72	36.31
Ensemble Tuning: 3 Metrics		
B-M-R	***36.36***	***37.37***
B-M-T	**36.22**	36.89
B-R-T	35.97	36.72
Ensemble Tuning: >3 Metrics		
B-M-R-T	35.94	36.84
B-M-R-T-B3	***36.16***	**37.12**
B-M-R-T-B3-B2-B1	***36.08***	***37.24***

Table 2: BLEU Scores on MTA (4 refs) and ISI (1 ref) test sets using the standard *mteval* script. Boldface scores indicate scores that are comparable to or better than the baseline BLEU-only tuning. *Italicized* scores indicate statistically significant differences at p-value 0.05 computed with bootstrap significance test.

Among the different MMO methods the ensemble tuning performs better than lateen or union approaches. In terms of the number of metrics being optimized jointly, we see substantial gains when using a small number (typically 2 or 3) of metrics. Results seem to suffer beyond this number; probably because there might not be a space that contain solution(s) optimal for *all* the metrics that are jointly optimized.

We hypothesize that each metric correlates well

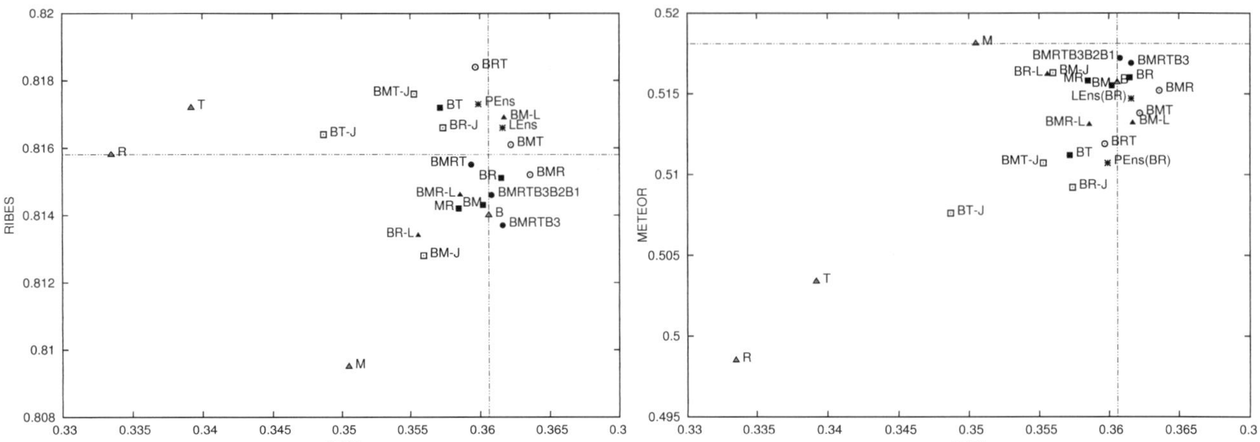

(a) BLEU-RIBES scores

(b) BLEU-METEOR scores

Figure 3: MTA 4-refs testset: Comparison of different MMO approaches. The dashed lines correspond to baseline scores tuned on the respective metrics in the axes. The union of metrics method is identified with the suffix J and lateen with suffix L.

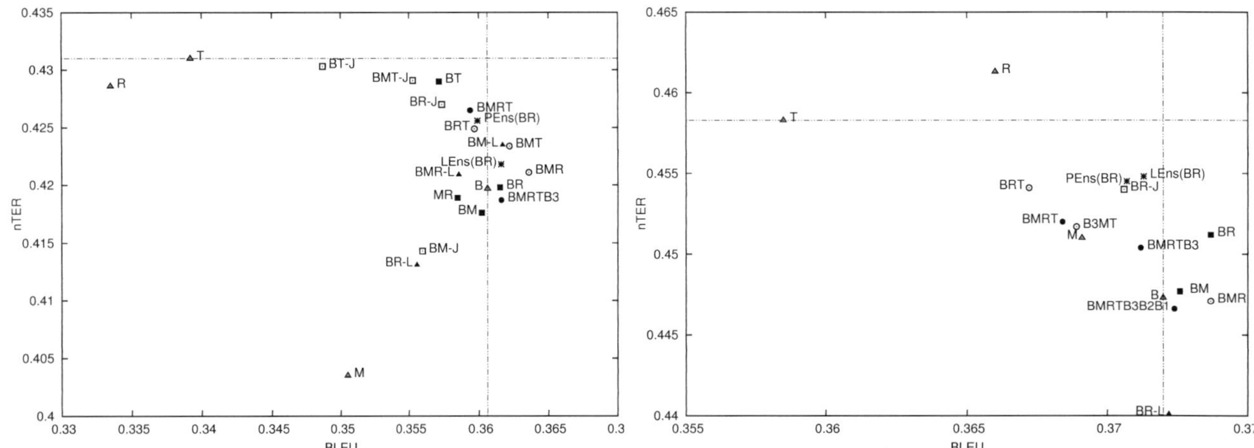

(a) MTA (4-refs)

(b) ISI (1-ref)

Figure 4: BLEU-TER scores: Comparison of different MMO approaches. We plot nTER (1-TER) scores for easy reading of the plots. The dashed lines correspond to baseline scores tuned on the respective metrics in the axes.

(in a looser sense) with few others, but not all. For example, union optimizations BR-J and BMT-J perform close to or better than RIBES and TER baselines, but get very poor score in METEOR. On the other hand BM-J is close to the METEOR baseline, while doing poorly on the RIBES and TER. This behaviour is also evident from the single-metric baselines, where R and T-only settings are clearly distinguished from the M-only system. It is not clear if such distinct classes of metrics could be bridged by some optimal solution and the *metric dichotomy* requires further study as this is key to practical multi-metric tuning in SMT.

The lateen and union approaches appear to be very sensitive to the number of metrics and they generally perform well for two metrics case and show degradation for more metrics. Unlike other approaches, the union approach failed to improve over the baseline BLEU and this could be attributed to the conflict of interest among the metrics, while choosing example points for the optimization step. The positive example preferred by a particular metric could be a negative example for the other metric. This would only confuse the optimizer resulting in poor solutions. Our future line of work would be to study the effect of avoiding such of conflicting examples in the union approach.

For the single-reference (ISI) dataset, we only plot the BLEU-TER case in Figure 4(b) due to lack of space. The results are similar to the multiple references set indicating that MMO approaches are equally effective for single references[5]. Table 2

[5]One could argue that MMO methods require multiple references since each metric might be picking out a different ref-

Metric	Single-metric Tuning		Ensemble Tuning
	B-only	M-only	B-M-R
BLEU	37.89	37.18	***39.01***
HBLEU	51.93	**53.59**	53.14
METEOR	61.31	61.56	**61.68**
HMETEOR	72.35	72.39	**72.74**
TER	0.520	0.532	***0.516***
HTER	0.361	0.370	**0.346**

Table 3: Post-editing Human Evaluation: Regular (untargeted) and human-targeted scores. Human targeted scores are computed against the post-edited reference and regular scores are computed with the original references. **Best** scores are in boldface and *statistically significant* ones (at $p = 0.05$) are italicized.

shows the BLEU scores for our ensemble tuning method (for various combinations) and we again see improvements over the baseline BLEU-only tuning.

6.3 Human Evaluation

So far we have shown that multi-metric optimization can improve over single-metric tuning on a single metric like BLEU and we have shown that our methods find a tuned model that performs well with respect to multiple metrics. Is the output that scores higher on multiple metrics actually a better translation? To verify this, we conducted a post-editing human evaluation experiment. We compared our ensemble tuning approach involving BLEU, METEOR and RIBES (B-M-R) with systems optimized for BLEU (B-only) and METEOR (M-only).

We selected 100 random sentences (that are at least 15 words long) from the Arabic-English MTA (4 references) test set and translated them using the three systems (two single metric systems and BMR ensemble tuning). We shuffled the resulting translations and split them into 3 sets such that each set has equal number of the translations from three systems. The translations were edited by three human annotators in a post-editing setup, where the goal was to edit the translations to make them as close to the references as possible, using the Post-Editing Tool: PET (Aziz et al., 2012). The annotators were not Arabic-literate and relied only on the reference translations during post-editing. The identifiers that link each translation to the system that generated it are removed to avoid annotator bias.

In the end we collated post-edited translations for each system and then computed the system-level human-targeted (HBLEU, HMETEOR, HTER) scores, by using respective post-edited translations as the reference. First comparing the HTER (Snover et al., 2006) scores shown in Table 3, we see that the single-metric system optimized for METEOR performs slightly worse than the one optimized for BLEU, despite using METEOR-hter version (Denkowski and Lavie, 2011). Ensemble tuning-based system optimized for three metrics (B-M-R) improves HTER by 4% and 6.3% over BLEU and METEOR optimized systems respectively.

The single-metric system tuned with M-only setting scores high on HBLEU, closely followed by the ensemble system. We believe this to be caused by chance rather than any systematic gains by the M-only tuning; the ensemble system scores high on HMETEOR compared to the M-only system. While HTER captures the edit distance to the targeted reference, HMETEOR and HBLEU metrics capture missing content words or synonyms by exploiting n-grams and paraphrase matching.

We also computed the regular variants (BLEU, METEOR and TER), which are scored against original references. The ensemble system outperformed the single-metric systems in all the three metrics. The improvements were also statistically significant at p-value of 0.05 for BLEU and TER.

7 Conclusion

We propose and present a comprehensive study of several multi-metric optimization (MMO) methods in SMT. First, by exploiting the idea of ensemble decoding (Razmara et al., 2012), we propose an effective way to combine multiple Pareto-optimal model weights from previous MMO methods (e.g. Duh et al. (2012)), obviating the need for manually trading off among metrics. We also proposed two new variants: lateen-style MMO and union of metrics.

We also extended ensemble decoding to a new tuning algorithm called *ensemble tuning*. This method demonstrates statistically significant gains for BLEU and RIBES with modest reduction in METEOR and TER. Further, in our human evaluation, ensemble tuning obtains the best HTER among competing baselines, confirming that optimizing on multiple metrics produces human-preferred translations compared to the conventional optimization approach involving a single metric.

erence sentence. Our experiment shows that even with a single reference MMO methods can work.

References

Michael Auli and Adam Lopez. 2011. Training a log-linear parser with loss functions via softmax-margin. In *Proceedings of the 2011 Conference on Empirical Methods in Natural Language Processing*, pages 333–343, Edinburgh, Scotland, UK., July. Association for Computational Linguistics.

Wilker Aziz, Sheila Castilho Monteiro de Sousa, and Lucia Specia. 2012. PET: a tool for post-editing and assessing machine translation. In *Proceedings of the Eight International Conference on Language Resources and Evaluation (LREC'12)*, Istanbul, Turkey, may. European Language Resources Association (ELRA).

Marzieh Bazrafshan, Tagyoung Chung, and Daniel Gildea. 2012. Tuning as linear regression. In *Proceedings of the 2012 Conference of the North American Chapter of the ACL: Human Language Technologies*, pages 543–547, Montréal, Canada. ACL.

Chris Callison-Burch, Philipp Koehn, Christof Monz, and Omar Zaidan. 2011. Findings of the 2011 workshop on statistical machine translation. In *Proceedings of the Sixth Workshop on Statistical Machine Translation*, pages 22–64, Edinburgh, Scotland, July. ACL.

Daniel Cer, Christopher D. Manning, and Daniel Jurafsky. 2010. The best lexical metric for phrase-based statistical mt system optimization. In *Human Language Technologies: The 2010 Annual Conference of the North American Chapter of the ACL*, pages 555–563. ACL.

Boxing Chen, Roland Kuhn, and Samuel Larkin. 2012. Port: a precision-order-recall mt evaluation metric for tuning. In *Proceedings of the 50th Annual Meeting of the ACL (Volume 1: Long Papers)*, pages 930–939, Jeju Island, Korea. ACL.

Colin Cherry and George Foster. 2012. Batch tuning strategies for statistical machine translation. In *Proceedings of the 2012 Conference of the North American Chapter of the ACL: Human Language Technologies*, pages 427–436, Montréal, Canada. ACL.

David Chiang, Yuval Marton, and Philip Resnik. 2008. Online large-margin training of syntactic and structural translation features. In *Proceedings of the Conference on Empirical Methods in Natural Language Processing*, pages 224–233. ACL.

David Chiang. 2007. Hierarchical phrase-based translation. *Computational Linguistics*, 33.

Michael Denkowski and Alon Lavie. 2011. Meteor 1.3: Automatic Metric for Reliable Optimization and Evaluation of Machine Translation Systems. In *Proceedings of the Sixth Workshop on Statistical Machine Translation*, Edinburgh, Scotland, July. ACL.

Jacob Devlin and Spyros Matsoukas. 2012. Trait-based hypothesis selection for machine translation. In *Proceedings of the 2012 Conference of the North American Chapter of the ACL: Human Language Technologies*, pages 528–532. ACL.

Kevin Duh, Katsuhito Sudoh, Xianchao Wu, Hajime Tsukada, and Masaaki Nagata. 2012. Learning to translate with multiple objectives. In *Proceedings of the 50th Annual Meeting of the ACL*, Jeju Island, Korea. ACL.

Chris Dyer, Hendra Setiawan, Yuval Marton, and Philip Resnik. 2009. The university of maryland statistical machine translation system for the fourth workshop on machine translation. In *Proc. of the Fourth Workshop on Machine Translation.*

Kevin Gimpel and Noah A. Smith. 2012. Structured ramp loss minimization for machine translation. In *Proceedings of the 2012 Conference of the North American Chapter of the ACL: Human Language Technologies*, pages 221–231, Montréal, Canada. ACL.

Keith Hall, Ryan T. McDonald, Jason Katz-Brown, and Michael Ringgaard. 2011. Training dependency parsers by jointly optimizing multiple objectives. In *Proceedings of the Empirical Methods in Natural Language Processing*, pages 1489–1499.

Xiaodong He and Li Deng. 2012. Maximum expected bleu training of phrase and lexicon translation models. In *Proceedings of the 50th Annual Meeting of the Association for Computational Linguistics (Volume 1: Long Papers)*, pages 292–301, Jeju Island, Korea. ACL.

Yifan He and Andy Way. 2009. Improving the objective function in minimum error rate training. In *MT Summit*.

Mark Hopkins and Jonathan May. 2011. Tuning as ranking. In *Proceedings of the 2011 Conference on Empirical Methods in Natural Language Processing*, Edinburgh, Scotland. ACL.

Hideki Isozaki, Tsutomu Hirao, Kevin Duh, Katsuhito Sudoh, and Hajime Tsukada. 2010. Automatic evaluation of translation quality for distant language pairs. In *Proceedings of the 2010 Conference on Empirical Methods in Natural Language Processing*, pages 944–952, Cambridge, MA. ACL.

Thorsten Joachims. 2006. Training linear svms in linear time. In *Proceedings of the 12th ACM SIGKDD international conference on Knowledge discovery and data mining*, pages 217–226.

Alon Lavie and Michael J. Denkowski. 2009. The meteor metric for automatic evaluation of machine translation. *Machine Translation*, 23(2-3):105–115.

Chang Liu, Daniel Dahlmeier, and Hwee Tou Ng. 2011. Better evaluation metrics lead to better machine translation. In *Proceedings of the Conference on Empirical Methods in Natural Language Processing*.

R. T. Marler and J. S. Arora. 2004. Survey of multi-objective optimization methods for engineering. *Structural and Multidisciplinary Optimization*, 26(6):369–395, April.

Arne Mauser, Saša Hasan, and Hermann Ney. 2008. Automatic evaluation measures for statistical machine translation system optimization. In *International Conference on Language Resources and Evaluation*, Marrakech, Morocco.

Franz Josef Och. 2003. Minimum error rate training in statistical machine translation. In *Proceedings of the 41st Annual Meeting of the ACL*, pages 160–167. ACL.

Sebastian Padó, Daniel Cer, Michel Galley, Dan Jurafsky, and Christopher D. Manning. 2009. Measuring machine translation quality as semantic equivalence: A metric based on entailment features. *Machine Translation*, 23(2-3):181–193.

Kishore Papineni, Salim Roukos, Todd Ward, and Wie-Jing Zhu. 2002. BLEU: a method for automatic evaluation of machine translation. In *Proceedings of Association of Computational Linguistics*, pages 311–318. ACL.

Majid Razmara, George Foster, Baskaran Sankaran, and Anoop Sarkar. 2012. Mixing multiple translation models in statistical machine translation. In *Proceedings of the 50th Annual Meeting of the ACL*, Jeju, Republic of Korea. ACL.

Baskaran Sankaran, Majid Razmara, and Anoop Sarkar. 2012. *Kriya* an end-to-end hierarchical phrase-based mt system. *The Prague Bulletin of Mathematical Linguistics (PBML)*, 97(97):83–98.

Christophe Servan and Holger Schwenk. 2011. Optimising multiple metrics with mert. *Prague Bull. Math. Linguistics*, 96:109–118.

Patrick Simianer, Stefan Riezler, and Chris Dyer. 2012. Joint feature selection in distributed stochastic learning for large-scale discriminative training in smt. In *Proceedings of the 50th Annual Meeting of the Association for Computational Linguistics (Volume 1: Long Papers)*, pages 11–21, Jeju Island, Korea. ACL.

Matthew Snover, Bonnie Dorr, Richard Schwartz, Linnea Micciulla, and John Makhoul. 2006. A study of translation edit rate with targeted human annotation. In *Proceedings of Association for Machine Translation in the Americas*, pages 223–231.

Valentin I. Spitkovsky, Hiyan Alshawi, and Daniel Jurafsky. 2011. Lateen EM: Unsupervised training with multiple objectives, applied to dependency grammar induction. In *Proceedings of the Empirical Methods in Natural Language Processing*, pages 1269–1280. Association of Computational Linguistics.

Taro Watanabe, Jun Suzuki, Hajime Tsukada, and Hideki Isozaki. 2007. Online large-margin training for statistical machine translation. In *Proceedings of the 2007 Joint Conference on Empirical Methods in Natural Language Processing and Computational Natural Language Learning (EMNLP-CoNLL)*, pages 764–773. ACL.

Taro Watanabe. 2012. Optimized online rank learning for machine translation. In *Proceedings of the 2012 Conference of the North American Chapter of the ACL: Human Language Technologies*, pages 253–262, Montréal, Canada, June. ACL.

Omar F. Zaidan. 2009. Z-MERT: A fully configurable open source tool for minimum error rate training of machine translation systems. *The Prague Bulletin of Mathematical Linguistics*, 91:79–88.

Daqi Zheng, Yifan He, Yang Liu, and Qun Liu. 2012. Maximum rank correlation training for statistical machine translation. In *MT Summit XIII*.

Grouping Language Model Boundary Words to Speed K–Best Extraction from Hypergraphs

Kenneth Heafield[*,†] **Philipp Koehn**[*] **Alon Lavie**[†]

[*] School of Informatics
University of Edinburgh
10 Crichton Street
Edinburgh EH8 9AB, UK
pkoehn@inf.ed.ac.uk

[†] Language Technologies Institute
Carnegie Mellon University
5000 Forbes Avenue
Pittsburgh, PA 15213, USA
{heafield,alavie}@cs.cmu.edu

Abstract

We propose a new algorithm to approximately extract top-scoring hypotheses from a hypergraph when the score includes an N–gram language model. In the popular cube pruning algorithm, every hypothesis is annotated with boundary words and permitted to recombine only if all boundary words are equal. However, many hypotheses share some, but not all, boundary words. We use these common boundary words to group hypotheses and do so recursively, resulting in a tree of hypotheses. This tree forms the basis for our new search algorithm that iteratively refines groups of boundary words on demand. Machine translation experiments show our algorithm makes translation 1.50 to 3.51 times as fast as with cube pruning in common cases.

1 Introduction

This work presents a new algorithm to search a packed data structure for high-scoring hypotheses when the score includes an N–gram language model. Many natural language processing systems have this sort of problem e.g. hypergraph search in hierarchical and syntactic machine translation (Mi et al., 2008; Klein and Manning, 2001), lattice rescoring in speech recognition, and confusion network decoding in optical character recognition (Tong and Evans, 1996). Large language models have been shown to improve quality, especially in machine translation (Brants et al., 2007; Koehn and Haddow, 2012). However, language models make search computationally expensive because they examine surface words without regard to the structure of the packed search space. Prior work, including cube pruning (Chiang, 2007), has largely treated the language model as a black box. Our new search algorithm groups hypotheses by common prefixes and suffixes, exploiting the tendency of the language model to score these hypotheses similarly. An example is shown in Figure 1. The result is a substantial improvement over the time-accuracy trade-off presented by cube pruning.

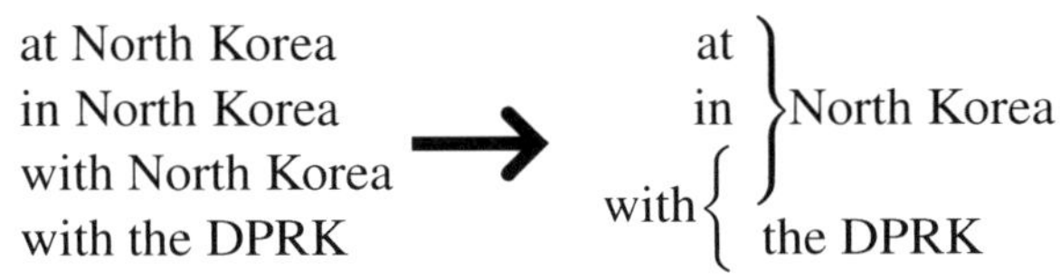

Figure 1: Hypotheses are grouped by common prefixes and suffixes.

The search spaces mentioned in the previous paragraph are special cases of a directed acyclic hypergraph. As used here, the difference from a normal graph is that an edge can go from one vertex to any number of vertices; this number is the *arity* of the edge. Lattices and confusion networks are hypergraphs in which every edge happens to have arity one. We experiment with parsing-based machine translation, where edges represent grammar rules that may have any number of non-terminals, including zero.

Hypotheses are paths in the hypergraph scored by a linear combination of features. Many features are *additive*: they can be expressed as weights on edges that sum to form hypothesis features. However, log probability from an N–gram language model is non-additive because it examines surface strings across edge and vertex boundaries. Non-additivity makes search difficult because locally optimal hypotheses may not be globally optimal.

In order to properly compute the language model score, each hypothesis is annotated with its boundary words, collectively referred to as its *state* (Li and Khudanpur, 2008). Hypotheses with equal state may be recombined, so a straightforward dynamic programming approach (Bar-Hillel et al., 1964) simply treats state as an additional dimension in the dynamic programming table. However, this approach quickly becomes intractable for large language models where the number of states is too large.

Beam search (Chiang, 2005; Lowerre, 1976) approximates the straightforward algorithm by remembering a *beam* of up to k hypotheses[1] in each vertex. It visits each vertex in bottom-up order, each time calling a *beam filling algorithm* to select k hypotheses. The parameter k is a time-accuracy trade-off: larger k increases both CPU time and accuracy.

We contribute a new beam filling algorithm that improves the time-accuracy trade-off over the popular cube pruning algorithm (Chiang, 2007) discussed in §2.3. The algorithm is based on the observation that competing hypotheses come from the same input, so their language model states are often similar. Grouping hypotheses by these similar words enables our algorithm to reason over multiple hypotheses at once. The algorithm is fully described in §3.

2 Related Work

2.1 Alternatives to Bottom-Up Search

Beam search visits each vertex in the hypergraph in bottom-up (topological) order. The hypergraph can also be searched in left-to-right order (Watanabe et al., 2006; Huang and Mi, 2010). Alternatively, hypotheses can be generated on demand with cube growing (Huang and Chiang, 2007), though we note that it showed little improvement in Moses (Xu and Koehn, 2012). All of these options are compatible with our algorithm. However, we only experiment with bottom-up beam search.

[1] We use K to denote the number of fully-formed hypotheses requested by the user and k to denote beam size.

2.2 Exhaustive Beam Filling

Originally, beam search was used with an exhaustive beam filling algorithm (Chiang, 2005). It generates every possible hypothesis (subject to the beams in previous vertices), selects the top k by score, and discards the remaining hypotheses. This is expensive: just one edge of arity a encodes $O(1 + a^k)$ hypotheses and each edge is evaluated exhaustively. In the worst case, our algorithm is exhaustive and generates the same number of hypotheses as beam search; in practice, we are concerned with the average case.

2.3 Baseline: Cube Pruning

Cube pruning (Chiang, 2007) is a fast approximate beam filling algorithm and our baseline. It chooses k hypotheses by popping them off the top of a priority queue. Initially, the queue is populated with hypotheses made from the best (highest-scoring) parts. These parts are an edge and a hypothesis from each vertex referenced by the edge. When a hypothesis is popped, several next-best alternatives are pushed. These alternatives substitute the next-best edge or a next-best hypothesis from one of the vertices.

Our work follows a similar pattern of popping one queue entry then pushing multiple entries. However, our queue entries are a group of hypotheses while cube pruning's entries are a single hypothesis.

Hypotheses are usually fully scored before being placed in the priority queue. An alternative prioritizes hypotheses by their *additive score*. The additive score is the edge's score plus the score of each component hypothesis, ignoring the non-additive aspect of the language model. When the additive score is used, the language model is only called k times, once for each hypothesis popped from the queue.

Cube pruning can produce duplicate queue entries. Gesmundo and Henderson (2010) modified the algorithm prevent duplicates instead of using a hash table. We include their work in the experiments.

Hopkins and Langmead (2009) characterized cube pruning as A* search (Hart et al., 1968) with an inadmissible heuristic. Their analysis showed deep and unbalanced search trees. Our work can be interpreted as a partial rebalancing of these search trees.

2.4 Exact Algorithms

A number of exact search algorithms have been developed. We are not aware of an exact algorithm that tractably scales to the size of hypergraphs and language models used in many modern machine translation systems (Callison-Burch et al., 2012).

The hypergraph and language model can be compiled into an integer linear program. The best hypothesis can then be recovered by taking the dual and solving by Lagrangian relaxation (Rush and Collins, 2011). However, that work only dealt with language models up to order three.

Iglesias et al. (2011) represent the search space as a recursive transition network and the language model as a weighted finite state transducer. Using standard finite state algorithms, they intersect the two automatons then exactly search for the highest-scoring paths. However, the intersected automaton is too large. The authors suggested removing low probability entries from the language model, but this form of pruning negatively impacts translation quality (Moore and Quirk, 2009; Chelba et al., 2010). Their work bears some similarity to our algorithm in that partially overlapping state will be collapsed and efficiently handled together. However, the key advatage to our approach is that groups have a score that can be used for pruning *before* the group is expanded, enabling pruning without first constructing the intersected automaton.

2.5 Coarse-to-Fine

Coarse-to-fine (Petrov et al., 2008) performs multiple pruning passes, each time with more detail. Search is a subroutine of coarse-to-fine and our work is inside search, so the two are compatible. There are several forms of coarse-to-fine search; the closest to our work increases the language model order each iteration. However, by operating inside search, our algorithm is able to handle hypotheses at different levels of refinement and use scores to choose where to further refine hypotheses. Coarse-to-fine decoding cannot do this because it determines the level of refinement before calling search.

3 Our New Beam Filling Algorithm

In our algorithm, the primary idea is to group hypotheses with similar language model state. The following sections formalize what these groups are (partial state), that the groups have a recursive structure (state tree), how groups are split (bread crumbs), using groups with hypergraph edges (partial edge), prioritizing search (scoring) and best-first search (priority queue).

3.1 Partial State

An N–gram language model (with order N) computes the probability of a word given the $N-1$ preceding words. The left state of a hypothesis is the first $N-1$ words, which have insufficient context to be scored. Right state is the last $N-1$ words; these might become context for another hypothesis. Collectively, they are known as *state*. State minimization (Li and Khudanpur, 2008) may reduce the size of state due to backoff in the language model.

For example, the hypothesis "the few nations that have diplomatic relations with North Korea" might have left state "the few" and right state "Korea" after state minimization determined that "North" could be elided. Collectively, the state is denoted (the few $\dashv \diamond \vdash$ Korea). The diamond $\diamond$ is a stand-in for elided words. Terminators $\dashv$ and $\vdash$ indicate when left and right state are exhausted, respectively[2].

Our algorithm is based on *partial state*. Partial state is simply state with more inner words elided. For example, (the $\diamond$ Korea) is a partial state for (the few $\dashv \diamond \vdash$ Korea). Terminators $\dashv$ and $\vdash$ can be elided just like words. Empty state is denoted using the customary symbol for empty string, ϵ. For example, ($\epsilon \diamond \epsilon$) is the empty partial state. The terminators serve to distinguish a completed state (which may be short due to state minimization) from an incomplete partial state.

3.2 State Tree

States (the few $\dashv \diamond \vdash$ Korea) and (the $\dashv \diamond \vdash$ Korea) have words in common, so the partial state (the $\diamond$ Korea) can be used to reason over both of them. Generalizing this notion to the set of hypotheses in a beam, we build a *state tree*. The root of the tree is the empty partial state ($\epsilon \diamond \epsilon$) that reasons

[2] A corner case arises for hypotheses with less than $N-1$ words. For these hypotheses, we still attempt state minimization and, if successful, the state is treated normally. If state minimization fails, a flag is set in the state. For purposes of the state tree, the flag acts like a different terminator symbol.

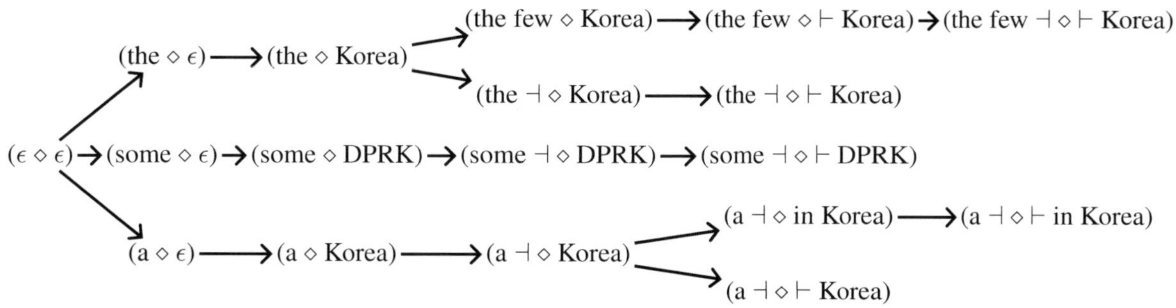

Figure 2: A state tree containing five states: (the few ⊣ ◇ ⊢ Korea), (the ⊣ ◇ ⊢ Korea), (some ⊣ ◇ ⊢ DPRK), (a ⊣ ◇ ⊢ in Korea), and (a ⊣ ◇ ⊢ Korea). Nodes of the tree are partial states. The branching order is the first word, the last word, the second word, and so on. If the left or right state is exhausted, then branching continues with the remaining state. For purposes of branching, termination symbols ⊣ and ⊢ act like normal words.

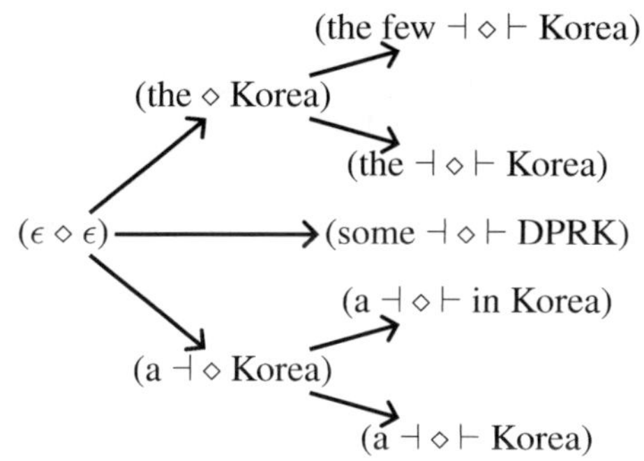

Figure 3: The optimized version of Figure 2. Nodes immediately reveal the longest shared prefix and suffix among hypotheses below them.

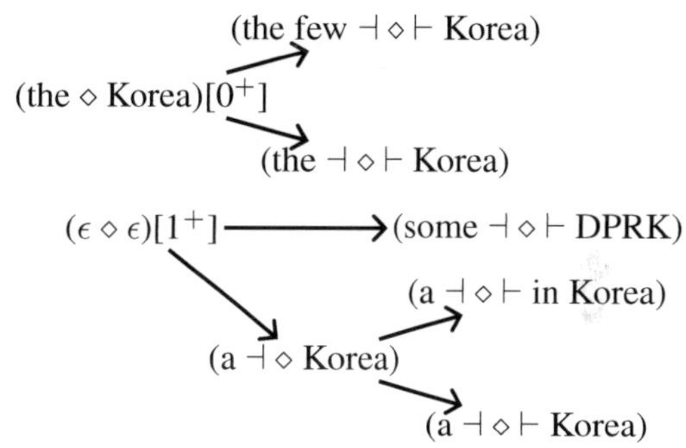

Figure 4: Visiting the root node partitions the tree into best child (the ◇ Korea)$[0^+]$ and bread crumb $(\epsilon \diamond \epsilon)[1^+]$. The data structure remains intact for use elsewhere.

over all hypotheses. From the root, the tree branches by the first word of state, the last word, the second word, the second-to-last word, and so on. If left or right state is exhausted, then branching continues using the remaining state. The branching order prioritizes the outermost words because these can be used to update the language model probability. The decision to start with left state is arbitrary. An example tree is shown in Figure 2.

As an optimization, each node determines the longest shared prefix and suffix of the hypotheses below it. The node reports these words immediately, rendering some other nodes redundant. This makes our algorithm faster because it will then only encounter nodes when there is a branching decision to be made. The original tree is shown in Figure 2 and the optimized version is shown in Figure 3. As a side effect of branching by left state first, the algorithm did not notice that states (the ◇ Korea) and (a ⊣ ◇ Korea) both end with Korea. We designed the tree building algorithm for speed and plan to experiment with alternatives as future work.

The state tree is built lazily. A node initially holds a flat array of all the hypotheses below it. When its children are first needed, the hypotheses are grouped by the branching word and an array of child nodes is built. In turn, these newly created children each initially hold an array of hypotheses. CPU time is saved because nodes containing low-scoring nodes may never construct their children.

Each node has a score. For leaves, this score is copied from the underlying hypothesis (or best hypothesis if some other feature prevented recombination). The score of an internal node is the maximum score of its children. As an example, the root node's score is the same as the highest-scoring hypothesis in the tree. Children are sorted by score.

3.3 Bread Crumbs

The state tree is explored in a best-first manner. Specifically, when the algorithm visits a node, it considers that node's best child. The best child reveals more words, so the score may go up or down when the language model is consulted. Therefore, simply following best children may lead to a poor hypothesis. Some backtracking mechanism is required, for which we use bread crumbs. Visiting a node results in two items: the best child and a bread crumb. The bread crumb encodes the node that was visited and how many children have already been considered. Figure 4 shows an example.

More formally, each node has an array of children sorted by score, so it suffices for the bread crumb to keep an index in this array. An index of zero denotes that no child has been visited. Continuing the example from Figure 3, $(\epsilon \diamond \epsilon)[0^+]$ denotes the root partial state with children starting at index 0 (i.e. all of them). Visiting $(\epsilon \diamond \epsilon)[0^+]$ yields best child (the $\diamond$ Korea)$[0^+]$ and bread crumb $(\epsilon \diamond \epsilon)[1^+]$. Later, the search algorithm may return to $(\epsilon \diamond \epsilon)[1^+]$, yielding best child (some $\dashv \diamond \vdash$ DPRK)$[0^+]$ and bread crumb $(\epsilon \diamond \epsilon)[2^+]$. If there is no remaining sibling, visiting yields only the best child.

The index serves to restrict the array of children to those with that index or above. Formally, let d map from a node or bread crumb to the set of leaves descended from it. The descendants of a node n are those of its children

$$d(n) = \bigsqcup_{i=0}^{|n|-1} d(n[i])$$

where $\sqcup$ takes the union of disjoint sets and $n[i]$ is the ith child. In a bread crumb with index c, only descendents by the remaining children are considered

$$d(n[c^+]) = \bigsqcup_{i=c}^{|n|-1} d(n[i])$$

It follows that the set of descendants is *partitioned* into two disjoint sets

$$d(n[c^+]) = d(n[c]) \bigsqcup d(n[c+1^+])$$

3.4 Partial Edge

The beam filling algorithm is tasked with selecting hypotheses given a number of hypergraph edges. Hypergraph edges are strings comprised of words and references to vertices (in parsing, terminals and non-terminals). A hypergraph edge is converted to a *partial edge* by replacing each vertex reference with the root node from that vertex. For example, the hypergraph edge "is v ." referencing vertex v becomes partial edge "is $(\epsilon \diamond \epsilon)[0^+]$."

Partial edges allow our algorithm to reason over a large set of hypotheses at once. Visiting a partial edge divides that set into two as follows. A heuristic chooses one of the non-leaf nodes to visit. Currently, this heuristic picks the node with the fewest words revealed. As a tie breaker, it chooses the leftmost node. The chosen node is visited (partitioned), yielding the best child and bread crumb as described in the previous section. These are substituted into separate copies of the partial edge. Continuing our example with the vertex shown in Figure 3, "is $(\epsilon \diamond \epsilon)[0^+]$." partitions into "is (the $\diamond$ Korea)$[0^+]$." and "is $(\epsilon \diamond \epsilon)[1^+]$."

3.5 Scoring

Every partial edge has a score that determines its search priority. Initially, this score is the sum of the edge's score and the scores of each bread crumb (defined below). As words are revealed, the score is updated to account for new language model context.

Each edge score includes a log language model probability and possibly additive features. Whenever there is insufficient context to compute the language model probability of a word, an estimate r is used. For example, edge "is v ." incorporates estimate

$$\log r(\text{is}) r(.)$$

into its score. The same applies to hypotheses: (the few $\dashv \diamond \vdash$ Korea) includes estimate

$$\log r(\text{the}) r(\text{few} \mid \text{the})$$

because the words in left state are those with insufficient context.

In common practice (Chiang, 2007; Hoang et al., 2009; Dyer et al., 2010), the estimate is taken from the language model: $r = p$. However, querying the language model with incomplete context leads

Kneser-Ney smoothing (Kneser and Ney, 1995) to assume that backoff has occurred. An alternative is to use average-case rest costs explicitly stored in the language model (Heafield et al., 2012). Both options are used in the experiments[3].

The score of a bread crumb is the maximum score of its descendants as defined in §3.3. For example, the bread crumb $(\epsilon \diamond \epsilon)[1^+]$ has a lower score than $(\epsilon \diamond \epsilon)[0^+]$ because the best child (the $\diamond$ Korea)$[0^+]$ and its descendants no longer contribute to the maximum.

The score of partial edge "is $(\epsilon \diamond \epsilon)[0^+]$." is the sum of scores from its two parts: edge "is v ." and bread crumb $(\epsilon \diamond \epsilon)[0^+]$. The edge's score includes estimated log probability $\log r(\text{is})r(.)$ as explained earlier. The bread crumb's score comes from its highest-scoring descendent (the few $\dashv \diamond \vdash$ Korea) and therefore includes estimate $\log r(\text{the})r(\text{few} \mid \text{the})$.

Estimates are updated as words are revealed. Continuing the example, "is $(\epsilon \diamond \epsilon)[0^+]$." has best child "is (the $\diamond$ Korea)$[0^+]$." In this best child, the estimate $r(.)$ is updated to $r(. \mid \text{Korea})$. Similarly, $r(\text{the})$ is replaced with $r(\text{the} \mid \text{is})$. Updates examine only words that have been revealed: $r(\text{few} \mid \text{the})$ remains unrevised.

Updates are computed efficiently by using pointers (Heafield et al., 2011) with KenLM. To summarize, the language model computes

$$\frac{r(w_n|w_1^{n-1})}{r(w_n|w_i^{n-1})}$$

in a single call. In the popular reverse trie data structure, the language model visits w_i^n while retrieving w_1^n, so the cost is the same as a single query. Moreover, when the language model earlier provided estimate $r(w_n|w_i^{n-1})$, it also returned a data-structure pointer $t(w_i^n)$. Pointers are retained in hypotheses, edges, and partial edges for each word with an estimated probability. When context is revealed, our algorithm queries the language model with new context w_1^{i-1} and pointer $t(w_i^n)$. The language model uses this pointer to immediately retrieve denominator $r(w_n|w_i^{n-1})$ and as a starting point to retrieve numerator $r(w_n|w_1^{n-1})$. It can therefore avoid looking up $r(w_n), r(w_n|w_{n-1}), \ldots, r(w_n|w_{i+1}^{n-1})$ as would normally be required with a reverse trie.

3.6 Priority Queue

Our beam filling algorithm is controlled by a priority queue containing partial edges. The queue is populated by converting all outgoing hypergraph edges into partial edges and pushing them onto the queue. After this initialization, the algorithm loops. Each iteration begins by popping the top-scoring partial edge off the queue. If all nodes are leaves, then the partial edge is converted to a hypothesis and placed in the beam. Otherwise, the partial edge is partitioned as described in §3.3. The two resulting partial edges are pushed onto the queue. Looping continues with the next iteration until the queue is empty or the beam is full. After the loop terminates, the beam is given to the root node of the state tree; other nodes will be built lazily as described in §3.2.

Overall, the algorithm visits hypergraph vertices in bottom-up order. Our beam filling algorithm runs in each vertex, making use of state trees in vertices below. The top of the tree contains full hypotheses. If a K-best list is desired, packing and extraction works the same way as with cube pruning.

4 Experiments

Performance is measured by translating the 3003-sentence German-English test set from the 2011 Workshop on Machine Translation (Callison-Burch et al., 2011). Two translation models were built, one hierarchical (Chiang, 2007) and one with target syntax. The target-syntax system is based on English parses from the Collins (1999) parser. Both were trained on Europarl (Koehn, 2005). The language model interpolates models built on Europarl, news commentary, and news data provided by the evaluation. Interpolation weights were tuned on the 2010 test set. Language models were built with SRILM (Stolcke, 2002), modified Kneser-Ney smoothing (Kneser and Ney, 1995; Chen and Goodman, 1998), default pruning, and order 5. Feature weights were tuned with MERT (Och, 2003), beam size 1000, 100-best output, and cube pruning. Systems were built with the Moses (Hoang et al., 2009) pipeline.

Measurements were collected by running the decoder on all 3003 sentences. For consistency, all

[3]We also tested upper bounds (Huang et al., 2012; Carter et al., 2012) but the result is still approximate due to beam pruning and initial experiments showed degraded performance.

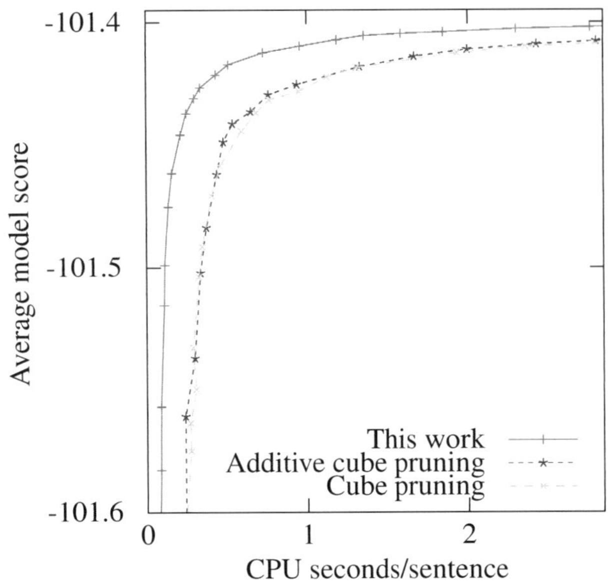

Figure 5: Hierarchial system in Moses with our algorithm, cube pruning with additive scores, and cube pruning with full scores (§2.3). The two baselines overlap.

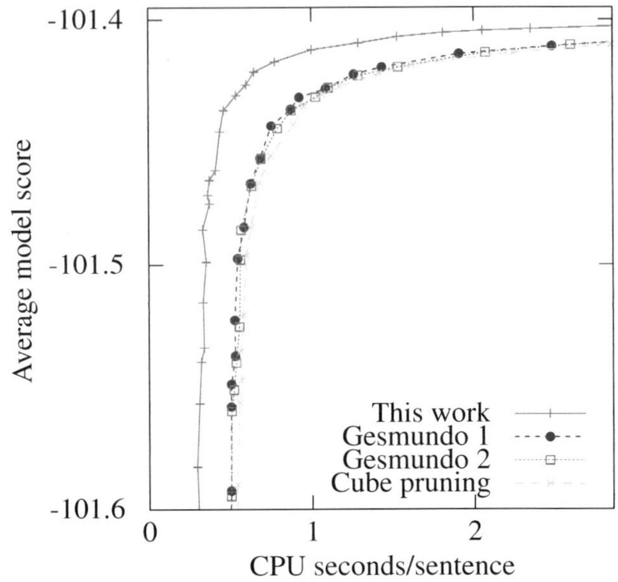

Figure 6: Hierarchical system in cdec with our algorithm, similarly-performing variants of cube pruning defined in Gesmundo and Henderson (2010), and the default.

relevant files were forced into the operating system disk cache before each run. CPU time is the total user and system time taken by the decoder minus loading time. Loading time was measured by running the decoder with empty input. In particular, CPU time includes the cost of parsing. Our test system has 32 cores and 64 GB of RAM; no run came close to running out of memory. While multi-threaded experiments showed improvements as well, we only report single-threaded results to reduce noise and to compare with cdec (Dyer et al., 2010). Decoders were compiled with the optimization settings suggested in their documentation.

Search accuracy is measured by average model score; higher is better. Only relative comparisons are meaningful because model scores have arbitrary scale and include constant factors. Beam sizes start at 5 and rise until a time limit determined by running the slowest algorithm with beam size 1000.

4.1 Comparison Inside Moses

Figure 5 shows Moses performance with this work and with cube pruning. These results used the hierarchical system with common-practice estimates (§3.5). The two cube pruning variants are explained in §2.3. Briefly, the queue can be prioritized using additive or full scores. Performance with additive scores is roughly the same as using full scores with half the beam size.

Our algorithm is faster for every beam size tested. It is also more accurate than additive cube pruning with the same beam size. However, when compared with full scores cube pruning, it is less accurate for beam sizes below 300. This makes sense because our algorithm starts with additive estimates and iteratively refines them by calling the language model. Moreover, when beams are small, there are fewer chances to group hypotheses. With beams larger than 300, our algorithm can group more hypotheses, overtaking both forms of cube pruning.

Accuracy improvements can be interpreted as speed improvements by asking how much time each algorithm takes to achieve a set level of accuracy. By this metric, our algorithm is 2.04 to 3.37 times as fast as both baselines.

4.2 Comparison Inside cdec

We also implemented our algorithm in cdec (Dyer et al., 2010). Figure 6 compares with two enhanced versions of cube pruning (Gesmundo and Henderson, 2010) and the cdec baseline. The model scores

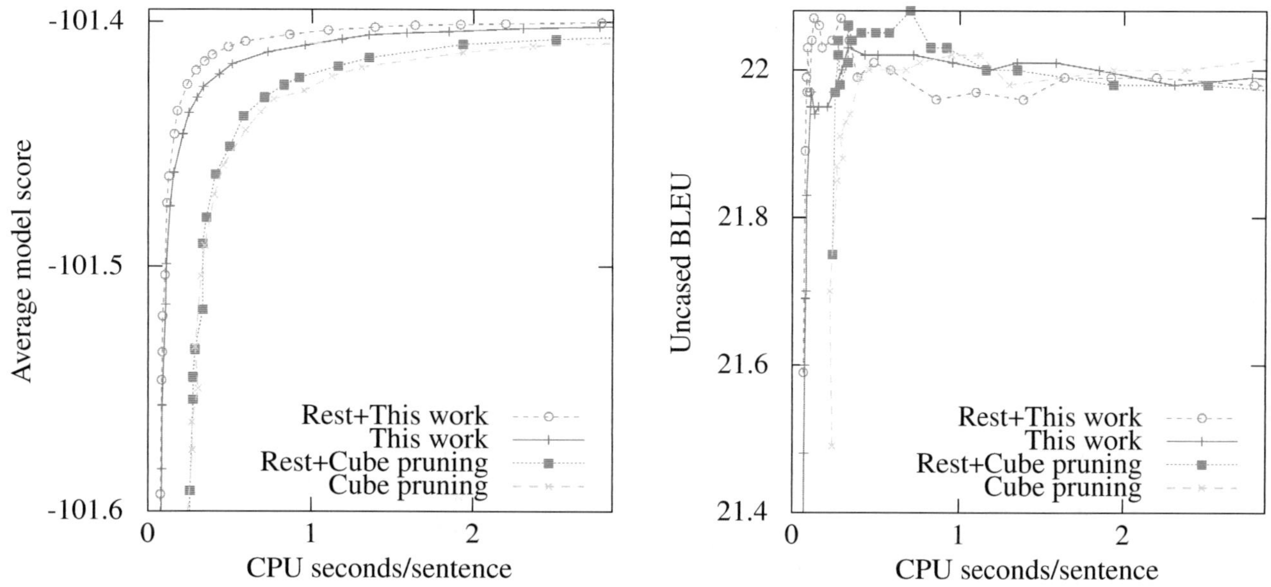

Figure 7: Effect of rest costs on our algorithm and on cube pruning in Moses. Noisy BLEU scores reflect model errors.

are comparable with Moses[4].

Measuring at equal accuracy, our algorithm makes cdec 1.56 to 2.24 times as fast as the best baseline. At first, this seems to suggest that cdec is faster. In fact, the opposite is true: comparing Figures 5 and 6 reveals that cdec has a higher parsing cost than Moses[5], thereby biasing the speed ratio towards 1. In subsequent experiments, we use Moses because it more accurately reflects search costs.

4.3 Average-Case Rest Costs

Previous experiments used the common-practice probability estimate described in §3.5. Figure 7 shows the impact of average-case rest costs on our algorithm and on cube pruning in Moses. We also looked at uncased BLEU (Papineni et al., 2002) scores, finding that our algorithm attains near-peak BLEU in less time. The relationship between model score and BLEU is noisy due to model errors.

Average-case rest costs impact our algorithm more than they impact cube pruning. For small beam sizes, our algorithm becomes more accurate, mostly eliminating the disadvantage reported in §4.1. Compared to the common-practice estimate with beam size 1000, rest costs made our algorithm 1.62 times as fast and cube pruning 1.22 times as fast.

Table 1 compares our best result with the best baseline: our algorithm and cube pruning, both with rest costs inside Moses. In this scenario, our algorithm is 2.59 to 3.51 times as fast as cube pruning.

4.4 Target-Syntax

We took the best baseline and best result from previous experiments (Moses with rest costs) and ran the target-syntax system. Results are shown in Figure 8. Parsing and search are far more expensive. For beam size 5, our algorithm attains equivalent accuracy 1.16 times as fast. Above 5, our algorithm is 1.50 to 2.00 times as fast as cube pruning. Moreover, our algorithm took less time with beam size 6900 than cube pruning took with beam size 1000.

A small bump in model score occurs around 15 seconds. This is due to translating "durchzogenen" as "criss-crossed" instead of passing it through, which incurs a severe penalty (-100). The only rule capable of doing so translates "X durchzogenen" as "criss-crossed *PP*"; a direct translation rule was not

[4]The glue rule builds hypotheses left-to-right. In Moses, glued hypotheses start with <s> and thus have empty left state. In cdec, sentence boundary tokens are normally added last, so intermediate hypotheses have spurious left state. Running cdec with the Moses glue rule led to improved time-accuracy performance. The improved version is used in all results reported. We accounted for constant-factor differences in feature definition i.e. whether <s> is part of the word count.

[5]In-memory phrase tables were used with both decoders. The on-disk phrase table makes Moses slower than cdec.

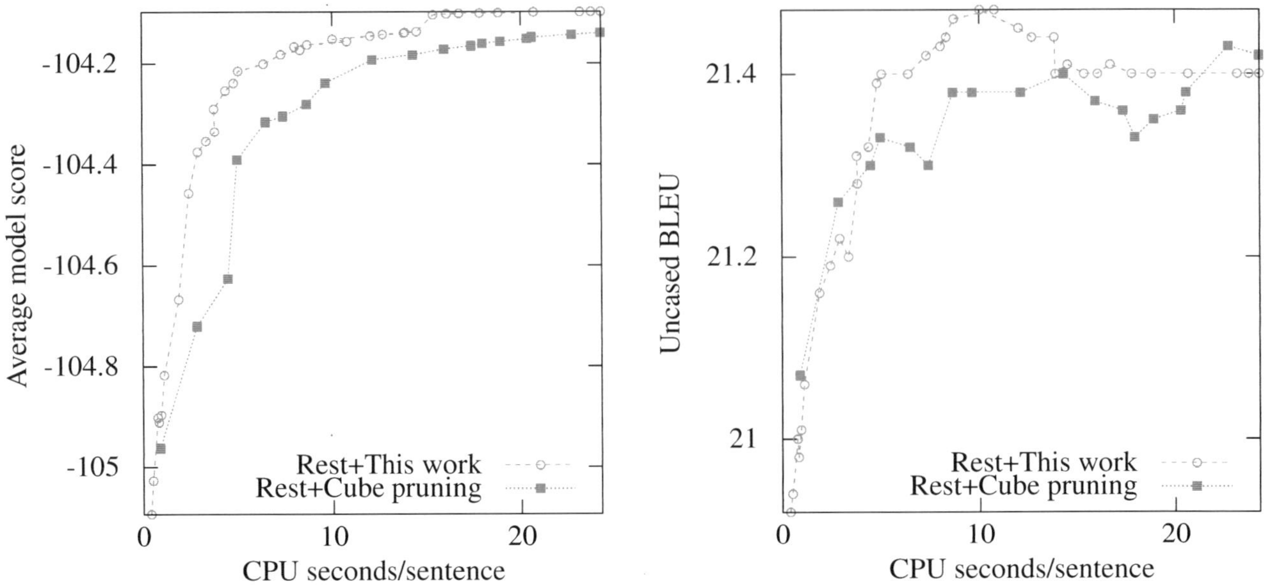

Figure 8: Performance of Moses with the target-syntax system.

extracted due to reordering. An appropriate prepositional phrase (PP) was pruned with smaller beam sizes because it is disfluent.

4.5 Memory

Peak virtual memory usage was measured before each process terminated. Compared with cube pruning at a beam size of 1000, our algorithm uses 160 MB more RAM in Moses and 298 MB less RAM in cdec. The differences are smaller with lower beam sizes and minor relative to 12-13 GB total size, most of which is the phrase table and language model.

	Rest+This work			Rest+Cube pruning		
k	CPU	Model	BLEU	CPU	Model	BLEU
5	0.068	-1.698	21.59	0.243	-1.667	21.75
10	0.076	-1.593	21.89	0.255	-1.592	21.97
50	0.125	-1.463	22.07	0.353	-1.480	22.04
75	0.157	-1.446	22.06	0.408	-1.462	22.05
100	0.176	-1.436	22.03	0.496	-1.451	22.05
500	0.589	-1.408	22.00	1.356	-1.415	22.00
750	0.861	-1.405	21.96	1.937	-1.409	21.98
1000	1.099	-1.403	21.97	2.502	-1.407	21.98

Table 1: Numerical results from the hierarchical system for select beam sizes k comparing our best result with the best baseline, both in Moses with rest costs enabled. To conserve space, model scores are shown with 100 added.

5 Conclusion

We have described a new search algorithm that achieves equivalent accuracy 1.16 to 3.51 times as fast as cube pruning, including two implementations and four variants. The algorithm is based on grouping similar language model feature states together and dynamically expanding these groups. In doing so, it exploits the language model's ability to estimate with incomplete information. Our implementation is available under the LGPL as a standalone from `http://kheafield.com/code/` and distributed with Moses and cdec.

Acknowledgements

This research work was supported in part by the National Science Foundation under grant IIS-0713402, by a NPRP grant (NPRP 09-1140-1-177) from the Qatar National Research Fund (a member of the Qatar Foundation), and by computing resources provided by the NSF-sponsored XSEDE program under grant TG-CCR110017. The statements made herein are solely the responsibility of the authors. The research leading to these results has received funding from the European Union Seventh Framework Programme (FP7/2007-2013) under grant agreements 287576 (CASMACAT), 287658 (EU BRIDGE), 287688 (MateCat), and 288769 (ACCEPT).

References

Yehoshua Bar-Hillel, Micha Perles, and Eli Shamir. 1964. *On Formal Properties of Simple Phrase Structure Grammars*. Hebrew University Students' Press.

Thorsten Brants, Ashok C. Popat, Peng Xu, Franz J. Och, and Jeffrey Dean. 2007. Large language models in machine translation. In *Proceedings of the 2007 Joint Conference on Empirical Methods in Natural Language Processing and Computational Language Learning*, pages 858–867, June.

Chris Callison-Burch, Philipp Koehn, Christof Monz, and Omar Zaidan. 2011. Findings of the 2011 workshop on statistical machine translation. In *Proceedings of the Sixth Workshop on Statistical Machine Translation*, pages 22–64, Edinburgh, Scotland, July. Association for Computational Linguistics.

Chris Callison-Burch, Philipp Koehn, Christof Monz, Matt Post, Radu Soricut, and Lucia Specia. 2012. Findings of the 2012 workshop on statistical machine translation. In *Proceedings of the Seventh Workshop on Statistical Machine Translation*, pages 10–51, Montréal, Canada, June. Association for Computational Linguistics.

Simon Carter, Marc Dymetman, and Guillaume Bouchard. 2012. Exact sampling and decoding in high-order hidden Markov models. In *Proceedings of the 2012 Joint Conference on Empirical Methods in Natural Language Processing and Computational Natural Language Learning*, pages 1125–1134, Jeju Island, Korea, July.

Ciprian Chelba, Thorsten Brants, Will Neveitt, and Peng Xu. 2010. Study on interaction between entropy pruning and Kneser-Ney smoothing. In *Proceedings of Interspeech*, pages 2242–2245.

Stanley Chen and Joshua Goodman. 1998. An empirical study of smoothing techniques for language modeling. Technical Report TR-10-98, Harvard University, August.

David Chiang. 2005. A hierarchical phrase-based model for statistical machine translation. In *Proceedings of the 43rd Annual Meeting on Association for Computational Linguistics*, pages 263–270, Ann Arbor, Michigan, June.

David Chiang. 2007. Hierarchical phrase-based translation. *Computational Linguistics*, 33:201–228, June.

Michael Collins. 1999. *Head-Driven Statistical Models for Natural Language Parsing*. Ph.D. thesis, University of Pennsylvania.

Chris Dyer, Adam Lopez, Juri Ganitkevitch, Johnathan Weese, Ferhan Ture, Phil Blunsom, Hendra Setiawan, Vladimir Eidelman, and Philip Resnik. 2010. cdec: A decoder, alignment, and learning framework for finite-state and context-free translation models. In *Proceedings of the ACL 2010 System Demonstrations*, ACLDemos '10, pages 7–12.

Andrea Gesmundo and James Henderson. 2010. Faster cube pruning. In *Proceedings of the International Workshop on Spoken Language Translation (IWSLT)*, pages 267–274.

Peter Hart, Nils Nilsson, and Bertram Raphael. 1968. A formal basis for the heuristic determination of minimum cost paths. *IEEE Transactions on Systems Science and Cybernetics*, 4(2):100–107, July.

Kenneth Heafield, Hieu Hoang, Philipp Koehn, Tetsuo Kiso, and Marcello Federico. 2011. Left language model state for syntactic machine translation. In *Proceedings of the International Workshop on Spoken Language Translation*, San Francisco, CA, USA, December.

Kenneth Heafield, Philipp Koehn, and Alon Lavie. 2012. Language model rest costs and space-efficient storage. In *Proceedings of the 2012 Joint Conference on Empirical Methods in Natural Language Processing and Computational Natural Language Learning*, Jeju Island, Korea.

Hieu Hoang, Philipp Koehn, and Adam Lopez. 2009. A unified framework for phrase-based, hierarchical, and syntax-based statistical machine translation. In *Proceedings of the International Workshop on Spoken Language Translation*, pages 152–159, Tokyo, Japan.

Mark Hopkins and Greg Langmead. 2009. Cube pruning as heuristic search. In *Proceedings of the 2009 Conference on Empirical Methods in Natural Language Processing*, pages 62–71, Singapore, August.

Liang Huang and David Chiang. 2007. Forest rescoring: Faster decoding with integrated language models. In *Proceedings of the 45th Annual Meeting of the Association for Computational Linguistics*, Prague, Czech Republic.

Liang Huang and Haitao Mi. 2010. Efficient incremental decoding for tree-to-string translation. In *Proceedings of the 2010 Conference on Empirical Methods in Natural Language Processing*, pages 273–283, Cambridge, MA, October.

Zhiheng Huang, Yi Chang, Bo Long, Jean-Francois Crespo, Anlei Dong, Sathiya Keerthi, and Su-Lin Wu. 2012. Iterative Viterbi A* algorithm for k-best sequential decoding. In *Proceedings of the 2012 Joint Conference on Empirical Methods in Natural Language Processing and Computational Natural Language Learning*, pages 1125–1134, Jeju Island, Korea, July.

Gonzalo Iglesias, Cyril Allauzen, William Byrne, Adrià de Gispert, and Michael Riley. 2011. Hierarchical phrase-based translation representations. In *Proceedings of the 2011 Conference on Empirical Methods in*

Natural Language Processing, pages 1373–1383, Edinburgh, Scotland, UK, July. Association for Computational Linguistics.

Dan Klein and Christopher D. Manning. 2001. Parsing and hypergraphs. In *Proceedings of the Seventh International Workshop on Parsing Technologies*, Beijing, China, October.

Reinhard Kneser and Hermann Ney. 1995. Improved backing-off for m-gram language modeling. In *Proceedings of the IEEE International Conference on Acoustics, Speech and Signal Processing*, pages 181–184.

Philipp Koehn and Barry Haddow. 2012. Towards effective use of training data in statistical machine translation. In *Proceedings of the Seventh Workshop on Statistical Machine Translation*, pages 317–321, Montréal, Canada, June. Association for Computational Linguistics.

Philipp Koehn. 2005. Europarl: A parallel corpus for statistical machine translation. In *Proceedings of MT Summit*.

Zhifei Li and Sanjeev Khudanpur. 2008. A scalable decoder for parsing-based machine translation with equivalent language model state maintenance. In *Proceedings of the Second ACL Workshop on Syntax and Structure in Statistical Translation (SSST-2)*, pages 10–18, Columbus, Ohio, June.

Bruce Lowerre. 1976. *The Harpy Speech Recognition System*. Ph.D. thesis, Carnegie Mellon University.

Haitao Mi, Liang Huang, and Qun Liu. 2008. Forest-based translation. In *Proceedings of ACL-08: HLT*, pages 192–199, Columbus, Ohio, June.

Robert C. Moore and Chris Quirk. 2009. Less is more: Significance-based n-gram selection for smaller, better language models. In *Proceedings of the 2009 Conference on Empirical Methods in Natural Language Processing*, pages 746–755, August.

Franz Josef Och. 2003. Minimum error rate training in statistical machine translation. In *ACL '03: Proceedings of the 41st Annual Meeting on Association for Computational Linguistics*, pages 160–167, Morristown, NJ, USA. Association for Computational Linguistics.

Kishore Papineni, Salim Roukos, Todd Ward, and Wei-Jing Zhu. 2002. BLEU: A method for automatic evalution of machine translation. In *Proceedings 40th Annual Meeting of the Association for Computational Linguistics*, pages 311–318, Philadelphia, PA, July.

Slav Petrov, Aria Haghighi, and Dan Klein. 2008. Coarse-to-fine syntactic machine translation using language projections. In *Proceedings of the 2008 Conference on Empirical Methods in Natural Language Processing*, pages 108–116, Honolulu, HI, USA, October.

Alexander Rush and Michael Collins. 2011. Exact decoding of syntactic translation models through lagrangian relaxation. In *Proceedings of the 49th Annual Meeting of the Association for Computational Linguistics*, pages 72–82, Portland, Oregon, USA, June.

Andreas Stolcke. 2002. SRILM - an extensible language modeling toolkit. In *Proceedings of the Seventh International Conference on Spoken Language Processing*, pages 901–904.

Xiang Tong and David A. Evans. 1996. A statistical approach to automatic OCR error correction in context. In *Proceedings of the Fourth Workshop on Very Large Corpora*, pages 88–100, Copenhagen, Denmark, April.

Taro Watanabe, Hajime Tsukada, and Hideki Isozaki. 2006. Left-to-right target generation for hierarchical phrase-based translation. In *Proceedings of the 21st International Conference on Computational Linguistics and 44th Annual Meeting of the ACL*, pages 777–784, Sydney, Australia, July.

Wenduan Xu and Philipp Koehn. 2012. Extending hiero decoding in Moses with cube growing. *The Prague Bulletin of Mathematical Linguistics*, 98:133–142.

A Systematic Bayesian Treatment of the IBM Alignment Models

Yarin Gal
Department of Engineering
University of Cambridge
Cambridge, CB2 1PZ, United Kingdom
yg279@cam.ac.uk

Phil Blunsom
Department of Computer Science
University of Oxford
Oxford, OX1 3QD, United Kingdom
Phil.Blunsom@cs.ox.ac.uk

Abstract

The dominant yet ageing IBM and HMM word alignment models underpin most popular Statistical Machine Translation implementations in use today. Though beset by the limitations of implausible independence assumptions, intractable optimisation problems, and an excess of tunable parameters, these models provide a scalable and reliable starting point for inducing translation systems. In this paper we build upon this venerable base by recasting these models in the non-parametric Bayesian framework. By replacing the categorical distributions at their core with hierarchical Pitman-Yor processes, and through the use of collapsed Gibbs sampling, we provide a more flexible formulation and sidestep the original heuristic optimisation techniques. The resulting models are highly extendible, naturally permitting the introduction of phrasal dependencies. We present extensive experimental results showing improvements in both AER and BLEU when benchmarked against Giza++, including significant improvements over IBM model 4.

1 Introduction

The IBM and HMM word alignment models (Brown et al., 1993; Vogel et al., 1996) have underpinned the majority of statistical machine translation systems for almost twenty years. The key attraction of these models is their principled probabilistic formulation, and the existence of (mostly) tractable algorithms for their training.

The dominant Giza++ implementation of the IBM models (Och and Ney, 2003) employs a variety of exact and approximate EM algorithms to optimise categorical alignment distributions. While effective, this parametric approach results in a significant number of parameters to be tuned and intractable summations over the space of alignments for models 3 and 4. Giza++ hides the hyper-parameters with defaults and approximates the intractable expectations using restricted alignment neighbourhoods. However this approach was shown to often return alignments with probabilities well below the true maxima (Ravi and Knight, 2010).

To overcome perceived limitations with the word based and non-syntactic nature of the IBM models many alternative approaches to word alignment have been proposed (e.g. (DeNero et al., 2008; Cohn and Blunsom, 2009; Levenberg et al., 2012)). While interesting results have been reported, these alternatives have failed to dislodge the IBM approach.

In this paper we proposed to retain the original generative stories of the IBM models, while replacing the inflexible categorical distributions with hierarchical Pitman-Yor (PY) processes – a mathematical tool which has been successfully applied to a range of language tasks (Teh, 2006b; Goldwater et al., 2006; Blunsom and Cohn, 2011). In the context of language modelling, the hierarchical PY process was shown to roughly correspond to interpolated Kneser-Ney (Kneser and Ney, 1995; Teh, 2006a). The key contribution of the hierarchical PY formulation is that it provides a principle probabilistic framework that easily extends to latent variable models, such as those used for alignment, for which a Kneser-Ney formulation is unclear. While Bayesian priors have previously been applied to IBM model 1 (Riley and Gildea, 2012), in this work we go considerably further by implementing non-parametric priors for the full Giza++ training pipeline.

Inference for the proposed models and their hyper-parameters is done with Gibbs sampling. This eliminates the intractable summations over alignments and the need for tuning hyper-parameters. Further, we exploit the highly extendible nature of the hierarchical PY process to implement improvements to the original models such as the introduction of phrasal dependencies.

We present extensive experimental results showing improvements in both BLEU scores and AER when compared to Giza++. The demonstrated improvements over IBM model 4 suggest that the heuristics used in the implementation of the EM algorithm for this model were suboptimal.

We begin with a formal presentation of the hierarchical PY process used in our Bayesian approach to replace the original categorical distributions. Section 3 introduces our Bayesian formulation of the word alignment models, while its inference scheme is presented in the following section. Finally, the experimental results evaluating our models against the originals are given in section 5, demonstrating the superiority of the non-parametric approach.

2 The hierarchical PY process

Before giving the formal definition for the hierarchical Pitman-Yor (PY) process, we first give some intuition into how this distribution works and why it is commonly used to model problems in natural language.

The hierarchical PY process is an atomic distribution that can share its atoms between different levels in a hierarchy. When used for language modelling it captures the probability of observing a word after any given sequence of n words. It does so by interpolating the observed frequency of the whole sequence followed by the word of interest, with the observed frequency of a shorter sequence followed by the word of interest. This interpolation is done in such a way that tokens in a more specific distribution are interpolated with types in a less specific one. If there is sufficient evidence for the whole word sequence, i.e. it is not sparse in the corpus, higher weight will be given to the frequency of the word of interest after the more specific sequence than the shorter one. If the sequence was not observed frequently and there is not enough information to model whether the word of interest follows after it frequently or not, the process will back-off to the shorter sequence and assign higher weight to its frequency instead. This is done in a recursive fashion, decreasing the sequence length by one every time until the probability is interpolated with the uniform distribution, much like interpolated Kneser-Ney, the state of the art for language modelling.

Unlike Kneser-Ney, the hierarchical PY approach naturally extends to model complicated conditional distributions involving latent variables. Moreover, almost all instances of priors with categorical distributions can be replaced by the PY process, where in its most basic representation (with no conditional) it provides a flexible model of power law frequencies.

The PY process generalises a number of simpler distributions. The Dirichlet distribution is a distribution over discrete probability mass functions of a certain given length which is often used to model prior beliefs on parameter sparsity in machine learning problems. The Dirichlet process generalises the Dirichlet distribution to a distribution over infinite sequences of non-negative reals that sum to one and is often used for nonparametric Bayesian inference. The PY process is used in the context of natural language processing as it further generalises the Dirichlet process by adding an additional degree of freedom that enables it to produce power-law discrete probability mass functions that resemble those seen experimentally in corpora (Goldwater et al., 2006).

Formally, draws from the PY process $G_1 \sim PY(d, \theta, G_0)$ with a discount parameter $0 \leq d < 1$, a strength parameter $\theta > -d$, and a base distribution G_0, are constructed using a Chinese restaurant process analogy as follows:

$$X_{n+1}|X_1, ..., X_n \sim \sum_{k=1}^{K} \frac{m_k - d}{\theta + n} \delta_{y_k} + \frac{\theta + dK}{\theta + n} G_0$$

Where m_k denotes the number of X_is (customers) assigned to y_k (a table) and K is the total number of y_ks drawn from G_0.

Hierarchical PY processes (Teh, 2006b), PY processes where the base distribution is itself a PY process, were developed as an extension which is often used in the context of natural language processing due to their relationship to back-off smoothing. Denoting a context of atoms $\mathbf{u}$ as $(w_{i-l}, ..., w_{i-1})$, the hierarchical PY process is defined using the above definition of the PY process by:

$$\begin{aligned} w_i &\sim G_{\mathbf{u}} \\ G_{\mathbf{u}} &\sim PY(d_{|\mathbf{u}|}, \theta_{|\mathbf{u}|}, G_{\pi(\mathbf{u})}) \\ &\dots \\ G_{(w_{i-1})} &\sim PY(d_1, \theta_1, G_\emptyset) \\ G_\emptyset &\sim PY(d_0, \theta_0, G_0) \end{aligned}$$

where $\pi(\mathbf{u}) = (w_{i-l+1}, ..., w_{i-1})$ is the suffix of $\mathbf{u}$, $|\mathbf{u}|$ denotes the length of context $\mathbf{u}$, and G_0 is a base distribution.

3 A Bayesian approach to word alignment

In this work we replace the categorical distributions at the heart of statistical alignment models with PY processes. We start by describing the revised models for IBM model 1 and the HMM alignment model, before continuing to the more advanced IBM models 3 and 4. Throughout this section, we assume that the base distributions in our models (denoted G_0, H_0, etc.) are uniform over all atoms, and omit the strength and concentration parameters of the PY process for clarity. We use subscripts to denote the hierarchy, and lower-case superscripts to denote a fixed condition (for example, G_0^m is the (uniform) base distribution that is determined uniquely for each possible foreign sentence length m).

3.1 Model 1 and the HMM alignment model

The most basic word alignment model, IBM model 1, can be described using the following generative process (Brown et al., 1993): Given an English sentence $E = e_1, ..., e_l$, first choose a length m for the foreign sentence F. Next, choose a vector of random word positions from the English sentence $A = a_1, ..., a_m$ to be the alignment, and then for each foreign word f_i choose a translation from the English word e_{a_i} aligned to it by A. The existence of a NULL word at the beginning of the English sentence is assumed, a word to which spurious words in the foreign sentence can align. From this generative process the following probability model is derived:

$$P(F, A|E) = p(m|l) \times \prod_{i=1}^{m} p(a_i)p(f_i|e_{a_i})$$

Where $p(a_i) = \frac{1}{l+1}$ is uniform over all alignments and $p(f_i|e_{a_i}) \sim$ *Categorical*.

In our approach we model these distributions using hierarchical PY processes instead of the categorical distributions. Thus we place the following assumptions on IBM model 1:

$$\begin{aligned} a_i|m &\sim G_0^m \\ f_i|e_{a_i} &\sim H_{e_{a_i}} \\ H_{e_{a_i}} &\sim PY(H_\emptyset) \\ H_\emptyset &\sim PY(H_0) \end{aligned}$$

In this probability modelling we assume that the alignment positions are determined using the uniform distribution, and that word translations are generated depending on the source word – the probability of translating to a specific foreign word depends on the observed frequency of pairs of the foreign word and the given source word. We back-off to the frequencies of the foreign words when the source word wasn't observed frequently.

The HMM alignment model uses the Hidden Markov Model to find word alignments. It treats the translations of the words of the English sentence as observables and the alignment positions as the latent variables to be discovered. Its generative process can be described in an abstract way as follows: we determine the length of the foreign sentence and then iterate over the words of the source sentence emitting translations for each word to fill-in the words in the foreign sentence from left to right.

The following probability model is derived for the HMM alignment model (Vogel et al., 1996):

$$P(F,A|E) = p(m|l) \times \prod_{i=1}^{m} p(a_i|a_{i-1}, m) \times p(f_i|e_{a_i})$$

For the HMM alignment model we replace the categorical translation distribution $p(f_i|e_{a_i})$ with the same one we used for model 1, and replace the categorical distribution for the transition $p(a_i|a_{i-1}, m)$ with a hierarchical PY process with a longer sequence of alignment positions in the conditional:

$$
\begin{aligned}
a_i|a_{i-1}, m &\sim G^m_{a_{i-1}} \\
G^m_{a_{i-1}} &\sim PY(G^m_\emptyset) \\
G^m_\emptyset &\sim PY(G^m_0)
\end{aligned}
$$

We use a unique distribution for each foreign sentence length, and condition the position on the previous alignment position, backing-off to the HMM's stationary distribution over alignment positions.

3.2 Models 3 and 4

IBM models 3 and 4 introduce the concept of a word's fertility, the number of foreign words that are generated from a specific English word. These models can be described using the following generative process. Given an English sentence E, first determine the length of the foreign sentence: for each word in the English sentence e_i choose a fertility, denoted ϕ_i. Every time a word is generated, an additional spurious word from the NULL word in the English sentence can be generated with a fixed probability. After the foreign sentence length is determined translate each English word into its foreign equivalent (including the NULL word) in the same way as for model 1. Finally, non-spurious words are rearranged into the final word positions and the spurious words inserted into the empty positions. In model 3 this is done with a zero order HMM, and in model 4 with two first order HMMs. One controls the distortion of the head of each English word (the first foreign word generated from it) relative to the centre (denoted here $\odot$) of the set of foreign words generated from the previous English word, and the other controls the distortion within the set itself by conditioning the word position on the previous word position.

For the probability model, we follow the notation of Och and Ney (2003) and define the alignment as a function from the source sentence positions i to $B_i \subset \{1, ..., m\}$ where the B_i's form a partition of the set $\{1, ..., m\}$. The fertility of the English word i is $\phi_i = |B_i|$, and we use $B_{i,k}$ to refer to the kth element of B_i in ascending order.

Using the above notation, the following probability model is derived (Och and Ney, 2003):

$$
\begin{aligned}
P(F, A|E) =& p(B_0|B_1, ..., B_l) \times \prod_{i=1}^{l} p(B_i|B_{i-1}, e_i) \\
& \times \prod_{i=0}^{l} \prod_{j \in B_i} p(f_j|e_i)
\end{aligned}
$$

For model 3 the dependence on previous alignment sets is ignored and the probability $p(B_i|B_{i-1}, e_i)$ is modelled as

$$
p(B_i|B_{i-1}, e_i) = p(\phi_i|e_i)\phi_i! \prod_{j \in B_i} p(j|i, m),
$$

whereas in model 4 it is modelled using two HMMs:

$$
\begin{aligned}
p(B_i|B_{i-1}, e_i) =& p(\phi_i|e_i) \times p_{=1}(B_{i,1} - \odot(B_{i-1})|\cdot) \\
& \times \prod_{k=2}^{\phi_i} p_{>1}(B_{i,k} - B_{i,k-1}|\cdot)
\end{aligned}
$$

For both these models the spurious word generation is controlled by a binomial distribution:

$$
p(B_0|B_1, ..., B_l) = \binom{m - \phi_0}{\phi_0} (1 - p_0)^{m - 2\phi_0} p_1^{\phi_0} \frac{1}{\phi_0!}
$$

for some parameters p_0 and p_1.

Replacing the categorical priors with hierarchical PY process ones, we set the translation and fertility probabilities $p(\phi_i|e_i) \prod_{j \in B_i} p(f_j|e_i)$ using a common prior that generates translation sequences:

$$
\begin{aligned}
(f^1, ..., f^{\phi_i})|e_i &\sim H_{e_i} \\
H_{e_i} &\sim PY(H^{FT}_{e_i}) \\
H^{FT}_{e_i}((f^1, ..., f^{\phi_i})) &= H^F_{e_i}(\phi_i) \prod_j H^T_{(f^{j-1}, e_i)}(f^j)
\end{aligned}
$$

$$
\begin{aligned}
H^F_{e_i} &\sim PY(H^F_\emptyset) & H^T_{(f^{j-1}, e_i)} &\sim PY(H^T_{e_i}) \\
H^F_\emptyset &\sim PY(H^F_0) & H^T_{e_i} &\sim PY(H^T_\emptyset) \\
& & H^T_\emptyset &\sim PY(H^T_0)
\end{aligned}
$$

Here we used superscripts for the indexing of words which do not have to occur sequentially in the sentence. We generate sequences instead of individual words and fertilities, and fall-back onto these only in sparse cases. For example, when aligning the English sentence "I don't speak French" to its

French translation "Je ne parle pas français", the word "not" will generate the phrase ("ne", "pas"), which will later on be distorted into its place around the verb.

The distortion probability for model 3, $p(j|i, m)$, is modelled simply as depending on the position of the source word i and its class:

$$\begin{aligned} j|(C(e_i), i), m &\sim G^m_{(C(e_i),i)} \\ G^m_{(C(e_i),i)} &\sim PY(G^m_i) \\ G^m_i &\sim PY(G^m_\emptyset) \\ G^m_\emptyset &\sim PY(G^m_0) \end{aligned}$$

where we back-off to the source word position and then to the frequencies of the alignment positions.

As opposed to this simple mechanism, in the distortion probability for IBM model 4 there exist two distinct probability distributions. The first probability distribution $p_{=1}$ controls the head distortion:

$$\begin{aligned} B_{i,1} - \odot(B_{i-1}) \mid (C(e_i), C(f_{B_{i,1}})), m & \\ \sim G^m_{(C(e_i),C(f_{B_{i,1}}))} & \\ G^m_{(C(e_i),C(f_{B_{i,1}}))} &\sim PY(G^m_{C(f_{B_{i,1}})}) \\ G^m_{C(f_{B_{i,1}})} &\sim PY(G^m_\emptyset) \\ G^m_\emptyset &\sim PY(G^m_0) \end{aligned}$$

In this probability modelling we model the jump size itself, as depending on the word class for the source word and the word class for the proposed foreign word, backing-off to the proposed foreign word class and then to the relative jump frequencies.

The second probability distribution $p_{>1}$ controls the distortion within the set of words:

$$\begin{aligned} B_{i,j} - B_{i,j-1}|C(f_{B_{i,j}}), m &\sim H^m_{C(f_{B_{i,j}})} \\ H^m_{C(f_{B_{i,j}})} &\sim PY(H^m_\emptyset) \\ H^m_\emptyset &\sim PY(H^m_0) \end{aligned}$$

Here we again model the jump size as depending on the word class for the proposed foreign word, backing-off to the relative jump frequencies.

Lastly, we add to this probability model a treatment for fertility and translation of NULL words. The fertility generation follows the idea of the original model, where the number of spurious words is determined by a binomial distribution created from a set of Bernoulli experiments, each one performed after the translation of a non-spurious word. We use an indicator function I to signal whether a spurious word was generated after a non-spurious word ($I = 1$) or not ($I = 0$).

$$\begin{aligned} I = 0, 1|l &\sim H^{NF}_l \\ H^{NF}_l &\sim PY(H^{NF}_\emptyset) \\ H^{NF}_\emptyset &\sim PY(H^{NF}_0) \end{aligned}$$

Then, the translation of spurious words is done in a straightforward manner:

$$\begin{aligned} f_i &\sim H^{NT}_\emptyset \\ H^{NT}_\emptyset &\sim PY(H^{NT}_0) \end{aligned}$$

4 Inference

The Gibbs sampling inference scheme together with the Chinese Restaurant Franchise process (Teh and Jordan, 2009) are used to induce alignments for a parallel corpus. A set of restaurants $\mathcal{S}$ is constructed and initialised either randomly or through a pipeline of alignment results from simpler models, and then at each iteration each alignment position is removed from the restaurants and re-sampled, conditioned on the rest of the alignment positions.

Denoting $\mathbf{e}, \mathbf{f}, \mathbf{a}$ the sets of all source sentences, their translations, and their corresponding alignments in our corpus, and denoting E, F, A a specific source sentence, its translation, and their corresponding alignment, where e_i is the i'th word of the source sentence and f_j, a_j are the j'th word in the foreign sentence and its alignment into the source sentence, we sample a new value for a_j using the univariate conditional distribution:

$$\begin{aligned} &P(a_j = i|E, F, A_{-j}, \mathbf{e}_{-E}, \mathbf{f}_{-F}, \mathbf{a}_{-A}, \mathcal{S}_{-a_j}) \\ &\propto P(F, (A_{-j}, a_j = i)|E, \mathbf{e}_{-E}, \mathbf{f}_{-F}, \mathbf{a}_{-A}, \mathcal{S}_{-a_j}) \end{aligned}$$

Where a minus sign in the subscript denotes the structure without the mentioned element, and $\mathcal{S}_{-a_j}$ denotes the configuration of the restaurants after removing the alignment a_j.

This univariate conditional distribution is proportional to the probability assigned by the different models to an alignment sequence, where the restaurants replace the counts of the alignment positions

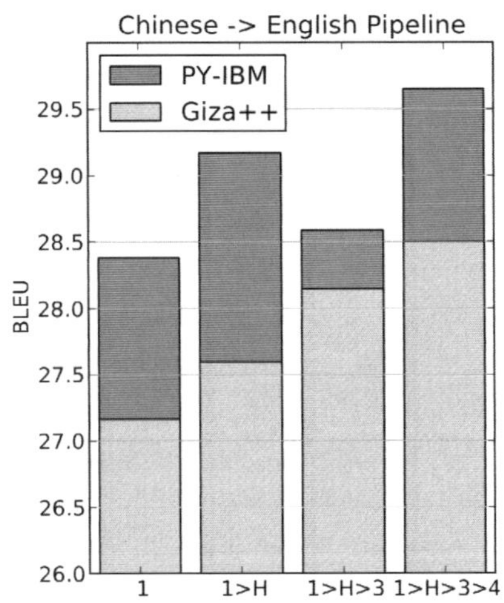

Figure 1: BLEU scores of pipelined Giza++ and pipelined PY-IBM translating from Chinese into English

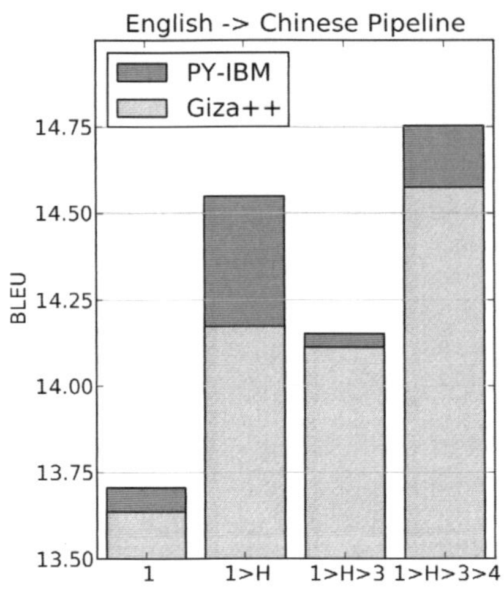

Figure 2: BLEU scores of pipelined Giza++ and pipelined PY-IBM translating from English into Chinese

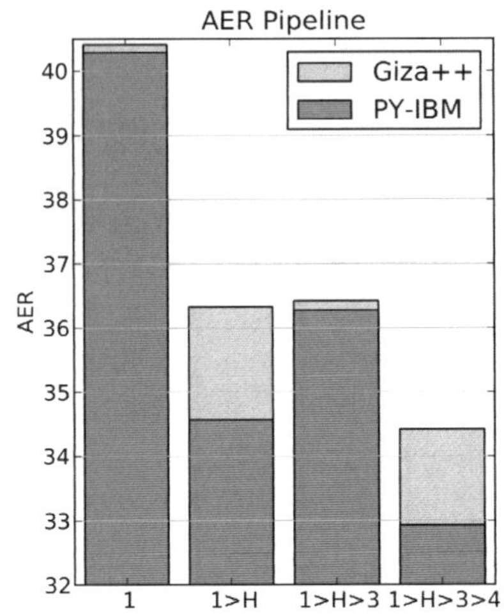

Figure 3: AER of pipelined Giza++ and pipelined PY-IBM aligning Chinese and English

in the prior. Maximum marginal decoding (Johnson and Goldwater, 2009) can then be used to get the MAP estimate of the probability distributions over the alignment positions for each sentence from the samples extracted from the Gibbs sampler.

In addition to sampling the alignments, we also place a uniform Beta prior on the discount parameters and a vague Gamma prior on the strength parameters, and sample them using slice sampling (Neal, 2003). The end result is that the alignment models have no free parameters to tune.

5 Experimental results

In order to assess our PY process alignment models (referred to as PY-IBM henceforth) several experiments were carried out to benchmark them against the original models (as implemented in Giza++). We evaluated the BLEU scores (Papineni et al., 2002) of translations from Chinese into English and from English into Chinese, as well as the alignment error rates (AER) of the induced symmetrised alignments compared to a human aligned dataset. Moses (Koehn et al., 2007) was used for the training of the SMT system and the symmetrisation (using the grow-diag-final procedure), with MERT (Och, 2003) used for tuning of the weights, and SRILM (Stolcke, 2002) to build the language model (5-grams based). The corpus used for training and evaluation was the Chinese FBIS corpus. MT02 was used for tuning, and MT03 was used for evaluation. In each case we used one reference sentence in Chinese and 4 reference sentences in English.

Most translation systems rely on the Giza++ package in which the implementation of the original models is done by combining them in a pipeline. Model 1 and the HMM alignment model are run sequentially each for 5 iterations; then models 3 and 4 are run sequentially for 3 iterations each. This follows the observation of Och and Ney (2003) that bootstrapping from previous results assists the fertility algorithms find the best alignment neighbourhood in order to estimate the expectations.

We assessed the proposed models against the original models in a pipeline experiment where both systems were trained on a corpus starting at model 1, and used the results of the previous run to initialise the next one – noting the BLEU scores and AER at each step. The Gibbs samplers for the pipelined PY-IBM models were run for 50 iterations for each model and started accumulating samples after a burn-in period of 10 iterations, each experiment was repeated three times and the results averaged. As can be seen in figures 1 to 3, the pipelined PY-IBM models achieved higher BLEU scores across all steps, with the highest improvement of 1.6 percentage points in the pipelined HMM alignment models when translating

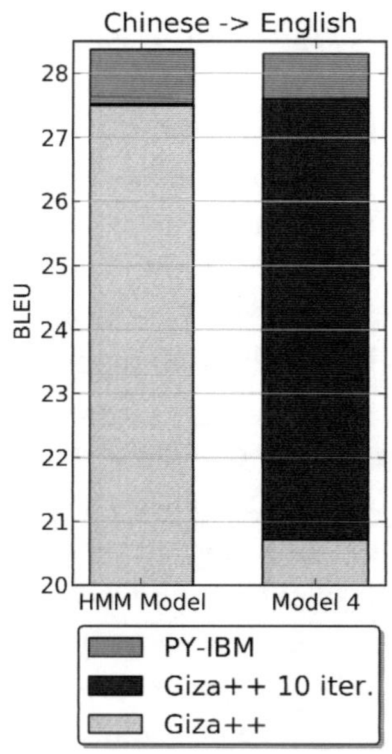

Figure 4: BLEU scores of Giza++'s and PY-IBM's HMM model and model 4 translating from Chinese into English

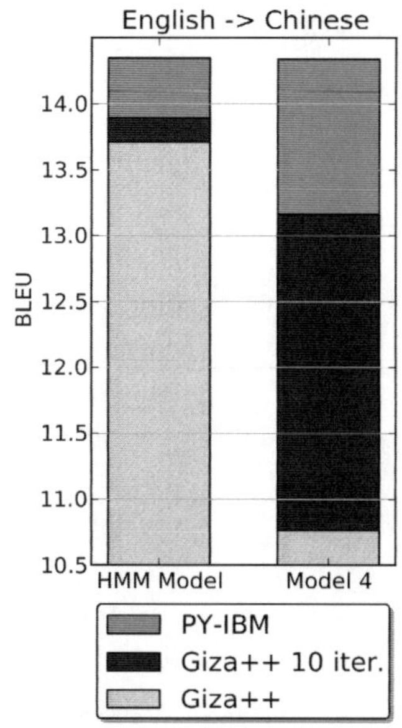

Figure 5: BLEU scores of Giza++'s and PY-IBM's HMM model and model 4 translating from English into Chinese

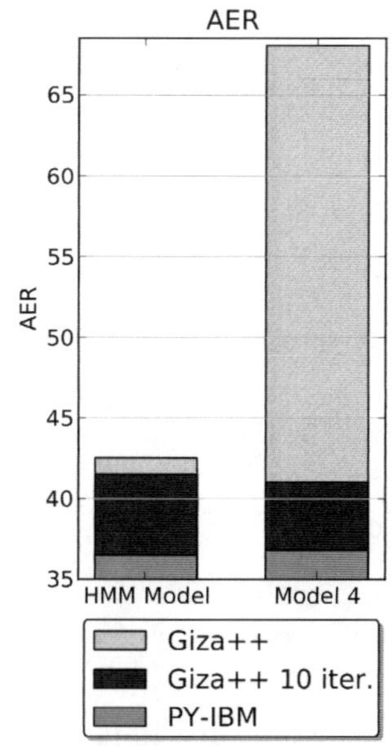

Figure 6: AER of Giza++'s and PY-IBM's HMM model and model 4 aligning Chinese and English

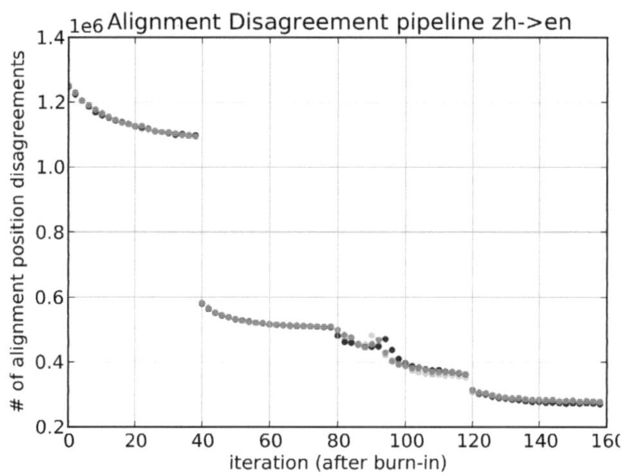

Figure 7: Alignment disagreement of the Chinese to English pipelined PY-IBM models for the 3 repetitions

from Chinese into English, and an improvement of 1.2 percentage points in the overall results after finishing the pipeline.

We also saw an improvement in AER for all models, where the pipelined PY-IBM model 4 achieved an error rate of 32.9, as opposed to the result obtained by the Giza++ pipelined model 4 of 34.4. We note an interesting observation that both Giza++ and PY-IBM model 3 underperformed compared to the previously run HMM alignment model, as seen in the English to Chinese pipeline results and the AER pipeline results.

The alignment disagreement (the number of changed alignment positions between subsequent iterations) of the Chinese to English pipelined PY-IBM models (1 to 4) can be seen in fig. 7. This graph shows that each model in the pipeline reaches an alignment disagreement equilibrium after about 20 iterations, and that earlier models have greater initial deviation from their equilibrium than later models – which have an overall lower disagreement.

In order to assess the dependence of the fertility based models on the initialisation step another set of experiments was carried out. The models were trained with a randomly initialised set of alignments and assessed after a set number of iterations for the Giza++ models (5 and 10 for the Giza++ HMM alignment model, and 3 and 10 for the Giza++ IBM model 4), or after 100 iterations with a burn-in period of 10 iterations for the PY-IBM ones (we report the average of three runs for both models).

The results, reported in figures 4 to 6, show again that the PY-IBM model outperformed the Giza++ implementations, and to a large extent in the case of IBM model 4. This provides further evidence that the supposition underlying the neighbourhood

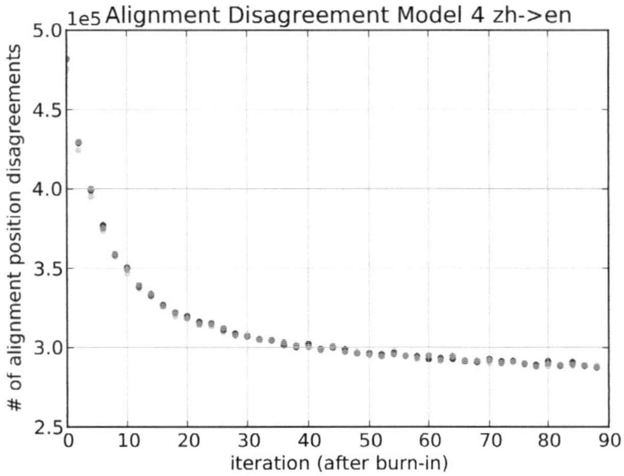

Figure 8: Alignment disagreement of the Chinese to English PY-IBM model 4 for the 3 repetitions

approximation for training models 3 and 4 – that there exists a small set of alignments on which most of the probability mass concentrates – is poor. An interesting observation to note is that the BLEU score of the non-pipelined PY-IBM model 4 is the same as the PY-IBM HMM model translating in both directions, as opposed to an improvement in the pipelined case. This suggests that the sampler might not have fully converged after 100 iterations for model 4 (the number of alignment disagreements for this experiment can be seen in figure 8). Further confirmation for this comes from the higher standard deviation of 0.54 observed for the PY-IBM model 4, as opposed to a standard deviation for the PY-IBM HMM model of 0.21 (which is still more significant than that of the pipelined PY-IBM model 4, whose standard deviation was 0.13).

Both the PY-IBM and the Giza++ trained models run in a linear time in the number of sentences, where due to the nature of MCMC sampling techniques, more iterations are required for its convergence. In our experiments, the running time of the unoptimised Gibbs sampler was 50 times slower than the optimised EM.

6 Discussion

The models described in this paper allow one to use non-parametric approaches to flexibly model word alignment distributions, overcoming a number of limitations of the EM algorithm for the fertility based alignment models. The models achieved a significant improvement in BLEU scores and AER on the tested corpus, and are easy to extend without the need for additional modelling tools.

The alignment models proposed mostly follow the original generative stories while introducing additional phrasal conditioning into models 3 and 4. However there are many other areas in which we could make use of hierarchical tools to introduce new dependencies easily without running into sparsity problems.

One example is the extension of the transition history used in the HMM alignment model: IBM model 1 uses a uniform distribution over transitions, model 2 conditions on relative sentence positions, and the HMM model uses a first order dependency. One extension would be to use longer histories of n previous positions, handling sparsity with back-off.

Previously proposed approaches to extend the HMM alignment model include Och and Ney (2003)'s use of word classes and smoothing, and the combination of part-of-speech information of the words surrounding the source word (Brunning et al., 2009). Using our hierarchical model one could easily introduce such dependencies on the context words of the word to be translated and their part-of-speech information. This could assist in both translation and reordering disambiguation, and would incorporate back-off by using smaller and smaller contexts when such information is sparse.

Further improvements to models 3 and 4 could be carried out by introducing longer dependencies in the fertility and distortion distributions. Instead of conditioning on the previous word, one could use further information such as PoS tags, previously translated words, or previous fertilities. Additional research would involve the use of more effective variational inference algorithms for hierarchical PY process based models.

The PY-IBM models described in this paper were implemented within the Giza++ code base, and are available as an open source package for further development and research.[1]

References

Phil Blunsom and Trevor Cohn. 2011. A hierarchical Pitman-Yor process HMM for unsupervised part of

[1]Available at `github.com/yaringal/Giza-sharp`

speech induction. In *Proceedings of the 49th Annual Meeting of the Association for Computational Linguistics: Human Language Technologies*, pages 865–874, Portland, Oregon, USA, June. Association for Computational Linguistics.

Peter F. Brown, Stephen A. Della Pietra, Vincent J. Della Pietra, and Robert L. Mercer. 1993. The mathematics of statistical machine translation: Parameter estimation. *Computational Linguistics*, 19(2):263–311.

Jamie Brunning, Adrià de Gispert, and William Byrne. 2009. Context-dependent alignment models for statistical machine translation. In *Proceedings of Human Language Technologies: The 2009 Annual Conference of the North American Chapter of the Association for Computational Linguistics*, NAACL '09, pages 110–118.

Trevor Cohn and Phil Blunsom. 2009. A Bayesian model of syntax-directed tree to string grammar induction. In *Proceedings of the 2009 Conference on Empirical Methods in Natural Language Processing*, pages 352–361, Singapore, August. Association for Computational Linguistics.

John DeNero, Alexandre Bouchard-Côté, and Dan Klein. 2008. Sampling alignment structure under a Bayesian translation model. In *Proceedings of the 2008 Conference on Empirical Methods in Natural Language Processing*, pages 314–323, Honolulu, Hawaii, October. Association for Computational Linguistics.

Sharon Goldwater, Tom Griffiths, and Mark Johnson. 2006. Interpolating between types and tokens by estimating power-law generators. In Y. Weiss, B. Schölkopf, and J. Platt, editors, *Advances in Neural Information Processing Systems 18*, pages 459–466. MIT Press, Cambridge, MA.

Mark Johnson and Sharon Goldwater. 2009. Improving nonparameteric Bayesian inference: experiments on unsupervised word segmentation with adaptor grammars. In *Proceedings of Human Language Technologies: The 2009 Annual Conference of the North American Chapter of the Association for Computational Linguistics*, NAACL '09, pages 317–325.

Reinhard Kneser and Hermann Ney. 1995. Improved backing-off for m-gram language modeling. *Acoustics, Speech, and Signal Processing, IEEE International Conference on*, 1:181–184.

Philipp Koehn, Hieu Hoang, Alexandra Birch, Chris Callison-Burch, Marcello Federico, Nicola Bertoldi, Brooke Cowan, Wade Shen, Christine Moran, Richard Zens, Chris Dyer, Ondrej Bojar, Alexandra Constantin, and Evan Herbst. 2007. Moses: Open source toolkit for statistical machine translation. In *Proc. of the 45th Annual Meeting of the ACL (ACL-2007)*, Prague.

Abby Levenberg, Chris Dyer, and Phil Blunsom. 2012. A Bayesian model for learning SCFGs with discontiguous rules. In *Proceedings of the 2012 Joint Conference on Empirical Methods in Natural Language Processing and Computational Natural Language Learning*, pages 223–232, Jeju Island, Korea, July. Association for Computational Linguistics.

Radford Neal. 2003. Slice sampling. *Annals of Statistics*, 31:705–767.

Franz Josef Och and Hermann Ney. 2003. A systematic comparison of various statistical alignment models. *Computational Linguistics*, 29(1):19–52.

Franz Josef Och. 2003. Minimum error rate training in statistical machine translation. In *Proc. of the 41st Annual Meeting of the ACL (ACL-2003)*, pages 160–167, Sapporo, Japan.

Kishore Papineni, Salim Roukos, Todd Ward, and Wei-Jing Zhu. 2002. Bleu: a method for automatic evaluation of machine translation. In *Proc. of the 40th Annual Meeting of the ACL and 3rd Annual Meeting of the NAACL (ACL-2002)*, pages 311–318, Philadelphia, Pennsylvania.

Sujith Ravi and Kevin Knight. 2010. Does Giza++ make search errors? *Computational Linguistics*, 36(3):295–302, September.

Darcey Riley and Daniel Gildea. 2012. Improving the ibm alignment models using variational bayes. In *Proceedings of the 50th Annual Meeting of the Association for Computational Linguistics: Short Papers - Volume 2*, ACL '12, pages 306–310.

A. Stolcke. 2002. SRILM – an extensible language modeling toolkit. In *Proc. of the International Conference on Spoken Language Processing*.

Y. W. Teh and M. I. Jordan, 2009. *Hierarchical Bayesian Nonparametric Models with Applications.* Cambridge University Press.

Yee Whye Teh. 2006a. A Bayesian interpretation of interpolated Kneser-Ney. Technical report, National University of Singapore School of Computing.

Yee Whye Teh. 2006b. A hierarchical bayesian language model based on pitman-yor processes. In *Proceedings of the 21st International Conference on Computational Linguistics and the 44th annual meeting of the Association for Computational Linguistics*, ACL-44, pages 985–992, Morristown, NJ, USA. Association for Computational Linguistics.

Stephen Vogel, Hermann Ney, and Christoph Tillmann. 1996. HMM-based word alignment in statistical translation. In *Proc. of the 16th International Conference on Computational Linguistics (COLING '96)*, pages 836–841, Copenhagen, Denmark, August.

Unsupervised Metaphor Identification Using Hierarchical Graph Factorization Clustering

Ekaterina Shutova
International Computer Science Institute and
Institute for Cognitive and Brain Sciences
University of California, Berkeley
katia@icsi.berkeley.edu

Lin Sun
Computer Laboratory
University of Cambridge
lin.sun@cl.cam.ac.uk

Abstract

We present a novel approach to automatic metaphor identification, that discovers both metaphorical associations and metaphorical expressions in unrestricted text. Our system first performs hierarchical graph factorization clustering (HGFC) of nouns and then searches the resulting graph for metaphorical connections between concepts. It then makes use of the salient features of the metaphorically connected clusters to identify the actual metaphorical expressions. In contrast to previous work, our method is fully unsupervised. Despite this fact, it operates with an encouraging precision (0.69) and recall (0.61). Our approach is also the first one in NLP to exploit the cognitive findings on the differences in organisation of abstract and concrete concepts in the human brain.

1 Introduction

Metaphor has traditionally been viewed as a form of linguistic creativity, that gives our expression more vividness, distinction and artistism. While this is true on the surface, the mechanisms of metaphor have a much deeper origin in our reasoning. Today metaphor is widely understood as a cognitive phenomenon operating at the level of mental processes, whereby one concept or domain is systematically viewed in terms of the properties of another (Lakoff and Johnson, 1980). Consider the examples (1) "He *shot down* all of my arguments" and (2) "He *attacked* every weak point in my argument". They demonstrate a metaphorical mapping of the concept of *argument* to that of *war*. The *argument*, which is the target concept, is viewed in terms of a *battle* (or a *war*), the source concept. The existence of such a link allows us to systematically describe *arguments* using the *war* terminology, thus leading to a number of metaphorical expressions. Lakoff and Johnson call such generalisations a source–target domain mapping, or *conceptual metaphor*.

The ubiquity of metaphor in language has been established in a number of corpus studies (Cameron, 2003; Martin, 2006; Steen et al., 2010; Shutova and Teufel, 2010) and the role it plays in human reasoning has been confirmed in psychological experiments (Thibodeau and Boroditsky, 2011). This makes metaphor an important research area for computational and cognitive linguistics, and its automatic processing indispensable for any semantics-oriented NLP application. The problem of metaphor modeling is gaining interest within NLP, with a growing number of approaches exploiting statistical techniques (Mason, 2004; Gedigian et al., 2006; Shutova, 2010; Shutova et al., 2010; Turney et al., 2011; Shutova et al., 2012). Compared to more traditional approaches based on hand-coded knowledge (Fass, 1991; Martin, 1990; Narayanan, 1997; Narayanan, 1999; Feldman and Narayanan, 2004; Barnden and Lee, 2002; Agerri et al., 2007), these more recent methods tend to have a wider coverage, as well as be more efficient, accurate and robust. However, even the statistical metaphor processing approaches so far often focused on a limited domain or a subset of phenomena (Gedigian et al., 2006; Krishnakumaran and Zhu, 2007), and only addressed one of the metaphor processing subtasks: identification of metaphorical mappings (Mason, 2004) or identification of metaphorical expressions (Shutova et al., 2010; Turney et al., 2011). In this paper, we present the first computational method that identifies the generalisations that govern the production of metaphorical expressions, i.e. conceptual metaphors, and then uses these generalisations to identify metaphorical expressions in unrestricted text. As opposed to previous works on statistical metaphor processing that were supervised or semi-supervised, and thus required training data, our method is fully unsupervised. It relies on building a hierarchical graph of concepts connected by their association strength (using hierarchical clustering) and then searching for metaphorical links in this graph.

Shutova et al. (2010) introduced the hypothesis of "clustering by association" and claimed that in the course of distributional noun clustering, abstract concepts tend to cluster together if they are associated with the same source domain, while concrete concepts cluster by meaning similarity. We share this intuition, but take this idea a significant step further. Our approach is theoretically grounded in the cognitive science findings suggesting that abstract and concrete concepts are organised differently in the human brain (Crutch and Warrington, 2005; Binder et al., 2005; Wiemer-Hastings and Xu, 2005; Huang et al., 2010; Crutch and Warrington, 2010; Adorni and Proverbio, 2012). According to Crutch and Warrington (2005), these differences emerge from their general patterns of relation with other concepts. However, most NLP systems to date treat abstract and concrete concepts as identical. In contrast, we incorporate this distinction into our model by creating a network (or a graph) of concepts, and automatically learning the different patterns of association of abstract and concrete concepts with other concepts. We expect that, while concrete concepts would tend to naturally organise into a tree-like structure (with more specific terms descending from the more general terms), abstract concepts would exhibit a more complex pattern of associations. Consider the example in Figure 1. The figure schematically shows a small portion of the graph describing the concepts of *mechanism* (concrete), *political system* and *relationship* (abstract) at two levels of generality. One can see from this graph that if concrete concepts, such as *bike* or *engine* tend to be connected to only one concept at the higher level in the hierarchy (*mechanism*), abstract concepts may have multiple higher-level associates: the literal ones and the metaphorical ones. For example, the abstract concept of *democracy* is literally associated with a more general concept of *political system*, as well as metaphorically associated with the concept of *mechanism*. Such multiple associations are due to the fact that *political systems* are metaphorically viewed as *mechanisms*, they can *function, break*, they can be *oiled* etc. We often discuss them using *mechanism* terminology, and thus a corpus-based distributional learning approach would learn that they share features with *political systems* (from their literal uses), as well as with *mechanisms* (from their metaphorical uses, as shown next to the respective graph edges in the figure). Our system discovers such association patterns within the graph and uses them to identify metaphorical connections between the concepts.

To the best of our knowledge, our method is the first one to use a hierarchical clustering model for the metaphor processing task. The original graph of concepts is built using hierarchical graph factorization clustering (HGFC) (Yu et al., 2006) of nouns, yielding a network of clusters with different levels of generality. The weights on the edges of the graph indicate association between the clusters (concepts). HGFC has not been previously employed for noun clustering in NLP, but showed successful results in the verb clustering task (Sun and Korhonen, 2011).

In summary, our system (1) builds a graph of concepts using HGFC, (2) traverses it to find metaphorical associations between clusters using weights on the edges of the graph, (3) generates lists of salient features for the metaphorically connected clusters and (4) searches the British National Corpus (BNC) (Burnard, 2007) for metaphorical expressions describing the target domain concepts using the verbs from the set of salient features. We evaluated the performance of the system with the aid of human judges in precision- and recall-oriented settings. In addition, we compared its performance to that of two baselines, an unsupervised baseline using agglomerative clustering (AGG) and a supervised baseline built upon WordNet (Fellbaum, 1998) (WN).

2 Method

2.1 Dataset and Feature Extraction

Our noun dataset used for clustering contains 2000 most frequent nouns in the BNC (Burnard, 2007).

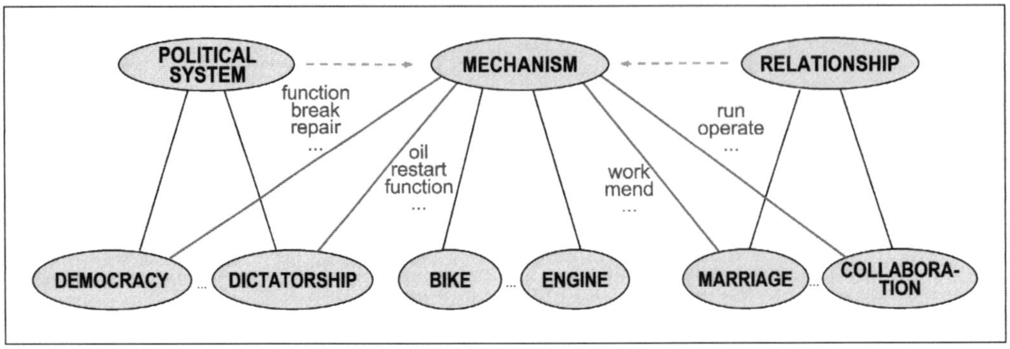

Figure 1: Organisation of the hierarchical graph of concepts

Following previous semantic noun classification experiments (Pantel and Lin, 2002; Bergsma et al., 2008), we use the grammatical relations (GRs) as features for clustering. We extracted the features from the Gigaword corpus (Graff et al., 2003), which was first parsed using the RASP parser (Briscoe et al., 2006). The verb lemmas in VERB–SUBJECT, VERB–DIRECT_OBJECT and VERB–INDIRECT_OBJECT relations with the nouns in the dataset were then extracted from the GR output of the parser. The feature values were the relative frequencies of the features.

2.2 Hierarchical Graph Factorization Clustering

The most widely used method for hierarchical word clustering is AGG (Schulte im Walde and Brew, 2001; Stevenson and Joanis, 2003; Ferrer, 2004; Devereux and Costello, 2005). The method treats each word as a singleton cluster and then successively merges two closest clusters until all the clusters have been merged into one. The cluster similarity is measured using linkage criteria (e.g. Ward (1963) measures the decrease in variance for the clusters being merged). As opposed to this, HGFC derives probabilistic bipartite graphs from the similarity matrix (Yu et al., 2006). Since we require a graph of concepts, our task is rather different from standard hierarchical word clustering that produces a tree of concepts. In a tree, each word can only have a unique parent cluster at each level. Our concept graph does not have this constraint: at any level a word can be associated with an arbitrary number of parent clusters. Therefore, not only HGFC outperformed agglomerative clustering methods in hierarchical clustering tasks (Yu et al., 2006; Sun and Korhonen, 2011), but its hierarchical graph output is also a more suitable representation of the concept graph. In addition, HGFC can detect the number of levels and the number of clusters on each level of the hierarchical graph automatically. This is essential for our task as these settings are difficult to predefine for a general-purpose concept graph.

Given a set of nouns, $V = \{v_n\}_{n=1}^N$, the similarity matrix W for HGFC is constructed using Jensen-Shannon Divergence. W can be encoded by an undirected graph G (Figure 2(a)), where the nouns are mapped to vertices and W_{ij} is the edge weight between vertices i and j. The graph G and the cluster structure can be represented by a bipartite graph $K(V, U)$. V are the vertices on G. $U = \{u_p\}_{p=1}^m$ represent the hidden m clusters. For example, looking at Figure 2(b), V on G can be grouped into three clusters u_1, u_2 and u_3. The matrix B denotes the $n \times m$ adjacency matrix, with b_{ip} being the connection weight between the vertex v_i and the cluster u_p. Thus, B represents the connections between clusters at an upper and lower level of clustering. A flat clustering algorithm can be induced by assigning a lower level node to the parent node that has the largest connection weight. The number of clusters at any level can be determined by only counting the number of non-empty nodes (namely the nodes that have at least one lower level node associated).

The bipartite graph K also induces a similarity (W') between v_i and v_j: $w'_{ij} = \sum_{p=1}^{m} \frac{b_{ip} b_{jp}}{\lambda_p} = (B\Lambda^{-1}B^T)_{ij}$ where $\Lambda = \text{diag}(\lambda_1, ..., \lambda_m)$. Therefore, B can be found by minimizing the divergence distance (ζ) between the similarity matrices W and W':

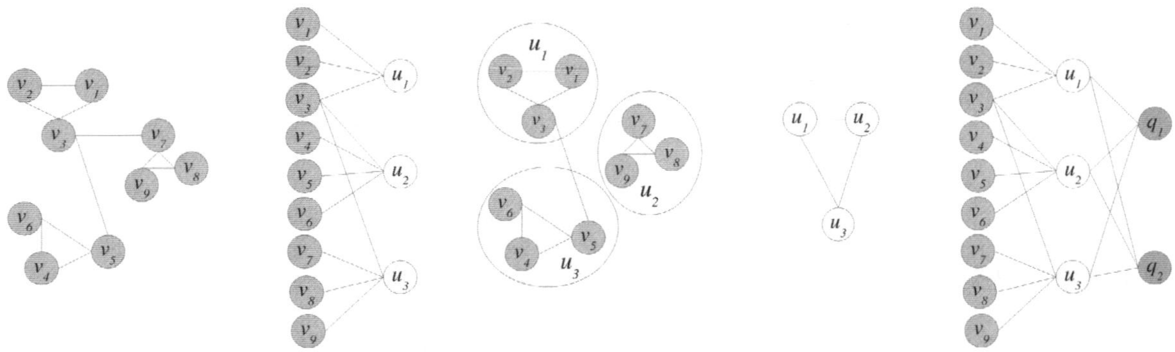

(a) (b) (c) (d) (e)

Figure 2: (a) An undirected graph G representing the similarity matrix; (b) The bipartite graph showing three clusters on G; (c) The induced clusters U; (d) The new graph G_1 over clusters U; (e) The new bipartite graph over G_1

$$\min_{H,\Lambda} \zeta(W, H\Lambda H^T), s.t. \sum_{i=1}^{n} h_{ip} = 1 \quad (1)$$

$$H = B\Lambda^{-1}; \zeta(X,Y) = \sum_{ij}(x_{ij} \log \frac{x_{ij}}{y_{ij}} - x_{ij} + y_{ij})$$

Yu et al. (2006) showed that this cost function is non-increasing under the update rule:

$$\tilde{h}_{ip} \propto h_{ip} \sum_j \frac{w_{ij}}{(H\Lambda H^T)_{ij}} \lambda_p h_{jp} \text{ s.t.} \sum_i \tilde{h}_{ip} = 1 \quad (2)$$

$$\tilde{\lambda}_p \propto \lambda_p \sum_j \frac{w_{ij}}{(H\Lambda H^T)_{ij}} h_{ip} h_{jp} \text{ s.t.} \sum_p \tilde{\lambda}_p = \sum_{ij} w_{ij} \quad (3)$$

The cost function can thus be optimized by updating h and λ alternately.

The similarity between clusters $p(u_p, u_q)$ can be induced from B, as follows:

$$\begin{aligned} p(u_p, u_q) &= p(u_p)p(u_p|u_q) = (B^T D^{-1} B)_{pq} \quad (4) \\ D &= \text{diag}(d_1, ..., d_n) \text{ where } d_i = \sum_{p=0}^{m} b_{ip} \end{aligned}$$

We can then construct a new graph G_1 (Figure 2(d)) with the clusters U as vertices, and the cluster similarity p as the connection weight. The clustering algorithm can now be applied again (Figure 2(e)). This process can go on iteratively, leading to a hierarchical graph.

The number of levels (L) and the number of clusters (m_l) are detected automatically, using the method of Sun and Korhonen (2011). Clustering starts with an initial setting of number of clusters (m_0) for the first level. In our experiment, we set the value of m_0 to 800. For the subsequent levels, m_l is set to the number of non-empty clusters (bipartite graph nodes) on the parent level. The matrices B and Λ are initialized randomly. We found that the actual initialization values have little impact on the final result. The rows in B are normalized after the initialization so the values in each row add up to one. For a word v_i, the probability of assigning it to cluster $x_p^{(l)} \in X_l$ at level l is given by:

$$\begin{aligned} p(x_p^{(l)}|v_i) &= \sum_{X_{l-1}} ... \sum_{x^{(1)} \in X_1} p(x_p^{(l)}|x^{(l-1)})...p(x^{(1)}|v_i) \\ &= (D_1^{(-1)} B_1 D_2^{-1} B_2 ... D_l^{-1} B_l)_{ip} \quad (5) \end{aligned}$$

Due to the random walk property of the graph, m_l is non-increasing for higher levels (Sun and Korhonen, 2011). The algorithm can thus terminate when all nouns are assigned to one cluster. We run 1000 iterations of updates of h and λ (equation 2 and 3) for each two adjacent levels.

The resulting graph is composed of a set of bipartite graphs defined by $B_l, B_{l-1}, ..., B_1$. A bipartite graph has a similar structure as in Figure 1. For a given noun, we can rank the clusters at any level according to the soft assignment probability (eq. 5). The clusters that have no member noun were hidden from the ranking since they do not explicitly represent any concept. However, these clusters are still part of the organisation of conceptual space within the model and they contribute to the probability for the clusters on upper levels (eq. 5). We call the *view* of the hierarchical graph where these empty clusters are hidden an *explicit graph*. The whole algorithm can be summarized as follows:

Require: N nouns V, initial number of clusters m_1
  Compute the similarity matrix W_0 from V
  Build the graph G_0 from W_0, $l \leftarrow 1$
  while $m_l > 1$ **do**
    Factorize G_{l-1} to obtain bipartite graph K_l with the adjacency matrix B_l (eq. 1, 2 and 3)
    Build a graph G_l with similarity matrix $W_l = B_l^T D_l^{-1} B_l$ according to equation 4
    $l \leftarrow l + 1$; $m_l \leftarrow$ No. non-empty clusters (eq. 5)
  end while
  return $B_l, B_{l-1} ... B_1$

2.3 Identification of Metaphorical Associations

Once we obtained the explicit graph of concepts, we can now identify metaphorical associations based on the weights connecting the clusters at different levels (eq. 5). Taking a single noun (e.g. *fire*) as input, the system computes the probability of its cluster membership for each cluster at each level, using these weights. We expect the cluster membership probabilities to indicate the level of association of the input noun with the clusters. The system can then rank the clusters at each level based on these probabilities. We chose level 3 as the optimal level of generality for our experiments, based on our qualitative analysis of the graph. The system selects 6 top-ranked clusters from this level (we expect an average source concept to have no more than 5 typical target associates) and excludes the literal cluster containing the input concept (e.g. *"fire flame blaze"*). The remaining clusters represent the target concepts associated with the input source concept. Example output for the input concepts of *fire* and *disease* is shown in Figure 3. One can see from the Figure that each of the noun-to-cluster mappings represents a new conceptual metaphor, e.g. EMOTION is FIRE, VIOLENCE is FIRE, CRIME is a DISEASE etc. These mappings are exemplified in language by a number of metaphorical expressions (e.g. "His anger will *burn* him", "violence *flared* again", "it's time they found a *cure* for corruption").

SOURCE: fire
TARGET 1: sense hatred emotion passion enthusiasm sentiment hope interest feeling resentment optimism hostility excitement anger
TARGET 2: coup violence fight resistance clash rebellion battle drive fighting riot revolt war confrontation volcano row revolution struggle
TARGET 3: alien immigrant
TARGET 4: prisoner hostage inmate

SOURCE: disease
TARGET 1: fraud outbreak offense connection leak count crime violation abuse conspiracy corruption terrorism suicide
TARGET 2: opponent critic rival
TARGET 3: execution destruction signing
TARGET 4: refusal absence fact failure lack delay

Figure 3: Discovered metaphorical associations

rage-ncsubj *engulf*-ncsubj *erupt*-ncsubj *burn*-ncsubj *light*-dobj *consume*-ncsubj *flare*-ncsubj *sweep*-ncsubj *spark*-dobj *battle*-dobj *gut*-idobj *smolder*-ncsubj *ignite*-dobj *destroy*-idobj *spread*-ncsubj *damage*-idobj *light*-ncsubj *ravage*-ncsubj *crackle*-ncsubj *open*-dobj *fuel*-dobj *spray*-idobj *roar*-ncsubj *perish*-idobj *destroy*-ncsubj *wound*-idobj *start*-dobj *ignite*-ncsubj *injure*-idobj *fight*-dobj *rock*-ncsubj *retaliate*-idobj *devastate*-idobj *blaze*-ncsubj *ravage*-idobj *rip*-ncsubj *burn*-idobj *spark*-ncsubj *warm*-idobj *suppress*-dobj *rekindle*-dobj

Figure 4: Salient features for *fire* and the *violence* cluster

2.4 Identification of Salient Features and Metaphorical Expressions

After extracting the source–target domain mappings, we now move on to the identification of the corresponding metaphorical expressions. The system does this by harvesting the salient features that lead to the input noun being strongly associated with the extracted clusters. The salient features are selected by ranking the features according to the joint probability of the feature (f) occurring both with the input noun (w) and the cluster (c). Under a simplified independence assumption, $p(w, c|f) = p(w|f) \times p(c|f)$. $p(w|f)$ and $p(c|f)$ are calculated as the ratio of the frequency of the feature f to the total frequency of the input noun and the cluster respectively. The features ranked higher are expected to represent the source domain vocabulary that can be used to metaphorically describe the target concepts. We selected the top 50 features from the ranked list. Example features (verbs and their grammatical relations) extracted for the source domain noun *fire* and the *violence* cluster are shown in Figure 4.

We then refined the lists of features by means of selectional preference (SP) filtering. We use SPs to

FEELING IS FIRE hope *lit* (Subj), anger *blazed* (Subj), optimism *raged* (Subj), enthusiasm *engulfed* them (Subj), hatred *flared* (Subj), passion *flared* (Subj), interest *lit* (Subj), *fuel* resentment (Dobj), anger *crackled* (Subj), feelings *roared* (Subj), hostility *blazed* (Subj), *light* with hope (Iobj)
CRIME IS A DISEASE *cure* crime (Dobj), abuse *transmitted* (Subj), *eradicate* terrorism (Dobj), *suffer from* corruption (Iobj), *diagnose* abuse (Dobj), *combat* fraud (Dobj), *cope with* crime (Iobj), *cure* abuse (Dobj), *eradicate* corruption

Figure 5: Identified metaphorical expressions for the mappings FEELING IS FIRE and CRIME IS A DISEASE

quantify how well the extracted features describe the source domain (e.g. *fire*). We extracted nominal argument distributions of the verbs in our feature lists for VERB–SUBJECT, VERB–DIRECT_OBJECT and VERB–INDIRECT_OBJECT relations. We used the algorithm of Sun and Korhonen (2009) to create SP classes and the measure of Resnik (1993) to quantify how well a particular argument class fits the verb. Resnik measures selectional preference strength $S_R(v)$ of a predicate as a Kullback-Leibler distance between two distributions: the prior probability of the noun class $P(c)$ and the posterior probability of the noun class given the verb $P(c|v)$. $S_R(v) = D(P(c|v)||P(c)) = \sum_c P(c|v) \log \frac{P(c|v)}{P(c)}$. In order to quantify how well a particular argument class fits the verb, Resnik defines selectional association as $A_R(v,c) = \frac{1}{S_R(v)} P(c|v) \log \frac{P(c|v)}{P(c)}$. We rank the nominal arguments of the verbs in our feature lists using their selectional association with the verb, and then only retain the features whose top 5 arguments contain the source concept. For example, the verb *start*, that is a common feature for both *fire* and the *violence* cluster (e.g. "start a war", "start a fire"), would be filtered out in this way, whereas the verbs *flare* or *blaze* would be retained as descriptive source domain vocabulary.

We then search the RASP-parsed BNC for grammatical relations, in which the nouns from the target domain cluster appear with the verbs from the source domain vocabulary (e.g. "war *blazed*" (subj), "to *fuel* violence" (dobj) for the mapping VIOLENCE is FIRE). The system thus annotates metaphorical expressions in text, as well as the corresponding conceptual metaphors, as shown in Figure 5.

3 Evaluation and Discussion

3.1 Baselines

AGG: the agglomerative clustering baseline is constructed using SciPy implementation (Oliphant, 2007) of Ward's linkage method (Ward, 1963). The output tree is cut according to the number of levels and the number of clusters of the explicit graph detected by HGFC. The resulting tree is converted into a graph by adding connections from each cluster to all the clusters one level above. The connection weight (the cluster distance) is measured using Jensen-Shannon Divergence between the cluster centroids. This graph is used in place of the HGFC graph in the metaphor identification experiments.
WN: in the WN baseline, the WordNet hierarchy is used as the underlying graph of concepts, to which the metaphor extraction method is applied. Given a source concept, the system extracts all its sense-1 hypernyms two levels above and subsequently all of their sister terms. The hypernyms themselves are considered to represent the literal sense of the source noun and are, therefore, removed. The sister terms are kept as potential target domains.

3.2 Evaluation of Metaphorical Associations

To create our dataset, we extracted 10 common source concepts that map to multiple targets from the Master Metaphor List (Lakoff et al., 1991) and linguistic analyses of metaphor (Lakoff and Johnson, 1980; Shutova and Teufel, 2010). These included FIRE, CHILD, SPEED, WAR, DISEASE, BREAKDOWN, CONSTRUCTION, VEHICLE, SYSTEM, BUSINESS. Each of the three systems identified 50 source–target domain mappings for the given source domains, resulting in a set of 150 conceptual metaphors (each representing a number of submappings since all the target concepts are clusters or synsets). These were then evaluated against human judgements in two different experimental settings.
Setting 1: The judges were presented with a set of conceptual metaphors identified by the three systems, randomized. They were asked to annotate the mappings they considered valid. In all our experiments, the judges were encouraged to rely on their own intuition of metaphor, but they also reviewed the metaphor annotation guidelines of Shutova and Teufel (2010). Two independent judges, both na-

tive speakers of English, participated in this experiment. Their agreement on the task was $\kappa = 0.60$ ($n = 2, N = 150, k = 2$) (Siegel and Castellan, 1988). The main differences in the annotators' judgements stem from the fact that some metaphorical associations are less obvious and common than others, and thus need more context (or imaginative effort) to establish. Such examples, where the judges disagreed included metaphorical mappings such as INTENSITY is SPEED, GOAL is a CHILD, COLLECTION is a SYSTEM, ILLNESS is a BREAKDOWN.

The system performance was then evaluated against these judgements in terms of precision (P), i.e. the proportion of the valid metaphorical mappings among those identified. We calculated system precision (in all experiments) as an average over both annotations. HGFC operates with a precision of $P = 0.69$, whereas the baselines attain $P = 0.36$ (AGG) and $P = 0.29$ (WN). The precision of annotator judgements against each other (the human ceiling) is $P = 0.80$, suggesting that this is a challenging task.

Setting 2: To measure recall, R, of the systems we asked two annotators (both native speakers with a background in metaphor, different from Setting 1) to write down up to 5 target concepts they strongly associated with each of the 10 source concepts. Their annotations were then aggregated into a single metaphor association gold standard, consisting of 63 mappings in total. The recall of the systems was measured against this gold standard, resulting in HGFC $R = 0.61$, AGG $R = 0.11$ and WN $R = 0.03$.

As expected, HGFC outperforms both AGG and WN baselines in both settings. AGG has been previously shown to be less accurate than HGFC in the verb clustering task (Sun and Korhonen, 2011). Our analysis of the noun clusters indicated that HGFC tends to produce more pure and complete clusters than AGG. Another important reason AGG fails is that it by definition organises all concepts into tree and optimises its solution locally, taking into account a small number of clusters at a time. However, being able to discover connections between more distant domains and optimising globally over all concepts is crucial for metaphor identification. This makes AGG less suitable for the task, as demonstrated by our results. However, AGG identified a number of interesting mappings missed by HGFC, e.g. CAREER IS A CHILD, LANGUAGE IS A SYSTEM, CORRUPTION IS A VEHICLE, EMPIRE IS A CONSTRUCTION, as well as a number of mappings in common with HGFC, e.g. DEBATE IS A WAR, DESTRUCTION IS A DISEASE. The WN system also identified a few interesting metaphorical mappings (e.g. COGNITION IS FIRE, EDUCATION IS CONSTRUCTION), but its output is largely dominated by the concepts similar to the source noun and contains some unrelated concepts. The comparison of HGFC to WN shows that HGFC identifies meaningful properties and relations of abstract concepts that can not be captured in a tree-like classification (even an accurate, manually created one). The latter is more appropriate for concrete concepts, and a more flexible representation is needed to model abstract concepts. The fact that both baselines identified some valid metaphorical associations, relying on less suitable conceptual graphs, suggests that our way of traversing the graph is a viable approach in principle.

HGFC identifies valid metaphorical associations for a range of source concepts. On of them (CRIME IS A VIRUS) happened to have been already validated in psychological experiments (Thibodeau and Boroditsky, 2011). The most frequent type of error of HGFC is the presence of target clusters similar or closely related to the source noun (e.g. the *parent* cluster for *child*). The clusters from the same domain can, however, be filtered out if their nouns frequently occur in the same documents with the source noun (in a large corpus), i.e. by topical similarity. The latter is less likely for the metaphorically connected nouns. We intend to implement this improvement in the future version of the system.

3.3 Evaluation of Metaphorical Expressions

For each of the identified conceptual metaphors, the three systems extracted a number of metaphorical expressions from the corpus (average of 430 for HGFC, 148 for AGG, and 855 for WN). The expressions were also evaluated against human judgements. The judges were presented with a set of randomly sampled sentences containing metaphorical expressions as annotated by the system and by the baselines (200 each), randomized. They were asked to mark the tagged expressions that were metaphorical in their judgement as correct. Their agreement on the task was $\kappa = 0.56$ ($n = 2, N = 600, k = 2$),

HLJ 26 [..] "effective action" was needed to **eradicate terrorism, drug-trafficking** and **corruption**.
EG0 275 In the 1930s the words "means test" was a curse, **fuelling the resistance** against it both among the unemployed and some of its administrators.
CRX 1054 [..] if the rehabilitative approach were demonstrably successful in **curing crime**.
HL3 1206 [..] he would strive to **accelerate progress** towards the economic integration of the Caribbean.
HXJ 121 [..] it is likely that some **industries will flourish** in certain countries as the **market widens**.

Figure 6: Metaphors tagged by the system (in bold)

whereby the main source of disagreement was the presence of lexicalized metaphors, e.g. verbs such as *impose, decline* etc. The system performance against these annotations is $P = 0.65$ (HGFC), $P = 0.47$ (AGG) and $P = 0.12$ (WN). The human ceiling for this task was measured at $P = 0.79$. Figure 6 shows example sentences annotated by HGFC. The performance of our unsupervised approach is close to the previous supervised systems of Mason (2004) (accuracy of 0.73) and Shutova et al. (2010) (precision of 0.79), however, the results are not directly comparable due to different experimental settings.

The system errors in this task stem from multiple word senses of the salient features or the source and target sharing some physical properties (e.g. one can "*die from* crime" and "*die from* a disease"). Some identified expressions invoke a chain of mappings (e.g. ABUSE IS A DISEASE, DISEASE IS AN ENEMY for "*combat* abuse"), however, such chains are not yet incorporated into the system. The performance of AGG is higher than in the mappings identification task, since it outputs only few expressions for the incorrect mappings. In contrast, WN tagged a large number of literal expressions due to the incorrect prior identification of the underlying associations.

Since there is no large metaphor-annotated corpus available, it was impossible for us to reliably evaluate the recall of metaphorical expressions. However, we estimated it as a recall of salient features. We manually compiled sets of typical features for the 10 source domains, and measured their recall among the top 50 HGFC features at $R = 0.70$. However, in practice the coverage in this task would directly depend on that of the metaphorical associations.

4 Related Work

One of the first attempts to identify and interpret metaphorical expressions in text is the met* system of Fass (1991), that utilizes hand-coded knowledge and detects non-literalness via selectional preference violation. In case of a violation, the respective phrase is first tested for being metonymic using hand-coded patterns (e.g. CONTAINER-FOR-CONTENT). If this fails, the system searches the knowledge base for a relevant analogy in order to discriminate metaphorical relations from anomalous ones. The system of Krishnakumaran and Zhu (2007) uses WordNet (the hyponymy relation) and word bigram counts to predict verbal, nominal and adjectival metaphors at the sentence level. The authors discriminate between conventional metaphors (included in WordNet) and novel metaphors. Birke and Sarkar (2006) present a sentence clustering approach that employs a set of seed sentences annotated for literalness and computes similarity between the new input sentence and all of the seed sentences. The system then tags the sentence as literal or metaphorical according to the annotation in the most similar seeds, attaining an f-score of 53.8%.

The first system to discover source–target domain mappings automatically is CorMet (Mason, 2004). It does this by searching for systematic variations in domain-specific verb selectional preferences. For example, *pour* is a characteristic verb in both LAB and FINANCE domains. In the LAB domain it has a strong preference for *liquids* and in the FINANCE domain for *money*. From this the system infers the domain mapping FINANCE – LAB and the concept mapping *money – liquid*. Gedigian et al. (2006) trained a maximum entropy classifier to discriminate between literal and metaphorical use. They annotated the sentences from PropBank (Kingsbury and Palmer, 2002) containing the verbs of MOTION and CURE for metaphoricity. They used PropBank annotation (arguments and their semantic types) as features for classification and report an accuracy of 95.12% (however, against a majority baseline of 92.90%). The metaphor identification system of Shutova et al. (2010) starts from a small seed set of metaphorical expressions, learns the analogies involved in their production and extends the set of analogies by means of verb and noun clustering. As a result, the system can recognize new metaphorical expressions in unrestricted text (e.g. from the seed "*stir* excitement" it infers that "*swallow* anger" is also a metaphor), achieving a precision of 79%.

Turney et al. (2011) classify verbs and adjectives as literal or metaphorical based on their level of concreteness or abstractness in relation to a noun they appear with. They learn concreteness rankings for words automatically (starting from a set of examples) and then search for expressions where a concrete adjective or verb is used with an abstract noun (e.g. "*dark* humour" is tagged as a metaphor and "dark hair" is not). They report an accuracy of 73%.

5 Conclusions and Future Directions

Previous research on metaphor addressed a number of different aspects of the phenomenon, and has shown that these aspects can be successfully modeled using statistical techniques. However, the methods often focused on a limited domain and needed manually-labeled training data. This made them difficult to apply in a real-world setting with the goal of improving semantic interpretation in NLP at large. Our method takes a step towards this direction. It is fully unsupervised, and thus more robust, and can perform accurate metaphor identification in unrestricted text. It identifies metaphor with a precision of 69% and a recall of 61%, which is a very encouraging result for an unsupervised method. We believe that this work has important implications for computational and cognitive modeling of metaphor, but is also applicable to a range of other semantic tasks within NLP. Integrating different representations of abstract and concrete concepts into NLP systems may improve their performance, as well as make the models more cognitively plausible.

One of our key future research objectives is to investigate the use and adaptation of the created conceptual graph to perform metaphor interpretation. In addition, we plan to extend this work to cover nominal and adjectival metaphors, by harvesting salient nominal and adjectival features.

Acknowledgments

This work was funded by the MetaNet project (grant number W911NF-12-C-0022) and the Dorothy Hodgkin Postgraduate Award.

References

Roberta Adorni and Alice Mado Proverbio. 2012. The neural manifestation of the word concreteness effect: An electrical neuroimaging study. *Neuropsychologia*, 50(5):880 – 891.

Rodrigo Agerri, John Barnden, Mark Lee, and Alan Wallington. 2007. Metaphor, inference and domain-independent mappings. In *Proceedings of RANLP-2007*, pages 17–23, Borovets, Bulgaria.

John Barnden and Mark Lee. 2002. An artificial intelligence approach to metaphor understanding. *Theoria et Historia Scientiarum*, 6(1):399–412.

Shane Bergsma, Dekang Lin, and Randy Goebel. 2008. Discriminative learning of selectional preference from unlabeled text. In *Proceedings of the Conference on Empirical Methods in Natural Language Processing*, EMNLP '08, pages 59–68, Honolulu, Hawaii.

Jeffrey R. Binder, Chris F. Westbury, Kristen A. McKiernan, Edward T. Possing, and David A. Medler. 2005. Distinct brain systems for processing concrete and abstract concepts. *Journal of Cognitive Neuroscience*, 17(6):905–917.

Julia Birke and Anoop Sarkar. 2006. A clustering approach for the nearly unsupervised recognition of nonliteral language. In *In Proceedings of EACL-06*, pages 329–336.

Ted Briscoe, John Carroll, and Rebecca Watson. 2006. The second release of the rasp system. In *Proceedings of the COLING/ACL on Interactive presentation sessions*.

Lou Burnard. 2007. *Reference Guide for the British National Corpus (XML Edition)*.

Lynne Cameron. 2003. *Metaphor in Educational Discourse*. Continuum, London.

Sebastian J. Crutch and Elizabeth K. Warrington. 2005. Abstract and concrete concepts have structurally different representational frameworks. *Brain*, 128(3):615–627.

Sebastian J Crutch and Elizabeth K Warrington. 2010. The differential dependence of abstract and concrete words upon associative and similarity-based information: Complementary semantic interference and facilitation effects. *Cognitive Neuropsychology*, 27(1):46–71.

Barry Devereux and Fintan Costello. 2005. Propane stoves and gas lamps: How the concept hierarchy influences the interpretation of noun-noun compounds. In *Proceedings of the Twenty-Seventh Annual Conference of the Cognitive Science Society*.

Dan Fass. 1991. met*: A method for discriminating metonymy and metaphor by computer. *Computational Linguistics*, 17(1):49–90.

Jerome Feldman and Srini Narayanan. 2004. Embodied meaning in a neural theory of language. *Brain and Language*, 89(2):385–392.

Christiane Fellbaum, editor. 1998. *WordNet: An Electronic Lexical Database (ISBN: 0-262-06197-X)*. MIT Press, first edition.

Eva E. Ferrer. 2004. Towards a semantic classification of spanish verbs based on subcategorisation information. In *Proceedings of the ACL 2004 workshop on Student research*, page 13. Association for Computational Linguistics.

Matt Gedigian, John Bryant, Srini Narayanan, and Branimir Ciric. 2006. Catching metaphors. In *In Proceedings of the 3rd Workshop on Scalable Natural Language Understanding*, pages 41–48, New York.

David Graff, Junbo Kong, Ke Chen, and Kazuaki Maeda. 2003. English gigaword. *Linguistic Data Consortium, Philadelphia.*

Hsu-Wen Huang, Chia-Lin Lee, and Kara D. Federmeier. 2010. Imagine that! erps provide evidence for distinct hemispheric contributions to the processing of concrete and abstract concepts. *NeuroImage*, 49(1):1116 – 1123.

Paul Kingsbury and Martha Palmer. 2002. From TreeBank to PropBank. In *Proceedings of LREC-2002*, pages 1989–1993, Gran Canaria, Canary Islands, Spain.

Saisuresh Krishnakumaran and Xiaojin Zhu. 2007. Hunting elusive metaphors using lexical resources. In *Proceedings of the Workshop on Computational Approaches to Figurative Language*, pages 13–20, Rochester, NY.

George Lakoff and Mark Johnson. 1980. *Metaphors We Live By*. University of Chicago Press, Chicago.

George Lakoff, Jane Espenson, and Alan Schwartz. 1991. The master metaphor list. Technical report, University of California at Berkeley.

James Martin. 1990. *A Computational Model of Metaphor Interpretation*. Academic Press Professional, Inc., San Diego, CA, USA.

James Martin. 2006. A corpus-based analysis of context effects on metaphor comprehension. In A. Stefanowitsch and S. T. Gries, editors, *Corpus-Based Approaches to Metaphor and Metonymy*, Berlin. Mouton de Gruyter.

Zachary Mason. 2004. Cormet: a computational, corpus-based conventional metaphor extraction system. *Computational Linguistics*, 30(1):23–44.

Srini Narayanan. 1997. Knowledge-based Action Representations for Metaphor and Aspect (KARMA). Technical report, PhD thesis, University of California at Berkeley.

Srini Narayanan. 1999. Moving right along: A computational model of metaphoric reasoning about events. In *Proceedings of AAAI 99)*, pages 121–128, Orlando, Florida.

Travis E. Oliphant. 2007. Python for scientific computing. *Computing in Science and Engineering*, 9:10–20.

Patrick Pantel and Dekang Lin. 2002. Discovering word senses from text. In *Proceedings of the eighth ACM SIGKDD international conference on Knowledge discovery and data mining*, pages 613–619. ACM.

Philip Resnik. 1993. *Selection and Information: A Class-based Approach to Lexical Relationships*. Ph.D. thesis, Philadelphia, PA, USA.

Sabine Schulte im Walde and Chris Brew. 2001. Inducing German semantic verb classes from purely syntactic subcategorisation information. In *ACL '02: Proceedings of the 40th Annual Meeting on Association for Computational Linguistics*, pages 223–230, Morristown, NJ, USA. Association for Computational Linguistics.

Ekaterina Shutova and Simone Teufel. 2010. Metaphor corpus annotated for source - target domain mappings. In *Proceedings of LREC 2010*, pages 3255–3261, Malta.

Ekaterina Shutova, Lin Sun, and Anna Korhonen. 2010. Metaphor identification using verb and noun clustering. In *Proceedings of Coling 2010*, pages 1002–1010, Beijing, China.

Ekaterina Shutova, Simone Teufel, and Anna Korhonen. 2012. Statistical Metaphor Processing. *Computational Linguistics*, 39(2).

Ekaterina Shutova. 2010. Automatic metaphor interpretation as a paraphrasing task. In *Proceedings of NAACL 2010*, pages 1029–1037, Los Angeles, USA.

Sidney Siegel and N. John Castellan. 1988. *Nonparametric statistics for the behavioral sciences*. McGraw-Hill Book Company, New York, USA.

Gerard J. Steen, Aletta G. Dorst, J. Berenike Herrmann, Anna A. Kaal, Tina Krennmayr, and Trijntje Pasma. 2010. *A method for linguistic metaphor identification: From MIP to MIPVU*. John Benjamins, Amsterdam/Philadelphia.

Suzanne Stevenson and Eric Joanis. 2003. Semi-supervised verb class discovery using noisy features. In *Proceedings of HLT-NAACL 2003*, pages 71–78.

Lin Sun and Anna Korhonen. 2009. Improving verb clustering with automatically acquired selectional preferences. In *Proceedings of EMNLP 2009*, pages 638–647, Singapore, August.

Lin Sun and Anna Korhonen. 2011. Hierarchical verb clustering using graph factorization. In *Proceedings of EMNLP*, pages 1023–1033, Edinburgh, UK.

Paul H. Thibodeau and Lera Boroditsky. 2011. Metaphors we think with: The role of metaphor in reasoning. *PLoS ONE*, 6(2):e16782, 02.

Peter D. Turney, Yair Neuman, Dan Assaf, and Yohai Cohen. 2011. Literal and metaphorical sense identification through concrete and abstract context. In *Proceedings of the Conference on Empirical Methods in Natural Language Processing*, EMNLP '11, pages 680–690, Stroudsburg, PA, USA. Association for Computational Linguistics.

Joe H. Ward. 1963. Hierarchical grouping to optimize an objective function. *Journal of the American statistical association*, 58(301):236–244.

Katja Wiemer-Hastings and Xu Xu. 2005. Content Differences for Abstract and Concrete Concepts. *Cognitive Science*, 29(5):719–736.

Kai Yu, Shipeng Yu, and Volker Tresp. 2006. Soft clustering on graphs. *Advances in Neural Information Processing Systems*, 18.

Three Knowledge-Free Methods for Automatic Lexical Chain Extraction

Steffen Remus and **Chris Biemann**
FG Language Technology
Department of Computer Science
Technische Universität Darmstadt
remus@kdsl.informatik.tu-darmstadt.de, biem@cs.tu-darmstadt.de

Abstract

We present three approaches to lexical chaining based on the LDA topic model and evaluate them intrinsically on a manually annotated set of German documents. After motivating the choice of statistical methods for lexical chaining with their adaptability to different languages and subject domains, we describe our new two-level chain annotation scheme, which rooted in the concept of cohesive harmony. Also, we propose a new measure for direct evaluation of lexical chains. Our three LDA-based approaches outperform two knowledge-based state-of-the art methods to lexical chaining by a large margin, which can be attributed to lacking coverage of the knowledge resource. Subsequent analysis shows that the three methods yield a different chaining behavior, which could be utilized in tasks that use lexical chaining as a component within NLP applications.

1 Introduction

A text that is understandable by its nature exhibits an underlying structure which makes the text coherent; that is, the structure is responsible for making the text "hang" together (Halliday and Hasan, 1976). The theoretic foundation of this structure is defined as *coherence* and *cohesion*. While the former is concerned with the meaning of a text, the latter can be seen as a collection of devices for creating it. Cohesion and coherence build the basis for most of the current natural language processing problems that deal with text understanding. *Lexical cohesion* ties together words or phrases that are semantically related. Once all the cohesive ties are identified the involved items can be grouped together to form so-called *lexical chains*, which form a theoretically well-founded building block in various natural language processing applications, such as word sense disambiguation (Okumura and Honda, 1994), summarization (Barzilay and Elhadad, 1997), malapropism detection and correction (Hirst and St-Onge, 1998), document hyperlinking (Green, 1996), text segmentation (Stokes et al., 2004), topic tracking (Carthy, 2004), and others. The performance of the individual task heavily depends on the quality of the identified lexical chains.

1.1 Motivation for Corpus-driven Approach

Previous approaches mainly focus on the use of knowledge resources like lexical semantic databases (Hirst and St-Onge, 1998) or thesauri (Morris and Hirst, 1991) as background information in order to resolve possible semantic relations. A major drawback of this strategy is the dependency on the coverage of the resource, which has a direct impact on the lexical chains. Their quality can be expected to be poor for resource-scarce languages or specialized application domains.

Statistical methods to modeling language semantics have proven to deliver good results in many natural language processing applications. In particular, probabilistic topic models have been successfully used for tasks such as summarization (Gong and Liu, 2001; Hennig, 2009), text segmentation (Misra et al., 2009), lexical substitution (Dinu and Lapata, 2010) or word sense disambiguation (Cai et al., 2007; Boyd-Graber et al., 2007).

In this work, we address the question, whether statistical methods for the extraction of lexical chains can yield better results than existing knowledge-based methods, especially for underresourced languages or domains, following principles of Structure Discovery (Biemann, 2012). To address this, we have developed a methodology for evaluating the quality of lexical chains intrinsically, have carried out an annotation study, and report results on a corpus of manually annotated German news documents.

After defining a measure for the comparison of (manually or automatically created) lexical chains in Section 2, Section 3 describes our annotation methodology and discusses issues regarding the inherent subjectivity of lexical chain annotation. In Section 4, three statistical approaches for lexical chaining are developed on the basis of the LDA topic model. Experiments that demonstrate the advantage of these approaches over a knowledge-baseline are conducted and evaluated in Section 5, and Section 6 concludes and provides an outlook future directions.

1.2 Previous Work on Lexical Chains

Morris and Hirst (1991) initially proposed an algorithm for lexical chaining based on Roget's thesaurus (Roget, 1852), and manually assessed the quality of their algorithm. Hirst and St-Onge (1998) first presented a computational approach to lexical chaining based on WordNet showing that the lexical database is a reasonable replacement to Roget's. The basic idea behind these algorithms is that semantically close words should be connected to form chains. Subsequent approaches mainly concentrated on disambiguation of words to WordNet concepts (WSD), since ambiguous words can lead to the overgeneration of connections. Barzilay and Elhadad (1997) improved the implicit word sense disambiguation (WSD) by keeping a list of different interpretations of the text and finally choosing the most plausible senses for chaining. Silber and McCoy (2002) introduced an efficient variant of the algorithm with linear complexity in the number of candidate terms. Galley and McKeown (2003) further improved accuracy by first performing WSD, and then using the remaining links between the disambiguated concepts only. They also introduced a so-called *disambiguation graph*, a representation that has also been utilized by the method of Medelyan (2007), where she applied a graph clustering algorithm to the disambiguation graph to cut weak links, performing implicit WSD. A combination of statistical and knowledge-based methods is presented by Marathe and Hirst (2010), who combine distributional co-occurrence information with semantic information from a lexicographic resource for extracting lexical chains and evaluate them by text segmentation. We are not aware of previous lexical chaining algorithms that do not rely on a lexicographic resource at all.

A major issue in developing a new lexical chaining algorithm is the comparison to previous systems. Most of previous approaches are validated by the evaluation in a certain task like summarization, word sense disambiguation, keyphrase extraction or information retrieval (Stairmand, 1996). Hence, these extrinsic evaluations are heavily influenced by the particular task at hand. We propose to re-consider lexical chaining as a task on its own, and propose objective criteria for directly comparing lexical chains to this end.

2 Comparing Lexical Chains

The comparison of lexical chains is a non-trivial task. We adopt the idea of interpreting lexical chains as clusters and a particular set of lexical chains as a clustering, and develop a suitable cluster comparison measure. As stated by Meilă (2005) and Amigó et al. (2009), a best clustering comparison measure for the general case does not exist. It should be stressed that the appropriate clustering measure highly depends on the task at hand.

After exploring a number of measures[1], we decided on a combination of the adjusted Rand index (ARI, Hubert and Arabie (1985)) and the *basic merge distance* (BMD, Menestrina et al. (2010)) for our new measure. Menestrina et al. (2010) introduced a linear time algorithm for computing the *generalized merge distance* (GMD), which counts

[1]Explored measures which are unsatisfactory for the given task are: Closest Cluster F_1 (Benjelloun et al., 2009), K (Ajmera et al., 2002), Pairwise F_1 (Manning et al., 2008), Variation of Information (Meilă, 2005), B^3(Bagga and Baldwin, 1998), V-Measure (Rosenberg and Hirschberg, 2007), Normalized Mutual Information (Strehl, 2002). The last two measures are equal. A proof of this can be found in the appendix.

split and *merge* cluster editing operations. Using a constant factor of 1 for both splits and merges gives the *basic merge distance* (BMD): Considering $\top$ as the most general clustering of a dataset D, where all elements are grouped into the same cluster, and further considering $\bot$ as the most specific clustering of D, where each element builds its own cluster, the *lattice* between $\top$ and $\bot$ spans all possible clusterings and the BMD can be interpreted as the *shortest path* from a clustering C to a clustering C' in the lattice with some restrictions (see Menestrina et al. (2010) for details). We normalize the BMD score by the maximum BMD[2] to the normalized basic merge distance ($NBMD$). ARI is is based on pair comparisons, and is computed as[3]:

$$index = TP$$

$$expected\ index = \frac{(TP + FP) \times (TP + FN)}{TP + TN + FP + FN}$$

$$max\ index = TP + \frac{1}{2}(FP + FN)$$

$$ARI(C, C') = \frac{index - expected\ index}{max\ index - expected\ index}$$

The reasons for choosing these two particular measures are the following: ARI is a well known measure which is adjusted (corrected) for decisions made by chance. But since it is based on pairwise element comparison it completely disregards singleton clusters (chains) and some types of errors are not adequately penalized. The NBMD on the other hand penalizes various errors almost equally.

We combine the two single measures into a new $lccm$ (lexical chain comparison measure), defined as the arithmetic mean between ARI and $1 - NBMD$. An $lccm$ of 1 indicates perfect congruence and an $lccm = 0$ indicates that not a single pair of items in C is found in a cluster together in C'.

$$lccm(C, C') = \frac{1}{2}\left[1 - NBMD(C, C') + ARI(C, C')\right] .$$

[2] $BMD(\top, \bot)$ for $|D| \leq 2$, $BMD(\top, \bot) + 1$ otherwise

[3] TP: pairs in D and D', FP: pairs in D' but not in D, FN: pairs in D but not in D', TN: pairs not in D and not in D', where D is the underlying dataset of C, D' is the underlying dataset of C', and pairs means all unique combinations of elements that are in the same cluster.

3 Annotating Lexical Chains

A challenge with the annotation of lexical chains is the subjective interpretation of the text by individual annotators (Morris and Hirst, 2004), which also substantiates the fact that currently no gold standard exist, and all previous automatic approaches are evaluated by performing a certain NLP task. Hollingsworth and Teufel (2005) as well as Cramer et al. (2008) conclude from their lexical chain annotation projects that high inter-annotator agreement is very hard to achieve. We argue that directly evaluating on lexical chains should enable us to optimize towards higher-quality chain annotations, which is a task of its own right and which has the potential to improve all subsequent applications. For this, we devise an annotation scheme that gets us reasonable inter-annotator agreement, inspired by the concept of *cohesive harmony* (Hasan, 1984), and report on an annotation project for German newswire texts.

Documents from the SALSA 2.0 (Burchardt et al., 2006) corpus were chosen to form the basis for the annotation of lexical chain information. SALSA is based on the semi-automatically annotated TIGER Treebank 2.1 (Brants et al., 2002). The TIGER treebank provides manual annotations, such as lemmas, part-of-speech tags, and syntactic structure, the SALSA part of the corpus is also partially annotated with FrameNet-style (Baker et al., 1998) frame annotation. The documents are general domain news articles from a German newspaper comprising about 1,550 documents and around 50,000 sentences in total, with a median document length of 275 tokens.

3.1 Annotation Scheme

In order to minimize the subjectiveness of choices by different annotators, annotation guidelines were developed comprising a total of ten pages. We decided to consider only nouns, noun compounds and non-compositional adjective noun phrases like "dirty money" as candidate terms for lexical chaining, which is consistent with the procedures of Hollingsworth and Teufel (2005) and Cramer et al. (2008). For annotation, we used the MMAX2[4] (Müller and Strube, 2006) tool.

We introduce the term *dense chain*, which refers to a type of lexical chain in which every element is

[4] http://mmax2.sourceforge.net

related to every other element in that chain. Terms are considered to be related if they share the same topic, i.e. common sense and knowledge of the language is needed to decide which terms belong together in the same topic and whether a chosen topic is neither too broad nor too narrow. A single dense chain can thus be assigned a definite topical description of its items. Whereas Hollingsworth and Teufel (2005) dealt with the inherent fuzziness of membership of terms to lexical chains by allowing terms to occur in different lexical chains, we follow the concept of *cohesive harmony* introduced by Hasan (1984) here, where complete chains can be linked to others. For this purpose, we introduce so-called *level two links*, which are cohesive ties between lexical items in distinct dense chains. Having such a link between two chains, both chains can be assigned a topical description which is broader than the description of the individual chains. This results in a two-level representation of chains. We report on dense lexical chains and merged lexical chains (dense chains are merged into a common chain if a level two link exists between them) separately.

In total, 100 documents were annotated by two expert annotators. Documents were chosen around the length median and consist of 248 – 304 tokens. The two rightmost columns of Table 3 show the characteristics of the annotated data set. It can be concluded that there is a moderate to high agreement regarding the annotator selections of candidate terms, which is ensured by preselection of candidate terms by part-of-speech patterns. A value of 81 % in the average agreement on lexical items (cf. Figure 1) shows that even though the choice of lexical items is limited to nouns and adjective noun phrases only, the decision on candidate termhood is somewhat different between the annotators, but compares favorably with previous findings of 63 % average pairwise agreement (Morris and Hirst, 2004).

Figure 2 shows the annotator agreement on the individual documents using the *lccm* (cf. Sec. 2), sorted in the same way as in Figure 1. In order to use the level two link information the figure also shows a second agreement score, which was computed on merged chains.

The agreement scores of the assignment of lexical items to lexical chains depend partially on the agreement scores of the identified lexical items themselves, which is a desired property. Across all documents, a perfect agreement was never achieved, which confirms the difficulty of annotating such a subjective task: The average $lccm$ per document on the manual annotations is 0.56 (dense chains), respectively 0.54 (merged chains). However, the considerable overlap between the annotators still enables us to evaluate automatic chaining methods, and the $lccm$ agreement score serves as an upper bound. Note that by performing no reconciliation of the annotations we explicitly allow the possibility of different interpretations which is in our opinion appropriate here due to the subjectiveness of the task itself. By doing so, we evaluate our algorithms against individual annotator interpretations.

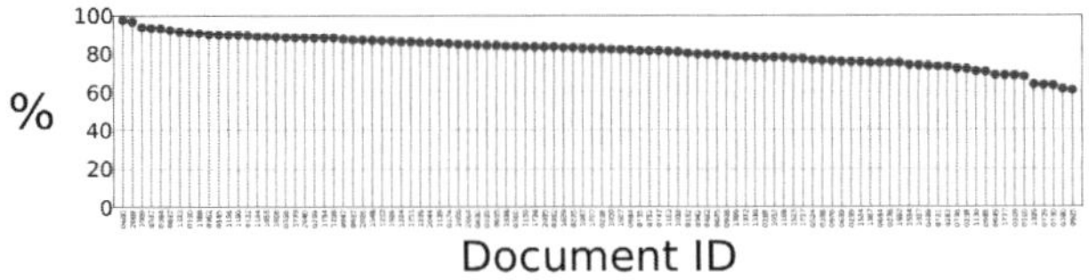

Figure 1: Agreement of lexical items annotated by annotator A and annotator B as a percentage of lexical items annotated by annotator A or annotator B. The average agreement is 81 %.

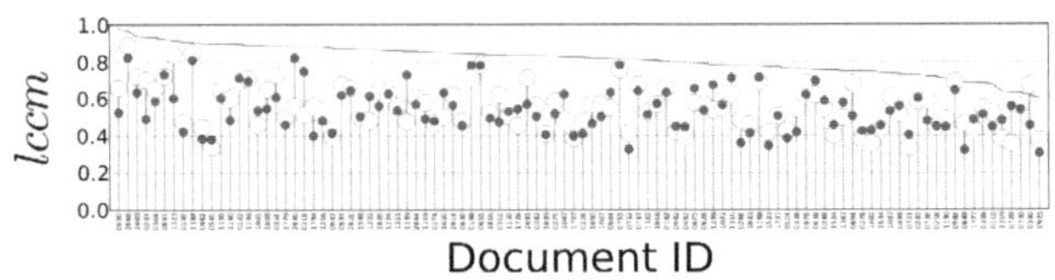

Figure 2: Individual annotator agreement scores on 100 documents sorted by their agreement on candidate terms. The red circles show the agreement of both annotators on the dense lexical chains disregarding the cohesive links, and the green dots show the agreement of both annotators on the merged lexical chains (via the cohesive links) both using the proposed *lexical chain comparison measure*.

4 Statistical Methods for Lexical Chaining

This work employs a well-studied statistical method for creating something that Barzilay (1997) called an *automatic thesaurus* which will then be adapted for lexical chaining. For our automatic approaches, candidate lexical items in a text are preselected by the same heuristic that is also applied in Section 3 for the annotation process.

Topic models (TMs) are a suite of unsupervised algorithms designed for unveiling some hidden structure in large data collections. The key idea is that documents can be represented as composites of so-called *topics* where a topic itself represents as a composite of words. Hofmann (1999) defined a topic to be a probability distribution over words and a document to be a probability distribution over a fixed set of topics. We use the *latent Dirichlet allocation* (LDA, Blei et al. (2003)) topic model for estimating the semantic closeness of candidate terms, and explore different ways of utilizing LDA's topic information in automatic lexical chainers. Specifically, we use the GibbsLDA++[5] framework for topic model estimation and inference, and examine the following LDA parameters: number of topics T, Dirichlet hyperparameters for document-topic distribution α and topic-term distribution β.

We now describe three LDA-based approaches to lexical chaining.

4.1 LDA Mode Method (LDA-MM)

The LDA-MM approach places all word tokens that share the same topic ID into the same chain. The point is now how to decide to which topic a word belongs to. Since single samples of topics per word exhibit a large variance (Riedl and Biemann, 2012), we follow these authors by sampling several times and using the mode (most frequently assigned) topic ID per word as the topic assignment. This strategy reduced the variance in the $lccm$ to a tenth[6].

More formally, let $samples^{(d,w)}$ be the vector of assignments that have been collected for a certain word w in a certain document d with each $samples_i^{(d,w)}$ referring to the i-th sampled topic ID for (d, w). In other words, $samples^{(d,w)}$ can be seen as the Markov chain for a particular word in a particular document. Further let $z^{(d,w)}$ be the topic ID that was most assigned to the word w with respect to the samples in $samples^{(d,w)}$. Precisely, $z^{(d,w)}$ is defined to be the sampled mode in $samples^{(d,w)}$ — in case of multiple modes a random mode is chosen, which never happened in our experiments.

$$z^{(d,w)} = \text{mode}\left(samples^{(d,w)}\right) \approx \arg\max_j \left(P(z = j|w, d)\right)$$

The LDA-MM assigns for every word w which is a candidate lexical item of a certain document d which is assigned the same topic $z^{(d,w)}$ to the same chain; hence implicitly disambiguating the terms.

The possibility to create level two links is given by taking the second most occurring topic for a given word if it exceeds a certain threshold.

4.2 LDA Graph Method (LDA-GM)

The LDA-GM algorithm creates a similarity graph based on the comparison of topic distributions for given words and then applies a clustering algorithm in order to find semantically related words.

Let $\psi^{(d,w)}$ be the per-word topic distribution $P(z|w, d)$. Analogously to the LDA-MM, $\psi^{(d,w)}$ can be obtained by counting the occurrences of a certain topic ID z in the sample collection $samples^{(d,w)}$ for a particular word w and document d.

The semantic relatedness between any two words w_i and w_j can then be measured by their similarity score of the topic distributions $\psi^{(d,w_i)}$ and $\psi^{(d,w_j)}$, which is stored in a term similarity matrix. This matrix can also be interpreted as an adjacency matrix of a graph, with candidate items being nodes and edges being weighted with the similarity value sim_{ij} for any two nodes $i, j : i \neq j \wedge i, j \in \{1, 2, \ldots, N_d\}$. We test two similarity measures: Euclidian (dis-)similarity and cosine similarity.

Let $G = (V, E)$ be the graph representation of a document with term vertices $V = \{v_1, \ldots, v_{Nd}\}$ and weighted edges $E = \{(v_1, v_2, sim_{12}), \ldots (v_{Nd}, v_{Nd-1}, sim_{N_d N_d - 1})\}$, where sim_{ij} is either the cosine or Euclidean similarity of term vectors. For simplicity, we reduce this representation to an unweighted graph by only retaining edges (of unit weight) that have a similarity above a parameter threshold ϵ_{sim}. To identify chains as clusters in this graph, we follow Medelyan (2007) and apply the *Chinese Whispers* graph clustering algorithm (CW, Biemann (2006)), which finds the number of clusters automatically. The CW algorithm implementation comes with

[5] `http://gibbslda.sourceforge.net`

[6] Preliminary experiments yielded a variance of 2.6×10^{-6} in $lccm$ using the mode method and 3.07×10^{-5} using a single sample for lexical chain assignment.

three parameters to regulate the node weight based on its degree, which influences cluster size and granularity. We test options "top", "dist log" and "dist lin".

The final chaining procedure is straightforward: The LDA-GM algorithm assigns every candidate lexical item w_i of a certain document d which is assigned the same class label c_i to the same chain. Level two links are drawn using the second dominant class of a vertex's neighborhood, which is provided by the CW implementation.

4.3 LDA Top-N Method (LDA-TM)

The LDA-TM method is different to the others in that it uses the information of the per-topic word distribution $\phi^{(z)} = P(w|z)$ and the per-document topic distribution $\theta^{(d)} = P(z|d)$. Given a parameter n referring to the top n topics to choose from $\theta^{(d)}$ and a parameter m referring to the top m words to choose from $\phi^{(z)}$ the main procedure can be described as follows: for all $z \in$ top n topics in $\theta^{(d)}$: chain the top m words in $\phi^{(z)}$.

Note that although the number of chains and chain members for each chain is bound and could lead to the same number and sizes of chains, in practice the number of generated chains as well as the number of chain members still varies considerably across documents: often some of the top m words for a (globally computed) topic do not even occur in a particular document. This implies that the parameters n and m must not be set globally but dependent on the particular document. To overcome this to some extent, additional thresholding parameters ϵ_θ and ϵ_ϕ are used for further bounding the respective n or m parameter. The procedure works like this: for all z $\in$ top n topics in $\theta^{(d)} \wedge \theta_z^{(d)} < \epsilon_\theta$: chain the top m words w in $\phi^{(z)} \wedge \phi_w^{(z)} < \epsilon_\phi$.

Level two links are created by computing the cosine similarity between every pair of the top n topic distributions, and thresholding with a link parameter.

4.4 Repetition Heuristic

All methods described above can be applied to new unseen documents that are not in the training set. To alleviate a possible vocabulary mismatch between training set and test set, which happens when terms in the test set have not been contained in our training documents, we add a heuristic that chains repetitions of (previously unknown) words as a post-processing step to all methods.

5 Empirical Analysis

In order to provide a realistic estimate of the quality of our methods to unseen material, we randomly split our annotated documents in two parts of 50 documents each. One part is used as a *development set* for optimizing the parameters of the methods (i.e. model selection), the other part forms our *test set* for evaluation.

The *training corpus*, on the other hand, consists of all 1,211 SALSA/Tiger documents that are not part of the development and test corpus and neither very long nor very short. These documents are taken from the German newspaper "Frankfurter Rundschau" around 1992. Additionally the training corpus is enriched with 12,264 news texts from the same newspaper around 1997 with similar characteristics[7], making up a total of 13,457 training documents for the estimation of topic models.

Input to the LDA model training are verbs, nouns and adjectives, as well as candidate terms as described in Section 3.1, all in their lemmatized form. We further filter words that occur in more than 1/3 of the training documents, as well as known stopwords, and words that occur in less than two documents which results in a vocabulary size of about 100K words.

5.1 Experimental Setup

For comparison, we implemented three baselines, which we describe below. One baseline is trivial, two baselines are state-of-the art knowledge-based systems adapted to German.

Random: Candidate lexical items are randomly tied together to form sets of lexical chains. Level two links are created analogously. We regulate the process to yield the same average number of chains and links as in the development and test data.

S&M GermaNet: Algorithm by Silber and McCoy (2002) with GermaNet as its knowledge resource.

[7] as provided by Projekt Deutscher Wortschatz, `http://wortschatz.uni-leipzig.de/`

G&M GermaNet: Algorithm by Galley and McKeown (2003), also using GermaNet.

GermaNet (Hamp and Feldweg, 1997) is a large WordNet-like resource for German, containing almost 100,000 lexical units and over 87,000 conceptual relations between synsets. While its size is only about half of WordNet, it is one of the largest non-English lexical semantic resources.

5.2 Model Selection

We optimize two sets of parameters: parameters for the LDA topic model (number of topics K, Dirichlet hyperparameters α and β) are optimized for the LDA-MM method only, and the same LDA model is used in the other two LDA-based methods. Parameters particular to the respective method are optimized individually. For LDA, we tested sensible combinations in the ranges $K = 50..1000$, $\alpha = 0.05/K..50/K$ and $\beta = 0.001..0.1$. The highest performance of the LDA-MM method was found for $K = 500$, $\alpha = 50/K$, $\beta = 0.001$, and the resulting topic model is used across all methods. The final parameter values for the other methods, found by exhaustive search, are summarized in Table 1.

Method	Parameter
LDA-GM	$similarityfunction$ = cosine similarity
	$labelweightscheme$ = dist log
	ϵ_{sim} = 0.95
LDA-TM	n = 10, m = 20, ϵ_θ = 0.2, ϵ_ϕ = 0.2

Table 1: Final parameter values.

5.3 Evaluation

For evaluation purposes, terms that consist of multiple words are mapped to its rightmost term which is assumed to be the head, e.g. "dirty money" is mapped to "money". Additionally, singleton chains, i.e. chains that contain only a single lexical item are omitted unless the respective lexical item is not linked by a level two link.

Dense Chains Comparative results of the approaches in terms of $lccm$ for both annotators are summarized in Table 2 (upper half). We observe that all our new methods beat the random baseline and the two knowledge-based baselines by a large margin. The knowledge-based baselines, both using GermaNet, produce very similar $lccm$ scores, which highlights the important role of the knowledge resource. Data analysis revealed that while chains produced by knowledge-based baselines are sensible, the main problem is a lack of coverage in terms of vocabulary and relations in GermaNet. Comparing the statistical methods, the LDA-GM method excels over the others.

	Anno A	Anno B	Average
LDA-MM	0.320	0.306	0.313
LDA-TM	0.307	0.299	0.303
LDA-GM	**0.328**	**0.314**	**0.321**
G&M	0.255	0.215	0.235
S&M	0.248	0.209	0.229
Random	0.126	0.145	0.135
LDA-MM	**0.316**	**0.300**	**0.308**
LDA-TM	0.303	0.280	0.291
LDA-GM	0.279	0.267	0.273
G&M	0.184	0.166	0.176
S&M	0.179	0.159	0.169
Random	0.196	0.205	0.201

Table 2: Results of the evaluation based on dense chains (upper half) and merged chains (lower half). The annotator agreement on the test set's chains = 0.585; on merged chains = 0.553

Level Two Links Table 2 (lower half) summarizes the evaluation results of the merged chains via level two links. Because of merging, a text now contains fewer chains with more lexical items each. Note that knowledge-based baselines do not construct level two links, which is why they are heavily penalized in this setup.

Again, the statistical methods beat the baselines by a substantial amount. In this evaluation, the random baseline performs above the knowledge-based methods, which is rooted in the fact that $lccm$ penalizes small, correct chains, whereas the random baseline with linking often produces very large chains containing most of the terms – something that we also observe for many manually annotated documents. The large overlap in the biggest chain then leads to the comparatively high random baseline score. In this evaluation, the LDA-MM is the clear winner, with LDA-GM being clearly inferior this time.

	LDA-MM	LDA-GM	LDA-TM	S&M	G&M	Anno A	Anno B
avg. num. of lexical items per doc.	38.20	29.32	30.82	14.40	15.29	38.66	38.96
avg. num. of chains per doc.	13.80	9.12	7.32	5.83	5.71	11.25	7.38
avg. num. of links per doc.	8.60	2.06	1.44	–	–	5.47	2.41
avg. size lexical chains	2.82	3.41	4.61	2.48	2.68	3.69	5.57
avg. num. of merged lexical chains	5.76	7.06	5.98	–	–	6.10	4.99
avg. size merged lexical chains	8.29	4.45	5.57	–	–	7.60	8.91

Table 3: Quantitiative characteristics of automatic and manual lexical chains. In average, a document contains 51.58 candidate terms as extracted by our noun phrase patterns

Davud Bouchehri, seit der letzten ***Spielzeit*** *als* ***Dramaturg*** *in Basel tätig, wechselt zur*
[Davud Bouchehri,] [since] [the] [last] [playing period] [as] [dramaturg] [in] [Basle] [acting,] [switches] [to the]

Saison *1996 / 97 als* ***künstlerischer Geschäftsführer*** *des* ***Schauspiels*** *an das* ***Staatstheater*** *Darmstadt. Der*
[1996 / 97 season] [as] [art] [director] [of the] [play] [to] [the] [state theater] [Darmstadt.] [The]

aus dem Iran stammende 34jährige soll daneben auch für ***spartenübergreifende Projekte*** *zuständig sein,*
[from] [the] [Iran] [coming] [34-year-old] [shall] [besides] [also] [for] [multi discipline] [projects] [responsible] [be,]

teilte das Basler ***Theater*** *am Donnerstag mit.*
[aquainted] [the] [Basle's] [theather] [on] [Thursday] [with.]

LDA-MM:
c_1: {*Spielzeit, Schauspiels, Staatstheater*}
c_2: {*Dramaturg, Theater*}
c_3: {*Saison*}
l_1: (*Theater* $\rightarrow$ *Spielzeit*)
l_2: (*Spielzeit* $\rightarrow$ *Saison*)

LDA-GM:
c_1: {*Dramaturg, Theater*}
c_2: {*Schauspiels, Staatstheater*}

LDA-TM:
c_1: {*Schauspiels, Staatstheater, Theater*}
c_2: {*Dramaturg*}
c_3: {*Spielzeit, Saison*}
l_1: (*Theater* $\rightarrow$ *Dramaturg*)

S&M-GermaNet:
–

G&M-GermaNet:
c_1: {*Staatstheater, Theater*}

Figure 3: Diverse output of the various lexical chaining systems after applying them on a short German example text from the used TIGER/SALSA corpus. For a better understanding the text is calqued. Candidate items are highlighted and the c_i are the resulting dense lexical chains and the l_i are the level two links produced by the various methods.

Data Analysis Table 3 shows quantitative numbers of the extracted lexical chains in the test set.

The LDA-MM approach chains and links a lot more items than the other statistical methods: it creates a lot more links between items that would otherwise be removed because they form unlinked singleton chains. As opposed to this, the graph method (LDA-GM), as well as the top-n method (LDA-TM) perform an implicit filtering on the candidate lexical items by creating less level two links, yet larger dense chains. The knowledge based algorithms by Silber and McCoy (2002) and Galley and McKeown (2003) extract fewer and smaller chains than the statistical approaches, which reflects GermaNet's sparsity issues. While higher lexical coverage in the underlying resource would increase the coverage of our knowledge-based systems, this is only one part of the story. The other part is rooted in the fact that lexical cohesion relations, which are used in lexical chains, encompass many more semantic relations than listed in today's lexical semantic networks. This especially holds for cases where several expressions refer to the same event or theme for which no well-defined relation exists, such as e.g. "captain" and "harbor".

Comparing the three LDA-based approaches, no overall best method could be determined. the LDA-MM seems especially suited for a high coverage and coarse (level two) chains, the LDA-GM appears most suited for dense chains, and LDA-TM produces the longest chains on average.

Figure 3 shows the resulting dense lexical chains and level two links after applying our chainers to a short example text from our corpus. In the example the LDA-TM produces the most adequate lexical chains, at least in our intuition. The LDA-GM and the LDA-MM produce slightly wrong chains, yet the LDA-MM additionally creates some meaningfull level two links which the LDA-GM does not. Both knowledge-based approaches perform poorly compared to the knowledge-free approaches, where the S&M algorithm creates no chains at all and the

G&M algorithm produces only a single chain containing only two words. This is mostly due to GermaNet's lacking lexical and relational coverage and the scope of the algorithms for finding relations between the words.

6 Conclusion

In this paper, we presented experiments for automatic lexical chain annotation and evaluated them directly on a manually annotated dataset for German. A new two-level annotation scheme for lexical chains was proposed and motivated by the concept of cohesive harmony. We further proposed a new measure for comparing lexical chain annotations that is especially suited for the characteristics of lexical chain annotations. Three variants of statistical lexical chaining methods based on the LDA topic model were proposed and evaluated against two knowledge-based baseline systems. Our statistical methods exhibit a substantially higher performance than the knowledge-based systems on our dataset. This can partially be attributed to missing relations, partially to the lack of lexical coverage of GermaNet, which was used in these systems. Since GermaNet is a large lexical-semantic net, however, this strengthens our main point: Especially for under-resourced languages or subject domains, statistical and data-driven methods should be preferred over their knowledge-based counterparts, since they do not require the development of lexical-semantic nets and adopt easily to subject domains by training their unsupervised models on an in-domain collection.

In future work, we would like to explore better ways of selecting candidate items. While our POS-pattern-based selection mechanism works for practical purposes, it currently only extracts noun phrases and over-generates on compositional adjective modifiers. We would like to define a better filter to reduce over-generation. Further, especially for compounding languages such as German, we would like to decompose one-word compounds as to be able to link their heads in lexical chains.

While we found it important to directly evaluate our lexical chaining algorithms on manually annotated data, a natural next step in this line of research is to use our lexical chaining methods as pre-processing steps for applications such as summarization, text segmentation or word sense disambiguation. This would enable to find out advantages and disadvantages of our three variants with respect to an application.

The manually annotated data, the open source annotation tool, the annotation guidelines and the implementations of all described methods and baselines are available for download[8].

Acknowledgments

This work has been supported by the Hessian research excellence program *Landes-Offensive zur Entwicklung Wissenschaftlich-ökonomischer Exzellenz (LOEWE)* as part of the research center *Digital Humanities*.

Proof: Equality of NMI and V

Using the standard notation from information retrieval $H(X)$= Entropy, $I(X,Y)$= Information, $H(X|Y)$= Conditional Entropy, NMI(X,Y)= Normalized Mutual Information, V(X,Y)= V-Measure:

$$V(C,K) = 2 \times \frac{h \times c}{h + c} \quad (1)$$

$$h = 1 - \frac{H(C|K)}{H(C)} \quad , \quad c = 1 - \frac{H(K|C)}{H(K)} \quad (2)$$

and

$$NMI(C,K) = \frac{I(C,K)}{\frac{H(C)+H(K)}{2}} = 2 \times \frac{I(C,K)}{H(C)+H(K)} \quad (3)$$

reformulate h and c using the fact that $I(C,K) = H(C) - H(C|K) = H(K) - H(K|C)$:

$$\begin{aligned} h &= 1 - \frac{H(C|K)}{H(C)} \\ &= \frac{H(C)}{H(C)} - \frac{H(C|K)}{H(C)} \quad (4) \\ &= \frac{I(C,K)}{H(C)} \end{aligned} \qquad \begin{aligned} c &= 1 - \frac{H(K|C)}{H(K)} \\ &= \frac{H(K)}{H(K)} - \frac{H(K|C)}{H(K)} \quad (5) \\ &= \frac{I(C,K)}{H(K)} \end{aligned}$$

simplifying $h \times c$ using (4) and (5):

$$\begin{aligned} h \times c &= \frac{I(C,K)}{H(C)} \times \frac{I(C,K)}{H(K)} \\ &= \frac{I(C,K)^2}{H(C)H(K)} \end{aligned} \quad (6)$$

simplifying $h + c$ using (4) and (5):

$$\begin{aligned} h + c &= \frac{I(C,K)}{H(C)} + \frac{I(C,K)}{H(K)} \\ &= \frac{I(C,K)H(K) + I(C,K)H(C)}{H(C)H(K)} \\ &= \frac{I(C,K)[(H(K) + H(C)]}{H(C)H(K)} \end{aligned} \quad (7)$$

simplifying $\frac{h \times c}{h+c}$ using (6) and (7):

$$\begin{aligned} \frac{h \times c}{h + c} &= \frac{I(C,K)^2}{H(C)H(K)} \times \frac{H(C)H(K)}{I(C,K)[H(K) + H(C)]} \\ &= \frac{I(C,K)}{H(K) + H(C)} \end{aligned} \quad (8)$$

[8] http://www.ukp.tu-darmstadt.de/data/lexical-chains-for-german/

substituting (8) into (1) shows that NMI and V are equal:

$$V(C,K) = 2\times\frac{h \times c}{h + c} = 2\times\frac{I(C,K)}{H(K) + H(C)} = NMI(C,K) \quad (9)$$

References

Jitendra Ajmera, Hervé Bourlard, and I. Lapidot. 2002. Unknown-Multiple Speaker clustering using HMM. In *Proceedings of the International Conference of Spoken Language Processing*, ICSLP '02, Denver, Colorado, USA.

Enrique Amigó, Julio Gonzalo, Javier Artiles, and Felisa Verdejo. 2009. A comparison of extrinsic clustering evaluation metrics based on formal constraints. *Information Retrieval*, 12:461–486.

Amit Bagga and Breck Baldwin. 1998. Algorithms for Scoring Coreference Chains. In *Proceedings of the Linguistic Coreference Workshop at The First International Conference on Language Resources and Evaluation*, LREC '98, pages 563–566, Granada, Spain.

Collin F. Baker, Charles J. Fillmore, and John B. Lowe. 1998. The Berkeley FrameNet Project. In *COLING '98: Proceedings of the 17th International Conference on Computational Linguistics*, volume 1, pages 86–90, Montreal, Quebec, Canada.

Regina Barzilay and Michael Elhadad. 1997. Using Lexical Chains for Text Summarization. In *Proceedings of the ACL Workshop on Intelligent Scalable Text Summarization*, pages 10–17, Madrid, Spain.

Regina Barzilay. 1997. Lexical Chains for Summarization. Master's thesis, Ben-Gurion University of the Negev, Beersheva, Israel.

Omar Benjelloun, Hector Garcia-Molina, David Menestrina, Qi Su, Steven Whang, and Jennifer Widom. 2009. Swoosh: a generic approach to entity resolution. *The VLDB Journal*, 18:255–276.

Chris Biemann. 2006. Chinese Whispers – an Efficient Graph Clustering Algorithm and its Application to Natural Language Processing. In *Proceedings of TextGraphs: the Second Workshop on Graph Based Methods for Natural Language Processing*, pages 73–80, New York City, USA.

Chris Biemann. 2012. *Structure Discovery in Natural Language*. Theory and Applications of Natural Language Processing. Springer Berlin / Heidelberg.

David M. Blei, Andrew Y. Ng, and Michael I. Jordan. 2003. Latent Dirichlet Allocation. *Journal of Machine Learning Research*, 3:993–1022.

Jordan Boyd-Graber, David M. Blei, and Xiaojin Zhu. 2007. A Topic Model for Word Sense Disambiguation. In *Proceedings of the 2007 Joint Conference on Empirical Methods in Natural Language Processing and Computational Natural Language Learning (EMNLP-CoNLL)*, pages 1024–1033, Prague, Czech Republic.

Sabine Brants, Stefanie Dipper, Silvia Hansen, Wolfgang Lezius, and George Smith. 2002. TIGER Treebank. In *Proceedings of the Workshop on Treebanks and Linguistic Theories (TLT02)*, Sozopol, Bulgaria.

Aljoscha Burchardt, Katrin Erk, Anette Frank, Andrea Kowalski, Sebastian Padó, and Manfred Pinkal. 2006. The SALSA Corpus: a German corpus resource for lexical semantics. In *Proceedings of the 5th international conference on Language Resources and evaluation (LREC-2006)*, Genoa, Italy.

Junfu Cai, Wee Sun Lee, and Yee Whye Teh. 2007. Improving Word Sense Disambiguation Using Topic Features. In *Proceedings of the 2007 Joint Conference on Empirical Methods in Natural Language Processing and Computational Natural Language Learning (EMNLP-CoNLL)*, pages 1015–1023, Prague, Czech Republic.

Joe Carthy. 2004. Lexical Chains versus Keywords for Topic Tracking. In A. Gelbukh, editor, *Computational Linguistics and Intelligent Text Processing*, volume 2945 of *Lecture Notes in Computer Science*, pages 507–510. Springer, Berlin / Heidelberg.

Irene Cramer, Marc Finthammer, Alexander Kurek, Lukas Sowa, Melina Wachtling, and Tobias Claas. 2008. Experiments on Lexical Chaining for German Corpora: Annotation, Extraction, and Application. *Journal for Language Technology and Computational Linguistics (JLCL)*, 23(2):34–48.

Georgiana Dinu and Mirella Lapata. 2010. Topic Models for Meaning Similarity in Context. In *COLING '10: Proceedings of the 23rd International Conference on Computational Linguistics: Posters*, pages 250–258, Beijing, China.

Michel Galley and Kathleen McKeown. 2003. Improving word sense disambiguation in lexical chaining. In *IJCAI'03: Proceedings of the 18th international joint conference on Artificial intelligence*, pages 1486–1488, Acapulco, Mexico.

Yihong Gong and Xin Liu. 2001. Generic Text Summarization Using Relevance Measure and Latent Semantic Analysis. In *SIGIR 2001: Proceedings of the 24th Annual International ACM SIGIR Conference on Research and Development in Information Retrieval*, pages 19–25, New Orleans, Louisiana, USA.

Stephen J. Green. 1996. Using Lexical Chains to Build Hypertext Links in Newspaper Articles. In *AAAI-96 Workshop on Internet-based Information Systems*, pages 115–141, Portland, Oregon, USA.

Michael A. K. Halliday and Ruqaiya Hasan. 1976. *Cohesion in English*. English language series. Longman, London.

Birgit Hamp and Helmut Feldweg. 1997. GermaNet - a Lexical-Semantic Net for German. In *Proceed-*

ings of the ACL/EACL-97 workshop Automatic Information Extraction and Building of Lexical Semantic Resources for NLP Applications, Madrid, Spain.

Ruqaiya Hasan. 1984. Coherence and Cohesive Harmony. In James Flood, editor, *Understanding Reading Comprehension*, Cognition, Language, and the Structure of Prose, pages 181–220. International Reading Association, Newark, Delaware, USA.

Leonhard Hennig. 2009. Topic-based multi-document summarization with probabilistic latent semantic analysis. In *Proceedings of the International Conference RANLP-2009*, pages 144–149, Borovets, Bulgaria.

Graeme Hirst and David St-Onge. 1998. Lexical Chains as representation of context for the detection and correction malapropisms. In Christiane Fellbaum, editor, *WordNet: An Electronic Lexical Database*, Language, Speech, and Communication, pages 305–332. The MIT Press, Cambridge, Massachusetts, USA.

Thomas Hofmann. 1999. Probabilistic Latent Semantic Analysis. In *Proceedings of the Fifteenth Conference on Uncertainty in Artificial Intelligence*, UAI '99, pages 289–296, Stockholm, Sweden.

William Hollingsworth and Simone Teufel. 2005. Human annotation of lexical chains: Coverage and agreement measures. In *Proceedings of the Workshop ELECTRA: Methodologies and Evaluation of Lexical Cohesion Techniques in Real-world Applications*, In Association with SIGIR '05, Salvador, Brazil.

Lawrence Hubert and Phipps Arabie. 1985. Comparing partitions. *Journal of Classification*, 2(1):193–218.

Christopher Manning, Prabhakar Raghavan, and Hinrich Schütze. 2008. *An Introduction to Information Retrieval.* Cambridge University Press, Cambridge, UK.

Meghana Marathe and Graeme Hirst. 2010. Lexical Chains Using Distributional Measures of Concept D. In *Proceedings of the 11th International Conference on Computational Linguistics and Intelligent Text Processing*, CICLing'10, pages 291–302, Iaşi, Romania.

Olena Medelyan. 2007. Computing lexical chains with graph clustering. In *Proceedings of the 45th Annual Meeting of the ACL: Student Research Workshop*, ACL '07, pages 85–90, Prague, Czech Republic.

Marina Meilă. 2005. Comparing clusterings: an axiomatic view. In *Proceedings of the 22nd International Conference on Machine Learning*, ICML '05, pages 577–584, Bonn, Germany.

David Menestrina, Steven Euijong Whang, and Hector Garcia-Molina. 2010. Evaluating entity resolution results. *Proceedings of the VLDB Endowment*, 3(1):208–219.

Hemant Misra, François Yvon, Joemon Jose, and Olivier Cappé. 2009. Text Segmentation via Topic Modeling: An Analytical Study. In *Proceedings of the 18th ACM Conference on Information and Knowledge Management*, CIKM 2009, pages 1553–1556, Hong Kong, China.

Jane Morris and Graeme Hirst. 1991. Lexical cohesion computed by thesaural relations as an indicator of the structure of text. *Computational Linguistics*, 17:21–48.

Jane Morris and Graeme Hirst. 2004. The Subjectivity of Lexical Cohesion in Text. In *Proceedings of the AAAI Spring Symposium on Exploring Attitude and Affect in Text: Theories and Applications*, Palo Alto, California, USA.

Christoph Müller and Michael Strube. 2006. Multi-level annotation of linguistic data with MMAX2. In Sabine Braun, Kurt Kohn, and Joybrato Mukherjee, editors, *Corpus Technology and Language Pedagogy: New Resources, New Tools, New Methods*, pages 197–214. Peter Lang, Frankfurt a.M., Germany.

Manabu Okumura and Takeo Honda. 1994. Word sense disambiguation and text segmentation based on lexical cohesion. In *COLING '94: Proceedings of the 15th Conference on Computational Linguistics*, volume 2, pages 755–761, Kyoto, Japan.

Martin Riedl and Chris Biemann. 2012. Sweeping through the Topic Space: Bad luck? Roll again! In *ROBUS-UNSUP 2012: Joint Workshop on Unsupervised and Semi-Supervised Learning in NLP held in conjunction with EACL 2012*, pages 19–27, Avignon, France.

Peter Mark Roget. 1852. *Roget's Thesaurus of English Words and Phrases.* Longman Group Ltd., Harlow, UK.

Andrew Rosenberg and Julia Hirschberg. 2007. V-measure: A conditional entropy-based external cluster evaluation measure. In *Proceedings of the 2007 Joint Conference on Empirical Methods in Natural Language Processing and Computational Natural Language Learning (EMNLP-CoNLL)*, pages 410–420, Prague, Czech Republic.

H. Gregory Silber and Kathleen F. McCoy. 2002. Efficiently computed lexical chains as an intermediate representation for automatic text summarization. *Computational Linguistics*, 28(4):487–496.

Mark A. Stairmand. 1996. *A Computational Analysis of Lexical Cohesion with Applications in Information Retrieval.* Ph.D. thesis, Center for Computational Linguistics, UMIST, Manchester.

Nicola Stokes, Joe Carthy, and Alan F. Smeaton. 2004. SeLeCT: A Lexical Cohesion Based News Story Segmentation System. *AI Communications*, 17(1):3–12.

Alexander Strehl. 2002. *Relationship-based Clustering and Cluster Ensembles for High-dimensional Data Mining.* Ph.D. thesis, University of Texas, Austin.

Combining Heterogeneous Models for Measuring Relational Similarity

Alisa Zhila*
Instituto Politecnico Nacional
Mexico City, Mexico
alisa.zhila@gmail.com

Wen-tau Yih **Christopher Meek**
Microsoft Research
Redmond, WA 98052, USA
{scottyih,meek}@microsoft.com

Geoffrey Zweig
Microsoft Research
Redmond, WA 98052, USA
gzweig@microsoft.com

Tomas Mikolov*
BRNO University of Technology
BRNO, Czech Republic
tmikolov@gmail.com

Abstract

In this work, we study the problem of measuring relational similarity between two word pairs (e.g., *silverware:fork* and *clothing:shirt*). Due to the large number of possible relations, we argue that it is important to combine multiple models based on heterogeneous information sources. Our overall system consists of two novel general-purpose relational similarity models and three specific word relation models. When evaluated in the setting of a recently proposed SemEval-2012 task, our approach outperforms the previous best system substantially, achieving a 54.1% relative increase in Spearman's rank correlation.

1 Introduction

The problem of measuring relational similarity is to determine the degree of correspondence between two word pairs. For instance, the analogous word pairs *silverware:fork* and *clothing:shirt* both exemplify well a *Class-Inclusion:Singular_Collective* relation and thus have high relational similarity. Unlike the problem of *attributional similarity*, which measures whether two words share similar attributes and is addressed in extensive research work (Budanitsky and Hirst, 2006; Reisinger and Mooney, 2010; Radinsky et al., 2011; Agirre et al., 2009; Yih and Qazvinian, 2012), measuring relational similarity is a relatively new research direction pioneered by Turney (2006), but with many potential applications. For instance, problems of identifying specific relations between words, such as synonyms, antonyms or associations, can be reduced to measuring relational similarity compared to prototypical word pairs with the desired relation (Turney, 2008). In scenarios like information extraction or question answering, where identifying the existence of certain relations is often the core problem, measuring relational similarity provides a more flexible solution rather than creating relational classifiers for pre-defined or task-specific categories of relations (Turney, 2006; Jurgens et al., 2012).

In order to promote this research direction, Jurgens et al. (2012) proposed a new shared task of measuring relational similarity in SemEval-2012 recently. In this task, each submitted system is required to judge the degree of a target word pair having a particular relation, measured by its relational similarity compared to a few prototypical example word pairs. The system performance is evaluated by its correlation with the human judgments using two evaluation metrics, Spearman's rank correlation and MaxDiff accuracy (more details of the task and evaluation metrics will be given in Sec. 3). Although participating systems incorporated substantial amounts of information from lexical resources (e.g., WordNet) and contextual patterns from large corpora, only one system (Rink and Harabagiu, 2012) is able to outperform a simple baseline that uses PMI (pointwise mutual information) scoring, which demonstrates the difficulty of this task.

In this paper, we explore the problem of measuring relational similarity in the same task setting. We argue that due to the large number of possible relations, building an ensemble of relational simi-

*Work conducted while interning at Microsoft Research.

larity models based on heterogeneous information sources is the key to advance the state-of-the-art on this problem. By combining two general-purpose relational similarity models with three specific word-relation models covering relations like IsA and synonymy/antonymy, we improve the previous state-of-the-art substantially – having a relative gain of 54.1% in Spearman's rank correlation and 14.7% in the MaxDiff accuracy!

Our main contributions are threefold. First, we propose a novel directional similarity method based on the vector representation of words learned from a recurrent neural network language model. The relation of two words is captured by their vector offset in the latent semantic space. Similarity of relations can then be naturally measured by a distance function in the vector space. This method alone already performs better than all existing systems. Second, unlike the previous finding, where SVMs learn a much poorer model than naive Bayes (Rink and Harabagiu, 2012), we show that using a highly-regularized log-linear model on simple contextual pattern features collected from a document collection of 20GB, a discriminative approach can learn a strong model as well. Third, we demonstrate that by augmenting existing word-relation models, which cover only a small number of relations, the overall system can be further improved.

The rest of this paper is organized as follows. We first survey the related work in Sec. 2 and formally define the problem in Sec. 3. We describe the individual models in detail in Sec. 4. The combination approach is depicted in Sec. 5, along with experimental comparisons to individual models and existing systems. Finally, Sec. 6 concludes the paper.

2 Related Work

Building a classifier to determine whether a relationship holds between a pair of words is a natural approach to the task of measuring relational similarity. While early work was mostly based on hand-crafted rules (Finin, 1980; Vanderwende, 1994), Rosario and Hearst (2001) introduced a machine learning approach to classify word pairs. They targeted classifying noun modifier pairs from the medical domain into 13 classes of semantic relations. Features for each noun modifier pair were constructed using large medical lexical resources and a multi-class classifier was trained using a feed-forward neural network with one hidden layer. This work was later extended by Nastase and Szpakowicz (2003) to classify general domain noun-modifier pairs into 30 semantic relations. In addition to extracting features using WordNet and Roget's Thesaurus, they also experimented with several different learners including decision trees, memory-based learning and inductive logic programming methods like RIPPER and FOIL. Using the same dataset as in (Nastase and Szpakowicz, 2003), Turney and Littman (2005) created a 128-dimentional feature vector for each word pair based on statistics of their co-occurrence patterns in Web documents and applied the k-NN method ($k = 1$ in their work).

Measuring relational similarity, which determines whether two word pairs share the same relation, can be viewed as an extension of classifying relations between two words. Treating a relational similarity measure as a distance metric, a testing pair of words can be judged by whether they have a relation that is *similar* to some prototypical word pairs having a particular relation. A multi-relation classifier can thus be built easily in this framework as demonstrated in (Turney, 2008), where the problems of identifying synonyms, antonyms and associated words are all reduced to finding good analogous word pairs. Measuring relational similarity has been advocated and pioneered by Turney (2006), who proposed a latent vector space model for answering SAT analogy questions (e.g., *mason:stone* vs. *carpenter:wood*). In contrast, we take a slightly different view when building a relational similarity measure. Existing classifiers for specific word relations (e.g., synonyms or Is-A) are combined with general relational similarity measures. Empirically, mixing heterogeneous models tends to make the final relational similarity measure more robust.

Although datasets for semantic relation classification or SAT analogous questions can be used to evaluate a relational similarity model, their labels are either binary or categorical, which makes the datasets suboptimal for determining the quality of a model when evaluated on instances of the same relation class. As a result, Jurgens et al. (2012) proposed a new task of "Measuring Degrees of Relational Similarity" at SemEval-2012, which includes 79 relation categories exemplified by three or four prototypical word pairs and a schematic description. For example, for the *Class-Inclusion:Taxonomic* relation, the schematic description is *"Y is a kind/type/instance of X"*. Using Amazon Mechanical Turk[1], they collected word pairs for each relation, as well as their degrees of being a good representative of a particular relation when compared with defining examples. Participants of this shared task proposed various kinds of approaches that leverage both lexical resources and general corpora. For instance, the Duluth systems (Pedersen, 2012) created word vectors based on WordNet and estimated the degree of a relation using cosine similarity. The BUAP system (Tovar et al., 2012) represented each word pair as a whole by a vector of 4 different types of features: context, WordNet, POS tags and the average number of words separating the two words in text. The degree of relation was then determined by the cosine distance of the target pair from the prototypical examples of each relation. Although their models incorporated a significant amount of information of words or word pairs, unfortunately, the performance were not much better than a random baseline, which indicates the difficulty of this task. In comparison, a supervised learning approach seems more promising. The UTD system (Rink and Harabagiu, 2012), which mined lexical patterns between co-occurring words in the corpus and then used them as features to train a Naive Bayes classifier, achieved the best results. However, potentially due to the large feature space, this strategy did not work as well when switching the learning algorithm to SVMs.

3 Problem Definition & Task Description

Following the setting of SemEval-2012 Task 2 (Jurgens et al., 2012), the problem of measuring the degree of relational similarity is to rate word pairs by the degree to which they are prototypical members of a given relation class. For instance, comparing to the prototypical word pairs, {*cutlery:spoon, clothing:shirt, vermin:rat*} of the *Class-Inclusion:Singular_Collective* relation, we would like to know among the input word pairs {*dish:bowl, book:novel, furniture:desk*}, which one best demonstrates the relation.

Because our approaches are evaluated using the data provided in this SemEval-2012 task, we describe briefly below how the data was collected, as well as the metrics used to evaluate system performance. The dataset consists of 79 relation classes that are chosen according to (Bejar et al., 1991) and broadly fall into 10 main categories, including *Class-Inclusion*, *Part-Whole*, *Similar* and more. With the help of Amazon Mechanical Turk, Jurgens et al. (2012) used a two-phase approach to collect word pairs and their degrees. In the first phase, a lexical schema, such as *"a Y is one item in a collection/group of X"* for the aforementioned relation *Class-Inclusion:Singular_Collective*, and a few prototypical pairs for each class were given to the workers, who were asked to provide approximately a list of 40 word pairs representing the same relation class. Naturally, some of these pairs were better examples than the others. Therefore, in the second phase, the goal was to measure the degree of their similarity to the corresponding relation. This was done using the MaxDiff technique (Louviere and Woodworth, 1991). For each relation, about one hundred questions were first created. Each question consists of four different word pairs randomly sampled from the list. The worker was then asked to choose the most and least representative word pairs for the specific relation in each question.

The set of 79 word relations were randomly split into *training* and *testing* sets. The former contains 10 relations and the latter has 69. Word pairs in all 79 relations were given to the task participants in advance, but only the human judgments of the *training* set were available for system development. In this work, we treat the training set as the validation set – all the model exploration and refinement is done using this set of data, as well as the hyper-parameter tuning when learning the final model combination.

The quality of a relational similarity measure is estimated by its correlation to human judgments. This is evaluated using two metrics in the task: the MaxDiff accuracy and Spearman's rank correlation coefficient (ρ). A system is first asked to pick the most and least representative word pairs of each question in the MaxDiff setting. The average accuracy of the predictions compared to the human answers is then reported. In contrast, Spearman's ρ

[1] http://www.mturk.com

measures the correlation between the total orderings of all word pairs of a relation, where the total ordering is derived from the MaxDiff answers (see (Jurgens et al., 2012) for the exact procedure).

4 Models for Relational Similarity

We investigate three types of models for relational similarity. Operating in a word vector space, the *directional similarity* model compares the vector differences of target and prototypical word pairs to estimate their relational similarity. The *lexical pattern* method collects contextual information of pairs of words when they co-occur in large corpora, and learns a highly regularized log-linear model. Finally, the *word relation* models incorporate existing, specific word relation measures for general relational similarity.

4.1 Directional Similarity Model

Our first model for relational similarity extends previous work on semantic word vector representations to a directional similarity model for pairs of words. There are many different methods for creating real-valued semantic word vectors, such as the distributed representation derived from a word co-occurrence matrix and a low-rank approximation (Landauer et al., 1998), word clustering (Brown et al., 1992) and neural-network language modeling (Bengio et al., 2003; Mikolov et al., 2010). Each element in the vectors conceptually represents some latent topicality information of the word. The goal of these methods is that words with similar meanings will tend to be close to each other in the vector space.

Although the vector representation of *single* words has been successfully applied to problems like semantic word similarity and text classification (Turian et al., 2010), the issue of how to represent and compare pairs of words in a vector space remains unclear (Turney, 2012). In a companion paper (Mikolov et al., 2013), we present a vector offset method which performs consistently well in identifying both syntactic and semantic regularities. This method measures the degree of the analogy "a is to b as c is to d" using the cosine score of $(\vec{v}_b - \vec{v}_a + \vec{v}_c, \vec{v}_d)$, where a, b, c, d are the four given words and $\vec{v}_a, \vec{v}_b, \vec{v}_c, \vec{v}_d$ are the corresponding vectors. In this paper, we propose a variant called the *directional similarity* model, which performs better for semantic relations. Let $\omega_i = (w_{i_1}, w_{i_2})$ and $\omega_j = (w_{j_1}, w_{j_2})$ be the two word pairs being compared. Suppose $(\vec{v}_{i_1}, \vec{v}_{i_2})$ and $(\vec{v}_{j_1}, \vec{v}_{j_2})$ are the corresponding vectors of these words. The *directional vectors* of ω_i and ω_j are defined as $\vec{v}_i \equiv \vec{v}_{i_2} - \vec{v}_{i_1}$ and $\vec{v}_j \equiv \vec{v}_{j_2} - \vec{v}_{j_1}$, respectively. Relational similarity of these two word pairs can be measured by some distance function of v_i and v_j, such as the cosine function:

$$\frac{\vec{v}_i \cdot \vec{v}_j}{\|\vec{v}_i\| \|\vec{v}_j\|}$$

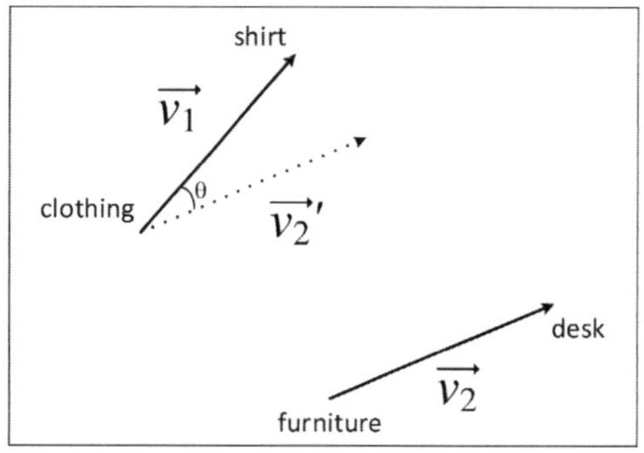

Figure 1: Directional vectors v_1 and v_2 capture the relations of *clothing:shirt* and *furniture:desk* respectively in this semantic vector space. The relational similarity of these two word pairs is estimated by the cosine of θ.

The rationale behind this variant is as follows. Because the difference of two word vectors reveals the change from one word to the other in terms of multiple topicality dimensions in the vector space, two word pairs having similar offsets (i.e., being relatively parallel) can be interpreted as they have similar relations. Fig. 1 further illustrates this method.

Compared to the original method, this variant places less emphasis on the similarity between words w_{j_1} and w_{j_2}. That similarity is necessary for syntactic relations where the words are often related by morphology, but not for semantic relations. On semantic relations studied in this paper, the *directional similarity* model performs about 18% relatively better in Spearman's ρ than the original one.

The quality of the directional similarity method depends heavily on the underlying word vector space model. We compared two choices with dif-

Word Embedding	Spearman's ρ	MaxDiff Acc. (%)
LSA-80	0.055	34.6
LSA-320	0.066	34.4
LSA-640	0.102	35.7
RNNLM-80	0.168	37.5
RNNLM-320	0.214	39.1
RNNLM-640	0.221	39.2
RNNLM-1600	0.234	41.2

Table 1: Results of measuring relational similarity using the directional similarity method, evaluated on the training set. The 1600-dimensional RNNLM vector space achieves the highest Spearman's ρ and MaxDiff accuracy.

ferent dimensionality settings: the word embedding learned from the recurrent neural network language model (RNNLM)[2] and the LSA vectors, both were trained using the same Broadcast News corpus of 320M words as described in (Mikolov et al., 2011). All the word vectors were first normalized to unit vectors before applying the directional similarity method. Given a target word pair, we computed its relational similarity compared with the prototypical word pairs of the same relation. The average of these measurements was taken as the final model score. Table 1 summarizes the results when evaluated on the training set. As shown in the table, the RNNLM vectors consistently outperform their LSA counterparts with the same dimensionality. In addition, more dimensions seem to preserve more information and lead to better performance. Therefore, we take the 1600-dimensional RNNLM vectors to construct our final directional similarity model.

4.2 Lexical Pattern Model

Our second model for measuring relational similarity is built based on lexical patterns. It is well-known that contexts in which two words co-occur often provide useful cues for identifying the word relation. For example, having observed frequent text fragments like *"X such as Y"*, it is likely that there is a *Class-Inclusion:Taxonomic* relation between *X* and *Y*; namely, *Y* is a type of *X*. Indeed, by mining lexical patterns from a large corpus, the UTD system (Rink and Harabagiu, 2012) managed to outperform other participants in the SemEval-2012 task of measuring relational similarity.

In order to find more co-occurrences of each pair of words, we used a large document set that consists of the Gigaword corpus (Parker et al., 2009), Wikipedia and LA Times articles[3], summing up to more than 20 Gigabytes of texts. For each word pair (w_1, w_2) that co-occur in a sentence, we collected the words in between as its *context* (or so-called "raw pattern"). For instance, *"such as"* would be the context extracted from *"X such as Y"* for the word pair (*X*, *Y*). To reduce noise, contexts with more than 9 words were dropped and 914,295 patterns were collected in total.

Treating each raw pattern as a feature where the value is the logarithm of the occurrence count, we then built a probabilistic classifier to determine the association of the context and relation. For each relation, we treated all its word pairs as positive examples and all the word pairs in other relations as negative examples[4]. 79 classifiers were trained in total, where each one was trained using 3,218 examples. The degree of relational similarity of each word pair can then be judged by the output of the corresponding classifier[5]. Although this seems like a standard supervised learning setting, the large number of features poses a challenge here. Using almost 1M features and 3,218 examples, the model could easily overfit if not regularized properly, which may explain why learning SVMs on pattern features performed poorly (Rink and Harabagiu, 2012). Instead of employing explicit feature selection methods, we used an efficient L_1 regularized log-linear model learner (Andrew and Gao, 2007) and chose the hyper-parameters based on model performance on the training data. The final models we chose were trained with $L_1 = 3$, where 28,065 features in average were selected automatically by the algo-

[2] http://www.fit.vutbr.cz/~imikolov/rnnlm

[3] We used a Nov-2010 dump of English Wikipedia, which contains approximately 917M words after pre-processing. The LA Times corpus consists of articles from 1985 to 2002 and has about 1.1B words.

[4] Given that not all word pairs belonging to the same relation category are equally good, removing those with low judgment scores may help improve the quality of the labeled data. We leave this study to future work.

[5] Training a separate classifier for each MaxDiff question using all words pairs except the four target pairs appears to be a better setting, as it would avoid including the target pairs in the training process. We did not use this setting because it is more complicated and performed roughly the same empirically.

rithm. The performance on the training data is 0.322 in Spearman's ρ and 41.8% in MaxDiff accuracy.

4.3 Word Relation Models

The directional similarity and lexical pattern models can be viewed as *general* purpose methods for relational similarity as they do not differentiate the specific relation categories. In contrast, for *specific* word relations, there exist several high-quality methods. Although they are designed for detecting specific relations between words, incorporating them could still improve the overall results. Next, we explore the use of some of these word relation models, including information encoded in the knowledge base and a lexical semantic model for synonymy and antonymy.

4.3.1 Knowledge Bases

Predetermined types of relations can often be found in existing lexical and knowledge databases, such as WordNet's Is-A taxonomy and the extensive relations stored in the NELL (Carlson et al., 2010) knowledge base. Although in theory, these resources can be directly used to solve the problem of relational similarity, such direct approaches often suffer from two practical issues. First, the word coverage of these databases is usually very limited and it is common that the relation of a given word pair is absent. Second, the degree of relation is often not included, which makes the task of measuring the degree of relational similarity difficult.

One counter example, however, is Probase (Wu et al., 2012), which is a knowledge base that establishes connections between more than 2.5 million concepts discovered automatically from the Web. For the *Is-A* and *Attribute* relations it encodes, Probase also returns the probability that two input words share the relation, based on the co-occurrence frequency. We used some relations in the training set to evaluate the quality of Probase. For instance, its Is-A model performs exceptionally well on the relation *Class-Inclusion:Taxonomic*, reaching a high Spearman's $\rho = 0.642$ and MaxDiff accuracy 55.8%. Similarly, its Attribute model performs better than our lexical pattern model on *Attribute:Agent_Attribute-State* with Spearman's $\rho = 0.290$ and MaxDiff accuracy 32.7%.

4.3.2 Lexical Semantics Measures

Most lexical semantics measures focus on the semantic similarity or relatedness of two words. Since our task focuses on distinguishing the difference between word pairs in the *same* relation category. The crude relatedness model does not seem to help in our preliminary experimental study. Instead, we leverage the recently proposed polarity-inducing latent semantic analysis (PILSA) model (Yih et al., 2012), which specifically estimates the degree of synonymy and antonymy. This method first forms a signed co-occurrence matrix using synonyms and antonyms in a thesaurus and then generalizes it using a low-rank approximation derived by SVD. Given two words, the cosine score of their PILSA vectors tend to be negative if they are antonymous and positive if synonymous. When tested on the *Similar:Synonymity* relation, it has a Spearman's $\rho = 0.242$ and MaxDiff accuracy 42.1%, both are better than those of our directional similarity and lexical pattern models.

5 Model Combination

In order to fully leverage the diverse models proposed in Sec. 4, we experiment with a model combination approach and conduct a model ablation study. Performance of the combined and individual models is evaluated using the *test* set and compared with existing systems.

We seek an optimal linear combination of all the individual models by treating their output as *features* and use a logistic regression learner to learn the weights[6]. The training setting is essentially the same as the one used to learn the lexical pattern model (Sec. 4.2). For each relation, we treat all the word pairs in this relation group as positive examples and all other word pairs as negative ones. Consequently, 79 sets of weights for model combination are learned in total. The average Spearman's ρ of the 10 training relations is used for selecting the values of the L_1 and L_2 regularizers[7]. Evaluated on the remaining 69 relations (i.e., the test set), the average results of each main relation group and the overall

[6]Nonlinear methods, such as MART (Friedman, 2001), do not perform better in our experiments (not reported here).

[7]We tested 15 combinations, where $L_1 \in \{0, 0.01, 0.1\}$ and $L_2 \in \{0, 0.001, 0.01, 1, 10\}$. The parameter setting that gave the highest Spearman rank correlation coefficient score on the training set was selected.

Relation Group	Rand.	BUAP	Duluth$_{V0}$	UTD$_{NB}$	DS	Pat.	IsA	Attr.	PILSA	Com.
Class-Inclusion	0.057	0.064	0.045	0.233	0.350	0.422	**0.619**	-0.137	0.029	0.519
Part-Whole	0.012	0.066	-0.061	0.252	0.317	0.244	-0.014	0.026	-0.010	**0.329**
Similar	0.026	-0.036	0.183	0.214	0.254	0.245	-0.020	0.133	0.058	**0.303**
Contrast	-0.049	0.000	0.142	0.206	0.063	**0.298**	-0.012	-0.032	-0.079	0.268
Attribute	0.037	-0.095	0.044	0.158	**0.431**	0.198	-0.008	0.016	-0.052	0.406
Non-Attribute	-0.070	0.009	0.079	0.098	0.195	0.117	0.036	0.078	-0.093	**0.296**
Case Relations	0.090	-0.037	-0.011	0.241	**0.503**	0.288	0.076	-0.075	0.059	0.473
Cause-Purpose	-0.011	0.114	0.021	0.183	**0.362**	0.234	0.044	-0.059	0.038	0.296
Space-Time	0.013	0.035	0.055	0.375	0.439	0.248	0.064	-0.002	-0.018	**0.443**
Reference	0.142	-0.001	0.028	**0.346**	0.301	0.119	0.033	-0.123	0.021	0.208
Average	0.018	0.014	0.050	0.229	0.324†	0.235	0.058‡	-0.010‡	-0.009‡	**0.353**‡

Relation Group	Rand.	BUAP	Duluth$_{V0}$	UTD$_{NB}$	DS	Pat.	IsA	Attr.	PILSA	Com.
Class-Inclusion	30.1	29.0	26.7	39.1	46.7	43.4	**59.6**	24.7	32.3	51.2
Part-Whole	31.9	35.1	29.4	40.9	**43.9**	38.1	31.3	29.5	31.0	42.9
Similar	31.5	29.1	37.1	39.8	38.5	38.4	30.8	36.3	34.2	**43.3**
Contrast	30.4	32.4	38.3	40.9	33.6	42.2	32.3	31.8	30.1	**42.8**
Attribute	30.2	29.2	31.9	36.5	47.9	38.3	30.7	31.0	28.8	**48.3**
Non-Attribute	28.9	30.4	36.0	36.8	38.7	36.7	32.3	32.8	27.7	**42.6**
Case Relations	32.8	29.5	28.2	40.6	**54.3**	42.2	32.8	25.7	31.0	50.6
Cause-Purpose	30.8	35.4	29.5	36.3	**45.3**	38.0	30.3	28.1	32.0	41.7
Space-Time	30.6	32.5	31.9	43.2	**50.0**	39.2	33.2	29.3	30.6	47.7
Reference	35.1	30.0	31.9	41.2	**45.7**	36.9	30.4	27.2	30.2	42.5
Average	31.2	31.7	32.4	39.4	44.5‡	39.2	33.3‡	29.8‡	30.7‡	**45.2**‡

Table 2: Average Spearman's ρ (Top) and MaxDiff accuracy (%) (Bottom) of each major relation group and all 69 testing relations. The best result in each row is highlighted in boldface font. Statistical significance tests are conducted by comparing each of our systems with the previous best performing system, UTD$_{NB}$. $\dagger$ and $\ddagger$ indicate the difference in the average results is statistically significant with 95% or 99% confidence level, respectively.

results are presented in Table 2. For comparison, we also show the performance of a random baseline and the best performing system of each participant in the SemEval-2012 task.

We draw two conclusions from this table. First, both of our general relational similarity models, the directional similarity (DS) and lexical pattern (Pat) models are fairly strong. The former outperforms the previous best system UTD$_{NB}$ in both Spearman's ρ and MaxDiff accuracy, where the differences are statistically significant[8]; the latter has comparable performance, where the differences are not statistically significant. In contrast, while the IsA relation from Probase is exceptionally good in identifying *Class-Inclusion* relations, with high Spearman's $\rho = 0.619$ and MaxDiff accuracy 59.6%, it does not have high correlations with human judgments in other relations. Like in the case of Probase Attribute and PILSA, specific word-relation models individually are not good measures for general relational similarity. Second, as expected, combining multiple diverse models (Com) is a robust strategy, which provides the best overall performance. It achieves superior results in both evaluation metrics compared to UTD$_{NB}$ and only a lower Spearman's ρ value in one of the ten relation groups (namely, *Reference*). The differences are statistically significant with p-value less than 10^{-3}.

In order to understand the interaction among different component models, we conducted an ablation study by iteratively removing one model from the final combination. The weights are re-trained using the same procedure that finds the best regularization parameters with the help of training data. Table 3 summarizes the results and compares them with the

[8]We conducted a paired-t test on the results of each of the 69 relation. The difference is considered statistically significant if the p-value is less than 0.05.

	Spearman's ρ						MaxDiff Accuracy (%)					
Relation Group	Com.	-Attr	-IsA	-PILSA	-DS	-Pat	Com.	-Attr	-IsA	-PILSA	-DS	-Pat
Class-Inclusion	0.519	0.557	0.467	**0.593**	0.490	0.570	51.2	53.7	49.2	54.6	49.3	**56.2**
Part-Whole	**0.329**	0.326	0.335	0.331	0.277	0.285	42.9	42.1	42.6	41.8	38.5	**42.9**
Similar	**0.303**	0.269	0.302	0.281	0.256	0.144	**43.3**	41.2	42.7	40.5	40.2	38.9
Contrast	0.268	0.234	0.267	**0.289**	0.260	0.156	**42.8**	42.0	42.4	41.5	42.7	38.1
Attribute	0.406	0.409	0.405	0.433	0.164	**0.447**	48.3	47.8	48.2	**49.1**	36.9	49.0
Non-Attribute	0.296	0.287	**0.296**	0.276	0.123	0.283	42.6	42.9	42.6	41.8	36.0	**43.0**
Case Relations	0.473	0.497	0.470	0.484	0.309	**0.498**	50.6	52.5	50.2	50.9	42.9	**53.2**
Cause-Purpose	0.296	0.282	0.299	**0.301**	0.205	0.296	41.7	41.6	41.6	41.2	36.6	**44.1**
Space-Time	**0.443**	0.425	0.443	0.420	0.269	0.431	47.7	47.2	47.7	46.9	40.5	**49.5**
Reference	0.208	**0.238**	0.205	0.168	0.102	0.210	42.5	42.3	**42.6**	41.8	36.1	41.4
Average	0.353	0.348	0.350	**0.354**	0.238‡	0.329	45.2	45.0	44.9‡	44.7	39.6‡	**45.4**

Table 3: Average Spearman's ρ and MaxDiff accuracy results of different model combinations. *Com* indicates combining all models, where other columns show the results when the specified model is removed. The best result in each row is highlighted in boldface font. Statistical significance tests are conducted by comparing each ablation configuration with *Com*. ‡ indicates the difference in the average results is statistically significant with 99% confidence level.

original combination model.

Overall, it is clear that the directional similarity method based on RNNLM vectors is the most critical component model. Removing it from the final combination decreases both the Spearman's ρ and MaxDiff accuracy by a large margin; both differences (Com vs. -DS) are statistically significant. The Probase IsA model also has an important impact on the performance on the *Class-Inclusion* relation group. Eliminating the IsA model makes the overall MaxDiff accuracy statistically significantly lower (Com vs. -IsA). Again, the benefits of incorporating Probase Attribute and PILSA models are not clear. Removing them from the final combination lowers the MaxDiff accuracy, but neither the difference in Spearman's ρ nor MaxDiff accuracy is statistically significant. Compared to the RNNLM directional similarity model, the lexical pattern model seems less critical. Removing it lowers the *Similar* and *Contrast* relation groups, but improves some other relation groups like *Class-Inclusion* and *Case Relations*. The final MaxDiff accuracy becomes slightly higher but the Spearman's ρ drops a little (Com vs. -Pat); neither is statistically significant.

Notice that the main purpose of the ablation study is to verify the importance of an individual component model when a significant performance drop is observed after removing it. However, occasionally the overall performance may go up slightly. Typically this is due to the fact that some models do not provide useful signals to a particular relation, but instead introduce more noise. Such effects can often be alleviated when there are enough quality training data, which is unfortunately not the case here.

6 Conclusions

In this paper, we presented a system that combines heterogeneous models based on different information sources for measuring relational similarity. Our two individual general-purpose relational similarity models, *directional similarity* and *lexical pattern* methods, perform strongly when compared to existing systems. After incorporating specific word-relation models, the final system sets a new state-of-the-art on the SemEval-2012 task 2 test set, achieving Spearman's $\rho = 0.353$ and MaxDiff accuracy 45.4% – resulting in 54.1% and 14.7% relative improvement in these two metrics, respectively.

Despite its simplicity, our directional similarity approach provides a robust model for relational similarity and is a critical component in the final system. When the lexical pattern model is included, our overall model combination method can be viewed as a two-stage learning system. As demonstrated in our work, with an appropriate regularization strategy, high-quality models can be learned in both stages. Finally, as we observe from the positive effect of adding the Probase IsA model, specific word-relation models can further help improve the system although they tend to cover only a small number of relations. Incorporating more such models could be a steady path to enhance the final system.

In the future, we plan to pursue several research directions. First, as shown in our experimental results, the model combination approach does not always outperform individual models. Investigating how to select models to combine for each specific relation or relation group individually will be our next step for improving this work. Second, because the labeling process of relational similarity comparisons is inherently noisy, it is unrealistic to request a system to correlate human judgments perfectly. Conducting some user study to estimate the performance ceiling in each relation category may help us focus on the weaknesses of the final system to enhance it. Third, it is intriguing to see that the directional similarity model based on the RNNLM vectors performs strongly, even though the RNNLM training process is not related to the task of relational similarity. Investigating the effects of different vector space models and proposing some theoretical justifications are certainly interesting research topics. Finally, we would like to evaluate the utility our approach in other applications, such as the SAT analogy problems proposed by Turney (2006) and question answering.

Acknowledgments

We thank Richard Socher for valuable discussions, Misha Bilenko for his technical advice and anonymous reviewers for their comments.

References

E. Agirre, E. Alfonseca, K. Hall, J. Kravalova, M. Paşca and A. Soroa. 2009. A study on similarity and relatedness using distributional and WordNet-based approaches. In *NAACL '09*, pages 19–27.

Galen Andrew and Jianfeng Gao. 2007. Scalable training of L1-regularized log-linear models. In *ICML '07*.

I.I. Bejar, R. Chaffin, and S.E. Embretson. 1991. *Cognitive and psychometric analysis of analogical problem solving*. Recent research in psychology. Springer-Verlag.

Y. Bengio, R. Ducharme, P. Vincent, and C. Jauvin. 2003. A neural probabilistic language model. *Journal of Machine Learning Research*, 3:1137–1155.

Peter F. Brown, Peter V. deSouza, Robert L. Mercer, Vincent J. Della Pietra, and Jenifer C. Lai. 1992. Class-based n-gram models of natural language. *Computational Linguistics*, 18:467–479.

A. Budanitsky and G. Hirst. 2006. Evaluating WordNet-based measures of lexical semantic relatedness. *Computational Linguistics*, 32:13–47, March.

Andrew Carlson, Justin Betteridge, Bryan Kisiel, Burr Settles, Estevam R. Hruschka Jr., and Tom M. Mitchell. 2010. Toward an architecture for never-ending language learning. In *Proceedings of the Twenty-Fourth Conference on Artificial Intelligence (AAAI 2010)*.

Timothy W. Finin. 1980. *The Semantic Interpretation of Compound Nominals*. Ph.D. thesis, University of Illinois at Urbana-Champaign.

J.H. Friedman. 2001. Greedy function approximation: a gradient boosting machine. *Ann. Statist*, 29(5):1189–1232.

David Jurgens, Saif Mohammad, Peter Turney, and Keith Holyoak. 2012. SemEval-2012 Task 2: Measuring degrees of relational similarity. In *Proceedings of the Sixth International Workshop on Semantic Evaluation (SemEval 2012)*, pages 356–364, Montréal, Canada, 7-8 June. Association for Computational Linguistics.

Thomas K. Landauer, Peter W. Foltz, and Darrell Laham. 1998. An introduction to latent semantic analysis. *Discourse Processes, 25*, pages 259–284.

Jordan J. Louviere and G. G. Woodworth. 1991. Best-worst scaling: A model for the largest difference judgments. Technical report, University of Alberta.

Tomas Mikolov, Martin Karafiát, Lukas Burget, Jan Cernocký, and Sanjeev Khudanpur. 2010. Recurrent neural network based language model. In *INTERSPEECH*, pages 1045–1048.

Tomas Mikolov, Anoop Deoras, Daniel Povey, Lukas Burget, and Jan Cernocky. 2011. Strategies for training large scale neural network language models. In *ASRU*.

Tomas Mikolov, Wen tau Yih, and Geoffrey Zweig. 2013. Linguistic regularities in continuous space word representations. In *Proceedings of NAACL-HLT*.

Vivi Nastase and Stan Szpakowicz. 2003. Exploring noun-modifier semantic relations. In *Proceedings of the 5th International Workshop on Computational Semantics*.

Robert Parker, David Graff, Junbo Kong, Ke Chen, and Kazuaki Maeda. 2009. English Gigaword fourth edition. Technical report, Linguistic Data Consortium, Philadelphia.

Ted Pedersen. 2012. Duluth: Measuring degrees of relational similarity with the gloss vector measure of semantic relatedness. In *Proceedings of the Sixth International Workshop on Semantic Evaluation (SemEval*

2012), pages 497–501, Montréal, Canada, 7-8 June. Association for Computational Linguistics.

K. Radinsky, E. Agichtein, E. Gabrilovich, and S. Markovitch. 2011. A word at a time: computing word relatedness using temporal semantic analysis. In *WWW '11*, pages 337–346.

J. Reisinger and R. Mooney. 2010. Multi-prototype vector-space models of word meaning. In *NAACL '10*.

Bryan Rink and Sanda Harabagiu. 2012. UTD: Determining relational similarity using lexical patterns. In *Proceedings of the Sixth International Workshop on Semantic Evaluation (SemEval 2012)*, pages 413–418, Montréal, Canada, 7-8 June. Association for Computational Linguistics.

Barbara Rosario and Marti Hearst. 2001. Classifying the semantic relations in noun compounds via a domain-specific lexical hierarchy. In *Proceedings of the 2001 Conference on Empirical Methods in Natural Language Processing (EMNLP-01*, pages 82–90.

Mireya Tovar, J. Alejandro Reyes, Azucena Montes, Darnes Vilariño, David Pinto, and Saul León. 2012. BUAP: A first approximation to relational similarity measuring. In *Proceedings of the Sixth International Workshop on Semantic Evaluation (SemEval 2012)*, pages 502–505, Montréal, Canada, 7-8 June. Association for Computational Linguistics.

J. Turian, L. Ratinov, and Y. Bengio. 2010. Word representations: a simple and general method for semi-supervised learning. In *Proceedings of Association for Computational Linguistics (ACL 2010)*.

Peter Turney and Michael Littman. 2005. Corpus-based learning of analogies and semantic relations. *Machine Learning, 60 (1-3)*, pages 251–278.

P. D. Turney. 2006. Similarity of semantic relations. *Computational Linguistics*, 32(3):379–416.

Peter Turney. 2008. A uniform approach to analogies, synonyms, antonyms, and associations. In *International Conference on Computational Linguistics (COLING)*.

Peter D. Turney. 2012. Domain and function: A dual-space model of semantic relations and compositions. *Journal of Artificial Intelligence Research (JAIR)*, 44:533–585.

Lucy Vanderwende. 1994. Algorithm for automatic interpretation of noun sequences. In *Proceedings of COLING-94*, pages 782–788.

Wentao Wu, Hongsong Li, Haixun Wang, and Kenny Q. Zhu. 2012. Probase: a probabilistic taxonomy for text understanding. In *Proceedings of the 2012 ACM SIGMOD International Conference on Management of Data*, pages 481–492, May.

Wen-tau Yih and Vahed Qazvinian. 2012. Measuring word relatedness using heterogeneous vector space models. In *Proceedings of NAACL-HLT*, pages 616–620, Montréal, Canada, June.

Wen-tau Yih, Geoffrey Zweig, and John Platt. 2012. Polarity inducing latent semantic analysis. In *Proceedings of NAACL-HLT*, pages 1212–1222, Jeju Island, Korea, July.

Broadly Improving User Classification via Communication-Based Name and Location Clustering on Twitter

Shane Bergsma, Mark Dredze, Benjamin Van Durme, Theresa Wilson, David Yarowsky
Department of Computer Science and Human Language Technology Center of Excellence
Johns Hopkins University
Baltimore, MD 21218, USA
shane.a.bergsma@gmail.com, mdredze@cs.jhu.edu, vandurme@cs.jhu.edu, taw@jhu.edu, yarowsky@cs.jhu.edu

Abstract

Hidden properties of social media users, such as their ethnicity, gender, and location, are often reflected in their observed attributes, such as their first and last names. Furthermore, users who communicate with each other often have similar hidden properties. We propose an algorithm that exploits these insights to cluster the observed attributes of hundreds of millions of Twitter users. Attributes such as user names are grouped together if users with those names communicate with other similar users. We separately cluster millions of unique first names, last names, and user-provided locations. The efficacy of these clusters is then evaluated on a diverse set of classification tasks that predict hidden users properties such as ethnicity, geographic location, gender, language, and race, using only profile names and locations when appropriate. Our readily-replicable approach and publicly-released clusters are shown to be remarkably effective and versatile, substantially outperforming state-of-the-art approaches and human accuracy on each of the tasks studied.

1 Introduction

There is growing interest in automatically classifying users in social media by various hidden properties, such as their gender, location, and language (e.g. Rao et al. (2010), Cheng et al. (2010), Bergsma et al. (2012)). Predicting these and other properties for users can enable better advertising and personalization, as well as a finer-grained analysis of user opinions (O'Connor et al., 2010), health (Paul and Dredze, 2011), and sociolinguistic phenomena (Eisenstein et al., 2011). Classifiers for user properties often rely on information from a user's social network (Jernigan and Mistree, 2009; Sadilek et al., 2012) or the textual content they generate (Pennacchiotti and Popescu, 2011; Burger et al., 2011).

Here, we propose and evaluate classifiers that better exploit the *attributes* that users explicitly provide in their user profiles, such as names (e.g., first names like *Mary*, last names like *Smith*) and locations (e.g., *Brasil*). Such attributes have previously been used as "profile features" in supervised user classifiers (Pennacchiotti and Popescu, 2011; Burger et al., 2011; Bergsma et al., 2012). There are several motivations for exploiting these data. Often the only information available for a user is a name or location (e.g. for a new user account). Profiles also provide an orthogonal or complementary source of information to a user's social network and textual content; gains based on profiles alone should therefore add to gains based on other data. The decisions of profile-based classifiers could also be used to bootstrap training data for other classifiers that use complementary features.

Prior work has encoded profile attributes via lexical or character-based features (e.g. Pennacchiotti and Popescu (2011), Burger et al. (2011), Bergsma et al. (2012)). Unfortunately, due to the long-tailed distribution of user attributes, a profile-based classifier will encounter many examples at test time that were not observed during training. For example, suppose a user *wassim hassan* gives their location as *tanger*. If the attribute tokens *wassim*, *hassan*, and *tanger* do not occur in training (nor indicative substrings), then a classifier can only guess at the user's ethnicity and location. In social media, the prevalence of fake names and large variations in spelling, slang, and language make matters worse.

Our innovation is to enhance attribute-based classifiers with new data, derived from the communications of Twitter users with those attributes. Users with the name tokens *wassim* and *hassan* often talk to users with Arab names like *abdul* and *hussein*. Users listing their location as *tanger* often talk to users from *morocco*. Since users who communicate often share properties such as ethnicity and location (§8), the user *wassim hassan* might be an Arab who uses the French spelling of the city *Tangier*.

Our challenge is to encode these data in a form readily usable by a classifier. Our approach is to represent each unique profile attribute (e.g. *tanger* or *hassan*) as a vector that encodes the communication pattern of users with that attribute (e.g. how often they talk to users from *morocco*, etc.); we then cluster the vectors to discover latent groupings of similar attributes. Based on transitive (third party) connections, *tanger* and *tangier* can appear in the same cluster, even if no two users from these locations talk directly. To use the clusters in an attribute-based classifier, we add new features that indicate the cluster memberships of the attributes. Clustering thus lets us convert a high-dimensional space of all attribute pairs to a low-dimensional space of cluster memberships. This makes it easier to share our data, yields fewer parameters for learning, and creates attribute groups that are interpretable to humans.

We cluster names and locations in a very large corpus of 168 million Twitter users (§2) and use a distributed clustering algorithm to separately cluster millions of first names, last names, and user-provided locations (§3). We evaluate the use of our cluster data as a novel feature in supervised classifiers, and compare our result to standard classifiers using character and token-level features (§4). The cluster data enables significantly improved performance in predicting the gender, location, and language of social media users, exceeding both existing state-of-the-art machine and human performance (§6). Our cluster data can likewise improve performance in other domains, on both established and new NLP tasks as further evaluated in this paper (§6). We also propose a way to enhance a geolocation system by using communication patterns, and show strong improvements over a hand-engineered baseline (§7). We share our clusters with the community to use with other tasks. The clusters, and other experimental data, are available for download from `www.clsp.jhu.edu/~sbergsma/TwitterClusters/`.

First names: maria, david, ana, daniel, michael, john, alex, jessica, carlos, jose, chris, sarah, laura, juan
Last names: silva, santos, smith, garcia, oliveira, rodriguez, jones, williams, johnson, brown, gonzalez
Locations: brasil, indonesia, philippines, london, jakarta, são paulo, rio de janeiro, venezuela, brazil

Table 1: Most frequent profile attributes for our collection of 168 million Twitter users, in descending order

2 Attribute Associations on Twitter

Data and Processing Our raw Twitter data comprises the union of 2.2 billion tweets from 05/2009 to 10/2010 (O'Connor et al., 2010), 1.8 billion tweets collected from 07/2011 to 08/2012, and 80 million tweets collected from followers of 10 thousand location and language-specific Twitter feeds.

We implemented each stage of processing using MapReduce (Dean and Ghemawat, 2008). The total computation (from extracting profiles to clustering attributes) was 1300 days of wall-clock CPU time.

Attribute Extraction Tweets provide the name and self-reported location of the tweeter. We find 126M unique users with these attributes in our data. When tweets mention other users via an *@user* construction, Twitter also includes the profile name of the mentioned user; we obtain a further 42M users from these cases. We then normalize the extracted attributes by converting to lower-case, deleting symbols, numbers, and punctuation, and removing common honorifics and suffixes like *mr/mrs* and *jr/sr*. Common prefixes like *van* and *de la* are joined to the last-name token.[1] This processing yields 8.3M

[1] `www.clsp.jhu.edu/~sbergsma/TwitterClusters/` also provides our scripts for normalizing attributes. The scripts can be used to ensure consistency/compatibility between arbitrary datasets and our shared cluster data. Note we use no special processing for the companies, organizations, and spammers among our users, nor for names arising from different conventions (e.g. 1-word names, reversed first/last names).

henrik: fredrik 5.87, henrik 5.82, anders 5.73, johan 5.69, andreas 5.59, martin 5.54, magnus 5.41
courtney: taylor 8.03, ashley 7.92, courtney 7.92, emily 7.91, lauren 7.82, katie 7.72, brittany 7.69
ilya: sergey 5.85, alexey 5.62, alexander 5.59, dmitry 5.51, Александр 5.46, anton 5.44, andrey 5.40

Table 2: Top associates and PMIs for three first names.

unique locations, 7.4M unique last names, and 5.5M unique first names. These three sets provide the target attributes that we cluster in §3. Table 1 shows the most frequent names in each of these three sets.

User-User Links We extract each user mention as an undirected communication link between the user tweeting and the mentioned user (including self-mentions but not retweets). We consider each user-user link as a single event; we count it once no matter how often two specific users interact. We extract 436M user-user links in total.

Attribute-Attribute Pairs We use our profile data to map each user-user link to an attribute-attribute pair; we separately count each pair of first names, last names, and locations. For example, the first-name pair (*henrik,fredrik*) occurs 181 times. Rather than using the raw count, we calculate the association between attributes a_1 and a_2 via their pointwise mutual information (PMI), following prior work in distributional clustering (Lin and Wu, 2009):

$$\mathrm{PMI}(a_1, a_2) = \log \frac{\mathrm{P}(a_1, a_2)}{\mathrm{P}(a_1)\mathrm{P}(a_2)}$$

PMI essentially normalizes the co-occurrence by what we would expect if the attributes were independently distributed. We smooth the PMI by adding a count of 0.5 to all co-occurrence events.

The most highly-associated name attributes reflect similarities in ethnicity and gender (Table 2). The most highly-ranked associates for locations are often nicknames and alternate/misspellings of those locations. For example, the locations *charm city*, *bmore*, *balto*, *westbaltimore*, *b a l t i m o r e*, *baltimoreee*, and *balitmore* each have the U.S. city of *baltimore* as their highest-PMI associate. We show how this can be used to help geolocate users (§7).

3 Attribute Clustering

Representation We first represent each target attribute as a feature vector, where each feature corresponds to another attribute of the same type as the target and each value gives the PMI between this attribute and the target (as in Table 2).[2] To help cluster the long-tail of infrequent attributes, we also include orthographic features. For first and last names, we have binary features for the last 2 characters in the string. For locations, we have binary features for (a) any ideographic characters in the string and (b) each token (with diacritics removed) in the string. We normalize the feature vectors to unit length.

Distributed K-Means Clustering Our approach to clustering follows Lin and Wu (2009) who used k-means to cluster tens of millions of phrases. We also use cosine similarity to compute the closest centroid (i.e., we use the *spherical* k-means clustering algorithm (Dhillon and Modha, 2001)). We keep track of the average cosine similarity between each vector and its nearest centroid; this average is guaranteed to increase at each iteration.

Like Lin and Wu (2009), we parallelize the algorithm using MapReduce. Each mapper finds the nearest centroids for a portion of the vectors, while also computing the partial sums of the vectors assigned to each centroid. The mappers emit the centroid IDs as keys and the partial sums as values. The Reducer aggregates the partial sums from each partition and re-normalizes each sum vector to unit length to obtain the new centroids. We also use an inverted index at each iteration that, for each input feature, lists which centroids each feature belongs to. Using this index greatly speeds up the centroid similarity computations.

Clustering Details We cluster with nine separate configurations: over first names, last names, and locations, and each with 50, 200, and 1000 cluster centroids (denoted C^{50}, C^{200}, and C^{1000}). Since k-

[2] We decided to restrict the features for a target to be attributes of the same type (e.g., we did not use *last name* associations for a *first name* target) because each attribute type conveys distinct information. For example, first names convey gender and age more than last names. By separately clustering representations using first names, last names, and locations, each clustering can capture its own distinct latent-class associations.

Cluster 463 (Serbian): pavlović, jovanovic, jovanović, stanković, srbija, marković, petrović, radovic, nenad, milenkovic, nikolic, sekulic, todorovic, stojanovic, petrovic, aleksic, ilic, markovic
Cluster 544 (Black South African): ngcobo, nkosi, dlamini, ndlovu, mkhize, mtshali, sithole, mathebula, mthembu, khumalo, ngwenya, shabangu, nxumalo, buthelezi, radebe, mabena, zwane, mbatha, sibiya
Cluster 449 (Turkish): şahin, çelik, öztürk, koç, çakır, karataş, aktaş, güngör, özkan, balcı, gümüş, akkaya, genç, sarı, yüksel, güneş, yiğit, yalçın, orhan, sağlam, güler, demirci, küçük, yavuz, bayrak, özcan, altun
Cluster 656 (Indonesian): utari, oktaviana, apriani, mustika, septiana, febrianti, kurniawati, indriani, nurjanah, septian, cahya, anggara, yuliani, purnamasari, sukma, wijayanti, pramesti, ningrum, yanti, wulansari

Table 3: Example C^{1000} last-name clusters

Cluster 56 [sim=0.497]: gregg, bryn, bret, stewart, lyndsay, howie, elyse, jacqui, becki, rhett, meaghan, kirstie, russ, jaclyn, zak, katey, seamus, brennan, fraser, kristie, stu, jaimie, kerri, heath, carley, griffin
Cluster 104 [sim=0.442]: stephon, devonte, deion, demarcus, janae, tyree, jarvis, donte, dewayne, javon, destinee, tray, janay, tyrell, jamar, iesha, chyna, jaylen, darion, lamont, marquise, domonique, alexus
Cluster 132 [sim=0.292]: moustafa, omnya, mennatallah, إسلام, shorouk, ragab, لؤي, radwa, moemen, mohab, hazem, yehia, حرية, اسراء, mennah, مصري, abdelrahman, مصطفي, حزب, تامر, nermeen, hebatallah
...

Table 4: C^{200} soft clustering for first name *yasmeen*

means is not guaranteed to reach a global optimum, we use ten different random initializations for each configuration, and select the one with the highest average similarity after 20 iterations. We run this one for an additional 30 iterations and take the output as our final set of centroids for that configuration.

The resulting clusters provide data that could help classify hidden properties of social media users. For example, Table 3 shows that last names often cluster by ethnicity, even at the sub-national level (e.g. Zulu tribe surnames *nkosi*, *dlamini*, *mathebula*, etc.). Note the Serbian names include two entries that are not last names: *srbija*, the Serbian word for *Serbia*, and *nenad*, a common Serbian first name.

Soft Clustering Rather than assigning each attribute to its single highest-similarity cluster, we can assign each vector to its N most similar clusters. These soft-cluster assignments often reflect different social groups where a name or location is used. For example, the name *yasmeen* is similar to both common American names (Cluster 56), African American names (Cluster 104), and Arabic names (Cluster 132) (Table 4). As another example, the C^{1000} assignments for the location *trujillo* comprise separate clusters containing towns and cities in Peru, Venezuela, Colombia, etc., reflecting the various places in the Latin world with this name. In general, the soft cluster assignment is a low-dimensional representation of each of our attributes. Although it can be interpretable to humans, it need not be in order to be useful to a classifier.

4 Classification with Cluster Features

Our motivating problem is to classify users for hidden properties such as their gender, location, race, ethnicity, and language. We adopt a discriminative solution. We encode the relevant data for each instance in a feature vector and train a (linear) support vector machine classifier (Cortes and Vapnik, 1995). SVMs represent the state-of-the-art on many NLP classification tasks, but other classifiers could also be used. For multi-class classification, we use a one-versus-all strategy, a competitive approach on most multi-class problems (Rifkin and Klautau, 2004).

The input to our system is one or more observed user attributes (e.g. name and location fields from a user profile). We now describe how features are created from these attributes in both state-of-the-art systems and via our new cluster data.

Token Features (*Tok*) are binary features that indicate the presence of a specific attribute (e.g., *first-name=bob*). Burger et al. (2011) and Bergsma et al. (2012) used *Tok* features to encode user profile features. For multi-token fields (e.g. location), our *Tok* features also indicate the specific position of each token (e.g., loc_1=*são*, loc_2=*paulo*, loc_N=*brasil*).

Character N-gram Features (*Ngm*) give the count of all character n-grams of length 1-to-4 in the input. *Ngm* features have been used in user classification (Burger et al., 2011) and represent the state-of-the-art in detecting name ethnicity (Bhargava and Kondrak, 2010). We add special begin/end characters to the attributes to mark the prefix and suffix positions. We also use a smoothed log-count; we found this to be most effective in preliminary work.

Cluster Features (*Clus*) indicate the soft-cluster memberships of the attributes. We have features for the top-2, 5, and 20 most similar clusters in the C^{50}, C^{200}, and C^{1000} clusterings, respectively. Like Lin and Wu (2009), we "side-step the matter of choosing the optimal value k in k-means" by using features from clusterings at different granularities. Our feature dimensions correspond to cluster IDs; feature values give the similarity to the cluster centroid. Other strategies (e.g. hard clustering, binary features) were less effective in preliminary work.

5 Classification Experiments

5.1 Methodology

Our main objective is to assess the value of using cluster features (*Clus*). We add these features to classifiers using *Tok+Ngm* features, which represents the current state-of-the-art. We compare these feature settings on both Twitter tasks (§5.2) and tasks not related to social-media (§5.3). For each task, we randomly divide the gold standard data into 50% train, 25% development and 25% test, unless otherwise noted. As noted above, the gold-standard datasets for all of our experiments are available for download. We train our SVM classifiers using the LIBLINEAR package (Fan et al., 2008). We optimize the classifier's regularization parameter on development data, and report our final results on the held-out test examples. We report *accuracy*: the proportion of test examples classified correctly. For comparison, we report the accuracy of a majority-class baseline on each task (*Base*).

Classifying hidden properties of social media users is challenging (Table 5). Pennacchiotti and Popescu (2011) even conclude that "profile fields do not contain enough good-quality information to be directly used for user classification." To provide insight into the difficulty of the tasks, we had two humans annotate 120 examples from each of the test sets, and we average their results to give a "*Human*" performance number. The two humans are experts in this domain and have very wide knowledge of global names and locations.

Country: 53 possible countries		
United States	courtland dante	cali baby
United States	tinas twin	on the court
Brazil	thamires gomez	macapá ap
Denmark	marte clason	NONE
Lang. ID: 9 confusable languages		
Bulgarian	valentina getova	NONE
Russian	borisenko yana	edinburgh
Bulgarian	NONE	blagoevgrad
Ukrainian	andriy kupyna	ternopil
Farsi	kambiz barahouei	NONE
Urdu	musadiq sanwal	jammu
Ethnicity: 13 European ethnicities		
German	dennis hustadt	
Dutch	bernhard hofstede	
French	david coste	
Swedish	mattias bjarsmyr	
Portuguese	helder costa	
Race: black or white		
black	kerry swain	
black	darrell foskey	
white	ty j larocca	
black	james n jones	
white	sean p farrell	

Table 5: Examples of class (left) and input (names, locations) for some of our evaluation tasks.

5.2 Twitter Applications

Country A number of recent papers have considered the task of predicting the geolocation of users, using both user content (Cheng et al., 2010; Eisenstein et al., 2010; Hecht et al., 2011; Wing and Baldridge, 2011; Roller et al., 2012) and social network (Backstrom et al., 2010; Sadilek et al., 2012).

Here, we first predict user location at the level of the user's location *country*. To our knowledge, we are the first to exploit user locations *and* names for this prediction. For this task, we obtain gold data from the portion of Twitter users who have GPS enabled (geocoded tweets). We were able to obtain a very large number of gold instances for this task, so selected only 10K for testing, 10K for development, and retained the remaining 782K for training.

Language ID Identifying the language of users is an important prerequisite for building language-specific social media resources (Tromp and Pechenizkiy, 2011; Carter et al., 2013). Bergsma et al. (2012) recently released a corpus of tweets marked for one of nine languages grouped into three confusable character sets: Arabic, Farsi, and Urdu tweets written in Arabic characters; Hindi, Nepali, and Marathi written in Devanagari, and Russian, Bulgarian, and Ukrainian written in Cyrillic. The tweets were marked for language by native speakers via Amazon Mechanical Turk. We again discard the tweet content and extract each user's first name, last name, and user location as our input data, while taking the annotated language as the class label.

Gender We predict whether a Twitter user is male or female using data from Burger et al. (2011). This data was created by linking Twitter users to structured profile pages on other websites where users must select their gender. Unlike prior systems using this data (Burger et al., 2011; Van Durme, 2012), we make the predictions using only user names.

5.3 Other Applications

Origin Knowing the origin of a name can improve its automatic pronunciation (Llitjos and Black, 2001) and transliteration (Bhargava and Kondrak, 2010). We evaluate our cluster data on name-origin prediction using a corpus of names marked as either Indian or non-Indian by Bhargava and Kondrak (2010). Since names in this corpus are not marked for entity type, we include separate cluster features from both our first and last name clusters.

Ethnicity We also evaluate on name-origin data from Konstantopoulos (2007). This data derives from lists of football players on European national teams; it marks each name (with diacritics removed) as arising from one of 13 European languages. Following prior work, we test in two settings: (1) using last names only, and (2) using first and last names.

Race We also evaluate our ability to identify ethnic groups at a sub-national level. To obtain data for this task, we mined the publicly-available arrest records on `mugshots.com` for the U.S. state of New Jersey (a small but diverse and densely-populated area). Over 99% of users were listed as either *black* or *white*, and we structure the task as a binary classification problem between these two classes. We predict the race of each person based purely on their name; this contrasts with prior work in social media which looked at identifying African Americans on the basis of their Twitter *content* (Eisenstein et al., 2011; Pennacchiotti and Popescu, 2011).

6 Classification Results

Table 6 gives the results on each task. The system incorporating our novel *Clus* features consistently improves over the *Ngm+Tok* system; all differences between *All* and *Ngm+Tok* are significant (McNemar's, $p<0.01$). The relative reduction in error from adding *Clus* features ranges between 7% and 51%. The *All* system including *Clus* features also exceeds human performance on all studied tasks.

On **Country**, the U.S. is the majority class, occurring in 42.5% of cases.[3] It is impressive that *All* so significantly exceeds *Tok+Ngm* (86.7% vs. 84.8%); with 782K training examples, we did not expect such room for improvement. Both names and locations play an important role: *All* achieves 66% using names alone and 70% with only location. On the subset of data where all three attributes are non-empty, the full system achieves 93% accuracy.

Both feature classes are likewise important for **Lang. ID**; *All* achieves 67% with only first+last names, 72% with just locations, but 83% with both.

Our smallest improvement is on **Gender**. This task is easier (with higher human/system accuracy) and has plenty of training data (more data *per class* than any other task); there is thus less room to improve. Looking at the feature weights, the strongest-weighted *female* cluster apparently captures a sub-community of Justin Bieber fans (showing loyalty with "first names" *jbieber*, *belieb*, *biebz*, *beliebing*, *jbiebs*, etc.). Just because a first name like *madison* has a high similarity to this cluster does not imply girls named *Madison* are Justin Bieber fans; it simply means that Madisons have similar names to the *friends* of Justin Bieber fans (who tend to be girls). Also, note that while the majority of the 34K users in our training data are assigned this cluster somewhere in their soft clustering, only 6 would be assigned this

[3]We tried other baselines: e.g., we predict countries if they are substrings of the location (otherwise predicting U.S.); and we predict countries if they often occur as a string following the given location in our profile data (e.g., we predict *Spain* for *Madrid* since *Madrid, Spain* is common). Variations on these approaches consistently performed between 48% and 56%.

Task	Input	Num. Train	Num. Class	*Base*	*Human*	*Tok*	*Ngm*	*Clus*	*Tok+ Ngm*	*All*	Δ
Country	first+last+loc	781920	53	42.5	71.7	83.0	84.5	80.2	84.8	**86.7**	12.5
Lang. ID	first+last+loc	2492	9	27.0	74.2	74.6	80.6	71.1	80.4	**82.7**	11.7
Gender	first+last	33805	2	52.4	88.3	85.3	88.6	79.5	89.5	**90.2**	6.7
Origin	entity name	500	2	52.4	80.4	-	75.6	81.2	75.6	**88.0**	50.8
Ethnicity	last	6026	13	20.8	47.9	-	54.6	48.5	54.6	**62.4**	17.2
Ethnicity	first+last	7457	13	21.2	53.3	67.6	77.5	73.6	78.4	**81.3**	13.4
Race	first+last	7977	2	54.7	71.4	80.4	81.6	84.6	82.4	**84.6**	12.5

Table 6: Task details and accuracy (%) for attribute-based classification tasks. Δ = relative error reduction (%) of *All* (*Tok+Ngm+Clus*) over *Ngm+Tok*. *All* always exceeds both *Tok+Ngm* and the human performance.

cluster in a *hard* clustering. This clearly illustrates the value of the soft clustering representation.

Note the *All* system performed between 83% and 90% on each Twitter task. This level of performance strongly refutes the prevailing notion that Twitter profile information is useless in general (Pennacchiotti and Popescu, 2011) and especially for geolocation (Cheng et al., 2010; Hecht et al., 2011).

We now move to applications beyond social media. Bhargava and Kondrak (2010) have the current state-of-the-art on **Origin** and **Ethnicity** based on an SVM using character-n-gram features; we reimplemented this as *Ngm*. We obtain a huge improvement over their work using *Clus*, especially on **Origin** where we reduce error by >50%.[4] This improvement can partly be attributed to the small amount of training data; with fewer parameters to learn, *Clus* learns more from limited data than *Ngm*. We likewise see large improvements over the state-of-the-art on **Ethnicity**, on both last name and full name settings.

Finally, *Clus* features also significantly improve accuracy on the new **Race** task. Our cluster data can therefore help to classify names into sub-national groups, and could potentially be used to infer other interesting communities such as castes in India and religious divisions in many countries.

In general, the relative value of our cluster models varies with the amount of training data; we see huge gains on the smaller **Origin** data but smaller gains on the large **Gender** set. Figure 1 shows how performance of *Clus* and *Ngm* varies with training data on **Race**. Again, *Clus* is especially helpful with less data; thousands of training examples are needed for *Ngm* to rival the performance of *Clus* using only a handful. Since labeled data is generally expensive to obtain or in short supply, our method for exploiting unlabeled Twitter data can both save money and improve top-end performance.

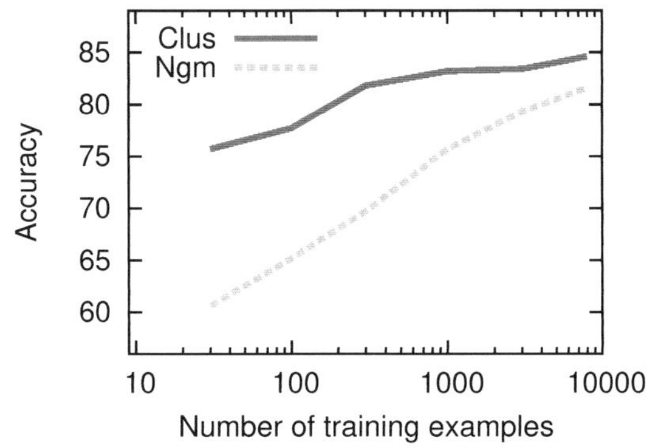

Figure 1: Learning curve on Race: *Clus* perform as well with 30 training examples as *Ngm* features do with 1000.

7 Geolocation by Association

There is a tradition in computational linguistics of grouping words both by the similarity of their context vectors (Hindle, 1990; Pereira et al., 1993; Lin, 1998) and directly by their statistical association in text (Church and Hanks, 1990; Brown et al., 1992). While the previous sections explored clusters built by vector similarity, we now explore a direct application of our attribute association data (§2).

We wish to use this data to improve an existing Twitter geolocation system based on user profile locations. The system operates as follows: 1) normal-

[4]Note *Tok* is not used here because the input is a single token and training and test splits have distinct instances.

ize user-provided locations using a set of regular expressions (e.g. remove extra spacing, punctuation); 2) look up the normalized location in an *alias list*; 3) if found, map the alias to a unique string (target location), corresponding to a structured location object that includes geo-coordinates.

The alias list we are currently using is based on extensive work in hand-writing aliases for the most popular Twitter locations. For example, the current aliases for *Nashville, Tennessee* include *nashville*, *nashville tn*, *music city*, etc. Our objective is to improve on this human-designed list by automatically generating aliases using our association data.

Aliases by Association For each target, we propose new aliases from the target's top-PMI associates (§2). To become an alias, the PMI between the alias and target must be above a threshold, the alias must occur more than a fixed number of times in our profile data, the alias must be within the top-N_1 associates of the target, and the target must be within the top-N_2 associates of the alias. We merge our automatic aliases with the manually-written aliases. The new aliases for *Nashville, Tennessee* include *east nashville*, *nashville tenn*, *music city usa*, *nashvegas*, *cashville tn*, etc.

Experiments To evaluate the geolocation system, we use tweets from users with GPS enabled (§5.2). For each tweet, we resolve the location using the system and compare to the gold coordinates. The system can skip a location if it does not match the alias list; more than half of the locations are skipped, which is consistent with prior work (Hecht et al., 2011). We evaluate the alias lists using two measures: (1) its coverage: the percentage of locations it resolves, and (2) its precision: of the ones resolved, the percentage that are correct. We define a *correct* resolution to be one where the resolved coordinates are within 50 miles of the gold coordinates.

We use 56K gold tweets to tune the parameters of our automatic alias-generator, trading off coverage and precision. We tune such that the system using these aliases obtains the highest possible coverage, while being at least as precise as the baseline system. We then evaluate both the baseline set of aliases and our new set on 56K held-out examples.

Results On held-out test data, the geolocation system using baseline aliases has a coverage of 38.7% and a precision of 59.5%. Meanwhile, the system using the new aliases has a coverage of 44.6% and a precision of 59.4%. With virtually the same precision, the new aliases are thus able to resolve 15% more users. This provides an immediate benefit to our existing Twitter research efforts.

Note that our alias lists can be viewed as *clusters* of locations. In ongoing work, we are exploring techniques based on discriminative learning to infer alias lists using not only *Clus* information but also *Ngm* and *Tok* features as in the previous sections.

8 Related Work

In both real-world and online social networks, "people socialize with people who are like them in terms of gender, sexual orientation, age, race, education, and religion" (Jernigan and Mistree, 2009). Social media research has exploited this for two main purposes: (1) to predict friendships based on user properties, and (2) to predict user properties based on friendships. Friendship prediction systems (e.g. Facebook's *friend suggestion tool*) use features such as whether both people are computer science majors (Taskar et al., 2003) or whether both are at the same location (Crandall et al., 2010; Sadilek et al., 2012). The inverse problem has been explored in the prediction of a user's location given the location of their peers (Backstrom et al., 2010; Cho et al., 2011; Sadilek et al., 2012). Jernigan and Mistree (2009) predict a user's sexuality based on the sexuality of their Facebook friends, while Garera and Yarowsky (2009) predict a user's gender partly based on the gender of their conversational partner. Jha and Elhadad (2010) predict the cancer stage of users of an online cancer discussion board; they derive complementary information for prediction from both the text a user generates and the cancer stage of the people that a user interacts with.

The idea of clustering data in order to provide features for supervised systems has been successfully explored in a range of NLP tasks, including named-entity-recognition (Miller et al., 2004; Lin and Wu, 2009; Ratinov and Roth, 2009), syntactic chunking (Turian et al., 2010), and dependency parsing (Koo et al., 2008; Täckström et al., 2012). In each case, the clusters are derived from the distribution of the words or phrases in text, not from their communication pattern. It would be interesting to see whether prior distributional clusters can be combined with our communication-based clusters to achieve even better performance. Indeed, there is evidence that features derived from text can improve the prediction of name ethnicity (Pervouchine et al., 2010).

There has been an explosion of work in recent years in predicting user properties in social networks. Aside from the work mentioned above that analyzes a user's social network, a large amount of work has focused on inferring user properties based on the content they generate (e.g. Burger and Henderson (2006), Schler et al. (2006), Rao et al. (2010), Mukherjee and Liu (2010), Pennacchiotti and Popescu (2011), Burger et al. (2011), Van Durme (2012)).

9 Conclusion and Future Work

We presented a highly effective and readily replicable algorithm for generating language resources from Twitter communication patterns. We clustered user attributes based on both the communication of users with those attributes as well as substring similarity. Systems using our clusters significantly outperform state-of-the-art algorithms on each of the tasks investigated, and exceed human performance on each task as well. The power and versatility of our clusters is exemplified by the fact we reduce error by a larger margin on each of the non-Twitter tasks than on any Twitter task itself.

Twitter provides a remarkably large sample and effectively a partial census of much of the world's population, with associated metadata, descriptive content and sentiment information. Our ability to accurately assign numerous often unspecified properties such as race, gender, language and ethnicity to such a large user sample substantially increases the sociological insights and correlations one can derive from such data.

References

Lars Backstrom, Eric Sun, and Cameron Marlow. 2010. Find me if you can: improving geographical prediction with social and spatial proximity. In *Proc. WWW*, pages 61–70.

Shane Bergsma, Paul McNamee, Mossaab Bagdouri, Clayton Fink, and Theresa Wilson. 2012. Language identification for creating language-specific Twitter collections. In *Proceedings of the Second Workshop on Language in Social Media*, pages 65–74.

Aditya Bhargava and Grzegorz Kondrak. 2010. Language identification of names with SVMs. In *Proc. HLT-NAACL*, pages 693–696.

Peter F. Brown, Vincent J. Della Pietra, Peter V. de Souza, Jennifer C. Lai, and Robert L. Mercer. 1992. Class-based n-gram models of natural language. *Computational Linguistics*, 18(4):467–479.

John D. Burger and John C. Henderson. 2006. An exploration of observable features related to blogger age. In *Proc. AAAI Spring Symposium: Computational Approaches to Analyzing Weblogs*, pages 15–20.

John D. Burger, John Henderson, George Kim, and Guido Zarrella. 2011. Discriminating gender on Twitter. In *Proc. EMNLP*, pages 1301–1309.

Simon Carter, Wouter Weerkamp, and Manos Tsagkias. 2013. Microblog Language Identification: Overcoming the Limitations of Short, Unedited and Idiomatic Text. *Language Resources and Evaluation Journal*. (forthcoming).

Zhiyuan Cheng, James Caverlee, and Kyumin Lee. 2010. You are where you tweet: a content-based approach to geo-locating Twitter users. In *Proc. CIKM*, pages 759–768.

Eunjoon Cho, Seth A. Myers, and Jure Leskovec. 2011. Friendship and mobility: user movement in location-based social networks. In *Proc. KDD*, pages 1082–1090.

Kenneth W. Church and Patrick Hanks. 1990. Word association norms, mutual information, and lexicography. *Computational Linguistics*, 16(1):22–29.

Corinna Cortes and Vladimir Vapnik. 1995. Support-vector networks. *Mach. Learn.*, 20(3):273–297.

David J. Crandall, Lars Backstrom, Dan Cosley, Siddharth Suri, Daniel Huttenlocher, and Jon Kleinberg. 2010. Inferring social ties from geographic coincidences. *Proceedings of the National Academy of Sciences*, 107(52):22436–22441.

Jeffrey Dean and Sanjay Ghemawat. 2008. MapReduce: simplified data processing on large clusters. *Commun. ACM*, 51(1):107–113.

Inderjit S. Dhillon and Dharmendra S. Modha. 2001. Concept decompositions for large sparse text data using clustering. *Mach. Learn.*, 42(1-2):143–175.

Jacob Eisenstein, Brendan O'Connor, Noah A. Smith, and Eric P. Xing. 2010. A latent variable model for geographic lexical variation. In *Proc. EMNLP*, pages 1277–1287.

Jacob Eisenstein, Noah A. Smith, and Eric P. Xing. 2011. Discovering sociolinguistic associations with structured sparsity. In *Proc. ACL*, pages 1365–1374.

Rong-En Fan, Kai-Wei Chang, Cho-Jui Hsieh, Xiang-Rui Wang, and Chih-Jen Lin. 2008. LIBLINEAR: A library for large linear classification. *J. Mach. Learn. Res.*, 9:1871–1874.

Nikesh Garera and David Yarowsky. 2009. Modeling latent biographic attributes in conversational genres. In *Proc. ACL-IJCNLP*, pages 710–718.

Brent Hecht, Lichan Hong, Bongwon Suh, and Ed H. Chi. 2011. Tweets from Justin Bieber's heart: the dynamics of the location field in user profiles. In *Proc. CHI*, pages 237–246.

Donald Hindle. 1990. Noun classification from predicate-argument structures. In *Proc. ACL*, pages 268–275.

Carter Jernigan and Behram F. T. Mistree. 2009. Gaydar: Facebook friendships expose sexual orientation. *First Monday*, 14(10). [Online].

Mukund Jha and Noemie Elhadad. 2010. Cancer stage prediction based on patient online discourse. In *Proc. 2010 Workshop on Biomedical Natural Language Processing*, pages 64–71.

Stasinos Konstantopoulos. 2007. What's in a name? In *Proc. Computational Phonology Workshop, RANLP*.

Terry Koo, Xavier Carreras, and Michael Collins. 2008. Simple semi-supervised dependency parsing. In *Proc. ACL-08: HLT*, pages 595–603.

Dekang Lin and Xiaoyun Wu. 2009. Phrase clustering for discriminative learning. In *Proc. ACL-IJCNLP*, pages 1030—1038.

Dekang Lin. 1998. Automatic retrieval and clustering of similar words. In *Proc. Coling-ACL*, pages 768–774.

Ariadna Font Llitjos and Alan W. Black. 2001. Knowledge of language origin improves pronunciation accuracy of proper names. In *Proceedings of EuroSpeech-01*, pages 1919–1922.

Scott Miller, Jethran Guinness, and Alex Zamanian. 2004. Name tagging with word clusters and discriminative training. In *Proc. HLT-NAACL*, pages 337–342.

Arjun Mukherjee and Bing Liu. 2010. Improving gender classification of blog authors. In *Proc. EMNLP*, pages 207–217.

Brendan O'Connor, Ramnath Balasubramanyan, Bryan R. Routledge, and Noah A. Smith. 2010. From tweets to polls: Linking text sentiment to public opinion time series. In *Proc. ICWSM*, pages 122–129.

Michael Paul and Mark Dredze. 2011. You are what you tweet: Analyzing Twitter for public health. In *Proc. ICWSM*, pages 265–272.

Marco Pennacchiotti and Ana-Maria Popescu. 2011. A machine learning approach to Twitter user classification. In *Proc. ICWSM*, pages 281–288.

Fernando Pereira, Naftali Tishby, and Lillian Lee. 1993. Distributional clustering of English words. In *Proc. ACL*, pages 183–190.

Vladimir Pervouchine, Min Zhang, Ming Liu, and Haizhou Li. 2010. Improving name origin recognition with context features and unlabelled data. In *Coling 2010: Posters*, pages 972–978.

Delip Rao, David Yarowsky, Abhishek Shreevats, and Manaswi Gupta. 2010. Classifying latent user attributes in Twitter. In *Proc. International Workshop on Search and Mining User-Generated Contents*, pages 37–44.

Lev Ratinov and Dan Roth. 2009. Design challenges and misconceptions in named entity recognition. In *Proc. CoNLL*, pages 147–155.

Ryan Rifkin and Aldebaro Klautau. 2004. In defense of one-vs-all classification. *J. Mach. Learn. Res.*, 5:101–141.

Stephen Roller, Michael Speriosu, Sarat Rallapalli, Benjamin Wing, and Jason Baldridge. 2012. Supervised text-based geolocation using language models on an adaptive grid. In *Proc. EMNLP-CoNLL*, pages 1500–1510.

Adam Sadilek, Henry Kautz, and Jeffrey P. Bigham. 2012. Finding your friends and following them to where you are. In *Proc. WSDM*, pages 723–732.

Jonathan Schler, Moshe Koppel, Shlomo Argamon, and James W. Pennebaker. 2006. Effects of age and gender on blogging. In *Proc. AAAI Spring Symposium: Computational Approaches to Analyzing Weblogs*, pages 199–205.

Oscar Täckström, Ryan McDonald, and Jakob Uszkoreit. 2012. Cross-lingual word clusters for direct transfer of linguistic structure. In *Proc. NAACL-HLT*, pages 477–487.

Ben Taskar, Ming-Fai Wong, Pieter Abbeel, and Daphne Koller. 2003. Link prediction in relational data. In *Proc. NIPS*, volume 15.

Erik Tromp and Mykola Pechenizkiy. 2011. Graph-based n-gram language identication on short texts. In *Proc. 20th Machine Learning conference of Belgium and The Netherlands*, pages 27–34.

Joseph Turian, Lev Ratinov, and Yoshua Bengio. 2010. Word representations: A simple and general method for semi-supervised learning. In *Proc. ACL*, pages 384–394.

Benjamin Van Durme. 2012. Streaming analysis of discourse participants. In *Proc. EMNLP-CoNLL*, pages 48–58.

Benjamin Wing and Jason Baldridge. 2011. Simple supervised document geolocation with geodesic grids. In *Proc. ACL*, pages 955–964.

To Link or Not to Link? A Study on End-to-End Tweet Entity Linking

Stephen Guo
Stanford University
sdguo@cs.stanford.edu

Ming-Wei Chang **Emre Kıcıman**
Microsoft Research
{minchang, emrek}@microsoft.com

Abstract

Information extraction from microblog posts is an important task, as today microblogs capture an unprecedented amount of information and provide a view into the pulse of the world. As the core component of information extraction, we consider the task of Twitter entity linking in this paper.

In the current entity linking literature, mention detection and entity disambiguation are frequently cast as equally important but distinct problems. However, in our task, we find that mention detection is often the performance bottleneck. The reason is that messages on micro-blogs are short, noisy and informal texts with little context, and often contain phrases with ambiguous meanings.

To rigorously address the Twitter entity linking problem, we propose a structural SVM algorithm for entity linking that jointly optimizes mention detection and entity disambiguation as a single end-to-end task. By combining structural learning and a variety of first-order, second-order, and context-sensitive features, our system is able to outperform existing state-of-the art entity linking systems by 15% F_1.

1 Introduction

Microblogging services, such as Twitter and Facebook, are today capturing the largest volume ever recorded of fine-grained discussions spanning a huge breadth of topics, from the mundane to the historic. The micro-blogging service Twitter reports that it alone captures over 340M short messages, or *tweets*, per day.[1] From such micro-blogging services' data streams, researchers have reported mining insights about a variety of domains, from election results (Tumasjan et al., 2010) and democracy movements (Starbird and Palen, 2012) to health issues and disease spreading (Paul and Dredze, 2011; Sadilek et al., 2012), as well as tracking product feedback and sentiment (Asur and Huberman, 2010).

A critical step in mining information from a micro-blogging service, such as Twitter, is the identification of entities in tweets. In order to mine the relationship between drugs, symptoms and side-effects, or track the popularity of politicians or sentiment about social issues, we must first be able to identify the topics and specific entities being discussed. The challenge is that messages on micro-blogs are short, noisy, and informal texts with little context, and often contain phrases with ambiguous meanings. For example, "one day" may be either a set phrase or a reference to a movie. Given such difficulties, current mining and analysis of micro-blogs lists limits its application to certain domains with easy-to-recognize, unambiguous entities in order to avoid noise in the extraction results.

We begin this paper with a thorough investigation of mention detection and entity disambiguation for social media, focused on the Twitter micro-blogging service. *Mention detection* is the task of extraction surface form candidates that can link to an entity in the domain of interest. *Entity disambiguation* is the task of linking an extracted mention to a specific definition or instance of an entity in a knowledge base.

[1] http://blog.twitter.com/2012/03/twitter-turns-six.html

While mention detection and entity disambiguation are frequently cast as equally important but distinct and separate problems, we find that mention detection is where today's systems and our baseline techniques incur the most failures. Detecting the correct entity mention is a significant challenge given mis-capitalizations, incorrect grammar, and ambiguous phrases. In (Ritter et al., 2011), the authors report their system achieves 0.64 to 0.67 F_1 on named entity segmentation results with 34K tokens of labeled examples. On the other hand, once the correct entity mention is detected, a trivial disambiguation that maps to the most popular entity[2] will achieve 85% accuracy in our set.

Our primary contribution in this paper is a recasting and merging of the tasks of mention detection and entity disambiguation into a single *end-to-end entity linking* task. We achieve significant improvements by applying structural learning techniques to jointly optimize the detection and disambiguation of entities. Treating detection and disambiguation as a single task also enables us to apply a large set of new features, conventionally used only for disambiguation, to the initial detection of mentions. These features, derived from external knowledge bases, include entity popularity and inter-entity relations from external knowledge bases, and are not well utilized in current mention detection systems. For example, consider the following partial tweet:

(1) The town is so, so good. And don't worry Ben, we already forgave you for Gigli. Really.

Determining whether or not "The town" is a mention of a location or other specific entity based solely on lexical and syntactic features is challenging. Knowing "The Town" is the name of a recent movie helps, and we can we be more confident if we know that Ben Affleck is an actor in the movie, and Gigli is another of his movies.

To train and evaluate our system, we created three separate annotated data sets of approximately 500 tweets each. These data sets are hand annotated with entity links to Wikipedia. We evaluate our system by comparing its performance at detecting entities to the performance of two state-of-the-art entity linking systems, Cucerzan (Cucerzan, 2007) and TagMe (Ferragina and Scaiella, 2010), and find that our system outperforms them significantly by 15% in absolute F_1.

The rest of this paper describes related work, our structured learning approach to entity linking, and our experimental results.

2 Related Work

Building an entity linking system requires solving two interrelated sub-problems: mention detection and entity disambiguation. The significant portion of recent work in the literature (Ratinov et al., 2011; Davis et al., 2012; Sil et al., 2012; Demartini et al., 2012; Wang et al., 2012; Han and Sun, 2011; Han et al., 2011) focuses solely upon the entity linking problem. The entity linking systems of these studies assume that entity mentions are provided by a separate mention detection system. In contrast, our study jointly identifies and disambiguates entity mentions within tweets (short text fragments).

A subset of existing literature targets end-to-end linking (Cucerzan, 2007; Milne and Witten, 2008; Kulkarni et al., 2009; Ferragina and Scaiella, 2010; Han and Sun, 2011; Meij et al., 2012), but there are quite a few differences between our work and each of these systems. Some systems (Milne and Witten, 2008; Kulkarni et al., 2009; Han and Sun, 2011) heavily depend on Wikipedia text and might not work well in short and noisy tweets. Many systems (Mihalcea and Csomai, 2007; Cucerzan, 2007; Milne and Witten, 2008; Ferragina and Scaiella, 2010) treat mention detection and entity disambiguation as two different problems. (Meij et al., 2012) is the most related to our paper. While their system also considers mention detection and entity disambiguation together, they do not consider entity-to-entity relationships and do not incorporate contextual words from tweets.

An area of work closely related to the mention detection problem is the Named Entity Recognition (NER) problem, the identification of textual phrases which belong to core categories (Person, Location, Organization). It is well-known that NER systems trained on well-written documents perform very poorly on short, noisy text, such as tweets (Rit-

[2] What we mean here is "the most linked entity". See Section 3 for details.

ter et al., 2011). There have been a few recent studies proposing Twitter-specific NER systems (Li et al., 2012; Ritter et al., 2011).

3 Preliminaries

For performing entity linking on Twitter, we choose Wikipedia as our external knowledge base of entities.

Entity We define an *entity* as a nonambiguous, terminal page (e.g., The Town (the film)) in Wikipedia (i.e., a Wikipedia page that is not a category, disambiguation, list, or redirect page). We define an *anchor phrase* (surface form) as the textual phrase (e.g., the town) which can potentially link to some entities. We define an *entity mention* as an anchor phrase *and* the context ("the town" in the example tweet in Section 1), where its semantic meaning umambiguously represents a specific entity. Note that an entity may be represented by multiple surface forms.

Wikipedia Lexicon Construction Following the assumptions used in most prior entity linking research, we assume that surface forms of entities can be found as anchor phrases in Wikipedia. In order to construct a Wikipedia lexicon, we first collect all anchors phases in Wikipedia. For each anchor phrase (surface form) s, we construct a lexicon entry by gathering the set of entities $\{e_1, e_2, \dots e_K\}$ that can be linked from s. We also collect the number of times anchor a links to the entity e_i, $d(s, e_i)$. We define $P(e_i|s) = d(s, e_i)/d(s)$, where $d(s)$ represents the number of times s appears in Wikipedia. We refer e' as *the most linked entity* for anchor s if $e' = \arg\max_e P(e_i|s)$.

Candidate Generation Given a tweet t, we extract all k-grams of size $\leq k$. For each k-gram, we find all entities where this k-gram is an anchor phrase. If a k-gram is an anchor phrase for at least one entity, then the k-gram is a *candidate* entity mention. In general, we identify many candidate phrase per tweet; let $U(t) = \{c_1, c_2, \dots\}$ denote the set of candidates in tweet t. We refer to $s(c)$ as the surface form (e.g., the anchor phrase) of c. Compared to the anchor phrase, the candidate also carries the context and position information. Let $E(c_i) = \{e_1, e_2, \dots, \textbf{NIL}\}$ denote the set of entities which candidate i may be linked to, plus the additional special token **NIL**. Note that the size of $E(c_i)$ is always at least 2.

Task Definition First, our system generates candidate entity mentions, textual phrases which can possibly be entity mentions. Our system then performs filtering and optimization to process the list of candidates. For each candidate, our system links the candidate to a special **NIL** token or links the candidate to its corresponding entity in Wikipedia. More formally, given a tweet t and its candidate set $U(t)$, the goal of the system is to predict $y_i \in E(c_i), \forall c_i \in U(t)$.

Comparison to the TAC KBP Competition It is important to state that our definition of the entity linking problem differs significantly from the entity linking problem as defined by the TAC KBP competition (Ji et al., 2010; Ji et al., 2011). In the TAC, there is no true mention detection problem; every candidate in the TAC is an entity mention that represents an entity. Another difference is that the TAC allows for an entity mention to map to an entity not in the external knowledge base (Wikipedia); our system does not provide special handling of this case.

Comparison to Named Entity Recognition There are also important differences between our task and the canonical NER task. For example, NER systems identify common names, such as "Robert," as entities. In our task, we only consider a prediction as a success if the system can determine which person in Wikipedia "Robert" is referring to. In other words, our definition of entities depends on the given knowledge base, rather than human judgment. Hence, it is difficult to make a fair system comparison of our system to NER systems.

4 Entity Linking as Structural Learning

In our framework, we use structural learning as a tool to capture the relationship between entities. We define y_i as the output for c_i, where $y_i \in E(c_i)$. Let $T = |U(t)|$ and $\mathbf{y} = \{y_1, y_2, \dots, y_T\}$. The feature function for the whole assignment can be written as $\Phi(t, U(t), \mathbf{y})$. The score for the assignment $\mathbf{y}$ can be obtained as the linear product between the weight vector $\mathbf{w}$ and the feature vector. For an input example, the prediction can be found by solving the inference problem:

$$\mathbf{y}' = \arg\max_{\mathbf{y}} \mathbf{w}^T \Phi(t, U(t), \mathbf{y}) \quad (1)$$

We use a Structural SVM (SSVM) (Taskar et al., 2004; Tsochantaridis et al., 2005; Chang et al., 2010) as our learning algorithm. To train the weight vector $\mathbf{w}$, we minimize the objective function of the SSVM

$$\min_{\mathbf{w}} \frac{\|\mathbf{w}\|^2}{2} + C \sum_{i=1}^{l} \xi_i^2 \quad (2)$$

where l is the number of labeled examples and

$$\begin{aligned} &\mathbf{w}^T \Phi(t_i, c(t_i), \mathbf{y}_i) \\ \geq &\Delta(\mathbf{y}_i, \mathbf{y}) + \mathbf{w}^T \Phi(t_i, c(t_i), \mathbf{y}) - \xi_i, \forall i, \mathbf{y} \end{aligned}$$

We denote $\mathbf{y}_i$ as the gold assignment for $\mathbf{x}_i$ and define $\Delta(\mathbf{y}_i, \mathbf{y})$ as the Hamming distance between two assignments $\mathbf{y}_i$ and $\mathbf{y}$.

4.1 Features

Feature definitions are very important as they define the shapes of the structures. Our feature vector is defined as

$$\Phi(t, U(t), \mathbf{y}) = \sum_i \phi(t, c_i, y_i) + \sum_{i<j} \phi(t, c_i, y_i, c_j, y_j)$$

where c_i and c_j is the i-th and j-th candidates in $U(t)$, respectively.

First, we assign $\Phi(t, c_i, \mathbf{NIL})$ to be a special bias feature. The corresponding weight value behaves as a threshold to cut-off mentions. Recall in our definition that $y_i = \mathbf{NIL}$ represents that the candidate c_i is not a mention.

The first order features for $\Phi(t, c_i, e)$ are described as follows. In general, we can classify our features into two types: mention-specific features and entity-specific features. For a given candidate c_i, mention-specific features only consider the surface form of c_i and the tweet t. Entity-specific features also consider the knowledge base content of the entity e. Prior work in the entity linking literature has primarily focused on entity-specific features, as most prior work solves entity disambiguation with given mentions.

Base and Capitalization Rate Our base features are from two resources. Let $s(c)$ denote the surface form of candidate c. The link probability $P_l(s(c))$ and $P(e|s(c))$ features are extracted from Wikipedia. We explained $P(e|s(c))$ in Section 3. Link probability $P_l(s(c))$ is the probability that a phrase is used as an anchor in Wikipedia. We also add a third feature that captures normalized link count. Besides these three features, we also have a feature to indicate if a is a stop word, and a feature indicating the number of tokens in a. The view count and $P(e|s)$ features are entity-specific, while the other three features are mention-specific.

For each phrase $s(c)$, we also collect statistics about the probability that a phrase is capitalized in Wikipedia. We refer to this feature as the capitalization rate feature, $P_c(s(c))$.

Popularity Feature We have access to 300GBs of Wikipedia page view counts, representing one months worth of page view information, we use this as popularity data.[3] As mentioned in Section 3, we find that the most often linked Wikipedia articles might not be the most popular ones on Twitter. Using page view statistics helps our system correct this bias. We define another probability based on page view statistics $P_v(e_i|c) = v(e_i)/(\sum_{e \in E(c)/\{\mathbf{NIL}\}} v(e))$, where $v(e)$ represents the view count for the page e.

Context Capitalization Our context capitalization features indicate if the current candidate, the word before, and the word after the candidate are capitalized.

Entity Type and Tf-idf We use the procedure proposed in (Ratinov et al., 2011) to extract keyword phrases from categories for each Wikipedia page, and then build a rule-based system using keyword phrases to classify if each entity page belongs to one of the following entity types: Person, Location, Organization, TV Show, Book/Magazine and Movie.[4] For a given candidate c and an entity e, the associated binary feature becomes active if the entity belongs to a specific entity type. There are six entity type features in our system.

[3] `http://dammit.lt/wikistats`

[4] The entity type prediction accuracy of our rule-based system on the development set is around 95%.

Features	Descriptions
Base	$P_l(s_i)$, $P(e\|s)$, normalized link counts, stop word, # tokens
Cap. Rate	$P_c(s_i)$
Popularity	$P_v(e\|s)$, normalized page view count, $P_v(e\|s)P(e\|s)$
Context Cap.	Three features indicating if the current candidate and the words before and after are capitalized
Entity Type	Six binary features for each entity type
Tf-idf	Two features for the similarity between the word vectors of the entity and the tweet
Second-Order	$Jac(e_i, e_j)$, $P(e_i\|s_i)P(e_j\|s_j)$, $P_c(s_i)P_c(s_j)$, $P_l(s_i)P_l(s_j)$

Table 1: Summary of the features used in our structural learning systems.

We also include tf-idf features in our system. For each Wikipedia page, we collect the top 100 tf-idf words. We add one feature that is the dot product between the tf-idf word vector of e and the words of tweet t. We include a second feature that represents the average tf-idf score of all words that appear in both e and t.

Second-order features We include four very simple second-order features $\phi(t, c_i, e_i, c_j, e_j)$ to capture more complex relations between entities and candidates. The first feature is the Jaccard distance between two Wikipedia pages e_i and e_j. Let $\Gamma(e_i)$ denote the set of Wikipedia pages that contain a hyperlink to e_i. We define the Jaccard distance between e_i and e_j as:

$$Jac(e_i, e_j) = \frac{|\Gamma(e_i) \cap \Gamma(e_j)|}{|\Gamma(e_i) \cup \Gamma(e_j)|}$$

This feature has a similar effect as the normalized Google distance (Cilibrasi and Vitanyi, 2007), which has been used for many entity linking systems. Let us use the following shorthand: $s_i = s(c_i)$ and $s_j = s(c_j)$. We have also included three features $P(e_i|s_i)P(e_j|s_j)$, $P_c(s_i)P_c(s_j)$ and $P_l(s_i)P_l(s_j)$ to increase the expressivity of our model.

4.2 Mining Additional Contextual Words

Unlike mention detection systems used in other NLP tasks, there are no lexical features in our system. Lexical features are important as they can capture semantic meaning precisely. However, given that we do not have many labeled examples, lexical features can lead to overfitting. The diverse language in tweets also make it more difficult to use lexical features.

Our solution for this problem is to use a very simple method to mine context words for different entities from a large, unlabeled tweet corpus. The algorithm works as follows:

1. Train an end-to-end entity linking system and then apply it to a large, unlabeled tweet corpus
2. Extract contextual words for each entity type based on the pseudo-labeled data.
3. Train the entity linking system again with new contextual features.

In this paper, we only use the word before and the word after as our contextual word for a candidate. Note that while there are ambiguous phrases on the surface (e.g., "friends" can be a TV show or just a regular phrase), certain phrases are unambiguous (e.g., "CSI : Miami"). As contextual words are often shared within the same entity type (e.g. "watching" is likely to appear before a tv show), those words can potentially improve our final system.

Let w_i denote the i-th word in the tweet and t_i denote the entity type for the i-th word.[5] We use a very simple rule to select a set of left context words $Q(R)$ for entity type R.

$$Q(R) = \{w_i \mid P(t_{i+1} = R|w_i) > r, d(w_i) > z\}$$

where $d(w_i)$ represent the number of times the word w_i appears in the unlabeled set. The first rule is to simply find a word which is more likely to be followed by an entity. The second rule filter outs noisy words (e.g., Twitter handles) in the unlabeled set. The right context words are also extracted in a similar way.

To train the second end-to-end entity linking system, we add one additional feature for the contextual words. For the feature vector $\Phi(t, c_i, e)$, the context feature is active if the candidate c_i is capitalized[6] and the context words around c_i belongs to $Q(R)$, given R is the entity type for the entity e.

[5]The tag t_i belongs to the entity type R if our system links a candidate c to an entity with type R and c covers the word w_i.

[6]The word "watching" can be a TV show while most of the time it is not. These common makes this contextual feature noisy. We found that the context feature can only be reliably applied when the candidate is capitalized.

4.3 Cohesiveness Score

There are several ways to consider entity-entity cohesiveness besides using the second-order features directly. In our model, we also consider a modified cohesiveness score proposed in (Ferragina and Scaiella, 2010). The idea behind the cohesiveness score is to estimate the correlations between different entities by using weighted Jaccard scores.[7]

There are two rounds in the procedure of computing the cohesiveness score. We first estimate approximately the most probable entity for each candidate given all the other candidates in the same tweet. In the second round, the cohesiveness score is then produced with respect to the most probable entity computed in the first round.

More formally, in the first round, we compute the relevance score for each candidate and entity pair:

$$Rel(e, c|t) = \frac{\sum_{c' \neq c} \sum_{e' \in E(c')} P(e'|c') Jac(e, e')}{|U(t)|}.$$

Then, the cohesiveness score is computed by

$$S_{coh}(e, c|t) = \frac{\sum_{c' \neq c} Jac(e, \bar{e}(c')) P(\bar{e}(c')|c')}{|U(t)|},$$

where the $\bar{e}(c') = \arg\max_{e \in E(c')} Rel(e, c'|t)$. We then put the cohesiveness score as a feature for each (e, c) pair. In practice, we found that the cohesiveness score in the model can significantly increase the disambiguation ability of the model without using the second-order information.

4.4 Inference

In order to train and test the SSVM model, one needs to solve both the inference problem Eq. (3) and the loss-augmented inference problem. Without second-order features, the inference and loss-augmented inference problems can be easily solved, given that each component can be solved independently by

$$y_i' = \arg\max_{y \in E(c_i)} \mathbf{w}^T \Phi(t, c_i, y) \quad (3)$$

While the inference problem can be solved independently, the training algorithm still considers the whole assignment together in the training procedure.

[7]In our experiments, we only apply the cohesiveness score technique on candidates which pass the filtering procedure. See section 5 for more details for our filtering process.

Data	#Tweets	#Cand	#Men.	P@1
Train	473	8212	218	85.3%
Test 1	500	8950	249	87.7%
Test 2	488	7781	332	89.6%

Table 2: Labeled example statistics. "#Cand" represents the total number of candidates we found in this dataset. "#Men." is the total number of mentions that disambiguate to an entity. The top-1 rate (P@1) represents the proportion of the mentions that disambiguate to the most linked entity in Wikipedia.

With the second-order features, the inference problem becomes NP-hard. While one can resort to using integer linear programming to find the optimal solution, we choose not to do so. We instead use the beam search algorithm. Our beam search algorithm first arranges the candidates from left to right, and then solve the inference problems approximately.

5 Experiments

We collected unlabeled Twitter data from two resources and then asked human annotators to label each tweet with a set of entities present. Our annotators ignored the following: duplicate entities per tweet, ambiguous entity mentions, and entities not present in Wikipedia. We next describe the two sets of Twitter data used as our training data and testing data. In addition to these two datasets, we also randomly sampled another 200 tweets as our development set.

Ritter We sampled 473 and 500 tweets[8] from the data used in (Ritter et al., 2011) to be our training data and test data, respectively. We did not use any labels generated by (Ritter et al., 2011); our annotators completely re-annotated each tweets with its set of entities. We refer to the first set as **Train** and the second set as **Test 1**.

Entertainment To check if our system has the ability to generalize across different domains, we sampled another 488 tweets related to entertainment entities. Our main focus was to extract tweets that contained TV shows, Movies, and

[8]We originally labeled 1000 tweets but then found 27 repeated tweets in the dataset. Therefore, we remove those 27 tweets in the training set.

Books/Magazines. Identifying tweets from a specific domain is a research topic on its own, so we followed (Dalvi et al., 2012), and used a keyword matching method.[9] After sampling this set of tweets, we asked our annotators to label the data in the same way as before (all entities are labeled, not just entertainment entities). We refer to this tweet set as **Test 2**.

After sampling, all tweets were then normalized in the following way. First, we removed all retweet symbols (RT) and special symbols, as these are tokens that may easily confuse NER systems. We treated punctuation as separate tokens. Hashtags (#) play a very important role in tweets as they often carry critical information. We used the following web service[10] to break the hashtags into tokens (e.g., the service will break "#TheCloneWars" into "the clone wars") (Wang et al., 2011).

The statistics of our labeled examples are presented in Table 2. First, note that the average number of mentions per tweet is well below 1. In fact, many tweets are personal conversations and do not carry any entities that can be linked to Wikipedia. Still, many candidates are generated (such as "really") for those tweets, given that those candidates can still potentially link to an entity ("really" could be a TV channel). Therefore, it is very important to include tweets without entities in the training set because we do not want our system to create unnecessary links to entities.

Another interesting thing to note is the percentage of entity mentions that disambiguate directly to their most often linked entities in Wikipedia. If we simply disambiguate each entity mention to its most linked entity in Wikipedia, we can already achieve 85% to 90% accuracy, if mention detection is perfectly accurate. However, mention detection is a difficult problem as only about 3% of candidates are valid entity mentions.

It is worthwhile to mention that, as per (Ferragina and Scaiella, 2010), for computational efficiency, we apply several preprocessing steps before running our entity linking system. First, for each anchor in Wikipedia, we gather all entities it can disambiguate to and remove from that anchor's entity set all entities that are linked less than 2% of the time. Second, we apply a modified filtering procedure similar to that proposed in (Ferragina and Scaiella, 2010) to filter the set of candidates per tweet.

Evaluation Our annotated datasets contain entities from many Wikipedia categories. For evaluation, we primarily focus on entities belonging to a set of six *core* categories (Person, Location, Organization, TV Show, Book/Magazine, Movie). We believe it is necessary to focus upon core entities, rather than considering all possible entities in Wikipedia. Most common words in the English language have their own Wikpedia page, but most words are not important enough to be considered entities. In general, there is a large degree of subjectivity when comparing different entity linking datasets; different researchers have their own interpretation of what constitutes an entity. For example, we examined the annotation used in (Meij et al., 2012) and found it to be extremely lenient, when compared to our own beliefs of what is an entity. Therefore, we believe evaluating performance on restricted entity types is the only fair way to compare different end-to-end entity linking systems.

We evaluate the performance of our system on a per-tweet basis, by comparing the set of annotated "gold" entities with the set of entities predicted by our system, and computing performance metrics (precision, recall, F_1). We choose to evaluate our system on a per-tweet basis, as opposed to a per-entity basis, because we wish to avoid the issue of matching segmentations. For example, it is quite common to observe multiple overlapping phrases in a tweet that should be linked to the same entity (e.g., "President Obama" and "Obama"). When evaluating our system, we compute performance metrics for both all entities and core entities.[11]

Parameters In our implementation, we fixed the regularization parameter $C = 10$. When beam-

[9]We use the following word list :"movie", "tv", "episode", "film", "actor", "actors", "actress", "director", "directors", "movies", "episodes", "book", "novel", "reading", "read", "watch", "watching", "show", "books", "novels", "movies", "author" and "authors".

[10]`http://web-ngram.research.microsoft.com/info/break.html`

[11]To decide if an entity is a core entity or not, we use the following procedure. For the gold entities, the annotators also annotate type of the entity. We decide the entity type of the predicted entities using the procedure described in Section 4.1.

Model	Test 1			Test 2		
	P	R	F_1	P	R	F_1
Cucerzan	64.8	42.2	51.1	64.9	39.7	49.5
TagMe	38.8	69.0	49.7	34.9	70.3	46.7
SSVM	78.8	59.9	**68.0**	75.0	57.7	**65.2**

Table 3: Comparisons between different end-to-end entity linking systems. We evaluate performance on core entities, as it is the only fair way to compare different systems.

Structural SVM	Test 1		Test 2	
	All	Core	All	Core
Base	35.9	42.9	47.7	52.5
+Cap. Rate	38.4	45.6	49.9	53.7
+Popularity	41.3	47.9	50.3	55.1
+Context Cap	43.7	52.0	50.7	54.8
+Entity Type	47.9	57.0	53.5	59.0
+Tfidf	53.2	63.1	56.8	61.9

Table 4: Feature Study: F_1 for entity linking performance. "All" means evaluation on all annotated entities. "Core" means evaluation only on our six entity types. Each row contains all additional features of the row above it.

search is used, the beam size is set to be 50, and we only consider the top 10 candidates for each candidate to speed the inference process. In the context word mining algorithm, $r = 0.5\%$ and $z = 1000$.

5.1 Results

In the following, we analyze the contributions of each component in our system and compare our final systems to other existing end-to-end entity linking systems.

System Comparison We compare our final system to other state-of-the-art systems in Table 3. CUCERZAN represents a modified implementation of the system in (Cucerzan, 2007). TagMe is an end-to-end linking system that focuses on short texts, including tweets. Our system significantly outperforms these two systems in both precision and recall. Note that CUCERZAN's system is a state-of-the-art system on well-written documents with provided entity mentions. The system (Cucerzan, 2007) has been extended by the authors and won the TAC KBP competition in 2010 (Ji et al., 2010).

There are two possible reasons to explain why our system outperforms CUCERZAN. First, their mention detection is a carefully designed system targeted toward documents, not tweets. Their system has segmentation issues when applied to Twitter, as it relies heavily upon capitalization when identifying candidate entity mentions. Second, their system heavily depends on the fact that related entities should appear together within documents. However, given that tweets are very short, some of their most important features are not suitable for the Twitter domain. Our system outperforms TagMe because we use a more sophisticated machine learning approach, as compared to their system. TagMe links too many spurious entity mentions for common words. This is a result of their algorithm's over-emphasis on entity-entity co-occurrence features.

Feature Study We study the contributions of each feature group in our system in Table 4. We summarize our discoveries as follows:

First, we find collecting statistics from a large corpus helps the system significantly. In addition to $P(e|s)$, we find that capitalization rate features offer around 3% to 4% F_1 improvement in Test 1. Similarly, popularity features are also important, as it corrects bias existing in Wikipedia link statistics. Compared to lexical features, using statistical features offers a great advantage of reducing the need for large amounts of labeled data.

We also find entity related features (Popularity, Entity Type, Tf-idf) are crucial. Given that between 85% to 90% of our mentions should directly disambiguate to the most often linked entities, one might think entity-specific features are not important in our task. Interestingly, entity-specific features are among the most important features. The discovery confirms our hypothesis: it is critical to consider mention detection and entity disambiguation as a single problem, rather than as separate problems in a two staged approach used by many other entity linking systems. Note that capitalization rate and context capitalization features are mention-specific. Additionally, we find that mixing mention-specific features and entity-specific features results in a better model.

Entity Type	Words appearing before the mention	Words appearing after the mention
Person	wr, dominating, rip, quarterback, singer, featuring, defender, rb, minister, actress, twitition, secretary	tarde, format, noite, suffers, dire, admits, senators, urges, performs, joins
TV Show	sbs, assistir, assistindo, otm, watching, nw, watchn, viagra, watchin, ver	skit, performances, premieres, finale, parody, marathon, season, episodes, spoilers, sketch

Table 5: An example of context words that are automatically extracted from 20 million unlabeled tweets. For the sake of brevity, we only display context words for two categories. Note that there are misspelled words (such as "watchn") and abbreviations (such as nw) that do not appear in well-written documents.

Advance Models	Test 1		Test 2	
	All	Core	All	Core
SSVM (Table 4)	53.2	63.1	56.8	61.9
+Context	53.9	64.6	58.6	63.4
+Cohesiveness	55.6	66.5	59.7	65.1
+2nd order	58.1	68.0	60.6	65.2

Table 6: Evaluation results (F_1) of the advanced models. "+ Context" is the model that uses additional context features extracted from 20 millions unlabeled tweets. "+ Cohesiveness" is the model with both additional context and cohesiveness features. "+2nd order" is our final model (which incorporates context, cohesiveness, and second-order features).

Mining Context Words We verify the effectiveness of adding contextual features that are extracted automatically from large unlabeled data. We apply our system (with all first-order features) on a set of 20 million unlabeled tweets we collected. Context words are then extracted using the simple rules described in Section 4. We list the top 10 words we extracted in Table 5. Due to space limitations, we only list the words for the Person and TV Show categories. The results are interesting as we are able to find common misspelled words and abbreviations used in Twitter. For example, we find that "watchn" means "watching" and "nw" means "now watching," and they are usually words found before TV shows. We also find tweeters frequently use abbreviations for people's jobs. For example, "wr" means "wide receiver" and "rb" means "running back." When mined context is added into our system, the performance improves significantly (Table 6). We note that extending context mining algorithms in a large-scale, principled approach is an important next research topic.

Capturing Entity-Entity Relationships In this paper, we use two methods to capture the relationship between entities: adding the cohesiveness score and using second order information. Until now, we only considered features that can be extracted from only one entity. Past research has shown that considering features that involve multiple entities can improve entity linking performance, given that related entities are more likely to appear together in a document. When these type of features are added, we need to perform beamsearch, as the exact inference procedure can be prohibitively expensive.

As displayed in Table 6, we find that either adding the cohesiveness score or using second order information can improve prediction. Using both methods improves the model even more. Comparing computation overhead, computing cohesiveness is significantly more cost-effective than using second-order information.

6 Conclusion

In this paper, we propose a structural SVM method to address the problem of end-to-end entity linking on Twitter. By considering mention detection and entity disambiguation together, we build a end-to-end entity linking system that outperforms current state-of-the-art systems.

There are plenty of research problems left to be addressed. Developing a better algorithm for mining contextual words is an important research topic. It would also be interesting to design a method that jointly learns NER models and entity linking models.

References

S. Asur and B.A. Huberman. 2010. Predicting the future with social media. *arXiv preprint arXiv:1003.5699*.

M. Chang, V. Srikumar, D. Goldwasser, and D. Roth. 2010. Structured output learning with indirect supervision. In *Proceedings of the International Conference on Machine Learning (ICML)*.

R.L. Cilibrasi and P.M.B. Vitanyi. 2007. The google similarity distance. *Knowledge and Data Engineering, IEEE Transactions on*, 19(3):370–383.

S. Cucerzan. 2007. Large-scale named entity disambiguation based on Wikipedia data. In *Proceedings of the 2007 Joint Conference of EMNLP-CoNLL*, pages 708–716.

N. Dalvi, R. Kumar, and B. Pang. 2012. Object matching in tweets with spatial models. In *Proceedings of the fifth ACM international conference on Web search and data mining*, WSDM '12, pages 43–52, New York, NY, USA. ACM.

A. Davis, A. Veloso, A. S. da Silva, W. Meira, Jr., and A. H. F. Laender. 2012. Named entity disambiguation in streaming data. In *Proceedings of the Annual Meeting of the Association for Computational Linguistics (ACL)*, pages 815–824, Stroudsburg, PA, USA. Association for Computational Linguistics.

G. Demartini, D. E. Difallah, and P. Cudré-Mauroux. 2012. Zencrowd: leveraging probabilistic reasoning and crowdsourcing techniques for large-scale entity linking. In *The International World Wide Web Conference*, pages 469–478, New York, NY, USA. ACM.

P. Ferragina and U. Scaiella. 2010. Tagme: on-the-fly annotation of short text fragments (by wikipedia entities). In *Proceedings of the 19th ACM international conference on Information and knowledge management*, CIKM '10, pages 1625–1628, New York, NY, USA. ACM.

X. Han and L. Sun. 2011. A generative entity-mention model for linking entities with knowledge base. In *Proceedings of the 49th Annual Meeting of the Association for Computational Linguistics: Human Language Technologies - Volume 1*, HLT '11, pages 945–954, Stroudsburg, PA, USA. Association for Computational Linguistics.

X. Han, L. Sun, and J. Zhao. 2011. Collective entity linking in web text: a graph-based method. In *Proceedings of the 34th international ACM SIGIR conference on Research and development in Information Retrieval*, SIGIR '11, pages 765–774, New York, NY, USA. ACM.

H. Ji, R. Grishman, H.T. Dang, K. Griffitt, and J. Ellis. 2010. Overview of the tac 2010 knowledge base population track. In *Proceedings of the TAC 2010 Workshop*.

H. Ji, R. Grishman, and Dang. 2011. Overview of the tac 2011 knowledge base population track. In *Proceedings of the TAC 2011 Workshop*.

S. Kulkarni, A. Singh, G. Ramakrishnan, and S. Chakrabarti. 2009. Collective annotation of wikipedia entities in web text. In *Proceedings of the 15th ACM SIGKDD international conference on Knowledge discovery and data mining*, Proceedings of International Conference on Knowledge Discovery and Data Mining (KDD), pages 457–466, New York, NY, USA. ACM.

C. Li, J. Weng, Q. He, Y. Yao, A. Datta, A. Sun, and B.-S. Lee. 2012. Twiner: named entity recognition in targeted twitter stream. In *Proceedings of the 35th international ACM SIGIR conference on Research and development in information retrieval*, Proceedings of International Conference on Research and Development in Information Retrieval, SIGIR, pages 721–730, New York, NY, USA. ACM.

E. Meij, W. Weerkamp, and M. de Rijke. 2012. Adding semantics to microblog posts. In *Proceedings of the fifth ACM international conference on Web search and data mining*, pages 563–572, New York, NY, USA. ACM.

R. Mihalcea and A. Csomai. 2007. Wikify!: linking documents to encyclopedic knowledge. In *Proceedings of ACM Conference on Information and Knowledge Management (CIKM)*, pages 233–242. ACM.

D. Milne and I. H. Witten. 2008. Learning to link with wikipedia. In *Proceedings of ACM Conference on Information and Knowledge Management (CIKM)*, pages 509–518, New York, NY, USA. ACM.

M.J. Paul and M. Dredze. 2011. You are what you tweet: Analyzing twitter for public health. In *Fifth International AAAI Conference on Weblogs and Social Media (ICWSM 2011)*.

L. Ratinov, D. Roth, D. Downey, and M. Anderson. 2011. Local and global algorithms for disambiguation to wikipedia. In *Proceedings of the Annual Meeting of the Association for Computational Linguistics (ACL)*, pages 1375–1384, Stroudsburg, PA, USA. Association for Computational Linguistics.

A. Ritter, S. Clark, Mausam, and O. Etzioni. 2011. Named entity recognition in tweets: an experimental study. In *Proceedings of the Conference on Empirical Methods for Natural Language Processing (EMNLP)*, pages 1524–1534, Stroudsburg, PA, USA. Association for Computational Linguistics.

A. Sadilek, H. Kautz, and V. Silenzio. 2012. Modeling spread of disease from social interactions. In *Sixth AAAI International Conference on Weblogs and Social Media (ICWSM)*.

A. Sil, E. Cronin, P. Nie, Y. Yang, A.-M. Popescu, and A. Yates. 2012. Linking named entities to any database. In *Proceedings of the Conference on Empirical Methods for Natural Language Processing (EMNLP)*, pages 116–127, Stroudsburg, PA, USA. Association for Computational Linguistics.

K. Starbird and L. Palen. 2012. (how) will the revolution be retweeted?: information diffusion and the 2011 egyptian uprising. In *Proceedings of the acm 2012 conference on computer supported cooperative work*, pages 7–16. ACM.

B. Taskar, C. Guestrin, and D. Koller. 2004. Max-margin markov networks. In *The Conference on Advances in Neural Information Processing Systems (NIPS)*.

I. Tsochantaridis, T. Joachims, T. Hofmann, and Y. Altun. 2005. Large margin methods for structured and interdependent output variables. *Journal of Machine Learning Research*, 6:1453–1484, September.

A. Tumasjan, T.O. Sprenger, P.G. Sandner, and I.M. Welpe. 2010. Predicting elections with twitter: What 140 characters reveal about political sentiment. In *Proceedings of the fourth international aaai conference on weblogs and social media*, pages 178–185.

K. Wang, C. Thrasher, and B.J.P. Hsu. 2011. Web scale nlp: a case study on url word breaking. In *The International World Wide Web Conference*, pages 357–366. ACM.

C. Wang, K. Chakrabarti, T. Cheng, and S. Chaudhuri. 2012. Targeted disambiguation of ad-hoc, homogeneous sets of named entities. In *The International World Wide Web Conference*, pages 719–728, New York, NY, USA. ACM.

A Latent Variable Model for Viewpoint Discovery from Threaded Forum Posts

Minghui Qiu
School of Information Systems
Singapore Management University
Singapore
minghui.qiu.2010@smu.edu.sg

Jing Jiang
School of Information Systems
Singapore Management University
Singapore
jingjiang@smu.edu.sg

Abstract

Threaded discussion forums provide an important social media platform. Its rich user generated content has served as an important source of public feedback. To automatically discover the viewpoints or stances on hot issues from forum threads is an important and useful task. In this paper, we propose a novel latent variable model for viewpoint discovery from threaded forum posts. Our model is a principled generative latent variable model which captures three important factors: viewpoint specific topic preference, user identity and user interactions. Evaluation results show that our model clearly outperforms a number of baseline models in terms of both clustering posts based on viewpoints and clustering users with different viewpoints.

1 Introduction

Threaded discussion forums provide an important social media platform that allows netizens to express their opinions, to ask for advice, and to form online communities. In particular, responses to major sociopolitical events and issues can often be found in discussion forums, which serve as an important source of public feedback. In such discussion threads, we often observe heated debates over a controversial issue, with different sides defending their viewpoints with different arguments. For example, after the presidential debate between Barack Obama and Mitt Romney, there were heated discussions in online forums like CreateDebate[1] where some people expressed their support for Obama while some others have their opposition to him. For a user who is not closely following an event or issue, instead of going through all the existing posts in a long thread, she may want to quickly get an overview of the major viewpoints and arguments given by the different sides. For policy makers who want to obtain public feedback on social issues from social media, it is also desirable to automatically summarize the viewpoints on an issue from relevant threads. In this paper, we study the problem of modeling and discovering different viewpoints in forum threads.

Recently there has been some work on finding contrastive viewpoints from text. The model proposed by Paul et al. (2010) assumes viewpoints and topics are orthogonal dimensions. Another model proposed by Fang et al. (2012) assumes that documents are already grouped by viewpoints and it focus on identifying contrastive viewpoint words under the same topic. However, these existing studies are not based on interdependent documents like threaded forum posts. As a result, at least two important characteristics of threaded forum data are not considered in these models. (1) **User identity**: The user or publisher of each forum post is known, and a user may publish several posts in the same thread. Since the same user's opinion on an issue usually remains unchanged, posts published by the same user are likely to contain the same viewpoint. (2) **User interactions**. A thread is like a conversation, where users not only directly comment on the issue under discussion but also comment on each other's posts. Users having different viewpoints may express their disagreement or even attack each other while users having the same viewpoint often support each other.

[1] http://www.createdebate.com/

The interaction expressions in forum posts may help us infer the relation between two users and subsequently infer the viewpoints of the corresponding posts.

In this paper, we propose a novel latent variable model for viewpoint discovery from threaded forum posts. Our model is based on the following observations: First, posts with different viewpoints tend to focus on different topics. To illustrate this point, we first apply the Latent Dirichlet Allocation (LDA) model (Blei et al., 2003) on a thread about "will you vote Obama" and obtain a set of topics. This thread comes from a data set that has each user's viewpoint annotated. Using the ground truth viewpoint labels, we group all posts published by users with viewpoint 1 (or viewpoint 2) and compute the topic proportions. The two topic distributions are shown in Figure 1. We can see that indeed the two viewpoints each have some dominating topics. Our second observations is that the same user tends to hold the same viewpoint. In our model, we use a user-level viewpoint distribution to capture this observation, and the experiments show that it works better than assuming a global viewpoint distribution. Third, users with the same viewpoint are likely to have positive interactions while users with different viewpoints tend to have negative interactions. Using a sentiment lexicon, we can first predict the polarity of interaction expressions. We then propose a novel way to incorporate this information into the latent variable model. In summary, we capture the three observations above in a principled generative latent variable model. We present the details of our model in Section 3.

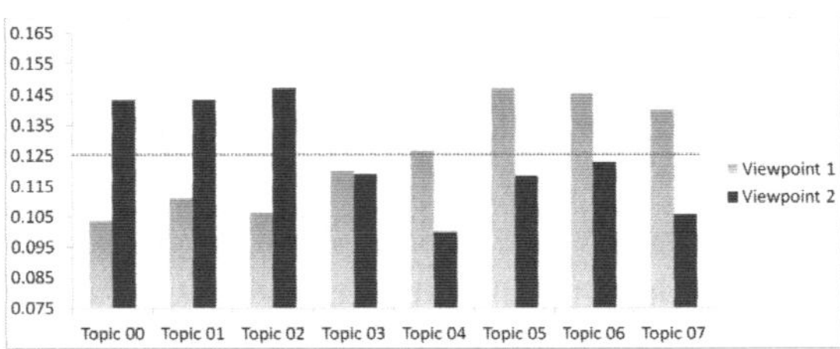

Figure 1: Topic distributions of two viewpoints for the thread "will you vote Obama?" The dotted line is the average topic probability.

We use two tasks to evaluate our model. In the first task, we evaluate how well posts with different viewpoints are separated. In the second task, we evaluate how well our model is able to group users with different viewpoints. For both tasks, we compare our model with an existing model as well as a few degenerate versions of our model. The results show that our model can clearly outperform the baselines in terms of three evaluation metrics. The experiments are presented in Section 5.

The contributions of our work are threefold: (1) We identify the importance of using user interactions to help infer viewpoints in forum posts. (2) We propose a principled latent variable model to jointly model topics, viewpoints and user interactions. (3) We empirically verify the validity of the three assumptions in our model using real data sets.

2 Related Work

There are a few different lines of work that are related to our work. For discovering different viewpoints from general text, Paul et al. (2010) used the model proposed by Paul and Girju (2010) to jointly model topics and viewpoints. They assume these two concepts are orthogonal and they do not consider user identity. In comparison, our model has the notion of topics and viewpoints, but we explicitly model the dependency of topics on viewpoints, i.e. we assume each viewpoint has a topic distribution. We also consider author identities as an important factor of our model. Fang et al. (2012) proposed a model that also combines topics and viewpoints. But they assume that documents are already grouped by viewpoints, which is not the case for forum posts. Therefore, their model cannot be directly applied to forum posts.

There has also been some work on finding viewpoints from social media. Somasundaran and Wiebe (2010) studied how to identify stances in online debates. They used a supervised approach for classifying stances in ideological debates. In comparison, our model is an unsupervised method. The same authors proposed an unsupervised method which relies on associations of aspects with topics indicative of stances mined from the Web for the task (Somasundaran and Wiebe, 2009). In contrast, our model is also an unsupervised one but we do not rely on any external knowledge.

Part of our work is related to detecting agreement/disagreement from text. For this task, normally supervised methods are used (Galley et al., 2004; Abbott et al., 2011), which require sufficient labeled training data. In our work, since we deal with different languages, we use a lexicon-based approach that does not need training data. Recently, Mukherjee and Liu (2012) proposed an unsupervised model to extract different types of expressions including agreement/disagreement expressions. However, our focus is not to detect agreement/disagreement expressions but to model the interplay between agreement/disagreement expressions and viewpoints. The work by Mukherjee and Liu (2012) can potentially be combined with our model.

Another line of related work is subgroup detection, which aims to separate users holding different viewpoints. This problem has recently been studied by Abu-Jbara and Radev (2012), Dasigi et al. (2012), Abu-Jbara et al. (2012) and Hassan et al. (2012), where a clustering based approach is used. Lu et al. (2012) studied both textual content and social interactions to find opposing network from online forums. In our experiments we show that our model can also be used for subgroup detection, but meanwhile we also directly identify viewpoints, which is not the goal of existing work on subgroup finding or opposing network extraction.

3 Model

3.1 Motivation

Before we formally present our latent variable model for viewpoint discovery, let us first look at the assumptions we would like to capture in the model.

Viewpoint-based topic distribution: The first assumption we have is that different viewpoints tend to touch upon different topics. This is because to support a viewpoint, users need to provide evidence and arguments, and for different viewpoints the arguments are likely different. To capture this assumption, in our model, we let each viewpoint have its own distribution of topics. Given the viewpoint of a post, the hidden topic of each word in the post is chosen according to the corresponding topic distribution associated with that viewpoint.

User identify: The second assumption we have is that the same user tends to talk from the same viewpoint, although there are also users who do not clearly have a viewpoint. In our model, we assume that there is a user-level viewpoint distribution. For each post by a user, its viewpoint is drawn from the corresponding viewpoint distribution.

User interaction: An important difference between threaded forum posts and regular document collections such as news articles is that posts in the same thread form a tree structure via the "reply-to" relations. Many reply posts start with an expression that comments on a previous post or directly addresses another user. These interaction expressions may carry positive or negative sentiment, indicating an agreement or a disagreement. For example, Table 1 shows the interaction expressions from a few sample posts with words such as "correct," "agree," and "delusional," implying the polarity of the interaction expressions. The polarity of these interaction expressions can help us infer whether two posts or two users hold the same viewpoint or not. In our model, we assume that the polarity of each interaction expression can be detected. Details of how we perform this detection are in Section 3.4.

	Post
$+$	You are **correct**. Obama got into office w/ everything $\cdots$ I **agree** with your post Dan. Obama is so $\cdots$
$-$	Most of your post is **delusional**, especially the part $\cdots$ Are you **freaking** nutz? Palin is a BIMBO!

Table 1: Sample posts with positive $(+)$ and negative$(-)$ interactions.

While the way to capture the first two assumptions discussed above is fairly standard, modeling user interactions is something new. In our model, we assume that the polarity of an interaction expression is generated based on the viewpoint of the current post and the viewpoint of post(s) that the current post replies to. The intuition is that if the viewpoints are the same, we are more likely to see a positive interaction whereas if the viewpoints are different we are more likely to see a negative interaction.

3.2 Model description

We use the following notation to represent our data. We consider a set of forum posts published by U different users on the same event or issue, where user u $(1 \leq u \leq U)$ has published N_u posts. Let $w_{u,n,l}$ $(1 \leq l \leq L_{u,n}$) denote the l-th word in the n-th post by user u, where $L_{u,n}$ is the number of words in the n-th post by user u. $w_{u,n,l}$ is represented by an index between 1 and V where V is the vocabulary size. Furthermore, we assume that some of the posts have user interaction expressions, where the polarity of the expression is known. Without loss of generality, let $s_{u,n} \in \{0, 1\}$ denote the polarity of the interaction expression of the n-th post by user u. In addition, for each post that has an interaction expression, we assume we also know the previous post(s) it replies to. (In the case when the current post replies to a user, we assume all that user's existing posts are being replied to.) We refer to these posts as the *parent posts* of the current post.

We assume that there are T topics where each topic is essentially a word distribution, denoted as ψ^t. We also assume that there are Y different viewpoints expressed in the collection of posts. For most controversial issues, Y can be set to 2. Each viewpoint y has a topic distribution θ^y over the T topics. While these T topics are meant to capture the topical differences between viewpoints, since these viewpoints are all about the same issue, there are also some words commonly used by different viewpoints. We therefore introduce a background topic ψ^B to capture these words. Finally, each user u has a distribution over the Y viewpoints, denoted as φ^u.

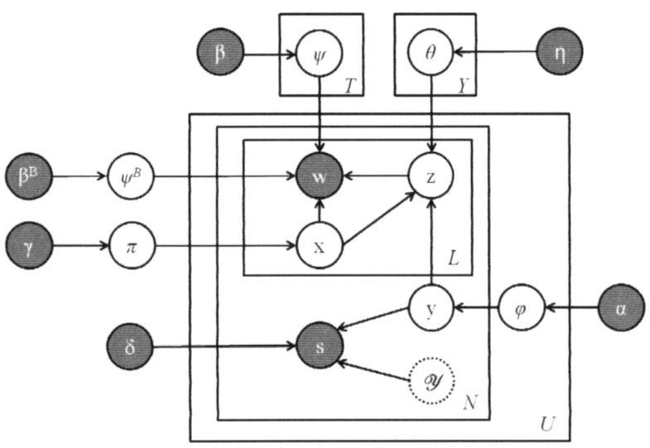

Figure 2: Plate notation of the Joint Viewpoint-Topic Model with User Interaction (JVTM-UI). The dotted circle for $\mathcal{Y}$ means the variables represented by $\mathcal{Y}$ are not new variables but a subset of the y variables.

Figure 2 shows the plate notation of the complete model. We assume the following generation process in our model. When user u generates her n-th post, she first samples a viewpoint from φ^u. Let this viewpoint be represented by a hidden variable $y_{u,n}$. For the l-th word in this post, she first samples an indicator variable $x_{u,n,l}$ from a Bernoulli distribution parameterized by π. If $x_{u,n,l} = 0$, then she draws $w_{u,n,l}$ from ψ^B. Otherwise, she first samples a topic, denoted as $z_{u,n,l}$, according to $\theta^{y_{u,n}}$, and then draws $w_{u,n,l}$ from $\psi^{z_{u,n,l}}$.

Furthermore, if this post is a reply to a previous post or another user, she may first comment on the parent post(s). The polarity of the interaction expression in the post is dependent on the viewpoint $y_{u,n}$ and the viewpoints of the previous post(s). Let us use $\mathcal{Y}_{u,n}$ to denote the set of y variables associated with the parent posts of the current post. The user draws $s_{u,n}$ according to following distribution:

$$p(s_{u,n} = 1|y_{u,n}, \mathcal{Y}_{u,n}, \delta) = \frac{\sum_{y' \in \mathcal{Y}_{u,n}} \mathbb{I}(y_{u,n} == y') + \delta}{|\mathcal{Y}_{u,n}| + 2\delta},$$
$$p(s_{u,n} = 0|y_{u,n}, \mathcal{Y}_{u,n}, \delta) = 1 - p(s_{u,n} = 1|y_{u,n}, \mathcal{Y}_{u,n}, \delta), \quad (1)$$

where $\mathbb{I}(\cdot)$ is 1 if the statement inside is true and 0 otherwise, and $\delta > 0$ is a smoothing parameter.

Finally, we assume that ψ^B, ψ^t, φ^u, θ^y and π all have some uniform Dirichlet priors.

3.3 Inference

We use collapsed Gibbs sampling to estimate the model parameters. In the initialization stage of Gibbs sampling, for a reply post to a recipient, we initialize its corresponding reply polarity s according to all the labeled polarity of interaction words. Specifically, if the majority of labeled interaction words are positive, we set $s = 1$, otherwise we set $s = 0$.

Let $\mathbf{Y}$ denote the set of all y variables, and $\mathbf{Y}_{\neg(u,n)}$ denote $\mathbf{Y}$ excluding $y_{u,n}$. Similar notation is used for the other variables. We sample $y_{u,n}$ using the following formula.

$$\begin{aligned}
&p(y_{u,n} = k|\mathbf{Y}_{\neg(u,n)}, \mathbf{Z}, \mathbf{S}, \mathbf{X}, \alpha, \eta, \delta) \\
\propto\ & \frac{p(y_{u,n} = k, \mathbf{Y}_{\neg(u,n)}|\alpha)}{p(\mathbf{Y}_{\neg(u,n)}|\alpha)} \cdot \frac{p(\mathbf{Z}|y_{u,n} = k, \mathbf{Y}_{\neg(u,n)}, \mathbf{X}, \eta)}{p(\mathbf{Z}_{\neg(u,n)}|\mathbf{Y}_{\neg(u,n)}, \mathbf{X}_{\neg(u,n)}, \eta)} \\
&\cdot p(\mathbf{S}|y_{u,n} = k, \mathbf{Y}_{\neg(u,n)}, \delta) \\
=\ & \frac{C^k_{u,\neg n} + \alpha}{C^{(\cdot)}_{u,\neg n} + Y\alpha} \cdot \frac{\prod_{t=1}^{T} \prod_{a=0}^{C^t_{u,n}-1} (C^t_{k,\neg(u,n)} + \eta + a)}{\prod_{b=0}^{C^{(\cdot)}_{u,n}-1} (C^{(\cdot)}_{k,\neg(u,n)} + T\eta + b)} \\
&\cdot p(\mathbf{S}|y_{u,n} = k, \mathbf{Y}_{\neg(u,n)}, \delta). \qquad (2)
\end{aligned}$$

Here all Cs are counters. $C^k_{u,\neg n}$ is the number of times we observe the viewpoint k from u's posts, excluding the n-th post, based on $\mathbf{Y}_{\neg(u,n)}$. $C^t_{u,n}$ is the number of times we observe topic t from user u's n-th post, based on $\mathbf{Z}_{u,n}$. And $C^t_{k,\neg(u,n)}$ is the number of times we observe topic t associated with viewpoint k, excluding user u's n-th post. Note that we need $\mathbf{X}$ to know which words are assigned to the background topic so we can exclude them for $C^t_{u,n}$ and $C^t_{k,\neg(u,n)}$. $C^{(\cdot)}_{u,\neg n}$ is the number of times we observe any viewpoint from u's posts, excluding the n-th post. $C^{(\cdot)}_{u,n}$ and $C^{(\cdot)}_{k,\neg(u,n)}$ are defined similarly.

The last term is further expanded as follows:

$$p(\mathbf{S}|y_{u,n} = k, \mathbf{Y}_{\neg(u,n)}, \delta) = p(s_{u,n}|y_{u,n} = k, \mathcal{Y}_{u,n}, \delta) \cdot p(\mathbf{S}_{\neg(u,n)}|y_{u,n} = k, \mathbf{Y}_{\neg(u,n)}, \delta). \quad (3)$$

Here $p(s_{u,n}|y_{u,n} = k, \mathcal{Y}_{u,n}, \delta)$ is computed according to Eqn. (1). For the latter term, we need to consider posts which reply to user u's n-th post because the value of $y_{u,n}$ affects these posts.

$$p(\mathbf{S}_{\neg(u,n)}|y_{u,n} = k, \mathbf{Y}_{\neg(u,n)}, \delta) \propto \prod_{(u',n'): y_{u,n} \in \mathcal{Y}_{u',n'}} p(s_{u',n'}|y_{u',n'}, \mathcal{Y}_{u',n'}, \delta). \quad (4)$$

Next, we show how we jointly sample $x_{u,n,l}$ and $z_{u,n,l}$. We jointly sample them because when $x_{u,n,l} = 0$, $z_{u,n,l}$ does not need a value. We have the following formulas:

$$p(x_{u,n,l} = 1, z_{u,n,l} = t|\mathbf{X}_{\neg(u,n,l)}, \mathbf{Z}_{\neg(u,n,l)}, \mathbf{Y}, \mathbf{W}, \gamma, \eta, \beta, \beta^B) \propto \frac{C^1_{\neg(u,n,l)} + \gamma}{C^{(\cdot)}_{\neg(u,n,l)} + 2\gamma} \cdot \frac{C^t_{y_{u,n,l},\neg(u,n,l)} + \eta}{C^{(\cdot)}_{y_{u,n,l},\neg(u,n,l)} + T\eta} \cdot \frac{C^{w_{u,n,l}}_{t,\neg(u,n,l)} + \beta}{C^{(\cdot)}_{t,\neg(u,n,l)} + V\beta}, \quad (5)$$

$$p(x_{u,n,l} = 0|\mathbf{X}_{\neg(u,n,l)}, \mathbf{Z}_{\neg(u,n,l)}, \mathbf{Y}, \mathbf{W}, \gamma, \eta, \beta, \beta^B) \propto \frac{C^0_{\neg(u,n,l)} + \gamma}{C^{(\cdot)}_{\neg(u,n,l)} + 2\gamma} \cdot \frac{C^{w_{u,n,l}}_{B,\neg(u,n,l)} + \beta^B}{C^{(\cdot)}_{B,\neg(u,n,l)} + V\beta^B}. \quad (6)$$

Here again the Cs are counters defined in similar ways as before. For example, $C^1_{\neg(u,n,l)}$ is the number of times we observe 1 assigned to an x variable, excluding $x_{u,n,l}$.

3.4 Interaction polarity prediction

The problem of detecting agreement and disagreement from forum posts is relatively new. One possible solution is to use supervised learning, which requires training data (Galley et al., 2004; Abbott et al., 2011; Andreas et al., 2012). However, training data are also likely domain and language dependent, which makes them hard for re-use. For our task, we take a simpler approach and use a sentiment lexicon together with some heuristics to predict the polarity of interaction expressions. Specifically, we first identify interaction sentences following the strategies from Hassan et al. (2012). We assume sentences containing mentions of the recipient of a post are interaction sentences. Next, we consider words within a text window of 8 words surrounding these mentions. We then use a subjectivity lexicon to label these words. To form an English lexicon, we combine three popular lexicons: the sentiment lexicon used by Hu and Liu (2004), Multi-Perspective Question Answering Subjectivity Lexicon by Wilson et al. (2005) and SentiWordNet by Baccianella et al. (2010). Since we also work with a Chinese data set, to form the Chinese sentiment lexicon, we use opinion words from HowNet[2] and NTUSD by Ku et al. (2007). To predict the polarity of an interaction expression, we simply check whether there are more positive sentiment words or more negative sentiment words in the expression, and label the interaction expression accordingly.

We would like to stress that since this interaction classification step is independent of the latent variable model, we can always apply a more accurate method, but this is not the focus of this work.

4 Models for Comparison

In our experiments, we compare our model, Joint Viewpoint-Topic Model with User Interaction (JVTM-UI), with the following baseline models.

JVTM: The model is shown in Figure 3(a), a variant of JVTM-UI that does not consider user interaction. Through comparison with it, we can check the effect of modeling user interactions.

JVTM-G: We consider JVTM-G in Figure 3(b), a variant of JVTM which assumes a global viewpoint distribution. Comparison with it allows us to check the usefulness of user identity in the task.

UIM: The third model we consider is a User Interaction Model (UIM) in Figure 3(c), where we rely on only the users' interactions to infer the viewpoints. We use it to check how well viewpoints can be discovered from only user interaction expressions.

[2] http://www.keenage.com/html/e_index.html

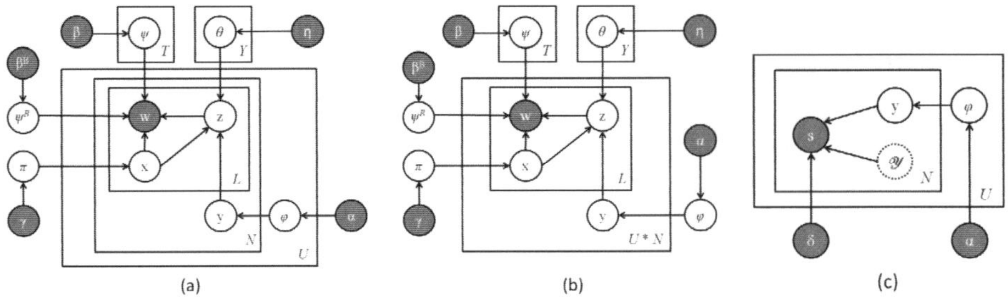

Figure 3: (a) JVTM: Joint Viewpoint-Topic Model. (b) JVTM-G: JVTM with a global viewpoint distribution. (c) UIM: User-Interaction Model.

TAM: The last model we consider is the one by Paul et al. (2010). As TAM is applied at document collections, we first concatenate all the posts by the same user into a pseudo document and then apply TAM.

5 Experiments and Analysis

In this section, we evaluate our model with a set of baseline models using two data sets.

Name	Issue	#Posts	#Users
EDS1	Vote for Obama	2599	197
EDS2	Arizona Immigration Law	738	59
EDS3	Tax Cuts	276	26
CDS1	Tencent and Qihoo dispute	30137	2507
CDS2	Fang Zhouzi questions Han Han	76934	1769
CDS3	Liu Xiang in London Olympics	29486	2774

Table 2: Some statistics of the data set.

5.1 Data Sets and Experimental Settings

We focus our work on finding users' viewpoints on a controversial issue, where we assume that there are two contradictory viewpoints. We use two data sets on controversial issues. The first data set comes from Abu-Jbara et al. (2012) and Hassan et al. (2012). This data set originally was used for finding subgroups of users, so the annotations were done at user level, i.e. for each user there is a label indicating which subgroup he/she belongs to. We use the top-3 mostly discussed threads with two subgroups for our study.

In reality, controversial issues are often discussed across threads. We thus constructed another large data set which contains more than one thread for each issue. We chose three hot issues from one of the most popular Chinese online forums — TianYa Club[3]. The three issues are "Fang Zhouzi questions Han Han"[4], "Tencent and Qihoo dispute"[5], and "Liu Xiang in London Olympics"[6]. All these issues triggered heated discussions on the forum and we found that most of the users were divided into two different groups.

We crawled the data set using the TianYa API[7]. The API allows users to issue queries and get threads most related to the queries. For each issue, we used entities involved in the event as queries and obtained 750 threads for each query. We then extracted all the posts in the threads. As there are users who posted irrelevant posts in the forum, we then filtered out those users who did not mention the entities or had fewer than 4 posts.

We refer to the first set of data in English as EDS1, EDS2 and EDS3, and the second set of data in Chinese as CDS1, CDS2 and CDS3. Some statistics of the resulting data set are shown in Table 2.

For all the models, we set $Y = 2$. We set $T = 10$ for the English data sets and $T = 40$ for the Chinese data sets. We run 400 iterations of Gibbs sampling as burn-in iterations and then take 100 samples with a gap of 5 to obtain our final results. We empirically set $\beta = 0.01$, $\beta^B = 0.1$, $\gamma = 10$ and $\delta = 0.1$ for our model on all the data sets. α and η are set through grid search where they take values in $\{0.01, 0.001\}$. For each data set, we choose the best setting for each model and report the corresponding results.

[3] http://en.wikipedia.org/wiki/Tianya_Club
[4] http://en.wikipedia.org/wiki/Fang_Zhouzi
[5] http://en.wikipedia.org/wiki/360_v._Tencent
[6] http://en.wikipedia.org/wiki/Liu_Xiang
[7] http://open.tianya.cn/index.php

5.2 Identification of viewpoints

We first evaluate the models on the task of identifying viewpoints. For fair comparison, each model will output a viewpoint label for each post. For JVTM-UI, JVTM, JVTM-G and UIM, after we learn the model, each post will directly have a viewpoint assignment. For TAM we cannot directly get each post's viewpoint as the model assumes a document-level viewpoint distribution. To estimate each post's viewpoint in this model, we use viewpoint assignment at the word level learnt from the model. Then for each post, we label its viewpoint as the viewpoint that has the majority count in the post.

Ideally, we would like to manually label all the posts to obtain the ground truth for evaluation. Since there are too many posts, we only labeled a sample of them. For each issue, we randomly selected 150 posts to label their viewpoints. For each post, we asked two different annotators to label its viewpoint. We made sure that the annotators understand the issue and the two major viewpoints before they annotated the posts. Specifically, as the Chinese data sets are about some controversial issues around the entities involved, we then defined two major viewpoints as *support* and *not support* the entity who initiated the event. The entities of data set CDS1, CDS2 and CDS3 are *Fang Zhouzi*, *Tencent* and *Liu Xiang* respectively. For each given post, the annotators were asked to judge whether the post has expressed viewpoints and if so, what is its corresponding viewpoint. We measure the agreement score using Cohen's kappa coefficient. The lowest agreement score for an issue is 0.61 in the data set, showing good agreement. We then used the set of posts that were labeled with the same viewpoint by the two annotators as our evaluation data for all the models.

Since our task is essentially a clustering problem, we use *purity* and *entropy* to measure the performance (Manning et al., 2008). Furthermore, we also use *accuracy* where we choose the better alignment of clusters with ground truth class labels and compute the percentage of posts that are "classified" correctly. For purity and accuracy, the higher the measure is the better the performance. For entropy, the lower the measure is the better the performance.

We give an overview of the all the averaged model results on the data sets in Figure 4. We observed that

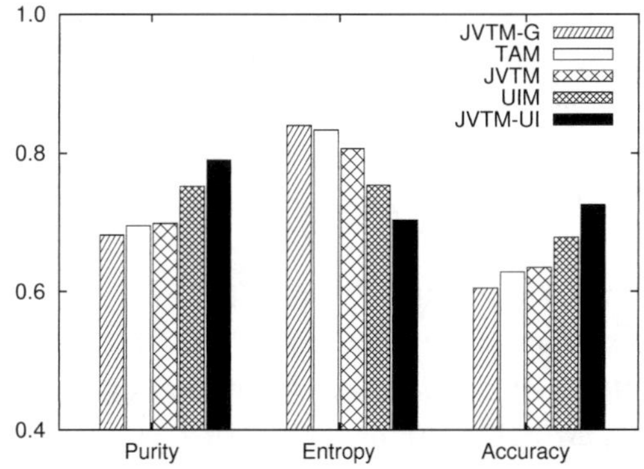

Figure 4: Averaged results of the models in identification of viewpoints.

UIM performs relatively better than other methods except our model. This shows user interactions are important features to identify post viewpoints. Overall, our model has a better performance as it is with higher purity and accuracy, and lower entropy.

		JVTM-UI	UIM	JVTM	TAM	JVTM-G
	P	**0.77**	0.74	0.64	0.65	0.63
EDS1	*E*	**0.72**	0.76	0.90	0.92	0.94
	A	**0.77**	0.74	0.61	0.60	0.57
	P	**0.82**	0.78	0.68	0.65	0.64
EDS2	*E*	**0.69**	0.73	0.79	0.86	0.90
	A	**0.81**	0.78	0.68	0.68	0.65
	P	**0.79**	0.73	0.65	0.64	0.62
EDS3	*E*	**0.67**	0.79	0.88	0.89	0.87
	A	**0.79**	0.73	0.65	0.64	0.62
	P	**0.87**	0.83	0.83	0.82	0.82
CDS1	*E*	**0.61**	0.64	0.65	0.66	0.64
	A	**0.60**	0.58	0.59	0.58	0.57
	P	**0.71**	0.65	0.61	0.63	0.60
CDS2	*E*	**0.80**	0.85	0.92	0.95	0.96
	A	**0.71**	0.65	0.61	0.61	0.59
	P	0.78	0.78	0.78	0.78	0.78
CDS3	*E*	0.73	0.75	**0.70**	0.72	0.73
	A	**0.67**	0.59	**0.67**	0.66	0.63

Table 3: Results on viewpoint identification on the all data sets.

Table 3 shows the detailed results on the data sets. We perform the 2-tailed paired t-test as used by Abu-Jbara et al. (2012) on the results. All the result differences are at 10% significance level if not with further clarification. First, JVTM has a better performance over JVTM-G, which shows it is important to consider user identity in the task. Second, JVTM and TAM have similar performance on

EDS1 and CDS2, but JVTM has a relatively better performance on EDS2, EDS3, CDS1 and CDS3. This shows it is helpful to consider each viewpoint's topic preference. Although as studied by Paul et al. (2010), by only using unigram features, TAM may not be able to cluster viewpoints accurately, our study shows that the results can be improved when adding each viewpoint's topic focus. Third, UIM has relatively better performance than the other models, which demonstrates that user interactions alone can do a decent job in inferring viewpoints. Finally, our proposed model has the best performance across the board in terms of all three evaluation metrics. Note that, our proposed model significantly outperforms other methods at 5% significance level except at 10% significance level over JVTM model. This shows by jointly modeling topics, viewpoints and user interactions, our model can better identify posts with different viewpoints.

5.3 Identification of user groups

We also use another task to evaluate our model. The task here is finding each user's viewpoint and subsequently grouping users by their viewpoints. This task has been studied by Abu-Jbara and Radev (2012), Dasigi et al. (2012), Abu-Jbara et al. (2012) and Hassan et al. (2012). For the English data set, the user-level group labels are provided by the original data set. For the Chinese data set, we randomly selected 150 users for each issue and manually labeled them according to their viewpoints as reflected by their posts. If a user's posts do not clearly suggest a viewpoint, we label her as neutral. Again we asked two human judges to do annotation. The agreement scores are above 0.70 for all issues, showing substantial agreement. This score is higher than viewpoint identification, which suggests that it is easier to judge a user's viewpoint than a single post's viewpoint. We use the set of users who have got the same labels by the two human judges for our experiments. Similarly we compute *purity*, *entropy* and *accuracy* to evaluate the clustering results.

Figure 5 shows the averaged results of all the models. Similar to previous experiment, our model has a better performance compared to the competing models.

The results on the each data set are shown in Table 4. The tables show that similar trends can be observed for the task of user group identification. We also perform the 2-tailed paired t-test on the results. We find our model significantly outperforms other models in terms of accuracy at 5% significance level, and purity and entropy at 10% significance level. Overall speaking, our joint model performed the best among all the models for this task for all three metrics. This shows that it is important to consider the topical preference of individual viewpoint, user's identify as well as the interactions between users.

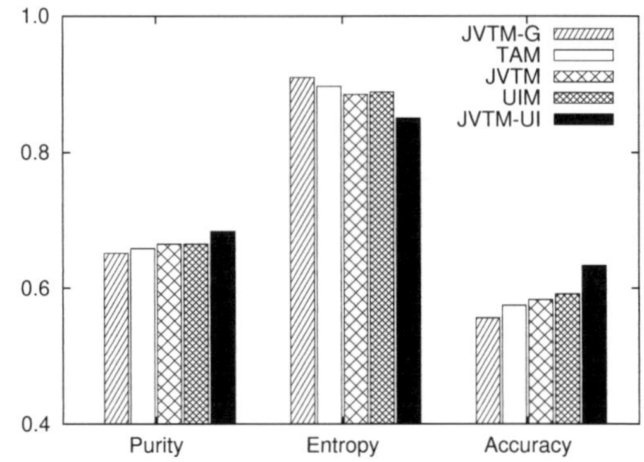

Figure 5: Averaged results of the models in identification of user groups.

		JVTM-UI	UIM	JVTM	TAM	JVTM-G
	P	0.67	0.67	0.67	0.67	0.67
EDS1	*E*	**0.85**	0.88	0.89	0.89	0.91
	A	**0.63**	0.59	0.58	0.59	0.57
	P	0.77	0.77	0.77	0.77	0.77
EDS2	*E*	**0.72**	0.76	0.74	0.75	0.76
	A	**0.62**	0.59	0.60	0.58	0.59
	P	**0.68**	0.63	0.61	0.61	0.58
EDS3	*E*	**0.90**	0.92	0.95	0.96	0.97
	A	**0.68**	0.63	0.61	0.58	0.57
	P	**0.64**	0.60	0.61	0.61	0.60
CDS1	*E*	**0.91**	0.97	0.96	0.96	0.97
	A	**0.61**	0.55	0.55	0.56	0.53
	P	0.69	0.69	0.69	0.69	0.69
CDS2	*E*	**0.83**	0.89	0.85	0.89	0.89
	A	**0.62**	0.57	0.56	0.58	0.54
	P	**0.67**	0.63	0.64	0.60	0.60
CDS3	*E*	**0.89**	0.91	0.92	0.93	0.96
	A	**0.64**	0.62	0.60	0.56	0.54

Table 4: Results on identification of user groups on the all the data sets.

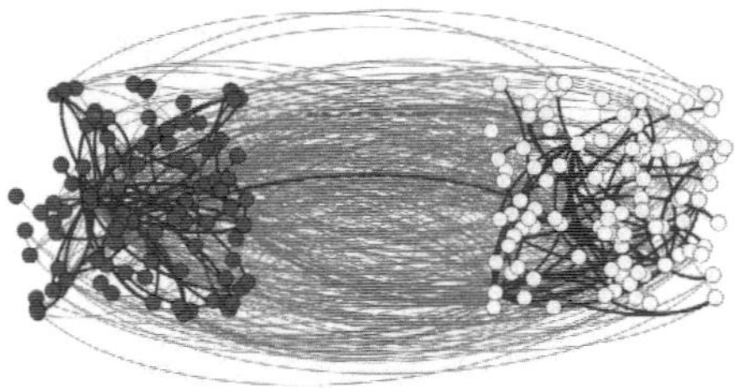

Figure 6: The user interaction network in a discussion thread about "will you vote obama." Green (left) and white (right) nodes represent users with two different viewpoints. Red (thin) and blue(thick) edges represent negative and positive interactions.

5.4 User interaction network

To gain some direct insight into our results, we show the user interaction network from one thread in Figure 6. Here each node denotes a user, and its color denotes the predicted viewpoint of that user. A link between a pair of users means these users have interactions and the interaction types have a dominant polarity. The polarities of these links are predicted using the interaction expressions and a sentiment lexicon, whereas the viewpoints of different users are learned by JVTM-UI, making use of the interaction polarities. The figure shows that clearly there are mostly positive interactions between users with the same viewpoint and mostly negative interactions between users with different viewpoints. Note that, our method to identify user interaction polarity is rule-based. As this step serves as a preprocessing step for our latent variable model, we can always use a more accurate method to improve the performances.

6 Conclusion

In this work, we proposed a novel latent variable model for viewpoint discovery from threaded forum posts. Our model is based on the three important factors: viewpoint specific topic preference, user identity and user interactions. Our proposed model captures these observations in a principled way. In particular, to incorporate the user interaction information, we proposed a novel generative process. Empirical evaluation on the real forum data sets showed that our model could cluster both posts and users with different viewpoints more accurately than the baseline models we consider. To the best of our knowledge, our work is the first to incorporate user interaction polarity into a generative model to discover viewpoints.

In this work, we only considered unigrams. As some previous work has shown, more complex lexical units such as n-grams (Mukherjee and Liu, 2012) and dependency triplets (Paul et al., 2010) may improve the performance of topic models. We will consider these strategies in our future work. Currently we use a simple heuristic-based classifier to predict interaction polarity. In our further work, we plan to consider more accurate methods using deeper linguistic analysis. We did not study how to summarize the discovered viewpoints in this work, which is also something we will look into in our future work.

Acknowledgments

We thank the reviewers for their valuable comments on this work. We also thank Shuang Xia for his help on processing and labeling the data sets.

References

Rob Abbott, Marilyn Walker, Pranav Anand, Jean E. Fox Tree, Robeson Bowmani, and Joseph King. 2011. How can you say such things?!?: Recognizing disagreement in informal political argument. In *Proceedings of the Workshop on Language in Social Media (LSM 2011)*, pages 2–11.

Amjad Abu-Jbara and Dragomir R. Radev. 2012. Subgroup detector: A system for detecting subgroups in online discussions. In *ACL (System Demonstrations)*, pages 133–138.

Amjad Abu-Jbara, Pradeep Dasigi, Mona Diab, and Dragomir R. Radev. 2012. Subgroup detection in ideological discussions. In *Proceedings of ACL 2012*, pages 399–409.

Jacob Andreas, Sara Rosenthal, and Kathleen McKeown. 2012. Annotating agreement and disagreement in threaded discussion. In *Proceedings of LREC'12*.

Stefano Baccianella, Andrea Esuli, and Fabrizio Sebastiani. 2010. Sentiwordnet 3.0: An enhanced lexical resource for sentiment analysis and opinion mining. In *LREC*.

David M. Blei, Andrew Y. Ng, and Michael I. Jordan. 2003. Latent dirichlet allocation. *J. Mach. Learn. Res.*, 3:993–1022.

Pradeep Dasigi, Weiwei Guo, and Mona T. Diab. 2012. Genre independent subgroup detection in online discussion threads: A study of implicit attitude using textual latent semantics. In *Proceedings of the 50th Annual Meeting of the Association for Computational Linguistics*, pages 65–69.

Yi Fang, Luo Si, Naveen Somasundaram, and Zhengtao Yu. 2012. Mining contrastive opinions on political texts using cross-perspective topic model. In *WSDM*, pages 63–72.

Michel Galley, Kathleen McKeown, Julia Hirschberg, and Elizabeth Shriberg. 2004. Identifying agreement and disagreement in conversational speech: Use of bayesian networks to model pragmatic dependencies. In *Proceedings of ACL'04, Main Volume*, pages 669–676.

Ahmed Hassan, Amjad Abu-Jbara, and Dragomir Radev. 2012. Detecting subgroups in online discussions by modeling positive and negative relations among participants. In *Proceedings of the 2012 EMNLP*, pages 59–70.

Minqing Hu and Bing Liu. 2004. Mining and summarizing customer reviews. In *Proceedings of the 10th ACM SIGKDD international conference on Knowledge discovery and data mining*, pages 168–177.

Lun-wei Ku, Yong-sheng Lo, and Hsin-hsi Chen. 2007. Using polarity scores of words for sentence-level opinion extraction. In *Proc. of the NTCIR-6 Workshop Meeting*, pages 316–322.

Yue Lu, Hongning Wang, ChengXiang Zhai, and Dan Roth. 2012. Unsupervised discovery of opposing opinion networks from forum discussions. In *Proceedings of the 21st ACM international conference on Information and knowledge management*, CIKM '12, pages 1642–1646, New York, NY, USA. ACM.

Christopher D. Manning, Prabhakar Raghavan, and Hinrich Schtze. 2008. *Introduction to Information Retrieval*. Cambridge University Press, July.

Arjun Mukherjee and Bing Liu. 2012. Modeling review comments. In *Proceedings of the 50th Annual Meeting of the Association for Computational Linguistics*, pages 320–329.

Michael J. Paul and Roxana Girju. 2010. A two-dimensional topic-aspect model for discovering multi-faceted topics. In *AAAI*.

Michael J. Paul, ChengXiang Zhai, and Roxana Girju. 2010. Summarizing contrastive viewpoints in opinionated text. In *EMNLP*, pages 66–76.

Swapna Somasundaran and Janyce Wiebe. 2009. Recognizing stances in online debates. In *Proceedings of the Joint Conference of the 47th Annual Meeting of the ACL and the 4th International Joint Conference on Natural Language Processing of the AFNLP*, pages 226–234.

Swapna Somasundaran and Janyce Wiebe. 2010. Recognizing stances in ideological on-line debates. In *Proceedings of the NAACL HLT 2010 Workshop on Computational Approaches to Analysis and Generation of Emotion in Text*, pages 116–124.

Theresa Wilson, Janyce Wiebe, and Paul Hoffmann. 2005. Recognizing contextual polarity in phrase-level sentiment analysis. In *HLT/EMNLP*.

Identifying Intention Posts in Discussion Forums

Zhiyuan Chen, Bing Liu

Department of Computer Science
University of Illinois at Chicago
Chicago, IL 60607, USA
czyuanacm@gmail.com, liub@cs.uic.edu

Meichun Hsu, Malu Castellanos, Riddhiman Ghosh
HP Labs
Palo Alto, CA 94304, USA
{meichun.hsu, malu.castellanos, riddhiman.ghosh}@hp.com

Abstract

This paper proposes to study the problem of identifying intention posts in online discussion forums. For example, in a discussion forum, a user wrote "I plan to buy a camera," which indicates a buying intention. This intention can be easily exploited by advertisers. To the best of our knowledge, there is still no reported study of this problem. Our research found that this problem is particularly suited to transfer learning because in different domains, people express the same intention in similar ways. We then propose a new transfer learning method which, unlike a general transfer learning algorithm, exploits several special characteristics of the problem. Experimental results show that the proposed method outperforms several strong baselines, including supervised learning in the target domain and a recent transfer learning method.

1 Introduction

Social media content is increasingly regarded as an information gold mine. Researchers have studied many problems in social media, e.g., sentiment analysis (Pang & Lee, 2008; Liu, 2010) and social network analysis (Easley & Kleinberg, 2010). In this paper, we study a novel problem which is also of great value, namely, *intention identification*, which aims to identify discussion posts expressing certain user intentions that can be exploited by businesses or other interested parties. For example, one user wrote, "*I am looking for a brand new car to replace my old Ford Focus*". Identifying such intention automatically can help social media sites to decide what ads to display so that the ads are more likely to be clicked.

This work focuses on identifying user posts with *explicit* intentions. By *explicit* we mean that the intention is explicitly stated in the text, no need to deduce (hidden or implicit intention). For example, in the above sentence, the author clearly expressed that he/she wanted to buy a car. On the other hand, an example of an implicit sentence is "*Anyone knows the battery life of iPhone*?" The person may or may not be thinking about buying an iPhone.

To our knowledge, there is no reported study of this problem in the context of text documents. The main related work is in Web search, where *user* (or *query*) *intent classification* is a major issue (Hu et al., 2009; Li, 2010; Li, Wang, & Acero, 2008). Its task is to determine what the user is searching for based on his/her keyword queries (2 to 3 words) and his/her click data. We will discuss this and other related work in Section 2.

We formulate the proposed problem as a two-class classification problem since an application may only be interested in a particular intention. We define *intention posts* (positive class) as the posts that explicitly express a particular intention of interest, e.g., the intention to buy a product. The other posts are *non-intention posts* (negative class). Note that we do not exploit intention specific knowledge since our aim is to propose a generic method applicable to different types of intentions.

There is an important feature about this problem which makes it amenable to transfer learning so that we do not need to label data in every domain. That is, for a particular kind of intention such as buying, the ways to express the intention in different domains are often very similar. This fact can be exploited to build a classifier based on labeled data in some domains and apply it to a new/target domain without labeling any training data in the target domain. However, this problem also has some special difficulties that existing general transfer learning methods do not deal with. The two special difficulties of the proposed problem are as follows:

1. In an intention post, the intention is typically expressed in only one or two sentences while most sentences do not express intention, which provide very noisy data for classifiers. Furthermore, words/phrases used for expressing intention are quite limited compared to other types of expressions. These mean that the set of shared (or common) features in different domains is very small. Most of the existing advanced transfer learning methods all try to extract and exploit these shared features. The small number of such features in our task makes it hard for the existing methods to find them accurately, which in turn learn poorer classifiers.
2. As mentioned above, in different domains, the ways to express the same intention are often similar. This means that only the positive (intention) features are shared among different domains, while features indicating the negative class in different domains are very diverse. We then have an imbalance problem, i.e., the shared features are almost exclusively features indicating the positive class. To our knowledge, none of the existing transfer learning methods deals with this imbalance problem of shared features, which also results in inaccurate classifiers.

We thus propose a new transfer learning (or domain adaptation) method, called Co-Class, which, unlike a general transfer learning method, is able to deal with these difficulties in solving the problem. Co-Class works as follows: we first build a classifier h using the labeled data from existing domains, called the source data, and then apply the classifier to classify the target (domain) data (which is unlabeled). Based on the target data labeled by h, we perform a feature selection on the target data. The selected set of features is used to build two classifiers, one (h_S) from the labeled source data and one (h_T) from the target data which has been labeled by h. The two classifiers (h_S and h_T) then work together to perform classification of the target data. The process then runs iteratively until the labels assigned to the target data stabilize. Note that in each iteration both classifiers are built using the same set of features selected from the target domain in order to focus on the target domain. The proposed Co-Class explicitly deals with the difficulties mentioned above (see Section 3). Our experiments using four real-life data sets extracted from four forum discussion sites show that Co-Class outperforms several strong baselines. What is also interesting is that it works even better than fully supervised learning in the target domain itself, i.e., using both training and test data in the target domain. It also outperforms a recent state-of-the-art transfer learning method (Tan et al., 2009), which has been successfully applied to the NLP task of sentiment classification.

In summary, this paper makes two main contributions:

1. It proposes to study the novel problem of intention identification. User intention is an important type of information in social media with many applications. To our knowledge, there is still no reported study of this problem.
2. It proposes a new transfer learning method Co-Class which is able to exploit the above two key issues/characteristics of the problem in building cross-domain classifiers. Our experimental results demonstrate its effectiveness.

2 Related Work

Although we have not found any paper studying intention classification of social media posts, there are some related works in the domain of Web search, where user or query intent classification is a major issue (Hu et al., 2009; Li, 2010; Li et al., 2008). The task there is to classify a query submitted to a search engine to determine what the user is searching for. It is different from our problem because they classify based on the user-submitted keyword queries (often 2 to 3 words) together with the user's click-through data (which represent the user's behavior). Such intents are typically implicit because people usually do not issue a search query like "*I want to buy a digital camera.*" Instead, they may just type the keywords "*digital camera*". Our interest is to identify *explicit* intents expressed in full text documents (forum posts). Another related problem is online commercial intention (OCI) identification (Dai et al.,

2006; Hu et al., 2009), which focuses on capturing commercial intention based on a user query and web browsing history. In this sense, OCI is still a user query intent problem.

In NLP, (Kanayama & Nasukawa, 2008) studied users' needs and wants from opinions. For example, they aimed to identify the user needs from sentences such as "*I'd be happy if it is equipped with a crisp LCD.*" This is clearly different from our explicit intention to buy or to use a product/service, e.g., "*I plan to buy a new TV.*"

Our proposed Co-Class technique is related to transfer learning or domain adaptation. The proposed method belongs to "*feature representation transfer*" from source domain to target domain (Pan & Yang, 2010). Aue & Gamon (2005) tried training on a mixture of labeled reviews from other domains where such data are available and test on the target domain. This is basically one of our baseline methods 3TR-1TE in Section 4. Their work does not do multiple iterations and does not build two separate classifiers as we do. Some related methods were also proposed in (W. Dai, Xue, Yang & Yu, 2007; Tan et al., 2007; Yang, Si & Callan, 2006). More sophisticated transfer learning methods try to find common features in both the source and target domains and then try to map the differences of the two domains (Blitzer, Dredze, & Pereira, 2007; Pan, et al, 2010; Bollegala, Weir & Carroll, 2011; Tan et al., 2009). Some researchers also used topic modeling of both domains to transfer knowledge (Gao & Li, 2011; He, Lin & Alani, 2011). However, none of these methods deals with the two problems/difficulties of our task. Co-Class tackles them explicitly and effectively (Section 4).

The proposed Co-Class method is also related to Co-Training method in (Blum & Mitchell, 1998). We will compare them in detail in Section 3.3.

3 The Proposed Technique

We now present the proposed technique. Our objective is to perform classification in the target domain by utilizing labeled data from the source domains. We use the term "source domains" as we can combine labeled data from multiple source domains. The target domain has no labeled data. Only the source domain data are labeled.

To deal with the first problem in Section 1 (i.e., the difficulty of finding common features across different domains), Co-Class avoids it by using an EM-based method to iteratively transfer from the source domains to the target domain while exploiting feature selection in the target domain to focus on important features in the target domain.

Since our ideas are developed starting from the EM (Expectation Maximization) algorithm and its shortcomings, we now introduce EM.

3.1 EM Algorithm

EM (Dempster, Laird, & Rubin, 1977) is a popular class of iterative algorithms for maximum likelihood estimation in problems with incomplete data. It is often used to address missing values in the data by computing expected values using existing values. The EM algorithm consists of two steps, the Expectation step (E-step) and the Maximization step (M-step). E-step basically fills in the missing data, and M-step re-estimates the parameters. This process iterates until convergence. Since our target data have no labels, which can be treated as missing values/data, the EM algorithm naturally applies. For text classification, each iteration of EM (Nigam, McCallum, Thrun, & Mitchell, 2000) usually uses the naïve Bayes (NB) classifier. Below, we first introduce the NB classifier.

Given a set of training documents D, each document $d_i \in D$ is an ordered list of words. We use $w_{d_i,k}$ to denote the word in the position k of d_i, where each word is from the vocabulary $V = \{w_1, \dots, w_{|v|}\}$, which is the set of all words considered in classification. We also have a set of classes $C = \{+, -\}$ representing positive and negative classes. For classification, we compute the posterior probability $\Pr(c_j|d_i)$. Based on the Bayes rule and multinomial model, we have:

$$\Pr(c_j) = \frac{\sum_{i=1}^{|D|} \Pr(c_j \mid d_i)}{|D|} \quad (1)$$

and with Laplacian smoothing:

$$\Pr(w_t \mid c_j) = \frac{1 + \sum_{i=1}^{|D|} N(w_t, d_i) \Pr(c_j \mid d_i)}{|V| + \sum_{s=1}^{|V|} \sum_{i=1}^{|D|} N(w_s, d_i) \Pr(c_j \mid d_i)} \quad (2)$$

where $N(w_t, d_i)$ is the number of times that the word w_t occurs in document d_i, and $\Pr(c_j|d_i) \in [0,1]$ is the probability of assigning class c_j to d_i. Assuming that word probabilities are independent given a class, we have the NB classifier:

$$\Pr(c_j \mid d_i) = \frac{\Pr(c_j)\prod_{k=1}^{|d_i|}\Pr(w_{d_i,k} \mid c_j)}{\sum_{r=1}^{|C|}\Pr(c_r)\prod_{k=1}^{|d_i|}\Pr(w_{d_i,k} \mid c_r)} \quad (3)$$

The EM algorithm basically builds a classifier iteratively using NB and both the labeled source data and the unlabeled target data. However, the major shortcoming is that the feature set, even with feature selection, may fit the labeled source data well but not the target data because the target data has no labels to be used in feature selection. Feature selection is shown to be very important for this application as we will see in Section 4.

3.2 FS-EM

Based on the discussion above, the key to solve the problem of EM is to find a way to reflect the features in the target domain during the iterations. We propose two alternatives, FS-EM (Feature Selection EM) and Co-Class (Co-Classification). This sub-section presents FS-EM.

EM can select features only before iterations using the labeled source data and keep using the same features in each iteration. However, these features only fit the labeled source data but not the target data. We then propose to select features during iterations, i.e., after each iteration, we re-do feature selection. For this, we use the predicted classes of the target data. In naïve Bayes, we define the predicted class for document d_i as

$$c = \operatorname*{argmax}_{c_j \in C} \Pr(c_j | d_i) \quad (4)$$

The detailed algorithm for FS-EM is given in Figure 1. First, we select a feature set from the labeled source data D_L and then build an initial NB classifier (lines 1 and 2). The feature selection is based on Information Gain, which will be introduced in Section 3.4. After that, we classify each document in the target data D_U to obtain its predicted class (lines 4-6). A new target data set D_P is produced in line 7, which is D_U with added classes (predicted in line 5). Line 8 selects a new feature set Δ from the data D' (which is discussed below), from which a new classifier h is built (line 9). The iteration stops when the predicted classes of D_U do not change any more (line 10).

We now turn to the data set D', which can be formed with one of the two methods:

1. $D' = D_L \cup D_P$
2. $D' = D_P$

The first method (called FS-EM1) merges the labeled source data D_L and the target data D_P (with predicted classes). However, this method does not work well because the labeled source data can dominate D' and the target domain features are still not well represented.

The second method ($D' = D_P$), denoted as FS-EM2, selects features from the target domain data D_P only based on the predicted classes. The classifiers are built in iterations (lines 3-10) using only the target domain data. The weakness of this is that it completely ignores the labeled source data after initialization, but the source data does contain some valuable information. Our final proposed method Co-Class is able to solve this problem.

3.3 Co-Class

Co-Class is our final proposed algorithm. It considers both the source labeled data and the target data with predicted classes. It uses the idea of FS-EM, but is also inspired by Co-Training in (Blum & Mitchell, 1998). It additionally deals with the second issue identified in Section 1 (i.e., the imbalance of shared positive and negative features).

Co-Training is originally designed for semi-supervised learning to learn from a small labeled and a large unlabeled set of training examples, which assumes the set of features in the data can be partitioned into two subsets, and each subset is sufficient for building an accurate classifier. The proposed Co-Class model is similar to Co-Training in that it also builds two classifiers. However, unlike Co-Training, Co-Class does not partition the feature space. Instead, one classifier is built based on the target data with predicted classes (D_P), and the other classifier is built using only the source labeled data (D_L). Both classifiers use the same features (this is an important point) that are selected from the target data D_P only, in order to focus on the target domain. The final classification is based on both classifiers. Furthermore, Co-Training only uses the data from the same domain.

The detailed Co-Class algorithm is given in Figure 2. Lines 1-6 are the same as lines 1, 2 and 4-7 in FS-EM. Line 8 selects new features Δ from D_P. Two naïve Bayes classifiers, h_L and h_P, are then built using the source data D_L and predicted target data D_P respectively with the same set of

Algorithm FS-EM

Input: Labeled data D_L and unlabeled data D_U

Select a feature set Δ based on IG from D_L;

Learn an initial naïve Bayes classifier h from D_L based on Δ (using Equations (1) and (2));

repeat

  for each document d_i in D_U **do**

    $c = h(d_i)$; // predict the class of d_i using h

  end

  Produce data D_P based on predicted class of D_U;

  Select a new feature set Δ from D';

  Learn a new classifier h on D' based on the new feature set Δ;

until the predicted classes of D_U stabilize

Return the classifier h from the last iteration.

Figure 1 – The FS-EM algorithm

Algorithm Co-Class

Input: Labeled data D_L and unlabeled data D_U

1 Select a feature set Δ based on IG from D_L;

2 Learn an initial naïve Bayes classifier h from D_L based on Δ (using Equations (1) and (2));

3 **for** each document d_i in D_U **do**

4   $c = h(d_i)$; // predict the class of d_i using h

5 **end**

6 Produce data D_P based on the predicted class of D_U;

7 **repeat**

8   Select a new feature set Δ from D_P;

9   Build a naïve Bayes classifier h_L using Δ and D_L;

10   Build a naïve Bayes classifier h_P using Δ and D_P;

11   **for** each document d_i in D_U **do**

12     $c_i = \Phi(h_L(d_i), h_P(d_i))$; // Aggregate function

13   **end**

14   Produce data D_P based on predicted class of D_U;

15 **until** the prediction classes of D_U stabilize

16 Return classifiers h_L and h_P from the last iteration.

Figure 2 – The Co-Class algorithm

features Δ (lines 9-10). Lines 11-13 classify each target domain document d_i using the two classifiers. $\Phi(h_L(d_i), h_P(d_i))$ is the aggregate function to combine the results of two classifiers. It is defined as:

$$\Phi(h_L(d_i), h_P(d_i)) = \begin{cases} + & h_L(d_i) = h_P(d_i) = + \\ - & Otherwise \end{cases}$$

This aims to deal with the imbalanced feature problem. As discussed before, the expressions for stating a particular intention (e.g., buying) are very similar across domains but the non-intention expressions across domains are highly diverse, which result in strong positive features and weak negative features. We then need to restrict the positive class by requiring both classifiers to give positive predictions. If we use the method in Co-Training (multiplying the probabilities of the two NB classifiers), the classification results deteriorate from iteration to iteration because the positive class recall gets higher and higher due to strong positive features, but the precision gets lower and lower.

Since we build and use two classifiers for the final classification, we call the method *Co-Class*, short for *Co-Classification*. Co-Class is different from EM (Nigam et al., 2000) in two main aspects. First, it integrates feature selection into the iterations, which has not been done before. Feature selection refines features to enhance the correlation between the features and classes. Second, two classifiers are built based on different domains and combined to improve the classification. Only one classifier is built in existing EM methods, which gives poorer results (Section 4).

3.4 Feature Selection

As feature selection is important for our task, we briefly introduce the Information Gain (IG) method given in (Yang & Pedersen, 1997), which is a popular feature selection algorithm for text classification. IG is based on entropy reflecting the purity of the categories or classes by knowing the presence or absence of each feature, which is defined as:

$$IG(f) = -\sum_{i=1}^{m} P(c_i)\log P(c_i) + \sum_{f,\bar{f}} P(f)\sum_{i=1}^{m} P(c_i \mid f)\log P(c_i \mid f)$$

Using the IG value of each feature f, all features can be ranked. As in normal classification tasks, the common practice is to use a set of top ranked features for classification.

4 Evaluation

We have conducted a comprehensive set of experiments to compare the proposed Co-Class method with several strong baselines, including a state-of-the-art transfer learning method.

4.1 Experiment Settings

Datasets: We created 4 different domain datasets crawled from 4 different forum discussion sites:

Cellphone: http://www.howardforums.com/forums.php
Electronics: http://www.avsforum.com/avs-vb/
Camera: http://forum.digitalcamerareview.com/

TV: http://www.avforums.com/forums/tvs/

For our experiments, we are interested in the intention to *buy*, which is our intention or positive class. For each dataset, we manually labeled 1000 posts.

Labeling: We initially labeled about one fifth of posts by two human annotators. We found their labels highly agreed. We then used only one annotator to complete the remaining labeling. The reason for the strong labeling agreement is that we are interested in only explicit buying intentions, which are clearly expressed in each post, e.g., "*I am in the market for a new smartphone*." There is little ambiguity or subjectivity in labeling.

To ensure that the task is realistic, for all datasets we keep their original class distributions as they are extracted from their respective websites to reflect the real-life situation. The intention class is always the minority class, which makes it much harder to predict due to the imbalanced class distribution. Table 1 gives the statistics of each dataset. On average, each post contains about 7.5 sentences and 122 words. We have made the datasets used in this paper publically available at the websites of the first two authors.

Evaluation measures: For all experiments, we use *precision*, *recall* and *F1-score* as the evaluation measures. They are suitable because our objective is to identify intention posts.

4.2 One Domain Learning

The objective of our work is to classify the target domain instances without labeling any target domain data. To set the background, we first give the results of one domain learning, i.e., assuming that there is labeled training data in the target domain (which is the traditional fully supervised learning). We want to see how the results of Co-Class compare with the fully supervised learning.

For this set of experiments, we use naïve Bayes and SVM. For naïve Bayes, we use the *Lingpipe* implementation (http://alias-i.com/lingpipe/). For SVM, we use *SVM*^{Light} (Joachims, 1999) from (http://svmlight.joachims.org/) with the linear kernel as it has been shown by many researchers that linear kernel is sufficient for text classification (Joachims, 1998; Yang and Liu, 1999).

Dataset	No. of Intention	No. of Non-Intention	Total No. of posts
Cellphone	184	816	1000
Electronics	280	720	1000
Camera	282	718	1000
TV	263	737	1000

Table 1: Datasets statistics with the buy intention

During labeling, we observed that the intention in an intention (positive) post is often expressed in the first few or the last few sentences. Hence, we tried to use the full post (denoted by Full), the first 5 sentences (denoted by (5, 0)), and first 5 and last 5 sentences (denoted by (5, 5)). We also experimented with the first 3 sentences, and first 3 and last 3 sentences but their results were poorer.

The experiments were done using 10-fold cross validation. For the number of selected features, we tried 500, 1000, 1500, 2000, 2500 and all. We also tried unigrams, bigrams, trigrams, and 4-grams. To compare naïve Bayes with SVM, we tried each combination, i.e. number of features and n-grams, and found the best model for each method. We found that naïve Bayes works best when using trigrams with 1500 selected features. Bigrams with 1000 features are the best combination for SVM. Figure 3 shows the comparison of the best results (F1-scores) of naïve Bayes and SVM.

From Figure 3, we make the following observations:

1. SVM does not do well for this task. We tuned the parameters of SVM, but the results were similar to the default setting, and all were worse than naïve Bayes. We believe the main reason is that the data for this application is highly noisy because apart from one or two intention sentences, other sentences in an intention post have little difference from those in a non-intention post. SVM does not perform well with very noisy data. When there are data points far away from their own classes, SVM

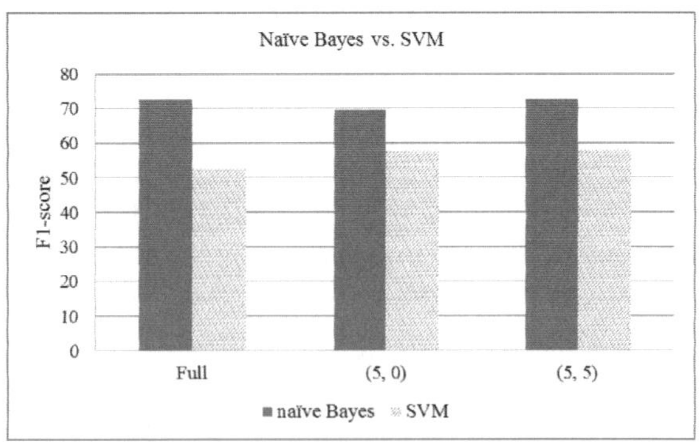

Figure 3 – Naïve Bayes vs. SVM

Naïve Bayes (n-grams, features)	Cellphone			Electronics			Camera			TV		
	Full	**5,0**	**5,5**	**Full**	**5,0**	**5,5**	**Full**	**5,0**	**5,5**	**Full**	**5,0**	**5,5**
Unigrams, 2000	59.91	55.21	56.76	71.31	70.10	71.24	71.57	71.53	75.78	74.96	74.45	74.13
Bigrams, 1500	61.97	54.29	59.17	70.71	71.46	72.48	77.02	74.12	77.38	79.76	77.71	79.72
Trigrams, 1500	**61.50**	**55.78**	**60.15**	**71.38**	**71.07**	**71.61**	**77.66**	**75.71**	**78.74**	**80.24**	**75.66**	**79.92**
4-grams, 2000	58.94	51.94	57.72	72.03	71.98	73.05	79.84	75.09	79.46	79.12	76.61	79.88

Table 2: One-domain learning using naïve Bayes with n-grams (with best no. of features)

Naïve Bayes (n-grams, features)	Cellphone			Electronics			Camera			TV		
	Full	**5,0**	**5,5**	**Full**	**5,0**	**5,5**	**Full**	**5,0**	**5,5**	**Full**	**5,0**	**5,5**
Trigrams, 2000	57.98	57.60	58.67	71.85	69.74	71.51	74.45	73.58	74.24	74.07	71.34	73.65
Trigrams, 2500	58.08	57.48	59.12	72.27	69.65	71.82	76.15	73.64	76.31	74.02	71.25	73.49
Trigrams, 3000	**56.74**	**56.94**	**56.74**	**72.27**	**70.76**	**72.43**	**77.62**	**74.65**	**77.62**	**75.64**	**71.65**	**74.73**
Trigrams, 3500	56.60	56.81	57.21	71.86	70.40	72.24	77.17	74.85	76.68	74.25	71.10	73.37
4-grams, 2000	58.94	51.94	57.72	72.03	71.98	73.05	79.84	75.09	79.46	79.12	76.61	79.88

Table 3: F1-scores of 3TR-1TE with trigrams and different no. of features

tends to be strongly affected by such points (Wu & Liu, 2007). Naïve Bayes is more robust in the presence of noise due to its probabilistic nature.

2. SVM using only the first few and/or last few sentences performs better than using full posts because full posts have more noise. However, it is still worse than naïve Bayes.
3. For naïve Bayes, using full posts and the first 5 and last 5 (5, 5) sentences give similar results, which is not surprising as (5, 5) has almost all the information needed. Without using the last 5 sentence (5, 0), the results are poorer.

We also found that without feature selection (using all features), the results are markedly worse for both naïve Bayes and SVM. This is understandable (as we discussed earlier) because most words and sentences in both intention and non-intention posts are very similar. Thus, feature selection is highly desirable for this application.

Effect of different combinations: Table 2 gives the detailed F1-score results of naïve Bayes with best results in different n-grams (with best number of features). We can see that using trigrams produces the best results on average, but bigrams and 4-grams are quite similar. It turns out that using trigrams with 1500 selected features performs the best. SVM results are not shown as they are poorer.

In summary, we say that naïve Bayes is more suitable than SVM for our application and feature selection is crucial. In our experiments reported below, we will only use naïve Bayes with feature selection.

4.3 Evaluation of Co-Class

We now compare Co-Class with the baseline methods listed below. Note that for this set of experiments, the source data all contain labeled posts from three domains and the target data contain unlabeled posts in one domain. That is, for each target domain, we merge three other domains for training and the target domain for testing. For example, for the target of "Cellphone", the model is built using the data from the other three domains (i.e., "Electronics", "Camera" and "TV"). The results are the classification of the model on the target domain "Cellphone". Several strong baselines are described as follows:

3TR-1TE: Use labeled data from three domains to train and then classify the target (test) domain. There is no iteration. This method was used in (Aue & Gamon, 2005).

EM: This is the algorithm in Section 3.1. The combined data from three domains are used as the labeled source data. The data of the remaining one domain are used as the unlabeled target data, which is also used as the test data (since it is unlabeled).

ANB: This is a recent transfer learning method (Tan et al., 2009). ANB uses *frequently co-occurring entropy* (FCE) to pick out generalizable (or shared) features that occur frequently in both the source and target domains. Then, a weighted transfer version of naïve Bayes classifier is applied. We chose this method for comparison as it is a recent method, also based on naïve Bayes, and has been applied to the NLP task of sentiment

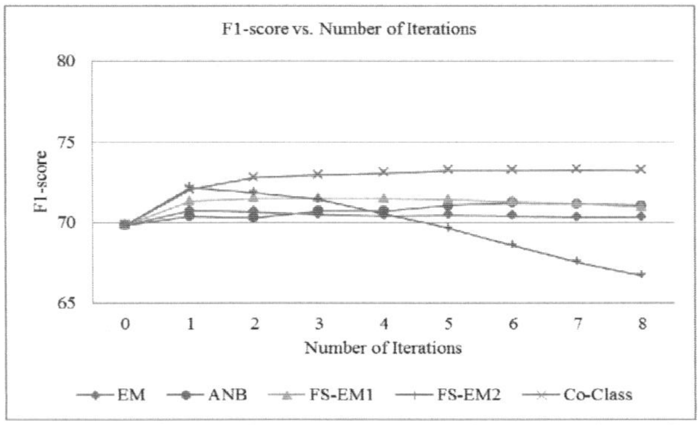

Figure 4 – Comparison EM, ANB, FS-EM1, FS-EM2, and Co-Class across iterations (0 is 3TR-1TE)

classification, which to some extend is related to the proposed task of intention classification. ANB was also shown to perform better than EM and naïve Bayes transfer learning method (Dai et al., 2007).

We look at the results of 3TR-1TE first, which are shown in Table 3. Due to space limitations, we only show the trigrams F1-scores as they perform the best on average. Table 3 gives the number of features with trigrams. We can observe that on average using 3000 features gives the best F1-score results. It has 1000 more features than one domain learning because we now combine three domains (3000 posts) for training and thus more useful features.

From Table 3, we observe that the F1-score results of 3TR-1TE are worse than those of one domain learning (Table 2), which is intuitive because no training data are used from the target domain. But the results are not dramatically worse which indicate that there are some common features in different domains, meaning people expressing the same intention in similar ways.

Since we found that trigrams with 3000 features perform the best on average, we run EM, FS-EM1, FS-EM2 and Co-Class based on trigrams with 3000 features. For the baseline ANB, we tuned the parameters using a development set (1/10 of the training data). We found that selecting 2000 generalizable/shared features gives the best results (the default is 500 in (Tan et al., 2009)). We kept ANB's other original parameter values. The F1-scores (averages over all 4 datasets) with the number of iterations are shown in Figure 4. Iteration 0 is the result of 3TR-1TE. From Figure 4, we can make the following observations:

1. EM makes a little improvement in iteration 1. After that, the results deteriorate. The gain of iteration 1 shows that incorporating the target domain data (unlabeled) is helpful. However, the selected features from source domains can only fit the labeled source data but not the target data, which was explained in Section 3.1.
2. ANB improves slightly from iteration 1 to iteration 6, but the results are all worse than those of Co-Class. We checked the generalizable/shared features of ANB and found that they were not suitable for our problem since they were mainly adjectives, nouns and sentiment verbs, which do not have strong correlation with intentions. This shows that it is hard to find the truly shared features indicating intentions. Furthermore, ANB's results are almost the same as those of EM.
3. FS-EM2 behaves similarly to FS-EM1. After two iterations, the results start to deteriorate. Selecting features only from the target domain makes sense since it can reflect target domain data well. However, it also becomes worse with the increased number of iterations, due to strong positive features. With increased iterations, positive features get stronger due to the imbalanced feature problem discussed in Section 1.
4. Co-Class performs much better than all other methods. With the increased number of iterations, the results actually improve. Starting from iteration 7, the results stabilize. Co-Class solves the problem of strong positive features by requiring strong conditions for positive classification and focusing on features in the target domain only. Although the detailed results of precision and recall are not shown, the Co-Class model actually improves the F1-score by improving both the precision and recall.

Significance of improvement: We now discuss the significance of improvements by comparing the results of Co-Class with other models. Table 4 summarizes the results among the models. For Co-Class, we use the converged models at iteration 7. We also include the One Domain learning results which are from fully supervised classification in the target domains with trigrams and 1500 features. The results of 3TR-1TE, EM, ANB, FS-EM1, and FS-EM2 are obtained based on their settings which give the best results in Figure 4.

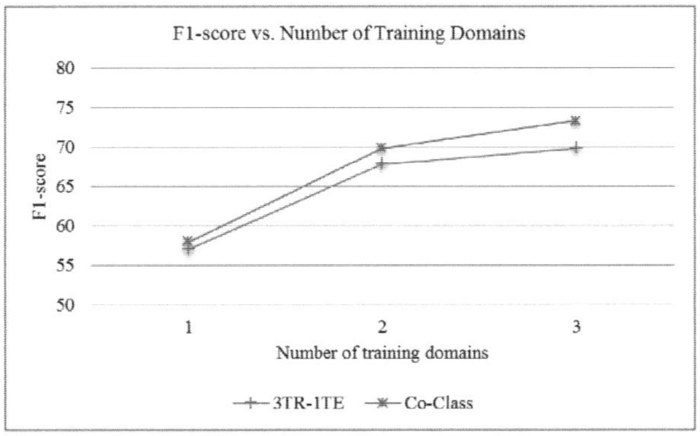

Figure 5 – Effect of number of source domains using 3TR-1TE and Co-Class.

It is clear from Table 4 that Co-Class is the best method in general. It is even better than the fully supervised One-Domain learning, although their results are not strictly comparable because One-Domain learning uses training and test data from the same domain via 10-fold cross validation, while all other methods use one domain as the test data (the labeled data are from the other three domains). One possible reason is that the labeled data are much bigger than those in One-Domain learning, which contain more expressions of buying intention. Note that FS-EM1 and FS-EM2 work slightly better than Co-Class in domain "Camera" because it is the least noisy domain with very short posts while other domains (as source data) are quite noisy. With good quality data, FS-EM1 and FS-EM2 (also proposed in this paper) can do slightly better than Co-Class. Statistical paired *t*-test shows that Co-Class performs significantly better than baseline methods 3TR-1TE, EM, ANB and FS-EM1 at the confidence level of 95%, and better than FS-EM2 at the confidence level of 94%.

Effect of the number of training domains: In our experiments above, we used 3 source domain data and tested on one target domain. We now show what happens if we use only one or two source domain data and test on one target domain. We tried all possible combinations of source and target data. Figure 5 gives the average results over the four target/test domains. We can see that using more source domains is better due to more labeled data. With more domains, Co-Class also improves more over 3TR-1TE.

5 Conclusion

This paper studied the problem of identifying intention posts in discussion forums. The problem has not been studied in the social media context. Due to special characteristics of the problem, we found that it is particularly suited to transfer learning. A new transfer learning method, called Co-Class, was proposed to solve the problem. Unlike a general transfer learning method, Co-Class can deal with two specific difficulties of the problem to produce more accurate classifiers. Our experimental results show that Co-Class outperforms strong baselines including classifiers trained using labeled data in the target domains and classifiers from a state-of-the-art transfer learning method.

Acknowledgments

This work was supported in part by a grant from National Science Foundation (NSF) under grant no. IIS-1111092, and a grant from HP Labs Innovation Research Program.

References

Aue, A., & Gamon, M. (2005). Customizing Sentiment Classifiers to New Domains: A Case Study. *Proceedings of Recent Advances in Natural Language Processing (RANLP).*

Blitzer, J., Dredze, M., & Pereira, F. (2007). Biographies, Bollywood, Boom-boxes and Blenders: Domain Adaptation for Sentiment Classification. *Proceedings of Annual Meeting of the Association for Computational Linguistics (ACL).*

Model	**Cellphone**			**Electronics**			**Camera**			**TV**		
	Full	**5,0**	**5,5**	**Full**	**5,0**	**5,5**	**Full**	**5,0**	**5,5**	**Full**	**5,0**	**5,5**
One-Domain	61.50	55.78	60.15	71.38	71.07	71.61	77.66	75.71	78.74	80.24	75.66	79.92
3TR-1TE	56.74	56.94	56.74	72.27	70.76	72.43	77.62	74.65	77.62	75.64	71.65	74.73
EM	60.28	59.59	60.45	70.47	69.90	71.33	79.38	77.01	80.31	74.96	70.76	74.31
ANB	62.53	59.29	62.41	66.58	68.29	68.36	78.37	77.49	78.83	78.70	75.73	78.26
FS-EM1	59.01	57.69	59.41	70.75	71.74	72.00	80.58	76.13	80.37	79.29	73.75	77.34
FS-EM2	59.54	60.09	61.33	71.19	72.09	72.07	80.14	77.93	81.09	78.90	74.21	77.53
Co-Class	**62.69**	**61.10**	**62.69**	**73.38**	**73.23**	**73.95**	**79.69**	**74.65**	**78.66**	**81.12**	**76.40**	**81.60**

Table 4: F1-score results of One-Domain, 3TR-1TE, EM, ANB, FS-EM1, FS-EM2, and Co-Class

Blum, A., & Mitchell, T. (1998). Combining Labeled and Unlabeled Data with Co-Training. COLT: *Proceedings of the eleventh annual conference on Computational learning theory*.

Bollegala, D., Weir, D. J., & Carroll, J. (2011). Using Multiple Sources to Construct a Sentiment Sensitive Thesaurus for Cross-Domain Sentiment Classification. *Proceedings of Annual Meeting of the Association for Computational Linguistics* (*ACL*).

Dai, H. K., Zhao, L., Nie, Z., Wen, J. R., Wang, L., & Li, Y. (2006). Detecting online commercial intention (OCI). *Proceedings of the 15th international conference on World Wide Web* (*WWW*).

Dai, W., Xue, G., Yang, Q., & Yu, Y. (2007). Transferring naive bayes classifiers for text classification. In *Proceedings of the 22nd AAAI Conference on Artificial Intelligence* (*AAAI*).

Dempster, A., Laird, N., & Rubin, D. (1977). Maximum likelihood from incomplete data via the EM algorithm. *Journal of the Royal Statistical Society*. Series B, 39(1), 1–38.

Easley, D., & Kleinberg, J. (2010). *Networks, Crowds, and Markets: Reasoning About a Highly Connected World*. Cambridge University Press.

Gao, S., & Li, H. (2011). A cross-domain adaptation method for sentiment classification using probabilistic latent analysis. *Proceedings of the 20th ACM international conference on Information and knowledge management* (*CIKM*).

He, Y., Lin, C., & Alani, H. (2011). Automatically Extracting Polarity-Bearing Topics for Cross-Domain Sentiment Classification. *Proceedings of the 49th Annual Meeting of the Association for Computational Linguistics: Human Language Technologies* (*ACL*).

Hu, D. H., Shen, D., Sun, J.-T., Yang, Q., & Chen, Z. (2009). Context-Aware Online Commercial Intention Detection. *Proceedings of the 1st Asian Conference on Machine Learning: Advances in Machine Learning* (*ACML*).

Hu, J., Wang, G., Lochovsky, F., tao Sun, J., & Chen, Z. (2009). Understanding user's query intent with wikipedia. *Proceedings of the 18th international conference on World wide web* (*WWW*).

Joachims, T. (1998). Text Categorization with Support Vector Machines: Learning with Many Relevant Features. *European Conference on Machine Learning* (*ECML*).

Joachims, T. (1999). Making large-Scale SVM Learning Practical. *Advances in Kernel Methods - Support Vector Learning*. MIT Press.

Kanayama, H., & Nasukawa, T. (2008). Textual Demand Analysis: Detection of Users' Wants and Needs from Opinions. *Proceedings of the 22nd International Conference on Computational Linguistics* (*COLING*).

Li, X. (2010). Understanding the Semantic Structure of Noun Phrase Queries. *Proceedings of Annual Meeting of the Association for Computational Linguistics* (*ACL*).

Li, X., Wang, Y.-Y., & Acero, A. (2008). Learning query intent from regularized click graphs. *Proceedings of the 31st annual international ACM SIGIR conference on Research and development in information retrieval* (*SIGIR*).

Liu, B. (2010). Sentiment Analysis and Subjectivity. (N. Indurkhya & F. J. Damerau, Eds.) *Handbook of Natural Language Processing*, 2nd ed.

Nigam, K., McCallum, A. K., Thrun, S., & Mitchell, T. (2000). Text Classification from Labeled and Unlabeled Documents using EM. *Mach. Learn.*, 39(2-3), 103–134.

Pan, S. J., Ni, X., Sun, J.-T., Yang, Q., & Chen, Z. (2010). Cross-domain sentiment classification via spectral feature alignment. *Proceedings of the 19th international conference on World wide web* (*WWW*).

Pan, S. J., & Yang, Q. (2010). A Survey on Transfer Learning. *IEEE Trans. Knowl. Data Eng.*, 22(10), 1345–1359.

Pang, B., & Lee, L. (2008). Opinion mining and sentiment analysis. *Foundations and Trends in Information Retrieval*, 2(1-2), 1–135.

Tan, S., Cheng, X., Wang, Y., & Xu, H. (2009). Adapting Naive Bayes to Domain Adaptation for Sentiment Analysis. *Proceedings of the 31th European Conference on IR Research on Advances in Information Retrieval* (*ECIR*).

Tan, S., Wu, G., Tang, H., & Cheng, X. (2007). A novel scheme for domain-transfer problem in the context of sentiment analysis. *Proceedings of the sixteenth ACM conference on Conference on information and knowledge management* (*CIKM*).

Wu, Y., & Liu, Y. (2007). Robust truncated-hinge-loss support vector machines. *Journal of the American Statistical Association*, 102(479), 974–983.

Yang, H., Si, L., & Callan, J. (2006). Knowledge Transfer and Opinion Detection in the TREC 2006 Blog Track. *Proceedings of TREC*.

Yang, Y., & Liu, X. (1999). A re-examination of text categorization methods. *Proceedings of the 22nd annual international ACM SIGIR conference on Research and development in information retrieval* (*SIGIR*).

Yang, Y., & Pedersen, J. O. (1997). A Comparative Study on Feature Selection in Text Categorization. *Proceedings of the Fourteenth International Conference on Machine Learning* (*ICML*).

Dependency-based empty category detection via phrase structure trees

Nianwen Xue
Brandeis University
Waltham, MA, USA
xuen@brandeis.edu

Yaqin Yang
Brandeis University
Waltham, MA, USA
yaqin@brandeis.edu

Abstract

We describe a novel approach to detecting empty categories (EC) as represented in dependency trees as well as a new metric for measuring EC detection accuracy. The new metric takes into account not only the position and type of an EC, but also the head it is a dependent of in a dependency tree. We also introduce a variety of new features that are more suited for this approach. Tested on a subset of the Chinese Treebank, our system improved significantly over the best previously reported results even when evaluated with this more stringent metric.

1 Introduction

In modern theoretical linguistics, empty categories (ECs) are an important piece of machinery in representing the syntactic structure of a sentence and they are used to represent phonologically null elements such as dropped pronouns and traces of dislocated elements. They have also found their way into large-scale treebanks which have played an important role in advancing the state of the art in syntactic parsing. In phrase-structure treebanks, ECs have been used to indicate long-distance dependencies, discontinuous constituents, and certain dropped elements (Marcus et al., 1993; Xue et al., 2005). Together with labeled brackets and function tags, they make up the full syntactic representation of a sentence.

The use of ECs captures some cross-linguistic commonalities and differences. For example, while both the Penn English TreeBank (PTB) (Marcus et al., 1993) and the Chinese TreeBank (CTB) (Xue et al., 2005) use traces to represent the extraction site of a dislocated element, dropped pronouns (represented as ***pro***s) are much more widespread in the CTB. This is because Chinese is a pro-drop language (Huang, 1984) that allows the subject to be dropped in more contexts than English does. While detecting and resolving traces is important to the interpretation of the syntactic structure of a sentence in both English and Chinese, the prevalence of dropped nouns in Chinese text gives EC detection added significance and urgency. They are not only an important component of the syntactic parse of a sentence, but are also essential to a wide range of NLP applications. For example, any meaningful tracking of entities and events in natural language text would have to include those represented by dropped pronouns. If Chinese is translated into a different language, it is also necessary to render these dropped pronouns explicit if the target language does not allow pro-drop. In fact, Chung and Gildea (2010) reported preliminary work that has shown a positive impact of automatic EC detection on statistical machine translation.

Some ECs can be resolved to an overt element in the same text while others only have a generic reference that cannot be linked to any specific entity. Still others have a plausible antecedent in the text, but are not annotated due to annotation limitations. A common practice is to resolve ECs in two separate stages (Johnson, 2002; Dienes and Dubey, 2003b; Dienes and Dubey, 2003a; Campbell, 2004; Gabbard et al., 2006; Schmid, 2006; Cai et al., 2011). The first stage is *EC detection*, where empty categories are first located and typed. The second stage is *EC resolution*, where empty categories are linked to an overt element if possible.

In this paper we describe a novel approach to detecting empty categories in Chinese, using the CTB as training and test data. More concretely, EC detection involves (i) identifying the position of the EC, relative to some overt word tokens in the same sentence, and (ii) determining the type of EC, e.g., whether it is a dropped pronoun or a trace. We focus on EC detection here because most of the ECs in the Chinese Treebank are either not resolved to an overt element or linked to another EC. For example, dropped pronouns (***pro***) are not resolved, and traces (***T***) in relative clauses are linked to an empty relative pronoun (***OP***).

In previous work, ECs are either represented linearly, where ECs are indexed to the following word (Yang and Xue, 2010) or attached to nodes in a phrase structure tree (Johnson, 2002; Dienes and Dubey, 2003b; Gabbard et al., 2006). In a linear representation where ECs are indexed to the following word, it is difficult to represent consecutive ECs because that will mean more than one EC will be indexed to the same word (making the classification task more complicated). While in English consecutive ECs are relatively rare, in Chinese this is very common. For example, it is often the case that an empty relative pronoun (***OP***) is followed immediately by a trace (***T***). Another issue with the linear representation of ECs is that it leaves unspecified where the EC should be attached, and crucial dependencies between ECs and other elements in the syntactic structure are not represented, thus limiting the utility of this task.

In a phrase structure representation, ECs are attached to a hierarchical structure and the problem of multiple ECs indexed to the same word token can be avoided because linearly consecutive ECs may be attached to different non-terminal nodes in a phrase structure tree. In a phrase structure framework, ECs are evaluated based on their linear position as well as on their contribution to the overall accuracy of the syntactic parse (Cai et al., 2011).

In the present work, we propose to look at EC detection in a dependency structure representation, where we define EC detection as (i) determining its linear position relative to the following word token, (ii) determining its head it is a dependent of, and (iii) determining the type of EC. Framing EC detection this way also requires a new evaluation metric. An EC is considered to be correctly detected if its linear position, its head, and its type are all correctly determined. We report experimental results that show even using this more stringent measure, our EC detection system achieved performance that improved significantly over the state-of-the-art results.

The rest of the paper is organized as follows. In Section 2, we will describe how to represent ECs in a dependency structure in detail and present our approach to EC detection. In Section 3, we describe how linguistic information is encoded as features. In Section 4, we discuss our experimental setup and present our results. In Section 5, we describe related work. Section 6 concludes the paper.

2 Approach

In order to detect ECs anchored in a dependency tree, we first convert the phrase structure trees in the CTB into dependency trees. After the conversion, each word token in a dependency tree, including the ECs, will have one and only one head (or parent). We then train a classifier to predict the position and type of ECs in the dependency tree. Let W be a sequence of word tokens in a sentence, and T is syntactic parse tree for W, our task is to predict whether there is a tuple (h, t, e), such that h and t are word tokens in W, e is an EC, h is the head of e, and t immediately follows e. When EC detection is formulated as a classification task, each classification instance is thus a tuple (h, t). The input to our classifier is T, which can either be a phrase structure tree or a dependency tree. We choose to use a phrase structure tree because phrase structure parsers trained on the Chinese Treebank are readily available, and we also hypothesize that phrase structure trees have a richer hierarchical structure that can be exploited as features for EC detection.

2.1 Empty categories in the Chinese Treebank

According to the CTB bracketing guidelines (Xue and Xia, 2000), there are seven different types of ECs in the CTB. Below is a brief description of the empty categories:

1. ***pro***: small pro, used to represent dropped pronouns.

2. ***PRO***: big PRO, used to represent shared elements in control structures or elements that have generic references.
3. ***OP***: null operator, used to represent empty relative pronouns.
4. ***T***: trace left by movement such as topicalization and relativization.
5. ***RNR***: right node raising.
6. *: trace left by passivization and raising.
7. ***?***: missing elements of unknown category.

An example parse tree with ECs is shown in Figure 1. In the example, there are two ECs, an empty relative pronoun (*OP*) and a trace (*T*), a common syntactic pattern for relative clauses in the CTB.

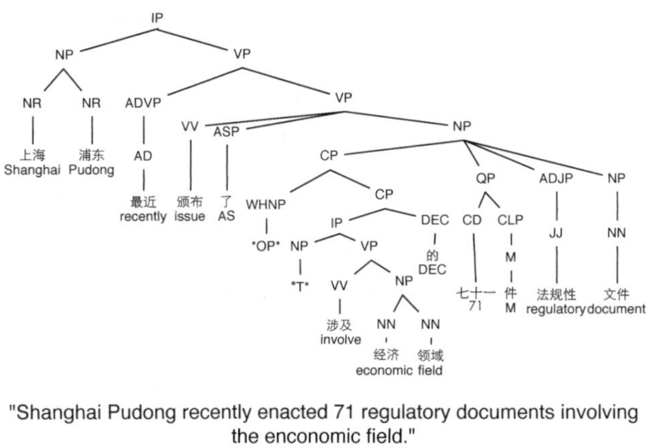

Figure 1: Empty categories in a phrase structure tree

2.2 Converting phrase structure to dependency structure

We convert the phrase structure parses in the CTB to dependency trees using the conversion tool that generated the Chinese data sets for the CoNLL 2009 Shared Task on multilingual dependency parsing and semantic role labeling (Hajič et al., 2009)[1]. While the Chinese data of CoNLL 2009 Shared Task does not include ECs, the tool has an option of preserving the ECs in the conversion process. As an example, the dependency tree in Figure 2 is converted from the phrase structure tree in Figure 1, with the ECs preserved.

In previous work EC detection has been formulated as a classification problem with the target of the classification being word tokens (Yang and Xue, 2010; Chung and Gildea, 2010), or constituents in a parse tree (Gabbard et al., 2006). When word tokens are used as the target of classification, the task is to determine whether there is an EC before each word token, and what type EC it is. One shortcoming with that representation is that more than one EC can precede the same word token, as is the case in the example in Figure 1, where both *OP* and *T* precede 涉及 ("involve"). In fact, (Yang and Xue, 2010) takes the last EC when there is a sequence of ECs and as a result, some ECs will never get the chance to be detected. Notice that this problem can be avoided in a dependency structure representation if we make the target of classification a tuple that consists of the following word token and the head of the EC. From Figure 2, it should be clear that while *OP* and *T* both precede the same word token 涉及 ("involve"), they have different heads, which are 的 (DE) and 涉及 respectively.

Dependency-based EC detection also has other nice properties. For ECs that are arguments of their verbal head, when they are resolved to some overt element, the dependency between the referent of the EC and its head will be naturally established. This can be viewed as an alternative to the approach adopted by Levy and Manning (2004), where phrase structure parses are augmented to recover non-local dependencies. Dependency structures are also easily decomposable into head/dependency pairs and this makes the evaluation more straightforward. Each classification instance can be evaluated independently of other parts of the dependency structure.

2.3 One pass vs two passes

With pairs of tokens (h, t) as the classification target, all possible pairs in a sentence will have to be considered and there will be a large number of (h, t) tuples that are not associated with an EC, leading to a highly imbalanced data set. One can conceive a two-pass scenario where we first make a binary decision of whether there is an empty category associated with the head in the first pass and then determine whether there is an EC associated with the tuple as well as the EC type in the second pass. The alternative is to have a one-pass model in which we

[1]The tool can be downloaded at http://www.cs.brandeis.edu/ clp/ctb/ctb.html.

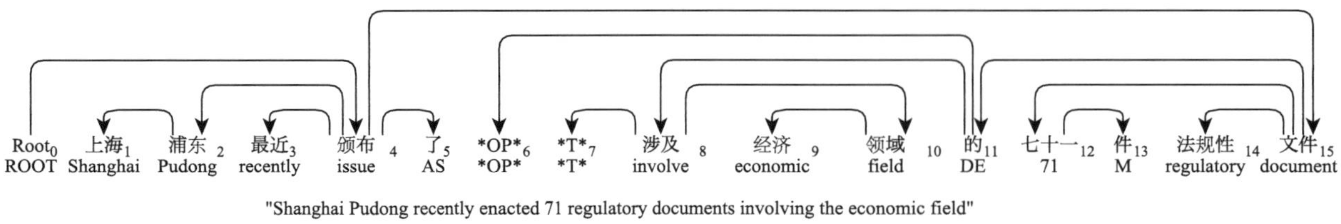

Figure 2: Empty categories in a dependency structure tree

add a NONE category indicating there is no EC associated with the tuple. With the seven EC types presented earlier in this section, this will be an eight-way classification problem. There are reasons for either model: the one-pass model is simpler but in the two-pass model we can bring different sources of information to bear on each sub-problem. Ultimately which model leads to better accuracy is an empirical question. We experimented with both models and it turned out that they led to very similar results. In this paper, we report results from the simpler one-pass model.

3 Features

We explored a wide range of features, all derived from the phrase structure parse tree (T). With each classification instance being a tuple (h, t), the "pivots" for these features are h the head, t the word token following the EC, and p, the word token preceding the EC. The features we tried fall into six broad groups that are all empirically confirmed to have made a positive contribution to our classification task. These are (i) horizontal features, (ii) vertical features, (iii) targeted grammatical constructions, (iv) head information, (v) transitivity features, and (vi) semantic role features. We obviously have looked at features used in previous work on Chinese EC detection, most notably (Yang and Xue, 2010), which has also adopted a classification-based approach, but because we frame our classification task very differently, we have to use very different features. However, there is a subset of features we used here that has at least a partial overlap with their features, and such features are clearly indicated with $*$.

3.1 Horizontal features

The first group of features we use can be described as horizontal features that exploit lexical context of the head (h), the word token following the EC (t), and the word token before the EC (p) . These include different combinations of h, t and p, as well as their parts-of-speech. They also include various linear distance features between h and t. Below is the full list of lexical features:

1. $*$The token string representation of h, t and p, as well as their part-of-speech tag (POS).
2. $*$The POS combination of h and t, the POS combination of t and p.
3. The normalized word distance between h and t, with the values of this feature being $same$, $immediately\ before$, $immediately\ after$, $near\ before$, and $near\ after$, and $other$.
4. The verb distance between h and t, defined as the number of verbs that occur between h and t.
5. The comma distance between h and t, defined as the number of commas that occur between h and t.

3.2 Vertical features

Vertical features are designed to exploit the hierarchical structure of the syntactic tree. Our hierarchical features are based on the following observations. An empty category is always located between its *left frontier* and *right frontier*, anchored by t and p. Given the lowest common ancestor A of p and t, the right frontier is the path from t to A and the left frontier is the path from the p to A. We also define a path feature from h to t, which constrains the distance between the EC and its head, just as it constrains the distance between a predicate and its argument in the semantic role labeling task (Gildea and Jurafsky, 2002). Given the lowest common ancestor A' of h and t, the path from h to t is the path from h to A' and from A' to t.

In Figure 3, assuming that t is 迅速 ("rapidly") and h is 崛起 ("take off"), the vertical features ex-

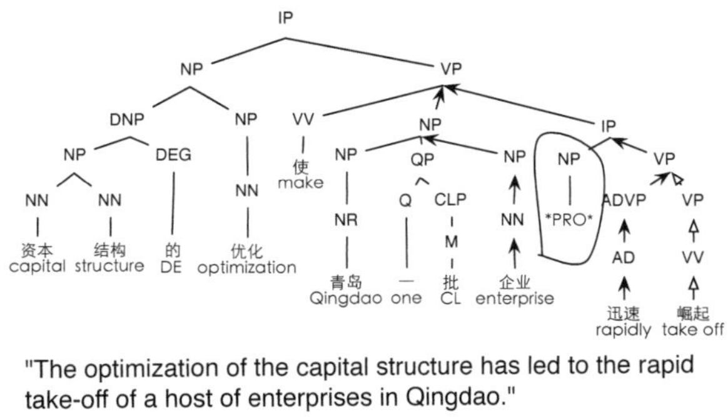

Figure 3: Empty category on the right frontier

tracted include:

1. The string representation of the right frontier, AD↑ADVP↑VP↑IP↑VP
2. The path from the head t to h, AD↑ADVP↑VP↓VP↓VV
3. The path from the head h to A, VV↑VP↑VP↑IP↑VP. Notice there is not always a path from h to A.

The vertical features are really a condensed representation of a certain syntactic configuration that helps to predict the presence or absence of an empty category as well as the empty category type. For example, the right frontier of **PRO** in Figure 3 AD↑ADVP↑VP↑IP↑VP represents a subjectless IP. Had there been an overt subject in the place of the **PRO**, the right frontier would have been AD↑ADVP↑VP↑IP. Therefore, the vertical features are discriminative features that can help detect the presence or absence of an empty category.

3.3 Targeted grammatical constructions

The third group of features target specific, linguistically motivated grammatical constructions. The majority of features in this group hinge on the immediate IP (roughly corresponds to S in the PTB) ancestor of t headed by h. These features are only invoked when t starts (or is on the left edge of) the immediate IP ancestor, and they are designed to capture the context in which the IP ancestor is located. This context can provide discriminative clues that may help identify the types of empty category. For example, both **pro**s and **PRO**s tend to occur in the subject position of an IP, but the larger context of the IP often determines the exact empty category type. In Figure 3, the IP that has a **PRO** subject is the complement of a verb in a canonical object-control construction. An IP can also be a sentential subject, the complement of a preposition or a localizer (also called postposition in the literature), or the complement in a CP (roughly SBAR in the PTB), etc. These different contexts tend to be associated with different types of empty categories. The full list of features that exploit these contexts include:

1. $*$Whether t starts an IP
2. $*$Whether t starts a subjectless IP
3. The left sisters of the immediate IP parent that t starts
4. The right sisters of the immediate IP parent that t starts
5. The string representation of the governing verb of the immediate IP parent that t starts
6. Whether the IP started by t is the complement of a localizer phrase
7. Whether the immediate IP parent that t starts is a sentential subject

3.4 Head information

Most ECs have a verb as its head, but when there is a coordination VP structure where more than one VP share an EC subject, only one such verb can be the head of this EC. The phrase structure to dependency structure conversion tool designates the first verb as the head of the coordinated VP and thus the head of the EC subject in the dependency structure. Other verbs have no chance of being the head. We use a VP head feature to capture this information. It is a binary feature indicating whether a verb can be a head.

3.5 Transitivity features

A transitivity lexicon has been extracted from the Chinese Treebank and it is used to determine the transitivity value of a word. A word can be $transitive$, $intransitive$, or $unknown$ if it is not a verb. Ditransitive verbs are small in number and are folded into transitive verbs. Transitivity features are defined on h and constrained by word distance: it is only used when h immediately precedes t. This feature category is intended to capture transitive verbs that are missing an object.

3.6 Semantic role features

There are apparent connections between semantic role labeling and EC detection. The task of semantic role labeling is typically defined as one of detecting and classifying arguments for verbal or nominal predicates, with more work done so far on verbal than nominal predicates. Although empty categories are annotated as arguments to verbal predicates in linguistic resources such as the English (Palmer et al., 2005) and Chinese (Xue and Palmer, 2009) Propbanks, they are often left out in semantic role labeling systems trained on these resources. This is because the best performing semantic role labeling systems rely on syntactic features extracted from automatic parses (Gildea and Palmer, 2002; Punyakanok et al., 2005) and the parsers that produce them do not generally reproduce empty categories. As a result, current semantic role labeling systems can only recover explicit arguments. However, assuming that all the explicit arguments to a predicate are detected and classified, one can infer the empty arguments of a predicate from its explicit arguments, given a list of *expected* arguments for the predicate. The list of expected arguments can be found in the "frame files" that are used to guide probank annotation. We defined a semantic role feature category on h when it is a verb and the value of this feature is the semantic role labels for the EC arguments. Like transitivity features, this feature category is also constrained by word distance. It is only used when h immediately precedes t.

To extract semantic role features, we retrained a Chinese semantic role labeling system on the Chinese Propbank. We divided the Chinese Propbank data into 10 different subsets, and automatically assigned semantic roles to each subset with a system trained on the other nine subsets. Using the frame files for the Chinese Propbank, we are able to infer the semantic roles for the missing arguments and use them as features.

4 Experimental Results

4.1 Experimental setup

Our EC detection models are trained and evaluated on a subset of the Chinese TreeBank 6.0. The training/development/test data split in our experiments is recommended in the CTB documentation. The CTB file IDs for training, development and testing are listed in Table 1. The development data is used for feature selection and tuning, and results are reported on the test set.

Train	Dev	Test
81-325, 400-454, 500-554 590-596, 600-885, 900	41-80	1-40 901-931

Table 1: Data set division.

As discussed in Section 2, the gold standard dependency structure parses are converted from the CTB parse trees, with the ECs preserved. From these gold standard parse trees, we extract triples of (e, h, t) where e is the EC type, h is (the position of) the head of the EC, and t is (the position of) the word token following the EC. During the training phrase, features are extracted from automatic phrase structure parses and paired with these triples. The automatic phrase structure parses are produced by the the Berkeley parser[2] with a 10-fold cross-validation, which each fold parsed using a model trained on the other nine folds. Measured by the ParsEval metric (Black et al., 1991), the parsing accuracy on the CTB test set stands at 83.63% (F-score), with a precision of 85.66% and a recall of 81.69%. We chose to train a Maximum Entropy classifier using the Mallet toolkit[3] (McCallum, 2002) to detect ECs.

4.2 Evaluation metric

We use standard metrics of precision, recall and F-measure in our evaluation. In a dependency structure representation, evaluation is very straightforward because individual arcs from the dependency tree can be easily decomposed. An EC is considered to be correctly detected if it is attached to the correct head h, correctly positioned relative to t, and correctly typed. This is a more stringent measure than metrics proposed in previous work, which evaluates EC detection based on its position and type without considering the head it is a dependent of.

4.3 Results

There are 1,838 total EC instances in the test set, and if we follow (Yang and Xue, 2010) and collapse all

[2] `http://code.google.com/p/berkeleyparser`
[3] `http://mallet.cs.umass.edu`

consecutive ECs before the same word token to one, we will end up with a total EC count of 1,352, and this is also the EC count used by (Cai et al., 2011) in their evaluation. On the dependency-based representation adopted here, after collapsing all consecutive ECs before the same word token AND attached to the same head to one, we end up with a total EC count of 1,765. The distribution of the ECs in the test set are presented in Table 2, with the EC count per type from (Yang and Xue, 2010) in parenthesis if it is different. The number of *OP*s, in particular, has increased dramatically from 134 to 527, and this is because a null relative pronoun (*OP*) immediately followed by a trace (*T*) in the subject position of a relative clause is a very common pattern in the Chinese Treebank, as illustrated in Figure 2. In (Yang and Xue, 2010), the *OP*-*T* sequences are collapsed into one, and only the *T*s are counted. That leads to the much smaller count of *OP*s.

type	count	type	count
pro	298 (290)	*PRO*	305 (299)
OP	527 (134)	*T*	584 (578)
*	19	*RNR*	32
?	0	total	(1352)/1765/(1838)

Table 2: EC distribution in the CTB test set

Our results are shown in Table 3. These results are achieved by using the full feature set presented in Section 3. The overall accuracy by F1-measure is 0.574 if we assume there can only be one EC associated with a given (h, t) tuple and hence the total EC count in the gold standard is 1,765, or 0.561 if we factor in all the EC instances and use the higher total count of 1,838, which lowers the recall. If instead we use the total EC count of 1,352 that was used in previous work (Yang and Xue, 2010; Cai et al., 2011), then the F1-measure is 0.660 because the lower total count greatly improves the recall. This is a significant improvement over the best previous result reported by Cai et al (2011), which is an F1 measure of 0.586 on the same test set but based on a less stringent metric of just comparing the EC position and type, without considering whether the EC is attached to the correct head.

There are several observations worth noting from these results. One is that our method performs particularly well on null relative pronouns (*OP*) and

class	correct	prec	rec	F1
pro	46	.397	.154	.222
PRO	162	.602	.531	.564
OP	344	.724	.653	.687
T	331	.673	.567	.615
*	0	0	0	0
RNR	20	.714	.625	.667
all	903	.653	.512 (.491) (.668)	.574 (.561) (.660)
CCG		.660	.545	.586

Table 3: EC detection results on the CTB test set and comparison with (Cai et al., 2011) [CCG]

traces (*T*), indicating that our features are effective in capturing information from relative clause constructions. This accounts for most of the gain compared with previous approaches. The *OP* category, in particular, benefits most from the dependency representation because it is collapsed to the immediately following *T* in previous approaches and does not even get a chance to be detected. On the other hand, our model did poorly on dropped pronouns (*pro*). One possible explanation is that *pro*s generally occupy subject positions in a sentence and is attached as an immediate child of an IP, which is the top-level structure of a sentence that an automatic parser tends to get wrong. Unlike *PRO*, it is not constrained to well-defined grammatical constructions such as subject- and object-control structures.

To evaluate the effectiveness of our features, we also did an ablation study on the contribution of different feature groups. The most effective features are the ones when taken out lead to the most drop in accuracy. As should be clear from Table 4, the most effective features are the horizontal features, followed by vertical structures. Features extracted from targeted grammatical constructions and features representing whether h is the head of a coordinated VP lead to modest improvement. Transitivity and semantic role features make virtually no difference at all. We believe it is premature to conclude that they are not useful. Possible explanations for their lack of effectiveness is that they are used in very limited context and the accuracy of the semantic role labeling system is not sufficient to make a difference.

class	correct	prec	rec	F1
all	903	.653	.512	.574 (.561)
-Horizontal	827	.627	.469	.536 (.524)
-Vertical	865	.652	.490	.559 (.547)
-Gr Cons	887	.646	.483	.565 (.552)
-V head	891	.651	.505	.569 (.556)
-Trans	899	.654	.509	.573 (.560)
-SRL	900	.657	.510	.574 (.561)

Table 4: Contribution of feature groups

5 Related Work

The work reported here follows a fruitful line of research on EC detection and resolution, mostly in English. Empty categories have initially been left behind in research on syntactic parsing (Collins, 1999; Charniak, 2001) for efficiency reasons, but more recent work has shown that EC detection can be effectively integrated into the parsing process (Schmid, 2006; Cai et al., 2011). In the meantime, both pre-processing and post-processing approaches have been explored in previous work as alternatives. Johnson (2002) has showed that empty categories can be added to the skeletal parses with reasonable accuracy with a simple pattern-matching algorithm in a postprocessing step. Dienes and Dubey (2003b; 2003a) achieved generally superior accuracy using a machine learning framework without having to refer to the syntactic structure in the skeletal parses. They described their approach as a pre-processing step for parsing because they only use as features morpho-syntactic clues (passives, gerunds and to-infinitives) that can be found in certain function words and part-of-speech tags. Even better results, however, were obtained by Campbell (2004) in a postprocessing step that makes use of rules inspired by work in theoretical linguistics. Gabbard et al (2006) reported further improvement largely by recasting the Campbell rules as features to seven different machine learning classifiers.

We adopted a machine-learning based postprocessing approach based on insights gained from prior work in English and on Chinese-specific considerations. All things being equal, we believe that a machine learning approach that can exploit partial information is more likely to succeed than deterministic rules that have to make reference to morpho-syntactic clues such as to-infinitives and gerunds that are largely non-existent in Chinese. Without these clues, we believe a preprocessing approach that does not take advantage of skeletal parses is unlikely to succeed either. The work we report here also builds on emerging work in Chinese EC detection. Yang and Xue (2010) reported work on detecting just the presence and absence of empty categories without further classifying them. Chung and Gildea (2010) reported work on just detecting just a small subset of the empty categories posited in the Chinese Tree-Bank. Kong and Zhou (2010) worked on Chinese zero anaphora resolution, where empty category detection is a subtask. More recently, Cai et al (2011) has successfully integrated EC detection into phrase-structure based syntactic parsing and reported state-of-the-art results in both English and Chinese.

6 Conclusions and Future Work

We described a novel approach to detecting empty categories (EC) represented in dependency trees and a new metric for measuring EC detection accuracy. The new metric takes into account not only the position and type of an EC, but also the head it is a dependent of in a dependency structure. We also proposed new features that are more suited for this new approach. Tested on a subset of the Chinese Treebank, we show that our system improved significantly over the best previously reported results despite using a more stringent evaluation metric, with most of the gain coming from an improved representation. In the future, we intend to work toward resolving ECs to their antecedents when EC detection can be done with adequate accuracy. We also plan to test our approach on the Penn (English) Treebank, with the first step being converting the Penn Treebank to a dependency representation with the ECs preserved.

Acknowledgments

This work is supported by the National Science Foundation via Grant No. 0910532 entitled "Richer Representations for Machine Translation". All views expressed in this paper are those of the authors and do not necessarily represent the view of the National Science Foundation.

References

E. Black, S. Abney, D. Flickinger, C. Gdaniec, R. Grishman, P. Harrison, D. Hindle, R. Ingria, F. Jelinek, J. Klavans, M. Liberman, M. Marcus, S. Roukos, B. Santorini, and T. Strzalkowski. 1991. A procedure for quantitively comparing the syntactic coverage of English grammars. In *Proceedings of the DARPA Speech and Natural Language Workshop*, pages 306–311.

Shu Cai, David Chiang, and Yoav Goldberg. 2011. Language-independent parsing with empty elements. In *Proceedings of the 49th Annual Meeting of the Association for Computational Linguistics: Human Language Technologies*, pages 212–216, Portland, Oregon, USA, June. Association for Computational Linguistics.

Richard Campbell. 2004. Using linguistic principles to recover empty categories. In *Proceedings of the 42nd Annual Meeting on Association For Computational Linguistics*.

E. Charniak. 2001. Immediate-head Parsing for Language Models. In *ACL-01*.

Tagyoung Chung and Daniel Gildea. 2010. Effects of empty categories on machine translation. In *Proceedings of the 2010 Conference on Empirical Methods in Natural Language Processing*, pages 636–645, Cambridge, MA.

Michael Collins. 1999. *Head-driven Statistical Models for Natural Language Parsing*. Ph.D. thesis, University of Pennsylvania.

Péter Dienes and Amit Dubey. 2003a. Antecendant Recovery: Experiments with a Trace Tagger. In *Proceedings of the Conference on Empirical Methods in Natural Language Processing* , Sapporo, Japan.

Péter Dienes and Amit Dubey. 2003b. Deep syntactic processing by combining shallow methods. In *Proceedings of the 41st Annual Meeting of the Association for Computational Linguistics*, Sapporo, Japan.

Ryan Gabbard, Seth Kulick, and Mitchell Marcus. 2006. Fully parsing the penn treebank. In *Proceedings of HLT-NAACL 2006*, pages 184–191, New York City.

D. Gildea and D. Jurafsky. 2002. Automatic labeling for semantic roles. *Computational Linguistics*, 28(3):245–288.

Dan Gildea and Martha Palmer. 2002. The Necessity of Parsing for Predicate Argument Recognition. In *Proceedings of the 40th Meeting of the Association for Computational Linguistics*, Philadelphia, PA.

Jan Hajič, Massimiliano Ciaramita, Richard Johansson, Daisuke Kawahara, Maria Antònia Martí, Lluís Màrquez, Adam Meyers, Joakim Nivre, Sebastian Padó, Jan Štěpánek, Pavel Straňák, Mihai Surdeanu, Nianwen Xue, and Yi Zhang. 2009. The CoNLL-2009 shared task: Syntactic and semantic dependencies in multiple languages. In *Proceedings of the 13th Conference on Computational Natural Language Learning (CoNLL-2009), June 4-5*, Boulder, Colorado, USA.

James C.T. Huang. 1984. On the distribution and reference of empty pronouns. *Linguistics Inquiry*, 15:531–574.

Mark Johnson. 2002. A simple pattern-matching algorithm for recovering empty nodes and their antecedents. In *Proceedings of the 40th Annual Meeting of the Association for Computational Linguistics*.

Fang Kong and Guodong Zhou. 2010. A Tree Kernel-based unified framework for Chinese zero anaphora resolution. In *Proceedings of the 2010 Conference on Empirical Methods in Natural Language Processing*, MIT, Massachusetts.

Roger Levy and Christopher Manning. 2004. Deep dependencies from context-free statistical parsers: correcting the surface dependency approximation. In *Proceedings of the ACL*.

M. Marcus, B. Santorini, and M. A. Marcinkiewicz. 1993. Building a Large Annotated Corpus of English: the Penn Treebank. *Computational Linguistics*.

Andrew Kachites McCallum. 2002. Mallet: A machine learning for language toolkit. http://mallet.cs.umass.edu.

Martha Palmer, Daniel Gildea, and Paul Kingsbury. 2005. The Proposition Bank: An annotated corpus of semantic roles. *Computational Linguistics*, 31(1):71–106.

Vasin Punyakanok, Dan Roth, and W. Yih. 2005. The Necessity of Syntactic Parsing for Semantic Role Labeling. In *Proceedings of IJCAI-2005*, pages 1124–1129, Edinburgh, UK.

Helmut Schmid. 2006. Trace prediction and recovery with unlexicalized PCFGs and slash features. In *Proc of ACL*.

Nianwen Xue and Martha Palmer. 2009. Adding semantic roles to the Chinese Treebank. *Natural Language Engineering*, 15(1):143–172.

Nianwen Xue and Fei Xia. 2000. The Bracketing Guidelines for Penn Chinese Treebank Project. Technical Report IRCS 00-08, University of Pennsylvania.

Nianwen Xue, Fei Xia, Fu dong Chiou, and Martha Palmer. 2005. The Penn Chinese TreeBank: Phrase Structure Annotation of a Large Corpus. *Natural Language Engineering*, 11(2):207–238.

Yaqin Yang and Nianwen Xue. 2010. Chasing the Ghost: Recovering Empty Categories in the Chinese Treebank. In *Proceedings of the 23rd International Conference on Computational Linguistics (COLING)*, Beijing, China.

Target Language Adaptation of Discriminative Transfer Parsers

Oscar Täckström*
SICS | Uppsala University
Sweden
oscar@sics.se

Ryan McDonald
Google
New York
ryanmcd@google.com

Joakim Nivre*
Uppsala University
Sweden
joakim.nivre@lingfil.uu.se

Abstract

We study multi-source transfer parsing for resource-poor target languages; specifically methods for target language adaptation of delexicalized discriminative graph-based dependency parsers. We first show how recent insights on selective parameter sharing, based on typological and language-family features, can be applied to a discriminative parser by carefully decomposing its model features. We then show how the parser can be relexicalized and adapted using unlabeled target language data and a learning method that can incorporate diverse knowledge sources through ambiguous labelings. In the latter scenario, we exploit two sources of knowledge: arc marginals derived from the base parser in a self-training algorithm, and arc predictions from multiple transfer parsers in an ensemble-training algorithm. Our final model outperforms the state of the art in multi-source transfer parsing on 15 out of 16 evaluated languages.

1 Introduction

Many languages still lack access to core NLP tools, such as part-of-speech taggers and syntactic parsers. This is largely due to the reliance on *fully supervised* learning methods, which require large quantities of manually annotated training data. Recently, methods for *cross-lingual transfer* have appeared as a promising avenue for overcoming this hurdle for both part-of-speech tagging (Yarowsky et al., 2001; Das and Petrov, 2011) and syntactic dependency parsing (Hwa et al., 2005; Zeman and Resnik, 2008; Ganchev et al., 2009; McDonald et al., 2011; Naseem et al., 2012). While these methods do not yet compete with fully supervised approaches, they can drastically outperform both *unsupervised* methods (Klein and Manning, 2004) and *weakly supervised* methods (Naseem et al., 2010; Berg-Kirkpatrick and Klein, 2010).

A promising approach to cross-lingual transfer of syntactic dependency parsers is to use multiple source languages and to tie model parameters across related languages. This idea was first explored for weakly supervised learning (Cohen and Smith, 2009; Snyder et al., 2009; Berg-Kirkpatrick and Klein, 2010) and recently by Naseem et al. (2012) for multi-source cross-lingual transfer. In particular, Naseem et al. showed that by *selectively sharing* parameters based on typological features of each language, substantial improvements can be achieved, compared to using a single set of parameters for all languages. However, these methods all employ generative models with strong independence assumptions and weak feature representations, which upper bounds their accuracy far below that of feature-rich discriminative parsers (McDonald et al., 2005; Nivre, 2008).

In this paper, we improve upon the state of the art in cross-lingual transfer of dependency parsers from multiple source languages by adapting feature-rich discriminatively trained parsers to a specific target language. First, in §4 we show how selective sharing of model parameters based on typological traits can be incorporated into a delexicalized discriminative graph-based parsing model. This requires a careful decomposition of features into language-generic and language-specific sets in order to tie specific target language parameters to their relevant source language counterparts. The resulting parser outperforms the method of Naseem et al. (2012) on 12 out of 16 evaluated languages. Second, in §5 we introduce a train-

* Work primarily carried out while at Google, NY.

ing method that can incorporate diverse knowledge sources through ambiguously predicted labelings of unlabeled target language data. This permits effective relexicalization and target language adaptation of the transfer parser. Here, we experiment with two different knowledge sources: arc sets, which are filtered by marginal probabilities from the cross-lingual transfer parser, are used in an *ambiguity-aware self-training* algorithm (§5.2); these arc sets are then combined with the predictions of a different transfer parser in an *ambiguity-aware ensemble-training* algorithm (§5.3). The resulting parser provides significant improvements over a strong baseline parser and achieves a 13% relative error reduction on average with respect to the best model of Naseem et al. (2012), outperforming it on 15 out of the 16 evaluated languages.

2 Multi-Source Delexicalized Transfer

The methods proposed in this paper fall into the *delexicalized transfer* approach to multilingual syntactic parsing (Zeman and Resnik, 2008; McDonald et al., 2011; Cohen et al., 2011; Søgaard, 2011). In contrast to *annotation projection* approaches (Yarowsky et al., 2001; Hwa et al., 2005; Ganchev et al., 2009; Spreyer and Kuhn, 2009), delexicalized transfer methods do not rely on any bitext. Instead, a parser is trained on annotations in a source language, relying solely on features that are available in both the source and the target language, such as "universal" part-of-speech tags (Zeman and Resnik, 2008; Naseem et al., 2010; Petrov et al., 2012), cross-lingual word clusters (Täckström et al., 2012) or type-level features derived from bilingual dictionaries (Durrett et al., 2012).[1] This parser is then directly used to parse the target language. For languages with similar typology, this method can be quite accurate, especially when compared to purely unsupervised methods. For instance, a parser trained on English with only part-of-speech features can correctly parse the Greek sentence in Figure 1, even without knowledge of the lexical items since the sequence of part-of-speech tags determines the syntactic structure almost unambiguously.

Learning with multiple languages has been shown to benefit unsupervised learning (Cohen and Smith,

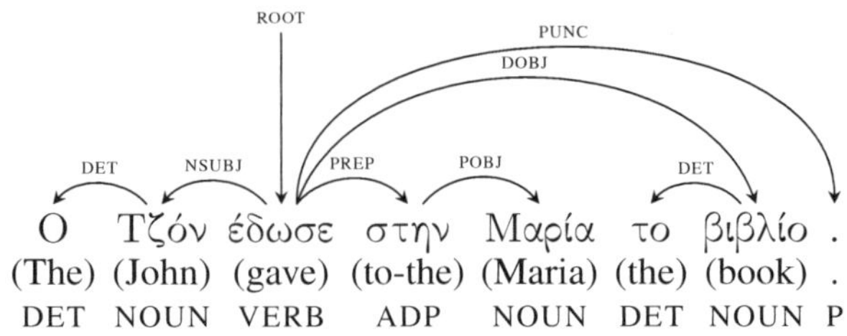

Figure 1: A Greek sentence which is correctly parsed by a delexicalized English parser, provided that part-of-speech tags are available in both the source and target language.

2009; Snyder et al., 2009; Berg-Kirkpatrick and Klein, 2010). Annotations in multiple languages can be combined in delexicalized transfer as well, as long as the parser features are available across the involved languages. This idea was explored by McDonald et al. (2011), who showed that target language accuracy can be improved by simply concatenating delexicalized treebanks in multiple languages. In similar work, Cohen et al. (2011) proposed a mixture model in which the parameters of a generative target language parser is expressed as a linear interpolation of source language parameters, whereas Søgaard (2011) showed that target side language models can be used to selectively subsample training sentences to improve accuracy. Recently, inspired by the phylogenetic prior of Berg-Kirkpatrick and Klein (2010), Søgaard and Wulff (2012) proposed — among other ideas — a typologically informed weighting heuristic for linearly interpolating source language parameters. However, this weighting did not provide significant improvements over uniform weighting.

The aforementioned approaches work well for transfer between similar languages. However, their assumptions cease to hold for typologically divergent languages; a target language can rarely be described as a linear combination of data or model parameters from a set of source languages, as languages tend to share varied typological traits; this critical insight is discussed further in §4. To account for this issue, Naseem et al. (2012) recently introduced a novel generative model of dependency parsing, in which the generative process is factored into separate steps for the *selection* of dependents and their *ordering*. The parameters used in the selection step are all language independent, capturing only head-dependent attachment preferences. In the ordering step, however, parameters are *selectively shared* between subsets of

[1]Note that Täckström et al. (2012) and Durrett et al. (2012) do require bitext or a bilingual dictionary. The same holds for most cross-lingual representations, e.g., Klementiev et al. (2012).

Feature	Description
81A	Order of Subject, Object and Verb
85A	Order of Adposition and Noun
86A	Order of Genitive and Noun
87A	Order of Adjective and Noun
88A	Order of Demonstrative and Noun
89A	Order of Numeral and Noun

Table 1: Typological features from WALS (Dryer and Haspelmath, 2011), proposed for selective sharing by Naseem et al. (2012). Feature 89A has the same value for all studied languages, while 88A differs only for Basque. These features are therefore subsequently excluded.

source languages based on typological features of the languages extracted from WALS — the World Atlas of Language Structures (Dryer and Haspelmath, 2011) — as shown in Table 1. In the transfer scenario, where no supervision is available in the target language, this parser achieves the hitherto best published results across a number of languages; in particular for target languages with a word order divergent from the source languages.

However, the generative model of Naseem et al. is quite impoverished. In the fully supervised setting, it obtains substantially lower accuracies compared to a standard arc-factored graph-based parser (McDonald et al., 2005). Averaged across 16 languages,[2] the generative model trained with full supervision on the target language obtains an accuracy of 67.1%. A comparable lexicalized discriminative arc-factored model (McDonald et al., 2005) obtains 84.1%. Even when delexicalized, this model reaches 78.9%. This gap in supervised accuracy holds for all 16 languages. Thus, while selective sharing is a powerful device for transferring parsers across languages, the underlying generative model used by Naseem et al. (2012) restricts its potential performance.

3 Basic Models and Experimental Setup

Inspired by the superiority of discriminative graph-based parsing in the supervised scenario, we investigate whether the insights of Naseem et al. (2012) on selective parameter sharing can be incorporated into such models in the transfer scenario. We first review the basic graph-based parser framework and the experimental setup that we will use throughout. We then delve into details on how to incorporate selective sharing in this model in §4. In §5, we show how learning with ambiguous labelings in this parser can be used for further target language adaptation, both through self-training and through ensemble-training.

[2]Based on results in Naseem et al. (2012), excluding English.

3.1 Discriminative Graph-Based Parser

Let x denote an input sentence and let $y \in \mathcal{Y}(x)$ denote a dependency tree, where $\mathcal{Y}(x)$ is the set of well-formed dependency trees spanning x. Henceforth, we restrict $\mathcal{Y}(x)$ to projective dependency trees, but all our methods are equally applicable in the non-projective case. Provided a vector of model parameters θ, the probability of a dependency tree $y \in \mathcal{Y}(x)$, conditioned on a sentence x, has the following form:

$$p_\theta(y \mid x) = \frac{\exp\left\{\theta^\top \Phi(x, y)\right\}}{\sum_{y' \in \mathcal{Y}(x)} \exp\left\{\theta^\top \Phi(x, y')\right\}} .$$

Without loss of generality, we restrict ourselves to first-order models, where the feature function $\Phi(x, y)$ factors over individual arcs (h, m) in y, such that

$$\Phi(x, y) = \sum_{(h,m) \in y} \phi(x, h, m) ,$$

where $h \in [0, |x|]$ and $m \in [1, |x|]$ are the indices of the head word and the dependent word of the arc; $h = 0$ represents a dummy ROOT token. The model parameters are estimated by maximizing the log-likelihood of the training data $\mathcal{D} = \{(x_i, y_i)\}_{i=1}^n$,

$$\mathcal{L}(\theta; \mathcal{D}) = \sum_{i=1}^{n} \log\, p_\theta(y_i \mid x_i) .$$

We use the standard gradient-based L-BFGS algorithm (Liu and Nocedal, 1989) to maximize the log-likelihood. Eisner's algorithm (Eisner, 1996) is used for inference of the Viterbi parse and arc-marginals.

3.2 Data Sets and Experimental Setup

To facilitate comparison with the state of the art, we use the same treebanks and experimental setup as Naseem et al. (2012). Notably, we use the mapping proposed by Naseem et al. (2010) to map from fine-grained treebank specific part-of-speech tags to coarse-grained "universal" tags, rather than the more recent mapping proposed by Petrov et al. (2012). For

Delexicalized MSTParser	Bare	Selectively shared
$\mathtt{d} \otimes \mathtt{l}$; $[\mathtt{d} \otimes \mathtt{l}] \otimes \mathtt{h.p}$; $[\mathtt{d} \otimes \mathtt{l}] \otimes \mathtt{m.p}$	$\mathtt{l}$	$\mathtt{d} \otimes \mathtt{w.81A} \otimes \mathbb{1}[\mathtt{h.p} = \mathtt{VERB} \wedge \mathtt{m.p} = \mathtt{NOUN}]$
$[\mathtt{d} \otimes \mathtt{l}] \otimes \mathtt{h.p} \otimes \mathtt{m.p}$	$[\mathtt{l}] \otimes \mathtt{h.p}$	$\mathtt{d} \otimes \mathtt{w.81A} \otimes \mathbb{1}[\mathtt{h.p} = \mathtt{VERB} \wedge \mathtt{m.p} = \mathtt{PRON}]$
$[\mathtt{d} \otimes \mathtt{l}] \otimes \mathtt{h.p} \otimes \mathtt{h_{+1}.p} \otimes \mathtt{m_{-1}.p} \otimes \mathtt{m.p}$	$[\mathtt{l}] \otimes \mathtt{m.p}$	$\mathtt{d} \otimes \mathtt{w.85A} \otimes \mathbb{1}[\mathtt{h.p} = \mathtt{ADP} \wedge \mathtt{m.p} = \mathtt{NOUN}]$
$[\mathtt{d} \otimes \mathtt{l}] \otimes \mathtt{h_{-1}.p} \otimes \mathtt{h.p} \otimes \mathtt{m_{-1}.p} \otimes \mathtt{m.p}$	$[\mathtt{l}] \otimes \mathtt{h.p} \otimes \mathtt{m.p}$	$\mathtt{d} \otimes \mathtt{w.85A} \otimes \mathbb{1}[\mathtt{h.p} = \mathtt{ADP} \wedge \mathtt{m.p} = \mathtt{PRON}]$
$[\mathtt{d} \otimes \mathtt{l}] \otimes \mathtt{h.p} \otimes \mathtt{h_{+1}.p} \otimes \mathtt{m.p} \otimes \mathtt{m_{+1}.p}$		$\mathtt{d} \otimes \mathtt{w.86A} \otimes \mathbb{1}[\mathtt{h.p} = \mathtt{NOUN} \wedge \mathtt{m.p} = \mathtt{NOUN}]$
$[\mathtt{d} \otimes \mathtt{l}] \otimes \mathtt{h_{-1}.p} \otimes \mathtt{h.p} \otimes \mathtt{m.p} \otimes \mathtt{m_{+1}.p}$		$\mathtt{d} \otimes \mathtt{w.87A} \otimes \mathbb{1}[\mathtt{h.p} = \mathtt{NOUN} \wedge \mathtt{m.p} = \mathtt{ADJ}]$
$\mathtt{h.p} \otimes \mathtt{between.p} \otimes \mathtt{m.p}$		

Figure 2: Arc-factored feature templates for graph-based parsing. Direction: $\mathtt{d} \in \{\mathtt{LEFT}, \mathtt{RIGHT}\}$; dependency length: $\mathtt{l} \in \{1, 2, 3, 4, 5+\}$; part of speech of head / dependent / words between head and dependent: $\mathtt{h.p}$ / $\mathtt{m.p}$ / $\mathtt{between.p} \in \{\mathtt{NOUN}, \mathtt{VERB}, \mathtt{ADJ}, \mathtt{ADV}, \mathtt{PRON}, \mathtt{DET}, \mathtt{ADP}, \mathtt{NUM}, \mathtt{CONJ}, \mathtt{PRT}, \mathtt{PUNC}, \mathtt{X}\}$; token to the left / right of $\mathtt{z}$: $\mathtt{z_{-1}}$ / $\mathtt{z_{+1}}$; WALS features: $\mathtt{w.X}$ for $\mathtt{X} = \mathtt{81A}, \mathtt{85A}, \mathtt{86A}, \mathtt{87A}$ (see Table 1). $[\cdot]$ denotes an optional template, e.g., $[\mathtt{d} \otimes \mathtt{l}] \otimes \mathtt{h.p} \otimes \mathtt{m.p}$ expands to templates $\mathtt{d} \otimes \mathtt{l} \otimes \mathtt{h.p} \otimes \mathtt{m.p}$ and $\mathtt{h.p} \otimes \mathtt{m.p}$, so that the template also falls back on its undirectional variant.

each target language evaluated, the treebanks of the remaining languages are used as *labeled* training data, while the target language treebank is used for testing only (in §5 a different portion of the target language treebank is additionally used as *unlabeled* training data). We refer the reader to Naseem et al. (2012) for detailed information on the different treebanks. Due to divergent treebank annotation guidelines, which makes fine-grained evaluation difficult, all results are evaluated in terms of unlabeled attachment score (UAS). In line with Naseem et al. (2012), we use gold part-of-speech tags and evaluate only on sentences of length 50 or less excluding punctuation.

3.3 Baseline Models

We compare our models to two multi-source baseline models. The first baseline, *NBG*, is the generative model with selective parameter sharing from Naseem et al. (2012).[3] This model is trained without target language data, but we investigate the use of such data in §5.4. The second baseline, *Delex*, is a delexicalized projective version of the well-known graph-based MSTParser (McDonald et al., 2005). The feature templates used by this model are shown to the left in Figure 2. Note that there is no selective sharing in this model.

The second and third columns of Table 2 show the unlabeled attachment scores of the baseline models for each target language. We see that *Delex* performs well on target languages that are related to the majority of the source languages. However, for languages that diverge from the Indo-European majority family, the selective sharing model, *NBG*, achieves substantially higher accuracies.

4 Feature-Based Selective Sharing

The results for the baseline models are not surprising considering the feature templates used by *Delex*. There are two fundamental issues with these features when used for direct transfer. First, all but one template include the arc direction. Second, some features are sensitive to local word order; e.g., $[\mathtt{d} \otimes \mathtt{l}] \otimes \mathtt{h.p} \otimes \mathtt{h_{+1}.p} \otimes \mathtt{m_{-1}.p} \otimes \mathtt{m.p}$, which models direction as well as word order in the local contexts of the head and the dependent. Such features do not transfer well across typologically different languages.

In order to verify that these issues are the cause of the poor performance of the *Delex* model, we remove all directional features and all features that model local word order from *Delex*. The feature templates of the resulting *Bare* model are shown in the center of Figure 2. These features only model selectional preferences and dependency length, analogously to the selection component of *NBG*. The performance of *Bare* is shown in the fourth column of Table 2. The removal of most of the features results in a performance drop on average. However, for languages outside of the Indo-European family, *Bare* is often more accurate, especially for Basque, Hungarian and Japanese, which supports our hypothesis.

4.1 Sharing Based on Typological Features

After removing all directional features, we now carefully reintroduce them. Inspired by Naseem et al.

[3] Model "D-,T_o" in Table 2 from Naseem et al. (2012).

		Graph-Based Models				
Lang.	NBG	Delex	Bare	Share	Similar	Family
ar	**57.2**	43.3	43.1	52.7	<u>52.7</u>	<u>52.7</u>
bg	**67.6**	64.5	56.1	65.4	62.4	65.4
ca	71.9	72.0	58.1	66.1	**80.2**	77.6
cs	43.9	40.5	43.1	42.5	**45.3**	43.5
de	54.0	57.0	49.3	55.2	58.1	**59.2**
el	61.9	63.2	57.7	62.9	59.9	**63.2**
es	62.3	66.9	52.6	59.3	**69.0**	67.1
eu	39.7	29.5	43.3	**46.8**	<u>**46.8**</u>	<u>**46.8**</u>
hu	56.9	56.2	60.5	**64.5**	<u>**64.5**</u>	<u>**64.5**</u>
it	68.0	70.8	55.7	63.5	**74.6**	72.5
ja	62.3	38.9	50.6	57.1	64.6	**65.9**
nl	56.2	**57.9**	51.6	55.0	51.8	56.8
pt	76.2	77.5	63.0	72.7	**78.4**	**78.4**
sv	52.0	61.4	55.9	58.8	48.8	**63.5**
tr	59.1	37.4	36.0	41.7	**59.5**	59.4
zh	**59.9**	45.1	47.9	54.8	<u>54.8</u>	<u>54.8</u>
avg	59.3	55.1	51.5	57.4	60.7	**62.0**

Table 2: Unlabeled attachment scores of the multi-source transfer models. Boldface numbers indicate the best result per language. Underlined numbers indicate languages whose group is not represented in the training data (these default to *Share* under *Similarity* and *Family*). *NBG* is the "D-,T_o" model in Table 2 from Naseem et al. (2012).

(2012), we make use of the typological features from WALS (Dryer and Haspelmath, 2011), listed in Table 1, to selectively share directional parameters between languages. As a natural first attempt at sharing parameters, one might consider forming the cross-product of all features of *Delex* with all WALS properties, similarly to a common domain adaptation technique (Daumé III, 2007; Finkel and Manning, 2009). However, this approach has two issues. First, it results in a huge number of features, making the model prone to overfitting. Second, and more critically, it ties together languages via features for which they are not typologically similar. Consider English and French, which are both prepositional and thus have the same value for WALS property 85A. These languages will end up sharing a parameter for the feature $[\texttt{d} \otimes \texttt{l}] \otimes \texttt{h.p} = \texttt{NOUN} \otimes \texttt{m.p} = \texttt{ADJ} \otimes \texttt{w.85A}$; yet they have the exact opposite direction of attachment preference when it comes to nouns and adjectives. This problem applies to any method for parameter mixing that treats all the parameters as equal.

Like Naseem et al. (2012), we instead share parameters more selectively. Our strategy is to use the relevant part-of-speech tags of the head and dependent to select which parameters to share, based on very basic linguistic knowledge. The resulting features are shown to the right in Figure 2. For example, there is a shared directional feature that models the order of Subject, Object and Verb by conjoining WALS feature 81A with the arc direction and an indicator feature that fires only if the head is a verb and the dependent is a noun. These features would not be very useful by themselves, so we combine them with the *Bare* features. The accuracy of the resulting *Share* model is shown in column five of Table 2. Although this model still performs worse than *NBG*, it is an improvement over the *Delex* baseline and actually outperforms the former on 5 out of the 16 languages.

4.2 Sharing Based on Language Groups

While *Share* models selectional preferences and arc directions for a subset of dependency relations, it does not capture the rich local word order information captured by *Delex*. We now consider two ways of selectively including such information based on language similarity. While more complex sharing could be explored (Berg-Kirkpatrick and Klein, 2010), we use a flat structure and consider two simple groupings of the source and target languages.

First, the *Similar* model consists of the features used by *Share* together with the features from *Delex* in Figure 2. The latter are conjoined with an indicator feature that fires only when the source and target languages share values for all the WALS features in Table 1. This is accomplished by adding the template

$$\texttt{f} \otimes [\texttt{w.81A} \otimes \texttt{w.85A} \otimes \texttt{w.86A} \otimes \texttt{w.87A} \otimes \texttt{w.88A}]$$

for each template f in *Delex*. This groups: 1) Catalan, Italian, Portuguese and Spanish; 2) Bulgarian, Czech and English; 3) Dutch, German and Greek; and 4) Japanese and Turkish. The remaining languages do not share all WALS properties with at least one source language and thus revert to *Share*, since they cannot exploit these grouped features.

Second, instead of grouping languages according to WALS, the *Family* model is based on a simple subdivision into Indo-European languages (Bulgarian, Catalan, Czech, Greek, English, Spanish, Italian,

Dutch, Portuguese, Swedish) and Altaic languages (Japanese, Turkish). This is accomplished with indicator features analogous to those used in *Similar*. The remaining languages are again treated as isolates and revert to *Similar*.

The results for these models are given in the last two columns of Table 2. We see that by adding these rich features back into the fold, but having them fire only for languages in the same group, we can significantly increase the performance — from 57.4% to 62.0% on average when considering *Family*. If we consider our original *Delex* baseline, we see an absolute improvement of 6.9% on average and a relative error reduction of 15%. Particular gains are seen for non-Indo-European languages; e.g., Japanese increases from 38.9% to 65.9%. Furthermore, *Family* achieves a 7% relative error reduction over the *NBG* baseline and outperforms it on 12 of the 16 languages. This shows that a discriminative graph-based parser can achieve higher accuracies compared to generative models when the features are carefully constructed.

5 Target Language Adaptation

While some higher-level linguistic properties of the target language have been incorporated through selective sharing, so far no features specific to the target language have been employed. Cohen et al. (2011) and Naseem et al. (2012) have shown that using expectation-maximization (EM) to this end can in some cases bring substantial accuracy gains. For discriminative models, self-training has been shown to be quite effective for adapting monolingual parsers to new domains (McClosky et al., 2006), as well as for *relexicalizing* delexicalized parsers using unlabeled target language data (Zeman and Resnik, 2008). Similarly Täckström (2012) used self-training to adapt a multi-source direct transfer named-entity recognizer (Täckström et al., 2012) to different target languages, "relexicalizing" the model with word cluster features. However, as discussed in §5.2, standard self-training is not optimal for target language adaptation.

5.1 Ambiguity-Aware Training

In this section, we propose a related training method: *ambiguity-aware training*. In this setting a discriminative probabilistic model is induced from automatically inferred *ambiguous labelings* over unlabeled target language data, in place of gold-standard dependency trees. The ambiguous labelings can combine multiple sources of evidence to guide the estimation or simply encode the underlying uncertainty from the base parser. This uncertainty is marginalized out during training. The structure of the output space, e.g., projectivity and single-headedness constraints, along with regularities in the feature space, can together guide the estimation, similar to what occurs with the expectation-maximization algorithm.

Core to this method is the idea of an *ambiguous labeling* $\tilde{\boldsymbol{y}}(x) \subseteq \mathcal{Y}(x)$, which encodes a set of possible dependency trees for an input sentence x. In subsequent sections we describe how to define such labelings. Critically, $\tilde{\boldsymbol{y}}(x)$ should be large enough to capture the correct labeling, but on the other hand small enough to provide concrete guidance for model estimation. Ideally, $\tilde{\boldsymbol{y}}(x)$ will capture heterogenous knowledge that can aid the parser in target language adaptation. In a first-order arc-factored model, we define $\tilde{\boldsymbol{y}}(x)$ in terms of a collection of *ambiguous arc sets* $\mathcal{A}(x) = \{\mathcal{A}(x,m)\}_{m=1}^{|x|}$, where $\mathcal{A}(x,m)$ denotes the set of ambiguously specified heads for the mth token in x. Then, $\tilde{\boldsymbol{y}}(x)$ is defined as the set of all projective dependency trees spanning x that can be assembled from the arcs in $\mathcal{A}(x)$.

Methods for learning with ambiguous labelings have previously been proposed in the context of multi-class classification (Jin and Ghahramani, 2002), sequence-labeling (Dredze et al., 2009), log-linear LFG parsing (Riezler et al., 2002), as well as for discriminative reranking of generative constituency parsers (Charniak and Johnson, 2005). In contrast to Dredze et al., who allow for weights to be assigned to partial labels, we assume that the ambiguous arcs are weighted uniformly. For target language adaptation, these weights would typically be derived from unreliable sources and we do not want to train the model to simply mimic their beliefs. Furthermore, with this assumption, learning is simply achieved by maximizing the *marginal* log-likelihood of the ambiguous training set $\widetilde{\mathcal{D}} = \{(x_i, \tilde{\boldsymbol{y}}(x_i))\}_{i=1}^{n}$,

$$\mathcal{L}(\theta; \widetilde{\mathcal{D}}) = \sum_{i=1}^{n} \log \left\{ \sum_{y \in \tilde{\boldsymbol{y}}(x_i)} p_\theta(y \mid x_i) \right\} - \lambda \left\| \theta \right\|_2^2 .$$

In maximizing the marginal log-likelihood, the model is free to distribute probability mass among the trees in the ambiguous labeling to its liking, as long as the marginal log-likelihood improves. The same objective function is used by Riezler et al. (2002) and Charniak and Johnson (2005). A key difference is that in these works, the ambiguity is constrained through a supervised signal, while we use ambiguity as a way to achieve self-training, using the base-parser itself, or some other potentially noisy knowledge source as the sole constraints. Note that we have introduced an ℓ_2-regularizer, weighted by λ. This is important as we are now training *lexicalized* target language models which can easily overfit. In all experiments, we optimize parameters with L-BFGS. Note also that the marginal likelihood is non-concave, so that we are only guaranteed to find a local maximum.

5.2 Ambiguity-Aware Self-Training

In standard self-training — hereafter referred to as *Viterbi self-training* — a base parser is used to label each unlabeled sentence with its most probable parse tree to create a self-labeled data set, which is subsequently used to train a supervised parser. There are two reasons why this simple approach may work. First, if the base parser's errors are not too systematic and if the self-training model is not too expressive, self-training can reduce the variance on the new domain. Second, self-training allows for features in the new domain with low support — or no support in the case of lexicalized features — in the base parser to be "filled in" by exploiting correlations in the feature representation. However, a potential pitfall of this approach is that the self-trained parser is encouraged to blindly mimic the base parser, which leads to error reinforcement. This may be particularly problematic when relexicalizing a transfer parser, since the lexical features provide the parser with increased power and thereby an increased risk of overfitting to the noise. To overcome this potential problem, we propose an *ambiguity-aware self-training* (AAST) method that is able to take the noise of the base parser into account.

We use the arc-marginals of the base parser to construct the ambiguous labeling $\tilde{\boldsymbol{y}}(x)$ for a sentence x. For each token $m \in [1, |x|]$, we first sort the set of arcs in which m is the dependent, $\{(h, m)\}_{h=0}^{|x|}$, by the marginal probabilities of the arcs:

$$p_\theta(h, m \mid x) = \sum_{\{y \in \mathcal{Y}(x) \,|\, (h,m) \in y\}} p_\theta(y \mid x)$$

We next construct the ambiguous arc set $\mathcal{A}(x, m)$ by adding arcs (h, m) in order of decreasing probability, until their cumulative probability exceeds σ, i.e. until

$$\sum_{(h,m) \in \mathcal{A}(x,m)} p_\theta(h, m \mid x) \geq \sigma .$$

Lower values of σ result in more aggressive pruning, with $\sigma = 0$ corresponding to including no arc and $\sigma = 1$ corresponding to including all arcs. We always add the highest scoring tree $\hat{y}$ to $\tilde{\boldsymbol{y}}(x)$ to ensure that it contains at least one complete projective tree.

Figure 3 outlines an example of how (and why) AAST works. In the Greek example, the genitive phrase Η παραμονή σκαφών (*the stay of vessels*) is incorrectly analyzed as a flat noun phrase. This is not surprising given that the base parser simply observes this phrase as DET NOUN NOUN. However, looking at the arc marginals we can see that the correct analysis is available during AAST, although the actual marginal probabilities are quite misleading. Furthermore, the genitive noun σκαφών also appears in other less ambiguous contexts, where the base parser correctly predicts it to modify a noun and not a verb. This allows the training process to add weight to the corresponding lexical feature pairing σκαφών with a noun head and away from the feature pairing it with a verb. The resulting parser correctly predicts the genitive construction.

5.3 Ambiguity-Aware Ensemble-Training

While ambiguous labelings can be used as a means to improve self-training, any information that can be expressed as hard arc-factored constraints can be incorporated, including linguistic expert knowledge and annotation projected via bitext. Here we explore another natural source of information: the predictions of other transfer parsers. It is well known that combining several diverse predictions in an ensemble often leads to improved predictions. However, in most ensemble methods there is typically no learning involved once the base learners have been trained (Sagae and Lavie, 2006). An exception is the method of Sagae and Tsujii (2007), who combine the outputs of many parsers on unlabeled data to train a parser for a new domain. However, in that work the learner is not exposed to the underlying ambiguity of the base parsers; it is only given the Viterbi parse of the combination system as the gold standard. In contrast,

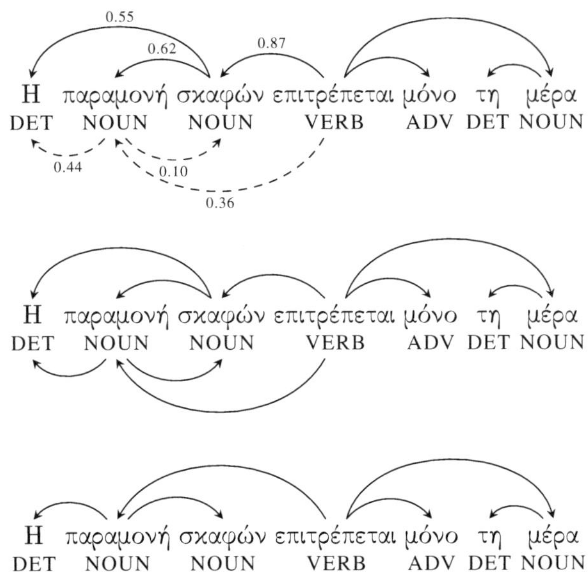

Figure 3: An example of ambiguity-aware self-training (AAST) on a sentence from the Greek self-training data. The sentence roughly translates to *The stay of vessels is permitted only for the day*. **Top:** Arcs from the base model's Viterbi parse are shown above the sentence. When only the part-of-speech tags are observed, the parser tends to treat everything to the left of the verb as a head-final noun phrase. The dashed arcs below the sentence are the arcs for the true genitive construction *stay of vessels*. These arcs and the corresponding incorrect arcs in the Viterbi parse are marked with their marginal probabilities. **Middle:** The ambiguous labeling $\tilde{\boldsymbol{y}}(x)$, which is used as supervision in AAST. Additional non-Viterbi arcs are present in $\tilde{\boldsymbol{y}}(x)$; for clarity, these are not shown. When learning with AAST, probability mass will be pushed towards any tree consistent with $\tilde{\boldsymbol{y}}(x)$. Marginal probabilities are ignored at this stage, so that all arcs in $\tilde{\boldsymbol{y}}(x)$ are treated as equals. **Bottom:** The Viterbi parse of the AAST model, which has selected the correct arcs from $\tilde{\boldsymbol{y}}(x)$.

we propose an *ambiguity-aware ensemble-training* (AAET) method that treats the union of the ensemble predictions for a sentence x as an ambiguous labeling $\tilde{\boldsymbol{y}}(x)$. An additional advantage of this approach is that the ensemble is compiled into a single model and therefore does not require multiple models to be stored and used at runtime.

It is straightforward to construct $\tilde{\boldsymbol{y}}(x)$ from multiple parsers. Let $\mathcal{A}_k(x, m)$ be the set of arcs for the mth token in x according to the kth parser in the ensemble. When arc-marginals are used to construct the ambiguity set, $|\mathcal{A}_k(x, m)| \geq 1$, but when the Viterbi-parse is used, $\mathcal{A}_k(x, m)$ is a singleton. We next form $\mathcal{A}(x, m) = \bigcup_k \mathcal{A}_k(x, m)$ as the ensemble arc ambiguity set from which $\tilde{\boldsymbol{y}}(x)$ is assembled. In this study, we combine the arc sets of two base parsers: first, the arc-marginal ambiguity set of the base parser (§5.2); and second, the Viterbi arc set from the *NBG* parser of Naseem et al. (2012) in Table 2.[4] Thus, the latter will have singleton arc ambiguity sets, but when combined with the arc-marginal ambiguity sets of our base parser, the result will encode uncertainty derived from both parsers.

5.4 Adaptation Experiments

We now study the different approaches to target language adaptation empirically. As in Naseem et al. (2012), we use the CoNLL training sets, stripped of all dependency information, as the unlabeled target language data in our experiments. We use the *Family* model as the base parser, which is used to label the unlabeled target data with the Viterbi parses as well as with the ambiguous labelings. The final model is then trained on this data using standard lexicalized features (McDonald et al., 2005). Since labeled training data is unavailable in the target language, we cannot tune any hyper-parameters and simply set $\lambda = 1$ and $\sigma = 0.95$ throughout. Although the latter may suggest that $\tilde{\boldsymbol{y}}(x)$ contains a high degree of ambiguity, in reality, the marginal distributions of the base model have low entropy and after filtering with $\sigma = 0.95$, the average number of potential heads per dependent ranges from 1.4 to 3.2, depending on the target language.

The ambiguity-aware training methods, that is ambiguity-aware self-training *(AAST)* and ambiguity-aware ensemble-training *(AAET)*, are compared to three baseline systems. First, *NBG+EM* is the generative model of Naseem et al. (2012) trained with expectation-maximization on additional unlabeled target language text. Second, *Family* is the best discriminative model from the previous section. Third, *Viterbi* is the basic Viterbi self-training model. The results of each of these models are shown in Table 3.

There are a number of things that can be observed. First, *Viterbi* self-training helps slightly on average, but the gains are not consistent and there are even drops in accuracy for some languages. Second, *AAST* outperforms the *Viterbi* variant on all languages and

[4]We do not have access to the marginals of *NBG*.

Lang.	NBG+EM	Family	Target Adaptation		
			Viterbi	AAST	AAET
ar	**59.3**	52.7	52.6	53.5	58.7
bg	67.0	65.4	66.4	67.9	**73.0**
ca	71.7	77.6	78.0	**79.9**	76.1
cs	44.3	43.5	43.6	44.4	**48.3**
de	54.1	59.2	59.7	**62.5**	61.5
el	67.9	63.2	64.5	65.5	**69.6**
es	62.0	67.1	68.2	**68.5**	66.9
eu	47.8	46.8	47.5	48.6	**49.4**
hu	58.6	64.5	64.6	65.6	**67.5**
it	65.6	72.5	71.6	72.4	**73.4**
ja	64.1	65.9	65.7	68.8	**72.0**
nl	56.6	56.8	57.9	58.1	**60.2**
pt	75.8	78.4	79.9	**80.7**	79.9
sv	61.7	63.5	63.4	**65.5**	**65.5**
tr	59.4	59.4	59.5	64.1	**64.2**
zh	51.0	54.8	54.8	57.9	**60.7**
avg	60.4	62.0	62.4	64.0	**65.4**

Table 3: Target language adaptation using unlabeled target data. *AAST*: ambiguity-aware self-training. *AAET*: ambiguity-aware ensemble-training. Boldface numbers indicate the best result per language. Underlined numbers indicate the best result, excluding *AAET*. *NBG+EM* is the "D+,T_o" model from Naseem et al. (2012).

nearly always improves on the base parser, although it sees a slight drop for Italian. *AAST* improves the accuracy over the base model by 2% absolute on average and by as much as 5% absolute for Turkish. Comparing this model to the *NBG+EM* baseline, we observe an improvement by 3.6% absolute, outperforming it on 14 of the 16 languages. Furthermore, ambiguity-aware self-training appears to help more than expectation-maximization for generative (unlexicalized) models. Naseem et al. observed an increase from 59.3% to 60.4% on average by adding unlabeled target language data and the gains were not consistent across languages. *AAST*, on the other hand, achieves consistent gains, rising from 62.0% to 64.0% on average. Third, as shown in the rightmost column of Table 3, ambiguity-aware ensemble-training is indeed a successful strategy; *AAET* outperforms the previous best self-trained model on 13 and *NB&G+EM* on 15 out of 16 languages. The relative error reduction with respect to the base *Family* model is 9% on average, while the average reduction with respect to *NBG+EM* is 13%.

Before concluding, two additional points are worth making. First, further gains may potentially be achievable with feature-rich discriminative models. While the best generative transfer model of Naseem et al. (2012) approaches its upper-bounding supervised accuracy (60.4% vs. 67.1%), our relaxed self-training model is still far below its supervised counterpart (64.0% vs. 84.1%). One promising statistic along these lines is that the oracle accuracy for the ambiguous labelings of *AAST* is 75.7%, averaged across languages, which suggests that other training algorithms, priors or constraints could improve the accuracy substantially. Second, relexicalization is a key component of self-training. If we use delexicalized features during self-training, we only observe a small average improvement from 62.0% to 62.1%.

6 Conclusions

We contributed to the understanding of multi-source syntactic transfer in several complementary ways. First, we showed how selective parameter sharing, based on typological features and language family membership, can be incorporated in a discriminative graph-based model of dependency parsing. We then showed how ambiguous labelings can be used to integrate heterogenous knowledge sources in parser training. Two instantiations of this framework were explored. First, an ambiguity-aware self-training method that can be used to effectively relexicalize and adapt a delexicalized transfer parser using unlabeled target language data. Second, an ambiguity-aware ensemble-training method, in which predictions from different parsers can be incorporated and further adapted. On average, our best model provides a relative error reduction of 13% over the state-of-the-art model of Naseem et al. (2012), outperforming it on 15 out of 16 evaluated languages.

Acknowledgments We thank Alexander Rush for help with the hypergraph framework used for inference. Tahira Naseem kindly provided us with her data sets and the predictions of her systems. This work benefited from many discussions with Yoav Goldberg and members of the Google parsing team. We finally thank the three anonymous reviewers for their valuable feedback. The work of the first author was partly funded by the Swedish National Graduate School of Language Technology (GSLT).

References

Taylor Berg-Kirkpatrick and Dan Klein. 2010. Phylogenetic grammar induction. In *Proceedings of ACL*.

Eugene Charniak and Mark Johnson. 2005. Coarse-to-fine n-best parsing and maxent discriminative reranking. In *Proceedings of ACL*.

Shay B. Cohen and Noah A. Smith. 2009. Shared logistic normal distributions for soft parameter tying in unsupervised grammar induction. In *Proceedings of NAACL*.

Shay B. Cohen, Dipanjan Das, and Noah A. Smith. 2011. Unsupervised structure prediction with non-parallel multilingual guidance. In *Proceedings of EMNLP*.

Dipanjan Das and Slav Petrov. 2011. Unsupervised part-of-speech tagging with bilingual graph-based projections. In *Proceedings of ACL-HLT*.

Hal Daumé III. 2007. Frustratingly easy domain adaptation. In *Proceedings of ACL*.

Mark Dredze, Partha Pratim Talukdar, and Koby Crammer. 2009. Sequence learning from data with multiple labels. In *Proceedings of the ECML/PKDD Workshop on Learning from Multi-Label Data*.

Matthew S. Dryer and Martin Haspelmath, editors. 2011. *The World Atlas of Language Structures Online*. Munich: Max Planck Digital Library. http://wals.info/.

Greg Durrett, Adam Pauls, and Dan Klein. 2012. Syntactic transfer using a bilingual lexicon. In *Proceedings of EMNLP-CoNLL*.

Jason Eisner. 1996. Three new probabilistic models for dependency parsing: an exploration. In *Proceedings of COLING*.

Jenny Rose Finkel and Christopher D. Manning. 2009. Hierarchical Bayesian domain adaptation. In *Proceedings of HLT-NAACL*.

Kuzman Ganchev, Jennifer Gillenwater, and Ben Taskar. 2009. Dependency grammar induction via bitext projection constraints. In *Proceedings of ACL-IJCNLP*.

Rebecca Hwa, Philip Resnik, Amy Weinberg, Clara Cabezas, and Okan Kolak. 2005. Bootstrapping parsers via syntactic projection across parallel texts. *Natural Language Engineering*, 11(03):311–325.

Rong Jin and Zoubin Ghahramani. 2002. Learning with multiple labels. In *Proceedings of NIPS*.

Dan Klein and Chris D. Manning. 2004. Corpus-based induction of syntactic structure: models of dependency and constituency. In *Proceedings of ACL*.

Alexandre Klementiev, Ivan Titov, and Binod Bhattarai. 2012. Inducing crosslingual distributed representations of words. In *Proceedings of COLING*.

Dong C. Liu and Jorge Nocedal. 1989. On the limited memory BFGS method for large scale optimization. *Mathematical Programming*, 45.

David McClosky, Eugene Charniak, and Mark Johnson. 2006. Reranking and self-training for parser adaptation. In *Proceedings of ACL*.

Ryan McDonald, Koby Crammer, and Fernando Pereira. 2005. Online large-margin training of dependency parsers. In *Proceedings of ACL*.

Ryan McDonald, Slav Petrov, and Keith Hall. 2011. Multi-source transfer of delexicalized dependency parsers. In *Proceedings of EMNLP*.

Tahira Naseem, Harr Chen, Regina Barzilay, and Mark Johnson. 2010. Using universal linguistic knowledge to guide grammar induction. In *Proceedings of EMNLP*.

Tahira Naseem, Regina Barzilay, and Amir Globerson. 2012. Selective sharing for multilingual dependency parsing. In *Proceedings of ACL*.

Joakim Nivre. 2008. Algorithms for deterministic incremental dependency parsing. *Computational Linguistics*, 34(4):513–553.

Slav Petrov, Dipanjan Das, and Ryan McDonald. 2012. A universal part-of-speech tagset. In *Proceedings of LREC*.

Stefan Riezler, Tracy H. King, Ronald M. Kaplan, Richard Crouch, John T. Maxwell, III, and Mark Johnson. 2002. Parsing the Wall Street Journal using a lexical-functional grammar and discriminative estimation techniques. In *Proceedings of ACL*.

Kenji Sagae and Alon Lavie. 2006. Parser combination by reparsing. In *Proceedings of NAACL*.

Kenji Sagae and Jun'ichi Tsujii. 2007. Dependency parsing and domain adaptation with LR models and parser ensembles. In *Proceedings of EMNLP-CoNLL*.

Benjamin Snyder, Tahira Naseem, Jacob Eisenstein, and Regina Barzilay. 2009. Adding more languages improves unsupervised multilingual part-of-speech tagging: A Bayesian non-parametric approach. In *Proceedings of NAACL*.

Anders Søgaard and Julie Wulff. 2012. An empirical study of non-lexical extensions to delexicalized transfer. In *Proceedings of COLING*.

Anders Søgaard. 2011. Data point selection for cross-language adaptation of dependency parsers. In *Proceedings of ACL*.

Kathrin Spreyer and Jonas Kuhn. 2009. Data-driven dependency parsing of new languages using incomplete and noisy training data. In *Proceedings of CONLL*.

Oscar Täckström, Ryan McDonald, and Jakob Uszkoreit. 2012. Cross-lingual word clusters for direct transfer of linguistic structure. In *Proceedings of NAACL-HLT*.

Oscar Täckström. 2012. Nudging the envelope of direct transfer methods for multilingual named entity recognition. In *Proceedings of the NAACL-HLT 2012 Workshop on Inducing Linguistic Structure (WILS 2012)*.

David Yarowsky, Grace Ngai, and Richard Wicentowski. 2001. Inducing multilingual text analysis tools via robust projection across aligned corpora. In *Proceedings of HLT*.

Daniel Zeman and Philip Resnik. 2008. Cross-language parser adaptation between related languages. In *IJCNLP Workshop: NLP for Less Privileged Languages*.

Emergence of Gricean Maxims from Multi-Agent Decision Theory

Adam Vogel, Max Bodoia, Christopher Potts, and **Dan Jurafsky**
Stanford University
Stanford, CA, USA
{acvogel,mbodoia,cgpotts,jurafsky}@stanford.edu

Abstract

Grice characterized communication in terms of the *cooperative principle*, which enjoins speakers to make only contributions that serve the evolving conversational goals. We show that the cooperative principle and the associated maxims of relevance, quality, and quantity emerge from multi-agent decision theory. We utilize the Decentralized Partially Observable Markov Decision Process (Dec-POMDP) model of multi-agent decision making which relies only on basic definitions of rationality and the ability of agents to reason about each other's beliefs in maximizing joint utility. Our model uses cognitively-inspired heuristics to simplify the otherwise intractable task of reasoning jointly about actions, the environment, and the nested beliefs of other actors. Our experiments on a cooperative language task show that reasoning about others' belief states, and the resulting emergent Gricean communicative behavior, leads to significantly improved task performance.

1 Introduction

Grice (1975) famously characterized communication among rational agents in terms of an overarching *cooperative principle* and a set of more specific maxims, which enjoin speakers to make contributions that are truthful, informative, relevant, clear, and concise. Since then, there have been many attempts to derive the maxims (or perhaps just their effects) from more basic cognitive principles concerning how people make decisions, formulate plans, and collaborate to achieve goals. This research traces to early work by Lewis (1969) on signaling systems. It has recently been the subject of extensive theoretical discussion (Clark, 1996; Merin, 1997; Blutner, 1998; Parikh, 2001; Beaver, 2002; van Rooy, 2003; Benz et al., 2005; Franke, 2009) and has been tested experimentally using one-step games in which the speaker produces a message and the hearer ventures a guess as to its intended referent (Rosenberg and Cohen, 1964; Dale and Reiter, 1995; Golland et al., 2010; Stiller et al., 2011; Frank and Goodman, 2012; Krahmer and van Deemter, 2012; Degen and Franke, 2012; Rohde et al., 2012).

To date, however, these theoretical models and experiments have not been extended to multi-step interactions extending over time and involving both language and action together, which leaves this work relatively disconnected from research on planning and goal-orientation in artificial agents (Perrault and Allen, 1980; Allen, 1991; Grosz and Sidner, 1986; Bratman, 1987; Hobbs et al., 1993; Allen et al., 2007; DeVault et al., 2005; Stone et al., 2007; DeVault, 2008). We attribute this in large part to the complexity of Gricean reasoning itself, which requires agents to model each other's belief states. Tracking these as they evolve over time in response to experiences is extremely demanding. Our approach complements slot-filling dialog systems, where the focus is on managing speech recognition uncertainty (Young et al., 2010; Thomson and Young, 2010).

However, recent years have seen significant advances in multi-agent decision-theoretic models and their efficient implementation. With the current paper, we seek to show that the Decentralized Partially Observable Markov Decision Process (Dec-POMDP) provides a robust, flexible foundation for implementing agents that communicate in a Gricean manner. Dec-POMDPs are multi-agent, partially-observable models in which agents maintain belief distributions over the underlying, hidden world state, including the beliefs of the other players, and speech actions change those beliefs. In this setting, informative, relevant communication emerges as the best way to maximize joint utility.

The complexity of pragmatic reasoning is still forbidding, though. Correspondingly, optimal decision making in Dec-POMDPs is NEXP complete (Bernstein et al., 2002). To manage this issue, we introduce several cognitively-plausible approximations which allow us to simplify the Dec-POMDP to a single-agent POMDP, for which relatively efficient solvers exist (Spaan and Vlassis, 2005). We demonstrate our algorithms on a variation of the Cards task, a partially-observable collaborative search problem (Potts, 2012). Spatial language comprises the bulk of communication in the Cards task, and we discuss a model of spatial semantics in Section 3. Using this task and a model of the meaning of spatial language, we next discuss two agents that play the game: *ListenerBot* (Section 4) makes decisions using a single-agent POMDP that does not take into account the beliefs or actions of its partner, whereas *DialogBot* (Section 5) maintains a model of its partner's beliefs. As a result of the cooperative structure of the underlying model and the effects of communication within it, DialogBot's contributions are relevant, truthful, and informative, which leads to significantly improved task performance.

2 The Cards Task and Corpus

The Cards corpus consists of 1,266 transcripts[1] from an online, two-person collaborative game in which two players explore a maze-like environment, communicating with each other via a text chat window (Figure 1). A deck of playing cards has been distributed randomly around the environment, and the players' task is to find six consecutive cards of the same suit. Our implemented agents solve a simplified version of this task in which the two agents

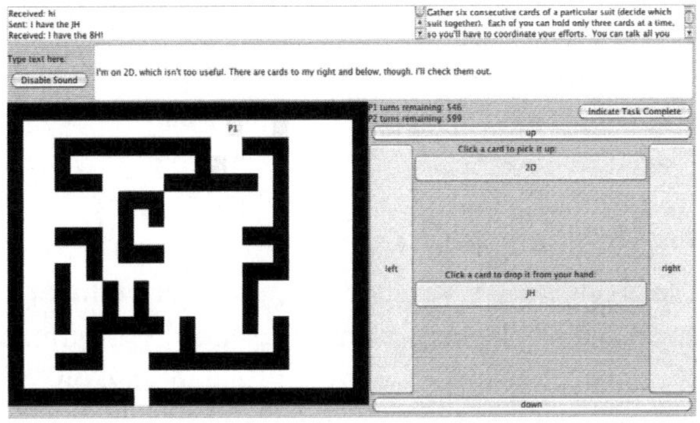

Figure 1: The Cards corpus gameboard. Player 1's location is marked "P1". The nearby yellow boxes mark card locations. The dialogue history and chat window are at the top. This board, the one we use throughout, consists of 231 open grid squares.

must both end up co-located with a single card, the Ace of Spades (AS). This is much simpler than the six-card version from the human–human corpus, but it involves the same kind of collaborative goal and forces our agents to deal with the same kind of partial knowledge about the world as the humans did. Each agent knows its own location, but not his partner's, and a player can see the AS only when co-located with it. The agents use (simplified) English to communicate with each other.

3 Spatial Semantics

Much of the communication in the Cards task involves referring to spatial locations on the board. Accordingly, we focus on spatial language for our artificial agents. In this section, we present a model of spatial semantics, which we create by leveraging the human–human Cards transcripts. We discuss the spatial semantic representation, how we classify the semantics of new locative expressions, and our use of spatial semantics to form a high-level state space for decision making.

3.1 Semantic Representation

Potts (2012) released annotations, derived from the Cards corpus, which reduce 599 of the players' statements about their locations to formulae of the form $\delta(\varphi_1 \wedge \cdots \wedge \varphi_k)$, where δ is a *domain* and $\varphi_1, \ldots, \varphi_k$ are semantic literals. For example, the utterance "(I'm) at the top right of the board" is annotated as BOARD(top $\wedge$ right), and "(I'm) in bottom

[1]Released by Potts (2012) at `http://cardscorpus.christopherpotts.net`

of the C room" is annotated as C_room(bottom). Table 1 lists the full set of semantic primitives that appear as domain expressions and literals.

Because the Cards transcripts are so highly structured, we can interpret these expressions in terms of the Cards world itself. For a given formula $\sigma = \delta(\varphi_1 \wedge \cdots \wedge \varphi_k)$, we compute the number of times that a player identified its location with (an utterance translated as) σ while standing on grid square (x,y). These counts are smoothed using a simple 2D-smoothing scheme, detailed in (Potts, 2012), and normalized in the usual manner to form a distribution over board squares $\Pr((x,y)|\sigma)$. These grounded interpretations are the basis for communication between the artificial agents we define in Section 4.

BOARD, SQUARE, right, middle, top, left, bottom, corner, approx, precise, entrance, C_room, hall, room, sideways_C, loop, reverse_C, U_room, T_room, deadend, wall, sideways_F

Table 1: The spatial semantic primitives.

3.2 Semantics Classifier

Using the corpus examples of utterances paired with their spatial semantic representations, we learn a set of classifiers to predict a spatial utterance's semantic representation. We train a binary classifier for each semantic primitive φ_i using a log-linear model with simple bag of words features. The words are not normalized or stemmed and we use whitespace tokenization. We additionally train a multi-class classifier for all possible domains δ. At test time, we use the domain classifier and each primitive binary classifier to produce a semantic representation.

3.3 Semantic State Space

The decision making algorithms that we discuss in Section 4 are highly sensitive to the size of the state space. The full representation of the game board consists of 231 squares. Representing the location of both players and the location of the card requires $323^3 = 12,326,391$ states, well beyond the capabilities of current decision-making algorithms.

To ameliorate this difficulty, we cluster squares together using the spatial referring expression corpus. This approach follows from research that shows that humans' mental spatial representations are influenced by their language (Hayward and Tarr, 1995). Our intuition is that human players do not consider all possible locations of the card and players, but instead lump them into semantically coherent states, such as "the card is in the top right corner." Following this intuition, we cluster states together which have similar referring expressions, allowing our agents to use language as a *cognitive technology* and not just a tool for communication.

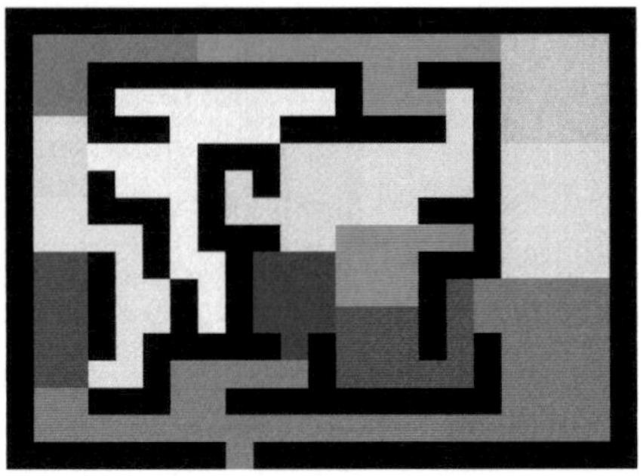

Figure 2: Semantic state space clusters with $k = 16$.

For each board square (x,y) we form a vector $\phi(x,y)$ with $\phi_i(x,y) = \Pr((x,y)|\sigma_i)$, where σ_i is the ith distinct semantic representation in the corpus. This forms a 136-dimensional vector for each board square. We then use k-means clustering with a Euclidean distance metric in this semantic space to cluster states which are referred to similarly.

Figure 2 shows a clustering for $k = 16$ which we utilize for the remainder of the paper. Denoting the board regions by $\{1,\ldots,N_{\text{regions}}\}$, we compute the probability of an expression σ referring to a region r by averaging over the squares in the region:

$$\Pr(r|\sigma_i) \propto \sum_{(x,y)\in \text{ region } r} \frac{\Pr((x,y)|\sigma_i)}{|\{(x,y)|(x,y) \in \text{ region } r\}|}$$

4 ListenerBot

We first introduce ListenerBot, an agent that does not take into account the actions or beliefs of its partner. ListenerBot decides what actions to take using a *Partially Observable Markov Decision Process* (POMDP). This allows ListenerBot to track its beliefs about the location of the card and to incorporate linguistic advice. However, ListenerBot does not produce utterances.

A POMDP is defined by a tuple $(S, A, T, O, \Omega, R, b_0, \gamma)$. We explicate each component with examples from our task. Figure 3(a) provides the POMDP influence diagram.

States S is the finite state space of the world. The state space S of ListenerBot consists of the location of the player p and the location of the card c. As discussed above in Section 3.3, we cluster squares of the board into N_{regions} semantically coherent regions, denoted by $\{1, \ldots, N_{\text{regions}}\}$. The state space over these regions is defined as

$$S := \{(p,c) | p, c \in \{1, \ldots, N_{\text{regions}}\}\}$$

Two regions r_1 and r_2 are called *adjacent*, written $\text{adj}(r_1, r_2)$, if any of their constituent squares touch.

Actions A is the set of actions available to the agent. ListenerBot can only take physical actions and has no communicative ability. Physical actions in our region-based state space are composed of two types: traveling to a region and searching a region.

- $\text{travel}(r)$: travel to region r
- search: player exhaustively searches the current region

Transition Distributions The transition distribution $T(s'|a,s)$ models the dynamics of the world. This represents the ramifications of physical actions such as moving around the map. For a state $s = (p,c)$ and action $a = \text{travel}(r)$, the player moves to region r if it is adjacent to p, and otherwise stays in the same place:

$$T((p',c')|\text{travel}(r),(p,c)) = \begin{cases} 1 & \text{adj}(r,p) \wedge p' = r \\ & \wedge c = c' \\ 1 & \neg\text{adj}(r,p) \wedge p = p' \\ & \wedge c = c' \\ 0 & \text{otherwise} \end{cases}$$

Search actions are only concerned with observations and do not change the state of the world:[2]

$$T((p',c')|\text{search},(p,c)) = \mathbb{1}\left[p' = p \wedge c' = c\right]$$

The travel and search high-level actions are translated into low-level (up, down, left, right) actions using a simple A* path planner.

Observations Agents receive observations from a set O according to an observation distribution $\Omega(o|s',a)$. Observations include properties of the physical world, such as the location of the card, and also natural language utterances, which serve to indirectly change agents' beliefs about the world and the beliefs of their interlocutors.

Search actions generate two possible observations: o_{here} and $o_{\neg\text{here}}$, which denote the presence or absence of the card from the current region.

$$\Omega(o_{\text{here}}|(p',c'),\text{search}) = \mathbb{1}\left[p' = c'\right]$$
$$\Omega(o_{\neg\text{here}}|(p',c'),\text{search}) = \mathbb{1}\left[p' \neq c'\right]$$

Travel actions do not generate meaningful observations:

$$\Omega(o_{\neg\text{here}}|(p',c'),\text{travel}) = 1$$

Linguistic Advice We model linguistic advice as another form of observation. Agents receive messages from a finite set Σ, and each message $\sigma \in \Sigma$ has a *semantics*, or distribution over the state space $\Pr(s|\sigma)$. In the Cards task, we use the semantic distributions defined in Section 3. To combine the semantics of language with the standard POMDP observation model, we apply Bayes' rule:

$$\Pr(\sigma|s) = \frac{\Pr(s|\sigma)\Pr(\sigma)}{\sum_{\sigma'} \Pr(s|\sigma')\Pr(\sigma')} \quad (1)$$

The prior, $\Pr(\sigma)$, can be derived from corpus data. By treating language as just another form of observation, we are able to leverage existing POMDP solution algorithms. This approach contrasts with previous work on communication in Dec-POMDPs, where agents directly share their perceptual observations (Pynadath and Tambe, 2002; Spaan et al., 2008), an assumption which does not fit natural language.

Reward The reward function $R(s,a) : S \to \mathbb{R}$ represents the goals of the agent, who chooses actions to maximize reward. The goal of the Cards task is for both players to be on top of the card, so any action that leads to this state receives a high reward R^+. All other actions receive a small negative reward R^-, which gives agents an incentive to finish the task as quickly as possible.

$$R((p,c),a) = \begin{cases} R^+ & p = c \\ R^- & p \neq c \end{cases}$$

Lastly, $\gamma \in [0,1)$ is the discount factor, specifying the trade-off between immediate and future rewards.

[2] $\mathbb{1}[Q]$ is the indicator function, which is 1 if proposition Q is true and 0 otherwise.

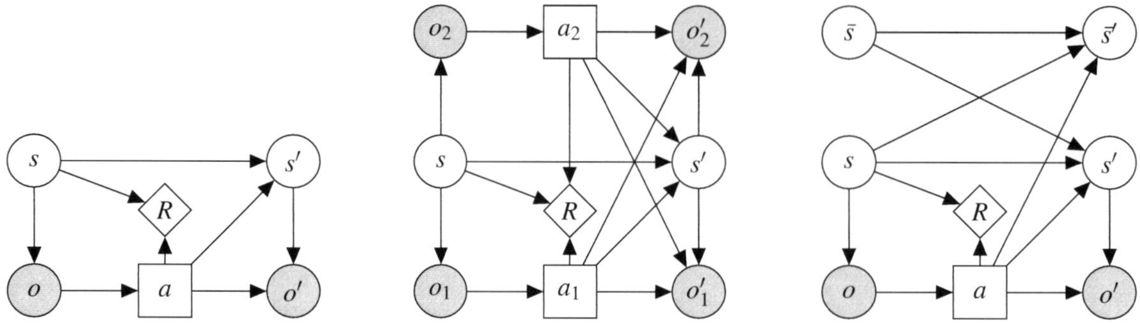

(a) ListenerBot POMDP (b) Full Dec-POMDP (c) DialogBot POMDP

Figure 3: The decision diagram for the ListenerBot POMDP, the full Dec-POMDP, and the DialogBot approximation POMDP. The ListenerBot (a) only considers his own location p and the card location c. In the full Dec-POMDP (b), both agents receive individual observations and choose actions independently. Optimal decision making requires tracking all possible histories of beliefs of the other agent. In diagram (c), DialogBot approximates the full Dec-POMDP as single-agent POMDP. At each time step, DialogBot marginalizes out the possible observations $\bar{o}$ that ListenerBot received, yielding an *expected belief state* $\bar{b}$.

Initial Belief State The initial belief state, $b_0 \in \Delta(S)$, is a distribution over the state space S. ListenerBot begins each game with a known initial location p_0 but a uniform distribution over the location of the card c:

$$b_0(p,c) \propto \begin{cases} \frac{1}{N_{\text{regions}}} & p = p_0 \\ 0 & \text{otherwise} \end{cases}$$

Belief Update and Decision Making The key decision making problem in POMDPs is the construction of a policy $\pi : \Delta(S) \rightarrow A$, a function from beliefs to actions which dictates how the agent acts. Decision making in POMDPs proceeds as follows. The world starts in a hidden state $s_0 \sim b_0$. The agent executes action $a_0 = \pi(b_0)$. The underlying hidden world state transitions to $s_1 \sim T(s'|a_0, s_0)$, the world generates observation $o_0 \sim \Omega(o|s_1, a_0)$, and the agent receives reward $R(s_0, a_0)$. Using the observation o_0, the agent constructs a new belief $b_1 \in \Delta(S)$ using Bayes' rule:

$$\begin{aligned} b_{t+1}^{a_t,o_t}(s') &= \Pr(s'|a_t, o_t, b_t) \\ &= \frac{\Pr(o_t|a_t, s', b_t)\Pr(s'|a_t, b_t)}{\Pr(o_t|b_t, a_t)} \\ &= \frac{\Omega(o_t|s', a_t)\sum_{s\in S} T(s'|a_t, s)b_t(s)}{\sum_{s''}\Omega(o_t|s'', a_t)\sum_{s\in S} T(s''|a_t, s)b_t(s)} \end{aligned}$$

This process is referred to as *belief update* and is analogous to the forward algorithm in HMMs. To incorporate communication into the standard POMDP model, we consider observations $(o, \sigma) \in O \times \Sigma$ which are a combination of a perceptual observation o and a received message σ. The semantics of the message σ is included in the belief update equation using $\Pr(s|\sigma)$, derived in Equation 1:

$$b_{t+1}^{a_t,o_t,\sigma_t}(s') = \frac{\Omega(o|s',a)\frac{\Pr(s'|\sigma)\Pr(\sigma)}{\sum_{\sigma'\in\Sigma}\Pr(s'|\sigma')\Pr(\sigma')}\sum_{s\in S} T(s'|a,s)b_t(s)}{\sum_{s''\in S}\Omega(o|s'',a)\frac{\Pr(s''|\sigma)\Pr(\sigma)}{\sum_{\sigma'\in\Sigma}\Pr(s''|\sigma')\Pr(\sigma')}\sum_{s\in S} T(s''|a,s)b_t(s)}$$

Using this new belief state b_1, the agent selects an action $a_1 = \pi(b_1)$, and the process continues.

An initial belief state b_0 and a policy π together define a Markov chain over pairs of states and actions. For a given policy π, we define a *value function* $V^\pi : \Delta(S) \rightarrow \mathbb{R}$ which represents the expected discounted reward with respect to that Markov chain:

$$V^\pi(b_0) = \sum_{t=0}^{\infty} \gamma^t\, \mathbb{E}[R(b_t, a_t)|b_0, \pi]$$

The goal of the agent is find a policy π^* which maximizes the value of the initial belief state:

$$\pi^* = \arg\max_\pi V^\pi(b_0)$$

Exact computation of π^* is PSPACE-complete (Papadimitriou and Tsitsiklis, 1987), making approximation algorithms necessary for all but the simplest problems. We use Perseus (Spaan and Vlassis, 2005), an anytime approximate point-based value iteration algorithm.

5 DialogBot

We now introduce DialogBot, a Cards agent which is capable of producing linguistic advice. To decide when and how to speak, DialogBot maintains a distribution over its partner's beliefs and reasons about the effects his utterances will have on those beliefs. To handle these complexities, DialogBot models the world as a *Decentralized Partially Observable Markov Decision Process* (Dec-POMDP) (Bernstein et al., 2002). See Figure 3(b) for the influence diagram. The definition of Dec-POMDPs mirrors that of the POMDP, with the following changes.

There is a finite set I of agents, which we restrict to two. Each agent takes an action a_i at each time step, forming a joint action $\vec{a} = (a_1, a_2)$. Each agent receives its own observation o_i according to $\Omega(o_1, o_2 | a_1, a_2, s')$. The transition distributions $T(s'|a_1, a_2, s)$ and the reward $R(s, a_1, a_2)$ both depend on both agents' actions.

Optimal decision making in Dec-POMDPs requires maintaining a probability distribution over all possible sequences of actions and observations $(\bar{a}_1, \bar{o}_1, \ldots, \bar{a}_t, \bar{o}_t)$ that the other player might have received. As t increases, we have an exponential increase in the belief states an agent must consider. Confirming this informal intuition, decision making in Dec-POMDPs is NEXP-complete, a complexity class above P-SPACE (Bernstein et al., 2002). This computational complexity limits the application of Dec-POMDPs to very small problems. To address this difficulty we make several simplifying assumptions, allowing us to construct a single-agent POMDP which approximates the full Dec-POMDP.

Firstly, we assume that other agents do not take into account our own beliefs, i.e., the other agent acts like a ListenerBot. This bypasses the infinitely nested belief problem by assuming that other agents track one less level of nested beliefs, a common approach (Goodman and Stuhlmüller, 2012; Gmytrasiewicz and Doshi, 2005).

Secondly, instead of tracking the full tree of possible observation histories, we maintain a point estimate $\bar{b}$ of the other agent's beliefs, which we term the *expected belief state*. Rather than tracking each possible observation/action history of the other agent, at each time step we marginalize out the observations they could have received. Figure 4 compares this approach with exact belief update.

Thirdly, we assume that the other agent acts according to a variant of the Q_{MDP} approximation (Littman et al., 1995). Under this approximation, the other agent solves a fully-observable MDP version of the ListenerBot POMDP, yielding an MDP policy $\bar{\pi} : S \to A$. This critically allows us to approximate the other agent's belief update using a specially formed POMDP, which we detail next.

State Space To construct the approximate single-agent POMDP from the full Dec-POMDP problem, we formulate the state space as $S \times S$. (See Figure 3(c) for the influence diagram.) We write a state $(s, \bar{s}) \in S \times S$, where s is DialogBot's beliefs about the true state of the world, and $\bar{s}$ is DialogBot's estimate of the other agent's beliefs.

Transition Distribution The main difficulty in constructing the approximate single-agent POMDP is specifying the transition distribution $T((s', \bar{s}')|a, (s, \bar{s}))$. To address this, we break this distribution into two components: $T((s', \bar{s}')|a, (s, \bar{s})) = \bar{T}(\bar{s}'|s', a, (s, \bar{s}))T(s'|a, s, \bar{s})$. The first term dictates how DialogBot updates its beliefs about the other agent's beliefs:

$$\begin{aligned}\bar{T}(\bar{s}'|s', a, (s, \bar{s})) &= \Pr(\bar{s}'|s', a, (s, \bar{s})) \\ &= \sum_{\bar{o} \in O} \Pr(\bar{s}'|a, \bar{o}, \bar{s}, s) \Pr(\bar{o}|s', a, \bar{\pi}(\bar{s})) \\ &= \sum_{\bar{o} \in O} \left(\frac{\Omega(\bar{o}|\bar{s}', a, \bar{\pi}(\bar{s}))T(\bar{s}'|a, \bar{\pi}(\bar{s}), \bar{s})}{\sum_{\bar{s}''} \Omega(\bar{o}|\bar{s}'', a, \bar{\pi}(\bar{s}))T(\bar{s}''|a, \bar{\pi}(\bar{s}), \bar{s})} \right. \\ &\qquad \left. \times\, \Omega(\bar{o}|s', a, \bar{\pi}(\bar{s})) \right)\end{aligned}$$

We sum over all observations $\bar{o}$ the other agent could have received, updating our probability of $\bar{s}'$ as ListenerBot would have, multiplied by the probability that ListenerBot would have received that observation, $\Omega(\bar{o}|s', \bar{\pi}(\bar{s}))$. The Q_{MDP} approximation allows us to simulate ListenerBot's belief update in $\bar{T}(\bar{s}'|s', a, (s, \bar{s}))$. Exact belief update would require access to $\bar{b}$: by using $\bar{\pi}(\bar{s})$ we can estimate the action that ListenerBot would have taken.

In cases where $\bar{s}$ contradicts s such that for all $\bar{o}$ either $\Omega(\bar{o}|s', \bar{\pi}(\bar{s})) = 0$ or $\Omega(\bar{o}|\bar{s}', \bar{\pi}(\bar{s})) = 0$, we redistribute the belief mass uniformly: $\bar{T}(\bar{s}'|s', a, (s, \bar{s})) \propto$

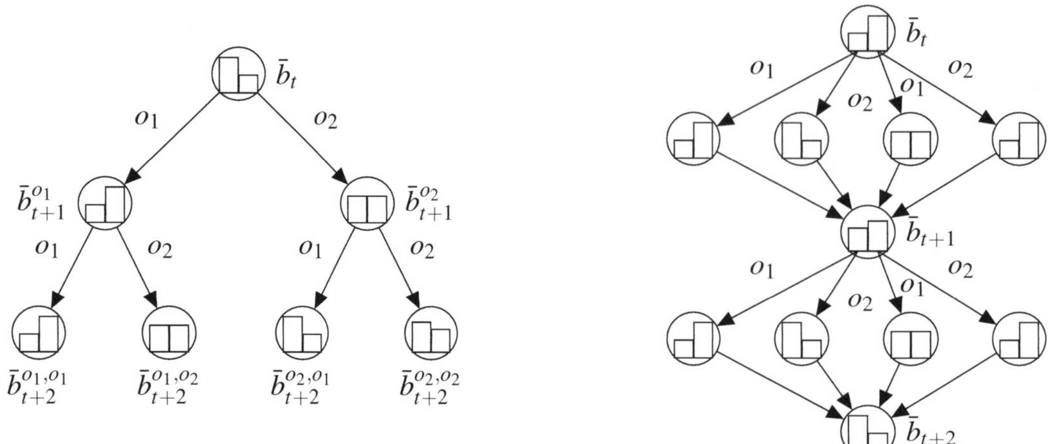

(a) Exact multi-agent belief tracking

(b) Approximate multi-agent belief tracking

Figure 4: Exact multi-agent belief tracking compared with our approximate approach. Each node represents a belief state. In exact tracking (a), the agent tracks every possible history of observations that its partner could have received, which grows exponentially in time. In approximate update (b), the agent considers each possible observation and then averages the resulting belief states, weighted by the probability the other agent received that observation, resulting in a single summary belief state $\bar{b}_{t+1}$. Under the Q_{MDP} approximation, the agent considers what action the other agent would have taken if it completely believed the world was in a certain state. Thus, there are four belief states resulting from $\bar{b}_t$, as opposed to two in the exact case.

$1\ \forall \bar{s}' \neq \bar{s}$. This approach to managing contradiction is analogous to logical belief revision (Alchourronón et al., 1985; Gärdenfors, 1988; Fermé and Hansson, 2011).

Speech Actions Speech actions are modeled by how they change the beliefs of the other agent. The effects of a speech actions are modeled in $\bar{T}(\bar{s}'|s', a, (s, \bar{s}))$, our model of how ListenerBot's beliefs change. For a speech action $a = \text{say}(\sigma)$ with $\sigma \in \Sigma$,

$$\bar{T}(\bar{s}'|s', a, (s, \bar{s})) = \sum_{\bar{o} \in O} \left(\frac{\Omega(\bar{o}|\bar{s}', a, \bar{\pi}(\bar{s})) \Pr(\sigma|\bar{s}') T(\bar{s}'|a, \bar{\pi}(\bar{s}), \bar{s})}{\sum_{\bar{s}''} \Omega(\bar{o}|\bar{s}'', a, \bar{\pi}(\bar{s})) \Pr(\sigma|\bar{s}'') T(\bar{s}''|a, \bar{\pi}(\bar{s}), \bar{s})} \times \Omega(\bar{o}|s', a, \bar{\pi}(\bar{s})) \right)$$

DialogBot is equipped with the five most frequent speech actions: BOARD(middle), BOARD(top), BOARD(bottom), BOARD(left), and BOARD(right). It produces concrete utterances by selecting a sentence from the training corpus with the desired semantics.

Reward DialogBot receives a large reward when both it and its partner are located on the card, and a negative cost when moving or speaking:

$$R((p, c, \bar{p}, \bar{c}), a) = \begin{cases} R^+ & p = c \wedge \bar{p} = c \\ R^- & p \neq c \vee \bar{p} \neq c \end{cases}$$

DialogBot's reward is not dependent on the beliefs of the other player, only the true underlying state of the world.

6 Experimental Results

We now experimentally evaluate our semantic classifiers and the agents' task performance.

6.1 Spatial Semantics Classifiers

We report the performance of our spatial semantics classifiers, although their accuracy is not the focus of this paper. We use 10-fold cross validation on a corpus of 577 annotated utterances. We used simple bag-of-words features, so overfitting the data with cross validation is not a pressing concern. Of the 577 utterances, our classifiers perfectly labeled 325 (56.3% accuracy). The classifiers correctly predicted the domain δ of 515 (89.3%) utterances. The precision of our binary semantic primitive classifiers was $\frac{969}{1126} = .861$ and recall $\frac{969}{1242} = .780$, yielding F_1 measure .818.

6.2 Cards Task Evaluation

We evaluated our ListenerBot and DialogBot agents in the Cards task. Using 500 randomly generated initial player and card locations, we tested each combination of ListenerBot and DialogBot partners. Agents succeeded at a given initial position if they both reached the card within 50 moves. Table 2 shows how many trials each dyad won and how many high-level actions they took to do so.

Agents	% Success	Moves
LB & LB	84.4%	19.8
LB & DB	87.2%	17.5
DB & DB	90.6%	16.6

Table 2: The evaluation for each combination of agents. LB = ListenerBot; DB = DialogBot.

Collaborating DialogBots performed the best, completing more trials and using fewer moves than the ListenerBots. The DialogBots initially explore the space in a similar manner to the ListenerBots, but then share card location information. This leads to shorter interactions, as once the DialogBot finds the card, the other player can find it more quickly. In the combination of ListenerBot and DialogBot, we see about half of the improvement over two ListenerBots. Roughly 50% of the time, the ListenerBot finds the card first, which doesn't help the DialogBot find the card any faster.

7 Emergent Pragmatics

Grice's original model of pragmatics (Grice, 1975) involves the cooperative principle and four maxims: quality ("say only what you know to be true"), relation ("be relevant"), quantity ("be as informative as is required; do not say more than is required"), and manner (roughly, be clear and concise).

In most interactions, DialogBot searches for the card and then reports its location to the other agent. These reports obey quality in that they are made only when based on actual observations. The behavior is not hard-coded, but rather emerges, because only accurate information serves the agents' goals. In contrast, sub-optimal policies generated early in the POMDP solving process sometimes lie about card locations. Since this behavior confuses the other agent and thus has a lower utility, it gets replaced by truthful communication as the policies improve.

We also capture the effects of relation and the first clause of quantity, because the nature of the reward function and the nested belief structures ensure that DialogBot offers only relevant, informative information. For instance, when DialogBot finds the card in the lower left corner, it alternates saying "left" and "bottom", effectively overcoming its limited generation capabilities. Again, early sub-optimal policies sometimes do not report the location of the card at all, thereby failing to fulfill these maxims.

We expect these models to produce behavior consistent with manner and the second clause of quantity, but evaluating this claim will require a richer experimental paradigm. For example, if DialogBot had a larger and more structured vocabulary, it would have to choose between levels of specificity as well as more or less economical forms.

8 Conclusion

We have shown that cooperative pragmatic behavior can arise from multi-agent decision-theoretic models in which the agents share a joint utility function and reason about each other's belief states. Decision-making in these models is intractable, which has been a major obstacle to achieving experimental results in this area. We introduced a series of approximations to manage this intractability: (i) combining low-level states into semantically coherent high-level ones; (ii) tracking only an averaged summary of the other agent's potential beliefs; (iii) limiting belief state nesting to one level, and (iv) simplifying each agent's model of the other's beliefs so as to reduce uncertainty. These approximations bring the problems under sufficient control that they can be solved with current POMDP approximation algorithms. Our experimental results highlight the rich pragmatic behavior this gives rise to and quantify the communicative value of such behavior. While there remain insights from earlier theoretical proposals and logic-based methods that we have not fully captured, our current results support the notion that probabilistic decision-making methods can yield robust, widely applicable models that address the real-world difficulties of partial observability and uncertainty.

Acknowledgments

This research was supported in part by ONR grants N00014-10-1-0109 and N00014-13-1-0287 and ARO grant W911NF-07-1-0216.

References

Carlos E. Alchourronón, Peter Gärdenfors, and David Makinson. 1985. On the logic of theory change: Partial meets contradiction and revision functions. *Journal of Symbolic Logic*, 50(2):510–530.

James F. Allen, Nathanael Chambers, George Ferguson, Lucian Galescu, Hyuckchul Jung, Mary Swift, and William Taysom. 2007. PLOW: A collaborative task learning agent. In *Proceedings of the Twenty-Second AAAI Conference on Artificial Intelligence*, pages 1514–1519. AAAI Press, Vancouver, British Columbia, Canada.

James F. Allen. 1991. *Reasoning About Plans*. Morgan Kaufmann, San Francisco.

David Beaver. 2002. Pragmatics, and that's an order. In David Barker-Plummer, David Beaver, Johan van Benthem, and Patrick Scotto di Luzio, editors, *Logic, Language, and Visual Information*, pages 192–215. CSLI, Stanford, CA.

Anton Benz, Gerhard Jäger, and Robert van Rooij, editors. 2005. *Game Theory and Pragmatics*. Palgrave McMillan, Basingstoke, Hampshire.

Daniel S. Bernstein, Robert Givan, Neil Immerman, and Shlomo Zilberstein. 2002. The complexity of decentralized control of Markov decision processes. *Mathematics of Operations Research*, 27(4):819–840.

Reinhard Blutner. 1998. Lexical pragmatics. *Journal of Semantics*, 15(2):115–162.

Michael Bratman. 1987. *Intentions, Plans, and Practical Reason*. Harvard University Press.

Herbert H. Clark. 1996. *Using Language*. Cambridge University Press, Cambridge.

Robert Dale and Ehud Reiter. 1995. Computational interpretations of the Gricean maxims in the generation of referring expressions. *Cognitive Science*, 19(2):233–263.

Judith Degen and Michael Franke. 2012. Optimal reasoning about referential expressions. In *Proceedings of SemDIAL 2012*, Paris, September.

David DeVault, Natalia Kariaeva, Anubha Kothari, Iris Oved, and Matthew Stone. 2005. An information-state approach to collaborative reference. In *Proceedings of the ACL Interactive Poster and Demonstration Sessions*, pages 1–4, Ann Arbor, MI, June. Association for Computational Linguistics.

David DeVault. 2008. *Contribution Tracking: Participating in Task-Oriented Dialogue under Uncertainty*. Ph.D. thesis, Rutgers University, New Brunswick, NJ.

Eduardo Fermé and Sven Ove Hansson. 2011. AGM 25 years: Twenty-five years of research in belief change. *Journal of Philosophical Logic*, 40(2):295–331.

Michael C. Frank and Noah D. Goodman. 2012. Predicting pragmatic reasoning in language games. *Science*, 336(6084):998.

Michael Franke. 2009. *Signal to Act: Game Theory in Pragmatics*. ILLC Dissertation Series. Institute for Logic, Language and Computation, University of Amsterdam.

Peter Gärdenfors. 1988. *Knowledge in Flux: Modeling the Dynamics of Epistemic States*. MIT Press.

Piotr J. Gmytrasiewicz and Prashant Doshi. 2005. A framework for sequential planning in multi-agent settings. *Journal of Artificial Intelligence Research*, 24:24–49.

Dave Golland, Percy Liang, and Dan Klein. 2010. A game-theoretic approach to generating spatial descriptions. In *Proceedings of the 2010 Conference on Empirical Methods in Natural Language Processing*, pages 410–419, Cambridge, MA, October. ACL.

Noah D. Goodman and Andreas Stuhlmüller. 2012. Knowledge and implicature: Modeling language understanding as social cognition. In *Proceedings of the Thirty-Fourth Annual Conference of the Cognitive Science Society*.

H. Paul Grice. 1975. Logic and conversation. In Peter Cole and Jerry Morgan, editors, *Syntax and Semantics*, volume 3: Speech Acts, pages 43–58. Academic Press, New York.

Barbara J. Grosz and Candace L. Sidner. 1986. Attention, intentions, and the structure of discourse. *Comput. Linguist.*, 12(3):175–204, July.

William G. Hayward and Michael J. Tarr. 1995. Spatial language and spatial representation. *Cognition*, 55:39–84.

Jerry Hobbs, Mark Stickel, Douglas Appelt, and Paul Martin. 1993. Interpretation as abduction. *Artificial Intelligence*, 63(1–2):69–142.

Emiel Krahmer and Kees van Deemter. 2012. Computational generation of referring expressions: A survey. *Computational Linguistics*, 38(1):173–218.

David Lewis. 1969. *Convention*. Harvard University Press, Cambridge, MA. Reprinted 2002 by Blackwell.

Michael L. Littman, Anthony R. Cassandra, and Leslie Pack Kaelbling. 1995. Learning policies for partially observable environments: Scaling up. In Armand Prieditis and Stuart J. Russell, editors, *ICML*, pages 362–370. Morgan Kaufmann.

Arthur Merin. 1997. If all our arguments had to be conclusive, there would be few of them. Arbeitspapiere SFB 340 101, University of Stuttgart, Stuttgart.

Christos Papadimitriou and John N. Tsitsiklis. 1987. The complexity of markov decision processes. *Math. Oper. Res.*, 12(3):441–450, August.

Prashant Parikh. 2001. *The Use of Language*. CSLI, Stanford, CA.

C. Raymond Perrault and James F. Allen. 1980. A plan-based analysis of indirect speech acts. *American Journal of Computational Linguistics*, 6(3–4):167–182.

Christopher Potts. 2012. Goal-driven answers in the Cards dialogue corpus. In Nathan Arnett and Ryan Bennett, editors, *Proceedings of the 30th West Coast Conference on Formal Linguistics*, Somerville, MA. Cascadilla Press.

David V. Pynadath and Milind Tambe. 2002. The communicative multiagent team decision problem: Analyzing teamwork theories and models. *Journal of Artificial Intelligence Research*, 16:2002.

Hannah Rohde, Scott Seyfarth, Brady Clark, Gerhard Jäger, and Stefan Kaufmann. 2012. Communicating with cost-based implicature: A game-theoretic approach to ambiguity. In *The 16th Workshop on the Semantics and Pragmatics of Dialogue*, Paris, September.

Robert van Rooy. 2003. Questioning to resolve decision problems. *Linguistics and Philosophy*, 26(6):727–763.

Seymour Rosenberg and Bertram D. Cohen. 1964. Speakers' and listeners' processes in a word communication task. *Science*, 145:1201–1203.

Matthijs T. J. Spaan and Nikos Vlassis. 2005. Perseus: Randomized point-based value iteration for POMDPs. *Journal of Artificial Intelligence Research*, 24(1):195–220, August.

Matthijs T. J. Spaan, Frans A. Oliehoek, and Nikos Vlassis. 2008. Multiagent planning under uncertainty with stochastic communication delays. In *In Proc. of the 18th Int. Conf. on Automated Planning and Scheduling*, pages 338–345.

Alex Stiller, Noah D. Goodman, and Michael C. Frank. 2011. Ad-hoc scalar implicature in adults and children. In *Proceedings of the 33rd Annual Meeting of the Cognitive Science Society*, Boston, July.

Matthew Stone, Richmond Thomason, and David DeVault. 2007. Enlightened update: A computational architecture for presupposition and other pragmatic phenomena. To appear in Donna K. Byron; Craige Roberts; and Scott Schwenter, *Presupposition Accommodation*.

Blaise Thomson and Steve Young. 2010. Bayesian update of dialogue state: A pomdp framework for spoken dialogue systems. *Comput. Speech Lang.*, 24(4):562–588, October.

Steve Young, Milica Gašić, Simon Keizer, François Mairesse, Jost Schatzmann, Blaise Thomson, and Kai Yu. 2010. The hidden information state model: A practical framework for pomdp-based spoken dialogue management. *Comput. Speech Lang.*, 24(2):150–174, April.

Open Dialogue Management for Relational Databases

Ben Hixon
Computer Science & Engineering
University of Washington
Seattle, WA 98195, USA
bhixon@cs.washington.edu

Rebecca J. Passonneau
Center for Computational Learning Systems
Columbia University
New York, New York, USA
becky@ccls.columbia.edu

Abstract

We present open dialogue management and its application to relational databases. An open dialogue manager generates dialogue states, actions, and default strategies from the semantics of its application domain. We define three open dialogue management tasks. First, vocabulary selection finds the intelligible attributes in each database table. Second, focus discovery selects candidate dialogue foci, tables that have the most potential to address basic user goals. Third, a focus agent is instantiated for each dialogue focus with a default dialogue strategy governed by efficiency. We demonstrate the portability of open dialogue management on three very different databases. Evaluation of our system with simulated users shows that users with realistically limited domain knowledge have dialogues nearly as efficient as those of users with complete domain knowledge.

1 Introduction

This paper presents *open dialogue management.* An open dialogue manager (ODM) generates dialogue states, actions, and strategies from knowledge it computes about the semantics of its domain. A *dialogue strategy* is the procedure by which a system chooses its next action given the current state of the dialogue. The system's *dialogue policy* completely specifies which strategy to use in any dialogue state. Strategies can be handcrafted or learned. Reinforcement learning, the leading method for dialogue strategy learning, can yield powerful results but relies on small sets of states and actions predefined by the researcher. This reliance on domain expertise limits machine learned dialogue managers to the domains for which they were specifically designed, and contributes to the prevalence of handcrafted strategies over machine learning approaches for dialogue management in commercial applications (Paek & Pieraccini, 2008). We argue that open dialogue management, which exploits the semantics and contents of its database to generate actions, states and default strategies, is a step towards a dialogue manager that operates across domains.

As a first step to open dialogue management we present ODDMER (OPEN-DOMAIN DIALOGUE MANAGER), the first dialogue system to generate its own dialogue strategy from relational databases. ODDMER's vocabulary selection module uses supervised learning to determine each table's *intelligible* attributes, those most likely to be in the user's vocabulary. Its focus discovery module finds *candidate dialogue foci,* tables that have the most potential to address basic user goals. Foci are identified with *schema summarization* through a random walk over the database schema that ranks tables by size, linguistic information, and connectivity. For each candidate focus, ODDMER instantiates a *focus agent* that prompts users for values of intelligible attributes ordered by efficiency.

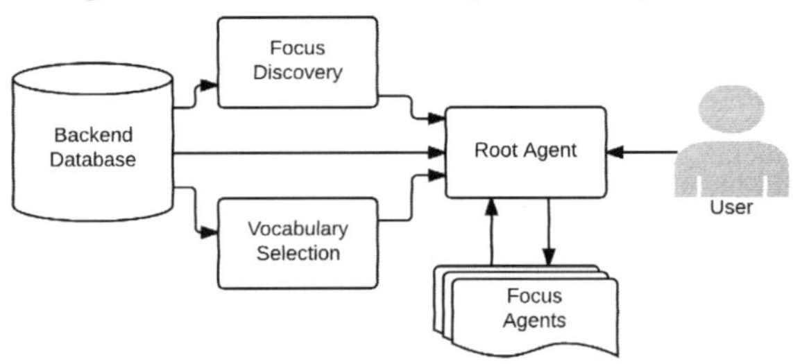

Figure 1. ODDMER uses focus discovery and vocabulary selection to choose its states, actions, and strategy.

This paper addresses a particular type of information-seeking dialogue in which the user's goal is to select a tuple from a table. Tuples are identified by *constraints,* attribute-value pairs elicited from a user during the dialogue. A typical user, however, cannot supply all values with equal readiness. For example, attributes such as primary or foreign keys are irrelevant or unintelligible to users. This results in a *vocabulary problem*, a mismatch between system and user vocabulary (Furnas et al., 1987). Furthermore, tables differ in their relevance to users. Tables that contain little semantic information have less potential to address user goals. Dialogue systems for relational databases often rely on manual pre-processing to select the attributes a typical user can most readily supply and identify the tables with the most relevance to basic user goals. An open dialogue system obviates this manual step by exploiting the database semantics.

For example, *Heiskell* is a library database that includes a table for books (BOOK) and a table for book subject headings (HEADING). A typical patron wants a book, not a heading. Due to BOOK's larger size, its greater number of intelligible attributes, and its higher connectivity to other tables, ODDMER recognizes that a BOOK tuple satisfies a more basic user goal. BOOK has 32 attributes, most of which are numeric fields familiar to a librarian but arcane to the user. ODDMER selects the table's intelligible attributes as its vocabulary. It recognizes that a book's author and title are intelligible, but the book's ISBN is not. Consequently, ODDMER will not ask the user for the ISBN.

ODDMER assumes a user of the Heiskell database will be likely to know one or more intelligible attributes of books. ODDMER ranks intelligible attribute-value pairs by their *semantic specificity,* the degree to which they uniquely identify a tuple. To demonstrate the benefit of pre-computing this semantic information, we test ODDMER on three databases with simulated users of two knowledge levels. *Complete-knowledge* users know all attribute values. They have no vocabulary problem, will always be able to supply a requested constraint, and require no vocabulary selection to achieve maximum dialogue efficiency. *Incomplete-knowledge* users have a more realistic vocabulary. They know values for different attributes with different probabilities. Without vocabulary selection, these users have long, inefficient dialogues. Given ODDMER's vocabulary selection and efficient dialogue strategy, these users achieve their goals nearly as efficiently as complete-knowledge users.

2 Related Work

ODDMER is the first dialogue system to examine a database and choose which tables and attributes to use in dialogue. We envision open dialogue management as a suite of domain-independent procedures through which a dialogue manager can exploit its knowledge base. Hastie, Liu, and Lemon (2009) also generate policies from databases. They do not consider multiple tables, and they depend on handcrafted Business Process Models that explicitly specify the dialogue flow for the domain. This limits their method to domains with available models. Polifroni, Chung, and Seneff (2003) also argue for the importance of generic, domain-independent dialogue managers. Their portable information presentation strategies cluster attribute values to summarize database contents for users. Neither of these works considers how to choose attributes or find which domain entities are likely objects of dialogue goals. Chotimongkol and Rudnicky (2008) use unsupervised learning to automatically acquire task-specific information from a corpus of in-domain human-human dialogue transcripts. They require a large corpus whereas we need only the underlying database.

The vocabulary problem has received relatively little attention in dialogue research, and no method to automatically identify intelligible constraints has been previously demonstrated. Demberg and Moore (2006) choose constraints with a user model that records user importance, such as 'price' for a student in a restaurant domain. They require a manually crafted user model and must match model to user. Polifroni and Walker (2006) use attribute entropy to order system initiative prompts, but assume that both the table and the relevant attributes are known a priori. Varges, Weng, and Pon-Barry (2006) develop a WOZ system in which a wizard recommends to real users what constraint to provide that will best narrow down results. Each of these works assumes all constraints are intelligible.

Two recent works concentrate more closely on the vocabulary problem. Janarthanam and Lemon (2010) build a system that determines a user's level of referring expression expertise, but manually determine the set of possible expressions. Selfridge and Heeman (2010) simulate users with different levels of domain knowledge. A novice has a 10% chance to know any constraint, and an expert a 90% chance. They do not consider users who know different constraints with different probabilities as we do, and do not consider databases that contain attributes likely to be unintelligible to most users.

Reinforcement learning, the leading approach for learning a dialogue strategy, demonstrates powerful results. For example, Rieser and Lemon (2009) find the optimal size of a list of tuples that match a user's constraints and when to display it in different user environments. A dialogue strategy is treated as a *policy*, a function that maps states to actions. Policy optimization is a Markov decision process. Paek and Pieraccini (2008) argue that reinforcement learning is limited by its reliance upon small sets of manually defined states and actions, with no standard method to determine these. ODDMER identifies dialogue states and actions automatically. Its default strategy could be optimized with reinforcement learning.

Portability is an important research area in natural-language interfaces to databases (NLIDBs). An NLIDB parses a user utterance into a logical form, which is transformed into a database query. Users typically know the database structure and contents. TEAM (Grosz, 1983), the first portable NLIDB, questions a domain expert to acquire linguistic knowledge for new databases. More recently, the ORAKEL interface (Cimiano et al., 2008) partially derives a domain-specific lexicon from a generic ontology. Here we do not focus on parsing of user questions, but on the acquisition of dialogue states, actions, and strategies from a database.

3 The ODDMER Dialogue System

ODDMER's *vocabulary selection* module finds each table's intelligible attributes. Its *focus discovery* module identifies candidate foci. A *focus agent* module instantiates dialogue agents for each focus. Their default strategy elicits attribute values from users in order of semantic specificity.

3.1 Vocabulary Selection

A *vocabulary* is the set of words and expressions used to discuss a domain. Domain entities can be identified by their *descriptions*, or sets of attribute-value pairs. In order for a system and a user to profitably engage in a natural language dialogue about database items, descriptions should consist of attributes and values understood by both system and user. We define the *vocabulary selection task* as the automatic selection of attribute-value pairs that the system expects its users will use to describe domain entities.

Successful vocabulary selection solves the vocabulary problem. The vocabulary problem is a bottleneck to portability because the attributes a user is likely to know must be predetermined for existing systems. ODDMER learns a classifier to determine a table's intelligible attributes. An attribute is *intelligible* if its values are in a user's vocabulary. A user interested in a particular item but unfamiliar with the structure of a database is more likely to recognize an intelligible attribute, and to know all or part of the relevant value.

To determine intelligible attributes, ODDMER currently relies on a binary classifier that takes as input the values of each attribute found in a particular instantiation of a relational database. To train the classifier, we labeled a set of 84 attributes belonging to tables taken from the Microsoft AdventureWorks Cycle Company database, a benchmark database packaged with Microsoft SQL Server. An attribute was labeled as intelligible if its values were likely to be known to a user. Four annotators worked independently to label the attributes. Pairwise agreement was 69%, and Krippendorff's alpha (Krippendorff, 1980) was 0.42. The low agreement can be attributed in part to the many ways to interpret the question annotators were to answer. The instructions indicated that the goal was to identify attributes corresponding to common-sense knowledge, but for a given table, annotators were shown all the attributes and asked whether they would know a value. For an employee table, annotators disagreed on attributes such as birthdate, hire date, and organization level. If they had instead been asked whether anyone without access to the table might know a value, there may have been more agreement.

Ratio of unique to total characters in all values
Mean ratio of unique to total characters per value
Ratio of numeric to total characters in all values
Ratio of unique to total values
Ratio of unique to total words in all values
Total number of characters in all values

Table 1. Representative features for attribute classification used in the best-performing intelligibility classifier.

The training data for the classifier consisted of 67 attributes that at least three annotators agreed on (22 intelligible, 45 not intelligible); pairwise agreement was 0.81 and Krippendorff's alpha was 0.61. They represented 8 tables and contained a total of 393,520 values, 123,901 of which were unique. For each attribute we extracted 17 features to represent the linguistic *expressiveness* of the attributes' values. An attribute whose values are more like natural language is more intelligible. Table 1 lists the features of the best classifier.

We tested several binary classifiers in Weka (Hall et al., 2009). ADTree (Freund & Mason, 1999) with ten boosting iterations performed best, with 91% recall and 91% precision under 10-fold cross-validation. However, the ADTree models were overfitted to the AdventureWorks domain. The RIPPER rule-learning algorithm (Cohen, 1995) achieved 77% precision and 78% recall. Because its learned model of three simple rules generalizes better to our domains, ODDMER uses the RIPPER intelligibility classifier.

Given a table, the vocabulary selection module returns which of its attributes should be in the system's vocabulary. For the Heiskell Library domain, the 32 attributes of the BOOK table include many internal codes understood by librarians but not by users. Only the seven attributes shown in Table 2 are classified as intelligible. Dialogues with only intelligible attributes should be more efficient for users with incomplete domain knowledge, because they will be more likely to know their values.

ODDMER's vocabulary selection module also computes the *semantic specificity* score of each attribute (Hixon, Passonneau, & Epstein, 2012). Semantic specificity rates an attribute on a scale from 0 to 1 according to how unambiguously its values map to rows in the database. More specific attributes are expected to be more efficient prompts. Table 2 lists the specificity values of the intelligible attributes for BOOK.

Intelligible Attributes	Specificity
ANNOTATION	0.958
TITLE	0.878
SORTTITLE	0.878
AUTHOR	0.300
NARRATOR	0.018
PUBLISHER	0.016
SERIES	0.003

Table 2. Intelligible attributes for BOOK sorted by specificity. (SORTTITLE is a duplicate of TITLE.)

3.2 Candidate Dialogue Focus Discovery

Information-seeking dialogues address diverse dialogue goals. For example, users may want to identify a tuple in a table ("I want a certain book by Stephen King."), retrieve the value of an attribute for a given tuple ("Is my plane on time?" "Who wrote *Moby Dick*?"), aggregate over a set of tuples ("How many Italian restaurants are in this neighborhood?"), or compare values of different tuples ("Which restaurant is more expensive?"). Each of these dialogue goals represents a distinct information need. However, not all possible information needs in a domain are equally likely. For example, a user is unlikely to ask for the value of a primary key attribute, or to select a tuple from a table that contains only primary and foreign keys. A dialogue system should place less priority on addressing these peripheral dialogue goals.

Given a particular domain, we assume that some goals are more *basic* than others. For example, the basic function of a library is to provide books to borrowers. Some libraries will also provide other material, or perform reference functions, but these are less basic. This notion of a basic goal is related to the basic categories proposed by Rosch (1978), who claimed that not all categories are equally useful for cognition. Basic categories are more differentiated from other categories, and have attributes that are common to all or most members of the category, thus provide us with more information (the principle of *cognitive economy*). Basic categories also mirror the structure of the perceptual and functional attributes of the natural world, thus serve us better in our daily activities. Typically a domain expert will identify the basic dialogue goals in a domain, but we suggest that the basic dialogue goals are *discoverable* in the underlying database. While a difficult problem, we are motivated by work in the database literature to identify and rank the most likely queries for an arbitrary database (Jayapandian & Jagadish, 2008).

We approach the problem of recovering dialogue goals from a database by restricting our attention to the tuple selection task, a commonly studied type of information-seeking dialogue in which the user's goal is to select a tuple from a table. A relational database typically consists of multiple tables, and each table can satisfy different user goals. Given a database composed of multiple tables, an open dialogue system calculates which tables are larger, have more natural language content, and greater connectivity to other tables. We refer to these tables as *candidate dialogue foci.* This notion of candidate focus for a dialogue is similar to focus of attention (Grosz & Sidner, 1986) in that information-seeking dialogues can be segmented to reflect the table both participants focus their attention on at a given time. We denote the task of identifying candidate foci in a relational database as *focus discovery.*

ODDMER's focus discovery module returns an ordered list of candidate foci, the *focal summary.* The highest ranked focus is the most relevant to basic user goals, those goals that pertain to the most information-rich and intelligible table. For our tuple-selection task, the highest-ranked focus is the table from which the system predicts a user will most likely want to select a tuple. A system that begins a dialogue by first mentioning the most relevant tables communicates the structure of the database better than does a system that lists all tables in a random order. Users with more specialized goals may be interested in more peripheral tables. For these users, more effort will be required to establish a dialogue focus: several tables may be proposed by the system and rejected before the user agrees to consider a given table. In tests with real users, we would expect them to find it acceptable for a specialized goal to take more effort than a basic goal.

We use *schema summarization* to find candidate focus tables. According to Yu and Jagadish (2006), a schema summary should convey a concise understanding of the underlying database schema. They identify table importance and coverage as criteria for good schema summaries. Their summaries for XML databases rank entities with higher cardinality (number of rows) and connectivity (number of joins) as more important. Yang, Procopiuc, and Srivastava (2009) extend schema summarization to relational databases. We closely follow the Yang algorithm but make modifications for dialogue to account for attribute intelligibility.

A database *schema* is an undirected graph G = <R,E> where each node r ∈ R corresponds to a table in a database and each edge e ∈ E denotes a join between two tables. A *schema summary* is a set of the most important nodes in the schema. Yang and colleagues compute the importance of a table as a function of its size, total entropy of its attributes, and connectivity to other tables. To incorporate connectivity, they employ a random walk over the schema graph. The most important tables maintain the highest information content in the steady state of a random walk over the schema.

A significant feature of their algorithm is that a table's high-entropy attributes largely determine its importance. It is possible to artificially inflate a table's importance under the Yang algorithm by introducing a new column of distinct integer values; numeric and linguistic values contribute equally to importance. For dialogue applications, this is undesirable. A table with more intelligible attributes is a more likely candidate focus because it can more readily be discussed. We therefore modify the Yang algorithm to compute table *verbality.* Verbality is similar to importance except that where Yang and colleagues use all attributes, we use intelligible attributes identified by vocabulary selection.

A table's verbality score is a function of its cardinality, the entropy of its intelligible attributes, and its connectivity to other tables. We apply vocabulary selection to find natural language attributes. To calculate the verbality of a table T, let A be the attributes of T and let $A' \subseteq A$ be those attributes of T whose values are intelligible, found by the classifier described previously. For BOOK, A' consists of the attributes shown in Table 2. Define V, the verbal information content of a table, as

$$V(T) = \log(|T|) + \sum_{a \in A'} H(a)$$

where $|T|$ is the cardinality of the table and $H(a)$ is the entropy of the attribute a in A'. The entropy of a is given by $H(a) = -\sum_{k \in K} p_k \log p_k$ where K is the set of distinct values of a and p_k is the fraction of rows in T for which a=k. If table T has no joins, $V(T)$ is the final verbality score of T. Table 3 shows $V(T)$ for each T in *Heiskell*.

To incorporate connectivity into verbality, we create a matrix of transition probabilities between every pair of nodes in the schema and determine which table maintains the highest information. Let $J \subseteq A$ be the attributes of T that join to other tables. The *information transfer* (IT) over the join $j \in J$ is

$$IT(j) = \frac{H(j)}{V(T) + \sum_{a \in A} q_a H(a)}$$

where q_a is the number of joins in which attribute a participates. Let P(T,R) be the transition probability from table T to table R. For $T \neq R$, P(T,R) is the sum of $IT(j)$ for all joins j between T and R. These probabilities represent the flow of information between tables over their joins. The diagonal entries of the transition matrix are given by

$$P(T,T) = 1 - \sum_{T \neq R} P(T,R),$$

the information that stays within table T. We then define the *verbality* of table T_i to be the ith element in the stable distribution of a random walk over the NxN matrix whose elements are $P(T_i,T_j)$ for $i,j \in$ N. We follow Yang and colleagues and use power iteration to find the stable distribution.

T	V(T)	Verbality(T)
Book	88.2	45.4
Heading	31.7	22.4
BibHeadingLink	19.2	23.6
CirculationHistory	17.9	24.9
Holding Stats	15.2	24.0
Patron Properties	12.7	21.9
Reserve	12.2	25.5
Patron	9.0	18.6

Table 3. Verbalities of *Heiskell*. V(T) is the verbal information of T. Verbality(T) incorporates connectivity.

Table 3 illustrates the verbalities of *Heiskell* before and after information transfer. BOOK clearly dominates. Before information transfer there is more verbal information V in BOOK than in the next four tables combined. After information transfer reaches a steady state, its connectivity with other tables increases their verbality, but BOOK remains the leading candidate by a large margin. HEADING's verbality decreases sharply after information transfer because of its low connectivity.

The focus discovery module returns a *focal summary,* a list of the top k tables with the highest verbalities. The focal summary is similar to the intensional summary described by Polifroni and Walker (2008), which communicates the contents of a single table to a user. A key difference is that the focal summary pertains to the entire database.

ODDMER is currently limited to the table and attribute labels assigned by the database designer. For example, the Heiskell 'BOOK' table was labeled 'BIBREC' by the database designers, for Bibliographic Record. We renamed this table prior to its use as a backend for the dialogue system. But ODDMER has no way to determine if labels are meaningful. In many cases there is a disincentive towards meaningful table names to avoid conflicts with SQL keywords. Future work will explore how to infer more meaningful table and attribute labels from a database instantiation, for example by consulting external knowledge bases to predict the entity a table represents.

3.3 Focus agent generation

Focus discovery fits naturally into an agent-based or agenda-based approach to dialogue management (Bohus & Rudnicky, 2009; Nguyen & Wobcke, 2005). At the onset of a dialogue, ODDMER's root agent announces the focal summary and prompts the user for her goal. Upon receipt of a user reply, it launches the appropriate *focus agent*, a finite state machine based on Information State Update (Traum & Larsson, 2003), whose parameters are a table, its list of intelligible attributes, and their computed specificity scores. The agent elicits constraints from the user until the current goal is satisfied or the user abandons the focus. Control over the dialogue then returns to the root, which queries the user for a new focus or ends the dialogue. Figure 2 shows a sample dialogue.

1. S: Hello, I can help you find a Book. Would you like to find a Book?
2. U: I'd like a Book.
3. S: Do you know the annotation?
4: U: No.
5: S: Do you know the title?
6. U: It's *Gone with the Wind*

Figure 2. ODDMER's root agent gives the focal summary (k=1) in line 1. The BOOK focus agent launches in line 3 and prompts for the value of the most specific intelligible attribute.

The default strategy of the focus agent is to elicit the most specific, intelligible constraints first. While intelligible attributes are more likely to be known by users, they are not equally valuable as item descriptions. As shown in Table 2, the specificities of NARRATOR, PUBLISHER, and SERIES are so low that a strategy involving them will likely lead to inefficient dialogues and unsatisfied users. The focus agent therefore orders its prompts for constraints by their specificity, and requests the most specific attributes first. Because specificity is a function of the database instantiation and not user knowledge, we expect that this strategy will lead to shorter, more efficient dialogues for all users.

The dialogue starts with the root agent in control of the dialogue. The root agent announces the focal summary, the k tables with highest verbality.

Here we let k=1. The root agent parses the user's reply to determine the focus of interest and launches the appropriate agent. The agent interacts with the user to find a tuple from the table. Its default strategy elicits constraints from the user in order of semantic specificity. Because semantic specificity can apply to combinations of attributes, future work will investigate tradeoffs between efficiency and user effort in prompts for multiple attributes.

The focus agent queries the database upon receipt of each new constraint. If the return size is small enough (here, a single tuple) it announces the result. Otherwise it continues to elicit constraints until all intelligible attributes have elicited values, at which point it announces all matching results.

ODDMER deals with three goal setbacks: (1) disambiguation, in which a query is under-constrained and matches multiple tuples; (2) over-constrained queries that have no matching tuple; and (3) attributes whose values are unknown to the user. The third setback is particularly prevalent in real-world databases. Our system addresses these setbacks with specific, intelligible vocabulary.

4 Evaluation

ODDMER finds foci and vocabulary for any relational database. We evaluate it on three very different domains. These databases were chosen for their variety, and are not equally suitable for dialogue. Our primary domain of consideration is *Heiskell,* the database of the Heiskell Library. *Heiskell* has eight tables. The largest table is CIRCULATION HISTORY, which contains 16 attributes with 244,072 rows. However, focus discovery identifies BOOK as the top candidate focus, which matches our intuition. Though BOOK is smaller at only 71,166 rows, it has 32 attributes of which seven are classified as intelligible. The classifier finds none of CIRCULATION HISTORY's attributes intelligible. Manual inspection revealed CIRCULATION HISTORY to consist primarily of alphanumeric codes relevant to the library rather than to users.

The second domain we consider is *Grocery*, a small supermarket database used as a teaching tool in an undergraduate class at Hunter College. Grocery has 20 tables. Their cardinalities range from 7 to 197 rows. The top focus in *Grocery* represents the products sold in the store. It was the largest table with the greatest connectivity, and makes intuitive sense; it is the table a supermarket customer would most likely want to talk about.

To challenge our system we consider *Eve,* a freely available database for the virtual game Eve Online, a massively multiplayer online role-playing game with over 400,000 subscribers. *Eve* has 78 tables and the game's active community regularly accesses it to determine in-game goals and objects of interest. *Eve* is a challenge for ODDMER because it primarily contains numeric data for objects in the game world. These numeric attributes are of great interest to players but confound our assumption that dialogue goals correlate with high verbality. Moreover, connectivity plays no role in table verbality because *Eve* contains no joins. Focus discovery on *Eve* identifies INVTYPES, a table that represents in-game inventory items, as the best focus, even though vocabulary selection identifies only three of its 15 attributes as intelligible. The 12 unintelligible attributes were all numeric. In general, focus discovery and vocabulary selection proved less effective on *Eve* than on *Heiskell*. In *Eve* the verbality scores of the top tables were close together without one outstanding focus candidate.

4.1 Simulating the vocabulary problem

A typical evaluation of a spoken dialogue system provides users with all the information needed to carry out a dialogue. Such a *completely knowledgeable* user can unrealistically describe objects in the domain with the same vocabulary that the system uses. This means it does not experience the vocabulary problem. To test vocabulary selection, we simulate users with *incomplete* domain knowledge. In contrast with Selfridge and Heeman (2010), our limited-knowledge users are more likely to know some attributes than others.

User simulation is often used to stand in for real user dialogues, but it is a concern whether the dialogues are sufficiently realistic (Schatzmann, Georgila, & Young, 2005). Here, we use simulation to exercise each dialogue system with a large number of cases in a highly controlled fashion. For simulated users, we can specify exactly what each user knows about the domain, thus simulation makes it possible to hold everything else the same while contrasting users with complete versus incomplete domain knowledge. We view this as a preliminary step towards evaluation with real users, which we hope to do in future work.

	Heiskell	*Grocery*	*Eve*
C/N/R	15.9 ± 0.4	11.1 ± 0.2	16.3 ± 0.4
C/N/S	9.0 ± 0.0	9.0 ± 0.0	9.0 ± 0.0
C/V/R	11.5 ± 0.2	11.1 ± 0.3	10.6 ± 0.1
C/V/S	9.5 ± 0.1	9.0 ± 0.0	9.0 ± 0.0
L/N/R	25.3 ± 0.8	13.1 ± 0.2	17.7 ± 0.5
L/N/S	16.5 ± 0.6	9.3 ± 0.1	9.4 ± 0.1
L/V/R	12.4 ± 0.2	12.2 ± 0.1	10.7 ± 0.1
L/V/S	11.3 ± 0.2	9.7 ± 0.1	9.0 ± 0.0

Table 4. Mean dialogue length across domains. C/*/*: complete-knowledge user; L/*/*: incomplete-knowledge user; */N/*: no vocabulary selection; */V/*: with vocabulary selection; */*/R: random order; */*/S: order by specificity. Intervals are 95% confidence.

Our simulated user knows each attribute's value with a different probability. Ideally we might estimate these probabilities from a language model of a corpus in the domain. Unfortunately our domains contain many obscure names and non-verbal values for which we need non-zero probabilities. Instead, we estimate a probability for attribute value knowledge by calculating the frequency of total value occurrences in a subset of the New York Times portion of the English Gigaword corpus (Parker et al., 2011), a 4 million word corpus of news articles. These frequency values could have been used during vocabulary selection but we chose to reserve them for evaluation.

The probability that the limited-knowledge user knows a particular value is the normalized frequency that the attribute's values appear in Gigaword. We tokenized attribute values in our databases to remove punctuation and case. We ignored word order so that, for example, the author values "King, Stephen" and "Stephen King" are equivalent. For each value, we counted the articles in which all the value's tokens co-occurred. For each attribute, we took the sum of these counts over all its values, and took its log to represent the probability that the user knows that attribute. We then normalized by the log of the highest-frequency attribute to enforce our assumption that the user usually knows at least one piece of information about her goal. This method is robust to attributes with missing values. Probabilities for the BOOK attributes were 100% for TITLE, 78% for AUTHOR, 75% for PLACE PUBLISHED, and 73% for PUBLISHER. ISBN has a 0% probability because none of its values occur in the corpus. ANNOTATIONS, whose values are brief plot descriptions of each book, has a low 37%. Although its values contained many common words, the words in a single annotation rarely co-occurred in one article.

4.2 Testing the impact of domain knowledge

We evaluate dialogue efficiency with two simulated users as measured by number of turns. The first user, C, has complete domain knowledge and always knows every constraint. The second, L, has limited, incomplete domain knowledge. When confronted with the focal summary, the simulated user always chooses the top suggested focus. The dialogue ends when either a single tuple matching the constraints is found, or all constraints have been requested, in which case all matching tuples are announced. We measure average dialogue length of 1000 simulated dialogues for each user with vocabulary selection (V) and without (N), and with prompts ordered randomly (R) or by specificity (S). Table 4 shows the results. ANOVAs of all pairs of comparisons were highly significant.

The longest dialogues for both users occur without vocabulary selection and with prompts in random order (*/N/R). The more attributes there are, the longer it takes a random order to achieve a constraint combination that forms a key, so C has long dialogues even though it knows every constraint. L experiences much longer dialogues because it is prompted for inefficient constraints, and is unlikely to know most of them. This difference is particularly noticeable in *Heiskell*. On average, L's dialogues are ten turns longer.

Ordering prompts by specificity without vocabulary selection (*/N/S) yields a sharp increase in efficiency for both users. C's dialogues achieve the minimum number of turns because it is immediately asked for the most specific constraint, which it always knows. In *Heiskell*, specificity decreases L's average length from 25.3 to 16.5, a large increase in efficiency but still much worse than C. For *Eve*, L performs better in the absence of vocabulary selection. Specificity alone brings its average efficiency near optimum. This is because for *Eve*'s INVTYPES table, the most specific intelligible attribute is the item's NAME, which our domain knowledge model predicts L will always know.

Vocabulary selection is more effective than specificity for L on *Heiskell*. L is much more likely to know the selected attributes and its efficiency increases even when prompted for intelligible attributes in a random order. Vocabulary selection is less effective than specificity for C because C knows every attribute, but in general the intelligible attributes are also more specific, so selection increases C's efficiency even with random prompts. Vocabulary selection combined with specificity (*/V/S) leads to a small *decrease* in efficiency for C on *Heiskell* over specificity alone. This is because the most specific intelligible attribute is slightly ambiguous, and C must occasionally supply extra constraints to disambiguate. However, with both specificity and vocabulary selection, L achieves a mean dialogue length of 11.3, requiring only two turns more than C to order a book.

For *Eve*, vocabulary selection and order-by-specificity are each effective individually, and yield similar dialogues for both L and C. This is because INVTYPES has only three intelligible attributes, so the dialogue ends after at most three prompts. Our domain knowledge model predicts close to 100% knowledge for two of these.

A comparison of the order-by-specificity strategy used here with the order-by-entropy strategy described by Polifroni and Walker (2006) yielded no significant difference in dialogue length. The two strategies produce similar attribute orders.

5 Conclusion and Open Questions

We have demonstrated an open dialogue management system, ODDMER, which formulates a dialogue strategy by computing *metaknowledge* about its database: table verbality, attribute intelligibility, and attribute specificity. Candidate dialogue foci are the tables with high verbality. For each candidate focus, ODDMER chooses an intelligible domain vocabulary and generates a default strategy that orders prompts by specificity. A simulated user facing the vocabulary problem achieves more efficient dialogues with vocabulary selection. Our method works well on the Heiskell Library database, which has a particularly prominent candidate focus showing a clear separation between intelligible and unintelligible attributes. Focus discovery and vocabulary selection are less effective for numeric databases without clear dialogue goals. For example, *Eve*'s top focus scored the highest verbality, even though the table contained only three intelligible attributes.

Questions that arise from this work include how to extend focus discovery and vocabulary selection to numerical databases, how to extract strategies for goals other than tuple-selection from a database, and how to automatically infer intelligible table and attribute labels. We are also interested in discovery of less rigid dialogue goals, for example, a library patron who would be satisfied by an alternative book, and goals involving information aggregation where user utterances map to sophisticated queries. We would like to investigate how optimal policies learned through reinforcement learning vary across domains. Future work will also scale to mixed-initiative open dialogue management, explore more sophisticated models of user domain knowledge, and evaluate portability on more databases.

ODDMER uses the semantics of its domain representation to discover what to talk about and how to talk about it. We envision a rich toolkit that enables a system to explore its database for knowledge to exploit in collaborative dialogues with its users.

Acknowledgements

The first author was supported in part by NSF grant IIS-0803481, ONR grant N00014-11-1-0294, and DARPA contract FA8750-09-C-0179. The second author was supported by the NSF grant IIS-0745369. This research was carried out at Columbia University. We thank Susan Epstein, Oren Etzioni, Wlodek Zadrozny, and the anonymous reviewers for helpful comments. We thank Luis Gravano for valuable literature suggestions, and Susan Epstein for use of the Grocery database.

References

Bohus, D., & Rudnicky, A. (2009). The RavenClaw Dialog Management Framework: Architecture and systems. *Computer Speech and Language 23*(3), 332-361.

Chotimongkol, A., & Rudnicky, A. I. (2008). *Acquiring Domain-Specific Dialog Information from Task-Oriented Human-Human Interaction through an Unsupervised Learning*. Paper presented at the Conference on Empirical Methods in Natural Language Processing (EMNLP '08).

Cimiano, P., Haase, P., Heizmann, J., Mantel, M., & Studer, R. (2008). Towards Portable Natural Language Interfaces to Knowledge Bases - The case of the ORAKEL system. *Data & Knowledge Engineering, 65*(2), 325-354.

Cohen, W. W. (1995). *Fast Effective Rule Induction.* Paper presented at the Twelfth International Conference on Machine Learning.

Demberg, V., & Moore, J. D. (2006). *Information Presentation in Spoken Dialogue Systems.* Paper presented at the 11th Conference of the European Chapter of the Association of Computational Linguistics (EACL 2006).

Freund, Y., & Mason, L. (1999). *The Alternating Decision Tree Learning Algorithm.* Paper presented at the Sixteenth International Conference on Machine Learning (ICML).

Furnas, G. W., Landauer, T. K., Gomez, L. M., & Dumais, S. T. (1987). The Vocabulary Problem in Human-System Communication. *Communications of the ACM, 30*(11), 964-971.

Grosz, B. J. (1983). *TEAM: a Transportable Natural-Language Interface System.* Paper presented at the First conference on Applied natural language processing.

Grosz, B. J., & Sidner, C. L. (1986). Attention, intentions, and the structure of discourse. *Computational Linguistics, 12*(3), 175-204.

Hall, M., Frank, E., Holmes, G., Pfahringer, B., Reutemann, P., & Witten, I. H. (2009). The WEKA Data Mining Software: An Update. *SIGKDD Explorations, 11*(1).

Hastie, H., Liu, X., & Lemon, O. (2009). *Automatic Generation of Information State Update Dialogue Systems that Dynamically Create Voice XML, as Demonstrated on the iPhone.* Paper presented at the 10th Annual SIGdial Meeting on Discourse and Dialogue (SIGdial 2009).

Hixon, B., Passonneau, R. J., & Epstein, S. L. (2012). *Semantic Specificity in Spoken Dialogue Requests.* Paper presented at the 13th Annual SIGdial Meeting on Discourse and Dialogue (SIGdial 2012).

Janarthanam, S., & Lemon, O. (2010). *Learning to Adapt to Unknown Users: Referring Expression Generation in Spoken Dialogue Systems.* Paper presented at the 48th Annual Meeting of the Association for Computational Linguistics (ACL 2010), Uppsala, Sweden.

Jayapandian, M., & Jagadish, H. V. (2008). *Automated creation of a forms-based database query interface.* Paper presented at the 34th international conference on Very large data bases (VLDB '08).

Krippendorff, K. (1980). *Content Analysis: An Introduction to its Methodology.* Beverly Hills, CA: Sage Publications.

Nguyen, A., & Wobcke, W. (2005). *An Agent-based Approach to Dialogue Management in Personal Assistants.* Paper presented at the 10th international conference on Intelligent user interfaces (IUI '05), New York.

Paek, T., & Pieraccini, R. (2008). Automating Spoken Dialogue Management Design Using Machine Learning: An Industry Perspective. *Speech Communication, 50*, 716-729.

Parker, R., Graff, D., Kong, J., Chen, K., & Maeda, K. (2011). *English Gigaword Fifth Edition.* Philadelphia: Linguistic Data Consortium.

Polifroni, J., Chung, G., & Seneff, S. (2003). *Towards the Automatic Generation of Mixed-Initiative Dialogue Systems from Web Content.* Paper presented at the Eurospeech 2003.

Polifroni, J., & Walker, M. (2006). *Learning Database Content for Spoken Dialogue System Design.* Paper presented at the 5th International Conference on Language Resources and Evaluation (LREC).

Polifroni, J., & Walker, M. (2008). *Intensional Summaries as Cooperative Responses in Dialogue: Automation and Evaluation.* Paper presented at the ACL-HLT.

Rieser, V., & Lemon, O. (2009). Does this list contain what you were searching for? Learning Adaptive Dialogue Strategies for Interactive Question Answering. *Natural Language Engineering, 15*(1), 55-72.

Rosch, E. (1978). Principles of Categorization. In E. Rosch & B. Lloyd (Eds.), *Cognition and Categorization* (pp. 27-48). Hillsdale, NJ: Lawrence Erlbaum.

Schatzmann, J., Georgila, K., & Young, S. (2005). *Quantitative Evaluation of User Simulation Techniques for Spoken Dialogue Systems.* Paper presented at the 6th SIGdial Workshop on Discourse and Dialogue.

Selfridge, E., & Heeman, P. (2010). *Importance-Driven Turn-Bidding for Spoken Dialogue Systems.* Paper presented at the 48th Annual Meeting of the Association for Computational Linguistics (ACL 2010).

Traum, D., & Larsson, S. (2003). The Information State Approach to Dialogue Management. In Jan van Kuppevelt and Ronnie Smith (Eds.), *Current and new directions in discourse and dialogue.* Kluwer: 325-353.

Varges, S., Weng, F., & Pon-Barry, H. (2006). *Interactive Question Answering and Constraint Relaxation in Spoken Dialogue Systems.* Paper presented at the 7th Annual SIGdial Meeting on Discourse and Dialogue (SIGdial 2006).

Yang, X., Procopiuc, C. M., & Srivastava, D. (2009). *Summarizing Relational Databases.* Paper presented at the 35th international conference on Very large data bases (VLDB '09).

Yu, C., & Jagadish, H. V. (2006). *Schema Summarization.* Paper presented at the 32nd international conference on Very large data bases (VLDB '06).

A method for the approximation of incremental understanding of explicit utterance meaning using predictive models in finite domains

David DeVault and **David Traum**
Institute for Creative Technologies, University of Southern California,
12015 Waterfront Dr., Playa Vista, CA 90094 USA
{devault,traum}@ict.usc.edu

Abstract

This paper explores the relationship between explicit and predictive models of incremental speech understanding in a dialogue system that supports a finite set of user utterance meanings. We present a method that enables the approximation of explicit understanding using information implicit in a predictive understanding model for the same domain. We show promising performance for this method in a corpus evaluation, and discuss its practical application and annotation costs in relation to some alternative approaches.

1 Introduction

In recent years, there has been a growing interest among researchers in methods for incremental natural language understanding (NLU) for spoken dialogue systems; see e.g. (Skantze and Schlangen, 2009; Sagae et al., 2009; Schlangen et al., 2009; Heintze et al., 2010; DeVault et al., 2011a; Selfridge et al., 2012). This work has generally been motivated by a desire to make dialogue systems more efficient and more natural, by enabling them to provide lower latency responses (Skantze and Schlangen, 2009), human-like feedback such as backchannels that indicate how well the system is understanding user speech (DeVault et al., 2011b; Traum et al., 2012), and more interactive response capabilities such as collaborative completions of user utterances (DeVault et al., 2011a), more adaptive handling of interruptions (Buschmeier et al., 2012), and others.

This paper builds on techniques developed in previous work that has adopted a *predictive* approach to incremental NLU (DeVault et al., 2011a). On this approach, at specific moments while a user's speech is in progress, an attempt is made to predict what the full meaning of the complete user utterance will be. Predictive models can be contrasted with *explicit* approaches to incremental NLU. We use the term *explicit* understanding to refer to approaches that attempt to determine the meaning that has been expressed explicitly in the user's partial utterance so far (without predicting further aspects of meaning to come). Explicit understanding of partial utterances can be implemented using statistical classification or sequential tagging models (Heintze et al., 2010).

Both predictive and explicit incremental NLU capabilities can be valuable in a dialogue system. Prediction can support specific response capabilities, such as system completion of user utterances (DeVault et al., 2011a) and reduced response latency.[1] However, explicit models support additional and complementary capabilities. For instance, depending on the application domain (Heintze et al., 2010) and on the individual utterance (DeVault et al., 2011b), it may be difficult for a system to predict a user's impending meaning with confidence. Nevertheless, it may often be possible for systems to determine the meaning of what a user has said so far, and to take action based on this partial understanding. As one example, items in a user interface could be highlighted when mentioned by a user (Buß and Schlangen, 2011). Another capability would be to provide grounding feedback, such as verbal back-channels or head nods (in embodied systems), to indicate when the system is understanding the user's meaning (Traum et al., 2012). Explicit utterance meanings also allow a system to distinguish between meaning that has been expressed and meaning that is merely implied or inferred, which may be less reliable. In the near future, as incremental processing capabilities in dialogue systems grow, it may prove valuable for dialogue systems to combine both predictive and explicit incremental understanding capabilities.

In this paper, we present a technique for approximating a user's explicit meaning using an existing predictive understanding framework (DeVault et al., 2011a). The specific new contributions in this paper are (1) to show that

[1] A simple approach to reducing response latency is to begin to plan a response to the predicted meaning while the user is still speaking.

an estimate of a user's explicit utterance meaning can be derived from this kind of predictive understanding model (Section 2); (2) to quantify the performance of this new method in a corpus evaluation (Section 3); (3) to provide concrete examples and discussion of the annotation costs associated with implementing this technique, in relation to some alternative approaches to explicit understanding (Section 4). Our results and discussion show that the proposed method offers promising performance, has relatively low annotation costs, and enables explicit and predictive understanding to be easily combined within a dialogue system. It may therefore be a useful incremental understanding technique for some dialogue systems.

2 Technical Approach and Data Set

In Sections 2.1-2.3, we briefly summarize the data set and approach to predictive incremental NLU (DeVault et al., 2011a) that serves as the starting point for the new work in this paper. Sections 2.4 and 2.5 present our new approach to explicit understanding based on this approach.

2.1 Data set

For the experiments reported here, we use a corpus of user utterances collected with the SASO-EN spoken dialogue system (Hartholt et al., 2008; Traum et al., 2008). Briefly, this system is designed to allow a trainee to practice multi-party negotiation skills by engaging in face to face negotiation with virtual humans. The scenario involves a negotiation about the possible re-location of a medical clinic in an Iraqi village. A human trainee plays the role of a US Army captain, and there are two virtual humans that he negotiates with: Doctor Perez, the head of an NGO clinic, and a local village elder, al-Hassan. The captain's main objective is to convince the doctor and the elder to move the clinic out of an unsafe marketplace area.

The corpus used for the experiments in this paper includes 3,826 training and 449 testing utterances drawn from user dialogues in this domain. The corpus and its semantic annotation are described in (DeVault et al., 2010; DeVault et al., 2011a). All user utterances have been audio recorded, transcribed, and manually annotated with the correct NLU output frame for the entire utterance. (We discuss the cost of this annotation in Section 4.) Each NLU output frame contains a set of attributes and values that represent semantic information linked to a domain-specific ontology and task model (Traum, 2003). Examples of the NLU output frames are included in Figures 2, 3, and 5.

2.2 Predictive incremental NLU

This approach uses a predictive incremental NLU module, mxNLU (Sagae et al., 2009; DeVault et al., 2011a), which is based on maximum entropy classification. The approach treats entire individual frames as output classes, and extracts input features from partial ASR results. To define the incremental understanding problem, the audio of the utterances in the training data were fed through an ASR module, PocketSphinx (Huggins-Daines et al., 2006), in 200 millisecond chunks, and each partial ASR result produced by the ASR was recorded. Each partial ASR result then serves as an incremental input to mxNLU. NLU is predictive in the sense that, for each partial ASR result, the task of mxNLU is to produce as output the *complete* frame that has been associated by a human annotator with the user's *complete* utterance, even if that utterance has not yet been fully processed by the ASR.

The human annotation defines a finite set $\mathcal{S} = \{S_1, ..., S_N\}$ of possible NLU output frames, where each frame $S_i = \{e_1, ..., e_n\}$ is a set of key-value pairs or *frame elements*. For notation, a user utterance u generally creates a sequence of m partial ASR results $\langle r_1, ..., r_m \rangle$, where each ASR result r_j is a partial text such as *we need to move*. Let G_u denote the correct (or "gold") frame for the complete utterance u. For each result r_j and for each complete frame S_i, the maximum entropy model provides $P(G_u = S_i | r_j)$. The NLU output frame S_j^{NLU} is the complete frame for which this probability is highest.

2.3 Performance of predictive incremental NLU

The performance of this predictive incremental NLU framework has been evaluated using the training and test portions of the SASO-EN data set described in Section 2.1. Performance is quantified by looking at precision, recall, and F-score of the frame elements that compose the predicted (S_j^{NLU}) and correct (G_u) frames for each partial ASR result. When evaluated over all the 5,736 partial ASR results for the 449 test utterances, the precision/recall/F-Score of this predictive NLU, in relation to the complete frames, are 0.67/0.47/0.56, respectively. When evaluated on only the ASR results for complete test utterances, these scores increase to 0.81/0.71/0.76, respectively.

2.4 Assigning probability to frame elements

An interesting question is whether we can use this model to attach useful probabilities not only to complete predicted frames but also to the individual frame elements that make up those frames. To explore this, for each partial ASR result r_j in each utterance u, and for each frame element e in SASO-EN, let us model the probability that e will be part of the correct frame for the complete utterance as:

$$P(e \in G_u | r_j) = \sum_{S_i : e \in S_i} P(G_u = S_i | r_j) \qquad (1)$$

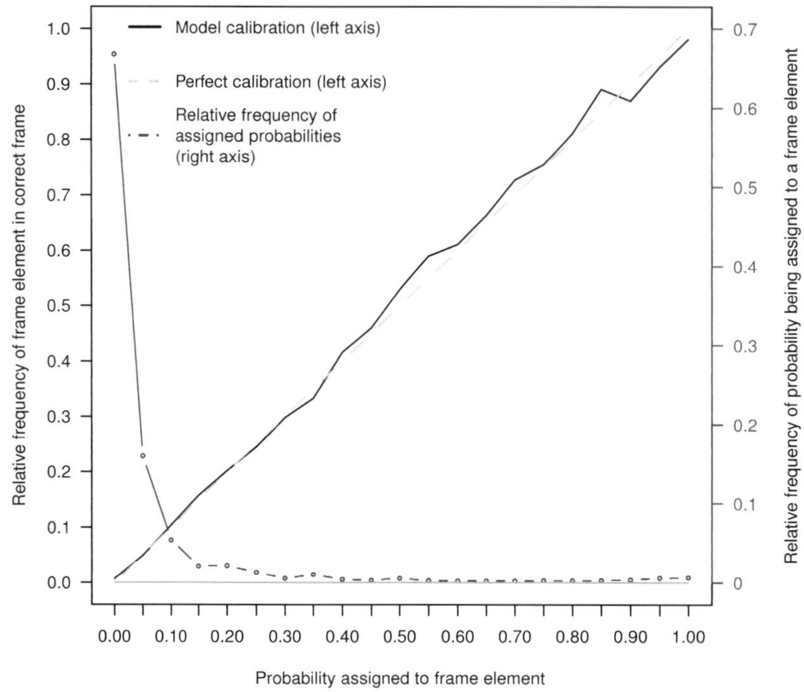

Figure 1: Calibration of frame element probabilities.

This method derives the probability of frame elements from the probabilities assigned to the possible frames that contain them. Computing this sum is straightforward in a finite semantic domain such as SASO-EN.

We computed this probability for all frame elements e and all partial ASR results r_j in our test set, yielding approximately 478,000 probability values. We grouped these probability values into bins of size 0.05, and calculated the frequency with which the frame elements in each bin were indeed present in the correct frame G_u for the relevant utterance u. The results are presented in Figure 1, which shows that the probability values derived from Equation (1) are relatively "well calibrated", in the sense that the relative frequency with which a frame element is in the final frame is very close to the numeric probability assigned by Equation (1). The figure also shows how frequently the model assigns various probability ranges to frame elements (blue dotted line, plotted against the secondary right axis). Note that most frame elements are assigned very little probability for most partial ASR results.

We conclude from these observations that the probabilities assigned by (1) could indeed carry useful information about the likelihood that individual key values will be present in the complete utterance meaning.

2.5 Selecting probable frame elements

In exploring the model of frame element probabilities given in Equation (1), we observed that often the reason a frame element has lower probability, at a given point within a user utterance, is that it is a *prediction* rather than something that has been expressed explicitly. Building on this observation, our technique for estimating the user's explicit meaning uses a probability threshold to select those individual frame elements which are most likely to be in the frame for a complete utterance, according to the predictive model. That is, at each partial result r_j, we estimate the user's explicit meaning using a constructed frame:

$$S_j^{\text{SUB}} = \{e|P(e \in G_u|r_j) \geq \tau\} \tag{2}$$

This approximation could work well if, in practice, the most probable frame elements prove to match fairly closely the user's non-incremental utterance meaning at the point this frame is constructed. We evaluate this in the next section.

Note that, in general, the returned subset of frame elements may not be identical to any complete frame $S_i \in \mathcal{S}$; rather it will correspond to parts of these complete frames or "subframes".

3 Performance Evaluation

To evaluate this technique, we constructed subsets of frame elements or "explicit subframes" using Equation (2) and various minimum probability thresholds τ for partial ASR results in our test set. We then compared the resulting subframes both to the final complete frame G_u for each utterance u, and also to manually annotated sub-

Explicit subframe (with frame element probabilities)	**Predicted complete frame**	**Annotated subframe**
Partial ASR result: *hello*		
0.813 <S>.sem.speechact.type greeting	<S>.sem.speechact.type greeting <S>.addressee doctor-perez	<S>.sem.speechact.type greeting
Partial ASR result: *hello elder*		
0.945 <S>.sem.speechact.type greeting 0.934 <S>.addressee elder-al-hassan	<S>.sem.speechact.type greeting <S>.addressee elder-al-hassan	<S>.sem.speechact.type greeting <S>.addressee elder-al-hassan

Figure 2: Explicit subframes and predicted complete frames for two partial ASR results in a user utterance of *hello elder*.

frames that represent human judgments of explicit incremental utterance meaning.

To collect these judgments, we hand-annotated a word-meaning alignment for 50 random utterances in our test set.[2] To perform this annotation, successively larger prefixes of each utterance transcript were mapped to successively larger subframes of the full frame for the complete utterance. The annotated subframes for each utterance prefix were selected to be *explicit*; they include only those frame elements that are explicitly expressed in the corresponding prefix of the user's utterance. (We discuss the cost of this annotation in Section 4.)

We provide a simple concrete example in Figure 2. This example shows two partial ASR results during an utterance of *hello elder* by a user. For each partial ASR result, three frames are indicated horizontally. At the right, labeled "Annotated subframe", we show the human judgment of explicit incremental utterance meaning for this partial utterance. Our human judge has indicated that the word *hello* corresponds to the frame element `<S>.sem.speechact.type greeting`, and that the words *hello elder* correspond to an expanded frame that includes the frame element `<S>.addressee elder-al-hassan`.

At the left, labeled "Explicit subframe", we show the subframe selected by Equation (2) for each partial ASR result, with threshold $\tau = 0.5$. A relevant background fact for this example is that in this scenario, the user can generally address either of two virtual humans who are present, Doctor Perez or Elder Al-Hassan. After the user has said *hello*, the frame element `<S>.sem.speechact.type greeting` is assigned probability 0.813 by Equation (1), and only this frame element appears in the explicit subframe.

In the middle, labeled "Predicted complete frame", the figure also shows the full predicted frame from mxNLU at each point. After the user has said *hello*, the full predicted output includes an additional frame element, `<S>.addressee doctor-perez`, indicating a prediction that the addressee of this user utterance will be Doctor Perez rather than Elder al-Hassan. However, the probability assigned to this prediction by Equation (1) is less than 0.5, and so this predicted frame element is excluded from the explicit subframe. And indeed, this is the correct *explicit* representation of the meaning of *hello* in this system.

This simple example illustrates how our proposed technique can enable a dialogue system to have access to both explicit and predicted utterance meaning as a user's utterance progresses. An excerpt from a more complex utterance is given in Figure 3. This example shows incremental outputs for two partial ASR results during a user utterance of *we will provide transportation at no cost*. In this example, the explicit subframe for *we will* includes frame elements that convey that the captain (i.e. the user) is promising to do something. This subframe does not exactly match the human judgment of explicit meaning at the right, which does not include at this point the `<S>.sem.agent captain-kirk` and `<S>.sem.type event` frame elements. However, the explicit subframe more closely matches the human judgment than does the predicted complete frame from mxNLU (middle column), which includes an incorrect prediction that the captain is promising to deliver medical supplies (represented by the key values `<S>.sem.event deliver` and `<S>.sem.theme medical-supplies`). For the next partial ASR result shown in the figure, the explicit subframe correctly adds several additional frame elements which formalize the meaning of the phrase *provide transportation* in this scenario as having the army move the clinic out of the market area.

To understand more quantitatively how well this technique works, we evaluated this technique in the SASO-EN test corpus, using different probability thresholds in the range [0.5,1.0). We present the results in Figure 4. To understand the effect of the threshold τ, note that, in general, the effect of selecting a higher threshold should be to "cherry pick" those frame elements which are most likely to appear in the complete frame G_u, thereby increasing precision while decreasing recall of the frame elements in S_j^{SUB} in relation to G_u. In the figure, we can see that this is indeed the case. The lines marked "(complete frame)"

[2]Note that no utterances in our *training* set were annotated.

Explicit subframe (with frame element probabilities)	**Predicted complete frame**	**Annotated subframe**
Partial ASR result: *we will*		
0.856 <S>.mood declarative	<S>.mood declarative	<S>.mood declarative
0.824 <S>.sem.agent captain-kirk	<S>.sem.agent captain-kirk	<S>.sem.modal.intention will
0.663 <S>.sem.modal.intention will	<S>.sem.event deliver	<S>.sem.speechact.type promise
0.663 <S>.sem.speechact.type promise	<S>.sem.modal.intention will	
0.776 <S>.sem.type event	<S>.sem.speechact.type promise	
	<S>.sem.theme medical-supplies	
	<S>.sem.type event	
Partial ASR result: *we will provide transportation*		
0.991 <S>.mood declarative	<S>.mood declarative	<S>.mood declarative
0.990 <S>.sem.agent captain-kirk	<S>.sem.agent captain-kirk	<S>.sem.agent captain-kirk
0.927 <S>.sem.event move	<S>.sem.event move	<S>.sem.event move
0.905 <S>.sem.instrument us-army	<S>.sem.instrument us-army	<S>.sem.instrument us-army
0.964 <S>.sem.modal.intention will	<S>.sem.modal.intention will	<S>.sem.modal.intention will
0.927 <S>.sem.source market	<S>.sem.source market	<S>.sem.source market
0.964 <S>.sem.speechact.type promise	<S>.sem.speechact.type promise	<S>.sem.speechact.type promise
0.928 <S>.sem.theme clinic	<S>.sem.theme clinic	<S>.sem.theme clinic
0.989 <S>.sem.type event	<S>.sem.type event	<S>.sem.type event

Figure 3: Explicit subframes and predicted complete frames for two partial ASR results in a user utterance of we *will provide transportation at no cost*.

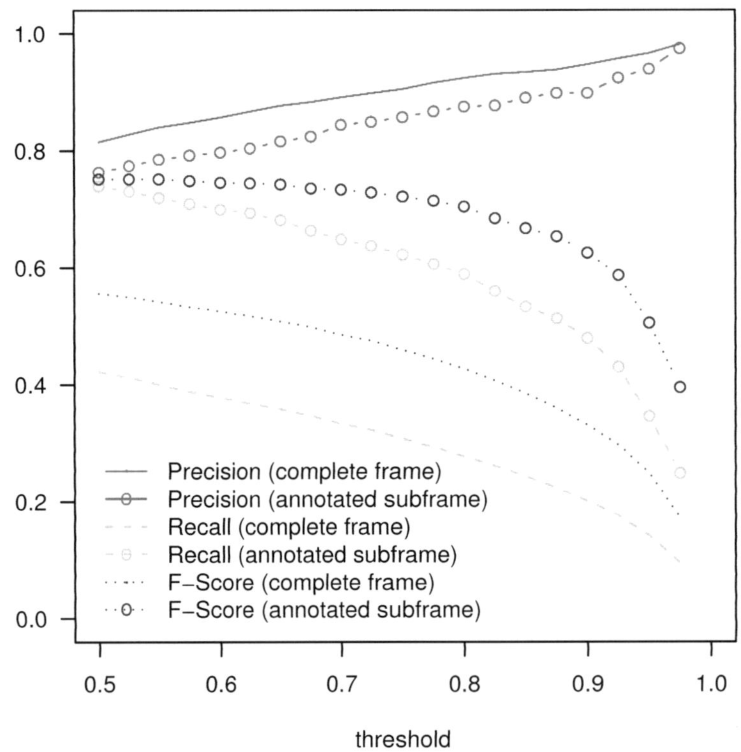

Figure 4: The effect of threshold on precision, recall, and F-Score of explicit subframes. All scores are measured in relation to complete utterance frames and annotated subframes.

in the figure evaluate the returned subframes in relation to the complete frame G_u associated with the user's *complete* utterance. We see that this method enables us to select subsets of frame elements that are most likely to appear in G_u: by increasing the threshold, it is possible to return subframes which are of increasingly higher precision in relation to the final frame G_u, but that also have lower recall.

We also evaluated the returned subframes in relation to the hand-annotated subframes, to assess its performance at identifying the user's explicit meaning. For an utterance u that generates partial ASR results $\langle r_1, ..., r_m \rangle$, we denote the hand-annotated subframe corresponding to partial ASR result r_j by G_j^{SUB}. In the lines marked "(annotated subframe)", we show the precision, recall, and F-score of the explicit subframe for each ASR result r_j in relation to the annotated subframe G_j^{SUB}.

As a first observation, note that at any threshold level, the explicit subframes do better at recalling the hand-annotated subframe elements than they do at recalling the complete frame elements. This means our new method is better at recalling what has been said already by the user than it is at predicting what will be said, as intended. We have seen two examples of this already, for the partial ASR result *hello* in Figure 2, and for the partial ASR result *we will* in Figure 3.

A second observation in Figure 4 is that precision remains better against the complete utterance frame than against the hand-annotated subframe (at all threshold levels). This indicates that the explicit subframes are often still predicting some aspects of the full frame. An example of this is given in Figure 5, where the user's partial utterance *we need to* is assigned an explicit subframe that includes frame elements describing an event of moving the clinic, which the user has not said explicitly. This happens because, in the SASO-EN domain, in fact there is nothing else that the interlocutors need to do besides move the clinic. So based on the NLU training data, the data-driven probabilities assigned by Equation (1) describe the additional frame elements as about as probable as the ones capturing the *we need to* part of the semantics (given at the right).

Finally, a third observation is that overall, the precision, recall, and F-score results against the annotated subframes using our method are surprisingly strong. For example, when evaluating the explicit subframes over all partial ASR results, an F-score of 0.75 is attained at thresholds in the range 0.5-0.55. This F-score is substantially better than the F-score of our predictive NLU in relation to the final full frames, which is 0.56 when evaluated over all partial ASR results. This means that our proposed model works better as an explicit incremental NLU than mxNLU works as a predictive incremental NLU. Further, we observe that this F-score of 0.75 against hand-annotated subframes is approximately as good as the F-score of 0.76 that is achieved when mxNLU is used to interpret complete utterances. We therefore conclude that the proposed model is a promising and viable approach to explicit incremental NLU in SASO-EN.

4 Discussion and Related Approaches

In this section, we discuss some of the practical aspects of using the technique presented here, in relation to some alternative approaches.

An important consideration for NLU techniques is the cost, in both time and knowledge, of the annotation that is needed. One attractive aspect of our technique is that the only semantic annotation that is required is the association of complete user utterances with complete NLU output frames. This task can be performed by anyone familiar with the scenario and the semantic frame format, such as a system developer or scenario designer. In fact, the annotation of the SASO-EN data set we use in this paper has been described in (DeVault et al., 2010), which reports that the overall corpus of 4678 token utterances was semantically annotated at an average rate of about 10 seconds per unique utterance.

The model in Equation (2) is what (Heintze et al., 2010) call a *hybrid output* approach, in which larger and larger frames are provided as partial input grows, but in which a detailed alignment between surface text and frames is not provided by the incremental NLU component. They contrast hybrid output systems with techniques that deliver either *whole-frame output* (like the predictive mxNLU) or *aligned output* that connects individual words to their meanings. A data-driven approach to providing aligned outputs would involve preparing a more detailed annotated corpus that aligns individual words and surface expressions to their corresponding frame elements. Given such a word-aligned corpus, one could train several kinds of models to produce the aligned outputs incrementally. One strategy would be to use a sequential tagging model such as a CRF to tag partial utterances with the frame elements that capture their explicit meaning, as in (Heintze et al., 2010).

Using a machine learning approach that models a more detailed alignment between surface text and frames would be one way to more cleanly separate explicit from predictive aspects of meaning. Preparing the training data for such models, however, would create additional annotation costs. As part of creating the annotated subframes for the evaluation presented in Section 3, we measured the time requirement for such annotation of word-meaning alignments at about 30 seconds per unique utterance. Performing full word-meaning alignment therefore takes about three times as much time as the complete utterance annotation needed for our technique. Ad-

Explicit subframe (with frame element probabilities)	**Predicted complete frame**	**Annotated subframe**
Partial ASR result: *we*		
0.753 <S>.mood declarative 0.687 <S>.sem.agent captain-kirk 0.692 <S>.sem.type event	<S>.mood declarative <S>.sem.agent captain-kirk <S>.sem.event deliver <S>.sem.modal.possibility can <S>.sem.speechact.type offer <S>.sem.theme medical-supplies <S>.sem.type event	
Partial ASR result: *we need to*		
0.945 <S>.mood declarative 0.928 <S>.sem.agent captain-kirk 0.900 <S>.sem.event move 0.816 <S>.sem.modal.deontic must 0.900 <S>.sem.source market 0.900 <S>.sem.speechact.type statement 0.906 <S>.sem.theme clinic 0.930 <S>.sem.type event	<S>.mood declarative <S>.sem.agent captain-kirk <S>.sem.event move <S>.sem.modal.deontic must <S>.sem.source market <S>.sem.speechact.type statement <S>.sem.theme clinic <S>.sem.type event	<S>.mood declarative <S>.sem.modal.deontic must <S>.sem.speechact.type statement

Figure 5: Explicit subframes and predicted complete frames for two partial ASR results in a user utterance of *we need to move the clinic*.

ditionally, this task requires a greater degree of linguistic knowledge and sophistication, as the annotator must be able to segment the utterance and align specific surface segments with potentially complex aspects of meaning such as modality, polarity, speech act types, and others. An example of the kinds of complexities that arise is illustrated in Figure 3, where the relationship between specific words like "provide" and "transportation" to frame elements like `<S>.sem.event move` and `<S>.sem.theme clinic` is not transparent, even if it is straightforward to mark the whole utterance as conveying that meaning in this domain. We have generally found this alignment task challenging for people without advanced linguistics training.

The reason we describe the method in this paper as an *approximation* of explicit NLU is that, partly because it is trained without detailed word-meaning alignments, it can be expected to occasionally include some predictive aspects of user utterance meaning. An example of this is the method's explicit subframe output for the phrase *we need to* in Figure 5.

Another way to approximate explicit NLU would be using the method (Heintze et al., 2010) call an *ensemble of classifiers*; it involves training an individual classifier for each frame key. Like the method presented here, an ensemble of classifiers can be easily trained to predict those frame elements that will appear in the *final* frame G_u for each utterance. And like our method, prediction with an ensemble of classifiers does not require detailed annotation of word-meaning alignment in the training data. One difference is that, with our method, by selecting an appropriate threshold, it is easy to enforce certain consistency properties on subframe outputs. In an ensemble of classifiers approach, there is no immediate guarantee that the output frame constructed by the independent classifiers will be internally consistent from the standpoint of downstream system modules (Heintze et al., 2010). For example, in the SASO-EN domain, an NLU frame should not contain frame elements that mix aspects of events and states in the SASO-EN ontology; e.g., the frame element `<S>.sem.type event` should not co-occur in an NLU output frame with the frame element `<S>.sem.object-id market` (which would be appropriate for a state frame but not for an event frame). With the method proposed here, if we select a threshold τ that is greater than 0.5, and if none of the complete NLU frames contain incompatible key values (which is relatively easy to enforce as part of the annotation task), then it will be mathematically impossible for two incompatible frame elements to be returned in a subframe.[3]

Ultimately, a classification method that is trained on word-meaning aligned data and that uses additional techniques to ensure that only valid, grammatical output frames are produced could prove to be an attractive approach. In future work, we will explore such techniques, and compare both their performance as well as their annotation and development costs to the approximation technique presented here.

5 Conclusion

The analysis in this paper has explored a method of approximating explicit incremental NLU using predictive

[3]Suppose frame element e_i is incompatible with e_j, and that $P(e_i \in G_u|r_j) > 0.5$. By stipulation, no complete frame $S \in \mathcal{S}$ such that $e_i \in S$ will also contain e_j. Since we know that the total probability of all the frames containing e_i must be greater than 0.5 in order for e_i to be selected, we can infer that the total probability of all frames including e_j must be less than 0.5, and thus that e_j will not be selected.

techniques in finite semantic domains. We have shown that an estimate of a user's explicit utterance meaning can be derived from an existing predictive understanding model in an example domain. We have quantified the performance of this new method in a corpus evaluation, showing that the method returns incremental explicit subframes with performance – as measured by precision, recall, and F-Score against hand-annotated subframes – that is competitive with a current statistical, data-driven approach for understanding complete spoken utterances in the same domain. We have provided examples that illustrate its strengths and weaknesses, and discussed the annotation costs associated with implementing this technique in relation to some alternative approaches. The method requires no additional annotation beyond what is needed for training an NLU module to understand complete spoken utterances. (Hand annotation of word-meaning alignment for a small number of utterances may be performed in order to tune the selected threshold and evaluate explicit understanding performance.) The method provides a free parameter that can be used to target the most advantageous levels of precision and recall for a particular dialogue system application. In future work, we will explore additional machine learning models that leverage richer training data, and investigate further the combination of explicit and predictive techniques.

Acknowledgments

The project or effort described here has been sponsored by the U.S. Army Research, Development, and Engineering Command (RDECOM). Statements and opinions expressed do not necessarily reflect the position or the policy of the United States Government, and no official endorsement should be inferred. This material is based upon work supported by the National Science Foundation under Grant No. IIS-1219253. Any opinions, findings, and conclusions or recommendations expressed in this material are those of the author(s) and do not necessarily reflect the views of the National Science Foundation.

References

Hendrik Buschmeier, Timo Baumann, Benjamin Dosch, Stefan Kopp, and David Schlangen. 2012. Combining incremental language generation and incremental speech synthesis for adaptive information presentation. In *Proceedings of the 13th Annual Meeting of the Special Interest Group on Discourse and Dialogue*, pages 295–303, Seoul, South Korea, July. Association for Computational Linguistics.

Okko Buß and David Schlangen. 2011. Dium - an incremental dialogue manager that can produce self-corrections. In *Proceedings of the 15th Workshop on the Semantics and Pragmatics of Dialogue (SemDial)*.

David DeVault, Susan Robinson, and David Traum. 2010. IORelator: A graphical user interface to enable rapid semantic annotation for data-driven natural language understanding. In *Fifth Joint ISO-ACL/SIGSEM Workshop on Interoperable Semantic Annotation*.

David DeVault, Kenji Sagae, and David Traum. 2011a. Incremental interpretation and prediction of utterance meaning for interactive dialogue. *Dialogue & Discourse*, 2(1).

David DeVault, Kenji Sagae, and David R. Traum. 2011b. Detecting the status of a predictive incremental speech understanding model for real-time decision-making in a spoken dialogue system. In *Interspeech*, pages 1021–1024.

Arno Hartholt, Thomas Russ, David Traum, Eduard Hovy, and Susan Robinson. 2008. A common ground for virtual humans: Using an ontology in a natural language oriented virtual human architecture. In European Language Resources Association (ELRA), editor, *Proc. LREC*, Marrakech, Morocco, may.

Silvan Heintze, Timo Baumann, and David Schlangen. 2010. Comparing local and sequential models for statistical incremental natural language understanding. In *The 11th Annual Meeting of the Special Interest Group in Discourse and Dialogue (SIGDIAL 2010)*.

David Huggins-Daines, Mohit Kumar, Arthur Chan, Alan W. Black, Mosur Ravishankar, and Alex I. Rudnicky. 2006. Pocketsphinx: A free, real-time continuous speech recognition system for hand-held devices. In *Proceedings of ICASSP*.

Kenji Sagae, Gwen Christian, David DeVault, and David R. Traum. 2009. Towards natural language understanding of partial speech recognition results in dialogue systems. In *NAACL HLT*.

David Schlangen, Timo Baumann, and Michaela Atterer. 2009. Incremental reference resolution: The task, metrics for evaluation, and a bayesian filtering model that is sensitive to disfluencies. In *SIGDIAL*.

Ethan O. Selfridge, Iker Arizmendi, Peter A. Heeman, and Jason D. Williams. 2012. Integrating incremental speech recognition and pomdp-based dialogue systems. In *Proceedings of the 13th Annual Meeting of the Special Interest Group on Discourse and Dialogue*, pages 275–279, Seoul, South Korea, July. Association for Computational Linguistics.

Gabriel Skantze and David Schlangen. 2009. Incremental dialogue processing in a micro-domain. In *Proceedings of EACL 2009*.

David Traum, Stacy Marsella, Jonathan Gratch, Jina Lee, and Arno Hartholt. 2008. Multi-party, multi-issue, multi-strategy negotiation for multi-modal virtual agents. In *Proc. of Intelligent Virtual Agents Conference IVA-2008*.

David Traum, David DeVault, Jina Lee, Zhiyang Wang, and Stacy C. Marsella. 2012. Incremental dialogue understanding and feedback for multi-party, multimodal conversation. In *The 12th International Conference on Intelligent Virtual Agents (IVA)*, Santa Cruz, CA, September.

David Traum. 2003. Semantics and pragmatics of questions and answers for dialogue agents. In *Proc. of the International Workshop on Computational Semantics*, pages 380–394, January.

Paving the Way to a Large-scale Pseudosense-annotated Dataset

Mohammad Taher Pilehvar and **Roberto Navigli**
Department of Computer Science
Sapienza University of Rome
{pilehvar,navigli}@di.uniroma1.it

Abstract

In this paper we propose a new approach to the generation of pseudowords, i.e., artificial words which model real polysemous words. Our approach simultaneously addresses the two important issues that hamper the generation of large pseudosense-annotated datasets: semantic awareness and coverage. We evaluate these pseudowords from three different perspectives showing that they can be used as reliable substitutes for their real counterparts.

1 Introduction

A fundamental problem in computational linguistics is the paucity of manually annotated data, such as part-of-speech tagged sentences, treebanks, and logical forms, which exist only for few languages (Ide et al., 2010). A case in point is the lack of abundant sense annotated data, which hampers the performance and coverage of lexical semantic tasks such as Word Sense Disambiguation (Navigli, 2009; Navigli, 2012, WSD) and semantic role labeling (Gildea and Jurafsky, 2002). A possible way to break this bottleneck is to use pseudowords, i.e., artificial words constructed by conflating a set of unambiguous words, with the aim of modeling polysemy in real ambiguous words. The idea of pseudowords was originally proposed by Gale et al. (1992) and Schütze (1992) for WSD evaluation, but later found application in other tasks such as selectional preferences (Erk, 2007; Bergsma et al., 2008; Chambers and Jurafsky, 2010), Word Sense Induction (Bordag, 2006; Di Marco and Navigli, 2013) or studies concerning the effects of the amount of data on machine learning for natural language disambiguation (Banko and Brill, 2001). Being made up of monosemous words, pseudowords can potentially be used to create large amounts of pseudosense-annotated data at virtually no cost, hence enabling large-scale studies in lexical semantics. Unfortunately, though, the extent of their usability for such a purpose is hampered by two main issues: semantic awareness and wide coverage.

Semantic awareness corresponds to the constraint that pseudowords, in order to be realistic, are expected to have senses which are in a semantic relationship (thus modeling systematic polysemy). Recent work has focused on this issue and, by exploiting either specific lexical hierarchies (Nakov and Hearst, 2003; Lu et al., 2006), or the WordNet structure (Otrusina and Smrz, 2010), have succeeded in generating pseudowords which are comparable to real words in terms of disambiguation difficulty. The second challenge is coverage, which corresponds to the number of distinct pseudowords an algorithm can generate. When coupled with the semantic awareness issue, wide coverage is hampered by the difficulty in generating thousands of pseudowords which mimic existing polysemous words.

Unfortunately, none of the existing approaches to the generation of pseudowords can meet both these challenges simultaneously, and this has hindered the generation of a large pseudosense-annotated dataset. For instance, approaches which exploit the monosemous neighbors of a target sense in WordNet (Otrusina and Smrz, 2010) can be used to generate pseudowords with good semantic awareness, but they have low coverage of ambiguous nouns when many pseudosense-tagged sentences are needed (cf. Section 2.1.1).

In this paper we propose a new approach, based on Personalized PageRank, which simultaneously addresses the two above-mentioned issues concerning the generation of pseudowords (i.e., semantic awareness and coverage), and hence enables the generation of large-scale pseudosense-annotated datasets. We perform three different experiments to show that our pseudowords are good at modeling existing ambiguous words in terms of disambiguation difficulty, representativeness of real senses and distinguishability of the artificial senses. As a byproduct of this work, we generate a large dataset that provides 1000 tagged sentences for each of the 15,935 pseudowords modeled after real ambiguous nouns in WordNet 3.0.

2 Pseudowords

A pseudoword $p = w_1{*}w_2{*}\ldots{*}w_n$ is an artificially-generated ambiguous word of polysemy degree n which is usually created by conflating n unique unambiguous words w_i called pseudosenses. For instance, *airplane*river* is a pseudoword with two meanings explicitly identified by its pseudosenses: *airplane* and *river*. Pseudowords are particularly interesting as they can be used to introduce controlled artificial ambiguity into a corpus. Given a pseudoword p and an untagged corpus C, this artificial tagging is achieved by substituting all occurrences of w_i in C with p for each pseudosense $i \in \{1, \ldots, n\}$. As a result, each occurrence of the pseudoword p is tagged with the underlying sense w_i. As an example, consider the following two sentences:

a1. The Wright brothers invented the *airplane*.

a2. The Nile is the longest *river* in the world.

If we replace the individual occurrences of *airplane* and *river* with the pseudoword *airplane*river* while noting the replaced term as the corresponding sense, we obtain the following pseudosense-tagged sentences:

b1. The Wright brothers invented the ***airplane*****river*.

b2. The Nile is the longest *airplane*****river*** in the world.

As a result of this procedure, we obtain a corpus of sentences containing the occurrences of an artificially ambiguous word p, for each of which we know its correct sense annotation w_i. Virtually any number of pseudowords can be created, resulting in a large pseudosense-annotated corpus. An obvious restriction on the choice of pseudosenses is that they need to be unambiguous, so as to avoid the introduction of uncontrolled ambiguity. Another constraint is that the constituent w_i must satisfy a minimum occurrence frequency in the corpus C. This minimum frequency corresponds to the number of annotated sentences that are requested for the task of interest which will exploit the resulting annotated corpus.

An immediate way of generating a pseudoword would be to randomly select its constituents from the set of all monosemous words given by a lexicon (e.g., WordNet). However, constructing a pseudoword by merely combining a random set of unambiguous words selected on the basis of their falling in the same range of occurrence frequency (Schütze, 1992), or leveraging homophones and OCR ambiguities (Yarowsky, 1993), does not provide a suitable model of a real polysemous word (Gaustad, 2001; Nakov and Hearst, 2003). This is because in the real world different senses, unless they are homonymous, share some semantic or pragmatic relation. Therefore, random pseudowords will typically model only homonymous distinctions (such as the *centimeter* vs. *curium* senses of *cm*), while they will fall short of modeling systematic polysemy (such as the *lack* vs. *insufficiency* senses of *deficiency*).

2.1 Semantically-aware Pseudowords

In order to cope with the above-mentioned limits of random pseudowords, an artificial word has to model an existing word by providing a one-to-one correspondence between each pseudosense and a corresponding sense of the modeled word. For instance, the pseudoword *lack*shortfall* is a good model of the real word *deficiency* in that its pseudosenses preserve the meanings of their corresponding real word's senses. We call this kind of artificial words semantically-aware pseudowords.

In the next two subsections, we will describe two techniques (the second of which is presented for the first time in this paper) for the generation of

Minimum Frequency	Polysemy 2	3	4	5	6	7	8	9	10	11	12	>12	Overall
0	87	82	74	71	67	70	60	64	45	46	44	28	83
500	41	31	24	15	12	13	10	7	7	0	0	0	35
1000	31	20	16	7	4	6	4	3	0	0	0	0	25

Table 1: Ambiguous noun coverage percentage of vicinity-based pseudowords by degree of polysemy for different values of minimum pseudosense occurrence frequency in Gigaword.

semantically-aware pseudowords. In what follows we focus on nominal pseudowords, and leave the extension to other parts of speech to future work.

2.1.1 Vicinity-based Pseudowords

A computational lexicon such as WordNet (Fellbaum, 1998) can be used as the basis for the automatic generation of semantically-aware pseudowords, an idea which was first proposed by Otrusina and Smrz (2010). WordNet can be viewed as a graph in which synsets act as nodes and the lexical and semantic relationships among them as edges. Given a sense, the approach looks into its surrounding synsets in the WordNet graph in order to find a related monosemous term that can represent that sense. As search space, the approach considers: the other literals in the same synset, the genus phrase from its textual definition, direct siblings, and direct hyponyms. If no monosemous candidate can be found, this space is further extended to hypernyms and meronyms. Hereafter, we term this approach as vicinity-based.

For example, consider the generation process of the vicinity-based pseudoword corresponding to the term *coke*, which has three senses in WordNet 3.0. There exist multiple monosemous candidates for each sense: dozens of candidates (such as *biomass* and *butane*) in the direct siblings' vicinity of the first sense, *coca_cola*, *pepsi*, and *pepsi_cola* for the second sense, and *nose_candy* and *coca_cola* for the third sense. Among these candidates Otrusina and Smrz (2010) select those whose occurrence frequency ratio in a given text corpus is most similar to that of the senses of the corresponding real word as given by a sense-annotated corpus. Clearly, a sufficiently large sense-tagged corpus is required for calculating the occurrence frequency of the individual senses of a word. This is a limitation of the vicinity-based approach.

In addition, as we mentioned earlier, we need pseudowords that can enable the generation of large-scale pseudosense-tagged corpora. For this to be achieved, each pseudosense is required to occur with a relatively high frequency in a given text corpus. The vicinity-based approach can, however, identify at best only a few representatives for each pseudosense, thus undermining its ability to cover many ambiguous nouns. Table 1 shows the percentage of ambiguous nouns in WordNet that can be modeled using the vicinity-based approach when different minimum numbers of annotated sentences are requested, i.e. each pseudosense is required to occur in at least 0 (i.e., no minimum frequency restriction), 500, or 1000 unique sentences in the reference corpus (we use Gigaword (Graff and Cieri, 2003) in our experiments). In the Table, beside the overall coverage percentage, we present the coverage by degree of polysemy and for three different values of minimum pseudosense occurrence frequency. Even though the overall coverage is over 80% when no restriction on minimum frequency is considered (first row in the Table), this high coverage drops rapidly when we request some hundred sentences per sense. For instance, only 25% of the ambiguous nouns in WordNet can be modeled using this approach when a minimum frequency of 1000 noun occurrences is required (last row of Table 1), with most of the covered words having low polysemy (in fact about 93% of them are either 2- or 3-sense nouns). This severe limitation of the vicinity-based approach hinders a wide-coverage modeling of ambiguous nouns in WordNet, thus preventing it from being an option for the generation of a large-scale pseudosense-annotated dataset.

With a view to addressing the above-mentioned issues and to enable wide coverage, in the next subsection we propose a flexible approach for the generation of semantically-aware pseudowords.

2.1.2 Similarity-based Pseudowords

The vicinity-based pseudoword generation approach works on local subgraphs of WordNet, considering mostly all those candidates which are in a direct relationship with a real sense s_i, and treating them as potentially good representatives of s_i. We propose an extension to this approach which exploits the WordNet semantic network in its entirety, hence enabling us to determine a graded degree of similarity between s_i and all the senses of all other words in WordNet.

We chose a graph-based similarity measure for two reasons: firstly, it comes as a natural extension of the vicinity-based method, and, secondly, alternative context-based methods such as Lin's measure (Lin, 1998) have been shown to require a wide-coverage sense-tagged dataset in order to calculate similarities on a sense-by-sense basis for all words in the lexicon (Otrusina and Smrz, 2010). As our similarity measure we selected the Personalized PageRank (Haveliwala, 2002, PPR) algorithm. PPR basically computes the probability according to which a random walker at a specific node in a graph would visit an arbitrary node in the same graph. The algorithm estimates, for a specific node in a graph, a probability distribution (called PPR vector) which determines the importance of any given node in the graph for that specific node. When applied to a semantic graph, this importance can be interpreted as semantic similarity. PPR has previously been used as a core component for semantic similarity[1] (Hughes and Ramage, 2007; Agirre et al., 2009) and Word Sense Disambiguation (Agirre and Soroa, 2009).

Algorithm 1 shows the procedure for the generation of our similarity-based pseudowords. The algorithm takes an ambiguous word w as input, and outputs its corresponding similarity-based pseudoword P_w whose i^{th} pseudosense models the ith sense of w, together with a confidence score which we detail below.

Given w, the algorithm iterates over the synsets corresponding to its individual senses (lines 4-13) and finds the most suitable pseudosenses for P_w. For

[1]Top-ranking synsets will contain words which are most likely similar to the target sense, whereas we move to a graded notion of relatedness as far as lower-ranking ones are concerned (Agirre et al., 2009).

Algorithm 1 Generate a similarity-based pseudoword

Input: an ambiguous word w in WordNet
Output: a "similarity-based" pseudoword P_w
a confidence score *averageRank*

1: $P_w \leftarrow \emptyset$
2: *totalRank* $\leftarrow 0$
3: $i \leftarrow 1$
4: **for each** $s \in$ *Synsets*(w)
5: *similarSynsets* $\leftarrow$ *PersonalizedPageRank*(s)
6: sort *similarSynsets* in descending order
7: **for each** $s' \in$ *similarSynsets*
8: *totalRank* $\leftarrow$ *totalRank* $+ 1$
9: **for each** $w' \in$ *SynsetLiterals*(s')
10: **if** $|$*Synsets*$(w')|$=1 **&** *Freq*(w')>*minFreq* **then**
11: $P_w \leftarrow P_w \cup \{(i, w')\}$
12: **break**
13: $i \leftarrow i + 1$
14: *averageRank* $\leftarrow$ *totalRank*$/|$*Synsets*$(w)|$
15: **return** $(P_w,$ *averageRank*$)$

each synset s of w, we start the PPR algorithm from s (line 5) and collect the probability distribution vector output by PPR (*similarSynsets* in the algorithm), which determines the probability of reaching each synset in WordNet starting from s. We then sort this vector (line 6) and check if each of its nominal synsets (s') contains a monosemous word (line 10). This search continues until a suitable candidate is found that satisfies a certain minimum occurrence frequency *minFreq*. When this occurs, the selected monosemous candidate w' is saved as the corresponding pseudosense for the ith sense of P_w (line 11). We iterate these steps for all synsets of w.

In line 14 we calculate the *averageRank*, a value given by the average of synset positions in the *similarSynsets* lists from which the pseudosenses of P_w are picked out. We later use this value as a confidence score while evaluating our pseudowords. Finally, the algorithm returns the corresponding pseudoword P_w along with its *averageRank* score (line 15). We show in Table 2 some examples of ambiguous words together with their similarity-based pseudowords.

Thanks to the large search space of our similarity-based approach, we are always able to select a monosemous candidate for each pseudosense, thus resolving the coverage issue regarding vicinity-based pseudowords. A question that arises here is that of how often our algorithm needs to resort to lower-ranking items in the *similarSynsets* list. To

Word	Similarity-based Pseudoword
bernoulli	physicist*mathematician***astronomer**
coach	football_coach*tutor*passenger_car*clarence*public_transport
green	**greenery***common*labor_leader*green_party*river*golf_course*greens***max**
horoscope	forecast*diagram
sunray	sunbeam***vine***sunlight
lifter	athlete*thief

Table 2: Similarity-based pseudowords generated for six different nouns in WordNet 3.0 (with minimum frequency of 1000 occurrences in Gigaword). Pseudosenses which could not be modeled using the vicinity-based approach are shown in bold.

verify this, we analyzed the *averageRank* values output by Algorithm 1. Table 3 shows for each polysemy degree and for three different values of *minFreq*, the mean and mode statistics of the *averageRank* scores of the generated similarity-based pseudowords for all the 15,935 polysemous nouns in WordNet 3.0. As expected, the higher the number of required sentences per pseudosense (*minFreq*), the further the algorithm descends through the list *similarSynsets* to select a pseudosense. However, as can be seen from the mode statistics in the Table, even when *minFreq* is set to a large value, most of the pseudosenses are picked from the highest-ranking positions in the *similarSynsets* list.

3 Evaluation

Our novel similarity-based algorithm for the generation of pseudowords inherently tackles the coverage issue. To test whether our generated pseudowords also cope with the issue of semantic awareness we carried out three separate evaluations so as to assess their strength in modeling semantic properties of their corresponding real senses from different perspectives. These will be described in the next three subsections. Since our aim was to leverage pseudowords for the creation of a large-scale pseudosense-annotated dataset, we performed evaluations on pseudowords generated with *minFreq* per pseudosense set to 1000 (i.e., we can generate at least 1000 annotated sentences for each pseudosense).

minFreq	**0**		**500**		**1000**	
poly.	**mean**	**mode**	**mean**	**mode**	**mean**	**mode**
2	2.0	1.0	14.8	2.0	25.4	4.0
3	2.3	1.7	13.4	2.7	21.0	5.5
4	2.3	1.8	12.3	5.8	19.8	6.8
5	2.3	1.8	12.9	5.6	20.0	10.0
6	2.4	2.0	13.7	4.5	18.7	8.8
7	2.3	2.1	11.5	6.3	16.0	6.1
8	2.2	1.8	11.3	9.6	17.2	10.8
9	2.4	2.0	10.7	10.9	15.6	15.1
10	2.2	2.0	10.1	7.0	14.3	12.1
11	2.4	2.1	10.2	7.1	14.2	17.3
12	2.5	2.4	11.0	4.4	14.4	14.4
>12	2.6	1.0	9.3	2.0	13.7	4.0
overall	2.1	1.0	14.1	2.0	23.4	4.0

Table 3: Statistics of *averageRank* scores for the full set of 15,935 similarity-based pseudowords modeled after ambiguous nouns in WordNet 3.0: we show mean and mode statistics for three different values of minimum occurrence frequency (0, 500, and 1000). We show the average value in the case of multiple modes.

3.1 Disambiguation Difficulty of Pseudowords

Our first experiment is an extrinsic evaluation of pseudowords. Ideally, pseudowords are expected to show a similar degree of difficulty to real ambiguous words in a disambiguation task (Otrusina and Smrz, 2010; Lu et al., 2006). We thus experimentally tested this assumption on similarity-based and random pseudowords. Given its low coverage, we excluded the vicinity-based approach from this experiment.

Starting from a sense-tagged lexical sample dataset for a set of ambiguous nouns, for each such noun and for each kind of pseudoword, we automatically generated a pseudosense-annotated dataset by enforcing the same sense distribution as the corresponding real ambiguous noun. This constraint was particularly important for random pseudowords since they do not model the corresponding real ambiguous words (see Section 2). An analysis was then performed to compare the disambiguation performance of a supervised WSD system on a given ambiguous word against its corresponding pseudoword.

Specifically, for our manually sense-tagged corpus we used the Senseval-3 English lexical sample dataset (Mihalcea et al., 2004), which contains 3593 and 1807 sense-tagged sentences for 20 ambiguous nouns (with an average polysemy degree of 5.8) in its training and test sets, respectively. We generated, with *minFreq* = 1000, the similarity-based pseudowords corresponding to these 20 nouns, as well as a set of 20 random pseudowords with the same polysemy degrees. We note that, in this setting, the vicinity-based approach could only generate pseudowords corresponding to 5 of the 20 nouns.

In order to create the datasets for our experiments, for each of our similarity-based and random pseudowords, we sampled unique sentences from the English Gigaword corpus (Graff and Cieri, 2003) according to the same sense distributions given by the Senseval-3 training and test datasets for the corresponding real word. Next, we performed WSD on our three datasets, namely: the Senseval-3 dataset of real words, and the two artificially sense-tagged datasets for the similarity-based and random pseudowords. As our WSD system for this experiment, we used It Makes Sense (IMS), a state-of-the-art supervised WSD system (Zhong and Ng, 2010).

WSD recall[2] performance values on the above-mentioned datasets are shown in Table 4. For the random setting, in order to ensure stability, the results are averaged on a set of 25 different pseudowords modeling a given ambiguous noun. We can see from the Table that the overall system performance with the similarity-based pseudowords (75.14%) is much closer to the real setting (73.26%) than it is with random pseudowords (78.80%). For random pseudowords, the overall recall over 25 runs ranges from 75.40% to 80.80%.

Moreover, the similarity-based approach exhibits a closer WSD recall performance to that of real data (|RE−SB| column in the table) for 15 of the 20 nouns (shown in bold in the Table). Accordingly, the overall sum of the differences (distance) between the recall values is 129.3 for similarity-based pseudowords, which is considerably lower than the 196.4 for random pseudowords (averaged over 25 runs whose distances range from 158.3 to 262.0).

To further corroborate our findings, we calculated the Pearson's r correlation between recall values on real words with those obtained on the corresponding pseudowords. Similarity-based pseudowords obtain the high correlation of 0.74, whereas this value drops to 0.54 for random pseudowords. Even worse, we

[2]Since in our experiments the WSD system always provides an answer for each item in the test set, the values of precision, recall and $F1$ will be equal.

Word	**RE**	**SB**	**RND**	**|RE−SB|**	**|RE−RND|**
argument	50.44	68.79	77.15	**18.35**	26.71
arm	92.30	85.69	88.11	6.61	**4.19**
atmosphere	70.52	69.15	80.44	**1.37**	10.32
audience	81.28	73.74	83.76	7.54	**4.22**
bank	85.76	83.07	82.46	**2.69**	3.99
degree	78.42	81.58	80.59	**3.16**	4.35
difference	62.46	61.43	75.17	**1.03**	12.90
difficulty	52.72	51.82	67.23	**0.90**	14.97
disc	78.62	76.48	78.07	**2.14**	6.18
image	71.78	75.76	81.50	**3.98**	10.02
interest	77.34	73.19	71.70	**4.15**	6.85
judgment	55.64	66.87	59.64	11.23	**9.01**
organization	80.36	72.86	78.65	7.50	**3.65**
paper	60.84	66.29	73.14	**5.45**	12.59
party	82.94	80.00	81.04	**2.94**	3.74
performance	58.56	64.76	73.86	**6.20**	15.52
plan	88.42	85.41	87.39	**3.01**	3.12
shelter	58.48	74.75	80.21	**16.27**	21.73
sort	67.64	88.15	77.37	20.51	**9.73**
source	63.46	67.74	66.26	**4.28**	7.03
overall	73.26	75.14	78.80	**129.31**	196.35

Table 4: Recall percentage of IMS on the 20 nouns of the Senseval-3 lexical-sample test set (RE) compared to the corresponding similarity-based (SB) and random (RND) pseudowords. The last 2 columns show absolute differences between the real and the two pseudoword settings.

observed a high variation of correlation (in the range of [0.18, 0.67]) over the 25 sets of random pseudowords (0.54 being the average).

3.2 Representative Power of Pseudosenses

The ideal case for pseudosenses would be that of being in a synonymous relationship with the corresponding real sense, i.e., selected from the same WordNet synset. But given that many of the WordNet synsets do not contain monosemous terms, the similarity-based approach often needs to look further into other related synsets to find a suitable pseudosense. To get a clear idea of the exact statistics, we went through all our similarity-based pseudowords and, for each pseudosense w_i, checked the relationship in WordNet between the synset containing w_i and the corresponding real sense. Table 5 shows for three values of *minFreq* the distribution of pseudosenses across different types of WordNet relationships, also including indirect ones. As can be seen in the Table, when *minFreq* is set to 0, a large portion of pseudosenses (around 75%) are selected from synonyms or generalization/specialization relations

	minFreq	0	500	1000
Relation type	Synonyms	33.0	7.6	5.4
	Hypernyms	33.4	16.1	13.0
	Hyponyms	9.1	6.1	4.9
	Meronyms	0.2	0.2	0.2
	Siblings	8.2	17.2	16.6
	Indirect relations	16.1	52.8	59.9

Table 5: Percentage of similarity-based pseudosenses obtained from different types of WordNet relations.

(hypernym and hyponyms). However, this percentage drops to about 23% when *minFreq* = 1000. This suggests that many of our pseudosenses are modeled from indirect relations when higher values of *minFreq* are used. This can potentially increase the risk of an undesirable modeling in which meanings are not properly preserved. For this reason, we carried out another experiment to assess the representative power of similarity-based pseudosenses. To this end, we randomly sampled 110 pseudowords (from the entire set of 15,935 pseudowords generated with minimum frequency of 1000), 10 for each degree of polysemy, from 2 to 12, totaling 770 pseudosenses. Then we presented each of these pseudowords[3] to two annotators who were asked to judge the degree of representativeness of its pseudosenses based on the following scores: 1: completely unrelated, 2: somewhat related, 3: good substitute, or 4: perfect substitute.

As an example, the scores assigned by the two annotators to different pseudosenses of the pseudoword generated for the noun *representative* are shown in Table 6. The overall representativeness score for each pseudoword is calculated by averaging the scores assigned to its individual pseudosenses. For instance, the overall scores calculated for the pseudoword *representative* are 3.75 and 3.50 (as given by the two annotators). The first row in Table 7 shows the average representativeness scores for each degree of polysemy on the full set of 770 pseudosenses. It can be seen that the score remains around 3.0 for all polysemy degrees from 2 to 12. Despite the fact that only one fifth of pseudosenses are taken from synonyms, hypernyms and hyponyms (when *minFreq* is 1000, cf. Table 5), the overall

[3]For each pseudoword, we provided annotators with the corresponding real word, as well as its synsets and glosses as given by WordNet.

Sense Definition (in short) **{Synset}** **> Corresponding Pseudosense**	**Score 1**	**Score 2**
a person who represents others {representative} > negotiator	3	3
an advocate who represents someone else's policy {spokesperson, interpreter, representative, voice} > spokesperson	4	4
a member of the U.S. House of Representatives {congressman, congresswoman, representative} > congressman	4	4
an item of information that is typical of a group {example, illustration, instance, representative} > case_in_point	4	3
average score	3.75	3.50

Table 6: Examples of representativeness scores assigned by the annotators to pseudosenses of the term *representative*.

representativeness score of 3.12 shows that most of these pseudosenses can be considered as good substitutes for their corresponding real senses. Therefore we conclude that not only does our similarity-based pseudoword generation approach extend the coverage of the vicinity-based method from 25% to 100% (when *minFreq* = 1000), but also that the pseudosenses coming from more distant synsets as ranked by PPR are still good representatives on average.

3.3 Distinguishability of Pseudosenses

In addition to assessing the representativeness of pseudosenses, their degree of distinguishability has to be determined. In other words, we have to determine how easily each pseudosense can be distinguished from the others in a pseudoword. Our reason for having such an experiment is readily illustrated by way of an example: consider the similarity-based pseudoword *philanthropist*benefactor*[4] corresponding to the noun *donor*[5]. Even though both pseudosenses are good representatives for their corresponding senses, the distinguishability of the two

[4]From WordNet: "Philanthropist: someone who makes charitable donations intended to increase human well-being"; "Benefactor: a person who helps people or institutions (especially with financial help)".

[5]*donor* has 2 senses according to WordNet 3.0: (1) "person who makes a gift of property"; (2) "(medicine) someone who gives blood or tissue or an organ to be used in another person".

Polysemy	2	3	4	5	6	7	8	9	10	11	12	Overall
Representativeness score	3.3	3.4	3.1	3.1	2.9	3.1	2.9	2.8	3.3	3.1	3.3	3.12
Distinguishability score	0.90	0.83	0.83	0.82	0.81	0.77	0.75	0.73	0.80	0.71	0.70	0.79

Table 7: Average representativeness and distinguishability scores for pseudosenses of different polysemy classes (scores range from 1 to 4 for representativeness and from 0 to 1 for distinguishability evaluation).

real senses is not preserved in the pseudoword. For instance, *benefactor* is a suitable pseudosense for both senses of *donor*, whereas *philanthropist* cannot be used in the blood donation sense.

Therefore we carried out another manual evaluation to test the efficacy of pseudowords in preserving the distinguishability of senses of real words. To this end, for each pseudoword P_w (from the same set of 110 sampled pseudowords used in Section 3.2) we presented its corresponding pseudosenses in random order to two annotators and asked them to associate each pseudosense with the most appropriate WordNet sense of the real word w. Then we calculated a distinguishability score for each polysemy degree by dividing the number of correct mappings by the total number of senses.

For instance, for the similarity-based pseudoword corresponding to the word *representative* (shown in Table 6), we provided the shuffled list of pseudosenses [*spokesperson, case_in_point, negotiator, congressman*] to each annotator and asked them to sort the list according to the WordNet sense inventory of *representative* (i.e., map each pseudosense to its most suitable real sense). Both annotators correctly mapped all pseudosenses of this pseudoword; hence, the distinguishability score given by each annotator for this pseudoword was 4/4 = 1.

The average distinguishability scores for each degree of polysemy, as well as the overall score, is shown in Table 7 (second row). Each value is an average of the scores obtained from the two annotators. It can be seen that the distinguishability score decreases for higher degrees of polysemy. The score, however, remains above 0.70 with highly-polysemous pseudowords. The overall score of 0.79 shows that similarity-based pseudowords effectively preserve the distinguishability of senses of their real counterparts. In other words, they do not tend to have over-generalized pseudosenses which cover more than one sense.

4 Related Work

The idea of pseudowords dates back to 1992, when it was first proposed as a means of generating large amounts of artificially annotated evaluation data for WSD algorithms (Gale et al., 1992; Schütze, 1992). However, as mentioned earlier in Section 2, constructing a pseudoword by combining a random set of unambiguous words, as was done in these early works, can not model systematic polysemy (Gaustad, 2001; Nakov and Hearst, 2003), since different senses of a real ambiguous word, unless it is homonymous, share some semantic or pragmatic relation.

Several researchers addressed the issue of producing semantically-aware pseudowords that can model semantic relationships between senses. Nakov and Hearst (2003) used lexical category membership from a medical term hierarchy (extracted from MeSH[6] (Medical Subject Headings)) to create "more plausibly-motivated" pseudowords. By considering the frequency distributions from lexical category co-occurrence, they produced a set of pseudowords which were closer to real ambiguous words in terms of disambiguation difficulty than random pseudowords. However, this approach requires a specific hierarchical lexicon and falls short of creating many pseudowords with high polysemy (the authors report generating pseudowords with two senses only).

More recent work has focused on the identification of monosemous representatives in the surrounding of a sense, i.e., selected among concepts directly related to the given sense. Lu et al. (2006) modeled senses of a real ambiguous word by picking out the most similar monosemous morpheme from a Chinese hierarchical lexicon. Pseudowords are then constructed by conflating these morphemes accordingly. However, this method leverages a specific Chinese hierarchical lexicon, in which different lev-

[6] http://www.nlm.nih.gov/mesh

els of the hierarchy correspond to different levels of sense granularity. A more flexible technique is proposed by Otrusina and Smrz (2010) who model ambiguous words in WordNet. Their vicinity-based approach searches the surroundings of each particular sense in the WordNet graph in order to find an unambiguous representative for that sense. However, as we described in Section 2.1.1, while the approach addresses the semantic awareness issue, it falls short of providing a high coverage, an issue which we tackle in our novel similarity-based approach.

5 Conclusion and Future Work

In this paper we proposed a new technique for the generation of pseudowords which, in contrast to existing work, can simultaneously tackle the two major issues associated with pseudowords, i.e., semantic awareness and coverage. Our approach can be used to model any given ambiguous noun in WordNet, hence enabling the generation of large-scale pseudosense-annotated datasets for thousands of pseudowords. We performed three experiments to evaluate the reliability of our pseudowords. We showed that the similarity-based pseudowords are highly correlated with their real counterparts in terms of disambiguation difficulty. Further evaluations demonstrated that this approach is able to provide a good semantic modeling of individual senses of real words while preserving their distinguishability.

We are releasing to the research community the entire set of 15,935 pseudowords, i.e., for all WordNet polysemous nouns (`http://lcl.uniroma1.it/pseudowords/`). This set of pseudowords (together with the English Gigaword corpus) can be used to generate a large pseudosense-tagged dataset containing $\geq$1000 annotated sentences for every sense of all the pseudowords modeled after real ambiguous nouns in WordNet. The resulting dataset could be a good complement for MASC (Ide et al., 2010) which, being human-created, can provide 1000 sense-annotated sentences for just a few words.

We hope that the availability of this resource will enable large-scale experiments in tasks such as semantic role labeling, semantic parsing, and Word Sense Disambiguation. Specifically, as future work, we plan to utilize the generated pseudosense-tagged dataset to perform an in-depth study of different WSD paradigms. We also plan to extend our work to other part-of-speech tags.

Acknowledgments

The authors gratefully acknowledge the support of the ERC Starting Grant MultiJEDI No. 259234.

References

Eneko Agirre and Aitor Soroa. 2009. Personalizing PageRank for word sense disambiguation. In *Proceedings of the 12th Conference of the European Chapter of the Association for Computational Linguistics*, EACL '09, pages 33–41, Athens, Greece.

Eneko Agirre, Enrique Alfonseca, Keith Hall, Jana Kravalova, Marius Paşca, and Aitor Soroa. 2009. A study on similarity and relatedness using distributional and WordNet-based approaches. In *Proceedings of Human Language Technologies: The 2009 Annual Conference of the North American Chapter of the Association for Computational Linguistics*, NAACL '09, pages 19–27, Boulder, Colorado.

Michele Banko and Eric Brill. 2001. Scaling to very very large corpora for natural language disambiguation. In *Proceedings of the 39th Annual Meeting on Association for Computational Linguistics*, ACL '01, pages 26–33, Toulouse, France.

Shane Bergsma, Dekang Lin, and Randy Goebel. 2008. Discriminative learning of selectional preference from unlabeled text. In *Proceedings of the Conference on Empirical Methods in Natural Language Processing*, EMNLP '08, pages 59–68, Honolulu, Hawaii.

Stefan Bordag. 2006. Word Sense Induction: Triplet-based clustering and automatic evaluation. In *Proceedings of the 11th Conference on European chapter of the Association for Computational Linguistics*, EACL '06, pages 137–144, Trento, Italy.

Nathanael Chambers and Dan Jurafsky. 2010. Improving the use of pseudo-words for evaluating selectional preferences. In *Proceedings of the 48th Annual Meeting of the Association for Computational Linguistics*, ACL '10, pages 445–453, Uppsala, Sweden.

Antonio Di Marco and Roberto Navigli. 2013. Clustering and diversifying Web search results with graph-based Word Sense Induction. *Computational Linguistics*, 39(4).

Katrin Erk. 2007. A simple, similarity-based model for selectional preferences. In *Proceedings of the 45th*

Annual Meeting of the Association of Computational Linguistics, ACL '07, pages 216–223, Prague, Czech Republic.

Christiane Fellbaum, editor. 1998. *WordNet: An Electronic Database*. MIT Press, Cambridge, MA.

William Gale, Kenneth Church, and David Yarowsky. 1992. Work on statistical methods for Word Sense Disambiguation. In *Proceedings of the AAAI Fall Symposium on Probabilistic Approaches to Natural Language*, pages 54–60, Menlo Park, CA.

Tanja Gaustad. 2001. Statistical corpus-based Word Sense Disambiguation: Pseudowords vs real ambiguous words. In *Companion Volume to the Proceedings of the 39th Annual Meeting of the Association for Computational Linguistics Proceedings ot the Student Research Workshop*, ACL/EACL '01, pages 61–66, Toulouse, France.

Daniel Gildea and Daniel Jurafsky. 2002. Automatic labeling of semantic roles. *Computational Linguistics*, 28(3):245–288.

David Graff and Christopher Cieri. 2003. English Gigaword, LDC2003T05. In *Linguistic Data Consortium*, Philadelphia.

Taher H. Haveliwala. 2002. Topic-sensitive PageRank. In *Proceedings of* 11th *International Conference on World Wide Web*, WWW '02, pages 517–526, Honolulu, Hawaii, USA.

Thad Hughes and Daniel Ramage. 2007. Lexical semantic relatedness with random graph walks. In *Proceedings of the 2007 Joint Conference on Empirical Methods in Natural Language Processing and Computational Natural Language Learning*, EMNLP-CoNLL '07, pages 581–589, Prague, Czech Republic.

Nancy Ide, Collin F. Baker, Christiane Fellbaum, and Rebecca J. Passonneau. 2010. The manually annotated sub-corpus: A community resource for and by the people. In *Proceedings of the 48th Annual Meeting of the Association for Computational Linguistics (Short Papers)*, pages 68–73, Uppsala, Sweden.

Dekang Lin. 1998. An information-theoretic definition of similarity. In *Proceedings of the Fifteenth International Conference on Machine Learning*, ICML '98, pages 296–304, Madison, USA.

Zhimao Lu, Haifeng Wang, Jianmin Yao, Ting Liu, and Sheng Li. 2006. An equivalent pseudoword solution to Chinese Word Sense Disambiguation. In *Proceedings of the 21st International Conference on Computational Linguistics and the 44th annual meeting of the Association for Computational Linguistics*, ACL '06, pages 457–464, Sydney, Australia.

Rada Mihalcea, Timothy Chklovski, and Adam Kilgarriff. 2004. The Senseval-3 English lexical sample task. In *Proceedings of Senseval-3: The Third International Workshop on the Evaluation of Systems for the Semantic Analysis of Text*, pages 25–28, Barcelona, Spain.

Preslav I. Nakov and Marti A. Hearst. 2003. Category-based pseudowords. In *Proceedings of the Conference of the North American Chapter of the Association of Computational Linguistics – short papers*, HLT-NAACL '03, pages 67–69, Edmonton, Canada.

Roberto Navigli. 2009. Word Sense Disambiguation: A survey. *ACM Computing Surveys*, 41(2):1–69.

Roberto Navigli. 2012. A quick tour of word sense disambiguation, induction and related approaches. In *Proceedings of the 38th Conference on Current Trends in Theory and Practice of Computer Science*, SOFSEM '12, pages 115–129, Spindleruv Mlyn, Czech Republic.

Lubomir Otrusina and Pavel Smrz. 2010. A new approach to pseudoword generation. In *Proceedings of the International Conference on Language Resources and Evaluation*, LREC'10, pages 1195–1199, Valletta, Malta.

Hinrich Schütze. 1992. Dimensions of meaning. In *Supercomputing '92: Proceedings of the 1992 ACM/IEEE conference on Supercomputing*, pages 787–796, Minneapolis, Minnesota, USA.

David Yarowsky. 1993. One sense per collocation. In *Proceedings of the 3rd DARPA Workshop on Human Language Technology*, pages 266–271, Princeton, New Jersey.

Zhi Zhong and Hwee Tou Ng. 2010. It makes sense: A wide-coverage Word Sense Disambiguation system for free text. In *Proceedings of the 48th Annual Meeting of the Association for Computational Linguistics, ACL'10*, pages 78–83, Uppsala, Sweden.

Labeling the Languages of Words in Mixed-Language Documents using Weakly Supervised Methods

Ben King
Department of EECS
University of Michigan
Ann Arbor, MI
benking@umich.edu

Steven Abney
Department of Linguistics
University of Michigan
Ann Arbor, MI
abney@umich.edu

Abstract

In this paper we consider the problem of labeling the languages of words in mixed-language documents. This problem is approached in a weakly supervised fashion, as a sequence labeling problem with monolingual text samples for training data. Among the approaches evaluated, a conditional random field model trained with generalized expectation criteria was the most accurate and performed consistently as the amount of training data was varied.

1 Introduction

Language identification is a well-studied problem (Hughes et al., 2006), but it is typically only studied in its canonical text-classification formulation, identifying a document's language given sample texts from a few different languages. But there are several other interesting and useful formulations of the problem that have received relatively little attention. Here, we focus on the problem of labeling the languages of individual words within a multilingual document. To our knowledge, this is the first paper to specifically address this problem.

Our own motivation for studying this problem stems from issues encountered while attempting to build language resources for minority languages. In trying to extend parts of Kevin Scannell's Crúbadán project (Scannell, 2007), which automatically builds minority language corpora from the Web, we found that the majority of webpages that contain text in a minority language also contain text in other languages. Since Scannell's method builds these corpora by bootstrapping from the pages that were retrieved, the corpus-building process can go disastrously wrong without accounting for this problem. And any resources, such as a lexicon, created from the corpus will also be incorrect.

In this paper, we explore techniques for performing language identification at the word level in mixed language documents. Our results show that one can do better than independent word language classification, as there are clues in a word's context: words of one language are frequently surrounded by words in the same language, and many documents have patterns that may be marked by the presence of certain words or punctuation. The methods in this paper also outperform sentence-level language identification, which is too coarse to capture most of the shifts between language.

To evaluate our methods, we collected and manually annotated a corpus of over 250,000 words of bilingual (though mostly non-parallel) text from the web. After running several different weakly-supervised learning methods, we found that a conditional random field model trained with generalized expectation criteria is the most accurate and performs quite consistently as the amount of training data is varied.

In section 2, we review the related work. In section 3, we define the task and describe the data and its annotation. Because the task of language identification for individual words has not been explicitly studied in the literature, and because of its importance to the overall task, we examine the features and methods that work best for independent word language identification in section 4. We begin to examine the larger problem of labeling the language of words in context in section 5 by describing our methods. In section 6, we describe the evaluation and present the results. We present our error analysis in section 7 and conclude in section 8.

2 Related Work

Language identification is one of the older NLP problems (Beesley, 1988), especially in regards to spoken language (House and Neuburg, 1977), and has received a fair share of attention through the years (Hughes et al., 2006). In its standard formulation, language identification assumes monolingual documents and attempts to classify each document according to its language from some closed set of known languages.

Many approaches have been proposed, such as Markov models (Dunning, 1994), Monte Carlo methods (Poutsma, 2002), and more recently support vector machines with string kernels, but nearly all approaches use the *n*-gram features first suggested by (Cavnar and Trenkle, 1994). Performance of language identification is generally very high with large documents, usually in excess of 99% accuracy, but Xia et al. (2009) mention that current methods still can perform quite poorly when the class of potential languages is very large or the texts to be classified are very short.

This paper attempts to address three of the ongoing issues specifically mentioned by Hughes et al. (2006) in their survey of textual language identification: supporting minority languages, sparse or impoverished training data, and multilingual documents.

A number of methods have been proposed in recent years to apply to the problems of unsupervised and weakly-supervised learning. Excluding self- and co-training methods, these methods can be categorized into two broad classes: those which bootstrap from a small number of tokens (sometimes called prototypes) (Collins and Singer, 1999; Haghighi and Klein, 2006), and those which impose constraints on the underlying unsupervised learning problem (Chang et al., 2007; Bellare et al., 2009; Druck et al., 2008; Ganchev et al., 2010).

Constraint-based weakly supervised learning has been applied to some sequence labeling problems, through such methods as contrastive estimation (Smith and Eisner, 2005), generalized expectation criteria (Mann and McCallum, 2008), alternating projections (Singh et al., 2010), and posterior regularization (Ganchev et al., 2010).

Perhaps the work that is most similar to this work is the study of *code-switching* within NLP literature. Most of the work done has been on automatically identifying code-switch points (Joshi, 1982; Solorio and Liu, 2008). The problem of identifying language in the presence of code-switching has seen the most attention in the realm of speech processing (Chu et al., 2007; Lyu and Lyu, 2008), among many others. Though code-switching has been well-studied linguistically, it is only one possible reason to explain why a document contains multiple languages, and is actually one of the less common causes observed in our corpus. For that reason, we approach this problem more generally, assuming no specific generative process behind multilingual text.

3 Task Definition

The task we describe in this paper is a sequence labeling problem, labeling a word in running text according to the language to which it belongs. In the interest of being able to produce reliable human annotations, we limit ourselves to texts with exactly two languages represented, though the techniques developed in this paper would certainly be applicable to documents with more than two languages. The two languages represented in the paper are known *a priori* by the labeler and the only training data available to the labeler is a small amount of sample text in each of the two languages represented.

In most NLP sequence labeling problems, the researchers can safely assume that each sequence (but not each item in the sequence) is independent and identically distributed (*iid*) according to some underlying distribution common to all the documents. For example, it is safe to assume that a sentence drawn from WSJ section 23 can be labeled by a model trained on the other sections. With the task of this paper we cannot assume that sequences from different documents are *iid*, (*e.g.* One document may have 90% of its words in Basque, while another only has 20%), but we do make the simplifying assumption that sequences within the same document are *iid*.

Because of this difference, the labeler is presented each document separately and must label its words independently of any other document. And the training data for this task is not in the form of labeled sequences. Rather, the models in this task are given two monolingual example texts which are used only to learn a model for individual instances. Any sequential dependencies between words must be bootstrapped from the document. It is this aspect of the problem that makes it well-suited for weakly-supervised learning.

It is worth considering whether this problem is best approached at the word level, or if perhaps sentence- or paragraph-level language identification would suffice for this task. In those cases, we could easily segment the text at the sentence or paragraph level and feed those segments to an existing language identifier. To answer this question we segmented our corpus into sentences by splitting at every period, exclamation point, or question mark (an overly agressive approximation of sentence segmentation). Even if every sentence was given the correct majority label under this sentence segmentation, the maximum possible word-level accuracy that a sentence-level classifier could achieve is 85.8%, and even though this number reflects quite optimistic conditions, it is still much lower than the methods of this paper are able to achieve.

3.1 Evaluation Data

To build a corpus of mixed language documents, we used the BootCat tool (Baroni and Bernardini, 2004) seeded with words from a minority language. BootCat is designed to automatically collect webpages on a specific topic by repeatedly searching for keywords from a topic-specific set of seed words. We found that this method works equally well for languages as for topics, when seeded with words from a specific language. Once BootCat returned a collection of documents, we manually identified documents from the set that contained text in both the target language and in English, but did not contain text in any other languages. Since the problem becomes trivial when the languages do not share a character set, we limited ourselves to languages with a Latin orthography.

Language	# words	Language	# words
Azerbaijani	4114	Lingala	1359
Banjar	10485	Lombard	18512
Basque	5488	Malagasy	6779
Cebuano	17994	Nahuatl	1133
Chippewa	15721	Ojibwa	24974
Cornish	2284	Oromo	28636
Croatian	17318	Pular	3648
Czech	886	Serbian	2457
Faroese	8307	Slovak	8403
Fulfulde	458	Somali	11613
Hausa	2899	Sotho	8198
Hungarian	9598	Tswana	879
Igbo	11828	Uzbek	43
Kiribati	2187	Yoruba	4845
Kurdish	531	Zulu	20783

Table 1: Languages present in the corpus and their number of words before separating out English text.

We found that there was an important balance to be struck concerning the popularity of a language. If a language is not spoken widely enough, then there is little chance of finding any text in that language on the Web. Conversely if a language is too widely spoken, then it is difficult to find mixed-language pages for it. The list of languages present in the corpus and the number of words in each language reflects this balance as seen in Table 1.

For researchers who wish to make use this data, the set of annotations used in this paper is available from the first author's website[1].

3.2 Annotation

Before the human annotators were presented with the mixed-language documents fetched by BootCat, the documents were first stripped of all HTML markup, converted to Unicode, and had HTML escape sequences replaced with the proper Unicode characters. Documents that had any encoding errors (*e.g.* original page used a mixture of encodings) were excluded from the corpus.

[1] `http://www-personal.umich.edu/~benking/resources/mixed-language-annotations-release-v1.0.tgz`

ENG:	because of LUTARU.Thank you ntate T.T! Sevice...
SOT:	Retselisitsoemonethi ekare jwale hotla sebetswa ...
ENG:	Lesotho is heading 4 development #big-ups Mr ...
SOT:	Basotho bare monoana hao its'upe.
ENG:	Just do the job and lets see what you are made ...
SOT:	Malerato Mokoena Ntate Thabane, molimo ...
ENG:	It is God who reigns and if God is seen in your ...
SOT:	Mathabo Letsie http://www.facebook.com/taole. ...
ENG:	As Zuma did he should introduce a way of we can ...
SOT:	Msekhotho Matona a rona ha a hlomamisoe, re ...

Table 2: An example of text from an annotated English-Sotho web page.

Since there are many different reasons that the language in a document may change (*e.g.* code-switching, change of authors, borrowing) and many variations thereof, we attempted to create a broad set of annotation rules that would cover many cases, rather than writing a large number of very specific rules. In cases when the language use was ambiguous, the annotators were instructed simply to make their best guess. Table 2 shows an example of an annotated document.

Generally, only well-digested English loanwords and borrowings were to be marked as belonging to the foreign language. If a word appeared in the context of both languages, it was permissible for that word to receive different labels at different times, depending on its context.

Ordinary proper names (like "John Williams" or "Chicago") were to be marked as belonging to the language of the context in which they appear. This rule also applied to abbreviations (like "FIFA" or "BBC"). The exception to this rule was proper names composed of common nouns (like "Stairway to Heaven" or "American Red Cross") and to abbreviations that spelled out English words, which were to be marked as belonging to the language of the words they were composed of.

The annotators were instructed not to assign labels to numbers or punctuation, but they were allowed to use numbers as punctuation as clues for assigning other labels.

3.3 Human Agreement

To verify that the annotation rules were reasonable and led to a problem that could potentially be solved by a computer, we had each of the annotators mark up a small shared set of a few hundred words from each of eight documents, in order to measure the inter-annotator agreement.

The average actual agreement was 0.988, with 0.5 agreement expected by chance for a kappa of 0.975.

Language	# words	Language	# words
Azerbaijani	211	Lingala	1816
Banjar	450	Lombard	2955
Basque	1378	Malagasy	4038
Cebuano	1898	Nahuatl	3544
Chippewa	92	Ojibwa	167
Cornish	2096	Oromo	1443
Croatian	1505	Pular	1285
Czech	1503	Serbian	1515
English	16469	Slovak	1504
Faroese	1585	Somali	1871
Fulfulde	1097	Sotho	2154
Hausa	2677	Tswana	2191
Hungarian	1541	Uzbek	1533
Igbo	2079	Yoruba	2454
Kiribati	1891	Zulu	1075
Kurdish	1674		

Table 3: Number of total words of training data for each language.

3.4 Training Data

Following Scannell (2007), we collected small monolingual samples of 643 languages from four sources: the Universal Declaration of Human Rights[2], non-English Wikipedias[3], the Jehovah's Witnesses website[4], and the Rosetta project (Landsbergen, 1989).

Only 30 of these languages ended up being used in experiments. Table 3 shows the sizes of the monolingual samples of the languages used in this paper.

[2]The Universal Declaration of Human Rights is a document created by the United Nations and translated into many languages. As of February 2011 there were 365 versions available from `http://www.unicode.org/udhr/`

[3]As of February 2011, there were 113 Wikipedias in different languages. Current versions of Wikipedia can be accessed from `http://meta.wikimedia.org/wiki/List_of_Wikipedias`

[4]As of February 2011, there were 310 versions of the site available at `http://www.watchtower.org`

They range from 92 for Chippewa to 16469 for English. Most of the languages have between 1300 and 1600 words in their example text. To attempt to mitigate variation caused by the sizes of these language samples, we sample an equal number of words with replacement from each of English and a second language to create the training data.

4 Word-level Language Classification

We shift our attention momentarily to a subproblem of the overall task: independent word-level language classification. While the task of language identification has been studied extensively at the document, sentence, and query level, little or no work has been done at the level of an individual word. For this reason, we feel it is prudent to formally evaluate the features and classifiers which perform most effectively at the task of word language classification (ignoring any sequential dependencies at this point).

4.1 Features

We used a logistic regression classifier to experiment with combinations of the following features: character unigrams, bigrams, trigrams, 4-grams, 5-grams, and the full word. For these experiments, the training data consisted of 1000 words sampled uniformly with replacement from the sample text in the appropriate languages. Table 4 shows the accuracies that the classifier achieved when using different sets of features averaged over 10 independent runs.

Features	**Accuracy**
Unigrams	0.8056
Bigrams	0.8783
Trigrams	0.8491
4-grams	0.7846
5-grams	0.6977
{1,2,3,4,5}-grams	0.8817
{1,2,3,4,5}-grams, word	0.8819

Table 4: Logistic regression accuracy when trained using varying features.

The use of all available features seems to be the best option, and we use the full set of features in all proceeding experiments. This result also concurs with the findigs of (Cavnar and Trenkle, 1994), who found 1-5-grams to be most effective for document language classification.

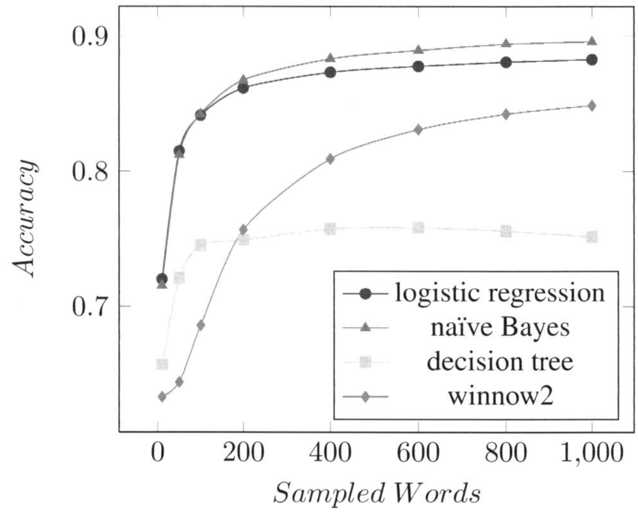

Figure 1: Learning curves for logistic regression, naïve Bayes, decision tree, and Winnow2 on the independent word classification problem as the number of sampled words in each training example changes from 10 to 1000.

4.2 Classifiers

Using all available features, we compare four MALLET (McCallum, 2002) classifiers: logistic regression, naïve Bayes, decision tree, and Winnow2. Figure 1 shows the learning curves for each classifier as the number of sampled words comprising each training example is varied from 10 to 1000.

Since a naïve Bayes classifier gave the best performance in most experiments, we use naïve Bayes as a representative word classifier for the rest of the paper.

5 Methods

Moving onto the main task of this paper, labeling *sequences* of words in documents according to their languages, we use this section to describe our methods.

Since training data for this task is limited and is of a different type than the evaluation data (labeled instances from monolingual example texts *vs.* labeled sequences from the multilingual document), we approach the problem with weakly- and semi-supervised methods.

The sequence labeling methods are presented with a few new sequence-relevant features, which are not applicable to independent word classification (since these features do not appear in the training data):

- a feature for the presence of each possible non-word character (punctuation or digit) between the previous and the current words
- a feature for the presence of each possible non-word character between the current and next words

In addition to independent word classification, which was covered in section 4, we also implement a conditional random field model trained with generalized expectation criteria, a hidden Markov model (HMM) trained with expectation maximization (EM), and a logistic regression model trained with generalized expectation criteria.

We had also considered that a semi-Markov CRF (Sarawagi and Cohen, 2004) could be useful if we could model segment lengths (a non-Markovian feature), but we found that gold-standard segment lengths did not seem to be distributed according to any canonical distribution, and we did not have a reliable way to estimate these segment lengths.

5.1 Conditional Random Field Model trained with Generalized Expectation

Generalized expectation (GE) criteria (Druck et al., 2008) are terms added to the objective function of a learning algorithm which specify preferences for the learned model. When the model is a linear chain conditional random field (CRF) model, we can straightforwardly express these criteria in the objective function with a KL-divergence term between the expected values of the current model $\tilde{p}$ and the preferred model $\hat{p}$ (Mann and McCallum, 2008).

$$\mathcal{O}(\theta; D, U) = \sum_d \log p_\theta(y^{(d)}|x^{(d)}) - \frac{\sum_k \theta_k}{2\sigma^2} - \lambda D(\hat{p}||\tilde{p}_\theta)$$

Practically, to compute these expectations, we produce the smoothed MLE on the output label distribution for every feature observed in the training data. For example, the trigram "ter" may occur 27 times in the English sample text and 34 times in the other sample text, leading to an MLE of $\hat{p}(\texttt{eng}|\texttt{ter}) \approx 0.44$.

Because we do not expect the true marginal label distribution to be uniform (*i.e.* the document may not have equal numbers of words in each language), we first estimate the expected marginal label distribution by classifying each word in the document independently using naïve Bayes and taking the resulting counts of labels produced by the classifier as an MLE estimate for it: $\hat{p}(\texttt{eng})$ and $\hat{p}(\texttt{non})$.

We use these terms to bias the expected label distributions over each feature. Let $\mathcal{F}_{eng}$ and $\mathcal{F}_{non}$ respectively be the collections of all training data features with the two labels. For every label $l \in \mathcal{L} = \{\texttt{eng}, \texttt{non}\}$ and every feature $f \in \mathcal{F}_{eng} \cup \mathcal{F}_{non}$, we calculate

$$p(l|f) = \frac{count(f, \mathcal{F}_l) + \delta}{count(f, \bigcup_i \mathcal{F}_i) + \delta|\mathcal{L}|} \times \frac{\hat{p}(l)}{p_{uniform}(l)},$$

the biased maximum likelihood expected output label distribution. To avoid having $p(l|f) = 0$, which can cause the KL-divergence to be undefined, we perform additive smoothing with $\delta = 0.5$ on the counts before multiplying with the biasing term.

We use the implementation of CRF with GE criteria from MALLET (McCallum, 2002), which uses a gradient descent algorithm to optimize the objective function. (Mann and McCallum, 2008; Druck, 2011)

5.2 Hidden Markov Model trained with Expectation Maximization

A second method we used was a hidden Markov model (HMM) trained iteratively using the Expectation Maximization algorithm (Dempster et al., 1977). Here an HMM is preferable to a CRF because it is a generative model and therefore uses parameters with simple interpretations. In the case of an HMM, it is easy to estimate emission and transition probabilities using an external method and then set these directly.

To initialize the HMM, we use a uniform distribution for transition probabilities, and produce the emission probabilities by using a naïve Bayes classifier trained over the two small language samples.

In the expectation step, we simply pass the document through the HMM and record the labels it produces for each word in the document.

In the maximization step, we produce maximum-likelihood estimates for transition probabilities from the transitions between the labels produced. To estimate emission probabilities, we retrain a naïve Bayes classifier on the small language samples along the set of words from the document that were labeled as being in the respective language. We iterated this process until convergence, which usually took fewer than 10 iterations.

We additionally experimented with a naïve Bayes classifier trained by EM in the same fashion, except that it had no transition probabilities to update. This classifier's performance was almost identical to that of the GE-trained MaxEnt method mentioned in the following section, so we omit it from the results and analysis for that reason.

5.3 Logistic Regression trained with Generalized Expectation

GE criteria can also be straightforwardly applied to the weakly supervised training of logistic regression models. The special case where the constraints specified are over marginal label distributions, is called *label regularization*.

As with the CRF constraint creation, here we first use an ordinary supervised naïve Bayes classifier in order to estimate the marginal label distributions for the document, which can be used to create more accurate output label expectations that are biased to the marginal label distributions over all words in the document.

We use the MALLET implementation of a GE-trained logistic regression classifier, which optimizes the objective function using a gradient descent algorithm.

5.4 Word-level Classification

Our fourth method served as a baseline and did not involve any sequence labeling, only independent classification of words. Since naïve Bayes was the best performer among word classification methods, we use that the representative of independent word classification methods. The implementation of the naïve Bayes classifier is from MALLET.

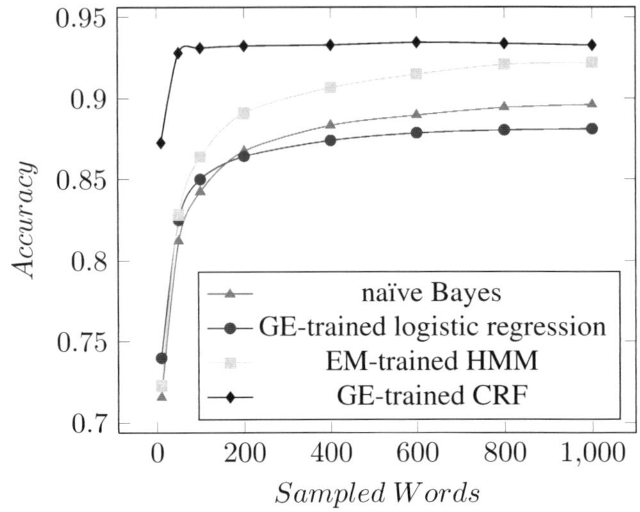

Figure 2: Learning curves for naïve Bayes, logistic regression trained with GE, HMM trained with EM, and CRF trained with GE as the number of sampled words in each training example changes from 10 to 1000.

We also implemented a self-trained CRF, initially trained on the output of this naïve Bayes classifier, and trained on its own output in subsequent iterations. This method was not able to consistently outperform the naïve Bayes classifier after any number of iterations.

6 Evaluation and Results

We evaluated each method using simple token-level accuracy, *i.e.* whether the correct label was assigned to a word in the document. Word boundaries were defined by punctuation or whitespace, and no tokens containing a digit were included. Figure 2 displays the accuracy for each method as the number of sampled words from each language example is varied from 10 to 1000.

In all the cases we tested, CRF trained with GE is clearly the most accurate option among the methods examined, though the EM-trained HMM seemed to be approaching a similar accuracy with large amounts of training data. With a slight edge in efficiency also in its favor, we think the GE+CRF approach, rather than EM+HMM, is the best approach for this problem because of its consistent performance across a wide range of training data sizes. In its favor, the EM+HMM approach has a slightly lower variance in its performance across different files, though not at a statistically significant level.

Contrary to most of the results in (Mann and McCallum, 2010), a logistic regression classifier trained with GE did not outperform a standard supervised naïve Bayes classifier. We suspect that this is due to the different nature of this problem as compared to most other sequence labeling problems, with the classifier bootstrapping over a single document only. In the problems studied by Mann and McCallum, the GE-trained classifier was able to train over the entire training set, which was on average about 50,000 instances, far more than the number of words in the average document in this set (2,500).

7 Error Analysis

In order to analyze the types of mistakes that the models made we performed an error analysis on ten randomly selected files, looking at each mislabeled word and classifying the error according to its type. The results of this analysis are in Table 5. The three classes of errors are (1) named entity errors, when a named entity is given a label that does not match the label it was given in the original annotation, (2) shared word errors, when a word that could belong to either language is classified incorrectly, and (3) other, a case that covers all other types of errors.

Method	NE	SW	Other
GE+CRF	41%	10%	49%
EM+HMM	50%	14%	35%
GE+MaxEnt	37%	12%	51%
Naïve Bayes	42%	17%	40%

Table 5: Types of errors and their proportions among the different methods. NE stands for Named Entity, SW stands for Shared Word, and Other covers all other types of errors.

Our annotation rules for named entities specified that named entities should be given a label matching their context, but this was rather arbitrary, and not explicitly followed by any of the methods, which treat a named entity as if it was any other token. This was the one of most frequent types of error made by each of the methods and in our conclusion in section 8, we discuss ways to improve it.

In a regression analysis to determine which factors had the greatest correlations with the GE-trained CRF performance, the estimated proportion of named entities in the document had by far the greatest correlation with CRF accuracy of anything we measured. Following that in decreasing order of correlation strength were the cosine similarity between English and the document's second language, the number of words in the monolingual example text (even though we sampled from it), and the average length of gold-standard monolingual sequences in the document.

The learning curve for GE-trained CRF in Figure 2 is somewhat atypical as far as most machine learning methods are concerned: performance is typically non-decreasing as more training data is made available.

We believe that the model is becoming overconstrained as more words are used to create the constraints. The GE method does not have a way to specify that some of the soft constraints (for the labels observed most frequently in the sample text) should be more important than other constraints (those observed less frequently). When we measure the KL-divergence between the label distributions predicted by the constraints and the true label distribution, we find that this divergence seems to reach its minimum value between 600 and 800 words, which is where the GE+CRF also seems to reach its maximum performance.

The step with a naïve Bayes classifier estimating the marginal label distribution ended up being quite important overall. Without it, the accuracy dropped by more than a full percentage point absolute. But the problem of inaccurate constraint estimation is one that needs further consideration. Some possible ways to address it may be to prune the constraints according to their frequency or perhaps according to a metric like entropy, or to vary the GE-criteria coefficient in the objective function in order to penalize the model less for varying from the expected model.

8 Conclusion

This paper addresses three of the ongoing issues specifically mentioned by Hughes et al. (2006) in their survey of textual language identification. Our approach is able to *support minority languages*; in fact, almost all of the languages we tested on would be considered minority languages. We also address the issue of *sparse or impoverished training data*. Because we use weakly-supervised methods, we are able to successfully learn to recognize a language with as few as 10 words of training data[5]. The last and most obvious point we address is that of *multilingual documents*, which is the focus of the paper.

We present a weakly-supervised system for identifying the languages of individual words in mixed-language documents. We found that across a broad range of training data sizes, a CRF model trained with GE criteria is an accurate sequence classifier and is preferable to other methods for several reasons.

One major issue to be improved upon in future work is how named entities are handled. A straightforward way to approach this may be to create another label for named entities, which (for the purposes of evaluation) would be considered not to belong to any of the languages in the document. We could simply choose not to evaluate a system on the named entity tokens in a document. Alternatively, the problem of language-independent named entity recognition has received some attention in the past (Tjong Kim Sang and De Meulder, 2003), and it may be beneficial to incorporate such a system in a robust word-level language identification system.

Going forward, an issue that needs to be addressed with this method is its dependence on knowing the set of possible languages *a priori*. Because we don't see an easy way to adapt this method to accurately label words in documents from a possible set of thousands of languages when the document itself may only contain two or three languages, we would propose the following future work.

We propose a two-step approach to general word-level language identification. The first step would be to examine a multilingual document, and with high accuracy, list the languages that are present in the document. The second step would be identical to the approach described in this paper (but with the two-language restriction lifted), and would be responsible for labeling the languages of individual words, using the set of languages provided by the first step.

[5]With only 10 words of each language as training data, the CRF approach correctly labels 88% of words

References

Marco Baroni and Silvia Bernardini. 2004. Bootcat: Bootstrapping corpora and terms from the web. In *Proceedings of the Fourth International Conference on Langauge Resources and Evaluation (LREC 2004)*, volume 4, pages 1313–1316, Lisbon, Portugal.

Kenneth R. Beesley. 1988. Language identifier: A computer program for automatic natural-language identification of on-line text. In *Proceedings of the 29th Annual Conference of the American Translators Association*, volume 47, page 54.

Kedar Bellare, Gregory Druck, and Andrew McCallum. 2009. Alternating projections for learning with expectation constraints. In *Proceedings of the Twenty-Fifth Conference on Uncertainty in Artificial Intelligence*, pages 43–50. AUAI Press.

William B. Cavnar and John M. Trenkle. 1994. N-gram-based text categorization. In *Proceedings of the Third Annual Symposium on Document Analysis and Information (SDAIR 94)*, pages 161–175, Las Vegas, Nevada.

Ming-Wei Chang, Lev Ratinov, and Dan Roth. 2007. Guiding semi-supervision with constraint-driven learning. In *Proceedings of the 45th Annual Meeting of the Association of Computational Linguistics*, pages 280–287, Prague, Czech Republic, June. Association for Computational Linguistics.

Chyng-Leei Chu, Dau-cheng Lyu, and Ren-yuan Lyu. 2007. Language identification on code-switching speech. In *Proceedings of ROCLING*.

Michael Collins and Yoram Singer. 1999. Unsupervised models for named entity classification. In *Proceedings of the Joint SIGDAT Conference on Empirical Methods in Natural Language Processing and Very Large Corpora*, pages 100–110.

Arthur P. Dempster, Nan M. Laird, and Donald B. Rubin. 1977. Maximum likelihood from incomplete data via the em algorithm. *Journal of the Royal Statistical Society. Series B (Methodological)*, pages 1–38.

Gregory Druck, Gideon Mann, and Andrew McCallum. 2008. Learning from labeled features using generalized expectation criteria. In *Proceedings of the 31st annual international ACM SIGIR conference on Research and development in information retrieval (SIGIR 2008)*, pages 595–602. ACM.

Gregory Druck. 2011. *Generalized Expectation Criteria for Lightly Supervised Learning*. Ph.D. thesis, University of Massachusetts Amherst.

Ted Dunning. 1994. Statistical identification of language. Technical report.

Kuzman Ganchev, João Graça, Jennifer Gillenwater, and Ben Taskar. 2010. Posterior regularization for structured latent variable models. *The Journal of Machine Learning Research*, 11:2001–2049.

Aria Haghighi and Dan Klein. 2006. Prototype-driven learning for sequence models. In *Proceedings of the Human Language Technology Conference of the NAACL, Main Conference*, pages 320–327, New York City, USA, June. Association for Computational Linguistics.

A.S. House and E.P. Neuburg. 1977. Toward automatic identification of the language of an utterance. i. preliminary methodological considerations. *The Journal of the Acoustical Society of America*, 62:708.

Baden Hughes, Timothy Baldwin, Steven Bird, Jeremy Nicholson, and Andrew MacKinlay. 2006. Reconsidering language identification for written language resources. In *Proc. International Conference on Language Resources and Evaluation*, pages 485–488.

Aravind K. Joshi. 1982. Processing of sentences with intra-sentential code-switching. In *Proceedings of the 9th conference on Computational linguistics-Volume 1*, pages 145–150. Academia Praha.

Jan Landsbergen. 1989. The rosetta project. pages 82–87, Munich, Germany.

Dau-Cheng Lyu and Ren-Yuan Lyu. 2008. Language identification on code-switching utterances using multiple cues. In *Ninth Annual Conference of the International Speech Communication Association.*

Gideon S. Mann and Andrew McCallum. 2008. Generalized expectation criteria for semi-supervised learning of conditional random fields. In *Proceedings of ACL-08: HLT*, pages 870–878, Columbus, Ohio, June. Association for Computational Linguistics.

Gideon S. Mann and Andrew McCallum. 2010. Generalized expectation criteria for semi-supervised learning with weakly labeled data. *The Journal of Machine Learning Research*, pages 955–984.

Andrew McCallum. 2002. Mallet: A machine learning for language toolkit. http://mallet.cs.umass.edu.

Arjen Poutsma. 2002. Applying monte carlo techniques to language identification. *Language and Computers*, 45(1):179–189.

Sunita Sarawagi and William W. Cohen. 2004. Semi-markov conditional random fields for information extraction. *Advances in Neural Information Processing Systems (NIPS 2004)*, 17:1185–1192.

Kevin P. Scannell. 2007. The crúbadán project: Corpus building for under-resourced languages. In *Building and Exploring Web Corpora: Proceedings of the 3rd Web as Corpus Workshop*, volume 4, pages 5–15, Louvain-la-Neuve, Belgium.

Sameer Singh, Dustin Hillard, and Chris Leggetter. 2010. Minimally-supervised extraction of entities from text advertisements. In *Human Language Technologies: The 2010 Annual Conference of the North American Chapter of the Association for Computational Linguistics*, pages 73–81, Los Angeles, California, June. Association for Computational Linguistics.

Noah A. Smith and Jason Eisner. 2005. Contrastive estimation: Training log-linear models on unlabeled data. In *Proceedings of the 43rd Annual Meeting of the Association for Computational Linguistics (ACL'05)*, pages 354–362, Ann Arbor, Michigan, June. Association for Computational Linguistics.

Thamar Solorio and Yang Liu. 2008. Learning to predict code-switching points. In *Proceedings of the 2008 Conference on Empirical Methods in Natural Language Processing*, pages 973–981, Honolulu, Hawaii, October. Association for Computational Linguistics.

Erik F. Tjong Kim Sang and Fien De Meulder. 2003. Introduction to the conll-2003 shared task: Language-independent named entity recognition. In Walter Daelemans and Miles Osborne, editors, *Proceedings of the Seventh Conference on Natural Language Learning at HLT-NAACL 2003*, pages 142–147.

Fei Xia, William Lewis, and Hoifung Poon. 2009. Language ID in the context of harvesting language data off the web. In *Proceedings of the 12th Conference of the European Chapter of the ACL (EACL 2009)*, pages 870–878, Athens, Greece, March. Association for Computational Linguistics.

Learning Whom to Trust with MACE

Dirk Hovy[1] **Taylor Berg-Kirkpatrick**[2] **Ashish Vaswani**[1] **Eduard Hovy**[3]
(1) Information Sciences Institute, University of Southern California, Marina del Rey
(2) Computer Science Division, University of California at Berkeley
(3) Language Technology Institute, Carnegie Mellon University, Pittsburgh
{dirkh,avaswani}@isi.edu, tberg@cs.berkeley.edu, hovy@cmu.edu

Abstract

Non-expert annotation services like Amazon's Mechanical Turk (AMT) are cheap and fast ways to evaluate systems and provide categorical annotations for training data. Unfortunately, some annotators choose bad labels in order to maximize their pay. Manual identification is tedious, so we experiment with an item-response model. It learns in an unsupervised fashion to a) identify which annotators are trustworthy and b) predict the correct underlying labels. We match performance of more complex state-of-the-art systems and perform well even under adversarial conditions. We show considerable improvements over standard baselines, both for predicted label accuracy and trustworthiness estimates. The latter can be further improved by introducing a prior on model parameters and using Variational Bayes inference. Additionally, we can achieve even higher accuracy by focusing on the instances our model is most confident in (trading in some recall), and by incorporating annotated control instances. Our system, MACE (Multi-Annotator Competence Estimation), is available for download[1].

1 Introduction

Amazon's MechanicalTurk (AMT) is frequently used to evaluate experiments and annotate data in NLP (Callison-Burch et al., 2010; Callison-Burch and Dredze, 2010; Jha et al., 2010; Zaidan and Callison-Burch, 2011). However, some turkers try to maximize their pay by supplying quick answers that have nothing to do with the correct label. We refer to this type of annotator as a *spammer*. In order to mitigate the effect of spammers, researchers typically collect multiple annotations of the same instance so that they can, later, use de-noising methods to infer the best label. The simplest approach is majority voting, which weights all answers equally. Unfortunately, it is easy for majority voting to go wrong. A common and simple spammer strategy for categorical labeling tasks is to always choose the same (often the first) label. When multiple spammers follow this strategy, the majority can be incorrect. While this specific scenario might seem simple to correct for (remove annotators that always produce the same label), the situation grows more tricky when spammers do not annotate consistently, but instead choose labels at random. A more sophisticated approach than simple majority voting is required.

If we knew whom to trust, *and when*, we could reconstruct the correct labels. Yet, the only way to be sure we know whom to trust is if we knew the correct labels ahead of time. To address this circular problem, we build a generative model of the annotation process that treats the correct labels as latent variables. We then use unsupervised learning to estimate parameters directly from redundant annotations. This is a common approach in the class of unsupervised models called *item-response* models (Dawid and Skene, 1979; Whitehill et al., 2009; Carpenter, 2008; Raykar and Yu, 2012). While such models have been implemented in other fields (e.g., vision), we are not aware of their availability for NLP tasks (see also Section 6).

Our model includes a binary latent variable that explicitly encodes if and *when* each annotator is spamming, as well as parameters that model the annotator's specific spamming "strategy". Impor-

[1]Available under http://www.isi.edu/publications/licensed-sw/mace/index.html

tantly, the model assumes that labels produced by an annotator when spamming are independent of the true label (though, a spammer can still produce the correct label by chance).

In experiments, our model effectively differentiates dutiful annotators from spammers (Section 4), and is able to reconstruct the correct label with high accuracy (Section 5), even under extremely adversarial conditions (Section 5.2). It does not require any annotated instances, but is capable of including varying levels of supervision via token constraints (Section 5.2). We consistently outperform majority voting, and achieve performance equal to that of more complex state-of-the-art models. Additionally, we find that thresholding based on the posterior label entropy can be used to trade off coverage for accuracy in label reconstruction, giving considerable gains (Section 5.1). In tasks where correct answers are more important than answering every instance, e.g., when constructing a new annotated corpus, this feature is extremely valuable. Our contributions are:

- We demonstrate the effectiveness of our model on real world AMT datasets, matching the accuracy of more complex state-of-the-art systems
- We show how posterior entropy can be used to trade some coverage for considerable gains in accuracy
- We study how various factors affect performance, including number of annotators, annotator strategy, and available supervision
- We provide MACE (Multi-Annotator Competence Estimation), a Java-based implementation of a simple and scalable unsupervised model that identifies malicious annotators and predicts labels with high accuracy

2 Model

We keep our model as simple as possible so that it can be effectively trained from data where annotator quality is unknown. If the model has too many parameters, unsupervised learning can easily pick up on and exploit coincidental correlations in the data. Thus, we make a modeling assumption that keeps our parameterization simple. We assume that an annotator always produces the correct label when he tries to. While this assumption does not reflect the reality of AMT, it allows us to focus the model's power where it's important: explaining away labels that are not correlated with the correct label.

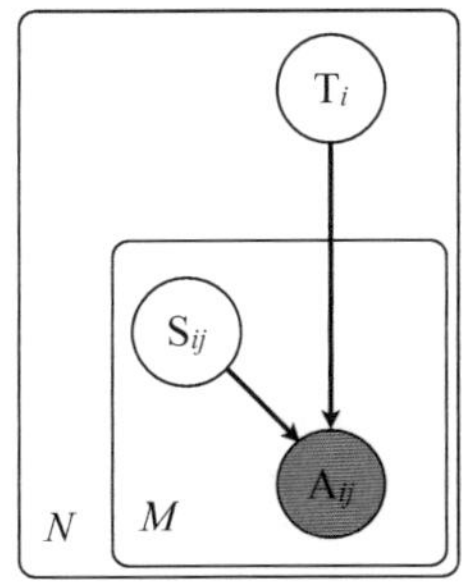

Figure 1: **Graphical model**: Annotator j produces label A_{ij} on instance i. Label choice depends on instance's true label T_i, and whether j is spamming on i, modeled by binary variable S_{ij}. $N = |instances|$, $M = |annotators|$.

$$
\begin{aligned}
&\text{for } i = 1 \ldots N: \\
&\quad T_i \sim \text{Uniform} \\
&\quad \text{for } j = 1 \ldots M: \\
&\qquad S_{ij} \sim \text{Bernoulli}(1 - \theta_j) \\
&\qquad \text{if } S_{ij} = 0: \\
&\qquad\quad A_{ij} = T_i \\
&\qquad \text{else}: \\
&\qquad\quad A_{ij} \sim \text{Multinomial}(\xi_j)
\end{aligned}
$$

Figure 2: **Generative process**: see text for description.

Our model generates the observed annotations as follows: First, for each instance i, we sample the true label T_i from a uniform prior. Then, for each annotator j we draw a binary variable S_{ij} from a Bernoulli distribution with parameter $1 - \theta_j$. S_{ij} represents whether or not annotator j is spamming on instance i. We assume that when an annotator is not spamming on an instance, i.e. $S_{ij} = 0$, he just copies the true label to produce annotation A_{ij}. If $S_{ij} = 1$, we say that the annotator is spamming on the current instance, and A_{ij} is sampled from a multinomial with parameter vector ξ_j. Note that in this case the annotation A_{ij} *does not* depend on the true label T_i. The annotations A_{ij} are observed, while the true labels T_i and the spamming indicators S_{ij} are unobserved. The graphical model is shown in Figure 1 and the generative process is described in Figure 2.

The model parameters are θ_j and ξ_j. θ_j specifies the probability of trustworthiness for annotator j (i.e. the probability that he is not spamming on any given instance). The learned value of θ_j will prove useful later when we try to identify reliable annotators (see Section 4). The vector ξ_j determines how annotator j behaves when he is spamming. An annotator can produce the correct answer even while spamming, but this can happen only by chance since the annotator must use the same multinomial parameters ξ_j across all instances. This means that we only learn annotator biases *that are not correlated with the correct label*, e.g., the strategy of the spammer who always chooses a certain label. This contrasts with previous work where additional parameters are used to model the biases that even dutiful annotators exhibit. Note that an annotator can also choose not to answer, which we can naturally accommodate because the model is generative. We enhance our generative model by adding Beta and Dirichlet priors on θ_j and ξ_j respectively which allows us to incorporate prior beliefs about our annotators (section 2.1).

2.1 Learning

We would like to set our model parameters to maximize the probability of the observed data, i.e., the marginal data likelihood:

$$P(A;\theta,\xi) = \sum_{T,S}\Big[\prod_{i=1}^{N} P(T_i)\cdot\prod_{j=1}^{M} P(S_{ij};\theta_j)\cdot P(A_{ij}|S_{ij},T_i;\xi_j)\Big]$$

where A is the matrix of annotations, S is the matrix of competence indicators, and T is the vector of true labels.

We maximize the marginal data likelihood using Expectation Maximization (EM) (Dempster et al., 1977), which has successfully been applied to similar problems (Dawid and Skene, 1979). We initialize EM randomly and run for 50 iterations. We perform 100 random restarts, and keep the model with the best marginal data likelihood. We smooth the M-step by adding a fixed value δ to the fractional counts before normalizing (Eisner, 2002). We find that smoothing improves accuracy, but, overall, learning is robust to varying δ, and set $\delta = \frac{0.1}{\text{num labels}}$.

We observe, however, that the average annotator proficiency is usually high, i.e., most annotators answer correctly. The distribution learned by EM, however, is fairly linear. To improve the correlation between model estimates and true annotator proficiency, we would like to add priors about the annotator behavior into the model. A straightforward approach is to employ Bayesian inference with Beta priors on the proficiency parameters, θ_j. We thus also implement Variational-Bayes (VB) training with symmetric Beta priors on θ_j and symmetric Dirichlet priors on the strategy parameters, ξ_j. Setting the shape parameters of the Beta distribution to 0.5 favors the extremes of the distribution, i.e., either an annotator tried to get the right answer, or simply did not care, but (almost) nobody tried "a little". With VB training, we observe improved correlations over all test sets with no loss in accuracy. The hyper-parameters of the Dirichlet distribution on ξ_j were clamped to 10.0 for all our experiments with VB training. Our implementation is similar to Johnson (2007), which the reader can refer to for details.

3 Experiments

We evaluate our method on existing annotated datasets from various AMT tasks. However, we also want to ensure that our model can handle adversarial conditions. Since we have no control over the factors in existing datasets, we create synthetic data for this purpose.

3.1 Natural Data

In order to evaluate our model, we use the datasets from (Snow et al., 2008) that use discrete label values (some tasks used continuous values, which we currently do not model). Since they compared AMT annotations to experts, gold annotations exist for these sets. We can thus evaluate the accuracy of the model as well as the proficiency of each annotator. We show results for word sense disambiguation (WSD: 177 items, 34 annotators), recognizing textual entailment (RTE: 800 items, 164 annotators), and recognizing temporal relation (Temporal: 462 items, 76 annotators).

3.2 Synthetic Data

In addition to the datasets above, we generate synthetic data in order to control for different factors. This also allows us to create a gold standard to which we can compare. We generate data sets with 100 items, using two or four possible labels.

For each item, we generate answers from 20 different annotators. The "annotators" are functions that return one of the available labels according to some strategy. Better annotators have a smaller chance of guessing at random.

For various reasons, usually not all annotators see or answer all items. We thus remove a randomly selected subset of answers such that each item is only answered by 10 of the annotators. See Figure 3 for an example annotation of three items.

	annotators									
items	–	0	0	1	–	0	–	–	0	–
	1	–	–	0	–	1	0	–	–	0
	–	–	0	–	0	1	–	0	–	0

Figure 3: Annotations: 10 annotators on three items, labels $\{1, 0\}$, 5 annotations/item. Missing annotations marked '–'

3.3 Evaluations

First, we want to know which annotators to trust. We evaluate whether our model's learned trustworthiness parameters θ_j can be used to identify these individuals (Section 4).

We then compare the label predicted by our model and by majority voting to the correct label. The results are reported as accuracy (Section 5). Since our model computes posterior entropies for each instance, we can use this as an approximation for the model's confidence in the prediction. If we focus on predictions with high confidence (i.e., low entropy), we hope to see better accuracy, even at the price of leaving some items unanswered. We evaluate this trade-off in Section 5.1. In addition, we investigate the influence of the number of spammers and their strategy on the accuracy of our model (Section 5.2).

4 Identifying Reliable Annotators

One of the distinguishing features of the model is that it uses a parameter for each annotator to estimate whether or not they are spamming. Can we use this parameter to identify trustworthy individuals, to invite them for future tasks, and block untrustworthy ones?

	RTE	**Temporal**	**WSD**
raw agreement	0.78	0.73	0.81
Cohen's κ	0.70	0.80	0.13
G-index	0.76	0.73	0.81
MACE-EM	0.87	0.88	0.44
MACE-VB $_{(0.5,0.5)}$	**0.91**	**0.90**	**0.90**

Table 1: Correlation with annotator proficiency: Pearson ρ of different methods for various data sets. MACE-VB's trustworthiness parameter (trained with Variational Bayes with $\alpha = \beta = 0.5$) correlates best with true annotator proficiency.

It is natural to apply some form of weighting. One approach is to assume that reliable annotators agree more with others than random annotators. Inter-annotator agreement is thus a good candidate to weigh the answers. There are various measures for inter-annotator agreement.

Tratz and Hovy (2010) compute the average agreement of each annotator and use it as a weight to identify reliable ones. Raw agreement can be directly computed from the data. It is related to majority voting, since it will produce high scores for all members of the majority class. Raw agreement is thus a very simple measure.

In contrast, Cohen's κ corrects the agreement between two annotators for chance agreement. It is widely used for inter-annotator agreement in annotation tasks. We also compute the κ values for each pair of annotators, and average them for each annotator (similar to the approach in Tratz and Hovy (2010)). However, whenever one label is more prevalent (a common case in NLP tasks), κ overestimates the effect of chance agreement (Feinstein and Cicchetti, 1990) and penalizes disproportionately. The G-index (Gwet, 2008) corrects for the number of labels rather than chance agreement.

We compare these measures to our learned trustworthiness parameters θ_j in terms of their ability to select reliable annotators. A better measure should lend higher score to annotators who answer correctly more often than others. We thus compare the ratings of each measure to the true proficiency of each annotator. This is the percentage of annotated items the annotator answered correctly. Methods that can identify reliable annotators should highly correlate to the annotator's proficiency. Since the methods use different scales, we compute Pearson's ρ for the correlation coefficient, which is scale-invariant. The correlation results are shown in Table 1.

The model's θ_j correlates much more strongly with annotator proficiency than either κ or raw agreement. The variant trained with VB performs consistently better than standard EM training, and yields the best results. This show that our model detects reliable annotators much better than any of the other measures, which are only loosely correlated to annotator proficiency.

The numbers for WSD also illustrate the low κ score resulting when all annotators (correctly) agree on a small number of labels. However, all inter-annotator agreement measures suffer from an even more fundamental problem: removing/ignoring annotators with low agreement will always improve the overall score, irrespective of the quality of their annotations. Worse, there is no natural stopping point: deleting the most egregious outlier always improves agreement, until we have only one annotator with perfect agreement left (Hovy, 2010). In contrast, MACE does not discard any annotators, but weighs their contributions differently. We are thus not losing information. This works well even under adversarial conditions (see Section 5.2).

5 Recovering the Correct Answer

	RTE	Temporal	WSD
majority	0.90	0.93	0.99
Raykar/Yu 2012	0.93	0.94	—
Carpenter 2008	0.93	—	—
MACE-EM/VB	0.93	0.94	0.99
MACE-EM@90	0.95	0.97	0.99
MACE-EM@75	0.95	0.97	1.0
MACE-VB@90	0.96	0.97	1.0
MACE-VB@75	0.98	0.98	1.0

Table 2: Accuracy of different methods on data sets from (Snow et al., 2008). MACE-VB uses Variational Bayes training. Results @n use the $n\%$ items the model is most confident in (Section 5.1). Results below double line trade coverage for accuracy and are thus not comparable to upper half.

The previous sections showed that our model reliably identifies trustworthy annotators. However, we also want to find the most likely correct answer. Using majority voting often fails to find the correct label. This problem worsens when there are more than two labels. We need to take relative majorities into account or break ties when two or more labels receive the same number of votes. This is deeply unsatisfying.

Figure 2 shows the accuracy of our model on various data sets from Snow et al. (2008). The model outperforms majority voting on both RTE and Temporal recognition sets. It performs as well as majority voting for the WSD task. This last set is somewhat of an exception, though, since almost all annotators are correct all the time, so majority voting is trivially correct. Still, we need to ensure that the model does not perform worse under such conditions. The results for RTE and Temporal data also rival those reported in Raykar and Yu (2012) and Carpenter (2008), yet were achieved with a much simpler model.

Carpenter (2008) models instance difficulty as a parameter. While it seems intuitively useful to model which items are harder than other, it increases the parameter space more than our trustworthiness variable. We achieve comparable performance without modeling difficulty, which greatly simplifies inference. The model of Raykar and Yu (2012) is more similar to our approach, in that it does not model item difficulty. However, it adds an extra step that learns priors from the estimated parameters. In our model, this is part of the training process. For more details on both models, see Section 6.

5.1 Trading Coverage for Accuracy

Sometimes, we want to produce an answer for every item (e.g., when evaluating a data set), and sometimes, we value good answers more than answering all items (e.g., when developing an annotated corpus). Jha et al. (2010) have demonstrated how to achieve better coverage (i.e., answer more items) by relaxing the majority voting constraints. Similarly, we can improve accuracy if we only select high quality annotations, even if this incurs lower coverage.

We provide a parameter in MACE that allows users to set a threshold for this trade-off: the model only returns a label for an instance if it is sufficiently confident in its answer. We approximate the model's confidence by the posterior entropy of

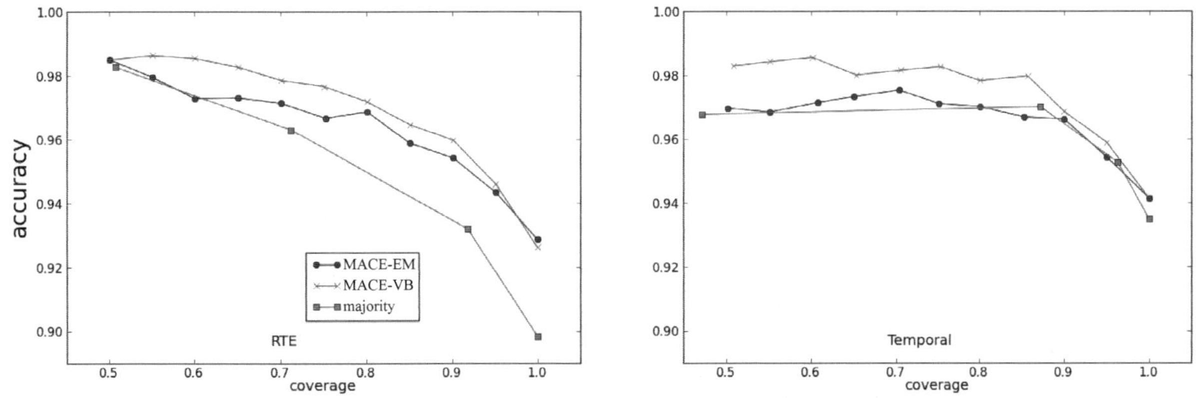

Figure 4: Tradeoff between coverage and accuracy for RTE (left) and temporal (right). Lower thresholds lead to less coverage, but result in higher accuracy.

each instance. However, entropy depends strongly on the specific makeup of the dataset (number of annotators and labels, etc.), so it is hard for the user to set a specific threshold.

Instead of requiring an exact entropy value, we provide a simple thresholding between 0.0 and 1.0 (setting the threshold to 1.0 will include all items). After training, MACE orders the posterior entropies for all instances and selects the value that covers the selected fraction of the instances. The threshold thus roughly corresponds to coverage. It then only returns answers for instances whose entropy is below the threshold. This procedure is similar to precision/recall curves.

Jha et al. (2010) showed the effect of varying the relative majority required, i.e., requiring that at least n out of 10 annotators have to agree to count an item. We use that method as baseline comparison, evaluating the effect on coverage and accuracy when we vary n from 5 to 10.

Figure 4 shows the tradeoff between coverage and accuracy for two data sets. Lower thresholds produce more accurate answers, but result in lower coverage, as some items are left blank. If we produce answers for all items, we achieve accuracies of 0.93 for RTE and 0.94 for Temporal, but by excluding just the 10% of items in which the model is least confident, we achieve accuracies as high as 0.95 for RTE and 0.97 for Temporal. We omit the results for WSD here, since there is little headroom and they are thus not very informative. Using Variational Bayes inference consistently achieves higher results for the same coverage than the standard implementation. Increasing the required majority also improves accuracy, although not as much, and the loss in coverage is larger and cannot be controlled. In contrast, our method allows us to achieve better accuracy at a smaller, controlled loss in coverage.

5.2 Influence of Strategy, Number of Annotators, and Supervision

Adverse Strategy We showed that our model recovers the correct answer with high accuracy. However, to test whether this is just a function of the annotator pool, we experiment with varying the trustworthiness of the pool. If most annotators answer correctly, majority voting is trivially correct, as is our model. What happens, however, if more and more annotators are unreliable? While some agreement can arise from randomness, majority voting is bound to become worse—can our model overcome this problem? We set up a second set of experiments to test this, using synthetic data. We choose 20 annotators and vary the amount of good annotators among them from 0 to 10 (after which the trivial case sets in). We define a *good* annotator as one who answers correctly 95% of the time.[2] Adverse annotators select their answers randomly or always choose a certain value (minimal annotators). These are two frequent strategies of spammers.

For different numbers of labels and varying percentage of spammers, we measure the accuracy

[2]The best annotators on the Snow data sets actually found the correct answer 100% of the time.

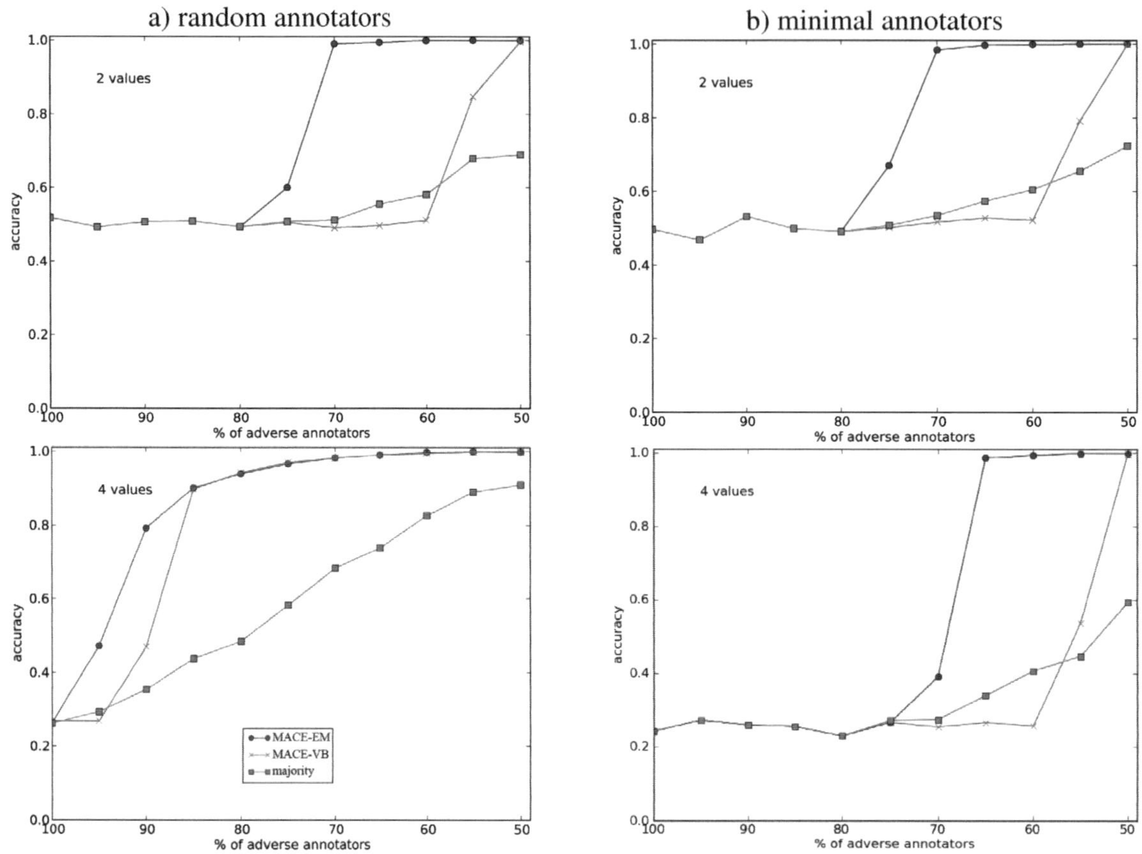

Figure 5: Influence of adverse annotator strategy on label accuracy (y-axis). Number of possible labels varied between 2 (top row) and 4 (bottom row). Adverse annotators either choose at random (a) or always select the first label (b). MACE needs fewer good annotators to recover the correct answer.

Figure 6: Varying number of annotators: effect on prediction accuracy. Each point averaged over 10 runs. Note different scale for WSD.

of our model and majority voting on 100 items, averaged over 10 runs for each condition. Figure 5 shows the effect of annotator proficiency on both majority voting and our method for both kinds of spammers. Annotator pool strategy affects majority voting more than our model. Even with few good annotators, our model learns to dismiss the spammers as noise. There is a noticeable point on each graph where MACE diverges from the majority voting line. It thus reaches good accuracy much faster than majority voting, i.e., with fewer good annotators. This divergence point happens earlier with more label values when adverse annotators label randomly. In general, random annotators are easier to deal with than the ones always choosing the first label. Note that in cases where we have a majority of adversarial annotators, VB performs worse than EM, since this condition violates the implicit assumptions we encoded with the priors in VB. Under these conditions, setting different priors to reflect the annotator pool should improve performance.

Obviously, both of these pools are extremes: it is unlikely to have so few good or so many malicious annotators. Most pools will be somewhere in between. It does show, however, that our model can pick up on reliable annotators even under very unfavorable conditions. The result has a practical upshot: AMT allows us to require a minimum rating for annotators to work on a task. Higher ratings improve annotation quality, but delay completion, since there are fewer annotators with high ratings. The results in this section suggest that we can find the correct answer even in annotator pools with low overall proficiency. We can thus waive the rating requirement and allow more annotators to work on the task. This considerably speeds up completion.

Number of Annotators Figure 6 shows the effect different numbers of annotators have on accuracy. As we increase the number of annotators, MACE and majority voting achieve better accuracy results. We note that majority voting results level or even drop when going from an odd to an even number. In these cases, the new annotator does not improve accuracy if it goes with the previous majority (i.e., going from 3:2 to 4:2), but can force an error when going against the previous majority (i.e., from 3:2 to 3:3), by creating a tie. MACE-EM and MACE-VB dominate majority voting for RTE and Temporal. For WSD, the picture is less clear, where majority voting dominates when there are fewer annotators. Note that the differences are minute, though (within 1 percentage point). For very small pool sizes (< 3), MACE-VB outperforms both other methods.

Amount of Supervision So far, we have treated the task as completely unsupervised. MACE does not require any expert annotations in order to achieve high accuracy. However, we often have annotations for some of the items. These annotated data points are usually used as control items (by removing annotators that answer them incorrectly). If such annotated data is available, we would like to make use of it. We include an option that lets users supply annotations for some of the items, and use this information as token constraints in the E-step of training. In those cases, the model does not need to estimate the correct value, but only has to adjust the trust parameter. This leads to improved performance.[3]

We explore for RTE and Temporal how performance changes when we vary the amount of supervision in increments of 5%.[4] We average over 10 runs for each value of n, each time supplying annotations for a random set of n items. The baseline uses the annotated label whenever supplied, otherwise the majority vote, with ties split at random.

Figure 7 shows that, unsurprisingly, all methods improve with additional supervision, ultimately reaching perfect accuracy. However, MACE uses the information more effectively, resulting in higher accuracy for a given amount of supervision. This gain is more pronounced when only little supervision is available.

6 Related Research

Snow et al. (2008) and Sorokin and Forsyth (2008) showed that Amazon's MechanicalTurk use in providing non-expert annotations for NLP tasks. Various models have been proposed for predicting correct annotations from noisy non-expert annotations and for estimating annotator trustworthiness. These models divide naturally into two categories: those that use expert annotations for supervised learning (Snow et al., 2008; Bian et al., 2009), and completely unsupervised ones. Our method falls into the latter category because it learns from the redundant non-expert annotations themselves, and makes no use of expertly annotated data.

Most previous work on unsupervised models belongs to a class called "Item-response models", used in psychometrics. The approaches differ with respect to which aspect of the annotation process

[3] If we had annotations for all items, accuracy would be perfect and require no training.

[4] Given the high accuracy for the WSD data set even in the fully unsupervised case, we omit the results here.

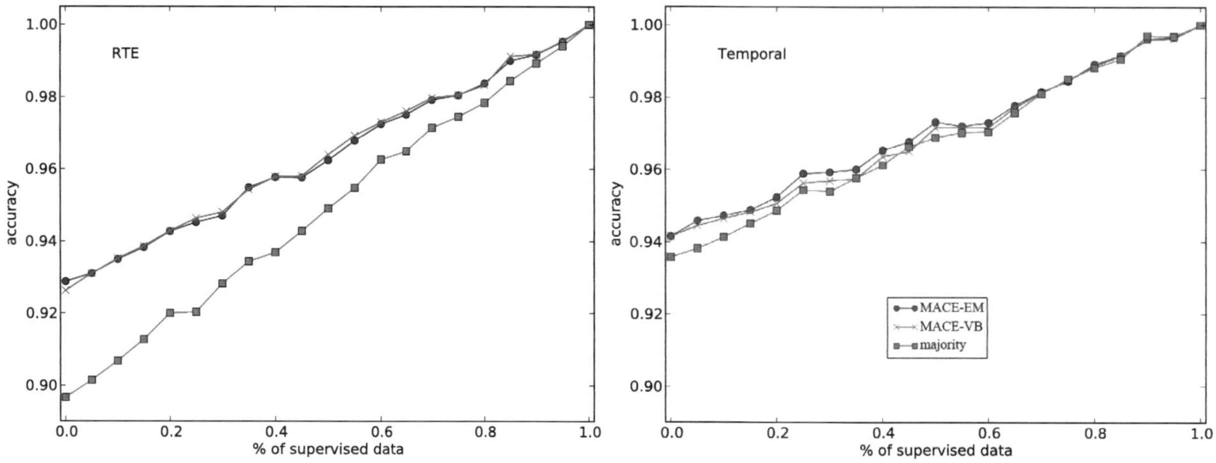

Figure 7: Varying the amount of supervision: effect on prediction accuracy. Each point averaged over 10 runs. MACE uses supervision more efficiently.

they choose to focus on, and the type of annotation task they model. For example, many methods explicitly model annotator bias in addition to annotator competence (Dawid and Skene, 1979; Smyth et al., 1995). Our work models annotator bias, but only when the annotator is suspected to be spamming.

Other methods focus modeling power on instance difficulty to learn not only which annotators are good, but which instances are hard (Carpenter, 2008; Whitehill et al., 2009). In machine vision, several models have taken this further by parameterizing difficulty in terms of complex features defined on each pairing of annotator and annotation instance (Welinder et al., 2010; Yan et al., 2010). While such features prove very useful in vision, they are more difficult to define for the categorical problems common to NLP. In addition, several methods are specifically tailored to annotation tasks that involve ranking (Steyvers et al., 2009; Lee et al., 2011), which limits their applicability in NLP.

The method of Raykar and Yu (2012) is most similar to ours. Their goal is to identify and filter out annotators whose annotations are not correlated with the gold label. They define a function of the learned parameters that is useful for identifying these spammers, and then use this function to build a prior. In contrast, we use simple priors, but incorporate a model parameter that explicitly represents the probability that an annotator is spamming. Our simple model achieves the same accuracy on gold label predictions as theirs.

7 Conclusion

We provide a Java-based implementation, MACE, that recovers correct labels with high accuracy, and reliably identifies trustworthy annotators. In addition, it provides a threshold to control the accuracy/coverage trade-off and can be trained with standard EM or Variational Bayes EM. MACE works fully unsupervised, but can incorporate token constraints via annotated control items. We show that even small amounts help improve accuracy.

Our model focuses most of its modeling power on learning trustworthiness parameters, which are highly correlated with true annotator reliability (Pearson ρ 0.9). We show on real-world and synthetic data sets that our method is more accurate than majority voting, even under adversarial conditions, and as accurate as more complex state-of-the-art systems. Focusing on high-confidence instances improves accuracy considerably. MACE is freely available for download under `http://www.isi.edu/publications/licensed-sw/mace/index.html`.

Acknowledgements

The authors would like to thank Chris Callison-Burch, Victoria Fossum, Stephan Gouws, Marc Schulder, Nathan Schneider, and Noah Smith for invaluable discussions, as well as the reviewers for their constructive feedback.

References

Jiang Bian, Yandong Liu, Ding Zhou, Eugene Agichtein, and Hongyuan Zha. 2009. Learning to recognize reliable users and content in social media with coupled mutual reinforcement. In *Proceedings of the 18th international conference on World wide web*, pages 51–60. ACM.

Chris Callison-Burch and Mark Dredze. 2010. Creating speech and language data with amazon's mechanical turk. In *Proceedings of the NAACL HLT 2010 Workshop on Creating Speech and Language Data with Amazon's Mechanical Turk*, pages 1–12, Los Angeles, June. Association for Computational Linguistics.

Chris Callison-Burch, Philipp Koehn, Christof Monz, Kay Peterson, Mark Przybocki, and Omar Zaidan. 2010. Findings of the 2010 joint workshop on statistical machine translation and metrics for machine translation. In *Proceedings of the Joint Fifth Workshop on Statistical Machine Translation and MetricsMATR*, pages 17–53, Uppsala, Sweden, July. Association for Computational Linguistics.

Bob Carpenter. 2008. Multilevel Bayesian models of categorical data annotation. *Unpublished manuscript*.

A. Philip Dawid and Allan M. Skene. 1979. Maximum likelihood estimation of observer error-rates using the EM algorithm. *Applied Statistics*, pages 20–28.

Arthur P. Dempster, Nan M. Laird, and Donald B. Rubin. 1977. Maximum likelihood from incomplete data via the EM algorithm. *Journal of the Royal Statistical Society. Series B (Methodological)*, 39(1):1–38.

Jason Eisner. 2002. An interactive spreadsheet for teaching the forward-backward algorithm. In *Proceedings of the ACL-02 Workshop on Effective tools and methodologies for teaching natural language processing and computational linguistics-Volume 1*, pages 10–18. Association for Computational Linguistics.

Alvan R. Feinstein and Domenic V. Cicchetti. 1990. High agreement but low kappa: I. the problems of two paradoxes. *Journal of Clinical Epidemiology*, 43(6):543–549.

Kilem Li Gwet. 2008. Computing inter-rater reliability and its variance in the presence of high agreement. *British Journal of Mathematical and Statistical Psychology*, 61(1):29–48.

Eduard Hovy. 2010. Annotation. A Tutorial. In *48th Annual Meeting of the Association for Computational Linguistics*.

Mukund Jha, Jacob Andreas, Kapil Thadani, Sara Rosenthal, and Kathleen McKeown. 2010. Corpus creation for new genres: A crowdsourced approach to pp attachment. In *Proceedings of the NAACL HLT 2010 Workshop on Creating Speech and Language Data with Amazon's Mechanical Turk*, pages 13–20. Association for Computational Linguistics.

Mark Johnson. 2007. Why doesn't EM find good HMM POS-taggers. In *Proceedings of the 2007 Joint Conference on Empirical Methods in Natural Language Processing and Computational Natural Language Learning (EMNLP-CoNLL)*, pages 296–305.

Michael D. Lee, Mark Steyvers, Mindy de Young, and Brent J. Miller. 2011. A model-based approach to measuring expertise in ranking tasks. In L. Carlson, C. Hölscher, and T.F. Shipley, editors, *Proceedings of the 33rd Annual Conference of the Cognitive Science Society*, Austin, TX. Cognitive Science Society.

Vikas C. Raykar and Shipeng Yu. 2012. Eliminating Spammers and Ranking Annotators for Crowdsourced Labeling Tasks. *Journal of Machine Learning Research*, 13:491–518.

Padhraic Smyth, Usama Fayyad, Mike Burl, Pietro Perona, and Pierre Baldi. 1995. Inferring ground truth from subjective labelling of Venus images. *Advances in neural information processing systems*, pages 1085–1092.

Rion Snow, Brendan O'Connor, Dan Jurafsky, and Andrew Y. Ng. 2008. Cheap and fast—but is it good? Evaluating non-expert annotations for natural language tasks. In *Proceedings of the Conference on Empirical Methods in Natural Language Processing*, pages 254–263. Association for Computational Linguistics.

Alexander Sorokin and David Forsyth. 2008. Utility data annotation with Amazon Mechanical Turk. In *IEEE Computer Society Conference on Computer Vision and Pattern Recognition Workshops, CVPRW '08*, pages 1–8. IEEE.

Mark Steyvers, Michael D. Lee, Brent Miller, and Pernille Hemmer. 2009. The wisdom of crowds in the recollection of order information. *Advances in neural information processing systems*, 23.

Stephen Tratz and Eduard Hovy. 2010. A taxonomy, dataset, and classifier for automatic noun compound interpretation. In *Proceedings of the 48th Annual Meeting of the Association for Computational Linguistics*, pages 678–687. Association for Computational Linguistics.

Peter Welinder, Steve Branson, Serge Belongie, and Pietro Perona. 2010. The multidimensional wisdom of crowds. In *Neural Information Processing Systems Conference (NIPS)*, volume 6.

Jacob Whitehill, Paul Ruvolo, Tingfan Wu, Jacob Bergsma, and Javier Movellan. 2009. Whose vote should count more: Optimal integration of labels from labelers of unknown expertise. *Advances in Neural Information Processing Systems*, 22:2035–2043.

Yan Yan, Rómer Rosales, Glenn Fung, Mark Schmidt, Gerardo Hermosillo, Luca Bogoni, Linda Moy, and

Jennifer Dy. 2010. Modeling annotator expertise: Learning when everybody knows a bit of something. In *International Conference on Artificial Intelligence and Statistics*.

Omar F. Zaidan and Chris Callison-Burch. 2011. Crowdsourcing translation: Professional quality from non-professionals. In *Proceedings of the 49th Annual Meeting of the Association for Computational Linguistics: Human Language Technologies*, pages 1220–1229, Portland, Oregon, USA, June. Association for Computational Linguistics.

Supervised All-Words Lexical Substitution using Delexicalized Features

György Szarvas[1] Chris Biemann[2] Iryna Gurevych[3,4]
(1) Nuance Communications Deutschland GmbH
Kackertstrasse 10, D-52072 Aachen, Germany
(2) FG Language Technology
Department of Computer Science, Technische Universität Darmstadt
(3) Ubiquitous Knowledge Processing Lab (UKP-TUDA)
Department of Computer Science, Technische Universität Darmstadt
(4) Ubiquitous Knowledge Processing Lab (UKP-DIPF)
German Institute for Educational Research and Educational Information
http://www.nuance.com, http://www.ukp.tu-darmstadt.de

Abstract

We propose a supervised lexical substitution system that does not use separate classifiers per word and is therefore applicable to any word in the vocabulary. Instead of learning word-specific substitution patterns, a global model for lexical substitution is trained on delexicalized (i.e., non lexical) features, which allows to exploit the power of supervised methods while being able to generalize beyond target words in the training set. This way, our approach remains technically straightforward, provides better performance and similar coverage in comparison to unsupervised approaches. Using features from lexical resources, as well as a variety of features computed from large corpora (n-gram counts, distributional similarity) and a ranking method based on the posterior probabilities obtained from a Maximum Entropy classifier, we improve over the state of the art in the LexSub Best-Precision metric and the Generalized Average Precision measure. Robustness of our approach is demonstrated by evaluating it successfully on two different datasets.

1 Introduction

In recent years, the task of automatically providing lexical substitutions in context (McCarthy and Navigli, 2007) received much attention. The premise to be able to replace words in a sentence without changing its meaning gave rise to applications like linguistic steganography (Topkara et al., 2006; Chang and Clark, 2010), semantic text similarity (Agirre et al., 2012), and plagiarism detection (Gipp et al., 2011).

Lexical substitution, a special form of contextual paraphrasing where only a single word is replaced, is closely related to word sense disambiguation (WSD): polysemous words have possible substitutions reflecting several senses, and the correct sense has to be picked to avoid spurious system behavior. However, no explicit word sense inventory is required for lexical substitution (Dagan et al., 2006).

The prominent tasks in a lexical substitution system are *generation* and *ranking*, i.e. to generate a set of possible substitutions for the target word and then to rank this set of possible substitutions according to their contextual fitness. The task to generate a high quality set of possible substitutions is challenging in itself, for two reasons. First, the available lexical resources are seldom complete in listing synonyms. Second, manually annotated substitutions show that not all synonyms of a word are appropriate in a given context, and many good substitutions have other lexical relation than synonymy to the original word.

In this work, we present a supervised lexical substitution system that, unlike the usual *lexical sample* supervised approaches, can produce substitutions for targets that are not contained in the training material. We reach this by using non-lexical features from heterogeneous evidence, including lexical-semantic resources and distributional similarity, n-gram and shallow syntactic features based on large, unannotated background corpora. In light of the existence of lexical resources such as WordNet (Fellbaum, 1998) or machine readable dictionaries that can serve as the source for lexical information, and with the ever-increasing availability of large unannotated corpora for many languages and domains, our proposal enables us to leverage the quality gain of supervised machine learning while generalizing over a large vocabulary through the avoidance of lexicalized features. Using a single classifier for all substitution targets in this way results in an all-words substitution system. As our results demonstrate, our model improves over the state of the art in lexical substitution with practically no open parameters that have to be optimized and selected carefully according to the dataset at hand.

2 Related Work

Previous works in lexical substitution either address both the *generation* and the *ranking* tasks, and are therefore applicable to any word without prelabeled data (c.f. the Semeval 2007 task (McCarthy and Navigli, 2007) and related work) or focus on the more challenging ranking step only (c.f. Erk and Padó (2008) and related work). The latter approaches take the list of possible substitutions directly from the testing data as a workaround to generating the possible substitutions, and merely evaluate the ranking capabilities of these methods.

The most accurate lexical substitution systems use supervised machine learning to train (and test) a separate classifier per target word, using lexical and shallow syntactic features. These systems rely on the existence of a large number of annotated examples (i.e. sentences together with the contextually valid substitutions) for each word. Biemann (2012) describes a supervised lexical substitution system for frequent nouns. Exploiting a large amount of sense tagged examples and (sense-specific) data annotated with substitutions, an accurate coarse-grained WSD model is trained and then the most frequent substitutions of the predicted sense are assigned to the new occurrences of the target words. The results demonstrate that lexical substitution of noun targets can be attained with very high precision (over 90%) if sufficient training material is available. However, due to high annotation costs, methods that do not require labeled training data per target scale better to a large vocabulary.

Knowledge-based systems like e.g. by Hassan et al. (2007), who use a number of knowledge-based and unsupervised methods and combine these clues using a voting scheme, do not need training data per target. The combination of different signals, however, has to be done manually. Unsupervised systems that rely on distributional similarity (Thater et al., 2011) or topic models (Li et al., 2010) are single signals in this sense, and their development is guided by the performance and observations on standard datasets. Such signals, however, can also be kept simple avoiding any task-specific optimization and can be integrated in a single model for all words using a limited amount of training data and delexicalized features, as in Senselearner (Mihalcea and Csomai, 2005) for weakly supervised all-words disambiguation. This way, task specific development can be replaced by a machine learning component and the resulting model applies also to unseen words, similar to the knowledge-based approaches.

2.1 Full Lexical Substitution Systems

Related works that address the lexical substitution problem according to the settings established by the *English Lexical Substitution Task* (McCarthy and Navigli, 2007) at Semeval 2007 (LexSub) typically employ a simple ranking strategy based on local n-gram frequencies and focus on finding an optimal source of possible substitutions, as the selection of lexical resources has largest impact on the overall system performance: Sinha and Mihalcea (2009) systematically explored the benefits of multiple lexical resources and found that a supervised combination of several resources lead to statistically significant improvements in accuracy (about 3.5% points over the best single resource, WordNet). They tested LSA (Deerwester et al., 1990), ESA (Gabrilovich and Markovitch, 2007) and n-gram frequencies for contextualization and found n-gram frequencies to be more effective than dimensionality reduction techniques by a large margin. Their improvements were obtained by supervised learning on the *combination* of several lexical resources. Our work, on the other hand, is concerned with using more advanced features and we obtain significant improvements based on a diverse set of features and a different learning setup: we train a *model for contextualization*, rather than to combine substitutions from several different resources.

A recent work by Sinha and Mihalcea (2011) used an approach based on graph centrality to rank the candidates and achieved comparable performance to n-gram-frequency-based ranking. To summarize, the use of n-gram frequencies for ranking and WordNet as the (most appropriate single) source of synonyms is competitive to more complex solutions and provides a simple and strong lexical substitution system. This motivated the follow-up work by Chang and Clark (2010) to use WordNet and n-grams in a linguistic steganography application and this motivates us to use this method as our baseline.

2.2 Ranking Word Meaning in Context

Another prominent line of related work focused solely on the accurate ranking of a pre-given set of possible synonyms, according to their plausibility as a substitution in a given context. Typically, lexical substitution data is used for evaluation purposes, taking the candidate substitutions directly from the test data. This choice is motivated by the assumption that better semantic models should rank near-synonyms more accurately according to how they fit in the original word's context.

Erk and Padó (2008) proposed the use of multiple vector representations of words, where the basic representation corresponds to a standard co-occurrence vector, while further vectors are used to characterize words according to their inverse selectional preference statistics for typical dependency relations. The representation of a word in its context is computed via combining the basic representation of a word with the inverse selectional preference vectors of its related words from the context. Ranking is done by comparing vectors of possible substitutions with the substitution target. Thater et al. (2010) took a similar approach but used second order co-occurrence vectors and report improved performance.

An exemplar-based approach is presented by Erk and Padó (2010) and Reisinger and Mooney (2010b) to model word meaning with respect to its context: instead of representing the word and the context as separate vectors and combining them, a set of word occurrences in similar contexts is picked first, and then only these exemplars are used to represent the word in context. While this approach provides good results with relatively simple and transparent models, each occurrence of a word has a unique representation (that can only be computed at testing time), and it is computationally expensive to scale these models to a large number of examples.

Dinu and Lapata (2010) used a bag of words latent variable model to characterize the meaning of a word as a distribution over a set of latent variables (that is, probabilistic senses). Contextualized representation of word meaning is then attained by conditioning the model on the context words in which the target word occurs. A similar approach has been evaluated for word similarity (Reisinger and Mooney, 2010a) and word sense disambiguation (Li et al., 2010).

Although our main goal here is to develop a full-fledged lexical substitution system, we mainly focus on the construction of better ranking models based on supervised machine learning and delexicalized features that scale well for unseen words. This approach has similar properties (applicability to all words without word-specific training data) to the knowledge-based and unsupervised models described above, so we will also refer to these systems for comparison.

3 Datasets

In our work, we use two major freely available datasets that contain human-annotated substitutions for single words in their full-sentence context.

3.1 LexSub dataset

This dataset was introduced in the Lexical Substitution task at Semeval 2007[1]. It consists of 2002 sentences for a total of 201 words (10 sentences per word, but 8 sentences does not have gold standard labels). Each sentence was assigned to 5 native speaker annotators, who entered as many paraphrases or substitutions as they found appropriate for the word in context. Paraphrases are assigned a weight (or frequency) that denotes how many annotators suggested that particular word as a substitute.

3.2 TWSI

A similar, but larger dataset is the Turk Bootstrap Word Sense Inventory (TWSI[2], (Biemann, 2012)). The data was collected through a three-step crowdsourcing process and comprises 24,647 sentences

[1] download at http://nlp.cs.swarthmore.edu/semeval/tasks/task10/data.shtml

[2] http://www.ukp.tu-darmstadt.de/data/lexical-resources/twsi-lexical-substitutions/

for a total of 1,012 target nouns, where crowdworkers have provided substitutions for a target word in context. We did not use the roughly 150,000 sense-labeled contexts and the sense inventory of this resource, i.e. this dataset – as used in this study – is transparent to the LexSub data. For the majority of the data, responses from 3 annotators were collected per context, and there are on average 24 sentences per target word in the dataset. Due to this, the average weight of good substitutions is somewhat lower than in the LexSub dataset (1.27 vs. 1.58 in LexSub), but the average number of unique substitutions per target word is slightly higher in TWSI (average of 22 words / target vs. 17 in LexSub).

	LexSub		TWSI	
source	WN	Gold St.	WN	Gold St.
# words	201	201	908	1007
#inst	2002	2002	22543	24643
avg. set	21	17	7.5	22
# empty	508	17	11165	620
#0	39465	27300	151538	443993
#1	1302	4698	10678	77417
#2	582	1251	4171	17585
#3	308	571	2069	5629
#4	212	319	74	325
#5+	129	179	121	411

Table 1: Details of the datasets: WN=WordNet

3.3 Source of Possible Substitutions

In our lexical substitution system, we used WordNet as the source for candidate synonyms. For each substitution target, we took all synonyms from all of the word's WordNet synsets as candidates, together with the words from synsets in *similar to, entailment* and *also see* relation to these synsets[3]. In order to evaluate and compare our ranking methodology in a transparent way with those studies that focused just on the candidate ranking task, we also performed experiments where we pooled the set of candidates from the gold standard dataset. This setting ensures that each set contains a positive candidate, and that all human-suggested paraphrases are available as positive examples for a given sentence.

The main characteristics of the datasets (with both WordNet or the gold standard as the source of candidate substitutions) are summarized in Table 1. The rows in the table indicate the source of possible substitutions, number of target words, instances with at least one non-multiword possible substitution, average size of candidate sets, and number of instances with no good candidate and frequency of different labels. The labels denote how many annotators proposed a particular word as substitution in the given context and can be interpreted as a measure of goodness: the higher the value, the better the candidate fits in the context. Similarly, the label 0 denotes the total number of negative examples in our datasets, i.e. bad substitutions – words that belong to the candidate set for a particular target word, but are not listed as good substitutions in the given context in the dataset.

4 Methodology

4.1 Experimental Setup and Evaluation

We follow previous works in lexical substitution and evaluate our models using the Generalized Average Precision (GAP) (Kishida, 2005) measure which assesses the quality of the entire ranked list. In addition, we also provide the precision of our system at the first rank (P@1), i.e. the percentage of correct paraphrases at rank 1. This is a realistic evaluation criterion for many applications, such as paraphrasing for linguistic steganography: it is the highest-ranked candidate that can be used to replace the original word (the manipulated text should preserve the original meaning) and there is no straightforward way to exploit multiple correct answers. In addition, we also provide the Semeval 2007 *best precision*[4] metric (McCarthy and Navigli, 2007) for the LexSub dataset for comparison to Semeval 2007 participants. This metric also evaluates the first guess of a system (per context), but gives less credit to easier contexts, where several good options exist. This fact motivates us to use P@1 rather than the *best precision* metric in all other experiments.

[3]This candidate set was found best for WordNet by Martinez et al. (2007).

[4]Since our system always provides an answer, the Semeval 2007 *best recall* equals *best precision*.

4.2 Machine Learning on Delexicalized Features

After the list of potential substitutions is obtained, lexical substitution is cast as a ranking task where the goal is to prefer contextually plausible substitutions over implausible ones. The goal of this study is to learn a ranking model that is applicable to any word, for which a list of synonyms is available. A supervised model can generalize over the example target words in the datasets, if aggregate features can be defined that have the same semantics regardless of the actual context, target word or candidate substitution they are computed from. Having such a representation, one can expect to learn patterns that generalize over the words/contexts seen in the training dataset, and thus the setup constitutes a supervised all-word system.

To simulate an all-word scenario, we perform a 10-fold cross validation in our experiments, splitting the dataset into equal-sized folds randomly on the *target word* level. That is, all sentences for a particular target word fall into the same fold and thus either the training or the test set (but never both). This way we always train and test the model on disjoint sets of words and as such, the learnt models cannot exploit word-specific properties. This makes our results realistic estimates of an open vocabulary paraphrasing system, where we would apply the models (mostly) to words that were not in the training material.

4.2.1 Machine Learning Model

In our experiments, we used a Maximum Entropy (MaxEnt) classifier model implemented in the Mallet (McCallum, 2002) package and trained a binary classifier to predict if a given substitution is valid in a particular context or not.

We chose to use Maximum Entropy models for two main reasons: MaxEnt is not sensitive to parameter settings and handles correlated features well, which is crucial in our situation where many features are highly correlated.

Due to the low number of positive examples in the datasets (see Table 1, labels 1-5+) and to emphasize better paraphrases suggested by several annotators, we assigned a weight to positive instances during the training process equal to their score (the number of annotators suggesting that paraphrase; the weight of negative instances was set to 1).

The output of the MaxEnt classifier is a posterior probability distribution for each target/substitution pair, denoting the probabilities of the instance to be a good or a bad substitution, given the feature values that describe both the words and their context. The ranking over a set of candidates can be naturally induced based on their posterior scores for the positive class, i.e. a number that denotes 'how good the candidate is, given the context'. That is, the best substitution candidate s (characterized by a set of features $\mathbf{F}$) from a set of candidates $\mathbf{S}$ is obtained as $argmax_{s \in \mathbf{S}}[P(good|\mathbf{F})]$, the next best as the $argmax$ of the remaining elements, and so on.

This pointwise approach to subset ranking (Cossock and Zhang, 2008) is arguably simplistic, but several studies (c.f. Li et al. (2007; Busa-Fekete et al. (2011)) found this approach to perform reasonably well given that the model provides accurate probability estimates, which is the case for MaxEnt.

4.3 Delexicalized Features

We use heterogeneous sources of information to describe each target word/candidate substitution pair in its context. The most important features describe the syntagmatic coherence of the substitute in context, measured as local n-gram frequencies obtained from web data, in a sliding window around the target word. In addition we use features to describe the (non-positional, i.e. non-local) distributional similarity of the target and its candidate substitution in terms of sentence level co-occurrence statistics collected from newspaper texts. A further set of features captures the properties of the target and candidate word in a lexical resource (WordNet), such as their number of senses, how frequent senses are synonymous, etc. Lastly, we use part of speech patterns to describe the target word in context. This way, unlike many other methods suggested in previous works (Thater et al., 2011; Erk and Padó, 2008), our model does not require deep syntactic analysis of the test sentences in order to rank the candidates. Even though we make intensive use of WordNet to compute some of our feature functions, this is not a severe restriction for a practical paraphrasing system: one has to have a decent lexical resource in order to mine a reasonable set of candidate synonyms and such a resource can also serve as a source for features in the classifier. The rest of the feature functions exploit only large unannotated corpora and a POS tagger at application time.

For a target word t, and candidate substitution s_i from a set of candidates S, we used the features below. Each numeric feature is used both in the form given below, and set-wise scaled to $[0, 1]$ (we leave it to the classifier to pick the more useful form of information). For the LexSub dataset, each feature is defined once for all instances, and once specific to the four POS categories in the dataset. That is each instance would have the described features defined twice, once the general form (defined for every instance) and once the form according to the *predicted* POS category of the target word. This allows the model to learn general and also POS-specific patterns based on the information described below (i.e. frequency thresholds, distributional properties etc. for nouns or verbs etc. in particular). We denote the left and right contexts around t and all words in the sentence except t with c_l, c_r and c, respectively)

4.3.1 Lexical Resource Features

We used Wordnet 3.0 as the source for substitution candidates and as a source for delexicalized features. We found the measure of ambiguity and the sense number to provide useful information in a more general context: it is informative how many senses a word has, and it is informative from which sense number of the substitution target the substitution candidate came from, since they are ordered by corpus frequency. In addition, we used the synsets IDs of the words' hypernyms as features, which can capture more general semantics (the word to replace is 'animate', 'abstract', etc.). The following features were extracted from WordNet:

- number of senses of t and s_i in WordNet
- the sense numbers of t and s_i which are synonymous (in case they are direct synonyms, c.f. WN sense numbers encode sense frequencies)
- binary features for synset IDs of the hypernyms of the synset containing t and s_i (this feature type did not significantly improve results)

4.3.2 Corpus-based Features

In order to create a Distributional Thesaurus (DT) similar to Lin (1998), we parsed a source corpus of 120M sentence English newspaper texts from the LCC[5] (Richter et al., 2006) with the Stanford parser (de Marneffe et al., 2006) and used dependencies to extract features for words: each dependency triple $(w1, r, w2)$ denoting a dependency of type r between words $w1$ and $w2$ results in a feature $(r, w2)$ characterizing $w1$, and a feature $(w1, r)$ characterizing $w2$[6]. After counting the frequency of each feature for each word, we apply a significance measure (log-likelihood test (LL), (Dunning, 1993)), rank features per word according to their significance, and prune the data, keeping only the 1000 most salient features (F_w) per word[7]. The similarity of two words is then given by the number of their common features. Our distributional thesaurus provides a list of the 1000 most salient features and a ranked list of up to 200 similar words (sim_w, based on the number of shared features) for all words above a certain frequency in the source corpus. We compute the following features to characterize a target word / substitution pair:

- To what extent the context c characterizes s_i: $\frac{\sum_{c \in F_{s_i}} LL(F_{s_i}(c))}{\sum_{s_j \in S} \sum_{c \in F_{s_j}} LL(F_{s_j}(c))}$
- percentage of shared words among the top k similar words to t and to s_i: $\frac{|sim_t|_k \cap |sim_{s_i}|_k}{max(|sim_t|_k, |sim_{s_i}|_k)}$, for $k = 1, 5, 10, 20, 50, 100, 200$[8]
- percentage of shared salient features among the top k features of t and s_i, globally and restricted to the words from the target sentence: $\frac{|F_t|_k \cap |F_{s_i}|_k}{max(|F_t|_k, |F_{s_i}|_k)}$ and $\frac{|F_t|_k \cap |F_{s_i}|_k \cap |c|}{|c|}$, for $k = 1, 5, 10, 20, 50, 100, 1000$
- boolean feature indicating whether $s_i \in sim_t$ or not (in top 100 similar words)

[5] http://corpora.informatik.uni-leipzig.de/

[6] open source implementation and data available at http://sourceforge.net/p/jobimtext

[7] The pruning operation greatly reduces runtime at thesaurus collection, rendering memory reduction techniques like (Charikar et al., 2004) as unnecessary.

[8] The various values for k trade off the salience of this feature for coverage: only very few substitutions have overlap in the top 1-5 similar words set, but if this happens, it is a very strong indicator of contextual fitness, whereas overlap within the top 100-200 similar words is present for much more target/substitution pairs, but it is a weaker indicator of fitness.

4.3.3 Local n-gram Features (from Web 1T)

Syntagmatic coherence, measured as the n-gram frequency of the context with the candidate substitution serves as the basis of ranking in the best Semeval 2007 system (Giuliano et al., 2007), which is also our baseline method here. We use the same n-grams as features in our supervised model:

- 1-5-gram frequencies in a sliding window around t: $freq(c_l s_i c_r)/freq(c_l t c_r)$, normalized w.r.t t
- 1-5-gram frequencies in a sliding window around t: $freq(c_l s_i c_r)/\sum freq(c_l S c_r)$, normalized w.r.t. S
- for each of x in {*'and', 'or', ','*}, 3-5-gram frequencies in a sliding window around t: $freq(c_l t x s_i c_r)/freq(c_l t c_r)$ (how frequently the target and candidate are part of a list or conjunctive phrase)

4.3.4 Shallow Syntactic Features

We also use part of speech information (from TreeTagger (Schmid, 1994)) as features, in order to enable the model to learn POS-specific patterns. This is especially important for the LexSub dataset, which contains examples from all major parts of speech (the TWSI dataset contains only noun targets). Specifically, we use:

- 1-3-grams of main POS categories in a window around t, e.g. *NVV* for a noun, verb, verb context
- Penn Treebank POS code of t

4.3.5 Example

For clarity, we exemplify our delexicalized features briefly. Using WordNet as a source for the word *bright*, we considered the 11 words *brilliant, vivid, smart, burnished, lustrous, shining, shiny, undimmed, brilliant, hopeful, promising* from the synsets of *bright*, and 64 further words from its related synsets (e.g. *intelligent, glimmery, polished, happy, ...*) as potential paraphrases. That is, for the sentence "He was **bright** and independent and proud.", where the human annotators listed *intelligent, clever* as suitable paraphrases, our system had 1 correct (*intelligent*) and 74 incorrect substituions in the candidate set (that is, *clever* is not found in WordNet in the above described way). The substitution *intelligent* in this context is characterized by a total of 178 active features. Of those, 112 features are based on local n-gram features (Sect. 4.3.3), where the large number stems from different n in n-gram, as well as the different variants of normalization and copies for the particular POS (here: JJ) and for all POS. For instance, "bright" and "intelligent" are frequently occurring in comma-separated enumerations, and "intelligent" fits well in the target context based on n-gram probabilities. The second largest block of features is constituted by 48 active distributional similarity features (Sect. 4.3.2), which are also available per POS and for different normalizations. Here is e.g. captured that the candidate has a high distributional similarity to the target with respect to our background corpus. The 12 shallow syntatic features (Sect 4.3.4) capture various present POS patterns around the target, and the 6 resource-based features (Sect. 4.3.1) e.g. inform about the number of senses of the target (10) and the candidate (4).

4.4 Results

Now, we describe our results in detail. First we compare our system on two datasets with a competitive baseline, which uses the same candidate set as our ML-based model, and the simple and effective ranking function based on Google n-grams described by Giuliano et al. (2007). Later on we analyze how the four major feature groups contribute to the results in a feature ablation experiment, and then we provide a detailed and thorough comparison to earlier works that are similar to the model presented here and used the same dataset (LexSub) for evaluation.

4.4.1 Semeval 2007 Lexical Substitution

In Table 2 we report results on the LexSub dataset. As can be seen, our model outperforms the baseline by a significant margin ($p < 0.01$ for all measures, using a paired t-test for significance). Both the overall rankings and the P@1 scores are of higher quality than the rankings based only on n-grams.

4.4.2 Turk Bootstrap Word Sense Inventory

The results on the TWSI dataset are provided in Table 3. Our model outperforms the baseline in all

	cand. from WN		from Gold St.	
	GAP	P@1	GAP	P@1
Baseline	36.8	31.1	46.9	49.5
Our model	43.8	40.2	52.4	57.7

Table 2: Comparison to the baseline on LexSub 2007.

	cand. from WN		from Gold St.	
	GAP	P@1	GAP	P@1
Baseline	33.8	28.2	44.4	44.5
Our model	36.6	32.4	47.2	49.5

Table 3: Comparison to the baseline on the TWSI dataset.

the comparisons similar to the LexSub dataset. The differences are not so pronounced but still highly significant ($p < 0.01$). This is consistent with the observation by several Semeval 2007 participants and with a per-POS analysis of our results on LexSub: the ranking task seems to be more challenging for nouns than for other parts of speech. When using WordNet, for about half (11165/22543) of the instances, individual scores are 0 (cf. Table 1). For the other half, avg. P@1 score is around 0.7, which results in 0.324 overall. Note that the task of ranking in avg. 7.5 items is considerably easier than ranking in avg. 22 items, which explains the high P@1 scores for cases where good candidates exist – also, a random ranker would score higher in this case.

These results demonstrate that the proposed delexicalized approach is superior to a competitive baseline across two datasets.

4.5 Feature Exploration

We explored the contribution of our various feature types on the LexSub dataset with candidate set from the gold standard. Our MaxEnt model relying only on local n-gram frequency features, i.e. the same information as the baseline model, achieved a GAP score of 48.3 and P@1 of 52.1, respectively. This result is significantly better than the baseline ($p < 0.01$), i.e. the machine learnt ranking model is better than a state-of-the-art handcrafted ranker based on the same data. All single feature groups, when combined with n-grams, lead to significant improvements ($p < 0.01$), which proves the usefulness of each feature group. In order to assess the contribution of each group to the *overall* system performance, we performed a feature ablation experiment. That is, we trained the MaxEnt model with using all feature groups (this equals the model in Table 2) and then with leaving each of the feature groups out once. As can be seen, all feature groups improve the overall results in a noticeable way, i.e. their contribution is complementary.

	GAP	P@1
w/o n-gram features	47.3	48.9
w/o distr. thesaurus	49.8	55.0
w/o POS features	51.6	56.3
w/o WN features	51.7	57.0
Our model (all)	**52.4**	**57.7**

Table 4: Feature ablation experiment (on LexSub dataset, with candidates from Gold Standard).

4.5.1 Comparison to Previous Works

In Table 5 we compare our method with previous works in the field, using the LexSub dataset.

candidates from WN		from Gold Standard	
	Best-P		GAP
		PadóErk10	38.6
Giuliano	12.93	DinuLapata	42.9
Martinez	12.68	Thater10	46.0
Sinha	13.60	Thater11	51.7
Baseline	11.75	Baseline	46.9
Our model	**15.94**	Our model	**52.4**

Table 5: Comparison to previous works (LexSub dataset).

In the left column of Table 5, we compare the performance of our system to representative Semeval 2007 participants, namely Martinez et al. (2007) and Giuliano et al. (2007). In order to make a fair comparison, we report scores for the official test data of Semeval 2007, using a 10-fold cross-validation scheme. Martinez et al. (2007) developed their system based on WordNet and we use the same candidate set here that they proposed in their system description. Our reimplementation of (Giuliano et al., 2007) performs below the original scores, due to the more restricted source of substitution candidates (they use more lexical resources), yet uses the same ranking methodology based on Google n-grams that we adopted here as our baseline. We also report the best previous result for this task, which was achieved via the (supervised) combination of lexical resources to improve the performance (Sinha and Mihalcea, 2009). Our model outperforms this result by a large margin for the best-precision evaluation (mode-P, precision measured on those examples where there is a clear best substitution provided by humans was 26.3%, compared to 21.3% reported by Sinha and Mihalcea (2009). This is especially promising in light of the fact that we use only a single source (WordNet) for synonyms and achieve our improvements through more advanced delexicalized features in an improved ranking model. Sinha and Mihalcea (2009), on the other hand, used comparably simple features for contextualization, of which n-gram features were deemed most successful. As Sinha and Mihalcea (2009) showed improvements through utilizing several synonym sources, a combination of their approach with ours should allow for further improvements in the future.

In the right column of Table 5, we compare our model to previous works that addressed only the ranking task, and report performance on the whole dataset (i.e. trial and test). As can be seen, the methodology proposed here outperforms previous ranking models, without the need to develop a high-quality ranking model by hand, and without the need to parse the test sentences. Our delexicalized supervised model only requires the development of features, and achieves excellent results without major task-specific tuning or customization: we omitted the optimization of the feature set and the parameters of the learning model. This fact makes us assume that the proposed model can be applied more quickly and easily than previous models that have several important design aspects to choose from.

5 Conclusion and Future Work

In this study, we presented a supervised approach to all-words lexical substitution based on delexicalized features, which enables us to fully exploit the power of supervised models while ensuring applicability to a large, open vocabulary.

Results demonstrate the feasibility of this method: our MaxEnt-based ranking approach improved over the baseline in all settings and yielded – to our knowledge – the best scores for lexical substitution with automatically gathered synonyms on the Semeval 2007 LexSub dataset. Also, it performed slightly better than the state of the art for candidates pooled from the gold standard without any parameter tuning or empirical design choices.

In this study, we established transparency between Semeval-style and ranking-only studies in lexical substitution – two lines of work that were difficult to compare in the past. Further, we observe similar improvements on two different datasets, showing the robustness of the approach.

While previous works showed the potential of more/improved lexical resources for lexical substitution, we improved over the best Semeval-style performance just by exploiting an improved ranking model over a standard WordNet-based candidate set. These results indicate that improvements from lexical resources and better ranking models are additive, thus we want to add more lexical resources in our system in the future.

Of course there are several other ways to improve further the work described here. First of all, similar to the best ranking approaches (e.g. Thater et al. (2011)), one could use contextualized feature functions to make global information from the distributional thesaurus more accurate. Instead of using globally calculated similarities, information from the distributional thesaurus could be contextualized via constraining the statistics with words from the context.

Other natural ways to improve the model described here are to make heavier use of parser information or to employ pair-wise or list-wise machine learning models (Cao et al., 2007), which are specifically designed for subset ranking. Lastly, while intrinsic evaluation of lexical substitution is important, we would like to show its practicability in tasks such as steganography or information retrieval.

Acknowledgements

This work has been supported by the Hessian research excellence program Landes-Offensive zur Entwicklung Wissenschaftlich-ökonomischer Exzellenz (LOEWE) as part of the research center *Digital Humanities*, and by the German Ministry of Education and Research under grant *SiDiM* (grant no. 01IS10054G).

References

Eneko Agirre, Daniel Cer, Mona Diab, and Aitor Gonzalez-Agirre. 2012. Semeval-2012 task 6: A pilot on semantic textual similarity. In **SEM 2012: The First Joint Conference on Lexical and Computational Semantics – Volume 1: Proceedings of the main conference and the shared task, and Volume 2: Proceedings of the Sixth International Workshop on Semantic Evaluation (SemEval 2012)*, pages 385–393, Montréal, Canada.

Chris Biemann. 2012. Creating a System for Lexical Substitutions from Scratch using Crowdsourcing. *Language Resources and Evaluation: Special Issue on Collaboratively Constructed Language Resources*, 46(2).

Róbert Busa-Fekete, Balázs Kégl, Éltető Yamás, and Györgi Szarvas. 2011. A robust ranking methodology based on diverse calibration of adaboost. In *European Conference on Machine Learning*, volume LNCS, 6911, pages 263–279.

Zhe Cao, Tao Qin, Tie-Yan Liu, Ming-Feng Tsai, and Hang Li. 2007. Learning to rank: from pairwise approach to listwise approach. In *Proceedings of the 24rd International Conference on Machine Learning*, pages 129–136.

Ching-Yun Chang and Stephen Clark. 2010. Practical linguistic steganography using contextual synonym substitution and vertex colour coding. In *Proceedings of the 2010 Conference on Empirical Methods in Natural Language Processing*, pages 1194–1203, Cambridge, MA.

Moses Charikar, Kevin Chen, and Martin Farach-Colton. 2004. Finding frequent items in data streams. *Theor. Comput. Sci.*, 312(1):3–15.

D. Cossock and T. Zhang. 2008. Statistical analysis of Bayes optimal subset ranking. *IEEE Transactions on Information Theory*, 54(11):5140–5154.

Ido Dagan, Oren Glickman, Alfio Gliozzo, Efrat Marmorshtein, and Carlo Strapparava. 2006. Direct word sense matching for lexical substitution. In *Proceedings of the 21st International Conference on Computational Linguistics and the 44th annual meeting of the Association for Computational Linguistics*, ACL-44, pages 449–456, Sydney, Australia.

Marie-Catherine de Marneffe, Bill MacCartney, and Christopher D. Manning. 2006. Generating typed dependency parses from phrase structure parses. In *LREC 2006*, Genova, Italy.

Scott Deerwester, Susan T. Dumais, George W. Furnas, Thomas K. Landauer, and Richard Harshman. 1990. Indexing by latent semantic analysis. *Journal of the American Society for Information Science*, 41(6):391–407.

Georgiana Dinu and Mirella Lapata. 2010. Measuring distributional similarity in context. In *Proceedings of the 2010 Conference on Empirical Methods in Natural Language Processing*, pages 1162–1172, Cambridge, MA.

Ted Dunning. 1993. Accurate methods for the statistics of surprise and coincidence. *Computational Linguistics*, 19(1):61–74.

Katrin Erk and Sebastian Padó. 2008. A structured vector space model for word meaning in context. In *Proceedings of the 2008 Conference on Empirical Methods in Natural Language Processing*, pages 897–906, Honolulu, Hawaii.

Katrin Erk and Sebastian Padó. 2010. Exemplar-based models for word meaning in context. In *Proceedings of the ACL 2010 Conference Short Papers*, pages 92–97, Uppsala, Sweden.

Christiane Fellbaum. 1998. *WordNet: An Electronic Lexical Database*. MIT Press.

Evgeniy Gabrilovich and Shaul Markovitch. 2007. Computing Semantic Relatedness using Wikipedia-based Explicit Semantic Analysis. In *Proceedings of the 20th International Joint Conference on Artificial Intelligence*, pages 1606–1611.

Bela Gipp, Norman Meuschke, and Joeran Beel. 2011. Comparative Evaluation of Text- and Citation-based Plagiarism Detection Approaches using GuttenPlag. In *Proceedings of 11th ACM/IEEE-CS Joint Conference on Digital Libraries (JCDL'11)*, pages 255–258, Ottawa, Canada. ACM New York, NY, USA. Available at http://sciplore.org/pub/.

Claudio Giuliano, Alfio Gliozzo, and Carlo Strapparava. 2007. FBK-irst: Lexical substitution task exploiting domain and syntagmatic coherence. In *Proceedings of the Fourth International Workshop on Semantic Evaluations (SemEval-2007)*, pages 145–148, Prague, Czech Republic.

Samer Hassan, Andras Csomai, Carmen Banea, Ravi Sinha, and Rada Mihalcea. 2007. UNT: SubFinder: Combining knowledge sources for automatic lexical substitution. In *Proceedings of the Fourth International Workshop on Semantic Evaluations (SemEval-2007)*, pages 410–413, Prague, Czech Republic.

Kazuaki Kishida. 2005. *Property of Average Precision and Its Generalization: An Examination of Evaluation Indicator for Information Retrieval Experiments*. NII technical report. National Institute of Informatics.

Ping Li, Christopher J.C. Burges, and Qiang Wu. 2007. McRank: Learning to rank using multiple classification and gradient boosting. In *Advances in Neural Information Processing Systems*, volume 19, pages 897–904. The MIT Press.

Linlin Li, Benjamin Roth, and Caroline Sporleder. 2010. Topic models for word sense disambiguation and token-based idiom detection. In *Proceedings of the 48th Annual Meeting of the Association for Computational Linguistics*, ACL '10, pages 1138–1147.

Dekang Lin. 1998. Automatic retrieval and clustering of similar words. In *Proceedings of the 36th Annual Meeting of the Association for Computational Linguistics and the 17th International Conference on Computational Linguistics*, volume 2 of *ACL '98*, pages 768–774, Montreal, Quebec, Canada.

David Martinez, Su Nam Kim, and Timothy Baldwin. 2007. MELB-MKB: Lexical substitution system based on relatives in context. In *Proceedings of the Fourth International Workshop on Semantic Evaluations (SemEval-2007)*, pages 237–240, Prague, Czech Republic.

Andrew Kachites McCallum. 2002. *MALLET: A Machine Learning for Language Toolkit*. http://mallet.cs.umass.edu.

Diana McCarthy and Roberto Navigli. 2007. Semeval-2007 task 10: English lexical substitution task. In *Proceedings of the Fourth International Workshop on Semantic Evaluations (SemEval-2007)*, pages 48–53, Prague, Czech Republic.

Rada Mihalcea and Andras Csomai. 2005. Senselearner: word sense disambiguation for all words in unrestricted text. In *Proceedings of the ACL 2005 on Interactive poster and demonstration sessions*, ACLdemo '05, pages 53–56.

Joseph Reisinger and Raymond Mooney. 2010a. A mixture model with sharing for lexical semantics. In *Proceedings of the 2010 Conference on Empirical Methods in Natural Language Processing*, pages 1173–1182, Cambridge, MA.

Joseph Reisinger and Raymond J. Mooney. 2010b. Multi-prototype vector-space models of word meaning. In *Human Language Technologies: The 2010 Annual Conference of the North American Chapter of the Association for Computational Linguistics*, pages 109–117, Los Angeles, California.

M. Richter, U. Quasthoff, E. Hallsteinsdóttir, and C. Biemann. 2006. Exploiting the leipzig corpora collection. In *Proceesings of the IS-LTC 2006. Ljubljana, Slovenia.*

Helmut Schmid. 1994. Probabilistic part-of-speech tagging using decision trees. In *Proceedings of the International Conference on New Methods in Language Processing*, Manchester, UK.

Ravi Sinha and Rada Mihalcea. 2009. Combining lexical resources for contextual synonym expansion. In *Proceedings of the International Conference RANLP-2009*, pages 404–410, Borovets, Bulgaria.

Ravi Som Sinha and Rada Flavia Mihalcea. 2011. Using centrality algorithms on directed graphs for synonym expansion. In R. Charles Murray and Philip M. McCarthy, editors, *FLAIRS Conference*. AAAI Press.

Stefan Thater, Hagen Fürstenau, and Manfred Pinkal. 2010. Contextualizing semantic representations using syntactically enriched vector models. In *Proceedings of the 48th Annual Meeting of the Association for Computational Linguistics*, pages 948–957, Uppsala, Sweden.

Stefan Thater, Hagen Fürstenau, and Manfred Pinkal. 2011. Word meaning in context: A simple and effective vector model. In *Proceedings of the Fifth International Joint Conference on Natural Language Processing : IJCNLP 2011*, pages 1134–1143, Chiang Mai, Thailand. MP, ISSN 978-974-466-564-5.

Umut Topkara, Mercan Topkara, and Mikhail J. Atallah. 2006. The hiding virtues of ambiguity: quantifiably resilient watermarking of natural language text through synonym substitutions. In *Proceedings of the 8th workshop on Multimedia and security*, pages 164–174, New York, NY, USA. ACM.

A Tensor-based Factorization Model of Semantic Compositionality

Tim Van de Cruys
IRIT – UMR 5505
CNRS
Toulouse, France
tim.vandecruys@irit.fr

Thierry Poibeau[⋆]
LaTTiCe – UMR 8094
CNRS & ENS
Paris, France
thierry.poibeau@ens.fr

Anna Korhonen
Computer Laboratory & DTAL[⋆]
University of Cambridge
United Kingdom
anna.korhonen@cl.cam.ac.uk

Abstract

In this paper, we present a novel method for the computation of compositionality within a distributional framework. The key idea is that compositionality is modeled as a multi-way interaction between latent factors, which are automatically constructed from corpus data. We use our method to model the composition of *subject verb object* triples. The method consists of two steps. First, we compute a latent factor model for nouns from standard co-occurrence data. Next, the latent factors are used to induce a latent model of three-way *subject verb object* interactions. Our model has been evaluated on a similarity task for transitive phrases, in which it exceeds the state of the art.

1 Introduction

In the course of the last two decades, significant progress has been made with regard to the automatic extraction of lexical semantic knowledge from large-scale text corpora. Most work relies on the distributional hypothesis of meaning (Harris, 1954), which states that words that appear within the same contexts tend to be semantically similar. A large number of researchers have taken this dictum to heart, giving rise to a plethora of algorithms that try to capture the semantics of words by looking at their distribution in text. Up till now, however, most work on the automatic acquisition of semantics only deals with individual words. The modeling of meaning beyond the level of individual words – i.e. the combination of words into larger units – is to a large degree left unexplored.

The principle of compositionality, often attributed to Frege, is the principle that states that the meaning of a complex expression is a function of the meaning of its parts and the way those parts are (syntactically) combined (Frege, 1892). It is the fundamental principle that allows language users to understand the meaning of sentences they have never heard before, by constructing the meaning of the complex expression from the meanings of the individual words. Recently, a number of researchers have tried to reconcile the framework of distributional semantics with the principle of compositionality (Mitchell and Lapata, 2008; Baroni and Zamparelli, 2010; Coecke et al., 2010; Socher et al., 2012). However, the absolute gains of the systems remain a bit unclear, and a simple method of composition – vector multiplication – often seems to produce the best results (Blacoe and Lapata, 2012).

In this paper, we present a novel method for the joint composition of a verb with its subject and direct object. The key idea is that compositionality is modeled as a multi-way interaction between latent factors, which are automatically constructed from corpus data. In order to adequately model the multi-way interaction between a verb and its subject and objects, a significant part of our method relies on tensor algebra. Additionally, our method makes use of a factorization model appropriate for tensors.

The remainder of the paper is structured as follows. In section 2, we give an overview of previous work that is relevant to the task of computing compositionality within a distributional framework. Section 3 presents a detailed description of our method, including an overview of the necessary mathematical machinery. Section 4 illustrates our method with a number of detailed examples. Section 5 presents a quantitative evaluation, and compares our method to other models of distributional compositionality. Section 6, then, concludes and lays out a number of directions for future work.

2 Previous Work

In recent years, a number of methods have been developed that try to capture compositional phenomena within a distributional framework. One of the first approaches to tackle compositional phenomena in a systematic way is Mitchell and Lapata's (2008) approach. They explore a number of different models for vector composition, of which vector addition (the sum of each feature) and vector multiplication (the elementwise multiplication of each feature) are the most important. They evaluate their models on a noun-verb phrase similarity task, and find that the multiplicative model yields the best results, along with a weighted combination of the additive and multiplicative model.

Baroni and Zamparelli (2010) present a method for the composition of adjectives and nouns. In their model, an adjective is a linear function of one vector (the noun vector) to another vector (the vector for the adjective-noun pair). The linear transformation for a particular adjective is represented by a matrix, and is learned automatically from a corpus, using partial least-squares regression.

Coecke et al. (2010) present an abstract theoretical framework in which a sentence vector is a function of the Kronecker product of its word vectors, which allows for greater interaction between the different word features. A number of instantiations of the framework are tested experimentally in Grefenstette and Sadrzadeh (2011a) and Grefenstette and Sadrzadeh (2011b). The key idea is that relational words (e.g. adjectives or verbs) have a rich (multi-dimensional) structure that acts as a filter on their arguments. Our model uses an intuition similar to theirs.

Socher et al. (2012) present a model for compositionality based on recursive neural networks. Each node in a parse tree is assigned both a vector and a matrix; the vector captures the actual meaning of the constituent, while the matrix models the way it changes the meaning of neighbouring words and phrases.

Closely related to the work on compositionality is research on the computation of word meaning in context. Erk and Padó (2008, 2009) make use of selectional preferences to express the meaning of a word in context; the meaning of a word in the presence of an argument is computed by multiplying the word's vector with a vector that captures the inverse selectional preferences of the argument. Thater et al. (2009, 2010) extend the approach based on selectional preferences by incorporating second-order co-occurrences in their model. And Dinu and Lapata (2010) propose a probabilistic framework that models the meaning of words as a probability distribution over latent factors. This allows them to model contextualized meaning as a change in the original sense distribution. Dinu and Lapata use non-negative matrix factorization (NMF) to induce latent factors. Similar to their work, our model uses NMF – albeit in a slightly different configuration – as a first step towards our final factorization model.

In general, latent models have proven to be useful for the modeling of word meaning. One of the best known latent models of semantics is Latent Semantic Analysis (Landauer and Dumais, 1997), which uses singular value decomposition in order to automatically induce latent factors from term-document matrices. Another well known latent model of meaning, which takes a generative approach, is Latent Dirichlet Allocation (Blei et al., 2003).

Tensor factorization has been used before for the modeling of natural language. Giesbrecht (2010) describes a tensor factorization model for the construction of a distributional model that is sensitive to word order. And Van de Cruys (2010) uses a tensor factorization model in order to construct a three-way selectional preference model of verbs, subjects, and objects. Our underlying tensor factorization – Tucker decomposition – is the same as Giesbrecht's; and similar to Van de Cruys (2010), we construct a latent model of verb, subject, and object interactions. The way our model is constructed, however, is significantly different. The former research does not use any syntactic information for the construction of the tensor, while the latter makes use of a more restricted tensor factorization model, viz. parallel factor analysis (Harshman and Lundy, 1994).

The idea of modeling compositionality by means of tensor (Kronecker) product has been proposed in the literature before (Clark and Pulman, 2007; Coecke et al., 2010). However, the method presented here is the first that tries to capture compositional phenomena by exploiting the multi-way interactions between latent factors, induced by a suitable tensor factorization model.

3 Methodology

3.1 Mathematical preliminaries

The methodology presented in this paper requires a number of concepts and mathematical operations from tensor algebra, which are briefly reviewed in this section. The interested reader is referred to Kolda and Bader (2009) for a more thorough introduction to tensor algebra (including an overview of various factorization methods).

A *tensor* is a multidimensional array; it is the generalization of a matrix to more than two dimensions, or *modes*. Whereas matrices are only able to capture two-way co-occurrences, tensors are able to capture *multi-way* co-occurrences.[1] Following prevailing convention, tensors are represented by boldface Euler script notation ($\boldsymbol{\mathcal{X}}$), matrices by boldface capital letters ($\mathbf{X}$), vectors by boldface lower case letters ($\mathbf{x}$), and scalars by italic letters (x).

The *n-mode product* of a tensor $\boldsymbol{\mathcal{X}} \in \mathbb{R}^{I_1 \times I_2 \times \ldots \times I_N}$ with a matrix $\mathbf{U} \in \mathbb{R}^{J \times I_n}$ is denoted by $\boldsymbol{\mathcal{X}} \times_n \mathbf{U}$, and is defined elementwise as

$$(\boldsymbol{\mathcal{X}} \times_n \mathbf{U})_{i_1 \ldots i_{n-1} j i_{n+1} \ldots i_N} = \sum_{i_n=1}^{I_n} x_{i_1 i_2 \ldots i_N} u_{j i_n} \quad (1)$$

The *Kronecker product* of matrices $\mathbf{A} \in \mathbb{R}^{I \times J}$ and $\mathbf{B} \in \mathbb{R}^{K \times L}$ is denoted by $\mathbf{A} \otimes \mathbf{B}$. The result is a matrix of size $(IK) \times (JL)$, and is defined by

$$\mathbf{A} \otimes \mathbf{B} = \begin{bmatrix} a_{11}\mathbf{B} & a_{12}\mathbf{B} & \cdots & a_{1J}\mathbf{B} \\ a_{21}\mathbf{B} & a_{22}\mathbf{B} & \cdots & a_{2J}\mathbf{B} \\ \vdots & \vdots & \ddots & \vdots \\ a_{I1}\mathbf{B} & a_{I2}\mathbf{B} & \ldots & a_{IJ}\mathbf{B} \end{bmatrix} \quad (2)$$

[1]In this research, we limit ourselves to three-way co-occurrences of verbs, subject, and objects, modelled using a three-mode tensor.

A special case of the Kronecker product is the *outer product* of two vectors $\mathbf{a} \in \mathbb{R}^I$ and $\mathbf{b} \in \mathbb{R}^J$, denoted $\mathbf{a} \circ \mathbf{b}$. The result is a matrix $\mathbf{A} \in \mathbb{R}^{I \times J}$ obtained by multiplying each element of $\mathbf{a}$ with each element of $\mathbf{b}$.

Finally, the *Hadamard product*, denoted $\mathbf{A} * \mathbf{B}$, is the elementwise multiplication of two matrices $\mathbf{A} \in \mathbb{R}^{I \times J}$ and $\mathbf{B} \in \mathbb{R}^{I \times J}$, which produces a matrix that is equally of size $I \times J$.

3.2 The construction of latent noun factors

The first step of our method consists in the construction of a latent factor model for nouns, based on their context words. For this purpose, we make use of non-negative matrix factorization (Lee and Seung, 2000). Non-negative matrix factorization (NMF) minimizes an objective function – in our case the Kullback-Leibler (KL) divergence – between an original matrix $\mathbf{V}_{I \times J}$ and $\mathbf{W}_{I \times K}\mathbf{H}_{K \times J}$ (the matrix multiplication of matrices $\mathbf{W}$ and $\mathbf{H}$) subject to the constraint that all values in the three matrices be non-negative. Parameter K is set $\ll I, J$ so that a reduction is obtained over the original data. The factorization model is represented graphically in figure 1.

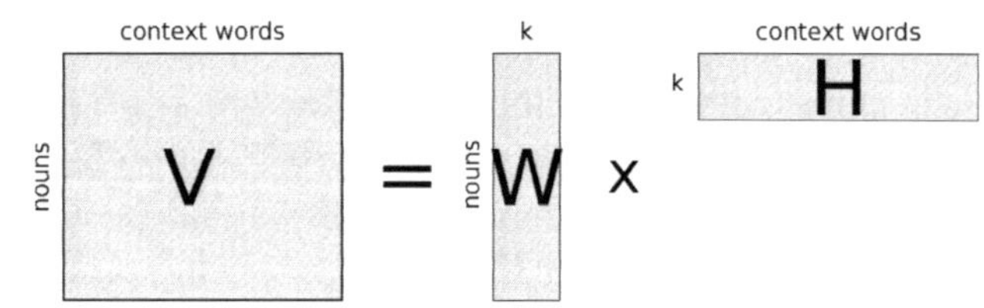

Figure 1: Graphical representation of NMF

NMF can be computed fairly straightforwardly, alternating between the two iterative update rules represented in equations 3 and 4. The update rules are guaranteed to converge to a local minimum in the KL divergence.

$$\mathbf{H}_{a\mu} \leftarrow \mathbf{H}_{a\mu} \frac{\sum_i \mathbf{W}_{ia} \frac{\mathbf{V}_{i\mu}}{(\mathbf{WH})_{i\mu}}}{\sum_k \mathbf{W}_{ka}} \quad (3)$$

$$\mathbf{W}_{ia} \leftarrow \mathbf{W}_{ia} \frac{\sum_\mu \mathbf{H}_{a\mu} \frac{\mathbf{V}_{i\mu}}{(\mathbf{WH})_{i\mu}}}{\sum_v \mathbf{H}_{av}} \quad (4)$$

3.3 Modeling multi-way interactions

In our second step, we construct a multi-way interaction model for *subject verb object* (*svo*) triples, based on the latent factors induced in the first step. Our latent interaction model is inspired by a tensor factorization model called Tucker decomposition (Tucker, 1966), although our own model instantiation differs significantly. In order to explain our method, we first revisit Tucker decomposition, and subsequently explain how our model is constructed.

3.3.1 Tucker decomposition

Tucker decomposition is a multilinear generalization of the well-known singular value decomposition, used in Latent Semantic Analysis. It is also known as higher order singular value decomposition (HOSVD, De Lathauwer et al. (2000)). In Tucker decomposition, a tensor is decomposed into a core tensor, multiplied by a matrix along each mode. For a three-mode tensor $\mathcal{X} \in \mathbb{R}^{I \times J \times L}$, the model is defined as

$$\mathcal{X} = \mathcal{G} \times_1 \mathbf{A} \times_2 \mathbf{B} \times_3 \mathbf{C} \quad (5)$$

$$= \sum_{p=1}^{P} \sum_{q=1}^{Q} \sum_{r=1}^{R} g_{pqr} \mathbf{a}_p \circ \mathbf{b}_q \circ \mathbf{c}_r \quad (6)$$

Setting $P, Q, R \ll I, J, L$, the core tensor $\mathcal{G}$ represents a compressed, latent version of the original tensor $\mathcal{X}$; matrices $\mathbf{A} \in \mathbb{R}^{I \times P}$, $\mathbf{B} \in \mathbb{R}^{J \times Q}$, and $\mathbf{C} \in \mathbb{R}^{L \times R}$ represent the latent factors for each mode, while $\mathcal{G} \in \mathbb{R}^{P \times Q \times R}$ indicates the level of interaction between the different latent factors. Figure 2 shows a graphical representation of Tucker decomposition.[2]

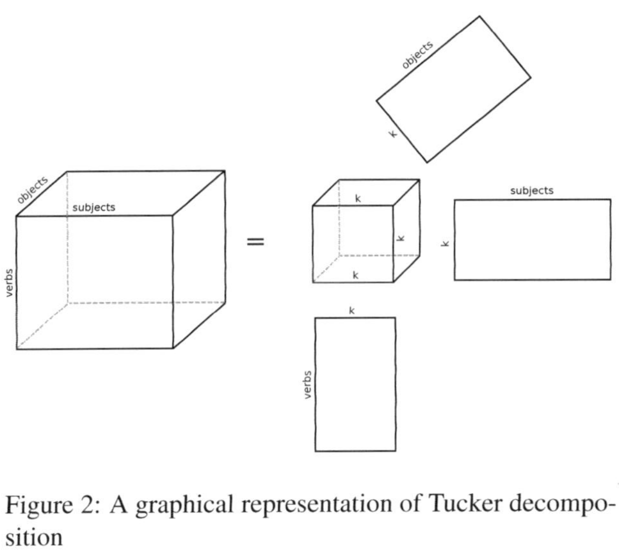

Figure 2: A graphical representation of Tucker decomposition

[2]where $P = Q = R = K$, i.e. the same number of latent factors K is used for each mode

3.3.2 Reconstructing a Tucker model from two-way factors

Computing the Tucker decomposition of a tensor is rather costly in terms of time and memory requirements. Moreover, the decomposition is not unique: the core tensor $\mathcal{G}$ can be modified without affecting the model's fit by applying the inverse modification to the factor matrices. These two drawbacks led us to consider an alternative method for the construction of the Tucker model. Specifically, we consider the factor matrices as given (as the output from our first step), and proceed to compute the core tensor $\mathcal{G}$. Additionally, we do not use a latent representation for the first mode, which means that the first mode is represented by its original instances.

Our model can be straightforwardly applied to language data. The core tensor $\mathcal{G}$ models the latent interactions between verbs, subject, and objects. $\mathcal{G}$ is computed by applying the n-mode product to the appropriate mode of the original tensor (equation 7),

$$\mathcal{G} = \mathcal{X} \times_2 \mathbf{W}^T \times_3 \mathbf{W}^T \quad (7)$$

where $\mathcal{X}^{V \times N \times N}$ is our original data tensor, consisting of the weighted co-occurrence frequencies of *svo* triples (extracted from corpus data), and $\mathbf{W}^{N \times K}$ is our latent factor matrix for nouns. Note that we do not use a latent representation for the verb mode. To be able to efficiently compute the similarity of verbs (both within and outside of compositional phrases), only the *subject* and *object* mode are represented by latent factors, while the *verb* mode is represented by its original instances. This means that our core tensor $\mathcal{G}$ will be of size $V \times K \times K$.[3] A graphical representation is given in figure 3.

Note that both tensor $\mathcal{X}$ and factor matrices $\mathbf{W}$ are non-negative, which means our core tensor $\mathcal{G}$ will also be non-negative.

3.4 The composition of *svo* triples

In order to compute the composition of a particular subject verb object triple $\langle s, v, o \rangle$, we first extract the appropriate subject vector $\mathbf{w}_s$ and object vector $\mathbf{w}_o$ (both of length K) from our factor matrix $\mathbf{W}$, and

[3]It is straightforward to also construct a latent factor model for verbs using NMF, and include it in the construction of our core tensor; we believe such a model might have interesting applications, but we save this as an exploration for future work.

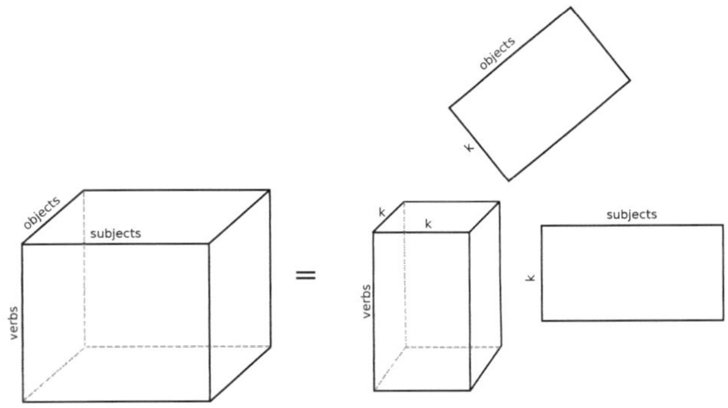

Figure 3: A graphical representation of our model instantiation without the latent verb mode

compute the outer product of both vectors, resulting in a matrix $\mathbf{Y}$ of size $K \times K$.

$$\mathbf{Y} = \mathbf{w}_s \circ \mathbf{w}_o \tag{8}$$

Our second and final step is then to weight the original verb matrix $\mathbf{G}_v$ of latent interactions (the appropriate verb slice of tensor $\mathcal{G}$) with matrix $\mathbf{Y}$, containing the latent interactions of the specific subject and object. This is carried out by taking the Hadamard product of $\mathbf{G}_v$ and $\mathbf{Y}$.

$$\mathbf{Z} = \mathbf{G}_v * \mathbf{Y} \tag{9}$$

4 Example

In this section, we present a number of example computations that clarify how our model is able to capture compositionality. All examples come from actual corpus data, and are computed in a fully automatic and unsupervised way.

Consider the following two sentences:

(1) The athlete runs a race.

(2) The user runs a command.

Both sentences contain the verb *run*, but they represent clearly different actions. When we compute the composition of both instances of *run* with their respective subject and object, we want our model to show this difference.

To compute the compositional representation of sentences (1) and (2), we proceed as follows. First, we extract the latent vectors for subject and object ($\mathbf{w}_{athlete}$ and $\mathbf{w}_{race}$ for the first sentence, $\mathbf{w}_{user}$ and $\mathbf{w}_{command}$ for the second sentence) from matrix $\mathbf{W}$. Next, we compute the outer product of subject and object – $\mathbf{w}_{athlete} \circ \mathbf{w}_{race}$ and $\mathbf{w}_{user} \circ \mathbf{w}_{command}$ – which yields matrices $\mathbf{Y}_{\langle athlete,race \rangle}$ and $\mathbf{Y}_{\langle user,command \rangle}$. By virtue of the outer product, the matrices $\mathbf{Y}$ – of size $K \times K$ – represent the level of interaction between the latent factors of the subject and the latent factors of the object. We can inspect these interactions by looking up the factor pairs (i.e. matrix cells) with the highest values in the matrices $\mathbf{Y}$. Table 1 presents the factor pairs with highest value for matrix $\mathbf{Y}_{\langle athlete,race \rangle}$; table 2 represents the factor pairs with highest value for matrix $\mathbf{Y}_{\langle user,command \rangle}$. In order to render the factors interpretable, we include the three most salient words for the various factors (i.e. the words with the highest value for a particular factor).

The examples in tables 1 and 2 give an impression of the effect of the outer product: semantic features of the subject combine with semantic features of the object, indicating the extent to which these features interact within the expression. In table 1, we notice that animacy features (28, 195) and a sport feature (25) combine with a 'sport event' feature (119). In table 2, we see that similar animacy features (40, 195) and technological features (7, 45) combine with another technological feature (89).

Similarly, we can inspect the latent interactions of the verb *run*, which are represented in the tensor slice $\mathbf{G}_{run}$. Note that this matrix contains the verb semantics computed over the complete corpus. The most salient factor interactions for $\mathbf{G}_{run}$ are represented in table 3.

Table 3 illustrates that different senses of the verb *run* are represented within the matrix $\mathbf{G}_{run}$. The first two factor pairs hint at the 'organize' sense of the verb (*run a seminar*). The third factor pair represents the 'transport' sense of the verb (*the bus runs every hour*).[4] And the fourth factor pair represents the 'execute' or 'deploy' sense of *run* (*run Linux, run a computer program*). Note that we only show the factor pairs with the highest value; matrix $\mathbf{G}$ contains a value for each pairwise combination of the latent factors, effectively representing a rich latent semantics for the verb in question.

The last step is to take the Hadamard product of matrices $\mathbf{Y}$ with verb matrix $\mathbf{G}$, which yields our final

[4]Obviously, *hour* is not an object of the verb, but due to parsing errors it is thus represented.

factors	subject	object	value
$\langle 195,119\rangle$	*people* (.008), *child* (.008), *adolescent* (.007)	*cup* (.007), *championship* (.006), *final* (.005)	.007
$\langle 25,119\rangle$	*hockey* (.007), *poker* (.007), *tennis* (.006)	*cup* (.007), *championship* (.006), *final* (.005)	.004
$\langle 90,119\rangle$	*professionalism* (.007), *teamwork* (.007), *confidence* (.006)	*cup* (.007), *championship* (.006), *final* (.005)	.003
$\langle 28,119\rangle$	*they* (.004), *pupil* (.003), *participant* (.003)	*cup* (.007), *championship* (.006), *final* (.005)	.003

Table 1: Factor pairs with highest value for matrix $\mathbf{Y}_{\langle athlete,race\rangle}$

factors	subject	object	value
$\langle 7,89\rangle$	*password* (.009), *login* (.007), *username* (.007)	*filename* (.007), *null* (.006), *integer* (.006)	.010
$\langle 40,89\rangle$	*anyone* (.004), *reader* (.004), *anybody* (.003)	*filename* (.007), *null* (.006), *integer* (.006)	.007
$\langle 195,89\rangle$	*people* (.008), *child* (.008), *adolescent* (.007)	*filename* (.007), *null* (.006), *integer* (.006)	.006
$\langle 45,89\rangle$	*website* (.004), *Click* (.003), *site* (.003)	*filename* (.007), *null* (.006), *integer* (.006)	.006

Table 2: Factor pairs with highest value for matrix $\mathbf{Y}_{\langle user,command\rangle}$

matrices, $\mathbf{Z}_{run,\langle athlete,race\rangle}$ and $\mathbf{Z}_{run,\langle user,command\rangle}$. The Hadamard product will act as a bidirectional filter on the semantics of both the verb and its subject and object: interactions of semantic features that are present in both matrix **Y** and **G** will be highlighted, while the other interactions are played down. The result is a representation of the verb's semantics tuned to its particular subject-object combination. Note that this final step can be viewed as an instance of function application (Baroni and Zamparelli, 2010). Also note the similarity to Grefenstette and Sadrzadeh's (2011a,2011b) approach, who equally make use of the elementwise matrix product in order to weight the semantics of the verb.

We can now go back to our original tensor $\mathcal{G}$, and compute the most similar verbs (i.e. the most similar tensor slices) for our newly computed matrices **Z**.[5]

If we do this for matrix $\mathbf{Z}_{run,\langle athlete,race\rangle}$, our model comes up with verbs *finish* (.29), *attend* (.27), and *win* (.25). If, instead, we compute the most similar verbs for $\mathbf{Z}_{run,\langle user,command\rangle}$, our model yields *execute* (.42), *modify* (.40), *invoke* (.39).

Finally, note that the design of our model naturally takes into account word order. Consider the following two sentences:

(3) man damages car

(4) car damages man

Both sentences contain the exact same words, but the process of damaging described in sentences (3) and (4) is of a rather different nature. Our model is able to take this difference into account: if we compute $\mathbf{Z}_{damage,\langle man,car\rangle}$ following sentence (3), our model yields *crash* (.43), *drive* (.35), *ride* (.35) as most similar verbs. If we do the same for $\mathbf{Z}_{damage,\langle car,man\rangle}$ following sentence (4), our model instead yields *scare* (.26), *kill* (.23), *hurt* (.23).

5 Evaluation

5.1 Methodology

In order to evaluate the performance of our tensor-based factorization model of compositionality, we make use of the sentence similarity task for transitive sentences, defined in Grefenstette and Sadrzadeh (2011a). This is an extension of the similarity task for compositional models developed by Mitchell and Lapata (2008), and constructed according to the same guidelines. The dataset contains 2500 similarity judgements, provided by 25 participants, and is publicly available.[6]

The data consists of transitive verbs, each paired with both a subject and an object noun – thus forming a small transitive sentence. Additionally, a 'landmark' verb is provided. The idea is to compose both the target verb and the landmark verb with subject and noun, in order to form two small compositional

[5]Similarity is calculated by measuring the cosine of the vectorized and normalized representation of the verb matrices.

[6]`http://www.cs.ox.ac.uk/activities/CompDistMeaning/GS2011data.txt`

factors	subject	object	value
$\langle 128, 181 \rangle$	*Mathematics* (.004), *Science* (.004), *Economics* (.004)	*course* (.005), *tutorial* (.005), *seminar* (.005)	.058
$\langle 293, 181 \rangle$	*organization* (.007), *association* (.007), *federation* (.006)	*course* (.005), *tutorial* (.005), *seminar* (.005)	.053
$\langle 60, 140 \rangle$	*rail* (.011), *bus* (.009), *ferry* (.008)	*third* (.004), *decade* (.004), *hour* (.004)	.038
$\langle 268, 268 \rangle$	*API* (.008), *Apache* (.007), *Unix* (.007)	*API* (.008), *Apache* (.007), *Unix* (.007)	.038

Table 3: Factor combinations for $\mathbf{G}_{run}$

phrases. The system is then required to come up with a suitable similarity score for these phrases. The correlation of the model's judgements with human judgements (scored 1–7) is then calculated using Spearman's ρ. Two examples of the task are provided in table 4.

p	target	subject	object	landmark	sim
19	meet	system	criterion	visit	1
21	write	student	name	spell	6

Table 4: Two example judgements from the phrase similarity task defined by Grefenstette and Sadrzadeh (2011a)

Grefenstette and Sadrzadeh (2011a) seem to calculate the similarity score contextualizing both the target verb and the landmark verb. Another possibility is to contextualize only the target verb, and compute the similarity score with the non-contextualized landmark verb. In our view, the latter option provides a better assessment of the model's similarity judgements, since contextualizing low-similarity landmarks often yields non-sensical phrases (e.g. *system visits criterion*). We provide scores for both contextualized and non-contextualized landmarks.

We compare our results to a number of different models. The first is Mitchell and Lapata's (2008) model, which computes the elementwise vector multiplication of verb, subject and object. The second is Grefenstette and Sadrzadeh's (2011b) best scoring model instantiation of the categorical distributional compositional model (Coecke et al., 2010). This model computes the outer product of the subject and object vector, the outer product of the verb vector with itself, and finally the elementwise product of both results. It yields the best score on the transitive sentence similarity task reported to date.

As a baseline, we compute the non-contextualized similarity score for target verb and landmark. The upper bound is provided by Grefenstette and Sadrzadeh (2011a), based on interannotator agreement.

5.2 Implementational details

All models have been constructed using the UKWAC corpus (Baroni et al., 2009), a 2 billion word corpus automatically harvested from the web. From this data, we accumulate the input matrix **V** for our first NMF step. We use the 10K most frequent nouns, cross-classified by the 2K most frequent context words.[7] Matrix **V** is weighted using pointwise mutual information (PMI, Church and Hanks (1990)).

A parsed version of the corpus is available, which has been parsed with MaltParser (Nivre et al., 2006). We use this version in order to extract our *svo* triples. From these triples, we construct our tensor $\mathcal{X}$, using 1K verbs $\times$ 10K subjects $\times$ 10K objects. Note once again that the subject and object instances in the second step are exactly the same as the noun instances in the first step. Tensor $\mathcal{X}$ has been weighted using a three-way extension of PMI, following equation 10 (Van de Cruys, 2011).

$$pmi3(x,y,z) = \log \frac{p(x,y,z)}{p(x)p(y)p(z)} \quad (10)$$

We set $K = 300$ as our number of latent factors. The value was chosen as a trade-off between a model that is both rich enough, and does not require an excessive amount of memory (for the modeling of the core tensor). The algorithm runs fairly efficiently. Each NMF step is computed in a matter of seconds, with convergence after 50–100 iterations. The construction of the core tensor is somewhat more

[7]We use a context window of 5 words, both before and after the target word; a stop list was used to filter out grammatical function words.

evolved, but does not exceed a wall time of 30 minutes. Results have been computed on a machine with Intel Xeon 2.93Ghz CPU and 32GB of RAM.

5.3 Results

The results of the various models are presented in table 5; *multiplicative* represents Mitchell and Lapata's (2008) multiplicative model, *categorical* represents Grefenstette and Sadrzadeh's (2011b) model, and *latent* represents the model presented in this paper.

model	contextualized	non-contextualized
baseline	.23	
multiplicative	**.32**	.34
categorical	**.32**	.35
latent	**.32**	**.37**
upper bound	.62	

Table 5: Results of the different compositionality models on the phrase similarity task

In the contextualized version of the similarity task (in which the landmark is combined with subject and object), all three models obtain the same result (.32). However, in the non-contextualized version (in which only the target verb is combined with subject and object), the models differ in performance. These differences are statistically significant.[8] As mentioned before, we believe the non-contextualized version of the task gives a better impression of the systems' ability to capture compositionality. The contextualization of the landmark verb often yields non-sensical combinations, such as *system visits criterion*. We therefore deem it preferable to compute the similarity of the target verb in composition (*system meets criterion*) to the non-contextualized semantics of the landmark verb (*visit*).

Note that the scores presented in this evaluation (including the baseline score) are significantly higher than the scores presented in Grefenstette and Sadrzadeh (2011b). This is not surprising, since the corpus we use – UKWAC – is an order of magnitude larger than the corpus used in their research – the British National Corpus (BNC). Presumably, the scores are also favoured by our weighting measure. In our experience, PMI performs better than weighting with conditional probabilities.[9]

6 Conclusion

In this paper, we presented a novel method for the computation of compositionality within a distributional framework. The key idea is that compositionality is modeled as a multi-way interaction between latent factors, which are automatically constructed from corpus data. We used our method to model the composition of *subject verb object* combinations. The method consists of two steps. First, we compute a latent factor model for nouns from standard co-occurrence data. Next, the latent factors are used to induce a latent model of three-way *subject verb object* interactions, represented by a core tensor. Our model has been evaluated on a similarity task for transitive phrases, in which it matches and even exceeds the state of the art.

We conclude with a number of future work issues. First of all, we would like to extend our framework in order to incorporate more compositional phenomena. Our current model is designed to deal with the latent modeling of *subject verb object* combinations. We would like to investigate how other compositional phenomena might fit within our latent interaction framework, and how our model is able to tackle the computation of compositionality across a differing number of modes.

Secondly, we would like to further explore the possibilities of our model in which all three modes are represented by latent factors. The instantiation of our model presented in this paper has two latent modes, using the original instances of the verb mode in order to efficiently compute verb similarity. We think a full-blown latent interaction model might prove to have interesting applications in a number of NLP tasks, such as the paraphrasing of compositional expressions.

Finally, we would like to test our method using a number of different evaluation frameworks. We think tasks of similarity judgement have their merits, but in a way are also somewhat limited. In our opinion, research on the modeling of compositional phenomena within a distributional framework would substantially

[8] $p < 0.01$; model differences have been tested using stratified shuffling (Yeh, 2000).

[9] Contrary to the findings of Mitchell and Lapata (2008), who report a high correlation with human similarity judgements.

benefit from new evaluation frameworks. In particular, we think of a lexical substitution or paraphrasing task along the lines of McCarthy and Navigli (2009), but specifically aimed at the assessment of compositional phenomena.

Acknowledgements

Tim Van de Cruys and Thierry Poibeau are supported by the *Centre National de la Recherche Scientifique* (CNRS, France), Anna Korhonen is supported by the *Royal Society* (UK).

References

Brett W. Bader, Tamara G. Kolda, et al. 2012. Matlab tensor toolbox version 2.5. `http://www.sandia.gov/~tgkolda/TensorToolbox/`.

Marco Baroni and Roberto Zamparelli. 2010. Nouns are vectors, adjectives are matrices: Representing adjective-noun constructions in semantic space. In *Proceedings of the 2010 Conference on Empirical Methods in Natural Language Processing*, pages 1183–1193, Cambridge, MA, October. Association for Computational Linguistics.

Marco Baroni, Silvia Bernardini, Adriano Ferraresi, and Eros Zanchetta. 2009. The wacky wide web: A collection of very large linguistically processed web-crawled corpora. *Language Resources and Evaluation*, 43(3):209–226.

William Blacoe and Mirella Lapata. 2012. A comparison of vector-based representations for semantic composition. In *Proceedings of the 2012 Joint Conference on Empirical Methods in Natural Language Processing and Computational Natural Language Learning*, pages 546–556, Jeju Island, Korea, July. Association for Computational Linguistics.

David M. Blei, Andrew Y. Ng, and Michael I. Jordan. 2003. Latent dirichlet allocation. *The Journal of Machine Learning Research*, 3:993–1022.

Kenneth W. Church and Patrick Hanks. 1990. Word association norms, mutual information & lexicography. *Computational Linguistics*, 16(1):22–29.

Stephen Clark and Stephen Pulman. 2007. Combining symbolic and distributional models of meaning. In *Proceedings of the AAAI Spring Symposium on Quantum Interaction*, pages 52–55.

Bob Coecke, Mehrnoosh Sadrzadeh, and Stephen Clark. 2010. Mathematical foundations for a compositional distributed model of meaning. *Lambek Festschrift, Linguistic Analysis, vol. 36*, 36.

Lieven De Lathauwer, Bart De Moor, and Joseph Vandewalle. 2000. A multilinear singular value decomposition. *SIAM Journal on Matrix Analysis and Applications*, 21(4):1253–1278.

Georgiana Dinu and Mirella Lapata. 2010. Measuring distributional similarity in context. In *Proceedings of the 2010 Conference on Empirical Methods in Natural Language Processing*, pages 1162–1172, Cambridge, MA, October.

Katrin Erk and Sebastian Padó. 2008. A structured vector space model for word meaning in context. In *Proceedings of the Conference on Empirical Methods in Natural Language Processing*, pages 897–906, Waikiki, Hawaii, USA.

Katrin Erk and Sebastian Padó. 2009. Paraphrase assessment in structured vector space: Exploring parameters and datasets. In *Proceedings of the Workshop on Geometrical Models of Natural Language Semantics*, pages 57–65, Athens, Greece.

Gottlob Frege. 1892. Über Sinn und Bedeutung. *Zeitschrift für Philosophie und philosophische Kritik*, 100:25–50.

Eugenie Giesbrecht. 2010. Towards a matrix-based distributional model of meaning. In *Proceedings of the NAACL HLT 2010 Student Research Workshop*, pages 23–28. Association for Computational Linguistics.

Edward Grefenstette and Mehrnoosh Sadrzadeh. 2011a. Experimental support for a categorical compositional distributional model of meaning. In *Proceedings of the 2011 Conference on Empirical Methods in Natural Language Processing*, pages 1394–1404, Edinburgh, Scotland, UK., July. Association for Computational Linguistics.

Edward Grefenstette and Mehrnoosh Sadrzadeh. 2011b. Experimenting with transitive verbs in a discocat. In *Proceedings of the GEMS 2011 Workshop on GEometrical Models of Natural Language Semantics*, pages 62–66, Edinburgh, UK, July. Association for Computational Linguistics.

Zellig S. Harris. 1954. Distributional structure. *Word*, 10(23):146–162.

Richard A Harshman and Margaret E Lundy. 1994. Parafac: Parallel factor analysis. *Computational Statistics & Data Analysis*, 18(1):39–72.

Tamara G. Kolda and Brett W. Bader. 2009. Tensor decompositions and applications. *SIAM Review*, 51(3):455–500, September.

Tamara G. Kolda and Jimeng Sun. 2008. Scalable tensor decompositions for multi-aspect data mining. In *ICDM 2008: Proceedings of the 8th IEEE International Conference on Data Mining*, pages 363–372, December.

Thomas Landauer and Susan Dumais. 1997. A solution to Plato's problem: The Latent Semantic Analysis theory of the acquisition, induction, and representation of knowledge. *Psychology Review*, 104:211–240.

Daniel D. Lee and H. Sebastian Seung. 2000. Algorithms for non-negative matrix factorization. In *Advances in Neural Information Processing Systems 13*, pages 556–562.

Diana McCarthy and Roberto Navigli. 2009. The English lexical substitution task. *Language resources and evaluation*, 43(2):139–159.

Jeff Mitchell and Mirella Lapata. 2008. Vector-based models of semantic composition. *proceedings of ACL-08: HLT*, pages 236–244.

Joakim Nivre, Johan Hall, and Jens Nilsson. 2006. Maltparser: A data-driven parser-generator for dependency parsing. In *Proceedings of LREC-2006*, pages 2216–2219.

Richard Socher, Brody Huval, Christopher D. Manning, and Andrew Y. Ng. 2012. Semantic compositionality through recursive matrix-vector spaces. In *Proceedings of the 2012 Joint Conference on Empirical Methods in Natural Language Processing and Computational Natural Language Learning*, pages 1201–1211, Jeju Island, Korea, July. Association for Computational Linguistics.

Stefan Thater, Georgiana Dinu, and Manfred Pinkal. 2009. Ranking paraphrases in context. In *Proceedings of the 2009 Workshop on Applied Textual Inference*, pages 44–47, Suntec, Singapore.

Stefan Thater, Hagen Fürstenau, and Manfred Pinkal. 2010. Contextualizing semantic representations using syntactically enriched vector models. In *Proceedings of the 48th Annual Meeting of the Association for Computational Linguistics*, pages 948–957, Uppsala, Sweden.

Ledyard R. Tucker. 1966. Some mathematical notes on three-mode factor analysis. *Psychometrika*, 31(3):279–311.

Tim Van de Cruys. 2010. A non-negative tensor factorization model for selectional preference induction. *Natural Language Engineering*, 16(4):417–437.

Tim Van de Cruys. 2011. Two multivariate generalizations of pointwise mutual information. In *Proceedings of the Workshop on Distributional Semantics and Compositionality*, pages 16–20, Portland, Oregon, USA, June. Association for Computational Linguistics.

Alexander Yeh. 2000. More accurate tests for the statistical significance of result differences. In *Proceedings of the 18th conference on Computational linguistics*, pages 947–953, Saarbrücken, Germany.

A Participant-based Approach for Event Summarization Using Twitter Streams

Chao Shen[1], **Fei Liu**[2], **Fuliang Weng**[2], **Tao Li**[1]
[1]School of Computing and Information Sciences, Florida International University
Miami, Florida 33199, USA
[2]Research and Technology Center, Robert Bosch LLC
Palo Alto, California 94304, USA
{cshen001, taoli}@cs.fiu.edu
{fei.liu, fuliang.weng}@us.bosch.com

Abstract

Twitter offers an unprecedented advantage on live reporting of the events happening around the world. However, summarizing the Twitter event has been a challenging task that was not fully explored in the past. In this paper, we propose a participant-based event summarization approach that "zooms-in" the Twitter event streams to the participant level, detects the important sub-events associated with each participant using a novel mixture model that combines the "burstiness" and "cohesiveness" properties of the event tweets, and generates the event summaries progressively. We evaluate the proposed approach on different event types. Results show that the participant-based approach can effectively capture the sub-events that have otherwise been shadowed by the long-tail of other dominant sub-events, yielding summaries with considerably better coverage than the state-of-the-art.

1 Introduction

Twitter has increasingly become a critical source of information. People report the events they are experiencing or publish comments on a wide variety of events happening around the world, ranging from the unexpected natural disasters, regional riots, to many scheduled events, such as sports games, political debates, local festivals, and even academic conferences. The Twitter data streams thus cover a broad range of events and broadcast these information in a live manner. Event summarization in this paper aims to generate a representative and concise textual description of the *scheduled* events that are being lively reported on Twitter, providing people with an alternative means of observing the world beyond the traditional journalism. Specifically, we investigate scheduled events of different types, including six of the NBA (National Basketball Association) sports games and a representative conference event, namely the Apple CEO's keynote speech in the Apple Worldwide Developers Conference (WWDC 2012)[1]. All these events have excited great discussion among the Twitter community.

Summarizing the Twitter event is a challenging task that has yet been fully explored in the past. Most previous summarization studies focus on the well-formatted news documents, as driven by the annual DUC[2] and TAC[3] evaluations. In contrast, the Twitter messages (a.k.a., tweets) are very short and noisy, containing nonstandard terms such as abbreviations, acronyms, emoticons, etc. (Liu et al., 2011b; Liu et al., 2012; Eisenstein, 2013). The noisy contents also cause great difficulties to the traditional NLP tools such as NER and dependency parser (Ritter et al., 2011; Foster et al., 2011), limiting the possibility of applying finer-grained event analysis tools. In nature, the event tweets are closely associated with the timeline and are drastically different from a static collection of news documents. The tweets converge into text streams that pulse along the timeline and cluster around the important moments or sub-events. These "sub-events" are of crucial importance since they represent a surge of interest from the Twitter audience and the correspond-

[1]https://developer.apple.com/wwdc/
[2]http://duc.nist.gov/
[3]http://www.nist.gov/tac/

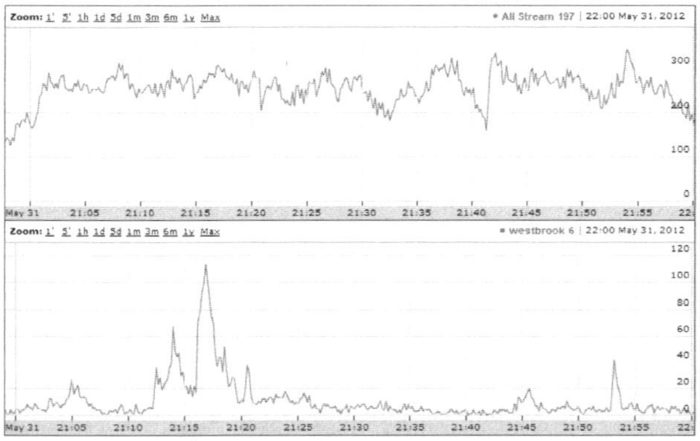

Figure 1: Example Twitter event stream (upper) and participant stream (lower). Event stream contains tweets related to an NBA basketball game (Spurs vs Thunder) scheduled on May 31, 2012; participant stream contains tweets corresponding to the player Russell Westbrook in team Thunder. X-axis denotes the timeline and y-axis represents the number of tweets per 10-second interval.

ing key information must be reflected in the event summary. As such, event summarization research has been focusing on developing accurate sub-event detection systems and generating text descriptions that can best summarize the sub-events in a progressive manner (Chakrabarti and Punera, 2011; Nichols et al., 2012; Zubiaga et al., 2012).

In Figure 1, we show an example Twitter event stream and one of its "participant" streams. The event stream contains all the tweets related to an NBA basketball game Spurs vs Thunder; while the participant stream contains only tweets corresponding to the player Russell Westbrook in this game. Previous research on event summarization focuses on identifying the important moments from the coarse-level event stream. This may yield several side effects: first, the spike patterns are not clearly identifiable from the overall event stream, though they are more clearly seen if we "zoom-in" to the participant level; second, it is arguable whether the important sub-events can be accurately detected based solely on the tweet volume change; third, a popular participant or sub-event can elicit huge volume of tweets which dominant the event discussion and shield less prominent sub-events. For example, in the NBA games, discussions about the key players (e.g., "LeBron James", "Kobe Bryant") can heavily shadow other important participants or sub-events, resulting in an event summary with repetitive descriptions about the dominant players.

In this work, we propose a novel participant-based event summarization approach, which dynamically identifies the participants from data streams, then "zooms-in" the event stream to participant level, detects the important sub-events related to each participant using a novel time-content mixture model, and generates the event summary progressively by concatenating the descriptions of the important sub-events. Results show that the mixture model-based sub-event detection approach can efficiently incorporate the "burstiness" and "cohesiveness" of the participant streams, and the participant-based event summarization can effectively capture the sub-events that have otherwise been shadowed by the long-tail of other dominant sub-events, yielding summaries with considerably better coverage than the state-of-the-art approach.

2 Related Work

Mining Twitter for event information has received increasing attention in recent years. Many research studies focus on identifying the trending events from Twitter and providing a concise and dynamic visualization of the information. The identified events are often represented using a set of keywords. (Petrovic et al., 2010) proposed an algorithm based on locality-sensitive hashing for detecting new events from a stream of Twitter posts. (O'Connor et al., 2010; Becker et al., 2011b; Becker et al., 2011a; Weng et al., 2011) proposed demo systems to display the event-related themes and popular tweets, allowing the users to navigate through their topic of interest. (Zhao et al., 2011) described an effort to perform data collection and event recognition despite various limits to the free access of Twitter data. (Diao et al., 2012) integrated both temporal information and users' personal interests for bursty topic detection from the microblogs. (Ritter et al., 2012) described an open-domain event-extraction and categorization system, which extracts an open-domain calendar of significant events from Twitter.

With the identified events of interest, there is an ever-increasing demand for event summarization, which distills the huge volume of Twitter discussions into a concise and representative textual description of the events. Many studies start with the text summarization approaches that have been shown to perform well on the news documents and develop adaptations to fit these methods to a collection of event tweets. (Sharifi et al., 2010b) proposed a graph-based phrase reinforcement algorithm to build a one-sentence summary from a collection of topic tweets. (Sharifi et al., 2010a; Inouye and Kalita, 2011) presented a hybrid TF-IDF approach to extract one- or multiple-sentence summary for each topic. (Liu et al., 2011a) proposed to use the concept-based ILP framework for summarizing the Twitter trending topics, using both tweets and the webpages linked from the tweets as input text sources. (Harabagiu and Hickl, 2011) introduced a generative framework that incorporates event structure and user behavior information in summarizing multiple microblog posts related to the same topic.

Regarding summarizing the data streams, (Marcus et al., 2011) introduced a "TwitInfo" system to visually summarize and track the events on Twitter. They proposed an automatic peak detection and labeling algorithm for the social streams. (Takamura et al., 2011) proposed a summarization model based on the facility location problem, which generates summary for a stream of short documents along the timeline. (Chakrabarti and Punera, 2011) proposed an event summarization algorithm based on learning an underlying hidden state representation of the event via hidden Markov models. (Louis and Newman, 2012) presented a method for summarizing a collection of tweets related to a business. The proposed procedure aggregates tweets into subtopic clusters which are then ranked and summarized by a few representative tweets from each cluster. (Nichols et al., 2012; Zubiaga et al., 2012) focused on real-time event summarization, which detects the sub-events by identifying those moments where the tweet volume has increases sharply, then uses various weighting schemes to perform tweet selection and finally generates the event summary.

Our work is different from the above research studies in three folds: first, we propose to "zoom-in" the Twitter event streams to the participant level, which allows us to clearly identify the important sub-events associated with each participant and generate a balanced event summary with comprehensive coverage of all the important sub-events; second, we propose a novel time-content mixture model approach for sub-event detection, which effectively leverages the "burstiness" and "cohesiveness" of the event tweets and accurately detects the participant-level sub-events. Third, we evaluate the participant-based event summarization system on different event types and demonstrate that the proposed approach outperforms the state-of-the-art method by a considerable margin.

3 Participant-based Event Summarization

We propose a novel participant-centered event summarization approach that consists of three key components: (1) "Participant Detection" dynamically identifies the event participants and divides the entire event stream into a number of participant streams (Section 3.1); (2) "Sub-event Detection" introduces a novel time-content mixture model approach to identify the important sub-events associated with each participant; these "participant-level sub-events" are then merged along the timeline to form a set of "global sub-events"[4], which capture all the important moments in the event stream (Section 3.2); (3) "Summary Tweet Extraction" extracts the representative tweets from the global sub-events and forms a comprehensive coverage of the event progress (Section 3.3).

3.1 Participant Detection

We define event participants as the entities that play a significant role in shaping the event progress. "Participant" is a general concept to denote the event participating persons, organizations, product lines, etc., each of which can be captured by a set of correlated proper nouns. For example, the NBA player "*LeBron Raymone James*" can be represented by $\{$*LeBron James, LeBron, LBJ, King James, L. James*$\}$, where each proper noun represents a unique mention of the participant. In this work, we automatically identify the proper nouns from tweet streams, filter out the infrequent ones using a threshold ψ, and cluster them into individual event participants. This process allows us to dynamically identify the key participating entities and provide a full-coverage for these participants in the event summary.

[4]We use "**participant sub-events**" and "**global sub-events**" respectively to represent the important moments happened on the participant-level and on the entire event-level. A "global sub-event" may consist of one or more "participant sub-events". For example., the "steal" action in the basketball game typically involves both the defensive and offensive players, and can be generated by merging the two participant-level sub-events.

We formulate the participant detection in a hierarchical agglomerative clustering framework. The CMU TweetNLP tool (Gimpel et al., 2011) was used for proper noun tagging. The proper nouns (a.k.a., mentions) are grouped into clusters in a bottom-up fashion. Two mentions are considered similar if they share (1) lexical resemblance, and (2) contextual similarity. For example, in the following two tweets "*Gotta respect Anthony Davis, still rocking the unibrow*", "*Anthony gotta do something about that unibrow*", the two mentions *Anthony Davis* and *Anthony* are referring to the same participant and they share both character overlap ("anthony") and context words ("unibrow", "gotta"). We use $sim(c_i, c_j)$ to represent the similarity between two mentions c_i and c_j, defined as:

$$sim(c_i, c_j) = lex\_sim(c_i, c_j) \times cont\_sim(c_i, c_j)$$

where the lexical similarity ($lex\_sim(\cdot)$) is defined as a binary function representing whether a mention c_i is an abbreviation, acronym, or part of another mention c_j, or if the character edit distance between the two mentions is less than a threshold θ[5]:

$$lex\_sim(c_i, c_j) = \begin{cases} 1 & c_i(c_j) \text{ is part of } c_j(c_i) \\ 1 & \text{EditDist}(c_i, c_j) < \theta \\ 0 & \text{Otherwise} \end{cases}$$

We define the context similarity ($cont\_sim(\cdot)$) of two mentions as the cosine similarity between their context vectors $\vec{v}_i$ and $\vec{v}_j$. Note that on the tweet stream, two temporally distant tweets can be very different even though they are lexically similar, e.g., two slam dunk shots performed by the same player at different time points are different. We therefore restrain the context to a segment of the tweet stream $|S_k|$ and then take the weighted average of the segment-based similarity as the final context similarity. To build the context vector, we use term frequency (TF) as the term weight and remove all the stopwords. We use $|D|$ to represent the total tweets in the event stream.

$$cont\_sim_{|S_k|}(c_i, c_j) = \cos(\vec{v}_i, \vec{v}_j)$$

$$cont\_sim(c_i, c_j) = \sum_k \frac{|S_k|}{|D|} \times cont\_sim_{|S_k|}(c_i, c_j)$$

[5] θ was empirically set as $0.2 \times min\{|c_i|, |c_j|\}$

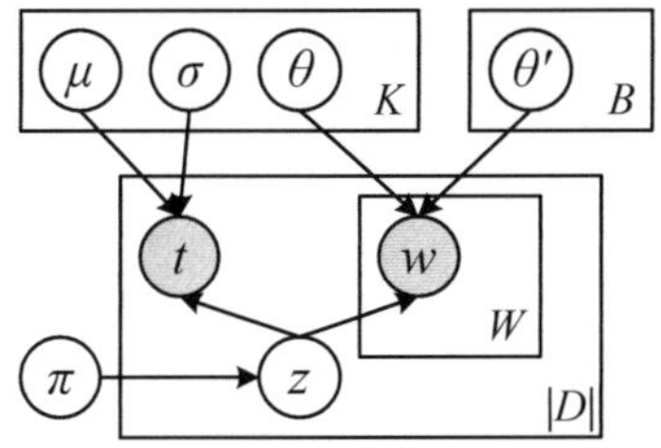

Figure 2: Plate notation of the mixture model.

Similarity between two clusters of mentions are defined as the maximum possible similarity between a pair of mentions, each from one cluster:

$$sim(C_i, C_j) = \max_{c_i \in C_i, c_j \in C_j} sim(c_i, c_j)$$

We perform bottom-up agglomerative clustering on the mentions until a stopping threshold δ has been reached for $sim(C_i, C_j)$. The clustering approach naturally groups the frequent proper nouns into participants. The **participant streams** are then formed by gathering the tweets that contain one or more mentions in the participant cluster.

3.2 Mixture Model-based Sub-event Detection

A sub-event corresponds to a topic that emerges from the data stream, being intensively discussed during a short period, and then gradually fades away. The tweets corresponding to a sub-event thus demand not only "temporal burstiness" but also a certain degree of "lexical cohesiveness". To incorporate both the time and content aspects of the sub-events, we propose a mixture model approach for sub-event detection. Figure 2 shows the plate notation.

In the proposed model, each tweet d in the data stream D is generated from a topic z, weighted by π_z. Each topic is characterized by both its content and time aspects. The content aspect is captured by a multinomial distribution over the words, parameterized by θ; while the time aspect is characterized by a Gaussian distribution, parameterized by μ and σ, with μ represents the average time point that the sub-event emerges and σ determines the duration of the sub-event. These distributions bear similarities with the previous work (Hofmann, 1999; Allan, 2002; Haghighi and Vanderwende, 2009). In addition, there are often background or "noise" topics that are being constantly discussed over the entire event evolvement process and do not present the desired "burstiness" property. We use a uniform distribution $U(t_b, t_e)$ to model the time aspect of these "background" topics, with t_b and t_e being the event beginning and end time points. The content aspect of a background topic is modeled by similar multinomial distribution, parameterized by θ'. We use the maximum likelihood parameter estimation. The data likelihood can be represented as:

$$L(D) = \prod_{d \in D} \sum_{z} \{\pi_z p_z(t_d) \prod_{w \in d} p_z(w)\}$$

where $p_z(t_d)$ models the timestamp of tweet d under the topic z; $p_z(w)$ corresponds to the word distribution in topic z. They are defined as:

$$p_z(t_d) = \begin{cases} N(t_d; \mu_z, \sigma_z) & \text{if } z \text{ is a sub-event topic} \\ U(t_b, t_e) & \text{if } z \text{ is background topic} \end{cases}$$

$$p_z(w) = \begin{cases} p(w; \theta_z) & \text{if } z \text{ is a sub-event topic} \\ p(w; \theta'_z) & \text{if } z \text{ is background topic} \end{cases}$$

where both $p(w; \theta_z)$ and $p(w; \theta'_z)$ are multinomial distributions over the words. Initially, we assume there are K sub-event topics and B background topics and use the EM algorithm for model fitting. The EM equations are listed below:

E-step:

$$p(z_d = j) \propto \begin{cases} \pi_j N(d; \mu_j, \sigma_j) \prod_{w \in d} p(w; \theta_j) & \text{if } j <= K \\ \pi_j U(t_b, t_e) \prod_{w \in d} p(w; \theta'_j) & \text{else} \end{cases}$$

M-step:

$$\pi_j \propto \sum_d p(z_d = j)$$

$$p(w; \theta_j) \propto \sum_d p(z_d = j) \times c(w, d)$$

$$p(w; \theta'_j) \propto \sum_d p(z_d = j) \times c(w, d)$$

$$\mu_j = \frac{\sum_d p(z_d = j) \times t_d}{\sum_{j=1}^{K} \sum_d p(z_d = j)}$$

$$\sigma_j^2 = \frac{\sum_d p(z_d = j) \times (t_d - \mu_j)^2}{\sum_{j=1}^{K} \sum_d p(z_d = j)}$$

To process the data stream D, we divide the data into 10-second bins and process each bin at a time. The peak time of a sub-event was determined as the bin that has the most tweets related to this sub-event. During EM initialization, the number of sub-event topics K was empirically decided by scanning through the data stream and examine tweets in every 3-minute stream segment. If there was a spike[6], we add a new sub-event to the model and use the tweets in this segment to initialize the value of μ, σ, and θ. Initially, we use a fixed number of background topics with $B = 4$. A topic re-adjustment was performed after the EM process. We merge two sub-events in a data stream if they (1) locate closely in the timeline, with peaks times within a 2-minute window; and (2) share similar word distributions: among the top-10 words with highest probability in the word distributions, there are over 5 words overlap. We also convert the sub-event topics to background topics if their σ values are greater than a threshold β[7]. We then re-run the EM to obtain the updated parameters. The topic re-adjustment process continues until the number of sub-events and background topics do not change further.

We obtain the "**participant sub-events**" by applying this sub-event detection approach to each of the participant streams. The "**global sub-events**" are obtained by merging the participant sub-events along the timeline. We merge two participant sub-events into a global sub-event if (1) their peaks are within a 2-minute window, and (2) the Jaccard similarity (Lee, 1999) between their associated tweets is greater than a threshold (set to 0.1 empirically). The tweets associated with each global sub-event are the ones with $p(z|d)$ greater than a threshold γ, where z is one of the participant sub-events and γ was set to 0.7 empirically. After the sub-event detection process, we obtain a set of global sub-events and their associated event tweets.[8]

3.3 Summary Tweet Extraction

We extract a representative tweet from each of the global sub-events and concatenate them to form an informative event summary. Note that our goal in this work is to identify all the important moments

[6] We use the algorithm described in (Marcus et al., 2011) as a baseline and ad hoc spike detection algorithm.

[7] β was set to 5 minutes in our experiments.

[8] We empirically set some threshold values in the topic re-adjustment and sub-event merging process. In future, we would like to explore more principled way of parameter selection.

Event		Date	Duration	#Tweets
N B A	Lakers vs Okc	05/19/2012	3h10m	218,313
	Celtics vs 76ers	05/23/2012	3h30m	245,734
	Celtics vs Heat	05/30/2012	3h30m	345,335
	Spurs vs Okc	05/31/2012	3h	254,670
	Heat vs Okc (1)	06/12/2012	3h30m	331,498
	Heat vs Okc (2)	06/21/2012	3h30m	332,223
Apple's WWDC'12 Conf.		06/11/2012	3h30m	163,775

Table 1: Statistics of the data set, including six NBA basketball games and the WWDC 2012 conference event.

for event summarization, but not on proposing new methods for tweet selection. We thus use the Hybrid TF-IDF approach (Sharifi et al., 2010a; Liu et al., 2011a) to extract the representative sentences from a collection of tweets. In this approach, each tweet was considered as a sentence. The sentences were ranked according to the average TF-IDF score of the consisting words; top weighted sentences were iteratively extracted, while excluding those that have high cosine similarity with the existing summary sentences. (Inouye and Kalita, 2011) showed the Hybrid TF-IDF approach performs constantly better than the phrase reinforcement algorithm and other traditional summarization systems.

4 Data Corpus

We evaluate the proposed event summarization approach on six NBA basketball games and a representative conference event, namely the Apple CEO's keynote speech in the Apple Worldwide Developers Conference (WWDC 2012)[9]. We use the heterogeneous event types to verify that the proposed approach can robustly and efficiently produce summaries on different event streams. The tweet streams corresponding to these events are collected using the Twitter Streaming API[10] with pre-defined keyword set. For NBA games, we use the team names, first name and last name of the players and head coaches as keywords for retrieving the event tweets; for the WWDC conference, the keyword set contains about 20 terms related to the Apple event, such as "wwdc", "apple", "mac", etc. We crawl the tweets in real-time when these scheduled events are taking place; nevertheless, certain non-event tweets could be mis-included due to the broad coverage of the used keywords. During preprocessing, we filter out the tweets containing URLs, non-English tweets, and retweets since they are less likely containing new information regarding the event progress. Table 1 shows statistics of the event tweets after the filtering process. In total, there are over 1.8 million tweets used in the event summarization experiments.

Time	Action (Sub-event)	Score
9:22	Chris Bosh misses 10-foot two point shot	7-2
9:22	Serge Ibaka defensive rebound	7-2
9:11	Kevin Durant makes 15-foot two point shot	9-2
8:55	Serge Ibaka shooting foul (Shane Battier draws the foul)	9-2
8:55	Shane Battier misses free throw 1 of 2	9-2
8:55	Miami offensive team rebound	9-2
8:55	Shane Battier makes free throw 2 of 2	9-3

Table 2: An example clip of the play-by-play live coverage of an NBA game (Heat vs Okc). "Time" corresponds to the minutes left in the current quarter of the game; "Score" shows the score between the two teams.

We use the play-by-play live coverage collected from the ESPN[11] and MacRumors[12] websites as reference, which provide detailed descriptions of the NBA and WWDC events as they unfold. Table 2 shows an example clip of the play-by-play descriptions of an NBA game. Ideally, each item in the live coverage descriptions may correspond to a sub-event in the tweet streams, but in reality, not all actions would attract enough attention from the Twitter audience. We use a human annotator to manually filter out the actions that did not lead to any spike in the corresponding participant stream. The rest items are projected to the participant and event streams as the goldstandard sub-events. The projection was manually performed since the "game clock" associated with the goldstandard (first column in Table 2) does not align well with the "wall clock" due to the game rules such as timeout and halftime rest. To evaluate the participant detection performance, we ask the annotator to manually group the proper noun mentions into clusters, each cluster corresponds to a participant. The mentions that do not correspond to any participant are discarded. The goldstandard event summaries are generated by manually selecting one representative tweet from each of the groundtruth global sub-events. We choose not to use the play-by-play descriptions as reference summaries since their vocabulary is rather limited and do not overlap with the tweet language.

[9] https://developer.apple.com/wwdc/

[10] https://dev.twitter.com/docs/streaming-apis

[11] http://espn.go.com/nba/scoreboard

[12] http://www.macrumorslive.com/archive/wwdc12/

Example Participants - NBA game
westbrook, russell westbrook
stephen jackson, steven jackson, jackson
james, james harden, harden
ibaka, serge ibaka
oklahoma city thunder, oklahoma
gregg popovich, greg popovich, popovich
kevin durant, kd, durant
thunder, okc, #okc, okc thunder, #thunder

Example Participants - WWDC Conference
macbooks, mbp, macbook pro, macbook air,...
google maps, google, apple maps
wwdc, apple wwdc, #wwdc
os, mountain, os x mountain, os x
iphone 4s, iphone 3gs, iphone

Table 3: Example participants automatically detected from the NBA game Spurs vs Okc (2012-5-31) and the WWDC'12 conference.

5 Experimental Results

We evaluate the participant-based event summarization in a cascaded fashion and present results for each of the three components, including the participant detection (Section 5.1), sub-event detection (Section 5.2), and quantitative and qualitative evaluation of example event summaries (Section 5.3).

5.1 Participant Detection Results

In Table 3, we show example participants that were automatically detected by the proposed hierarchical agglomerative clustering approach. We note that the clusters include various mentions of the same event participant, e.g., "*gregg popovich*", "*greg popovich*", and "*popovich*" are both referring to the head coach of the team Spurs; "*macbooks*", "*macbook pro*", "*mbp*" are referring to a line of products from Apple. Quantitatively, we evaluate the participant detection results on both participant- and mention-level. Assume the system-detected and the goldstandard participant clusters are T_s and T_g respectively. We define a **correct participant** as a system detected participant with more than half of its associated mentions are included in a goldstandard participant (referred to as the **hit participant**). As a result, we can define the participant-level precision and recall as below:

$$\text{participant-prec} = \#\text{correct-participants}/|T_s|$$
$$\text{participant-recall} = \#\text{hit-participants}/|T_g|$$

Note that a correct participant may include incorrect mentions, and that more than one correct participants may correspond to the same hit participant, both of which are undesired. In the latter case, we use **representative participant** to refer to the correct participant which contains the most mentions in the hit participant. In this way, we build a 1-to-1 mapping from the detected participants to the groundtruth participants. Next, we define **correct mentions** as the union of the overlapping mentions between all pairs of representative and hit participants. Then we calculate the mention-level precision and recall as the number of correct mentions divided by the total mentions in the system or goldstandard participant clusters.

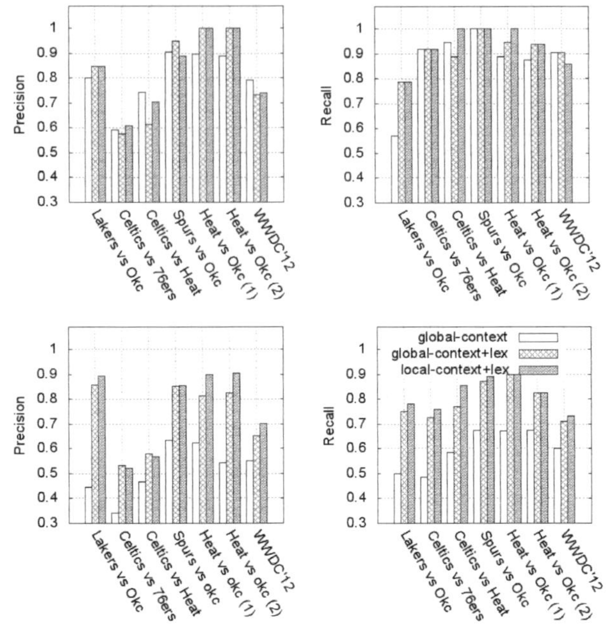

Figure 3: Participant detection performance. The upper figures represent the participant-level precision and recall scores; while the lower figures represent the mention-level precision and recall. X-axis corresponds to the six NBA games and the WWDC conference.

Figure 3 shows the participant- and mention-level precision and recall scores. We experimented with different similarity measures for the agglomerative clustering approach[13]. The "global context" means that the context vectors are created from the entire data stream; this may not perform well since different participants can share similar global context. E.g., the terms "shot", "dunk", "rebound" can appear in the context of any NBA players and are not

[13]The stopping threshold δ was set to 0.15, local context length is 3 minutes, and frequency threshold ψ was set to 200.

Event	Participant-level Sub-event Detection								Global Sub-event Detection									
	#P	#S	Spike			MM			#S	Spike			Participant + Spike			Participant + MM		
			R	P	F	R	P	F		R	P	F	R	P	F	R	P	F
Lakers vs Okc	9	65	0.75	0.31	**0.44**	0.71	0.39	**0.50**	48	0.67	0.38	0.48	**0.94**	0.19	0.32	**0.88**	0.40	**0.55**
Celtics vs 76ers	10	88	0.52	0.39	**0.45**	0.53	0.43	**0.47**	60	0.65	0.51	0.57	**0.72**	0.18	0.29	**0.78**	0.39	**0.52**
Celtics vs Heat	14	152	0.53	0.29	**0.37**	0.50	0.38	**0.43**	67	0.57	0.41	0.48	**0.97**	0.21	0.35	**0.91**	0.28	**0.43**
Spurs vs Okc	12	98	0.78	0.46	**0.58**	0.84	0.57	**0.68**	81	0.41	0.42	0.41	**0.88**	0.35	0.50	**0.91**	0.54	**0.68**
Heat vs Okc (1)	15	123	0.75	0.27	**0.40**	0.72	0.35	**0.47**	85	0.41	0.47	0.44	**0.94**	0.20	0.33	**0.96**	0.34	**0.50**
Heat vs okc (2)	13	153	0.74	0.36	**0.48**	0.76	0.43	**0.55**	92	0.41	0.33	0.37	**0.88**	0.21	0.34	**0.87**	0.38	**0.53**
WWDC'12	10	56	0.64	0.14	**0.23**	0.59	0.33	**0.42**	43	0.53	0.26	0.35	**0.77**	0.14	0.24	**0.70**	0.31	**0.43**
Average	**12**	**105**	0.67	0.32	**0.42**	0.66	0.41	**0.50**	**68**	0.52	0.40	0.44	**0.87**	0.21	0.34	**0.86**	0.38	**0.52**

Table 4: Sub-event detection results on both participant and the event streams. "Spike" corresponds to the spike detection algorithm proposed in (Marcus et al., 2011); "MM" represents our proposed time-content mixture model approach. "#P" and "#S" list the number of participants and sub-events in each event stream.

discriminative enough. We found that adding the lexical similarity measure greatly boosted the clustering performance, especially on the mention-level, and that combining the lexical similarity with the local context is even more helpful for some events. We notice that two events (celtics vs 76ers and celtics vs heat) yield relatively low precision on both participant- and mention-level. Taking a close look at the data, we found that these two events accidentally co-occurred with other popular events, namely the TV program "American Idol" finale and the NBA Draft. The keyword based data crawler thus includes many noisy tweets in the event streams, leading to some false participants being detected.

5.2 Sub-event Detection Results

We compare our proposed time-content mixture model (noted as "MM") against the spike detection algorithm proposed in (Marcus et al., 2011) (noted as "Spike") . The spike algorithm is based on the tweet volume change. It uses 10 seconds as a time unit, calculates the tweet arrival rate in each unit, and identifies the rates that are significantly higher than the mean tweet rate. For these rate spikes, the algorithm finds the local maximum of tweet rate and identify a window surrounding the local maximum. We tune the parameter of the "Spike" approach (set $\tau = 4$) so that it yields similar recall values as the mixture model approach. We then apply the "MM" and "Spike" approaches to both the participant and event streams and evaluate the sub-event detection performance. Results are shown in Table 4. A system detected sub-event is considered to match the goldstandard sub-event if its peak time is within a 2-minute window of the goldstandard.

We first apply the "Spike" and "MM" approach to the participant streams. The participant streams on which we cannot detect any meaningful sub-events have been excluded, the resulting number of participants are listed in Table 4 and denoted as "#P". In general, we found the "MM" approach can perform better since it inherently incorporates both the "burstiness" and "lexical cohesiveness" of the event tweets, while the "Spike" approach relies solely on the "burstiness" property. Note that although we divide the entire event stream into participant streams, some key participants still own huge amount of discussion and the spike patterns are not always clearly identifiable. The time-content mixture model gains advantages in these cases.

We apply three settings to detect global sub-events on the data streams. "Spike" directly applies the spike algorithm on the entire event stream; the "Participant + Spike" and "Participant + MM" approaches first perform sub-event detection on the participant streams and then merge the detected sub-events along the timeline to generate global sub-events. Note that there are fewer goldstandard sub-events ("#S") on the global streams since each global sub-event may correspond to one or multiple participant-level sub-events. Because of the averaging effect, spike patterns on the entire event stream is less obvious than those on the participant streams. As a result, few spikes have been detected on the event stream using the "Spike" algorithm, which leads to low recall as compared to other participant-based approaches. It also indicates that, by dividing the entire event stream into participant streams, we have a better chance of identifying the sub-events that have otherwise been shadowed by the dominant sub-events or participants. The two participant-based methods yield similar recall but "Participant

+ Spike" yields slightly worse precision, since it is very sensitive to the spikes on the participant-level, leading to the rise of false alarms. The "Participant + MM" approach is much better in precision, which is consistent to our findings on the participant streams.

5.3 Summarization Results

Summarization evaluation has been a longstanding issue in the literature (Nenkova and Mckeown, 2011; Liu and Liu, 2010). There are even less studies focusing on evaluating the event summaries generated from data streams. Since the summary annotation takes quite some effort, we sample a 10-minute segment from each of the seven event streams and ask a human annotator to select representative tweets for each segment. We then compare the system summaries against the manual summaries using the ROUGE-1 (Lin, 2004) metric. The quantitative results and qualitative analysis are presented in Table 5 and Table 6 respectively. Note that the ROUGE scores are based solely on the n-gram overlap between the system and reference summaries, which may not be the most appropriate measure for evaluating the Twitter event summaries. However, we do notice that the accurate sub-event detection performance can successfully translate into a gain of the ROUGE scores. Qualitatively, the participant-based event summarization approach focus more on extracting tweets associated with the targeted participants, which could lead to better text coherence.

Event	Method	R(%)	P(%)	F(%)
NBA Average	Spike	14.73	23.24	**16.87**
	Participant + Spike	54.60	14.65	**22.40**
	Participant + MM	54.36	23.06	**31.53**
WWDC Conf.	Spike	26.58	39.62	**31.82**
	Participant + Spike	49.37	25.16	**33.33**
	Participant + MM	42.77	31.73	**36.07**

Table 5: ROUGE-1 scores of summarization

Method	Summary
Manual	Good drive for *durant* Pretty shot by *Duncan* Good 3 point *tony parker* Nice move *westbrook* Good shot *Westbrook*
Spike	Game 3. Spurs vs. OKC Okc and spurs game.
Participant + Spike	OKLAHOMA CITY THUNDER vs san antonio spurs!! YA I hope okc win the series. Ill hate too see the heat play San Antonio we aint in San Antonio anymore. NBA: SA 0 OKC 8, 9:11 1st.#TeamOkc San antonio spurs for 21 consecutive win? #nba Somebody Should Stop *Tim Duncan*. Pass the damn ball *Westbrook* Good 3 pointer *tony parker*!
Participant + MM	*Tim Duncan* shot is so precise *Tim Duncan* is gettin started Good 3 pointer *tony parker*! Sefalosa guarding *tony parker*. Good fucking move coach brooks *Westbrook* = 2 Fast 2 Furious Niggas steady letting *Tim Duncan* shoot *Westbrook* mid range shot is automatic

Table 6: Example summaries for an event segment. Participants are marked using *italicized* text.

6 Conclusion and Future Work

In this work, we made an initial attempt to generate event summaries using Twitter data streams. We proposed a participant-based event summarization approach which "zooms-in" the Twitter event streams to the participant level, detects the important sub-events associated with each participant using a novel mixture model that incorporates both the "burstiness" and "cohesiveness" of tweets, and generates the event summaries progressively. Results show that the proposed approach can effectively capture the sub-events that have otherwise been shadowed by the long-tail of other dominant sub-events, yielding summaries with considerably better coverage. Without loss of generality, we report results on the entire event streams, though the proposed approach can well be applied in an online fashion.

There are many challenges left in this line of research. Having a standardized evaluation metric for event summaries is one of them. In the current work, we employed ROUGE-1 for summary evaluation, since it has been shown to correlate well with the human judgements on noisy text genres (Liu and Liu, 2010). We would like to explore other evaluation metrics (e.g., ROUGE-2, -SU4, Pyramid (Nenkova et al., 2007)) and the human evaluation in future. We will also explore better ways of integrating the sub-event detection and summarization approaches.

Acknowledgments

Part of this work was done during the first author's internship in Bosch Research and Technology Center. The work is also partially supported by NSF grants DMS-0915110 and HRD-0833093.

References

James Allan. 2002. Topic detection and tracking: Event-based information organization. *Kluwer Academic Publishers Norwell, MA, USA.*

Hila Becker, Feiyang Chen, Dan Iter, Mor Naaman, and Luis Gravano. 2011a. Automatic identification and presentation of twitter content for planned events. In *Proceedings of the Fifth International AAAI Conference on Weblogs and Social Media (ICWSM)*, pages 655–656.

Hila Becker, Mor Naaman, and Luis Gravano. 2011b. Beyond trending topics: Real-world event identification on twitter. In *Proceedings of the Fifth International AAAI Conference on Weblogs and Social Media (ICWSM)*, pages 438–441.

Deepayan Chakrabarti and Kunal Punera. 2011. Event summarization using tweets. In *Proceedings of the Fifth International AAAI Conference on Weblogs and Social Media (ICWSM)*, pages 66–73.

Qiming Diao, Jing Jiang, Feida Zhu, and Ee-Peng Lim. 2012. Finding bursty topics from microblogs. In *Proceedings of the 50th Annual Meeting of the Association for Computational Linguistics (ACL)*, pages 536–544.

Jacob Eisenstein. 2013. What to do about bad language on the internet. In *Proceedings of the 2013 Conference of the North American Chapter of the Association for Computational Linguistics: Human Language Technologies (NAACL/HLT)*.

Jennifer Foster, Ozlem Cetinoglu, Joachim Wagner, Joseph Le Roux, Stephen Hogan, Joakim Nivre, Deirdre Hogan, and Josef van Genabith. 2011. #hardtoparse: POS tagging and parsing the twitterverse. In *Proceedings of the AAAI Workshop on Analyzing Microtext*, pages 20–25.

Kevin Gimpel, Nathan Schneider, Brendan O'Connor, Dipanjan Das, Daniel Mills, Jacob Eisenstein, Michael Heilman, Dani Yogatama, Jeffrey Flanigan, and Noah A. Smith. 2011. Part-of-speech tagging for twitter: Annotation, features, and experiments. In *Proceedings of the 49th Annual Meeting of the Association for Computational Linguistics: Human Language Technologies (ACL-HLT)*, pages 42–47.

Aria Haghighi and Lucy Vanderwende. 2009. Exploring content models for multi-Document summarization. In *Proceedings of Human Language Technologies: The 2009 Annual Conference of the North American Chapter of the Association for Computational Linguistics (NAACL)*, pages 362–370.

Sanda Harabagiu and Andrew Hickl. 2011. Relevance modeling for microblog summarization. In *Proceedings of the Fifth International AAAI Conference on Weblogs and Social Media (ICWSM)*, pages 514–517.

Thomas Hofmann. 1999. Probabilistic latent semantic analysis. In *Proceedings of Uncertainty in Artificial Intelligence (UAI)*.

David Inouye and Jugal K. Kalita. 2011. Comparing twitter summarization algorithms for multiple post summaries. In *Proceedings of 2011 IEEE Third International Conference on Social Computing*, pages 290–306.

Lillian Lee. 1999. Measures of distributional similarity. In *Proceedings of the 37th Annual Meeting of the Association for Computational Linguistics (ACL)*, pages 25–32.

Chin-Yew Lin. 2004. ROUGE: A package for automatic evaluation of summaries. In *Workshop on Text Summarization Branches Out*.

Feifan Liu and Yang Liu. 2010. Exploring correlation between ROUGE and human evaluation on meeting summaries. *IEEE Transactions on Audio, Speech, and Language Processing*, 18(1):187–196.

Fei Liu, Yang Liu, and Fuliang Weng. 2011a. Why is "SXSW" trending? Exploring multiple text sources for twitter topic summarization. In *Proceedings of the ACL Workshop on Language in Social Media (LSM)*, pages 66–75.

Fei Liu, Fuliang Weng, Bingqing Wang, and Yang Liu. 2011b. Insertion, deletion, or substitution? Normalizing text messages without pre-categorization nor supervision. In *Proceedings of the 49th Annual Meeting of the Association for Computational Linguistics (ACL)*, pages 71–76.

Fei Liu, Fuliang Weng, and Xiao Jiang. 2012. A broad-coverage normalization system for social media language. In *Proceedings of the 50th Annual Meeting of the Association for Computational Linguistics (ACL)*, pages 1035–1044.

Annie Louis and Todd Newman. 2012. Summarization of business-related tweets: A concept-based approach. In *Proceedings of the 24th International Conference on Computational Linguistics (COLING)*.

Adam Marcus, Michael S. Bernstein, Osama Badar, David R. Karger, Samuel Madden, and Robert C. Miller. 2011. Twitinfo: Aggregating and visualizing microblogs for event exploration. In *Proceedings of the SIGCHI Conference on Human Factors in Computing Systems*, pages 227–236.

Ani Nenkova and Kathleen Mckeown. 2011. Automatic summarization. *Foundations and Trends in Information Retrieval*, 5(2–3):103–233.

Ani Nenkova, Rebecca Passonneau, and Kathleen Mckeown. 2007. The pyramid method: Incorporating human content selection variation in summarization evaluation. *ACM Transactions on Speech and Language Processing*, 4(2).

Jeffrey Nichols, Jalal Mahmud, and Clemens Drews. 2012. Summarizing sporting events using twitter. In *Proceedings of the 2012 ACM Interntional Conference on Intelligent User Interfaces (IUI)*, pages 189–198.

Brendan O'Connor, Michel Krieger, and David Ahn. 2010. TweetMotif: Exploratory search and topic summarization for twitter. In *Proceedings of the Fourth International AAAI Conference on Weblogs and Social Media (ICWSM)*, pages 384–385.

Sasa Petrovic, Miles Osborne, and Victor Lavrenko. 2010. Streaming first story detection with application to twitter. In *Proceedings of the 2010 Annual Conference of the North American Chapter of the Association for Computational Linguistics (NAACL)*, pages 181–189.

Alan Ritter, Sam Clark, Mausam, and Oren Etzioni. 2011. Named entity recognition in tweets: An experimental study. In *Proceedings of the Conference on Empirical Methods in Natural Language Processing (EMNLP)*, pages 1524–1534.

Alan Ritter, Mausam, Oren Etzioni, and Sam Clark. 2012. Open domain event extraction from twitter. In *Proceedings of the 18th ACM SIGKDD International Conference on Knowledge Discovery and Data Mining*, pages 1104–1112.

Beaux Sharifi, Mark-Anthony Hutton, and Jugal K. Kalita. 2010a. Experiments in microblog summarization. In *Proceedings of the 2010 IEEE Second International Conference on Social Computing*, pages 49–56.

Beaux Sharifi, Mark-Anthony Hutton, and Jugal K. Kalita. 2010b. Summarizing microblogs automatically. In *Proceedings of the 2010 Annual Conference of the North American Chapter of the Association for Computational Linguistics (NAACL)*, pages 685–688.

Hiroya Takamura, Hikaru Yokono, and Manabu Okumura. 2011. Summarizing a document stream. In *Proceedings of the 33rd European Conference on Advances in Information Retrieval (ECIR)*, pages 177–188.

Jui-Yu Weng, Cheng-Lun Yang, Bo-Nian Chen, Yen-Kai Wang, and Shou-De Lin. 2011. Imass: An intelligent microblog analysis and summarization system. In *Proceedings of the 49th Annual Meeting of the Association for Computational Linguistics: Human Language Technologies (ACL-HLT)*, pages 133–138.

Siqi Zhao, Lin Zhong, Jehan Wickramasuriya, and Venu Vasudevan. 2011. Human as real-time sensors of social and physical events: A case study of twitter and sports games. *Technical Report TR0620-2011, Rice University and Motorola Labs.*

Arkaitz Zubiaga, Damiano Spina, Enrique Amigó, and Julio Gonzalo. 2012. Towards real-time summarization of scheduled events from twitter streams. In *Proceedings of the 23rd ACM Conference on Hypertext and Social Media*, pages 319–320.

Towards Coherent Multi-Document Summarization

Janara Christensen, Mausam, Stephen Soderland, Oren Etzioni
Computer Science & Engineering
University of Washington
Seattle, WA 98195, USA
{janara,mausam,soderlan,etzioni}@cs.washington.edu

Abstract

This paper presents G-FLOW, a novel system for coherent extractive multi-document summarization (MDS).[1] Where previous work on MDS considered sentence selection and ordering separately, G-FLOW introduces a joint model for selection and ordering that balances coherence and salience. G-FLOW's core representation is a graph that approximates the discourse relations across sentences based on indicators including discourse cues, deverbal nouns, co-reference, and more. This graph enables G-FLOW to estimate the coherence of a candidate summary.

We evaluate G-FLOW on Mechanical Turk, and find that it generates dramatically better summaries than an extractive summarizer based on a pipeline of state-of-the-art sentence selection and reordering components, underscoring the value of our joint model.

1 Introduction

The goal of multi-document summarization (MDS) is to produce high quality summaries of collections of related documents. Most previous work in extractive MDS has studied the problems of sentence selection (*e.g.*, (Radev, 2004; Haghighi and Vanderwende, 2009)) and sentence ordering (*e.g.*, (Lapata, 2003; Barzilay and Lapata, 2008)) separately, but we believe that a joint model is necessary to produce coherent summaries. The intuition is simple: if the sentences in a summary are first selected—without regard to coherence—then a satisfactory ordering of the selected sentences may not exist.

[1]System and data at http://knowitall.cs.washington.edu/gflow/

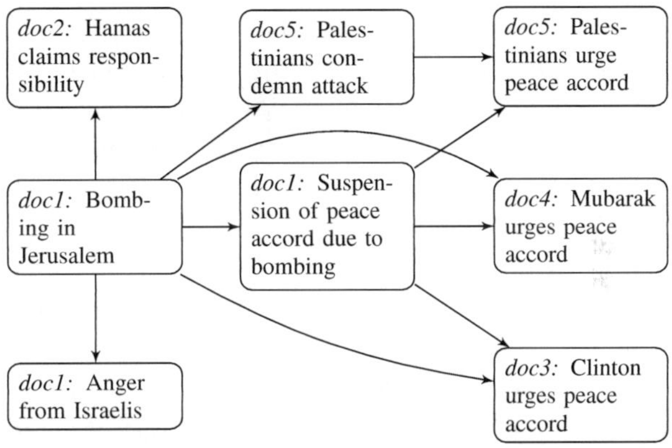

Figure 1: An example of a discourse graph covering a bombing and its aftermath, indicating the source document for each node. A coherent summary should begin with the bombing and then describe the reactions. Sentences are abbreviated for compactness.

An extractive summary is a subset of the sentences in the input documents, ordered in some way.[2] Of course, most *possible* summaries are incoherent. Now, consider a directed graph where the nodes are sentences in the collection, and each edge represents a pairwise ordering constraint necessary for a coherent summary (see Figure 1 for a sample graph). By definition, any *coherent* summary must obey the constraints in this graph.

Previous work has constructed similar graphs automatically for single document summarization and manually for MDS (see Section 2). Our system, G-FLOW extends this research in two important ways. First, it tackles automatic graph construction for MDS, which requires novel methods for identifying inter-document edges (Section 3). It uses this

[2]We focus exclusively on extractive summaries, so we drop the word "extractive" henceforth.

State-of-the-art MDS system	G-FLOW
• The attack took place Tuesday near Cailaco in East Timor, a former Portuguese colony, according to a statement issued by the pro-independence Christian Democratic Union of East Timor. • The United Nations does not recognize Indonesian claims to East Timor.	• In a decision welcomed as a landmark by Portugal, European Union leaders Saturday backed calls for a referendum to decide the fate of East Timor, the former Portuguese colony occupied by Indonesia since 1975. • Indonesia invaded East Timor in 1975 and annexed it the following year.
• Bhichai Rattakul, deputy prime minister and president of the Bangkok Asian Games Organizing Committee, asked the Foreign Ministry to urge the Saudi government to reconsider withdrawing its 105-strong team. • The games will be a success.	• Thailand won host rights for the quadrennial games in 1995, but setbacks in preparations led officials of the Olympic Council of Asia late last year to threaten to move the games to another country. • Thailand showed its nearly complete facilities for the Asian Games to a tough jury Thursday - the heads of the organizing committees from the 43 nations competing in the December event.

Table 1: Pairs of sentences produced by a pipeline of a state-of-the-art sentence extractor (Lin and Bilmes, 2011) and sentence orderer (Li et al., 2011a), and by G-FLOW.

graph to estimate coherence of a candidate summary. Second, G-FLOW introduces a novel methodology for joint sentence selection and ordering (Section 4). It casts MDS as a constraint optimization problem where salience and coherence are soft constraints, and redundancy and summary length are hard constraints. Because this optimization problem is NP-hard, G-FLOW uses local search to approximate it.

We report on a Mechanical Turk evaluation that directly compares G-FLOW to state-of-the-art MDS systems. Using DUC'04 as our test set, we compare G-FLOW against a combination of an extractive summarization system with state-of-the-art ROUGE scores (Lin and Bilmes, 2011) followed by a state-of-the-art sentence reordering scheme (Li et al., 2011a). We also compare G-FLOW to a combination of an extractive system with state-of-the-art coherence scores (Nobata and Sekine, 2004) followed by the reordering system. In both cases participants substantially preferred G-FLOW. Participants chose G-FLOW 54% of the time when compared to Lin, and chose Lin's system 22% of the time. When compared to Nobata, participants chose G-FLOW 60% of the time, and chose Nobata only 20% of the time. The remainder of the cases were judged equivalent.

A further analysis shows that G-FLOW's summaries are judged superior along several dimensions suggested in the DUC'04 evaluation (including coherence, repetitive text, and referents). A comparison against manually written, gold standard summaries, reveals that while the gold standard summaries are preferred in direct comparisons, G-FLOW has nearly equivalent scores on almost all dimensions suggested in the DUC'04 evaluation.

The paper makes the following contributions:

- We present G-FLOW, a novel MDS system that jointly solves the sentence selection and ordering problems to produce coherent summaries.
- G-FLOW automatically constructs a domain-independent graph of ordering constraints over sentences in a document collection, based on syntactic cues and redundancy across documents. This graph is the backbone for estimating the coherence of a summary.
- We perform human evaluation on blind test sets and find that G-FLOW dramatically outperforms state-of-the-art MDS systems.

2 Related Work

Most existing research in multi-document summarization (MDS) focuses on sentence selection for increasing coverage and does not consider coherence of the summary (Section 2.1). Although coherence has been used in ordering of summary sentences (Section 2.2), this work is limited by the quality of summary sentences given as input. In contrast, G-FLOW incorporates coherence in both selection and ordering of summary sentences.

G-FLOW can be seen as an instance of discourse-driven summarization (Section 2.3). There is prior work in this area, but primarily for summarization of single documents. There is some preliminary work on the use of manually-created discourse models in MDS. Our approach is fully automated.

2.1 Subset Selection in MDS

Most extractive summarization research aims to increase the coverage of concepts and entities while reducing redundancy. Approaches include the use of maximum marginal relevance (Carbonell and Goldstein, 1998), centroid-based summarization (Saggion and Gaizauskas, 2004; Radev et al., 2004), covering weighted scores of concepts (Takamura and Okumura, 2009; Qazvinian et al., 2010), formulation as minimum dominating set problem (Shen and Li, 2010), and use of submodularity in sentence selection (Lin and Bilmes, 2011). Graph centrality has also been used to estimate the salience of a sentence (Erkan and Radev, 2004). Approaches to content analysis include generative topic models (Haghighi and Vanderwende, 2009; Celikyilmaz and Hakkani-Tur, 2010; Li et al., 2011b), and discriminative models (Aker et al., 2010).

These approaches do not consider coherence as one of the desiderata in sentence selection. Moreover, they do not attempt to organize the selected sentences into an intelligible summary. They are often evaluted by ROUGE (Lin, 2004), which is coherence-insensitive. In practice, these approaches often result in incoherent summaries.

2.2 Sentence Reordering

A parallel thread of research has investigated taking a set of summary sentences as input and reordering them to make the summary fluent. Various algorithms use some combination of topic-relatedness, chronology, precedence, succession, and entity coherence for reordering sentences (Barzilay et al., 2001; Okazaki et al., 2004; Barzilay and Lapata, 2008; Bollegala et al., 2010). Recent work has also used event-based models (Zhang et al., 2010) and context analysis (Li et al., 2011a).

The hypothesis in this research is that a pipelined combination of subset selection and reordering will produce high-quality summaries. Unfortunately, this is not true in practice, because sentences are selected primarily for coverage without regard to coherence. This methodology often leads to an inadvertent selection of a set of disconnected sentences, which cannot be put together in a coherent summary, irrespective of how the succeeding algorithm reorders them. In our evaluation, reordering had limited impact on the quality of the summaries.

2.3 Coherence Models and Summarization

Research on discourse analysis of documents provides a basis for modeling coherence in a document. Several theories have been developed for modeling discourse, *e.g.*, Centering Theory, Rhetorical Structure Theory (RST), Penn Discourse TreeBank (Grosz and Sidner, 1986; Mann and Thompson, 1988; Wolf and Gibson, 2005; Prasad et al., 2008). Numerous discourse-guided summarization algorithms have been developed (Marcu, 1997; Mani, 2001; Taboada and Mann, 2006; Barzilay and Elhadad, 1997; Louis et al., 2010). However, these approaches have been applied to single document summarization and not to MDS.

Discourse models have seen some application to summary generation in MDS, for example, using a detailed semantic representation of the source texts (McKeown and Radev, 1995; Radev and McKeown, 1998). A multi-document extension of RST is Cross-document Structure Theory (CST), which has been applied to MDS (Zhang et al., 2002; Jorge and Pardo, 2010). However, these systems require a stronger input, such as a manual CST-annotation of the set of documents. Our work can be seen as an instance of summarization based on lightweight CST. However, a key difference is that our proposed algorithm is completely automated and does not require any additional human annotation. Additionally, while incorporating coherence into selection, this work does not attempt to order the sentences coherently, while our approach performs joint selection and ordering.

Discourse models have also been used for evaluating summary quality (Barzilay and Lapata, 2008; Louis and Nenkova, 2009; Pitler et al., 2010). Finally, there is work on generating coherent summaries in specific domains, such as scientific articles (Saggion and Lapalme, 2002; Abu-Jbara and Radev, 2011) using domain-specific cues like citations. In contrast, our work generates summaries without any domain-specific knowledge. Other research has focused on identifying coherent threads of *documents* rather than sentences (Shahaf and Guestrin, 2010).

3 Discourse Graph

As described in Section 1, our goal is to identify pairwise ordering constraints over a set of input sentences. These constraints specify a multi-document discourse graph, which is used by G-FLOW to evaluate the coherence of a candidate summary.

In this graph G, each vertex is a sentence and an edge from s_i to s_j indicates that s_j can be placed right after s_i in a coherent summary. In other words, the two share a discourse relationship. In the following three sentences (from possibly different documents) there should be an edge from s_1 to s_2, but not between s_3 and the other sentences:

s_1 *Militants attacked a market in Jerusalem.*

s_2 *Arafat condemned the bombing.*

s_3 *The Wye River Accord was signed in Oct.*

Discourse theories have proposed a variety of relationships between sentences such as background and interpretation. RST has 17 such relations (Mann and Thompson, 1988) and PDTB has 16 (Prasad et al., 2008). While we seek to identify pairs of sentences that have a relationship, we do not attempt to label the edges with the exact relation.

We use textual cues from the discourse literature in combination with the redundancy inherent in related documents to generate edges. Because this methodology is noisy, the graph used by G-FLOW is an approximation, which we refer to as an approximate discourse graph (ADG). We first describe the construction of this graph, and then discuss the use of the graph for summary generation (Section 4).

3.1 Deverbal Noun Reference

Often, the main description of an event is mentioned in a verbal phrase and subsequent references use deverbal nouns (nominalization of verbs) (*e.g.*, 'attacked' and 'the attack'). In this example, the noun is derivationally related to the verb, but that is not always the case. For example, 'bombing' in s_2 above refers to 'attacked' in s_1.

We identify verb-noun pairs with this relationship as follows. First, we locate a set of candidate pairs from WordNet: for each verb v, we determine potential noun references n using a path length of up to two in WordNet (moving from verb to noun is possible via WordNet's 'derivationally related' links).

This set captures verb-noun pairs such as ('to attack', 'bombing'), but also includes generic pairs such as ('to act', 'attack'). To filter such errors we score the candidate references. Our goal is to emphasize common pairs and to deemphasize pairs with common verbs or verbs that map to many nouns. To this end, we score pairs by $(c/p) * (c/q)$, where c is the number of times the pair (v, n) appears in adjacent sentences, p is the number of times the verb appears, and q is the number of times that v appears with a different noun. We generate these statistics over a background corpus of 60,000 articles from the New York Times and Reuters, and filter out candidate pairs scoring below a threshold identified over a small training set.

We construct edges in the ADG between pairs of sentences containing these verb to noun mappings. To our knowledge, we are the first to use deverbal nouns for summarization.

3.2 Event/Entity Continuation

Our second indicator is related to lexical chains (Barzilay and Lapata, 2008). We add an edge in the ADG from a sentence s_i to s_j if they contain the same event or entity and the timestamp of s_i is less than or equal to the timestamp of s_j (timestamps generated with (Chang and Manning, 2012)).

3.3 Discourse Markers

We use 36 explicit discourse markers (*e.g.*, 'but', 'however', 'moreover') to identify edges between two adjacent sentences of a document (Marcu and Echihabi, 2002). This indicator lets us learn an edge from s_4 to s_5 below:

s_4 *Arafat condemned the bombing.*

s_5 ***However,*** *Netanyahu suspended peace talks.*

3.4 Inferred Edges

We exploit the redundancy of information in MDS documents to infer edges to related sentences. An edge (s, s'') can be inferred if there is an existing edge (s, s') and s' and s'' express similar information. As an example, the edge (s_6, s_7) can be inferred based on edge (s_4, s_5):

s_6 *Arafat condemned the attack.*

s_7 *Netanyahu has suspended the talks.*

To infer edges we need an algorithm to identify sentences expressing similar information. To identify these pairs, we extract Open Information Extraction (Banko et al., 2007) relational tuples for each sentence, and we mark any pair of sentences with an equivalent relational tuple as redundant (see Section 4.3). The inferred edges allow us to propagate within-document discourse information to sentences from other documents.

3.5 Co-referent Mentions

A sentence s_j will not be clearly understood in isolation and may need another sentence s_i in its context, if s_j has a general reference (*e.g.*, 'the president') pointing to a specific entity or event in s_i (*e.g.*, 'President Bill Clinton'). We construct edges based on coreference mentions, as predicted by Stanford's coreference system (Lee et al., 2011). We are able to identify syntactic edge (s_8, s_9):

s_8 *Pres. Clinton expressed sympathy for Israel.*

s_9 ***He** said the attack should not derail the deal.*

3.6 Edge Weights

We weight each edge in the ADG by adding the number of distinct indicators used to construct that edge – if sentences s and s' have an edge because of a discourse marker and a deverbal reference, the edge weight $w_G(s, s')$ will be two. We also include negative edges in the ADG. $w_G(s, s')$ is negative if s' contains a deverbal noun reference, a discourse marker, or a co-reference mention that is not fulfilled by s. For example, if s' contains a discourse marker, and s is neither the sentence directly preceding s' and there is no inferred discourse link between s and s', then we will add a negative edge $w_G(s, s')$.

3.7 Preliminary Graph Evaluation

We evaluated the quality of the ADG used by G-FLOW, which is important not only for its use in MDS, but also because the ADG may be used for other applications like topic tracking and decomposing an event into sub-events. One author randomly chose 750 edges and labeled an edge correct if the pair of sentences did have a discourse relationship between them and incorrect otherwise. 62% of the edges accurately reflected a discourse relationship. Our ADG has on average 31 edges per sentence for a dataset in which each document cluster has on average 253 sentences. This evaluation includes only the positive edges.

4 Summary Generation

We denote a candidate summary X to be a sequence of sentences $\langle x_1, x_2, \ldots, x_{|X|}\rangle$. G-FLOW's summarization algorithm searches through the space of ordered summaries and scores each candidate summary along the dimensions of coherence (Section 4.1), salience (Section 4.2) and redundancy (Section 4.3). G-FLOW returns the summary that maximizes a joint objective function (Section 4.4).

weight	feature
-0.037	position in document
0.033	from first three sentences
-0.035	number of people mentions
0.111	contains money
0.038	sentence length > 20
0.137	length of sentence
0.109	#sentences verbs appear in (any form)
0.349	#sentences common nouns appear in
0.355	#sentences proper nouns appear in

Table 2: Linear regression features for salience.

4.1 Coherence

G-FLOW estimates coherence of a candidate summary via the ADG. We define coherence as the sum of edge weights between successive summary sentences. For disconnected sentence pairs, the edge weight is zero.

$$Coh(X) = \sum_{i=1..|X|-1} w_{G+}(x_i, x_{i+1}) + \lambda w_{G-}(x_i, x_{i+1})$$

w_{G+} represents positive edges and w_{G-} represents negative edge weights. λ is a tradeoff coefficient for positive and negative weights, which is tuned using the methodology described in Section 4.4.

4.2 Salience

Salience is the inherent value of each sentence to the documents. We compute salience of a summary ($Sal(X)$) as the sum of the saliences of individual sentences ($\sum_i Sal(x_i)$).

To estimate salience of a sentence, G-FLOW uses a linear regression classifier trained on ROUGE scores over the DUC'03 dataset. The classifier uses surface features designed to identify sentences that cover important concepts. The complete list of features and learned weights is in Table 2. The classifier finds a sentence more salient if it mentions nouns or verbs that are present in more sentences across the documents. The highest ranked features are the last three – number of other sentences that mention a noun or a verb in the given sentence. We use the same procedure as in deverbal nouns for detecting verb mentions that appear as nouns in other sentences (Section 3.1).

4.3 Redundancy

We also wish to avoid redundancy. G-FLOW first processes each sentence with a state-of-the-art Open Information extractor OLLIE (Mausam et al., 2012), which converts a sentence into its component relational tuples of the form (arg1, relational phrase, arg2).[3] For example, it finds (Militants, bombed, a marketplace) as a tuple from sentence s_{12}.

Two sentences will express redundant information if they both contain the same or synonymous component fact(s). Unfortunately, detecting synonymy even at relational tuple level is very hard. G-FLOW approximates this synonymy by considering two relational tuples synonymous if the relation phrases contain verbs that are synonyms of each other, have at least one synonymous argument, and are timestamped within a day of each other. Because the input documents cover related events, these relatively weak rules provide good performance. The same algorithm is used for inferring edges for the ADG (Section 3.4). This algorithm can detect that the following sentences express redundant information:

s_{12} *Militants bombed a marketplace in Jerusalem.*

s_{13} *He alerted Arafat after assailants attacked the busy streets of Mahane Yehuda.*

4.4 Objective Function

The objective function needs to balance coherence, salience and redundancy and also honor the given budget, *i.e.*, maximum summary length B. G-FLOW treats redundancy and budget as hard constraints and coherence and salience as soft. Coherence is necessarily soft as the graph is approximate. While previous MDS systems specifically maximized coverage, in preliminary experiments on a development set, we found that adding a coverage term did not improve G-FLOW's performance. We optimize:

$$\begin{aligned} \textbf{maximize:} \quad & F(x) \triangleq Sal(X) + \alpha Coh(X) - \beta|X| \\ s.t. \quad & \textstyle\sum_{i=1..|X|} len(x_i) < B \\ & \forall x_i, x_j \in X : \text{redundant}(x_i, x_j) = 0 \end{aligned}$$

Here len refers to the sentence length. We add $|X|$ term (the number of sentences in the summary) to avoid picking many short sentences, which may increase coherence and salience scores at the cost of overall summary quality.

The parameters α, β and λ (see Section 4.1) are tuned automatically using a grid search over a development set as follows. We manually generate *extractive* summaries for each document cluster in our development set (DUC'03) and choose the parameter setting that minimizes $|F(X_{\text{G-FLOW}}) - F(X^*)|$ summed over all document clusters. F is the objective function, $X_{\text{G-FLOW}}$ is the summary produced by G-FLOW and X^* is the manual summary.

This constraint optimization problem is NP hard, which can be shown by using a reduction of the longest path problem. For this reason, G-FLOW uses local search to reach an approximation of the optimum. G-FLOW employs stochastic hill climbing with random restarts as the base search algorithm. At each step, the search either adds a sentence, removes a sentence, replaces a sentence by another, or reorders a pair of sentences. The initial summary for random restarts is constructed as follows. We first pick the highest salience sentence with no incoming negative edges as the first sentence. The following sentences are probabilistically added one at a time based on the summary score up to that sentence. The initial summary is complete when there are no possible sentences left to fit within the budget. Intuitively, this heuristic chooses a good starting point by selecting a first sentence that does not rely on context and subsequent sentences that build a high scoring summary. As with all local search algorithms, this algorithm is highly scalable and can easily apply to large collections of related documents, but does not guarantee global optima.

5 Experiments

Because summaries are intended for human consumption we focused on human evaluations. We hired workers on Amazon Mechanical Turk (AMT) to evaluate the summaries. Our evaluation addresses the following questions: (1) how do G-FLOW summaries compare against the state-of-the-art in MDS (Section 5.2)? (2) what is G-FLOW's performance along important summarization dimensions such as coherence and redundancy (Section 5.3)? (3) how does G-FLOW perform on coverage as measured by ROUGE (Section 5.3.1)? (4) how much do the components of G-FLOW's objective function contribute to performance (Section 5.4)? (5) how do G-FLOW's summaries compare to human summaries?

5.1 Data and Systems

We evaluated the systems on the Task 2 DUC'04 multi-document summarization dataset. This dataset consists of 50 clusters of related documents, each of which contains 10 documents. Each cluster of doc-

[3] Available from http://ollie.cs.washington.edu

uments also includes four gold standard summaries used for evaluation. As in the DUC'04 competition, we allowed 665 bytes for each summary including spaces and punctuation. We used DUC'03 as our development set, which contains 30 document clusters, again with approximately 10 documents each.

We compared G-FLOW against four systems. The first is a recent MDS extractive summarizer, which we choose for its state-of-the-art ROUGE scores (Lin and Bilmes, 2011).[4] The second is a pipeline of Lin's system followed by a reimplementation of a state-of-the-art sentence reordering system (Li et al., 2011a). We refer to these systems as LIN and LIN-LI, respectively. This second baseline allows us to quantify the advantage of using coherence as a factor in both sentence extraction and ordering.

We also compare against the system that had the highest coherence ratings at DUC'04 (Nobata and Sekine, 2004), which we refer to as NOBATA. As this system did not preform sentence ordering on its output, we also compare against a pipeline of Nobata's system and the sentence reordering system. We refer to this system as NOBATA-LI.

Lastly, to evaluate how well the system performs against human generated summaries, we compare against the gold standard summaries provided by DUC.

5.2 Overall Summary Quality

Following (Haghighi and Vanderwende, 2009) and (Celikyilmaz and Hakkani-Tur, 2010), to compare overall summary quality, we asked AMT workers to compare two candidate system summaries. The workers first read a gold standard summary, followed by the two system summaries, and were then asked to choose the better summary from the pair. The system summaries were shown in a random order to remove any bias.

To ensure that workers provided high quality data we added two quality checks. First, we restricted to workers who have an overall approval rating of over 95% on AMT. Second, we asked the workers to briefly describe the main events of the summary. We manually filtered out work where this description was incorrect.

[4]We thank Lin and Bilmes for providing us with their code. Unfortunately, we were unable to obtain other recent MDS systems from their authors.

Six workers compared each pair of summaries. We recorded the scores for each cluster, and report three numbers: the percentages of clusters where a system is more often preferred over the other and the percentage where the two systems are tied. G-FLOW is preferred almost three times as often as LIN:

G-FLOW	Indifferent	LIN
56%	24%	20%

Next, we compared G-FLOW and LIN-LI. Sentence reordering improves performance, but G-FLOW is still overwhelmingly preferred:

G-FLOW	Indifferent	LIN-LI
54%	24%	22%

These results suggest that incorporating coherence in sentence extraction adds significant value to a summarization system. In these experiments, LIN and LIN-LI are preferred in some cases. We analyzed those summaries more carefully, and found that occasionally, G-FLOW will sacrifice a small amount of coverage for coherence, resulting in lower performance in those cases (see Section 5.3.1).

We also compared LIN and LIN-LI, and found that reordering does not improve performance by much.

LIN-LI	Indifferent	LIN
32%	38%	30%

While the scores presented above represent comparisons between G-FLOW and a summarization system with state-of-the-art ROUGE scores, we also compared against a summarization system with state-of-the-art coherence scores – the system with the highest coherence scores from DUC'04, (Nobata and Sekine, 2004). We found that G-FLOW was again preferred:

G-FLOW	Indifferent	NOBATA
68%	10%	22%

Adding in sentence ordering again improved the scores for the comparison system somewhat:

G-FLOW	Indifferent	NOBATA-LI
60%	20%	20%

While these scores show a significant improvement over previous sytems, they do not convey how well G-FLOW compares to the gold standard – manually generated summaries. As a final experiment, we compared G-FLOW and a second, manually generated summary:

G-FLOW	Indifferent	Gold
14%	18%	68%

While we were pleased that in 32% of the cases, Turkers either preferred G-FLOW or were indifferent, there is clearly a lot of room for improvement despite the gains reported over previous sytems.

5.3 Comparison along Summary Dimensions

A high quality summary needs to be good along several dimensions. We asked AMT workers to rate summaries using the quality questions enumerated in DUC'04 evaluation scheme.[5] These questions concern: (1) coherence, (2) useless, confusing, or repetitive text, (3) redundancy, (4) nouns, pronouns, and personal names that are not well-specified (5) entities rementioned in an overly explicit way, (6) ungrammatical sentences, and (7) formatting errors.

We evaluated G-FLOW LIN-LI and NOBATA-LI against the gold standard summaries, using the same AMT scheme as in the previous section. To assess automated performance with respect to the standards set by human summaries, we also evaluated a (different) gold standard summary for each document cluster, using the same Mechanical Turk scheme as in the previous section. The 50 summaries produced by each system were evaluated by four workers. The results are shown in Figure 2.

G-FLOW was rated significantly better than LIN-LI in all categories except 'Redundancy' and significant better than NOBATA-LI on 'Coherence' and 'Referents'. The ratings for 'Coherence', 'Referents', and 'OverlyExplicit' are not surprising given G-FLOW's focus on coherence. The results for 'UselessText' may also be due to G-FLOW's focus on coherence which ideally prevents it from getting off topic. Lastly, G-FLOW may perform better on 'Grammatical' and 'Formatting' because it tends to choose longer sentences than other systems, which are less likely to be sentence segmentation errors. There may also be some bleeding from one dimension to the other – if a worker likes one summary she may score it highly for many dimensions.

Finally, somewhat surprisingly, we find G-FLOW's performance to be nearly that of human summaries. G-FLOW is rated statistically significantly lower than the gold summaries on only 'Redundancy'. Given the results from the previous section, G-FLOW is likely performing worse on categories not conveyed in these scores, such as Coverage, which we examine next.

[5]http://duc.nist.gov/duc2004/quality.questions.txt

System	R	F
NOBATA	30.44	34.36
Best system in DUC-04	38.28	37.94
Takamura and Okumura (2009)	38.50	-
LIN	39.35	38.90
G-FLOW	37.33	37.43
Gold Standard Summaries	**40.03**	**40.03**

Table 3: ROUGE-1 recall and F-measure results (%) on DUC-04. Some values are missing because not all systems reported both F-measure and recall.

5.3.1 Coverage Evaluation using ROUGE

Most recent research has focused on the ROUGE evaluation, and thus implicitly on coverage of information in a summary. To estimate the coverage of G-FLOW, we compared the systems on ROUGE (Lin, 2004). We calculated ROUGE-1 scores for G-FLOW, LIN, and NOBATA.[6] As sentence ordering does not matter for ROUGE, we do not include LIN-LI or NOBATA-LI in this evaluation. Because our algorithm does not explicitly maximize coverage while LIN does, we expected G-FLOW to perform slightly worse than LIN.

The ROUGE-1 scores for G-FLOW, LIN, NOBATA and other recent MDS systems are listed in Table 3. We also include the ROUGE-1 scores for the gold summaries (compared to the other gold summaries). G-FLOW has slightly lower scores than LIN and the gold standard summaries, but much higher scores than NOBATA. G-FLOW only scores significantly lower than LIN and the gold standard summaries.

We can conclude that good summaries have both the characteristics listed in the quality dimensions, and good coverage. The gold standard summaries outperform G-FLOW on both ROUGE scores and the quality dimension scores, and therefore, outperform G-FLOW on overall comparison. However, G-FLOW is preferred to LIN-LI in addition to NOBATA-LI indicating that its quality scores outweigh its ROUGE scores in that comparison. An improvement to G-FLOW may focus on increasing

[6]ROUGE version 1.5.5 with options: -a -c 95 -b 665 -m -n 4 -w 1.2

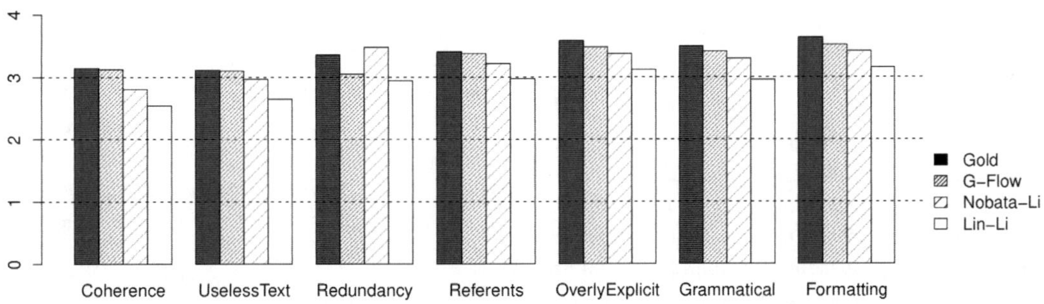

Figure 2: Ratings for the systems. 0 is the lowest possible score and 4 is the highest possible score. G-FLOW is rated significantly higher than LIN-LI on all categories, except for 'Redundancy', and significantly higher than NOBATA-LI on 'Coherence' and 'Referents'. G-FLOW is only significantly lower than the gold standard on 'Redundancy'.

coverage while retaining strengths such as coherence.

5.4 Ablation Experiments

In this ablation study, we evaluated the contribution of the main components of G-FLOW – coherence and salience. The details of the experiments are the same as in the experiment described in Section 5.2.

We first measured the importance of coherence in summary generation. This system G-FLOW-SAL is identical to the full system except that it does not include the coherence term in the objective function (see Section 4.4). The results show that coherence is very important to G-FLOW's performance:

G-FLOW	Indifferent	G-FLOW-SAL
54%	26%	20%

Similarly, we evaluated the contribution of salience. This system G-FLOW-COH does not include the salience term in the objective function:

G-FLOW	Indifferent	G-FLOW-COH
60%	20%	20%

Without salience, the system produces readable, but highly irrelevant summaries.

5.5 Agreement of Expert & AMT Workers

Because summary evaluation is a relatively complex task, we compared AMT workers' annotations with expert annotations from DUC'04. We randomly selected ten summaries from each of the seven DUC'04 annotators, and asked four Turk workers to annotate them on the DUC'04 quality questions. For each DUC'04 annotator, we selected all pairs of summaries where one summary was judged more than one point better than the other summary. We compared whether the workers (voting as in Section 5.2) likewise judged that summary better than the second summary. We found that the annotations agreed in 75% of cases. When we looked only at pairs more than two points different, the agreement was 80%. Thus, given the subjective nature of the task, we feel reasonably confident that the AMT annotations are informative, and that the dramatic preference of G-FLOW over the baseline systems is due to a substantial improvement in its summaries.

6 Conclusion

In this paper, we present G-FLOW, a multi-document summarization system aimed at generating coherent summaries. While previous MDS systems have focused primarily on salience and coverage but not coherence, G-FLOW generates an ordered summary by jointly optimizing coherence and salience. G-FLOW estimates coherence by using an approximate discourse graph, where each node is a sentence from the input documents and each edge represents a discourse relationship between two sentences. Manual evaluations demonstrate that G-FLOW generates substantially better summaries than a pipeline of state-of-the-art sentence selection and reordering components. ROUGE scores, which measure summary coverage, show that G-FLOW sacrifices a small amount of coverage for overall readability and coherence. Comparisons to gold standard summaries show that G-FLOW must improve in coverage to equal the quality of manually written summaries. We believe this research has applications to other areas of summarization such as update summarization and query based summarization, and we are interested in investigating these topics in future work.

Acknowledgements

We thank Luke Zettlemoyer, Lucy Vanderwende, Hal Daume III, Pushpak Bhattacharyya, Chris Quirk, Erik Frey, Tony Fader, Michael Schmitz, Alan Ritter, Melissa Winstanley, and the three anonymous reviewers for helpful conversations and feedback on earlier drafts. We also thank Lin and Bilmes for providing us with the code for their system. This research was supported in part by NSF grant IIS-0803481, ONR grant N00014-11-1-0294, and DARPA contract FA8750-13-2-0019, and carried out at the University of Washington's Turing Center. This paper was also supported in part by the Intelligence Advanced Research Projects Activity (IARPA) via Air Force Research Laboratory (AFRL) contract number FA8650-10-C-7058. The U.S. Government is authorized to reproduce and distribute reprints for Governmental purposes notwithstanding any copyright annotation thereon. The views and conclusions contained herein are those of the authors and should not be interpreted as necessarily representing the official policies or endorsements, either expressed or implied, of IARPA, AFRL, or the U.S. Government.

References

Amjad Abu-Jbara and Dragomir R. Radev. 2011. Coherent citation-based summarization of scientific papers. In *Proceedings of ACL 2011*, pages 500–509.

Ahmet Aker, Trevor Cohn, and Robert Gaizauskas. 2010. Multi-document summarization using A * search and discriminative training. In *Proceedings of EMNLP 2010*.

Michele Banko, Michael Cafarella, Stephen Soderland, Matt Broadhead, and Oren Etzioni. 2007. Open information extraction from the web. In *Proceedings of IJCAI 2007*, pages 68–74.

Regina Barzilay and Michael Elhadad. 1997. Using lexical chains for text summarization. In *Proceedings of the ACL Workshop on Intelligent Scalable Text Summarization*, pages 10–17.

Regina Barzilay and Mirella Lapata. 2008. Modeling local coherence: An entity-based approach. *Computational Linguistics*, 34(1):1–34.

Regina Barzilay, Noemie Elhadad, and Kathleen R McKeown. 2001. Sentence ordering in multidocument summarization. In *Proceedings of HLT 2001*, pages 1–7.

Danushka Bollegala, Naoaki Okazaki, and Mitsuru Ishizuka. 2010. A bottom-up approach to sentence ordering for multi-document summarization. *Information Process Management*, 46(1):89–109.

Jaime Carbonell and Jade Goldstein. 1998. The use of MMR, diversity-based reranking for reordering documents and producing summaries. In *Proceedings of SIGIR 1998*, pages 335–336.

Asli Celikyilmaz and Dilek Hakkani-Tur. 2010. A hybrid hierarchical model for multi-document summarization. In *Proceedings of ACL 2010*, pages 815–824.

Angel Chang and Christopher Manning. 2012. SUTIME: A library for recognizing and normalizing time expressions. In *Proceedings of LREC 2012*.

Gunes Erkan and Dragomir R Radev. 2004. LexRank: Graph-based centrality as salience in text summarization. *Journal of Artificial Intelligence Research*, 22(1):457–479.

Barbara Grosz and Candace Sidner. 1986. Attention, intentions, and the structure of discourse. *Computational Linguistics*, 12(3):175–204.

Aria Haghighi and Lucy Vanderwende. 2009. Exploring content models for multi-document summarization. *Proceedings of NAACL 2009*, pages 362–370.

Maria Lucia Castro Jorge and Thiago Alexandre Salgueiro Pardo. 2010. *Multi-Document Summarization: Content Selection based on CST Model (Cross-document Structure Theory)*. Ph.D. thesis, Núcleo Interinstitucional de Lingüística Computacional (NILC).

Mirella Lapata. 2003. Probabilistic text structuring: Experiments with sentence ordering. In *Proceedings of ACL 2003*, pages 545–552.

Heeyoung Lee, Yves Peirsman, Angel Chang, Nathanael Chambers, Mihai Surdeanu, and Dan Jurafsky. 2011. Stanford's multi-pass sieve coreference resolution system at the CoNLL-2011 shared task. In *CoNLL 2011 Shared Task*.

Peifeng Li, Guangxi Deng, and Qiaoming Zhu. 2011a. Using context inference to improve sentence ordering for multi-document summarization. In *Proceedings of IJCNLP 2011*, pages 1055–1061.

Peng Li, Yinglin Wang, Wei Gao, and Jing Jiang. 2011b. Generating aspect-oriented multi-document summarization with event-aspect model. In *Proceedings of EMNLP 2011*, pages 1137–1146.

Hui Lin and Jeff Bilmes. 2011. A class of submodular functions for document summarization. In *Proceedings of ACL 2011*, pages 510–520.

Chin-Yew Lin. 2004. ROUGE: A package for automatic evaluation of summaries. In *Text Summarization Branches Out: Proceedings of the ACL-04 Workshop*, pages 74–81.

Annie Louis and Ani Nenkova. 2009. Automatic summary evaluation without using human models. In *Proceedings of EMNLP 2009*, pages 306–314.

Annie Louis, Aravind Joshi, Rashmi Prasad, and Ani Nenkova. 2010. Using entity features to classify implicit discourse relations. In *Proceedings of SIGDIAL 2010*, pages 59–62.

Inderjeet Mani. 2001. *Automatic Summarization*. John Benjamins Publishing Co, Amsterdam/Philadelphia.

William C. Mann and Sandra A. Thompson. 1988. Rhetorical structure theory: Toward a functional theory of text organization. *Text*, 8(3):243–281.

Daniel Marcu and Abdessamad Echihabi. 2002. An unsupervised approach to recognizing discourse relations. In *Proceedings of ACL 2002*, pages 368–375.

Daniel Marcu. 1997. From discourse structures to text summaries. In *Proceedings of the ACL Workshop on Intelligent Scalable Text Summarization*, pages 82–88.

Mausam, Michael Schmitz, Robert Bart, Stephen Soderland, and Oren Etzioni. 2012. Open language learning for information extraction. In *Proceedings of EMNLP 2012*, pages 523–534.

Kathleen McKeown and Dragomir Radev. 1995. Generating summaries of multiple news articles. In *Proceedings of SIGIR 1995*, pages 74–82.

Chikashi Nobata and Satoshi Sekine. 2004. Crl/nyu summarization system at duc-2004. In *Proceedings of DUC 2004*.

Naoaki Okazaki, Yutaka Matsuo, and Mitsuru Ishizuka. 2004. Improving chronological sentence ordering by precedence relation. In *Proceedings of COLING 2004*, pages 750–756.

Emily Pitler, Annie Louis, and Ani Nenkova. 2010. Automatic evaluation of linguistic quality in multi-document summarization. In *Proceedings of ACL 2010*, pages 544–554.

Rashmi Prasad, Nikhil Dinesh, Alan Lee, Eleni Miltsakaki, Livio Robaldo, Aravind Joshi, and Bonnie Webber. 2008. The Penn Discourse TreeBank 2.0. In *Proceedings of LREC 2008*.

Vahed Qazvinian, Dragomir R. Radev, and Arzucan Özgür. 2010. Citation summarization through keyphrase extraction. In *Proceedings of COLING 2010*, pages 895–903.

Dragomir R. Radev and Kathleen R. McKeown. 1998. Generating natural language summaries from multiple on-line sources. *Computational Linguistics*, 24(3):469–500.

Dragomir R. Radev, Hongyan Jing, Malgorzata Stys, and Daniel Tam. 2004. Centroid-based summarization of multiple documents. *Information Processing and Management*, 40(6):919–938.

Dragomir R. Radev. 2004. LexRank: Graph-based lexical centrality as salience in text summarization. *Journal of Artificial Intelligence Research*, 22(1):457–479.

Horacio Saggion and Robert Gaizauskas. 2004. Multi-document summarization by cluster/profile relevance and redundancy removal. In *Proceedings of DUC 2004*.

Horacio Saggion and Guy Lapalme. 2002. Generating indicative-informative summaries with sumUM. *Computational Linguistics*, 28(4):497–526.

Dafna Shahaf and Carlos Guestrin. 2010. Connecting the dots between news articles. In *Proceedings of KDD 2010*, pages 623–632.

Chao Shen and Tao Li. 2010. Multi-document summarization via the minimum dominating set. In *Proceedings of Coling 2010*, pages 984–992.

Maite Taboada and William C. Mann. 2006. Applications of rhetorical structure theory. *Discourse Studies*, 8(4):567–588.

Hiroya Takamura and Manabu Okumura. 2009. Text summarization model based on maximum coverage problem and its variant. In *Proceedings of EACL 2009*, pages 781–789.

Florian Wolf and Edward Gibson. 2005. Representing discourse coherence: A corpus-based study. *Computational Linguistics*, 31(2):249–288.

Zhu Zhang, Sasha Blair-Goldensohn, and Dragomir R. Radev. 2002. Towards CST-enhanced summarization. In *Proceedings of AAAI 2002*, pages 439–445.

Renxian Zhang, Li Wenjie, and Lu Qin. 2010. Sentence ordering with event-enriched semantics and two-layered clustering for multi-document news summarization. In *Proceedings of COLING 2010*, pages 1489–1497.

Generating Expressions that Refer to Visible Objects

Margaret Mitchell
Johns Hopkins HLTCOE
m.mitchell@jhu.edu

Kees van Deemter
University of Aberdeen
k.vdeemter@abdn.ac.uk

Ehud Reiter
University of Aberdeen
e.reiter@abdn.ac.uk

Abstract

We introduce a novel algorithm for generating referring expressions, informed by human and computer vision and designed to refer to visible objects. Our method separates absolute properties like color from relative properties like size to stochastically generate a diverse set of outputs. Expressions generated using this method are often overspecified and may be underspecified, akin to expressions produced by people. We call such expressions *identifying descriptions*. The algorithm outperforms the well-known Incremental Algorithm (Dale and Reiter, 1995) and the Graph-Based Algorithm (Krahmer et al., 2003; Viethen et al., 2008) across a variety of images in two domains. We additionally motivate an evaluation method for referring expression generation that takes the proposed algorithm's non-determinism into account.

1 Introduction

Referring expression generation (REG) is the task of generating an expression that can identify a referent to a listener. These expressions generally take the form of a definite noun phrase such as "the large orange plate" or "the furry running dog". Research in REG primarily focuses on the subtask of selecting a set of properties that may be used to construct the final surface expression, e.g., ⟨color:orange, size:large, type:plate⟩. This property selection task is optimized to meet different goals: for example, to be identical to those a person would generate in the same situation, or to be unique to the intended referent and no other item in the discourse.

We focus on the task of generating referring expressions for visible objects, specifically with the goal of generating descriptive, human-like referring expressions. We are motivated by the desire to connect this algorithm to input from a computer vision system, and discuss how this may work throughout the paper. Computer vision (CV) does not yet reliably provide features for some of the most frequent properties that people use in visual description (in particular, size-based features), and so we use a gold-standard visual input, evaluating purely on REG. The proposed algorithm, which we call the Visible Objects Algorithm, is designed to approximate human variation identifying an object in a group of visible, real world objects.

Our primary contributions are the following. Background for each issue is provided in Section 2:

1. An approach accounting for overspecification, underspecification, and some of the known effects of vision on reference.
2. A function to approximate the stochastic nature of reference. This reflects that people will produce different references to the same object.
3. A separation between absolute properties like color, which may be detected directly by CV, from relative properties like size and location, which require reasoning over visual features to determine an appropriate form (e.g., height/width and distance features between pixels are available from a visual input; saying an object is "tall" requires further reasoning).
4. An evaluation method for non-deterministic REG that aligns generated and observed data and calculates accuracy over alignments.

2 Motivation & Overview

Most implemented algorithms for referring expression generation focus on unique identification of a referent, determining the set of properties that distinguish a particular target object from the other objects in the scene (the *contrast set*) (Dale, 1989; Reiter and Dale, 1992; Dale and Reiter, 1995; Krahmer et al., 2003; Areces et al., 2008). This view of reference was first outlined by Olson (1970), "the specification of an intended referent relative to a set of alternatives". A substantial body of evidence now shows that contrastive value relative to alternatives is not the only factor motivating speakers' property choices, specifically in visual domains. The phenomena of *overspecification* and *redundancy*, where speakers select properties that have little or no contrastive value, was observed in early developmental studies in visual domains (Ford and Olson, 1975; Whitehurst, 1976; Sonnenschein, 1985) as well as later studies on adult speakers in visual domains (Pechmann, 1989; Engelhardt et al., 2006; Koolen et al., 2011). The related phenomenon of *underspecification*, where speakers select a set of properties that do not linguistically specify the referent, has also received some attention, particularly in visual domains (Clark et al., 1983; Kelleher et al., 2005).

These findings make sense in light of visual evidence that some properties "pop out" in the scene (Treisman and Gelade, 1980), and speakers may begin referring before scanning the full set of scene objects (Pechmann, 1989), selecting those properties that are salient for them (Horton and Keysar, 1996; Bard et al., 2009) without spending a great amount of cognitive effort considering the perception of a hearer (Keysar and Henly, 2002).

We take this evidence to suggest an approach for a visual reference algorithm that generates natural, human-like reference by generating visual properties that are salient for a speaker.[1] We can understand what is salient visually (what does the visual system first respond to, what guides attention?), linguistically (what do people tend to mention in visual scenes?), and cognitively, which we will not have room to discuss in this paper (what is atypical for this object?); as well as in terms of broader notions of salience, e.g., discourse salience (Krahmer and Theune, 2002).

Figure 1: Relative properties, like size and location, are difficult to obtain from a two-dimensional image. We find it easy to perceive the background object as larger than the one in the front; but they are technically the same size in the image (from Murray et al. (2006)).

This suggests a paradigm shift in the generation task when referring to visible objects, if the goal is to produce human-like reference. In particular, this suggests moving from selecting properties that *rule out* other scene objects to selecting properties that are salient for the speaker (visually, conversationally, based on previous experiences, etc.). This mirrors related research on the tradeoff between audience design and egocentrism in language production (Clark and Murphy, 1982; Horton and Keysar, 1996; Bard et al., 2009; Gann and Barr, 2013). Under- and overspecification naturally fall out from such an approach, with no need to specifically model either phenomenon.

Perhaps unsurprisingly, the set of properties that are visually salient and the set of properties that are linguistically salient largely overlap. Color is the first property our visual system processes, followed soon after by size (Murray et al., 2006; Fang et al., 2008; Schwarzkopf et al., 2010); and people tend to use color (Pechmann, 1989; Viethen et al., 2012) and size when identifying objects, with size common when there is another object of the same type in the scene (Brown-Schmidt and Tanenhaus, 2006).

Following this, our algorithm gives a privileged position to these properties, processing them first. Using computer vision techniques to determine an object's color works reasonably well (Berg et al., 2011), and the relevant visual features for this task may be useful in future work to return several possible color labels that capture differences in lexical choice (cf. Reiter and Sripada (2002)).

Detecting size does not work well (Forsyth,

[1]We can also add functionality to ensure that a referent is uniquely identified against the contrast set (whether or not that reflects what a person would do), which we will describe.

2011); and when it does, it will likely not take the form supposed in recent generation work. Most REG algorithms use a predefined single-featured value, such as "big"; however, given an image-based input, obtaining such a value requires (1) determining how the object is situated in a three-dimensional space, difficult to obtain from a two-dimensional image (see Figure 1); and (2) determining what the value should be: object detectors currently can provide the height and width of the location where an object is likely to exist (its bounding box), as well as the x- and y-axis locations of the pixels within the object detection; but a value from these features like "big", "tall", or "long" requires further reasoning. As such, we incorporate the top-performing size algorithm introduced in Mitchell et al. (2011), which takes as input the height and widths of objects in the image and outputs a size value or NONE, indicating that size should not be used to describe the object.

In addition to color and size, location and orientation begin to be processed early on in the visual system (Treisman, 1985; Itti and Koch, 2001), with our first perception of location corresponding to basic cues of where an object is relative to our focus of attention. For an input image, this simple type of location corresponds to surface forms such as, e.g., "on the right of the image" or "at the top of the image". Along with size, location and orientation make up the three primary relative properties that we aim to generate language for.

After the simple forms for color, size, location, and orientation properties are processed, our visual system feeds forward to two parallel pathways, the so-called "what" and "where" pathways (Ungerleider and Mishkin, 1982), which process properties with growing complexity. The "what" pathway includes absolute properties like shape and material, which computer vision has had some success detecting (Ferrari and Zisserman, 2007; Farhadi et al., 2009) while the "where" pathway corresponds to more complex spatial orientation and location information, such as where objects are relative to one another and which way they are facing.

To begin connecting this process to the generation of human-like descriptions of visible objects, we start with the following simplification: Color and size have a privileged status, the first properties processed. These are followed by the relative properties

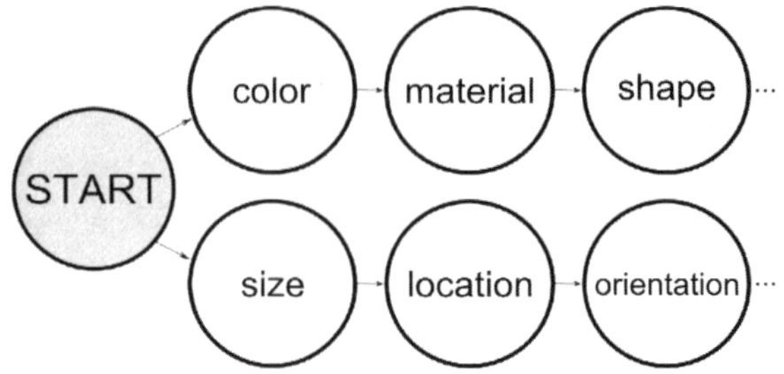

Figure 2: Initial model for generating visual reference.

of location and orientation, which may feed forward to more complex location and orientation properties in one pathway; and absolute properties following color, like material and shape, which may be processed in another pathway.

This gives us the basic model for generating reference to visible objects shown in Figure 2. To generate reference in this model, nodes correspond to general visual *attributes* and may generate forms for visual *properties* (attribute:value pairs). That is, a property such as color:red is generated from the attribute node color and a property such as size:tall is generated from the attribute node size. We are limited by existing REG corpora in which properties we can evaluate; in this paper, we examine the effect of the independent selection of color and size, followed by location and orientation.[2]

Generating human-like expressions in this setting begins to be possible by adopting recent proposals that REG handle speaker variation (Viethen and Dale, 2010) and the non-deterministic nature of reference (van Gompel et al., 2012; van Deemter et al., 2012b). We can capture such variation simply by estimating α_{att}, the likelihood that an attribute att generates a corresponding visual property. During generation, the algorithm passes through each attribute node, and uses this estimate to stochastically add each property to the output property set.

Such a non-deterministic process means that the algorithm will not return the same output every time, which offers new challenges for evaluation. If we run the algorithm 1,000 times, we have a distribution over several possible output property sets. From this we can obtain the majority set and check if it matches the majority observed set. Similarly, we can

[2]We have also built an algorithm and corpus with more complex properties in order to tease out further details of visual reference, but must leave these details for follow up work; for now, we focus on the properties common to REG corpora.

run the algorithm for as many instances as we have in our test data, and see how well the property sets it produces aligns to the observed property sets. We discuss evaluation using both methods in Section 6.

3 The State of the Art in REG

3.1 Algorithms

In order to understand how this approach compares to the state of the art in REG, we evaluate against two of the most well-known algorithms, the Incremental Algorithm (Dale and Reiter, 1995) and the Graph-Based Algorithm (Krahmer et. al, 2003, as implemented in Viethen et al., 2008). Details on these algorithms are available in their corresponding papers. As a brief summary, both algorithms formalize the objects in the discourse as a set of properties (attribute:value pairs). For example, one object may be represented as ⟨type:box, color:red, size:large⟩. The task is to find the set of properties that uniquely specify the referent. This is known as a content selection problem, and the set of properties chosen by the algorithm is called a *distinguishing description.*

The Incremental Algorithm (IA) proceeds by iterating through attributes in a predefined order (a preference order), and for each attribute, it checks whether specifying a value would rule out at least one item in the contrast set that has not already been ruled out. If it will, the attribute:value is added to the distinguishing description. This process continues until all contrast items (distractors) are ruled out or all available properties have been checked. We use the implementation of the IA available from the NLTK (Bird et al., 2009).[3]

In the Graph-Based Algorithm (GB), the objects in the discourse are represented within a labeled directed graph, and content selection is a subgraph construction problem. Each object is represented as a vertex, with properties for an object represented as self-edges on the object vertex, and spatial relations between objects represented as edges between vertices. The algorithm seeks to find the cheapest subgraph, calculated from the edge costs. We use the implementation available from Viethen et al. (2008), which adds a preference order to decide between edges with the same cost during search. This has been one of the best-performing systems in recent generation challenges (Gatt and Belz, 2008; Gatt et al., 2009).

An important commonality between these algorithms, and much of the work on REG that they have influenced, is the focus on *unique identification* and operating *deterministically.* Both produce one property set (and only one), and stop once a target item has been uniquely identified (or else fail). Their driving goal is to rule out distractor objects.

In the approach introduced here, the algorithm produces a distribution over several possible outputs, and the initial driving mechanism is based on likelihood estimates for each attribute independent of the other objects in the scene, rather than ruling out all distractors. This offers a way to capture some aspects of human-like reference, including under- and overspecification and speaker variation. Due to the fundamentally different objective of this algorithm, we will call the kind of expression it generates an *identifying description*, following Searle (1969). This is a description that the system finds (1) useful to describe the referent and (2) true of the referent.

4 The Algorithm

The Visible Objects Algorithm iterates through lists of visible attributes, stochastically adding properties to the property set it will generate. After this initial search, the algorithm then scans through the objects in the scene, roughly corresponding to how people scan a scene when referring (Pechmann, 1989). The target referent type, corresponding to the head noun in the final generated description, is added to the property set at the end of the algorithm.

We represent the basic components of the algorithm graphically in Figure 3. Full code is available online.[4] After START, the algorithm proceeds in parallel through a list of absolute attributes and a list of relative attributes. The likelihood of generating a property is a function of the prior likelihood α_{att} and γ, a penalty on the length of the constructed property set up to that point. This ensures that only a few properties are generated for a referent, and the expression will not be too complex. This is also in line with recent research suggesting that there are rarely more than three adjectives in a visual noun phrase

[3] https://github.com/nltk/nltk_contrib/blob/master/nltk_contrib/referring.py retrieved 1.Aug.2012.

[4] https://github.com/itallow/VisibleObjectsAlgorithm.

(Berg et al., 2011). Once the algorithm hits END, it scans through the objects in the scene. If it finds an object that is the same type as the referent object, the algorithm checks through the attributes again in a preference order akin to the IA, comparing the object's properties against the referent's and generating properties as a function of the length penalty alone. If the algorithm does not find an object that it is the same type, no further properties are added.

4.1 Requirements

The algorithm requires the following:

1. Prior likelihood estimates on the inclusion of different attributes. Represented as α_{att}.
2. Ordered list of absolute attributes beyond color. Represented as `AP`.
3. Ordered list of relative attributes beyond size. Represented as `RP`.
4. Ordered list of all attributes. Represented as `P`.
5. Ordered list specifying the order in which to scan through other scene objects. The current implementation uses the order in which the objects are listed in the corpora it is run on.

(1) is similar to the cost functions for GB, but attributes are selected non-deterministically using prior likelihoods. (2), (3), and (4) are similar to the IA's and GB's preference order. For our evaluation corpora, `AP` is empty and `RP` contains location and orientation. (5) is novel to this algorithm, defining an order in which to compare the target object against other objects in the scene. This is inspired by the process of incremental speech production (Pechmann, 1989), where speakers scan objects during naming, incrementally producing properties.

4.2 The Stochastic Process

Generally speaking, we want to penalize longer descriptions and encourage the attributes that we know people are likely to use. We can encourage a likely attribute by using its prior likelihood as an estimate of whether to include it. We can penalize longer descriptions with a penalty proportional to the length of the property set under construction. In other words, given a prior likelihood estimate for including an attribute att, α_{att}, and the property set constructed so far A, we compute whether to add a property for att to A as a function of α_{att} and the length-based penalty γ:

a. b.

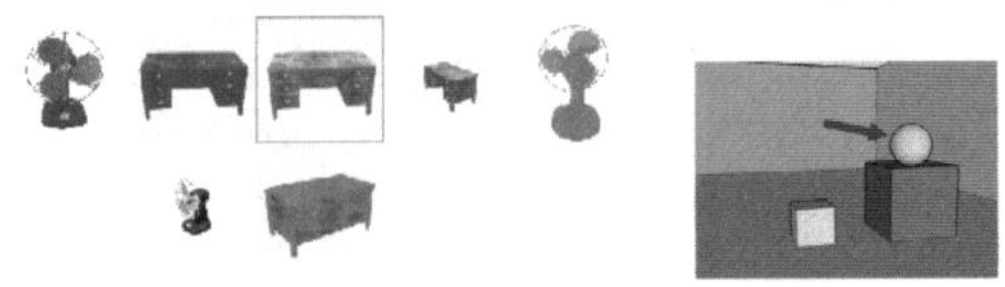

TUNA corpus **GRE3D3 corpus**

Figure 4: Example scenes from corpora.

$$f(A \cup \{x\}) = \gamma\alpha_{att}$$

where

$$\gamma = \begin{cases} \frac{1}{\lambda|A|} & \text{if } |A| > 0 \\ 1 & \text{otherwise} \end{cases}$$

and λ is an empirically determined weight. The algorithm then chooses a random number n, $0 \leq n \leq 1$. If $n < f(A \cup \{x\})$, it adds the property.

4.3 Scanning Through Objects

After the initial pass through the properties, the algorithm compares each object in the scene that is the same type as the target. If the values for an attribute are different, then the corresponding property is added to the property set based on the length penalty alone; when the goal is unique identification, the algorithm can use no penalty. In development, we found that incrementally scanning through objects after initially adding properties resulted in better performance than an algorithm that did not contain this step.

4.4 Worked Example

Suppose the input in Figure 6 (visualized in Figure 4a), with the goal of referring to obj_1 by producing a property set A. First, the algorithm scans through color and size in parallel. For color, it finds the corresponding value grey; with a computer vision input, this would be possible using the object pixels as features. There is no length penalty at this point ($|A|$=0), so it adds the property color:grey to A with likelihood α_{color}. For our evaluation domains, α_{color} is around .90 across folds, and so a color property is usually added.

For size, the algorithm finds an appropriate value using the Size Algorithm from Mitchell et al. (2011). The Size Algorithm uses the average height and

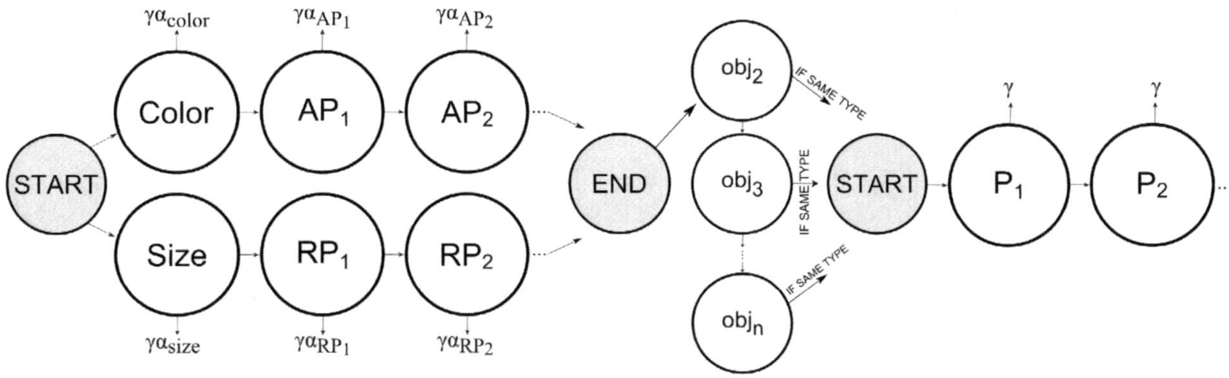

Figure 3: Basic model for generating visual reference.

width of all objects that are the same type as the referent object; in this case, obj2, obj3, obj4. This returns a size value large, and so the property size:large is added to A with likelihood α_{size} (around .40 to .70 across folds, depending on the domain).

The most likely property set at this point is simply ⟨color:grey⟩. The next most likely is ⟨color:grey, size:large⟩, then ⟨size:large⟩. There are no further absolute properties in this example, but there are values for the relative attributes loc (location) and ori (orientation). Assuming RP=⟨location, orientation⟩, the algorithm first analyzes location, then orientation. A location property is added to A with likelihood α_{loc} multiplied by the length penalty $\gamma=\frac{1}{(\lambda\times1)}$ if A=⟨color:grey⟩; $\gamma=\frac{1}{(\lambda\times2)}$ if A=⟨color:grey, size:large⟩, etc.; and an orientation property is added to A with likelihood α_{ori} multiplied by the length penalty $\gamma=\frac{1}{(\lambda\times1)}$ if the property set is ⟨color:grey⟩, etc. At this point, the likelihood of adding further properties quickly diminishes.

Once all properties have been analyzed, the algorithm scans through the objects in the scene. For each object obj2...objn, if the object is the same type as the target object obj1, then any different property of the target referent is added to A with a likelihood based on the length penalty alone γ. ⟨type:desk⟩ is added at the end.

For this example scene, the algorithm will generate the property sets ⟨color:grey, type:desk⟩, ⟨color:grey, size:large, type:desk⟩, ⟨size:large, type:desk⟩, ⟨color:grey, ori:front, type:desk⟩, ⟨color:grey, loc:(3, 1), type:desk⟩, etc., with different frequencies. Due to the length penalty, generated property sets will almost never have more than 3 properties.

tg	color:yellow	size:(63,63)	type:ball	loc:right-hand
lm	color:red	size:(345,345)	type:cube	loc:right-hand
obj3	color:yellow	size:(70,70)	type:cube	loc:left-hand

Figure 5: Example input scene: GRE3D3 corpus. For IA And GB, gold-standard size values are provided rather than measurements (small, large).

obj1	colour:grey	size:(454,454)	type:desk	loc:(3,1)	ori:front
obj2	colour:blue	size:(454,454)	type:desk	loc:(2,1)	ori:front
obj3	colour:red	size:(454,454)	type:desk	loc:(3,2)	ori:back
obj4	colour:green	size:(254,254)	type:desk	loc:(4,1)	ori:left
obj5	colour:blue	size:(454,454)	type:fan	loc:(1,1)	ori:front
obj6	colour:red	size:(454,454)	type:fan	loc:(5,1)	ori:back
obj7	colour:green	size:(254,254)	type:fan	loc:(2,2)	ori:left

Figure 6: Example input scene: TUNA corpus. For IA And GB, gold-standard size values are provided rather than measurements (small, large).

As such, although ⟨color:grey, type:desk⟩ would sufficiently distinguish the intended referent, we instead produce a variety of sets, overspecifying in some instances (e.g., ⟨color:grey, ori:front, type:desk⟩), and with a small chance of underspecifying in others (e.g., ⟨size:large, type:desk⟩).

5 Evaluation Algorithms & Corpora

5.1 Corpora

We evaluate on two well-known REG corpora, the GRE3D3 corpus (Viethen and Dale, 2008) and the singular furniture section of the TUNA corpus (van Deemter et al., 2006). Both corpora contain expressions elicited to computer-generated objects, and so provide a reasonable starting point for evaluating reference to visible objects. For all algorithms, we evaluate on the selection of referent attributes. Lexical choice and word order are not taken into account. Example images from GRE3D3 and TUNA are shown in Figure 4, and example algorithm input from these corpora are shown in Figures 5 and 6.

In GRE3D3, we evaluate on the selection of type, color, size, and location, but leave aside properties of relatum objects, which are not currently addressed by this algorithm or the IA. In TUNA, we evaluate on the selection of type, color, size and orientation.[5]

5.2 Algorithms

5.2.1 The Incremental Algorithm

The Incremental Algorithm requires a preference order list (PO) specifying the order to iterate through scene attributes. We determine the preference order from corpus frequencies using cross-validation to hold out a test scene and list attributes from the training scenes in descending order. We find that color precedes size in the preference orders, in line with recent research showing that this allows the algorithm to perform optimally on the TUNA corpus (van Deemter et al., 2012a). In development, we find that IA performs best with type as the last attribute in the PO, and report on numbers with this approach.

5.2.2 The Graph-Based Algorithm

The version of the Graph-Based Algorithm that we use is available from Viethen et al. (2008). This algorithm requires (1) a set of cost functions for each edge, and (2) a PO for deciding between properties in the case of a tie. For (1), we use the method from Theune et al. (2011) to assign two costs (0, 1) to the edges. We first determine the relative frequency with which each property is mentioned for a target object, and then create costs for each property using k-means clustering (k=2) in the Weka toolkit (Hall et al., 2009). We refer interested readers to the Theune et al. paper for further details. For (2), we follow the same method as for the Incremental Algorithm.

5.2.3 The Visual Objects Algorithm

The proposed algorithm requires α_{att}, which we estimate as the relative frequency of each attribute att in the training data. The ordered attribute lists for the algorithm (AP, RP and P) are built in the same way as the preference order list for the IA and GB, listing attributes from the training data in order of descending frequency. For these corpora, there are not absolute properties beyond color, so AP is empty.

6 Evaluation

Previous evaluation of REG algorithms have used measurements such as Uniqueness, Minimality, Dice (Belz and Gatt, 2008), and Accuracy (Gatt et al., 2009; Reiter and Belz, 2009). *Uniqueness* is the proportion of outputs that identify the referent uniquely, and *Minimality* is the proportion of outputs that are both minimal and unique. As our goal is to mimic human reference, these metrics are not as useful for the evaluations as the others.

The *Dice* metric provides a value for the similarity between a generated description and a human-produced description, and therefore serves as a reasonable objective measure for how human-like the produced sets are. Given the generated property set (D_S) and the human-produced property set (D_H), Dice is calculated as:

$$\frac{2 \times |D_S \cap D_H|}{|D_S| + |D_H|}$$

For each input domain, we evaluate over boolean values (included or excluded) for the attributes D (see Table 1). Note that this means the specific values for the attributes are not compared. In this formulation based on boolean values, $|D_S|$=$|D_H|$=$|D|$ and Dice reduces to:

$$\frac{|D_S \cap D_H|}{|D|}$$

Calculating Dice over the same number of attributes for both the observed and generated data has the nice mathematical property of making Dice equal to other common metrics for evaluating a model, including Accuracy, Precision, and Recall.[6]

Since the proposed algorithm is stochastic, this introduces a problem in using a metric that compares single expressions. We therefore seek to find the best alignment between the set of expressions produced by the algorithm and the set of expressions produced by people. We formulate this alignment as an assignment problem weighted by Dice. For the corpus of observed property sets H and the corpus of generated property sets S, we find the best align-

[5] We remove location from evaluation in this corpus. Location is not annotated directly, but split such that only x-dimension or y-dimension may be marked for a reference.

[6] A false positive is a false negative, and there are no true negatives, so all four metrics are equivalent.

Example Expression	Corresponding Property Set	Evaluated Property Set
the red ball	⟨color:red, type:ball⟩	type:1 color:1 size:0 loc:0

Table 1: Example human expression and corresponding boolean-valued property set for evaluation in GRE3D3, with D={type, color, size, and location}.

ment x out of all possible alignments X between the corpora:

$$\arg\max_{x \in X} \sum_{(S,H) \in x} \text{Dice}(D_S, D_H)$$

This may be solved in polynomial time using the Hungarian method (Kuhn, 1955; Munkres, 1957). Note that because IA and GB are deterministic, finding an optimal alignment is trivial. We call this method ALIGNED DICE.

It is an open question whether an alignment-based evaluation is fair: the proposed algorithm has more than one chance to match the human descriptions. In the second evaluation method (MAJORITY) we address this issue, comparing how often the *most frequent* generated set compares with the most frequent observed set. We run the proposed algorithm 1,000 times, and the generated property sets are ordered by frequency. The most frequent generated set is compared against the most frequent human-produced set. The majority score is the percentage of folds where these two sets match. For IA and FB, the most frequent generated set is the only generated set. This is a simple way to fairly compare the output of deterministic and non-deterministic algorithms. There are no ties in the generated sets, but in the case of a tie in the observed data, we count a match if any match the most frequent generated set.

6.1 GRE3D3

We randomly select two scenes (7, 9) from Set 1 and their mirrored counterparts in Set 2 (17, 19) for development. We empirically determine λ=5 for the length-based penalty γ in the proposed algorithm.

We use the eight remaining scenes in each Set for eight-fold cross-validation, estimating parameters for the algorithms on the seven training scenes in each fold, as discussed in Section 5.2.

For ALIGNED DICE, we run the proposed algorithm five times in each fold and report the average score. Results are shown in Table 2.[7]

Algorithm	ALIGNED DICE		MAJORITY	
	Set 1	Set 2	Set 1	Set 2
Proposed Alg.	**88.23**	**90.06**	62.50	**50.00**
IA	87.71	85.13	62.50	25.00
GB	87.71	88.73	62.50	**50.00**

Table 2: GRE3D3: Results (in %).

The proposed Visible Objects Algorithm achieves higher accuracy than either version of the Incremental Algorithm or the Graph-Based Algorithm using ALIGNED DICE. In MAJORITY, the Graph-Based and the Visible Objects Algorithm both predict the majority property set in this evaluation at least 50% of the time. The algorithm is competitive with the state of the art on this corpus.

6.2 TUNA

TUNA is split into two conditions: subjects discouraged to use location (-LOC) or not (+LOC). We randomly hold out two scenes from both conditions (1 and 2), and find a value of λ=5 again works well on the development data.

As in the GRE3D3 corpus, we use the TUNA scenes in five-fold cross-validation, estimating parameters on the four training scenes in each fold. For ALIGNED DICE, we average over five runs of the algorithm, and for MAJORITY, we run the proposed algorithm 1,000 times for each test scene.

Algorithm	ALIGNED DICE		MAJORITY	
	+LOC	-LOC	+LOC	-LOC
Proposed Alg.	**88.75**	**86.07**	**40.00**	40.00
IA	81.79	81.55	0.00	**100.00**
GB	75.36	66.04	20.00	20.00

Table 3: TUNA: Results (in %).

Results are shown in Table 3. Again we see that the proposed Visible Objects Algorithm is competitive with the IA and GB for both ALIGNED DICE and MAJORITY. GB performs poorly here, and this may be due to the data sparsity issue that arises when requiring the algorithm to train on properties.[8] In

[7] We do not report statistical significance; the proposed algorithm produces several possible outputs for one input, while the IA and GB produce only one.

[8] The original property-based weighting approach (Theune et al., 2011; Koolen et al., 2012, see Section 5.2) trained on object collections that were identical to their test data in all properties except x- and y-dimension, and so this was less of an issue. We hope to explore whether basing weights on attributes alone

MAJORITY, the Visible Objects Algorithm is relatively stable across conditions, generating the majority property set in 40% of the test scenes. It does not outperform the IA in the -LOC condition, but the IA has a large range across the two conditions (0% and 100%).

7 Conclusions and Future Work

We have introduced a new algorithm for generating referring expressions, inspired by human and computer vision and aiming to refer in a human-like way to visible objects. The algorithm successfully generates the most common attributes that people choose for different objects, and offers a varied output to capture speaker variation. In contrast to most algorithms for the generation of referring expressions, which have aimed to produce distinguishing descriptions when these exist (Krahmer and van Deemter, 2012), the core idea behind this algorithm is to generate what is likely for a speaker in a visual domain. Since the driving mechanism behind the algorithm is not to uniquely identify the object, but rather to pipeline the analysis of properties in a way similar to human visual processing, the generated expression may be overspecified or underspecified.

We are limited by available REG corpora to reliably assess methods for generating more complex absolute properties like shape and material, but adding such properties would help advance the generation of human-like reference in visual scenes and offers further points of connection between the generation process and computer vision property detection. Models for generating more complex spatial relations are currently available, and are a natural extension to this framework (e.g., those of Kelleher and Costello (2009)) as object detection becomes more robust.

We may also be able to build more sophisticated graphical models as larger corpora become available. For example, modeling the conditional probability of generating reference for a property v_n given the previously generated context $p(v_n|v_1 \ldots v_{n-1})$ may bring us closer to human-like output.

There are several additional issues that do not arise in this evaluation, but we expect must be accounted for when referring to naturalistic objects in visual domains. These include:

- The interconnected nature of properties, where some properties entail others; for example, a wooden object is likely to be called *wooden*, referring to its material, rather than *tan* or *brown*.
- The role of typicality, where properties are selected because they are atypical for the object.
- Referring to more complex properties, e.g., material, texture, etc., and object parts.
- Better methods for determining the length penalty and attribute likelihoods.

We hope to discuss extensions to this algorithm covering these aspects of reference in future work.

improves performance.

Acknowledgments

Funding for this research has been provided by SICSA and ORSAS. We thank the anonymous reviewers for useful comments on this paper.

References

Carlos Areces, Alexander Koller, and Kristina Striegnitz. 2008. Referring expressions as formulas of description logic. *Proceedings of the 5th International Natural Language Generation Conference (INLG 2008)*, pages 42–29.

Ellen Gurman Bard, Robin Hill, Manabu Arai, and Mary Ellen Foster. 2009. Accessibility and attention in situated dialogue: Roles and regulations. *Proceedings of the Workshop on the Production of Referring Expressions (PRE-CogSci 2009)*.

Anja Belz and Albert Gatt. 2008. Intrinsic vs. extrinsic evaluation measures for referring expression generation. *Proceedings of the 46th Annual Meeting of the Association for Computational Linguistics (ACL 2008)*, pages 197–200.

Alexander C. Berg, Tamara L. Berg, Hal Daumé III, Jesse Dodge, Amit Goyal, Xufeng Han, Alyssa Mensch, Margaret Mitchell, Karl Stratos, and Kota Yamaguchi. 2011. An exploration of how to learn from visually descriptive text. *JHU-CLSP Summer Workshop Whitepaper*.

Steven Bird, Edward Loper, and Ewan Klein. 2009. *Natural Language Processing with Python*. O'Reilly Media Inc., Sebastopol, CA.

Sarah Brown-Schmidt and Michael K. Tanenhaus. 2006. Watching the eyes when talking about size: An investigation of message formulation and utterance planning. *Journal of Memory and Language*, 54:592–609.

Herbert H. Clark and Gregory L. Murphy. 1982. Audience Design in Meaning and Reference. In J. F. LeNy and W. Kintsch, editors, *Language and Comprehension*, volume 9 of *Advances in Psychology*, pages 287–299. North-Holland, Amsterdam.

Herbert H. Clark, Robert Schreuder, and Samuel Buttrick. 1983. Common ground and the understanding of demonstrative reference. *Journal of Verbal Learning and Verbal Behavior*, 22:245–258.

Robert Dale and Ehud Reiter. 1995. Computational interpretations of the gricean maxims in the generation of referring expressions. *Cognitive Science*, 19:233–263.

Robert Dale. 1989. Cooking up referring expressions. *Proceedings of the 27th Annual Meeting of the Association for Computational Linguistics (ACL 1989).*

P. E. Engelhardt, K. Bailey, and F. Ferreira. 2006. Do speakers and listeners observe the gricean maxim of quantity? *Journal of Memory and Language*, 54:554–573.

Fang Fang, Huseyin Boyaci, Daniel Kersten, and Scott O. Murray. 2008. Attention-dependent representation of a size illusion in human V1. *Current biology*, 18(21):1707–1712.

Ali Farhadi, Ian Endres, Derek Hoiem, and David Forsyth. 2009. Describing objects by their attributes. *Proceedings of IEEE Conference on Computer Vision and Pattern Recognition (CVPR 2009).*

V. Ferrari and A. Zisserman. 2007. Learning visual attributes. *Advances in Neural Information Processing Systems (NIPS 2007).*

William Ford and David Olson. 1975. The elaboration of the noun phrase in children's description of objects. *The Journal of Experimental Child Psychology*, 19:371–382.

David A. Forsyth. 2011. Personal communication. Video clip of communication available from: http://vimeo.com/40553150. At 1:06:46.

T. M. Gann and D. J. Barr. 2013. Speaking from experience: Audience design as expert performance. *Language and Cognitive Processes*. In press.

Albert Gatt and Anja Belz. 2008. Attribute selection for referring expression generation: New algorithms and evaluation methods. *Proceedings of 5th International Natural Language Generation Conference (INLG 2008)*, pages 50–58.

Albert Gatt, Anja Belz, and Eric Kow. 2009. The TUNA REG challenge 2009: Overview and evaluation results. *Proceedings of the 12th European Workshop on Natural Language Generation (ENLG 2009)*, pages 174–182.

Mark Hall, Eibe Frank, Geoffrey Holmes, Bernhard Pfahringer, Peter Reutemann, and Ian H. Witten. 2009. The weka data mining software: An update. *SIGKDD Explorations*, 11(1).

William S. Horton and Boaz Keysar. 1996. When do speakers take into account common ground? *Cognition*, 59(1):91–117.

Laurent Itti and Christof Koch. 2001. Computational modelling of visual attention. *Nature Reviews Neuroscience*, 2:194–203.

John Kelleher and Fintan Costello. 2009. Applying computational models of spatial prepositions to visually situated dialog. *Computational Linguistics*, 35(2):271–306.

John Kelleher, Fintan Costello, and Josef van Genabith. 2005. Dynamically structuring, updating and interrelating representations of visual and linguistic discourse context. *Artificial Intelligence*, 167:62–102.

Boaz Keysar and Anne S. Henly. 2002. Speakers' overestimation of their effectiveness. *Psychological Science*, 13(3):207–212.

Ruud Koolen, Martijn Goudbeek, and Emiel Krahmer. 2011. Effects of scene variation on referential overspecification. *Proceedings of the 33rd Annual Meeting of the Cognitive Science Society (CogSci 2011).*

Ruud Koolen, Emiel Krahmer, and Mariët Theune. 2012. Learning preferences for referring expression generation: Effects of domain, language and algorithm. *Proceedings of the 7th International Workshop on Natural Language Generation (INLG 2012).*

Emiel Krahmer and Mariët Theune. 2002. Efficient context-sensitive generation of referring expressions. *Information Sharing: Reference and Presupposition in Language Generation and Interpretation*, 143:223–263.

Emiel Krahmer and Kees van Deemter. 2012. Computational generation of referring expressions: A survey. *Computational Linguistics*, 38:173–218.

Emiel Krahmer, Sebastiaan van Erk, and André Verleg. 2003. Graph-based generation of referring expressions. *Computational Linguistics*, 29(1):53–72.

H. W. Kuhn. 1955. The hungarian method for the assignment problem. *Naval Research Logistics Quarterly*, 2:83–97.

Margaret Mitchell, Kees van Deemter, and Ehud Reiter. 2011. Two approaches for generating size modifiers. *Proceedings of the 13th European Workshop on Natural Language Generation (ENLG 2011).*

James Munkres. 1957. Algorithms for the assignment and transportation problems. *Journal of Industrial and Applied Mathematics*, 5(1):32–38.

Scott O. Murray, Huseyin Boyaci, and Daniel Kersten. 2006. The representation of perceived angular size in human primary visual cortex. *Nature Neuroscience*, 9(3):429–434.

David R. Olson. 1970. Language and thought: Aspects of a cognitive theory of semantics. *Psychological Review*, 77:257–273.

Thomas Pechmann. 1989. Incremental speech production and referential overspecification. *Linguistics*, 27:89–110.

Ehud Reiter and Anja Belz. 2009. An investigation into the validity of some metrics for automatically evaluating natural language generation systems. *Computational Linguistics*, 35(4):529–558.

Ehud Reiter and Robert Dale. 1992. A fast algorithm for the generation of referring expressions. *Proceedings of the 14th International Conference on Computational Linguistics (COLING 1992)*, 1:232–238.

Ehud Reiter and Somayajulu Sripada. 2002. Human variation and lexical choice. *Computational Linguistics*, 28:545–553.

D. Samuel Schwarzkopf, Chen Song, and Geraint Rees. 2010. The surface area of human V1 predicts the subjective experience of object size. *Nature Neuroscience*, 14(1):28–30.

J. R. Searle. 1969. *Speech Acts: An Essay in the Philosophy of Language*. Cambridge University Press, Cambridge.

Susan Sonnenschein. 1985. The development of referential communication skills: Some situations in which speakers give redundant messages. *Journal of Psycholinguistic Research*, 14:489–508.

Mariët Theune, Ruud Koolen, Emiel Krahmer, and Sander Wubben. 2011. Does size matter – how much data is required to train a REG algorithm? *Proceedings of the 49th Annual Meeting of the Association for Computational Linguistics (ACL 2011)*.

Anne M. Treisman and Garry Gelade. 1980. A feature integration theory of attention. *Cognitive Psychology*, 12:97–13.

Anne Treisman. 1985. Preattentive processing in vision. *Computer Vision, Graphics, and Image Processing*, 31:156177.

L. G. Ungerleider and M. Mishkin. 1982. Two Cortical Visual Systems. In D. J. Ingle, M. Goodale, and R. J. W. Mansfield, editors, *Analysis of Visual Behaviour*, chapter 18, pages 549–586. The MIT Press.

Kees van Deemter, Ielka van der Sluis, and Albert Gatt. 2006. Building a semantically transparent corpus for the generation of referring expressions. *Proceedings of the 4th International Conference on Natural Language Generation (INLG 2006)*.

Kees van Deemter, Albert Gatt, Ielka van der Sluis, and Richard Power. 2012a. Generation of referring expressions: Assessing the incremental algorithm. *Cognitive Science*, 36(5):799–836.

Kees van Deemter, Emiel Krahmer, Roger van Gompel, and Albert Gatt. 2012b. Towards a computational psycholinguistics of reference production. *TopiCS: Production of Referring Expressions - Bridging the Gap between Computational and Empirical Approaches to Reference*.

Roger P. G. van Gompel, Albert Gatt, Emiel Krahmer, and Kees van Deemter. 2012. PRO: A computational model of referential overspecification. *Architectures and Mechanisms for Language Processing (AMLaP 2012)*.

Jette Viethen and Robert Dale. 2008. The use of spatial relations in referring expression generation. *Proceedings of the 5th International Natural Language Generation Conference (INLG 2008)*, pages 59–67.

Jette Viethen and Robert Dale. 2010. Speaker-dependent variation in content selection for referring expression generation. *Proceedings of the 8th Australasian Language Technology Workshop (ALTW 2010)*, pages 81–89.

Jette Viethen, Robert Dale, Emiel Krahmer, Mariët Theune, and Pascal Touset. 2008. Controlling redundancy in referring expressions. *Proceedings of the 6th International Conference on Language Resources and Evaluation (LREC 2008)*.

Jette Viethen, Martijn Goudbeek, and Emiel Krahmer. 2012. The impact of colour difference and coloure codability on reference production. *Proceedings of the 34th Annual Meeting of the Cognitive Science Society (CogSci 2012)*.

G. J. Whitehurst. 1976. The development of communication: Changes with age and modeling. *Child Development*, 47:473–482.

Supervised Learning of Complete Morphological Paradigms

Greg Durrett*
Computer Science Division
University of California, Berkeley
gdurrett@cs.berkeley.edu

John DeNero
Google, Inc.
denero@google.com

Abstract

We describe a supervised approach to predicting the set of all inflected forms of a lexical item. Our system automatically acquires the orthographic transformation rules of morphological paradigms from labeled examples, and then learns the contexts in which those transformations apply using a discriminative sequence model. Because our approach is completely data-driven and the model is trained on examples extracted from Wiktionary, our method can extend to new languages without change. Our end-to-end system is able to predict complete paradigms with 86.1% accuracy and individual inflected forms with 94.9% accuracy, averaged across three languages and two parts of speech.

1 Introduction

For natural languages with rich morphology, knowledge of how to inflect base forms is critical for both text generation and analysis. Hand-engineered, rule-based methods for predicting inflections can offer extremely high accuracy, but they are laborious to construct and do not exist with full lexical coverage in all languages. By contrast, a large number of example inflections are freely available in a semi-structured format on the Web. The English Wiktionary[1] is a crowd-sourced lexical resource that includes complete inflection tables for many lexical items in many languages. We present a supervised system that, given only data from Wiktionary, automatically discovers and learns to apply the orthographic transformations governing a language's inflectional morphology.[2]

Our data-driven approach is designed to extend to any language for which we have a substantial number of example inflection tables. The design of our model is guided by three structural assumptions:

1. The inflections of many lexical items are governed by a few repeated morphological paradigms.
2. A morphological paradigm can be decomposed into independent orthographic transformation rules (including prefix, suffix, and stem changes), which are triggered by orthographic context.
3. A base form is transformed in consistent, correlated ways to produce its inflected variants.

Learning proceeds in two stages that both utilize the same training set of labeled inflection tables. First, an inventory of interpretable transformation rules is generated by aligning each base form to all of its inflected forms. Second, a semi-Markov conditional random field (CRF) (Sarawagi and Cohen, 2004) is trained to apply these rules correctly to unseen base forms. As we demonstrate experimentally, the CRF is most effective when jointly predicting all inflected forms of a lexical item together, forcing the system to adopt a single consistent analysis of each base form.

*Research conducted during an internship at Google.
[1]http://en.wiktionary.org

[2]See http://eecs.berkeley.edu/~gdurrett for our datasets and code.

Previous work has also described supervised and semi-supervised approaches to predicting inflectional morphology (Yarowsky and Wicentowski, 2000; Wicentowski, 2004; Dreyer and Eisner, 2011). Our approach differs primarily in its use of automatically extracted morphological rules and our discriminative prediction method which jointly models entire inflection tables. These modeling choices are directly inspired by the data setting: Wiktionary contains complete inflection tables for many lexical items in each of a large number of languages, so it is natural to make full use of this information with a joint model of all inflected forms.

We evaluate our predictions on held-out Wiktionary inflection tables for three languages and two parts of speech. Our language-independent method predicts inflections for unseen base forms with accuracies ranging from 88.9% (German nouns) to 99.7% (Spanish verbs). For comparability with previous work, we also evaluate our approach on German verb forms in the CELEX lexical database (Baayen et al., 1995). Our approach outperforms the semi-supervised hierarchical Bayesian model of Dreyer and Eisner (2011), while employing scalable exact inference and interpretable transformation rules.

2 Background: Inflectional Morphology

Among the valid words W and parts of speech P in a language, the base forms $B \subset W \times P$ are the canonical forms of the language's lexical items. A base form relates to an inflected form via an inflectional relation (b, w, a), where $b \in B$ is a base form, $w \in W$ is the inflected form, and a is a vector of morphological attributes. An inflection table $T(b)$ is the set of all such relations for a base form b.

Two partial inflection tables are shown in Table 1, for the base forms (infinitives) of the German verbs *machen* and *schleichen*, containing such inflectional relations as (*machen*, *mache*, [1P,PRES,SING]) and (*machen*, *gemacht*, [PAST PART.]). Only a small sample of the valid attribute combinations are shown; a full inflection table for a German verb in our Wiktionary dataset contains 27 relations.

The goal of this paper is to learn how to map b to $T(b)$. We generate candidate inflection tables by applying compact, interpretable orthographic transformation rules that have been extracted from example tables. As an example of our rule application process, to inflect *machen* appropriately in the forms listed in Table 1, one could apply the following rules:

INFINITIVE	machen	schleichen
1P,PRES,SING	mache	schleiche
2P,PRES,SING	machst	schleichst
3P,PRES,SING	macht	schleicht
PAST PART.	gemacht	geschlichen
...	...	...

Table 1: Two partial inflection tables for the German verbs *machen* (to make) and *schleichen* (to crawl).

1. Replace a suffix *-en* with *-e* for first person, *-st* for second person, *-t* for third person, and *-t* for the past participle.

2. Add a prefix *ge-* for the past participle.

To inflect *schleichen*, one could apply a larger set of three rules:

1. Replace a suffix *-en* with *-e* for first person, *-st* for second person, *-t* for third person, and *-en* for the past participle.

2. Add a prefix *ge-* for the past participle.

3. Delete the first *e* for the past participle.

The inflection tables of other German verbs can be generated using precisely the same rules above, and different inflection patterns may share rules, such as the repeated rule 2. This example illustrates one of our chief assumptions, that the inflections of many base forms can be modeled with a small number of such rules, applied in various combinations.

3 Learning Transformation Rules

From a training set of inflection tables $\{T(b_1), ..., T(b_n)\}$, our system learns a set of orthographic transformation rules. A rule is a function $R : s, a \rightarrow s'$ that takes as input a substring s of a base form and an attribute vector a and outputs a replacement substring s'. The suffix transformation from Section 2 for *machen* can be described using a

Algorithm 1 Learning rules from examples.

Input: n training instances $T(b_1), \ldots, T(b_n)$
Rule set $\mathcal{R} \leftarrow \{\}$
for $i \leftarrow 1$ to n **do**
  Changed source spans $C \leftarrow \{\}$
  for all $a \in A$ **do**
    $C_a \leftarrow$ PROJECTSPANS(ALIGN($b_i, T_a(b_i)$))
    $C \leftarrow$ UNIONSPANS(C, C_a)
  end for
  for all $c \in C$ **do**
    $\mathcal{R} \leftarrow \mathcal{R} \cup \{$EXTRACTRULE($c$)$\}$
  end for
end for
return $\mathcal{R}$

rule with four entries:

$$R(en, [\text{1P,PRES,SING}]) = e$$
$$R(en, [\text{2P,PRES,SING}]) = st$$
$$R(en, [\text{3P,PRES,SING}]) = t$$
$$R(en, [\text{PAST PART.}]) = t$$

Our method for learning rules from examples is described in Algorithm 1 and depicted in Figure 1. We extract rules from each observed inflection table $T(b_i)$ independently, and the final set of rules is simply the union of the sets of rules learned from each example. The procedure for a single inflection table has three steps:

Alignment: Align each inflected form to the base form with an iterated edit-distance algorithm.

Span Merging: Extract the set of spans of the base form that changed to produce the inflected form, and take their union across all attribute vectors to identify maximal changed spans.

Rule Extraction: Extract a rule for each maximal changed span.

Alignment. For each setting of attributes a, we find the lowest-cost transformation of the base form b into the corresponding inflected form $T_a(b)$ using single-character insertions, deletions, and substitutions. This minimum edit distance calculation is computed via the following recurrence, where i is an index into the base form b and j is an index into an inflected form $T_a(b)$:

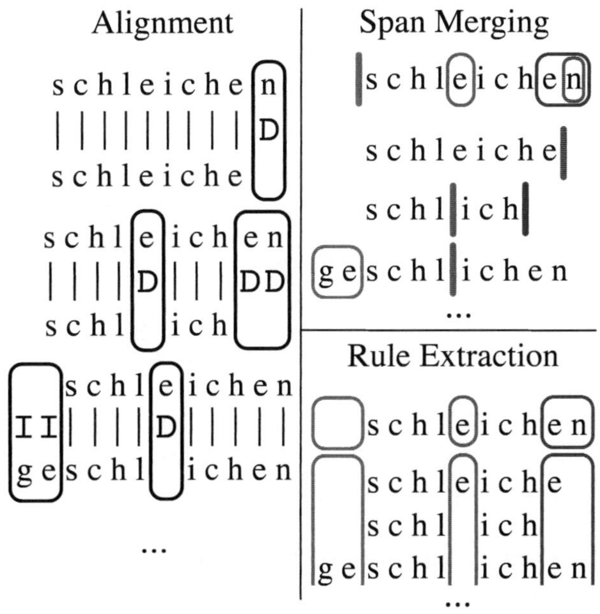

Figure 1: Demonstration of the rule extraction algorithm with the base form *schleichen* and three inflected forms: *schleiche* (first person singular present), *schlich* (first person singular past), and *geschlichen* (past participle). We ideally want to extract appropriate transformation rules like those described in Section 2. In the alignment step, we minimize the edit distance between each inflected form and the base form to identify changed spans. In the span merging step, we project changes onto the base form and take the union of adjacent or overlapping spans. In the rule extraction step, we project these spans back onto the inflected forms to identify transformation rules.

$$\begin{aligned} L(i,j) = \min\{ & L(i,j-1) + I, \\ & L(i-1,j) + D, \\ & L(i-1,j-1) + S(i,j)\} \end{aligned}$$

I, D, and S are insertion, deletion, and substitution costs, respectively. Tracing the computation of $L(\text{len}(b), \text{len}(T_a(b)))$ yields an optimal sequence of edit operations. The alignments output by this procedure are depicted in the first panel of Figure 1.

The most typical cost scheme sets $I = 1$, $D = 1$, and $S(i,j) = (1 - \mathbb{I}[\text{match}(i,j)])$, i.e. 0 if the ith character of b is the same as the jth character of $T_a(b)$, and 1 otherwise. However, this cost scheme did not yield intuitive alignments for some of our training instances. For example, in the case of the verb *denken* aligning to its past participle *gedacht*, the initial d and g will be aligned and the following e's will be aligned, preventing the algorithm from recognizing the addition of the prefix *ge-*. To solve this problem, we use a dynamic edit distance cost scheme in which I, D, and unmatched substitutions all have a cost of 0. Matched substitutions have a negative cost $-c_i$, where i is the index in the base form and c_i is the number of other inflected forms for which i is aligned to a matching character. The inflected forms are iteratively realigned with the base form until the c_i converge (Eisner, 2002; Oncina and Sebban, 2006). This cost scheme encourages a single consistent analysis of the base form as it aligns to all of its inflected forms.

Span Merging. From each aligned pair of words, the PROJECTSPANS procedure identifies sequences of character edit operations with contiguous spans of the base form. We construct a set of changed spans C_a of b as follows: include the span (i, j) if and only if no characters between i and j were aligned to matching characters in $T_a(b)$ and no smaller span captures the same set of changes. Projected spans for the inflected forms of *schleichen* are shown in the "Span Merging" panel of Figure 1.

The UNIONSPANS procedure combines two sets of spans by iteratively merging any two spans that are overlapping or adjacent. Repeating this procedure to accumulate spans for each setting of a yields the set C of maximal changed spans for a base form. Any span in C is bordered either by word boundaries or by characters that are match-aligned in every inflected form, meaning that we have isolated a region characterized by a particular orthographic transformation.

Rule Extraction. The final step of Algorithm 1 extracts one rule for each maximal changed span of the base form. The Rule Extraction panel of Figure 1 depicts how maximal changed spans in the base form correspond to transformation rules. Because UNIONSPANS guarantees that match-aligned characters border each maximal changed span, there is no ambiguity about the segmentation of transformations. The EXTRACTRULE procedure produces one rule $R(s, a)$ corresponding to each changed span.

Table 2 contains examples of the transformation rules we extract from German verbs. The extracted rules are interpretable descriptions of common inflection patterns.

Attributes	Suffix				Stem	Pre.
INFINITIVE	en	en	en	n	e	
1P,PRES,SING	e	e	e	e	e	
1P,PAST,SING	te	te		te		
2P,PRES,SING	st	t	st	st	e	
2P,PAST,SING	test	test	st	test		
3P,PRES,SING	t	t	t	t	e	
3P,PAST,SING	te	te		te		
PAST PART.	t	t	en	t		ge
...	...	...	...	...	...	...
Label	$R_{\text{suf},1}$	$R_{\text{suf},2}$	$R_{\text{suf},3}$	$R_{\text{suf},4}$	$R_{\text{st},1}$	$R_{\text{pre},1}$

Table 2: Each column is an example of a morphological transformation rule extracted by our approach. The first four are suffix changes; these apply to, in order, regular verbs such as *machen*, verbs ending in *-zen* or *-sen* such as *setzen*, verbs such as *schleichen* and *beheben*, and verbs ending in *-ern* or *-eln* such as *sprenkeln*. The stem change occurs in strong verbs of the first class such as *schleichen*, *greifen*, and *streiten*. Finally, we learn that *ge-* can be added as a prefix to indicate the past participle.

4 Applying Transformation Rules

For a novel base form b, the inventory of learned transformation rules $\mathcal{R} = \{R(s, a)\}$ can typically generate many candidate inflection tables $T(b)$ for us to choose between. A rule can potentially apply to a base form in a number of places; we define an anchored rule $A = (R, i, j, b)$ to be the application of R to a span (i, j) in b. A is only a valid anchoring if the substring of b between i and j matches the input of rule R.

Given a set $\mathcal{A}$ of non-overlapping anchored rules for b, each entry of $T(b)$ can be deterministically produced by rewriting each anchored rule's span (i, j) using the rule R. Therefore, the task of predicting $T(b)$ is equivalent to selecting a coherent subset $\mathcal{A}$ of anchored rules from the set of all possible anchored rules for this base form. By coherent, we mean that the selected rules are anchored to non-overlapping, non-adjacent[3] spans of b. Figure 2a shows two coherent anchored rule subsets for *schleichen* (the top one being correct). Underlining indi-

[3]During rule extraction, any adjacent changed spans are merged into a single rule. Disallowing adjacent spans here therefore prevents us from synthesizing new rules.

cates length-one spans $S = (i, i+1, b)$ that are not part of any anchored rule in $\mathcal{A}$. We denote the set of such spans by $\mathcal{S}(\mathcal{A})$; this set is uniquely defined for the given base form by the selected anchored rules.

We use a log-linear model to place a conditional distribution over valid anchored rule subsets $\mathcal{A}$ given the base form b:

$$p_w(\mathcal{A}|b) \propto \exp w^T \left(\sum_{A \in \mathcal{A}} \phi(A) + \sum_{S \in \mathcal{S}(\mathcal{A})} \psi(S) \right)$$

where w is a weight vector, $\phi(A)$ computes a feature vector for anchored rule A, and $\psi(S)$ computes a feature vector for preserved spans S. We train this model to maximize the regularized conditional log-likelihood of the training data, which consists of base forms b_i and gold subsets of anchored rules $\mathcal{A}_i^*$ derived using Algorithm 1 on the gold inflection tables.

$$L(w) = \sum_{i=1}^{n} \log p(\mathcal{A}_i^*|b_i) + \frac{\gamma}{2}\|w\|^2.$$

We find $w^* = \arg\max_w L(w)$ using L-BFGS (Liu and Nocedal, 1989), which requires computing $\frac{\partial L}{\partial w}$. This gradient takes the standard form of the difference between gold feature counts and expected feature counts under the model:

$$\frac{\partial L}{\partial w} = \sum_{i=1}^{n} \left[\left(\sum_{A \in \mathcal{A}_i^*} \phi(A) + \sum_{S \in \mathcal{S}(\mathcal{A}_i^*)} \psi(S) \right) - \left(\sum_{A \in \mathcal{A}(\mathcal{R},b)} \mathbb{E}_{p_w}\phi(A) + \sum_{S \in \mathcal{S}(b)} \mathbb{E}_{p_w}\psi(S) \right) \right] - \gamma w$$

where, by a slight abuse of notation, $\mathcal{S}(b)$ is the set of all length-one spans of b.

In general, the normalizer of p_w and the expectation over p_w cannot be computed directly, since there may be exponentially many coherent subsets of anchored rules. However, we note that $\mathcal{A}$ and its corresponding $\mathcal{S}(\mathcal{A})$ form a segmentation of the base form b, with features decomposing over individual segments. Our model can therefore be viewed a semi-Markov model over b (Sarawagi and Cohen, 2004); more precisely, a zeroth-order semi-Markov model, since we do not include features on state transitions. At training time, we can use the

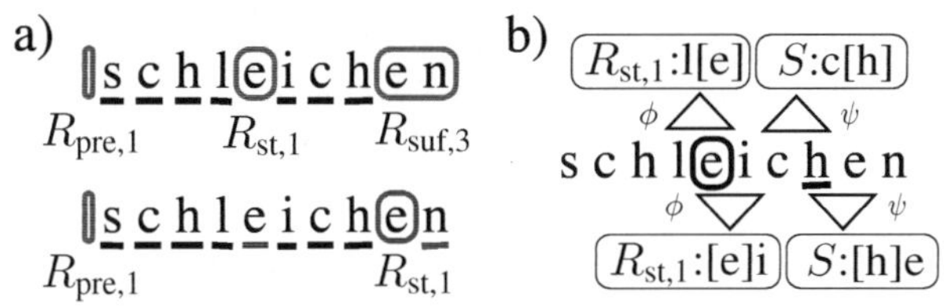

Figure 2: a) Two possible anchored rule sets for *schleichen*. The indicated rules are prefix, stem, and suffix rules as found in Table 2. The top anchoring is correct, while the bottom misplaces the stem change and does not include a suffix change. Underlined letters indicate preserved spans S. b) Bigram context features computed by $\phi(R_{st,1})$, where the stem change is applied to the highlighted *e*, and similar features computed by $\psi(S)$ for the underlined *h*, which is unchanged by the applied rules.

forward-backward algorithm for semi-Markov models to compute the gradient of p_w, and at test time, the Viterbi algorithm can exactly find the best rule subset under the model: $\hat{A} = \arg\max_{\mathcal{A}} p_w(\mathcal{A}|b)$.

Features. The feature function ϕ captures contextual information in the base form surrounding the site of the anchored rule application. It is well understood that different morphological rules may require examining different amounts of context to apply correctly (Kohonen, 1986; Torkkola, 1993; Shalonova and Golénia, 2010); to this end, we will use local character n-gram features, which have been successfully applied to related problems (Jiampojamarn et al., 2008; Dinu et al., 2012).

A sketch of our feature computation scheme is shown in Figure 2b. Our basic feature template is an indicator on a character n-gram with some offset from the rule application site, conjoined with the identity of the rule R being applied. Our features look at variable amounts of context: we include features on unigrams through 4-grams, starting up to five letters behind the anchored rule span and ending up to five letters past the anchored rule span. These features can model most hand-coded morphological rules, but are in many cases more numerous than necessary. However, we find that regularization is effective at balancing high model capacity with generalization, and reducing the size of the feature set empirically harms overall accuracy.

We also employ factored features that only look at predictions over particular inflected forms; these are coarser features that are shared between two rules when they predict the same orthographic change for a particular setting of attributes. These features are indicators on R_a (the restriction of R to attributes a), the context n-gram, and its offset from the span.

The feature function ψ is almost identical to ϕ, but instead of indicating a rule appearing in some context, it instead indicates that a particular length-one span is being preserved in its n-gram context. Examples of ψ features are shown in Figure 2b.

Pruning. Thus far, the only requirement on an anchoring A is that the source side of its rule R must match the span it is anchored to in the base form b. We further filter the set of possible A as follows: if every occurrence of R in the training set is preceded by the same character (including a start-of-word character) or followed by the same character (including an end-of-word character), any anchoring A must be preceded or followed accordingly. This stipulation is most useful in restricting prefixing or suffixing insertions, which have an empty source side, to apply only at the beginnings or ends of base forms (rather than at arbitrary points throughout). In doing so, we prune out many erroneous anchored rules and speed up inference substantially without prohibiting correct rule applications.

5 Wiktionary Morphology Data

Our primary source of supervised inflection table data is English Wiktionary. The collective editors of English Wiktionary have created complete, consistent inflection tables for many lexical items in many languages. Previous work has successfully parsed other information from Wiktionary, such as parts of speech, glosses, and etymology (Zesch et al., 2008; Li et al., 2012); however, to our knowledge, inflection tables have not previously been extracted in a format easily amenable to natural language processing applications. These inflection tables are challenging to extract because the layout of tables varies substantially by language (beyond the expected changes due to differing sets of relevant morphological attributes), and some tables contain annotations in addition to word forms.

In order to extract this data, we built a Wiktionary scraper which generates fully structured output by interpreting the templates that generate the rendered inflection tables. Table 3 gives statistics for the number of base forms and inflected forms extracted from Wikitionary. When multiple forms were listed in an inflection table for the same base form and attribute vector, we selected the first in linear order; applying the same principle, we also kept only the first inflection table when more than one was listed for a given base form. Furthermore, base forms and inflected forms separated by spaces, hyphens, or colons were discarded. As a result, we discarded German verb-preposition compounds such as *ablehnen*[4] and Spanish reflexives such as *lavarse*.

Lang/POS	Base forms	Infl. forms per base
DE-NOUNS	2764	8
DE-VERBS	2027	27
ES-VERBS	4055	57
FI-NOUNS	40589	28
FI-VERBS	7249	53

Table 3: Number of full morphology tables extracted from Wiktionary for each language and part of speech pair that we considered, as well as the number of inflected forms associated with each base form.

6 Experiments

We evaluate our model under two experimental conditions. First, we use the German verb lexicon in the CELEX lexical database (Baayen et al., 1995) with the same train/test splits as Dreyer and Eisner (2011). Second, we train on our Wiktionary data described in Section 5 and evaluate on held-out forms from this same dataset.

In each case, we evaluate two variants of our model in order to examine the importance of jointly modeling the production of the entire inflection table. Our JOINT model is exactly as defined in Section 4. For our FACTORED model, the dictionary of rules is extracted separately for each setting of the attributes a; i.e., we run the entire procedure in Section 3 with only one inflected form at a time and forego the UNIONSPANS step. A separate prediction model is trained for each a and so features are not shared across multiple predictions as they are in the JOINT case. Note that this FACTORED approach

[4] This class of verbs was also ignored by Dreyer and Eisner (2011).

	No. of training examples		
	50	100	200
NAÏVE	87.61	87.70	87.70
FACTORED	89.61	91.40	92.64
JOINT	**90.47**	**92.31**	**93.18**
DE11	89.9	91.5	
DE11+CORPUS	90.9	92.2	
ORACLE	*95.47*	*96.09*	*96.77*

Table 4: Accuracies on reconstructing individual inflected forms in CELEX, averaged over the 5415 inflection tables in each of 10 test sets. Three training set sizes are reported. DE11 indicates a reported result from Dreyer and Eisner (2011), with blank results unreported in that work. Our FACTORED model is able to do approximately as well as the DE11 baseline method, and our JOINT model performs better yet, performing comparably to DE11+CORPUS, which uses additional monolingual text. All models substantially outperform the NAÏVE suffixing baseline. The relatively low ORACLE accuracy indicates that some errors arise from failing to apply rules that are not attested in these small training sets.

can produce inflection tables that the JOINT model cannot, due to its ability to "mix and match" orthographic changes in the same inflection table.

We also evaluate a NAÏVE method for applying the joint rules which selects the most common suffix rule available after pruning.[5] Finally, we report the ORACLE accuracy attainable with the morphological rule dictionary of the JOINT model.

For our conditional likelihood objective, we use $\gamma = 0.0002$; this parameter and the feature set were tuned on a small development set and held fixed for all experiments.

6.1 CELEX Experiments

Dreyer and Eisner (2011) construct ten train/test splits of the 5615 German verb forms in the CELEX lexical database, keeping 200 forms for training in each case, which they further subsample. These random splits serve to control for instability due to the small training set sizes. Each infinitive verb form has 22 corresponding inflected forms capturing variation such as person, number, mood, and tense.

Table 4 shows our results compared to those of Dreyer and Eisner (2011). The FACTORED model performs on par with the DE11 baseline model, but the stronger performance of the JOINT model indicates that making joint predictions is important. With 100 training examples, our model is able to equal the performance of DE11+CORPUS, which additionally uses ten million tokens of monolingual German text.

We emphasize that this is not the data condition for which our model was designed. It is unfavorable for two reasons: first, feature-rich models can be learned more stably on larger training sets, and second, the train/test splits are chosen randomly, and therefore the test sets may contain completely irregular verbs using morphological rules that we have never observed. As can be seen from the ORACLE results in Table 4, a substantial fraction of the missed test examples cannot be produced using our extracted rules simply because we have not seen the relevant examples; in many cases, even a human could not generalize correctly from the given examples without exploiting external knowledge of the German language.

6.2 Held-Out Wiktionary Data

Our algorithm was designed with the fundamental assumption that the training set should be a comprehensive description of the morphology of a given language, which is not true for the CELEX data. In order to evaluate on a broader set of languages under these training conditions, we turn to our Wiktionary data. For each language and part of speech, we train on all but 400 inflection tables, holding back 200 examples as a development set and 200 examples as a blind test set.[6] The forms selected for the development and test data were purposely chosen not to be among the 200 most frequently occurring forms in the language, since these common cases can be easily memorized from Wiktionary.

Results are shown in Table 5. As with the CELEX results, we see that the joint prediction improves accuracy over the factored model, obtaining a 9% error reduction on individual forms and a 35% error reduction on exact match. The more pronounced

[5] For example, for German verbs ending in *-en*, this applies the most regular *-en* suffix change, that exhibited by *machen* and many other verbs.

[6] For Finnish nouns, because there were so many inflection tables, we trained only on the first 6000 examples. Using more examples did not significantly change performance.

	Exact table match				Individual form accuracy			
Lang/POS	NAÏVE	FACT.	JOINT	ORACLE	NAÏVE	FACT.	JOINT	ORACLE
DE-VERBS	42.0	74.5	**85.0**	*99.5*	89.13	94.76	**96.19**	*99.98*
DE-NOUNS	12.0	74.0	**79.5**	*98.5*	49.06	88.31	**88.94**	*99.25*
ES-VERBS	81.5	93.5	**95.0**	*99.5*	97.20	99.61	**99.67**	*99.99*
FI-VERBS	33.5	82.0	**87.5**	*99.5*	75.32	**97.23**	96.43	*99.86*
FI-NOUNS	31.0	69.0	**83.5**	*100.0*	61.23	92.14	**93.41**	*100.00*
AVG	40.0	78.6	**86.1**	*99.4*	74.39	94.41	**94.93**	*99.81*

Table 5: Accuracies on reconstructing complete inflection tables and individual inflected forms for held-out base forms in our Wiktionary dataset. Results are shown for our fully JOINT model, a FACTORED model that predicts individual inflected forms independently, a NAÏVE baseline that picks the most common applicable suffix rule, and an ORACLE that selects the best inflection table within our model's capacity. For each language and part of speech, regardless of training set size, evaluation is based on a blind test set of 200 held-out forms.

improvement on exact match is unsurprising, since we expect that the joint predictions should get inflection tables correct in an "all-or-nothing" fashion, whereas factored predictions are more likely to reflect divergent feature weights of the different component models. The NAÏVE baseline performs rather poorly overall, indicating our algorithm is being sophisticated about applying more than just the most common changes. Finally, we note that the ORACLE performance is much higher in this case than on the CELEX data, confirming our intuition that with the appropriate level of supervision our model at least has the capacity to make correct predictions in almost every case.

6.3 Error Analysis

We conducted an error analysis on the output of our JOINT model on German nouns. From 2364 paradigms, we learn 53 different orthographic transformation rules, of which our 200-example development set exhibits 14.[7]

On our development set, 196 inflection tables are within the capacity of our model. Of those 196, 159 are exactly correct. In Table 6, we show the top six rules by frequency in the development set, along with the precision, recall, and F-measure that our model attains for each rule.[8] These rules are mostly interpretable: for example, the first two columns correspond to common suffix rules for feminine and masculine nouns, respectively. Our model's performance is consistently high for each of the rules shown, including a stem change (*a* changing to *ä* in plural forms), providing further evidence that our model is useful for modeling rarer morphological

NOM,SING			a		
NOM,PL	n	e	ä		en
ACC,SING			a		
ACC,PL	n	e	ä		en
DAT,SING			a		
DAT,PL	n	en	ä	n	en
GEN,SING		es	a	s	
GEN,PL	n	e	ä		en
Example	Klasse	Krieg	Haus	Nutzer	Frau
Gold	49	48	26	26	20
Prec	95.7	72.9	88.0	82.8	87.0
Rec	91.8	89.6	84.6	92.3	100.0
F1	93.8	80.4	86.3	87.3	93.0

Table 6: Breakdown of errors by morphological rule being applied by the JOINT model on the DE-NOUNS development set. We show the rule itself, treating the nominative singular as the base form, an example of a German word using that rule, and then the model's accuracy at predicting applications of that rule. Errors are spread out over many rules, but it generally appears that common rules are to blame for the errors that are made, due in large part to gender confusion in this case.

[7]Nineteen of our 53 extracted rules only occur on one example; this suggests a few reasons that fewer rules are applied than are extracted. First, very common base forms with irregular morphology may give rise to completely irregular rules. Second, our edit distance alignment procedure can sometimes merge two adjacent rules if the orthographic context is such that there are multiple minimum-cost analyses. Finally, errors and inconsistencies in Wiktionary can yield nonsense rules that are never applied elsewhere.

[8]Gold rules are obtained by running our rule extraction procedure over the examples in question.

paradigms as well as more common ones.

As a concrete example of an error our model does make, *Löwe* (lion) is incorrectly predicted to have the first suffix, instead of the correct suffix (not shown) which adds an *-n* for accusative, genitive, and dative singular as well. However, making this prediction correctly is essentially beyond the capacity of a model based purely on orthography. Words ending in *-e* are commonly feminine, and none of our other training examples end in *-we*, so guessing that *Löwe* follows a common feminine inflection pattern is reasonable (though *Löwe* is, in fact, masculine). Disambiguating this case requires either features on observed genders, a more complex model of the German language, or observing the word in a large corpus. Generally, when the model fails, as in this case, it is because of a fundamental linguistic information source that it does not have access to.

7 Related Work

Much of the past work on morphology has focused on concatenative morphology using unsupervised methods (Goldsmith, 2001; Creutz and Lagus, 2007; Monson, 2008; Poon et al., 2009; Goldwater et al., 2009) or weak forms of supervision (Snyder and Barzilay, 2008). These methods can handle aspects of derivational morphology that we cannot, such as compounding, but we can handle a much larger subset of inflectional morphology, including more complex prefix and suffix rules, stem changes, and irregular forms. Some unsupervised work has specifically targeted these sorts of phenomena by, for example, learning spelling rules for mildly nonconcatenative cases (Dasgupta and Ng, 2007; Naradowsky and Goldwater, 2009) or mining lemma-base form pairs from a corpus (Schone and Jurafsky, 2001), but it is extremely difficult to make unsupervised methods perform as well as supervised approaches like ours.

Past supervised work on nonconcatenative inflectional morphology has typically targeted individual pairs of base forms and inflected forms for the purposes of inflection (Clark, 2001) or lemmatization (Yarowsky and Wicentowski, 2000; Wicentowski, 2004; Lindén, 2008; Toutanova and Cherry, 2009). Some of these methods may use analysis (Lindén, 2008) or decoding (Toutanova and Cherry, 2009) steps similar to those of our model, but none attempt to jointly predict a complete inflection table based on automatically extracted rules.

Some previous work has addressed the joint analysis (Zajac, 2001; Monson, 2008) or prediction (Lindén and Tuovila, 2009; Dinu et al., 2012) of whole inflection tables, as we do, but rarely are both aspects addressed simultaneously and most approaches are tuned to one particular language or use language-specific, curated resources. In overall setup, our work most closely resembles that of Dreyer and Eisner (2011), but they focus on incorporating large amounts of raw text data rather than using large training sets effectively.

Broadly similar techniques are also employed in systems to filter candidate rules and aid in human annotation of paradigms (Zajac, 2001; Forsberg et al., 2006; Détrez and Ranta, 2012) for resources such as Grammatical Framework (Ranta, 2011).

8 Conclusion

In this work, we presented a method for inflecting base forms in morphologically rich languages: we first extract orthographic transformation rules from observed inflection tables, then learn to apply these rules to new base forms based on orthographic features. Training examples for our supervised method can be collected from Wiktionary for a large number of languages and parts of speech. The changes we extract are interpretable and can be associated with particular classes of words. Moreover, our model can successfully apply these changes to unseen base forms with high accuracy, allowing us to rapidly generate lexicons for new languages of interest.

Our Wiktionary datasets and an open-source version of our code are available at `http://eecs.berkeley.edu/~gdurrett`

Acknowledgments

We are grateful to Klaus Macherey and David Talbot for assistance with the examples and helpful discussions throughout the course of this work. We would also like to thank the three anonymous reviewers for their useful comments.

References

R. H. Baayen, R. Piepenbrock, and L. Gulikers. 1995. The CELEX Lexical Database (Release 2). Linguistic Data Consortium, University of Pennsylvania.

Alexander Clark. 2001. Partially Supervised Learning of Morphology with Stochastic Transducers. In *Proceedings of Natural Language Processing Pacific Rim Symposium*, pages 341–348, Tokyo, Japan.

Mathias Creutz and Krista Lagus. 2007. Unsupervised Models for Morpheme Segmentation and Morphology Learning. *ACM Transactions on Speech and Language Processing*, 4(1):3:1–3:34, Feb.

Sajib Dasgupta and Vincent Ng. 2007. High Performance, Language-Independent Morphological Segmentation. In *Proceedings of the North American Chapter of the Association for Computational Linguistics*.

Grégoire Détrez and Aarne Ranta. 2012. Smart Paradigms and the Predictability and Complexity of Inflectional Morphology. In *Proceedings of the European Chapter of the Association for Computational Linguistics*.

Liviu P. Dinu, Vlad Niculae, and Octavia-Maria Şulea. 2012. Learning How to Conjugate the Romanian Verb: Rules for Regular and Partially Irregular Verbs. In *Proceedings of the European Chapter of the Association for Computational Linguistics*.

Markus Dreyer and Jason Eisner. 2011. Discovering Morphological Paradigms from Plain Text Using a Dirichlet Process Mixture Model. In *Proceedings of Empirical Methods in Natural Language Processing*, pages 616–627, Edinburgh, Scotland, UK.

Jason Eisner. 2002. Parameter Estimation for Probabilistic Finite-State Transducers. In *Proceedings of the Association for Computational Linguistics*.

Markus Forsberg, Harald Hammarström, and Aarne Ranta. 2006. Morphological Lexicon Extraction from Raw Text Data. In *Proceedings of Advances in Natural Language Processing*.

John Goldsmith. 2001. Unsupervised Learning of the Morphology of a Natural Language. *Computational Linguistics*, 27(2):153–198, June.

Sharon Goldwater, Thomas L. Griffiths, and Mark Johnson. 2009. A Bayesian Framework for Word Segmentation: Exploring the Effects of Context. *Cognition*, 112(1):21–54.

Sittichai Jiampojamarn, Colin Cherry, and Grzegorz Kondrak. 2008. Joint Processing and Discriminative Training for Letter-to-Phoneme Conversion. In *Proceedings of the Association for Computational Linguistics*.

Teuvo Kohonen. 1986. Dynamically Expanding Context, With Application to the Correction of Symbol Strings in the Recognition of Continuous Speech. In *Proceedings of the International Conference on Pattern Recognition*.

Shen Li, João V. Graça, and Ben Taskar. 2012. Wiki-ly Supervised Part-of-speech Tagging. In *Proceedings of Empirical Methods in Natural Language Processing*.

Krister Lindén and Jussi Tuovila. 2009. Corpus-based Paradigm Selection for Morphological Entries. In *Proceedings of the Nordic Conference of Computational Linguistics*.

Krister Lindén. 2008. A Probabilistic Model for Guessing Base Forms of New Words by Analogy. In *Proceedings of Computational Linguistics and Intelligent Text Processing*.

Dong C. Liu and Jorge Nocedal. 1989. On the limited memory BFGS method for large scale optimization. *Mathematical Programming*, 45(3):503–528, December.

Christian Monson. 2008. ParaMor: From Paradigm Structure to Natural Language Morphology Induction. *Ph.D. thesis, Carnegie Mellon University*.

Jason Naradowsky and Sharon Goldwater. 2009. Improving Morphology Induction by Learning Spelling Rules. In *Proceedings of the International Joint Conferences on Artificial Intelligence*.

Jose Oncina and Marc Sebban. 2006. Learning Stochastic Edit Distance: Application in Handwritten Character Recognition. *Pattern Recognition*, 39(9):1575–1587, September.

Hoifung Poon, Colin Cherry, and Kristina Toutanova. 2009. Unsupervised Morphological Segmentation with Log-Linear Models. In *Proceedings of the North American Chapter of the Association for Computational Linguistics*.

Aarne Ranta. 2011. *Grammatical Framework: Programming with Multilingual Grammars*. CSLI Publications, Stanford.

Sunita Sarawagi and William W. Cohen. 2004. Semi-Markov Conditional Random Fields for Information Extraction. In *Advances in Neural Information Processing Systems 17*.

Patrick Schone and Daniel Jurafsky. 2001. Knowledge-Free Induction of Inflectional Morphologies. In *Proceedings of the North American Chapter of the Association for Computational Linguistics*.

Ksenia Shalonova and Bruno Golénia. 2010. Weakly Supervised Morphology Learning for Agglutinating Languages Using Small Training Sets. In *Proceedings of the Conference on Computational Linguistics*.

Benjamin Snyder and Regina Barzilay. 2008. Unsupervised Multilingual Learning for Morphological Segmentation. In *Proceedings of the Association for Computational Linguistics*.

Kari Torkkola. 1993. An Efficient Way to Learn English Grapheme-to-Phoneme Rules Automatically. In *Proceedings of the International Conference on Acoustics, Speech, and Signal Processing: Speech Processing - Volume II*.

Kristina Toutanova and Colin Cherry. 2009. A Global Model for Joint Lemmatization and Part-of-Speech Prediction. In *Proceedings of the Association for Computational Linguistics*.

Richard Wicentowski. 2004. Multilingual Noise-Robust Supervised Morphological Analysis Using the Word-Frame Model. In *Proceedings of the ACL Special Interest Group in Computational Phonology*.

David Yarowsky and Richard Wicentowski. 2000. Minimally Supervised Morphological Analysis by Multimodal Alignment. In *Proceedings of the Association for Computational Linguistics*.

Rémi Zajac. 2001. Morpholog: Constrained and Supervised Learning of Morphology. In *Proceedings of the Conference on Natural Language Learning*.

Torsten Zesch, Christof Müller, and Iryna Gurevych. 2008. Extracting Lexical Semantic Knowledge from Wikipedia and Wiktionary. In *Proceedings of Language Resources and Evaluation*.

Optimal Data Set Selection: An Application to Grapheme-to-Phoneme Conversion

Young-Bum Kim and Benjamin Snyder
University of Wisconsin-Madison
{ybkim,bsnyder}@cs.wisc.edu

Abstract

In this paper we introduce the task of unlabeled, optimal, data set selection. Given a large pool of unlabeled examples, our goal is to select a small subset to label, which will yield a high performance supervised model over the entire data set. Our first proposed method, based on the rank-revealing QR matrix factorization, selects a subset of words which span the entire word-space effectively. For our second method, we develop the concept of *feature coverage* which we optimize with a greedy algorithm. We apply these methods to the task of grapheme-to-phoneme prediction. Experiments over a data-set of 8 languages show that in all scenarios, our selection methods are effective at yielding a small, but optimal set of labelled examples. When fed into a state-of-the-art supervised model for grapheme-to-phoneme prediction, our methods yield average error reductions of 20% over randomly selected examples.

1 Introduction

Over the last 15 years, supervised statistical learning has become the dominant paradigm for building natural language technologies. While the accuracy of supervised models can be high, expertly annotated data sets exist for a small fraction of possible tasks, genres, and languages. The would-be tool builder is thus often faced with the prospect of annotating data, using crowd-sourcing or domain experts. With limited time and budget, the amount of data to be annotated might be small, especially in the prototyping stage, when the exact specification of the prediction task may still be in flux, and rapid prototypes are desired.

In this paper, we propose the problem of unsupervised, optimal data set selection. Formally, given a large set $\mathcal{X}$ of n unlabeled examples, we must select a subset $\mathcal{S} \subset \mathcal{X}$ of size $k \ll n$ to label. Our goal is to select such a subset which, when labeled, will yield a high performance supervised model over the entire data set $\mathcal{X}$. This task can be thought of as a zero-stage version of active learning: we must choose a single batch of examples to label, without the benefit of any prior labelled data points. This problem definition avoids the practical complexity of the active learning set-up (many iterations of learning and labeling), and ensures that the labeled examples are not tied to one particular model class or task, a well-known danger of active learning (Settles, 2010). Alternatively, our methods may be used to create the initial seed set for the active learner.

Our initial testbed for optimal data set selection is the task of grapheme-to-phoneme conversion. In this task, we are given an out-of-vocabulary word, with the goal of predicting a sequence of phonemes corresponding to its pronunciation. As training data, we are given a pronunciation dictionary listing words alongside corresponding sequences of phones, representing canonical pronunciations of those words. Such dictionaries are used as the final bridge between written and spoken language for technologies that span this divide, such as speech recognition, text-to-speech generation, and speech-to-speech language translation. These dictionaries are necessary: the pronunciation of words continues to evolve after their written form has been fixed, leading to a large number of rules and irregularities. While large pronunciation dictionaries of over 100,000 words exist for several major languages, these resources are entirely lacking for the majority of the world's languages. Our goal is to automatically select a small but optimal subset of words to be annotated with pronunciation data.

The main intuition behind our approach is that the subset of selected data points should efficiently cover the range of phenomena most commonly observed across the pool of unlabeled examples. We consider two methods. The first comes from a line of research initiated by the numerical linear algebra community (Golub, 1965) and taken up by computer science theoreticians (Boutsidis et al., 2009), with the name COLUMN SUBSET SELECTION PROBLEM (CSSP). Given a matrix A, the goal of CSSP is to select a subset of k columns whose span most closely captures the range of the full matrix. In particular, the matrix $\tilde{A}$ formed by orthogonally projecting A onto the k-dimensional space spanned by the selected columns should be a good approximation to A. By defining A^T to be our data matrix, whose rows correspond to words and whose columns correspond to features (character 4-grams), we can apply the CSSP randomized algorithm of (Boutsidis et al., 2009) on A to obtain a subset of k words which best span the entire space of words.

Our second approach is based on a notion of *feature coverage*. We assume that the benefit of seeing a feature f in a selected word bears some positive relationship to the frequency of f in the unlabeled pool. However, we further assume that the lion's share of benefit accrues the first few times that we label a word with feature f, with the marginal utility quickly tapering off as more such examples have been labeled. We formalize this notion and provide an exact greedy algorithm for selecting the k data points with maximal feature coverage.

To assess the benefit of these methods, we apply them to a suite of 8 languages with pronunciation dictionaries. We consider ranges from 500 to 2000 selected words and train a start-of-the-art grapheme-to-phoneme prediction model (Bisani and Ney, 2008). Our experiments show that both methods produce significant improvements in prediction quality over randomly selected words, with our feature coverage method consistently outperforming the randomized CSSP algorithm. Over the 8 languages, our method produces average reductions in error of 20%.

2 Background

Grapheme-to-phoneme Prediction The task of grapheme-to-phoneme conversion has been considered in a variety of frameworks, including neural networks (Sejnowski and Rosenberg, 1987), rule-based FSA's (Kaplan and Kay, 1994), and pronunciation by analogy (Marchand and Damper, 2000). Our goal here is not to compare these methods, so we focus on the probabilistic joint-sequence model of Bisani and Ney (2008). This model defines a joint distribution over a grapheme sequence $\boldsymbol{g} \in G^*$ and a phoneme sequence $\boldsymbol{\phi} \in \Phi^*$, by way of an unobserved *co-segmentation* sequence $\boldsymbol{q}$. Each co-segmentation unit q_i is called a *graphone* and consists of an aligned pair of zero or one graphemes and zero or one phonemes: $q_i \in G \cup \{\epsilon\} \times \Phi \cup \{\epsilon\}$.[1] The probability of a joint grapheme-phoneme sequence is then obtained by summing over all possible co-segmentations:

$$P(\boldsymbol{g}, \boldsymbol{\phi}) = \sum_{\boldsymbol{q} \in S(\boldsymbol{g}, \boldsymbol{\phi})} P(\boldsymbol{q})$$

where $S(\boldsymbol{g}, \boldsymbol{\phi})$ denotes the set of all graphone sequences which yield $\boldsymbol{g}$ and $\boldsymbol{\phi}$. The probability of a graphone sequence of length K is defined using an h-order Markov model with multinomial transitions:

$$P(\boldsymbol{q}) = \prod_{i=1}^{k+1} P(q_i | q_{i-h}, \ldots, q_{i-1})$$

where special start and end symbols are assumed for $q_{j<1}$ and q_{k+1}, respectively.

To deal with the unobserved co-segmentation sequences, the authors develop an EM training regime that avoids overfitting using a variety of smoothing and initialization techniques. Their model produces state-of-the-art or comparable accuracies across a

[1]The model generalizes easily to graphones consisting of more than one grapheme or phoneme, but in both (Bisani and Ney, 2008) and our initial experiments we found that the 01-to-01 model always performed best.

wide range of languages and data sets.[2] We use the publicly available code provided by the authors.[3] In all our experiments we set $h = 4$ (i.e. a 5-gram model), as we found that accuracy tended to be flat for $h > 4$.

Active Learning for G2P Perhaps most closely related to our work are the papers of Kominek and Black (2006) and Dwyer and Kondrak (2009), both of which use active learning to efficiently bootstrap pronunciation dictionaries. In the former, the authors develop an active learning word selection strategy for inducing pronunciation rules. In fact, their greedy n-gram selection strategy shares some of the some intuition as our second data set selection method, but they were unable to achieve any accuracy gains over randomly selected words without active learning.

Dwyer and Kondrak use a Query-by-Bagging active learning strategy over decision tree learners. They find that their active learning strategy produces higher accuracy across 5 of the 6 languages that they explored (English being the exception). They extract further performance gains through various refinements to their model. Even so, we found that the Bisani and Ney grapheme-to-phoneme (G2P) model (Bisani and Ney, 2008) always achieved higher accuracy, even when trained on random words. Furthermore, the relative gains that we observe using our optimal data set selection strategies (without any active learning) are much larger than the relative gains of active learning found in their study.

Data Set Selection and Active Learning Eck et al (2005) developed a method for training compact Machine Translation systems by selecting a subset of sentences with high n-gram coverage. Their selection criterion essentially corresponds to our feature coverage selection method using coverage function cov_2 (see Section 3.2). As our results will show, the use of a geometric feature discount (cov_3) provided better results in our task.

Otherwise, we are not aware of previous work proposing optimal data set selection as a general research problem. Of course, active learning strategies can be employed for this task by starting with a small random seed of examples and incrementally adding small batches. Unfortunately, this can lead to datasets that are biased to work well for one particular class of models and task, but may otherwise perform worse than a random set of examples (Settles, 2010, Section 6.6). Furthermore the active learning setup can be prohibitively tedious and slow. To illustrate, Dwyer and Kondrak (2009) used 190 iterations of active learning to arrive at 2,000 words. Each iteration involves bootstrapping 10 different samples, and training 10 corresponding learners. Thus, in total, the underlying prediction model is trained 1,900 times. In contrast, our selection methods are fast, can select any number of data points in a single step, and are not tied to a particular prediction task or model. Furthermore, these methods can be combined with active learning in selecting the initial seed set.

Unsupervised Feature Selection Finally, we note that CSSP and related spectral methods have been applied to the problem of *unsupervised feature selection* (Stoppiglia et al., 2003; Mao, 2005; Wolf and Shashua, 2005; Zhao and Liu, 2007; Boutsidis et al., 2008). These methods are related to dimensionality reduction techniques such as Principal Components Analysis (PCA), but instead of truncating features in the eigenbasis representation (where each feature is a linear combination of all the original features), the goal is to remove dimensions in the standard basis, leading to a compact set of interpretable features. As long as the discarded features can be well approximated by a (linear) function of the selected features, the loss of information will be minimal.

Our first method for optimal data-set creation applies a randomized CSSP approach to the transpose of the data matrix, A^T. Equivalently, it selects the optimal k *rows* of A for embedding the full set of unlabeled examples. We use a recently developed randomized algorithm (Boutsidis et al., 2009), and an underlying rank-revealing QR factorization (Golub, 1965).

[2]We note that the discriminative model of Jiampojamarn and Kondrak (2010) outperforms the Bisani and Ney model by an average of about 0.75 percentage points across five data sets.

[3]`http://www-i6.informatik.rwth-aachen.de/web/Software/g2p.html`

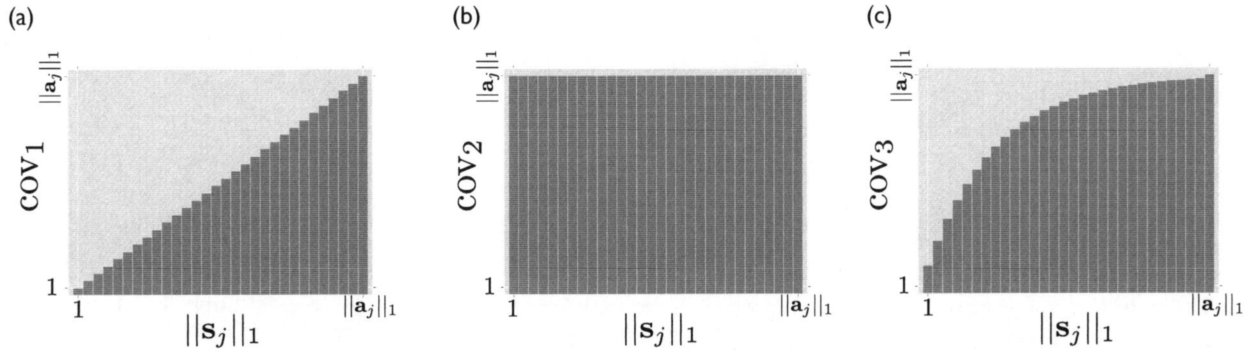

Figure 1: Various versions of the feature coverage function. Panel (a) shows cov_1 (Equation 5). Panel (b) shows cov_2 (Equation 6). Panel (c) shows cov_3 (Equation 7) with discount factor $\eta = 1.2$.

3 Two Methods for Optimal Data Set Selection

In this section we detail our two proposed methods for optimal data set selection. The key intuition is that we would like to pick a subset of data points which broadly and efficiently cover the features of the full range of data points. We assume a large pool $\mathcal{X}$ of n unlabeled examples, and our goal is to select a subset $\mathcal{S} \subset \mathcal{X}$ of size $k \ll n$ for labeling. We assume that each data point $x \in \mathcal{X}$ is a vector of m feature values. Our first method applies to any real or complex feature space, while our second method is specialized for binary features. We will use the $(n \times m)$ matrix A to denote our unlabeled data: each row is a data point and each column is a feature. In all our experiments, we used the presence (1) or absence (0) of each character 4-gram as our set of features.

3.1 Method 1: Row Subset Selection

To motivate this method, first consider the task of finding a rank k approximation to the data matrix A. The SVD decomposition yields:

$$A = U \Sigma V^T$$

- U is $(n \times n)$ orthogonal and its columns form the eigenvectors of AA^T
- V is $(m \times m)$ orthogonal and its columns form the eigenvectors of $A^T A$
- Σ is $(n \times m)$ diagonal, and its diagonal entries are the singular values of A (the square roots of the eigenvalues of both AA^T and $A^T A$).

To obtain a rank k approximation to A, we start by rewriting the SVD decomposition as a sum:

$$A = \sum_{i=1}^{\rho} \sigma_i \mathbf{u}_i \mathbf{v}_i^T \quad (1)$$

where $\rho = \min(m, n)$, σ_i is the ith diagonal entry of Σ, $\mathbf{u}_i$ is the ith column of U, and $\mathbf{v}_i$ is the ith column of V. To obtain a rank k approximation to A, we simply truncate the sum in equation 1 to its first k terms, yielding A_k. To evaluate the quality of this approximation, we can measure the Frobenius norm of the residual matrix $||A - A_k||_F$.[4] The Eckart-Young theorem (Eckart and Young, 1936) states that A_k is optimal in the following sense:

$$A_k = \underset{\tilde{A} \ s.t. \ \text{rank}(\tilde{A})=k}{\text{argmin}} ||A - \tilde{A}||_F \quad (2)$$

In other words, truncated SVD gives the best rank k approximation to A in terms of minimizing the Frobenius norm of the residual matrix. In CSSP, the goal is similar, with the added constraint that the approximation to A must be obtained by projecting onto the subspace spanned by a k-subset of the original rows of A.[5] Formally, the goal is to produce a $(k \times m)$ matrix S formed from rows of A, such that

$$||A - AS^+S||_F \quad (3)$$

[4]The Frobenius norm $||M||_F$ is defined as the entry-wise L_2 norm: $\sqrt{\sum_{i,j} m_{ij}^2}$

[5]Though usually framed in terms of column selection, we switch to row selection here as our goal is to select data points rather than features.

is minimized over all $\binom{n}{k}$ possible choices for S. Here S^+ is the $(m \times k)$ Moore-Penrose pseudo-inverse of S, and S^+S gives the orthogonal projector onto the rowspace of S. In other words, our goal is to select k data points which serve as a good approximate basis for *all* the data points. Since AS^+S can be at most rank k, the constraint considered here is stricter than that of Equation 1, so the truncated SVD A_k gives a lower bound on the residual.

Boutsidis et al (2009) develop a randomized algorithm that produces a submatrix S (consisting of k rows of A) which, with high probability, achieves a residual bound of:

$$||A - AS^+S||_F \leq O(k\sqrt{\log k})||A - A_k||_F \quad (4)$$

in running time $O(\min\{mn^2, m^2n\})$. The algorithm proceeds in three steps: first by computing the SVD of A, then by randomly sampling $O(k \log k)$ rows of A with importance weights carefully computed from the SVD, and then applying a deterministic rank-revealing QR factorization (Golub, 1965) to select k of the sampled rows. To give some intuition, we now provide some background on rank revealing factorizations.

Rank revealing QR / LQ (RRQR) Every real $(n \times m)$ matrix can be factored as $A = LQ$, where Q is $(m \times m)$ orthogonal and L is $(n \times m)$ lower triangular.[6] It is important to notice that in this triangular factorization, each successive row of A introduces exactly one new basis vector from Q. We can thus represent row i as a linear combination of the first $i - 1$ rows along with the ith row of Q.

A *rank-revealing* factorization is one which displays the numerical rank of the matrix — defined to be the singular value index r such that

$$\sigma_r \gg \sigma_{r+1} = O(\epsilon)$$

for machine precision ϵ. In the case of the LQ factorization, our goal is to order the rows of A such that each successive row has decreasing representational importance as a basis for the future rows. More formally, If there exists a row permutation Π such that ΠA has a triangular factorization $\Pi A = LQ$ with $L = \begin{bmatrix} L_{11} & 0 \\ L_{21} & L_{22} \end{bmatrix}$, where the smallest singular value of L_{11} is much greater than the spectral norm of L_{22}, which is itself almost zero:

$$\sigma_{min}(L_{11}) \gg ||L_{22}||_2 = O(\epsilon)$$

then we say that $\Pi A = LQ$ is a *rank-revealing LQ factorization*. Both L_{11} and L_{22} will be lower triangular matrices and if L_{11} is $(r \times r)$ then A has numerical rank r (Hong and Pan, 1992).

[6] We replace the standard upper triangular QR factorization with an equivalent lower triangular factorization LQ to focus intuition on the rowspace of A.

Language	Training	Test	Total
Dutch	11,622	104,589	116,211
English	11209	100891	112100
French	2,748	24,721	27,469
Frisian	6,198	55,778	61,976
German	4,942	44,460	49,402
Italian	7,529	79,133	86,662
Norwegian	4,172	37,541	41,713
Spanish	3,150	28,341	31,491

Table 1: Pronunciation dictionary size for each of the languages.

Implementation In our implementation of the CSSP algorithm, we first prune away 4-gram features that appear in fewer than 3 words, then compute the SVD of the pruned data matrix using the PROPACK package,[7] which efficiently handles sparse matrixes. After sampling $k \log k$ words from A (with sampling weights calculated from the top-k singular vectors), we form a submatrix B consisting of the sampled words. We then use the RRQR implementation from ACM Algorithm 782 (Bischof and Quintana-Ortí, 1998) (routine DGEQPX) to compute $\Pi B = LQ$. We finally select the first k rows of ΠB as our optimal data set. Even for our largest data sets (English and Dutch), this entire procedure runs in less than an hour on a 3.4Ghz quad-core i7 desktop with 32 GB of RAM.

3.2 Method 2: Feature Coverage Maximization

In our previous approach, we adopted a general method for approximating a matrix with a subset of rows (or columns). Here we develop a novel objective function with the specific aim of optimal data set selection. Our key assumption is that the benefit of

[7] http://soi.stanford.edu/~rmunk/PROPACK/

seeing a new feature f in a selected data point bears a positive relationship to the frequency of f in the unlabeled pool of words. However, we further assume that the lion's share of benefit accrues quickly, with the marginal utility quickly tapering off as we label more and more examples with feature f. Note that for this method, we assume a boolean feature space.

To formalize this intuition, we will define the *coverage* of a selected $(k \times m)$ submatrix S consisting of rows of A, with respect to a feature index j. For illustration purposes, we will list three alternative definitions:

$$\mathrm{cov}_1(S;j) = ||\mathbf{s}_j||_1 \tag{5}$$

$$\mathrm{cov}_2(S;j) = ||\mathbf{a}_j||_1 \, \mathbb{I}\big(||\mathbf{s}_j||_1 > 0\big) \tag{6}$$

$$\mathrm{cov}_3(S;j) = ||\mathbf{a}_j||_1 - \frac{||\mathbf{a}_j||_1}{\eta^{||\mathbf{s}_j||_1}} \, \mathbb{I}\big(||\mathbf{s}_j||_1 < ||\mathbf{a}_j||_1\big) \tag{7}$$

In all cases, $\mathbf{s}_j$ refers the jth column of S, $\mathbf{a}_j$ refers the jth column of A, $\mathbb{I}(\cdot)$ is a 0-1 indicator function, and η is a scalar discount factor.[8]

Figure 1 provides an intuitive explanation of these functions: cov_1 simply counts the number of selected data points with boolean feature j. Thus, full coverage ($||\mathbf{a}_j||$: the entire number of data points with the feature) is only achieved when *all* data points with the feature are selected. cov_2 lies at the opposite extreme. Even a single selected data point with feature j triggers coverage of the entire feature. Finally, cov_3 is designed so that the coverage scales monotonically as additional data points with feature j are selected. The first selected data point will capture all but $\frac{1}{\eta}$ of the total coverage, and each further selected data point will capture all but $\frac{1}{\eta}$ of whatever coverage remains. Essentially, the coverage for a feature scales as a geometric series in the number of selected examples having that feature.

To ensure that the total coverage ($|||\mathbf{a}_j||_1$) is achieved when all the data points are selected, we add an indicator function for the case of $||\mathbf{c}_j||_1 = ||\mathbf{a}_j||_1$.[9]

[8] Chosen to be 5 in all our experiments. We experimented with several values between 2 and 10, without significant differences in results.

[9] Otherwise, the geometric coverage function would converge to $||\mathbf{a}_j||$ only as $||\mathbf{c}_j|| \to \infty$.

	500 Words			2000 Words		
	RAND	CSSP	FEAT	RAND	CSSP	FEAT
Dut	48.2	50.8	**59.3**	69.8	75.0	**77.8**
Eng	25.4	26.5	**29.5**	40.3	40.1	**42.8**
Fra	66.9	69.2	**72.1**	81.2	82.0	**84.8**
Fri	42.7	48.0	**53.6**	62.2	65.3	**68.5**
Ger	55.2	58.6	**65.0**	74.2	78.6	**80.8**
Ita	80.6	82.8	**82.8**	85.3	86.1	**86.8**
Nor	48.1	49.5	**55.0**	66.1	69.9	**71.6**
Spa	90.7	**96.8**	95.0	98.1	98.4	**99.0**
avg	57.2	60.3	**64.0**	72.2	74.4	**76.5**

Table 2: Test word accuracy across the 8 languages for randomly selected words (RAND), CSSP matrix subset selection (CSSP), and Feature Coverage Maximization (FEAT). We show results for 500 and 2000 word training sets.

Setting our feature coverage function to cov_3, we can now define the overall feature coverage of the selected points as:

$$\mathbf{coverage}(S) = \frac{1}{||A||_1} \sum_j \mathrm{cov}_3(S;j) \tag{8}$$

where $||A||_1$ is the L_1 entrywise matrix norm, $\sum_{i,j} |A_{ij}|$, which ensures that $0 \leq \mathbf{coverage}(S) \leq 1$ with equality only achieved when $S = A$, i.e. when all data points have been selected.

We provide a brief sketch of our optimization algorithm: To pick the subset S of k words which optimizes Equation 8, we incrementally build optimal subsets $S' \subset S$ of size $k' < k$. At each stage, we keep track of the unclaimed coverage associated with each feature j:

$$\mathrm{unclaimed}(j) = ||\mathbf{a}_j||_1 - \mathrm{cov}_3(S';j)$$

To add a new word, we scan through the pool of remaining words, and calculate the additional coverage that selecting word w would achieve:

$$\Delta(w) \quad = \sum_{\text{feature } j \text{ in } w} \mathrm{unclaimed}(j) \left(\frac{\eta - 1}{\eta}\right)$$

We greedily select the word which adds the most coverage, remove it from the pool, and update the unclaimed feature coverages. It is easy to show that this greedy algorithm is globally optimal.

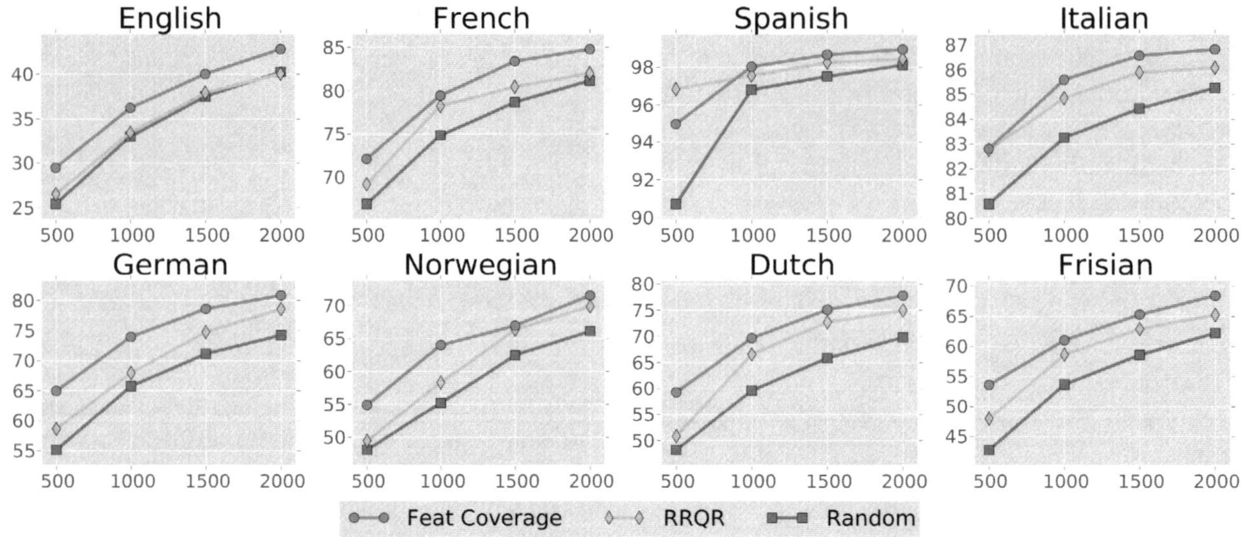

Figure 2: Test word accuracy across the 8 languages for (1) feature coverage, (2) CSSP matrix subset selection, (3) and randomly selected words.

4 Experiments and Analysis

To test the effectiveness of the two proposed data set selection methods, we conduct grapheme-to-phoneme prediction experiments across a test suite of 8 languages: Dutch, English, French, Frisian, German, Italian, Norwegian, and Spanish. The data was obtained from the PASCAL Letter-to-Phoneme Conversion Challenge,[10] and was processed to match the setup of Dwyer and Kondrak (2009). The data comes from a range of sources, including CELEX for Dutch and German (Baayen et al., 1995), BRULEX for French (Mousty et al., 1990), CMUDict for English,[11] the Italian Festival Dictionary (Cosi et al., 2000), as well as pronunciation dictionaries for Spanish, Norwegian, and Frisian (original provenance not clear).

As Table 1 shows, the size of the dictionaries ranges from 31,491 words (Spanish) up to 116,211 words (Dutch). We follow the PASCAL challenge training and test folds, treating the training set as our pool of words to be selected for labeling.

Results We consider training subsets of sizes 500, 1000, 1500, and 2000. For our baseline, we train the G2P model (Bisani and Ney, 2008) on randomly selected words of each size, and average the results over 10 runs. We follow the same procedure for our two data set selection methods. Figure 2 plots the word prediction accuracy for all three methods across the eight languages with varying training sizes, while Table 2 provides corresponding numerical results. We see that in all scenarios the two data set selection strategies fare better than random subsets of words.

In all but one case, the feature coverage method yields the best performance (with the exception of Spanish trained with 500 words, where the CSSP yields the best results). Feature coverage achieves average error reduction of 20% over the randomly selected training words across the different languages and training set sizes.

Coverage variants We also experimented with the other versions of the feature coverage function discussed in Section 3.2 (see Figure 1). While cov_1 tended to perform quite poorly (usually worse than random), cov_2 — which gives full credit for each feature the first time it is seen — yields results just slightly worse than the CSSP matrix method on average, and always better than random. In the 2000 word scenario, for example, cov_2 achieves average accuracy of 74.0, just a bit below the 74.4 accuracy of the CSSP method. It is also possible that more

[10] `http://pascallin.ecs.soton.ac.uk/Challenges/PRONALSYL/`

[11] `http://www.speech.cs.cmu.edu/cgi-bin/cmudict`

	RAND	CSSP	FEAT	SVD
Fra	0.66	0.62	0.65	0.51
Fry	0.75	0.72	0.75	0.6
Ger	0.71	0.67	0.71	0.55
Ita	0.64	0.61	0.67	0.49
Nor	0.7	0.61	0.64	0.5
Spa	0.65	0.67	0.68	0.53
avg	0.69	0.65	0.68	0.53

Table 3: Residual matrix norm across 6 languages for randomly selected words (RAND), CSSP matrix subset selection (CSSP), feature coverage maximization (FEAT), and the rank k SVD (SVD). Lower is better.

	RAND	CSSP	FEAT
Dut	0.66	0.72	0.81
Eng	0.52	0.58	0.69
Fra	0.68	0.74	0.81
Fry	0.7	0.79	0.84
Ger	0.68	0.74	0.81
Ita	0.79	0.84	0.9
Nor	0.7	0.79	0.84
Spa	0.67	0.75	0.8
avg	0.68	0.74	0.81

Table 4: Feature coverage across the 8 languages for randomly selected words (RAND), CSSP matrix subset selection (CSSP), and feature coverage maximization (FEAT). Higher is better.

careful tuning of the discount factor η of cov_3 would yield further gains.

Optimization Analysis Both the CSSP and feature coverage methods have clearly defined objective functions — formulated in Equations 3 and 8, respectively. We can therefore ask how well each methods fares in optimizing either one of the two objectives.

First we consider the objective of the CSSP algorithm: to find k data points which can accurately embed the entire data matrix. Once the data points are selected, we compute the orthogonal projection of the data matrix onto the submatrix, obtaining an approximation matrix $\tilde{A}$. We can then measure the residual norm as a fraction of the original matrix norm:

$$\frac{||A - \tilde{A}||_F}{||A||_F} \tag{9}$$

As noted in Section 3.1, truncated SVD minimizes the residual over all rank k matrices, so we can compare our three methods — random selections, CSSP, and feature coverage — all of which select k examples as a basis, against the lower bound given by SVD. Table 3 shows the result of this analysis for $k = 2000$ (Note that we were unable to compute the projection matrices for English and Dutch due to the size of the data and memory limitations). As expected, SVD fares the best, with CSSP as a somewhat distant second. On average, feature coverage seems to do a bit better than random.

A similar analysis for the feature coverage objective function is shown in Table 4. Unsurprisingly, this objective is best optimized by the feature coverage method. Interestingly though, CSSP seems to perform about halfway between random and the feature coverage method. This makes some sense, as good basis data points will tend to have frequent features, while at the same time being maximally spread out from one another. We also note that the poor coverage result for English in Table 4 mirrors its overall poor performance in the G2P prediction task – not only are the phoneme labels unpredictable, but the input data itself is wild and hard to compress.

CSSP	FEAT	FEAT-SLS
fettered	internationalization	rating
exceptionally	underestimating	overs
gellert	schellinger	nation
daughtry	barristers	scherman
blowed	constellations	olinger
harmonium	complementing	anderson
cassini	bergerman	inter
rupees	characteristically	stated
tewksbury	heatherington	press
ley	overstated	conner

Table 5: Top 10 words selected by CSSP, feature coverage (FEAT), and feature coverage with stratified length sampling (FEAT-SLS)

Stratified length sampling As Table 5 shows, the top 10 words selected by the feature coverage method are mostly long and unusual, averaging 13.3 characters in length. In light of the potential annotation burden, we developed a stratified sampling strategy to ensure typical word lengths. Before selecting each new word, we first sample a word length according to the empirical word length distribution. We then choose among words of the sampled length according to the feature coverage criterion. This results in more typical words of average length, with only a very small drop in performance.

5 Conclusion and Future Work

In this paper we proposed the task of optimal data set selection in the unsupervised setting. In contrast to active learning, our methods do not require repeated training of multiple models and iterative annotations. Since the methods are unsupervised, they also avoid tying the selected data set to a particular model class (or even task).

We proposed two methods for optimally selecting a small subset of examples for labeling. The first uses techniques developed by the numerical linear algebra and theory communities for approximating matrices with subsets of columns or rows. For our second method, we developed a novel notion of *feature coverage*. Experiments on the task of grapheme-to-phoneme prediction across eight languages show that our method yields performance improvements in all scenarios, averaging 20% reduction in error. For future work, we intend to apply the data set selection strategies to other NLP tasks, such as the optimal selection of sentences for tagging and parsing.

Acknowledgments

The authors thank the reviewers and acknowledge support by the NSF (grant IIS-1116676) and a research gift from Google. Any opinions, findings, or conclusions are those of the authors, and do not necessarily reflect the views of the NSF.

References

RH Baayen, R. Piepenbrock, and L. Gulikers. 1995. The celex lexical database (version release 2)[cd-rom]. *Philadelphia, PA: Linguistic Data Consortium, University of Pennsylvania.*

Maximilian Bisani and Hermann Ney. 2008. Joint-sequence models for grapheme-to-phoneme conversion. *Speech Communication*, 50(5):434–451, 5.

C.H. Bischof and G. Quintana-Ortí. 1998. Algorithm 782: codes for rank-revealing qr factorizations of dense matrices. *ACM Transactions on Mathematical Software (TOMS)*, 24(2):254–257.

C. Boutsidis, M.W. Mahoney, and P. Drineas. 2008. Unsupervised feature selection for principal components analysis. In *Proceeding of the 14th ACM SIGKDD international conference on Knowledge discovery and data mining*, pages 61–69.

C. Boutsidis, M. W. Mahoney, and P. Drineas. 2009. An improved approximation algorithm for the column subset selection problem. In *Proceedings of the twentieth Annual ACM-SIAM Symposium on Discrete Algorithms*, pages 968–977. Society for Industrial and Applied Mathematics.

P. Cosi, R. Gretter, and F. Tesser. 2000. Festival parla italiano. *Proceedings of GFS2000, Giornate del Gruppo di Fonetica Sperimentale, Padova.*

K. Dwyer and G. Kondrak. 2009. Reducing the annotation effort for letter-to-phoneme conversion. In *Proceedings of the ACL*, pages 127–135. Association for Computational Linguistics.

Matthias Eck, Stephan Vogel, and Alex Waibel. 2005. Low cost portability for statistical machine translation based on n-gram coverage. In *Proceedings of the Machine Translation Summit X.*

C. Eckart and G. Young. 1936. The approximation of one matrix by another of lower rank. *Psychometrika*, 1(3):211–218.

G. Golub. 1965. Numerical methods for solving linear least squares problems. *Numerische Mathematik*, 7(3):206–216.

Yoo Pyo Hong and C-T Pan. 1992. Rank-revealing factorizations and the singular value decomposition. *Mathematics of Computation*, 58(197):213–232.

S. Jiampojamarn and G. Kondrak. 2010. Letter-phoneme alignment: An exploration. In *Proceedings of the ACL*, pages 780–788. Association for Computational Linguistics.

R.M. Kaplan and M. Kay. 1994. Regular models of phonological rule systems. *Computational linguistics*, 20(3):331–378.

J. Kominek and A. W. Black. 2006. Learning pronunciation dictionaries: language complexity and word selection strategies. In *Proceedings of the NAACL*, pages 232–239. Association for Computational Linguistics.

K.Z. Mao. 2005. Identifying critical variables of principal components for unsupervised feature selection. *Systems, Man, and Cybernetics, Part B: Cybernetics, IEEE Transactions on*, 35(2):339–344.

Y. Marchand and R.I. Damper. 2000. A multistrategy approach to improving pronunciation by analogy. *Computational Linguistics*, 26(2):195–219.

P. Mousty, M. Radeau, et al. 1990. Brulex. une base de données lexicales informatisée pour le français écrit et parlé. *L'année psychologique*, 90(4):551–566.

T.J. Sejnowski and C.R. Rosenberg. 1987. Parallel networks that learn to pronounce english text. *Complex systems*, 1(1):145–168.

Burr Settles. 2010. Active learning literature survey. Technical Report TR1648, Department of Computer Sciences, University of Wisconsin-Madison.

H. Stoppiglia, G. Dreyfus, R. Dubois, and Y. Oussar. 2003. Ranking a random feature for variable and feature selection. *The Journal of Machine Learning Research*, 3:1399–1414.

L. Wolf and A. Shashua. 2005. Feature selection for unsupervised and supervised inference: The emergence of sparsity in a weight-based approach. *The Journal of Machine Learning Research*, 6:1855–1887.

Z. Zhao and H. Liu. 2007. Spectral feature selection for supervised and unsupervised learning. In *Proceedings of the ICML*, pages 1151–1157.

Knowledge-Rich Morphological Priors for Bayesian Language Models

Victor Chahuneau Noah A. Smith Chris Dyer
Language Technologies Institute
Carnegie Mellon University
Pittsburgh, PA 15213, USA
{vchahune,nasmith,cdyer}@cs.cmu.edu

Abstract

We present a morphology-aware nonparametric Bayesian model of language whose prior distribution uses manually constructed finite-state transducers to capture the word formation processes of particular languages. This relaxes the word independence assumption and enables sharing of statistical strength across, for example, stems or inflectional paradigms in different contexts. Our model can be used in virtually any scenario where multinomial distributions over words would be used. We obtain state-of-the-art results in language modeling, word alignment, and unsupervised morphological disambiguation for a variety of morphologically rich languages.

1 Introduction

Despite morphological phenomena's salience in most human languages, many NLP systems treat fully inflected forms as the atomic units of language. By assuming independence of lexical stems' various surface forms, this *avoidance approach* exacerbates the problem of data sparseness. If it is employed at all, morphological analysis of text tends to be treated as a preprocessing step to other NLP modules. While this latter *disambiguation approach* helps address data sparsity concerns, it has substantial drawbacks: it requires supervised learning from expert-annotated corpora, and determining the optimal morphological granularity is labor-intensive (Habash and Sadat, 2006).

Neither approach fully exploits the finite-state transducer (FST) technology that has been so successful for modeling the mapping between surface forms and their morphological analyses (Karttunen and Beesley, 2005), and the mature collections of high quality transducers that already exist for many languages (e.g., Turkish, Russian, Arabic). Much linguistic knowledge is encoded in such FSTs.

In this paper, we develop morphology-aware nonparametric Bayesian language models that bring together hand-written FSTs with statistical modeling and require no token-level annotation. The sparsity issue discussed above is addressed by hierarchical priors that share statistical strength across different inflections of the same stem by backing off to word formation models that piece together morphemes using FSTs. Furthermore, because of the nonparametric formulation of our models, the regular morphological patterns found in the long tail of word types will rely more heavily on deeper analysis, while frequent and idiosyncratically behaved forms are modeled opaquely.

Our prior can be used in virtually any generative model of language as a replacement for multinomial distributions over words, bringing morphological awareness to numerous applications. For various morphologically rich languages, we show that:

- our model can provide rudimentary unsupervised disambiguation for a highly ambiguous analyzer;
- integrating morphology into n-gram language models allows better generalization to unseen words and can improve the performance of applications that are truly open vocabulary; and
- bilingual word alignment models also benefit greatly from sharing translation information

across stems.

We are particularly interested in low-resource scenarios, where one has to make the most of the small quantity of available data, and overcoming data sparseness is crucial. If analyzers exist in such settings, they tend to be highly ambiguous, and annotated data for learning to disambiguate are also likely to be scarce or non-existent. Therefore, in our experiments with Russian, we compare two analyzers: a rapidly-developed *guesser*, which models regular inflectional paradigms but contains no lexicon or irregular forms, and a high-quality analyzer.

2 Word Models with Morphology

In this section, we describe a generative model of word formation based on Pitman-Yor processes that generates word types using a finite-state morphological generator. At a high level, the process first produces lexicons of stems and inflectional patterns; then it generates a lexicon of inflected forms using the finite-state generator. Finally, the inflected forms are used to generate observed data. Different independence assumptions can be made at each of these levels to encode beliefs about where stems, inflections, and surface forms should share statistical strength.

2.1 Pitman-Yor Processes

Our work relies extensively on Pitman-Yor processes, which provide a flexible framework for expressing backoff and interpolation relationships and extending standard models with richer word distributions (Pitman and Yor, 1997). They have been shown to match the performance of state-of-the-art language models and to give estimates that follow appropriate power laws (Teh, 2006).

A draw from a Pitman-Yor process (PYP), denoted $G \sim \text{PY}(d, \theta, G_0)$, is a discrete distribution over a (possibly infinite) set of events, which we denote abstractly $\mathcal{E}$. The process is parameterized by a discount parameter $0 \leq d < 1$, a strength parameter $\theta > -d$, and a base distribution G_0 over the event space $\mathcal{E}$.

In this work, our focus is on the base distribution G_0. We place vague priors on the hyperparameters $d \sim \mathbb{U}([0, 1])$ and $(\theta + d) \sim \text{Gamma}(1, 1)$. Inference in PYPs is discussed below.

2.2 Unigram Morphology Model

The most basic expression of our model is a unigram model of text. So far, we only assume that each word can be analyzed into a stem and a sequence of morphemes forming an inflection pattern. Let G_s be a distribution over stems, G_p be a distribution over inflectional patterns, and let GENERATE be a deterministic mapping from $\langle \text{stem}, \text{pattern} \rangle$ pairs to inflected word forms.[1] An inflected word *type* is generated with the following process, which we designate $\text{MP}(G_s, G_d, \text{GENERATE})$:

$$\begin{aligned} \text{stem} &\sim G_s \\ \text{pattern} &\sim G_p \\ \text{word} &= \text{GENERATE}(\text{stem}, \text{pattern}) \end{aligned}$$

For example, in Russian, we might sample stem = прочий,[2] pattern = STEM+Adj+Pl+Dat, and obtain word = прочим.

This model could be used directly to generate observed tokens. However, we have said nothing about G_s and G_p, and the assumption that stems and patterns are independent is clearly unsatisfying. We therefore assume that both the stem and the pattern distributions are generated from PY processes, and that $\text{MP}(G_s, G_p, \text{GENERATE})$ is itself the base distribution of a PYP.

$$\begin{aligned} G_s &\sim \text{PY}(d_s, \theta_s, G_s^0) \\ G_p &\sim \text{PY}(d_p, \theta_p, G_p^0) \\ G_w &\sim \text{PY}(d, \theta, \text{MP}(G_s, G_p, \text{GENERATE})) \end{aligned}$$

A draw G_w from this PYP is a unigram distribution over tokens.

2.3 Base Stem Model G_s^0

In general there are an unbounded number of stems possible in any language, so we set G_s^0 to be character trigram model, which we statically estimate, with Kneser-Ney smoothing, from a large corpus of word types in the language being modeled. While using fixed parameters estimated to maximize likelihood is

[1] The assumption of determinism is only inappropriate in cases of inflectional spelling variants (e.g., *modeled* vs. *modelled*) or pronunciation variants (e.g., reduced forms in certain environments).

[2] прочий (pronounced [prɐtɕij]) = *other*

questionable from the perspective of Bayesian learning, it is tremendously beneficial for computational reasons. For some applications (e.g., word alignment), the set of possible stems for a corpus S can be precomputed, so we will also experiment with using a uniform stem distribution based on this set.

2.4 Base Pattern Model G_p^0

Several choices are possible for the base pattern distribution:

MP$_0$ We can assume a uniform G_p^0 when the number of patterns is small.

MP$_1$ To be able to generalize to new patterns, we can draw the length of the pattern from a Poisson distribution and generate morphemes one by one from a uniform distribution.

MP$_2$ A more informative prior is a Markov chain of morphemes, where each morpheme is generated conditional on the preceding morpheme.

The choice of the base pattern distribution could depend on the complexity of the inflectional patterns produced by the morphological analyzer, reflecting the type of morphological phenomena present in a given language. For example, the number of possible patterns can practically be considered finite in Russian, but this assumption is not valid for languages with more extensive derivational morphology like Turkish.

2.5 Posterior Inference

For most applications, rather than directly generating from a model using the processes outlined above, we seek to infer posterior distributions over latent parameters and structures, given a sample of data.

Although there is no known analytic form of the PYP density, it is possible to marginalize the draws from it and to work directly with observations. This marginalization produces the classical Chinese restaurant process representation (Teh, 2006). When working with the morphology models we are proposing, we also need to marginalize the different latent forms (stems s and patterns p) that may have given rise to a given word w. Thus, we require that the inverse relation of GENERATE is available to compute the marginal base word distribution:

$$p(w \mid G_w^0) = \sum_{\textsc{Generate}(s,p)=w} p(s \mid G_s)\, p(p \mid G_p)$$

Since our approach encodes morphology using FSTs, which are invertible, this poses no problem.

To illustrate, consider the Russian word прочим, which may be analyzed in several ways:

прочий	+Adj +Sg +Neut +Instr
прочий	+Adj +Sg +Masc +Instr
прочий	+Adj +Pl +Dat
прочить	+Verb +Pl +1P
прочее	+Pro +Sg +Ins

Because the set of possible analyses is in general small, marginalization is fast and complex blocked sampling is not necessary.

Finally, to infer hyperparameter values $(d, \theta, \ldots)$, a Metropolis-Hastings update is interleaved with Gibbs sampling steps for the rest of the hidden variables.[3]

Having described a model for generating words, we now show its usage in several contexts.

3 Unsupervised Morphological Disambiguation

Given a rule-based morphological analyzer encoded as an unweighted FST and a corpus on which the analyzer has been run – possibly generating multiple analyses for each token – we can use our unigram model to learn a probabilistic model of disambiguation in an unsupervised setting (i.e., without annotated examples). The corpus is assumed to be generated from the unigram distribution G_w, and the base stem model is set to a fixed character trigram model.[4] After learning the parameters of the model, we can find for each word in the vocabulary its most likely analysis and use this as a crude disambiguation step.

[3]The proposal distribution for Metropolis-Hastings is a Beta distribution (d) or a Gamma distribution ($\theta + d$) centered on the previous parameter values.

[4]Experiments suggest that this is important to constrain the model to realistic stems.

3.1 Morphological Guessers

Finite-state morphological analyzers are usually specified in three parts: a **stem lexicon**, which defines the words in the language and classifies them into several categories according to their grammatical function and their morphological properties; a set of **prefixes and suffixes** that can be applied to each category to form surface words; and possibly **alternation rules** that can encode exceptions and spelling variations. The combination of these parts provides a powerful framework for defining a generative model of words. Such models can be reversed to obtain an analyzer. However, while the two latter parts can be relatively easy to specify, enumerating a comprehensive stem lexicon is a time consuming and necessarily incomplete process, as some categories are truly open-class.

To allow unknown words to be analyzed, one can use a *guesser* that attempts to analyze words missing in the lexicon. Can we eliminate the stem lexicon completely and use only the guesser? This is what we try to do by designing a lexicon-free analyzer for Russian. A guesser was developed in three hours; it is prone to over-generation and produces ambiguous analyses for most words but covers a large number of morphological phenomena (gender, case, tense, etc.). For example, the word иврите[5] can be correctly analyzed as `иврит+Noun+Masc+Prep+Sg` but also as the incorrect forms: `ивритъ+Verb+Pres+2P+Pl`, `иврита+Noun+Fem+Dat+Sg`, `иврития+Noun+Fem+Prep+Sg`, and more.

3.2 Disambiguation Experiments

We train the unigram model on a 1.7M-word corpus of TED talks transcriptions translated into Russian (Cettolo et al., 2012) and evaluate our analyzer against a test set consisting of 1,500 gold-standard analyses obtained from the morphology disambiguation task of the DIALOG 2010 conference (Lyaševskaya et al., 2010).[6]

Each analysis is composed of a lemma (`иврит`), a part of speech (`Noun`), and a sequence of additional functional morphemes (`Masc,Prep,Sg`). We consider only open-class categories: nouns, adjectives, adverbs and verbs, and evaluate the output of our model with three metrics: the lemma accuracy, the part-of-speech accuracy, and the morphology F-measure.[7]

As a baseline, we consider picking a random analysis from output of the analyzer or choosing the most frequent lemma and the most frequent morphological pattern.[8] Then, we use our model with each of the three versions of the pattern model described in §2.2. Finally, as an upper bound, we use the gold standard to select one of the analyses produced by the guesser.

Since our evaluation is not directly comparable to the standard for this task, we use for reference a high-quality analyzer from Xerox[9] disambiguated with the MP_0 model (all of the models have very close accuracy in this case).

Model	Lemma	POS	Morph.
Random	29.8	70.9	50.2
Frequency	31.1	74.4	48.8
Guesser MP_0	60.0	82.2	66.3
Guesser MP_1	58.9	82.5	69.5
Guesser MP_2	59.9	82.4	65.5
Guesser oracle	68.4	84.9	83.0
Xerox MP_0	83.6	96.4	78.1

Table 1: Russian morphological disambiguation.

Considering the amount of effort put in developing the guesser, the baseline POS tagging accuracy is relatively good. However, the disambiguation is largely improved by using our unigram model with respect to all the evaluation categories. We are still far from the performance of a high-quality analyzer but, in absence of such a resource, our technique might be a sensible option. We also note that there is no clear winner in terms of pattern model, and conclude that this choice is task-specific.

[5] иврите = *Hebrew* (masculine noun, prepositional case)

[6] `http://ru-eval.ru`

[7] F-measure computed for the set of additional morphemes and averaged over the words in the corpus.

[8] We estimate these frequencies by assuming each analysis of each token is uniformly likely, then summing fractional counts.

[9] `http://open.xerox.com/Services/fst-nlp-tools/Pages/morphology`

4 Open Vocabulary Language Models

We now integrate our unigram model in a hierarchical Pitman-Yor n-gram language model (Fig. 1). The training corpus words are assumed to be generated from a distribution G_w^n drawn from $\text{PY}(d_n, \theta_n, G_w^{n-1})$, where G_w^{n-1} is defined recursively down to the base model G_w^0. Previous work Teh (2006) simply used $G_w^0 = \mathbb{U}(V)$ where V is the word vocabulary, but in our case G_w^0 is the MP defined in §2.2.

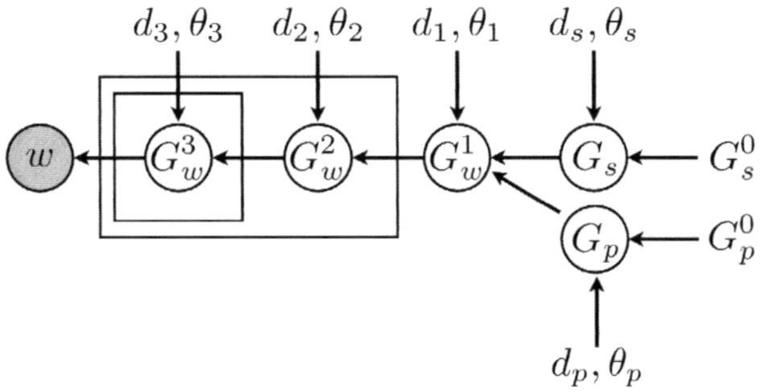

Figure 1: The trigram version of our language model represented as a graphical model. G_w^1 is the unigram model of §2.2.

We are interested in evaluating our model in an open vocabulary scenario where the ability to explain new unseen words matters. We expect our model to be able to generalize better thanks to the combination of a morphological analyzer and a stem distribution which is less sparse than the word distribution (for example, for the 1.6M word Turkish corpus, $|V| \approx 3.5|S| \approx 140\text{k}$).

To integrate out-of-vocabulary words in our evaluation, we use infinite base distributions: G_w^0 (in the baseline model) or G_s^0 (in the MP) are character trigram models. We define perplexity of a held-out test corpus in the standard way:

$$\text{ppl} = \exp\left(-\frac{1}{N}\sum_{i=1}^{N}\log p\left(w_i \mid w_{i-n+1}\cdots w_{i-1}\right)\right)$$

but compared to the common practice, we do not need to discount OOVs from this sum since the model vocabulary is infinite. Note that we also marginalize by summing over all the possible analyses for a given word when computing its base probability according to the MP.

4.1 Language Modeling Experiments

We train several trigram models on the Russian TED talks corpus used in the previous section. Our baseline is a hierarchical PY trigram model with a trigram character model as the base word distribution. We compare it with our model using the same character model for the base *stem* distribution. Both of the morphological analyzers described in the previous section help obtaining perplexity reductions (Table 2). We ran a similar experiment on the Turkish version of this corpus (1.6M words) with a high-quality analyzer (Oflazer, 1994) and obtain even larger gains (Table 3).

Model	ppl
PY-character LM	563
Guesser MP_2	530
Xerox MP_2	522

Table 2: Evaluation of the Russian n-gram model.

Model	ppl
PY-character LM	1,640
Oflazer MP_2	1,292

Table 3: Evaluation of the Turkish n-gram model.

These results can partly be attributed to the high OOV rate in these conditions: 4% for the Russian corpus and 6% for the Turkish corpus.

4.2 Predictive Text Input

It is difficult to know whether a decrease in perplexity, as measured in the previous section, will result in a performance improvement in downstream applications. As a confirmation that correctly modeling new words matters, we consider a predictive task with a truly open vocabulary and that requires *only* a language model: predictive text input.

Given some text, we encode it using a lossy deterministic character mapping, and try to recover the original content by computing the most likely word sequence. This task is inspired by predictive text input systems available on cellphones with a 9-key keypad. For example, the string `gave me a cup` is encoded as `4283 63 2 287`, which could also be decoded as: `hate of a bus`.

Silfverberg et al. (2012) describe a system designed for this task in Finnish, which is composed of a weighted finite-state morphological analyzer trained on IRC logs. However, their system is restricted to words that are encoded in the analyzer's lexicon and does not use context for disambiguation.

In our experiments, we use the same Turkish TED talks corpus as the previous section. As a baseline, we use a trigram character language model. We produce a character lattice which encodes all the possible interpretations for a word and compose it with a finite-state representation of the character LM using OpenFST (Allauzen et al., 2007). Alternatively, we can use a unigram word model to decode this lattice, backing off to the character language model if no solution is found. Finally, to be able to make use of word context, we can extract the k most likely paths according to the character LM and produce a word lattice, which is in turn decoded with a language model defined over the extracted vocabulary.

Model	WER	CER
Character LM	48.37	16.72
1-gram + character LM	8.50	3.28
1-gram MP_2	**6.46**	**2.37**
3-gram + character LM	7.86	3.07
3-gram MP_2	**5.73**	**2.15**

Table 4: Evaluation of Turkish predictive text input.

We measure word and character error rate (WER, CER) on the predicted word sequence and observe large improvements in both of these metrics by modeling morphology, both at the unigram level and when context is used (Table 4).

Preliminary experiments with a corpus of 1.6M Turkish tweets, an arguably more appropriate domain this task, show smaller but consistent improving: the trigram word error rate is reduced from 26% to 24% when our model is used.

4.3 Limitations

While our model is an important step forward in practical modeling of OOVs using morphological processes, we have made the linguistically naive assumption that morphology applies inside the language's lexicon but has no effect on the process that put inflected lexemes together into sentences. In this regard, our model is a minor variant on traditional n-gram models that work with "opaque" word forms. How to best relax this assumption in a computationally tractable way is an important open question left for future work.

5 Word Alignment Model

Monolingual models of language are not the only models that can benefit from taking into account morphology. In fact, alignment models are a good candidate for using richer word distributions: they assume a target word distribution conditioned on each source word. When the target language is morphologically rich, classic independence assumptions produce very weak models unless some kind of preprocessing is applied to one side of the corpus. An alternative is to use our unigram model as a word translation distribution for each source word in the corpus.

Our alignment model is based on a simple variant of IBM Model 2 where the alignment distribution is only controlled by two parameters, λ and p_0 (Dyer et al., 2013). p_0 is the probability of the null alignment. For a source sentence f of length n, a target sentence e of length m and a latent alignment a, we define the following alignment link probabilities ($j \neq 0$):

$$p(a_i = j \mid n, m) \propto (1 - p_0) \exp\left(-\lambda \left|\frac{i}{m} - \frac{j}{n}\right|\right)$$

λ controls the flatness of this distribution: larger values make the probabilities more peaked around the diagonal of the alignment matrix.

Each target word is then generated given a source word and a latent alignment link from the word translation distribution $p(e_i \mid f_{a_i}, G_w)$. Note that this is effectively a unigram distribution over target words, albeit conditioned on the source word f_j. Here is where our model differs from classic alignment models: the unigram distribution G_w is assumed be generated from a PY process. There are two choices for the base word distribution:

- As a baseline, we use a uniform base distribution over the target vocabulary: $G_w^0 = \mathbb{U}(V)$.
- We define a stem distribution $G_s[f]$ for each source word f, a shared pattern distribution G_p, and set $G_w^0[f] = \text{MP}(G_s[f], G_p)$. In this case,

we obtain the model depicted in Fig. 2. The stem and the pattern models are also given PY priors with uniform base distribution ($G_s^0 = \mathbb{U}(S)$).

Finally, we put uninformative priors on the alignment distribution parameters: $p_0 \sim \text{Beta}(\alpha, \beta)$ is collapsed and $\lambda \sim \text{Gamma}(k, \theta)$ is inferred using Metropolis-Hastings.

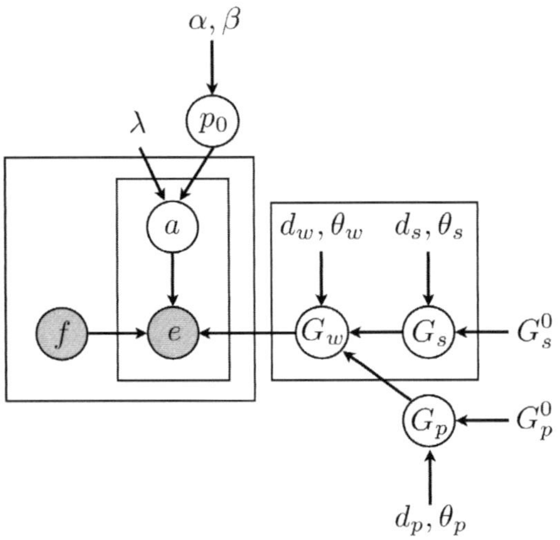

Figure 2: Our alignment model, represented as a graphical model.

Experiments

We evaluate the alignment error rate of our models for two language pairs with rich morphology on the target side. We compare to alignments inferred using IBM Model 4 trained with EM (Brown et al., 1993),[10] a version of our baseline model (described above) without PY priors (learned using EM), and the PY-based baseline. We consider two language pairs.

English-Turkish We use a 2.8M word cleaned version of the South-East European Times corpus (Tyers and Alperen, 2010) and gold-standard alignments from Çakmak et al. (2012). Our morphological analyzer is identical to the one used in the previous sections.

English-Czech We use the 1.3M word News Commentary corpus and gold-standard alignments from Bojar and Prokopová (2006). The morphological analyzer is provided by Xerox.

Results Results are shown in Table 5. Our lightly parameterized model performs much better than IBM Model 4 in these small-data conditions. With an identical model, we find PY priors outperform traditional multinomial distributions. Adding morphology further reduced the alignment error rate, for both languages.

	AER	
Model	en-tr	en-cs
Model 4	52.1	34.5
EM	43.8	28.9
PY-$\mathbb{U}(V)$	39.2	25.7
PY-$\mathbb{U}(S)$	**33.8**	**24.8**

Table 5: Word alignment experiments on English-Turkish (en-tr) and English-Czech (en-cs) data.

As an example of how our model generalizes better, consider the sentence pair in Fig. 3, taken from the evaluation data. The two words composing the Turkish sentence are not found elsewhere in the corpus, but several related inflections occur.[11] It is therefore trivial for the stem-base model to find the correct alignment (marked in black), while all the other models have no evidence for it and choose an arbitrary alignment (gray points).

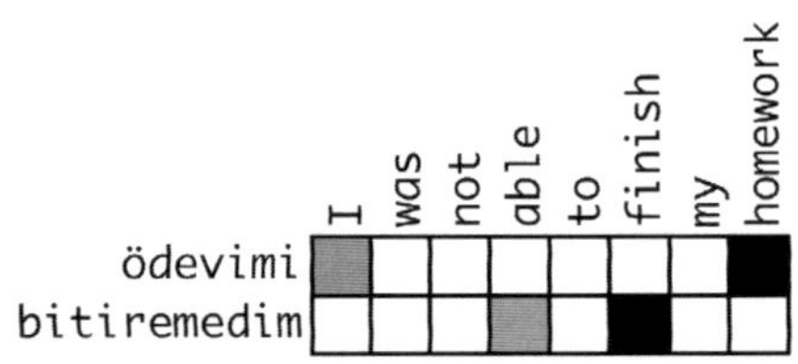

Figure 3: A complex Turkish-English word alignment (alignment points in gray: EM/PY-$\mathbb{U}(V)$; black: PY-$\mathbb{U}(S)$).

6 Related Work

Computational morphology has received considerable attention in NLP since the early work on *two-level morphology* (Koskenniemi, 1984; Kaplan and

[10] We use the default GIZA++ stage training scheme: Model 1 + HMM + Model 3 + Model 4.

[11] ödevinin, ödevini, ödevleri; bitmez, bitirileceğinden, bitmesiyle, ...

Kay, 1994). It is now widely accepted that finite-state transducers have sufficient power to express nearly all morphological phenomena, and the XFST toolkit (Beesley and Karttunen, 2003) has contributed to the practical adoption of this modeling approach. Recently, open-source tools have been released: in this paper, we used Foma (Hulden, 2009) to develop the Russian guesser.

Since some inflected forms have several possible analyses, there has been a great deal of work on selecting the intended one in context (Hakkani-Tür et al., 2000; Hajič et al., 2001; Habash and Rambow, 2005; Smith et al., 2005; Habash et al., 2009). Our disambiguation model is closely related to generative models used for this purpose (Hakkani-Tür et al., 2000).

Rule-based analysis is not the only approach to modeling morphology, and many unsupervised models have been proposed.[12] Heuristic segmentation approaches based on the minimum description length principle (Goldsmith, 2001; Creutz and Lagus, 2007; de Marcken, 1996; Brent et al., 1995) have been shown to be effective, and Bayesian model-based versions have been proposed as well (Goldwater et al., 2011; Snyder and Barzilay, 2008; Snover and Brent, 2001). In §3, we suggested a third way between rule-based approaches and fully unsupervised learning that combines the best of both worlds.

Morphological analysis or segmentation is crucial to the performance of several applications: machine translation (Goldwater and McClosky, 2005; Al-Haj and Lavie, 2010; Oflazer and El-Kahlout, 2007; Minkov et al., 2007; Habash and Sadat, 2006, *inter alia*), automatic speech recognition (Creutz et al., 2007), and syntactic parsing (Tsarfaty et al., 2010). Several methods have been proposed to integrate morphology into n-gram language models, including factored language models (Bilmes and Kirchhoff, 2003), discriminative language modeling (Arısoy et al., 2008), and more heuristic approaches (Monz, 2011).

Despite the fundamentally open nature of the lexicon (Heaps, 1978), there has been distressingly little attention to the general problem of open vocabulary language modeling problem (most applications make a closed-vocabulary assumption). The classic exploration of open vocabulary language modeling is Brown et al. (1992), which proposed the strategy of interpolating between word- and character-based models. Character-based language models are reviewed by Carpenter (2005). So-called *hybrid* models that model both words and sublexical units have become popular in speech recognition (Shaik et al., 2012; Parada et al., 2011; Bazzi, 2002). Open-vocabulary language language modeling has also recently been explored in the context of assistive technologies (Roark, 2009).

Finally, Pitman-Yor processes (PYPs) have become widespread in natural language processing since they are natural power-law generators. It has been shown that the widely used modified Kneser-Ney estimator (Chen and Goodman, 1998) for n-gram language models is an approximation of the posterior predictive distribution of a language model with hierarchical PYP priors (Goldwater et al., 2011; Teh, 2006).

7 Conclusion

We described a generative model which makes use of morphological analyzers to produce richer word distributions through sharing of statistical strength between stems. We have shown how it can be integrated into several models central to NLP applications and have empirically validated the effectiveness of these changes. Although this paper mostly focused on languages that are well studied and for which high-quality analyzers are available, our models are especially relevant in low-resource scenarios because they do not require disambiguated analyses. In future work, we plan to apply these techniques to languages such as Kinyarwanda, a resource-poor but morphologically rich language spoken in Rwanda. It is our belief that knowledge-rich models can help bridge the gap between low- and high-resource languages.

Acknowledgments

We thank Kemal Oflazer for making his Turkish language morphological analyzer available to us and Brendan O'Connor for gathering the Turkish tweets used in

[12] Developing a high-coverage analyzer can be a time-consuming process even with the simplicity of modern toolkits, and unsupervised morphology learning is an attractive problem for computational cognitive science.

the predictive text experiments. This work was sponsored by the U. S. Army Research Laboratory and the U. S. Army Research Office under contract/grant number W911NF-10-1-0533.

References

H. Al-Haj and A. Lavie. 2010. The impact of Arabic morphological segmentation on broad-coverage English-to-Arabic statistical machine translation. *Proc. of AMTA*.

Cyril Allauzen, Michael Riley, Johan Schalkwyk, Wojciech Skut, and Mehryar Mohri. 2007. OpenFst: A general and efficient weighted finite-state transducer library. In *Implementation and Application of Automata*, pages 11–23.

Ebru Arısoy, Brian Roark, Izhak Shafran, and Murat Saraçlar. 2008. Discriminative n-gram language modeling for Turkish. In *Proc. of Interspeech*.

Issam Bazzi. 2002. *Modelling out-of-vocabulary words for robust speech recognition*. Ph.D. thesis, MIT.

K.R. Beesley and L. Karttunen. 2003. *Finite-state morphology: Xerox tools and techniques*. CSLI, Stanford.

Jeff A. Bilmes and Katrin Kirchhoff. 2003. Factored language models and generalized parallel backoff. In *Proc. of NAACL*.

Ondřej Bojar and Magdalena Prokopová. 2006. Czech-English word alignment. In *Proc. of LREC*.

Michael R. Brent, Sreerama K. Murthy, and Andrew Lundberg. 1995. Discovering morphemic suffixes: A case study in MDL induction. In *Proceedings of the Fifth International Workshop on Artificial Intelligence and Statistics*.

Peter F. Brown, Vincent J. Della Pietra, Stephen A. Della Pietra, Robert L. Mercer, and Jennifer C. Lai. 1992. An estimate of an upper bound for the entropy of English. *Computational Linguistics*, 18(1):31–40.

P. F. Brown, V. J. D. Pietra, S. A. D. Pietra, and R. L. Mercer. 1993. The mathematics of statistical machine translation: Parameter estimation. *Computational Linguistics*, 19(2):263–311.

Bob Carpenter. 2005. Scaling high-order character language models to gigabytes. In *Proceedings of the ACL Workshop on Software*.

Mauro Cettolo, Christian Girardi, and Marcello Federico. 2012. WIT3: Web inventory of transcribed and translated talks. In *Proc. of EAMT*.

Stanley F. Chen and Joshua Goodman. 1998. An empirical study of smoothing techniques for language modeling. Technical Report TR-10-98, Harvard University.

Mathias Creutz and Krista Lagus. 2007. Unsupervised models for morpheme segmentation and morphology learning. *ACM Transactions on Speech and Language Processing*, 4(1).

M. Creutz, T. Hirsimäki, M. Kurimo, A. Puurula, J. Pylkkönen, V. Siivola, M. Varjokallio, E. Arisoy, M. Saraçlar, and A. Stolcke. 2007. Morph-based speech recognition and modeling of out-of-vocabulary words across languages. *ACM Transactions on Speech and Language Processing*, 5(1):3.

Carl G. de Marcken. 1996. *Unsupervised Language Acquisition*. Ph.D. thesis, MIT.

Chris Dyer, Victor Chahuneau, and Noah A. Smith. 2013. A simple, fast, and effective reparameterization of IBM Model 2. In *Proc. of NAACL*.

J. Goldsmith. 2001. Unsupervised learning of the morphology of a natural language. *Computational Linguistics*, 27(2):153–198.

S. Goldwater and D. McClosky. 2005. Improving statistical MT through morphological analysis. In *Proc. of EMNLP*.

Sharon Goldwater, Thomas L. Griffiths, and Mark Johnson. 2011. Producing power-law distributions and damping word frequencies with two-stage language models. *Journal of Machine Learning Research*, 12:2335–2382.

Nizar Habash and Owen Rambow. 2005. Arabic tokenization, part-of-speech tagging, and morphological disambiguation in one fell swoop. In *Proc. of ACL*.

Nizar Habash and Fatiha Sadat. 2006. Arabic preprocessing schemes for statistical machine translation. In *Proc. of NAACL*.

Nizar Habash, Owen Rambow, and Ryan Roth. 2009. MADA+TOKAN: A toolkit for Arabic tokenization, diacritization, morphological disambiguation, POS tagging, stemming and lemmatization. In *Proceedings of the Second International Conference on Arabic Language Resources and Tools*.

Jan Hajič, P. Krbec, P. Květoň, K. Oliva, and V. Petrovič. 2001. Serial combination of rules and statistics. In *Proc. of ACL*.

D. Z. Hakkani-Tür, Kemal Oflazer, and G. Tür. 2000. Statistical morphological disambiguation for agglutinative languages. In *Proc. of COLING*.

Harold Stanley Heaps. 1978. *Information Retrieval: Computational and Theoretical Aspects*. Academic Press.

M. Hulden. 2009. Foma: a finite-state compiler and library. In *Proc. of EACL*.

Ronald M. Kaplan and Martin Kay. 1994. Regular models of phonological rule systems. *Computational Linguistics*, 20(3):331–378.

Lauri Karttunen and Kenneth R. Beesley. 2005. Twenty-five years of finite-state morphology. In *Inquiries into Words, Constraints and Contexts*, pages 71–83. CSLI.

Kimmo Koskenniemi. 1984. A general computational model for word-form recognition and production. In *Proc. of ACL-COLING*.

O. Lyaševskaya, I. Astaf'yeva, A. Bonch-Osmolovskaya, A. Garejšina, Y. Grišina, V. D'yačkov, M. Ionov, A. Koroleva, M. Kudrinskij, A. Lityagina, Y. Lučina, Y. Sidorova, S. Toldova, S. Savčuk, and S. Koval'. 2010. Ocenka metodov avtomatičeskogo analiza teksta: morfologičeskie parseri russkogo yazyka. *Komp'juternaya lingvistika i intellektual'nye texnologii (Computational linguistics and intellectual technologies).*

Einat Minkov, Kristina Toutanova, and Hisami Suzuki. 2007. Generating complex morphology for machine translation. In *Proc. of ACL.*

Christof Monz. 2011. Statistical machine translation with local language models. In *Proc. of EMNLP.*

Kemal Oflazer and İlknur Durgar El-Kahlout. 2007. Exploring different representational units in English-to-Turkish statistical machine translation. In *Proc. of StatMT.*

K. Oflazer. 1994. Two-level description of Turkish morphology. *Literary and Linguistic Computing*, 9(2):137–148.

Carolina Parada, Mark Dredze, Abhinav Sethy, and Ariya Rastrow. 2011. Learning sub-word units for open vocabulary speech recognition. In *Proc. of ACL.*

Jim Pitman and Marc Yor. 1997. The two-parameter Poisson-Dirichlet distribution derived from a stable subordinator. *Annals of Probability*, 25(2):855–90.

Brian Roark. 2009. Open vocabulary language modeling for binary response typing interfaces. Technical Report CSLU-09-001, Oregon Health & Science University.

M. Ali Basha Shaik, David Rybach, Stefan Hahn, Ralf Schluüter, and Hermann Ney. 2012. Hierarchical hybrid language models for open vocabulary continuous speech recognition using wfst. In *Proc. of SAPA.*

M. Silfverberg, K. Lindén, and M. Hyvärinen. 2012. Predictive text entry for agglutinative languages using unsupervised morphological segmentation. In *Proc. of Computational Linguistics and Intelligent Text Processing.*

Noah A. Smith, David A. Smith, and Roy W. Tromble. 2005. Context-based morphological disambiguation with random fields. In *Proc. of EMNLP.*

Matt G. Snover and Michael R. Brent. 2001. A Bayesian model for morpheme and paradigm identification. In *Proc. of ACL.*

Benjamin Snyder and Regina Barzilay. 2008. Unsupervised multilingual learning for morphological segmentation. In *Proc. of ACL.*

Yee Whye Teh. 2006. A hierarchical Bayesian language model based on Pitman-Yor processes. In *Proc. of ACL.*

Reut Tsarfaty, Djamé Seddah, Yoav Goldberg, Sandra Kübler, Marie Candito, Jennifer Foster, Yannick Versley, Ines Rehbein, and Lamia Tounsi. 2010. Statistical parsing of morphologically rich languages: What, how and whither. In *Proc. of Workshop on Statistical Parsing of Morphologically Rich Languages.*

F. Tyers and M.S. Alperen. 2010. South-east european times: A parallel corpus of Balkan languages. In *Proceedings of the LREC workshop on Exploitation of multilingual resources and tools for Central and (South) Eastern European Languages.*

M. Talha Çakmak, Süleyman Acar, and Gülşen Eryiğit. 2012. Word alignment for English-Turkish language pair. In *Proc. of LREC.*

Author Index

Association for Computational Linguistics
209 N. Eighth Street
Stroudsburg, Pennsylvania 18360

CURRAN ASSOCIATES INC
proceedings.com